The Broadview Anthology of

BRITISH LITERATURE

Volume 4
The Age of Romanticism
Third Edition

The Broadview Anthology of British Literature

The Broadview Anthology of

BRITISH LITERATURE

Volume 4
The Age of Romanticism
Third Edition

GENERAL EDITORS

Joseph Black, University of Massachusetts
Leonard Conolly, Trent University
Kate Flint, University of Southern California
Isobel Grundy, University of Alberta
Don LePan, Broadview Press
Roy Liuzza, University of Tennessee
Jerome J. McGann, University of Virginia
Anne Lake Prescott, Barnard College
Barry V. Qualls, Rutgers University
Claire Waters, University of California, Davis

broadview press

PRESS — www.broadviewpress.com
Ontario, Canada

1985, Broadview Press remains a wholly independent publishing house. Broadview's focus is on academic our titles are accessible to university and college students as well as scholars and general readers. With over 800 print, Broadview has become a leading international publisher in the humanities, with world-wide distribution. ew is committed to environmentally responsible publishing and fair business practices.

018 Broadview Press
printed with corrections 2022

LIBRARY AND ARCHIVES CANADA CATALOGUING IN PUBLICATION

The Broadview anthology of British literature / general editors, Joseph Black (University of Massachusetts), Leonard Conolly (Trent University), Kate Flint (University of Southern California), Isobel Grundy (University of Alberta), Don LePan (Broadview Press), Roy Liuzza (University of Tennessee), Jerome J. McGann (University of Virginia), Anne Lake Prescott (Barnard College), Barry V. Qualls (Rutgers University), Claire Waters (University of California, Davis). — Third edition.

(Broadview anthology of British literature)
Includes bibliographical references and indexes.
Contents: Volume 4. The age of romanticism.
ISBN 978-1-55481-311-7 (v. 4 : paperback)

1. English literature. I. Black, Joseph, 1962-, editor II. Title: British literature. III. Series: Broadview anthology of British literature (Series)

PR1109.B772 2014   820.8   C2014-907235-X

Broadview Press handles its own distribution in North America
PO Box 1243, Peterborough, Ontario K9J 7H5, Canada
555 Riverwalk Parkway, Tonawanda, NY 14150, USA
Tel: (705) 743-8990; Fax: (705) 743-8353
email: customerservice@broadviewpress.com

For all territories outside of North America, distribution is handled by Eurospan Group.

Broadview Press acknowledges the financial support of the Government of Canada for our publishing activities.

Canada

Typeset by Kathryn Brownsey
Cover design by Lisa Brawn

PRINTED IN CANADA

CONTRIBUTING EDITORS AND WRITERS

MANAGING EDITOR	Laura Buzzard
DEVELOPMENTAL EDITOR	Jennifer McCue
GENERAL ACADEMIC AND TEXTUAL EDITORS	Laura Cardiff, Joe Davies, Colleen Franklin, Don LePan, Bethany Qualls, Nora Ruddock
DESIGN COORDINATOR	Kathryn Brownsey

CONTRIBUTING EDITORS

Katherine O. Acheson
Suzy Anger
Phanuel Antwi
Melissa Bachynski
Robert Barrett
Gisele Baxter
Donald Beecher
Sandra Bell
Emily Bernhard Jackson
Joseph Black
Carol Blessing
Robert Boenig
Sarika Bose
Matthieu Boyd
Andrew Bretz
Benjamin Bruch
Laura Buzzard
Michael Calabrese
Laura Cardiff
Lisa Chevalier
Mita Choudhury
Youngjin Chung
Massimo Ciavolella
Anna Clark
Elisha Cohn
Thomas J. Collins
Leonard Conolly
Matthew Davis
Darryl Domingo
Annmarie Dru
Dianne Dzie
Siân Finster
R. Eisendrath
ett Epp
Michael Faletra
Emily Farrell

Christina Fawcett
Christina Fitzgerald
Adrienne Fitzpatrick
Andrew Fleck
Melissa Free
Maura Giles-Watson
Stephen Glosecki
Amanda Goldrick-Jones
Katie Gramich
Erik Gray
John Greenwood
Isobel Grundy
Stephen Guy-Bray
Douglas Hayes
Peter C. Herman
Heather Hill-Vasquez
Erika Hodges
John Holmes
Diane Jakacki
Eleanor Johnson
Ian Johnston
Essaka Joshua
Susan Kattwink
Michael K
Amy Hausner
Kleinman
Chris Koenig-Woodyard
Gary Kuchar
Roger P. Kuin
Lydia K. Lake
Wendy Lee
Don LePan
Ruth Lexton
Roy Liuzza
Kirsten Lodge
Marie Loughlin
D.L. Macdonald
Hugh Magennis

Anne McWhir
Tobias Menely
Britt Mize
Alexander Mueller
Ian Munro
Sarah Neville
Meghan Nieman
David Oakleaf
Maureen Okun
Philip S. Palmer
Virginia Philipson
Jude Polsky
Kristen Pond
Anne LakePrescott
Joyce Rappaport
Andrew Rszitnyk
Joseph Reek
Shelby Richardson
Terry Robnson
Herbert Rosengarten
Nora Ruddock
Jason Rudy
Janice Schroeder
Chester Scoville
John T. Sebastian
Helena Snopek
Kelly Stage
Emily Steiner
Ashley Streeter
Martha Stoddard-Holmes
Julie Sutherland
David Swain
Carol Symes
Andrew Tayl
Peggy T
Jane

Melissa Valiska Gregory
Martine van Elk
Fred Waage
Andrea Walkden
Craig Walker

Claire Waters
David Watt
William Weaver
Vivienne Westbrook

Dan White
David Williams
Adrienne Williams Boyarin
James Winny

CONTRIBUTING WRITERS

Victoria Abboud
Jane Beal
Jennifer Beauvais
Rachel Bennett
Emily Bernhard Jackson
Rebecca Blasco
Matthieu Boyd
Julie Brennan
Andrew Bretz
Laura Buzzard
Laura Cardiff
Emily Cargan
Adrienne Eastwood
Wendy Eberle-Sinatra
Zachary Edwards
Peter Enman
Emily Farrell
Christina Fawcett
Joanne Findon
Jane Grove

Camille Isaacs
Erik Isford
John Geddert
Shoshannah Jones Square
Stephanie King
Chris Koenig-Woodyard
Gabrielle L'Archeveque
Don LePan
Anna Lepine
John McIntyre
Carrie Nartkler
Byron Nelson
Robin Norris
Kenna Olsen
Kendra O'Neal Smith
Laura Pellerine
Virginia Philipson
Jude Polky
Nora Ruddock
Jason Rudy

Anne Salo
Janice Schroeder
Carrie Shanafelt
Nicole Shukin
Helena Snopek
James Soderholm
Anne Sorbie
Jenna Stook
Ashley Streeter
Alexandria Stuart
Candace Taylor
Yevgeniya Traps
David Van Belle
Sarah Vickers
Deirdra Wadden
Shari Watling
Matthew Williams
Bj Wray
Nicole Zylstra

LAYOUT AND TYPESETTING

Kathryn Brownsey

ILLUSTRATION FORMATTING AND ASSISTANCE

Cheryl Baldwin

Lisa Brawn

Eileen Eckert

PRODUCTION COORDINATORS

Tara Lowes

Tara Trueman

PERMISSIONS COORDINATORS

Emily Cargan
Amy Nimegeer

Jennifer Elsayed

Merilee Atos
Chris Griffin

PROOFREADERS

Jennifer Bingham
Joe Davies
Ann Fraser
Neufeld

Martin Boyne
Judith Earnshaw
Anne Hodgetts
Bethany Qualls

Nancy Conolly
Eckert-Jantzie
feld

Editorial Advisors

CONTENTS

Please note that content is continually being added to the website component of this anthology, and some materials available online may not be listed here.

[Note to Instructors: *The Private Memoirs and Confessions of a Justified Sinner* is among over 400 available editions from Broadview, any one of which may be packaged together with this anthology volume.]

[Note to Instructors: *Lyrical Ballads: 1798 and 1800* is among over 400 available editions from Broadview, any one of which may be packaged together with this anthology volume.]

[Note to Instructors: *Pride and Prejudice* is among over 400 available editions from Broadview, any one of which may be packaged together with this anthology volume.]

APPENDICES

PREFACE

A FRESH APPROACH

The publication of the first edition of this anthology in 2006 was widely hailed as an exciting achievement, with many academics concluding that its comprehensiveness, its consistency, its visual appeal, and its fresh approach made the Broadview the "new standard" in anthologies of British literature. We have also been taking a fresh approach in issuing new editions of the anthology's volumes. Rather than publishing new editions of each of the six volumes simultaneously, we are publishing new editions of the individual volumes at the rate of approximately one per year. Each volume thus appears in a new edition roughly every six years. We recognize that our two main competitors have in recent years made it a practice to issue new editions much more frequently than that, but our feeling is that it is better to allow several years to elapse between editions—not least of all, as a new edition may represent a considerable inconvenience to academics teaching from the anthology. (The approach also has real practical advantages for a smaller publisher such as Broadview; rather than gearing up for a massive process of revision every few years and then gearing down again in the wake of publication, we can proceed at a steady pace with the work of updating and revising.)

The third edition of this volume features a great deal of new material. Some of the most significant additions involve complete longer texts; new to this edition, for example, is Maria Edgeworth's early historical novel *Castle Rackrent*. Byron's *The Giaour* and Keats's *Hyperion: A Fragment* are also new to the volume, and we now include Blake's *Songs of Innocence and of Experience* in its entirety. With each volume of the anthology's third edition we are striving to offer improved representation of Irish, Welsh, and Scottish literature; to that end, in addition to *Castle Rackrent*, we are also including selections from James Macpherson's *Fragments of*

Ancient Poetry and a number of poems by Thomas Moore. We have strengthened our representation of the Gothic, too, with a substantial new "Contexts" section representing developments in Gothic literature through the period. The "Contexts" section on "Slavery and Its Abolition" now addresses the Haitian Revolution in relation to Britain's abolitionist movement; the "Contexts" section on the French Revolution, which now appears in the bound-book portion of the anthology, has also been revised and expanded, with the addition of writings by Edmund Burke, Mary Wollstonecraft, and William Godwin. Our representation of Wollstonecraft is further augmented by portions of her *Letters Written During a Short Residence*, as well as by an "In Context" section offering excerpts of Godwin's biography of her. We have also refreshed our coverage of many poets with the addition of one or two short pieces: these pages feature additional poems by Anna Laetitia Barbauld; Charlotte Smith; Robert Burns; Joanna Baillie; Sir Walter Scott; Dorothy Wordsworth; Samuel Taylor Coleridge; George Gordon, Lord Byron; Percy Bysshe Shelley; Felicia Hemans; John Clare; John Keats; and Letitia Elizabeth Landon.

Cuts, of course, have been necessary to make room for this new material. A few authors whom we have found to be taught infrequently—Sir William Jones, William Taylor, and Matthew Gregory Lewis—are no longer represented by individual sections in the bound book, and the "Contexts" section addressing "India and the Orient" has been moved to the online component. Academics wishing to teach any material that has been dropped from the bound book component should note that, in every case, this material remains available as part of the anthology's online component.

One advantage of the anthology's website component is that it can be updated continually; a range of additions to the website are planned in association with this new edition. Here, we have found a place for several important authors for whom space could not be found in the bound book, including Robert Southey; Leigh Hunt; Hannah More; Sydney Owenson, Lady Morgan; and Jane Cave. The website also now features several long works that could not be accommodated in the bound book, including short fiction by James Hogg and by Scott, Landon's long poem "The Improvisatrice," and Byron's *Manfred*. Several new "Contexts" sections are also projected, addressing the subjects of religion (edited by Dan White); of disability (edited by Essaka Joshua); and of Irish oppression.

As with all volumes of *The Broadview Anthology of British Literature*, many people outside the group of General Editors have made important contributions to the preparation of the book's contents. For this volume particular thanks should go, in addition to those mentioned above, to Daniel Burgoyne, Julie Nash, Heidi Kaufman, Andrew Bretz, Joe Davies, Bethany Qualls, Judith Earnshaw, Nora Ruddock, Helena Snopek, Sarah Vickers, Andrew Reszitnyk, Kathryn Brownsey, and Jennifer McCue.

Enlisting the help of a substantial number of people is entirely consistent with the approach we have followed from the start with *The Broadview Anthology*. Rather than dividing up the vast amount of work entailed in preparing such a large anthology among a relatively small number of academics, and asking each of them to handle on their own the work of choosing, annotating, and preparing introductions to texts in their own areas of specialization, we chose to involve a large number of contributors in the process (as the pages following the title page to this volume attest), and to encourage a high degree of collaboration at every level. First and foremost are the distinguished academics who serve as our General Editors for the project, but in all there have literally been hundreds of people involved at various stages in researching, drafting headnotes or annotations, reviewing material, editing material, and carrying out the work of designing and typesetting the texts and other materials. That approach allowed us to draw on a diverse range of talent, and to prepare the first edition of a large anthology with extraordinary efficiency. It has also facilitated the maintenance of a high

degree of consistency. Material has been reviewed and revised in-house at Broadview, by outside editors, by a variety of academics with an extraordinarily diverse range of backgrounds and academic specialities, and by our team of General Editors for the project as a whole. The aim has been not only to ensure accuracy but also to make sure that the same standards are applied throughout the anthology to matters such as coverage provided in introductions, level of annotation, tone of writing, and student accessibility.

As with the first and second editions, several core principles have guided the selection of texts for this volume. We have endeavored to provide a selection that is broadly representative, while also being mindful of the importance of choosing texts that have the capacity to engage readers' interest today. We have for the most part made it a policy to include long works in their entirety or not at all; readers will find complete in *The Broadview Anthology* works such as *Utopia*, "Beachy Head," *Lady Susan*, *The History of Mary Prince*, and *In Memoriam* that are often excerpted in (or omitted from) other anthologies. Where editions of works are available separately in our acclaimed Broadview Editions series, we have often decided to omit them from the anthology, on the grounds that those wishing to teach one or more such works may easily do so in a combination package with the anthology.

Any discussion of what is distinctive about *The Broadview Anthology of British Literature* must focus above all on the contents. In every volume of the anthology there is material that is distinctive and fresh— including not only selections by lesser-known writers but also less familiar selections from canonical writers. The anthology takes a fresh approach too to a great many canonical texts. The first volume of the anthology includes not only Roy Liuzza's translation of *Beowulf* (widely acclaimed as the most engaging and reliable translation available), but also new translations by Liuzza of many other works of Old English poetry and prose. Unique to the first volume of this anthology are a new verse translation of *Judith* by Stephen Glosecki and new translations by Claire Waters of several of the *Lais* of Marie de France. And so on through all six volumes.

In a number of these cases the distinctive form of the anthology facilitates the presentation of content in an engaging and practical fashion. Notably, the adoption of a two-column format allows for some translations (the Marie de France *Lais*, the James Winny translation of *Sir Gawain and the Green Knight*, poetry in Old Irish and other Celtic languages) to be presented in parallel column format alongside the original texts, allowing readers to experience something of the flavor of the original, while providing convenient access to an accessible translation. Similarly, passages from four translations of the Bible are laid out parallel to each other for ready comparison.

The large trim-size, two-column format also allows for greater flexibility in the presentation of visual materials. Throughout our intent is to make this an anthology that is fully alive to the connections between literary and visual culture, from the discussion of the CHI-RHO page of the Lindisfarne Gospels in the first volume of the anthology (and the accompanying color illustration) to the inclusion in Volume 6 of a number of selections (including Graham Greene's "The Basement Room," Tom Stoppard's "Professional Foul," and several skits from "Monty Python's Flying Circus") that may be discussed in connection with film or television versions. Along the way appear several full-page illustrations from the Ellesmere manuscript of Chaucer's *Canterbury Tales* and illustrations to a wide variety of other works, from *Robinson Crusoe* and *Gulliver's Travels* to *The Adventure of the Speckled Band* and *The Road to Wigan Pier*.

CONTEXTUAL MATERIALS

Visual materials are also included in the background materials that form an important part of the anthology. These materials are presented in two ways. Several "Contexts" sections on particular topics or themes appear in each volume of the anthology, presented independent of any particular text or author. These include broadly based groupings of material on such topics as "Religion and Spiritual Life," "Print Culture,"

"India and the Orient," "The Abolition of Slavery," "The New Art of Photography," and "The End of Empire." The groups of "In Context" materials each relate to a particular text or author. They range from the genealogical tables provided as a supplement to *Beowulf*; to materials on "The Eighteenth-Century Sexual Imagination" (presented in conjunction with Haywood's *Fantomina*); to a selection of materials relating to the Peterloo massacre (presented in conjunction with Percy Shelley's "The Mask of Anarchy"); to materials on "'The Vilest Scramble for Loot' in Central Africa" (presented in conjunction with Conrad's "An Outpost of Progress"). For the most part these contextual materials are, as the word suggests, included with a view to setting texts in their broader literary, historical, and cultural contexts; in some cases, however, the materials included in "Contexts" sections are themselves literary works of a high order. The autobiographical account by Eliza M. of nineteenth-century life in Cape Town, for example (included in the section in Volume 5 on "Race and Empire"), is as remarkable for its literary qualities as it is for the light it sheds on the realities of colonial life. In the inclusion of texts such as these, as well as in other ways, the anthology aims to encourage readers to explore the boundaries of the literary and the non-literary, and the issue of what constitutes a "literary text."

TEXTS BY WOMEN WRITERS

A central element of the broadening of the canon of British literature in recent generations has of course been a great increase in the attention paid to texts by women writers. As one might expect from a publisher that has played an important role in making neglected works by women writers widely available, this anthology reflects the broadening of the canon quantitatively, by including a substantially larger number of women writers than have earlier anthologies of British literature. But it also reflects this broadening in other ways. In many anthologies of literature (anthologies of British literature, to be sure, but also anthologies of literature of a variety of other sorts) women writers are still too often set somewhat apart, referenced in introductions and headnotes only in relation to issues of gender, and treated as important only for the fact of their being women writers. *The Broadview Anthology* strenuously resists such segregation; while women writers are of course discussed in relation to gender issues, their texts are also presented and discussed alongside those by men in a wide variety of other contexts, including seventeenth-century religious and political controversies, the abolitionist movement, and World War I pacifism. Texts by women writers are front and center in the discussion of the development of realism in nineteenth-century fiction. And when it comes to the twentieth century, both Virginia Woolf and Dorothy Richardson are included alongside James Joyce as practitioners of groundbreaking modernist narrative techniques.

"BRITISH," "ENGLISH," "IRISH," "SCOTTISH," "WELSH," "OTHER"

The broadening of English Studies, in conjunction with the expansion and subsequent contraction of British power and influence around the world, has considerably complicated the issue of exactly how inclusive anthologies should be. In several respects this anthology (like its two main competitors) is significantly more inclusive than its title suggests, including a number of non-British writers whose works connect in important ways with the traditions of British literature. We endeavor to portray the fluid and multilingual reality of the medieval period through the inclusion not only of works in Old and Middle English but also of works in Latin, in French, in Irish, in Welsh, and in Scots. This approach extends into the early modern period with the inclusion of works from the literatures of Ireland, Gaelic Scotland, and Wales.

In later periods the word "British" becomes deeply problematic in different respects, but on balance we have preferred it to the only obvious alternative, "English." There are several objections to the latter in this context. Perhaps most obviously, "English" excludes authors or texts not only from Ireland but also from

Scotland and from Wales, both of which retain to this day cultures quite distinct from that of the English. "English literature," of course, may also be taken to mean "literature written in English," but since the anthology does not cover *all* literature written in English (most obviously in excluding American literature), the ambiguity would not in this case be helpful.

The inclusion of Irish writers presents a related but even more tangled set of issues. At the beginning of the period covered by the six volumes of this anthology we find works, such as the *Book of Kells*, that may have been created in what is now England, in what is now Scotland, in what is now Ireland—or in some combination of these. Through most of the seventeenth, eighteenth, and nineteenth centuries almost the whole of Ireland was under British control—but for the most part unwillingly. In the period covered in the last of the six volumes Ireland was partitioned, with Northern Ireland becoming a part of the United Kingdom and the Republic of Ireland declared independent of Britain on 6 December 1921. Less than two months earlier, James Joyce had completed *Ulysses*, which was first published as a complete work the following year (in Paris, not in Britain). It would be obviously absurd to regard Joyce as a British writer up to just before the publication of *Ulysses*, and an Irish writer thereafter. And arguably he and other Irish writers should never be regarded as British, whatever the politics of the day. If on no other grounds than their overwhelming influence on and connection to the body of literature written in the British Isles, however, we have included Irish writers—among them Swift, Sheridan, Edgeworth, Wilde, Shaw, Beckett, Bowen, Muldoon, and Heaney as well as Joyce—throughout this anthology. We have also endeavored to give a real sense in the introductions to the six volumes of the anthology, in the headnotes to individual authors, and in the annotations to the texts themselves, of the ways in which the histories and the cultures of England, Ireland, Scotland, and Wales, much as they interact with one another, are also distinct.

Also included in this anthology are texts by writers from areas that are far removed geographically from the British Isles but that are or have been British posses-

XL THE BROADVIEW ANTHOLOGY OF BRITISH LITERATURE

sions. Writers such as Mary Rowlandson, Olaudah Equiano, and Phillis Wheatley are included, as they spent all or most of their lives living in what were then British colonial possessions. Writers who came of age in an independent United States, on the other hand, are not included, unless (like T.S. Eliot) they subsequently put down roots in Britain and became important British literary figures. Substantial gray areas, of course, surround such issues. One might well argue, for example, that Henry James merits inclusion in an anthology of British literature, or that W.H. Auden and Thom Gunn are more American poets than British ones. But the chosen subject matter of James's work has traditionally been considered to mark him as having remained an American writer, despite having spent almost two-thirds of his life in England. And both Auden and Gunn so clearly made a mark in Britain before crossing the Atlantic that it would seem odd to exclude them from these pages on the grounds of their having lived the greater part of their adult lives in America. One of our competitors includes Sylvia Plath in their anthology of British literature; Plath lived in England for only five of her thirty years, though, and her poetry is generally agreed to have more in common with the traditions of Lowell, Merwin, and Sexton than with the currents of British poetry in the 1950s and '60s.

As a broad principle, we have been open to the inclusion of twentieth and twenty-first century work in English not only by writers from the British Isles but also by writers from British possessions overseas, and by writers from countries that were once British possessions and have remained a part of the British Commonwealth. In such cases we have often chosen selections that relate in one way or another to the tradition of British literature and the British colonial legacy. Of the Judith Wright poems included here, several relate to her coming to terms with the British colonial legacy in Australia; similarly, both the Margaret Atwood and the Alice Munro selections include work in which these Canadian authors attempt to recreate imaginatively the experience of British emigrants to Canada in the nineteenth century; the Chinua Achebe story in the anthology concerns the divide between British colonial culture and traditional Nigerian culture; and so on. For convenience we have also grouped most of the post-World War II non-British authors together, following the "Contexts: The End of Empire" section. (For the most part, the table of contents for the anthology is arranged chronologically according to the birthdate of each author.)

THE HISTORY OF LANGUAGE, AND OF PRINT CULTURE

Among the liveliest discussions we had at meetings of our General Editors were those concerning the issue of whether or not to bring spelling and punctuation into accord with present-day practice. We finally decided that, in the interests of making the anthology accessible to the introductory student, we should *in most cases* bring spelling and punctuation in line with present-day practice. An important exception has been made for works in which modernizing spelling and punctuation would alter the meaning or the aural and metrical qualities. In practice this means that works before the late sixteenth century tend to be presented either in their original form or in translation, whereas later texts tend to have spelling and punctuation modernized. But where spelling and punctuation choices in later texts are known (or believed on reliable authority) to represent conscious choice on the part of the author rather than simply the common practice of the time, we have in those cases, too, made an exception and retained the original spelling and punctuation. (Among these are texts by Edmund Spenser; by William Cowper; by William Blake, John Clare, and several other poets of the Romantic era; by George Bernard Shaw; and by contemporary figures such as Linton Kwesi Johnson.)

Beyond this, we all agreed that we should provide for readers a real sense of the development of the language and of print culture. To that end we have included in each volume examples of texts in their original form—in some cases through the use of pages shown in facsimile, in others by providing short passages in which spelling and punctuation have not been modernized. A list of these appears near the beginning of each volume of the anthology.

We have also included a section of the history of the language as part of the introduction to each volume. And throughout the anthology we include materials—visual as well as textual—relating to the history of print culture.

A DYNAMIC AND FLEXIBLE ANTHOLOGY

Almost all major book publishing projects nowadays are accompanied by an adjunct website, and most large-scale anthologies are accompanied by websites that provide additional materials in electronic form. Since this anthology's inception, we have viewed its website component as precisely that—a *component* of the anthology itself. The notion of a website of this sort grew organically out of the process of trying to winnow down the contents of the first edition of the anthology to a manageable level—the point at which all the material to be included would fit within the covers of bound books that would not be overwhelmingly heavy. And we simply could not do it. After we had made a very substantial round of cuts we were still faced with a table of contents in which each volume was at least 200 or 300 pages longer than our agreed-upon maximum. Our solution was not to try to cut anything more, but rather to select a range of material to be made available in a website component of the anthology. This material is in every way produced according to the same high standards of the material in the bound books; the editorial standards, the procedures for annotation, the author introductions, and the page design and layout—all are the same. The texts on the web, in short, are not "extra" materials; they are an integral part of the full anthology. In accordance with that principle, we have been careful to include a wide range of texts by lesser-known writers within the bound books, and a number of texts by canonical writers within the web component of the anthology.

The latter may be used in a variety of ways. Most obviously, readings from the web component are

available to any purchaser of the book. Instructors who adopt *The Broadview Anthology of British Literature* as a course text are also granted permission to reproduce any web material for which Broadview holds copyright in a supplementary coursepack. An alternative for instructors who want to "create their own" anthology is to visit the "Custom Texts" page on the Broadview website or contact the publisher directly; Broadview can make available to students through their university bookstore a custom-made coursepack with precisely the desired materials included. Other options are available too. Volumes of the anthology itself may of course be shrink-wrapped together at special prices in any desired combination. They may also be combined in a shrink-wrapped package with one of the over 400 volumes in the Broadview Editions series, at no additional cost to the student (or with more than one volume for a modest additional charge).

We anticipate that over the years the web-based component of the anthology will continue to grow — every year there will be a greater choice of web-based texts in the anthology. But we never foresee a day when the web will be the only option; we expect physical books always to remain central to Broadview's approach to publishing.

THE BROADVIEW LIST

One of the reasons we were able to bring a project of this sort to fruition in such a relatively short time was that we were able to draw on the resources of the full Broadview list: the many titles in the Broadview Editions series, and also the considerable range of other Broadview anthologies. As the contributors' pages and the permissions acknowledgments pages indicate, a number of Broadview authors have acted as contributing editors to this volume, providing material from other volumes that has been adapted to suit the needs of the present anthology; we gratefully acknowledge their contribution.

As it has turned out, the number of cases where we have been able to draw on the resources of the

Broadview list in the full sense, using in these pages texts and annotations in very much the same form in which they appear elsewhere, has been relatively small; whether because of an issue such as the level of textual modernization or one of style of annotation, we have more often than not ended up deciding that the requirements of this anthology were such that we could not use material from another Broadview source as-is. But even in these cases we often owe a debt of gratitude to the many academics who have edited outstanding editions and anthologies for Broadview. For even where we have not drawn directly from them, we have often been inspired by them—inspired to think of a wider range of texts as possibilities than we might otherwise have done, inspired to think of contextual materials in places where we might otherwise not have looked, inspired by the freshness of approach that so many of these titles exemplify.

EDITORIAL PROCEDURES AND CONVENTIONS, APPARATUS

The in-house set of editorial guidelines for *The Broadview Anthology of British Literature* runs to over 40 pages, covering everything from conventions for the spacing of marginal notes, to the use of small caps for the abbreviations CE and BCE, to the approach we have adopted to references in author headnotes to name changes. Perhaps the most important core principle in the introductions to the various volumes, in the headnotes for each author, in the introductions in "Contexts" sections, and in annotations throughout the anthology, is to endeavor to provide a sufficient amount of information to enable students to read and interpret these texts, but without making evaluative judgments or imposing particular interpretations. In practice that is all a good deal more challenging than it sounds; it is often extremely difficult to describe why a particular author is considered to be important without using language that verges on the interpretive or the evaluative. But it is a fine line that we have all agreed is worth trying to walk; we hope that readers will find that the anthology achieves an appropriate balance.

ANNOTATION: It is also often difficult to make judgments as to where it is appropriate to provide an explanatory annotation for a word or phrase. Our policy has been to annotate where we feel that most first- or second-year students are likely to have difficulty understanding the denotative meaning. (We have made it a practice not to provide notes discussing connotative meanings.) But in practice the vocabularies and levels of verbal facility of first- and second-year students may vary enormously, both from institution to institution and within any given college or university class. On the whole, we provide somewhat more annotation than our competitors, and somewhat less interpretation. Again, we hope that readers will find that the anthology has struck an appropriate balance.

THE ETHICS AND POLITICS OF ANNOTATION: On one issue regarding annotation we have felt that principles are involved that go beyond the pedagogical. Most anthologies of British literature allow many words or phrases of a racist, sexist, anti-Semitic, or homophobic nature either to pass entirely without comment, or to be glossed with apologist comments that leave the impression that such comments were excusable in the past, and may even be unobjectionable in the present. Where derogatory comments about Jewish people and money-lending are concerned, for example, anthologies often leave the impression that money-lending was a pretty unsavory practice that Jewish people entered by choice; it has been all too rare to provide readers with any sense of the degree to which English society consistently discriminated against Jews, expelling them entirely for several centuries, requiring them to wear physical marks identifying their Jewish status, prohibiting them from entering most professions, and so on. *The Broadview Anthology* endeavors in such cases, first of all, not to allow such words and phrases to pass without comment; and second, to gloss without glossing over.

DATES: We make it a practice to include the date when a work was first made public, whether publication in print or, in the case of dramatic works, made public through the first performance of the play. Where that date is known to differ substantially from the date of composition, a note to this effect is included in parentheses. With medieval works, where there is no equivalent to the "publication" of later eras, where texts often vary greatly from one manuscript copy to another, and where knowledge as to date of original composition is usually imprecise, the date that appears at the end of each work is an estimate of the date of the work's origin in the written form included in the anthology. Earlier oral or written versions are of course in some cases real possibilities.

TEXTS: Where translations appear in this anthology, a note at the bottom of the first page indicates what translation is being used. Similar notes also address overall textual issues where choice of copy text is particularly significant. Reliable editions of most works are listed in the bibliography for the anthology, which is included as part of the website component rather than in the bound books, to facilitate ready revision. (In addition to information as to reliable editions, the bibliography provides for each author and for each of the six periods select lists of important or useful historical and critical works.) Copyright information for texts not in the public domain, however, is provided within the bound books in a section listing Permissions Acknowledgments.

INTRODUCTIONS: In addition to the introductory headnotes for each author included in the anthology, each "Contexts" section includes a substantial introduction, and each volume includes an introduction to the period as a whole. These introductions to the six volumes of the anthology endeavor to provide a sense not only of the broad picture of literary developments in the period, but also of the historical, social, and political background, and of the cultural climate. Readers should be cautioned that, while there is inevitably some overlap between information presented here and information presented in the author headnotes, an effort has been made to avoid such repetition as much as possible; the general introduction to each period should thus be read in conjunction with the author headnotes. The general introductions aim not only to provide an overview of

ways in which texts and authors included in these pages may connect with one another, but also to give readers a sense of connection with a range of other writers and texts of the period.

READING POETRY: For much of the glossary and for the "Reading Poetry" section that appears as part of the appendices to each volume we have drawn on the superb material prepared by Herbert Rosengarten and Amanda Goldrick-Jones for *The Broadview Anthology of Poetry*; this section provides a concise but comprehensive introduction to the study of poetry. It includes discussions of diction, imagery, poetic figures, and various poetic forms, as well as offering an introduction to prosody.

MAPS: Also appearing within each of the bound books are maps especially prepared for this anthology, including, for each volume, a map of Britain showing towns and features of relevance during the pertinent period; a map showing the counties of Britain and of Ireland; maps both of the London area and of the inner city; and world maps indicating the locations of some of the significant places referenced in the anthology, and for later volumes showing the extent of Britain's overseas territories.

GLOSSARY: Some other anthologies of British literature include both glossaries of terms and essays introducing students to various political and religious categories in British history. Similar information is included in *The Broadview Anthology of British Literature*, but we have adopted a more integrated approach, including political and religious terms along with literary ones in a convenient general glossary. While we recognize that looking to resources such as Wikipedia for information of this sort is often the student's first resort (and we recognize too the value of searching the web for the wealth of background reference information available there), we also recognize that not all online sources are equally reliable; it is our intent, through this glossary, through our introductions and headnotes, and through the wealth of accessible annotation in the anthology, to provide as part of the anthology a reliable core of information in the most convenient and accessible form possible.

OTHER MATERIALS: A chart of Monarchs and Prime Ministers is also provided within these pages. A range of other adjunct materials may be accessed through *The Broadview Anthology of British Literature* website. "Texts and Contexts" charts for each volume provide a conve-

nient parallel reference guide to the dates of literary texts and historical developments. "Money in Britain" provides a thumbnail sketch of the world of pounds, shillings, and pence, together with a handy guide to estimating the current equivalents of monetary values from earlier eras. And the website offers, too, a variety of further aids for the student and the instructor. An up-to-date list of these appears on the site.

ACKNOWLEDGMENTS

The names of those on the Editorial Board that shaped this anthology appear on the title page, and those of the many who contributed directly to the writing, editing, and production of the project on the following two pages. Special acknowledgment for this new edition should go to Developmental Editor Jennifer McCue, who has been instrumental in tying together all the vast threads of this project and in making it a reality; to General Academic and Textual Editor Nora Ruddock, who has played a key role in drafting introductory materials and annotations for the new material, and done so with great skill and unfailing grace; to Kathryn Brownsey, who has been responsible for design and typesetting, and has continued to do an outstanding job and to maintain her good spirits even when faced with near-impossible demands; to Joe Davies and Bethany Qualls for the range of their general knowledge as well as for their keen eyes as our primary proofreaders for the entire project; and to Merilee Atos, who has done superb work on the vast job of clearing permissions for the anthology.

The academic general editors and all of us in-house at Broadview owe an enormous debt of gratitude to the hundreds of academics who have offered assistance at various stages of this project. In particular we would like to express our appreciation and our thanks to the following:

Rachel Ablow, University of Rochester
Katherine Acheson, University of Waterloo
Kenet Adamson, Southwestern Community College
Bryan Alexander, Middlebury College
Sharon Alker, Whitman College
James Allard, Brock University
Ella Allen, St. Thomas University
Rosemary Allen, Georgetown College
Laurel Amtower, San Diego State University
Robert Anderson, Oakland University
Christopher Armitage, University of North Carolina, Chapel Hill
Clinton Atchley, Henderson State University
Gerry Baillargeon, University of Victoria
John Baird, University of Toronto
William Baker, Northern Illinois University
Karen Bamford, Mount Allison University
John Batchelor, University of Newcastle
Lynn Batten, University of California, Los Angeles
Stephen Behrendt, University of Nebraska
Alexandra Bennett, Northern Illinois University

John Beynon, California State University, Fresno
Daniel Bivona, Arizona State University
Robert E. Bjork, Arizona State University
John Black, Moravian College
Scott Black, Villanova University
Rita Bode, Trent University
Robert Boenig, Texas A & M University
Matthew Borushko, Stonehill College
Rick Bowers, University of Alberta
Patricia Brace, Columbus State University
David Brewer, Ohio State University
William Brewer, Appalachian State University
Glen Brewster, Westfield State University
Susan Brown, University of Guelph
Sylvia Brown, University of Alberta
Sheila Burgar, University of Victoria
Catherine Burroughs, Wells College
Rebecca Bushnell, University of Pennsylvania
Michael Calabrese, California State University
Elizabeth Campbell, Oregon State University
Katey Castellano, James Madison University

Gregory Castle, Arizona State University

Cynthia Caywood, University of San Diego

Jane Chance, Rice University

Ranita Chatterjee, California State University, Northridge

William Christmas, San Francisco State University

Nancy Cirillo, University of Illinois, Chicago

Eric Clarke, University of Pittsburgh

Jeanne Clegg, University of Aquila, Italy

Thomas J. Collins, University of Western Ontario

Thomas L. Cooksey, Armstrong Atlantic State University

Kevin Cope, Louisiana State University

David Cowart, University of South Carolina

Catherine Craft-Fairchild, University of St. Thomas

Jenny Crisp, Dalton State College

Laura Dabundo, Kennesaw State University

Roger Davis, Red Deer College

Carol Davison, University of Windsor

JoEllen DeLucia, Central Michigan University

Alexander Dick, University of British Columbia

Len Diepeveen, Dalhousie University

Mary Dockray-Miller, Lesley College

James Doelman, Brescia University College, University of Western Ontario

Frank Donoghue, Ohio State University

Chris Downs, Saint James School

Alfred Drake, Chapman University

Ian Duncan, University of California, Berkeley

Julie Early, University of Alabama, Huntsville

Roxanne Eberle, University of Georgia

Siân Echard, University of British Columbia

Garrett Epp, University of Alberta

Joshua Eyler, Columbus State University

Ruth Feingold, St. Mary's College, Maryland

Dino Franco Felluga, Perdue University

Joanne Findon, Trent University

Larry Fink, Hardin Simmons University

Daniel Fischlin, University of Guelph

Christina Fitzgerald, University of Toledo

Verlyn Flieger, University of Maryland

Robert Forman, St. John's University

Allyson Foster, Hunter College

Lorcan Fox, University of British Columbia

Peter Francev, Victor Valley College

Roberta Frank, Yale University

Jeff Franklin, University of Colorado, Denver

Maria Frawley, George Washington University

Mark Fulk, Buffalo State College

Christine Gallant, Georgia State University

Andrew Galloway, Cornell University

Michael Gamer, University of Pennsylvania

Barbara Gates, University of Delaware

Laura George, Eastern Michigan University

Denise Gigante, Stanford University

Jonathan C. Glance, Mercer University

Susan Patterson Glover, Laurentian University

Jennifer Golightly, University of Denver

Daniel Gonzalez, University of New Orleans

Jan Gorak, University of Denver

Chris Gordon-Craig, University of Alberta

Evan Gottlieb, Oregon State University

Ann-Barbara Graff, Georgia Tech University

Bruce Graver, Providence College

Mary Griffin, Kwantlen University College

Michael Griffin, formerly of Southern Illinois University

George C. Grinnell, University of British Columbia, Okanagan

Jonathan Gross, DePaul University

Elisabeth Gruner, University of Richmond

Bonnie Gunzenhauser, Roosevelt University

Kevin Gustafson, University of Texas at Arlington

Stephen Guy-Bray, University of British Columbia

Ruth Haber, Worcester State College

Dorothy Hadfield, University of Guelph

Margaret Hadley, University of Calgary

Robert Hampson, Royal Holloway University of London

Carol Hanes, Howard College

Michael Hanly, Washington State University

Lila Harper, Central Washington State University

Joseph Harris, Harvard University

Katherine Harris, San Jose State University

Anthony Harrison, North Carolina State University

John Hart, Motlow State Community College

Douglas Hayes, Lakehead University

Jennifer Hellwarth, Allegheny University

David Herman, Ohio State University
Peter Herman, San Diego State University
Jillian Hess, Bronx Community College, CUNY
Kathy Hickock, Iowa State University
John Hill, US Naval Academy
Thomas Hill, Cornell University
Elizabeth Hodgson, University of British Columbia
Jim Hood, Guilford College
Joseph Hornsby, University of Alabama
Scott Howard, University of Denver
Jennifer Hughes, Averett University
Sylvia Hunt, Georgian College
Tara Hyland-Russell, St. Mary's College
Catherine Innes-Parker, University of Prince Edward
    Island
Jacqueline Jenkins, University of Calgary
John Johansen, University of Alberta
Gordon Johnston, Trent University
Essaka Joshua, University of Notre Dame
Richard Juang, Susquehanna University
Michael Keefer, University of Guelph
Sarah Keefer, Trent University
Lloyd Kermode, California State University,
    Long Beach
Brandon Kershner, University of Florida
Jon Kertzer, University of Calgary
Waqas Khwaja, Agnes State College
Helen Killoran, Ohio University
Gordon Kipling, University of California, Los Angeles
Anne Klinck, University of New Brunswick
Elizabeth Kraft, University of Georgia
Mary Kramer, University of Massachusetts, Lowell
Scott Krawczyk, United States Military Academy
Wai-Leung Kwok, San Francisco State University
Marilyn Lantz, East Mississippi Community College
Kate Lawson, University of Waterloo
Nathanial Leach, Cape Breton University
Linda Leeds, Bellevue Community College
Mary Elizabeth Leighton, University of Victoria
Eric Lindstrom, University of Vermont
Harriet Linkin, New Mexico State University
William Liston, Ball State University
Sharon Locy, Loyola Marymount University

Ross MacKay, Malaspina University-College
Peter Mallios, University of Maryland
Arnold Markley, Penn State University
Louis Markos, Houston Baptist University
Nick Mason, Brigham Young University
Pamela McCallum, University of Calgary
Patricia McCormack, Itawamba Community College
Kristen McDermott, Central Michigan University
John McGowan, University of North Carolina
Brian McHale, Ohio State University
Jim McKeown, McLennan Community College
Thomas McLean, University of Otago, New Zealand
Susan McNeill-Bindon, University of Alberta
Jodie Medd, Carleton University
Rod Michell, Thompson Rivers University
David Miller, Mississippi College
Kitty Millett, San Francisco State University
Britt Mize, Texas A&M University
Richard Moll, University of Western Ontario
Amy L. Montz, Texas A&M University
Monique Morgan, McGill University
John Morillo, North Carolina State University
Lucy Morrison, Salisbury University
Lorri Nandrea, University of Wisconsin-Steven's Point
Mara Narain, Texas Christian University
Byron Nelson, West Virginia University
Carolyn Nelson, West Virginia University
Claudia Nelson, Southwest Texas State University
Holly Faith Nelson, Trinity Western University
John Niles, University of Wisconsin, Madison
Michael North, University of California, Los Angeles
Mary Anne Nunn, Central Connecticut State University
David Oakleaf, University of Calgary
Tamara O'Callaghan, Northern Kentucky University
Karen Odden, Assistant Editor for *Victorian Literature
    and Culture* (formerly of University of Wisconsin,
    Milwaukee)
Erika Olbricht, Pepperdine University
Patrick O'Malley, Georgetown University
Patricia O'Neill, Hamilton College
Delilah Orr, Fort Lewis College
John Pagano, Barnard College
Kirsten Parkinson, Hiram College

XLVIII   THE BROADVIEW ANTHOLOGY OF BRITISH LITERATURE

Diana Patterson, Mount Royal College
Cynthia Patton, Emporia State University
Russell Perkin, St. Mary's University
Marjorie G. Perloff, Stanford University
Jim Persoon, Grand Valley State University
John Peters, University of North Texas
Todd Pettigrew, Cape Breton University
Alexander Pettit, University of North Texas
Jennifer Phegley, The University of Missouri,
    Kansas City
John Pollock, San Jose State University
Mary Poovey, New York University
Gautam Premnath, University of Massachusetts,
    Boston
Regina Psaki, University of Oregon
Laura Quinney, Brandeis University
Katherine Quinsey, University of Windsor
Tilottama Rajan, University of Western Ontario
Geoff Rector, University of Ottawa
Walter Reed, Emory University
Margaret Reeves, Atkinson College, York University
Cedric Reverand, University of Wyoming
Gerry Richman, Suffolk University
John Rickard, Bucknell University
Michelle Risdon, Lake Tahoe Community College
David Robinson, University of Arizona
Solveig C. Robinson, Pacific Lutheran University
Laura Rotunno, Pennsylvania State University, Altoona
Brian Rourke, New Mexico State University
Christopher Rovee, Lousiana State University
Nicholas Ruddick, University of Regina
Jason Rudy, University of Maryland
Shannon Russell, John Cabot University
Donelle Ruwe, Northern Arizona University
Jon Saklofske, Acadia University
Michelle Sauer, Minot State University
John Savarese, University of Waterloo
SueAnn Schatz, Lock Haven University of Pennsylvania
Dan Schierenbeck, Central Missouri State University
Norbert Schürer, California State University,
    Long Beach
Debora B. Schwartz, California Polytechnic University
Janelle A. Schwartz, Loyola University

John T. Sebastian, Loyola Marymount University
David Seed, University of Liverpool
Karen Selesky, University College of the Fraser Valley
Carol Senf, Georgia Tech University
Sharon Setzer, North Carolina State University
Lynn Shakinovsky, Wilfrid Laurier University
John Sider, Westmont College
Judith Slagle, East Tennessee State University
Johanna Smith, University of Texas at Arlington
Sharon Smulders, Mount Royal College
Jason Snart, College of DuPage
Malinda Snow, Georgia State University
Yasmin Solomonescu, University of Georgia
Goran Stanivukovic, St. Mary's University
Thomas Steffler, Carleton University
Richard Stein, University of Oregon
Eric Sterling, Auburn University Montgomery
James Stokes, University of Wisconsin, Stevens Point
Mary-Ann Stouck, Simon Fraser University
Nathaniel Strout, Hamilton College
Brad Sullivan, Western New England College
Lisa Surridge, University of Victoria
Joyce A. Sutphen, Gustavus Adolphus College
Beth Sutton-Ramspeck, Ohio State University
Nanora Sweet, University of Missouri, St. Louis
Dana Symons, Simon Fraser University
Andrew Taylor, University of Ottawa
Elizabeth Teare, University of Dayton
Doug Thorpe, University of Saskatchewan
Jane Toswell, University of Western Ontario
Kim Trainor, University of British Columbia
Herbert Tucker, University of Virginia
John Tucker, University of Victoria
Mark Turner, King's College, University of London
Eleanor Ty, Wilfrid Laurier University
Deborah Tyler-Bennett, Loughborough University
Kirsten Uszkalo, University of Alberta
Lisa Vargo, University of Saskatchewan
Gina Luria Walker, The New School, New York City
Kim Walker, Victoria University of Wellington
Miriam Wallace, New College of Florida
Orrin Wang, University of Maryland
Hayden Ward, West Virginia State University

David Watt, University of Manitoba
Ruth Wehlau, Queen's University
Lynn Wells, University of Regina
Dan White, University of Toronto
Patricia Whiting, Carleton University
Thomas Willard, University of Arizona
Tara Williams, Oregon State University
Chris Willis, Birkbeck University of London
Lisa Wilson, SUNY College at Potsdam
Ed Wiltse, Nazareth College
Anne Windholz, Augustana College

Rosemary Winslow, The Catholic University of
   America
Susan Wolfson, Princeton University
Kenneth Womack, Pennsylvania State University
Gillen Wood, University of Illinois,
   Urbana-Champaign
Carolyn Woodward, University of New Mexico
Julia Wright, Wilfrid Laurier University
Julian Yates, University of Delaware
Arlene Young, University of Manitoba
Lisa Zeitz, University of Western Ontario

THE AGE OF ROMANTICISM

Perhaps the spirit and ethos of the Romantic era and its creative output are nowhere better captured than in the evolution of clothing during the period. When the artistic, literary, and political changes that are usually associated with Romanticism began in the 1780s, the heavy and elaborate costumes of the eighteenth century still prevailed, constricting their wearers into a rigid formality and mirroring contemporaneous social and aesthetic structures. In the heady years surrounding the French Revolution, when the possibility of greater freedom seemed within reach, these stiff garments gave way to loose, flowing dresses for women, clothes cut from muslins and patterned cottons that had been rendered relatively inexpensive by increasing British imperial control in the East and by technological advances in weaving in Britain itself. During the same period, local militiamen, sporting magnificent military uniforms, demonstrated Britain's growing national pride, all the while masking persistent fear of French invasion. By the time the Romantic period drew to a close in the mid-1830s, these looser fashions and glittering uniforms had themselves been superseded by the tightly laced corsets, salt-and-pepper trousers, and bell skirts heavily supported by hoops and petticoats that are now inextricably associated with English Victorianism.

Morning dress, c. 1800.

Ball dress, c. 1800.

Richard Dighton, *George "Beau" Brummell*, 1805. Brummell, the leading "dandy" of the age, brought into fashion a new style of dress coat, pantaloons, and black evening dress for men. Brummell was fastidious about cleanliness as well as clothing, but denounced perfume for men and any form of showy display.

As the combination of freedom and militarism expressed by Romantic fashions suggests, the fifty years between the French Revolution and the reign of Queen Victoria were neither historically simple nor culturally straightforward. Despite its seeming cohesiveness and unity, the Romantic period was a complex nexus of revolution and conservatism, of bold iconoclasm and hidebound conventionality. Revolutions played a central role in shaping the Romantic period—and continue to shape our perceptions of it. The form and structure of the British Romantic era, as well as the very concept of "Romanticism," have changed radically in recent decades. What in the mid-twentieth century was seen as a literary period centered on five or six major poets—all male—and a select number of prose writers—also all male—has gradually come to be seen as an era made up of writers and thinkers of different genders, beliefs, and social backgrounds. Whereas familiarity with British Romantic poetry once meant having read only William Blake, William Wordsworth, Samuel Taylor Coleridge, Lord Byron, Percy Bysshe Shelley, and John Keats (collectively known as "The Big Six"), today, the voices of Mary Robinson, Anna Laetitia Barbauld, Felicia Hemans, and Letitia Landon—all respected and popular in their day but largely unstudied for much of the twentieth century—are seen as integral to a proper understanding of the period's verse. So too with Romantic non-fiction, which was once seen as consisting of the prose of Coleridge, Charles Lamb, and William Hazlitt, but now encompasses the proto-feminist writing of Mary Wollstonecraft, the didactic prose of Hannah More and Maria Edgeworth, and the natural sketches and observations of Dorothy Wordsworth. The prose fiction of the period (aside from a nod or two acknowledging Jane Austen and Sir Walter Scott) was once given short shrift; the drama was, generally, neglected. At this moment, Mary Shelley's novels—particularly *Frankenstein* (1818) and *The Last Man* (1826)—receive at least as much critical attention as do the works of her husband Percy Shelley, with *Frankenstein* probably being read more widely than any other single work of the Romantic period; Austen's works are now seen to hold a central position in the history of the novel; and the work of other writers of fiction—from William Godwin to Mary Hays, Amelia Opie, Mary Robinson, and Charlotte Smith—has been much more fully and more favorably assessed. In the study of drama, a similar, if less marked, shift has occurred, with the importance of the work of Hannah Cowley, Elizabeth Inchbald, and Joanna Baillie, as well as that of Percy Shelley and of Byron, being broadly recognized.

If the past several decades have brought a substantial shift in the emphasis placed on various authors in the study of the Romantic period, they have also brought a shift in the way the period as a whole is perceived. Whereas Romantic literature in English was once discussed far more with reference to nature and to the imagination than it was with reference to politics or to ideology, a broader perspective is now almost universally acknowledged as essential to a more comprehensive sense of the period. Not everything has changed however; it is still almost universally accepted that the Romantic mindset and the literary works it produced were shaped, above all, by the French Revolution and the Industrial Revolution.

For Romanticism, the French Revolution was epoch-making. When the Bastille fell on 14 July 1789 and the French National Constituent Assembly issued its democratic, anti-monarchical *Declaration of the Rights of Man and Citizen* on 27 August of the same year, it seemed to the people of Great Britain, a mere 21 miles across the Channel, that a new dawn was on the horizon. For liberals and for many authors, artists, and intellectuals this dawn was a rosy one, promising not only greater equality and better government in France itself, but also the beginning of a thoroughgoing transformation of the world. Mary Robinson's "Ainsi Va Le Monde" (1791) provides a vivid sense of the degree to which a fervent faith in and enthusiasm for freedom knew no bounds in the breasts of many writers of the time:

> Hark! "Freedom" echoes thro' the vaulted skies.
> The goddess speaks! O mark the blest decree,—
> Tyrants Shall Fall—Triumphant Man Be Free!

Wordsworth, present in France during the early days of the Revolution, famously wrote of it later, "Bliss was it in that dawn to be alive!" while his friend and fellow poet Robert Southey recalled that "a visionary world seemed to open … [N]othing was dreamt of but regeneration of the human race." Mary Wollstonecraft, who had recently published *A Vindication of the Rights of Woman*, moved to Paris in 1792, inspired by revolutionary idealism. The Revolution became a central Romantic metaphor, as well as a central psychological influence on the first generation of Romantic writers.

The younger generation too, particularly Byron and Percy Shelley, were stirred by revolutionary fervor. What these poets hoped for, however, was a continuation of the *spirit* of the French Revolution. For, in actuality,

Wordsworth's new dawn soon darkened into a terrible thunderstorm and a rain of blood. In August of 1792, the leaders of the Revolution overthrew the French monarchy, and, a month later, a Parisian mob massacred more than a thousand prisoners whom they believed to be Royalist conspirators. Extremist Jacobins[1] now prevailed over more moderate Girondins,[2] and the Revolution turned into the Reign of Terror (1793–94). In January 1793, King Louis XVI went to the guillotine; Marie Antoinette followed him in October. France declared war on Britain in 1793, and Britain quickly reciprocated the declaration. As the Terror progressed under the guidance of Maximilien Robespierre, thousands of aristocrats, clergy, and alleged opponents of the Revolution were guillotined including, eventually, Robespierre himself. In 1794, France offered to support any and all revolutions abroad, and proceeded to invade its neighbors. In 1799, Napoleon had himself named First Consul for life, and, in 1804, he crowned himself Emperor. When he invaded the Iberian Peninsula in 1807, Britain intervened to aid the Spanish and Portuguese. The Napoleonic Wars, as these military conflicts came to be known, did not end until Napoleon was thoroughly routed at the Battle of Waterloo in 1815.

What had begun as a movement for democracy, then, had become a military dictatorship. Looking back from a distance of 24 years, Byron wrote, in *Childe Harold's Pilgrimage* (1812–18), that the French made themselves a fearful monument:

> The wreck of old opinions …
> … the veil they rent
> And what behind it lay all earth shall view.

---

[1] The term "Jacobin" was used throughout the Romantic period to denote those in sympathy with the radical, revolutionary ideals associated with the French Revolution. Those opposing the Revolution were termed "anti-Jacobins." The ideological differences between the radical Jacobins and the conservative anti-Jacobins were often played out in the novels of the late eighteenth and early nineteenth centuries.

[2] A loosely affiliated coalition of moderate republicans, the Girondins controlled the French Legislative Assembly from late 1791 to late 1792, when they were ousted by more radical politicians. Many Girondin leaders were summarily executed during the Reign of Terror.

William Heath, *The Battle of Waterloo* (detail), 1815. British infantrymen to the right are firing into the ranks of the French cavalry. The full battle involved approximately 75,000 French troops under Napoleon; the Duke of Wellington commanded an allied force of well over 100,000. The casualties totaled over 50,000—60 per cent of them French.

> But good with ill they also overthrew,
> Leaving but ruins, wherewith to rebuild
> Upon the same foundation, and renew
> Dungeons and thrones …   (*Childe Harold* 3.82)

The Revolution's promise of freedom died in a frenzy of oppression, destruction, violence, and imperialism, and many of Britain's intellectuals watched in horror, gradually turning from bold liberalism to a cautious conservatism they saw as both pragmatic and necessary. To use the political terminology that first developed out of the seating arrangements in the French National Constituent Assembly in 1789, they moved from the left of center to the right of center; Wordsworth, Coleridge, and Southey, all radical thinkers in their youth, were firm conservatives by the end of their lives. Others—such as Barbauld—remained politically on the left but became disillusioned, both by the course that revolution had taken in France and by the failure of the

British to embrace the principles of freedom. Barbauld surveyed what seemed to her a decadent and oppressive England in "Eighteen Hundred and Eleven" (1812)— "The worm is in thy core, thy glories pass away"—and Percy Shelley despaired in "England in 1819" (composed in 1819, but not published until 1839) at "Rulers who neither see nor feel nor know, / But leechlike to their fainting country cling."

The British government's response to the developments in France had been swift and repressive. In 1794, the right of habeas corpus—which required the state to show legitimate cause for imprisonment and to carry out trials in a timely manner—was suspended. As a result, those accused of crimes could be held for an indefinite period. In 1795, Parliament passed the Treasonable Practices Act, which made criticism of the government a crime; in the same year, it passed an act that limited the size of public meetings and the places in which they could be held. The Combination Acts of 1799 and

1800 forbade workers to associate for the purposes of collective bargaining. To enforce all these restrictive measures, the government set loose a herd of spies, many of whom acted as *agents provocateurs*, infiltrating liberal and radical groups and prompting them to commit criminal acts they otherwise might not have committed. In at least one important case, that of the Cato Street Conspiracy of 1820—a scheme to murder cabinet ministers and stage a government coup—these government agents first urged on and then exposed conspirators who were punished with hanging or with transportation to Australia. (In Scotland and Ireland, authoritarianism could be even more severe.)

If the French Revolution and the 22 years of war with France that followed produced ruinous government authoritarianism, they also acted to create for the first time a widespread sense—among the English, at least—that England, Wales, Scotland and, to a lesser extent, Ireland, formed one cohesive nation: Great Britain. Scotland had been linked to England by the Union of 1707, while union with Ireland, which had been firmly under English control since the time of Cromwell, was made official with the Acts of Union in 1800. (This sense of England, Scotland, Wales, and Ireland forming a cohesive whole was rarely if ever to be found in many areas of Scotland, Wales, or Ireland—of which more will be said below.) The wars with France allowed the populace to see themselves as leading a larger body defending liberty and freedom (even if that liberty and freedom were now, ironically, defined by a conservative authoritarian mind-set). At the same time, the wars raised very real threats of invasion—there were scares in 1778, 1796–98, and 1803, and Wales was actually invaded in a very modest fashion in 1797 (though the drama of that episode quickly dissolved into farce).

The threats from without acted to foster cohesion within. Foreign travel was out of the question for all but the very rich or the very brave; interest among the English in all things British rose. Sir Walter Scott's collection of folk-songs and ballads, *Minstrelsy of the Scottish Border* (1802–03); Thomas Moore's *Irish Melodies* (1807–34); and Felicia Hemans's *Welsh Melodies* (1822) gave their readers a sense of a rich past,

T.W. Huffram, *Theobald Wolfe Tone*, date unknown. Tone is shown in French uniform.

James Gillray, *United Irishmen in Training*, 1798. The famous English caricaturist here portrays the Irish as cruel buffoons; they are assaulting a British uniform stuffed with straw.

while simultaneously celebrating the blend of cultures that went into making up Great Britain. Regional poets such as Robert Burns and John Clare gave proud voice

Thomas Girtin, *Westminster from Lambeth*, c. 1800. Girtin's watercolor was one of a series of sketches for a panorama of London (now lost).

to local cultures, so that the individual nations which made up the one great nation were simultaneously celebrated for their respective traditions and recognized as within the British fold. Long poetical works such as John Thelwall's *The Hope of Albion; or Edwin of Northumbria* (1801) expanded the sense of an epic British mythology, while collections such as Hemans's *Tales and Historic Scenes* (1819), a celebration of military valor, fostered a sense of pride in present-day accomplishments.

The history of the very words *English* and *British* offers another indication of the change. Until 1780 the word *English* appeared in English books at least three times as often as did the word *British*; by 1800 that ratio had slipped to 2:1, and by 1840 it had slipped to 1.5:1. (Not until just after the Second World War did the two terms begin to be used with roughly the same frequency.)

The sense of a larger Britain with England at its center further strengthened the English belief that England itself was particularly, even divinely, favored. Such notions were perhaps given their most memorable, if also most ambivalent, expression in the opening to William Blake's "Preface" to *Milton* (1804), in which ancient England is linked with Christ:

> And did those feet in ancient time
> Walk upon England's mountains green?
> And was the Holy Lamb of God
> On England's pleasant pastures seen?
> And did the countenance divine
> Shine forth upon our clouded hills?[1]

Although Blake leaves it up to his reader to determine whether the answers to these rhetorical questions are yes or no, the stanza that follows explicitly figures England as a land worthy of being the new Jerusalem (if only sometime in the future):

---

[1] The opening two stanzas of this poem (a total of 16 lines) were set to music by Charles H.H. Parry in 1916; under the title "Jerusalem," these verses have become an unofficial national anthem for the English.

I will not cease from mental fight,
Nor shall my sword sleep in my hand,
Till we have built Jerusalem
In England's green and pleasant land.

Between these invocations of the divine in England, however, Blake inserts an insidious question, one that began to plague English writers and citizens more and more as the Romantic period progressed: "was Jerusalem builded here / Among these dark Satanic mills?" The phrase "dark Satanic mills" has become the most famous description of the force at the center of the Industrial Revolution. Even as the French Revolution changed the consciousness of the British people, this other revolution in their own country had as much impact on them as did any conflagration abroad.

In the sixteenth and seventeenth centuries, the British Isles, and England in particular, had begun to undergo extensive changes in economic structure. The pace of change increased dramatically as the eighteenth century progressed. From being a largely rural nation with a largely agricultural economy, Britain became an urban nation with an economy based in manufacturing. James Watt's refinement of the steam engine and James Hargreaves's invention of the Spinning Jenny (a machine that allowed cotton to be spun on several spindles simultaneously) were only the most famous of a host of changes that produced a boom in industrialization. Factories sprang up in what had once been countryside, and the populations of towns and cities, particularly those associated with manufacture, swelled. At the beginning of the 1770s, about a quarter of England's population lived in urban centers, but by 1801 that proportion had risen to one-third, and by the 1840s half of the English population resided in cities. In 1750, the total English population was roughly 5.5 million; by the time of the first census in 1800, it had grown to 8 million, while the population of Scotland and Ireland totaled more than 6.5 million. By 1831, the total population of Great Britain was thus approximately 14 million. This increase fueled the Industrial Revolution from both ends, supplying more consumers eager to acquire goods and more bodies to work in factories that produced those goods.

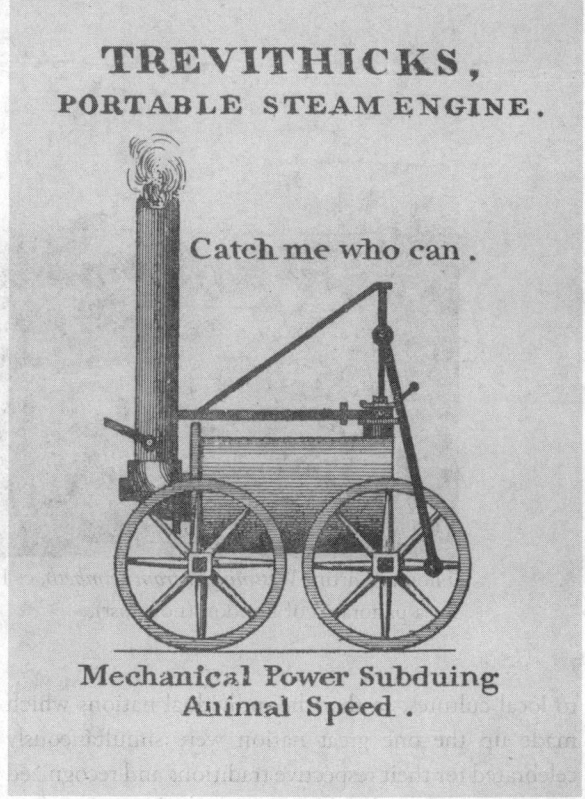

Illustration of an early locomotive engine, 1808.

Industrialization also contributed to an important shift in the country's social structure. The paradigm of classes and ranks that placed the nobility at the top with everyone else keeping to their places beneath had begun to change as early as the seventeenth century, with those involved in business and commerce growing wealthy enough to exert power of their own. The process was greatly accelerated in the late eighteenth and early nineteenth centuries as more and more industrialists and business owners—the majority of whom were men, and a disproportionate number of whom were non-conformist[1]—amassed larger and larger fortunes. Still, the road that led from newly acquired wealth to social acceptance remained a long and circuitous one. An inherited

---

[1] The term *non-conformist* was applied to Methodists, Baptists, Quakers, and others whose religious beliefs did not accord with the doctrines of the established church—the Church of England.

George and I.R. Cruikshank, *Sporting a Toe at Almacks*, 1821. Many clubs were restricted to men; Almack's was an exclusive London club controlled by a group of society women. During "the season" a fashionable ball was held at Almack's every week.

fortune stemming from longstanding ownership of large amounts of land—and the rents thereby produced—remained the most respectable form of wealth. To possess a good deal of money as a result not of belonging to the "landed gentry" but rather of having amassed it through commercial activity was considered more than faintly disreputable. It might take two or three generations before the taint of anyone in the family having been "in trade" (a term applied to industrialists as much as to tradespeople) was removed, and the source of the family fortune forgotten. The social nuances involved in such transitions were vividly captured in the novels of Jane Austen; here, for example, is her description of the Bingley sisters in *Pride and Prejudice* (1813):

They were rather handsome, had been educated in one of the first private seminaries in town, had a fortune of twenty thousand pounds, were in the habit of spending more than they ought, and of associating with people of rank; and were therefore in every respect entitled to think well of themselves, and meanly of others. They were of a respectable family in the north of England; a circumstance more deeply impressed on their memories than that their brother's fortune and their own had been acquired by trade.

Fine gradations of respectability were attached to every occupation, with social position often at odds with financial circumstances. Members of the clergy and their families, for instance, though sometimes impecunious, were generally respected; whether members of the gentry or born into the working class, they often moved in elevated social circles. Physicians, defined as those medical men who had a degree from a university, could sometimes move in the "best circles" in a community, although apothecaries and surgeons, who gained their knowledge through apprenticeship, could not.

The Romantic literary world reflected the increased social mobility possible during the period. John Keats, for example, was the son of a stable keeper who had increased his financial standing by marrying the daughter of the stable owner. Keats trained as a surgeon-apothecary (a job that combined the duties of a present-day pharmacist, general practitioner, and surgeon), but, at the age of 18, he came into an inheritance and was able to devote himself entirely to literature. He wrote to a friend that he thought he would "be among the English poets" after his death, and, as it turned out, no social barriers could prevent that from occurring. Similarly, Samuel Taylor Coleridge, a parson's son who attended a London charity school as a child, ended his life lauded and respected as "The Sage of Highgate."

The Industrial Revolution may have increased social mobility; it certainly allowed goods to be produced more efficiently. But it also devastated large portions of England's underclasses, the agricultural laborers and peasants who had benefited, however slightly, from the land-based economy that was passing away. In Wordsworth's "Tintern Abbey" (1798), the reference to "vagrant dwellers in the houseless woods" describes a very real phenomenon. In the late eighteenth and early nineteenth centuries, a series of Enclosure Acts resulted in the continued conversion of formerly common land into large, privately held farms.[1] To be fair, enclosures did often result in an increase in agricultural production, but they also often spelled ruin for thousands of small farmers. Large landholders benefited from their enlarged acreage, but many of those who had heretofore been able to eke out a living from a tiny patch of land and sell their modest surpluses now lost all ability to support themselves. These smallholders and their families were forced either to labor for others for meager wages, to migrate to the city and enter the manufacturing workforce, or to turn to begging or thievery. Poor harvests in 1794–95, 1799–1800, and 1810–11 wors-

ened the plight of the rural poor even further. The proliferation of vandals, vagrants, and beggars in the writing of this era thus reflected a growing social reality.

The leading literary figures of the day were, for the most part, sympathetic to the plight of the poor in a time of growing inequity, but, beyond that, they held widely divergent attitudes concerning these developments, and concerning the commoners themselves. Anna Laetitia Barbauld was one writer who sought to ameliorate the inequities that had become so characteristic of English life; she condemned the power relations involved, harshly criticizing the privileged, and took a view of commoners that saw them as prey to vice as a result of the circumstances in which they had been placed through economic hardship and lack of education. As she wrote in *Thoughts on the Inequality of Conditions* (1800),

Power enables the indolent and the useless not only to retain, but to add to their possessions, by taking from the industrious the natural reward of their labour, and applying it to their own use. … It is not sufficiently considered how many virtues depend upon comfort, and cleanliness, and decent apparel. Destroy dirt and misery, and you will destroy at once a great many vices.

It is the approach of William Wordsworth, however, that has more often been taken to characterize British Romanticism. That approach posits nature as central to human experience—nature in its simpler or wilder forms, not distorted by human artifice. Wordsworth was interested not only in "the beautiful and permanent forms of nature" but also in the ways in which human passions are excited by these forms; he describes "the mind" (rather than nature) as "My haunt, and the main region of my song." He was vitally interested, too, in the minds of those whom he saw as most closely connected to the natural world. If Barbauld's focus was very largely on the struggle to ameliorate conditions for the poor, Wordsworth's was more on the worth inherent in the hearts and minds of rural common folk—and on the associated poetic value. In the same year as Barbauld wrote her *Thoughts on the Inequality of Conditions*,

---

[1] The process of enclosure was not new; it had been occurring since the late Middle Ages, in response to population pressures and as Britain was transformed first into a largely mercantile economy and then into an industrial society.

Wordsworth expressed his ideals in the 1800 "Preface" to *Lyrical Ballads*:

> The principal object, then, proposed in these Poems was to choose incidents and situations from common life. … Humble and rustic life was generally chosen, because, in that condition, the essential passions of the heart find a better soil in which they can attain their maturity, are less under restraint, and speak a plainer and more emphatic language; because in that condition of life our elementary feelings coexist in a state of greater simplicity, and, consequently, may be more accurately contemplated, and more forcibly communicated; because the manners of rural life germinate from those elementary feelings, and, from the necessary character of rural occupations, are more easily comprehended, and are more durable; and, lastly, because in that condition the passions of men are incorporated with the beautiful and permanent forms of nature.

Poems such as "Michael," "The Ruined Cottage," "The Idiot Boy," and "Resolution and Independence," represent Wordsworth's attempt to put those ideals into practice. In "Resolution and Independence," the poet encounters an old, poor, itinerant leech-gatherer, ending the poem by admiring "In that decrepit Man so firm a mind." Whereas Barbauld regarded theft as a justifiable response to the oppression of extreme poverty in an iniquitous social system, Wordsworth pays homage to the old leech-gatherer for earning an "honest maintenance" despite the "many hardships" he must endure.

If the rural working-poor fared badly during these years, life for the workers in the cities and the unemployed-poor was just as bad. In 1815, at the instigation of large land holders, who stood to benefit from high prices for grain, the government passed the Corn Laws to institute a substantial tariff on imports of grain from foreign countries, making such imports much more expensive.[1] The tariff was effective in protecting British grain producers; at the same time, it inflated the price of bread and other foodstuffs for the consumer. The poor in the cities suffered particularly,

and, from 1815 until the Corn Laws were finally repealed in 1845, they remained a lightning rod for political dissent.

Had conditions for the urban poor been better in other respects, the Corn Laws might have had less impact. The British government, however, assured by Adam Smith's highly influential work of economic philosophy, *The Wealth of Nations* (1776), that the best way to encourage national economic success was to leave businesses free to grow without hindrance, for the most part adopted a laissez-faire[2] approach to regulating treatment of employees and working conditions during this period. In practice, "laissez-faire" ultimately meant shifts of as much as 15 hours at a stretch, often for very young children. Wages were kept as low as manufacturers could manage and injuries were common; children were the preferred workers for clearing jams in mechanized looms, for example, and the frequent result was the loss of the tiny fingers and hands that made them ideal for the job. Workers' health was often ruined by unsanitary working and living conditions—employers often owned not only the factories, but the slums in which their workers lived—and by unfettered pollution.

It is often assumed that the worst extremes of the Industrial Revolution in Britain occurred during the Victorian era, but, by the time Victoria came to the throne, Parliament had already been pressed to take a succession of measures to restrict the abuse of children: the largely ineffectual Health and Morals of Apprentices Act (1802), the Regulation of Cotton Mills and Factories Act (1819), and the Act to Regulate the Labour of Children and Young Persons in the Mills and Factories of the United Kingdom (1833). Even after the passage of this last, children as young as nine could be forced to work nine-hour days, and thirteen-year-olds to work twelve-hour days; still, this represented a degree of improvement from the late eighteenth and early nineteenth centuries. Robert Blincoe, for example, an orphan raised in a London workhouse and transported in 1799, at the age of seven, to work in the Lowdham Mill near Nottingham, described his life at the mill to John Brown in 1822:

---

[1] In Britain, corn denotes grain, most commonly wheat; what North Americans call corn is referred to in Britain as maize.

[2] French: allow to do.

Blincoe heard the burring sound [of the machinery] before he reached the portals and smelt the fumes of the oil with which the axles of twenty-thousand wheels and spindles were bathed the moment he entered the doors. The noise appalled him, and the stench seemed intolerable. It was the custom at Lowdham Mills, as it is in most water mills, to make the apprentices work up lost time [i.e., time when the machines had been unable to run during regular working hours], by working over hours. ... When children of seven years of age had to work fourteen hours every day in the week, Sundays excepted, any addition was severely felt. ... Almost from the first hour [Blincoe] entered the Mill, till he arrived at a state of manhood, it was one continual round of cruel and arbitrary punishment. ... I asked him if he could state the average number of times in which he might safely say he had suffered corporal punishment in a week. His answer invariably was, that his punishments were so various and so frequent, it was impossible to state with anything approaching to accuracy. ... Supper consisted of milk-porridge, of a very blue complexion [together with] bread partly made of rye—very black, and so soft they could scarcely swallow it, as it stuck like bird-lime to their teeth.

If the government addressed such outrages only with reluctance—sometimes parliamentary committees looking into allegations would not hear any direct testimony from the workers—many citizens found them harder to ignore. Demonstrations of popular dissatisfaction were frequent and took various forms. Luddites, followers of the imaginary "General Ned Ludd," attacked and broke machinery during the years 1811–16, sometimes to force concessions from their employers but sometimes simply to express their dissatisfaction with creeping mechanization. After the bad harvests and the passage of the Corn Laws in 1815, food riots occurred across the country. Coercion Acts were passed in 1817 to try to stifle dissent, but they provoked strong antagonism, and both in London and in parts of Scotland some republican groups advocated revolution. Throughout the 1820s, farm workers staged violent protests, culminating in mass barn-burnings in 1830. Perhaps the most famous popular uprising was the 1819 gathering of

A

MEMOIR

OF

ROBERT BLINCOE,

An Orphan Boy;

SENT FROM THE WORKHOUSE OF ST. PANCRAS, LONDON,

AT SEVEN YEARS OF AGE,

TO ENDURE

THE HORRORS OF A COTTON-MILL,

THROUGH HIS INFANCY AND YOUTH.

WITH A MINUTE DETAIL OF HIS SUFFERINGS.

BEING

THE FIRST MEMOIR OF THE KIND PUBLISHED.

BY JOHN BROWN.

London:

PRINTED AND PUBLISHED BY RICHARD CARLILE,
62, FLEET STREET.

Price One Shilling.

Title page, *A Memoir of Robert Blincoe*, first published in 1828, re-issued in 1832. Demonstrations in 1832 and 1833 for factory reform frequently cited the evidence of factory conditions that he had provided, and Blincoe testified before the Royal Commission that investigated the issue of child labor in 1833.

roughly 80,000 mill workers at St. Peter's Field, near Manchester. A peaceful demonstration that ended with an address to the crowd by Henry Hunt,[1] this gathering so alarmed the local gentry that they sent drunken, armed militiamen to break it up and arrest Hunt. The militiamen attacked the crowd with their sabers when it jeered them, and the ensuing melee left 11 dead—including one trampled child—and more than 400 injured, many from saber wounds.

---

[1] Known as the "Orator," Hunt (1773–1835) was a radical speaker and agitator, renowned for his advocacy of parliamentary reform and the abolition of the Corn Laws.

"Peterloo," as it came to be dubbed by the radical press, in reference to the British victory at Waterloo four years earlier, was a seminal event in nineteenth-century politics and economics. Parliament did nothing to relieve the sufferings of these poor or the hundreds of thousands like them, instead strengthening its repressive powers by passing the Six Acts at the end of 1819. These Acts made it a crime to demonstrate; gave magistrates the power to enter private homes to search for weapons; outlawed meetings of more than 50 people unless all th[...] s of the parish in w[...] ectively curtailing [...] ed the guidelines [...] nous or treasonous [...] thereby cutting the [...] radical newspaper[...]

[handwritten annotation: • English gov. out of tune with lower classes in this period (Tories from 1783 – 1830) · 6 acts]

POLITICAL PARTIES AND ROYAL ALLEGIANCES

For most of this period, the upheavals among the lower classes found little reflection in the English government, where the Tories held sway from 1783 to 1830, with only one short interruption. The Tories were the conservative party: they saw themselves as upholders of law and tradition, determined to preserve the prevailing political and social order. From 1793 to 1801, and again from 1804 to 1806, the Tories—and the country—were led by Prime Minister William Pitt, whose fiscal restraint and willingness to suppress political protest (sometimes with open brutality) made him a hero to some and a villain to many others. After Pitt died in office in 1806, certainly of overwork and probably of alcoholism—his last words were, depending on the source, either, "Oh, my country! how I leave my country!" or "I think I could eat one of Bellamy's veal pies"—the Tories continued in power, on their own or in coalition, until 1830.

The Whigs, who remained the party of opposition during this time, presented themselves against the Tories as advocates of greater civil and religious liberty. In reality, neither party would have been called "Liberals" or "Democrats" by today's standards, but the Whigs did advocate the abolition of the slave trade, Catholic emancipation (which would allow greater political participation to Catholics, heretofore barred from a role in government), and parliamentary reform. From 1782 to 1806, the leader of the Whigs was the charismatic Charles James Fox, gambler, gourmand, and political colossus, whose political machinations made him as many enemies as friends. Not until 1806, a year after Fox's death, would the Whigs participate in government—and then for only a relatively short period, as part of a coalition. They would not gain power in their own right until 1830. They were then at last able to pass the Reform Act of 1832 (also known as the Great Reform Act), which extended voting rights to a broader spectrum of propertied males,[2] redistributed parliamentary seats, and brought significantly fairer political representation.

While the politicians plotted and schemed, the British royal family suffered its own difficulties. George III, who had ascended the throne in 1760, embodied Toryism both politically and personally; traditionalist, ponderous, and domestic, he produced a large family, embraced conservative politics, and allegedly liked to wander the countryside incognito, chatting with farmers. In 1788, however, he suffered a bout of mental illness that lasted until early 1789. This illness, now believed to be the result of the hereditary blood disease porphyria, reappeared in 1810, leaving him permanently insane. In 1811, when it became apparent that the king would not recover, his eldest son was declared regent.

Monarchs of the House of Hanover traditionally clashed with their eldest sons, and George III and the prince who would become George IV were no different. The regent was a stark contrast to his thrifty father; in

---

[1] The Six Acts ultimately proved repugnant to certain members of the liberal Whig party—who subsequently became politically powerful—and led to the liberal Reform Act of 1832. Thus, the long-term result of the massacre was modest relief from the extraordinarily repressive measures it had spawned.

[2] The changes are estimated to have altered the composition of the electorate to approximately one in seven males from fewer than one in ten.

Sir Thomas Lawrence, *The Prince Regent in Profile*, c. 1814. The prince knighted Lawrence, the leading English portraitist of the day, in 1815, saying that he was "proud in conferring a mark of his favour on one who had raised the character of British art in the estimation of all Europe."

Sir _____ _____ zabeth of Br_____

1787, when he was 25, his debts totaled more than £160,000 (equivalent to about £8,000,000 today). He lived with a Roman Catholic mistress whom he later married, secretly and unconstitutionally, before abandoning her for a series of other mistresses. Later, to secure relief from debts, he married his cousin Caroline of Brunswick, a woman he found so instantly and completely loathsome that his first words upon seeing her were "I am not well; pray get me a glass of brandy." Although they did manage to produce one daughter, Charlotte, who later died in childbirth, the prince and his wife never lived together, and his attempt to divorce her after his accession in 1820 was one of the great scandals of the period.

George IV was not without redeeming virtues; notably, he was a keen patron of the arts, particularly architecture. In addition to a magnificent pavilion in Brighton, he and his architects built Trafalgar Square, modified and improved Buckingham House into Buckingham Palace, and created parks, streets, and crescents throughout London. He was an enthusiastic reader and promoter of literature, as well as a generous patron of the sciences, establishing several fellowships and prizes. Nonetheless, the prince became a figure of increasing public contempt. Leigh Hunt described him as "a libertine head over heels in debt and disgrace, a despiser of domestic ties"; Percy Shelley called him, in prose, an "overgrown bantling [infant]," and, in poetry, "the dregs of [his] dull race." When he died in 1830, *The Times* wrote, "There never was an individual less regretted by his fellow creatures than this dead King."

IMPERIAL EXPANSION

Even as Britain was experiencing its own internal power struggles and upheavals, the nation was expanding its presence around the globe. Throughout the first half of the nineteenth century, Britain was well on its way to forging the empire that would reach full flower in the Victorian period. The East India Company, founded by a group of London merchants in 1600, controlled most of eastern India by 1765, and thereafter continued to extend its administrative and governmental control over the sub-continent. British interest in China began in the late eighteenth century, when Britain began to import the tea that would soon become a staple of the British table, and that interest rose throughout the 1800s. Increased contact with—and domination of—various parts of the Far East led to increased fascination with its cultures, a fascination widely reflected in literature. "Eastern" influence pervades the prose and poetry of this period, from William Beckford's novel *The History of the Caliph Vathek* (1786), to Byron's *Eastern Tales* (1813–14), to Percy Shelley's *Alastor* (1816), where the protagonist makes his way

> through Arabie
> And Persia, and the wild Carmanian waste,
> And o'er the aerial mountains which pour down
> Indus and Oxus from their icy caves,
> In joy and exultation [he] held his icy way,
> Till in the vale of Cashmire ...
>   he stretched
> His languid limbs.

Wearing her India cotton frock, sipping her tea from Canton, coffee from Yemen, or chocolate from Mexico, the English consumer of the Romantic period felt the influence of imperial expansion everywhere, from the commodities she purchased to the pages she turned.

But if the British Empire brought rewards to the nation's citizens, it all too often entailed exploitation and horror in the colonies themselves. Chief amongst these was the slavery that fueled the economy of the British West Indies. The mass of sugar required to sweeten Britain's tea, coffee, and chocolate was culti-vated, cut, and processed on these islands by enslaved people who worked under inhuman conditions until they literally wore out—at which point their white masters simply purchased fresh replacements. Over the course of the eighteenth century, British slavers transported some three million enslaved people to the West Indies and other agricultural colonies; the economic success of the port towns Bristol and Liverpool was based in large part on the important part they played in the English slave trade—and the trade in sugar from plantations that relied on the labor of enslaved people.[1]

Arguably the strongest resistance to slavery in the West Indies came from the enslaved people themselves. The British invaded the formerly French island of Saint-Domingue in 1793 in order to aid in the suppression of an uprising by enslaved people led by Toussaint Louverture, but they withdrew five years later, having sent more troops to the West Indies over that period than they had sent to America during the War of Independence. When a subsequent effort by Napoleon also failed, the formerly enslaved people founded the Republic of Haiti in 1804, sending the message that emancipation was inevitable.

Emancipation was also spurred by a widespread and effective protest movement within Britain. Between 1787, when protests first began, and 1791, abolitionists gathered 500 petitions against slavery from across Britain. In all some 400,000 signatures were collected; this was Britain's first large-scale petition campaign. The abolitionist movement attracted support from Evangelicals, from Whig politicians, and from radicals, and has been described as the first British political movement in the modern sense. The leading figures in the movement were abolitionists Thomas Clarkson, Granville Sharp, and William Wilberforce, but it also drew considerable support from the poets of the day, among them William Cowper, Hannah More, William Blake, Mary Robinson, Anna Laetitia Barbauld, and Ann Yearsley (whose *A Poem on the Inhumanity of the Slave Trade* [1788] inveighed against the very business that supported her home town of Bristol).

---

[1] At the start of the American Revolution, British imports from the largest sugar plantation center, Jamaica, were worth five times more than British imports from the Thirteen Colonies.

James Gillray, *Fashionable Contrasts, or the Duchess' Little Shoe Yielding to the Magnitude of the Duke's Foot*, 1792. At the time this print was published the press had been fawning over Princess Frederica Charlotte Ulrica Catherina, who had just married Frederick Augustus, Duke of York; the daintiness of her feet had been particularly praised.

James Gillray, *The Plum Pudding in Danger*, 1805. Napoleon and British Prime Minister William Pitt are shown carving up the globe, with Napoleon skewering Europe and Pitt helping himself to the ocean. (1805 saw both the Battle of Trafalgar, at which the British under Lord Nelson established dominance at sea, and the Battle of Austerlitz, at which Napoleon defeated Russian and Austrian armies to cement his control of the continent.)

Sir Charles D'Oyly, *The Emporium of Taylor & Co. in Calcutta*, c. 1825–28.

Central to the literature of the abolitionist movement were books written by formerly enslaved people, such as Olaudah Equiano and Mary Prince, which laid out plainly the horrors of enslavement and openly sought sympathy and fellow-feeling from readers. In his autobiography, *The Interesting Narrative of the Life of Olaudah Equiano* (1786), Equiano described conditions both in the West Indies and in America. As he observed with telling effect, the system bred degradation for "free negroes" as well as for enslaved people:

I have often seen slaves, particularly those who were meagre, in different islands, put into scales and weighed; and then sold from three pence to six pence to nine pence a pound. My master, however, whose humanity was shocked at this mode, used to sell by the lump. And at or after a sale it was not uncommon to see negroes taken from their wives, wives taken from their husbands, and children from their parents, and sent off to other islands, and wherever else their merciless lords chose, and probably never more during life to see each other! …

[Free negroes] live in constant alarm for their liberty; and even this is but nominal, for they are universally insulted and plundered without the possibility of redress; for such is the equity of West Indian laws, that no free negro's evidence will be admitted in their courts of justice.

Such accounts, coupled with a determined and prolonged campaign and with the effects of the growth of the Asian sugar trade, led to the abolition of the slave trade in 1806–07, and (following another uprising, this time in Jamaica in 1831–32) to an act in 1833 that provided for the full abolition of slavery. The persecution of blacks by whites, however, continued both in the West Indies and throughout the British Empire.

Several of the leading names of English Romantic poetry are noticeably absent from the list of writers who wrote frequently and explicitly in favor of abolition. Wordsworth,[1] Coleridge, Byron, Percy Shelley, and Keats were in general all sympathetic to the aims of the abolitionist movement, and Coleridge in particular spoke out strongly both against slavery itself and against the maintenance of the slave trade, memorably writing that "a slave is a person perverted into a thing," and slavery not so much "a deviation from justice as an absolute subversion of all morality." (Coleridge's views regarding slavery became significantly more conservative, however, later in his life.) It has been plausibly suggested that some major works of Romantic poetry (notably Coleridge's "The Rime of the Ancient Mariner" [1798] and Keats's "Lamia" [1819]) may usefully be read in relation to the slave trade. But directly pressing for the abolition of slavery through verse in the manner of Cowper, Robinson, and Yearsley was never a significant part of these poets' agendas.

SCOTLAND, IRELAND, WALES

The Jacobite Rising of 1745 and the 1746 Battle of Culloden that put an end to it cast a shadow over Scotland well into the nineteenth century. The defeat of the Scottish rebels by the English (led with brutal efficiency by the Duke of Cumberland) initiated a long period of repression and of social and economic upheaval. Thousands who had been active in the Jacobite uprising were killed either during the battle or shortly thereafter (those who lay wounded on the battlefield were bayonetted to death rather than taken prisoner); many more died in prison, and many others were transported to colonies overseas to work as servants. Various new laws placed restrictions on "highland dress," on the carrying of arms, and on public gather-

ings, and the use of Gaelic was discouraged even more thoroughly than it had been previously. Some of these cultural restrictions were repealed in the 1780s, but the structural changes to the legal and economic systems that were introduced following the crushing of the rebellion were permanent. The powers of the Highland chieftains were drastically curtailed, and the clan system itself severely undermined—as was the old system of tenant farming. That system had been a largely cooperative one under which strips of farming land were rotated from one tenant to another (so as to ensure fairness), and tenants had shared access to grazing land; multiple tenants worked under the management of supervisors known as tucksmen. Under the new system the tucksmen were gradually eliminated—and so too were many of the tenants; evictions became common, and farms became larger (and fewer in number), with much of the land cleared not for common use but for the grazing of herds under single ownership. Those tenants who remained became crofters holding small individual plots; many others left for the cities—or for North America. English interventions created tremendous poverty among those displaced by "the clearances"; more broadly, the traditions of Highland Scotland that had formed the guiding principles of economic and social life were reduced by the English to little more than cultural trappings.

The great irony here is that (as touched on above), at the very point at which the English had succeeded in destroying much of the Gaelic culture of Highland Scotland, the English began to display an unprecedented interest in Scottish traditional culture. They embraced with tremendous enthusiasm the sort of romanticized portrayal of Highland culture generally (and of the doomed rebellion of '45 in particular) that Sir Walter Scott presented. In his postscript to *Waverley* (1814), Scott described "the present people of Scotland" as "a class of beings as different from their grandfathers as the existing English are from those of Queen Elizabeth's time." Glossing over the extent of British oppression, he described the changes time had wrought as "steadily and rapidly progressive" while yet lamenting the fading away of those

---

[1] In *The Prelude*, Wordsworth admits that in the 1790s "this particular strife had wanted power / To rivet my affections." He did write two sonnets (one to Clarkson, one to Toussaint Louverture) in 1807, the year in which abolition of the slave trade was accomplished.

who still cherished a lingering, though hopeless, attachment to the house of Stewart. This race has almost entirely vanished from the land, and with it … many living examples of … attachment to the principles of loyalty which they received from their fathers, and of old Scottish faith, hospitality, worth, and honour.

It was my accidental lot, though not born a Highlander (which may be an apology for much bad Gaelic) to reside, during my childhood and youth, among persons of the above description; and now, for the purpose of preserving some of the ancient manners of which I have witnessed the almost total extinction, I have embodied in imaginary scenes, and ascribed to fictitious characters, a part of the incidents which I then received from those who were actors in them. Indeed, the most romantic parts of the narrative are precisely those which have a foundation in fact.

The culture romanticized by Scott and so many others was primarily that of Gaelic-speaking Highland Scotland, just as the socio-economic system that had been largely destroyed by the English was that of Highland Scotland. Scots-speaking and English-speaking Lowland Scotland was a different story—far less romanticized, far more connected to English social, intellectual, and economic life, and far less oppressed.

Economically, Scottish inventors and engineers (most prominent among them James Watt, famous for his steam engine) made highly significant contributions to the industrialization of Britain. Scottish cities became world leaders in industries such as ship-building and engine-making. Politically too, Scots were often highly influential. Most notably, Henry Brougham played a key role in reforming the British legal system and in securing passage of the Reform Bill of 1832.

Intellectually, authors from the Scottish Lowlands—first Robert Burns, writing both in Scots and in English, and later Walter Scott—had arguably as great an impact on the English literary world as they did on that of Scotland. So too did two Scottish-based journals. The *Edinburgh Review*, revived by Francis Jeffrey and others in 1802, quickly became the most interesting and most influential literary, cultural, and political journal of its

era. The *Edinburgh Review*'s political leanings were always towards the progressive side; as a counter, conservative book publisher William Blackwood in 1817 founded a rival journal (originally the *Edinburgh Monthly Magazine*, later *Blackwood's Edinburgh Magazine*). Though less "highbrow" than *The Edinburgh Review*, *Blackwood's* too became a significant force in the cultural and political life of England as well as Scotland.

If English oppression, rebellion, and displacement of the local populace from lands occupied for centuries are central threads of the history of Scotland in this period, they are if anything even more central to the history of Ireland. In the wake of Cromwell's seventeenth-century campaign of conquest, a great many Catholic landowners had been forced to forfeit their land so that it could be given to English Protestants. Further restrictions had followed; a series of early eighteenth-century laws made it illegal for Catholics to inherit or to purchase land—or to lease land for any period longer than 31 years. The laws had the desired effect: by 1778 no more than 7 per cent of Ireland was still owned by Catholics. In some cases those Catholics with the means to do so went abroad; more commonly those who had been displaced were effectively forced to become tenant farmers on lands now held by Protestant English or Anglo-Irish landowners—or else to face desperate poverty, even starvation.

Even for those who did become established as tenant farmers, starvation remained a real possibility through most of the eighteenth and nineteenth centuries. The import and export restrictions that enforced Irish economic dependence on England helped to keep prices high, and absentee landlords often failed to maintain their properties, increasing the level of hardship suffered by tenant farmers.

Throughout this period, then, the Protestant, English-speaking Anglo-Irish class dominated and exploited the much larger native Irish population, which spoke Irish Gaelic (often referred to as simply as *Irish*) and was predominantly Catholic. Confiscation of land and severe economic hardship for the Irish Catholic majority were only the most visible manifestations of deprivation at the hands of Protestant English and Anglo-Irish rule; a wide range of Penal Laws discriminated against

Catholics in myriad ways. By the 1790s some of the more extreme of the Penal Laws imposed in the seventeenth and eighteenth centuries had been weakened or repealed, but the weight of the system was still overwhelmingly oppressive for the Catholic majority. In such circumstances it can hardly be surprising that the possibility of rebellion was continually mooted.

The figure who became the leading voice for sweeping change was a Protestant rather than a Catholic; the young lawyer Wolfe Tone's idealistic vision was of an Ireland freed from the yoke of English control—an Ireland in which Catholic and Protestant (including not only Anglicans but also Presbyterians, who had, like the Catholics, been disenfranchised) could live side by side on an equal footing, and at peace. In 1791 Tone became one of the founders of the Society of United Irishmen, a group devoted to bringing those ideals to fruition. Within a few years the group—which by 1797 numbered over 300,000—began to contemplate seriously the possibility of an armed insurrection, and major rebellions were planned both in 1796 and 1798. The first of these foundered when bad weather threw off a planned invasion by a large French fleet; the second did indeed become a major rebellion, but the French provided far less support than the rebels had hoped for, and the uprising was suppressed in short order by government forces. Most of the leaders were captured and executed (Tone slit his own throat in prison before he could be hanged), but the spirit of rebellion was not extinguished; guerrilla attacks occurred periodically, and another rebellion briefly broke out in 1803.

Though Ireland had long been effectively under English control, the Irish had always been allowed a separate Parliament—and a new Irish constitution in 1782 had granted that Parliament a greater degree of autonomy than it had previously possessed. (Here it is important to remember that the "Irish" Parliament was in fact open only to the Anglo-Irish; the native Irish population was entirely excluded from political life.) Even before the rebellion of 1798 many in England felt that the Anglo-Irish were doing a poor job of running Ireland, and that English as well as Anglo-Irish interests would be better served by uniting Ireland with England—thereby bringing Ireland under the direct control of the English. The rebellion strengthened those feelings, and in 1800 Acts of Union were introduced in both the English and Irish Parliaments.

Whether or not to support the Acts was an issue that to some extent cut across established lines. Many in England who were essentially anti-Irish felt that "the Irish" had to be brought under tighter control, and that this was the way to do it. But supporters of the Acts of Union were also to be found among those who believed that a fair deal for Catholics in Ireland would come sooner from an English Parliament than an Anglo-Irish one, and that union would put an end to many of the trade restrictions and other forms of economic discrimination that had held back the Irish economy. In Ireland, these arguments were not as well received; the remnants of the United Irishmen were of course against greater English control—but so was the conservative Anglo-Irish aristocracy that the United Irishmen had so bitterly opposed in the rebellion. The idea was so unpopular among the Anglo-Irish elite that the English resorted to outright bribery in order to ensure that an Act of Union was passed by the Irish Parliament.

The union continued throughout the century to be highly unpopular in Ireland, and periodic attempts were made over the succeeding decades to have it repealed and a "Kingdom of Ireland" restored, such that Ireland would retain some control over its domestic affairs, with England continuing to act on its behalf in foreign affairs. (By 1840 the cause of bringing a measure of independence to Ireland had come to be known as "Home Rule.") Increasingly, however, such efforts were led not by Anglo-Irish leaders but by Catholic ones—most notably Daniel O'Connell. O'Connell achieved a partial success with the passage in 1829 of the Roman Catholic Relief Act, which repealed the last of the Penal Laws, allowing Catholics to be elected to Parliament and to be accorded the same civil rights as Protestants. There was, however, a catch; in conjunction with the Roman Catholic Relief Act, Parliament also passed the Parliamentary Elections (Ireland) Act, which effectively disenfranchised most of the Catholic population by quintupling the financial qualification required to qualify as a voter. (Prior to 1829 the vote was available to men owning or renting land worth two pounds; with the 1829 act the amount was increased to ten pounds.)

A success so qualified was still an enormous step forward; not for nothing did O'Connell come to be referred to as "The Liberator" and "The Emancipator." O'Connell was known too for the power of his rhetoric; aesthetically as well as politically, Ireland was for O'Connell (and for most other Irish people) a nation unto itself:

> Among the nations of the earth, Ireland stands number one in the physical strength of her sons and in the beauty and purity of her daughters. Ireland, land of my forefathers, how my mind expands, and my spirit walks abroad in something of majesty, when I contemplate the high qualities, inestimable virtues, and true purity and piety and religious fidelity of the inhabitants of your green fields.... Nature herself has written her character with the finest beauty in the verdant plains that surround us. Let any man run around the horizon with his eye, and tell me if created nature ever produced anything so green and so lovely, so undulating, so teeming with production.

Pride in Ireland may have remained strong through this era, but the Irish language was in steady decline. In 1800 a majority of the Irish peasantry were able to speak English, but most spoke Irish too; in western counties such as Kerry and Donegal many spoke only Irish. By 1850, it is estimated that those able to speak Irish were in the minority, and almost no one was a unilingual Irish-speaker.

Given the degree to which Irish was discouraged, it is hardly surprising that the Irish literature of the era is almost entirely in English. The novels of Maria Edgeworth and of Gerald Griffin; the novels, plays, and poems of John Banim (most notably the short fiction collected in the three volumes of *Tales of the O'Hara Family*); and the poems of Thomas Moore—all these were written in English. So too was *Pizarro*, the last work of Richard Brinsley Sheridan, an author usually associated with the literature of the previous era. The five-act play, first performed in 1799, became one of the most popular dramatic works of the entire nineteenth century. Set during the Spanish Conquest of Peru, *Pizarro* dramatizes English fears of invasion by Revolutionary France, but also engages critically with Britain's colonial exploits abroad.

Though the history and culture of Wales are arguably as distinct from that of England as are the histories and cultures of Scotland and Ireland, Wales experienced a period of relative calm through the late eighteenth and early nineteenth centuries. English control of Wales assumed softer forms in this era, without brutal oppression or violent rebellion. A majority appear to have been fluent in Welsh (education in Welsh was not prohibited), but as in Scotland and Ireland, published literature was almost exclusively written in English; indeed, the most significant Welsh writer of the period—Felicia Hemans[1]—became known in the later nineteenth and early twentieth centuries above all for her patriotic poems "Casabianca" and "The Homes of England." Other notable writers of the period include the poet Jane Cave and the poet and hymn-writer Ann Griffiths.

The greatest conflicts in Wales during the period were religious in nature. Methodism and Calvinism had grown in Wales throughout much of the eighteenth and early nineteenth centuries, and in 1811 the Welsh branch of the Church of England seceded from the larger body. By 1823 the Presbyterian Church of Wales had been formed—and various other forms of nonconforming Protestantism had also developed deep roots.

Like Scotland, Wales was far more affected by the Industrial Revolution in the late eighteenth and early nineteenth centuries than was Ireland. Mining—and in particular the coal mining industry—drove economic growth, especially in the cities of Cardiff and Swansea. Overall, the population of Wales increased from little more than a half million in the late eighteenth century to more than a million by 1840.

---

[1] Though Hemans was born in Liverpool and is sometimes treated as an English poet, she considered herself Welsh and spent most of her life in Wales.

LXX THE BROADVIEW ANTHOLOGY OF BRITISH LITERATURE

THE ROMANTIC MIND AND ITS LITERARY PRODUCTIONS

It is not surprising that in a world overwhelmingly concerned with change, revolution, and freedom the makers of literature should be similarly preoccupied; as has already been discussed, the French Revolution and its aftermath lent vital force to the Romantic impulse. That force, though, was not exerted on all the literary minds in the Romantic era with equal force or in quite the same direction. For several of the leading figures of English Romanticism, the freedom that animated the poetic imagination was only tangentially related to the collectivist enterprise that the revolution in France had represented. Instead, it was very much an *individual freedom*; the freeing of the individual mind and the individual soul took pride of place. Subjective experience and the role that it played in the individual's response to and experience of reality are dominant themes in the works of the Romantics. Wordsworth's "Ode: Intimations of Immortality" (1807) surveys what becomes of the "heaven-born freedom" with which every individual who enters the world is born. Percy Shelley's *Mont Blanc* (1817) is an extended exploration of power and creativity, and Keats's various odes continually express their author's fascination with the connection between physical experience and the individual human imagination. In Byron's work, subjectivity, creativity, and epistemological questing all find expression in a series of heroes for whom the power of the will is a central concern. The question of what it means to be an individual looms large in the works of all these authors.

Nature became a fulcrum in the balancing of subjective and objective in the Romantic construction of reality, and most of the period's leading writers were particularly preoccupied with the relationship between the natural world and the individual mind. Percy Shelley appealed to the wind, "Make me thy lyre, even as the forest is," and, in "Tintern Abbey," Wordsworth recognized nature as

> The anchor of my purest thoughts, the nurse,
> The guide, the guardian of my heart, and soul
> Of all my moral being.

This commingling of self and nature was, at least in part, an expression of the late eighteenth- and early nineteenth-century tendency to see the natural world in opposition to the human world. In the same poem, for example, Wordsworth describes himself as coming to nature

> more like a man
> Flying from something that he dreads than one
> Who sought the thing he loved.

Less frequently did poets of the Romantic period comment on the relationship between humans and nature as an objective reality. The focus was much more often on what non-human nature had to offer to the individual human soul than on how humans in aggregate were reshaping the natural world. Barbauld was unusual in observing and commenting on the latter clearly; in her grim survey of England in "Eighteen Hundred and Eleven," she described how

> Science and Art urge on the useful toil,
> New mould a climate and create the soil, …
> On yielding Nature urge their new demands,
> And ask not gifts but tribute at her hands.

Such clear-eyed observations of human manipulation of nature were few and far between.

The importance of the subjective sense of reality to the Romantic imagination also comes out clearly in the widespread fascination with the visions experienced in dreams, in nightmares, and other altered states. The question Keats poses at the end of "Ode to a Nightingale" (1819)—"Was it a vision, or a waking dream?"—is of a sort that occurs frequently in the literature of Romanticism. Among the many works of the period that touch on this theme are Coleridge's fragment "Kubla Khan" (which he claimed came to him during a drug-induced sleep); Keats's visionary *The Fall of Hyperion: A Dream*; Mary Shelley's *Frankenstein* (the story of which she claimed came to her in a "waking dream," and in which Victor Frankenstein acquires the habit of taking "every night a small quantity of laudanum" in order to "gain the rest necessary for the preservation of life"); and De Quincey's *Confessions of an English Opium-Eater*.

If thou would'st view fair Melrose aright,
Go visit it by the pale Moonlight...

Lay of the last Minstrel

J.M.W. Turner, *Melrose Abbey*, 1822. Courtesy of the Clark Art Institute, Williamstown, MA.

In the work of female writers of the period, interest in the individual and the mind often took different forms from those that engaged the interest of male writers. Many were concerned with education: Hannah More produced a series of Cheap Repository Tracts designed to enlighten the poor, while Maria Edgeworth gained fame as a children's writer and educationalist. Mary Wollstonecraft authored not only her famous *Vindication of the Rights of Woman*, but also *Thoughts on the Education of Daughters* (1787) and *The Female Reader* (1789). The Romantic period abounded in outspoken female writers who engaged with the issues of their day and sought to make a difference in their world. While Wollstonecraft would eventually be condemned for supposed sexual immorality, another more conservative group of educated women were derided as "Bluestockings," unnatural women who revealed their prudishness through their interest in intellectual pursuits. In their own day, the writings of these authors made little, if any, difference to the social, legal, and economic position of women, who remained little more than property in the eyes of the law for many more years. But over the longer term their impact was considerable; Wollstonecraft and the Bluestockings laid the intellectual foundations for the social and political progress of women that would slowly be achieved over the next 200 years and more.

It would be a mistake to think of the female writers of the Romantic period as solely concerned with women's rights and with the stereotypical "female arenas" of education and religion, however. Much of the writing by women in this period is as broadly engaged in the issues of the time as anything produced by their male counterparts, and many women writers exerted a significant shaping effect on the style and substance of Romantic literature. Mary Robinson, for example—famous first as an actress and mistress of the Prince of Wales, then as a successful poet and novelist—earned the admiration of both Wordsworth and Coleridge (who called her "an undoubted genius") and preceded them in the writing of poetry concerned with the poor and disenfranchised. In her influential *Elegiac Sonnets* (1784), Charlotte Smith modeled an approach to

emotional intensity and incisive self-examination that has come to be associated with the male Romantics—and did so more than a decade before the publication of *Lyrical Ballads*. Poet Felicia Hemans rivaled (indeed, perhaps surpassed) Byron in popularity. Playwright Joanna Baillie, famous for producing works that, as she put it, "delineate the progress of the higher passions in the human breast," was considered by Walter Scott to be "the best dramatic writer since the days of Shakespeare."

One area of common ground for almost all Romantic writers, male and female, was a strong interest in the "Imagination," the creative power by which an individual took the raw material of the physical world and transformed it into art. Although "Imagination" was recognized as being distinct from religious inspiration, descriptions of imaginative or poetic power often took on strong religious overtones, as in Blake's assertion that "One Power alone makes a Poet: Imagination, the Divine Vision." Coleridge, Blake, and Wordsworth were all deeply invested in the notion of the poet as *vates*, or prophet. And the imagination was seen as invested with moral as well as prophetic power, as the Romantics saw the realms of the aesthetic and the moral as being closely bound up with each other. Earlier ages, too, had linked the aesthetic and the moral, but had tended to see literature as expressing truths emanating from elsewhere and the ethical element of literature as inhering in its ability to illustrate virtues and vices and point out moral lessons. In contrast, leading Romantics tended to locate the moral aspects of literature—and life itself—largely in the imagination, and tended to see the imagination as embodying truth as well as morality. "The great instrument of moral good," wrote Percy Shelley in his *Defence of Poetry* (1821), "is the imagination," while Keats proclaimed that "what the imagination seizes as Beauty must be truth."[1] More broadly, a belief took root among poets—the most prominent male Romantic poets in particular—that the aesthetic and imaginative truths of

---

[1] Keats's notion of the value of "negative capability—that is, when a man is capable of being in uncertainties, mysteries, doubts, without any irritable reaching after fact and reason"—destabilizes in interesting ways the connections that he and other Romantics drew between morality and the imagination and between the imagination and truth.

poetry were possessed of a transcendent status, a status that placed such insights above the historical or scientific truths of the ordinary world.

Another opposition that animates the literature of the Romantic period is that between sense and sensibility—a tension with parallels to that between reason and emotion in the intellectual landscape of any age, but also one possessing elements particular to the late eighteenth and early nineteenth centuries. In this era, the terms "sentiment," "sentimentality," "sentimentalism," and "sensibility" were all widely used (and to some extent overlapped in meaning), but none was more used than "sensibility." The concept of "sensibility" entailed strong emotional responsiveness, with life and literary work animated by powerful feeling. Indeed, "sensibility" was frequently associated with emotional excess: when Jane Austen describes Marianne's "excess of sensibility" in *Sense and Sensibility* (1811), she is using the notion of sensibility in ways that would have been familiar to any late eighteenth- or early nineteenth-century reader:

> She was sensible and clever; but eager in every thing; her sorrows, her joys, could have no moderation. She was generous, amiable, interesting: she was every thing but prudent. The resemblance between her and her mother was strikingly great. Elinor saw, with concern, the excess of her sister's sensibility; but by Mrs. Dashwood it was valued and cherished.

It may well be that most educated Britons of the period privileged sense over sensibility in very much the way that Austen appears to do. But it is also true that the feelings associated with Romantic sensibility—above all, as they were expressed in poetry—became the defining passions of the age. And the poetry of sensibility carried ideological as well as aesthetic force; for a considerable period it stood in the vanguard of the movement for social and political change.

That is not to say that the distinction separating poets of sensibility from the rest was entirely clear; far from it. Rather in the way that competing factions today will sometimes each accuse the other of being controlled by their emotions rather than their reason, many in the late eighteenth century tried to situate sensibility in a

natural alliance with political views they opposed. Anti-Jacobins suggested there was a natural affinity between the supposed excesses of sensibility and those of political radicalism, while radicals often portrayed sensibility as associated with reactionary political views. In truth, the language of sensibility was used by both sides.

Also among the oppositions that occur throughout the literature of the Romantic period is that between the natural and the artificial, which was sometimes linked to the opposition between the original and the imitative. If "artificial" is taken simply to mean "human-made," of course, the distinction between the natural and the artificial is purely a matter of physical process. But "artificial" and "natural" as matters of taste and of style have more fluid meanings. As the culture of sentiment and of sensibility grew over the course of the eighteenth century, "artificial" came to be used less and less frequently to mean "displaying special art or skill" and more and more frequently to mean "contrived, shaped in a way not spontaneous or natural," or even "not expressive of reality." The divide between natural and artificial was felt to connect with that between "novelty" of thought and expression—"originality," as we would call it—and the "servility" of the stale or overly imitative. Whereas the Neoclassical poets had proudly imitated classical models, often devoting themselves to translating Classical works into English poetry, Romantic writers—and the leading Romantic poets in particular—had little interest in seeing the work of earlier eras as models to be imitated. They might admire the poets of earlier eras, they might be inspired by them—by Shakespeare and by Milton above all—and they might aspire to similar glory, but they had no interest in taking the same path to glory. If not entirely for the first time, then certainly to an unprecedented degree, originality came in the Romantic period to be seen as a criterion of poetic achievement.

Even at the beginning of the period we find originality embraced as an aesthetic value. A 1791 assessment of a volume of Robinson's poetry, for example, praises originality, even as it sets up an opposition between the original and the natural—two qualities often assumed to normally accompany each other:

The attempt at originality is in all pursuits laudable. Invention is a noble attribute of the mind. But the danger is, lest, by pursuing it too intensely, we deviate so far from ease and nature, that the real object of Poetry, that of touching the heart, be lost.

A more familiar set of oppositions involving the natural and the artificial, the "original" and the imitative, is put forward by William Hazlitt in his *The Spirit of the Age* (1825), as he assesses at the end of the Romantic period the place of Wordsworth in the poetry and the intellectual life of the age:

> His popular, inartificial style gets rid (at a blow) of all the trappings of verse, of all the high places of poetry: "the cloud-capt towers, the solemn temples, the gorgeous palaces," are swept to the ground. … All the traditions of learning, all the superstitions of age, are obliterated and effaced. We begin *de novo* on a *tabula rasa* of poetry. … He chooses to have his subject a foil to his invention, to owe nothing but to himself. … Taught by political opinions to say to the vain pomp and glory of the world, "I hate ye," seeing the path of classical and artificial poetry blocked up by the cumbrous ornaments of style and turgid common-places, so that nothing more could be achieved in that direction but by the most ridiculous bombast or the tamest servility, he has … struck into the sequestered vale of humble life, sought out the muse among sheep-cotes and hamlets, and the peasant's mountain-haunts, has discarded all the tinsel pageantry of verse, and endeavored (not in vain) to … add the charm of novelty to the familiar.

In passages such as this one, we may see the paradigms according to which the literature of the Romantic period is still largely seen being articulated even before the period had ended. On the one side are the natural, the spontaneous, the original, fresh and new; on the other, the artificial, the studied, the imitative, the tired, and traditional. On the one side, imagination and sensibility; on the other, excessive rationalism. On the one side, a passion for freedom, especially, aesthetic freedom and freedom of the spirit; on the other, restraint, reaction, oppression. On the one side, in short,

the Romantic; on the other, the classical, the Neoclassical, the conservative.

If these sets of oppositions often bear some correspondence to reality, it is important to recognize that the correspondences are just as often loose and unreliable. Romantic literature—the Romantic period itself—is filled with unexpected parallels, with surprising evolutions, with unexpected paradoxes, with outright contradictions. The Della Cruscans[1] and their followers, for example, have often been taken to task for the supposed artificiality of their verse. Wordsworth, usually seen as the great poet of a natural world set apart from the oppressive workings of the human-made world of cities and factories, wrote, in 1833, that "Steamboats, Viaducts, and Railways … Nature doth embrace / Her lawful offspring in Man's art." Coleridge, who in the early 1790s felt strongly the attractions of sensibility and planned to establish a community in Pennsylvania founded on revolutionary democratic ideals, became in later life as dismissive of sensibility as he was of revolutionary fervor. Byron, the paradigmatic Romantic figure, professed to reject many of the impulses at the core of the Romantic movement; in "To Romance" (1807), he vows to leave the realms of romance "for those of truth":

> Romance! disgusted with deceit,
> Far from thy motley court I fly,
> Where Affection holds her seat,
> And sickly Sensibility …

Keats, for his part, is perhaps at his most enthusiastic when he exclaims not over nature or freedom but over the experience of classical literature ("On First Looking into Chapman's Homer" [1816]) and classical art ("On Seeing the Elgin Marbles" [1817], "Ode on a Grecian Urn" [1819]). The distinctions made in the attempt to define the essence of the Romantic, in short, often become elusive or indistinct when it comes to particulars; indeed, such divisions can be downright misleading. Throughout most of the nineteenth and twentieth

---

1   The Della Cruscans were poets of sensibility who, in the late 1780s and early 1790s, took the lead in exuberantly embracing revolutionary freedom in the wake of the French Revolution.

centuries, literary critics and theorists tended to accept very much at face value the Romantics' self-representations of the nature and importance of their work; more recently, these self-representations have been frequently problematized and widely challenged.

There have been few challenges, however, to the view that this was a period of revolutionary developments—or to the notion that at the center of those developments (so far as English literature is concerned) was an extraordinary body of verse. Looking back, in 1832, Letitia Landon was among those who identified poetry as a particular locus of change:

> Already there is a wide gulf between the last century and the present. In religion, in philosophy, in politics, in manners, there has passed a great change; but in none has been worked a greater change than in poetry, whether as regards the art itself, or the general feeling towards it.

Poetic ambition was in itself central to the spirit of Romanticism. When they spoke of the confident outpouring of Romantic verse, Romantic poets did not hesitate to compare their own work to that of the great poets of the past—and to feel themselves capable of such greatness. "I would sooner fail than not be among the greatest," wrote Keats.

The tendencies of our own age, when poetry is usually taken in small doses and the lyric mode predominates, sometimes lead modern readers to place far less emphasis than did the Romantics themselves on their longer works. The shorter poems of the Romantic canon are justly celebrated—among them Smith's *Elegiac Sonnets* (1784–97), Blake's *Songs of Innocence and of Experience* (1794), several of the sonnets in Robinson's *Sappho and Phaon* sequence (1796), Wordsworth's "The World Is Too Much with Us" and "I Wandered Lonely as a Cloud" (both 1807), Coleridge's "Dejection: An Ode" (1802), Byron's "She Walks in Beauty" (1814), Percy Shelley's "To a Skylark" (1820), Barbauld's "The Caterpillar" (1825), and Keats's odes and sonnets. Wordsworth and Coleridge's *Lyrical Ballads* is rightly seen as the era's most significant single volume of literature. But even as these works retain

pride of place, it is important to give full notice to the vast range of the ambitions of the Romantic poets—ambitions that found their fullest expression in extended poetic work. Blake's long prophetic poems charted new territory for English verse, both in the poetry itself and in his unique marriage of the verbal and the visual. Robinson's more substantial works include the series of longer poems on related themes that were eventually published as the sequence *The Progress of Liberty* (1806). Landon was arguably best known in her lifetime for long works such as "The Improvisatrice" (1824), a series of love narratives linked by a larger narrative frame. Over the course of some 50 years, Wordsworth reworked his poetic autobiography, *The Prelude*, into an 8,000-line epic. Coleridge's narrative poems "The Rime of the Ancient Mariner" and "Christabel" (1800) are works of modest extent by comparison with these—but still long by modern standards. Byron gave extraordinary new life to the epic romance with *Childe Harold*, broke new ground poetically with what he termed the "epic satire" of *Don Juan* (1824), and wrote seven full-length poetic dramas. Mary Tighe published little other than her long poem *Psyche* (1805), but that poem alone was enough to establish her as a significant poet. Percy Shelley's long works encompass not only the complex allegorical drama *Prometheus Unbound* (1820) but also the poems "The Mask of Anarchy" (1819) and "Adonais"[1] (1821) and the poetic drama *The Cenci* (1819). Keats's *Endymion* (1818) is another memorable work of epic proportions. And, though Keats abandoned both the original epic-length version of his *Hyperion* (1819) and the later *The Fall of Hyperion: A Dream* (1821), what remains of both also constitutes a very substantial poetic achievement. Charlotte Smith's monumental poem of history, nature, and the self, "Beachy Head" (1807), is a landmark in early nineteenth-century poetry, while George Crabbe's *The Borough* (1810) memorialized village life in meticulous detail. Felicia Hemans's most significant works are the poetic drama *The Siege of Valencia* (1823) and the 19 poems that together comprise *Records of Woman* (1828).

---

[1] Subtitled "An Elegy on the Death of John Keats," the poem is a pastoral elegy, written by Shelley upon hearing of Keats's death.

The ambitions of the Romantic poets extended, too, to poetic theory and criticism; to a heretofore unprecedented degree, the leading writers of the time were also the leading critics and theorists. Wordsworth's "Preface" to the *Lyrical Ballads*, in its various versions; Shelley's *A Defence of Poetry*; Coleridge's enormously influential body of literary theory and criticism; Baillie's "Introductory Discourse" to her *Plays on the Passions* (1798); Barbauld's extensive body of critical commentary on the novel; Landon's reviews for *The Critical Gazette*; and Keats's critically insightful letters have all long been regarded as central documents in the literature of Romanticism.

The novel, dramatic writing, and the essay all flourished alongside poetry in the Romantic period, even if these genres were not accorded the same degree of respect as poetry. Barbauld commented wryly on the situation of the novel in 1810:

> A collection of novels has a better chance of giving pleasure than of commanding respect. Books of this description are condemned to the grave and despised by the fastidious; but their leaves are seldom found unopened, and they occupy the parlour and the dressing-room while productions of higher name are often gathering dust upon the shelf.

Though such laments reflected the perception of the novel fairly accurately, the novel nonetheless became increasingly popular, and the changes and innovations to the form arising during the Romantic period continue to reverberate and resonate to this day.

The Romantic era saw the decline of that mainstay of eighteenth-century prose, the epistolary novel, and the development and proliferation of other forms of fiction. James Hogg produced one of the great masterpieces of psychological literature, *The Private Memoirs and Confessions of a Justified Sinner* (1824). This period also saw the development and increasing popularity of historical novels. Maria Edgeworth's widely read *Castle Rackrent* (1800), a work considered by many to be the first in the genre, displays attributes of the comedy of manners alongside qualities of the nascent historical novel; in the Irish dialect of its quirky unreliable narra-

tor, *Castle Rackrent* recounts the moral and financial failures of the Anglo-Irish Rackrent family. Edgeworth's novel was followed by works such as Sydney Owenson's *The Wild Irish Girl* (1806) and Jane Porter's *Scottish Chiefs* (1810), which similarly celebrated specific nationhood within Britain. Inspired by Edgeworth's work in particular, Sir Walter Scott developed the historical novel into the genre we now recognize, reshaping notions not just of "the historical novel" but of the novel itself. After beginning his career as a highly successful poet, he switched to long fiction in 1814 and produced a succession of extraordinarily popular novels, including *Waverley* (1814), *Rob Roy* (1817), and *Ivanhoe* (1819), the first modern bestsellers. Using his works to explore the ongoing political struggles of the time—the clash between traditionalism and progress, the tempting attractions of an idealized past that is really a cover for abuse and exploitation, the struggles and missteps that characterize the creation of a just society—Scott at the same time created vivid, entirely engrossing characters. Indeed, one hallmark of his writing is his ability to use these fully realized individuals to give human expression to broad social and political issues.

Scott produced more than twenty-five full length novels, as well as a number of other works. His use of dialect (following Edgeworth) and his decision to set his works almost exclusively in Scotland validated the language and folklore of regional and marginalized people at a time when "British" was increasingly equated with "English." His use of editorial personae, interlocutors, mediated (sometimes twice-mediated) story presentation, and complexly constructed authorial selves raise questions about the natures of authority and authorship, the difficulty of interpretation, and the concept of truth itself. Scott not only largely created the now well-known version of "Scotland" as a land of kilts and clans, with fierce rivalries fought out against a backdrop of misty mountains and purple heather, filled with eccentric but kind-hearted peasants, he also anticipated or pioneered many of the devices associated with modern and post-modern literature.

Many novels of the period, including Scott's, had roots in an earlier form of long prose fiction, the romance. Whereas "romance novel" today usually denotes a form of pulp fiction focused on romantic love as wish-fulfillment, the tradition of romance literature has its roots in medieval tales of the supernatural, of chivalry, and of courtly love, in which a sense of the extraordinary or the fantastic continually colors the narrative. The genre of romance made its influence felt in several different sorts of literary work in the Romantic era, but none more so than the Gothic. Gothic works of the late eighteenth and early nineteenth centuries—novels, but also poems, short stories, and plays—typically investigate human responses to real or apparent supernatural occurrences, or those things thought to be "impossible," thanks to the advances of science and natural history. These works tend to feature stereotypical characters and to take place in worlds temporally or geographically distant from England. The surrounding landscape is often highly symbolic, reflecting the psychological world of the characters, and the heroine's plight—and the protagonist was almost without fail a heroine—is usually rendered in highly expressive rhetoric, full of rhapsodic feeling. The structure of Gothic literary work frequently corresponds to the political and social tensions that result from the integration of long-ago, remotely historical time—preserved in ancient castles or abbeys—into an otherwise modern world. The Gothic setting of Charlotte Smith's *Emmeline, the Orphan of the Castle* (1788), for example, allows for the exploration of social concerns such as English laws of primogeniture[1] and women's social status and identity within the frame of a courtship novel. Her novel illustrates the ways in which the frightening, distorted world of the Gothic could also serve as a forum for social commentary—as it also does in William Godwin's *Caleb Williams* (1794) and in Eliza Fenwick's *Secresy* (1795). Gothic novels such as Matthew Lewis's *The Monk* (1796), Charlotte Dacre's *Zofloya, or The Moor* (1806), Charles Maturin's *Melmoth the Wanderer* (1820), and Ann Radcliffe's series of highly successful Gothic novels, including *The Romance of the Forest* (1791) and *The Mysteries of Udolpho* (1794), welcomed their readers into a world marked by sexual perversity, threatened female virtue,

and grotesque sights and experiences. Concerned with revealing what lay repressed or hidden behind the mask of middle-class conformity, the Gothic also often veered into savagery and melodrama, tendencies captured perfectly in the following exchange from *The Vampyre* (1819), by John Polidori, in which a mysterious villain extracts a promise from his traveling companion:

> "Swear!" cried the dying man raising himself with exultant violence. "Swear by all your soul reveres, by all your nature fears, swear that for a year and a day you will not impart your knowledge of my crimes or death to any living being in any way, whatever may happen, or whatever you may see."—His eyes seemed bursting from their sockets; "I swear!" said Aubrey; he sunk laughing upon his pillow, and breathed no more.

If the heightened atmosphere of the Gothic novel often tends toward imaginative excess, it can also foster literary art of the highest order—as *Frankenstein*, Mary Shelley's famous first novel, amply demonstrates. The story of a "monster" who turns against his creator Victor Frankenstein, *Frankenstein* is, on one level, a gripping tale of adventure, written with apparent simplicity. But it is also a text that brings together virtually all the great themes of the era: freedom and oppression; science and nature; society and the individual; knowledge and power; gender and sexuality; dream and reality; creation and destruction; self-deception and self-discovery; death and life; God and the universe.

If one strand of the tradition of romance literature runs through the evolution of the Gothic novel, a strand also runs through the development of the courtship novel in the Romantic period. From Frances Burney's *Camilla* (1796) to Elizabeth Susan Ferrier's *The Inheritance* (1824), the pages of Romantic fiction are filled with young people who are misguided, thwarted, and, ultimately, united in marriage. It seems no exaggeration to say that no author of the period was as successful with the courtship genre as was Jane Austen. Between 1811 and 1817, her six major novels were published, all of them warmly engaging yet sharply observant and often satirical, telling of courtship, social class, and domestic

---

[1] Primogeniture refers to the common law right of the first-born son to inherit the entire estate, to the exclusion of female and younger male siblings.

life. Much as her novels do not engage directly or obviously with the large issues of her age, Austen reveals a shrewd awareness of both politics and economics, particularly as they concern women; her novels emphasize the limited possibilities open to women during the period in which she wrote. Within this frame, Austen provides a vividly three-dimensional picture of the shaping of character, of the inner world of the emotions as much as the outer world of social behavior. Austen's heroines are preoccupied with wooing, marriage, and the minutiae of income, entailment,[1] and other details of domestic and marital economy, precisely because these dominated and defined the lives of middle- and upper-class women of the period, while her concentration on "3 or 4 Families in a country village" (as she famously remarked to her niece) draws attention to the geographical and physical constraints imposed on such women during this time. Even the happy endings that have delighted generations of Austenites are undercut by the obvious and acknowledged fictionality of the novels—emphasized through authorial asides, direct appeals to the reader, and other devices—by means of which Austen suggests that all happy endings may be mere fictions.

Austen was a skilled stylist, as well a keen-eyed social critic, bringing to her novels an unprecedented range of novelistic technique. With *Lady Susan* (an early novella, written around 1794 but not published until 1871), she proved herself adept at epistolary narrative; with *Sense and Sensibility, Pride and Prejudice,* and *Emma* (1815), she brought new flexibility to the use of the third person narrative voice, demonstrating perfect pitch in a variety of ironic tones, and pioneering the technique now known as free indirect discourse. In this mode of narration, the apparently independent third-person narrative voice temporarily assumes the viewpoint of one or more of the characters—or indeed of an entire social class, as is the case with the famous opening to *Pride and Prejudice*: "It is a truth universally acknowledged, that a single man in possession of a good fortune, must be in want of a wife." In her tone, Austen is at a

great remove from the leading poets of the Romantic period, but in the importance she places on the exercise of moral imagination—both by her characters and through her own narrative style—she is very much at one with the age.

Other Romantic novels sought to reflect social and political concerns in fiction more directly than did either most Gothic novels or most courtship novels; a number of writers used the novel as a means of challenging prevailing beliefs and mores. Maria Edgeworth's series of Irish novels—*Castle Rackrent* (1800), *Ennui* (1809), *The Absentee* (1812), and *Ormond* (1817)— explored the colonial relationship between England and Ireland. William Godwin's *Caleb Williams* (1794) sought to reveal, in the author's words, the "perfidiousness exercised by the powerful members of the community against those who are more privileged than themselves." Hogg's *Private Memoirs* was a powerful indictment of the smug superiority that could be engendered by religious zeal. And Mary Hays's *The Victim of Prejudice* (1799), a passionate tale of a young woman who dares to resist the pressure put upon her to marry the man who has raped her, was among those novels that spoke powerfully of injustice in a male-dominated society. Conservative voices also spoke out loudly through the medium of prose fiction; important anti-Jacobin novels of the period include Jane West's *A Tale of the Times* (1799), Elizabeth Hamilton's *Memoirs of Modern Philosophers* (1800), and Charles Lucas's *The Infernal Quixote* (1801). And a number of novelists used the novel as a means of making politically pointed connections with other parts of the world, whether to cast a critical eye on the course of European imperialism—as in Sydney Owenson's *The Missionary* (1811)— or to criticize aspects of British society by presenting them through the view of an outsider—as in Hamilton's *Translations of the Letters of a Hindoo Rajah* (1796).

While the novel prospered and evolved, so too did the genre of non-fiction prose. With the rise of the periodical (see "The Business of Literature" section below) came the rise of first critical and then more general essays, designed to engage, enlighten, and entertain the reader. William Hazlitt, originally intended for the Church and later an aspiring painter and philoso-

---

[1] Entailment refers to a common law placing restrictions on how a property was to be used and who could inherit it; in practice, entailment was most frequently used to keep property in the hands of male heirs.

pher, turned his hand to writing and became the most trenchant cultural critic of his time. His works include dramatic, literary, and art criticism, as well as political journalism, general essays, and his famous work *The Spirit of the Age* (1824), a collection of pieces on important figures of the eighteenth century and the Romantic period. His friend Charles Lamb rivaled Hazlitt's renown as an essayist, although his style was very different. Where Hazlitt used plain language and popular modes of construction to express his points cleanly and carefully, Lamb cultivated a more genteel style, rich in allusions and puns, with the resulting prose emerging as both thoughtful and rhetorically complex. Together, the two played a central role in the development of the essay during the Romantic period, but they were far from the only practitioners of the art. From Francis Jeffrey, whose pieces in the *Edinburgh Review* made literary criticism an exercise in stylish perspicacity, to Thomas De Quincey, whose psychological probing anticipates Freud, and Mary Wollstonecraft, whose work anticipates twentieth-century feminism as well as displaying "robust and unwavering" aesthetic judgment, Romantic essay writers worked with a vast range of styles and subjects.

In the field of drama, the Romantic period is traditionally seen as an era of great "closet dramas."[1] In contrast to the drama of the Restoration and early eighteenth century—or that of the later nineteenth and twentieth centuries—serious dramatic writing in the Romantic period was very largely in verse. The period produced Byron's powerful verse drama, *Manfred* (1816–17); his iconoclastic meditation on sin and damnation, *Cain* (1822); and Percy Shelley's mythographic masterpiece, *Prometheus Unbound*; its reputation as a breeding ground for rich, multi-layered poetic theatricals is well deserved. Other serious plays failed on the stage but were widely read and highly praised as literature. Chief among these was Joanna Baillie's series of tragedies, collectively entitled *Plays on the Passions* (1798–1812); depicting the passions "in their rise and progress in the heart" was Baillie's intent, and she believed that such drama could have a moral purpose,

though she made no transcendent claims for the moral value of the imagination. Drama, in her view, "improves us by the knowledge we acquire of our own minds, from the natural desire we have to look into the thoughts, and observe the behaviour of others." Baillie's explorations in psychology harked back to Enlightenment concepts, but her plays also engaged powerfully with the issues of her own day, including the question of women's rights.

In Byron's view, the distaste many serious writers felt for the public theater in this period was entirely justified:

> When I first entered upon theatrical affairs, I had some idea of writing for the [play]house myself, but soon became a convert to Pope's opinion of that subject. Who would condescend to the drudgery of the stage, and enslave himself to the humours, the caprices, the taste or tastelessness, of the age? Besides, one must write for particular actors, have them continually in one's eye, sacrifice character to the personating of it, cringe to some favourite of the public, neither give him too many nor too few lines to spout[.] …

Baillie was rather more charitable, attributing the low tolerance of audiences for serious drama to an escapism born of a desire to find refuge from the "commercial hurricane" of the age—and locating a good deal of the problem in the poor acoustics and lighting of the theaters of the day:

> The Public have now to choose between what we shall suppose are well-written and well-acted plays, the words of which are not heard, or heard but imperfectly by two-thirds of the audience, while the finer and more pleasing traits of the acting are by a still greater proportion lost altogether; and splendid pantomime, or pieces whose chief object is to produce striking scenic effect, which can be seen and comprehended by the whole.

As both Byron's and Baillie's comments indicate, the theater in this period was, in some sense at least, thriving. People thronged to the theaters, where they saw work by such popular and prolific career playwrights as

---

[1] Closet dramas are plays written not for the stage but for private performance—in a private room or "closet"—or to be read.

Thomas Rowlandson, *Dr. Syntax and a Bookseller*, 1812.

Hannah Cowley and Elizabeth Inchbald. Writers perhaps better known for other genres also wrote successful plays, such as Samuel Taylor Coleridge's *Remorse* (1812) and Charles Maturin's *Bertram* (1816). The Stage Licensing Act of 1737 meant that, in London, only a few theaters—Covent Garden and Drury Lane, and, in the summer, the Haymarket—were permitted to present "legitimate" drama, but this in no way limited theatrical production. Stage entertainments of all sorts were held in venues from pubs to tents. In cities and provinces outside London, theaters sprang up to meet the demands of an increasing audience: a survey completed in 1804 counted 280 playhouses throughout the nation. The Licensing Act also required the texts of plays to be submitted to the Lord Chamberlain for censorship before performance. As a result, many works intended for the stage were forced into the closet; perhaps the most famous example is Percy Shelley's *The Cenci*, a verse drama that features not only father-daughter incest but also parricide. Many new plays, however, were permitted, and a roll call of drama produced between 1780 and 1834 includes everything from light comedy to melodramatic tragedy and from pantomimes to operas, as well as spectacles that featured impressive special effects.

THE BUSINESS OF LITERATURE

The thriving literary scene of the period is intimately tied to developments in the worlds of book publishing, bookselling, and book marketing. The most influential of these was the rise of the periodical. By the 1760s, there were more than 30 periodicals in London alone, including monthly journals, quarterly magazines, and collections of reviews and essays, all designed to inform and stimulate their readers. This boom in the periodical press meant increased employment for those who sought to establish themselves as writers; the demand for articles often outweighed the supply. For readers and publishers, it meant an ever-growing number of publications in which reviews of the latest books might appear. Bound volumes of new books were expensive—a three-volume novel could cost a total of between nine and sixteen shillings—equivalent to $100 or more today.[1] Reviews often printed long extracts, and thus readers who could not afford to buy a book could to some extent experience it through the review. But new books re-

---

[1] Given that working- and middle-class people in Britain tended to have far less purchasing power than they do now, this price put book-buying out of the reach of most people; if considered relative to the wages of an average British worker, spending nine shillings would be akin to spending several hundred or even several thousand dollars today.

Henry Fuseli, *The Nightmare*, 1790–91. The Swiss-born artist Fuseli (1741–1825) moved to England in 1779, and soon became one of the leading artistic figures of the day. Beginning in 1781, Fuseli painted several different versions of *The Nightmare*, for which he became famous; it remains an iconic image of the Gothic sensibility, and of Romantic interest in what we now term "the unconscious."

Fuseli moved in London's artistic and intellectual circles through the 1790s, and was briefly involved romantically with Mary Wollstonecraft before her marriage to William Godwin.

Anne-Louis Girodet de Roussy-Trioson, *Sommeil d'Endymion* (*The Sleep of Endymion*), 1791. According to Greek myth, the mortal man Endymion was so beautiful that he attracted the love of the goddess Diana (associated with chastity and the moon). Zeus placed Endymion in an eternal sleep, but also gave him eternal youth to preserve his appearance. Girodet's painting depicts the slumbering Endymion, visited by Diana in the form of a moonbeam, as Amor (Cupid) watches disguised as Zephyr (the west wind). Girodet, a student of the important Neoclassical artist Jacques-Louis David (1748–1825), signaled his independence from David and established his reputation with this work, which played an influential role in the development of early Romantic painting.

Jacques-Louis David, *Bonaparte*, 1798.

Artist unknown, *A Stoppage to a Stride over the Globe*, 1803.

William Blake, "The Sun Standing at His Eastern Gate," illustration to John Milton's "L'Allegro," c. 1816–20.

William Blake, "The Sick Rose," from *Songs of Experience*, 1794.

Philip James de Loutherbourg, *Coalbrookdale by Night*, 1801. The small Shropshire town of Coalbrookdale has been sometimes described as the birthplace of the Industrial Revolution. Located in a gorge on the River Severn, it was the site of the first ironworks that used the modern method of smelting with coke rather than charcoal (an innovation of Joseph Darby in 1709). Together with the adjacent towns of Madeley, Ironbridge, Jackfield, and Coalport, Coalbrookdale was part of an early industrial powerhouse; at the end of the eighteenth century it had a greater concentration of furnaces and forges than anywhere else in the world. Darby's son Abraham also constructed the world's first iron bridge nearby in 1779; the bridge and much of the old ironworks remain today, and the Ironbridge Gorge has been declared a World Heritage Site.

Thomas Phillips, *George Gordon, Lord Byron*, 1813. Byron is wearing clothing of a sort native to the region of Epirus (then part of Albania, now part of northern Greece); he had bought this outfit while traveling through the area in 1809.

John Martin, *The Bard*, 1817. According to legend, when Edward I conquered Wales for England in the late thirteenth century, he ordered the killing of all the Welsh bards—professional poet-musicians and keepers of Welsh history and tradition. The story of "the massacre of the bards" inspired a number of writers and artists of the eighteenth and nineteenth centuries, including John Martin, whose painting above depicts a survivor of the massacre; the English army is also visible in the lower foreground. Martin, born in poverty in rural Northumberland, achieved enormous popular success during his lifetime with his large-scale paintings, many of which depict biblical scenes.

Elizabeth Leveson-Gower, *Mountain Landscape*, c. 1830. Leveson-Gower published two volumes based on her watercolor images of Scottish landscapes, the first a collection of etchings, *Views of Orkney and the North-Eastern Coast of Scotland* (1807), and the second a volume of twenty aquatints, *Views on the Northern and Western Coasts of Sutherland* (1833). The artist intended that various of the wide Sutherland images be joined together to form 360 degree scenic panoramas.

Louis Édouard Fournier, *The Funeral of Shelley*, 1889. To the left stand Shelley's friends Edward Trelawny, Leigh Hunt, and George Gordon, Lord Byron. According to Trelawny's account, Shelley's heart "would not take the flame." It was said to have been given initially to Leigh Hunt and then to Mary Shelley; Shelley's other remains were buried in Rome.

Shelley's funeral occurred on 16 August 1822. We know that this much later image is in some respects inaccurate; Leigh Hunt, for example, remained in the carriage throughout the ceremony. (National Museums, Liverpool)

John Orlando Parry, *A London Street Scene*, 1835. This watercolor shows the posters in extraordinary detail, and shows, too, a number of small details of human life in the activities of the figures—among them a pickpocket, a guard, a chimney sweep, and a woman selling roasted chestnuts.

J.M.W. Turner, *The Burning of the Houses of Parliament*, 1835. In the 1830s it became Turner's practice to send unfinished work (often with only rough underpainting completed) to the Royal Academy in advance of its annual exhibition. During the period devoted (in the case of other artists) to the varnishing of already-completed work, Turner would complete the painting itself, often watched by a sizeable crowd. An eyewitness, E.V. Rippingille, described Turner completing *The Burning of the Houses of Parliament* in 1835:

> For [the] three hours I was there … he never ceased to work, or even once looked or turned from the wall in which his picture was hung. A small box of colors, a few very small brushes, and a vial or two, were at his feet … In one part of the mysterious proceedings Turner, who worked almost entirely with his palette knife, was observed to be rolling and spreading a half-transparent stuff over his picture, the size of a finger in length and thickness. As Callcott was looking on I ventured to say … "What is that he is plastering his picture with?" to which enquiry it was replied, "should be sorry to be the man to ask him" … Presently the work was finished: Turner gathered his tools together, put them into and shut the box, and then with his face still turned to the wall, and at the same distance from it, went sidelong off, without speaking a word to anybody … Maclise, who stood near, remarked, "There, that's masterly, he does not stop to look at his work; he knows it is done, and he is off!"

J.M.W. Turner, *Slavers Throwing Overboard the Dead and Dying—Typhoon Coming On*, 1840. Turner's painting depicts a 1781 incident in which Captain Luke Collingwood of the slave ship *Zong*, with his ship running short of water and other supplies when it had been blown off-course during a severe storm, ordered that all sick and dying enslaved people be thrown overboard; 133 were killed as a result. Insurance was a factor in Collingwood's decision; compensation could be claimed for property lost or jettisoned in storms, but not for enslaved people killed by disease or other natural causes. The incident became widely publicized and spurred support for the abolitionist movement. In the ensuing legal case the court upheld the insurance company's financial liability; no criminal charges were brought against the captain. In the twentieth century the incident became the basis for several literary works, including a long poem by David Dabydeen and a novel by Fred D'Aguiar.

J. Bluck, after Augustus Charles Pugin, *Ackermann's Art Library* (detail), c. 1812–15. Rudolf Ackermann (1764–1834) moved to London from his native Germany and opened a print shop in London on the Strand in 1795, selling books and artist supplies as well as prints, and exhibiting paintings. He later also began to publish color-plate books, the most notable of which was *The Microcosm of London*, a three-volume set with 104 hand-colored aquatint plates by various artists (including Thomas Rowlandson and Augustus Pugin), published between 1808 and 1811.

mained expensive throughout the period; that a great growth in reading and in book buying nevertheless occurred from 1774 (when the old "perpetual copyright" regime ended) onwards is attributable very largely to the publication of cheap octavo editions of works no longer protected by copyright—what literary historian William St. Clair has termed "the old canon" of works by seventeenth- and eighteenth-century authors no longer living.

At the same time as the number of books and of periodicals increased, so did ways of obtaining them. Between 1740 and 1790, the number of outlets nearly doubled. Most obviously, books could be bought: well-established bookshops flourished in cities all over the nation. In provincial towns and villages, where book-selling was not profitable on its own, literature was often sold side by side with stationery, patent medicines, and even groceries. Because the cost of books put them outside the means of many readers, however, some booksellers began to lend volumes to customers for a small fee, thus initiating the circulating library. Payment of a yearly fee enabled patrons to borrow books as they pleased.

Although both circulating and subscription libraries offered a good value, they still lay outside the financial resources of those below the lower middle classes. For these readers, there were other alternatives. Peddlers[1]

---

[1] Peddlers are travelers who make their living by selling small items they carry with them in a pack.

and hawkers sold street literature that included ballads, sermons, and tracts. Those who could not afford library subscriptions but who wished to read something more than broadsheet ballads or pamphlets often formed book clubs in which a number of people contributed money to buy a single copy of a new book, which they would then share. After all had read the book, it might well be sold to a local bookseller, with the proceeds put toward the price of a new one. Slightly more formally, in numerous towns and villages, the local male elite came together to select and discuss books and pamphlets, usually on a controversial topic of the day. This literature, too, was sold on, often by means of an auction among members at the end of the year.

Perhaps as a result of these efforts in group reading, or perhaps simply because people enjoyed it, reading aloud remained a feature of the Romantic era. The fiction and the non-fiction of the period abounds in scenes of communal reading, and the visions that come down to us range from Countess Granville's admission that when her husband read *Don Juan* to her "I roared till I could neither hear nor see" to Henry Austen's description of his sister Jane as one who "read aloud with very great taste and effect. Her own works, probably, were never heard to such advantage as from her own mouth." Writers of the Romantic period were not very far removed from a time when illiteracy was more common than literacy, a time when literature was still an oral art. It is worth bearing in mind that many of them wrote texts intended to be read aloud, and many of their works gain luster from being heard.

"ROMANTIC"

Of the six periods into which the history of British literature has long been conventionally divided, the era of Romanticism is by far the briefest, extending over less than 40 years. Arguably it is also the most intense, particularly during the years 1789 to 1815: the era not only of the French Revolution and the Napoleonic Wars but also of the most tumultuous literary developments—and an extraordinary number of lasting literary achievements.

This was unquestionably an age of contradiction. It was a period in which political consciousness spread through society in unprecedented ways, with a great growth in collective awareness not only among those whose hearts resonated with revolutionary developments on the continent but also amongst workers, the disenfranchised poor, women, and antislavery activists. It was also a time of unprecedented growth in awareness of humans as individuals, of a rights-based political individualism, and of the individualism of the soul.

Applying a broad title to any literary or historical period is always risky. As much as any group of authors and thinkers may at first appear to have in common, deeper examination tends to reveal complexities and complications. Literature, like history, does not occur in isolation. One idea bleeds into another: revolutions are often old ideas returning under new names; factions develop, and their members deny that they are in any way related to the members of other factions. In its own time, Romanticism—a label never used by any of its writers, but rather first applied by the Victorians looking back on the period—was very frequently a house divided. "Lakers"[1] such as Wordsworth and Southey denounced the "Satanic School"[2] of Percy Shelley and Byron, who in turn produced vicious satires of these elders. "The Cockney School"[3] of Londoners Leigh Hunt and John Keats was derided by critics of the day, while writers who were later ignored, such as Hannah More, Samuel Rogers, and Thomas Moore, were lauded for their skill and rewarded with tremendous popularity. The Romantic era gains richness and interest if we view it not as a perfect stream but rather more accurately as a thick murmuring torrent of powerful voices that

---

[1] The Lake Poets were so known because they resided in the Lake District of northwest England; the three most famous Lake Poets were Wordsworth, Coleridge, and Southey. The name "the Lake School of Poetry" was first used—derisively—in the *Edinburgh Review*.

[2] The name "Satanic School" was first used by Southey in *A Vision of Judgment* (1821), as a condemnation of writers, Byron and Shelley foremost among them, whose literary output was "characterized by a Satanic spirit of pride and audacious impiety."

[3] The term "Cockney School" first appeared in negative reviews of Hunt's poetry in *Blackwood's Magazine* in 1817. John Scott, the editor of *The Statesman*, a literary journal founded by Hunt, died in a duel fought over the contemptuous "Cockney" designation.

chorused and clashed, that simultaneously sought and struggled. These mingled tones together make up the voice of a movement that changed English literature.

A Changing Language

Of all the places in which the political clashes of the Romantic period made themselves felt, perhaps the most surprising was in the arena of linguistics. Concern with questions of nationalism and political loyalties affected the very language of Britain. From 1750 onward, the book market was flooded with pronunciation guides, a deluge inspired by the belief that standardized pronunciation would foster a sense of national unity. In this case, "standard" pronunciation meant the speech of educated urban dwellers. Even as many adhered to the essentially Tory belief that this supposedly standard speech was superior, there grew up a precisely opposite point of view, largely expressed by radical publishers and writers, that in the everyday speech of the common people one might find all that was best and most true about England: honesty, frankness, and English liberty given verbal form. In his *Classical Dictionary of the Vulgar Tongue* (1785), Francis Grose transcribed and celebrated the speech of commoners in their many regional variations, and, in 1818, the radical William Cobbett published his *Grammar of the English Language*, a book which explicitly treated language as a political matter. Cobbett took issue with the "false grammar" that he saw as having been put forward by eighteenth-century "authorities" such as Samuel Johnson, and attacked the grammatical slips as well as the privileged position of kings and nobles in a chapter entitled "Errors and Nonsense in a King's Speech." He addressed his work to the less privileged classes, who he believed should be enabled to participate in political discussions—"to assert with effect the rights and liberties of [their] country." As Cobbett saw it, "tyranny has no enemy so formidable as the pen."

Evidence of the Romantic celebration of "common language" can be found throughout the literature of the period. It accounts in part for the huge popularity of Robert Burns—a poet whose greatest effects come from his mixing of standard English dialect with his native Scots dialect. But it finds its most famous expression in the "Preface" to the 1800 edition of *Lyrical Ballads*. There, Wordsworth writes that

> "men" in "low and rustic life" hourly communicate with the best objects from which the best part of language is originally derived; and because, from their rank in society and the sameness and narrow circle of intercourse, being less under the influence of social vanity they convey their feelings and notions in simple and unelaborated expressions. Accordingly, such language, rising out of repeated experience and regular feelings, is a more permanent, and a far more philosophical language[.] …

Still, it is important to note that Wordsworth's opinions on this point represented a minority view, and the Romantic belief in the "philosophical language" of "low and rustic life" was altogether short-lived, becoming less and less widely held. Fifteen years later, one finds Wordsworth's collaborator on *Lyrical Ballads*, Coleridge, writing that

> The best part of human language, properly so called, is derived from reflection on the acts of the mind itself. It is formed by a voluntary appropriation of fixed symbols to internal acts, to processes and results of imagination, the greater part of which have no place in the consciousness of the uneducated man …

As the Romantic period slid into the Victorian and the vogue for rustic or uneducated authors passed away, so the point of view represented in Coleridge's remark came to dominate, and "standard" educated English became more and more widely accepted as an ideal to which all should aspire. However, even as the varieties of English were to some extent dissolving into the form of standard English over the course of this period, many regional variations persisted, and the form of standard English itself was far from unchanging.

In pronunciation, the most significant change in "standard British English" was the disappearance of the / r / sound before many consonants, and before a pause, so that in words such as "harm" or "person," for example, the "r" has since the late eighteenth century been flattened into the smooth "hahm" or "pehson" associated with modern "standard English" pronunciation. Interesting geographical variations have developed over this change, however. In Scotland and in Ireland, as in Canada and most of the United States, the "r" has continued to be sounded in such contexts; these varieties of English are referred to by linguists as "rhotic." In Australia, New Zealand, and South Africa, on the other hand, as well as in some parts of the United States, for instance in Massachusetts and some other parts of New England, non-rhotic forms have come to predominate in much the same way as they have in England.

As the rhymes of English poetry reveal, there were also changes in the sounding of some vowels in the late eighteenth century. In the early eighteenth century, for example, Alexander Pope rhymed "tea" with "obey"; other rhymes suggest that "sea" was pronounced in a manner closer to "say" than to "see." By 1797, however, Coleridge could rhyme "sea" with "free"; and by the end of the Romantic period the older pronunciations of such words had almost certainly died out.

Eighteenth-century habits of capitalization and punctuation were also largely abandoned during this period. Capitalization and typography had generally been considered the business of the compositor rather than that of the author, and the tendency in the early and mid-eighteenth century had been to capitalize (or sometimes italicize) a wide range of nouns. By the end of the century, patterns of usage were coming to approximate the conventions of modern English.

Paragraphing remained less strongly conventionalized than it is now—many writers tended to start new paragraphs very infrequently—and the conventions for writing direct speech were still unstable, with the practice of using double quotation marks surrounding the exact words spoken starting to become common at the end of the eighteenth century. The practice of using single rather than double quotation marks did not become common in Britain until later in the nineteenth century and did not become entirely standardized as British usage until the twentieth century.

HISTORY OF THE LANGUAGE
AND OF PRINT CULTURE

In an effort to provide for readers a direct sense of the development of the language and of print culture, examples of texts in their original form (and of illustrations) have been provided in each volume of this anthology. A list of these within the present volume appears below. Overviews of "the business of literature," and of developments in the history of language during this period appear on pages lxxx to lxxxii, and a "Contexts" section on various aspects of "Reading, Writing, Publishing" appears on pages 461 to 474 of this anthology.

John Brown, title page for *A Memoir of Robert Blincoe*, 1832, p. lx.

Thomas Rowlandson, *Dr. Syntax and a Bookseller*, 1812, p. lxxx.

J. Bluck, *Ackermann's Art Library*, c.1812–15, p. lxxxi.

Charlotte Smith, all poems (1784–1807) in original spelling and punctuation, pp. 46–63.

William Blake, all poems (1789–1807) in original spelling and punctuation, pp. 89–123.

William Blake, *Songs of Innocence and of Experience*, 1789–94, title page for the full work, p. 89; "The Little Black Boy," p. 91; title page for *Songs of Experience*, p. 97; frontispiece, *Songs of Experience*, p. 97; "The Tyger," p. 102. See also the color insert pages.

William Blake, *The Marriage of Heaven and Hell*, 1793, illustrated plates, pp. 115–19.

Mary Robinson, all poems (1795–1804) in original spelling and punctuation, pp. 129–34.

Robert Burns, all poems (1783–99) in original spelling and punctuation, pp. 197–225.

Illustration for *The Mysteries of Udolpho*, 1803, p. 266.

Frontispiece and title page for *The True and Affecting History of the Duchess of C*****, 1803, p. 272.

Frontispiece for *The Midnight Assassin*, 1802, p. 273.

Theodor von Holst, frontispiece for *Frankenstein; or, the Modern Prometheus*, 1831, p. 282.

Maria Edgeworth, *Castle Rackrent*, 1800, passage in original spelling and punctuation, p. 294.

William Wordsworth, "I wandered lonely as a Cloud," 1807, facsimile of page from *Poems in Two Volumes* with manuscript additions, p. 409.

Samuel Taylor Coleridge, all poems (1795–1836) in original spelling and punctuation, pp. 558–91.

Jane Austen, *Lady Susan*, 1871, passage in original spelling and punctuation, pp. 622–23.

William Blake, illustrations for John Stedman, *Narrative of Five Years' Expedition against the Revolted Negroes of Surinam*, 1796, p. 748.

George Gordon, Lord Byron, personal writings (1809–21) in original spelling and punctuation, pp. 902–18.

John Clare, all material (written 1821–48) in original spelling and punctuation, pp. 1062–81.

John Keats, all poems (1816–20) in original spelling and punctuation, pp. 1084–1139.

JAMES MACPHERSON
1736 – 1798

"Except the Bible and Shakespeare, there is not any book that sells better than Ossian," wrote the Scottish antiquarian George Chalmers in 1805. The person responsible for the popular phenomenon of the "Ossian poems" was James Macpherson, who claimed to have translated them from manuscripts he had discovered by the legendary Celtic poet Ossian (Gaelic: Oisín). Though a controversy arose when Macpherson, unable to produce the original manuscripts in question, was suspected of forgery, the poems awakened a nationalistic enthusiasm for Scottish history and Highland culture, as well as an international interest in its mythology. The Ossian poems have ensured the enduring significance of Macpherson as a contributor not only to Scottish national identity but also to the development of literary Romanticism throughout Europe.

James Macpherson was born in 1736 in the village of Ruthven, Scotland. His father, a farmer who was poor but of a distinguished family, had ambitions for his son to become a minister; Macpherson attended various schools and universities, though he never completed a degree. He appears to have acquired his interest in Scottish history and Highland culture early in his life, and by 1756 he had begun to make use of his native Gaelic on his travels throughout Scotland, collecting various oral and written ballads. By 1758, he had moved to Edinburgh and dedicated himself to becoming a writer.

One of Macpherson's earliest published poems, *The Highlander* (1758), already displays his keen interest in the culture and history of his native country, relaying a semi-fictional battle between the Scots and the Danes. But it was at the request of a friend, the successful writer John Home, that he made his first translation of a Gaelic-language poem, which he called "The Death of Oscur." "The Death of Oscur" received positive feedback from Home and his literati friends, and Macpherson followed it with others. 1760 saw the publication of what would be his first volume of Ossian poems: *Fragments of Ancient Poetry, Collected in the Highlands of Scotland, and Translated from the Gaelic or Erse Language*. Macpherson claimed that the collection, described in its preface as "the genuine remains of ancient Scottish poetry," offered literal translations of the surviving manuscript fragments of what had once been a complete epic by Ossian.

The poems immediately created a sensation. Macpherson's work was not only a popular success but also a source of excitement in the literary world, attracting the support of such prominent members of the Scottish intelligentsia as Adam Smith and David Hume, as well as the English poet Thomas Gray. In part the enthusiasm derived from the Ossian poems' extraction of national heroes for Scotland from Celtic myth; Ossian himself was one such legendary figure, as were his father (the mythical Fionn Mac Cumhail, translated by Macpherson as "Fingal") and Ossian's son Oscar, both of whom appear in the poems. The volume also presented an ancient national history the people of Scotland could be proud of: according to a later critical essay by Macpherson, the history recorded by Ossian's epic rivaled that of Greece and Rome. This culture, he claimed, had until now apparently lacked a parallel to the great chroniclers, such as Herodotus and Thucydides, who had so beautifully preserved ancient Greek history—but Ossian was now found to have fulfilled that function. He was even called "the Homer of Scotland" by Voltaire. Members of Edinburgh's literary elite, attracted by the idea of a complete Scottish epic that might serve as a point of resistance against the encroachment of English upon Scottish culture, funded a research trip for Macpherson the autumn after *Fragments* was published. By the time of his return in January 1761, Macpherson claimed to have discovered "a pretty complete poem," which he published as *Fingal* later that year. *Temora*, another Ossian epic, followed in 1763.

Soon, however, questions regarding the authenticity of Macpherson's discoveries began to gain traction. To those who were not completely enthralled by their enthusiasm for the idea of an Ossian, the fact that Macpherson could never produce the originals upon which his translations were based was problematic. The degree to which the authenticity of the translations was doubted varied from critic to critic. Some merely speculated as to the extent of Macpherson's poetic license, disputing the completeness and accuracy of his translations; others suggested that the project was wholly Macpherson's fabrication. Hume himself had doubted the poems' genuineness from the outset, and Samuel Johnson, one of many English readers who were perhaps biased by anti-Scottish sentiment, was among Macpherson's most significant detractors. Macpherson's work was also criticized by Irish readers, who were upset that Macpherson had combined material from the Ulster Cycle and the Fenian Cycle, two separate sources of Celtic myth—and that he had made a Scottish claim to Irish heroes. (The former charge may have been more warranted than the latter; Macpherson did indeed combine elements from the two cycles, but there is substantial overlap between Irish and Scottish Gaelic mythological traditions.)

After the publication of *Temora*, Macpherson's life began to take a turn toward the political. In the early 1760s he moved to colonial America to become the Governor's secretary in West Florida. His brief time there was followed by a tour of the West Indies, and a subsequent return to London. By 1765, he was employed as a writer of propaganda for the Tory government. He continued, however, his historical pursuits, writing *An Introduction to the History of Great Britain and Ireland* (1771), as well as publishing a prose translation of Homer's *Iliad* (1773) that was poorly received outside Scotland. Macpherson's later years were spent as a Member of Parliament for Camelford, Cornwall, an office in which he served from 1780 until his death in 1796. He was buried, at his own expense, in the Poets' Corner of Westminster Abbey, and had a monument erected at his home in Badenoch.

In 1797, a committee was assigned to inquire into the question of the Ossian poems' authenticity. After researching until 1805, the committee decided that the poems were far from literal translations—but that they had been based upon real manuscript and oral sources, albeit ones not nearly so ancient as Macpherson had claimed. These were then rearranged, adapted, and freely added to by Macpherson. Twenty-first-century scholars of Macpherson tend to be less interested in the potential authenticity or inauthenticity of his work than they are in the profound influence the Ossian poems had on the burgeoning Romantic movement; their melancholy expressiveness and sublime natural settings were taken up by many Romantic writers, including such influential figures as Goethe and Byron.

⌘ ⌘ ⌘

from *Fragments of Ancient Poetry*

FRAGMENT 8

By the side of a rock on the hill, beneath the aged trees, old Ossian sat on the moss; the last of the race of Fingal.[1] Sightless are his aged eyes; his beard is waving in the wind. Dull through the leafless trees he heard the voice of the north. Sorrow revived in his soul: he began and lamented the dead.

How hast thou fallen like an oak, with all thy branches round thee! Where is Fingal the King? where is Oscur[2] my son? where are all my race? Alas! in the earth they lie. I feel their tombs with my hands. I hear the river below murmuring hoarsely over the stones. What dost thou, O river, to me? Thou bringest back the memory of the past.

The race of Fingal stood on thy banks, like a wood in a fertile soil. Keen were their spears of steel. Hardy was he who dared to encounter their rage. Fillan[3] the great was there. Thou Oscur wert there, my son! Fingal himself was there, strong in the grey locks of years. Full rose his sinewy limbs; and wide his shoulders spread. The unhappy met with his arm, when the pride of his wrath arose.

The son of Morny came; Gaul, the tallest of men. He stood on the hill like an oak; his voice was like the streams of the hill. Why reigneth alone, he cries, the son of the mighty Corval? Fingal is not strong to save: he is no support for the people. I am strong as a storm in the ocean; as a whirlwind on the hill. Yield, son of Corval; Fingal, yield to me.

Oscur stood forth to meet him; my son would meet the foe. But Fingal came in his strength, and smiled at the vaunter's[4] boast. They threw their arms round each other; they struggled on the plain. The earth is ploughed with their heels. Their bones crack as the boat on the ocean, when it leaps from wave to wave. Long did they toil; with night, they fell on the sounding plain; as two oaks, with their branches mingled, fall crashing from the hill. The tall son of Morny is bound; the aged overcame. Fair with her locks of gold, her smooth neck, and her breasts of snow; fair, as the spirits of the hill when at silent noon they glide along the heath; fair, as the rainbow of heaven; came Minvane the maid. Fingal! she softly saith, loose me[5] my brother Gaul. Loose me the hope of my race, the terror of all but Fingal. Can I, replies the King, can I deny the lovely daughter of the hill? take thy brother, O Minvane, thou fairer than the snow of the north!

Such, Fingal! were thy words; but thy words I hear no more. Sightless I sit by thy tomb. I hear the wind in the wood; but no more I hear my friends. The cry of the hunter is over. The voice of war is ceased.

FRAGMENT 9

Thou askest, fair daughter of the isles! whose memory is preserved in these tombs? The memory of Ronnan the bold, and Connan the chief of men; and of her, the fairest of maids, Rivine the lovely and the good. The wing of time is laden with care. Every moment hath woes of its own. Why seek we our grief from afar? or give our tears to those of other times? But thou commandest, and I obey, O fair daughter of the isles! Conar was mighty in war. Caul was the friend of strangers. His gates were open to all; midnight darkened not on his barred door. Both lived upon the sons of the mountains. Their bow was the support of the poor.

Connan was the image of Conar's soul. Caul was renewed in Ronnan his son. Rivine the daughter of Conar was the love of Ronnan; her brother Connan was his friend. She was fair as the harvest-moon setting in

---

[1] *Fingal* Ossian's father.

[2] *Oscur* Ossian's son. In the previous fragments, Oscur and his friend Dermid both love the same woman, who chooses Oscur. In despair, Dermid forces Oscur to kill him; Oscur then tricks his lover into killing him as well.

[3] *Fillan* Another of Fingal's sons, mentioned earlier in the *Fragments*.

[4] *vaunter* Braggart.

[5] *loose me* Release to me.

the seas of Molochasquir. Her soul was settled on Ronnan; the youth was the dream of her nights.

Rivine, my love! says Ronnan, I go to my king in Norway.[1] A year and a day shall bring me back. Wilt thou be true to Ronnan?

Ronnan! a year and a day I will spend in sorrow. Ronnan, behave like a man, and my soul shall exult in thy valour. Connan my friend, says Ronnan, wilt thou preserve Rivine thy sister? Durstan is in love with the maid; and soon shall the sea bring the stranger to our coast.

Ronnan, I will defend: Do thou securely go.—He went. He returned on his day. But Durstan returned before him.

Give me thy daughter, Conar, says Durstan; or fear and feel my power.

He who dares attempt[2] my sister, says Connan, must meet this edge of steel. Unerring in battle is my arm: my sword, as the lightning of heaven.

Ronnan the warrior came; and much he threatened Durstan.

But, saith Euran the servant of gold, Ronnan! by the gate of the north shall Durstan this night carry thy fair-one away. Accursed, answers Ronnan, be this arm if death meet him not there.

Connan! saith Euran, this night shall the stranger carry thy sister away. My sword shall meet him, replies Connan, and he shall lie low on earth.

The friends met by night, and they fought. Blood and sweat ran down their limbs as water on the mossy rock. Connan falls; and cries, O Durstan, be favourable to Rivine!—And is it my friend, cries Ronnan, I have slain? O Connan! I knew thee not.

He went, and he fought with Durstan. Day began to rise on the combat, when fainting they fell, and expired. Rivine came out with the morn; and—O what detains my Ronnan!—She saw him lying pale in his blood; and her brother lying pale by his side.

What could she say? what could she do? her complaints were many and vain. She opened this grave for the warriors; and fell into it herself, before it was closed; like the sun snatched away in a storm.

Thou hast heard this tale of grief, O fair daughter of the isles! Rivine was fair as thyself: shed on her grave a tear.

—1760

---

1 [Macpherson's note]   Supposed to be Fergus II. This fragment is reckoned not altogether so ancient as most of the rest.

2 *attempt*   I.e., attempt to obtain; seduce.

THOMAS PAINE
1737 – 1809

Born in relative obscurity and buried in ignominy 72 years later, Thomas Paine played a major role in the histories of three nations. After failing in numerous early careers, Paine became an overnight success with the publication of his first pamphlet in the American colonies, *Common Sense* (1776), and his talent for political rhetoric and persuasion made him an important influence in the Revolutionary War effort in America, in the drafting of Jefferson's Declaration of Independence, and in the formation of the French National Assembly.

Paine was born in the town of Thetford, Norfolk, the only son of a Quaker couple, Joseph Pain (a shopkeeper of modest means who made and sold "stays" or corsets) and his wife Frances (Cocke) Pain. (At some point before 1769 Paine added an "e" to his surname.) His early life was marked by a series of personal and professional setbacks. He enlisted twice, briefly, on British privateers; and he attempted careers as a stay-maker, excise officer, teacher, and shopkeeper. His first wife died in childbirth (in 1760) and he formally separated from his second wife (in 1774) after his shop had failed and he had been threatened with debtor's prison. Paine set out for America with letters of introduction from his friend Benjamin Franklin and hopes for greater success.

In Philadelphia Paine was hired to edit a new publication, the *Pennsylvania Magazine*. The magazine enjoyed some success, and Paine began to contribute pieces himself, beginning in March 1775 with an essay on "African Slavery in America," in which he argued that those who had been enslaved had "a natural, perfect right" to freedom. As hostilities between Britain and its American colonies escalated, Paine put his writing skills to further use; on 9 January 1776 he issued the pamphlet *Common Sense*. Reaching an extraordinarily large readership (Paine estimated that over 150,000 copies were distributed), it spread the argument for independence throughout the would-be nation. Paine called on ordinary people to give their energy to a higher purpose—the creation of America. His accessible prose, simple but persuasive style, compelling logic, and gift for dismissing opposing arguments made him for a time the American Revolution's most adept promoter. Dubbing Britain a "tyrannical oppressor," *Common Sense* argues that government, at best "a necessary evil," should serve to protect its citizens and preserve their freedom. A subsequent series of letters, entitled *The American Crisis* (1776–83), continued to muster support for the revolution in the face of military setbacks and public fear and despondency. One such letter's rousing rhetoric—"These are the times that try men's souls. ..."—was read to Washington's troops on Christmas Eve to boost their morale.

After the Revolutionary War concluded, Paine traveled between Britain, France, and America, rather lacking in direction until the publication of Edmund Burke's conservative pamphlet attacking the French Revolution, *Reflections on the Revolution in France* (1790), spurred him to publish a rebuttal, based largely on the account of the Revolution he had been working on at the time. Part 1 of Paine's *Rights of Man* (1791) came in the midst of a pamphlet storm of replies to Burke, amongst which one of the most famous was Mary Wollstonecraft's *A Vindication of the Rights of Men*.

Demonstrating once again his powers of persuasion, and leaning on the weight of his experience in the American Revolution (the work was dedicated to George Washington), Paine challenged Burke's scathing criticism of the French Revolution. *Rights of Man* insists that each generation, rather than being ruled by preceding generations, "must be as free to act for itself, in all cases, as the ages and generations which preceded it." He argues, against Burke, that men have certain natural rights, existent from birth and given by their creator, which society is formed to protect and enforce through civil rights. Part 2 of *Rights of Man* (1792) went farther still, adding that American independence had set in motion changes that would bring down the tyranny of hereditary government in Europe. This attack on the monarchy and aristocracy saw him charged with treason in England and resulted in his departure for France, where he had been made an honorary citizen.

Paine's efforts to assist the emerging French revolutionary government resulted eventually in his imprisonment by Maximilien Robespierre and the Jacobins during the Reign of Terror (1793–94). Paine narrowly avoided death, but was released following Robespierre's execution in 1794. While in France, however, he had been convicted in absentia of treason in England. Unable to return to his country of birth, he fled once again to the United States.

Once in America, Paine—whose opinionated nature, self-aggrandizing attitude, and apparently flagrant spending habits had cost him many friends and supporters—again found himself at the center of controversy, this time for his last major work, *The Age of Reason* (1794–95). This Deist denunciation of the Bible and organized Christianity (along with religious institutions of all denominations) resulted in his being labeled an infidel and an atheist, despite his professed belief at the work's outset in "one God." As a result, when years of heavy drinking and ill-health led to his death in 1809, he was denied burial in the Quaker burial-ground (and any other consecrated burial). Ten years after he was interred in his New Rochelle farm (under a tombstone stating simply—at his request—"The author of *Common Sense*"), a fellow revolutionary exhumed his remains, hoping to see them placed under a grand monument in England. When this request was later denied by the British government, however, Paine's remains were lost somewhere in England, and have yet to be recovered.

⌘ ⌘ ⌘

from *Common Sense*

OF THE ORIGIN AND DESIGN OF GOVERNMENT IN GENERAL. WITH CONCISE REMARKS ON THE ENGLISH CONSTITUTION

Some writers have so confounded society with government, as to leave little or no distinction between them; whereas they are not only different, but have different origins. Society is produced by our wants, and government by our wickedness; the former promotes our happiness positively by uniting our affections, the latter negatively by restraining our vices. The one encourages intercourse, the other creates distinctions. The first is a patron, the last a punisher.

Society in every state is a blessing, but government, even in its best state, is but a necessary evil; in its worst state, an intolerable one. For when we suffer, or are exposed to the same miseries by a *government* which we might expect in a country *without government*, our calamity is heightened by reflecting that we furnish the means by which we suffer. Government, like dress, is the badge of lost innocence; the palaces of kings are built on the ruins of the bowers of paradise. For were the impulses of conscience clear, uniform, and irresistibly obeyed, man would need no other lawgiver; but that not being the case, he finds it necessary to surrender up a part of his property to furnish means for the protection of the rest; and this he is induced to do by the same prudence which in every other case advises him out of two evils to choose the least. *Wherefore* security being the true design and end of government, it unanswerably follows, that whatever *form* thereof appears most likely to ensure it to us, with the least expense and greatest benefit, is preferable to all others. …

I draw my idea of the form of government from a principle in nature, which no art can overturn, viz. that the more simple anything is the less liable it is to be disordered, and the easier repaired when disordered; and with this maxim in view, I offer a few remarks on the so much boasted constitution of England. That it was noble for the dark and slavish times in which it was erected, is granted. When the world was overrun with tyranny, the least remove therefrom was a glorious risk. But that it is imperfect, subject to convulsions, and incapable of producing what it seems to promise, is easily demonstrated.

Absolute governments (though the disgrace of human nature) have this advantage with them, that they are simple; if the people suffer, they know the head from which their suffering springs, know likewise the remedy, and are not bewildered by a variety of causes and cures. But the constitution of England is so exceedingly complex, that the nation may suffer for years together without being able to discover in which part the fault lies; some will say in one and some in another, and every political physician will advise a different medicine.

I know it is difficult to get over local or long standing prejudices, yet if we will suffer ourselves to examine the component parts of the English constitution, we shall find them to be the base remains of two ancient tyrannies, compounded with some new republican materials.

First.—The remains of monarchical tyranny in the person of the king.

Secondly.—The remains of aristocratical tyranny in the persons of the peers.

Thirdly.—The new republican materials, in the persons of the commons, on whose virtue depends the freedom of England.

The two first, by being hereditary, are independent of the people; wherefore in a *constitutional sense* they contribute nothing towards the freedom of the state.

To say that the constitution of England is a *union* of three powers reciprocally *checking* each other, is farcical; either the words have no meaning, or they are flat contradictions.

To say that the commons is a check upon the king, presupposes two things.

First.—That the king is not to be trusted without being looked after, or in other words, that a thirst for absolute power is the natural disease of monarchy.

Secondly.—That the commons, by being appointed for that purpose, are either wiser or more worthy of confidence than the crown.

But as the same constitution which gives the commons a power to check the king by withholding the supplies, gives afterwards the king a power to check the commons, by empowering him to reject their other bills; it again supposes that the king is wiser than those whom it has already supposed to be wiser than him. A mere absurdity!

There is something exceedingly ridiculous in the composition of monarchy; it first excludes a man from the means of information, yet empowers him to act in cases where the highest judgment is required. The state of a king shuts him from the world, yet the business of a king requires him to know it thoroughly; wherefore the different parts, unnaturally opposing and destroying each other, prove the whole character to be absurd and useless.

Some writers have explained the English constitution thus; the king, say they, is one, the people another; the peers are an house in behalf of the king; the commons in behalf of the people; but this hath all the distinctions of an house divided against itself; and though the expressions be pleasantly arranged, yet when examined they appear idle and ambiguous; and it will always happen, that the nicest construction that words are capable of, when applied to the description of something which either cannot exist, or is too incomprehensible to be within the compass of description, will be words of sound only, and though they may amuse the ear, they cannot inform the mind, for this explanation includes a previous question, viz. *How came the king by a power which the people are afraid to trust, and always obliged to check?* Such a power could not be the gift of a wise people, neither can any power, which needs checking, be from God; yet the provision, which the constitution makes, supposes such a power to exist.

But the provision is unequal to the task; the means either cannot or will not accomplish the end, and the whole affair is a *felo de se*;[1] for as the greater weight will always carry up the less, and as all the wheels of a machine are put in motion by one, it only remains to know which power in the constitution has the most weight, for that will govern; and though the others, or a part of them, may clog, or, as the phrase is, check the rapidity of its motion, yet so long as they cannot stop it, their endeavours will be ineffectual; the first moving power will at last have its way, and what it wants in speed is supplied by time.

That the crown is this overbearing part in the English constitution needs not be mentioned, and that it derives its whole consequence merely from being the giver of places and pensions is self-evident, wherefore, though we have been wise enough to shut and lock a door against absolute monarchy, we at the same time have been foolish enough to put the crown in possession of the key.

The prejudice of Englishmen, in favour of their own government by king, lords, and commons, arises as much or more from national pride than reason. Individuals are undoubtedly safer in England than in some other countries, but the *will* of the king is as much the *law* of the land in Britain as in France, with this difference, that instead of proceeding directly from his mouth, it is handed to the people under the most formidable shape of an act of parliament. For the fate of Charles the First, hath only made kings more subtle—

not more just.[2]

Wherefore, laying aside all national pride and prejudice in favour of modes and forms, the plain truth is, that *it is wholly owing to the constitution of the people, and not to the constitution of the government* that the crown is not as oppressive in England as in Turkey.

An inquiry into the *constitutional errors* in the English form of government is at this time highly necessary; for as we are never in a proper condition of doing justice to others, while we continue under the influence of some leading partiality, so neither are we capable of doing it to ourselves while we remain fettered by any obstinate prejudice. And as a man who is attached to a prostitute is unfitted to choose or judge of a wife, so any prepossession in favour of a rotten constitution of government will disable us from discerning a good one.

OF MONARCHY AND HEREDITARY SUCCESSION

Mankind being originally equals in the order of creation, the equality could only be destroyed by some subsequent circumstance; the distinctions of rich, and poor, may in a great measure be accounted for, and that without having recourse to the harsh, ill-sounding names of oppression and avarice. Oppression is often the *consequence*, but seldom or never the *means* of riches; and though avarice will preserve a man from being necessitously poor, it generally makes him too timorous to be wealthy.

But there is another and greater distinction for which no truly natural or religious reason can be assigned, and that is, the distinction of men into kings and subjects. Male and female are the distinctions of nature, good and bad the distinctions of heaven; but how a race of men came into the world so exalted above the rest, and distinguished like some new species, is worth inquiring into, and whether they are the means of happiness or of misery to mankind. In the early ages of the world, according to the scripture chronology, there

---

[1] *felo de se* Latin: suicide or self murder; here, negating contradictions, and so absurdities.

[2] *For the fate ... more just* Charles I (1600–49), English king who was executed by parliamentary order in 1649.

were no kings; the consequence of which was there were no wars; it is the pride of kings which throws mankind into confusion. Holland without a king hath enjoyed more peace for this last century than any of the monarchical governments in Europe. Antiquity favours the same remark; for the quiet and rural lives of the first patriarchs have a happy something in them, which vanishes when we come to the history of Jewish royalty.

Government by kings was first introduced into the world by the Heathens, from whom the children of Israel copied the custom. It was the most prosperous invention the Devil ever set on foot for the promotion of idolatry. The heathens paid divine honours to their deceased kings, and the Christian world hath improved on the plan by doing the same to their living ones. How impious is the title of *sacred majesty* applied to a worm, who in the midst of his splendour is crumbling into dust.

As the exalting one man so greatly above the rest cannot be justified on the equal rights of nature, so neither can it be defended on the authority of scripture; for the will of the Almighty, as declared by Gideon and the prophet Samuel, expressly disapproves of government by kings.[1] All anti-monarchical parts of scripture have been very smoothly glossed over in monarchical governments, but they undoubtedly merit the attention of countries which have their governments yet to form. "*Render unto Caesar the things which are Caesar's*" is the scriptural doctrine of courts, yet it is no support of monarchical government, for the Jews at that time were without a king, and in a state of vassalage to the Romans. …

To the evil of monarchy we have added that of hereditary succession; and as the first is a degradation and lessening of ourselves, so the second, claimed as a matter of right, is an insult and imposition on posterity. For all men being originally equals, no *one* by *birth* could have a right to set up his own family in perpetual preference to all others forever, and though himself might deserve *some* decent degree of honours of his cotemporaries, yet his descendants might be far too

unworthy to inherit them. One of the strongest *natural* proofs of the folly of hereditary right in kings, is, that nature disapproves it, otherwise she would not so frequently turn it into ridicule, by giving mankind an *ass for a lion*.[2]

Secondly, as no man at first could possess any other public honours than were bestowed upon him, so the givers of those honours could have no power to give away the right of posterity, and though they might say "We choose you for *our* head," they could not, without manifest injustice to their children, say "that your children and your children's children shall reign over *ours* forever." Because such an unwise, unjust, unnatural compact might (perhaps) in the next succession put them under the government of a rogue or a fool. Most wise men, in their private sentiments, have ever treated hereditary right with contempt; yet it is one of those evils, which when once established is not easily removed: many submit from fear, others from superstition, and the more powerful part shares with the king the plunder of the rest.

This is supposing the present race of kings in the world to have had an honourable origin; whereas it is more than probable that could we take off the dark covering of antiquity, and trace them to their first rise, that we should find the first of them nothing better than the principal ruffian of some restless gang, whose savage manners or pre-eminence in subtlety obtained him the title of chief among plunderers; and who by increasing in power, and extending his depredations, over-awed the quiet and defenceless to purchase their safety by frequent contributions. Yet his electors could have no idea of giving hereditary right to his descendants, because such a perpetual exclusion of themselves was incompatible with the free and unrestrained principles they professed to live by. Wherefore, hereditary succession in the early ages of monarchy could not take place as a matter of claim, but as something casual or complimental; but as few or no records were extant in those days,

---

[1] *for the will … by kings* See Judges 6–8.

[2] *ass for a lion* In Aesop's fable "The Ass in the Lion's Skin," a lonely ass terrorizes flocks and herds after he discovers and dons a lion's skin. The owner, however, recognizes the ass by his ears and beats him.

and traditionary history stuffed with fables, it was very easy, after the lapse of a few generations, to trump up some superstitious tale, conveniently timed, Mahomet[1] like, to cram hereditary right down the throats of the vulgar. Perhaps the disorders which threatened, or seemed to threaten on the decease of a leader and the choice of a new one (for elections among ruffians could not be very orderly) induced many at first to favour hereditary pretensions; by which means it happened, as it hath happened since, that what was first submitted to as a convenience, was afterwards claimed as a right.

England, since the conquest,[2] hath known some few good monarchs, but groaned beneath a much larger number of bad ones, yet no man in his senses can say that their claim under William the Conqueror is a very honorable one. A French bastard landing with an armed banditti, and establishing himself king of England against the consent of the natives, is in plain terms a very paltry rascally original.—It certainly hath no divinity in it. However, it is needless to spend much time in exposing the folly of hereditary right, if there are any so weak as to believe it, let them promiscuously worship the ass and lion, and welcome. I shall neither copy their humility, nor disturb their devotion.

Yet I should be glad to ask how they suppose kings came at first? The question admits but of three answers, viz. either by lot, by election, or by usurpation. If the first king was taken by lot, it establishes a precedent for the next, which excludes hereditary succession. Saul was by lot yet the succession was not hereditary, neither does it appear from that transaction there was any intention it ever should.[3] If the first king of any country was by election, that likewise establishes a precedent for the next; for to say, that the *right* of all future generations is

taken away by the act of the first electors, in their choice not only of a king, but of a family of kings forever, hath no parallel in or out of scripture but the doctrine of original sin, which supposes the free will of all men lost in Adam; and from such comparison, and it will admit of no other, hereditary succession can derive no glory. For as in Adam all sinned, and as in the first electors all men obeyed; as in the one all mankind were subjected to Satan, and in the other to Sovereignty; as our innocence was lost in the first, and our authority in the last; and as both disable us from re-assuming some former state and privilege, it unanswerably follows that original sin and hereditary succession are parallels. Dishonorable rank! Inglorious connection! Yet the most subtle sophist cannot produce a juster simile.

As to usurpation, no man will be so hardy as to defend it; and that William the Conqueror was an usurper is a fact not to be contradicted. The plain truth is, that the antiquity of English monarchy will not bear looking into.

But it is not so much the absurdity as the evil of hereditary succession which concerns mankind. Did it ensure a race of good and wise men it would have the seal of divine authority, but as it opens a door to the *foolish*, the *wicked*, and the *improper*, it hath in it the nature of oppression. Men who look upon themselves born to reign, and others to obey, soon grow insolent; selected from the rest of mankind, their minds are early poisoned by importance; and the world they act in differs so materially from the world at large, that they have but little opportunity of knowing its true interests, and when they succeed to the government are frequently the most ignorant and unfit of any throughout the dominions.

Another evil which attends hereditary succession is, that the throne is subject to be possessed by a minor at any age; all which time the regency, acting under the cover of a king, have every opportunity and inducement to betray their trust. The same national misfortune happens when a king, worn out with age and infirmity, enters the last stage of human weakness. In both these cases the public becomes a prey to every miscreant who

---

[1] *Mahomet* Mohammed (c. 570–632 CE), founder of Islam. Like other contemporary Protestants, Paine associates Islam with superstition.

[2] *England, since the conquest* I.e., the Norman Conquest of 1066, under the command of William I (c. 1021–87), "the Conqueror."

[3] *Saul was by lot ... should* See 1 Samuel 10.20–24. Paine's interpretation of Samuel's succession "by lot" is dubious, as in the story the latter is chosen by God.

can tamper successfully with the follies either of age or infancy.

The most plausible plea which hath ever been offered in favour of hereditary succession is that it preserves a nation from civil wars; and were this true, it would be weighty; whereas it is the most barefaced falsity ever imposed upon mankind. The whole history of England disowns the fact. Thirty kings and two minors have reigned in that distracted kingdom since the conquest, in which time there have been (including the Revolution) no less than eight civil wars and nineteen rebellions. Wherefore instead of making for peace, it makes against it, and destroys the very foundation it seems to stand on.

The contest for monarchy and succession, between the houses of York and Lancaster, laid England in a scene of blood for many years.[1] Twelve pitched battles, besides skirmishes and sieges, were fought between Henry and Edward. Twice was Henry prisoner to Edward, who in his turn was prisoner to Henry. And so uncertain is the fate of war and the temper of a nation, when nothing but personal matters are the ground of a quarrel, that Henry was taken in triumph from a prison to a palace, and Edward obliged to fly from a palace to a foreign land; yet, as sudden transitions of temper are seldom lasting, Henry in his turn was driven from the throne, and Edward recalled to succeed him. The parliament always following the strongest side.

This contest began in the reign of Henry the Sixth, and was not entirely extinguished till Henry the Seventh, in whom the families were united. Including a period of 67 years, viz. from 1422 to 1489.

In short, monarchy and succession have laid (not this or that kingdom only) but the world in blood and ashes. 'Tis a form of government which the word of God bears testimony against, and blood will attend it.

If we inquire into the business of a king, we shall find that in some countries they may have none; and after sauntering away their lives without pleasure to themselves or advantage to the nation, withdraw from the scene, and leave their successors to tread the same idle round. In absolute monarchies the whole weight of business civil and military lies on the king; the children of Israel in their request for a king, urged this plea, "that he may judge us, and go out before us and fight our battles." But in countries where he is neither a judge nor a general, as in E—d, a man would be puzzled to know what is his business.

The nearer any government approaches to a republic the less business there is for a king. It is somewhat difficult to find a proper name for the government of E—. Sir William Meredith[2] calls it a republic; but in its present state it is unworthy of the name, because the corrupt influence of the crown, by having all the places in its disposal, hath so effectually swallowed up the power, and eaten out the virtue of the house of commons (the republican part in the constitution) that the government of England is nearly as monarchical as that of France or Spain. Men fall out with names without understanding them. For it is the republican and not the monarchical part of the constitution of England which Englishmen glory in, viz. the liberty of choosing an house of commons from out of their own body—and it is easy to see that when republican virtues fail, slavery ensues. Why is the Constitution of E—d sickly, but because monarchy hath poisoned the republic; the crown has engrossed the commons?

In England a k— hath little more to do than to make war and give away places; which in plain terms, is to impoverish the nation and set it together by the ears. A pretty business indeed for a man to be allowed eight hundred thousand sterling a year for, and worshipped into the bargain! Of more worth is one honest man to society, and in the sight of God, than all the crowned ruffians that ever lived.

---

[1] *The contest for ... many years* The Wars of the Roses—the struggle for the English crown between the houses of Lancaster and York—raged for 32 years before Henry VII of Lancaster established the Tudor claim, and brought about a period of relative calm.

[2] *William Meredith* English politician (c. 1724–90).

THOUGHTS OF THE PRESENT STATE OF AMERICAN AFFAIRS

In the following pages I offer nothing more than simple facts, plain arguments, and common sense; and have no other preliminaries to settle with the reader than that he will divest himself of prejudice and prepossession, and suffer his reason and his feelings to determine for themselves; that he will put *on*, or rather that he will not put *off* the true character of a man, and generously enlarge his views beyond the present day.

Volumes have been written on the subject of the struggle between England and America. Men of all ranks have embarked in the controversy, from different motives, and with various designs; but all have been ineffectual, and the period of debate is closed. Arms, as the last resource, decide the contest; the appeal was the choice of the king, and the continent hath accepted the challenge.

It hath been reported of the late Mr. Pelham[1] (who though an able minister was not without his faults) that on his being attacked in the house of commons on the score, that his measures were only of a temporary kind, replied, "*they will last my time.*" Should a thought so fatal and unmanly possess the colonies in the present contest, the name of ancestors will be remembered by future generations with detestation.

The sun never shined on a cause of greater worth. 'Tis not the affair of a city, a country, a province, or a kingdom, but of a continent—of at least one eighth part of the habitable globe. 'Tis not the concern of a day, a year, or an age; posterity are virtually involved in the contest, and will be more or less affected, even to the end of time, by the proceedings now. Now is the seed time of continental union, faith and honour. The least fracture now will be like a name engraved with the point of a pin on the tender rind of a young oak; the wound will enlarge with the tree, and posterity read it in full grown characters.

By referring the matter from argument to arms, a new era for politics is struck; a new method of thinking hath arisen. All plans, proposals, etc. prior to the nineteenth of April, i.e., to the commencement of hostilities,[2] are like the almanacs of the last year; which, though proper then, are superseded and useless now. Whatever was advanced by the advocates on either side of the question then, terminated in one and the same point, viz. a union with Great Britain; the only difference between the parties was the method of effecting it; the one proposing force, the other friendship; but it hath so far happened that the first hath failed, and the second hath withdrawn her influence.

As much hath been said of the advantages of reconciliation, which, like an agreeable dream, hath passed away and left us as we were, it is but right that we should examine the contrary side of the argument, and inquire into some of the many material injuries which these colonies sustain, and always will sustain, by being connected with, and dependant on Great Britain. To examine that connection and dependence, on the principles of nature and common sense, to see what we have to trust to, if separated, and what we are to expect, if dependant.

I have heard it asserted by some, that as America hath flourished under her former connection with Great Britain, that the same connection is necessary towards her future happiness, and will always have the same effect. Nothing can be more fallacious than this kind of argument. We may as well assert, that because a child has thrived upon milk, that it is never to have meat; or that the first twenty years of our lives is to become a precedent for the next twenty. But even this is admitting more than is true, for I answer roundly, that America would have flourished as much, and probably much more, had no European power had anything to do with her. The commerce by which she hath enriched herself are the necessaries of life, and will always have a market while eating is the custom of Europe.

---

[1] *Mr. Pelham* Henry Pelham (1694–1754), English prime minister from 1743 until his death.

[2] *commencement of hostilities* On 19 April 1775, 15 months before the Declaration of Independence, British and American forces clashed in what is often thought of as the first battle of the American Revolution.

But she has protected us, say some. That she hath engrossed us is true, and defended the continent at our expense as well as her own is admitted, and she would have defended Turkey from the same motive, viz. the sake of trade and dominion.

Alas, we have been long led away by ancient prejudices and made large sacrifices to superstition. We have boasted the protection of Great Britain, without considering that her motive was *interest* not *attachment*; that she did not protect us from *our enemies* on *our account*, but from *her enemies* on *her own account*, from those who had no quarrel with us on any *other account*, and who will always be our enemies on the *same account*. Let Britain wave her pretensions to the continent, or the continent throw off the dependence, and we should be at peace with France and Spain were they at war with Britain. The miseries of Hanover's last war, ought to warn us against connections.[1]

It hath lately been asserted in parliament, that the colonies have no relation to each other but through the parent country, i.e., that Pennsylvania and the Jerseys, and so on for the rest, are sister colonies by the way of England; this is certainly a very roundabout way of proving relationship, but it is the nearest and only true way of proving enemyship, if I may so call it. France and Spain never were, nor perhaps ever will be our enemies as *Americans*, but as our being the *subjects of Great Britain*.

But Britain is the parent country, say some. Then the more shame upon her conduct. Even brutes do not devour their young; nor savages make war upon their families; wherefore the assertion, if true, turns to her reproach; but it happens not to be true, or only partly so, and the phrase *parent* or *mother country* hath been jesuitically[2] adopted by the king and his parasites, with a low papistical design of gaining an unfair bias on the credulous weakness of our minds. Europe, and not England, is the parent country of America. This new world hath been the asylum for the persecuted lovers of civil and religious liberty from *every part* of Europe. Hither have they fled, not from the tender embraces of the mother, but from the cruelty of the monster; and it is so far true of England, that the same tyranny which drove the first emigrants from home pursues their descendants still.

In this extensive quarter of the globe, we forget the narrow limits of three hundred and sixty miles (the extent of England) and carry our friendship on a larger scale; we claim brotherhood with every European Christian, and triumph in the generosity of the sentiment.

It is pleasant to observe by what regular gradations we surmount the force of local prejudice, as we enlarge our acquaintance with the world. A man born in any town in England divided into parishes, will naturally associate most with his fellow parishioners (because their interests in many cases will be common) and distinguish him by the name of *neighbour*; if he meet him but a few miles from home, he drops the narrow idea of a street, and salutes him by the name of *townsman*; if he travels out of the county, and meet him in any other, he forgets the minor divisions of street and town, and calls him *countryman*; i.e., *countyman*; but if in their foreign excursions they should associate in France or any other part of *Europe*, their local remembrance would be enlarged into that of *Englishmen*. And by a just parity of reasoning, all Europeans meeting in America, or any other quarter of the globe, are *countrymen*; for England, Holland, Germany, or Sweden, when compared with the whole, stand in the same places on the larger scale, which the divisions of street, town, and county do on the smaller ones; distinctions too limited for continental minds. Not one third of the inhabitants, even of this province, are of English descent. Wherefore, I reprobate the phrase of parent or mother country applied to England only, as being false, selfish, narrow and ungenerous.

But admitting that we were all of English descent, what does it amount to? Nothing. Britain, being now an

---

1 *The miseries ... connections* I.e., the Seven Years' War (1756–63), a major military conflict that involved a number of European powers, including Britain and France.

2 *jesuitically* For contemporary Protestants like Paine, the Jesuits—a Catholic religious order—was a byword for deceit and conniving behavior.

open enemy, extinguishes every other name and title: And to say that reconciliation is our duty, is truly farcical. The first king of England, of the present line (William the Conqueror) was a Frenchman, and half the Peers of England are descendants from the same country; wherefore by the same method of reasoning, England ought to be governed by France.

Much hath been said of the united strength of Britain and the colonies, that in conjunction they might bid defiance to the world. But this is mere presumption; the fate of war is uncertain, neither do the expressions mean anything; for this continent would never suffer itself to be drained of inhabitants to support the British arms in either Asia, Africa, or Europe.

Besides, what have we to do with setting the world at defiance? Our plan is commerce, and that, well attended to, will secure us the peace and friendship of all Europe; because it is the interest of all Europe to have America a *free port*. Her trade will always be a protection, and her barrenness of gold and silver secure her from invaders.

I challenge the warmest advocate for reconciliation to show a single advantage that this continent can reap, by being connected with Great Britain. I repeat the challenge, not a single advantage is derived. Our corn will fetch its price in any market in Europe, and our imported goods must be paid for by them where we will.

But the injuries and disadvantages we sustain by that connection are without number; and our duty to mankind at large, as well as to ourselves, instruct us to renounce the alliance. Because, any submission to, or dependence on Great Britain, tends directly to involve this continent in European wars and quarrels, and sets us at variance with nations who would otherwise seek our friendship, and against whom we have neither anger nor complaint. As Europe is our market for trade, we ought to form no partial connection with any part of it. It is the true interest of America to steer clear of European contentions, which she never can do, while by her dependence on Britain, she is made the make weight in the scale of British politics.

Europe is too thickly planted with kingdoms to be long at peace, and whenever a war breaks out between England and any foreign power, the trade of America goes to ruin, *because of her connection with Britain*. The next war may not turn out like the last, and should it not, the advocates for reconciliation now will be wishing for separation then, because neutrality in that case would be a safer convoy than a man of war. Every thing that is right or natural pleads for separation. The blood of the slain, the weeping voice of nature cries, 'TIS TIME TO PART. Even the distance at which the Almighty hath placed England and America is a strong and natural proof, that the authority of the one, over the other, was never the design of Heaven. The time likewise at which the continent was discovered, adds weight to the argument, and the manner in which it was peopled increases the force of it. The reformation was preceded by the discovery of America, as if the Almighty graciously meant to open a sanctuary to the persecuted in future years, when home should afford neither friendship nor safety.

The authority of Great Britain over this continent is a form of government, which sooner or later must have an end: And a serious mind can draw no true pleasure by looking forward, under the painful and positive conviction, that what he calls "the present constitution" is merely temporary. As parents, we can have no joy, knowing that *this government* is not sufficiently lasting to ensure any thing which we may bequeath to posterity: And by a plain method of argument, as we are running the next generation into debt, we ought to do the work of it, otherwise we use them meanly and pitifully. In order to discover the line of our duty rightly, we should take our children in our hand, and fix our station a few years farther into life; that eminence will present a prospect, which a few present fears and prejudices conceal from our sight.

Though I would carefully avoid giving unnecessary offence, yet I am inclined to believe, that all those who espouse the doctrine of reconciliation, may be included within the following descriptions: Interested men, who are not to be trusted; weak men who *cannot* see; prejudiced men who *will not* see; and a certain set of moderate men, who think better of the European world than it deserves; and this last class by an ill-judged deliberation, will be the cause of more calamities to this continent than all the other three.

It is the good fortune of many to live distant from the scene of sorrow; the evil is not sufficiently brought to *their* doors to make *them* feel the precariousness with which all American property is possessed. But let our imaginations transport us for a few moments to Boston, that seat of wretchedness will teach us wisdom, and instruct us for ever to renounce a power in whom we can have no trust. The inhabitants of that unfortunate city, who but a few months ago were in ease and affluence, have now no other alternative than to stay and starve, or turn out to beg. Endangered by the fire of their friends if they continue within the city, and plundered by the soldiery if they leave it. In their present condition they are prisoners without the hope of redemption, and in a general attack for their relief, they would be exposed to the fury of both armies.

Men of passive tempers look somewhat lightly over the offenses of Britain, and, still hoping for the best, are apt to call out, "*Come, come, we shall be friends again for all this.*" But examine the passions and feelings of mankind. Bring the doctrine of reconciliation to the touchstone of nature, and then tell me whether you can hereafter love, honour, and faithfully serve the power that hath carried fire and sword into your land? If you cannot do all these, then are you only deceiving yourselves, and by your delay bringing ruin upon posterity. Your future connection with Britain, whom you can neither love nor honour, will be forced and unnatural, and being formed only on the plan of present convenience, will in a little time fall into a relapse more wretched than the first. But if you say you can still pass the violations over, then I ask, Hath your house been burnt? Hath your property been destroyed before your face? Are your wife and children destitute of a bed to lie on, or bread to live on? Have you lost a parent or a child by their hands, and yourself the ruined and wretched survivor? If you have not, then are you not a judge of those who have. But if you have, and can still shake hands with the murderers, then are you unworthy the name of husband, father, friend, or lover, and whatever may be your rank or title in life, you have the heart of a coward, and the spirit of a sycophant.

This is not inflaming or exaggerating matters, but trying them by those feelings and affections which nature justifies, and without which, we should be incapable of discharging the social duties of life, or enjoying the felicities of it. I mean not to exhibit horror for the purpose of provoking revenge, but to awaken us from fatal and unmanly slumbers, that we may pursue determinately some fixed object. It is not in the power of Britain or of Europe to conquer America, if she do not conquer herself by *delay* and timidity. The present winter is worth an age if rightly employed, but if lost or neglected, the whole continent will partake of the misfortune; and there is no punishment which that man will not deserve, be he who, or what, or where he will, that may be the means of sacrificing a season so precious and useful.

It is repugnant to reason, to the universal order of things, to all examples from the former ages, to suppose, that this continent can longer remain subject to any external power. The most sanguine in Britain does not think so. The utmost stretch of human wisdom cannot, at this time, compass a plan short of separation, which can promise the continent even a year's security. Reconciliation is now a fallacious dream. Nature hath deserted the connection, and Art cannot supply her place. For, as Milton wisely expresses, "never can true reconcilement grow where wounds of deadly hate have pierced so deep."[1]

Every quiet method for peace hath been ineffectual. Our prayers have been rejected with disdain; and only tended to convince us, that nothing flatters vanity, or confirms obstinacy in kings more than repeated petitioning—and nothing hath contributed more than that very measure to make the kings of Europe absolute: Witness Denmark and Sweden. Wherefore since noth-

---

[1] *never can true … so deep* From John Milton's *Paradise Lost* (1667, 1674), 4.98–99.

ing but blows will do, for God's sake, let us come to a final separation, and not leave the next generation to be cutting throats, under the violated unmeaning names of parent and child.

To say, they will never attempt it again is idle and visionary, we thought so at the repeal of the stamp act,[1] yet a year or two undeceived us; as well may we suppose that nations, which have been once defeated, will never renew the quarrel.

As to government matters, it is not in the powers of Britain to do this continent justice: the business of it will soon be too weighty, and intricate, to be managed with any tolerable degree of convenience by a power so distant from us, and so very ignorant of us; for if they cannot conquer us, they cannot govern us. To be always running three or four thousand miles with a tale or a petition, waiting four or five months for an answer, which when obtained requires five or six more to explain it in, will in a few years be looked upon as folly and childishness—There was a time when it was proper, and there is a proper time for it to cease.

Small islands not capable of protecting themselves, are the proper objects for kingdoms to take under their care; but there is something very absurd, in supposing a continent to be perpetually governed by an island. In no instance hath nature made the satellite larger than its primary planet, and as England and America, with respect to each other, reverses the common order of nature, it is evident they belong to different systems: England to Europe—America to itself.

I am not induced by motives of pride, party, or resentment to espouse the doctrine of separation and independence; I am clearly, positively, and conscientiously persuaded that it is the true interest of this continent to be so; that everything short of *that* is mere patchwork, that it can afford no lasting felicity,—that it is leaving the sword to our children, and shrinking back

at a time when a little more, a little farther, would have rendered this continent the glory of the earth. …

But where, say some, is the King of America? I'll tell you Friend, he reigns above, and doth not make havoc of mankind like the Royal Brute of Britain. Yet that we may not appear to be defective even in earthly honours, let a day be solemnly set apart for proclaiming the charter; let it be brought forth placed on the divine law, the word of God; let a crown be placed thereon, by which the world may know, that so far as we approve of monarchy, that in America THE LAW IS KING. For as in absolute governments the King is law, so in free countries the law *ought* to be King; and there ought to be no other. But lest any ill use should afterwards arise, let the crown at the conclusion of the ceremony be demolished, and scattered among the people whose right it is.

A government of our own is our natural right: And when a man seriously reflects on the precariousness of human affairs, he will become convinced, that it is infinitely wiser and safer, to form a constitution of our own in a cool deliberate manner, while we have it in our power, than to trust such an interesting event to time and chance. If we omit it now, some Massenello[2] may hereafter arise, who laying hold of popular disquietudes, may collect together the desperate and the discontented, and by assuming to themselves the powers of government, may sweep away the liberties of the continent like a deluge. Should the government of America return again into the hands of Britain, the tottering situation of things will be a temptation for some desperate adventurer to try his fortune; and in such a case, what relief can Britain give? Ere she could hear the news the fatal business might be done, and ourselves suffering like the wretched Britons under the oppression of the Conqueror. Ye that oppose independence now, ye know not what ye do; ye are opening a door to eternal tyranny, by keeping vacant the seat of government. There are thousands and tens of thousands, who would think it glorious to expel from the continent that barbarous and

---

[1] *the stamp act* Controversial 1765 act that imposed a tax on printed material (such as newspapers and legal documents) throughout the American colonies. Although it was soon repealed, the Stamp Act is often viewed as an important precursor to the Declaration of Independence.

---

[2] *Massenello* Tommaso Anielo (1620–47), a fisher and leader of a popular but short-lived revolt against the Spanish nobles who ruled Naples.

hellish power, which hath stirred up the Indians and Negroes to destroy us; the cruelty hath a double guilt, it is dealing brutally by us, and treacherously by them.

To talk of friendship with those in whom our reason forbids us to have faith, and our affections (wounded through a thousand pores) instruct us to detest, is madness and folly. Every day wears out the little remains of kindred between us and them, and can there be any reason to hope, that as the relationship expires, the affection will increase, or that we shall agree better, when we have ten times more and greater concerns to quarrel over than ever?

Ye that tell us of harmony and reconciliation, can ye restore to us the time that is past? Can ye give to prostitution its former innocence? Neither can ye reconcile Britain and America. The last cord now is broken, the people of England are presenting addresses against us. There are injuries which nature cannot forgive; she would cease to be nature if she did. As well can the lover forgive the ravisher of his mistress, as the continent forgive the murders of Britain. The Almighty hath implanted in us these inextinguishable feelings for good and wise purposes. They are the guardians of his image in our hearts. They distinguish us from the herd of common animals. The social compact would dissolve, and justice be extirpated from the earth, or have only a casual existence were we callous to the touches of affection. The robber and the murderer would often escape unpunished, did not the injuries which our tempers sustain, provoke us into justice.

O ye that love mankind! Ye that dare oppose, not only the tyranny, but the tyrant, stand forth! Every spot of the old world is overrun with oppression. Freedom hath been hunted round the globe. Asia, and Africa, have long expelled her—Europe regards her like a stranger, and England hath given her warning to depart. O! receive the fugitive, and prepare in time an asylum for mankind. …

—1776

from *Rights of Man*

PART 2

INTRODUCTION

What Archimedes[1] said of the mechanical powers, may be applied to reason and liberty: "*Had we,*" said he, "*a place to stand upon, we might raise the world.*"

The revolution in America presented in politics what was only theory in mechanics. So deeply rooted were all the governments of the old world, and so effectually had the tyranny and the antiquity of habit established itself over the mind, that no beginning could be made in Asia, Africa or Europe, to reform the political condition of man. Freedom had been hunted round the globe: reason was considered as rebellion; and the slavery of fear had made men afraid to think.

But such is the irresistible nature of truth, that all it asks, and all it wants, is the liberty of appearing. The sun needs no inscription to distinguish him from darkness, and no sooner did the American governments display themselves to the world, than despotism felt a shock, and man began to contemplate redress.

The independence of America, considered merely as a separation from England, would have been a matter but of little importance, had it not been accompanied by a revolution in the principles and practice of government. She made a stand, not for herself only, but for the world, and looked beyond the advantages which *she* could receive. Even the Hessian,[2] though hired to fight against her, may live to bless his defeat; and England, condemning the viciousness of its government, rejoice in its miscarriage.

As America was the only spot in the political world where the principles of universal reformation could begin, so also was it the best in the natural world. An assemblage of circumstances conspired, not only to give

---

[1] *Archimedes* Greek mathematician, engineer, and inventor (287–212 BCE).

[2] *Hessian* German soldiers who served Britain in the eighteenth century.

birth, but to add gigantic maturity to its principles. The scene which that country presents to the eye of the spectator, has something in it which generates and enlarges great ideas. Nature appears to him in magnitude. The mighty objects he beholds, act upon his mind by enlarging it, and he partakes of the greatness he contemplates. Its first settlers were emigrants from different European nations, and of diversified professions of religion, retiring from the governmental persecutions of the old world, and meeting in the new, not as enemies, but as brothers. The wants which necessarily accompany the cultivation of a wilderness, produced among them a state of society which countries long harassed by the quarrels and intrigues of governments had neglected to cherish. In such a situation man becomes what he ought to be. He sees his species, not with the inhuman idea of a natural enemy, but as kindred; and the example shows to the artificial world, that man must go back to nature for information.

From the rapid progress which America makes in every species of improvement, it is rational to conclude that if the governments of Asia, Africa and Europe, had begun on a principle similar to that of America, or had they not been very early corrupted therefrom, those countries must by this time have been in a far superior condition to what they are. Age after age has passed away, for no other purpose than to behold their wretchedness. Could we suppose a spectator who knew nothing of the world, and who was put into it merely to make his observations, he would take a great part of the old world to be new, just struggling with the difficulties and hardships of an infant settlement. He could not suppose that the hordes of miserable poor, with which old countries abound, could be any other than those who had not yet been able to provide for themselves. Little would he think they were the consequence of what in such countries is called government.

If, from the more wretched parts of the old world, we look at those which are in an advanced state of improvement, we still find the greedy hand of government thrusting itself into every corner and crevice of industry, and grasping the spoil of the multitude. Invention is continually exercised, to furnish new pretences for revenue and taxation. It watches prosperity as its prey, and permits none to escape without a tribute.

As revolutions have begun, (and as the probability is always greater against a thing beginning, than of proceeding after it has begun) it is natural to expect that other revolutions will follow. The amazing and still increasing expenses with which old governments are conducted, the numerous wars they engage in or provoke, the embarrassments they throw in the way of universal civilization and commerce, and the oppression and usurpation acted at home, have wearied out the patience, and exhausted the property of the world. In such a situation, and with such examples already existing, revolutions are to be looked for. They are become subjects of universal conversation, and may be considered as the *order of the day*.

If systems of government can be introduced less expensive, and more productive of general happiness, than those which have existed, all attempts to oppose their progress will in the end prove fruitless. Reason, like time, will make its own way, and prejudice will fall in the combat with interest. If universal peace, harmony, civilization and commerce are ever to be the happy lot of man, it cannot be accomplished but by a revolution in the present system of governments. All the monarchical governments are military. War is their trade, plunder and revenue their objects. While such governments continue, peace has not the absolute security of a day. What is the history of all monarchical governments but a disgustful picture of human wretchedness, and the accidental respite of a few years' repose? Wearied with war, and tired with human butchery, they sat down to rest and called it peace. This certainly is not the condition that heaven intended for man; and if *this be monarchy*, well might monarchy be reckoned among the sins of the Jews.

The revolutions which formerly took place in the world, had nothing in them that interested the bulk of mankind. They extended only to a change of persons and measures, but not of principles, and rose or fell among the common transactions of the moment. What we now behold, may not improperly be called a "counter revolution." Conquest and tyranny, at some early period, dispossessed man of his rights, and he is now recovering them. And as the tide of human affairs has its ebb and flow in directions contrary to each other, so also is it in this. Government founded on a *moral theory, on a system of universal peace, on the indefeasible, hereditary rights of man*, is now revolving from west to east by a stronger impulse than the government of the sword revolved from east to west. It interests not particular individuals but nations in its progress, and promises a new era to the human race.

The danger to which the success of revolutions is most exposed, is that of attempting them before the principles on which they proceed, and the advantages to result from them, are sufficiently understood. Almost every thing appertaining to the circumstances of a nation has been absorbed and confounded under the general and mysterious word *government*. Though it avoids taking to its account the errors it commits, and the mischiefs it occasions, it fails not to arrogate to itself whatever has the appearance of prosperity. It robs industry of its honours by pedantically making itself the cause of its effects; and purloins from the general character of man the merits that appertain to him as a social being.

It may therefore be of use, in this day of revolutions, to discriminate between those things which are the effect of government, and those which are not. This will best be done by taking a review of society and civilization, and the consequences resulting therefrom, as things distinct from what are called governments. By beginning with this investigation, we shall be able to assign effects to their proper causes, and analyze the mass of common errors.

from Chapter 3:
Of the Old and New Systems of Government

… Though it might be proved that the system of government now called the *new*, is the most ancient in principle of all that have existed, being founded on the original inherent rights of man: yet, as tyranny and the sword have suspended the exercise of those rights for many centuries past, it serves better the purpose of

distinction to call it the new, than to claim the right of calling it the old.

The first general distinction between those two systems, is, that the one now called the old is hereditary, either in whole or in part; and the new is entirely representative. It rejects all hereditary government:

1st, As being an imposition on mankind.

2nd, As inadequate to the purposes for which government is necessary.

With respect to the first of these heads—It cannot be proved by what right hereditary government could begin: neither does there exist within the compass of mortal power, a right to establish it. Man has no authority over posterity in matters of personal right; and therefore, no man, or body of men, had, or can have, a right to set up hereditary government. Were even ourselves to come again into existence, instead of being succeeded by posterity, we have not now the right of taking from ourselves the rights which would then be ours. On what ground, then, do we pretend to take them from others?

All hereditary government is in its nature tyranny. An heritable crown, or an heritable throne, or by what other fanciful name such things may be called, have no other significant explanation than that mankind are heritable property. To inherit a government, is to inherit the people, as if they were flocks and herds.

With respect to the second head, that of being inadequate to the purposes for which government is necessary, we have only to consider what government essentially is, and compare it with the circumstances to which hereditary government is subject.

Government ought to be a thing always in full maturity. It ought to be so constructed as to be superior to all the accidents to which individual man is subject: and, therefore, hereditary succession, by being *subject to them all*, is the most irregular and imperfect of all the systems of government.

We have heard the *rights of man* called a *levelling* system; but the only system to which the word *levelling* is truly applicable, is the hereditary monarchical system. It is a system of *mental levelling*. It indiscriminately admits every species of character to the same authority.

Vice and virtue, ignorance and wisdom, in short, every quality, good or bad, is put on the same level. Kings succeed each other, not as rationals, but as animals. Can we then be surprised at the abject state of the human mind in monarchical countries, when the government itself is formed on such an abject levelling system?—It has no fixed character. Today it is one thing; and tomorrow it is something else. It changes with the temper of every succeeding individual, and is subject to all the varieties of each. It is government through the medium of passions and accidents. It appears under all the various characters of childhood, decrepitude, dotage, a thing at nurse, in leading strings, and on crutches. It reverses the wholesome order of nature. It occasionally puts children over men, and the conceits of nonage over wisdom and experience. In short, we cannot conceive a more ridiculous figure of government, than hereditary succession, in all its cases, presents.

Could it be made a decree in nature, or an edict registered in heaven, and man could know it, that virtue and wisdom should invariably appertain to hereditary succession, the objections to it would be removed; but when we see that nature acts as if she disowned and sported with the hereditary system; that the mental characters of successors, in all countries, are below the average of human understanding; that one is a tyrant, another an idiot, a third insane, and some all three together, it is impossible to attach confidence to it, when reason in man has power to act.

It is not to the abbe Sieyes[1] that I need apply this reasoning; he has already saved me that trouble by giving his own opinion on the case. "If it be asked," says he, "what is my opinion with respect to hereditary right, I answer, without hesitation, that, in good theory, an hereditary transmission of any power or office, can never accord with the laws of true representation. Hereditary-ship is, in this sense, as much an attaint upon principle, as an outrage upon society. But let us," continues he, "refer to the history of all elective monarchies and principalities; is there one in which the elective mode is not worse than the hereditary succession?"

As to debating on which is the worst of the two, it is admitting both to be bad; and herein we are agreed. The preference which the abbe has given is a condemnation of the thing he prefers. Such a mode of reasoning on such a subject is inadmissible, because it finally amounts to an accusation of providence, as if she had left to man no other choice with respect to government, than between two evils, the best of which he admits to be, "*an attaint upon principle, and an outrage upon society.*"

Passing over, for the present, all the evils and mischiefs which monarchy has occasioned in the world, nothing can more effectually prove its uselessness in a state of *civil government*, than making it hereditary. Would we make any office hereditary that required wisdom and abilities to fill it? And where wisdom and abilities are not necessary, such an office, whatever it may be, is superfluous or insignificant.

Hereditary succession is a burlesque upon monarchy. It puts it in the most ridiculous light, by presenting it as an office which any child or idiot may fill. It requires some talents to be a common mechanic; but to be a king, requires only the animal figure of a man—a sort of breathing automaton. This sort of superstition may last a few years more, but it cannot long resist the awakened reason and interest of man.

As to Mr. Burke, he is a stickler for monarchy, not altogether as a pensioner, if he is one, which I believe, but as a political man. He has taken up a contemptible opinion of mankind, who, in their turn, are taking up the same of him. He considers them as a herd of beings that must be governed by fraud, effigy, and show; and an idol would be as good a figure of monarchy with him, as a man. I will, however, do him the justice to say, that, with respect to America, he has been very complimentary. He always contended, at least in my hearing, that the people of America were more enlightened than those of England, or of any country in Europe; and that therefore the imposition of show was not necessary in their governments. ...

[1] *abbe Sieyes* Emmanuel Joseph Sieyès (1748–1838), French Roman Catholic abbé (abbot) and clergyman, and one of the chief theorists of the French Revolution.

Having thus glanced at a few of the defects of the old, or hereditary systems of government, let us compare it with the new or representative system.

The representative system takes society and civilization for its basis; nature, reason, and experience for its guide.

Experience, in all ages, and in all countries, has demonstrated, that it is impossible to control nature in her distribution of mental powers. She gives them as she pleases. Whatever is the rule by which she, apparently to us, scatters them among mankind, that rule remains a secret to man. It would be as ridiculous to attempt to fix the hereditaryship of human beauty, as of wisdom.

Whatever wisdom constituently is, it is like a seedless plant; it may be reared when it appears; but it cannot be voluntarily produced. There is always a sufficiency somewhere in the general mass of society for all purposes; but with respect to the parts of society, it is continually changing its place. It rises in one today, in another tomorrow, and has most probably visited in rotation every family of the earth, and again withdrawn.

As this is the order of nature, the order of government must necessarily follow it, or government will, as we see it does, degenerate into ignorance. The hereditary system, therefore, is as repugnant to human wisdom, as to human rights; and is as absurd as it is unjust.

As the republic of letters brings forward the best literary productions, by giving to genius a fair and universal chance; so the representative system of government is calculated to produce the wisest laws, by collecting wisdom where it can be found. I smile to myself when I contemplate the ridiculous insignificance into which literature and all the sciences would sink, were they made hereditary; and I carry the same idea into governments. An hereditary governor is as inconsistent as an hereditary author. I know not whether Homer[1] or Euclid[2] had sons; but I will venture an opinion, that if they had, and had left their works unfinished, those sons could not have completed them.

Do we need a stronger evidence of the absurdity of hereditary government, than is seen in the descendants of those men, in any line of life, who once were famous? Is there scarcely an instance in which there is not a total reverse of the character? It appears as if the tide of mental faculties flowed as far as it could in certain channels, and then forsook its course, and arose in others. How irrational then is the hereditary system which establishes channels of power, in company with which wisdom refuses to flow! By continuing this absurdity, man is in perpetual contradiction with himself; he accepts, for a king, or a chief magistrate, or a legislator, a person whom he would not elect for a constable.

It appears to general observation, that revolutions create genius and talents; but those events do no more than bring them forward. There exists in man a mass of sense lying in a dormant state, and which, unless something excites it to action, will descend with him, in that condition, to the grave. As it is to the advantage of society that the whole of its faculties should be employed, the construction of government ought to be such as to bring forward, by a quiet and regular operation, all that extent of capacity which never fails to appear in revolutions.

This cannot take place in the insipid state of hereditary government, not only because it prevents, but because it operates to benumb. When the mind of a nation is bowed down by any political superstition in its government, such as hereditary succession is, it loses a considerable portion of its powers on all other subjects and objects. Hereditary succession requires the same obedience to ignorance as to wisdom; and when once the mind can bring itself to pay this indiscriminate reverence, it descends below the stature of mental manhood. It is fit to be great only in little things. It acts a treachery upon itself, and suffocates the sensations that urge to detection.

Though the ancient governments present to us a miserable picture of the condition of man, there is one which above all others exempts itself from the general description. I mean the democracy of the Athenians. We see more to admire and less to condemn, in that great,

1 *Homer* Legendary Greek poet (c. 8th century BCE).
2 *Euclid* Greek mathematician (c. 3rd century BCE).

extraordinary people, than in any thing which history affords.

Mr. Burke is so little acquainted with constituent principles of government, that he confounds democracy and representation together. Representation was a thing unknown in the ancient democracies. In those the mass of the people met and enacted laws (grammatically speaking) in the first person. Simple democracy was no other than the common hall of the ancients. It signifies the *form*, as well as the public principle of the government. As these democracies increased in population, and the territory extended, the simple democratical form became unwieldy and impracticable; and as the system of representation was not known, the consequence was, they either degenerated convulsively into monarchies, or became absorbed into such as then existed. Had the system of representation been then understood, as it now is, there is no reason to believe that those forms of government, now called monarchical or aristocratical, would ever have taken place. It was the want of some method to consolidate the parts of society, after it became too populous, and too extensive for the simple democratical form, and also the lax and solitary condition of shepherds and herdsmen in other parts of the world, that afforded opportunities to those unnatural modes of government to begin.

As it is necessary to clear away the rubbish of errors, into which the subject of government has been thrown, I shall proceed to remark on some others.

It has always been the political craft of courtiers and court governments, to abuse something which they called republicanism; but what republicanism was, or is, they never attempt to explain. Let us examine a little into this case.

The only forms of government are, the democratical, the aristocratical, the monarchical, and what is now called the representative.

What is called a *republic*, is not any *particular form* of government. It is wholly characteristical of the purport, matter, or object for which government ought to be instituted, and on which it is to be employed, *res-publica*, the public affairs, or the public good; or, literally translated, the *public thing*. It is a word of a good original, referring to what ought to be the character and business of government; and in this sense it is naturally opposed to the word *monarchy*, which has a base original signification. It means arbitrary power in an individual person; in the exercise of which, himself, and not the *res-publica*, is the object.

Every government that does not act on the principle of a republic, or, in other words, that does not make the *res-publica* its whole and sole object, is not a good government. Republican government is no other than government established and conducted for the interest of the public, as well individually as collectively. It is not necessarily connected with any particular form, but it most naturally associates with the representative form, as being best calculated to secure the end for which a nation is at the expense of supporting it.

Various forms of government have affected to style themselves republics. Poland calls itself a republic, but is in fact an hereditary aristocracy, with what is called an elective monarchy. Holland calls itself a republic, which is chiefly aristocratical, with an hereditary stadtholdership. But the government of America, which is wholly on the system of representation, is the only real republic in character and practice, that now exists. Its government has no other object than the public business of the nation, and therefore it is properly a republic; and the Americans have taken care that *this*, and no other, shall be the object of their government, by their rejecting every thing hereditary, and establishing government on the system of representation only.

Those who have said that a republic is not a *form* of government calculated for countries of great extent, mistook, in the first place, the *business* of a government, for a *form* of government; for the *res-publica* equally appertains to every extent of territory and population. And, in the second place, if they meant any thing with respect to *form*, it was the simple democratical form, such as was the mode of government in the ancient democracies, in which there was no representation. The case, therefore, is not that a republic cannot be extensive, but that it cannot be extensive on the simple democratic form; and the question naturally presents itself, *What is the best form of government for conducting the Res-publica or Public Business of a nation, after it becomes too extensive and populous for the simple democratical form?*

It cannot be monarchy, because monarchy is subject to an objection of the same amount to which the democratical form was subject.

It is possible that an individual may lay down a system of principles, on which government shall be constitutionally established to any extent of territory. This is no more than an operation of the mind acting by its own powers. But the practice upon those principles, as applying to the various and numerous circumstances of a nation, its agriculture, manufactures, trade, commerce, &c., requires a knowledge, of a different kind, and which can be had only from the various parts of society. It is an assemblage of practical knowledge, which no one individual can possess; and therefore the monarchical form is as much limited, in useful practice, from the incompetency of knowledge, as was the democratical form, from the multiplicity of population. The one degenerates, by extension, into confusion; the other into ignorance and incapacity, of which all the great monarchies are an evidence. The monarchical form, therefore, could not be a substitute for the democratical, because it has equal inconveniences.

Much less could it when made hereditary. This is the most effectual of all forms to preclude knowledge. Neither could the high democratical mind have voluntarily yielded itself to be governed by children and idiots, and all the motley insignificance of character, which attends such a mere animal system, the disgrace and the reproach of reason and of man.

As to the aristocratical form, it has the same vices and defects with the monarchical, except that the chance of abilities is better from the proportion of numbers, but there is still no security for the right use and application of them.

Referring, then, to the original simple democracy, it affords the true data from which government on a large scale can begin. It is incapable of extension, not from its principle, but from the inconvenience of its form; and monarchy and aristocracy from their incapacity. Retain-

ing, then, democracy as the ground, and rejecting the corrupt systems of monarchy and aristocracy, the representative system naturally presents itself; remedying at once the defects of the simple democracy as to form, and the incapacity of the other two with regard to knowledge.

Simple democracy was society governing itself without the use of secondary means. By ingrafting representation upon democracy, we arrive at a system of government capable of embracing and confederating all the various interests and every extent of territory and population; and that also with advantages as much superior to hereditary government, as the republic of letters is to hereditary literature.

It is on this system that the American government was founded. It is representation ingrafted upon democracy. It has settled the form by a scale parallel in all cases to the extent of the principle. What Athens was in miniature, America will be in magnitude. The one was the wonder of the ancient world—the other is becoming the admiration and model of the present. It is the easiest of all the forms of government to be understood, and the most eligible in practice; and excludes at once the ignorance and insecurity of the hereditary mode, and the inconvenience of the simple democracy.

It is impossible to conceive a system of government capable of acting over such an extent of territory, and such a circle of interests, as is produced by the operation of representation. France, great and populous as it is, is but a spot in the capaciousness of the system. It adapts itself to all possible cases. It is preferable to simple democracy even in small territories. Athens, by representation, would have surpassed her own democracy.

That which is called government, or rather that which we ought to conceive government to be, is no more than some common centre, in which all the parts of society unite. This cannot be established by any method so conducive to the various interests of the community, as by the representative system. It concentrates the knowledge necessary to the interests of the parts, and of the whole. It places government in a state of constant maturity. It is, as has already been observed, never young, never old.[1] It is subject neither to nonage nor dotage. It is never in the cradle nor on crutches. It admits not of a separation between knowledge and power, and is superior, as government ought always to be, to all the accidents of individual man, and is therefore superior to what is called monarchy.

A nation is not a body, the figure of which is to be represented by the human body; but is like a body contained within a circle, having a common centre, in which every radius meets; and that centre is formed by representation. To connect representation with what is called monarchy, is eccentric government. Representation is of itself the delegated monarchy of a nation, and cannot debase itself by dividing it with another.

Mr. Burke has two or three times in his parliamentary speeches, and in his publications, made use of a jingle of words that conveyed no ideas. Speaking of government, he says, "It is better to have monarchy for its basis, and republicanism for its corrective, than republicanism for its basis, and monarchy for its corrective." If he means that it is better to correct folly with wisdom, than wisdom with folly, I will no otherwise contend with him, than to say it would be much better to reject the folly altogether.

But what is this thing which Mr. Burke calls monarchy? Will he explain it: all mankind can understand what representation is; and that it must necessarily include a variety of knowledge and talents. But what security is there for the same qualities on the part of monarchy? Or, when this monarchy is a child, where then is the wisdom? What does it know about government? Who then is the monarch? or where is the monarchy? If it is to be performed by regency, it proves to be a farce. A regency is a mock species of republic,

and the whole of monarchy deserves no better appellation. It is a thing as various as imagination can paint. It has none of the stable character that government ought to possess. Every succession is a revolution, and every regency a counter-revolution. The whole of it is a scene of perpetual court cabal and intrigue, of which Mr. Burke is himself an instance.

Whether I have too little sense to see, or too much to be imposed upon: whether I have too much or too little pride, or of anything else, I leave out of the question; but certain it is, that what is called monarchy, always appears to me a silly, contemptible thing. I compare it to something kept behind a curtain, about which there is a great deal of bustle and fuss, and a wonderful air of seeming solemnity; but when, by any accident, the curtain happens to be open and the company see what it is, they burst into laughter.

In the representative system of government, nothing like this can happen. Like the nation itself, it possesses a perpetual stamina, as well of body as of mind, and presents itself on the open theatre of the world in a fair and manly manner. Whatever are its excellencies or its defects, they are visible to all. It exists not by fraud and mystery; it deals not in cant and sophistry; but inspires a language, that, passing from heart to heart, is felt and understood.

We must shut our eyes against reason, we must basely degrade our understanding, not to see the folly of what is called monarchy. Nature is orderly in all her works; but this is a mode of government that counteracts nature. It turns the progress of the human faculties upside down. It subjects age to be governed by children, and wisdom by folly.

On the contrary, the representative system is always parallel with the order and immutable laws of nature, and meets the reason of man in every part. For example:

In the American federal government, more power is delegated to the president of the United States, than to any other individual member of congress. He cannot, therefore, be elected to this office under the age of thirty-five years. By this time the judgment of man becomes matured, and he has lived long enough to become acquainted with men and things, and the

[1] *It places government ... never old* In *Reflections*, Burke argued that "Our political system is placed in a just correspondence and symmetry with the order of the world, and with the mode of existence decreed to a permanent body composed of transitory parts; wherein, by the disposition of stupendous wisdom, molding together the great mysterious incorporation of the human race, the whole, at one time, is never old, or middle-aged, or young, but in a condition of unchanged constancy, moves on through the varied tenour of perpetual decay, fall, renovation, and progression."

country with him. But on the monarchical plan (exclusive of the numerous chances there are against every man born into the world, of drawing a prize in the lottery of human faculties) the next in succession, whatever he may be, is put at the head of a nation, and of a government, at the age of eighteen years. Does this appear like an act of wisdom? Is it consistent with the proper dignity and the manly character of a nation? Where is the propriety of calling such a lad the father of the people?—In all other cases, a person is a minor until the age of twenty-one years. Before this period he is not trusted with the management of an acre of land, or with the heritable property of a flock of sheep, or an herd of swine; but wonderful to tell! he may at the age of eighteen years, be trusted with a nation.

That monarchy is all a bubble, a mere court artifice to procure money is evident (at least to me) in every character in which it can be viewed. It would be almost impossible, on the rational system of representative government, to make out a bill of expenses to such an enormous amount as this deception admits. Government is not of itself a very chargeable institution. The whole expense of the federal government of America, founded, as I have already said, on the system of representation, and extending over a country nearly ten times as large as England, is but six hundred thousand dollars, or one hundred and thirty thousand pounds sterling.

I presume that no man in his sober senses will compare the character of any of the kings of Europe, with that of general Washington.[1] Yet, in France, and also in England, the expense of the civil list only, for the support of one man, is eight times greater than the whole expense of the federal government of America. To assign a reason for this appears almost impossible. The generality of people in America, especially the poor, are more able to pay taxes, than the generality of people either in France or England.

But the case is, that the representative system diffuses such a body of knowledge throughout the nation, on the subject of government, as to explode ignorance and preclude imposition. The craft of courts cannot be acted on that ground. There is no place for mystery; nowhere for it to begin. Those who are not in the representation, know as much of the nature of business as those who are. An affectation of mysterious importance would there be scouted. Nations can have no secrets; and the secrets of courts, like those of individuals, are always their defects.

In the representative system, the reason for everything must publicly appear. Every man is a proprietor in government, and considers it a necessary part of his business to understand. It concerns his interest because it affects his property. He examines the cost, and compares it with the advantages; and above all, he does not adopt the slavish custom of following what in other governments are called *leaders*.

It can only be by blinding the understanding of man, and making him believe that government is some wonderful mysterious thing, that excessive revenues are obtained. Monarchy is well calculated to ensure this end. It is the popery of government; a thing kept up to amuse the ignorant, and quiet them into paying taxes.

The government of a free country, properly speaking, is not in the persons, but in the laws. The enacting of those requires no great expense; and when they are administered, the whole of civil government is performed—the rest is all court contrivance.

—1792

---

[1] *Washington*   Commander of the Continental Army in the Revolutionary War and the first President of the United States of America (1732–99).

ANNA LAETITIA BARBAULD
1743 – 1825

William Blake admired Anna Laetitia Barbauld's poetry, as did Samuel Taylor Coleridge, who walked forty miles to meet her, and William Wordsworth, who said about the Barbauld poem "Life": "I am not in the habit of grudging people their good things, but I wish I had written those [final] lines." Although born in the provinces, Barbauld was a leading figure in London literary life, as well as a prominent educator and a committed political and social activist. She composed innovative and influential poetry, hymns, children's literature, political pamphlets, essays, and works of literary criticism.

Anna Laetitia Aikin was born in Leicestershire to Jane Jennings and John Aikin, a nonconformist Presbyterian minister and schoolteacher at the Warrington Dissenting Academy in Yorkshire. Schooled by her father, she was a precocious child who studied the classics early in life. In her late teens she became acquainted with the influential educator and scientist Joseph Priestley and developed a lasting friendship with him and his wife. He was impressed by her poetry and eventually encouraged her to publish her first volume, *Poems* (1773). This collection of lyrics, hymns, epistles, and mock-heroic poems, published under her birth name, went through five editions in four years and received considerable critical acclaim, *The Monthly Review* calling it a "great accession to the literary world." That same year Barbauld printed *Miscellaneous Pieces in Prose* with her brother, John Aikin (later the editor of a radical journal, *Monthly Magazine*).

Living at Warrington Academy prepared Barbauld to run her own boys' boarding school, which she started with her husband, the dissenting clergy member Rochemont Barbauld, whom she married in 1774. During this period she wrote her popular and influential *Lessons for Children* (1787–88) and *Hymns in Prose for Children* (1787), designed for the very young. Both went through many printings and continued to be widely read in the United States and England for more than a century. By 1785 her husband's mental instability required them to close the school (he eventually became violent and later died by suicide), and from this point on, Barbauld committed herself solely to literary work.

In her political pamphlets and essays of the 1790s, Barbauld addressed ethics, education, and political economy, and argued for freedom of religion and conscience—a cause dear to the hearts of Dissenters. She also argued strongly for the abolition of slavery (at a moment when the movement had suffered a setback) in her verse *Epistle to William Wilberforce* (1791); and in the essay *Sins of Government, Sins of Nation* (1793) she derided the British government for its involvement in the war against France. Barbauld then turned to editorial work, producing the first collection of *The Correspondence of Samuel Richardson* (1804), which includes her biography of the author. She also published *The British Novelists* (1810), a fifty-volume collection featuring the work of 28 novelists, along with Barbauld's biographical and critical prefaces. In her general introduction to *On the Origin and Progress of Novel-Writing*, she argued for the value of novels for both education and enjoyment. This was pioneering in its recognition of the novel as a serious genre.

In 1812 Barbauld published the prophetic poem *Eighteen Hundred and Eleven*. Written in a pessimistic tone, the poem traces the cyclical rise and fall of national empires, indicts Britain for its involvement in the war with France, and predicts the fall of the British Empire. At the end of the poem, "Genius" leaves for America, the nation Barbauld suggests will replace Britain as the new empire. The poem elicited widespread criticism for what was deemed its "anti-patriotism." John Wilson Croker's abusive attack in the *Quarterly Review* used to be credited with effectively ending Barbauld's publishing career, but this is not accurate: she continued writing into the 1820s. After her death in 1825 her niece published two collections of her works.

⌘ ⌘ ⌘

Summer Evening's Meditation

One sun by day, by night ten thousand shine.
　　　　　　　　　　　　—Young.

'Tis past! The sultry tyrant of the south
　Has spent his short-lived rage; more grateful
　　hours
Move silent on; the skies no more repel
The dazzled sight, but with mild maiden beams
5　Of tempered lustre, court the cherished eye
To wander o'er their sphere; where hung aloft
Dian's bright crescent, like a silver bow
New strung in heaven, lifts high its beamy horns
Impatient for the night, and seems to push
10　Her brother down the sky. Fair Venus shines
E'en in the eye of the day; with sweetest beam
Propitious shines, and shakes a trembling flood
Of softened radiance from her dewy locks.
The shadows spread apace; while meekened° *made meek*
　　Eve,
15　Her cheek yet warm with blushes, slow retires
Through the Hesperian gardens of the west,
And shuts the gates of day. 'Tis now the hour
When Contemplation, from her sunless haunts,
The cool damp grotto, or the lonely depth
20　Of unpierced woods, where wrapt in solid shade
She mused away the gaudy hours of noon,
And fed on thoughts unripened by the sun,
Moves forward; and with radiant finger points

To yon blue concave swelled by breath divine,
25　Where, one by one, the living eyes of heaven
Awake, quick kindling o'er the face of ether
One boundless blaze; ten thousand trembling fires,
And dancing lustres, where th'unsteady eye
Restless and dazzled, wanders unconfined
30　O'er all this field of glories: spacious field!
And worthy of the master: he, whose hand
With hieroglyphics elder than the Nile,
Inscribed the mystic tablet; hung on high
To public gaze, and said, adore, O man!
35　The finger of thy God. From what pure wells
Of milky light, what soft o'erflowing urn,
Are all these lamps so filled? these friendly lamps,
For ever streaming o'er the azure deep
To point our path, and light us to our home.
40　How soft they slide along their lucid spheres!
And silent as the foot of time, fulfill
Their destined courses: Nature's self is hushed,
And, but a scattered leaf, which rustles through
The thick-wove foliage, not a sound is heard
45　To break the midnight air; though the raised ear,
Intensely listening, drinks in every breath.
How deep the silence, yet how loud the praise!
But are they silent all? or is there not
A tongue in every star that talks with man,
50　And woos him to be wise; nor woos in vain:
This dead of midnight is the noon of thought,
And wisdom mounts her zenith with the stars.
At this still hour the self-collected soul

Turns inward, and beholds a stranger there
55 Of high descent, and more than mortal rank;
An embryo God; a spark of fire divine,
Which must burn on for ages, when the sun,
(Fair transitory creature of a day!)
Has closed his golden eye, and wrapt in shades
60 Forgets his wonted° journey through   *customary*
      the east.
Ye citadels of light, and seats of Gods!
Perhaps my future home, from whence the soul
Revolving° periods past, may oft look back   *considering*
With recollected tenderness, on all
65 The various busy scenes she left below,
Its deep laid projects and its strange events,
As on some fond and doting tale that soothed
Her infant hours; O be it lawful now
To tread the hallowed circle of your courts,
70 And with mute wonder and delighted awe
Approach your burning confines. Seized in thought,
On fancy's wild and roving wing I sail,
From the green borders of the peopled earth,
And the pale moon, her duteous fair attendant;
75 From solitary Mars; from the vast orb
Of Jupiter, whose huge gigantic bulk
Dances in ether like the lightest leaf;
To the dim verge, the suburbs of the system,
Where chearless Saturn 'midst his wat'ry moons
80 Girt with a lucid zone,° in gloomy pomp,   *belt*
Sits like an exiled monarch: fearless thence
I launch into the trackless deeps of space,
Where, burning round, ten thousand suns appear,
Of elder beam; which ask no leave to shine
85 Of our terrestrial star, nor borrow light
From the proud regent of our scanty day;
Sons of the morning, first-born of creation,
And only less than him who marks their track,

And guides their fiery wheels. Here must I stop,
90 Or is there aught beyond? What hand unseen
Impels me onward through the glowing orbs
Of habitable nature; far remote,
To the dread confines of eternal night,
To solitudes of vast unpeopled space,
95 The deserts of creation, wide and wild;
Where embryo systems and unkindled suns
Sleep in the womb of chaos; fancy droops,
And thought astonished stops her bold career.
But oh though mighty mind! whose powerful word
100 Said, thus let all things be, and thus they were,
Where shall I seek thy presence? how unblamed
Invoke thy dread perfection?
Have the broad eye-lids of the morn beheld thee?
Or does the beamy shoulder of Orion
105 Support thy throne? O look with pity down
On erring guilty man; not in thy names
Of terror clad; not with those thunders armed
That conscious Sinai felt, when fear appalled
The scattered tribes; thou hast a gentler voice,
110 That whispers comfort to the swelling heart,
Abashed, yet longing to behold her Maker.
      But now my soul unused to stretch her powers
In flight so daring, drops her weary wing,
And seeks again the known accustomed spot,
115 Drest up with sun, and shade, and lawns, and streams,
A mansion fair and spacious for its guest,
And full replete with wonders. Let me here
Content and grateful, wait th'appointed time
And ripen for the skies: the hour will come
120 When all these splendours bursting on my sight
Shall stand unveiled, and to my ravished sense
Unlock the glories of the world unknown.
—1773

The Groans of the Tankard[1]

Dulci digne mero![2] —Horat.

O f strange events I sing, and portents dire;
　The wond'rous themes a reverent ear require;
Though strange the tale, the faithful Muse believe,
And what she says with pious awe receive.
5　　'Twas at the solemn, silent, noon-tide hour,[3]
When hunger rages with despotic power,
When the lean student quits his Hebrew roots[4]
For the gross nourishment of English fruits,
And throws unfinished airy systems by
10　For solid pudding[5] and substantial pie,
When hungry poets the glad summons own,
And leave spare fast to dine with Gods alone;[6]
Our sober meal dispatched with silent haste,
The decent grace concludes the short repast:
15　Then urged by thirst we cast impatient eyes
Where deep, capacious, vast, of ample size,
The tankard stood, replenished to the brink
With the cold beverage blue-eyed Naiads[7] drink.
But lo! a sudden prodigy appears,
20　And our chilled hearts recoil with startling fears;
Its yawning mouth disclosed the deep profound,
And in low murmurs breathed a sullen sound;

Cold drops of dew did on the sides appear;
No finger touched it, and no hand was near;
25　At length th' indignant vase its silence broke,
First heaved deep hollow groans, and then distinctly
　　spoke.[8]
　　"How changed the scene![9] for what unpardoned
　　crimes
Have I survived to these degenerate times?
I, who was wont the festal board to grace,
30　And midst the circle lift my honest face,
White o'er with froth, like Etna[10] crowned with snow,
Which mantled o'er the brown abyss below,
Where Ceres[11] mingled with her golden store
The richer spoils of either India's[12] shore,
35　The dulcet reed[13] the Western islands boast,
And spicy fruit from Banda's[14] fragrant coast.
At solemn feasts the nectared draught I poured,
And often journeyed round the ample board:
The portly Alderman, the stately Mayor,
40　And all the furry tribe[15] my worth declare;
And the keen Sportsman oft, his labours done,
To me retreating with the setting sun,
Deep draughts imbibed, and conquered land and sea,
And overthrew the pride of France—by me.
45　　"Let meaner clay contain the limpid wave,
The clay for such an office nature gave;
Let China's earth,[16] enriched with coloured stains,

---

[1] *Tankard* A drinking vessel, formerly made of wooden staves and hooped; now especially a tall one-handled jug or mug, usually of pewter, sometimes with a lid: used chiefly for drinking beer.

[2] *Dulci digne mero!* From Horace, "The Spring of Bandusia," *Odes*, 3.13.2: "Worthy of sweet wine!" Horace is known to have admired the beauty of fountains, and this ode celebrates the beauty of a spring.

[3] *'Twas at … noon-tide hour* Adapted from David Mallet's "William and Margaret" (1723): "'Twas at the silent, solemn hour, / When night and morning meet; / In glided Margaret's grimly ghost, / And stood at William's feet" (1–4).

[4] *Hebrew roots* Both in the sense of linguistic origins and ascetic diet.

[5] *solid pudding* From Alexander Pope's mock-epic poem *The Dunciad* (1728), 3.5.2.

[6] *Gods alone* Adapted from John Milton's "Il Pensoroso" (1645): "Spare Fast, that oft with gods doth diet" (46).

[7] *Naiads* In Greek mythology, nymphs who presided over fountains, wells, springs, and streams.

---

[8] *th'indignant vase … distinctly spoke* Cf. Keats's "Ode on a Grecian Urn" (1819).

[9] *How changed the scene!* Adapted from Satan's speech to his fellow fallen angels in Book I of Milton's *Paradise Lost* (1667, 1674).

[10] *Etna* Sicilian volcano.

[11] *Ceres* In Roman mythology, the goddess of agriculture and motherly love; she is known as Demeter in Greek mythology.

[12] *either India* The West Indies in the Caribbean and the East Indies in Southeast Asia.

[13] *dulcet reed* West Indian sugar.

[14] *Banda's* The Banda Islands in the East Indies; until the mid-nineteenth century, the Banda Islands were the only known source of nutmeg (here referred to as "spicy fruit").

[15] *furry tribe* The Alderman and the Mayor, both public officials, would wear ermine fur robes.

[16] *China's earth* Chinaware.

Penciled with gold, and streaked with azure veins,
The grateful flavour of the Indian leaf,[1]
50   Or Mocho's sunburnt berry[2] glad receive;
The nobler metal claims more generous use,
And mine should flow with more exalted juice.
Did I for this my native bed resign,
In the dark bowels of Potosi's mine?[3]
55   Was I for this with violence torn away,
And dragged to regions of the upper day?
For this the rage of torturing furnace bore,
From foreign dross to purge the bright'ning ore?
For this have I endured the fiery test,
60   And was I stamped for this with Britain's lofty crest?[4]
     "Unblest the day, and luckless was the hour
Which doomed me to a Presbyterian's power;
Fated to serve the Puritanic race,
Whose slender meal is shorter than their grace;
65   Whose moping sons no jovial orgies keep;
Where evening brings no summons——but to sleep;
No Carnival is even Christmas here,
And one long Lent involves the meagre year.
Bear me, ye pow'rs! to some more genial scene,
70   Where on soft cushions lolls the gouty Dean,
Or rosy Prebend,[5] with cherubic face,
With double chin, and paunch of portly grace,
Who lulled in downy slumbers shall agree
To own no inspiration but from me.
75   Or to some spacious mansion, Gothic, old,
Where Comus'[6] sprightly train their vigils hold;
There oft exhausted, and replenished oft,
Oh! let me still supply th' eternal draught;
Till care within the deep abyss be drowned,
80   And thought grows giddy at the vast profound."

More had the goblet spoke, but lo! appears
An ancient Sybil[7] furrowed o'er with years;
Her aspect sour, and stern ungracious look
With sudden damp the conscious vessel struck;
85   Chilled at her touch its mouth it slowly closed,
And in long silence all its griefs reposed:
Yet still low murmurs creep along the ground,
And the air vibrates with the silver sound.
—1773

from *Hymns in Prose for Children*

Hymn V

The glorious sun is set in the west; the night dews fall; and the air, which was sultry, becomes cool.

The flowers fold up their coloured leaves; they fold themselves up, and hang their heads on the slender stalk.

The chickens are gathered under the wing of the hen, and are at rest; the hen herself is at rest also.

The little birds have ceased their warbling; they are asleep on the boughs; each one has his head behind his wing.

There is no murmur of bees around the hive, or among the honeyed woodbines;[8] they have done their work, and lie close in their waxen cells.

The sheep rest upon their soft fleeces, and their loud bleating is no more heard amongst the hills.

There is no sound of a number of voices, or of children at play, or the trampling of busy feet, and of people hurrying to and fro.

The smith's hammer is not heard upon the anvil;[9] nor the harsh saw of the carpenter.

---

[1]   *Indian leaf*   Tea.

[2]   *Mocho's sunburnt berry*   Coffee.

[3]   *Potosi's mine*   The richest silver mine in Bolivia.

[4]   *Britain's lofty crest*   The Britannia, a female figure representing Great Britain. Originally a Roman goddess, she became a figure of national personification for Britain.

[5]   *Prebend*   Like the Dean, an officer of the Anglican Church.

[6]   *Comus'*   In Greek mythology, Comus is the god of festivity and night-time dalliances.

[7]   *ancient Sybil*   In ancient Greece, a prophetess or seer consulted about the future.

[8]   *woodbines*   Climbing vines or shrubs.

[9]   *anvil*   Forging tool used by blacksmiths to hammer and mold a heated piece of metal into its desired shape.

All men are stretched on their quiet beds; and the child sleeps upon the breast of its mother.

Darkness is spread over the skies, and darkness is upon the ground; every eye is shut, and every hand is still.

Who taketh care of all people when they are sunk in sleep; when they cannot defend themselves, nor see if danger approacheth?

There is an eye that never sleepeth; there is an eye that seeth in dark night, as well as in the bright sunshine.

When there is no light of the sun, nor of the moon; when there is no lamp in the house, nor any little star twinkling through the thick clouds; that eye seeth everywhere, in all places, and watcheth continually over all the families of the earth.

The eye that sleepeth not, is God's; his hand is always stretched out over us.

He made sleep to refresh us when we are weary: he made night that we might sleep in quiet.

As the mother moveth about the house with her finger on her lips, and stilleth every little noise, that[1] her infant be not disturbed; as she draweth the curtains around its bed, and shutteth out the light from its tender eyes, so God draweth the curtains of darkness around us; so he maketh all things to be hushed and still, that his large family may sleep in peace.

Labourers, spent[2] with toil, and young children, and every little humming insect, sleep quietly, for God watcheth over you.

You may sleep, for he never sleeps; you may close your eyes in safety, for his eye is always open to protect you.

When the darkness is passed away, and the beams of the morning sun strike through your eyelids, begin the day with praising God, who hath taken care of you through the night.

Flowers, when you open again, spread your leaves, and smell sweet to his praise.

Birds, when you awake, warble your thanks amongst the green boughs; sing to Him before you sing to your mates.

Let his praise be in our hearts, when we lie down; let his praise be on our lips, when we awake.
—1781

Autumn
A Fragment

Farewell the softer hours, Spring's opening blush
And Summer's deeper glow, the shepherd's pipe
Tuned to the murmurs of a weeping spring,
And song of birds, and gay enameled fields—
Farewell! 'Tis now the sickness of the year,   5
Not to be medicined by the skillful hand.
Pale suns arise that like weak kings behold
Their predecessor's empire moulder° from them; *decay*
While swift-increasing spreads the black domain
Of melancholy Night—no more content   10
With equal sway, her stretching shadows gain
On the bright morn, and cloud the evening sky.
Farewell the careless lingering walk at eve,
Sweet with the breath of kine° and new-spread hay; *cows*
And slumber on a bank, where the lulled youth,   15
His head on flowers, delicious languor feels
Creep in the blood. A different season now
Invites a different song. The naked trees
Admit the tempest; rent is Nature's robe;
Fast, fast, the blush of Summer fades away   20
From her wan cheek, and scarce a flower remains
To deck her bosom; Winter follows close,
Pressing impatient on, and with rude breath
Fans her discoloured tresses. Yet not all
Of grace and beauty from the falling year   25
Is torn ungenial. Still the taper fir
Lifts its green spire, and the dark holly edged
With gold, and many a strong perennial plant,
Yet cheer the waste: nor does yon knot of oaks

[1] *that* So that.

[2] *spent* Exhausted.

30   Resign its honours to the infant blast.
     This is the time, and these the solemn walks,
     When inspiration rushes o'er the soul
     Sudden, as through the grove the rustling breeze.
     —1825 (WRITTEN C. 1780)

To the Poor[1]

C hild of distress, who meet'st the bitter scorn
     Of fellow men to happier prospects born,
     Doomed art and nature's various stores to see
     Flow in full cups of joy—and not for thee,
5   Who seest the rich, to heaven and fate resigned,
     Bear *thy* afflictions with a patient mind;
     Whose bursting heart disdains unjust control,
     Who feel'st oppression's iron in thy soul,
     Who drag'st the load of faint and feeble years,
10   Whose bread is anguish and whose water tears[2]—
     Bear, bear thy wrongs, fulfil thy destined hour,
     Bend thy meek neck beneath the foot of power!
     But when thou feel'st the great deliverer nigh,
     And thy freed spirit mounting seeks the sky,
15   Let no vain fears thy parting hour molest,
     No whispered terrors shake thy quiet breast,
     Think not their threats can work thy future woe,
     Nor deem the Lord above, like Lords below.
     Safe in the bosom of that love repose
20   By whom the sun gives light, the ocean flows,
     Prepare to meet a father undismayed,
     Nor fear the God whom priests and kings have made.
     —1795

---

[1]   *To the Poor* Lucy Aikin, in her edition of Barbauld's *Works*, notes
that the poem was motivated by Barbauld's indignation at a sermon
demanding relief for the poor after a bad harvest in 1794 led to bread
riots among the impoverished.

[2]   *Whose bread … whose water tears* See Isaiah 30.20: "And though
the Lord give you the bread of adversity, and the water of affliction,
yet shall not thy teachers be removed into a corner any more, but thine
eyes shall see thy teachers."

Washing Day

          … and their voice,
     Turning again towards childish treble, pipes
     And whistles in its sound.[3]

T he Muses[4] are turned gossips; they have lost
     The buskined step,[5] and clear high-sounding phrase,
     Language of gods. Come, then, domestic Muse,
     In slipshod measure loosely prattling on
5   Of farm or orchard, pleasant curds and cream,
     Or drowning flies, or shoe lost in the mire
     By little whimpering boy, with rueful face;
     Come, Muse, and sing the dreaded Washing-Day.
     Ye who beneath the yoke of wedlock bend,
10   With bowed soul, full well ye ken° the day   *know*
     Which week, smooth sliding after week, brings on
     Too soon; for to that day nor peace belongs
     Nor comfort; ere the first grey streak of dawn,
     The red-armed washers come and chase repose.
15   Nor pleasant smile, nor quaint device of mirth,
     E'er visited that day; the very cat,
     From the wet kitchen scared, and reeking hearth,
     Visits the parlour, an unwonted° guest.   *infrequent*
     The silent breakfast meal is soon dispatched
20   Uninterrupted, save by anxious looks
     Cast at the lowering sky, if sky should lower.
     From that last evil, O preserve us, heavens!
     For should the skies pour down, adieu to all
     Remains of quiet; then expect to hear
25   Of sad disasters—dirt and gravel stains
     Hard to efface, and loaded lines at once
     Snapped short—and linen-horse° by dog   *clotheshorse*
          thrown down,
     And all the petty miseries of life.

---

[3]   *and their voice … sound* Cf. Shakespeare's *As You Like It*
2.7.161–63: "and his big manly voice, / Turning again toward childish
treble, pipes / And whistles in his sound."

[4]   *Muses* In classical mythology, nine goddesses who presided over
learning and the arts.

[5]   *buskined step* I.e., tragic mode. Actors in Athenian tragedy wore
buskins, or high, thick-soled boots.

Saints have been calm while stretched upon the rack,
30 And Guatimozin[1] smiled on burning coals;
But never yet did housewife notable
Greet with a smile a rainy washing-day.
But grant the welkin° fair, require not thou   *sky*
Who call'st thyself perchance the master there,
35 Or study swept, or nicely dusted coat,
Or usual 'tendance; ask not, indiscreet,
Thy stockings mended, though the yawning rents
Gape wide as Erebus,[2] nor hope to find
Some snug recess impervious; should'st thou try
40 The 'customed garden walks, thine eye shall rue
The budding fragrance of thy tender shrubs,
Myrtle or rose, all crushed beneath the weight
Of coarse checked apron, with impatient hand
Twitched off when showers impend: or crossing lines
45 Shall mar thy musings, as the wet cold sheet
Flaps in thy face abrupt. Woe to the friend
Whose evil stars have urged him forth to claim
On such a day the hospitable rites;
Looks, blank at best, and stinted courtesy,
50 Shall he receive. Vainly he feeds his hopes
With dinner of roast chicken, savoury pie,
Or tart or pudding:—pudding he nor tart
That day shall eat; nor, though the husband try,
Mending what can't be helped, to kindle mirth
55 From cheer deficient, shall his consort's brow
Clear up propitious; the unlucky guest
In silence dines, and early slinks away.
I well remember, when a child, the awe
This day struck into me; for then the maids,
60 I scarce knew why, looked cross, and drove me from
        them;
Nor soft caress could I obtain, nor hope
Usual indulgencies; jelly or creams,
Relic of costly suppers, and set by
For me their petted one; or buttered toast,

65 When butter was forbid; or thrilling tale
Of ghost, or witch, or murder—so I went
And sheltered me beside the parlour fire:
There my dear grandmother, eldest of forms,
Tended the little ones, and watched from harm,
70 Anxiously fond, though oft her spectacles
With elfin cunning hid, and oft the pins
Drawn from her ravelled stocking, might have soured
One less indulgent.—
At intervals my mother's voice was heard,
75 Urging dispatch; briskly the work went on,
All hands employed to wash, to rinse, to wring,
To fold, and starch, and clap, and iron, and plait.[3]
Then would I sit me down, and ponder much
Why washings were. Sometimes through hollow
        bole°   *bowl*
80 Of pipe amused we blew, and sent aloft
The floating bubbles, little dreaming then
To see, Mongolfier,[4] thy silken ball
Ride buoyant through the clouds—so near approach
The sports of children and the toils of men.
85 Earth, air, and sky, and ocean, hath its bubbles,[5]
And verse is one of them—this most of all.
—1797

Eighteen Hundred and Eleven,[6] A Poem

Still the loud death drum, thundering from afar,
O'er the vext nations pours the storm of war:
To the stern call still Britain bends her ear,
Feeds the fierce strife, the alternate hope and fear;

---

[3] *clap* Smooth; *plait* Fold.

[4] *Mongolfier* Montgolfier brothers, from Annonay, France, who invented and launched the first hot-air balloon in 1783.

[5] *Earth … bubbles* Cf. Shakespeare's *Macbeth* 1.3.83: "The earth hath bubbles, as the water has."

[6] *Eighteen Hundred and Eleven* Britain's war [...] 1793, would not end until the Battle of Water[loo ...] Russia, Austria, and Spain, Britain's allies, had already capitulated to the strength of Napoleon's army; Britain was in financial distress; and King George III had been declared insane.

---

[1] *Guatimozin* Cuauhtémoc, the last Aztec emperor (c. 1495–1522), was captured and tortured by Cortés's Spanish conquistadors when they invaded the Aztec capital (now Mexico City).

[2] *Erebus* In Greek mythology, a place below the earth that the dead pass through on their way to Hades, or the underworld.

5   Bravely, though vainly, dares to strive with fate,
    And seeks by turns to prop each sinking state.
    Colossal Power[1] with overwhelming force
    Bears down each fort of freedom in its course;
    Prostrate she lies beneath the despot's sway,
10 While the hushed nations curse him—and obey.
        Bounteous in vain, with frantic man at strife,
    Glad Nature pours the means—the joys of life;
    In vain with orange blossoms scents the gale,
    The hills with olives clothes, with corn the vale;
15 Man calls to Famine,[2] nor invokes in vain,
    Disease and Rapine° follow in her train;   *plunder*
    The tramp of marching hosts disturbs the plough,
    The sword, not sickle, reaps the harvest now,[3]
    And where the soldier gleans the scant supply,
20 The helpless peasant but retires to die;
    No laws his hut from licensed outrage shield,
    And war's least horror is the ensanguined° field.   *blood-stained*
        Fruitful in vain, the matron counts with pride
    The blooming youths that grace her honoured side;
25 No son returns to press her widowed hand,
    Her fallen blossoms strew a foreign strand.
    —Fruitful in vain, she boasts her virgin race,
    Whom cultured arts adorn and gentlest grace;
    Defrauded of its homage, Beauty mourns,
30 And the rose withers on its virgin thorns.
    Frequent, some stream obscure, some uncouth name
    By deeds of blood is lifted into fame;
    Oft o'er the daily page some soft one bends
    To learn the fate of husband, brothers, friends,
35 Or the spread map with anxious eye explores,
    Its dotted boundaries and penciled shores,
    Asks where the spot that wrecked her bliss is found,
    And learns its name but to detest the sound.

        And think'st thou, Britain, still to sit at ease,
40 An island queen amidst thy subject seas,
    While the vext billows, in their distant roar,
    But soothe thy slumbers, and but kiss thy shore?
    To sport in wars, while danger keeps aloof,
    Thy grassy turf unbruised by hostile hoof?
45 So sing thy flatterers; but, Britain, know,
    Thou who hast shared the guilt must share the woe.
    Nor distant is the hour; low murmurs spread,
    And whispered fears, creating what they dread;
    Ruin, as with an earthquake shock, is here,
50 There, the heart-witherings of unuttered fear,
    And that sad death, whence most affection bleeds,
    Which sickness, only of the soul, precedes.
    Thy baseless wealth dissolves in air away,[4]
    Like mists that melt before the morning ray:
55 No more on crowded mart or busy street
    Friends, meeting friends, with cheerful hurry greet;
    Sad, on the ground thy princely merchants bend
    Their altered looks, and evil days portend,
    And fold their arms, and watch with anxious breast
60 The tempest blackening in the distant West.[5]
        Yes, thou must droop; thy Midas dream is o'er;
    The golden tide of Commerce leaves thy shore,
    Leaves thee to prove the alternate ills that haunt
    Enfeebling Luxury and ghastly Want;
65 Leaves thee, perhaps, to visit distant lands,
    And deal the gifts of Heaven with equal hands.
        Yet, O my country, name beloved, revered,
    By every tie that binds the soul endeared,
    Whose image to my infant senses came
70 Mixt with Religion's light and Freedom's holy flame!
    If prayers may not avert, if 'tis thy fate
    To rank amongst the names that once were great,

---

[1] *Colossal Power* Napoleon Bonaparte (1769–1821), emperor of France.

[2] *Famine* In 1811 there was widespread hunger in Britain and much of Europe due to crop failures in the preceding years, as well as the necessity of providing food for soldiers.

[3] *The sword ... now* Napoleon sent his soldiers out unencumbered with provisions; consequently, most of them were starving and were forced to steal food.

---

[4] *Thy baseless wealth ... away* 1810 saw the failure of many British businesses, and in 1811, the country itself was threatened with financial collapse.

[5] *The tempest ... West* Relations had been strained between England and the United States since the French Revolution; Barbauld here foresees the beginning of the War of 1812.

Not like the dim cold crescent[1] shalt thou fade,
Thy debt to Science and the Muse unpaid;
75 Thine are the laws surrounding states revere,
Thine the full harvest of the mental year,
Thine the bright stars in Glory's sky that shine,
And arts that make it life to live are thine.
If westward streams the light that leaves thy shores,
80 Still from thy lamp the streaming radiance pours.
Wide spreads thy race from Ganges[2] to the pole,
O'er half the western world thy accents roll:
Nations beyond the Appalachian hills[3]
Thy hand has planted and thy spirit fills:
85 Soon as their gradual progress shall impart
The finer sense of morals and of art,
Thy stores of knowledge the new states shall know,
And think thy thoughts, and with thy fancy glow;
Thy Lockes, thy Paleys[4] shall instruct their youth,
90 Thy leading star direct their search for truth;
Beneath the spreading platan's[5] tent-like shade,
Or by Missouri's rushing waters laid,
"Old father Thames" shall be the poet's theme,
Of Hagley's woods[6] the enamoured virgin dream,
95 And Milton's tones the raptured ear enthrall,
Mixt with the roar of Niagara's fall;
In Thomson's glass[7] the ingenuous youth shall learn
A fairer face of Nature to discern;
Nor of the bards that swept the British lyre
100 Shall fade one laurel, or one note expire.

Then, loved Joanna,[8] to admiring eyes
Thy storied groups in scenic pomp shall rise;
Their high souled strains and Shakespeare's noble rage
Shall with alternate passion shake the stage.
105 Some youthful Basil[9] from thy moral lay
With stricter hand his fond desires shall sway;
Some Ethwald,[10] as the fleeting shadows pass,
Start at his likeness in the mystic glass;
The tragic Muse resume her just control,
110 With pity and with terror purge the soul,
While wide o'er transatlantic realms thy name
Shall live in light, and gather all its fame.
     Where wanders Fancy down the lapse of years
Shedding o'er imaged woes untimely tears?
115 Fond moody Power! as hopes—as fears prevail,
She longs, or dreads, to lift the awful veil,
On visions of delight now loves to dwell,
Now hears the shriek of woe or Freedom's knell:
Perhaps, she says, long ages past away,
120 And set in western waves our closing day,
Night, Gothic night, again may shade the plains
Where Power is seated, and where Science reigns;
England, the seat of arts, be only known
By the gray ruin and the mouldering stone;
125 That time may tear the garland from her brow,
And Europe sit in dust, as Asia now.
     Yet then the ingenuous youth whom Fancy fires
With pictured glories of illustrious sires,
With duteous zeal their pilgrimage shall take
130 From the Blue Mountains,° or Ontario's lake,   *in Pennsylvania*
With fond adoring steps to press the sod
By statesmen, sages, poets, heroes trod;
On Isis' banks[11] to draw inspiring air,
From Runnymede[12] to send the patriot's prayer;

---

[1] *crescent* Symbol of the Ottoman Empire, which had been in decline throughout the eighteenth and into the nineteenth century.

[2] *Ganges* Sacred river of India.

[3] *Appalachian hills* Mountain range in the eastern United States.

[4] *Lockes … Paleys* Men as eminent as John Locke and William Paley. John Locke (1632–1704), English philosopher who wrote about political, intellectual, and religious freedom and William Paley (1743–1805), English theologian and moral philosopher, who defended Christianity in many of his texts.

[5] *platan* Plane tree.

[6] *Hagley's woods* Cf. *The Seasons*, "Spring," in which James Thomson writes about Lord Lyttleton's lush estate in Worcestershire.

[7] *glass* Mirror; i.e., nature as reflected in Thomson's *The Seasons*.

---

[8] *Joanna* Scottish playwright Joanna Baillie (1762–1851), who was often compared with Shakespeare.

[9] *Basil* Character in Baillie's tragedy *Count Basil* (1798).

[10] *Ethwald* Character in Baillie's tragedy *Ethwald* (1802).

[11] *Isis' banks* The River Thames at Oxford was known as the Isis.

[12] *Runnymede* Site where King John signed the Magna Carta (1215).

135 In pensive thought, where Cam's[1] slow waters wind,
To meet those shades that ruled the realms of mind;
In silent halls to sculptured marbles bow,
And hang fresh wreaths round Newton's[2] awful brow.
Oft shall they seek some peasant's homely shed,
140 Who toils, unconscious of the mighty dead,
To ask where Avon's[3] winding waters stray,
And thence a knot of wild flowers bear away;
Anxious enquire where Clarkson,[4] friend of man,
Or all-accomplished Jones[5] his race began;
145 If of the modest mansion aught remains
Where Heaven and Nature prompted Cowper's[6] strains;
Where Roscoe, to whose patriot breast belong
The Roman virtue and the Tuscan song,
Led Ceres to the black and barren moor
150 Where Ceres never gained a wreath before:[7]
With curious search their pilgrim steps shall rove
By many a ruined tower and proud alcove,
Shall listen for those strains that soothed of yore
Thy rock, stern Skiddaw, and thy fall, Lodore;[8]
155 Feast with Dun Edin's° classic brow their sight,   *Edinburgh's*
And visit "Melrose by the pale moonlight."[9]
    But who their mingled feelings shall pursue
When London's faded glories rise to view?
The mighty city, which by every road,

160 In floods of people poured itself abroad;
Ungirt by walls, irregularly great,
No jealous drawbridge, and no closing gate;
Whose merchants (such the state which commerce brings)
Sent forth their mandates to dependant kings;
165 Streets, where the turbaned Moslem, bearded Jew,
And woolly Afric, met the brown Hindu;
Where through each vein spontaneous plenty flowed,
Where Wealth enjoyed, and Charity bestowed.
Pensive and thoughtful shall the wanderers greet
170 Each splendid square, and still, untrodden street;
Or of some crumbling turret, mined by time,
The broken stairs with perilous step shall climb,
Thence stretch their view the wide horizon round,
By scattered hamlets trace its ancient bound,
175 And, choked no more with fleets, fair Thames survey
Through reeds and sedge pursue his idle way.
    With throbbing bosoms shall the wanderers tread
The hallowed mansions of the silent dead,
Shall enter the long isle and vaulted dome
180 Where Genius and where Valour find a home;[10]
Awestruck, midst chill sepulchral marbles breathe,
Where all above is still, as all beneath;
Bend at each antique shrine, and frequent turn
To clasp with fond delight some sculptured urn,
185 The ponderous mass of Johnson's[11] form to greet,
Or breathe the prayer at Howard's[12] sainted feet.
    Perhaps some Briton, in whose musing mind
Those ages live which Time has cast behind,
To every spot shall lead his wondering guests
190 On whose known site the beam of glory rests:
Here Chatham's eloquence in thunder broke,
Here Fox persuaded, or here Garrick[13] spoke;

[1] *Cam* River at Cambridge.

[2] *Newton* Sir Isaac Newton (1642–1727), mathematician, physicist, and professor at Cambridge University.

[3] *Avon* River that runs through Stratford, where Shakespeare was born.

[4] *Clarkson* Thomas Clarkson (1760–1846), abolitionist, whose work helped to end the British slave trade in 1807.

[5] *Jones* Sir William Jones (1746–94), judge and scholar, who promoted Asian and Sanskrit studies.

[6] *Cowper* William Cowper (1731–1800), English poet.

[7] *Roscoe … before* William Roscoe (1753–1831), historian and MP, who promoted the use of the moors for agriculture; *Ceres* Roman goddess of agriculture.

[8] *Skiddaw … Lodore* Mountain and waterfall in the Lake District, England.

[9] *Melrose … moonlight* Site of the beautiful Melrose Abbey ruins in the Scottish Borderlands; cf. Sir Walter Scott's *The Lay of the Last Minstrel* 2.1: "If thou woud'st view fair Melrose aright, / Go visit it by the pale moonlight."

[10] *vaulted dome … home* St. Paul's Cathedral, home to statues of eminent British men and women.

[11] *Johnson* Samuel Johnson (1709–84), scholar and author.

[12] *Howard* John Howard (1726–90), prison reformer and philanthropist.

[13] *Chatham* William Pitt, 1st Earl of Chatham (1708–78), prime minister and famous patriot and orator; *Fox* Charles James Fox (1749–1806), parliamentarian and orator; *Garrick* David Garrick (1717–79), famous English actor and dramatist.

Shall boast how Nelson, fame and death in view,
To wonted victory led his ardent crew,
In England's name enforced, with loftiest tone,
Their duty—and too well fulfilled his own:[1]
How gallant Moore,[2] as ebbing life dissolved,
But hoped his country had his fame absolved.[3]
Or call up sages whose capacious mind
Left in its course a track of light behind;
Point where mute crowds on Davy's[4] lips reposed,
And Nature's coyest secrets were disclosed;
Join with their Franklin, Priestley's[5] injured name,
Whom, then, each continent shall proudly claim.

Oft shall the strangers turn their eager feet
The rich remains of ancient art to greet,
The pictured walls with critic eye explore,
And Reynolds be what Raphael[6] was before.
On spoils from every clime their eyes shall gaze,
Egyptian granites and the Etruscan vase;
And when midst fallen London, they survey
The stone where Alexander's ashes lay,[7]
Shall own with humbled pride the lesson just
By Time's slow finger written in the dust.

215 There walks a Spirit o'er the peopled earth,
Secret his progress is, unknown his birth;
Moody and viewless° as the changing wind,   *invisible*
No force arrests his foot, no chains can bind;
Where'er he turns, the human brute awakes,
220 And, roused to better life, his sordid hut forsakes:
He thinks, he reasons, glows with purer fires,
Feels finer wants, and burns with new desires:
Obedient Nature follows where he leads;
The steaming marsh is changed to fruitful meads;
225 The beasts retire from man's asserted reign,
And prove his kingdom was not given in vain.
Then from its bed is drawn the ponderous ore,
Then Commerce pours her gifts on every shore.
Then Babel's towers[8] and terraced gardens rise,
230 And pointed obelisks invade the skies;
The prince commands, in Tyrian purple drest,
And Egypt's virgins weave the linen vest.
Then spans the graceful arch the roaring tide,
And stricter bounds the cultured fields divide.
235 Then kindles Fancy, then expands the heart,
Then blow° the flowers of Genius and of Art;   *blossom*
Saints, Heroes, Sages, who the land adorn,
Seem rather to descend than to be born;
Whilst History, midst the rolls consigned to fame,
240 With pen of adamant inscribes their name.

The Genius now forsakes the favoured shore,
And hates, capricious, what he loved before;
Then empires fall to dust, then arts decay,
And wasted realms enfeebled despots sway;
245 Even Nature's changed; without his fostering smile
Ophir[9] no gold, no plenty yields the Nile;
The thirsty sand absorbs the useless rill,°   *stream*
And spotted plagues from putrid fens distill.
In desert solitudes then Tadmor[10] sleeps,

---

[1] *Nelson ... his own* Admiral Horatio Nelson, English war hero, spoke these famous words before he died at the Battle of Trafalgar in 1805: "England expects that every man will do his duty."

[2] *Moore* Sir John Moore (1761–1809), general who led a retreat during the Napoleonic Wars; he saved his troops, but died in the process.

[3] [Barbauld's note] "I hope England will be satisfied," were the last words of General Moore.

[4] *Davy* Sir Humphrey Davy (1778–1829), physicist and chemist, whose lectures were renowned.

[5] *Franklin* Benjamin Franklin (1706–90), American scientist, inventor, and politician; *Priestley* Joseph Priestley (1733–1804), English scientist and theologian, whose correspondence with Franklin led to Priestley's experimentation with and discoveries regarding electricity; Priestley was persecuted for his support of the French and American Revolutions, which led to his emigration from England to America.

[6] *Reynolds ... Raphael* Sir Joshua Reynolds (1723–92), eminent English portrait artist, and Raphael (1483–1520), famous Italian Renaissance painter and architect.

[7] *stone ... lay* The British Museum mistakenly believed it had purchased the tomb of Alexander the Great.

[8] *Babel's towers* Cf. Genesis 11.3–9. The Babylonians attempted to create a tower that would reach heaven; God punished them by giving them different languages and scattering them around the earth.

[9] *Ophir* Cf. 1 Kings 9.28: "And they came to Ophir, and fetched from thence gold."

[10] *Tadmor* Biblical land in ancient Syria.

250 Stern Marius then o'er fallen Carthage weeps;[1]
    Then with enthusiast love the pilgrim roves
    To seek his footsteps in forsaken groves,
    Explores the fractured arch, the ruined tower,
    Those limbs disjointed of gigantic power;
255 Still at each step he dreads the adder's sting,
    The Arab's javelin, or the tiger's spring;
    With doubtful caution treads the echoing ground,
    And asks where Troy or Babylon[2] is found.
        And now the vagrant Power no more detains
260 The vale of Tempe, or Ausonian plains;[3]
    Northward he throws the animating ray,
    O'er Celtic nations bursts the mental day:
    And, as some playful child the mirror turns,
    Now here now there the moving lustre burns;
265 Now o'er his changeful fancy more prevail
    Batavia's dykes than Arno's[4] purple vale,
    And stinted suns, and rivers bound with frost,
    Than Enna's plains or Baia's[5] viny coast;
    Venice the Adriatic weds in vain,
270 And Death sits brooding o'er Campania's[6] plain;
    O'er Baltic shores and through Hercynian groves,[7]
    Stirring the soul, the mighty impulse moves;
    Art plies his tools, and Commerce spreads her sail,
    And wealth is wafted in each shifting gale.
275 The sons of Odin[8] tread on Persian looms,
    And Odin's daughters breathe distilled perfumes;
    Loud minstrel bards, in Gothic halls, rehearse

    The Runic rhyme, and "build the lofty verse:"[9]
    The Muse, whose liquid notes were wont to swell
280 To the soft breathings of the Aeolian shell,[10]
    Submits, reluctant, to the harsher tone,
    And scarce believes the altered voice her own.
    And now, where Caesar saw with proud disdain
    The wattled hut and skin of azure stain,[11]
285 Corinthian columns rear their graceful forms,
    And light verandas brave the wintry storms,
    While British tongues the fading fame prolong
    Of Tully's eloquence and Maro's[12] song.
    Where once Bonduca whirled the scythed car,
290 And the fierce matrons raised the shriek of war,[13]
    Light forms beneath transparent muslins float,
    And tutored voices swell the artful note.
    Light-leaved acacias and the shady plane
    And spreading cedar grace the woodland reign;
295 While crystal walls the tenderer plants confine,
    The fragrant orange and the nectared pine;
    The Syrian grape there hangs her rich festoons,
    Nor asks for purer air, or brighter noons:
    Science and Art urge on the useful toil,
300 New mold a climate and create the soil,
    Subdue the rigour of the northern Bear,[14]
    O'er polar climes shed aromatic air,
    On yielding Nature urge their new demands,
    And ask not gifts but tribute at her hands.
305   London exults:—on London Art bestows

---

[1] *Marius ... weeps* Gaius Marius (157–86 BCE), Roman Consul and general who was once called the "savior of Rome"; upon aging and falling from power, he was said to have wept among the ruins of Carthage.

[2] *Troy* Ancient city in Asia Minor, subject of the Trojan War in Homer's *Iliad*; *Babylon* Ancient Mesopotamian city known for its wealth and beauty, destroyed in 689 BCE.

[3] *vale of Tempe* Valley in Greece celebrated by ancient poets for its beauty; *Ausonian plains* Virgil called Italy "Ausonia."

[4] *Batavia* Republic, now the Netherlands; *Arno* River in Italy.

[5] *Enna* Sicilian valley; *Baia* Italian village on the Bay of Naples, celebrated for its spas in Roman times.

[6] *Campania* Italian province whose plains were marshy and malarial.

[7] *Hercynian groves* Black Forest in Germany.

[8] *Odin* Supreme Norse god.

[9] *build the lofty verse* From Milton's *Lycidas* (10–11): "He knew / Himself to sing, and build the lofty rhyme."

[10] *Aeolian shell* Aeolian harp, a musical instrument that produces sound when the wind passes over its strings.

[11] *Caesar ... stain* Cf. Julius Caesar's *The Gallic Wars* 5.14: "All the Britains, indeed, dye themselves with wood, which occasions a bluish color, and thereby have a more terrible appearance in fight."

[12] *Tully* Marcus Tullius Cicero (106–43 BCE), Roman orator, philosopher, and politician; *Maro* Publius Vergilius Maro, or Virgil (70–19 BCE), Roman poet, author of the *Aeneid*.

[13] *Bonduca ... war* Queen of the ancient Iceni Celts, Boadicea (sometimes written as "Bonduca" or "Boudicca") led a massive rebellion against the Romans in about 60 CE; she died by suicide upon the failure of the mission.

[14] *northern Bear* The constellation Ursa Major (Latin: Great Bear).

Her summer ices and her winter rose;
Gems of the East her mural crown adorn,
And Plenty at her feet pours forth her horn;[1]
While even the exiles her just laws disclaim,
310 People a continent, and build a name:
August she sits, and with extended hands
Holds forth the book of life to distant lands.
    But fairest flowers expand but to decay;
The worm is in thy core, thy glories pass away;
315 Arts, arms and wealth destroy the fruits they bring;
Commerce, like beauty, knows no second spring.
Crime walks thy streets, Fraud earns her unblest bread,
O'er want and woe thy gorgeous robe is spread,
And angel charities in vain oppose:
320 With grandeur's growth the mass of misery grows.
For see,—to other climes the Genius soars,
He turns from Europe's desolated shores;
And lo, even now, midst mountains wrapt in storm,
On Andes' heights he shrouds his awful form;
325 On Chimborazo's[2] summits treads sublime,
Measuring in lofty thought the march of Time;
Sudden he calls:—"'Tis now the hour!" he cries,
Spreads his broad hand, and bids the nations rise.
La Plata[3] hears amidst her torrents' roar,
330 Potosi[4] hears it, as she digs the ore:
Ardent, the Genius fans the noble strife,
And pours through feeble souls a higher life,
Shouts to the mingled tribes from sea to sea,
And swears—Thy world, Columbus, shall be free.
    —1812

On the Death of the Princess Charlotte[5]

Yes, Britain mourns, as with electric touch
   For youth, for love, for happiness destroyed,
Her universal population melts
In grief spontaneous, and hard hearts are moved,
5 And rough unpolished natures learn to feel
For those they envied, leveled in the dust
By Fate's impartial stroke; and pulpits sound
With vanity and woe to earthly goods,
And urge and dry the tear. Yet one there is
10 Who midst this general burst of grief remains
In strange tranquility;[6] whom not the stir
And long drawn murmurs of the gathering crowd,
That by his very windows trail the pomp
Of hearse,[7] and blazoned arms, and long array
15 Of sad funereal rites, nor the loud groans
And deep-felt anguish of a husband's[8] heart,
Can move to mingle with this flood of tear.
In careless apathy, perhaps in mirth
He wears the day. Yet is he near in blood,
20 The very stem on which this blossom grew,
And at his knees she fondled, in the cha[...]
And grace spontaneous which alone belongs
To untaught infancy. Yet oh forbear!
Nor deem him hard of heart; or awestruck
25 By heaven's severest visitation sad,
Like a scathed oak amidst the forest trees,
Lonely he stands—leaves, and root, and fall;
He holds no sympathy in living nature
Or time's thought is busy with the woes
30 Whi[...]

---

[1] horn Horn of plenty, or cornucopia, contains an abu[...]
essentials and luxuries of life.
[2] Chimborazo Volcanic mountain in Ecuador [...] silver [...]
[3] La Plata City in Argentina.
[4] Potosi City in Bolivia. All three co[...]
resistant to colonial rule. The regio[...]
deposits.

[...] Charlotte The popular Princess C[...]
[...]6–1817), daughter of the Prince of Wales [...] to his feud
[...] V, died at the age of 21 of complication[...]
[6] one there is ... tranquility Charl[...] ttend his daughter's
expressed his disdain of his own C[...]
with her mother.
[7] by his ... hearse [...]
funeral.
[8] husband [...]
1816.

And restless cares of poor humanity,
Think then, oh think of him, and breathe one prayer,
From the full tide of sorrow spare one tear
For him who does not weep!
—1819

To a Little Invisible Being Who Is Expected
Soon to Become Visible

Germ of new life, whose powers expanding slow
  For many a moon their full perfection wait,—
Haste, precious pledge of happy love, to go
Auspicious borne through life's mysterious gate.

5   What powers lie folded in thy curious frame,—
Senses from objects locked, and mind from thought!
How little canst thou guess thy lofty claim
To grasp at all the worlds the Almighty wrought!

And see, the genial season's warmth to share,
10   Fresh younghgs shoot, and opening roses glow!
Swarms of new life exulting fill the air,—
Haste, infant bud of being, haste to blow!°   blossom

For thee the nurse prepares her lulling songs,
The eager matron counts the lingering day;
15   But far the mostly anxious mother longs
On thy soft cheek mother's kiss to lay.

She only asks to lay her burden down,
That her glad arms that burden may
And nature's sharpest pangs her wishes
That free thee living from thy living tomb.

To fold to her maternal breast
Fed yet to herself unknown;
te the stranger guest,
25   Bask in through many a tedious moon.

nce of love!
's eye!

Nor wit nor eloquence her heart shall move
Like the first accents of thy feeble cry.

Haste, little captive, burst thy prison doors!
30   Launch on the living world, and spring to light!
Nature for thee displays her various stores,
Opens her thousand inlets of delight.

If charmed verse or muttered prayers had power,
With favouring spells to speed thee on thy way,
35   Anxious I'd bid my beads° each passing hour,   pray
Till thy wished smile thy mother's pangs o'erpay.
—1825

Life

Animula, vagula, blandula.[1]

Life! I know not what thou art,
  But know that thou and I must part;
And when, or how, or where we met,
I own to me's a secret yet.
5   But this I know, when thou art fled,
Where'er they lay these limbs, this head,
No clod so valueless shall be,
As all that then remains of me.
O whither, whither dost thou fly,
10   Where bend unseen thy trackless course,
  And in this strange divorce,
Ah, tell where I must seek this compound I?

To the vast ocean of empyreal flame,[2]
  From whence thy essence came,
15   Dost thou thy flight pursue, when freed
From matter's base encumbering weed?
  Or dost thou, hid from sight,

, vagula, blandula   Latin: Gentle wandering soul. First lin
ieved to have been composed by the Roman emper
before his death in 138 CE.
ame Empyrean, or highest sphere of heaven

Wait, like some spellbound knight,
Through blank oblivious years th'appointed hour,
20 To break thy trance and reassume thy power?
Yet canst thou without thought or feeling be?
O say what art thou, when no more thou'rt thee?

Life! we've been long together,
Through pleasant and through cloudy weather;
25 'Tis hard to part when friends are dear;
    Perhaps 'twill cost a sigh, a tear;
    Then steal away, give little warning,
        Choose thine own time;
Say not good night, but in some brighter clime
30   Bid me good morning.
—1825

The Rights of Woman[1]

Yes, injured Woman! rise, assert thy right!
Woman! too long degraded, scorned, opprest;
O born to rule in partial° Law's despite,   *biased*
Resume thy native empire o'er the breast!

5 Go forth arrayed in panoply[2] divine;
That angel pureness which admits no stain;
Go, bid proud Man his boasted rule resign,
And kiss the golden sceptre of thy reign.

Go, gird thyself with grace; collect thy store
10 Of bright artillery glancing from afar;
Soft melting tones thy thundering cannon's roar,
Blushes and fears thy magazine° of war.   *storehouse*

Thy rights are empire: urge no meaner claim,—
Felt, not defined, and if debated, lost;
15 Like sacred mysteries, which withheld from fame,
Shunning discussion, are revered the most.

Try all that wit and art suggest to bend
Of thy imperial foe the stubborn knee;
Make treacherous Man thy subject, not thy friend;
20 Thou mayst command, but never canst be free.

Awe the licentious, and restrain the rude;
Soften the sullen, clear the cloudy brow:
Be, more than princes' gifts, thy favours sued;—
She hazards all, who will the least allow.

25 But hope not, courted idol of mankind,
On this proud eminence secure to stay;
Subduing and subdued, thou soon shalt find
Thy coldness soften, and thy pride give way.

Then, then, abandon each ambitious thought,
30 Conquest or rule thy heart shall feebly move,
In Nature's school, by her soft maxims taught,
That separate rights are lost in mutual love.
—1825

The Baby-House

Dear Agatha,[3] I give you joy,
And much admire your pretty toy,
A mansion in itself complete
And fitted to give guests a treat;
5 With couch and table, chest and chair,
The bed or supper to prepare;
We almost wish to change ourselves
To fairy forms of tripping elves,
To press the velvet couch and eat
10 From tiny cups the sugared meat.
    I much suspect that many a sprite
Inhabits it at dead of night;
That, as they dance, the listening ear
The pat of fairy feet might hear;
15 That, just as you have said your prayers,

---

[1] *The Rights of Woman* Cf. Mary Wollstonecraft's *A Vindication of the Rights of Woman* (1792).

[2] *panoply* Lavish ceremonial attire.

[3] *Agatha* Though Agatha has not been definitively identified, she is believed to have been the daughter of a friend of Barbauld's.

They hurry-scurry down the stairs:
And you'll do well to try to find
Tester[1] or ring they've left behind.
    But think not, Agatha, you own
20 That toy, a Baby-house, alone;
For many a sumptuous one is found
To press an ampler space of ground.
The broad-based Pyramid that stands
Casting its shade in distant lands,
25 Which asked some mighty nation's toil
With mountain-weight to press the soil,
And there has raised its head sublime
Through eras of uncounted time—
Its use if asked, 'tis only said,
30 A Baby-house to lodge the dead.
Nor less beneath more genial skies
The domes of pomp and folly rise,
Whose sun through diamond windows streams,
While gems and gold reflect his beams;
35 Where tapestry clothes the storied wall,
And fountains spout and waters fall;
The peasant faints beneath his load,
Nor tastes the grain his hands have sowed,
While scarce a nation's wealth avails
40 To raise thy Baby-house, Versailles.[2]
And Baby-houses oft appear
On British ground, of prince or peer;
Awhile their stately heads they raise,
The admiring traveller stops to gaze;
45 He looks again—where are they now?
Gone to the hammer[3] or the plough.
Then trees, the pride of ages, fall,
And naked stands the pictured wall;
And treasured coins from distant lands
50 Must feel the touch of sordid hands;
And gems, of classic stores the boast,
Fall to the cry of—Who bids most?

Then do not, Agatha, repine
That cheaper Baby-house is thine.
—1825

The First Fire
October 1st 1815

Ha, old acquaintance! many a month has past
Since last I viewed thy ruddy face; and I,
Shame on me! had mean time well nigh forgot
That such a friend existed. Welcome now!—
5 When summer suns ride high, and tepid airs
Dissolve in pleasing languor; then indeed
We think thee needless, and in wanton pride
Mock at thy grim attire and sooty jaws,
And breath sulphureous, generating spleen,—
10 As Frenchmen say; Frenchmen, who never knew
The sober comforts of a good coal fire.[4]
—Let me imbibe thy warmth, and spread myself
Before thy shrine adoring:—magnet thou
Of strong attraction, daily gathering in
15 Friends, brethren, kinsmen, variously dispersed,
All the dear charities of social life,
To thy close circle. Here a man might stand,
And say, This is my world! Who would not bleed
Rather than see thy violated hearth
20 Prest by a hostile[5] foot? The winds sing shrill;
Heap on the fuel! Not the costly board,
Nor sparkling glass, nor wit, nor music, cheer
Without thy aid. If thrifty thou dispense
Thy gladdening influence, in the chill saloon
25 The silent shrug declares the unpleased guest.
—How grateful to belated traveller
Homeward returning, to behold the blaze

---

[1] *Tester* Sixpence coin.

[2] *Versailles* The famously self-indulgent palace of the French king Louis XIV (1638–1715).

[3] *the hammer* Auctioneer's gavel; that is, auctioned for sale.

[4] *As Frenchmen … coal fire* The reference is to Alexandre de La Rochefoucauld's *A Frenchman's Year in Suffolk* (1784): "At Dover I first burnt coal and found it very inconvenient. I regretted … that we had no firewood…. Coal is much better for warming a room. But I found the smell of coal extremely disagreeable."

[5] *hostile* Though the Napoleonic Wars ended in 1815, anti-French sentiment remained common in England.

From cottage window, rendering visible
The cheerful scene within! There sits the sire,
Whose wicker chair, in sunniest nook enshrined,
His age's privilege,—a privilege for which
Age gladly yields up all precedence else
In gay and bustling scenes,—supports his limbs.
Cherished by thee, he feels the grateful warmth
Creep through his feeble frame and thaw the ice
Of fourscore years, and thoughts of youth arise.
—Nor less the young ones press within, to see
Thy face delighted, and with husk of nuts,
Or crackling holly, or the gummy pine,
Feed thy immortal hunger: cheaply pleased
They gaze delighted, while the leaping flames
Dart like an adder's tongue upon their prey;
Or touch with lighted reed thy wreaths of smoke;
Or listen, while the matron sage remarks
Thy bright blue scorching flame and aspect clear,
Denoting frosty skies. Thus pass the hours,
While Winter spends without his idle rage.
—Companion of the solitary man,
From gayer scenes withheld! With thee he sits,
Converses, moralizes; musing asks
How many eras of uncounted time
Have rolled away since thy black unctuous food
Was green with vegetative life,[1] and what
This planet then: or marks, in sprightlier mood,
Thy flickering smiles play round the illumined room,
And fancies gay discourse, life, motion, mirth,
And half forgets he is a lonely creature.
—Nor less the bashful poet loves to sit
Snug, at the midnight hour, with only thee
Of his lone musings conscious. Oft he writes,
And blots, and writes again; and oft, by fits,
Gazes intent with eyes of vacancy
On thy bright face;[2] and still at intervals,

65 Dreading the critic's scorn, to thee commits,
Sole confidant and safe, his fancies crude.
—O wretched he, with bolts and massy bars
In narrow cell immured, whose green damp walls,
That weep unwholesome dews, have never felt
Thy purifying influence! Sad he sits
70 Day after day, till in his youthful limbs
Life stagnates, and the hue of hope is fled
From his wan cheek.—And scarce less wretched he—
When wintry winds blow loud and frosts bite keen,—
The dweller of the clay-built tenement,
75 Poverty-struck, who, heartless, strives to raise
From sullen turf, or stick plucked from the hedge,
The short-lived blaze; while chill around him spreads
The dreary fen, and Ague,[3] sallow-faced,
Stares through the broken pane;—Assist him, ye
80 On whose warm roofs the sun of plenty shines,
And feel a glow beyond material fire!
—1825

The Caterpillar

No, helpless thing, I cannot harm thee now;
Depart in peace, thy little life is safe,
For I have scanned thy form with curious eye,
Noted the silver line that streaks thy back,
5 The azure and the orange that divide
Thy velvet sides; thee, houseless wanderer,
My garment has enfolded, and my arm
Felt the light pressure of thy hairy feet;
Thou hast curled round my finger; from its tip,
10 Precipitous descent! with stretched out neck,
Bending thy head in airy vacancy,
This way and that, inquiring, thou hast seemed
To ask protection; now, I cannot kill thee.
Yet I have sworn perdition to thy race,
15 And recent from the slaughter am I come
Of tribes and embryo nations: I have sought
With sharpened eye and persecuting zeal,

---

[1] *black unctuous food … vegetative life* Barbauld's nephew Arthur Aikin discusses the vegetable origins of coal in his *Manual of Minerology* (1814).

[2] *the bashful poet … bright face* Adapted from Samuel Taylor Coleridge's "Frost at Midnight" (1798). "The First Fire" is thought to correspond with Coleridge's poem.

[3] *Ague* An acute or violent fever.

Where, folded in their silken webs they lay
Thriving and happy; swept them from the tree
20   And crushed whole families beneath my foot;
Or, sudden, poured on their devoted heads
The vials of destruction.[1]—This I've done,
Nor felt the touch of pity: but when thou—
A single wretch, escaped the general doom,
25   Making me feel and clearly recognise
Thine individual existence, life,
And fellowship of sense with all that breathes—
Present'st thyself before me, I relent,
And cannot hurt thy weakness.—So the storm
30   Of horrid war, o'erwhelming cities, fields,

And peaceful villages, rolls dreadful on:
The victor shouts triumphant; he enjoys
The roar of cannon and the clang of arms,
And urges, by no soft relentings stopped,
35   The work of death and carnage. Yet should one,
A single sufferer from the field escaped,
Panting and pale, and bleeding at his feet,
Lift his imploring eyes—the hero weeps;
He is grown human, and capricious Pity,
40   Which would not stir for thousands, melts for one
With sympathy spontaneous: 'Tis not Virtue,
Yet 'tis the weakness of a virtuous mind.
—1825

---

[1] *vials of destruction* I.e., pesticides.

CHARLOTTE SMITH
1749 – 1806

Charlotte Smith was, as Wordsworth wrote, "a lady to whom English is under greater obligations than are likely to be acknowledged or remembered." As a poet, she initiated a revival of the sonnet by demonstrating its potential to capture quintessentially Romantic emotional experiences. As a novelist, she contributed significantly to debates surrounding the French Revolution and other issues of importance to liberals of her time. Her work was enormously popular in her own day and exerted a strong influence on other Romantic poets. By the middle of the nineteenth century, however, her poems and novels had fallen out of fashion, and it was not until the late twentieth century that they once again received substantial critical attention and a more extensive readership.

Smith (née Turner) was born into the landed gentry in 1749 in London; her father was a country gentleman in Sussex, to which county Smith remained devoted throughout her life. Charlotte was the second of three children and her mother died giving birth to her brother when Charlotte was three years old. Her education was typical for someone of her gender and social class; she attended a fashionable boarding school between the ages of eight and twelve, at which point she left school and entered "society." Her father remarried in 1764, and it was arranged that Charlotte would marry the following year, at the age of 15. Her husband, Benjamin Smith, was the son of a West Indian merchant and was living beyond his means. Her father-in-law died in 1776, leaving a will that attempted to prevent his legacy from being wasted by his wayward son. The document was so complicated, however, that Smith was to spend the rest of her life going to the courts to fight for her children's inheritance. (Her case became well known in London, and it is probably the basis for the unending, impoverishing, and misery-inducing law case in Dickens's *Bleak House*.) Benjamin Smith continued his spendthrift ways and was imprisoned for debt in 1783. For a time, Smith and their growing family lived with him in prison.

In 1784, when Smith first turned to writing professionally, she was 35 years old and had nine living children. Desperate for money while her husband was still in prison, she composed *Elegiac Sonnets*. These remarkable sonnets, famous for their melancholy, pessimism, and pathos, represent an important stylistic achievement in their ability to convey a highly personal effect through an understated and impersonal style. This volume was extremely popular, and she later repeatedly rearranged and enlarged the collection. Among the additions were many poems supposedly written by characters in the novels she wrote later. By 1851 her sonnets had gone through 11 editions. Both Wordsworth and Coleridge learned from her, admiring her more in their youth than they were later willing to admit. Both used Smith's work as a model for working out their new style of Romantic self-expression.

More money troubles were to follow for Smith. When her husband was released from prison in 1785, he fled to France to escape his creditors and Smith followed with the family. While in France, she discovered Antoine-François Prévost's controversial novel *Manon Lescaut* and translated it into English.

In 1785 Smith returned to England with her children; she separated from her husband one year later. From this point onward, she was the sole supporter of her family, a position made more difficult by the fact that at this date everything earned by a wife legally belonged to her husband. In 1788 her first novel, *Emmeline*, was published; from then on she published almost a novel a year. Smith drew on the circumstances of her own life for her fiction: she often portrayed women married to cruel or dissolute husbands, and still more often grasping or incompetent lawyers, while scenes from her stay in debtor's prison appear both in *Ethelinde* and in *Marchmont*. If her own life figured frequently in her work, however, so did many of the great public issues of the day; her fiction is sharply critical of empire, the slave trade, the class system, and marriage laws. She was a strong early supporter of the French Revolution, but was also sensitive to the plight of French emigrés in England after the Terror; in 1793 she published the 800-line blank-verse poem *The Emigrants*.

Although she came to be known primarily as a novelist and, in the later part of her life, as a children's author, Smith continued to write poetry. *Beachy Head*, one of her finest poems, was published the year after her death, in 1807.

⌘ ⌘ ⌘

from *Elegiac Sonnets*

1

The partial Muse,[1] has from my earliest hours
    Smil'd on the rugged path I'm doom'd to tread,
And still with sportive° hand has snatch'd   *playful*
    wild flowers,
    To weave fantastic garlands for my head:
5   But far, far happier is the lot of those
        Who never learn'd her dear delusive art,
    Which while it decks the head with many a rose,
        Reserves the thorn, to fester in the heart.
    For still she bids° soft Pity's melting eye   *commands*
10 Stream o'er the ills she knows not to remove,
    Points° every pang, and deepens every sigh   *sharpens*
        Of mourning friendship, or unhappy love.
    Ah! then, how dear° the Muse's favors cost,   *expensive*
    If those paint sorrow best—who feel it most![2]

2
Written at the Close of Spring

The garlands fade that Spring so lately wove,
    Each simple flower which she had nursed in dew,
Anemonies,[3] that spangled every grove,
    The primrose wan, and hare-bell[4] mildly blue.
5   No more shall violets linger in the dell,°   *wooded valley*
        Or purple orchis variegate[5] the plain,
    Till Spring again shall call forth every bell,°   *flowering plant*
        And dress° with humid hands her   *prepare*
        wreaths again.—
    Ah! poor Humanity! so frail, so fair,
10   Are the fond visions of thy early day,
    Till tyrant Passion,° and corrosive Care,   *suffering*
        Bid° all thy fairy colours fade away!   *orders*
    Another May new buds and flowers shall bring;
    Ah! why has happiness—no second Spring?

---

1   *partial* Showing favoritism; *Muse* Goddess of poetic inspiration, the invocation of which is a tradition going back to Classical antiquity.

2   [Smith's note]   "The well-sung woes shall soothe my pensive ghost; / He best can paint them who shall feel them most." Pope's "Eloisa to Abelard." 366th line.

3   [Smith's note] Anemonies. *Anemony Nemeroso.* The wood Anemone. [Flowering plant having brilliant blossoms, common to Great Britain.]

4   *primrose* Wild flowering plant noted for its yellow blossoms; *harebell* Wild hyacinth, blue-bell.

5   *orchis* Orchids; *variegate* Make varied.

3
To a Nightingale[1]

Poor, melancholy bird—that all night long
Tell'st to the Moon thy tale of tender woe;
   From what sad cause can such sweet sorrow flow,
And whence this mournful melody of song?
Thy poet's musing fancy would translate
   What mean the sounds that swell thy little breast,
   When still at dewy eve thou leavest thy nest,
Thus to the listening Night to sing thy fate?
Pale Sorrow's victims wert thou once among,
   Tho' now released in woodlands wild to rove?
   Say—hast thou felt from friends some cruel wrong,
Or died'st thou—martyr of disastrous love?
Ah! songstress sad! that such my lot might be,
To sigh and sing at liberty—like thee!

8
To Spring

Again the wood, and long-withdrawing vale,
   In many a tint of tender green are drest,
Where the young leaves, unfolding, scarce conceal
   Beneath their early shade, the half-formed nest
5 Of finch or woodlark; and the primrose pale,
   And lavish cowslip,[2] wildly scatter'd round,
Give their sweet spirits to the sighing gale.
   Ah! season of delight!—could aught be found
   To soothe awhile the tortur'd bosom's pain,
10 Of Sorrow's rankling° shaft to cure   *rotting*
      the wound,
   And bring life's first delusions once again,
'Twere surely met in thee!—thy prospect fair,
Thy sounds of harmony, thy balmy air,
Have power to cure all sadness—but despair.[3]

II
To Sleep

Come, balmy Sleep! tired Nature's soft resort![4]
   On these sad temples all thy poppies[5] shed;
And bid gay dreams, from Morpheus'[6] airy court,
   Float in light vision round my aching head![7]
5 Secure of all thy blessings, partial° Power!   *favorable, prejudiced*
   On his hard bed the peasant throws him down;
And the poor sea-boy, in the rudest° hour,   *most harsh*
   Enjoys thee more than he who wears a crown.[8]
Clasp'd in her faithful shepherd's guardian arms,
10   Well may the village-girl sweet slumbers prove;
And they, O gentle Sleep! still taste thy charms,
   Who wake to labour, liberty, and love.
But still thy opiate aid dost thou deny
To calm the anxious breast, to close the streaming eye.

39
To Night

I love thee, mournful, sober-suited°   *darkly clothed*
   Night!
   When the faint moon, yet lingering in her wane,
And veil'd in clouds, with pale uncertain light
   Hangs o'er the waters of the restless main.°   *sea*
5 In deep depression sunk, the enfeebled mind
   Will to the deaf cold elements complain,
   And tell the embosom'd grief, however vain,
To sullen[9] surges and the viewless wind.
Tho' no repose on thy dark breast I find,
10   I still enjoy thee—cheerless as thou art;
   For in thy quiet gloom the exhausted heart

[1] [Smith's note] The idea from the 43[r]d Sonnet of Petrarch. Secondo parte. "Quel rosignuol, che si soave piagne." [Italian: "That nightingale, who so gently weeps." From Francesco Petrarca's (1304–74) *Il Canzoniere*, "Sonnet 311."]

[2] *cowslip* Wild plant with fragrant yellow flowers.

[3] *Have power … despair* Cf. Milton's *Paradise Lost* 4.154–56.

[4] *balmy* Soothing; *resort* Escape.

[5] *poppies* Opium, which induces sleep, is made from poppies.

[6] *Morpheus* God of dreams.

[7] [Smith's note] "Float in light vision round the poet's head." Mason. [Cf. line 12 of William Mason's "Elegy V. On the Death of a Lady" (1760).]

[8] [Smith's note] "Wilt thou upon the high and giddy mast / Seal up the ship boy's eyes, and rock his brains / In cradle of the rude impetuous surge?" Shakespeare's *Henry IV*. [Cf. *2 Henry IV*, 3.1.18–20. Smith here substitutes "impetuous," for the original "imperious."]

[9] *sullen* Make sluggish or slow.

Is calm, tho' wretched; hopeless, yet resign'd.
While to the winds and waves its sorrows given,
May reach—tho' lost on earth—the ear of Heaven!

44
Written in the Church-yard at Middleton in Sussex

Press'd by the Moon, mute arbitress° of   female judge
    tides,
  While the loud equinox[1] its power combines,
  The sea no more its swelling surge confines,
But o'er the shrinking land sublimely rides.
5 The wild blast, rising from the Western cave,
  Drives the huge billows from their heaving bed;
  Tears from their grassy tombs the village dead,[2]
And breaks the silent sabbath of the grave!
With shells and sea-weed mingled, on the shore
10   Lo! their bones whiten in the frequent wave;
  But vain to them the winds and waters rave;
They hear the warring elements no more:
While I am doom'd—by life's long storm opprest,
To gaze with envy, on their gloomy rest.

59
Written September 1791, during a remarkable thunder storm, in which the moon was perfectly clear, while the tempest gathered in various directions near the earth

What awful pageants° crowd the   majestic displays
    evening sky!
  The low horizon gathering vapours shroud;
  Sudden, from many a deep-embattled cloud
Terrific thunders burst, and lightnings fly—
5 While in serenest azure,° beaming high,   intense blue

---

[1] *equinox* Time of year at which the sun crosses the equator, rendering day and night of equal length.

[2] [Smith's note] Middleton is a village on the margin of the sea, in Sussex, containing only two or three houses. There were formerly several acres of ground between its small church and the sea, which now, by its continual encroachments, approaches within a few feet of this half-ruined and humble edifice. The wall, which once surrounded the church-yard, is entirely swept away, many of the graves broken up, and the remains of bodies interred washed into the sea; whence human bones are found among the sand and shingles on the shore.

Night's regent,° of her calm pavilion proud,   moon
Gilds the dark shadows that beneath her lie,
  Unvex'd by all their conflicts fierce and loud.
—So, in unsullied dignity elate,
10   A spirit conscious of superior worth,
In placid elevation firmly great,
  Scorns the vain cares that give Contention birth;
And blest with peace above the shocks of Fate,
  Smiles at the tumult of the troubled earth.

70
On being cautioned against walking on an headland overlooking the sea, because it was frequented by a lunatic

Is there a solitary wretch who hies°   hastens
  To the tall cliff, with starting° pace or slow,   fitful
And, measuring, views with wild and hollow eyes
  Its distance from the waves that chide° below;   scold
5 Who, as the sea-born gale with frequent sighs
  Chills his cold bed upon the mountain turf,
With hoarse, half-utter'd lamentation, lies
  Murmuring responses to the dashing surf?
In moody sadness, on the giddy° brink,   dizzying
10   I see him more with envy than with fear;
He has no *nice felicities*° that shrink[3]   good fortunes
  From giant horrors; wildly wandering here,
He seems (uncursed with reason) not to know
The depth or the duration of his woe.

74
The Winter Night

"Sleep, that knits up the ravell'd sleeve of care,"[4]
  Forsakes me, while the chill and sullen blast,
  As my sad soul recalls its sorrows past,
Seems like a summons, bidding me prepare
5 For the last sleep of death.—Murmuring I hear

---

[3] [Smith's note] "This delicate felicity that shrinks / When rocking winds are loud." Walpole. [See Horace Walpole's 1768 play *The Mysterious Mother* 2.3.]

[4] [Smith's note] Shakespeare. [Cf. *Macbeth* 2.2.36.]

The hollow wind around the ancient towers,[1]
While night and silence reign; and cold and drear
    The darkest gloom of Middle Winter lours;°   *scowls*
But wherefore° fear existence such as mine,   *why*
    To change for long and undisturb'd repose?
Ah! when this suffering being I resign,
    And o'er my miseries the tomb shall close,
By her,[2] whose loss in anguish I deplore,   10
I shall be laid, and feel that loss no more!

84
To the Muse[3]

W ilt thou forsake me who in life's bright May
    Lent warmer lustre to the radiant morn;
    And even o'er Summer scenes by tempests torn,
Shed with illusive light the dewy ray
Of pensive pleasure?—Wilt thou, while the day
    Of saddening Autumn closes, as I mourn
In languid, hopeless sorrow, far away
    Bend° thy soft step, and never more return?—   *aim*
Crush'd to the earth, by bitterest anguish pressed,
    From my faint eyes thy graceful form recedes;
    Thou canst not heal an heart like mine that bleeds;
But, when in quiet earth that heart shall rest,
    Haply° may'st thou one sorrowing vigil keep,   *by chance*
    Where Pity and Remembrance bend° and weep![4] *kneel*
—1784–97

Beachy Head

O n thy stupendous summit, rock sublime!
    That o'er the channel rear'd, half way at sea

The mariner at early morning hails,[5]
I would recline; while Fancy° should go forth,   *imagination*
And represent the strange and awful hour   5
Of vast concussion; when the Omnipotent[6]
Stretch'd forth his arm, and rent the solid hills,
Bidding the impetuous main flood° rush between   *sea*
The rifted shores, and from the continent
Eternally divided this green isle.   10
Imperial lord of the high southern coast!
From thy projecting head-land I would mark[7]
Far in the east the shades of night disperse,
Melting and thinned, as from the dark blue wave
Emerging, brilliant rays of arrowy light   15
Dart from the horizon; when the glorious sun
Just lifts above it his resplendent orb.
Advances now, with feathery silver touched,
The rippling tide of flood; glisten the sands,
While, inmates of the chalky clefts that scar   20
Thy sides precipitous, with shrill harsh cry,
Their white wings glancing in the level beam,
The terns, and gulls, and tarrocks, seek their food,[8]
And thy rough hollows echo to the voice
Of the gray choughs, and ever restless daws,[9]   25
With clamour, not unlike the chiding hounds,
While the lone shepherd, and his baying dog,
Drive to thy turfy° crest his bleating flock.   *grassy*

The high meridian of the day° is past,   *noon*
And Ocean now, reflecting the calm Heaven,   30
Is of cerulean° hue; and murmurs low   *sky blue*
The tide of ebb, upon the level sands.
The sloop,[10] her angular canvas shifting still,
Catches the light and variable airs°   *breezes*

---

1 [Smith's note]   These lines were written in a residence among ancient public buildings.

2 *her* Smith's daughter, Anna Augusta (d. 1795). Cf. Smith's "Sonnet 65," not included in this anthology.

3 *Muse* Goddess of poetic inspiration, the invocation of whom is a tradition going back to Classical antiquity.

4 [Smith's note]   "Where melancholy friendship bends and weeps." Thomas Gray. [Cf. "Epitaph on Sir William Williams," line 12, by Thomas Gray (1716–71).]

5 [Smith's note]   In crossing the Channel from the coast of France, Beachy-Head is the first land made.

6 *concussion* Violent shaking; *Omnipotent* God.

7 *mark* Observe.

8 [Smith's note]   Terns. *Sterna hirundo*, or Sea Swallow. Gulls. *Larus canus*. Tarrocks. *Larus tridactylus*. [All varieties of sea birds.]

9 [Smith's note]   Gray choughs. *Corvus Graculus*, Cornish Choughs, or, as these birds are called by the Sussex people, Saddle-backed Crows, build in great numbers on this coast. [*daws* Small crow-like birds.]

10 *sloop* Small, single-masted sailing vessel.

35　That but a little crisp the summer sea,
　　Dimpling its tranquil surface.

　　　　　　　　　　　　　　　　Afar off,
　　And just emerging from the arch immense
　　Where seem to part the elements, a fleet
　　Of fishing vessels stretch their lesser sails;
40　While more remote, and like a dubious spot
　　Just hanging in the horizon, laden deep,
　　The ship of commerce richly freighted, makes
　　Her slower progress, on her distant voyage,
　　Bound to the orient° climates, where the sun　　　*eastern*
45　Matures the spice within its odorous shell,
　　And, rivalling the gray worm's filmy toil,°　　　*silk making*
　　Bursts from its pod the vegetable down;[1]
　　Which in long turban'd wreaths, from torrid heat
　　Defends the brows of Asia's countless castes.
50　There the Earth hides within her glowing breast
　　The beamy adamant,[2] and the round pearl
　　Enchased[3] in rugged covering; which the slave,
　　With perilous and breathless toil, tears off
　　From the rough sea-rock, deep beneath the waves.
55　These are the toys of Nature; and her sport
　　Of little estimate in Reason's eye:
　　And they who reason, with abhorrence see
　　Man, for such gauds and baubles,[4] violate
　　The sacred freedom of his fellow man—
60　Erroneous estimate! As Heaven's pure air,
　　Fresh as it blows on this aërial height,
　　Or sound of seas upon the stony strand,°　　　*shore*
　　Or inland, the gay harmony of birds,
　　And winds that wander in the leafy woods;
65　Are to the unadulterate° taste more worth　　　*uncorrupted*
　　Than the elaborate harmony, brought out

From fretted stop, or modulated airs[5]
Of vocal science.—So the brightest gems,
Glancing resplendent on the regal crown,
70　Or trembling in the high born beauty's ear,
Are poor and paltry,° to the lovely light　　　*insignificant, trivial*
Of the fair star,° that as the day declines,　　　*Venus*
Attendant on her queen, the crescent moon,
Bathes her bright tresses in the eastern wave.
75　For now the sun is verging to the sea,
And as he westward sinks, the floating clouds
Suspended, move upon the evening gale,
And gathering round his orb, as if to shade
The insufferable brightness, they resign
80　Their gauzy whiteness; and more warm'd, assume
All hues of purple. There, transparent gold
Mingles with ruby tints, and sapphire gleams,
And colours, such as Nature through her works
Shows only in the ethereal canopy.°　　　*heavens*
85　Thither aspiring Fancy fondly soars,
Wandering sublime thro' visionary vales,
Where bright pavilions rise, and trophies,[6] fann'd
By airs celestial; and adorn'd with wreaths
Of flowers that bloom amid elysian bowers.[7]
90　Now bright, and brighter still the colours glow,
Till half the lustrous orb within the flood
Seems to retire: the flood reflecting still
Its splendor, and in mimic° glory drest;　　　*imitating*
Till the last ray shot upward, fires the clouds
95　With blazing crimson; then in paler light,
Long lines of tenderer radiance, lingering yield
To partial darkness; and on the opposing side
The early moon distinctly rising, throws
Her pearly brilliance on the trembling tide.

---

[1]　[Smith's note]　Cotton. *Gossypium herbaceum.*

[2]　[Smith's note]　Diamonds, the hardest and most valuable of precious stones. For the extraordinary exertions of the Indians in diving for the pearl oysters, see the account of the pearl fisheries in Percival's *View of Ceylon.*

[3]　*Enchased*　Ornamented or inlaid decoration.

[4]　*gauds … baubles*　Insignificant but showy trinkets or toys.

[5]　*fretted stop*　Ridges set across the fingerboard of a stringed instrument; *modulated airs*　Harmonic melodies varying in pitch and/or tone, here referring specifically to vocal melodies.

[6]　*trophies*　Structure erected, usually on a battlefield, to commemorate a victory.

[7]　*elysian*　Having the qualities of the Elysium, the resting place of the blessed after death in Greek mythology; *bowers*　Wooded enclosures.

The fishermen, who at set seasons pass
Many a league[1] off at sea their toiling night,
Now hail their comrades, from their daily task
Returning; and make ready for their own,
With the night tide commencing:—The night tide
Bears a dark vessel on, whose hull° and sails   *body*
Mark her a coaster[2] from the north. Her keel
Now ploughs the sand; and sidelong now she leans,
While with loud clamours her athletic crew
Unload her; and resounds the busy hum
Along the wave-worn rocks. Yet more remote,
Where the rough cliff hangs beetling°   *overhanging*
    o'er its base,
All breathes repose; the water's rippling sound
Scarce heard; but now and then the sea-snipe's[3] cry
Just tells that something living is abroad;
And sometimes crossing on the moonbright line,
Glimmers the skiff,[4] faintly discern'd awhile,
Then lost in shadow.

                    Contemplation here,
High on her throne of rock, aloof may sit,
And bid recording Memory unfold
Her scroll voluminous—bid her retrace
The period, when from Neustria's hostile shore[5]
The Norman launch'd his galleys,[6] and the bay
O'er which that mass of ruin[7] frowns even now

In vain and sullen menace, then received
The new invaders; a proud martial race,
Of Scandinavia[8] the undaunted sons,

---

[1] *league* Measurement of distance roughly equal to three miles.

[2] *coaster* Ship that sails along the coast, especially one trading from port to port in the same country.

[3] [Smith's note] In crossing the Channel this bird is heard at night, uttering a short cry, and flitting along near the surface of the waves. The sailors call it the Sea Snipe; but I can find no species of sea bird of which this is the vulgar name. A bird so called inhabits the Lake of Geneva.

[4] *skiff* Open boat with flat bottom, having a squared stern and pointed bow.

[5] *Neustria's ... shore* Neustria was the western Frankish kingdom from c. 6th century CE to 8th century CE. After the ninth century, the name was applied to Normandy, the area of northwestern France.

[6] *The Norman* William the Conqueror, the king who led the Norman invasion of England and conquered the country at the historic Battle of Hastings in 1066; *galleys* Large medieval ships used in war or commerce.

[7] [Smith's note] Pevensey Castle.

[8] [Smith's note] The Scandinavians (modern Norway, Sweden, Denmark, Lapland, &c.) and other inhabitants of the north, began towards the end of the 8th century to leave their inhospitable climate in search of the produce of more fortunate countries.

The North-men made inroads on the coasts of France; and carrying back immense booty, excited their compatriots to engage in the same piratical voyages: and they were afterwards joined by numbers of necessitous and daring adventurers from the coasts of Provence and Sicily.

In 844, these wandering innovators had a great number of vessels at sea; and again visiting the coasts of France, Spain, and England, the following year they penetrated even to Paris: and the unfortunate Charles the Bald, King of France, purchased at a high price the retreat of the banditti he had no other means of repelling.

These successful expeditions continued for some time; till Rollo [First Duke of Normandy (c. 860–932 CE), ancestor of William the Conqueror], otherwise Raoul, assembled a number of followers, and after a descent on England, crossed the Channel, and made himself master of Rouen, which he fortified. Charles the Simple [Charles III of France (879–929 CE)], unable to contend with Rollo, offered to resign to him some of the northern provinces, and to give him his daughter in marriage. Neustria, since called Normandy, was granted to him, and afterwards Brittany. He added the more solid virtues of the legislator to the fierce valour of the conqueror—converted to Christianity, he established justice, and repressed the excesses of his Danish subjects, till then accustomed to live only by plunder. His name became the signal for pursuing those who violated the laws; as well as the cry of Haro, still so usual in Normandy. The Danes and Francs produced a race of men celebrated for their valour; and it was a small party of these that in 983, having been on a pilgrimage to Jerusalem, arrived on their return at Salerno, and found the town surrounded by Mahometans [Islamic soldiers], whom the Salernians were bribing to leave their coast. The Normans represented to them the baseness and cowardice of such submission; and notwithstanding the inequality of their numbers, they boldly attacked the Saracen [Islamic] camp, and drove the infidels to their ships. The prince of Salerno, astonished at their successful audacity, would have loaded them with the marks of his gratitude; but refusing every reward, they returned to their own country, from whence, however, other bodies of Normans passed into Sicily (anciently called Trinacria); and many of them entered into the service of the Emperor of the East [Basil II (976–1025 CE), of the Eastern Roman, or Byzantine Empire], others of the Pope [either Pope Benedict VII or Pope John XIV], and the Duke of Naples was happy to engage a small party of them in defence of his newly founded duchy. Soon afterwards three brothers of Coutance [Coutances, a district in Normandy], the sons of Tancred de Hauteville [Norman noble illustrious for the deeds of his sons], Guillaume Fier-a-bras [William Iron-Arm (d. 1046 CE)], Drogon [d. 1051 CE], and Humfroi [d. 1057 CE], joining the Normans established at Aversa, became masters of the fertile island of   [continued ...]

Whom Dogon, Fier-a-bras, and Humfroi led
To conquest: while Trinacria to their power
Yielded her wheaten garland; and when thou,
130   Parthenope! within thy fertile bay
Receiv'd the victors—

           In the mailed ranks
Of Normans landing on the British coast
Rode Taillefer; and with astounding voice
Thunder'd the war song daring Roland sang
135   First in the fierce contention: vainly brave,
One not inglorious struggle England made—
But failing, saw the Saxon heptarchy[1]
Finish for ever.—Then the holy pile,[2]
Yet seen upon the field of conquest, rose,
140   Where to appease heaven's wrath for so much blood,
The conqueror bade unceasing prayers ascend,
And requiems[3] for the slayers and the slain.
But let not modern Gallia form from hence[4]
Presumptuous hopes, that ever thou again,
145   Queen of the isles!° shalt crouch to foreign arms.   *England*
The enervate sons of Italy may yield;

And the Iberian, all his trophies torn
And wrapp'd in Superstition's monkish
      weed,°   *monastic clothing*
May shelter his abasement, and put on
150   Degrading fetters.[5] Never, never thou!
Imperial mistress of the obedient sea;
But thou, in thy integrity secure,
Shalt now undaunted meet a world in arms.

England! 'twas where this promontory rears
155   Its rugged brow above the channel wave,
Parting the hostile nations,[6] that thy fame,
Thy naval fame was tarnish'd, at what time
Thou, leagued with the Batavian, gavest to France[7]
One day of triumph—triumph the more loud,
160   Because even then so rare. Oh! well redeem'd,
Since, by a series of illustrious men,
Such as no other country ever rear'd,
To vindicate her cause. It is a list
Which, as Fame echoes it, blanches° the cheek   *makes pale*

Sicily; and Robert Guiscard [another of de Hauteville's sons, Guiscard (1015–85 CE) was the most successful and well-known of the Normans who conquered southern Italy] joining them, the Normans became sovereigns both of Sicily and Naples (Parthenope). How William, the natural son of Robert, duke of Normandy, possessed himself of England, is too well known to be repeated here. William sailing from St. Valori, landed in the bay of Pevensey; and at the place now called Battle, met the English forces under Harold [Harold II (c. 1022–66), King of England killed at the Battle of Hastings]: an esquire (*ecuyer*) called Taillefer, mounted on an armed horse, led on the Normans, singing in a thundering tone the war song of Rollo. He threw himself among the English, and was killed on the first onset. In a marsh not far from Hastings, the skeletons of an armed man and horse were found a few years since, which are believed to have belonged to the Normans, as a party of their horse, deceived in the nature of the ground, perished in the morass.

[1]   *Saxon heptarchy* Seven kingdoms of the Anglo-Saxons: Northumbria, Mercia, Kent, East Anglia, Wessex (West Saxons), Essex (East Saxons), and Sussex (South Saxons).

[2]   [Smith's note] Battle Abbey was raised by the Conqueror, and endowed with an ample revenue, that masses might be said night and day for the souls of those who perished in battle.

[3]   *requiems* Masses for the deceased.

[4]   *Gallia* France; *hence* This reason.

[5]   *The enervate ... fetters* By the time Smith wrote *Beachy Head*, Napoleon (1769–1821) had already established his empire, conquering both Italy and the Iberian Peninsula (Spain and Portugal).

[6]   *hostile nations* France and England, who had almost constantly been at violent odds since the Norman Conquest through the end of the Hundred Years' War.

[7]   [Smith's note] In 1690, King William being then in Ireland, Tourville, the French admiral, arrived on the coast of England. His fleet consisted of seventy-eight large ships, and twenty-two fire-ships. Lord Torrington, the English admiral, lay at St. Helens, with only forty English and a few Dutch ships; and conscious of the disadvantage under which he should give battle, he ran up between the enemy's fleet and the coast, to protect it. The Queen's council, dictated to by Russell, persuaded her to order Torrington to venture a battle. The order Torrington appears to have obeyed reluctantly: his fleet now consisted of twenty-two Dutch and thirty-four English ships. Evertson, the Dutch admiral, was eager to obtain glory; Torrington, more cautious, reflected on the importance of the stake. The consequence was, that the Dutch rashly sailing on were surrounded, and Torrington, solicitous to recover this false step, placed himself with difficulty between the Dutch and the French; but three Dutch ships were burnt, two of their admirals killed, and almost all their ships disabled. The English and the Dutch declining a second engagement, retired towards the mouth of the Thames. The French, from ignorance of the coast, and misunderstanding among each other, failed to take all the advantage they might have done of this victory.

Of bold Ambition; while the despot feels
The extorted sceptre tremble in his grasp.

From even the proudest roll[1] by glory fill'd,
How gladly the reflecting mind returns
To simple scenes of peace and industry,
Where, bosom'd° in some valley of the hills   enclosed
Stands the lone farm; its gate with tawny ricks[2]
Surrounded, and with granaries and sheds,
Roof'd with green mosses, and by elms and ash
Partially shaded; and not far remov'd
The hut of sea-flints° built; the humble home   sea stones
Of one, who sometimes watches on the heights,[3]
When hid in the cold mist of passing clouds,
The flock, with dripping fleeces, are dispers'd
O'er the wide down; then from some ridged point
That overlooks the sea, his eager eye
Watches the bark° that for his signal waits   small ship
To land its merchandise:—Quitting for this
Clandestine traffic his more honest toil,
The crook° abandoning, he braves himself   shepherd's staff
The heaviest snow-storm of December's night,
When with conflicting winds the ocean raves,
And on the tossing boat, unfearing mounts
To meet the partners of the perilous trade,
And share their hazard. Well it were for him,
If no such commerce of destruction known,
He were content with what the earth affords
To human labour; even where she seems
Reluctant most. More happy is the hind,°   farm laborer
Who, with his own hands rears on some black moor,
Or turbary,[4] his independent hut
Cover'd with heather, whence the slow white smoke

Of smouldering peat[5] arises——A few sheep,
His best possession, with his children share
The rugged shed when wintry tempests blow;
200 But, when with Spring's return the green blades rise
Amid the russet heath,[6] the household live
Joint tenants of the waste° throughout   uncultivated wilderness
     the day,
And often, from her nest, among the swamps,
Where the gemm'd sun-dew grows, or fring'd buck-bean,[7]
205 They scare the plover,[8] that with plaintive cries
Flutters, as sorely wounded, down the wind.
Rude,° and but just remov'd from savage life   common, rustic
Is the rough dweller among scenes like these,
(Scenes all unlike the poet's[9] fabling dreams
210 Describing Arcady[10])—But he is free;
The dread that follows on illegal acts
He never feels; and his industrious mate
Shares in his labour. Where the brook is traced
By crowding osiers, and the black coot[11] hides
215 Among the plashy° reeds, her diving brood,   boggy
The matron wades; gathering the long green rush[12]
That well prepar'd hereafter lends its light
To her poor cottage, dark and cheerless else
Thro' the drear hours of Winter. Otherwhile
220 She leads her infant group where charlock[13] grows
"Unprofitably gay,"[14] or to the fields,
Where congregate the linnet° and the finch,   song bird
That on the thistles, so profusely spread,

---

[1] *roll* Rolled parchment (scroll) generally used for official documents, in this case likely a chronicle.

[2] *ricks* Bales of hay or grain.

[3] [Smith's note] The shepherds and laborers of this tract of country, a hardy and athletic race of men, are almost universally engaged in the contraband trade, carried on for the coarsest and most destructive spirits, with the opposite coast. When no other vessel will venture to sea, these men hazard their lives to elude the watchfulness of the Revenue officers, and to secure their cargoes.

[4] *turbary* Area of land from whence turf can be harvested for fuel.

[5] *peat* Moss found in bogs and swamps that is used for fuel.

[6] *heath* Open, uncultivated ground.

[7] [Smith's note] Sun-dew. *Drosera rotundifolia*. [Botanical found in boggy areas, which secretes dew-like drops of liquid;] buck-bean *Menyanthes trifoliatum*. [Pinkish-white flowered water plant.]

[8] [Smith's note] Plover. *Tringa vanellus*. [Water bird.]

[9] *poet* Sir Philip Sidney (1554–86), prominent Elizabethan poet who wrote the prose romance *Arcadia*.

[10] *Arcady* Ideal land of the pastoral tradition.

[11] *osiers* Willow trees; [Smith's note] Coot. *Fulita aterrima*. [Swimming bird.]

[12] *rush* Water rush dried and used for light.

[13] *charlock* Field mustard.

[14] [Smith's note] "With blossom'd furze, unprofitably gay." Goldsmith. [Cf. *The Deserted Village*, line 194, by Oliver Goldsmith (1728–74).]

Feast in the desert; the poor family
225 Early resort, extirpating[1] with care
These, and the gaudier mischief of the ground;
Then flames the high rais'd heap; seen afar off
Like hostile war-fires flashing to the sky.[2]
Another task is theirs: On fields that show
230 As° angry Heaven had rain'd sterility,   *as if*
Stony and cold, and hostile to the plough,
Where clamouring loud, the evening curlew[3] runs
And drops her spotted eggs among the flints;
The mother and the children pile the stones
235 In rugged pyramids;—and all this toil
They patiently encounter; well content
On their flock bed to slumber undisturb'd
Beneath the smoky roof they call their own.
Oh! little knows the sturdy hind, who stands
240 Gazing, with looks where envy and contempt
Are often strangely mingled, on the car°   *carriage*
Where prosperous Fortune sits; what secret care
Or sick satiety is often hid,
Beneath the splendid outside: *He* knows not
245 How frequently the child of Luxury
Enjoying nothing, flies from place to place
In chase of pleasure that eludes his grasp;
And that content is e'en less found by him,
Than by the labourer, whose pick-axe smooths
250 The road before his chariot; and who doffs
What *was* an hat; and as the train pass on,
Thinks how one day's expenditure, like this,
Would cheer him for long months, when to his toil
The frozen earth closes her marble breast.

255 Ah! who *is* happy? Happiness! a word
That like false fire, from marsh effluvia[4] born,
Misleads the wanderer, destin'd to contend
In the world's wilderness, with want or woe—

Yet *they* are happy, who have never ask'd
260 What good or evil means. The boy
That on the river's margin gaily plays,
Has heard that Death is there—He knows not Death,
And therefore fears it not; and venturing in
He gains a bullrush, or a minnow—then,
265 At certain peril, for a worthless prize,
A crow's, or raven's nest, he climbs the boll°   *trunk*
Of some tall pine; and of his prowess proud,
Is for a moment happy. Are *your* cares,
Ye who despise him, never worse applied?
270 The village girl is happy, who sets forth
To distant fair, gay in her Sunday suit,
With cherry colour'd knots,[5] and flourish'd shawl,
And bonnet newly purchas'd. So is he
Her little brother, who his mimic drum
275 Beats, till he drowns her rural lovers' oaths
Of constant faith, and still increasing love;
Ah! yet a while, and half those oaths believ'd,
Her happiness is vanish'd; and the boy
While yet a stripling,° finds the sound   *inexperienced youth*
     he lov'd
280 Has led him on, till he has given up
His freedom, and his happiness together.
I once was happy, when while yet a child,
I learn'd to love these upland solitudes,
And, when elastic as the mountain air,
285 To my light spirit, care was yet unknown
And evil unforeseen:—Early it came,
And childhood scarcely passed, I was condemned,
A guiltless exile, silently to sigh,
While Memory, with faithful pencil, drew
290 The contrast; and regretting, I compared
With the polluted smoky atmosphere
And dark and stifling streets, the southern hills
That to the setting Sun, their graceful heads
Rearing, o'erlook the frith, where Vecta[6] breaks

---

1 *extirpating* Removing by pulling up by the roots.

2 [Smith's note] The Beacons formerly lighted up the hills to give notice of the approach of an enemy. These signals would still be used in case of alarm, if the Telegraph [system of semaphore signals] now substituted could not be distinguished on account of fog or darkness.

3 [Smith's note] Curlew. *Charandrius oedienemus.* [Shore bird.]

4 *false fire* Hovering phosphorescence created by gases in swampy areas; *effluvia* Emissions (usually vapor or gas).

---

5 *knots* I.e., of ribbon.

6 *frith* Firth, narrow sea inlet; [Smith's note] Vecta. The Isle of Wight [island in the English Channel, off the south-central coast], which breaks the force of the waves when they are driven by south-west winds against this long and open coast. It is somewhere described as "Vecta shouldering the Western Waves."

5   With her white rocks, the strong impetuous tide,
    When western winds the vast Atlantic urge
    To thunder on the coast—Haunts[1] of my youth!
    Scenes of fond day dreams, I behold ye yet!
0   Where 'twas so pleasant by thy northern slopes
    To climb the winding sheep-path, aided oft
    By scattered thorns: whose spiny branches bore
    Small woolly tufts, spoils of the vagrant lamb
    There seeking shelter from the noon-day sun;
    And pleasant, seated on the short soft turf,
5   To look beneath upon the hollow way[2]
    While heavily upward moved the labouring wain,°   *wagon*
    And stalking slowly by, the sturdy hind
    To ease his panting team, stopped with a stone
    The grating wheel.

             Advancing higher still
0   The prospect° widens, and the village church   *view*
    But little, o'er the lowly roofs around
    Rears its gray belfry, and its simple vane;
    Those lowly roofs of thatch[3] are half concealed
    By the rude arms of trees, lovely in spring,[4]
5   When on each bough, the rosy-tinctured bloom
    Sits thick, and promises autumnal plenty.
    For even those orchards round the Norman farms,
    Which as their owners mark the promised fruit,
    Console them for the vineyards of the south,
20   Surpass not these.

             Where woods of ash, and beech,
    And partial copses, fringe the green hill foot,
    The upland shepherd rears his modest home,
    There wanders by, a little nameless stream
    That from the hill wells forth, bright now and clear,
25   Or after rain with chalky mixture gray,

But still refreshing in its shallow course,
The cottage garden; most for use designed,
Yet not of beauty destitute. The vine
Mantles the little casement; yet the briar[5]
330 Drops fragrant dew among the July flowers;
And pansies rayed, and freak'd° and mottled pinks *flecked*
Grow among balm, and rosemary and rue:[6]
There honeysuckles flaunt, and roses blow[7]
Almost uncultured:° Some with dark   *uncultivated*
    green leaves
335 Contrast their flowers of pure
    unsullied° white;   *spotlessly pure*
Others, like velvet robes of regal state
Of richest crimson, while in thorny moss
Enshrined and cradled, the most lovely, wear
The hues of youthful beauty's glowing cheek.
340 With fond regret I recollect e'en now
In Spring and Summer, what delight I felt
Among these cottage gardens, and how much
Such artless nosegays,° knotted with a rush *small bouquets*
By village housewife or her ruddy° maid, *rosy*
345 Were welcome to me; soon and simply pleased

An early worshipper at Nature's shrine,
I loved her rudest scenes—warrens, and heaths,
And yellow commons,° and birch-shaded *common lands*
    hollows,
And hedge rows, bordering unfrequented lanes
350 Bowered with wild roses, and the clasping woodbine[8]
Where purple tassels of the tangling vetch[9]
With bittersweet, and bryony inweave,[10]

---

[1] *Haunts* Places frequently visited.

[2] *hollow way* Path through a gorge.

[3] *thatch* Plant stalks used for roofing.

[4] [Smith's note] Every cottage in this country has its orchard; and I imagine that not even those of Herefordshire, or Worcestershire, exhibit a more beautiful prospect, when the trees are in bloom, and the "Primavera candida e vermiglia" [cf. Petrarch's Sonnet 310, line 4 ("Pure and rosy spring")], is every where so enchanting.

---

[5] *Mantles* Dresses; *casement* Window sash opening outwards; *briar* Small shrub or tree with hardy wooden roots.

[6] *balm … rue* Culinary and medicinal herbs.

[7] *blow* Bloom, blossom.

[8] *woodbine* Climbing vine, such as the honeysuckle.

[9] [Smith's note] Vetch. *Vicia sylvatica.* [Plant with tendrils ending in small flowers of various colors.]

[10] [Smith's note] Bittersweet. *Solanum dulcamara.* [Common shrub.] Bryony. *Bryonia alba.* [Tendril-bearing vine.]

And the dew fills the silver bindweed's[1] cups—
I loved to trace the brooks whose humid banks
355   Nourish the harebell, and the freckled pagil;[2]
And stroll among o'ershadowing woods of beech,
Lending in Summer, from the heats of noon
A whispering shade; while haply there reclines
Some pensive lover of uncultur'd flowers,
360   Who, from the tumps[3] with bright green mosses clad,
Plucks the wood sorrel,[4] with its light thin leaves,
Heart-shaped, and triply folded; and its root
Creeping like beaded coral; or who there
Gathers, the copse's pride, anémones,[5]
365   With rays like golden studs on ivory laid
Most delicate: but touch'd with purple clouds,
Fit crown for April's fair but changeful brow.

Ah! hills so early loved! in fancy still
I breathe your pure keen air; and still behold
370   Those widely spreading views, mocking alike
The Poet and the Painter's utmost art.
And still, observing objects more minute,
Wondering remark the strange and foreign forms
Of sea-shells; with the pale calcareous° soil   *chalky*
375   Mingled, and seeming of resembling substance.[6]

Tho' surely the blue Ocean (from the heights
Where the downs westward trend,[7] but dimly seen)
Here never roll'd its surge. Does Nature then
Mimic, in wanton° mood, fantastic shapes   *unruly*
380   Of bivalves, and inwreathed volutes,[8] that cling
To the dark sea-rock of the wat'ry world?
Or did this range of chalky mountains, once
Form a vast basin, where the Ocean waves
Swell'd fathomless? What time these fossil shells,
385   Buoy'd° on their native-element, were thrown   *floated*
Among the imbedding calx:[9] when the huge hill
Its giant bulk heaved, and in strange ferment
Grew up a guardian barrier, 'twixt the sea
And the green level of the sylvan weald.°   *upland*

390   Ah! very vain is Science' proudest boast,
And but a little light its flame yet lends
To its most ardent votaries;[10] since from whence
These fossil forms are seen, is but conjecture,
Food for vague theories, or vain dispute,
395   While to his daily task the peasant goes,
Unheeding such inquiry; with no care
But that the kindly change of sun and shower,
Fit for his toil the earth he cultivates.
As little recks° the herdsman of the hill,   *cares*
400   Who on some turfy knoll,° idly reclined,   *small hill*
Watches his wether° flock; that deep beneath   *castrated ram*
Rest the remains of men, of whom is left[11]
No traces in the records of mankind,
Save what these half obliterated mounds

---

1 [Smith's note] Bindweed. *Convolvulus sepium.* [Trailing or twining weedy plant with cup-shaped blossoms.]

2 [Smith's note] Harebell. *Hyacinthus non scriptus.* [Plant having bell-shaped white or blue flowers.] Pagil. *Primula veris.* [Primrose.]

3 *tumps* Hillocks.

4 [Smith's note] Sorrel. *Oxalis acetosella.* [Culinary herb having a sour taste.]

5 [Smith's note] Anémones. *Anemone nemorosa.* [Flowering plant having brilliant blossoms, common to Great Britain.] It appears to be settled on late and excellent authorities, that this word should not be accented on the second syllable, but on the penultima [second to last]. I have however ventured the more known accentuation, as more generally used, and suiting better the nature of my verse.

6 [Smith's note] Among the crumbling chalk I have often found shells, some quite in a fossil state and hardly distinguishable from chalk. Others appeared more recent; cockles, muscles, and periwinkles, I well remember, were among the number; and some whose names I do not know. A great number were like those of small land snails. It is now many years since I made these observations. The appearance of sea-shells so far from the sea excited my surprise, though I then knew nothing of natural history. I have never read any of the late theories of the earth, nor was I ever satisfied with the attempts to explain many of the phenomena which call forth conjecture in those books I happened to have had access to on this subject.

7 *downs* Chalky uplands of south and southwest England; *westward trend* Move in a westerly direction.

8 *bivalves* Mollusks, such as oysters and clams, having two hinged shells; *volutes* Mollusks with spiral-shaped shells, such as conchs.

9 *calx* Residue remaining after a metal or mineral has been burned.

10 *votaries* Persons bound by solemn oaths, usually to religious orders.

11 [Smith's note] These Downs are not only marked with traces of encampments, which from their forms are called Roman or Danish; but there are numerous tumuli [burial mounds] among them. Some of which having been opened a few years ago, were supposed by a learned antiquary to contain the remains of the original natives of the country.

And half fill'd trenches doubtfully impart
To some lone antiquary;[1] who on times remote,
Since which two thousand years have roll'd away,
Loves to contemplate. He perhaps may trace,
Or fancy he can trace, the oblong square
Where the mail'd legions, under Claudius,[2] rear'd
The rampire, or excavated fosse[3] delvcd;
What time the huge unwieldly Elephant[4]
Auxiliary reluctant, hither led,
From Afric's forest glooms and tawny sands,
First felt the Northern blast, and his vast frame

Sunk useless; whence in after ages found,
The wondering hinds, on those enormous bones
Gaz'd; and in giants[5] dwelling on the hills
Believed and marvell'd—

                  Hither, Ambition, come!
420 Come and behold the nothingness of all
For which you carry thro' the oppressed Earth,
War, and its train° of horrors—see where tread   *retinue*
The innumerous hoofs of flocks above the works
By which the warrior sought to register
425 His glory, and immortalize his name—
The pirate Dane,[6] who from his circular camp
Bore in destructive robbery, fire and sword
Down thro' the vale, sleeps unremember'd here;
And here, beneath the green sward,° rests alike   *meadow*
430 The savage native,[7] who his acorn meal
Shar'd with the herds, that ranged the pathless woods;
And the centurion, who on these wide hills
Encamping, planted the Imperial Eagle.°   *Roman emblem*
All, with the lapse of Time, have passed away,
435 Even as the clouds, with dark and dragon shapes,
Or like vast promontories crown'd with towers,
Cast their broad shadows on the downs: then sail
Far to the northward, and their transient gloom
Is soon forgotten.

              But from thoughts like these,
440 By human crimes suggested, let us turn
To where a more attractive study courts
The wanderer of the hills; while shepherd girls

---

1 *antiquary* Recorder of antiquities.

2 [Smith's note] That the legions of Claudius [10 BCE–54 CE] were in this part of Britain appears certain. Since this emperor received the submission of Cantii, Atrebates, Irenobates, and Regni [Celtic tribes in pre-Roman Britain], in which latter denomination were included the people of Sussex.

3 *rampire* Ramparts or barriers; *fossé* Ditch.

4 [Smith's note] In the year 1740, some workmen digging in the park at Burton in Sussex, discovered, nine feet below the surface, the teeth and bones of an elephant; two of the former were seven feet eight inches in length. There were besides these, tusks, one of which broke in removing it, a grinder not at all decayed, and a part of the jaw-bone, with bones of the knee and thigh, and several others. Some of them remained very lately at Burton House, the seat of John Biddulph, Esq. Others were in possession of the Rev. Dr. Langrish, minister of Petworth at that period, who was present when some of these bones were taken up, and gave it as his opinion, that they had remained there since the universal deluge [Biblical flood of Noah's time]. The Romans under the Emperor Claudius probably brought elephants into Britain. Milton, in the second book of his History, in speaking of the expedition, says that "he [who waiteth ready with a huge preparation, as if not safe enough amidst the flower of all his Romans,] like a great eastern king, with armed elephants, marched [marches] through Gallia." This is given on the authority of Dion Cassius, in his Life of the Emperor Claudius. It has therefore been conjectured, that the bones found at Burton might have been those of one of these elephants, who perished there soon after its landing; or dying on the high downs, one of which, called Duncton Hill, rises immediately above Burton Park, the bones might have been washed down by the torrents of rain, and buried deep in the soil. They were not found together, but scattered at some distance from each other. The two tusks were twenty feet apart. I had often heard of the elephant's bones at Burton, but never saw them; and I have no books to refer to. I think I saw, in what is now called the National Museum at Paris, the very large bones of an elephant, which were found in North America: though it is certain that this enormous animal is never seen in its natural state, but in the countries under the torrid zone of the old world. I have, since making this note, been told that the bones of the rhinoceros and hippopotamus have been found in America.

5 [Smith's note] The peasants believe that the large bones sometimes found belonged to giants, who formerly lived on the hills. The devil also has a great deal to do with the remarkable forms of hill and vale: the Devil's Punch Bowl, the Devil's Leaps, and the Devil's Dyke, are names given to deep hollows, or high and abrupt ridges, in this and the neighboring county.

6 [Smith's note] The incursions of the Danes were for many ages the scourge of this island.

7 [Smith's note] The Aborigines of this country lived in woods, unsheltered but by trees and caves; and were probably as truly savage as any of those who are now termed so.

Will from among the fescue[1] bring him flowers,
Of wonderous mockery; some resembling bees
445 In velvet vest, intent on their sweet toil,[2]
While others mimic flies,[3] that lightly sport
In the green shade, or float along the pool,
But here seem perch'd upon the slender stalk,
And gathering honey dew. While in the breeze
450 That wafts the thistle's plumed seed along,
Blue bells wave tremulous. The mountain thyme[4]
Purples the hassock of the heaving mole,[5]
And the short turf is gay with tormentil,[6]
And bird's foot trefoil, and the lesser tribes
455 Of hawkweed;[7] spangling it with fringed stars.—
Near where a richer tract of cultur'd land
Slopes to the south; and burnished by the sun,

Bend in the gale of August, floods of corn;
The guardian of the flock, with watchful care,[8]
460 Repels by voice and dog the encroaching sheep—
While his boy visits every wired trap[9]
That scars the turf; and from the pit-falls takes
The timid migrants,[10] who from distant wilds,
Warrens, and stone quarries, are destined thus
465 To lose their short existence. But unsought
By Luxury yet, the Shepherd still protects
The social bird,[11] who from his native haunts
Of willowy current, or the rushy pool,
Follows the fleecy crowd, and flirts and skims,
470 In fellowship among them.

                      Where the knoll
More elevated takes the changeful winds,
The windmill rears its vanes; and thitherward
With his white load,° the master travelling,   *grain*
Scares the rooks° rising slow on whispering wings,   *crows*
475 While o'er his head, before the summer sun
Lights up the blue expanse, heard more than seen,
The lark sings matins;° and above   *morning worship*
   the clouds
Floating, embathes his spotted breast in dew.

---

[1] [Smith's note]   The grass called Sheep's Fescue, (*Festuca ovina*)
clothes these Downs with the softest turf.

[2] [Smith's note]   *Ophrys apifera*, Bee Ophrys, or Orchis found
plentifully on the hills, as well as the next.

[3] [Smith's note]   *Ophrys muscifera*. Fly Orchis. Linnaeus, misled by
the variations to which some of this tribe are really subject, has perhaps
too rashly esteemed all those which resemble insects, as forming only
one species, which he terms Ophrys insectifera. See *English Botany*
[written by James Sowerby in 36 volumes from 1791 to 1814].

[4] [Smith's note]   Blue bells. *Campanula rotundifolia*. Mountain
thyme. *Thymus serpyllum*. "It is a common notion, that the flesh of
sheep which feed upon aromatic plants, particularly wild thyme, is
superior in flavour to other mutton. The truth is, that sheep do not
crop these aromatic plants, unless now and then by accident, or when
they are first turned on hungry to downs, heaths, or commons; but the
soil and situations favourable to aromatic plants, produce a short sweet
pasturage, best adapted to feeding sheep, whom nature designed for
mountains, and not for turnip grounds and rich meadows. The
attachment of bees to this, and other aromatic plants, is well known."
Martyn's Miller [Thomas Martyn's edition of Philip Miller's *The
Gardener's and Botanist's Dictionary*, 1797–1807].

[5] *hassock … mole*   Clump of grass thrust up by the tunneling of a
mole.

[6] [Smith's note]   Tormentil. *Tormentilla reptans*. [Plant with yellow
flowers and bitter roots.]

[7] [Smith's note]   Bird's foot trefoil. *Trifolium ornithopoides*. [Plant
having claw-shaped pods.] Hawkweed. *Hieracium*, many sorts. [Hairy
plants having dandelion-like blossoms.]

[8] [Smith's note]   The downs, especially to the south, where they are
less abrupt, are in many places under the plough; and the attention of
the shepherds is there particularly required to keep the flocks from
trespassing.

[9] [Smith's note]   Square holes cut in the turf, into which a wire noose
is fixed, to catch Wheatears. Mr. White [*The Natural History of
Selbourne* (1789)] says, that these birds (*Motacilla oenanthe*) are never
taken beyond the river Adur, and Beding Hill; but this is certainly a
mistake.

[10] [Smith's note]   These birds are extremely fearful, and on the
slightest appearance of a cloud, run for shelter to the first rut, or heap
of stone, that they see.

[11] [Smith's note]   The Yellow Wagtail. *Motacilla flava*. It frequents
the banks of rivulets in winter, making its nest in meadows and corn-
fields. But after the breeding season is over, it haunts downs and
sheepwalks, and is seen constantly among the flocks, probably for the
sake of the insects it picks up. In France the shepherds call it *La
Bergeronette*, and say it often gives them, by its cry, notice of approaching danger.

Beneath the shadow of a gnarled thorn,
Bent by the sea blast,[1] from a seat of turf
With fairy nosegays strewn, how wide the view![2]
Till in the distant north it melts away,
And mingles indiscriminate with clouds:
But if the eye could reach so far, the mart
Of England's capital, its domes and spires
Might be perceived—Yet hence the distant range
Of Kentish hills,[3] appear in purple haze;
And nearer, undulate the wooded heights,
And airy summits, that above the mole[4]
Rise in green beauty; and the beacon'd ridge
Of Black-down[5] shagg'd with heath, and swelling rude
Like a dark island from the vale; its brow
Catching the last rays of the evening sun
That gleam between the nearer park's old oaks,
Then lighten up the river, and make prominent
The portal, and the ruin'd battlements[6]
Of that dismantled fortress; rais'd what time
The Conqueror's° successors fiercely fought,   *William I*
Tearing with civil feuds the desolate land.
But now a tiller of the soil dwells there,
And of the turret's loop'd and rafter'd halls
Has made an humbler homestead—Where he sees,
Instead of armed foemen, herds that graze

Along his yellow meadows; or his flocks
At evening from the upland driv'n to fold—   505

In such a castellated mansion once
A stranger chose his home; and where hard by
In rude disorder fallen, and hid with brushwood
Lay fragments gray of towers and buttresses,
Among the ruins, often he would muse—   510
His rustic meal soon ended, he was wont°   *accustomed*
To wander forth, listening the evening sounds
Of rushing milldam,[7] or the distant team,
Or night-jar, chasing fern-flies:[8] the tir'd hind
Pass'd him at nightfall, wondering he should sit   515
On the hill top so late: they from the coast
Who sought bye paths with their clandestine
        load,°   *smugglers*
Saw with suspicious doubt, the lonely man
Cross on their way: but village maidens thought
His senses injur'd; and with pity say   520
That he, poor youth! must have been cross'd in love—
For often, stretch'd upon the mountain turf
With folded arms, and eyes intently fix'd
Where ancient elms and firs obscured a grange,°   *farm*
Some little space within the vale below,   525

---

[1] [Smith's note] The strong winds from the south-west occasion almost all the trees, which on these hills are exposed to it, to grow the other way.

[2] [Smith's note] So extensive are some of the views from these hills, that only the want of power in the human eye to travel so far, prevents London itself being discerned. Description falls so infinitely short of the reality, that only here and there, distinct features can be given.

[3] [Smith's note] A scar of chalk in a hill beyond Sevenoaks in Kent, is very distinctly seen of a clear day.

[4] [Smith's note] The hills about Dorking in Surrey; over almost the whole extent of which county the prospect extends; *mole* Cliffs leading down to sea.

[5] [Smith's note] This is an high ridge, extending between Sussex and Surrey. It is covered with heath, and has almost always a dark appearance. On it is a telegraph.

[6] [Smith's note] In this country there are several of the fortresses or castles built by Stephen of Blois [British king (r. 1135–54)], in his contention for the kingdom, with the daughter of Henry the First, the Empress Matilda. Some of these are now converted into farm houses.

[7] *milldam* Dam erected in a stream in order to power a mill.

[8] [Smith's note] Dr. Aikin remarks, I believe, in his essay "On the Application of Natural History to the Purposes of Poetry [1777]," how many of our best poets have noticed the same circumstance, the hum of the Dor Beetle (*Scaraboeus stercorarius*) among the sounds heard by the evening wanderer. I remember only one instance in which the more remarkable, though by no means uncommon noise, of the Fern Owl, or Goatsucker, is mentioned. It is called the Night Hawk, the Jar Bird, the Churn Owl, and the Fern Owl, from its feeding on the *Scaraboeus solstitialis*, or Fern Chafer, which it catches while on the wing with its claws, the middle toe of which is long and curiously serrated, on purpose to hold them. It was this bird that was intended to be described in the Forty-second Sonnet [Smith's *Sonnets*]. I was mistaken in supposing it as visible in November; it is a migrant, and leaves this country in August. I had often seen and heard it, but I did not then know its name or history. It is called Goatsucker (*Caprimulgus*), from a strange prejudice taken against it by the Italians, who assert that it sucks their goats; and the peasants of England still believe that a disease in the backs of their cattle, occasioned by a fly, which deposits its eggs under the skin, and raises a boil, sometimes fatal to calves, is the work of this bird, which they call a Puckeridge. Nothing can convince them that their beasts are not injured by this bird, which they therefore hold in abhorrence.

They heard him, as complaining of his fate,
And to the murmuring wind, of cold neglect
And baffled hope he told.—The peasant girls
These plaintive sounds remember, and even now
530   Among them may be heard the stranger's songs.

   Were I a Shepherd on the hill
      And ever as the mists withdrew
   Could see the willows of the rill°   *brook*
   Shading the footway to the mill
535   Where once I walk'd with you—

   And as away Night's shadows sail,
      And sounds of birds and brooks arise,
   Believe, that from the woody vale
   I hear your voice upon the gale
540   In soothing melodies;

   And viewing from the Alpine height,
      The prospect dress'd in hues of air,
   Could say, while transient colours bright
   Touch'd the fair scene with dewy light,
545   'Tis, that *her* eyes are there!

   I think, I could endure my lot
      And linger on a few short years,
   And then, by all but you forgot,
   Sleep, where the turf that clothes the spot
550   May claim some pitying tears.

   For 'tis not easy to forget
      One, who thro' life has lov'd you still,
   And you, however late, might yet
   With sighs to Memory giv'n, regret
555   The Shepherd of the Hill.

Yet otherwhile it seem'd as if young Hope
Her flattering pencil gave to Fancy's hand,
And in his wanderings, rear'd to sooth his soul
Ideal bowers of pleasure—Then, of Solitude
560   And of his hermit life, still more enamour'd,
His home was in the forest; and wild fruits
And bread sustain'd him. There in early spring

The Barkmen[1] found him, e'er° the sun arose;   *before*
There at their daily toil, the Wedgecutters[2]
565   Beheld him thro' the distant thicket move.
The shaggy dog following the truffle hunter,[3]
Bark'd at the loiterer; and perchance at night
Belated villagers from fair or wake,
While the fresh night-wind let the moonbeams in
570   Between the swaying boughs, just saw him pass,
And then in silence, gliding like a ghost
He vanish'd! Lost among the deepening gloom.—
But near one ancient tree, whose wreathed roots
Form'd a rude couch, love-songs and scatter'd rhymes,
575   Unfinish'd sentences, or half erased,
And rhapsodies like this, were sometimes found—

   Let us to woodland wilds repair
      While yet the glittering night-dews seem
   To wait the freshly-breathing air,
580   Precursive° of the morning beam,   *preparatory*
   That rising with advancing day,
   Scatters the silver drops away.

   An elm, uprooted by the storm,
      The trunk with mosses gray and green,
585   Shall make for us a rustic form,
      Where lighter grows the forest scene;
   And far among the bowery° shades,   *leafy*
   Are ferny lawns and grassy glades.

   Retiring May to lovely June
590   Her latest garland now resigns;

---

[1] [Smith's note]   As soon as the sap begins to rise, the trees intended for felling are cut and barked [bark is removed from the trees], at which time the men who are employed in that business pass whole days in the woods.

[2] [Smith's note]   The wedges used in ship-building are made of beech wood, and great numbers are cut every year in the woods near the Downs.

[3] [Smith's note]   Truffles [rare exotic mushrooms growing underground] are found under the beech woods, by means of small dogs trained to hunt them by the scent.

The banks with cuckoo-flowers[1] are strewn,
    The woodwalks blue with columbines,[2]
And with its reeds, the wandering stream
Reflects the flag-flower's[3] golden gleam.

There, feathering down the turf to meet,   620
    Their shadowy arms the beeches spread,
While high above our sylvan seat,
    Lifts the light ash its airy head;
And later leaved, the oaks between
Extend their bows of vernal° green.   spring-like   625

The slender birch its paper rind
    Seems offering to divided love,
And shuddering even without a wind
    Aspens, their paler foliage move,   630
As if some spirit of the air
Breath'd a low sigh in passing there.

The Squirrel in his frolic mood,
    Will fearless bound among the boughs;
Yaffils[4] laugh loudly thro' the wood,   635
    And murmuring ring doves tell their vows;
While we, as sweetest woodscents rise,
Listen to woodland melodies.

And I'll contrive a sylvan room
    Against the time of summer heat,   640
Where leaves, inwoven in Nature's loom,
    Shall canopy our green retreat;

And gales that "close the eye of day"[5]
Shall linger, e'er they die away.

And when a sear[6] and sallow hue
    From early frost the bower receives,
I'll dress the sand rock cave for you,
    And strew the floor with heath and leaves,
That you, against the autumnal air
May find securer shelter there.

The Nightingale will then have ceas'd
    To sing her moonlight serenade;
But the gay bird with blushing breast,[7]
    And Woodlarks[8] still will haunt the shade,
And by the borders of the spring
Reed-wrens[9] will yet be carolling.

The forest hermit's lonely cave
    None but such soothing sounds shall reach,
Or hardly heard, the distant wave
    Slow breaking on the stony beach;
Or winds, that now sigh soft and low,
Now make wild music as they blow.

And then, before the chilling North
    The tawny foliage falling light,
Seems, as it flits along the earth,
    The footfall of the busy Sprite,[10]
Who wrapt in pale autumnal gloom,
Calls up the mist-born Mushroom.

---

1 [Smith's note] Cuckoo-flowers. *Lychnis dioica.* Shakespeare describes the Cuckoo buds as being yellow [cf. *Love's Labour's Lost* 5.2.894]. He probably meant the numerous Ranunculi, or March marigolds (*Caltha palustris*), which so gild the meadows in Spring; but poets have never been botanists. The Cuckoo flower is the *Lychnis floscuculi.*

2 [Smith's note] Columbines. *Aquilegia vulgaris.* [Plant with showy blooms featuring variously colored petals surrounded by hollow spurs.]

3 [Smith's note] Flag-flower. *Iris pseudacorus.*

4 [Smith's note] Yaffils. Woodpeckers (*Picus*); three or four species in Britain.

5 [Smith's note] "And [Thy] liquid notes that close the eye of day." Milton [from Sonnet 1, "O nightingale," line 5]. The idea here meant to be conveyed is one of the evening wind, so welcome after a hot day of Summer, and which appears to soothe and lull all nature into tranquillity.

6 *sear* Sere, dry.

7 [Smith's note] The Robin, (*Motacilla rubecula*), which is always heard after other songsters have ceased to sing.

8 [Smith's note] The Woodlark (*Alauda nemorosa*) sings very late.

9 [Smith's note] Reed-wrens (*Motacilla arundinacea*) sing all the summer and autumn, and are often heard during the night.

10 *Sprite* Elusive mythical woodland creature.

Oh! could I hear your soft voice there,
  And see you in the forest green
645 All beauteous as you are, more fair
  You'd look, amid the sylvan scene,
And in a wood-girl's simple guise,
Be still more lovely in mine eyes.

Ye phantoms of unreal delight,
650   Visions of fond delirium born!
Rise not on my deluded sight,
  Then leave me drooping and forlorn
To know, such bliss can never be,
Unless Amanda loved like me.

655 The visionary, nursing dreams like these,
Is not indeed unhappy. Summer woods
Wave over him, and whisper as they wave,
Some future blessings he may yet enjoy.
And as above him sail the silver clouds,
660 He follows them in thought to distant climes,
Where, far from the cold policy of this,
Dividing him from her he fondly loves,
He, in some island of the southern sea,[1]
May haply build his cane-constructed[2] bower
665 Beneath the bread-fruit,[3] or aspiring palm,
With long green foliage rippling in the gale.
Oh! let him cherish his ideal bliss—
For what is life, when Hope has ceas'd to strew
Her fragile flowers along its thorny way?
670 And sad and gloomy are his days, who lives
Of Hope abandon'd!

    Just beneath the rock
Where Beachy overpeers the channel wave,

Within a cavern mined by wintry tides
Dwelt one,[4] who long disgusted with the world
675 And all its ways, appear'd to suffer life
Rather than live; the soul-reviving gale,
Fanning the bean-field, or the thymy heath,
Had not for many summers breathed on him;
And nothing mark'd to him the season's change,
680 Save that more gently rose the placid sea,
And that the birds which winter on the coast
Gave place to other migrants; save that the fog,
Hovering no more above the beetling cliffs
Betray'd not then the little careless sheep[5]
685 On the brink grazing, while their headlong fall
Near the lone Hermit's flint-surrounded home,
Claim'd unavailing pity; for his heart
Was feelingly alive to all that breath'd;
And outraged as he was, in sanguine[6] youth,
690 By human crimes, he still acutely felt
For human misery.

    Wandering on the beach,
He learn'd to augur° from the clouds of heaven, *predict*
And from the changing colours of the sea,
And sullen murmurs of the hollow cliffs,
695 Or the dark porpoises,[7] that near the shore
Gambol'd° and sported on the level brine *leapt playfully*
When tempests were approaching: then at night
He listen'd to the wind; and as it drove
The billows with o'erwhelming vehemence
700 He, starting from his rugged couch, went forth
And hazarding a life, too valueless,

---

[1] [Smith's note] An allusion to the visionary delights of the newly discovered islands [those in the South Pacific such as Tahiti], where it was at first believed men lived in a state of simplicity and happiness; but where, as later enquiries have ascertained, that exemption from toil, which the fertility of their country gives them, produces the grossest vices; and a degree of corruption that late navigators think will end in the extirpation of the whole people in a few years.

[2] *cane-constructed* Built of cane, the thin flexible stems from bamboo and rattan.

[3] *bread-fruit* Evergreen tree having large edible fruits.

[4] [Smith's note] In a cavern almost immediately under the cliff called Beachy Head, there lived, as the people of the country believed, a man of the name of Darby, who for many years had no other abode than this cave, and subsisted almost entirely on shell-fish. He had often administered assistance to ship-wrecked mariners; but venturing into the sea on this charitable mission during a violent equinoctial storm, he himself perished. As it is above thirty years since I heard this tradition of parson Darby (for so I think he was called), it may now perhaps be forgotten.

[5] [Smith's note] Sometimes in thick weather the sheep feeding on the summit of the cliff miss their footing, and are killed by the fall.

[6] *sanguine* Cheerfully optimistic.

[7] [Smith's note] Dark porpoises. *Delphinus phocoena*.

He waded thro' the waves, with plank or pole,
Towards where the mariner in conflict dread
Was buffeting for life the roaring surge;
5 And now just seen, now lost in foaming gulfs,
The dismal gleaming of the clouded moon
Show'd the dire peril. Often he had snatch'd
From the wild billows, some unhappy man
Who liv'd to bless the hermit of the rocks.
10 But if his generous cares were all in vain,
And with slow swell the tide of morning bore
Some blue swol'n cor'se° to land; the pale recluse   *corpse*
Dug in the chalk a sepulchre—above
Where the dank sea-wrack[1] mark'd the utmost tide,
15 And with his prayers perform'd the obsequies°   *funeral rites*
For the poor helpless stranger.

                              One dark night
The equinoctial wind blew south by west,
Fierce on the shore;—the bellowing cliffs were shook
Even to their stony base, and fragments fell
720 Flashing and thundering on the angry flood.
At day-break, anxious for the lonely man,
His cave the mountain shepherds visited,
Tho' sand and banks of weeds had chok'd their way—
He was not in it; but his drowned cor'se
725 By the waves wafted, near his former home
Receiv'd the rites of burial. Those who read
Chisel'd within the rock, these mournful lines,
Memorials of his sufferings, did not grieve,
That dying in the cause of charity
730 His spirit, from its earthly bondage freed,
Had to some better region fled for ever.
                                        —1807

---
[1] *sea-wrack* Shipwreck.

THE FRENCH REVOLUTION
CONTEXTS

Debate about the French Revolution, which was to open English eyes to the possibility of political change in their own country, began shortly after the 14 July 1789 storming of the Bastille (during which a Parisian crowd swarmed the prison in search of ammunition, freeing seven prisoners and killing the governor in the process). The Revolution forced English men and women to re-examine their most basic societal tenets: their system of government and their handling of issues such as individual civil rights and liberties, rights of inheritance, and sufferance. Discussion of the Revolution triggered a massive increase in the production of written materials. On the pages of novels, periodicals, sermons, chapbooks, handbills, song sheets, and poetry, English writers debated their new relationship with France and its implications for issues of social and political reform at home.

On 4 November 1789, moral philosopher, mathematician, and dissenting preacher Richard Price delivered a sermon venerating the French Revolution and equating it with England's Glorious Revolution of 1688–89, the bloodless revolution in which James II was replaced by William III and Mary II—a key moment in the evolution of constitutional monarchy in Britain. "Struggle no longer against increasing light and liberality," he warned. "Restore to mankind their rights; and consent to the correction of abuses, before they and you are destroyed together." Such views became more and more widespread over the course of the next few months. On 14 July 1790, Parisians gathered near the ruins of the Bastille to celebrate the Revolution's first anniversary, and there was celebrating in Britain too; according to the London *Times*, the anniversary gathering represented "a magnificent association of FREE MEN, emancipated from the shackles of despotism within so short a space of time." The newspaper declared the Revolution "a Phenomenon on which surrounding empires look with admiration." Such feelings ran counter to age-old habit; since 1688, the English had tended to think of themselves as progressive guardians of liberty and the French as intolerant and slavish in their Catholicism. To many in Britain, however, English attitudes did not seem to have changed. Rather, the French Revolution merely represented their long-overdue and much-needed Glorious Revolution.

To be sure, English support for the ideals of the French Revolution was far from being universal. The most important expression of early opposition to those ideals was that of politician and writer Edmund Burke, whose *Reflections on the Revolution in France* was published on 1 November 1790. Burke had been reluctant to condemn the American revolutionaries fifteen years earlier, and he surprised many with his vigorous condemnation of the French Revolution as undermining the foundations of constitutional monarchy. In Burke's view, the suggestion of Price and others that a monarch owes his lawful authority solely "to the choice of the people" was either "nonsense, and therefore neither true nor false, or it affirms a most unfounded, dangerous, illegal and unconstitutional position."

Burke's long essay came to be regarded as a classic statement of conservative principles, and one of the works written in answer to it, Thomas Paine's *Rights of Man*, as a classic expression of Enlightenment principles of human liberty. The voice of Paine, an expatriate from England who had moved to America in 1774, was joined in Britain by voices such as those of William Godwin, Mary Wollstonecraft, and other prominent reformers who were later labeled "Jacobins." Condemning Burke's allegiance to "canonized forefathers," Wollstonecraft accused him of clinging to an ideology of inherited rights: "any personal present convenience should prevent a struggle for the most estimable advantages. This is sound reasoning," she quipped, "in the mouth of the rich and short-sighted."

In 1792, a Republic was declared in France, and the Revolution's violence escalated. In May, the English government, fearing rebellion on its own soil, vowed to eradicate "wicked and seditious writings"; shortly thereafter, it banned Paine's *Rights of Man (Part II)*. In August, Louis XVI and Marie Antoinette were marched out of the Palace of the Tuileries and placed under house arrest—and an increasing number of English began to feel alienated from their French neighbors. Within the conservative English imagination, the French were becoming savages, choosing anarchy over liberty. Even some reformers began to reconsider their view of the Revolution, although they continued to lobby in England for expanded suffrage, electoral reform, and the natural rights of citizens. British attitudes toward the concept of revolution were further complicated by the similarly violent events of the Haitian Revolution (1791–1804), in which Black enslaved people rose up against the island's French colonizers and eventually created an independent state.[1]

In late 1792, Maximilien Robespierre and his Committee for Public Safety took control of Paris and brutally demonstrated their intolerance for any enemy of the republic. The Committee put Louis XVI on trial, and the King and Queen soon joined the list of beheaded aristocrats, clergy, and counter-revolutionary suspects. The English anti-Jacobin movement gathered momentum as citizens expressed horror at these "un-English" acts. By this time other European nations had been considering intervention in France for more than two years. In April 1792, France declared war on Austria; after the execution of the King in early 1793, other countries (Britain included) joined to form the "First Coalition" against France. Over the next several years, the French government remained in a state of turmoil, but French forces held their own against their various enemies, with a young general named Napoleon Bonaparte playing an increasingly important military role. In 1799, Bonaparte seized power, and, for the next fifteen years, the powerful Corsican dominated the European stage.

For some in England, the French by that time had lost their way. In William Wordsworth's view, the oppressed had, in a few short years, "become Oppressors in their turn," and had "changed a war of self-defence / For one of conquest, losing sight of all / Which they had struggled for." Yet, as Godwin noted, all "the great points embraced by the revolution remain entire: hereditary government is gone; hereditary nobility is extinguished; the hierarchy of the Gallican church is no more; the feudal rights, the oppressive immunities of a mighty aristocracy, are banished never to return."

⌘ ⌘ ⌘

---

[1] See "The Haitian Revolution" in "Contexts: Slavery and Its Abolition," elsewhere in this volume.

from Richard Price, *A Discourse on the Love of Our Country, Delivered on Nov. 4, 1789, at the Meeting-House in the Old Jewry, to the Society for Commemorating the Revolution in Great Britain*

Richard Price (1723–91) was a well-known dissenting preacher, mathematician, and political thinker. This sermon initiated England's debate about the French Revolution by likening it to England's Glorious Revolution of 1688.

The love of our country has in all times been a subject of warm commendations; and it is certainly a noble passion; but, like all other passions, it requires regulation and direction. There are mistakes and prejudices by which, in this instance, we are in particular danger of being misled. I will briefly mention some of these to you, and observe,

First, That by our country is meant, in this case, not the soil or the spot of earth on which we happen to have been born; not the forests and fields, but that community of which we are members; or that body of companions and friends and kindred who are associated with us under the same constitution of government, protected by the same laws, and bound together by the same civil polity.

Secondly, It is proper to observe, that even in this sense of our country, that love of it which is our duty, does not imply any conviction of the superior value of it to other countries, or any particular preference of its laws and constitution of government. ... All our attachments should be accompanied, as far as possible, with right opinions.—We are too apt to confine wisdom and virtue within the circle of our own acquaintance and party. Our friends, our country, and in short every thing related to us, we are disposed to overvalue. A wise man will guard himself against this delusion. He will study to think of all things as they are, and not suffer any partial affections to blind his understanding. ...

Thirdly, It is proper I should desire you particularly to distinguish between the love of our country and that spirit of rivalship and ambition which has been common among nations.—What has the love of their country hitherto been among mankind? What has it been but a love of domination; a desire of conquest, and a thirst for grandeur and glory, by extending territory, and enslaving surrounding countries? What has it been but a blind and narrow principle, producing in every country a contempt of other countries, and forming men into combinations and factions against their common rights and liberties? ... As most of the evils which have taken place in private life, and among individuals, have been occasioned by the desire of private interest overcoming the public affections; so most of the evils which have taken place among bodies of men have been occasioned by the desire of their own interest overcoming the principle of universal benevolence: and leading them to attack one another's territories, to encroach on one another's rights, and to endeavour to build their own advancement on the degradation of all within the reach of their power. ...

... I have just observed, that there is a submission due to the executive officers of government, which is our duty; but you must not forget what I have also observed, that it must not be a blind and slavish submission. ... [T]he tendency of every government is to despotism; and in this the best constituted governments must end, if the people are not vigilant, ready to take alarms, and determined to resist abuses as soon as they begin. ... This vigilance, therefore, it is our duty to maintain. Whenever it is withdrawn, and a people cease to reason about their rights and to be awake to encroachments, they are in danger of being enslaved, and their *servants* will soon become their *masters*.

... We have, therefore, on this occasion, peculiar reasons for thanksgiving—But let us remember that we ought not to satisfy ourselves with thanksgivings. ... Let us, in particular, take care not to forget the principles of the Revolution.[1] ...

First; The right to liberty of conscience in religious matters.

Secondly; The right to resist power when abused. And,

---

[1] *Revolution* England's Glorious Revolution of 1688, which ended the reign of King James II and limited the monarch's power under a constitutional monarchy.

Thirdly; The right to choose our own governors; to cashier them for misconduct; and to frame a government for ourselves. ...

I would farther direct you to remember, that though the Revolution was a great work, it was by no means a perfect work; and that all was not then gained which was necessary to put the kingdom in the secure and complete possession of the blessings of liberty. ...

But the most important instance of the imperfect state in which the Revolution left our constitution, is the INEQUALITY OF OUR REPRESENTATION. ... When the representation is partial, a kingdom possesses liberty only partially ... but if not only extremely partial, but corruptly chosen, and under corrupt influence after being chosen, it becomes a *nuisance,* and produces the worst of all forms of government—a government by corruption. ... We are, at present, I hope, at a great distance from it. But it cannot be pretended that there are no advances towards it, or that there is no reason for apprehension and alarm.

The inadequateness of our representation has long been a subject of complaint. But all attention to it seems now lost, and the probability is, that this inattention will continue, and that nothing will be done towards gaining for us this essential blessing, till some great calamity again alarms our fears, or till some great abuse of power again provokes our resentment; or, perhaps, till the acquisition of a pure and equal representation by other countries ... kindles our shame. ...

What an eventful period is this! I am thankful that I have lived to it. ... I have lived to see a diffusion of knowledge, which has undermined superstition and error—I have lived to see the rights of men better understood than ever; and nations panting for liberty, which seemed to have lost the idea of it. I have lived to see THIRTY MILLIONS of people, indignant and resolute, spurning at slavery, and demanding liberty with an irresistible voice; their king led in triumph, and an arbitrary monarch surrendering himself to his subjects. —After sharing in the benefits of one Revolution, I have been spared to be a witness to two other Revolutions,

both glorious.[1]—And now, methinks, I see the ardour for liberty catching and spreading; a general amendment beginning in human affairs; the dominion of kings changed for the dominion of laws, and the dominion of priests giving way to the dominion of reason and conscience.

Be encouraged, all ye friends of freedom, and writers in its defence! ... Behold kingdoms, admonished by you, starting from sleep, breaking their fetters, and claiming justice from their oppressors! Behold, the light you have struck out, after setting AMERICA free, reflected to FRANCE, and there kindled into a blaze that lays despotism in ashes, and warms and illuminates EUROPE!

Tremble all ye oppressors of the world! Take warning all ye supporters of slavish governments, and slavish hierarchies! Call no more (absurdly and wickedly) REFORMATION, innovation. You cannot now hold the world in darkness. Struggle no longer against increasing light and liberality. Restore to mankind their rights; and consent to the correction of abuses, before they and you are destroyed together.

from Edmund Burke, *Reflections on the Revolution in France* (1790)

A political writer and politician, Edmund Burke (1729–97) wrote the *Reflections* as a rebuttal to Price's *Discourse on the Love of Our Country.* Burke's conservative critique of the revolution was published two years before Louis XVI was executed, and it set the tone for the loyalist side of England's revolution debate.

... When I see the spirit of liberty in action, I see a strong principle at work; and this, for a while, is all I can possibly know of it. The wild *gas,* the fixed air, is plainly broke loose: but we ought to suspend our judgment until the first effervescence is a little subsided, till the liquor is cleared, and until we see something deeper than the agitation of a troubled and frothy surface. I must be

---

[1] *After sharing ... both glorious* Price refers first to the Glorious Revolution, then to the American and French revolutions.

tolerably sure, before I venture publicly to congratulate men upon a blessing, that they have really received one. Flattery corrupts both the receiver and the giver; and adulation is not of more service to the people than to kings. I should therefore suspend my congratulations on the new liberty of France, until I was informed how it had been combined with government; with public force; with the discipline and obedience of armies; with the collection of an effective and well-distributed revenue; with morality and religion; with the solidity of property; with peace and order; with civil and social manners. All these (in their way) are good things too; and, without them, liberty is not a benefit whilst it lasts, and is not likely to continue long. The effect of liberty to individuals is that they may do what they please: we ought to see what it will please them to do, before we risk congratulations, which may be soon turned into complaints. Prudence would dictate this in the case of separate, insulated, private men; but liberty, when men act in bodies, is *power.* Considerate people, before they declare themselves, will observe the use which is made of *power*; and particularly of so trying a thing as *new* power in *new* persons, of whose principles, tempers, and dispositions they have little or no experience. …

   It appears to me as if I were in [the midst of] a great crisis, not of the affairs of France alone, but of all Europe, perhaps of more than Europe. All circumstances taken together, the French Revolution is the most astonishing that has hitherto happened in the world. The most wonderful[1] things are brought about in many instances by means the most absurd and ridiculous; in the most ridiculous modes; and, apparently, by the most contemptible instruments. Everything seems out of nature in this strange chaos of levity and ferocity, and of all sorts of crimes jumbled together with all sorts of follies. In viewing this monstrous tragi-comic scene, the most opposite passions necessarily succeed, and sometimes mix with each other in the mind; alternate contempt and indignation; alternate laughter and tears; alternate scorn and horror. …

Whatever may be the success of evasion in explaining away the gross error of fact, which supposes that his Majesty (though he holds it in concurrence with the wishes) owes his crown to the choice of his people, yet nothing can evade their full, explicit declaration concerning the principle of a right in the people to choose—which right is directly maintained, and tenaciously adhered to. … The political divine proceeds dogmatically to assert that, by the principles of the Revolution,[2] the people of England have acquired three fundamental rights …: that we have acquired a right

1. "To choose our own governors."
2. "To cashier[3] them for misconduct."
3. "To frame a government for ourselves."

This new, and hitherto unheard-of bill of rights, though made in the name of the whole people, belongs to those gentlemen and their faction[4] only. The body of the people of England have no share in it. They utterly disclaim it. They will resist the practical assertion of it with their lives and fortunes. They are bound to do so by the laws of their country, made at the time of that very Revolution which is appealed to in favour of the fictitious rights claimed by the society which abuses its name. …

   The people of England will not ape the fashions they have never tried, nor go back to those which they have found mischievous on trial.[5] They look upon the legal hereditary succession of their crown as among their rights, not as among their wrongs; as a benefit, not as a grievance; as a security for their liberty, not as a badge of servitude. They look on the frame of their common-

---

[1] *wonderful* Remarkable, extraordinary (not necessarily with any positive connotation).

[2] *the Revolution* The English Revolution of 1688, known as the Glorious Revolution. This revolution led to the passing of the Bill of Rights in 1689, limiting the authority of the monarch and laying out rights for English citizens and Parliament. Richard Price believed the Glorious Revolution to have paved the way for the French Revolution, which he supported.

[3] *cashier* Depose.

[4] *those gentlemen and their faction* I.e., Richard Price and those thinkers who agree with him.

[5] *which they have found mischievous on trial* Which they have, after having tried them, found to be productive of bad results.

wealth,[1] such as it stands, to be of inestimable value, and they conceive the undisturbed succession of the crown[2] to be a pledge of the stability and perpetuity of all the other members of our constitution.[3] …

You will observe, that from Magna Charta to the Declaration of Right,[4] it has been the uniform policy of our constitution to claim and assert our liberties, as an *entailed*[5] *inheritance* derived to us from our forefathers, and to be transmitted to our posterity; as an estate specially belonging to the people of this kingdom, without any reference whatever to any other more general or prior right. By this means our constitution preserves a unity in so great a diversity of its parts. We have an inheritable crown; an inheritable peerage;[6] and a House of Commons[7] and a people inheriting privileges, franchises, and liberties, from a long line of ancestors.

This policy appears to me to be the result of profound reflection; or rather the happy effect of following nature, which is wisdom without reflection, and above it. A spirit of innovation is generally the result of a selfish temper, and confined views. People will not look forward to posterity, who never look backward to their ancestors. Besides, the people of England well know, that the idea of inheritance furnishes a sure principle of conservation, and a sure principle of transmission; without at all excluding a principle of improvement. It leaves acquisition free; but it secures what it acquires. Whatever advantages are obtained by a state proceeding on these maxims, are locked fast as in a sort of family settlement; grasped as in a kind of mortmain[8] for ever. By a constitutional policy, working after the pattern of nature, we receive, we hold, we transmit our government and our privileges, in the same manner in which we enjoy and transmit our property and our lives. The institutions of policy, the goods of fortune, the gifts of providence, are handed down to us, and from us, in the same course and order. Our political system is placed in a just correspondence and symmetry with the order of the world, and with the mode of existence decreed to a permanent body composed of transitory parts; wherein, by the disposition of a stupendous wisdom, moulding together the great mysterious incorporation of the human race, the whole, at one time, is never old, or middle-aged, or young, but, in a condition of unchangeable constancy, moves on through the varied tenor of perpetual decay, fall, renovation, and progression. Thus, by preserving the method of nature in the conduct of the state, in what we improve, we are never wholly new; in what we retain, we are never wholly obsolete. By adhering in this manner and on those principles to our forefathers, we are guided not by the superstition of antiquarians, but by the spirit of philosophic analogy. In this choice of inheritance we have given to our frame of polity the image of a relation in blood; binding up the constitution of our country with our dearest domestic ties; adopting our fundamental laws into the bosom of our family affections; keeping inseparable, and cherishing with the warmth of all their combined and mutually reflected charities, our state, our hearths, our sepulchres, and our altars.

Through the same plan of a conformity to nature in our artificial institutions, and by calling in the aid of her unerring and powerful instincts, to fortify the fallible and feeble contrivances of our reason, we have derived several other, and those no small benefits, from considering our liberties in the light of an inheritance. Always acting as if in the presence of canonized forefathers, the spirit of freedom, leading in itself to misrule and excess, is tem-

[1] *frame of their commonwealth* Political structure of their kingdom.

[2] *undisturbed succession of the crown* Uninterrupted hereditary succession of monarchs.

[3] *perpetuity* Permanence; *members of our constitution* Various documents, such as the Magna Carta, comprising the body politic of England, which has no single codified constitution.

[4] *Magna Charta* England's Great Charter of 1215 was a precedent-setting document that limited the power of King John; *Declaration of Right* Brought about by the Glorious Revolution, this bill increased the power of Parliament and is fundamental to English constitutional law.

[5] *entailed* Alludes to the legal concept of the entail, a form of inheritance in which property is inherited according to a pre-existing rule of succession, from which one may not legally deviate.

[6] *peerage* Nobility.

[7] *House of Commons* Lower house of Parliament, to which representatives from various districts are elected.

[8] *mortmain* Legal term for the perpetual tenure of land by a corporation (often ecclesiastical).

pered with an awful[1] gravity. This idea of a liberal descent inspires us with a sense of habitual native dignity, which prevents that upstart insolence almost inevitably adhering to and disgracing those who are the first acquirers of any distinction. By this means our liberty becomes a noble freedom. It carries an imposing and majestic aspect. It has a pedigree and illustrating ancestors. It has its bearings and its ensigns armorial. It has its gallery of portraits; its monumental inscriptions; its records, evidences, and titles. We procure reverence to our civil institutions on the principle upon which nature teaches us to revere individual men; on account of their age, and on account of those from whom they are descended. All your sophisters[2] cannot produce anything better adapted to preserve a rational and manly freedom than the course that we have pursued, who have chosen our nature rather than our speculations, our breasts rather than our inventions, for the great conservatories and magazines[3] of our rights and privileges. …

History will record, that on the morning of the 6th of October, 1789, the king and queen of France, after a day of confusion, alarm, dismay, and slaughter, lay down, under the pledged security of public faith, to indulge nature in a few hours of respite, and troubled, melancholy repose. From this sleep the queen was first startled by the voice of the sentinel at her door, who cried out her to save herself by flight—that this was the last proof of fidelity he could give—that they were upon him, and he was dead. Instantly he was cut down. A band of cruel ruffians and assassins, reeking with his blood, rushed into the chamber of the queen, and pierced with a hundred strokes of bayonets and poniards the bed, from whence this persecuted woman had but just time to fly almost naked, and, through ways unknown to the murderers, had escaped to seek refuge at the feet of a king and husband, not secure of his own life for a moment.

This king, to say no more of him, and this queen, and their infant children, (who once would have been the pride and hope of a great and generous people,) were then forced to abandon the sanctuary of the most splendid palace in the world, which they left swimming in blood, polluted by massacre, and strewed with scattered limbs and mutilated carcasses. Thence they were conducted into the capital of their kingdom. Two had been selected from the unprovoked, unresisted, promiscuous slaughter, which was made of the gentlemen of birth and family who composed the king's body guard. These two gentlemen, with all the parade of an execution of justice, were cruelly and publicly dragged to the block, and beheaded in the great court of the palace. Their heads were stuck upon spears, and led the procession; whilst the royal captives who followed in the train were slowly moved along, amidst the horrid yells, and shrilling screams, and frantic dances, and infamous contumelies,[4] and all the unutterable abominations of the furies of hell, in the abused shape of the vilest of women. After they had been made to taste, drop by drop, more than the bitterness of death, in the slow torture of a journey of twelve miles, protracted to six hours, they were, under a guard, composed of those very soldiers who had thus conducted them through this famous triumph, lodged in one of the old palaces of Paris, now converted into a Bastile[5] for kings.

Is this a triumph to be consecrated at altars? to be commemorated with grateful thanksgiving? to be offered to the divine humanity with fervent prayer and enthusiastic ejaculation? …

It is now sixteen or seventeen years since I saw the queen of France, then the dauphiness, at Versailles; and surely never lighted on this orb,[6] which she hardly seemed to touch, a more delightful vision. I saw her just above the horizon, decorating and cheering the elevated sphere she just began to move in,—glittering like the morning-star, full of life, and splendour, and joy. Oh!

---

[1] *awful* Inspiring awe or reverence (not necessarily with a negative connotation).

[2] *sophisters* People who make skillfully persuasive but fallacious arguments.

[3] *magazines* Warehouses.

[4] *contumelies* Humiliations, abuses.

[5] *Bastile* Name of the major political prison in France.

[6] *then the dauphiness* Marie Antoinette was Dauphine of France from April 1770 until May 1774, as the wife of Louis-Auguste, Dauphin of France, prior to his ascension to the throne; *this orb* The earth.

what a revolution! and what a heart must I have to contemplate without emotion that elevation and that fall! Little did I dream when she added titles of veneration to those of enthusiastic, distant, respectful love, that she should ever be obliged to carry the sharp antidote against disgrace concealed in that bosom; little did I dream that I should have lived to see such disasters fallen upon her in a nation of gallant men, in a nation of men of honour, and of cavaliers. I thought ten thousand swords must have leaped from their scabbards to avenge even a look that threatened her with insult. But the age of chivalry is gone. That of sophisters, economists, and calculators, has succeeded; and the glory of Europe is extinguished for ever. Never, never more shall we behold that generous loyalty to rank and sex,[1] that proud submission, that dignified obedience, that subordination of the heart, which kept alive, even in servitude itself, the spirit of an exalted freedom. The unbought grace of life, the cheap defence of nations, the nurse[2] of manly sentiment and heroic enterprise, is gone! It is gone, that sensibility of principle, that charity of honour, which felt a stain like a wound, which inspired courage whilst it mitigated ferocity, which ennobled whatever it touched, and under which vice itself lost half its evil, by losing all its grossness.

This mixed system of opinion and sentiment had its origin in the ancient chivalry; and the principle, though varied in its appearance by the varying state of human affairs, subsisted and influenced through a long succession of generations, even to the time we live in. If it should ever be totally extinguished, the loss I fear will be great. It is this [system] which has given its character to modern Europe. It is this which has distinguished it under all its forms of government, and distinguished it to its advantage, from the states of Asia, and possibly from those states which flourished in the most brilliant periods of the antique world. It was this, which, without con-

founding ranks, had produced a noble equality, and handed it down through all the gradations of social life. It was this opinion which mitigated kings into companions, and raised private men to be fellows with kings. Without force or opposition, it subdued the fierceness of pride and power; it obliged sovereigns to submit to the soft collar of social esteem. ...

But now all is to be changed. All the pleasing illusions, which made power gentle and obedience liberal, which harmonized the different shades of life, and which, by a bland[3] assimilation, incorporated into politics the sentiments which beautify and soften private society, are to be dissolved by this new conquering empire of light and reason. All the decent drapery of life is to be rudely torn off. All the superadded ideas, furnished from the wardrobe of a moral imagination, which the heart owns, and the understanding ratifies, as necessary to cover the defects of our naked, shivering nature, and to raise it to dignity in our own estimation, are to be exploded as a ridiculous, absurd, and antiquated fashion.

On this scheme of things, a king is but a man, a queen is but a woman; a woman is but an animal, and an animal not of the highest order. All homage paid to the sex in general as such,[4] ..., is to be regarded as romance and folly. Regicide, and parricide, and sacrilege,[5] are but fictions of superstition, corrupting jurisprudence by destroying its simplicity. The murder of a king, or a queen, or a bishop, or a father, are only common homicide; and if the people are by any chance, or in any way, gainers by it, a sort of homicide much the most pardonable, and into which we ought not to make too severe a scrutiny.

On the scheme of this barbarous philosophy, which is the offspring of cold hearts and muddy understandings, and which is as void of solid wisdom as it is destitute of all taste and elegance, laws are to be supported only by their own terrors, and by the concern which each individual may find in them from his own private

---

[1] *generous loyalty to rank and sex* I.e., chivalric reverence due to those of the upper classes and of the female sex; *generous* Noble, magnanimous.

[2] *cheap defence of nations* Often erroneously quoted as "Education is the cheap defence of nations"; *cheap* Unbought, costing nothing; *nurse* That which nurtures.

[3] *bland* Pleasant, soothing.

[4] *to the sex ... as such* To women, inherently because of their womanhood.

[5] *Regicide, and parricide, and sacrilege* Killing of one's king, killing of one's father, and violation of the sacred.

speculations, or can spare to them from his own private interests. In the groves of their academy, at the end of every vista, you see nothing but the gallows. Nothing is left which engages the affections on the part of the commonwealth. On the principles of this mechanic philosophy, our institutions can never be embodied, if I may use the expression, in persons; so as to create in us love, veneration, admiration, or attachment. But that sort of reason which banishes the affections is incapable of filling their place. These public affections, combined with manners, are required sometimes as supplements, sometimes as correctives, always as aids to law. The precept given by a wise man, as well as a great critic, for the construction of poems, is equally true as to states:— *Non satis est pulchra esse poemata, dulcia sunto.*[1] There ought to be a system of manners in every nation, which a well-formed mind would be disposed to relish. To make us love our country, our country ought to be lovely.

But power, of some kind or other, will survive the shock in which manners and opinions perish; and it will find other and worse means for its support. The usurpation which, in order to subvert ancient institutions, has destroyed ancient principles, will hold power by arts similar to those by which it has acquired it. When the old feudal and chivalrous spirit of fealty, which, by freeing kings from fear, freed both kings and subjects from the precautions of tyranny,[2] shall be extinct in the minds of men, plots and assassinations will be anticipated by preventive murder and preventive confiscation, and that long roll of grim and bloody maxims, which form the political code of all power, not standing on its own honour, and the honour of those who are to obey it. Kings will be tyrants from policy, when subjects are rebels from principle.

When ancient opinions and rules of life are taken away, the loss cannot possibly be estimated. From that moment we have no compass to govern us; nor can we know distinctly to what port we steer. Europe, undoubtedly, taken in a mass, was in a flourishing condition the day on which your revolution was completed. How much of that prosperous state was owing to the spirit of our old manners and opinions is not easy to say; but as such causes cannot be indifferent in their operation, we must presume, that, on the whole, their operation was beneficial.

We are but too apt to consider things in the state in which we find them, without sufficiently adverting to[3] the causes by which they have been produced, and possibly may be upheld. Nothing is more certain, than that our manners, our civilization, and all the good things which are connected with manners and with civilization, have, in this European world of ours, depended for ages upon two principles; and were indeed the result of both combined; I mean the spirit of a gentleman, and the spirit of religion. The nobility and the clergy, the one by profession, the other by patronage, kept learning in existence, even in the midst of arms and confusions, and whilst governments were rather in their causes than formed. Learning paid back what it received to nobility and to priesthood, and paid it with usury,[4] by enlarging their ideas, and by furnishing their minds. Happy if they had all continued to know their indissoluble union, and their proper place! Happy if learning, not debauched by ambition, had been satisfied to continue the instructor, and not aspired to be the master! Along with its natural protectors and guardians, learning will be cast into the mire, and trodden down under the hoofs of a swinish multitude.[5] …

We know, and what is better, we feel inwardly, that religion is the basis of civil society, and the source of all good and of all comfort. In England we are so convinced of this, that there is no rust of superstition, with which the accumulated absurdity of the human mind might

---

[1] *Non satis … dulcia sunto* Latin: It is insufficient for poems to be beautiful; they should also be sweetly pleasing (quoted from Horace's *Ars Poetica* or *The Poetic Arts*).

[2] *precautions of tyranny* Anticipatory acts (such as are mentioned a few words on—preventive murder, etc.).

[3] *adverting to* Taking note of; paying attention to.

[4] *usury* Interest, especially at an exorbitantly high rate.

[5] *swinish multitude* This became one of Burke's most infamous and frequently-cited comments. Though Burke is probably here referring to a particular faction of extremists, and not to average citizens, many reformers took this comment as proof of arrogance on the part of Burke and the conservative faction.

have crusted it over in the course of ages, that ninety-nine in a hundred of the people of England would not prefer to impiety. …

If our religious tenets should ever want a further elucidation, we shall not call on atheism to explain them. We shall not light up our temple from that unhallowed fire. It will be illuminated with other lights. It will be perfumed with other incense, than the infectious stuff which is imported by the smugglers of adulterated metaphysics. If our ecclesiastical establishment should want a revision, it is not avarice or rapacity, public or private, that we shall employ for the audit, or receipt, or application of its consecrated revenue. Violently condemning neither the Greek nor the Armenian, nor, since heats are subsided, the Roman system of religion,[1] we prefer the Protestant; not because we think it has less of the Christian religion in it, but because, in our judgment, it has more. We are Protestants, not from indifference, but from zeal.

We know, and it is our pride to know, that man is by his constitution a religious animal; that atheism is against, not only our reason, but our instincts; and that it cannot prevail long. But if, in the moment of riot, and in a drunken delirium from the hot spirit drawn out of the alembic[2] of hell, which in France is now so furiously boiling, we should uncover our nakedness, by throwing off that Christian religion which has hitherto been our boast and comfort, and one great source of civilization amongst us, and amongst many other nations, we are apprehensive (being well aware that the mind will not endure a void) that some uncouth, pernicious, and degrading superstition might take place of it. …

When the people have emptied themselves of all the lust of selfish will, which without religion it is utterly impossible they ever should, when they are conscious that they exercise, and exercise perhaps in a higher link of the order of delegation, the power, which to be legitimate must be according to that eternal, immutable

which will and reason are the same, they will be more careful how they place power in base[3] and incapable hands. In their nomination to office they will not appoint to the exercise of authority, as to a pitiful job, but as to a holy function; not according to their sordid, selfish interest, nor to their wanton caprice, nor to their arbitrary will; but they will confer that power (which any man may well tremble to give or to receive) on those only, in whom they may discern that predominant proportion of active virtue and wisdom, taken together and fitted to the charge, such, as in the great and inevitable mixed mass of human imperfections and infirmities, is to be found.

To avoid therefore the evils of inconstancy and versatility,[4] ten thousand times worse than those of obstinacy and the blindest prejudice, we have consecrated the state, that no man should approach to look into its defects or corruptions but with due caution; that he should never dream of beginning its reformation by its subversion; that he should approach to the faults of the state as to the wounds of a father, with pious awe and trembling solicitude. By this wise prejudice we are taught to look with horror on those children of their country, who are prompt rashly to hack that aged parent in pieces, and put him into the kettle of magicians, in hopes that by their poisonous weeds, and wild incantations, they may regenerate the paternal constitution, and renovate their father's life.

Society is indeed a contract. … may be dissolved … to be considered as … agreement in a trade of … bacco, or some other such … for a little temporary inter- … the fancy of the parties. It is to … reverence; because it is not a … subservient only to the gross … of a temporary and perishable nature. It … in all science; a partnership in all art; a …

---

[1] *neither the Greek … religion* Neither the … Orthodox churches, nor Roman Catholicism; … branches of Christianity other than Protesta… official religion of England.

[2] *alembic* Alchemical device which distills su…

… ommon, not of noble rank.

… utility I.e., in the sense of being changeable or fickle.

… Coarse, material.

partnership in every virtue, and in all perfection. As the ends of such a partnership cannot be obtained in many generations, it becomes a partnership not only between those who are living, but between those who are living, those who are dead, and those who are to be born. Each contract of each particular state is but a clause in the great primeval contract of eternal society, linking the lower with the higher natures, connecting the visible and invisible world, according to a fixed compact sanctioned by the inviolable oath which holds all physical and all moral natures, each in their appointed place. …

But am I so unreasonable as to see nothing at all that deserves commendation in the indefatigable labours of this Assembly?[1] I do not deny that, among an infinite number of acts of violence and folly, some good may have been done. They who destroy everything certainly will remove some grievance. They who make everything new, have a chance that they may establish something beneficial. To give them credit for what they have done in virtue of the authority they have usurped, or which can excuse them in the crimes by which that authority has been acquired, it must appear, that the same things could not have been accomplished without producing ... a revolution. Most assuredly they might. … The ... ements of the National Assembly are superficial, ... fundamental.

recom... ...they are, I wish my countrymen rather to constitut... ...neighbours the example of the British improvem... ...take models from them for the invaluable th... ...In the former they have got an causes of appre... not owe to their... ...ot, I think, without some I think our happy... the wh...aint; but these they do ...the ...eat measu... their own conduct. ...eviews and ... r constitution; we have altered or super... ...part singly; employment enough for ...nding in independent spirit, in guardi... what violation. …

I have little to recommend my opinions but long observation and much impartiality. They come from one who has been no tool of power, no flatterer of greatness; and who in his last acts does not wish to belie the tenor of his life. They come from one, almost the whole of whose public exertion has been a struggle for the liberty of others; from one in whose breast no anger durable or vehement has ever been kindled, but by what he considered as tyranny. …

from Mary Wollstonecraft, *A Vindication of the Rights of Men, in a Letter to the Right Honourable Edmund Burke; Occasioned by His* Reflections on the Revolution in France (1790)

The primary purpose of this pamphlet by Mary Wollstonecraft (1759–97) was the defense of Richard Price, whom Edmund Burke described as a radical in his *Reflections on the Revolution in France* (1790). Price, like Wollstonecraft, advocated republicanism in opposition to Burke's championing of constitutional monarchy. In the following excerpts, Wollstonecraft challenges Burke's conservative attachment to tradition and his enshrinement of hereditary private property as essential to civilized life.

Sir,
… I perceive, from the whole tenor of your Reflections, that you have a mortal antipathy to reason; but, if there is any thing like argument, or first principles, in your wild declamation, behold the result: that we are to reverence the rust of antiquity, and term the unnatural customs, which ignorance and mistaken self-interest have consolidated, the sage fruit of experience: nay, that, if we do discover some errors, our *feelings* should lead us to excuse, with blind love, or unprincipled filial affection, the venerable vestiges of ancient days. These are gothic notions of beauty—the ivy is beautiful, but, when it insidiously destroys the trunk from which it receives support, who would not grub it up?[2]

Further, that we ought cautiously to remain for ever frozen inactivity, because a thaw, whilst it nourishes the soil, spreads a temporary inundation; and the fear of risking any personal present convenience should prevent a struggle for the most estimable advantages. This is sound reasoning, I grant, in the mouth of the rich and short-sighted.

Yes, Sir, the strong gained riches, the few have sacrificed the many to their vices; and, to be able to pamper their appetites, and supinely exist without exercising mind or body, they have ceased to be men. Lost to the relish of true pleasure, such beings would, indeed, deserve compassion, if injustice was not softened by the tyrant's plea—necessity; if prescription was not raised as an immortal boundary against innovation. Their minds, in fact, instead of being cultivated, have been so warped by education, that it may require some ages to bring them back to nature, and enable them to see their true interest, with that degree of conviction which is necessary to influence their conduct.

The civilization which has taken place in Europe has been very partial,[1] and, like every custom that an arbitrary point of honour has established, refines the manners at the expense of morals, by making sentiments and opinions current in conversation that have no root in the heart, or weight in the cooler resolves of the mind. And what has stopped its progress?—hereditary property—hereditary honours. …

And what is this mighty revolution in property?[2] The present incumbents only are injured, or the hierarchy of the clergy, an ideal part of the constitution, which you have personified, to render your affection more tender. How has posterity been injured by a distribution of the property snatched, perhaps, from innocent hands, but accumulated by the most abominable violation of every sentiment of justice and piety? Was the monument of former ignorance and iniquity to be held sacred, to enable the present possessors of enormous benefices[3] to

dissolve in indolent pleasures? Was not their convenience, for they have not been turned adrift on the world, to give place to a just partition of the land belonging to the state? And did not the respect due to the natural equality of man require this triumph over Monkish rapacity?[4] Were those monsters to be reverenced on account of their antiquity, and their unjust claims perpetuated to their ideal children, the clergy, merely to preserve the sacred majesty of Property inviolate, and to enable the Church to retain her pristine splendor? Can posterity be injured by individuals losing the chance of obtaining great wealth, without meriting it, by its being diverted from a narrow channel, and disembogued[5] into the sea that affords clouds to water all the land? Besides, the clergy not brought up with the expectation of great revenues will not feel the loss; and if bishops should happen to be chosen on account of their personal merit, religion may be benefited by the vulgar nomination.[6] …

But, among all your plausible arguments, and witty illustrations, your contempt for the poor always appears conspicuous, and rouses my indignation. The following paragraph in particular struck me, as breathing the most tyrannic spirit, and displaying the most factitious feelings. "Good order is the foundation of all good things. To be enabled to acquire, the people, without being servile, must be tractable and obedient. The magistrate must have his reverence, the laws their authority. The body of the people must not find the principles of natural subordination by art rooted out of their minds. *They must respect that property of which they cannot partake. They must labour to obtain what by labour can be obtained; and when they find, as they commonly do, the success disproportioned to the endeavour, they must be taught their consolation in the final proportions of eternal justice.* Of this consolation, whoever deprives them, deadens their industry, and strikes at the root of all acquisition as of all conservation. He that does this, is the

---

[1] *partial* Incomplete.

[2] *mighty revolution in property* Speaking of the French Revolution, Burke wrote in his *Reflections* that "few barbarous conquerors have ever made so terrible a revolution in property."

[3] *enormous benefices* Rich livings (of property and money) given to the clergy of the Catholic church. During the French Revolution, church lands were confiscated and made over to the state; in 1790, the

Civil Constitution of the Clergy was passed, which officially subordinated the Church to the French state, and which mandated that bishops and priests be elected by the people.

[4] *Monkish rapacity* Clerical greed.

[5] *disembogued* Emptied out (from a river mouth).

[6] *vulgar nomination* Popular vote.

cruel oppressor, the merciless enemy, of the poor and wretched; at the same time that, by his wicked speculations, he exposes the fruits of successful industry, and the accumulations of fortune," (ah! there's the rub)[1] "to the plunder of the negligent, the disappointed, and the unprosperous."

This is contemptible hard-hearted sophistry, in the specious form of humility, and submission to the will of Heaven. It is, Sir, *possible* to render the poor happier in this world, without depriving them of the consolation which you gratuitously grant them in the next. They have a right to more comfort than they at present enjoy; and more comfort might be afforded them, without encroaching on the pleasures of the rich: not now waiting to enquire whether the rich have any right to exclusive pleasures. What do I say?—encroaching! No; if an intercourse were established between them, it would impart the only true pleasure that can be snatched in this land of shadows, this hard school of moral discipline. …

Your real or artificial affection for the English constitution seems to me to resemble the brutal affection of some weak characters. They think it a duty to love their relations with a blind, indolent tenderness, that *will not* see the faults it might assist to correct, if their affection had been built on rational grounds. They love they know not why, and they will love to the end of the chapter.

Is it absolute blasphemy to doubt of the omnipotence of the law, or to suppose that religion might be more pure if there were fewer baits for hypocrites in the church? But our manners, you tell us, are drawn from the French, though you had before celebrated our native plainness. If they were, it is time we broke loose from Dependence—Time that Englishmen drew water from their own springs; for, if manners are not a painted substitute for morals, we have only to cultivate our reason, and we shall not feel the want of an arbitrary model. Nature will suffice; but I forget myself: Nature

and Reason, according to your system, are all to give place to authority; and the gods, as Shakespeare makes a frantic wretch exclaim, seem to kill us for their sport, as men do flies.[2] …

from Thomas Paine, *Rights of Man* (1791 and 1792)

Thomas Paine (1737–1809) was indicted for treason because of his unflinching reformist reply to Burke's *Reflections on the Revolution in France*. After fleeing to France, he was imprisoned for not supporting Louis XVI's execution. He was spared the guillotine, and spent the rest of his years in America.

There is scarcely an epithet of abuse to be found in the English language, with which Mr. Burke has not loaded the French Nation and the National Assembly. Every thing which rancour, prejudice, ignorance, or knowledge, could suggest, are poured forth in the copious fury of near four hundred pages. In the strain, and on the plan Mr. Burke was writing, he might have written on to as many thousands. When the tongue or the pen is let loose in a frenzy of passion, it is the man, and not the subject, that becomes exhausted. …

As Mr. Burke occasionally applies the poison drawn from his horrid principles, not only to the English nation, but to the French Revolution and the National Assembly, and charges that august, illuminated and illuminating body of men with the epithet of *usurpers,* I shall, *sans cérémonie,* place another system of principles in opposition to his.

The English Parliament of 1688 did a certain thing, which, for themselves and their constituents, they had a right to do, and which it appeared right should be done: But, in addition to this right, which they possessed by delegation, *they set up another right by assumption,* that

---

[1] *there's the rub* Therein lies the difficulty. Cf. *Hamlet* 3.1.65.

[2] *the gods … as men do flies* Cf. *King Lear* 4.1.36–37.

"THE RIGHTS OF MAN;—or—TOMMY PAINE, the little American Taylor, taking the Measure of the CROWN, for a new Pair of Revolution-Breeches." *Humbly dedicated to the Jacobine Clubs of France & England!!! by Common Sense*, 1791. This anti-Jacobin caricature suggests that Thomas Paine, who was once a tailor, is no match for the enormous legacy of the English monarchy.

of binding and controlling posterity to the end of time. The case, therefore, divides itself into two parts; the right which they possessed by delegation, and the right which they set up by assumption. The first is admitted; but, with respect to the second, I reply—

There never did, there never will, and there never can exist a parliament, or any description of men, or any generation of men, in any country, possessed of the right or the power of binding and controlling posterity to the *"end of time,"* or of commanding forever how the world shall be governed, or who shall govern it; and therefore,

all such clauses, acts, or declarations, by which the makers of them attempt to do what they have neither the right nor the power to do, nor the power to execute, are in themselves null and void. Every age and generation must be as free to act for itself, *in all cases*, as the ages and generations which preceded it. The vanity and presumption of governing beyond the grave, is the most ridiculous and insolent of all tyrannies. ... It is the living, and not the dead, that are to be accommodated. When man ceases to be, his power and his wants cease with him; and having no longer any participation in the concerns of this world, he has no longer any authority in directing who shall be its governors, or how its government shall be organized, or how administered. ...

While I am writing this, there are accidentally before me some proposals for a declaration of rights by the Marquis de la Fayette[1] (I ask his pardon for using his former address, and do it only for distinction's sake) to the National Assembly, on the 11th of July 1789, three days before the taking of the Bastile; and I cannot but remark with astonishment how opposite the sources are from which that Gentleman and Mr. Burke draw their principles. Instead of referring to musty records and mouldy parchments to prove that the rights of the living are lost, "renounced and abdicated forever," by those who are now no more, as Mr. Burke has done, M. de la Fayette applies to the living world, and emphatically says, "Call to mind the sentiments which Nature has engraved in the heart of every citizen, and which take a new force when they are solemnly recognized by all:—For a nation to love liberty, it is sufficient that she knows it; and to be free, it is sufficient that she wills it." ...

It was not against Louis the XVIth, but against the despotic principles of the government, that the nation revolted. These principles had not their origin in him, but in the original establishment, many centuries back[.] ... Perhaps no man, bred up in the stile of an absolute King, ever possessed a heart so little disposed to the exercise of that species of power as the present King of France. But the principles of the government itself still

---

[1] *Marquis de la Fayette* Vice president of the National Assembly. La Fayette composed the initial draft of the *Declaration of the Rights of Man and of the Citizen*.

The Contrast, by Thomas Rowlandson, after a drawing by Lord George Murray, 1792.

remained the same. The Monarch and the Monarchy were distinct and separate things; and it was against the established despotism of the latter, and not against the person or principles of the former, that the revolt commenced, and the revolution has been carried.

… When despotism has established itself for ages in a country, as in France, it is not in the person of the King only that it resides. It has the appearance of being so in show, and in nominal authority; but it is not so in practice, and in fact. It has its standard everywhere. Every office and department has its despotism, founded upon custom and usage. Every place has its Bastile, and every Bastile its despot. The original hereditary despo-

tism, resident in the person of the King, divides and subdivides itself into a thousand shapes and forms, till at last the whole of it is acted by deputation. This was the case in France; and against this species of despotism, proceeding on through an endless labyrinth of office, till the source of it is scarcely perceptible, there is no mode of redress. It strengthens itself by assuming the appearance of duty, and tyrannises under the pretense of obeying. …

As to the tragic paintings, by which Mr. Burke has outraged his own imagination, and seeks to work upon that of his readers, they are very well calculated for theatrical representation, where facts are manufactured for the sake of show, and accommodated to produce, through the weakness of sympathy, a weeping effect. But Mr. Burke should recollect that he is writing history, and not *plays*; and that his readers will expect truth, and not the spouting rant of high-toned exclamation. ...

Not one glance of compassion, not one commiserating reflection, that I can find throughout his whole book, has he bestowed on those who lingered out the most wretched of lives, a life without hope, in the most miserable of prisons. ... His hero or his heroine must be a tragedy-victim expiring in show, and not the real prisoner of misery, sliding into death in the silence of a dungeon.

As Mr. Burke has passed over the whole transaction of the Bastile (and his silence is nothing in his favour), and has entertained his readers with reflections on supposed facts distorted into real falsehoods, I will give, since he has not, some account of the circumstances which preceded that transaction. They will serve to show, that less mischief could scarcely have accompanied such an event, when considered with the treacherous and hostile aggravations of the enemies of the Revolution. ...

The mind can hardly picture to itself a more tremendous scene than what the city of Paris exhibited at the time of taking the Bastile, and for two days before and after, nor conceive the possibility of its quieting so soon. At a distance, this transaction has appeared only as an act of heroism, standing on itself; and the close political connection it had with the Revolution is lost in the brilliancy of the achievement. But we are to consider it as the strength of the parties, brought man to man, and contending for the issue. The Bastile was to be either the prize or the prison of the assailants. The downfall of it included the idea of the downfall of Despotism. ...

That the Bastile was attacked with an enthusiasm of heroism, such only as the highest animation of liberty could inspire, and carried in the space of a few hours, is an event which the world is fully possessed of. I am not undertaking a detail of the attack; but bringing into view the conspiracy against the nation which provoked it, and which fell with the Bastile. The prison to which the new ministry were dooming the National Assembly, in addition to its being the high altar and castle of despotism, became the proper object to begin with. This enterprise broke up the new ministry, who began now to fly from the ruin they had prepared for others. ...

During the latter part of the time in which this confusion was acting, the King and Queen were in public at the balcony, and neither of them concealed for safety's sake, as Mr. Burke insinuates. Matters being thus appeased, and tranquillity restored, a general acclamation broke forth, of *Le Roi à Paris—Le Roi à Paris*—The King to Paris. It was the shout of peace, and immediately accepted on the part of the King. By this measure, the King and his family reached Paris in the evening, and were congratulated on their arrival by Mr. Bailley, the Mayor of Paris, in the name of the citizens. ...

The French constitution says, *There shall be no titles*; and, of consequence, all that class of equivocal generation, which in some countries is called "*aristocracy*" and in others "*nobility*" is done away, and the *peer*[1] is exalted into MAN. ...

It is, properly, from the elevated mind of France that the folly of titles has fallen. It has outgrown the baby-clothes of *Count* and *Duke*, and breeched itself in manhood. France has not levelled; it has exalted. It has put down the dwarf, to set up the man. The puny-ism of a senseless word like *Duke*, or *Count*, or *Earl*, has ceased to please. Even those who possessed them have disowned the gibberish; and, as they outgrew the rickets, have despised the rattle. The genuine mind of man, thirsting for its native home, society, contemns the gewgaws[2] that separate him from it. Titles are like circles drawn by the magician's wand, to contract the sphere of man's felicity. He lived immured within the Bastile of a word, and surveys at a distance the envied life of man. ...

The patriots of France have discovered, in good time, that rank and dignity in society must take a new ground. The old one has fallen through. It must now take the substantial ground of character, instead of the chimerical ground of titles; and they have brought their titles to the

---

[1] *peer* Member of the hereditary nobility.

[2] *gewgaws* Gaudy baubles.

altar, and made of them a burnt-offering to Reason.

If no mischief had annexed itself to the folly of titles, they would not have been worth a serious and formal destruction, such as the National Assembly have decreed them; and this makes it necessary to enquire farther into the nature and character of aristocracy. ...

Nothing can appear more contradictory, than the principle on which the old governments began, and the condition to which society, civilization, and commerce, are capable of carrying mankind. Government, on the old system, is an assumption of power, for the aggrandisement of itself; on the new, a delegation of power, for the common benefit of society. The former supports itself by keeping up a system of war; the latter promotes a system of peace, as the true means of enriching a nation. The one encourages national prejudices; the other promotes universal society, as the means of universal commerce. The one measures its prosperity, by the quantity of revenue it extorts; the other proves its excellence, by the small quantity of taxes it requires. ...

Never did so great an opportunity offer itself to England, and to all Europe, as is produced by the two Revolutions of America and France. By the former, freedom has a national champion in the Western world; and by the latter, in Europe. When another nation shall join France, despotism and bad government will scarcely dare to appear. To use a trite expression, the iron is becoming hot all over Europe. The insulted German and the enslaved Spaniard, the Russ and the Pole, are beginning to think. The present age will hereafter merit to be called the Age of Reason, and the present generation will appear to the future as the Adam of a new world.

from William Godwin, *An Enquiry Concerning Political Justice and Its Influence on General Virtue and Happiness* (1793)

Political philosopher, novelist, and anarchist William Godwin (1756–1836) was a leading figure in radical circles in London. In *Enquiry Concerning Political Justice*, he sought to give philosophical grounding to the ideas of Paine and Rousseau, and to oppose the

arguments in Burke's conservative *Reflections on the Revolution in France* (1790). In the following selections, Godwin considers the responsibilities of the citizen in society, as well as the best mode of effecting revolutionary change, particularly such fundamental change as the abolishment of private property.

from BOOK 4: MISCELLANEOUS PRINCIPLES
from CHAPTER 2: OF REVOLUTIONS

SECTION 1: DUTIES OF A CITIZEN

No question can be more important than that which respects the best mode of effecting revolutions. Before we enter upon it however, it may be proper to remove a difficulty which has suggested itself to the minds of some men, how far we ought generally speaking to be the friends of revolution; or, in other words, whether it be justifiable in a man to be the enemy of the constitution of his country.

"We live," it will be said, "under the protection of this constitution; and protection, being a benefit conferred, obliges us to a reciprocation of support in return."

To this it may be answered, first, that this protection is a very equivocal thing; and, till it can be shown that the vices, from the effects of which it protects us, are not for the most part the produce of that constitution, we shall never sufficiently understand the quantity of benefit it includes.

Secondly, gratitude, as has already been proved,[1] is a vice and not a virtue. Every man and every collection of men ought to be treated by us in a manner founded upon their intrinsic qualities and capacities, and not according to a rule which has existence only in relation to ourselves.

Add to this, thirdly, that no motive can be more equivocal than the gratitude here recommended. Grati-

---

[1] *has already been proved*   See Book 2.2, "On Justice": "Gratitude ... a principle which has so often been the theme of the moralist and the poet, is no part either of justice or virtue. By gratitude I understand a sentiment, which would lead me to prefer one man to another, from some other consideration than that of his superior usefulness or worth: that is, which would make something true to me ... which cannot be true to another man, and is not true in itself."

tude to the constitution, an abstract idea, an imaginary existence, is altogether unintelligible. Affection to my countrymen will be much better proved, by my exertions to procure them a substantial benefit, than by my supporting a system which I believe to be fraught with injurious consequences.

He who calls upon me to support the constitution must found his requisition[1] upon one or two principles. It has a claim upon my support either because it is good, or because it is British.

Against the requisition in the first sense there is nothing to object. All that is necessary is to prove the goodness which is ascribed to it. But perhaps it will be said, "that, though not absolutely good, more mischief will result from an attempt to overturn it, than from maintaining it with its mixed character of partly right and partly wrong." If this can be made evident, undoubtedly I ought to submit. Of this mischief however I can be no judge but in consequence of enquiry. To some the evils attendant on a revolution will appear greater, and to others less. Some will imagine that the vices with which the English constitution is pregnant are considerable, and some that it is nearly innocent. Before I can decide between these opposite opinions and balance the existing and the possible evils, I must examine for myself. But examination in its nature implies uncertainty of result. Were I to determine before I sat down on which side the decision should be, I could not strictly speaking be said to examine at all. He that desires a revolution for its own sake is to be regarded as a madman. He that desires it from a thorough conviction of its usefulness and necessity has a claim upon us for candour and respect.

As to the demand upon me for support to the English constitution, because it is English, there is little plausibility in this argument. It is of the same nature as the demand upon me to be a Christian, because I am a Briton, or a Mahometan,[2] because I am a native of Turkey. Instead of being an expression of respect, it argues contempt of all government, religion and virtue, and every thing that is sacred among men. If there be

such a thing as truth, it must be better than error. If there be such a faculty as reason, it ought to be exerted. But this demand makes truth a matter of absolute indifference, and forbids us the exercise of our reason. If men reason and reflect, it must necessarily happen that either the Englishman or the Turk will find his government to be odious and his religion false. For what purpose employ his reason, if he must for ever conceal the conclusions to which it leads him? How would man have arrived at his present attainments, if he had always been contented with the state of society in which he happened to be born? In a word, either reason is the curse of our species, and human nature is to be regarded with horror; or it becomes us to employ our understanding and to act upon it, and to follow truth wherever it may lead us. It cannot lead us to mischief, since utility, as it regards percipient beings,[3] is the only basis of moral and political truth.

SECTION 2: MODE OF EFFECTING REVOLUTION

To return to the enquiry respecting the mode of effecting revolutions. If no question can be more important, there is fortunately no question perhaps that admits of a more complete and satisfactory general answer. The revolutions of states, which a philanthropist would desire to witness, or in which he would willingly co-operate, consist principally in a change of sentiments and dispositions in the members of those states. The true instruments for changing the opinions of men are argument and persuasion. The best security for an advantageous issue[4] is free and unrestricted discussion. In that field truth must always prove the successful champion. If then we would improve the social institutions of mankind, we must write, we must argue, we must converse. To this business there is no close; in this pursuit there should be no pause. Every method should be employed, not so much positively to allure the attention of mankind, or persuasively to invite them to the adoption of our opinions, as to remove every restraint upon thought, and

---

[1] *requisition* Request.

[2] *Mahometan* Muslim.

[3] *percipient beings* Conscious and perceptive beings.

[4] *issue* Outcome.

to throw open the temple of science and the field of enquiry to all the world.

Those instruments will always be regarded by the discerning mind as suspicious, which may be employed with equal prospect of success on both sides of every question. This consideration should make us look with aversion upon all resources of violence. When we descend into the listed field,[1] we of course desert the vantage ground of truth, and commit the decision to uncertainty and caprice. The phalanx[2] of reason is invulnerable; it advances with deliberate and determined pace; and nothing is able to resist it. But when we lay down our arguments, and take up our swords, the case is altered. Amidst the barbarous pomp of war and the clamorous din of civil brawls, who can tell whether the event[3] shall be prosperous or miserable?

We must therefore carefully distinguish between informing the people and inflaming them. Indignation, resentment and fury are to be deprecated; and all we should ask is sober thought, clear discernment and intrepid discussion. Why were the revolutions of America and France a general concert of all orders and descriptions of men, without so much (if we bear in mind the multitudes concerned) as almost a dissenting voice; while the resistance against our Charles the first divided the nation into two equal parts?[4] Because the latter was the

affair of the seventeenth century, and the former happened in the close of the eighteenth. Because in the case of America and France philosophy had already developed some of the great principles of political truth, and Sydney and Locke and Montesquieu and Rousseau[5] had convinced a majority of reflecting and powerful minds of the evils of usurpation. If these revolutions had happened still later, not one drop of the blood of one citizen would have been shed by the hands of another, nor would the event have been marked so much perhaps as with one solitary instance of violence and confiscation.

There are two principles therefore which the man who desires the regeneration of his species ought ever to bear in mind, to regard the improvement of every hour as essential in the discovery and dissemination of truth, and willingly to suffer the lapse of years before he urges the reducing his theory into actual execution. With all his caution it is possible that the impetuous multitude will run before the still and quiet progress of reason; nor will he sternly pass sentence upon every revolution that shall by a few years have anticipated the term that wisdom would have prescribed. But, if his caution be firmly exerted, there is no doubt that he will supersede many abortive attempts, and considerably prolong the general tranquility. …

---

[1] *listed field*   Ground enclosed for jousting or dueling (i.e., a place for settling disagreement with physical force).

[2] *phalanx*   Group of soldiers arranged in a classical military formation.

[3] *event*   Outcome.

[4] *two equal parts*   The English Civil War (1642–51) was a series of armed conflicts between Royalists (loyal to Charles I) and Parliamentarians (who fought for a constitutional monarchy rather than an absolute monarchy). The Parliamentarians conquered the armies of Charles I in the end, leading to the execution of the king in 1649.

[5] *Sydney … Rousseau*   Eighteenth-century philosophers whose ideals of reason, liberty, and equality were influential in shaping the American and French Revolutions.

from BOOK 8: OF PROPERTY
from CHAPTER 8: OF THE MEANS OF INTRODUCING
THE GENUINE SYSTEM OF PROPERTY[1]

... No idea has excited greater horror in the minds of a multitude of persons, than that of the mischiefs that are to ensue from the dissemination of what they call levelling principles.[2] They believe "that these principles will inevitably ferment in the minds of the vulgar, and that the attempt to carry them into execution will be attended with every species of calamity."[3] They represent to themselves "the uninformed and uncivilized part of mankind, as let loose from all restraint, and hurried into every kind of excess. Knowledge and taste, the improvements of intellect, the discoveries of sages, the beauties of poetry and art, are trampled under foot and extinguished by barbarians. It is another inundation of Goths and Vandals,[4] with this bitter aggravation, that the viper that stings us to death was warmed in our own bosoms."

They conceive of the scene as "beginning in massacre." They suppose "all that is great, preeminent and illustrious as ranking among the first victims. Such as are distinguished by peculiar elegance of manners or energy of diction and composition, will be the inevitable objects of envy and jealousy. Such as intrepidly exert themselves to succour the persecuted, or to declare to the public those truths which they are least inclined, but which are most necessary for them to hear, will be marked out for assassination."

Let us not, from any partiality to the system of equality delineated in this book, shrink from the picture here exhibited. Massacre is the too possible attendant upon revolution, and massacre is perhaps the most hateful scene, allowing for its momentary duration, that any imagination can suggest. The fearful, hopeless expectation of the defeated, and the bloodhound fury of their conquerors, is a complication of mischief that all which has been told of infernal regions[5] cannot surpass. The cold-blooded massacres that are perpetrated under the name of criminal justice fall short of these in their most frightful aggravations. The ministers and instruments of law have by custom reconciled their minds to the dreadful task they perform, and bear their respective parts in the most shocking enormities, without being sensible to the passions allied to those enormities. But the instruments of massacre are actuated with all the sentiments of fiends. Their eyes emit flashes of cruelty and rage. They pursue their victims from street to street and from house to house. They tear them from the arms of their fathers and their wives. They glut themselves with barbarity and insult, and utter shouts of horrid joy at the spectacle of their tortures.

We have now contemplated the tremendous picture; what is the conclusion it behooves us to draw? Must we shrink from reason, from virtue and happiness? Suppose that the inevitable consequence of communicating truth were the temporary introduction of such a scene as has just been described, must we on that account refuse to communicate it? The crimes that were perpetrated would in no just estimate appear to be the result of truth, but of the error which had previously been infused. The impartial enquirer would behold them as the last struggles of expiring despotism, which, if it had survived, would have produced mischiefs, scarcely less atrocious in the hour of their commission, and infinitely more calamitous by the length of their duration. If we would judge truly, even admitting the unfavourable supposition above stated, we must contrast a moment of horror and distress with ages of felicity. No imagination can sufficiently conceive the mental improvement and the tranquil virtue that would succeed, were property once permitted to rest upon its genuine basis. ...

It being then sufficiently evident that truth must be told at whatever expense, let us proceed to consider the

---

[1] *GENUINE SYSTEM OF PROPERTY* For Godwin, this means a system of property based on just principles (i.e., an egalitarian society in which property is abolished).

[2] *levelling principles* Ideas that promote social equality.

[3] *that these ... of calamity* The sources of this and the following two quotations are unknown; they may be real quotations, or they may be invented statements summarizing positions held by conservative politicians.

[4] *Goths and Vandals* Germanic tribes that fought against the Roman Empire; the Vandals conquered Rome in 455. These tribes were long thought of as barbarians seeking to destroy Roman culture.

[5] *infernal regions* Hell.

precise amount of that expense, to enquire how much of confusion and violence is inseparable from the transit which mind has to accomplish. And here it plainly appears that mischief is by no means inseparable from the progress. In the mere circumstances of our acquiring knowledge and accumulating one truth after another there is no direct tendency to disorder. Evil can only spring from the clash of mind with mind, from one body of men in the community outstripping another in their ideas of improvement, and becoming impatient of the opposition they have to encounter. ...

No maxim can be more pernicious than that which would teach us to consult the temper of the times, and to tell only so much as we imagine our contemporaries will be able to bear. This practise is at present almost universal, and it is the mark of a very painful degree of depravity. We retail[1] and mangle truth. We impart it to our fellows, not with the liberal measure with which we have received it, but with such parsimony as our own miserable prudence may chance to prescribe. We pretend that truths fit to be practised in one country, nay, truths which we confess to be eternally right, are not fit to be practised in another. That we may deceive others with a tranquil conscience, we begin deceiving ourselves. We put shackles on our minds, and dare not trust ourselves at large in the pursuit of truth. This practise took its commencement from the machinations of party,[2] and the desire of one wise and adventurous leader to carry a troop of weak, timid and selfish supporters in his train. There is no reason why I should not declare in any assembly upon the face of the earth that I am a republican. There is no more reason why, being a republican under a monarchial government, I should enter into a desperate faction to invade the public tranquillity, than if I were monarchial under a republic. Every community of men, as well as every individual, must govern itself according to its ideas of justice. What I should desire is, not by violence to change its institutions, but by reason to change its ideas. I have no business with factions or

intrigue; but simply to promulgate the truth, and to wait the tranquil progress of conviction. ...

Samuel Taylor Coleridge, Letter to Charles Heath (1794)

Romantic poets Robert Southey (1774–1843) and Samuel Taylor Coleridge (1772–1834), inspired by the social and political idealism manifested across the channel, planned an English utopian settlement (or "Pantisocracy," as they called it) in Pennsylvania in 1794—a plan that Coleridge outlines below in his letter to Charles Heath. The following poems by Coleridge and Southey demonstrate the profound sense of hope and optimism typical of English radicals in the 1790s. This hope was to fade as both men became disillusioned with the French Revolution later in their lives.

29 August, 1794
Jesus College, Cambridge

Sir,

Your brother has introduced my name to you; I shall therefore offer no apology for this letter. A small but liberalized party have formed a scheme of emigration on the principles of an abolition of individual property. Of their political creed, and the arguments by which they support and elucidate it, they are preparing a few copies—not as meaning to publish them, but for private distribution. In this work they will have endeavoured to prove the exclusive justice of the system and its practicability; nor will they have omitted to sketch out the code of contracts necessary for the internal regulation of the society; all of which will of course be submitted to the improvements and approbation of each component member. As soon as the work is printed, one or more copies shall be transmitted to you. Of the characters of the individuals who compose the party, I find it embarrassing to speak; yet, vanity apart, I may assert with truth,

---

[1] *retail* Parcel out, sell.

[2] *party* Political party.

that they have each a sufficient strength of head to make the virtues of the heart respectable; and that they are all highly charged with that enthusiasm which results from strong perceptions of moral rectitude, called into life and action by ardent feelings. With regard to pecuniary matters it is found necessary, if twelve men with their families emigrate on this system, that 2000£ should be the aggregate of their contributions; but infer not from hence that each man's quota is to be settled with the littleness of arithmetical accuracy. No; *all* will strain *every* nerve, and then I trust the surplus money of some will supply the deficiencies of others. The minutiae of topographical information we are daily endeavouring to acquire; at present our plan is, to settle at a distance, but at a convenient distance, from Cooper's Town on the banks of the Susquehannah. This, however, will be the object of future investigation. For the time of emigration we have fixed on next March. In the course of the winter those of us whose bodies, from habits of sedentary study or academic indolence, have not acquired their full tone and strength, intend to learn the theory and practice of agriculture and carpentry, according as situation and circumstances make one or the other convenient.

Your fellow Citizen,
S.T. Coleridge

Samuel Taylor Coleridge, "Pantisocracy" (1794)

No more my visionary soul shall dwell
On joys that were; no more endure to weigh
The shame and anguish of the evil day,
Wisely forgetful! O'er the ocean swell
5 Sublime of Hope, I seek the cottag'd dell
Where Virtue calm with careless step may stray,
And dancing to the moonlight roundelay,
The wizard Passions weave an holy spell.
Eyes that have ach'd with Sorrow! Ye shall weep
10 Tears of doubt-mingled joy, like theirs who start
From Precipices of distemper'd sleep,
On which the fierce-eyed Fiends their revels keep,
And see the rising Sun, and feel it dart
New rays of pleasance trembling to the heart.

Robert Southey, "On the Prospect of Establishing a Pantisocracy in America" (1794)

Whilst pale Anxiety, corrosive Care,
The tear of Woe, the gloom of sad Despair,
And deepen'd Anguish generous bosoms rend;—
Whilst patriot souls their country's fate lament;
5 Whilst mad with rage demoniac, foul intent,
Embattled legions Despots vainly send
To arrest the immortal mind's expanding ray
Of, everlasting Truth;—I other climes
Where dawns, with hope serene, a brighter day
10 Than e'er saw Albion° in her happiest times,   *England*
With mental eye exulting now explore,
And soon with kindred minds shall haste to enjoy
(Free from the ills which here our peace destroy)
Content and Bliss on Transatlantic shore.

WILLIAM BLAKE
1757 – 1827

"I labor upwards into futurity," etched William Blake onto the back of one of the copper plates that constituted the "tablets" of his visionary art. A poet and artist whose work was sorely undervalued during his own lifetime, Blake recognized that his was a genius before its time. The mysterious and powerful poetry that he crafted to convey his vision would eventually come to be appreciated for its revolutionary significance; for the past century or more Blake has been widely considered to be among the greatest poets of the Romantic era.

Blake was born one November evening in 1757 above his parents' hosiery shop in the Soho district of London. James and Catherine Blake, religious Dissenters whose non-compromising beliefs were those of a growing number of tradespeople, allowed their son to pursue a program of self study that saved him from being schooled under the institutional authorities he instinctively abhorred. Although his parents were generally indulgent, there are hints that Blake balked even under their natural expressions of authority. He received a thrashing for declaring he had seen the face of God, and was accused of lying when he reported passing a tree bespangled with angels. Since his family could not afford the expense of artistic training, he was apprenticed at fourteen to a highly respected engraver, with whom he lived for seven years while learning the trade which would thereafter earn him his living.

During the period of his apprenticeship, Blake began writing the poems that were eventually collected in *Poetical Sketches* (1783)—the only volume of his verse originally printed by letterpress rather than by the "illuminated" methods he later originated. Of his parents and three siblings, Blake retained lasting affection only for his younger brother, Robert. Blake claimed to communicate daily with the spirit of Robert after his early death from tuberculosis. Indeed, the unique style of relief etching or "Illuminated Printing" which Blake later devised was imparted, he claimed, by Robert in a visitation. Etching words backwards into copper plates so that they would reverse to normal upon printing, Blake in 1788 produced his first illuminated texts with "All Religions Are One" and "There Is No Natural Religion." It was a defining moment for him, one in which words and images converged into prophetic expression. He soon applied his new method of printing to a larger project, the poetic and pictorial depiction of a young soul descending into the realm of matter, recounted in *The Book of Thel*.

Blake's words and designs "interanimate each other," in the words of one critic; a master of color, he achieved unearthly effects in his hand-tinted books, of which no two copies were exactly the same. Rather than reflecting the tones of the natural world, Blake's color—and indeed the vividness of his verse—aim toward the supernatural. Similarly, what separates his poetry from that of contemporaries, such as Wordsworth and Coleridge, is his lack of interest in "painting Nature." For Blake, the true aim of art was to tune the senses and the imaginative faculties to the higher pitch of a spiritual reality, not to the natural world. For this reason, Blake detested what he called the "muddy" colors, nuanced shade work, and secular sensibilities of an artist such as Rembrandt, while revering the determined outlines, bright colors, and unequivocal contrasts of light and dark achieved by High Renaissance painters such as Michelangelo and Raphael.

The bold, declarative, and (to some modern eyes) exaggerated style that Blake admired in painting is paralleled in many of his literary preferences. His work has close associations with the declamatory traditions of prophecy, aphorism, political writing, and proverb. *The Marriage of Heaven and Hell* (1790) contains some of his most chiseled epigrams, such as "The cut worm forgives the plow" and "The tigers of wrath are wiser than the horses of instruction." The Bible was a tremendous imaginative reserve upon which he drew all of his life. He admired Dante, Milton, Spenser, and Shakespeare, supplied commissioned designs for editions of Milton's *L'Allegro*, *Il Penseroso*, *Paradise Lost*, and *Paradise Regained*, and left behind an unfinished series of watercolors illustrating Dante's work. He was also influenced by the architecture and sepulchral art of Westminster Abbey and by the literary gothic of Edward Young's *Night Thoughts* and Robert Blair's *The Grave*, versions of which he illustrated. If he was in many respects an outsider to his own culture, Blake was fully a man of the times in his love of the popular "forgeries" of James Macpherson (author of the "Ossian" poems) and Thomas Chatterton, as well as in his enjoyment of works of Gothic fiction such as Ann Radcliffe's *The Mysteries of Udolpho* (1794).

On at least two occasions Blake struck out to earn a reputation as an artist in his own right. The first occasion came at the end of his apprenticeship, when he submitted a portfolio to the Royal Academy of Arts (under the presidency of Sir Joshua Reynolds) and was accepted into the Academy. Yet he failed to emerge out of obscurity, and was forced to set up an engraver's shop. For twenty years, Blake would resign himself to the grueling schedule of a copy engraver, recognized only by a few of his friends as a formidably original artist, and almost wholly overlooked as a poet. In 1809, energized by a gallery showing of works by Dürer, Michelangelo, Giulio Romano, and others, Blake renewed his association with the Royal Academy to launch a solo exhibition of his own work. With the exception of a caustic review or two, the public remained unmoved by the idiosyncratic light Blake cast upon subjects such as "The Body of Abel found by Adam and Eve."

Blake found his soul mate in Catherine Boucher, the illiterate daughter of a market gardener. He taught her to read and trained her in the preparation of copper plates, the hand coloring of prints, and the stitching of pages into bound copies. Catherine was evidently a submissive, devoted wife, and some have denigrated Blake's traditional and even misogynist approach to marriage, citing his pronouncement that "the female ... lives from the light of the male." At the same time, however, Blake approved of the arguments for sexual equality made by Mary Wollstonecraft in *A Vindication of the Rights of Woman* (1792). He also radically proposed that carnal pleasure was a portal to the divine. In *Visions of the Daughters of Albion* (1793), Blake abjures sexual domination and celebrates "the moment of desire!" in a manner highly unconventional at the time. Visitors to the Blake home reported coming across the couple reading naked in a garden house in their back yard, enjoying the innocence of their private Eden and rejecting the narratives of shame and the Fall.

The rewriting of the biblical drama of the Creation and Fall that underlies nearly all of Blake's work was influenced by radical Dissenters who celebrated nudity as a symbol of unfallen humanity. Blake was also influenced by the mystical systems of Emanuel Swedenborg and Jacob Boehme, and he tapped into veins of esoteric knowledge related to the cabbalistic teachings of the Freemasons, the Rosicrucians, and Paracelsus. He also had associations with decidedly non-mystical political movements that were bravely calling for democratic reforms at a time when the English monarchy was intent on quashing sympathizers with the American War of Independence and the French Revolution.

Blake, however, never fully participated in an organized movement of any kind, be it religious or political. His was "a voice crying in the wilderness," urging men and women to realize their "human form divine." Unwilling to conform to any system not of his own creation, Blake's language grew increasingly esoteric and opaque in later major prophecies such as *The Four Zoas*, *Milton* (1804), and *Jerusalem* (1804–20).

One vision that Blake explores over and over again is that of an earthly Eden triumphing over forces of repression. This is the common theme of *The French Revolution* (1791), *America: A Prophecy* (1793), *Europe: A Prophecy* (1794), and *The Book of Urizen* (1794). When Blake summons Albion, figure of the human form divine in *Jerusalem*, to "Awake!" he is calling for a spiritual revolution in which humanity awakens to the knowledge that the republic of heaven is immanent.

Blake imagined the spiritual dimensions of the geography of London in particularly vivid detail. That the material double of his holy city was corrupt lends a sharp edge to Blake's vision. As one Blake biographer writes, "it was a time when mobs and rioters often controlled large areas of the city; there were riots by sailors, silk-weavers, coal-heavers, hatters, glass-grinders ... and bloody demonstrations over the price of bread." The biting simplicity of "The Chimney Sweeper" and "The Little Black Boy" in Blake's *Songs of Innocence and of Experience* (1789–94) are testimony to his acute sensitivity to the realities of poverty and exploitation that accompanied the "dark satanic mills" of the Industrial Revolution.

In this London, Blake admitted to living in fear that his artistic vision and eccentric tendency to converse with angels and ghosts would land him in trouble with the authorities—a fear horribly realized in 1803. The Blakes had been generously invited by William Hayley, an eminent poet and wealthy patron of the arts, to live in a country cottage at Felpham. One day a private in the Royal Dragoons, John Scofield, while drunk fell into a heated argument with Blake at his garden gate. Blake physically evicted the abusive soldier from the premises. Scofield subsequently accused Blake of making seditious remarks against the Crown, an offense punishable by death. Hayley generously paid for his friend's bail and his defense, and Blake was eventually acquitted, to the thunderous approval of the court. However, the incident stamped itself upon his sensitive mind; he raised it to mythological proportions in the convoluted poetic symbology of *Jerusalem*, where the Law is figured as the nauseous region of "Bowlahoola," while Scofield and his cohorts appear as "ministers of evil."

As the culture around him placed increasing faith in the physical laws of natural science, Blake's insistence on the incorruptible coordinates of imaginative truth cast him as an increasing oddity. Many of Blake's contemporaries considered him insane. London was shifting to a secular orientation under the rise of industrial culture. Against the grain of the times, Blake continued producing labor-intensive printings of illuminated books, none of which proved to be a commercial success. Only twenty-eight copies of *Songs of Innocence and of Experience* are known to exist, sixteen of *The Book of Thel*, nine of *The Marriage of Heaven and Hell*, and five of *Jerusalem*.

In his last years, just as he had reconciled himself to poverty and obscurity, Blake attracted the first following he had ever enjoyed, a small group of painters called "the Ancients." Charles Lamb and a few other writers of the period also expressed admiration, but the glimmerings of a full-fledged "Blake industry" did not appear until years after his death, when his art and poetry were discovered by Dante Gabriel Rossetti and the Pre-Raphaelites. Rossetti and, later, William Butler Yeats edited volumes of Blake's poems, and appreciation grew of his powerful poetic as well as painterly achievements. By the middle of the twentieth century, academics around the world were devoting themselves to the scholarly study of Blake's work, which was also exerting a profound influence on the literary and popular culture of the time. Blake was an inspiration to the generation of Beat poets clustered around Allen Ginsberg and to many in the 1960s' counterculture who took up his call to open the "doors of perception" (words straight from *The Marriage of Heaven and Hell*), trying everything from the hallucinogenic drugs proposed by Aldous Huxley, to communal living and free love to approximate his visionary universe. The future had finally caught up with William Blake.

⌘ ⌘ ⌘

Songs of Innocence and of Experience
Showing the Two Contrary States of the
Human Soul[1]

Songs of Innocence

Title page, *Songs of Innocence and of Experience.*

Introduction

Piping down the valleys wild
  Piping songs of pleasant glee
On a cloud I saw a child,
And he laughing said to me,

5 "Pipe a song about a Lamb":
So I piped with merry chear.
"Piper pipe that song again"
So I piped, he wept to hear.

"Drop thy pipe thy happy pipe
10 Sing thy songs of happy chear."
So I sung the same again,
While he wept with joy to hear

"Piper sit thee down and write
In a book that all may read—"
15 So he vanish'd from my sight
And I pluck'd a hollow reed,

And I made a rural pen,
And I stain'd the water clear,
And I wrote my happy songs,
20 Every child may joy to hear.

The Shepherd

How sweet is the Shepherd's sweet lot!
  From the morn to the evening he strays:
He shall follow his sheep all the day
And his tongue shall be filled with praise.

---

[1] *Songs of Innocence ... Soul* The usual practice of this anthology regarding modernization of spelling and punctuation has not been followed in the case of Blake; his idiosyncrasies have been retained.

5   For he hears the lamb's innocent call,
And he hears the ewe's tender reply.
He is watchful while they are in peace,
For they know when their Shepherd is nigh.

The Ecchoing Green

The Sun does arise,
And make happy the skies.
The merry bells ring
To welcome the Spring.
5   The sky-lark and thrush,
The birds of the bush,
Sing louder around,
To the bells' chearful sound.
While our sports shall be seen
10   On the Ecchoing Green.

Old John with white hair
Does laugh away care,
Sitting under the oak,
Among the old folk.
15   They laugh at our play,
And soon they all say,
"Such such were the joys,
When we all girls & boys,
In our youth-time were seen,
20   On the Ecchoing Green."

Till the little ones weary
No more can be merry
The sun does descend,
And our sports have an end:
25   Round the laps of their mothers.
Many sisters and brothers,
Like birds in their nest,
Are ready for rest:
And sport no more seen,
30   On the darkening Green.

The Lamb[1]

Little Lamb who made thee
Dost thou know who made thee
Gave thee life & bid thee feed,
By the stream & o'er the mead;
5   Gave thee clothing of delight,
Softest clothing wooly bright;
Gave thee such a tender voice,
Making all the vales rejoice:
   Little Lamb who made thee
10   Dost thou know who made thee

   Little Lamb I'll tell thee,
   Little Lamb I'll tell thee:
He is called by thy name,
For he calls himself a Lamb:
15   He is meek & he is mild,[2]
He became a little child:
I a child & thou a lamb,
We are called by his name.
   Little Lamb God bless thee:
20   Little Lamb God bless thee.

The Little Black Boy

My mother bore me in the southern wild,
And I am black, but O! my soul is white.
White as an angel is the English child:
But I am black as if bereav'd of light.

5   My mother taught me underneath a tree
And sitting down before the heat of day.
She took me on her lap and kissed me.
And pointing to the east began to say.

"Look on the rising sun! there God does live
10   And gives his light and gives his heat away.

---

[1] *The Lamb*   The question-and-answer form of this poem recalls the Church of England's catechism for children.

[2] *He … mild*   Cf. Charles Wesley's hymn, "Gentle Jesus, Meek and Mild" (1742).

Title page, *Songs of Experience*.

Frontispiece, *Songs of Experience*.

"Turn away no more:
Why wilt thou turn away
The starry floor[1]
The watry shore
20   Is giv'n thee till the break of day."

Earth's Answer

Earth rais'd up her head,
From the darkness dread & drear.
Her light fled:
Stony dread!
5   And her locks cover'd with grey despair.

"Prison'd on watry shore
Starry Jealousy does keep my den
Cold and hoar°   *grey-haired*
Weeping o'er
10   I hear the Father of the ancient men."[2]

"Selfish father of men
Cruel jealous selfish fear
Can delight
Chain'd in night
15   The virgins of youth and morning bear."

"Does spring hide its joy
When buds and blossoms grow?
Does the sower?
Sow by night?
20   Or the plowman in darkness plow?"

"Break this heavy chain,
That does freeze my bones around
Selfish! Vain!
Eternal bane!
25   That free Love with bondage bound."

The Clod & the Pebble

"Love seeketh not Itself to please.
Nor for itself hath any care;
But for another gives its ease,
And builds a Heaven in Hell's despair."

5   So sang a little Clod of Clay,
Trodden with the cattle's feet;
But a Pebble of the brook,
Warbled out these metres meet.

"Love seeketh only Self to please,
10   To bind another to Its delight;
Joys in another's loss of ease,
And builds a Hell in Heaven's despite."[3]

Holy Thursday

Is this a holy thing to see,
In a rich and fruitful land,
Babes reducd to misery,
Fed with cold and usurous hand?[4]

5   Is that trembling cry a song?
Can it be a song of joy?
And so many children poor?
It is a land of poverty!

And their sun does never shine.
10   And their fields are bleak & bare.
And their ways are fill'd with thorns.
It is eternal winter there.

For where-e'er the sun does shine,
And where-e'er the rain does fall:
15   Babe can never hunger there,
Nor poverty the mind appall.

---

[1]   *starry floor*   The sky, the floor of heaven.

[2]   *Father of the ancient men*   In Blake's prophetic works, this figure is called "Urizen": he embodies conventional reason and law and is depicted as an old bearded man. He bears tools for constraining people and nets in which to trap them.

---

[3]   *builds … despite*   In Milton's *Paradise Lost* (1.254–55), Satan declares, "The mind is its own place, and in itself / Can make a Heaven of Hell, a Hell of Heaven."

[4]   *usurous hand*   I.e., the hand of someone engaged in lending money at interest.

The Little Girl Lost

In futurity
I prophetic see,
That the earth from sleep,
(Grave the sentence deep)

5   Shall arise and seek
For her maker meek:
And the desert wild
Become a garden mild.

In the southern clime,
10   Where the summer's prime
Never fades away;
Lovely Lyca lay.

Seven summers old
Lovely Lyca told,
15   She had wander'd long,
Hearing wild birds' song.

"Sweet sleep come to me
Underneath this tree.
Do father, mother weep.—
20   'Where can Lyca sleep.'

"Lost in desart wild
Is your little child.
How can Lyca sleep,
If her mother weep.

25   "If her heart does ake,°   ache
Then let Lyca wake;
If my mother sleep,
Lyca shall not weep.

"Frowning frowning night,
30   O'er this desart bright,
Let thy moon arise,
While I close my eyes."

Sleeping Lyca lay:
While the beasts of prey,
35   Come from caverns deep,
View'd the maid asleep.

The kingly lion stood
And the virgin view'd,
Then he gamboll'd round
40   O'er the hallow'd ground;

Leopards, tygers play,
Round her as she lay;
While the lion old,
Bow'd his mane of gold.

45   And her bosom lick,
And upon her neck,
From his eyes of flame,
Ruby tears there came;

While the lioness
50   Loos'd her slender dress.
And naked they convey'd
To caves the sleeping maid.

The Little Girl Found

All the night in woe,
Lyca's parents go:
Over valleys deep
While the desarts weep.

5   Tired and woe-begone,
Hoarse with making moan:
Arm in arm seven days
They trac'd the desart ways.

Seven nights they sleep,
10   Among shadows deep:
And dream they see their child
Starv'd in desart wild.

Pale thro' pathless ways
The fancied image strays,
15 Famish'd, weeping, weak
With hollow piteous shriek.

Rising from unrest,
The trembling woman prest,
With feet of weary woe;
20 She could no further go.

In his arms he bore,
Her arm'd with sorrow sore;
Till before their way,
A couching lion lay.

25 Turning back was vain,
Soon his heavy mane
Bore them to the ground;
Then he stalk'd around.

Smelling to his prey,
30 But their fears allay,
When he licks their hands:
And silent by them stands.

They look upon his eyes
Fill'd with deep surprise:
35 And wondering behold,
A spirit arm'd in gold.

On his head a crown,
On his shoulders down
Flow'd his golden hair.
40 Gone was all their care.

"Follow me" he said,
"Weep not for the maid;
In my palace deep,
Lyca lies asleep."

45 Then they followed
Where the vision led:

And saw their sleeping child,
Among tygers wild.

To this day they dwell
50 In a lonely dell,
Nor fear the wolfish howl,
Nor the lions' growl.

The Chimney Sweeper

A little black thing among the snow:
Crying "weep, weep," in notes of woe!
"Where are thy father & mother? say?"
"They are both gone up to the church to pray.

5 "Because I was happy upon the heath.
And smil'd among the winters snow:
They clothed me in the clothes of death,
And taught me to sing the notes of woe.

"And because I am happy & dance & sing,
10 They think they have done me no injury:
And are gone to praise God & his Priest & King
Who make up a heaven of our misery."

Nurse's Song

When the voices of children are heard on the
green
And whisp'rings are in the dale:
The days of my youth rise fresh in my mind,
My face turns green and pale.

5 Then come home my children, the sun is gone down
And the dews of night arise
Your spring & your day are wasted in play
And your winter and night in disguise.

The Sick Rose

O Rose thou art sick.
The invisible worm,
That flies in the night
In the howling storm:

5 Has found out thy bed
Of crimson joy:
And his dark secret love
Does thy life destroy.

The Fly

Little Fly
Thy summer's play,
My thoughtless hand
Has brush'd away.

5 Am not I
A fly like thee?[1]
Or art not thou
A man like me?

For I dance
10 And drink & sing:
Till some blind hand
Shall brush my wing.

If thought is life
And strength & breath:
15 And the want
Of thought is death;[2]

Then am I
A happy fly,
If I live,
20 Or if I die.

---

[1] *Am ... thee* Cf. Shakespeare, *King Lear* 4.1.36–37: "As flies to wanton boys, are we to the gods, / They kill us for their sport."

[2] *If thought ... death* Cf. René Descartes's statement "Cogito, ergo sum" ("I think, therefore I am").

The Angel

I Dreamt a Dream! what can it mean?
And that I was a maiden Queen:
Guarded by an Angel mild:
Witless woe, was ne'er beguil'd!

5 And I wept both night and day
And he wip'd my tears away
And I wept both day and night
And hid from him my heart's delight:

So he took his wings and fled:
10 Then the morn blush'd rosy red:
I dried my tears & arm'd my fears
With ten thousand shields and spears.

Soon my Angel came again:
I was arm'd, he came in vain;
15 For the time of youth was fled,
And grey hairs were on my head.

The Tyger

Tyger Tyger, burning bright,
In the forests of the night;
What immortal hand or eye,
Could frame thy fearful symmetry?

5 In what distant deeps or skies,
Burnt the fire of thine eyes?
On what wings dare he aspire?[3]
What the hand, dare seize the fire?[4]

And what shoulder, & what art,
10 Could twist the sinews of thy heart?
And when thy heart began to beat,
What dread hand? & what dread feet?

---

[3] *what ... aspire* In Greek mythology, Icarus attempted to fly using wings fashioned from wax and feathers; these melted when he flew too close to the sun.

[4] *What ... fire* Prometheus stole fire from heaven to give to humans.

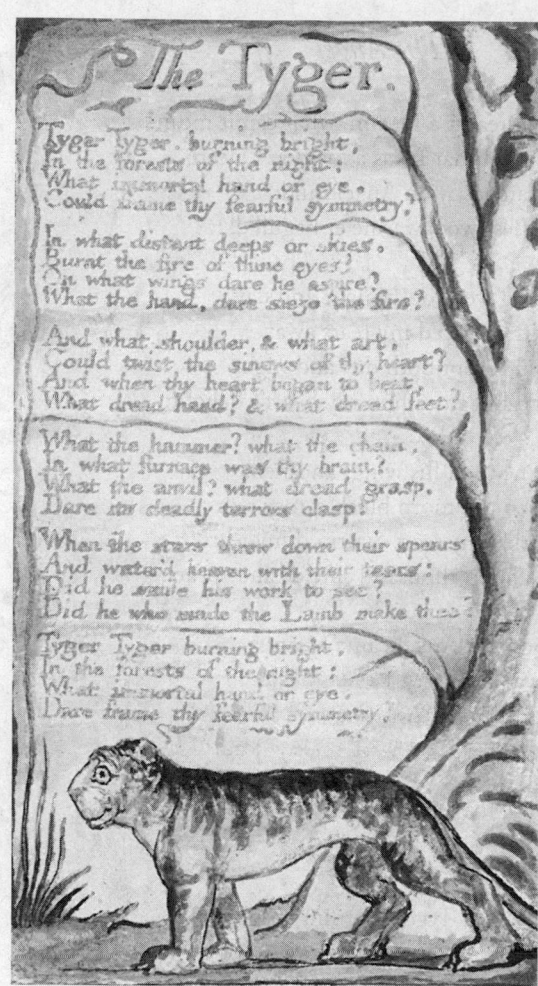

Did he smile his work to see?
20   Did he who made the Lamb make thee?

Tyger Tyger burning bright,
In the forests of the night:
What immortal hand or eye,
Dare frame thy fearful symmetry?

My Pretty Rose Tree

A flower was offer'd to me:
Such a flower as May never bore.
But I said I've a Pretty Rose-tree,
And I passed the sweet flower o'er.

5   Then I went to my Pretty Rose-tree:
To tend her by day and by night,
But my Rose turned away with jealousy:
And her thorns were my only delight.

Ah! Sun-Flower

Ah Sun-flower! weary of time,
Who countest the steps of the Sun:
Seeking after that sweet golden clime
Where the traveller's journey is done.

5   Where the Youth pined away with desire,
And the pale Virgin shrouded in snow:
Arise from their graves and aspire,
Where my Sun-flower wishes to go.

The Lilly

The modest Rose puts forth a thorn:
The humble Sheep, a threat'ning horn:
While the Lilly white, shall in Love delight,
Nor a thorn nor a threat stain her beauty bright.

What the hammer? what the chain,
In what furnace was thy brain?
15   What the anvil? what dread grasp,
Dare its deadly terrors clasp!

When the stars threw down their spears[1]
And water'd heaven with their tears:

---

[1] *threw down their spears* Either in surrender or as an act of rebellion—it is uncertain which.

The Garden of Love

I went to the Garden of Love,
  And saw what I never had seen:
A Chapel was built in the midst,
Where I used to play on the green.

5 And the gates of this Chapel were shut,
And "Thou shalt not"[1] writ over the door;
So I turn'd to the Garden of Love,
That so many sweet flowers bore.

And I saw it was filled with graves,
10 And tomb-stones where flowers should be:
And Priests in black gowns were walking their
    rounds,
And binding with briars,[2] my joys & desires.

The Little Vagabond

Dear Mother, dear Mother, the Church is cold,
  But the Ale-house is healthy & pleasant & warm;
Besides I can tell where I am used well,
Such usage in heaven will never do well.

5 But if at the Church they would give us some Ale,
And a pleasant fire, our souls to regale:
We'd sing and we'd pray all the live-long day:
Nor ever once wish from the Church to stray.

Then the Parson might preach & drink & sing,
10 And we'd be as happy as birds in the spring;

And modest dame Lurch, who is always at Church
Would not have bandy children, nor fasting nor
    birch.[3]

And God like a father rejoicing to see
His children as pleasant and happy as he:
15 Would have no more quarrel with the Devil or the
    Barrel,
But kiss him & give him both drink and apparel.

London

I wander thro' each charter'd[4] street,
  Near where the charter'd Thames does flow,
And mark in every face I meet
Marks of weakness, marks of woe.

5 In every cry of every Man,
In every Infants cry of fear,
In every voice; in every ban.
The mind-forg'd manacles I hear

How the Chimney-sweepers cry
10 Every blackning Church appalls,
And the hapless Soldier's sigh
Runs in blood down Palace walls.

But most thro' midnight streets I hear
How the youthful Harlot's curse[5]
15 Blasts the new born Infant's tear[6]
And blights with plagues the Marriage hearse.

---

[1] *Thou shalt not* The phrase that introduces most of the Ten Commandments (Exodus 20.3–17).

[2] *binding with briars* Prior to the nineteenth century, binding graves with briars was a common practice.

[3] *bandy* Bandy-legged, having legs that are curved outwards at the calf; while some cases of bandy legs are caused by disease, many are caused by malnutrition (vitamin D deficiency); *birch* Rods of birch were used to beat children.

[4] *charter'd* Subject to a charter, a document granting rights to a group of people (either to all the people of a state or to a privileged class) or a document certifying the ownership of a property. "Chartered" could also mean "mapped" or "hired out."

[5] *Harlot's curse* Referring both to the oaths she utters and the venereal diseases she spreads.

[6] *Blasts ... tear* A reference to the blindness caused in infants if they contract certain venereal diseases (such as gonorrhea) from the mother.

The Human Abstract

Pity would be no more,
  If we did not make somebody Poor:
And Mercy no more could be,
If all were as happy as we;

5 And mutual fear brings peace;
Till the selfish loves increase.
Then Cruelty knits a snare,
And spreads his baits with care.

He sits down with holy fears,
10 And waters the ground with tears:
Then Humility takes its root
Underneath his foot.

Soon spreads the dismal shade
Of Mystery over his head;
15 And the Catterpiller and Fly,
Feed on the Mystery.

And it bears the fruit of Deceit,
Ruddy and sweet to eat;
And the Raven his nest has made
20 In its thickest shade.

The Gods of the earth and sea,
Sought thro' Nature to find this Tree
But their search was all in vain:
There grows one in the Human Brain.

Infant Sorrow

My mother groand! my father wept.
  Into the dangerous world I leapt:
Helpless, naked, piping loud;
Like a fiend hid in a cloud.

5 Struggling in my father's hands:
Striving against my swadling bands:
Bound and weary I thought best
To sulk upon my mother's breast.

A Poison Tree[1]

I was angry with my friend:
  I told my wrath, my wrath did end.
I was angry with my foe:
I told it not, my wrath did grow.

5 And I waterd it in fears,
Night & morning with my tears:
And I sunned it with smiles,
And with soft deceitful wiles.

And it grew both day and night,
10 Till it bore an apple bright.
And my foe beheld it shine,
And he knew that it was mine.

And into my garden stole,
When the night had veild the pole;
15 In the morning glad I see.
My foe outstretched beneath the tree.

A Little Boy Lost

"Nought loves another as itself,
  Nor venerates another so.
Nor is it possible to Thought
A greater than itself to know:

5 "And Father, how can I love you,
Or any of my brothers more?
I love you like the little bird
That picks up crumbs around the door."

The Priest sat by and heard the child,
10 In trembling zeal he seiz'd his hair:
He led him by his little coat:
And all admir'd the Priestly care.

---

[1] *A Poison Tree* A manuscript version of this poem is entitled "Christian Forbearance."

And standing on the altar high,
"Lo what a fiend is here!" said he:
5   "One who sets reason up for judge
Of our most holy Mystery."

The weeping child could not be heard,
The weeping parents wept in vain:
They strip'd him to his little shirt,
20   And bound him in an iron chain.

And burn'd him in a holy place,
Where many had been burn'd before:
The weeping parents wept in vain.
Are such things done on Albion's° shore.   *England's*

A Little Girl Lost

Children of the future Age,
Reading this indignant page:
Know that in a former time,
Love! sweet Love! was thought a crime.

5   In the Age of Gold,
Free from winter's cold:
Youth and maiden bright,
In the holy light,
Naked in the sunny beams' delight.

10   Once a youthful pair
Fill'd with softest care,
Met in garden bright,
Where the holy light,
Had just remov'd the curtains of the night.

15   There in rising day,
On the grass they play:
Parents were afar:
Strangers came not near:
And the maiden soon forgot her fear.

20   Tired with kisses sweet
They agree to meet,

When the silent sleep
Waves o'er heaven's deep:
And the weary tired wanderers weep.

25   To her father white
Came the maiden bright:
But his loving look,
Like the holy book,
All her tender limbs with terror shook.

30   "Ona![1] pale and weak!
To thy father speak:
O the trembling fear!
O the dismal care!
That shakes the blossoms of my hoary° hair!"   *grey*
—1794

To Tirzah [2]

Whate'er is Born of Mortal Birth,
Must be consumed with the Earth
To rise from Generation free:
Then what have I to do with thee?[3]

5   The Sexes sprung from Shame & Pride
Blow'd° in the morn; in evening died,   *bloomed*
But Mercy chang'd Death into Sleep:
The Sexes rose to work & weep.

Thou Mother of my Mortal part,
10   With cruelty didst mould my Heart:
And with false self-deceiving tears,
Didst bind my Nostrils Eyes & Ears.

---

[1] *Ona* In Blake's mythology, Ona is one of the daughters of Urizen, an elderly figure embodying conventional reason and law.

[2] *Tirzah* Hebrew name meaning "she is my delight." In Blake's mythology, Tirzah is a figure symbolic of worldliness and the physical senses (as opposed to spiritual perception). This poem was added to a later edition of *Songs of Experience* in 1805.

[3] *Then what ... with thee?* In John 2.4, Jesus says to his mother, "Woman, what have I to do with thee? mine hour is not yet come."

Didst close my Tongue in senseless clay,
And me to Mortal Life betray:
15   The Death of Jesus set me free.
Then what have I to do with thee?
—1805

The School Boy

I love to rise in a summer morn,
When the birds sing on every tree;
The distant huntsman winds° his horn,   *blows*
And the sky-lark sings with me.
5   O! what sweet company.

But to go to school in a summer morn,
O! it drives all joy away;
Under a cruel eye outworn,
The little ones spend the day,
10   In sighing and dismay.

Ah! then at times I drooping sit,
And spend many an anxious hour,
Nor in my book can I take delight,
Nor sit in learning's bower,
15   Worn thro' with the dreary shower.

How can the bird that is born for joy,
Sit in a cage and sing.
How can a child when fears annoy
But droop his tender wing,
20   And forget his youthful spring.

O! father & mother, if buds are nip'd,
And blossoms blown away,
And if the tender plants are strip'd
Of their joy in the springing day,
25   By sorrow and care's dismay,

How shall the summer arise in joy,
Or the summer fruits appear.
Or how shall we gather what griefs destroy,
Or bless the mellowing year,
30   When the blasts of winter appear.
—1794

The Voice of the Ancient Bard

Youth of delight come hither,
And see the opening morn,
Image of truth new-born.
Doubt is fled & clouds of reason,
5   Dark disputes & artful teazing.
Folly is an endless maze,
Tangled roots perplex her ways.
How many have fallen there!
They stumble all night over bones of the dead:
10   And feel they know not what but care:
And wish to lead others when they should be led.
—1805

———————

A Cradle Song[1]

Sleep, Sleep beauty bright
Dreaming o'er the joys of night
Sleep Sleep: in thy sleep
Little sorrows sit & weep

5   Sweet Babe in thy face
Soft desires I can trace
Secret joys & secret smiles
Little pretty infant wiles

———————

[1] *A Cradle Song*   This poem is found in Blake's Notebook, a
commonplace book containing sketches and poems, including many
drafts for poems eventually included in *Songs of Experience*. "A Cradle
Song" is found among these drafts in the Notebook, but it was never
published in the engraved versions of *Songs of Experience*.

Hell, is because he was a true Poet and of the Devils party without knowing it.

A Memorable Fancy[1]

As I was walking among the fires of hell, delighted with the enjoyments of Genius; which to Angels look like torment and insanity. I collected some of their Proverbs: thinking that as the sayings used in a nation. mark its character, so the Proverbs of Hell, shew the nature of Infernal wisdom better than any description of buildings or garments

When I came home; on the abyss of the five senses. where a flat sided steep frowns over the present world. I saw a mighty Devil folded in black clouds, hovering on the sides of the rock, with corroding [Plate 7] fires[2] he wrote the following sentence now percieved by the minds of men, & read by them on earth.

> How do you know but ev'ry Bird that cuts the airy way,
> Is an immense world of delight, clos'd by your
>   senses five?[3]

Proverbs of Hell[4]

In seed time learn, in harvest teach, in winter enjoy.
Drive your cart and your plow over the bones of the
    dead.
The road of excess leads to the palace of wisdom.
Prudence is a rich ugly old maid courted by Incapacity.
5 He who desires but acts not, breeds pestilence.
The cut worm forgives the plow.
Dip him in the river who loves water.

A fool sees not the same tree that a wise man sees.
He whose face gives no light, shall never become a star.
10 Eternity is in love with the productions of time.
The busy bee has no time for sorrow.
The hours of folly are measur'd by the clock, but of
    wisdom: no clock can measure.
All wholsom food is caught without a net or a trap.
Bring out number weight, & measure in a year of dearth
15 No bird soars too high. if he soars with his own wings.
A dead body. revenges not injuries.
The most sublime act is to set another before you.
If the fool would persist in his folly he would become
    wise
Folly is the cloke of knavery.
20 Shame is Prides cloke.

[Plate 8]

Prisons are built with stones of Law, Brothels with
    bricks of Religion.
The pride of the peacock is the glory of God.
The lust of the goat is the bounty of God.
The wrath of the lion is the wisdom of God.
5 The nakedness of woman is the work of God.
Excess of sorrow laughs. Excess of joy weeps.
The roaring of lions, the howling of wolves, the raging
    of the stormy sea, and the destructive sword. are
    portions of eternity too great for the eye of man.
The fox condemns the trap, not himself.
Joys impregnate. Sorrows bring forth.
10 Let man wear the fell of the lion. woman the fleece of
    the sheep.
The bird a nest. the spider a web. man friendship.
The selfish smiling fool & the sullen frowning fool.
    shall be both thought wise. that they may be a rod.
What is now proved was once only imagin'd.
The rat, the mouse, the fox, the rabbet; watch the roots,
    the lion. the tyger. the horse. the elephant. watch
    the fruits.
15 The cistern contains: the fountain overflows
One thought. fills immensity.
Always be ready to speak your mind, and a base man
    will avoid you.

---

[1] *Memorable Fancy* Blake's "Memorable Fancies" are modeled on the "Memorable Relations" in which Swedenborg recounts his visionary experiences.

[2] *corroding fires* A reference to Blake's use of acids to etch the copper plates from which he printed his poems. More extended accounts of the printing process occur on plates 14 and 15.

[3] *How do ... five* Cf. Thomas Chatterton, *Bristowe Tragedie, or the Dethe of Syr Charles Bawdin* (1768): "How dydd I know that ev'ry darte / That cutte the airie waie / Myghte nott find passage toe my harte / And close myne eyes for aie?" (133–36).

[4] *Proverbs of Hell* A diabolical version of the Old Testament's Book of Proverbs.

Every thing possible to be believ'd is an image of truth.
The eagle never lost so much time as when he
    submitted to learn of the crow.

[Plate 9]

The fox provides for himself. but God provides for the
    lion.
Think in the morning. Act in the noon, Eat in the
    evening, Sleep in the night,
He who has sufferd you to impose on him knows you.
As the plow follows words, so God rewards prayers.
5 Thy tygers of wrath are wiser than the horses of
    instruction
Expect poison. from the standing water.
You never know what is enough unless you know what
    is more than enough.
Listen to the fools reproach! it is a kingly title!
The eyes of fire, the nostrils of air, the mouth of water,
    the beard of earth.
10 The weak in courage is strong in cunning.
The apple tree never asks the beech how he shall grow,
    nor the lion the horse, how he shall take his prey.
The thankful reciever bears a plentiful harvest.
If others had not been foolish, we should be so.
The soul of sweet delight, can never be defil'd,
15 When thou seest an Eagle. thou seest a portion of
    Genius. lift up thy head!
As the caterpiller chooses the fairest leaves to lay her eggs
    on. so the priest lays his curse on the fairest joys.
To create a little flower is the labour of ages.
Damn. braces. Bless relaxes.
The best wine is the oldest. the best water the newest.
20 Prayers plow not! Praises reap not!
Joys laugh not! Sorrows weep not!

[Plate 10]

The head Sublime, the heart Pathos, the genitals
    Beauty. the hands & feet Proportion.
As the air to a bird or the sea to a fish, so is contempt to
    the contemptible.
The crow wish'd every thing was black, the owl, that
    every thing was white.

Exuberance is Beauty.
5 If the lion was advised by the fox. he would be cunning.
Improvement makes strait roads, but the crooked roads
    without Improvement. are roads of Genius.
Sooner murder an infant in its cradle than nurse
    unacted desires
Where man is not nature is barren.
Truth can never be told so as to be understood. and not
    be believ'd.
10   Enough! or Too much

[Plate 11]

The ancient Poets animated all sensible objects with
Gods or Geniuses, calling them by the names and
adorning them with the properties of woods, rivers,
mountains, lakes, cities, nations, and whatever their
enlarged & numerous senses could perceive.
    And particularly they studied the genius of each city
& country. placing it under its mental deity.
    Till a system was formed, which some took
advantage of & enslav'd the vulgar by attempting to
realize or abstract the mental deities from their objects:
thus began Priesthood.
    Choosing forms of worship from poetic tales.
    And at length they pronounced that the Gods had
ordered such things.
    Thus men forgot that All deities reside in the human
breast.

[Plate 12]

A Memorable Fancy

The Prophets Isaiah and Ezekiel dined with me, and
I asked them how they dared so roundly to assert. that
God spoke to them; and whether they did not think at
the time, that they would be misunderstood, & so be
the cause of imposition.
    Isaiah answer'd. "I saw no God. nor heard any, in a
finite organical perception; but my senses discover'd the
infinite in every thing, and as I was then perswaded. &
remain confirm'd; that the voice of honest indignation is
the voice of God, I cared not for consequences but wrote"

Then I asked: "does a firm perswasion that a thing is so, make it so?"

He replied, "All poets believe that it does. & in ages of imagination this firm perswasion removed mountains; but many are not capable of a firm perswasion of any thing"

Then Ezekiel said. The philosophy of the east taught the first principles of human perception some nations held one principle for the origin & some another, we of Israel taught that the Poetic Genius (as you now call it) was the first principle and all the others merely derivative, which was the cause of our despising the Priests & Philosophers of other countries, and prophecying that all Gods [Plate 13] would at last be proved to originate in ours & to be the tributaries of the Poetic Genius, it was this. that our great poet King David desired so fervently & invokes so patheticly, saying by this he conquers enemies & governs kingdoms; and we so loved our God. that we cursed in his name all the deities of surrounding nations, and asserted that they had rebelled; from these opinions the vulgar came to think that all nations would at last be subject to the jews.

"This" said he, "like all firm perswasions, is come to pass, for all nations believe the jews code and worship the jews god, and what greater subjection can be"

I heard this with some wonder, & must confess my own conviction. After dinner I ask'd Isaiah to favour the world with his lost works, he said none of equal value was lost. Ezekiel said the same of his.

I also asked Isaiah what made him go naked and barefoot three years? he answered, "the same that made our friend Diogenes the Grecian."[1]

I then asked Ezekiel. why he eat dung, & lay so long on his right & left side?[2] he answered. "the desire of raising other men into a perception of the infinite this the North American tribes practise, & is he honest who resists his genius or conscience. only for the sake of present ease or gratification?"

[Plate 14]

The ancient tradition that the world will be consumed in fire at the end of six thousand years[3] is true. as I have heard from Hell.

For the cherub with his flaming sword is hereby commanded to leave his guard at tree of life, and when he does, the whole creation will be consumed, and appear infinite. and holy whereas it now appears finite & corrupt.

This will come to pass by an improvement of sensual enjoyment.

But first the notion that man has a body distinct from his soul, is to be expunged; this I shall do, by printing in the infernal method, by corrosives, which in Hell are salutary and medicinal, melting apparent surfaces away, and displaying the infinite which was hid.[4]

If the doors of perception were cleansed every thing would appear to man as it is, infinite.

For man has closed himself up, till he sees all things thro' narrow chinks of his cavern.[5]

[Plate 15]

A Memorable Fancy

I was in a Printing House in Hell & saw the method in which knowledge is transmitted from generation to generation

In the first chamber was a Dragon-Man. clearing away the rubbish from a caves mouth; within, a number

---

[1] *Diogenes the Grecian*   Founder of the Cynic school of philosophers, who advocated and practiced a lifestyle of extreme simplicity. In Isaiah 20.2–3, Isaiah is commanded by the Lord to walk "naked and barefoot" for three years.

[2] *why … side*   As he was instructed by the Lord in Ezekiel 4.4–6.

[3] *The ancient … years*   In Genesis 8.21, just after the Flood, God promises not to destroy the world again. The New Testament, however, contains several prophecies that it will be destroyed, this time by fire (Luke 12.49, 2 Peter 3.5–7). The traditional figure of six thousand years seems to have been obtained by combining the six days it took to make the world (Genesis 1) and the idea "that one day is with the Lord as a thousand years" (2 Peter 3.8).

[4] *this I … hid*   In conventional etching, only the lines of the design are burned away by the acid, the rest of the plate being protected by an acid-proof substance such as wax. In Blake's relief etching process, however, almost the whole surface of the plate is burned away, leaving the lines in relief.

[5] *chinks … cavern*   Cf. the allegory of the cave in Plato, *Republic*, and the image of the camera obscura in John Locke (1632–1704), *An Essay Concerning Human Understanding*.

of Dragons were hollowing the cave,

In the second chamber was a Viper folding round the rock & the cave, and others adorning it with gold silver and precious stones

In the third chamber was an Eagle with wings and feathers of air, he caused the inside of the cave to be infinite, around were numbers of Eagle like men, who built palaces in the immense cliffs.

In the fourth chamber were Lions of flaming fire raging around & melting the metals into living fluids.

In the fifth chamber were Unnam'd forms, which cast the metals into the expanse.

There they were reciev'd by Men who occupied the sixth chamber, and took the forms of books & were arranged in libraries.

[Plate 16]

The Giants who formed this world into its sensual existence and now seem to live in it in chains, are in truth. the causes of its life & the sources of all activity, but the chains are, the cunning of weak and tame minds. which have power to resist energy. according to the proverb, the weak in courage is strong in cunning.

Thus one portion of being, is the Prolific. the other, the Devouring; to the devourer it seems as if the producer was in his chains, but it is not so, he only takes portions of existence and fancies that the whole.

But the Prolific would cease to be Prolific unless the Devourer as a sea received the excess of his delights.

Some will say, "Is not God alone the Prolific?" I answer, "God only Acts & Is. in existing beings or Men."

These two classes of men are always upon earth. & they should be enemies; whoever tries [Plate 17] to reconcile them seeks to destroy existence.

Religion is an endeavour to reconcile the two.

Note. Jesus Christ did not wish to unite but to seperate them, as in the Parable of sheep and goats![1] &

he says "I came not to send Peace but a Sword."[2]

Messiah or Satan or Tempter was formerly thought to be one of the Antediluvians[3] who are our Energies.

A Memorable Fancy

An Angel came to me and said. "O pitiable foolish young man! O horrible! O dreadful state! consider the hot burning dungeon thou art preparing for thyself to all eternity, to which thou art going in such career."

I said. "perhaps you will be willing to shew me my eternal lot & we will contemplate together upon it and see whether your lot or mine is most desirable."

So he took me thro' a stable & thro a church & down into the church vault at the end of which was a mill; thro' the mill; we went. and came to a cave. down the winding cavern we groped our tedious way till a void boundless as a nether sky appeard beneath us & we held by the roots of trees and hung over this immensity, but I said, "if you please we will commit ourselves to this void, and see whether providence is here also, if you will not I will?" but he answerd. "do not presume O young-man but as we here remain behold thy lot which will soon appear when the darkness passes away."

So I remaind with him sitting in the twisted [Plate 18] root of an oak. he was suspended in a fungus which hung with the head downward into the deep;

By degrees we beheld the infinite Abyss, fiery as the smoke of a burning city; beneath us at an immense distance was the sun, black but shining round it were fiery tracks on which revolv'd vast spiders. crawling after their prey; which flew or rather swum in the infinite deep, in the most terrific shapes of animals sprung from corruption. & the air was full of them, & seemd composed of them; these are Devils. and are called Powers of the air, I now asked my companion which was my eternal lot? he said, "between the black & white spiders."

But now, from between the black & white spiders a cloud and fire burst and rolled thro' the deep blackning all beneath, so that the nether deep grew black as a sea & rolled with a terrible noise: beneath us was nothing

---

[1] *Parable ... goats* Cf. Matthew 25.32–46. God divides the nations "as a shepherd divideth his sheep from his goats," placing the sheep, who are to be saved, on his right hand, and the goats, who are damned, on his left.

[2] *I ... Sword* From Matthew 10.34.

[3] *Antediluvians* Those who existed before the Flood.

now to be seen but a black tempest, till looking east between the clouds & the waves. we saw a cataract of blood mixed with fire and not many stones throw from us appeard and sunk again the scaly fold of a monstrous serpent at last to the east, distant about three degrees[1] appeard a fiery crest above the waves slowly it reared like a ridge of golden rocks till we discoverd two globes of crimson fire. from which the sea fled away in clouds of smoke, and now we saw, it was the head of Leviathan,[2] his forehead was divided into streaks of green & purple like those on a tygers forehead: soon we saw his mouth & red gills hang just above the raging foam tinging the black deep with beams of blood, advancing toward [Plate 19] us with all the fury of a spiritual existence.

My friend the Angel climb'd up from his station into the mill; I remain'd alone, & then this appearance was no more, but I found myself sitting on a pleasant bank beside a river by moon light hearing a harper who sung to the harp. & his theme was, "The man who never alters his opinion is like standing water, & breeds reptiles of the mind."

But I arose. and sought for the mill, & there I found my Angel, who surprised asked me, how I escaped?

I answered. "All that we saw was owing to your metaphysics: for when you ran away, I found myself on a bank by moonlight hearing a harper, But now we have seen my eternal lot, shall I shew you yours?" he laughd at my proposal; but I by force suddenly caught him in my arms, & flew westerly thro' the night, till we were elevated above the earths shadow: then I flung myself with him directly into the body of the sun, here I clothed myself in white,[3] & taking in my hand Swedenborgs volumes sunk from the glorious clime, and passed all the planets till we came to saturn, here I staid to rest & then

leap'd into the void. between saturn & the fixed stars.[4]

"Here" said I! "is your lot, in this space, if space it may be calld," Soon we saw the stable and the church, & I took him to the altar and open'd the Bible, and lo! it was a deep pit, into which I descended driving the Angel before me, soon we saw seven houses of brick,[5] one we entred; in it were a [Plate 20] number of monkeys. baboons, & all of that species chaind by the middle, grinning and snatching at one another. but witheld by the shortness of their chains; however I saw that they sometimes grew numerous, and then the weak were caught by the strong and with a grinning aspect, first coupled with & then devourd, by plucking off first one limb and then another till the body was left a helpless trunk. this after grinning & kissing it with seeming fondness they devourd too; and here & there I saw one savourily picking the flesh off his own tail; as the stench terribly annoyd us both we went into the mill, & I in my hand brought the skeleton of a body, which in the mill was Aristotles Analytics.[6]

So the Angel said: "thy phantasy has imposed upon me & thou oughtest to be ashamed."

I answered: "we impose on one another, & it is but lost time to converse with you whose works are only Analytics."

Opposition is True Friendship

[Plate 21]

I have always found that Angels have the vanity to speak of themselves as the only wise; this they do with a confident insolence sprouting from systematic reasoning;

Thus Swedenborg boasts that what he writes is new; tho' it is only the Contents or Index of already publish'd books.

A man carried a monkey about for a shew. & because he was a little wiser than the monkey, grew vain.

[1] *three degrees*   Paris is three degrees east of London.

[2] *Leviathan*   The beast Leviathan is described in Job 4.1; Psalms 104.26; Isaiah 27.1; Revelation 11.7, 12.9, 13.2, 20.1–3. Blake may also be thinking of Thomas Hobbes's *Leviathan; or, The Matter, Form, and Power of a Commonwealth, Ecclesiastical and Civil.*

[3] *clothed … white*   Cf. Revelation 7.9, in which those who have been redeemed are clothed in white when they appear before Christ's throne.

[4] *void … stars*   In the Ptolemaic world system, Saturn was the outermost planet, and bordered on the sphere of the fixed stars.

[5] *seven … brick*   John addresses the book of Revelation to the "seven churches which are in Asia" (Revelation 1.4).

[6] *Analytics*   Aristotle's two treatises on logic.

and conceiv'd himself as much wiser than seven men. It is so with Swedenborg; he shews the folly of churches & exposes hypocrites, till he imagines that all are religious. & himself the single [Plate 22] one on earth that ever broke a net.

Now hear a plain fact: Swedenborg has not written one new truth: Now hear another: he has written all the old falshoods.

And now hear the reason. He conversed with Angels who are all religious. & conversed not with Devils who all hate religion, for he was incapable thro' his conceited notions.

Thus Swedenborgs writings are a recapitulation of all superficial opinions, and an analysis of the more sublime. but no further.

Have now another plain fact: Any man of mechanical talents may from the writings of Paracelsus or Jacob Behmen,[1] produce ten thousand volumes of equal value with Swedenborg's. and from those of Dante or Shakespear. an infinite number.

But when he has done this, let him not say that he knows better than his master, for he only holds a candle in sunshine.

A Memorable Fancy

Once I saw a Devil in a flame of fire. who arose before an Angel that sat on a cloud. and the Devil uttered these words.

"The worship of God is. Honouring his gifts in other men, each according to his genius. and loving the [Plate 23] greatest men best, those who envy or calumniate great men hate God, for there is no other God."

The Angel hearing this became almost blue but mastering himself he grew yellow, & at last white pink & smiling, and then replied,

"Thou Idolater, is not God One? & is not he visible in Jesus Christ? and has not Jesus Christ given his sanction to the law of ten commandments and are not all other men fools. sinners, & nothings?"

The Devil answer'd; "bray a fool in a morter with wheat. yet shall not his folly be beaten out of him:[2] if Jesus Christ is the greatest man. you ought to love him in the greatest degree; now hear how he has given his sanction to the law of ten commandments: did he not mock at the sabbath,[3] and so mock the sabbaths God? murder those who were murderd because of him?[4] turn away the law from the woman taken in adultery?[5] steal the labor of others to support him?[6] bear false witness when he omitted making a defence before Pilate?[7] covet when he pray'd for his disciples, and when he bid them shake off the dust of their feet against such as refused to lodge them?[8] I tell you, no virtue can exist without breaking these ten commandments: Jesus was all virtue, and acted from impulse.[Plate 24] not from rules."

When he had so spoken: I beheld the Angel who stretched out his arms embracing the flame of fire & he was consumed and arose as Elijah.[9]

Note. This Angel, who is now become a Devil, is my particular friend: we often read the Bible together in its infernal or diabolical sense which the world shall have if they behave well

I have also: The Bible of Hell:[10] which the world shall have whether they will or no.

One Law for the Lion & Ox is Oppression
—1793

---

1 *Paracelsus* Philippus Aureolus, Theophrastus Bombastus von Hohenheim (1493–1541), Swiss physician and alchemist; *Behmen* Jakob Boehme (1575–1624), German mystic.

2 *bray … him* Proverbs 27.22. This devil can quote scripture to his purpose; *bray* Crush.

3 *mock … sabbath* In Exodus 20.8–11; Matthew 12.8–12; Mark 2.27, 3.2–4; Luke 14.3–5; John 5.16.

4 *murder … him* In Exodus 20.13; see the martyrdom of Stephen (Acts 7.58–60).

5 *turn … adultery* In Exodus 20.14; John 8.3–11.

6 *steal … him* Cf. Exodus 20.15; Matthew 26.6–13.

7 *bear … Pilate* Cf. Exodus 20.16; Matthew 27.11–14; Mark 15.2–5.

8 *covet … them* Cf. Exodus 20.17; Matthew 10.14; Luke 9.5.

9 *who … Elijah* Cf. 2 Kings 2.11: "There appeared a chariot of fire, and … Elijah went up by a whirlwind into heaven."

10 *Bible of Hell* A reference to Blake's own work. In addition to the Proverbs of Hell (plates 7–10), this bible is sometimes said to include such later works as The [First] Book of Urizen, The Book of Ahania, and The Book of Los (1794–95).

1

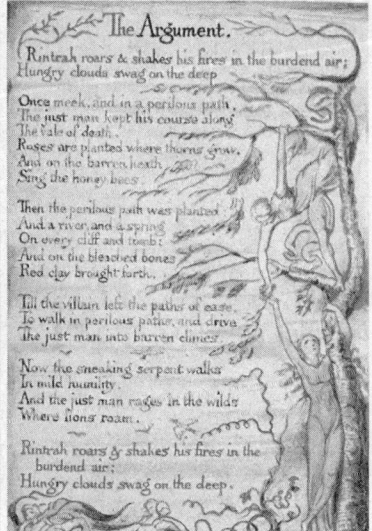

The Argument.

Rintrah roars & shakes his fires in the burdend air;
Hungry clouds swag on the deep

Once meek, and in a perilous path,
The just man kept his course along
The vale of death.
Roses are planted where thorns grow,
And on the barren heath
Sing the honey bees.

Then the perilous path was planted
And a river, and a spring
On every cliff and tomb;
And on the bleached bones
Red clay brought forth.

Till the villain left the paths of ease,
To walk in perilous paths, and drive
The just man into barren climes.

Now the sneaking serpent walks
In mild humility.
And the just man rages in the wilds
Where lions roam.

Rintrah roars & shakes his fires in the
burdend air;
Hungry clouds swag on the deep.

2

As a new heaven is begun, and it is now thir-
ty-three years since its advent: the Eternal Hell
revives. And lo! Swedenborg is the Angel sitting
at the tomb; his writings are the linen clothes folded
up. Now is the dominion of Edom, & the return of
Adam into Paradise; see Isaiah XXXIV & XXXV Chap.
Without Contraries is no progression. Attraction
and Repulsion, Reason and Energy, Love and
Hate, are necessary to Human existence.
From these contraries spring what the religious call
Good & Evil. Good is the passive that obeys Reason
Evil is the active springing from Energy.
Good is Heaven. Evil is Hell.

3

All Bibles or sacred codes, have been the
causes of the following Errors.
1. That Man has two real existing principles Viz: a Body & a Soul.
2. That Energy, calld Evil, is alone from the
Body, & that Reason, calld Good, is alone from
the Soul.
3. That God will torment Man in Eternity
for following his Energies.
But the following Contraries to these are True
1. Man has no Body distinct from his Soul
for that calld Body is a portion of Soul discernd
by the five Senses, the chief inlets of Soul in this
age.
2. Energy is the only life and is from the Body
and Reason is the bound or outward circumference
of Energy.
3. Energy is Eternal Delight.

4

Those who restrain desire, do so because theirs
is weak enough to be restrained; and the restrainer or
reason usurps its place & governs the unwilling.
And being restrained it by degrees becomes passive
till it is only the shadow of desire.
The history of this is written in Paradise Lost, & the
Governor or Reason is calld Messiah.
And the original Archangel or possessor of the com-
mand of the heavenly host, is calld the Devil or Satan
and his children are calld Sin & Death
But in the Book of Job Miltons Messiah is calld
Satan.
For this history has been adopted by both parties.
It indeed appeard to Reason as if Desire was
cast out, but the Devils account is that the Messi-

5

in hell & formed a heaven of what he stole from the
Abyss.
This is shewn in the Gospel, where he prays to the
Father to send the comforter or Desire that Reason
may have Ideas to build on, the Jehovah of the Bible
being no other than he who dwells in flaming fire.
Know that after Christs death, he became Jehovah.
But in Milton; the Father is Destiny, the Son, a
Ratio of the five senses, & the Holy-ghost, Vacuum!
Note. The reason Milton wrote in fetters when
he wrote of Angels & God, and at liberty when of
Devils & Hell, is because he was a true Poet and
of the Devils party without knowing it.

A Memorable Fancy

As I was walking among the fires of hell, delighted with the enjoyments of Genius; which to Angels look like torment and insanity. I collected some
of their Proverbs: thinking that as the sayings used
in a nation, mark its character, so the Proverbs of
Hell shew the nature of Infernal wisdom better
than any description of buildings or garments
When I came home; on the abyss of the five senses, where a flat sided steep frowns over the present world. I saw a mighty Devil folded in black
clouds, hovering on the sides of the rock, with cor-

10

6

roding fires he wrote the following sentence now perceived by the minds of men, & read by them on earth.

How do you know but ev'ry Bird that cuts the airy way,
Is an immense world of delight, clos'd by your senses five?

Proverbs of Hell

In seed time learn, in harvest teach, in winter enjoy.
Drive your cart and your plow over the bones of the dead.
The road of excess leads to the palace of wisdom.
Prudence is a rich ugly old maid courted by Incapacity.
He who desires but acts not, breeds pestilence.
The cut worm forgives the plow.
Dip him in the river who loves water.
A fool sees not the same tree that a wise man sees.
He whose face gives no light, shall never become a star.
Eternity is in love with the productions of time.
The busy bee has no time for sorrow.
The hours of folly are measur'd by the clock, but of wis-
dom: no clock can measure.
All wholsom food is caught without a net or a trap.
Bring out number weight & measure in a year of dearth.
No bird soars too high. if he soars with his own wings.
A dead body. revenges not injuries.
The most sublime act is to set another before you.
If the fool would persist in his folly he would become
wise.
Folly is the cloke of knavery.
Shame is Prides cloke.

7

Proverbs of Hell

Prisons are built with stones of Law, Brothels with
bricks of Religion.
The pride of the peacock is the glory of God.
The lust of the goat is the bounty of God.
The wrath of the lion is the wisdom of God.
The nakedness of woman is the work of God.
Excess of sorrow laughs. Excess of joy weeps.
The roaring of lions, the howling of wolves, the raging
of the stormy sea, and the destructive sword. are
portions of eternity too great for the eye of man.
The fox condemns the trap, not himself.
Joys impregnate. Sorrows bring forth.
Let man wear the fell of the lion. woman the fleece of
the sheep.
The bird a nest, the spider a web, man friendship.
The selfish smiling fool. & the sullen frowning fool. shall
be both thought wise. that they may be a rod.
What is now proved was once, only imagin'd.
The rat, the mouse, the fox, the rabbet; watch the roots;
the lion, the tyger, the horse, the elephant, watch
the fruits.
The cistern contains: the fountain overflows.
One thought. fills immensity.
Always be ready to speak your mind, and a base man
will avoid you.
Every thing possible to be believ'd is an image of truth.
The eagle never lost so much time, as when he submit-
-ted to learn of the crow.
The

8

Proverbs of Hell

The fox provides for himself, but God provides for the lion.
Think in the morning. Act in the noon. Eat in the even-
ing, Sleep in the night.
He who has suffer'd you to impose on him knows you.
As the plow follows words, so God rewards prayers.
The tygers of wrath are wiser than the horses of in-
struction.
Expect poison from the standing water.
You never know what is enough unless you know what is
more than enough.
Listen to the fools reproach! it is a kingly title!
The eyes of fire, the nostrils of air, the mouth of water,
the beard of earth.
The weak in courage is strong in cunning.
The apple tree never asks the beech how he shall grow,
nor the lion, the horse; how he shall take his prey.
The thankful reciever bears a plentiful harvest.
If others had not been foolish. we should be so.
The soul of sweet delight, can never be defil'd.
When thou seest an Eagle. thou seest a portion of Ge-
-nius. lift up thy head!
As the catterpiller chooses the fairest leaves to lay
her eggs on, so the priest lays his curse on
the fairest joys.
To create a little flower is the labour of ages.
Damn braces. Bless relaxes.
The best wine is the oldest. the best water the newest.
Prayers plow not. Praises reap not.
Joys laugh not. Sorrows weep not.

9

Proverbs of Hell

The head Sublime, the heart Pathos, the genitals Beauty,
the hands & feet Proportion.
As the air to a bird or the sea to a fish, so is contempt
to the contemptible.
The crow wish'd every thing was black, the owl, that eve-
-ry thing was white.
Exuberance is Beauty.
If the lion was advised by the fox. he would be cunning.
Improvent makes strait roads, but the crooked roads
without Improvement, are roads of Genius.
Sooner murder an infant in its cradle than nurse unact-
ed desires.
Where man is not nature is barren.
Truth can never be told so as to be understood, and
not be believ'd.
Enough! or Too much.

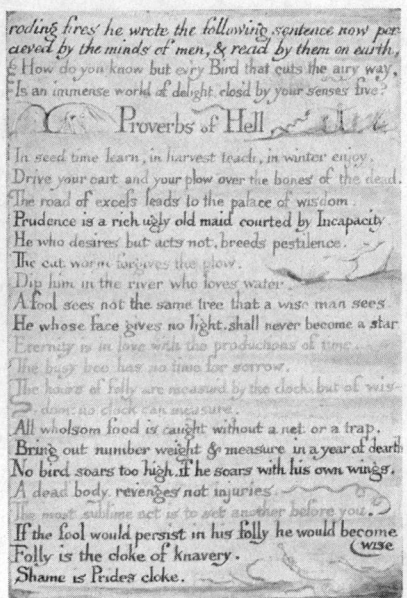

10

The ancient Poets animated all sensible objects
with Gods or Geniuses, calling them by the names and
adorning them with the properties of woods, rivers,
mountains, lakes, cities, nations, and whatever their
enlarged & numerous senses could perceive.
And particularly they studied the genius of each
city & country. placing it under its mental deity.
Till a system was formed, which some took advantage of & enslav'd the vulgar by attempting to
realize or abstract the mental deities from their
objects: thus began Priesthood.
Choosing forms of worship from poetic tales.
And at length they pronounced that the Gods
had order'd such things.
Thus men forgot that All deities reside
in the human breast.

11

A Memorable Fancy

The Prophets Isaiah and Ezekiel dined with
me, and I asked them how they dared so roundly to
assert, that God spoke to them; and whether they
did not think at the time, that they would be misunderstood, & so be the cause of imposition.
Isaiah answer'd. I saw no God, nor heard
any, in a finite organical perception; but my senses discover'd the infinite in every thing, and as I
was then perswaded, & remain confirm'd; that the
voice of honest indignation is the voice of God. I
cared not for consequences but wrote.
Then I asked: does a firm perswasion that a
thing is so, make it so?
He replied. All poets believe that it does, &
in ages of imagination this firm perswasion removed mountains; but many are not capable of a
firm perswasion of any thing.
Then Ezekiel said. The philosophy of the east
taught the first principles of human perception.
some nations held one principle for the origin &
some another, we of Israel taught that the Poetic
Genius (as you now call it) was the first principle
and all the others merely derivative which was the
cause of our despising the Priests & Philosophers
of other countries, and prophecying that all Gods
would

12

would at last be proved to originate in ours & to be the tributaries of the Poetic Genius. it was this. that our great poet King David desired so fervently & invokes so pathetically. saying by this he conquers enemies & governs kingdoms; and we so loved our God. that we cursed in his name all the deities of surrounding nations. and asserted that they had rebelled; from these opinions the vulgar came to think that all nations would at last be subject to the jews.

This said he. like all firm perswasions, is come to pass, for all nations believe the jews code and worship the jews god, and what greater subjection can be

I heard this with some wonder. & must confess my own conviction. After dinner I askd Isaiah to favour the world with his lost works, he said none of equal value was lost. Ezekiel said the same of his.

I also asked Isaiah what made him go naked and barefoot three years? he answerd, the same that made our friend Diogenes the Grecian.

I then asked Ezekiel. why he eat dung, & lay so long on his right & left side? he answerd. the desire of raising other men into a perception of the infinite this the North American tribes practise. & is he honest who resists his genius or conscience. only for the sake of present ease or gratification?

13

The ancient tradition that the world will be consumed in fire at the end of six thousand years is true, as I have heard from Hell.

For the cherub with his flaming sword is hereby commanded to leave his guard at tree of life, and when he does, the whole creation will be consumed, and appear infinite. and holy whereas it now appears finite & corrupt.

This will come to pass by an improvement of sensual enjoyment.

But first the notion that man has a body distinct from his soul. is to be expunged; this I shall do. by printing in the infernal method. by corrosives, which in Hell are salutary and medicinal. melting apparent surfaces away, and displaying the infinite which was hid.

If the doors of perception were cleansed every thing would appear to man as it is: infinite.

For man has closed himself up, till he sees all things thro' narrow chinks of his cavern.

14

A Memorable Fancy

I was in a Printing house in Hell & saw the method in which knowledge is transmitted from generation to generation.

In the first chamber was a Dragon-Man, clearing away the rubbish from a caves mouth; within, a number of Dragons were hollowing the cave.

In the second chamber was a Viper folding round the rock & the cave, and others adorning it with gold silver and precious stones.

In the third chamber was an Eagle with wings and feathers of air, he caused the inside of the cave to be infinite, around were numbers of Eagle like men, who built palaces in the immense cliffs.

In the fourth chamber were Lions of flaming fire raging around & melting the metals into living fluids.

In the fifth chamber were Unnam'd forms, which cast the metals into the expanse.

There they were received by Men who occupied the sixth chamber, and took the forms of books & were arranged in libraries.

15

The Giants who formed this world into its sensual existence and now seem to live in it in chains; are in truth. the causes of its life & the sources of all activity, but the chains are. the cunning of weak and tame minds. which have power to resist energy. according to the proverb, the weak in courage is strong in cunning.

Thus one portion of being. is the Prolific. the other. the Devouring: to the devourer it seems as if the producer was in his chains. but it is not so. he only takes portions of existence and fancies that the whole.

But the Prolific would cease to be Prolific unless the Devourer as a sea received the excess of his delights.

Some will say. Is not God alone the Prolific? I answer. God only Acts & Is. in existing beings or Men.

These two classes of men are always upon earth. & they should be enemies; whoever tries to

16

to reconcile them seeks to destroy existence.

Religion is an endeavour to reconcile the two.

Note. Jesus Christ did not wish to unite but to separate them. as in the Parable of sheep and goats. & he says I came not to send Peace but a Sword.

Messiah or Satan or Tempter was formerly thought to be one of the Antediluvians who are our Energies.

A Memorable Fancy

An Angel came to me and said. O pitiable foolish young man! O horrible! O dreadful state! consider the hot burning dungeon thou art preparing for thyself to all eternity, to which thou art going in such career.

I said. perhaps you will be willing to shew me my eternal lot & we will contemplate together upon it and see whether your lot or mine is most desirable

So he took me thro' a stable & thro' a church & down into the church vault at the end of which was a mill: thro' the mill we went. and came to a cave. down the winding cavern we groped our tedious way till a void boundless as a nether sky appeard beneath us & we held by the roots of trees and hung over this immensity; but I said. if you please we will commit ourselves to this void, and see whether providence is here also. if you will not I will? but he answerd. do not presume O young-man but as we here remain behold thy lot which will soon appear when the darkness passes away

So I remained with him sitting in the twisted

17

root of an oak. he was suspended. in a fungus which hung with the head downward into the deep:

By degrees we beheld the infinite Abyss, fiery as the smoke of a burning city. beneath us at an immense distance was the sun, black but shining round it were fiery tracks on which revolved vast spiders. crawling after their prey; which flew or rather swum in the infinite deep. in the most terrific shapes of animals sprung from corruption. & the air was full of them, & seemd composed of them; these are Devils. and are called Powers of the air, I now asked my companion which was my eternal lot? he said. between the black & white spiders

But now. from between the black & white spiders a cloud and fire burst and rolled thro' the deep blackning all beneath. so that the nether deep grew black as a sea & rolled with a terrible noise: beneath us was nothing now to be seen but a black tempest. till looking east between the clouds & the waves. we saw a cataract of blood mixed with fire and not many stones throw from us appeard and sunk again the scaly fold of a monstrous serpent. at last to the east. distant about three degrees appeard a fiery crest above the waves slowly it reared like a ridge of golden rocks till we discovered two globes of crimson fire. from which the sea fled away in clouds of smoke, and now we saw. it was the head of Leviathan. his forehead was divided into streaks of green & purple like those on a tygers forehead: soon we saw his mouth & red gills hang just above the raging foam tinging the black deep with beams of blood, advancing toward us

18

...us with all the...

My friend the Angel climb'd up from his station into the mill; I remain'd alone, & then this appearance was no more, but I found myself sitting on a pleasant bank beside a river by moonlight hearing a harper who sung to the harp, & his theme was, The man who never alters his opinion is like standing water, & breeds reptiles of the mind.

But I arose, and sought for the mill & there I found my Angel, who surprised asked me how I escaped?

I answered. All that we saw was owing to your metaphysics; for when you ran away, I found myself on a bank by moonlight hearing a harper. But now we have seen my eternal lot, shall I shew you yours? he laughd at my proposal; but I by force suddenly caught him in my arms, & flew westerly thro' the night, till we were elevated above the earths shadow; then I flung myself with him directly into the body of the sun, here I clothed myself in white, & taking in my hand Swedenborgs volumes sunk from the glorious clime, and passed all the planets till we came to saturn, here I staid to rest & then leapd into the void, between saturn & the fixed stars.

Here said I! is your lot, in this space, if space it may be calld, Soon we saw the stable and the church, & I took him to the altar and opend the Bible, and lo! it was a deep pit, into which I descended driving the Angel before me, soon we saw seven houses of brick, one we enterd; in it were a num-

19

number of monkeys, baboons, & all of that species chaind by the middle, grinning and snatching at one another, but witheld by the shortness of their chains; however I saw that they sometimes grew numerous, and then the weak were caught by the strong and with a grinning aspect, first coupled with & then devourd, by plucking off first one limb and then another till the body was left a helpless trunk, this after grinning & kissing it with seeming fondness they devourd too; and here & there I saw one savourily picking the flesh off of his own tail; as the stench terribly annoyd us both we went into the mill, & I in my hand brought the skeleton of a body, which in the mill was Aristotles Analytics.

So the Angel said: thy phantasy has imposed upon me & thou oughtest to be ashamed.

I answerd: we impose on one another, & it is but lost time to converse with you whose works are only Analytics

20

I have always found that Angels have the vanity to speak of themselves as the only wise; this they do with a confident insolence sprouting from systematic reasoning.

Thus Swedenborg boasts that what he writes is new; tho' it is only the Contents or Index of already publish'd books.

A man carried a monkey about for a shew, & because he was a little wiser than the monkey, grew vain, and conceiv'd himself as much wiser than seven men. It is so with Swedenborg; he shews the folly of churches & exposes hypocrites, till he imagines that all are religious, & himself the single one

21

one on earth that ever broke a net.

Now hear a plain fact: Swedenborg has not written one new truth: Now hear another: he has written all the old falshoods.

And now hear the reason. He conversed with Angels who are all religious, & conversed not with Devils who all hate religion for he was incapable thro' his conceited notions.

Thus Swedenborgs writings are a recapitulation of all superficial opinions, and an analysis of the more sublime, but no further.

Have now another plain fact: Any man of mechanical talents may from the writings of Paracelsus or Jacob Behmen, produce ten thousand volumes of equal value with Swedenborgs, and from those of Dante or Shakespear, an infinite number.

But when he has done this, let him not say that he knows better than his master, for he only holds a candle in sunshine.

A Memorable Fancy

Once I saw a Devil in a flame of fire, who arose before an Angel that sat on a cloud, and the Devil utterd these words.

The worship of God is. Honouring his gifts in other men each according to his genius. and loving the great-

22

greatest men best, those who envy or calumniate great men hate God, for there is no other God.

The Angel hearing this became almost blue but mastering himself he grew yellow, & at last white pink & smiling, and then replied,

Thou Idolater, is not God One? & is not he visible in Jesus Christ? and has not Jesus Christ given his sanction to the law of ten commandments and are not all other men fools, sinners, & nothings?

The Devil answer'd; bray a fool in a morter with wheat, yet shall not his folly be beaten out of him: if Jesus Christ is the greatest man, you ought to love him in the greatest degree; now hear how he has given his sanction to the law of ten commandments: did he not mock at the sabbath, and so mock the sabbaths God? murder those who were murderd because of him? turn away the law from the woman taken in adultery? steal the labor of others to support him? bear false witness when he omitted making a defence before Pilate? covet when he prayd for his disciples, and when he bid them shake off the dust of their feet against such as refused to lodge them? I tell you, no virtue can exist without breaking these ten commandments: Jesus was all virtue, and acted from im-pulse

23

pulse, not from rules.

When he had so spoken, I beheld the Angel who stretched out his arms embracing the flame of fire & he was consumed and arose as Elijah.

Note. This Angel, who is now become a Devil, is my particular friend; we often read the Bible together in its infernal or diabolical sense which the world shall have if they behave well.

I have also: The Bible of Hell: which the world shall have whether they will or no.

One Law for the Lion & Ox is Oppression

24

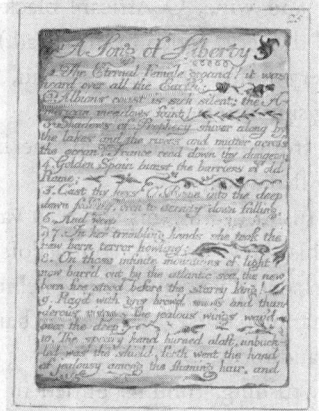
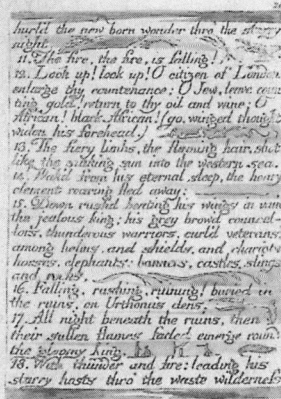
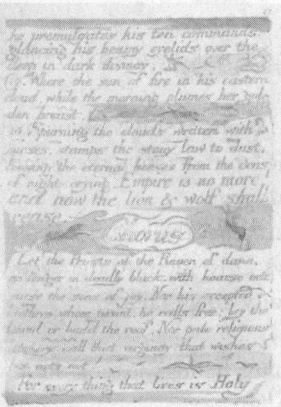

25   26   27

A Song of Liberty

Engraved circa 1792 and appended as the conclusion (plates 25, 26, and 27) to *The Marriage of Heaven and Hell* (1790–93), "A Song of Liberty" is an important part of Blake's canon. The poem reiterates and anticipates a number of themes significant to the artist; perhaps most prominent among these are the myth of revolution announced in the cry of "Empire is no more!"—and the prophetic belief in salvation through religious faith. The song can be seen as a key founding document of British Romanticism in its celebration of freedom, its rejection of reason as the focus of human existence, and its insistence on equality. Blake's engravings of vegetative motifs—looped vines, various leaves, branches, flame-like foliage—and two soaring birds to accompany the textual manuscript further contribute to the Romantic vision of the text.

Although the "Song" invariably appears as the last verse in all extant manuscript copies of *The Marriage of Heaven and Hell*, recent criticism suggests that the poem may not have been intended originally to serve as part of the longer work; some scholars have noted the sometimes striking differences in style and content between "A Song of Liberty" and the preceding plates, while others have suggested that the "Song" was to have been published as a separate pamphlet.

⌘ ⌘ ⌘

A Song of Liberty[1]

1. The Eternal Female[2] groand! it was heard over all the Earth:

2. Albions[3] coast is sick silent; the American meadows faint!

3. Shadows of Prophecy shiver along by the lakes and the rivers and mutter across the ocean? France rend down thy dungeon

4. Golden Spain burst the barriers of old Rome;[4]

5. Cast thy keys O Rome into the deep down falling, even to eternity down falling,

6. And weep[5]

7. In her trembling hands she took the new born terror howling:

8. On those infinite mountains of light now barr'd out by the atlantic sea, the new born fire stood before the starry king!

9. Flag'd with grey browd snows and thunderous visages the jealous wings wav'd over the deep.

10. The speary hand burned aloft, unbuckled was the shield, forth went the hand of jealousy among the flaming hair. and[6] hurl'd the new born wonder thro' the starry night.

11. The fire, the fire, is falling!

12. Look up! look up! O citizen of London enlarge thy countenance; O Jew, leave counting gold![7] return to thy oil and wine; O African! black African! (go, winged thought, widen his forehead.)

13. The fiery limbs, the flaming hair, shot like the sinking sun into the western sea.

14. Wak'd from his eternal sleep, the hoary element roaring fled away;

15. Down rushd beating his wings in vain the jealous king; his grey brow'd councellors, thunderous warriors, curl'd veterans, among helms, and shields, and chariots, horses, elephants: banners, castles, slings, and rocks,

16. Falling, rushing, ruining! buried in the ruins, on Urthona's[8] dens;

17. All night beneath the ruins, then their sullen flames faded emerge round the gloomy king.

18. With thunder and fire: leading his starry hosts thro' the waste wilderness[9] he promulgates his ten commands,[10] glancing his beamy eyelids over the deep in dark dismay,

19. Where the son of fire in his eastern cloud, while the morning plumes her golden breast.

20. Spurning the clouds written with curses. stamps the stony law to dust. loosing the eternal horses from the

---

[1] *A Song of Liberty*   The poem appears as the last three plates (25–27) of *The Marriage of Heaven and Hell* (1790–93), Blake's long prophetic poem, composed in the period following the French Revolution.

[2] *Eternal Female*   The Eternal Female appears in a variety of guises in Blake's poetry; cf. "Earth" and "Earth's Answer" in the opening poems of the *Songs of Experience* (1789), and the "nameless shadowy female" in the Preludium to *Europe* (1794). Here, it seems to birth the revolutionary spirit itself.

[3] *Albion*   Ancient name for the island of Great Britain. Loosely influenced by Greek myth and British folklore, Blake developed his own mythological vision of the figure of Albion as an ancient man who is the father of all humankind.

[4] *old Rome*   The center of religious authority for Catholics.

[5] *weep*   "and bow thy reverend locks!" was deleted from the copper plate following "weep." These five words are absent in all extant manuscript copies except Copy L (now in the collection of Robert N. Essick) and Copy M (in the collection of E.B. Bentley and G.E. Bentley, Jr.); these two manuscripts consist of plates 25–27 only, with plate 25 in its first state.

[6] *and*   This marks the end of Plate 25 in manuscripts of *The Marriage of Heaven and Hell*.

[7] *Jew … counting gold*   Since the Middle Ages, European Christian society has condemned Jews for the practice of money-lending, which was in most European countries one of the few professions that Jews were allowed to follow. Blake's anti-Semitic image reflects a stereotypical association, commonly held in England at the time, of Jews with greed.

[8] *Urthona*   In later works such as *The Four Zoas* and *Milton a Poem* (1804), Blake develops Urthona as one of the four "Zoas," divisions that result from the fall of Albion; he is linked to the imagination, inspiration, and creativity. Urthona's female counterpart is "Enitharmon," and his fallen form is "Los," usually depicted as a blacksmith. The three other Zoas are "Urizen" (incarnation of law and reason), "Tharmas" (nature, instinct, and unity), and "Luvah" (passion and love).

[9] *wilderness*   This marks the end of Plate 26.

[10] *ten commands*   Blake repeatedly rejects the Ten Commandments throughout *The Marriage of Heaven and Hell*, a stance consistent with his antinomian position, which discards social law and morality in favor of individual faith, associated for Blake with energy and joy.

dens of night, crying Empire is no more! and now the lion & wolf shall cease.[1]

Chorus

Let the Priests of the Raven[2] of dawn. no longer in deadly black, with hoarse note curse the sons of joy. Nor his accepted brethren whom tyrant, he calls free: lay the bound or build the roof: Nor pale religions letchery call that virginity that wishes but acts not!

    For everything that lives is Holy[3]

—1792–93

Auguries of Innocence[4]

To see a World in a Grain of Sand
    And a Heaven in a Wild Flower
Hold Infinity in the palm of your hand
And Eternity in an hour
5 A Robin Red breast in a Cage
Puts all Heaven in a Rage
A Dove house filld with Doves & Pigeons
Shudders Hell thro all its regions
A dog starvd at his Masters Gate
10 Predicts the ruin of the State
A Horse misusd upon the Road
Calls to Heaven for Human blood
Each outcry of the hunted Hare
A fibre from the Brain does tear
15 A Skylark wounded in the wing
A Cherubim° does cease to sing   angel

The Game Cock clipd & armd[5] for fight
Does the Rising Sun affright
Every Wolfs & Lions howl
20 Raises from Hell a Human Soul
The wild deer wandring here & there
Keeps the Human Soul from Care
The Lamb misusd breeds Public strife
And yet forgives the Butchers Knife
25 The Bat that flits at close of Eve
Has left the Brain that wont Believe
The Owl that calls upon the Night
Speaks the Unbelievers fright
He who shall hurt the little Wren
30 Shall never be belovd by Men
He who the Ox to wrath has movd
Shall never be by Woman lovd
The wanton Boy that kills the Fly
Shall feel the Spiders enmity
35 He who torments the Chafers sprite[6]
Weaves a Bower in endless Night
The Caterpiller on the Leaf
Repeats to thee thy Mothers grief
Kill not the Moth nor Butterfly
40 For the Last judgment draweth nigh
He who shall train the Horse to War
Shall never pass the Polar Bar[7]
The Beggers Dog & Widows Cat
Feed them & thou wilt grow fat
45 The Gnat that sings his Summers song
Poison gets from Slanders tongue
The poison of the Snake & Newt
Is the sweat of Envys Foot
The Poison of the Honey Bee
50 Is the Artists Jealousy
The Princes Robes & Beggars Rags

---

[1] *Empire is no more! … shall cease* Cf. Plate 6 of Blake's *America* (1793): "For Empire is no more, and now the Lion & Wolf shall cease" (15).

[2] *Priests of the Raven* The Raven represents the fear of death; in its association here with the "priests," the Raven is connected to orthodoxy and its emphasis on such fear.

[3] *For everything that lives is Holy* Cf. Plate 8 of Blake's *America*: "For every thing that lives is holy, life delights in life" (13).

[4] *Auguries of Innocence* This poem is found in the Pickering Manuscript, a notebook containing ten poems, seven of which, including *Auguries*, are unique to the manuscript. The poem presented here is a transcription from the manuscript.

[5] *Game Cock* Rooster trained for cockfighting; *clipd* "Clipped" roosters have their wattles and combs cut off for fighting; *armd* Game cocks are "armed" with sharp metal spurs on their legs.

[6] *Chafers sprite* Beetle's spirit.

[7] *Polar Bar* In book 13 of Homer's *Odyssey*, the cave of the Naiads has two gates, the northern and the southern; the northern gate is the way mortals enter (cf. "the northern bar" in *The Book of Thel*, Plate VI, line 1). In Blake's mythology, the "northern" or "polar" bar is a threshold mortals must cross to enter the spiritual realm.

Are Toadstools on the Misers Bags[1]
A truth thats told with bad intent
Beats all the Lies you can invent
55 It is right it should be so
Man was made for Joy & Woe
And when this we rightly know
Thro the World we safely go
Joy & Woe are woven fine
60 A Clothing for the soul divine
Under every grief & pine°   sorrow
Runs a joy with silken twine[2]
The Babe is more than swadling Bands[3]
Throughout all these Human Lands
65 Tools were made & Born were hands
Every Farmer Understands
Every Tear from Every Eye
Becomes a Babe in Eternity
This is caught by Females bright
70 And returnd to its own delight
The Bleat the Bark Bellow & Roar
Are Waves that Beat on Heavens Shore
The Babe that weeps the Rod beneath
Writes Revenge in realms of death
75 The Beggars Rags fluttering in Air
Does to Rags the Heavens tear
The Soldier armd with Sword & Gun
Palsied strikes the Summers Sun[4]
The poor Mans Farthing[5] is worth more
80 Than all the Gold on Africs° Shore.   Africa's
One Mite[6] wrung from the Labrers° hands   Laborer's
Shall buy & sell the Misers Lands
Or if protected from on high
Does that whole Nation sell & buy
85 He who mocks the Infants Faith
Shall be mock'd in Age & Death
He who shall teach the Child to Doubt

The rotting Grave shall neer° get out   never
He who respects the Infants faith
90 Triumphs over Hell & Death
The Childs Toys & the Old Mans Reasons
Are the Fruits of the Two seasons
The Questioner who sits so sly
Shall never know how to Reply
95 He who replies to words of Doubt
Doth put the Light of Knowledge out
The Strongest Poison ever known
Came from Caesars Laurel Crown[7]
Nought can Deform the Human Race
100 Like to the Armours iron brace
When Gold & Gems adorn the Plow
To peaceful Arts shall Envy Bow
A Riddle or the Crickets Cry
Is to Doubt a fit Reply
105 The Emmets° Inch & Eagles Mile   ant's
Make Lame Philosophy to smile
He who Doubts from what he sees
Will neer Believe do what you Please
If the Sun & Moon should Doubt
110 Theyd immediately Go out
To be in a Passion you Good may do
But no Good if a Passion is in you
The Whore & Gambler by the State
Licencd build that Nations Fate
115 The Harlots cry from Street to Street
Shall weave Old Englands winding Sheet[8]
The Winners Shout the Losers Curse
Dance before dead Englands Hearse
Every Night & every Morn
120 Some to Misery are Born
Every Morn & every Night
Some are Born to sweet delight
Some are Born to sweet delight

---

1 *Misers Bags* Money bags of someone who hoards wealth.

2 *twine* String made of two threads twisted together.

3 *swadling Bands* Swaddling blankets.

4 *Palsied … Sun* Renders the summer sun powerless, as though it had suffered a stroke.

5 *Farthing* Quarter of a penny.

6 *Mite* Coin of very low value.

7 *Caesars Laurel Crown* Roman commanders were crowned with laurel wreaths during celebrations of their military victories; when Julius Caesar became dictator, he was awarded the honor of wearing a laurel wreath all the time, not just during a celebration. Caesar's seizure of power and resulting assassination led to the end of the Roman Republic and the beginning of autocratic rule under the emperors.

8 *winding Sheet* Sheet that wraps a corpse; a burial sheet or shroud.

Some are Born to Endless Night
25 We are led to Believe a Lie
When we see not Thro the Eye
Which was Born in a Night to perish in a Night
When the Soul Slept in Beams of Light
God Appears & God is Light

130 To those poor Souls who dwell in Night
But does a Human Form Display
To those who Dwell in Realms of day
—1863 (MANUSCRIPT 1807)

In Context

"A Most Extraordinary Man"

Contemporary documents provide a vivid sense of the degree to which Blake was an extraordinary original. Following are excerpts from a letter written by Charles Lamb to Bernard Barton in 1824, and from a biography by John Thomas Smith of the sculptor Joseph Nollekens, in which Smith published as part of a supplement recollections of Blake, whom he had been acquainted with for some 40 years.

from Charles Lamb, Letter to Bernard Barton,[1] 15 May 1824

Dear B.B.,

… **B**lake is a real name, I assure you, and a most extraordinary man, if he be still living. He is the Robert Blake whose wild designs accompany a splendid folio edition of the Night Thoughts, which you may have seen, in one of which he pictures the parting of soul and body by a solid mass of human form floating off, God knows how, from a lumpish mass (facsimile to itself) left behind on the dying bed. He paints in water colours, marvellous strange pictures, visions of his brain which he asserts that he has seen. They have great merit. He has *seen* the old Welch bards on Snowdon[2]—he has seen the Beautifullest, the Strongest, and the Ugliest Man, left alone from the Massacre of the Britons by the Romans, and has painted them from memory (I have seen his paintings) and asserts them to be as good as the figures of Raphael and Angelo, but not better, as they had precisely the same retro-visions and prophetic visions with himself. The painters in oil (which he will have it that neither of them practised) he affirms to have been the ruin of art, and affirms that all the while he was engaged in his water-paintings, Titian[3] was disturbing him, Titian the Ill Genius of Oil Painting. His pictures, one

---

[1] *Bernard Barton* Barton had seen a copy of Blake's "The Chimney Sweeper" when Lamb submitted it for publication as part of a project undertaken by the Society for Ameliorating the Condition of Infant Chimney-Sweepers. Barton assumed "Blake" to be a pseudonym of Lamb's. Here Lamb corrects him, though he also gets Blake's first name wrong (Robert was the name of Blake's brother) and confuses Blake's *Night Thoughts* engravings with his engravings for Robert Blair's poem *The Grave*.

[2] *Snowdon* Mountain in northern Wales, under which, according to legend, Arthur and his knights lie sleeping.

[3] *Titian* Italian painter of the sixteenth century.

in particular, the Canterbury Pilgrims (far above Stothard's),[1] have great merit, but hard, dry, yet with grace. He has written a catalogue of them, with a most spirited criticism on Chaucer, but mystical and full of vision. His poems have been sold hitherto only in manuscript. I never read them, but a friend at my desire procured the Sweep Song. There is one to a Tiger, which I have heard recited, beginning

> Tiger Tiger burning bright
> Thro' the deserts of the night—

which is glorious. But alas! I have not the book, for the man is flown, whither I know not, to Hades, or a mad house—but I must look on him as one of the most extraordinary persons of the age. ...

Yours ever truly,

C.L.

from John Thomas Smith, *Nollekens and His Times*[2] (1828)

Much about this time,[3] Blake wrote many other songs, to which he also composed tunes. These he would occasionally sing to his friends; and though, according to his confession, he was entirely unacquainted with the science of music, his ear was so good that his tunes were sometimes most singularly beautiful, and were noted down by musical professors. As for his later poetry, if it may be so called, attached to his plates, though it was certainly in some parts enigmatically curious as to its application, yet it was not always wholly uninteresting; and I have unspeakable pleasure in being able to state that, though I admit he did not for the last forty years attend any place of divine worship, yet he was not a freethinker,[4] as some invidious detractors have thought proper to assert, nor was he ever in any degree irreligious. Through life, his Bible was every thing with him. ...

In his choice of subjects, and in his designs in art, perhaps no man had higher claim to originality, nor ever drew with a closer adherence to his own conception; and from what I knew of him, and have heard related by his friends, I most firmly believe few artists have been guilty of less plagiarisms than he. It is true, I have seen him admire and heard him expatiate upon the beauties of Marcantonio and of Albrecht Dürer;[5] but I verily believe not with any view of borrowing an idea. ...

After his marriage, which took place at Battersea, and which proved a mutually happy one, he instructed his *beloved,* for so he most frequently called his Kate, and allowed her, till the last moment of his practice, to take off his proof impressions and print his works, which she did most carefully, and ever delighted in the task: nay, she became a draughtswoman; and as a convincing proof that she and her husband were born for each other's comfort, she not only entered cheerfully into his views,

---

[1] *Stothard*   London painter and engraver.

[2] *Nollekens ... Times*   Smith added memoirs of other noted artists such as Blake to his biography of portrait sculptor Joseph Nollekens.

[3] *this time*   Around 1780.

[4] *freethinker*   One who refuses to allow his or her reason to be dominated by religious faith.

[5] *Marcantonio*   Marcantonio Raimondi, a sixteenth-century Italian engraver known for his skill at reproducing pieces of artwork in prints, and for his method of cross-hatching to produce the appearance of depth; *Albrecht Dürer*   Sixteenth-century printmaker and art theorist from Nuremberg.

but, what is curious, possessed a similar power of imbibing ideas, and has produced drawings equally original, and, in some respects, interesting.

Blake's peace of mind, as well as that of his Catherine, was much broken by the death of their brother Robert,[1] who was a most amicable link in their happiness; and, as a proof how much Blake respected him, whenever he beheld him in his visions, he implicitly attended to his opinion and advice as to his future projected works. I should have stated that Blake was supereminently endowed with the power of disuniting all other thoughts from his mind whenever he wished to indulge in thinking of any particular subject; and so firmly did he believe, by this abstracting power, that the objects of his compositions were before him in his mind's eye, that he frequently believed them to be speaking to him. This I shall now illustrate by the following narrative.

Blake, after deeply perplexing himself as to the mode of accomplishing the publication of his illustrated songs, without their being subject to the expense of letter-press, his brother Robert stood before him in one of his visionary imaginations, and so decidedly directed him in the way in which he ought to proceed, that he immediately followed his advice by writing his poetry, and drawing his marginal subjects of embellishments in outline, upon the copper-plate with an impervious liquid, and then eating the plain parts or lights away with aquafortis considerably below them, so that the outlines were left as a stereotype. The plates in this state were then printed in any tint that he wished, to enable him or Mrs. Blake to colour the marginal figures up by hand in imitation of drawings. …

Blake and his wife were known to have lived so happily together, that they might unquestionably have been registered at Dunmow.[2] "Their hopes and fears were to each other known," and their days and nights were passed in each other's company, for he always painted, drew, engraved and studied in the same room where they grilled, boiled, stewed, and slept; and so steadfastly attentive was he to his beloved tasks, that for the space of two years he had never once been out of his house; and his application was often so incessant that in the middle of the night he would, after thinking deeply upon a particular subject, leap from his bed and write for two hours or more; and for many years he made a constant practice of lighting the fire and putting on the kettle for breakfast before his Kate awoke.

During his last illness, which was occasioned by the gall mixing with his blood, he was frequently bolstered-up in his bed to complete his drawings, for his intended illustration of Dante; an author so great a favourite with him, that though he agreed with Fuseli and Flaxman[3] in thinking Carey's translation superior to all others, yet, at the age of sixty-three years, he learned the Italian language purposely to enjoy Dante in the highest possible way. For this intended work, he produced seven engraved plates of an imperial quarto size, and nearly one hundred finished drawings of a size considerably larger; which will do equal justice to his wonderful mind, and the liberal heart of their possessor, who engaged him upon so delightful a task at a time when few persons would venture to give him employment, and whose kindness softened, for the remainder of his life, his lingering bodily sufferings, which he was seen to support with the most Christian fortitude.

On the day of his death, August 12th, 1827, he composed and uttered songs to his Maker so sweetly to the ear of his Catherine, that when she stood to hear him, he, looking upon her most

---

[1] *death … Robert*   In 1787.

[2] *Dunmow*   To this day, the village of Dunmow awards a side of bacon every four years to any couple who can prove that they have lived in complete harmony for a year and a day.

[3] *Fuseli and Flaxman*   Henry Fuseli (1741–1825), a painter and art critic, and John Flaxman, an English sculptor and designer (1755–1826).

affectionately, said, "My beloved, they are not mine—no—they are not mine." He expired at six in the evening, with the most cheerful serenity. Some short time before his death, Mrs. Blake asked him where he should like to be buried, and whether he would have the dissenting minister, or the clergyman of the Church of England, to read the service. His answers were, that as far as his own feelings were concerned, they might bury him where she pleased, adding that as his father, mother, aunt, and brother were buried in Bunhill row, perhaps it would be better to lie there, but as to service, he should wish for that of the Church of England.

MARY ROBINSON
1758 – 1800

Mary Robinson was the author of an extraordinary body of work—groundbreaking poetry, important novels and plays, and influential works of prose non-fiction. Increasingly, she is coming to be recognized as one of the most important writers of the Romantic period. To some extent her genius was recognized in her own time (admirers of her poetry included Samuel Coleridge and William Wordsworth), and certainly her work enjoyed considerable popularity. But both during her lifetime and for several succeeding generations interest in her personal life far exceeded interest in her literary work. The wife of a husband so profligate that he at one point forced his entire family into debtors' prison, Robinson became an independent woman who supported herself through writing and acting. Eventually she also became the acknowledged mistress of some of the leading men of the day, including the future king of England. Inevitably, her independent behavior became fuel for gossip—but her battle to support herself also provided fuel for her non-fiction writings that argued against the subordination of women.

Mary Darby was born in Bristol in 1758, the third of five children. Her father was a naval captain who soon deserted the family, supporting them only sporadically thereafter. Their strained finances led to an irregular education for the young girl. She was taught some Latin, French, and Italian, and for a time she attended school. She was forced to help support the family by teaching English in a school her mother had opened. In 1774, at the age of 15, she was duped into marrying Thomas Robinson, whom she believed to be a man of means. It was only after the marriage had taken place that she found out that he was the illegitimate son of a man who had made no promises to leave him any inheritance. Thomas Robinson was in serious financial straits, and the couple had to flee London to Wales to escape his creditors. It was there that their daughter Mary was born later that year. Creditors soon caught up with them, however, forcing the family to reside in King's Bench prison for 15 months. While in prison Robinson began composing poetry, in part to raise funds. The resulting volume, *Captivity, A Poem* (1775), prompted the Duchess of Devonshire to become her patron.

On her release Robinson began to work in the theater to support herself. She made her acting debut as Shakespeare's Juliet and was on the stage for four years, garnering considerable fame. She also began to write for the stage and in 1778 played a role in one of her own plays, *The Lucky Escape*. In 1779, she became known as "the exquisite Perdita" for her role in *A Winter's Tale*. After seeing her performance, the young Prince of Wales requested an audience and soon was insisting she become his mistress (she was then separated from her husband). During this period of her life she was more notorious for her relationship with the Prince than she was renowned for her writing, and the press and cartoonists had a field day with the very public affair: "The Perdita is a prodigious fine clean bottomed vessel, and had taken many prizes during her cruise, particularly the Florizel [i.e., the

Prince], a most valuable ship belonging to the Crown, but which was immediately released, after taking out the cargo."

Robinson became the mistress of other men—most notably Banastre Tarleton, a distinguished but dissolute officer—in subsequent years, and she returned to writing to support herself. In the early 1790s she published a substantial amount of non-fiction prose, two books of poetry, several plays, and six novels, supporting herself, her mother, and her young daughter (and often Tarleton) on the proceeds. Novels such as *Vancenza* (1792), *The Widow* (1794), *Angelina* (1796), and *Walsingham* (1797) were lucrative and popular, and went through many editions as well as translations into German and French.

Robinson's poetry came to be seen as embodying the characteristics of the Della Cruscan movement. Here is how those characteristics were described in a July 1791 notice reviewing Robinson's first volume of poems in the *Critical Review*:

> Within a very few years, a race of versifiers has sprung up, determined to claim ... the merit of novelty in expression, in unusual figure and striking combination. Rejecting the accustomed modes of description and phraseology, these fastidious writers seem fond of introducing uncommon terms and ideas, to provoke attention and excite admiration.

It is an interesting reflection of the times that these comments were intended to be taken as highly *critical* of the Della Cruscan School. Subsequent generations, when they did not ignore the Della Cruscans altogether, also tended to deride them for what was claimed to be a tendency toward poetic extravagance and emotional excess. Not all eras respond negatively to "novelty in expression, in unusual figure and striking combination," however, and the theatricality of Della Cruscan verse has in recent years begun to excite critical interest and admiration rather than ridicule. Moreover, it has increasingly come to be recognized that, above and beyond the element of theatricality in Robinson's verse, the feelings conveyed by it are powerful and convincing; she is among the leading poets of sensibility—of intelligent feeling and of intellect.

Nowhere in Robinson's poetry is that union more powerfully expressed than in her 1796 volume *Sappho and Phaon*, a sequence of 44 sonnets that offers an expressive treatment of the story of the Greek poet from the Island of Lesbos who, according to legend, fell desperately in love with Phaon and leapt from a cliff to her death after he abandoned her. The sequence provides an extended passionate discourse on the themes of reason and passion, love and art.

Robinson's last collection was a volume she described as consisting "of Tales, serious and gay, on a variety of subjects in the manner of Wordsworth's Lyrical Ballads." There are indeed close links between the two volumes; Robinson's "All Alone" parallels Wordsworth's "We Are Seven," her "Golfre" parallels Coleridge's "Rime of the Ancient Mariner," and so on. It would be a mistake, however, to regard the tales merely as derivative. Less bucolic than those of Wordsworth, they are more closely in touch with life's often grim realities. They are also in some respects more political; certainly "The Negro Girl" is a notable expression of abolitionist as well as of romantic sentiment. Robinson's strongest political statements, however, were on the subject of gender equality. In *A Letter to the Women of England, on the Injustice of the Marital Insubordination* (1791, published originally under the pseudonym Anne Francis Randall), she argued strongly and persuasively against the oppression of women through marriage.

Robinson suffered ill health in her last 15 years, and although she published *Lyrical Tales* in 1800, by the spring she was too ill to write, and she died later that year. Her unfinished memoirs were published by her daughter after her death.

⌘ ⌘ ⌘

January, 1795

1

Pavement slip'ry; people sneezing;
  Lords in ermine, beggars freezing;
Nobles, scarce the wretched heeding;
  Gallant soldiers—fighting!—bleeding!

2

5 Lofty mansions, warm and spacious;
  Courtiers, cringing and voracious:
Titled gluttons, dainties carving;
  Genius, in a garret, starving!

3

Wives, who laugh at passive spouses;
10 Theatres, and meeting-houses;
Balls, where simp'ring misses languish;
  Hospitals, and groans of anguish.

4

Arts and sciences bewailing;
  Commerce drooping, credit failing!
15 Placemen,[1] mocking subjects loyal;
  Separations; weddings royal!

5

Authors, who can't earn a dinner;
  Many a subtle° rogue, a winner!   crafty
Fugitives, for shelter seeking,
20 Misers hoarding, tradesmen breaking!

6

Ladies gambling, night and morning;
  Fools, the works of genius scorning!

Ancient dames for girls mistaken,
  Youthful damsels—quite forsaken!

7

25 Some in luxury delighting;
  More in talking than in fighting;
Lovers old, and beaux decrepit;
  Lordlings, empty and insipid.

8

Poets, painters, and musicians;
30 Lawyers, doctors, politicians;
Pamphlets, newspapers, and odes,
  Seeking fame, by diff'rent roads.

9

Taste and talents quite deserted;
  All the laws of Truth perverted;
35 Arrogance o'er merit soaring!
  Merit, silently deploring!

10

Gallant souls with empty purses;
  Gen'rals, only fit for nurses!
Schoolboys, smit with martial spirit,
40 Taking place of vet'ran merit!

11

Honest men, who can't get place;
  Knaves, who show unblushing faces;
Ruin hasten'd, peace retarded!
  Candour spurn'd, and art° rewarded.   artifice
—1795

---

[1] *Placemen* Men appointed to positions of power, often because of self-interested motives.

from *Sappho and Phaon: In a Series of Legitimate Sonnets, with Thoughts on Poetical Subjects, and Anecdotes of the Grecian Poetess*

4

Why, when I gaze on Phaon's[1] beauteous eyes,
    Why does each thought in wild disorder stray?
    Why does each fainting faculty decay,
And my chill'd breast in throbbing tumults rise?
5 Mute, on the ground my lyre neglected lies,
    The Muse forgot, and lost the melting lay;[2]
    My down-cast looks, my faltering lips betray,
That stung by hopeless passion, Sappho[3] dies!
    Now, on a bank of cypress[4] let me rest;
10 Come, tuneful maids, ye pupils of my care,[5]
    Come, with your dulcet numbers soothe my breast;
    And, as the soft vibrations float on air,
    Let pity waft my spirit to the blest,
To mock the barb'rous triumphs of despair!

12

Now, o'er the tessellated pavement[6] strew
    Fresh saffron, steep'd in essence of the rose,
    While down yon agate column gently flows
A glitt'ring streamlet of ambrosial[7] dew!
5 My Phaon smiles! the rich carnation's hue,
    On his flush'd cheek in conscious lustre glows,
    While o'er his breast enamour'd Venus[8] throws
Her starry mantle of celestial blue!
    Breathe soft, ye dulcet flutes, among the trees

Where clust'ring boughs with golden citron twine;
    While slow vibrations, dying on the breeze,
Shall soothe his soul with harmony divine!
    Then let my form his yielding fancy seize,
And all his fondest wishes, blend with mine.

18

Why art thou chang'd? O Phaon! tell me why?
    Love flies reproach, when passion feels decay;
    Or, I would paint the raptures of that day,
When, in sweet converse, mingling sigh with sigh,
5 I mark'd the graceful languor of thine eye
    As on a shady bank entranc'd we lay:
    O! Eyes! whose beamy radiance stole away
As stars fade trembling from the burning sky!
    Why art thou chang'd? dear source of all my woes?
10 Though dark my bosom's tint, through ev'ry vein
    A ruby tide of purest lustre flows,
Warm'd by thy love, or chill'd by thy disdain;
    And yet no bliss this sensate being knows;
Ah! why is rapture so allied to pain?

30

O'er the tall cliff that bounds the billowy main
    Shad'wing the surge that sweeps the lonely
        strand,°   *shore*
    While the thin vapours break along the sand,
Day's harbinger unfolds the liquid plain.
5 The rude sea murmurs, mournful as the strain
    That love lorn minstrels strike with trembling hand,
    While from their green beds rise the Siren band[9]
With tongues aerial° to repeat my pain!   *ethereal*
    The vessel rocks beside the pebbly shore,
10 The foamy curls its gaudy trappings lave;°   *wash*
    Oh! Bark[10] propitious! bear me gently o'er,
Breathe soft, ye winds; rise slow, O! swelling wave!
    Lesbos;[11] these eyes shall meet thy sands no more:
I fly, to seek my lover, or my grave!

---

[1] *Phaon* Boatman with whom Sappho was said to be in love.

[2] *melting lay* Touching song.

[3] *Sappho* In Roman legend, the poet Sappho (630 BCE) was Phaon's lover. When he rejected her, she threw herself off a cliff into the sea and drowned.

[4] *cypress* Cypress was a symbol of mourning.

[5] *tuneful maids ... care* According to legend, Sappho was head of a girls' school.

[6] *tessellated pavement* Paving stones arranged like a mosaic.

[7] *ambrosial* Ambrosia is the drink of the gods.

[8] *Venus* Roman goddess of love.

[9] *Siren band* Mythological sea nymphs who lured sailors to their deaths with their enchanting singing.

[10] *Bark* Small ship.

[11] *Lesbos* Island in the Aegean sea; home of Sappho.

37

When, in the gloomy mansion of the dead,
    This with'ring heart, this faded form shall sleep:
    When these fond[1] eyes, at length shall cease to weep,
And earth's cold lap receive this fev'rish head:
5 Envy shall turn away, a tear to shed,
    And Time's obliterating pinions° sweep   *feathers*
    The spot, where poets shall their vigils keep,
To mourn and wander near my freezing bed!
    Then, my pale ghost, upon th' Elysian shore,[2]
10 Shall smile, releas'd from ev'ry mortal care;
    While, doom'd love's victim to repine°   *complain*
      no more,
My breast shall bathe in endless rapture there!
    Ah! no! my restless shade would still deplore,
Nor taste that bliss, which Phaon did not share.
—1796

The Poor, Singing Dame

Beneath an old wall, that went round an old castle,
    For many a year, with brown ivy o'erspread;
A neat little hovel, its lowly roof raising,
    Defied the wild winds that howled over its shed:
5 The turrets, that frowned on the poor simple dwelling,
    Were rocked to and fro, when the tempest would
      roar,
And the river, that down the rich valley was swelling,
    Flowed swiftly beside the green step of its door.
The summer sun gilded the rushy-roof[3] slanting,
10   The bright dews bespangled its ivy-bound hedge
And above, on the ramparts, the sweet birds were
      chanting,
    And wild buds thick dappled the clear river's edge.
When the castle's rich chambers were haunted, and
      dreary,
    The poor little hovel was still, and secure;
15 And no robber e'er entered, nor goblin nor fairy,

For the splendours of pride had no charms to allure.
The lord of the castle, a proud, surly ruler,
    Oft heard the low dwelling with sweet music ring:
For the old dame that lived in the little hut
    cheerly,°   *cheerfully*
20 Would sit at her wheel, and would merrily sing:
When with revels the castle's great hall was resounding,
    The old dame was sleeping, not dreaming of fear;
And when over the mountains the huntsmen were
      bounding
    She would open her wicket,[4] their clamours to hear.
25 To the merry-toned horn, she would dance on the
      threshold;
    And louder, and louder, repeat her old song:
And when winter its mantle of frost was displaying
    She carolled, undaunted, the bare woods among:
She would gather dry fern, ever happy and singing,
30   With her cake of brown bread, and her jug of brown
      beer,
And would smile when she heard the great castle-bell
      ringing,
    Inviting the proud—to their prodigal[5] cheer.
Thus she lived, ever patient and ever contented,
    Till envy the lord of the castle possessed,
35 For he hated that poverty should be so cheerful,
    While care could the fav'rites of fortune molest;
He sent his bold yeomen with threats to prevent her,
    And still would she carol her sweet roundelay;[6]
At last, an old steward relentless he sent her—
40   Who bore her, all trembling, to prison away!
Three weeks did she languish, then died broken-hearted,
    Poor dame! how the death-bell did mournfully
      sound!
And along the green path six young bachelors[7] bore her,
    And laid her, for ever, beneath the cold ground!
45 And the primroses pale 'mid the long grass were growing,
    The bright dews of twilight bespangled her grave
And morn heard the breezes of summer soft blowing

---

1 *fond* Infatuated, foolish.

2 *Elysian shore* In Greek mythology, Elysium was a section of the underworld where virtuous souls went after death.

3 *rushy-roof* Thatched roof made with bundles of straw or rush.

4 *wicket* Small gate or door.

5 *prodigal* Lavish or extravagant in their use of money and resources.

6 *roundelay* Song with a recurring phrase or refrain.

7 *bachelors* Here, knights in service to the lord of the castle.

To bid the fresh flow'rets° in sympathy   *small flowers*
    wave.
The lord of the castle, from that fatal moment
50   When poor singing Mary was laid in her grave,
Each night was surrounded by screech-owls appalling,
    Which o'er the black turrets their pinions°   *wings*
    would wave!
On the ramparts that frowned on the river, swift flowing,
    They hovered, still hooting a terrible song,
55 When his windows would rattle, the winter blast
    blowing,
    They would shriek like a ghost, the dark alleys
    among!
Wherever he wandered they followed him crying,
    At dawnlight, at eve, still they haunted his way!
When the moon shone across the wide common, they
    hooted,
60   Nor quitted his path, till the blazing of day.
His bones began wasting, his flesh was decaying,
    And he hung his proud head, and he perished with
    shame;
And the tomb of rich marble, no soft tear displaying,
    O'ershadows the grave, of the poor singing dame!
—1800

The Haunted Beach

Upon a lonely desert beach
    Where the white foam was scatter'd,
A little shed uprear'd its head
    Though lofty barks[1] were shatter'd.
5 The seaweeds gathering near the door,
    A sombre path display'd;
And, all around, the deafening roar,
Re-echo'd on the chalky shore,
    By the green billows° made.   *waves*

10 Above, a jutting cliff was seen
    Where sea birds hover'd, craving;

And all around, the crags were bound
    With weeds, forever waving.
And here and there, a cavern wide
15   Its shad'wy jaws display'd;
And near the sand, at ebb of tide,
A shiver'd mast was seen to ride
    Where the green billows stray'd.

And often, while the morning wind
20   Stole o'er the summer ocean,
The moonlight scene was all serene,
    The waters scarce in motion:
Then, while the smoothly slanting sand
    The tall cliff wrapp'd in shade,
25 The fisherman beheld a band
Of spectres,° gliding hand in hand,   *ghosts*
    Where the green billows play'd.

And pale their faces were, as snow,
    And sullenly they wander'd;
30 And to the skies, with hollow eyes
    They look'd, as tho' they ponder'd.
And sometimes from their hammock shroud,[2]
    They dismal howlings made,
And while the blast blew strong and loud
35 The clear moon mark'd the ghastly crowd,
    Where the green billows play'd!

And then, above the haunted hut
    The curlews,[3] screaming, hover'd;
And the low door with furious roar
40   The frothy breakers cover'd.
For, in the fisherman's lone shed
    A murder'd man was laid,
With ten wide gashes on his head
And deep was made his sandy bed
45   Where the green billows play'd.

A shipwreck'd mariner was he,
    Doom'd from his home to sever;

---

1   *barks*   Small ships.

2   *hammock shroud*   Hammocks were used as shrouds to bury corpses at sea.

3   *curlews*   Long-legged seabirds, similar to sandpipers.

Who swore to be thro' wind and sea
    Firm and undaunted ever!
50 And when the wave resistless roll'd,
    About his arm he made
A packet rich of Spanish gold,
And, like a British sailor, bold,
    Plung'd where the billows play'd!

55 The spectre band, his messmates brave
    Sunk in the yawning ocean,
While to the mast he lash'd him fast
    And brav'd the storm's commotion.
The winter moon, upon the sand
60   A silv'ry carpet made,
And mark'd the sailor reach the land,
And mark'd his murd'rer wash his hand
    Where the green billows play'd.

And since that hour the fisherman
65   Has toil'd, and toil'd in vain!
For all the night, the moony light
    Gleams on the spectre'd main!
And when the skies are veil'd in gloom,
    The murd'rer's liquid way
70 Bounds o'er the deeply yawning tomb,
And flashing fires the sands illume,
    Where the green billows play!

Full thirty years his task has been,
    Day after day, more weary;
75 For heav'n design'd his guilty mind
    Should dwell on prospects dreary.
Bound by a strong and mystic chain,
    He has not power to stray;
But destin'd mis'ry to sustain,
80 He wastes, in solitude and pain,
    A loathsome life away.
    —1800

London's Summer Morning

Who has not wak'd to list° the busy sounds   *hear*
    Of summer's morning, in the sultry smoke
Of noisy London? On the pavement hot
The sooty chimney-boy, with dingy face
5 And tatter'd covering, shrilly bawls his trade,
Rousing the sleepy housemaid. At the door
The milk-pail rattles, and the tinkling bell
Proclaims the dustman's[1] office; while the street
Is lost in clouds impervious. Now begins
10 The din of hackney-coaches,[2] wagons, carts;
While tinmen's shops, and noisy trunk-makers,
Knife-grinders, coopers, squeaking cork-cutters,
Fruit-barrows, and the hunger-giving cries
Of vegetable vendors, fill the air.
15 Now ev'ry shop displays its varied trade,
And the fresh-sprinkled pavement cools the feet
Of early walkers. At the private door
The ruddy house-maid twirls the busy mop,
Annoying the smart 'prentice,° or neat girl   *apprentice*
20 Tripping with band-box[3] lightly. Now the sun
Darts burning splendor on the glitt'ring pane,
Save where the canvas awning throws a shade
On the gay merchandise. Now, spruce and trim,
In shops (where beauty smiles with industry)
25 Sits the smart damsel; while the passenger
Peeps through the window, watching ev'ry charm.
Now pastry dainties catch the eyes minute
Of humming insects, while the slimy snare
Waits to enthral them. Now the lamp-lighter
30 Mounts the slight ladder, nimbly venturous,
To trim the half-fill'd lamp; while at his feet
The pot-boy[4] yells discordant! All along
The sultry pavement, the old-clothes-man cries
In tone monotonous, and side-long views
35 The area for his traffic: now the bag

---

[1] *dustman* Garbage collector.

[2] *hackney-coaches* Horse-drawn carriages for hire.

[3] *band-box* Box for collars, hats, gloves, and other items.

[4] *pot-boy* Boy employed by a tavern to bring beer to customers at their tables.

Is slyly open'd, and the half-worn suit
(Sometimes the pilfer'd treasure of the base
Domestic spoiler)[1] for one half its worth,
Sinks in the green abyss. The porter now
40   Bears his huge load along the burning way;
And the poor poet wakes from busy dreams,
To paint the summer morning.
—1804

from *A Letter to the Women of England*

Custom, from the earliest periods of antiquity, has endeavoured to place the female mind in the subordinate ranks of intellectual sociability. WOMAN has ever been considered as a lovely and fascinating part of the creation, but her claims to mental equality have not only been questioned, by envious and interested sceptics; but, by a barbarous policy in the other sex, considerably depressed, for want of liberal and classical cultivation. I will not expatiate largely on the doctrines of certain philosophical sensualists, who have aided in this destructive oppression, because an illustrious British female, (whose death has not been sufficiently lamented, but to whose genius posterity will render justice) has already written volumes in vindication of *The Rights of Woman*.[2] But I shall endeavour to prove that, under the present state of mental subordination, universal knowledge is not only benumbed and blighted, but true happiness, originating in enlightened manners, retarded in its progress. Let WOMAN once assert her proper sphere, unshackled by prejudice, and unsophisticated by vanity; and pride (the noblest species of pride), will

establish her claims to the participation of power, both mentally and corporeally. ...

In what is woman inferior to man? In some instances, but not always, in corporeal strength; in activity of mind, she is his equal. Then, by this rule, if she is to endure oppression in proportion as she is deficient in muscular power *only*, through all the stages of animation the weaker should give precedence to the stronger. Yet we should find a Lord of the Creation with a puny frame, reluctant to confess the superiority of a lusty peasant girl whom nature had endowed with that bodily strength of which luxury had bereaved him.

The question is simply this: is woman persecuted and oppressed because she is the *weaker* creature? Supposing that to be the order of Nature, let me ask these human despots whether a woman of strong mental and corporeal powers is born to yield obedience, merely because she is a woman, to those shadows of mankind who exhibit the effeminacy of women united with the mischievous foolery of monkeys? I remember once to have heard one of those modern Hannibals[3] confess that he had changed his regiments three times because the regimentals were unbecoming.

If woman be the weaker creature, why is she employed in laborious avocations? Why compelled to endure the fatigue of household drudgery; to scrub, to scour, to labour, both late and early, while the powdered lackey only waits at the chair, or behind the carriage of his employer? Why are women, in many parts of the kingdom, permitted to follow the plough; to perform the laborious business of the dairy; to work in our manufactories; to wash, to brew, and to bake, while men are employed in measuring lace and ribands; folding gauzes; composing artificial bouquets; fancying feathers, and mixing cosmetics for the preservation of beauty? I have seen, and every inhabitant of the metropolis may, during the summer season, behold strong Welsh girls carrying on their heads strawberries, and other fruits from the vicinity of London to Covent-Garden market, in heavy loads which they repeat three, four, and five

---

[1]   *base / Domestic spoiler*   Unscrupulous thieving servant.

[2]   [Robinson's note]   The writer of this letter, though avowedly of the same school, disdains the drudgery of servile imitation. The same subject may be argued in a variety of ways; and though this letter may not display the philosophical reasoning with which "The Rights of Woman" abounded; it is not less suited to the purpose. For it requires a *legion of Wollstonecrafts* to undermine the poisons of prejudice and malevolence. [See chapter 2 of Mary Wollstonecraft's *A Vindication of the Rights of Woman* for a discussion of the dangers male philosophies posed to women.]

---

[3]   *Hannibal*   Fearless Carthaginian general of the Second Punic War.

times, daily, for a very small pittance; while the male domestics of our nobility are revelling in luxury, to which even their lords are strangers. Are women thus compelled to labour, because they are of the weaker sex?

In my travels some years since through France and Germany, I often remember having seen stout girls, from the age of seventeen to twenty-five, employed in the most fatiguing and laborious avocations; such as husbandry,[1] watering horses, and sweeping the public streets. Were they so devoted to toil because they were the weaker creatures? and would not a modern *petit maître*[2] have fainted beneath the powerful grasp of one of these rustic or domestic Amazons?[3] …

It is not by precept but by example that conviction strikes deeply into the thinking mind. Man is supposed to be the more wise and more rational creature; his faculties are more liberally expanded by classical education; he is supposed to be more enlightened by an unlimited intercourse with society. He is permitted to assert the dignity of his character, to punish those who assail his reputation, and to assume a superiority over all his fellow creatures. He is not accountable to any mortal for the actions of his life; he may revel in the follies, indulge the vices of his superior nature. He pursues the pleasures or the eccentricities of his imagination with an avidity insatiable, and he perpetually proves that human passions subjugate him to the degradations of human frailty; while woman, the *weaker* animal, she whose enjoyments are limited, whose education, knowledge, and actions are circumscribed by the potent rule of prejudice, she is expected to *resist* temptation; to be invincible in fortitude, strong in prescient and reflecting powers, subtle in the defence of her own honor, and forbearing under all the conflicts of the passions. Man first degrades, and then deserts her. Yet, if driven by famine, insult, shame, and persecution, she rushes forth like the wolf for prey; if, like Millwood, she finds it "necessary to be rich" in this sordid, selfish world,[4] she is shunned, abhorred, condemned to the very lowest scenes of vile debasement; to exist in misery, or to perish unlamented. No kindred breast will pity her misfortunes; no pious tear embalm her ashes: she rushes into the arms of death as her last, her only, asylum from the monsters who have destroyed her.

Woman is destined to pursue no path in which she does not find an enemy. If she is liberal, generous, careless of wealth, friendly to the unfortunate, and bountiful to persecuted merit, she is deemed prodigal, and over-much profuse; all the good she does, every tear she steals from the downcast eye of modest worth, every sigh she converts into a throb of joy, in grateful bosoms, is, by the world, forgotten; while the ingenuous liberality of her soul excites the imputation of folly and extravagance. If, on the contrary, she is wary, shrewd, thrifty, economical, and eager to procure and to preserve the advantages of independence, she is condemned as narrow-minded, mean, unfeeling, artful, mercenary, and base: in either case she is exposed to censure. If liberal, unpitied; if sordid, execrated! In a few words, a generous woman is termed a fool; a prudent one, a miser. …

Had fortune enabled me, I would build an university for women, where they should be politely, and at the same time classically, educated; the depth of their studies should be proportioned to their mental powers; and those who were incompetent to the labours of knowledge should be dismissed after a fair trial of their capabilities and allotted to the more humble paths of life, such as domestic and useful occupations. The wealthy part of the community who neglected to educate their female offspring at this seminary of learning should pay a fine, which should be appropriated to the maintenance of the unportioned scholars. In

---

[1] *husbandry* Farming; agricultural labor.

[2] *petit maître* French: little master, i.e., dandy, fop.

[3] *Amazons* Mythical race of female warriors.

[4] *if … world* Reference to George Lillo's play *The London Merchant* (1731), in which Millwood seduces a young merchant's apprentice and convinces him first to steal money from his master, and then to kill his uncle and steal his fortune for her. In Act 4, she explains her actions by saying, "My soul disdained, and yet disdains, dependence and contempt. Riches, no matter by what means obtained, I saw secured the worst of men from both. I found it, therefore, necessary to be rich, and to that end I summoned all my arts."

half a century there would be a sufficient number of learned women to fill all the departments of the university, and those who excelled in an eminent degree should receive honorary medals, which they should wear as an Order of Literary Merit.

O! my unenlightened country-women! Read, and profit, by the admonition of Reason. Shake off the trifling, glittering shackles which debase you. Resist those fascinating spells, which, like the petrifying torpedo,[1] fasten on your mental faculties. Be less the slaves of vanity, and more the converts of Reflection. Nature has endowed you with personal attractions: she has also given you the mind capable of expansion. Seek not the visionary triumph of universal conquest; know yourselves equal to greater, nobler, acquirements: and by prudence, temperance, firmness, and reflection, subdue that prejudice which has, for ages past, been your inveterate enemy. Let your daughters be liberally, classically, philosophically, and usefully educated; let them speak and write their opinions freely; let them read and think like rational creatures, adapt their studies to their strength of intellect, expand their minds, and purify their hearts, by teaching them to feel their mental equality with their imperious rulers. By such laudable exertions you will excite the noblest emulation; you will explode the superstitious tenets of bigotry and fanaticism, confirm the intuitive immortality of the soul, and give them that genuine glow of conscious virtue which will grace them to posterity.

There are men who affect to think lightly of the literary productions of women: and yet no works of the present day are so universally read as theirs. The best novels that have been written since those of Smollett, Richardson, and Fielding[2] have been produced by women; and their pages have not only been embellished with the interesting events of domestic life, portrayed with all the elegance of phraseology and all the refinement of sentiment, but with forcible and eloquent political, theological, and philosophical reasoning. To the genius and labours of some enlightened British women posterity will also be indebted for the purest and best translations from the French and German languages. I need not mention Mrs. Dobson, Mrs. Inchbald, Miss Plumptre,[3] &c., &c. Of the more profound researches in the dead languages, we have many female classics of the first celebrity: Mrs. Carter, Mrs. Thomas (late Miss Parkhurst), Mrs. Francis, the Hon. Mrs. Damer,[4] &c., &c.

Of the drama, the wreath of fame has crowned the brows of Mrs. Cowley, Mrs. Inchbald, Miss Lee, Miss Hannah More,[5] and others of less celebrity. Of biography, Mrs. Dobson, Mrs. Thicknesse, Mrs. Piozzi, Mrs. Montagu, Miss Helen Williams, have given specimens highly honourable to their talents.[6] Poetry has unquestionably risen high in British literature from the productions of female pens; for many English women have produced such original and beautiful compositions that the first critics and scholars of the age have wondered, while they applauded.

—1799

[1] *torpedo* Type of flat fish now more commonly referred to as the electric ray.

[2] *Smollett* Tobias Smollett (1721–71); *Richardson* Samuel Richardson (1689–1761); *Fielding* Henry Fielding (1707–54).

[3] *Mrs. ... Plumptre* Three well-known translators: Susannah Dobson (?–1795) is known primarily for her *Life of Petrarch* (1775), translated from Jacques de Sade's original French, Elizabeth Inchbald (1753–1821) and Ann Plumptre both translated August von Kotzbue's German plays.

[4] *Mrs. Carter ... Damer* Elizabeth Carter (1717–1806) and Anne Francis were translators of classic Greek and Hebrew texts, respectively, while Anne Seymour Damer (1748–1828) was a famous sculptor and the niece of Horace Walpole.

[5] *Cowley* Hannah Cowley (1743–1809); *Inchbald* Elizabeth Inchbald (1753–1821); *Lee* Sophia Lee (1750–1824); *More* Hannah More (1745–1833).

[6] *Of biography ... talents* Susannah Dobson (?–1795) translated Jacques de Sade's *Life of Petrarch*; Ann Ford Thicknesse (1737–1824) wrote *Sketches of the Lives and Writings of the Ladies of France* (1778); Hester Lynch Thrale Piozzi (1741–1821) was best known for her *Anecdotes of the Late Samuel Johnson* (1786); Elizabeth Montagu (1720–1800) published *An Essay on the Writing and Genius of Shakespeare* (1769); and Helen Maria Williams (1761–1827) wrote *Memoirs of M. and Mme. Du Fossé*.

MARY WOLLSTONECRAFT
1759 – 1797

"Independence," Mary Wollstonecraft said, "I have long considered as the grand blessing of life." A key founder of feminist thought, Wollstonecraft was an unwavering advocate for political reform, for reducing the "unnatural distinctions" of class, and for educating women so they could achieve greater independence. When she died in 1797, she was a literary celebrity; her husband William Godwin wrote that she was "the firmest champion … her sex ever had to boast." Wollstonecraft has long been acknowledged as an important late eighteenth-century philosopher and writer, and *A Vindication of the Rights of Woman*, in particular, is widely read as a core text in the Western liberal tradition.

Wollstonecraft was born in London on 27 April 1759 to Elizabeth Dixon and Edward Wollstonecraft; she was the eldest daughter among seven children. The Wollstonecrafts were a middle-class, modestly prosperous family whose fortunes went into a gradual decline. Edward attempted to transform himself into a gentleman farmer, moving the family to Epping, to Barking, and finally to Beverley in Yorkshire. These moves exacerbated the family's financial difficulties. Wollstonecraft's father was also a violent man. As a child, Wollstonecraft frequently intervened in her father's outbursts in order to try to protect her mother. For solace and respite, she turned to her close friend Jane Arden. Arden's father, John, was a teacher and philosopher who encouraged Wollstonecraft's self-education and provided her with access to his library.

When Wollstonecraft was 15 the family moved to Hoxton, on the outskirts of London. Here, Wollstonecraft was befriended by her next-door neighbors, the Reverend and Mrs. Clare. They became her surrogate family and were responsible for introducing her to Fanny Blood, with whom she would develop an intensely passionate and possibly romantic friendship. Years later, Wollstone-craft described her connection to Blood as "a friendship so fervent, as for years to have constituted the ruling passion of my mind." Blood became the model for Ann in Wollstonecraft's autobiographical novel, *Mary, A Fiction.*

In 1778, Wollstonecraft made the decision to leave home and earn her own living. Now 19, she took a job as a paid companion to a Mrs. Dawson, a widow in Bath. When her mother became ill in 1781, however, Wollstonecrtaft returned to London to nurse her. After months of pain, Elizabeth Wollstonecraft died, and Mary took up residence with the Bloods. Shortly afterwards Wollstonecraft's sister Eliza married Meredith Bishop, a well-to-do shipwright. After Eliza gave birth to a daughter in 1783, she fell into a deep postpartum depression that Wollstonecraft attributed to Bishop's cruelty. Wanting to rescue her sister, Wollstonecraft convinced Eliza to run away from her husband and child. (At the time, children legally belonged to the father.) Bishop eventually gave up his attempts to bring his wife back, and their daughter died just days before her first birthday.

Wollstonecraft soon realized that she and Eliza would need to find their own source of financial support. In 1784, together with Fanny Blood, they opened a school at Newington Green, north of

London. Here, Wollstonecraft met Richard Price, a preacher and a leader of the Dissenters. His congregation was a Unitarian-like group whose political positions on freedom and equality influenced Wollstonecraft's developing ideas. In 1785, Fanny Blood left Newington Green to marry her longtime suitor, Hugh Skeys, in Lisbon. Wollstonecraft joined them several months later when she heard that Fanny was having trouble with her first pregnancy, but despite her efforts both Fanny and her child died a few days after the birth. Wollstonecraft returned to London where her school's financial problems had worsened during her absence. To raise money, she wrote her first book, *Thoughts on the Education of Daughters*. Joseph Johnson, a leading radical bookseller and a fellow Dissenter, published the book in 1787. The book's modest success was not enough to save the school, but it did establish Wollstonecraft in the debate on women's education.

Following the collapse of the school, Wollstonecraft became a governess to the Kingsborough family in Ireland, but it was not a happy development; she was doubtless drawing on experience when she later wrote that governesses "are not always treated in a manner calculated to render them respectable in the eyes of their pupils." She did, however, exert an apparently life-long influence on one of her pupils, who grew up to be a public champion of women's rights. Wollstonecraft soon fell into a depression that was diagnosed as nervous fever. She continued writing, though, beginning work on *Mary, A Fiction*. When she was dismissed from her position as governess, still within the year 1787, she returned to London and convinced Johnson to publish *Mary*. He also hired her as a reviewer for the *Analytical Review*, a monthly progressive periodical. Through her reviews she became an influential voice in the decade of ferment that was coming. Through Johnson, Wollstonecraft met Henry Fuseli, an artist and self-described genius. Although Fuseli was married, Wollstonecraft felt he was her soulmate, and they soon began an affair.

Wollstonecraft embraced the start of the French Revolution with excitement. When Edmund Burke published his *Reflections on the Revolution in France* (1790), a treatise that attacked revolutionary ideas, Johnson urged Wollstonecraft to write a reply. She quickly crafted *A Vindication of the Rights of Men*, published anonymously less than a month after the appearance of Burke's book. A few weeks later, a second edition was published under her name, and this solidified her reputation as a radical. In early 1792, she became famous throughout Europe when her new book, *A Vindication of the Rights of Woman*, was published. Written in only six weeks, *A Vindication* presented the case for universal rights, social equality, and women's economic independence. As Wollstonecraft pointed out, the refusal of those who had espoused revolutionary principles of equality to extend rights to women represented a betrayal of those supposedly universal principles.

Eager to obtain first-hand knowledge about the Revolution, and just as eager to escape her deteriorating affair with Fuseli, Wollstonecraft traveled to France in December 1792. There she met Gilbert Imlay, an American and a fellow radical whose lover she soon became. When she discovered she was pregnant, Imlay registered her at the American Embassy as his wife, even though they were not married, so that she could claim the protection of American citizenship. In May 1794, she gave birth to a daughter whom she called Fanny, and two months later Imlay returned to England, leaving mother and child alone. Wollstonecraft's *An Historical and Moral View of the French Revolution* was published in London later that year.

Wollstonecraft's relationship with Imlay was strained, and when she returned to London in April 1795 she discovered he had been unfaithful. Distraught, she attempted suicide but was prevented by him. As a way of distancing himself from her, as well as tracking some bothersome financial losses, Imlay sent her (with Fanny) to Scandinavia on a business trip. She returned to England in September to find him living with another woman. Outraged and increasingly depressed, Wollstonecraft

women in each, this hint is, for the present, sufficient; and I have only alluded to the subject because it appears to me to be the very essence of an introduction to give a cursory account of the contents of the work it introduces.

My own sex, I hope, will excuse me if I treat them like rational creatures, instead of flattering their fascinating graces and viewing them as if they were in a state of perpetual childhood, unable to stand alone. I earnestly wish to point out in what true dignity and human happiness consists: I wish to persuade women to endeavour to acquire strength, both of mind and body, and to convince them that the soft phrases, susceptibility of heart, delicacy of sentiment, and refinement of taste are almost synonymous with epithets of weakness, and that those beings who are only the objects of pity and that kind of love, which has been termed its sister, will soon become objects of contempt.

Dismissing then those pretty feminine phrases, which the men condescendingly use to soften our slavish dependence, and despising that weak elegancy of mind, exquisite sensibility, and sweet docility of manners supposed to be the sexual characteristics of the weaker vessel, I wish to show that elegance is inferior to virtue; that the first object of laudable ambition is to obtain a character as a human being, regardless of the distinction of sex; and that secondary views should be brought to this simple touchstone.

This is a rough sketch of my plan; and should I express my conviction with the energetic emotions that I feel whenever I think of the subject, the dictates of experience and reflection will be felt by some of my readers. Animated by this important object, I shall disdain to cull[1] my phrases or polish my style: I aim at being useful, and sincerity will render me unaffected; for, wishing rather to persuade by the force of my arguments than dazzle by the elegance of my language, I shall not waste my time in rounding periods,[2] or in fabricating the turgid bombast of artificial feelings, which, coming from the head, never reach the heart. I shall be employed about things, not words—and, anxious to render my sex more respectable members of society, I shall try to avoid that flowery diction which has slid from essays into novels, and from novels into familiar letters and conversation.

These pretty superlatives, dropping glibly from the tongue, vitiate[3] the taste and create a kind of sickly delicacy that turns away from simple unadorned truth; and a deluge of false sentiments and over-stretched feelings, stifling the natural emotions of the heart, render the domestic pleasures insipid that ought to sweeten the exercise of those severe duties that educate a rational and immortal being for a nobler field of action.

The education of women has, of late, been more attended to than formerly; yet they are still reckoned a frivolous sex, and ridiculed or pitied by the writers who endeavour by satire or instruction to improve them. It is acknowledged that they spend many of the first years of their lives in acquiring a smattering of accomplishments; meanwhile strength of body and mind are sacrificed to libertine[4] notions of beauty, to the desire of establishing themselves—the only way women can rise in the world—by marriage. And this desire making mere animals of them, when they marry they act as such children may be expected to act: they dress, they paint,[5] and nickname God's creatures.[6] Surely these weak beings are only fit for a seraglio![7] Can they be expected to govern a family with judgment, or take care of the poor babes whom they bring into the world?

If then it can be fairly deduced from the present conduct of the sex, from the prevalent fondness for pleasure—which takes place of ambition and those nobler passions that open and enlarge the soul—that the instruction which women have hitherto received has

---

[1] *cull* Choose carefully.

[2] *rounding periods* Crafting graceful sentences.

[3] *vitiate* Render impure, corrupt.

[4] *libertine* Licentious.

[5] *paint* I.e., wear make-up.

[6] *they dress … God's creatures* From Shakespeare's *Hamlet* 3.1.142–46: "I have heard of your paintings, well enough. God hath given you one face, and you make yourselves another. You jig and amble, and you lisp, you nickname God's creatures and make your wantonness your ignorance."

[7] *seraglio* Harem.

only tended, with the constitution of civil society, to render them insignificant objects of desire—mere propagators of fools! If it can be proved that in aiming to accomplish them without cultivating their understandings they are taken out of their sphere of duties, and made ridiculous and useless when the short-lived bloom of beauty is over,[1] I presume that rational men will excuse me for endeavouring to persuade them to become more masculine and respectable.

Indeed the word masculine is only a bugbear:[2] there is little reason to fear that women will acquire too much courage or fortitude, for their apparent inferiority with respect to bodily strength must render them, in some degree, dependent on men in the various relations of life; but why should it be increased by prejudices that give a sex to virtue and confound simple truths with sensual reveries?

Women are, in fact, so much degraded by mistaken notions of female excellence that I do not mean to add a paradox when I assert that this artificial weakness produces a propensity to tyrannize, and gives birth to cunning, the natural opponent of strength, which leads them to play off those contemptible infantine airs that undermine esteem even whilst they excite desire. Let men become more chaste and modest, and if women do not grow wiser in the same ratio, it will be clear that they have weaker understandings. It seems scarcely necessary to say that I now speak of the sex in general. Many individuals have more sense than their male relatives; and as nothing preponderates[3] where there is a constant struggle for an equilibrium without[4] it has naturally more gravity, some women govern their husbands without degrading themselves because intellect will always govern.

Chapter 2
The Prevailing Opinion of a Sexual Character Discussed

To account for, and excuse, the tyranny of man, many ingenious arguments have been brought forward to prove that the two sexes, in the acquirement of virtue, ought to aim at attaining a very different character: or, to speak explicitly, women are not allowed to have sufficient strength of mind to acquire what really deserves the name of virtue. Yet it should seem, allowing them to have souls, that there is but one way appointed by Providence to lead mankind to either virtue or happiness.

If then women are not a swarm of ephemeron[5] triflers, why should they be kept in ignorance under the specious name of innocence? Men complain, and with reason, of the follies and caprices[6] of our sex, when they do not keenly satirize our headstrong passions and grovelling vices. Behold, I should answer, the natural effect of ignorance! The mind will ever be unstable that has only prejudices to rest on, and the current will run with destructive fury when there are no barriers to break its force. Women are told from their infancy, and taught by the example of their mothers, that a little knowledge of human weakness, justly termed cunning, softness of temper, outward obedience, and a scrupulous attention to a puerile kind of propriety, will obtain for them the protection of man; and should they be beautiful, every thing else is needless for, at least, twenty years of their lives.

Thus Milton describes our first frail mother; though when he tells us that women are formed for softness and sweet attractive grace,[7] I cannot comprehend his meaning; unless, in the true Mahometan strain, he meant to deprive us of souls and insinuate that we were beings only designed by sweet attractive grace, and docile blind

---

[1] [Wollstonecraft's note]   A lively writer, I cannot recollect his name, asks what business women turned of forty have to do in the world? [Wollstonecraft is perhaps referring to a remark made by a libertine character in Frances Burney's *Evelina*, Lord Merton.]

[2] *bugbear*   Imaginary creature invoked to cause fear.

[3] *preponderates*   Weighs more, predominates.

[4] *without*   Unless.

[5] *ephemeron*   Short-lived.

[6] *caprices*   Whims, fancies.

[7] *Milton … grace*   John Milton contrasts Adam and Eve, the first man and woman, in *Paradise Lost* (1667): "For contemplation he and valour formed, / For softness she and sweet attractive grace" (4.297–98).

obedience, to gratify the senses of man when he can no longer soar on the wing of contemplation.

How grossly do they insult us who thus advise us only to render ourselves gentle, domestic brutes! For instance, the winning softness so warmly, and frequently, recommended that governs by obeying. What childish expressions, and how insignificant is the being—can it be an immortal one?—who will condescend to govern by such sinister methods! "Certainly," says Lord Bacon, "man is of kin to the beasts by his body; and if he be not of kin to God by his spirit, he is a base and ignoble creature!"[1] Men, indeed, appear to me to act in a very unphilosophical manner when they try to secure the good conduct of women by attempting to keep them always in a state of childhood. Rousseau[2] was more consistent when he wished to stop the progress of reason in both sexes, for if men eat of the tree of knowledge,[3] women will come in for a taste; but, from the imperfect cultivation which their understandings now receive, they only attain a knowledge of evil.

Children, I grant, should be innocent; but when the epithet is applied to men, or women, it is but a civil term for weakness. For if it be allowed that women were destined by Providence to acquire human virtues and, by the exercise of their understandings, that stability of character which is the firmest ground to rest our future hopes upon, they must be permitted to turn to the fountain of light, and not forced to shape their course by the twinkling of a mere satellite.[4] Milton, I grant, was of a very different opinion; for he only bends to the indefeasible[5] right of beauty, though it would be difficult to render two passages, which I now mean to

contrast, consistent. But into similar inconsistencies are great men often led by their senses.

> To whom thus Eve with *perfect beauty* adorn'd.
> My Author and Disposer, what thou bidst
> *Unargued* I obey; so God ordains;
> God *is thy law, thou mine*: to know no more
> Is Woman's *happiest* knowledge and her *praise*.[6]

These are exactly the arguments that I have used to children; but I have added, "Your reason is now gaining strength, and, until it arrives at some degree of maturity, you must look up to me for advice—then you ought to think and only rely on God."

Yet in the following lines Milton seems to coincide with me when he makes Adam thus expostulate[7] with his Maker.

> Hast thou not made me here thy substitute,
> And these inferior far beneath me set?
> Among *unequals* what society
> Can sort, what harmony or true delight?
> Which must be mutual, in proportion due
> Giv'n and receiv'd; but in *disparity*
> The one intense, the other still remiss
> Cannot well suit with either, but soon prove
> Tedious alike: of *fellowship* I speak
> Such as I seek, fit to participate
> All rational delight[8]—

In treating, therefore, of the manners of women, let us, disregarding sensual arguments, trace what we should endeavour to make them in order to co-operate, if the expression be not too bold, with the supreme Being.

By individual education, I mean—for the sense of the word is not precisely defined—such an attention to a child as will slowly sharpen the senses, form the temper, regulate the passions as they begin to ferment, and set the understanding to work before the body

---

[1] *Certainly … creature* Francis Bacon (1561–1626), English philosopher, jurist, and political figure, author of *Essays or Counsels Civil and Moral* (1625). The quotation is from Essay 16, "Of Atheism."

[2] *Rousseau* Jean-Jacques Rousseau (1712–78), Geneva-born philosopher, composer, and essayist.

[3] *tree of knowledge* In Genesis 2.17, God forbids Adam and Eve to eat of the tree of the knowledge of good and evil; tempted by the serpent, Eve disobeys and Adam follows suit.

[4] *satellite* Subordinate, secondary planet orbiting round a larger one.

[5] *indefeasible* Incapable of being defeated.

[6] *To whom … praise* Milton, *Paradise Lost*, 4.634–38. [Wollstonecraft's italics.]

[7] *expostulate* Remonstrate, argue.

[8] *Hast … delight* Milton, *Paradise Lost*, 8.381–91. [Wollstonecraft's italics.]

arrives at maturity; so that the man may only have to proceed, not to begin, the important task of learning to think and reason.

To prevent any misconstruction, I must add that I do not believe that a private education can work the wonders which some sanguine[1] writers have attributed to it. Men and women must be educated, in a great degree, by the opinions and manners of the society they live in. In every age there has been a stream of popular opinion that has carried all before it, and given a family character, as it were, to the century. It may then fairly be inferred that until society be differently constituted, much cannot be expected from education. It is, however, sufficient for my present purpose to assert that whatever effect circumstances have on the abilities, every being may become virtuous by the exercise of its own reason; for if but one being was created with vicious inclinations that is positively bad, what can save us from atheism? Or, if we worship a God, is not that God a devil?

Consequently, the most perfect education, in my opinion, is such an exercise of the understanding as is best calculated to strengthen the body and form the heart. Or, in other words, to enable the individual to attain such habits of virtue as will render it independent. In fact, it is a farce to call any being virtuous whose virtues do not result from the exercise of its own reason. This was Rousseau's opinion respecting men:[2] I extend it to women, and confidently assert that they have been drawn out of their sphere by false refinement and not by an endeavour to acquire masculine qualities. Still the regal homage which they receive is so intoxicating that until the manners of the times are changed and formed on more reasonable principles, it may be impossible to convince them that the illegitimate power, which they obtain by degrading themselves, is a curse, and that they must return to nature and equality if they wish to secure the placid satisfaction that unsophisticated affections impart. But for this epoch we must wait—wait, perhaps, until kings and nobles, enlightened by reason, and

preferring the real dignity of man to childish state, throw off their gaudy hereditary trappings: and if then women do not resign the arbitrary power of beauty, they will prove that they have less mind than man.

I may be accused of arrogance; still I must declare what I firmly believe: that all the writers who have written on the subject of female education and manners from Rousseau to Dr. Gregory[3] have contributed to render women more artificial, weak characters than they would otherwise have been; and, consequently, more useless members of society. I might have expressed this conviction in a lower key, but I am afraid it would have been the whine of affectation and not the faithful expression of my feelings, of the clear result which experience and reflection have led me to draw. When I come to that division of the subject, I shall advert[4] to the passages that I more particularly disapprove of in the works of the authors I have just alluded to; but it is first necessary to observe that my objection extends to the whole purport[5] of those books, which tend, in my opinion, to degrade one half of the human species and render women pleasing at the expense of every solid virtue.

Though, to reason on Rousseau's ground, if man did attain a degree of perfection of mind when his body arrived at maturity, it might be proper, in order to make a man and his wife one, that she should rely entirely on his understanding; and the graceful ivy, clasping the oak that supported it, would form a whole in which strength and beauty would be equally conspicuous. But, alas! Husbands, as well as their helpmates, are often only overgrown children; nay, thanks to early debauchery, scarcely men in their outward form—and if the blind lead the blind,[6] one need not come from heaven to tell us the consequence.

---

[1] *sanguine*   Cheerfully optimistic.

[2] *Rousseau's ... men*   Jean-Jacques Rousseau, *Émile* (1762), Book One.

[3] *Dr. Gregory*   John Gregory (1724–73), Scottish physician, author of *A Father's Legacy to His Daughters* (1774), an influential conduct book for young women.

[4] *advert*   Take notice.

[5] *purport*   Intention.

[6] *blind lead the blind*   Matthew 15.14: "And if the blind lead the blind, both shall fall into the ditch."

Many are the causes that, in the present corrupt state of society, contribute to enslave women by cramping their understandings and sharpening their senses. One, perhaps, that silently does more mischief than all the rest is their disregard of order.

To do every thing in an orderly manner is a most important precept which women, who generally speaking receive only a disorderly kind of education, seldom attend to with that degree of exactness that men, who from their infancy are broken into method, observe. This negligent kind of guess-work—for what other epithet can be used to point out the random exertions of a sort of instinctive common sense, never brought to the test of reason?—prevents their generalizing matters of fact: so they do today what they did yesterday, merely because they did it yesterday.

This contempt of the understanding in early life has more baneful[1] consequences than is commonly supposed; for the little knowledge which women of strong minds attain is, from various circumstances, of a more desultory[2] kind than the knowledge of men, and it is acquired more by sheer observations on real life than from comparing what has been individually observed with the results of experience generalized by speculation. Led by their dependent situation and domestic employments more into society, what they learn is rather by snatches; and as learning is with them, in general, only a secondary thing, they do not pursue any one branch with that persevering ardour necessary to give vigour to the faculties and clearness to the judgment. In the present state of society, a little learning is required to support the character of a gentleman; and boys are obliged to submit to a few years of discipline. But in the education of women, the cultivation of the understanding is always subordinate to the acquirement of some corporeal accomplishment; even while enervated[3] by confinement and false notions of modesty, the body is prevented from attaining that grace and beauty which relaxed half-formed limbs never exhibit. Besides, in youth their faculties are not brought forward by emulation; and having no serious scientific study, if they have natural sagacity it is turned too soon on life and manners. They dwell on effects, and modifications, without tracing them back to causes; and complicated rules to adjust behaviour are a weak substitute for simple principles.

As a proof that education gives this appearance of weakness to females, we may instance the example of military men who are, like them, sent into the world before their minds have been stored with knowledge or fortified by principles. The consequences are similar; soldiers acquire a little superficial knowledge, snatched from the muddy current of conversation, and, from continually mixing with society, they gain what is termed a knowledge of the world; and this acquaintance with manners and customs has frequently been confounded[4] with a knowledge of the human heart. But can the crude fruit of casual observation, never brought to the test of judgment, formed by comparing speculation and experience, deserve such a distinction? Soldiers, as well as women, practice the minor virtues with punctilious[5] politeness. Where is then the sexual difference when the education has been the same? All the difference that I can discern arises from the superior advantage of liberty, which enables the former to see more of life.

It is wandering from my present subject, perhaps, to make a political remark; but, as it was produced naturally by the train of my reflections, I shall not pass it silently over.

Standing armies can never consist of resolute, robust men; they may be well-disciplined machines, but they will seldom contain men under the influence of strong passions or with very vigorous faculties. And as for any depth of understanding, I will venture to affirm that it is as rarely to be found in the army as amongst women; and the cause, I maintain, is the same. It may be further observed that officers are also particularly attentive to their persons, fond of dancing, crowded rooms, adven-

---

[1] *baneful* Destructive, poisonous.

[2] *desultory* Irregular, unmethodical.

[3] *enervated* Mentally weakened.

[4] *confounded* Disordered, confused.

[5] *punctilious* Carefully polite.

tures, and ridicule.[1] Like the fair sex, the business of their lives is gallantry. They were taught to please, and they only live to please. Yet they do not lose their rank in the distinction of sexes, for they are still reckoned superior to women, though in what their superiority consists, beyond what I have just mentioned, it is difficult to discover.

The great misfortune is this: that they both acquire manners before morals, and a knowledge of life before they have, from reflection, any acquaintance with the grand ideal outline of human nature. The consequence is natural; satisfied with common nature, they become a prey to prejudices, and taking all their opinions on credit, they blindly submit to authority. So that, if they have any sense, it is a kind of instinctive glance that catches proportions and decides with respect to manners, but fails when arguments are to be pursued below the surface, or opinions analyzed.

May not the same remark be applied to women? Nay, the argument may be carried still further, for they are both thrown out of a useful station by the unnatural distinctions established in civilized life. Riches and hereditary honours have made ciphers[2] of women to give consequence to the numerical figure; and idleness has produced a mixture of gallantry and despotism into society which leads the very men who are the slaves of their mistresses to tyrannize over their sisters, wives, and daughters. This is only keeping them in rank and file, it is true. Strengthen the female mind by enlarging it and there will be an end to blind obedience, but, as blind obedience is ever sought for by power, tyrants and sensualists are in the right when they endeavour to keep women in the dark, because the former only want slaves, and the latter a play-thing. The sensualist, indeed, has been the most dangerous of tyrants, and women have been duped by their lovers, as princes by their ministers, whilst dreaming that they reigned over them.

I now principally allude to Rousseau, for his character of Sophia[3] is, undoubtedly, a captivating one, though it appears to me grossly unnatural; however, it is not the superstructure but the foundation of her character, the principles on which her education was built, that I mean to attack; nay, warmly as I admire the genius of that able writer, whose opinions I shall often have occasion to cite, indignation always takes place of admiration, and the rigid frown of insulted virtue effaces the smile of complacency, which his eloquent periods are wont to raise when I read his voluptuous reveries. Is this the man who, in his ardour for virtue, would banish all the soft arts of peace and almost carry us back to Spartan discipline?[4] Is this the man who delights to paint the useful struggles of passion, the triumphs of good dispositions, and the heroic flights which carry the glowing soul out of itself? How are these mighty sentiments lowered when he describes the pretty foot and enticing airs of his little favourite! But, for the present, I wave the subject, and, instead of severely reprehending[5] the transient effusions of overweening[6] sensibility, I shall only observe that whoever has cast a benevolent eye on society must often have been gratified by the sight of humble mutual love, not dignified by sentiment, or strengthened by a union in intellectual pursuits. The domestic trifles of the day have afforded matters for cheerful converse, and innocent caresses have softened toils which did not require great exercise of mind or stretch of thought: yet, has not the sight of this moderate felicity excited more tenderness than respect? An emotion similar to what we feel when children are playing, or animals sporting,[7] whilst the contemplation

---

[1] [Wollstonecraft's note] Why should women be censured with petulant acrimony, because they seem to have a passion for a scarlet coat? Has not education placed them more on a level with soldiers than any other class of men? [See Jonathan Swift's "The Furniture of a Woman's Mind."]

[2] *ciphers* Neutral symbols which can change the value of other numbers depending on their position.

[3] *Sophia* Character in Jean-Jacques Rousseau, *Émile*, Book Five.

[4] *Spartan discipline* The militaristic Greek city-state of Sparta was infamous for its harsh laws, outlined in Plutarch's account of Lycurgus (*Lives*), which controlled nearly every aspect of the lives of its citizens.

[5] *reprehending* Finding fault with.

[6] *overweening* Arrogant.

[7] [Wollstonecraft's note] Similar feelings has Milton's pleasing picture of paradisiacal happiness ever raised in my mind; yet, instead of envying the lovely pair, I have, with conscious dignity, or Satanic pride, turned to hell for sublimer objects. In the same style, when viewing some noble monument of human art, I have traced the

of the noble struggles of suffering merit has raised admiration and carried our thoughts to that world where sensation will give place to reason.

Women are, therefore, to be considered either as moral beings, or so weak that they must be entirely subjected to the superior faculties of men.

Let us examine this question. Rousseau declares that a woman should never, for a moment, feel herself independent, that she should be governed by fear to exercise her natural cunning, and made a coquettish slave in order to render her a more alluring object of desire, a sweeter companion to man whenever he chooses to relax himself.[1] He carries the arguments, which he pretends to draw from the indications of nature, still further and insinuates that truth and fortitude, the corner stones of all human virtue, should be cultivated with certain restrictions, because, with respect to the female character, obedience is the grand lesson which ought to be impressed with unrelenting rigour.

What nonsense! When will a great man arise with sufficient strength of mind to puff away the fumes which pride and sensuality have thus spread over the subject! If women are by nature inferior to men, their virtues must be the same in quality, if not in degree, or virtue is a relative idea; consequently, their conduct should be founded on the same principles and have the same aim.

Connected with man as daughters, wives, and mothers, their moral character may be estimated by their manner of fulfilling those simple duties; but the end, the grand end of their exertions should be to unfold their own faculties and acquire the dignity of conscious virtue. They may try to render their road pleasant, but ought never to forget, in common with man, that life yields not the felicity which can satisfy an immortal soul. I do not mean to insinuate that either sex should be so lost in abstract reflections or distant views as to forget the affections and duties that lie before

them, and are, in truth, the means appointed to produce the fruit of life; on the contrary, I would warmly recommend them, even while I assert that they afford most satisfaction when they are considered in their true, sober light.

Probably the prevailing opinion, that woman was created for man,[2] may have taken its rise from Moses's poetical story;[3] yet, as very few, it is presumed, who have bestowed any serious thought on the subject ever supposed that Eve was, literally speaking, one of Adam's ribs,[4] the deduction must be allowed to fall to the ground; or, only be so far admitted as it proves that man, from the remotest antiquity, found it convenient to exert his strength to subjugate his companion, and his invention to show that she ought to have her neck bent under the yoke because the whole creation was only created for his convenience or pleasure.

Let it not be concluded that I wish to invert the order of things; I have already granted that, from the constitution of their bodies, men seem to be designed by Providence to attain a greater degree of virtue. I speak collectively of the whole sex; but I see not the shadow of a reason to conclude that their virtues should differ in respect to their nature. In fact, how can they, if virtue has only one eternal standard? I must, therefore, if I reason consequentially, as strenuously maintain that they have the same simple direction as that there is a God.

It follows then that cunning should not be opposed to wisdom, little cares to great exertions, or insipid softness, varnished over with the name of gentleness, to that fortitude which grand views alone can inspire.

emanation of the Deity in the order I admired, till, descending from that giddy height, I have caught myself contemplating the grandest of all human sights;—for fancy quickly placed, in some solitary recess, an outcast of fortune, rising superior to passion and discontent.

[1] *Rousseau ... himself* See Jean-Jacques Rousseau, *Émile*, Book Five.

[2] *woman ... man* "And the Lord God said, It is not good that the man should be alone; I will make him an helpmeet for him" (Genesis 2.18–25).

[3] *Moses's ... story* I.e., Genesis. Moses was believed to be the author of the Pentateuch, the first five books of the Bible: Genesis, Exodus, Leviticus, Numbers, and Deuteronomy.

[4] *Adam's ribs* "And the Lord God caused a deep sleep to fall upon Adam, and he slept: and he took one of his ribs, and closed up the flesh instead thereof; And the rib, which the Lord God had taken from man, made he a woman, and brought her unto the man" (Genesis 2.22–23).

I shall be told that woman would then lose many of her peculiar graces, and the opinion of a well-known poet might be quoted to refute my unqualified assertion. For Pope[1] has said, in the name of the whole male sex:

> Yet ne'er so sure our passion to create,
> As when she touch'd the brink of all we hate.[2]

In what light this sally[3] places men and women, I shall leave to the judicious to determine; meanwhile I shall content myself with observing that I cannot discover why, unless they are mortal, females should always be degraded by being made subservient to love or lust.

To speak disrespectfully of love is, I know, high treason against sentiment and fine feelings; but I wish to speak the simple language of truth, and rather to address the head than the heart. To endeavour to reason love out of the world would be to out Quixote Cervantes[4] and equally offend against common sense; but an endeavour to restrain this tumultuous passion, and to prove that it should not be allowed to dethrone superior powers, or to usurp the sceptre which the understanding should ever coolly wield, appears less wild.

Youth is the season for love in both sexes; but in those days of thoughtless enjoyment, provision should be made for the more important years of life when reflection takes place of sensation. But Rousseau, and most of the male writers who have followed his steps, have warmly inculcated[5] that the whole tendency of female education ought to be directed to one point: to render them pleasing.

Let me reason with the supporters of this opinion who have any knowledge of human nature: do they imagine that marriage can eradicate the habitude of life? The woman who has only been taught to please will soon find that her charms are oblique sunbeams, and that they cannot have much effect on her husband's heart when they are seen every day, when the summer is passed and gone. Will she then have sufficient native energy to look into herself for comfort and cultivate her dormant faculties? Or, is it not more rational to expect that she will try to please other men; and, in the emotions raised by the expectation of new conquests, endeavour to forget the mortification her love or pride has received? When the husband ceases to be a lover—and the time will inevitably come—her desire of pleasing will then grow languid, or become a spring of bitterness; and love, perhaps, the most evanescent of all passions, gives place to jealousy or vanity.

I now speak of women who are restrained by principle or prejudice; such women, though they would shrink from an intrigue with real abhorrence, yet, nevertheless, wish to be convinced by the homage of gallantry that they are cruelly neglected by their husbands; or, days and weeks are spent in dreaming of the happiness enjoyed by congenial souls until their health is undermined and their spirits broken by discontent. How then can the great art of pleasing be such a necessary study? It is only useful to a mistress; the chaste wife, and serious mother, should only consider her power to please as the polish of her virtues, and the affection of her husband as one of the comforts that render her task less difficult and her life happier. But, whether she be loved or neglected, her first wish should be to make herself respectable, and not to rely for all her happiness on a being subject to like infirmities with herself.

The worthy Dr. Gregory fell into a similar error. I respect his heart, but entirely disapprove of his celebrated *Legacy to his Daughters*.

He advises them to cultivate a fondness for dress,[6] because a fondness for dress, he asserts, is natural to them. I am unable to comprehend what either he or Rousseau mean when they frequently use this indefinite term. If they told us that in a pre-existent state the soul

---

[1] *Pope* Alexander Pope (1688–1744), English poet and satirist.

[2] *Yet ... hate* Alexander Pope, "Epistle II: To a Lady (Of the Characters of Women)," from "Epistles to Several Persons," *Works*, lines 51–52 (1735).

[3] *sally* Sudden attack on an enemy.

[4] *out Quixote Cervantes* I.e., even more than the hero of Cervantes's picaresque novel, *Don Quixote* (1605–15), be determined to carry out a lofty albeit impossible goal.

[5] *inculcated* Taught through force or persistence.

[6] *fondness for dress* Gregory, *A Father's Legacy to His Daughters*, lines 55–57.

was fond of dress, and brought this inclination with it into a new body, I should listen to them with a half smile, as I often do when I hear a rant about innate elegance. But if he only meant to say that the exercise of the faculties will produce this fondness—I deny it. It is not natural; but arises, like false ambition in men, from a love of power.

Dr. Gregory goes much further; he actually recommends dissimulation,[1] and advises an innocent girl to give the lie to her feelings, and not dance with spirit, when gaiety of heart would make her feel eloquent without making her gestures immodest. In the name of truth and common sense, why should not one woman acknowledge that she can take more exercise than another? Or, in other words, that she has a sound constitution; and why, to damp innocent vivacity, is she darkly to be told that men will draw conclusions which she little thinks of? Let the libertine draw what inference he pleases; but I hope that no sensible mother will restrain the natural frankness of youth by instilling such indecent cautions. Out of the abundance of the heart the mouth speaketh;[2] and a wiser than Solomon[3] hath said that the heart should be made clean, and not trivial ceremonies observed,[4] which it is not very difficult to fulfil with scrupulous exactness when vice reigns in the heart.

Women ought to endeavour to purify their heart; but can they do so when their uncultivated understandings make them entirely dependent on their senses for employment and amusement, when no noble pursuit sets them above the little vanities of the day, or enables them to curb the wild emotions that agitate a reed over which every passing breeze has power? To gain the affections of a virtuous man is affectation necessary?

Nature has given woman a weaker frame than man; but, to ensure her husband's affections, must a wife—who, by the exercise of her mind and body whilst she was discharging the duties of a daughter, wife, and mother, has allowed her constitution to retain its natural strength, and her nerves a healthy tone—is she, I say, to condescend to use art and feign a sickly delicacy in order to secure her husband's affection? Weakness may excite tenderness and gratify the arrogant pride of man; but the lordly caresses of a protector will not gratify a noble mind that pants for and deserves to be respected. Fondness is a poor substitute for friendship!

In a seraglio, I grant that all these arts are necessary; the epicure[5] must have his palate tickled or he will sink into apathy; but have women so little ambition as to be satisfied with such a condition? Can they supinely[6] dream life away in the lap of pleasure, or the languor of weariness, rather than assert their claim to pursue reasonable pleasures and render themselves conspicuous by practising the virtues which dignify mankind? Surely she has not an immortal soul who can loiter life away, merely employed to adorn her person, that she may amuse the languid hours, and soften the cares of a fellow-creature who is willing to be enlivened by her smiles and tricks when the serious business of life is over.

Besides, the woman who strengthens her body and exercises her mind will, by managing her family and practising various virtues, become the friend and not the humble dependent of her husband; and if she, by possessing such substantial qualities, merit his regard, she will not find it necessary to conceal her affection, nor to pretend to an unnatural coldness of constitution to excite her husband's passions. In fact, if we revert to history, we shall find that the women who have distinguished themselves have neither been the most beautiful nor the most gentle of their sex.

Nature, or, to speak with strict propriety, God, has made all things right; but man has sought him out many inventions to mar the work. I now allude to that part of Dr. Gregory's treatise where he advises a wife never to

---

[1] *dissimulation* Concealment, feigning; Gregory, *A Father's Legacy to His Daughters*, lines 57–58.

[2] *Out of … speaketh* "O generation of vipers, how can ye, being evil, speak good things? For out of the abundance of the heart the mouth speaketh" (Matthew 12.34).

[3] *a wiser than Solomon* I.e., Jesus; see Luke 11.31.

[4] *the heart … observed* Matthew 23.25: "Woe unto you, scribes and Pharisees, hypocrites! For ye make clean the outside of the cup and of the platter, but within they are full of extortion and excess."

[5] *epicure* One devoted to physical pleasures.

[6] *supinely* Indolently, literally on one's back.

let her husband know the extent of her sensibility or affection.[1] Voluptuous precaution, and as ineffectual as absurd. Love, from its very nature, must be transitory. To seek for a secret that would render it constant would be as wild a search as for the philosopher's stone, or the grand panacea:[2] and the discovery would be equally useless, or rather pernicious, to mankind. The most holy band of society is friendship. It has been well said, by a shrewd satirist, "that rare as true love is, true friendship is still rarer."[3]

This is an obvious truth, and the cause, not lying deep, will not elude a slight glance of inquiry.

Love, the common passion in which chance and sensation take place of choice and reason, is, in some degree, felt by the mass of mankind; for it is not necessary to speak, at present, of the emotions that rise above or sink below love. This passion, naturally increased by suspense and difficulties, draws the mind out of its accustomed state and exalts the affections; but the security of marriage, allowing the fever of love to subside, a healthy temperature is thought insipid only by those who have not sufficient intellect to substitute the calm tenderness of friendship, the confidence of respect, instead of blind admiration and the sensual emotions of fondness.

This is, must be, the course of nature—friendship or indifference inevitably succeeds love—and this constitution seems perfectly to harmonize with the system of government which prevails in the moral world. Passions are spurs to action and open the mind; but they sink into mere appetites, become a personal and momentary gratification, when the object is gained and the satisfied mind rests in enjoyment. The man who had some virtue whilst he was struggling for a crown often becomes a voluptuous tyrant when it graces his brow; and, when

the lover is not lost in the husband, the dotard,[4] a prey to childish caprices and fond jealousies, neglects the serious duties of life, and the caresses which should excite confidence in his children are lavished on the overgrown child, his wife.

In order to fulfil the duties of life, and to be able to pursue with vigour the various employments which form the moral character, a master and mistress of a family ought not to continue to love each other with passion. I mean to say that they ought not to indulge those emotions which disturb the order of society and engross the thoughts that should be otherwise employed. The mind that has never been engrossed by one object wants vigour—if it can long be so, it is weak.

A mistaken education, a narrow, uncultivated mind, and many sexual prejudices tend to make women more constant than men; but, for the present, I shall not touch on this branch of the subject. I will go still further and advance, without dreaming of a paradox, that an unhappy marriage is often very advantageous to a family, and that the neglected wife is, in general, the best mother. And this would almost always be the consequence if the female mind were more enlarged: for it seems to be the common dispensation[5] of Providence that what we gain in present enjoyment should be deducted from the treasure of life—experience; and that when we are gathering the flowers of the day and revelling in pleasure, the solid fruit of toil and wisdom should not be caught at the same time. The way lies before us, we must turn to the right or left; and he who will pass life away in bounding from one pleasure to another must not complain if he acquire neither wisdom nor respectability of character.

Supposing, for a moment, that the soul is not immortal, and that man was only created for the present scene; I think we should have reason to complain that love, infantine fondness, ever grew insipid and palled upon the sense. Let us eat, drink, and love, for tomorrow we die,[6] would be, in fact, the language of

---

[1]   *never to let ... affection*   Gregory, *A Father's Legacy to His Daughters*, lines 87–88.

[2]   *wild a search ... panacea*   Alchemists believed in the existence of a philosopher's stone, a substance which could turn base metals into gold, as well as a grand panacea, a medicine that could cure all illnesses.

[3]   *that rare ... rarer*   François de La Rochefoucauld (1613–80), French essayist, author of *Réflexions; ou Sentences et maximes morales* (1665).

[4]   *dotard*   Senile person.

[5]   *dispensation*   Divine ordering of the world.

[6]   *Let us ... die*   Isaiah 22.13.

reason, the morality of life; and who but a fool would part with a reality for a fleeting shadow? But, if awed by observing the improbable powers of the mind, we disdain to confine our wishes or thoughts to such a comparatively mean field of action that only appears grand and important, as it is connected with a boundless prospect and sublime hopes, what necessity is there for falsehood in conduct, and why must the sacred majesty of truth be violated to detain a deceitful good that saps the very foundation of virtue? Why must the female mind be tainted by coquettish arts to gratify the sensualist and prevent love from subsiding into friendship, or compassionate tenderness, when there are not qualities on which friendship can be built? Let the honest heart show itself, and reason teach passion to submit to necessity; or, let the dignified pursuit of virtue and knowledge raise the mind above those emotions which rather embitter than sweeten the cup of life when they are not restrained within due bounds.

I do not mean to allude to the romantic passion which is the concomitant[1] of genius. Who can clip its wing? But that grand passion not proportioned to the puny enjoyments of life is only true to the sentiment and feeds on itself. The passions which have been celebrated for their durability have always been unfortunate. They have acquired strength by absence and constitutional melancholy—the fancy has hovered round a form of beauty dimly seen—but familiarity might have turned admiration into disgust; or, at least, into indifference, and allowed the imagination leisure to start fresh game. With perfect propriety, according to this view of things, does Rousseau make the mistress of his soul, Eloisa, love St. Preux[2] when life was fading before her; but this is no proof of the immortality of the passion.

Of the same complexion is Dr. Gregory's advice respecting delicacy of sentiment,[3] which he advises a woman not to acquire if she have determined to marry. This determination, however, perfectly consistent with his former advice, he calls indelicate, and earnestly persuades his daughters to conceal it, though it may govern their conduct—as if it were indelicate to have the common appetites of human nature.

Noble morality!, and consistent with the cautious prudence of a little soul that cannot extend its views beyond the present minute division of existence. If all the faculties of woman's mind are only to be cultivated as they respect her dependence on man; if, when a husband be obtained, she have arrived at her goal and, meanly proud, rests satisfied with such a paltry crown, let her grovel contentedly, scarcely raised by her employments above the animal kingdom; but if, struggling for the prize of her high calling, she look beyond the present scene, let her cultivate her understanding without stopping to consider what character the husband may have whom she is destined to marry. Let her only determine, without being too anxious about present happiness, to acquire the qualities that ennoble a rational being, and a rough inelegant husband may shock her taste without destroying her peace of mind. She will not model her soul to suit the frailties of her companion, but to bear with them: his character may be a trial, but not an impediment to virtue.

If Dr. Gregory confined his remark to romantic expectations of constant love and congenial feelings, he should have recollected that experience will banish what advice can never make us cease to wish for, when the imagination is kept alive at the expense of reason.

I own it frequently happens that women who have fostered a romantic, unnatural delicacy of feeling waste their lives in imagining how happy they should have been with a husband who could love them with a fervid increasing affection every day, and all day. But they might as well pine married as single—and would not be a jot more unhappy with a bad husband than longing for a good one. That a proper education or, to speak

---

[1] *concomitant* Accompaniment.

[2] *Eloisa … St. Preux* Eloisa/Julie is the heroine of Rousseau's epistolary novel *Julie, ou, La Nouvelle Héloïse* (1761). Julie falls in love with her tutor, St. Preux, but is forced to marry her father's friend, Wolmar. St. Preux and Julie meet again many years later, and Julie ultimately admits on her deathbed that she has never stopped loving him.

[3] *advice … sentiment* Gregory, *A Father's Legacy to His Daughters*, lines 116–19.

with more precision, a well stored mind would enable a woman to support a single life with dignity, I grant; but that she should avoid cultivating her taste lest her husband should occasionally shock it, is quitting a substance for a shadow. To say the truth, I do not know of what use is an improved taste if the individual be not rendered more independent of the casualties of life; if new sources of enjoyment, only dependent on the solitary operations of the mind, are not opened. People of taste, married or single, without distinction, will ever be disgusted by various things that touch not less observing minds. On this conclusion the argument must not be allowed to hinge; but in the whole sum of enjoyment is taste to be denominated a blessing?

The question is whether it procures most pain or pleasure? The answer will decide the propriety of Dr. Gregory's advice, and show how absurd and tyrannical it is thus to lay down a system of slavery; or to attempt to educate moral beings by any other rules than those deduced from pure reason, which apply to the whole species.

Gentleness of manners, forbearance, and long-suffering[1] are such amiable Godlike qualities that in sublime poetic strains the Deity has been invested with them; and, perhaps, no representation of his goodness so strongly fastens on the human affections as those that represent him abundant in mercy and willing to pardon.[2] Gentleness, considered in this point of view, bears on its front all the characteristics of grandeur combined with the winning graces of condescension;[3] but what a different aspect it assumes when it is the submissive demeanour of dependence, the support of weakness that loves, because it wants protection, and is forbearing, because it must silently endure injuries, smiling under the lash at which it dare not snarl. Abject

as this picture appears, it is the portrait of an accomplished woman, according to the received opinion of female excellence, separated by specious reasoners from human excellence. Or, they kindly restore the rib and make one moral being of a man and woman—not forgetting to give her all the "submissive charms."

How women are to exist in that state where there is to be neither marrying nor giving in marriage,[4] we are not told. For though moralists have agreed that the tenor[5] of life seems to prove that man is prepared by various circumstances for a future state, they constantly concur in advising woman only to provide for the present. Gentleness, docility, and a spaniel-like affection are, on this ground, consistently recommended as the cardinal virtues of the sex; and, disregarding the arbitrary economy of nature, one writer has declared that it is masculine for a woman to be melancholy. She was created to be the toy of man, his rattle, and it must jingle in his ears whenever, dismissing reason, he chooses to be amused.

To recommend gentleness, indeed, on a broad basis is strictly philosophical. A frail being should labour to be gentle. But when forbearance confounds right and wrong, it ceases to be a virtue; and, however convenient it may be found in a companion, that companion will ever be considered as an inferior and only inspire a vapid tenderness, which easily degenerates into contempt. Still, if advice could really make a being gentle, whose natural disposition admitted not of such a fine polish, something towards the advancement of order would be attained; but if, as might quickly be demonstrated, only affectation be produced by this indiscriminate counsel, which throws a stumbling-block in the way of gradual improvement and true melioration[6] of temper, the sex is not much benefited by sacrificing solid virtues to the attainment of superficial graces, though for a few years they may procure the individuals regal sway.

---

[1] *Gentleness ... long-suffering* "But the fruit of the Spirit is love, joy, peace, longsuffering, gentleness, goodness, faith, meekness, temperance: against such there is no law" (Galatians 5.22–23).

[2] *abundant ... pardon* "Let the wicked forsake his way, and the unrighteous man his thoughts: and let him return unto the Lord, and he will have mercy upon him; and to our God, for he will abundantly pardon" (Isaiah 55.7).

[3] *condescension* Gracious behavior shown to a social inferior.

[4] *neither ... marriage* "For in the resurrection they neither marry, nor are given in marriage, but are as the angels of God in heaven" (Matthew 22.30).

[5] *tenor* Continuous meaning.

[6] *melioration* Betterment.

As a philosopher, I read with indignation the plausible epithets which men use to soften their insults; and, as a moralist, I ask what is meant by such heterogeneous associations as fair defects, amiable weaknesses, &c.? If there be but one criterion of morals, but one archetype for man, women appear to be suspended by destiny, according to the vulgar tale of Mahomet's coffin;[1] they have neither the unerring instinct of brutes, nor are allowed to fix the eye of reason on a perfect model. They were made to be loved, and must not aim at respect, lest they should be hunted out of society as masculine.

But to view the subject in another point of view. Do passive, indolent women make the best wives? Confining our discussion to the present moment of existence, let us see how such weak creatures perform their part. Do the women who, by the attainment of a few superficial accomplishments, have strengthened the prevailing prejudice merely contribute to the happiness of their husbands? Do they display their charms merely to amuse them? And have women, who have early imbibed notions of passive obedience, sufficient character to manage a family or educate children? So far from it that, after surveying the history of woman, I cannot help agreeing with the severest satirist, considering the sex as the weakest as well as the most oppressed half of the species. What does history disclose but marks of inferiority, and how few women have emancipated themselves from the galling yoke of sovereign man? So few that the exceptions remind me of an ingenious conjecture respecting Newton: that he was probably a being of a superior order accidentally caged in a human body.[2] Following the same train of thinking, I have been led to imagine that the few extraordinary women who have rushed in eccentrical directions out of the orbit prescribed to their sex were male spirits, confined by

mistake in female frames. But if it be not philosophical to think of sex when the soul is mentioned, the inferiority must depend on the organs; or the heavenly fire, which is to ferment the clay, is not given in equal portions.

But avoiding, as I have hitherto done, any direct comparison of the two sexes collectively, or frankly acknowledging the inferiority of woman, according to the present appearance of things, I shall only insist that men have increased that inferiority until women are almost sunk below the standard of rational creatures. Let their faculties have room to unfold, and their virtues to gain strength, and then determine where the whole sex must stand in the intellectual scale. Yet let it be remembered that for a small number of distinguished women I do not ask a place.

It is difficult for us purblind[3] mortals to say to what height human discoveries and improvements may arrive when the gloom of despotism subsides, which makes us stumble at every step; but, when morality shall be settled on a more solid basis, then, without being gifted with a prophetic spirit, I will venture to predict that woman will be either the friend or slave of man. We shall not, as at present, doubt whether she is a moral agent or the link which unites man with brutes. But, should it then appear that, like the brutes, they were principally created for the use of man, he will let them patiently bite the bridle and not mock them with empty praise; or, should their rationality be proved, he will not impede their improvement merely to gratify his sensual appetites. He will not, with all the graces of rhetoric, advise them to submit implicitly their understanding to the guidance of man. He will not, when he treats of[4] the education of women, assert that they ought never to have the free use of reason, nor would he recommend cunning and dissimulation to beings who are acquiring, in like manner as himself, the virtues of humanity.

Surely there can be but one rule of right, if morality has an eternal foundation; and whoever sacrifices virtue, strictly so called, to present convenience, or whose duty

---

[1] *Mahomet's coffin*   It was believed that Mohammed's coffin was suspended in mid-air at his tomb in Medina, Saudi Arabia.

[2] *Newton ... body*   Newton and his scientific discoveries were held in extremely high regard during the eighteenth century; consider, for example, Pope's *Epitaph. Intended for Sir Isaac Newton, in Westminster-Abbey* (1730): "Nature and nature's laws lay hid in night; / God said 'Let Newton be' and all was light."

---

[3] *purblind*   Imperfectly sighted.

[4] *treats of*   Discourses on.

it is to act in such a manner,[1] lives only for the passing day and cannot be an accountable creature.

The poet then should have dropped his sneer when he says:

If weak women go astray,
The stars are more in fault than they.[2]

For that they are bound by the adamantine[3] chain of destiny is most certain, if it be proved that they are never to exercise their own reason, never to be independent, never to rise above opinion, or to feel the dignity of a rational will that only bows to God—and often forgets that the universe contains any being but itself and the model of perfection to which its ardent gaze is turned—to adore attributes that, softened into virtues, may be imitated in kind, though the degree overwhelms the enraptured mind.

If, I say, for I would not impress by declamation when Reason offers her sober light, if they be really capable of acting like rational creatures, let them not be treated like slaves, or like the brutes who are dependent on the reason of man when they associate with him; but cultivate their minds, give them the salutary, sublime curb of principle, and let them attain conscious dignity by feeling themselves only dependent on God. Teach them, in common with man, to submit to necessity, instead of giving, to render them more pleasing, a sex to morals.

Further, should experience prove that they cannot attain the same degree of strength of mind, perseverance, and fortitude, let their virtues be the same in kind, though they may vainly struggle for the same degree; and the superiority of man will be equally clear, if not clearer; and truth, as it is a simple principle, which admits of no modification, would be common to both. Nay, the order of society as it is at present regulated would not be inverted, for woman would then only have the rank that reason assigned her, and arts could not be practised to bring the balance even, much less to turn it.

These may be termed Utopian dreams—thanks to that Being who impressed them on my soul and gave me sufficient strength of mind to dare to exert my own reason until, becoming dependent only on him for the support of my virtue, I view, with indignation, the mistaken notions that enslave my sex.

I love man as my fellow; but his sceptre, real or usurped, extends not to me, unless the reason of an individual demands my homage; and even then the submission is to reason, and not to man. In fact, the conduct of an accountable being must be regulated by the operations of its own reason, or on what foundation rests the throne of God?

It appears to me necessary to dwell on these obvious truths because females have been insulated, as it were; and, while they have been stripped of the virtues that should clothe humanity, they have been decked with artificial graces that enable them to exercise a short-lived tyranny. Love, in their bosoms, takes the place of every nobler passion; their sole ambition is to be fair, to raise emotion instead of inspiring respect; and this ignoble desire, like the servility in absolute monarchies, destroys all strength of character. Liberty is the mother of virtue, and if women be, by their very constitution, slaves, and not allowed to breathe the sharp invigorating air of freedom, they must ever languish like exotics, and be reckoned beautiful flaws in nature.

As to the argument respecting the subjection in which the sex has ever been held, it retorts on[4] man. The many have always been enthralled by the few; and monsters, who scarcely have shown any discernment of human excellence, have tyrannized over thousands of their fellow-creatures. Why have men of superior endowments submitted to such degradation? For is it not universally acknowledged that kings, viewed collectively, have ever been inferior, in abilities and virtue, to the same number of men taken from the common mass of mankind—yet have they not, and are they not still treated with a degree of reverence that is an insult to reason? China is not the only country where a living

---

[1] *to act in such a manner*   I.e., to sacrifice duty to convenience.

[2] *If weak ... they*   "Hans Carvel" (1700) by Matthew Prior.

[3] *adamantine*   Unbreakable.

[4] *retorts on*   Answers back.

man has been made a God.[1] Men have submitted to superior strength to enjoy with impunity[2] the pleasure of the moment; women have only done the same, and therefore until it is proved that the courtier, who servilely resigns the birthright of a man, is not a moral agent, it cannot be demonstrated that woman is essentially inferior to man because she has always been subjugated.

Brutal force has hitherto governed the world; and that the science of politics is in its infancy is evident from philosophers scrupling to give the knowledge most useful to man that determinate distinction.

I shall not pursue this argument any further than to establish an obvious inference: that as sound politics diffuse liberty, mankind, including woman, will become more wise and virtuous.

from CHAPTER 3
THE SAME SUBJECT CONTINUED

... I wish to sum up what I have said in a few words, for I here throw down my gauntlet and deny the existence of sexual virtues, not excepting modesty. For man and woman, truth—if I understand the meaning of the word—must be the same; yet for the fanciful female character, so prettily drawn by poets and novelists demanding the sacrifice of truth and sincerity, virtue becomes a relative idea, having no other foundation than utility, and of that utility men pretend arbitrarily to judge, shaping it to their own convenience.

Women, I allow, may have different duties to fulfil; but they are human duties, and the principles that should regulate the discharge of them, I sturdily maintain, must be the same.

To become respectable, the exercise of their understanding is necessary; there is no other foundation for independence of character. I mean explicitly to say that they must only bow to the authority of reason instead of being the modest slaves of opinion.

In the superior ranks of life how seldom do we meet with a man of superior abilities, or even common acquirements? The reason appears to me clear: the state they are born in was an unnatural one. The human character has ever been formed by the employments that the individual, or class, pursues; and if the faculties are not sharpened by necessity, they must remain obtuse. The argument may fairly be extended to women; for, seldom occupied by serious business, the pursuit of pleasure gives that insignificancy to their character which renders the society of the great so insipid. The same want of firmness, produced by a similar cause, forces them both to fly from themselves to noisy pleasures, and artificial passions, until vanity takes place of every social affection, and the characteristics of humanity can scarcely be discerned. Such are the blessings of civil governments, as they are at present organized, that wealth and female softness equally tend to debase mankind and are produced by the same cause; but allowing women to be rational creatures, they should be incited to acquire virtues which they may call their own, for how can a rational being be ennobled by any thing that is not obtained by its own exertions?

—1792

---

[1] *China ... God* See *A Discourse on the Love of Our Country* (1789) by Richard Price (1723–91), English philosopher and writer.

[2] *impunity* Safety from punishment.

IN CONTEXT

Contemporary Reviews of *A Vindication of the Rights of Woman*

Early reviews of *A Vindication of the Rights of Woman* divided largely along party lines. Reviewers from *The Analytical Review* and *The Monthly Review*, for example, praised the work while more conservative papers such as *The Critical Review*, *The General Magazine*, and *The Gentleman's Magazine* attacked it. Excerpts from *The Analytical Review* and *The Critical Review* are reprinted below.

from *The Analytical Review* (1792)

... It is with some reluctance that for the present we take our leave of this singular, and, on the whole, excellent production. The subjects which it investigates, are of the utmost importance to human nature, and we should be wanting in our engagements, and in our duty, if we passed it over too slightly. This circumstance makes it necessary to defer the further analysis to a future Review, when we shall proceed to the remaining topics of this volume.

It might have been supposed that Mrs. W. had taken advantage of the popular topic of the "Rights of Man" in calling her work "A Vindication of the Rights of Woman," had she not already published a work, one of the first answers that appeared to Mr. Burke, under the title of "A Vindication of the Rights of Man." But in reality the present work is an elaborate *treatise* of *female education*. The lesser wits will probably affect to make themselves merry at the title and apparent object of this publication; but we have no doubt if even her contemporaries should fail to do her justice, posterity will compensate the defect; and have no hesitation in declaring, that if the bulk of the great truths which this publication contains were reduced to practice, the nation would be better, wiser and happier, than it is upon the wretched, trifling, useless and absurd system of education which is now prevalent.

from *The Critical Review* (1792)

One of the strictest proofs in mathematical demonstrations, is the reducing the questions to an absurdity; by allowing, for instance, that the proposition is not true, and then showing that this would lead to the most obvious inconsistencies. Miss Wollstonecraft has converted this method of proceeding with the same success: reasoning on the boasted principles of the Rights of Man, she finds they lead very clearly to the object of her work, a Vindication of the Rights of Woman; and, by the absurdity of many of her conclusions, shows, while we admit the reasoning, that the premises must be, in some respects, fallacious.

Dismissing then those pretty feminine phrases, which the men condescendingly use to soften our slavish dependence, and despising that weak elegancy of mind, exquisite sensibility, and sweet docility of manners, supposed to be the sexual characteristics of the weaker vessel, I wish to shew that elegance is inferior to virtue, that the first object of laudable ambition is to obtain a character as a human being, regardless of the distinction of sex; and that secondary views should be brought to this simple touchstone.

This is the outline of her plan; but before she proceeds to show that this change would be suitable, useful, advantageous, it will be first necessary to prove that there is no sexual distinction of character; that the female mind is equally fitted for the more arduous mental operations; that women are equally able to pursue the toilsome road of minute, laborious, investigation; that their judgments are equally sound, their resolution equally strong. After this is done, the benefit derived must be considered; and, when all are strong, to whom must the weaker operations belong? The female Plato will find it unsuitable to "the dignity of her virtue" to dress the child, and descend to the disgusting offices of a nurse: the new Archimedes will measure the shirts by means of the altitude taken by a quadrant; and the young lady, instead of studying the softer and more amiable arts of pleasing, must contend with her lover for superiority of mind, for greater dignity of virtue; and before she condescends to become his wife, must prove herself his equal or superior.—It may be fancy, prejudice, or obstinacy, we contend not for a name, but we are infinitely better pleased with the present system; and, in truth, dear young lady, for by the appellation sometimes prefixed to your name we must suppose you to be young, endeavour to attain "the weak elegancy of mind," the "sweet docility of manners," "the exquisite sensibility," the former ornaments of your sex; we are certain you will be more pleasing, and we dare pronounce that you will be infinitely happier. Mental superiority is not an object worth contending for, if happiness be the aim. But, as this is the first female combatant in the new field of the Rights of Woman, if we smile only, we shall be accused of wishing to decline the contest; if we content ourselves with paying a compliment to her talents, it will be styled inconsistent with "true dignity," and as showing that we want to continue the "slavish dependence."—We must contend then with this new Atalanta; and who knows whether, in this modern instance, we may not gain two victories by the contest? There is more than one bachelor in our corps; and, if we should succeed, Miss Wollstonecraft may take her choice.

This work is dedicated to M. Talleyrand-Perigord, late bishop of Autun, who, in his treatise on National Education, does not seem to be perfectly convinced that the rights of man extend to woman; yet in France the diffusion of knowledge, our author asserts, is greater than in any other European nation, on account of the more unreserved communication between the sexes, though what the ladies have gained in knowledge they seem confessedly to have lost in delicacy. The following passage we must transcribe, for we confess we do not fully understand it.

Contending for the rights of woman, my main argument is built on this simple principle, that if she be not prepared by education to become the companion of man, she will stop the progress of knowledge, for truth must be common to all, or it will be inefficacious with respect to its influence on general practice. And how can woman be expected to co-operate unless she know why she ought to be virtuous! unless freedom strengthen her reason till she comprehend her duty, and see in what manner it is connected with her real good? If children are to be educated to understand the true principle of patriotism, their mother must be a patriot; and the love of mankind, from which an orderly train of virtues spring, can only be produced by considering the moral and civil interest of mankind; but the education and situation of woman, at present, shuts her out from such investigations.

In this work I have produced many arguments, which to me were conclusive, to prove that the prevailing notion respecting a sexual character was subversive of morality, and I have contended, that to render the human body and mind more perfect, chastity must more universally prevail, and that chastity will never be respected in the male world till the person of a woman is not, as it were, idolized, when little virtue or sense embellish it with the grand traces of mental beauty, or the interesting simplicity of affection.

The first sentence is erroneous in fact and in reasoning: it is contradicted by the experience of ages, the practice of different nations. The second sentence is a curious one—How can she be supposed to co-operate (we *suppose* in the progress of knowledge) unless she know why she ought to be *virtuous?* Virtuous! Here must be some mistake: what has virtue to do with the progress of knowledge? As to freedom, strengthening the reason, &c. we see no occasion for metaphysical investigation on this subject: that virtue is connected with prosperity and happiness, and vice with misfortune and misery, she might learn, not from Locke, but the New Testament. The concluding sentence of the first paragraph is still more strange. Patriotism may be very properly instilled by a *father,* and we must beg leave to differ in opinion from this lady in another point: we are confident, from frequent and extensive observation, no arguments can confute the opinion that we have formed, and we must still persist in thinking, that the education and situation of women, *at present,* really and effectually *inspire* the *love* of *mankind.* We do believe with Miss Wollstonecraft, that chastity will be respected more, when the person of a woman ceases to be idolized, and the grand traces of mental beauty are principally conspicuous. ...

from *Letters Written during a Short Residence in Sweden, Norway, and Denmark*[1]

ADVERTISEMENT

The writing travels, or memoirs, has ever been a pleasant employment; for vanity or sensibility always renders it interesting. In writing these desultory letters, I found I could not avoid, being continually the first person—"the little hero of each tale."[2] I tried to correct this fault, if it be one, for they were designed for publication; but in proportion as I arranged my thoughts, my letter, I found, became stiff and affected: I, therefore, determined to let my remarks and reflec-tions flow unrestrained, as I perceived that I could not give a just description of what I saw, but by relating the effect different objects had produced on my mind and feelings, whilst the impression was still fresh.

A person has a right, I have sometimes thought, when amused by a witty or interesting egotist, to talk of himself when he can win on our attention by acquiring our affection. Whether I deserve to rank amongst this privileged number, my readers alone can judge—and I give them leave to shut the book, if they do not wish to become better acquainted with me.

My plan was simply to endeavour to give a just view of the present state of the countries I have passed through, as far as I could obtain information during so short a residence; avoiding those details which, without being very useful to travellers who follow the same route, appear very insipid to those who only accompany you in their chair.

---

[1] *Letters Written ... Denmark*   In 1795, Wollstonecraft traveled with her one-year-old daughter Fanny through Scandinavia. The letters in this volume were composed for publication as a travel narrative and memoir; the text is drawn from her journals and from letters she had sent to her lover, Gilbert Imlay (1754–1828), while in Scandinavia.

[2] *"the little hero of each tale"*   Cf. Edward Young's 1725–28 satirical poem *Love of Fame, The Universal Passion* 1.115–16: "It [love of fame] makes *dear self* on well-bred tongues prevail, / And *I* the *little hero* of each Tale."

LETTER I

Eleven days of weariness on board a vessel not intended for the accommodation of passengers have so exhausted my spirits, to say nothing of the other causes,[1] with which you are already sufficiently acquainted, that it is with some difficulty I adhere to my determination of giving you my observations, as I travel through new scenes, whilst warmed with the impression they have made on me.

The captain, as I mentioned to you, promised to put me on shore at Arendall,[2] or Gothenburg, in his way to Elsineur;[3] but contrary winds obliged us to pass both places during the night. In the morning, however, after we had lost sight of the entrance of the latter bay, the vessel was becalmed; and the captain, to oblige me, hanging out a signal for a pilot,[4] bore down towards the shore.

My attention was particularly directed to the lighthouse; and you can scarcely imagine with what anxiety I watched two long hours for a boat to emancipate me—still no one appeared. Every cloud that flitted on the horizon was hailed as a liberator, till approaching nearer, like most of the prospects sketched by hope, it dissolved under the eye into disappointment.

Weary of expectation, I then began to converse with the captain on the subject; and, from the tenor of the information my questions drew forth, I soon concluded, that, if I waited for a boat, I had little chance of getting on shore at this place. Despotism, as is usually the case, I found had here cramped the industry of man. The pilots being paid by the king, and scantily, they will not run into any danger, or even quit their hovels, if they can possibly avoid it, only to fulfill what is termed their duty. How different is it on the English coast, where, in

the most stormy weather, boats immediately hail you, brought out by the expectation of extraordinary profit. Disliking to sail for Elsineur, and still more to lie at anchor, or cruise about the coast for several days, I exerted all my rhetoric to prevail on the captain to let me have the ship's boat; and though I added the most forcible of arguments, I for a long time addressed him in vain.

It is a kind of rule at sea, not to send out a boat. The captain was a good-natured man; but men with common minds seldom break through general rules. Prudence is ever the resort of weakness; and they rarely go as far as they may in any undertaking, who are determined not to go beyond it on any account. If, however, I had some trouble with the captain, I did not lose much time with the sailors; for they, all alacrity, hoisted out the boat, the moment I obtained permission, and promised to row me to the lighthouse.

I did not once allow myself to doubt of obtaining a conveyance from thence round the rocks—and then away for Gothenburg—confinement is so unpleasant. The day was fine; and I enjoyed the water till, approaching the little island, poor Marguerite,[5] whose timidity always acts as a feeler before her adventuring spirit, began to wonder at our not seeing any inhabitants. I did not listen to her. But when, on landing, the same silence prevailed, I caught the alarm, which was not lessened by the sight of two old men, whom we forced out of their wretched hut. Scarcely human in their appearance, we with difficulty obtained an intelligible reply to our questions—the result of which was, that they had no boat, and were not allowed to quit their post, on any pretence. But, they informed us, that there was at the other side, eight or ten miles over, a pilot's dwelling; two guineas[6] tempted the sailors to risk the captain's displeasure, and once more embark to row me over.

The weather was pleasant, and the appearance of the shore so grand, that I should have enjoyed the two hours it took to reach it, but for the fatigue which was too visible in the countenances of the sailors who,

---

[1] *other causes*   The month previous to her setting out for Scandinavia, Wollstonecraft had attempted suicide, in large part because Imlay had become involved with another woman.

[2] [Wollstonecraft's note]   In Norway.

[3] *Gothenburg* Göteborg, a city in Sweden; *Elsineur* Elsinore, a city in Denmark.

[4] *pilot* A navigator who is temporarily taken on board a ship to guide it into, or out of, a port.

[5] *Marguerite* Wollstonecraft's maid, Marguerite Fournée.

[6] *guineas* British coins worth twenty-one shillings each.

instead of uttering a complaint, were, with the thought-less hilarity peculiar to them, joking about the possibil-ity of the captain's taking advantage of a slight westerly breeze, which was springing up, to sail without them. Yet, in spite of their good humour, I could not help growing uneasy when the shore, receding, as it were, as we advanced, seemed to promise no end to their toil. This anxiety increased when, turning into the most picturesque bay I ever saw, my eyes sought in vain for the vestige of a human habitation. Before I could determine what step to take in such a dilemma, for I could not bear to think of returning to the ship, the sight of a barge relieved me, and we hastened towards it for information. We were immediately directed to pass some jutting rocks when we should see a pilot's hut.

There was a solemn silence in this scene, which made itself be felt. The sunbeams that played on the ocean, scarcely ruffled by the lightest breeze, contrasted with the huge, dark rocks, that looked like the rude materials of creation forming the barrier of unwrought space, forcibly struck me; but I should not have been sorry if the cottage had not appeared equally tranquil. Approaching a retreat where strangers, especially women, so seldom appeared, I wondered that curiosity did not bring the beings who inhabited it to the win-dows or door. I did not immediately recollect that men who remain so near the brute creation, as only to exert themselves to find the food necessary to sustain life, have little or no imagination to call forth the curiosity necessary to fructify the faint glimmerings of mind which entitles them to rank as lords of the creation. Had they either, they could not contentedly remain rooted in the clods they so indolently cultivate.

Whilst the sailors went to seek for the sluggish inhabitants, these conclusions occurred to me; and, recollecting the extreme fondness which the Parisians ever testify for novelty, their very curiosity appeared to me a proof of the progress they had made in refinement. Yes; in the art of living—in the art of escaping from the cares which embarrass the first steps towards the attain-ment of the pleasures of social life.

The pilots informed the sailors that they were under the direction of a lieutenant retired from the service,

who spoke English; adding, that they could do nothing without his orders; and even the offer of money could hardly conquer their laziness, and prevail on them to accompany us to his dwelling. They would not go with me alone which I wanted them to have done, because I wished to dismiss the sailors as soon as possible. Once more we rowed off, they following tardily, till, turning round another bold protuberance of the rocks, we saw a boat making towards us, and soon learnt that it was the lieutenant himself, coming with some earnestness to see who we were.

To save the sailors any further toil, I had my baggage instantly removed into his boat; for, as he could speak English, a previous parley was not necessary; though Marguerite's respect for me could hardly keep her from expressing the fear, strongly marked on her counte-nance, which my putting ourselves into the power of a strange man excited. He pointed out his cottage; and, drawing near to it, I was not sorry to see a female figure, though I had not, like Marguerite, been thinking of robberies, murders, or the other evil[1] which instantly, as the sailors would have said, runs foul of a woman's imagination.

On entering, I was still better pleased to find a clean house, with some degree of rural elegance. The beds were of muslin, coarse it is true, but dazzlingly white; and the floor was strewed over with little sprigs of juniper (the custom, as I afterwards found, of the country), which formed a contrast with the curtains and produced an agreeable sensation of freshness, to soften the ardour of noon. Still nothing was so pleasing as the alacrity of hospitality—all that the house afforded was quickly spread on the whitest linen. Remember I had just left the vessel, where, without being fastidious, I had continually been disgusted. Fish, milk, butter, and cheese, and I am sorry to add, brandy, the bane of this country, were spread on the board. After we had dined, hospitality made them, with some degree of mystery, bring us some excellent coffee. I did not then know that it was prohibited.[2]

---

[1] *the other evil* Rape.

[2] *prohibited* A coffee ban had been imposed by the Swedish state in 1794.

The good man of the house apologized for coming in continually, but declared that he was so glad to speak English, he could not stay out. He need not have apologized; I was equally glad of his company. With the wife I could only exchange smiles; and she was employed observing the make of our clothes. My hands, I found, had first led her to discover that I was the lady. I had, of course, my quantum of reverences; for the politeness of the north seems to partake of the coldness of the climate, and the rigidity of its iron sinewed rocks. Amongst the peasantry, there is, however, so much of the simplicity of the golden age in this land of flint—so much overflowing of heart, and fellow-feeling, that only benevolence, and the honest sympathy of nature, diffused smiles over my countenance when they kept me standing, regardless of my fatigue, whilst they dropt courtesy after courtesy.

The situation of this house was beautiful, though chosen for convenience. The master being the officer who commanded all the pilots on the coast, and the person appointed to guard wrecks, it was necessary for him to fix on a spot that would overlook the whole bay. As he had seen some service, he wore, not without a pride I thought becoming, a badge to prove that he had merited well of his country. It was happy, I thought, that he had been paid in honour; for the stipend he received was little more than twelve pounds a year. I do not trouble myself or you with the calculation of Swedish ducats. Thus, my friend, you perceive the necessity of *perquisites*.[1] This same narrow policy runs through every thing. I shall have occasion further to animadvert in[2] it.

Though my host amused me with an account of himself, which gave me an idea of the manners of the people I was about to visit, I was eager to climb the rocks to view the country, and see whether the honest tars[3] had regained their ship. With the help of the lieutenant's telescope, I saw the vessel underway with a fair though gentle gale. The sea was calm, playful even as the most shallow stream, and on the vast basin I did not see a dark speck to indicate the boat. My conductors were consequently arrived.

Straying further, my eye was attracted by the sight of some heart's-ease[4] that peeped through the rocks. I caught at it as a good omen, and going to preserve it in a letter that had not conveyed balm to my heart, a cruel remembrance suffused my eyes; but it passed away like an April shower. If you are deep read in Shakspeare, you will recollect that this was the little western flower tinged by love's dart, which "maidens call love in idleness."[5] The gaiety of my babe[6] was unmixed; regardless of omens or sentiments, she found a few wild strawberries more grateful than flowers or fancies.

The lieutenant informed me that this was a commodious bay. Of that I could not judge, though I felt its picturesque beauty. Rocks were piled on rocks, forming a suitable bulwark to the ocean. Come no further, they emphatically said, turning their dark sides to the waves to augment the idle roar. The view was sterile; still little patches of earth, of the most exquisite verdure, enamelled with the sweetest wild flowers, seemed to promise the goats and a few straggling cows luxurious herbage. How silent and peaceful was the scene. I gazed around with rapture, and felt more of that spontaneous pleasure which gives credibility to our expectation of happiness, than I had for a long, long time before. I forgot the horrors I had witnessed in France,[7] which had cast a gloom over all nature, and suffering the enthusiasm of my character, too often, gracious God! damped by the tears of disappointed affection, to be lighted up afresh, care took wing while simple fellow feeling expanded my heart.

---

[1] *perquisites* Casual profits attached to a given position (from smuggling, for example).

[2] *animadvert in* Comment critically about.

[3] *tars* Familiar term for sailors.

[4] *heart's-ease* Common European wildflower. Sometimes called "wild pansy," the flower is the progenitor of cultivated pansies.

[5] *"maidens call love in idleness"* Cf. *A Midsummer Night's Dream* 2.1.166–68. Oberon uses the phrase to describe the pansy, the juice of which he will use to enchant Titania's eyes.

[6] *my babe* Fanny Imlay (1794–1816), Wollstonecraft and Imlay's daughter.

[7] *horrors … in France* Wollstonecraft was living in France during the Terror (September 1793–July 1794), a period of the French Revolution during which there were over 16,000 death sentences issued in France; in Paris alone, thousands were executed by guillotine.

To prolong this enjoyment, I readily assented to the proposal of our host to pay a visit to a family, the master of which spoke English, who was the drollest dog in the country, he added, repeating some of his stories, with a hearty laugh.

I walked on, still delighted with the rude beauties of the scene; for the sublime often gave place imperceptibly to the beautiful, dilating the emotions which were painfully concentrated.

When we entered this abode, the largest I had yet seen, I was introduced to a numerous family; but the father, from whom I was led to expect so much entertainment, was absent. The lieutenant consequently was obliged to be the interpreter of our reciprocal compliments. The phrases were awkwardly transmitted, it is true; but looks and gestures were sufficient to make them intelligible and interesting. The girls were all vivacity, and respect for me could scarcely keep them from romping with my host, who, asking for a pinch of snuff, was presented with a box, out of which an artificial mouse, fastened to the bottom, sprung. Though this trick had doubtless been played time out of mind, yet the laughter it excited was not less genuine.

They were overflowing with civility; but to prevent their almost killing my babe with kindness, I was obliged to shorten my visit; and two or three of the girls accompanied us, bringing with them a part of whatever the house afforded to contribute towards rendering my supper more plentiful; and plentiful in fact it was, though I with difficulty did honour to some of the dishes, not relishing the quantity of sugar and spices put into every thing. At supper my host told me bluntly that I was a woman of observation, for I asked him *men's questions*.

The arrangements for my journey were quickly made; I could only have a car with post-horses,[1] as I did not choose to wait till a carriage could be sent for to Gothenburg. The expense of my journey, about one or two and twenty English miles, I found would not amount to more than eleven or twelve shillings, paying,

he assured me, generously. I gave him a guinea and a half. But it was with the greatest difficulty that I could make him take so much, indeed any thing for my lodging and fare. He declared that it was next to robbing me, explaining how much I ought to pay on the road. However, as I was positive, he took the guinea for himself; but, as a condition, insisted on accompanying me, to prevent my meeting with any trouble or imposition on the way.

I then retired to my apartment with regret. The night was so fine, that I would gladly have rambled about much longer; yet recollecting that I must rise very early; I reluctantly went to bed: but my senses had been so awake, and my imagination still continued so busy, that I sought for rest in vain. Rising before six, I scented the sweet morning air; I had long before heard the birds twittering to hail the dawning day, though it could scarcely have been allowed to have departed.

Nothing, in fact, can equal the beauty of the northern summer's evening and night; if night it may be called that only wants[2] the glare of day, the full light which frequently seems so impertinent; for I could write at midnight very well without a candle. I contemplated all nature at rest; the rocks, even grown darker in their appearance, looked as if they partook of the general repose, and reclined more heavily on their foundation. What, I exclaimed, is this active principle which keeps me still awake? Why fly my thoughts abroad when every thing around me appears at home? My child was sleeping with equal calmness—innocent and sweet as the closing flowers. Some recollections, attached to the idea of home, mingled with reflections respecting the state of society I had been contemplating that evening, made a tear drop on the rosy cheek I had just kissed; and emotions that trembled on the brink of ecstasy and agony gave a poignancy to my sensations, which made me feel more alive than usual.

What are these imperious sympathies? How frequently has melancholy and even misanthropy taken possession of me, when the world has disgusted me, and friends have proved unkind. I have then considered

---

[1] *post-horses* Horses available for hire. A traveler could move more quickly by exchanging exhausted post horses for fresh ones at posting-houses and inns throughout the country.

[2] *wants* Lacks.

myself as a particle broken off from the grand mass of mankind; I was alone, till some involuntary sympathetic emotion, like the attraction of adhesion, made me feel that I was still a part of a mighty whole, from which I could not sever myself—not, perhaps, for the reflection has been carried very far, by snapping the thread of an existence which loses its charms in proportion as the cruel experience of life stops or poisons the current of the heart. Futurity, what hast thou not to give to those who know that there is such a thing as happiness! I speak not of philosophical contentment, though pain has afforded them the strongest conviction of it.

After our coffee and milk, for the mistress of the house had been roused long before us by her hospitality, my baggage was taken forward in a boat by my host, because the car could not safely have been brought to the house.

The road at first was very rocky and troublesome; but our driver was careful, and the horses accustomed to the frequent and sudden acclivities and descents; so that not apprehending any danger, I played with my girl, whom I would not leave to Marguerite's care, on account of her timidity.

Stopping at a little inn to bait[1] the horses, I saw the first countenance in Sweden that displeased me, though the man was better dressed than any one who had as yet fallen in my way. An altercation took place between him and my host, the purport of which I could not guess, excepting that I was the occasion of it, be it what it would. The sequel was his leaving the house angrily; and I was immediately informed that he was the custom-house officer.[2] The professional had indeed effaced the national character, for living as he did with these frank hospitable people, still only the exciseman[3] appeared, the counterpart of some I had met with in England and France. I was unprovided with a passport, not having entered any great town. At Gothenburg I knew I could immediately obtain one, and only the trouble made me object to the searching my trunks. He blustered for money; but the lieutenant was determined to guard me, according to promise, from imposition.

To avoid being interrogated at the town-gate, and obliged to go in the rain to give an account of myself, merely a form, before we could get the refreshment we stood in need of, he requested us to descend, I might have said step, from our car, and walk into town.

I expected to have found a tolerable inn, but was ushered into a most comfortless one; and, because it was about five o'clock, three or four hours after their dining hour, I could not prevail on them to give me any thing warm to eat.

The appearance of the accommodations obliged me to deliver one of my recommendatory letters, and the gentleman, to whom it was addressed, sent to look out for a lodging for me whilst I partook of his supper. As nothing passed at this supper to characterize the country, I shall here close my letter.

Your's truly.

from LETTER 19

Business having obliged me to go a few miles out of town[4] this morning, I was surprised at meeting a crowd of people of every description; and inquiring the cause, of a servant who spoke French, I was informed that a man had been executed two hours before, and the body afterwards burnt. I could not help looking with horror around—the fields lost their verdure—and I turned with disgust from the well-dressed women, who were returning with their children from this sight. What a spectacle for humanity! The seeing such a flock of idle gazers, plunged me into a train of reflections, on the pernicious effects produced by false notions of justice. And I am persuaded that till capital punishments be entirely abolished, executions ought to have every appearance of horror given to them; instead of being, as they are now, a scene of amusement for the gaping crowd, where sympathy is quickly effaced by curiosity.

---

[1] *bait* Feed.

[2] *custom-house officer* Official appointed by the government to collect border taxes.

[3] *exciseman* Tax collector.

---

[4] *town* Copenhagen, then capital of Denmark and Norway. Wollstonecraft had recently arrived in the city (described in Letter 18).

I have always been of opinion that the allowing actors to die, in the presence of the audience, has an immoral tendency; but trifling when compared with the ferocity acquired by viewing the reality as a show; for it seems to me, that in all countries the common people go to executions to see how the poor wretch plays his part, rather than to commiserate his fate, much less to think of the breach of morality which has brought him to such a deplorable end. Consequently executions, far from being useful examples to the survivors, have, I am persuaded, a quite contrary effect, by hardening the heart they ought to terrify. Besides, the fear of an ignominious death, I believe, never deferred anyone from the commission of a crime; because, in committing it, the mind is roused to activity about present circumstances. It is a game at hazard,[1] at which all expect the turn of the die in their own favour; never reflecting on the chance of ruin, till it comes. In fact, from what I saw, in the fortresses of Norway,[2] I am more and more convinced that the same energy of character, which renders a man a daring villain, would have rendered him useful to society, had that society been well organized. When a strong mind is not disciplined by cultivation, it is a sense of injustice that renders it unjust.

Executions, however, occur very rarely at Copenhagen; for timidity, rather than clemency, palsies all the operations of the present government. The malefactor who died this morning would not, probably, have been punished with death at any other period; but an incendiary excites universal execration; and as the greater part of the inhabitants are still distressed by the late conflagration,[3] an example was thought absolutely necessary; though, from what I can gather, the fire was accidental. ...

I forgot to mention to you, that I was informed, by a man of veracity, that two persons came to the stake to drink a glass of the criminal's blood, as an infallible remedy for the apoplexy.[4] And when I animadverted in the company, where it was mentioned, on such a horrible violation of nature, a Danish lady reproved me very severely, asking how I knew that it was not a cure for the disease? adding, that every attempt was justifiable in search of health. I did not, you may imagine, enter into an argument with a person the slave of such a gross prejudice. And I allude to it not only as a trait of the ignorance of the people, but to censure the government, for not preventing scenes that throw an odium on the human race.

Empiricism[5] is not peculiar to Denmark; and I know no way of rooting it out, though it be a remnant of exploded witchcraft, till the acquiring a general knowledge of the component parts of the human frame becomes a part of public education. ...

If travelling, as the completion of a liberal education, were to be adopted on rational grounds, the northern states ought to be visited before the more polished parts of Europe, to serve as the elements even of the knowledge of manners, only to be acquired by tracing the various shades in different countries. But, when visiting distant climes, a momentary social sympathy should not be allowed to influence the conclusions of the understanding; for hospitality too frequently leads travellers, especially those who travel in search of pleasure, to make a false estimate of the virtues of a nation; which, I am now convinced, bear an exact proportion to their scientific improvements.

—Adieu.

—1796

---

[1] *game at hazard* Game of chance, a gamble.

[2] *fortresses of Norway* In Letter 7, Wollstonecraft visits the House of Detention in Christiania (now Oslo), Norway. After praising the leniency of the laws in Norway more generally, Wollstonecraft also notes recent reforms to the prison that limited the corporal punishments inflicted on the prisoners.

[3] *incendiary* Arsonist; *late conflagration* Three months before Wollstonecraft arrived in Copenhagen there had been a fire that destroyed a quarter of the city and left thousands homeless.

[4] *apoplexy* Stroke or epileptic fit depriving the sufferer of sense and movement.

[5] *Empiricism* Used here in a depreciative sense, meaning "ignorance."

from *Maria; or The Wrongs of Woman*

CHAPTER 5

"My Father," said Jemima, "seduced my mother, a pretty girl, with whom he lived fellow-servant; and she no sooner perceived the natural, the dreaded consequence, than the terrible conviction flashed on her—that she was ruined. Honesty, and a regard for her reputation, had been the only principles inculcated by her mother; and they had been so forcibly impressed that she feared shame more than the poverty to which it would lead. Her incessant importunities[1] to prevail upon my father to screen her from reproach by marrying her, as he had promised in the fervour of seduction, estranged him from her so completely that her very person became distasteful to him; and he began to hate, as well as despise me, before I was born.

"My mother, grieved to the soul by his neglect, and unkind treatment, actually resolved to famish herself and injured her health by the attempt; though she had not sufficient resolution to adhere to her project, or renounce it entirely. Death came not at her call; yet sorrow, and the methods she adopted to conceal her condition, still doing the work of a house-maid, had such an effect on her constitution that she died in the wretched garret where her virtuous mistress had forced her to take refuge in the very pangs of labour; though my father, after a slight reproof,[2] was allowed to remain in his place—allowed by the mother of six children who, scarcely permitting a footstep to be heard during her month's indulgence,[3] felt no sympathy for the poor wretch denied every comfort required by her situation.

"The day my mother died, the ninth after my birth, I was consigned to the care of the cheapest nurse my father could find; who suckled her own child at the same time, and lodged as many more as she could get in two cellar-like apartments.

"Poverty, and the habit of seeing children die off her hands, had so hardened her heart that the office of a mother did not awaken the tenderness of a woman; nor were the feminine caresses which seem a part of the rearing of a child ever bestowed on me. The chicken has a wing to shelter under; but I had no bosom to nestle in, no kindred warmth to foster me. Left in dirt, to cry with cold and hunger till I was weary, and sleep without ever being prepared by exercise, or lulled by kindness to rest, could I be expected to become any thing but a weak and rickety babe? Still, in spite of neglect, I continued to exist, to learn to curse existence, [her countenance grew ferocious as she spoke,] and the treatment that rendered me miserable seemed to sharpen my wits. Confined then in a damp hovel, to rock the cradle of the succeeding tribe, I looked like a little old woman, or a hag shrivel-ing into nothing. The furrows of reflection and care contracted the youthful cheek, and gave a sort of super-natural wildness to the ever-watchful eye. During this period, my father had married another fellow-servant, who loved him less and knew better how to manage his passion than my mother. She likewise proving with child, they agreed to keep a shop: my stepmother—if, being an illegitimate offspring, I may venture thus to characterize her—having obtained a sum of a rich relation for that purpose.

"Soon after her lying-in,[4] she prevailed on my father to take me home, to save the expense of maintaining me, and of hiring a girl to assist her in the care of the child. I was young, it was true, but appeared a knowing little thing and might be made handy. Accordingly I was brought to her house; but not to a home—for a home I never knew. Of this child, a daughter, she was extrava-gantly fond; and it was a part of my employment to assist to spoil her, by humouring all her whims and bearing all her caprices. Feeling her own consequence before she could speak, she had learned the art of tormenting me, and if I ever dared to resist, I received blows, laid on with no compunctious hand,[5] or was sent to bed dinnerless, as well as supperless. I said that it was

---

1   *importunities*   Attempts to get attention.

2   *reproof*   Rebuke.

3   *during her month's indulgence*   I.e., during the period when she herself had been recovering after childbirth.

4   *lying-in*   Period of rest following childbirth.

5   *compunctious hand*   I.e., Jemima was beaten without pity, or indeed any concern.

a part of my daily labour to attend this child with the servility of a slave; still it was but a part. I was sent out in all seasons, and from place to place, to carry burdens far above my strength, without being allowed to draw near the fire, or ever being cheered by encouragement or kindness. No wonder then, treated like a creature of another species, that I began to envy, and at length to hate, the darling of the house. Yet, I perfectly remember that it was the caresses, and kind expressions of my step-mother, which first excited my jealous discontent. Once, I cannot forget it, when she was calling in vain her wayward child to kiss her, I ran to her, saying, 'I will kiss you, ma'am!'; and how did my heart, which was in my mouth, sink, what was my debasement of soul, when pushed away with—'I do not want you, pert thing!' Another day, when a new gown had excited the highest good humour, and she uttered the appropriate *dear*, addressed unexpectedly to me, I thought I could never do enough to please her; I was all alacrity,[1] and rose proportionably in my own estimation.

"As her daughter grew up, she was pampered with cakes and fruit, while I was, literally speaking, fed with the refuse of the table, with her leavings. A liquorish tooth[2] is, I believe, common to children, and I used to steal any thing sweet that I could catch up with a chance of concealment. When detected, she was not content to chastise me herself at the moment, but, on my father's return in the evening (he was a shopman), the principal discourse was to recount my faults, and attribute them to the wicked disposition which I had brought into the world with me, inherited from my mother. He did not fail to leave the marks of his resentment on my body, and then solaced himself by playing with my sister. I could have murdered her at those moments. To save myself from these unmerciful corrections, I resorted to falsehood, and the untruths which I sturdily maintained were brought in judgment against me, to support my tyrant's inhuman charge of my natural propensity to vice. Seeing me treated with contempt, and always being

fed and dressed better, my sister conceived a contemptuous opinion of me that proved an obstacle to all affection; and my father, hearing continually of my faults, began to consider me as a curse entailed[3] on him for his sins: he was therefore easily prevailed on to bind me apprentice to one of my step-mother's friends, who kept a slop shop[4] in Wapping.[5] I was represented (as it was said) in my true colours; but she 'warranted,'[6] snapping her fingers, 'that she should break my spirit or heart.'

"My mother replied, with a whine, 'that if any body could make me better, it was such a clever woman as herself; though, for her own part, she had tried in vain, but good nature was her fault.'

"I shudder with horror when I recollect the treatment I had now to endure. Not only under the lash of my task-mistress, but the drudge of the maid, apprentices, and children, I never had a taste of human kindness to soften the rigour of perpetual labour. I had been introduced as an object of abhorrence into the family; as a creature of whom my step-mother, though she had been kind enough to let me live in the house with her own child, could make nothing. I was described as a wretch whose nose must be kept to the grinding stone—and it was held there with an iron grasp. It seemed indeed the privilege of their superior nature to kick me about like the dog or cat. If I were attentive, I was called fawning, if refractory,[7] an obstinate mule, and like a mule I received their censure on my loaded back. Often has my mistress, for some instance of forgetfulness, thrown me from one side of the kitchen to the other, knocked my head against the wall, spit in my face, with various refinements on barbarity that I forbear to enumerate, though they were all acted over again by the servant, with additional insults, to which the appellation of *bastard* was commonly added with taunts or sneers. But I will not attempt to give you an adequate idea of my situation, lest you, who probably have never

---

[1] *alacrity* Readiness.

[2] *liquorish tooth* Sweet tooth, i.e., fondness for sweets.

[3] *entailed* Irrevocably attached.

[4] *slop shop* Shop that sold inexpensive, ready-made clothing.

[5] *Wapping* District of East London.

[6] *warranted* Guaranteed.

[7] *refractory* Stubborn, non-compliant.

been drenched with the dregs of human misery, should think I exaggerate.

"I stole now—from absolute necessity—bread; yet whatever else was taken, which I had it not in my power to take, was ascribed to me. I was the filching cat, the ravenous dog, the dumb brute who must bear all; for if I endeavoured to exculpate[1] myself, I was silenced without any enquiries being made, with 'Hold your tongue, you never tell truth.' Even the very air I breathed was tainted with scorn; for I was sent to the neighbouring shops with Glutton, Liar, or Thief written on my forehead. This was, at first, the most bitter punishment; but sullen pride, or a kind of stupid desperation, made me, at length, almost regardless of the contempt which had wrung from me so many solitary tears at the only moments when I was allowed to rest.

"Thus was I the mark of cruelty till my sixteenth year; and then I have only to point out a change of misery, for a period I never knew. Allow me first to make one observation. Now I look back, I cannot help attributing the greater part of my misery to the misfortune of having been thrown into the world without the grand support of life—a mother's affection. I had no one to love me, or to make me respected, to enable me to acquire respect. I was an egg dropped on the sand; a pauper by nature, hunted from family to family, who belonged to nobody—and nobody cared for me. I was despised from my birth, and denied the chance of obtaining a footing for myself in society. Yes; I had not even the chance of being considered as a fellow-creature—yet all the people with whom I lived, brutalized as they were by the low cunning of trade, and the despicable shifts of poverty, were not without bowels,[2] though they never yearned for me. I was, in fact, born a slave, and chained by infamy[3] to slavery during the whole of existence, without having any companions to alleviate it by sympathy, or teach me how to rise above it by their example. …

"At sixteen, I suddenly grew tall, and something like comeliness[4] appeared on a Sunday, when I had time to wash my face and put on clean clothes. My master had once or twice caught hold of me in the passage; but I instinctively avoided his disgusting caresses. One day however, when the family were at a Methodist meeting, he contrived to be alone in the house with me, and by blows—yes, blows and menaces—compelled me to submit to his ferocious desire; and, to avoid my mistress's fury, I was obliged in future to comply, and skulk to my loft at his command, in spite of increasing loathing.

"The anguish which was now pent up in my bosom seemed to open a new world to me: I began to extend my thoughts beyond myself and grieve for human misery, until I discovered, with horror—ah! what horror!—that I was with child. I know not why I felt a mixed sensation of despair and tenderness, excepting that, ever called a bastard, a bastard appeared to me an object of the greatest compassion in creation.

"I communicated this dreadful circumstance to my master, who was almost equally alarmed at the intelligence; for he feared his wife and public censure at the meeting. After some weeks of deliberation had elapsed, I in continual fear that my altered shape would be noticed, my master gave me a medicine in a phial which he desired me to take, telling me, without any circumlocution,[5] for what purpose it was designed. I burst into tears, I thought it was killing myself—yet was such a self as I worth preserving? He cursed me for a fool, and left me to my own reflections. I could not resolve to take this infernal potion; but I wrapped it up in an old gown, and hid it in a corner of my box.

"Nobody yet suspected me, because they had been accustomed to view me as a creature of another species. But the threatening storm at last broke over my devoted head—never shall I forget it! One Sunday evening when I was left, as usual, to take care of the house, my master came home intoxicated, and I became the prey of his brutal appetite. His extreme intoxication made him

---

[1] *exculpate* Clear oneself from blame.

[2] *bowels* Heart, compassion.

[3] *infamy* Scandalous reputation.

[4] *comeliness* Beauty.

[5] *circumlocution* Indirect speaking.

forget his customary caution, and my mistress entered and found us in a situation that could not have been more hateful to her than me. Her husband was 'pot-valiant,'[1] he feared her not at the moment, nor had he then much reason, for she instantly turned the whole force of her anger another way. She tore off my cap, scratched, kicked, and buffeted me until she had exhausted her strength, declaring, as she rested her arm, 'that I had wheedled[2] her husband from her. But, could any thing better be expected from a wretch whom she had taken into her house out of pure charity?' What a torrent of abuse rushed out, until, almost breathless, she concluded with saying, 'that I was born a strumpet;[3] it ran in my blood, and nothing good could come to those who harboured me.'

"My situation was, of course, discovered, and she declared that I should not stay another night under the same roof with an honest family. I was therefore pushed out of doors, and my trumpery[4] thrown after me, when it had been contemptuously examined in the passage lest I should have stolen any thing.

"Behold me then in the street, utterly destitute! Whither could I creep for shelter? To my father's roof I had no claim when not pursued by shame—now I shrunk back as from death from my mother's cruel reproaches, my father's execrations.[5] I could not endure to hear him curse the day I was born, though life had been a curse to me. Of death I thought, but with a confused emotion of terror, as I stood leaning my head on a post and starting at every footstep, lest it should be my mistress coming to tear my heart out. One of the boys of the shop passing by heard my tale, and immediately repaired to his master to give him a description of my situation; and he touched the right key—the scandal it would give rise to if I were left to repeat my tale to every enquirer. This plea came home to his reason, who

had been sobered by his wife's rage, the fury of which fell on him when I was out of her reach, and he sent the boy to me with half-a-guinea,[6] desiring him to conduct me to a house where beggars, and other wretches, the refuse of society, nightly lodged.

"This night was spent in a state of stupefaction, or desperation. I detested mankind, and abhorred myself.

"In the morning I ventured out, to throw myself in my master's way, at his usual hour of going abroad. I approached him, he 'damned me for a b——, declared I had disturbed the peace of the family, and that he had sworn to his wife never to take any more notice of me.' He left me; but, instantly returning, he told me that he should speak to his friend, a parish-officer,[7] to get a nurse for the brat I laid to him; and advised me, if I wished to keep out of the house of correction, not to make free with his name.

"I hurried back to my hole, and, rage giving place to despair, sought for the potion that was to procure abortion and swallowed it, with a wish that it might destroy me at the same time that it stopped the sensations of new-born life, which I felt with indescribable emotion. My head turned round, my heart grew sick, and in the horrors of approaching dissolution,[8] mental anguish was swallowed up. The effect of the medicine was violent, and I was confined to my bed several days; but, youth and a strong constitution prevailing, I once more crawled out to ask myself the cruel question, 'Whither I should go?' I had but two shillings[9] left in my pocket, the rest had been expended, by a poor woman who slept in the same room, to pay for my lodging and purchase the necessaries of which she partook.

"With this wretch I went into the neighbouring streets to beg, and my disconsolate appearance drew a few pence from the idle, enabling me still to command a bed; until, recovering from my illness, and taught to

[1]   *pot-valiant*   Courageous due to the effects of alcohol.
[2]   *wheedled*   Seduced by flattery or gentle coaxing.
[3]   *strumpet*   Derogatory term for a woman who has a number of sexual partners.
[4]   *trumpery*   Worthless clothing goods.
[5]   *execrations*   Expressions of intense loathing.

[6]   *half-a-guinea*   Gold coin.
[7]   *parish-officer*   General term for person holding any one of several elected positions within a parish, including churchwarden, surveyor, overseer of the poor, constable, etc.; overseers of the poor set and collected poor rates, as well as administering benefits to those in need.
[8]   *dissolution*   Death.
[9]   *shillings*   Coins of small value.

put on my rags to the best advantage, I was accosted from different motives, and yielded to the desire of the brutes I met with the same detestation that I had felt for my still more brutal master. I have since read in novels of the blandishments[1] of seduction, but I had not even the pleasure of being enticed into vice.

"I shall not," interrupted Jemima, "lead your imagination into all the scenes of wretchedness and depravity which I was condemned to view, or mark the different stages of my debasing misery. Fate dragged me through the very kennels[2] of society: I was still a slave, a bastard, a common property. Become familiar with vice, for I wish to conceal nothing from you, I picked the pockets of the drunkards who abused me; and proved by my conduct that I deserved the epithets with which they loaded me at moments when distrust ought to cease.

"Detesting my nightly occupation, though valuing, if I may so use the word, my independence, which only consisted in choosing the street in which I should wander, or the roof, when I had money, in which I should hide my head, I was some time before I could prevail on myself to accept of a place in a house of ill fame[3] to which a girl, with whom I had accidentally conversed in the street, had recommended me. I had been hunted almost into a fever by the watchmen[4] of the quarter of the town I frequented; one, whom I had unwittingly offended, giving the word to the whole pack. You can scarcely conceive the tyranny exercised by these wretches: considering themselves as the instruments of the very laws they violate, the pretext which steels their conscience hardens their heart. Not content with receiving from us, outlaws of society (let other women talk of favours), a brutal gratification gratuitously as a privilege of office, they extort a tithe[5] of prostitution, and harass with threats the poor creatures whose occupation affords not the means to silence the growl of avarice. To escape from this persecution, I once more entered into servitude.

"A life of comparative regularity restored my health; and—do not start[6]—my manners were improved in a situation where vice sought to render itself alluring, and taste was cultivated to fashion the person, if not to refine the mind. Besides, the common civility of speech, contrasted with the gross vulgarity to which I had been accustomed, was something like the polish of civilization. I was not shut out from all intercourse[7] of humanity. Still I was galled[8] by the yoke of service, and my mistress often flying into violent fits of passion made me dread a sudden dismission, which I understood was always the case. I was therefore prevailed on, though I felt a horror of men, to accept the offer of a gentleman, rather in the decline of years, to keep his house, pleasantly situated in a little village near Hampstead.[9]

"He was a man of great talents, and of brilliant wit; but, a worn-out votary of voluptuousness,[10] his desires became fastidious in proportion as they grew weak, and the native tenderness of his heart was undermined by a vitiated[11] imagination. A thoughtless career of libertinism[12] and social enjoyment had injured his health to such a degree that, whatever pleasure his conversation afforded me (and my esteem was ensured by proofs of the generous humanity of his disposition), the being his mistress was purchasing it at a very dear rate. With such a keen perception of the delicacies of sentiment, with an imagination invigorated by the exercise of genius, how could he sink into the grossness of sensuality!

"But, to pass over a subject which I recollect with pain, I must remark to you, as an answer to your often-repeated question—'Why my sentiments and language were superior to my station?'—that I now began to read,

[1] *blandishments* Flattering words.

[2] *kennels* Gutters.

[3] *house of ill fame* Brothel.

[4] *watchmen* Before the Police Act of 1839, men were formally appointed to guard city and town streets from sunset to sunrise.

[5] *tithe* Tenth of one's earnings.

[6] *do not start* I.e., do not be startled, shocked.

[7] *intercourse* Social interaction or communication.

[8] *galled* Irritated, chafed.

[9] *Hampstead* North London suburb.

[10] *votary of voluptuousness* Person devoted to sensuality.

[11] *vitiated* Rendered impure, soiled.

[12] *libertinism* Unrestrained, licentious conduct.

to beguile[1] the tediousness of solitude, and to gratify an inquisitive, active mind. I had often, in my childhood, followed a ballad-singer to hear the sequel of a dismal story, though sure of being severely punished for delaying to return with whatever I was sent to purchase. I could just spell and put a sentence together, and I listened to the various arguments, though often mingled with obscenity, which occurred at the table where I was allowed to preside: for a literary friend or two frequently came home with my master to dine and pass the night. Having lost the privileged respect of my sex, my presence, instead of restraining, perhaps gave the reins to their tongues; still I had the advantage of hearing discussions from which, in the common course of life, women are excluded.

"You may easily imagine that it was only by degrees that I could comprehend some of the subjects they investigated, or acquire from their reasoning what might be termed a moral sense. But my fondness of reading increasing, and my master occasionally shutting himself up in this retreat for weeks together to write, I had many opportunities of improvement. At first, considering money (I was right!" exclaimed Jemima, altering her tone of voice) "as the only means, after my loss of reputation, of obtaining respect, or even the toleration of humanity, I had not the least scruple to secrete a part of the sums entrusted to me, and to screen myself from detection by a system of falsehood. But, acquiring new principles, I began to have the ambition of returning to the respectable part of society, and was weak enough to suppose it possible. The attention of my unassuming instructor, who, without being ignorant of his own powers, possessed great simplicity of manners, strengthened the illusion. Having sometimes caught up hints for thought from my untutored remarks, he often led me to discuss the subjects he was treating, and would read to me his productions, previous to their publication, wishing to profit by the criticism of unsophisticated feeling. The aim of his writings was to touch the simple springs of the heart; for he despised the would-be oracles, the self-elected philosophers, who fright away fancy while sifting each grain of thought to prove that slowness of comprehension is wisdom.

"I should have distinguished this as a moment of sunshine, a happy period in my life, had not the repugnance the disgusting libertinism of my protector inspired daily become more painful. And, indeed, I soon did recollect it as such with agony, when his sudden death (for he had recourse to the most exhilarating cordials to keep up the convivial tone of his spirits) again threw me into the desert of human society. Had he had any time for reflection, I am certain he would have left the little property in his power to me: but, attacked by the fatal apoplexy[2] in town, his heir, a man of rigid morals, brought his wife with him to take possession of the house and effects before I was even informed of his death—'to prevent,' as she took care indirectly to tell me, 'such a creature as she supposed me to be from purloining[3] any of them, had I been apprized of the event in time.'

"The grief I felt at the sudden shock the information gave me, which at first had nothing selfish in it, was treated with contempt, and I was ordered to pack up my clothes; and a few trinkets and books, given me by the generous deceased, were contested, while they piously hoped, with a reprobating[4] shake of the head, 'that God would have mercy on his sinful soul!' With some difficulty, I obtained my arrears of wages; but asking—such is the spirit-grinding consequence of poverty and infamy—for a character[5] for honesty and economy, which God knows I merited, I was told by this—why must I call her woman?—'that it would go against her conscience to recommend a kept mistress.' Tears started in my eyes, burning tears; for there are situations in which a wretch is humbled by the contempt they are conscious they do not deserve.

"I returned to the metropolis; but the solitude of a poor lodging was inconceivably dreary after the society I had enjoyed. To be cut off from human converse, now

----

1   *beguile* Charm away.

2   *apoplexy* Stroke.

3   *purloining* Stealing.

4   *reprobating* Condemning.

5   *character* I.e., formal reference from an employer.

I had been taught to relish it, was to wander a ghost among the living. Besides, I foresaw, to aggravate the severity of my fate, that my little pittance would soon melt away. I endeavoured to obtain needlework; but, not having been taught early, and my hands being rendered clumsy by hard work, I did not sufficiently excel to be employed by the ready-made linen shops when so many women, better qualified, were suing[1] for it. The want of a character prevented my getting a place; for, irksome as servitude would have been to me, I should have made another trial had it been feasible. Not that I disliked employment, but the inequality of condition to which I must have submitted. I had acquired a taste for literature during the five years I had lived with a literary man, occasionally conversing with men of the first abilities of the age; and now to descend to the lowest vulgarity was a degree of wretchedness not to be imagined unfelt. I had not, it is true, tasted the charms of affection, but I had been familiar with the graces of humanity.

"One of the gentlemen, whom I had frequently dined in company with while I was treated like a companion, met me in the street and enquired after my health. I seized the occasion, and began to describe my situation; but he was in haste to join, at dinner, a select party of choice spirits; therefore, without waiting to hear me, he impatiently put a guinea into my hand, saying, 'It was a pity such a sensible woman should be in distress—he wished me well from his soul.'

"To another I wrote, stating my case and requesting advice. He was an advocate for unequivocal sincerity; and had often, in my presence, descanted[2] on the evils which arise in society from the despotism of rank and riches.

"In reply, I received a long essay on the energy of the human mind with continual allusions to his own force of character. He added, 'That the woman who could write such a letter as I had sent him could never be in want of resources, were she to look into herself and exert her powers; misery was the consequence of indolence,

and, as to my being shut out from society, it was the lot of man to submit to certain privations.'[3]

"How often have I heard," said Jemima, interrupting her narrative, "in conversation, and read in books, that every person willing to work may find employment? It is the vague assertion, I believe, of insensible[4] indolence when it relates to men; but, with respect to women, I am sure of its fallacy, unless they will submit to the most menial bodily labour; and even to be employed at hard labour is out of the reach of many whose reputation misfortune or folly has tainted.

"How writers, professing to be friends to freedom and the improvement of morals, can assert that poverty is no evil, I cannot imagine."

"No more can I," interrupted Maria, "yet they even expatiate[5] on the peculiar happiness of indigence,[6] though in what it can consist, excepting in brutal rest, when a man can barely earn a subsistence, I cannot imagine. The mind is necessarily imprisoned in its own little tenement; and, fully occupied by keeping it in repair, has not time to rove abroad for improvement. The book of knowledge is closely clasped against those who must fulfill their daily task of severe manual labour or die; and curiosity, rarely excited by thought or information, seldom moves on the stagnate lake of ignorance."

"As far as I have been able to observe," replied Jemima, "prejudices, caught up by chance, are obstinately maintained by the poor to the exclusion of improvement; they have not time to reason or reflect to any extent, or minds sufficiently exercised to adopt the principles of action, which form perhaps the only basis of contentment in every station."

"And independence," said Darnford, "they are necessarily strangers to, even the independence of despising their persecutors. If the poor are happy, or can be happy, *things are very well as they are*. And I cannot conceive on what principle those writers contend for a change of

---

[1] *suing* Asking, applying.

[2] *descanted* Commented on.

[3] *privations* Absence of comforts.

[4] *insensible* Incapable of feeling.

[5] *expatiate* Write or speak copiously on a subject.

[6] *indigence* Poverty.

system who support this opinion. The authors on the other side of the question are much more consistent who grant the fact; yet, insisting that it is the lot of the majority to be oppressed in this life, kindly turn them over to another, to rectify the false weights and measures of this, as the only way to justify the dispensations of Providence.[1] I have not," continued Darnford, "an opinion more firmly fixed by observation in my mind than that, though riches may fail to produce proportionate happiness, poverty most commonly excludes it by shutting up all the avenues to improvement."

"And as for the affections," added Maria, with a sigh, "how gross,[2] and even tormenting do they become, unless regulated by an improving mind! The culture of the heart ever, I believe, keeps pace with that of the mind. But pray go on," addressing Jemima, "though your narrative gives rise to the most painful reflections on the present state of society."

"Not to trouble you," continued she, "with a detailed description of all the painful feelings of unavailing[3] exertion, I have only to tell you that at last I got recommended to wash in a few families, who did me the favour to admit me into their houses without the most strict enquiry, to wash from one in the morning till eight at night for eighteen or twenty-pence a day. On the happiness to be enjoyed over a washing-tub I need not comment; yet you will allow me to observe that this was a wretchedness of situation peculiar to my sex. A man with half my industry, and, I may say, abilities, could have procured a decent livelihood and discharged some of the duties which knit mankind together; whilst I, who had acquired a taste for the rational—nay, in honest pride let me assert it, the virtuous enjoyments of life—was cast aside as the filth of society. Condemned to labour, like a machine, only to earn bread, and scarcely that, I became melancholy and desperate.

"I have now to mention a circumstance which fills me with remorse, and fear it will entirely deprive me of your esteem. A tradesman became attached to me, and

visited me frequently, and I at last obtained such a power over him that he offered to take me home to his house. Consider, dear madam, I was famishing; wonder not that I became a wolf! The only reason for not taking me home immediately was the having a girl in the house with child by him; and this girl, I advised him—yes, I did! Would I could forget it!—to turn out of doors: and one night he determined to follow my advice. Poor wretch! She fell upon her knees, reminded him that he had promised to marry her, that her parents were honest! What did it avail? She was turned out.

"She approached her father's door in the skirts of London, listened at the shutters, but could not knock. A watchman had observed her go and return several times—Poor wretch! (The remorse Jemima spoke of seemed to be stinging her to the soul, as she proceeded.)

"She left it, and, approaching a tub where horses were watered, she sat down in it, and, with desperate resolution, remained in that attitude[4]—till resolution was no longer necessary!

"I happened that morning to be going out to wash, anticipating the moment when I should escape from such hard labour. I passed by, just as some men, going to work, drew out the stiff, cold corpse—let me not recall the horrid moment! I recognized her pale visage; I listened to the tale told by the spectators, and my heart did not burst. I thought of my own state, and wondered how I could be such a monster! I worked hard; and, returning home, I was attacked by a fever. I suffered both in body and mind. I determined not to live with the wretch. But he did not try[5] me; he left the neighbourhood. I once more returned to the wash tub.

"Still this state, miserable as it was, admitted of aggravation. Lifting one day a heavy load, a tub fell against my shin and gave me great pain. I did not pay much attention to the hurt until it became a serious wound, being obliged to work as usual or starve. But, finding myself at length unable to stand for any time, I thought of getting into an hospital. Hospitals, it should seem (for they are comfortless abodes for the sick), were

---

[1] *dispensations of Providence* Providential management of the world.

[2] *gross* Unrefined, lacking sensitivity.

[3] *unavailing* Of no avail, no use or hope.

[4] *attitude* Posture, bodily position.

[5] *try* Put to the test.

expressly endowed for the reception of the friendless; yet I, who had on that plea a right to assistance, wanted the recommendation of the rich and respectable, and was several weeks languishing for admittance; fees were demanded on entering; and, what was still more unreasonable, security for burying me—that expense not coming into the letter of the charity. A guinea was the stipulated sum—I could as soon have raised a million; and I was afraid to apply to the parish for an order, lest they should have passed me I knew not whither.[1] The poor woman at whose house I lodged, compassionating[2] my state, got me into the hospital; and the family where I received the hurt sent me five shillings, three and sixpence of which I gave at my admittance—I know not for what.

"My leg grew quickly better; but I was dismissed before my cure was completed because I could not afford to have my linen washed to appear decently, as the virago[3] of a nurse said, when the gentlemen (the surgeons) came. I cannot give you an adequate idea of the wretchedness of an hospital; everything is left to the care of people intent on gain. The attendants seem to have lost all feeling of compassion in the bustling discharge of their offices; death is so familiar to them that they are not anxious to ward it off. Everything appeared to be conducted for the accommodation of the medical men and their pupils, who came to make experiments on the poor for the benefit of the rich. One of the physicians, I must not forget to mention, gave me half-a-crown, and ordered me some wine, when I was at the lowest ebb. I thought of making my case known to the lady-like matron;[4] but her forbidding countenance prevented me. She condescended to look on the patients, and make general enquiries, two or three times a week;

but the nurses knew the hour when the visit of ceremony would commence, and every thing was as it should be.

"After my dismission, I was more at a loss than ever for a subsistence, and, not to weary you with a repetition of the same unavailing attempts, unable to stand at the washing-tub, I began to consider the rich and poor as natural enemies, and became a thief from principle. I could not now cease to reason, but I hated mankind. I despised myself, yet I justified my conduct. I was taken, tried, and condemned to six months' imprisonment in a house of correction. My soul recoils with horror from the remembrance of the insults I had to endure until, branded with shame, I was turned loose in the street, penniless. I wandered from street to street until, exhausted by hunger and fatigue, I sunk down senseless at a door where I had vainly demanded a morsel of bread. I was sent by the inhabitant to the work-house, to which he had surlily bid me go, saying, he 'paid enough in conscience to the poor' when, with parched tongue, I implored his charity. If those well-meaning people who exclaim against beggars were acquainted with the treatment the poor receive in many of these wretched asylums, they would not stifle so easily involuntary sympathy by saying that they have all parishes to go to, or wonder that the poor dread to enter the gloomy walls. What are the common run of workhouses but prisons, in which many respectable old people, worn out by immoderate labour, sink into the grave in sorrow to which they are carried like dogs!"

Alarmed by some indistinct noise, Jemima rose hastily to listen, and Maria, turning to Darnford, said, "I have indeed been shocked beyond expression when I have met a pauper's funeral. A coffin carried on the shoulders of three or four ill-looking wretches, whom the imagination might easily convert into a band of assassins hastening to conceal the corpse and quarrelling about the prey on their way. I know it is of little consequence how we are consigned to the earth;[5] but I am led by this brutal insensibility, to what even the animal creation appears forcibly to feel, to advert to[6] the

---

[1] *I was afraid … whither* One applied for poor relief from the parish in which one was last legally settled; terms of legal settlement included being born into a parish, renting property of a certain value, working for over a year and a day, serving an apprenticeship of seven years or more, marrying into the parish, etc. If one applied for poor relief without meeting the settlement requirements, one would be sent back to a parish in which one did.

[2] *compassionating* Having compassion for.

[3] *virago* Bold woman, scold.

[4] *matron* Woman in charge of the nurses.

[5] *how we are consigned to the earth* I.e., how we are buried.

[6] *advert to* Pay attention to.

wretched, deserted manner in which they died."

"True," rejoined Darnford, "and until the rich will give more than a part of their wealth, until they will give time and attention to the wants of the distressed, never let them boast of charity. Let them open their hearts, and not their purses, and employ their minds in the service if they are really actuated by humanity; or charitable institutions will always be the prey of the lowest order of knaves."

Jemima returning, seemed in haste to finish her tale. "The overseer farmed[1] the poor of different parishes, and out of the bowels of poverty was wrung the money with which he purchased this dwelling, as a private receptacle for madness. He had been a keeper at a house of the same description, and conceived that he could make money much more readily in his old occupation. He is a shrewd—shall I say it?—villain. He observed something resolute in my manner, and offered to take me with him and instruct me how to treat the disturbed minds he meant to entrust to my care. The offer of forty pounds a year, and to quit a workhouse, was not to be despised, though the condition of shutting my eyes and hardening my heart was annexed[2] to it.

"I agreed to accompany him; and four years have I been attendant on many wretches, and"—she lowered her voice—"the witness of many enormities.[3] In solitude my mind seemed to recover its force, and many of the sentiments which I imbibed in the only tolerable period of my life returned with their full force. Still, what should induce me to be the champion for suffering humanity? Who ever risked any thing for me? Who ever acknowledged me to be a fellow-creature?"

Maria took her hand, and Jemima, more overcome by kindness than she had ever been by cruelty, hastened out of the room to conceal her emotions.

Darnford soon after heard his summons, and, taking leave of him, Maria promised to gratify his curiosity, with respect to herself, at the first opportunity.
—1798

---

1 *farmed* Contracted out care or maintenance for a fee.

2 *annexed* Included as a condition.

3 *enormities* Gross breaches of law or morals.

IN CONTEXT

Mary Wollstonecraft's Biography

The year after Wollstonecraft died, her husband and colleague William Godwin (1756–1836) published his biography of her, *Memoirs of the Author of a Vindication of the Rights of Woman*. Godwin believed that "individual histories" of remarkable people were important revolutionary tools, contributing to the gradual improvement of mind that would lead, ultimately, to social reform. In keeping with these ideals, he did not hesitate to write a clear account of Wollstonecraft's life, including her unconventional relationships and two suicide attempts. While the resulting work has since come to be recognized as an important contribution to the genre, his frankness was not well-received by contemporaries. Readers were shocked. For conservative reactionaries the publication of *Memoirs* sealed a link between radical politics, especially feminist politics, and sexual immorality, and Godwin's book adversely affected Wollstonecraft's reputation, as well as his own, for decades to come.

from William Godwin, *Memoirs of the Author of a Vindication of the Rights of Woman* (1798)

from CHAPTER I
1759–1775

... Mary was distinguished in early youth by some portion of that exquisite sensibility, soundness of understanding, and decision of character, which were the leading features of her mind through the whole course of her life. She experienced in the first period of her existence but few of those indulgences and marks of affection which are principally calculated to sooth the subjection and sorrows of our early years. She was not the favourite either of her father or mother. Her father was a man of quick, impetuous disposition, subject to alternate fits of kindness and cruelty. In his family he was a despot, and his wife appears to have been the first, and most submissive of his subjects. ...

When, in the *Wrongs of Woman*, Mary speaks of "the petty cares which obscured the morning of her heroine's life; continual restraint in the most trivial matters; unconditional submission to orders, which, as a mere child, she soon discovered to be unreasonable, because inconsistent and contradictory; and the being often obliged to sit, in the presence of her parents, for three or four hours together, without daring to utter a word;"[1] she is, I believe, to be considered as copying the outline of the first period of her own existence.

But it was in vain that the blighting winds of unkindness or indifference seemed destined to counteract the superiority of Mary's mind. It surmounted every obstacle; and, by degrees, from a person little considered in the family, she became in some sort its director and umpire. The despotism of her education cost her many a heart-ache. She was not formed to be the contented and unresisting subject of a despot; but I have heard her remark more than once, that, when she felt she had done wrong, the reproof or chastisement of her mother, instead of being a terror to her, she found to be the only thing capable of reconciling her to herself. The blows of her father on the contrary, which were the mere ebullitions of a passionate temper, instead of humbling her, roused her indignation.

---

[1] *the petty ... utter a word* Cf. Chapter 7 of Wollstonecraft's novel *Maria; or The Wrongs of Woman* (1798).

Upon such occasions she felt her superiority, and was apt to betray marks of contempt. The quickness of her father's temper, led him sometimes to threaten similar violence towards his wife. When that was the case, Mary would often throw herself between the despot and his victim, with the purpose to receive upon her own person the blows that might be directed against her mother. She has even laid whole nights upon the landing place near their chamber-door, when, mistakenly, or with reason, she apprehended that her father might break out into paroxysms of violence. ...

from CHAPTER 6
1790–1792

Hitherto the literary career of Mary had for the most part been silent; and had been productive of income to herself, without apparently leading to the wreath of fame. From this time she was destined to attract the notice of the public, and perhaps no female writer ever obtained so great a degree of celebrity throughout Europe. It cannot be doubted that, while, for three years of literary employment, she "held the noiseless tenor of her way,"[1] her mind was insensibly advancing towards a vigorous maturity. The uninterrupted habit of composition gave a freedom and firmness to the expression of her sentiments. The society she frequented nourished her understanding, and enlarged her mind. The French revolution, while it gave a fundamental shock to the human intellect through every region of the globe, did not fail to produce a conspicuous effect in the progress of Mary's reflections. The prejudices of her early years suffered a vehement concussion. Her respect for establishments was undermined. ...

The event immediately introductory to the rank which from this time she held in the lists of literature was the publication of Burke's *Reflections on the Revolution in France*. This book, after having been long promised to the world, finally made its appearance on the first of November 1790; and Mary, full of sentiments of liberty, and impressed with a warm interest in the struggle that was now going on, seized her pen in the first burst of indignation, an emotion of which she was strongly susceptible. She was in the habit of composing with rapidity, and her answer,[2] which was the first of the numerous ones that appeared, obtained extraordinary notice. Marked as it is with the vehemence and impetuousness of its eloquence, it is certainly chargeable with a too contemptuous and intemperate treatment of the great man against whom its attack is directed. But this circumstance was not injurious to the success of the publication. Burke had been warmly loved by the most liberal and enlightened friends of freedom, and they were proportionably inflamed and disgusted by the fury of his assault upon what they deemed to be its sacred cause. ...

It is probable that the applause which attended her Answer to Burke elevated the tone of her mind. She had always felt much confidence in her own powers; but it cannot be doubted that the actual perception of a similar feeling respecting us in a multitude of others must increase the confidence and stimulate the adventure of any human being. Mary accordingly proceeded, in a short time after, to the composition of her most celebrated production, the *Vindication of the Rights of Woman*.

Never did any author enter into a cause with a more ardent desire to be found, not a flourishing and empty declaimer, but an effectual champion. She considered herself as standing forth in defence

---

[1] *held the ... her way*   Adapted from Thomas Gray's 1751 poem "Elegy Written in a Country Church Yard" l.76.

[2] *her answer*   Wollstonecraft's *Vindication of the Rights of Men, in a Letter to the Right Honourable Edmund Burke* (1790). A selection from this work is reprinted elsewhere in this anthology; see "Contexts: The French Revolution."

of one half of the human species, labouring under a yoke which, through all the records of time, had degraded them from the station of rational beings, and almost sunk them to the level of the brutes. ...

The *Vindication of the Rights of Woman* is undoubtedly a very unequal performance, and eminently deficient in method and arrangement. When tried by the hoary[1] and long established laws of literary composition, it can scarcely maintain its claim to be placed in the first class of human productions. But when we consider the importance of its doctrines, and the eminence of genius it displays, it seems not very improbable that it will be read as long as the English language endures. The publication of this book forms an epoch in the subject to which it belongs; and Mary Wollstonecraft will perhaps hereafter be found to have performed more substantial service for the cause of her sex than all the other writers, male or female, that ever felt themselves animated in the behalf of oppressed and injured beauty. ...

from CHAPTER 8
1795, 1796

In April 1795, Mary returned once more to London, being requested to do so by Mr. Imlay,[2] who even sent a servant to Paris to wait upon her in the journey, before she could complete the necessary arrangements for her departure. But, notwithstanding these favourable appearances, she came to England with a heavy heart, not daring, after all the uncertainties and anguish she had endured, to trust to the suggestions of hope.

The gloomy forebodings of her mind were but too faithfully verified. Mr. Imlay had already formed another connection; as it is said, with a young actress from a strolling company of players. His attentions therefore to Mary were formal and constrained, and she probably had but little of his society. This alteration could not escape her penetrating glance. He ascribed it to pressure of business, and some pecuniary embarrassments which, at that time, occurred to him; it was of little consequence to Mary what was the cause. She saw but too well, though she strove not to see, that his affections were lost to her for ever.

It is impossible to imagine a period of greater pain and mortification than Mary passed, for about seven weeks, from the sixteenth of April to the sixth of June, in a furnished house that Mr. Imlay had provided for her. ... Her reception by Mr. Imlay was cold and embarrassed. Discussions ("explanations" they were called) followed; cruel explanations, that only added to the anguish of a heart already overwhelmed in grief! They had small pretensions indeed to explicitness; but they sufficiently told that the case admitted not of remedy.

Mary was incapable of sustaining her equanimity in this pressing emergency. "Love, dear, delusive love!" as she expressed herself to a friend some time afterwards, "rigorous reason had forced her to resign; and now her rational prospects were blasted, just as she had learned to be contented with rational enjoyments." Thus situated, life became an intolerable burthen. While she was absent from Mr. Imlay, she could talk of purposes of separation and independence. But, now that they were in the same house, she could not withhold herself from endeavours to revive their mutual cordiality; and unsuccessful endeavours continually added fuel to the fire that destroyed her. She formed a desperate purpose to die.

[1] *hoary* I.e., ancient.

[2] *Mr. Imlay* Gilbert Imlay (1754–1828) was an American writer and businessman. He and Wollstonecraft met in 1793 and became lovers; Fanny Imlay, their daughter, was born in 1794. In 1795 Imlay left Wollstonecraft and formed a new relationship, though Wollstonecraft continued to hope for their reconciliation until October of that year.

This part of the story of Mary is involved in considerable obscurity. I only know that Mr. Imlay became acquainted with her purpose at a moment when he was uncertain whether or no it were already executed, and that his feelings were roused by the intelligence. It was perhaps owing to his activity and representations[1] that her life was at this time saved. She determined to continue to exist. Actuated by this purpose, she took a resolution worthy both of the strength and affectionateness of her mind. Mr. Imlay was involved in a question of considerable difficulty respecting a mercantile adventure in Norway.[2] It seemed to require the presence of some very judicious agent to conduct the business to its desired termination. Mary determined to make the voyage, and take the business into her own hands. Such a voyage seemed the most desirable thing to recruit her health, and, if possible, her spirits, in the present crisis. …

The narrative of this voyage is before the world,[3] and perhaps a book of travels that so irresistibly seizes on the heart never, in any other instance, found its way from the press. The occasional harshness and ruggedness of character that diversify her *Vindication of the Rights of Woman*, here totally disappear. If ever there was a book calculated to make a man in love with its author, this appears to me to be the book. She speaks of her sorrows in a way that fills us with melancholy and dissolves us in tenderness, at the same time that she displays a genius which commands all our admiration. …

from CHAPTER 9
1796, 1797
[MARRIAGE TO WILLIAM GODWIN]

… Ours was not an idle happiness, a paradise of selfish and transitory pleasures. It is perhaps scarcely necessary to mention that, influenced by the ideas I had long entertained upon the subject of cohabitation, I engaged an apartment, about twenty doors from our house in the Polygon, Somers Town, which I designed for the purpose of my study and literary occupations. Trifles however will be interesting to some readers, when they relate to the last period of the life of such a person as Mary. I will add therefore, that we were both of us of opinion that it was possible for two persons to be too uniformly in each other's society. Influenced by that opinion, it was my practice to repair to the apartment I have mentioned as soon as I rose, and frequently not to make my appearance in the Polygon till the hour of dinner. We agreed in condemning the notion, prevalent in many situations in life, that a man and his wife cannot visit in mixed society, but[4] in company with each other; and we rather sought occasions of deviating from, than of complying with, this rule. By these means, though, for the most part, we spent the latter half of each day in one another's society, yet we were in no danger of satiety. We seemed to combine, in a considerable degree, the novelty and lively sensation of a visit with the more delicious and heart-felt pleasures of domestic life.

Whatever may be thought, in other respects, of the plan we laid down to ourselves, we probably derived a real advantage from it, as to the constancy and uninterruptedness of our literary pursuits. …

[1] *representations* Arguments, expostulations.

[2] *mercantile adventure in Norway* Wollstonecraft took on the role of mediator in a lawsuit Imlay was involved in with a Norwegian shipmaster, Peder Ellefson. Ellefson had been hired by Imlay to convey a shipload of silver from Le Havre to Sweden, and the ship and the silver had disappeared. Wollstonecraft was to investigate and negotiate a settlement on Imlay's behalf.

[3] *narrative … world* Wollstonecraft published an epistolary travel memoir, *Letters Written during a Short Residence in Sweden, Norway, and Denmark* (1796), selections from which are included in this anthology.

[4] *but* Except.

from CHAPTER 10
[1797]
[WOLLSTONECRAFT DIES AFTER CHILDBIRTH]

... The loss of the world in this admirable woman, I leave to other men to collect; my own I well know, nor can it be improper to describe it. I do not here allude to the personal pleasures I enjoyed in her conversation: these increased every day, in proportion as we knew each other better, and as our mutual confidence increased. They can be measured only by the treasures of her mind, and the virtues of her heart. But this is a subject for meditation, not for words. What I purposed alluding to, was the improvement that I have for ever lost.

We had cultivated our powers (if I may venture to use this sort of language) in different directions; I chiefly an attempt at logical and metaphysical distinction, she a taste for the picturesque. ...

The strength of her mind lay in intuition. She was often right, by this means only, in matters of mere speculation. Her religion, her philosophy (in both of which the errors were comparatively few, and the strain dignified and generous) were, as I have already said, the pure result of feeling and taste. She adopted one opinion, and rejected another, spontaneously, by a sort of tact, and the force of a cultivated imagination; and yet, though perhaps, in the strict sense of the term, she reasoned little, it is surprising what a degree of soundness is to be found in her determinations. But, if this quality was of use to her in topics that seem the proper province of reasoning, it was much more so in matters directly appealing to the intellectual taste. In a robust and unwavering judgment of this sort, there is a kind of witchcraft; when it decides justly, it produces a responsive vibration in every ingenuous mind. In this sense, my oscillation and scepticism were fixed by her boldness. When a true opinion emanated in this way from another mind, the conviction produced in my own assumed a similar character, instantaneous and firm. ...

This light was lent to me for a very short period, and is now extinguished for ever! ...

WOMEN AND SOCIETY
CONTEXTS

I n the later eighteenth century, women's education and social status became a topic of heated debate
among philanthropists, political and educational theorists, and many middle- and upper-class
parents. As the first excerpt in this section, from William Blackstone's *Commentaries on the Laws of
England*, shows, women's identity in marriage was subsumed under that of their husbands—as it was
subsumed under that of their fathers before marriage. Women could not conduct business, own
property (unless widowed), reject their fathers' choice of husbands for them, or choose to divorce their
husbands. Without legal status they had no representation in Parliament; the idea of female suffrage
was one entertained by only the most radical thinkers.

A common concern voiced by educational theorists at the time was that the fashion of educating
women in "accomplishments" would help them to attract a husband but would not equip them to
fulfill their roles as capable wives or mothers. Instead, many began to stress moral, religious, and
domestic training. While more radical feminists, such as Mary Wollstonecraft, insisted that changes
in gender roles and assumptions about female nature were essential to improving the status of women,
these ideas were not generally accepted. Nevertheless, many of those who supported traditional
notions of female roles and behavior advocated education reform along similar lines—insisting that
practical education for women would benefit society as a whole. The excerpts printed here from
Catharine Macaulay's *Letters on Education*, a series of letters to a fictional friend, Hortensia, criticize
the idea that women's education "should be of an opposite kind to that of males." The weaknesses
that were typically considered natural in women were a result of education and situation only, she
argues, and women should not accept this assumption of inferiority. She proposes one standard of
rational conduct by which both sexes should be judged and attacks traditional gender ideologies and
the often-praised female art of "coquetry," by which women attempt to manipulate men. These ideas
align Macaulay with Wollstonecraft, who was deeply influenced by the work, and later praised
Macaulay in her *Vindication of the Rights of Woman* (1792). Others were less sympathetic, however;
upon publication, Macaulay's *Letters* made her the subject of many personal attacks. In general, the
work was more influential in France than in England.

The next excerpt is taken from French novelist and playwright Olympe de Gouges's *The Rights
of Woman*, a piece with many similarities to Wollstonecraft's work of the following year. De Gouges's
pamphlet also emphasizes the importance of female education and professional opportunities to the
betterment of society and compares women's situation with that of enslaved people, demonstrating
the corrupting effect on men of such arbitrary power over both groups. De Gouges's political
agitation extended far beyond women's rights, and during the French Revolution she published
writings that criticized the violent actions of the revolutionaries and were viewed as sympathetic
towards the monarchy. When her expression of these opinions led to her arrest and execution, the
newspaper of the Committee of Public Safety declared, "She wanted to be a statesman, and it seems
the law has punished this conspiratress for having forgotten the virtues befitting her sex."

Like de Gouges, Wollstonecraft saw that to espouse revolutionary principles of equality but refuse
to extend rights to women represented a betrayal of those supposedly universal principles. Her

Vindication of the Rights of Woman presents the case for women's social equality and economic independence, and argues that education should prepare women to lead rational, virtuous lives. Written in only six weeks, *A Vindication* made Wollstonecraft famous throughout Europe.

A more conservative approach to female education is exemplified in novelist Maria Edgeworth and her father Richard Lovell Edgeworth's *Practical Education*, excerpted here, which emphasizes moral education (as opposed to the acquisition of accomplishments). Conservative thinkers such as the Edgeworths tended to advocate women's training in "traditional female virtues" of modesty, piety, and obedience; such an education consisted of instruction in domestic duties and Christian principles. Quaker philanthropist Priscilla Wakefield's *Reflections on the Present Condition of the Female Sex* proceeds along similar lines, positing that women will be better able to fulfill their roles as wives and mothers if given opportunities for education and professional advancement. She also helps to bring to public attention the plight of many genteel women faced with social and economic difficulties while lacking the skills or opportunities that would enable them to help themselves.

Reverend Richard Polwhele's poem "The Unsexed Females" was part of the backlash against thinkers such as Macaulay and Wollstonecraft that occurred at the turn of the century, following a decade of debate initiated by those two women's works. While Polwhele's poem celebrates women he sees as modestly virtuous, it depicts Wollstonecraft and her followers as unnatural, anti-Christian women driven by a godless "Reason." His poem contains numerous footnotes (most of which are included here) that extend and amplify his arguments.

Hannah More's *Strictures on the Modern System of Female Education*, excerpted here, advocates separate spheres for men and women and emphasizes the education of young women in Christian virtue, morality, and rational education in practical matters. Like most conservative thinkers, More believed that social divisions of class and gender were ordained by God and should not be challenged. Though her ideas for the education of women are, practically speaking, similar to Wollstonecraft's, More insisted on female subordination to men.

The penultimate piece excerpted here, William Thompson and Anna Wheeler's *Appeal of One Half the Human Race*, challenges those utilitarians who overlooked women in their search for universal happiness, as did many of Thompson and Wheeler's fellow reformers. It also argues for female suffrage and takes issue with the misogynist belief that women's interests are best represented by those of their husbands. Written primarily by Thompson but with key passages by Wheeler, the *Appeal* extends many of the ideas developed by Wollstonecraft in her *Vindication*. It examines the faults in the economic system that help to create the social iniquities Wollstonecraft examines, and extends Wollstonecraft's comparison of women's oppression to slavery, comparing the status of enslaved people on New World plantations and in Turkish harems with that of Englishwomen.

⌘ ⌘ ⌘

from William Blackstone, *Commentaries on the Laws of England* (1765)

from BOOK 1, CHAPTER 15: OF HUSBAND AND WIFE

By marriage, the husband and wife are one person in law: that is, the very being or legal existence of the woman is suspended during the marriage, or at least is incorporated and consolidated into that of the husband, under whose wing, protection, and *cover* she performs everything; and is therefore called in our law-French[1] a *feme-covert*; is said to be a *covert-baron*, or under the

[1] *law-French*   Corrupt dialect of Norman French used in English law books until the reign of Edward III (1327–77).

protection and influence of her husband, her *baron*, or lord; and her condition during her marriage is called her *coverture*. Upon this principle, of a union of person in husband and wife, depend almost all the legal rights, duties, and disabilities that either of them acquire by the marriage. I speak not at present of the rights of property, but of such as are merely *personal*. For this reason, a man cannot grant anything to his wife, or enter into covenant with her; for the grant would be to suppose her separate existence, and to covenant with her would be only to covenant with himself. And therefore it is also generally true that all compacts made between husband and wife when single are voided by the intermarriage. A woman indeed may be attorney for her husband; for that implies no separation from, but is rather a representation of, her lord. And a husband may also bequeath anything to his wife by will; for that cannot take effect till the coverture is determined[1] by his death. The husband is bound to provide his wife with necessaries by law, as much as himself; and if he contracts debts for them, he is obliged to pay them: but for anything besides necessaries he is not chargeable. Also, if a wife elopes, and lives with another man, the husband is not chargeable even for necessaries—at least if the person who furnishes them is sufficiently apprized of her elopement. If the wife be indebted before marriage, the husband is bound afterwards to pay the debt; for he has adopted her and her circumstances together. If the wife be injured in her person or her property, she can bring no action for redress without her husband's concurrence, and in his name as well as her own; neither can she be sued without making the husband a defendant. ...

These are the chief legal effects of marriage during the coverture, upon which we may observe that even the disabilities which the wife lies under are for the most part intended for her protection and benefit. So great a favourite is the female sex of the laws of England.[2]

---

[1] *determined* Terminated.

[2] *So great ... England* Not until 1870, with the Married Woman's Property Act, did women gain the right to retain their earnings. In 1882, amendments to this Act allowed them to keep personal property that they brought to or acquired during a marriage. They also finally gained a legal identity separate from their husbands', and could then enter into legal contracts and seek restitution in courts.

from Catharine Macaulay, *Letters on Education* (1790)

from LETTER 21:
MORALS MUST BE TAUGHT ON IMMUTABLE PRINCIPLES

... In order to take from public sentiment a reproach which leaves a deep stain on the human character, and to correct many irregularities, and even enormities, which arise from incorrect systems of ethics, it ought to be the first care of education to teach virtue on immutable principles, and to avoid that confusion which must arise from confounding the laws and customs of society with those obligations which are founded on correct principles of equity. But as you have had patience to go through my whole plan of education, from infancy to manhood, it is but fair that I should attend to your objections, and examine whether my plan is founded on error, or on the principles of reason and truth. Know then, good Hortensia, that I have given similar rules for male and female education, on the following grounds of reasoning.

First, that there is but one rule of right for the conduct of all rational beings; consequently that true virtue in one sex must be equally so in the other, whenever a proper opportunity calls for its exertion, and, *vice versa*, what is vice in one sex cannot have a different property when found in the other.

Secondly, that true wisdom, which is never found at variance with rectitude, is as useful to women as to men, because it is necessary to the highest degree of happiness, which can never exist with ignorance.

Lastly, that as on our first entrance into another world our state of happiness may possibly depend on the degree of perfection we have attained in this, we cannot justly lessen, in one sex or the other, the means by which perfection, that is another word for wisdom, is acquired.

It would be paying you a bad compliment, Hortensia, were I to answer all the frivolous objections which prejudice has framed against the giving a learned education to women; for I know of no learning worth having that does not tend to free the mind from error and enlarge our stock of useful knowledge. Thus much it may be proper to observe, that those hours which are spent in studious retirement by learned women will not in all probability intrude so much on the time for useful avocation as the wild and spreading dissipations of the present day; that levity and ignorance will always be found in opposition to what is useful and graceful in life; and that the contrary may be expected from a truly enlightened understanding. However, Hortensia, to throw some illustration on what I have advanced on this subject, it may be necessary to show you that all those vices and imperfections which have been generally regarded as inseparable from the female character do not in any manner proceed from sexual causes, but are entirely the effects of situation and education. But these observations must be left to further discussion.

from LETTER 22:
NO CHARACTERISTIC DIFFERENCE IN SEX

… It must be confessed that the virtues of the males among the human species, though mixed and blended with a variety of vices and errors, have displayed a bolder and a more consistent picture of excellence than female nature has hitherto done. It is on these reasons that when we compliment the appearance of a more than ordinary energy in the female mind, we call it masculine; and hence it is that Pope has elegantly said "a perfect woman's but a softer man."[1] And if we take in the consideration that there can be but one rule of moral excellence for beings made of the same materials, organized after the same manner, and subjected to similar laws of nature, we must either agree with Mr. Pope, or we must reverse the proposition, and say that "a perfect man is a woman formed after a coarser mold." The difference that actually does subsist between the sexes is too flattering for men to be willingly imputed to accident; for what accident occasions, wisdom might correct, and it is better, says Pride, to give up the

advantages we might derive from the perfection of our fellow associates than to own that nature has been just in the equal distribution of her favours. These are the sentiments of the men; but mark how readily they are yielded to by the women—not from humility, I assure you, but merely to preserve with character those fond vanities on which they set their hearts. No; suffer them to idolize their persons, to throw away their life in the pursuit of trifles, and to indulge in the gratification of the meaner passions, and they will heartily join in the sentence of their degradation.

Among the most strenuous asserters of a sexual difference in character, Rousseau[2] is the most conspicuous, both on account of that warmth of sentiment which distinguishes all his writings, and the eloquence of his compositions: but never did enthusiasm and the love of paradox, those enemies to philosophical disquisition, appear in more strong opposition to plain sense than in Rousseau's definition of this difference. He sets out with a supposition that Nature intended the subjection of the one sex to the other; that consequently there must be an inferiority of intellect in the subjected party; but as man is a very imperfect being, and apt to play the capricious tyrant, Nature, to bring things nearer to an equality, bestowed on the woman such attractive graces, and such an insinuating address, as to turn the balance on the other scale. Thus Nature, in a giddy mood, recedes from her purposes, and subjects prerogative to an influence which must produce confusion and disorder in the system of human affairs. Rousseau saw this objection, and in order to obviate it he has made up a moral person of the union of the two sexes, which, for contradiction and absurdity, outdoes every metaphysical riddle that was ever formed in the schools. In short, it is not reason, it is not wit; it is pride and sensuality that speak in Rousseau, and, in this instance, has lowered the man of genius to the licentious pedant.

But whatever might be the wise purpose intended by Providence in such a disposition of things, certain it is that some degree of inferiority, in point of corporal

[1] *a perfect … man* Reference to Alexander Pope, "Epistle 2: To a Lady, on the Characters of Women" (1735), lines 271–72: "Heaven, when it strives to polish all it can / Its last best work, but forms a softer man."

[2] *Rousseau* In his *Émile* (1762), French philosopher Jean-Jacques Rousseau argues that female children should be educated, but should be taught to remain subordinate and submissive to men.

strength, seems always to have existed between the two sexes; and this advantage, in the barbarous ages of mankind, was abused to such a degree as to destroy all the natural rights of the female species and reduce them to a state of abject slavery. What accidents have contributed in Europe to better their condition would not be to my purpose to relate, for I do not intend to give you a history of women; I mean only to trace the sources of their peculiar foibles and vices, and these I firmly believe to originate in situation and education only: for so little did a wise and just Providence intend to make the condition of slavery an unalterable law of female nature, that in the same proportion as the male sex have consulted the interest of their own happiness, they have relaxed in their tyranny over women; and such is their use in the system of mundane creation, and such their natural influence over the male mind, that were these advantages properly exerted, they might carry every point of any importance to their honour and happiness. However, till that period arrives in which women will act wisely, we will amuse ourselves in talking of their follies.

The situation and education of women, Hortensia, is precisely that which must necessarily tend to corrupt and debilitate both the powers of mind and body. From a false notion of beauty and delicacy, their system of nerves is depraved before they come out of their nursery; and this kind of depravity has more influence over the mind, and consequently over morals, than is commonly apprehended. But it would be well if such causes only acted towards the debasement of the sex; their moral education is, if possible, more absurd than their physical. The principles and nature of virtue, which is never properly explained to boys, is kept quite a mystery to girls. They are told, indeed, that they must abstain from those vices which are contrary to their personal happiness, or they will be regarded as criminals, both by God and man; but all the higher parts of rectitude, everything that ennobles our being, and that renders us both innoxious and useful, is either not taught, or is taught in

such a manner as to leave no proper impression on the mind. This is so obvious a truth that the defects of female education have ever been a fruitful topic of declamation for the moralist; but not one of this class of writers have laid down any judicious rules for amendment. Whilst we still retain the absurd notion of a sexual excellence, it will militate against the perfecting a plan of education for either sex. The judicious Addison animadverts on the absurdity of bringing a young lady up with no higher idea of the end of education than to make her agreeable to a husband, and confining the necessary excellence for this happy acquisition to the mere graces of person.[1]

Every parent and tutor may not express himself in the same manner as is marked out by Addison; yet certain it is that the admiration of the other sex is held out to women as the highest honour they can attain; and whilst this is considered as their *summum bonum*,[2] and the beauty of their persons the chief *desideratum*[3] of men, Vanity and its companion Envy must taint, in their characters, every native and every acquired excellence. Nor can you, Hortensia, deny that these qualities, when united to ignorance, are fully equal to the engendering and rivetting all those vices and foibles which are peculiar to the female sex—vices and foibles which have caused them to be considered, in ancient times, as beneath cultivation, and in modern days have subjected them to the censure and ridicule of writers of all descriptions, from the deep thinking philosopher to the man of ton and gallantry, who, by the by,[4] sometimes distinguishes himself by qualities which are not greatly superior to those he despises in women. ...

---

[1] *judicious Addison ... person* Reference to an article in *Spectator* No. 66 (16 May 1711) actually written by Richard Steele; *animadverts* Comments critically.

[2] *summum bonum* Latin: greatest good.

[3] *desideratum* Latin: thing desired.

[4] *by the by* Incidentally; as a side issue.

from Olympe de Gouges, *The Rights of Woman* [1]
(1791)

Man, are you able to be just? It is a woman who asks you the question; you will not take that right, at least, away from her. Tell me: what has given you the sovereign power to oppress my sex? your strength? your talents? Observe the Creator in His wisdom; survey nature in all its grandeur, to which you seem to want to compare yourself, and give me, if you dare, an example of this tyrannical power. Go back to the animals, consult the elements, study the vegetables, cast a glance, finally, over all the modifications of organized matter; and submit to the evidence when I give you the means to; search, excavate, and distinguish the sexes, if you can, in the government of nature. Everywhere you will find them mingled, everywhere they cooperate as a harmonious consort in this immortal masterpiece.

Man alone has dressed up this exception as a principle. Bizarre, blind, bloated with sciences and degenerated, in this age of enlightenment and wisdom, into the crassest ignorance, he wants to rule like a despot over a sex which has received all the intellectual faculties; he pretends to rejoice in the revolution, and to claim his rights to equality, in order to say no more about it.

DECLARATION OF THE RIGHTS OF WOMAN AND OF THE FEMALE CITIZEN

To be decreed by the National Assembly in its last sessions or in that of the next legislature.

PREAMBLE

The mothers, daughters, sisters, representatives of the nation, demand to be formed into a national assembly. Considering that ignorance, neglect, or contempt of the rights of woman are the sole causes of public misfortunes and the corruption of governments, have resolved to set forth in a solemn declaration the natural, inalienable, and sacred rights of woman, that this declaration, being constantly present to all the members of the body social, may ever remind them of their rights and their duties; that the acts of the power of women, and those of the power of men, being capable of being every moment compared with the end of all political institutions, may be more respected; that the claims of the female citizens, founded hereafter on simple and incontestable principles, may always tend to the maintenance of the constitution and of good morals, and to the general happiness.

Accordingly, the sex that is as superior in beauty as in courage, in the sufferings of maternity, recognizes and declares, in the presence and under the auspices of the Supreme Being, the following Rights of Woman and of the Female citizen.

FIRST ARTICLE

Woman is born free and remains equal to man in rights. Social distinctions can only be founded on common utility.

2

The end of all political association is the preservation of the natural and imprescriptible [2] rights of woman and of man: these rights are liberty, property, security, and above all resistance to oppression.

3

The principle of all sovereignty resides essentially in the Nation, which is nothing more than the union of woman and man: no body, no individual, can exercise an authority which does not emanate expressly from it.

---

[1] *The Rights of Woman* Translated from the French by D.L. Macdonald.

[2] *imprescriptible* That cannot legally be taken away.

4

Liberty and justice consist in rendering to others all that belongs to them; thus the exercise of the natural rights of woman has no other limits than the perpetual tyranny that man opposes to it; these limits should be reformed by the laws of nature and of reason.

5

The laws of nature and of reason prohibit all actions hurtful to society: nothing that is not prohibited by these laws, wise and divine, may be hindered, nor may anyone be compelled to do what they do not enjoin.

6

The law should be the expression of the general will; all the female and male citizens should concur personally, or by their representatives, in its formation; it should be the same for all: all the female and all the male citizens, being equal in its eyes, should be equally admissible to all honours, positions, and public employments, according to their capacities, and without any other distinctions than those of their virtues and their talents.

7

No woman is exempt; she is accused, arrested, and detained in cases determined by the law. Women, like men, obey this rigorous law.

8

The law should impose only those penalties which are strictly and evidently necessary, and no one can be punished except by virtue of a law established and promulgated previously to the offense and legally applied to women.

9

Whenever a woman is declared guilty, all rigour is exercised by the law.

10

No one should be molested for their opinions, even fundamental ones; woman has the right to mount the scaffold; she should equally have the right to mount the tribune,[1] provided that her actions do not disturb the public order established by the law.

11

The free communication of thoughts and opinions is one of the most precious rights of woman, since this liberty ensures that fathers acknowledge their children. Every female citizen may therefore say freely, I am the mother of a child who belongs to you, without a barbarous prejudice to force her to conceal the truth, provided she is held responsible for the abuse of this liberty in the cases determined by the law.

12

The good of the majority is necessary in order to secure the rights of woman and the female citizen; this security should be instituted for the advantage of all, and not for the particular good of those women to whom it is entrusted.

13

For the maintenance of the public force, and for the expenses of government, the contributions of woman and man are equal; she takes part in all the drudgery, in all the laborious tasks; she should therefore take the same part in the distribution of positions, of employments, of commissions, of honours, and of business.

14

The female and male citizens have the right to determine, by themselves or by their representatives, the necessity of public contributions. The female citizens cannot enjoy this right except by being allowed an equal

---

[1]   *tribune*   Raised platform or dais for addressing an assembly.

share, not only in wealth, but also in public administration, and by being allowed to determine the amount, the basis, the collection, and the duration of taxation.

15

The mass of women, united for the purposes of taxation with that of men, has the right to demand of all its public agents an account of their administration.

16

Every society in which the security of rights is not assured, and the separation of powers is not determined, has no constitution; the constitution is null and void if the majority of the individuals who make up the nation has not cooperated in drawing it up.

17

Property belongs to both sexes, individually or collectively; it is everyone's inviolable and sacred right; as it is a true patrimony of nature, no one may be deprived of it, except when public necessity, legally ascertained, evidently demands it, and on condition of a previously established and just indemnity.

from Maria Edgeworth and Richard Lovell Edgeworth, *Practical Education* (1798)

from PRUDENCE AND ECONOMY

In the education of girls we must teach them much more caution than is necessary to boys: their prudence must be more the result of reasoning than of experiment; they *must* trust to the experience of others; they cannot always have recourse to what *ought to be*, they must adapt themselves to what is. They cannot rectify the material mistakes in their conduct. Timidity, a certain tardiness of decision, and reluctance to act in public situations are not considered as defects in a woman's character; her pausing prudence does not to a man of discernment denote imbecility, but appears to him the graceful auspicious characteristic of female virtue. There is always more probability that women should endanger their own happiness by precipitation than by forbearance.

Promptitude of choice is seldom expected from the female sex; they should avail themselves of the leisure that is permitted to them for reflection. "Begin nothing of which you have not well considered the end," was the piece of advice for which the Eastern Sultan paid a purse of gold, the price set upon it by a sage. The monarch did not repent of his purchase. This maxim should be engraved upon the memory of our female pupils by the repeated lessons of education. We should even in trifles avoid every circumstance which can tend to make girls venturesome, which can encourage them to trust to their good fortune, instead of relying on their own prudence. ...

In the choice of friends, and on all matters of taste, young women should be excited to reason about their own feelings. "There is no reasoning about taste," is a pernicious maxim; if there was more reasoning, there would be disputation upon this subject. If women questioned their own minds, or allowed their friends to question them concerning the reasons of their "preferences and aversions," there would not probably be so many love matches, and so few love marriages. It is in vain to expect that young women should begin to reason miraculously, at the very moment that reason is wanted in the guidance of their conduct. We should also observe that women are called upon for the exertion of their prudence at an age when young men are scarcely supposed to possess that virtue; therefore women should be more early, and more carefully educated for the purpose. The important decisions of a woman's life are often made before she is twenty; a man does not come upon the theatre of public life, where most of his prudence is shown, till he is much older.

from Priscilla Wakefield, *Reflections on the Present Condition of the Female Sex; With Suggestions for Its Improvement* (1798)

from Chapter 3
The Necessity of Women Being Educated for the Exercise of Lucrative Employments Shown, and the Absurdity of a Woman Honourably Earning a Support Being Excluded from Society, Exposed

In the education of females, the same view actuates every rank: an advantageous settlement on marriage is the universal prize, for which parents of all classes enter their daughters upon the lists; and partiality or self-complacency assures to every competitor the most flattering prospect of success. To this one point tends the principal part of female instruction; for the promotion of this design, their best years for improvement are sacrificed to the attainment of attractive qualities, showy superficial accomplishments, polished manners, and, in one word, the whole science of pleasing, which is cultivated with unceasing assiduity as an object of the most essential importance.

The end is laudable, and deserving of every effort that can be exerted to secure it; a happy marriage may be estimated among the rarest felicities of human life, but it may be doubted whether the means used to accomplish it are adequate to the purpose, as the making a first impression is by no means effectual to determine the preference of a wise man. It is not then sufficient that a girl be qualified to excite admiration; her own happiness, and that of the man to whom she devotes the remainder of her days, depend upon her possession of those virtues, which alone can preserve lasting esteem and confidence.

The offices of a wife are very different from those of the mere pageant of a ballroom; and as their nature is more exalted, the talents they require are of a more noble kind: something far beyond the elegant trifler is wanted in a companion for life. A young woman is very ill-adapted to enter into the most solemn of social contracts who is not prepared, by her education, to become the participator of her husband's cares, the consoler of his sorrows, his stimulator to every praiseworthy undertaking, his partner in the labours and vicissitudes of life, the faithful and economical manager of his affairs, the judicious superintendant of his family, the wife and affectionate mother of his children, the preserver of his honour, his chief counsellor, and, to sum up all, the chosen friend of his bosom. If a modern female education be not calculated to produce these effects, as few surely will judge it to be, who reflect upon its tendency, it is incompetent to that very purpose, which is confessedly its main object, and must therefore be deemed imperfect, and require reformation. …

from Chapter 6
Lucrative Employments for the First and Second Classes Suggested … With Strictures on a Theatrical Life

Transitions in private life from affluence to poverty, like the sable pageantry of death, from their frequency produce no lasting impressions on the beholders. Unexpected misfortunes befall an acquaintance who has been caressed in the days of prosperity: the change is lamented, and she is consoled by the visits of her friends, in the first moments of affliction; she sinks gradually into wretchedness; she becomes obscure, and is forgotten. … A few remarks upon the nature of those employments which are best adapted to the higher classes of the sex, when reduced to necessitous circumstances, may, perhaps, afford useful hints to those who are languishing under the pressure of misfortune, and induce abler pens to treat a subject hitherto greatly neglected.

The most renowned actress of the day was Sarah Siddons (1755–1831), born into the theatrical family of Roger Kemble. Siddons's most famous role was that of Lady Macbeth, which she first played in 1785. Above left is a detail from a painting (c. 1790) of her playing the role opposite her brother; at right is George Henry Harlow's *Sarah Siddons in the Scene of Lady Macbeth Sleepwalking*, 1814. Siddons's farewell stage performance had been as Lady Macbeth in 1812.

Numerous difficulties arise in the choice of occupations for the purpose. They must be such as are neither laborious nor servile, and they must of course be productive, without requiring a capital.

For these reasons, pursuits which require the exercise of intellectual rather than bodily powers are generally the most eligible.

Literature affords a respectable and pleasing employment for those who possess talents and an adequate degree of mental cultivation. For although the emolument is precarious, and seldom equal to a maintenance, yet if the attempt be tolerably successful, it may yield a comfortable assistance in narrow circumstances and beguile many hours, which might otherwise be passed in solitude or unavailing regret. The fine arts offer a mode of subsistence congenial to the delicacy of the most refined minds, and they are peculiarly adapted, by their elegance, to the gratification of taste. The perfection of every species of painting is attainable by women, from the representation of historic facts to the minute execution of the miniature portrait, if they will bestow sufficient time and application for the acquisition of the principles of the art, in the study of those models which have been the means of transmitting the names and character of so many men to the admiration of posterity. The successful exercise of this imitative art requires invention, taste, and judgment: in the two first, the sex are allowed to excel, and the last may be obtained by a perseverance in examining, comparing, and reflecting upon the works of those masters who have copied nature in her most graceful forms. ...

The stage is a profession to which many women of refined manners and a literary turn of mind have had recourse. Since it has been customary for females to assume dramatic characters, there appears to have been full as great a proportion of women who have attained celebrity among those who have devoted themselves to a theatrical life, as of the other sex—a fact which argues that there is no inequality of genius in the sexes for the imitative arts. The observation may operate as a stimulant to women to those pursuits which are less objectionable than the stage, which is not mentioned for the purpose of recommending it, but of proving that the abilities of the female sex are equal to nobler labours than are usually undertaken by women. The profession of an actress is indeed most unsuitable to the sex in every point of view, whether it be considered with respect to the courage requisite to face an audience, or the variety of situations incident to it, which expose moral virtue to the most severe trials. Let the daughters of a happier destiny, whilst they lament the evils to which some of their sex are exposed, remember those unpropitious circumstances that have cast them into a line of life in which it is scarcely possible to preserve that purity of sentiment and conduct which characterizes female excellence. When their errors are discussed, let the harsh voice of censure be restrained by the reflection that she who has made the greatest advances towards perfection might have fallen, had she been surrounded by the same influences.

That species of agriculture which depends upon skill in the management of the nursery ground, in rearing the various kinds of shrubs and flowers for the supply of gentlemen's gardens and pleasure grounds, would supply an elegant means of support to those women who are able to raise a capital for carrying on a work of that magnitude. Ornamental gardening, and the laying out of pleasure grounds and parks with the improvement of natural landscape, one of the refinements of modern times, may likewise afford an eligible maintenance to some of those females who, in the days of their prosperity, displayed their taste in the embellishment of their own domains.

The presiding over seminaries for female education is likewise a suitable employment for those whose minds have been enlarged by liberal cultivation, whilst the under parts of that profession may be more suitably filled by persons whose early views have been contracted within narrower limits. After all that can be suggested by general remarks, the different circumstances of individuals must decide the profession most convenient to them. But it is a consolatory reflection that amidst the daily vicissitudes of human life, from which no rank is exempt, there are resources from which aid may be drawn, without derogating from the true dignity of a rational being.

from Richard Polwhele, "The Unsexed Females: A Poem, Addressed to the Author of *The Pursuits of Literature*"[1] (1798)

Survey with me, what ne'er our fathers saw,
A female band despising Nature's law,[2]
As "proud defiance"[3] flashes from their arms,
And vengeance smothers all their softer charms.
5   I shudder at the new unpictured scene,
Where unsexed woman vaunts the imperious
    mien;°   *bearing*
Where girls, affecting to dismiss the heart,
Invoke the Proteus of petrific[4] art;
With equal ease, in body or in mind,
10 To Gallic freaks or Gallic faith resigned,
The crane like neck, as Fashion bids, lay bare,
Or frizzle,[5] bold in front, their borrowed hair;
Scarce by a gossamery film carest,

Sport,[6] in full view, the meretricious° breast;[7]   *whorish*
15 Loose the chaste cincture,[8] where the graces shone,
And languished all the Loves, the ambrosial zone;
As lordly domes inspire dramatic rage,
Court prurient Fancy to the private stage;
With bliss botanic[9] as their bosoms heave,
20 Still pluck forbidden fruit, with mother Eve,
For puberty in sighing florets pant,
Or point the prostitution of a plant;
Dissect[10] its organ of unhallowed lust,
And fondly gaze the titillating dust;
25 With liberty's sublimer views expand,

---

[1] *the Author … Literature* Thomas James Mathias, whose extremely popular satirical poem *The Pursuits of Literature* (1794–97) reacted against radical politics, particularly against feminists such as Mary Wollstonecraft. Polwhele draws on Mathias's comment in the poem's preface that "our *unsexed* female writers now instruct, or confuse, us and themselves, in the labyrinth of politics, or turn us wild with Gallic frenzy" (i.e., ideas inspired by the French Revolution).

[2] [Polwhele's note] Nature is the grand basis of all laws human and divine: and the woman who has no regard to nature, either in decoration of her person or the culture of her mind, will soon "walk after the flesh in the lust of uncleanness, and despise government." [Polwhele quotes from 2 Peter 2.10.]

[3] [From Polwhele's note] "A troop came next, who crowns and armour wore / And proud defiance in their looks they bore" Pope. The Amazonian band—the female Quixotes of the new philosophy are here too justly characterised. … [Polwhele quotes Alexander Pope's "The Temple of Fame" (1711), lines 342–43. *Amazons* Members of a legendary race of warrior women from Scythia; *Quixotes* Idealists, dreamers. "Female Quixotes" refers more specifically to Charlotte Lennox's famous novel of 1752, *The Female Quixote*.]

[4] *Proteus* God who could change shape at will; *petrific* Able to turn to stone, or to turn something else to stone.

[5] *frizzle* Curl in small curls.

[6] [Polwhele's note] To "sport a face" is a cant phrase in one of our universities, by which is meant an impudent obtrusion of a man's person in company. It is not applicable, perhaps, to the open bosom—a fashion which we have never invited or sanctioned.

[7] [From Polwhele's note] The fashions of France, which have been always imitated by the English, were, heretofore, unexceptionable in a moral point of view; since, however ridiculous or absurd, they were innocent. But they have now their source among prostitutes—among women of the most abandoned character. …

[8] *cincture* Girdle for the waist, sometimes surrounding the breasts as well.

[9] [Polwhele's note] Botany has lately become a fashionable amusement with the ladies. But how the study of the sexual system can accord with female modesty, I am not able to comprehend. I had at first, written, "More eager for illicit knowledge pant, / With lustful boys anatomise a plant; / The virtues of its dust prolific speak, / Or point its pistil with unblushing cheek." I have, several times, seen boys and girls botanizing together.

[10] [Polwhele's note] Miss Wollstonecraft does not blush to say, in an introduction to a book designed for the use of young ladies, that, "in order to lay the axe at the root of corruption, it would be proper to familiarize the sexes to an unreserved discussion of those topics which are generally avoided in conversation from a principle of false delicacy; and that it would be right to speak of the organs of generation as freely as we mention our eyes or our hands." To such language our botanizing girls are doubtless familiarized; and they are in a fair way of becoming worthy disciples of Miss W. If they do not take heed to their ways, they will soon exchange the blush of modesty for the bronze of impudence. [Polwhele refers to Mary Wollstonecraft's "Introductory Address to Parents," from her *Elements of Morality, for the Use of Children* (1792), but he misrepresents her argument, which is that children can be discouraged from masturbating by being taught about the sexual organs and by having explained to them "the noble use which they were designed for." In her *Vindication of the Rights of Woman* (1792) she also argues that the study of botany can be consistent with female modesty.]

And o'er the wreck of kingdoms[1] sternly stand;
And, frantic, midst the democratic storm,
Pursue, Philosophy! thy phantom-form.[2]
    Far other is the female shape and mind,
30 By modest luxury heightened and refined;
Those limbs, that figure, though by Fashion[3] graced,
By Beauty polished, and adorned by Taste;
That soul, whose harmony perennial flows,
In Music trembles, and in Color glows;
35 Which bids sweet Poesy reclaim the praise
With faery light to gild fastidious days,
From sullen clouds relieve domestic care,
And melt in smiles the withering frown of war.
Ah! once the female Muse,[4] to *Nature* true,
40 The unvalued store from *Fancy*, *Feeling* drew;
Won, from the grasp of woe, the roseate hours,
Cheered life's dim vale, and strewed the grave with
    flowers.
But lo! where, pale amidst the wild,[5] she draws
Each precept cold from sceptic Reason's[6] vase;

45 Pours with rash arm the turbid stream along,
And in the foaming torrent whelms the throng.[7] …
See Wollstonecraft, whom no decorum checks,
Arise, the intrepid champion of her sex;
O'er humbled man assert the sovereign claim,
50 And slight the timid blush[8] of virgin fame.

from Hannah More, *Strictures on the Modern System of Female Education, With a View of the Principles and Conduct Prevalent among Women of Rank and Fortune* (1799)

from VOLUME 1, CHAPTER 4:
COMPARISON OF THE MODE OF FEMALE EDUCATION
IN THE LAST AGE WITH THE PRESENT AGE

A young lady may excel in speaking French and Italian, may repeat a few passages from a volume of extracts; play like a professor, and sing like a siren;[9] have her dressing-room decorated with her own drawings, tables, stands, screens, and cabinets; nay, she may dance like Sempronia[10] herself, and yet may have been very badly educated. I am far from meaning to set no value whatever on any or all of these qualifications; they are all of them elegant, and many of them properly tend to the perfecting of a polite education. These things, in

---

[1] [Polwhele's note] The female advocates of democracy in this country, though they have had no opportunity of imitating the French ladies in their acts of atrocious cruelty, have yet assumed a stern serenity in the contemplation of those savage excesses. "To express their abhorrence of royalty, they (the French ladies) threw away the character of their sex, and bit the amputated limbs of their murdered countrymen. I say this on the authority of a young gentleman who saw it. I am sorry to add that the relation, accompanied with looks of horror and disgust, only provoked a contemptuous smile from an illuminated British fair-one." See Robison—p.219. [John Robison's *Proofs of a Conspiracy Against All the Religions and Governments of Europe* (1797).]

[2] [From Polwhele's note] Philosophism, the false image of philosophy. …

[3] [Polwhele's note] I admit that we are quickly reconciled to the fashion of the day, and often consider it as graceful, if it offends not against delicacy.

[4] *Muse* One of nine daughters of Zeus and Mnemosyne, each of whom presided over and provided inspiration for an aspect of arts and sciences.

[5] [Polwhele's note] "A wild, where flowers and weeds promiscuous shoot; / A garden tempting with forbidden fruit" Pope. [From Alexander Pope's *Essay on Man* (1733) 1.7–8.]

[6] [Polwhele's note] A troubled stream only can proceed from the vase of skepticism; if it be not "the broken cistern that will hold no water" [from Jeremiah 2.13].

[7] [Polwhele's note] "Raging waves, foaming out their own shame"—St. Jude. Such were those infamous publications of Paine and others, which, like the torrents of December, threatened to sweep all before them—to overwhelm the multitude. [Polwhele quotes from Jude 1.13 and refers to Thomas Paine's *Rights of Man* (1791–92), his reply to an attack on the French Revolutionaries by Edmund Burke.]

[8] [Polwhele's note] That Miss Wollstonecraft was a sworn enemy to the blushes, I need not remark. But many of my readers, perhaps, will be astonished to hear that at several of our boarding schools for young ladies, a blush incurs a penalty.

[9] *siren* Mythical creature, part woman and part bird, whose enchanted songs were said to lure sailors to their destruction.

[10] *Sempronia* Infamous woman of ancient Rome, known for her loose morals, who was said to have taken part in Cataline's conspiracy to overthrow the government in 63 BCE. According to Roman historian Sallust, Sempronia "had greater skill in lyre playing and dancing than there is any need for a respectable woman to acquire. There was nothing that she set a smaller value on than seemliness and chastity."

their measure and degree, may be done, but there are others which should not be left undone. Many things are becoming, but "one thing is needful." Besides, as the world seems to be fully apprized of the value of whatever tends to embellish life, there is less occasion here to insist on its importance.

But, though a well bred young lady may lawfully learn most of the fashionable arts, yet it does not seem to be the true end of education to make women of fashion dancers, singers, players, painters, actresses, sculptors, gilders, varnishers, engravers, and embroiderers. Most men are commonly destined to some profession, and their minds are consequently turned each to its respective object. Would it not be strange if they were called out to exercise their profession, or to set up their trade, with only a little general knowledge of the trades of all other men, and without any previous definite application to their own peculiar calling? The profession of ladies, to which the bent of their instruction should be turned, is that of daughters, wives, mothers, and mistresses of families. They should be therefore trained with a view to these several conditions, and be furnished with a stock of ideas and principles, and qualifications ready to be applied and appropriated, as occasion may demand, to each of these respective situations: for though the arts which merely embellish life must claim admiration, yet when a man of sense comes to marry, it is a companion whom he wants, and not an artist. It is not merely a creature who can paint, and play, and dress, and dance; it is a being who can comfort and counsel him; one who can reason and reflect, and feel, and judge, and discourse, and discriminate; one who can assist him in his affairs, lighten his cares, soothe his sorrows, strengthen his principles, and educate his children.

from VOLUME 1, CHAPTER 6: ON THE EARLY FORMING OF HABITS. ON THE NECESSITY OF FORMING THE JUDGMENT TO DIRECT THOSE HABITS

An early habitual restraint is peculiarly important to the future character and happiness of women. They should when very young be inured to contradiction. Instead of

hearing their bon-mots[1] treasured up and repeated to the guests till they begin to think it dull when they themselves are not the little heroine of the theme, they should be accustomed to receive but little praise for their vivacity or their wit, though they should receive just commendation for their patience, their industry, their humility, and other qualities which have more worth than splendour. They should be led to distrust their own judgment; they should learn not to murmur at expostulation, but should be accustomed to expect and to endure opposition. It is a lesson with which the world will not fail to furnish them, and they will not practice it the worse for having learnt it the sooner. It is of the last importance to their happiness in life that they should early acquire a submissive temper and a forbearing spirit. They must even endure to be thought wrong sometimes when they cannot but feel they are right. And while they should be anxiously aspiring to do well, they must not expect always to obtain the praise of having done so. But while a gentle demeanor is inculcated, let them not be instructed to practise gentleness merely on the low ground of its being decorous and feminine, and pleasing, and calculated to attract human favour; but let them be carefully taught to cultivate it on the high principle of obedience to Christ.

from William Thompson and Anna Wheeler, *Appeal of One Half the Human Race, Women, Against the Pretensions of the Other Half, Men, to Retain Them in Political, and Thence in Civil and Domestic Slavery* (1825)

from INTRODUCTORY LETTER TO MRS. WHEELER

With you I would equally elevate both sexes. Really enlightened women, disdaining equally the submissive tricks of the slave and the caprices of the despot, breathing freely only in the air of the esteem of equals, and of mutual, *unbought*, *uncommanded* affection, would find it difficult to meet with associates

[1] *bon-mots* French: witticisms.

worthy of them in men as now formed, full of ignorance and vanity, priding themselves on a *sexual* superiority, entirely independent of any merit, any superior qualities, or pretensions to them, claiming respect from the strength of their arm and the lordly faculty of producing beards attached by nature to their chins! No: unworthy of, as incapable of appreciating, the delight of the society of such women, are the great majority of the existing race of men. The pleasures of mere animal appetite, the pleasures of commanding (the prettier and more helpless the slave, the greater these pleasures of the brute) are the only pleasures which the majority of men seek for from women, are the only pleasures which their education and the hypocritical system of morals with which they have been necessarily imbued, permit them to expect. ...

Even under the present arrangements of society, founded as they all are on the basis of individual competition, nothing could be more easy than to put the *rights* of women, political and civil, on a perfect equality with those of men. It is only to abolish all prohibitory and exclusive laws—statute or what are called "common"—the remnants of the barbarous customs of our ignorant ancestors; particularly the horrible and odious inequality and indissolubility of that disgrace of civilization, the present marriage code. Women then might exert in a free career with men their faculties of mind and body, to whatever degree developed, in pursuit of happiness by means of exertion, as men do. But this would not raise women to an equality of happiness with men: their rights might be equal, but not their happiness, because unequal powers under free competition must produce unequal effects.

In truth, the system of the most enlightened of the school of those reformers called political economists is still founded on exclusions. Its basis is too narrow for human happiness. A more comprehensive system, founded on equal benevolence, on the true development of the principle of Utility, is wanting.[1] Let the *competitive* political economists be satisfied with the praise of causing the removal of some of the rubbish of

ignorant restrictions, under the name of laws, impeding the development of human exertion in the production of wealth. To build up a new fabric of social happiness, comprehending equally the interests of all existing human beings, has never been contemplated by them, and is altogether beyond the scope of their little theories; aiming at the utmost at increasing the number of what they style the happy middling orders, but leaving the great bulk of human beings to eternal ignorance and toil, requited by the mere means of prolonging from day to day an unhealthy and precarious existence. To a new science, the *social science*, or the science of promoting human happiness, that of political economy, or the mere science of producing wealth by individual competition, must give way.

from PART 2

As soon as adult daughters become wives, their civil rights disappear; they fall back again, and remain all their lives—should their owners and directors live so long—into the state of children or idiots, the passive property of their owners; protected by the law in some few respects only, like other slaves, from the excessive abuse of despotic power.

Woman is then compelled, in marriage, by the possession of superior strength on the part of men, by the want of knowledge, skill, and wealth, by the positive, cruel, partial, and cowardly enactments of law, by the terrors of superstition, by the mockery of a pretended vow of obedience, and to crown all, and as the result of all, by the force of an unrelenting, unreasoning, unfeeling public opinion, to be the literal unequivocal *slave* of the man who may be styled her husband. I say emphatically the slave; for a slave is a person whose actions and earnings, instead of being under his own control, liable only to equal laws, to public opinion, and to his own calculations, under these, of his own interest, are under the arbitrary control of any other human being, by whatever name called. This is the essence of slavery, and what distinguishes it from freedom. A domestic, a civil, a political slave, in the plain unsophisticated sense of the word—in no meta-

---

[1] *principle of Utility* Central principle of utilitarianism, an ethical theory developed by Jeremy Bentham and others; *wanting* Lacking.

phorical sense—is every married woman. No matter with what wealth she may be surrounded, with what dainties she may be fed, with what splendor of trappings adorned, with what voluptuousness her corporeal, mental, or moral sweets may be gathered; that high prerogative of human nature, the faculty of self-government, the basis of intellectual development, without which no moral conduct can exist, is to her wanting. … Till laws afford married women the same protection against the restraints and violence of the men to whom they are married, that they affect to afford them against all other individuals; till they afford them the same protection against the restraints and violence of their husbands, that their husbands enjoy against their caprices and violence, the social condition of the civilized wife will remain more completely slavish than that of the female slave of the West Indies. …

Be consistent, men! Ye stronger half of the race, be at length rational! Three or four thousand years have worn threadbare your vile cloak of hypocrisy. Even women, your poor, weak, contented slaves, at whose impotence of penetration, the result of your vile exclusions, you have been accustomed to laugh, begin to see through it and to shudder at the loathsomeness beneath. Cast aside this tattered cloak before it leaves you naked and exposed. Clothe yourselves with the new garments of sincerity. Be rational human beings, not mere male sexual creatures. Cast aside the ferocious brute of your nature: give up the pleasures of the brute, those of mere lust and command, for the pleasures of the rational being. So shall you enjoy the love of your *equals*, enlightened, benevolent, graceful, like yourselves, founded on an appreciation of your real merits: so shall you be happy. For the intercourse of the *bought* prostitute, or of the *commanded* household slave, you shall have full and equal participation in the compounded and associated pleasures of sense, intellect, and benevolence. To the highest enjoyments of which your nature is susceptible, there is no shorter road than the simple road of equal justice. …

Women of England! women, in whatever country ye breathe—wherever ye breathe, degraded—awake! Awake to the contemplation of the happiness that awaits you when all your faculties of mind and body shall be fully cultivated and developed; when every path in which ye can exercise those improved faculties shall be laid open and rendered delightful to you, even as to them who now ignorantly enslave and degrade you. …

Isabel Pagan, "Account of the Author's Lifetime" (1803)

I was born near four miles from Nith-head,[1]
Where fourteen years I got my bread;
My learning it can soon be told,
Ten weeks when I was seven years old
5   With a good old religious wife,
Who lived a quiet and sober life;
Indeed she took of me more pains
Than some docs now of forty bairns.°   children
With my attention, and her skill,
10   I read the Bible no' that ill;
And when I grew a wee thought mair,°   bigger
I read when I had time to spare.
But a' the whole tract of my time,
I found myself inclined to rhyme;
15   When I see merry company,
I sing a song with mirth and glee,
And sometimes I the whisky pree,°   taste, sample
But 'deed its best to let it be.
A' my faults I will not tell,
20   I scarcely ken them a' mysel;
I've come thro' various scenes of life,
Yet never was a married wife.

---

[1] *Nith-head* Head of the Scottish river Nith.

ROBERT BURNS
1759 – 1796

There is a riddle among certain linguists: "What is the difference between a language and a dialect?" Answer: "A language is a dialect that has an army and a navy." The point is well taken, and the prevalence of the British language across the planet no doubt is connected to the huge successes of the British navy in the last two and a half centuries. But when we sing Robert Burns's "Auld Lang Syne" on New Year's Eve we repeat a dialect piece that made good without the backing of an army or a navy. No doubt the distinctive resonance of Burns's Ayrshire dialect has helped to make the words of "Auld Lang Syne" memorable, but its popularity also rests on the degree to which it speaks the language of the heart, conveying a strong sense of mortality and of the blessings of memory itself.

Burns was born in Ayrshire, a county in southwestern Scotland, and spent his early years laboring with his father, a tenant-farmer who died in 1784. Intending to accept a position on a plantation in Jamaica, Burns gave up on this scheme when his first volume of poems, *Poems, Chiefly in the Scottish Dialect* (1786), brought him instant acclaim and the means to a more comfortable life. The Scottish dialect in which he wrote was descended from the Northumbrian dialect of Old English and had been known originally as "Inglis." In the eighteenth century it came to be called "Scots." Burns owes his reputation as "Heaven-taught plowman" to his ear for his Scots dialect, but he also knew how to write using English diction.

In some of his best poems, broad Scots and formal English alternate—indeed, nearly overlap. Burns's most famous narrative poem, the mock-heroic "Tam O'Shanter," is one in which we may see and hear the double-fluency of the poet, his broad Scots dialect giving way to "pure English." Many readers not fluent in Scots, both in Burns's time and in our own, have felt some relief when the poetry gives us a brief shower of more familiar language. But by not forsaking the richness of his dialect, Burns was helping to ensure his future status as Scotland's national poet—and dealing a blow to the class prejudice against him that was always present, despite the Edinburgh aristocracy's celebration of him when *Poems* first appeared.

Burns's *Poems* became known as the "Kilmarnock edition," after the place in which the book was published. At twenty-seven, Burns had already written his most famous poems, and he spent much of the rest of his short life helping to formalize an oral tradition in Scotland, contributing many of the works collected in James Johnson's *The Scots Musical Museum* and in George Thomson's *Select Collection of Original Scottish Airs*. Although never a wealthy man, Burns refused any money for his contribution to this work.

Burns's reputation as a lover for a time rivaled his fame as a poet. Having fathered several illegitimate children, he finally settled down in 1788 with a former lover, Jean Armour, in the town of Dumfries, where he received a commission as an excise (tax) officer. Thereafter he seems to have enjoyed relative prosperity in the last years of his life. Burns's love songs often express both his love of women and his feeling for his craft, as in "Green Grow the Rashes": "Auld nature swears, the lovely dears / Her noblest work she classes, O: / Her prentice han' she tries on man, / An' then she made the lasses, O." Burns also collected all the bawdy songs he inherited and invented in *The Merry Muses of Caledonia*, published shortly after his death (and subjected to expurgation and suppression even today).

A rebel in religion (he chafed against his strict Calvinist upbringing, although he attended church his entire life) and a sympathizer with the revolutions in America and France, Burns often wrote politically charged poems. In "Robert Bruce's March to Bannockburn" (popularly known as "Scots, wha hae"), for example, we hear a war-cry for emancipation: "Lay the proud usurpers low! / Tyrants fall in every foe! / Liberty's in every blow! / Let us do, or die!" Burns could also see the world from the lowliest, humblest places, even to the point of reckoning the mischief and malice of plowing up a field mouse from its home and seeing the calamity from the mouse's point of view ("To a Mouse").

Burns drew heavily on oral tradition, using the ballad form to produce what many consider his masterpiece: "Love and Liberty: A Cantata," commonly known as "The Jolly Beggars" (published posthumously in 1799). The cantata is a series of songs sung by a group of vagabonds, who recall past events in their lives. Burns was strongly influenced by his literary predecessors—perhaps most notably the Scottish Chaucerians of the fifteenth and sixteenth centuries (Gavin Douglas, William Dunbar), and the eighteenth-century Scottish poets Allan Ramsay and Robert Fergusson, whose work supplied him with materials and forms for his comprehensive refashioning of the lyric tradition in Scotland.

Burns was only thirty-seven when he died from an attack of rheumatic fever in 1796, on the day that his wife gave birth to the couple's ninth child. He was buried in St. Michael's Churchyard, Dumfries, Scotland, but his remains were later moved to a mausoleum. Scottish people around the world continue to celebrate Burns's birthday each year on 25 January.

⌘ ⌘ ⌘

Green Grow the Rashes[1]

Green grow the rashes O,
    Green grow the rashes O;
The sweetest hours that e'er I spend,
    Are spent amang the lasses O!

5 There's nought but care on ev'ry han',
    In ev'ry hour that passes O;
What signifies the life o' man,
    An'° 'twere na° for the lasses O.   *if / not*

The war'ly° race may riches chase,   *worldly*
10   An' riches still may fly° them O;   *escape*
An' tho' at last they catch them fast,
    Their hearts can ne'er enjoy them O.

But gie° me a canny° hour at e'en,   *give / quiet*
    My arms about my dearie O;
15 An' warly cares, an' warly men,
    May a' gae tapsalteerie° O!   *topsy-turvy*

For you sae douce,° ye sneer at this,   *wise*
    Ye're nought but senseless asses O:
The wisest man the warl' ere saw,
20   He dearly lov'd the lasses O.

Auld nature swears, the lovely dears
    Her noblest work she classes, O:
Her prentice han' she tried on man,
    An' then she made the lasses O.
—1783

---

[1] *Rashes* Rushes.

To a Mouse, On Turning Her Up in Her Nest with the Plough

Wee, sleekit, cowrin, tim'rous beastie,
O, what a panic's in thy breastie!
Thou need na start awa sae hasty,
    Wi' bickerin' brattle![1]
5 I wad be laith° to rin an' chase thee,   *loathe*
    Wi' murd'ring pattle!°   *plough spade*

I'm truly sorry man's dominion
Has broken nature's social union,
An' justifies that ill opinion,
10   Which makes thee startle,
At me, thy poor, earth-born companion,
    An' fellow mortal!

I doubt na, whyles,° but thou may thieve;   *at times*
What then? poor beastie, thou maun° live!   *must*
15 A daimen icker in a thrave[2]
    'S a sma' request;
I'll get a blessin wi' the lave,°   *rest*
    An' never miss't!

Thy wee-bit housie, too, in ruin!
20 It's silly wa's° the win's are strewin!   *walls*
An' naething, now, to big° a new ane,   *build*
    O' foggage° green!   *moss*
An' bleak December's winds ensuin,
    Baith snell° an' keen!   *bitter*

25 Thou saw the fields laid bare an' waste,
An's weary winter comin fast,
An' cozie here, beneath the blast,
    Thou thought to dwell,
Till crash! the cruel coulter° past   *plow blade*
30   Out thro' thy cell.

That wee-bit hcap o' leaves an' stibble,
Has cost thee monie a weary nibble!
Now thou's turn'd out, for a' thy trouble,
    But° house or hald,°   *without / belongings*
35 To thole° the winter's sleety dribble,   *bear*
    An' cranreuch° cauld!   *hoar frost*

But, Mousie, thou art no thy lane,[3]
In proving foresight may be vain:
The best-laid schemes o' mice an' men
40   Gang aft agley,[4]
An' lea'e us nought but grief an' pain,
    For promis'd joy!

Still thou art blest, compar'd wi' me!
The present only toucheth thee:
45 But, Och! I backward cast my e'e
    On prospects drear!
An' forward, tho' I canna see,
    I guess an' fear!
—1785

To a Louse, On Seeing One on a Lady's Bonnet, at Church

Ha! Whare ye gaun, ye crowlan ferlie![5]
    Your impudence protects you sairly:°   *sorely*
I canna say but ye strunt° rarely,   *strut*
    Owre *gawze* and *lace*;
5 Tho' faith, I fear ye dine but sparely,
    On sic° a place.   *such*

    Ye ugly, creepan, blastet wonner,
Detested, shunn'd, by saunt an' sinner,
How daur ye set your fit° upon her,   *feet*
10   Sae fine a *Lady*!
Gae somewhere else and seek your dinner,
    On some poor body.

---

1 *bickerin' brattle* Hurrying scurry.

2 *A daimen icker in a thrave* The odd ear in twenty-four sheaves of corn.

3 *no thy lane* Not alone.

4 *Gang aft agley* Go oft awry.

5 *crowlan ferlie* Crawling wonder.

Swith,° in some beggar's haffet°   *away / temple*
    squattle;°   *settle*
There ye may creep, and sprawl, and sprattle,°   *scramble*
Wi' ither kindred, jumping cattle,
    In shoals and nations;
Whaur *horn* nor *bane*[1] ne'er daur unsettle,
    Your thick plantations.

Now haud° you there, ye're out o' sight,   *stay*
Below the fatt'rels,[2] snug and tight,
Na faith ye yet! ye'll no be right,
    Till ye've got on it,
The vera tapmost, towrin height
    O' *Miss's bonnet.*

My sooth! right bauld ye set your nose out,
As plump an' gray as onie grozet:°   *gooseberry*
O for some rank, mercurial rozet,°   *resin*
    Or fell,° red smeddum,[3]   *deadly*
I'd gie you sic a hearty dose o't,
    Wad dress your droddum![4]

I wad na been surpriz'd to spy
You on an auld wife's *flainen° toy;*[5]   *flannel*
Or aiblins° some bit duddie° boy,   *maybe / shabby*
    On's *wylecoat;°*   *waistcoat*
But Miss's fine *Lunardi,*[6] fye!
    How daur ye do't?

O *Jenny* dinna toss your head,
An' set your beauties a' abroad!°   *abroad*
Ye little ken° what cursed speed   *know*
    The blastie's makin!

---

[1] *horn nor bane* Horn nor bone; i.e., the materials of a lady's hair-comb.

[2] *fatt'rels* Loose ends of ribbons.

[3] *smeddum* Fine powder used to kill vermin.

[4] *dress your droddum* Give you a thrashing; *droddum* Buttocks.

[5] *toy* Style of head-dress, worn in Scotland mainly by lower-class women.

[6] *Lunardi* Style of tall, balloon-shaped bonnet fashionable in Scotland in the late 1700s, named after the Italian aeronaut Vincenzo Lunardi.

Thae *winks* and *finger-ends*, I dread,
    Are notice takin!

O wad some Pow'r the giftie gie° us   *give*
To see oursels as others see us!
It wad frae monie[7] a blunder free us
    An' foolish notion:
What airs in dress an' gait wad lae'e° us,   *leave*
    And ev'n Devotion!
—1786

The Fornicator

Ye jovial boys who love the joys,
    The blissful joys of lovers;
Yet dare avow with dauntless brow,
    When th'bony lass discovers;
I pray draw near and lend an ear,
    And welcome in a frater,°   *brother*
For I've lately been on quarantine,
    A proven Fornicator.

Before the congregation wide
    I pass'd the muster fairly,
My handsome Betsey by my side,
    We gat our ditty° rarely;   *sermon*
But my downcast eye by chance did spy
    What made my lips to water,
Those limbs so clean where I, between
    Commenc'd a Fornicator.

With rueful face and signs of grace
    I pay'd the buttock-hire,[8]
The night was dark and thro the park
    I could not but convoy her;
A parting kiss, what could I less,
    My vows began to scatter,
My Betsey fell—lal de dal lal lal,
    I am a Fornicator.

---

[7] *frae monie* From many.

[8] *buttock-hire* Church fine charged to fornicators.

ROBERT BURNS   199

25 But for her sake this vow I make,
        And solemnly I swear it,
    That while I own a single crown,
        She's welcome for to share it;
    And my roguish boy his mother's joy,
30   And the darling of his pater,°   *father*
    For him I boast my pains and cost,
        Although a Fornicator.

    Ye wenching blades whose hireling jades°   *prostitutes*
        Have tipt ye off blue-joram,[1]
35 I tell ye plain, I do disdain
        To rank ye in the quorum;
    But a bony lass upon the grass
        To teach her esse mater,[2]
    And no reward but for regard,
40   O that's a Fornicator.

    Your warlike kings and heroes bold,
        Great captains and commanders;
    Your mighty Caesars fam'd of old,
        And conquering Alexanders;
45 In fields they fought and laurels[3] bought
        And bulwarks strong did batter,
    But still they grac'd our noble list
        And ranked Fornicator!!!
    —1785

The Holy Fair[4]

A robe of seeming truth and trust
Hid crafty Observation;
And secret hung, with poison'd crust,
The dirk° of Defamation: *dagger*

---

[1] *tipt ye off blue-joram* Given you the pox.

[2] *esse mater* Latin: to be a mother.

[3] *laurels* Leaves of the bay laurel tree were once a symbol of victory in battle.

[4] *Holy Fair* Celebration of Holy Communion, which in eighteenth-century Scotland was held a small number of times per year. The event was conducted outside to accommodate the large numbers of attendees, both from within the parish and from the rural areas beyond it; many treated the Holy Fair as a holiday rather than a solemn occasion.

A mask that like the gorget[5] show'd,
Dye-varying on the pigeon;
And for a mantle large and broad,
He wrapt him in Religion.
HYPOCRISY A-LA-MODE

Upon a simmer° Sunday morn,   *summer*
    When Nature's face is fair,
I walked forth to view the corn,
    An' snuff the caller° air.   *cool*
5   The risin' sun, owre Galston muirs,[6]
    Wi' glorious light was glintin;
    The hares were hirplin° down the furrs,° *hobbling | furrows*
    The lav'rocks° they were chantin   *larks*
        Fu' sweet that day.

10 As lightsomely I glowr'd abroad,
    To see a scene sae gay,
    Three Hizzies,° early at the road,   *hussies*
    Cam skelpin° up the way.   *skipping*
    Twa had manteels° o' doleful black,   *shawls*
15 But ane° wi' lyart° lining;   *one | gray*
    The third, that gaed a wee a-back,°   *behind*
    Was in the fashion shinin
        Fu' gay that day.

    The twa appear'd like sisters twin,
20 In feature, form, an' claes;°   *clothes*
    Their visage wither'd, lang an' thin,
    An' sour as only slaes:°   *sloes*
    The third cam up, hap-step-an'-lowp,[7]
    As light as ony lambie,°   *lamh*
25 An' wi' a curchie° low did stoop,   *curtsy*
    As soon as e'er she saw me,
        Fu' kind that day.

    Wi' bonnet aff, quoth I, "Sweet lass,
    I think ye seem to ken° me;   *know*
30 I'm sure I've seen that bonie face,
    But yet I canna name ye."

---

[5] *gorget* Colorful patch on an animal's throat.

[6] *Galston muirs* Moors in East Ayrshire, Scotland; *muirs* Moors.

[7] *hap-step-an'-lowp* Hop, step, and leap.

Quo'° she, an' laughin' as she spak,   *quoth*
An' takes me by the han's,   65
"Ye, for my sake, hae gi'en the feck°   *bulk*
Of a' the ten comman's
        A screed° some day.   *rapid reading*

"My name is Fun—your cronie° dear,   *close friend*
The nearest friend ye hae;   70
An' this is Superstition here,
An' that's Hypocrisy.
I'm gaun to Mauchline[1] Holy Fair,
To spend an hour in daffin:°   *larking*
Gin ye'll go there, yon runkl'd° pair,   *wrinkled*   75
We will get famous laughin
        At them this day."

Quoth I, "With a' my heart, I'll do't;
I'll get my Sunday's sark° on,   *shirt*
An' meet you on the holy spot;   80
Faith, we'se hae fine remarkin!"
Then I gaed hame at crowdie-time,°   *breakfast-time*
An' soon I made me ready;
For roads were clad, frae side to side,
Wi' monie a wearie bodie,
        In droves that day.

Here, farmers gash,° in ridin graith°   *well-dressed / gear*
Gaed hoddin by their cotters;[2]   85
There, swankies young, in braw braid-claith,[3]
Are springin owre the gutters.
The lasses, skelpin barefit, thrang,°   *thronged*
In silks an' scarlets glitter;
Wi' sweet-milk cheese, in monie a whang,°   *large slice*
An' farls,[4] bak'd wi' butter,
        Fu' crump° that day.   *crunchy*

When by the plate we set our nose,
Weel heaped up wi' ha'pence,   65
A greedy glowr Black Bonnet[5] throws,
An' we maun° draw our tippence.   *must*
Then in we go to see the show,
On ev'ry side they're gath'rin,
Some carryin dails,° some chairs an' stools,   *planks*   70
An' some are busy bleth'rin
        Right loud that day.

Here stands a shed to fend the show'rs,
An' screen our countra gentry,
There, racer Jess,[6] an' twa-three whores,   75
Are blinkin at the entry.
Here sits a raw° o' tittlin jades,°   *row / prostitutes*
Wi' heaving breast an' bare neck,
An' there, a batch o' wabster° lads,   *weaver*
Blackguarding frae Kilmarnock[7]   80
        For fun this day.

Here, some are thinkin on their sins,
An' some upo' their claes;
Ane curses feet that fyl'd his shins,[8]
Anither sighs an' prays: 85
On this hand sits a chosen swatch,
Wi' screw'd up, grace-proud faces;
On that, a set o' chaps, at watch,
Thrang° winkin on the lasses   *busy*
        To chairs that day.   90

O happy is that man an' blest!
Nae wonder that it pride him!
Wha's ain dear lass, that he likes best,
Comes clinkin down beside him!
Wi' arm repos'd on the chair-back,   95

---

[1] *Mauchline* Town in East Ayrshire.

[2] *hoddin* Jostling up and down (as they travel by horse); *cotters* Peasants, many of whom rented from land-owning farmers.

[3] *swankies* Strapping, intelligent young men; *braw braid-claith* Fancy broad-cloth.

[4] *farls* Thin cakes made of oatmeal.

[5] *Black Bonnet* I.e., the church member holding the collection plate.

[6] *racer Jess* Daughter of Poosie Nansie, a Mauchline tavern-owner who plays a role in Burns's poem "The Jolly Beggars." Burns describes Jess as "half-witted" and "a great pedestrian" (i.e., a remarkably fast runner).

[7] *Blackguarding* Acting like vagabonds and scoundrels; *Kilmarnock* Burgh in Ayrshire.

[8] *fyl'd his shins* Soiled his shoes.

He sweetly does compose him;
Which, by degrees, slips round her neck,
An's loof° upon her bosom   *palm*
    Unkend° that day.   *unknown*

100 Now a' the congregation o'er
Is silent expectation;
For Moodie[1] speels° the holy door,   *climbs*
Wi' tidings o' damnation
Should Hornie,° as in ancient days,   *the devil*
105 'Mang sons o' God present him,
Ther vera sight o' Moodie's face,
To's ain het° hame had sent him   *hot*
    Wi' fright that day.

Hear how he clears the points o' faith
110 Wi' rattlin an' wi' thumpin!
Now meekly calm, now wild in wrath,
He's stampin an' he's jumpin!
His lengthen'd chin, his turned-up snout,
His eldritch° squeel an' gestures,   *unearthly*
115 O how they fire the heart devout,
Like cantharidian plasters,[2]
    On sic a day!

But, hark! the tent has chang'd its voice;
There's peace an' rest nae langer:
120 For a' the real judges rise,
They canna sit for anger.
Smith opens out his cauld harangues,
On practice and on morals;
An' aff the godly pour in thrangs,
125 To gie the jars an' barrels
    A lift that day.

What signifies his barren shine
Of moral pow'rs an' reason?

His English style, an' gesture fine,
130 Are a' clean out o' season.
Like Socrates or Antonine,[3]
Or some auld pagan Heathen,
The moral man he does define,
But ne'er a word o' faith in
135   That's right that day.

In guid° time comes an antidote   *good*
Against sic poisoned nostrum;°   *quack remedy*
For Peebles, frae the water-fit,[4]
Ascends the holy rostrum:°   *platform*
140 See, up he's got the word o' God
An' meek an' mim° has view'd it,   *mild*
While Common Sense has ta'en the road,
An' aff, an' up the Cowgate
    Fast, fast, that day.

145 Wee Miller, neist,° the Guard relieves,   *next*
An' Orthodoxy raibles,°   *recites*
Tho' in his heart he weel believes,
An' thinks it auld wives' fables:
But, faith! the birkie° wants a manse,[5]   *man*
150 So, cannilie° he hums them;   *astutely*
Altho' his carnal wit an' sense
Like hafflins-wise° o'ercomes him   *halfway*
    At times that day.

Now, butt an' ben,[6] the Change-house fills,
155 Wi' yill-caup° Commentators: *ale-cup*
Here's crying out for bakes° an' gills,[7]   *cakes*
An' there the pint-stowp° clatters;   *pint tankard*
While thick an' thrang, an' loud an' lang,

---

1 *Moodie* Minister from Riccarton, another parish in East Ayrshire. It was common for visiting ministers to preach at the celebration of Holy Communion; all the preachers named in the poem were real ministers from East Ayrshire and the surrounding areas.

2 *cantharidian plasters* Medicinal, emollient spreads composed of cantharides, a kind of acid.

3 *Socrates* Ancient Athenian philosopher (470/69–399 BCE), considered one of the cofounders of Western philosophy; *Antonine* Marcus Aurelius Antoninus (121–180 CE), Roman emperor and famous Stoic philosopher.

4 *water-fit* River mouth. William Peebles was from Newton on Ayr, South Ayrshire, which was located near the mouth of a river.

5 *manse* House provided to a minster by the church.

6 *butt an' ben* In the outer and inner apartment, i.e., in both (or all) parts of the house.

7 *gills* Measures of alcohol.

Wi' logic, an' wi' Scripture,
190 They raise a din, that in the end,
Is like to breed a rupture
    O' wrath that day.

Leeze me on[1] Drink! it gi'es us mair
Than either School or College:
165 It kindles Wit, it waukens° Lair,°   *wakens / learning*
It pangs us fou o' Knowledge.
Be't whisky gill, or penny wheep,[2]
Or ony stronger potion,
It never fails, on drinkin' deep,
170 To kittle up[3] our notion
    By night or day.

The lads an' lasses, blythely bent
To mind baith saul an' body,
Sit roun the table, weel content,
175 An' steer about the toddy.[4]
On this ane's dress, an' that ane's leuk,°   *look*
They're makin observations;
While some are cozie i' the neuk,°   *nook*
An' formin assignations
180   To meet some day.

But now the Lord's ain trumpet touts,
Till a' the hills are rairin,
An' echoes back return the shouts;
Black Russel is na spairin:
185 His piercing words, like Highlan swords,
Divide the joint an' marrow;
His talk o' Hell, whare devils dwell,
Our vera "sauls does harrow"[5]
    Wi' fright that day!

190 A vast, unbottom'd, boundless Pit,
Fill'd fou o' lowin brunstane,°   *brimstone*

Wha's ragin flame, an' scorchin heat,
Wad melt the hardest whun-stane!°   *whinstone*
The half asleep start up wi' fear,
195 An' think they hear it roarin,
When presently it does appear,
'Twas but some neebor snorin
    Asleep that day.

'Twad be owre lang a tale to tell
200 How monie stories past,
An' how they crowded to the yill,°   *ale*
When they were a' dismist:
How drink gaed round, in cogs[6] an' caups,
Amang the furms° and benches;   *long benches*
205 An' cheese an' bread, frac women's laps,
Was dealt about in lunches,°   *chunks*
    An' dawds° that day.   *large slices*

In comes a gaucie,[7] gash Guidwife,
An' sits down by the fire,
210 Syne draws her kebbuck° an' her knife;   *cheese*
The lasses they are shyer.
The auld Guidmen, about the grace,
Frae side to side they bother,
Till some ane by his bonnet lays,
215 An' gi'es them't like a tether,
    Fu' lang that day.

Waesucks!° for him that gets nae lass,   *alas*
Or lasses that hae naething!
Sma' need has he to say a grace,
220 Or melvie[8] his braw claithing!
O Wives, be mindfu', ance yoursel
How bonie lads ye wanted,
An' dinna, for a kebbuck-heel,[9]
Let lasses be affronted
225   On sic a day!

---

1 *Leeze me on* I love.

2 *penny wheep* Small beer (cheaper and weaker than regular beer).

3 *kittle up* Rouse.

4 *toddy* Beverage made with alcohol and hot water.

5 *sauls does harrow* Cf. *Hamlet* 1.5.16.

---

6 *cogs* Large drinking vessels.

7 *gaucie* Fat and jolly-looking.

8 *melvie* Cover with meal.

9 *kebbuck-heel* Last crust of cheese.

Now Clinkumbell,[1] wi' rattling tow,
    Begins to jow[2] an' croon;
Some swagger hame, the best they dow,°   *are able*
Some wait the afternoon.
230 At slaps the billies° halt a blink,   *companions*
    Till lasses strip their shoon:°   *shoes on*
Wi' faith an' hope, an' love an' drink,
They're a' in famous tune
    For crack that day.

235 How monie hearts this day converts
O' sinner and o' lasses!
Their hearts o' stane, gin night, are gane
As saft as ony flesh is.
There's some are fou o' love divine,
240 There's some are fou o' brandy;
An' monie jobs that day begin,
May end in Houghmagandie°   *fornication*
    Some ither day.
    —1785

Halloween

Yes! let the rich deride, the proud disdain,
The simple pleasure of the lowly train;
To me more dear, congenial to my heart,
One native charm, than all the gloss of art.[3]
            —GOLDSMITH

1

Upon that night, when fairies light
    On Cassilis Downans[4] dance,
Or owre the lays, in splendid blaze,
    On sprightly coursers° prance;   *horses*
5 Or for Colean° the rout is ta'en,   *cavern*
    Beneath the moon's pale beams;
There, up the cove, to stray an' rove,

Amang the rocks and streams
    To sport that night.

2

Amang the bonie winding banks,
    Where Doon rins, wimplin,[5] clear;
Where Bruce[6] ance rul'd the martial ranks,
    An' shook his Carrick[7] spear;
Some merry, friendly, countra-folks
15   Together did convene,
To burn their nits, an' pou[8] their stocks,
    An' haud° their Halloween   *hold*
    Fu' blythe° that night.   *merry*

3

The lasses feat,° an' cleanly neat,   *well-dressed*
20   Mair braw° than when they're fine;   *handsome*
Their faces blythe, fu' sweetly kythe,°   *displayed*
    Hearts leal,° an' warm, an' kin':   *loyal / kind*
The lads sae trig,° wi' wooer-babs   *neat*
    Weel-knotted on their garten;[9]
25 Some unco blate,[10] an' some wi' gabs°   *mouths*
    Gar° lasses' hearts gang startin   *cause*
    Whiles fast at night.

4

Then, first an' foremost, thro' the kail,
    Their stocks maun° a' be sought ance;°   *must / once*
30 They steek° their een,° and grape an' wale   *close / eyes*
    For muckle anes,[11] an' straught anes.
Poor hav'rel° Will fell aff the drift,[12]   *half-wit*
    An' wandered thro' the bow-kail,°   *cabbage*
An' pou't° for want o' better shift°   *pulled / choice*

---

[1] *Clinkumbell* One who rings a bell.

[2] *jow* Toll a bell.

[3] *Yes! … art* From Oliver Goldsmith's *The Deserted Village* (1770), 251–54.

[4] *Cassilis Downans* Small hills in Ayrshire County, Scotland.

[5] *Doon rins, wimplin* The river Doon runs, winding.

[6] *Bruce* Scottish hero Robert the Bruce (1274–1329).

[7] *Carrick* District in Ayrshire.

[8] *nits* Nuts; *pou* Pull.

[9] *wooer-babs … garten* Garters worn in a particular way in order to announce that the wearer is wooing the person he is visiting.

[10] *unco blate* Extremely shy.

[11] *They steek … anes* They shut their eyes, and grope and choose / For big ones.

[12] *fell aff the drift* Wandered away.

A runt° was like a sow-tail   *cabbage stalk*
    Sae bow't° that night.   *bent*

5

Then, straught or crooked, yird° or nane,°   *earth / none*
    They roar an' cry a' throu'ther;°   *recklessly*
The vera wee-things, toddlin, rin,
    Wi' stocks out owre their shouther:
An' gif° the custock's° sweet or sour,   *if / kale-stock*
    Wi' joctelegs° they taste them;   *pocket knives*
Syne° coziely, aboon° the door,   *then / above*
    Wi' cannie care, they've plac'd them
        To lie that night.

6

The lassies staw frae[1] 'mang them a',
    To pou their stalks o' corn;
But Rab slips out, an' jinks° about,   *dodges*
    Behint the muckle° thorn: *great*
He grippit Nelly hard and fast:
    Loud skirl'd° a' the lasses: *shrieked*
But her tap-pickle[2] maist° was lost,   *most*
    What kiutlan° in the fause-house[3]   *fondling*
        Wi' him that night.

7

The auld guid-wife's° weel-hoordit° nits *landlady's / hoarded*
    Are round an' round divided,
An' mony lads an' lasses' fates
    Are there that night decided:
Some kindle couthie° side by side,   *comfortably*
    And burn thegither° trimly;   *together*
Some start awa wi' saucy pride,
    An' jump out owre the chimlie°   *chimney*
        Fu' high that night.

8

Jean slips in twa, wi' tentie° e'e;   *watchful*
    Wha 'twas, she wadna tell;

But this is Jock, an' this is me,
    She says in to hersel':
He bleez'd owre her, an' she owre him,
    As they wad never mair part:
Till fuff! he started up the lum,°   *chimney*
    An' Jean had e'en a sair° heart   *sore*
        To see't that night.

9

Poor Willie, wi' his bow-kail runt,
    Was brunt° wi' primsie° Mallie;   *burned / prim*
An' Mary, nae doubt, took the drunt,[4]
    To be compar'd to Willie:
Mall's nit lap° out, wi' pridefu' fling,   *leaped*
    An' her ain fit,[5] it brunt it;
While Willie lap, and swore by jing,
    'Twas just the way he wanted
        To be that night.

10

Nell had the fause-house wi' her min',
    She pits hersel an' Rob in;
In loving bleeze they sweetly join,
    Till white in ase° they're sobbin: *ash*
Nell's heart was dancin at the view;
    She whisper'd Rob to leuk for't:
Rob, stownlins,° prie'd° her bonie mou', *stealthily / kissed*
    Fu' cozie in the neuk° for't,   *nook*
        Unseen that night.

11

But Merran sat behint their backs,
    Her thoughts on Andrew Bell:
She lea'es them gashin at their cracks,[6]
    An' slips out-by hersel':
She thro' the yard the nearest taks,
    An' for the kiln she goes then,
An' darklins grapit for the bauks,[7]

---

[1] *staw frae* Steal from.

[2] *tap-pickle* Grain at the top of the stalk.

[3] *fause-house* Hollow in a large stack of corn stalks, created for drying the corn.

[4] *took the drunt* Sulked.

[5] *ain fit* Own foot.

[6] *gashin at their cracks* Gossiping.

[7] *darklins grapit for the bauks* In the darkness grabbed for the beams.

And in the blue-clue[1] throws then,
　　　　Right fear't that night.

12

100 An' ay she win't,° an' ay she swat°—   *wound / sweated*
　　　　I wat° she made nae jaukin;°   *know / dawdling*
Till something held within the pat,
　　　　Good Lord! but she was quaukin!
But whether 'twas the deil himsel,
105 　　　　Or whether 'twas a bauk-en',°   *beam end*
Or whether it was Andrew Bell,
　　　　She did na wait on talkin
　　　　　　To spier° that night.   *inquire*

13

Wee Jenny to her graunie says,
110 　　　　"Will ye go wi' me, graunie?
I'll eat the apple at the glass,
　　　　I gat frae uncle Johnie":
She fuff't° her pipe wi' sic a lunt,[2]   *puffed*
　　　　In wrath she was sae vap'rin,
115 She notic't na an aizle° brunt   *hot ember*
　　　　Her braw, new, worset apron
　　　　　　Out thro' that night.

14

"Ye little skelpie-limmer's° face!   *naughty girl's*
　　　　I daur you try sic sportin,
120 As seek the foul thief° ony place,   *devil*
　　　　For him to spae° your fortune: *tell*
Nae doubt but ye may get a sight!
　　　　Great cause ye hae to fear it;
For mony a ane has gotten a fright,
125 　　　　An' liv'd an' died deleerit,°   *delirious*
　　　　　　On sic° a night.   *such*

15

"Ae hairst° afore the Sherra-moor,   *harvest*
　　　　I mind't as weel's yestreen—
I was a gilpcy° then, I'm sure   *young girl*
130 　　　　I was na past fyfteen:

The simmer had been cauld an' wat,
　　　　An' stuff was unco green;
An' eye a rantin kirn[3] we gat,
　　　　An' just on Halloween
135 　　　　　　It fell that night.

16

"Our stibble-rig° was Rab M'Graen,   *chief harvester*
　　　　A clever, sturdy fallow;
His sin° gat Eppie Sim wi' wean,°   *son / child*
　　　　That lived in Achmacalla:
140 He gat hemp-seed, I mind° it weel,   *remember*
　　　　An' he made unco light o't;
But mony a day was by himsel',
　　　　He was sae sairly frighted
　　　　　　That vera night."

17

145 Then up gat fechtin° Jamie Fleck,   *fighting*
　　　　An' he swoor by his conscience,
That he could saw° hemp-seed a peck;   *sow*
　　　　For it was a' but nonsense:
The auld guidman raught° down the pock,°   *reached / bag*
150 　　　　An' out a handfu' gied° him;   *gave*
Syne bad[4] him slip frae' mang the folk,
　　　　Sometime when nae ane see'd him,
　　　　　　An' try't that night.

18

He marches thro' amang the stacks,
155 　　　　Tho' he was something sturtin;°   *frightened*
The graip° he for a harrow taks,   *pitchfork*
　　　　An' haurls° at his curpin:[5]   *drags*
And ev'ry now an' then, he says,
　　　　"Hemp-seed I saw thee,
160 An' her that is to be my lass
　　　　Come after me, an' draw thee
　　　　　　As fast this night."

1　*clue*　Clew; ball of yarn.

2　*lunt*　Smoke column.

3　*rantin kirn*　Boisterous party.

4　*Syne bad*　Soon bade.

5　*at his curpin*　Behind him (at his buttocks).

19

He wistl'd up Lord Lennox' March
    To keep his courage cherry;
Altho' his hair began to arch,
    He was sae fley'd° an' eerie: *terrified*
Till presently he hears a squeak,
    An' then a grane an' gruntle;
He by his shouther gae a keek,°   *glanced*
    An' tumbled wi' a wintle°   *somersaulted*
        Out-owre that night.

20

He roar'd a horrid murder-shout,
    In dreadfu' desperation!
An' young an' auld come rinnin out,
    An' hear the sad narration:
He swoor 'twas hilchin'° Jean M'Craw,   *limping*
    Or crouchie° Merran Humphie—   *hunchbacked*
Till stop! she trotted thro' them a',
    And wha was it but grumphie°   *a pig*
        Asteer that night!

21

Meg fain° wad to the barn gaen,°   *gladly | have gone*
    To winn° three wechts° o' naething;   *winnow | sieves*
But for to meet the deil her lane,[1]
    She pat but little faith in:
She gies the herd° a pickle° nits,   *shepherd | few*
    An' twa red cheekit apples,
To watch, while for the barn she sets,
    In hopes to see Tam Kipples
        That vera night.

22

She turns the key wi' cannie thraw,[2]
    An' owre the threshold ventures;
But first on Sawnie° gies a ca',   *sandy*
    Syne baudly in she enters:
A ratton° rattl'd up the wa',   *rat*
    An' she cry'd Lord preserve her!
An' ran thro' midden-hole° an' a',   *dung pile*

An' pray'd wi' zeal and fervour,
        Fu' fast that night.

23

They hoy't° out Will, wi' sair advice;   *urged*
    They hecht° him some fine braw ane;   *promised*
It chanc'd the stack he faddom't thrice
    Was timmer-propt° for thrawin: *propped up*
He taks a swirlie auld moss-oak
    For some black, grousome carlin;°   *witch*
An' loot a winze,[3] an' drew a stroke,
    Till skin in blypes° cam haurlin   *shreds*
        Aff's nieves° that night.   *fists*

24

A wanton widow Leezie was,
    As cantie° as a kittlen;°   *lively | kitten*
But och! that night, amang the shaws,°   *woods*
    She gat a fearfu' settlin!
She thro' the whins,° an' by the cairn,   *gorse bushes*
    An' owre the hill gaed scrievin;°   *running swiftly*
Whare three lairds' lan's met at a burn,
    To dip her left sark°-sleeve in,   *shirt*
        Was bent that night.

25

Whiles owre a linn° the burnie° plays,   *waterfall | brook*
    As thro' the glen it wimpl't;
Whiles round a rocky scar° it strays,   *cliff*
    Whiles in a wiel° it dimpl't;   *eddy*
Whiles glitter'd to the nightly rays,
    Wi' bickerin', dancin' dazzle;
Whiles cookit° underneath the braes,   *hidden*
    Below the spreading hazel
        Unseen that night.

26

Amang the brachens, on the brae,
    Between her an' the moon,
The deil, or else an outler quey,[4]
    Gat up an' ga'e a croon:

---

1 *her lane* Alone.

2 *cannie thraw* Careful turn.

3 *loot a winze* Cursed.

4 *outler quey* Cow in the field.

230 Poor Leezie's heart maist lap the hool;[1]
    　　Near lav'rock°-height she jumpit,　　　　*lark*
    But mist a fit, an' in the pool
    　　Out-owre the lugs° she plumpit,　　　　*ears*
    　　　　Wi' a plunge that night.

27

235 In order, on the clean hearth-stane,
    　　The luggies° three are ranged;　　　*wooden dishes*
    An' ev'ry time great care is ta'en
    　　To see them duly changed:
    Auld uncle John, wha wedlock's joys
240 　　Sin' Mar's-year[2] did desire,
    Because he gat the toom° dish thrice,　　　*empty*
    　　He heav'd them on the fire
    　　　　In wrath that night.

28

    Wi' merry sangs, an' friendly cracks,
245 　　I wat they did na weary;
    And unco tales, an' funnie jokes—
    　　Their sports were cheap an' cheery:
    Till butter'd sowens,[3] wi' fragrant lunt,°　　　*steam*
    　　Set a' their gabs a-steerin;[4]
250 Syne, wi' a social glass o' strunt,°　　　*liquor*
    　　They parted aff careerin
    　　　　Fu' blythe that night.
    —1786

---

[1] *maist lap the hool* Almost jumped out of her skin.

[2] *Mar's-year* 1715, the year of the Jacobite Rebellion.

[3] *butter'd sowens* Puddings.

[4] *gabs a-steerin* Tongues wagging.

Address to the De'il[5]

O Prince, O chief of many throned pow'rs,
That led th'embattled Seraphim to war[6]—
　　　　　　　　MILTON

O Thou, whatever title suit thee!
　　Auld Hornie, Satan, Nick, or Clootie,[7]
Wha in yon cavern grim an' sooty
　　Closed under hatches,
5 Spairges about the brunstane cootie,[8]
　　To scaud° poor wretches!　　　　*scald*

Hear me, auld Hangie,° for a wee,　　　*hangman*
An' let poor, damned bodies bee;
I'm sure sma' pleasure it can gie,
10 　　Ev'n to a de'il,
To skelp° an' scaud poor dogs like me,　　　*strike*
　　An' hear us squeel!

Great is thy pow'r, an' great thy fame;
Far ken'd,° an' noted is thy name;　　　*known*
15 An' tho' yon lowan heugh's[9] thy hame,
　　Thou travels far;
An' faith! thou's neither lag° nor lame,　　　*slow*
　　Nor blate° nor scaur.°　　　*shy / scared*

Whyles,° ranging like a roaring lion,　　　*sometimes*
20 For prey, a' holes an' corners tryin;
Whyles, on the strong-wing'd tempest flyin,
　　Tirlan the kirks;[10]
Whyles, in the human bosom pryin,
　　Unseen thou lurks.

25 I've heard my rev'rend Graunie° say,　　　*grandmother*
In lanely° glens ye like to stray;　　　*lonely*

---

[5] *De'il* Devil.

[6] *O Prince … war* From Milton's *Paradise Lost* 1.128–29.

[7] *Clootie* Scottish slang name for the devil; it alludes to his cloven feet.

[8] *Spairges … cootie* Splashes about the brimstone vat.

[9] *lowan heugh* Flaming pit.

[10] *Tirlan the kirks* Unroofing the churches.

Or where auld, ruined castles, gray,
　　　Nod to the moon,
Ye fright the nightly wand'rer's way,
　　　Wi' eldritch croon.[1]

30

When twilight did my Graunie summon,
To say her pray'rs, douse,° honest woman,　　grave
Aft 'yont° the dyke she's heard you bumman　　beyond
　　　Wi' eerie drone;
35　　Or, rustling, thro' the boortries° coman,　　elder shrubs
　　　Wi' heavy groan.

Ae dreary, windy, winter night,
The stars shot down wi' sklentan° light,　　slanting
Wi' you, mysel, I gat a fright
40　　　Ayont the lough;°　　lake
Ye, like a rash-buss,[2] stood in sight,
　　　Wi' waving sugh:°　　sound

The cudgel in my nieve° did shake,　　fist
Each bristl'd hair stood like a stake,
45　　When wi' an eldritch, stoor,° quaick, quaick,　　hoarse
　　　Amang the springs,
Awa ye squatter'd° like a drake,　　fluttered
　　　On whistling wings.

Let warlocks grim, an' wither'd hags,
50　　Tell, how wi' you, on ragweed nags,[3]
They skim the muirs° an' dizzy crags,　　moors
　　　Wi' wicked speed;
And in kirk-yards renew their leagues,
　　　Owre howcket° dead.　　dug up

55　　Thence, countra° wives, wi' toil an' pain,　　country
May plunge an' plunge the kirn° in vain;　　churn
For och! the yellow treasure's taen,°　　taken
　　　By witching skill;

An' dawtit, twal-pint Hawkie's gane
60　　　As yell's the bill.[4]

Thence, mystic knots mak great abuse,
On young guidmen,° fond, keen an'　　husbands
　　　croose;°　　spirited
When the best warklum° i' the house,　　tool
　　　By cantraip° wit,　　enchanted
65　　Is instant made no worth a louse,
　　　Just at the bit.°　　final moment

When thowes° dissolve the snawy hoord,°　　thaws / hoard
An' float the jinglan° icy boord,°　　crackling / shore
Then, water-kelpies haunt the foord,[5]
70　　　By your direction,
An' nighted trav'llers are allur'd
　　　To their destruction.

An' aft your moss-traversing spunkies°　　will-o'-the-wisps
Decoy the wight° that late an' drunk is,　　person
75　　The bleezan,° curst, mischievous monkies　　blazing
　　　Delude his eyes,
Till in some miry slough he sunk is,
　　　Ne'er mair to rise.

When Masons'[6] mystic word an' grip,
80　　In storms an' tempests raise you up,
Some cock, or cat, your rage maun° stop,　　must
　　　Or, strange to tell!
The youngest brother ye wad whip
　　　Aff straught to H-ll.

85　　Lang syne[7] in Eden's bonie yard,
When youthfu' lovers first were pair'd,
An' all the soul of love they shar'd,
　　　The raptured hour,

1　*eldritch croon*　Ghastly moan.

2　*rash-buss*　Bunch of rushes.

3　*ragweed nags*　Broomsticks.

4　*dawtit … bill*　Pampered twelve-pint cow's gone / As milkless as the bull.

5　*water-kelpies … foord*　Water spirits haunt the rivers.

6　*Masons*　Freemasons; members of an organization, formerly of stone masons, with secret codes and rites.

7　*Lang syne*　Long ago.

Sweet on the fragrant, flow'ry swaird,°   *surface*
90   In shady bow'r:

Then you, ye auld, snick°-drawing dog!   *latch*
Ye cam to Paradise incog,°   *disguised*
An' play'd on a man a cursed brogue,°   *trick*
     (Black be your fa'!)
95 An' gied° the infant warld a shog,°   *gave / shock*
     'Maist° ruin'd a'.   *almost*

D'ye mind that day, when in a bizz,°   *flurry*
Wi' reeket duds, an' reestet gizz,[1]
Ye did present your smoutie phiz[2]
100   'Mang better folk,
An' sklented on the man of Uz[3]
     Your spitefu' joke?

An' how ye gat him i' your thrall,
An' brak him out o' house an' hal',
105 While scabs an' botches° did him gall,   *tumor*
     Wi' bitter claw,
An' lows'd° his ill-tongu'd, wicked scawl[4]   *loosed*
     Was warst ava?[5]

But a' your doings to rehearse,
110 Your wily snares an' fechtin° fierce,   *fighting*
Sin' that day Michael did you pierce,[6]
     Down to this time,
Wad ding° a' Lallan° tongue, or Erse,   *overcome / Lowland*
     In prose or rhyme

115 An' now, auld cloots, I ken ye're thinkan,
A certain bardie's° rantin, drinkin,   *poet's*
Some luckless hour will send him linkan,°   *running*
     To your black pit;

But faith! he'll turn a corner jinkan,°   *ducking*
120   An' cheat you yet.

But fare you weel, auld Nickie-ben!°   *Devil*
O wad ye tak a thought an' men'!°   *mend*
Ye aiblins° might—I dinna ken—   *perhaps*
     Still hae a stake[7]—
125 I'm wae° to think upo' yon den,   *sad*
     Ev'n for your sake.
—1786

Holy Willie's Prayer[8]

And send the Godly in a pet to pray—
ALEXANDER POPE

O Thou, wha in the Heavens dost dwell,
   Wha, as it pleases best thysel',
Sends ane° to heaven and ten to hell,   *one*
     A' for thy glory,
5 And no for ony guid° or ill   *good*
     They've done afore thee![9]

I bless and praise thy matchless might,
Whan thousands thou hast left in night,
That I am here afore thy sight,
10   For gifts an' grace

---

[1] *reeket … gizz* Smoky clothes and singed face.

[2] *smoutie phiz* Dirty face.

[3] *man of Uz* Job, the man of Uz, was a righteous man who lost everything when God and Satan challenged his faith. See Job 1.1.

[4] *scawl* Scolding wife.

[5] *warst ava* Worst of all.

[6] *Michael did you pierce* See Milton's *Paradise Lost* 6.321–25, in which Satan stabs the angel Michael with a sword.

[7] *hae a stake* Have a chance.

[8] *Holy Willie's Prayer* Willie Fisher was a church elder in Mauchline, East Ayrshire, where Burns briefly lived in the 1780s. Seen by Burns as a religious fanatic and hypocrite, Fisher accused Burns's landlord Gavin Hamilton of stealing from church elders (as well as of various other "sins" such as tilling his land on the Sabbath) when he was found to have allowed poor community members to default on their taxes to the church. The matter was brought before the Presbytery of Ayr, a governing body of church elders; Fisher ultimately lost the case to Hamilton.

[9] *as it pleases … afore thee!* This stanza alludes to the Calvinist belief in predestination held by many members of the Church of Scotland during Burns's time. According to this view, God has preordained the salvation or damnation of human souls; in some interpretations, predestination effectively means that the fate of one's soul is fixed regardless of one's moral actions in life.

A burnin' an' a shinin' light,
       To a' this place.

What was I, or my generation,
That I should get sic° exaltation?   *such*
15 I, wha deserve most just damnation,
       For broken laws,
Sax thousand years 'fore my creation,
       Thro' Adam's cause.[1]

When frae my mither's womb I fell,
20 Thou might hae plungèd me in hell,
To gnash my gums, to weep and wail,
       In burnin' lakes,
Whar damnèd devils roar and yell,
       Chain'd to their stakes;

25 Yet I am here a chosen sample,
To show thy grace is great and ample;
I'm here a pillar in thy temple,
       Strong as a rock,
A guide, a buckler,[2] an example
30   To a' thy flock.

O Lord, thou kens° what zeal I bear,   *knows*
When drinkers drink, and swearers swear,
And singin' there and dancin' here,
       Wi' great an' sma':
35 For I am keepit by thy fear
       Free frae them a'.

But yet, O Lord! confess I must
At times I'm fash'd° wi' fleshy lust;   *troubled*
An' sometimes too, in wardly trust,
40   Vile self gets in;

But thou remembers we are dust,[3]
       Defil'd in sin.

O Lord! yestreen,° thou kens, wi' Meg—.   *yesternight*
Thy pardon I sincerely beg;
45 O! may't ne'er be a livin' plague
       To my dishonour,
An' I'll ne'er lift a lawless leg
       Again upon her.

Besides I farther maun° allow,   *must*
50 Wi' Lizzie's lass, three times I trow°—   *trust*
But, Lord, that Friday I was fou,°   *drunk*
       When I cam near her,
Or else thou kens thy servant true
       Wad never steer her.

55 May be thou lets this fleshly thorn
Beset thy servant e'en and morn
Lest he owre high and proud should turn,
       That he's sae gifted;
If sae, thy hand maun e'en be borne,
60   Until thou lift it.

Lord, bless thy chosen in this place,
For here thou hast a chosen race;
But God confound their stubborn face,
       And blast their name,
65 Wha bring thy elders to disgrace
       An' public shame.

Lord, mind Gawn Hamilton's deserts,
He drinks, an' swears, an' plays at cartes,
Yet has sae mony° takin' arts,   *many*
70   Wi' grit an' sma',[4]
Frae God's ain priest the people's hearts
       He steals awa'.

---

[1]   *broken laws ... Adam's cause*   Allusion to the Biblical narrative of Genesis, in which Adam and Eve disobey God in the Garden of Eden and thus originate human sin. Christian belief generally holds this "original sin" to be carried through the generations, rendering all humans corrupt from birth.

[2]   *buckler*   Shield or protector.

---

[3]   *we are dust*   Cf. Genesis 3.19: "In the sweat of thy face shalt thou eat bread, till thou return unto the ground; for out of it wast thou taken: for dust thou art, and unto dust shalt thou return."

[4]   *grit an' sma'*   Great and small.

An' when we chasten'd him therefor,
Thou kens how he bred sic a splore°   *commotion*
75   As set the warld in a roar
          O' laughin' at us;
Curse thou his basket and his store,
          Kail° and potatoes.   *kale*

Lord, hear my earnest cry an' pray'r,
80   Against that presbyt'ry o' Ayr;
Thy strong right hand, Lord, make it bare
          Upo' their heads;
Lord, weigh it down, and dinna spare,
          For their misdeeds.

85   O Lord my God, that glib-tongu'd Aiken,[1]
My very heart and soul are quakin',
To think how we stood sweatin', shakin',
          An' piss'd wi' dread,
While he, wi' hingin' lips and snakin',°   *sneering*
90   Held up his head.

Lord, in the day of vengeance try him;
Lord, visit them wha did employ him,
And pass not in thy mercy by them,
          Nor hear their pray'r:
95   But, for thy people's sake, destroy them,
          And dinna spare.

But, Lord, remember me and mine
Wi' mercies temp'ral° and divine,   *earthly*
That I for gear and grace may shine
100   Excell'd by nane,
And a' the glory shall be thine,
          Amen, Amen!
          —1789

---

[1] *Aiken*   Robert Aiken, Hamilton's counsel in the dispute.

Tam O'Shanter, A Tale

When chapmen billies[2] leave the street,
    And drouthy° neebors, neebors meet,   *thirsty*
As market-days are wearing late,
And folk begin to tak the gate;
5   While we sit bowsing° at the nappy,°   *boozing / ale*
And getting fou,° and unco° happy,   *drunk / very*
We think na on the long Scots miles,[3]
The waters, mosses,° slaps[4] and styles,   *bogs*
That lie between us and our hame,
10   Where sits our sulky sullen dame,
Gathering her brows, like gathering storm,
Nursing her wrath to keep it warm.

    This truth fand honest Tam o'Shanter,
As he frae Ayr[5] ae° night did canter;   *one*
15   (Auld Ayr, wham ne'er a town surpasses
For honest men and bonnie lasses.)

    O Tam! hadst thou but been sae wise
As taen thy ain wife Kate's advice!
She tauld thee weel, thou was a skellum,°   *scoundrel*
20   A bletherin, busterin drunken blellum;°   *blabber*
That frae November till October,
Ae market-day thou was na sober;
That ilka° melder,[6] wi' the miller,   *each*
Thou sat as long as thou had siller°   *silver*
25   That every naig° was ca'd° a shoe on,   *nag / nailed*
The smith and thee gat roarin fou on;
That at the L——d's house, even on Sunday,
Thou drank wi' Kirkton Jean till Monday.—
She prophesied that, late or soon,
30   Thou wad be found deep-drown'd in Doon;[7]

---

[2] *chapmen billies*   Pedlar friends.

[3] *long Scots miles*   A Scots mile was about 300 yards longer than an English mile.

[4] *slaps*   Gaps in fences or hedges.

[5] *Ayr*   Seaport in southwest Scotland.

[6] *melder*   Time when grain is taken to be ground at a mill.

[7] *Doon*   River in southwest Scotland that flows through Ayr.

Or catch'd wi' warlocks in the mirk
By Aloway's old haunted kirk.°   *church*

     Ah, gentle dames! it gars° me greet,°   *makes / cry*
To think how mony counsels sweet,
35 How mony lengthen'd sage advices,
The husband frae the wife despises!

     But to our tale:—Ae market-night,
Tam had got planted unco right,
Fast by an ingle° bleezing finely,   *fire*
40 Wi' reamin swats¹ that drank divinely;
And at his elbow souter° Johnie,   *shoemaker*
His ancient trusty, drouthy cronie;
Tam lo'ed him like a vera brither,
They had been fou for weeks tegither.—
45 The night drave on wi' sangs and clatter,
And ay the ale was growing better:
The landlady and Tam grew gracious,
With favors secret, sweet, and precious:
The souter tauld his queerest stories;
50 The landlord's laugh was ready chorus:
The storm without might rair and rustle,
Tam did na mind the storm a whistle.—
Care, mad to see a man sae happy,
E'en drown'd himsel amang the nappy:
55 As bees flee hame, wi' lades o' treasure,
The minutes wing'd their way wi' pleasure:
Kings may be blest, but Tam was glorious,
O'er a' the ills o' life victorious!

     But pleasures are like poppies spread,
60 You seize the flower, its bloom is shed;
Or like the snow falls in the river,
A moment white—then melts for ever;
Or like the borealis² race,
That flit ere you can point their place;
65 Or like the rainbow's lovely form,
Evanishing amid the storm.—
Nae man can tether time or tide,

The hour approaches Tam maun° ride;   *must*
That hour o' night's black arch the key-stane,
70 That dreary hour he mounts his beast in;
And fie a night he taks the road in
As ne'er poor sinner was abroad in.

     The wind blew, as 'twad blawn its last;
The rattling showers rose on the blast;
75 The speedy gleams the darkness swallow'd
Loud, deep, and lang, the thunder bellow'd:
That night, a child might understand
The deil° had business on his hand.   *devil*

     Weel mounted on his grey meare, Meg,
80 A better never lifted leg,
Tam skepit° on thro' dub° and mire,   *hurried / bog*
Despising wind, and rain, and fire:
Whyles holding fast his gude blue bonnet;
Whyles crooning o'er an auld Scots sonnet;
85 Whyles glowring round wi' prudent cares,
Lest bogles° catch him unawares;   *phantoms*
Kirk-Aloway was drawing nigh,
Where ghaists and houlets° nightly cry.   *owls*

     By this time he was cross the ford,
90 Where in the snaw the chapman smoor'd;° *was smothered*
And past the birks and meikle stane,³
Where drunken Charlie brak's neck-bane;⁴
And thro' the whins,° and by the   *thorns*
    cairn,°   *stone monument*
Where hunters fand the murder'd bairn;°   *child*
95 And near the tree, aboon° the well,   *above*
Where Mungo's mither hang'd hersel:
Before him, Doon pours all his floods;
The doubling storm roars thro' the woods;
The light'nings flash from pole to pole;
100 Near, and more near, the thunders roll;
When glimmering thro' the groaning trees,
Kirk-Aloway seem'd in a bleeze;°   *blaze*

---

¹ *reamin swats* Foaming ale.
² *borealis* Aurora borealis, also called "northern lights."

---

³ *birks and meikle stane* Birch trees and large stone.
⁴ *brak's neck-bane* Broke his neckbone.

Thro' ilka bore° the beams were glancing,   *crack*
And loud resounded mirth and dancing.

105   Inspiring, bold John Barleycorn![1]
What dangers thou canst make us scorn:
Wi' tippeny,° we fear nae evil;   *twopenny ale*
Wi' usquebae,° we'll face the devil!   *whisky*
The swats sae ream'd in Tammie's noddle,°   *head*
110   Fair-play, he car'd na deils a boddle:[2]
But Maggy stood, right fair astonish'd,
Till by the heel and hand admonish'd,
She ventur'd forward on the light,
And, wow! Tam saw an unco° sight!   *strange*

115   Warlocks and witches in a dance,
Nae cotillion brent new[3] frae France,
But hornpipes, jigs, strathspeys and reels,[4]
Put life and mettle in their heels.—
At winnock-bunker in the East,
120   There sat auld Nick° in shape o' beast;   *Satan*
A towzie tyke,[5] black, grim, and large;
To gie them music was his charge:
He screw'd the pipes° and gart°   *bagpipes | made*
    them skirl,°   *squeal*
Till roof and rafters a' did dirl.°—   *shake*
125   Coffins stood round, like open presses,°   *cupboards*
That shaw'd the dead in their last dresses;
And (by some devilish cantraip° slight)   *magic spell*
Each in its cauld hand held a light;
By which heroic Tam was able
130   To note upon the haly table,[6]
A murderer's banes, in gibbet-airns;[7]

Twa span-lang, wee, unchirsten'd bairns;°   *children*
A thief, new cutted frae a rape,°   *rope*
Wi' his last gasp his gab° did gape;   *mouth*
135   Five tomahawks, wi' blood red-rusted;
Five scimitars, wi' murder crusted;
A garter which a babe had strangled;
A knife a father's throat had mangled,
Whom his ain son of life bereft,
140   The grey hairs yet stack° to the heft:°   *stuck | handle*
Wi' mair° of horrible and awefu',   *more*
That even to name wad be unlawfu':—
Three lawyers' tongues, turn'd inside out,
Wi' lies seam'd like a beggar's clout;°   *patchcloth*
145   Three priests' hearts, rotten, black as muck,
Lay stinking vile in every neuk.°   *nook*

As Tammie glowr'd, amaz'd and curious,
The mirth and fun grew fast and furious:
The piper loud and louder blew;
150   The dancers quick and quicker flew;
They reel'd, they set, they cross'd, they
    cleekit,°   *linked arms*
Till ilka Carlin° swat and reekit,[8]
And coost° her duddies° to the wark,°   *cast | clothes | work*
And linket at it in her sark.[9]—

155   Now Tam! O Tam! had thae been
    queans,°   *young women*
A' plump and strappin in their teens!
Their sarks, instead o' creeshie flainen,[10]
Been snaw white, seventeen-hunder linen;
This breeks° o' mine, my only pair,   *trousers*
160   That ance were plush o' gude blue hair,
I wad hae gien them off my hurdies°   *haunches*
For ae blink o' the bonie burdies!°   *girls*
But withered beldams,° auld and droll,   *hags*
Rigwoodie[11] hags wad spean° a foal,   *wean*

---

[1] *John Barleycorn* Personification of barley, and of beer and whisky made from barley.

[2] *he car'd … boddle* He didn't care a farthing about devils.

[3] *cotillion* Highly organized group dance of eighteenth-century French origin; *brent new* Very new.

[4] *hornpipes … reels* Types of traditional Scottish dance.

[5] *towzie tyke* Scruffy dog. In British folklore, the figure of the black dog is an omen of death and associated with Satan.

[6] *haly table* Holy table, i.e., altar.

[7] *gibbet-airns* Gibbet irons, used to display the body of an executed person.

[8] *ilka … reekit* Each witch sweated and steamed.

[9] *And … sark* And danced nimbly around it in her undergarments.

[10] *creeshie flainen* Greasy flannel.

[11] *Rigwoodie* Possibly "gnarled." Literally, a rigwiddy is a band made from twigs twisted together, used as part of a harness for a cart-horse.

65 Loupin° and flingin on a crumock,°   *leaping / staff*
I wonder did na turn thy stomach.—

   But Tam kend° what was what fu'   *knew*
      brawlie;°   *well*
There was ae winsome wench and walie,°   *handsome*
That night enlisted in the core,
70 (Lang after kend on Carrick shore;
For mony a beast to dead she shot,
And perish'd mony a bonnie boat,
And shook baith meikle corn and bear°   *barley*
And kept the country-side in fear)—
75 Her cutty-sark° o' Paisley harn,°   *short underdress / linen*
That while a lassie she had worn,
In longitude tho' sorely scanty,°   *meager*
It was her best, and she was vauntie.°—   *vain*
Ah! little thought thy reverend graunie,
80 That sark she cost for her wee Nannie
Wi' twa pund Scots ('twas a' her riches)
Should ever grac'd a dance o' witches!

   But here my Muse her wing maun cour,°   *lower*
Sic° flights are far beyond her power;   *such*
85 To sing how Nannie lap° and flang,°   *leapt / danced*
(A souple jad° she was and strang,)   *disreputable woman*
And how Tam stood like ane bewitch'd,
And thought his very een° enrich'd;   *eyes*
Even Satan glowr'd, and fidg'd fu' fain,[1]
90 And hotch'd,° and blew wi' might and main;   *jerked*
Till first ae caper—syne° anither—   *then*
Tam tint° his reason a'thegither,   *lost*
And roars out—"Weel done, cutty-sark!"
And in an instant all was dark;
95 And scarcely had he Maggie rallied,
When out the hellish legion sallied.—

   As bees bizz out wi' angry fyke,°   *commotion*
When plundering herds assail their byke;°   *hive*
As open pussie's° mortal foes,   *hare's*
200 When, pop, she starts before their nose;
As eager rins the market-croud,
When "catch the thief!" resounds aloud;
So Maggy rins, the witches follow,
Wi' mony an eldritch° shout and hollo.—   *ghastly*

205 Ah Tam! ah Tam! thou'll get thy fairin![2]
In hell they'll roast thee like a herrin!
In vain thy Kate awaits thy comin,
Kate soon will be a woefu' woman!
Now, do thy speedy utmost, Meg!
210 And win the key-stane o' the brig;°   *bridge*
There at them thou thy tail may toss,
A running stream they dare na cross!
But ere the key-stane she could make,
The fient° a tale she had to shake;   *fiend, devil*
215 For Nannie, far before the rest,
Hard upon noble Maggy prest,
And flew at Tam with furious ettle,°   *intent*
But little kend she Maggy's mettle!
Ae spring brought off her master hale,°   *whole*
220 But left behind her ain gray tail:
The carlin claught her by the rump,
And left poor Maggy scarce a stump.

   Now wha this Tale o' truth shall read,
Ilk man and mother's son, take heed:
225 Whene'er to drink you are inclin'd,
Or cutty-sarks rin in your mind,
Think, ye may buy the joys o'er dear;
Remember TAM O'SHANTER'S MEARE!
—1791

---

[1] *fidg'd fu' fain* Quivered with excitement.

[2] *fairin* I.e., just deserts.

Fareweel to a' Our Scottish Fame[1]

Fareweel to a' our Scottish fame,
   Fareweel our ancient glory,
Fareweel even to the Scottish name,
   Sae fam'd in martial story!
5 Now Sark rins o'er the Solway[2] sands,
   And Tweed[3] rins to the ocean,
To mark where England's province stands;
   Such a parcel°[4] of rogues in a nation!   *pack*

What guile or force could not subdue,
10   Through many warlike ages,[5]
Is wrought now by a coward few,
   For hireling traitors' wages.
The English steel we could disdain,
   Secure in valour's station.
15 But English gold has been our bane;
   Such a parcel of rogues in a nation!

O would, ere I had seen the day
   That treason thus could sell us,
My auld grey head had lien in clay,
20   Wi' Bruce and loyal Wallace![6]
But pith° and power, till my last hour   *strength*
   I'll mak this declaration,

We're bought and sold for English gold:
   Such a parcel of rogues in a nation!
—1791

Flow gently, sweet Afton[7]

Flow gently, sweet Afton, among thy green
   braes!°   *banks*
Flow gently, I'll sing thee a song in thy praise!
My Mary's asleep by thy murmuring stream—
Flow gently, sweet Afton, disturb not her dream!

5 Thou stock-dove whose echo resounds thro' the glen,
Ye wild whistling blackbirds in yon thorny den,
Thou green-crested lapwing, thy screaming forbear—
I charge you, disturb not my slumbering fair!

How lofty, sweet Afton, thy neighbouring hills,
10 Far mark'd with the courses of clear, winding rills!°   *brooks*
There daily I wander, as noon rises high,
My flocks and my Mary's sweet cot° in my eye.   *cottage*

How pleasant thy banks and green valleys below,
Where wild in the woodlands the primroses blow;
15 There oft, as mild ev'ning weeps over the lea,
The sweet-scented birk° shades my Mary and me.   *birch*

Thy crystal stream, Afton, how lovely it glides,
And winds by the cot where my Mary resides!
How wanton thy waters her snowy feet lave,°   *wash*
20 As, gathering sweet flowerets, she stems thy clear wave.

Flow gently, sweet Afton, among thy green braes!
Flow gently, sweet river, the theme of my lays!°   *song*
My Mary's asleep by thy murmuring stream—
Flow gently, sweet Afton, disturb not her dream!
—1792

---

[1] *Fareweel to … Scottish Fame* This poem references the Acts of Union between England and Scotland, (passed in 1706 by the English Parliament, and in 1707 by the Scottish Parliament), under the terms of which the previously separate states became a single kingdom (named Great Britain). Many suspected that members of the Scottish Parliament had been bribed by the English to support the Union.

[2] *Sark* River that runs partway along the border between England and Scotland; *Solway* Moss or bog in England, near the Scottish border, the site of the Battle of Solway Moss in 1542.

[3] *Tweed* River that runs along the eastern part of the Scottish-English border.

[4] *parcel* Pack.

[5] *Through many warlike ages* English armies had made many attempts to conquer Scotland, beginning in the twelfth century.

[6] *Bruce … Wallace* Alludes to Robert the Bruce, the Scottish king, and William Wallace, both leaders in the fourteenth-century Wars of Scottish Independence, and revered as Scottish national heroes.

---

[7] *Afton* River that runs through southwestern Scotland.

Ae Fond Kiss[1]

Ae° fond kiss, and then we sever;   *one*
   Ae fareweel, alas, forever!
Deep in heart-wrung tears I'll pledge thee,
Warring sighs and groans I'll wage thee.
5 Who shall say that Fortune grieves him,
While the star of hope she leaves him?
Me, nae cheerful twinkle lights me;
Dark despair around benights me.

I'll ne'er blame my partial fancy,
10 Naething could resist my Nancy:
But to see her was to love her;
Love but her, and love forever.
Had we never lov'd sae kindly,
Had we never lov'd sae blindly,
15 Never met—or never parted,
We had ne'er been brokenhearted.

Fare-thee-weel, thou first and fairest!
Fare-thee-weel, thou best and dearest!
Thine be ilka° joy and treasure,   *every*
20 Peace, Enjoyment, Love and Pleasure!
Ae fond kiss, and then we sever!
Ae fareweel, alas, forever!
Deep in heart-wrung tears I'll pledge thee,
Warring sighs and groans I'll wage thee.
—1792

Robert Bruce's March to Bannockburn[2]

Scots, wha hae° wi' Wallace[3] bled,   *who have*
  Scots, wham° Bruce has aften led,   *whom*

Welcome to your gory bed,
   Or to victorie!

5 Now's the day, and now's the hour;
See the front o' battle lour;°   *threaten*
See approach proud Edward's power—
   Chains and slaverie!

Wha will be a traitor knave?
10 Wha can fill a coward's grave?
Wha sae base as be a slave?
   Let him turn and flee!

Wha, for Scotland's King and Law,
Freedom's sword will strongly draw,
15 Free-man stand, or Free-man fa',
   Let him on wi' me!

By Oppression's woes and pains!
By your Sons in servile chains!
We will drain our dearest veins,
20 But they shall be free!

Lay the proud usurpers low!
Tyrants fall in every foe!
Liberty's in every blow!—
   Let us Do or Die!
—1795

A Man's a Man for A' That

Is there for honest poverty
   That hings° his head, an' a'° that;   *hangs | all*
The coward slave—we pass him by,
   We dare be poor for a' that!
5 For a' that, an' a' that.
   Our toils obscure an' a' that,
The rank is but the guinea's stamp,
   The Man's the gowd° for a' that.   *gold*

---

1 *Ae Fond Kiss* Burns wrote this love song for Nancy McLehose (the two called each other "Sylvander" and "Clarinda"), when she left England to reunite with her husband in Jamaica.

2 *Robert Bruce … Bannockburn* In 1314, Robert the Bruce, King of the Scots, fought successfully for a free Scotland in a battle against the English under Edward II at Bannockburn.

3 *Wallace* Sir William Wallace led numerous battles against the English under King Edward I.

What though on hamely° fare we dine,   *simple*
10   Wear hoddin grey,[1] an' a that;
Gie° fools their silks, and knaves their wine;   *give*
    A Man's a Man for a' that:
For a' that, and a' that,
    Their tinsel show, an' a' that;
15 The honest man, tho' e'er sae° poor,   *so*
    Is king o' men for a' that.

Ye see yon birkie,[2] ca'd° "a lord,"   *called*
    Wha struts, an' stares, an' a' that;
Tho' hundreds worship at his word,
20   He's but a coof° for a' that: *fool*
For a' that, an' a' that,
    His ribband,° star,[3] an' a' that: *ribbon*
The man o' independent mind
    He looks an' laughs at a' that.

25 A prince can mak a belted knight,
    A marquis, duke, an' a' that;
But an honest man's aboon° his might,   *above*
    Gude faith, he mauna fa' that![4]
For a' that, an' a' that,
30   Their dignities an' a' that;
The pith° o' sense, an' pride o' worth,   *importance*
    Are higher rank than a' that.

Then let us pray that come it may,
    As come it will for a' that,
35 That sense and worth, o'er a' the earth,
    Shall bear the gree,[5] an' a' that.
For a' that, an' a' that,
    It's coming yet for a' that,
That Man to Man, the world o'er,
40   Shall brithers be for a' that.
    —1795

---

[1] *hoddin grey* Coarse, woolen peasant cloth.

[2] *birkie* Conceited, swaggering fellow.

[3] *ribband, star* Emblems of nobility.

[4] *mauna fa' that* Musn't have that befall him.

[5] *bear the gree* Have the victory.

Comin' thro' the Rye

CHORUS

O, Jenny's a' weet,[6] poor body,
  Jenny's seldom dry;
She draigl't[7] a' her petticoatie
    Comin thro' the rye!

5 Comin thro' the rye, poor body,
    Comin thro' the rye,
She draigl't a' her petticoatie
    Comin thro' the rye!

Gin° a body meet a body   *suppose*
10   Comin thro' the rye,
Gin a body kiss a body,
    Need a body cry?

Gin a body meet a body
    Comin thro' the glen,
15 Gin a body kiss a body,
    Need the warld ken?°   *know*

CHORUS

O, Jenny's a' weet, poor body,
  Jenny's seldom dry;
She draigl't a' her petticoatie
20   Comin thro' the rye!
—1796

---

[6] *a' weet* All wet.

[7] *draigl't* Draggled; dragged through the mud.

A Red, Red Rose

O, my luve's like a red, red rose,
  That's newly sprung in June;
O, my luve's like the melodie,
    That's sweetly play'd in tune.

5 As fair art thou, my bonie lass,
    So deep in luve am I;

And I will luve thee still, my dear,
 Till a' the seas gang° dry.   *go*

Till a' the seas gang dry, my dear,
10 And the rocks melt wi' the sun;
And I will luve thee still, my dear,
 While the sands o' life shall run.

And fare thee weel, my only luve!
 And fare thee weel, a while!
15 And I will come again, my luve,
 Tho' 'twere ten thousand mile!
 —1796

Auld Lang Syne[1]

Should auld acquaintance be forgot,
 And never brought to mind?
Should auld acquaintance be forgot,
 And auld lang syne!

CHORUS

5 For auld lang syne, my dear,
  For auld lang syne.
 We'll tak a cup o' kindness yet,
  For auld lang syne.

And surely ye'll be° your pint stowp![2]   *raise*
10 And surely I'll be mine!
And we'll tak a cup o' kindness yet,
 For auld lang syne.

CHORUS

We twa° hae run about the braes,°   *two / hills*
 And pou'd° the gowans° fine;   *pulled / daisies*
15 But we've wander'd mony a weary fit,°   *foot*
 Sin'° auld lang syne.   *since*

---

1 *Auld Lang Syne* Times long since passed.
2 *stowp* Drinking glass.

CHORUS

We twa hae paidl'd in the burn,°   *stream*
 Frae morning sun till dine;
But seas between us braid° hae roar'd   *broad*
20 Sin' auld lang syne.

CHORUS

And there's a hand, my trusty fiere!°   *friend*
 And gie's° a hand o' thine!   *give us*
And we'll tak a right gude willie-waught,[3]
 For auld lang syne.

CHORUS

—1796

Love and Liberty. A Cantata[4]

RECITATIVO

When lyart° leaves bestrow the yird,° *decayed / ground*
 Or wavering like the bauckie-bird,°   *bat*
 Bedim cauld Boreas' blast;[5]
When hailstanes drive wi' bitter skyte,°   *lash*
5 And infant frosts begin to bite,
 In hoary cranreuch[6] drest;
Ae night at e'en a merry core°   *corps*
 O' randie, gangrel° bodies,   *vagrant*
In Poosie Nansie's[7] held the splore,°   *drinking spree*
10 To drink their orra duddies;[8]
  Wi' quaffing an' laughing,
   They ranted an' they sang,

---

3 *gude willie-waught* Hearty glass of draught beer.
4 *Love and Liberty. A Cantata* Commonly known by the title "The Jolly Beggars."
5 *Boreas' blast* North wind (Boreas is the Greek god of the north wind).
6 *hoary cranreuch* Hoar frost.
7 *Poosie Nansie's* Scottish tavern where Burns found the inspiration for "The Jolly Beggars."
8 *orra duddies* Extra rags.

Wi' jumping an' thumping,
　　The vera girdle[1] rang,

15　First, neist° the fire, in auld red rags,　　　　　　　　*next*
　　Ane sat, weel brac'd wi' mealy bags,[2]
　　　　And knapsack a' in order;
　　His doxy° lay within his arm;　　　　　　　　　　*wench*
　　Wi' usquebae° an' blankets warm　　　　　　　　*whisky*
20　　　She blinkit on her sodger;
　　An' aye he gies the tozie drab[3]
　　　　The tither skelpin'[4] kiss,
　　While she held up her greedy gab,°　　　　　　　*mouth*
　　　　Just like an aumous° dish;　　　　　　　　　*alms*
25　　　Ilk° smack still, did crack still,　　　　　　*each*
　　　　Just like a cadger's[5] whip;
　　　　Then staggering an' swaggering
　　　　　He roar'd this ditty up—

AIR

　　I am a son of Mars[6] who have been in many wars,
30　　　And show my cuts and scars wherever I come;
　　This here was for a wench, and that other in a trench,
　　　　When welcoming the French at the sound of the
　　　　　drum.
　　　　　　　　　　　　　　　Lal de daudle, &c.

　　My 'prenticeship I past where my leader breath'd his
　　　　last,
35　　　When the bloody die was cast on the heights of
　　　　　Abram:[7]
　　And I scrved out my trade when the gallant game was
　　　　play'd,

And the Moro[8] low was laid at the sound of the
　　drum.

　　I lastly was with Curtis[9] among the floating batt'ries,
　　　And there I left for witness an arm and a limb;
40　Yet let my country need me, with Elliot[10] to head me,
　　　I'd clatter on my stumps at the sound of a drum.

And now tho' I must beg, with a wooden arm and leg,
　　And many a tatter'd rag hanging over my bum,
I'm as happy with my wallet, my bottle, and my
　　callet,°　　　　　　　　　　　　　　　*whore*
45　As when I used in scarlet to follow a drum.

What tho' with hoary locks, I must stand the winter
　　shocks,
　　Beneath the woods and rocks oftentimes for a home,
When the t'other bag I sell, and the t'other bottle tell,
　　I could meet a troop of hell, at the sound of a drum.

RECITATIVO

50　He ended; and the kebars° sheuk,　　　　　　　*rafters*
　　　Aboon° the chorus roar;　　　　　　　　　　*above*
　　While frighted rattons° backward leuk,　　　　　*rats*
　　　An' seek the benmost° bore:　　　　　　　　*innermost*
　　A fairy fiddler frae the neuk,
55　　He skirl'd out, *Encore!*
　　But up arose the martial chuck,°　　　　　　　*camp whore*
　　　An' laid the loud uproar.

AIR

　　I once was a maid, tho' I cannot tell when,
　　And still my delight is in proper young men;
60　Some one of a troop of dragoons was my daddie,
　　No wonder I'm fond of a sodger laddie,
　　　　　　　　　　　　　Sing, lal de lal, &c.

---

[1] *vera girdle*　Very griddle.

[2] *weel brac'd wi' mealy bags*　Well fed with porridge.

[3] *tozie drab*　Drunken slut.

[4] *tither skelpin'*　Other smacking.

[5] *cadger*　Salesman who traveled with a horse and cart.

[6] *Mars*　Roman god of war.

[7] *heights of Abram*　In 1759, British general James Wolfe's troops won the Battle of the Plains of Abraham against the French in Quebec; Wolfe and the opposing general, Montcalm, both died in the battle.

[8] *Moro*　El Moro was a castle on the island of Santiago, Cuba, which was stormed by the British in 1762.

[9] *Curtis*　Rear Admiral Sir Roger Curtis, who took part in the battle of 1782 against the Spanish off the coast of Gibraltar.

[10] *Elliot*　Sir George Augustus Elliot, who also helped defend Gibraltar.

The first of my loves was a swaggering blade,
To rattle the thundering drum was his trade;
His leg was so tight, and his cheek was so ruddy,
Transported I was with my sodger laddie.

But the godly old chaplain left him in the lurch;
The sword I forsook for the sake of the church:
He ventur'd the soul, and I risked the body,
'Twas then I proved false to my sodger laddie.

Full soon I grew sick of my sanctified sot,
The regiment at large for a husband I got;
From the gilded spontoon° to the fife I was ready,   weapon
I asked no more but a sodger laddie.

But the peace it reduc'd me to beg in despair,
Till I met my old boy in a Cunningham fair,
His rags regimental, they flutter'd so gaudy,
My heart it rejoic'd at a sodger laddie.

And now I have liv'd—I know not how long,
And still I can join in a cup and a song;
But whilst with both hands I can hold the glass steady,
Here's to thee, my hero, my sodger laddie.

RECITATIVO

Poor Merry-Andrew,[1] in the neuk,
    Sat guzzling wi' a tinkler-hizzie;°   tinker-hussy
They mind't na wha the chorus teuk,
    Between themselves they were sae busy:
    At length, wi' drink an' courting dizzy,
He stoiter'd° up an' made a face;   staggered
    Then turn'd an' laid a smack on Grizzie,
Syne° tun'd his pipes wi' grave grimace.   then

AIR

Sir Wisdom's a fool when he's fou;°   drunk
    Sir Knave is a fool in a session;
He's there but a 'prentice I trow,°   trust
    But I am a fool by profession.

My grannie she bought me a beuk,
    An' I held° awa to the school;   went
I fear I my talent misteuk,
    But what will ye hae of a fool?

For drink I would venture my neck;
    A hizzie's the half of my craft;
But what could ye other expect
    Of ane that's avowedly daft?

I ance was tied up like a stirk,°   young cow
    For civilly swearing and quaffin;[2]
I ance was abus'd i' the kirk,°   church
    For towsing a lass i' my daffin.[3]

Poor Andrew that tumbles for sport,
    Let naebody name wi' a jeer;
There's even, I'm tauld, i' the Court
    A tumbler ca'd the Premier.

Observ'd ye yon reverend lad
    Mak faces to tickle the mob;
He rails at our mountebank[4] squad—
    It's rivalship just i' the job.

And now my conclusion I'll tell,
    For faith I'm confoundedly dry;
The chiel° that's a fool for himsel',   young boy
    Guid Lord! he's far dafter than I.

RECITATIVO

Then niest° outspak a raucle carlin,[5]   next
Wha kent fu' weel to cleek° the sterlin;°   steal / money
For mony a pursie she had hooked,
An' had in mony a well been douked;°   ducked
Her love had been a Highland laddie,
But weary fa' the waefu' woodie!°   dolt

[1] *Merry-Andrew* Clown, joker, buffoon.

[2] *quaffin* Drinking large amounts of alcohol.

[3] *towsing a lass i' my daffin* Literally, disheveling a woman in merriment; obliquely, having sex out of wedlock.

[4] *mountebank* Itinerant seller of supposed remedies.

[5] *raucle carlin* Stout hag.

125   Wi' sighs an' sobs she thus began
       To wail her braw° John Highlandman.   *handsome*

AIR

       A Highland lad my love was born,
       The Lalland° laws he held in scorn;   *lowland*
       But he still was faithfu' to his clan,
130   My gallant, braw John Highlandman.

CHORUS

       Sing hey my braw John Highlandman!
       Sing ho my braw John Highlandman!
       There's not a lad in a' the lan'
       Was match for my John Highlandman.

135   With his philibeg° an' tartan plaid,   *kilt*
       An' guid claymore° down by his side,   *sword*
       The ladies' hearts he did trepan,°   *entrap*
       My gallant, braw John Highlandman.
            Sing hey, &c.

140   We ranged a' from Tweed to Spey,
       An' liv'd like lords an' ladies gay;
       For a Lalland face he feared none—
       My gallant, braw John Highlandman.
            Sing hey, &c.

145   They banish'd him beyond the sea.
       But ere the bud was on the tree,
       Adown my cheeks the pearls ran,
       Embracing my John Highlandman.
            Sing hey, &c.

150   But, och! they catch'd him at the last,
       And bound him in a dungeon fast:
       My curse upon them every one,
       They've hang'd my braw John Highlandman!
            Sing hey, &c.

155   And now a widow, I must mourn
       The pleasures that will ne'er return:
       The comfort but a hearty can,

       When I think on John Highlandman.
            Sing hey, &c.

RECITATIVO

160   A pigmy scraper wi' his fiddle,
       Wha us'd at trystes° an' fairs to driddle.°   *markets / dawdle*
       Her strappin limb and gausy° middle   *plump*
            (He reach'd nae higher)
       Had hol'd his heartie like a riddle,
165   An' blawn't° on fire.   *blown it*

       Wi' hand on hainch, and upward e'e,
       He croon'd his gamut, one, two, three,
       Then in an arioso key,
            The wee Apollo[1]
170   Set off wi' allegretto glee
            His giga° solo.   *jig*

AIR

       Let me ryke° up to dight° that tear,   *reach / wipe*
       An' go wi' me an' be my dear;
       An' then your every care an' fear
175   May whistle owre the lave° o't.   *rest*

CHORUS

       I am a fiddler to my trade,
       An' a' the tunes that e'er I played,
       The sweetest still to wife or maid,
       Was whistle owre the lave o't.

180   At kirns° an' weddins we'se be there,   *harvest feasts*
       An' O sae nicely's we will fare!
       We'll bowse° about till Daddie Care   *drink*
            Sing whistle owre the lave o't.
            I am, &c.

185   Sae merrily's the banes° we'll pyke,°   *bones / pick*
       An' sun oursel's about the dyke;
       An' at our leisure, when ye like,
            We'll whistle owre the lave o't.
            I am, &c.

---

1   *Apollo*   Greek god of music.

190 But bless me wi' your heav'n o' charms,
An' while I kittle° hair on thairms,[1]   *tickle*
Hunger, cauld, an' a' sic° harms,   *such*
 May whistle owre the lave o't.
  I am, &c.

RECITATIVO

195 Her charms had struck a sturdy caird,°   *tinker*
 As weel as poor gut-scraper;
He taks the fiddler by the beard,
 An' draws a roosty° rapier—   *rusty*
He swoor, by a' was swearing worth,
200 To speet° him like a pliver,°   *pierce / plover*
Unless he would from that time forth
 Relinquish her forever.

Wi' ghastly e'e° poor tweedle-dee   *eye*
 Upon his hunkers° bended,   *haunches*
205 An' pray'd for grace wi' ruefu' face,
 An' so the quarrel ended.
But tho' his little heart did grieve
 When round the tinkler prest her,
He feign'd to snirtle° in his sleeve,   *snicker*
210 When thus the caird address'd her:

AIR

My bonie lass, I work in brass,
 A tinkler is my station:
I've travell'd round all Christian ground
 In this my occupation;
215 I've taen the gold, an' been enrolled
 In many a noble squadron;
But vain they search'd when off I march'd
 To go an' clout° the cauldron.   *patch*

Despise that shrimp, that wither'd imp,
220 With a' his noise an' cap'rin;
An' take a share with those that bear
 The budget° and the apron!   *pouch*
And by that stowp!° my faith an' houp,   *cup*

And by that dear Kilbaigie![2]
225 If e'er ye want, or meet wi' scant,
 May I ne'er weet° my craigie.°   *wet / throat*

RECITATIVO

The caird prevail'd—th' unblushing fair
 In his embraces sunk;
Partly wi' love o'ercome sae sair,
230 An' partly she was drunk:
Sir Violino, with an air
 That show'd a man o' spunk,
Wish'd unison between the pair,
 An' made the bottle clunk
235   To their health that night.

But hurchin° Cupid shot a shaft,   *urchin*
 That play'd a dame a shavie°—   *trick*
The fiddler rak'd her, fore and aft,
 Behint the chicken cavie.°   *coop*
240 Her lord, a wight° of Homer's craft,   *creature*
 Tho' limpin wi' the spavie,[3]
He hirpl'd° up, an' lap° like daft,   *limped / leapt*
 An' shor'd° them Dainty Davie[4]   *offered*
  O' boot[5] that night.

245 He was a care-defying blade[6]
 As ever Bacchus[7] listed!
Tho' Fortune sair upon him laid,
 His heart, she ever miss'd it.
He had no wish but—to be glad,
250 Nor want but—when he thirsted;
He hated nought but—to be sad,
 An' thus the muse suggested
  His sang that night.

---

[1] *hair on thairms* Fiddle strings.

[2] *Kilbaigie* Brand of whisky.

[3] *spavie* Tumorous bone disease.

[4] *Dainty Davie* Lovemaking; Dainty Davie is the subject of a Scottish song about David Williamson, who was said to have been given refuge by the Laird of Cherrytrees. The Laird hid the man in his daughter's bed, and the girl was later discovered to be pregnant.

[5] *O' boot* For free.

[6] *blade* Good-natured fellow.

[7] *Bacchus* Roman god of wine.

AIR

I am a Bard of no regard,
255 Wi' gentle folks an' a' that;
But Homer—like, the glowrin byke,°   *crowd*
Frae town to town I draw that.

CHORUS

For a' that, an' a' that,
An' twice as muckle's° a' that;   *much*
260 I've lost but ane, I've twa behin',
I've wife eneugh for a' that.

I never drank the Muses'[1] stank,°   *pool*
Castalia's[2] burn,° an' a' that;   *brewing water*
But there it streams an' richly reams,
265 My Helicon[3] I ca' that.
For a' that, &c.

Great love I bear to a' the fair,
Their humble slave an' a' that;
But lordly will, I hold it still
270 A mortal sin to thraw° that.   *thwart*
For a' that, &c.

In raptures sweet, this hour we meet,
Wi' mutual love an' a' that;
But for how lang the flie may stang,
275 Let inclination law that.
For a' that, &c.

Their tricks an' craft hae put me daft,
They've taen me in, an' a' that;
But clear your decks, and here's—"The Sex!"
280 I like the jads° for a' that.   *young ladies*

CHORUS

For a' that, an' a' that,
An' twice as muckle's a' that;

My dearest bluid,° to do them guid,   *blood*
They're welcome till't° for a' that.   *to it*

RECITATIVO

285 So sang the bard—and Nansie's wa's
Shook with a thunder of applause,
Re-echo'd from each mouth!
They toom'd° their pocks,° they pawn'd   *emptied / pockets*
their duds,
They scarcely left to co'er their fuds,°   *behinds*
290 To quench their lowin drouth:[4]
Then owre again, the jovial thrang
The poet did request
To lowse his pack an' wale° a sang,   *choose*
A ballad o' the best;
295 He rising, rejoicing,
Between his twa Deborahs,[5]
Looks round him, an' found them
Impatient for the chorus.

AIR

See the smoking bowl before us,
300 Mark our jovial ragged ring!
Round and round take up the chorus,
And in raptures let us sing—

CHORUS

A fig for those by law protected!
Liberty's a glorious feast!
305 Courts for cowards were erected,
Churches built to please the priest.

What is title, what is treasure,
What is reputation's care?
If we lead a life of pleasure,
310 'Tis no matter how or where!
A fig for, &c.

With the ready trick and fable,
Round we wander all the day;

---

1 *Muses* In Greek mythology, the nine daughters of Zeus and Mnemosyne, each of whom presided over and provided inspiration for an aspect of learning or the arts.

2 *Castalia* Spring on Mount Parnassus that was sacred to the Muses.

3 *Helicon* Mountain dedicated to the Muses.

4 *lowin drouth* Burning thirst.

5 *twa Deborahs* The two Deborahs of the Bible.

And at night in barn or stable,
   Hug our doxies° on the hay.   *mistresses*

15
      A fig for, &c.

Does the train-attended carriage
   Thro' the country lighter rove?
Does the sober bed of marriage

20
   Witness brighter scenes of love?
      A fig for, &c.

Life is all a variorum,[1]
   We regard not how it goes;
Let them cant about decorum,

25
   Who have character to lose.
      A fig for, &c.

Here's to budgets, bags and wallets!
   Here's to all the wandering train.
Here's our ragged brats and callets,°   *whores*

330
   One and all cry out, Amen!

A fig for those by law protected!
   Liberty's a glorious feast!
Courts for cowards were erected,
   Churches built to please the priest.

—1799

---

[1] *variorum*   Changing scene, variation.

JOANNA BAILLIE
1762 – 1851

An important and influential figure of the Romantic era, Joanna Baillie was, according to Sir Walter Scott, "the best dramatic writer whom Britain has produced since the days of Shakespeare and Massinger." Baillie also produced a significant work of literary criticism—she included an "Introductory Discourse" to her *Plays on the Passions* (1798) (published the same year as Wordsworth's famous "Preface" to *Lyrical Ballads*), in which she analyzed Enlightenment drama and critiqued its discourse of tragedy.

Joanna Baillie was born in 1762 to Dorothea Hunter and James Baillie, a Presbyterian minister, in Lanarkshire, Scotland. Her mother was known as a good storyteller, a talent that Baillie picked up at an early age. Despite this interest, she shunned reading until she was ten years old, preferring to spend her time outdoors. In 1768 she left the rural area in which she was born when her father was transferred to a church in Hamilton, a nearby town on the banks of the Clyde River.

Baillie was sent to boarding school in Glasgow in 1772. Four years later the rest of her family joined her when her father was hired as Professor of Divinity at the University of Glasgow. At boarding school, she proved herself to be vivacious and outgoing, studying music, visual art, mathematics, and reading. In addition to her studies, she was active in the school's artistic life, helping to stage plays. The family returned to Lanarkshire when her father died in 1778. While her brother Matthew left to study at Oxford, Baillie pursued her own studies privately. (Universities would remain a male preserve in England until the mid-nineteenth century.)

In 1784 the family moved again, this time to London. There Baillie began to publish, releasing a small book in 1790 entitled *Poems: Wherein It Is Attempted to Describe Certain Views of Nature*. She published *Poems* anonymously, as was common for women writers at the time. The book had little impact, but Baillie's plays proved much more successful. She wrote mainly closet dramas—plays intended to be read, not performed. Nevertheless, some of her plays did make it to the stage, and were performed by prominent actors such as John Kemble, Sarah Siddons, and Edmund Kean.

In 1798 the first of her six-volume *A Series of Plays* (now commonly referred to as *Plays on the Passions*) was published. The volume, composed of three plays, was the beginning of an investigation into the strongest human passions, such as love, fear, hatred, and jealousy. Each passion was to be the subject of one comedy and one tragedy. *Count Basil*, a meditation on love, is a tragedy about a man caught between his responsibilities as a military general and his love for a woman—*The Tryal* is its comic counterpart. The third play, and arguably her most distinguished work, is *De Monfort*, a meditation on hatred. The "Introductory Discourse" to the volume is an important piece of early Romantic literary criticism. In it, Baillie argues for a grounded, psychologically based treatment of dramatic characters, urging authors not to rely on overblown rhetoric or scenes of extreme emotion to convey the passions of their characters.

Baillie published the first volume of *A Series of Plays* anonymously, and there was considerable public discussion over the identity of the author. Most readers immediately assumed that the author was male (although several women—Hester Thrale, for one—guessed otherwise); the plays were widely attributed to Sir Walter Scott and later the "Introductory Discourse" to Baillie's brother, Matthew. At the time, many took as an article of faith Voltaire's dictum that "the composition of a tragedy requires *testicles*." It was with reference to this notion that Byron remarked in admiration of her work: "Lord knows what Joanna Baillie does—I suppose she borrows them." She went on to release five further volumes in the series under her own name, in 1802, 1812, and 1836.

Many other prominent literary figures of the time came to visit Baillie, including Lord Byron, William Wordsworth, Maria Edgeworth, and Sir Walter Scott. Through her friendship with Scott, Baillie had the opportunity to return to Scotland in 1807 and 1820. The visit had a profound effect on her writing. She began to use a Scottish idiom in some of her work, and chose to include Scottish figures such as William Wallace and Lady Grisell Baillie (a possible ancestor) in her *Metrical Legends of Exalted Characters* (1821).

Even as she outlived many of her contemporaries, Baillie continued to produce new work. She addressed religious matters in *A View of the General Tenor of the New Testament Regarding the Nature and Dignity of Jesus Christ* (1831), and in 1836 she published a three-volume collection of dramas. These were followed by the poetry collection *Fugitive Pieces* (1840) and *Ahalya Baee: A Poem* (1849). Baillie supervised the publication of her own complete works, *The Dramatic and Poetical Works of Joanna Baillie*, which were released a few weeks before her death, at the age of 88, in 1851.

⌘ ⌘ ⌘

A Mother to Her Waking Infant

Now in thy dazzling half-op'd eye,
　Thy curled nose, and lip awry,
Thy up-hoist arms, and noddling head,
And little chin with crystal spread,
5　Poor helpless thing! what do I see,
　　That I should sing of thee?

From thy poor tongue no accents come,
Which can but rub thy toothless gum:
Small understanding boast thy face,
10　Thy shapeless limbs nor step, nor grace:
A few short words thy feats may tell,
　　And yet I love thee well.

When sudden wakes the bitter shriek,
And redder swells thy little cheek;
15　When rattled keys thy woe beguile,

And through the wet eye gleams the smile,
Still for thy weakly self is spent
　　Thy little silly plaint.°　　　　　　*complaint*

But when thy friends are in distress,
20　Thou'lt laugh and chuckle ne'er the less;
Nor e'en with sympathy be smitten,
Tho' all are sad but thee and kitten;
Yet little varlet° that thou art,　　　　*rascal*
　　Thou twitchest at the heart.

25　Thy rosy cheek so soft and warm;
Thy pinky hand, and dimpled arm;
Thy silken locks that scantly peep,
With gold-tipped ends, where circle deep
Around thy neck in harmless grace
30　So soft and sleekly hold their place,
Might harder hearts with kindness fill,
　　And gain our right good will.

Each passing clown° bestows his blessing,   *rustic*
Thy mouth is worn with old wives' kissing:
35 E'en lighter looks the gloomy eye
Of surly sense, when thou art by;
And yet I think whoe'er they be,
   They love thee not like me.

Perhaps when time shall add a few
40 Short years to thee, thou'lt love me too.
Then wilt thou through life's weary way
Become my sure and cheering stay:
Wilt care for me, and be my hold,°   *protector*
   When I am weak and old.

45 Thou'lt listen to my lengthened tale,
And pity me when I am frail—
But see, the sweepy° spinning fly   *sweeping*
Upon the window takes thine eye.
Go to thy little senseless play—
50   Thou dost not heed my lay.°   *song*
 —1790

A Child to His Sick Grandfather

Grand-dad, they say you're old and frail,
 Your stocked[1] legs begin to fail:
Your knobbed stick (that was my horse)
Can scarce support your bended corse;°   *body*
5 While back to wall, you lean so sad,
   I'm vexed to see you, dad.

You used to smile, and stroke my head,
And tell me how good children did;
But now I wot° not how it be,   *know*
10 You take me seldom on your knee;
Yet ne'ertheless I am right glad
   To sit beside you, dad.

How lank and thin your beard hangs down!
Scant are the white hairs on your crown:
15 How wan° and hollow are your cheeks!   *unhealthy*
Your brow is rough with crossing breaks;
But yet, for all his strength is fled,
   I love my own old dad.

The housewives round their potions brew,
20 And gossips come to ask for you:
And for your weal° each neighbour cares,   *well-being*
And good men kneel, and say their pray'rs:
And ev'rybody looks so sad,
   When you are ailing, dad.

25 You will not die, and leave us then?
Rouse up and be our dad again.
When you are quiet and laid in bed,
We'll doff our shoes and softly tread;
And when you wake we'll aye° be near,   *always*
30   To fill old dad his cheer.

When through the house you shift your stand,
I'll lead you kindly by the hand:
When dinner's set, I'll with you bide,
And aye be serving by your side:
35 And when the weary fire burns blue,
   I'll sit and talk with you.

I have a tale both long and good,
About a partlet° and her brood;   *hen*
And cunning greedy fox, that stole,
40 By dead of midnight through a hole,
Which slyly to the hen-roost led—
   You love a story, dad?

And then I have a wond'rous tale
Of men all clad in coats of mail,
45 With glitt'ring swords—you nod, I think?
Your fixed eyes begin to wink:
Down on your bosom sinks your head:
   You do not hear me, dad.
 —1790

---

[1] *stocked* Dressed in stockings.

A Winter Day

The cock, warm roosting 'midst his feathered dames
  Now lifts his beak and snuffs the morning air,
Stretches his neck and claps his heavy wings,
Gives three hoarse crows, and glad his task is done;
5 Low, chuckling, turns himself upon the roost,
Then nestles down again amongst his mates.
The lab'ring hind,° who on his bed of straw,   *servant*
Beneath his home-made coverings, coarse, but warm,
Locked in the kindly arms of her who spun them,
10 Dreams of the gain that next year's crop should bring;
Or at some fair disposing° of his wool,   *sale*
Or by some lucky and unlooked-for bargain,
Fills his skin purse with heaps of tempting gold,
Now wakes from sleep at the unwelcome call,
15 And finds himself but just the same poor man
  As when he went to rest.
He hears the blast against his window beat,
And wishes to himself he were a lord,
  That he might lie a-bed.
20 He rubs his eyes, and stretches out his arms;
Heigh ho! Heigh ho! He drawls with gaping mouth,
Then most unwillingly creeps out of bed,
And without looking-glass puts on his clothes.
With rueful face he blows the smothered fire,
25 And lights his candle at the red'ning coal;
First sees that all be right amongst his cattle,
Then hies° him to the barn with heavy tread,   *goes*
Printing his footsteps on the new fall'n snow.
From out the heap of corn he pulls his sheaves,
30 Dislodging the poor red-breast° from his shelter,   *robin*
Where all the live-long night he slept secure;
But now affrighted, with uncertain flight
He flutters round the walls, to seek some hole,
At which he may escape out to the frost.
35 And now the flail, high whirling o'er his head,
Descends with force upon the jumping sheave,
Whilst every rugged wall, and neighb'ring cot°   *cottage*
Re-echoes back the noise of his strokes.

    The fam'ly cares call next upon the wife
40 To quit her mean° but comfortable bed.   *simple*

And first she stirs the fire, and blows the flame,
Then from her heap of sticks, for winter stored,
An armful brings; loud crackling as they burn,
Thick fly the red sparks upward to the roof,
45 While slowly mounts the smoke in wreathy clouds.
On goes the seething pot with morning cheer,
For which some little wishful hearts await,
Who, peeping from the bed-clothes, spy, well pleased,
The cheery light that blazes on the wall,
50   And bawl for leave to rise.
Their busy mother knows not where to turn,
Her morning work comes now so thick upon her.
One she must help to tie his little coat,
Unpin his cap, and seek another's shoe.
55 When all is o'er, out to the door they run,
With new combed sleeky hair, and glist'ning cheeks,
Each with some little project in his head.
One on the ice must try his new soled shoes:
To view his well-set trap another hies,
60 In hopes to find some poor unwary bird
(No worthless prize) entangled in his snare;
While one, less active, with round rosy face,
Spreads out his purple fingers to the fire,
And peeps, most wishfully, into the pot.

65   But let us leave the warm and cheerful house,
To view the bleak and dreary scene without,
And mark the dawning of a winter day.
For now the morning vapour, red and grumly,°   *dense*
Rests heavy on the hills; and o'er the heav'ns
70 Wide spreading forth in lighter gradual shades,
Just faintly colours the pale muddy sky.
Then slowly from behind the southern hills,
Enlarged and ruddy looks the rising sun,
Shooting his beams askance the hoary waste,
75 Which gild the brow of ev'ry swelling height,
And deepen every valley with a shade.
The crusted window of each scattered cot,
The icicles that fringe the thatched roof,
The new swept slide upon the frozen pool,
80 All lightly glance, new kindled with his rays;
And e'en the rugged face of scowling Winter
Looks somewhat gay. But for a little while

He lifts his glory o'er the bright'ning earth,
Then hides his head behind a misty cloud.

85   The birds now quit their holes and lurking sheds,
Most mute and melancholy, where through night
All nestling close to keep each other warm,
In downy sleep they had forgot their hardships;
But not to chant and carol in the air,
90 Or lightly swing upon some waving bough,
And merrily return each other's notes;
No; silently they hop from bush to bush,
Yet find no seeds to stop their craving want,
Then bend their flight to the low smoking cot,
95 Chirp on the roof, or at the window peck,
To tell their wants to those who lodge within.
The poor lank° hare flies homeward to his den,   *thin*
But little burthened with his nightly meal
Of withered greens grubbed from the farmer's garden;
100 A poor and scanty portion snatched in fear;
And fearful creatures, forced abroad by want,
Are now to ev'ry enemy a prey.

        The husbandman lays bye his heavy flail,
And to the house returns, where on him wait
105 His smoking breakfast and impatient children;
Who, spoon in hand, and longing to begin,
Towards the door cast many a weary look
To see their dad come in.
Then round they sit, a cheerful company,
110 All eagerly begin, and with heaped spoons
Besmear from ear to ear their rosy cheeks.
The faithful dog stands by his master's side
Wagging his tail, and looking in his face;
While humble puss pays court to all around,
115 And purrs and rubs them with her furry sides;
Nor goes this little flattery unrewarded.
But the laborious sit not long at table;
The grateful father lifts his eyes to heav'n
To bless his God, whose ever bounteous hand
120 Him and his little ones doth daily feed;
Then rises satisfied to work again.

        The cheerful rousing noise of industry
Is heard, with varied sounds, through all the village.
The humming wheel, the thrifty housewife's tongue,
125 Who scolds to keep her maidens at their work,
Rough grating cards,[1] and voice of squalling children
Issue from every house.
But hark! The sportsman from the neighb'ring hedge
His thunder sends! Loud bark each village cur;°   *dog*
130 Up from her wheel each curious maiden starts,
And hastens to the door, whilst matrons chide,
Yet run to look themselves, in spite of thrift,[2]
And all the little town is in a stir.

        Strutting before, the cock leads forth his train,
135 And, chuckling near the barn among the straw,
Reminds the farmer of his morning's service;
His grateful master throws a lib'ral handful;
They flock about it, whilst the hungry sparrows
Perched on the roof, look down with envious eye,
140 Then, aiming well, amidst the feeders light,
And seize upon the feast with greedy bill,
Till angry partlets° peck them off the field.   *hens*
But at a distance, on the leafless tree,
All woebegone, the lonely blackbird sits;
145 The cold north wind ruffles his glossy feathers;
Full oft' he looks, but dare not make approach;
Then turns his yellow bill to peck his side,
And claps his wings close to his sharpened breast.
The wand'ring fowler, from behind the hedge,
150 Fastens his eye upon him, points his gun,
And firing wantonly as at a mark,
E'en lays him low in that same cheerful spot
Which oft' hath echoed with his ev'ning's song.

        The day now at its height, the pent-up kine°   *cattle*
155 Are driven from their stalls to take the air.
How stupidly they stare! and feel how strange!
They open wide their smoking mouths to low,

---

[1] *cards* Combs for carding, or dressing, raw material such as wool
before it can be woven.

[2] *thrift* I.e., in spite of their commitment to their work, their ideas
of household economy would suggest to them that they stay busy and
avoid idling or gossip.

But scarcely can their feeble sound be heard;
Then turn and lick themselves, and step by step
60 Move dull and heavy to their stalls again.
In scattered groups the little idle boys
With purple fingers, moulding in the snow
Their icy ammunition, pant for war;
And drawing up in opposite array,
65 Send forth a mighty shower of well aimed balls,
Whilst little heroes try their growing strength,
And burn to beat the en'my off the field.
Or on the well worn ice in eager throngs,
Aiming their race, shoot rapidly along,
70 Trip up each other's heels, and on the surface
With knotted shoes, draw many a chalky line.
Untired of play, they never cease their sport
Till the faint sun has almost run his course,
And threat'ning clouds, slow rising from the north,
75 Spread grumly darkness o'er the face of heav'n;
Then, by degrees, they scatter to their homes,
With many a broken head and bloody nose,
To claim their mothers' pity, who, most skilful,
Cures all their troubles with a bit of bread.

80   The night comes on apace—
Chill blows the blast, and drives the snow in wreaths.
Now ev'ry creature looks around for shelter,
And, whether man or beast, all move alike
Towards their several° homes; and happy they   different
85 Who have a house to screen them from the cold!
Lo, o'er the frost a rev'rend form advances!
His hair white as the snow on which he treads,
His forehead marked with many a care-worn furrow,
Whose feeble body, bending o'er a staff,
90 Still show that once it was the seat of strength,
Though now it shakes like some old ruined tow'r.
Clothed indeed, but not disgraced with rags,
He still maintains that decent dignity
Which well becomes those who have served their
      country.
95 With tott'ring steps he to the cottage moves:
The wife within, who hears his hollow cough,
And patt'ring of his stick upon the threshold,
Sends out her little boy to see who's there.

The child looks up to view the stranger's face,
200 And seeing it enlightened with a smile,
Holds out his little hand to lead him in.
Roused from her work, the mother turns her head,
And sees them, not ill-pleased.
The stranger whines not with a piteous tale,
205 But only asks a little, to relieve
A poor old soldier's wants.
The gentle matron brings the ready chair,
And bids him sit, to rest his wearied limbs,
And warm himself before her blazing fire.
210 The children, full of curiosity,
Flock round, and with their fingers in their mouths,
Stand staring at him; whilst the stranger, pleased,
Takes up the youngest boy upon his knee.
Proud of its seat, it wags its little feet,
215 And prates,° and laughs, and plays with his   chatters
      white locks.
But soon the soldier's face lays off its smiles;
His thoughtful mind is turned on other days,
When his own boys were wont to play around him,
Who now lie distant from their native land
220 In honourable, but untimely graves.
He feels how helpless and forlorn he is,
And bitter tears gush from his dim-worn eyes.
His toilsome daily labour at an end,
In comes the wearied master of the house,
225 And marks with satisfaction his old guest,
With all his children round.
His honest heart is filled with manly kindness;
He bids him stay, and share their homely meal,
And take with them his quarters for the night.
230 The weary wanderer thankfully accepts,
And, seated with the cheerful family,
Around the plain but hospitable board,
Forgets the many hardships he has passed.

When all are satisfied, about the fire
235 They draw their seats, and form a cheerful ring.
The thrifty housewife turns her spinning wheel;
The husband, useful even in his rest,
A little basket weaves of willow twigs,
To bear her eggs to town on market days;

240 And work but serves t'enliven conversation.
Some idle neighbours now come straggling in,
Draw round their chairs, and widen out the circle.
Without a glass the tale and jest go round;
And every one, in his own native way,
245 Does what he can to cheer the merry group.
Each tells some little story of himself,
That constant subject upon which mankind,
Whether in court or country, love to dwell.
How at a fair he saved a simple clown°   rustic
250 From being tricked in buying of a cow;
Or laid a bet upon his horse's head
Against his neighbour's, bought for twice his price,
Which failed not to repay his better skill:
Or on a harvest day, bound in an hour
255 More sheaves of corn than any of his fellows,
Though ne'er so keen, could do in twice the time.
But chief the landlord, at his own fire-side,
Doth claim the right of being listened to;
Nor dares a little bawling tongue be heard,
260 Though but in play, to break upon his story.
The children sit and listen with the rest;
And should the youngest raise its little voice,
The careful mother, ever on the watch,
And always pleased with what her husband says,
265 Gives it a gentle tap upon the fingers,
Or stops its ill timed prattle with a kiss.
The soldier next, but not unasked, begins,
And tells in better speech what he has seen;
Making his simple audience to shrink
270 With tales of war and blood. They gaze upon him,
And almost weep to see the man so poor,
So bent and feeble, helpless and forlorn,
That oft' has stood undaunted in the battle
Whilst thund'ring cannons shook the quaking earth,
275 And showering bullets hissed around his head.
With little care they pass away the night,
Till time draws on when they should go to bed;
Then all break up, and each retires to rest
With peaceful mind, nor torn with vexing cares,
280 Nor dancing with the unequal beat of pleasure.

But long accustomed to observe the weather,
The labourer cannot lay him down in peace
Till he has looked to mark what bodes the night.
He turns the heavy door, thrusts out his head,
285 Sees wreathes of snow heaped up on ev'ry side,
And black and grumly all above his head,
Save when a red gleam shoots along the waste
To make the gloomy night more terrible.
Loud blows the northern blast—
290 He hears it hollow grumbling from afar,
Then, gath'ring strength, roll on with doubled might,
And break in dreadful bellowings o'er his head;
Like pithless saplings bend the vexed trees,
And their wide branches crack. He shuts the door,
295 And, thankful for the roof that covers him,
Hies him to bed.
—1790

A Summer Day

The dark-blue clouds of night in dusky lines,
    Drawn wide and streaky o'er the purer sky,
Wear faint the morning purple on their skirts.
The stars that full and bright shone in the west,
5 But dimly twinkle to the steadfast eye;
And seen, and vanishing, and seen again,
Like dying tapers° smoth'ring in their sockets,   candles
Appear at last shut from the face of heav'n;
Whilst every lesser flame which shone by night,
10 The flashy meteor from the op'ning cloud,
That shoots full oft' across the dusky sky;
Or wand'ring fire which looks across the marsh,[1]
Beaming like candle in a lonely cot,°   cottage
To cheer the hopes of the benighted trav'ller,
15 Till swifter than the very change of thought,
It shifts from place to place, escapes his glance,
And makes him wond'ring rub his doubtful eyes;
Or humble glow-worm, or the silver moth,
Which cast a feeble glimm'ring o'er the green,

---

[1] wand'ring fire … marsh I.e., will-o'-the-wisps, flickering lights
that are seen at night, especially over marshes, and may spontaneously
move or vanish.

All die away.——
For now the sun, slow moving in his grandeur,
Above the eastern mountains lifts his head.
The webs of dew spread o'er the hoary[1] lawn,
The smooth clear bosom of the settled pool,
The polished ploughshare on the distant field,
Catch fire from him, and dart their new got beams
Upon the dazzled eye.

    The new-waked birds upon the branches hop,
Peck their soft down, and bristle out their feathers;
Then stretch their throats and tune their morning song;
Whilst stately crows, high swinging o'er their heads,
Upon the topmost boughs, in lordly pride,
Mix their hoarse croaking with the linnet's note;
Till gathered closer in a sable band,
They take their flight to seek their daily food.
The village labourer, with careful mind,
As soon as doth the morning light appear,
Opens his eyes with the first darting ray
That pierces through the window of his cot,
And quits his easy bed; then o'er the field,
With lengthened swinging strides, betakes his way,
Bearing his spade and hoe across his shoulder,
Seen from afar clear glancing in the sun,
And with good will begins his daily work.
The sturdy sun-burnt boy drives forth the cattle,
And vain of power, bawls to the lagging kine,°   *cattle*
Who fain would stay to crop the tender shoots
Of the green tempting hedges as they pass;
Or beats the glist'ning bushes with his club,
To please his fancy with a shower of dew,
And frighten the poor birds who lurk within.
At ev'ry open door, through all the village,
Half naked children, half awake, are seen
Scratching their heads, and blinking to the light;
Till roused by degrees, they run about,
Or rolling in the sun, amongst the sand
Build many a little house, with heedful art.
The housewife tends within, her morning care;
And stooping 'midst her tubs of curdled milk,

With busy patience, draws the clear green whey
From the pressed sides of the pure snowy curd;[2]
Whilst her brown dimpled maid, with tucked-up sleeve,
And swelling arm, assists her in her toil.
Pots smoke, pails rattle, and the warm confusion
Still thickens on them, till within its mould,
With careful hands, they press the well-wrought curd.

    So goes the morning, till the pow'rful sun
High in the heav'ns sends forth his strengthened beams,
And all the freshness of the morn is fled.
The sweating trav'ller throws his burden down,
And leans his weary shoulder 'gainst a tree.
The idle horse upon the grassy field
Rolls on his back, nor heeds the tempting clover.
The swain[3] leaves off his labour, and returns
Slow to his house with heavy sober steps,
Where on the board his ready breakfast placed,
Invites the eye, and his right cheerful wife
Doth kindly serve him with unfeigned good will.
No sparkling dew-drops hang upon the grass;
Forth steps the mower with his glitt'ring scythe,
In snowy shirt, and doublet all unbraced,[4]
White moves he o'er the ridge, with sideling bend,
And lays the waving grass in many a heap.
In ev'ry field, in ev'ry swampy mead,°   *meadow*
The cheerful voice of industry is heard;
The hay-cock° rises, and the frequent rake   *hay pile*
Sweeps on the yellow hay, in heavy
    wreaths,°   *curved motions*
Leaving the smooth green meadow bare behind.
The old and young, the weak and strong are there,
And, as they can, help on the cheerful work.
The father jeers his awkward half-grown lad,
Who trails his tawdry armful o'er the field,
Nor does he fear the jeering to repay.
The village oracle, and simple maid,
Jest in their turns, and raise the ready laugh;

---

[1] *hoary* White (here, with frost).

[2] *stooping … snowy curd* I.e., the housewife is removing the whey (the liquid portion of the milk) from cheese curds (the solidified portion) in order to make cheese.

[3] *swain* Farm worker.

[4] *doublet all unbraced* Jacket all undone.

For there authority, hard favoured, frowns not;
All are companions in the gen'ral glee,
And cheerful complaisance still through their roughness,
With placid look enlightens ev'ry face.
100   Some more advanced raise the tow'ring rick,°   *haystack*
Whilst on its top doth stand the parish toast[1]
In loose attire, and swelling ruddy cheek;
With taunts and harmless mock'ry she receives
The tossed-up heaps from the brown gaping youth,
105   Who staring at her, takes his aim awry,
Whilst half the load comes tumbling on himself.
Loud is her laugh, her voice is heard afar;
Each mower, busied in the distant field,
The carter, trudging on his distant way,
110   The shrill sound know, cast up their hats in air,
And roar across the fields to catch her notice:
She waves her arm, and shakes her head at them,
And then renews her work with double spirit.
Thus do they jest, and laugh away their toil,
115   Till the bright sun, full in his middle course,
Shoots down his fiercest beams, which none may brave.
The stoutest arm hangs listless by its side,
And the broad shouldered youth begins to fail.
But to the weary, lo! there comes relief!
120   A troop of welcome children, o'er the lawn,
With slow and wary steps, their burthens bring.
Some bear upon their heads large baskets, heaped
With piles of barley bread, and gusty° cheese,   *delicious*
And some full pots of milk and cooling whey.
125   Beneath the branches of a spreading tree,
Or by the shad'wy side of the tall rick,
They spread their homely fare, and seated round,
Taste all the pleasure that a feast can give.

A drowsy indolence now hangs on all,
130   And ev'ry creature seeks some place of rest,
Screened from the violence of the oppressive heat.
No scattered flocks are seen upon the lawn,
Nor chirping birds among the bushes heard.
Within the narrow shadow of the cot
135   The sleepy dog lies stretched on his side,
Nor heeds the heavy-footed passenger;

At noise of feet but half his eye-lid lifts,
Then gives a feeble growl, and sleeps again:
Whilst puss, less nice,[2] e'en in the scorching window,
140   On t'other side, sits winking to the sun.
No sound is heard but humming of the bee,
For she alone retires not from her labour,
Nor leaves a meadow flower unsought for gain.

Heavy and slow so pass the mid-day hours,
145   Till gently bending on the ridge's top,
The heavy seeded grass begins to wave,
And the high branches of the slender poplar
Shiver aloft in air their rustling leaves.
Cool breathes the rising breeze, and with it wakes
150   The worn out spirit from its state of stupor.
The lazy boy springs from his mossy bed,
To chase the gaudy tempting butterfly,
Who spreading on the grass its mealy wings,
Oft lights within his reach, e'en at his feet,
155   Yet still eludes his grasp, and o'er his head
Light hov'ring round, or mounted high in air
Temps his young eye, and wearies out his limbs.
The drowsy dog, who feels the kindly breeze
That passing o'er him, lifts his shaggy ear,
160   Begins to stretch him, on his legs half-raised,
Till fully waked, with bristling cocked-up tail,
He makes the village echo to his bark.

But let us not forget the busy maid
Who, by the side of the clear pebbly stream,
165   Spreads out her snowy linens to the sun,
And sheds with lib'ral hand the crystal show'r
O'er many a fav'rite piece of fair attire,
Revolving in her mind her gay appearance
In all this dress, at some approaching fair.
170   The dimpling half-checked smile, and mutt'ring lip
Betray the secret workings of her fancy,
And flattering thoughts of the complacent mind.
There little vagrant bands of truant boys
Amongst the bushes try their harmless tricks;
175   Whilst some a sporting in the shallow stream

---

[1] *parish toast* I.e., belle of the parish.

[2] *nice* Of refined taste; difficult to please.

Toss up the lashing water round their heads,
Or strive with wily art to catch the trout,
Or 'twixt their fingers grasp the slipp'ry eel.
The shepherd-boy sits singing on the bank,
To pass away the weary lonely hours,
Weaving with art his little crown of rushes,
A guiltless easy crown that brings no care,
Which having made he places on his head,
And leaps and skips about, and bawls full loud
To some companion, lonely as himself,
Far in the distant field; or else delighted
To hear the echoed sound of his own voice
Returning answer from the neighboring rock,
Holds no unpleasing converse with himself.

Now weary labourers perceive, well-pleased,
The shadows lengthen, and th' oppressive day
With all its toil fast wearing to an end.
The sun, far in the west, with side-long beam
Plays on the yellow head of the round hay-cock,
And fields are checkered with fantastic shapes
Or tree, or shrub, or gate, or rugged stone,
All lengthened out, in antic° disproportion,   grotesque
Upon the darkened grass.——
They finish out their long and toilsome talk.
Then, gathering up their rakes and scattered coats,
With the less cumb'rous fragments of their feast,
Return right gladly to their peaceful homes.

The village, lone and silent through the day,
Receiving from the fields its merry bands,
Sends forth its evening sound, confused but cheerful;
Whilst dogs and children, eager housewives' tongues,
And true love ditties, in no plaintive strain,
By shrill voiced maid, at open window sung;
The lowing of the home-returning kine,
The herd's low droning trump, and tinkling bell
Tied to the collar of his fav'rite sheep,
Make no contemptible variety
To ears not over nice.——
With careless lounging gait, the saunt'ring youth
Upon his sweetheart's open window leans,
And as she turns about her buzzing wheel

Diverts her with his jokes and harmless taunts.
Close by the cottage door, with placid mien,°   countenance
The old man sits upon his seat of turf,
His staff with crooked head laid by his side,
Which oft the younger race in wanton sport,
Gambolling round him, slyly steal away,
And straddling o'er it, shew their horsemanship
By raising round the clouds of summer sand,
While still he smiles, yet chides them for the trick.
His silver locks upon his shoulders spread,
And not ungraceful is his stoop of age.
No stranger passes him without regard;
And ev'ry neighbour stops to wish him well,
And ask him his opinion of the weather.
They fret not at the length of his discourse,
But listen with respect to his remarks
Upon the various seasons he remembers;
For well he knows the many divers signs
Which do foretell high winds, or rain, or drought,
Or aught that may affect the rising crop.
The silken clad, who courtly breeding boast,
Their own discourse still sweetest to their ears,
May grumble at the old man's lengthened story,
But here it is not so.——

From ev'ry chimney mounts the curling smoke,
Muddy and gray, of the new ev'ning fire;
On ev'ry window smokes the fam'ly supper,
Set out to cool by the attentive housewife,
While cheerful groups at every door convened
Bawl cross the narrow lane the parish news,
And oft the bursting laugh disturbs the air.
But see who comes to set them all agag!
The weary-footed pedlar with his pack.
How stiff he bends beneath his bulky load!
Covered with dust, slip-shod, and out at elbows;[1]
His greasy hat sits backward on his head;
His thin straight hair divided on his brow
Hangs lank on either side his glist'ning cheeks,
And woe-begone, yet vacant is his face.
His box he opens and displays his ware.

---
[1] *out at elbows* Raggedly dressed.

Full many a varied row of precious stones
Cast forth their dazzling lustre to the light.
To the desiring maiden's wishful eye
260 The ruby necklace shews its tempting blaze:
The china buttons, stamped with love device,
Attract the notice of the gaping youth;
Whilst streaming garters,[1] fastened to a pole,
Aloft in air their gaudy stripes display,
265 And from afar the distant stragglers lure.
The children leave their play and round him flock;
E'en sober aged grand-dame quits her seat,
Where by the door she twines her lengthened threads,
Her spindle stops, and lays her distaff[2] by,
270 Then joins with step sedate the curious throng.
She praises much the fashions of her youth,
And scorns each gaudy nonsense of the day;
Yet not ill-pleased the glossy riband° views,   *ribbon*
Uprolled, and changing hues with ev'ry fold,
275 New measured out to deck her daughter's head.

Now red, but languid, the last weakly beams
Of the departing sun, across the lawn
Deep gild the top of the long sweepy° ridge,   *sweeping*
And shed a scattered brightness, bright but cheerless,
280 Between the op'nings of the rifted hills;
Which like the farewell looks of some dear friend,
That speaks him kind, yet sadden as they smile,
But only serve to deepen the low vale,
And make the shadows of the night more gloomy.
285 The varied noises of the cheerful village
By slow degrees now faintly die away,
And more distinct each feeble sound is heard
That gently steals adown the river's bed,
Or through the wood comes with the ruffling breeze.
290 The white mist rises from the swampy glens,
And from the dappled skirting of the heav'ns
Looks out the ev'ning star.——
The lover skulking in the neighb'ring copse°   *thicket*
(Whose half-seen form shewn through the
          thickened air,

295 Large and majestic, makes the tray'ller start,
And spreads the story of the haunted grove)
Curses the owl, whose loud ill-omened scream,
With ceaseless spite, robs from his watchful ear
The well known footsteps of his darling maid;
300 And fretful, chases from his face the night-fly,
Who buzzing round his head doth often skim,
With flutt'ring wing, across his glowing cheek:
For all but him in deep and balmy sleep
Forget the toils of the oppressive day;
305 Shut is the door of ev'ry scattered cot,
And silence dwells within.
—1790

from *Plays on the Passions* [3]

INTRODUCTORY DISCOURSE

It is natural for a writer, who is about to submit his works to the public, to feel a strong inclination, by some preliminary address, to conciliate the favour of his reader, and dispose him, if possible, to peruse them with a favourable eye. I am well aware, however, that his endeavours are generally fruitless: in his situation our hearts revolt from all appearance of confidence, and we consider his diffidence as hypocrisy. Our own word is frequently taken for what we say of ourselves, but very rarely for what we say of our works. Were these three plays, which this small volume contains, detached pieces only, and unconnected with others that do not yet appear, I should have suppressed this inclination altogether, and have allowed my reader to begin what is before him, and to form what opinion of it his taste or his humour might direct, without any previous trespass upon his time or his patience. But they are part of an extensive design; of one which, as far as my information goes, has nothing exactly similar to it in any language; of one which a whole life time will be limited enough to accomplish; and which has, therefore, a considerable

---

[1] *garters* Bands worn around the legs to hold up stockings.

[2] *spindle* Tool used to spin yarn or thread; *distaff* Simple device used to hold unspun fibers when spinning.

[3] *Plays on the Passions* This volume, first published in 1798, included *Count Basil: A Tragedy* and *The Tryal: A Comedy*, as well as *De Monfort: A Tragedy*.

chance of being cut short by that hand which nothing can resist.

Before I explain the plan of this work, I must make a demand upon the patience of my reader, whilst I endeavour to communicate to him those ideas regarding human nature, as they in some degree affect almost every species of moral writings, but particularly the dramatic, that induced me to attempt it; and, as far as my judgment enabled me to apply them, has directed me in the execution of it.

From that strong sympathy which most creatures, but the human above all, feel for others of their kind, nothing has become so much an object of man's curiosity as man himself. We are all conscious of this within ourselves, and so constantly do we meet with it in others, that like every circumstance of continually repeated occurrence, it thereby escapes observation. Every person who is not deficient in intellect, is more or less occupied in tracing, amongst the individuals he converses with, the varieties of understanding and temper which constitute the characters of men; and receives great pleasure from every stroke of nature that points out to him those varieties. This is, much more than we are aware of, the occupation of children, and of grown people also, whose penetration is but lightly esteemed; and that conversation which degenerates with them into trivial and mischievous tattling takes its rise not infrequently from the same source that supplies the rich vein of the satirist and the wit. That eagerness so universally shown for the conversation of the latter, plainly enough indicates how many people have been occupied in the same way with themselves. Let any one, in a large company, do or say what is strongly expressive of his peculiar character, or of some passion or humour of the moment, and it will be detected by almost every person present. How often may we see a very stupid countenance animated with a smile, when the learned and the wise have betrayed some native feature of their own minds! And how often will this be the case when they have supposed it to be concealed under a very sufficient disguise! From this constant employment of their minds, most people, I believe, without being conscious of it, have stored up in idea the greater part of those strong marked varieties of human character, which may be said to divide it into classes; and in one of those classes they involuntarily place every new person they become acquainted with.

I will readily allow that the dress and the manners of men, rather than their characters and disposition, are the subjects of our common conversation, and seem chiefly to occupy the multitude. But let it be remembered that it is much easier to express our observations upon these. It is easier to communicate to another how a man wears his wig and cane, what kind of house he inhabits, and what kind of table he keeps, than from what slight traits in his words and actions we have been led to conceive certain impressions of his character: traits that will often escape the memory, when the opinions that were founded upon them remain. Besides, in communicating our ideas of the characters of others, we are often called upon to support them with more expense of reasoning than we can well afford, but our observations on the dress and appearance of men seldom involve us in such difficulties. For these and other reasons too tedious to mention, the generality of people appear to us more trifling than they are, and I may venture to say that, but for this sympathetic curiosity towards others of our kind, which is so strongly implanted within us, the attention we pay to the dress and the manners of men would dwindle into an employment as insipid as examining the varieties of plants and minerals is to one who understands not natural history.

In our ordinary intercourse with society, this sympathetic propensity of our minds is exercised upon men, under the common occurrences of life, in which we have often observed them. Here vanity and weakness put themselves forward to view, more conspicuously than the virtues: here men encounter those smaller trials, from which they are not apt to come off victorious; and here, consequently, that which is marked with the whimsical and ludicrous will strike us most forcibly, and make the strongest impression on our memory. To this sympathetic propensity of our minds, so exercised, the genuine and pure comic of every composition, whether drama, fable, story, or satire is addressed.

If man is an object of so much attention to man,

engaged in the ordinary occurrences of life, how much more does he excite his curiosity and interest when placed in extraordinary situations of difficulty and distress? It cannot be any pleasure we receive from the sufferings of a fellow creature which attracts such multitudes of people to a public execution, though it is the horror we conceive for such a spectacle that keeps so many more away. To see a human being bearing himself up under such circumstances, or struggling with the terrible apprehensions which such a situation impresses must be the powerful incentive which makes us press forward to behold what we shrink from, and wait with trembling expectation for what we dread. For though few at such a spectacle can get near enough to distinguish the expression of face or the minuter parts of a criminal's behaviour, yet from a considerable distance will they eagerly mark whether he steps firmly; whether the motions of his body denote agitation or calmness; and if the wind does but ruffle his garment, they will, even from that change upon the outline of his distant figure, read some expression connected with his dreadful situation. Though there is a greater proportion of people in whom this strong curiosity will be overcome by other dispositions and motives, though there are many more who will stay away from such a sight than will go to it, yet there are very few who will not be eager to converse with a person who has beheld it, and to learn, very minutely, every circumstance connected with it, except the very act itself of inflicting death. To lift up the roof of his dungeon, like the *Diable boiteux*,[1] and look upon a criminal the night before he suffers, in his still hours of privacy, when all that disguise, which respect for the opinion of others, the strong motive by which even the lowest and wickedest of men still continue to be moved, would present an object to the mind of every person, not withheld from it by great timidity of character, more powerfully attractive than almost any other.

Revenge, no doubt, first began amongst the savages of America that dreadful custom of sacrificing their prisoners of war. But the perpetration of such hideous cruelty could never have become a permanent national custom, but for this universal desire in the human mind to behold man in every situation, putting forth his strength against the current of adversity, scorning all bodily anguish, or struggling with those feelings of nature, which, like a beating stream, will oft times burst through the artificial barriers of pride. Before they begin those terrible rites they treat their prisoner kindly; and it cannot be supposed that men, alternately enemies and friends to so many neighbouring tribes in manners and appearance like themselves, should so strongly be actuated by a spirit of public revenge. This custom, therefore, must be considered as a grand and terrible game, which every tribe plays against another, where they try not the strength of the arm, the swiftness of the feet, nor the acuteness of the eye, but the fortitude of the soul. Considered in this light, the excess of cruelty exercised upon their miserable victim, in which every hand is described as ready to inflict its portion of pain, and every head ingenious in the contrivance of it, is no longer to be wondered at. To put into his measure of misery one agony less would be, in some degree, betraying the honour of their nation; would be doing a species of injustice to every hero of their own tribe who had already sustained it, and to those who might be called upon to do so; amongst whom each of these savage tormentors has his chance of being one, and has prepared himself for it from his childhood. Nay, it would be a species of injustice to the haughty victim himself, who would scorn to purchase his place amongst the heroes of his nation, at an easier price than his undaunted predecessors.

Amongst the many trials to which the human mind is subjected, that of holding intercourse,[2] real or imaginary, with the world of spirits, of finding itself alone with a being terrific and awful, whose nature and power are unknown, has been justly considered as one of the most severe. The workings of nature in this situation, we all know, have ever been the object of our most eager enquiry. No man wishes to see the ghost himself, which would certainly procure him the best information on the

---

[1] *Diable boiteux*   1707 novel by Alain René Lesage, in which the devil removes the roofs of houses in order to show a student the vices that are occurring within.

[2] *intercourse*   Conversation.

subject, but every man wishes to see one who believes that he sees it, in all the agitation and wildness of that species of terror. To gratify this curiosity how many people have dressed up hideous apparitions to frighten the timid and superstitious! And have done it at the risk of destroying their happiness or understanding forever. For the instances of intellect being destroyed by this kind of trial are more numerous, perhaps, in proportion to the few who have undergone it than by any other.

How sensible are we of this strong propensity within us when we behold any person under the pressure of great and uncommon calamity! Delicacy and respect for the afflicted will indeed make us turn ourselves aside from observing him, and cast down our eyes in his presence; but the first glance we direct to him will involuntarily be one of the keenest observation, how hastily soever it may be checked; and often will a returning look of enquiry mix itself by stealth with our sympathy and reserve.

But it is not in situations of difficulty and distress alone that man becomes the object of this sympathetic curiosity; he is no less so when the evil he contends with arises in his own breast, and no outward circumstance connected with him either awakens our attention or our pity. What human creature is there, who can behold a being like himself under the violent agitation of those passions which all have, in some degree, experienced, without feeling himself most powerfully excited by the sight? I say, all have experienced; for the bravest man on earth knows what fear is as well as the coward, and will not refuse to be interested for one under the dominion of this passion, provided there be nothing in the circumstances attending it to create contempt. Anger is a passion that attracts less sympathy than any other, yet the unpleasing and distorted features of an angry man will be more eagerly gazed upon by those who are no wise concerned with his fury or the objects of it than the most amiable placid countenance in the world. Every eye is directed to him, every voice hushed to silence in his presence. Even children will leave off their gambols[1] as he passes, and gaze after him more eagerly than the

gaudiest equipage.[2] The wild tossings of despair; the gnashing of hatred and revenge; the yearnings of affection, and the softened mien[3] of love; all that language of the agitated soul, which every age and nation understands, is never addressed to the dull nor inattentive.

It is not merely under the violent agitations of passion, that man so rouses and interests us; even the smallest indications of an unquiet mind, the restless eye, the muttering lip, the half-checked exclamation, and the hasty start, will set our attention as anxiously upon the watch, as the first distant flashes of a gathering storm. When some great explosion of passion bursts forth, and some consequent catastrophe happens, if we are at all acquainted with the unhappy perpetrator, how minutely will we endeavour to remember every circumstance of his past behaviour! And with what avidity[4] will we seize upon every recollected word or gesture that is in the smallest degree indicative of the supposed state of his mind, at the time when they took place. If we are not acquainted with him, how eagerly will we listen to similar recollections from another! Let us understand, from observation or report, that any person harbours in his breast concealed from the world's eye some powerful rankling passion of what kind soever it may be; we will observe every word, every motion, every look, even the distant gait of such a man, with a constancy and attention bestowed upon no other. Nay, should we meet him unexpectedly on our way, a feeling will pass across our minds as though we found ourselves in the neighbourhood of some secret and fearful thing. If invisible, would we not follow him into his lonely haunts, into his closet, into the midnight silence of his chamber? There is, perhaps, no employment which the human mind will with so much avidity pursue as the discovery of concealed passion, as the tracing the varieties and progress of a perturbed soul.

It is to this sympathetic curiosity of our nature, exercised upon mankind in great and trying occasions and under the influence of the stronger passions when

[1] *gambols* Games.

[2] *equipage* Carriage and horses, with attendants.
[3] *mien* Here, expression of the face.
[4] *avidity* Ardent desire.

the grand, the generous, the terrible attract our attention far more than the base and depraved, that the high and powerfully tragic, of every composition, is addressed.

This propensity is universal. Children begin to show it very early; it enters into many of their amusements, and that part of them too, for which they show the keenest relish. It tempts them many times, as well as the mature in years, to be guilty of tricks, vexations, and cruelty; yet God Almighty has implanted it within us, as well as all our other propensities and passions, for wise and good purposes. It is our best and most powerful instructor. From it we are taught the proprieties and decencies of ordinary life, and are prepared for distressing and difficult situations. In examining others we know ourselves. With limbs untorn, with head unsmitten, with senses unimpaired by despair, we know what we ourselves might have been on the rack, on the scaffold, and in the most afflicting circumstances of distress. Unless when accompanied with passions of the dark and malevolent kind, we cannot well exercise this disposition without becoming more just, more merciful, more compassionate; and as the dark and malevolent passions are not the predominant inmates of the human breast, it hath produced more deeds—many more—of kindness than of cruelty. It holds up for our example a standard of excellence, which, without its assistance, our inward consciousness of what is right and becoming might never have dictated. It teaches us, also, to respect ourselves, and our kind; for it is a poor mind, indeed, that from this employment of its faculties learns not to dwell upon the noble view of human nature rather than the mean.

Universal, however, as this disposition undoubtedly is, with the generality of mankind it occupies itself in a passing and superficial way. Though a native trait of character or of passion is obvious to them as well as to the sage, yet to their minds it is but the visitor of a moment; they look upon it singly and unconnected. And though this disposition, even so exercised, brings instruction as well as amusement, it is chiefly by storing up in their minds those ideas to which the instructions of others refer, that it can be eminently useful. Those who reflect and reason upon what human nature holds out to their observation, are comparatively but few. No stroke of nature which engages their attention stands insulated and alone. Each presents itself to them with many varied connections; and they comprehend not merely the immediate feeling which gave rise to it, but the relation of that feeling to others which are concealed. We wonder at the changes and caprices of men; they see in them nothing but what is natural and accountable. We stare upon some dark catastrophe of passion, as the Indians did upon an eclipse of the moon; they, conceiving the track of ideas through which the impassioned mind has passed, regard it like the philosopher who foretold the phenomenon. Knowing what situation of life he is about to be thrown into, they perceive in the man, who, like Hazael,[1] says, "is thy servant a dog that he should do this thing?" the foul and ferocious murderer. A man of this contemplative character partakes, in some degree, of the entertainment of the Gods, who were supposed to look down upon this world and the inhabitants of it, as we do upon a theatrical exhibition; and if he is of a benevolent disposition, a good man struggling with and triumphing over adversity will be to him also the most delightful spectacle. But though this eagerness to observe their fellow creatures in every situation leads not the generality of mankind to reason and reflect, and those strokes of nature which they are so ready to remark, stand single and unconnected in their minds, yet they may be easily induced to do both; and there is no mode of instruction which they will so eagerly pursue as that which lays open before them in a more enlarged and connected view than their individual observations are capable of supplying, the varieties of the human mind. Above all, to be well exercised in this study will fit a man more particularly for the most important situations of life. He will prove for it the better judge, the better magistrate, the better advocate; and as a ruler or conductor of other men, under every occurring circumstance, he will find himself the better enabled to fulfill his duty, and accomplish his designs. He will perceive the natural effect of every order that he issues upon the minds of his soldiers,

---

[1] *Hazael* King of Damascus. The quotation is his response to Elisha's prophecy that he will commit atrocities on the people of Israel. See 2 Kings 8.11–13.

his subjects, or his followers, and he will deal to others judgment tempered with mercy; that is to say truly just, for justice appears to us severe only when it is imperfect.

In proportion as moral writers of every class have exercised within themselves this sympathetic propensity of our nature, and have attended to it in others, their works have been interesting and instructive. They have struck the imagination more forcibly, convinced the understanding more clearly, and more lastingly impressed the memory. If unseasoned with any reference to this, the fairy bowers[1] of the poet, with all his gay images of delight, will be admired and forgotten; the important relations of the historian, and even the reasonings of the philosopher will make a less permanent impression.

The historian points back to the men of other ages, and from the gradually clearing mist in which they are first discovered, like the mountains of a far distant land, the generations of the world are displayed to our mind's eye in grand and regular procession. But the transactions of men become interesting to us only as we are made acquainted with men themselves. Great and bloody battles are to us battles fought in the moon if it is not impressed upon our minds, by some circumstances attending them, that men subject to like weaknesses and passions with ourselves were the combatants.[2] The

establishments of policy make little impression upon us if we are left ignorant of the beings whom they affected. Even a very masterly drawn character will but slightly imprint upon our memory the great man it belongs to, if, in the account we receive of his life, those lesser circumstances are entirely neglected, which do best of all point out to us the dispositions and tempers of men. Some slight circumstance characteristic of the particular turn of a man's mind, which at first sight seems but little connected with the great events of his life, will often explain some of those events more clearly to our understanding than the minute details of ostensible policy. A judicious selection of those circumstances which characterize the spirit of an associated mob, paltry and ludicrous as some of them may appear, will oftentimes convey to our minds a clearer idea why certain laws and privileges were demanded and agreed to than a methodical explanation of their causes. A historian who has examined human nature himself, and likewise attends to the pleasure which developing and tracing it does ever convey to others, will employ our understanding as well as our memory with his pages; and if this is not done, he will impose upon the latter a very difficult task, in retaining what she is concerned with alone.

In argumentative and philosophical writings, the effect which the author's reasoning produces on our minds depends not entirely on the justness of it. The images and examples that he calls to his aid to explain and illustrate his meaning will very much affect the attention we are able to bestow upon it, and consequently the quickness with which we shall apprehend, and the force with which it will impress us. These are selected from animated and unanimated nature, from the habits, manners, and characters of men; and though that image or example, whatever it may be in itself which brings out his meaning most clearly, ought to be preferred before every other, yet of two equal in this

---

1 *bowers* Dwellings.

2 [Baillie's note] Let two great battles be described to us with all the force and clearness of the most able pen. In the first let the most admirable exertions of military skill in the General, and the most unshaken courage in the soldiers, gain over an equal or superiour number of brave opponents a compleat and glorious victory. In the second let the General be less scientifick, and the soldiers less dauntless. Let them go into the field for a cause that is dear to them, and fight with the ardour which such motives inspire; till discouraged with the many deaths around them, and the renovated pressure of the foe, some unlooked-for circumstance, trifling in itself, strikes their imagination at once; they are visited with the terrours of nature; their national pride, the honour of soldiership is forgotten; they fly like a fearful flock. Let some beloved chief then step forth, and call upon them by the love of their country, by the memory of their valiant fathers, by every thing that kindles in the bosom of man the high and generous passions: they stop; they gather round him; and goaded by shame and indignation, returning again to the charge, with the fury of wild beasts rather than the courage of soldiers, bear down every thing before them. Which of these two battles will interest us the most? and

which of them shall we remember the longest? The one will stand forth in the imagination of the reader like a rock of the desert, which points out to the far-removed traveller the country through which he has passed, when its lesser objects are obscured in the distance; whilst the other leaves no traces behind it, but in the minds of the scientifick in war.

respect, that which is drawn from the most interesting source will please us the most at the time, and most lastingly take hold of our minds. An argument supported with vivid and interesting illustration will long be remembered when many equally important and clear are forgotten; and a work where many such occur will be held in higher estimation by the generality of men than one its superior, perhaps, in acuteness, perspicuity, and good sense.

Our desire to know what men are in the closet as well as the field, by the blazing hearth, and at the social board,[1] as well as in the council and the throne, is very imperfectly gratified by real history; romance writers, therefore, stepped boldly forth to supply the deficiency, and tale writers and novel writers of many descriptions followed after. If they have not been very skilful in their delineations of nature, if they have represented men and women speaking and acting as men and women never did speak or act, if they have caricatured both our virtues and our vices, if they have given us such pure and unmixed, or such heterogeneous combinations of character as real life never presented, and yet have pleased and interested us, let it not be imputed to the dullness of man in discerning what is genuinely natural in himself. There are many inclinations belonging to us, besides this great master propensity of which I am treating. Our love of the grand, the beautiful, the novel, and above all of the marvellous, is very strong; and if we are richly fed with what we have a good relish for, we may be weaned to forget our native and favourite aliment.[2] Yet we can never so far forget it, but that we will cling to, and acknowledge it again, whenever it is presented before us. In a work abounding with the marvellous and unnatural, if the author has anyhow stumbled upon an unsophisticated genuine stroke of nature, we will immediately perceive and be delighted with it, though we are foolish enough to admire at the same time all the nonsense with which it is surrounded. After all the wonderful incidents, dark mysteries, and secrets revealed, which eventful novel so liberally pres-

---

[1] *social board* Table.
[2] *aliment* Food.

ents to us; after the beautiful fairy ground, and even the grand and sublime scenes of nature with which descriptive novel so often enchants us; those works which most strongly characterize human nature in the middling and lower classes of society, where it is to be discovered by stronger and more unequivocal marks, will ever be the most popular. For though great pains have been taken in our higher sentimental novels to interest us in the delicacies, embarrassments, and artificial distresses of the more refined part of society, they have never been able to cope in the public opinion with these. The one is a dressed and beautiful pleasure ground, in which we are enchanted for a while, amongst the delicate and unknown plants of artful cultivation, the other is a rough forest of our native land: the oak, the elm, the hazel, and the bramble are there, and amidst the endless varieties of its paths we can wander for ever. Into whatever scenes the novelist may conduct us, what objects soever he may present to our view, still is our attention most sensibly awake to every touch faithful to nature, still are we upon the watch for every thing that speaks to us of ourselves.

The fair field of what is properly called poetry is enriched with so many beauties that in it we are often tempted to forget what we really are, and what kind of beings we belong to. Who in the enchanted regions of simile, metaphor, allegory and description, can remember the plain order of things in this everyday world? From heroes whose majestic forms rise like a lofty tower, whose eyes are lightning, whose arms are irresistible, whose course is like the storms of heaven, bold and exalted sentiments we will readily receive, and will not examine them very accurately by that rule of nature which our own breast prescribes to us. A shepherd whose sheep, with fleeces of the purest snow, browse the flowery herbage of the most beautiful valleys, whose flute is ever melodious, and whose shepherdess is ever crowned with roses, whose every care is love, will not be called very strictly to account for the loftiness and refinement of his thoughts. The fair nymph, who sighs out her sorrows to the conscious and compassionate wilds, whose eyes gleam like the bright drops of heaven, whose loose tresses stream to the breeze, may say what she pleases with impunity. I will venture, however, to say, that amidst all this decoration and ornament, all this loftiness and refinement, let one simple trait of the human heart, one expression of passion genuine and true to nature be introduced, and it will stand forth alone in the boldness of reality, whilst the false and unnatural around it fades away upon every side, like the rising exhalations of the morning. With admiration, and often with enthusiasm, we proceed on our way through the grand and the beautiful images, raised to our imagination by the lofty epic muse, but what even here are those things that strike upon the heart, that we feel and remember? Neither the descriptions of war, the sound of the trumpet, the clanging of arms, the combat of heroes, nor the death of the mighty, will interest our minds like the fall of the feeble stranger, who simply expresses the anguish of his soul, at the thoughts of that far-distant home which he must never return to again, and closes his eyes, amongst the ignoble and forgotten; like the timid stripling[1] goaded by the shame of reproach, who urges his trembling steps to the fight, and falls like a tender flower before the first blast of winter. How often will some simple picture of this kind be all that remains upon our minds of the terrific and magnificent battle, whose description we have read with admiration! How comes it that we relish so much the episodes of an heroic poem? It cannot merely be that we are pleased with a resting-place, where we enjoy the variety of contrast; for were the poem of the simple and familiar kind, and an episode after the heroic style introduced into it, ninety readers out of an hundred would pass over it altogether. Is it not that we meet such a story, so situated, with a kind of sympathetic good will, as in passing through a country of castles and of palaces, we should pop unawares upon some humble cottage, resembling the dwellings of our own native land, and gaze upon it with affection. The highest pleasures we receive from poetry, as well as from the real objects which surround us in the world, are derived from the sympathetic interest we all take in beings like ourselves; and I will even venture to say, that were the grandest scenes which can enter into the imagination of man,

presented to our view, and all reference to man completely shut out from our thoughts, the objects that composed it would convey to our minds little better than dry ideas of magnitude, colour, and form; and the remembrance of them would rest upon our minds like the measurement and distances of the planets.

If the study of human nature then is so useful to the poet, the novelist, the historian, and the philosopher, of how much greater importance must it be to the dramatic writer? To them it is a powerful auxiliary, to him it is the centre and strength of the battle. If characteristic views of human nature enliven not their pages, there are many excellencies with which they can, in some degree, make up for the deficiency; it is what we receive from them with pleasure rather than demand. But in his works no richness of invention, harmony of language, nor grandeur of sentiment will supply the place of faithfully delineated nature. The poet and the novelist may represent to you their great characters from the cradle to the tomb. They may represent them in any mood or temper, and under the influence of any passion which they see proper, without being obliged to put words into their mouths, those great betrayers of the feigned and adopted. They may relate every circumstance however trifling and minute, that serves to develop their tempers and dispositions. They tell us what kind of people they intend their men and women to be, and as such we receive them. If they are to move us with any scene of distress, every circumstance regarding the parties concerned in it, how they looked, how they moved, how they sighed, how the tears gushed from their eyes, how the very light and shadow fell upon them, is carefully described, and the few things that are given them to say along with all this assistance must be very unnatural indeed if we refuse to sympathize with them. But the characters of the drama must speak directly for themselves. Under the influence of every passion, humour, and impression, in the artificial veilings of hypocrisy and ceremony, in the openness of freedom and confidence, and in the lonely hour of meditation they speak. He who made us hath placed within our breast a judge that judges instantaneously of every thing they say. We expect to find them creatures

---

[1] *stripling* Adolescent.

like ourselves; and if they are untrue to nature, we feel that we are imposed upon, as though the poet had introduced to us for brethren creatures of a different race, beings of another world.

As in other works deficiency in characteristic truth may be compensated by excellencies of a different kind. In the drama characteristic truth will compensate every other defect. Nay, it will do what appears a contradiction; one strong genuine stroke of nature will cover a multitude of sins even against nature herself. When we meet in some scene of a good play a very fine stroke of this kind, we are apt to become so intoxicated with it, and so perfectly convinced of the author's great knowledge of the human heart, that we are unwilling to suppose that the whole of it has not been suggested by the same penetrating spirit. Many well-meaning enthusiastic critics have given themselves a great deal of trouble in this way, and have shut their eyes most ingeniously against the fair light of nature for the very love of it. They have converted, in their great zeal, sentiments palpably false, both in regard to the character and situation of the persons who utter them, sentiments which a child or a clown[1] would detect, into the most skilful depictments of the heart. I can think of no stronger instance to show how powerfully this love of nature dwells within us.

Formed as we are with these sympathetic propensities in regard to our own species, it is not at all wonderful that theatrical exhibition has become the grand and favourite amusement of every nation into which it has been introduced. Savages will, in the wild contortions of a dance, shape out some rude story expressive of character or passion, and such a dance will give more delight to his companions than the most artful exertions of agility. Children in their gambols will make out a mimic representation of the manners, characters, and passions of grown men and women, and such a pastime will animate and delight them much more than a treat of the daintiest sweetmeats, or the handling of the gaudiest toys. Eagerly as it is enjoyed by the rude[2] and the young,

to the polished and the ripe in years it is still the most interesting amusement. Our taste for it is durable as it is universal. Independently of those circumstances which first introduced it, the world would not have long been without it. The progress of society would soon have brought it forth; and men in the whimsical decorations of fancy would have displayed the characters and actions of their heroes, the folly and absurdity of their fellow-citizens, had no Priests of Bacchus[3] ever existed.

In whatever age or country the drama might have its rise, tragedy would have been the first-born of its children. For every nation has its great men, and its great events upon record; and to represent their own forefathers struggling with those difficulties, and braving those dangers, of which they have heard with admiration, and the effects of which they still perhaps experience would certainly have been the most animating subject for the poet and the most interesting for his audience, even independently of the natural inclination we all so universally show for scenes of horror and distress, of passion and heroic exertion. Tragedy would have been the first child of the drama, for the same reasons that have made heroic ballad, with all its battles, murders and disasters, the earliest poetical compositions of every country.

We behold heroes and great men at a distance, unmarked by those small but distinguishing features of the mind, which give a certain individuality to such an infinite variety of similar beings, in the near and familiar intercourse of life. They appear to us from this view like distant mountains, whose dark outlines we trace in the clear horizon, but the varieties of whose roughened sides, shaded with heath and brushwood, and seamed with many a cleft, we perceive not. When accidental anecdote reveals to us any weakness or peculiarity belonging to them, we start upon it like a discovery. They are made known to us in history only, by the great events they are connected with, and the part they have taken in extraordinary or important transactions. Even in poetry and romance, with the exception of some love story interwoven with the main events of their lives, they

---

[1] *clown* Rustic, country dweller.

[2] *rude* Uneducated

[3] *Priests of Bacchus* I.e., Baccants, or revelers.

are seldom more intimately made known to us. To tragedy it belongs to lead them forward to our nearer regard, in all the distinguishing varieties which nearer inspection discovers; with the passions, the humours, the weaknesses, the prejudices of men. It is for her to present to us the great and magnanimous hero, who appears to our distant view as a superior being, as a God, softened down with those smaller frailties and imperfections which enable us to glory in and claim kindred to his virtues. It is for her to exhibit to us the daring and ambitious man, planning his dark designs, and executing his bloody purposes, marked with those appropriate characteristics, which distinguish him as an individual of that class, and agitated with those varied passions, which disturb the mind of man when he is engaged in the commission of such deeds. It is for her to point out to us the brave and impetuous warrior struck with those visitations of nature, which, in certain situations, will unnerve the strongest arm, and make the boldest heart tremble. It is for her to show the tender, gentle, and unassuming mind animated with that fire which, by the provocation of circumstances, will give to the kindest heart the ferocity and keenness of a tiger. It is for her to present to us the great and striking characters that are to be found amongst men, in a way which the poet, the novelist, and the historian can but imperfectly attempt. But above all, to her, and to her only it belongs to unveil to us the human mind under the dominion of those strong and fixed passions, which, seemingly unprovoked by outward circumstances, will from small beginnings brood within the breast, till all the better dispositions, all the fair gifts of nature are borne down before them. Those passions which conceal themselves from the observation of men, which cannot unbosom themselves even to the dearest friend, and can often times only give their fullness vent in the lonely desert, or in the darkness of midnight. For who hath followed the great man into his secret closet, or stood by the side of his nightly couch, and heard those exclamations of the soul which heaven alone may hear, that the historian should be able to inform us? And what form of story, what mode of rehearsed speech will communicate to us those feelings, whose irregular bursts, abrupt transitions, sudden pauses, and half-uttered suggestions, scorn all harmony of measured verse, all method and order of relation? …

How little credit soever, upon perusing these plays, the reader may think me entitled to in regard to the execution of the work, he will not, I flatter myself, deny me some credit in regard to the plan. I know of no series of plays, in any language, expressly descriptive of the different passions; and I believe there are few plays existing in which the display of one strong passion is the chief business of the drama, so written that they could properly make part of such a series. I do not think that we should, from the works of various authors, be able to make a collection which would give us any thing exactly of the nature of that which is here proposed. If the reader, in perusing it, perceives that the abilities of the author are not proportioned to the task which is imposed upon them, he will wish in the spirit of kindness rather than of censure, as I most sincerely do, that they had been more adequate to it. However, if I perform it ill, I am still confident that this (pardon me if I call it noble) design will not be suffered to fall to the ground, some one will arise after me who will do it justice; and there is no poet, possessing genius for such a work, who will not at the same time possess that spirit of justice and of candour, which will lead him to remember me with respect.

I have now only to thank my reader, whoever he may be, who has followed me through the pages of this discourse, for having had the patience to do so. May he, in going through what follows (a wish the sincerity of which he cannot doubt) find more to reward his trouble than I dare venture to promise him; and for the pains he has already taken, and that, which he intends to take for me, I request that he will accept of my grateful acknowledgments.

—1798

GOTHIC LITERATURE, 1764–1830

CONTEXTS

An ancient castle full of mysteries; a blood-soaked specter; a beautiful woman pursued through an underground passage; a nefarious monk; an atmosphere of fear and suspense: many of the ingredients that make up what we now call Gothic literature solidified into a recognizable formula during the Romantic era. For readers, the Gothic at its best offered an imaginative escape and, through fear, a sublime encounter with the limits of rational understanding. For critics, the Gothic at its worst represented the degradation of public taste and morality.

The Gothic as a literary genre—with its castles, monasteries, dungeons, and graveyards—stemmed in part from what is known as the Gothic Revival, a faux medieval trend in architecture and interior decoration that became the dominant style of church architecture in the nineteenth century. One particularly influential early example is Strawberry Hill House (1749–76), an ordinary house that, under the direction of its owner, Horace Walpole, was transformed through a decades-long series of renovations into a fantastically ornate imitation Gothic castle. Not coincidentally, Walpole was living at Strawberry Hill when he wrote what is widely considered the first Gothic novel, *The Castle of Otranto* (1764). This novel established many of the conventions that came to be associated with the genre—supernatural occurrences, a heightened sense of the dramatic, atmospheric castles with secret passages, young heroines persecuted by villainous men.

Much as present-day readers may trace the history of "the Gothic novel" back to *Otranto*, writers and readers at the time did not use this term. To be sure, Walpole subtitled his book "A Gothic Story," but by *Gothic* he meant *medieval*, and, by extension, *irrational* and *uncivilized*, without many of the associations that came to be regarded as characteristic of the genre. And he would have been less likely to describe his work as a "novel" than as a "romance," a term used in reference to long narratives that could include elements of the fantastic. In his preface to the second edition of *Otranto*, Walpole described it as "an attempt to blend the two kinds of romance, the ancient and the modern. In the former, all was imagination and improbability: in the latter, nature is always intended to be, and sometimes has been, copied with success." The supernatural elements of "ancient" romances and the realism of "modern" novels proved to be a compelling combination, and *The Castle of Otranto* has never been out of print since its first publication. Walpole followed it with *The Mysterious Mother* (1768), an incest tragedy too shocking to be staged at the time; it is usually described as the first Gothic drama.

A few works inspired by Walpole were published in the decades immediately following *Otranto*, but the real vogue for Gothic fiction did not emerge until the enormously influential successes of Ann Radcliffe in the 1790s. Foreboding castles and persecuted heroines still figure prominently in Radcliffe's fiction, but her work also emphasizes sublime landscapes, and gives what was then a new twist to stories of the supernatural: a logical conclusion. In most of Radcliffe's novels, seemingly supernatural events are eventually revealed to have rational causes, and to be much less frightening than they had first appeared to be. The success of this approach—and especially of her fourth novel, *The Mysteries of Udolpho* (1794)—made Radcliffe the highest-earning writer of the decade. It also inspired a remarkable number of followers, often described as the "Radcliffe school."

Radcliffe herself was viewed with some degree of critical respect, though many critics were disappointed by her tendency to rationalize the supernatural out of existence; one anonymous reviewer (probably Mary Wollstonecraft) complained that "[a]fter being awakened to wonder by the rumbling of a mountain, the reader has an unpleasant sensation of being tricked … when he perceives only a mouse creep out." Far greater critical ire, however, was reserved for the "crowd of copyists," as Walter Scott described them, "who came forward in imitation of Mrs. Radcliffe, and assumed her magic wand, without having the power of wielding it with effect."

While Radcliffe's closest emulators followed her in writing stories of the "explained supernatural," other writers of the period took the frightening aspects of the Gothic in an opposite direction, leaving fantastical events unexplained and amplifying their horrific qualities. The "horror" stream of Gothic fiction is best exemplified by Matthew Lewis's *The Monk: A Romance* (1796), a staggeringly popular success. That book's evocative descriptions of sexual content and of graphic violence, together with its unflattering depiction of religion, caused Coleridge to condemn it as "a poison for youth, and a provocative for the debauchee." In her posthumously published essay "On the Supernatural in Poetry" (1826), Radcliffe too disparaged such works of "horror," arguing that their explicit evocation of objects of fear "nearly annihilates" the faculties, while works of "terror," presumably such as her own, "expan[d] the soul" with material more suggestive of the sublime.

Lewis and writers like him were often inspired by their reading in German literature—and in part for that reason were sometimes referred to as members of the "German school." However, the importance of German literary influence was often overstated by critics who felt that the graphic and subversive content of their works was opposed to British values. Such content was undeniably attractive to many readers, though; for that reason, numerous British writers falsely subtitled their original work as having been translated or adapted "from the German." (In fairness, it should be noted that members of the much larger "Radcliffe school" were also sometimes associated with foreign degeneracy—an association created by their stories being sent to the European Continent.)

Gothic novels were generally multi-volume affairs, but Gothic fiction was also available to those without the time, money, or literacy skills to enjoy a full-length novel. Any novel with a degree of popularity was likely to be pirated into a "chapbook" or "bluebook" abridgment—a short, cheap, pamphlet-style narrative that could be purchased on the street. Periodicals and collections might feature even shorter Gothic "tales," as well as "fragments," brief pieces of great dramatic intensity that commenced in the middle of the narrative action and ended before the plot was resolved.

The Gothic also appeared in a range of genres far beyond prose fiction. The work of Matthew Lewis illustrates the spread of the Gothic across genres: Lewis was also an influential writer of supernatural ballads, some of which were incorporated into *The Monk*, and he authored an extremely popular play, *The Castle Spectre* (1797), which thrilled audiences with the appearance of a ghost in a blood-stained white dress.

The Castle Spectre, along with theatrical adaptations of Radcliffe's works, contributed to a fashion for Gothic drama that paralleled that for the Gothic novel. Many of the most successful or important plays of the era—Joanna Baillie's *De Monfort* (1800), Coleridge's *Remorse* (1813), and Charles Maturin's *Bertram* (1816) among them—can be considered part of the genre. As with the novel, Gothic drama was not defined as such at the time, but it incorporated the same recognizable set of conventional elements, from gloomy foreign castles to persecuted heroines. It too was sometimes disparaged as an un-British reflection of the degraded tastes of the masses. Wordsworth, for example, quipped that *The Castle Spectre* "fitted the taste of the audience like a glove," and a critic in the *Monthly Review* expressed a commonplace complaint with his remark that "German spectres have almost driven Shakespeare and [the early-eighteenth-century English playwright William] Congreve from the stage." (Shakespeare, however, was also claimed by defenders of the Gothic, who pointed to his use of the supernatural in *Macbeth* as a model.)

The case against Gothic fiction and drama was in part based on the sheer number of works in the Gothic mode. As Clara Reeve, herself an author of Gothic novels, complained, "[e]very work of merit produced a swarm of imitators, till they became a public evil, and the institution of circulating libraries, conveyed them in the cheapest manner to every bodies hand." Circulating libraries, where books could be borrowed for a small fee, were commonplace by the close of the eighteenth century. This development meant that readers could read more books, and might choose them less discriminately, than if they had to buy them outright. Even if the phrase "Gothic novel" was not yet common, borrowers at circulating libraries knew that a book title referencing a castle, a monk, or a mystery promised a certain set of enjoyments. It is no accident that William Lane, the proprietor of a major circulating library, was also the owner of Minerva Press, a prolific publisher of Gothic novels. The disdain many felt for such novels is reflected in an unsubstantiated rumor widely repeated at the time that Minerva Press would pay £5 for any writer's manuscript, regardless of quality, so long as the story adhered to a certain set of conventions.

Concern regarding the proliferation of Gothic writing was compounded by the assumption, suggested by many reviewers, that the audience of the Gothic was primarily impressionable young women (who were assumed to be particularly sensitive to the Gothic's corrupting and frivolous qualities). Yet when Henry Tilney in Jane Austen's *Northanger Abbey* (1817) declares his liking for *The Mysteries of Udolpho*, he asserts that young men read "nearly as many" novels as women; he himself has read "hundreds and hundreds." The records of circulating libraries suggest that Henry's habits resembled those of many real male readers: borrowing practices appear to have been close to equal between the sexes. To be sure, many of the *writers* of Gothic novels, chapbooks, tales, and dramas were women—though, again, perhaps not as high a percentage as the critics suggested.

Critical condemnation of the Gothic as a corrupted and feminine form of low culture was increasingly complicated from the late 1790s onwards by the degree to which its influence permeated more "highbrow" literature. Coleridge, Wordsworth, Byron, Keats, and Baillie, for example, all wrote Gothic works, and Mary Robinson, Charlotte Smith, and Percy Shelley were Gothic novelists as well as poets.[1] Interestingly, strong Gothic influences in a writer's own work sometimes did little to mitigate that author's critical stance towards other writers more strongly associated with the Gothic. Byron was one of the few Romantic poets to openly express admiration for Walpole and other Gothic writers; Coleridge wrote scornful reviews of works by both Radcliffe and Lewis, while Wordsworth

---

[1] The following is an incomplete list of works with Gothic elements appearing elsewhere in this anthology: Charlotte Smith, *Elegiac Sonnets* 39, 44, 70, and 74; Mary Robinson, "The Haunted Beach"; Robert Burns, "Halloween" and "Tam O'Shanter, A Tale"; Joanna Baillie, *De Monfort*; William Taylor, "Ellenore"; James Hogg, "The Expedition to Hell," "The Brownie of the Black Haggs," and "The Mysterious Bride"; William Wordsworth, "The Thorn"; Sir Walter Scott, "The Eve of St. John," "Glenfinlas," and "The Tapestried Chamber"; Samuel Taylor Coleridge, *The Rime of the Ancient Mariner* and "Christabel"; Matthew Lewis, "The Anaconda" and "The Captive"; George Gordon, Lord Byron, "Darkness" and *The Giaour*; Percy Shelley, *Alastor*; John Keats, "The Eve of St. Agnes," "La Belle Dame sans Merci," "La Belle Dame sans Mercy," "Lamia," and "This Living Hand"; John William Polidori, *The Vampyre*; Mary Shelley, from *The Last Man* and "The Mortal Immortal." (Some of these selections may be found in the anthology's online component; most appear in the bound book.)

was likely thinking of the Gothic when he condemned contemporary readers for their "degrading thirst after outrageous stimulation." More than a decade later, Keats disparaged the failure of "[d]arkness, and worms, and shrouds, and sepulchres" to "lift the thoughts of man."

Though Gothic elements abound in Romantic poetry more broadly, the poems most strongly associated with the Gothic during the period were those written in the 1790s as part of a medieval and folk ballad revival movement. As Walter Scott later reflected in his "Essay on Imitations of the Ancient Ballad" (1830), contributors to the ballad revival tended to attempt one of two things. What Scott called "real imitation[s] of the old ballads" aimed to replicate what their authors saw as the appealing simplicity of ballads of the past. What he called "legendary poems," on the other hand, appropriated aspects of the old ballads and attempted "to engraft modern refinement upon" them. This movement built on the work of slightly earlier poets and collectors, such as Robert Burns (1759–96) and Thomas Percy (1729–1811), but it was at its most overtly Gothic in the very late eighteenth and very early nineteenth centuries. The role of the Gothic in ballad writing intensified in 1796, when a flurry of interest developed surrounding Gottfried August Bürger's poem "Lenore" (1774), a German supernatural ballad that was published in five different English translations that year.[1] Another key event in 1796 was the publication of Matthew Lewis's poem "Alonzo the Brave and Fair Imogine," which was praised for bringing modern metric sophistication to the old ballad style. Building on this success, Lewis published a collection of ballads, *Tales of Wonder* (1800), that included translations and adaptations of older ballads alongside "original" works by himself and such ballad revival poets as Scott and Robert Southey. *Tales of Wonder* was a resounding critical failure, and it marked a change in direction for the poets involved; Scott, for example, abandoned his "German-mad" writings and began to focus more exclusively on Scottish history, while Southey went so far as to have his ballads removed from the second edition of *Tales*.

The popularity of the Gothic began to wane as the nineteenth century progressed, though this by no means signalled an end to the creation of important Gothic works. Some of the most widely acclaimed Gothic novels—including Mary Shelley's *Frankenstein* (1818), Charles Maturin's *Melmoth the Wanderer* (1820), and James Hogg's *The Private Memoirs and Confessions of a Justified Sinner* (1824)—were written long after enthusiasm for the Radcliffe school and the medieval-style ballad had dimmed. And many of the Gothic tropes established in the late eighteenth century would provide creative fodder for centuries to come—for Victorian classics such as *Strange Case of Dr Jekyll and Mr Hyde* (1886) and *Dracula* (1897), and for the "horror" films and novels of the twentieth and twenty-first centuries.

⌘ ⌘ ⌘

---

[1] William Taylor's translation, arguably the most influential, is reprinted in the online component of this anthology; Walter Scott's adaptation, "William and Helen," is included in the website component of this "Contexts" section.

from Horace Walpole, *The Castle of Otranto*[1] (1764)

English antiquarian, writer, and politician Horace Walpole (1717–97) is best known as the author of *The Castle of Otranto*; among his other literary accomplishments are books on such subjects as history, gardening, and his own Gothic Revival home, Strawberry Hill.

In its first printing, Walpole published *The Castle of Otranto* under a pseudonym and presented it as a translation of a sixteenth century southern Italian manuscript "found in the library of an ancient Catholic family in the north of England." After the popular success of the first edition, he confessed to being the author. *Otranto* provoked highly disparate critical responses—including in one case from the same reviewer, who praised it as a translation but condemned its "preposterous phenomena" upon learning it was an original work.

from CHAPTER 1

Manfred, Prince of Otranto, had one son and one daughter. The latter, a most beautiful virgin, aged eighteen, was called Matilda. Conrad, the son, was three years younger, a homely youth, sickly, and of no promising disposition; yet he was the darling of his father, who never showed any symptoms of affection to Matilda. Manfred had contracted a marriage for his son with the Marquis of Vicenza's daughter, Isabella, and she had already been delivered by her guardians into the hands of Manfred, that he might celebrate the wedding as soon as Conrad's infirm state of health would permit. Manfred's impatience for this ceremonial was remarked by his family and neighbours. The former, indeed, apprehending the severity of their prince's disposition, did not dare to utter their surmises on this precipitation. Hippolita, his wife, an amiable lady, did sometimes venture to represent the danger of marrying their only son so early, considering his great youth and greater infirmities, but she never received any other answer than reflections on her own sterility, who had given him but one heir. His tenants and subjects were less cautious in their discourses: they attributed this hasty wedding to the prince's dread of seeing accomplished an ancient prophecy, which was said to have pronounced that *the castle and lordship of Otranto should pass from the present family, whenever the real owner should be grown too large to inhabit it*. It was difficult to make any sense of this prophecy; and still less easy to conceive what it had to do with the marriage in question. Yet these mysteries, or contradictions, did not make the populace adhere the less to their opinion.

Young Conrad's birthday was fixed for his espousals. The company was assembled in the chapel of the castle, and everything ready for beginning the divine office, when Conrad himself was missing. Manfred, impatient of the least delay, and who had not observed his son retire, dispatched one of his attendants to summon the young prince. The servant, who had not stayed long enough to have crossed the court to Conrad's apartment, came running back breathless, in a frantic manner, his eyes staring, and foaming at the mouth. He said nothing, but pointed to the court. The company were struck with terror and amazement. The princess Hippolita, without knowing what was the matter, but anxious for her son, swooned away. Manfred, less apprehensive than enraged at the procrastination of the nuptials and at the folly of his domestic, asked imperiously what was the matter. The fellow made no answer, but continued pointing towards the courtyard; and at last, after repeated questions put to him, cried out,

"Oh! the helmet! the helmet!"

In the meantime, some of the company had run into the court, from whence was heard a confused noise of shrieks, horror, and surprise. Manfred, who began to be alarmed at not seeing his son, went himself to get information of what occasioned this strange confusion. Matilda remained, endeavouring to assist her mother, and Isabella stayed for the same purpose, and to avoid showing any impatience for the bridegroom, for whom, in truth, she had conceived little affection.

The first thing that struck Manfred's eyes was a group of his servants endeavouring to raise something

---

[1] *The Castle of Otranto* Please note that the complete text of *The Castle of Otranto* is available in the online component of this anthology.

that appeared to him a mountain of sable plumes. He gazed without believing his sight. "What are ye doing?" cried Manfred wrathfully, "where is my son?"

A volley of voices replied, "Oh, my Lord! the prince! the prince! the helmet! the helmet!"

Shocked with these lamentable sounds and dreading he knew not what, he advanced hastily—but what a sight for a father's eyes! He beheld his child dashed to pieces and almost buried under an enormous helmet, an hundred times more large than any casque[1] ever made for human being, and shaded with a proportionable quantity of black feathers.

The horror of the spectacle, the ignorance of all around how this misfortune had happened, and, above all, the tremendous phenomenon before him, took away the prince's speech. Yet his silence lasted longer than even grief could occasion. He fixed his eyes on what he wished in vain to believe a vision, and seemed less attentive to his loss than buried in meditation on the stupendous object that had occasioned it. He touched, he examined the fatal casque; nor could even the bleeding mangled remains of the young prince divert the eyes of Manfred from the portent before him. All who had known his partial[2] fondness for young Conrad were as much surprised at their prince's insensibility as thunderstruck themselves at the miracle of the helmet. ...

[Later the same day, Manfred requests that Isabella, his son's intended bride, be brought to him.]

"I sent for you, Lady," said he, and then stopped under great appearance of confusion.

"My Lord!"

"Yes, I sent for you on a matter of great moment," resumed he. "Dry your tears, young Lady. You have lost your bridegroom—yes, cruel fate, and I have lost the hopes of my race!—but Conrad was not worthy of your beauty."

"How, my Lord!" said Isabella. "Sure you do not suspect me of not feeling the concern I ought? My duty and affection would have always—"

"Think no more of him," interrupted Manfred. "He was a sickly, puny child, and Heaven has perhaps taken him away that I might not trust the honours of my house on so frail a foundation. The line of Manfred calls for numerous supports. My foolish fondness for that boy blinded the eyes of my prudence—but it is better as it is. I hope, in a few years, to have reason to rejoice at the death of Conrad."

Words cannot paint the astonishment of Isabella. At first she apprehended that grief had disordered Manfred's understanding. Her next thought suggested that this strange discourse was designed to ensnare her: she feared that Manfred had perceived her indifference for his son, and in consequence of that idea she replied, "Good my Lord, do not doubt my tenderness; my heart would have accompanied my hand. Conrad would have engrossed all my care, and wherever fate shall dispose of me, I shall always cherish his memory and regard your highness and the virtuous Hippolita as my parents."

"Curse on Hippolita!" cried Manfred. "Forget her from this moment, as I do. In short, Lady, you have missed a husband undeserving of your charms; they shall now be better disposed of. Instead of a sickly boy, you shall have a husband in the prime of his age who will know how to value your beauties, and who may expect a numerous offspring."

"Alas, my Lord," said Isabella, "my mind is too sadly engrossed by the recent catastrophe in your family to think of another marriage. If ever my father returns and it shall be his pleasure, I shall obey, as I did when I consented to give my hand to your son. But until his return permit me to remain under your hospitable roof, and employ the melancholy hours in assuaging yours, Hippolita's, and the fair Matilda's affliction."

"I desired you once before," said Manfred angrily, "not to name that woman; from this hour she must be a stranger to you, as she must be to me. In short, Isabella, since I cannot give you my son, I offer you myself."

"Heavens!" cried Isabella, waking from her delusion. "What do I hear! You, my Lord! You! My father-in-law! the father of Conrad! the husband of the virtuous and tender Hippolita!—"

---

[1] *casque* Military helmet.

[2] *partial* Preferential.

"I tell you," said Manfred imperiously, "Hippolita is no longer my wife; I divorce her from this hour. Too long has she cursed me by her unfruitfulness. My fate depends on having sons, and this night I trust will give a new date to my hopes."

At those words he seized the cold hand of Isabella, who was half-dead with fright and horror. She shrieked and started from him. Manfred rose to pursue her, when the moon, which was now up and gleamed in at the opposite casement, presented to his sight the plumes of the fatal helmet, which rose to the height of the windows, waving backwards and forwards in a tempestuous manner, and accompanied with a hollow and rustling sound.

Isabella, who gathered courage from her situation, and who dreaded nothing so much as Manfred's pursuit of his declaration, cried, "Look, my Lord! see, Heaven itself declares against your impious intentions!"

"Heaven nor hell shall impede my designs," said Manfred, advancing again to seize the princess. At that instant the portrait of his grandfather, which hung over the bench where they had been sitting, uttered a deep sigh and heaved its breast.

Isabella, whose back was turned to the picture, saw not the motion, nor knew whence the sound came, but started and said, "Hark, my Lord! What sound was that?" and at the same time made towards the door. Manfred, distracted between the flight of Isabella, who had now reached the stairs, and yet unable to keep his eyes from the picture, which began to move, had however advanced some steps after her, still looking backwards on the portrait, when he saw it quit its panel and descend on the floor with a grave and melancholy air.

"Do I dream?" cried Manfred, returning, "or are the devils themselves in league against me? Speak, infernal spectre! Or, if thou art my grandsire, why dost thou too conspire against thy wretched descendant, who too dearly pays for—" Ere he could finish the sentence the vision sighed again, and made a sign to Manfred to follow him.

"Lead on!" cried Manfred. "I will follow thee to the gulf of perdition." The spectre marched sedately, but dejected, to the end of the gallery, and turned into a chamber on the right hand. Manfred accompanied him at a little distance, full of anxiety and horror, but resolved. As he would have entered the chamber, the door was clapped-to with violence by an invisible hand. The prince, collecting courage from this delay, would have forcibly burst open the door with his foot, but found that it resisted his utmost efforts.

"Since hell will not satisfy my curiosity," said Manfred, "I will use the human means in my power for preserving my race. Isabella shall not escape me."

The lady, whose resolution had given way to terror the moment she had quitted Manfred, continued her flight to the bottom of the principal staircase. There she stopped, not knowing whither to direct her steps, nor how to escape from the impetuosity of the prince. The gates of the castle she knew were locked, and guards placed in the court. Should she, as her heart prompted her, go and prepare Hippolita for the cruel destiny that awaited her, she did not doubt but Manfred would seek her there, and that his violence would incite him to double the injury he meditated, without leaving room for them to avoid the impetuosity of his passions. Delay might give him time to reflect on the horrid measures he had conceived, or produce some circumstance in her favour, if she could, for that night, at least, avoid his odious purpose. Yet where conceal herself? How avoid the pursuit he would infallibly make throughout the castle? As these thoughts passed rapidly through her mind, she recollected a subterraneous passage which led from the vaults of the castle to the church of St. Nicholas. Could she reach the altar before she was overtaken, she knew even Manfred's violence would not dare to profane the sacredness of the place; and she determined, if no other means of deliverance offered, to shut herself up for ever among the holy virgins, whose convent was contiguous to the cathedral. In this resolution, she seized a lamp that burned at the foot of the staircase, and hurried towards the secret passage.

The lower part of the castle was hollowed into several intricate cloisters, and it was not easy for one under so much anxiety to find the door that opened into the cavern. An awful silence reigned throughout those subterraneous regions, except now and then some blasts of wind that shook the doors she had passed, and which, grating on the rusty hinges, were re-echoed through that long labyrinth of darkness. Every murmur struck her with new terror, yet more she dreaded to hear the wrathful voice of Manfred urging his domestics to pursue her. ...

Strawberry Hill and Fonthill Abbey

Horace Walpole's Strawberry Hill House (1749–76) is an early example of Gothic Revival architecture. A modest and ordinary building when he purchased it, Strawberry Hill became a decades-long project for Walpole, who enjoyed, as he wrote, the "satisfaction of imprinting the gloomth of abbeys and cathedrals on one's house." Strawberry Hill House was in no way an authentic Gothic building; even most of the stone used was artificial.

In a letter to a friend, Walpole wrote explicitly of the connections between Strawberry Hill and *The Castle of Otranto*: "You will even have found some traits [in the novel] to put you in mind of this place. When you read of the picture quitting its panel, did you recollect the portrait of Lord Falkland all in white in my gallery?"

Fonthill Abbey (1796–1807), a later and even more extravagant Gothic Revival home, was the creation of the architect James Wyatt and the art collector, writer, and politician William Beckford. Fonthill took Gothic artificiality to impractical extremes, featuring a cavernous dining room that could not be effectively heated and a tower so tall that it collapsed and had to be rebuilt multiple times. Beckford was also, like Walpole, an early participant in Gothic literature; his Orientalist Gothic novel *Vathek* is excerpted below.

Paul Sandby, *Strawberry Hill from the Southeast*, c. late eighteenth century.

J. Godfrey, "Library at Strawberry Hill," illustration from Horace Walpole, *Description of the Villa of Mr. Horace Walpole, Youngest Son of Sir Robert Walpole Earl of Orford, at Strawberry-Hill near Twickenham, Middlesex, with an Inventory of the Furniture, Pictures, Curiosities, &c.,* 1784.

Edward Edwards and James Newton, "Staircase at Strawberry Hill," illustration from *Description of the Villa of Mr. Horace Walpole.*

L. Martin and T. Higham, "Fonthill Abbey. View of the West & North Fronts," illustration from John Rutter, *Delineations of Fonthill and Its Abbey,* 1823.

G. Cattermole and M. Dubourg, "Fonthill Abbey, S. End of St. Michael's Gallery," illustration from *Delineations of Fonthill and Its Abbey.*

G. Cattermole and J.C. Varrall, "Fonthill Abbey. Interior of the Great Western Hall," illustration from *Delineations of Fonthill and Its Abbey*.

from Anna Laetitia Aikin (later Barbauld) and John Aikin, "On the Pleasure Derived from Objects of Terror; with Sir Bertrand, a Fragment" (1773)

> The following selection first appeared in *Miscellaneous Pieces, in Prose*, a collection of fiction and essays by the siblings John Aikin (1747–1822) and Anna Laetitia Aikin (1743–1825)—the latter a poet who would become better known by her married name, Barbauld. "On the Pleasure Derived from Objects of Terror" offers one of the first critical defenses of what would become the Gothic genre. It is followed by one of the first examples of a Gothic fragment: "Sir Bertrand," which became a popular piece frequently reprinted in magazines. Its success inspired a number of similar "fragments."

... [T]he apparent delight with which we dwell upon objects of pure terror, where our moral feelings are not in the least concerned, and no passion seems to be excited but the depressing one of fear, is a paradox of the heart. ...

The reality of this source of pleasure seems evident from daily observation. The greediness with which the tales of ghosts and goblins, of murders, earthquakes, fires, shipwrecks, and all the most terrible disasters attending human life, are devoured by every ear, must have been generally remarked. Tragedy, the most favourite work of fiction, has taken a full share of those scenes. ...

How are we then to account for the pleasure derived from such objects? I have often been led to imagine that there is a deception in these cases; and that the avidity with which we attend is not a proof of our receiving real pleasure. The pain of suspense, and the irresistible desire of satisfying curiosity, when once raised, for our eagerness to go quite through an adventure, though we suffer actual pain during the whole course of it. We rather choose to suffer the smart pang of a violent emotion than the uneasy craving of an unsatisfied desire. That this principle, in many instances, may involuntarily carry us through what we dislike, I am convinced from experience. This is the impulse which renders the poorest and most insipid narrative interesting when

once we get fairly into it; and I have frequently felt it with regard to our modern novels, which, if lying on my table, and taken up in an idle hour, have led me through the most tedious and disgusting pages, while, like Pistol[1] eating his leek, I have swallowed and execrated to the end. And it will not only force us through dullness, but through actual torture—through the relation of a Damien's execution, or an inquisitor's act of faith.[2] When children, therefore, listen with pale and mute attention to the frightful stories of apparitions, we are not, perhaps, to imagine that they are in a state of enjoyment, any more than the poor bird which is dropping into the mouth of the rattlesnake—they are chained by the ears, and fascinated by curiosity. This solution, however, does not satisfy me with respect to the well-wrought scenes of artificial terror which are formed by a sublime and vigorous imagination. Here, though we know before-hand what to expect, we enter into them with eagerness, in quest of a pleasure already experienced. This is the pleasure constantly attached to the excitement of surprise from new and wonderful objects. A strange and unexpected event awakens the mind, and keeps it on the stretch; and where the agency of invisible beings is introduced, of "forms unseen, and mightier far than we,"[3] our imagination, darting forth, explores with rapture the new world which is laid open to its view, and rejoices in the expansion of its powers. Passion and fancy cooperating elevate the soul to its highest pitch; and the pain of terror is lost in amazement.

Hence the more wild, fanciful, and extraordinary are the circumstance of a scene of horror, the more pleasure we receive from it; and where they are too near common nature, though violently borne by curiosity through the

---

[1] *Pistol* Comic character who, in *Henry V* 5.1, is forced to eat a raw leek.

[2] *Damien* Robert-François Damiens (1715–57), who was gruesomely tortured before his execution for the attempted assassination of King Louis XV of France; *inquisitor's act of faith* The term used by the Spanish Inquisition for the sentencing of heretics was "auto-da-fé," meaning "act of faith." Potential punishments included various forms of torture, as well as execution by burning at the stake.

[3] *forms ... than we* Paraphrased from Alexander Pope, *Essay on Man* 3.251.

adventure, we cannot repeat it or reflect on it, without an overbalance of pain. In the *Arabian Nights*[1] are many most striking examples of the terrible joined with the marvellous: the story of Alladin, and the travels of Sinbad, are particularly excellent. *The Castle of Otranto* is a very spirited modern attempt upon the same plan of mixed terror, adapted to the model of Gothic romance. The best conceived, and most strongly worked-up scene of mere natural horror that I recollect, is in Smollett's *Ferdinand Count Fathom*;[2] where the hero, entertained in a lone house in a forest, finds a corpse just slaughtered in the room where he is sent to sleep, and the door of which is locked upon him. It may be amusing for the reader to compare his feelings upon these, and from thence form his opinion of the justness of my theory. The following fragment, in which both these manners are attempted to be in some degree united, is offered to entertain a solitary winter's evening.

——————————————————

——————————————————

—————————— After this adventure, Sir Bertrand turned his steed towards the wolds, hoping to cross these dreary moors before the curfew.[3] But ere he had proceeded half his journey, he was bewildered by the different tracks, and not being able, as far as the eye could reach, to espy any object but the brown heath surrounding him, he was at length quite uncertain which way he should direct his course. Night overtook him in this situation. It was one of those nights when the moon gives a faint glimmering of light through the thick black clouds of a lowering sky. Now and then she suddenly emerged in full splendour from her veil; and then instantly retired behind it, having just served to give the forlorn Sir Bertrand a wide extended prospect over the desolate waste. Hope and native courage a while urged him to

push forwards, but at length the increasing darkness and fatigue of body and mind overcame him; he dreaded moving from the ground he stood on, for fear of unknown pits and bogs, and, alighting from his horse in despair, he threw himself on the ground. He had not long continued in that posture when the sullen toll of a distant bell struck his ears—he started up, and turning towards the sound discerned a dim twinkling light.

Instantly he seized his horse's bridle, and with cautious steps advanced towards it. After a painful march he was stopt by a moated ditch surrounding the place from whence the light proceeded; and by a momentary glimpse of moon-light he had a full view of a large antique mansion, with turrets at the corners, and an ample porch in the centre. The injuries of time were strongly marked on every thing about it. The roof in various places was fallen in, the battlements were half demolished, and the windows broken and dismantled. A drawbridge, with a ruinous gateway at each end, led to the court before the building—He entered, and instantly the light, which proceeded from a window in one of the turrets, glided along and vanished; at the same moment the moon sunk beneath a black cloud, and the night was darker than ever. All was silent—Sir Bertrand fastened his steed under a shed, and approaching the house traversed its whole front with light and slow footsteps—All was still as death—He looked in at the lower windows, but could not distinguish a single object through the impenetrable gloom. After a short parley with himself, he entered the porch, and seizing a massy iron knocker at the gate, lifted it up, and hesitating, at length struck a loud stroke. The noise resounded through the whole mansion with hollow echoes. All was still again—He repeated the strokes more boldly and louder—another interval of silence ensued—A third time he knocked, and a third time all was still. He then fell back to some distance that he might discern whether any light could be seen in the whole front—It again appeared in the same place and quickly glided away as before—at the same instant a deep sullen toll sounded from the turret. Sir Bertrand's heart made a fearful stop—He was a while motionless; then terror impelled

---

[1] *Arabian Nights*   Title sometimes used to refer to *One Thousand and One Nights*, a Middle Eastern folktale collection that was first translated from the Arabic into French and English in the early eighteenth century.

[2] *Ferdinand Count Fathom*   1753 picaresque novel detailing episodes in the life of its villainous and depraved title character.

[3] *wolds*   I.e., moors; *curfew*   Hour of the evening at which, during the Middle Ages, a bell was rung to indicate that open fires were no longer permitted.

him to make some hasty steps toward his steed—but shame stopt his flight; and urged by honour, and a resistless desire of finishing the adventure, he returned to the porch; and working up his soul to a full steadiness of resolution, he drew forth his sword with one hand, and with the other lifted up the latch of the gate. The heavy door, creaking upon its hinges, reluctantly yielded to his hand—he applied his shoulder to it and forced it open—he quitted it and stept forward—the door instantly shut with a thundering clap. Sir Bertrand's blood was chilled—he turned back to find the door, and it was long ere his trembling hands could seize it—but his utmost strength could not open it again. After several ineffectual attempts, he looked behind him, and beheld, across a hall, upon a large staircase, a pale bluish flame which cast a dismal gleam of light around. He again summoned forth his courage and advanced towards it—It retired. He came to the foot of the stairs, and after a moment's deliberation ascended. He went slowly up, the flame retiring before him, till he came to a wide gallery—The flame proceeded along it, and he followed in silent horror, treading lightly, for the echoes of his footsteps startled him. It led him to the foot of another staircase, and then vanished—At the same instant another toll sounded from the turret—Sir Bertrand felt it strike upon his heart. He was now in total darkness, and with his arms extended, began to ascend the second staircase. A dead cold hand met his left hand and firmly grasped it, drawing him forcibly forwards—he endeavoured to disengage himself, but could not—he made a furious blow with his sword, and instantly a loud shriek pierced his ears, and the dead hand was left powerless in his—He dropt it, and rushed forwards with a desperate valour. The stairs were narrow and winding, and interrupted by frequent breaches, and loose fragments of stone. The staircase grew narrower and narrower and at length terminated in a low iron grate. Sir Bertrand pushed it open—it led to an intricate winding passage, just large enough to admit a person upon his hands and knees. A faint glimmering of light served to show the nature of the place. Sir Bertrand entered—A deep hollow groan resounded from a distance through the vault—He went forwards, and

proceeding beyond the first turning, discerned the same blue flame[1] which had before conducted him. He followed it. The vault, at length, suddenly opened into a lofty gallery, in the midst of which a figure appeared, completely armed, thrusting forwards the bloody stump of an arm, with a terrible frown and menacing gesture, and brandishing a sword in his hand. Sir Bertrand undauntedly sprung forwards; and aiming a fierce blow at the figure, it instantly vanished, letting fall a massy iron key. The flame now rested upon a pair of ample folding doors at the end of the gallery. Sir Bertrand went up to it, and applied the key to a brazen lock—with difficulty he turned the bolt—instantly the doors flew open, and discovered[2] a large apartment, at the end of which was a coffin rested upon a bier, with a taper[3] burning on each side of it. Along the room on both sides were gigantic statues of black marble, attired in the Moorish[4] habit, and holding enormous sabres in their right hands. Each of them reared his arm, and advanced one leg forwards, as the knight entered; at the same moment the lid of the coffin flew open, and the bell tolled. The flame still glided forwards, and Sir Bertrand resolutely followed, till he arrived within six paces of the coffin. Suddenly, a lady in a shroud and black veil rose up in it, and stretched out her arms towards him—at the same time the statues clashed their sabres and advanced. Sir Bertrand flew to the lady and clasped her in his arms—she threw up her veil and kissed his lips; and instantly the whole building shook as with an earthquake, and fell asunder with a horrible crash. Sir Bertrand was thrown into a sudden trance, and on recovering, found himself seated on a velvet sofa, in the most magnificent room he had ever seen, lighted with innumerable tapers, in lustres of pure crystal. A sumptuous banquet was set in the middle. The doors opening to soft music, a lady of incomparable beauty, attired with amazing splendour entered, surrounded by a troop of gay nymphs far more fair than the

---

[1] *blue flame* According to tradition, blue flame is a sign of ghosts.

[2] *discovered* Revealed.

[3] *taper* Candle.

[4] *Moorish* I.e., North African.

Graces[1]—She advanced on the knight, and falling on her knees thanked him as her deliverer. The nymphs placed a garland of laurel on his head, and the lady led him by the hand to the banquet, and sat beside him. The nymphs placed themselves at the table, and a numerous train of servants entering, served up the feast; delicious music playing all the time. Sir Bertrand could not speak for astonishment—he could only return their honours by courteous looks and gestures. After the banquet was finished, all retired but the lady, who leading back the knight to the sofa, addressed him in these words:———————————————

————————————————————————

————————————————————————

from Clara Reeve, *The Old English Baron: A Gothic Story* (1777, revised 1778)

The Old English Baron is the best-known work by writer and translator Clara Reeve (1729–1807). First published in Essex in 1777 as *The Champion of Virtue: A Gothic Story*, Reeve's novel was revised by Martha Bridgen (Samuel Richardson's daughter) and issued a year later in London as *The Old English Baron: A Gothic Story*. Reprinted more than a dozen times in the following decade, it was an important contribution to the development and popularization of the Gothic genre.

PREFACE

... **T**his story is the literary offspring of *The Castle of Otranto*, written upon the same plan, with a design to unite the most attractive and interesting circumstances of the ancient romance and modern novel, at the same time it assumes a character and manner of its own, that differs from both; it is distinguished by the appellation of a Gothic Story, being a picture of Gothic times and manners. Fictitious stories have been the delight of all times and all countries, by oral tradition in barbarous, by writing in more civilized ones; and although some persons of wit and learning have condemned them indiscriminately, I would venture to affirm, that even those who so much affect to despise them under one form, will receive and embrace them under another. ...

... *The Castle of Otranto*[,...] as already has been observed, is an attempt to unite the various merits and graces of the ancient romance and modern novel. To attain this end, there is required a sufficient degree of the marvellous to excite the attention; enough of the manners of real life to give an air of probability to the work; and enough of the pathetic[2] to engage the heart in its behalf.

The book we have mentioned is excellent in the two last points, but has a redundancy in the first; the opening excites the attention very strongly; the conduct of the story is artful and judicious; the characters are admirably drawn and supported; the diction polished and elegant; yet, with all these brilliant advantages, it palls upon the mind (though it does not upon the ear); and the reason is obvious, the machinery[3] is so violent that it destroys the effect it is intended to excite. Had the story been kept within the utmost verge of probability, the effect had been preserved, without losing the least circumstance that excites or detains the attention. For instance; we can conceive, and allow of, the appearance of a ghost; we can even dispense with an enchanted sword and helmet; but then they must keep within certain limits of credibility: A sword so large as to require an hundred men to lift it; a helmet that by its own weight forces a passage through a court-yard into an arched vault, big enough for a man to go through; a picture that walks out of its frame; a skeleton ghost in a hermit's cowl—When your expectation is wound up to the highest pitch, these circumstances take it down with a witness, destroy the work of imagination, and, instead of attention, excite laughter. I was both surprised and vexed to find the enchantment dissolved, which I wished might continue to the end of the book; and

---

[1] *nymphs* Beautiful young women; *Graces* In Greek mythology, three goddesses of beauty and charm.

[2] *pathetic* Emotionally affecting.

[3] *machinery* Elements—especially supernatural elements—inserted to advance the plot or increase the effectiveness of a narrative.

several of its readers have confessed the same disappointment to me: The beauties are so numerous, that we cannot bear the defects, but want it to be perfect in all respects.

In the course of my observations upon this singular book, it seemed to me that it was possible to compose a work upon the same plan, wherein these defects might be avoided; and the keeping,[1] as in painting, might be preserved. …

from THE OLD ENGLISH BARON
A GOTHIC STORY

[The events of *The Old English Baron* surround an estate in western England that once belonged to the Lovel family. Early in the novel, readers learn that, years ago, Lord Lovel was killed in battle and his pregnant wife died of grief; his estate was inherited by a cousin and immediately sold to the Fitz-Owen family. Much of the novel concerns Edmund Twyford, a peasant whose "'uncommon merit, and gentleness of manners, distinguish him from those of his own class,'" who is employed by the Fitz-Owens as a servant and companion to the young men of the family.

Edmund is challenged to spend three nights in the east apartment of the house, which is said to be haunted. The following excerpt describes the second night of the challenge, which Edmund spends with Father Oswald, a priest, and with Joseph, a serving man. Immediately before this passage, Joseph tells a story suggesting that Lord Lovel was in fact murdered, that his wife gave birth before she died, and that Edmund may be Lovel's son.]

Here a silence of several minutes ensued; when, suddenly, they were awakened from their reverie by a violent noise in the rooms underneath them. It seemed like the clashing of arms, and something seemed to fall down with violence.

They started, and Edmund rose up with a look full of resolution and intrepidity.

"I am called!" said he; "I obey the call!"

He took up a lamp, and went to the door that he had opened the night before. Oswald followed with his rosary in his hand, and Joseph last with trembling steps. The door opened with ease, and they descended the stairs in profound silence.

The lower rooms answered exactly to those above; there were two parlours and a large closet. They saw nothing remarkable in these rooms, except two pictures, that were turned with their faces to the wall. Joseph took the courage to turn them. "These," said he, "are the portraits of my lord and lady. Father, look at this face; do you know who is like it?"

"I should think," said Oswald, "it was done for Edmund!"

"I am," said Edmund, "struck with the resemblance myself; but let us go on; I feel myself inspired with unusual courage. Let us open the closet door."

Oswald stopped him short.

"Take heed," said he, "lest the wind of the door put out the lamp. I will open this door."

He attempted it without success; Joseph did the same, but to no purpose; Edmund gave the lamp to Joseph; he approached the door, tried the key, and it gave way to his hand in a moment.

"This adventure belongs," said he, "to me only; that is plain—bring the lamp forward."

Oswald repeated the paternoster,[2] in which they all joined, and then entered the closet.

The first thing that presented itself to their view, was a complete suit of armour, that seemed to have fallen down on an heap.

"Behold!" said Edmund; "this made the noise we heard above." They took it up, and examined it piece by piece; the inside of the breast plate was stained with blood.

"See here!" said Edmund; "what think you of this?"

"'Tis my Lord's armour," said Joseph; "I know it well—here has been bloody work in this closet!"

Going forward, he stumbled over something; it was a ring with the arms of Lovel engraved upon it.

---

[1] *keeping* Harmonious relationship between the components of a painting's composition.

[2] *paternoster* Latin for "our father," a well-known Christian prayer.

"This is my Lord's ring," said Joseph; "I have seen him wear it; I give it to you, sir, as the right owner; and most religiously do I believe you his son."

"Heaven only knows that," said Edmund; "and, if it permits, I will know who was my father before I am a day older."

While he was speaking, he shifted his ground, and perceived that the boards rose up on the other side of the closet; upon farther examination they found that the whole floor was loose, and a table that stood over them concealed the circumstance from a casual observer.

"I perceive," said Oswald, "that some great discovery is at hand."

"God defend us!" said Edmund, "but I verily believe that the person that owned this armour lies buried under us."

Upon this, a dismal hollow groan was heard, as if from underneath. A solemn silence ensued, and marks of fear were visible upon all three; the groan was thrice heard; Oswald made signs for them to kneel, and he prayed audibly, that Heaven would direct them how to act; he also prayed for the soul of the departed, that it might rest in peace. After this, he arose; but Edmund continued kneeling—he vowed solemnly to devote himself to the discovery of this secret, and the avenging the death of the person there buried. He then rose up. "It would be to no purpose," said he, "for us to examine further now; when I am properly authorised, I will have this place opened; I trust that time is not far off." ...

from William Beckford, *Vathek*[1] (1786)

While most Gothic works of the late eighteenth century take place in an imagined medieval Europe, *Vathek* transports the Gothic's atmospheric qualities and villainous characters to an imagined Middle East. *Vathek* is the best-known work by William Beckford (1760–1844), an English writer, collector, and politician who studied Arabic but never traveled farther east than the European continent. It presents a series of excessive and often bizarre episodes in the life of the powerful Caliph Vathek, including a series of reprehensible tasks, including human sacrifices, he performs in order to reach the Hall of Eblis, the Devil. The excerpts below describe what Vathek and his wife, Nouronihar, find when they finally reach the Hall of Eblis.

... The Caliph and Nouronihar beheld each other with amazement, at finding themselves in a place which, though roofed with a vaulted ceiling, was so spacious and lofty that, at first, they took it for an immeasurable plain. But their eyes, at length, growing familiar to the grandeur of the surrounding objects, they extended their view to those at a distance; and discovered rows of columns and arcades, which gradually diminished, till they terminated in a point radiant as the sun, when he darts his last beams athwart the ocean. The pavement, strewed over with gold dust and saffron, exhaled so subtle an odour as almost overpowered them. They, however, went on, and observed an infinity of censers, in which ambergris[2] and the wood of aloes were continually burning. Between the several columns were placed tables, each spread with a profusion of viands,[3] and wines of every species, sparkling in vases of crystal. A throng of genii, and other fantastic spirits, of either sex, danced lasciviously at the sound of the music which issued from beneath.

In the midst of this immense hall, a vast multitude was incessantly passing, who severally kept their right hands on their hearts, without once regarding any thing around them. They had, all, the livid paleness of death. Their eyes, deep sunk in their sockets, resembled those phosphoric meteors that glimmer by night in places of interment.[4] Some stalked slowly on, absorbed in profound reverie; some, shrieking with agony, ran

---

[1] *Vathek*   Beckford wrote *Vathek* in French and helped his friend Samuel Henley to translate it; Henley then had the translation published without Beckford's consent, prompting Beckford to publish the original French version later the same year. The following excerpt incorporates Beckford's corrections to Henley's translation.

[2] *censers*   Vessel used to hold incense; *ambergris*   Substance used as perfume.

[3] *viands*   Foods.

[4] *phosphoric ... interment*   Will-o'-the-wisps, phosphorescent lights sometimes seen hovering over bogs or graveyards.

furiously about, like tigers wounded with poisoned arrows; whilst others, grinding their teeth in rage, foamed along, more frantic than the wildest maniac. They all avoided each other; and, though surrounded by a multitude that no one could number, each wandered at random, unheedful of the rest, as if alone on a desert which no foot had trodden.

Vathek and Nouronihar, frozen with terror at a sight so baleful, demanded of the Giaour[1] what these appearances might mean; and why these ambulating spectres never withdrew their hands from their hearts? "Perplex not yourselves with so much at once," replied he bluntly; "you will soon be acquainted with all: let us haste, and present you to Eblis." They continued their way through the multitude; but, notwithstanding their confidence at first, they were not sufficiently composed to examine, with attention, the various perspective of halls and of galleries that opened on the right hand and left; which were all illuminated by torches and braziers, whose flames rose in pyramids to the centre of the vault. At length they came to a place where long curtains, brocaded with crimson and gold, fell from all parts in striking confusion. Here, the choirs and dances were heard no longer. The light which glimmered came from afar.

After some time, Vathek and Nouronihar perceived a gleam brightening through the drapery, and entered a vast tabernacle hung round with the skins of leopards. An infinity of elders with streaming beards, and afrits[2] in complete armour, had prostrated themselves before the ascent of a lofty eminence, on the top of which, upon a globe of fire, sat the formidable Eblis. His person was that of a young man, whose noble and regular features seemed to have been tarnished by malignant vapours. In his large eyes appeared both pride and despair: his flowing hair retained some semblance to that of an angel of light. In his hand, which thunder had blasted, he swayed the iron sceptre that causes the

monster Ouranbad,[3] the afrits, and all the powers of the abyss to tremble. At his presence, the heart of the Caliph sunk within him; and he fell prostrate on his face. Nouronihar, however, though greatly dismayed, could not help admiring the person of Eblis: for she expected to have seen some stupendous giant. Eblis, with a voice more mild than might be imagined, but such as penetrated the soul and filled it with the deepest melancholy, said: "Creatures of clay, I receive you into mine empire: ye are numbered amongst my adorers: enjoy whatever this palace affords. …"

[Vathek and Nouronihar begin to explore, but soon learn that they only have a few days to do so before they are tormented for eternity, with their hearts engulfed in flames.]

… Nouronihar fell back, like one petrified, into the arms of Vathek, who cried out with a convulsive sob: "O Giaour! whither hast thou brought us! Allow us to depart, and I will relinquish all thou hast promised. O Mahomet! remains there no more mercy?"—"None! none!" replied the malicious dive.[4] "Know, miserable Prince! thou art now in the abode of vengeance and despair. Thy heart, also, will be kindled like those of the other votaries of Eblis. A few days are allotted thee, previous to this fatal period: employ them as thou wilt; recline on these heaps of gold; command the infernal potentates; range, at thy pleasure, through these immense subterranean domains: no barrier shall be shut against thee. As for me, I have fulfilled my mission: I now leave thee to thyself." At these words he vanished. The Caliph and Nouronihar remained in the most abject affliction. Their tears were unable to flow, and scarcely could they support themselves. At length, taking each other despondingly by the hand, they went faltering from this fatal hall, indifferent which way they turned their steps. Every portal opened at their approach. The dives fell prostrate before them. Every

---

1 *Giaour* Derogatory term for a non-Muslim. The "Giaour" helped Vathek gain entry to the Hall of Eblis, and is now acting as his guide.

2 *afrits* In Islamic folklore, a supernatural being associated with fire, death, and the underworld.

3 *Ouranbad* Voracious flying monster associated with Ahriman, the spirit of evil in Zoroastrianism.

4 *dive* Evil supernatural beings in Zoroastrianism and Persian folklore.

reservoir of riches was disclosed to their view: but they no longer felt the incentives of curiosity, of pride, or avarice. With like apathy they heard the chorus of genii, and saw the stately banquets prepared to regale them. They went wandering on, from chamber to chamber; hall to hall; and gallery to gallery; all without bounds or limit; all distinguishable by the same lowering gloom; all adorned with the same awful grandeur; all traversed by persons in search of repose and consolation, but who sought them in vain; for every one carried within him a heart tormented in flames. Shunned by these various sufferers, who seemed by their looks to be upbraiding the partners of their guilt, they withdrew from them to wait, in direful suspense, the moment which should render them to each other the like objects of terror. …

[Vathek and Nouronihar run out of time and their sentence is enacted.]

… Their hearts immediately took fire, and they, at once, lost the most precious gift of heaven—HOPE. These unhappy beings recoiled, with looks of the most furious distraction. Vathek beheld in the eyes of Nouronihar nothing but rage and vengeance; nor could she discern aught in his but aversion and despair. …

Such was, and such should be, the punishment of unrestrained passions and atrocious actions! Such shall be the chastisement of that blind curiosity, which would transgress those bounds the wisdom of the Creator has prescribed to human knowledge; and such the dreadful disappointment of that restless ambition which, aiming at discoveries reserved for beings of a supernatural order, perceives not, through its infatuated pride, that the condition of man upon earth is to be—humble and ignorant.

Thus the Caliph Vathek, who, for the sake of empty pomp and forbidden power, had sullied himself with a thousand crimes, became a prey to grief without end, and remorse without mitigation. …

from Ann Radcliffe, *The Mysteries of Udolpho, a Romance* (1794)

The works of Ann Radcliffe (1764–1823) were tremendously popular, and inaugurated a period of proliferation of novels of "terror." None was more successful than *The Mysteries of Udolpho*, for which Radcliffe was paid a copyright fee of £500, about fifty times the price of an average manuscript. Radcliffe received even more for her next novel, *The Italian* (1797), after which she retired from writing—a decision that prompted unfounded but persistent rumors that she had been driven mad by her own work. Her last novel, *Gaston de Blondeville* (1826), was published posthumously.

The plot of *The Mysteries of Udolpho* concerns Emily St. Aubert, a young woman whose prospects for marriage and fortune are manipulated by her aunt and her aunt's new husband, the sinister Montoni. All of the following excerpts relate to a mysteriously veiled object at Udolpho, Montoni's castle; they begin as Emily is examining paintings in the castle with her aunt's maid, Annette.

VOLUME 2
from CHAPTER 5

… **P**assing the light hastily over several other pictures, she came to one concealed by a veil of black silk. The singularity of the circumstance struck her, and she stopped before it, wishing to remove the veil, and examine what could thus carefully be concealed, but somewhat wanting courage. "Holy Virgin! what can this mean?" exclaimed Annette. "This is surely the picture they told me of at Venice."

"What picture?" said Emily. "Why a picture—a picture," replied Annette, hesitatingly—"but I never could make out exactly what it was about, either."

"Remove the veil, Annette."

"What! I, ma'amselle!—I! not for the world!" Emily, turning round, saw Annette's countenance grow pale. "And pray, what have you heard of this picture, to terrify you so, my good girl?" said she. "Nothing, ma'amselle: I have heard nothing, only let us find our way out."

"Certainly: but I wish first to examine the picture; take the light, Annette, while I lift the veil." Annette took the light, and immediately walked away with it, disregarding Emily's call to stay, who, not choosing to be left alone in the dark chamber, at length followed her. "What is the reason of this, Annette?" said Emily, when she overtook her, "what have you heard concerning that picture, which makes you so unwilling to stay when I bid you?"

"I don't know what is the reason, ma'amselle," replied Annette, "nor any thing about the picture, only I have heard there is something very dreadful belonging to it—and that it has been covered up in black EVER SINCE—and that nobody has looked at it for a great many years—and it somehow has to do with the owner of this castle before Signor Montoni came to the possession of it—and—"

"Well, Annette," said Emily, smiling, "I perceive it is as you say—that you know nothing about the picture."

"No, nothing, indeed, ma'amselle, for they made me promise never to tell:—but—"

"Well," rejoined Emily, who observed that she was struggling between her inclination to reveal a secret, and her apprehension for the consequence, "I will inquire no further—"

"No, pray, ma'am, do not."

"Lest you should tell all," interrupted Emily. ...

from CHAPTER 6

... To withdraw her thoughts ... from the subject of her misfortunes, she attempted to read, but her attention wandered from the page, and, at length, she threw aside the book, and determined to explore the adjoining chambers of the castle. Her imagination was pleased with the view of ancient grandeur, and an emotion of melancholy awe awakened all its powers, as she walked through rooms, obscure and desolate, where no footsteps had passed probably for many years, and remembered the strange history of the former possessor of the edifice. This brought to her recollection the veiled picture, which had attracted her curiosity, on the preceding night, and she resolved to examine it. As she passed through the chambers, that led to this, she found herself somewhat agitated; its connection with the late lady of the castle, and the conversation of Annette, together with the circumstance of the veil, throwing a mystery over the subject, that excited a faint degree of terror. But a terror of this nature, as it occupies and expands the mind, and elevates it to high expectation, is purely sublime, and leads us, by a kind of fascination, to seek even the object, from which we appear to shrink.

Emily passed on with faltering steps, and having paused a moment at the door, before she attempted to open it, she then hastily entered the chamber, and went towards the picture, which appeared to be enclosed in a frame of uncommon size, that hung in a dark part of the room. She paused again, and then, with a timid hand, lifted the veil; but instantly let it fall—perceiving that what it had concealed was no picture, and, before she could leave the chamber, she dropped senseless on the floor.

When she recovered her recollection, the remembrance of what she had seen had nearly deprived her of it a second time. ...

VOLUME 3
from CHAPTER 1

[Emily is locked into a room at Udolpho, and is afraid for the well-being of her aunt, as well as her own safety.]

... When her spirits had overcome the first shock of her situation, she held up the lamp to examine, if the chamber afforded a possibility of an escape. It was a spacious room, whose walls, wainscoted with rough oak, shewed no casement but the grated one, which Emily had left, and no other door than that, by which she had entered. The feeble rays of the lamp, however, did not allow her to see at once its full extent; she perceived no furniture, except, indeed, an iron chair, fastened in the centre of the chamber, immediately over which, depending on a chain from the ceiling, hung an iron ring. Having gazed upon these, for some time, with wonder and horror, she next observed iron bars below, made for the purpose of confining the feet, and on the arms of the chair were rings of the same metal. As she continued to survey them, she concluded, that they were instruments of torture, and it struck her, that some poor wretch had once been fastened in this chair, and had there been starved to death. She was chilled by the thought; but, what was her agony, when, in the next moment, it occurred to her, that her aunt might have been one of these victims, and that she herself might be the next! An acute pain seized her head, she was scarcely able to hold the lamp, and, looking round for support, was seating herself, unconsciously, in the iron chair itself; but suddenly perceiving where she was, she started from it in horror, and sprung towards a remote end of the room. Here again she looked round for a seat to sustain her, and perceived only a dark curtain, which, descending from the ceiling to the floor, was drawn along the whole side of the chamber. Ill as she was, the appearance of this curtain struck her, and she paused to gaze upon it, in wonder and apprehension.

It seemed to conceal a recess of the chamber; she wished, yet dreaded, to lift it, and to discover what it veiled: twice she was withheld by a recollection of the terrible spectacle her daring hand had formerly unveiled in an apartment of the castle, till, suddenly conjecturing, that it concealed the body of her murdered aunt, she seized it, in a fit of desperation, and drew it aside. Beyond, appeared a corpse, stretched on a kind of low couch, which was crimsoned with human blood, as was the floor beneath. The features, deformed by death, were ghastly and horrible, and more than one livid wound appeared in the face. Emily, bending over the body, gazed, for a moment, with an eager, frenzied eye; but, in the next, the lamp dropped from her hand, and she fell senseless at the foot of the couch. …

from CHAPTER 17

… It may be remembered, that, in a chamber of Udolpho, hung a black veil, whose singular situation had excited Emily's curiosity, and which afterwards disclosed an object, that had overwhelmed her with horror; for, on lifting it, there appeared, instead of the picture she had expected, within a recess of the wall, a human figure of ghastly paleness, stretched at its length, and dressed in the habiliments of the grave. What added to the horror of the spectacle, was, that the face appeared partly decayed and disfigured by worms, which were visible on the features and hands. On such an object, it will be readily believed, that no person could endure to look twice. Emily, it may be recollected, had, after the first glance, let the veil drop, and her terror had prevented her from ever after provoking a renewal of such suffering, as she had then experienced. Had she dared to look again, her delusion and her fears would have vanished together, and she would have perceived, that the figure before her was not human, but formed of wax. The history of it is somewhat extraordinary, though not without example in the records of that fierce severity, which monkish superstition has sometimes inflicted on mankind. A member of the house of Udolpho, having committed some offence against the prerogative of the church, had been condemned to the penance of contemplating, during certain hours of the day, a waxen image, made to resemble a human body in the state, to which it is reduced after death. This penance, serving as a memento of the condition at which he must himself arrive, had been designed to reprove the pride of the Marquis of Udolpho, which had formerly so much exasperated that of the Romish[1] church; and he had not only superstitiously observed this penance himself, which, he had believed, was to obtain a pardon for all his sins, but had made it a condition in his will, that his descendants should preserve the image, on pain of forfeiting to the church a certain part of his domain, that they also might profit by the humiliating moral it conveyed. The figure, therefore, had been suffered to retain its station in the wall of the chamber, but his descendants excused themselves from observing the penance, to which he had been enjoined.

This image was so horribly natural, that it is not surprising Emily should have mistaken it for the object it resembled. …

---

[1] *Romish* I.e., Roman Catholic.

Illustration from *The Mysteries of Udolpho*, 1803 edition. This illustration, from the fifth edition of Radcliffe's novel, depicts the scene from Volume 3, Chapter 1 reprinted above.

from Matthew Gregory Lewis, *The Monk: A Romance*[1] (1796)

When *The Monk* was first published, anonymously, there was little indication that it would become one of the most notorious novels of its period; it was well received by critics as well as by general readers. Critical opinion, however, changed drastically later that year after Matthew Lewis (1775–1818) chose to publish the second edition under his own name—

"M.G. Lewis, Esq., M.P."—and reviewers learned that the author of the novel was a person of significant stature. Coleridge, who condemned the book in the *Critical Review*, noted that "the author of the Monk signs himself a LEGISLATOR! We stare and tremble." Lewis would likely have faced criminal charges for obscene or blasphemous libel if he had not published a fourth edition of *The Monk* in which, as he wrote, he "expunged every syllable on which could be grounded the slightest construction of immorality." None of this seems to have diminished *The Monk*'s popularity; the novel appeared in several editions, as well as in numerous pirated chapbook abridgments and dramatic adaptations, in the years following its publication.

The following selections commence with a conversation between the nobleman Don Raymond (also called Alphonso) and Agnes, a noblewoman whose family wants to force her to become a nun.

VOLUME 2
from CHAPTER I

"... **B**ut can you possibly have lived at Lindenberg for three whole months without hearing of the bleeding nun?"

"You are the first who ever mentioned the name to me. Pray, who may the lady be?"

"That is more than I can pretend to tell you. All my knowledge of her history comes from an old tradition in this family, which has been handed down from father to son, and is firmly credited throughout the baron's domains. Nay, the baron believes it himself; and as for my aunt who has a natural turn for the marvellous, she would sooner doubt the veracity of the Bible than of the bleeding nun. Shall I tell you this history?"

I answered that she would oblige me much by relating it: she resumed her drawing, and then proceeded as follows in a tone of burlesqued gravity:[2]

"It is surprising that in all the chronicles of past times this remarkable personage is never once mentioned. Fain would I recount to you her life; but unluckily till after her death she was never known to

[1]   *The Monk: A Romance*   Further selections from *The Monk* are available on the website component of this anthology.

[2]   *burlesqued gravity*   Seriousness exaggerated for comic effect.

have existed. Then first did she think it necessary to make some noise in the world, and with that intention she made bold to seize upon the Castle of Lindenberg. Having a good taste, she took up her abode in the best room of the house; and once established there, she began to amuse herself by knocking about the tables and chairs in the middle of the night. Perhaps she was a bad sleeper, but this I have never been able to ascertain. According to the tradition, this entertainment commenced about a century ago. It was accompanied with shrieking, howling, groaning, swearing, and many other agreeable noises of the same kind. But though one particular room was more especially honoured with her visits, she did not entirely confine herself to it. She occasionally ventured into the old galleries, paced up and down the spacious halls; or, sometimes stopping at the doors of the chambers, she wept and wailed there to the universal terror of the inhabitants. In these nocturnal excursions she was seen by different people, who all describe her appearance as you behold it here traced by the hand of her unworthy historian."[1]

The singularity of this account insensibly engaged my attention.

"Did she never speak to those who met her?" said I.

"Not she. The specimens indeed, which she gave nightly of her talents for conversation, were by no means inviting. Sometimes the castle rung with oaths and execrations: a moment after she repeated her paternoster:[2] now she howled out the most horrible blasphemies, and then chaunted De profundis,[3] as orderly as if still in the choir. In short she seemed a mighty capricious being: but whether she prayed or cursed, whether she was impious or devout, she always contrived to terrify her auditors[4] out of their senses. The castle became scarcely habitable; and its lord was so frightened by these midnight revels, that one fine morning he was found dead in his bed. This success seemed to please the nun mightily, for now she made more noise than ever. But the next baron proved too cunning for her. He made his appearance with a celebrated exorciser in his hand, who feared not to shut himself up for a night in the haunted chamber. There it seems that he had a hard battle with the ghost before she would promise to be quiet. She was obstinate, but he was more so, and at length she consented to let the inhabitants of the castle take a good night's rest. For some time after no news was heard of her. But at the end of five years the exorciser died, and then the nun ventured to peep abroad again. However, she was now grown much more tractable and well-behaved. She walked about in silence, and never made her appearance above once in five years. This custom, if you will believe the baron, she still continues. He is fully persuaded, that on the fifth of May of every fifth year, as soon as the clock strikes one, the door of the haunted chamber opens. (Observe, that this room has been shut up for near a century.) Then out walks the ghostly nun with her lamp and dagger: she descends the staircase of the eastern tower; and crosses the great hall. On that night the porter always leaves the gates of the castle open, out of respect to the apparition: not that this is thought by any means necessary, since she could easily whip through the keyhole if she chose it; but merely out of politeness, and to prevent her from making her exit in a way so derogatory to the dignity of her ghostship."

"And whither does she go on quitting the castle?"

"To heaven, I hope; but if she does, the place certainly is not to her taste, for she always returns after an hour's absence. The lady then retires to her chamber, and is quiet for another five years."

"And you believe this, Agnes?"

"How can you ask such a question? No, no, Alphonso! I have too much reason to lament superstition's influence to be its victim myself. ..."

[Raymond and Agnes confess their love for each other. Agnes decides to disguise herself as the bleeding nun so as to escape her family and elope with Raymond:]

---

[1] *as you behold ... historian* Raymond is looking at Agnes's drawing of the bleeding nun.

[2] *paternoster* Latin for "our father," a well-known Christian prayer.

[3] *chaunted* Intoned, especially in the style of traditional liturgical music; *De profundis* Conventional Latin title of Psalm 130, which in English begins "Out of the depths have I cried unto thee, O Lord."

[4] *auditors* Hearers.

... She was habited exactly as she had described the spectre. A chaplet of beads hung upon her arm; her head was enveloped in a long white veil; her nun's dress was stained with blood; and she had taken care to provide herself with a lamp and dagger. She advanced towards the spot where I stood. I flew to meet her, and clasped her in my arms.

"Agnes!" said I, while I pressed her to my bosom,

> Agnes! Agnes! thou art mine!
> Agnes! Agnes! I am thine!
> In my veins while blood shall roll,
> Thou art mine!
> I am thine!
> Thine my body! thine my soul!

Terrified and breathless, she was unable to speak: She dropped her lamp and dagger, and sank upon my bosom in silence. I raised her in my arms, and conveyed her to the carriage. ...

[The lovers' carriage crashes, and Raymond is knocked unconscious; when he comes to his senses, Agnes is gone. He is assisted by some peasants, who take him to an inn to recover.]

... According to the physician's order, I swallowed a composing medicine; and as soon as the night shut in, my attendants withdrew, and left me to repose.

That repose I wooed in vain. The agitation of my bosom chased away sleep. Restless in my mind, in spite of the fatigue of my body, I continued to toss about from side to side, till the clock in a neighbouring steeple struck "one." As I listened to the mournful hollow sound, and heard it die away in the wind, I felt a sudden chillness spread itself over my body. I shuddered without knowing wherefore; cold dews poured down my forehead, and my hair stood bristling with alarm. Suddenly I heard slow and heavy steps ascending the staircase. By an involuntary movement I started up in my bed, and drew back the curtain. A single rush-light, which glimmered upon the hearth, shed a faint gleam through the apartment, which was hung with tapestry.

The door was thrown open with violence. A figure entered, and drew near my bed with solemn measured steps. With trembling apprehension I examined this midnight visitor. God Almighty! It was the bleeding nun! It was my lost companion! Her face was still veiled, but she no longer held her lamp and dagger. She lifted up her veil slowly. What a sight presented itself to my startled eyes! I beheld before me an animated corse.[1] Her countenance was long and haggard; her cheeks and lips were bloodless; the paleness of death was spread over her features; and her eye-balls, fixed steadfastly upon me, were lustreless and hollow.

I gazed upon the spectre with horror too great to be described. My blood was frozen in my veins. I would have called for aid, but the sound expired ere it could pass my lips. My nerves were bound up in impotence, and I remained in the same attitude inanimate as a statue.

The visionary nun looked upon me for some minutes in silence: there was something petrifying in her regard. At length, in a low sepulchral voice, she pronounced the following words:

> Raymond! Raymond! Thou art mine!
> Raymond! Raymond! I am thine!
> In thy veins while blood shall roll,
> I am thine!
> Thou art mine!
> Mine thy body! Mine thy soul!——

Breathless with fear, I listened while she repeated my own expressions. The apparition seated herself opposite to me at the foot of the bed, and was silent. Her eyes were fixed earnestly upon mine: they seemed endowed with the property of the rattlesnake's, for I strove in vain to look off her. My eyes were fascinated, and I had not the power of withdrawing them from the spectre's.

In this attitude she remained for a whole long hour without speaking or moving; nor was I able to do either. At length the clock struck two. The apparition rose from her seat, and approached the side of the bed. She

---

[1] *corse* Corpse.

grasped with her icy fingers my hand which hung lifeless upon the coverture, and pressing her cold lips to mine, again repeated,

> Raymond! Raymond! Thou art mine!
> Raymond! Raymond!
> I am thine! &c.—

She then dropped my hand, quitted the chamber with slow steps, and the door closed after her. ...

Matthew Gregory Lewis, "Alonzo the Brave and Fair Imogine" (1796)

The following poem first appeared as part of Lewis's *The Monk*, where a character discovers it in "a volume of old Spanish ballads." An author's footnote in that volume indicates that the ballad is "[b]ased loosely on Gottfried August Bürger, 'Lenore' (1773)." "Alonzo the Brave" was reprinted independently in a number of magazines after *The Monk*'s publication, becoming a favorite for many readers and an inspiration for other ballad poets.

A warrior so bold and a virgin so bright,
  Conversed, as they sat on the green;
They gazed on each other with tender delight:
Alonzo the Brave was the name of the knight,
5 The maid's was the Fair Imogine.

"And, oh!" said the youth, "since to-morrow I go
  To fight in a far distant land,
Your tears for my absence soon leaving to flow,
Some other will court you, and you will bestow
10 On a wealthier suitor your hand."

"Oh! hush these suspicions," Fair Imogine said,
  "Offensive to love and to me!
For, if you be living, or if you be dead,
I swear by the Virgin that none in your stead
15 Shall husband of Imogine be.

"And if e'er for another my heart should decide,
  Forgetting Alonzo the Brave,
God grant that, to punish my falsehood and pride,
Your ghost at the marriage may sit by my side,
20 May tax me with perjury, claim me as bride,
  And bear me away to the grave!"

To Palestine hastened the hero so bold;
  His love she lamented him sore:
But scarce had a twelvemonth elapsed, when behold,
25 A baron all covered with jewels and gold
  Arrived at Fair Imogine's door.

His treasures, his presents, his spacious domain,
  Soon made her untrue to her vows:
He dazzled her eyes; he bewildered her brain;
30 He caught her affections so light and so vain,
  And carried her home as his spouse.

And now had the marriage been blessed by the priest;
  The revelry now was begun:
The tables they groaned with the weight of the feast;
35 Nor yet had the laughter and merriment ceased,
  When the bell at the castle tolled—one.

Then first with amazement Fair Imogine found
  That a stranger was placed by her side:
His air was terrific; he uttered no sound;
40 He spoke not, he moved not, he looked not around,
  But earnestly gazed on the bride.

His vizor was closed, and gigantic his height;
  His armor was sable to view;
All pleasure and laughter were hushed at his sight;
45 The dogs, as they eyed him, drew back in affright;
  The lights in the chamber burnt blue![1]

His presence all bosoms appeared to dismay;
  The guests sat in silence and fear:
At length spoke the bride, while she trembled: "I pray,

---

[1] *burnt blue* According to tradition, blue flame is a sign of ghosts.

50 Sir knight, that your helmet aside you would lay,
　　And deign to partake of our cheer."

The lady is silent: the stranger complies,
　　His visor he slowly unclosed:
Oh! then what a sight met Fair Imogine's eyes!
55 What words can express her dismay and surprise,
　　When a skeleton's head was exposed!

All present then uttered a terrified shout,
　　All turned with disgust from the scene.
The worms they crept in, and the worms they crept out,
60 And sported his eyes and his temples about,
　　While the spectre addressed Imogine:

"Behold me, thou false one, behold me!" he cried,
　　"Remember Alonzo the Brave!
God grants that, to punish thy falsehood and pride,
65 My ghost at thy marriage should sit by thy side;
Should tax thee with perjury, claim thee as bride,
　　And bear thee away to the grave!"

Thus saying, his arms round the lady he wound,
　　While loudly she shrieked in dismay;
70 Then sunk with his prey through the wide-yawning
　　　　ground,
Nor ever again was Fair Imogine found,
　　Or the spectre that bore her away.

Not long lived the baron: and none since that time,
　　To inhabit the castle presume;
75 For chronicles tell that, by order sublime,
There Imogine suffers the pain of her crime,
　　And mourns her deplorable doom.

At midnight four times in each year does her sprite,
　　When mortals in slumber are bound,
80 Arrayed in her bridal apparel of white,
Appear in the hall with the skeleton-knight,
　　And shriek as he whirls her around.

While they drink out of skulls newly torn from the
　　　　grave,

85 Dancing round them pale spectres are seen:
Their liquor is blood, and this horrible stave
They howl: "To the health of Alonzo the Brave,
　　And his consort, the False Imogine!"

from Matthew Gregory Lewis, "Giles Jollup the Grave and Brown Sally Green: A Parody" (1798)

The following parody of Lewis's own poem "Alonzo the Brave and the Fair Imogine" first appeared as a footnote to the poem in the fourth edition of *The Monk*. Lewis prefaced it with the following statement: "After this raw-head and bloody-bones history, perhaps it may be agreeable to some readers to peruse the following parody. I must observe that the lines in italics, and the original idea of making a brewer of the baron, and a physician of the knight, are borrowed from another parody which appeared in the newspapers under the title of 'Pil-Garlic[1] the Brave, and Brown Celestine.'"

A doctor so prim and a sempstress so tight
　　Hob-a-nobbed in some right marasquin;[2]
They sucked up the cordial with truest delight:
Giles Jollup the Grave *was just five feet in height,*
5　　*And four feet the brown Sally Green.*

"And as," said Giles Jollup, "to-morrow I go
　　To physic a feverish land,
At some sixpenny hop,° or perhaps the　　　　　*dance*
　　　　Mayor's show,[3]
You'll tumble in love with some smart city-beau,
10　　And with him share your shop in the Strand."[4]

"Lord! how can you think so?" brown Sally Green said;
　　"You must know mighty little of me;
For if you be living, or if you be dead,

---

[1] *Pil-Garlic* Bald, bedraggled, or slovenly.
[2] *marasquin* Cherry liqueur.
[3] *Mayor's show* Parade in honor of the swearing-in of the Lord Mayor of London.
[4] *Strand* London street known in the eighteenth century for its theaters, taverns, and brothels.

I swear, 'pon my honour, that none in your stead
    Shall husband of Sally Green be.

"And if e'er for another my heart should decide,
    False to you and the faith which I gave,
God grant that, at dinner too amply supplied,
Over-eating may give me a pain in my side;
May your ghost then bring rhubarb[1] to physic the bride,
    And send her well-dosed to the grave!"

Away went poor Giles, to what place is not told;
    Sally wept till she blew her nose sore!
But scarce had a twelvemonth elapsed, when behold!
A brewer, quite stylish, his gig that way rolled,
    And stopped it at Sally Green's door.

His wealth, his pot-belly, and whisky of cane,
    Soon made her untrue to her vows:
The steam of strong beer now bewildering her brain,
He caught her while tipsy! Denials were vain,
    So her carried her home as his spouse.

And now the roast beef has been blest by the priest,
    To cram now the guests had begun:
Tooth and nail like a wolf fell the bride on the feast;
Nor yet had the clash of her knife and fork ceased,
    When a bell –('twas the dustman's)[2] –tolled– "one"!

Then first with amazement brown Sally Green found
    That a stranger was stuck by her side:
His cravat and ruffles with snuff were embrowned;
He ate not, he drank not, but, turning him round,
    Sent some pudding away to be fried!!!

His wig was turned forwards, and short was his height;
    His apron was dirty to view:
The women (oh! wondrous) were hushed at his sight:
45 *The cats, as they eyed him, drew back (well they might),*
    For his body was pea-green and blue! …

Gothic Chapbooks and Bluebooks

As much as critics condemned the proliferation of Gothic novels, they condemned even more vehemently a related form of fiction that became popular around the same time: short Gothic tales printed individually and sold cheaply. Initially, these tales were part of a more general trade in chapbooks—pamphlets or short books made available for purchase on the street—but they developed into a more specific subgenre known as "bluebooks" for the bright blue covers that identified them. Often authored by hack writers, bluebooks typically sold for sixpence or a shilling; they were cheaply produced, with the expectation that they would fall apart after reading. Many were unapologetically pirated condensations of longer, popular Gothic works (there are, for example, five surviving bluebook versions of *The Monk*), while others offered original stories that made use of the same plot conventions found in the full-length novels. The length of a bluebook—usually between twenty and seventy-five pages—encouraged a focus on action at the expense of description and character. Such publications often had very long titles, making it clear to readers exactly what thrills the book promised.

---

[1] *rhubarb* Rhubarb root was commonly used in medicine as a laxative, as a treatment for upset stomach, and for other purposes.

[2] *dustman* Garbage collector.

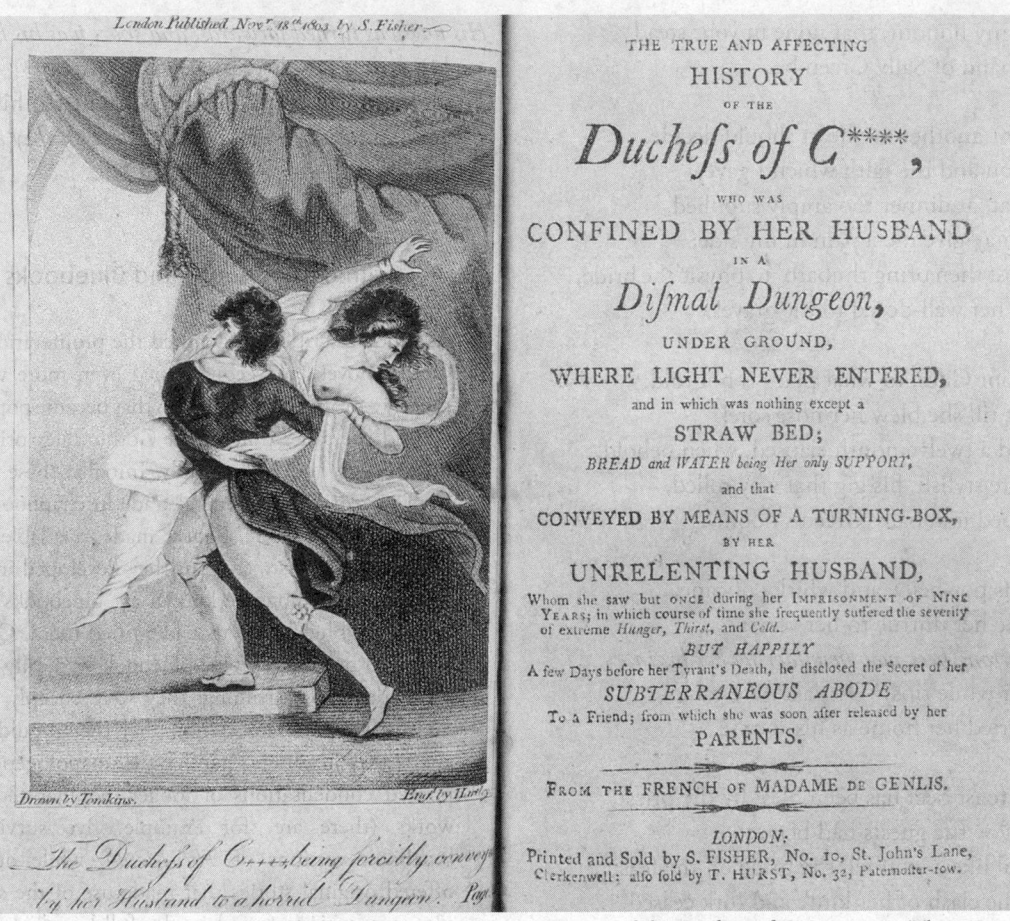

Frontispiece and title page from *The True and Affecting History of the Duchess of C*****, 1803. This is one of several English retellings of the French novelist Stéphanie Félicité's *Histoire de le duchesse de C**** (1782). The description on the title page reads as follows: "The true and affecting history of the Duchess of C****, who was confined by her husband in a dismal dungeon, under ground, where light never entered, and in which was nothing except a straw bed; bread and water being her only support, and that conveyed by means of a turning-box, by her unrelenting husband, whom she saw but once during her imprisonment of nine years; in which course of time she frequently suffered the severity of extreme hunger, thirst, and cold. But happily a few days before her tyrant's death, he disclosed the secret of her subterraneous abode to a friend; from which she was soon after released by her parents."

Frontispiece from *The Midnight Assassin: or, The Confessions of the Monk Rinaldi, Containing a Complete History of His Diabolical Machinations and Unparalleled Ferocity. Together with a Circumstantial Account of that Scourge of Mankind the Inquisition, with the Manner of Bringing to Trial Those Unfortunate Beings Who Are at Its Disposal*, 1802. This frontispiece, from a condensation of Radcliffe's *The Italian, or the Confessional of the Black Penitents* (1797), depicts the moment at which the villainous Catholic priest Schedoni is about to stab the virtuous orphan Ellena. He forbears when he sees that she is wearing a locket containing his picture and concludes that she must be his daughter.

from Anonymous, "Terrorist Novel Writing," *The Spirit of the Public Journals* (1797)

The following anonymous piece advances points that were commonly raised by critics of the burgeoning genre of "terror" fiction. A footnote attached to the title explained that "the satire of this letter is particularly levelled at a literary lady of considerable talents"—that is, Ann Radcliffe—and claimed that "[t]he *system of terror* which she has adopted is not the only reproach to which she is liable. Besides the tedious monotony of her descriptions, she affects in the most disgusting manner a knowledge of languages, countries, customs, and objects of art, of which she is lamentably ignorant. … This shows how well a lady understands the wants of her sex [i.e., what is lacking in her gender.]"

I never complain of fashion, when it is confined to externals; to the form of a cap, or the cut of a lapel; to the colour of a wig, or the tune of a ballad; but when I perceive that there is such a thing as fashion, even in composing books, it is, perhaps, full time that some attempt should be made to recall writers to the old boundaries of common sense.

I allude, Sir, principally to the great quantity of novels with which our circulating libraries are filled, and our parlour tables covered, in which it has been the fashion to make *terror* the *order of the day*, by confining the heroes and heroines in old gloomy castles, full of spectres, apparitions, ghosts, and dead men's bones. This is now so common that a novelist blushes to bring about a marriage by ordinary means, but conducts the happy pair through long and dangerous galleries, where the light burns blue,[1] the thunder rattles, and the great window at the end presents the hideous visage of a *murdered* man, *uttering* piercing groans, and developing shocking mysteries. If a curtain is withdrawn, there is a bleeding body behind it; if a chest is opened, it contains a skeleton; if a noise is heard, somebody is receiving a deadly blow; and if a candle goes out, its place is sure to

---

[1] *light burns blue* According to tradition, blue flame is a sign of ghosts.

be supplied by a flash of lightning. Cold hands grasp us in the dark, statues are seen to move, and suits of armour walk off their pegs, while the wind whistles louder than one of Handel's choruses, and the still air is more melancholy than the dead march in Saul.[1]

Such are the dresses and decorations of a modern novel, which, as Bayes says, is calculated to "elevate and surprise"; but in doing so, carries the young reader's imagination into such a confusion of terrors as must be hurtful. It is to no great purpose, indeed, that we have forbidden our servants from telling the children stories of ghosts and hobgoblins, if we cannot put a novel into their hands which is not filled with monsters of the imagination, more frightful than are to be found in Glanvil,[2] the famous *bug-a-boo* of our forefathers.

A novel, if at all useful, ought to be a representation of human life and manners, with a view to direct the conduct in the important duties of life, and to correct its follies. But what instruction is to be reaped from the distorted ideas of lunatics, I am at a loss to conceive. Are we come to such a pass that the only commandment necessary to be repeated is, "Thou shalt do no murder"? Are the duties of life so changed that all the instruction necessary for a young person is to learn to walk at night upon the battlements of an old castle, to creep hands and feet along a narrow passage, and meet the devil at the end of it? Is the corporeal frame of the female sex so masculine and hardy that it must be softened down by the touch of dead bodies, clay-cold hands, and damp sweats? Can our young ladies be taught nothing more necessary in life than to sleep in a dungeon with venomous reptiles, walk through a ward with assassins, and carry bloody daggers in their pockets, instead of pin-cushions and needle-books?

Every absurdity has an end; and as I observe that almost all novels are of the terrific cast, I hope the insipid repetition of the same bugbears will at length work a cure. In the mean time, should any of your female readers be desirous of catching the season of terrors, she may compose two or three very pretty volumes from the following recipe:

Take—
An old castle, half of it ruinous.
A long gallery, with a great many doors, some secret ones.
Three murdered bodies, quite fresh.
As many skeletons, in chests and presses.
An old woman hanging by the neck, with her throat cut.
Assassins and desperadoes, *quant. suff.*[3]
Noises, whispers, and groans, threescore at least.

Mix them together, in the form of three volumes, to be taken at any of the watering-places before going to bed.
PROBATUM EST.[4]

from Charlotte Dacre, *Zofloya; Or, the Moor* (1806)

Charlotte Dacre was the pseudonym of Charlotte King (1771 or 72–1825), the daughter of a notorious Jewish moneylender. Rather than belonging to the women-dominated "Radcliffe school" of novels, Dacre's work is more closely aligned with the works of a primarily male category of writers, such as Matthew Lewis and the Marquis de Sade, whose approach to sexuality and horror was frequently condemned as obscene.

Critics were not pleased to see such "disgusting depravity" from a woman writer. While one reviewer suggested that "our fair authoress is afflicted with the dismal malady of maggots in the brain," another declared that "we never read a more odious and indecent performance" than *Zofloya* and urged Dacre "to leave the profession of romance writing to females who possess more delicacy of mind, more facility of style and purity of sentiments, than she, in the present work, has exhibited." The reading public

---

[1] *Handel* George Frideric Handel (1685–1759), German-born British composer known for such works as the "Hallelujah" chorus; *the dead march in Saul* The "Dead March" from Handel's oratorio *Saul* (1739) is a sorrowful piece of music frequently played at important funerals.

[2] *Glanvil* Joseph Glanvill's *Saducismus Triumphatus* (1681) compiled descriptions of the deeds of witches and argued that they had real supernatural abilities.

[3] *quant. suff* Abbreviation for the Latin "quantum sufficit," meaning "of sufficient quantity."

[4] *PROBATUM EST* Latin phrase placed at the conclusion of a recipe to indicate that the recipe has been tested and shown to work.

did not entirely share those critics' views, however; *Zofloya* was a considerable popular success.

CHAPTER 2

Before we proceed, some account must be given of Count Ardolph, as to the bent of his principles and character; as to his introduction amid the ill-fated family of Loredani, may be ascribed the origin of those misfortunes which subsequently overwhelmed them.

By birth he was German: being left early in life, from the death of an only surviving parent, to his own disposal, he quitted his native country, and visited France and England; in both places, instigated at once by inclinations naturally vicious, and the contamination of bad example, he plunged into such a stream of depravity as rendered him in a few years callous to every sentiment of honour and delicacy; but the species of crime, the dreadful and diabolical triumph which gratified his worthless heart, was to destroy, not the fair fame of an innocent, unsullied female—not to deceive and abandon a trusting, yielding maid—no, he loved to take higher and more destructive aim- his was the savage delight to intercept the happiness of wedded love—to wean from an adoring husband the regards of a pure and faithful wife—to blast with his baleful breath the happiness of a young and rising family—to seduce the best, the noblest affections of the heart, and to glory and to exult in the wide-spreading havoc he had caused. Endowed with a form cast in nature's finest mould, blest, or rather cursed, with abilities to astonish and enslave, possessed of every grace and every charm that could render a man the most dangerous, or the most perfect of his sex, he employed these rare and fascinating qualities, as a demon would put on the semblance of an angel, to mislead and to betray. Yet, even of perpetual conquest the heart of man will grow weary. Ardolph, as the fury of passion or excitement of vanity became gratified and assuaged, sunk into inanity; and, despising all he had acquired, disdaining those females whose blandishments, while they had momentarily enchanted his senses, had been incapable of touching his heart, he quitted Paris, the hot-bed of his vices and profligacy, in

disgust, and hoped by change of scene to give a zest to those feelings which excessive and unlimited gratification had blunted and almost destroyed. Yet, in change of scene, he had as yet failed of finding what he sought with an anxious and impatient curiosity—a woman who should be capable of inspiring his *heart* with continued sensation; for the proud Ardolph denied, in his mind, the possibility of the existence of such a woman. He analysed and investigated, with too contemptuous and prejudiced an eye, not to find in the sex an infinity of folly, weakness, and inconsistency. Thus it was, that having triumphed over them, he disdained his conquest, and disdained himself to have been attracted by them. …

It was one evening, that, straying pensively down an avenue in the garden, [Laurina] suddenly encountered [Ardolph]; not, however, accidentally on his side, who was forming, unconsciously to herself, a portion of her thoughts: he appeared before her, pale, haggard, and with an expression of wretchedness on his countenance deeper than any he had yet worn. Involuntarily she stopped; and, looking with kindness in his face, asked, in a soothing voice, if he were ill. An enquiry into the cause of his complaint was all he had anxiously desired, but had not yet ventured to expect: thrown for once, however, off his guard, no longer master of his violent emotions, he threw himself at her feet, and acknowledged, in hurried accents, the passion with which she had filled up his heart. Confounded, bewildered, and overcome, the trembling Laurina knew not how to fly; yet to remain an instant after an avowal so base, would, she felt, be infamous, and participating in its guilt. She made an agitated attempt to disengage herself from the Count, who on his knees grasped wildly between his hands one of hers. But in admitting to her *thoughts, even for an instant, any other man than her husband*—in listening for an instant to an acknowledgment of the passion with which she had inspired him, the unhappy Laurina had advanced one step in the path of vice, and to recede required an energy and resolution almost incompatible with the weakness of which she had been already guilty!—At length, inspired with sudden resolution, touched, as it were, by a keen sense of the impropriety of her situation, she snatched her hand from the deluding Ardolph, and, flying from his presence, sought, in the solitude of her chamber, vent to her emotions.

There, sunk in shame, and absorbed in retrospection, she dared not analyse the feelings excited in her bosom: a thousand times did she wish that Count Ardolph had never entered the Pallazzo Loredani; but the reigning, the only foible of her nature, whispered to her the brilliant triumph of captivating such an heart as his, whose every smile, whose every look, seemed a condescension from the superiority of his nature.

Oh! self-love!—dangerous and resistless flatterer!—thou immolatest at thy shrine more victims than all the artifices of man!

Earnestly did Laurina desire to be virtuous, earnestly did she pray for fortitude to preserve her from the power of temptation; but she had not strength to fly from it, and in that alone her safety would have consisted. Her mind became torn with conflicting sentiments; her reason, her gratitude, the secret and powerful ties of early habit, taught her to adore her husband; but the insidious Ardolph daily led her senses wandering, and corrupted the purity of her heart. In his company she became thoughtful and embarrassed; in his absence, restless and unhappy. The cruel Ardolph perceived his advantage, and pursued it: like a keen blood-hound he hunted the wretched victim of his pursuit, even to the brink of destruction—no friendly hand extended to save her, no guardian angel hovered nigh; and, ere she knew the extent of her danger, she was far beyond the reach of preservation.

from Jane Austen, *Northanger Abbey* (1817)

Northanger Abbey was largely written in 1798, but was kept out of print for many years as a result of a contractual dispute with the prospective publisher. Austen's brother, Henry Austen, finally purchased the rights back from that publisher in 1816, and Austen revised the manuscript that same year. She died in July of 1817, and the novel was published posthumously under Henry's oversight.

The work incorporates elements of many genres, from sentimental novel to parody; some of its most

memorable scenes mock the works of Radcliffe and her imitators. The titular abbey is the family home of "a very gentlemanlike young man" named Henry Tilney, where the novel's protagonist, a young woman named Catherine, is invited to visit. A voracious reader of Gothic novels, she comes to act—with Henry's sly encouragement—as though she is a heroine in one.

from CHAPTER 6

The following conversation, which took place between the two friends [Catherine and Isabella] in the pump-room[1] one morning, after an acquaintance of eight or nine days, is given as a specimen of their very warm attachment, and of the delicacy, discretion, originality of thought, and literary taste which marked the reasonableness of that attachment. …

"… But, my dearest Catherine, what have you been doing with yourself all this morning? Have you gone on with Udolpho?"

"Yes, I have been reading it ever since I woke; and I am got to the black veil."[2]

"Are you, indeed? How delightful! Oh! I would not tell you what is behind the black veil for the world! Are not you wild to know?"

"Oh! Yes, quite; what can it be? But do not tell me—I would not be told upon any account. I know it must be a skeleton, I am sure it is Laurentina's skeleton. Oh! I am delighted with the book! I should like to spend my whole life in reading it. I assure you, if it had not been to meet you, I would not have come away from it for all the world."

"Dear creature! How much I am obliged to you; and when you have finished Udolpho, we will read the Italian[3] together; and I have made out a list of ten or

---

[1] *pump-room* Fashionable establishment in Bath where waters from the hot springs were distributed for drinking.

[2] *Udolpho … black veil* In Ann Radcliffe's novel *The Mysteries of Udolpho* (excerpted above), the protagonist lifts a black veil to discover what she comes to believe is the corpse of the murdered Signora Laurentini. It is later revealed that she saw only a "waxen image" of a dead body.

[3] *the Italian* Another Radcliffe novel, published in 1797.

twelve more of the same kind for you."

"Have you, indeed! How glad I am! What are they all?"

"I will read you their names directly; here they are, in my pocketbook. Castle of Wolfenbach, Clermont, Mysterious Warnings, Necromancer of the Black Forest, Midnight Bell, Orphan of the Rhine, and Horrid Mysteries.[1] Those will last us some time."

"Yes, pretty well; but are they all horrid, are you sure they are all horrid?"

"Yes, quite sure; for a particular friend of mine, a Miss Andrews, a sweet girl, one of the sweetest creatures in the world, has read every one of them. ..."

from CHAPTER 21

[Catherine is a guest at Northanger Abbey. In the previous chapter, Henry teasingly predicts that she will gain entry to "a small vaulted room" in which she will find "a large, old-fashioned cabinet of ebony and gold" containing a manuscript, but will be unable to read it before her lamp extinguishes itself.]

... The fire ... died away, and Catherine, having spent the best part of an hour in her arrangements, was beginning to think of stepping into bed, when, on giving a parting glance round the room, she was struck by the appearance of a high, old-fashioned black cabinet, which, though in a situation conspicuous enough, had never caught her notice before. Henry's words, his description of the ebony cabinet which was to escape her observation at first, immediately rushed across her; and though there could be nothing really in it, there was something whimsical, it was certainly a very remarkable coincidence! She took her candle and looked closely at the cabinet. It was not absolutely ebony and gold; but it was Japan,[2] black and yellow Japan of the handsomest kind; and as she held her candle, the yellow had very much the effect of gold. The key was in the door, and she had a strange fancy to look into it; not, however, with the smallest expectation of finding any thing, but

[1] *Castle of ... Mysteries* Titles of Gothic novels published between 1793 and 1798.

[2] *Japan* Wood lacquered in a Japanese style.

it was so very odd, after what Henry had said. In short, she could not sleep till she had examined it. So, placing the candle with great caution on a chair, she seized the key with a very tremulous hand and tried to turn it; but it resisted her utmost strength. Alarmed, but not discouraged, she tried it another way; a bolt flew, and she believed herself successful; but how strangely mysterious!—the door was still immovable. She paused a moment in breathless wonder. The wind roared down the chimney, the rain beat in torrents against the windows, and every thing seemed to speak the awfulness of her situation. To retire to bed, however, unsatisfied on such a point, would be vain, since sleep must be impossible with the consciousness of a cabinet so mysteriously closed in her immediate vicinity. Again, therefore, she applied herself to the key, and after moving it in every possible way for some instants with the determined celerity of hope's last effort, the door suddenly yielded to her hand: her heart leaped with exultation at such a victory, and having thrown open each folding door, the second being secured only by bolts of less wonderful construction than the lock, though in that her eye could not discern any thing unusual, a double range of small drawers appeared in view, with some larger drawers above and below them; and in the centre, a small door, closed also with a lock and key, secured in all probability a cavity of importance.

Catherine's heart beat quick, but her courage did not fail her. With a cheek flushed by hope, and an eye straining with curiosity, her fingers grasped the handle of a drawer and drew it forth. It was entirely empty. With less alarm and greater eagerness she seized a second, a third, a fourth; each was equally empty. Not one was left unsearched, and in not one was any thing found. Well read in the art of concealing a treasure, the possibility of false linings to the drawers did not escape her, and she felt round each with anxious acuteness in vain. The place in the middle alone remained now unexplored; and though she had "never from the first had the smallest idea of finding any thing in any part of the cabinet, and was not in the least disappointed at her ill success thus far, it would be foolish not to examine it thoroughly while she was about it." It was some time however before she could unfasten the door, the same difficulty occurring in the management of this inner lock as of the outer; but at length it did open; and not vain, as hitherto, was her search; her quick eyes directly fell on a roll of paper pushed back into the further part of the cavity, apparently for concealment, and her feelings at that moment were indescribable. Her heart fluttered, her knees trembled, and her cheeks grew pale. She seized, with an unsteady hand, the precious manuscript, for half a glance sufficed to ascertain written characters; and while she acknowledged with awful sensations this striking exemplification of what Henry had foretold, resolved instantly to peruse every line before she attempted to rest.

The dimness of the light her candle emitted made her turn to it with alarm; but there was no danger of its sudden extinction; it had yet some hours to burn; and that she might not have any greater difficulty in distinguishing the writing than what its ancient date might occasion, she hastily snuffed it.[1] Alas! it was snuffed and extinguished in one. A lamp could not have expired with more awful effect. Catherine, for a few moments, was motionless with horror. It was done completely; not a remnant of light in the wick could give hope to the rekindling breath. Darkness impenetrable and immovable filled the room. A violent gust of wind, rising with sudden fury, added fresh horror to the moment. Catherine trembled from head to foot. In the pause which succeeded, a sound like receding footsteps and the closing of a distant door struck on her affrighted ear. Human nature could support no more. A cold sweat stood on her forehead, the manuscript fell from her hand, and groping her way to the bed, she jumped hastily in, and sought some suspension of agony by creeping far underneath the clothes. To close her eyes in sleep that night, she felt must be entirely out of the question. With a curiosity so justly awakened, and feelings in every way so agitated, repose must be absolutely impossible. The storm too abroad so dreadful!—She had not been used to feel alarm from wind, but now every blast seemed fraught with awful intelligence. The manuscript so wonderfully found, so wonderfully accomplishing the morning's prediction, how was it to be accounted for?—What could it contain?—to whom could it relate?—by what means could it have been so long concealed?—and how singularly strange that it should fall to her lot to discover it! Till she had made herself mistress of its contents, however, she could have neither repose nor comfort; and with the sun's first rays she was determined to peruse it. But many were the tedious hours which must yet intervene. She shuddered, tossed about in her bed, and envied every quiet sleeper. The storm still raged, and various were the noises, more terrific even than the wind, which struck at intervals on her startled ear. The very curtains of her bed seemed at one moment in motion, and at another the lock of her door was agitated, as if by the attempt of somebody to enter. Hollow murmurs seemed to creep along the gallery, and more than once her blood was chilled by the sound of distant moans. Hour after hour passed away, and the wearied Catherine had heard three proclaimed by all the clocks in the house before the tempest subsided or she unknowingly fell fast asleep.

CHAPTER 22

The housemaid's folding back her window-shutters at eight o'clock the next day was the sound which first roused Catherine; and she opened her eyes, wondering that they could ever have been closed, on objects of cheerfulness; her fire was already burning, and a bright morning had succeeded the tempest of the night. Instantaneously, with the consciousness of existence, returned her recollection of the manuscript; and springing from the bed in the very moment of the maid's going away, she eagerly collected every scattered sheet which had burst from the roll on its falling to the ground, and flew back to enjoy the luxury of their perusal on her pillow. She now plainly saw that she must not expect a manuscript of equal length with the generality of what she had shuddered over in books, for the roll, seeming to consist entirely of small disjointed

---

[1] *snuffed it* Remove the burnt portion of the candle wick (so as to allow the flame to burn more brightly).

sheets, was altogether but of trifling size, and much less than she had supposed it to be at first.

Her greedy eye glanced rapidly over a page. She started at its import. Could it be possible, or did not her senses play her false?—An inventory of linen, in coarse and modern characters, seemed all that was before her! If the evidence of sight might be trusted, she held a washing-bill in her hand. She seized another sheet, and saw the same articles with little variation; a third, a fourth, and a fifth presented nothing new. Shirts, stockings, cravats, and waistcoats faced her in each. Two others, penned by the same hand, marked an expenditure scarcely more interesting, in letters, hair-powder, shoe-string, and breeches ball.[1] And the larger sheet, which had enclosed the rest, seemed by its first cramp line, "To poultice chestnut mare"—a farrier's bill! Such was the collection of papers (left perhaps, as she could then suppose, by the negligence of a servant in the place whence she had taken them) which had filled her with expectation and alarm, and robbed her of half her night's rest! She felt humbled to the dust. Could not the adventure of the chest have taught her wisdom? A corner of it, catching her eye as she lay, seemed to rise up in judgment against her. Nothing could now be clearer than the absurdity of her recent fancies. To suppose that a manuscript of many generations back could have remained undiscovered in a room such as that, so modern, so habitable!—or that she should be the first to possess the skill of unlocking a cabinet, the key of which was open to all!

from Mary Shelley, *Frankenstein; or, the Modern Prometheus* (1818)

Mary Shelley (1797–1851) began *Frankenstein* in the summer of 1816, while staying in Switzerland with her husband and several friends; the novel was inspired by a suggestion from Lord Byron, one of the company, that each of the authors present should write a "ghost story." Two nights later,

according to Shelley's account in the preface to her novel's 1831 edition, she dreamed of the monster who would feature in *Frankenstein*, and awoke with the inspiration for her story.

Frankenstein was first published anonymously in 1818, and was immediately well-received by critics as well as by the public; Sir Walter Scott, for example, praised its "philosophical and refined use of the supernatural." The following excerpt, from the novel's first edition, offers Victor Frankenstein's account of the creation of his monster.

CHAPTER 3

... Remember, I am not recording the vision of a madman. The sun does not more certainly shine in the heavens, than that which I now affirm is true. Some miracle might have produced it, yet the stages of the discovery were distinct and probable. After days and nights of incredible labour and fatigue, I succeeded in discovering the cause of generation and life; nay, more, I became myself capable of bestowing animation upon lifeless matter. ...

I see by your eagerness, and the wonder and hope which your eyes express, my friend, that you expect to be informed of the secret with which I am acquainted; that cannot be: listen patiently until the end of my story, and you will easily perceive why I am reserved upon that subject. I will not lead you on, unguarded and ardent as I then was, to your destruction and infallible misery. Learn from me, if not by my precepts, at least by my example, how dangerous is the acquirement of knowledge, and how much happier that man is who believes his native town to be the world, than he who aspires to become greater than his nature will allow.

When I found so astonishing a power placed within my hands, I hesitated a long time concerning the manner in which I should employ it. Although I possessed the capacity of bestowing animation, yet to prepare a frame for the reception of it, with all its intricacies of fibres, muscles, and veins, still remained a work of inconceivable difficulty and labour. I doubted at first whether I should attempt the creation of a being like myself or one of simpler organization; but my

---

[1] *breeches-ball* Ball of colored substance used to cover stains on breeches.

imagination was too much exalted by my first success to permit me to doubt of my ability to give life to an animal as complex and wonderful as man. The materials at present within my command hardly appeared adequate to so arduous an undertaking; but I doubted not that I should ultimately succeed. I prepared myself for a multitude of reverses; my operations might be incessantly baffled, and at last my work be imperfect: yet, when I considered the improvement which every day takes place in science and mechanics, I was encouraged to hope my present attempts would at least lay the foundations of future success. Nor could I consider the magnitude and complexity of my plan as any argument of its impracticability. It was with these feelings that I began the creation of a human being. As the minuteness of the parts formed a great hindrance to my speed, I resolved, contrary to my first intention, to make the being of a gigantic stature; that is to say, about eight feet in height, and proportionably large. After having formed this determination, and having spent some months in successfully collecting and arranging my materials, I began.

No one can conceive the variety of feelings which bore me onwards, like a hurricane, in the first enthusiasm of success. Life and death appeared to me ideal bounds, which I should first break through, and pour a torrent of light into our dark world. A new species would bless me as its creator and source; many happy and excellent natures would owe their being to me. No father could claim the gratitude of his child so completely as I should deserve theirs. Pursuing these reflections, I thought, that if I could bestow animation upon lifeless matter, I might in process of time (although I now found it impossible) renew life where death had apparently devoted the body to corruption.

These thoughts supported my spirits, while I pursued my undertaking with unremitting ardour. My cheek had grown pale with study, and my person had become emaciated with confinement. Sometimes, on the very brink of certainty, I failed; yet still I clung to the hope which the next day or the next hour might realize. One secret which I alone possessed was the hope to which I had dedicated myself; and the moon gazed on my midnight labours, while, with unrelaxed and breathless eagerness, I pursued nature to her hiding places. Who shall conceive the horrors of my secret toil, as I dabbled among the unhallowed damps of the grave, or tortured the living animal to animate the lifeless clay? My limbs now tremble, and my eyes swim with the remembrance; but then a resistless, and almost frantic impulse, urged me forward; I seemed to have lost all soul or sensation but for this one pursuit. It was indeed but a passing trance, that only made me feel with renewed acuteness so soon as, the unnatural stimulus ceasing to operate, I had returned to my old habits. I collected bones from charnel houses; and disturbed, with profane fingers, the tremendous secrets of the human frame. In a solitary chamber, or rather cell, at the top of the house, and separated from all the other apartments by a gallery and staircase, I kept my workshop of filthy creation; my eyeballs were starting from their sockets in attending to the details of my employment. The dissecting room and the slaughter-house furnished many of my materials; and often did my human nature turn with loathing from my occupation, whilst, still urged on by an eagerness which perpetually increased, I brought my work near to a conclusion.

The summer months passed while I was thus engaged, heart and soul, in one pursuit. It was a most beautiful season; never did the fields bestow a more plentiful harvest, or the vines yield a more luxuriant vintage: but my eyes were insensible to the charms of nature. And the same feelings which made me neglect the scenes around me caused me also to forget those friends who were so many miles absent, and whom I had not seen for so long a time. I knew my silence disquieted them; and I well remembered the words of my father: "I know that while you are pleased with yourself, you will think of us with affection, and we shall hear regularly from you. You must pardon me, if I regard any interruption in your correspondence as a proof that your other duties are equally neglected."

I knew well therefore what would be my father's feelings; but I could not tear my thoughts from my employment, loathsome in itself, but which had taken an irresistible hold of my imagination. I wished, as it were, to procrastinate all that related to my feelings of

GOTHIC LITERATURE, 1764–1830   281

affection until the great object, which swallowed up every habit of my nature, should be completed.

I then thought that my father would be unjust if he ascribed my neglect to vice, or faultiness on my part; but I am now convinced that he was justified in conceiving that I should not be altogether free from blame. A human being in perfection ought always to preserve a calm and peaceful mind, and never to allow passion or a transitory desire to disturb his tranquillity. I do not think that the pursuit of knowledge is an exception to this rule. If the study to which you apply yourself has a tendency to weaken your affections, and to destroy your taste for those simple pleasures in which no alloy can possibly mix, then that study is certainly unlawful, that is to say, not befitting the human mind. If this rule were always observed; if no man allowed any pursuit whatsoever to interfere with the tranquillity of his domestic affections, Greece had not been enslaved; Cæsar would have spared his country; America would have been discovered more gradually; and the empires of Mexico and Peru had not been destroyed.

But I forget that I am moralizing in the most interesting part of my tale; and your looks remind me to proceed.

My father made no reproach in his letters; and only took notice of my silence by inquiring into my occupations more particularly than before. Winter, spring, and summer, passed away during my labours; but I did not watch the blossom or the expanding leaves—sights which before always yielded me supreme delight, so deeply was I engrossed in my occupation. The leaves of that year had withered before my work drew near to a close; and now every day shewed me more plainly how well I had succeeded. But my enthusiasm was checked by my anxiety, and I appeared rather like one doomed by slavery to toil in the mines, or any other unwholesome trade, than an artist occupied by his favourite employment. Every night I was oppressed by a slow fever, and I became nervous to a most painful degree; a disease that I regretted the more because I had hitherto enjoyed most excellent health, and had always boasted of the firmness of my nerves. But I believed that exercise and amusement would soon drive away such symptoms; and I promised myself both of these, when my creation should be complete.

CHAPTER 4

It was on a dreary night of November, that I beheld the accomplishment of my toils. With an anxiety that almost amounted to agony, I collected the instruments of life around me, that I might infuse a spark of being into the lifeless thing that lay at my feet. It was already one in the morning; the rain pattered dismally against the panes, and my candle was nearly burnt out, when, by the glimmer of the half-extinguished light, I saw the dull yellow eye of the creature open; it breathed hard, and a convulsive motion agitated its limbs.

How can I describe my emotions at this catastrophe, or how delineate the wretch whom with such infinite pains and care I had endeavoured to form? His limbs were in proportion, and I had selected his features as beautiful. Beautiful!—Great God! His yellow skin scarcely covered the work of muscles and arteries beneath; his hair was of a lustrous black, and flowing; his teeth of a pearly whiteness; but these luxuriances only formed a more horrid contrast with his watery eyes, that seemed almost of the same colour as the dun white sockets in which they were set, his shrivelled complexion, and straight black lips.

The different accidents of life are not so changeable as the feelings of human nature. I had worked hard for nearly two years, for the sole purpose of infusing life into an inanimate body. For this I had deprived myself of rest and health. I had desired it with an ardour that far exceeded moderation; but now that I had finished, the beauty of the dream vanished, and breathless horror and disgust filled my heart. Unable to endure the aspect of the being I had created, I rushed out of the room, and continued a long time traversing my bed-chamber, unable to compose my mind to sleep. At length lassitude succeeded to the tumult I had before endured; and I threw myself on the bed in my clothes, endeavouring to seek a few moments of forgetfulness. But it was in vain: I slept indeed, but I was disturbed by the wildest dreams. I thought I saw Elizabeth,[1] in the bloom of

---

[1] *Elizabeth* Elizabeth Lavenza, Victor's cousin, who is raised alongside him. He marries her later in the novel, but the monster murders her on their wedding night.

Theodor von Holst, frontispiece from the 1831 edition of *Frankenstein*. A caption placed below this image in the 1831 edition reads "By the glimmer of the half-extinguished light, I saw the dull, yellow eye of the creature open: it breathed hard, and a convulsive motion agitated its limbs. ... I rushed out of the room."

health, walking in the streets of Ingolstadt. Delighted and surprised, I embraced her; but as I imprinted the first kiss on her lips, they became livid with the hue of death; her features appeared to change, and I thought that I held the corpse of my dead mother in my arms; a shroud enveloped her form, and I saw the grave-worms crawling in the folds of the flannel. I started from my

sleep with horror; a cold dew covered my forehead, my teeth chattered, and every limb became convulsed; when, by the dim and yellow light of the moon, as it forced its way through the window-shutters, I beheld the wretch—the miserable monster whom I had created. He held up the curtain of the bed; and his eyes, if eyes they may be called, were fixed on me. His jaws opened, and he muttered some inarticulate sounds, while a grin wrinkled his cheeks. He might have spoken, but I did not hear; one hand was stretched out, seemingly to detain me, but I escaped, and rushed down stairs. I took refuge in the court-yard belonging to the house which I inhabited; where I remained during the rest of the night, walking up and down in the greatest agitation, listening attentively, catching and fearing each sound as if it were to announce the approach of the demoniacal corpse to which I had so miserably given life. …

from Charles Maturin, *Melmoth the Wanderer* (1820)

Charles Robert Maturin (1782–1824) attempted to combine a career in the Irish Anglican clergy with a clandestine career as a Gothic novelist and playwright; not surprisingly, the balancing act proved difficult to sustain. *Melmoth the Wanderer*, the work for which Maturin is best known, received a lukewarm reception upon its publication, but toward the end of the nineteenth century came to be widely appreciated as Maturin's best work—and as one of the greatest Gothic novels of its period. The novel takes the form of a series of nested stories discovered by John Melmoth, who attempts to understand the mystery of his ancestor, the titular "Wanderer." As readers eventually learn, Melmoth the Wanderer has made a bargain with the devil to gain 150 years of mortal life—which will end in his damnation unless he is able to convince another person to take his place.

At the beginning of the novel, John Melmoth sees a 170-year-old portrait of an ancestor in the home of his dying uncle, who tells him that "the original is still alive." Upon his uncle's death, Melmoth finds instructions in the will asking that the portrait be destroyed.

CHAPTER 3

… [Melmoth] saw the picture gazing at him from its canvas. He was within ten inches of it as he sat, and the proximity appeared increased by the strong light that was accidentally thrown on it, and its being the only representation of a human figure in the room. Melmoth felt for a moment as if he were about to receive an explanation from its lips.

He gazed on it in return—all was silent in the house—they were alone together. The illusion subsided at length; and as the mind rapidly passes to opposite extremes, he remembered the injunction of his uncle to destroy the portrait. He seized it; his hand shook at first, but the mouldering canvas appeared to assist him in the effort. He tore it from the frame with a cry half terrific, half triumphant; it fell at his feet, and he shuddered as it fell. He expected to hear some fearful sounds, some unimaginable breathings of prophetic horror, follow this act of sacrilege, for such he felt it, to tear the portrait of his ancestor from his native walls. He paused and listened—"There was no voice, nor any that answered"[1]—but as the wrinkled and torn canvas fell to the floor, its undulations gave the portrait the appearance of smiling. Melmoth felt horror indescribable at this transient and imaginary resuscitation of the figure. He caught it up, rushed into the next room, tore, cut, and hacked it in every direction, and eagerly watched the fragments that burned like tinder in the turf-fire which had been lit in his room. As Melmoth saw the last blaze, he threw himself into bed, in hope of a deep and intense sleep. He had done what was required of him, and felt exhausted both in mind and body; but his slumber was not so sound as he had hoped for. The sullen light of the turf-fire, burning but never blazing, disturbed him every moment. He turned and turned, but still there was the same red light glaring on, but not illuminating, the dusky furniture of the apartment. The wind was high that night, and as the creaking door swung on its hinges, every noise seemed like the sound of a hand struggling with the lock, or of a foot pausing on the threshold. But (for Melmoth never could decide) was it in a dream or not, that he saw the figure of his ancestor appear at the door?—hesitatingly as he saw him at first on the night of his uncle's death—saw him enter the room, approach his bed, and heard him whisper, "You have burned me,

---

[1] *There was … answered* See 1 Kings 18.26.

then; but those are flames I can survive. I am alive—I am beside you." Melmoth started, sprung from his bed—it was broad day-light. He looked round—there was no human being in the room but himself. He felt a slight pain in the wrist of his right arm. He looked at it, it was black and blue, as from the recent gripe of a strong hand. ...

from Ann Radcliffe, "On the Supernatural in Poetry" (1826)

A few years after Radcliffe died, the following essay was published in *The New Monthly*. Taking the form of a conversation between characters named W—— and S——, the essay draws most of its examples from depictions of the supernatural in Shakespeare's tragedies; the following excerpt contrasts the depictions of ghosts in *Macbeth* and *Hamlet*. In making this contrast, Radcliffe draws her famous distinction between "horror" and "terror."

... [W——:] "... Who ever suffered for the ghost of Banquo,[1] the gloomy and sublime kind of terror, which that of *Hamlet*[2] calls forth? ... There, though deep pity mingles with our surprise and horror, we experience a far less degree of interest, and that interest too of an inferior kind. The union of grandeur and obscurity, which Mr. Burke[3] describes as a sort of tranquillity

tinged with terror, and which causes the sublime, is to be found only in *Hamlet*; or in scenes where circumstances of the same kind prevail."

"That may be," said Mr. S——, "and I perceive you are not one of those who contend that obscurity does not make any part of the sublime."

"They must be men of very cold imaginations," said W——, "with whom certainty is more terrible than surmise. Terror and horror are so far opposite, that the first expands the soul, and awakens the faculties to a high degree of life; the other contracts, freezes, and nearly annihilates them. I apprehend that neither Shakespeare nor Milton by their fictions, nor Mr. Burke by his reasoning, anywhere looked to positive horror as a source of the sublime, though they all agree that terror is a very high one; and where lies the great difference between horror and terror, but in the uncertainty and obscurity, that accompany the first, respecting the dreaded evil?" ...

---

[1] *Banquo* Character in *Macbeth* whose ghost appears in Act 3, Scene 4.

[2] *Hamlet* Hamlet's father's ghost appears in *Hamlet* 1.1, 1.4–5, and 3.4.

[3] *Mr. Burke* See Edmund Burke, *A Philosophical Enquiry into the Origin of Our Ideas of the Sublime and Beautiful* (1757), especially the excerpts from Part 2 included elsewhere in this anthology.

MARIA EDGEWORTH
1768 – 1849

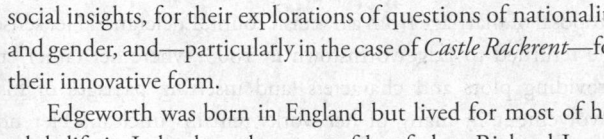

A leading Anglo-Irish writer and intellectual for over half a century, Maria Edgeworth was and is best known for her novels, which in her own time were as widely read as those of her contemporaries Walter Scott and Jane Austen. Her works of fiction have been highly valued for their social insights, for their explorations of questions of nationality and gender, and—particularly in the case of *Castle Rackrent*—for their innovative form.

Edgeworth was born in England but lived for most of her adult life in Ireland on the estate of her father, Richard Lovell Edgeworth—who was himself a leading intellectual, as well as an inventor and, briefly, a politician. She was the third child of Anna Maria Elers Edgeworth, who died in 1773, shortly after giving birth to her fifth child; Richard Lovell Edgeworth was married three times more, and became father to twenty-one children in all. Maria spent most of the years 1773–82 in boarding school, first in Derby and later in London. She received little of her father's attentions until 1782, when she joined her father, stepmother, and siblings at the Edgeworth's Irish estate at Edgeworthstown. Young Maria helped her father with estate business, and began to forge a professional and intellectual partnership with him that would last the remainder of his life.

In 1795 Edgeworth brought out her first publication, *Letters to Literary Ladies*, a series of letters about the importance of educating women—a subject of personal importance to Edgeworth, who was responsible for the education of thirteen of her younger siblings. The following year she published a collection for children, *The Parent's Assistant*, offering a series of rigorously didactic moral stories and a play. Other works for children followed: *Moral Tales for Young People* (1801), for example, offered tales for older children, this time in a less didactic narrative mode. Together with her father, Edgeworth also produced a series of *Essays on Practical Education* (1798).

Edgeworth achieved considerable literary success with her first work of fiction for adults: *Castle Rackrent, An Hibernian Tale Taken from the Facts and from the Manners of the Irish Squires Before the Year 1782* (1800). She first published this short novel anonymously, revealing herself as the author only with the publication of the third edition of 1801.

Her second novel was the three-volume *Belinda* (1801), a work that is as much about female friendship as is about the search for marriage. It attracted considerable attention purely for its literary qualities—in Austen's *Northanger Abbey* it is grouped along with two novels by Frances Burney as examples of works "in which the greatest powers of the mind are displayed, in which the most thorough knowledge of human nature, the happiest delineation of its varieties, the liveliest effusions of wit and humour, are conveyed to the world in the best-chosen language." It also attracted considerable attention for its depictions of inter-racial romance; in the early editions of the novel the heroine agrees to marry a mixed race landowner, whose black servant Juba is to wed an English farm girl. When Edgeworth prepared a new edition for inclusion in Anna Laetitia Barbauld's "English

Novelists" series, however, she revised the work substantially so as to remove these controversial romantic links. She explained the 1810 revisions in the following way in a letter to Barbauld:

> My father says that gentlemen have horrors upon this subject, and would draw conclusions very unfavourable to a female writer who appeared to recommend such unions; as I do not understand the subject, I trust to his better judgement.

As a result of their joint literary success, father and daughter increasingly began to move in literary circles. In 1802, the Edgeworths visited Brussels and Paris, where Maria received—and declined—a proposal of marriage from a Swedish count, Edelcrantz. Her sense of duty to her family prevailed and she returned to Edgeworthstown in 1803, where her father encouraged her writings, sometimes providing plots and characters, and inserting passages of his own. (The precise extent of his involvement in many of her works remains unclear.) Her novels continued to earn handsome royalties, particularly the six-volume *Tales of Fashionable Life*. With *The Absentee* (1812) she returned to the topic of Irish landlords and their tenants. That novel helped to inspire Edgeworth's friend Sir Walter Scott to write *Waverley* (the first of his own historical novels); Scott later wrote that his hope had been "in some distant degree to emulate the admirable Irish portraits drawn by Miss Edgeworth."

Edgeworth's *Patronage* (1814), in some respects her most ambitious novel, was published in four volumes. In 1817 she published two shorter novels—*Ormond*, in which she further broadened her depiction of Irish life; and *Harrington*. She had been prompted to write *Harrington* after receiving a letter from a reader, Rachel Mordecai, who noted Edgeworth's tendency to portray Jews in unsympathetic fashion in her fiction and wondered that a writer "who on all other subjects shows such justice and liberality, should on one [subject] appear biased by prejudice." In *Harrington* Edgeworth responded with sympathetic portrayals of Jewish characters and, in her title character, with a portrayal of a virulent anti-Semite who comes to see the error of his ways.

In 1817 Edgeworth's father died, and she completed his *Memoirs* on his behalf. In 1826 she resumed the management of the family estate in Ireland on behalf of her brother, but she continued to write. Among her later works were *Helen* (1834), her last novel, and *Orlandino* (1848), a story that she sold to "earn a little money for our parish poor." This was during the Great Famine (1845–49); though Edgeworth's political sympathies had become more conservative with the years, she was still concerned to raise awareness of the plight of the Irish peasantry—and to ameliorate their distress. She died at home in Edgeworthstown, aged 81, after complaining of heart trouble.

The popularity of most of Edgeworth's writings declined significantly in the Victorian era, and—though *Castle Rackrent* continued to find readers in every era—she remained a largely neglected writer until the latter part of the twentieth century. Since the 1980s, however, she has begun to again attract a wide readership—and to receive a great deal of attention from scholars. An extraordinarily wide-ranging writer and thinker, she continues to fascinate in part because of apparent contradictions. Courageous innovation; dutiful obeisance to patriarchal authority; impassioned advocacy for the poor and the oppressed; sincere respect for aristocratic convention; extraordinary open-mindedness on issues of gender, nationality, and race—all these are characteristic of Edgeworth and her highly individual genius.

Castle Rackrent

Castle Rackrent—Maria Edgeworth's first novel, and the work for which she was and is best known—occupies a most unusual place in the history of English fiction. It has sometimes been called the first historical novel in English literature, yet in its tone it more closely resembles a comedy of manners than anything in the genre that has come to be known as "the historical novel." It has been identified as the first of other lines as well—the first English novel written in a non-standard dialect, the first "provincial" or "regional" novel, and the first in what developed into the "big house" tradition of novels focused on the lives of the Anglo-Irish Protestant landholding class that dominated much of Ireland for centuries. Its innovative use of an unreliable narrator makes it also, arguably, an important milestone in the development of the novel form as a whole.

On its publication at the dawn of the nineteenth century, *Castle Rackrent* was taken by many English readers to be little more than a sort of amusing exhibition of Irish manners and life—"a very pleasant, good-humoured and successful representation of the eccentricities of our Irish neighbours," to quote one reviewer. It was reported that King George III, upon first reading the novel, announced, "I know something now of my Irish subjects." By 1831, Edgeworth was being gently criticized for her supposed "careful avoidance of political topics, the bearing of which on Irish society is too marked and important to be altogether neglected." In the late twentieth and twenty-first centuries, on the other hand, many literary scholars have seen the novel as being highly subversive—as "a critique of patriarchy," a novel that "undermines every convention of the realist novel," and a work that challenges "the entire social system" of the time.[1]

One thing readers of every era have agreed on is that the novel accomplished something fresh in its portrayal of the Irish dialect and overall "Irishness." Walter Scott was persuaded to embark on his *Waverley* series of historical novels set in Scotland in part because of Edgeworth's example. The warm reception that *Castle Rackrent* and others of Edgeworth's novels had met with—not as historical novels in the sense that he ended up writing them, but as novels of Irish life—encouraged him to think he might, as an Anglo-Scottish writer, do for Scotland what Edgeworth had done for Ireland:

> Something might be attempted for my own country, of the same kind [as] that which Miss Edgeworth so fortunately achieved for Ireland—something which might introduce her natives to those of the sister kingdom, in a more favourable light than they had been placed hitherto, and tend to procure sympathy for their virtues and indulgence for their foibles.

Castle Rackrent chronicles the declining fortunes and ultimate ruin of the Rackrent family through the mishandling of the estate by a series of incompetent and irresponsible heirs. The family name itself references the Rackrents' failings as landlords, "rack-rent" being rent set at an extortionately high level—akin to putting tenants on the "rack," an ancient torture device. Such practices were typical of the Anglo-Irish landlords, the Protestant English-speaking families living or holding land in Ireland (a class also sometimes referred to as the Protestant Ascendancy, or simply the Ascendancy). Edgeworth, herself Anglo-Irish, had firsthand knowledge on which to found her novel, having assisted her father in the operation of the family estate at Edgeworthstown, which had suffered from mismanagement during a period of several years when the family had been absentee landlords.

The Edgeworths' own circumstances in many ways reflected those of the Anglo-Irish landlord class as a whole. The family had been granted the estate in 1585 by the English government in one of a long series of moves by the English designed to establish complete control over Ireland. In order to encourage colonization by established English families, vast tracts of land were confiscated from native Gaelic Irish owners, who were also predominantly Catholic; with their land handed over to

---

[1] See, respectively, Sandra Gilbert and Susan Gubar, *The Madwoman in the Attic*, 1979; Katherine O'Donnell, "Castle Stopgap: Historical Reality, Literary Realism, and Oral Culture," *Eighteenth Century Fiction* 22.1, 2009; and Marilyn Butler, "Edgeworth's Ireland: History, Popular Culture, and Secret Codes," *NOVEL: A Forum on Fiction* 34.2, 2001.

English Protestants, the previous owners were forced to move elsewhere, or to become tenants on the land they had previously owned. Such grants were often very large—the Edgeworths' estate amounted to 600 acres—and by 1700 the Anglo-Irish owned more than four-fifths of Ireland, though they constituted less than one fifth of the population.[1]

If the Edgeworths' background was typical of Anglo-Irish landholders, though, the manner in which they managed the estate from 1782 onwards was much less so. The comic degree of mismanagement depicted in *Castle Rackrent* is no doubt exaggerated, but it is an exaggeration of truth; whether controlled by absentee owners or not, a great many Irish estates seem to have been irresponsibly managed for generation after generation. The Edgeworths, by contrast, made significant investments to improve both the productivity of the estate and the living conditions of the tenants, made efforts to help the workers educate themselves, and endeavored to assist the children of their tenants in finding employment if they left the estate.

To what degree the tales of past generations of Rackrents may have been based on tales of past generations of Edgeworths is not entirely clear; Edgeworth herself attested in a letter she wrote years later[2] that "the only character drawn from the life" in the novel is Thady Quirk, whose character she based on John Langan, the Irish steward at Edgeworthstown. Thady, the novel's unreliable narrator, is in several respects at the heart of *Castle Rackrent*. While the various Rackrent men and women are memorable characters, it is the comic narrative style of "Old Thady," the family servant, that carries the novel. The comedy of his narration, however, often conflicts with the horrific content being narrated—"middle men who grind the face of the poor," a lord who keeps his wife under lock and key for seven years, and so on. Many readers have wondered how to interpret Thady's own attitude toward these events. Is he as naïve as he sometimes seems? Is he truly as devoted as he maintains to the feckless family he serves? Or does he, as some critics have suggested, merely act the part?

One of Thady's most immediately entertaining qualities is his way with words. In recent generations it has become commonplace for novels written in English to reproduce more or less faithfully a dialect likely to be unfamiliar to many readers, but in 1800 it was unheard-of for a novelist to portray characters speaking in regional or colloquial dialect—let alone to have an entire novel narrated by such a character. Conceptually, some of the ground had been prepared for this sort of development by what Wordsworth described as the "experiments" he and Coleridge put forward in *Lyrical Ballads* (1798): poems "written chiefly with a view to ascertain how far the language of conversation of the middle and lower classes [may be] adapted for the purposes of poetic pleasure." But the poems in that volume, much as they eschew elevated language, are not written in dialect; indeed, the vocabulary employed by Wordsworth and Coleridge includes few words that would not have been immediately clear to any educated reader. Edgeworth was truly breaking ground in writing an entire novel in the voice of a narrator who speaks in a non-standard dialect—and thereby preparing the way not only for Scott but also for Emily Brontë, Charles Dickens, and many others who followed.

Edgeworth was evidently concerned that the approach she had taken linguistically might be considered *too* unusual; she initially included numerous footnotes and then added an extensive glossary,[3] ostensibly to make "intelligible to the English reader" various "terms and idiomatic

---

[1] For an overview of relevant developments in Irish history during this period, see the introduction to the "In Context" materials for this text, available in the online portion of the anthology.

[2] See the "In Context" materials mentioned above.

[3] The glossary was added almost literally at the last minute; the body of the book had already been typeset and sent to press. It was at that time common practice to set and print the prefatory material to a book last; such material would always be paginated separately, in Roman numerals, so that last minute additions to this material   [continued ...]

phrases." In some cases—*canting*, for example, or *barrack-room*—the glossary does exactly that, and nothing more. But in many of the entries the explanations and commentary go far beyond simple glosses. Such is the case, for example, with what the editor terms "the feudal custom" of duty work, some of the practices associated with which are described as "the height of absurd injustice."

The glossary and annotations are only part of the extensive framing material that surrounds the novel; the body of the novel also begins with a "Preface" and concludes with four paragraphs in which the reader is again addressed directly. All this framing material is by "the editor," which prompts a number of questions. Are we to take what is written by "the editor" as representing the views of Edgeworth herself? Has she created in the persona of the editor another filter, whose commentary we should no more take to be reliable than we should that of Thady?

Discussions of the ways in which the framing material may relate to the body of the novel have very largely focused on the context in which the book was written. Thady's narrative ends almost twenty years before *Castle Rackrent*'s publication; the plot concludes in 1782, the year Edgeworth arrived in Ireland as a youth, and also the year in which a new constitution granted the Irish Parliament a larger degree of independence from England. The editor's comments in the Preface suggest that readers are to take the stories of the Rackrents—and, by extension, of the Irish generally—as reflective of a bygone era: "the manners depicted in the following pages are not those of the present age." Yet the first of the editor's four paragraphs appended to the conclusion of Thady's account seem to imply that the account offers a "specimen of manners and characters" in Ireland that are far from having entirely disappeared.

Much has been made of the book being issued shortly before the vote regarding the Acts of Union, which would abolish the Irish Parliament and create the United Kingdom of Great Britain and Ireland. Edgeworth's English "editor" refers to the proposed union both in the final sentence of the preface and in the novel's penultimate paragraph: "It is a problem of difficult solution to determine whether a union will hasten or retard the amelioration of this country." Is Edgeworth herself likely to have shared the view of her "editor" that whether or not the union was a good idea was simply "a problem of difficult solution"? She has often been presumed to have favored a union between England and Ireland, on the grounds that the Irish majority would have a better chance of being treated well by the English than by the Anglo-Irish Ascendancy, and that remains a plausible view. But there is no firm evidence that she supported the Acts of Union—let alone that she intended *Castle Rackrent* to be interpreted as in any way arguing for their passage. (Her father, Richard Lovell Edgeworth, is on record as having favored closer ties between England and Ireland in principle, and, as a member of the Irish Parliament, was in a position to vote on the measure; put off by the strong-arm tactics the British used to ensure passage of the bill in the Irish Parliament, however, he did not cast a vote.)

It seems entirely safe to conclude that Edgeworth genuinely intended the novel to portray the Irish in ways that would lead her readers to better understand Irish manners—and to feel some sympathy for the Irish people as a whole. But should the novel also be read as a far stronger statement—as an indictment of the systemic cruelty with which the Irish peasantry were exploited? To what extent did the book's tone lead early nineteenth-century readers to gloss over whatever political content it may contain? And for readers of any era, might the text—despite, or perhaps in part because of its entertaining comedy—be read less as sympathetic than as condescending (in the modern sense of the word) towards the Irish people? *Castle Rackrent* is a text that continues to support multiple readings—and to prompt difficult questions.

---

would not affect pagination of the body of the book. The first edition of *Castle Rackrent* included the glossary at the end of this prefatory material; it is only in later editions that the glossary appears where one would expect it to be, at the back of the book.

A Note on the Text

The first edition of *Castle Rackrent* was published anonymously in January 1800. The book enjoyed considerable success from the start and went through numerous editions in the first three decades of the century. These were for the most part reprints with at most a small number of corrections made; Edgeworth (whose name first appeared on the title page with the publication of the third edition in 1801) worked with publishers to correct minor mistakes and in a few cases alter wording. For the 1832 collected edition of *Tales and Novels of Maria Edgeworth*, published by Baldwin & Craddock, she made many revisions to the punctuation to bring the book more in line with what had become modern practice. In early editions, Thady's narrative is punctuated by numerous dashes (see page 294 for a sample); Edgeworth eliminated many of these in the 1832 edition. Though the present editors gave some consideration to using an early edition as a base text, there can be little question that the 1832 edition is considerably more readable for a twenty-first-century audience. Given that the dialect already presents significant barriers for modern readers, the editors of this anthology have decided to do as other modern editors have done, and use the 1832 edition as a base text. Beyond that, the editors have very largely followed the general anthology practice of modernizing spelling and punctuation, but have left some of the original punctuation in place to try to convey something of the flavor of the original, and have retained Edgeworth's practice of not starting a new paragraph for each new speaker in passages of direct speech.

⌘ ⌘ ⌘

Castle Rackrent
An Hibernian[1] Tale Taken from Facts, and from the Manners of the Irish Squires, Before the Year 1782

PREFACE[2]

The prevailing taste of the public for anecdote has been censured and ridiculed by critics, who aspire to the character of superior wisdom: but if we consider it in a proper point of view, this taste is an incontestable proof of the good sense and profoundly philosophic temper of the present times. Of the numbers who study, or at least who read history, how few derive any advantage from their labours! The heroes of history are so decked out by the fine fancy of the professed historian; they talk in such measured prose, and act from such sublime[3] or such diabolical motives, that few have sufficient taste, wickedness or heroism, to sympathize in their fate. Besides, there is much uncertainty even in the best authenticated ancient or modern histories; and that love of truth, which in some minds is innate and immutable, necessarily leads to a love of secret memoirs and private anecdotes. We cannot judge either of the feelings or of the characters of men with perfect accuracy from their actions or their appearance in public; it is from their careless conversations, their half finished sentences, that we may hope with the greatest probability of success to discover their real characters. The life of a great or of a little man written by himself, the familiar letters, the diary of any individual published by his friends, or by his enemies after his decease, are esteemed important literary curiosities. We are surely justified in

---

[1] *Hibernian* Hibernia was the ancient Roman name for the island of Ireland; it began to be used again in the eighteenth century.

[2] *PREFACE* It was once thought that the Preface to *Castle Rackrent* might have been largely written by Maria Edgeworth's father, R.L. Edgeworth, who is known to have helped to shape a number of her other writings. Recent scholars, however, have generally concluded that, while Edgeworth may well have consulted her father, the preface and other paratextual materials accompanying *Castle Rackrent* are—like the text itself—Edgeworth's own work, and not the product of a full collaboration with her father.

[3] *sublime* Lofty.

this eager desire to collect the most minute facts relative to the domestic lives, not only of the great and good, but even of the worthless and insignificant, since it is only by a comparison of their actual happiness or misery in the privacy of domestic life, that we can form a just estimate of the real reward of virtue, or the real punishment of vice. That the great are not as happy as they seem, that the external circumstances of fortune and rank do not constitute felicity, is asserted by every moralist; the historian can seldom, consistently with his dignity, pause to illustrate this truth: it is therefore to the biographer we must have recourse. After we have beheld splendid characters playing their parts on the great theatre of the world, with all the advantages of stage effect and decoration, we anxiously beg to be admitted behind the scenes, that we may take a nearer view of the actors and actresses.

Some may perhaps imagine, that the value of biography depends upon the judgment and taste of the biographer; but on the contrary it may be maintained, that the merits of a biographer are inversely as the extent of his intellectual powers and of his literary talents. A plain unvarnished tale is preferable to the most highly ornamented narrative. Where we see that a man has the power, we may naturally suspect that he has the will to deceive us, and those who are used to literary manufacture know how much is often sacrificed to the rounding of a period or the pointing of an antithesis.

That the ignorant may have their prejudices as well as the learned cannot be disputed, but we see and despise vulgar errors: we never bow to the authority of him who has no great name to sanction his absurdities. The partiality which blinds a biographer to the defects of his hero, in proportion as it is gross[1] ceases to be dangerous; but if it be concealed by the appearance of candour, which men of great abilities best know how to assume, it endangers our judgment sometimes, and sometimes our morals. If her Grace the Duchess of Newcastle, instead of penning her lord's elaborate eulogium, had undertaken to write the life of Savage, we should not have been in any danger of mistaking an idle,

ungrateful libertine, for a man of genius and virtue.[2] The talents of a biographer are often fatal to his reader. For these reasons the public often judiciously countenances those who, without sagacity to discriminate character, without elegance of style to relieve the tediousness of narrative, without enlargement of mind to draw any conclusions from the facts they relate, simply pour forth anecdotes and retail[3] conversations, with all the minute prolixity of a gossip in a country town.

The author[4] of the following memoirs has upon these grounds fair claims to the public favour and attention: he was an illiterate old steward, whose partiality to *the family* in which he was bred and born must be obvious to the reader. He tells the history of the Rackrent family in his vernacular idiom,[5] and in the full confidence that Sir Patrick, Sir Murtagh, Sir Kit, and Sir Condy Rackrent's affairs will be as interesting to all the world as they were to himself. Those who were acquainted with the manners of a certain class of the gentry of Ireland some years ago will want no evidence of the truth of honest Thady's narrative; to those who are totally unacquainted with Ireland, the following memoirs will perhaps be scarcely intelligible, or probably they may appear perfectly incredible. For the information of the *ignorant* English reader a few notes have been subjoined by the editor, and he had it once in contemplation to translate the language of Thady into plain English; but Thady's idiom is incapable of translation, and besides, the authenticity of his story would have been more exposed to doubt if it were not told in his own characteristic manner. Several years ago he related to the editor the history of the Rackrent family, and it was with some difficulty that he

1 *gross* Obvious or conspicuous.

2 *If her Grace ... genius and virtue* English poet and scientist Margaret Cavendish, Duchess of Newcastle-upon-Tyne, in 1667 published a flattering biography of her husband, William Cavendish. Samuel Johnson was similarly sympathetic to his subject in his *Life of Savage* (1744), a biography of the author's friend, poet Richard Savage, who became renowned as a murderer after mortally wounding his opponent in a brawl; *eulogium* Tribute to or high praise of a person; *libertine* Immoral, sensually indulgent person (usually a man).

3 *retail* Recount.

4 *The author* I.e., the narrator, Thady Quirk.

5 *idiom* Particular mode of speech of an individual or of a group of people.

was persuaded to have it committed to writing; however, his feelings for "*the honour of the family*," as he expressed himself, prevailed over his habitual laziness, and he at length completed the narrative which is now laid before the public.

The editor hopes his readers will observe, that these are "tales of other times"; that the manners depicted in the following pages are not those of the present age: the race of the Rackrents has long since been extinct in Ireland, and the drunken Sir Patrick, the litigious Sir Murtagh, the fighting Sir Kit, and the slovenly Sir Condy are characters which could no more be met with at present in Ireland, than Squire Western or Parson Trulliber[1] in England. There is a time when individuals can bear to be rallied[2] for their past follies and absurdities, after they have acquired new habits and a new consciousness. Nations as well as individuals gradually lose attachment to their identity, and the present generation is amused rather than offended by the ridicule that is thrown upon their ancestors.

Probably we shall soon have it in our power, in a hundred instances, to verify the truth of these observations.

When Ireland loses her identity by an union with Great Britain, she will look back with a smile of good-humoured complacency on the Sir Kits and Sir Condys of her former existence.

1800

Castle Rackrent

Monday Morning*[3]

Having, out of friendship for the family, upon whose estate, praised be Heaven! I and mine have lived rent-

---

free time out of mind, voluntarily undertaken to publish the *Memoirs of the Rackrent Family*, I think it my duty to say a few words, in the first place, concerning myself. My real name is Thady Quirk, though in the family I have always been known by no other than "honest Thady"—afterwards, in the time of Sir Murtagh, deceased, I remember to hear them calling me "old Thady;" and now I'm come to "poor Thady"—for I wear a long great coat[4] winter and summer, which is very handy, as I never put my arms into the sleeves; they are as good as new, though come Holantide[5] next, I've had it these seven years; it holds on by a single button

[4] [Edgeworth's note]   The cloak, or mantle, as described by Thady, is of high antiquity. Spenser, in his *View of the State of Ireland*, proves that it is not, as some have imagined, peculiarly derived from the Scythians, but that "most nations of the world anciently used the mantle; for the Jews used it, as you may read of Elias's mantle, &c.; the Chaldees also used it, as you may read in Diodorus; the Egyptians likewise used it, as you may read in Herodotus, and may be gathered by the description of Berenice, in the Greek Commentary upon Callimachus; the Greeks also used it anciently, as appeareth by Venus's mantle lined with stars, though afterwards they changed the form thereof into their cloaks, called Pallai, as some of the Irish also use; and the ancient Latins and Romans used it, as you may read in Virgil, who was a very great antiquary, that Evander, when Æneas came to him at his feast, did entertain and feast him, sitting on the ground, and lying on mantles; insomuch as he useth the very word "mantile" for a mantle—Humi mantilia sternunt—so that it seemeth that the mantle was a general habit to most nations, and not proper to the Scythians only."

Spenser knew the convenience of the said mantle, as housing, bedding, and clothing:

Iren. Because the commodity doth not countervail the discommodity; for the inconveniences which thereby do arise, are much more many; for it is is a fit house for an outlaw, a meet bed for a rebel, and an apt cloak for a thief. First—the outlaw being, for his many crimes and villainies, banished from the towns and houses of honest men, and wandering in waste places, far from danger of law—maketh his mantle his house, and under it covereth himself from the wrath of Heaven, from the offence of the earth, and from the sight of men. When it raineth, it is his penthouse; when it bloweth, it is his tent; when it freezeth, it is his tabernacle. In summer he can wear it loose; in winter he can wrap it close; at all times he can use it—never heavy, never cumbersome. Likewise for a rebel it is as serviceable; for in this war that he maketh (if at least it deserve the name of war), when he still flieth from his foe, and lurketh in the *thick woods*, (this should be *black bogs*) and straight passages waiting for advantages; it is his bed, yea, and almost his household-stuff.

[5] *Holantide*   Period from the end of October to beginning of November during which Halloween and other Christian observances occur.

---

[1] *Squire Western or Parson Trulliber*   Squire Western is the wealthy but simple-minded father of the heroine in English author Henry Fielding's comic novel *Tom Jones* (1749), while Parson Trulliber is the country parson in Fielding's *Joseph Andrews* (1742).

[2] *rallied*   Teased.

[3] *Monday Morning*   Words and phrases discussed in the glossary Edgeworth appended to the body of the novel are marked with an asterisk.

round my neck, cloak fashion. To look at me, you would hardly think "poor Thady" was the father of attorney Quirk: he is a high gentleman, and never minds what poor Thady says, and having better than 1500 a-year, landed estate, looks down upon honest Thady; but I wash my hands of his doings, and as I have lived so will I die, true and loyal to the family. The family of the Rackrents is, I am proud to say, one of the most ancient in the kingdom. Everybody knows this is not the old family name, which was O'Shaughlin, related to the Kings of Ireland—but that was before my time. My grandfather was driver to the great Sir Patrick O'Shaughlin, and I heard him, when I was a boy, telling how the Castle Rackrent estate came to Sir Patrick; Sir Tallyhoo Rackrent was cousin-german[1] to him, and had a fine estate of his own, only never a gate upon it, it being his maxim, that a car was the best gate. Poor gentleman! He lost a fine hunter and his life, at last, by it, all in one day's hunt. But I ought to bless that day, for the estate came straight into *the* family, upon one condition, which Sir Patrick O'Shaughlin at the time took sadly to heart, they say, but thought better of it afterwards, seeing how large a stake depended upon it, that he should, by Act of Parliament, take and bear the surname and arms of Rackrent.[2]

Now it was that the world was to see what was *in* Sir Patrick. On coming into the estate, he gave the finest entertainment ever was heard of in the country: not a man could stand after supper but Sir Patrick himself, who could sit out the best man in Ireland, let alone the three kingdoms[3] itself.* He had his house, from one year's end to another, as full of company as ever it could hold, and fuller; for rather than be left out of the parties at Castle Rackrent, many gentlemen, and those men of the first consequence and landed estates in the country,

such as the O'Neills of Ballynagrotty, and the Money-gawls of Mount Juliet's Town, and O'Shannons of New Town Tullyhog, made it their choice, often and often, when there was no room to be had for love or money, in long winter nights, to sleep in the chicken house, which Sir Patrick had fitted up for the purpose of accommodating his friends and the public in general, who honoured him with their company unexpectedly at Castle Rackrent; and this went on, I can't tell you how long—the whole country rang with his praises!—Long life to him! I'm sure I love to look upon his picture, now opposite to me; though I never saw him, he must have been a portly gentleman—his neck something short, and remarkable for the largest pimple on his nose, which, by his particular desire, is still extant in his picture, said to be a striking likeness, though taken when young. He is said also to be the inventor of raspberry whiskey, which is very likely, as nobody has ever appeared to dispute it with him, and as there still exists a broken punch-bowl at Castle Rackrent, in the garret, with an inscription to that effect—a great curiosity. A few days before his death he was very merry; it being his honour's birthday, he called my great grandfather in, God bless him! to drink the company's health, and filled a bumper[4] himself, but could not carry it to his head, on account of the great shake in his hand; on this he cast his joke, saying, "What would my poor father say to me if he was to pop out of the grave, and see me now? I remember, when I was a little boy, the first bumper of claret[5] he gave me after dinner, how he praised me for carrying it so steady to my mouth. Here's my thanks to him—a bumper toast." Then he fell to singing the favourite song he learned from his father—for the last time, poor gentleman—he sung it that night as loud and hearty as ever, with a chorus:

He that goes to bed, and goes to bed sober,
Falls as the leaves do, falls as the leaves do, and
    dies in October—
But he that goes to bed, and goes to bed mellow

---

[1] *cousin-german* First cousin (a cousin sharing the same grandparents).

[2] *he should … of Rackrent* It is likely that Sir Patrick took on the name of Rackrent in conjunction with a conversion from the Catholic Church to the Protestant Church of Ireland; at the time of this narrative, under a variety of Penal Laws, Irish Catholics were barred from numerous public offices and generally penalized in society.

[3] *the three kingdoms* I.e., Ireland, Scotland, and England.

[4] *bumper* Large glass.

[5] *claret* Red wine.

> Lives as he ought to do, lives as he ought to do,
> and dies an honest fellow.[1]

Sir Patrick died that night; just as the company rose to drink his health with three cheers, he fell down in a sort of a fit, and was carried off. They sat it out, and were surprised, on enquiry, in the morning, to find it was all over with poor Sir Patrick. Never did any gentleman live and die more beloved in the country by rich and poor; his funeral was such a one as was never known before nor since in the county! All the gentlemen in the three counties were at it—far and near, how they flocked! My great grandfather said that to see all the women even[2] in their red cloaks, you would have taken them for the army drawn out. Then such a fine whillaluh!* you might have heard it to the farthest end of the county, and happy the man who could get but a sight of the hearse! But who'd have thought it? Just as all was going on right, through his own town they were passing, when the body was seized for debt—a rescue was apprehended from the mob, but the heir who attended the funeral was against that, for fear of consequences, seeing that those villains who came to serve acted under the disguise of the law. So, to be sure, the law must take its course—and little gain had the creditors for their pains. First and foremost, they had the curses of the country; and Sir Murtagh Rackrent, the new heir, in the next place, on account of this affront to the body, refused to pay a shilling of the debts, in which he was countenanced by all the best gentlemen of property, and others of his acquaintance, Sir Murtagh alleging in all companies that he all along meant to pay his father's debts of honour; but the moment the law was taken of him, there was an end of honour to be sure. It was whispered—but none but the enemies of the family believe it—that this was all a sham

seizure to get quit of the debts, which he had bound himself to pay in honour.

It's a long time ago, there's no saying how it was, but this for certain, the new man did not take at all after the old gentleman—The cellars were never filled after his death—and no open house, or any thing as it used to be—the tenants even were sent away without their whiskey*—I was ashamed myself, and knew not what to say for the honour of the family—But I made the best of a bad case, and laid it all at my lady's door, for I did not like *her* any how, nor any body else—she was of the family of the Skinflints, and a widow—It was a strange match for Sir Murtagh; the people in the country thought he demeaned himself greatly*—but *I* said nothing—I knew how it was—Sir Murtagh was a great lawyer, and looked to the great Skinflint estate; there, however, he overshot himself; for though one of the co-heiresses, he was never the better for her, for she outlived him many's the long day—he could not foresee that, to be sure, when he married her.

I must say for her, she made him the best of wives, being a very notable stirring woman, and looking close to everything. But I always suspected she had Scotch blood in her veins;[3] anything else I could have looked over[4] in her from a regard to the family. She was a strict observer for self and servants of Lent,[5] and all fast days, but not holidays. One of the maids having fainted three times the last day of Lent, to keep soul and body together we put a morsel of roast beef into her mouth, which came from Sir Murtagh's dinner, who never fasted, not he; but somehow or other it unfortunately reached my lady's ears, and the priest of the parish had a complaint made of it the next day, and the poor girl was forced as soon as she could walk to do penance for it, before she could get any peace or absolution in the house or out of it. However, my lady was very charitable

---

[1] *He that goes to bed … honest fellow*   This traditional song (sometimes referred to as "Come Landlord Fill the Flowing Bowl," sometimes as "Three Jolly Coachmen") exists in several versions. Parts of the song appear to have their origin in rhymes included in Act 2, Scene 2 of *Rollo, Duke of Normandy, or The Bloody Brother*, an early seventeenth-century play by John Fletcher ("And he that will to bed go sober / Falls with the leaf in October").

[2] *even*   Lined up.

[3] *Scotch blood in her veins*   A slur against Scottish people, who were long stereotyped as stingy (or as "skinflints").

[4] *looked over*   Overlooked.

[5] *for self and servants of Lent*   Lent is the forty-day period preceding Easter that, in Christian observance, is meant as a time of penitence and fasting. Masters had the power to enforce such religious observances on their servants.

in her own way. She had a charity school for poor children, where they were taught to read and write gratis,[1] and where they were kept well to spinning gratis for my lady in return; for she had always heaps of duty yarn[2] from the tenants, and got all her household linen out of the estate from first to last; for after the spinning, the weavers on the estate took it in hand for nothing, because of the looms my lady's interest could get from the Linen Board[3] to distribute gratis. Then there was a bleach yard near us, and the tenant dare refuse my lady nothing, for fear of a lawsuit Sir Murtagh kept hanging over him about the watercourse.[4] With these ways of managing, 'tis surprising how cheap my lady got things done, and how proud she was of it. Her table the same way, kept for next to nothing; duty fowls, and duty turkeys, and duty geese,* came as fast as we could eat 'em, for my lady kept a sharp look out, and knew to a tub of butter everything the tenants had, all round. They knew her way, and what with fear of driving for rent and Sir Murtagh's lawsuits, they were kept in such good order, they never thought of coming near Castle Rackrent without a present of something or other— nothing too much or too little for my lady—eggs, honey, butter, meal, fish, game, grouse, and herrings, fresh or salt: all went for something. As for their young pigs, we had them, and the best bacon and hams they could make up, with all young chickens in spring; but they were a set of poor wretches, and we had nothing but misfortunes with them, always breaking and running away. This, Sir Murtagh and my lady said, was all their former landlord Sir Patrick's fault, who let 'em all get the half year's rent into arrear; there was something in that, to be sure. But Sir Murtagh was as much the contrary way; for let alone making English tenants* of them, every soul, he was always driving and driving, and pounding and pounding, and canting and canting,* and replevying and replevying,[5] and he made a good living of trespassing cattle—there was always some tenant's pig, or horse, or cow, or calf, or goose, trespassing, which was so great a gain to Sir Murtagh, that he did not like to hear me talk of repairing fences. Then his heriots[6] and duty work* brought him in something: his turf was cut,[7] his potatoes set and dug, his hay brought home, and in short all the work about his house done for nothing; for in all our leases there were strict clauses with heavy penalties, which Sir Murtagh knew well how to enforce; so many days' duty work of man and horse, from every tenant, he was to have, and had, every year; and when a man vexed him, why the finest day he could pitch on, when the cratur[8] was getting in his own harvest, or thatching his cabin, Sir Murtagh made it a principle to call upon him and his horse; so he taught 'em all, as he said, to know the law of landlord and tenant. As for law, I believe no man, dead or alive, ever loved it so well as Sir Murtagh. He had once sixteen suits[9] pending at a time, and I never saw him so much himself; roads, lanes, bogs, wells, ponds, eel-wires, orchards, trees, tythes, vagrants, gravel-pits, sandpits, dung-hills, and nuisances, everything upon the face of the earth furnished him good matter for a suit. He used to boast that he had a lawsuit for every letter in the alphabet. How I used to wonder to see Sir Murtagh in the midst of the papers in his office! Why, he could hardly turn about for them. I made bold to shrug my shoulders once in his presence, and thanked my stars I was not born a gentleman to so much toil and trouble, but Sir Murtagh took me up short with his old

---

[1] *gratis* At no charge.

[2] *duty yarn* Yarn that tenants were required to supply to their landlords.

[3] *Linen Board* At the time, linen produced from Irish-grown flax was one of Ireland's most important products.

[4] *watercourse* I.e., the right of watercourse, a tenant's right to make use of the channel of water which runs through the land on which he or she lives.

[5] *pounding* Impounding (stray livestock); *replevying* Restoring to a person goods or chattel which have previously been seized in order to obtain due rent, with an agreement that the matter will be tried in court.

[6] *heriots* Tenant's best animals, live or dead, which were considered to be owed to a landlord upon the tenant's death.

[7] *turf was cut* Turf, the traditional source of fuel and fire in Ireland, is prepared by cutting pieces from peat bogs, and then leaving it to dry in the sun; eventually it forms hard, dry, earthen blocks.

[8] *the finest … the cratur* The finest day he could settle on, when the creature.

[9] *suits* I.e., lawsuits.

proverb, "learning is better than house or land."[1] Out of forty-nine suits which he had, he never lost one but seventeen;* the rest he gained with costs, double costs, treble costs[2] sometimes; but even that did not pay. He was a very learned man in the law, and had the character of it; but how it was I can't tell, these suits that he carried cost him a power of money; in the end he sold some hundreds a year of the family estate; but he was a very learned man in the law, and I know nothing of the matter except having a great regard for the family. I could not help grieving when he sent me to post up notices of the sale of the fee simple of the lands and appurtenances[3] of Timoleague. "I know, honest Thady," says he to comfort me, "what I'm about better than you do; I'm only selling to get the ready money wanting,[4] to carry on my suit with spirit with the Nugents of Carrickashaughlin."

He was very sanguine[5] about that suit with the Nugents of Carrickashaughlin. He would have gained it, they say, for certain, had it pleased Heaven to have spared him to us, and it would have been at the least a plump two thousand a year in his way; but things were ordered otherwise, for the best to be sure. He dug up a fairy mount*[6] against my advice, and had no luck afterwards. Though a learned man in the law, he was a little too incredulous[7] in other matters. I warned him that I heard the very Banshee[8] that my grandfather heard, before I was born long, under Sir Patrick's window a few days before his death. But Sir Murtagh thought nothing of the Banshee, nor of his cough with a spitting of blood, brought on, I understand, by catching cold in attending the courts, and overstraining his chest with making himself heard in one of his favourite causes. He was a great speaker, with a powerful voice; but his last speech was not in the courts at all. He and my lady, though both of the same way of thinking in some things, and though she was as good a wife and great economist as you could see, and he the best of husbands, as to looking into his affairs, and making money for his family; yet I don't know how it was, they had a great deal of sparring and jarring between them. My lady had her privy purse;[9] and she had her weed ashes,* and her sealing money* upon the signing of all the leases, with something to buy gloves besides; and besides again often took money from the tenants, if offered properly, to speak for them to Sir Murtagh about abatements[10] and renewals. Now the weed ashes and the glove money he allowed her clear perquisites; though once when he saw her in a new gown saved out of the weed ashes, he told her to my face (for he could say a sharp thing), that she should not put on her weeds before her husband's death. But it grew more serious when they came to the renewal businesses. At last, in a dispute about an abatement, my lady would have the last word, and Sir Murtagh grew mad;* I was within hearing of the door, and now wish I had made bold to step in. He spoke so loud, the whole kitchen was out on the stairs.* All on a sudden he stopped, and my lady too.

---

[1] *learning is … or land* Proverb appearing in David Garrick's prologue to Oliver Goldsmith's play *She Stoops to Conquer* (1773).

[2] *costs … treble costs* I.e., the Judge would include in his judgment an award of the legal costs—or sometimes up to three times the cost of bringing the lawsuit.

[3] *fee simple* Absolute title to an estate in land (considered to belong to the owner's descendants in perpetuity); *appurtenances* Minor properties or rights.

[4] *wanting* (That I am) lacking.

[5] *sanguine* Confident or hopeful.

[6] [Edgeworth's note] These fairy mounts are called ant-hills in England. They are held in high reverence by the common people in Ireland. A gentleman, who in laying out his lawn had occasion to level one of these hillocks, could not prevail upon any of his labourers to begin the ominous work. He was obliged to take a *loy* [narrow spade] from one of their reluctant hands, and began the attack himself. The labourers agreed that the vengeance of the fairies would fall upon the head of the presumptuous mortal, who first disturbed them in their retreat.

[7] *incredulous* Unbelieving.

[8] [Edgeworth's note] The Banshee is a species of aristocratic fairy who in the shape of a little hideous old woman has been known to appear, and heard to sing in a mournful supernatural voice under the windows of great houses, to warn the family that some of them are soon to die. In the last century every great family in Ireland had a Banshee, who attended regularly, but latterly their visits and songs have been discontinued.

[9] *privy purse* Literally, funds collected from public revenues for the private expenses of a sovereign.

[10] *abatements* Decreases in rent.

Something has surely happened, thought I—and so it was, for Sir Murtagh in his passion broke a blood-vessel, and all the law in the land could do nothing in that case. My lady sent for five physicians, but Sir Murtagh died, and was buried. She had a fine jointure[1] settled upon her, and took herself away, to the great joy of the tenantry. I never said anything, one way or the other, whilst she was part of the family, but got up to see her go at three o'clock in the morning. "It's a fine morning, honest Thady," says she; "good bye to ye"—and into the carriage she stepped, without a word more, good or bad, or even half-a-crown;[2] but I made my bow, and stood to see her safe out of sight for the sake of the family.

Then we were all bustle in the house, which made me keep out of the way, for I walk slow and hate a bustle, but the house was all hurry-skurry, preparing for my new master. Sir Murtagh, I forgot to notice, had no childer,[3] so the Rackrent estate went to his younger brother—a young dashing officer, who came amongst us before I knew for the life of me whereabouts I was, in a gig or some of them things, with another spark[4] along with him, and led horses, and servants, and dogs, and scarce a place to put any Christian of them into; for my late[5] lady had sent all the feather-beds off before her, and blankets, and household linen, down to the very knife cloths, on the cars to Dublin, which were all her own, lawfully paid for out of her own money. So the house was quite bare, and my young master, the moment ever he set foot in it out of his gig, thought all those things must come of themselves, I believe, for he never looked after anything at all, but harum-scarum called for everything as if we were conjurers, or he in a public-house. For my part, I could not bestir myself

anyhow; I had been so used to my late master and mistress, all was upside down with me, and the new servants in the servants' hall were quite out of my way; I had nobody to talk to, and if it had not been for my pipe and tobacco should, I verily believe, have broke my heart for poor Sir Murtagh.

But one morning my new master caught a glimpse of me as I was looking at his horse's heels, in hopes of a word from him. "And is that old Thady?" says he, as he got into his gig. I loved him from that day to this, his voice was so like the family; and he threw me a guinea[6] out of his waistcoat pocket, as he drew up the reins with the other hand, his horse rearing too; I thought I never set my eyes on a finer figure of a man, quite another sort from Sir Murtagh, though withal *to me*, a family likeness. A fine life we should have led, had he stayed amongst us, God bless him! He valued a guinea as little as any man; money to him was no more than dirt, and his gentleman and groom, and all belonging to him, the same; but the sporting season over, he grew tired of the place, and having got down[7] a great architect for the house, and an improver for the grounds, and seen their plans and elevations, he fixed a day for settling with the tenants, but went off in a whirlwind to town, just as some of them came into the yard in the morning. A circular letter came next post from the new agent, with news that the master was sailed for England, and he must remit £500 to Bath[8] for his use, before a fortnight was at an end. Bad news still for the poor tenants, no change still for the better with them. Sir Kit Rackrent, my young master, left all to the agent, and though he had the spirit of a prince, and lived away to the honour of his country abroad, which I was proud to hear of, what were we the better for that at home? The agent was

[1] *jointure* Estate that becomes the possession of a woman upon the death of her husband.

[2] *or even half-a-crown* Or even a tip. A half crown (or 2½ shillings) in 1800 would be a very generous tip.

[3] [Edgeworth's note] *Childer*—this is the manner in which many of Thady's rank, and others in Ireland, *formerly* pronounced the word *children*.

[4] *spark* Lively young gentleman of fashion.

[5] *late* Former.

[6] *guinea* Gold coin valued at twenty-one shillings, equivalent to just over one pound sterling.

[7] *got down* Brought in.

[8] *circular letter* Official letter addressed to a group of people, to be circulated among them; *Bath* City in the southwest of England, at the time a fashionable spa resort.

one of your middlemen,[1] who grind the face of the poor, and can never bear a man with a hat upon his head;[2] he ferreted the tenants out of their lives;[3] not a week without a call for money; drafts upon drafts from Sir Kit; but I laid it all to the fault of the agent; for, says I, what can Sir Kit do with so much cash, and he a single man? But still it went. Rents must be all paid up to the day, and afore; no allowance for improving tenants; no consideration for those who had built upon their farms. No sooner was a lease out, but the land was advertised to the highest bidder; all the old tenants turned out, when they had spent their substance in the hope and trust of a renewal from the landlord. All was now set at the highest penny to a parcel of poor wretches who meant to run away, and did so, after taking two crops out of the ground. Then fining down the year's rent* came into fashion; any thing for the ready penny, and with all this, and presents to the agent and the driver,* there was no such thing as standing it. I said nothing, for I had a regard for the family, but I walked about, thinking if his honour Sir Kit (long may he live to reign over us!) knew all this, it would go hard with him, but he'd see us righted—not that I had any thing for my own share to complain of, for the agent was always very civil to me, when he came down into the country, and took a great deal of notice of my son Jason. Jason Quirk, though he be my son, I must say, was a good scholar from his birth, and a very 'cute[4] lad; I thought to make him a priest,* but he did better for himself. Seeing how he was as good a clerk as any in the country, the agent gave him his rent accounts to copy, which he did first of all for the pleasure of obliging the gentleman, and would take nothing at all for his trouble, but was always proud to serve the family. By and by, a good farm bounding us to the east fell into his honour's hands, and my son put in a proposal for it; why shouldn't he as well as another? The proposals all went over to the master at the Bath, who knowing no more of the land than the child unborn, only having once been out a grousing[5] on it before he went to England; and the value of lands, as the agent informed him, falling every year in Ireland, his honour wrote over in all haste a bit of a letter, saying he left it all to the agent, and that he must set it as well as he could to the best bidder, to be sure, and send him over £200 by return of post: with this the agent gave me a hint, and I spoke a good word for my son, and gave out in the country, that nobody need bid against us. So his proposal was just the thing, and he a good tenant; and he got a promise of an abatement in the rent, after the first year, for advancing the half year's rent at signing the lease, which was wanting to complete the agent's £200, by the return of the post, with all which my master wrote back he was well satisfied. About this time we learned from the agent, as a great secret, how the money went so fast, and the reason of the thick coming of the master's drafts: he was a little too fond of play, and Bath, they say, was no place for a young man of his fortune, where there were so many of his own countrymen too haunting him up and down, day and night, who had nothing to lose. At last, at Christmas, the agent wrote over to stop the

---

[1] [Edgeworth's note] *Middlemen*—There was a class of men termed middlemen in Ireland, who took large farms on long leases from gentlemen of landed property, and set the land again in small portions to the poor, as under tenants, at exorbitant rents. The *head-landlord*, as he *was* called, seldom saw his *under tenants*, but if he could not get the *middleman to pay him his rent punctually, he went to the land, and drove the land for his rent*, that is to say, he sent his steward or bailiff, or driver, to the land, to seize the cattle, hay, corn, flax, oats, or potatoes, belonging to the under-tenants, and proceeded to sell these for his rent; it sometimes happened that these unfortunate tenants paid their rent twice over, once to *the middleman, and once to the head landlord*.

The characteristics of a middleman *were* servility to his superiors and tyranny towards his inferiors: the poor detested this race of beings. In speaking to them, however, they always used the most abject language, and the most humble tone and posture. "*Please your honour;* and *please your honour's honour*," they knew must be repeated as a charm at the beginning and end of every equivocating, exculpatory, or supplicatory sentence; and they were much more alert in doffing their caps to these new men, than to those of what they call *good old families*. A witty carpenter once termed these middlemen *journeymen gentlemen*.

[2] *can never bear ... hat upon his head* Always insist upon servility. Removing one's cap in the presence of "one's betters" was considered a sign of respect.

[3] *ferreted the ... of their lives* Dug away at the livelihoods of the tenants.

[4] *'cute* Acute; clever.

[5] *grousing* Grouse hunting.

drafts, for he could raise no more money on bond or mortgage, or from the tenants, or any how, nor had he any more to lend himself, and desired at same time to decline the agency for the future, wishing Sir Kit his health and happiness, and the compliments of the season, for I saw the letter before ever it was sealed, when my son copied it. When the answer came, there was a new turn in affairs, and the agent was turned out; and my son Jason, who had corresponded privately with his honour occasionally on business, was forthwith desired by his honour to take the accounts into his own hands, and took them over till further orders. It was a very spirited letter, to be sure: Sir Kit sent his service, and the compliments of the season, in return to the agent, and he would fight him with pleasure tomorrow, or any day, for sending him such a letter, if he was born a gentleman, which he was sorry (for both their sakes) to find (too late) he was not. Then, in a private postscript, he condescended to tell us that all would be speedily settled to his satisfaction, and we should turn over a new leaf, for he was going to be married in a fortnight to the grandest heiress in England, and had only immediate occasion at present for £200, as he would not choose to touch his lady's fortune for travelling expenses home to Castle Rackrent, where he intended to be, wind and weather permitting, early in the next month, and desired fires, and the house to be painted, and the new building to go on as fast as possible, for the reception of him and his lady before that time; with several words besides in the letter, which we could not make out, because—God bless him!—he wrote in such a flurry. My heart warmed to my new lady when I read this; I was almost afraid it was too good news to be true; but the girls fell to scouring, and it was well they did, for we soon saw his marriage in the paper to a lady with I don't know how many tens of thousand pounds to her fortune; then I watched the post-office for his landing, and the news came to my son of his and the bride being in Dublin, and on the way home to Castle Rackrent. We had bonfires all over the country, expecting him down the next day, and we had his coming of age still to celebrate, which he had not time to do properly before he left the country; therefore a great ball was expected, and great

doings upon his coming, as it were, fresh to take possession of his ancestors' estate. I never shall forget the day he came home: we had waited and waited all day long till eleven o'clock at night, and I was thinking of sending the boy to lock the gates, and giving them up for that night, when there come the carriages thundering up to the great hall door. I got the first sight of the bride; for when the carriage door opened, just as she had her foot on the steps, I held the flam[1]* full in her face to light her, at which she shuts her eyes, but I had a full view of the rest of her, and greatly shocked I was, for by that light she was little better than a blackamoor,[2] and seemed crippled, but that was only sitting so long in the chariot.[3] "You're kindly welcome to Castle Rackrent, my lady," says I, (recollecting who she was). "Did your honour hear of the bonfires?" His honour spoke never a word, nor so much as handed her up the steps; he looked to me no more like himself than nothing at all; I know I took him for the skeleton of his honour. I was not sure what to say next to one or t'other, but seeing she was a stranger in a foreign country, I thought it but right to speak cheerful to her, so I went back again to the bonfires. "My lady," says I, as she crossed the hall, "there would have been fifty times as many, but for fear of the horses and frightening your ladyship, Jason and I forbid them, please your honour." With that she looked at me a little bewildered. "Will I have a fire lighted in the state room tonight?" was the next question I put to her; but never a word she answered, so I concluded she could not speak a word of English, and was from foreign parts. The short and the long of it was, I couldn't tell what to make of her, so I left her to herself, and went straight down to the servants' hall to learn something for certain about her. Sir Kit's own man was tired, but the groom[4] set him a-talking at last, and

---

[1] *flam* Torch.

[2] *little better than a blackamoor* The word *blackamoor* was already in 1800 an archaic term; it denoted any dark-skinned person, generally of African descent. With the phrase "little better than" Thady signals his prejudice.

[3] *only sitting so long in the chariot* Only the result of sitting so long in the carriage.

[4] *groom* Servant responsible for dealing with horses.

we had it all out before ever I closed my eyes that night. The bride might well be a great fortune; she was a *Jewish* by all accounts, who are famous for their great riches. I had never seen any of that tribe or nation before, and could only gather that she spoke a strange kind of English of her own, that she could not abide pork or sausages,[1] and went neither to church nor mass. Mercy upon his honour's poor soul, thought I; what will become of him and his, and all of us, with this heretic blackamoor at the head of the Castle Rackrent estate! I never slept a wink all night for thinking of it, but before the servants I put my pipe in my mouth and kept my mind to myself; for I had a great regard for the family, and after this when strange gentlemen's servants came to the house, and would begin to talk about the bride, I took care to put the best foot foremost, and passed her for a nabob,[2] in the kitchen, which accounted for her dark complexion, and every thing.

The very morning after they came home, however, I saw how things were, plain enough, between Sir Kit and my lady, though they were walking together arm in arm after breakfast, looking at the new buildings and the improvements. "Old Thady," said my master, just as he used to do, "how do you do?" "Very well, I thank your honour's honour," said I, but I saw he was not well pleased, and my heart was in my mouth as I walked along after him. "Is the large room damp, Thady?" said his honour. "Oh, damp, your honour! How should it but be as dry as a bone," says I, "after all the fires we have kept in it day and night? It's the barrack-room* your honour's talking on." "And what is a barrack-room, pray, my dear?" were the first words I ever heard out of my lady's lips. "No matter, my dear," said he, and went on talking to me, ashamed like I should witness her ignorance. To be sure, to hear her talk, one might have taken her for an innocent,* for it was "what's this, Sir Kit?" and "what's that, Sir Kit?" all the way we went. To be sure, Sir Kit had enough to do to answer her. "And what do you call that, Sir Kit?" said she, "that,

that looks like a pile of black bricks, pray Sir Kit?" "My turf stack,[3] my dear," said my master, and bit his lip. Where have you lived, my lady, all your life, not to know a turf stack when you see it, thought I, but I said nothing. Then, by-and-by, she takes out her glass[4] and begins spying over the country. "And what's all that black swamp out yonder, Sir Kit?" says she. "My bog, my dear," says he, and went on whistling. "It's a very ugly prospect, my dear," said she. "You don't see it, my dear," says he, "for we've planted it out, when the trees grow up, in summer time," says he. "Where are the trees," said she, "my dear?" still looking through her glass. "You are blind, my dear," says he, "what are these under your eyes?" "These shrubs?" said she. "Trees," said he. "Maybe they are what you call trees in Ireland, my dear," says she, "but they are not a yard high, are they?" "They were planted out but last year, my lady," says I, to soften matters between them, for I saw she was going the way to make his honour mad with her. "They are very well grown for their age, and you'll not see the bog of Allyballycarricko'shaughlin at-all-at-all through the screen, when once the leaves come out. But, my lady, you must not quarrel with any part or parcel of Allyballycarricko'shaughlin, for you don't know how many hundred years that same bit of bog has been in the family; we would not part with the bog of Allyballycarricko'shaughlin upon no account at all. It cost the late Sir Murtagh two hundred good pounds to defend his title to it, and boundaries, against the O'Learys, who cut a road through it." Now one would have thought this would have been hint enough for the lady, but she fell to laughing like one out of their right mind, and made me say the name of the bog over for her to get it by heart, a dozen times; then she must ask me how to spell it, and what was the meaning of it in English—Sir Kit standing by whistling all the while—I verily believe she laid the corner-stone of all her future misfortunes at that very instant; but I said no more, only looked at Sir Kit.

[1] *pork or sausages* The Jewish religion prohibits the consumption of pork.

[2] *passed her for a nabob* Took her to be a person distinguished by conspicuous wealth acquired in India.

[3] *turf stack* Stack of blocks of peat (for use as fuel).

[4] *glass* Field glass, similar to binoculars.

There were no balls, no dinners, no doings, the country was all disappointed; Sir Kit's gentleman said, in a whisper to me, it was all my lady's own fault, because she was so obstinate about the cross. "What cross?" says I, "is it about her being a heretic?"[1] "Oh, no such matter," says he, "my master does not mind her heresies, but her diamond cross, it's worth I can't tell you how much, and she has thousands of English pounds concealed in diamonds about her, which she as good as promised to give up to my master before he married, but now she won't part with any of them, and she must take the consequences."

Her honeymoon, at least her Irish honeymoon, was scarcely well over, when his honour one morning said to me, "Thady, buy me a pig!" and then the sausages were ordered, and here was the first open breaking out of my lady's troubles. My lady came down herself into the kitchen to speak to the cook about the sausages, and desired never to see them more at her table. Now my master had ordered them, and my lady knew that; the cook took my lady's part, because she never came down into the kitchen, and was young and innocent in housekeeping, which raised her pity; besides, said she, at her own table, surely, my lady should order and disorder what she pleases; but the cook soon changed her note, for my master made it a principle to have the sausages, and swore at her for a Jew herself, till he drove her fairly out of the kitchen; then, for fear of her place, and because he threatened that my lady should give her no discharge without the sausages, she gave up, and from that day forward always sausages or bacon, or pig meat, in some shape or other, went up to table; upon which my lady shut herself up in her own room, and my master said she might stay there, with an oath; and to make sure of her, he turned the key in the door, and kept it ever after in his pocket. We none of us ever saw or heard her speak for seven years after that:[2] he carried

her dinner himself. Then his honour had a great deal of company to dine with him, and balls in the house, and was as gay and gallant, and as much himself as before he was married; and at dinner he always drank my Lady Rackrent's good health, and so did the company, and he sent out always a servant, with his compliments to my Lady Rackrent, and the company was drinking her

___

questioned the maid-servant who lived with Colonel M'Guire during the time of Lady Cathcart's imprisonment. Her Ladyship was locked up in her own house for many years; during which period her husband was visited by the neighbouring gentry, and it was his regular custom at dinner to send his compliments to Lady Cathcart, informing her that the company had the honour to drink her ladyship's health, and begging to know whether there was any thing at table that she would like to eat. The answer was always—"Lady Cathcart's compliments, and she has everything she wants."

An instance of honesty in a poor Irishwoman deserves to be recorded. Lady Cathcart had some remarkable fine diamonds, which she had concealed from her husband, and which she was anxious to get out of the house, lest he should discover them; she had neither servant nor friend to whom she could entrust them, but she had observed a poor beggar-woman who used to come to the house. She spoke to her from the window of the room in which she was confined; the woman promised to do what she desired, and Lady Cathcart threw a parcel, containing the jewels, to her. The poor woman carried them to the person to whom they were directed, and several years afterwards, when Lady Cathcart recovered her liberty, she received her diamonds safely. [Elizabeth Malyn (1691?–1789) was married four times; her third marriage was to Lord Cathcart, and her fourth, in 1745, to Hugh Macguire, a colonel who owned an estate in Tempo in northern Ireland. The obituary published in the August 1789 issue of *The Gentleman's Magazine* provides considerable detail concerning Macguire (said to have died "in or about 1764," a date which would make it impossible for Edgeworth herself to have been "acquainted with Colonel M'Guire"), the marriage, Macguire's imprisoning of his wife, and the story of the jewels. In her letter to Mrs. Stark (see the "In Context" materials available in the anthology's website component), Edgeworth asserts that she had known little of the actual case.]

At Colonel M'Guire's death, her ladyship was released. The Editor, within this year, saw the gentleman who accompanied her to England after her husband's death. When she first was told of his death, she imagined that the news was not true, and that it was told only with an intention of deceiving her. At his death she had scarcely clothes sufficient to cover her; she wore a red wig, looked scared, and her understanding seemed stupified; she said she scarcely knew one human creature from another. Her imprisonment lasted about twenty years. These circumstances may appear strange to the English reader, but there is no danger in the present times that any individual should exercise such tyranny as Colonel M'Guire's with impunity, the power being now all in the hands of government, and there being no possibility of obtaining from Parliament an act of indemnity for any cruelties.

___

[1] *a heretic* I.e., not a Christian.

[2] [Edgeworth's note] This part of the history of the Rackrent family can scarcely be thought credible; but in justice to honest Thady, it is hoped the reader will recollect the history of the celebrated Lady Cathcart's conjugal imprisonment. The Editor was acquainted with Colonel M'Guire, Lady Cathcart's husband; he has lately seen and

ladyship's health, and begged to know if there was any thing at table he might send her; and the man came back, after the sham errand, with my Lady Rackrent's compliments, and she was very much obliged to Sir Kit: she did not wish for any thing, but drank the company's health. The country, to be sure, talked and wondered at my lady's being shut up, but nobody chose to interfere or ask any impertinent questions, for they knew my master was a man very apt to give a short answer himself, and likely to call a man out[1] for it afterwards; he was a famous shot—had killed his man before he came of age—and nobody scarce dare look at him whilst at Bath. Sir Kit's character was so well known in the country, that he lived in peace and quietness ever after, and was a great favourite with the ladies, especially when in process of time, in the fifth year of her confinement, my Lady Rackrent fell ill, and took entirely to her bed, and he gave out that she was now skin and bone, and could not last through the winter. In this he had two physicians' opinions to back him (for now he called in two physicians for her), and tried all his arts to get the diamond cross from her on her deathbed, and to get her to make a will in his favour of her separate possessions; but she was there too tough for him. He used to swear at her behind her back, after kneeling to her to her face, and call her, in the presence of his gentleman, his stiff-necked Israelite, though before he married her, that same gentleman told me he used to call her (how he could bring it out I don't know!) "my pretty Jessica."[2] To be sure, it must have been hard for her to guess what sort of a husband he reckoned to make her. When she was lying, to all expectation, on her deathbed, of a broken heart, I could not but pity her, though she was a Jewish; and considering too it was no fault of hers to be taken with my master so young as she was at the Bath, and so fine a gentleman as Sir Kit was when he courted her; and considering too, after all they had heard and seen of him as a husband, there were now no less than three ladies in our county talked of for his

second wife, all at daggers drawing with[3] each other, as his gentleman swore, at the balls, for Sir Kit for their partner—I could not but think them bewitched, but they all reasoned with themselves, that Sir Kit would make a good husband to any Christian, but a Jewish, I suppose, and especially as he was now a reformed rake;[4] and it was not known how my lady's fortune was settled in her will, nor how the Castle Rackrent estate was all mortgaged, and bonds out against him, for he was never cured of his gaming tricks—but that was the only fault he had, God bless him!

My lady had a sort of fit, and it was given out she was dead, by mistake; this brought things to a sad crisis for my poor master—one of the three ladies showed his letters to her brother, and claimed his promises, whilst another did the same. I don't mention names. Sir Kit, in his defence, said he would meet any man who dared question his conduct, and as to the ladies, they must settle it amongst them who was to be his second, and his third, and his fourth, whilst his first was still alive, to his mortification and theirs. Upon this, as upon all former occasions, he had the voice of the country with him, on account of the great spirit and propriety he acted with. He met and shot the first lady's brother; the next day he called out the second, who had a wooden leg, and their place of meeting by appointment being in a new ploughed field, the wooden leg man stuck fast in it. Sir Kit seeing his situation, with candour fired his pistol over his head, upon which the seconds interposed, and convinced the parties there had been a slight misunderstanding between them, thereupon they shook hands cordially, and went home to dinner together. This gentleman, to show the world how they stood together, and by the advice of the friends of both parties to re-establish his sister's injured reputation, went out with Sir Kit as his second, and carried his message next day to the last of his adversaries. I never saw him in such fine spirits as that day he went out; sure enough he was within ames-ace[5] of getting quit handsomely of all his

---

[1] *call a man out* Challenge a man to a duel.

[2] *pretty Jessica* From Shakespeare's *The Merchant of Venice* 5.1.21; in *The Merchant of Venice*, Jessica, the daughter of Jewish moneylender Shylock, is also the love interest and later wife of Lorenzo.

[3] *at daggers drawing with* On the verge of fighting with.

[4] *rake* Fashionable, promiscuous man of morally questionable habits.

[5] *ames-ace* Lowest possible dice throw; thus, the shortest possible distance.

enemies; but unluckily, after hitting the toothpick out of his adversary's finger and thumb, he received a ball in a vital part, and was brought home, in little better than an hour after the affair, speechless, on a hand-barrow,[1] to my lady; we got the key out of his pocket the first thing we did, and my son Jason ran to unlock the barrack-room, where my lady had been shut up for seven years, to acquaint her with the fatal accident. The surprise bereaved her of her senses at first, nor would she believe but we were putting some new trick upon her, to entrap her out of her jewels, for a great while, till Jason bethought himself of taking her to the window, and showed her the men bringing Sir Kit up the avenue upon the hand-barrow, which had immediately the desired effect; for directly she burst into tears, and pulling her cross from her bosom, she kissed it with as great devotion as ever I witnessed, and lifting up her eye to Heaven, uttered some ejaculation, which none present heard; but I take the sense of it to be, she returned thanks for this unexpected interposition in her favour, when she had least reason to expect it. My master was greatly lamented; there was no life in him when we lifted him off the barrow, so he was laid out immediately, and waked[2] the same night. The country was all in an uproar about him, and not a soul but cried shame upon his murderer, who would have been hanged surely, if he could have been brought to his trial whilst the gentleman in the country were up about it, but he very prudently withdrew himself to the continent before the affair was made public. As for the young lady who was the immediate cause of the fatal accident, however innocently, she could never show her head after at the balls in the county or any place, and by the advice of her friends and physicians she was ordered soon after to Bath, where it was expected, if any where on this side of the grave, she would meet with the recovery of her health and lost peace of mind. As a proof of his great popularity, I need only add, that there was a song made upon my master's untimely death in the newspapers,

which was in every body's mouth, singing up and down through the country, even down to the mountains, only three days after his unhappy exit. He was also greatly bemoaned at the Curragh,* where his cattle were well known, and all who had taken up his bets formerly were particularly inconsolable for his loss to society. His stud[3] sold at the cant* at the greatest price ever known in the country; his favourite horses were chiefly disposed of amongst his particular friends, who would give any price for them for his sake; but no ready money was required by the new heir, who wished not to displease any of the gentlemen of the neighbourhood just upon his coming to settle amongst them; so a long credit was given where requisite, and the cash has never been gathered in from that day to this.

But to return to my lady: she got surprisingly well after my master's decease. No sooner was it known for certain that he was dead, than all the gentlemen within twenty miles of us came in a body as it were, to set my lady at liberty, and to protest against her confinement, which they now for the first time understood was against her own consent. The ladies too were as attentive as possible, striving who should be foremost with their morning visits; and they that saw the diamonds spoke very handsomely of them, but thought it a pity they were not bestowed, if it had so pleased God, upon a lady who would have become them better. All these civilities wrought little with my lady, for she had taken an unaccountable prejudice against the country and every thing belonging to it, and was so partial to her native land, that after parting with the cook, which she did immediately upon my master's decease, I never knew her easy one instant, night or day, but when she was packing up to leave us. Had she meant to make any stay in Ireland, I stood a great chance of being a great favourite with her, for when she found I understood the weathercock,[4] she was always finding some pretence to be talking to me, and asking me which way the wind blew, and was it likely, did I think, to continue fair for England. But when I saw she had made up her mind to

---

[1] *hand-barrow* Flat frame with bars at either end, used for carrying loads; comparable to a modern stretcher.

[2] *waked* Honored in a night-time vigil held over the dead body prior to burial.

[3] *stud* Horses kept for breeding.

[4] *understood the weathercock* Understood which way the wind was blowing. (A weathercock is a weathervane in the shape of a rooster.)

spend the rest of her days upon her own income and jewels in England, I considered her quite as a foreigner, and not at all any longer as part of the family. She gave no vails[1] to the servants at Castle Rackrent at parting, notwithstanding the old proverb of "*as rich as a Jew*," which she being a Jewish, they built upon with reason.[2] But from first to last she brought nothing but misfortunes amongst us; and if it had not been all along with her, his honour Sir Kit would have been now alive in all appearance. Her diamond cross was, they say, at the bottom of it all; and it was a shame for her, being his wife, not to show more duty, and to have given it up when he condescended to ask so often for such a bit of a trifle in his distresses, especially when he all along made it no secret he had married for money. But we will not bestow another thought upon her. This much I thought to lay upon my conscience to say, in justice to my poor master's memory.

'Tis an ill wind that blows nobody no good—the same wind that took the Jew Lady Rackrent over to England brought over the new heir to Castle Rackrent.

Here let me pause for breath in my story, for though I had a great regard for every member of the family, yet without compare Sir Conolly, commonly called for short amongst his friends Sir Condy Rackrent, was ever my great favourite, and indeed the most universally beloved man I had ever seen or heard of, not excepting his great ancestor Sir Patrick, to whose memory he, amongst other instances of generosity, erected a handsome marble stone in the church of Castle Rackrent, setting forth in large letters his age, birth, parentage, and many other virtues, concluding with the

compliment so justly due, that "Sir Patrick Rackrent lived and died a monument of old Irish hospitality."

CONTINUATION OF THE MEMOIRS OF THE RACKRENT FAMILY HISTORY OF SIR CONOLLY RACKRENT

Sir Condy Rackrent, by the grace of God heir at law to the Castle Rackrent estate, was a remote branch of the family: born to little or no fortune of his own, he was bred to the bar,[3] at which having many friends to push him, and no mean natural abilities of his own, he doubtless would in process of time, if he could have borne the drudgery of that study, have been rapidly made king's counsel at the least. But things were disposed of otherwise, and he never went the circuit but twice,[4] and then made no figure for want of a fee, and being unable to speak in public. He received his education chiefly in the college of Dublin;[5] but before he came to years of discretion, lived in the country in a small but slated house, within view of the end of the avenue. I remember him bare-footed and headed, running through the street of O'Shaughlin's Town, and playing at pitch and toss, ball, marbles, and what not, with the boys of the town, amongst whom my son Jason was a great favourite with him. As for me, he was ever my white-headed boy[6]—often's the time when I would call in at his father's, where I was always made welcome, he would slip down to me in the kitchen, and love to sit on my knee whilst I told him stories of the family and the blood from which he was sprung, and how he might look forward, if the *then* present man should die without childer, to being at the head of the Castle Rackrent estate. This was then spoke quite and clear at random to

---

[1] *vails* Tips usually given to servants by guests when they are leaving a house.

[2] *gave no vails … with reason* The stereotype of Jews as both wealthy and stingy was as deeply entrenched in Ireland at the time as it was in England. Its roots were (and are) in a history of anti-Semitic oppression: Jews had for many centuries been prohibited from engaging in almost every respectable occupation; moneylending (which Christians regarded as unethical) was one of the few jobs Jews were allowed to perform in those European societies that did not expel all Jews outright (as England did from the fourteenth to the mid-seventeenth centuries). Edgeworth's personal history of anti-Semitic prejudice is discussed in the introduction.

[3] *bred to the bar* Bred to become a lawyer.

[4] *circuit* Route that judges and other legal professionals travel so as to conduct hearings throughout the area the court serves; *he never went the circuit but twice* He did not travel the circuit more than twice.

[5] *the college of Dublin* Trinity College, at that time the only university in Ireland.

[6] [Edgeworth's note] *White-headed boy*—is used by the Irish as an expression of fondness. It is upon a par with the English term *crony*. We are at a loss for the derivation of this term.

please the child, but it pleased Heaven to accomplish my prophecy afterwards, which gave him a great opinion of my judgment in business. He went to a little grammar school with many others, and my son amongst the rest, who was in his class, and not a little useful to him in his book learning, which he acknowledged with gratitude ever after. These rudiments of his education thus completed, he got a-horseback, to which exercise he was ever addicted, and used to gallop over the country whilst yet but a slip of a boy, under the care of Sir Kit's huntsman, who was very fond of him, and often lent him his gun and took him out a shooting under his own eye. By these means he became well acquainted and popular amongst the poor in the neighbourhood early, for there was not a cabin at which he had not stopped some morning or other along with the huntsman, to drink a glass of burnt whiskey out of an egg-shell, to do him good, and warm his heart, and drive the cold out of his stomach. The old people always told him he was a great likeness of Sir Patrick, which made him first have an ambition to take after him, as far as his fortune should allow. He left us when of an age to enter the college, and there completed his education and nineteenth year; for as he was not born to an estate, his friends[1] thought it incumbent on them to give him the best education which could be had for love or money, and a great deal of money consequently was spent upon him at College and Temple.[2] He was very little altered for the worse, by what he saw there of the great world, for when he came down into the country to pay us a visit we thought him just the same man as ever, hand and glove with every one, and as far from high,[3] though not without his own proper share of family pride, as any man ever you see. Latterly, seeing how Sir Kit and the Jewish lived together, and that there was no one between him and the Castle Rackrent estate, he neglected to apply to the law as much as was expected of him, and secretly many of the tenants, and others, advanced him

cash upon his note of hand value received, promising bargains of leases and lawful interest should he ever come into the estate. All this was kept a great secret, for fear the present man, hearing of it, should take it into his head to take it ill of poor Condy, and so should cut him off for ever by levying a fine, and suffering a recovery to dock the entail.[4] Sir Murtagh would have been the man for that, but Sir Kit was too much taken up philandering to consider the law in this case, or any other. These practices I have mentioned account for the state of his affairs, I mean Sir Condy's, upon his coming into the Castle Rackrent estate. He could not command a penny of his first year's income, which, and keeping no accounts, and the great sight of company he did, with many other causes too numerous to mention, was the origin of his distresses. My son Jason, who was now established agent, and knew everything, explained matters out of the face to Sir Conolly, and made him sensible of his embarrassed[5] situation. With a great nominal rent-roll, it was almost all paid away in interest, which being for convenience suffered to run on, soon doubled the principal, and Sir Condy was obligated to pass new bonds for the interest, now grown principal, and so on. Whilst this was going on, my son requiring to be paid for his trouble, and many years service in the family gratis, and Sir Condy not willing to take his affairs into his own hands, or to look them even in the face, he gave my son a bargain of some acres which fell out of lease at a reasonable rent; Jason set the land as soon as his lease was sealed to under-tenants, to make the rent, and got two hundred a year profit rent, which was little enough, considering his long agency. He bought the land at twelve years purchase two years afterwards, when Sir Condy was pushed for money on an execution, and was at the same time allowed for his improvements thereon. There was a sort of hunting lodge upon the estate convenient to my son Jason's

[1] *friends* I.e., supporters (here used in reference to family members).
[2] *Temple* The Temple Bar area is adjacent to Trinity College, Dublin. In the eighteenth century it was something of a seedy area with a reputation as a center of prostitution.
[3] *as far from high* As little affected by superciliousness or arrogance.
[4] *entail* Fixed rule of succession for an estate, requiring that ownership be transmitted only to certain persons (for instance, the direct male descendants of the original lord) and that the estate cannot be bequeathed to any person at the will of any one possessor. "Docking the entail" is the legal procedure by which such restrictions are lifted.
[5] *embarrassed* Financially difficult.

land, which he had his eye upon about this time; and he was a little jealous of Sir Condy, who talked of setting it to a stranger, who was just come into the country. Captain Moneygawl was the man; he was son and heir to the Moneygawls of Mount Juliet's Town, who had a great estate in the next county to ours, and my master was loth[1] to disoblige the young gentleman, whose heart was set upon the lodge; so he wrote him back that the lodge was at his service, and if he would honour him with his company at Castle Rackrent, they could ride over together some morning and look at it before signing the lease. Accordingly the Captain came over to us, and he and Sir Condy grew the greatest friends ever you see, and were for ever out a-shooting or a-hunting together, and were very merry in the evenings, and Sir Condy was invited of course to Mount Juliet's Town, and the family intimacy that had been in Sir Patrick's time was now recollected, and nothing would serve Sir Condy but he must be three times a week at the least with his new friends, which grieved me, who knew by the Captain's groom and gentleman how they talked of him at Mount Juliet's Town, making him quite, as one may say, a laughing stock and a butt for the whole company: but they were soon cured of *that* by an accident that surprised 'em not a little, as it did me. There was a bit of a scrawl found upon the waiting maid[2] of old Mr. Moneygawl's youngest daughter Miss Isabella, that laid open the whole; and her father, they say, was like one out of his right mind, and swore it was the last thing he ever should have thought of when he invited my master to his house, that his daughter should think of such a match. But their talk signified not a straw;[3] for as Miss Isabella's maid reported, her young mistress was fallen over head and ears in love with Sir Condy, from the first time that ever her brother brought him into the house to dinner: the servant who waited that day behind my master's chair was the first who knew it, as he says; though it's hard to believe him, for

he did not tell till a great while afterwards; but however, it's likely enough as the thing turned out that he was not far out of the way; for towards the middle of dinner, as he says, they were talking of stage plays, having a play-house and being great play actors at Mount Juliet's Town, and Miss Isabella turns short to my master and says, "Have you seen the play-bill, Sir Condy?" "No, I have not," said he. "Then more shame for you," said the Captain her brother, "not to know that my sister is to play Juliet tonight, who plays it better than any woman on or off the stage in all Ireland." "I am very happy to hear of it," said Sir Condy, and there the matter dropped for the present; but Sir Condy all this time, and a great while afterwards, was at a terrible nonplus,[4] for he had no liking, not he, to stage plays, nor to Miss Isabella either; to his mind, as it came out over a bowl of whiskey punch at home, his little Judy M'Quirk, who was daughter to a sister's son of mine, was worth twenty of Miss Isabella. He had seen her often when he stopped at her father's cabin to drink whiskey out of the egg-shell, out of hunting, before he came to the estate, and as she gave out was under something like a promise of marriage to her. Any how I could not but pity my poor master, who was so bothered between them, and he an easy-hearted man that could not disoblige nobody, God bless him. To be sure it was not his place to behave ungenerous to Miss Isabella, who had disobliged all her relations for his sake, as he remarked; and then she was locked up in her chamber and forbid to think of him any more, which raised his spirit, because his family was, as he observed, as good as theirs at any rate, and the Rackrents a suitable match for the Moneygawls any day in the year; all which was true enough; but it grieved me to see that upon the strength of all this Sir Condy was growing more in the mind to carry off Miss Isabella to Scotland,[5] in spite of her relations, as she desired.

---

[1] *Mount Juliet's Town* Thomastown, County Kilkenny, in south-east Ireland; *loth* Reluctant.

[2] *a bit of a ... waiting maid* A letter discovered to be in the possession of the serving maid.

[3] *signified not a straw* Was of no importance whatsoever.

[4] *nonplus* State of inaction; standstill.

[5] *carry off ... to Scotland* As English law required parental consent to marriage if one party were under the age of twenty-one, it was common practice for young English couples to elope to Scotland, where marriage was legal without parental consent for girls of twelve and for boys of fourteen.

"It's all over with our poor Judy!" said I, with a heavy sigh, making bold to speak to him one night when he was a little cheerful, and standing in the servant's hall all alone with me, as was often his custom. "Not at all," said he, "I never was fonder of Judy than at this present speaking, and to prove it to you," said he, and he took from my hand a halfpenny, change that I had just got along with my tobacco, "and to prove it to you, Thady," says he, "it's a toss up with me which I shall marry this minute, her or Mr. Moneygawl of Mount Juliet's Town's daughter—so it is." "Oh, boo! boo!"[1] says I, making light of it, to see what he would go on to next, "your honour's joking, to be sure, there's no compare between our poor Judy and Miss Isabella, who has a great fortune, they say." "I'm not a man to mind a fortune, nor never was," said Sir Condy proudly, "whatever her friends may say; and to make short of it," says he, "I'm come to a determination upon the spot;" with that he swore such a terrible oath, as made me cross myself: "And by this book," said he, snatching up my ballad book mistaking it for my prayer-book, which lay in the window, "and by this book," said he, "and by all the books that ever were shut and opened, it's come to a toss up with me, and I'll stand or fall by the toss, and so, Thady, hand me over that *pin*[2] out of the inkhorn," and he makes a cross on the smooth side of the halfpenny; "Judy M'Quirk," said he, "her mark."[3] God bless him! his hand was a little unsteadied by all the whiskey punch he had taken, but it was plain to see his heart was for poor Judy. My heart was all as one as in my mouth, when I saw the halfpenny up in the air, but

I said nothing at all, and when it came down, I was glad I had kept myself to myself, for to be sure now it was all over with poor Judy. "Judy's out a luck," said I, striving to laugh. "I'm out a luck," said he, and I never saw a man look so cast down; he took up the halfpenny off the flag,[4] and walked away quite sober-like by the shock. Now though as easy a man you would think as any in the wide world, there was no such thing as making him unsay one of these sort of vows,[5] which he had learned to reverence when young, as I well remember teaching him to toss up for bog berries on my knee. So I saw the affair was as good as settled between him and Miss Isabella, and I had no more to say but to wish her joy, which I did the week afterwards upon her return from Scotland with my poor master.

My new lady was young, as might be supposed of a lady that had been carried off by her own consent to Scotland, but I could only see her at the first through her veil, which, from bashfulness or fashion, she kept over her face. "And am I to walk through all this crowd of people, my dearest love?" said she to Sir Condy, meaning us servants and tenants, who had gathered at the back gate. "My dear," said Sir Condy, "there's nothing for it but to walk, or to let me carry you as far as the house, for you see the back road's too narrow for a carriage, and the great piers have tumbled down across the front approach, so there's no driving the right way by reason of the ruins." "Plato, thou reasonest well!"[6] said she, or words to that effect, which I could no ways understand; and again, when her foot stumbled against a broken bit of a car wheel, she cried out, "Angels and

---

[1] [Edgeworth's note] *Boo! Boo!*—an exclamation equivalent to *pshaw!* or *nonsense.*

[2] [Edgeworth's note] *Pin,* read *pen*—it formerly was vulgarly pronounced *pin* in Ireland.

[3] [Edgeworth's note] *Her mark*—It *was* the custom in Ireland for those who could not write, to make a cross to stand for their signature, as was formerly the practice of our English monarchs. The editor inserts the facsimile of an Irish mark, which may hereafter be valuable to a judicious antiquary—

Her
Judy x M'Quirk
Mark.

In bonds or notes, signed in this manner, a witness is requisite, as the name is frequently written by him or her.

[4] *flag* Flagstone.

[5] [Edgeworth's note] *Vows*—It has been maliciously and unjustly hinted, that the lower classes of the people in Ireland pay but little regard to oaths; yet it is certain that some oaths or vows have great power over their minds. Sometimes they swear they will be revenged on some of their neighbours; this is an oath they never are known to break. But what is infinitely more extraordinary and unaccountable, they sometimes make a vow against whiskey; these vows are usually limited for a short time. A woman who has a drunken husband is the most fortunate if she can prevail upon him to go to the priest, and make a vow against whiskey for a year, or a month, or a week, or a day.

[6] *Plato, thou reasonest well!* From Joseph Addison's *Cato, a Tragedy* 5.1.1 (1713).

ministers of grace, defend us!"[1] Well, thought I, to be sure if she's no Jewish like the last, she is a mad woman for certain, which is as bad: it would have been as well for my poor master to have taken up with poor Judy, who is in her right mind any how.

She was dressed like a mad woman, moreover, more than like any one I ever saw afore or since, and I could not take my eyes off her, but still followed behind her, and her feathers on the top of her hat were broke going in at the low back door, and she pulled out her little bottle out of her pocket to smell to when she found herself in the kitchen and said, "I shall faint with the heat of this odious, odious place." "My dear, it's only three steps across the kitchen, and there's a fine air if your veil was up," said Sir Condy, and with that threw back her veil, so that I had then a full sight of her face; she had not at all the colour of one going to faint, but a fine complexion of her own, as I then took it to be, though her maid told me after it was all put on;[2] but even complexion and all taken in, she was no way, in point of good looks, to compare to Judy; and with all she had a quality toss with her,[3] but may be it was my over-partiality to Judy, into whose place I may say she stepped, that made me notice all this. To do her justice, however, she was, when we came to know her better, very liberal in housekeeping, nothing at all of the skin-flint in her; she left every thing to the housekeeper, and her own maid, Mrs. Jane, who went with her to Scotland, gave her the best of characters for generosity; she seldom or ever wore a thing twice the same way, Mrs. Jane told us, and was always pulling her things to pieces, and giving them away, never being used in her father's house to think of expense in any thing; and she reckoned, to be sure, to go on the same way at Castle Rackrent; but when I came to enquire, I learned that her father was so mad with her for running off after his locking her up, and forbidding her to think any more of

Sir Condy, that he would not give her a farthing;[4] and it was lucky for her she had a few thousands of her own, which had been left to her by a good grandmother, and these were very convenient to begin with. My master and my lady set out in great style; they had the finest coach and chariot, and horses and liveries,[5] and cut the greatest dash in the county, returning their wedding visits!—and it was immediately reported that her father had undertaken to pay all my master's debts, and of course all his tradesmen gave him a new credit, and every thing went on smack smooth, and I could not but admire my lady's spirit, and was proud to see Castle Rackrent again in all its glory. My lady had a fine taste for building and furniture, and play-houses, and she turned every thing topsy-turvy, and made the barrack-room into a theatre, as she called it, and she went on as if she had a mint of money at her elbow; and to be sure I thought she knew best, especially as Sir Condy said nothing to it one way or the other. All he asked, God bless him! was to live in peace and quietness, and have his bottle or his whiskey punch at night to himself. Now this was little enough, to be sure, for any gentleman, but my lady couldn't abide the smell of the whiskey punch. "My dear," says he, "you liked it well enough before we were married, and why not now?" "My dear," said she, "I never smelt it, or I assure you I should never have prevailed upon myself to marry you." "My dear, I am sorry you did not smell it, but we can't help that now," returned my master, without putting himself in a passion, or going out of his way, but just fair and easy helped himself to another glass, and drank it off to her good health. All this the butler told me, who was going backwards and forwards unnoticed with the jug, and hot water, and sugar, and all he thought wanting. Upon my master's swallowing the last glass of whiskey punch, my lady burst into tears, calling him an ungrateful, base, barbarous wretch! and went off into a fit of hysterics, as I think Mrs. Jane called it, and my poor master was greatly frightened, this being the first thing of the kind he had seen; and he fell straight on his knees before her,

---

1   *Angels and … defend us!*   From Shakespeare's *Hamlet* 1.4.39.

2   *it was all put on*   It was achieved through the use of make-up. (The use of cosmetics by younger women was often disapproved of in eighteenth-century Britain.)

3   *she had … toss with her*   She had upper-class mannerisms.

4   *farthing*   Coin valued at a quarter of a penny.

5   *coach … and liveries*   Four-wheel carriage and two-wheel carriage, and horses and stables.

and, like a good-hearted cratur as he was, ordered the whiskey punch out of the room, and bid 'em throw open all the windows, and cursed himself, and then my lady came to herself again, and when she saw him kneeling there, bid him get up, and not forswear himself any more, for that she was sure he did not love her, nor never had: this we learnt from Mrs. Jane, who was the only person left present at all this. "My dear," returns my master, thinking to be sure of Judy, as well he might, "whoever told you so is an incendiary, and I'll have 'em turned out of the house this minute, if you'll only let me know which of them it was." "Told me what?" says my lady, starting upright in her chair. "Nothing, nothing at all," said my master, seeing he had overshot himself, and that my lady spoke at random, "but what you said just now that I did not love you, Bella; who told you that?" "My own sense," she said, and she put her handkerchief to her face, and leant back upon Mrs. Jane, and fell to sobbing as if her heart would break. "Why now Bella, this is very strange of you," said my poor master, "if nobody has told you nothing, what is it you are taking on for at this rate, and exposing yourself and me for this way?" "Oh say no more, say no more, every word you say kills me," cried my lady; and she ran on like one, as Mrs. Jane says, raving. "Oh Sir Condy, Sir Condy! I that had hoped to find in you—" "Why now faith this is a little too much; do Bella, try to recollect yourself, my dear; am not I your husband, and of your own choosing, and is not that enough?" "Oh, too much! too much!" cried my lady, wringing her hands. "Why, my dear, come to your right senses for the love of heaven. See, is not the whiskey punch, jug and bowl and all, gone out of the room long ago? What is it in the wide world you have to complain of?" But still my lady sobbed and sobbed, and called herself the most wretched of women; and among other out-of-the-way provoking things, asked my master, was he fit company for her, and he drinking all night? This nettling[1] him, which it was hard to do, he replied, that as to drinking all night, he was then as sober as she was herself, and that it was no matter how much a man drank, provided

it did no ways affect or stagger him; that as to being fit company for her, he thought himself of a family to be fit company for any lord or lady in the land; but that he never prevented her from seeing and keeping what company she pleased, and that he had done his best to make Castle Rackrent pleasing to her since her marriage, having always had the house full of visitors, and if her own relations were not amongst them, he said, that was their own fault, and their pride's fault, of which he was sorry to find her ladyship had so unbecoming a share. So concluding, he took his candle and walked off to his room, and my lady was in her tantarums[2] for three days after; and would have been so much longer, no doubt, but some of her friends, young ladies and cousins and second cousins, came to Castle Rackrent, by my poor master's express invitation, to see her, and she was in a hurry to get up, as Mrs. Jane called it, a play for them, and so got well, and was as finely dressed and as happy to look at as ever; and all the young ladies who used to be in her room dressing of her, said, in Mrs. Jane's hearing, that my lady was the happiest bride ever they had seen, and that to be sure a love match was the only thing for happiness, where the parties could any way afford it.

As to affording it, God knows it was little they knew of the matter; my lady's few thousands could not last for ever, especially the way she went on with them; and letters from tradesfolk came every post thick and three-fold, with bills as long as my arm, of years and years standing; my son Jason had 'em all handed over to him, and the pressing letters were all unread by Sir Condy, who hated trouble, and could never be brought to hear talk of business, but still put it off and put it off, saying, settle it any how, or bid 'em call again tomorrow, or speak to me about it some other time. Now it was hard to find the right time to speak, for in the mornings he was a-bed and in the evenings over his bottle, where no gentleman chooses to be disturbed. Things in a twelve-month or so came to such a pass, there was no making a shift to go on any longer, though we were all of us well enough used to live from hand to mouth at Castle

---

[1] *nettling* Irritating or provoking.

[2] *tantarums* Tantrums.

Rackrent. One day, I remember, when there was a power of company, all sitting after dinner in the dusk, not to say dark, in the drawing-room, my lady having rung five times for candles and none to go up, the housekeeper sent up the footman, who went to my mistress, and whispered behind her chair how it was. "My lady," says he, "there are no candles in the house." "Bless me," says she, "then take a horse and gallop off as fast as you can to Carrick O'Fungus and get some." "And in the mean time tell them to step into the play-house, and try if there are not some bits left," added Sir Condy, who happened to be within hearing. The man was sent up again to my lady, to let her know there was no horse to go but one that wanted a shoe. "Go to Sir Condy then; I know nothing at all about the horses," said my lady, "why do you plague me with these things?" How it was settled I really forget, but to the best of my remembrance, the boy was sent down to my son Jason's to borrow candles for the night. Another time in the winter, and on a desperate cold day, there was no turf in for the parlour and above stairs, and scarce enough for the cook in the kitchen. The little *gossoon*[1] was sent off to the neighbours to see and beg or borrow some, but none could he bring back with him for love or money; so as needs must we were forced to trouble Sir Condy. "Well, and if there's no turf to be had in the town or country, why what signifies talking any more about it; can't ye go and cut down a tree?" "Which tree, please your honour?" I made bold to say. "Any tree at all that's good to burn," said Sir Condy; "send off smart and get one down and the fires lighted before my lady gets up to breakfast, or the house will be too hot to hold us." He was always very considerate in all things about my lady, and she wanted for nothing whilst he had it to give. Well, when things were tight with them about this time, my son Jason put in a word again about the lodge, and made a genteel offer to lay

down the purchase money to relieve Sir Condy's distresses. Now Sir Condy had it from the best authority, that there were two writs[2] come down to the Sheriff against his person, and the Sheriff, as ill luck would have it, was no friend of his, and talked how he must do his duty, and how he would do it, if it was against the first man in the county, or even his own brother, let alone one who had voted against him at the last election, as Sir Condy had done. So Sir Condy was fain[3] to take the purchase money of the lodge from my son Jason to settle matters; and sure enough it was a good bargain for both parties, for my son bought the fee simple of a good house for him and his heirs for ever for little or nothing, and by selling of it for that same my master saved himself from a gaol. Every way it turned out fortunate for Sir Condy; for before the money was all gone there came a general election, and he being so well beloved in the county, and one of the oldest families, no one had a better right to stand candidate for the vacancy; and he was called upon by all his friends, and the whole county I may say, to declare himself against the old member, who had little thought of a contest. My master did not relish the thoughts of a troublesome canvas,[4] and all the ill will he might bring upon himself by disturbing the peace of the county, besides the expense, which was no trifle; but all his friends called upon one another to subscribe,[5] and formed themselves into a committee, and wrote all his circular letters for him, and engaged all his agents, and did all the business unknown to him; and he was well pleased that it should be so at last, and my lady herself was very sanguine about the election; and there was open house kept night and day at Castle Rackrent, and I thought I never saw my lady look so well in her life as she did at that time; there were grand dinners, and all the gentlemen drinking success to Sir Condy till they were carried off; and then dances and balls, and the ladies all finishing with a raking pot of tea* in the morning. Indeed it was well the company

[1] [Edgeworth's note] *Gossoon*—a little boy—from the French word *Garçon*. In most Irish families there used to be a bare-footed gossoon, who was slave to the cook and the butler, and who in fact, without wages, did all the hard work of the house. Gossoons were always employed as messengers. The Editor has known a gossoon to go on foot, without shoes or stockings, fifty-one English miles between sunrise and sunset.

[2] *writs* Summonses.
[3] *fain* Obligated.
[4] *of a troublesome canvas* Of taking the trouble to canvas the constituency (i.e., to call on individuals to solicit their support).
[5] *subscribe* Contribute money (to Sir Condy's election campaign).

made it their choice to sit up all nights, for there was not half beds enough for the sights of people that were in it, though there were shakedowns[1] in the drawing-room always made up before sunrise, for those that liked it. For my part, when I saw the doings that were going on, and the loads of claret that went down the throats of them that had no right to be asking for it, and the sights of meat that went up to table and never came down, besides what was carried off to one or t'other below stairs, I couldn't but pity my poor master who was to pay for all, but I said nothing for fear of gaining myself ill will. The day of election will come some time or other, says I to myself, and all will be over; and so it did, and a glorious day it was as any I ever had the happiness to see. "Huzza! huzza! Sir Condy Rackrent for ever!" was the first thing I hears in the morning, and the same and nothing else all day, and not a soul sober only just when polling, enough to give their votes as became 'em, and to stand the brow-beating of the lawyers, who came tight enough upon us; and many of our freeholders were knocked off;[2] having never a freehold that they could safely swear to, and Sir Condy was not willing to have any man perjure himself for his sake, as was done on the other side, God knows, but no matter for that. Some of our friends were dumbfounded, by the lawyers asking them: had they ever been upon the ground where their freeholds lay? Now Sir Condy being tender of the consciences of them that had not been on the ground, and so could not swear to a freehold when cross-examined by them lawyers, sent out for a couple of cleaves[3]-full of the sods of his farm of Gulteeshinnagh; and as soon as the sods came into town, he set each man upon his sod, and so then ever after, you know, they could fairly swear they had been upon the ground.[4] We gained

the day by this piece of honesty.* I thought I should have died in the streets for joy when I seed my poor master chaired, and he bare-headed, and it raining as hard as it could pour; but all the crowds following him up and down, and he bowing and shaking hands with the whole town. "Is that Sir Condy Rackrent in the chair?" says a stranger man in the crowd. "The same," says I, "who else should it be? God bless him!" "And I take it, then, you belong to him," says he. "Not at all," says I, "but I live under him, and have done so these two hundred years and upwards, me and mine." "It's lucky for you, then," rejoins he, "that he is where he is; for was he any where else but in the chair this minute he'd be in a worse place, for I was sent down on purpose to put him up,[5] and here's my order for so doing in my pocket." It was a writ that villain the wine merchant had marked against my poor master, for some hundreds of an old debt which it was a shame to be talking of at such a time as this. "Put it in your pocket again, and think no more of it any ways for seven years to come, my honest friend," says I, "he's a member of Parliament now, praised be God, and such as you can't touch him;[6] and if you'll take a fool's advice, I'd have ye keep out of the way this day, or you'll run a good chance of getting your deserts amongst my master's friends, unless you choose to drink his health like every body else." "I've no objection to that in life," said he; so we went into one of the public houses kept open for my master, and we had a great deal of talk about this thing and that. "And how is it," says he, "your master keeps on so well upon his legs? I heard say he was off Holantide twelve-month past." "Never was better or heartier in his life," said I. "It's not that I'm after speaking of," said he, "but there was a great report of his being ruined." "No matter," says I,

---

[1] *shakedowns*   Makeshift beds, probably consisting of straw gathered on the floor.

[2] *many of our … knocked off*   Many of those who had been listed as eligible to vote were knocked off the list. Only those males who owned property—or "freeholds"—valued at two pounds or more were eligible to vote.

[3] *cleaves*   Baskets.

[4] [Edgeworth's note]   This was actually done at an election in Ireland.

[5] [Edgeworth's note]   *To put him up*—to put him in gaol. [Until well into the nineteenth century, those unable to pay a debt were liable to imprisonment.]

[6] *he's a member of Parliament now … you can't touch him*   Whereas "parliamentary privilege" today is a narrow concept providing immunity from prosecution for statements made in the House of Commons, in the eighteenth century much wider privileges were claimed by members of Parliament; not until 1831 was it "established generally," (according to the House of Commons Committee of Privileges) that privilege was "not claimable for any indictable offence."

"the Sheriffs two years running were his particular friends, and the sub-sheriffs were both of them gentlemen, and were properly spoken to; and so the writs lay snug with them, and they, as I understand by my son Jason the custom in them cases is, returned the writs as they came to them to those that sent 'em, much good may it do them, with word in Latin that no such person as Sir Condy Rackrent, Bart.,[1] was to be found in those parts." "Oh, I understand all those ways better, no offence, than you," says he, laughing, and at the same time filling his glass to my master's good health, which convinced me he was a warm friend in his heart after all, though appearances were a little suspicious or so at first. "To be sure," says he, still cutting his joke, "when a man's over head and shoulders in debt, he may live the faster for it, and the better if he goes the right way about it; or else how is it so many live on so well, as we see every day, after they are ruined?" "How is it," says I, being a little merry at the time, "how is it but just as you see the ducks in the kitchen yard, just after their heads are cut off by the cook, running round and round faster than when alive?" At which conceit he fell a laughing, and remarked he had never had the happiness yet to see the chicken yard at Castle Rackrent. "It won't be long so, I hope," says I, "you'll be kindly welcome there, as every body is made by my master; there is not a freer spoken gentleman or a better beloved, high or low, in all Ireland." And of what passed after this I'm not sensible, for we drank Sir Condy's good health and the downfall of his enemies till we could stand no longer ourselves. And little did I think at the time, or till long after, how I was harbouring my poor master's greatest of enemies myself. This fellow had the impudence, after coming to see the chicken-yard, to get me to introduce him to my son Jason; little more than the man that never was born did I guess at his meaning by this visit; he gets him a correct list fairly drawn out from my son Jason of all my master's debts, and goes straight round to the creditors and buys them all up, which he did easy enough, seeing the half of them never expected to see their money out

of Sir Condy's hands.[2] Then, when this base-minded limb of the law, as I afterwards detected him in being, grew to be sole creditor over all, he takes him out a custodiam[3] on all the denominations and sub-denominations, and every carton and half carton* upon the estate; and not content with that, must have an execution against the master's goods and down to the furniture, though little worth, of Castle Rackrent itself. But this is a part of my story I'm not come to yet, and it's bad to be forestalling—ill news flies fast enough all the world over.

To go back to the day of the election, which I never think of but with pleasure and tears of gratitude for those good times; after the election was quite and clean over, there comes shoals[4] of people from all parts, claiming to have obliged my master with their votes, and putting him in mind of promises which he could never remember himself to have made: one was to have a freehold for each of his four sons; another was to have a renewal of a lease; another an abatement; one came to be paid ten guineas for a pair of silver buckles sold my master on the hustings,[5] which turned out to be no better than copper gilt; another had a long bill for oats, the half of which never went into the granary to my certain knowledge, and the other half was not fit for the cattle to touch; but the bargain was made the week before the election, and the coach and saddle-horses were got into order for the day, besides a vote fairly got by them oats; so no more reasoning on that head; but then there was no end to them that were telling Sir

---

[1]   *Bart.*   Abbreviation for Baronet.

[2]   *all my master's debts … Sir Condy's hands*   It was a common eighteenth-century practice for individuals acting as debt collectors (the precursors of today's collection agencies) to buy up debts that creditors had been unable to settle, at prices that would in each case be far below the amount owed. In the event of the debt collector being able to arrange for the debt to be finally paid in full, he would thus turn a substantial profit.

[3]   *custodiam*   In Ireland, a lease-grant of Crown land, giving the lessee the right to collect rent from the property.

[4]   *shoals*   Crowds.

[5]   *on the hustings*   Hustings were platforms from which candidates for election spoke to the electors; by extension, "on the hustings" came to be used to mean "during the election campaign."

Condy he had engaged to make their sons excisemen,[1] or high constables, or the like; and as for them that had bills to give in for liquor, and beds, and straw, and ribbons, and horses, and post-chaises[2] for the gentlemen freeholders that came from all parts and other counties to vote for my master, and were not, to be sure, to be at any charges, there was no standing against all these; and, worse than all the gentlemen of my master's committee, who managed all for him, and talked how they'd bring him in without costing him a penny, and subscribed by hundreds very genteelly, forgot to pay their subscriptions, and had laid out in agents and lawyers, fees and secret service money, the Lord knows how much; and my master could never ask one of them for their subscription, you are sensible, nor for the price of a fine horse he had sold one of them, so it all was left at his door. He could never, God bless him again, I say, bring himself to ask a gentleman for money, despising such sort of conversation himself; but others, who were not gentlemen born, behaved very uncivil in pressing him at this very time, and all he could do to content 'em all was to take himself out of the way as fast as possible to Dublin, where my lady had taken a house as fitting for him, a Member of Parliament, to attend his duty in there all the winters. I was very lonely when the whole family was gone, and all the things they had ordered to go and forgot sent after them by the stage.[3] There was then a great silence in Castle Rackrent, and I went moping from room to room, hearing the doors clap for want of right locks, and the wind through the broken windows that the glazier never would come to mend, and the rain coming through the roof and best ceilings all over the house, for want of the slater whose bill was not paid; besides our having no slates or shingles for that part of the old building which was shingled, and burnt when the chimney took fire, and had been open to the weather ever since. I took myself to the servants' hall in the evening to smoke my pipe as usual, but missed the bit of talk we used to have there sadly, and ever after was content to stay in the kitchen and boil my little potatoes,[4] and put up my bed there, and every post day I looked in the newspaper, but no news of my master in the house. He never spoke good or bad; but, as the butler wrote down word to my son Jason, was very ill-used by the government about a place that was promised him and never given, after his supporting them against his conscience very honourably, and being greatly abused for it, which hurt him greatly, he having the name of a great patriot in the country before. The house and living in Dublin too was not to be had for nothing, and my son Jason said, "Sir Condy must soon be looking out for a new agent, for I've done my part, and can do no more: if my lady had the bank of Ireland to spend, it would go all in one winter, and Sir Condy would never gainsay[5] her, though he does not care the rind of a lemon for her all the while."

Now I could not bear to hear Jason giving out after this manner against the family, and twenty people standing by in the street. Ever since he had lived at the lodge of his own he looked down, howsomever, upon poor old Thady, and was grown quite a great gentleman, and had none of his relations near him; no wonder he was no kinder to poor Sir Condy than to his own kith or kin.[6] In the spring it was the villain that got the list of the debts from him brought down the custodiam, Sir Condy still attending his duty in Parliament; and I could scarcely believe my own old eyes, or the spectacles with which I read it, when I was shown my son Jason's name joined in the custodiam; but he told me it was only for form's sake, and to make things easier, than if all the land was under the power of a total stranger. Well, I did not know what to think; it was hard to be talking ill of my own, and I could not but grieve for my poor master's fine estate, all torn by these vultures of the

[1] *excisemen* Officers who collect excise taxes on the sale and production of goods within a country.

[2] *post-chaise* Hired coach that could be used for long-distance travel.

[3] *stage* Stagecoach, used for mail and passenger transport.

[4] [Edgeworth's note] *My little potatoes*—Thady does not mean by this expression that his potatoes were less than other people's, or less than the usual size; *little* is here used only as an Italian diminutive, expressive of fondness.

[5] *gainsay* Contradict.

[6] [Edgeworth's note] *Kith and kin*—family or relations. *Kin* from *Kind*; *Kith* from we know not what.

law; so I said nothing, but just looked on to see how it would all end.

It was not till the month of June that he and my lady came down to the country. My master was pleased to take me aside with him to the brewhouse that same evening, to complain to me of my son and other matters, in which he said he was confident I had neither art nor part; he said a great deal more to me, to whom he had been fond to talk ever since he was my white-headed boy before he came to the estate; and all that he said about poor Judy I can never forget, but scorn to repeat. He did not say an unkind word of my lady, but wondered, as well he might, her relations would do nothing for him or her, and they in all this great distress. He did not take any thing long to heart, let it be as it would, and had no more malice or thought of the like in him than the child that can't speak; this night it was all out of his head before he went to his bed. He took his jug of whiskey punch; my lady was grown quite easy about the whiskey punch by this time, and so I did suppose all was going on right betwixt them, till I learnt the truth through Mrs. Jane, who talked over the affairs to the housekeeper, and I within hearing. The night my master came home, thinking of nothing at all, but just making merry, he drank his bumper toast "to the deserts of that old curmudgeon my father-in-law, and all enemies at Mount Juliet's Town." Now my lady was no longer in the mind she formerly was, and did no ways relish hearing her own friends abused in her presence, she said. "Then why don't they show themselves your friends," said my master, "and oblige me with the loan of the money I condescended, by your advice, my dear, to ask? It's now three posts since I sent off my letter, desiring in the postscript a speedy answer by the return of the post, and no account at all from them yet." "I expect they'll write to *me* next post," says my lady, and that was all that passed then; but it was easy from this to guess there was a coolness betwixt them, and with good cause.

The next morning, being post day, I sent off the *gossoon* early to the post-office, to see was there any letter likely to set matters to rights, and he brought back one with the proper post-mark upon it, sure enough, and I

had no time to examine, or make any conjecture more about it, for into the servants' hall pops Mrs. Jane with a blue bandbox[1] in her hand, quite entirely mad. "Dear Ma'am, and what's the matter?" says I. "Matter enough," says she, "don't you see my bandbox is wet through, and my best bonnet here spoiled, besides my lady's, and all by the rain coming in through that gallery window, that you might have got mended if you'd had any sense, Thady, all the time we were in town in the winter." "Sure, I could not get the glazier, Ma'am," says I. "You might have stopped it up anyhow," says she. "So I did, Ma'am, to the best of my ability; one of the panes with the old pillow-case, and the other with a piece of the old stage green curtain; sure I was as careful as possible all the time you were away, and not a drop of rain came in at that window of all the windows in the house, all winter, Ma'am, when under my care; and now the family's come home, and it's summertime, I never thought no more about it to be sure; but dear, it's a pity to think of your bonnet, Ma'am; but here's what will please you, Ma'am, a letter from Mount Juliet's Town for my lady." With that she snatches it from me without a word more, and runs up the back stairs to my mistress; I follows with a slate to make up the window. This window was in the long passage, or gallery, as my lady gave out orders to have it called, in the gallery leading to my master's bed-chamber and hers, and when I went up with the slate, the door having no lock, and the bolt spoilt, was a-jar after Mrs. Jane, and as I was busy with the window, I heard all that was saying within.

"Well, what's in your letter, Bella, my dear?" says he, "you're a long time spelling it over."[2] "Won't you shave this morning, Sir Condy," says she, and put the letter in her pocket. "I shaved the day before yesterday," says he, "my dear, and that's not what I'm thinking of now; but anything to oblige you, and to have peace and quietness, my dear"—and presently I had a glimpse of him at the cracked glass over the chimney piece, standing up shaving himself to please my lady. But she took no notice, but went on reading her book, and Mrs. Jane

---

[1] *bandbox* Small box for storing caps, ruffs, and other accessories.

[2] *spelling it over* Reading through it slowly.

doing her hair behind. "What is it you're reading there, my dear?—phoo, I've cut myself with this razor; the man's a cheat that sold it me, but I have not paid him for it yet. What is it you're reading there? did you hear me asking you, my dear?" "The Sorrows of Werter,"[1] replies my lady, as well as I could hear. "I think more of the sorrows of Sir Condy," says my master, joking like. "What news from Mount Juliet's Town?" "No news," says she, "but the old story over again; my friends all reproaching me still for what I can't help now." "Is it for marrying me?" said my master, still shaving; "what signifies, as you say, talking of that when it can't be helped now?"

With that she heaved a great sigh, that I heard plain enough in the passage. "And did not you use me basely, Sir Condy," says she, "not to tell me you were ruined before I married you?" "Tell you, my dear," said he, "did you ever ask me one word about it? and had not you friends enough of your own, that were telling you nothing else from morning to night, if you'd have listened to them slanders?" "No slanders, nor are my friends slanderers; and I can't bear to hear them treated with disrespect as I do," says my lady, and took out her pocket handkerchief, "they are the best of friends, and if I had taken their advice—but my father was wrong to lock me up, I own; that was the only unkind thing I can charge him with; for if he had not locked me up, I should never have had a serious thought of running away as I did." "Well, my dear," said my master, "don't cry and make yourself uneasy about it now, when it's all over, and you have the man of your own choice in spite of 'em all." "I was too young, I know, to make a choice at the time you ran away with me, I'm sure," says my lady, and another sigh, which made my master, half shaved as he was, turn round upon her in surprise. "Why Bella," says he, "you can't deny what you know as well as I do, that it was at your own particular desire, and that twice under your own hand and seal expressed,

that I should carry you off as I did to Scotland, and marry you there." "Well, say no more about it, Sir Condy," said my lady, pettish like,[2] "I was a child then, you know." "And as far as I know, you're little better now, my dear Bella, to be talking in this manner to your husband's *face*; but I won't take it ill of you, for I know it's something in that letter you put in your pocket just now, that has set you against me all on a sudden, and imposed upon your understanding." "It is not so very easy as you think it, Sir Condy, to impose upon *my* understanding," said my lady. "My dear," says he, "I have, and with reason, the best opinion of your understanding of any man now breathing, and you know I have never set my own in competition with it; till now, my dear Bella," says he, taking her hand from her book as kind as could be, "till now when I have the great advantage of being quite cool, and you not; so don't believe one word your friends say against your own Sir Condy, and lend me the letter out of your pocket, till I see what it is they can have to say." "Take it then," says she, "and as you are quite cool, I hope it is a proper time to request you'll allow me to comply with the wishes of all my own friends, and return to live with my father and family, during the remainder of my wretched existence, at Mount Juliet's Town."

At this my poor master fell back a few paces, like one that had been shot. "You're not serious, Bella," says he, "and could you find it in your heart to leave me this way in the very middle of my distresses, all alone?" But recollecting himself after his first surprise, and a moment's time for reflection, he said, with a great deal of consideration for my lady, "Well, Bella, my dear, I believe you are right; for what could you do at Castle Rackrent, and an execution against the goods coming down, and the furniture to be canted, and an auction in the house all next week?[3] So you have my full consent to go, since that is your desire, only you must not think of my accompanying you, which I could not in honour do upon the terms I always have been since our marriage

---

[1] *The Sorrows of Werter* Johann Wolfgang von Goethe's *The Sorrows of Young Werther* (*Die Leiden des Jungen Werthers*, 1774). The epistolary novel, which presents a powerfully melodramatic story of romance and strong emotion, was extremely popular in the late eighteenth and early nineteenth centuries.

[2] *pettish like* Petulantly.

[3] *and an execution against the goods … next week* Given that a legal order for the goods is to be executed, and the furniture and other possessions are to be auctioned off next week.

with your friends; besides I have business to transact at home; so in the mean time, if we are to have any breakfast this morning, let us go down and have it for the last time in peace and comfort, Bella."

Then as I heard my master coming to the passage door, I finished fastening up my slate against the broken pane, and when he came out, I wiped down the window seat with my wig,[1] bade him a good morrow as kindly as I could, seeing he was in trouble, though he strove and thought to hide it from me. "This window is all racked and tattered," says I, "and it's what I'm striving to mend." "It *is* all racked and tattered plain enough," says he, "and never mind mending it, honest old Thady," says he, "it will do well enough for you and I, and that's all the company we shall have left in the house by-and-bye." "I'm sorry to see your honour so low this morning," says I, "but you'll be better after taking your breakfast." "Step down to the servants' hall," says he, "and bring me up the pen and ink into the parlour, and get a sheet of paper from Mrs. Jane, for I have business that can't brook to be delayed,[2] and come into the parlour with the pen and ink yourself, Thady, for I must have you to witness my signing a paper I have to execute in a hurry." Well, while I was getting of the pen and inkhorn, and the sheet of paper, I ransacked my brains to think what could be the papers my poor master could have to execute in such a hurry, he that never thought of such a thing as doing business afore breakfast in the whole course of his life for any man living; but this was for my lady, as I afterwards found, and the more genteel of him after all her treatment.

I was just witnessing the paper that he had scrawled over, and was shaking the ink out of my pen upon the carpet, when my lady came in to breakfast, and she started as if it had been a ghost, as well she might, when she saw Sir Condy writing at this unseasonable hour. "That will do very well, Thady," says he to me, and took the paper I had signed to, without knowing what upon the earth it might be, out of my hands, and walked, folding it up, to my lady.

"You are concerned in this, my Lady Rackrent," says he, putting it into her hands, "and I beg you'll keep this memorandum safe, and show it to your friends the first thing you do when you get home, but put it in your pocket now, my dear, and let us eat our breakfast, in God's name." "What is all this?" said my lady, opening the paper in great curiosity. "It's only a bit of a memorandum of what I think becomes me to do whenever I am able," says my master; "you know my situation, tied hand and foot at the present time being, but that can't last always, and when I'm dead and gone, the land will be to the good,[3] Thady, you know; and take notice it's my intention your lady should have a clear five hundred a year jointure off the estate, afore any of my debts are paid." "Oh, please your honour," says I, "I can't expect to live to see that time, being now upwards of fourscore and ten[4] years of age, and you a young man, and likely to continue so, by the help of God." I was vexed to see my lady so insensible too, for all she said was, "This is very genteel of you, Sir Condy. You need not wait any longer, Thady." So I just picked up the pen and ink that had tumbled on the floor, and heard my master finish with saying, "You behaved very genteel to me, my dear, when you threw all the little you had in your own power, along with yourself, into my hands; and as I don't deny but what you may have had some things to complain of," (to be sure he was thinking then of Judy, or of the whiskey punch, one or t'other, or both); "and as I don't deny but you may have had something to complain of, my dear, it is but fair you should have something in the form of compensation to look forward

---

1   [Edgeworth's note]   Wigs were formerly used instead of brooms in Ireland, for sweeping or dusting tables, stairs, &c. The Editor doubted the fact, till he saw a labourer of the old school sweep down a flight of stairs with his wig; he afterwards put it on his head again with the utmost composure, and said, "Oh please your honour, it's never a bit the worse."

It must be acknowledged that these men are not in any danger of catching cold by taking off their wigs occasionally, because they usually have fine crops of hair growing under their wigs. The wigs are often yellow, and the hair which appears from beneath them black; the wigs are usually too small, and are raised up by the hair beneath, or by the ears of the wearers.

2   *that can't ... be delayed*   So urgent that it can't be delayed.

3   *the land ... to the good*   The value of the land will exceed the value of the debts that will need to be paid.

4   *fourscore and ten*   Ninety (a "score" being twenty).

to agreeably in future; besides, it's an act of justice to myself, that none of your friends, my dear, may ever have it to say against me I married for money, and not for love." "That is the last thing I should ever have thought of saying of you, Sir Condy," said my lady, looking very gracious. "Then, my dear," said Sir Condy, "we shall part as good friends as we met, so, all's right."

I was greatly rejoiced to hear this, and went out of the parlour to report it all to the kitchen. The next morning my lady and Mrs. Jane set out for Mount Juliet's Town in the jaunting car;[1] many wondered at my lady's choosing to go away, considering all things, upon the jaunting car, as if it was only a party of pleasure; but they did not know till I told them, that the coach was all broke in the journey down, and no other vehicle but the car to be had; besides, my lady's friends were to send their coach to meet her at the cross roads; so it was all done very proper.

My poor master was in great trouble after my lady left us. The execution came down, and every thing at Castle Rackrent was seized by the gripers,[2] and my son Jason, to his shame be it spoken, amongst them; I wondered, for the life of me, how he could harden himself to do it, but then he had been studying the law, and had made himself attorney Quirk; so he brought down at once a heap of accounts upon my master's head. To cash lent, and to ditto, and to ditto, and to ditto, and oats, and bills paid at the milliner's and linen-draper's, and many dresses for the fancy balls in Dublin for my lady, and all the bills to the workmen and tradesmen for the scenery of the theatre, and the chandler's[3] and grocer's bills, and tailor's, besides butcher's and baker's, and worse than all, the old one of that base wine-merchant's, that wanted to arrest my poor master for the amount on the election day, for which amount Sir Condy afterwards passed his note of hand, bearing lawful interest from the date thereof; and the interest and compound interest was now mounted to a terrible deal on many other notes and bonds for money bor-

rowed, and there was besides hush-money to the sub-sheriffs, and sheets upon sheets of old and new attorneys' bills, with heavy balances, *as per former account furnished*, brought forward with interest thereon; then there was a powerful deal due to the Crown for sixteen years arrear of quit-rent of the town lands of Carrick-shaughlin, with drivers' fees, and a compliment to the receiver every year for letting the quit-rent run on, to oblige Sir Condy and Sir Kit afore him. Then there was bills for spirits, and ribbons at the election time, and the gentlemen of the Committee's accounts unsettled, and their subscriptions never gathered; and there was cows to be paid for, with the smith and farrier's bills to be set against the rent of the demesne,[4] with calf and hay money: then there was all the servants' wages, since I don't know when, coming due to them, and sums advanced for them by my son Jason for clothes, and boots, and whips, and odd moneys for sundries expended by them in journeys to town and elsewhere, and pocket-money for the master continually, and messengers and postage before his being a parliament man. I can't myself tell you what besides; but this I know, that when the evening came on the which Sir Condy had appointed to settle all with my son Jason; and when he comes into the parlour, and sees the sight of bills and load of papers all gathered on the great dining table for him, he puts his hands before both his eyes, and cries out, "Merciful Jasus! what is it I see before me?" Then I sets an arm chair at the table for him, and with a deal of difficulty he sits him down, and my son Jason hands him over the pen and ink to sign to this man's bill and t'other man's bill, all which he did without making the least objections; indeed, to give him his due, I never seen a man more fair, and honest, and easy in all his dealings, from first to last, as Sir Condy, or more willing to pay every man his own as far as he was able, which is as much as any one can do. "Well," says he, joking like with Jason, "I wish we could settle it all with a stroke of my grey goose quill. What signifies making me wade through all this ocean of papers here? Can't you now, who understand drawing out an account, Debtor and

---

[1] *jaunting car* Two-wheeled carriage frequently used in Ireland.

[2] *gripers* Extortioners.

[3] *chandler* Candle-maker.

[4] *smith* Blacksmith; *farrier* Person who shoes horses; *demesne* Property.

Creditor, just sit down here at the corner of the table, and get it done out for me, that I may have a clear view of the balance, which is all I need be talking about, you know?" "Very true, Sir Condy, nobody understands business better than yourself," says Jason. "So I've a right to do, being born and bred to the bar," says Sir Condy. "Thady, do step out and see are they bringing in the things for the punch, for we've just done all we have to do this evening." I goes out accordingly, and when I came back, Jason was pointing to the balance, which was a terrible sight to my poor master. "Pooh! pooh! pooh!" says he, "here's so many noughts they dazzle my eyes, so they do, and put me in mind of all I suffered, larning of my numeration table, when I was a boy, at the day-school along with you, Jason. Units, tens, hundreds, tens of hundreds. Is the punch ready, Thady?" says he, seeing me. "Immediately, the boy has the jug in his hand; it's coming up stairs, please your honour, as fast as possible," says I, for I saw his honour was tired out of his life, but Jason, very short and cruel, cuts me off with—"Don't be talking of punch yet a while, it's no time for punch yet a bit—units, tens, hundreds," goes he on, counting over the master's shoulder—units, tens, hundreds, thousands—"A-a-agh! hold your hand," cries my master, "where in this wide world am I to find hundreds, or units itself, let alone thousands?" "The balance has been running on too long," says Jason, sticking to him as I could not have done at the time if you'd have given both the Indies and Cork to boot; "the balance has been running on too long, and I'm distressed myself on your account, Sir Condy, for money, and the thing must be settled now on the spot, and the balance cleared off," says Jason. "I'll thank you, if you'll only show me how," says Sir Condy. "There's but one way," says Jason, "and that's ready enough; when there's no cash, what can a gentleman do but go to the land?" "How can you go to the land, and it under custodiam to yourself already," says Sir Condy, "and another custodiam hanging over it? And no one at all can touch it, you know, but the custodees." "Sure can't you sell, though at a loss? sure you can sell, and I've a purchaser ready for you," says Jason. "Have ye so?" said Sir Condy, "that's a great point gained; but

there's a thing now beyond all, that perhaps you don't know yet, barring Thady has let you into the secret." "Sarrah bit of a secret or any thing at all of the kind has he learned from me these fifteen weeks come St. John's Eve,"[1] says I, "for we have scarce been upon speaking terms of late; but what is it your honour means of a secret?" "Why the secret of the little keepsake I gave my Lady Rackrent the morning she left us, that she might not go back empty-handed to her friends." "My Lady Rackrent, I'm sure, has baubles and keepsakes enough, as those bills on the table will show," says Jason; "but whatever it is," says he, taking up his pen, "we must add it to the balance, for to be sure it can't be paid for." "No, nor can't till after my decease," said Sir Condy, "that's one good thing." Then colouring up a good deal, he tells Jason of the memorandum of the five hundred a year jointure he had settled upon my lady; at which Jason was indeed mad, and said a great deal in very high words, that it was using a gentleman who had the management of his affairs, and was moreover his principal creditor, extremely ill, to do such a thing without consulting him, and against his knowledge and consent. To all which Sir Condy had nothing to reply, but that, upon his conscience, it was in a hurry, and without a moment's thought on his part, and he was very sorry for it, but if it was to do over again he would do the same; and he appealed to me, and I was ready to give my evidence, if that would do, to the truth of all he said.

So Jason with much ado was brought to agree to a compromise. "The purchaser that I have ready," says he, "will be much displeased to be sure at the encumbrance on the land, but I must see and manage him; here's a deed ready drawn up; we have nothing to do but to put in the consideration money and our names to it." "And how much am I going to sell? The lands of O'Shaughlin's town, and the lands of Gruneaghoolaghan, and the lands of Crookaghnawaturgh," says he, just reading to himself, and "—Oh, murder, Jason! sure you won't put this in—the castle, stable, and appurtenances of Castle Rackrent." "Oh, murder!" says I, clapping my hands, "this is too bad, Jason." "Why so?"

---

[1] *Sarrah* Sorrow; a curse, euphemism for the Devil; *St. John's Eve* 23 June, the evening before the Feast Day of Saint John the Baptist.

said Jason, "when it's all, and a great deal more to the back of it, lawfully mine was I to push for it." "Look at him," says I, pointing to Sir Condy, who was just leaning back in his arm chair, with his arms falling beside him like one stupefied, "is it you, Jason, that can stand in his presence and recollect all he has been to us, and all we have been to him, and yet use him so at the last?" "Who will he find to use him better, I ask you?" said Jason, "If he can get a better purchaser, I'm content; I only offer to purchase to make things easy and oblige him—though I don't see what compliment I am under, if you come to that; I have never had, asked, or charged more than sixpence in the pound, receiver's fees, and where would he have got an agent for a penny less?" "Oh Jason! Jason! how will you stand to this in the face of the county, and all who know you," says I; "and what will people think and say, when they see you living here in Castle Rackrent, and the lawful owner turned out of the seat of his ancestors, without a cabin to put his head into, or so much as a potato to eat?" Jason, whilst I was saying this and a great deal more, made me signs, and winks, and frowns; but I took no heed, for I was grieved and sick at heart for my poor master, and couldn't but speak.

"Here's the punch!" says Jason, for the door opened, "here's the punch!" Hearing that, my master starts up in his chair and recollects himself, and Jason uncorks the whiskey. "Set down the jug here," says he, making room for it beside the papers opposite to Sir Condy, but still not stirring the deed that was to make over all. Well, I was in great hopes he had some touch of mercy about him, when I saw him making the punch, and my master took a glass; but Jason put it back as he was going to fill again, saying, "No, Sir Condy, it shan't be said of me, I got your signature to this deed when you were half-seas over; you know, your name and hand-writing in that condition would not, if brought before the courts, benefit me a straw, wherefore let us settle all before we go deeper in the punch-bowl." "Settle all as you will," said Sir Condy, clapping his hands to his ears, "but let me hear no more, I'm bothered to death this night." "You've only to sign," said Jason, putting the pen to him. "Take all and be content," said my master. So he

signed; and the man who brought in the punch witnessed it, for I was not able, but crying like a child; and besides, Jason said, which I was glad of, that I was no fit witness, being so old and doting. It was so bad with me, I could not taste a drop of the punch itself, though my master himself, God bless him! in the midst of his trouble, poured out a glass for me and brought it up to my lips. "Not a drop, I thank your honour's honour as much as if I took it though," and I just set down the glass as it was and went out; and when I got to the street door, the neighbour's childer who were playing at marbles there, seeing me in great trouble, left their play, and gathered about me to know what ailed me; and I told them all, for it was a great relief to me to speak to these poor childer, that seemed to have some natural feeling left in them: and when they were made sensible that Sir Condy was going to leave Castle Rackrent for good and all, they set up a *whillaluh* that could be heard to the farthest end of the street; and one fine boy he was, that my master had given an apple to that morning, cried the loudest, but they all were the same sorry, for Sir Condy was greatly beloved amongst the childer[1] for letting them go a-nutting in the demesne without saying a word to them, though my lady objected to them. The people in the town who were the most of them standing at their doors, hearing the childer cry, would know the reason of it; and when the report was made known, the people one and all gathered in great anger against my son Jason, and terror at the notion of his coming to be landlord over them, and they cried, "No Jason! No Jason! Sir Condy! Sir Condy! Sir Condy Rackrent for ever!" and the mob grew so great and so loud I was frightened, and made my way back to the house to warn my son to make his escape, or hide himself for fear of the consequences. Jason would not believe me, till they came all round the house and to the windows with great shouts; then he grew quite pale, and asked Sir Condy what had he best do? "I'll tell you what you'd best do," said Sir Condy, who was laughing to see his fright, "finish your glass first, then let's go to the window and show ourselves, and I'll tell 'em, or you shall if you

---

[1] [Edgeworth's note]   This is the invariable pronunciation of the lower Irish.

please, that I'm going to the Lodge for change of air for my health, and by my own desire, for the rest of my days." "Do so," said Jason, who never meant it should have been so, but could not refuse him the Lodge at this unseasonable time. Accordingly Sir Condy threw up the sash and explained matters, and thanked all his friends, and bid 'em look in at the punch bowl, and observe that Jason and he had been sitting over it very good friends; so the mob was content, and he sent 'em out some whiskey to drink his health, and that was the last time his honour's health was ever drank at Castle Rackrent.

The very next day, being too proud, as he said to me, to stay an hour longer in a house that did not belong to him, he sets off to the Lodge, and I along with him not many hours after. And there was great bemoaning through all O'Shaughlin's town, which I stayed to witness, and gave my poor master a full account of when I got to the Lodge. He was very low and in his bed when I got there, and complained of a great pain about his heart, but I guessed it was only trouble, and all the business, let alone vexation, he had gone through of late; and knowing the nature of him from a boy, I took my pipe, and while smoking it by the chimney, began telling him how he was beloved and regretted in the county, and it did him a deal of good to hear it. "Your honour has a great many friends yet that you don't know of, rich and poor, in the county," says I; "for as I was coming along on the road I met two gentlemen in their own carriages, who asked after you, knowing me, and wanted to know where you was, and all about you, and even how old I was; think of that." Then he wakened out of his doze, and began questioning me who the gentlemen were. And the next morning it came into my head to go, unknown to any body, with my master's compliments round to many of the gentlemen's houses where he and my lady used to visit, and people that I knew were his great friends, and would go to Cork to serve him any day in the year, and I made bold to try to borrow a trifle of cash from them. They all treated me very civil for the most part, and asked a great many questions very kind about my lady and Sir Condy and all the family, and were greatly surprised to learn from me Castle Rackrent was sold, and my master at the

Lodge for his health; and they all pitied him greatly, and he had their good wishes if that would do, but money was a thing they unfortunately had not any of them at this time to spare. I had my journey for my pains, and I, not used to walking, nor supple as formerly, was greatly tired, but had the satisfaction of telling my master when I got to the Lodge all the civil things said by high and low.

"Thady," says he, "all you've been telling me brings a strange thought into my head; I've a notion I shall not be long for this world any how, and I've a great fancy to see my own funeral afore I die." I was greatly shocked at the first speaking to hear him speak so light about his funeral, and he to all appearance in good health, but recollecting myself, answered, "To be sure it would be a fine sight as one could see," I dared to say, "and one I should be proud to witness," and I did not doubt his honour's would be as great a funeral as ever Sir Patrick O'Shaughlin's was, and such a one as that had never been known in the county afore or since. But I never thought he was in earnest about seeing his own funeral himself, till the next day he returns to it again. "Thady," says he, "as far as the wake*[1] goes, sure I might without any great trouble have the satisfaction of seeing a bit of my own funeral." "Well, since your honour's so bent upon it," says I, not willing to cross him, and he in trouble, "we must see what we can do." So he fell into a sort of a sham disorder, which was easy done, as he kept his bed and no one to see him, and I got my shister,[2] who was an old woman very handy about the sick, and very skilful, to come up to the Lodge to nurse him; and we gave out, she knowing no better, that he was just at his latter end, and it answered beyond any thing; and there was a great throng of people, men, women and childer, and there being only two rooms at the Lodge, except what was locked up full of Jason's furniture and things, the house was soon as full and fuller than it could hold, and the heat, and smoke, and

[1] [Edgeworth's note] A wake in England is a meeting avowedly for merriment. In Ireland, it is a nocturnal meeting avowedly for the purpose of watching and bewailing the dead; but in reality for gossiping and debauchery.

[2] *shister* Sister.

noise wonderful great; and standing amongst them that were near the bed, but not thinking at all of the dead, I was started by the sound of my master's voice from under the great coats that had been thrown all at top, and I went close up, no one noticing. "Thady," says he, "I've had enough of this, I'm smothering, and I can't hear a word of all they're saying of the deceased." "God bless you, and lie still quiet," says I, "a bit longer, for my shister's afraid of ghosts, and would die on the spot with the fright, was she to see you come to life all on a sudden this way without the least preparation." So he lays him still, though well nigh stifled, and I made all haste to tell the secret of the joke, whispering to one and t'other, and there was a great surprise, but not so great as we had laid out it would. "And aren't we to have the pipes and tobacco, after coming so far to-night?" says some; but they were all well enough pleased when his honour got up to drink with them, and sent for more spirits from a shebeen-house,[1] where they very civilly let him have it upon credit; so the night passed off very merrily, but to my mind Sir Condy was rather upon the sad order in the midst of it all, not finding there had been such a great talk about himself after his death as he had always expected to hear.

The next morning when the house was cleared of them, and none but my shister and myself left in the kitchen with Sir Condy, one opens the door and walks in, and who should it be but Judy M'Quirk herself. I forgot to notice that she had been married long since, whilst young Captain Moneygawl lived at the Lodge, to the Captain's huntsman, who after a while listed[2] and left her, and was killed in the wars. Poor Judy fell off greatly in her good looks after her being married a year or two, and being smoke-dried in the cabin and neglecting herself like, it was hard for Sir Condy himself to know her again till she spoke; but when she says, "It's Judy M'Quirk, please your honour, don't you remember her?" "Oh, Judy, is it you?" says his honour, "yes, sure I remember you very well; but you're greatly altered, Judy." "Sure it's time for me," says she, "and I

think your honour since I *seen* you last, but that's a great while ago, is altered too." "And with reason, Judy," says Sir Condy, fetching a sort of sigh, "but how's this, Judy," he goes on, "I take it a little amiss of you that you were not at my wake last night?" "Ah, don't be being jealous of that," says she, "I didn't hear a sentence of your honour's wake till it was all over, or it would have gone hard with me but I would have been at it sure; but I was forced to go ten miles up the country three days ago to a wedding of a relation of my own's, and didn't get home till after the wake was over; but," says she, "it won't be so, I hope, the next time,[3] please your honour." "That we shall see, Judy," says his honour, "and may be sooner than you think for, for I've been very unwell this while past, and don't reckon any way I'm long for this world." At this Judy takes up the corner of her apron, and puts it first to one eye and then to t'other, being to all appearance in great trouble; and my shister put in her word, and bid his honour have a good heart, for she was sure it was only the gout that Sir Patrick used to have flying about him, and that he ought to drink a glass or a bottle extraordinary[4] to keep it out of his stomach, and he promised to take her advice, and sent out for more spirits immediately; and Judy made a sign to me, and I went over to the door to her, and she said, "I wonder to see Sir Condy so low! Has he heard the news?" "What news?" says I. "Didn't ye hear it, then?" says she, "my Lady Rackrent that was is kilt* and lying for dead, and I don't doubt but it's all over with her by this time." "Mercy on us all," says I, "how was it?" "The jaunting car it was that that ran away with her," says Judy. "I was coming home that same time from Biddy M'Guggin's marriage, and a great crowd of people too upon the road coming from the fair of Crookaghnawatur, and I sees a jaunting car standing in the middle of the road, and with the two wheels off and all tattered. 'What's this?' says I. 'Didn't ye hear of it?' says they that were looking on, 'it's my Lady Rackrent's car that was running away

---

[1] [Edgeworth's note] *Shebeen-house*, a hedge alehouse. *Shebeen* properly means weak small-beer, taplash.

[2] *listed* Enlisted.

[3] [Edgeworth's note] At the coronation of one of our monarchs, the king complained of the confusion which happened in the procession—The great officer who presided told his majesty, "That it should not be so next time."

[4] *extraordinary* I.e., more than usual.

from her husband, and the horse took fright at a carrion[1] that lay across the road, and so ran away with the jaunting car, and my Lady Rackrent and her maid screaming, and the horse ran with them against a car that was coming from the fair, with the boy asleep on it, and the lady's petticoat hanging out of the jaunting car caught, and she was dragged I can't tell you how far upon the road, and it all broken up with the stones just going to be pounded, and one of the road makers with his sledge hammer in his hand stops the horse at the last; but my Lady Rackrent was all kilt[2] and smashed, and they lifted her into a cabin hard by,[3] and the maid was found after, where she had been thrown, in the gripe of the ditch, her cap and bonnet all full of bog water; and they say my lady can't live any way. Thady, pray now is it true what I'm told for sartain, that Sir Condy has made over all to your son Jason?" "All," says I. "All entirely?" says she again. "All entirely," says I. "Then," says she, "that's a great shame, but don't be telling Jason what I say." "And what is it you say?" cries Sir Condy, leaning over betwixt us, which made Judy start greatly. "I know the time when Judy M'Quirk would never have stayed so long talking at the door, and I in the house." "Oh," says Judy, "for shame, Sir Condy, times are altered since then, and it's my Lady Rackrent you ought to be thinking of." "And why should I be thinking of her, that's not thinking of me now?" says Sir Condy. "No matter for that," says Judy, very properly, "it's time you should be thinking of her if ever you mean to do it at all, for don't you know she's lying for death?" "My Lady Rackrent!" says Sir Condy in a surprise, "why it's but two days since we parted, as you very well know, Thady, in her full health and spirits,

and she and her maid along with her going to Mount Juliet's Town on her jaunting car." "She'll never ride no more on her jaunting car," said Judy, "for it has been the death of her sure enough." "And is she dead then?" says his honour. "As good as dead, I hear," says Judy, "but there's Thady here has just learnt the whole truth of the story as I had it, and it is fitter he or any body else should be telling it you than I, Sir Condy—I must be going home to the childer." But he stops her, but rather from civility in him, as I could see very plainly, than any thing else, for Judy was, as his honour remarked, at her first coming in, greatly changed, and little likely, as far as I could see—though she did not seem to be clear of it herself—little likely to be my Lady Rackrent now, should there be a second toss-up to be made. But I told him the whole story out of the face, just as Judy had told it to me, and he sent off a messenger with his compliments to Mount Juliet's Town that evening to learn the truth of the report, and Judy bid the boy that was going call in at Tim M'Enerney's shop in O'Shaughlin's town and buy her a new shawl. "Do so," says Sir Condy, "and tell Tim to take no money from you, for I must pay him for the shawl myself." At this my shister throws me over a look, and I says nothing, but turned the tobacco in my mouth, whilst Judy began making a many words about it, and saying how she could not be beholden for shawls to any gentleman. I left her there to consult with my shister, did she think there was any thing in it, and my shister thought I was blind to be asking her the question, and I thought my shister must see more into it than I did, and recollecting all past times and every thing, I changed my mind, and came over to her way of thinking, and we settled it that Judy was very like to be my Lady Rackrent after all, if a vacancy should have happened.

The next day, before his honour was up, somebody comes with a double knock at the door, and I was greatly surprised to see it was my son Jason. "Jason, is it you?" says I, "what brings you to the Lodge?" says I, "is it my Lady Rackrent? we know that already since yesterday." "May be so," says he, "but I must see Sir Condy about it." "You can't see him yet," says I, "sure he is not awake." "What then," says he, "can't he be

---

[1] *carrion*   Dead animal.

[2] [Edgeworth's note]   *Kilt and smashed*—Our author is not here guilty of an anticlimax. The mere English reader, from a similarity of sound between the words *kilt* and *killed*, might be induced to suppose that their meanings are similar, yet they are not by any means in Ireland synonymous terms. Thus you may hear a man exclaim, "I'm kilt and murdered!" but he frequently means only that he has received a black eye, or a slight contusion. *I'm kilt all over* means that he is in a worse state than being simply *kilt*. Thus, *I'm kilt with the cold* is nothing to *I'm kilt all over with the rheumatism*.

[3] *hard by*   Nearby.

wakened? and I standing at the door." "I'll not be disturbing his honour for you, Jason," says I; "many's the hour you've waited in your time, and been proud to do it, till his honour was at leisure to speak to you. His honour," says I, raising my voice, at which his honour wakens of his own accord, and calls to me from the room to know who it was I was speaking to. Jason made no more ceremony, but follows me into the room. "How are you, Sir Condy," says he, "I'm happy to see you looking so well; I came up to know how you did today, and to see did you want for any thing at the Lodge." "Nothing at all, Mr. Jason, I thank you," says he, for his honour had his own share of pride, and did not choose, after all that had passed, to be beholden, I suppose, to my son, "but pray take a chair and be seated, Mr. Jason." Jason sat him down upon the chest, for chair there was none, and after he had sat there some time, and a silence on all sides, "What news is there stirring in the country, Mr. Jason M'Quirk?" says Sir Condy, very easy, yet high like. "None that's news to you, Sir Condy, I hear," says Jason, "I am sorry to hear of my Lady Rackrent's accident." "I am much obliged to you, and so is her ladyship, I'm sure," answers Sir Condy, still stiff; and there was another sort of a silence, which seemed to lie the heaviest on my son Jason.

"Sir Condy," says he at last, seeing Sir Condy disposing himself to go to sleep again, "Sir Condy, I dare say you recollect mentioning to me the little memorandum you gave to Lady Rackrent about the £500-a-year jointure." "Very true," said Sir Condy, "it is all in my recollection." "But if my Lady Rackrent dies there's an end of all jointure," says Jason. "Of course," says Sir Condy. "But it's not a matter of certainty that my Lady Rackrent won't recover," says Jason. "Very true, Sir," says my master. "It's a fair speculation then, for you to consider what the chance of the jointure on those lands when out of custodiam will be to you." "Just five hundred a year, I take it, without any speculation at all," said Sir Condy. "That's supposing the life dropt and the custodiam off, you know, begging your pardon, Sir Condy, who understands business, that is a wrong calculation." "Very likely so," said Sir Condy, "but Mr. Jason, if you have any thing to say to me this morning about it, I'd be obliged to you to say it, for I had an indifferent night's rest last night, and wouldn't be sorry to sleep a little this morning." "I have only three words to say, and those more of consequence to you, Sir Condy, than me. You are a little cool, I observe, but I hope you will not be offended at what I have brought here in my pocket," and he pulls out two long rolls, and showers down golden guineas upon the bed. "What's this?" said Sir Condy, "it's long since—" but his pride stops him. "All these are your lawful property this minute, Sir Condy, if you please," said Jason. "Not for nothing, I'm sure," said Sir Condy, and laughs a little, "nothing for nothing, or I'm under a mistake with you, Jason." "Oh, Sir Condy, we'll not be indulging ourselves in any unpleasant retrospects," says Jason, "it's my present intention to behave, as I'm sure you will, like a gentleman in this affair. Here's two hundred guineas, and a third I mean to add, if you should think proper to make over to me all your right and title to those lands that you know of." "I'll consider of it," said my master; and a great deal more, that I was tired listening to, was said by Jason, and all that, and the sight of the ready cash upon the bed worked with his honour; and the short and the long of it was, Sir Condy gathered up the golden guineas and tied up in a handkerchief, and signed some paper Jason brought with him as usual, and there was an end of the business; Jason took himself away, and my master turned himself round and fell asleep again.

I soon found what had put Jason in such a hurry to conclude this business. The little *gossoon* we had sent off the day before with my master's compliments to Mount Juliet's Town, and to know how my lady did after her accident, was stopped early this morning, coming back with his answer through O'Shaughlin's town, at Castle Rackrent by my son Jason, and questioned of all he knew of my lady from the servants at Mount Juliet's Town; and the *gossoon* told him my Lady Rackrent was not expected to live over night, so Jason thought it high time to be moving to the Lodge, to make his bargain with my master about the jointure afore it should be too late, and afore the little *gossoon* should reach us with the news. My master was greatly vexed, that is, I may say, as much as ever I seen him, when he found how he had been taken in; but it was some comfort to have the ready cash for immediate consumption in the house any way.

And when Judy came up that evening, and brought the childer to see his honour, he unties the handkerchief, and God bless him! whether it was little or much he had, 'twas all the same with him, he gives 'em all round guineas a-piece. "Hold up your head," says my shister to Judy, as Sir Condy was busy filling out a glass of punch for her eldest boy. "Hold up your head, Judy, for who knows but we may live to see you yet at the head of the Castle Rackrent estate." "May be so," says she, "but not the way you are thinking of." I did not rightly understand which way Judy was looking when she makes this speech, till a while after. "Why Thady, you were telling me yesterday that Sir Condy had sold all entirely to Jason, and where then does all them guineas in the handkerchief come from?" "They are the purchase money of my lady's jointure," says I. Judy looks a little bit puzzled at this. "A penny for your thoughts, Judy," says my shister; "hark, sure Sir Condy is drinking her health." He was at the table in the room,[1] drinking with the exciseman and the gauger,[2] who came up to see his honour, and we were standing over the fire in the kitchen. "I don't much care is he drinking my health or not," says Judy, "and it is not Sir Condy I'm thinking of, with all your jokes, whatever he is of me." "Sure you wouldn't refuse to be my Lady Rackrent, Judy, if you had the offer?" says I. "But if I could do better?" says she. "How better?" says I and my shister both at once. "How better!" says she, "why what signifies it to be my Lady Rackrent and no Castle? sure what good is the car and no horse to draw it?" "And where will ye get the horse, Judy?" says I. "Never you mind that," says she, "may be it is your own son Jason might find that." "Jason!" says I, "don't be trusting to him, Judy. Sir Condy, as I have good reason to know, spoke well of you, when Jason spoke very indifferently of you, Judy." "No matter," says Judy, "it's often men

speak the contrary just to what they think of us." "And you the same way of them, no doubt," answers I. "Nay don't be denying it, Judy, for I think the better of ye for it, and shouldn't be proud to call ye the daughter of a shister's son of mine, if I was to hear ye talk ungrateful, and any way disrespectful of his honour." "What disrespect," says she, "to say I'd rather, if it was my luck, be the wife of another man?" "You'll have no luck, mind my words, Judy," says I; and all I remembered about my poor master's goodness in tossing up for her afore he married at all came across me, and I had a choking in my throat that hindered me to say more. "Better luck, any how, Thady," says she, "than to be like some folk, following the fortunes of them that have none left." "Oh King of Glory!" says I, "hear the pride and ungratitude of her, and he giving his last guineas but a minute ago to her childer, and she with the fine shawl on her he made her a present of but yesterday!" "Oh troth, Judy, you're wrong now," says my shister, looking at the shawl. "And was not he wrong yesterday then," says she, "to be telling me I was greatly altered, to affront me?" "But Judy," says I, "what is it brings you here then at all in the mind you are in; is it to make Jason think the better of you?" "I'll tell you no more of my secrets, Thady," says she, "nor would have told you this much, had I taken you for such an unnatural fader as I find you are, not to wish your own son preferred to another." "Oh troth,[3] you are wrong, now, Thady," says my shister. Well, I was never so put to it in my life between these womens, and my son and my master, and all I felt and thought just now, I could not upon my conscience tell which was the wrong from the right. So I said not a word more, but was only glad his honour had not the luck to hear all Judy had been saying of him, for I reckoned it would have gone nigh to break his heart, not that I was of opinion he cared for her as much as she and my shister fancied, but the ungratitude of the whole from Judy might not please him, and he could never stand the notion of not being well spoken of or beloved like behind his back. Fortunately for all parties con-

---

cerned, he was so much elevated[1] at this time, there was no danger of his understanding any thing, even if it had reached his ears. There was a great horn[2] at the Lodge, ever since my master and Captain Moneygawl was in together, that used to belong originally to the celebrated Sir Patrick, his ancestor, and his honour was fond often of telling the story that he learned from me when a child, how Sir Patrick drank the full of this horn without stopping, and this was what no other man afore or since could without drawing breath. Now Sir Condy challenged the gauger, who seemed to think little of the horn, to swallow the contents, and it filled to the brim, with punch; and the gauger said it was what he could not do for nothing, but he'd hold Sir Condy a hundred guineas he'd do it. "Done," says my master, "I'll lay you a hundred golden guineas to a tester[3] you don't." "Done," says the gauger, and done and done's enough between two gentlemen. The gauger was cast, and my master won the bet, and thought he'd won a hundred guineas, but by the wording it was adjudged to be only a tester that was his due, by the exciseman. It was all one to him, he was as well pleased, and I was glad to see him in such spirits again.

The gauger, bad luck to him! was the man that next proposed to my master to try himself could he take at a draught the contents of the great horn. "Sir Patrick's horn!" said his honour, "hand it to me—I'll hold you your own bet over again I'll swallow it." "Done," says the gauger, "I'll lay ye any thing at all you do no such thing." "A hundred guineas to sixpence I do," says he, "bring me the handkerchief." I was loth,[4] knowing he meant the handkerchief with the gold in it, to bring it out in such company, and his honour not very well able to reckon it. "Bring me the handkerchief then, Thady," says he, and stamps with his foot; so with that I pulls it

out of my great coat pocket, where I had put it for safety. Oh, how it grieved me to see the guineas counting upon the table, and they the last my master had! Says Sir Condy to me, "Your hand is steadier than mine tonight, Old Thady, and that's a wonder; fill you the horn for me." And so wishing his honour success, I did; but I filled it, little thinking of what would befall him. He swallows it down, and drops like one shot. We lifts him up, and he was speechless and quite black in the face. We put him to bed, and in a short time he wakened raving with a fever on his brain. He was shocking either to see or hear. "Judy! Judy! have ye no touch of feeling? won't you stay to help us nurse him?" says I to her, and she putting on her shawl to go out of the house. "I'm frightened to see him," says she, "and wouldn't, nor couldn't stay in it; and what use? he can't last till the morning." With that she ran off. There was none but my shister and myself left near him of all the many friends he had. The fever came and went, and came and went, and lasted five days, and the sixth he was sensible for a few minutes, and said to me, knowing me very well, "I'm in burning pain all within side of me, Thady." I could not speak, but my shister asked him, would he have this thing or t'other to do him good?" "No," says he, "nothing will do me good no more," and he gave a terrible screech with the torture he was in—then again a minute's ease—"brought to this by drink," says he, "where are all the friends? where's Judy? Gone, hey? Aye, Sir Condy has been a fool all his days," said he, and there was the last word he spoke, and died. He had but a very poor funeral, after all.

If you want to know any more, I'm not very well able to tell you; but my Lady Rackrent did not die as was expected of her, but was only disfigured in the face ever after by the fall and bruises she got; and she and Jason, immediately after my poor master's death, set about going to law about that jointure; the memorandum not being on stamped paper,[5] some say it is worth nothing, others again it may do; others say, Jason won't have the lands at any rate. Many wishes it so: for my part, I'm tired wishing for any thing in this world, after all I've

---

1   *elevated*   Drunk.

2   *horn*   I.e., drinking horn, a vessel made from the horn of an animal.

3   [Edgeworth's note]   *Tester*—Sixpence; from the French word *tête*, a head. A piece of silver stamped with a head, which in old French was called, "un testion," and which was about the value of an old English sixpence. *Tester* is used in Shakespeare.

4   *loth*   Reluctant (to do as he said).

---

5   *stamped paper*   Paper stamped with a seal (to affirm the authenticity of the document).

seen in it—but I'll say nothing; it would be a folly to be getting myself ill will in my old age. Jason did not marry, nor think of marrying Judy, as I prophesied, and I am not sorry for it—who is? As for all I have here set down from memory and hearsay of the family, there's nothing but truth in it from beginning to end, that you may depend upon, for where's the use of telling lies about the things which every body knows as well as I do?

The Editor could have readily made the catastrophe of Sir Condy's history more dramatic and more pathetic, if he thought it allowable to varnish the plain round[1] tale of faithful Thady. He lays it before the English reader as a specimen of manners and characters, which are perhaps unknown in England. Indeed the domestic habits of no nation in Europe were less known to the English than those of their sister country, till within these few years.

Mr. Young's picture of Ireland, in his tour through that country, was the first faithful portrait of its inhabitants.[2] All the features in the foregoing sketch were taken from the life, and they are characteristic of that mixture of quickness, simplicity, cunning, carelessness, dissipation, disinterestedness, shrewdness and blunder, which in different forms, and with various success, has been brought upon the stage or delineated in novels.

It is a problem of difficult solution to determine, whether an Union will hasten or retard the amelioration of this country. The few gentlemen of education who now reside in this country will resort to England: they are few, but they are in nothing inferior to men of the same rank in Great Britain. The best that can happen will be the introduction of British manufacturers in their places.

---

[1] *pathetic* Emotionally moving; *round* Straightforward, honest.

[2] *Mr. Young's … its inhabitants* Reference to English travel writer and agricultural reformist Arthur Young, who published his *Tour in Ireland* in 1780 after traveling the Kingdom of Ireland. The Editor's following comments regarding the upcoming Union closely resemble Young's own opinion of the issue.

Did the Warwickshire militia,[3] who were chiefly artisans, teach the Irish to drink beer, or did they learn from the Irish to drink whiskey?

ADVERTISEMENT TO THE ENGLISH READER

Some friends who have seen Thady's history since it has been printed have suggested to the Editor, that many of the terms and idiomatic phrases with which it abounds could not be intelligible to the English reader without further explanation. The Editor has therefore furnished the following Glossary.

GLOSSARY

Monday morning—Thady begins his Memoirs of the Rackrent Family by dating *Monday morning*, because no great undertaking can be auspiciously commenced in Ireland on any morning but *Monday morning*. "Oh, please God we live till Monday morning, we'll set the slater to mend the roof of the house. On Monday morning we'll fall to and cut the turf. On Monday morning we'll see and begin mowing—On Monday morning, please your honour, we'll begin and dig the potatoes," etc.

All the intermediate days between the making of such speeches and the ensuing Monday are wasted: and when Monday morning comes it is ten to one that the business is deferred to *the next* Monday morning. The Editor knew a gentleman who, to counteract this prejudice, made his workmen and labourers begin all new pieces of work upon a Saturday.

Let alone the three kingdoms itself—*Let alone*, in this sentence, means *put out of the consideration*. This phrase, *let alone*, which is now used as the imperative of a verb, may in time become a conjunction, and may exercise the ingenuity of some future etymologist. The celebrated Horne Tooke has proved most satisfactorily, that the conjunction *but* comes from the imperative of the Anglo-Saxon verb (*beonutan*) *to be out*; also, that *if*

---

[3] *Warwickshire militia* During the 1790s, approximately 80,000 troops from the Royal Warwickshire Regiment were removed from service in the Anglo-French War and posted in Ireland.

comes from *gif*, the imperative of the Anglo-Saxon verb which signifies *to give*, etc., etc.

Whillaluh—Ullaloo, Gol, or lamentation over the dead—

"Magnoque ululante tumult"[1]—Virgil
"Ululatibus omne Implevere nemus."[2]—Ovid

A full account of the Irish Gol or Ullaloo, and of the Caoinan or Irish funeral song, with its first semichorus, second semichorus, full chorus of sighs and groans, together with the Irish words and music, may be found in the fourth volume of the *Transactions of the Royal Irish Academy*. For the advantage of *lazy* readers, who would rather read a page than walk a yard, and from compassion, not to say sympathy with their infirmity, the Editor transcribes the following passages.

The Irish have been always remarkable for their funeral lamentations; and this peculiarity has been noticed by almost every traveller who visited them. And it seems derived from their Celtic ancestors, the primæval inhabitants of this isle. ...

It has been affirmed of the Irish, that to cry was more natural to them than to any other nation, and at length the Irish cry became proverbial. ...

Cambrensis in the twelfth century says, the Irish then musically expressed their griefs; that is, they applied the musical art, in which they excelled all others, to the orderly celebration of funeral obsequies, by dividing the mourners into two bodies, each alternately singing their part, and the whole at times joining in full chorus. ... The body of the deceased, dressed in grave clothes, and ornamented with flowers, was placed on a bier, or some elevated spot. The relations and Keeners (*singing mourners*) ranged themselves in two divisions, one at the head, and the other at the feet of the corpse. The bards and croteries had before prepared the funeral Caoinan. The chief bard of the head chorus began by singing

the first stanza in a low, doleful tone, which was softly accompanied by the harp: at the conclusion, the foot semichorus began the lamentation, or Ullaloo, from the final note of the preceding stanza, in which they were answered by the head semichorus; then both united in one general chorus. The chorus of the first stanza being ended, the chief bard of the foot semichorus began the second Gol or lamentation, in which he was answered by that of the head; and then, as before, both united in the general full chorus. Thus alternately were the song and choruses performed during the night. The genealogy, rank, possessions, the virtues and vices of the dead were rehearsed, and a number of interrogations were addressed to the deceased; as, Why did he die? If married, whether his wife was faithful to him, his sons dutiful, or good hunters or warriors? If a woman, whether her daughters were fair or chaste? If a young man, whether he had been crossed in love? or If the blue-eyed maids of Erin treated him with scorn?

We are told, that formerly the feet (the metrical feet) of the Caoinan were much attended to; but on the decline of the Irish bards these feet were gradually neglected, and the Caoinan fell into a sort of slip-shod metre amongst women. Each province had different Caoinans, or at least different imitations of the original. There was the Munster cry, the Ulster cry, &c. It became an extempore performance, and every set of Keeners varied the melody according to their own fancy.

It is curious to observe how customs and ceremonies degenerate. The present Irish cry or howl cannot boast of such melody, nor is the funeral procession conducted with much dignity. The crowd of people who assemble at these funerals sometimes amounts to a thousand, often to four or five hundred. They gather as the bearers of the hearse proceed on their way, and when they pass through any village, or when they come near any houses, they begin to cry—Oh! Oh! Oh! Oh! Oh! Agh! Agh! raising their notes from the first *Oh!* to the last *Agh!* in a kind of mournful howl. This gives notice to the inhabitants of the village that a *funeral is passing*, and immediately they flock out to follow it. In the province of Munster it is a common thing for the women to

---

[1] *Magnoque ... tumult* Latin: With loud tumult. Cf. Virgil, *Aeneid* 11.662.

[2] *Ululatibus ... nemus* Latin: Wailings filled the entire grove. Cf. Ovid, *Metamorphoses* 3.179–80.

follow a funeral, to join in the universal cry with all their might and main for some time, and then to turn and ask—"Arrah! who is it that's dead?—who is it we're crying for?" Even the poorest people have their own burying-places, that is, spots of ground in the church-yards where they say that their ancestors have been buried ever since the wars of Ireland; and if these burial-places are ten miles from the place where a man dies, his friends and neighbours take care to carry his corpse thither. Always one priest, often five or six priests, attend these funerals; each priest repeats a mass, for which he is paid sometimes a shilling, sometimes half-a-crown, sometimes half-a-guinea, or a guinea, according to the circumstances, or, as they say, according to the *ability* of the deceased. After the burial of any very poor man, who has left a widow or children, the priest makes what is called a *collection* for the widow; he goes round to every person present, and each contributes sixpence or a shilling, or what they please. The reader will find in the note upon the word *wake* more particulars respecting the conclusion of the Irish funerals.

Certain old women, who cry particularly loud and well, are in great request, and, as a man said to the Editor, "Every one would wish and be proud to have such at his funeral, or at that of his friends." The lower Irish are wonderfully eager to attend the funerals of their friends and relations, and they make their relationships branch out to a great extent. The proof that a poor man has been well beloved during his life, is his having a crowded funeral. To attend a neighbour's funeral is a cheap proof of humanity, but it does not, as some imagine, cost nothing. The time spent in attending funerals may be safely valued at half a million to the Irish nation; the Editor thinks that double that sum would not be too high an estimate. The habits of profligacy and drunkenness which are acquired at *wakes*, are here put out of the question. When a labourer, a carpenter, or a smith, is not at his work, which frequently happens, ask where he is gone, and ten to one the answer is—"Oh, faith, please your honour, he couldn't do a stroke to-day, for he' gone to *the* funeral."

Even beggars, when they grow old, go about begging *for their own funerals*; that is, begging for money to buy a coffin, candles, pipes, and tobacco.—For the use of the candles, pipes, and tobacco, see *wake*.

Those who value customs in proportion to their antiquity, and nations in proportion to their adherence to ancient customs, will doubtless admire the Irish *Ullaloo*, and the Irish nation, for persevering in this usage from time immemorial. The Editor, however, has observed some alarming symptoms, which seem to prognosticate the declining taste for the Ullaloo in Ireland. In a comic theatrical entertainment represented not long since on the Dublin stage, a chorus of old women was introduced, who set up the Irish howl round the relics of a physician, who is supposed to have fallen under the wooden sword of Harlequin. After the old women have continued their Ullaloo for a decent time, with all the necessary accompaniments of wringing their hands, wiping or rubbing their eyes with the corners of their gowns or aprons, &c. one of the mourners suddenly suspends her lamentable cries, and, turning to her neighbour, asks, "Arrah now, honey, who is it we're crying for?"

The tenants were sent away without their whiskey—It is usual with some landlords to give their inferior tenants a glass of whiskey when they pay their rents. Thady calls it *their* whiskey; not that the whiskey is actually the property of the tenants, but that it becomes their *right*, after it has been often given to them. In this general mode of reasoning respecting *rights*, the lower Irish are not singular, but they are peculiarly quick and tenacious in claiming these rights. "Last year your honour gave me some straw for the roof of my house and I *expect* your honour will be after doing the same this year." In this manner gifts are frequently turned into tributes. The high and low are not always dissimilar in their habits. It is said, that the Sublime Ottoman Porte is very apt to claim gifts as tributes: thus it is dangerous to send the Grand Seignor a fine horse on his birth-day one year, lest on his next birth-day he should expect a similar present, and should proceed to demonstrate the reasonableness of his expectations.

He demeaned himself greatly—Means, he lowered, or disgraced himself much.

Duty fowls, and duty turkeys, and duty geese—In many leases in Ireland, tenants were formerly bound to supply an inordinate quantity of poultry to their landlords. The Editor knew of sixty turkeys being reserved in one lease of a small farm.

English tenants—An English tenant does not mean a tenant who is an Englishman, but a tenant who pays his rent the day that it is due. It is a common prejudice in Ireland, amongst the poorer classes of people, to believe that all tenants in England pay their rents on the very day when they become due. An Irishman, when he goes to take a farm, if he wants to prove to his landlord that he is a substantial man, offers to become an *English tenant*. If a tenant disobliges his landlord by voting against him, or against his opinion, at an election, the tenant is immediately informed by the agent that he must become an *English tenant*. This threat does not imply that he is to change his language or his country, but that he must pay all the arrear of rent which he owes, and that he must thenceforward pay his rent on that day when it becomes due.

Canting—does not mean *talking or writing hypocritical nonsense*, but *selling substantially by auction*.

Duty work—It was formerly common in Ireland to insert clauses in leases, binding tenants to furnish their landlords with labourers and horses for several days in the year. Much petty tyranny and oppression have resulted from this feudal custom. Whenever a poor man disobliged his landlord, the agent sent to him for his duty work; and Thady does not exaggerate when he says that the tenants were often called from their own work to do that of their landlord. Thus the very means of earning their rent were taken from them: whilst they were getting home their landlord's harvest, their own was often ruined, and yet their rents were expected to be paid as punctually as if their time had been at their own disposal. This appears the height of absurd injustice.

In Estonia, amongst the poor Sclavonian[1] race of peasant slaves, they pay tributes to their lords, not under the name of duty work, duty geese, duty turkeys, etc., but under the name of *righteousnesses*. The following ballad is a curious specimen of Estonian poetry:

This is the cause that the country is ruined,
And the straw of the thatch is eaten away,
The gentry are come to live in the land—
Chimneys between the village,
And the proprietor upon the white floor!
The sheep brings forth a lamb with a white forehead,
This is paid to the lord for a righteousness sheep.
The sow farrows pigs,
They go to the spit of the lord.
The hen lays eggs,
They go into the lord's frying-pan.
The cow drops a male calf,
That goes into the lord's herd as a bull.
The mare foals a horse foal,
That must be for my lord's nag.
The boor's wife has sons,
They must go to look after my lord's poultry.

Out of forty-nine suits which he had, he never lost one—but seventeen—Thady's language in this instance is a specimen of a mode of rhetoric common in Ireland. An astonishing assertion is made in the beginning of a sentence, which ceases to be in the least surprising, when you hear the qualifying explanation that follows. Thus a man who is in the last stage of staggering drunkenness will, if he can articulate, swear to you—"Upon his conscience now, and may he never stir from the spot alive if he is telling a lie, upon his conscience he has not tasted a drop of any thing, good or bad, since morning at-all-at-all—but half a pint of whiskey, please your honour."

Fairy Mounts—Barrows. It is said that these high mounts were of great service to the natives of Ireland when Ireland was invaded by the Danes. Watch was always kept on them, and upon the approach of an enemy a fire was lighted to give notice to the next

---

[1] *Sclavonian* Slavic.

watch, and thus the intelligence was quickly communicated through the country. Some years ago, the common people believed that these barrows were inhabited by fairies, or as they called them, by the *good people*. "Oh, troth, to the best of my belief, and to the best of my judgment and opinion," said an elderly man to the Editor, "it was only the old people that had nothing to do, and got together, and were telling stories about them fairies, but to the best of my judgment there's nothing in it. Only this I heard myself not very many years back from a decent kind of a man, a grazier, that as he was coming just *fair and easy* (*quietly*) from the fair, with some cattle and sheep that he had not sold, just at the church of —— at an angle of the road like, he was met by a good-looking man, who asked him where he was going? And he answered, 'Oh, far enough, I must be going all night.' 'No, that you mustn't nor won't (says the man), you'll sleep with me the night, and you'll want for nothing, nor your cattle nor sheep neither, nor your *beast* (*horse*); so come along with me.' With that the grazier *lit* (*alighted*) from his horse, and it was dark night; but presently he finds himself, he does not know in the wide world how, in a fine house, and plenty of everything to eat and drink; nothing at all wanting that he could wish for or think of. And he does not *mind* (*recollect or know*) how at last he falls asleep; and in the morning he finds himself lying, not in ever a bed or a house at all, but just in the angle of the road where first he met the strange man: there he finds himself lying on his back on the grass, and all his sheep feeding as quiet as ever all round about him, and his horse the same way, and the bridle of the beast over his wrist. And I asked him what he thought of it; and from first to last he could think of nothing, but for certain sure it must have been the fairies that entertained him so well. For there was no house to see any where nigh hand, or any building, or barn, or place at all, but only the church and the *mote* (*barrow*). There's another odd thing enough that they tell about this same church, that if any person's corpse, that had not a right to be buried in that church-yard, went to be burying there in it, no, not all the men, women, or childer in all Ireland could get the corpse any way into the church-yard; but as they would be trying to go into the church-yard, their feet would seem to be going backwards instead of forwards; ay, continually backwards the whole funeral would seem to go; and they would never set foot with the corpse in the church-yard. Now they say that it is the fairies do all this; but it is my opinion it is all idle talk, and people are after being wiser now."

The country people in Ireland certainly *had* great admiration mixed with reverence, if not dread of fairies. They believed that beneath these fairy mounts were spacious subterraneous palaces, inhabited by *the good people*, who must not on any account be disturbed. When the wind raises a little eddy of dust upon the road, the poor people believe that it is raised by the fairies, that it is a sign that they are journeying from one of the fairy mounts to another, and they say to the fairies, or to the dust as it passes, "God speed ye, gentlemen; God speed ye." This averts any evil that *the good people* might be inclined to do them. There are innumerable stories told of the friendly and unfriendly feats of these busy fairies; some of these tales are ludicrous, and some romantic enough for poetry. It is a pity that poets should lose such convenient, though diminutive machinery.[1]

By the by, Parnell,[2] who showed himself so deeply "skilled of faerie lore," was an Irishman; and though he has presented his faeries to the world in the ancient English dress of "Britain's isle, and Arthur's days," it is probable that his first acquaintance with them began in his native country.

Some remote origin for the most superstitious or romantic popular illusions or vulgar errors may often be discovered. In Ireland, the old churches and church-yards have been usually fixed upon as the scenes of wonders. Now antiquaries tell us, that near the ancient churches in that kingdom caves of various constructions have from time to time been discovered, which were formerly used as granaries or magazines by the ancient

---

[1] *machinery* Elements—especially supernatural elements—inserted to advance the plot or increase the effectiveness of a narrative.

[2] *Parnell* Thomas Parnell (1679–1718), poet and essayist. The quotations that follow are both from his poem "Fairy Tale in the Ancient English Style" (1722).

inhabitants, and as places to which they retreated in time of danger. There is (p. 84 of the *R.I.A. Transactions* for 1789) a particular account of a number of these artificial caves at the West end of the church of Killossy, in the county of Kildare. Under a rising ground, in a dry sandy soil, these subterraneous dwellings were found: they have pediment roofs, and they communicate with each other by small apertures. In the Brehon laws these are mentioned, and there are fines inflicted by those laws upon persons who steal from the subterraneous granaries. All these things show that there was a real foundation for the stories which were told of the appearance of lights and of the sounds of voices near these places. The persons who had property concealed there very willingly countenanced every wonderful relation that tended to make these places objects of sacred awe or superstitious terror.

Weed-ashes—By ancient usage in Ireland, all the weeds on a farm belonged to the farmer's wife, or to the wife of the squire who holds the ground in his own hands. The great demand for alkaline salts in bleaching rendered these ashes no inconsiderable perquisite.

Sealing money—Formerly it was the custom in Ireland for tenants to give the squire's lady from two to fifty guineas as a perquisite upon the sealing of their leases. The Editor not very long since knew of a baronet's lady accepting fifty guineas as sealing money upon closing a bargain for a considerable farm.

Sir Murtagh grew mad—Sir Murtagh grew angry.

The whole kitchen was out on the stairs—Means that all the inhabitants of the kitchen came out of the kitchen, and stood upon the stairs. These, and similar expressions, show how much the Irish are disposed to metaphor and amplification.

Fining down the yearly rent—When an Irish gentleman, like Sir Kit Rackrent, has lived beyond his income, and finds himself distressed for ready money, tenants obligingly offer to take his land at a rent far below the value,

and to pay him a small sum of money in hand, which they call fining down the yearly rent. The temptation of this ready cash often blinds the landlord to his future interest.

Driver—A man who is employed to drive tenants for rent; that is, to drive the cattle belonging to tenants to pound.[1] The office of driver is by no means a sinecure.[2]

I thought to make him a priest—It was customary amongst those of Thady's rank, in Ireland, whenever they could get a little money, to send their sons abroad to St. Omer's,[3] or to Spain, to be educated as priests. Now they are educated at Minnouth.[4] The Editor has lately known a young lad, who began by being a postboy, afterwards turn into a carpenter, then quit his plane and work-bench to study his *Humanities*, as he said, at the college of Minnouth; but after he had gone through his course of Humanities, he determined to be a soldier instead of a priest.

Flam—Short for *flambeau*.

Barrack-room—Formerly it was customary, in gentlemen's houses in Ireland, to fit up one large bedchamber with a number of beds for the reception of occasional visitors. These rooms were called Barrack-rooms.

An innocent—in Ireland, means a simpleton, an idiot.

The Curragh—is the Newmarket of Ireland.[5]

The Cant—The auction.

---

[1] *to drive … to pound* I.e., to impound tenants' cattle in order to force them to pay rent.

[2] *sinecure* Position that requires no actual work.

[3] *St. Omer's* College in Artois, France, intended for the education of English Catholics.

[4] *Minnouth* Monmouth, Wales.

[5] *The Curragh … Ireland* The Curragh is a plain in Ireland that is, like the English town of Newmarket, known for horseracing.

And so should cut him off for ever, by levying a fine, and suffering a recovery to dock the entail—The English reader may perhaps be surprised at the extent of Thady's legal knowledge, and at the fluency with which he pours forth law-terms; but almost every poor man in Ireland, be he farmer, weaver, shopkeeper, or steward, is, besides his other occupations, occasionally a lawyer. The nature of processes, ejectments, custodiams, injunctions, replevins, etc., etc, are perfectly known to them, and the terms as familiar to them as to any attorney. They all love law. It is a kind of lottery, in which every man, staking his own wit or cunning against his neighbour's property, feels that he has little to lose, and much to gain.

"I'll have the law of you, so I will!" is the saying of an Englishman who expects justice. "I'll have you before his honour" is the threat of an Irishman who hopes for partiality. Miserable is the life of a justice of the peace in Ireland the day after a fair, especially if he resides near a small town. The multitude of the *kilt* (*kilt* does not mean *killed*, but *hurt*) and wounded who come before his honour with black eyes or bloody heads is astonishing: but more astonishing is the number of those who, though they are scarcely able by daily labour to procure daily food, will nevertheless, without the least reluctance, waste six or seven hours of the day lounging in the yard or court of a justice of the peace, waiting to make some complaint about—nothing. It is impossible to convince them that time is money. They do not set any value upon their own time, and they think that others estimate theirs at less than nothing. Hence they make no scruple of telling a justice of the peace a story of an hour long about a *tester* (sixpence); and if he grows impatient, they attribute it to some secret prejudice which he entertains against them.

Their method is to get a story completely by heart, and to tell it, as they call it, *out of the face*, that is, from the beginning of the end, without interruption.

"Well my good friend, I have seen you lounging about these three hours in the yard; what is your business?"

"Please your honour, it is what I want to speak one word to your honour."

"Speak then, but be quick—What is the matter?"

"The matter, please your honour, is nothing at-all-at-all, only just about the grazing of a horse, please your honour, that this man here sold me at the fair of Gurtishannon last Shrove fair, which lay down three times with myself, please your honour, and *kilt* me; not to be telling your honour of how, no later back than yesterday night, he lay down in the house there within, and all the childer standing round, and it was God's mercy he did not fall a'-top of them, or into the fire to burn himself. So please your honour, to-day I took him back to this man, which owned him, and after a great deal to do I got the mare again I *swopped* (*exchanged*) him for; but he won't pay the grazing of the horse for the time I had him, though he promised to pay the grazing in case the horse didn't answer;[1] and he never did a day's work, good or bad, please your honour, all the time he was with me, and I had the doctor to him five times, any how. And so, please your honour, it is what I expect your honour will stand my friend, for I'd sooner come to your honour for justice than to any other in all Ireland. And so I brought him here before your honour, and expect your honour will make him pay me the grazing, or tell me, can I process him for it at the next assizes, please your honour?"

The defendant now turning a quid of tobacco with his tongue into some secret cavern in his mouth, begins his defence with—

"Please your honour, under favour, and saving your honour's presence, there's not a word of truth in all this man has been saying from beginning to end, upon my conscience, and I wouldn't for the value of the horse itself, grazing and all, be after telling your honour a lie. For please your honour, I have a dependence upon your honour that you'll do me justice, and not be listening to him or the like of him. Please your honour, it's what he has brought me before your honour, because he had a spite against me about some oats I sold your honour, which he was jealous of, and a shawl his wife got at my shister's shop there without, and never paid for; so I offered to set the shawl against the grazing, and give him

---

[1] *answer* Respond to commands.

a receipt in full of all demands, but he wouldn't out of spite, your honour; so he brought me before your honour, expecting your honour was mad with me for cutting down the tree in the horse park, which was none of my doing, please your honour—ill luck to them that went and belied me to your honour behind my back!– So if your honour is pleasing, I'll tell you the whole truth about the horse that he swopped against my mare, out of the face. Last Shrove fair I met this man, Jemmy Duffy, please your honour, just at the corner of the road, where the bridge is broken down that your honour is to have the presentment for this year—long life to you for it! And he was at that time coming from the fair of Gurtishannon, and I the same way. 'How are you, Jemmy?' says I. 'Very well, I thank ye kindly, Bryan,' says he; 'shall we turn back to Paddy Salmon's and take a naggin of whiskey to our better acquaintance?' 'I don't care if I did, Jemmy,' says I; 'only it is what I can't take the whiskey, because I'm under an oath against it for a month.' Ever since, please your honour, the day your honour met me on the road, and observed to me I could hardly stand I had taken so much—though upon my conscience your honour wronged me greatly that same time; ill luck to them that belied me behind my back to your honour! Well, please your honour, as I was telling you, as he was taking the whiskey, and we talking of one thing or t'other, he makes me an offer to swop his mare that he couldn' sell at the fair of Gurtishannon, because nobody would be troubled with the beast, please your honour, against my horse, and to oblige him I took the mare—sorrow take her! and him along with her! She kicked me a new car, that was worth three pounds ten, to tatters the first time I ever put her into it, and I expect your honour will make him pay me the price of the car, any how, before I pay the grazing, which I've no right to pay at-all-at-all, only to oblige him. But I leave it all to your honour—and the whole grazing he ought to be charging for the beast is but two and eight pence half-penny, anyhow, please your honour. So I'll abide by what your honour says, good or bad. I'll leave it all to your honour."

"I'll leave it all to your honour" literally means, "I'll leave all the trouble to your honour."

The Editor knew a justice of the peace in Ireland, who had such a dread of having it all left to his honour that he frequently gave the complainants the sum about which they were disputing, to make peace between them, and to get rid of the trouble of hearing their stories out of the face. But he was soon cured of this method of buying off disputes, by the increasing multitude of those who, out of pure regard to his honour, came "to get justice from him, because they would sooner come before him than before any man in all Ireland."

A raking pot of tea—We should observe, this custom has long since been banished from the higher orders of Irish gentry. The mysteries of a raking pot of tea, like those of the Bona Dea,[1] are supposed to be sacred to females; but now and then it has happened, that some of the male species, who were either more audacious, or more highly favoured than the rest of their sex, have been admitted by stealth to these orgies. The time when the festive ceremony begins varies according to circumstances, but it is never earlier than twelve o'clock at night; the joys of a raking pot of tea depending on its being made in secret, and at an unseasonable hour. After a ball, when the more discreet part of the company had departed to rest, a few chosen female spirits, who have footed it till they can foot it no longer, and till the sleepy notes expire under the slurring hand of the musician, retire to a bed-chamber, call the favourite maid, who alone is admitted, bid her put down the kettle, lock the door, and amidst as much giggling and scrambling as possible, they get round a tea-table, on which all manner of things are huddled together. Then begin mutual railleries and mutual confidences amongst the young ladies, and the faint scream and the loud laugh is heard, and the romping for letters and pocket-books begins, and gentlemen are called by their surnames, or by the general name of fellows—pleasant fellows! charming fellows! odious fellows! abominable fellows!—and then all prudish decorums are forgotten, and then we might be convinced how much the satirical poet was mistaken

---

[1] Bona Dea Roman goddess whose rites were performed exclusively by women.

when he said, "There is no woman where there's no reserve." The merit of the original idea of a raking pot of tea evidently belongs to the washerwoman and the laundry-maid. But why should not we have *Low life above stairs*, as well as *High life below stairs*?

We gained the day by this piece of honesty—In a dispute which occurred some years ago in Ireland, between Mr. E and Mr. M, about the boundaries of a farm, an old tenant of Mr. M's cut a sod from Mr. M's land, and inserted it in a spot prepared for its reception in Mr. E's land; so nicely was it inserted, that no eye could detect the junction of the grass. The old man, who was to give his evidence as to the property, stood upon the inserted sod when the viewers came, and swore that the ground he then stood upon belonged to his landlord, Mr. M.

The Editor had flattered himself that the ingenious contrivance which Thady records, and the similar subterfuge of this old Irishman, in the dispute concerning boundaries, were instances of 'cuteness unparalleled in all but Irish story: an English friend, however, has just mortified the Editor's national vanity by an account of the following custom, which prevails in part of Shropshire. It is discreditable for women to appear abroad after the birth of their children till they have been churched.[1] To avoid this reproach, and at the same time to enjoy the pleasure of gadding,[2] whenever a woman goes abroad before she has been to church, she takes a tile from the roof of her house, and puts it upon her head: wearing this panoply all the time she pays her visits, her conscience is perfectly at ease; for she can afterwards safely declare to the clergyman, that she "has never been from under her own roof till she came to be churched."

Carton, or half Carton—Thady means *cartron* or *half cartron*. "According to the old record in the black book of Dublin, a *cantred* is said to contain 30 *villatas terras*, which are also called *quarters* of land (quarterons, *cartrons*); every one of which quarters must contain so

much ground as will pasture 400 cows, and 17 ploughlands. A knight's fee was composed of 8 hydes, which amount to 160 acres, and that is generally deemed about a *plough-land*."

The Editor was favoured by a learned friend with the above extract, from a ms. of Lord Totness's in the Lambeth library.

Wake—A wake, in England, means a festival held upon the anniversary of the Saint of the parish. At these wakes, rustic games, rustic conviviality, and rustic courtship, are pursued with all the ardour and all the appetite which accompany such pleasures as occur but seldom. In Ireland a wake is a midnight meeting, held professedly for the indulgence of holy sorrow, but usually it is converted into orgies of unholy joy. When an Irish man or woman of the lower order dies, the straw which composed the bed, whether it has been contained in a bag to form a mattress, or simply spread upon the earthen floor, is immediately taken out of the house, and burned before the cabin door, the family at the same time setting up the death howl. The ears and eyes of the neighbours being thus alarmed, they flock to the house of the deceased, and by their vociferous sympathy excite and at the same time soothe the sorrows of the family.

It is curious to observe how good and bad are mingled in human institutions. In countries which were thinly inhabited, this custom prevented private attempts against the lives of individuals, and formed a kind of coroner's inquest upon the body which had recently expired, and burning the straw upon which the sick man lay became a simple preservative against infection. At night the dead body is waked, that is to say, all the friends and neighbours of the deceased collect in a barn or stable, where the corpse is laid upon some boards, or an unhinged door, supported upon stools, the face exposed, the rest of the body covered with a white sheet. Round the body are stuck in brass candlesticks, which have been borrowed perhaps at five miles distance, as many candles as the poor person can beg or borrow, observing always to have an odd number. Pipes and tobacco are first distributed, and then, according to the

---

[1] *churched* Ceremonially blessed in a rite held forty days after childbirth.

[2] *gadding* Wandering about for pleasure.

ability of the deceased, cakes and ale, and sometimes whiskey, are *dealt* to the company:

> Deal on, deal on, my merry men all,
>   Deal on your cakes and your wine,
> For whatever is dealt at her funeral to-day
>   Shall be dealt to-morrow at mine.

After a fit of universal sorrow, and the comfort of a universal dram, the scandal of the neighbourhood, as in higher circles, occupies the company. The young lads and lasses romp with one another, and when the fathers and mothers are at last overcome with sleep and whiskey (*vino & somno*), the youth become more enterprising and are frequently successful. It is said that more matches are made at wakes than at weddings.

Kilt—This word frequently occurs in the following pages, where it means not *killed*, but much *hurt*. In Ireland, not only cowards, but the brave "die many times before their death." There, *killing is no murder*. —1800

The Grateful Negro[1]

In the island of Jamaica there lived two planters, whose methods of managing their slaves were as different as possible. Mr. Jefferies considered the negroes as an inferior species, incapable of gratitude, disposed to treachery, and to be roused from their natural indolence only by force; he treated his slaves, or rather suffered his overseer to treat them, with the greatest severity.

Jefferies was not a man of a cruel, but of a thoughtless and extravagant temper. He was of such a sanguine disposition, that he always calculated upon having a fine season, and fine crops on his plantation; and never had the prudence to make allowance for unfortunate accidents: he required, as he said, from his overseer produce and not excuses.

Durant, the overseer, did not scruple to use the most cruel and barbarous methods of forcing the slaves to exertions beyond their strength. Complaints of his brutality, from time to time, reached his master's ears; but though Mr. Jefferies was moved to momentary compassion, he shut his heart against conviction: he hurried away to the jovial banquet, and drowned all painful reflections in wine.

He was this year much in debt; and, therefore, being more than usually anxious about his crop, he pressed his overseer to exert himself to the utmost.

The wretched slaves upon his plantation thought themselves still more unfortunate when they compared their condition with that of the negroes on the estate of Mr. Edwards. This gentleman treated his slaves with all possible humanity and kindness. He wished that there was no such thing as slavery in the world, but he was convinced, by the arguments of those who have the best means of obtaining information, that the sudden emancipation of the negroes would rather increase than diminish their miseries. His benevolence, therefore, confined itself within the bounds of reason. He adopted those plans for the amelioration of the state of the slaves which appeared to him the most likely to succeed without producing any violent agitation or revolution. For instance, his negroes had reasonable and fixed daily tasks; and when these were finished, they were permitted to employ their time for their own advantage or amusement. If they chose to employ themselves longer for their master, they were paid regular wages for their extra work. This reward, for as such it was considered, operated most powerfully upon the slaves. Those who are animated by hope can perform what would seem impossibilities to those who are under the depressing influence of fear. The wages which Mr. Edwards promised, he took care to see punctually paid.

He had an excellent overseer, of the name of Abraham Bayley, a man of a mild but steady temper, who was attached not only to his master's interests but to his

---

[1] *The Grateful Negro* In a note accompanying this story, Edgeworth acknowledges planter and politician Bryan Edwards's *History, Civil and Commercial, of the British Colonies in the West Indies* (1793) as a source for much of her background information concerning Jamaica.

virtues; and who, therefore, was more intent upon seconding his humane views than upon squeezing from the labour of the negroes the utmost produce. Each negro had, near his cottage, a portion of land, called his provision-ground; and one day in the week was allowed for its cultivation.

It is common in Jamaica for the slaves to have provision-grounds, which they cultivate for their own advantage; but it too often happens, that, when a good negro has successfully improved his little spot of ground, when he has built himself a house, and begins to enjoy the fruits of his industry, his acquired property is seized upon by the sheriff's officer for the payment of his master's debts; he is forcibly separated from his wife and children, dragged to public auction, purchased by a stranger, and perhaps sent to terminate his miserable existence in the mines of Mexico; excluded for ever from the light of heaven; and all this without any crime or imprudence on his part, real or pretended. He is punished because his master is unfortunate!

To this barbarous injustice the negroes on Mr. Edwards' plantation were never exposed. He never exceeded his income; he engaged in no wild speculations; he contracted no debts; and his slaves, therefore, were in no danger of being seized by a sheriff's officer: their property was secured to them by the prudence as well as by the generosity of their master.

One morning, as Mr. Edwards was walking in that part of his plantation which joined to Mr. Jefferies' estate, he thought he heard the voice of distress at some distance. The lamentations grew louder and louder as he approached a cottage, which stood upon the borders of Jefferies' plantation.

This cottage belonged to a slave of the name of Caesar, the best negro in Mr. Jefferies' possession. Such had been his industry and exertion that, notwithstanding the severe tasks imposed by Durant, the overseer, Caesar found means to cultivate his provision-ground to a degree of perfection nowhere else to be seen on this estate. Mr. Edwards had often admired this poor fellow's industry, and now hastened to inquire what misfortune had befallen him.

When he came to the cottage, he found Caesar standing with his arms folded, and his eyes fixed upon the ground. A young and beautiful female negro was weeping bitterly, as she knelt at the feet of Durant, the overseer, who, regarding her with a sullen aspect, repeated, "He must go. I tell you, woman, he must go. What signifies all this nonsense?"

At the sight of Mr. Edwards, the overseer's countenance suddenly changed, and assumed an air of obsequious civility. The poor woman retired to the farther corner of the cottage, and continued to weep. Caesar never moved. "Nothing is the matter, sir," said Durant, "but that Caesar is going to be sold. That is what the woman is crying for. They were to be married; but we'll find Clara another husband, I tell her; and she'll get the better of her grief, you know, sir, as I tell her, in time."

"Never! never!" said Clara.

"To whom is Caesar going to be sold, and for what sum?"

"For what can be got for him," replied Durant, laughing; "and to whoever will buy him. The sheriff's officer is here, who has seized him for debt, and must make the most of him at market."

"Poor fellow!" said Mr. Edwards; "and must he leave this cottage which he has built, and these bananas which he has planted?"

Caesar now for the first time looked up, and fixing his eyes upon Mr. Edwards for a moment, advanced with an intrepid rather than an imploring countenance, and said, "Will you be my master? Will you be her master? Buy both of us. You shall not repent of it. Caesar will serve you faithfully."

On hearing these words Clara sprang forward, and clasping her hands together, repeated, "Caesar will serve you faithfully."

Mr. Edwards was moved by their entreaties, but he left them without declaring his intentions. He went immediately to Mr. Jefferies, whom he found stretched on a sofa, drinking coffee. As soon as Mr. Edwards mentioned the occasion of his visit, and expressed his sorrow for Caesar, Jefferies exclaimed, "Yes, poor devil! I pity him from the bottom of my soul. But what can I do? I leave all those things to Durant. He says the sheriff's officer has seized him; and there's an end of the matter. You know, money must be had. Besides, Caesar is not worse off than any other slave sold for debt. What signifies talking about the matter, as if it were something that never happened before! Is not it a case that occurs every day in Jamaica?"

"So much the worse," replied Mr. Edwards.

"The worse for them, to be sure," said Jefferies. "But, after all, they are slaves, and are used to be treated as such; and they tell me the negroes are a thousand times happier here, with us, than they ever were in their own country."

"Did the negroes tell you so themselves?"

"No; but people better informed than negroes have told me so; and, after all, slaves there must be; for indigo,[1] and rum, and sugar, we must have."

"Granting it to be physically impossible that the world should exist without rum, sugar, and indigo, why could they not be produced by freemen as well as by slaves? If we hired negroes for labourers, instead of purchasing them for slaves, do you think they would not work as well as they do now? Does any negro, under the fear of the overseer, work harder than a Birmingham journeyman, or a Newcastle collier,[2] who toil for themselves and their families?"

"Of that I don't pretend to judge. All I know is, that the West India planters would be ruined if they had no slaves; and I am a West India planter."

"So am I; yet I do not think they are the only people whose interests ought to be considered in this business."

"Their interests, luckily, are protected by the laws of the land; and though they are rich men, and white men, and freemen, they have as good a claim to their rights as the poorest black slave on any of our plantations."

"The law, in our case, seems to make the right; and the very reverse ought to be done—the right should make the law."

"Fortunately for us planters, we need not enter into such nice distinctions. You could not, if you would, abolish the trade. Slaves would be smuggled into the islands."

"What, if nobody would buy them? You know that you cannot smuggle slaves into England. The instant a slave touches English ground he becomes free. Glorious privilege! Why should it not be extended to all her dominions? If the future importation of slaves into these islands were forbidden by law, the trade must cease. No man can either sell or possess slaves without its being known: they cannot be smuggled like lace or brandy."

"Well, well!" retorted Jefferies, a little impatiently, "as yet the law is on our side. I can do nothing in this business, nor can you."

"Yes, we can do something; we can endeavour to make our negroes as happy as possible."

"I leave the management of these people to Durant."

"That is the very thing of which they complain; forgive me for speaking to you with the frankness of an old acquaintance."

"Oh! you can't oblige me more: I love frankness of all things! To tell you the truth, I have heard complaints of Durant's severity; but I make it a principle to turn a deaf ear to them, for I know nothing can be done with these fellows without it. You are partial to negroes; but even you must allow they are a race of beings naturally inferior to us. You may in vain think of managing a black as you would a white. Do what you please for a negro, he will cheat you the first opportunity he finds. You know what their maxim is: 'God gives black men what white men forget.'"

To these common-place desultory observations Mr. Edwards made no reply; but recurred to poor Caesar, and offered to purchase both him and Clara, at the highest price the sheriff's officer could obtain for them at market. Mr. Jefferies, with the utmost politeness to his neighbour, but with the most perfect indifference to the happiness of those whom he considered of a different species from himself, acceded to this proposal. Nothing could be more reasonable, he said; and he was happy to have it in his power to oblige a gentleman for whom he had such a high esteem.

The bargain was quickly concluded with the sheriff's officer; for Mr. Edwards willingly paid several dollars more than the market price for the two slaves. When

---

[1] *indigo* I.e., indigo dye.

[2] *journeyman* I.e., a hireling. Birmingham was a major industrial center at this time; *collier* Coal miner. Newcastle was the chief exporter of coal during the Industrial Revolution.

Caesar and Clara heard that they were not to be separated, their joy and gratitude were expressed with all the ardour and tenderness peculiar to their different characters. Clara was an Eboe, Caesar a Koromantyn negro:[1] the Eboes are soft, languishing, and timid; the Koromantyns are frank, fearless, martial, and heroic.

Mr. Edwards took his new slaves home with him, desired Bayley, his overseer, to mark out a provision-ground for Caesar, and to give him a cottage, which happened at this time to be vacant.

"Now, my good friend," said he to Caesar, "you may work for yourself, without fear that what you earn may be taken from you; or that you should ever be sold, to pay your master's debts. If he does not understand what I am saying," continued Mr. Edwards, turning to his overseer, "you will explain it to him."

Caesar perfectly understood all that Mr. Edwards said; but his feelings were at this instant so strong that he could not find expression for his gratitude: he stood like one stupefied! Kindness was new to him; it overpowered his manly heart; and at hearing the words "my good friend," the tears gushed from his eyes: tears which no torture could have extorted! Gratitude swelled in his bosom; and he longed to be alone, that he might freely yield to his emotions.

He was glad when the conch-shell sounded to call the negroes to their daily labour, that he might relieve the sensations of his soul by bodily exertion. He performed his task in silence; and an inattentive observer might have thought him sullen.

In fact, he was impatient for the day to be over, that he might get rid of a heavy load which weighed upon his mind.

The cruelties practised by Durant, the overseer of Jefferies' plantation, had exasperated the slaves under his dominion.

They were all leagued together in a conspiracy, which was kept profoundly secret. Their object was to extirpate[2] every white man, woman, and child, in the island. Their plans were laid with consummate art; and the negroes were urged to execute them by all the courage of despair.

The confederacy extended to all the negroes in the island of Jamaica, excepting those on the plantation of Mr. Edwards. To them no hint of the dreadful secret had yet been given; their countrymen, knowing the attachment they felt to their master, dared not trust them with these projects of vengeance. Hector, the negro who was at the head of the conspirators, was the particular friend of Caesar, and had imparted to him all his designs. These friends were bound to each other by the strongest ties. Their slavery and their sufferings began in the same hour; they were both brought from their own country in the same ship. This circumstance alone forms, amongst the negroes, a bond of connection not easily to be dissolved. But the friendship of Caesar and Hector commenced even before they were united by the sympathy of misfortune; they were both of the same nation, both Koromantyns. In Africa they had both been accustomed to command; for they had signalized themselves by superior fortitude and courage. They respected each other for excelling in all which they had been taught to consider as virtuous; and with them revenge was a virtue!

Revenge was the ruling passion of Hector: in Caesar's mind it was rather a principle instilled by education. The one considered it as a duty, the other felt it as a pleasure. Hector's sense of injury was acute in the extreme; he knew not how to forgive. Caesar's sensibility was yet more alive to kindness than to insult. Hector would sacrifice his life to extirpate an enemy. Caesar would devote himself for the defence of a friend; and Caesar now considered a white man as his friend.

He was now placed in a painful situation. All his former friendships, all the solemn promises by which he was bound to his companions in misfortune, forbade him to indulge that delightful feeling of gratitude and affection, which, for the first time, he experienced for one of that race of beings whom he had hitherto considered as detestable tyrants—objects of implacable and just revenge!

Caesar was most impatient to have an interview with

---

[1] *Eboe*   Name applied, in the West Indies, to those from Benin; *Koromantyn negro*   An African from the Gold Coast.

[2] *extirpate*   Exterminate; destroy.

Hector, that he might communicate his new sentiments, and dissuade him from those schemes of destruction which he meditated. At midnight, when all the slaves except himself were asleep, he left his cottage, and went to Jefferies' plantation, to the hut in which Hector slept. Even in his dreams Hector breathed vengeance. "Spare none! Sons of Africa, spare none!" were the words he uttered in his sleep, as Caesar approached the mat on which he lay. The moon shone full upon him. Caesar contemplated the countenance of his friend, fierce even in sleep. "Spare none! Oh, yes! There is one that must be spared. There is one for whose sake all must be spared."

He wakened Hector by this exclamation. "Of what were you dreaming?" said Caesar.

"Of that which, sleeping or waking, fills my soul—revenge! Why did you waken me from my dream? It was delightful. The whites were weltering in their blood! But silence! we may be overheard."

"No; every one sleeps but ourselves," replied Caesar. "I could not sleep without speaking to you on—a subject that weighs upon my mind. You have seen Mr. Edwards?"

"Yes. He that is now your master."

"He that is now my benefactor—my friend!"

"Friend! Can you call a white man friend?" cried Hector, starting up with a look of astonishment and indignation.

"Yes," replied Caesar, with firmness. "And you would speak, ay, and would feel, as I do, Hector, if you knew this white man. Oh, how unlike he is to all of his race, that we have ever seen! Do not turn from me with so much disdain. Hear me with patience, my friend."

"I cannot," replied Hector, "listen with patience to one who between the rising and the setting sun can forget all his resolutions, all his promises; who by a few soft words can be so wrought upon as to forget all the insults, all the injuries he has received from this accursed race; and can even call a white man friend!"

Caesar, unmoved by Hector's anger, continued to speak of Mr. Edwards with the warmest expressions of gratitude; and finished by declaring he would sooner forfeit his life than rebel against such a master. He conjured Hector to desist from executing his designs;

but all was in vain. Hector sat with his elbows fixed upon his knees, leaning his head upon his hands, in gloomy silence.

Caesar's mind was divided between love for his friend and gratitude to his master: the conflict was violent and painful. Gratitude at last prevailed: he repeated his declaration, that he would rather die than continue in a conspiracy against his benefactor!

Hector refused to except him from the general doom. "Betray us if you will!" cried he. "Betray our secrets to him whom you call your benefactor; to him whom a few hours have made your friend! To him sacrifice the friend of your youth, the companion of your better days, of your better self! Yes, Caesar, deliver me over to the tormentors: I can endure more than they can inflict. I shall expire without a sigh, without a groan. Why do you linger here, Caesar? Why do you hesitate? Hasten this moment to your master; claim your reward for delivering into his power hundreds of your countrymen! Why do you hesitate? Away! The coward's friendship can be of use to none. Who can value his gratitude? Who can fear his revenge?"

Hector raised his voice so high, as he pronounced these words, that he wakened Durant, the overseer, who slept in the next house. They heard him call out suddenly, to inquire who was there: and Caesar had but just time to make his escape, before Durant appeared. He searched Hector's cottage; but finding no one, again retired to rest. This man's tyranny made him constantly suspicious; he dreaded that the slaves should combine against him; and he endeavoured to prevent them, by every threat and every stratagem he could devise, from conversing with each other.

They had, however, taken their measures, hitherto, so secretly, that he had not the slightest idea of the conspiracy which was forming in the island. Their schemes were not yet ripe for execution; but the appointed time approached. Hector, when he coolly reflected on what had passed between him and Caesar, could not help admiring the frankness and courage with which he had avowed his change of sentiments. By this avowal, Caesar had in fact exposed his own life to the most imminent danger, from the vengeance of the conspirators, who might be tempted to assassinate him who had their lives in his power. Notwithstanding the contempt with which, in the first moment of passion, he had treated his friend, he was extremely anxious that he should not break off all connection with the conspirators. He knew that Caesar possessed both intrepidity and eloquence, and that his opposition to their schemes would perhaps entirely frustrate their whole design. He therefore determined to use every possible means to bend him to their purposes.

He resolved to have recourse to one of those persons who, amongst the negroes, are considered as sorceresses.[1] Esther, an old Koromantyn negress, had obtained by her skill in poisonous herbs, and her knowledge of venomous reptiles, a high reputation amongst her countrymen. She soon taught them to believe her to be possessed of supernatural powers; and she then worked their imagination to what pitch and purpose she pleased.

She was the chief instigator of this intended rebellion. It was she who had stimulated the revengeful temper of Hector almost to frenzy. She now promised him that her arts should be exerted over his friend; and it was not long before he felt their influence. Caesar soon perceived an extraordinary change in the countenance and manner of his beloved Clara. A melancholy hung over her, and she refused to impart to him the cause of her dejection. Caesar was indefatigable in his exertions to cultivate and embellish the ground near his cottage, in hopes of making it an agreeable habitation for her; but she seemed to take no interest in anything. She would stand beside him immoveable, in a deep reverie; but when he inquired whether she was ill, she would answer no, and endeavour to assume an air of gaiety: but this cheerfulness was transient; she soon relapsed into despondency. At length, she endeavoured to avoid her lover, as if she feared his farther inquiries.

Unable to endure this state of suspense, he one

evening resolved to bring her to an explanation. "Clara," said he, "you once loved me: I have done nothing, have I, to forfeit your confidence?"

"I once loved you!" said she, raising her languid eyes, and looking at him with reproachful tenderness; "and can you doubt my constancy? Oh, Caesar, you little know what is passing in my heart! You are the cause of my melancholy!"

She paused and hesitated, as if afraid that she had said too much; but Caesar urged her with so much vehemence, and so much tenderness, to open to him her whole soul, that, at last, she could not resist his eloquence. She reluctantly revealed to him that secret of which she could not think without horror. She informed him, that unless he complied with what was required of him by the sorceress Esther, he was devoted to die. What it was that Esther required of him, Clara knew not: she knew nothing of the conspiracy. The timidity of her character was ill suited to such a project; and everything relating to it had been concealed from her with the utmost care.

When she explained to Caesar the cause of her dejection, his natural courage resisted these superstitious fears; and he endeavoured to raise Clara's spirits. He endeavoured in vain: she fell at his feet; and with tears, and the most tender supplications, conjured him to avert the wrath of the sorceress, by obeying her commands, whatever they might be!

"Clara," replied he, "you know not what you ask!"

"I ask you to save your life!" said she. "I ask you, for my sake, to save your life, while yet it is in your power!"

"But would you, to save my life, Clara, make me the worst of criminals? Would you make me the murderer of my benefactor?"

Clara started with horror.

"Do you recollect the day, the moment, when we were on the point of being separated for ever, Clara? Do you remember the white man's coming to my cottage? Do you remember his look of benevolence—his voice of compassion? Do you remember his generosity? Oh! Clara, would you make me the murderer of this man?"

"Heaven forbid!" said Clara. "This cannot be the will of the sorceress!"

---

[1] *who, amongst ... sorceresses* Edgeworth's original text contains a long note here (largely excerpted from Edwards's *History, Civil and Commercial, of the British Colonies in the West Indies*) recounting tales of *Obeah* practices, a type of witchcraft or folk medicine practiced in the English-speaking Caribbean at this time.

"It is," said Caesar. "But she shall not succeed, even though she speaks with the voice of Clara. Urge me no further; my resolution is fixed. I should be unworthy of your love if I were capable of treachery and ingratitude."

"But is there no means of averting the wrath of Esther?" said Clara. "Your life—"

"Think, first, of my honour," interrupted Caesar. "Your fears deprive you of reason. Return to this sorceress, and tell her that I dread not her wrath. My hands shall never be imbrued in the blood of my benefactor. Clara! can you forget his look when he told us that we should never more be separated?"

"It went to my heart," said Clara, bursting into tears. "Cruel, cruel Esther! Why do you command us to destroy such a generous master?"

The conch sounded to summon the negroes to their morning's work. It happened this day, that Mr. Edwards, who was continually intent upon increasing the comforts and happiness of his slaves, sent his carpenter, while Caesar was absent, to fit up the inside of his cottage; and when Caesar returned from work, he found his master pruning the branches of a tamarind tree that over-hung the thatch. "How comes it, Caesar," said he, "that you have not pruned these branches?"

Caesar had no knife. "Here is mine for you," said Mr. Edwards. "It is very sharp," added he, smiling; "but I am not one of those masters who are afraid to trust their negroes with sharp knives."

These words were spoken with perfect simplicity: Mr. Edwards had no suspicion, at this time, of what was passing in the negro's mind. Caesar received the knife without uttering a syllable; but no sooner was Mr. Edwards out of sight than he knelt down, and, in a transport of gratitude, swore that, with this knife, he would stab himself to the heart sooner than betray his master!

The principle of gratitude conquered every other sensation. The mind of Caesar was not insensible to the charms of freedom: he knew the negro conspirators had so taken their measures that there was the greatest probability of their success. His heart beat high at the idea of recovering his liberty: but he was not to be seduced from his duty, not even by this delightful hope;

nor was he to be intimidated by the dreadful certainty that his former friends and countrymen, considering him as a deserter from their cause, would become his bitterest enemies. The loss of Hector's esteem and affection was deeply felt by Caesar. Since the night that the decisive conversation relative to Mr. Edwards passed, Hector and he had never exchanged a syllable.

This visit proved the cause of much suffering to Hector, and to several of the slaves on Jefferies' plantation. We mentioned that Durant had been awakened by the raised voice of Hector. Though he could not find anyone in the cottage, yet his suspicions were not dissipated; and an accident nearly brought the whole conspiracy to light. Durant had ordered one of the negroes to watch a boiler of sugar: the slave was overcome by the heat, and fainted. He had scarcely recovered his senses when the overseer came up, and found that the sugar had fermented, by having remained a few minutes too long in the boiler. He flew into a violent passion, and ordered that the negro should receive fifty lashes. His victim bore them without uttering a groan; but, when his punishment was over, and when he thought the overseer was gone, he exclaimed, "It will soon be our turn!"

Durant was not out of hearing. He turned suddenly, and observed that the negro looked at Hector when he pronounced these words, and this confirmed the suspicion that Hector was carrying on some conspiracy. He immediately had recourse to that brutality which he considered as the only means of governing black men: Hector and three other negroes were lashed unmercifully; but no confessions could be extorted.

Mr. Jefferies might perhaps have forbidden such violence to be used, if he had not been at the time carousing with a party of jovial West Indians, who thought of nothing but indulging their appetites in all the luxuries that art and nature could supply. The sufferings which had been endured by many of the wretched negroes to furnish out this magnificent entertainment were never once thought of by these selfish epicures.[1] Yet so false are the general estimates of

---

[1] *epicures* Those devoted to the pursuit of sensual pleasures.

character, that all these gentlemen passed for men of great feeling and generosity! The human mind, in certain situations, becomes so accustomed to ideas of tyranny and cruelty, that they no longer appear extraordinary or detestable: they rather seem part of the necessary and immutable order of things.

Mr. Jefferies was stopped, as he passed from his dining-room into his drawing-room, by a little negro child, of about five years old, who was crying bitterly. He was the son of one of the slaves who were at this moment under the torturer's hand. "Poor little devil!" said Mr. Jefferies, who was more than half intoxicated. "Take him away; and tell Durant, some of ye, to pardon his father—if he can."

The child ran, eagerly, to announce his father's pardon; but he soon returned, crying more violently than before. Durant would not hear the boy; and it was now no longer possible to appeal to Mr. Jefferies, for he was in the midst of an assembly of fair ladies, and no servant belonging to the house dared to interrupt the festivities of the evening. The three men, who were so severely flogged to extort from them confessions, were perfectly innocent: they knew nothing of the confederacy; but the rebels seized the moment when their minds were exasperated by this cruelty and injustice, and they easily persuaded them to join the league. The hope of revenging themselves upon the overseer was a motive sufficient to make them brave death in any shape.

Another incident, which happened a few days before the time destined for the revolt of the slaves, determined numbers who had been undecided. Mrs. Jefferies was a languid beauty, or rather a languid fine lady who had been a beauty, and who spent all that part of the day which was not devoted to the pleasures of the table, or to reclining on a couch, in dress. She was one day extended on a sofa, fanned by four slaves, two at her head and two at her feet, when news was brought that a large chest, directed to her, was just arrived from London.

This chest contained various articles of dress of the newest fashions. The Jamaica ladies carry their ideas of magnificence to a high pitch: they willingly give a hundred guineas for a gown, which they perhaps wear but once or twice. In the elegance and variety of her ornaments, Mrs. Jefferies was not exceeded by any lady in the island, except by one who had lately received a cargo from England. She now expected to outshine her competitor, and desired that the chest should be unpacked in her presence.

In taking out one of the gowns, it caught on a nail in the lid, and was torn. The lady, roused from her natural indolence by this disappointment to her vanity, instantly ordered that the unfortunate female slave should be severely chastised. The woman was the wife of Hector; and this fresh injury worked up his temper, naturally vindictive, to the highest point. He ardently longed for the moment when he might satiate his vengeance.

The plan the negroes had laid was to set fire to the canes,[1] at one and the same time, on every plantation; and when the white inhabitants of the island should run to put out the fire, the blacks were to seize this moment of confusion and consternation to fall upon them, and make a general massacre. The time when this scheme was to be carried into execution was not known to Caesar; for the conspirators had changed their day, as soon as Hector told them that his friend was no longer one of the confederacy. They dreaded he should betray them; and it was determined that he and Clara should both be destroyed, unless they could be prevailed upon to join the conspiracy.

Hector wished to save his friend, but the desire of vengeance overcame every other feeling. He resolved, however, to make an attempt, for the last time, to change Caesar's resolution.

For this purpose, Esther was the person he employed: she was to work upon his mind by means of Clara. On returning to her cottage one night, she found suspended from the thatch one of those strange fantastic charms with which the Indian sorceresses terrify those whom they have proscribed. Clara, unable to conquer her terror, repaired again to Esther, who received her first in mysterious silence; but, after she had implored her forgiveness for the past, and with all possible humility conjured her to grant her future protection, the

---

[1] *canes* Sugar-cane fields.

sorceress deigned to speak. Her commands were that Clara should prevail upon her lover to meet her, on this awful spot, the ensuing night.

Little suspecting what was going forward on the plantation of Jefferies, Mr. Edwards that evening gave his slaves a holiday. He and his family came out at sunset, when the fresh breeze had sprung up, and seated themselves under a spreading palm-tree, to enjoy the pleasing spectacle of this negro festival. His negroes were all well clad, and in the gayest colours, and their merry countenances suited the gaiety of their dress. While some were dancing, and some playing on the tambourine, others appeared amongst the distant trees, bringing baskets of avocado pears, grapes, and pine-apples, the produce of their own provision-grounds; and others were employed in spreading their clean trenchers, or the calabashes, which served for plates and dishes. The negroes continued to dance and divert themselves till late in the evening. When they separated and retired to rest, Caesar, recollecting his promise to Clara, repaired secretly to the habitation of this sorceress. It was situated in the recess of a thick wood. When he arrived there, he found the door fastened; and he was obliged to wait some time before it was opened by Esther.

The first object he beheld was his beloved Clara, stretched on the ground, apparently a corpse! The sorceress had thrown her into a trance by a preparation of deadly nightshade.[1] The hag burst into an infernal laugh, when she beheld the despair that was painted in Caesar's countenance. "Wretch!" cried she, "you have defied my power: behold its victim!"

Caesar, in a transport of rage, seized her by the throat: but his fury was soon checked.

"Destroy me," said the fiend, "and you destroy your Clara. She is not dead: but she lies in the sleep of death, into which she has been thrown by magic art, and from which no power but mine can restore her to the light of life. Yes! look at her, pale and motionless! Never will she rise from the earth, unless, within one hour, you obey my commands. I have administered to Hector and his companions the solemn fetish oath, at the sound of

which every negro in Africa trembles! You know my object."

"Fiend, I do!" replied Caesar, eyeing her sternly; "but, while I have life, it shall never be accomplished."

"Look yonder!" cried she, pointing to the moon; "in a few minutes that moon will set: at that hour Hector and his friends will appear. They come armed—armed with weapons which I shall steep in poison for their enemies. Themselves I will render invulnerable. Look again!" continued she; "if my dim eyes mistake not, yonder they come. Rash man, you die if they cross my threshold."

"I wish for death," said Caesar. "Clara is dead!"

"But you can restore her to life by a single word."

Caesar, at this moment, seemed to hesitate.

"Consider! Your heroism is vain," continued Esther. "You will have the knives of fifty of the conspirators in your bosom, if you do not join them; and, after you have fallen, the death of your master is inevitable. Here is the bowl of poison, in which the negro knives are to be steeped. Your friends, your former friends, your countrymen, will be in arms in a few minutes; and they will bear down every thing before them—Victory, Wealth, Freedom, and Revenge, will be theirs."

Caesar appeared to be more and more agitated. His eyes were fixed upon Clara. The conflict in his mind was violent: but his sense of gratitude and duty could not be shaken by hope, fear, or ambition; nor could it be vanquished by love. He determined, however, to appear to yield. As if struck with panic, at the approach of the confederate negroes, he suddenly turned to the sorceress, and said, in a tone of feigned submission, "It is in vain to struggle with fate. Let my knife, too, be dipped in your magic poison."

The sorceress clapped her hands with infernal joy in her countenance. She bade him instantly give her his knife, that she might plunge it to the hilt in the bowl of poison, to which she turned with savage impatience. His knife was left in his cottage, and, under pretence of going in search of it, he escaped. Esther promised to prepare Hector and all his companions to receive him with their ancient cordiality on his return. Caesar ran with the utmost speed along a by-path out of the wood,

---

[1] *deadly nightshade* I.e., *Atropa belladonna*, a type of poisonous plant.

met none of the rebels, reached his master's house, scaled the wall of his bedchamber, got in at the window, and wakened him, exclaiming, "Arm—arm yourself, my dear master! Arm all your slaves! They will fight for you, and die for you; as I will the first. The Koromantyn yell of war will be heard in Jefferies plantation this night! Arm—arm yourself, my dear master, and let us surround the rebel leaders while it is yet time. I will lead you to the place where they are all assembled, on condition that their chief, who is my friend, shall be pardoned."

Mr. Edwards armed himself and the negroes on his plantation, as well as the whites; they were all equally attached to him. He followed Caesar into the recesses of the wood.

They proceeded with all possible rapidity, but in perfect silence, till they reached Esther's habitation: which they surrounded completely before they were perceived by the conspirators.

Mr. Edwards looked through a hole in the wall; and, by the blue flame of a cauldron, over which the sorceress was stretching her shrivelled hands, he saw Hector and five stout negroes standing, intent upon her incantations. These negroes held their knives in their hands, ready to dip them into the bowl of poison. It was proposed, by one of the whites, to set fire immediately to the hut, and thus to force the rebels to surrender. The advice was followed; but Mr. Edwards charged his people to spare their prisoners. The moment the rebels saw that the thatch of the hut was in flames, they set up the Koromantyn yell of war, and rushed out with frantic desperation.

"Yield! You are pardoned, Hector," cried Mr. Edwards, in a loud voice.

"You are pardoned, my friend!" repeated Caesar.

Hector, incapable at this instant of listening to anything but revenge, sprang forwards, and plunged his knife into the bosom of Caesar. The faithful servant staggered back a few paces: his master caught him in his arms. "I die content," said he. "Bury me with Clara."

He swooned from loss of blood as they were carrying him home; but when his wound was examined, it was found not to be mortal. As he recovered from his swoon, he stared wildly round him, trying to recollect where he was, and what had happened. He thought that he was still in a dream when he saw his beloved Clara standing beside him. The opiate, which the pretended sorceress had administered to her, had ceased to operate; she wakened from her trance just at the time the Koromantyn yell commenced. Caesar's joy!—we must leave that to the imagination.

In the meantime, what became of the rebel negroes, and Mr. Edwards?

The taking of the chief conspirators prisoners did not prevent the negroes upon Jefferies' plantation from insurrection. The moment they heard the war-whoop, the signal agreed upon, they rose in a body; and, before they could be prevented, either by the whites on the estate, or by Mr. Edwards' adherents, they had set fire to the overseer's house, and to the canes. The overseer was the principal object of their vengeance—he died in tortures, inflicted by the hands of those who had suffered most by his cruelties. Mr. Edwards, however, quelled the insurgents before rebellion spread to any other estates in the island. The influence of his character, and the effect of his eloquence upon the minds of the people, were astonishing: nothing but his interference could have prevented the total destruction of Mr. Jefferies and his family, who, as it was computed, lost this night upwards of fifty thousand pounds. He was never afterwards able to recover his losses, or to shake off his constant fear of a fresh insurrection among his slaves. At length, he and his lady returned to England, where they were obliged to live in obscurity and indigence. They had no consolation in their misfortunes but that of railing at the treachery of the whole race of slaves. Our readers, we hope, will think that at least one exception may be made, in favour of the Grateful Negro.

—1804

JAMES HOGG
1770 – 1835

Best known for *The Private Memoirs and Confessions of a Justified Sinner* (1824), the Scottish poet, novelist, and short-story writer James Hogg embodied the Romantic ideal of the "natural poet," an author thought to be capable of representing a pure, unspoiled view of life. Virtually illiterate until his early twenties, Hogg was a self-taught writer who became acquainted with Sir Walter Scott, perhaps the most famous Scottish writer of his generation, as well as a number of other prominent Romantics, and was memorialized by William Wordsworth upon his death. Still, Hogg was often mocked for his accent and manner during his own lifetime, and his work fell by the wayside to the extent that it was almost completely neglected for much of the twentieth century.

Born on a small farm near Ettrick, Scotland in 1770, Hogg had minimal formal education, leaving school at the age of seven as a result of the family's bankruptcy. However, his mother, Margaret Hogg, was an enthusiastic collector of Scottish ballads, and she frequently recited popular songs and tales to her son. At the age of eight, Hogg became a shepherd. His employer offered to aid his attempts at self-improvement by making books available to him. A quick study, Hogg would later claim that he began writing almost as soon as he began to read.

In 1797, Hogg discovered the work of Robert Burns, a fellow Scot whose poetry, Hogg later wrote in his *Memoir of the Author's Life* (1832), "formed a new epoch of [his] life." Introduced by his employer to Sir Walter Scott, Hogg eventually became involved in Scott's projects, helping to collect ballads for *The Minstrelsy of the Scottish Border* (1802–03). By 1807, Hogg published his own collection of verse, *The Mountain Bard*. That volume was largely ignored, but *The Queen's Wake*, published in 1813, became a success, and Hogg was recruited to write for *Blackwood's Magazine*. The triumph was short-lived, however; as the magazine gained in popularity and influence, Hogg found himself marginalized and excluded by more cosmopolitan and politically savvy writers. Depicted as the Ettrick Shepherd in popular *Blackwood's* "Noctes Ambroianae" dialogues, Hogg was derided as a rural simpleton-savant. His reputation declined; with a young wife and son to support, he soon found himself desperate for money.

Hogg's attempt to salvage his failing farm led to the writing of *The Private Memoirs and Confessions of a Justified Sinner*. The tale of a young man who encounters a shape-shifting devil did not fare well, due largely to its unconventional, unclassifiable style, its curious amalgamation of genres, and its themes of persecution and tormented consciousness. Hogg's subsequent attempts at prose were, generally, little understood and ill-received. Even Scott, who remained a life-long friend and champion, confided in a letter to his friend John Murray that "Hogg's Tales are a great failure to be sure. With a very considerable portion of original genius he is sadly deficient not only in correct taste but in common tact." At the time of his death in 1835, Hogg was largely dismissed as a writer of raw but uncultivated talent. In a note to his "Extempore Effusion upon the Death of James Hogg"

(1835), Wordsworth remarked that while Hogg "was undoubtedly a man of original genius," he was "of coarse manners and low and offensive opinions."

Bowdlerized in the nineteenth century, Hogg's work was largely neglected in the twentieth, until the rediscovery of *The Private Memoirs and Confessions of a Justified Sinner* by the French writer André Gide. Since then, critics have increasingly begun to acknowledge the power of Hogg's novel and to celebrate its seeming anticipation of postmodernism and its influence on works including Robert Louis Stevenson's *Strange Case of Dr. Jekyll and Mr. Hyde* (1886). The renewed attention has brought a new focus to Hogg's oeuvre as well as recognition of his place in the literature of Scotland and the history of Romanticism.

⌘ ⌘ ⌘

The Brownie of the Black Haggs [1]

When the Sprots were lairds[2] of Wheelhope, which is now a long time ago, there was one of the ladies who was very badly spoken of in the country. People did not just openly assert that Lady Wheelhope was a witch, but every one had an aversion even at hearing her named; and when by chance she happened to be mentioned, old men would shake their heads and say, "Ah! let us alane o' her! The less ye meddle wi' her the better." Auld wives would give over spinning, and, as a pretence for hearing what might be said about her, poke in the fire with the tongs, cocking up their ears all the while; and then, after some meaning coughs, hems, and haws, would haply say, "Hech-wow,[3] sirs! An a' be true that's said!" or something equally wise and decisive as that.

In short, Lady Wheelhope was accounted a very bad woman. She was an inexorable tyrant in her family, quarrelled with her servants, often cursing them, striking them, and turning them away; especially if they were religious, for these she could not endure, but suspected them of every thing bad. Whenever she found out any of the servant men of the laird's establishment for religious characters, she soon gave them up to the military, and got them shot; and several girls that were regular in their devotions, she was supposed to have popped off with poison. She was certainly a wicked woman, else many good people were mistaken in her character, and the poor persecuted Covenanters[4] were obliged to unite in their prayers against her.

As for the laird, he was a stump. A big, dun-faced, pluffy[5] body, that cared neither for good nor evil, and did not well know the one from the other. He laughed at his lady's tantrums and barley-hoods;[6] and the greater the rage that she got into, the laird thought it the better sport. One day, when two servant maids came running to him, in great agitation, and told him that his lady had felled one of their companions, the laird laughed heartily at them, and said he did not doubt it.

"Why, sir, how can you laugh?" said they. "The poor girl is killed."

"Very likely, very likely," said the laird. "Well, it will teach her to take care who she angers again."

"And, sir, your lady will be hanged."

---

[1] *The Brownie of the Black Haggs*   The story first appeared in the October 1828 edition of *Blackwood's Magazine*; *Brownie*   A benevolent spirit or goblin of shaggy appearance that is supposed to haunt old houses, especially farmhouses, in Scotland, and sometimes to perform useful household work while the family is asleep; in Scottish folklore, brownies typically leave the house if the owner abuses them; *Haggs*   A hedge; a wooded enclosure; a coppice or copse.

[2] *lairds*   Landed proprietors.

[3] *Hech-wow*   An exclamation expressive of various feelings, chiefly of surprise, sorrow, or fatigue.

[4] *Covenanters*   Extremist Presbyterians; the remnants of a politico-religious movement in Scotland that successfully opposed Charles I.

[5] *pluffy*   Having a puffed-up appearance; puffy; fat, swollen, fleshy.

[6] *barley-hoods*   Fits of drunkenness, or of ill humor or temper, brought on by drinking.

"Very likely; well, it will learn her how to strike so rashly again—Ha, ha, ha! Will it not, Jessy?"

But when this same Jessy died suddenly one morning, the laird was greatly confounded, and seemed dimly to comprehend that there had been unfair play going. There was little doubt that she was taken off by poison; but whether the lady did it through jealousy or not, was never divulged; but it greatly bamboozled and astonished the poor laird, for his nerves failed him, and his whole frame became paralytic. He seems to have been exactly in the same state of mind with a colley[1] that I once had. He was extremely fond of the gun as long as I did not kill any thing with her, (there being no game laws in Ettrick Forest in those days,) and he got a grand chase after the hares when I missed them. But there was one day that I chanced for a marvel to shoot one dead, a few paces before his nose. I'll never forget the astonishment that the poor beast manifested. He stared one while at the gun, and another while at the dead hare, and seemed to be drawing the conclusion, that if the case stood thus, there was no creature sure of its life. Finally, he took his tail between his legs, and ran away home, and never would face a gun all his life again.

So was it precisely with Laird Sprot of Wheelhope. As long as his lady's wrath produced only noise and splutter among the servants, he thought it fine sport; but when he saw what he believed the dreadful effects of it, he became like a barrel organ out of tune, and could only discourse one note, which he did to every one he met. "I wish she maunna hae gotten something she has been the waur of."[2] This note he repeated early and late, night and day, sleeping and waking, alone and in company, from the moment that Jessy died till she was buried; and on going to the churchyard as chief mourner, he whispered it to her relations by the way. When they came to the grave, he took his stand at the head, nor would he give place to the girl's father; but there he stood, like a huge post, as though he neither saw nor heard; and when he had lowered her late comely head into the grave, and dropped the cord, he slowly lifted his hat with one hand, wiped his dim eyes with the back of the other, and said, in a deep tremulous tone, "Poor lassie! I wish she didna get something she had been the waur of."

This death made a great noise among the common people; but there was no protection for the life of the subject in those days; and provided a man or woman was a true loyal subject, and a real Anti-Covenanter, any of them might kill as many as they liked. So there was no one to take cognizance of the circumstances relating to the death of poor Jessy.

After this, the lady walked softly for the space of two or three years. She saw that she had rendered herself odious, and had entirely lost her husband's countenance, which she liked worst of all. But the evil propensity could not be overcome; and a poor boy, whom the laird, out of sheer compassion, had taken into his service, being found dead one morning, the country people could no longer be restrained; so they went in a body to the Sheriff, and insisted on an investigation. It was proved that she detested the boy, had often threatened him, and had given him brose[3] and butter the afternoon before he died; but the cause was ultimately dismissed, and the pursuers fined.

No one can tell to what height of wickedness she might now have proceeded, had not a check of a very singular kind been laid upon her. Among the servants that came home at the next term, was one who called himself Merodach; and a strange person he was. He had the form of a boy, but the features of one a hundred years old, save that his eyes had a brilliancy and restlessness, which was very extraordinary, bearing a strong resemblance to the eyes of a well-known species of monkey. He was froward[4] and perverse in all his actions, and disregarded the pleasure or displeasure of any person; but he performed his work well, and with apparent ease. From the moment that he entered the house, the lady conceived a mortal antipathy against him, and besought the laird to turn him away. But the

---

[1] colley Breed of dog.

[2] maunna hae May have not; waur of Worse of.

[3] brose Dish made by pouring boiling water (or milk) on oatmeal (or oat-cake) seasoned with salt and butter.

[4] froward Disposed to go counter to what is demanded or what is reasonable; perverse, difficult to deal with, hard to please.

laird, of himself, never turned away any body, and moreover he had hired him for a trivial wage, and the fellow neither wanted activity nor perseverance. The natural consequence of this arrangement was, that the lady instantly set herself to make Merodach's life as bitter as it was possible, in order to get early quit of a domestic every way so disgusting. Her hatred of him was not like a common antipathy entertained by one human being against another,—she hated him as one might hate a toad or an adder; and his occupation of jotteryman (as the laird termed his servant of all work) keeping him always about her hand, it must have proved highly disagreeable.

She scolded him, she raged at him, but he only mocked her wrath, and giggled and laughed at her, with the most provoking derision. She tried to fell him again and again, but never, with all her address, could she hit him; and never did she make a blow at him, that she did not repent it. She was heavy and unwieldy, and he as quick in his motions as a monkey; besides, he generally had her in such an ungovernable rage, that when she flew at him, she hardly knew what she was doing. At one time she guided her blow towards him, and he at the same instant avoided it with such dexterity, that she knocked down the chief hind, or foreman; and then Merodach giggled so heartily, that, lifting the kitchen poker, she threw it at him with a full design of knocking out his brains; but the missile only broke every plate and ashet[1] on the kitchen dresser.

She then hasted to the laird, crying bitterly, and telling him she would not suffer that wretch Merodach, as she called him, to stay another night in the family. "Why, then, put him away, and trouble me no more about him," said the laird.

"Put him away!" exclaimed she; "I have already ordered him away a hundred times, and charged him never to let me see his horrible face again; but he only flouts me, and tells me he'll see me at the devil first."

The pertinacity of the fellow amused the laird exceedingly; his dim eyes turned upwards into his head with delight; he then looked two ways at once, turned

round his back, and laughed till the tears ran down his dun cheeks, but he could only articulate "You're fitted now."

The lady's agony of rage still increasing from this derision, she flew on the laird, and said he was not worthy the name of a man, if he did not turn away that pestilence, after the way he had abused her.

"Why, Shusy, my dear, what has he done to you?"

"What done to me! has he not caused me to knock down John Thomson, and I do not know if ever he will come to life again?"

"Have you felled your favourite John Thomson?" said the laird, laughing more heartily than before; "you might have done a worse deed than that. But what evil has John done?"

"And has he not broke every plate and dish on the whole dresser?" continued the lady, disregarding the laird's question; "and for all this devastation, he only mocks at my displeasure, absolutely mocks me, and if you do not have him turned away, and hanged or shot for his deeds, you are not worthy the name of man."

"O alack! What a devastation among the china metal!" said the laird; and calling on Merodach, he said, "Tell me, thou evil Merodach of Babylon,[2] how thou dared'st knock down thy lady's favourite servant, John Thomson?"

"Not I, your honour. It was my lady herself, who got into such a furious rage at me, that she mistook her man, and felled Mr. Thomson; and the good man's skull is fractured."

"That was very odd," said the laird, chuckling; "I do not comprehend it. But then, what the devil set you on smashing all my lady's delft and china ware?—That was a most infamous and provoking action."

"It was she herself, your honour. Sorry would I have been to have broken one dish belonging to the house. I take all the house-servants to witness, that my lady

---

[1] *ashet* Dish or large flat plate.

[2] *evil Merodach of Babylon* The son and successor of Nebuchadnezzar, king of Babylon, King Evil-Merodach reigned for only two years (562–560 BCE). He is best known for showing kindness to King Jehoiachin of Judah, who had been a prisoner in Babylon for 37 years, releasing him and speaking kindly to him.

smashed all the dishes with a poker, and now lays the blame on me."

The laird turned his dim and delighted eyes on his lady, who was crying with vexation and rage, and seemed meditating another personal attack on the culprit, which he did not at all appear to shun, but rather encourage. She, however, vented her wrath in threatenings of the most deep and desperate revenge, the creature all the while assuring her that she would be foiled, and that in all her encounters and contests with him, she would uniformly come to the worst. He was resolved to do his duty, and there before his master he defied her.

The laird thought more than he considered it prudent to reveal; but he had little doubt that his wife would wreak that vengeance on his jotteryman which she avowed, and as little of her capability. He almost shuddered when he recollected one who had taken *something that she had been the waur of.*

In a word, the Lady of Wheelhope's inveterate malignity against this one object, was like the rod of Moses,[1] that swallowed up the rest of the serpents. All her wicked and evil propensities seemed to be super-seded by it, if not utterly absorbed in its virtues. The rest of the family now lived in comparative peace and quietness; for early and late her malevolence was venting itself against the jotteryman, and him alone. It was a delirium of hatred and vengeance, on which the whole bent and bias of her inclination was set. She could not stay from the creature's presence, for in the intervals when absent from him, she spent her breath in curses and execrations, and then not able to rest, she ran again to seek him, her eyes gleaming with the anticipated delights of vengeance, while, ever and anon, all the scaith,[2] the ridicule, and the harm, redounded on herself.

Was it not strange that she could not get quit of this sole annoyance of her life? One would have thought she easily might. But by this time there was nothing farther

from her intention; she wanted vengeance, full, ade-quate, and delicious vengeance, on her audacious opponent. But he was a strange and terrible creature, and the means of retaliation came always, as it were, to his hand.

Bread and sweet milk was the only fare that Merodach cared for, and he having bargained for that, would not want it, though he often got it with a curse and with ill will. The lady having intentionally kept back his wonted allowance for some days, on the Sabbath morning following, she set him down a bowl of rich sweet milk, well drugged with a deadly poison, and then she lingered in a little anteroom to watch the success of her grand plot, and prevent any other creature from tasting of the potion. Merodach came in, and the house-maid says to him, "There is your breakfast, creature."

"Oho! my lady has been liberal this morning," said he; "but I am beforehand with her.—Here, little Missie, you seem very hungry to-day— take you my breakfast." And with that he set the beverage down to the lady's little favourite spaniel. It so happened that the lady's only son came at that instant into the anteroom, seeking her, and teazing his mamma about something which took her attention from the hall-table for a space. When she looked again, and saw Missie lapping up the sweet milk, she burst from her lobby like a dragon, screaming as if her head had been on fire, kicked the bowl and the remainder of its contents against the wall, and lifting Missie in her bosom, she retreated hastily, crying all the way.

"Ha, ha, ha—I have you now!" cried Merodach, as she vanished from the hall.

Poor Missie died immediately, and very privately; indeed, she would have died and been buried, and never one have seen her, save her mistress, had not Merodach, by a luck that never failed him, popped his nose over the flower garden wall, just as his lady was laying her favourite in a grave of her own digging. She, not per-ceiving her tormentor, plied on at her task, apostrophiz-ing the insensate little carcass, "Ah! poor dear little creature, thou hast had a hard fortune, and hast drank

[1] *rod of Moses* In Exodus, the rod of Moses is used to call down the ten plagues on Egypt. In the first plague, the rod, thrown in front of the pharaoh, becomes a serpent.

[2] *scaith* Hurt, harm, damage.

of the bitter potion that was not intended for thee; but he shall drink it three times double, for thy sake!"

"Is that little Missie?" said the eldrich[1] voice of the jotteryman, close at the lady's ear. She uttered a loud scream, and sunk down on the bank. "Alack for poor little Missie!" continued the creature in a tone of mockery, "My heart is sorry for Missie. What has befallen her—whose breakfast cup did she drink?"

"Hence with thee, thou fiend!" cried the lady; "what right hast thou to intrude on thy mistress's privacy? Thy turn is coming yet, or may the nature of woman change within me."

"It is changed already," said the creature, grinning with delight; "I have thee now, I have thee now! And were it not to shew my superiority over thee, which I do every hour, I should soon see thee strapped like a mad cat, or a worrying bratch.[2] What wilt thou try next?"

"I will cut thy throat, and if I die for it, will rejoice in the deed; a deed of charity to all that dwell on the face of the earth. Go about thy business."

"I have warned thee before, dame, and I now warn thee again, that all thy mischief meditated against me will fall double on thine own head."

"I want none of your warning, and none of your instructions, fiendish cur. Hence with your elvish face, and take care of yourself."

It would be too disgusting and horrible to relate or read all the incidents that fell out between this unaccountable couple. Their enmity against each other had no end, and no mitigation; and scarcely a single day passed over on which her acts of malevolent ingenuity did not terminate fatally for some favourite thing of the lady's, while all these doings never failed to appear as her own act. Scarcely was there a thing, animate or inanimate, on which she set a value, left to her, that was not destroyed; and yet scarcely one hour or minute could she remain absent from her tormentor, and all the while, it seems, solely for the purpose of tormenting him.

But while all the rest of the establishment enjoyed peace and quietness from the fury of their termagant[3] dame, matters still grew worse and worse between the fascinated pair. The lady haunted the menial, in the same manner as the raven haunts the eagle, for a perpetual quarrel, though the former knows that in every encounter she is to come off the loser. But now noises were heard on the stairs by night, and it was whispered among the menials, that the lady had been seeking Merodach's bed by night, on some horrible intent. Several of them would have sworn that they had seen her passing and repassing on the stair after midnight, when all was quiet; but then it was likewise well known, that Merodach slept with well fastened doors, and a companion in another bed in the same room, whose bed, too, was nearest the door. Nobody cared much what became of the jotteryman, for he was an unsocial and disagreeable person; but some one told him what they had seen, and hinted a suspicion of the lady's intent. But the creature only bit his upper lip, winked with his eyes, and said, "She had better let alone; she will be the first to rue that."

Not long after this, to the horror of the family and the whole country side, the laird's only son was found murdered in his bed one morning, under circumstances that manifested the most fiendish cruelty and inveteracy on the part of his destroyer. As soon as the atrocious act was divulged, the lady fell into convulsions, and lost her reason; and happy had it been for her had she never recovered either the use of reason, or her corporeal functions any more, for there was blood upon her hand, which she took no care to conceal, and there was too little doubt that it was the blood of her own innocent and beloved boy, the sole heir and hope of the family.

This blow deprived the laird of all power of action; but the lady had a brother, a man of the law, who came and instantly proceeded to an investigation of this unaccountable murder; but before the Sheriff arrived, the housekeeper took the lady's brother aside, and told him he had better not go on with the scrutiny, for she was sure the crime would be brought home to her

---

[1] *eldrich* Weird, ghostly, unnatural.

[2] *bratch* Kind of hound that hunts by scent; always feminine, and extended to any kind of hound; a bitch-hound.

[3] *termagant* Violent, overbearing, turbulent, brawling, quarrelsome woman; a virago, shrew, vixen.

unfortunate mistress; and after examining into several corroborative circumstances, and viewing the state of the raving maniac, with the blood on her hand and arm, he made the investigation a very short one, declaring the domestics all exculpated.

The laird attended his boy's funeral, and laid his head in the grave, but appeared exactly like a man walking in a trance, an automaton, without feelings or sensations, oftentimes gazing at the funeral procession, as on something he could not comprehend. And when the death-bell of the parish church fell a-tolling, as the corpse approached the kirk[1]-stile, he cast a dim eye up towards the belfry, and said hastily, "What, what's that? Och ay, we're just in time, just in time." And often was he hammering over the name of "Evil Mcrodach, King of Babylon," to himself. He seemed to have some far-fetched conception that his unaccountable jotteryman had a hand in the death of his only son, and other lesser calamities, although the evidence in favour of Merodach's innocence was as usual quite decisive.

This grievous mistake of Lady Wheelhope (for every landward laird's wife was then styled Lady) can only be accounted for, by supposing her in a state of derangement, or rather under some evil influence, over which she had no control; and to a person in such a state, the mistake was not so very unnatural. The mansion-house of Wheelhope was old and irregular. The stair had four acute turns, all the same, and four landing-places, all the same. In the uppermost chamber slept the two domestics,—Merodach in the bed farthest in, and in the chamber immediately below that, which was exactly similar, slept the young laird and his tutor, the former in the bed farthest in; and thus, in the turmoil of raging passions, her own hand made herself childless.

Merodach was expelled the family forthwith, but refused to accept of his wages, which the man of law pressed upon him, for fear of farther mischief; but he went away in apparent sullenness and discontent, no one knowing whither.

When his dismissal was announced to the lady, who was watched day and night in her chamber, the news

had such an effect on her, that her whole frame seemed electrified; the horrors of remorse vanished, and another passion, which I neither can comprehend nor define, took the sole possession of her distempered spirit. "He *must* not go! He *shall* not go!" she exclaimed. "No, no, no—he shall not—he shall not he shall not!" and then she instantly set herself about making ready to follow him, uttering all the while the most diabolical expressions, indicative of anticipated vengeance. "Oh, could I but snap his nerves one by one, and birl[2] among his vitals! Could I but slice his heart off piecemeal in small messes, and see his blood lopper and bubble, and spin away in purple slays; and then to see him grin, and grin, and grin, and grin! Oh—oh—oh How beautiful and grand a sight it would be to see him grin, and grin, and grin!" And in such a style would she run on for hours together.

She thought of nothing, she spake of nothing, but the discarded jotteryman, whom most people now began to regard as a creature that was not canny. They had seen him eat, and drink, and work like other people; still he had that about him that was not like other men. He was a boy in form, and an antediluvian in feature. Some thought he was a mule, between a Jew and an ape; some a wizard, some a kelpie,[3] or a fairy, but most of all, that he was really and truly a Brownie. What he was I do not know, and therefore will not pretend to say; but be that as it may, in spite of locks and keys, watching and waking, the Lady of Wheelhope soon made her escape and eloped after him. The attendants, indeed, would have made oath that she was carried away by some invisible hand, for that it was impossible she could have escaped on foot like other people; and this edition of the story took in the country; but sensible people viewed the matter in another light.

As for instance, when Wattie Blythe, the laird's old shepherd, came in from the hill one morning, his wife Bessie thus accosted him. "His presence be about us,

[1] *kirk* Church.

[2] *birl* To prick, pierce, or stab.

[3] *kelpie* The Lowland Scottish name of a fabled water-spirit or demon assuming various shapes, but usually appearing in that of a horse; it is reputed to haunt lakes and rivers, and to take delight in or even to bring about the drowning of travelers and others.

Wattie Blythe! have ye heard what has happened at the ha'? Things are aye turning waur and waur there, and it looks like as if Providence had gi'en up our laird's house to destruction. This grand estate maun now gang frae the Sprots, for it has finished them."

"Na, na, Bessie, it isna the estate that has finished the Sprots, but the Sprots that hae finished it, an' themsells into the boot. They hae been a wicked and degenerate race, an' aye the langer the waur, till they hae reached the utmost bounds o' earthly wickedness; an it's time the deil were looking after his am."

"Ah, Wattie Blythe, ye never said a truer say. An' that's just the very point where your story ends, and mine commences; for hasna the deil, or the fairies, or the brownies, ta'en away our lady bodily, an' the haul country is running and riding in search o' her; and there is twenty hunder merks offered to the first that can find her, an' bring her safe back. They hae ta'en her away, skin an' bane, body an' soul, an' a', Wattie!"

"Hech-wow! but that is awsome! And where is it thought they have ta'en her to, Bessie?"

"O, they hae some guess at that frae her am hints afore. It is thought they hae carried her after that Satan of a creature, wha wrought sae muckle wae about the house. It is for him they are a looking, for they ken weel, that where they get the tane they will get the tither."

"Whew! Is that the gate o't, Bessie? Why, then, the awfu' story is nouther mair nor less than this, that the leddy has made a lopment, as they ca't, and run away after a blackgaird jotteryman. Hech-wow! wae's me for human frailty! But that's just the gate! When aince the deil gets in the point o' his finger, he will soon have in his haul hand. Ay, he wants but a hair to make a tether of, ony day. I hae seen her a braw sonsy lass, but even then I feared she was devoted to destruction, for she aye mockit at religion, Bessie, an' that's no a good mark of a young body. An' she made a' its servants her enemies; an think you these good men's prayers were a' to blaw away i' the wind, and be nae mair regarded? Na, na, Bessie, my woman, take ye this mark baith o' our am bairns and ither folk's—If ever ye see a young body that disregards the Sabbath, and makes a mock at the ordinances o' religion, ye will never see that body come

to muckle good. A braw hand she has made o' her gibes an' jeers at religion, an' her mockeries o' the poor persecuted hill-folk!—sunk down by degrees into the very dregs o' sin and misery! run away after a scullion!"[1]

"Fy, fy, Wattie, how can ye say sae? It was wed kenn'd that she hatit him wi' a perfect an' mortal hatred, an' tried to make away wi' him mae ways."

"Aha, Bessie; but nipping an' scarting[2] are Scots folk's wooing; an' though it is but right that we suspend our judgments, there will naebody persuade me, if she be found alang wi' the creature, but that she has run away after him in the natural way, on her twa shanks, without help either frae fairy or brownie."

"I'll never believe sic a thing of any woman born, let be a lady wee[3] up in years."

"Od help ye, Bessie! ye dinna ken the stretch o' corrupt nature. The best o' us, when left to oursells, are nae better than strayed sheep, that will never find the way back to their am pastures; an' of a' things made o' mortal flesh, a wicked woman is the warst."

"Alack-a-day! we get the blame o' muckle that we little deserve. But, Wattie, keep ye a gayan sharp look-out about the cleuchs[4] and the caves o' our glen, or hope, as ye ca't; for the lady kens them a gayan weel; and gin the twenty hunder merks wad come our way, it might gang a waur gate. It wad tocher[5] a' our bonny lasses."

"Ay, weel I wat, Bessie, that's nae lee. And now, when ye bring me amind o't, the Lord forgie me gin I didna hear a creature up in the Brock-holes this morning, skirting as if something war cutting its throat. It gars a' the hairs stand on my head when I think it may hae been our leddy, an' the droich of a creature murdering her. I took it for a battle of wulcats, and wished they

---

[1]   *scullion*   Domestic servant of the lowest rank.

[2]   *nipping*   To pinch, bite, squeeze sharply; *scarting*   To scratch, scrape.

[3]   *wee*   Way.

[4]   *cleuchs*   Gorges or ravines with precipitous and usually rocky sides, generally that of a stream or torrent.

[5]   *tocher*   The marriage portion that a wife brings to her husband; dowry.

might pu' out ane anither's thrapples;[1] but when I think on it again, they war unco like some o our leddy's unearthly screams."

"His presence be about us, Wattie! Haste ye. Pit on your bonnet—take your staff in your hand, and gang an' see what it is."

"Shame fa' me, if I daur gang, Bessie."

"Hout, Wattie, trust in the Lord."

"Aweel, sae I do. But ane's no to throw himself ower a linn,[2] an trust that the Lord's to kep him in a blanket; nor hing himself up in a raip,[3] an' expect the Lord to come and cut him down. An' it's nae muckle safer for an auld stiff man to gang away out to a wild remote place, where there is ae body murdering another.—What is that I hear, Bessie? Haud the lang tongue o' you, and rin to the door, an' see what noise that is."

Bessie ran to the door, but soon returned an altered creature, with her mouth wide open, and her eyes set in her head.

"It is them, Wattie! it is them! His presence be about us! What will we do?"

"Them? whaten them?"

"Why, that blackguard creature, coming here, leading our leddy be the hair o' the head, an' yerking her wi' a stick. I am terrified out o' my wits. What will we do?"

"We'll see what they sad," said Wattie, manifestly in as great terror as his wife; and by a natural impulse, or as a last resource, he opened the Bible, not knowing what he did, and then hurried on his spectacles; but before he got two leaves turned over, the two entered, a frightful-looking couple indeed. Merodach, with his old withered face, and ferret eyes, leading the Lady of Wheelhope by the long hair, which was mixed with grey, and whose face was all bloated with wounds and bruises, and having stripes of blood on her garments.

"How's this!—How's this, sirs?" said Wattie Blythe.

"Close that book, and I will tell you, goodman," said Merodach.

"I can hear what you hae to say wi' the beuk open, sir," said Wattie, turning over the leaves, as if looking for some particular passage, but apparently not knowing what he was doing. "It is a shamefu' business this, but some will hae to answer for't. My leddy, I am unco grieved to see you in sic a plight. Ye hae surely been dooms sair left to yourself."

The lady shook her head, uttered a feeble hollow laugh, and fixed her eyes on Merodach. But such a look! It almost frightened the simple aged couple out of their senses. It was not a look of love nor of hatred exclusively; neither was it of desire or disgust, but it was a combination of them all. It was such a look as one fiend would cast on another, in whose everlasting destruction he rejoiced. Wattie was glad to take his eyes from such countenances, and look into the Bible, that firm foundation of all his hopes and all his joy.

"I request that you will shut that book, sir," said the horrible creature; "or if you do not, I will shut it for you with a vengeance"; and with that he seized it, and flung it against the wall. Bessie uttered a scream, and Wattie was quite paralysed; and although he seemed disposed to run after his best friend, as he called it, the hellish looks of the Brownie interposed, and glued him to his seat.

"Hear what I have to say first," said the creature, "and then pore your fill on that precious book of yours. One concern at a time is enough. I came to do you a service. Here, take this cursed, wretched woman, whom you style your lady, and deliver her up to the lawful authorities, to be restored to her husband and her place in society. She is come upon one that hates her, and never said one kind word to her in his life, and though I have beat her like a dog, still she clings to me, and will not depart, so enchanted is she with the laudable purpose of cutting my throat. Tell your master and her brother, that I am not to be burdened with their maniac. I have scourged, I have spurned and kicked her, afflicting her night and day, and yet from my side she will not depart. Take her. Claim the reward in full, and your fortune is made, and so farewell."

The creature bowed and went away, but the moment his back was turned the lady fell a-screaming and

---

struggling like one in an agony, and, in spite of all the old couple's exertions, she forced herself out of their hands, and ran after the retreating Merodach. When he saw better would not be, he turned upon her, and, by one blow with his stick, struck her down; and, not content with that, he continued to kick and baste her in such a manner as to all appearance would have killed twenty ordinary persons. The poor devoted dame could do nothing, but now and then utter a squeak like a half-worried cat, and writhe and grovel on the sward, till Wattie and his wife came up and withheld her tormentor from further violence. He then bound her hands behind her back with a strong cord, and delivered her once more to the charge of the old couple, who contrived to hold her by that means and take her home.

Wattie had not the face to take her into the hall, but into one of the outhouses, where he brought her brother to receive her. The man of the law was manifestly vexed at her reappearance, and scrupled not to testify his dissatisfaction; for when Wattie told him how the wretch had abused his sister, and that, had it not been for Bessie's interference and his own, the lady would have been killed outright.

"Why, Walter, it is a great pity that he did not kill her outright," said he. "What good can her life now do to her, or of what value is her life to any creature living? After one has lived to disgrace all connected with them, the sooner they are taken off the better."

The man, however, paid old Walter down his two thousand merks, a great fortune for one like him in those days; and not to dwell longer on this unnatural story, I shall only add, very shortly, that the Lady of Wheelhope soon made her escape once more, and flew, as by an irresistible charm, to her tormentor. Her friends looked no more after her; and the last time she was seen alive, it was following the uncouth creature up the water of Daur, weary, wounded, and lame, while he was all the way beating her, as a piece of excellent amusement.

A few days after that, her body was found among some wild haggs, in a place called Crook-burn, by a party of the persecuted Covenanters that were in hiding there, some of the very men whom she had exerted herself to destroy, and who had been driven, like David of old, to pray for a curse and earthly punishment[1] upon her. They buried her like a dog at the Yetts of Keppel, and rolled three huge stones upon her grave, which are lying there to this day. When they found her corpse, it was mangled and wounded in a most shocking manner, the fiendish creature having manifestly tormented her to death. He was never more seen or heard of in this kingdom, though all that country-side was kept in terror for him many years afterwards; and to this day, they will tell you of THE BROWNIE OF THE BLACK HAGGS, which title he seems to have acquired after his disappearance.

This story was told to me by an old man, named Adam Halliday, whose great grandfather, Thomas Halliday, was one of those that found the body and buried it. It is many years since I heard it; but, however ridiculous it may appear, I remember it made a dreadful impression on my young mind. I never heard any story like it, save one of an old fox-hound that pursued a fox through the Grampians for a fortnight, and when at last discovered by the Duke of Athole's people, neither of them could run, but the hound was still continuing to walk after the fox, and when the latter lay down the other lay down beside him, and looked at him steadily all the while, though unable to do him the least harm. The passion of inveterate malice seems to have influenced these two exactly alike. But, upon the whole, I scarcely believe the tale can be true.

—1828

---

[1] *David of old ... earthly punishment* David issues the following curse: "May Yahweh repay the one who does evil according to his own evil."

WILLIAM WORDSWORTH
1770 – 1850

Since about 1815, William Wordsworth has been acknowledged as a central figure in the English Romantic Movement. *Lyrical Ballads*, produced in conjunction with Samuel Taylor Coleridge though largely Wordsworth's project, marks a decisive break with the formalism and neo-classicism of eighteenth-century literature. It became the touchstone of a new literary sensibility that gave its faith to the benevolence of feeling, and of the vehicle it associated most with feeling: a poetry of sincerity. And it established the idea of Nature as the measure by which to judge whether a poem's expression of feeling was genuine or not. Wordworth's poems respond powerfully to the major developments of his day—including the French Revolution, war, and industrialization. That response, however, was marked by many tensions and contradictions.

Wordsworth was born in the Lake District of England, in West Cumberland, and spent his boyhood absorbing the natural beauty around him. The death of his mother when he was eight, and of his father only five years later, unsettled the lives of William and his four siblings. Their situation was worsened by the fact that the only substantial legacy their father left was a sum owed to him by his employer, Lord Lonsdale, who withheld the money until his own death in 1802. Along with his three brothers, William was sent to school at Hawkshead. His sister, Dorothy—later his confidante and source of inspiration, in addition to being a fellow writer whose work would influence his—found herself shifting among various relatives.

At Hawkshead Wordsworth and his brothers boarded at the home of Ann Tyson, who became a surrogate mother to Wordsworth, encouraging his love of nature and tolerating his habit of roaming the countryside. Wordsworth paid close attention to and frequently conversed with the town's working people. His observations would inform the representation of many of the humble rural characters who appear in his poetry. Leaving the Lake District for the first time in 1787, he entered St. John's College, Cambridge. During this period he made two walking tours with his friend Robert Jones, first through France and the Alps during a crucial period of the French Revolution, and later through Wales (excursions described in Books Six and Fourteen respectively of the 1850 *Prelude*).

These adventures quickened Wordsworth's belief in the healing powers of nature and of his own responsive imagination, and they also awakened radical sentiments. While traveling in France in 1791–92 he was swept up in the heady excitement that followed the French Revolution (1789). Young Wordsworth also fell in love with Annette Vallon, whose politics (Royalist) and religion (Catholic) he did not share, and they produced a daughter, Caroline, out of wedlock. Too poor to remain in France, which was now at war with England, Wordsworth returned to his country a divided man, his disillusionment growing as France fell into the Reign of Terror.

Financial concerns fed Wordsworth's doubts about his political convictions and his choice of vocation. In 1795, however, Wordsworth received a legacy of £900 from a friend, Raisley Calvert, whom he had nursed through his final illness. When, in 1797, other friends offered a rent-free cottage in Alfoxden, this sum enabled Wordsworth and his sister Dorothy to set up housekeeping there, with his friend Coleridge not far away at Nether Stowey. (Describing his relationship with Coleridge in an 1832 letter to a friend, Wordsworth declared, "He and my beloved sister are the two beings to whom my intellect is most indebted.") Long walks and talks with Coleridge resulted in an extraordinary literary collaboration, *Lyrical Ballads, with a Few Other Poems* (1798), a slender, anonymously published volume that opens with Coleridge's literary ballad "The Rime of the Ancient Mariner" and closes with Wordsworth's blank-verse meditation "Lines, Composed a Few Miles above Tintern Abbey." The volume sought to combat what the authors saw as the increasingly marginal position of the poet in society, and the overly artificial language on which poetry relied.

As Coleridge and Wordsworth had expected, critics attacked the tone and subject matter of the volume. In the Preface to the Second Edition (1800)—perhaps the most famous poetic manifesto in the language—Wordsworth explained and defended the decision he made "to choose incidents and situations from common life, and to relate or describe them, throughout, as far as was possible, in a selection of language really used by men." In poems such as "Michael" and "The Brothers" (added to the 1800 edition of *Lyrical Ballads*), Wordsworth depicts the Lake District's inhabitants as strong and dignified in the face of hardship, living in harmony with the natural world, removed from the taint of urban superficiality. Wordsworth was thus in an important sense what he is often taken to be, a "poet of nature." But his main object was not to depict directly "the beautiful and permanent forms of nature" but rather to explore how "the passions of men are incorporated with" such forms, and to depict the "ennobling interchange" between the natural world and the mental world. It is the mind, ultimately, that was Wordsworth's "haunt, and the main region of my song."

After a brief, inhospitable stay in Germany in 1798–99, during which Wordsworth wrote the "Lucy" poems (the identity of "Lucy" is unknown) and Coleridge assimilated German philosophy, Wordsworth and his sister returned to England and took up residence at Dove Cottage in Grasmere. Here Dorothy kept journals that have since become famous in their own right, and Wordsworth composed some of his finest lyrics, including "Resolution and Independence," "The Solitary Reaper" (a memorial of his walking tour through Scotland), and "Ode: Intimations of Immortality from Recollections of Early Childhood," all of which were later published in his *Poems, in Two Volumes* (1807).

In 1802, Wordsworth married a childhood friend, Mary Hutchinson, and began a period of relative tranquility and poetic fruitfulness, although these years were not without grief and disappointment. By 1812, two of his five children were dead, his brother John had been lost at sea, his friendship with Coleridge (whose health was deteriorating as his opium addiction deepened) had become strained, and *Poems, in Two Volumes* had suffered damaging reviews.

Then in 1814 Wordsworth published *The Excursion*, a long blank-verse meditation that was a forecast and first installment of his planned epic, *The Recluse*. The book was poorly reviewed, even ridiculed. Nevertheless, Wordsworth by this time had gained a growing audience of devoted admirers, and his reputation from this low point began to establish itself firmly.

Like *The Excursion*, *The Prelude*, which Wordsworth had begun in 1799, was intended as a subsidiary piece that would be incorporated into *The Recluse*. He completed a two-book version of *The Prelude* in 1799 and a much expanded thirteen-book poem in 1805. He then continued to revise the poem for the rest of his life. This epic in blank verse—which Coleridge, upon hearing it, declared a "prophetic Lay"—describes the growth of the poet's mind from earliest memories to adulthood. By the end of his journey in the poem, Wordsworth reaffirms both providential design and the revolutionary potential of the imagination. *The Prelude* is a great, long lesson showing "how the mind of Man becomes / A thousand times more beautiful than the earth / On which he dwells."

In 1813, the Wordsworth household left Grasmere for the more expansive environs of Rydal Mount. There the poet, his beloved sister, and his wife lived out their days. The move was made possible by Wordsworth's improved financial situation, the result of a literary patronage granted by Lord Lonsdale and a position as Stamp Distributor for Westmorland. In the eyes of the younger generation (including Percy Shelley, Lord Byron, and Robert Browning), the patronage and the government position seemed to transform the once radical poet into a hypocritical and complacent hireling. As they saw it, Wordsworth had abandoned his early commitment to be the voice of the disenfranchised and the poor. Increasingly skeptical of external revolutions and political agitation, Wordsworth saw himself not as having abandoned his ideals but rather as having internalized—or spiritualized—his commitment to truth and liberty.

During his middle and old age Wordsworth wrote numerous sonnets, including *Ecclesiastical Sketches* (1822), which takes England's religious history as a primary subject. Having begun as a poetic and political revolutionary, he ended his life an iconic figure of the early Victorian era. Queen Victoria crowned him her Poet Laureate in 1843, and admirers flocked to the Lake District to seek him out in his home. The influence of his poetic style remained strong until well into the twentieth century, and Victorian writers of prose and poetry alike—including Tennyson, Charles Dickens, George Eliot, and Elizabeth Gaskell—acknowledged their debt to the life he had breathed into ways of thinking about nature, poetic feeling, and the human imagination.

⌘ ⌘ ⌘

from *Lyrical Ballads, 1798*

ADVERTISEMENT

It is the honourable characteristic of Poetry that its materials are to be found in every subject which can interest the human mind. The evidence of this fact is to be sought, not in the writings of Critics, but in those of Poets themselves.

The majority of the following poems are to be considered as experiments. They were written chiefly with a view to ascertain how far the language of conversation in the middle and lower classes of society is adapted to the purposes of poetic pleasure. Readers accustomed to the gaudiness and inane phraseology of many modern writers, if they persist in reading this book to its conclusion, will perhaps frequently have to struggle with feelings of strangeness and awkwardness: they will look round for poetry, and will be induced to enquire by what species of courtesy these attempts can be permitted to assume that title. It is desirable that

such readers, for their own sakes, should not suffer the solitary word Poetry, a word of very disputed meaning, to stand in the way of their gratification; but that, while they are perusing this book, they should ask themselves if it contains a natural delineation of human passions, human characters, and human incidents; and if the answer be favourable to the author's wishes, that they should consent to be pleased in spite of that most dreadful enemy to our pleasures, our own pre-established codes of decision.

Readers of superior judgment may disapprove of the style in which many of these pieces are executed. It must be expected that many lines and phrases will not exactly suit their taste. It will perhaps appear to them that, wishing to avoid the prevalent fault of the day, the author has sometimes descended too low, and that many of his expressions are too familiar, and not of sufficient dignity. It is apprehended that the more conversant the reader is with our elder writers, and with those in modern times who have been the most successful in painting manners and passions, the fewer complaints of this kind will he have to make.

An accurate taste in poetry, and in all the other arts, Sir Joshua Reynolds[1] has observed, is an acquired talent, which can only be produced by severe thought, and a long continued intercourse with the best models of composition. This is mentioned not with so ridiculous a purpose as to prevent the most inexperienced reader from judging for himself; but merely to temper the rashness of decision, and to suggest that if poetry be a subject on which much time has not been bestowed, the judgment may be erroneous, and that in many cases it necessarily will be so.

The tale of Goody Blake and Harry Gill is founded on a well-authenticated fact which happened in Warwickshire. Of the other poems in the collection, it may be proper to say that they are either absolute inventions of the author, or facts which took place within his personal observation or that of his friends. The poem of the Thorn, as the reader will soon discover, is not supposed to be spoken in the author's own person: the character of the loquacious narrator will sufficiently show itself in the course of the story. The Rime of the Ancyent Marinere was professedly written in imitation of the style, as well as of the spirit of the elder poets; but with a few exceptions, the Author believes that the language adopted in it has been equally intelligible for these three last centuries. The lines entitled Expostulation and Reply, and those which follow, arose out of conversation with a friend who was somewhat unreasonably attached to modern books of moral philosophy.

Goody Blake, and Harry Gill, a True Story

Oh! what's the matter? what's the matter?
  What is't that ails young Harry Gill?
That evermore his teeth they chatter,
Chatter, chatter, chatter still.
5 Of waistcoats° Harry has no lack,   *vest*
Good duffle[2] grey, and flannel fine;

He has a blanket on his back,
And coats enough to smother nine.

In March, December, and in July,
10 'Tis all the same with Harry Gill;
The neighbours tell, and tell you truly,
His teeth they chatter, chatter still.
At night, at morning, and at noon,
'Tis all the same with Harry Gill;
15 Beneath the sun, beneath the moon,
His teeth they chatter, chatter still.

Young Harry was a lusty° drover,[3]   *hearty, active*
And who so stout of limb as he?
His cheeks were red as ruddy clover,[4]
20 His voice was like the voice of three.
Auld Goody[5] Blake was old and poor,
Ill fed she was, and thinly clad;
And any man who passed her door,
Might see how poor a hut she had.

25 All day she spun in her poor dwelling,
And then her three hours' work at night!
Alas! 'twas hardly worth the telling,
It would not pay for candle-light.
—This woman dwelt in Dorsetshire,[6]
30 Her hut was on a cold hill-side,
And in that country coals are dear,
For they come far by wind and tide.

By the same fire to boil their pottage,[7]
Two poor old dames, as I have known,
35 Will often live in one small cottage,
But she, poor woman, dwelt alone.

[1] *Sir Joshua Reynolds* Renowned portrait and history painter, and first president of the Royal Academy (1723–92).

[2] *duffle* Rough wool cloth.

[3] *drover* Livestock driver.

[4] *ruddy clover* Red clover, a wild plant with a pinkish-red flower.

[5] *Goody* Short for "Goodwife," an honorific often used to address laboring-class women.

[6] *Dorsetshire* Predominantly agricultural county on the coast of southwest England.

[7] *pottage* Soup or stew made from whatever vegetables, grains, or meats were available at the time. Pottage was commonly consumed by poor families in Britain.

'Twas well enough when summer came,
The long, warm, lightsome summer-day,
Then at her door the *canty*[1] dame
Would sit, as any linnet[2] gay.

But when the ice our streams did fetter,
Oh! then how her old bones would shake!
You would have said, if you had met her,
'Twas a hard time for Goody Blake.
Her evenings then were dull and dead;
Sad case it was, as you may think,
For very cold to go to bed,
And then for cold not sleep a wink.

Oh joy for her! when e'er in winter
The winds at night had made a rout,
And scattered many a lusty splinter,
And many a rotten bough about.
Yet never had she, well or sick,
As every man who knew her says,
A pile before-hand, wood or stick,
Enough to warm her for three days.

Now, when the frost was past enduring,
And made her poor old bones to ache,
Could any thing be more alluring,
Than an old hedge to Goody Blake?
And now and then, it must be said,
When her old bones were cold and chill,
She left her fire, or left her bed,
To seek the hedge of Harry Gill.

Now Harry he had long suspected
This trespass of old Goody Blake,
And vowed that she should be detected,
And he on her would vengeance take.
And oft from his warm fire he'd go,
And to the fields his road would take,
And there, at night, in frost and snow,
He watched to seize old Goody Blake.

And once; behind a rick of barley,
Thus looking out did Harry stand;
75   The moon was full and shining clearly,
And crisp with frost the stubble-land.
—He hears a noise—he's all awake—
Again?—on tip-toe down the hill
He softly creeps—'Tis Goody Blake,
80   She's at the hedge of Harry Gill.

Right glad was he when he beheld her:
Stick after stick did Goody pull,
He stood behind a bush of elder,[3]
Till she had filled her apron full.
85   When with her load she turned about,
The bye-road back again to take,
He started forward with a shout,
And sprang upon poor Goody Blake.

And fiercely by the arm he took her,
90   And by the arm he held her fast,
And fiercely by the arm he shook her,
And cried, "I've caught you then at last!"
Then Goody, who had nothing said,
Her bundle from her lap let fall;
95   And kneeling on the sticks, she prayed
To God that is the judge of all.

She prayed, her withered hand uprearing,
While Harry held her by the arm—
"God! who art never out of hearing,
100   O may he never more be warm!"
The cold, cold moon above her head,
Thus on her knees did Goody pray,
Young Harry heard what she had said,
And icy-cold he turned away.

105   He went complaining all the morrow
That he was cold and very chill:
His face was gloom, his heart was sorrow,
Alas! that day for Harry Gill!
That day he wore a riding-coat,

---

[1]   *canty*   British dialect slang: lively, energetic.

[2]   *linnet*   Small songbird of the finch family.

[3]   *elder*   Common hedge tree. In English folklore, elder is thought to keep evil at bay.

110 But not a whit the warmer he:
Another was on Thursday brought,
And ere the Sabbath he had three.

'Twas all in vain, a useless matter,
And blankets were about him pinned;
115 Yet still his jaws and teeth they clatter,
Like a loose casement[1] in the wind.
And Harry's flesh it fell away;
And all who see him say 'tis plain,
That, live as long as live he may,
120 He never will be warm again.

No word to any man he utters,
A-bed or up, to young or old;
But ever to himself he mutters,
"Poor Harry Gill is very cold."
125 A-bed or up, by night or day;
His teeth they chatter, chatter still.
Now think, ye farmers all, I pray,
Of Goody Blake and Harry Gill.

Simon Lee, the Old Huntsman, with an Incident in Which He Was Concerned

In the sweet shire of Cardigan,[2]
Not far from pleasant Ivor-hall,[3]
An old man dwells, a little man,
I've heard he once was tall.
5 Of years he has upon his back,
No doubt, a burthen weighty;
He says he is three score and ten,[4]
But others say he's eighty.

A long blue livery-coat[5] has he,
10 That's fair behind, and fair before;
Yet, meet him where you will, you see
At once that he is poor.
Full five and twenty years he lived
A running huntsman merry;
15 And, though he has but one eye left,
His cheek is like a cherry.

No man like him the horn could sound,
And no man was so full of glee;
To say the least, four counties round
20 Had heard of Simon Lee;
His master's dead, and no one now
Dwells in the hall of Ivor;
Men, dogs, and horses, all are dead;
He is the sole survivor.

25 His hunting feats have him bereft
Of his right eye, as you may see:
And then, what limbs those feats have left
To poor old Simon Lee!
He has no son, he has no child,
30 His wife, an aged woman,
Lives with him, near the waterfall,
Upon the village common.[6]

And he is lean and he is sick,
His little body's half awry,
35 His ankles they are swol'n and thick;
His legs are thin and dry.
When he was young he little knew
Of husbandry° or tillage;[7]   *farming*
And now he's forced to work, though weak,
40 —The weakest in the village.

He all the country could outrun,
Could leave both man and horse behind;

---

1 *casement*   Window that hinges open.

2 *Cardigan*   County in midwest Wales.

3 *Ivor-hall*   Probably a reference to the ruined hall of fourteenth-century nobleman Ifor Hael (Ifor the Generous), who, according to tradition, was an important patron of Welsh literature.

4 *three score and ten*   I.e., seventy; one score is twenty.

5 *livery-coat*   Part of a uniform; the position of "huntsman" was that of a high-status servant.

6 *village common*   Expanse of open land, held in common by all members of a village.

7 *tillage*   Preparation of soil for agricultural use.

And often, ere the race was done,
He reeled and was stone-blind.
And still there's something in the world
At which his heart rejoices;
For when the chiming hounds are out,
He dearly loves their voices!

Old Ruth works out of doors with him,
And does what Simon cannot do;
For she, not over stout of limb,
Is stouter of the two.
And though you with your utmost skill
From labour could not wean them,
Alas! 'tis very little, all
Which they can do between them.

Beside their moss-grown hut of clay,
Not twenty paces from the door,
A scrap of land they have, but they
Are poorest of the poor.
This scrap of land he from the heath
Enclosed[1] when he was stronger;
But what avails the land to them,
Which they can till no longer?

Few months of life has he in store,
As he to you will tell,
For still, the more he works, the more
His poor old ankles swell.
My gentle reader, I perceive
How patiently you've waited,
And I'm afraid that you expect
Some tale will be related.

O reader! had you in your mind
Such stores as silent thought can bring,
O gentle reader! you would find
A tale in every thing.
What more I have to say is short,
I hope you'll kindly take it;
It is no tale; but should you think,
Perhaps a tale you'll make it.

One summer-day I chanced to see
This old man doing all he could
About the root of an old tree,
A stump of rotten wood.
The mattock[2] tottered in his hand;
So vain was his endeavour
That at the root of the old tree
He might have worked for ever.

"You're overtasked, good Simon Lee,
Give me your tool" to him I said;
And at the word right gladly he
Received my proffered aid.
I struck, and with a single blow
The tangled root I severed,
At which the poor old man so long
And vainly had endeavoured.

The tears into his eyes were brought,
And thanks and praises seemed to run
So fast out of his heart, I thought
They never would have done.
—I've heard of hearts unkind, kind deeds
With coldness still returning.
Alas! the gratitude of men
Has oftner left me mourning.

[1] *Enclosed* Enclosure denotes the fencing and deeding of land, thus making private what was once public or common. Between the mid-eighteenth and mid-nineteenth centuries a great deal of previously common land was enclosed—mostly to form farms unlike the small property that Simon Lee possesses. [...] allowed for more efficient farming practices, but it also drove rural farmers into even greater poverty.

[2] [...] an ax or adze, used for digging or chopping.

We Are Seven

A simple child, dear brother Jim,
   That lightly draws its breath,
And feels its life in every limb,
What should it know of death?

5 I met a little cottage girl,
   She was eight years old, she said;
Her hair was thick with many a curl
That cluster'd round her head.

She had a rustic, woodland air,
10   And she was wildly clad;
Her eyes were fair, and very fair
  —Her beauty made me glad.

"Sisters and brothers, little maid,
  How many may you be?"
15 "How many? seven in all," she said,
  And wondering looked at me.

"And where are they, I pray you tell?"
  She answered, "Seven are we,
And two of us at Conway[1] dwell,
20   And two are gone to sea.

"Two of us in the church yard lie,
  My sister and my brother,
And in the church-yard cottage, I
  Dwell near them with my mother."

25 "You say that two at Conway dwell,
  And two are gone to sea,
Yet you are seven; I pray you tell
  Sweet Maid, how this may be?"

Then did the little Maid reply,
30   "Seven boys and girls are we;
Two of us in the church-yard lie,
  Beneath the church-yard tree."

35 "You run about, my little maid,
  Your limbs they are alive;
If two are in the church-yard laid,
  Then ye are only five."

"Their graves are green, they may be seen,"
  The little Maid replied,
"Twelve steps or more from my mother's door,
40   And they are side by side.

"My stockings there I often knit,
  My 'kerchief there I hem;
And there upon the ground I sit—
  I sit and sing to them.

45 "And often after sunset, Sir,
  When it is light and fair,
I take my little porringer,[2]
  And eat my supper there.

"The first that died was little Jane;
50   In bed she moaning lay,
Till God released her of her pain,
  And then she went away.

"So in the church-yard she was laid,
  And all the summer dry,
55 Together round her grave we played,
  My brother John and I.

"And when the ground was white with snow,
  And I could run and slide,
My brother John was forced to go,
60   And he lies by her side."

"How many are you then," said I,
  "If they two are in Heaven?"
The little Maiden did reply,
  "O Master! we are seven."

[1] *Conway* Seaport of northern Wales.

[2] *porringer* Small metal or earthenware basin from which broth or porridge is eaten.

65 "But they are dead; those two are dead!
   Their spirits are in heaven!"
   'Twas throwing words away; for still
   The little Maid would have her will,
   And said, "Nay, we are seven!"

Lines Written in Early Spring

I heard a thousand blended notes,
   While in a grove I sat reclined,
In that sweet mood when pleasant thoughts
Bring sad thoughts to the mind.

5 To her fair works did nature link
   The human soul that through me ran;
   And much it griev'd my heart to think
   What man has made of man.

   Through primrose-tufts, in that sweet bower,
10 The periwinkle trail'd its wreathes;
   And 'tis my faith that every flower
   Enjoys the air it breathes.

   The birds around me hopp'd and play'd:
   Their thoughts I cannot measure,
15 But the least motion which they made,
   It seem'd a thrill of pleasure.

   The budding twigs spread out their fan,
   To catch the breezy air;
   And I must think, do all I can,
20 That there was pleasure there.

   If I these thoughts may not prevent,
   If such be of my creed the plan,
   Have I not reason to lament
   What man has made of man?

The Thorn[1]

1

There is a thorn;° it looks so old,   *thorn bush*
   In truth you'd find it hard to say,
How it could ever have been young,
   It looks so old and grey.
5 Not higher than a two-years' child,
   It stands erect this aged thorn;
No leaves it has, no thorny points;
   It is a mass of knotted joints,
   A wretched thing forlorn.
10 It stands erect, and like a stone
   With lichens it is overgrown.

2

Like rock or stone, it is o'ergrown
   With lichens to the very top,
And hung with heavy tufts of moss,
15 A melancholy crop:
Up from the earth these mosses creep,
And this poor thorn they clasp it round
So close, you'd say that they were bent
   With plain and manifest intent,
20 To drag it to the ground;
And all had joined in one endeavour
To bury this poor thorn for ever.

3

High on a mountain's highest ridge,
   Where oft the stormy winter gale
25 Cuts like a scythe, while through the clouds
   It sweeps from vale to vale;
Not five yards from the mountain-path,
   This thorn you on your left espy;
And to the left, three yards beyond,
30 You see a little muddy pond
   Of water, never dry;

---

[1] [Wordsworth's note]   Arose from my observing, on the ridge of
Quantock Hill, on a stormy day a thorn which I had often passed in
calm and bright weather without noticing it. I said to myself, "Cannot
I by some invention do as much to make this Thorn permanently an
impressive object as the storm has made it to my eyes at this moment?"

I've measured it from side to side:
'Tis three feet long, and two feet wide.

4

And close beside this aged thorn,
35 There is a fresh and lovely sight,
A beauteous heap, a hill of moss,
Just half a foot in height.
All lovely colours there you see,
All colours that were ever seen,
40 And mossy network too is there,
As if by hand of lady fair
The work had woven been,
And cups,° the darlings of the eye,   *blossoms*
So deep is their vermilion° dye.   *red*

5

45 Ah me! what lovely tints are there!
Of olive-green and scarlet bright,
In spikes, in branches, and in stars,
Green, red, and pearly white.
This heap of earth o'ergrown with moss,
50 Which close beside the thorn you see,
So fresh in all its beauteous dyes,
Is like an infant's grave in size
As like as like can be:
But never, never any where,
55 An infant's grave was half so fair.

6

Now would you see this aged thorn,
This pond and beauteous hill of moss,
You must take care and choose your time
The mountain when to cross.
60 For oft there sits, between the heap
That's like an infant's grave in size,
And that same pond of which I spoke,
A woman in a scarlet cloak,
And to herself she cries,
65 "Oh misery! oh misery!
Oh woe is me! oh misery!"

7

At all times of the day and night
This wretched woman thither goes,
And she is known to every star,
70 And every wind that blows;
And there beside the thorn she sits
When the blue day-light's in the skies,
And when the whirlwind's on the hill,
Or frosty air is keen and still,
75 And to herself she cries,
"Oh misery! oh misery!
Oh woe is me! oh misery!"

8

"Now wherefore thus, by day and night,
In rain, in tempest, and in snow,
80 Thus to the dreary mountain-top
Does this poor woman go?
And why sits she beside the thorn
When the blue day-light's in the sky,
Or when the whirlwind's on the hill,
85 Or frosty air is keen and still,
And wherefore does she cry?
Oh wherefore? wherefore? tell me why
Does she repeat that doleful cry?"

9

I cannot tell; I wish I could;
90 For the true reason no one knows,
But if you'd gladly view the spot,
The spot to which she goes;
The heap that's like an infant's grave,
The pond—and thorn, so old and grey;
95 Pass by her door—'tis seldom shut—
And if you see her in her hut,
Then to the spot away!
I never heard of such as dare
Approach the spot when she is there.

10

100 "But wherefore to the mountain-top
Can this unhappy woman go,
Whatever star is in the skies,

Whatever wind may blow?"
Nay rack your brain—'tis all in vain,
I'll tell you every thing I know;
But to the thorn, and to the pond
Which is a little step beyond,
I wish that you would go:
Perhaps when you are at the place
You something of her tale may trace.

11

I'll give you the best help I can:
Before you up the mountain go,
Up to the dreary mountain-top,
I'll tell you all I know.
'Tis now some two and twenty years,
Since she (her name is Martha Ray)
Gave with a maiden's true good will
Her company to Stephen Hill;
And she was blithe and gay,
And she was happy, happy still
Whene'er she thought of Stephen Hill.

12

And they had fix'd the wedding-day,
The morning that must wed them both;
But Stephen to another maid
Had sworn another oath;
And with this other maid to church
Unthinking Stephen went—
Poor Martha! on that woeful day
A cruel, cruel fire, they say,
Into her bones was sent:
It dried her body like a cinder,
And almost turn'd her brain to tinder.[1]

13

They say, full six months after this,
While yet the summer leaves were green,
She to the mountain-top would go,
And there was often seen.
'Tis said, a child was in her womb,
As now to any eye was plain;

___
[1] *tinder* Dry, flammable substance that will take fire from a spark.

She was with child, and she was mad,
Yet often she was sober sad
From her exceeding pain.
Oh me! ten thousand times I'd rather
That he had died, that cruel father!

14

Sad case for such a brain to hold
Communion with a stirring child!
Sad case, as you may think, for one
Who had a brain so wild!
Last Christmas when we talked of this,
Old Farmer Simpson did maintain,
That in her womb the infant wrought
About its mother's heart, and brought
Her senses back again:
And when at last her time drew near,
Her looks were calm, her senses clear.

15

No more I know, I wish I did,
And I would tell it all to you;
For what became of this poor child
There's none that ever knew:
And if a child was born or no,
There's no one that could ever tell;
And if 'twas born alive or dead,
There's no one knows, as I have said,
But some remember well,
That Martha Ray about this time
Would up the mountain often climb.

16

And all that winter, when at night
The wind blew from the mountain-peak,
'Twas worth your while, though in the dark,
The church-yard path to seek:
For many a time and oft were heard
Cries coming from the mountain-head,
Some plainly living voices were,
And others, I've heard many swear,
Were voices of the dead:

175 I cannot think, whate'er they say,
    They had to do with Martha Ray.

17

    But that she goes to this old thorn,
    The thorn which I've described to you,
    And there sits in a scarlet cloak,
180 I will be sworn is true.
    For one day with my telescope,
    To view the ocean wide and bright,
    When to this country first I came,
    Ere I had heard of Martha's name,
185 I climbed the mountain's height:
    A storm came on, and I could see
    No object higher than my knee.

18

    'Twas mist and rain, and storm and rain,
    No screen, no fence could I discover,
190 And then the wind! in faith, it was
    A wind full ten times over.
    I looked around, I thought I saw
    A jutting crag, and off I ran,
    Head-foremost, through the driving rain,
195 The shelter of the crag to gain,
    And, as I am a man,
    Instead of jutting crag, I found
    A woman seated on the ground.

19

    I did not speak—I saw her face,
200 Her face it was enough for me;
    I turned about and heard her cry,
    "O misery! O misery!"
    And there she sits, until the moon
    Through half the clear blue sky will go,
205 And when the little breezes make
    The waters of the pond to shake,
    As all the country know,
    She shudders and you hear her cry,
    "Oh misery! oh misery!"

20

210 "But what's the thorn? and what's the pond?
    And what's the hill of moss to her?
    And what's the creeping breeze that comes
    The little pond to stir?"
    I cannot tell; but some will say
215 She hanged her baby on the tree,
    Some say she drowned it in the pond,
    Which is a little step beyond,
    But all and each agree,
    The little babe was buried there,
220 Beneath that hill of moss so fair.

21

    I've heard the scarlet moss is red
    With drops of that poor infant's blood;
    But kill a new-born infant thus!
    I do not think she could.
225 Some say, if to the pond you go,
    And fix on it a steady view,
    The shadow of a babe you trace,
    A baby and a baby's face,
    And that it looks at you;
230 Whene'er you look on it, 'tis plain
    The baby looks at you again.

22

    And some had sworn an oath that she
    Should be to public justice brought;
    And for the little infant's bones
235 With spades they would have sought.
    But then the beauteous hill of moss
    Before their eyes began to stir;
    And for full fifty yards around,
    The grass it shook upon the ground;
240 But all do still aver
    The little babe is buried there,
    Beneath that hill of moss so fair.

23

    I cannot tell how this may be,
    But plain it is, the thorn is bound
245 With heavy tufts of moss, that strive

To drag it to the ground.
And this I know, full many a time,
When she was on the mountain high,
By day, and in the silent night,
When all the stars shone clear and bright,
That I have heard her cry,
"Oh misery! oh misery!
Oh woe is me! oh misery!"

The Idiot Boy[1]

'Tis eight o'clock,—a clear March night,
  The moon is up—the sky is blue,
The owlet in the moonlight air,
He shouts from nobody knows where;
He lengthens out his lonely shout,
Halloo! halloo! a long halloo!

—Why bustle thus about your door,
What means this bustle, Betty Foy?
Why are you in this mighty fret?
And why on horseback have you set
Him whom you love, your idiot boy?

Beneath the moon that shines so bright,
Till she is tired, let Betty Foy
With girt[2] and stirrup fiddle-faddle;
But wherefore set upon a saddle
Him whom she loves, her idiot boy?

There's scarce a soul that's out of bed;
Good Betty! put him down again;
His lips with joy they burr at you,
But, Betty! what has he to do
With stirrup, saddle, or with rein?

The world will say 'tis very idle,
Bethink you of the time of night;
There's not a mother, no not one,
But when she hears what you have done,
Oh! Betty she'll be in a fright.

But Betty's bent on her intent,
For her good neighbour, Susan Gale,
Old Susan, she who dwells alone,
Is sick, and makes a piteous moan,
As if her very life would fail.

There's not a house within a mile,
No hand to help them in distress:
Old Susan lies a bed in pain,
And sorely puzzled are the twain,°   two
For what she ails they cannot guess.

And Betty's husband's at the wood,
Where by the week he doth abide,
A woodman in the distant vale;
There's none to help poor Susan Gale,
What must be done? what will betide?

And Betty from the lane has fetched
Her pony, that is mild and good,
Whether he be in joy or pain,
Feeding at will along the lane,
Or bringing faggots[3] from the wood.

And he is all in travelling trim,
And by the moonlight, Betty Foy
Has up upon the saddle set,
The like was never heard of yet,
Him whom she loves, her idiot boy.

And he must post without delay
Across the bridge that's in the dale,
And by the church, and o'er the down,
To bring a doctor from the town,
Or she will die, old Susan Gale.

---

1 *Idiot Boy* I.e., boy with an intellectual disability; in the eighteenth century the term "idiot" did not always carry the offensive connotation it has in the twenty-first.

2 *girt* Strap that passes under a horse's ribcage to hold a saddle in place.

---

3 *faggots* Sticks bundled for use as firewood.

There is no need of boot or spur,
There is no need of whip or wand,
For Johnny has his holly-bough,
60 And with a hurly-burly° now   *noisy confusion*
He shakes the green bough in his hand.

And Betty o'er and o'er has told
The boy who is her best delight,
Both what to follow, what to shun,
65 What do, and what to leave undone,
How turn to left, and how to right.

And Betty's most especial charge,
Was, "Johnny! Johnny! mind that you
Come home again, nor stop at all,
70 Come home again, whate'er befall,
My Johnny do, I pray you do."

To this did Johnny answer make,
Both with his head, and with his hand,
And proudly shook the bridle too,
75 And then! his words were not a few,
Which Betty well could understand.

And now that Johnny is just going,
Though Betty's in a mighty flurry,
She gently pats the pony's side,
80 On which her idiot boy must ride,
And seems no longer in a hurry.

But when the pony moved his legs,
Oh! then for the poor idiot boy!
For joy he cannot hold the bridle,
85 For joy his head and heels are idle,
He's idle all for very joy.

And while the pony moves his legs,
In Johnny's left-hand you may see,
The green bough's motionless and dead;
90 The moon that shines above his head
Is not more still and mute than he.

His heart it was so full of glee,
That till full fifty yards were gone,
He quite forgot his holly whip,
And all his skill in horsemanship,
95 Oh! happy, happy, happy John.

And Betty's standing at the door,
And Betty's face with joy o'erflows,
Proud of herself, and proud of him,
100 She sees him in his travelling trim;
How quietly her Johnny goes.

The silence of her idiot boy,
What hopes it sends to Betty's heart!
He's at the guide-post—he turns right,
105 She watches till he's out of sight,
And Betty will not then depart.

Burr, burr—now Johnny's lips they burr,
As loud as any mill, or near it,
Meek as a lamb the pony moves,
110 And Johnny makes the noise he loves,
And Betty listens, glad to hear it.

Away she hies to Susan Gale:
And Johnny's in a merry tune,
The owlets hoot, the owlets curr,
115 And Johnny's lips they burr, burr, burr,
And on he goes beneath the moon.

His steed and he right well agree,
For of this pony there's a rumour,
That should he lose his eyes and ears,
120 And should he live a thousand years,
He never will be out of humour.

But then he is a horse that thinks!
And when he thinks his pace is slack;
Now, though he knows poor Johnny well,
125 Yet for his life he cannot tell
What he has got upon his back.

So through the moonlight lanes they go,
And far into the moonlight dale,
And by the church, and o'er the down,
30   To bring a doctor from the town,
To comfort poor old Susan Gale.

And Betty, now at Susan's side,
Is in the middle of her story,
What comfort Johnny soon will bring,
35   With many a most diverting thing,
Of Johnny's wit and Johnny's glory.

And Betty's still at Susan's side:
By this time she's not quite so flurried;
Demure with porringer° and plate   °dish
40   She sits, as if in Susan's fate
Her life and soul were buried.

But Betty, poor good woman! she,
You plainly in her face may read it,
Could lend out of that moment's store
45   Five years of happiness or more,
To any that might need it.

But yet I guess that now and then
With Betty all was not so well,
And to the road she turns her ears,
50   And thence full many a sound she hears,
Which she to Susan will not tell.

Poor Susan moans, poor Susan groans,
"As sure as there's a moon in heaven,"
Cries Betty, "he'll be back again;
55   They'll both be here, 'tis almost ten,
They'll both be here before eleven."

Poor Susan moans, poor Susan groans,
The clock gives warning for eleven;
'Tis on the stroke—"If Johnny's near,"
60   Quoth Betty "he will soon be here,
As sure as there's a moon in heaven."

The clock is on the stroke of twelve,
And Johnny is not yet in sight,
The moon's in heaven, as Betty sees,
165   But Betty is not quite at ease;
And Susan has a dreadful night.

And Betty, half an hour ago,
On Johnny vile reflections cast;
"A little idle sauntering thing!"
170   With other names, an endless string,
But now that time is gone and past.

And Betty's drooping at the heart,
That happy time all past and gone,
"How can it be he is so late?
175   The doctor he has made him wait,
Susan! they'll both be here anon."°   °soon

And Susan's growing worse and worse,
And Betty's in a sad quandary;
And then there's nobody to say
180   If she must go or she must stay:
—She's in a sad quandary.

The clock is on the stroke of one;
But neither Doctor nor his guide
Appear along the moonlight road,
185   There's neither horse nor man abroad,
And Betty's still at Susan's side.

And Susan she begins to fear
Of sad mischances not a few,
That Johnny may perhaps be drowned,
190   Or lost perhaps, and never found;
Which they must both for ever rue.

She prefaced half a hint of this
With, "God forbid it should be true!"
At the first word that Susan said
195   Cried Betty, rising from the bed,
"Susan, I'd gladly stay with you.

"I must be gone, I must away,
Consider, Johnny's but half-wise;
Susan, we must take care of him,
200   If he is hurt in life or limb"—
"Oh God forbid!" poor Susan cries.

"What can I do?" says Betty, going,
"What can I do to ease your pain?
Good Susan tell me, and I'll stay;
205   I fear you're in a dreadful way,
But I shall soon be back again."

"Good Betty go, good Betty go,
There's nothing that can ease my pain."
Then off she hies, but with a prayer
210   That God poor Susan's life would spare,
Till she comes back again.

So, through the moonlight lane she goes,
And far into the moonlight dale;
And how she ran, and how she walked,
215   And all that to herself she talked,
Would surely be a tedious tale.

In high and low, above, below,
In great and small, in round and square,
In tree and tower was Johnny seen,
220   In bush and brake, in black and green,
'Twas Johnny, Johnny, every where.

She's past the bridge that's in the dale,
And now the thought torments her sore,
Johnny perhaps his horse forsook,
225   To hunt the moon that's in the brook,
And never will be heard of more.

And now she's high upon the down,
Alone amid a prospect wide;
There's neither Johnny nor his horse,
230   Among the fern or in the gorse;°   *thorny shrub*
There's neither doctor nor his guide.

"Oh saints! what is become of him?
Perhaps he's climbed into an oak,
Where he will stay till he is dead;
235   Or sadly he has been misled,
And joined the wandering gypsy-folk.

"Or him that wicked pony's carried
To the dark cave, the goblin's hall,
Or in the castle he's pursuing,
240   Among the ghosts, his own undoing;
Or playing with the waterfall."

At poor old Susan then she railed,
While to the town she posts away;
"If Susan had not been so ill,
245   Alas! I should have had him still,
My Johnny, till my dying day."

Poor Betty! in this sad distemper,
The doctor's self would hardly spare,
Unworthy things she talked and wild,
250   Even he, of cattle° the most mild,   *livestock*
The pony had his share.

And now she's got into the town,
And to the doctor's door she hies;
'Tis silence all on every side;
255   The town so long, the town so wide,
Is silent as the skies.

And now she's at the doctor's door,
She lifts the knocker, rap, rap, rap,
The doctor at the casement° shews,   *window*
260   His glimmering eyes that peep and doze;
And one hand rubs his old night-cap.

"Oh Doctor! Doctor! where's my Johnny?"
"I'm here, what is't you want with me?"
"Oh Sir! you know I'm Betty Foy,
265   And I have lost my poor dear boy,
You know him—him you often see;

"He's not so wise as some folks be,"
"The devil take his wisdom!" said
The Doctor, looking somewhat grim,
"What, woman! should I know of him?"
And, grumbling, he went back to bed.

"O woe is me! O woe is me!
Here will I die; here will I die;
I thought to find my Johnny here,
But he is neither far nor near,
Oh! what a wretched mother I!"

She stops, she stands, she looks about,
Which way to turn she cannot tell.
Poor Betty! it would ease her pain
If she had heart to knock again;
—The clock strikes three—a dismal knell!

Then up along the town she hies,
No wonder if her senses fail,
This piteous news so much it shocked her,
She quite forgot to send the Doctor,
To comfort poor old Susan Gale.

And now she's high upon the down,
And she can see a mile of road,
"Oh cruel! I'm almost three-score;
Such night as this was ne'er before,
There's not a single soul abroad."

She listens, but she cannot hear
The foot of horse, the voice of man;
The streams with softest sound are flowing,
The grass you almost hear it growing,
You hear it now if e'er you can.

The owlets through the long blue night
Are shouting to each other still:
Fond lovers, yet not quite hob nob,°   *together, close*
They lengthen out the tremulous sob,
That echoes far from hill to hill.

Poor Betty now has lost all hope,
Her thoughts are bent on deadly sin;
A green-grown pond she just has passed,
305 And from the brink she hurries fast,
Lest she should drown herself therein.

And now she sits her down and weeps;
Such tears she never shed before;
"Oh dear, dear pony! my sweet joy!
310 Oh carry back my idiot boy!
And we will ne'er o'erload thee more."

A thought is come into her head;
"The pony he is mild and good,
And we have always used him well;
315 Perhaps he's gone along the dell,
And carried Johnny to the wood."

Then up she springs as if on wings;
She thinks no more of deadly sin;
If Betty fifty ponds should see,
320 The last of all her thoughts would be,
To drown herself therein.

Oh reader! now that I might tell
What Johnny and his horse are doing!
What they've been doing all this time,
325 Oh could I put it into rhyme,
A most delightful tale pursuing!

Perhaps, and no unlikely thought!
He with his pony now doth roam
The cliffs and peaks so high that are,
330 To lay his hands upon a star,
And in his pocket bring it home.

Perhaps he's turned himself about,
His face unto his horse's tail,
And still and mute, in wonder lost,
335 All like a silent horseman-ghost,
He travels on along the vale.

And now, perhaps, he's hunting sheep,
A fierce and dreadful hunter he!
Yon valley, that's so trim and green,
340   In five month's time, should he be seen,
A desert wilderness will be.

Perhaps, with head and heels on fire,
And like the very soul of evil,
He's galloping away, away,
345   And so he'll gallop on for aye,
The bane of all that dread the devil.

I to the muses have been bound,
These fourteen years, by strong indentures;
Oh gentle muses! let me tell
350   But half of what to him befell,
For sure he met with strange adventures.

Oh gentle muses! is this kind?
Why will ye thus my suit repel?
Why of your further aid bereave me?
355   And can ye thus unfriended leave me?
Ye muses! whom I love so well.

Who's yon, that, near the waterfall,
Which thunders down with headlong force,
Beneath the moon, yet shining fair,
360   As careless as if nothing were,
Sits upright on a feeding horse?

Unto his horse, that's feeding free,
He seems, I think, the rein to give;
Of moon or stars he takes no heed;
365   Of such we in romances read,
—'Tis Johnny! Johnny! as I live.

And that's the very pony too.
Where is she, where is Betty Foy?
She hardly can sustain her fears;
370   The roaring water-fall she hears,
And cannot find her idiot boy.

Your pony's worth his weight in gold,
Then calm your terrors, Betty Foy!
She's coming from among the trees,
375   And now, all full in view, she sees
Him whom she loves, her idiot boy.

And Betty sees the pony too:
Why stand you thus Good Betty Foy?
It is no goblin, 'tis no ghost,
380   'Tis he whom you so long have lost,
He whom you love, your idiot boy.

She looks again—her arms are up—
She screams—she cannot move for joy;
She darts as with a torrent's force,
385   She almost has o'erturned the horse,
And fast she holds her idiot boy.

And Johnny burrs and laughs aloud,
Whether in cunning or in joy,
I cannot tell; but while he laughs,
390   Betty a drunken pleasure quaffs,
To hear again her idiot boy.

And now she's at the pony's tail,
And now she's at the pony's head,
On that side now, and now on this,
395   And almost stifled with her bliss,
A few sad tears does Betty shed.

She kisses o'er and o'er again,
Him whom she loves, her idiot boy,
She's happy here, she's happy there,
400   She is uneasy every where;
Her limbs are all alive with joy.

She pats the pony, where or when
She knows not, happy Betty Foy!
The little pony glad may be,
405   But he is milder far than she,
You hardly can perceive his joy.

"Oh! Johnny, never mind the Doctor;
You've done your best, and that is all."
She took the reins, when this was said,
10 And gently turned the pony's head
From the loud water-fall.

By this the stars were almost gone,
The moon was setting on the hill,
So pale you scarcely looked at her:
15 The little birds began to stir,
Though yet their tongues were still.

The pony, Betty, and her boy,
Wind slowly through the woody dale:
And who is she, be-times° abroad,   *early*
20 That hobbles up the steep rough road?
Who is it, but old Susan Gale?

Long Susan lay deep lost in thought,
And many dreadful fears beset her,
Both for her messenger and nurse;
25 And as her mind grew worse and worse,
Her body it grew better.

She turned, she tossed herself in bed,
On all sides doubts and terrors met her;
Point after point did she discuss;
30 And while her mind was fighting thus,
Her body still grew better.

"Alas! what is become of them?
These fears can never be endured,
I'll to the wood."—The word scarce said,
35 Did Susan rise up from her bed,
As if by magic cured.

Away she posts up hill and down,
And to the wood at length is come,
She spies her friends, she shouts a greeting;
40 Oh me! it is a merry meeting,
As ever was in Christendom.

The owls have hardly sung their last,
While our four travellers homeward wend;
The owls have hooted all night long,
445 And with the owls began my song,
And with the owls must end.

For while they all were travelling home,
Cried Betty, "Tell us Johnny, do,
Where all this long night you have been,
450 What you have heard, what you have seen,
And Johnny, mind you tell us true."

Now Johnny all night long had heard
The owls in tuneful concert strive;
No doubt too he the moon had seen;
455 For in the moonlight he had been
From eight o'clock till five.

And thus to Betty's question, he
Made answer, like a traveller bold,
(His very words I give to you,)
460 "The cocks did crow to-whoo, to-whoo,
And the sun did shine so cold."
—Thus answered Johnny in his glory,
And that was all his travel's story.

Expostulation and Reply[1]

"Why William, on that old grey stone,
Thus for the length of half a day,
Why William, sit you thus alone,
And dream your time away?

5 "Where are your books? that light bequeath'd
To beings else forlorn and blind!
Up! Up! and drink the spirit breath'd
From dead men to their kind.

---

[1] *Expostulation ar* ... *tise-*
ment to *Lyrical Ba* ... *had*
with the writer an...

"You look round on your mother earth,
10 As if she for no purpose bore you;
As if you were her first-born birth,
And none had lived before you!"

One morning thus, by Esthwaite lake,[1]
When life was sweet I knew not why,
15 To me my good friend Matthew spake,
And thus I made reply.

"The eye it cannot choose but see,
We cannot bid the ear be still;
Our bodies feel, where'er they be,
20 Against, or with our will.

"Nor less I deem that there are powers,
Which of themselves our minds impress,
That we can feed this mind of ours,
In a wise passiveness.

25 "Think you, mid all this mighty sum
Of things for ever speaking,
That nothing of itself will come,
But we must still be seeking?

"—Then ask not wherefore, here, alone,
30 Conversing as I may,
I sit upon this old grey stone,
And dream my time away."

The Tables Turned
An Evening Scene on the Same Subject

Up! up! my friend, and clear your looks,
Why all this toil and trouble?

Up! up! my friend, and quit your books,
Or surely you'll grow double.[2]

5 The sun above the mountain's head,
A freshening lustre mellow,
Through all the long green fields has spread,
His first sweet evening yellow.

Books! 'tis a dull and endless strife,
10 Come, hear the woodland linnet,
How sweet his music; on my life
There's more of wisdom in it.

And hark! how blithe the throstle° sings!   thrush
And he is no mean preacher;
15 Come forth into the light of things,
Let Nature be your teacher.

She has a world of ready wealth,
Our minds and hearts to bless—
Spontaneous wisdom breathed by health,
20 Truth breathed by cheerfulness.

One impulse from a vernal wood
May teach you more of man;
Of moral evil and of good,
Than all the sages can.

25 Sweet is the lore which nature brings;
Our meddling intellect
Mishapes the beauteous forms of things
—We murder to dissect.

Enough of science and of art;
30 Close up these barren leaves;
Come forth, and bring with you a heart
That watches and receives.

---

1 *Esthwaite lake*   Located at Hawkshead (in England's Lake District), where Wordsworth attended grammar school. The real conversation that inspired the poem took place not at Hawkshead but at Alfoxden.

---

2 *double*   Doubled over.

Lines Written a Few Miles above Tintern Abbey

On Revisiting the Banks of the Wye during a Tour, July 13, 1798[1]

Five years have passed; five summers, with the length
Of five long winters! and again I hear
These waters, rolling from their mountain-springs
With a sweet inland murmur.[2] Once again
5   Do I behold these steep and lofty cliffs,
Which on a wild secluded scene impress
Thoughts of more deep seclusion; and connect
The landscape with the quiet of the sky.
The day is come when I again repose
10 Here, under this dark sycamore, and view
These plots of cottage-ground, these orchard-tufts,
Which, at this season, with their unripe fruits,
Among the woods and copses lose themselves,
Nor, with their green and simple hue, disturb
15 The wild green landscape. Once again I see
These hedge-rows, hardly hedge-rows, little lines
Of sportive wood run wild; these pastoral farms
Green to the very door; and wreaths of smoke
Sent up, in silence, from among the trees,
20 With some uncertain notice, as might seem,
Of vagrant dwellers in the houseless woods,
Or of some hermit's cave, where by his fire
The hermit sits alone.
                          Though absent long,
These forms of beauty have not been to me
25 As is a landscape to a blind man's eye:
But oft, in lonely rooms, and 'mid the din
Of towns and cities, I have owed to them,
In hours of weariness, sensations sweet,

Felt in the blood, and felt along the heart,
30 And passing even into my purer mind
With tranquil restoration—feelings too
Of unremembered pleasure; such, perhaps,
As may have had no trivial influence
On that best portion of a good man's life;
35 His little, nameless, unremembered acts
Of kindness and of love. Nor less, I trust,
To them I may have owed another gift,
Of aspect more sublime; that blessed mood,
In which the burthen of the mystery,
40 In which the heavy and the weary weight
Of all this unintelligible world
Is lightened—that serene and blessed mood,
In which the affections gently lead us on,
Until, the breath of this corporeal frame,[3]
45 And even the motion of our human blood
Almost suspended, we are laid asleep
In body, and become a living soul:
While with an eye made quiet by the power
Of harmony, and the deep power of joy,
50 We see into the life of things.
                          If this
Be but a vain belief, yet, oh! how oft,
In darkness, and amid the many shapes
Of joyless daylight; when the fretful stir
Unprofitable, and the fever of the world,
55 Have hung upon the beatings of my heart,
How oft, in spirit, have I turned to thee
O sylvan Wye! Thou wanderer through the woods, }
How often has my spirit turned to thee!

And now, with gleams of half-extinguished thought,
60 With many recognitions dim and faint,
And somewhat of a sad perplexity,
The picture of the mind revives again:
While here I stand, not only with the sense
Of present pleasure, but with pleasing thoughts
65 That in this moment there is life and food
For future years. And so I dare to hope
Though changed, no doubt, from what I was, when first

---

[1] *Lines … 1798*   In a later commentary on this poem, Wordsworth writes that "No poem of mine was composed under circumstances more pleasant for me to remember than this. I began it upon leaving Tintern, after crossing the Wye, and concluded it just as I was entering Bristol in the evening, after a ramble of 4 or 5 days, with my sister. Not a line of it was altered, and not any part of it was written down till I reached Bristol."

[2] [Wordsworth's note]   The river is not affected by the tides a few miles above Tintern.

[3] *corporeal frame*   Physical body.

I came among these hills; when like a roe°   *deer*
I bounded o'er the mountains, by the sides
70   Of the deep rivers, and the lonely streams,
Wherever nature led; more like a man
Flying from something that he dreads, than one
Who sought the thing he loved. For nature then
(The coarser pleasures of my boyish days,
75   And their glad animal movements all gone by)
To me was all in all.—I cannot paint
What then I was. The sounding cataract
Haunted me like a passion: the tall rock,
The mountain, and the deep and gloomy wood,
80   Their colours and their forms, were then to me
An appetite: a feeling and a love,
That had no need of a remoter charm,
By thought supplied, or any interest
Unborrowed from the eye. That time is past,
85   And all its aching joys are now no more,
And all its dizzy raptures. Not for this
Faint[1] I, nor mourn nor murmur: other gifts
Have followed, for such loss, I would believe,
Abundant recompence. For I have learned
90   To look on nature, not as in the hour
Of thoughtless youth, but hearing oftentimes
The still, sad music of humanity,
Not harsh nor grating, though of ample power
To chasten and subdue. And I have felt
95   A presence that disturbs me with the joy
Of elevated thoughts; a sense sublime
Of something far more deeply interfused,
Whose dwelling is the light of setting suns,
And the round ocean, and the living air,
100 And the blue sky, and in the mind of man,
A motion and a spirit, that impels
All thinking things, all objects of all thought,
And rolls through all things. Therefore am I still
A lover of the meadows and the woods
105 And mountains; and of all that we behold
From this green earth; of all the mighty world
Of eye and ear, both what they half create,
And what perceive; well pleased to recognize

In nature and the language of the sense,[2]
110 The anchor of my purest thoughts, the nurse,
The guide, the guardian of my heart, and soul
Of all my moral being.
                              Nor, perchance,
If I were not thus taught, should I the more
Suffer my genial° spirits to decay: *creative*
115 For thou art with me, here, upon the banks
Of this fair river; thou, my dearest Friend,[3]
My dear, dear Friend, and in thy voice I catch
The language of my former heart, and read
My former pleasures in the shooting lights
120 Of thy wild eyes. Oh! yet a little while
May I behold in thee what I was once,
My dear, dear Sister! And this prayer I make,
Knowing that Nature never did betray
The heart that loved her; 'tis her privilege,
125 Through all the years of this our life, to lead
From joy to joy: for she can so inform
The mind that is within us, so impress
With quietness and beauty, and so feed
With lofty thoughts, that neither evil tongues,
130 Rash judgments, nor the sneers of selfish men,
Nor greetings where no kindness is, nor all
The dreary intercourse of daily life,
Shall e'er prevail against us, or disturb
Our cheerful faith that all which we behold
135 Is full of blessings. Therefore let the moon
Shine on thee in thy solitary walk;
And let the misty mountain winds be free
To blow against thee: and in after years,
When these wild ecstasies shall be matured
140 Into a sober pleasure, when thy mind
Shall be a mansion for all lovely forms,
Thy memory be as a dwelling-place
For all sweet sounds and harmonies; Oh! then,
If solitude, or fear, or pain, or grief,
145 Should be thy portion,[4] with what healing thoughts

---

1   *Faint*   Lose heart; grow weak.

2   *the language of the sense*   What the senses tell us.

3   *my dearest Friend*   I.e., Dorothy Wordsworth, Wordsworth's sister.

4   *portion*   Alloted fate.

Of tender joy wilt thou remember me,
And these my exhortations! Nor, perchance,
If I should be, where I no more can hear
Thy voice, nor catch from thy wild eyes these gleams
Of past existence, wilt thou then forget
That on the banks of this delightful stream
We stood together; and that I, so long
A worshipper of Nature, hither came,
Unwearied in that service: rather say
With warmer love, oh! with far deeper zeal
Of holier love. Nor wilt thou then forget,
That after many wanderings, many years
Of absence, these steep woods and lofty cliffs,
And this green pastoral landscape, were to me
More dear, both for themselves, and for thy sake.
—1798

from *Lyrical Ballads, 1800, 1802*

from PREFACE[1]

The first Volume of these Poems has already been submitted to general perusal. It was published as an experiment, which, I hoped, might be of some use to ascertain how far, by fitting to metrical arrangement a selection of the real language of men in a state of vivid sensation, that sort of pleasure and that quantity of pleasure may be imparted, which a Poet may rationally endeavour to impart.

I had formed no very inaccurate estimate of the probable effect of those Poems: I flattered myself that they who should be pleased with them would read them with more than common pleasure: and, on the other hand, I was well aware that by those who should dislike them they would be read with more than common dislike. The result has differed from my expectation in this only, that I have pleased a greater number than I ventured to hope I should please.

For the sake of variety, and from a consciousness of my own weakness, I was induced to request the assistance of a Friend,[2] who furnished me with the Poems of the *Ancient Mariner*, the *Foster-Mother's Tale*, the *Nightingale*, and the Poem entitled *Love*. I should not, however, have requested this assistance, had I not believed that the Poems of my Friend would in a great measure have the same tendency as my own, and that, though there would be found a difference, there would be found no discordance in the colours of our style; as our opinions on the subject of poetry do almost entirely coincide.

Several of my Friends are anxious for the success of these Poems from a belief that, if the views with which they were composed were indeed realized, a class of Poetry would be produced, well adapted to interest mankind permanently, and not unimportant in the multiplicity, and in the quality of its moral relations: and on this account they have advised me to prefix a systematic defence of the theory upon which the poems were written. But I was unwilling to undertake the task, because I knew that on this occasion the Reader would look coldly upon my arguments, since I might be suspected of having been principally influenced by the selfish and foolish hope of *reasoning* him into an approbation of these particular Poems: and I was still more unwilling to undertake the task, because, adequately to display my opinions, and fully to enforce my arguments, would require a space wholly disproportionate to the nature of a preface. For to treat the subject with the clearness and coherence of which I believe it susceptible, it would be necessary to give a full account of the present state of the public taste in this country, and to determine how far this taste is healthy or depraved; which, again, could not be determined without pointing out in what manner language and the human mind act and re-act on each other, and without retracing the revolutions, not of literature alone, but likewise of society itself. I have therefore altogether declined to enter regularly upon this defence; yet I am sensible that there would be some impropriety in abruptly obtruding upon the Public, without a few words of introduction,

---

[1] *PREFACE* This preface first appeared in the 1800 edition of *Lyrical Ballads*, and was revised for the 1802 edition.

[2] *Friend* Samuel Taylor Coleridge (1772–1834). Coleridge gives his account of their plan in his *Biographia Literaria*, Chapter 14.

Low + rustic life primarily chosen

Poems so materially different from those upon which general approbation is at present bestowed.

It is supposed, that by the act of writing in verse an Author makes a formal engagement that he will gratify certain known habits of association; that he not only thus apprizes the Reader that certain classes of ideas and expressions will be found in his book, but that others will be carefully excluded. This exponent or symbol held forth by metrical language must in different areas of literature have excited very different expectations: for example, in the age of Catullus, Terence, and Lucretius and that of Statius or Claudian;[1] and in our own country, in the age of Shakespeare and Beaumont and Fletcher, and that of Donne and Cowley, or Dryden, or Pope.[2] I will not take upon me to determine the exact import of the promise which by the act of writing in verse an Author, in the present day, makes to his Reader; but, I am certain, it will appear to many persons that I have not fulfilled the terms of an engagement thus voluntarily contracted. They who have been accustomed to the gaudiness and inane phraseology of many modern writers, if they persist in reading this book to its conclusion, will, no doubt, frequently have to struggle with feelings of strangeness and awkwardness: they will look round for poetry, and will be induced to inquire by what species of courtesy these attempts can be permitted to assume that title. I hope therefore the Reader will not censure me if I attempt to state what I have proposed to myself to perform; and also (as far as the limits of a preface will permit) to explain some of the chief reasons which have determined me in the choice of my purpose: that at least he may be spared any unpleasant feeling of disappointment, and that I myself may be protected from the most dishonorable accusation which can be brought against an Author, namely, that of an indolence

which prevents him from endeavouring to ascertain what is his duty, or, when his duty is ascertained, prevents him from performing it.

The principal object, then, which I proposed to myself in these Poems was to choose incidents and situations from common life, and to relate or describe them, throughout, as far as was possible, in a selection of language really used by men; and, at the same time, to throw over them a certain colouring of imagination, whereby ordinary things should be presented to the mind in an unusual way; and, further, and above all, to make these incidents and situations interesting by tracing in them, truly though not ostentatiously, the primary laws of our nature: chiefly as far as regards the manner in which we associate ideas in a state of excitement. Low and rustic life was generally chosen because, in that condition, the essential passions of the heart find a better soil in which they can attain their maturity, are less under restraint, and speak a plainer and more emphatic language; because in that condition of life our elementary feelings co-exist in a state of greater simplicity, and, consequently, may be more accurately contemplated, and more forcibly communicated; because the manners of rural life germinate from those elementary feelings; and, from the necessary character of rural occupations, are more easily comprehended, and are more durable; and lastly, because in that condition the passions of men are incorporated with the beautiful and permanent forms of nature. The language, too, of these men is adopted (purified indeed from what appear to be its real defects, from all lasting and rational causes of dislike or disgust) because such men hourly communicate with the best objects from which the best part of language is originally derived; and because, from their rank in society and the sameness and narrow circle of their intercourse, being less under the influence of social vanity they convey their feelings and notions in simple and unelaborated expressions. Accordingly, such a language, arising out of repeated experience and regular feelings, is a more permanent, and a far more philosophical language, than that which is frequently substituted for it by Poets, who think that they are conferring honour upon themselves and their art, in proportion as

---

[1] *Catullus, Terence, and Lucretius*   Roman poets of the first and second centuries BCE; *Statius or Claudian*   Roman epic poets of the first and fourth centuries CE, respectively.

[2] *Shakespeare and Beaumont and Fletcher*   The age of Renaissance drama, during which Shakespeare, Francis Beaumont, and John Fletcher wrote; *Donne and Cowley*   John Donne and Abraham Cowley, poets of the seventeenth century; *Dryden*   John Dryden, Poet Laureate from 1668 to 1688; *Pope*   Alexander Pope, a major poet of the eighteenth century.

they separate themselves from the sympathies of men, and indulge in arbitrary and capricious habits of expression, in order to furnish food for fickle tastes, and fickle appetites, of their own creation.[1]

I cannot, however, be insensible of the present outcry against the triviality and meanness both of thought and language, which some of my contemporaries have occasionally introduced into their metrical compositions; and I acknowledge that this defect, where it exists, is more dishonorable to the Writer's own character than false refinement or arbitrary innovation, though I should contend at the same time that it is far less pernicious in the sum of its consequences. From such verses the Poems in these volumes will be found distinguished at least by one mark of difference, that each of them has a worthy *purpose*. Not that I mean to say that I always began to write with a distinct purpose formally conceived; but I believe that my habits of meditation have so formed my feelings, as that my descriptions of such objects as strongly excite those feelings will be found to carry along with them a *purpose*. If in this opinion I am mistaken, I can have little right to the name of a Poet. For all good poetry is the spontaneous overflow of powerful feelings: but though this be true, Poems to which any value can be attached, were never produced on any variety of subjects but by a man who, being possessed of more than usual organic sensibility, had also thought long and deeply. For our continued influxes of feeling are modified and directed by our thoughts, which are indeed the representatives of all our past feelings; and, as by contemplating the relation of these general representatives to each other we discover what is really important to men, so, by the repetition and continuance of this act, our feelings will be connected with important subjects, till at length, if we be originally possessed of much sensibility, such habits of mind will be produced, that, by obeying blindly and mechanically the impulses of those habits, we shall describe objects, and utter sentiments, of such a nature and in such connection with each other, that

the understanding of the being to whom we address ourselves, if he be in a healthful state of association, must necessarily be in some degree enlightened, and his affections ameliorated.

I have said that each of these poems has a purpose. I have also informed my Reader what this purpose will be found principally to be: namely to illustrate the manner in which our feelings and ideas are associated in a state of excitement. But, speaking in language somewhat more appropriate, it is to follow the fluxes and refluxes of the mind when agitated by the great and simple affections of our nature. This object I have endeavoured in these short essays to attain by various means; by tracing the maternal passion through many of its more subtle windings, as in the poems of the *Idiot Boy* and the *Mad Mother*; by accompanying the last struggles of a human being, at the approach of death, cleaving in solitude to life and society, as in the Poem of the *Forsaken Indian*; by showing, as in the Stanzas entitled *We Are Seven*, the perplexity and obscurity which in childhood attend our notion of death, or rather our utter inability to admit that notion; or by displaying the strength of fraternal, or to speak more philosophically, of moral attachment when early associated with the great and beautiful objects of nature, as in *The Brothers*; or, as in the *Incident of Simon Lee*, by placing my Reader in the way of receiving from ordinary moral sensations another and more salutary impression than we are accustomed to receive from them. It has also been part of my general purpose to attempt to sketch characters under the influence of less impassioned feelings, as in the *Two April Mornings*, *The Fountain*, *The Old Man Travelling*, *The Two Thieves*, &c., characters of which the elements are simple, belonging rather to nature than to manners, such as exist now, and will probably always exist, and which from their constitution may be distinctly and profitably contemplated. I will not abuse the indulgence of my Reader by dwelling longer upon this subject; but it is proper that I should mention one other circumstance which distinguishes these Poems from the popular Poetry of the day; it is this, that the feeling therein developed gives importance to the action and situation, and not the action and situation to the

---

[1] [Wordsworth's note] It is worth while here to observe that the affecting parts of Chaucer are almost always expressed in language pure and universally intelligible even to this day.

[handwritten annotation: City life → zombies seeking extravagant simulation from modern poetry]

feeling. My meaning will be rendered perfectly intelligible by referring my Reader to the Poems entitled *Poor Susan* and the *Childless Father*, particularly to the last Stanza of the latter Poem.

I will not suffer a sense of false modesty to prevent me from asserting that I point my Reader's attention to this mark of distinction, far less for the sake of these particular Poems than from the general importance of the subject. The subject is indeed important! For the human mind is capable of being excited without the application of gross and violent stimulants; and he must have a very faint perception of its beauty and dignity who does not know this, and who does not further know that one being is elevated above another, in proportion as he possesses this capability. It has therefore appeared to me that to endeavour to produce or enlarge this capability is one of the best services in which, at any period, a Writer can be engaged; but this service, excellent at all times, is especially so at the present day. For a multitude of causes, unknown to former times, are now acting with a combined force to blunt the discriminating powers of the mind, and unfitting it for all voluntary exertion to reduce it to a state of almost savage torpor. The most effective of these causes are the great national events which are daily taking place,[1] and the increasing accumulation of men in cities, where the uniformity of their occupations produces a craving for extraordinary incident, which the rapid communication of intelligence hourly gratifies. To this tendency of life and manners the literature and theatrical exhibitions of the country have conformed themselves. The invaluable works of our elder writers, I had almost said the works of Shakespeare and Milton, are driven into neglect by frantic novels, sickly and stupid German Tragedies, and deluges of idle and extravagant stories in verse.[2] When I think upon this degrading thirst after outrageous stimulation, I am almost ashamed to have spoken of the feeble effort with which I have endeavoured to counteract it; and, reflecting upon the magnitude of the general evil, I should be oppressed with no dishonorable melancholy, had I not a deep impression of certain inherent and indestructible qualities of the human mind, and likewise of certain powers in the great and permanent objects that act upon it which are equally inherent and indestructible; and did I not further add to this impression a belief that the time is approaching when the evil will be systematically opposed, by men of greater powers, and with far more distinguished success.

Having dwelt thus long on the subjects and aim of these Poems, I shall request the Reader's permission to apprize him of a few circumstances relating to their *style*, in order, among other reasons, that I may not be censured for not having performed what I never attempted. The Reader will find that personifications of abstract ideas rarely occur in these volumes; and, I hope, are utterly rejected as an ordinary device to elevate the style, and raise it above prose. I have proposed to myself to imitate, and, as far as is possible, to adopt, the very language of men; and assuredly such personifications do not make any natural or regular part of that language. They are, indeed, a figure of speech occasionally prompted by passion, and I have made use of them as such; but I have endeavoured utterly to reject them as a mechanical device of style, or as a family language which Writers in metre seem to lay claim to by prescription. I have wished to keep my Reader in the company of flesh and blood, persuaded that by so doing I shall interest him. I am, however, well aware that others who pursue a different track may interest him likewise; I do not interfere with their claim, I only wish to prefer a different claim of my own. There will also be found in these volumes little of what is usually called poetic diction; I have taken as much pains to avoid it as others ordinarily take to produce it; this I have done for the reason already alleged, to bring my language near to the language of men, and further, because the pleasure which I have proposed to myself to impart is of a kind very different from that which is supposed by many persons to be the proper object of poetry. I do not know how

---

[1] *great national ... place* I.e., the wars against France and the Irish Rebellion.

[2] *frantic novels ... verse* References to popular Gothic novels of the time, such as Matthew Gregory Lewis's *The Monk* (1796) and the novels of Ann Radcliffe, and to the German sentimental melodramas translated and staged during the 1780s.

without being culpably particular I can give my Reader a more exact notion of the style in which I wished these poems to be written than by informing him that I have at all times endeavoured to look steadily at my subject; consequently, I hope that there is in these Poems little falsehood of description, and that my ideas are expressed in language fitted to their respective importance. Something I must have gained by this practice, as it is friendly to one property of all good poetry, namely, good sense; but it has necessarily cut me off from a large portion of phrases and figures of speech which from father to son have long been regarded as the common inheritance of Poets. I have also thought it expedient to restrict myself still further, having abstained from the use of many expressions, in themselves proper and beautiful, but which have been foolishly repeated by bad Poets, till such feelings of disgust are connected with them as it is scarcely possible by any art of association to overpower.

If in a Poem there should be found a series of lines, or even a single line, in which the language, though naturally arranged and according to the strict laws of metre, does not differ from that of prose, there is a numerous class of critics, who, when they stumble upon these prosaisms, as they call them, imagine that they have made a notable discovery, and exult over the Poet as over a man ignorant of his own profession. Now these men would establish a canon of criticism which the Reader will conclude he must utterly reject, if he wishes to be pleased with these volumes. And it would be a most easy task to prove to him that not only the language of a large portion of every good poem, even of the most elevated character, must necessarily, except with reference to the metre, in no respect differ from that of good prose, but likewise that some of the most interesting parts of the best poems will be found to be strictly the language of prose, when prose is well written. The truth of this assertion might be demonstrated by innumerable passages from almost all the poetical writings, even of Milton himself. I have not space for much quotation; but, to illustrate the subject in a general manner, I will here adduce a short composition of

Gray,[1] who was at the head of those who by their reasonings have attempted to widen the space of separation betwixt Prose and Metrical composition, and was more than any other man curiously elaborate in the structure of his own poetic diction.

In vain to me the smiling mornings shine,
And reddening Phoebus[2] lifts his golden fire:
The birds in vain their amorous descant join,
Or cheerful fields resume their green attire:
These ears alas! for other notes repine;
A different object do these eyes require;
My lonely anguish melts no heart but mine;
And in my breast the imperfect joys expire;
Yet Morning smiles the busy race to cheer,
And new-born pleasure brings to happier men;
The fields to all their wonted tribute bear;
To warm their little loves the birds complain.
I fruitless mourn to him that cannot hear
And weep the more because I weep in vain.

It will easily be perceived that the only part of this Sonnet which is of any value is the lines printed in Italics: it is equally obvious that, except in the rhyme, and in the use of the single word "fruitless" for fruitlessly, which is so far a defect, the language of these lines does in no respect differ from that of prose.

By the foregoing quotation I have shown that the language of Prose may yet be well adapted to Poetry; and I have previously asserted that a large portion of the language of every good poem can in no respect differ from that of good Prose. I will go further. I do not doubt that it may be safely affirmed that there neither is, nor can be, any essential difference between the language of prose and metrical composition. …

I ask what is meant by the word Poet? What is a Poet? To whom does he address himself? And what language is to be expected from him? He is a man speaking to men: a man, it is true, endued with more lively sensibility, more enthusiasm and tenderness, who has a greater knowledge of human nature, and a more

---

[1] *Gray* Thomas Gray (1716–71). Wordsworth quotes his *Sonnet on the Death of Richard West.*

[2] *Phoebus* Apollo, god of the sun and of poetry.

comprehensive soul, than are supposed to be common among mankind; a man pleased with his own passions and volitions, and who rejoices more than other men in the spirit of life that is in him; delighting to contemplate similar volitions and passions as manifested in the goings-on of the Universe, and habitually impelled to create them where he does not find them. To these qualities he has added a disposition to be affected more than other men by absent things as if they were present; an ability of conjuring up in himself passions, which are indeed far from being the same as those produced by real events, yet (especially in those parts of the general sympathy which are pleasing and delightful) do more nearly resemble the passions produced by real events than any thing which, from the motions of their own minds merely, other men are accustomed to feel in themselves; whence, and from practice, he has acquired a greater readiness and power in expressing what he thinks and feels, and especially those thoughts and feelings which, by his own choice, or from the structure of his own mind, arise in him without immediate external excitement.

But, whatever portion of this faculty we may suppose even the greatest Poet to possess, there cannot be a doubt but that the language which it will suggest to him must, in liveliness and truth, fall far short of that which is uttered by men in real life, under the actual pressure of those passions, certain shadows of which the Poet thus produces, or feels to be produced, in himself. However exalted a notion we would wish to cherish of the character of a Poet, it is obvious that, while he describes and imitates passions, his situation is altogether slavish and mechanical, compared with the freedom and power of real and substantial action and suffering. So that it will be the wish of the Poet to bring his feelings near to those of the persons whose feelings he describes—nay, for short spaces of time, perhaps, to let himself slip into an entire delusion, and even confound and identify his own feelings with theirs; modifying only the language which is thus suggested to him, by a consideration that he describes for a particular purpose, that of giving pleasure. Here, then, he will apply the principle on which I have so much insisted, namely, that of selection; on this he will depend for removing what would otherwise be painful or disgusting in the passion; he will feel that there is no necessity to trick out or to elevate nature: and, the more industriously he applies this principle, the deeper will be his faith that no words which his fancy or imagination can suggest will be to be compared with those which are the emanations of reality and truth. ...

It is not, then, in the dramatic parts of composition that we look for this distinction of language; but still it may be proper and necessary where the Poet speaks to us in his own person and character. To this I answer by referring my Reader to the description which I have before given of a Poet. Among the qualities which I have enumerated as principally conducting to form a Poet, is implied nothing differing in kind from other men, but only in degree. The sum of what I have there said is that the Poet is chiefly distinguished from other men by a greater promptness to think and feel without immediate external excitement, and a greater power in expressing such thoughts and feelings as are produced in him in that manner. But these passions and thoughts and feelings are the general passions and thoughts and feelings of men. And with what are they connected? Undoubtedly with our moral sentiments and animal sensations, and with the causes which excite these; with the operations of the elements and the appearances of the visible universe; with storm and sunshine, with the revolutions of the seasons, with cold and heat, with loss of friends and kindred, with injuries and resentments, gratitude and hope, with fear and sorrow. These, and the like, are the sensations and objects which the Poet describes, as they are the sensations of other men, and the objects which interest them. The Poet thinks and feels in the spirit of the passions of men. How, then, can his language differ in any material degree from that of all other men who feel vividly and see clearly? It might be *proved* that it is impossible. But supposing that this were not the case, the Poet might then be allowed to use a peculiar language when expressing his feelings for his own gratification, or that of men like himself. But Poets do not write for Poets alone, but for men. Unless therefore we are advocates for that admiration which depends upon ignorance, and that pleasure which arises from hearing what we do not understand, the Poet must descend from this supposed height, and, in order to excite rational sympathy, he must express himself as other men express themselves. To this it may be added, that while he is only selecting from the real language of men, or, which amounts to the same thing, composing accurately in the spirit of such selection, he is treading upon safe ground, and we know what we are to expect from him. Our feelings are the same with respect to metre; for, as it may be proper to remind the Reader, the distinction of metre is regular and uniform, and not like that which is produced by what is usually called poetic diction, arbitrary, and subject to infinite caprices upon which no calculation whatever can be made. In the one case, the Reader is utterly at the mercy of the Poet respecting what imagery or diction he may choose to connect with the passion, whereas, in the other, the metre obeys certain laws, to which the Poet and Reader both willingly submit because they are certain, and because no interference is made by them with the passion but such as the concurring testimony of ages has shown to heighten and improve the pleasure which co-exists with it.

It will now be proper to answer an obvious question, namely, why, professing these opinions, have I written in verse? To this, in addition to such answer as is included in what I have already said, I reply in the first place, because, however I may have restricted myself, there is still left open to me what confessedly constitutes the most valuable object of all writing whether in prose or verse, the great and universal passions of men, the most general and interesting of their occupations, and the entire world of nature, from which I am at liberty to supply myself with endless combinations of forms and imagery. Now, supposing for a moment that whatever is interesting in these objects may be as vividly described in prose, why am I to be condemned, if to such description I have endeavoured to superadd the charm which, by the consent of all nations, is acknowledged to exist in metrical language? To this, by such as are unconvinced by what I have already said, it may be answered that a very small part of the pleasure given by Poetry depends upon the metre, and that it is injudicious to write in metre, unless it be accompanied with the other artificial distinctions of style with which metre is usually accompanied, and that by such deviation more will be lost from the shock which will be thereby given to the Reader's associations than will be counterbalanced by any pleasure which he can derive from the general power of numbers. In answer to those who still contend for the necessity of accompanying metre with certain appropriate colours of style in order to the accomplishment of its appropriate end, and who also, in my opinion, greatly under-rate the power of metre in itself, it might perhaps, as far as relates to these Poems, have been almost sufficient to observe that poems are extant, written upon more humble subjects, and in a more naked and simple style than I have aimed at, which poems have continued to give pleasure from generation to generation. Now, if nakedness and simplicity be a defect, the fact here mentioned affords a strong presumption that poems somewhat less naked and simple are capable of affording pleasure at the present day; and, what I wished *chiefly* to attempt, at present, was to justify myself for having written under the impression of this belief.

But I might point out various causes why, when the style is manly, and the subject of some importance, words metrically arranged will long continue to impart such a pleasure to mankind as he who is sensible of the extent of that pleasure will be desirous to impart. The end of Poetry is to produce excitement in co-existence with an overbalance of pleasure. Now, by the supposition, excitement is an unusual and irregular state of the mind; ideas and feelings do not in that state succeed each other in accustomed order. But, if the words by which this excitement is produced are in themselves powerful, or the images and feelings have an undue proportion of pain connected with them, there is some danger that the excitement may be carried beyond its proper bounds. Now the co-presence of something regular, something to which the mind has been accustomed in various moods and in a less excited state, cannot but have great efficacy in tempering and restraining the passion by an intertexture of ordinary feeling, and of feeling not strictly and necessarily connected with the passion. This is unquestionably true, and hence, though the opinion will at first appear paradoxical, from the tendency of metre to divest language in a certain degree of its reality, and thus to throw a sort of half consciousness of unsubstantial existence over the whole composition, there can be little doubt but that more pathetic situations and sentiments—that is, those which have a greater proportion of pain connected with them—may be endured in metrical composition, especially in rhyme, than in prose. The metre of the old Ballads is very artless; yet they contain many passages which would illustrate this opinion, and, I hope, if the following Poems be attentively perused, similar instances will be found in them. ...

I have said that Poetry is the spontaneous overflow of powerful feelings: it takes its origin from emotion recollected in tranquillity: the emotion is contemplated till by a species of reaction the tranquillity gradually disappears, and an emotion, kindred to that which was before the subject of contemplation, is gradually produced, and does itself actually exist in the mind. In this mood successful composition generally begins, and in a mood similar to this it is carried on; but the emotion, of whatever kind and in whatever degree, from various causes is qualified by various pleasures, so that in describing any passions whatsoever, which are voluntarily described, the mind will upon the whole be in a state of enjoyment. Now, if Nature be thus cautious in preserving in a state of enjoyment a being thus employed, the Poet ought to profit by the lesson thus held forth to him, and ought especially to take care that whatever passions he communicates to his Reader, those passions, if his Reader's mind be sound and vigorous, should always be accompanied with an overbalance of pleasure. Now the music of harmonious metrical language, the sense of difficulty overcome, and the blind association of pleasure which has been previously received from works of rhyme or metre of the same or similar construction, an indistinct perception perpetually renewed of language closely resembling that of real life, and yet, in the circumstance of metre, differing from it so widely, all these imperceptibly make up a complex feeling of delight, which is of the most impor-

tant use in tempering the painful feeling which will always be found intermingled with powerful descriptions of the deeper passions. This effect is always produced in pathetic and impassioned poetry; while, in lighter compositions, the ease and gracefulness with which the Poet manages his numbers[1] are themselves confessedly a principal source of the gratification of the Reader. I might perhaps include all which it is *necessary* to say upon this subject by affirming what few persons will deny, that, of two descriptions, either of passions, manners, or characters, each of them equally well executed, the one in prose and the other in verse, the verse will be read a hundred times where the prose is read once. We see that Pope, by the power of verse alone, has contrived to render the plainest common sense interesting, and even frequently to invest it with the appearance of passion. ...

I know that nothing would have so effectually contributed to further the end which I have in view as to have shown of what kind the pleasure is, and how that pleasure is produced, which is confessedly produced by metrical composition essentially different from that which I have here endeavoured to recommend: for the Reader will say that he has been pleased by such composition; and what can I do more for him? The power of any art is limited; and he will suspect that, if I propose to furnish him with new friends, it is only upon condition of his abandoning his old friends. Besides, as I have said, the Reader is himself conscious of the pleasure which he has received from such composition, composition to which he has peculiarly attached the endearing name of Poetry; and all men feel an habitual gratitude, and something of an honorable bigotry for the objects which have long continued to please them: we not only wish to be pleased, but to be pleased in that particular way in which we have been accustomed to be pleased. There is a host of arguments in these feelings; and I should be the less able to combat them successfully, as I am willing to allow that, in order entirely to enjoy the Poetry which I am recommending, it would be necessary to give up much of what is ordinarily enjoyed. But,

---

[1] *numbers* Meter.

would my limits have permitted me to point out how this pleasure is produced, I might have removed many obstacles, and assisted my Reader in perceiving that the powers of language are not so limited as he may suppose; and that it is possible that poetry may give other enjoyments, of a purer, more lasting, and more exquisite nature. This part of my subject I have not altogether neglected; but it has been less my present aim to prove that the interest excited by some other kinds of poetry is less vivid, and less worthy of the nobler powers of the mind, than to offer reasons for presuming that, if the object which I have proposed to myself were adequately attained, a species of poetry would be produced which is genuine poetry; in its nature well adapted to interest mankind permanently, and likewise important in the multiplicity and quality of its moral relations.

From what has been said, and from a perusal of the Poems, the Reader will be able clearly to perceive the object which I have proposed to myself: he will determine how far I have attained this object; and, what is a much more important question, whether it be worth attaining; and upon the decision of these two questions will rest my claim to the approbation of the public.

[*There was a Boy*]

There was a Boy, ye knew him well, ye Cliffs
And Islands of Winander![1] many a time,
At evening, when the stars began
To move along the edges of the hills,
5   Rising or setting, would he stand alone,
Beneath the trees, or by the glimmering lake,
And there, with fingers interwoven, both hands
Press'd closely palm to palm and to his mouth
Uplifted, he, as through an instrument,
10   Blew mimic hootings to the silent owls
That they might answer him. And they would shout
Across the wat'ry vale and shout again
Responsive to his call, with quivering peals,
And long halloos, and screams, and echoes loud

---

[1]   *Winander*   Windermere, the largest lake in England's Lake District.

15   Redoubled and redoubled, a wild scene
Of mirth and jocund din. And, when it chanced
That pauses of deep silence mock'd his
Then, sometimes, in that silence, while
Listening, a gentle shock of mild surpris
20   Has carried far into his heart the voice
Of mountain torrents, or the visible scene
Would enter unawares into his mind
With all its solemn imagery, its rocks,
Its woods, and that uncertain heaven, receiv'd
25   Into the bosom of the steady lake.

    Fair are the woods, and beauteous is the spot,
The vale where he was born: the Church-yard hangs
Upon a slope above the village school,[2]
And there along that bank when I have pass'd
30   At evening, I believe, that near his grave
A full half-hour together I have stood,
Mute—for he died when he was ten years old.

[*Strange fits of passion I have known*][3]

Strange fits of passion I have known,
    And I will dare to tell,
But in the Lover's ear alone,
    What once to me befell.

5   When she I lov'd, was strong and gay
    And like a rose in June,
I to her cottage bent my way,
    Beneath the evening moon.

Upon the moon I fix'd my eye,
10   All over the wide lea;°   *meadow*
My horse trudg'd on, and we drew nigh
    Those paths so dear to me.

---

[2]   *the village school*   Hawkshead Grammar School in Esthwaite.

[3]   *Strange ... known*   This and the following two lyrics are part of a group of five lyrics now commonly called the "Lucy poems," all of which were composed during the winter of 1798–99, when Wordsworth and his sister were in Germany. The identity of Lucy is unknown (if she existed at all); she is not the Lucy of Wordsworth's poem *Lucy Gray* (1800). Some critics believe that in these poems Wordsworth attempts to express his feelings for his sister.

And now we reach'd the orchard plot,
And, as we climb'd the hill,
15   Towards the roof of Lucy's cot°   cottage
The moon descended still.

In one of those sweet dreams I slept,
Kind Nature's gentlest boon!
And, all the while, my eyes I kept
20   On the descending moon.

My horse mov'd on; hoof after hoof
He rais'd and never stopp'd:
When down behind the cottage roof
At once the planet dropp'd.

25   What fond and wayward thoughts will slide
Into a Lover's head—
"O mercy!" to myself I cried,
"If Lucy should be dead!"[1]

Song [She dwelt among th'untrodden ways]

She dwelt among th'untrodden ways
Beside the springs of Dove,[2]
A Maid whom there were none to praise
    And very few to love.

5   A violet by a mossy stone
    Half-hidden from the Eye!
—Fair, as a star when only one
    Is shining in the sky.

She liv'd unknown, and few could know
10   When Lucy ceas'd to be;
But she is in her Grave, and Oh!
    The difference to me.

[A slumber did my spirit seal][3]

A slumber did my spirit seal,
    I had no human fears:
She seem'd a thing that could not feel
    The touch of earthly years.

5   No motion has she now, no force
    She neither hears nor sees
Roll'd round in earth's diurnal° course   daily
    With rocks and stones and trees!

Lucy Gray[4]

Oft I had heard of Lucy Gray,
    And when I cross'd the Wild,
I chanc'd to see at break of day
    The solitary child.

5   No Mate, no comrade Lucy knew;
    She dwelt on a wide Moor,
The sweetest Thing that ever grew
    Beside a human door!

You yet may spy the Fawn at play,
10   The Hare upon the Green;
But the sweet face of Lucy Gray
    Will never more be seen.

---

[3]   *A slumber ... seal*   Of this poem, Coleridge wrote to a friend in April 1799: "Some months ago Wordsworth transmitted to me a most sublime epitaph. ... Whether it had any reality, I cannot say. Most probably, in some gloomier moment he had fancied the moment in which his sister might die."

[4]   *Lucy Gray*   Based on an account of a drowned girl told to Wordsworth by his sister. In his note, Wordsworth says that after the girl had become lost in a snowstorm, "her footsteps were traced by her parents to the middle of the lock of a canal, and no other vestige of her, backward or forward, could be traced. The body, however, was found in the canal. The way in which the incident was treated and the spiritualizing of the character might furnish hints for consulting the imaginative influences which I have endeavoured to throw over common life with Crabbe's matter of fact style of treating subjects of the same kind." (Wordsworth refers to the poet George Crabbe [1754–1832].)

---

[1]   *If ... dead*   In an earlier manuscript version, another stanza followed: "I told her this: her laughter light / Is ringing in my ears; / And when I think upon that night / My eyes are dim with tears."

[2]   *Dove*   Name of numerous rivers in England, one of which is in the Lake District.

"To-night will be a stormy night,
You to the Town must go,
And take a lantern, Child, to light
Your Mother thro' the snow."

"That, Father! will I gladly do;
'Tis scarcely afternoon—
The Minster°-clock has just struck two,   church
And yonder is the Moon!"

At this the Father rais'd his hook,
And snapp'd a faggot-band;[1]
He plied his work, and Lucy took
The lantern in her hand.

Not blither° is the mountain roe,   more merry
With many a wanton° stroke   frolicsome
Her feet disperse the powd'ry snow,
That rises up like smoke.

The storm came on before its time,
She wander'd up and down,
And many a hill did Lucy climb:
But never reach'd the Town.

The wretched Parents all that night
Went shouting far and wide;
But there was neither sound nor sight
To serve them for a guide.

At day-break on a hill they stood
That overlook'd the Moor;
And thence they saw the Bridge of Wood,
A furlong[2] from their door.

And now they homeward turn'd, and cry'd
"In Heaven we all shall meet!"
When in the snow the Mother spied
The print of Lucy's feet.

45 Then downward from the steep hill's edge
They track'd the footmarks small;
And through the broken hawthorn-hedge,
And by the long stone-wall;

And then an open field they cross'd,
50 The marks were still the same;
They track'd them on, nor ever lost,
And to the Bridge they came.

They follow'd from the snowy bank
Those footmarks, one by one,
55 Into the middle of the plank,
And further there were none.

Yet some maintain that to this day
She is a living Child,
That you may see sweet Lucy Gray
60 Upon the lonesome Wild.

O'er rough and smooth she trips along,
And never looks behind;
And sings a solitary song
That whistles in the wind.

Nutting

It seems a day,
(I speak of one from many singled out)
One of those heavenly days which cannot die,
When forth I sallied from our cottage-door,
5 And with a wallet° o'er my shoulder slung,   knapsack
A nutting crook[3] in hand, I turn'd my steps
Towards the distant woods, a Figure quaint,
Trick'd out in proud disguise of Beggar's weeds°   garments
Put on for the occasion, by advice
10 And exhortation of my frugal Dame.[4]
Motley accoutrements! of power to smile

---

[1] *faggot-band*   Cord for binding a bundle of firewood.

[2] *furlong*   Measurement equal to 220 yards, or one-eighth of a mile.

[3] *nutting crook*   Hooked instrument for gathering nuts.

[4] *my frugal Dame*   Ann Tyson, at whose house Wordsworth boarded
during his school years.

At thorns, and brakes,° and brambles, and,   *thickets*
   in truth,
More ragged than need was. Among the woods,
And o'er the pathless rocks, I forc'd my way
15 Until, at length, I came to one dear nook
Unvisited, where not a broken bough
Droop'd with its wither'd leaves, ungracious sign
Of devastation, but the hazels rose
Tall and erect, with milk-white clusters hung,
20 A virgin scene!—A little while I stood,
Breathing with such suppression of the heart
As joy delights in; and with wise restraint
Voluptuous, fearless of a rival, eyed
The banquet, or beneath the trees I sat
25 Among the flowers, and with the flowers I play'd;
A temper known to those, who, after long
And weary expectation, have been bless'd
With sudden happiness beyond all hope.
—Perhaps it was a bower beneath whose leaves
30 The violets of five seasons re-appear
And fade, unseen by any human eye,
Where fairy water-breaks[1] do murmur on
For ever, and I saw the sparkling foam,
And with my cheek on one of those green stones
35 That, fleec'd with moss, beneath the shady trees,
Lay round me scatter'd like a flock of sheep,
I heard the murmur and the murmuring sound,
In that sweet mood when pleasure loves to pay
Tribute to ease, and, of its joy secure
40 The heart luxuriates with Indifferent things,
Wasting its kindliness on stocks° and stones,   *stumps*
And on the vacant air. Then up I rose,
And dragg'd to earth both branch and bough, with crash
And merciless ravage; and the shady nook
45 Of hazels, and the green and mossy bower
Deform'd and sullied, patiently gave up
Their quiet being: and unless I now
Confound my present feelings with the past,

Even then, when from the bower I turn'd away,
50 Exulting, rich beyond the wealth of kings
I felt a sense of pain when I beheld
The silent trees and the intruding sky.

Then, dearest Maiden![2] move along these shades
In gentleness of heart with gentle hand
55 Touch—for there is a Spirit in the woods.

Michael

Wordsworth said this pastoral poem is founded on two real incidents, one of "the son of an old couple having become dissolute, and run away from his parents" and the other of "an old shepherd having been seven years in building up a sheepfold in a solitary valley." In combining these tales, he said in a letter to Thomas Poole, "I have attempted to give a picture of a man of strong mind and lively sensibility, agitated by two of the most powerful affections of the human heart—parental affection and the love of property, landed property, including the feelings of inheritance, home, and personal and family independence." As in his poem "Brothers," Wordsworth writes "with a view to show that men who do not wear fine clothes can feel deeply" and attempts "to draw a picture of the domestic affections, as I know they exist among a class of men who are now almost confined to the north of England. They are small independent proprietors of land, here called 'states-men,' men of respectable education, who daily labor on their own little properties. The domestic affections will always be strong amongst men who live in a country not crowded with population, if these men are placed above poverty. … Their little tract of land serves as a kind of permanent rallying point for their domestic feelings, as a tablet on which they are written, which makes them objects of memory in a thousand instances, when they would otherwise be forgotten."

---

[1] *water-breaks* Places where the water flow is broken by underlying rocks.

[2] *Maiden* In a longer manuscript draft of the poem, a passage originally intended to lead up to "Nutting" describes a maiden named Lucy ravaging a bower.

Michael

A Pastoral Poem

I f from the public way you turn your steps
   Up the tumultuous brook of Green-head Gill,[1]
You will suppose that with an upright path
Your feet must struggle; in such bold ascent
5 The pastoral Mountains front you, face to face.
But, courage! for beside that boisterous Brook
The mountains have all open'd out themselves,
And made a hidden valley of their own.
No habitation can be seen; but such
10 As journey thither find themselves alone
With a few sheep, with rocks and stones, and kites[2]
That overhead are sailing in the sky.

It is in truth an utter solitude,
Nor should I have made mention of this Dell
15 But for one object which you might pass by,
Might see and notice not. Beside the brook
There is a straggling heap of unhewn stones!
And to that place a story appertains,
Which, though it be ungarnish'd with events,
20 Is not unfit, I deem, for the fire-side,
Or for the summer shade. It was the first,
The earliest of those tales that spake to me
Of Shepherds, dwellers in the valleys, men
Whom I already lov'd, not verily
25 For their own sakes, but for the fields and hills
Where was their occupation and abode.
And hence this Tale, while I was yet a boy
Careless of books, yet having felt the power
Of Nature, by the gentle agency
30 Of natural objects led me on to feel
For passions that were not my own, and think
At random and imperfectly indeed
On man; the heart of man and human life.
Therefore, although it be a history
35 Homely and rude, I will relate the same

---

[1] *Gill* Steep, narrow valley with a stream running through it. Green-head Gill is near Wordsworth's cottage at Grasmere.

[2] *kites* Small falcon-like birds of prey.

Why doesn'e share this story?

For the delight of a few natural hearts,
And with yet fonder feeling, for the sake
Of youthful Poets, who among these Hills
Will be my second self when I am gone.

40 Upon the Forest-side in Grasmere Vale
There dwelt a Shepherd, Michael was his name,
An old man, stout of heart, and strong of limb.
His bodily frame had been from youth to age
Of an unusual strength: his mind was keen
45 Intense and frugal, apt for all affairs,
And in his Shepherd's calling he was prompt
And watchful more than ordinary men.
Hence he had learn'd the meaning of all winds,
Of blasts of every tone, and often-times
50 When others heeded not, He heard the South[3]
Make subterraneous music, like the noise
Of Bagpipers on distant Highland hills;
The Shepherd, at such warning, of his flock
Bethought him, and he to himself would say
55 The winds are now devising work for me!
And truly at all times the storm, that drives
The Traveller to a shelter, summon'd him
Up to the mountains: he had been alone
Amid the heart of many thousand mists
60 That came to him and left him on the heights.
So liv'd he till his eightieth year was pass'd.

And grossly that man errs, who should suppose
That the green Valleys, and the Streams and Rocks
Were things indifferent to the Shepherd's thoughts.
65 Fields, where with cheerful spirits he had breath'd
The common air; the hills, which he so oft
Had climb'd with vigorous steps; which had impress'd
So many incidents upon his mind
Of hardship, skill or courage, joy or fear;
70 Which like a book preserv'd the memory
Of the dumb animals, whom he had sav'd,
Had fed or shelter'd, linking to such acts,
So grateful in themselves, the certainty
Of honorable gains; these fields, these hills

---

[3] *South* South wind.

Which were his living Being, even more
Than his own Blood—what could they less? had laid
Strong hold on his affections, were to him
A pleasurable feeling of blind love,
The pleasure which there is in life itself.

80   He had not passed his days in singleness.
He had a Wife, a comely Matron, old
Though younger than himself full twenty years.
She was a woman of a stirring life
Whose heart was in her house: two wheels she had
85   Of antique form, this large for spinning wool,
That small for flax, and if one wheel had rest,
It was because the other was at work.
The Pair had but one Inmate in their house,
An only Child, who had been born to them
90   When Michael telling° o'er his years began   *counting*
To deem that he was old, in Shepherd's phrase,
With one foot in the grave. This only son,
With two brave sheep dogs tried in many a storm,
The one of an inestimable worth,
95   Made all their Household. I may truly say,
That they were as a proverb in the vale
For endless industry. When day was gone,
And from their occupations out of doors
The Son and Father were come home, even then
100   Their labour did not cease, unless when all
Turn'd to their cleanly supper-board,[1] and there
Each with a mess of pottage[2] and skimm'd milk,
Sat round their basket pil'd with oaten cakes,
And their plain home-made cheese. Yet when their meal
105   Was ended, LUKE (for so the Son was nam'd)
And his old Father, both betook themselves
To such convenient work, as might employ
Their hands by the fire-side; perhaps to card[3]
Wool for the House-wife's spindle, or repair
110   Some injury done to sickle, flail,[4] or scythe,
Or other implement of house or field.

---

[1] *supper-board* Table.

[2] *pottage* Stew of vegetables, and sometimes meat, boiled in water.

[3] *card* Comb out impurities.

[4] *flail* Tool for threshing corn.

Down from the ceiling by the chimney's edge,
Which in our ancient uncouth country style
Did with a huge projection overbrow°   *overhang*
115   Large space beneath, as duly as the light
Of day grew dim, the House-wife hung a lamp;
An aged utensil, which had perform'd
Service beyond all others of its kind.
Early at evening did it burn and late,
120   Surviving Comrade of uncounted Hours
Which going by from year to year had found
And left the Couple neither gay perhaps
Nor cheerful, yet with objects and with hopes
Living a life of eager industry.
125   And now, when LUKE was in his eighteenth year,
There by the light of this old lamp they sat,
Father and Son, while late into the night
The House-wife plied her own peculiar work,
Making the cottage thro' the silent hours
130   Murmur as with the sound of summer flies.
Not with a waste of words, but for the sake
Of pleasure, which I know that I shall give
To many living now, I of this Lamp
Speak thus minutely: for there are no few
135   Whose memories will bear witness to my tale.
The Light was famous in its neighbourhood,
And was a public Symbol of the life,
The thrifty Pair had liv'd. For, as it chanc'd,
Their Cottage on a plot of rising ground
140   Stood single, with large prospect North and South,
High into Easedale, up to Dunmal-Raise,
And Westward to the village near the Lake.
And from this constant light so regular
And so far seen, the House itself by all
145   Who dwelt within the limits of the vale,
Both old and young, was nam'd The Evening Star.

Thus living on through such a length of years,
The Shepherd, if he lov'd himself, must needs
Have lov'd his Help-mate; but to Michael's heart
150   This Son of his old age was yet more dear—
Effect which might perhaps have been produc'd
By that instinctive tenderness, the same
Blind Spirit, which is in the blood of all,

Or that a child, more than all other gifts,
165 Brings hope with it, and forward-looking thoughts,
And stirrings of inquietude, when they
By tendency of nature needs must fail.
From such, and other causes, to the thoughts
Of the old Man his only Son was now
170 The dearest object that he knew on earth.
Exceeding was the love he bare to him,
His Heart and his Heart's joy! For oftentimes
Old Michael, while he was a babe in arms,
Had done him female service, not alone
175 For dalliance and delight, as is the use
Of Fathers, but with patient mind enforc'd
To acts of tenderness; and he had rock'd
His cradle with a woman's gentle hand.

And in a later time, ere yet the Boy
180 Had put on Boy's attire, did Michael love,
Albeit of a stern unbending mind,
To have the young one in his sight, when he
Had work by his own door, or when he sat
With sheep before him on his Shepherd's stool,
185 Beneath that large old Oak, which near their door
Stood, and from its enormous breadth of shade
Chosen for the Shearer's covert from the sun,
Thence in our rustic dialect was call'd
The CLIPPING° TREE, a name which yet it bears.   *shearing*
190 There, while they two were sitting in the shade,
With others round them, earnest all and blithe,
Would Michael exercise his heart with looks
Of fond correction and reproof bestow'd
Upon the child, if he disturb'd the sheep
195 By catching at their legs, or with his shouts
Scar'd them, while they lay still beneath the shears.
And when by Heaven's good grace the Boy grew up
A healthy Lad, and carried in his cheek
Two steady roses that were five years old,
200 Then Michael from a winter coppice[1] cut
With his own hand a sapling, which he hoop'd
With iron, making it throughout in all
Due requisites a perfect Shepherd's Staff,
And gave it to the Boy; wherewith equipp'd

---

[1] *coppice* Thicket of small trees.

195 He as a Watchman oftentimes was plac'd
At gate or gap, to stem or turn the flock,
And to his office prematurely call'd
There stood the urchin, as you will divine,
Something between a hindrance and a help,
200 And for this cause not always, I believe,
Receiving from his Father hire of praise.
Though nought was left undone which staff, or voice,
Or looks, or threatening gestures, could perform.
But soon as Luke, full ten years old, could stand
205 Against the mountain blasts, and to the heights,
Not fearing toil, nor length of weary ways,
He with his Father daily went, and they
Were as companions, why should I relate
That objects which the Shepherd loved before
210 Were dearer now? that from the Boy there came
Feelings and emanations, things which were
Light to the sun and music to the wind;
And that the Old Man's heart seemed born again?
Thus in his Father's sight the Boy grew up:
215 And now when he had reached his eighteenth year,
He was his comfort and his daily hope.

While this good household thus were living on
From day to day, to Michael's ear there came
Distressful tidings. Long before the time
220 Of which I speak, the Shepherd had been bound
In surety for his Brother's Son, a man
Of an industrious life, and ample means,
But unforeseen misfortunes suddenly
Had press'd upon him, and old Michael now
225 Was summon'd to discharge the forfeiture,
A grievous penalty, but little less
Than half his substance. This un-look'd for claim
At the first hearing, for a moment took
More hope out of his life than he supposed
230 That any old man ever could have lost.
As soon as he had gather'd so much strength
That he could look his trouble in the face,

It seem'd that his sole refuge was to sell
A portion of his patrimonial fields.
235 Such was his first resolve; he thought again,
And his heart fail'd him. "Isabel," said he,
Two evenings after he had heard the news,
"I have been toiling more than seventy years,
And in the open sunshine of God's love
240 Have we all liv'd, yet if these fields of ours
Should pass into a Stranger's hand, I think
That I could not lie quiet in my grave.
Our lot is a hard lot; the Sun itself
Has scarcely been more diligent than I,
245 And I have liv'd to be a fool at last
To my own family. An evil Man
That was, and made an evil choice, if he
Were false to us; and if he were not false,
There are ten thousand to whom loss like this
250 Had been no sorrow. I forgive him—but
'Twere better to be dumb than to talk thus.
When I began, my purpose was to speak
Of remedies and of a cheerful hope.
Our Luke shall leave us, Isabel; the land
255 Shall not go from us, and it shall be free,[1]
He shall possess it, free as is the wind
That passes over it. We have, thou knowest,
Another Kinsman, he will be our friend
In this distress. He is a prosperous man,
260 Thriving in trade, and Luke to him shall go,
And with his Kinsman's help and his own thrift,
He quickly will repair this loss, and then
May come again to us. If here he stay,
What can be done? Where every one is poor
265 What can be gain'd?" At this, the old man paus'd,
And Isabel sat silent, for her mind
Was busy, looking back into past times.
There's Richard Bateman, thought she to herself,[2]
He was a parish-boy[3]—at the church-door
270 They made a gathering for him, shillings, pence,

---

[1] *free*   I.e., not mortgaged.

[2] [Wordsworth's note]   The story alluded to here is well known in
the country. The chapel is called Ings Chapel and is on the road
leading from Kendal to Ambleside.

[3] *parish-boy*   Youth cared for and supported by the parish.

And halfpennies, wherewith the Neighbours bought
A Basket, which they fill'd with Pedlar's wares,
And with this Basket on his arm, the Lad
Went up to London, found a Master there,
275 Who out of many chose the trusty Boy
To go and overlook his merchandise
Beyond the seas, where he grew wond'rous rich,
And left estates and monies to the poor,
And at his birth-place built a Chapel, floor'd
280 With Marble, which he sent from foreign lands.
These thoughts, and many others of like sort,
Pass'd quickly thro' the mind of Isabel,
And her face brighten'd. The Old Man was glad,
And thus resum'd. "Well! Isabel, this scheme
285 These two days has been meat and drink to me.
Far more than we have lost is left us yet.
—We have enough—I wish indeed that I
Were younger, but this hope is a good hope.
—Make ready Luke's best garments, of the best
290 Buy for him more, and let us send him forth
To-morrow, or the next day, or to-night:
—If he could go, the Boy should go to-night."

Here Michael ceas'd, and to the fields went forth
With a light heart. The House-wife for five days
295 Was restless morn and night, and all day long
Wrought on with her best fingers to prepare
Things needful for the journey of her Son.
But Isabel was glad when Sunday came
To stop her in her work; for, when she lay
300 By Michael's side, she for the last two nights
Heard him, how he was troubled in his sleep:
And when they rose at morning she could see
That all his hopes were gone. That day at noon
She said to Luke, while they two by themselves
305 Were sitting at the door, "Thou must not go,
We have no other Child but thee to lose,
None to remember—do not go away,
For if thou leave thy Father he will die."
The Lad made answer with a jocund voice,
310 And Isabel, when she had told her fears,
Recover'd heart. That evening her best fare
Did she bring forth, and all together sat

Like happy people round a Christmas fire.
Next morning Isabel resum'd her work,
And all the ensuing week the house appear'd
As cheerful as a grove in Spring: at length
The expected letter from their Kinsman came,
With kind assurances that he would do
His utmost for the welfare of the Boy,
To which requests were added that forthwith
He might be sent to him. Ten times or more
The letter was read over; Isabel
Went forth to shew it to the neighbours round:
Nor was there at that time on English land
A prouder heart than Luke's. When Isabel
Had to her house return'd, the Old Man said,
"He shall depart to-morrow." To this word
The House-wife answered, talking much of things
Which, if at such short notice he should go,
Would surely be forgotten. But at length
She gave consent, and Michael was at ease.

Near the tumultuous brook of Green-head Gill,
In that deep Valley, Michael had design'd
To build a Sheep-fold,[1] and, before he heard
The tidings of his melancholy loss,
For this same purpose he had gathered up
A heap of stones, which close to the brook side
Lay thrown together, ready for the work.
With Luke that evening thitherward he walk'd;
And soon as they had reach'd the place he stopp'd,
And thus the Old Man spake to him. "My Son,
To-morrow thou wilt leave me; with full heart
I look upon thee, for thou art the same
That wert a promise to me ere thy birth,
And all thy life hast been my daily joy.
I will relate to thee some little part
Of our two histories; 'twill do thee good
When thou art from me, even if I should speak
Of things thou canst not know of.——After thou
First cam'st into the world, as it befalls
To new-born infants, thou didst sleep away
Two days, and blessings from thy Father's tongue

355 Then fell upon thee. Day by day pass'd on,
And still I lov'd thee with encreasing love.
Never to living ear came sweeter sounds
Than when I heard thee by our own fire-side
First uttering without words a natural tune,
When thou, a feeding babe, didst in thy joy
360 Sing at thy Mother's breast. Month follow'd month,
And in the open fields my life was pass'd
And in the mountains, else I think that thou
Hadst been brought up upon thy father's knees.
—But we were playmates, Luke; among these hills,
As well thou know'st, in us the old and young
365 Have play'd together, nor with me didst thou
Lack any pleasure which a boy can know."

Luke had a manly heart; but at these words
He sobb'd aloud; the Old Man grasp'd his hand,
And said, "Nay, do not take it so—I see
370 That these are things of which I need not speak.
—Even to the utmost I have been to thee
A kind and a good Father: and herein
I but repay a gift which I myself
Receiv'd at others hands, for, though now old
375 Beyond the common life of man, I still
Remember them who lov'd me in my youth.
Both of them sleep together: here they liv'd
As all their Forefathers had done, and when
At length their time was come, they were not loth
380 To give their bodies to the family mold.
I wish'd that thou should'st live the life they liv'd.
But 'tis a long time to look back, my Son,
And see so little gain from sixty years.
These fields were burthen'd° when they   mortgaged
    came to me;
385 'Till I was forty years of age, not more
Than half of my inheritance was mine.
I toil'd and toil'd; God bless'd me in my work,
And 'till these three weeks past the land was free.
—It looks as if it never could endure
390 Another Master. Heaven forgive me, Luke,
If I judge ill for thee, but it seems good
That thou should'st go." At this the Old Man paus'd,
Then, pointing to the Stones near which they stood,

---

[1] *Sheep-fold* Stone-walled pen for sheep.

Thus, after a short silence, he resum'd:
395 "This was a work for us, and now, my Son,
It is a work for me. But, lay one Stone—
Here, lay it for me, Luke, with thine own hands.
Nay, Boy, be of good hope: we both may live
To see a better day. At eighty-four
400 I still am strong and stout; do thou thy part,
I will do mine. I will begin again
With many tasks that were resign'd to thee;
Up to the heights, and in among the storms,
Will I without thee go again, and do
405 All works which I was wont to do alone,
Before I knew thy face. Heaven bless thee, Boy!
Thy heart these two weeks has been beating fast
With many hopes—it should be so—yes—yes—
I knew that thou could'st never have a wish
410 To leave me, Luke, thou hast been bound to me
Only by links of love, when thou art gone
What will be left to us! But, I forget
My purposes. Lay now the corner-stone,
As I requested, and hereafter, Luke,
415 When thou art gone away, should evil men
Be thy companions, let this Sheep-fold be
Thy anchor and thy shield; amid all fear
And all temptation, let it be to thee
An emblem of the life thy Fathers liv'd,
420 Who, being innocent, did for that cause
Bestir them in good deeds. Now, fare thee well—
When thou return'st, thou in this place wilt see
A work which is not here, a covenant
'Twill be between us——but whatever fate
425 Befall thee, I shall love thee to the last,
And bear thy memory with me to the grave."

The Shepherd ended here; and Luke stoop'd down,
And as his Father had requested, laid
The first stone of the Sheep-fold; at the sight
430 The Old Man's grief broke from him, to his heart
He press'd his Son, he kissed him and wept;
And to the House together they return'd.
Next morning, as had been resolv'd, the Boy
Began his journey, and when he had reach'd
435 The public Way, he put on a bold face;

And all the Neighbours as he pass'd their doors
Came forth, with wishes and with farewell pray'rs,
That follow'd him 'till he was out of sight.
A good report did from their Kinsman come,
440 Of Luke and his well-doing; and the Boy
Wrote loving letters, full of wond'rous news,
Which, as the House-wife phrased it, were throughout
The prettiest letters that were ever seen.
Both parents read them with rejoicing hearts.
445 So, many months pass'd on: and once again
The Shepherd went about his daily work
With confident and cheerful thoughts; and now
Sometimes when he could find a leisure hour
He to that valley took his way, and there
450 Wrought at the Sheep-fold. Meantime Luke began
To slacken in his duty, and at length
He in the dissolute city gave himself
To evil courses: ignominy and shame
Fell on him, so that he was driven at last
455 To seek a hiding-place beyond the seas.

There is a comfort in the strength of love;
'Twill make a thing endurable, which else
Would break the heart: Old Michael found it so.
I have convers'd with more than one who well
460 Remember the Old Man, and what he was
Years after he had heard this heavy news.
His bodily frame had been from youth to age
Of an unusual strength. Among the rocks
He went, and still look'd up upon the sun,
465 And listen'd to the winds; and as before
Perform'd all kinds of labour for his Sheep,
And for the land his small inheritance.
And to that hollow Dell from time to time
Did he repair, to build the Fold of which
470 His flock had need. 'Tis not forgotten yet
The pity which was then in every heart
For the Old Man—and 'tis believ'd by all
That many and many a day he thither went,
And never lifted up a single stone.

475 There, by the Sheep-fold, sometimes was he seen
Sitting alone, with that his faithful Dog,

Then old, beside him, lying at his feet.
The length of full seven years from time to time
He at the building of this Sheep-fold wrought,
30 And left the work unfinished when he died.

Three years, or little more, did Isabel,
Survive her Husband: at her death the estate
Was sold, and went into a Stranger's hand.
The Cottage which was nam'd The Evening Star
35 Is gone, the ploughshare has been through the ground
On which it stood; great changes have been wrought
In all the neighbourhood, yet the Oak is left
That grew beside their Door; and the remains
Of the unfinished Sheep-fold may be seen
40 Beside the boisterous brook of Green-head Gill.
—1800 (PREFACE REVISED 1802)

The Ruined Cottage[1]

FIRST PART

'Twas summer and the sun was mounted high.
Along the south the uplands feebly glared
Through a pale steam, and all the northern downs[2]
In clearer air ascending shewed far off
5 Their surfaces with shadows dappled o'er
Of deep embattled clouds: far as the sight

Could reach those many shadows lay in spots
Determined and unmoved, with steady beams
Of clear and pleasant sunshine interposed;
10 Pleasant to him who on the soft cool moss
Extends his careless limbs beside the root
Of some huge oak whose aged branches make
A twilight of their own, a dewy shade
Where the wren warbles while the dreaming man,
15 Half-conscious of that soothing melody,
With side-long eye looks out upon the scene,
By those impending branches made more soft,
More soft and distant. Other lot was mine.
Across a bare wide Common[3] I had toiled
20 With languid feet which by the slipp'ry ground
Were baffled still, and when I stretched myself
On the brown earth my limbs from very heat
Could find no rest nor my weak arm disperse
The insect host which gathered round my face
25 And joined their murmurs to the tedious noise
Of seeds of bursting gorse[4] that crackled round.
I rose and turned towards a group of trees
Which midway in that level stood alone,
And thither come at length, beneath a shade
30 Of clustering elms that sprang from the same root
I found a ruined house, four naked walls
That stared upon each other. I looked round
And near the door I saw an aged Man,
Alone, and stretched upon the cottage bench;
35 An iron-pointed staff lay at his side.
With instantaneous joy I recognized
That pride of nature and of lowly life,
The venerable Armytage, a friend
As dear to me as is the setting sun.
40   Two days before
We had been fellow-travellers. I knew
That he was in this neighbourhood and now
Delighted found him here in the cool shade.
He lay, his pack of rustic merchandize[5]

[1] *The Ruined Cottage* Wordsworth revised this poem several times before publishing it in 1814 as Book 1 of *The Excursion*. MS B is the earliest complete manuscript of the poem that we have; it was written over 1797–98 and first published in 1949 (in *The Poetical Works of William Wordsworth*, volume 5, edited by Ernest de Selincourt and Helen Derbishire). MS D, which is the version printed here, was completed between 1799 and 1800. The manuscript was copied out by Dorothy Wordsworth, with the occasional blank space penciled in by Wordsworth's hand (the text appearing here includes Wordsworth's additions). In MS D, Wordsworth removed material about the narrator's history and added a concluding passage (lines 492–537). While scholars continue to debate the various merits of the different versions of this poem, many have agreed with Jonathan Wordsworth's argument, in his book *The Music of Humanity* (1969), that MS D is the strongest text. The version Wordsworth published in *The Excursion* (1814) can be found on the website component of this anthology.

[2] *downs* Areas of open, elevated land.

[3] *Common* Area of public land.

[4] *gorse* Type of prickly shrub. Its seed pods burst with a popping sound, spraying seeds.

[5] *pack … merchandize* Armytage is a pedlar, a trader who travels door-to-door selling small goods.

45 Pillowing his head—I guess he had no thought
    Of his way-wandering life. His eyes were shut;
    The shadows of the breezy elms above
    Dappled his face. With thirsty heat oppress'd
    At length I hailed him, glad to see his hat
50 Bedewed with water-drops, as if the brim
    Had newly scoop'd a running stream. He rose
    And pointing to a sun-flower bade me climb
    The [   ]¹ wall where that same gaudy flower
    Looked out upon the road. It was a plot
55 Of garden-ground, now wild, its matted weeds
    Marked with the steps of those whom as they pass'd,
    The goose-berry trees that shot in long lank slips,
    Or currants hanging from their leafless stems
    In scanty strings, had tempted to o'erleap
60 The broken wall. Within that cheerless spot,
    Where two tall hedgerows of thick willow boughs
    Joined in a damp cold nook, I found a well
    Half-choked with willow flowers and weeds.
    I slaked my thirst and to the shady bench
65 Returned, and while I stood unbonneted
    To catch the motion of the cooler air
    The old Man said, "I see around me here
    Things which you cannot see: we die, my Friend,
    Nor we alone, but that which each man loved
70 And prized in his peculiar nook of earth
    Dies with him or is changed, and very soon
    Even of the good is no memorial left.
    The Poets in their elegies and songs
    Lamenting the departed call the groves,
75 They call upon the hills and streams to mourn,
    And senseless rocks, nor idly; for they speak
    In these their invocations with a voice
    Obedient to the strong creative power
    Of human passion. Sympathies there are
80 More tranquil, yet perhaps of kindred birth,
    That steal upon the meditative mind
    And grow with thought. Beside yon spring I stood
    And eyed its waters till we seemed to feel
    One sadness, they and I. For them a bond
85 Of brotherhood is broken: time has been

When every day the touch of human hand
Disturbed their stillness, and they ministered
To human comfort. When I stooped to drink,
A spider's web hung to the water's edge,
90 And on the wet and slimy foot-stone lay
The useless fragment of a wooden bowl;
It moved my very heart. The day has been
When I could never pass this road but she
Who lived within these walls, when I appeared,
95 A daughter's welcome gave me, and I loved her
As my own child. O Sir! the good die first,
And they whose hearts are dry as summer dust
Burn to the socket. Many a passenger°   *traveler*
Has blessed poor Margaret for her gentle looks
100 When she upheld the cool refreshment drawn
From that forsaken spring, and no one came
But he was welcome,² no one went away
But that it seemed she loved him. She is dead,
The worm is on her cheek, and this poor hut,
105 Stripp'd of its outward garb of household flowers,
Of rose and sweet-briar, offers to the wind
A cold bare wall whose earthy top is tricked°   *decorated*
With weeds and the rank³ spear-grass. She is dead,
And nettles rot and adders sun themselves
110 Where we have sate together while she nurs'd
Her infant at her breast. The unshod Colt,
The wandring heifer and the Potter's ass,
Find shelter now within the chimney-wall
Where I have seen her evening hearth-stone blaze
115 And through the window spread upon the road
Its cheerful light. —You will forgive me, Sir,
But often on this cottage do I muse
As on a picture, till my wiser mind
Sinks, yielding to the foolishness of grief.
120 She had a husband, an industrious man,
Sober and steady; I have heard her say
That he was up and busy at his loom
In summer ere the mower's scythe had swept
The dewy grass, and in the early spring
125 Ere the last star had vanished. They who pass'd

---

¹ *[ ]* Brackets such as these indicate blank spaces in the manuscript.

² *no one … welcome* I.e., everyone who came was welcome.

³ *rank* Thickly growing.

At evening, from behind the garden-fence
Might hear his busy spade, which he would ply
After his daily work till the day-light
Was gone and every leaf and flower were lost
30 In the dark hedges. So they pass'd their days
In peace and comfort, and two pretty babes
Were their best hope next to the God in Heaven.
—You may remember, now some ten years gone,
Two blighting seasons when the fields were left
35 With half a harvest.[1] It pleased heaven to add
A worse affliction in the plague of war:
A happy land was stricken to the heart;
'Twas a sad time of sorrow and distress:
A wanderer among the cottages,
40 I with my pack of winter raiment saw
The hardships of that season: many rich
Sunk down as in a dream among the poor,
And of the poor did many cease to be,
And their place knew them not. Meanwhile,
    abridg'd°   *deprived*
Of daily comforts, gladly reconciled
45 To numerous self-denials, Margaret
Went struggling on through those calamitous years
With chearful hope: but ere the second autumn
A fever seized her husband. In disease
He lingered long, and when his strength returned
50 He found the little he had stored to meet
The hour of accident or crippling age
Was all consumed. As I have said, 'twas now
A time of trouble; shoals of artisans
Were from their daily labour turned away
55 To hang° for bread on parish charity,   *beg*
They and their wives and children—happier far
Could they have lived as do the little birds
That peck along the hedges or the kite°   *bird of prey*
That makes her dwelling in the mountain rocks.
60 Ill fared it now with Robert, he who dwelt
In this poor cottage; at his door he stood
And whistled many a snatch of merry tunes
That had no mirth in them, or with his knife

Carved uncouth figures on the heads of sticks,
165 Then idly sought about through every nook
Of house or garden any casual task
Of use or ornament, and with a strange,
Amusing but uneasy novelty
He blended where he might the various tasks
170 Of summer, autumn, winter, and of spring.
But this endured not; his good-humour soon
Became a weight in which no pleasure was,
And poverty brought on a petted° mood   *sulky*
And a sore temper: day by day he drooped,
175 And he would leave his home, and to the town
Without an errand would he turn his steps
Or wander here and there among the fields.
One while he would speak lightly of his babes
And with a cruel tongue: at other times
180 He played with them wild freaks of merriment:
And 'twas a piteous thing to see the looks
Of the poor innocent children. 'Every smile,'
Said Margaret to me here beneath these trees,
'Made my heart bleed.'" At this the old Man paus'd
185 And looking up to those enormous elms
He said, "'Tis now the hour of deepest noon.
At this still season of repose and peace,
This hour when all things which are not at rest
Are chearful, while this multitude of flies
190 Fills all the air with happy melody,
Why should a tear be in an old man's eye?
Why should we thus with an untoward mind
And in the weakness of humanity
From natural wisdom turn our hearts away,
195 To natural comfort shut our eyes and ears,
And feeding on disquiet thus disturb
The calm of Nature with our restless thoughts?"

End of the First Part

SECOND PART

He spake with somewhat of a solemn tone:
But when he ended there was in his face
200 Such easy chearfulness, a look so mild
That for a little time it stole away
All recollection, and that simple tale

---

[1] *Two blighting … half a harvest* In 1794–95 a bad harvest was followed by an extremely harsh winter, which killed the seed and caused bread prices to double.

Passed from my mind like a forgotten sound.
A while on trivial things we held discourse,
205 To me soon tasteless. In my own despite[1]
I thought of that poor woman as of one
Whom I had known and loved. He had rehearsed
Her homely tale with such familiar power,
With such an active countenance, an eye
210 So busy, that the things of which he spake
Seemed present, and, attention now relaxed,
There was a heartfelt chillness in my veins.
I rose, and turning from that breezy shade
Went out into the open air and stood
215 To drink the comfort of the warmer sun.
Long time I had not stayed ere, looking round
Upon that tranquil ruin, I returned
And begged of the old man that for my sake
He would resume his story. He replied,
220 "It were a wantonness and would demand
Severe reproof, if we were men whose hearts
Could hold vain dalliance with the misery
Even of the dead, contented thence to draw
A momentary pleasure never marked
225 By reason, barren of all future good.
But we have known that there is often found
In mournful thoughts, and always might be found,
A power to virtue friendly; were't not so,
I am a dreamer among men, indeed
230 An idle dreamer. 'Tis a common tale,
By moving accidents uncharactered,[2]
A tale of silent suffering, hardly clothed
In bodily form, and to the grosser sense
But ill adapted, scarcely palpable
235 To him who does not think. But at your bidding
I will proceed.
                    While thus it fared with them
To whom this cottage till that hapless year
Had been a blessed home, it was my chance
To travel in a country far remote,

240 And glad I was when, halting by yon gate
That leads from the green lane, again I saw
These lofty elm-trees. Long I did not rest:
With many pleasant thoughts I cheer'd my way
O'er the flat common. At the door arrived,
245 I knocked, and when I entered with the hope
Of usual greeting, Margaret looked at me
A little while, then turned her head away
Speechless, and sitting down upon a chair
Wept bitterly. I wist° not what to do   *knew*
250 Or how to speak to her. Poor wretch! at last
She rose from off her seat—and then, oh Sir!
I cannot tell how she pronounced my name:
With fervent love, and with a face of grief
Unutterably helpless, and a look
255 That seem'd to cling upon me, she enquir'd
If I had seen her husband. As she spake
A strange surprize and fear came to my heart,
Nor had I power to answer ere she told
That he had disappeared—just two months gone.
260 He left his house; two wretched days had passed,
And on the third by the first break of light,
Within her casement° full in view she saw   *window*
A purse of gold. 'I trembled at the sight,'
Said Margaret, 'for I knew it was his hand
265 That placed it there, and on that very day
By one, a stranger, from my husband sent,
The tidings came that he had joined a troop
Of soldiers going to a distant land.
He left me thus—Poor Man! he had not heart
270 To take a farewell of me, and he feared
That I should follow with my babes, and sink
Beneath the misery of a soldier's life.'
This tale did Margaret tell with many tears:
And when she ended I had little power
275 To give her comfort, and was glad to take
Such words of hope from her own mouth as serv'd
To cheer us both: but long we had not talked
Ere we built up a pile of better thoughts,
And with a brighter eye she looked around
280 As if she had been shedding tears of joy.
We parted. It was then the early spring;
I left her busy with her garden tools;

---

1 *In my own despite*   In spite of myself.

2 *By moving accidents uncharactered*   Unmarked by sensational events or accidents. Cf. *Othello* 1.3.155–56, where Othello describes his life story as one "of most disastrous chances, / Of moving accidents by flood and field."

And well remember, o'er that fence she looked,
And while I paced along the foot-way path
5 Called out, and sent a blessing after me
With tender chearfulness and with a voice
That seemed the very sound of happy thoughts.
    I roved o'er many a hill and many a dale
With this my weary load, in heat and cold,
0 Through many a wood, and many an open ground,
In sunshine or in shade, in wet or fair,
Now blithe, now drooping, as it might befal,
My best companions now the driving winds
And now the 'trotting brooks'¹ and whispering trees
5 And now the music of my own sad steps,
With many a short lived thought that pass'd between
And disappeared. I came this way again
Towards the wane of summer, when the wheat
Was yellow, and the soft and bladed grass
0 Sprang up afresh and o'er the hay-field spread
Its tender green. When I had reached the door
I found that she was absent. In the shade
Where now we sit I waited her return.
Her cottage in its outward look appeared
5 As chearful as before; in any shew
Of neatness little changed, but that I thought
The honeysuckle crowded round the door
And from the wall hung down in heavier wreathes,
And knots of worthless stone-crop² started out
0 Along the window's edge, and grew like weeds
Against the lower panes. I turned aside
And stroll'd into her garden.—It was chang'd:
The unprofitable bindweed³ spread his bells
From side to side and with unwieldy wreaths
5 Had dragg'd the rose from its sustaining wall
And bent it down to earth; the border-tufts—
Daisy and thrift⁴ and lowly chamomile
And thyme—had straggled out into the paths

---

¹ *trotting brooks* Adapted from Robert Burns, "To William Simpson, Ochiltree" (1786).

² *stone-crop* Type of succulent plant.

³ *bindweed* Hardy and rapidly spreading vine-like weed with trumpet-shaped flowers. It often wraps itself around plants and pulls them over.

⁴ *thrift* Common garden plant that usually bears pink flowers.

Which they were used to deck. Ere this an hour
320 Was wasted. Back I turned my restless steps,
And as I walked before the door it chanced
A stranger passed, and guessing whom I sought
He said that she was used to ramble⁵ far.
The sun was sinking in the west, and now
325 I sate with sad impatience. From within
Her solitary infant cried aloud.
The spot though fair seemed very desolate,
The longer I remained more desolate.
And, looking round, I saw the corner-stones,
330 Till then unmark'd, on either side the door
With dull red stains discoloured and stuck o'er
With tufts and hairs of wool, as if the sheep
That feed upon the commons thither came
Familiarly and found a couching-place
335 Even at her threshold.—The house clock struck eight;
I turned and saw her distant a few steps.
Her face was pale and thin, her figure too
Was chang'd. As she unlocked the door she said,
'It grieves me you have waited here so long,
340 But in good truth I've wandered much of late
And sometimes, to my shame I speak, have need
Of my best prayers to bring me back again.'
While on the board she spread our evening meal
She told me she had lost her elder child,
345 That he for months had been a serving-boy
Apprenticed by the parish.⁶ 'I perceive
You look at me, and you have cause. Today
I have been travelling far, and many days
About the fields I wander, knowing this
350 Only, that what I seek I cannot find.
And so I waste my time: for I am changed;
And to myself,' said she, 'have done much wrong,
And to this helpless infant. I have slept
Weeping, and weeping I have waked; my tears
355 Have flow'd as if my body were not such
As others are, and I could never die.
But I am now in mind and in my heart

---

⁵ *was used to ramble* Habitually rambled.

⁶ *Apprenticed by the parish* The parish had the authority to take children away from parents who were deemed unable to care for them; such children were apprenticed to members of the community.

More easy, and I hope,' said she, 'that heaven
Will give me patience to endure the things
360   Which I behold at home.' It would have grieved
Your very heart to see her. Sir, I feel
The story linger in my heart. I fear
'Tis long and tedious, but my spirit clings
To that poor woman: so familiarly
365   Do I perceive her manner, and her look
And presence, and so deeply do I feel
Her goodness, that not seldom in my walks
A momentary trance comes over me;
And to myself I seem to muse on one
370   By sorrow laid asleep or borne away,
A human being destined to awake
To human life, or something very near
To human life, when he shall come again
For whom she suffered. Sir, it would have griev'd
375   Your very soul to see her: evermore
Her eye-lids droop'd, her eyes were downward cast;
And when she at her table gave me food
She did not look at me. Her voice was low,
Her body was subdued. In every act
380   Pertaining to her house-affairs appeared
The careless stillness which a thinking mind
Gives to an idle matter—still she sighed,
But yet no motion of the breast was seen,
No heaving of the heart. While by the fire
385   We sate together, sighs came on my ear;
I knew not how, and hardly whence they came.
I took my staff, and when I kissed her babe
The tears stood in her eyes. I left her then
With the best hope and comfort I could give;
390   She thanked me for my will, but for my hope
It seemed she did not thank me.
                                        I returned
And took my rounds along this road again
Ere on its sunny bank the primrose flower
Had chronicled the earliest day of spring.
395   I found her sad and drooping; she had learn'd
No tidings of her husband: if he lived
She knew not that he lived; if he were dead
She knew not he was dead. She seemed the same

In person [and][1] appearance, but her house
400   Bespoke a sleepy hand of negligence;
The floor was neither dry nor neat, the hearth
Was comfortless [   ],
The windows too were dim, and her few books,
Which, one upon the other, heretofore
405   Had been piled up against the corner-panes
In seemly order, now with straggling leaves
Lay scattered here and there, open or shut
As they had chanced to fall. Her infant babe
Had from its mother caught the trick of grief
410   And sighed among its playthings. Once again
I turned towards the garden-gate and saw
More plainly still that poverty and grief
Were now come nearer to her: the earth was hard,
With weeds defaced and knots of withered grass;
415   No ridges there appeared of clear black mould,°   soil
No winter greenness; of her herbs and flowers
It seemed the better part were gnawed away
Or trampled on the earth; a chain of straw
Which had been twisted round the tender stem
420   Of a young apple-tree[2] lay at its root;
The bark was nibbled round by truant sheep.
Margaret stood near, her infant in her arms,
And seeing that my eye was on the tree
She said, 'I fear it will be dead and gone
425   Ere Robert come again.' Towards the house
Together we returned, and she inquired
If I had any hope. But for her Babe
And for her little friendless Boy, she said,
She had no wish to live, that she must die
430   Of sorrow. Yet I saw the idle loom
Still in its place. His Sunday garments hung
Upon the self-same nail, his very staff
Stood undisturbed behind the door. And when
I passed this way beaten by Autumn winds
435   She told me that her little babe was dead
And she was left alone. That very time,
I yet remember, through the miry lane

---

[1] *[and]* In the manuscript, the word "or" was erased here; later
manuscripts read "and."

[2] *chain of straw ... apple-tree* Straw was wound around young apple
trees to prevent rabbits and other animals from eating them.

She walked with me a mile, when the bare trees
Trickled with foggy damps, and in such sort
40 That any heart had ached to hear her begg'd
That wheresoe'er I went I still would ask
For him whom she had lost. We parted then,
Our final parting, for from that time forth
Did many seasons pass ere I returned
45 Into this tract again.
                        Five tedious years
She lingered in unquiet widowhood,
A wife and widow. Needs must it have been
A sore heart-wasting. I have heard, my friend,
That in that broken arbour she would sit
50 The idle length of half a sabbath day—
There, where you see the toadstool's lazy head—
And when a dog passed by she still would quit
The shade and look abroad. On this old Bench
For hours she sate, and evermore her eye
55 Was busy in the distance, shaping things
Which made her heart beat quick. Seest thou that path?
(The green-sward[1] now has broken its grey line)
There to and fro she paced through many a day
Of the warm summer, from a belt of flax
60 That girt her waist spinning the long-drawn thread
With backward steps.—Yet ever as there passed
A man whose garments shewed the Soldier's red,
Or crippled Mendicant in Sailor's garb,
The little child who sate to turn the wheel
65 Ceased from his toil, and she with faltering voice,
Expecting still to learn her husband's fate,
Made many a fond inquiry; and when they
Whose presence gave no comfort were gone by,
Her heart was still more sad. And by yon gate
70 Which bars the traveller's road she often stood
And when a stranger horseman came, the latch
Would lift, and in his face look wistfully,
Most happy if from aught discovered there
Of tender feeling she might dare repeat
75 The same sad question. Meanwhile her poor hut
Sunk to decay, for he was gone whose hand
At the first nippings of October frost

Closed up each chink and with fresh bands of straw
Chequered the green-grown thatch. And so she lived
480 Through the long winter, reckless and alone,
Till this reft° house by frost, and thaw, and rain   *bereft*
Was sapped; and when she slept the nightly damps
Did chill her breast, and in the stormy day
Her tattered clothes were ruffled by the wind
485 Even at the side of her own fire. Yet still
She loved this wretched spot, nor would for worlds
Have parted hence; and still that length of road
And this rude bench one torturing hope endeared,
Fast rooted at her heart, and here, my friend,
490 In sickness she remained, and here she died,
Last human tenant of these ruined walls."

        The old Man ceased: he saw that I was mov'd;
From that low Bench, rising instinctively,
I turned aside in weakness, nor had power
495 To thank him for the tale which he had told.
I stood, and leaning o'er the garden-gate
Reviewed that Woman's suff'rings, and it seemed
To comfort me while with a brother's love
I blessed her in the impotence of grief.
500 At length [towards] the [Cottage I returned][2]
Fondly, and traced with milder interest
That secret spirit of humanity
Which, 'mid the calm oblivious tendencies
Of nature, 'mid her plants, her weeds, and flowers,
505 And silent overgrowings, still survived.
The old man, seeing this, resumed and said,
"My Friend, enough to sorrow have you given,
The purposes of wisdom ask no more;
Be wise and chearful, and no longer read
510 The forms of things with an unworthy eye.
She sleeps in the calm earth, and peace is here.
I well remember that those very plumes,
Those weeds, and the high spear-grass on that wall,
By mist and silent rain-drops silver'd o'er,
515 As once I passed did to my heart convey
So still an image of tranquillity,

---

1 *green-sward* Grassy area.

2 *At length ... I returned* Before it was erased in the manuscript, this line had read "At length upon the hut I fix'd my eyes." The blanks were left in MS D; the text appearing here follows MS E and *The Excursion*.

So calm and still, and looked so beautiful
Amid the uneasy thoughts which filled my mind,
That what we feel of sorrow and despair
520 From ruin and from change, and all the grief
The passing shews of being leave behind,
Appeared an idle dream that could not live
Where meditation was. I turned away
And walked along my road in happiness."
525   He ceased. By this the sun declining shot
A slant and mellow radiance which began
To fall upon us where beneath the trees
We sate on that low bench, and now we felt,
Admonished thus, the sweet hour coming on.
530 A linnet warbled from those lofty elms,
A thrush sang loud, and other melodies,
At distance heard, peopled the milder air.
The old man rose and hoisted up his load.
Together casting then a farewell look
535 Upon those silent walls, we left the shade
And ere the stars were visible attained
A rustic inn, our evening resting-place.
—1949 (MANUSCRIPT C. 1797–1800)

[*I griev'd for Buonaparté*][1]

I griev'd for Buonaparté, with a vain
And an unthinking grief! the vital blood
Of that Man's mind what can it be? What food
Fed his first hopes? What knowledge could *He* gain?
5 'Tis not in battles that from youth we train
The Governor who must be wise and good,
And temper with the sternness of the brain
Thoughts motherly, and meek as womanhood.
Wisdom doth live with children round her knees:
10 Books, leisure, perfect freedom, and the talk
Man holds with week-day man in the hourly walk
Of the mind's business: these are the degrees

By which true Sway doth mount; this is the stalk
True Power doth grow on; and her rights are these.
—1802

[*My heart leaps up*]

My heart leaps up when I behold
A Rainbow in the sky:
So was it when my life began;
So is it now I am a Man;
5 So be it when I shall grow old,
    Or let me die!
The Child is Father of the Man;
And I could wish my days to be
Bound each to each by natural piety.
—1804

Ode to Duty

Stern Daughter of the Voice of God![2]
O Duty! if that name thou love
Who art a Light to guide, a Rod
To check the erring, and reprove;
5 Thou, who art victory and law
When empty terrors overawe;
From vain temptations dost set free;
From strife and from despair; a glorious ministry.

There are who ask not if thine eye
10 Be on them; who, in love and truth,
Where no misgiving is, rely
Upon the genial° sense° of youth: *natural / vitality*
Glad Hearts! without reproach or blot;
Who do thy work, and know it not:
15 May joy be theirs while life shall last!
And Thou, if they should totter, teach them to stand
    fast!

---

[1] *I ... Buonaparté* According to Dorothy Wordsworth, this sonnet was composed in 1802, the year that Napoleon Bonaparte declared himself First Consul of France for life.

[2] *Stern ... God* Cf. Milton, *Paradise Lost* 9.652–54: "God so commanded, and left that Command / Sole Daughter of His voice; the rest, we live / Law to ourselves, our Reason is our Law."

Serene will be our days and bright,
And happy will our nature be,
When love is an unerring light,
20 And joy its own security.
And bless'd are they who in the main
This faith, even now, do entertain:
Live in the spirit of this creed;
Yet find that other strength, according to their need.

25 I, loving freedom, and untried;
No sport of every random gust,
Yet being to myself a guide,
Too blindly have reposed my trust:
Resolved that nothing e'er should press
30 Upon my present happiness,
I shoved unwelcome tasks away;
But thee I now would serve more strictly, if I may.

Through no disturbance of my soul,
Or strong compunction in me wrought,
35 I supplicate for thy control;
But in the quietness of thought:
Me this uncharter'd freedom tires;
I feel the weight of chance desires:
My hopes no more must change their name,
40 I long for a repose that ever is the same.

Yet not the less would I throughout
Still act according to the voice
Of my own wish; and feel past doubt
That my submissiveness was choice:
45 Not seeking in the school of pride
For "precepts over dignified,"
Denial and restraint I prize
No farther than they breed a second Will more wise.

Stern Lawgiver! yet thou dost wear
50 The Godhead's most benignant grace;
Nor know we anything so fair
As is the smile upon thy face:
Flowers laugh before thee on their beds;
And Fragrance in thy footing treads;
55 Thou dost preserve the Stars from wrong;

And the most ancient Heavens, through Thee are fresh
    and strong.

To humbler functions, awful Power!
I call thee: I myself commend
Unto thy guidance from this hour;
60 Oh! let my weakness have an end!
Give unto me, made lowly wise,
The spirit of self-sacrifice;
The confidence of reason give;
And in the light of truth thy Bondman let me live!
—1807

Resolution and Independence

There was a roaring in the wind all night;
    The rain came heavily and fell in floods;
But now the sun is rising calm and bright;
The birds are singing in the distant woods;
5 Over his own sweet voice the Stock dove°   *wild pigeon*
    broods;
The Jay makes answer as the Magpie chatters;
And all the air is fill'd with pleasant noise of waters.

All things that love the sun are out of doors;
The sky rejoices in the morning's birth;
10 The grass is bright with rain-drops; on the moors
The Hare is running races in her mirth;
And with her feet she from the plashy[1] earth
Raises a mist; which, glittering in the sun,
Runs with her all the way, wherever she doth run.

15 I was a Traveller then upon the moor;
I saw the Hare that rac'd about with joy;
I heard the woods, and distant waters, roar;
Or heard them not, as happy as a Boy:
The pleasant season did my heart employ:
20 My old remembrances went from me wholly;
And all the ways of men, so vain and melancholy.

---

[1] *plashy* Having many puddles or pools of water; wet.

But, as it sometimes chanceth, from the might
Of joy in minds that can no farther go,
As high as we have mounted in delight
25 In our dejection do we sink as low,
To me that morning did it happen so;
And fears, and fancies, thick upon me came;
Dim sadness, and blind thoughts I knew not nor could
    name.

I heard the Sky-lark singing in the sky;
30 And I bethought me of the playful Hare:
Even such a happy Child of earth am I;
Even as these blissful Creatures do I fare;
Far from the world I walk, and from all care;
But there may come another day to me,
35 Solitude, pain of heart, distress, and poverty.

My whole life I have liv'd in pleasant thought,
As if life's business were a summer mood;
As if all needful things would come unsought
To genial faith, still rich in genial good;
40 But how can He expect that others should
Build for him, sow for him, and at his call
Love him, who for himself will take no heed at all?

I thought of Chatterton,[1] the marvellous Boy,
The sleepless Soul that perish'd in its pride;
45 Of Him who walk'd in glory and in joy
Behind his plough, upon the mountain-side:[2]
By our own spirits are we deified;
We Poets in our youth begin in gladness;
But thereof comes in the end despondency and
    madness.

50 Now, whether it were by peculiar grace,
A leading from above, a something given,
Yet it befel, that, in this lonely place,
When up and down my fancy thus was driven,

And I with these untoward thoughts had striven,
55 I saw a Man before me unawares:
The oldest man he seem'd that ever wore grey hairs.

My course I stopped as soon as I espied
The Old Man in that naked wilderness:
Close by a Pond, upon the further side,
60 He stood alone: a minute's space I guess
I watch'd him, he continuing motionless:
To the Pool's further margin then I drew;
He being all the while before me full in view.

As a huge Stone is sometimes seen to lie
65 Couch'd on the bald top of an eminence;
Wonder to all who do the same espy
By what means it could thither come, and whence;
So that it seems a thing endued with sense:
Like a Sea-beast crawl'd forth, which on a shelf
70 Of rock or sand reposeth, there to sun itself.

Such seem'd this Man, not all alive nor dead,
Nor all asleep; in his extreme old age:
His body was bent double, feet and head
Coming together in their pilgrimage;
75 As if some dire constraint of pain, or rage
Of sickness felt by him in times long past,
A more than human weight upon his frame had cast.

Himself he propp'd, his body, limbs, and face,
Upon a long grey Staff of shaven wood:
80 And, still as I drew near with gentle pace,
Beside the little pond or moorish flood
Motionless as a Cloud the Old Man stood;
That heareth not the loud winds when they call;
And moveth altogether, if it move at all.

85 At length, himself unsettling, he the Pond
Stirred with his Staff, and fixedly did look
Upon the muddy water, which he conn'd,°   studied
As if he had been reading in a book:
And now such freedom as I could I took;
90 And, drawing to his side, to him did say,
"This morning gives us promise of a glorious day."

---

[1] *Chatterton* Poet Thomas Chatterton (1752–70), who, after failing
to make a living as a poet in London, poisoned himself at the age of
seventeen.

[2] *Of Him … mountain-side* Scottish poet Robert Burns (1759–96),
known as "the Ploughman Poet" because of his farming background.

A gentle answer did the Old Man make,
In courteous speech which forth he slowly drew:
And him with further words I thus bespake,
95   "What kind of work is that which you pursue?
This is a lonesome place for one like you."
He answer'd me with pleasure and surprise;
And there was, while he spake, a fire about his eyes.

His words came feebly, from a feeble chest,
00   Yet each in solemn order follow'd each,
With something of a lofty utterance drest;
Choice word, and measured phrase; above the reach
Of ordinary men; a stately speech!
Such as grave Livers[1] do in Scotland use,
05   Religious men, who give to God and Man their dues.

He told me that he to this pond had come
To gather Leeches,[2] being old and poor:
Employment hazardous and wearisome!
And he had many hardships to endure:
10   From Pond to Pond he roam'd, from moor to moor,
Housing, with God's good help, by choice or chance:
And in this way he gain'd an honest maintenance.

The old Man still stood talking by my side;
But now his voice to me was like a stream
15   Scarce heard; nor word from word could I divide;
And the whole Body of the man did seem
Like one whom I had met with in a dream;
Or like a Man from some far region sent;
To give me human strength, and strong admonishment.

120 My former thoughts return'd: the fear that kills;
The hope that is unwilling to be fed;
Cold, pain, and labour, and all fleshly ills;
And mighty Poets in their misery dead.
And now, not knowing what the Old Man had said,
125 My question eagerly did I renew,
"How is it that you live, and what is it you do?"

He with a smile did then his words repeat;
And said that, gathering Leeches, far and wide
He travelled; stirring thus about his feet
130 The waters of the Ponds where they abide.
"Once I could meet with them on every side;
But they have dwindled long by slow decay;
Yet still I persevere, and find them where I may."

While he was talking thus, the lonely place,
135 The Old Man's shape, and speech, all troubled me:
In my mind's eye I seem'd to see him pace
About the weary moors continually,
Wandering about alone and silently.
While I these thoughts within myself pursued,
140 He, having made a pause, the same discourse renewed.

And soon with this he other matter blended,
Cheerfully uttered, with demeanour kind,
But stately in the main; and, when he ended,
I could have laugh'd myself to scorn, to find
145 In that decrepit Man so firm a mind.
"God," said I, "be my help and stay° secure;   *support*
I'll think of the Leech-gatherer on the lonely moor."
—1807

---

[1] *grave Livers* I.e., those who live seriously.

[2] *Leeches* Used at this time by doctors for drawing the blood of patients. A leech gatherer would find leeches by standing in shallow water and allowing them to attach themselves to his legs.

Composed upon Westminster Bridge
Sept. 3, 1803[1]

Earth has not any thing to show more fair:
Dull would he be of soul who could pass by
A sight so touching in its majesty:
This City now doth like a garment wear
5   This beauty of the morning; silent, bare,
Ships, towers, domes, theatres, and temples lie
Open unto the fields, and to the sky;
All bright and glittering in the smokeless air.
Never did sun more beautifully steep
10   In his first splendor valley, rock, or hill;
Ne'er saw I, never felt, a calm so deep!
The river glideth at his own sweet will:
Dear God! the very houses seem asleep;
And all that mighty heart is lying still!
—1807

[The world is too much with us]

The world is too much with us; late and soon,
Getting and spending, we lay waste our powers:
Little we see in nature that is ours;
We have given our hearts away, a sordid boon!
5   The Sea that bares her bosom to the moon;
The Winds that will be howling at all hours
And are up-gathered now like sleeping flowers;
For this, for every thing, we are out of tune;
It moves us not. Great God! I'd rather be
10   A Pagan suckled in a creed outworn;
So might I, standing on this pleasant lea,
Have glimpses that would make me less forlorn;

Have sight of Proteus coming from the sea;
Or hear old Triton blow his wreathed horn.[2]
—1807

[It is a beauteous Evening]

It is a beauteous Evening, calm and free;
The holy time is quiet as a Nun
Breathless with adoration; the broad sun
Is sinking down in its tranquillity;
5   The gentleness of heaven is on the Sea:
Listen! the mighty Being is awake
And doth with his eternal motion make
A sound like thunder—everlastingly.
Dear Child! dear Girl![3] that walkest with me here,
10   If thou appear'st untouch'd by solemn thought,
Thy nature is not therefore less divine:
Thou liest in Abraham's bosom[4] all the year;
And worshipp'st at the Temple's inner shrine,
God being with thee when we know it not.
—1807

London
1802[5]

Milton! thou should'st be living at this hour:
England hath need of thee: she is a fen
Of stagnant waters: altar, sword, and pen,
Fireside, the heroic wealth of hall and bower,
5   Have forfeited their ancient English dower

---

[2]   *Proteus*   Shape-changing sea god; *Triton … horn*   Sea god with the head and torso of a man and the tail of a fish. He was usually depicted blowing on a conch shell.

[3]   *Dear … Girl*   Wordsworth's daughter Caroline.

[4]   *Abraham's bosom*   The resting place for souls bound for heaven. See Luke 16.22: "And it came to pass, that the beggar died, and was carried by the angels into Abraham's bosom."

[5]   *London 1802*   Written immediately after Wordsworth's return from France, when he was struck by the differences between his native country and France after the Revolution. Milton died in 1674.

[1]   *Composed … 1803*   Wordsworth misremembered the date of composition, which was actually (according to Dorothy Wordsworth's *Grasmere Journals*) 1802, when Wordsworth took a brief trip to France, where his former lover Annette Vallon lived with their daughter, Caroline.

Of inward happiness. We are selfish men;
Oh! raise us up, return to us again;
And give us manners, virtue, freedom, power.
Thy soul was like a Star and dwelt apart:
10 Thou hadst a voice whose sound was like the sea;
Pure as the naked heavens, majestic, free,
So didst thou travel on life's common way,
In cheerful godliness; and yet thy heart
The lowliest duties on itself did lay.
—1807

The Solitary Reaper[1]

Behold her, single in the field,
  Yon solitary Highland Lass!
Reaping and singing by herself;
Stop here, or gently pass!
5 Alone she cuts, and binds the grain,
And sings a melancholy strain;
O listen! for the Vale profound
Is overflowing with the sound.

No Nightingale did ever chaunt
10 So sweetly to reposing bands
Of Travellers in some shady haunt,

Among Arabian Sands:
No sweeter voice was ever heard
In spring-time from the Cuckoo-bird,
15 Breaking the silence of the seas
Among the farthest Hebrides.

Will no one tell me what she sings?
Perhaps the plaintive numbers° flow   *verses*
For old, unhappy, far-off things,
20 And battles long ago:
Or is it some more humble lay,
Familiar matter of today?
Some natural sorrow, loss, or pain,
That has been, and may be again!

25 Whate'er the theme, the Maiden sang
As if her song could have no ending;
I saw her singing at her work,
And o'er the sickle bending;
I listen'd till I had my fill:
30 And, as I mounted up the hill,
The music in my heart I bore,
Long after it was heard no more.
—1807

---

[1] *The Solitary Reaper*   Suggested by the following passage in Thomas Wilkinson's *Tours to the British Mountains* (1824): "Passed a female who was reaping alone: she sung in Erse [a Gaelic language] as she bended over her sickle; the sweetest human voice I ever heard: her strains were tenderly melancholy, and felt delicious, long after they were heard no more."

IN CONTEXT

"I wandered lonely as a Cloud":
Stages in the Life of a Poem

The earliest version of this poem was composed in 1804 and first published in 1807. It was evidently inspired by an entry in Dorothy Wordsworth's journal from two years earlier, describing a scene at Glencoyne Bay, Ullswater, observed by Dorothy and William on their way back to Grasmere after a long ramble. Appearing below are the scene as described by Dorothy in the journal; William's first version of the poem; a facsimile of the page in the copy of *Poems, in Two Volumes* in which William began to compose an additional stanza to the poem; a transcription of his handwritten jottings; and William's revised version, with the added stanza and some other changes (which was not published until 1815).

from Dorothy Wordsworth, *Grasmere Journal* (Thursday, 15 April 1802)

When we were in the woods beyond Gowbarrow park we saw a few daffodils close to the water side. We fancied that the lake had floated the seeds ashore and that the little colony had so sprung up. But as we went along there were more and yet more and at last under the boughs of the trees, we saw that there was a long belt of them along the shore, about the breadth of a country turnpike road. I never saw daffodils so beautiful. They grew among the mossy stones about and about them, some rested their heads upon these stones as on a pillow for weariness and the rest tossed and reeled and danced and seemed as if they verily laughed with the wind that blew upon them over the lake, they looked so gay ever glancing ever changing. This wind blew directly over the lake to them. There was here and there a little knot and a few stragglers a few yards higher up but they were so few as not to disturb the simplicity and unity and life of that one busy highway.

[*I wandered lonely as a Cloud*]

I wandered lonely as a Cloud
　That floats on high o'er Vales and Hills,
When all at once I saw a crowd
A host of dancing Daffodils;
5　Along the Lake, beneath the trees,
Ten thousand dancing in the breeze.

The waves beside them danced, but they
Outdid the sparkling waves in glee—
A Poet could not but be gay
10　In such a laughing company:
I gazed—and gaz'd—but little thought
What wealth the show to me had brought:

For oft when on my couch I lie
In vacant or in pensive mood,
15　They flash upon that inward eye
Which is the bliss of solitude,
And then my heart with pleasure fills,
And dances with the Daffodils.
—1807

I wandered lonely as a cloud[1]

1

A host of golden Daffodi ls

Beside

~~Along~~ the Lake beneath the trees

                                vernal

All dancing ~~dancing~~ in the breeze

  Continuous

            { ed
~~Close crowd~~ { ing, [?like]

~~As numerous~~ ˄ as the stars that shine

  and twinkle

            on
At midnight, in } the milky way

            { a
They stretch'd { in } never ending line

Along the margin of a bay

Ten thousand saw I at a glance

Tossing their heads in spritely dance

[*I wandered lonely as a cloud*]

I wandered lonely as a cloud
    That floats on high o'er vales and hills,
When all at once I saw a crowd,
A host, of golden daffodils;
5   Beside the lake, beneath the trees,
Fluttering and dancing in the breeze.

Continuous as the stars that shine
And twinkle on the milky way,
They stretched in never-ending line
10   Along the margin of a bay:
Ten thousand saw I at a glance,
Tossing their heads in sprightly dance.

The waves beside them danced, but they
Outdid the sparkling waves in glee:
15   A poet could not but be gay,
In such a jocund company;
I gazed—and gazed—but little thought
What wealth the show to me had brought:

For oft, when on my couch I lie
20   In vacant or in pensive mood,
They flash upon that inward eye
Which is the bliss of solitude;
And then my heart with pleasure fills,
And dances with the daffodils.

—1815

---

[1]   *I wandered … cloud*   Transcription of Wordsworth's manuscript
(see previous page for facsimile).

Elegiac Stanzas

*Suggested by a Picture of Peele Castle, in a Storm, painted
by Sir George Beaumont*[1]

I was thy Neighbour once, thou rugged Pile!°   *castle*
  Four summer weeks I dwelt in sight of thee:
I saw thee every day; and all the while
Thy Form was sleeping on a glassy sea.

5 So pure the sky, so quiet was the air!
So like, so very like, was day to day!
Whene'er I look'd, thy Image still was there;
It trembled, but it never pass'd away.

How perfect was the calm! it seem'd no sleep;
10 No mood, which season takes away, or brings:
I could have fancied that the mighty Deep
Was even the gentlest of all gentle Things.

Ah! THEN, if mine had been the Painter's hand,
To express what then I saw; and add the gleam,
15 The light that never was, on sea or land,
The consecration, and the Poet's dream;

I would have planted thee, thou hoary Pile!
Amid a world how different from this!
Beside a sea that could not cease to smile;
20 On tranquil land, beneath a sky of bliss:

Thou shouldst have seem'd a treasure-house, a mine
Of peaceful years; a chronicle of heaven—
Of all the sunbeams that did ever shine
The very sweetest had to thee been given.

25 A Picture had it been of lasting ease,
Elysian[2] quiet, without toil or strife;
No motion but the moving tide, a breeze,
Or merely silent Nature's breathing life.

Such, in the fond delusion of my heart,
30 Such Picture would I at that time have made:
And seen the soul of truth in every part;
A faith, a trust, that could not be betray'd.

So once it would have been—'tis so no more;
I have submitted to a new control:
35 A power is gone, which nothing can restore;
A deep distress hath humaniz'd my Soul.

Not for a moment could I now behold
A smiling sea and be what I have been:
The feeling of my loss will ne'er be old;
40 This, which I know, I speak with mind serene.

Then, Beaumont, Friend! who would have been the
    Friend,
If he had lived, of Him whom I deplore,°   *mourn*
This Work of thine I blame not, but commend;
This sea in anger, and that dismal shore.

45 Oh 'tis a passionate Work!—yet wise and well;
Well chosen is the spirit that is here;
That Hulk which labours in the deadly swell,
This rueful sky, this pageantry of fear!

And this huge Castle, standing here sublime,
50 I love to see the look with which it braves,
Cased in the unfeeling armour of old time,
The light'ning, the fierce wind, and trampling waves.

Farewell, farewell the Heart that lives alone,
Hous'd in a dream, at distance from the Kind![3]
55 Such happiness, wherever it be known,
Is to be pitied; for 'tis surely blind.

---

[1] *Suggested by … Beaumont* In 1794, Wordsworth spent a month in
Rampside, Lancashire, which is located across the Morecambe Bay
from the Furness Peninsula, where the ruins of Peele Castle stand. In
1806 he saw the two pictures of this castle that had been painted by Sir
George Beaumont, a landscape painter who was Wordsworth's friend
and patron. Wordsworth's youngest brother, a captain with the East
India Company, drowned when his ship sank off the Bill of Portland
in February 1805.

[2] *Elysian* Blissful. Referring to Elysium, where, according to classical
mythology, the blessed, virtuous, or heroic reside after death.

[3] *Kind* Human race.

But welcome fortitude, and patient cheer,
And frequent sights of what is to be born!
Such sights, or worse, as are before me here.
60 Not without hope we suffer and we mourn.
—1807

Ode
[Intimations of Immortality]

In an 1843 letter to Isabella Fenwick, Wordsworth explained the experiences from his own life on which this ode is based, saying, "Nothing was more difficult for me in childhood than to admit the notion of death as a state applicable to my own being. … I used to brood over the stories of Enoch and Elijah, and almost to persuade myself that, whatever might become of others, I should be translated, in something of the same way, to heaven. With a feeling congenial to this, I was often unable to think of external things as having external existence, and I communed with all that I saw as something not apart from, but inherent in, my own immaterial nature. Many times while going to school have I grasped at a wall or tree to recall myself from this abyss of idealism to the reality. At that time I was afraid of such processes. In later periods of life I have deplored, as we have all reason to do, a subjugation of an opposite character, and have rejoiced over the remembrances, as is expressed in the lines—

> Obstinate questionings
> Of sense and outward things,
> Fallings from us, vanishings; etc."[1]

Wordsworth wrote the first four stanzas of the poem in 1802, and two years elapsed before he completed the poem in 1804. In 1815 he changed the title to "Ode: Intimations of Immortality from Recollections of Early Childhood," its more common title today. He also replaced the Latin epigram from Virgil with the last three lines from "My heart leaps up": "The Child is Father to the Man: / And I could wish my days to be / Bound each to each by natural piety."

Ode
[Intimations of Immortality from Recollections of Early Childhood]

Paulo majora canamus.[2]

There was a time when meadow, grove, and stream,
    The earth, and every common sight,
            To me did seem
        Apparelled in celestial light,
5 The glory and the freshness of a dream.
It is not now as it has been of yore;—
        Turn wheresoe'er I may,
            By night or day,
The things which I have seen I now can see no more.

10   The Rainbow comes and goes,
        And lovely is the Rose,
        The Moon doth with delight
Look round her when the heavens are bare;
        Waters on a starry night
15   Are beautiful and fair;
    The sunshine is a glorious birth;
        But yet I know, where'er I go,
That there hath passed away a glory from the earth.

Now, while the Birds thus sing a joyous song,
20   And while the young Lambs bound
            As to the tabor's[3] sound,
To me alone there came a thought of grief:
A timely utterance gave that thought relief,
        And I again am strong.
25 The Cataracts blow their trumpets from the steep,
No more shall grief of mine the season wrong;
I hear the Echoes through the mountains throng,
The Winds come to me from the fields of sleep,

---

[1] *Obstinate … etc.* Lines 144–46.

[2] *Paulo majora canamus* Latin: Let us sing of loftier things. From Virgil's Fourth Eclogue.

[3] *tabor* Small drum.

And all the earth is gay,
　　Land and sea
30 Give themselves up to jollity,
　　And with the heart of May
Doth every Beast keep holiday,
　　Thou Child of Joy
35 Shout round me, let me hear thy shouts, thou happy
　　Shepherd Boy!

Ye blessed Creatures, I have heard the call
　　Ye to each other make; I see
The heavens laugh with you in your jubilee;
　　My heart is at your festival,
40 　　My head hath its coronal,° wreath
The fullness of your bliss, I feel—I feel it all.
　　Oh evil day! if I were sullen
　　While Earth herself is adorning,
　　　This sweet May-morning,
45 　　And the Children are pulling,
　　　On every side,
In a thousand valleys far and wide,
Fresh flowers; while the sun shines warm,
And the Babe leaps up on his mother's arm:—
50 　I hear, I hear, with joy I hear!
　—But there's a Tree, of many one,
A single Field which I have looked upon,
Both of them speak of something that is gone:
　　The Pansy at my feet
55 　　Doth the same tale repeat:
Whither is fled the visionary gleam?
Where is it now, the glory and the dream?

Our birth is but a sleep and a forgetting:
The Soul that rises with us, our life's Star,
60 　Hath had elsewhere its setting,
　　And cometh from afar:
　　Not in entire forgetfulness,
　　And not in utter nakedness,
But trailing clouds of glory do we come
65 　　From God, Who is our home:
Heaven lies about us in our infancy!
Shades of the prison-house begin to close
　　Upon the growing Boy,

70 But he beholds the light, and whence it flows,
　　He sees it in his joy;
The Youth, who daily farther from the East
　　Must travel, still is Nature's Priest,
　　And by the vision splendid
　　Is on his way attended;
75 At length the Man perceives it die away,
And fade into the light of common day.

Earth fills her lap with pleasures of her own;
Yearnings she hath in her own natural kind,
And, even with something of a Mother's mind,
80 　　And no unworthy aim,
　The homely° Nurse doth all she can simple
To make her Foster-child, her Inmate Man,
　Forget the glories he hath known,
And that imperial palace whence he came.
85 Behold the Child among his new-born blisses,
A four year's Darling of a pigmy size!
See, where 'mid work of his own hand he lies,
Fretted by sallies of his Mother's kisses,
With light upon him from his Father's eyes!
90 See, at his feet, some little plan or chart,
Some fragment from his dream of human life,
Shaped by himself with newly-learned art;
　　A wedding or a festival,
　　A mourning or a funeral;
95 　　And this hath now his heart,
　And unto this he frames his song:
　　Then will he fit his tongue
To dialogues of business, love, or strife;
　　But it will not be long
100 　　Ere this be thrown aside,
　　And with new joy and pride
The little Actor cons another part,
Filling from time to time his "humourous stage"[1]
With all the Persons, down to palsied Age,
105 That Life brings with her in her Equipage;

---

[1] *humourous stage* From Elizabethan poet Samuel Daniel's *Muso-philus* (1599), in reference to the different character types (defined by their dominant temperaments, or "humors") depicted in Renaissance drama.

As if his whole vocation
Were endless imitation.

Thou, whose exterior semblance doth belie
    Thy Soul's immensity;
110 Thou best Philosopher, who yet dost keep
Thy heritage, thou Eye among the blind,
That, deaf and silent, read'st the eternal deep,
Haunted for ever by the eternal mind—
    Mighty Prophet! Seer blest!
115   On whom those truths do rest,
Which we are toiling all our lives to find;
Thou, over whom thy Immortality
Broods like the Day, a Master o'er a Slave,
A Presence which is not to be put by;
120   To whom the grave
Is but a lonely bed without the sense or sight
    Of day or the warm light,
A place of thought where we in waiting lie;
Thou little Child, yet glorious in the might
125 Of untamed pleasures, on thy Being's height,
Why with such earnest pains dost thou provoke
The Years to bring the inevitable yoke,
Thus blindly with thy blessedness at strife?
Full soon thy Soul shall have her earthly freight,
130 And custom lie upon thee with a weight,
Heavy as frost, and deep almost as life!

    O joy! that in our embers
    Is something that doth live,
    That nature yet remembers
135   What was so fugitive!
The thought of our past years in me doth breed
Perpetual benedictions: not indeed
For that which is most worthy to be blest;
Delight and liberty, the simple creed
140 Of Childhood, whether fluttering or at rest,
With new-born hope for ever in his breast:—
    Not for these I raise
    The song of thanks and praise;
    But for those obstinate questionings
145   Of sense and outward things,
    Fallings from us, vanishings;

    Blank misgivings of a Creature
Moving about in worlds not realized,[1]
High instincts, before which our mortal Nature
150 Did tremble like a guilty Thing surprised:
    But for those first affections,
    Those shadowy recollections,
    Which, be they what they may,
Are yet the fountain light of all our day,
155 Are yet a master light of all our seeing;
    Uphold us, cherish us, and make
Our noisy years seem moments in the being
Of the eternal Silence: truths that wake,
    To perish never;
160 Which neither listlessness, nor mad endeavour,
    Nor Man nor Boy,
Nor all that is at enmity with joy,
Can utterly abolish or destroy!
    Hence, in a season of calm weather,
165   Though inland far we be,
Our Souls have sight of that immortal sea
    Which brought us hither,
    Can in a moment travel thither,
And see the Children sport upon the shore,
170 And hear the mighty waters rolling evermore.

Then, sing ye Birds, sing, sing a joyous song!
    And let the young Lambs bound
    As to the tabor's sound!
We in thought will join your throng,
175   Ye that pipe and ye that play,
    Ye that through your hearts to day
    Feel the gladness of the May!
What though the radiance which was once so bright
Be now for ever taken from my sight,
180   Though nothing can bring back the hour
Of splendour in the grass, of glory in the flower;
    We will grieve not, rather find
    Strength in what remains behind,
    In the primal sympathy
185   Which having been must ever be,
    In the soothing thoughts that spring
    Out of human suffering,

---

[1] *realized* Seeming real.

In the faith that looks through death,
In years that bring the philosophic mind.

90 And oh ye Fountains, Meadows, Hills, and Groves,
Think not of any severing of our loves!
Yet in my heart of hearts I feel your might;
I only have relinquished one delight
To live beneath your more habitual sway.
95 I love the Brooks which down their channels fret,
Even more than when I tripped lightly as they;
The innocent brightness of a new-born Day
        Is lovely yet;
The Clouds that gather round the setting sun
100 Do take a sober colouring from an eye
That hath kept watch o'er man's mortality;
Another race hath been, and other palms[1] are won.
Thanks to the human heart by which we live,
Thanks to its tenderness, its joys, and fears,
105 To me the meanest flower that blows can give
Thoughts that do often lie too deep for tears.
—1807

Surprised by Joy

Surprised by joy—impatient as the Wind
I turned to share the transport—Oh! with whom
But Thee,[2] deep buried in the silent tomb,
That spot which no vicissitude can find?
5 Love, faithful love, recalled thee to my mind—
But how could I forget thee? Through what power,
Even for the least division of an hour,
Have I been so beguiled as to be blind
To my most grievous loss?—That thought's return
10 Was the worst pang that sorrow ever bore,
Save one, one only, when I stood forlorn,
Knowing my heart's best treasure was no more;
That neither present time, nor years unborn
Could to my sight that heavenly face restore.
—1815

Mutability[3]

From low to high doth dissolution climb,
    And sink from high to low, along a scale
Of awful° notes, whose concord shall not fail; *awe-inspiring*
A musical but melancholy chime,
5 Which they can hear who meddle not with crime,
Nor avarice, nor over-anxious care.
Truth fails not; but her outward forms that bear
The longest date do melt like frosty rime,
That in the morning whitened hill and plain
10 And is no more; drop like the tower sublime
Of yesterday, which royally did wear
His crown of weeds, but could not even sustain
Some casual shout that broke the silent air,
Or the unimaginable touch of Time.
—1822

Steamboats, Viaducts, and Railways

Motions and Means, on land and sea at war
    With old poetic feeling, not for this,
Shall ye, by Poets even, be judged amiss!
Nor shall your presence, howsoe'er it mar
5 The loveliness of Nature, prove a bar
To the Mind's gaining that prophetic sense
Of future change, that point of vision whence
May be discovered what in soul ye are.
In spite of all that beauty may disown
10 In your harsh features, Nature doth embrace
Her lawful offspring in Man's art; and Time,
Pleased with your triumphs o'er his brother Space,
Accepts from your bold hands the proffered crown
Of hope, and smiles on you with cheer sublime.
—1835

---

[1] *palms* Prizes. In ancient Greece, palm branches or wreaths were often awarded to the winners of foot races.

[2] *Thee* Catherine, the Wordsworths' daughter, who died in June 1812 at the age of three.

[3] *Mutability* From *Ecclesiastical Sonnets*, a sequence of poems dealing with the history of the Church of England.

IN CONTEXT

Visual Depictions of "Man's Art"

While one artistic tradition emphasized the "harsh features" of the products of the Industrial Revolution, many painters in the first half of the nineteenth century depicted such subjects as viaducts and railways in ways which suggested that, like Wordsworth, they saw these as nature's "lawful offspring."

John Sell Cotman, *Chirk Aqueduct*, 1806–07.
The aqueduct, built between 1796 and 1801, is 70 feet high.

J.M.W. Turner, *Rain, Steam and Speed*, 1844.

The Prelude

Wordsworth first began this blank-verse epic poem—generally regarded as his crowning achievement—in 1798, as a preface to his projected masterpiece, *The Recluse*, a philosophical poem that was never completed. Throughout his life Wordsworth referred to *The Prelude* simply as "the poem on my life," "the poem on the growth of my mind," or "the poem to Coleridge." It was his wife, Mary, who, publishing the piece a few months after his death, gave it the title by which it is now known.

The history of *The Prelude* is a long and complex one, spanning over forty years of revisions that saw several preliminary versions before the final, fourteen-book poem was completed in 1839. Wordsworth began *The Prelude* in 1798, during a lonely, cold winter in Germany, during which he and his sister Dorothy struggled with homesickness. This first part, which deals with Wordsworth's early childhood, and a second part describing his adolescence (composed after Wordsworth's return to England in 1799) formed the two books of the 1799 *Prelude*.

Wordsworth returned to *The Prelude* again in 1804, expanding the piece to five books that covered his life through his residence at Cambridge. Around this time, he began to envision the project as a poem of epic proportions that would re-examine his life and convictions. In the expanded version of thirteen books, Wordsworth revisits France of the 1790s in his imagination, reliving those painful years and showing how, in the face of disappointment at the failure of the French Revolution and the growth of tyranny in Europe, he was restored through his ties with nature. This version, completed in May of 1805, begins with echoes of Milton's *Paradise Lost* as Wordsworth describes his vision of the fallen world in which he began his quest to develop his poetic imagination. Still spanning Wordsworth's childhood and maturity, the work no longer proceeds chronologically, but instead moves continuously between past and present as the poet recollects events and then examines their effects on his development. By the poem's end, he emerges from these events transformed and with his poetic sensibilities fully developed.

Wordsworth continued to revise *The Prelude* until 1839, when Dora Wordsworth (the poet's daughter) prepared a beautiful copy of the poem in its fourteen-book version. When *The Prelude* was first released in 1850, critics were often puzzled as to how it should be classified. In part, the poem is a familiar verse epistle to Coleridge and a testament to the power of friendship. At the same time, it is a personal narrative of spiritual journey. Yet the prophetic narrator and the deliberate parallels with other epics elevate the work above the merely personal and provide a representative story of a naive English adolescent who, maturing during the aftermath of a failed revolution, learns to celebrate his heritage.

It was not until the twentieth century that the earlier 1799 and 1805 versions of *The Prelude* were discovered. Both of these have since received much independent critical attention and have been seen by some critics as superior to the final version.

The Two-Part *Prelude* (1799)

FIRST PART

Was it for this
That one, the fairest of all rivers, loved
To blend his murmurs with my Nurse's song,
And from his alder[1] shades, and rocky falls,
5   And from his fords and shallows, sent a voice
That flowed along my dreams? For this didst thou
O Derwent, travelling over the green plains
Near my "sweet birth-place,"[2] didst thou beauteous
   Stream
Make ceaseless music through the night and day,
10   Which with its steady cadence tempering
Our human waywardness, composed my thoughts
To more than infant softness, giving me,
Among the fretful dwellings of mankind,

A knowledge, a dim earnest of the calm
15   Which Nature breathes among the fields and groves?
   Beloved Derwent! fairest of all Streams!
Was it for this that I, a four year's child,
A naked Boy, among thy silent pools
Made one long bathing of a summer's day?
20   Basked in the sun, or plunged into thy streams,
Alternate, all a summer's day, or coursed
Over the sandy fields, and dashed the flowers
Of yellow grunsel,[3] or when crag and hill,
The woods and distant Skiddaw's[4] lofty height
25   Were bronzed with a deep radiance, stood alone,
A naked Savage in the thunder shower?
   And afterwards, 'twas in a later day
Though early, when upon the mountain-slope
The frost and breath of frosty wind had snapped
30   The last autumnal crocus, 'twas my joy
To wander half the night among the cliffs

John "Warwick" Smith, *Ulls-water in Paterdale*, 1792–95.

---

[1] *alder*   Tree resembling a birch and usually found in wet places.

[2] *sweet birth-place*   From Coleridge's *Frost at Midnight* (1798). Wordsworth's childhood home was in Cockermouth, Cumberland, through which the Derwent River flows.

[3] *grunsel*   Groundsel, a common weed.

[4] *Skiddaw*   Mountain in Cumberland.

And the smooth hollows, where the woodcocks ran
Along the moonlight turf. In thought and wish,
That time, my shoulder all with springes° hung,   snares
35 I was a fell destroyer. Gentle Powers!
Who give us happiness and call it peace!
When scudding on from snare to snare I plied
My anxious visitation, hurrying on,
Still hurrying hurrying onward, how my heart
40 Panted; among the scattered yew-trees, and the crags
That looked upon me, how my bosom beat
With expectation. Sometimes strong desire,
Resistless, overpowered me, and the bird
Which was the captive of another's toils[1]
45 Became my prey; and when the deed was done
I heard among the solitary hills
Low breathings coming after me, and sounds
Of undistinguishable motion, steps
Almost as silent as the turf they trod.
50   Nor less, in spring-time, when on southern banks
The shining sun had from his knot of leaves
Decoyed the primrose-flower, and when the vales
And woods were warm, was I a rover then
In the high places, on the lonesome peaks,
55 Among the mountains and the winds. Though mean
And though inglorious were my views, the end°   result
Was not ignoble. Oh, when I have hung
Above the raven's nest, by knots of grass,
Or half-inch fissures in the slipp'ry rock,
60 But ill sustained, and almost, as it seemed,
Suspended by the blast which blew amain,°   violently
Shouldering the naked crag, oh at that time,
While on the perilous ridge I hung alone,
With what strange utterance did the loud dry wind
65 Blow through my ears! the sky seemed not a sky
Of earth, and with what motion moved the clouds!
      The mind of man is fashioned and built up
Even as a strain of music: I believe
That there are spirits, which, when they would form
70 A favoured being, from his very dawn
Of infancy do open out the clouds
As at the touch of lightning, seeking him

With gentle visitation; quiet Powers!
Retired and seldom recognized, yet kind,
75 And to the very meanest not unknown;
With me, though rarely, in my early days
They communed: others too there are who use,
Yet haply aiming at the self-same end,
Severer interventions, ministry
80 More palpable, and of their school was I.
      They guided me: one evening, led by them,
I went alone into a Shepherd's boat,
A skiff that to a willow-tree was tied
Within a rocky cave, its usual home;
85 The moon was up, the lake was shining clear
Among the hoary mountains: from the shore
I pushed, and struck the oars, and struck again
In cadence, and my little Boat moved on
Just like a man who walks with stately step
90 Though bent on speed. It was an act of stealth
And troubled pleasure; not without the voice
Of mountain-echoes did my boat move on,
Leaving behind her still on either side
Small circles glittering idly in the moon
95 Until they melted all into one track
Of sparkling light. A rocky steep uprose
Above the cavern of the willow tree,
And now, as suited one who proudly rowed
With his best skill, I fixed a steady view
100 Upon the top of that same craggy ridge,
The bound of the horizon, for behind
Was nothing—but the stars and the grey sky.
—She was an elfin pinnace;[2] twenty times
I dipped my oars into the silent lake,
105 And, as I rose upon the stroke, my Boat
Went heaving through the water, like a swan—
When from behind that rocky steep, till then
The bound of the horizon, a huge Cliff,
As if with voluntary power instinct,°   imbued
110 Upreared its head: I struck, and struck again,
And, growing still in stature, the huge cliff
Rose up between me and the stars, and still
With measured motion, like a living thing,

---

[1] *toils* Meaning both "snares" and "labor."

[2] *pinnace* Small boat typically used to service larger vessels.

Strode after me. With trembling hands I turned,
15   And through the silent water stole my way
Back to the cavern of the willow-tree.
There, in her mooring-place I left my bark,°   *boat*
And through the meadows homeward went with grave
And serious thoughts: and after I had seen
20   That spectacle, for many days my brain
Worked with a dim and undetermined sense
Of unknown modes of being: in my thoughts
There was a darkness, call it solitude
Or blank desertion; no familiar shapes
25   Of hourly objects, images of trees,
Of sea or sky, no colours of green fields:
But huge and mighty forms, that do not live
Like living men, moved slowly through my mind
By day, and were the trouble of my dreams.
30   Ah! not in vain ye Beings of the hills!
And ye that walk the woods and open heaths
By moon or star-light, thus from my first dawn
Of childhood did ye love to intertwine
The passions that build up our human soul,
35   Not with the mean and vulgar° works of man,   *ordinary*
But with high objects, with eternal things,
With life and nature, purifying thus
The elements of feeling and of thought,
And sanctifying by such discipline
40   Both pain and fear, until we recognise
A grandeur in the beatings of the heart.
        Nor was this fellowship vouchsafed to me
With stinted kindness. In November days,
When vapours, rolling down the valleys, made
45   A lonely scene more lonesome, among woods
At noon, and 'mid the calm of summer nights
When by the margin of the trembling lake
Beneath the gloomy hills I homeward went
In solitude, such intercourse was mine.
50   And in the frosty season when the sun
Was set, and, visible for many a mile,
The cottage windows through the twilight blazed,
I heeded not the summons: clear and loud
The village clock tolled six; I wheeled about
55   Proud and exulting like an untired horse
That cares not for its home.—All shod with steel

We hissed along the polished ice, in games
Confederate, imitative of the chase
And woodland pleasures, the resounding horn,
160   The pack loud bellowing, and the hunted hare.
So through the darkness and the cold we flew,
And not a voice was idle: with the din,
Meanwhile, the precipices rang aloud,
The leafless trees and every icy crag
165   Tinkled like iron, while the distant hills
Into the tumult sent an alien sound
Of melancholy not unnoticed while the stars,
Eastward, were sparkling clear, and in the west
The orange sky of evening died away.
170   Not seldom from the uproar I retired
Into a silent bay, or sportively
Glanced sideway leaving the tumultuous throng
To cut across the shadow° of a star   *reflection*
That gleamed upon the ice: and oftentimes
175   When we had given our bodies to the wind
And all the shadowy banks on either side
Came sweeping through the darkness, spinning still
The rapid line of motion, then at once
Have I, reclining back upon my heels,
180   Stopped short; yet still the solitary cliffs
Wheeled by me, even as if the earth had rolled
With visible motion her diurnal° round;   *daily*
Behind me did they stretch in solemn train
Feebler and feebler, and I stood and watched
185   Till all was tranquil as a summer sea.
        Ye Powers of earth! ye Genii of the springs!
And ye that have your voices in the clouds
And ye that are Familiars of the lakes
And of the standing pools, I may not think
190   A vulgar hope was yours when ye employed
Such ministry, when ye through many a year
Thus by the agency of boyish sports
On caves and trees, upon the woods and hills,
Impressed upon all forms the characters°   *signs*
195   Of danger or desire, and thus did make
The surface of the universal earth
With meanings of delight, of hope and fear,
Work° like a sea.   *seethe*
            Not uselessly employed

I might pursue this theme through every change
200 Of exercise and sport to which the year
Did summon us in its delightful round.
We were a noisy crew: the sun in heaven
Beheld not vales more beautiful than ours
Nor saw a race in happiness and joy
205 More worthy of the fields where they were sown.
I would record with no reluctant voice
Our home amusements by the warm peat fire
At evening, when with pencil, and with slate
In square divisions parcelled out, and all
210 With crosses and with cyphers scribbled o'er,[1]
We schemed and puzzled, head opposed to head
In strife too humble to be named in verse,
Or round the naked table, snow-white deal,°   pine
Cherry or maple, sat in close array
215 And to the combat—Lu or Whist—led on
A thick-ribbed army,[2] not as in the world
Discarded and ungratefully thrown by
Even for the very service they had wrought,
But husbanded through many a long campaign.
220 Oh with what echoes on the board they fell—
Ironic diamonds, hearts of sable hue,
Queens gleaming through their splendour's last decay,
Knaves wrapt in one assimilating gloom,
And Kings indignant at the shame incurr'd
225 By royal visages. Meanwhile abroad
The heavy rain was falling, or the frost
Raged bitterly with keen and silent tooth,
And interrupting the impassioned game
Oft from the neighbouring lake the splitting ice
230 While it sank down towards the water sent
Among the meadows and the hills its long
And frequent yellings, imitative some
Of wolves that howl along the Bothnic main.[3]
       Nor with less willing heart would I rehearse
235 The woods of autumn and their hidden bowers

With milk-white clusters hung; the rod and line,
True symbol of the foolishness of hope,
Which with its strong enchantment led me on
By rocks and pools where never summer-star
240 Impressed its shadow, to forlorn cascades
Among the windings of the mountain-brooks;
The kite, in sultry calms from some high hill
Sent up, ascending thence till it was lost
Among the fleecy clouds, in gusty days
245 Launched from the lower grounds, and suddenly
Dash'd headlong—and rejected by the storm.
All these and more with rival claims demand
Grateful acknowledgement. It were a song
Venial,° and such as if I rightly judge   pardonable
250 I might protract unblamed; but I perceive
That much is overlooked, and we should ill
Attain our object if from delicate fears
Of breaking in upon the unity
Of this my argument I should omit
255 To speak of such effects as cannot here
Be regularly classed, yet tend no less
To the same point, the growth of mental power
And love of Nature's works.
                                   Ere I had seen
Eight summers (and 'twas in the very week
260 When I was first transplanted to thy vale,
Beloved Hawkshead![4] when thy paths, thy shores
And brooks were like a dream of novelty
To my half-infant mind) I chanced to cross
One of those open fields which, shaped like ears,
265 Make green peninsulas on Esthwaite's lake.
Twilight was coming on, yet through the gloom
I saw distinctly on the opposite shore
Beneath a tree and close by the lake side
A heap of garments, as if left by one
270 Who there was bathing: half an hour I watched
And no one owned them: meanwhile the calm lake
Grew dark with all the shadows on its breast,
And now and then a leaping fish disturbed
The breathless stillness. The succeeding day
275 There came a company, and in their boat

---

[1] *With crosses ... o'er* See Milton's *Paradise Lost* 8.83: "With centric and eccentric scribbled o'er." Here Wordsworth uses this heroic diction to describe a game of tick-tack-toe.

[2] *Lu or Whist* Popular card games; *thick-ribbed army* Pack of cards made of thick cardboard.

[3] *Bothnic main* Gulf of Bothnia, between Sweden and Finland.

[4] *Hawkshead* Where Wordsworth attended grammar school.

Sounded with iron hooks and with long poles.
At length the dead man 'mid that beauteous scene
Of trees, and hills, and water, bolt upright
Rose with his ghastly face.[1] I might advert
280 To numerous accidents in flood or field,
Quarry or moor, or 'mid the winter snows,
Distresses and disasters, tragic facts
Of rural history that impressed my mind
With images, to which in following years
285 Far other feelings were attached, with forms
That yet exist with independent life
And, like their archetypes, know no decay.

There are in our existence spots of time
Which with distinct pre-eminence retain
290 A fructifying virtue,[2] whence, depressed
By trivial occupations and the round
Of ordinary intercourse, our minds
(Especially the imaginative power)
Are nourished, and invisibly repaired.
295 Such moments chiefly seem to have their date
In our first childhood. I remember well
('Tis of an early season that I speak,
The twilight of rememberable life)
While I was yet an urchin, one who scarce
300 Could hold a bridle, with ambitious hopes
I mounted, and we rode towards the hills;
We were a pair of horsemen: honest James[3]
Was with me, my encourager and guide.
We had not travelled long ere some mischance
305 Disjoined me from my comrade, and through fear
Dismounting, down the rough and stony moor
I led my horse and, stumbling on, at length
Came to a bottom where in former times
A man, the murderer of his wife, was hung
310 In irons; mouldered° was the gibbet[4] mast,   *decayed*
The bones were gone, the iron and the wood,

Only a long green ridge of turf remained
Whose shape was like a grave. I left the spot,
And, reascending the bare slope, I saw
315 A naked pool that lay beneath the hills,
The beacon on the summit, and more near
A girl who bore a pitcher on her head
And seemed with difficult steps to force her way
Against the blowing wind. It was in truth
320 An ordinary sight but I should need
Colours and words that are unknown to man
To paint the visionary dreariness
Which, while I looked all round for my lost guide,
Did, at that time, invest the naked pool,
325 The beacon on the lonely eminence,
The woman and her garments vexed and tossed
By the strong wind. Nor less I recollect
(Long after, though my childhood had not ceased)
Another scene which left a kindred power
330 Implanted in my mind.

One Christmas time,
The day before the holidays began,
Feverish, and tired and restless, I went forth
Into the fields, impatient for the sight
Of those three horses which should bear us home,
335 My Brothers and myself. There was a crag,
An eminence which from the meeting point
Of two highways ascending overlooked
At least a long half-mile of those two roads,
By each of which the expected steeds might come,
340 The choice uncertain. Thither I repaired
Up to the highest summit; 'twas a day
Stormy, and rough, and wild, and on the grass
I sat, half-sheltered by a naked wall;
Upon my right hand was a single sheep,
345 A whistling hawthorn on my left, and there,
Those two companions at my side, I watched
With eyes intensely straining as the mist
Gave intermitting prospects of the wood
And plain beneath. Ere I to school returned
350 That dreary time, ere I had been ten days
A dweller in my Father's house, he died,[5]

---

[1] *At length ... face* In June 1779, shortly after Wordsworth arrived at Hawkshead, a schoolmaster from a neighboring village drowned while swimming in Esthwaite Water.

[2] *fructifying virtue* I.e., power to make fruitful.

[3] *honest James* Most likely the family's servant.

[4] *gibbet* Structure similar to a gallows from which the bodies of people sentenced to execution are suspended, often inside a metal cage.

[5] *ere I ... died* Wordsworth's father died on 30 December 1783. His mother had died five years earlier.

And I and my two Brothers, orphans then,
Followed his body to the grave. The event
With all the sorrow which it brought appeared
355 A chastisement, and when I called to mind
That day so lately passed when from the crag
I looked in such anxiety of hope,
With trite reflections of morality
Yet with the deepest passion I bowed low
360 To God, who thus corrected my desires;
And afterwards the wind, and sleety rain,
And all the business of the elements,
The single sheep, and the one blasted tree,
And the bleak music of that old stone wall,
365 The noise of wood and water, and the mist
Which on the line of each of those two roads
Advanced in such indisputable shapes,
All these were spectacles and sounds to which
I often would repair, and thence would drink
370 As at a fountain, and I do not doubt
That in this later time when storm and rain
Beat on my roof at midnight, or by day
When I am in the woods, unknown to me
The workings of my spirit thence are brought.
375   Nor sedulous° as I have been to trace   *diligent*
How Nature by collateral° interest   *indirect*
And by extrinsic passion peopled first
My mind with forms, or beautiful or grand,
And made me love them, may I well forget
380 How other pleasures have been mine, and joys
Of subtler origin, how I have felt
Not seldom, even in that tempestuous time,
Those hallowed and pure motions of the sense
Which seem in their simplicity to own
385 An intellectual charm, that calm delight
Which, if I err not, surely must belong
To those first-born affinities that fit
Our new existence to existing things
And in our dawn of being constitute
390 The bond of union betwixt life and joy.
    Yes, I remember when the changeful earth
And twice five seasons on my mind had stamped
The faces of the moving year, even then,
A Child, I held unconscious intercourse

395 With the eternal Beauty, drinking in
A pure organic pleasure from the lines
Of curling mist or from the level plain
Of waters coloured by the steady clouds.
    The sands of Westmoreland, the creeks and bays
400 Of Cumbria's[1] rocky limits, they can tell
How when the sea threw off his evening shade
And to the Shepherd's hut beneath the crags
Did send sweet notice of the rising moon,
How I have stood to images like these
405 A stranger, linking with the spectacle
No body of associated forms
And bringing with me no peculiar sense
Of quietness or peace, yet I have stood
Even while my eye has moved o'er three long leagues
410 Of shining water, gathering, as it seemed,
Through the wide surface of that field of light
New pleasure, like a bee among the flowers.
    Thus often in those fits of vulgar joy
Which through all seasons on a child's pursuits
415 Are prompt attendants, 'mid that giddy bliss
Which like a tempest works along the blood
And is forgotten, even then I felt
Gleams like the flashing of a shield; the earth
And common face of Nature spake to me
420 Rememberable things: sometimes, 'tis true,
By quaint associations, yet not vain
Nor profitless if haply° they impressed   *by chance*
Collateral[2] objects and appearances,
Albeit lifeless then, and doomed to sleep
425 Until maturer seasons called them forth
To impregnate and to elevate the mind
——And if the vulgar joy by its own weight
Wearied itself out of the memory,
The scenes which were a witness of that joy
430 Remained, in their substantial lineaments
Depicted on the brain, and to the eye
Were visible, a daily sight: and thus
By the impressive agency of fear,

---

[1] *Westmoreland ... Cumbria* Westmorland and Cumbria (usually called "Cumberland") were counties in the Lake District.

[2] *Collateral* I.e., indirect, lying aside from the main interests of the poet.

By pleasure and repeated happiness,
35 So frequently repeated, and by force
Of obscure feelings representative
Of joys that were forgotten, these same scenes
So beauteous and majestic in themselves,
Though yet the day was distant, did at length
40 Become habitually dear, and all
Their hues and forms were by invisible links
Allied to the affections.
                 I began
My story early, feeling, as I fear,
The weakness of a human love for days
45 Disowned by memory, ere the birth of spring
Planting my snow-drops among winter snows.
Nor will it seem to thee, my Friend,[1] so prompt
In sympathy, that I have lengthened out
With fond and feeble tongue a tedious tale.
50 Meanwhile my hope has been that I might fetch
Reproaches from my former years, whose power
May spur me on, in manhood now mature,
To honourable toil. Yet, should it be
That this is but an impotent desire,
55 That I by such inquiry am not taught
To understand myself, nor thou to know
With better knowledge how the heart was framed
Of him thou lovest, need I dread from thee
Harsh judgements if I am so loath to quit
60 Those recollected hours that have the charm
Of visionary things,[2] and lovely forms
And sweet sensations that throw back our life
And make our infancy a visible scene
On which the sun is shining?

SECOND PART

Thus far my Friend, have we retraced the way
Through which I travelled when I first began
To love the woods and fields: the passion yet
Was in its birth, sustained as might befall
5 By nourishment that came unsought, for still

From week to week, from month to month, we lived
A round of tumult: duly° were our games   *fittingly*
Prolonged in summer till the day-light failed;
No chair remained before the doors, the bench
10 And threshold steps were empty, fast asleep
The labourer and the old man who had sat
A later lingerer, yet the revelry
Continued and the loud uproar: at last
When all the ground was dark, and the huge clouds
15 Were edged with twinkling stars, to bed we went
With weary joints and with a beating mind.
Ah! is there one who ever has been young
And needs a monitory voice to tame
The pride of virtue and of intellect,
20 And is there one, the wisest and the best
Of all mankind, who does not sometimes wish
For things which cannot be, who would not give,
If so he might, to duty and to truth
The eagerness of infantine desire?
25 A tranquillizing spirit presses now
On my corporeal frame, so wide appears
The vacancy between me and those days
Which yet have such self-presence in my heart
That sometimes when I think of them I seem
30 Two consciousnesses, conscious of myself
And of some other being. A grey stone
Of native rock, left midway in the square
Of our small market-village, was the home
And centre of these joys, and when, returned
35 After long absence, thither I repaired,
I found that it was split and gone to build
A smart assembly-room that perked and flared
With wash and rough-cast,[3] elbowing the ground
Which had been ours. But let the fiddle scream
40 And be ye happy! yet I know, my Friends,
That more than one of you will think with me
Of those soft starry nights and that old dame
From whom the stone was named, who there had sat
And watched her table with its huckster's wares,
45 Assiduous, for the length of sixty years.
    —We ran a boisterous race, the year span round

---

[1] *my Friend*   Coleridge.

[2] *visionary things*   Things seen in the imagination.

[3] *smart assembly-room*   Hawkshead Town Hall, built in 1790; *wash* Whitewash; *rough-cast*   Plaster made of lime and gravel.

With giddy motion. But the time approached
That brought with it a regular desire
For calmer pleasures, when the beauteous scenes
50 Of nature were collaterally attached
To every scheme of holiday delight
And every boyish sport, less grateful° else   *pleasing*
And languidly pursued.
                              When summer came
It was the pastime of our afternoons
55 To beat along the plain of Windermere
With rival oars; and the selected bourn°   *goal*
Was now an island musical with birds
That sang for ever, now a sister isle
Beneath the oak's umbrageous° covert sown   *shady*
60 With lilies of the valley like a field,
And now a third small island[1] where remained
An old stone table and one mouldered cave,
A hermit's history. In such a race,
So ended, disappointment could be none,
65 Uneasiness, or pain, or jealousy;
We rested in the shade all pleased alike,
Conquered and conqueror. Thus our selfishness
Was mellowed down, and thus the pride of strength
And the vain-glory of superior skill
70 Were interfused with objects which subdued
And tempered them, and gradually produced
A quiet independence of the heart.
And to my Friend who knows me I may add,
Unapprehensive of reproof, that hence
75 Ensued a diffidence and modesty,
And I was taught to feel, perhaps too much,
The self-sufficing power of solitude.
        No delicate viands sapped our bodily strength;
More than we wished we knew the blessing then
80 Of vigorous hunger, for our daily meals
Were frugal, Sabine fare![2] and then exclude
A little weekly stipend, and we lived

Through three divisions of the quartered year
In penniless poverty. But now to school
85 Returned from the half-yearly holidays,
We came with purses more profusely filled,
Allowance which abundantly sufficed
To gratify the palate with repasts
More costly than the Dame of whom I spake,
90 That ancient woman, and her board° supplied,   *table*
Hence inroads into distant vales, and long
Excursions far away among the hills;
Hence rustic dinners on the cool green ground
Or in the woods or by a river-side
95 Or fountain,° festive banquets that provoked   *spring*
The languid action° of a natural scene   *effect*
By pleasure of corporeal appetite.
        Nor is my aim neglected if I tell
How twice in the long length of those half-years
100 We from our funds perhaps with bolder hand
Drew largely, anxious for one day at least
To feel the motion of the galloping steed;
And with the good old Innkeeper in truth
I needs must say that sometimes we have used
105 Sly subterfuge, for the intended bound
Of the day's journey was too distant far
For any cautious man, a Structure famed
Beyond its neighbourhood, the antique walls
Of a large Abbey[3] with its fractured arch,
110 Belfry, and images, and living trees,
A holy scene! Along the smooth green turf
Our horses grazed: in more than inland peace
Left by the winds that overpass the vale
In that sequestered ruin trees and towers
115 Both silent, and both motionless alike,
Hear all day long the murmuring sea that beats
Incessantly upon a craggy shore.
        Our steeds remounted, and the summons given,
With whip and spur we by the Chantry[4] flew
120 In uncouth race, and left the cross-legged Knight
And the stone Abbot, and that single wren

---

[1] *third small island* Island of Lady Holm, where a chapel dedicated
to the Virgin Mary was formerly located.

[2] *Sabine fare* The Sabines were an ancient Italian mountain tribe
known for their austere living habits. "Sabine fare" may also refer to
the sort of rustic food that would have been prepared at the Roman
poet Horace's country estate, often called the "Sabine farm."

[3] *a large Abbey* Furness Abbey, a ruined abbey located approximately
25 miles south of Hawkshead.

[4] *Chantry* Altar or chapel which has been endowed for daily masses
to be sung for the donor.

Which one day sang so sweetly in the nave
Of the old church that, though from recent showers
The earth was comfortless, and touched by faint
Internal breezes from the roofless walls
The shuddering ivy dripped large drops, yet still
So sweetly 'mid the gloom the invisible bird
Sang to itself that there I could have made
My dwelling-place, and lived for ever there
To hear such music. Through the walls we flew
And down the valley, and, a circuit made
In wantonness of heart, through rough and smooth
We scampered homeward. O ye rocks and streams
And that still spirit of the evening air,
Even in this joyous time I sometimes felt
Your presence, when with slackened step we breathed[1]
Along the sides of the steep hills, or when,
Lightened by gleams of moonlight from the sea,
We beat with thundering hoofs the level sand.

    There was a row of ancient trees, since fallen,
That on the margin of a jutting land
Stood near the lake of Coniston and made
With its long boughs above the water stretched
A gloom through which a boat might sail along
As in a cloister. An old Hall[2] was near,
Grotesque and beautiful, its gavel° end   *gable*
And huge round chimneys to the top o'ergrown
With fields of ivy. Thither we repaired,
'Twas even a custom with us, to the shore
And to that cool piazza. They who dwelt
In the neglected mansion-house supplied
Fresh butter, tea-kettle, and earthen-ware,
And chafing-dish with smoking coals, and so
Beneath the trees we sat in our small boat
And in the covert eat° our delicate meal   *ate*
Upon the calm smooth lake. It was a joy
Worthy the heart of one who is full grown
To rest beneath those horizontal boughs
And mark the radiance of the setting sun,
Himself unseen, reposing on the top
Of the high eastern hills. And there I said,
That beauteous sight before me, there I said

(Then first beginning in my thoughts to mark
That sense of dim similitude which links
165 Our moral feelings with external forms)
That in whatever region I should close
My mortal life I would remember you,
Fair scenes! that dying I would think on you,
My soul would send a longing look to you:
170 Even as that setting sun while all the vale
Could nowhere catch one faint memorial gleam
Yet with the last remains of his last light
Still lingered, and a farewell lustre threw
On the dear mountain-tops where first he rose.
175 'Twas then my fourteenth summer, and these words
Were uttered in a casual access
Of sentiment, a momentary trance
That far outran the habit of my mind.
    Upon the eastern shore of Windermere,
180 Above the crescent of a pleasant bay,
There was an Inn,[3] no homely-featured shed,
Brother of the surrounding cottages,
But 'twas a splendid place, the door beset
With chaises, grooms, and liveries, and within
185 Decanters, glasses, and the blood-red wine.
In ancient times, or ere the Hall[4] was built
On the large island, had the dwelling been
More worthy of a poet's love, a hut
Proud of its one bright fire and sycamore shade.
190 But though the rhymes were gone which once inscribed
The threshold, and large golden characters
On the blue-frosted sign-board had usurped
The place of the old Lion in contempt
And mockery of the rustic painter's hand,
195 Yet to this hour the spot to me is dear
With all its foolish pomp. The garden lay
Upon a slope surmounted by the plain
Of a small bowling-green; beneath us stood
A grove, with gleams of water through the trees
200 And over the tree-tops; nor did we want
Refreshment, strawberries and mellow cream,
And there through half an afternoon we played

---

[1] *breathed* I.e., let the horses catch their breath.

[2] *old Hall* Coniston Hall, built in 1580.

---

[3] *an Inn* The White Lion Inn, which was located in Bowness Village.

[4] *the Hall* Built on Belle Isle in Lake Windermere in the early 1780s.

On the smooth platform, and the shouts we sent
Made all the mountains ring. But ere the fall
205 Of night, when in our pinnace we returned
Over the dusky lake, and to the beach
Of some small island steered our course with one,
The minstrel of our troop, and left him there
And rowed off gently while he blew his flute
210 Alone upon the rock—oh then the calm
And dead still water lay upon my mind
Even with a weight of pleasure, and the sky,
Never before so beautiful, sank down
Into my heart and held me like a dream.
215   Thus day by day my sympathies increased
And thus the common range of visible things
Grew dear to me: already I began
To love the sun, a Boy I loved the sun
Not, as I since have loved him, as a pledge
220 And surety of my earthly life, a light
Which while I view I feel I am alive,
But for this cause, that I had seen him lay
His beauty on the morning hills, had seen
The western mountain touch his setting orb
225 In many a thoughtless hour, when from excess
Of happiness my blood appeared to flow
With its own pleasure and I breathed with joy.
And from like feelings, humble though intense,
To patriotic and domestic love
230 Analogous, the moon to me was dear,
For I would dream away my purposes
Standing to look upon her while she hung
Midway between the hills as if she knew
No other region but belonged to thee,
235 Yea, appertained by a peculiar right
To thee and thy grey huts,[1] my native vale.
    Those incidental charms which first attached
My heart to rural objects day by day
Grew weaker, and I hasten on to tell
240 How nature, intervenient° till this time   extraneous
And secondary, now at length was sought
For her own sake. But who shall parcel out
His intellect by geometric rules,

---
[1] *grey huts* Gray stone cottages.

Split like a province into round and square;
245 Who knows the individual hour in which
His habits were first sown, even as a seed;
Who that shall point as with a wand and say,
This portion of the river of my mind
Came from yon fountain? Thou, my Friend, art one
250 More deeply read in thy own thoughts, no slave
Of that false secondary power by which
In weakness we create distinctions, then
Believe our puny boundaries are things
Which we perceive and not which we have made.
255 To thee, unblinded by these outward shows,
The unity of all has been revealed,
And thou wilt doubt with me, less aptly skilled
Than many are to class the cabinet
Of their sensations and in voluble phrase
260 Run through the history and birth of each
As of a single independent thing.
Hard task to analyse a soul in which
Not only general habits and desires
But each most obvious and particular thought,
265 Not in a mystical and idle sense
But in the words of reason deeply weighed,
Hath no beginning.
                Bless'd the infant Babe
(For with my best conjectures I would trace
The progress of our being) blest the Babe
270 Nursed in his Mother's arms, the Babe who sleeps
Upon his Mother's breast, who when his soul
Claims manifest kindred with an earthly soul
Doth gather passion from his Mother's eye!
Such feelings pass into his torpid life
275 Like an awakening breeze, and hence his mind
Even in the first trial of its powers
Is prompt and watchful, eager to combine
In one appearance all the elements
And parts of the same object, else detached
280 And loath to coalesce. Thus day by day
Subjected to the discipline of love
His organs and recipient faculties
Are quickened, are more vigorous, his mind spreads
Tenacious of the forms which it receives.
285 In one beloved presence, nay, and more,

In that most apprehensive habitude[1]
And those sensations which have been derived
From this beloved presence, there exists
A virtue which irradiates and exalts
All objects through all intercourse of sense.
No outcast he, bewildered and depressed:
Along his infant veins are interfused
The gravitation and the filial bond
Of nature that connect him with the world.
Emphatically such a being lives
An inmate of this *active* universe;
From nature largely he receives, nor so
Is satisfied but largely gives again,
For feeling has to him imparted strength,
And powerful in all sentiments of grief,
Of exultation, fear and joy, his mind,
Even as an agent of the one great mind,
Creates, creator and receiver both,
Working but in alliance with the works
Which it beholds. Such verily is the first
Poetic spirit of our human life,
By uniform control of after years
In most abated and suppressed, in some
Through every change of growth or of decay
Preeminent till death.
          From early days,
Beginning not long after that first time
In which, a Babe, by intercourse of touch
I held mute dialogues with my Mother's heart,
I have endeavoured to display the means
Whereby this infant sensibility,
Great birth-right of our being, was in me
Augmented and sustained. Yet is a path
More difficult before me, and I fear
That in its broken windings we shall need
The Chamois'[2] sinews and the Eagle's wing:
For now a trouble came into my mind
From obscure causes. I was left alone
Seeking this visible world, nor knowing why:

The props of my affections were removed[3]
325 And yet the building stood as if sustained
By its own spirit. All that I beheld
Was dear to me, and from this cause it came
That now to Nature's finer influxes°   *influences*
My mind lay open, to that more exact
330 And intimate communion which our hearts
Maintain with the minuter properties
Of objects which already are beloved,
And of those only. Many are the joys
Of youth, but oh! what happiness to live
335 When every hour brings palpable access
Of knowledge, when all knowledge is delight,
And sorrow is not there. The seasons came
And every season brought a countless store
Of modes and temporary qualities
340 Which but for this most watchful power of love
Had been neglected, left a register
Of permanent relations, else unknown:
Hence life, and change, and beauty, solitude
More active even than "best society,"[4]
345 Society made sweet as solitude
By silent inobtrusive sympathies
And gentle agitations of the mind
From manifold distinctions, difference
Perceived in things where to the common eye
350 No difference is: and hence from the same source
Sublimer joy; for I would walk alone
In storm and tempest or in starlight nights
Beneath the quiet heavens, and at that time
Would feel whate'er there is of power in sound
355 To breathe an elevated mood by form
Or image unprofaned: and I would stand
Beneath some rock listening to sounds that are
The ghostly language of the ancient earth
Or make their dim abode in distant winds.
360 Thence did I drink the visionary power.
I deem not profitless these fleeting moods
Of shadowy exaltation, not for this,

---

1 *apprehensive habitude* Disposition most suited to learning.

2 *Chamois* Agile goat-antelope found primarily in the mountains of Europe.

---

3 *The props ... removed* Wordsworth's mother died just before his eighth birthday.

4 *best society* See Milton's *Paradise Lost* 9.249: "For solitude sometimes is the best society."

That they are kindred to our purer mind
And intellectual life, but that the soul
365 Remembering how she felt, but what she felt
Remembering not, retains an obscure sense
Of possible sublimity to which
With growing faculties she doth aspire,
With faculties still growing, feeling still
370 That whatsoever point they gain, they still
Have something to pursue.

                              And not alone
In grandeur and in tumult, but no less
In tranquil scenes, that universal power
And fitness in the latent qualities
375 And essences of things, by which the mind
Is moved with feelings of delight, to me
Came strengthened with a superadded soul,
A virtue not its own. My morning walks
Were early; oft before the hours of school
380 I travelled round our little lake, five miles
Of pleasant wandering, happy time more dear
For this, that one was by my side, a Friend
Then passionately loved;[1] with heart how full
Will he peruse these lines, this page, perhaps
385 A blank to other men, for many years
Have since flowed in between us, and, our minds
Both silent to each other, at this time
We live as if those hours had never been.
Nor seldom did I lift our cottage latch
390 Far earlier, and before the vernal° thrush   *spring-time*
Was audible, among the hills I sat
Alone upon some jutting eminence
At the first hour of morning when the vale
Lay quiet in an utter solitude.
395 How shall I trace the history, where seek
The origin of what I then have felt?
Oft in those moments such a holy calm
Did overspread my soul that I forgot
The agency of sight, and what I saw
400 Appeared like something in myself—a dream,
A prospect° in my mind. 'Twere long to tell   *view*
What spring and autumn, what the winter-snows

---

[1] *Friend ... passionately loved* John Fleming, Wordsworth's friend at
Hawkshead.

And what the summer-shade, what day and night,
The evening and the morning, what my dreams
405 And what my waking thoughts supplied, to nurse
That spirit of religious love in which
I walked with nature. But let this at least
Be not forgotten, that I still retained
My first creative sensibility,
410 That by the regular action of the world
My soul was unsubdued. A plastic° power   *formative*
Abode with me, a forming hand, at times
Rebellious, acting in a devious mood,
A local spirit of its own, at war
415 With general tendency, but for the most
Subservient strictly to the external things
With which it communed. An auxiliar light
Came from my mind which on the setting sun
Bestowed new splendour, the melodious birds,
420 The gentle breezes, fountains that ran on
Murmuring so sweetly in themselves, obeyed
A like dominion, and the midnight storm
Grew darker in the presence of my eye.
Hence my obeisance, my devotion hence,
425 And *hence* my transport.°   *exaltation*
                              Nor should this perchance
Pass unrecorded, that I still° had loved   *always*
The exercise and produce of a toil
Than analytic industry to me
More pleasing, and whose character, I deem,
430 Is more poetic, as resembling more
Creative agency: I mean to speak
Of that interminable building reared
By observation of affinities
In objects where no brotherhood exists
435 To common minds. My seventeenth year was come,
And whether from this habit rooted now
So deeply in my mind, or from excess
Of the great social principle of life
Coercing all things into sympathy,
440 To unorganic natures I transferred
My own enjoyments, or, the power of truth
Coming in revelation, I conversed
With things that really are. I at this time
Saw blessings spread around me like a sea.

Thus did my days pass on, and now at length
From Nature and her overflowing soul
I had received so much that all my thoughts
Were steeped in feeling; I was only then
Contented when with bliss ineffable
I felt the sentiment of being spread
O'er all that moves, and all that seemeth still,
O'er all that, lost beyond the reach of thought
And human knowledge, to the human eye
Invisible, yet liveth to the heart,
O'er all that leaps, and runs, and shouts and sings
Or beats the gladsome air, o'er all that glides
Beneath the wave, yea, in the wave itself
And mighty depth of waters: wonder not
If such my transports were, for in all things
I saw one life and felt that it was joy.
One song they sang, and it was audible,
Most audible then when the fleshly ear,
O'ercome by grosser prelude of that strain,
Forgot its functions, and slept undisturbed.

If this be error, and another faith
Find easier access to the pious mind,
Yet were I grossly destitute of all
Those human sentiments which make this earth
So dear, if I should fail with grateful voice
To speak of you, ye mountains! and ye lakes
And sounding cataracts! ye mists and winds
That dwell among the hills where I was born.
If, in my youth, I have been pure in heart,
If, mingling with the world, I am content
With my own modest pleasures, and have lived
With God and Nature communing, removed
From little enmities and low desires,
The gift is yours: if in these times[1] of fear,
This melancholy waste° of hopes o'erthrown,   wasteland
If, 'mid indifference and apathy
And wicked exultation, when good men

On every side fall off we know not how
To selfishness disguised in gentle names
Of peace, and quiet, and domestic love,
485 Yet mingled, not unwillingly, with sneers
On visionary minds, if in this time
Of dereliction and dismay I yet
Despair not of our nature, but retain
A more than Roman confidence, a faith
490 That fails not, in all sorrow my support,
The blessing of my life, the gift is yours,
Ye Mountains! thine, O Nature! thou hast fed
My lofty speculations, and in thee
For this uneasy heart of ours I find
495 A never-failing principle of joy
And purest passion.

Thou, my Friend, wast reared
In the great city 'mid far other scenes,[2]
But we, by different roads, at length have gained
The self-same bourne. And from this cause to thee
500 I speak unapprehensive of contempt,
The insinuated scoff of coward tongues,
And all that silent language which so oft
In conversation betwixt man and man
Blots from the human countenance all trace
505 Of beauty and of love. For thou hast sought
The truth in solitude, and thou art one,
The most intense of Nature's worshippers,
In many things my brother, chiefly here
In this my deep devotion.

Fare thee well!
510 Health and the quiet of a healthful mind
Attend thee! seeking oft the haunts of men
But yet more often living with thyself
And for thyself, so haply shall thy days
Be many and a blessing to mankind.
—1799

[1] *in these times* I.e., following the failure of the French Revolution, by which time many radicals were recanting. In a 1799 letter to Wordsworth, Coleridge asks him to write something about those who "have thrown up all hopes of the amelioration of mankind, and are sinking into an almost epicurean selfishness, disguising the same under the soft titles of domestic attachment and contempt for visionary *philosophes*."

[2] *Thou ... other scenes* See Coleridge's "Frost at Midnight" 50–52, in which the speaker addresses his child: "thou shalt learn far other lore, / And in far other scenes! For I was reared / In the great city, pent 'mid cloisters dim."

from The Fourteen-Book *Prelude* (1850)

BOOK FIRST
INTRODUCTION, CHILDHOOD, AND SCHOOL-TIME

O there is blessing in this gentle breeze,
  A visitant that while he fans my cheek
Doth seem half-conscious of the joy it brings
From the green fields, and from yon azure sky.
5 Whate'er its mission, the soft breeze can come
To none more grateful than to me; escaped
From the vast city,[1] where I long had pined
A discontented sojourner: now free,
Free as a bird to settle where I will.
10 What dwelling shall receive me? in what vale
Shall be my harbour? underneath what grove
Shall I take up my home? and what clear stream
Shall with its murmur lull me into rest?
The earth is all before me.[2] With a heart
15 Joyous, nor scared at its own liberty,
I look about; and should the chosen guide
Be nothing better than a wandering cloud,
I cannot miss my way. I breathe again!
Trances of thought and mountings of the mind
20 Come fast upon me: it is shaken off,
That burthen of my own unnatural self,
The heavy weight of many a weary day
Not mine, and such as were not made for me.
Long months of peace (if such bold word accord
25 With any promises of human life),
Long months of ease and undisturbed delight
Are mine in prospect; whither shall I turn
By road or pathway, or through trackless field,
Up hill or down, or shall some floating thing
30 Upon the river point me out my course?

    Dear Liberty! Yet what would it avail
But for a gift that consecrates the joy?
For I, methought, while the sweet breath of heaven

Was blowing on my body, felt within
35 A correspondent breeze, that gently moved
With quickening virtue, but is now become
A tempest, a redundant° energy,   *abounding*
Vexing its own creation. Thanks to both,
And their congenial powers, that, while they join
40 In breaking up a long-continued frost,
Bring with them vernal° promises, the hope *spring-time*
Of active days urged on by flying hours—
Days of sweet leisure, taxed with patient thought
Abstruse, nor wanting° punctual[3] service high, *lacking*
45 Matins and vespers,[4] of harmonious verse!

    Thus far, O Friend![5] did I, not used to make
A present joy the matter of a song,
Pour forth that day my soul in measured strains
That would not be forgotten, and are here
50 Recorded: to the open fields I told
A prophecy: poetic numbers° came   *verses*
Spontaneously to clothe in priestly robe
A renovated spirit singled out,
Such hope was mine, for holy services.
55 My own voice cheered me, and, far more, the mind's
Internal echo of the imperfect sound;
To both I listened, drawing from them both
A cheerful confidence in things to come.

    Content, and not unwilling now to give
60 A respite to this passion, I paced on
With brisk and eager steps; and came at length,
To a green shady place, where down I sat
Beneath a tree, slackening my thoughts by choice,
And settling into gentler happiness.
65 'Twas autumn, and a clear and placid day,
With warmth, as much as needed, from a sun
Two hours declined towards the west; a day
With silver clouds, and sunshine on the grass,
And in the sheltered and the sheltering grove
70 A perfect stillness. Many were the thoughts

---

1 *the vast city* I.e., London.

2 *The earth … me* See Milton's *Paradise Lost* 12.646. Milton writes that following the expulsion of Adam and Eve from Eden, "The world was all before them."

3 *punctual* Appropriately timed.

4 *Matins and vespers* Morning and evening prayer services, respectively.

5 *O Friend* The addressee is Samuel Taylor Coleridge.

Encouraged and dismissed, till choice was made
Of a known Vale,[1] whither my feet should turn,
Nor rest till they had reached the very door
Of the one cottage which methought I saw.
No picture of mere memory ever looked
So fair; and while upon the fancied scene
I gazed with growing love, a higher power
Than Fancy gave assurance of some work
Of glory there forthwith to be begun,
Perhaps too there performed.[2] Thus long I mused,
Nor e'er lost sight of what I mused upon,
Save when, amid the stately grove of oaks,
Now here, now there, an acorn, from its cup
Dislodged, through sere leaves rustled, or at once
To the bare earth dropped with a startling sound.
From that soft couch I rose not, till the sun
Had almost touched the horizon; casting then
A backward glance upon the curling cloud
Of city smoke, by distance ruralized;
Keen as a Truant or a Fugitive,
But as a Pilgrim resolute, I took,
Even with the chance equipment of that hour
The road that pointed toward the chosen Vale.
It was a splendid evening, and my Soul
Once more made trial of her strength, nor lacked
Æolian visitations;[3] but the harp
Was soon defrauded, and the banded host
Of harmony dispersed in straggling sounds,
And lastly utter silence! "Be it so;
Why think of any thing but present good?"
So, like a home-bound labourer I pursued
My way beneath the mellowing sun, that shed
Mild influence;[4] nor left in me one wish

105 Again to bend the Sabbath[5] of that time
To a servile yoke. What need of many words?
A pleasant loitering journey, through three days
Continued, brought me to my hermitage.
I spare to tell of what ensued, the life
110 In common things—the endless store of things,
Rare, or at least so seeming every day
Found all about me in one neighbourhood—
The self-congratulation,[6] and, from morn
To night, unbroken cheerfulness serene.
115 But speedily an earnest longing rose
To brace myself to some determined aim,
Reading or thinking; either to lay up
New stores, or rescue from decay the old
By timely interference: and therewith
120 Came hopes still higher, that with outward life
I might endue some airy phantasies
That had been floating loose about for years,
And to such beings temperately deal forth
The many feelings that oppressed my heart.
That hope hath been discouraged; welcome light
125 Dawns from the East, but dawns to disappear
And mock me with a sky that ripens not
Into a steady morning: if my mind,
Remembering the bold promise of the past,
Would gladly grapple with some noble theme,
130 Vain is her wish: where'er she turns she finds
Impediments from day to day renewed.

And now it would content me to yield up
Those lofty hopes awhile, for present gifts
Of humbler industry. But, oh, dear Friend!
135 The Poet, gentle creature as he is,
Hath, like the Lover, his unruly times;
His fits when he is neither sick nor well,
Though no distress be near him but his own
Unmanageable thoughts: his mind, best pleased
140 While she, as duteous as the mother dove,

---

[1] *a known Vale*   Grasmere, where Wordsworth and his sister moved in 1799.

[2] *some work ... performed*   A planned poem, *The Recluse*, which was intended to be Wordsworth's major work. *The Prelude* was intended to be the first third of *The Recluse*; most of the rest was never written.

[3] *Æolian visitations*   Influences that act on the poet's soul as winds act on an Aeolian harp, which makes music when touched by a breeze.

[4] *influence*   Reference to astrological influence, exerted by the stars over human life.

---

[5] *Sabbath*   Time of rest, especially one of religious significance.

[6] *self-congratulation*   Self-rejoicing.

Sits brooding,[1] lives not always to that end,
But, like the innocent bird, hath goadings on
That drive her as in trouble through the groves;
With me is now such passion, to be blamed
145 No otherwise than as it lasts too long.

When, as becomes a Man who would prepare
For such an arduous work, I through myself
Make rigorous inquisition, the report
Is often cheering; for I neither seem
150 To lack that first great gift, the vital soul,
Nor general Truths, which are themselves a sort
Of Elements and Agents, Under-powers,
Subordinate helpers of the living mind:
Nor am I naked of external things,
155 Forms, images, nor numerous other aids
Of less regard, though won perhaps with toil
And needful to build up a Poet's praise.
Time, place, and manners° do I seek, and these   *habits*
Are found in plenteous store, but nowhere such
160 As may be singled out with steady choice;
No little band of yet remembered names
Whom I, in perfect confidence, might hope
To summon back from lonesome banishment,
And make them dwellers in the hearts of men
165 Now living, or to live in future years.
Sometimes the ambitious Power of choice, mistaking
Proud spring-tide swellings for a regular sea,
Will settle on some British theme, some old
Romantic tale by Milton left unsung;[2]
170 More often turning to some gentle place
Within the groves of Chivalry, I pipe
To shepherd swains,° or seated, harp in hand,   *lovers*
Amid reposing knights by a river side
Or fountain, listen to the grave reports
175 Of dire enchantments faced and overcome
By the strong mind, and tales of warlike feats,
Where spear encountered spear, and sword with sword

Fought, as if conscious of the blazonry
That the shield bore, so glorious was the strife;
180 Whence inspiration for a song that winds
Through ever changing scenes of votive quest[3]
Wrongs to redress, harmonious tribute paid
To patient courage and unblemished truth,
To firm devotion, zeal unquenchable,
185 And Christian meekness hallowing faithful loves.[4]
Sometimes, more sternly moved, I would relate
How vanquished Mithridates northward passed,
And, hidden in the cloud of years, became
Odin, the Father of a race by whom
190 Perished the Roman Empire:[5] how the friends
And followers of Sertorius,[6] out of Spain
Flying, found shelter in the Fortunate Isles;
And left their usages, their arts and laws,
To disappear by a slow gradual death,
195 To dwindle and to perish one by one,
Starved in those narrow bounds: but not the soul
Of Liberty, which fifteen hundred years
Survived, and, when the European came
With skill and power that might not be withstood,
200 Did, like a pestilence, maintain its hold
And wasted down by glorious death that race
Of natural heroes: or I would record
How, in tyrannic times, some high-souled man,
Unnamed among the chronicles of kings,
205 Suffered in silence for Truth's sake: or tell

---

1 *While she ... brooding* See Milton's *Paradise Lost* 1.21–22, in which the narrator invokes the Holy Spirit, who, at the time of Creation, "Dovelike satst brooding on the vast Abyss / And madst it pregnant."

2 *some old ... unsung* In *Paradise Lost* 9.24–41, Milton writes that he chose to compose a biblical rather than a romantic epic.

3 *votive quest* Quest undertaken as the result of a vow.

4 *And Christian ... loves* Reference to Spenser's *Faerie Queene* 1.1.9: "Fierce warres and faithful loves shall moralize my song."

5 *How vanquished ... Empire* Mithridates was a king of Pontus (in present-day Turkey) who was defeated by the Romans in 66 BCE. In *Decline and Fall of the Roman Empire* (1776–88), Edward Gibbon associates the story of King Mithridates's downfall with the unsubstantiated tale of Odin, a chieftain who led his tribe out of Asia to establish the first European settlement of Goths. In the early fifth century CE, Goths played a major role in the fall of the Roman Empire.

6 *Sertorius* Roman general and ally of Mithridates who conquered much of Spain but was assassinated in 72 BCE. His followers were said to have emigrated to the Canary Islands (the "Fortunate Isles") to escape the Romans, and to have survived there until the fifteenth century, when they were defeated by the invading Spaniards.

How that one Frenchman,[1] through continued force
Of meditation on the inhuman deeds
Of those who conquered first the Indian Isles,
Went single in his ministry across
The Ocean; not to comfort the oppressed,
But, like a thirsty wind, to roam about,
Withering the Oppressor: how Gustavus sought
Help at his need in Dalecarlia's mines:[2]
How Wallace[3] fought for Scotland; left the name
Of Wallace to be found, like a wild flower,
All over his dear Country; left the deeds
Of Wallace, like a family of Ghosts,
To people the steep rocks and river banks,
Her natural sanctuaries, with a local soul
Of independence and stern liberty.
Sometimes it suits me better to invent
A tale from my own heart, more near akin
To my own passions, and habitual thoughts;
Some variegated story, in the main
Lofty, but the unsubstantial structure melts
Before the very sun that brightens it,
Mist into air dissolving! Then a wish,
My best and favourite aspiration, mounts
With yearning toward some philosophic song
Of Truth that cherishes our daily life;
With meditations passionate from deep
Recesses in man's heart, immortal verse
Thoughtfully fitted to the Orphean lyre;[4]
But from this awful° burthen I full soon   awe-inspiring
Take refuge and beguile myself with trust
That mellower years will bring a riper mind
And clearer insight. Thus my days are passed

In contradiction; with no skill to part
Vague longing, haply° bred by want of power,   by chance
240 From paramount impulse not to be withstood,
A timorous capacity from prudence,
From circumspection, infinite delay.
Humility and modest awe themselves
Betray me, serving often for a cloak
245 To a more subtle selfishness; that now
Locks every function up in blank° reserve,°total / inaction
Now dupes me, trusting to an anxious eye
That with intrusive restlessness beats off
Simplicity and self-presented truth.
250 Ah! better far than this, to stray about
Voluptuously,° through fields and rural walks,   luxuriously
And ask no record of the hours, resigned
To vacant musing, unreproved neglect
Of all things, and deliberate holiday.
255 Far better never to have heard the name
Of zeal and just ambition, than to live
Baffled and plagued by a mind that every hour
Turns recreant to her task; takes heart again,
Then feels immediately some hollow thought
260 Hang like an interdict° upon her hopes.   prohibition
This is my lot; for either still I find
Some imperfection in the chosen theme,
Or see of absolute accomplishment
Much wanting, so much wanting, in myself,
265 That I recoil and droop, and seek repose
In listlessness from vain perplexity,
Unprofitably travelling toward the grave,
Like a false steward who hath much received,
And renders nothing back.[5]
              Was it for this[6]
270 That one, the fairest of all rivers, loved
To blend his murmurs with my nurse's song,
And, from his alder[7] shades and rocky falls,
And from his fords and shallows, sent a voice
That flowed along my dreams? For this, didst thou,

[1] [Wordsworth's note] Dominique de Gourgues, a French gentleman who went in 1569 to Florida to avenge the massacre of the French by the Spaniards there.

[2] *Gustavus ... mines* Gustav Vasa (1496–1560) became King of Sweden after leading a successful revolt in Sweden against the ruling Danes. He found support for the revolt in the mining town of Dalecarlia.

[3] *Wallace* William Wallace (c. 1270–1305), Scottish hero who fought for the freedom of his country but was executed by Edward I in 1305.

[4] *Orphean lyre* Lyre of Orpheus, the poet of Greek myth who could charm all living things with his music.

[5] *false steward ... back* Reference to the biblical parable of the false steward, who wastes what his lord gives him (see Matthew 25.14–30).

[6] *Was it for this* For lines 269–498, cf. *The Two-Part Prelude of 1799* 1.1–247.

[7] *alder* Tree resembling a birch and usually found in wet places.

O Derwent![1] winding among grassy holms[2]
Where I was looking on, a babe in arms,
Make ceaseless music that composed my thoughts
To more than infant softness, giving me
Amid the fretful dwellings of mankind
A foretaste, a dim earnest, of the calm
That Nature breathes among the hills and groves?
When he had left the mountains and received
On his smooth breast the shadow of those towers
That yet survive, a shattered monument
Of feudal sway, the bright blue river passed
Along the margin of our terrace walk;
A tempting playmate whom we dearly loved.
Oh, many a time have I, a five years' child,
In a small mill-race[3] severed from his stream,
Made one long bathing of a summer's day;
Basked in the sun, and plunged and basked again
Alternate, all a summer's day, or scoured
The sandy fields, leaping through flowery groves
Of yellow ragwort; or when rock and hill,
The woods, and distant Skiddaw's[4] lofty height,
Were bronzed with deepest radiance, stood alone
Beneath the sky, as if I had been born
On Indian plains, and from my mother's hut
Had run abroad in wantonness, to sport
A naked savage, in the thunder shower.

Fair seed-time[5] had my soul, and I grew up
Fostered alike by beauty and by fear:
Much favoured in my birth-place, and no less
In that beloved Vale[6] to which erelong
We were transplanted—there were we let loose
For sports of wider range. Ere I had told

Ten birth-days, when among the mountain slopes
Frost, and the breath of frosty wind, had snapped
The last autumnal crocus, 'twas my joy
With store of springes[7] o'er my shoulder hung
To range the open heights where woodcocks° run   *game birds*
Along the smooth green turf. Through half the night,
Scudding[8] away from snare to snare, I plied
That anxious visitation; moon and stars
Were shining o'er my head. I was alone,
And seemed to be a trouble to the peace
That dwelt among them. Sometimes it befell
In these night wanderings, that a strong desire
O'erpowered my better reason, and the bird
Which was the captive of another's toil[9]
Became my prey; and when the deed was done
I heard among the solitary hills
Low breathings coming after me, and sounds
Of undistinguishable motion, steps
Almost as silent as the turf they trod.

Nor less when spring had warmed the cultured Vale,
Moved we as plunderers where the mother-bird
Had in high places built her lodge; though mean
Our object and inglorious, yet the end°   *result*
Was not ignoble. Oh! when I have hung
Above the raven's nest, by knots of grass
And half-inch fissures in the slippery rock
But ill sustained, and almost (so it seemed)
Suspended by the blast that blew amain,°   *with full force*
Shouldering the naked crag, oh, at that time
While on the perilous ridge I hung alone,
With what strange utterance did the loud dry wind
Blow through my ear! the sky seemed not a sky
Of earth—and with what motion moved the clouds!

Dust as we are, the immortal spirit grows
Like harmony in music; there is a dark
Inscrutable workmanship that reconciles

---

1 *Derwent* Wordsworth was born and spent some childhood years in a house overlooking this river in Cockermouth, Cumberland, on the edge of the English Lake District.

2 *holms* Areas of flat ground beside a river.

3 *mill-race* Channel or stream that feeds a mill wheel.

4 *Skiddaw* Mountain in Cumberland.

5 *seed-time* Sowing season.

6 *Vale* Probably Hawkshead, in the English Lake District. Wordsworth attended Hawkshead Grammar School after his mother's death in 1778.

7 *springes* Snares. (The word was pronounced with two syllables: *sprin-jez*.)

8 *Scudding* Moving quickly and smoothly.

9 *toil* A pun, meaning both "snare" and "labor."

275
280
285
290
295
300
305
310
315
320
325
330
335
340

Discordant elements, makes them cling together
In one society. How strange that all
The terrors, pains, and early miseries,
Regrets, vexations, lassitudes° interfused   *exhaustions*
Within my mind, should e'er have borne a part,
And that a needful part, in making up
The calm existence that is mine when I
Am worthy of myself! Praise to the end!
Thanks to the means which Nature deigned to employ;
Whether her fearless visitings, or those
That came with soft alarm, like hurtless light
Opening the peaceful clouds; or she may use
Severer interventions, ministry
More palpable, as best might suit her aim.

    One summer evening (led by her) I found
A little boat tied to a willow tree
Within a rocky cave, its usual home.
Straight I unloosed her chain, and stepping in
Pushed from the shore. It was an act of stealth
And troubled pleasure, nor without the voice
Of mountain-echoes did my boat move on;
Leaving behind her still, on either side,
Small circles glittering idly in the moon,
Until they melted all into one track
Of sparkling light. But now, like one who rows,
Proud of his skill, to reach a chosen point
With an unswerving line, I fixed my view
Upon the summit of a craggy ridge,
The horizon's utmost boundary; far above
Was nothing but the stars and the grey sky.
She was an elfin pinnace;[1] lustily
I dipped my oars into the silent lake,
And, as I rose upon the stroke, my boat
Went heaving through the water like a swan;
When, from behind that craggy steep till then
The horizon's bound, a huge peak, black and huge,
As if with voluntary power instinct°   *imbued*
Upreared its head. I struck and struck again,
And growing still in stature the grim shape
Towered up between me and the stars, and still,
For so it seemed, with purpose of its own

385 And measured motion like a living thing,
Strode after me. With trembling oars I turned,
And through the silent water stole my way
Back to the covert° of the willow tree;   *shelter*
There in her mooring-place I left my bark,°   *boat*
And through the meadows homeward went, in grave
390 And serious mood; but after I had seen
That spectacle, for many days, my brain
Worked with a dim and undetermined sense
Of unknown modes of being; o'er my thoughts
There hung a darkness, call it solitude
395 Or blank desertion. No familiar shapes
Remained, no pleasant images of trees,
Of sea or sky, no colours of green fields;
But huge and mighty forms, that do not live
Like living men, moved slowly through the mind
400 By day, and were a trouble to my dreams.

    Wisdom and Spirit of the universe!
Thou Soul that art the eternity of thought,
That givest to forms and images a breath
And everlasting motion, not in vain
405 By day or star-light thus from my first dawn
Of childhood didst thou intertwine for me
The passions that build up our human soul;
Not with the mean and vulgar works of man,
But with high objects, with enduring things—
410 With life and nature, purifying thus
The elements of feeling and of thought,
And sanctifying, by such discipline,
Both pain and fear, until we recognise
A grandeur in the beatings of the heart.
415 Nor was this fellowship vouchsafed to me
With stinted kindness. In November days,
When vapours rolling down the valley made
A lonely scene more lonesome, among woods
At noon, and 'mid the calm of summer nights,
420 When, by the margin of the trembling lake,
Beneath the gloomy hills homeward I went
In solitude, such intercourse was mine;
Mine was it in the fields both day and night,
And by the waters, all the summer long.

---

1 *pinnace* Small boat typically used to service larger vessels.

425   And in the frosty season, when the sun
        Was set, and visible for many a mile
        The cottage windows blazed through twilight gloom,
        I heeded not their summons: happy time
        It was indeed for all of us—for me
430   It was a time of rapture! Clear and loud
        The village clock tolled six—I wheeled about,
        Proud and exulting like an untired horse
        That cares not for his home. All shod with steel,[1]
        We hissed along the polished ice in games
435   Confederate,° imitative of the chase   *united*
        And woodland pleasures—the resounding horn,
        The pack loud chiming, and the hunted hare.
        So through the darkness and the cold we flew,
        And not a voice was idle; with the din
440   Smitten,° the precipices rang aloud;   *struck*
        The leafless trees and every icy crag
        Tinkled like iron; while far distant hills
        Into the tumult sent an alien sound
        Of melancholy not unnoticed, while the stars
445   Eastward were sparkling clear, and in the west
        The orange sky of evening died away.
        Not seldom from the uproar I retired
        Into a silent bay, or sportively
        Glanced sideway, leaving the tumultuous throng,
450   To cut across the reflex° of a star   *reflection*
        That fled, and, flying still before me, gleamed
        Upon the glassy plain; and oftentimes,
        When we had given our bodies to the wind,
        And all the shadowy banks on either side
455   Came sweeping through the darkness, spinning still
        The rapid line of motion, then at once
        Have I, reclining back upon my heels,
        Stopped short; yet still the solitary cliffs
        Wheeled by me—even as if the earth had rolled
460   With visible motion her diurnal° round!   *daily*
        Behind me did they stretch in solemn train,
        Feebler and feebler, and I stood and watched
        Till all was tranquil as a dreamless sleep.

        Ye Presences of Nature in the sky
465   And on the earth! Ye Visions of the hills!
        And Souls of lonely places! can I think
        A vulgar hope was yours when ye employed
        Such ministry, when ye through many a year
        Haunting me thus among my boyish sports,
470   On caves and trees, upon the woods and hills,
        Impressed upon all forms the characters
        Of danger or desire; and thus did make
        The surface of the universal earth
        With triumph and delight, with hope and fear,
475   Work° like a sea?   *move restlessly*
                        Not uselessly employed,
        Might I pursue this theme through every change
        Of exercise and play, to which the year
        Did summon us in his delightful round.

            We were a noisy crew; the sun in heaven
480   Beheld not vales more beautiful than ours;
        Nor saw a band in happiness and joy
        Richer, or worthier of the ground they trod.
        I could record with no reluctant voice
        The woods of autumn, and their hazel bowers
485   With milk-white clusters hung; the rod°   *fishing rod*
            and line,
        True symbol of hope's foolishness, whose strong
        And unreproved enchantment led us on
        By rocks and pools shut out from every star,
        All the green summer, to forlorn cascades
490   Among the windings hid of mountain brooks.
        —Unfading recollections! at this hour
        The heart is almost mine with which I felt,
        From some hill-top on sunny afternoons,
        The paper kite high among fleecy clouds
495   Pull at her rein like an impetuous courser;°   *horse*
        Or, from the meadows sent on gusty days,
        Beheld her breast[2] the wind, then suddenly
        Dashed headlong, and rejected by the storm.

            Ye lowly cottages wherein we dwelt,
500   A ministration of your own was yours;

---

[1] *All shod with steel* I.e., wearing ice skates.

[2] *breast* Reach the highest point of, as when climbing a mountain.

Can I forget you, being as you were
So beautiful among the pleasant fields
In which ye stood? or can I here forget
The plain and seemly countenance with which
Ye dealt out your plain comforts? Yet had ye
Delights and exultations of your own.
Eager and never weary we pursued
Our home-amusements by the warm peat-fire
At evening, when with pencil, and smooth slate
In square divisions parcelled out and all
With crosses and with cyphers scribbled o'er,[1]
We schemed and puzzled, head opposed to head
In strife too humble to be named in verse:
Or round the naked table, snow-white deal,°   pine
Cherry or maple, sat in close array,
And to the combat, Loo or Whist, led on
A thick-ribbed army;[2] not, as in the world,
Neglected and ungratefully thrown by
Even for the very service they had wrought,
But husbanded through many a long campaign.
Uncouth assemblage was it, where no few
Had changed their functions; some, plebeian cards[3]
Which Fate, beyond the promise of their birth,
Had dignified, and called to represent
The persons of departed potentates.
Oh, with what echoes on the board they fell!
Ironic diamonds—clubs, hearts, diamonds, spades,
A congregation piteously akin!
Cheap matter offered they to boyish wit,
Those sooty knaves, precipitated down
With scoffs and taunts, like Vulcan out of heaven:[4]
The paramount ace, a moon in her eclipse,

Queens gleaming through their splendour's last decay,
And monarchs surly at the wrongs sustained
535 By royal visages. Meanwhile abroad
Incessant rain was falling, or the frost
Raged bitterly, with keen and silent tooth;
And, interrupting oft that eager game,
From under Esthwaite's splitting fields of ice
540 The pent-up air, struggling to free itself,
Gave out to meadow grounds and hills a loud
Protracted yelling,[5] like the noise of wolves
Howling in troops along the Bothnic Main.[6]

Nor, sedulous° as I have been to trace[7]   careful
545 How Nature by extrinsic passion first
Peopled the mind with forms sublime or fair,
And made me love them, may I here omit
How other pleasures have been mine, and joys
Of subtler origin; how I have felt,
550 Not seldom even in that tempestuous time,
Those hallowed and pure motions of the sense
Which seem, in their simplicity, to own
An intellectual charm; that calm delight
Which, if I err not, surely must belong
555 To those first-born affinities that fit
Our new existence to existing things,
And, in our dawn of being, constitute
The bond of union between life and joy.

Yes, I remember when the changeful earth,
560 And twice five summers on my mind had stamped
The faces of the moving year, even then
I held unconscious intercourse with beauty
Old as creation, drinking in a pure
Organic pleasure from the silver wreaths
565 Of curling mist, or from the level plain
Of waters coloured by impending clouds.

---

[1] *With crosses ... o'er* See Milton's *Paradise Lost* 8.83: "With centric and eccentric scribbled o'er." Here Wordsworth uses this heroic diction to describe a game of tick-tack-toe.

[2] *Loo or Whist* Popular card games; *thick-ribbed army* Pack of cards made of thick cardboard.

[3] *plebeian cards* I.e., numbered cards, not face cards such as a queen, king, or jack. Also cf. Alexander Pope's *The Rape of the Lock* (1712, 1717): "Gained but one Trump and one Plebian Card" (3.54).

[4] *Vulcan out of heaven* Reference to the classical myth wherein the god Vulcan is thrown off Mount Olympus. In most versions of the story, he is cast out at birth by his mother, Juno, who is repulsed by his ugliness.

[5] *From under ... Protracted yelling* These lines describe the loud noises made by the ice as it breaks up in warming weather; *Esthwaite* Esthwaite Water, a lake near Hawkshead.

[6] *Bothnic Main* The Gulf of Bothnia, between Sweden and Finland.

[7] *Nor, sedulous ... to trace* For lines 544–635, cf. *The Two-Part Prelude of 1799* 1.378–468.

The sands of Westmoreland, the creeks and bays
Of Cumbria's¹ rocky limits, they can tell
How, when the Sea threw off his evening shade,
570 And to the shepherd's hut on distant hills
Sent welcome notice of the rising moon,
How I have stood, to fancies such as these
A stranger, linking with the spectacle
No conscious memory of a kindred sight,
575 And bringing with me no peculiar sense
Of quietness or peace; yet have I stood,
Even while mine eye hath moved o'er many a league
Of shining water, gathering as it seemed
Through every hair-breadth in that field of light
580 New pleasure like a bee among the flowers.

     Thus oft amid those fits of vulgar° joy   *everyday*
Which, through all seasons, on a child's pursuits
Are prompt attendants, 'mid that giddy bliss
Which, like a tempest, works along the blood
585 And is forgotten; even then I felt
Gleams like the flashing of a shield—the earth
And common face of Nature spake to me
Rememberable° things; sometimes, 'tis true.   *memorable*
By chance collisions and quaint accidents
590 (Like those ill-sorted unions, work supposed
Of evil-minded fairies), yet not vain
Nor profitless, if haply they impressed
Collateral° objects and appearances,   *indirect*
Albeit lifeless then, and doomed to sleep
595 Until maturer seasons called them forth
To impregnate and to elevate the mind.
—And if the vulgar joy by its own weight
Wearied itself out of the memory,
The scenes which were a witness of that joy
600 Remained in their substantial° lineaments   *material*
Depicted on the brain, and to the eye
Were visible, a daily sight; and thus
By the impressive² discipline of fear,
By pleasure and repeated happiness,
605 So frequently repeated, and by force

Of obscure feelings representative
Of things forgotten, these same scenes so bright,
So beautiful, so majestic in themselves,
Though yet the day was distant, did become
610 Habitually dear, and all their forms
And changeful colours by invisible links
Were fastened to the affections.
                                   I began
My story early—not misled, I trust,
By an infirmity of love for days
615 Disowned by memory—ere the breath of spring
Planting my snowdrops among winter snows:
Nor will it seem to thee, O Friend! so prompt
In sympathy, that I have lengthened out
With fond and feeble tongue a tedious tale.
620 Meanwhile, my hope has been, that I might fetch
Invigorating thoughts from former years;
Might fix the wavering balance° of my mind,   *scale*
And haply meet reproaches too, whose power
May spur me on, in manhood now mature,
625 To honourable toil. Yet should these hopes
Prove vain, and thus should neither I be taught
To understand myself, nor thou to know
With better knowledge how the heart was
          framed°   *constructed*
Of him thou lovest; need I dread from thee
630 Harsh judgments, if the song be loth to quit
Those recollected hours that have the charm
Of visionary things, those lovely forms
And sweet sensations that throw back our life,
And almost make remotest infancy
635 A visible scene, on which the sun is shining?

     One end at least hath been attained; my mind
Hath been revived, and if this genial mood
Desert me not, forthwith shall be brought down
Through later years the story of my life.
640 The road lies plain before me; 'tis a theme
Single and of determined bounds;³ and hence
I choose it rather at this time, than work
Of ampler or more varied argument,°   *subject matter*

---

¹ *Westmoreland ... Cumbria* Westmorland and Cumbria (usually called "Cumberland") were counties in the Lake District.

² *impressive* Capable of making an impression.

---

³ *determined bounds* Fixed boundaries.

Where I might be discomfited and lost:
And certain hopes are with me, that to thee
This labour will be welcome, honoured Friend!

from BOOK FIFTH
BOOKS

When Contemplation, like the night-calm felt
Through earth and sky, spreads widely, and sends deep
Into the soul its tranquillising power,
Even then I sometimes grieve for thee, O Man,
5   Earth's paramount Creature! not so much for woes
That thou endurest; heavy though that weight be,
Cloud-like it mounts, or touched with light divine
Doth melt away; but for those palms achieved,
Through length of time, by patient exercise
10   Of study and hard thought; there, there, it is
That sadness finds its fuel. Hitherto,
In progress through this Verse, my mind hath looked
Upon the speaking face of earth and heaven
As her prime Teacher, intercourse with man
15   Established by the sovereign Intellect,
Who through that bodily Image hath diffused,
As might appear to the eye of fleeting time,
A deathless spirit. Thou also, man! hast wrought,
For commerce of thy nature with herself,
20   Things that aspire to unconquerable life;
And yet we feel—we cannot choose but feel—
That they must perish. Tremblings of the heart
It gives, to think that our immortal being
No more shall need such garments; and yet man,
25   As long as he shall be the child of earth,
Might almost "weep to have"[1] what he may lose,
Nor be himself extinguished, but survive
Abject, depressed, forlorn, disconsolate.
A thought is with me sometimes, and I say—
30   Should the whole frame of earth by inward throes
Be wrenched, or fire come down from far to scorch
Her pleasant habitations, and dry up

Old Ocean in his bed, left singed and bare,
Yet would the living Presence still subsist
35   Victorious, and composure would ensue,
And kindlings like the morning—presage sure
Of day returning, and of life revived.
But all the meditations of mankind,
Yea, all the adamantine° holds°   indestructible / fortresses
   of truth
40   By reason built, or passion, which itself
Is highest reason in a soul sublime;
The consecrated works of Bard and Sage,
Sensuous or intellectual, wrought by men,
Twin labourers, and heirs of the same hopes;
45   Where would they be? Oh! why hath not the Mind
Some element to stamp her image on
In nature somewhat nearer to her own?
Why, gifted with such powers to send abroad
Her spirit, must it lodge in shrines so frail?

50   One day, when from my lips a like complaint
Had fallen in presence of a studious friend,
He with a smile made answer, that in truth
'Twas going far to seek disquietude
But on the front of his reproof, confessed
55   That he himself had oftentimes given way
To kindred hauntings. Whereupon I told,
That once in the stillness of a summer's noon,
While I was seated in a rocky cave,
By the sea-side, perusing, so it chanced,
60   The famous history of the errant knight
Recorded by Cervantes,[2] these same thoughts
Beset me, and to height unusual rose,
While listlessly I sat, and, having closed
The book, had turned my eyes toward the wide sea.
65   On poetry, and geometric truth,
And their high privilege of lasting life,
From all internal injury exempt,
I mused upon these chiefly: and, at length,
My senses yielding to the sultry air,
70   Sleep seized me, and I passed into a dream.

---

[1] *weep to have* See Shakespeare's Sonnet 64, lines 13–14: "This thought [of the destruction caused by time] is as a death, which cannot choose / But weep to have that which it fears to lose."

[2] *famous history … Cervantes* Miguel de Cervantes's *Don Quixote* (1605), in which the title character attempts to live as though he were a knight in a chivalric romance.

I saw before me stretched a boundless plain
Of sandy wilderness, all blank and void;
And as I looked around, distress and fear
Came creeping over me, when at my side,
75   Close at my side, an uncouth shape appeared
Upon a dromedary, mounted high.
He seemed an Arab of the Bedouin tribes:
A lance he bore, and underneath one arm
A stone; and, in the opposite hand, a shell
80   Of a surpassing brightness. At the sight
Much I rejoiced, not doubting but a Guide
Was present, one who with unerring skill
Would through the desert lead me; and while yet
I looked, and looked, self-questioned what this freight
85   Which the New-comer carried through the waste
Could mean, the Arab told me that the stone
(To give it in the language of the dream)
Was "Euclid's Elements";[1] and "This," said he,
"Is something of more worth"; and at the word
90   Stretched forth the shell, so beautiful in shape,
In color so resplendent, with command
That I should hold it to my ear. I did so,
And heard that instant in an unknown tongue,
Which yet I understood, articulate sounds,
95   A loud prophetic blast of harmony;
An Ode, in passion uttered, which foretold
Destruction to the children of the earth,
By deluge, now at hand. No sooner ceased
The song than the Arab with calm look declared
100 That all would come to pass of which the voice
Had given forewarning, and that he himself
Was going then to bury those two books:
The one that held acquaintance with the stars,
And wedded soul to soul in purest bond
105 Of reason, undisturbed by space or time;
The other, that was a god, yea many gods,
Had voices more than all the winds, with power
To exhilarate the spirit, and to soothe,
Through every clime, the heart of human kind.
110 While this was uttering, strange as it may seem,
I wondered not, although I plainly saw

The one to be a stone, the other a shell,
Nor doubted once but that they both were books;
Having a perfect faith in all that passed.
115 Far stronger now grew the desire I felt
To cleave unto this man; but when I prayed
To share his enterprise, he hurried on
Reckless° of me: I followed, not unseen,   *heedless*
For oftentimes he cast a backward look,
120 Grasping his twofold treasure. Lance in rest,
He rode, I keeping pace with him; and now
He, to my fancy, had become the knight
Whose tale Cervantes tells; yet not the Knight,
But was an Arab of the desert, too;
125 Of these was neither, and was both at once.
His countenance, meanwhile, grew more disturbed;
And looking backwards when he looked, mine eyes
Saw, over half the wilderness diffused,
A bed of glittering light: I asked the cause:
130 "It is," said he, "the waters of the deep
Gathering upon us"; quickening then the pace
Of the unwieldy creature he bestrode,
He left me: I called after him aloud;
He heeded not; but with his twofold charge
135 Still in his grasp, before me, full in view,
Went hurrying o'er the illimitable waste
With the fleet waters of a drowning world
In chase of him; whereat I waked in terror,
And saw the sea before me, and the book,
140 In which I had been reading, at my side.

     Full often, taking from the world of sleep
This Arab phantom, which I thus beheld,
This semi-Quixote, I to him have given
A substance, fancied him a living man,
145 A gentle dweller in the desert, crazed
By love and feeling, and internal thought
Protracted among endless solitudes;
Have shaped him wandering upon this quest!
Nor have I pitied him; but rather felt
150 Reverence was due to a being thus employed;
And thought that, in the blind and awful°   *awe-inspiring*
     lair
Of such a madness, reason did lie couched.

---

[1] *Euclid's Elements* Foundational geometry textbook by Euclid, a
Greek mathematician of the third century BCE.

Enow° there are on earth to take in charge   *enough*
Their wives, their children, and their virgin loves,
Or whatsoever else the heart holds dear;
Enow to stir for these; yea, will I say,
Contemplating in soberness the approach
Of an event so dire, by signs in earth
Or heaven made manifest, that I could share
That maniac's fond anxiety, and go
Upon like errand. Oftentimes, at least
Me hath such strong entrancement overcome,
When I have held a volume in my hand,
Poor earthly casket of immortal verse,
Shakespeare, or Milton, labourers divine!

    Great and benign, indeed, must be the power
Of living nature, which could thus so long
Detain me from the best of other guides
And dearest helpers, left unthanked, unpraised,
Even in the time of lisping infancy;
And later down, in prattling childhood even,
While I was travelling back among those days,
How could I ever play an ingrate's part?
Once more should I have made those bowers resound,
By intermingling strains of thankfulness
With their own thoughtless melodies; at least
It might have well beseemed me to repeat
Some simply fashioned tale, to tell again,
In slender accents of sweet verse, some tale
That did bewitch me then, and soothes me now.
O Friend! O Poet! brother of my soul,
Think not that I could pass along untouched
By these remembrances. Yet wherefore speak?
Why call upon a few weak words to say
What is already written in the hearts
Of all that breathe?—what in the path of all
Drops daily from the tongue of every child,
Wherever man is found? The trickling tear
Upon the cheek of listening Infancy
Proclaims it, and the insuperable look
That drinks as if it never could be full.

    That portion of my story I shall leave
There registered: whatever else of power

Or pleasure sown, or fostered thus, may be
195 Peculiar to myself, let that remain
Where still it works, though hidden from all search
Among the depths of time. Yet is it just
That here, in memory of all books which lay
Their sure foundations in the heart of man,
200 Whether by native prose, or numerous verse,[1]
That in the name of all inspirèd souls,
From Homer the great Thunderer, from the voice
That roars along the bed of Jewish song,
And that more varied and elaborate,
205 Those trumpet-tones of harmony that shake
Our shores in England—from those loftiest notes
Down to the low and wren-like warblings, made
For cottagers and spinners at the wheel,
And sun-burnt travellers resting their tired limbs,
210 Stretched under wayside hedge-rows, ballad tunes,
Food for the hungry ears of little ones,
And of old men who have survived their joys:
'Tis just that in behalf of these, the works,
And of the men that framed them, whether known,
215 Or sleeping nameless in their scattered graves,
That I should here assert their rights, attest
Their honours, and should, once for all, pronounce
Their benediction; speak of them as Powers
For ever to be hallowed; only less,
220 For what we are and what we may become,
Than Nature's self, which is the breath of God,
Or His pure Word by miracle revealed.

    Rarely and with reluctance would I stoop
To transitory themes; yet I rejoice,
225 And, by these thoughts admonished, will pour out
Thanks with uplifted heart, that I was reared
Safe from an evil which these days have laid
Upon the children of the land, a pest
That might have dried me up, body and soul.
230 This verse is dedicate to Nature's self,
And things that teach as Nature teaches: then,
Oh! where had been the Man, the Poet where,
Where had we been, we two, beloved Friend!
If in the season of unperilous choice,

---

1 *numerous verse* I.e., metrical verse (in which syllables are counted).

235　In lieu of wandering, as we did, through vales
　　　Rich with indigenous produce, open ground
　　　Of Fancy, happy pastures ranged at will,
　　　We had been followed, hourly watched, and noosed,
　　　Each in his several° melancholy walk　　　　　　*separate*
240　Stringed like a poor man's heifer at its feed,
　　　Led through the lanes in forlorn servitude;
　　　Or rather like a stallèd ox debarred
　　　From touch of growing grass, that may not taste
　　　A flower till it have yielded up its sweets
245　A prelibation to the mower's scythe.

　　　　　Behold the parent hen amid her brood,
　　　Though fledged and feathered, and well pleased to part
　　　And straggle from her presence, still a brood,
　　　And she herself from the maternal bond
250　Still undischarged; yet doth she little more
　　　Than move with them in tenderness and love,
　　　A centre to the circle which they make;
　　　And now and then, alike from need of theirs
　　　And call of her own natural appetites,
255　She scratches, ransacks up the earth for food,
　　　Which they partake at pleasure. Early died
　　　My honoured Mother, she who was the heart
　　　And hinge of all our learnings and our loves:
　　　She left us destitute, and, as we might,
260　Trooping together. Little suits it me
　　　To break upon the sabbath of her rest
　　　With any thought that looks at others' blame;
　　　Nor would I praise her but in perfect love.
　　　Hence am I checked: but let me boldly say,
265　In gratitude, and for the sake of truth,
　　　Unheard by her, that she, not falsely taught,
　　　Fetching her goodness rather from times past,
　　　Than shaping novelties for times to come,
　　　Had no presumption, no such jealousy,
270　Nor did by habit of her thoughts mistrust
　　　Our nature, but had virtual faith that He
　　　Who fills the mother's breast with innocent milk,
　　　Doth also for our nobler part provide,
　　　Under His great correction and control,
275　As innocent instincts, and as innocent food;
　　　Or draws for minds that are left free to trust

　　　In the simplicities of opening life
　　　Sweet honey out of spurned or dreaded weeds.
　　　This was her creed, and therefore she was pure
280　From anxious fear of error or mishap,
　　　And evil, overweeningly° so called;　　　　　　*arrogantly*
　　　Was not puffed up by false unnatural hopes,
　　　Nor selfish with unnecessary cares,
　　　Nor with impatience from the season asked
285　More than its timely produce; rather loved
　　　The hours for what they are, than from regard
　　　Glanced on their promises in restless pride.
　　　Such was she—not from faculties more strong
　　　Than others have, but from the times, perhaps,
290　And spot in which she lived, and through a grace
　　　Of modest meekness, simple-mindedness,
　　　A heart that found benignity and hope,
　　　Being itself benign. …

　　　　　There was a Boy: ye knew him well, ye cliffs[1]
365　And islands of Winander!—many a time
　　　At evening, when the earliest stars began
　　　To move along the edges of the hills,
　　　Rising or setting, would he stand alone
　　　Beneath the trees or by the glimmering lake,
370　And there, with fingers interwoven, both hands
　　　Pressed closely palm to palm, and to his mouth
　　　Uplifted, he, as through an instrument,
　　　Blew mimic hootings to the silent owls,
　　　That they might answer him; and they would shout
375　Across the watery vale, and shout again,
　　　Responsive to his call, with quivering peals,
　　　And long halloos and screams, and echoes loud,
　　　Redoubled and redoubled, concourse° wild　　　　*assembly*
　　　Of jocund° din; and, when a lengthened pause　　*cheery*
380　Of silence came and baffled his best skill,
　　　Then sometimes, in that silence while he hung
　　　Listening, a gentle shock of mild surprise
　　　Has carried far into his heart the voice
　　　Of mountain torrents; or the visible scene
385　Would enter unawares into his mind,
　　　With all its solemn imagery, its rocks,

---

[1] *There was … ye cliffs*　For lines 364–397, cf. "[There was a Boy]"
(1800), included in this anthology.

Its woods, and that uncertain heaven, received
Into the bosom of the steady lake.

This Boy was taken from his mates, and died
In childhood, ere he was full twelve years old.
Fair is the spot, most beautiful the vale
Where he was born; the grassy churchyard hangs
Upon a slope above the village school,
And through that churchyard when my way has led
On summer evenings, I believe that there
A long half hour together I have stood
Mute, looking at the grave in which he lies!
Even now appears before the mind's clear eye
That self-same village church; I see her sit
(The thronèd Lady whom erewhile we hailed)
On her green hill, forgetful of this Boy
Who slumbers at her feet—forgetful, too,
Of all her silent neighbourhood of graves,
And listening only to the gladsome sounds
That, from the rural school ascending, play
Beneath her and about her. May she long
Behold a race of young ones like to those
With whom I herded! (easily, indeed,
We might have fed upon a fatter soil
Of arts and letters—but be that forgiven)
A race of real children; not too wise,
Too learned, or too good; but wanton, fresh,
And bandied up and down by love and hate;
Not unresentful where self-justified;
Fierce, moody, patient, venturous, modest, shy;
Mad at their sports like withered leaves in winds;
Though doing wrong and suffering, and full oft
Bending beneath our life's mysterious weight
Of pain, and doubt, and fear, yet yielding not
In happiness to the happiest upon earth.
Simplicity in habit, truth in speech,
Be these the daily strengtheners of their minds;
May books and Nature be their early joy!
And knowledge, rightly honoured with that name—
Knowledge not purchased by the loss of power!

Well do I call to mind the very week
When I was first intrusted to the care

Of that sweet Valley; when its paths, its shores,
And brooks were like a dream of novelty
To my half-infant thoughts; that very week,
While I was roving up and down alone,
Seeking I knew not what, I chanced to cross
One of those open fields, which, shaped like ears,
Make green peninsulas on Esthwaite's Lake:
Twilight was coming on, yet through the gloom
Appeared distinctly on the opposite shore
A heap of garments, as if left by one
Who might have there been bathing. Long I watched,
But no one owned them; meanwhile the calm lake
Grew dark with all the shadows on its breast,
And, now and then, a fish up-leaping snapped
The breathless stillness. The succeeding day,
Those unclaimed garments telling a plain tale
Drew to the spot an anxious crowd; some looked
In passive expectation from the shore,
While from a boat others hung o'er the deep,
Sounding with grappling irons and long poles.
At last, the dead man, 'mid that beauteous scene
Of trees and hills and water, bolt upright
Rose, with his ghastly face, a spectre shape
Of terror; yet no soul-debasing fear,
Young as I was, a child not nine years old,
Possessed me, for my inner eye had seen
Such sights before, among the shining streams
Of faëry land, the forest of romance.
Their spirit hallowed the sad spectacle
With decoration of ideal grace;
A dignity, a smoothness, like the works
Of Grecian art, and purest poesy. ...

Here must we pause; this only let me add,
From heart-experience, and in humblest sense
Of modesty, that he, who in his youth
A daily wanderer among woods and fields
With living Nature hath been intimate,
Not only in that raw unpractised time
Is stirred to ecstasy, as others are,
By glittering verse; but further, doth receive,
In measure only dealt out to himself,
Knowledge and increase of enduring joy

From the great Nature that exists in works
595 Of mighty Poets. Visionary power
Attends the motions of the viewless° winds,   *invisible*
Embodied in the mystery of words:
There, darkness makes abode, and all the host
Of shadowy things work endless changes—there,
600 As in a mansion like their proper home,
Even forms and substances are circumfused
By that transparent veil with light divine,
And, through the turnings intricate of verse,
Present themselves as objects recognized,
605 In flashes, and with glory not their own.

from BOOK SIXTH
CAMBRIDGE AND THE ALPS

The leaves were fading when to Esthwaite's banks
And the simplicities of cottage life
I bade farewell; and, one among the youth
Who, summoned by that season, reunite
5 As scattered birds troop to the fowler's lure,
Went back to Granta's[1] cloisters, not so prompt
Or eager, though as gay and undepressed
In mind, as when I thence had taken flight
A few short months before. I turned my face
10 Without repining from the coves and heights
Clothed in the sunshine of the withering fern;
Quitted, not both, the mild magnificence
Of calmer lakes and louder streams; and you,
Frank-hearted maids of rocky Cumberland,
15 You and your not unwelcome days of mirth,
Relinquished, and your nights of revelry,
And in my own unlovely cell sate down
In lightsome mood—such privilege has youth
That cannot take long leave of pleasant thoughts.

20   The bonds of indolent society
Relaxing in their hold, henceforth I lived
More to myself. Two winters may be passed
Without a separate notice: many books
Were skimmed, devoured, or studiously perused,

25 But with no settled plan. I was detached
Internally from academic cares;
Yet independent study seemed a course
Of hardy disobedience towards friends
And kindred, proud rebellion and unkind.
30 This spurious° virtue, rather let it bear   *so-called*
A name it now deserves, this cowardice,
Gave treacherous sanction to that over-love
Of freedom which encouraged me to turn
From regulations even of my own
35 As from restraints and bonds. Yet who can tell—
Who knows what thus may have been gained, both then
And at a later season, or preserved;
What love of nature, what original strength
Of contemplation, what intuitive truths,
40 The deepest and the best, what keen research,
Unbiassed, unbewildered, and unawed?

    The Poet's soul was with me at that time;
Sweet meditations, the still overflow
Of present happiness, while future years
45 Lacked not anticipations, tender dreams,
No few of which have since been realised;
And some remain, hopes for my future life.
Four years and thirty, told this very week,[2]
Have I been now a sojourner on earth,
50 By sorrow not unsmitten; yet for me
Life's morning radiance hath not left the hills,
Her dew is on the flowers. Those were the days
Which also first emboldened me to trust
With firmness, hitherto but lightly touched
55 By such a daring thought, that I might leave
Some monument behind me which pure hearts
Should reverence. The instinctive humbleness,
Maintained even by the very name and thought
Of printed books and authorship, began
60 To melt away; and further, the dread awe
Of mighty names was softened down and seemed
Approachable, admitting fellowship
Of modest sympathy. Such aspect now,

---

[1] *Granta* Another name for the River Cam.

[2] *this very week* The week of 7 April 1804.

Though not familiarly, my mind put on,
Content to observe, to achieve, and to enjoy.

    All winter long, whenever free to choose,
Did I by night frequent the College groves
And tributary walks; the last, and oft
The only one, who had been lingering there
Through hours of silence, till the porter's bell,
A punctual follower on the stroke of nine,
Rang with its blunt unceremonious voice,
Inexorable summons! Lofty elms,
Inviting shades of opportune recess,
Bestowed composure on a neighbourhood
Unpeaceful in itself. A single tree
With sinuous trunk, boughs exquisitely wreathed,
Grew there; an ash which Winter for herself
Decked as in pride, and with outlandish grace:
Up from the ground, and almost to the top,
The trunk and every master branch were green
With clustering ivy, and the lightsome twigs
And outer spray profusely tipped with seeds
That hung in yellow tassels, while the air
Stirred them, not voiceless. Often have I stood
Foot-bound uplooking at this lovely tree
Beneath a frosty moon. The hemisphere
Of magic fiction, verse of mine perchance
May never tread; but scarcely Spenser's[1] self
Could have more tranquil visions in his youth,
Or could more bright appearances create
Of human forms with superhuman powers,
Than I beheld loitering on calm clear nights
Alone, beneath this fairy work of earth.

    On the vague reading of a truant youth
'Twere idle to descant.[2] My inner judgment
Not seldom differed from my taste in books,
As if it appertained to another mind,
And yet the books which then I valued most
Are dearest to me *now*; for, having scanned,
Not heedlessly, the laws, and watched the forms

Of Nature, in that knowledge I possessed
A standard, often usefully applied. ...

    When the third summer freed us from restraint,
A youthful friend, he too a mountaineer,
Not slow to share my wishes, took his staff,
And sallying forth, we journeyed side by side,
Bound to the distant Alps.[3] A hardy slight
Did this unprecedented course imply
Of college studies and their set rewards;
Nor had, in truth, the scheme been formed by me
Without uneasy forethought of the pain,
The censures, and ill-omening of those
To whom my worldly interests were dear.
But Nature then was sovereign in my mind,
And mighty forms, seizing a youthful fancy,
Had given a charter to irregular hopes.
In any age of uneventful calm
Among the nations, surely would my heart
Have been possessed by similar desire;
But Europe at that time was thrilled with joy,
France standing on the top of golden hours,[4]
And human nature seeming born again. ...

    'Tis not my present purpose to retrace
That variegated journey step by step.
A march it was of military speed,
And earth did change her images and forms
Before us, fast as clouds are changed in heaven.
Day after day, up early and down late,
From hill to vale we dropped, from vale to hill
Mounted—from province on to province swept,
Keen hunters in a chase of fourteen weeks,
Eager as birds of prey, or as a ship
Upon the stretch, when winds are blowing fair:
Sweet coverts did we cross of pastoral life,
Enticing valleys, greeted them and left
Too soon, while yet the very flash and gleam

---

[1] *Spenser* English poet Edmund Spenser (c. 1522–99), author of *The Faerie Queene.*

[2] *descant* Discuss in detail.

[3] *When ... Alps* In 1790 Wordsworth traveled with Robert Jones, a friend from Cambridge, to the French, Italian, and Swiss Alps.

[4] *France ... hours* In 1790 many English intellectuals were optimistic about the French Revolution, though most would change their views as the events of the Revolutionary period unfolded.

Of salutation were not passed away.
Oh! sorrow for the youth who could have seen
505 Unchastened, unsubdued, unawed, unraised
To patriarchal dignity of mind,
And pure simplicity of wish and will,
Those sanctified abodes of peaceful man;
Pleased (though to hardship born, and compassed round
510 With danger, varying as the seasons change),
Pleased with his daily tasks, or, if not pleased,
Contented, from the moment that the dawn
(Ah! surely not without attendant gleams
Of soul-illumination) calls him forth
515 To industry, by glistenings flung on rocks,
Whose evening shadows lead him to repose.

Well might a stranger look with bounding heart
Down on a green recess, the first I saw
Of those deep haunts, an aboriginal vale,
520 Quiet and lorded over and possessed
By naked huts, wood-built, and sown like tents,
Or Indian cabins over the fresh lawns
And by the river side.
                              That very day,
From a bare ridge we also first beheld
525 Unveiled the summit of Mont Blanc,[1] and grieved
To have a soulless image on the eye
That had usurped upon a living thought
That never more could be. The wondrous Vale
Of Chamouny[2] stretched far below, and soon
530 With its dumb° cataracts and streams of ice,   *unheard*
A motionless array of mighty waves,
Five rivers broad and vast, made rich amends,
And reconciled us to realities:
There small birds warble from the leafy trees,
535 The eagle soars high in the element,
There doth the reaper bind the yellow sheaf,
The maiden spread the haycock[3] in the sun,
While Winter like a well-tamed lion walks,

Descending from the Mountain to make sport
540 Among the Cottages by beds of flowers.

Whate'er in this wide circuit we beheld,
Or heard, was fitted to our unripe state
Of intellect and heart. With such a book
Before our eyes, we could not choose but read
545 Lessons of genuine brotherhood, the plain
And universal reason of mankind,
The truths of young and old. Nor, side by side
Pacing, two social pilgrims, or alone
Each with his humour,° could we fail to abound   *disposition*
550 In dreams and fictions, pensively composed,
Dejection taken up for pleasure's sake,
And gilded sympathies, the willow[4] wreath,
And sober posies° of funereal flowers   *bouquets*
Gathered among those solitudes sublime
555 From formal gardens of the lady Sorrow,
Did sweeten many a meditative hour.

Yet still in me with those soft luxuries
Mixed something of stern mood, an under-thirst
Of vigor seldom utterly allayed.
560 And from that source how different a sadness
Would issue, let one incident make known.
When from the Vallais[5] we had turned, and clomb
Along the Simplon's[6] steep and rugged road,
Following a band of Muleteers,° we reached   *mule drivers*
565 A halting-place, where all together took
Their noon-tide meal. Hastily rose our guide,
Leaving us at the board; awhile we lingered,
Then paced the beaten downward way that led
Right to a rough stream's edge, and there broke off;
570 The only track now visible was one
That from the torrent's further brink held forth
Conspicuous invitation to ascend
A loft mountain. After brief delay
Crossing the unbridged stream, that road we took,

---

[1] *Mont Blanc* The highest mountain in the Alps.

[2] *Vale / Of Chamouny* Valley located at the foot of Mont Blanc.
(The modern spelling is Chamonix.)

[3] *haycock* Conical pile of hay.

[4] *willow* Symbol of sadness.

[5] *Vallais* Canton in southern Switzerland, located in a valley
between ranges of the Alps.

[6] *Simplon* Mountain pass connecting the Valais with Piedmont,
Italy.

And clomb with eagerness, till anxious fears
Intruded, for we failed to overtake
Our comrades gone before. By fortunate chance,
While every moment added doubt to doubt,
A peasant met us, from whose mouth we learned
That to the spot which had perplexed us first
We must descend, and there should find the road,
Which in the stony channel of the stream
Lay a few steps, and then along its banks;
And that our future course, all plain to sight,
Was downwards, with the current of that stream.
Loth to believe what we so grieved to hear,
For still we had hopes that pointed to the clouds,
We questioned him again, and yet again;
But every word that from the peasant's lips
Came in reply, translated by our feelings,
Ended in this—*that we had crossed the Alps.*

    Imagination—here the Power so called
Through sad incompetence of human speech,
That awful° Power rose from the   *awe-inspiring*
    mind's abyss
Like an unfathered vapour that enwraps,
At once, some lonely traveller. I was lost;
Halted without an effort to break through;
But to my conscious soul I now can say—
"I recognise thy glory:" in such strength
Of usurpation, when the light of sense
Goes out, but with a flash that has revealed
The invisible world, doth greatness make abode,
There harbours; whether we be young or old,
Our destiny, our being's heart and home,
Is with infinitude, and only there;
With hope it is, hope that can never die,
Effort, and expectation, and desire,
And something evermore about to be.
Under such banners militant, the soul
Seeks for no trophies, struggles for no spoils
That may attest her prowess, blest in thoughts
That are their own perfection and reward,
Strong in herself and in beatitude
That hides her, like the mighty flood of Nile

615 Poured from his fount of Abyssinian clouds
    To fertilise the whole Egyptian plain.

    The melancholy slackening that ensued
Upon those tidings by the peasant given
Was soon dislodged. Downwards we hurried fast,
620 And, with the half-shaped road which we had missed,
Entered a narrow chasm. The brook and road
Were fellow-travellers in this gloomy strait,
And with them did we journey several hours
At a slow pace. The immeasurable height
625 Of woods decaying, never to be decayed,
The stationary blasts of waterfalls,
And in the narrow rent° at every turn   *steep gorge*
Winds thwarting winds, bewildered and forlorn,
The torrents shooting from the clear blue sky,
630 The rocks that muttered close upon our ears,
Black drizzling crags that spake by the way-side
As if a voice were in them, the sick sight
And giddy prospect of the raving stream,
The unfettered clouds and region of the Heavens,
635 Tumult and peace, the darkness and the light
Were all like workings of one mind, the features
Of the same face, blossoms upon one tree;
Characters of the great Apocalypse,
The types and symbols of Eternity,
640 Of first, and last, and midst, and without end. …

    Oh, most belovèd Friend! a glorious time,
755 A happy time that was; triumphant looks
Were then the common language of all eyes;
As if awaked from sleep, the Nations hailed
Their great expectancy: the fife of war
Was then a spirit-stirring sound indeed,
760 A black-bird's whistle in a budding grove.
We left the Swiss exulting in the fate
Of their near neighbours;[1] and, when shortening fast
Our pilgrimage, nor distant far from home,
We crossed the Brabant armies[2] on the fret

---

[1] *their near neighbours* I.e., the French.

[2] *Brabant armies* Armies of the Brabant Revolution (1789–90), in which the people of what is now Belgium, but was then part of the Holy Roman Empire, revolted and briefly established a republic.

765   For battle in the cause of Liberty.
     A stripling, scarcely of the household then
     Of social life, I looked upon these things
     As from a distance; heard, and saw, and felt,
     Was touched, but with no intimate concern;
770   I seemed to move along them, as a bird
     Moves through the air, or as a fish pursues
     Its sport, or feeds in its proper element;
     I wanted not that joy, I did not need
     Such help; the ever-living universe,
775   Turn where I might, was opening out its glories,
     And the independent spirit of pure youth
     Called forth, at every season, new delights
     Spread round my steps like sunshine o'er green fields.

from BOOK THIRTEENTH
IMAGINATION AND TASTE, HOW IMPAIRED AND
RESTORED (CONCLUDED)

     From Nature doth emotion come, and moods
     Of calmness equally are Nature's gift:
     This is her glory; these two attributes
     Are sister horns that constitute her strength.
5   Hence Genius, born to thrive by interchange
     Of peace and excitation,° finds in her   *stimulus*
     His best and purest friend, from her receives
     That energy by which he seeks the truth,
     From her that happy stillness of the mind
10   Which fits him to receive it, when unsought.

      Such benefit the humblest intellects
     Partake of, each in their degree: 'tis mine
     To speak, what I myself have known and felt;
     Smooth task! for words find easy way, inspired
15   By gratitude, and confidence in truth.
     Long time in search of knowledge did I range
     The field of human life, in heart and mind
     Benighted; but, the dawn beginning now
     To re-appear, 'twas proved that not in vain
20   I had been taught to reverence a Power
     That is the visible quality and shape
     And image of right reason; that matures

Her processes by steadfast laws; gives birth
     To no impatient or fallacious hopes,
25   No heat of passion or excessive zeal,
     No vain conceits, provokes to no quick turns
     Of self-applauding intellect; but trains
     To meekness, and exalts by humble faith;
     Holds up before the mind intoxicate
30   With present objects, and the busy dance
     Of things that pass away, a temperate show
     Of objects that endure; and by this course
     Disposes her, when over-fondly set
     On throwing off incumbrances, to seek
35   In man, and in the frame of social life,
     Whate'er there is desireable and good
     Of kindred permanence, unchanged in form
     And function, or, through strict vicissitude
     Of life and death, revolving. Above all
40   Were re-established now those watchful thoughts
     Which, seeing little worthy or sublime
     In what the Historian's pen so much delights
     To blazon—power and energy detached
     From moral purpose—early tutored me
45   To look with feelings of fraternal love
     Upon the unassuming things that hold
     A silent station in this beauteous world.

      Thus moderated, thus composed, I found
     Once more in Man an object of delight,
50   Of pure imagination, and of love;
     And, as the horizon of my mind enlarged,
     Again I took the intellectual° eye   *inner, spiritual*
     For my instructor, studious more to see
     Great truths, than touch and handle little ones.
55   Knowledge was given accordingly; my trust
     Became more firm in feelings that had stood
     The test of such a trial; clearer far
     My sense of excellence—of right and wrong:
     The promise of the present time retired
60   Into its true proportion; sanguine° schemes,   *confident*
     Ambitious projects, pleased me less; I sought
     For present good in life's familiar face,
     And built thereon my hopes of good to come.

With settling judgments now of what would last
5 And what must disappear, prepared to find
Presumption, folly, madness, in the men
Who thrust themselves upon the passive world
As Rulers of the world; to see in these,
Even when the public welfare is their aim,
0 Plans without thought, or built on theories
Vague and unsound; and having brought the books
Of modern statists° to their proper test,   *political theorists*
Life, human life, with all its sacred claims
Of sex and age, and heaven-descended rights,
5 Mortal, or those beyond the reach of death;
And having thus discerned how dire a thing
Is worshipped in that idol proudly named
"The Wealth of Nations,"[1] *where* alone that wealth
Is lodged, and how encreased; and having gained
0 A more judicious knowledge of the worth
And dignity of individual man,
No composition of the brain, but man
Of whom we read, the man whom we behold
With our own eyes—I could not but enquire—
5 Not with less interest than heretofore,
But greater, though in spirit more subdued,
Why is this glorious creature to be found
One only in ten thousand? What one is,
Why may not millions be? What bars are thrown
0 By Nature in the way of such a hope?
Our animal appetites and daily wants,
Are these obstructions insurmountable?
If not, then others vanish into air.
"Inspect the basis of the social pile:
5 Inquire," said I, "how much of mental Power
And genuine virtue they possess who live
By bodily toil, labour exceeding far
Their due proportion, under all the weight
Of that injustice which upon ourselves
0 Ourselves entail." Such estimate to frame
I chiefly looked (what need to look beyond?)
Among the natural abodes of men,
Fields with their rural works, recalled to mind
My earliest notices,° with these compared   *observations*

105 The observations made in later youth,
And to that day continued. For, the time
Had never been when throes of mighty Nations
And the world's tumult unto me could yield,
How far soe'er transported and possessed,
110 Full measure of content; but still I craved
An intermingling of distinct regards°   *sights*
And truths of individual sympathy
Nearer ourselves. Such often might be gleaned
From the great City, else it must have proved
115 To me a heart-depressing wilderness;
But much was wanting; therefore did I turn
To you, ye pathways, and ye lonely roads;
Sought you enriched with every thing I prized,
With human kindness and simple joys. …

Here, calling up to mind what then I saw,
A youthful traveller, and see daily now
In the familiar circuit of my home,
Here might I pause, and bend in reverence
225 To Nature, and the power of human minds,
To men as they are men within themselves.
How oft high service is performed within,
When all the external man is rude in show—
Not like a temple rich with pomp and gold,
230 But a mere mountain chapel, that protects
Its simple worshippers from sun and shower.
Of these, said I, shall be my song; of these,
If future years mature me for the task,
Will I record the praises, making verse
235 Deal boldly with substantial things; in truth
And sanctity of passion, speak of these,
That justice may be done, obeisance paid
Where it is due: thus haply° shall I teach,   *by chance*
Inspire, through unadulterated ears
240 Pour rapture, tenderness, and hope—my theme
No other than the very heart of man,
As found among the best of those who live,
Not unexalted by religious faith,
Nor uninformed by books, good books, though few,
245 In Nature's presence: thence may I select
Sorrow, that is not sorrow, but delight;
And miserable love, that is not pain

---

[1] *The … Nations* Reference to Adam Smith's *Inquiry into the Nature and Causes of the Wealth of Nations* (1776).

To hear of, for the glory that redounds
Therefrom to human kind, and what we are.
250 Be mine to follow with no timid step
Where knowledge leads me: it shall be my pride
That I have dared to tread this holy ground,
Speaking no dream, but things oracular;°   *prophetic*
Matter not lightly to be heard by those
255 Who to the letter of the outward promise
Do read the invisible soul;[1] by men adroit
In speech, and for communion with the world
Accomplished; minds whose faculties are then
Most active when they are most eloquent,
260 And elevated most when most admired.
Men may be found of other mould than these,
Who are their own upholders, to themselves
Encouragement, and energy, and will,
Expressing liveliest thoughts in lively words
265 As native passion dictates. Others, too,
There are among the walks of homely life
Still higher, men for contemplation framed,
Shy, and unpractised in the strife of phrase;
Meek men, whose very souls perhaps would sink
270 Beneath them, summoned to such intercourse:
Theirs is the language of the heavens, the power,
The thought, the image, and the silent joy:
Words are but under-agents in their souls;
When they are grasping with their greatest strength,
275 They do not breathe among them:[2] this I speak
In gratitude to God, Who feeds our hearts
For His own service; knoweth, loveth us,
When we are unregarded by the world.

     Also, about this time did I receive
280 Convictions still more strong than heretofore,
Not only that the inner frame is good,
And graciously composed, but that, no less,
Nature for all conditions wants° not power   *lacks*
To consecrate, if we have eyes to see,
285 The outside of her creatures, and to breathe

Grandeur upon the very humblest face
Of human life. I felt that the array
Of act and circumstance, and visible form,
Is mainly to the pleasure of the mind
290 What passion makes them; that meanwhile the forms
Of Nature have a passion in themselves,
That intermingles with those works of man
To which she summons him; although the works
Be mean, have nothing lofty of their own;
295 And that the Genius of the Poet hence
May boldly take his way among mankind
Wherever Nature leads; that he hath stood
By Nature's side among the men of old,
And so shall stand for ever. Dearest Friend!
300 If thou partake the animating faith
That Poets, even as Prophets, each with each
Connected in a mighty scheme of truth,
Have each his own peculiar° faculty,   *specific*
Heaven's gift, a sense that fits him to perceive
305 Objects unseen before, thou wilt not blame
The humblest of this band who dares to hope
That unto him hath also been vouchsafed
An insight that in some sort he possesses,
A privilege whereby a work of his,
310 Proceeding from a source of untaught things,
Creative and enduring, may become
A power like one of Nature's. To a hope
Not less ambitious once among the wilds
Of Sarum's Plain,[3] my youthful spirit was raised;
315 There, as I ranged at will the pastoral downs[4]
Trackless and smooth, or paced the bare white roads
Lengthening in solitude their dreary line,
Time with his retinue of ages fled
Backwards, nor checked his flight until I saw
320 Our dim ancestral Past in vision clear;
Saw multitudes of men, and, here and there,
A single Briton clothed in wolf-skin vest,

---

1 *to the letter ... soul* Form their opinion of the soul from the external qualities.

2 *They do ... them* I.e., such people do not exist ("breathe") in the realm of words.

3 *Sarum's Plain* Salisbury Plain, the site of Stonehenge and other Neolithic archeological features. Wordsworth's 1793 walk across the plain was an apparently profound experience that he referenced in his poem *Salisbury Plain* (written 1793–94, but later revised, expanded, and retitled to produce several other versions).

4 *downs* Chalky hills spanning much of southern England, including Salisbury Plain.

With shield and stone-axe, stride across the
    wold;°   *countryside*
The voice of spears was heard, the rattling spear
Shaken by arms of mighty bone, in strength,
Long mouldered, of barbaric majesty.
I called on Darkness—but before the word
Was uttered, midnight darkness seemed to take
All objects from my sight; and lo! again
The Desert[1] visible by dismal flames;
It is the sacrificial altar, fed
With living men[2]—how deep the groans! the voice
Of those that crowd the giant wicker thrills
The monumental hillocks,[3] and the pomp
Is for both worlds, the living and the dead.
At other moments (for through that wide waste
Three summer days I roamed) where'er the Plain
Was figured o'er with circles, lines, or mounds,[4]
That yet survive, a work, as some divine,°   *conjecture*
Shaped by the Druids, so to represent
Their knowledge of the heavens, and image forth
The constellations; gently was I charmed
Into a waking dream, a reverie
That, with believing eyes, where'er I turned,
Beheld long-bearded teachers, with white wands
Uplifted, pointing to the starry sky,
Alternately, and plain below, while breath
Of music swayed their motions, and the waste
Rejoiced with them and me in those sweet sounds.

    This for the past, and things that may be viewed
Or fancied in the obscurity of years
From monumental hints: and thou, O Friend!
Pleased with some unpremeditated strains

That served those wanderings to beguile,[5] hast said
355 That then and there my mind had exercised
Upon the vulgar forms of present things,
The actual world of our familiar days,
Yet higher power; had caught from them a tone,
An image, and a character, by books
360 Not hitherto reflected. Call we this
A partial judgment—and yet why? for *then*
We were as strangers; and I may not speak
Thus wrongfully of verse, however rude,
Which on thy young imagination, trained
365 In the great City, broke like light from far.
Moreover, each man's Mind is to herself
Witness and judge; and I remember well
That in life's every-day appearances
I seemed about this time to gain clear sight
370 Of a new world—a world, too, that was fit
To be transmitted, and to other eyes
Made visible; as ruled by those fixed laws
Whence spiritual dignity originates,
Which do both give it being and maintain
375 A balance, an ennobling interchange
Of action from without and from within;
The excellence, pure function, and best power
Both of the object seen, and eye that sees.

BOOK FOURTEENTH
CONCLUSION

In one of those excursions (may they ne'er
Fade from remembrance!) through the Northern tracts
Of Cambria ranging with a youthful friend,[6]
I left Bethgelert's huts at couching-time,°   *bedtime*
5 And westward took my way, to see the sun

---

[1] *Desert* Expanse of wilderness.

[2] *sacrificial ... living men* Druids were thought to have performed human sacrifices by placing the victims inside a giant wicker statue and setting it on fire.

[3] *monumental hillocks* I.e., burial mounds.

[4] *circles ... mounds* Marks on the plain, which are the results of prehistoric construction, burial mounds, field enclosures, and other archaeological remains.

[5] *some unpremeditated ... beguile* Some verse that Wordsworth wrote to pass the time during his walk across the plain. In 1796, less than a year after the poets had first met, Wordsworth sent Coleridge a copy of his *Adventures on Salisbury Plain* (1795), a revised and expanded version of his 1793–94 poem.

[6] *In one ... friend* The trip referred to was a 1791 walking tour through North Wales (Cambria) with Robert Jones, the same friend with whom Wordsworth crossed the Alps. In this passage, they ascend Mount Snowdon, the highest peak in Wales, from the village of Bethgellert.

Rise from the top of Snowdon. To the door
Of a rude cottage at the mountain's base
We came, and roused the shepherd who attends
The adventurous stranger's steps, a trusty guide;
10   Then, cheered by short refreshment, sallied forth.

It was a close, warm, breezeless summer night,
Wan, dull, and glaring,° with a dripping fog   *rainy*
Low-hung and thick, that covered all the sky;
But, undiscouraged, we began to climb
15   The mountain-side. The mist soon girt us round,
And, after ordinary travellers' talk
With our conductor, pensively we sank
Each into commerce with his private thoughts:
Thus did we breast the ascent, and by myself
20   Was nothing either seen or heard that checked
Those musings or diverted, save that once
The shepherd's lurcher,[1] who, among the crags,
Had to his joy unearthed a hedgehog, teased
His coiled-up prey with barkings turbulent.
25   This small adventure, for even such it seemed
In that wild place and at the dead of night,
Being over and forgotten, on we wound
In silence as before. With forehead bent
Earthward, as if in opposition set
30   Against an enemy, I panted up
With eager pace, and no less eager thoughts.
Thus might we wear a midnight hour away,
Ascending at loose distance each from each,
And I, as chanced, the foremost of the band:
35   When at my feet the ground appeared to brighten,
And with a step or two seemed brighter still;
Nor was time given to ask or learn the cause,
For instantly a light upon the turf
Fell like a flash, and lo! as I looked up,
40   The Moon hung naked in a firmament
Of azure without cloud, and at my feet
Rested a silent sea of hoary° mist.   *white*
A hundred hills their dusky backs upheaved
All over this still ocean; and beyond,
45   Far, far beyond, the solid vapours stretched,

In headlands, tongues, and promontory shapes,
Into the main Atlantic, that appeared
To dwindle, and give up his majesty,
Usurped upon far as the sight could reach.
50   Not so the ethereal vault; encroachment none
Was there, nor loss; only the inferior stars
Had disappeared, or shed a fainter light
In the clear presence of the full-orbed Moon,
Who, from her sovereign elevation, gazed
55   Upon the billowy ocean, as it lay
All meek and silent, save that through a rift—
Not distant from the shore whereon we stood,
A fixed, abysmal, gloomy breathing-place—
Mounted the roar of waters, torrents, streams
60   Innumerable, roaring with one voice!
Heard over earth and sea, and in that hour,
For so it seemed, felt by the starry heavens.

When into air had partially dissolved
That vision, given to spirits of the night,
65   And three chance human wanderers, in calm thought
Reflected, it appeared to me the type
Of a majestic intellect, its acts
And its possessions, what it has and craves,
What in itself it is, and would become.
70   There I beheld the emblem of a mind
That feeds upon infinity, that broods
Over the dark abyss, intent to hear
Its voices issuing forth to silent light
In one continuous stream; a mind sustained
75   By recognitions of transcendent power,
In sense, conducting to ideal form,
In soul of more than mortal privilege.
One function, above all, of such a mind
Had Nature shadowed there, by putting forth,
80   'Mid circumstances awful and sublime,
That mutual domination which she loves
To exert upon the face of outward things,
So moulded, joined, abstracted, so endowed
With interchangeable supremacy,
85   That men least sensitive see, hear, perceive,

---

[1]   *lurcher*   Rabbit-hunting dog.

And cannot choose but feel. The power, which all
Acknowledge when thus moved, which Nature thus
To bodily sense exhibits, is the express
Resemblance of that glorious faculty[1]
0   That higher minds bear with them as their own.
This is the very spirit in which they deal
With the whole compass of the universe:
They, from their native° selves, can send abroad   *natural*
Kindred mutations; for themselves create
5   A like existence, and whene'er it dawns
Created for them, catch it, or are caught
By its inevitable mastery,
Like angels stopped upon the wing by sound
Of harmony from heaven's remotest spheres.[2]
0   Them the enduring and the transient both
Serve to exalt; they build up greatest things
From least suggestions; ever on the watch,
Willing to work and to be wrought upon,
They need not extraordinary calls
5   To rouse them, in a world of life they live,
By sensible impressions not enthralled,
But by their quickening impulse made more prompt
To hold fit converse with the spiritual world,
And with the generations of mankind
0   Spread over time, past, present, and to come,
Age after age, till Time shall be no more.
Such minds are truly from the Deity,
For they are powers; and hence the highest bliss
That flesh can know is theirs—the consciousness
5   Of Whom they are, habitually infused
Through every image, and through every thought,
And all affections by communion raised
From earth to heaven, from human to divine;
Hence endless occupation for the Soul,
0   Whether discursive or intuitive;[3]
Hence cheerfulness for acts of daily life,

Emotions which best foresight need not fear,
Most worthy then of trust when most intense.
Hence, amid ills that vex, and wrongs that crush
125 Our hearts—if here the words of Holy Writ[4]
May with fit reverence be applied—that peace
Which passeth understanding,[5] that repose
In moral judgements which from this pure source
Must come, or will by Man be sought in vain.

130   Oh! who is he that hath his whole life long
Preserved, enlarged, this freedom in himself?
For this alone is genuine liberty:
Where is the favoured being who hath held
That course unchecked, unerring, and untired,
135 In one perpetual progress smooth and bright?—
A humbler destiny have we retraced,
And told of lapse and hesitating choice,
And backward wanderings along thorny ways:
Yet   compassed round by mountain solitudes,
140 Within whose solemn temple I received
My earliest visitations, careless then
Of what was given me; and which now I range,
A meditative, oft a suffering man—
Do I declare—in accents which, from truth
145 Deriving cheerful confidence, shall blend
Their modulation with these vocal streams—
That, whatsoever falls my better mind,
Revolving with the accidents of life,
May have sustained, that, howsoe'er misled,
150 Never did I, in quest of right and wrong,
Tamper with conscience from a private aim;
Nor was in any public hope the dupe
Of selfish passions; nor did ever yield
Wilfully to mean cares or low pursuits,
155 But shrunk with apprehensive
         jealousy°   *dedication, watchfulness*
From every combination which might aid
The tendency, too potent in itself,
Of use° and custom to bow down the soul   *habit*

---

[1] *that glorious faculty* I.e., imagination.

[2] *angels ... spheres* Reference to the concept of the "music of the spheres," a literal or figurative music produced by the movements of the planets and other objects in space; it is audible only to angels.

[3] *discursive or intuitive* In *Paradise Lost*, Milton distinguishes between "discursive" reason, normally held by humans, and "intuitive" reason, belonging to the angels; the two are "differing in degree, of kind the same" (5.490).

---

[4] *Holy Writ* Scripture.

[5] *that peace ... understanding* Cf. Philippians 4.7: "That peace of God, which passeth all understanding."

Under a growing weight of vulgar sense,
160 And substitute a universe of death[1]
For that which moves with light and life informed,
Actual, divine, and true. To fear and love,
To love as prime and chief, for there fear ends,
Be this ascribed; to early intercourse,
165 In presence of sublime or beautiful forms,
With the adverse principles of pain and joy—
Evil, as one is rashly named by men
Who know not what they speak. By love subsists
All lasting grandeur, by pervading love;
170 That gone, we are as dust. Behold the fields
In balmy spring-time full of rising flowers
And joyous creatures; see that pair, the lamb
And the lamb's mother, and their tender ways
Shall touch thee to the heart; thou callest this love,
175 And not inaptly so, for love it is,
Far as it carries thee. In some green bower
Rest, and be not alone, but have thou there
The One who is thy choice of all the world:
There linger, listening, gazing, with delight
180 Impassioned, but delight how pitiable!
Unless this love by a still higher love
Be hallowed, love that breathes not without awe;
Love that adores, but on the knees of prayer,
By heaven inspired; that frees from chains the soul,
185 Lifted, in union with the purest, best,
Of earth-born passions, on the wings of praise
Bearing a tribute to the Almighty's Throne.

    This spiritual Love acts not nor can exist
Without Imagination, which, in truth,
190 Is but another name for absolute power
And clearest insight, amplitude of mind,
And Reason in her most exalted mood.
This faculty hath been the feeding source
Of our long labour: we have traced the stream
195 From the blind cavern whence is faintly heard
Its natal murmur; followed it to light

And open day; accompanied its course
Among the ways of Nature, for a time
Lost sight of it bewildered and engulfed:
200 Then given it greeting as it rose once more
In strength, reflecting from its placid breast
The works of man and face of human life;
And lastly, from its progress have we drawn
Faith in life endless, the sustaining thought
205 Of human Being, Eternity, and God.

    Imagination having been our theme,
So also hath that intellectual° Love,   *inner, spiritual*
For they are each in each, and cannot stand
Dividually.° Here must thou be, O Man!   *divided*
210 Power to thyself; no Helper hast thou here;
Here keepest thou in singleness thy state:
No other can divide with thee this work:
No secondary hand can intervene
To fashion this ability; 'tis thine,
215 The prime and vital principle is thine
In the recesses of thy nature, far
From any reach of outward fellowship,
Else is not thine at all. But joy to him,
Oh, joy to him who here hath sown, hath laid
220 Here, the foundation of his future years!
For all that friendship, all that love can do,
All that a darling countenance can look
Or dear voice utter, to complete the man,
Perfect him, made imperfect in himself,
225 All shall be his: and he whose soul hath risen
Up to the height of feeling Intellect
Shall want no humbler tenderness; his heart
Be tender as a nursing mother's heart;
Of female softness shall his life be full,
230 Of humble cares and delicate desires,
Mild interests and gentlest sympathies.

    Child of my parents! Sister of my soul![2]
Thanks in sincerest verse have been elsewhere

---

[1] *a universe of death*   Cf. the description of hell in Milton's *Paradise Lost* 2.620–23: "many a Frozen, many a fiery Alp, / Rocks, Caves, Lakes, Fens, Bogs, Dens, and shades of death, / A Universe of death, which God by curse / Created evil."

[2] *Child of ... my soul!*   I.e., the poet's sister Dorothy.

Poured out for all the early tenderness
Which I from thee imbibed: and 'tis most true
That later seasons owed to thee no less;
For, spite of thy sweet influence and the touch
Of kindred hands that opened out the springs
Of genial thought in childhood, and in spite
Of all that unassisted I had marked
In life or nature of those charms minute
That win their way into the heart by stealth
(Still to the very going-out of youth),
I too exclusively esteemed *that* love,
And sought *that* beauty, which, as Milton sings,
Hath terror in it.[1] Thou didst soften down
This over-sternness; but for thee, dear Friend!
My soul, too reckless of[2] mild grace, had stood
In her original self too confident,
Retained too long a countenance severe;
A rock with torrents roaring, with the clouds
Familiar, and a favourite of the stars:
But thou didst plant its crevices with flowers,
Hang it with shrubs that twinkle in the breeze,
And teach the little birds to build their nests
And warble in its chambers. At a time
When Nature, destined to remain so long
Foremost in my affections, had fallen back
Into a second place, pleased to become
A handmaid to a nobler than herself,
When every day brought with it some new sense
Of exquisite regard for common things,
And all the earth was budding with these gifts
Of more refined humanity, thy breath,
Dear Sister! was a kind of gentler spring
That went before my steps. Thereafter came
One whom with thee friendship had early paired;[3]
She came, no more a phantom to adorn
A moment, but an inmate of the heart,

And yet a spirit, there for me enshrined
To penetrate the lofty and the low;
Even as one essence of pervading light
Shines, in the brightest of ten thousand stars,
And the meek worm° that feeds her lonely lamp   *glowworm*
Couched in the dewy grass.

                    With such a theme,
Coleridge! with this my argument, of thee
Shall I be silent? O capacious Soul!
Placed on this earth to love and understand,
And from thy presence shed the light of love,
Shall I be mute, ere thou be spoken of?
Thy kindred influence to my heart of hearts
Did also find its way. Thus fear relaxed
Her overweening° grasp; thus thoughts   *presumptuous*
    and things
In the self-haunting spirit learned to take
More rational proportions; mystery,
The incumbent mystery of sense and soul,
Of life and death, time and eternity,
Admitted more habitually a mild
Interposition[4]—a serene delight
In closelier gathering cares, such as become
A human creature, howsoe'er endowed,
Poet, or destined for a humbler name;
And so the deep enthusiastic joy,
The rapture of the hallelujah sent
From all that breathes and is, was chastened, stemmed,
And balanced by pathetic° truth, by trust   *emotional*
In hopeful reason, leaning on the stay
Of Providence; and in reverence for duty,
Here, if need be, struggling with storms, and there
Strewing in peace life's humblest ground with herbs,
At every season green, sweet at all hours.

    And now, O Friend! this history is brought
To its appointed close: the discipline
And consummation of a Poet's mind,

---

[1] *that beauty … it*   Cf. Satan's description of Eve in Milton's *Paradise Lost* 9.490–92: "She fair, divinely fair, fit Love for Gods, / Not terrible, though terror be in Love / And beauty."

[2] *reckless of*   Inattentive to.

[3] *One whom … paired*   Mary Hutchinson, the poet's wife, who was already a close friend of Dorothy's when the couple married.

[4] *Admitted … Interposition*   I.e., began to suffuse the poet's usual thoughts in a gentle, moderate way.

305 In every thing that stood most prominent,
Have faithfully been pictured; we have reached
The time (our guiding object from the first)
When we may, not presumptuously, I hope,
Suppose my powers so far confirmed, and such
310 My knowledge, as to make me capable
Of building up a Work that shall endure.
Yet much hath been omitted, as need was;
Of books how much! and even of the other wealth
That is collected among woods and fields,
315 Far more: for Nature's secondary grace
Hath hitherto been barely touched upon,
The charm more superficial that attends
Her works, as they present to Fancy's choice
Apt illustrations of the moral world,
320 Caught at a glance, or traced with curious pains.

    Finally, and above all, O Friend! (I speak
With due regret) how much is overlooked
In human nature and her subtle ways,
As studied first in our own hearts, and then
325 In life among the passions of mankind,
Varying their composition and their hue,
Where'er we move, under the diverse shapes
That individual character presents
To an attentive eye. For progress meet,
330 Along this intricate and difficult path,
Whate'er was wanting, something had I gained,
As one of many schoolfellows compelled,
In hardy independence, to stand up
Amid conflicting interests, and the shock
335 Of various tempers; to endure and note
What was not understood, though known to be;
Among the mysteries of love and hate,
Honour and shame, looking to right and left,
Unchecked by innocence too delicate,
340 And moral notions too intolerant,
Sympathies too contracted.° Hence,   *limited*
    when called
To take a station among men, the step
Was easier, the transition more secure,
More profitable also; for, the mind
345 Learns from such timely exercise to keep

In wholesome separation the two natures,
The one that feels, the other that observes.

    Yet one word more of personal concern—
Since I withdrew unwillingly from France,[1]
350 I led an undomestic wanderer's life,
In London chiefly harboured, whence I roamed,
Tarrying at will in many a pleasant spot
Of rural England's cultivated vales
Or Cambrian° solitudes. A youth (he bore   *Welsh*
355 The name of Calvert[2]—it shall live, if words
Of mine can give it life) in firm belief
That by endowments not from me withheld
Good might be furthered—in his last decay
By a bequest sufficient for my needs
360 Enabled me to pause for choice, and walk
At large and unrestrained, nor damped too soon
By mortal cares. Himself no Poet, yet
Far less a common follower of the world,
He deemed that my pursuits and labours lay
365 Apart from all that leads to wealth, or even
A necessary maintenance insures,
Without some hazard to the finer sense;
He cleared a passage for me, and the stream
Flowed in the bent of Nature.
                Having now
370 Told what best merits mention, further pains
Our present purpose seems not to require,
And I have other tasks. Recall to mind
The mood in which this labour was begun,
O Friend! The termination of my course
375 Is nearer now, much nearer; yet even then,
In that distraction and intense desire,
I said unto the life which I had lived,
Where art thou? Hear I not a voice from thee
Which 'tis reproach to hear? Anon° I rose   *then*
380 As if on wings, and saw beneath me stretched

---

1 *I withdrew … France* In 1792 financial pressures forced Wordsworth to return to England from France, leaving behind his lover,
Annette Vallon, who gave birth to their daughter in the same year.

2 *Calvert* Raisley Calvert, Wordsworth's friend, who died young of
tuberculosis. He left Wordsworth £900, enough for him to set up
house with his sister at Racedown Lodge and devote himself to his
poetry.

Vast prospect of the world which I had been
And was; and hence this Song, which like a lark
I have protracted,° in the unwearied heavens   *extended*
Singing, and often with more plaintive voice
5 To earth attempered° and her deep-drawn sighs, *adapted*
Yet centring all in love, and in the end
All gratulant,° if rightly understood.   *joyful*

Whether to me shall be allotted life,
And, with life, power to accomplish aught of worth,
0 That will be deemed no insufficient plea
For having given the story of myself,[1]
Is all uncertain: but, beloved Friend!
When, looking back, thou seest, in clearer view
Than any liveliest sight of yesterday,
5 That summer, under whose indulgent skies,
Upon smooth Quantock's[2] airy ridge we roved
Unchecked, or loitered 'mid her sylvan°   *wooded*
   combs,°   *valleys*
Thou in bewitching words, with happy heart,
Didst chaunt the vision of that Ancient Man,
0 The bright-eyed Mariner, and rueful woes
Didst utter of the Lady Christabel;
And I, associate with such labour, steeped
In soft forgetfulness the livelong hours,
Murmuring of him who, joyous hap,°   *chance*
   was found,
5 After the perils of his moonlight ride,
Near the loud waterfall;[3] or her who sat
In misery near the miserable Thorn;[4]
When thou dost to that summer turn thy thoughts,

And hast before thee all which then we were,
410 To thee, in memory of that happiness,
It will be known, by thee at least, my Friend!
Felt, that the history of a Poet's mind
Is labour not unworthy of regard:
To thee the work shall justify itself.

415   The last and later portions of this gift
Have been prepared, not with the buoyant spirits
That were our daily portion when we first
Together wantoned in wild Poesy,
But, under pressure of a private grief,[5]
420 Keen and enduring, which the mind and heart,
That in this meditative history
Have been laid open, needs must make me feel
More deeply, yet enable me to bear
More firmly; and a comfort now hath risen
425 From hope that thou art near, and wilt be soon
Restored to us in renovated health;
When, after the first mingling of our tears,
'Mong other consolations, we may draw
Some pleasure from this offering of my love.

430   Oh! yet a few short years of useful life,
And all will be complete, thy race be run,
Thy monument of glory will be raised;
Then, though (too weak to tread the ways of truth)
This age fall back to old idolatry,
435 Though men return to servitude as fast
As the tide ebbs, to ignominy and shame
By nations sink together, we shall still
Find solace—knowing what we have learnt to know,
Rich in true happiness if allowed to be
440 Faithful alike in forwarding a day
Of firmer trust, joint labourers in the work
(Should Providence such grace to us vouchsafe)
Of their deliverance, surely yet to come.
Prophets of Nature, we to them will speak
445 A lasting inspiration, sanctified
By reason, blest by faith: what we have loved,
Others will love, and we will teach them how;

---

[1] *Whether to … myself* Whether my life, abilities, and accomplishments will be considered to justify my writing about myself.

[2] *Quantock* Hills above Alfoxden House, in Somerset, where the Wordsworths moved for larger accommodations and to be closer to Coleridge. That summer while visiting them, Coleridge recited "The Rime of the Ancient Mariner" and "Christabel," both of which he had recently finished, and Wordsworth wrote "The Idiot Boy" and "The Thorn." Wordsworth and Coleridge published *Lyrical Ballads* the following year.

[3] *Murmuring … waterfall* In "The Idiot Boy," a boy with disabilities is sent to fetch a doctor and does not return; his mother finds him atop his horse near a waterfall.

[4] *In misery … Thorn* A refrain in the poem "The Thorn" is "'Oh misery! oh misery! / Oh woe is me! oh misery!'"

[5] *a private grief* Wordsworth's brother John died in a shipwreck in 1805.

Instruct them how the mind of man becomes
A thousand times more beautiful than the earth
450   On which he dwells, above this frame of things
(Which 'mid all revolutions in the hopes

And fears of men doth still remain unchanged)
In beauty exalted, as it is itself
Of quality and fabric more divine.
—1850

Benjamin Robert Haydon, *Wordsworth on Helvellyn*, 1842.

Reading, Writing, Publishing

CONTEXTS

During the Romantic period, questions concerning the definition of literature and the nature of its role in society pervaded print culture. Among the topics debated were definitions of intellectual property, the ways in which dissemination of texts should be encouraged or restrained, and the extent to which literature could effect social or political reform. For many, particularly in light of the French Revolution, literature was felt to hold a radical potential to change the world.

Some questioned whether women or members of the laboring classes should be allowed access to political tracts, and feared that less educated or less discerning minds could be easily swayed by the persuasive rhetoric of radicals. Daniel Isaac Eaton was among those whose powers of persuasion they feared; he had been tried nine times for publishing or writing radical texts and on one occasion had been sentenced to 18 months in jail. Here he satirizes the anti-revolutionaries' fear of the power of the press and the government's desire to control the circulation of potentially seditious material through legislation and taxes. Eaton's weekly magazine, *Politics for the People* (1793–95), was an important and popular organ of radical journalism; when he was placed in the pillory in 1812 for printing the third part of *Age of Reason*, he was cheered by a large crowd.

Thomas Spence, whose poem on the theme of repression appears next, was also well acquainted with the accusation of libel. He had been arrested four times and imprisoned twice between 1792 and 1794 alone. In the poem reproduced here, his parenthetical denials cleverly serve to protect him from such charges while simultaneously articulating radical criticism of the monarchy and aristocracy. The poem following Spence's, by an anonymous author, uses the sort of animal analogies that were commonly relied upon in political satire at the time. By exploiting traditional moral fables, writers could create poems that were clearly understood by their readers, yet were ambiguous enough to allow their authors to disavow any subversive intent.

The piece that follows emphasizes the importance of literature to revolutionary efforts. While Eaton had mocked anti-radicals' fear of the press, the anonymous author of "On the Characteristics of Poetry" links the feelings excited by poetry to powerful political action, and even to military victory.

The period was what John Stuart Mill called "a reading age"; there were more readers than ever before, and publishing was becoming a major industry. While many viewed this development as beneficial to society, others feared a proliferation of trivial works that would neither improve the minds of readers nor encourage them to pick up more challenging works. If too many books were produced each year for any one person to read, how could people hope to peruse them all and decide which were most worthy of their attention?

Voicing a common fear, the anonymous correspondent to the *Monthly Magazine* whose letter is excerpted here claims that the proliferation of writers has led to a decline in literary standards and a decreased appreciation for writers of true genius. In the following piece, Samuel Pratt proposes an effective solution to this problem in the form of literary journals, whose writers can together provide readers with a balanced critical appraisal. In a slightly later article, Isaac D'Israeli proposes another solution in the form of changes to copyright laws that would reward authors of true genius rather than benefiting only the "booksellers" (publishers), who in his view sought to publish trivial works of mass appeal.

Hannah More, in *Strictures on the Modern System of Female Education*, examines what she sees as the negative effects of the abundant novels and other "alluring little works" on the morals and intellects of young women. In a later excerpt, prolific novelist Anna Laetitia Barbauld, in her introduction to her edition of *The British Novelists*, celebrates the novel's ability to divert and entertain, a characteristic more important to the average reader than moral instruction.

In the final two excerpts, John Stuart Mill and William Hazlitt express opposing views on the future of British literature and culture. Hazlitt takes a more positive view of the commodification of literature, accepting what he sees as inevitable, while Mill predicts the downfall of a culture whose integrity he feared would soon be undermined by commercial society.

⌘ ⌘ ⌘

from Daniel Isaac Eaton, *The Pernicious Effects of the Art of Printing upon Society, Exposed* (1793)

Before this diabolical art was introduced among men, there was social order. ... In the times we are speaking of (the Golden Age), the feudal system prevailed—a system replete with blessings—by it the different orders of society were kept perfectly distinct and separate—there were kings, barons, priests, yeomanry, villains[1] or slaves; and they were, I believe, with regard to rank and power, in the order in which I have named them. The villains, or lowest class, were what Mr. Burke so elegantly terms the *Swinish Multitude*,[2] but of rights or privileges as men they had not an idea; we may with propriety style them the Jackals of the times: they tilled the earth, and performed all manual labour; but in return, their superiors allowed them sufficient of the produce for subsistence—permitted them to take some rest, in order that they might be strong. To bear hardship and fatigue took from them the trouble of thinking—indeed, from the very prudent manner in which they were brought up, I will not say

educated, they were little capable of thought, of course exempt from the mental fatigues of study and reflections. The Scriptures having declared gold to be the root of every evil, they were very humanely prevented from possessing any. As to religion, the clergy taught them as much as they thought necessary, and they were without doubt the best judges, being in general good scholars. ...

Since printing has been employed as the medium of diffusing sentiments, &c. government has become more difficult—the governors are frequently and insolently called upon to give an account of the national treasure, its expenditure, &c.—and if they are in any respect tardy, or should circumstances render evasion necessary, it is astonishing, with what boldness some men will dare to revile and insult them.

The lower orders begin to have ideas of rights, as men—to think that one man is as good as another; that society is at present founded upon false principles; that hereditary honours and distinctions are absurd, unjust, and oppressive; that abilities and morals only should recommend to the first officers in a state; that no regard should be paid to rank and titles; that instruction, sufficient to qualify a man for being a member of society, is a debt due to every individual, and that it is the duty of every state to take care that he receive it; that every man has a right to a share in the government, either in his own person, or that of his representative, and that no portion of his property or labour ought to be taxed without his consent, given either by himself, or

---

[1] *villains* I.e., villeins, serfs, or peasants.

[2] *Mr. Burke ... Multitude* Edmund Burke, probably in reference to a particular faction of extremists (rather than all members of the working classes), said that if learning was removed from the hierarchical social order in which it had originated, it would be "cast into the mire, and trodden down under the hoofs of a swinish multitude." Reformers took this comment as proof of the arrogance and superiority with which conservatives regarded the masses.

representative; that everyone should contribute to the support of the state in proportion to his ability, and that all partial exactions are oppressive; that laws should be the same to all, and that no one, whatever may be his rank or station, should be allowed to offend them with impunity; that freedom of speech is the equal right of all, and that the rich have no right to dictate to the poor what sentiments they shall adopt on any subject, or in any wise[1] prevent investigation and inquiry. This, with a great deal more such stuff, is called the rights of man—blessed fruits of the art of printing—the scum of the earth, the swinish multitude, talking of their rights! and insolently claiming, nay, almost demanding, that political liberty shall be the same to all—to the high and the low, the rich and the poor—what audacity!—what unparalleled effrontery!—it ought to meet correction. With similar mistaken notions of liberty, even many women are infatuated; and the press, that grand prolific source of evil, that fruitful mother of mischief, has already favoured the public with several female productions on this very popular subject—one in particular, called *Rights of Women*,[2] and in which, as one of their rights, a share in legislation is claimed and asserted —gracious heaven! to what will this fatal delusion lead, and in what will it terminate! …

For all these, and numberless other evils, the natural consequence of a diffusion of knowledge and science, some remedy must be found; the present administration have made some trifling feeble attempts to check their progress, such as additional duties upon advertisements and newspapers, which almost preclude cheap publications—of the same nature I suppose the late tax upon paper to be—but these remedies are totally inadequate, at least they will be so exceedingly slow in their operation, that the present race have but little prospect of living to see any of their good effects.

To rid ourselves of such a monster, some strong efficient measure must be had recourse to, something that will strike at the root, and have an almost instantaneous effect—such a one, I think, I can point out.

Let all printing presses be committed to the flames, all letter foundries be destroyed, schools and seminaries of learning abolished, dissenters of every denominations double and treble taxed, all discourse upon government and religion prohibited, political clubs and associations of every kind suppressed —excepting those formed for the express purpose of supporting government—and lastly, issue a proclamation against reading, and burn all private libraries. To carry some part of this plan into execution, it will be necessary to employ spies and informers, which by many (Jacobins and Republicans) are thought to be signs either of a weak or wicked and corrupt government; they say that governors, conscious of acting for the public good, of having it only in view in all their measure, would scorn using such unworthy and dishonourable means. I cannot be of this opinion, but am confident that if the measures I have proposed be but speedily adopted, and rigorously pursued, the happiest consequences would soon be experienced; all the wild, idle theories with which men are at present disturbed, would soon vanish—the lower orders would mind their work, become tractable and docile, and perhaps in less than half a century that desirable state of ignorance and darkness, which formerly prevailed, might again restore to this Island that happy state of society with which it once was blessed.

Thomas Spence, "Examples of Safe Printing," from *Pig's Meat*,[3] Volume 2 (1794)

To prevent misrepresentation in these prosecuting times, it seems necessary to publish every thing relating to tyranny and oppression, though only among brutes, in the most guarded manner.

The following are meant as specimens:

That tyger, or that other salvage wight°   *savage creature*
Is so exceeding furious and fell,°   *fierce*
As WRONG,

---

[1] *wise* Way.

[2] *Rights of Women* Mary Wollstonecraft's *A Vindication of the Rights of Woman* (1792).

[3] *Pig's Meat* The title is a reference to Burke's term "swinish multitude," which many radical writers adopted as an ironic definition of the working classes.

　　　[*Not meaning our most gracious sovereign*
5　　　*Lord the King, or the Government of this*
　　　country]
　　　when it hath arm'd himself with might;
Not fit 'mong men that do with reason mell,° 　　　*mix*
But 'mong wild beasts and salvage woods to dwell;
10　　Where still the stronger
　　　[*Not meaning the great men of this country*]
　　　doth the weak devour,
And they that most in boldness do excell,
　　　Are dreaded most, and feared by their power.
　　　　　　　　　　　　　　　—E. Spencer[1]

Joshua,[2] "Sonnet: The Lion," from *Moral and Political Magazine*, Volume 1 (1796)

Why grace we the stern lion with the name
　　That marks the chiefs of Europe? More of use
　　To man's assistance do the kine° produce; 　　　*cattle*
For bulk, behold the elephant's huge frame!
5　For agile beauty see the stately horse.
　　King of the forest HE, and doomed to reign,
　　Like earthly monarch, o'er the Lybian plain
For fierce pre-eminence in brutal force:
　　Before his tyrant rage the fleet° horse flies, 　　　*swift*
10　　The patient sheep avoids him, or he dies.
Stern bloody beast! they named thee well: thy right
　　Is to this royal title just and good;
Thou gain'dst it by thy savage joy in fight,
Thy brutal fury, and thy thirst for blood.

from Anonymous, "On the Characteristics of Poetry," No. 2, from the *Monthly Magazine* (1797)

In the course of our last discussion, we seemed to be unanimously of opinion that the grand characteristic, the *sine qua non*[3] of poetry, consists in its capacity of pressing the mind with the most vivid pictures. Indeed, the maxim *ut pictura poesis*[4] is amply illustrated whenever poetry is in any shape the subject of investigation. The terms of the painter's art then insensibly creep into the discourse and model our phraseology.

Pursuing, then, this idea, we may perhaps lay it down as the grand and leading end of poetry to make a strong and lively impression on the feelings. In her operations she hurries us far beyond the reach of the voice of sober judgment, and captivates by exciting the aid of the passions. Here, then, we see the cause of the mighty energy of verse, nor wonder at the efficaciousness that has been ascribed to the Muses.[5] For how easily are mankind guided by those that possess the happy art of awakening or allaying their feelings. Though all unconscious of being under the guidance of another, they turn obedient to the rein. They are roused to insurrection, or moderated to peace, by him who can touch, with a skilful hand, the master springs that regulate the motions of their minds. When Brutus[6] ascends the rostrum, the words of truth and soberness are heard, and plain integrity convinces the judgment. But, when Anthony[7] displays the bloody robe, and points to the wounds of Caesar, reminding the people that this was once their darling benefactor, the multitude are melted to sorrow, and at last roused from pity to fury and revenge.

Here, then, this essay might, perhaps, with propriety, have been closed. But I must rely upon your candour for the admission of a few more observations, which may, perhaps, tend to illustrate the point to which this enquiry has led us:

---

[1]　*E. Spencer*　I.e., Renaissance poet Edmund Spenser (1552?–99), whom the poet imitates in order to create historical distance from the referents of the poem.

[2]　*Joshua*　Biblical lieutenant of Moses who led the Israelites to victory over the Canaanites (see Joshua 1–12).

[3]　*sine qua non*　Latin: indispensable attribute.

[4]　*ut pictura poesis*　Latin: "as is painting, so is poetry" (from Horace, *Ars Poetica*).

[5]　*Muses*　Nine daughters of Zeus and Mnemosyne, each of whom presided over and provided inspiration for an aspect of the arts and sciences.

[6]　*Brutus*　One of the men who assassinated Julius Caesar, whom had become dictator of Rome for life.

[7]　*Anthony*　Marc Antony, consul who, after Caesar's assassination, aroused the mob against the conspirators, causing them to be driven from the city.

The end of poetry, it is said, is an impression upon the feelings. But as there is an intimate connection between feeling and action, so that where the one appears, the other "follows hard upon," if the foregoing observations be true, we may expect to find that the actions of mankind are, in some measure, influenced by the Muses.

And if we look to the simpler ages of society, when we can best distinguish the grand outlines of the human character, where the springs that actuate the conduct of man are, in a manner, bared for inspection, we shall find this to have been the case. In the infancy of states, poetry is a method equally captivating and efficacious of forming the dispositions of the people, and kindling in their hearts that love of glory which is their country's safeguard and defence. Whether we look to the cold regions of Scandinavia, or the delicious clime of Greece, we find that when society has made a certain progress, mankind are strongly influenced by a love of song, and listen, with raptured attention, to the strains that record the tale of other times, and the deeds of heroes of old. They listen till they imbibe the enthusiasm of warfare, and in the day of battle, the hero's arm has not unfrequently been nerved by the rough energy of the early bard. ...

But, indeed, what occasion have we to search into the dust of antiquity for examples of the influence of verse upon human conduct? The transactions of our own times may teach us that as strong feelings generate poetic language, so poetic language inspires the mind with at least a temporary enthusiasm, and thus impels to action. In this country, the fervour or loyalty has of late been blown into a blaze, and for this event the parties interested are not a little indebted to the assistance of the Muses. And when the Marseillaise Hymn[1] echoed through the ranks of the French army at the field of Jemappe,[2] we need not wonder that "the spear of liberty was wielded with classic grace," and that the energy of heroism was communicated with the sound.

[1] *Marseillaise Hymn* Composed by Claude Joseph Rouget de Lisle on 24 April 1792, "the Marseillaise" celebrated freedom and human rights and became a rallying cry for the French Revolutionaries. It was declared the French national anthem in 1795.

[2] *field of Jemappe* Where a Revolutionary victory occurred in 1792.

from Anonymous, Letter to the *Monthly Magazine* (24 October 1798)

Sir,

Literature is either less cultivated, or less valued in these days than it was in those of our ancestors, for certainly learning does not *now* receive the honours it *then* did. That it is less cultivated, cannot, I think, with any truth be asserted, because the present is denominated a learned age. It must be the universality then, with which it is diffused throughout society, that renders it less valuable—as articles grow cheap, not in proportion to their insignificancy, but their abundance. Great talents, indeed, in any condition of civilized society must inevitably confer a certain degree of power, inasmuch as they render their possessors either useful or formidable; but scarcely any literary attainments would, I apprehend, raise a writer in these days to the same degree of eminence and request as Petrarch, Erasmus, and Politiano[3] enjoyed in their respective times. We have now amongst us many scholars of great erudition (Parr, Wakefield, Professors Porson and White,[4] &c. &c.), men of distinguished abilities; yet I much question, as haughty as kings were under the feudal system, if any of the princes in being would contend with the same eagerness for their favour, as we learn the various sovereigns of Europe did for that of Petrarch or Erasmus.

It has been questioned by some whether the number of publications, which are annually poured upon the world, have contributed in any proportionable ratio to the increase of literature? In my opinion, they have *not*. To a liberal and cultivated mind there is certainly no indulgence equal to the luxury of books; but, in works

[3] *Petrarch* Francesco Petrarch, Italian poet and Humanist of the fourteenth century, famous for his sonnets; *Erasmus* Desiderius Erasmus, Dutch Humanist (1466–1536); *Politiano* Italian poet Angelo Poliziano (1454–94), who also served as professor of Greek and Latin at the University of Florence.

[4] *Parr* Samuel Parr (1747–1825), a Latin scholar, schoolmaster, minister, and vocal Whig supporter; *Wakefield* Gilbert Wakefield (1756–1801), a Biblical scholar and religious and political controversialist who also produced an edition of Virgil's *Georgics* (1788); *Professors Porson and White* Richard Porson (1759–1808), Greek professor at Cambridge, and Gilbert White (1720–93), noted naturalist.

of learning, may not the facilities of information be increased, until the powers of application and retention be diminished? After admitting that the present is a learned age, it may appear singular to doubt whether it affords[1] individuals as profoundly learned (at least, as far as Latin and Greek go), as some who flourished in the fifteenth and sixteenth centuries.

From these remarks, I would not be understood as wishing to make invidious comparisons between the learning of different ages, or to depreciate that of our own. Upon a fair investigation, there can be no doubt, I think, to which side the scale of general literature would incline. My object simply is, to show the different direction which letters take, and the different patronage they obtain, in different periods of society. Indeed, learning may more properly be said to *lead* than to *follow* the course of the world: since, though it may, at first, bend to the spirit of the age, it will in the end assuredly direct and govern it. The general stock of genius is, perhaps, always pretty equal; the opportunities of improving it, and the support it receives, vary with the times. Petrarch and Erasmus were caressed by popes and princes; Butler, Otway, and Chatterton,[2] not much inferior in merit, were absolutely starved; and Johnson,[3] whose moral works were calculated to delight and improve the age, lived long in distress, and at length received a scanty pension. In some ages, and upon some occasions, it must be admitted, a genius darts upon the world with intellectual powers that no industry, in the common course of things, can hope to equal. But this is a *particular* case, and is generally compensated some other way. If former times have enjoyed works of more fancy, and sublimity of imagination, than are given to us, we, in return, possess more useful acquisitions. If they have had their Spenser, Tasso, and Shakespeare, we

boast Newton, Locke,[4] and Johnson. Science, taste, and correction are indeed the characteristics of the present day. Everything is refined; everything is grand. We are actually misers in luxury and taste, and have left nothing for posterity. "*Venimus ad summum fortunae*"[5]—We learn our Greek from the Pursuits of Literature,[6] and our morality from Parissot, and I do not see how we are to be outdone either in learning or in dress.

I remain, Sir, &c., &c.

Ausonius[7]

from Samuel Pratt, *Gleanings in England: Descriptive of the Countenance, Mind, and Character of the Country* (1799)

There cannot be a doubt but that while the liberty of the press, as to the freedom of publication, shall be sacred—and on this side of licentiousness, it ought to be uncontrolled—it is equally just that the sense and nonsense which indiscriminately issue from the immense vehicle of communication should be subject to vigilant examination, otherwise the whole world would be over-run with abortions of the mind. We want the assistance of some guides who will take upon themselves the trouble of separating the good from the bad and wade through the troubled deep of literature in order, if we may be permitted a continuation of the figure, to collect the pearls and gems, and to describe the useless weeds, whether swimming on the surface or lying at the muddy bottom. A stupendous labour if we consider the great disproportion betwixt the former and the latter. Applying this to the case in point, and it is by no means

---

[1] *affords*   Is capable of producing.

[2] *Butler, Otway, and Chatterton*   Satirical poet Samuel Butler (1612–80), tragic dramatist Thomas Otway (1652–85), and young poet Thomas Chatterton (1752–70) all lived in dire poverty.

[3] *Johnson*   Samuel Johnson (1709–84), lexicographer, poet, and author of the journals *The Rambler* and *The Idler*. He struggled for financial security until 1762, when he was granted a pension for his work on the *Dictionary*.

[4] *Spenser*   English poet Edmund Spenser (c. 1552–99), author of *The Faerie Queene*; *Tasso*   Italian poet Torquato Tasso (1544–95); *Newton*   Mathematician and natural philosopher Sir Isaac Newton (1642–1727); *Locke*   Philosopher John Locke (1632–1704).

[5] *Venimus ... fortunae*   Latin: "We have come to the height of fortune" (Horace, *Epistles* 2.1).

[6] *Pursuits of Literature*   Four-part satirical poem by Thomas James Mathias concerning the nature of literature. Its publication (1794–97) aroused much debate.

[7] *Ausonius*   I.e., the author's pseudonym, referring to the Latin poet Dicimius Magmus Ausonius (c. 310–c. 393).

inapposite, a reader unused to such arduous undertakings can image to himself no task so overwhelming as that of being left unaided to search for instruction in the mass of productions which are every year piled, mountain high, before him. … For this reason, it would be proper that there should be some professional inspectors to direct our choice, even were literary excellence and defect nearly equal. But when the average is on a ratio of at least ninety in the hundred in the scale of compositions *deadweight*, there is not, perhaps, any office so necessary as his, who, with patient circumspection, will examine the great account betwixt wisdom and folly, and settle the balance.

It is not, therefore, possible to conceive a more useful institution than that of a literary journal, when conducted with various ability and inflexible justice; nor can it be denied that a great variety of articles, in every branch of literature, have been analysed on these principles, and a due proportion of good has thence resulted to the community.

We have to boast, even at this day, of great and noble critics; and from most, indeed, in all of our literary journals, we find substantial evidence of unimpeachable judgement and unwarped integrity. It is not, however, to be expected that any human association composed of many members should be conducted on principles uniformly sagacious and correct. Were they to write apart, and consult together ultimately, there must even then often be a clash of sentiment, a dissonance of opinion.

Yet I am persuaded the critics above-described are the very persons who must reprobate the virulences[1] and regret the errors for which they are made responsible. The literary body cannot be supposed to separate, or seem to move a limb independently—much less to commit themselves, and confederate against each other, by deploring the want of candour in some of their colleagues, and of capacity in others. Thus from their not being associated by congeniality, or chosen by consent—and yet under a kind of compact to hold together, and by the good faith that should be preserved

in all treaties, bound to support one another in the way of a common cause—the errors, incongruities, adulations, and virulences, which are observed occasionally to disfigure their journals, attach indiscriminately to all.

from Hannah More, *Strictures on the Modern System of Female Education* (1799)

from CHAPTER 8: ON FEMALE STUDY

Will it not be ascribed to a captious singularity, if I venture to remark that real knowledge and real piety, though they may have gained in many instances, have suffered in others from that profusion of little, amusing, sentimental books with which the youthful library overflows? Abundance has its dangers as well as scarcity. In the first place, may not the multiplicity of these alluring little works increase the natural reluctance to those more dry and uninteresting studies, of which, after all, the rudiments of every part of learning *must* consist? And, secondly, is there not some danger (though there are many honourable exceptions) that some of those engaging narratives may serve to infuse into the youthful heart a sort of spurious goodness, a confidence of virtue, a parade of charity? And that the benevolent actions with the recital of which they abound, when they are not made to flow from any source but *feeling*, may tend to inspire a self-complacency, a self-gratulation, a "stand by, for I am holier than thou?" May not the success with which the good deeds of the little heroes are uniformly crowned, the invariable reward which is made the instant concomitant of well-doing, furnish the young reader with false views of the condition of life, and the nature of the divine dealings with men? May they not help to suggest a false standard of morals, to infuse a love of popularity and an anxiety for praise, in the place of that simple and unostentatious rule of doing whatever good we do *because it is the will of God*? The universal substitution of this principle would tend to purify the worldly morality of many a popular little story. And there are few dangers which good parents will more carefully

---
[1] *virulences* Incidences of bitter hostility or antagonism.

guard against than that of giving their children a mere political piety—that sort of religion which just goes to make people more respectable, and to stand well with the world; a religion which is to save appearances without inculcating realities; a religion which affects to "preach peace and good will to men," but which forgets to give "glory to God in the highest."[1]

There is a certain precocity of mind which is much helped on by these superficial modes of instruction; for frivolous reading will produce its correspondent effect in much less time than books of solid instruction; the imagination being liable to be worked upon, and the feelings to be set a going, much faster than the understanding can be opened and the judgment enlightened. A talent for conversation should be the result of instruction, not its precursor: it is a golden fruit when suffered to ripen gradually on the tree of knowledge; but if forced in the hot-bed of a circulating library, it will turn out worthless and vapid in proportion as it was artificial and premature. Girls who have been accustomed to devour a multitude of frivolous books will converse and write with a far greater appearance of skill, as to style and sentiment, at twelve or fourteen years old, than those of a more advanced age who are under the discipline of severer studies; but the former having early attained to that low standard which had been held out to them, become stationary; while the latter, quietly progressive, are passing through just gradations to a higher strain of mind; and those who early begin with talking and writing like women, commonly end with thinking and acting like children.

… Who are those ever-multiplying authors that with unparalleled fecundity are overstocking the world with their quick-succeeding progeny? They are NOVEL-WRITERS, the easiness of whose productions is at once the cause of their own fruitfulness, and of the almost infinitely numerous race of imitators to whom they give birth. Such is the frightful facility of this species of composition, that every raw girl, while she reads, is tempted to fancy that she can also write. And as Alexan-der, on perusing the *Iliad*, found by congenial sympathy the image of Achilles stamped on his own ardent soul,[2] and felt himself the hero he was studying; and as Correggio,[3] on first beholding a picture which exhibited the perfection of the graphic art, prophetically felt all his own future greatness, and cried out in rapture, "And I, too, am a painter!" so a thorough-paced novel-reading Miss, at the close of every tissue of hackneyed adventures, feels within herself the stirring impulse of corresponding genius, and triumphantly exclaims, "And I, too, am an author!" The glutted imagination soon overflows with the redundance of cheap sentiment and plentiful incident, and by a sort of arithmetical proportion is enabled by the perusal of any three novels to produce a fourth; till every fresh production, like the prolific progeny of Banquo, is followed by "Another, and another, and another!"[4] Is a lady, however destitute of talents, education, or knowledge of the world, whose studies have been completed by a circulating library, in any distress of mind? the writing a novel suggests itself as the best soother of her sorrows! Does she labour under any depression of circumstances? writing a novel occurs as the readiest receipt for mending them! and she solaces her imagination with the conviction that the subscription which has been extorted by her importunity, or given to her necessities, has been offered as a homage to her genius; and this confidence instantly levies a fresh contribution for a succeeding work. Capacity and cultivation are so little taken into the account, that writing a book seems to be now considered as the only sure resource which the idle and the illiterate have always in their power

1 *preach peace … the highest* Quotations from Luke 2.14.

2 *Alexander … ardent soul* Reference to a famous anecdote recounting Alexander the Great's sympathy with Achilles, the Greek hero of Homer's *Iliad*.

3 *Correggio* Italian Renaissance painter Antonio Allegri (c. 1494–1534), called Correggio after his birthplace.

4 *prolific progeny … another* See *Macbeth* 4.1, in which Macbeth is frustrated by a vision of a nearly endless line of Banquo's royal heirs.

Anna Laetitia Barbauld, "On the Origin and Progress of Novel-Writing"[1] (1810)

A collection of novels has a better chance of giving pleasure than of commanding respect. Books of this description are condemned by the grave, and despised by the fastidious; but their leaves are seldom found unopened, and they occupy the parlour and the dressing-room while productions of higher name are often gathering dust upon the shelf. It might not perhaps be difficult to show that this species of composition is entitled to a higher rank than has been generally assigned it. Fictitious adventures, in one form or other, have made a part of the polite literature of every age and nation. These have been grafted upon the actions of their heroes; they have been interwoven with their mythology; they have been moulded upon the manners of the age—and, in return, have influenced the manners of the succeeding generation by the sentiments they have infused and the sensibilities they have excited.

If the end and object of this species of writing be asked, many no doubt will be ready to tell us that its object is to call in fancy to the aid of reason, to deceive the mind into embracing truth under the guise of fiction:

> Cosi a l'egro fanciul porgiamo aspersi
> Di soave licor gli orli del vaso,
> Succhi amari, ingannato in tanto ei beve,
> E da l'inganno suo vita riceve,[2]

with such-like reasons equally grave and dignified. For my own part, I scruple not to confess that when I take up a novel my end and object is entertainment; and as I suspect that to be the case with most readers, I hesitate not to say that entertainment is their legitimate end and object. To read the productions of wit and genius is a very high pleasure to all persons of taste, and the avidity with which they are read by all such shows sufficiently that they are calculated to answer this end. Reading is the cheapest of pleasures: it is a domestic pleasure. Dramatic exhibitions give a more poignant delight, but they are seldom enjoyed in perfection, and never without expense and trouble. Poetry requires in the reader a certain elevation of mind and a practiced ear. It is seldom relished unless a taste be formed for it pretty early. But the humble novel is always ready to enliven the gloom of solitude, to soothe the languor of debility and disease, to win the attention from pain or vexatious occurrences, to take man from himself (at many seasons the worst company he can be in), and, while the moving picture of life passes before him, to make him forget the subject of his own complaints. It is pleasant to the mind to sport in the boundless regions of possibility; to find relief from the sameness of everyday occurrences by expatiating amidst brighter skies and fairer fields; to exhibit love that is always happy, valour that is always successful; to feed the appetite for wonder by a quick succession of marvelous events; and to distribute, like a ruling Providence, rewards and punishments which fall just where they ought to fall.

It is sufficient, therefore, as an end, that these writings add to the innocent pleasures of life; and if they do no harm, the entertainment they give is a sufficient good. We cut down the tree that bears no fruit, but we ask nothing of a flower beyond its scent and its colour. The unpardonable sin in a novel is dullness: however grave or wise it may be, if its author possesses no powers of amusing, he has no business to write novels; he should employ his pen in some more serious part of literature.

from Isaac D'Israeli, *The Case of Authors Stated, Including the History of Literary Property* (1812)

Johnson has dignified the booksellers as "the patrons of literature,"[3] which was generous in that great

---

[1] *On the … Writing* From the introduction to Barbauld's fifty-volume edition of *The British Novelists*.

[2] *Cosi a … riceve* Italian: "So when the draught we give to the sick child, / The vessel's edge we touch with syrup sweet; / Cheated, he swift drinks down the bitter brew, / And from the cheat receives his life anew" (from Torquato Tasso's *Gerusalemme Liberata* [1575]).

[3] *Johnson … literature* According to James Boswell's *Life of Samuel Johnson* (1791), the lexicographer and author (whose father was a bookseller) referred to his publisher ("bookseller") as his "patron" in a letter to a friend. Johnson is also recorded as [continued …]

author, who had written well and lived but ill all his life on that patronage. Eminent booksellers, in their constant intercourse with the most enlightened class of the community, that is, with the best authors and the best readers, partake of the intelligence around them; their great capitals, too, are productive of good and evil in literature; useful when they carry on great works, and pernicious when they sanction indifferent ones. Yet are they but commercial men. A trader can never be deemed a patron, for it would be romantic to purchase what is not saleable; and where no favour is conferred, there is no patronage.

Authors continue poor, and booksellers become opulent; an extraordinary result! Booksellers are not agents for authors, but proprietors of their works, so that the perpetual revenues of literature are solely in the possession of the trade.[1]

Is it then wonderful that even successful authors are indigent? They are heirs to fortunes, but by a strange singularity they are disinherited at their birth; for, on the publication of their works, these cease to be their own property. Let that natural property be secured, and a good book would be an inheritance, a leasehold or a freehold, as you choose it; it might at least last out a generation, and descend to the author's blood, were they permitted to live on their father's glory, as in all other property they do on his industry. ...

The verbal and tasteless lawyers, not many years past, with legal metaphysics wrangled like the schoolmen,[2] inquiring of each other, "whether the *style* and *ideas* of an author were tangible things; or if these were *property*, how is *possession* to be taken, or any act of *occupancy* made on mere intellectual *ideas*." Nothing,

said they, can be an object of property but which has a corporeal substance; the air and the light, to which they compared an author's ideas, are common to all; ideas in the MS[3] state were compared to birds in a cage; while the author confines them in his own dominion, none but he has a right to let them fly; but the moment he allows the bird to escape from his hand, it is no violation of property in anyone to make it his own. And to prove that there existed no property after publication, they found an analogy in the gathering of acorns, or in seizing on a vacant piece of ground; and thus degrading that most refined piece of art formed in the highest state of society, a literary production, they brought us back to a state of nature, and seem to have concluded that literary property was purely ideal; a phantom which, as its author could neither grasp nor confine to himself, he must entirely depend on the public benevolence for his reward.[4]

The ideas, that is, the work of an author, are "tangible things." "There are works," to quote the words of a near and dear relative, "which require great learning, great industry, great labour, and great capital, in their preparation. They assume a palpable form. You may fill warehouses with them, and freight ships; and the tenure by which they are held is superior to that of all other property, for it is original. It is tenure which does not exist in a doubtful title; which does not spring from any adventitious circumstances; it is not found, it is not purchased, it is not prescriptive—it is original; so it is the most natural of all titles, because it is the most simple and least artificial. It is paramount and sovereign, because it is a tenure by creation."[5]

There were indeed some more generous spirits and better philosophers fortunately found on the same bench; and the identity of a literary composition was resolved into its sentiments and language, besides what was more obviously valuable to some persons, the print and paper. On this slight principle was issued the profound award which accorded a certain term of years

---

having said mockingly to the Earl of Chesterfield (the *Dictionary*'s intended patron, with whom Johnson had quarreled), "Is not a patron, my lord, one who looks with unconcern on a man struggling for life in the water and when he has reached ground encumbers him with help?"

[1] *Authors continue ... trade* The Statute of Anne (1710), generally considered the first copyright act, granted copyright protection to authors or proprietors for a fixed period of 14 years. The law generally protected publishers rather than authors.

[2] *schoolmen* I.e., the Scholastics, adherents of the Scholastic philosophy.

[3] *MS* Manuscript.

[4] [D'Israeli's note] Sir James Burrows's Reports on Literary Property.

[5] [D'Israeli's note] *Mirror of Parliament*, 3529.

to any work, however immortal. They could not diminish the immortality of a book, but only its reward. In all the litigations respecting literary property, authors were little considered—except some honourable testimonies due to genius, from the sense of Willes, and the eloquence of Mansfield.[1] Literary property was still disputed, like the rights of a parish common. An honest printer, who could not always write grammar, had the shrewdness to make a bold effort in this scramble, and perceiving that even by this last favourable award all literary property would necessarily centre with the booksellers, now stood forward for his own body—the printers. This rough advocate observed that "a few persons who call themselves *booksellers*, about the number of *twenty-five*, have kept the *monopoly of books and copies* in their hands, to the entire exclusion of all others, but more especially to the *printers*, whom they have always held it a rule never to let become purchasers in *copy*." Not a word for the *authors*! As for them, they were doomed by both parties as the fat oblation: they indeed sent forth some meek bleatings; but what were authors, between judges, booksellers, and printers? The sacrificed among the sacrificers. ...

As the matter now stands, let us address an arithmetical age—but my pen hesitates to bring down my subject to an argument fitted to "these coster-monger times."[2] On the present principle of literary property, it results that an author disposes of a leasehold property of twenty-eight years, often for less than the price of one year's purchase! How many living authors are the sad witnesses of this fact, who, like so many Esaus, have sold their inheritance for a meal![3] I leave the whole school of Adam Smith to calm their calculating emotions concerning "that unprosperous race of men" (sometimes this master-seer calls them "unproductive") "commonly called *men of letters*," who are pretty much in the situation which lawyers and physicians would be in, were these, as he tells us, in that state when "*a scholar* and *a beggar* seem to have been very nearly *synonymous terms*"[4]—and this melancholy fact that man of genius discovered, without the feather of his pen brushing away a tear from his lid—without one spontaneous and indignant groan!

Authors may exclaim, "we ask for justice, not charity." They would not need to require any favour, nor claim any other than that protection which an enlightened government, in its wisdom and its justice, must bestow. They would leave to the public disposition the sole appreciation of their works; their book must make its own fortune; a bad work may be cried up, and a good work may be cried down; but Faction will soon lose its voice, and Truth acquire one. The cause we are pleading is not the calamities of indifferent writers, but of those whose utility or whose genius long survives that limited term which has been so hardly wrenched from the penurious hand of verbal lawyers. Every lover of literature, and every votary of humanity has long felt indignant at that sordid state and all those secret sorrows to which men of the finest genius, or of sublime industry, are reduced and degraded in society. Johnson himself, who rejected that perpetuity of literary property which some enthusiasts seemed to claim at the time the subject was undergoing the discussion of the judges, is, however, for extending the copyright to a *century*. Could

---

[1] *Willes* Sir John Willes (1685–1761), who was the presiding judge in several copyright cases, and who believed that authors had a right to their intellectual property; *Mansfield* William Murray, first Earl of Mansfield (1705–93), a judge who upheld authors' perpetual common-law rights to their literary property in the influential copyright case *Millar v. Taylor* (1769, overturned in *Donaldson v. Beckett*, 1774).

[2] [D'Israeli's note] A coster-monger, or Costard-monger, is "A dealer in apples, which are so called because they are shaped like a costard, i.e., a man's head."—*Stevens*. Johnson explains the phrase eloquently: "In these times when the prevalence of trade has produced that meanness that rates the merit of everything by money."

[3] *Esaus ... meal* Cf. Hebrews 12.16: "Lest there be any fornicator, or profane person, as Esau, who for one morsel of meat sold his birthright."

[4] *Adam Smith ... terms* Reference to Adam Smith's *Wealth of Nations*, Book 1, Chapter 10, in which Smith discusses "that unprosperous race of men commonly called men of letters." He says these writers were generally educated for the Church, and then failed for some reason to take holy orders. "They have generally, therefore, been educated at the public expense, and their numbers are everywhere so great as commonly to reduce the price of their labor to a very paltry recompense."

authors secure this, their natural right, literature would acquire a permanent and a nobler reward; for great authors would then be distinguished by the very profits they would receive from that obscure multitude whose common disgraces they frequently participate, notwithstanding the superiority of their own genius. …

Authors now submit to have a shorter life than their own celebrity. While the book markets of Europe are supplied with the writings of English authors, and they have a wider diffusion in America than at home, it seems a national ingratitude to limit the existence of works for their authors to a short number of years, and then to seize on their possession for ever.

William Hazlitt, "A Review of *The St. James Chronicle, The Morning Chronicle, The Times, The New Times, The Courier, &c., Cobbett's Weekly Journal, The Examiner, The Observer, The Gentleman's Magazine, The New Monthly Magazine, The London, &c. &c.,*" from *The Edinburgh Review* (1823)

Literature formerly was a sweet Heremitress,[1] who fed on the pure breath of Fame in silence and in solitude, far from the madding strife, in sylvan shade or cloistered hall, she trimmed her lamp or turned her hourglass, pale with studious care, and aiming only to "make the age to come her own!"[2] She gave her life to the perfecting some darling work, and bequeathed it, dying, to posterity! Vain hope, perhaps; but the hope itself was fruition—calm, serene, blissful, unearthly! Modern literature, on the contrary, is a gay Coquette, fluttering, fickle, vain; followed by a train of flatterers; besieged by a crowd of pretenders; courted, she courts again; receives delicious praise, and dispenses it; is impatient for applause; pants for the breath of popularity; renounces eternal fame for a newspaper puff; trifles with all sorts of arts and sciences; coquettes with fifty accomplishments—*mille ornatus habet, mille decenter*[3]—is the subject of polite conversation; the darling of private parties; the go-between in politics; the directress of fashion; the polisher of manners; and, like her winged prototype in Spenser,

Now this now that, she tasteth tenderly,[4]

glitters, flutters, buzzes, spawns, dies—and is forgotten! But the very variety and superficial polish show the extent and height to which knowledge has been accumulated, and the general interest taken in letters.

To dig to the bottom of a subject through so many generations of authors is now impossible: the concrete mass is too voluminous and vast to be contained in any single head; and therefore, we must have essences and samples as substitutes for it. We have collected a superabundance of raw materials: the grand *desideratum*[5] now is, to fashion and render them portable. Knowledge is no longer confined to the few: the object therefore is, to make it accessible and attractive to the many. The *Monachism*[6] of literature is at an end; the cells of learning are thrown open and let in the light of universal day. We can no longer be churls of knowledge, ascetics in pretension. We must yield to the spirit of change (whether for the better or worse); and "to beguile the time, look like the time."[7] A modern author may (without much imputation of his wisdom) declare for a short life and a merry one. He may be a little gay, thoughtless, and dissipated. Literary immortality is now let on short leases, and he must be contented to succeed by rotation. A scholar of the olden time had resources, had consolations to support him under many privations and disadvantages. A light (that light which penetrates the most clouded skies) cheered him in his lonely cell, in the most obscure retirement; and, with the eye of faith,

---

[1] *Heremitress* I.e., female hermit.

[2] *make the … own* Cf. Abraham Cowley, "The Motto" (1656), line 2.

[3] *mille … decenter* Latin: "she has a thousand trifling things, a thousand things which are fitting to her." Reference to a quotation from the work of Roman elegiac poet Tibullus (c. 55–c. 19 BCE).

[4] *Now this … tenderly* From Edmund Spenser's "Muiopotmos, or The Fate of the Butterflie" (1590).

[5] *desideratum* Latin: thing desired.

[6] *Monachism* Monasticism.

[7] *to beguile … like the time* From Shakespeare's *Macbeth*, 1.5.62–63.

he could see the meanness of his garb exchanged for the wings of the Shining Ones, and the wedding-garment of the Spouse. Again, he lived only in the contemplation of old books and old events; and the remote and future became habitually present to his imagination, like the past. He was removed from low, petty vanity by the nature of his studies, and could wait patiently for his reward till after death. We exist in the bustle of the world, and cannot escape from the notice of our contemporaries. We must please to live, and therefore should live to please. We must look to the public for support. Instead of solemn testimonies from the learned, we require the smiles of the fair and the polite. If princes scowl upon us, the broad shining face of the people may turn to us with a favorable aspect. Is not this life (too) sweet? Would we change it for the former if we could? But the great point is that *we cannot*! Therefore, let reviews[1] flourish—let magazines increase and multiply—let the daily and weekly newspapers live forever! We are optimists in literature, and hold, with certain limitations that in this respect, whatever is, is right![2]

from John Stuart Mill, "The Present State of Literature" (16 November 1827)[3]

It is the demand, in literature as in most other things, which calls forth the supply. ... Assuming, therefore, as an indisputable truth, that the writers of every age are for the most part what the readers make them, it becomes important to the present question to consider who formed the reading public formerly, and who compose it now. The present age is very remarkably distinguished from all other ages by the number of persons who can read, and, what is of more consequence, by the number who do. Our working classes have learned to read, and our idle classes have learned to find pleasure in reading, and to devote a part of that

time to it which they formerly spent in amusements of a grosser kind. That human nature will be a gainer, and that in a high degree, by this change, no one can be more firmly convinced than I am—but it will perhaps be found that the benefit lies rather in the ultimate than in the immediate effects. Reading is necessary, but no wise or even sensible man was ever made by reading alone. The proper use of reading is to be subservient to thinking. It is by those who read to think that knowledge is advanced, prejudices dispelled, and the physical and moral condition of mankind is improved. I cannot, however, perceive that the general diffusion (so remarkable in our own day) of the taste for reading has yet been accompanied by any marked increase in taste for the severer exercises of the intellect; that such will one day be its effect, may fairly be presumed, but it has not yet declared itself: and it is to the immense multiplication in the present day of those who read but do not think, that I should be disposed to ascribe what I view as the degeneracy of our literature.

In former days the literati and the learned formed a class apart, and few concerned themselves with literature and philosophy except those who had leisure and inclination to form their philosophical opinions by study and meditation, and to cultivate their literary taste by the assiduous perusal of the most approved models. Those whose sole occupation was pleasure did not seek it in books, but in the gaieties of a court, or in field sports and debauchery. The public for which authors wrote was a small but, to a very considerable degree, an instructed public; and their suffrages were only to be gained by thinking to a certain extent profoundly and by writing well. The authors who were then in highest reputation are chiefly those to whom we now look back as the ablest thinkers and best writers of their time. No doubt there were many blockheads among the reading public in those days, as well as in our own, and the blockheads often egregiously misplaced their admiration, as blockheads are wont, but the applause of the blockheads was not then the object aimed at even by those who obtained it, and they did not constitute so large and so influential a class of readers as to tempt any writer of talent to lay himself out for their admiration.

---

[1] *reviews*   I.e., literary journals or periodicals.

[2] *whatever ... right*   Reference to Alexander Pope's *Essay on Man* (1733), Epistle 1, line 294: "One truth is clear: whatever is, is right."

[3] *The Present ... 1827*   From a speech delivered to the London Debating Society.

If an author failed of obtaining the suffrages of men of knowledge and taste, it was for want of powers, not from the misapplication of them. The case is now altered. We live in a refined age, and there is a corresponding refinement in our amusements. It is now the height of *mauvais ton*[1] to be drunk, neither is it any longer considered decorous among gentlemen that the staple of their conversation should consist of bawdy. Reading has become one of the most approved and

fashionable methods of killing time, and the number of persons who have skimmed the surface of literature is far greater than at any previous period of our history. Our writers therefore find that the greatest success is now to be obtained by writing for the many, and endeavouring all they can to bring themselves down to the level of the many, both in their matter and in the manner of expressing it.

---

[1] *mauvais ton*   French: bad form.

SIR WALTER SCOTT
1771 – 1832

Many of our modern notions of the "stern and wild" Scottish landscape and of the country's bloody past originate in the novels of Sir Walter Scott. Scott wrote 27 novels, many of them set in the Highlands or else on the borderland between Scotland and England, and is now remembered chiefly as the progenitor of the historical novel, but he began his literary career as a poet. Largely in order to raise funds for an extravagant castle he was building, Scott turned to novel-writing. He published all of his fiction anonymously, but it soon became widely known that he was the author of such popular books as *Waverley* (1814), *Rob Roy* (1818), and *Ivanhoe* (1819), and he became an internationally celebrated figure.

Scott was born in 1771 to Anne Rutherford and solicitor Walter Scott of Edinburgh. His grandparents, however, were stronger early influences, as was their land in the Border Country, where he had been sent to recuperate after contracting polio at the age of 18 months; it was an infirmity that left him with a lame leg but that rarely affected him in his robust adult years. On the farm, Scott acquired a passion for the landscape, history, and the traditional tales and ballads of southern Scotland. (Many of these ballads he eventually collected for *Minstrelsy of the Scottish Border*, published in 1802–03.) Scott studied law at Edinburgh University and made a lifelong career in the profession. While apprenticing in his father's firm, he met many clients from the Highlands who introduced him to the culture and traditions of the region that would figure prominently in both his poetry and his novels.

Scott married Charlotte Charpentier in 1795, and four years later he was appointed Deputy-Sheriff of Selkirk, a position that gave him much spare time and freedom to write. His first works were poetic: an adaptation of ballads by Gottfried August Burger (*The Chase, and William and Helen*, 1796) and a translation of Johann Wolfgang von Goethe's *Götz of Berlichingen with the Iron Hand* (1799). In 1805 Scott published *The Lay of the Last Minstrel* and thus embarked on a second career, one that was to be far more lucrative for him than was the legal profession. His next works were also in verse and included *Marmion* (1808) and *The Lady of the Lake* (1810); these, too, were extremely popular. Scott then decided to try his hand at fiction. By 1813 he was running short of funds. He had invested heavily in the printing and publishing ventures of his friends James and John Ballantyne, which were in a state of crisis, and he had committed himself to building a vast and hugely expensive estate at Abbotsford. In the hope of extricating himself from his financial difficulties he turned to writing novels—and enjoyed vast and immediate success. Thomas Carlyle said that his books were "faster written and better paid for than any other books in the world. … It must be granted, moreover, that they have a worth far surpassing what is usual in such cases." His first novel, *Waverley* (1814), a *tour de force* of historical fiction, would set the tone for Scott's novels, with a strong focus on a hero's conflicts between a romantic past and a progressive future, and on the relationship between Scottish and English culture.

Following this success, Scott produced at least one book a year (including others in the *Waverley* series) for the next ten years, all the while continuing his career in law, as well as pursuing editorial and critical work at a pace that seriously compromised his health. He also continued to suffer serious financial problems, having lived a lavish life at Abbotsford. He went bankrupt in the financial crash of 1826, after which he worked at an even more feverish pace in order to settle his debts, which were eventually paid off by profits from his books after his death in 1832. His obituary in the *Gentleman's Magazine* described him as "the proudest name in the modern annals of literature."

⌘ ⌘ ⌘

The Eve of St. John [1]

Smaylho'me, or Smallholm Tower, the scene of the following Ballad, is situated on the northern boundary of Roxburghshire, among a cluster of wild rocks, called Sandiknow-Crags, the property of Hugh Scott, Esq. of Harden. The tower is a high square building, surrounded by an outer wall, now ruinous. The circuit of the outer court being defended, on three sides, by a precipice and morass, is only accessible from the west, by a steep and rocky path. The apartments, as usual, in a Border Keep, or fortress, are placed one above another, and communicate by a narrow stair; on the roof are two bartizans, or platforms, for defence or pleasure. The inner door of the tower is wood, the outer an iron grate; the distance between them being nine feet, the thickness, namely, of the wall. From the elevated situation of Smaylho'me Tower, it is seen many miles in every direction. Among the crags by which it is surrounded, one more eminent is called the Watchfold, and is said to have been the station of a beacon in the times of war with England. Without the tower-court is a ruined Chapel.

The baron of Smaylho'me rose with day,
  He spurred his courser on,

Without stop or stay, down the rocky way,
  That leads to Brotherstone.

5 He went not with the bold Buccleuch,
    His banner broad to rear;
He went not 'gainst the English yew,
    To lift the Scottish spear.

Yet his plate-jack was braced, and his helmet was laced,
10   And his vaunt-brace of proof he wore;
At his saddle-gerthe was a good steel sperthe,[2]
    Full ten pound weight and more.

The Baron returned in three days' space,
    And his looks were sad and sour;
15 And weary was his courser's pace,
    As he reached his rocky tower.

He came not from where Ancram Moor
    Ran red with English blood;
Where the Douglas true, and the bold Buccleuch,
20   'Gainst keen Lord Evers stood.[3]

---

[1] *The Eve of St. John* St. John's Eve, the evening of 23 June, is the night before the Feast Day of St. John the Baptist, a celebration of the birth of St. John. The Feast Day coincides with the June solstice, also known as Midsummer's Day. Typically, the feast is celebrated with bonfires and prayers for the blessing of crops.

[2] *plate-jack* Coat of armor; *saddle-gerthe* Body armor; *sperthe* Battle-ax.

[3] *He came not ... Lord Evers stood* The battle of Ancrum Moor was fought in 1545, during the War of Rough Wooing, a term coined by Scott and H.E. Marshall to describe the series of conflicts between the English and the Scottish between 1544 and 1551. At Ancrum Moor, the Scottish, led by Archibald Douglas, Earl of Angus, and Sir Walter Scott of Buccleuch, temporarily ended the English incursion into the Scottish lowlands. The English were led by Sir Ralph Evers.

Yet was his helmet hacked and hewed,
    His action pierced and tore,
His axe and his dagger with blood imbrued,—
    But it was not English gore.

He lighted at the Chapellage,[1]
    He held him close and still;
And he whistled thrice for his little foot-page,
    His name was English Will.

"Come thou hither, my little foot-page,
    Come hither to my knee;
Though thou art young, and tender of age,
    I think thou art true to me.

"Come, tell me all that thou hast seen,
    And look thou tell me true!
Since I from Smaylho'me tower have been,
    What did thy lady do?"—

"My lady, each night, sought the lonely light,
    That burns on the wild Watchfold;
For, from height to height, the beacons bright
    Of the English foemen told.

"The bittern[2] clamoured from the moss,
    The wind blew loud and shrill;
Yet the craggy pathway she did cross
    To the eiry[3] Beacon Hill.

45 "I watched her steps, and silent came
    Where she sat her on a stone;—
No watchman stood by the dreary flame,
    It burned all alone.

"The second night I kept her in sight,
50   Till to the fire she came,
And, by Mary's might, an Armed Knight
    Stood by the lonely flame.

"And many a word that warlike lord
    Did speak to my lady there:
55 But the rain fell fast, and loud blew the blast,
    And I heard not what they were.

"The third night there the sky was fair,
    And the mountain-blast was still,
As again I watched the secret pair,
60   On the lonesome Beacon Hill.

"And I heard her name the midnight hour,
    And name this holy eve;
And say, 'Come this night to thy lady's bower;
    Ask no bold Baron's leave.

65 "'He lifts his spear with the bold Buccleuch;
    His lady is all alone;
The door she'll undo, to her knight so true,
    On the eve of good St. John.'—

"'I cannot come; I must not come,
70   I dare not come to thee;
On the eve of St. John I must wander alone:
    In thy bower I may not be.'—

"'Now, out on thee, faint-hearted knight!
    Thou shouldst not say me nay;
75 For the eve is sweet, and when lovers meet,
    Is worth the whole summer's day.

"'And I'll chain the blood-hound, and the warder shall
      not sound,
    And rushes shall be strewed on the stair;

---

[1] *Chapellage* Chapel stead; the chapel's precinct and its accessory buildings.

[2] *bittern* Type of bird similar to the heron, but smaller; noted for the loud "boom" it utters during the breeding season, and for frequenting marshland.

[3] *eiry* Scottish expression, referring to a feeling inspired by fear of ghostly apparitions.

So, by the black rood-stone,[1] and by Holy St. John,
80   I conjure thee, my love, to be there!'—

"'Though the blood-hound be mute, and the rush
            beneath my foot,
      And the warder his bugle should not blow,
Yet there sleepeth a priest in the chamber to the east,
      And my footstep he would know.'—

85   "'O fear not the priest, who sleepeth to the east!
      For to Dryburgh[2] the way he has ta'en;
And there to say mass, till three days do pass,
      For the soul of a knight that is slain.'—

"He turned him around, and grimly he frowned;
90   Then he laughed right scornfully—
'He who says the mass-rite for the soul of that knight,
      May as well say mass for me.

"'At the lone midnight hour, when bad spirits have power,
      In thy chamber will I be.'—
95   With that he was gone, and my lady left alone,
      And no more did I see."

Then changed, I trow, was that bold Baron's brow,
      From the dark to the blood-red high;
"Now, tell me the mien of the knight thou hast seen,
100   For, by Mary, he shall die!"—

"His arms shone full bright, in the beacon's red light;
      His plume it was scarlet and blue;
On his shield was a hound, in a silver leash bound,
      And his crest was a branch of the yew."—

105   "Thou liest, thou liest, thou little foot-page,
      Loud dost thou lie to me!

For that knight is cold, and low laid in the mould,
      All under the Eildon-tree."[3]

"Yet hear but my word, my noble lord!
110   For I heard her name his name;
And that lady bright, she called the knight
      Sir Richard of Coldinghame."—

The bold Baron's brow then changed, I trow,
      From high blood-red to pale—
115   "The grave is deep and dark, and the corpse is stiff
            and stark;
      So I may not trust thy tale.

"Where fair Tweed flows round holy Melrose,
      And Eildon slopes to the plain,
Full three nights ago, by some secret foe,
120   That gay gallant was slain.

"The varying light deceived thy sight,
      And the wild winds drowned the name;
For the Dryburgh bells ring, and the white monks
            do sing,
      For Sir Richard of Coldinghame!"—

125   He passed the court-gate, and he oped the tower-gate,
      And he mounted the narrow stair,
To the bartizan-seat, where, with maids that on her wait,
      He found his Lady fair.

That Lady sat in mournful mood;
130   Look'd over hill and vale;
Over Tweed's fair flood, and Mertoun's wood,
      And all down Teviotdale.

"Now hail, now hail, thou Lady bright!"—
      "Now hail, thou Baron true!
135   What news, what news, from Ancram fight?
      What news from the bold Buccleuch?"—

---

1 *black rood-stone* Sometimes referred to as the Holy Rood, it is
considered part of the cross on which Jesus died. It was kept in a black
case, which likely gives it the name of the Black Rood of Scotland. The
relic was thought to have been brought to Scotland by Saint Margaret
(c. 1045–93), the exiled English princess who married Malcolm III (d.
1093), the King of Scots.

2 *Dryburgh* Scottish village, famous for the ruins of Dryburgh
Abbey, destroyed in 1544.

3 *Eildon-tree* This spot is believed to have been the site where
Thomas the Rhymer, a thirteenth-century Scottish bard, uttered his
prophecies on the future and fate of Scotland.

"The Ancram Moor is red with gore,
    For many a Southron[1] fell;
And Buccleuch has charged us, evermore,
    To watch our beacons well."—

The Lady blushed red, but nothing she said:
    Nor added the Baron a word:
Then she stepped down the stair to her chamber fair,
    And so did her moody lord.

In sleep the Lady mourned, and the Baron tossed and
       turned,
    And oft to himself he said,—
"The worms around him creep, and his bloody grave
    is deep,
    It cannot give up the dead."—

It was near the ringing of matin bell,
    The night was well nigh done,
When a heavy sleep on that Baron fell,
    On the eve of good St. John.

The lady looked through the chamber fair,
    By the light of a dying flame;
And she was aware of a knight stood there,
    Sir Richard of Coldinghame.

"Alas! away, away!"—she cried,
    "For the holy Virgin's sake!"—
"Lady, I know who sleeps by thy side;
    But, lady, he will not awake.

"By Eildon-tree, for long nights three,
    In bloody grave have I lain;
The mass and the death-prayer are said for me,
    But, lady, they are said in vain.

"By the Baron's brand, near Tweed's fair strand,
    Most foully slain, I fell;
And my restless sprite on the beacon's height,
    For a space is doomed to dwell.

"At our trysting-place,[2] for a certain space,
    I must wander to and fro;
But I had not had power to come to thy bower
    Had'st thou not conjured me so."—

Love mastered fear—her brow she crossed;
    "How, Richard, hast thou sped?
And art thou saved, or art thou lost?"—
    The vision shook his head!

"Who spilleth life, shall forfeit life;
    So bid thy Lord believe;
That lawless love is guilt above,
    This awful sign receive."—

He laid his left palm on an oaken beam;
    His right upon her hand;
The lady shrunk, and fainting sunk,
    For it scorched like a fiery brand.[3]

The sable score, of fingers four,
    Remains on that board impressed,
And for evermore that Lady wore
    A covering on her wrist.

There is a nun in Melrose bower,
    Ne'er looks upon the sun;
There is a monk in Dryburgh tower,
    He speaketh word to none.

That nun, who ne'er beholds the day,
    That monk, who speaks to none,
That nun was Smaylho'me's Lady gay,
    That monk the bold Baron.
      —1799

---

[1] *Southron* Englishman.

[2] *trysting-place* Rendezvous point for romantic meetings.

[3] *For it … fiery brand* In later editions, this line reads, "For the touch was fiery warm."

Glenfinlas; or Lord Ronald's Coronach[1]

PREFACE

The simple tradition, upon which the following stanzas are founded, runs thus: While two Highland hunters were passing the night in a solitary *bothy*, (a hut, built for the purpose of hunting), and making merry over their venison and whiskey, one of them expressed a wish that they had pretty lasses to complete their party. The words were scarcely uttered, when two beautiful young women, habited in green, entered the hut, dancing and singing. One of the hunters was seduced by the siren[2] who attached herself particularly to him, to leave the hut: the other remained, and, suspicious of the fair seducers, continued to play upon a trump, or Jew's harp, some strain, consecrated to the Virgin Mary. Day at length came, and the temptress vanished. Searching in the forest, he found the bones of his unfortunate friend, who had been torn to pieces and devoured by the fiend into whose toils he had fallen. The place was from thence called the Glen of the Green Women.

Glenfinlas is a tract of forest-ground, lying in the Highlands of Perthshire, not far from Callender, in Menteith. It was formerly a royal forest, and now belongs to the Earl of Moray. This country, as well as the adjacent district of Balquidder, was, in times of yore, chiefly inhabited by the Macgregors. To the west of the Forest of Glenfinlas lies Loch[3] Katrine, and its romantic avenue, called the Trossachs. Benledi, Benmore, and Benvoirlich, are mountains in the same district, and at no great distance from Glenfinlas. The River Teith passes Callender and the Castle of Doune, and joins the Forth[4] near Stirling. The Pass of Lenny is immediately above Callender, and is the principal access to the Highlands, from that town. Glenartney is a forest, near Benvoirlich. The whole forms a sublime tract of Alpine scenery.

"For them the viewless forms of air obey,
    Their bidding heed, and at their beck repair;
They know what spirit brews the stormful day,
    And heartless oft, like moody madness stare,
To see the phantom-train their secret work prepare."[5]
—COLLINS

"Ohone a rie'![6] O hone a rie'!
    The pride of Albin's[7] line is o'er,
And fallen Glenartney's stateliest tree;
    We ne'er shall see Lord Ronald more!"

5 O! sprung from great Macgillianore,
    The chief that never feared a foe,
How matchless was thy broad claymore,°   *large sword*
    How deadly thine unerring bow!

Well can the Saxon° widows tell   *lowland*
10   How on the Teith's resounding shore
The boldest Lowland warriors fell,
    As down from Lenny's pass you bore.

But o'er his hills in festal° day   *festival*
    How blazed Lord Ronald's beltane-tree.°   *ritual bonfire*
15 While youths and maids the light strathspey°   *a dance*
    So nimbly danced with Highland glee!

Cheered by the strength of Ronald's shell,
    E'en age forgot his tresses hoar;°   *white (aged)*
But now the loud lament we swell,
20   O, ne'er to see Lord Ronald more!

From distant isles a chieftain came
    The joys of Ronald's halls to find,
And chase with him the dark-brown game
    That bounds o'er Albin's hills of wind.

---

[1] *Coronach* Lamentation for a fallen warrior.

[2] *siren* In Greek mythology, a sea nymph who would bewitch sailors with song and lure them to their deaths on the rocks.

[3] *Loch* Lake.

[4] *Forth* River in Scotland.

[5] *"For them … prepare."* From William Collins's "An Ode on the Popular Superstitions of the Highlands of Scotland, Considered as the Subject of Poetry."

[6] *hone a rie'* Lament.

[7] *Albin's* I.e., Alba's (Scotland's).

'Twas Moy; whom in Columba's isle[1]
   The seer's prophetic spirit[2] found,
As, with a minstrel's lyre the while,
   He waked his harp's harmonious sound.

Full many a spell to him was known
   Which wandering spirits shrink to hear;
And many a lay° of potent tone   *song*
   Was never meant for mortal ear.

For there, 'tis said, in mystic mood
   High converse with the dead they hold,
And oft espy the fated shroud
   That shall the future corpse enfold.

O, so it fell that on a day,
   To rouse the red deer from their den,
The chiefs have ta'en° their distant way,   *taken*
   And scoured the deep Glenfinlas glen.

No vassals[3] wait their sports to aid,
   To watch their safety, deck their board;
Their simple dress the Highland plaid,
   Their trusty guard the Highland sword.

Three summer days through brake° and dell   *thicket*
   Their whistling shafts successful flew;
And still when dewy evening fell
   The quarry to their hut they drew.

In gray Glenfinlas' deepest nook
   The solitary cabin stood,

Fast by Moneira's sullen brook,
   Which murmurs through that lonely wood.

Soft fell the night, the sky was calm,
   When three successive days had flown;
And summer mist in dewy balm
   Steeped heathy bank and mossy stone.

The moon, half-hid in silvery flakes,
   Afar her dubious radiance shed,
Quivering on Katrine's distant lakes,
   And resting on Benledi's head.

Now in their hut in social guise
   Their sylvan fare the chiefs enjoy;
And pleasure laughs in Ronald's eyes,
   As many a pledge he quaffs to Moy.

"What lack we here to crown our bliss,
   While thus the pulse of joy beats high?
What but fair woman's yielding kiss,
   Her panting breath and melting eye?

"To chase the deer of yonder shades,
   This morning left their father's pile
The fairest of our mountain maids,
   The daughters of the proud Glengyle.

"Long have I sought sweet Mary's heart,
   And dropped the tear and heaved the sigh:
But vain the lover's wily art
   Beneath a sister's watchful eye.

"But thou mayst teach that guardian fair,
   While far with Mary I am flown,
Of other hearts to cease her care,
   And find it hard to guard her own.

"Touch but thy harp, thou soon shalt see
   The lovely Flora of Glengyle,
Unmindful of her charge and me,
   Hang on thy notes 'twixt tear and smile.

[1] *Columba's isle* St. Columba's Isle, an ancient site on the Isle of Skye, Scotland. Many other Scottish place names appear in this poem; for the most part these have not been glossed.

[2] [Scott's note] I can only describe the second sight, by adopting Dr. Johnson's definition, who calls it, "An impression, either by the mind upon the eye, or the eye upon the mind, by which things distant and future are seen and perceived as if they were present." To which I would only add, that the spectral appearances, thus presented, usually presage misfortune; that the faculty is painful to those who suppose they possess it; and that they usually acquire it while themselves under the pressure of melancholy.

[3] *vassals* In the Scottish clan system, a vassal owed allegiance and homage to the clan chieftain.

85 "Or, if she choose a melting tale,
        All underneath the greenwood bough,
    Will good Saint Oran's rule[1] prevail,
        Stern huntsman of the rigid brow?"

    "Since Enrick's fight, since Morna's death,
90   No more on me shall rapture rise,
    Responsive to the panting breath,
        Or yielding kiss or melting eyes.

    "E'en then, when o'er the heath of woe
        Where sunk my hopes of love and fame,
95 I bade my harp's wild wailings flow,
        On me the seer's sad spirit came.

    "The last dread curse of angry heaven,
        With ghastly sights and sounds of woe
    To dash each glimpse of joy was given—
100   The gift the future ill to know.

    "The bark° thou saw'st, yon summer morn,   *boat*
        So gaily part from Oban's bay,
    My eye beheld her dashed and torn
        Far on the rocky Colonsay.

105 "Thy Fergus too—thy sister's son,
        Thou saw'st with pride the gallant's power,
    As marching 'gainst the Lord of Downe
        He left the skirts of huge Benmore.

    "Thou only saw'st their tartans wave
110   As down Benvoirlich's side they wound,

Heard'st but the pibroch[2] answering brave
    To many a target clanking round.

"I heard the groans, I marked the tears,
    I saw the wound his bosom bore,
115 When on the serried° Saxon spears   *crowded*
    He poured his clan's resistless roar.

"And thou, who bidst me think of bliss,
    And bidst my heart awake to glee,
And court like thee the wanton kiss—
120   That heart, O Ronald, bleeds for thee!

"I see the death-damps chill thy brow:
    I hear thy warning spirit cry;
The corpse-lights[3] dance—they're gone, and now—
    No more is given to gifted eye!"

125 "Alone enjoy thy dreary dreams,
    Sad prophet of the evil hour!
Say, should we scorn joy's transient beams
    Because tomorrow's storm may lour?°   *threaten*

"Or false or sooth thy words of woe,
130   Clangillian's chieftain ne'er shall fear;
His blood shall bound at rapture's glow,
    Though doomed to stain the Saxon spear.

"E'en now, to meet me in yon dell,
    My Mary's buskins° brush the dew."   *laced boots*
135 He spoke, nor bade the chief farewell,
    But called his dogs and gay withdrew.

Within an hour returned each hound,
    In rushed the rousers of the deer;
They howled in melancholy sound,
140   Then closely couched beside the seer.

No Ronald yet, though midnight came,
    And sad were Moy's prophetic dreams,

----

1 [Scott's note] St. Oran was a friend and follower of St. Columba, and is buried in Icolmkill. His pretensions to be a saint were rather dubious. According to the legend, he consented to be buried alive, in order to propitiate certain demons of the soil, who obstructed the attempts of Columba to build a chapel. Columba caused the body of his friend to be dug up, after three days had elapsed; when Oran, to the horror and scandal of the assistants, declared, that there was neither a God, a judgment, nor a future state! He had no time to make farther discoveries, for Columba caused the earth once more to be shoveled over him with the utmost dispatch. The chapel, however, and the cemetery, was called Relig Ouran; and, in memory of his rigid celibacy, no female was permitted to pay her devotions, or be buried, in that place. This is the rule alluded to in the poem.

2 *pibroch* Here, battle music played on a bagpipe.

3 *corpse-lights* Omen of death; illuminations thought to be souls or spirits of the dead.

As, bending o'er the dying flame,
    He fed the watch-fire's quivering gleams.

155 Sudden the hounds erect their ears,
    And sudden cease their moaning howl,
Close pressed to Moy, they mark their fears
    By shivering limbs and stifled growl.

160 Untouched the harp began to ring
    As softly, slowly, oped the door;
And shook responsive every string
    As light a footstep pressed the floor.

And by the watch-fire's glimmering light
    Close by the minstrel's side was seen
165 A huntress maid, in beauty bright,
    All dropping wet her robes of green.

All dropping wet her garments seem;
    Chilled was her cheek, her bosom bare,
As, bending o'er the dying gleam,
170   She wrung the moisture from her hair.

With maiden blush she softly said,
    "O gentle huntsman, hast thou seen,
In deep Glenfinlas' moonlight glade,
    A lovely maid in vest of green:

165 "With her a chief in Highland pride;
    His shoulders bear the hunter's bow,
The mountain dirk° adorns his side,   *dagger*
    Far on the wind his tartans flow?"—

"And who art thou? and who are they?"
170   All ghastly gazing, Moy replied:
"And why, beneath the moon's pale ray,
    Dare ye thus roam Glenfinlas' side?"

"Where wild Loch Katrine pours her tide,
    Blue, dark, and deep, round many an isle,
175 Our father's towers o'erhang her side,
    The castle of the bold Glengyle.

"To chase the dun Glenfinlas deer
    Our woodland course this morn we bore,
And haply met while wandering here
180   The son of great Macgillianore.

"O, aid me then to seek the pair,
    Whom, loitering in the woods, I lost;
Alone I dare not venture there,
    Where walks, they say, the shrieking ghost."

185 "Yes, many a shrieking ghost walks there:
    Then first, my own sad vow to keep,
Here will I pour my midnight prayer,
    Which still must rise when mortals sleep."

"O, first, for pity's gentle sake,
190   Guide a lone wanderer on her way!
For I must cross the haunted brake,
    And reach my father's towers ere day."

"First, three times tell each ave-bead,°   *prayer bead*
    And thrice a Paternoster[1] say;
195 Then kiss with me the holy rede;[2]
    So shall we safely wend our way."

"O, shame to knighthood, strange and foul!
    Go, doff the bonnet from thy brow,
And shroud thee in the monkish cowl,
200   Which best befits thy sullen vow.

"Not so, by high Dunlathmon's fire,
    Thy heart was froze to love and joy,
When gaily rung thy raptured lyre
    To wanton Morna's melting eye."

205 Wild stared the minstrel's eyes of flame
    And high his sable locks arose,
And quick his colour went and came
    As fear and rage alternate rose.

---

[1] *Paternoster* Latin: "Our Father." In Protestant tradition, "The Lord's Prayer."

[2] *rede* I.e., rood, or crucifix.

"And thou! when by the blazing oak
210   I lay, to her and love resigned,
Say, rode ye on the eddying smoke,
      Or sailed ye on the midnight wind?

"Not thine a race of mortal blood,
      Nor old Glengyle's pretended line;
215 Thy dame, the Lady of the Flood—
      Thy sire, the Monarch of the Mine."

He muttered thrice Saint Oran's rhyme,
      And thrice Saint Fillan's powerful prayer;[1]
Then turned him to the eastern clime,
220   And sternly shook his coal-black hair.

And, bending o'er his harp, he flung
      His wildest witch-notes on the wind;
And loud and high and strange they rung,
      As many a magic change they find.

225 Tall waxed the spirit's altering form,
      Till to the roof her stature grew;
Then, mingling with the rising storm,
      With one wild yell away she flew.

Rain beats, hail rattles, whirlwinds tear:
230   The slender hut in fragments flew;
But not a lock of Moy's loose hair
      Was waved by wind or wet by dew.

Wild mingling with the howling gale,
      Loud bursts of ghastly laughter rise;
235 High o'er the minstrel's head they sail
      And die amid the northern skies.

The voice of thunder shook the wood,
      As ceased the more than mortal yell;
And spattering foul a shower of blood
240   Upon the hissing firebrands fell.

Next dropped from high a mangled arm;
      The fingers strained a half-drawn blade:
And last, the life-blood streaming warm,
      Torn from the trunk, a gasping head.

245 Oft o'er that head in battling field
      Streamed the proud crest of high Benmore;
That arm the broad claymore could wield
      Which dyed the Teith with Saxon gore.

Woe to Moneira's sullen rills!
250   Woe to Glenfinlas' dreary glen!
There never son of Albin's hills
      Shall draw the hunter's shaft again!

E'en the tired pilgrim's burning feet
      At noon shall shun that sheltering den,
255 Lest, journeying in their rage, he meet
      The wayward Ladies of the Glen.

And we—behind the chieftain's shield
      No more shall we in safety dwell;
None leads the people to the field—
260   And we the loud lament must swell.

O hone a rie'! O hone a rie'!
      The pride of Albin's line is o'er!
And fallen Glenartney's stateliest tree;
      We ne'er shall see Lord Ronald more!
—1800

---

1 [Scott's note] St. Fillan has given his name to many chapels, holy fountains, &c. in Scotland. He was, according to Camerarius, an abbot of Pittenween, in Fife, from which situation he retired and died a hermit in the wilds of Glenurchy, 649 AD.

Lord Randal[1]

"O where hae° ye been, lord Randal, my son?   *have*
O where hae ye been, my handsome young man?"
"I hae been to the wild wood; mother, make my bed
    soon,
For I'm weary wi' hunting, and fain[2] wald°   *would*
    lie down."

5 "Where gat ye your dinner, lord Randal, my son?
Where gat ye your dinner, my handsome young man?"
"I dined wi' my true-love; mother, make my bed soon,
For I'm weary wi' hunting, and fain wald lie down."

"What gat ye to your dinner, lord Randal, my son,
10 What gat ye to your dinner, my handsome young man?"
"I gat eels boiled in broo'°; mother, make   *broth*
    my bed soon,
For I'm weary wi' hunting, and fain wald lie down."

"What became of your bloodhounds, lord Randal,
    my son?
What became of your bloodhounds, my handsome
    young man?"
15 "O they swelled and they died—mother, make my bed
    soon,
For I'm weary wi' hunting, and fain wald lie down."

"O I fear ye are poisoned, lord Randal, my son!
O I fear ye are poisoned, my handsome young man!"
"O yes! I am poisoned—mother, make my bed soon,
20 For I'm sick at the heart, and I fain wald lie down."
—1802

---

1 *Lord Randal* This is one of many anonymous border ballads that Scott compiled and reproduced in his collection *The Minstrelsy of the Scottish Border* (1802–03).

2 *fain* Willing or eager to.

from *The Lay of the Last Minstrel*[3]

Preface to the First Edition

The poem, now offered to the public, is intended to illustrate the customs and manners, which anciently prevailed on the Borders of England and Scotland. The inhabitants, living in a state partly pastoral, and partly warlike, and combining habits of constant depredation with the influence of a rude spirit of chivalry, were often engaged in scenes, highly susceptible of poetical ornament. As the description of scenery and manners was more the object of the author than a combined and regular narrative, the plan of the Ancient Metrical Romance[4] was adopted, which allows greater latitude, in this respect, than would be consistent with the dignity of a regular poem. The same model offered other facilities, as it permits an occasional alteration of measure, which, to some degree, authorizes the change of rhythm in the text. The machinery[5] also, adopted from popular belief, would have seemed puerile in a poem which did not partake of the rudeness of the old ballad, or metrical romance.

For these reasons, the poem was put into the mouth of an ancient Minstrel, the last of the race, who, as he is supposed to have survived the Revolution,[6] might have

---

3 *Lay* Ballad or narrative poem, especially one meant to be sung; *The Lay of the Last Minstrel* This poem relates the tale of a sixteenth-century Scottish Border feud as told by a wandering minstrel, the last of his kind, at the end of the seventeenth century. Weary from traveling, he receives hospitality from his patron, the Duchess of Buccleuch, and in return recites a tale concerning the Duchess's ancestors. Scott was descended from the Lords of Buccleuch, and thus the minstrel's tale, though fictional, incorporates aspects of Scott's own family history. The following selection focuses on the minstrel himself, rather than the tale he tells.

4 *Metrical Romance* I.e., medieval romance written in verse. Medieval romances typically detail the marvelous adventures of a chivalric hero; due to the episodic nature of the form, the plot can be stretched or contracted so the author can insert or remove any number of smaller, short adventures.

5 *machinery* I.e., supernatural elements incorporated into the plot.

6 *the Revolution* The "Glorious Revolution" (1688), in which the Catholic King James II (James VII of Scotland) was forced to abdicate and William of Orange, a Dutch Protestant, was made king.

caught somewhat of the refinement of modern poetry, without losing the simplicity of his original model. The date of the tale itself is about the middle of the sixteenth century, when most of the personages actually flourished. The time occupied by the action is three nights and three days.

INTRODUCTION

The way was long, the wind was cold,
  The Minstrel was infirm and old;
His withered cheek, and tresses gray,
Seemed to have known a better day;
5 The harp, his sole remaining joy,
Was carried by an orphan boy.
The last of all the Bards was he,
Who sung of Border chivalry;
For, welladay!° their date was fled,   *alas*
10 His tuneful brethren all were dead;
And he, neglected and oppressed,
Wished to be with them, and at rest.
No more on prancing palfrey° borne,   *saddle horse*
He carolled, light as lark at morn;
15 No longer courted and caressed,
High placed in hall, a welcome guest,
He poured, to lord and lady gay,
The unpremeditated lay:
Old times were changed, old manners gone;
20 A stranger filled the Stuarts' throne;[1]
The bigots of the iron time
Had called his harmless art a crime.[2]
A wandering Harper, scorned and poor,
He begged his bread from door to door,
25 And tuned, to please a peasant's ear,
The harp, a king had loved to hear.

He passed where Newark's[3] stately tower
Looks out from Yarrow's birchen bower:°   *arbor*
The Minstrel gazed with wishful eye—
30 No humbler resting-place was nigh.
With hesitating step at last,
The embattled portal arch he passed,
Whose ponderous grate and massy° bar   *massive*
Had oft rolled back the tide of war,
35 But never closed the iron door
Against the desolate and poor.
The Duchess[4] marked his weary pace,
His timid mien,° and reverend face,   *bearing*
And bade her page the menials tell,
40 That they should tend the old man well:
For she had known adversity,
Though born in such a high degree;
In pride of power, in beauty's bloom,
Had wept o'er Monmouth's bloody tomb!

45 When kindness had his wants supplied,
And the old man was gratified,
Began to rise his minstrel pride:
And he began to talk anon,
Of good Earl Francis, dead and gone,
50 And of Earl Walter,[5] rest him, God!
A braver ne'er to battle rode;
And how full° many a tale he knew,   *very*
Of the old warriors of Buccleuch:
And, would the noble Duchess deign
55 To listen to an old man's strain,
Though still his hand, his voice though weak,
He thought even yet, the sooth to speak,
That, if she loved the harp to hear,
He could make music to her ear.

---

[1] *A stranger ... throne* I.e., William of Orange had succeeded James II/VII, a Stuart.

[2] *The bigots ... time* The Puritans, who possessed a great deal of political power during the Commonwealth period (1649–60) and considered amusements sinful; *Had called ... a crime* Allusion to a 1656 ordinance that classified fiddlers and minstrels as "rogues, vagabonds, and sturdy beggars."

[3] *Newark* Castle located near the place where the Yarrow and Ettrick Rivers merge, in Selkirkshire, southern Scotland.

[4] *Duchess* Anne Scott, first Duchess of Buccleuch and Monmouth (1651–1732), owner of Newark Castle and widow of James, Duke of Monmouth, who was beheaded for treason in 1685 after leading a failed rebellion against James II.

[5] *Earl Francis* Francis Scott, Earl of Buccleuch, father of the Duchess; *Earl Walter* Walter Scott, Earl of Buccleuch, grandfather of the Duchess, and a celebrated warrior.

The humble boon was soon obtained;
The Aged Minstrel audience gained.
But, when he reached the room of state,[1]
Where she, with all her ladies, sate,
Perchance he wished his boon denied:
For, when to tune his harp he tried,
His trembling hand had lost the ease,
Which marks security[2] to please;
And scenes, long past, of joy and pain,
Came wildering° o'er his aged brain—   *bewilderingly*
He tried to tune his harp in vain!
The pitying Duchess praised its chime,
And gave him heart, and gave him time,
Till every string's according glee
Was blended into harmony.
And then, he said, he would full fain[3]
He could recall an ancient strain,
He never thought to sing again.
It was not framed for village churls,
But for high dames and mighty earls;
He had played it to King Charles the Good,
When he kept court in Holyrood;[4]
And much he wished, yet feared, to try
The long-forgotten melody.
Amid the strings his fingers strayed,
And an uncertain warbling made,
And oft he shook his hoary head.
But when he caught the measure wild,
The old man raised his face, and smiled;
And lightened up his faded eye,
With all a poet's ecstasy!
In varying cadence, soft or strong,
He swept the sounding chords along:
The present scene, the future lot,
His toils, his wants, were all forgot:
Cold diffidence, and age's frost,
In the full tide of song were lost;
Each blank, in faithless memory void,

The poet's glowing thought supplied;
And, while his harp responsive rung,
100 'Twas thus the LATEST MINSTREL sung. ...

from CANTO SIXTH

1

Breathes there the man, with soul so dead,
Who never to himself hath said,
    This is my own, my native land!
Whose heart hath ne'er within him burned,
5 As home° his footsteps he hath turned,   *homeward*
    From wandering on a foreign strand!
If such there breathe, go, mark him well;
For him no Minstrel raptures swell;
High though his titles, proud his name,
10 Boundless his wealth as wish can claim;
Despite those titles, power, and pelf,°   *riches*
The wretch, concentred° all in self,   *wrapped up*
Living, shall forfeit fair renown,
And, doubly dying, shall go down
15 To the vile dust, from whence he sprung,
Unwept, unhonoured, and unsung.

2

O Caledonia![5] stern and wild,
Meet° nurse for a poetic child!   *fitting*
Land of brown heath and shaggy wood,
20 Land of the mountain and the flood,
Land of my sires! what mortal hand
Can e'er untie the filial band,
That knits me to thy rugged strand!
Still as I view each well-known scene,
25 Think what is now, and what hath been,
Seems as, to me, of all bereft,
Sole friends thy woods and streams were left;
And thus I love them better still,
Even in extremity of ill.[6]
30 By Yarrow's streams still let me stray,
Though none should guide my feeble way;

---

[1] *room of state* Hall, receiving room.

[2] *security* Freedom from anxiety.

[3] *would full fain* Keenly wished; *fain* Gladly.

[4] *King Charles the Good* Charles I, crowned at Holyrood in 1633; *Holyrood* Royal Palace at Edinburgh.

[5] *Caledonia* Ancient Latin name for Scotland.

[6] *extremity of ill* Extreme misfortune.

Still feel the breeze down Ettrick break,
Although it chill my withered cheek;
Still lay my head by Teviot Stone,[1]
35   Though there, forgotten and alone,
The Bard may draw his parting groan. ...
—1805

Proud Maisie [2]

Proud Maisie is in the wood,
    Walking so early;
Sweet Robin sits on the bush,
    Singing so rarely.

5   "Tell me, thou bonny bird,
        When shall I marry me?"—
"When six braw° gentlemen   *fine*
    Kirkward[3] shall carry ye."

"Who makes the bridal bed,
10   Birdie, say truly?"—
"The gray-headed sexton
    That delves° the grave duly.   *digs*

"The glow-worm o'er grave and stone
    Shall light thee steady.
15 The owl from the steeple sing,
    'Welcome, proud lady.'"
—1818

---

[1] *Teviot Stone* Landmark stone located at the source of the River Teviot in the south of Scotland. The minstrel refers to the river and to the Teviot Stone in his lay.

[2] *Proud Maisie* Sung by a madwoman in Scott's novel *The Heart of Midlothian* (1818).

---

[3] *Kirkward* Toward the church.

DOROTHY WORDSWORTH
1771 – 1855

For Virginia Woolf, an ardent admirer of Dorothy Wordsworth's work, her journals have in them "the suggestive power which is the gift of the poet rather than of the naturalist, the power which, taking only the simplest facts, so orders them that the whole scene comes before us, heightened and composed, the lake in its quiet, the hills in their splendour." Wordsworth's exquisite observations on nature, her keen eye and ear for the details of the appearance and speech-patterns of the local populace—and her incisive sense of their harsh economic conditions and ingenious survival strategies—make her an important figure of Romanticism despite the fact that she published little under her own name during her lifetime. Her  writing is of interest not only in its own right but also for the influence she exerted on her more famous brother William, who consulted her journals for inspiration for many of his poems.

Dorothy Wordsworth was born on Christmas Day of 1771 to John Wordsworth, an attorney, and Ann (née Cookson), in Cockermouth, Cumberland, in the Lake District of England. Her mother died when Wordsworth was only six, and her father sent her to Yorkshire to live with relatives. She rarely saw her father again up to the day he, too, suffered an untimely death. Her childhood was spent happily among aunts and cousins, but at age fifteen she was sent to live with her stern grandparents; in the nine years she lived there she longed for the company of her four brothers. Her dream of living with William was realized when in 1795 he was bequeathed a legacy by a college friend, allowing the two siblings to secure a home together in Dorset in southwestern England. They were never again parted until William's death 55 years later.

The two made the acquaintance of Samuel Taylor Coleridge while in Somerset, and soon after that they moved to Alfoxden House to be nearer him. The bond the triad created was powerful, "three persons with one soul," according to Coleridge. This friendship marked the beginning of an intensely creative time for Coleridge and for William Wordsworth, culminating in their "*annus mirabilis*" that yielded the *Lyrical Ballads*. This alliance was productive for Dorothy Wordsworth, as well. She began her Alfoxden journal (the earliest of her journals that has survived) in 1798, chiefly for the enjoyment of her brother, who took great delight in reading it (and sometimes writing his own poems in it). Her sensitive descriptions of farm workers, beggars, leech gatherers, and a myriad of other characters, as well her vivid images of rural scenes, were also an invaluable resource for William, who would use them to spark his memory when he later "recollected in tranquility" an event the two had experienced. According to Woolf, "Dorothy stored the mood in prose, and later William came and bathed in it and made it into poetry." When the Wordsworths moved to Dove Cottage in the Lake District, Dorothy wrote in her Grasmere journal (1800–03): "I never saw daffodils so beautiful they grew among the mossy stones about and about them, some rested their heads upon these stones as on a pillow for weariness and the rest tossed and reeled and danced and seemed as if they verily laughed with the wind …, they looked so gay ever glancing ever changing." These words became the inspiration for William's description of daffodils in his poem "I Wandered Lonely as a Cloud."

Wordsworth remained with her brother in Grasmere even after his marriage in 1802. The two continued to take many excursions together, which she recorded in various travel journals. Her writing was curtailed in 1829, when she suffered the first of a series of ailments that eventually debilitated her both physically and mentally. By June of 1835 she was an invalid from dementia said to be caused by arteriosclerosis. She remained so, albeit with brief periods of lucidity, for the following two decades, but she was cared for lovingly by those whom she had once tended. She died in 1855, outliving her beloved William by five years.

Wordsworth's poems, letters, journals, and travelogues were published after her death. Once valued mainly as a resource for their insights into the work of the other poets in her circle, they are valued today for their descriptive power. Their author, according to Coleridge, possessed an "eye watchful in minutest observation of nature—and her taste a perfect electrometer—it bends, protrudes, and draws in at subtlest beauties and most recondite faults."

⌘ ⌘ ⌘

from *The Grasmere Journal*

May 14 1800 Wm. & John[1] set off into Yorkshire after dinner at ½ past 2 o'clock—cold pork in their pockets. I left them at the turning of the Low Wood bay[2] under the trees. My heart was so full that I could hardly speak to W. when I gave him a farewell kiss. I sat a long time upon a stone at the margin of the lake, and after a flood of tears my heart was easier. The lake looked to me I knew not why dull and melancholy, the weltering[3] on the shores seemed a heavy sound. I walked as long as I could amongst the stones of the shore. The wood rich in flowers. A beautiful yellow, palish yellow flower, that looked thick round and double, and smelt very sweet—I supposed it was a ranunculus—crowfoot, the grassy-leaved rabbit-toothed white flower, strawberries, geranium—scentless violet, anemones two kinds, orchises, primroses. The heckberry very beautiful as a low shrub. The crab coming out. Met a blind man driving a very large beautiful bull and a cow—he walked with two sticks. Came home by Clappersgate. The valley very green, many sweet views up to Rydale head when I could juggle away the fine

houses, but they disturbed me even more than when I have been happier—one beautiful view of the bridge, without Sir Michael's.[4] Sat down very often, though it was cold. I resolved to write a journal of the time till W. and J. return, and I set about keeping my resolve because I will not quarrel with myself, and because I shall give Wm. pleasure by it when he comes home again. At Rydale a woman of the village, stout and well-dressed, begged a halfpenny—she had never she said done it before—but these hard times! Arrived at home with a bad headache, set some slips of privet.[5] The evening cold had a fire—my face now flame-coloured. It is nine o'clock—I shall soon go to bed. A young woman begged at the door—she had come from Manchester on Sunday morn with two shillings and a slip of paper which she supposed a bank note—it was a cheat. She had buried her husband and three children within a year and a half—all in one grave—burying very dear—paupers all put in one place—20 shillings paid for as much ground as will bury a man—a grave stone to be put over it or the right will be lost—11/6[6] each time the ground is opened. Oh! that I had a letter from William!

---

[1] *Wm. & John* Dorothy Wordsworth's brothers, William (often written as "Wm." or "W.") and John.

[2] *Low Wood bay* In the Lake District, where Dorothy and William Wordsworth lived.

[3] *weltering* Tumbling (of waves).

[4] *bridge, without Sir Michael's* Pelter Bridge, beyond Rydal Hall, the chief seat of Sir Michael le Fleming, 4th Baronet of Rydal (1748–1806).

[5] *privet* Common hedge plant.

[6] *11/6* Eleven shillings and sixpence.

Friday 3rd October. Very rainy all the morning—little Sally[1] learning to mark. Wm. walked to Ambleside after dinner. I went with him part of the way—he talked much about the object of his essay for the second volume of LB.[2] I returned expecting the Simpsons—they did not come. I should have met Wm. but my teeth ached and it was showery and late—he returned after 10. Amos Cottle's[3] death in the morning Post. Wrote to S. Lowthian.[4]

N.B.[5] When Wm. and I returned from accompanying Jones we met an old man almost double—he had on a coat thrown over his shoulders above his waistcoat and coat. Under this he carried a bundle and had an apron on and a night cap. His face was interesting. He had dark eyes and a long nose—John who afterwards met him at Wythburn took him for a Jew. He was of Scotch parents but had been born in the army. He had had a wife "and a good woman and it pleased God to bless us with ten children"—all these were dead but one of whom he had not heard for many years, a sailor—his trade was to gather leeches but now leeches are scarce and he had not strength for it—he lived by begging and was making his way to Carlisle where he should buy a few godly books to sell. He said leeches were very scarce partly owing to this dry season, but many years they have been scarce—he supposed it owing to their being much sought after, that they did not breed fast, and were of slow growth. Leeches were formerly 2/6 100; they are now 30/. He had been hurt in driving a cart his leg broke his body driven over his skull fractured—he felt no pain till he recovered from his first insensibility. It was then late in the evening—when the light was just going away.

Saturday 11th A fine October morning—sat in the house working all the morning. Wm. composing—Sally Ashburner learning to mark. After dinner we walked up Greenhead Gill in search of a sheepfold. We went by Mr. Olliff's and through his woods. It was a delightful day and the views looked excessively cheerful and beautiful chiefly that from Mr. Oliff's field where our house is to be built. The colours of the mountains soft and rich, with orange fern. The cattle pasturing upon the hilltops kites[6] sailing as in the sky above our heads—sheep bleating and in lines and chains and patterns scattered over the mountains. They come down and feed on the little green islands in the beds of the torrents and so may be swept away. The sheepfold is falling away it is built nearly in the form of a heart unequally divided. Look down the brook and see the drops rise upwards and sparkle in the air, at the little falls, the higher sparkles the tallest. We walked along the turf of the mountain till we came to a cattle track—made by the cattle which come upon the hills. We drank tea at Mr. Simpson's returned at about nine—a fine mild night.

[November, 1801]

Tuesday 24th A rainy morning, We all were well except that my head ached a little and I took my breakfast in bed. I read a little of Chaucer, prepared the goose for dinner, and then we all walked out—I was obliged to return for my fur tippet and spenser[7] it was so cold. We had intended going to Easedale but we shaped our course to Mr. Gell's[8] cottage. It was very windy and we heard the wind everywhere about us as we went along the lane but the walls sheltered us—John Green's house looked pretty under Silver How[9]—as we were going along we were stopped at once, at the distance perhaps of 50 yards from our favorite birch tree. It was yielding to the gusty wind with all its tender twigs, the sun shone upon it and it glanced in the wind like a flying sunshiny shower—it was a tree in shape with stem and branches

---

[1] *little Sally* Sally Ashburner, daughter of the Wordsworths' neighbor.

[2] *LB Lyrical Ballads*, written with Samuel Taylor Coleridge (1798); William Wordsworth wrote a lengthy preface to the second edition, published in 1800.

[3] *Amos Cottle* Cottle was a poet, translator, and a member of the "Lake School," which included W. Wordsworth, Coleridge, and Southey; his brother, Joseph Cottle, was a poet and the publisher of Coleridge and W. Wordsworth's *Lyrical Ballads*.

[4] *S. Lowthian* Sally, one of Wordsworth's father's domestic staff.

[5] *N.B. Nota bene* : Note well (Latin); i.e., important note.

[6] *kites* Birds (of prey).

[7] *tippet and spenser* Shawl and jacket.

[8] *Mr. Gell* Anthropologist Sir William Gell.

[9] *Silver How* Hill near Grasmere.

but it was like a spirit of water. The sun went in and it resumed its purplish appearance the twigs still yielding to the wind but not so visibly to us. The other birch trees that were near it looked bright and cheerful—but it was a creature by its own self among them. We could not get into Mr. Gell's grounds—the old tree fallen from its undue exaltation above the gate. A shower came on when we were at Benson's. We went through the wood—it became fair, there was a rainbow which spanned the lake from the island house to the foot of Bainriggs. The village looked populous and beautiful. Catkins[1] are coming out palm trees budding—the alder with its plum coloured buds. We came home over the stepping stones—the lake was foamy with white waves. I saw a solitary butter flower[2] in the wood. *I* found it not easy to get over the stepping stones—reached home at dinner time. Sent Peggy Ashburner some goose. She sent me some honey—with a thousand thanks—"alas the gratitude of men has &c."[3] I went in to set her right about this and sat a while with her. She talked about Thomas's having sold his land—"Ay" says she, "I said many a time he's not come fra London to buy our land however." Then she told me with what pains and industry they had made up their taxes interest &c. &c. —how they all got up at 5 o'clock in the morning to spin and Thomas carded,[4] and that they had paid off a hundred pound of the interest. She said she used to take such pleasure in the cattle and sheep—"Oh how pleased I used to be when they fetched them down, and when I had been a bit poorly I would gang[5] out upon a hill and look ower t' fields and see them and it used to do me so much good you cannot think"—Molly said to me when I came in "poor body! She's very ill but one does not know how long she may last. Many a fair face may gang before her." We sat by the fire without work for some

time then Mary[6] read a poem of Daniel[7] upon learning. After tea Wm. read Spenser now and then a little aloud to us. We were making his waistcoat. We had a note from Mrs. C.[8] with bad news from poor C. very ill. William walked to John's grove—I went to meet him—moonlight but it rained. I met him before I had got as far as John Batys—he had been surprized and terrified by a sudden rushing of winds which seemed to bring earth sky and lake together, as if the whole were going to enclose him in—he was glad that he was in a high road.

In speaking of our walk on Sunday evening the 22nd November I forgot to notice one most impressive sight—it was the moon and the moonlight seen through hurrying driving clouds immediately behind the stone man upon the top of the hill on the forest side. Every tooth and every edge of rock was visible, and the man stood like a giant watching from the roof of a lofty castle. The hill seemed perpendicular from the darkness below it. It was a sight that I could call to mind at any time it was so distinct.

Friday 27th Snow upon the ground thinly scattered. It snowed after we got up and then the sun shone and it was very warm though frosty—now the sun shines sweetly. A woman came who was travelling with her husband—he had been wounded and was going with her to live at Whitehaven. She had been at Ambleside the night before, offered 4d at the Cock for a bed—they sent her to one Harrison's where she and her husband had slept upon the hearth and bought a pennyworth of chips for a fire. Her husband was gone before very lame. "Aye" says she, "I was once an officer's wife I, as you see me now. My first husband married me at Appleby. I had 18£ a year for teaching a school and because I had no fortune his father turned him out of doors. I have been in the West Indies—I lost the use of this finger. Just before he died he came to me and said he must bid farewell to his dear children and me—I had a muslin

---

[1] *Catkins* Cylindrical buds on birch and willow trees.

[2] *butter flower* Buttercup.

[3] *"alas ... &c."* From William Wordsworth's "Simon Lee" 95–96: "I've heard of hearts unkind, kind deeds / With coldness still returning; / Alas! the gratitude of men / Hath oftener left me mourning."

[4] *carded* Combed the wool.

[5] *gang* Go.

[6] *Mary* Mary Hutchinson, Wordsworth's friend and William's future wife; Wordsworth often refers to her as MH in the journals.

[7] *Daniel* Samuel Daniel (1562–1619).

[8] *Mrs. C.* Mrs. Coleridge.

gown on like yours—I seized hold of his coat as he went from me and slipped the joint of my finger—he was shot directly. I came to London and married this man. He was clerk to Judge Chambray, that man that's going on the road now. If he, Judge Chambray, had been at Kendal he would given us a guinea or two and made nought of it, for he is very generous."

Before dinner we set forward to walk intending to return to dinner. But as we had got as far as Rydale Wm. thought he would go on to Mr. Luffs. We accompanied him under Loughrigg, and parted near the stepping stones—it was very cold. Mary and I walked quick home. There was a fine gleam of sunshine upon the eastern side of Ambleside vale. We came up the old road and turning round we were struck with the appearance. Mary wrote to her aunt. We expected the Simpsons. I was sleepy and weary and went to bed—before tea. It came on wet in the evening and was very cold. We expected letters from C. and Sara[1]—Sara's came by the boy. But none from C.—a sad disappointment. We did not go to meet Wm. as we had intended—Mary was at work at Wm's warm waistcoat.

[December]

Tuesday 22nd Still thaw. I washed my head. Wm. and I went to Rydale for letters—the road was covered with dirty snow, rough and rather slippery. We had a melancholy letter from C. for he had been very ill, though he was better when he wrote. We walked home almost without speaking—Wm. composed a few lines of the Pedlar.[2] We talked about Lamb's tragedy[3] as we went down the White Moss. We stopped a long time in going to watch a little bird with a salmon coloured breast—a white cross or T upon its wings, and a brownish back with faint stripes. It was pecking the scattered dung upon the road—it began to peck at the distance of 4 yards from us and advanced nearer and nearer till it came within the length of Wm's stick without any

apparent fear of us. As we came up the White Moss we met an old man, who I saw was a beggar by his two bags hanging over his shoulder, but from a half laziness, half indifference and a wanting to *try* him if he would speak I let him pass. He said nothing, and my heart smote me. I turned back and said You are begging? "Ay" says he—I gave him a halfpenny. William, judging from his appearance joined in I suppose you were a Sailor? "Ay" he replied, "I have been fifty-seven years at sea, twelve of them on board a man-of-war[4] under Sir Hugh Palmer." Why have you not a pension? "I have no pension, but I could have got into Greenwich hospital[5] but all my officers are dead." He was seventy-five years of age, had a freshish colour in his cheeks, grey hair, a decent hat with a binding round the edge, the hat worn brown and glossy, his shoes were small thin shoes low in the quarters, pretty good—they had belonged to a gentleman. His coat was blue, frock shaped coming over his thighs, it had been joined up at the seams behind with paler blue to let it out, and there were three bell-shaped patches of darker blue behind where the buttons had been. His breeches were either of fustian[6] or grey cloth, with strings hanging down, whole and tight and he had a checked shirt on, and a small coloured handkerchief tied round his neck. His bags were hung over each shoulder and lay on each side of him, below his breast. One was brownish and of coarse stuff, the other was white with meal[7] on the outside, and his blue waistcoat was whitened with meal. In the coarse bag I guessed he put his scraps of meat &c. He walked with a slender stick decently stout, but his legs bowed outwards. We overtook old Fleming at Rydale, leading his little Dutchman-like grandchild along the slippery road. The same pace seemed to be natural to them both, the old man and the little child, and they went hand in hand, the grandfather cautious, yet looking proud of his charge. He had two patches of new cloth at the shoulder blades of his faded claret coloured coat, like eyes at each

---

[1] *C. and Sara* Samuel Taylor Coleridge and Sara Hutchinson, sister of William Wordsworth's future wife.

[2] *the Pedlar* "The Pedlar," a poem by William Wordsworth that was eventually incorporated into *The Excursion*.

[3] *Lamb's tragedy* Charles Lamb's play *John Woodvil* (1802).

[4] *man-of-war* Warship.

[5] *Greenwich hospital* Royal Naval Hospital, i.e., home for pensioned seamen.

[6] *fustian* Coarse cloth made of cotton and linen.

[7] *meal* Grain ground to a powder, like flour.

shoulder, not worn elsewhere. I found Mary at home in her riding-habit all her clothes being put up. We were very sad about Coleridge. Wm. walked further. When he came home he cleared a path to the necessary[1]—called me out to see it but before we got there a whole housetop full of snow had fallen from the roof upon the path and it echoed in the ground beneath like a dull beating upon it. We talked of going to Ambleside after dinner to borrow money of Luff, but we thought we would defer our visit to Eusemere a day. Half the seaman's nose was reddish as if he had been in his youth somewhat used to drinking, though he was not injured by it. We stopped to look at the stone seat at the top of the hill. There was a white cushion upon it round at the edge like a cushion and the rock behind looked soft as velvet, of a vivid green and so tempting! The snow too looked as soft as a down cushion. A young foxglove, like a star in the centre. There were a few green lichens about it and a few withered brackens of fern here and there and upon the ground near. All else was a thick snow—no foot mark to it, not the foot of a sheep. When we were at Thomas Ashburner's on Sunday Peggy talked about the Queen of Patterdale. She had been brought to drinking by her husband's unkindness and avarice. She was formerly a very nice tidy woman. She had taken to drinking but "that was better than if she had taken to something worse" (by this I suppose she meant killing herself). She said that her husband used to be out all night with other women and she used to hear him come in in the morning for they never slept together—"Many a poor body a wife like me, has had a working heart for her, as much stuff as she had." We sat snugly round the fire. I read to them the Tale of Custance and the Syrian Monarch, also some of the Prologues. It is the Man of Lawes Tale.[2] We went to bed early. It snowed and thawed.

Monday Morning 8th February 1802. It was very windy and rained very hard all the morning. William worked

at his poem and I read a little in Lessing[3] and the grammar. A chaise[4] came past to fetch Ellis the carrier[5] who had hurt his head. After dinner (i.e. we set off at about ½ past 4) we went towards Rydale for letters. It was a "*Cauld Clash*"[6]—the rain had been so cold that it hardly melted the snow. We stopped at Park's to get some straw in William's shoes. The young mother was sitting by a bright wood fire with her youngest child upon her lap and the other two sat on each side of the chimney. The light of the fire made them a beautiful sight, with their innocent countenances, their rosy cheeks and glossy curling hair. We sat and talked about poor Ellis, and our journey over the Hawes.[7] It had been reported that we came over in the night. Willy told us of three men who were once lost in crossing that way in the night—they had carried a lantern with them—the lantern went out at the tarn[8] and they all perished. Willy had seen their cloaks drying at the public house in Patterdale the day before their funeral. We walked on very wet through the clashy cold roads in bad spirits at the idea of having to go as far as Rydale, but before we had come again to the shore of the lake, we met our patient, bow-bent friend with his little wooden box at his back. "Where are you going?" said he, "To Rydale for letters"—"I have two for you in my box." We lifted up the lid and there they lay—poor fellow, he straddled and pushed on with all his might but we soon outstripped him far away when we had turned back with our letters. We were very thankful that we had not to go on, for we should have been sadly tired. In thinking of this I could not help comparing lots with him! He goes at that slow pace every morning, and after having wrought a hard day's work returns at night, however weary he may be, takes it all quietly, and though perhaps he neither feels thankfulness, nor pleasure when he eats his supper, and has no luxury to look forward to but

---

[1]   *necessary*   Outdoor toilet.

[2]   *Tale of Custance … Man of Lawes Tale*   From Geoffrey Chaucer's *The Canterbury Tales.*

[3]   *Lessing*   German author and critic Gotthold Ephraim Lessing (1729–81).

[4]   *chaise*   Light open carriage.

[5]   *carrier*   I.e., common carrier, a hired parcel delivery person.

[6]   *"Cauld Clash"*   Scottish phrase meaning a cold blow.

[7]   *the Hawes*   Grisedale Pass.

[8]   *tarn*   Small mountain lake.

falling asleep in bed, yet I daresay he neither murmurs nor thinks it hard. He seems mechanized to labour. We broke the seal of Coleridge's letter, and I had light enough just to see that he was not ill. I put it in my pocket but at the top of the White Moss I took it to my bosom, a safer place for it. The night was wild. There was a strange mountain lightness when we were at the top of the White Moss. I have often observed it there in the evenings, being between the two valleys. There is more of the sky there than any other place. It has a strange effect sometimes along with the obscurity of evening or night. It seems almost like a peculiar *sort* of light. There was not much wind till we came to John's Grove, then it roared right out of the grove, all the trees were tossing about. C's letter somewhat damped us, it spoke with less confidence about France.[1] William wrote to him. The other letter was from Montagu with 8£. William was very unwell, tired when he had written, he went to bed, and left me to write to M.H., Montagu and Calvert, and Mrs. Coleridge. I had written in his letter to Coleridge. We wrote to Calvert to beg him not to fetch us on Sunday. Wm left me with a *little* peat fire—it grew less—I wrote on and was starved.[2] At 2 o'clock I went to put my letters under Fletcher's door. I never felt such a cold night. There was a strong wind and it froze very hard. I collected together all the clothes I could find (for I durst not go into the pantry for fear of waking William). At first when I went to bed I seemed to be warm, I suppose because the cold air which I had just left no longer touched my body, but I soon found that I was mistaken. I could not sleep from sheer cold. I had baked pies and bread in the morning. Coleridge's letter contained prescriptions.

NB The moon came out suddenly when we were at John's Grove and "a star or two beside."[3]

[18 March]

Thursday A very fine morning. The sun shone but it was far colder than yesterday. I felt myself weak, and William charged me not to go to Mrs. Lloyds—I seemed indeed, to myself unfit for it but when he was gone I thought I would get the visit over if I could—so I ate a beefsteak thinking it would strengthen me, so it did, and I went off—I had a very pleasant walk. Rydale vale was full of life and motion. The wind blew briskly and the lake was covered all over with bright silver waves that were there each the twinkling of an eye, then others rose up and took their place as fast as they went away. The rocks glittered in the sunshine, the crows and the ravens were busy, and the thrushes and little birds sang—I went through the fields, and sat ½ an hour afraid to pass a cow. The cow looked at me and I looked at the cow and whenever I stirred the cow gave over eating. I was not very much tired when I reached Lloyds—I walked in the garden. Charles is all for agriculture. Mrs. L. in her kindest way. A parcel came in from Birmingham, with Lamb's play for us and for C. They came with me as far as Rydale. As we came along Ambleside vale in the twilight—it was a grave evening—there was something in the air that compelled me to serious thought—the hills were large, closed in by the sky. It was nearly dark when I parted from the Lloyds that is, night was come on and the moon was overcast. But as I climbed Moss the moon came out from behind a mountain mass of black clouds—O the unutterable darkness of the sky and the earth below the moon! and the glorious brightness of the moon itself! There was a vivid sparkling streak of light at this end of Rydale water but the rest was very dark and Loughrigg fell and Silver How were white and bright as if they were covered with hoar frost. The moon retired again and appeared and disappeared several times before I reached home. Once there was no moonlight to be seen but upon the island house and the promontory of the island where it stands, "That needs must be a holy place" &c.—&c. I had many very exquisite feelings when I saw this lowly building in the waters among the dark and lofty hills, with that bright soft light upon it—it made me more than half a poet. I was tired when I reached home. I

---

1 *it spoke … France* Regarding plans for the Wordsworths and Coleridges to move to France.

2 *starved* Frozen.

3 *a star or two beside* From Coleridge's "The Rime of the Ancient Mariner," Part IV.

could not sit down to reading and tried to write verses but alas! I gave up expecting William and went soon to bed. Fletcher's carts came home late.

[April]

Thursday 15th   It was a threatening misty morning—but mild. We set off after dinner from Eusemere—Mrs. Clarkson went a short way with us but turned back. The wind was furious, and we thought we must have returned. We first rested in the large boat-house, then under a furze bush[1] opposite Mr. Clarkson's—saw the plough going in the field. The wind seized our breath the lake was rough. There was a boat by itself floating in the middle of the Bay below Water Millock—We rested again in the Water Millock lane. The hawthorns are black and green, the birches here and there greenish but there is yet more of purple to be seen on the Twigs. We got over into a field to avoid some cows—people working, a few primroses by the roadside, woodsorrel flowers, the anemone, scentless violets, strawberries, and that starry yellow flower which Mrs. C. calls pile wort. When we were in the woods beyond Gowbarrow park we saw a few daffodils close to the water-side; we fancied that the lake had floated the seeds ashore and that the little colony had so sprung up. But as we went along there were more and yet more and at last under the boughs of the trees, we saw that there was a long belt of them along the shore, about the breadth of a country turnpike road. I never saw daffodils so beautiful they grew among the mossy stones about and about them, some rested their heads upon these stones as on a pillow for weariness and the rest tossed and reeled and danced and seemed as if they verily laughed with the wind that blew upon them over the lake, they looked so gay ever glancing ever changing. This wind blew directly over the lake to them. There was here and there a little knot and a few stragglers a few yards higher up but they were so few as not to disturb the simplicity and unity and life of that one busy highway. We rested again and again. The bays were stormy and we heard the waves at different distances and in the middle of the water like the

sea—rain came on, we were wet when we reached Luffs but we called in. Luckily all was cheerless and gloomy so we faced the storm—we *must* have been wet if we had waited—put on dry clothes at Dobson's. I was very kindly treated by a young woman, the landlady looked sour but it is her way. She gave us a goodish supper, excellent ham and potatoes. We paid 7/ when we came away. William was sitting by a bright fire when I came downstairs. He soon made his way to the library piled up in a corner of the window. He brought out a volume of Enfield's Speaker,[2] another miscellany, and an odd volume of Congreve's plays.[3] We had a glass of warm rum and water—we enjoyed ourselves and wished for Mary. It rained and blew when we went to bed. NB deer in Gowbarrow park like to skeletons.

Tuesday May 4th   William had slept pretty well and though he went to bed nervous and jaded in the extreme, he rose refreshed. I wrote the Leech Gatherer[4] for him which he had begun the night before and of which he wrote several stanzas in bed this Monday morning. It was very hot, we called at Mr. Simpson's door as we passed but did not go in. We rested several times by the way, read and repeated the Leech Gatherer. We were almost melted before we were at the top of the hill. We saw Coleridge on the Wytheburn side of the water, he crossed the beck[5] to us. Mr. Simpson was fishing there. William and I ate a luncheon, then went on towards the waterfall. It is a glorious wild solitude under that lofty purple crag. It stood upright by itself. Its own self and its shadow below, one mass—all else was sunshine. We went on further. A bird at the top of the crags was flying round and round and looked in thinness and transparency, shape and motion, like a moth. We climbed the hill but looked in vain for a shade except at the foot of the great waterfall, and there we did not like to stay on account of the loose stones above our heads. We came

---

[1]   *furze bush*   Common evergreen shrub.

[2]   *Enfield's Speaker*   William Enfield's *The Speaker; or Miscellaneous Pieces, Selected from the Best English Writers.*

[3]   *Congreve's plays*   Plays of William Congreve (1670–1729).

[4]   *wrote the Leech Gatherer*   Transcribed William's poem "Resolution and Independence."

[5]   *beck*   Stream.

down and rested upon a moss covered rock, rising out of the bed of the river. There we lay ate our dinner and stayed there till about 4 o'clock or later—Wm. and C. repeated and read verses. I drank a little brandy and water and was in heaven. The stag's horn is very beautiful and fresh springing upon the fells. Mountain ashes, green. We drank tea at a farm house. The woman had not a pleasant countenance, but was civil enough. She had a pretty boy a year old whom she suckled. We parted from Coleridge at Sara's crag after having looked at the letters which C. carved in the morning. I kissed them all. Wm. deepened the T with C's penknife. We sat afterwards on the wall, seeing the sun go down and the reflections in the still water. C. looked well and parted from us cheerfully, hopping up upon the side stones. On the rays we met a woman with 2 little girls one in her arms the other about 4 years old walking by her side, a pretty little thing, but half starved. She had on a pair of slippers that had belonged to some gentleman's child, down at the heels, but it was not easy to keep them on—but, poor thing! young as she was, she walked carefully with them. Alas too young for such cares and such travels. The mother when we accosted her told us that her husband had left her and gone off with another woman and how she "*pursued*" them. Then her fury kindled and her eyes rolled about. She changed again to tears. She was a Cockermouth woman—30 years of age a child at Cockermouth when I was—I was moved and gave her a shilling, I believe 6^d more than I ought to have given. We had the crescent moon with the "auld moon in her arms"[1]—We rested often:—always upon the bridges. Reached home at about 10 o'clock. The Lloyds had been here in our absence. We went soon to bed. I repeated verses to William while he was in bed—he was soothed and I left him. "This is the Spot"[2] over and over again.

[July]

Tuesday 26th Market day streets dirty, very rainy, did not leave Hull till 4 o'clock, and left Barton at about 6—rained all the way—almost—a beautiful village at the foot of a hill with trees—a gentleman's house converted into a lady's boarding school. We had a woman in bad health in the coach, and took in a lady and her daughter—supped at Lincoln. Duck and peas, and cream cheese—paid 2/-. We left Lincoln on Wednesday morning 27th July at six o'clock it rained heavily and we could see nothing but the ancientry of some of the buildings as we passed along. The night before, however, we had seen enough to make us regret this. The minster[3] stands at the edge of a hill, overlooking an immense plain. The country very flat as we went along—the day mended—We went to see the outside of the minster while the passengers were dining at Peterborough—the west end very grand. The little girl who was a great scholar, and plainly her mothers favorite though she had a large family at home had bought The Farmer's Boy.[4] She said it was written by a man without education and was very wonderful.

On Thursday morning, 29th, we arrived in London. Wm. left me at the inn—I went to bed &c. &c. &c. After various troubles and disasters we left London on Saturday morning at ½ past 5 or 6, the 31st of July (I have forgot which) we mounted the Dover coach at Charing Cross. It was a beautiful morning. The city, St. Paul's, with the river and a multitude of little boats, made a most beautiful sight as we crossed Westminster Bridge. The houses were not overhung by their cloud of smoke and they were spread out endlessly, yet the sun shone so brightly with such a pure light that there was even something like the purity of one of nature's own grand spectacles. We rode on cheerfully now with the Paris Diligence[5] before us, now behind—we walked up the steep hills, beautiful prospects everywhere, till we even reached Dover. At first the rich populous wide spreading woody country about London, then the river

---

[1] *auld moon in her arms* From the popular ballad "Sir Patrick Spens"; Coleridge also quoted this line in "Dejection: An Ode."

[2] *This is the Spot* From a poem by Dorothy Wordsworth, never published in her lifetime.

[3] *minster* Monastery church.

[4] *The Farmer's Boy* Long poem published by the laboring class poet Robert Bloomfield in 1800.

[5] *Diligence* Coach.

Thames, ships sailing, chalk cliffs, trees, little villages. Afterwards Canterbury, situated on a plain, rich and woody, but the city and cathedral disappointed me. Hop grounds on each side of the road some miles from Canterbury, then we came to a common, the race ground, an elevated plain, villages among trees in the bed of a valley at our right, and rising above this valley, green hills scattered over with wood—neat gentlemen's houses—one white house almost hid with green trees which we longed for and the parsons house as neat a place as could be which would just have suited Coleridge. No doubt we might have found one for Tom Hutchinson and Sara and a good farm too. We halted at a halfway house—fruit carts under the shade of trees, seats for guests, a tempting place to the weary traveller. Still as we went along the country was beautiful, hilly, with cottages lurking under the hills and their little plots of hop ground like vineyards. It was a bad hop-year—a woman on the top of the coach said to me "it is a sad thing for the poor people for the hop-gathering is the women's harvest, there is employment about the hops both for women and children." We saw the castle of Dover and the sea beyond four or five miles before we reached D. We looked at it through a long vale, the castle being upon an eminence, as it seemed at the end of this vale which opened to the sea. The country now became less fertile but near Dover it seemed more rich again. Many buildings stand on the flat fields, sheltered with tall trees. There is one old chapel that might have been there just in the same state in which it now is, when this vale was as retired and as little known to travellers, as our own Cumberland mountain wilds 30 years ago. There was also a very old building on the other side of the road which had a strange effect among the many new ones that are springing up everywhere. It seemed odd that it could have kept itself pure in its ancientry among so many upstarts. It was near dark when we reached Dover. We were told that the packet[1] was about to sail, so we went down to the Customhouse in half an hour, had our luggage examined &c. &c. and then we drank tea, with the honorable Mr. Knox and

his tutor. We arrived at Calais at 4 o'clock on Sunday morning the 31st of July. We stayed in the vessel till ½ past 7. Then Wm. went for letters, at about ½ past 8 or 9. We found out Annette and C.[2] chez Madame Avril dans la Rue de la Tête d'or. We lodged opposite two ladies in tolerably decent-sized rooms but badly furnished, and with large store of bad smells and dirt in the yard, and all about. The weather was very hot. We walked by the seashore almost every evening with Annette and Caroline or Wm. and I alone. I had a bad cold and could not bathe at first but William did. It was a pretty sight to see as we walked upon the sands when the tide was low, perhaps a hundred people bathing about ¼ of a mile distant from us, and we had delightful walks after the heat of the day was passed away—seeing far off in the west the coast of England like a cloud crested with Dover Castle, which was but like the summit of the cloud—the evening star and the glory of the sky. The reflections in the water were more beautiful than the sky itself, purple waves brighter than precious stones forever melting away upon the sands. The fort, a wooden building, at the entrance of the harbour at Calais, when the evening twilight was coming on, and we could not see anything of the building but its shape which was far more distinct than in perfect daylight, seemed to be reared upon pillars of ebony, between which pillars the sea was seen in the most beautiful colours that can be conceived. Nothing in romance was ever half so beautiful. Now came in view as the evening star sank down and the colours of the west faded away the two lights of England, lighted up by Englishmen in our country, to warn vessels of rocks or sands. These we used to see from the pier when we could see no other distant objects but the clouds the sky and the sea itself. All was dark behind. The town of Calais seemed deserted of the light of heaven, but there was always light, and life, and joy upon the sea. One night, though, I shall never forget, the day had been very hot, and William and I walked alone together upon the pier—the sea was gloomy for there was a blackness over all the sky

---

[1] *packet* Boat originally used to carry mail (packets).

[2] *Annette and C.* Annette Vallon, with whom William Wordsworth had had an affair when he visited France in his youth, and their daughter, Caroline.

except when it was overspread with lightning which often revealed to us a distant vessel. Near us the waves roared and broke against the pier, and as they broke and as they travelled towards us, they were interfused with greenish fiery light. The more distant sea always black and gloomy. It was, also beautiful on the calm hot nights to see the little Boats row out of harbour with wings of fire and the sail boats with the fiery track which they cut as they went along and which closed up after them with a hundred thousand sparkles balls shootings, and streams of glowworm light. Caroline was delighted.

On Sunday the 29th of August we left Calais at 12 o'clock in the morning and landed at Dover at 1 on Monday the 30th. I was sick all the way. It was very pleasant to me when we were in harbour at Dover to breathe the fresh air, and to look up and see the stars among the ropes of the vessel. The next day was very hot. We both bathed and sat upon the Dover cliffs and looked upon France with many a melancholy and tender thought. We could see the shores almost as plain as if it were but an English lake. We mounted the coach at ½ past 4 and arrived in London at 6 the 30th August. It was misty and we could see nothing. We stayed in London till Wednesday the 22nd of September, and arrived at Gallow Hill on Friday 24th September. Mary first met us in the avenue. She looked so fat and well that we were made very happy by the sight of her—then came Sara, and last of all Joanna. Tom was forking corn[1] standing upon the corn cart. We dressed ourselves immediately and got tea—the garden looked gay with asters and sweet peas—I looked at everything with tranquillity and happiness but I was ill both on Saturday and Sunday and continued to be poorly most of the time of our stay. Jack and George came on Friday evening 1st October. On Saturday 2nd we rode to Hackness, William Jack George and Sara single, I behind Tom.[2] On Sunday 3rd Mary and Sara were busy packing. On Monday 4th October 1802, my brother William was married to Mary Hutchinson. I slept a good deal of the night and rose fresh and well in the morning—at a little after 8 o'clock I saw them go down the avenue towards the church. William had parted from me upstairs. I gave him the wedding ring—with how deep a blessing! I took it from my forefinger where I had worn it the whole of the night before—he slipped it again onto my finger and blessed me fervently. When they were absent my dear little Sara prepared the breakfast. I kept myself as quiet as I could, but when I saw the two men running up the walk, coming to tell us it was over, I could stand it no longer and threw myself on the bed where I lay in stillness, neither hearing or seeing anything, till Sara came upstairs to me and said "They are coming." This forced me from the bed where I lay and I moved I knew not how straight forward, faster than my strength could carry me till I met my beloved William and fell upon his bosom. He and John Hutchinson led me to the house and there I stayed to welcome my dear Mary. As soon as we had breakfasted we departed. It rained when we set off. Poor Mary was much agitated when she parted from her brothers and sisters and her home. Nothing particular occurred till we reached Kirby. We had sunshine and showers, pleasant talk, love and cheerfulness. We were obliged to stay two hours at K. while the horses were feeding. We wrote a few lines to Sara and then walked out, the sun shone and we went to the churchyard, after we had put a letter into the post office for the York Herald. We sauntered about and read the gravestones. There was one to the memory of 5 children, who had all died within 5 years, and the longest lived had only lived 4 years. There was another stone erected to the memory of an unfortunate woman (as we supposed, by a stranger). The verses engraved upon it expressed that she had been neglected by her relations and counselled the readers of those words to look within and recollect their own frailties. We left Kirby at about ½ past 2. There is not much variety of prospect from K. to Helmsely but the country is very pleasant, being rich and woody, and Helmsely itself stands very sweetly at the foot of the rising grounds of Duncombe Park which is scattered over with tall woods and lifting itself above the common buildings of the town stands Helmsely Castle, now a ruin, formerly inhabited by the gay Duke of Buckingham. Every foot

---

[1] *corn* Grain.

[2] *Jack George and Sara … Tom* Mary Hutchinson's siblings.

of the road was, of itself interesting to us, for we had travelled along it on foot Wm. and I when we went to fetch our dear Mary, and had sat upon the turf by the roadside more than once. Before we reached Helmsely our driver told us that he could not take us any further, so we stopped at the same inn where we had slept before. My heart danced at the sight of its cleanly outside, bright yellow walls, casements overshadowed with jasmine and its low, double gavel-ended front. We were not shown into the same parlour where Wm. and I were, it was a small room with a drawing over the chimney piece which the woman told us had been bought at a sale. Mary and I warmed ourselves at the kitchen fire—we then walked into the garden, and looked over a gate up to the old ruin which stands at the top of a mount, and round about it the moats are grown up into soft green cradles, hollows surrounded with green grassy hillocks and these are overshadowed by old trees, chiefly ashes. I prevailed upon William to go up with me to the ruins. We left Mary sitting by the kitchen fire. The sun shone, it was warm and very pleasant. One part of the castle seems to be inhabited. There was a man mowing nettles in the open space which had most likely once been the castle court. There is one gateway exceedingly beautiful—children were playing upon the sloping ground. We came home by the street. After about an hour's delay we set forward again, had an excellent driver who opened the gates so dexterously that the horses never stopped. Mary was very much delighted with the view of the castle from the point where we had seen it before. I was pleased to see again the little path which we had walked upon, the gate I had climbed over, and the road down which we had seen the two little boys drag a log of wood, and a team of horses struggle under the weight of a great load of timber. We had felt compassion for the poor horses that were under the governance of oppressive and ill-judging drivers, and for the poor boys who seemed of an age to have been able to have dragged the log of wood merely out of the love of their own activity, but from poverty and bad food they panted for weakness and were obliged to fetch their father from the town to help them. Duncombe House looks well from the road—a large

building, though I believe only 2 thirds of the original design are completed. We rode down a very steep hill to Ryvaux valley, with woods all round us. We stopped upon the bridge to look at the abbey and again when we had crossed it. Dear Mary had never seen a ruined abbey before except Whitby. We recognized the cottages, houses, and the little valleys as we went along. We walked up a long hill, the road carrying us up the cleft or valley with woody hills on each side of us. When we *went* to G.H.[1] I had walked down this valley alone. Wm. followed me. It was not dark evening when we passed the little public house,[2] but before we had crossed the Hambledon hills and reached the point overlooking Yorkshire it was quite dark. We had not wanted, however, fair prospects before us, as we drove along the flat plain of the high hill, far far off us, in the western sky, we saw shapes of castles, ruins among groves, a great, spreading wood, rocks, and single trees, a minster with its tower unusually distinct, minarets in another quarter, and a round Grecian temple also—the colours of the sky of a bright grey and the forms of a sober grey, with a dome. As we descended the hill there was no distinct view, but of a great space, only near us, we saw the wild and (as the people say) bottomless tarn in the hollow at the side of the hill. It seemed to be made visible to us only by its own light, for all the hill about us was dark. Before we reached Thirsk we saw a light before us which we at first thought was the moon, then lime kilns, but when we drove into the market place it proved a large bonfire with lads dancing round it, which is a sight I dearly love. The inn was like an illuminated house— every room full. We asked the cause, and were told by the girl that it was "Mr. John Bell's Birthday, that he had heired his estate." The landlady was very civil. She did not recognise the despised foot-travellers. We rode nicely in the dark, and reached Leming Lane at 11 o'clock. I am always sorry to get out of a chaise when it is night. The people of the house were going to bed and we were not very well treated though we got a hot supper. We breakfasted the next morning and set off at

[1] *G.H.*   George Hutchinson.
[2] *public house*   Tavern.

about ½ past 8 o'clock. It was a cheerful sunny morning. We soon turned out of Leming Lane and passed a nice village with a beautiful church. We had a few showers, but when we came to the green fields of Wensley, the sun shone upon them all, and the Eure in its many windings glittered as it flowed along under the green slopes of Middleham and Middleham Castle. Mary looked about for her friend Mr. Place, and thought she had him sure on the contrary side of the vale from that on which we afterwards found that he lived. We went to a new built house at Leyburn, the same village where Wm. and I had dined with George Hutchinson on our road to Grasmere 2 years and ¾ ago, but not the same house. The landlady was very civil, giving us cake and wine but the horses being out we were detained at least 2 hours and did not set off till 2 o'clock. We paid for 35 miles, i.e. to Sedbergh, but the landlady did not encourage us to hope to get beyond Hawes. A shower came on just after we left the inn. While the rain beat against the windows we ate our dinners which M. and W. heartily enjoyed—I was not quite well. When we passed through the village of Wensly my heart was melted away with dear recollections, the bridge, the little waterspout the steep hill the church. They are among the most vivid of my own inner visions, for they were the first objects that I saw after we were left to ourselves, and had turned our whole hearts to Grasmere as a home in which we were to rest. The vale looked most beautiful each way. To the left the bright silver stream inlaid the flat and very green meadows, winding like a serpent. To the right we did not see it so far, it was lost among trees and little hills. I could not help observing as we went along how much more *varied* the prospects of Wensley Dale are in the summer time than I could have thought possible in the winter. This seemed to be in great measure owing to the trees being in leaf, and forming groves, and screens, and thence little openings upon recesses and concealed retreats which in winter only made a part of the one great vale. The *beauty* of the summertime here as much excels that of the winter as the variety, owing to the excessive greenness of the fields, and the trees in leaf half concealing, and where they do not conceal, softening

the hard bareness of the limey white roofs. One of our horses seemed to grow a little restive as we went through the first village, a long village on the side of a hill. It grew worse and worse, and at last we durst not go on any longer. We walked a while, and then the post-boy[1] was obliged to take the horse out and go back for another. We seated ourselves again snugly in the post chaise. The wind struggled about us and rattled the window and gave a gentle motion to the chaise, but we were warm and at our ease within. Our station was at the top of a hill, opposite Bolton Castle, the Eure flowing beneath. William has since wrote a sonnet on this our imprisonment—Hard was thy durance Queen compared with ours.[2] Poor Mary! Wm. fell asleep, lying upon my breast and I upon Mary. I lay motionless for a long time, but I was at last obliged to move. I became very sick and continued so for some time after the boy brought the horse to us. Mary had been a little sick but it soon went off. We had a sweet ride till we came to a public house on the side of a hill where we alighted and walked down to see the waterfalls. The sun was not set, and the woods and fields were spread over with the yellow light of evening, which made their greenness a thousand times more green. There was too much water in the river for the beauty of the falls, and even the banks were less interesting than in winter. Nature had entirely got the better in her struggles against the giants who first cast the mould of these works; for indeed it is a place that did not in winter remind one of God, but one could not help feeling as if there had been the agency of some "Mortal Instruments"[3] which nature had been struggling against without making a perfect conquest. There was something so wild and new in this feeling, knowing as we did in the inner man that God alone had laid his hand upon it that I could not help

---

[1] *post-boy* Boy who "rides post," i.e., a person who rides the leading horse and acts as guide or driver.

[2] *Hard ... with ours* Mary, Queen of Scots was imprisoned at Bolton Castle for six months in 1568–69. In 1817 William Wordsworth published "Lament of Mary Queen of Scots: On the Eve of a New Year," which dealt with the queen's imprisonment and execution.

[3] *Mortal Instruments* From Shakespeare's *Julius Caesar* 2.1 and W. Wordsworth's *The Borderers* 2.3.

regretting the want of it, besides it is a pleasure to a real lover of nature to give winter all the glory he can, for summer *will* make its own way, and speak its own praises. We saw the pathway which Wm. and I took at the close of evening, the path leading to the rabbit warren where we lost ourselves. The farm with its holly hedges was lost among the green hills and hedgerows in general, but we found it out and were glad to look at it again. When William had left us to seek the waterfalls Mary and I were frightened by a cow. At our return to the inn we found new horses and a new driver, and we went on nicely to Hawes where we arrived before it was quite dark. Mary and I got tea, and William had a partridge and mutton chops and tarts for his supper. Mary sat down with him. We had also a shilling's worth of negus[1] and Mary made me some broth for all which supper we were only charged 2/-. I could not sit up long. I vomited, and took the broth and then slept sweetly. We rose at 6 o'clock—a rainy morning. We had a good breakfast and then departed. There was a very pretty view about a mile from Hawes, where we crossed a bridge, bare, and very green fields with cattle, a glittering stream cottages, a few ill-grown trees, and high hills. The sun shone now. Before we got upon the bare hills there was a hunting lodge on our right exactly like Greta Hill, with fir plantations about it. We were very fortunate in the day, gleams of sunshine passing clouds, that travelled with their shadows below them. Mary was much pleased with Garsdale. It was a dear place to William and me. We noted well the public-house (Garsdale Hall) where we had baited and drunk our pint of ale, and afterwards the mountain which had been adorned by Jupiter[2] in his glory when we were here before. It was midday when we reached Sedbergh, and *market* day. We were in the same room where we had spent the evening together in our road to Grasmere. We had a pleasant ride to Kendal, where we arrived at about 2 o'clock—the day favored us—M. and I went to see the house where dear Sara had lived, then went to seek Mr. Bousfield's shop but we found him not—he had sold all his goods the day before. We then went to the pot woman's and bought 2 jugs and a dish, and some paper at Pennington's. When we came to the inn William was almost ready for us. The afternoon was not cheerful but it did not rain till we came near Windermere. I am always glad to see Stavely. It is a place I dearly love to think of—the first mountain village that I came to with Wm. when we first began our pilgrimage together. Here we drank a bason of milk at a public house, and here I washed my feet in the brook and put on a pair of silk stockings by Wm's advice. Nothing particular occurred till we reached Ing's chapel—the door was open and we went in. It is a neat little place, with a marble floor and marble communion table with a painting over it of the last supper, and Moses and Aaron on each side. The woman told us that "they had painted them as near as they could by the dresses as they are described in the Bible," and gay enough they are. The marble had been sent by Richard Bateman from Leghorn. The woman told us that a man had been at her house a few days before who told her he had helped to bring it down the Red Sea and she had believed him gladly. It rained very hard when we reached Windermere. We sat in the rain at Wilcock's to change horses, and arrived at Grasmere at about 6 o'clock on Wednesday Evening, the 6th of October 1802. Molly was overjoyed to see us,—for my part I cannot describe what I felt, and our dear Mary's feelings would I dare say not be easy to speak of. We went by candle light into the garden and were astonished at the growth of the brooms, Portugal laurels, &c. &c. &c.—The next day, Thursday, we unpacked the boxes. On Friday 8th we baked bread, and Mary and I walked, first upon the hill side, and then in John's Grove, then in view of Rydale, the first walk that I had taken with my sister.

—1897 (WRITTEN 1800–02)

---

[1] *negus* Hot drink made with wine or port.

[2] *Jupiter* Supreme Roman deity.

Grasmere—A Fragment

Peaceful our valley, fair and green,
  And beautiful her cottages,
Each in its nook, its sheltered hold,
Or underneath its tuft of trees

5   Many and beautiful they are;
But there is *one* that I love best,
A lowly shed, in truth, it is,
A brother of the rest.

Yet when I sit on rock or hill,
10   Down looking on the valley fair,
That cottage with its clustering trees
Summons my heart; it settles there.

Others there are whose small domain
Of fertile fields and hedgerows green
15   Might more seduce a wanderer's mind
To wish that *there* his home had been.

Such wish be his! I blame him not,
My fancies they perchance are wild
—I love that house because it is
20   The very mountains' child.

Fields hath it of its own, green fields,
But they are rocky steep and bare;
Their fence is of the mountain stone,
And moss and lichen flourish there.

25   And when the storm comes from the north
It lingers near that pastoral spot,
And, piping through the mossy walls,
It seems delighted with its lot.

And let it take its own delight;
30   And let it range the pastures bare;
Until it reach that group of trees,
—It may not enter there!

A green unfading grove it is,
Skirted with many a lesser tree,
35   Hazel and holly, beech and oak,
A bright and flourishing company.

Precious the shelter of those trees;
They screen the cottage that I love;
The sunshine pierces to the roof,
40   And the tall pine-trees tower above.

When first I saw that dear abode,
It was a lovely winter's day:
After a night of perilous storm
The west wind ruled with gentle sway;

45   A day so mild, it might have been
The first day of the gladsome spring;
The robins warbled, and I heard
One solitary throstle° sing.   song thrush

A stranger, Grasmere, in thy vale,
50   All faces then to me unknown,
I left my sole companion-friend
To wander out alone.

Lured by a little winding path,
I quitted soon the public road,
55   A smooth and tempting path it was,
By sheep and shepherds trod.

Eastward, towards the lofty hills,
This pathway led me on
Until I reached a stately rock,
60   With velvet moss o'ergrown.

With russet oak and tufts of fern
Its top was richly garlanded;
Its sides adorned with eglantine°   fragrant rose
Bedropped with hips° of glossy red.   rose berries

65   There, too, in many a sheltered chink
The foxglove's broad leaves flourished fair,

And silver birch whose purple twigs
Bend to the softest breathing air.

70 Beneath that rock my course I stayed,
And, looking to its summit high,
"Thou wear'st," said I, "a splendid garb,
Here winter keeps his revelry.

"Full long a dweller on the plains,
I grieved when summer days were gone;
75 No more I'll grieve; for Winter here
Hath pleasure gardens of his own.

"What need of flowers? The splendid moss
Is gayer than an April mead;°   meadow
More rich its hues of various green,
80 Orange, and gold, and glittering red."

—Beside that gay and lovely rock
There came with merry voice
A foaming streamlet glancing by;
It seemed to say "Rejoice!"

85 My youthful wishes all fulfilled,
Wishes matured by thoughtful choice,
I stood an inmate of this vale
How *could* I but rejoice?
—1892 (WRITTEN 1805)

Floating Island

Harmonious Powers with nature work
On sky, earth, river, lake and sea;
Sunshine and cloud, whirlwind and breeze,
All in one duteous task agree.[1]

5 Once did I see a slip of earth
(By throbbing waves long undermined)
Loosed from its hold; how, no one knew,
But all might see it float, obedient to the wind;

---
[1] *All ... agree* All work together to perform a task that is their duty.

Might see it, from the mossy shore
10 Dissevered,° float upon the Lake,   separated
Float with its crest of trees adorned
On which the warbling birds their pastime take.

Food, shelter, safety, there they find;
There berries ripen, flowerets° bloom;   small flowers
15 There insects live their lives, and die;
A peopled world it is; in size a tiny room.

And thus through many seasons' space
This little Island may survive;
But Nature, though we mark her not,
20 Will take away, may cease to give.

Perchance when you are wandering forth
Upon some vacant sunny day,
Without an object, hope, or fear,
Thither your eyes may turn—the Isle is passed away;

25 Buried beneath the glittering Lake,
Its place no longer to be found;
Yet the lost fragments shall remain
To fertilise some other ground.
—1842 (WRITTEN LATE 1820S)

Thoughts on My Sick-bed

And has the remnant of my life
Been pilfered of this sunny spring?
And have its own prelusive° sounds   introductory
Touched in my heart no echoing string?

5 Ah! say not so—the hidden life
Couchant° within this feeble frame   lying
Hath been enriched by kindred gifts,
That, undesired, unsought-for, came

With joyful heart in youthful days
10 When fresh each season in its round
I welcomed the earliest celandine°   yellow flower
Glittering upon the mossy ground;

With busy eyes I pierced the lane
In quest of known and *un*known things,
5 —The primrose a lamp on its fortress rock,
The silent butterfly spreading its wings,

The violet betrayed by its noiseless breath,
The daffodil dancing in the breeze,
The carolling thrush, on his naked perch,
0 Towering above the budding trees.

Our cottage-hearth no longer our home,
Companions of nature were we,
The stirring, the still, the loquacious, the mute—
To all we gave our sympathy.

5 Yet never in those careless days
When spring-time in rock, field, or bower
Was but a fountain of earthly hope
A promise of fruits and the *splendid* flower.

No! then I never felt a bliss
0 That might with *that* compare
Which, piercing to my couch of rest,
Came on the vernal° air.   *springtime*

When loving friends an offering brought,
The first flowers of the year,
5 Culled from the precincts of our home,
From nooks to memory dear.

With some sad thoughts the work was done,
Unprompted and unbidden,
But joy it brought to my *hidden* life,
0 To consciousness no longer hidden.

I felt a power unfelt before,
Controlling weakness, languor, pain;
It bore me to the terrace walk
I trod the hills again;—

45 No prisoner in this lonely room,
I *saw* the green banks of the Wye,
Recalling thy prophetic words,
Bard, brother, friend from infancy![1]

No need of motion, or of strength,
50 Or even the breathing air:
—I thought of nature's loveliest scenes;
And with memory I was there.
—1978 (WRITTEN 1832)

---

[1] *Recalling ... infancy* Wordsworth is referring to her brother William's poem "Lines Composed a Few Miles above Tintern Abbey."

The Natural and the Sublime

CONTEXTS

In "The Two Guides of Life: The Sublime and the Beautiful" (a poem translated into English by Edward Bulwer Lytton in 1844), the eighteenth-century German philosopher Friedrich Schiller identifies "two genii," present from birth till death, "to guide thee." These guides structure our existence; we are, the poem maintains, perpetually under the sway of the beautiful and the sublime. Schiller's notion of aesthetic experience as profoundly powerful, indeed as the central force of human life, would hardly come as a surprise to the Romantics, who placed the beautiful and the sublime, along with the picturesque, at the forefront of their creative and philosophical vision.

Of course, the impulse to catalogue and categorize encounters with the aesthetic has a long history, originating well before the eighteenth century. The ancient Greeks had a great deal to say about the beautiful; Plato's work, for example, frequently discusses the ideal of Beauty and its imperfect reflections in the world of sense. In *Peri Hypsous*, a treatise on writing, a first-century rhetorician known as Longinus deemed extraordinary works "sublime," identifying great thought, powerful emotion, elevated figure of speech, noble diction, and distinguished word arrangement as the sources of sublimity in writing. The sublime, Longinus noted, is a significant source of pleasure, one that is distinguishable from beauty, for the experience of the sublime involves astonishment, alarm, and even fear.

Longinus's commentary was rediscovered in the late sixteenth century, translated into French (in 1674) and subsequently into English (in 1680), and published as *On the Sublime*. The sustained intense interest in the beautiful and the sublime only became a defining feature of the eighteenth century and the Romantic era, however, when a number of important thinkers turned their attention to the principles and problems of aesthetics. At the same time, what had been formerly identified mainly as aspects of writing became more profoundly associated with the natural world. This evolution is evident in the definition of "sublime" in the *Oxford English Dictionary*, which notes, circa 1700, the first usage of the term as indicating "things in nature" that affect "the mind with a sense of overwhelming grandeur or irresistible power; calculated to inspire awe, deep reverence, or lofty emotion, by reason of its beauty, vastness, or grandeur." English writers, including Joseph Addison, the founder and editor of the popular *Spectator* magazine, and Anthony Ashley Cooper, the Earl of Shaftesbury, undertook the Grand Tour, a continental tour deemed necessary for learned young men, and wrote powerfully of crossing the Alps, extolling the mountains' greatness and testifying to their personal transformations through such experiences. They wrote, too, of the beauty of nature, remarking on "the pleasures of the imagination" in nature, as in the title of Addison's *Spectator* essays on the subject.

But it was Edmund Burke who, in *A Philosophical Enquiry into the Origin of Our Ideas of the Sublime and Beautiful* (1757), gave the project of categorizing "objects of experience" its most extensive theoretical treatment, initiating the era's myriad investigations into the underpinnings of the sublime and the beautiful. Burke's undertaking is significant in its insistence on the rigorous separation of the two qualities; they are, he proposed, in their effects, virtual opposites. Other thinkers, most notably the German philosopher Immanuel Kant, who wrote extensively on aesthetics, disputed some of Burke's premises, but Burke's ideas were immensely influential, shaping the representation of and reaction to the sublime and the beautiful in the writing of the Romantics. Particularly noteworthy in this context is Burke's focus on the empirical experience of the beauty and grandeur of nature, an emphasis that plays out in much eighteenth-century British poetry and travel writing.

A third aesthetic category bears mentioning. The "picturesque" became an obsession of sorts, a feature of published travelogues and of great interest to travelers everywhere. Here, in a passage from Jane Austen's *Pride and Prejudice* (1813), the novel's spirited heroine Elizabeth Bennet marvels at the picturesque splendor of an estate in Derbyshire:

> They gradually ascended for half a mile, and then found themselves at the top of a considerable eminence, where the wood ceased, and the eye was instantly caught by Pemberley House, situated on the opposite side of a valley, into which the road with some abruptness wound. It was a large, handsome, stone building, standing well on rising ground, and backed by a ridge of high woody hills;—and in front, a stream of some natural importance was swelled into greater, but without any artificial appearance. Its banks were neither formal, nor falsely adorned. Elizabeth was delighted.

Elizabeth so admires, we are told, "a place ... where natural beauty had been so little counteracted by an awkward taste." The scene is one of beauty, but its pleasures come from the seeming absence of human intervention. This appreciation for or awe of nature structures and informs the Romantic mindset. Nature was not simply a matter of inspiration but the object of aspiration, to be emulated and celebrated in its beauty, its sublimity, and its ability to mediate between the two.

⌘ ⌘ ⌘

from Dionysius Longinus, *On the Sublime*[1] (First Century CE)

Longinus's *On the Sublime* is one of the most significant classical explorations of aesthetics. The treatise's authorship is unknown—the name "Dionysius Longinus" seems to have been the misreading of a medieval copyist—but its importance to the development of ideas about the sublime and their application to literary criticism is undeniable.

In the passage below, Longinus explains how the sublime is achieved in writing and elucidates the sources of the sublime.

from SECTION I

... **B**ut I request you, my dear friend, to give me your opinion on whatever I advance, with that exactness

which is due to truth, and that sincerity, which is natural to yourself. For well did the sage answer the question, *in what do we most resemble the gods?* when he replied, *in doing good and speaking truth.* But since I write, my dear friend, to you, who are versed in every branch of polite learning, there will be little occasion to use many previous words in proving, that the sublime is a certain eminence or perfection of language, and that the greatest writers, both in verse and prose, have by this alone obtained the prize of glory, and filled all time with their renown. For the sublime not only persuades, but even throws an audience into transport. The marvelous always works with more surprising force, than that which barely persuades or delights. In most cases, it is wholly in our own power, either to resist or yield to persuasion. But the sublime, endued with strength irresistible, strikes home, and triumphs over every hearer. Dexterity of invention, and good order and economy in composition, are not to be discerned from one or two passages, nor scarcely sometimes from the

---

[1] *On the Sublime* The translation here is that of William Smith (1743).

whole texture of a discourse; but the sublime, when seasonably addressed, with the rapid force of lightning has borne down all before it, and shown at one stroke the compacted might of genius. ...

from SECTION 8

There are, if I may so express it, five very copious sources of the sublime, if we presuppose an ability of speaking well, as a common foundation for these five sorts, and indeed without it, any thing besides will avail but little.

1. The first and most excellent of these is a boldness and grandeur in the thoughts, as I have shown in my essay on Xenophon.[1]

2. The second is called the pathetic, or the power of raising the passions to a violent and even enthusiastic degree; and these two being genuine constituents of the sublime, are the gifts of nature, whereas the other sorts depend in some measure upon art.

3. The third consists in a skilful application of figures, which are two-fold, of sentiment and language.

4. The fourth is a noble and graceful manner of expression, which is not only to choose out significant and elegant words, but also to adorn and embellish the style, by the assistance of tropes.

5. The fifth source of the sublime, which completes all the preceding, is the structure or composition of all the periods, in all possible dignity and grandeur. ...

from Joseph Addison, "The Pleasures of the Imagination," *The Spectator* (1712)

Addison (1662–1719), the influential founder of *The Spectator*, contributed to the development of the eighteenth-century discourse on aesthetics and the imagination in a series of papers written in 1712. The essays departed from Addison's usual emphasis on the social and political and inspired later thinkers and poets, most notably Mark Akenside, who pub-

lished in 1744 his long poem also entitled *The Pleasures of the Imagination*.

from *The Spectator*, No. 411 (21 June 1712)

Our sight is the most perfect and most delightful of all our senses. It fills the mind with the largest variety of ideas, converses with its objects at the greatest distance, and continues the longest in action without being tired or satiated with its proper enjoyments. The sense of feeling can indeed give us a notion of extension, shape, and all other ideas that enter at the eye, except colours; but at the same time it is very much straitened and confined in its operations, to the number, bulk, and distance of its particular objects. Our sight seems designed to supply all these defects, and may be considered as a more delicate and diffusive kind of touch, that spreads itself over an infinite multitude of bodies, comprehends the largest figures, and brings into our reach some of the most remote parts of the universe.

It is this sense which furnishes the imagination with its ideas; so that by the pleasures of the imagination, or fancy (which I shall use promiscuously), I here mean such as arise from visible objects, either when we have them actually in our view, or when we call up their ideas into our minds by paintings, statues, descriptions, or any the like occasion. We cannot, indeed, have a single image in the fancy that did not make its first entrance through the sight; but we have the power of retaining, altering, and compounding those images, which we have once received, into all the varieties of picture and vision that are most agreeable to the imagination; for by this faculty a man in a dungeon is capable of entertaining himself with scenes and landscapes more beautiful than any that can be found in the whole compass of nature.

There are few words in the English language which are employed in a more loose and uncircumscribed sense than those of the fancy and the imagination. I therefore thought it necessary to fix and determine the notion of these two words, as I intend to make use of them in the thread of my following speculations, that the reader may conceive rightly what is the subject which I proceed

---

[1] *Xenophon* Contemporary and admirer of Socrates, Xenophon (c. 430–354 BCE) recorded many of the sayings of Socrates, documenting in the process the history of ancient Greece.

upon. I must therefore desire him to remember, that by the pleasures of the imagination, I mean only such pleasures as arise originally from sight, and that I divide these pleasures into two kinds: my design being first of all to discourse of those primary pleasures of the imagination, which entirely proceed from such objects as are before our eyes; and in the next place to speak of those secondary pleasures of the imagination which flow from the ideas of visible objects, when the objects are not actually before the eye, but are called up into our memories, or formed into agreeable visions of things that are either absent or fictitious.

The pleasures of the imagination, taken in their full extent, are not so gross as those of sense, nor so refined as those of the understanding. The last are, indeed, *more preferable*, because they are founded on some new knowledge or improvement in the mind of man; yet it must be confessed, that those of the imagination are as great and as transporting as the other. A beautiful prospect delights the soul, as much as a demonstration; and a description in Homer has charmed more readers than a chapter in Aristotle. Besides, the pleasures of the imagination have this advantage above those of the understanding, that they are more obvious, and more easy to be acquired. It is but opening the eye, and the scene enters. The colours paint themselves on the fancy, with very little attention of thought or application of mind in the beholder. We are struck, we know not how, with the symmetry of anything we see, and immediately assent to the beauty of an object, without inquiring into the particular causes and occasions of it.

A man of polite imagination is let into a great many pleasures, that the vulgar are not capable of receiving. He can converse with a picture, and find an agreeable companion in a statue. He meets with a secret refreshment in a description, and often feels a greater satisfaction in the prospect of fields and meadows, than another does in the possession. It gives him, indeed, a kind of property in everything he sees, and makes the most rude, uncultivated parts of nature administer to his pleasures: so that he looks upon the world, as it were in another light, and discovers in it a multitude of charms, that conceal themselves from the generality of mankind.

There are, indeed, but very few who know how to be idle and innocent, or have a relish of any pleasures that are not criminal: every diversion they take is at the expense of some one virtue or another, and their very first step out of business is into vice or folly. A man should endeavour, therefore, to make the sphere of his innocent pleasures as wide as possible, that he may retire into them with safety, and find in them such a satisfaction as a wise man would not blush to take. Of this nature are those of the imagination, which do not require such a bent of thought as is necessary to our more serious employments, nor, at the same time, suffer the mind to sink into that negligence and remissness, which are apt to accompany our more sensual delights, but, like a gentle exercise to the faculties, awaken them from sloth and idleness, without putting them upon any labour or difficulty.

We might here add, that the pleasures of the fancy are more conducive to health, than those of the understanding, which are worked out by dint of thinking, and attended with too violent a labour of the brain. Delightful scenes, whether in nature, painting, or poetry, have a kindly influence on the body, as well as the mind, and not only serve to clear and brighten the imagination, but are able to disperse grief and melancholy, and to set the animal spirits in pleasing and agreeable motions. …

from *The Spectator,* No. 412 (23 June 1712)

I shall first consider those pleasures of the imagination which arise from the actual view and survey of outward objects; and these, I think, all proceed from the sight of what is *great, uncommon,* or *beautiful.* There may indeed be something so terrible or offensive, that horror or loathsomeness of an object may overbear the pleasure which results from its *greatness, novelty,* or *beauty;* but still there will be such a mixture of delight in the very disgust it gives us, as any these three qualifications are most conspicuous and prevailing.

By *greatness,* I do not only mean the bulk of any single object, but the largeness of a whole view, considered as one entire piece. Such are the prospects of an open champaign country, a vast uncultivated desert, of huge heaps of mountains, high rocks and precipices, or a wide expanse of waters, where we are not struck with the novelty or beauty of the sight, but with that rude kind of magnificence which appears in many of these stupendous works of nature. Our imagination loves to be filled with an object, or to grasp at anything that is too big for its capacity. We are flung into a pleasing astonishment at such unbounded views, and feel a delightful stillness and amazement in the soul at the apprehension of them. The mind of man naturally hates everything that looks like a restraint upon it, and is apt to fancy itself under a sort of confinement, when the sight is pent up in a narrow compass, and shortened on every side by the neighbourhood of walls or mountains. On the contrary, a spacious horizon is an image of liberty, where the eye has room to range abroad, to expatiate at large on the immensity of its views, and to lose itself amidst the variety of objects that offer themselves to its observation. Such wide and undetermined prospects are as pleasing to the fancy, as the speculations of eternity or infinitude are to the understanding. But if there be a beauty or uncommonness joined with this grandeur, as in a troubled ocean, a heaven adorned with stars and meteors, or a spacious landscape cut out into rivers, woods, rocks, and meadows, the pleasure still grows upon us, as it arises from more than a single principle.

Every thing that is *new* or *uncommon* raises a pleasure in the imagination, because it fills the soul with an agreeable surprise, gratifies its curiosity, and gives it an idea of which it was not before possessed. We are indeed so often conversant with one set of objects, and tired out with so many repeated shows of the same things, that whatever is *new* or *uncommon* contributes a little to vary human life, and to divert our minds for a while with the strangeness of its appearance: it serves us for a kind of refreshment, and takes off from that satiety we are apt to complain of in our usual and ordinary entertainments. It is this that bestows charms on a monster, and makes even the imperfections of nature please us. It is this that recommends variety, where the mind is every instant called off to something new, and the attention not suffered to dwell too long and waste itself on any particu-

lar object. It is this, likewise, that improves what is great or beautiful, and makes it afford the mind a double entertainment. Groves, fields, and meadows are at any season of the year pleasant to look upon, but never so much as in the opening of the spring, when they are all new and fresh, with their first gloss upon them, and not yet too much accustomed and familiar to the eye. For this reason there is nothing that more enlivens a prospect than rivers, jetteaus, or falls of water, where the scene is perpetually shifting and entertaining the sight every moment with something that is new. We are quickly tired with looking upon hills and valleys, where everything continues fixed and settled in the same place and posture, but find our thoughts a little agitated and relieved at the sight of such objects as are ever in motion and sliding away from beneath the eye of the beholder.

But there is nothing that makes its way more directly to the soul than *beauty*, which immediately diffuses a secret satisfaction and complacency through the imagination, and gives a finishing to anything that is great or uncommon. The very first discovery of it strikes the mind with an inward joy, and spreads a cheerfulness and delight through all its faculties. There is not perhaps any real beauty or deformity more in one piece of matter than another, because we might have been so made, that whatsoever now appears loathsome to us, might have shown itself agreeable; but we find by experience, that there are several modifications of matter which the mind, without any previous consideration, pronounces at first sight beautiful or deformed. …

There is a second kind of *beauty* that we find in the several products of art and nature, which does not work in the imagination with that warmth and violence as the beauty that appears in our proper species, but is apt however to raise in us a secret delight, and kind of fondness for the places or objects in which we discover it. This consists either in the gaiety or variety of colours, in the symmetry and proportion of parts, in the arrangement and disposition of bodies or in a just mixture and concurrence of all together. Among these several kinds of beauty the eye takes most delight in colours. We nowhere meet with a more glorious or pleasing show in nature, than what appears in the heavens at the rising and setting of the sun which is wholly made up of those different stains of light that show themselves in clouds of a different situation. For this reason we find the poets, who are always addressing themselves to the imagination, borrowing more of their epithets from colours than from any other topic.

As the fancy delights in everything that is great, strange, or beautiful, and is still more pleased the more it finds of these perfections in the same object, so it is capable of receiving a new satisfaction by the assistance of another sense. Thus any continued sound, as the music of birds, or a fall of water, awakens every moment the mind of the beholder, and makes him more attentive to the several beauties of the place that lie before him. Thus if there arises a fragrancy of smells or perfumes, they heighten the pleasures of the imagination, and make even the colours and verdure of the landscape appear more agreeable; for the ideas of both senses recommend each other, and are pleasanter together than when they enter the mind separately: as the different colours of a picture, when they are well disposed, set off one another, and receive an additional beauty from the advantage of their situation.

from *The Spectator*, No. 413 (24 June 1712)

... One of the final causes of our delight in anything that is *great*, may be this. The Supreme Author of our being has so formed the soul of man, that nothing but himself can be its last, adequate, and proper happiness. Because, therefore, a great part of our happiness must arise from the contemplation of his being, that he might give our souls a just relish of such a contemplation, he has made them naturally delight in the apprehension of what is great or unlimited. Our admiration, which is a very pleasing motion of the mind, immediately rises at the consideration of any object that takes up a great deal of room in the fancy, and by consequence will improve into the highest pitch of astonishment and devotion when we contemplate his nature, that is neither circumscribed by time nor place, nor to be comprehended by the largest capacity of a created being.

He has annexed a secret pleasure to the idea of anything that is *new* or *uncommon*, that he might encourage us in the pursuit after knowledge, and engage us to search into the wonders of his creation; for every new idea brings such a pleasure along with it, as rewards any pains we have taken in its acquisition, and consequently serves as a motive to put us upon fresh discoveries.

He has made everything that is *beautiful in our own species* pleasant, that all creatures might be tempted to multiply their kind and fill the world with inhabitants; for 'tis very remarkable that wherever nature is crossed in the production of a monster (the result of any unnatural mixture) the breed is incapable of propagating its likeness and of founding a new order of creatures; so that unless all animals were allured by the beauty of their own species, generation would be at an end, and the earth unpeopled.

In the last place, he has made everything that is beautiful in all other objects pleasant, or rather has made so many objects appear beautiful, that he might render the whole creation more gay and delightful. He has given almost everything about us the power of raising an agreeable idea in the imagination: so that it is impossible for us to behold his works with coldness or indifference, and to survey so many beauties without secret satisfaction and complacency. Things would make but a poor appearance to the eye, if we saw them only in their proper figures and motions: and what reason can we assign for their exciting in us many of those ideas which are different from anything that exists in the objects themselves (for such are light and colours), were not it to add supernumerary ornaments to the universe, and make it more agreeable to the imagination? We are everywhere entertained with pleasing shows and apparitions, we discover imaginary glories in the heavens and in the earth, and see some of this visionary beauty poured out upon the whole creation; but what a rough unsightly sketch of nature should we be entertained with, did all her colouring disappear, and the several distinctions of light and shade vanish? In short, our souls are at present delightfully lost and bewildered in a pleasing delusion and we walk about like the enchanted hero of a romance who sees beautiful castles, woods, and meadows, and at the same time hears the warbling of birds and the purling of streams; but upon the finishing of some secret spell the fantastic scene breaks up, and the disconsolate knight finds himself on a barren heath or in a solitary desert. It is not improbable that some thing like this may be the state of the soul after its first separation, in respect of the images it will receive from matter; though indeed the ideas of colours are so pleasing and beautiful in the imagination, that it is possible the soul will not be deprived of them, but perhaps find them excited by some other occasional cause, as they are at present by the different impressions of the subtle matter on the organ of sight. ...

from Sir Jonathan Richardson the Elder, *An Essay on the Theory of Painting* (1725)

A notable early eighteenth-century portrait painter, Richardson (1667–1745) was also an important critic and theorist of art. In this excerpt from his *Essay on the Theory of Painting*, Richardson discusses the role of the sublime in the creation of art.

OF THE SUBLIME

... **B**y the sublime in general I mean the most excellent of what is excellent, as the excellent is the best of what is good. The dignity of a man consists chiefly in his capacity of thinking, and of communicating his ideas to another; *the greatest, and most noble thoughts, images, or sentiments, conveyed to us in the best chosen words*, I take therefore to be the perfect sublime in writing; the admirable, the marvellous.

But as there may be degrees even in the sublime, something short of the utmost may be also sublime.

Thought and language are two distinct excellencies: there are few that are capable of adding dignity to a great subject, or even of doing right to such a one; in some cases none; the bulk of mankind conceive not greatly, nor do they know how to utter the conceptions they have to the best advantage; and those that have higher capacities exert them but rarely, and on few

occasions: hence it is that we so justly admire what is so excellent, and so uncommon.

The great manner of thinking (as thought in general) is either pure invention, or what arises upon hints suggested from without. ...

As the thoughts, so the language of the sublime must be the most excellent; what that is is the question: whether it be confined to the florid, to magnificent, and sonorous words, tours, figures, &c. or whether brevity, simplicity, or even common, and low words are the best on some occasions.

Poetry, history, declamation, &c. have their peculiar styles, but the sublime (as our high court of parliament is not under the restrictions which inferior courts are) is not limited to any particular style: the best is the sublime language, and that is best that sets the idea in the strongest light; that is the great end, and use of words; but if those that please the ear do equally serve that purpose, no doubt they are preferable, but not otherwise. Plain and common words paint a great image sometimes stronger than any other. ...

The only reasons that can be given for a peculiarity of style in the sublime are, that as the thought must be great, the language must be so too as best expressing such thought; and because the music of the words serve to the same purpose, and moreover please. I own all this is generally true: why do we use the term *sublime*, and not *the very best*, both which express the same thing, only that one raises, and the other depresses the idea? But I deny it is always thus; and only contend that when low, common words, and a plain style best serves the main end of language, it is then, and only then the sublime style. And when this happens the pleasure that is wanting in the sound is abundantly recompensed by observing the judgment of him who made so wise a choice. ...

But the sublime, as the crown in the state hides all defects; it fills and satisfies the mind, nothing appears to be wanting; nothing to be amiss, or if it does it is easily forgiven. All faults die, and vanish in presence of the sublime, which when it appears is as *the sun traversing the vast desert of the sky*. ...

from Samuel Johnson, *A Dictionary of the English Language* (1755)

Samuel Johnson's (1709–84) famous dictionary offered not only a sense of the meaning of sublime, as it did for all its entries, but it also documented notable instances of the term's literary usage.

SUBLIME. *adj.* [*sublimis*, Latin.]

1. High in place; exalted aloft.

They furri'd their pens, and soaring th' air *sublime*
With clang despis'd the ground.   Milton.

Sublime on these a tow'r of steel is rear'd,
And dire Tisiphone there keeps the ward. Dryden.

2. High in excellence; exalted by nature.

My earthly strained to the height
In that celestial colloquy *sublime*.   Milton.

Can it be, that souls *sublime*
Return to visit our terrestrial clime;
And that the gen'rous mind releas'd by death,
Can cover lazy limbs?   Dryden.

3. High in stile or sentiment; lofty; grand.

Easy in stile, thy work in sense *sublime*.   Prior.

4. Elevated by joy.

All yet left of that revolted rout,
Heav'n-fall'n, in station stood or just array,
Sublime with expectation.   Milton.

Their hearts were jocund and *sublime*,
Drunk with idolatry, drunk with wine.   Milton.

5. Haughty; proud.

He was *sublime*, and almost tumorous in
his looks and gestures.   Wotton.

SUBLIME. *n.s.* The grand or lofty stile. *The sublime* is a Gallicism, but now naturalized.

Longinus strengthens all his laws,
And is himself the great *sublime* he draws.   Pope.

The *sublime* rises from the nobleness of thoughts, the magnificence of the words, or the harmonious and lively turn of the phrase; the perfect *sublime* arises from all three together.   Addison.

TO SUBLIME. *v.a.* [*sublimer*, Fr. from the adjective.]

1. To raise by a chemical fire.

Study our manuscripts, those myriads
Of letters, which have past 'twixt thee and me,

Thence write our annals, and in them lessons be
To all, whom love's *subliming* fire invades.   Donne.

2. To raise on high.

Although thy trunk be neither large nor strong,
Nor can thy head, not helpt, itself *sublime*,
Yet, like a serpent, a tall tree can climb.   Denham.

3. To exalt; to heighten; to improve.

Flow'rs, and the fruit,
Man's nourishment, by gradual scale *sublim'd*
To vital spirits aspire.   Milton.

The fancies of most are moved by the inward springs of the corporeal machine, which even in the most *sublime* intellectuals is dangerously influential.   Glanville.

Art being strengthened by the knowledge of things, may pass into nature by slow degrees, and so be *sublimed* into a pure genius which is capable of distinguishing betwixt the beauties of nature and that which is low in her.   Dryden's *Dufresnoy*.

Meanly they seek the blessing to confine,
And force that sun but on a part to shine;
Which not alone the southern wit *sublimes*,
But ripens spirits in cold northern climes.   Pope.

TO SUBLIME. *v.n.* To rise in the chemical vessel by the force of fire.

The particles of sal ammoniack in sublimation carry up the particles of antimony, which will not *sublime* alone.   Newton's *Optics*.

This salt is fixed in a gentle fire, and *sublimes* in a great one.   Arbuthnot on Aliments.

SUBLIMELY. *adv.* [from *sublime*.] Loftily; grandly.

This fustian's so *sublimely* bad;
It is not poetry, but prose run mad.   Pope.

SUBLIMITY. *n.s.* [from *sublime*; *sublimité*, Fr. *sublimitas*, Lat.]

1. Height of place; local elevation.

2. Height of nature; excellence.

As religion looketh upon him who in majesty and power is infinite, as we ought we account not of it, unless we esteem it even according to that very height of excellency which our hearts conceive, when divine *sublimity* itself is rightly considered.   Hooker.

In respect of God's incomprehensible *sublimity* and purity, this is also true, that God is neither a mind, nor a spirit like other spirits, nor a light such as can be discerned.   Raleigh.

3. Loftiness of style or sentiment.

Milton's distinguishing excellence lies in the *sublimity* of his thoughts, in the greatness of which he triumphs over all the poets, modern and ancient, Homer only excepted.   Addison.

from Edmund Burke, *A Philosophical Enquiry into the Origin of Our Ideas of the Sublime and Beautiful* (1757)

Burke's systematic investigation of the sublime and the beautiful marks perhaps the first eighteenth-century attempt to classify aesthetic feeling and effects. Like Longinus, Burke (1729–97) is interested in how the two categories are produced in writing; unlike Longinus, Burke fully separates the sublime and the beautiful, delineating their respective qualities.

from PART 1

OF THE SUBLIME

Whatever is fitted in any sort to excite the ideas of pain and danger, that is to say, whatever is in any sort terrible, or is conversant about terrible objects, or operates in a manner analogous to terror, is a source of the sublime; that is, it is productive of the strongest emotion which the mind is capable of feeling. I say the strongest emotion, because I am satisfied the ideas of pain are much more powerful than those which enter on the part of pleasure. Without all doubt, the torments which we may be made to suffer are much greater in their effect on the body and mind, than any pleasure which the most learned voluptuary could suggest, or than the liveliest imagination, and the most sound and exquisitely sensible body, could enjoy. Nay, I am in great doubt whether any man could be found, who would earn a life of the most perfect satisfaction, at the price of ending it in the torments, which justice inflicted in a few hours on the late unfortunate regicide in France.[1] But as pain is stronger in its operation than pleasure, so death is in general a much more affecting idea than pain; because there are very few pains, however exquisite, which are not preferred to death: nay, what generally makes pain itself, if I may say so, more painful, is, that it is considered as an emissary of this king of terrors. When danger or pain press too nearly, they are incapable of giving any delight, and are simply terrible; but at certain distances, and with certain modifications, they may be, and they are, delightful, as we every day experience. The cause of this I shall endeavour to investigate hereafter.

OF BEAUTY

The passion which belongs to generation, merely as such, is lust only. This is evident in brutes, whose passions are more unmixed, and which pursue their purposes more directly than ours. The only distinction they observe with regard to their mates, is that of sex. It is true, that they stick severally to their own species in preference to all others. But this preference, I imagine, does not arise from any sense of beauty which they find in their species, as Mr. Addison supposes, but from a law of some other kind, to which they are subject; and this we may fairly conclude, from their apparent want of choice amongst those objects to which the barriers of their species have confined them. But man, who is a creature adapted to a greater variety and intricacy of relation, connects with the general passion the idea of some *social* qualities, which direct and heighten the appetite which he has in common with all other animals; and as he is not designed like them to live at large, it is fit that he should have something to create a preference, and fix his choice; and this in general should be some sensible quality; as no other can so quickly, so powerfully, or so surely produce its effect. The object therefore of this mixed passion, which we call love, is the

[1] *Nay, I am … in France* Robert-François Damiens (1715–57) attempted to assassinate Louis XV on 5 January 1757; he was barbarously tortured and then executed later that year.

beauty of the *sex*. Men are carried to the sex in general, as it is the sex, and by the common law of nature; but they are attached to particulars by personal *beauty*. I call beauty a social quality; for where women and men, and not only they, but when other animals give us a sense of joy and pleasure in beholding them (and there are many that do so), they inspire us with sentiments of tenderness and affection towards their persons; we like to have them near us, and we enter willingly into a kind of relation with them, unless we should have strong reasons to the contrary. But to what end, in many cases, this was designed, I am unable to discover; for I see no greater reason for a connection between man and several animals who are attired in so engaging a manner, than between him and some others who entirely want this attraction, or possess it in a far weaker degree. But it is probable, that Providence did not make even this distinction, but with a view to some great end; though we cannot perceive distinctly what it is, as his wisdom is not our wisdom, nor our ways his ways.

from PART 2

OF THE PASSION CAUSED BY THE SUBLIME

The passion caused by the great and sublime in nature, when those causes operate most powerfully, is astonishment; and astonishment is that state of the soul, in which all its motions are suspended, with some degree of horror. In this case the mind is so entirely filled with its object, that it cannot entertain any other, nor by consequence reason on that object which employs it. Hence arises the great power of the sublime, that, far from being produced by them, it anticipates our reasonings, and hurries us on by an irresistible force. Astonishment, as I have said, is the effect of the sublime in its highest degree; the inferior effects are admiration, reverence, and respect.

TERROR

No passion so effectually robs the mind of all its powers of acting and reasoning as *fear*. For fear being an apprehension of pain or death, it operates in a manner that resembles actual pain. Whatever therefore is terrible, with regard to sight, is sublime too, whether this cause of terror be endued with greatness of dimensions or not; for it is impossible to look on anything as trifling, or contemptible, that may be dangerous. There are many animals, who though far from being large, are yet capable of raising ideas of the sublime, because they are considered as objects of terror. As serpents and poisonous animals of almost all kinds. And to things of great dimensions, if we annex an adventitious idea of terror, they become without comparison greater. A level plain of a vast extent on land, is certainly no mean idea; the prospect of such a plain may be as extensive as a prospect of the ocean: but can it ever fill the mind with anything so great as the ocean itself? This is owing to several causes; but it is owing to none more than this, that the ocean is an object of no small terror. Indeed, terror is in all cases whatsoever, either more openly or latently, the ruling principle of the sublime. Several languages bear a strong testimony to the affinity of these ideas. They frequently use the same word, to signify indifferently the modes of astonishment or admiration, and those of terror. θάμβος is in Greek, either fear or wonder; δεινός is terrible or respectable; αἰδέω, to reverence or to fear. *Vereor* in Latin, is what αἰδέω is in Greek. The Romans used the verb *stupeo*, a term which strongly marks the state of an astonished mind, to express the effect of simple fear, or of astonishment; the word *attonitus* (thunder-struck) is equally expressive of the alliance of these ideas; and do not the French *étonnement*, and the English *astonishment* and *amazement*, point out as clearly the kindred emotions which attend fear and wonder? They who have a more general knowledge of languages, could produce, I make no doubt, many other and equally striking examples.

VASTNESS

Greatness of dimension is a powerful cause of the sublime. This is too evident, and the observation too common, to need any illustration: it is not so common to consider in what ways greatness of dimension, vastness of extent or quantity, has the most striking effect. For certainly, there are ways and modes, wherein the same quantity of extension shall produce greater effects than it is found to do in others. Extension is either in length, height, or depth. Of these the length strikes least; an hundred yards of even ground will never work such an effect as a tower an hundred yards high, or a rock or mountain of that altitude. I am apt to imagine likewise, that height is less grand than depth; and that we are more struck at looking down from a precipice, than looking up at an object of equal height; but of that I am not very positive. A perpendicular has more force in forming the sublime, than an inclined plane; and the effects of a rugged and broken surface seem stronger than where it is smooth and polished. It would carry us out of our way to enter in this place into the cause of these appearances; but certain it is they afford a large and fruitful field of speculation. However, it may not be amiss to add to these remarks upon magnitude, that, as the great extreme of dimension is sublime, so the last extreme of littleness is in some measure sublime likewise: when we attend to the infinite divisibility of matter, when we pursue animal life into these excessively small, and yet organized beings, that escape the nicest inquisition of the sense; when we push our discoveries yet downward, and consider those creatures so many degrees yet smaller, and the still diminishing scale of existence, in tracing which the imagination is lost as well as the sense; we become amazed and confounded at the wonders of minuteness; nor can we distinguish in its effects this extreme of littleness from the vast itself. For division must be infinite as well as addition; because the idea of a perfect unity can no more be arrived at, than that of a complete whole, to which nothing may be added.

from PART 3

OF BEAUTY

It is my design to consider beauty as distinguished from the sublime; and, in the course of the inquiry, to examine how far it is consistent with it. But previous to this, we must take a short review of the opinions already entertained of this quality; which I think are hardly to be reduced to any fixed principles; because men are used to talk of beauty in a figurative manner, that is to say, in a manner extremely uncertain, and indeterminate. By beauty I mean that quality or those qualities in bodies, by which they cause love, or some passion similar to it. I confine this definition to the merely sensible qualities of things, for the sake of preserving the utmost simplicity in a subject, which must always distract us whenever we take in those various causes of sympathy which attach us to any persons or things from secondary considerations, and not from the direct force which they have merely on being viewed. I likewise distinguish love (by which I mean that satisfaction which arises to the mind upon contemplating anything beautiful, of whatsoever nature it may be) from desire or lust; which is an energy of the mind, that hurries us on to the possession of certain objects, that do not affect us as they are beautiful, but by means altogether different. We shall have a strong desire for a woman of no remarkable beauty; whilst the greatest beauty in men or in other animals, though it causes love, yet excites nothing at all of desire. Which shows that beauty, and the passion caused by beauty, which I call love, is different from desire, though desire may sometimes operate along with it; but it is to this latter that we must attribute those violent and tempestuous passions, and the consequent emotions of the body, which attend what is called love in some of its ordinary acceptations, and not to the effects of beauty merely as it is such.

THE REAL CAUSE OF BEAUTY

Having endeavoured to show what beauty is not, it remains that we should examine, at least with equal attention, in what it really consists. Beauty is a thing much too affecting not to depend upon some positive qualities. And, since it is no creature of our reason, since it strikes us without any reference to use, and even where no use at all can be discerned, since the order and method of nature is generally very different from our measures and proportions, we must conclude that beauty is, for the greater part, some quality in bodies acting mechanically upon the human mind by the intervention of the senses. We ought therefore to consider attentively in what manner those sensible qualities are disposed, in such things as by experience we find beautiful, or which excite in us the passion of love, or some correspondent affection.

The Sublime and Beautiful Compared

On closing this general view of beauty, it naturally occurs, that we should compare it with the sublime; and in this comparison there appears a remarkable contrast. For sublime objects are vast in their dimensions, beautiful ones comparatively small: beauty should be smooth and polished; the great, rugged and negligent; beauty should shun the right line, yet deviate from it insensibly; the great in many cases loves the right line, and when it deviates it often makes a strong deviation: beauty should not be obscure; the great ought to be dark and gloomy: beauty should be light and delicate; the great ought to be solid, and even massive. They are indeed ideas of a very different nature, one being founded on pain, the other on pleasure; and however they may vary afterwards from the direct nature of their causes, yet these causes keep up an eternal distinction between them, a distinction never to be forgotten by any whose business it is to affect the passions. In the infinite variety of natural combinations, we must expect to find the qualities of things the most remote imaginable from each other united in the same object. We must expect also to find combinations of the same kind in the works of art. But when we consider the power of an object upon our passions, we must know that when anything is intended to affect the mind by the force of some predominant property, the affection produced is like to be the more uniform and perfect, if all the other properties or qualities of the object be of the same nature, and tending to the same design, as the principal.

> If black and white blend, soften, and unite
> A thousand ways, are there no black and white?[1]

---

[1] *If black and ... black and white?* Misquoted slightly from Alexander Pope's *An Essay on Man* (1733–34), 2.213–14.

If the qualities of the sublime and beautiful are sometimes found united, does this prove that they are the same; does it prove that they are any way allied; does it prove even that they are not opposite and contradictory? Black and white may soften, may blend; but they are not therefore the same. Nor, when they are so softened and blended with each other, or with different colours, is the power of black as black, or of white as white, so strong as when each stands uniform and distinguished.

from Part 5

Of Words

Natural objects affect us, by the laws of that connection which Providence has established between certain motions and configurations of bodies, and certain consequent feelings in our mind. Painting affects us in the same manner, but with the superadded pleasure of imitation. Architecture affects by the laws of nature, and the law of reason: from which latter result the rules of proportion, which make a work to be praised or censured, in the whole or in some part, when the end for which it was designed is or is not properly answered. But as to words; they seem to me to affect us in a manner very different from that in which we are affected by natural objects, or by painting or architecture; yet words have as considerable a share in exciting ideas of beauty and of the sublime as many of those, and sometimes a much greater than any of them: therefore an inquiry into the manner by which they excite such emotions is far from being unnecessary in a discourse of this kind.

Effect of Words

If words have all their possible extent of power, three effects arise in the mind of the hearer. The first is, the *sound*; the second, the *picture*, or representation of the thing signified by the sound; the third is, the *affection* of the soul produced by one or by both of the foregoing. *Compounded abstract* words, of which we have been speaking, (honour, justice, liberty, and the like,) produce the first and the last of these effects, but not the second. *Simple abstracts* are used to signify some one simple idea, without much adverting to others which may chance to attend it, as blue, green, hot, cold, and the like; these are capable of affecting all three of the purposes of words; as the *aggregate* words, man, castle, horse, &c., are in a yet higher degree. But I am of opinion, that the most general effect, even of these words, does not arise from their forming pictures of the several things they would represent in the imagination; because, on a very diligent examination of my own mind, and getting others to consider theirs, I do not find that once in twenty times any such picture is formed, and when it is, there is most commonly a particular effort of the imagination for that purpose. But the aggregate words operate, as I said of the compound-abstracts, not by presenting any image to the mind, but by having from use the same effect on being mentioned, that their original has when it is seen. Suppose we were to read a passage to this effect: "The river Danube rises in a moist and mountainous soil in the heart of Germany, where winding to and fro, it waters several principalities, until, turning into Austria, and leaving the walls of Vienna, it passes into Hungary; there with a vast flood, augmented by the Saave and the Drave, it quits Christendom, and rolling through the barbarous countries which border on Tartary,[1] it enters by many mouths in the Black Sea." In this description many things are mentioned, as mountains, rivers, cities, the sea, &c. But let anybody examine himself, and see whether he has had impressed on his imagination any pictures of a river, mountain, watery soil, Germany, &c. Indeed it is impossible, in the rapidity and quick succession of words in conversation to have ideas both of the sound of the word, and of the thing represented: besides, some words, expressing real essences, are so mixed with others of a general and nominal import, that it is impracticable to jump from sense to thought, from particulars to generals, from things to words, in such a manner as to answer the purposes of life; nor is it necessary that we should.

---

[1] *Tartary* Vast region of eastern Europe and northern Asia controlled by the Mongols in the thirteenth and fourteenth centuries.

How Words Influence the Passions

Now, as words affect, not by any original power, but by representation, it might be supposed, that their influence over the passions should be but light; yet it is quite otherwise; for we find by experience, that eloquence and poetry are as capable, nay indeed much more capable, of making deep and lively impressions than any other arts, and even than nature itself in very many cases. And this arises chiefly from these three causes. First, that we take an extraordinary part in the passions of others, and that we are easily affected and brought into sympathy by any tokens which are shown of them; and there are no tokens which can express all the circumstances of most passions so fully as words; so that if a person speaks upon any subject, he can not only convey the subject to you, but likewise the manner in which he is himself affected by it. Certain it is, that the influence of most things on our passions is not so much from the things themselves, as from our opinions concerning them; and these again depend very much on the opinions of other men, conveyable for the most part by words only. Secondly, there are many things of a very affecting nature, which can seldom occur in the reality, but the words that represent them often do; and thus they have an opportunity of making a deep impression and taking root in the mind, whilst the idea of the reality was transient; and to some perhaps never really occurred in any shape, to whom it is notwithstanding very affecting, as war, death, famine, &c. Besides, many ideas have never been at all presented to the senses of any men but by words, as God, angels, devils, heaven, and hell, all of which have, however, a great influence over the passions. Thirdly, by words we have it in our power to make such *combinations* as we cannot possibly do otherwise. By this power of combining, we are able, by the addition of well-chosen circumstances, to give a new life and force to the simple object. In painting we may represent any fine figure we please; but we never can give it those enlivening touches which it may receive from words. To represent an angel in a picture, you can only draw a beautiful young man winged: but what painting can furnish out anything so grand as the addition of one word, "the angel of the *Lord*"? It is true, I have here no clear idea; but these words affect the mind more than the sensible image did; which is all I contend for. A picture of Priam dragged to the altar's foot, and there murdered, if it were well executed, would undoubtedly be very moving, but there are very aggravating circumstances, which it could never represent:

Sanguine fœdantem *quos ipse saeraverat ignes.*[1]

As a further instance, let us consider those lines of Milton, where he describes the travels of the fallen angels through their dismal habitation:

—O'er many a dark and dreary vale
They passed, and many a region dolorous;
O'er many a frozen, many a fiery Alp;
Rocks, caves, lakes, fens, bogs, dens, and shades of death,
A universe of death.[2]—

Here is displayed the force of union in

Rocks, caves, lakes, dens, bogs, fens, and shades;

Which yet would lose the greatest part of their effect, if they were not the

Rocks, caves, lakes, dens, bogs, fens, and shades—
——of *Death*.

This idea or this affection caused by a word, which nothing but a word could annex to the others, raises a very great degree of the sublime; and this sublime is raised yet higher by what follows, a *"universe of Death."* Here are again two ideas not presentable but by language; and an union of them great and amazing beyond conception; if they may properly be called ideas which present no distinct image to the mind:—but still it will be difficult to conceive how words can move the pas-

sions which belong to real objects, without representing these objects clearly. This is difficult to us, because we do not sufficiently distinguish, in our observations upon language, between a clear expression and a strong expression. These are frequently confounded with each other, though they are in reality extremely different. The former regards the understanding, the latter belongs to the passions. The one describes a thing as it is; the latter describes it as it is felt. Now, as there is a moving tone of voice, an impassioned countenance, an agitated gesture, which affect independently of the things about which they are exerted, so there are words, and certain dispositions of words, which being peculiarly devoted to passionate subjects; and always used by those who are under the influence of any passion, touch and move us more than those which far more clearly and distinctly express the subject matter. We yield to sympathy what we refuse to description. The truth is, all verbal description, merely as naked description, though never so exact, conveys so poor and insufficient an idea of the thing described, that it could scarcely have the smallest effect, if the speaker did not call in to his aid those modes of speech that mark a strong and lively feeling in himself. Then, by the contagion of our passions, we catch a fire already kindled in another, which probably might never have been struck out by the object described. Words, by strongly conveying the passions, by those means which we have already mentioned, fully compensate for their weakness in other respects. It may be observed, that very polished languages, and such as are praised for their superior clearness and perspicuity, are generally deficient in strength. The French language has that perfection and that defect, whereas the Oriental tongues, and in general the languages of most unpolished people, have a great force and energy of expression; and this is but natural. Uncultivated people are but ordinary observers of things, and not critical in distinguishing them; but, for that reason, they admire more, and are more affected with what they see, and therefore express themselves in a warmer and more passionate manner. If the affection be well conveyed, it will work its effect without any clear idea, often without any idea at all of the thing which has originally given rise to it.

---

[1] *Sanguine ... ignes* Cf. Virgil, *Aeneid*, 2.502. Latin: "Polluting with blood the flames that he [Priam, the king of Troy during the Trojan War] himself had sanctified."

[2] *O'er many ... universe of death* See John Milton, *Paradise Lost*, 2.618–22.

It might be expected from the fertility of the subject, that I should consider poetry, as it regards the sublime and beautiful, more at large; but it must be observed that in this light it has been often and well handled already. It was not my design to enter into the criticism of the sublime and beautiful in any art, but to attempt to lay down such principles as may tend to ascertain, to distinguish, and to form a sort of standard for them; which purposes I thought might be best effected by an inquiry into the properties of such things in nature, as raise love and astonishment in us; and by showing in what manner they operated to produce these passions. Words were only so far to be considered, as to show upon what principle they were capable of being the representatives of these natural things, and by what powers they were able to affect us often as strongly as the things they represent, and sometimes much more strongly.

from Immanuel Kant, *Observations on the Feeling of the Beautiful and Sublime* (1764; first English translation 1799)

German philosopher Immanuel Kant (1724–1804) argues that aesthetic experience and pleasure are always subjective; here he presents his observations on the feelings he associates with the beautiful and the sublime. Along with Edmund Burke, Kant is perhaps the most important eighteenth-century thinker on aesthetics.

from Section 1: Of the Distinct Objects of the Feeling of the Beautiful and Sublime

The various feelings of enjoyment or of displeasure rest not so much upon the nature of the external things that arouse them as upon each person's own disposition to be moved by these to pleasure or pain. This accounts for the joy of some people over things that cause aversion in others, or the amorous passion so often a puzzle to everybody, or the lively antipathy one person feels toward something that to another is quite indifferent. The field of observation of these peculiarities of human nature extends very wide, and still con-

ceals a rich source for discoveries that are just as pleasurable as they are instructive. For the present I shall cast my gaze upon only a few places that seem particularly exceptional in this area, and even upon these more with the eye of an observer than of a philosopher.

Because a person finds himself happy only so far as he gratifies an inclination, the feeling that makes him capable of enjoying great pleasures, without needing exceptional talents to do so, is certainly no trifle. Stout persons, whose favorite authors are their cooks and whose works of fine taste are in their cellars, will thrive on vulgar obscenities and on a coarse jest with just as lively a delight as that upon which persons of noble sensitivity pride themselves. An indolent man who loves having books read aloud to him because it is so pleasant to fall asleep that way, the merchant to whom all pleasures are trifling except those a clever man enjoys when he calculates his profits, one who loves the opposite sex only so far as he counts it among things to enjoy, the lover of the hunt, whether he hunt flies like Domitian[1] or ferocious beasts like A. … —all these have a feeling that makes them capable of enjoying pleasures after their own fashion, without presuming to envy others or even being able so much as to conceive of other pleasures. But to that kind of feeling, which can take place without any thought whatever, I shall here pay no attention. There is still another feeling of a more delicate sort, so described either because one can enjoy it longer without satiation and exhaustion; or because it presupposes a sensitivity of the soul, so to speak, which makes the soul fitted for virtuous impulses; or because it indicates talents and intellectual excellences. It is this feeling of which I wish to consider one aspect. I shall moreover exclude from it that inclination that is fixed upon high intellectual insights, and the thrill that was possible to a Kepler,[2] who, as Bayle[3] reports, would not have sold one of his discoveries for a princedom. The latter sensation is quite too delicate to belong in the

---

[1] *Domitian*   Titus Flavius Domitianus (51–96 CE), eleventh emperor of Rome.

[2] *Kepler*   Johannes Kepler (1571–1630), German mathematician, astronomer, and astrologer best known for articulating the laws of planetary motion, now named after him.

[3] *Bayle*   Pierre Bayle (1647–1706), French philosopher who advocated the separation of faith and reason.

present sketch, which will concern only the sensuous feeling of which also more ordinary souls are capable.

Finer feeling, which we now wish to consider, is chiefly of two kinds: the feeling of the *sublime* and that of the *beautiful*. The stirring of each is pleasant, but in different ways. The sight of a mountain whose snow-covered peaks rises above the clouds, the description of a raging storm, or Milton's portrayal of the infernal kingdom, arouse enjoyment but with horror; on the other hand, the sight of flower-strewn meadows, valleys with winding brooks and covered with grazing flocks, the description of Elysium, or Homer's portrayal of the girdle of Venus,[1] also occasion a pleasant sensation but one that is joyous and smiling. In order that the former impression could occur to us in due strength, we must have *a feeling of the sublime*, and, in order to enjoy the latter well, a *feeling of the beautiful*. Tall oaks and lonely shadows in a sacred grove are sublime; flower beds, low hedges and trees trimmed in figures are beautiful. Night is sublime, day is beautiful. Temperaments that possess a feeling for the sublime are drawn gradually, by the quiet stillness of a summer evening as the shimmering light of the stars breaks through the brown shadows of night and the lonely moon rises into view, into high feelings of friendship, of disdain for the world, of eternity. The shining day stimulates busy fervor and a feeling of gaiety. The sublime *moves*, the beautiful *charms*. The mien of a man who is undergoing the full feeling of the sublime is earnest, sometimes rigid and astonished. On the other hand the lively sensation of the beautiful proclaims itself through shining cheerfulness in the eyes, through smiling features, and often through audible mirth. The sublime is in turn of different kinds. Its feeling is sometimes accompanied with a certain dread, or melancholy; in some cases merely with quiet wonder; and in still others with a beauty completely pervading a sublime plan. The first I shall call the *terrifying sublime*, the second the *noble*, and the third the *splendid*. Deep loneliness is sublime, but in a way that stirs terror. Hence great far-reaching solitudes, like the colossal Komul Desert in Tartary,[2] have always given us occasion for peopling them with fearsome spirits, goblins, and ghouls.

The sublime must always be great; the beautiful can also be small. The sublime must be simple; the beautiful can be adorned and ornamented. A great height is just as sublime as a great depth, except that the latter is accompanied with the sensation of shuddering, the former with one of wonder. Hence the latter feeling can be the terrifying sublime, and the former the noble. The sight of an Egyptian pyramid, as Hasselquist[3] reports, moves one far more than one can imagine from all the descriptions; but its design is simple and noble. St. Peter's in Rome is splendid; because on its frame, which is large and simple, beauty is so distributed, for example, gold, mosaic work, and so on, that the feeling of the sublime still strikes through with the greatest effect; hence the object is called splendid. An arsenal must be noble and simple, a residence castle splendid, and a pleasure palace beautiful and ornamented.

A long duration is sublime. If it is of time past, then it is noble. If it is projected into an incalculable future, then it has something of the fearsome in it. A building of the remotest antiquity is venerable. Haller's[4] description of the coming eternity stimulates a mild horror, and of the past, transfixed wonder.

from Section 4: Of National Characteristics, So Far as They Depend upon the Distinct Feeling of the Beautiful and Sublime

Of the peoples of our part of the world, in my opinion those who distinguish themselves among all others by the feeling for the beautiful are the Italians and the French, but by the feeling for the sublime, the Germans, English, and Spanish. Holland can be considered as that land where the finer taste becomes largely unnoticeable. The beautiful itself is either fascinating and moving, or laughing and delightful. The first has something of the

---

[1] *Elysium … girdle of Venus*   In Greek mythology, Elysium, or the Elysian Fields, was the section of the Underworld reserved for the souls of the heroic and the virtuous. In Homer's *Iliad*, Hera thwarts Zeus's design to aid the Trojans by obtaining the magical girdle and seducing him.

[2] *Tartary*   Vast region of eastern Europe and northern Asia controlled by the Mongols in the thirteenth and fourteenth centuries.

[3] *Hasselquist*   Fredric Hasselquist (1722–52), Swedish traveler and naturalist.

[4] *Haller*   Albrecht von Haller (1708–77), Swiss anatomist, physiologist, naturalist, and poet.

sublime in it, and the mind in this feeling is thoughtful and enraptured, but in the second sort of feeling, smiling and joyful. The first sort of beautiful feeling seems to be excellently suited to the Italians, and the second, to the French. In the national character that bears the expression of the sublime, this is either that of the terrifying sort, which is a little inclined to the adventurous, or it is a feeling for the noble, or for the splendid. I believe I have reason to be able to ascribe the feeling of the first sort to the Spaniard, the second to the Englishman, and the third to the German. The feeling for the splendid is not original by nature, like the remaining kinds of taste; and although a spirit of imitation can be united with every other feeling, it really is more peculiar to the glittering sublime; for this is properly a mixed feeling combining the beautiful and the sublime, in which each taken by itself is colder, so that the mind is free enough by means of their combination to attend to examples, and in fact it stands in need of the impulsion of such examples. Accordingly, the German will have less feeling in respect to the beautiful than the Frenchman, and less of what pertains to the sublime than the Englishman; but instances in which both appear in combination will be more suitable to his feeling, as he will fortunately escape the faults into which an excessive strength of either of these sorts of feeling could fall.

from Mary Wollstonecraft, *A Vindication of the Rights of Men* (1790)

The primary purpose of this pamphlet by Mary Wollstonecraft (1759–97) was the defense of Richard Price, who Edmund Burke described as a radical in his *Reflections on the Revolution in France* (1790). Price, like Wollstonecraft, advocated republicanism, in opposition to Burke's championing of constitutional monarchy. In this excerpt, Wollstonecraft seeks to redefine, recast, and, perhaps most importantly, re-gender ideas about the sublime and the beautiful as they are laid out in Burke's *Enquiry*.

... **H**ad you been in a philosophising mood, had your heart or your reason been at home, you might have been convinced, by ocular demonstration, that madness is only the absence of reason. The ruling angel leaving its seat, wild anarchy ensues. You would have seen that the uncontrolled imagination often pursues the most regular course in its most daring flight; and that the eccentricities are boldly relieved when judgment no longer officiously arranges the sentiments, by bringing them to the test of principles. You would have seen every thing out of nature in that strange chaos of levity and ferocity, and of all sorts of follies jumbled together. You would have seen in that monstrous tragi-comic scene the most opposite passions necessarily succeed, and sometimes mix with each other in the mind; alternate contempt and indignation; alternate laughter and tears; alternate scorn and horror. This is a true picture of that chaotic state of mind, called madness; when reason gone, we know not where, the wild elements of passion clash, and all is horror and confusion. You might have heard the best turned conceits, flash following flash, and doubted whether the rhapsody was not eloquent, if it had not been delivered in an equivocal language, neither verse nor prose, if the sparkling periods had not stood alone, wanting force because they wanted concatenation.[1]

It is a proverbial observation, that a very thin partition divides wit and madness. Poetry therefore naturally addresses the fancy, and the language of passion is with great felicity borrowed from the heightened picture which the imagination draws of sensible objects concentrated by impassioned reflection. And, during this "fine frenzy," reason has no right to rein-in the imagination, unless to prevent the introduction of supernumerary images; if the passion is real, the head will not be ransacked for stale tropes and cold rodomontade. I now speak of the genuine enthusiasm of genius, which, perhaps, seldom appears, but in the infancy of civilization; for as this light becomes more luminous reason clips the wing of fancy—the youth becomes the man.

Whether the glory of Europe is set, I shall not now enquire; but probably the spirit of romance and chivalry is in the wane; and reason will gain by its extinction.

From observing several cold romantic characters I have been led to confine the term romantic to one definition—false, or rather artificial, feelings. Works of genius are read with a prepossession in their favour, and

---

1 *concatenation* I.e., connection.

sentiments imitated, because they were fashionable and pretty, and not because they were forcibly felt.

In modern poetry the understanding and memory often fabricate the pretended effusions of the heart, and romance destroys all simplicity; which, in works of taste, is but a synonymous word for truth. This romantic spirit has extended to our prose, and scattered artificial flowers over the most barren heath; or a mixture of verse and prose producing the strangest incongruities. The turgid bombast of some of your periods fully proves these assertions; for when the heart speaks we are seldom shocked by hyperbole, or dry raptures. …

Where is the dignity, the infallibility of sensibility, in the fair ladies, whom, if the voice of rumour is to be credited, the captive negroes curse in all the agony of bodily pain, for the unheard of tortures they invent? It is probable that some of them, after the sight of a flagellation, compose their ruffled spirits and exercise their tender feelings by the perusal of the last imported novel. How true these tears are to nature, I leave you to determine. But these ladies may have read your *Enquiry concerning the origin of our ideas of the Sublime and Beautiful,* and, convinced by your arguments, may have laboured to be pretty, by counterfeiting weakness.

You may have convinced them that *littleness* and *weakness* are the very essence of beauty; and that the Supreme Being, in giving women beauty in the most supereminent degree, seemed to command them, by the powerful voice of Nature, not to cultivate the moral virtues that might chance to excite respect, and interfere with the pleasing sensations they were created to inspire. Thus confining truth, fortitude, and humanity, within the rigid pale of manly morals, they might justly argue, that to be loved, woman's high end and distinction! they should "learn to lisp, to totter in their walk, and nickname God's creatures."[1] Never, they might repeat after you, was any man, much less a woman, rendered amiable by the force of those exalted qualities, fortitude, justice, wisdom, and truth; and thus forewarned of the sacrifice they must make to those austere, unnatural virtues, they would be authorised to turn all their attention to their persons, systematically neglecting morals to secure beauty. Some rational old woman indeed might chance to stumble at this doctrine, and hint, that in avoiding atheism you had not steered clear of the mussulman's[2] creed; but you could readily exculpate yourself by turning the charge on Nature, who made our idea of beauty independent of reason. Nor would it be necessary for you to recollect, that if virtue has any other foundation than worldly utility, you have clearly proved that one half of the human species, at least, have not souls; and that Nature, by making women *little, smooth, delicate, fair* creatures, never designed that they should exercise their reason to acquire the virtues that produce opposite, if not contradictory, feelings. The affection they excite, to be uniform and perfect, should not be tinctured with the respect which moral virtues inspire, lest pain should be blended with pleasure, and admiration disturb the soft intimacy of love. This laxity of morals in the female world is certainly more captivating to a libertine imagination than the cold arguments of reason, that give no sex to virtue. If beautiful weakness be interwoven in a woman's frame, if the chief business of her life be (as you insinuate) to inspire love, and Nature has made an eternal distinction between the qualities that dignify a rational being and this animal perfection, her duty and happiness in this life must clash with any preparation for a more exalted state. So that Plato and Milton were grossly mistaken in asserting that human love led to heavenly, and was only an exaltation of the same affection; for the love of the Deity, which is mixed with the most profound reverence, must be love of perfection, and not compassion for weakness. …

from Mary Wollstonecraft, *Letters Written during a Short Residence in Sweden, Norway, and Denmark* (1796)

In 1795, the prominent feminist writer and philosopher Mary Wollstonecraft (1759–97) traveled through Scandinavia with her one-year-old daughter, Fanny. *Letters Written during a Short Residence*

---

[1] *learn to … God's creatures* Loosely quoted from Shakespeare's *Hamlet*, 3.1.144–45.

[2] *mussulman* Muslim.

is a travel narrative and memoir recording her impressions of the journey; the text is drawn from her journals and from letters she had sent to her lover, Gilbert Imlay (1754–1828), while in Scandinavia. In the following excerpt, Wollstonecraft visits a waterfall near Frederikstad, Norway.

from LETTER 15

I left Christiania[1] yesterday. The weather was not very fine; and having been a little delayed on the road, I found that it was too late to go round, a couple of miles, to see the cascade near Fredericstadt, which I had determined to visit. Besides, as Fredericstadt is a fortress, it was necessary to arrive there before they shut the gate.

The road along the river is very romantic, though the views are not grand; and the riches of Norway, its timber, floats silently down the stream, often impeded in its course by islands and little cataracts, the offspring, as it were, of the great one I had frequently heard described.

I found an excellent inn at Fredericstadt, and was gratified by the kind attention of the hostess, who, perceiving that my clothes were wet, took great pains to procure me, as a stranger, every comfort for the night.

It had rained very hard, and we passed the ferry in the dark, without getting out of our carriage, which I think wrong, as the horses are sometimes unruly. Fatigue and melancholy, however, had made me regardless whether I went down or across the stream, and I did not know that I was wet before the hostess marked it. My imagination has never yet severed me from my griefs—and my mind has seldom been so free as to allow my body to be delicate.[2]

How I am altered by disappointment! When going to Lisbon,[3] the elasticity of my mind was sufficient to ward off weariness, and my imagination still could dip her brush in the rainbow of fancy, and sketch futurity in glowing colours. Now—but let me talk of something else—will you go with me to the cascade? …

I have often mentioned the grandeur, but I feel myself unequal to the task of conveying an idea of the beauty and elegance of the scene when the spiral tops of the pines are loaded with ripening seed, and the sun gives a glow to their light green tinge, which is changing into purple, one tree more or less advanced, contrasted with another. The profusion with which Nature has decked them, with pendant honours, prevents all surprise at seeing, in every crevice, some sapling struggling for existence. Vast masses of stone are thus encircled; and roots, torn up by the storms, become a shelter for a young generation. The pine and fir woods, left entirely to nature, display an endless variety; and the paths in the woods are not entangled with fallen leaves, which are only interesting whilst they are fluttering between life and death. The grey cobweb-like appearance of the aged pines is a much finer image of decay; the fibres whitening as they lose their moisture, imprisoned life seems to be stealing away. I cannot tell why—but death, under every form, appears to me like something getting free—to expand in I know not what element; nay, I feel that this conscious being must be as unfettered, have the wings of thought, before it can be happy.

Reaching the cascade, or rather cataract,[4] the roaring of which had a long time announced its vicinity, my soul was hurried by the falls into a new train of reflections. The impetuous dashing of the rebounding torrent from the dark cavities which mocked the exploring eye, produced an equal activity in my mind: my thoughts darted from earth to heaven, and I asked myself why I was chained to life and its misery? Still the tumultuous emotions this sublime object excited, were pleasurable; and, viewing it, my soul rose, with renewed dignity, above its cares—grasping at immortality—it seemed as impossible to stop the current of my thoughts, as of the always varying, still the same, torrent before me—I stretched out my hand to eternity, bounding over the

---

1 *Christiania* From 1625–1925, the name for Oslo, Norway. The city was named after King Christian IV after a fire in 1624; in 1925 the original Norwegian name was restored.

2 [Wollstonecraft's note] "When the mind's free, / The body's delicate." Vid. [see] *King Lear* [3.4.11–12].

3 *Lisbon* Wollstonecraft had gone to Lisbon in 1785 to visit her friend Fanny Skeys, who died in childbirth shortly after Wollstonecraft's arrival.

4 *cataract* A cataract is a waterfall of some prominence ("cascade," by contrast, can refer to a smaller waterfall). Cataracts also fall straight over a precipice, rather than more gently over a more gradual decline.

dark speck of life to come.

We turned with regret from the cascade. On a little hill, which commands the best view of it, several obelisks are erected to commemorate the visits of different kings. The appearance of the river above and below the falls is very picturesque, the ruggedness of the scenery disappearing as the torrent subsides into a peaceful stream. But I did not like to see a number of saw-mills crowded together close to the cataracts; they destroyed the harmony of the prospect.

The sight of a bridge erected across a deep valley, at a little distance, inspired very dissimilar sensations. It was most ingeniously supported by mast-like trunks, just stripped of their branches; and logs, placed one across the other, produced an appearance equally light and firm, seeming almost to be built in the air when we were below it, the height taking from the magnitude of the supporting trees give them a slender graceful look. ...

from Helen Maria Williams, *A Tour in Switzerland* (1798)

In the following excerpts, Helen Maria Williams (c. 1761–1827)—a novelist, poet, and political radical who was imprisoned in Paris during the Reign of Terror—describes the landscapes she encounters during her travels. Her record is notable for providing a female perspective, both on aesthetic experience and on the Grand Tour more readily associated with young educated men. The excerpts also demonstrate the possibility for locating both the sublime and the beautiful within the natural landscape.

from CHAPTER 4

... It was not without the most powerful emotion that, for the first time, I cast my eyes on that solemn, that majestic vision, the Alps! How often had the idea of those stupendous mountains filled my heart with enthusiastic awe! So long, so eagerly, had I desired to contemplate that scene of wonders, that I was unable to trace when first the wish was awakened in my bosom—it seemed from childhood to have made a part of my existence—I longed to bid adieu to the gaily-peopled landscapes of Zurich, and wander amidst those regions of mysterious sublimity, the solitudes of nature, where her eternal laws seem at all seasons to forbid more than the temporary visits of man, and where, sometimes, the dangerous passes to her frozen summits are inflexibly barred against mortal footsteps. The pleasure arising from the varying forms of smiling beauty with which we were surrounded, became a cold sensation, while expectation hung upon those vast gigantic shapes, that half-seen chaos which excited the stronger feelings of wonder, mingled with admiration. But I was obliged, with whatever regret, to relinquish for the present a nearer view of those tremendous objects, since private affairs left me only sufficient leisure to visit the cataract of the Rhine before I returned to Basle; whence, however, I soothed myself with the hope of being soon able to depart in search of the terrific scenes of the Alps, and the rich luxuriant graces of the Italian valleys of Switzerland. In the mean time we passed happily through Zurich, in our way to Schaffhausen, for although I had been assured that the cataract of the Rhine was "but a fall of water," it had excited so tormenting a curiosity, that I found I should be incapable of seeing any thing else with pleasure or advantage, till I had once gazed upon that object.

When we reached the summit of the hill which leads to the fall of the Rhine, we alighted from the carriage, and walked down the steep bank, whence I saw the river rolling turbulently over its bed of rocks, and heard the noise of the torrent, towards which we were descending, increasing as we drew near. My heart swelled with expectation—our path, as if formed to give the scene its full effect, concealed for some time the river from our view; till we reached a wooden balcony, projecting on the edge of the water, and whence, just sheltered from the torrent, it bursts in all its overwhelming wonders on the astonished sight. That stupendous cataract, rushing with wild impetuosity over those broken, unequal rocks, which, lifting up their sharp points amidst its sea of foam, disturb its headlong course, multiply its falls, and make the afflicted waters roar—that cadence of tumultuous sound, which had never till now struck upon my ear—those long feathery surges, giving the element a new aspect—that spray rising into clouds of vapour, and reflecting the prismatic colours, while it disperses itself over the hills—never, never can I forget the sensations of that moment! When with a sort of annihilation of self, with every part impression erased from my memory, I felt as if my heart were bursting with emotions too strong to be sustained—Oh, majestic torrent! which hast conveyed a new image of nature to my soul, the moments I have passed in contemplating thy sublimity will form an epoch in my short span!— thy course is coeval with time, and thou wilt rush down thy rocky walls when this bosom, which throbs with admiration of thy greatness, shall beat no longer!

What an effort does it require to leave, after a transient glimpse, a scene on which, while we meditate, we can take no account of time! Its narrow limits seem too confined for the expanded spirit; such objects appear to belong to immortality; they call the musing mind from all its little cares and vanities, to higher destinies and regions, more congenial than this world to the feelings they excite. I had been often summoned by my fellow-travelers to depart, had often repeated "but one moment more," and many "moments more" had elapsed, before I could resolve to tear myself from the balcony.

We crossed the river, below the fall, in a boat, and had leisure to observe the surrounding scenery. The cataract, however, had for me a sort of fascinating power, which, if I withdrew my eyes for a moment, again fastened them on its impetuous waters. In the background of the torrent a bare mountain lifts its head encircled with its blue vapours; on the right rises a steep cliff, of an enormous height, covered with wood, and upon its summit stands the Castle of Laussen, with its frowning towers, and encircled with its crannied wall; on the left, human industry has seized upon a slender thread of this mighty torrent in its fall, and made it subservient to the purposes of commerce. Foundries, mills, and wheels, are erected on the edge of the river, and a portion of the vast basin into which the cataract falls is confined by a dyke, which preserves the warehouses and the neighbouring huts from its inundations. Sheltered within this little nook, and accustomed to the neighbourhood of the torrent, the boatman unloads his merchandise, and the artisan pursues his toil, regardless

of the falling river, and inattentive to those thundering sounds which seem calculated to suspend all human activity in solemn and awful astonishment; while the imagination of the spectator is struck with the comparative littleness of fleeting man, busy with his trivial occupations, contrasted with the view of nature in all her vast, eternal, uncontrollable grandeur. ...

from Chapter 11

After winding for some time among these awful scenes, of which no painting can give an adequate description, and of which an imagination the most pregnant in sublime horrors could form but a very imperfect idea, we came within the sound of these cataracts of the Reuss[1] which announced our approach towards another operation of Satanic power, called the Devil's Bridge.[2] We were more struck with the august drapery of this supernatural work, than with the work itself. It seemed less marvellous than expectation had pictured it, and we were perhaps the more disappointed, as we remembered that "the wonderous art pontifical," was a part of architecture with which his infernal majesty was perfectly well acquainted; and the rocks of the valley of Schellenen were certainly as solid foundations for bridge building as "the aggregated soil solid, or flimsy," which was collected amidst the waste of chaos, and crowded drove "from each side shoaling towards the mouth of hell."[3]

On this spot we loitered for some time to contemplate the stupendous and terrific scenery. The mountainous rocks lifted their heads abrupt, and appeared to fix the limits of our progress at this point, unless we could climb the mighty torrent which was struggling impetuously for passage under our feet, after precipitating its afflicted waters with tremendous roar in successive cascades over the disjointed rocks, and filling the atmosphere with its foam.

[1] *Reuss* River in Switzerland.

[2] *Devil's Bridge* A number of European bridges were believed to have been constructed with the help of the devil.

[3] *the wonderous art ... mouth of hell* Phrases slightly misquoted from John Milton's *Paradise Lost*, 10.312–22, 293–96, and 288. In Book 10, Sin and Death enter the world following man's fall and punishment.

Separating ourselves with reluctance from these objects of overwhelming greatness, we turned an angle of the mountain at the end of the bridge, and proceeded along a way of difficult ascent, which led to a rock that seemed inflexibly to bar our passage. A bridge fastened to this rock by iron work, and suspended over the torrent, was formerly the only means of passing, but numerous accidents led the government to seek another outlet. The rock being too high to climb, and too weighty to remove, the engineer took the middle way, and bored a hole in the solid mass two hundred feet along, and about ten or twelve feet broad and high, through which he carried the road. The entrance into this subterranean passage is almost dark, and the little light that penetrates through a crevice in the rock, serves only to make its obscurity more visible. Filled with powerful images of the terrible and sublime, from the enormous objects which I had been contemplating for some hours past, objects, the forms of which were new to my imagination, it was not without a feeling of reluctance that I plunged into this scene of night, whose thick gloom heightened every sensation of terror.

After passing through this cavern, the view which suddenly unfolded itself appeared rather a gay illusion of the fancy than real nature. No magical wand was ever fabled to shift more instantaneously the scene, or call up forms of more striking contrast to those on which we had gazed. On the other side of the cavern we seemed amidst the chaos or the overthrow of nature; on this we beheld her dressed in all the loveliness of infancy or renovation, with every charm of soft and tranquil beauty. The rugged and stony interstices between the mountain and the road were here changed into smooth and verdant paths; the abrupt precipice and shagged rock were metamorphosed into gently sloping declivities; the barren and monotonous desert was transformed into a fertile and smiling plain. The long resounding cataract, struggling through the huge masses of granite, here became a calm and limpid current, gliding over fine beds of sand with gentle murmurs, as if reluctant to leave that enchanting abode. ...

from CHAPTER 40

... Whether the French Republic will accede to this invitation, and render the Pays de Vaud independent of Berne, is a secret which the book of destiny will perhaps ere long unfold.

In the mean time, it is natural to conclude, that the principles of that mighty revolution which have already diffused themselves over remote regions of the globe, cannot fail to expand in those countries which are placed immediately within their influence. Since the period of the French Revolution, ages have flitted before our eyes, and we have risen suddenly, like the offspring of Deucalion,[1] from infancy to manhood, not without indications it must be confessed, of the hardened origin whence we sprung. Like the traveller, who from the scorching plains, climbs the rocks that lead him to the regions of eternal snow, and finds that in the space of a few hours he has passed through every successive latitude, from burning heat to the confines of the frozen pole, the journey of months; so the human mind, placed within the sphere of the French Revolution, has bounded over the ruggedness of slow metaphysical researches, and reached at once, with an incredible effort, the highest probable attainments of political discovery. ...

from William Gilpin, *Three Essays: On Picturesque Beauty; On Picturesque Travel; and On Sketching Landscape* (1792)

William Gilpin (1724–1804) articulated the picturesque as "that kind of beauty which is agreeable in a picture" in his *Essay on Prints* (1768). In *Three Essays: On Picturesque Beauty; On Picturesque Travel; and On Sketching Landscape*, he further refined and explored the concept that would become of great importance to Romantic poets and painters.

---

[1] *Deucalion* In Greek mythology, Deucalion is the son of Prometheus who, like Noah, is warned of a coming flood, builds an ark, and so survives the devastation. He is then instructed to re-people the earth with his wife Pyrrha by throwing stones over their shoulders, with the cast stones forming men and women, respectively, according to the thrower's gender.

from Essay 1

Disputes about beauty might perhaps be involved in less confusion, if a distinction were established, which certainly exists, between such objects as are *beautiful*, and such as are *picturesque*—between those, which please the eye in their *natural state*; and those, which please from some quality, capable of being *illustrated by painting*.

Ideas of beauty vary with the objects, and with the eye of the spectator. The stonemason sees beauties in a well-jointed wall, which escape the architect, who surveys the building under a different idea. And thus the painter, who compares his object with the rules of his art, sees it in a different light from the man of general taste, who surveys it only as simply beautiful.

As this difference therefore between the *beautiful*, and the *picturesque* appears really to exist, and must depend on some peculiar construction of the object; it may be worthwhile to examine, what that peculiar construction is. We inquire not into the *general sources of beauty*, either in nature, or in representation. This would lead into a nice, and scientific discussion, in which it is not our purpose to engage. The question simply is, *What is that quality in objects, which particularly marks them as picturesque?*

In examining the *real object*, we shall find, one source of beauty arises from that species of elegance, which we call *smoothness*, or *neatness*; for the terms are nearly synonymous. The higher the marble is polished, the brighter the silver is rubbed, and the more the mahogany shines, the more each is considered as an object of beauty: as if the eye delighted in gliding smoothly over a surface.

In the class of larger objects the same idea prevails. In a pile of building we wish to see neatness in every part added to the elegance of the architecture. And if we examine a piece of improved pleasure-ground, every thing rough, and slovenly offends.

Mr. Burke, enumerating the properties of beauty, considers *smoothness* as one of the most essential. "A very considerable part of the effect of beauty, says he, is owing to this quality: indeed the most considerable: for take any beautiful object, and give it a broken, and rugged surface, and however well-formed it may be in other respects, it pleases no longer. Whereas, let it want ever so many of the other constituents, if it want not this, it becomes more pleasing, than almost all the others without it."[1] How far Mr. Burke may be right in making smoothness the most considerable source of beauty, I rather doubt. A considerable one it certainly is.

Thus then, we suppose, the matter stands with regard to *beautiful objects in general*. But in *picturesque representation* it seems somewhat odd, yet perhaps we shall find it equally true, that the reverse of this is the case; and that the ideas of *neat* and *smooth*, instead of being picturesque, in reality strip the object, in which they reside, of all pretensions to *picturesque beauty*. Nay, farther, we do not scruple to assert, that roughness forms the most essential point of difference between the *beautiful*, and the *picturesque*; as it seems to be that particular quality, which makes objects chiefly pleasing in painting. I use the general term *roughness*; but properly speaking roughness relates only to the surface of bodies: when we speak of their delineation, we use the word *ruggedness*. Both ideas however equally enter into the picturesque; and both are observable in the smaller, as well as in the larger parts of nature—in the outline, and bark of a tree, as in the rude summit, and craggy sides of a mountain.

Let us then examine our theory by an appeal to experience; and try how far these qualities enter into the idea of *picturesque beauty*; and how far they mark that difference among objects, which is the ground of our inquiry.

A piece of Palladian architecture[2] may be elegant in the last degree. The proportion of its parts—the propriety of its ornaments—and the symmetry of the whole may be highly pleasing. But if we introduce it in a picture, it immediately becomes a formal object, and ceases to please. Should we wish to give it picturesque beauty, we must use the mallet, instead of the chisel; we

---

[1] *A very considerable ... without it* From Edmund Burke's *A Philosophical Enquiry into the Origin of Our Ideas of the Sublime and Beautiful* (1757).

[2] *Palladian architecture* European architectural style, derived from the work of Andrea Palladio, a sixteenth-century Venetian architect. Palladio's work was in turn based on the classical temple architecture of ancient Greece and Rome.

must beat down one half of it, deface the other, and throw the mutilated members around in heaps. In short, from a *smooth* building we must turn it into a *rough* ruin. No painter, who had the choice of the two objects, would hesitate which to choose.

Again, why does an elegant piece of garden-ground make no figure on canvas? The shape is pleasing; the combination of the objects, harmonious; and the widening of the walk in the very line of beauty. All this is true, but the *smoothness* of the whole, though right, and as it should be in nature, offends in picture. Turn the lawn into a piece of broken ground: plant rugged oaks instead of flowing shrubs: break the edges of the walk: give it the rudeness of a road; mark it with wheel-tracks; and scatter around a few stones, and brushwood; in a word, instead of making the whole *smooth*, make it rough; and you make it also *picturesque*. All the other ingredients of beauty it already possessed. ...

Painting the Natural and the Sublime

French

The work of French artists of the Romantic period often displays a passionate flair for the dramatic, whether the subject be political, historical, or mythological; the sublime in nature is more often a backdrop for human drama than it is a subject in itself.

Jean-Antoine Gros, *Napoleon at the Battle of Eylau*, 1808. The Battle of Eylau was fought between the French and Russian armies in 1807; it resulted in the loss of between 25,000 and 50,000 lives, but with no clear victory on either side.

Jacques-Louis David, *Napoleon Crossing the Alps*, fifth version, c. 1805. This painting (also known as *Napoleon at the Saint-Bernard Pass* and as *Bonaparte Crossing the Alps*), which became the most widely reproduced image of Napoleon, exists in five different versions. Napoleon had led his army through the Saint-Bernard Pass in the Alps in 1800 as part of a campaign that concluded with the defeat of the Austrian army in the Battle of Marengo later that year. The French victory in Italy led to improved relations between France and Spain, and various gifts were exchanged between the French and Spanish leaders; the first version of *Napoleon Crossing the Alps* was one such gift. David, an ardent supporter of Napoleon, was commissioned by the French ambassador to Spain to paint the portrait and completed it in January 1801. Napoleon himself asked David to paint three more versions. David painted a fifth on his own initiative and retained it until his death. (Like the second version, it now belongs to the museum of the Palace of Versailles.)

Theodore Géricault, *The Raft of the Medusa*, 1819. Perhaps the best known of all French paintings of the Romantic era, this work is a monumental depiction (approximately 16 x 24 feet) of an incident that occurred in 1816. The *Medusa* was a French frigate captained by a political appointee lacking in experience; it ran aground on a sandbank some 60 miles from the African coast. The ship had too few lifeboats and almost 150 men and one woman ended up adrift on a makeshift raft with inadequate supplies. By the time the raft was sighted and the survivors rescued by a passing ship, the *Argus*, only 15 remained alive; the others had starved to death or, in some cases, been killed and eaten (Géricault also completed a much smaller work entitled *Cannibalism on the Raft of the Medusa*).

The painting depicts the survivors' despair as the *Argus* has been sighted but has not seen the raft and is sailing on. By chance, the *Argus* re-appeared again on the horizon some hours later on another tack, at which point the raft was finally sighted. The incident followed the restoration of the French monarchy after the defeat of Napoleon and was widely taken as a sign of the corruption, incompetence, and heartlessness of the new French regime, which had not bothered to instigate any search for the missing ship.

The painting, which was originally hung in Paris under the title *Scène de Naufrage* ("Scene of a Shipwreck"), was also controversial for its inclusion of a black man at the center of the composition; Géricault was an ardent abolitionist. When the work was exhibited in London for several months in 1820, it was received with tremendous enthusiasm and viewed by more than 40,000 people.

Eugène Delacroix, *Liberty Leading the People*, 1830. Delacroix's most famous painting celebrates the overthrow of Charles X in 1830, which led to the establishment of a constitutional monarchy under Louis-Phillippe. The figure of Liberty holds a tattered *tricoleur*—the flag of the French Revolution of 1789. The new government bought the painting in 1831; later, it became the inspiration for France's 1886 gift to the United States of the statue *Liberty Enlightening the World*.

German

The work of such Romantic-era German artists as Philipp Otto Runge and Caspar David Friedrich is infused with symbolism and spirituality; the supernatural (and often specifically the Christian) is portrayed as a deep presence in nature—in plants, in the hours of the day and the changing seasons, and in human nature as well. The nineteenth-century European tradition of painting in this vein has roots in the Academy at Copenhagen in Denmark (where Runge, Friedrich, and the Norwegian Romantic painter Johann Christian Dahl all studied) and in the work of the Danish artist Jens Juel.

Philipp Otto Runge, *The Child in the Meadow*, from *Morning*, 1809. *The Child in the Meadow* was conceived as one part of a larger picture, *Morning*, that was itself planned as part of a still-larger work, *Times of Day*. *Morning* was not quite complete when Runge died (aged 33); before he died he suggested that the unfinished work be cut up and the parts that had been completed be displayed independently. *The Child in the Meadow* was the title given to this fragment. The grand scheme of the larger work is suggestive both of Christian and of classical mythology. The fragment gives a turn to Christian iconography that is also expressive of two other elements central to Runge's vision: a belief in an overriding connection between humans and nature, and a faith in childhood as the human stage that stands closest to the force of creation.

Caspar David Friedrich, *The Wanderer above the Sea of Fog*, 1818. The title of this famous painting is also sometimes translated as *The Walker above the Mists*; in German the title is *Der Wanderer über dem Nebelmeer*; the German "Wanderer" can mean either wanderer or hiker.

Caspar David Friedrich, *Arctic Shipwreck* (also known as *Sea of Ice* or *Polar Sea*), 1824.

BRITISH

From the gentle vision of nature expressed in the late eighteenth-century work of Thomas Gainsborough, British artists moved in several directions. The vast scenes depicted by John Martin[1] are dark and theatrical; the Romantic sublime of Philip James de Loutherbourg is strangely unthreatening, even when terrible subjects are depicted. The work of the two most prominent Romantic-era British artists, J.M.W. Turner and John Constable, evolved markedly over the course of several decades.

Thomas Gainsborough, *Peasants Going to Market, Early Morning*, 1770.

Thomas Gainsborough, *Cottage Door with Girl and Pigs*, 1786.

---

[1] *John Martin*   See the color insert for work by Martin, as well as other examples of British painting during the Romantic era.

J.M.W. Turner, *Linlithgow Palace*, 1807. The palace where Mary, Queen of Scots had been born was by 1807 a picturesque ruin. The naked nymphs he added in the foreground are reminiscent of artistic styles of an earlier era, but the whole has an unmistakably Romantic cast.

J.M.W. Turner, *The Fighting Temeraire Tugged to Her Last Berth to Be Broken Up*, 1839. The *H.M.S. Temeraire* had played an important role in Nelson's victory over the French at Trafalgar in 1805; in 1838, it was towed to a scrap yard at the docks in East London.

J.M.W. Turner, *The Devil's Bridge*, 1841.

John Constable, *Dedham Vale*, 1802.

John Constable, *Brighton Beach, with Colliers*, 1824.

John Constable, *Old Sarum*, 1829. Old Sarum, near the site of present-day Salisbury, is the location of some of the earliest evidence of human settlement in Britain; it is known to have been inhabited over 3,000 years ago. By the early nineteenth century, however, the old hill fort was long-abandoned and Old Sarum was uninhabited.

Philip James de Loutherbourg, *Snowdon*, from *The Romantic and Picturesque Scenery of England and Wales*, 1805.

Philip James de Loutherbourg, *Storm off Margate*, from *The Romantic and Picturesque Scenery of England and Wales*, 1805.

David Cox, *Crossing Lancaster Sands*, 1841. Until 1857, when a railway line was built across the bay, people often made their way to Morecamb Bay at low tide across the Lancaster Sands. There were numerous dangers associated with the crossing (including quicksand as well as unpredictable and dangerous tides). The crossing inspired works by many artists, including J.M.W. Turner; the above painting is one of several depictions by the watercolorist David Cox.

THE PLACE OF HUMANS AND NON-HUMAN ANIMALS IN NATURE

CONTEXTS

Through much of the eighteenth century, philosophers debated the question of how non-human animals should be treated. The philosophical background on one side of the issue had been laid out by René Descartes, who asserted in his *Discourse on Method* (1637) that non-human animals "have no reason at all." Even in cases where they show greater ability or dexterity than humans, "it is nature which acts in them" rather than any mental activity of their own, "just as a clock, which is only composed of wheels and weights is able to tell the hours and measure the time more correctly than we can do with all our wisdom." John Locke argued in the other direction in his *Essay Concerning Human Understanding* (1690), asserting that it was far more difficult than Descartes had suggested to draw a clear line separating human and non-human animals. Locke also argued strongly that it was important to educate young people to treat non-human animals with consideration and kindness, which would become a recurring theme of eighteenth- and nineteenth-century writers. In the eighteenth century, Jean-Jacques Rousseau, while accepting that in some sense beasts could be machine-like, also argued that "every animal has ideas, since it has senses; it even combines those ideas in a certain degree; and it is only in degree that man differs, in this respect, from the brute." He, too, felt it important to inculcate in humans—children especially—feelings of kindness towards our fellow creatures.

As the horrific images in William Hogarth's *The Four Stages of Cruelty* suggest, such sentiments were often ignored in the eighteenth century. Indeed, it would be hard to argue that British society as a whole became less cruel toward animals over the course of the century. Animals such as cart horses and donkeys were routinely worked to death by their owners; poor farmers tied horses to plows by their tails to save the expense of a harness; sheep had their wool pulled off instead of sheared; sports such as bullbaiting and cockfighting flourished.

Yet some signs pointed in a different direction. Through the century, it became more and more common among better-off members of society to keep pets (Samuel Johnson's cat Hodge being perhaps the most famous example). In literature, we find powerful (if sometimes inconsistent) expressions of concern for the welfare of non-human animals from the likes of James Thomson, Alexander Pope, William Cowper, and Sarah Scott. In the Romantic era, such voices became more numerous; Anna Laetitia Barbauld was perhaps the most influential among them. As the language of Barbauld's "The Mouse's Petition" suggests, such views were to some degree connected to the revolutionary ferment of the time. Others—perhaps most notably Percy Shelley—went further and strongly advocated vegetarianism, often out of concern for the well-being of human as well as non-human animals. (A few went further still—see, for example, the author entry in the website component of this anthology for Lewis Gompertz.) Quite aside from any issues relating to the treatment of animals, there was also the question of what was natural; in Shelley's mind—and that of many others of his time—humans were not naturally meat eaters. (This is also the view suggested in Mary Shelley's *Frankenstein*; the monster decides to live on nuts and berries, thereby choosing a life that is "peaceful and human.")

Beginning with the introduction of a bill against bullbaiting in 1800, a political movement began to take shape, devoted to place legal limits on human cruelty against non-human animals. The movement attracted well-known supporters (including William Wilberforce and Richard Brinsley Sheridan), but it faced extremely strong opposition; the 1800 bill was defeated, and so were numerous others before the first piece of legislation against animal cruelty—An Act to Prevent the Cruel and Improper Treatment of Cattle—was passed in 1822.

⌘ ⌘ ⌘

from William Godwin, *Fleetwood: or, the New Man of Feeling* (1805)

Fleetwood, William Godwin's (1756–1836) third novel, assesses Rousseau's ideas about the virtue of the "natural man," finding its hero, raised in the natural world, far from ideal.

I loved the country, without feeling any partiality to what are called the sports of the country. My temper, as I have already said, was somewhat unsocial; and so far as related to the intercourse of my species, except when some strong stimulus of humanity called me into action, unenterprising. I was therefore no hunter. I was inaccessible to the pitiful ambition of showing, before a gang of rural squires, that I had a fine horse, and could manage him gracefully. I had not the motive, which ordinarily influences the inhabitants of the country to the cultivation of these sports—the want of occupation. I was young: the world was new to me: I abounded with occupation. In the scenery of Merionethshire I found a source of inexhaustible amusement. Science, history, poetry engaged me by turns, and into each of them my soul plunged itself with an ardour difficult to describe. In the train of these came my visions, my beloved and variegated inventions, the records, which to me appeared voluminous and momentous, of my past life, the plans of my future, the republics I formed, the seminaries of education for which I constructed laws, the figure I proposed hereafter

to exhibit in the eyes of a wondering world. I had a still further and more direct reason for my rejection for the sports of the field. I could not with patience regard torture, anguish, and death, as sources of amusement. My natural temper, or my reflective and undebauched habits as a solitaire, prevented me from overlooking the brutality and cruelty of such pursuits. In very early youth I had been seduced, first by a footman of my father, and afterward by my tutor, who was a great lover of the art, to join in an excursion of angling. But, after a short trial, I abjured the amusement for ever; and it was one among the causes of the small respect I entertained for my tutor, that he was devoted to so idle and unfeeling an avocation.

from John Locke, *Some Thoughts Concerning Education* (1693), Section 116

Locke (1632–1704) had argued in his *Essay Concerning Human Understanding* (1690) that reason is more important to what is human than is physical shape, and that several common human assumptions over how species and essences should be defined and delineated deserved to be challenged. In his influential *Some Thoughts Concerning Education*, he addressed the issue of cruelty toward animals.

Cruelty. One thing I have frequently observed in children, that when they have got possession of any poor creature, they are apt to use it ill: They often torment, and treat very roughly young birds, butterflies, and such other poor animals, which fall into their hands, and that with a seeming kind of pleasure. This I think should be watched in them, and if they incline to any such cruelty they should be taught the contrary usage. For the custom of tormenting and killing of beasts will, by degrees, harden their minds even towards men; and they who delight in the suffering and destruction of inferior creatures, will not be apt to be very compassionate or benign to those of their own kind. Our practice takes notice of this in the exclusion of *butchers* from juries of life and death. Children should from the beginning be bred up in an abhorrence of *killing*, or tormenting any living creature; and be taught not to *spoil* or destroy any thing, unless it be for the preservation or advantage of some other, that is nobler. ...

FIRST STAGE OF CRUELTY.

from William Hogarth, *The Four Stages of Cruelty* (1751)

In *The Four Stages of Cruelty*, painter, printmaker, satirist, and social critic William Hogarth (1697–1764) depicts four stages in the life of the fictional Tom Nero. In the first plate, Nero is shown as a child torturing a dog. Subsequent plates show him torturing a horse (Second Stage of Cruelty); engaging in a life of robbery, seduction, and murder (Cruelty in Perfection); and, finally, being mutilated by surgeons in an anatomical theater after he is executed for his crimes (The Reward of Cruelty). Hogarth's engravings thus suggest that childish cruelty to animals can quickly progress to depraved criminality.

Anna Laetitia Barbauld, "The Mouse's Petition" (1773)

Oh! Hear a pensive prisoner's prayer,
    For liberty that sighs;
And never let thine heart be shut
    Against the wretch's cries.

5   For here forlorn and sad I sit
    Within the wiry grate;
    And tremble at th'approaching morn,
    Which brings impending fate.

If e'er thy breast with freedom glowed
10   And spurned a tyrant's chain,
    Let not thy strong oppressive force
    A free-born mouse detain.[1]

---

[1] *If e'er ... detain* Barbauld may well be alluding here to political positions Joseph Priestley had taken in support of freedom. In 1769, Priestley (who eventually emigrated to the United States) had taken issue with the British government's "enslaving" of the American colonies, and had argued for "a just idea of natural and civil rights."

Oh! do not stain with guiltless blood
Thy hospitable hearth;
5 Nor triumph that thy wiles betrayed
A prize so little worth.

The scattered gleanings of a feast
My frugal meals supply;
But if thine unrelenting heart
10 That slender boon deny,

The chearful light, the vital air,
Are blessings widely given;
Let nature's commoners enjoy
The common gifts of heaven.

15 The well-taught philosophic mind
To all compassion gives;
Casts round the world an equal eye,
And feels for all that lives.

If mind, as ancient sages taught,
30 A never dying flame,
Still shifts through matter's varying forms,
In every form the same.

Beware, lest in the worm you crush,
A brother's soul you find;
35 And tremble lest thy luckless hand
Dislodge a kindred mind.

Or, if this transient gleam of day
Be *all* of life we share,
Let pity plead within thy breast
40 That little *all* to spare.

So may thy hospitable board
With health and peace be crowned;
And every charm of heartfelt ease
Beneath thy roof be found.

45 So, when destruction lurks unseen,
Which men, like mice, may share,

May some kind angel clear thy path,
And break the hidden snare.

from Anna Laetitia Barbauld, *Lessons for Children* (1778–88)

from LESSONS FOR CHILDREN, FROM TWO TO THREE YEARS OLD

Where is puss? Puss is got under the table. You cannot catch puss. Do not pull her by the tail, you hurt her. Stroke poor puss. You stroke her the wrong way. This is the right way. But puss, why did you kill the rabbit? You must catch mice; you must not kill rabbits. Well, what do you say, did you kill the rabbit? Why do you not speak, puss? Puss cannot speak. …

… Bread is to eat, you must not throw it away. Corn[1] makes bread. Corn grows in the fields. Grass grows in the fields. Cows eat grass, and sheep eat grass, and horses eat grass. Little boys do not eat grass: no, they eat bread and milk. …

There is a pretty butterfly. Come, shall we catch it. Butterfly, where are you going? It is flown over the hedge. He will not let us catch him. There is a bee sucking the flowers. Will the bee sting Charles? No, it will not sting you if you let it alone. Bees make wax and honey. Honey is sweet. Charles shall have some honey and bread for supper. Caterpillars eat cabbages. Here is a poor little snail crawling up the wall. Touch him with your little finger. Ah, the snail is crept into his shell. His shell is his house. Good night, snail. Let him alone, and he will soon come out again.

from LESSONS FOR CHILDREN OF THREE YEARS OLD, PART I

What has Billy got! He has got a nest of young birds. He has been climbing a high tree for them. Poor little birds! they have no feathers. Keep them warm. You must feed them with a quill. You must give them bread and milk. They are young goldfinches. They will be very pretty

---
[1] *Corn* Grain.

when they have got their red head and yellow wings. Do not let them die. The little birds papa and mamma will be very sorry if they come to die. …

It is September. Hark! somebody is letting off a gun. They are shooting the poor birds. Here is a bird dropped down just at your feet. It is all bloody. Poor thing! how it flutters. Its wing is broke. It cannot fly any further. It is going to die. What bird is it? It is a partridge. Are you not sorry, Charles? It was alive a little while ago.

from LESSONS FOR CHILDREN OF THREE YEARS OLD, PART II

Do you know why you are better than Puss? Puss can play as well as you; and Puss can drink milk, and lie upon the carpet; and she can run as fast as you, and faster too, a great deal; and she can climb trees better; and she can catch mice, which you cannot do. But can Puss talk? No. Can Puss read? No. Then that is the reason why you are better than Puss—because you can talk and read. Can Pierrot, your dog, read? No. Will you teach him? Take the pin and point to the words. No—he will not learn. I never saw a little dog or cat learn to read. But little boys can learn. If you do not learn, Charles, you are not good for half as much as Puss. You had better be drowned. …

Here is a seat of turf, and a bank almost covered with violets; we shall sit here, and you and Billy may lie on the carpet. The carpet is in the parlour. Yes, there is a carpet in the parlour, but there is a carpet here too. What is it? the grass is the carpet out of doors. Pretty green soft carpet! and it is very large, for it spreads every where, over all the fields, and over all the meadows: and it is very pleasant for the sheep and the lambs to lie upon. I do not know what they would do without it, for they have no feather-bed to sleep upon.

Samuel Taylor Coleridge, "To a Young Ass, Its Mother Being Tethered Near It" (1794)

While at Jesus College, Coleridge (1772–1834) frequently encountered a donkey grazing on the grass; the animal's mother was tethered to a log nearby, apparently unable to move toward fresh grass. Coleridge's pity for animals is consistent with the sympathies of many Romantic intellectuals, but his attraction to the donkey specifically may stem from its association in fable with spiritual merit, patience, humility, lowliness, and suffering that find favor in heaven.

At this stage of his life, Coleridge was in sympathy with the ideas of Barbauld (with whom he corresponded extensively) and others concerning appropriate human attitudes toward non-human animals. Later in life, as he became more conservative, he derided such views as overly sentimental.

Poor little Foal of an oppressèd Race!
I love the languid Patience of thy face:
And oft with gentle hand I give thee bread,
And clap thy ragged Coat, and pat thy head.
5   But what thy dullèd Spirits hath dismayed,
That never thou dost sport along the glade?
And (most unlike the nature of things young)
That earthward still thy moveless head is hung?
Do thy prophetic fears anticipate,
10 Meek Child of Misery! thy future fate?
The starving meal, and all the thousand aches
"Which patient Merit of the Unworthy takes"?[1]
Or is thy sad heart thrilled with filial pain
To see thy wretched Mother's shortened chain?
15 And truly, very piteous is *her* Lot—
Chained to a Log within a narrow spot,
Where the close-eaten Grass is scarcely seen,
While sweet around her waves the tempting Green!

Poor Ass! thy master should have learnt to show
20 Pity—best taught by fellowship of Woe!
For much I fear me that *He* lives like thee,
Half famished in a land of Luxury!

---

[1] *Which patient … Unworthy takes* From *Hamlet*, 3.1.74.

How *askingly* its footsteps hither bend!
It seems to say, "And have I then *one* friend?"
Innocent foal! thou poor despised Forlorn!
I hail thee *Brother*—spite of the fool's scorn!
And fain would take thee with me, in the Dell
Of Peace and mild Equality to dwell,
Where Toil shall call the charmer Health his bride,
And Laughter tickle Plenty's ribless side!
How thou wouldst toss thy heels in gamesome play,
And frisk about, as lamb or kitten gay!
Yea! and more musically sweet to me
Thy dissonant harsh bray of joy would be,
Than warbled melodies that soothe to rest
The aching of pale Fashion's vacant breast!

Percy Bysshe Shelley, *A Vindication of Natural Diet* (1813)

A strong crusader for Justice, particularly for the working classes, Shelley (1792–1822) was also an outspoken advocate of vegetarianism. He wrote a number of essays on the topic, of which *A Vindication of Natural Diet* is perhaps the most famous.

I hold that the depravity of the physical and moral nature of man originated in his unnatural habits of life. The origin of man, like that of the universe of which he is a part, is enveloped in impenetrable mystery. His generations either had a beginning, or they had not. The weight of evidence in favour of each of these suppositions seems tolerably equal; and it is perfectly unimportant to the present argument which is assumed. The language spoken however by the mythology of nearly all religions seems to prove, that at some distant period man forsook the path of nature, and sacrificed the purity and happiness of his being to unnatural appetites. The date of this event seems to have also been that of some great change in the climates of the earth, with which it has an obvious correspondence. The allegory of Adam and Eve eating of the tree of evil, and entailing upon their posterity the wrath of God, and the loss of everlasting life, admits of no other explanation, than the disease and crime that have flowed from unnatural diet. Milton was so well aware of this, that he makes Raphael thus exhibit to Adam the consequence of his disobedience:

Immediately a place,
Before his eyes appeared: sad, noisome, dark:
A lazar-house it seemed; wherein were laid
Numbers of all diseased: all maladies
Of ghastly spasm, or racking torture, qualms
Of heart-sick agony, all feverous kinds,
Convulsions, epilepsies, fierce catarrhs,
Intestine stone and ulcer, cholic pangs,
Dæmoniac frenzy, moping melancholy,
And moon-struck madness, pining atrophy,
Marasmus, and wide-wasting pestilence,
Dropsies, and asthmas, and joint-racking rheums.[1]

And how many thousand more might not be added to this frightful catalogue!

The story of Prometheus is one likewise which, although universally admitted to be allegorical, has never been satisfactorily explained. Prometheus stole fire from heaven, and was chained for this crime to mount Caucasus, where a vulture continually devoured his liver, that grew to meet its hunger. Hesiod says, that before the time of Prometheus, mankind were exempt from suffering; that they enjoyed a vigorous youth, and that death, when at length it came, approached like sleep, and gently closed their eyes. Again, so general was this opinion, that Horace, a poet of the Augustan age, writes:

Audax omnia perpeti,
Gens humana ruit per vetitum nefas,
Audax Iapeti genus
Ignem fraude mala gentibus intulit,
Post ignem ætheriâ domo
Subductum, macies et nova febrium
Terris incubuit cohors

[1] *Immediately a place … joint-racking rheums* From *Paradise Lost*, 10. 477–88.

Semotique prius tarda necessitas,
Lethi corripuit gradum.[1]

How plain a language is spoken by all this. Prometheus, (who represents the human race) effected some great change in the condition of his nature, and applied fire to culinary purposes; thus inventing an expedient for screening from his disgust the horrors of the shambles. From this moment his vitals were devoured by the vulture of disease. It consumed his being in every shape of its loathsome and infinite variety, inducing the soul-quelling sinkings of premature and violent death. All vice arose from the ruin of healthful innocence. Tyranny, superstition, commerce, and inequality, were then first known, when reason vainly attempted to guide the wanderings of exacerbated passion. I conclude this part of the subject with an extract from Mr. Newton's *Defence of Vegetable Regimen*, from whom I have borrowed this interpretation of the fable of Prometheus.

Making allowance for such transposition of the events of the allegory, as time might produce after the important truths were forgotten, which the portion of the ancient mythology was intended to transmit, the drift of the fable seems to be this: Man at his creation was endowed with the gift of perpetual youth; that is, he was not formed to be a sickly suffering creature as we now see him, but to enjoy health, and to sink by slow degrees into the bosom of his parent earth without disease or pain. Prometheus first taught the use of animal food (*primus bovem occidit Prometheus*) and of fire, with which to render it more digestible and pleasing to the taste. Jupiter, and the rest of the gods, foreseeing the consequences of the inventions, were amused or irritated at the short-sighted devices of the newly-formed creature, and left him to experience the sad effects of them. Thirst, the necessary concomitant of a flesh diet, (perhaps of all diet vitiated by culinary preparation) "ensued; water was resorted to, and man

forfeited the inestimable gift of health which he had received from heaven: he became diseased, the partaker of a precarious existence, and no longer descended slowly to his grave."[2]

But just disease to luxury succeeds,
And every death its own avenger breeds;
The fury passions from that blood began,
And turned on man a fiercer savage—Man.[3]

Man, and the animals whom he has infected with his society, or depraved by his dominion, are alone diseased. The wild hog, the mouflon,[4] the bison, and the wolf, are perfectly exempt from malady, and invariably die either from external violence, or natural old age. But the domestic hog, the sheep, the cow, and the dog, are subject to an incredible variety of distempers; and, like the corrupters of their nature, have physicians who thrive upon their miseries. The supereminence of man is like Satan's, a supereminence of pain; and the majority of his species, doomed to penury, disease, and crime, have reason to curse the untoward event, that by enabling him to communicate his sensations, raised him above the level of his fellow animals. But the steps that have been taken are irrevocable. The whole of human science is comprised in one question: How can the advantages of intellect and civilisation be reconciled with the liberty and pure pleasures of natural life? How can we take the benefits, and reject the evils of the system, which is now interwoven with all the fibres of our being? I believe that abstinence from animal food and spirituous liquors would in a great measure capacitate us for the solution of this important question.

Comparative anatomy teaches us that man resembles frugivorous[5] animals in everything, and carnivorous in

---

[1] *Audax omnia perpeti … corripuit gradum* Latin: "Men, ready for anything, are quick / Forbidden wickedness to find; / Prometheus by a dirty trick / Brought ready fire to humankind. / But after fire was brought down to earth / From its heavenly haven, with it a corps / Of new diseases came, and dearth, / So death, remote and slow before, / Sooner than necessary began" (Horace, *Odes*, 1.3.25–33).

[2] *Mr. Newton's … to his grave* John Frank Newton was the author of *Return to Nature, or Defence of Vegetable Regimen* (1811), the work from which the quoted passage is taken. Shelley met Newton in 1812 through the son of William Godwin. Newton's work included an account of his family's successful experiment with a vegetarian diet.

[3] *But just … Man* From Alexander Pope, *An Essay on Man*, 165–69.

[4] *mouflon* Subspecies of wild sheep.

[5] *frugivorous* Fruit-eating.

nothing; he has neither claws wherewith to seize his prey, nor distinct and pointed teeth to tear the living fibre. A Mandarin of the first class, with nails two inches long, would probably find them alone inefficient to hold even a hare. After every subterfuge of gluttony, the bull must be degraded into the ox, and the ram into the wether,[1] by an unnatural and inhuman operation, that the flaccid fibre may offer a fainter resistance to rebellious nature. It is only by softening and disguising dead flesh by culinary preparation that it is rendered susceptible of mastication or digestion, and that the sight of its bloody juices and raw horror, does not excite intolerable loathing and disgust. Let the advocate of animal food, force himself to a decisive experiment on its fitness, and as Plutarch[2] recommends, tear a living lamb with his teeth, and plunging his head into its vitals, slake his thirst with the steaming blood; when fresh from the deed of horror let him revert to the irresistible instincts of nature that would rise in judgment against it, and say, Nature formed me for such work as this. Then, and then only, would he be consistent.

Man resembles no carnivorous animal. There is no exception, except man be one, to the rule of herbivorous animals having cellulated colons.

The orang-outang perfectly resembles man both in the order and number of his teeth. The orang-outang is the most anthropomorphous of the ape tribe, all of which are strictly frugivorous. There is no other species of animals in which this analogy exists. In many frugivorous animals, the canine teeth are more pointed and distinct than those of man. The resemblance also of the human stomach to that of the orang-outang, is greater than to that of any other animal.

The intestines are also identical with those of herbivorous animals, which present a larger surface for absorption, and have ample and cellulated colons. The cæcum also, though short, is larger than that of carnivorous animals; and even here the orang-outang retains its accustomed similarity. The structure of the human frame then is that of one fitted to a pure vegetable diet,

in every essential particular. It is true, that the reluctance to abstain from animal food, in those who have been long accustomed to its stimulus, is so great in some persons of weak minds, as to be scarcely overcome; but this is far from bringing any argument in its favour. A lamb, which was fed for some time on flesh by a ship's crew, refused its natural diet at the end of the voyage. There are numerous instances of horses, sheep, oxen, and even wood-pigeons, having been taught to live upon flesh, until they have loathed their accustomed aliment. Young children evidently prefer pastry, oranges, apples, and other fruit, to the flesh of animals; until, by the gradual depravation of the digestive organs, the free use of vegetables has for a time produced serious inconveniences; *for a time*, I say, since there never was an instance wherein a change from spirituous liquors and animal food, to vegetables and pure water, has failed ultimately to invigorate the body, by rendering its juices bland and consentaneous, and to restore to the mind that cheerfulness and elasticity, which not one in fifty possess on the present system. A love of strong liquors is also with difficulty taught to infants. Almost everyone remembers the wry faces, which the first glass of port produced. Unsophisticated instinct is invariably unerring; but to decide on the fitness of animal food, from the perverted appetites which its constrained adoption produces, is to make the criminal a judge in his own cause: it is even worse, it is appealing to the infatuated drunkard in a question of the salubrity[3] of brandy.

What is the cause of morbid action in the animal system? Not the air we breathe, for our fellow denizens of nature, breathe the same uninjured; not the water we drink, if remote from the pollutions of man and his inventions, for the animals drink it too; not the earth we tread upon; not the unobscured sight of glorious nature, in the wood, the field, or the expanse of sky and ocean; nothing that we are or do in common, with the undiseased inhabitants of the forest. Something then wherein we differ from them: our habit of altering our food by fire, so that our appetite is no longer a just criterion for the fitness of its gratification. Except in

---

[1] *wether* Castrated male sheep or goat.

[2] *Plutarch* Lucius Mestrius Plutarchus (c. 46–120 CE), Greek biographer, historian, and essayist.

---

[3] *salubrity* Conduciveness to health and well-being.

children there remain no traces of that instinct, which determines in all other animals what aliment is natural or otherwise, and so perfectly obliterated are they in the reasoning adults of our species, that it has become necessary to urge considerations drawn from comparative anatomy to prove that we are naturally frugivorous.

Crime is madness. Madness is disease. Whenever the cause of disease shall be discovered, the root from which all vice and misery have so long overshadowed the globe, will lay bare to the axe. All the exertions of man, from that moment, may be considered as tending to the clear profit of his species. No sane mind in a sane body resolves upon a real crime. It is a man of violent passions, blood-shot eyes, and swollen veins, that alone can grasp the knife of murder. The system of a simple diet promises no Utopian advantages. It is no mere reform of legislation, whilst the furious passions and evil propensities of the human heart, in which it had its origin, are still unassuaged. It strikes at the root of all evil, and is an experiment which may be tried with success, not alone by nations, but by small societies, families, and even individuals. In no cases has a return to vegetable diet produced the slightest injury; in most it has been attended with changes undeniably beneficial. Should ever a physician be born with the genius of Locke,[1] I am persuaded that he might trace all bodily and mental derangements to our unnatural habits, as clearly as that philosopher has traced all knowledge to sensation. What prolific sources of disease are not those mineral and vegetable poisons that have been introduced for its extirpation! How many thousands have become murderers and robbers, bigots and domestic tyrants, dissolute and abandoned adventurers, from the use of fermented liquors; who, had they slaked their thirst only at the mountain stream, would have lived but to diffuse the happiness of their own unperverted feelings. How many groundless opinions and absurd institutions have not received a general sanction, from the sottishness[2] and intemperance of individuals! Who will assert, that had the populace of Paris drank at the pure source of the Seine, and satisfied their hunger at the ever-furnished table of vegetable nature, that they would have lent their brutal suffrage to the proscription-list of Robespierre?[3] Could a set of men, whose passions were not perverted by unnatural stimuli, look with coolness on an auto da fé?[4] Is it to be believed that a being of gentle feelings, rising from his meal of roots, would take delight in sports of blood? Was Nero a man of temperate life? Could you read calm health in his cheek, flushed with ungovernable propensities of hatred for the human race? Did Muley Ismael's[5] pulse beat evenly, was his skin transparent, did his eyes beam with healthfulness, and its invariable concomitants cheerfulness and benignity? Though history has decided none of these questions, a child could not hesitate to answer in the negative. Surely the bile-suffused cheek of Buonaparte,[6] his wrinkled brow, and yellow eye, the ceaseless inquietude of his nervous system, speak no less plainly the character of his unresting ambition than his murders and his victories. It is impossible, had Buonaparte descended from a race of vegetable feeders, that he could have had either the inclination or the power to ascend the throne of the Bourbons.[7] The desire of tyranny could scarcely be excited in the individual, the power to tyrannize would certainly not be delegated by a society, neither frenzied by inebriation, nor rendered impotent and irrational by disease. Pregnant indeed with inexhaustible calamity, is the renunciation of instinct, as it concerns our physical nature; arithmetic cannot enumerate, nor reason perhaps suspect, the multitudinous sources of disease in civilized life. Even common water,

---

[1] *Locke* John Locke (1632–1704), English philosopher, physician, and Enlightenment thinker.

[2] *sottishness* Drunkenness.

[3] *Robespierre* Maximilien François Marie Isidore de Robespierre (1758–94), prominent French revolutionary and architect of the Reign of Terror (1793–94).

[4] *auto da fé* Ritual of public penance for heretics and apostates during the Inquisition; literally, it translates to "act of faith." The most common example of auto da fé was burning at the stake.

[5] *Muley Ismael* I.e., Moulay Ismail, Moroccan sultan (c. 1645–1727), characterized by European writers as extremely cruel.

[6] *Buonaparte* Napoleon Bonaparte (1769–1821), military and political leader of France from 1799 to 1814.

[7] *Bourbons* Powerful and influential European royal family.

that apparently innoxious pabulum,[1] when corrupted by the filth of populous cities, is a deadly and insidious destroyer. Who can wonder that all the inducements held out by God himself in the Bible to virtue, should have been vainer than a nurse's tale; and that those dogmas, apparently favourable to the intolerant and angry passions, should have alone been deemed essential; whilst Christians are in the daily practice of all those habits, which have infected with disease and crime, not only the reprobate sons, but these favoured children of the common Father's love. Omnipotence itself could not save them from the consequences of this original and universal sin.

There is no disease, bodily or mental, which adoption of vegetable diet and pure water has not infallibly mitigated, wherever the experiment has been fairly tried. Debility is gradually converted into strength, disease into healthfulness; madness in all its hideous variety, from the ravings of the fettered maniac, to the unaccountable irrationalities of ill temper, that make a hell of domestic life, into a calm and considerate evenness of temper, that alone might offer a certain pledge of the future moral reformation of society. On a natural system of diet, old age would be our last and our only malady; the term of our existence would be protracted; we should enjoy life, and no longer preclude others from the enjoyment of it. All sensational delights would be infinitely more exquisite and perfect. The very sense of being would then be a continued pleasure, such as we now feel it in some few and favoured moments of our youth. By all that is sacred in our hopes for the human race, I conjure those who love happiness and truth, to give a fair trial to the vegetable system. Reasoning is surely superfluous on a subject, whose merits an experience of six months would set for ever at rest. But it is only among the enlightened and benevolent, that so great a sacrifice of appetite and prejudice can be expected, even though its ultimate excellence should not admit of dispute.

It is found easier, by the short-sighted victims of disease, to palliate their torments by medicine, than to prevent them by regimen. The vulgar of all ranks are invariably sensual and indocile; yet I cannot but feel myself persuaded, that when the benefits of vegetable diet are mathematically proved; when it is as clear, that those who live naturally are exempt from premature death, as that nine is not one, the most sottish of mankind will feel a preference towards a long and tranquil, contrasted with a short and painful life. On the average, out of sixty persons, four die in three years. In April 1814, a statement will be given, that sixty persons, all having lived more than three years on vegetables and pure water, are then *in perfect health*. More than two years have now elapsed; *not one of them has died*; no such example will be found in any sixty persons taken at random. Seventeen persons of all ages (the families of Dr. Lambe[2] and Mr. Newton) have lived for seven years on this diet, without a death and almost without the slightest illness. Surely when we consider that some of these were infants, and one a martyr to asthma now nearly subdued, we may challenge any seventeen persons taken at random in this city to exhibit a parallel case. Those who may have been excited to question the rectitude of established habits of diet, by these loose remarks, should consult Mr. Newton's luminous and eloquent essay. It is from that book, and from the conversation of its excellent and enlightened author, that I have derived the materials which I here present to the public.

When these proofs come fairly before the world, and are clearly seen by all who understand arithmetic, it is scarcely possible that abstinence from aliments demonstrably pernicious should not become universal.

In proportion to the number of proselytes, so will be the weight of evidence, and when a thousand persons can be produced living on vegetables and distilled water, who have to dread no disease but old age, the world will be compelled to regard animal flesh and fermented liquors, as slow, but certain poisons. The change which would be produced by simpler habits on political economy is sufficiently remarkable. The monopolizing

[1] *pabulum* Food, especially as a solution of nutrients suitable for absorption.

[2] *Dr. Lambe* William Lambe (1765–1847), author of *Reports on the Effects of Peculiar Regimen in Scirrhous Tumours and Cancerous Ulcers* (1809) and early advocate of a vegetarian diet.

eater of animal flesh would no longer destroy his constitution by devouring an acre at a meal, and many loaves of bread would cease to contribute to gout, madness and apoplexy,[1] in the shape of a pint of porter, or a dram of gin, when appeasing the long-protracted famine of the hard-working peasant's hungry babes. The quantity of nutritious vegetable matter, consumed in fattening the carcass of an ox, would afford ten times the sustenance, undepraving indeed, and incapable of generating disease, if gathered immediately from the bosom of the earth.

The most fertile districts of the habitable globe are now actually cultivated by men for animals, at a delay and waste of aliment absolutely incapable of calculation. It is only the wealthy that can, to any great degree, even now, indulge the unnatural craving for dead flesh, and they pay for the greater license of the privilege by subjection to supernumerary diseases. Again, the spirit of the nation that should take the lead in this great reform, would insensibly become agricultural; commerce, with all its vice, selfishness, and corruption, would gradually decline; more natural habits would produce gentler manners, and the excessive complication of political relations would be so far simplified, that every individual might feel and understand why he loved his country, and took a personal interest in its welfare. How would England, for example, depend on the caprices of foreign rulers, if she contained within herself all the necessaries, and despised whatever they possessed of the luxuries of life? How could they starve her into compliance with their views? Of what consequence would it be, that they refused to take her woolen manufactures, when large and fertile tracts of the island ceased to be allotted to the waste of pasturage? On a natural system of diet, we should require no spices from India; no wines from Portugal, Spain, France, or Madeira; none of those multitudinous articles of luxury, for which every corner of the globe is rifled, and which are the causes of so much individual rivalship, such calamitous and sanguinary national disputes.

In the history of modern times, the avarice of commercial monopoly, no less than the ambition of weak and wicked chiefs, seems to have fomented the universal discord, to have added stubbornness to the mistakes of cabinets, and indocility to the infatuation of the people. Let it ever be remembered, that it is the direct influence of commerce to make the interval between the richest and the poorest man wider and more unconquerable. Let it be remembered, that it is a foe to every thing of real worth and excellence in the human character. The odious and disgusting aristocracy of wealth, is built upon the ruins of all that is good in chivalry or republicanism; and luxury is the forerunner of a barbarism scarce capable of cure. Is it impossible to realize a state of society, where all the energies of man shall be directed to the production of his solid happiness?

Certainly, if this advantage (the object of all political speculation) be in any degree attainable, it is attainable only by a community, which holds out no factitious incentives to the avarice and ambition of the few, and which is internally organized for the liberty, security and comfort of the many. None must be entrusted with power (and money is the completest species of power) who do not stand pledged to use it exclusively for the general benefit. But the use of animal flesh and fermented liquors, directly militates with this equality of the rights of man. The peasant cannot gratify these fashionable cravings without leaving his family to starve. Without disease and war, those sweeping curtailers of population, pasturage would include a waste too great to be afforded. The labour requisite to support a family is far lighter than is usually supposed. The peasantry work, not only for themselves, but for the aristocracy, the army and the manufacturers.

The advantage of a reform in diet is obviously greater than that of any other. It strikes at the root of the evil. To remedy the abuses of legislation, before we annihilate the propensities by which they are produced, is to suppose, that by taking away the effect, the cause will cease to operate. But the efficacy of this system depends entirely on the proselytism of individuals, and grounds its merits as a benefit to the community, upon the total change of the dietetic habits in its members. It

---

[1]   *apoplexy*   Stroke.

proceeds securely from a number of particular cases, to one that is universal, and has this advantage over the contrary mode, that one error does not invalidate all that has gone before.

Let not too much, however, be expected from this system. The healthiest among us is not exempt from hereditary disease. The most symmetrical, athletic, and long-lived, is a being inexpressibly inferior to what he would have been, had not the unnatural habits of his ancestors accumulated for him a certain portion of malady and deformity. In the most perfect specimen of civilized man, something is still found wanting, by the physiological critic. Can a return to nature, then, instantaneously eradicate predispositions that have been slowly taking root in the silence of innumerable ages? Indubitably not. All that I contend for is, that from the moment of the relinquishing all unnatural habits, no new disease is generated; and that the predisposition to hereditary maladies, gradually perishes, for want of its accustomed supply. In cases of consumption, cancer, gout, asthma, and scrofula, such is the invariable tendency of a diet of vegetables and pure water.

Those who may be induced by these remarks to give the vegetable system a fair trial, should, in the first place, date the commencement of their practice from the moment of their conviction. All depends upon breaking through a pernicious habit, resolutely and at once. Dr. Trotter[1] asserts that no drunkard was ever reformed by gradually relinquishing his dram. Animal flesh in its effects on the human stomach is analogous to a dram. It is similar in the kind, though differing in the degree, of its operation. The proselyte to a pure diet, must be warned to expect a temporary diminution of muscular strength. The subtraction of a powerful stimulus will suffice to account for this event. But it is only temporary, and is succeeded by an equable capability for exertion, far surpassing his former various and fluctuating strength. Above all, he will acquire an easiness of breathing, by which the same exertion is performed, with a remarkable exemption from that painful and difficult panting now felt by almost every one, after hastily climbing an ordinary mountain. He will be equally capable of bodily exertion, or mental application, after as before his simple meal. He will feel none of the narcotic effects of ordinary diet. Irritability, the direct consequence of exhausting stimuli, would yield to the power of natural and tranquil impulses. He will no longer pine under the lethargy of ennui, that unconquerable weariness of life, more dreaded than death itself. He will escape the epidemic madness, that broods over its own injurious notions of the Deity, and "realizes the hell that priests and beldams feign."[2] Every man forms, as it were, his god from his own character; to the divinity of one of simple habits, no offering would be more acceptable than the happiness of his creatures. He would be incapable of hating or persecuting others for the love of God. He will find, moreover, a system of simple diet to be a system of perfect epicurism.[3] He will no longer be incessantly occupied in blunting and destroying those organs, from which he expects his gratification.

The pleasures of taste to be derived from a dinner of potatoes, beans, peas, turnips, lettuce, with a dessert of apples, gooseberries, strawberries, currants, raspberries, and in winter, oranges, apples and pears, is far greater than is supposed. Those who wait until they can eat this plain fare, with the sauce of appetite, will scarcely join with the hypocritical sensualist at a lord mayor's feast, who declaims against the pleasures of the table. Solomon[4] kept a thousand concubines, and owned in despair that all was vanity. The man whose happiness is constituted by the society of one amiable woman, would find some difficulty in sympathizing with the disappointment of this venerable debauchee.

I address myself not only to the young enthusiast: the ardent devotee of truth and virtue; the pure and

---

[1] *Dr. Trotter* Thomas Trotter (c. 1760–1832), a specialist in the nervous temperament and addiction, was an associate of William Lambe and a fellow advocate of a vegetarian diet.

[2] *realizes the hell ... beldams feign* From Shelley's *Queen Mab* (1813), 2.309, a philosophical poem in nine cantos.

[3] *epicurism* Devotion or adaptation to luxurious tastes, especially in drinking and eating.

[4] *Solomon* In the Bible, a king of Israel and son of David.

passionate moralist, yet unvitiated[1] by the contagion of the world. He will embrace a pure system, from its abstract truth, its beauty, its simplicity, and its promise of wide-extended benefit; unless custom has turned poison into food, he will hate the brutal pleasures of the chase by instinct; it will be a contemplation full of horror and disappointment to his mind, that beings capable of the gentlest and most admirable sympathies, should take delight in the death-pangs and last convulsions of dying animals. The elderly man, whose youth has been poisoned by intemperance, or who has lived with apparent moderation, and is afflicted with a variety of painful maladies, would find his account in a beneficial change produced without the risk of poisonous medicines. The mother, to whom the perpetual restlessness of disease, and unaccountable deaths incident to her children, are the causes of incurable unhappiness, would on this diet experience the satisfaction of beholding their perpetual healths and natural playfulness.

The most valuable lives are daily destroyed by diseases, that it is dangerous to palliate and impossible to cure by medicine. How much longer will man continue to pimp for the gluttony of death, his most insidious, implacable, and eternal foe? The proselyte to a simple and natural diet who desires health, must from the moment of his conversion attend to these rules—

NEVER TAKE ANY SUBSTANCE INTO THE STOMACH THAT ONCE HAD LIFE.
DRINK NO LIQUID BUT WATER RESTORED TO ITS ORIGINAL PURITY BY DISTILLATION.

from "An Act to Prevent the Cruel and Improper Treatment of Cattle" (1822)

This law was the first animal protection law passed by a national legislature. Largely the work of Member of Parliament Richard "Humanity Dick" Martin, the Act was the result of many years of effort on the part of Martin and others. It was significant not least of all for treating the offences it named as being

against the animals themselves, not against their owners; the implication of the Act was that non-human animals could have legal status other than as property. The bill was followed in 1835 and 1849 by other laws relating to the cruel and improper treatment of animals; provisions of those laws included the extension of legal protection to other animals, including bulls and dogs (though not to wild animals).

Whereas it is expedient to prevent the cruel and improper Treatment of Horses, Mares, Geldings, Mules, Asses, Cows, Heifers, Steers, Oxen, Sheep, and other Cattle: May it therefore please Your Majesty, by and with the Advice and Consent of the Lords Spiritual and Temporal, and Commons, in this present Parliament assembled, and by the Authority of the same, That if any person or persons shall wantonly and cruelly beat, abuse, or ill-treat any Horse, Mare, Gelding, Mule, Ass, Ox, Cow, Heifer, Steer, Sheep, or other Cattle, and Complaint on Oath thereof be made to any Justice of the Peace or other Magistrate within whose Jurisdiction such Offence shall be committed, it shall be lawful for such Justice of the Peace or other Magistrate to issue his Summons or Warrant, at his Discretion, to bring the party or parties so complained of before him, or any other Justice of the Peace or other Magistrate of the County, City, or place within which such Justice of the Peace or other Magistrate has Jurisdiction, who shall examine upon Oath any Witness or Witnesses who shall appear or be produced to give Information touching such Offence, (which Oath the said Justice of the Peace or other Magistrate is hereby authorized and required to administer); and if the party or parties accused shall be convicted of any such Offence, either by his, her, or their own Confession, or upon such Information as aforesaid, he, she, or they so convicted shall forfeit and pay any Sum not exceeding Five Pounds, not less than Ten Shillings, to His Majesty, His Heirs and Successors; and if the person or persons so convicted shall refuse or not be able forthwith to pay the Sum forfeited, every

[1] *unvitiated* Uncorrupted.

such Offender shall, by Warrant under the Hand and Seal of some Justice or Justices of the Peace or other Magistrate within whose Jurisdiction the person offending shall be Convicted, be committed to the House of Correction or some other Prison within the Jurisdiction within which the Offence shall have been committed, there to be kept without Bail or Mainprise[1] for any Time not exceeding Three Months.

---

[1] *Mainprise* Writ to a legal officer directing that security be held in order to ensure the appearance of a prisoner, who would then be released pending trial. Unlike bail, such securities might be other than monetary.

SAMUEL TAYLOR COLERIDGE

<u>1772 – 1834</u>

Samuel Taylor Coleridge is one of the most important figures of English Romanticism. Over the course of a few years, when in his mid-twenties, he composed poems that continue to be regarded as central to the English canon, among them "The Rime of the Ancient Mariner," "Frost at Midnight," and the fragment "Kubla Khan." Later in his life, his critical and philosophical writing earned him a place as one of the most profound thinkers of the nineteenth century.

Born in 1772, Coleridge was the youngest son of the vicar of Ottery St. Mary, the Rev. John Coleridge, and his wife, Anna Bowdon. He was a voracious reader with a mind that he described as "habituated to *the Vast*." When his father died, his mother arranged for nine-year-old Samuel to be sent to Christ's Hospital in London, a school founded to educate the promising sons of the poor. Although he received an excellent education at Christ's, Coleridge remained ambivalent about the school long after he left, continuing to feel injured by the fact that he had been a "charity boy."

In 1791, Coleridge entered Jesus College, Cambridge, where his intellectual abilities and academic success were matched only by his facility in running up debts and his increasing despair at his financial situation. He eventually attempted to escape his financial problems by enlisting (under the name Silas Tomkyn Comberbache), but he was rescued by his brother George from both the army and financial distress. In 1794 he met Robert Southey, then an Oxford undergraduate, and the two recognized a shared interest in poetry and radical political ideas. They hatched a plan to found a communitarian settlement in Pennsylvania to be run under a system they called "Pantisocracy." Both the plan and the friendship, however, foundered over the question of what role women and servants should play (Coleridge insisted on a completely egalitarian community; Southey did not). In his early exuberance for the scheme Coleridge became engaged to Sara Fricker, the sister of Southey's fiancée, and he felt bound to honor the commitment even though his feeling for her quickly waned. They married in 1795 but after a brief period of happiness they became progressively more miserable, finally separating in 1807. The marriage produced four children.

Coleridge began a short-lived liberal periodical in 1796 called *The Watchman*. He also published his first poetic collection, *Poems on Various Subjects*, which contained the poem that would later be titled "The Eolian Harp." Almost destitute, he was saved by a yearly pension granted him by Tom and Josiah Wedgwood, sons of the famous potter. The following year he and William Wordsworth began a troubled but lifelong friendship, the first fruit of which was the joint volume *Lyrical Ballads*, which opened with Coleridge's "The Rime of the Ancyent Marinere" (revised and retitled in 1817). Shortly afterward he accompanied Wordsworth and his sister Dorothy to Germany, where he immersed himself in German philosophy.

Returning to England in 1799, Coleridge joined Wordsworth in the Lake District. That same year he met Sara Hutchinson, Wordsworth's future sister-in-law, and became infatuated with her. The relationship between the two remained platonic, but it magnified Coleridge's estrangement from his wife, and the situation was made worse by his increasing dependence on laudanum, opium mixed with alcohol. From 1802 onward Coleridge spent only brief periods with his family. In 1804 he set off for Malta, where he took a post in the British government. From this time forth he became progressively more conservative, eventually going so far as to deny entirely his early liberal leanings. After a year and a half he returned to England penniless.

From 1808 to 1818, Coleridge intermittently delivered lectures with topics that ranged from German philosophy to current educational controversies. The highlight was a series he gave on Shakespeare and Milton, which displayed all the brilliance of his critical skills. These lectures offered incisive analyses of aspects of Shakespeare's plays, from a consideration of love in *Romeo and Juliet* to an anatomization of Hamlet's paradoxical psychology, and concluded with a masterful examination of *Paradise Lost*. During this period Coleridge, who had long been interested in newspaper writing, also undertook the most important of his journalistic ventures: *The Friend* (1809–10), a weekly newspaper he largely wrote himself. His drama, *Remorse*, was staged at the Drury Lane Theatre in 1813.

In 1816 Coleridge took up residence in Highgate with the family of the young doctor James Gillman. He asked to stay for a month; he remained for the rest of his life. The situation offered a stable environment, and Coleridge began publishing regularly. His Gothic ballad "Christabel," long known to other writers through private recitation (and an influence on Walter Scott's "The Lay of the Last Minstrel" and Lord Byron's "The Siege of Corinth"), was published in a collection with "Kubla Khan" and "The Pains of Sleep" in 1816, through Byron's enthusiastic support. Soon afterward Coleridge published *Sybilline Leaves*, a collection of his previous poems (including a newly revised *Ancient Mariner* with a marginal gloss) and the long work *Biographia Literaria*.

The first volume of *Biographia Literaria* is autobiographical, detailing (among other events) Coleridge's education and his first involvement with Wordsworth. The volume also begins to delve into literary analysis as, for example, in the famous passage in Chapter 13, in which Coleridge differentiates between imagination and fancy, defining the qualities of each and declaring imagination superior. The second volume consists almost entirely of literary criticism, both formal and philosophical, much of it focusing on Wordsworth's poetry. In both volumes, Coleridge anatomizes both poetry and poetic production, considering not only formal elements but also the psychology of the creative process.

Coleridge's genius and importance were gradually acknowledged by a considerable number of his contemporaries, and the "Sage of Highgate" began to be viewed as an important thinker. This opinion was cemented by the publication of *Aids to Reflection* (1825), which stressed the role of the personal in Christian faith, and *On the Constitution of Church and State* (1830), which emphasized the importance of national culture and defined the class of intellectuals needed to protect it. This latter book in particular had a profound influence on such authors as Matthew Arnold and Thomas Carlyle.

From 1832 onward Coleridge became increasingly ill, although this did not prevent him from helping to prepare *Poetica   oetry—he died shortly after its publication. *Table Talk*, a p   remarks on miscellaneous topics, appeared the following yea

Coleridge's poetry often presents Gothic story material in psychologically suggestive ways, delineating the mind as it explores itself and its relation to the larger world. His more uncanny poems, such as "The Rime of the Ancient Mariner," excite tension in the reader both through their handling of narrative and in the psychological complexity of their characters and relationships. Poems such as "Frost at Midnight" mingle contemplation and description to produce a richly interrelated whole, a style which influenced not only Wordsworth (specifically in "Tintern Abbey"), but also poets to the present day.

⌘ ⌘ ⌘

The Eolian Harp[1]

Composed at Clevedon, Somersetshire

My pensive Sara![2] thy soft cheek reclined
    Thus on mine arm, most soothing sweet it is
To sit beside our Cot,° our Cot o'ergrown   *cottage*
With white-flower'd Jasmin, and the broad-leav'd Myrtle,
5 (Meet emblems they of Innocence and Love!)
And watch the clouds, that late were rich with light,
Slow saddening round, and mark the star of eve
Serenely brilliant (such should Wisdom be)
Shine opposite! How exquisite the scents
10 Snatch'd from yon bean-field! and the world *so* hush'd!
The stilly murmur of the distant Sea
Tells us of silence.

           And that simplest Lute,
Placed length-ways in the clasping casement, hark!
How by the desultory breeze caress'd,
15 Like some coy maid half yielding to her lover,
It pours such sweet upbraiding, as must needs
Tempt to repeat the wrong! And now, its strings
Boldlier swept, the long sequacious° notes   *unvarying*
Over delicious surges sink and rise,
20 Such a soft floating witchery of sound
As twilight Elfins make, when they at eve
Voyage on gentle gales from Fairy-Land,
Where Melodies round honey-dropping flowers,

Footless and wild, like birds of Paradise,[3]
25 Nor pause, nor perch, hovering on untam'd wing!
O! the one Life within us and abroad,
Which meets all motion and becomes its soul,
A light in sound, a sound-like power in light,
Rhythm in all thought, and joyance every where—
30 Methinks, it should have been impossible
Not to love all things in a world so fill'd;
Where the breeze warbles, and the mute still air
Is Music slumbering on her instrument.

    And thus, my Love! as on the midway slope
35 Of yonder hill I stretch my limbs at noon,
Whilst through my half-clos'd eye-lids I behold
The sunbeams dance, like diamonds, on the main,
And tranquil muse upon tranquillity;
Full many a thought uncall'd and undetain'd,
40 And many idle flitting phantasies,
Traverse my indolent and passive brain,
As wild and various, as the random gales
That swell and flutter on this subject Lute!
    And what if all of animated nature
45 Be but organic Harps diversely fram'd,
That tremble into thought, as o'er them sweeps
Plastic and vast, one intellectual breeze,
At once the Soul of each, and God of all?
    But thy more serious eye a mild reproof
50 Darts, O belovéd Woman! nor such thoughts
Dim and unhallow'd dost thou not reject,

---

[1] *Eolian Harp* Musical instrument named after Æolus, Greek god of the winds; the music of the harp is created by exposure to the wind passing through it.

[2] *Sara* Sara Fricker, whom Coleridge had married in 1795.

---

[3] *birds of Paradise* New Guinean birds of brilliant plumage, thought by Europeans to have no feet.

And biddest me walk humbly with my God.
Meek Daughter in the family of Christ!
Well hast thou said and holily disprais'd
These shapings of the unregenerate mind;
Bubbles that glitter as they rise and break
On vain Philosophy's aye-babbling spring.
For never guiltless may I speak of Him,
The Incomprehensible! save when with awe
I praise Him, and with Faith that inly *feels*;
Who with His saving mercies healéd me,
A sinful and most miserable man,
Wilder'd and dark, and gave me to possess
Peace, and this Cot, and thee, heart-honour'd Maid!
—1795

Fears in Solitude

Written in April 1798, During the Alarm
of An Invasion[1]

A green and silent spot, amid the hills,
A small and silent dell! O'er stiller place
No singing sky-lark ever poised himself.
The hills are heathy, save that swelling slope,
Which hath a gay and gorgeous covering on,
All golden with the never-bloomless furze,°   *evergreen shrub*
Which now blooms most profusely: but the dell,
Bathed by the mist, is fresh and delicate
As vernal corn-field, or the unripe flax,
When, through its half-transparent stalks, at eve,
The level sunshine glimmers with green light.
O! 'tis a quiet spirit-healing nook!
Which all, methinks, would love; but chiefly he,
The humble man, who, in his youthful years,
Knew just so much of folly, as had made
His early manhood more securely wise!
Here he might lie on fern or withered heath,
While from the singing lark (that sings unseen
The minstrelsy that solitude loves best),
And from the sun, and from the breezy air,

Sweet influences trembled o'er his frame;
And he, with many feelings, many thoughts,
Made up a meditative joy, and found
Religious meanings in the forms of Nature!
And so, his senses gradually wrapt
In a half sleep, he dreams of better worlds,
And dreaming hears thee still, O singing lark,
That singest like an angel in the clouds!

My God! it is a melancholy thing
For such a man, who would full fain preserve
His soul in calmness, yet perforce must feel
For all his human brethren—O my God!
It weighs upon the heart, that he must think
What uproar and what strife may now be stirring
This way or that way o'er these silent hills—
Invasion, and the thunder and the shout,
And all the crash of onset; fear and rage,
And undetermined conflict—even now,
Even now, perchance, and in his native isle:
Carnage and screams beneath this blessed sun!
We have offended, O! my countrymen!
We have offended very grievously,
And have been tyrannous. From east to west
A groan of accusation pierces Heaven!
The wretched plead against us; multitudes
Countless and vehement, the sons of God,
Our brethren! like a cloud that travels on,
Steamed up from Cairo's swamps of pestilence,
Even so, my countrymen! have we gone forth
And borne to distant tribes slavery and pangs,
And, deadlier far, our vices, whose deep taint
With slow perdition murders the whole man,
His body and his soul! Meanwhile, at home,
All individual dignity and power
Engulfed in Courts, Committees, Institutions,
Associations and Societies,
A vain, speech-mounting, speech-reporting Guild,
One Benefit-Club for mutual flattery,
We have drunk up, demure as at a grace,
Pollutions from the brimming cup of wealth;
Contemptuous of all honourable rule,
Yet bartering freedom and the poor man's life

---
[1] *Invasion*   By the French, who threatened an attack on Wales.

For gold, as at a market! The sweet words
Of Christian promise, words that even yet
65 Might stem destruction, were they wisely preached,
Are muttered o'er by men, whose tones proclaim
How flat and wearisome they feel their trade:
Rank scoffers some, but most too indolent
To deem them falsehoods, or to know their truth.
70 O! blasphemous! the Book of Life is made
A superstitious instrument, on which
We gabble o'er the oaths we mean to break,
For all must swear[1]—all and in every place,
College and wharf, council and justice-court;
75 All, all must swear, the briber and the bribed,
Merchant and lawyer, senator and priest,
The rich, the poor, the old man and the young;
All, all make up one scheme of perjury,
That faith doth reel; the very name of God
80 Sounds like a juggler's charm; and bold with joy,
Forth from his dark and lonely hiding-place,
(Portentous sight!) the owlet Atheism,
Sailing on obscene wings athwart the noon,
Drops his blue-fringéd lids, and holds them close,
85 And hooting at the glorious sun in Heaven,
Cries out, "Where is it?"

                 Thankless too for peace,
(Peace long preserved by fleets and perilous seas)
Secure from actual warfare, we have loved
To swell the war-whoop, passionate for war!
90 Alas! for ages ignorant of all
Its ghastlier workings, (famine or blue plague,
Battle, or siege, or flight thro' wintry snows,)
We, this whole people, have been clamorous
For war and bloodshed; animating sports,
95 The which we pay for as a thing to talk of,
Spectators and not combatants! No guess
Anticipative of a wrong unfelt,
No speculation on contingency,
However dim and vague, too vague and dim
100 To yield a justifying cause; and forth,

---

[1] *all must swear* According to the Test and Corporation Acts, all public officials were required to swear allegiance to the Church of England. (Thus there would be no Catholics, Nonconformists, or Jews in office.)

(Stuffed out with big preamble, holy names,
And adjurations° of the God in Heaven,)   *appeal*
We send our mandates for the certain death
Of thousands and ten thousands! Boys and girls,
105 And women, that would groan to see a child
Pull off an insect's leg, all read of war,
The best amusement for our morning meal!
The poor wretch, who has learnt his only prayers
From curses, who knows scarcely words enough
110 To ask a blessing from his Heavenly Father,
Becomes a fluent phraseman, absolute
And technical in victories and defeats,
And all our dainty terms for fratricide;
Terms which we trundle smoothly o'er our tongues
115 Like mere abstractions, empty sounds to which
We join no feeling and attach no form!
As if the soldier died without a wound;
As if the fibres of this godlike frame
Were gored without a pang; as if the wretch,
120 Who fell in battle, doing bloody deeds,
Passed off to Heaven, translated and not killed;
As though he had no wife to pine for him,
No God to judge him! Therefore, evil days
Are coming on us, O my countrymen!
125 And what if all-avenging Providence,
Strong and retributive, should make us know
The meaning of our words, force us to feel
The desolation and the agony
Of our fierce doings?

                 Spare us yet awhile,
130 Father and God! O! spare us yet awhile!
Oh! let not English women drag their flight
Fainting beneath the burthen of their babes,
Of the sweet infants, that but yesterday
Laughed at the breast! Sons, brothers, husbands, all
135 Who ever gazed with fondness on the forms
Which grew up with you round the same fire-side,
And all who ever heard the sabbath-bells
Without the infidel's scorn, make yourselves pure!
Stand forth! be men! repel an impious foe,
140 Impious and false, a light yet cruel race,
Who laugh away all virtue, mingling mirth

With deeds of murder; and still promising
Freedom, themselves too sensual to be free,
Poison life's amities, and cheat the heart
Of faith and quiet hope, and all that soothes,
5 And all that lifts the spirit! Stand we forth;
Render them back upon the insulted ocean,
And let them toss as idly on its waves
As the vile sea-weed, which some mountain-blast
Swept from our shores! And oh! may we return
10 Not with a drunken triumph, but with fear,
Repenting of the wrongs with which we stung
So fierce a foe to frenzy!

              I have told,
O Britons! O my brethren! I have told
15 Most bitter truth, but without bitterness.
Nor deem my zeal or factious or mistimed;
For never can true courage dwell with them,
Who, playing tricks with conscience, dare not look
At their own vices. We have been too long
20 Dupes of a deep delusion! Some, belike,
Groaning with restless enmity, expect
All change from change of constituted power;
As if a Government had been a robe,
On which our vice and wretchedness were tagged
25 Like fancy-points and fringes, with the robe
Pulled off at pleasure. Fondly these attach
A radical causation to a few
Poor drudges of chastising Providence,
Who borrow all their hues and qualities
30 From our own folly and rank wickedness,
Which gave them birth and nursed them. Others,
    meanwhile,
Dote with a mad idolatry; and all
Who will not fall before their images,
And yield them worship, they are enemies
35 Even of their country!

            Such have I been deemed.—
But, O dear Britain! O my Mother Isle!
Needs must thou prove a name most dear and holy
To me, a son, a brother, and a friend,
A husband, and a father! who revere

180 All bonds of natural love, and find them all
Within the limits of thy rocky shores.
O native Britain! O my Mother Isle!
How shouldst thou prove aught else but dear and holy
To me, who from thy lakes and mountain-hills,
185 Thy clouds, thy quiet dales, thy rocks and seas,
Have drunk in all my intellectual life,
All sweet sensations, all ennobling thoughts,
All adoration of the God in nature,
All lovely and all honourable things,
190 Whatever makes this mortal spirit feel
The joy and greatness of its future being?
There lives nor form nor feeling in my soul
Unborrowed from my country! O divine
And beauteous island! thou hast been my sole
195 And most magnificent temple, in the which
I walk with awe, and sing my stately songs,
Loving the God that made me!—

              May my fears,
My filial fears, be vain! and may the vaunts
And menace of the vengeful enemy
200 Pass like the gust, that roared and died away
In the distant tree: which heard, and only heard
In this low dell, bowed not the delicate grass.

    But now the gentle dew-fall sends abroad
The fruit-like perfume of the golden furze:
205 The light has left the summit of the hill,
Though still a sunny gleam lies beautiful,
Aslant the ivied beacon. Now farewell,
Farewell, awhile, O soft and silent spot!
On the green sheep-track, up the heathy hill,
210 Homeward I wind my way; and lo! recalled
From bodings that have well-nigh wearied me,
I find myself upon the brow, and pause
Startled! And after lonely sojourning
In such a quiet and surrounded nook,
215 This burst of prospect, here the shadowy main,
Dim tinted, there the mighty majesty
Of that huge amphitheatre of rich
And elmy fields, seems like society—
Conversing with the mind, and giving it
220 A livelier impulse and a dance of thought!

And now, belovéd Stowey![1] I behold
Thy church-tower, and, methinks, the four huge elms
Clustering, which mark the mansion of my friend;
And close behind them, hidden from my view,
225   Is my own lowly cottage, where my babe ·
And my babe's mother dwell in peace! With light
And quickened footsteps thitherward I tend,
Remembering thee, O green and silent dell!
And grateful, that by nature's quietness
230   And solitary musings, all my heart
Is softened, and made worthy to indulge
Love, and the thoughts that yearn for human kind.
        —1798

Frost at Midnight

The Frost performs its secret ministry,
    Unhelped by any wind. The owlet's cry
Came loud—and hark, again! loud as before.
The inmates of my cottage, all at rest,
5   Have left me to that solitude, which suits
Abstruser musings: save that at my side
My cradled infant slumbers peacefully.
'Tis calm indeed! so calm, that it disturbs
And vexes meditation with its strange
10   And extreme silentness. Sea, hill, and wood,
This populous village! Sea, and hill, and wood,
With all the numberless goings-on of life,
Inaudible as dreams! the thin blue flame
Lies on my low-burnt fire, and quivers not;
15   Only that film,[2] which fluttered on the grate,
Still flutters there, the sole unquiet thing.
Methinks, its motion in this hush of nature
Gives it dim sympathies with me who live,
Making it a companionable form,
20   Whose puny flaps and freaks the idling Spirit
By its own moods interprets, every where
Echo or mirror seeking of itself,

And makes a toy of Thought.

                    But O! how oft,
How oft, at school, with most believing mind,
25   Presageful, have I gazed upon the bars,
To watch that fluttering *stranger*! and as oft
With unclosed lids, already had I dreamt
Of my sweet birth-place, and the old church-tower,
Whose bells, the poor man's only music, rang
30   From morn to evening, all the hot Fair-day,
So sweetly, that they stirred and haunted me
With a wild pleasure, falling on mine ear
Most like articulate sounds of things to come!
So gazed I, till the soothing things, I dreamt,
35   Lulled me to sleep, and sleep prolonged my dreams!
And so I brooded all the following morn,
Awed by the stern preceptor's° face, mine eye   teacher's
Fixed with mock study on my swimming book:
Save if the door half opened, and I snatched
40   A hasty glance, and still my heart leaped up,
For still I hoped to see the *stranger's* face,
Townsman, or aunt, or sister more beloved,
My play-mate when we both were clothed alike!

        Dear Babe, that sleepest cradled by my side,
45   Whose gentle breathings, heard in this deep calm,
Fill up the interspersed vacancies
And momentary pauses of the thought!
My babe so beautiful! it thrills my heart
With tender gladness, thus to look at thee,
50   And think that thou shalt learn far other lore,
And in far other scenes! For I was reared
In the great city, pent 'mid cloisters dim,
And saw nought lovely but the sky and stars.
But *thou*, my babe! shalt wander like a breeze
55   By lakes and sandy shores, beneath the crags
Of ancient mountain, and beneath the clouds,
Which image in their bulk both lakes and shores
And mountain crags: so shalt thou see and hear
The lovely shapes and sounds intelligible
60   Of that eternal language, which thy God
Utters, who from eternity doth teach
Himself in all, and all things in himself.

---

[1]   *Stowey*   Nether Stowey, a village in Somerset where Coleridge lived
for a few years.

[2]   [Coleridge's note]   In all parts of the kingdom these films are called
strangers and supposed to portend the arrival of some absent friend.

Great universal Teacher! he shall mould
Thy spirit, and by giving make it ask.

55   Therefore all seasons shall be sweet to thee,
Whether the summer clothe the general earth
With greenness, or the redbreast sit and sing
Betwixt the tufts of snow on the bare branch
Of mossy apple-tree, while the nigh thatch
70 Smokes in the sun-thaw; whether the eave-drops fall
Heard only in the trances of the blast,
Or if the secret ministry of frost
Shall hang them up in silent icicles,
Quietly shining to the quiet Moon.
—1798, 1829

from *The Rime of the Ancyent Marinere, in Seven Parts*[1]

ARGUMENT

How a Ship having passed the Line was driven by Storms to the cold Country towards the South Pole; and how from thence she made her course to the Tropical Latitude of the Great Pacific Ocean; and of the strange things that befell; and in what manner the Ancyent Marinere came back to his own Country.

PART I

It is an ancyent Marinere,
   And he stoppeth one of three:
"By thy long grey beard and thy glittering eye,
   "Now wherefore stoppest thou me?

5 "The Bridegroom's doors are open'd wide,
   "And I am next of kin;
"The Guests are met, the Feast is set—
   "May'st hear the merry din."

But still he holds the wedding-guest—
10   There was a Ship, quoth he—

"Nay, if thou'st got a laughsome tale,
   "Marinere! Come with me."

He holds him with his skinny hand,
   Quoth he, there was a Ship—
15 "Now get thee hence, thou grey-beard Loon!
   "Or my Staff shall make thee skip."[2]

He holds him with his glittering eye—
   The wedding-guest stood still,
And listens like a three year's child;
20   The Marinere hath his will.[3]

The wedding-guest sate on a stone,
   He cannot chuse but hear:
And thus spake on that ancyent man,
   The bright-eyed Marinere.

25 The Ship was cheer'd, the Harbour clear'd—
   Merrily did we drop
Below the Kirk,° below the Hill,   *church*
   Below the Light-house top.

The Sun came up upon the left,
30   Out of the Sea came he:
And he shone bright, and on the right
   Went down into the Sea.

Higher and higher every day,
   Till over the mast at noon—
35 The wedding-guest here beat his breast,
   For he heard the loud bassoon.

The Bride hath pac'd into the Hall,
   Red as a rose is she;
Nodding their heads before her goes
40   The merry Minstralsy.

The wedding-guest he beat his breast,
    Yet he cannot chuse but hear:
And thus spake on that ancyent Man,
    The bright-eyed Marinere.

45 Listen, Stranger! Storm and Wind,
    A Wind and Tempest strong!
For days and weeks it play'd us freaks—
    Like Chaff we drove along.

Listen, Stranger! Mist and Snow,
50   And it grew wond'rous cauld:
And Ice mast-high came floating by
    As green as Emerauld.

And thro' the drifts the snowy clifts
    Did send a dismal sheen;
55 Ne shapes of men ne beasts we ken—
    The Ice was all between.

The Ice was here, the Ice was there,
    The Ice was all around:
It crack'd and growl'd, and roar'd and howl'd—
60   Like noises of a swound!

At length did cross an Albatross,
    Thorough the Fog it came;
And an° it were a Christian Soul,   *as though*
    We hail'd it in God's name.

65 The Marineres gave it biscuit-worms,
    And round and round it flew:
The Ice did split with a Thunder-fit;
    The Helmsman steer'd us thro'.

And a good south wind sprung up behind,
70   The Albatross did follow;
And every day for food or play
    Came to the Marinere's hollo!

In mist or cloud on mast or shroud
    It perch'd for vespers nine,

75 Whiles all the night thro' fog-smoke white
    Glimmer'd the white moon-shine.

"God save thee, ancyent Marinere!
    "From the fiends that plague thee thus—
"Why look'st thou so?"—with my Cross-bow
80   I shot the Albatross.
   —1798

The Rime of the Ancient Mariner
In Seven Parts[1]

Facile credo, plures esse Naturas invisibiles quam visibiles in rerum universitate. Sed horum omnium familiam quis nobis enarrabit? et gradus et cognationes et discrimina et singulorum munera? Quid agunt? quæ loca habitant? Harum rerum notitiam semper ambivit ingenium humanum, nunquam attigit. Juvat, interea, non diffiteor, quandoque in animo, tanquam in Tabulâ, majoris et melioris mundi imaginem contemplari: ne mens assuefecta hodiernæ vitæ minutiis se contrahat nimis, & tota subsidat in pusillas cogitationes. Sed veritati interea invigilandum est, modusque servandus, ut certa ab incertis, diem a nocte, distinguamus.[2]*—*T. Burnet. *Archaeol. Phil.* p. 68.

PART I

It is an ancient Mariner,
  And he stoppeth one of three.
"By thy long grey beard and glittering eye,
Now wherefore stopp'st thou me?

An ancient Mariner meeteth three Gallants bidden to a wedding feast, and detaineth one.

---

[1] *The Rime … Parts* This version of the poem was published in 1817.

[2] *Facile … distinguamus* From Thomas Burnet's *Archaeologiae Philosophicae* (1692), translated by Mead and Foxton (1736): "I can easily believe, that there are more invisible than visible beings in the universe. But who will declare to us the family of all these, and acquaint us with the agreements, differences, and peculiar talents which are to be found among them? It is true, human wit has always desired a knowledge of these things, though it has never yet attained it. I will own that it is very profitable, sometimes to contemplate in the mind, as in a draught, the image of the greater and better world, lest the soul being accustomed to the trifles of this present life, should contract itself too much, and altogether rest in mean cogitations, but, in the meantime, we must take care to keep to the truth, and observe moderation, that we may distinguish certain from uncertain things, and day from night."

The Bridegroom's doors are opened wide,
And I am next of kin;
The guests are met, the feast is set:
May'st hear the merry din."

He holds him with his skinny hand,
"There was a ship," quoth he.
"Hold off! unhand me, grey-beard loon!"
Eftsoons[1] his hand dropt he.

He holds him with his glittering eye— *The wedding-guest is*
The Wedding-Guest stood still, *spellbound by the eye*
And listens like a three years' child: *of the old sea-faring*
The Mariner hath his will. *man, and constrained*
to hear his tale.

The Wedding-Guest sat on a stone:
He cannot choose but hear;
And thus spake on that ancient man,
The bright-eyed Mariner.

"The ship was cheered, the harbour cleared,
Merrily did we drop *The Mariner tells how*
Below the kirk,[2] below the hill, *the ship sailed southward*
Below the lighthouse top. *with a good wind and*
fair weather, till it
reached the line.

The Sun came up upon the left,
Out of the sea came he!
And he shone bright, and on the right
Went down into the sea.

Higher and higher every day,
Till over the mast at noon—"
The Wedding-Guest here beat his breast,
For he heard the loud bassoon.

The bride hath paced into the hall *The wedding-guest*
Red as a rose is she; *heareth the bridal*
Nodding their heads before her goes *music; but the*
The merry minstrelsy. *mariner continueth*
his tale.

The Wedding-Guest he beat his breast,
Yet he cannot choose but hear;
And thus spake on that ancient man,
40   The bright-eyed Mariner.

"And now the STORM-BLAST came, and he   *The ship drawn*
Was tyrannous and strong: *by a storm toward*
He struck with his o'ertaking wings,   *the south pole.*
And chased us south along.

45   With sloping masts and dipping prow,
As who pursued with yell and blow
Still treads the shadow of his foe,
And forward bends his head,
The ship drove fast, loud roared the blast,
50   And southward aye we fled.

And now there came both mist and snow,
And it grew wondrous cold:
And ice, mast-high, came floating by,
As green as emerald.

And through the drifts the snowy clifts   *The land of ice, and*
Did send a dismal sheen: *of fearful sounds,*
Nor shapes of men nor beasts we ken[3]—   *where no living*
The ice was all between.   *thing was to be seen.*

The ice was here, the ice was there,
60   The ice was all around:
It cracked and growled, and roared and howled,
Like noises in a swound![4]

At length did cross an Albatross,   *Till a great sea-bird,*
Thorough the fog it came;   *called the Albatross,*
65   As if it had been a Christian soul,   *came through the*
We hailed it in God's name.   *snow-fog, and was*
received with great
joy and hospitality.

It ate the food it ne'er had eat,
And round and round it flew.

---

[1] *Eftsoons* At once.

[2] *kirk* Church.

[3] *ken* Recognize.

[4] *swound* Swoon.

The ice did split with a thunder-fit;
70   The helmsman steered us through!

And a good south wind sprung up behind;
The Albatross did follow,
And every day, for food or play,
Came to the Mariner's hollo!

And lo! the Albatross proveth a bird of good omen, and followeth the ship as it returned northward, through fog and floating ice.

75   In mist or cloud, on mast or shroud,
It perched for vespers nine;[1]
Whiles all the night, through fog-smoke white,
Glimmered the white Moon-shine."

"God save thee, ancient Mariner!
80   From the fiends, that plague thee thus!—
Why look'st thou so?"—With my cross-bow
I shot the ALBATROSS.

The ancient Mariner inhospitably killed the pious bird of good omen.

PART 2

The Sun now rose upon the right:
Out of the sea came he,
85   Still hid in mist, and on the left
Went down into the sea.

And the good south wind still blew behind,
But no sweet bird did follow,
Nor any day for food or play
90   Came to the mariners' hollo!

And I had done a hellish thing,
And it would work 'em woe:
For all averred, I had killed the bird
That made the breeze to blow.
95   Ah wretch! said they, the bird to slay,
That made the breeze to blow!

His ship mates cry out against the ancient Mariner, for killing the bird of good luck.

Nor dim nor red, like God's own head,
The glorious Sun uprist:
Then all averred, I had killed the bird
100   That brought the fog and mist.

But when the fog cleared off, they justify the same—and thus make themselves accomplices in the crime.

'Twas right, said they, such birds to slay,
That bring the fog and mist.

The fair breeze blew, the white foam flew,
The furrow followed free;
105   We were the first that ever burst
Into that silent sea.

The fair breeze continues.

Down dropt the breeze, the sails dropt down,
'Twas sad as sad could be;
And we did speak only to break
110   The silence of the sea!

The ship enters the Pacific Ocean and sails northward, even till it reaches the Line.

All in a hot and copper sky,
The bloody Sun, at noon,
Right up above the mast did stand,
No bigger than the Moon.

The ship hath been suddenly becalmed.

115   Day after day, day after day,
We stuck, nor breath nor motion;
As idle as a painted ship
Upon a painted ocean.

Water, water, every where,
120   And all the boards did shrink;
Water, water, every where,
Nor any drop to drink.

And the Albatross begins to be avenged.

The very deep did rot: O Christ!
That ever this should be!
125   Yea, slimy things did crawl with legs
Upon the slimy sea.

About, about, in reel and rout
The death-fires[2] danced at night;
The water, like a witch's oils,
130   Burnt green, and blue and white.

A spirit has followed them; one of the invisible inhabitants of this planet, neither departed souls nor angels; concerning whom the learned Jew, Josephus [continued ...]

And some in dreams assuréd were
Of the Spirit that plagued us so;

---

[1] *vespers nine* I.e., nine evenings. Vespers are evening prayers.

[2] *death-fires* Possibly luminescent plankton.

Nine fathom deep he had followed us
From the land of mist and snow.

and the Platonic Constantinopolitan, Michael Psellus, may be consulted, and there is no climate or element without one or more.

5 And every tongue, through utter drought,
Was withered at the root;
We could not speak, no more than if
We had been choked with soot.

The shipmates in their sore distress, would fain throw the whole guilt on the ancient Mariner; in sign whereof they hang the dead seabird round his neck

Ah! well a-day! what evil looks
10 Had I from old and young!
Instead of the cross, the Albatross
About my neck was hung.

PART 3

There passed a weary time. Each throat
Was parched, and glazed each eye.

The ancient Mariner beholdeth a sign in the element afar off.

15 A weary time! a weary time!
How glazed each weary eye,
When looking westward, I beheld
A something in the sky.

At first it seemed a little speck,
20 And then it seemed a mist;
It moved and moved, and took at last
A certain shape, I wist.

A speck, a mist, a shape, I wist!
And still it neared and neared:
25 And as if it dodged a water-sprite,
It plunged and tacked and veered.

With throat unslacked, with black lips baked,
We could nor laugh nor wail;
Through utter drought all dumb we stood!

At its nearer approach, it seemeth him to be a ship; and at a dear ransom he freeth his speech from the bonds of thirst.

30 I bit my arm, I sucked the blood,
And cried, A sail! a sail!

With throat unslacked, with black lips
    baked,
Agape they heard me call:
Gramercy![1] they for joy did grin,

And all at once their breath drew in,
165 As they were drinking all.

A flash of joy.

See! see! (I cried) she tacks no more!
Hither to work us weal;[2]
Without a breeze, without a tide,
170 She steadies with upright keel!

And horror follows. For can it be a ship that comes onward without wind or tide?

The western wave was all a-flame.
The day was well nigh done!
Almost upon the western wave
Rested the broad bright Sun;
175 When that strange shape drove suddenly
Betwixt us and the Sun.

And straight the Sun was flecked with bars,
(Heaven's Mother send us grace!)
As if through a dungeon-grate he peered
180 With broad and burning face.

It seemeth him but the skeleton of a ship.

Alas! (thought I, and my heart beat loud)
How fast she nears and nears!
Are those *her* sails that glance in the Sun,
Like restless gossameres?

And its ribs are seen as bars on the face of the setting Sun. The spectre-woman and her death-mate, and no other on board the skeleton-ship.

185 Are those *her* ribs through which the Sun
Did peer, as through a grate?
And is that Woman all her crew?
Is that a DEATH? and are there two?
Is DEATH that woman's mate?

190 *Her* lips were red, *her* looks were free,
Her locks were yellow as gold:
Her skin was as white as leprosy,
The Night-mare LIFE-IN-DEATH was she,
Who thicks man's blood with cold.

Like vessel, like crew! Death and Life-in-Death have diced for the ship's crew, and she (the latter) winneth the ancient Mariner.

195 The naked hulk alongside came,
And the twain were casting dice;
"The game is done! I've won! I've won!"
Quoth she, and whistles thrice.

---

[1] *Gramercy* Grant mercy, i.e., may God reward you in his mercy.

[2] *work us weal* Benefit us.

The Sun's rim dips; the stars rush out:
200 At one stride comes the dark;
With far-heard whisper, o'er the sea,
Off shot the spectre-bark.

No twilight within the courts of the sun.

We listened and looked sideways up!
Fear at my heart, as at a cup,
205 My life-blood seemed to sip!
The stars were dim, and thick the night,
The steersman's face by his lamp gleamed white;
From the sails the dews did drip—
Till clomb above the eastern bar
210 The hornéd Moon, with one bright star
Within the nether tip.

At the rising of the Moon,

One after one, by the star-dogged Moon
Too quick for groan or sigh,
Each turned his face with a ghastly pang,
215 And cursed me with his eye.

One after another,

Four times fifty living men,
(And I heard nor sigh nor groan)
With heavy thump, a lifeless lump,
They dropped down one by one.

His ship-mates drop down dead.

220 The souls did from their bodies fly,—
They fled to bliss or woe!
And every soul, it passed me by,
Like the whiz of my cross-bow!

But Life-in-Death begins her work on the ancient Mariner.

PART 4

"I fear thee, ancient Mariner!
225 I fear thy skinny hand!
And thou art long, and lank, and brown,
As is the ribbed sea-sand.[1]

The wedding-guest feareth that a spirit is talking to him;

I fear thee and thy glittering eye,
And thy skinny hand, so brown."—

---

[1] [Coleridge's note] For the two last lines of this stanza, I am
indebted to Mr. WORDSWORTH. It was on a delightful walk from
Nether Stowey to Dulverton, with him and his sister, in the Autumn
of 1797, that this Poem was planned, and in part composed.

230 Fear not, fear not, thou Wedding-Guest!
This body dropt not down.

But the ancient Mariner assureth him of his bodily life, and proceedeth to relate his horrible penance.

Alone, alone, all, all alone,
Alone on a wide wide sea!
And never a saint took pity on
235 My soul in agony.

The many men, so beautiful!
And they all dead did lie:
And a thousand thousand slimy things
Lived on; and so did I.

He despiseth the creatures of the calm,

240 I looked upon the rotting sea,
And drew my eyes away;
I looked upon the rotting deck,
And there the dead men lay.

And envieth that they should live, and so many lie dead.

I looked to heaven, and tried to pray;
245 But or ever a prayer had gusht,
A wicked whisper came, and made
My heart as dry as dust.

I closed my lids, and kept them close,
And the balls like pulses beat;
250 For the sky and the sea, and the sea and the sky
Lay like a load on my weary eye,
And the dead were at my feet.

The cold sweat melted from their limbs,
Nor rot nor reek did they:
255 The look with which they looked on me
Had never passed away.

But the curse liveth for him in the eye of the dead men.

An orphan's curse would drag to hell
A spirit from on high;
But oh! more horrible than that
260 Is the curse in a dead man's eye!
Seven days, seven nights, I saw that curse,
And yet I could not die.

In his loneliness and fixedness, he yearneth towards the journeying Moon, and the stars that still [continued ...]

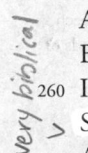

Very biblical

The moving Moon went up the sky,
And no where did abide:

By grace of the holy Mother, the ancient Mariner is refreshed with rain.

The silly[1] buckets on the deck,
That had so long remained,
...reamt that they were filled with dew;
...I awoke, it rained.

...were wet, my throat was cold,
...rments all were dank;
...I had drunken in my dreams,
...d still my body drank.

...moved, and could not feel my limbs:
...I was so light—almost
...I thought that I had died in sleep,
...And was a blesséd ghost.

He heareth sounds, and seeth strange sights and commotions in the sky and the elements.

And soon I heard a roaring wind:
It did not come anear;
310 But with its sound it shook the sails,
That were so thin and sere.

The upper air burst into life!
And a hundred fire-flags sheen,
To and fro they were hurried about!
And to and fro, and in and out,
315 The wan stars danced between.

And the coming wind did roar more loud,
And the sails did sigh like sedge;
And the rain poured down from one black cloud;
320 The Moon was at its edge.

The spell begins to break.

The thick black cloud was cleft, and still
The Moon was at its side:
Like waters shot from some high crag,
The lightning fell with never a jag,
325 A river steep and wide.

The bodies of the ship's crew are inspirited, and the ship moves on;

The loud wind never reached the ship,
Yet now the ship moved on!
Beneath the lightning and the Moon
330 The dead men gave a groan.

---

[1] *silly* Simple.

---

560 SAMUEL TAYLOR COLERIDGE

For gold, as at a market! The sweet words
Of Christian promise, words that even yet
65 Might stem destruction, were they wisely preached,
Are muttered o'er by men, whose tones proclaim
How flat and wearisome they feel their trade:
Rank scoffers some, but most too indolent
To deem them falsehoods, or to know their truth.
70 O! blasphemous! the Book of Life is made
A superstitious instrument, on which
We gabble o'er the oaths we mean to break,
For all must swear[1]—all and in every place,
College and wharf, council and justice-court;
75 All, all must swear, the briber and the bribed,
Merchant and lawyer, senator and priest,
The rich, the poor, the old man and the young;
All, all make up one scheme of perjury,
That faith doth reel; the very name of God
80 Sounds like a juggler's charm; and bold with joy,
Forth from his dark and lonely hiding-place,
(Portentous sight!) the owlet Atheism,
Sailing on obscene wings athwart the noon,
Drops his blue-fringéd lids, and holds them close,
85 And hooting at the glorious sun in Heaven,
Cries out, "Where is it?"

          Thankless too for peace,
(Peace long preserved by fleets and perilous seas)
Secure from actual warfare, we have loved
To swell the war-whoop, passionate for war!
90 Alas! for ages ignorant of all
Its ghastlier workings, (famine or blue plague,
Battle, or siege, or flight thro' wintry snows,)
We, this whole people, have been clamorous
For war and bloodshed; animating sports,
95 The which we pay for as a thing to talk of,
Spectators and not combatants! No guess
Anticipative of a wrong unfelt,
No speculation on contingency,
However dim and vague, too vague and dim
100 To yield a justifying cause; and forth,

(Stuffed out with big preamble, holy names,
And adjurations° of the God in Heaven,)   *appeal*
We send our mandates for the certain death
Of thousands and ten thousands! Boys and girls,
105 And women, that would groan to see a child
Pull off an insect's leg, all read of war,
The best amusement for our morning meal!
The poor wretch, who has learnt his only prayers
From curses, who knows scarcely words enough
110 To ask a blessing from his Heavenly Father,
Becomes a fluent phraseman, absolute
And technical in victories and defeats,
And all our dainty terms for fratricide;
Terms which we trundle smoothly o'er our tongues
115 Like mere abstractions, empty sounds to which
We join no feeling and attach no form!
As if the soldier died without a wound;
As if the fibres of this godlike frame
Were gored without a pang; as if the wretch,
120 Who fell in battle, doing bloody deeds,
Passed off to Heaven, translated and not killed;
As though he had no wife to pine for him,
No God to judge him! Therefore, evil days
Are coming on us, O my countrymen!
125 And what if all-avenging Providence,
Strong and retributive, should make us know
The meaning of our words, force us to feel
The desolation and the agony
Of our fierce doings?

          Spare us yet awhile,
130 Father and God! O! spare us yet awhile!
Oh! let not English women drag their flight
Fainting beneath the burthen of their babes,
Of the sweet infants, that but yesterday
Laughed at the breast! Sons, brothers, husbands, all
135 Who ever gazed with fondness on the forms
Which grew up with you round the same fire-side,
And all who ever heard the sabbath-bells
Without the infidel's scorn, make yourselves pure!
Stand forth! be men! repel an impious foe,
140 Impious and false, a light yet cruel race,
Who laugh away all virtue, mingling mirth

---

[1] *all must swear* According to the Test and Corporation Acts, all public officials were required to swear allegiance to the Church of England. (Thus there would be no Catholics, Nonconformists, or Jews in office.)

They groaned, they stirred, they all uprose,
Nor spake, nor moved their eyes;
It had been strange, even in a dream,
To have seen those dead men rise.

335 The helmsman steered, the ship moved on;
Yet never a breeze up-blew;
The mariners all 'gan work the ropes,
Where they were wont to do;
340 They raised their limbs like lifeless tools—
We were a ghastly crew.

The body of my brother's son
Stood by me, knee to knee:
The body and I pulled at one rope,
345 But he said nought to me.

"I fear thee, ancient Mariner!"
Be calm, thou Wedding-Guest!
'Twas not those souls that fled in pain,
Which to their corses¹ came again,
350 But a troop of spirits blest:

For when it dawned—they dropped their arms,
And clustered round the mast;
Sweet sounds rose slowly through their mouths,
And from their bodies passed.

355 Around, around, flew each sweet sound,
Then darted to the Sun;
Slowly the sounds came back again,
Now mixed, now one by one.

Sometimes a-dropping from the sky
360 I heard the sky-lark sing;
Sometimes all little birds that are,
How they seemed to fill the sea and air
With their sweet jargoning!

And now 'twas like all instruments,
Now like a lonely flute;

But not by the souls of the men, nor by dæmons of earth or middle air, but by a blessed troop of angelic spirits, sent down by the invocation of the guardian saint.

¹ corses Corpses.

365 And now it is an angel's song,
That makes the heavens be mute.

It ceased; yet still the sails made on
A pleasant noise till noon,
A noise like of a hidden brook
370 In the leafy month of June,
That to the sleeping woods all night
Singeth a quiet tune.

Till noon we quietly sailed on,
Yet never a breeze did breathe:
375 Slowly and smoothly went the ship,
Moved onward from beneath.

Under the keel nine fathom deep,
From the land of mist and snow,
380 The spirit slid: and it was he
That made the ship to go.
The sails at noon left off their tune,
And the ship stood still also.

The Sun, right up above the mast,
Had fixed her to the ocean:
385 But in a minute she 'gan stir,
With a short uneasy motion—
Backwards and forwards half her length
With a short uneasy motion.

Then like a pawing horse let go,
390 She made a sudden bound:
It flung the blood into my head,
And I fell down in a swound.

How long in that same fit I lay,
I have not to declare;
395 But ere my living life returned,
I heard and in my soul discerned
Two voices in the air.

The lonesome spirit from the south-pole carries on the ship as far as the line, in obedience to the angelic troop, but still requireth vengeance.

...fluences trembled o'er his frame;
...e, with many feelings, many thoughts,
...e up a meditative joy, and found
...igious meanings in the forms of Nature!
...nd so, his senses gradually wrapt
...n a half sleep, he dreams of better worlds,
And dreaming hears thee still, O singing lark,
That singest like an angel in the clouds!

My God! it is a melancholy thing
30 For such a man, who would full fain preserve
His soul in calmness, yet perforce must feel
For all his human brethren—O my God!
It weighs upon the heart, that he must think
What uproar and what strife may now be stirring
35 This way or that way o'er these silent hills—
Invasion, and the thunder and the shout,
And all the crash of onset; fear and rage,
And undetermined conflict—even now,
Even now, perchance, and in his native isle:
40 Carnage and screams beneath this blessed sun!
We have offended, O! my countrymen!
We have offended very grievously,
And have been tyrannous. From east to west
A groan of accusation pierces Heaven!
45 The wretched plead against us; multitudes
Countless and vehement, the sons of God,
Our brethren! like a cloud that travels on,
Steamed up from Cairo's swamps of pestilence,
Even so, my countrymen! have we gone forth
50 And borne to distant tribes slavery and pangs,
And, deadlier far, our vices, whose deep taint
With slow perdition murders the whole man,
His body and his soul! Meanwhile, at home,
All individual dignity and power
55 Engulfed in Courts, Committees, Institutions,
Associations and Societies,
A vain, speech-mounting, speech-reporting Guild,
One Benefit-Club for mutual flattery,
We have drunk up, demure as at a grace,
60 Pollutions from the brimming cup of wealth;
Contemptuous of all honourable rule,
Yet bartering freedom and the poor man's life

¹ Invasion By the French, who threatened an attack on Wales.

"Is it he?" quoth one, "Is this the man?
By Him who died on cross,
With his cruel bow he laid full low
The harmless Albatross.

The spirit who bideth by himself
In the land of mist and snow,
He loved the bird that loved the man
Who shot him with his bow."

The other was a softer voice,
As soft as honey-dew:
Quoth he, "The man hath penance done,
And penance more will do."

The Polar Spirit's fellow-dæmons, the invisible inhabitants of the element, take part in his wrong; and two of them relate, one to the other, that penance long and heavy for the ancient Mariner hath been accorded to the Polar Spirit, who returned southward.

PART 6

FIRST VOICE

"But tell me, tell me! speak again,
Thy soft response renewing—
What makes that ship drive on so fast?
What is the ocean doing?"

SECOND VOICE

"Still as a slave before his lord,
The ocean hath no blast;
His great bright eye most silently
Up to the Moon is cast—

If he may know which way to go;
For she guides him smooth or grim.
See, brother, see! how graciously
She looketh down on him."

FIRST VOICE

"But why drives on that ship so fast,
Without or wave or wind?"

SECOND VOICE

"The air is cut away before,
And closes from behind.

Fly, brother, fly! more high, more high!
Or we shall be belated:
For slow and slow that ship will go,
When the Mariner's trance is abated."

430 I woke, and we were sailing on
As in a gentle weather:
'Twas night, calm night, the Moon was high;
The dead men stood together.

All stood together on the deck,
435 For a charnel-dungeon[1] fitter:
All fixed on me their stony eyes,
That in the Moon did glitter.

The pang, the curse, with which they died,
Had never passed away:
440 I could not draw my eyes from theirs,
Nor turn them up to pray.

And now this spell was snapt: once more
I viewed the ocean green,
And looked far forth, yet little saw
445 Of what had else been seen—

Like one, that on a lonesome road
Doth walk in fear and dread,
And having once turned round, walks on,
And turns no more his head;
450 Because he knows, a frightful fiend
Doth close behind him tread.

But soon there breathed a wind on me,
Nor sound nor motion made:
Its path was not upon the sea,
455 In ripple or in shade.

It raised my hair, it fanned my cheek
Like a meadow-gale of spring—
It mingled strangely with my fears,
Yet it felt like a welcoming.

The Mariner hath been cast into a trance; for the angelic power causeth the vessel to drive north-ward, faster than human life could endure.

The supernatural motion is retarded; the Mariner awakes, and his penance begins anew.

The curse is finally expiated.

---

1 *charnel-dungeon* Mortuary; house of death.

460   Swiftly, swiftly flew the ship,
       Yet she sailed softly too:
       Sweetly, sweetly blew the breeze—
       On me alone it blew.

       Oh! dream of joy! is this indeed   And the ancient
465   The light-house top I see?   Mariner beholdeth
       Is this the hill? is this the kirk?   his native country.
       Is this mine own countree?

       We drifted o'er the harbour-bar,
       And I with sobs did pray—
470   O let me be awake, my God!
       Or let me sleep alway.

       The harbour-bay was clear as glass,
       So smoothly was it strewn!
       And on the bay the moonlight lay,
475   And the shadow of the Moon.

       The rock shone bright, the kirk no less,
       That stands above the rock:
       The moonlight steeped in silentness
       The steady weathercock.

480   And the bay was white with silent light,   The angelic spirits
       Till rising from the same,   leave the dead
       Full many shapes, that shadows were,   bodies,
       In crimson colours came.

       A little distance from the prow   And appear in their
485   Those crimson shadows were: own forms of light.
       I turned my eyes upon the deck—
       Oh, Christ! what saw I there!

       Each corse lay flat, lifeless and flat,
       And, by the holy rood!
490   A man all light, a seraph-man,[1]
       On every corse there stood.

This seraph-band, each waved his hand:
It was a heavenly sight!
They stood as signals to the land,
495   Each one a lovely light;

This seraph-band, each waved his hand,
No voice did they impart—
No voice; but oh! the silence sank
Like music on my heart.

500   But soon I heard the dash of oars,
I heard the Pilot's cheer;
My head was turned perforce away
And I saw a boat appear.

The Pilot and the Pilot's boy,
505   I heard them coming fast:
Dear Lord in Heaven! it was a joy
The dead men could not blast.

I saw a third—I heard his voice:
It is the Hermit good!
510   He singeth loud his godly hymns
That he makes in the wood.
He'll shrieve[2] my soul, he'll wash away
The Albatross's blood.

PART 7

This Hermit good lives in that wood   The Hermit of
515   Which slopes down to the sea.   the Wood.
How loudly his sweet voice he rears!
He loves to talk with marineres
That come from a far countree.

He kneels at morn, and noon, and eve—
520   He hath a cushion plump:
It is the moss that wholly hides
The rotted old oak-stump.

The skiff-boat neared: I heard them talk,
"Why, this is strange, I trow![3]

---

[1] *rood* Cross; *seraph-man* Angel.

[2] *shrieve* Give absolution to.

[3] *trow* Believe.

5 Where are those lights so many and fair,
That signal made but now?"

"Strange, by my faith!" the Hermit said—
"And they answered not our cheer!
The planks look warped! and see those sails,
0 How thin they are and sere!
I never saw aught like to them,
Unless perchance it were

Brown skeletons of leaves that lag
My forest-brook along;
5 When the ivy-tod[1] is heavy with snow,
And the owlet whoops to the wolf below,
That eats the she-wolf's young."

"Dear Lord! it hath a fiendish look"—
(The Pilot made reply)
0 "I am a-feared"—"Push on, push on!"
Said the Hermit cheerily.

The boat came closer to the ship,
But I nor spake nor stirred;
The boat came close beneath the ship,
45 And straight a sound was heard.

Under the water it rumbled on,
Still louder and more dread:
It reached the ship, it split the bay;
The ship went down like lead.

50 Stunned by that loud and dreadful sound,
Which sky and ocean smote,
Like one that hath been seven days drowned
My body lay afloat;
But swift as dreams, myself I found
55 Within the Pilot's boat.

Upon the whirl, where sank the ship,
The boat spun round and round;
And all was still, save that the hill
Was telling of the sound.

Approacheth the ship with wonder.

The ship suddenly sinketh.

The ancient Mariner is saved in the Pilot's boat.

560 I moved my lips—the Pilot shrieked
And fell down in a fit;
The holy Hermit raised his eyes,
And prayed where he did sit.

I took the oars: the Pilot's boy,
565 Who now doth crazy go,
Laughed loud and long, and all the while
His eyes went to and fro.
"Ha! ha!" quoth he, "full plain I see,
The Devil knows how to row."

570 And now, all in my own countree,
I stood on the firm land!
The Hermit stepped forth from the boat,
And scarcely he could stand.

"O shrieve me, shrieve me, holy man!"
575 The Hermit crossed his brow.
"Say quick," quoth he, "I bid thee say—
What manner of man art thou?"

Forthwith this frame of mine was wrenched
With a woful agony,
580 Which forced me to begin my tale;
And then it left me free.

Since then, at an uncertain hour,
That agony returns;
And till my ghastly tale is told,
585 This heart within me burns.

I pass, like night, from land to land;
I have strange power of speech;
That moment that his face I see,
I know the man that must hear me:
590 To him my tale I teach.

What loud uproar bursts from that door!
The wedding-guests are there:
But in the garden-bower the bride
And bride-maids singing are:

The ancient Mariner earnestly entreateth the Hermit to shrieve him; and the penance of life falls on him.

And ever and anon throughout his future life an agony constraineth him to travel from land to land.

---

[1] *ivy-tod* Bush.

595 And hark the little vesper bell,
Which biddeth me to prayer!

O Wedding-Guest! this soul hath been
Alone on a wide wide sea:
So lonely 'twas, that God Himself
600 Scarce seeméd there to be.

O sweeter than the marriage-feast,
'Tis sweeter far to me,
To walk together to the kirk
With a goodly company!—

605 To walk together to the kirk,
And all together pray,
While each to his great Father bends,
Old men, and babes, and loving friends
And youth and maidens gay!

610 Farewell, farewell! but this I tell
To thee, thou Wedding-Guest!

He prayeth well, who loveth well
Both man and bird and beast.

He prayeth best, who loveth best
615 All things both great and small;
For the dear God who loveth us,
He made and loveth all.

The Mariner, whose eye is bright,
Whose beard with age is hoar,[1]
620 Is gone: and now the Wedding-Guest
Turned from the bridegroom's door.

He went like one that hath been stunned,
And is of sense forlorn:
A sadder and a wiser man,
625 He rose the morrow morn.
—1817 (EARLIER VERSION PUBLISHED 1798)

And to teach by his own example, love and reverence to all things that God made and loveth.

In Context

The Origin of "The Rime of the Ancient Mariner"

from Samuel Taylor Coleridge, *Biographia Literaria*, Chapter 14 (1817)

Almost twenty years after the first publication of "The Rime of the Ancient Mariner," Coleridge gave the following account of the poem's origin and composition.

During the first year that Mr. Wordsworth and I were neighbours, our conversations turned frequently on the two cardinal points of poetry, the power of exciting the sympathy of the reader by a faithful adherence to the truth of nature, and the power of giving the interest of novelty by the modifying colours of imagination. The sudden charm, which accidents of light and shade, which moonlight or sunset diffused over a known and familiar landscape, appeared to represent the practicability of combining both. These are the poetry of nature. The thought suggested itself (to which of us I do not recollect) that a series of poems might be composed of two sorts. In the one, the

[1] *hoar* White, as with frost (hoarfrost).

incidents and agents were to be, in part at least supernatural; and the excellence aimed at was to consist in the interesting of the affections by the dramatic truth of such emotions, as would naturally accompany such situations, supposing them real. And real in *this* sense they have been to every human being who, from whatever source of delusion, has at any time believed himself under supernatural agency. For the second class, subjects were to be chosen from ordinary life; the characters and incidents were to be such, as will be found in every village and its vicinity where there is a meditative and feeling mind to seek after them, or to notice them, when they present themselves. In this idea originated the plan of the *Lyrical Ballads*; in which it was agreed, that my endeavours should be directed to persons and characters supernatural, or at least romantic; yet so as to transfer from our inward nature a human interest and a semblance of truth sufficient to procure for these shadows of imagination that willing suspension of disbelief for the moment, which constitutes poetic faith. Mr. Wordsworth, on the other hand, was to propose to himself as his object, to give the charm of novelty to things of every day, and to excite a feeling analogous to the supernatural, by awakening the mind's attention from the lethargy of custom, and directing it to the loveliness and the wonders of the world before us; an inexhaustible treasure, but for which, in consequence of the film of familiarity and selfish solicitude we have eyes, yet see not, and hearts that neither feel or understand. With this view I wrote "The Ancient Mariner," and was preparing among other poems, "The Dark Ladie," and the "Christabel" in which I should have more nearly realized my ideal than I had done in my first attempt.

from A Letter from the Reverend Alexander Dyce to Hartley Coleridge (1852)

In this letter to Samuel Taylor Coleridge's eldest son, Hartley, the Reverend Alexander Dyce quotes Wordsworth as saying the following about the inception of "The Rime of the Ancient Mariner":

"The Ancient Mariner" was founded on a strange dream, which a friend of Coleridge had, who fancied he saw a skeleton ship, with figures in it. We had both determined to write some poetry for a monthly magazine, the profits of which were to defray the expenses of a little excursion we were to make together. "The Ancient Mariner" was intended for this periodical, but was too long. I had very little share in the composition of it, for I soon found the style of Coleridge and myself would not assimilate. Beside the lines (in the fourth part) "And thou art long, and lank, and brown, / As in the ribbed sea-sand—" I wrote the stanza (in the first part) "He holds him with his glittering eye— / The Wedding-Guest stood still, / And listens like a three-years child: / The Mariner hath his will" and four or five lines more in different parts of the poem, which I could not now point out. The idea of shooting an albatross was mine; for I had been reading *Shelvocke's Voyages*, which probably Coleridge never saw. I also suggested the reanimation of the dead bodies, to work the ship.

This Lime-Tree Bower My Prison[1]

Addressed to Charles Lamb,
Of the India House, London

Well, they are gone, and here must I remain,
    This lime-tree bower my prison! I have lost
Beauties and feelings, such as would have been
Most sweet to my remembrance even when age
5 Had dimm'd mine eyes to blindness! They, meanwhile,
Friends, whom I never more may meet again,
On springy heath, along the hill-top edge,
Wander in gladness, and wind down, perchance,
To that still roaring dell, of which I told;
10 The roaring dell, o'erwooded, narrow, deep,
And only speckled by the mid-day sun;
Where its slim trunk the ash from rock to rock
Flings arching like a bridge;—that branchless ash,
Unsunn'd and damp, whose few poor yellow leaves
15 Ne'er tremble in the gale, yet tremble still,
Fann'd by the water-fall! and there my friends
Behold the dark green file of long lank weeds,[2]
That all at once (a most fantastic sight!)
Still nod and drip beneath the dripping edge
20 Of the blue clay-stone.

                Now, my friends emerge
Beneath the wide wide Heaven—and view again
The many-steepled tract magnificent
Of hilly fields and meadows, and the sea,
With some fair bark, perhaps, whose sails light up
25 The slip of smooth clear blue betwixt two Isles
Of purple shadow! Yes! they wander on
In gladness all; but thou, methinks, most glad,
My gentle-hearted Charles! for thou hast pined

And hunger'd after Nature, many a year,
30 In the great City pent, winning thy way
With sad yet patient soul, through evil and pain
And strange calamity![3] Ah! slowly sink
Behind the western ridge, thou glorious Sun!
Shine in the slant beams of the sinking orb,
35 Ye purple heath-flowers! richlier burn, ye clouds!
Live in the yellow light, ye distant groves!
And kindle, thou blue Ocean! So my friend
Struck with deep joy may stand, as I have stood,
Silent with swimming sense; yea, gazing round
40 On the wide landscape, gaze till all doth seem
Less gross than bodily; and of such hues
As veil the Almighty Spirit, when yet he makes
Spirits perceive his presence.

                A delight
Comes sudden on my heart, and I am glad
45 As I myself were there! Nor in this bower,
This little lime-tree bower, have I not mark'd
Much that has sooth'd me. Pale beneath the blaze
Hung the transparent foliage; and I watch'd
Some broad and sunny leaf, and lov'd to see
50 The shadow of the leaf and stem above
Dappling its sunshine! And that walnut-tree
Was richly ting'd, and a deep radiance lay
Full on the ancient ivy, which usurps
Those fronting elms, and now, with blackest mass
55 Makes their dark branches gleam a lighter hue
Through the late twilight: and though now the bat
Wheels silent by, and not a swallow twitters,
Yet still the solitary humble-bee
Sings in the bean-flower! Henceforth I shall know
60 That Nature ne'er deserts the wise and pure;
No plot so narrow, be but Nature there,
No waste so vacant, but may well employ
Each faculty of sense, and keep the heart
Awake to Love and Beauty! and sometimes
65 'Tis well to be bereft of promis'd good,
That we may lift the soul, and contemplate
With lively joy the joys we cannot share.

---

[1] [Coleridge's note] In the June of 1797 some long-expected friends [Charles Lamb and William and Dorothy Wordsworth] paid a visit to the author's cottage; and on the morning of their arrival, he met with an accident, which disabled him from walking during the whole time of their stay. One evening, when they had left him for a few hours, he composed the following lines in the garden-bower.

[2] [Coleridge's note] The *Asplenium Scolopendrium*, called in some countries the Adder's Tongue, in others the Hart's Tongue, but Withering gives the Adder's Tongue as the trivial name of the *Ophioglossum* only.

[3] *strange calamity* Charles Lamb's sister Mary, who suffered from periods of insanity, had fatally stabbed their mother.

My gentle-hearted Charles! when the last rook
Beat its straight path along the dusky air
Homewards, I blest it! deeming its black wing
(Now a dim speck, now vanishing in light)
Had cross'd the mighty Orb's dilated glory,
While thou stood'st gazing; or, when all was still,
Flew creeking o'er thy head, and had a charm[1]
For thee, my gentle-hearted Charles, to whom
No sound is dissonant which tells of Life.
—1800

Christabel

PREFACE

The first part of the following poem was written in the year 1797, at Stowey, in the county of Somerset. The second part, after my return from Germany, in the year 1800, at Keswick, Cumberland. Since the latter date, my poetic powers have been, till very lately, in a state of suspended animation. But as, in my very first conception of the tale, I had the whole present to my mind, with the wholeness, no less than with the liveliness of a vision; I trust that I shall be able to embody in verse the three parts yet to come, in the course of the present year.

It is probable that if the poem had been finished at either of the former periods, or if even the first and second part had been published in the year 1800, the impression of its originality would have been much greater than I dare at present expect. But for this, I have only my own indolence to blame. The dates are mentioned for the exclusive purpose of precluding charges of plagiarism or servile imitation from myself. For there is among us a set of critics, who seem to hold, that every possible thought and image is traditional; who have no notion that there are such things as fountains in the world, small as well as great; and who would therefore charitably derive every rill[2] they behold flowing from a perforation made in some other man's tank. I am confident however, that as far as the present poem is concerned, the celebrated poets whose writings I might be suspected of having imitated,[3] either in particular passages, or in the tone and the spirit of the whole, would be among the first to vindicate me from the charge, and who, on any striking coincidence, would permit me to address them in this doggerel version of two monkish Latin hexameters:

> 'Tis mine and it is likewise yours,
> But an if this will not do;
> Let it be mine, good friend! for I
> Am the poorer of the two.

I have only to add, that the metre of the Christabel is not, properly speaking, irregular, though it may seem so from its being founded on a new principle: namely, that of counting in each line the accents, not the syllables. Though the latter may vary from seven to twelve, yet in each line the accents will be found to be only four. Nevertheless this occasional variation in the number of syllables is not introduced wantonly, or for the mere ends of convenience, but in correspondence with some transition in the nature of the imagery or passion.

PART I

'Tis the middle of night by the castle clock,
        And the owls have awakened the crowing cock;
Tu—whit!—Tu—whoo!
And hark, again! the crowing cock,
How drowsily it crew.

Sir Leoline, the Baron rich,
Hath a toothless mastiff bitch;
From her kennel beneath the rock
She maketh answer to the clock,

---

1 [Coleridge's note] Some months after I had written this line, it gave me pleasure to find that Bartram had observed the same circumstance of the Savanna Crane. "When these Birds move their wings in flight, their strokes are slow, moderate and regular; and even when at a considerable distance or high above us, we plainly hear the quill-feathers: their shafts and webs upon one another creak as the joints or working of a vessel in a tempestuous sea."

2 *rill* Brook.

3 *celebrated poets … imitated* Lord Byron and Sir Walter Scott, both of whom had read "Christabel" in manuscript form and had been influenced by it in their own subsequent writings.

10 Four for the quarters, and twelve for the hour;
Ever and aye,° by shine and shower,   *always*
Sixteen short howls, not over loud;
Some say, she sees my lady's shroud.

Is the night chilly and dark?
15 The night is chilly, but not dark.
The thin gray cloud is spread on high,
It covers but not hides the sky.
The moon is behind, and at the full;
And yet she looks both small and dull.
20 The night is chill, the cloud is gray:
'Tis a month before the month of May,
And the Spring comes slowly up this way.

The lovely lady, Christabel,
Whom her father loves so well,
25 What makes her in the wood so late,
A furlong from the castle gate?
She had dreams all yesternight
Of her own betrothéd knight;
And she in the midnight wood will pray
30 For the weal° of her lover that's far away.   *well-being*

She stole along, she nothing spoke,
The sighs she heaved were soft and low,
And naught was green upon the oak
But moss and rarest misletoe:[1]
35 She kneels beneath the huge oak tree,
And in silence prayeth she.

The lady sprang up suddenly,
The lovely lady, Christabel!
It moaned as near, as near can be,
40 But what it is she cannot tell.—
On the other side it seems to be,
Of the huge, broad-breasted, old oak tree.

The night is chill; the forest bare;
Is it the wind that moaneth bleak?
45 There is not wind enough in the air

To move away the ringlet curl
From the lovely lady's cheek—
There is not wind enough to twirl
The one red leaf, the last of its clan,
50 That dances as often as dance it can,
Hanging so light, and hanging so high,
On the topmost twig that looks up at the sky.

Hush, beating heart of Christabel!
Jesu, Maria, shield her well!
55 She folded her arms beneath her cloak,
And stole to the other side of the oak.
      What sees she there?

There she sees a damsel bright,
Dressed in a silken robe of white,
60 That shadowy in the moonlight shone:
The neck that made that white robe wan,
Her stately neck, and arms were bare;
Her blue-veined feet unsandal'd were,
And wildly glittered here and there
65 The gems entangled in her hair.
I guess, 'twas frightful there to see
A lady so richly clad as she—
Beautiful exceedingly!

Mary mother, save me now!
70 (Said Christabel,) And who art thou?

The lady strange made answer meet,
And her voice was faint and sweet:—
Have pity on my sore distress,
I scarce can speak for weariness:
75 Stretch forth thy hand, and have no fear!
Said Christabel, How camest thou here?
And the lady, whose voice was faint and sweet,
Did thus pursue her answer meet:—

My sire is of a noble line,
80 And my name is Geraldine:
Five warriors seized me yestermorn,
Me, even me, a maid forlorn:
They choked my cries with force and fright,

---

[1] *misletoe* Plant considered sacred in ancient Britain when found growing on oak trees.

And tied me on a palfrey° white.   *saddle horse*
5   The palfrey was as fleet as wind,
And they rode furiously behind.

They spurred amain,° their steeds were white: *forcefully*
And once we crossed the shade of night.
As sure as Heaven shall rescue me,
10 I have no thought what men they be;
Nor do I know how long it is
(For I have lain entranced, I wis°)   *know*
Since one, the tallest of the five,
Took me from the palfrey's back,
95 A weary woman, scarce alive.
Some muttered words his comrades spoke:
He placed me underneath this oak;
He swore they would return with haste;
Whither they went I cannot tell—
100 I thought I heard, some minutes past,
Sounds as of a castle bell.
Stretch forth thy hand (thus ended she),
And help a wretched maid to flee.

Then Christabel stretched forth her hand,
105 And comforted fair Geraldine:
O well, bright dame! may you command
The service of Sir Leoline;
And gladly our stout° chivalry   *fierce*
Will he send forth and friends withal
110 To guide and guard you safe and free
Home to your noble father's hall.

She rose: and forth with steps they passed
That strove to be, and were not, fast.
Her gracious stars the lady blest,
115 And thus spake on sweet Christabel:
All our household are at rest,
The hall is silent as the cell;
Sir Leoline is weak in health,
And may not well awakened be,
120 But we will move as if in stealth,
And I beseech your courtesy,
This night, to share your couch with me.

They crossed the moat, and Christabel
Took the key that fitted well;
125 A little door she opened straight,
All in the middle of the gate;
The gate that was ironed within and without,
Where an army in battle array had marched out.
The lady sank, belike through pain,
130 And Christabel with might and main
Lifted her up, a weary weight,
Over the threshold of the gate:
Then the lady rose again,
And moved, as she were not in pain.

135 So free from danger, free from fear,
They crossed the court: right glad they were.
And Christabel devoutly cried
To the Lady by her side,
Praise we the Virgin all divine
140 Who hath rescued thee from thy distress!
Alas, alas! said Geraldine,
I cannot speak for weariness.
So free from danger, free from fear,
They crossed the court: right glad they were.

145 Outside her kennel, the mastiff old
Lay fast asleep, in moonshine cold.
The mastiff old did not awake,
Yet she an angry moan did make!
And what can ail the mastiff bitch?
150 Never till now she uttered yell
Beneath the eye of Christabel.
Perhaps it is the owlet's scritch:
For what can aid the mastiff bitch?

They passed the hall, that echoes still
155 Pass as lightly as you will!
The brands° were flat, the brands were dying,   *burning logs*
Amid their own white ashes lying;
But when the lady passed, there came
A tongue of light, a fit of flame;
160 And Christabel saw the lady's eye,
And nothing else saw she thereby,
Save the boss of the shield of Sir Leoline tall,

Which hung in a murky old niche in the wall.
O softly tread, said Christabel,
165   My father seldom sleepeth well.

Sweet Christabel her feet doth bare,
And jealous of the listening air
They steal their way from stair to stair,
Now in glimmer, and now in gloom,
170   And now they pass the Baron's room,
As still as death, with stifled breath!
And now have reached her chamber door;
And now doth Geraldine press down
The rushes of the chamber floor.

175   The moon shines dim in the open air,
And not a moonbeam enters here.
But they without its light can see
The chamber carved so curiously,
Carved with figures strange and sweet,
180   All made out of the carver's brain,
For a lady's chamber meet:°   suitable
The lamp with twofold silver chain
Is fastened to an angel's feet.

The silver lamp burns dead and dim;
185   But Christabel the lamp will trim.
She trimmed the lamp, and made it bright,
And left it swinging to and fro,
While Geraldine, in wretched plight,
Sank down upon the floor below.

190   O weary lady, Geraldine,
I pray you, drink this cordial wine!
It is a wine of virtuous powers;
My mother made it of wild flowers.

And will your mother pity me,
195   Who am a maiden most forlorn?
Christabel answered—Woe is me!
She died the hour that I was born.
I have heard the gray-haired friar tell
How on her death-bed she did say,
200   That she should hear the castle-bell

Strike twelve upon my wedding-day.
O mother dear! that thou wert here!
I would, said Geraldine, she were!

But soon with altered voice, said she—
205   "Off, wandering mother! Peak and pine!
I have power to bid thee flee."
Alas! what ails poor Geraldine?
Why stares she with unsettled eye?
Can she the bodiless dead espy?
210   And why with hollow voice cries she,
"Off, woman, off! this hour is mine—
Though thou her guardian spirit be,
Off, woman, off! 'tis given to me."

Then Christabel knelt by the lady's side,
215   And raised to heaven her eyes so blue—
Alas! said she, this ghastly ride—
Dear lady! it hath wildered you!
The lady wiped her moist cold brow,
And faintly said, "'tis over now!"

220   Again the wild-flower wine she drank:
Her fair large eyes 'gan glitter bright,
And from the floor whereon she sank,
The lofty lady stood upright:
She was most beautiful to see,
225   Like a lady of a far countrée.

And thus the lofty lady spake—
"All they who live in the upper sky,
Do love you, holy Christabel!
And you love them, and for their sake
230   And for the good which me befell,
Even I in my degree will try,
Fair maiden, to requite you well.
But now unrobe yourself; for I
Must pray, ere yet in bed I lie."

235   Quoth Christabel, So let it be!
And as the lady bade, did she.
Her gentle limbs did she undress
And lay down in her loveliness.

But through her brain of weal and woe
180 So many thoughts moved to and fro,
That vain it were her lids to close;
So half-way from the bed she rose,
And on her elbow did recline
To look at the lady Geraldine.

185 Beneath the lamp the lady bowed,
And slowly rolled her eyes around;
Then drawing in her breath aloud,
Like one that shuddered, she unbound
The cincture° from beneath her breast: _girdle_
190 Her silken robe, and inner vest,
Dropt to her feet, and full in view,
Behold! her bosom, and half her side—
A sight to dream of, not to tell!
O shield her! shield sweet Christabel!

195 Yet Geraldine nor speaks nor stirs;
Ah! what a stricken look was hers!
Deep from within she seems half-way
To lift some weight with sick assay,° _attempt_
And eyes the maid and seeks delay;
200 Then suddenly as one defied
Collects herself in scorn and pride,
And lay down by the Maiden's side!—
And in her arms the maid she took,
        Ah wel-a-day!
205 And with low voice and doleful look
These words did say:
"In the touch of this bosom there worketh a spell,
Which is lord of thy utterance, Christabel!
Thou knowest to-night, and wilt know to-morrow
210 This mark of my shame, this seal of my sorrow;
        But vainly thou warrest,
            For this is alone in
        Thy power to declare,
            That in the dim forest
215   Thou heard'st a low moaning,
And found'st a bright lady, surpassingly fair;
And didst bring her home with thee in love and in
        charity,
To shield her and shelter her from the damp air."

THE CONCLUSION TO PART 1

It was a lovely sight to see
280 The lady Christabel, when she
Was praying at the old oak tree.
        Amid the jaggéd shadows
        Of mossy leafless boughs,
        Kneeling in the moonlight,
285   To make her gentle vows;
Her slender palms together prest,
Heaving sometimes on her breast;
Her face resigned to bliss or bale°— _grief_
Her face, oh call it fair not pale,
290 And both blue eyes more bright than clear.
Each about to have a tear.

With open eyes (ah, woe is me!)
Asleep, and dreaming fearfully,
Fearfully dreaming, yet, I wis,
295 Dreaming that alone, which is—
O sorrow and shame! Can this be she,
The lady, who knelt at the old oak tree?
And lo! the worker of these harms,
That holds the maiden in her arms,
300 Seems to slumber still and mild,
As a mother with her child.

A star hath set, a star hath risen,
O Geraldine! since arms of thine
Have been the lovely lady's prison.
305 O Geraldine! one hour was thine—
Thou'st had thy will! By tairn° and rill, _mountain pool_
The night-birds all that hour were still.
But now they are jubilant anew,
From cliff and tower, tu—whoo! tu—whoo!
310 Tu—whoo! tu—whoo! from wood and fell!° _hill_

And see! the lady Christabel
Gathers herself from out her trance;
Her limbs relax, her countenance
Grows sad and soft; the smooth thin lids
315 Close o'er her eyes; and tears she sheds—
Large tears that leave the lashes bright!

And oft the while she seems to smile
As infants at a sudden light!

Yea, she doth smile, and she doth weep,
320 Like a youthful hermitess,
Beauteous in a wilderness,
Who, praying always, prays in sleep.
And, if she move unquietly,
Perchance, 'tis but the blood so free
325 Comes back and tingles in her feet.
No doubt, she hath a vision sweet.
What if her guardian spirit 'twere,
What if she knew her mother near?
But this she knows, in joys and woes,
330 That saints will aid if men will call:
For the blue sky bends over all!

PART 2

Each matin° bell, the Baron saith,   *morning*
Knells us back to a world of death.
These words Sir Leoline first said,
335 When he rose and found his lady dead:
These words Sir Leoline will say
Many a morn to his dying day!

And hence the custom and law began
That still at dawn the sacristan,°   *church sexton*
340 Who duly pulls the heavy bell,
Five and forty beads° must tell°   *rosary beads / count*
Between each stroke—a warning knell,
Which not a soul can choose but hear
From Bratha Head to Wyndermere.[1]

345 Saith Bracy the bard, So let it knell!
And let the drowsy sacristan
Still count as slowly as he can!
There is no lack of such, I ween,°   *suppose*
As well fill up the space between.
350 In Langdale Pike and Witch's Lair,
And Dungeon-ghyll so foully rent,

With ropes of rock and bells of air
Three sinful sextons' ghosts are pent,
Who all give back, one after t'other,
355 The death-note to their living brother;
And oft too, by the knell offended,
Just as their one! two! three! is ended,
The devil mocks the doleful tale
With a merry peal from Borodale.

360 The air is still! through mist and cloud
That merry peal comes ringing loud;
And Geraldine shakes off her dread,
And rises lightly from the bed;
Puts on her silken vestments white,
365 And tricks her hair in lovely plight,[2]
And nothing doubting of her spell
Awakens the lady Christabel.
"Sleep you, sweet lady Christabel?
I trust that you have rested well."

370 And Christabel awoke and spied
The same who lay down by her side—
O rather say, the same whom she
Raised up beneath the old oak tree!
Nay, fairer yet! and yet more fair!
375 For she belike hath drunken deep
Of all the blessedness of sleep!
And while she spake, her looks, her air
Such gentle thankfulness declare,
That (so it seemed) her girded vests
380 Grew tight beneath her heaving breasts.
"Sure I have sinn'd!" said Christabel,
"Now heaven be praised if all be well!"
And in low faltering tones, yet sweet,
Did she the lofty lady greet
385 With such perplexity of mind
As dreams too lively leave behind.

So quickly she rose, and quickly arrayed
Her maiden limbs, and having prayed
That He, who on the cross did groan,
390 Might wash away her sins unknown,

---

[1] *Bratha Head ... Wyndermere* In the Lake District.

[2] *plight* I.e., plait, or braid.

She forthwith led fair Geraldine
To meet her sire, Sir Leoline.

The lovely maid and the lady tall
Are pacing both into the hall,
5   And pacing on through page and groom,
Enter the Baron's presence-room.

The Baron rose, and while he prest
His gentle daughter to his breast,
With cheerful wonder in his eyes
0   The lady Geraldine espies,
And gave such welcome to the same,
As might beseem so bright a dame!

But when he heard the lady's tale,
And when she told her father's name,
5   Why waxed Sir Leoline so pale,
Murmuring o'er the name again,
Lord Roland de Vaux of Tryermaine?

Alas! they had been friends in youth;
But whispering tongues can poison truth;
0   And constancy lives in realms above;
And life is thorny; and youth is vain;
And to be wroth with one we love,
Doth work like madness in the brain.
And thus it chanced, as I divine,
5   With Roland and Sir Leoline.
Each spake words of high disdain
And insult to his heart's best brother:
They parted—ne'er to meet again!
But never either found another
0   To free the hollow heart from paining—
They stood aloof, the scars remaining,
Like cliffs which had been rent asunder;
A dreary sea now flows between;—
But neither heat, nor frost, nor thunder,
5   Shall wholly do away, I ween,
The marks of that which once hath been.

Sir Leoline, a moment's space,
Stood gazing on the damsel's face:

And the youthful Lord of Tryermaine
430   Came back upon his heart again.

O then the Baron forgot his age,
His noble heart swelled high with rage;
He swore by the wounds in Jesu's side,
He would proclaim it far and wide
435   With trump and solemn heraldry,
That they, who thus had wronged the dame,
Were base as spotted infamy!
"And if they dare deny the same,
My herald shall appoint a week,
440   And let the recreant traitors seek
My tourney° court—that there and then   *tournament*
I may dislodge their reptile souls
From the bodies and forms of men!"
He spake: his eye in lightning rolls!
445   For the lady was ruthlessly seized; and he
        kenned°   *recognized*
In the beautiful lady the child of his friend!

And now the tears were on his face,
And fondly in his arms he took
Fair Geraldine, who met the embrace,
450   Prolonging it with joyous look.
Which when she viewed, a vision fell
Upon the soul of Christabel,
The vision of fear, the touch and pain!
She shrunk and shuddered, and saw again—
455   (Ah, woe is me! Was it for thee,
Thou gentle maid! such sights to see?)

Again she saw that bosom old,
Again she felt that bosom cold,
And drew in her breath with a hissing sound:
460   Whereat the Knight turned wildly round,
And nothing saw, but his own sweet maid
With eyes upraised, as one that prayed.

The touch, the sight, had passed away,
And in its stead that vision blest,
465   Which comforted her after-rest.
While in the lady's arms she lay,

Had put a rapture in her breast,
And on her lips and o'er her eyes
Spread smiles like light!
                    With new surprise,
470 "What ails then my belovéd child?"
The Baron said—His daughter mild
Made answer, "All will yet be well!"
I ween, she had no power to tell
Aught else: so mighty was the spell.

475 Yet he, who saw this Geraldine,
Had deemed her sure a thing divine:
Such sorrow with such grace she blended,
As if she feared she had offended
Sweet Christabel, that gentle maid!
480 And with such lowly tones she prayed,
She might be sent without delay
Home to her father's mansion.
                       "Nay!
Nay, by my soul!" said Leoline.
"Ho! Bracy the bard, the charge be thine!
485 Go thou, with music sweet and loud,
And take two steeds with trappings proud,
And take the youth whom thou lov'st best
To bear thy harp, and learn thy song,
And clothe you both in solemn vest,
490 And over the mountains haste along,
Lest wandering folk, that are abroad,
Detain you on the valley road.

"And when he has crossed the Irthing flood,
My merry bard! he hastes, he hastes
495 Up Knorren Moor, through Halegarth Wood,
And reaches soon that castle good
Which stands and threatens Scotland's wastes.

"Bard Bracy! bard Bracy! your horses are fleet,
Ye must ride up the hall, your music so sweet,
500 More loud than your horses' echoing feet!
And loud and loud to Lord Roland call,
Thy daughter is safe in Langdale hall!
Thy beautiful daughter is safe and free—
Sir Leoline greets thee thus through me!

505 He bids thee come without delay
With all thy numerous array
And take thy lovely daughter home:
And he will meet thee on the way
With all his numerous array
510 White with their panting palfreys' foam:
And, by mine honour! I will say,
That I repent me of the day
When I spake words of fierce disdain
To Roland de Vaux of Tryermaine!—
515 —For since that evil hour hath flown,
Many a summer's sun hath shone;
Yet ne'er found I a friend again
Like Roland de Vaux of Tryermaine."

The lady fell, and clasped his knees,
520 Her face upraised, her eyes o'erflowing;
And Bracy replied, with faltering voice,
His gracious hail on all bestowing!—
"Thy words, thou sire of Christabel,
Are sweeter than my harp can tell;
525 Yet might I gain a boon° of thee,   *request*
This day my journey should not be,
So strange a dream hath come to me,
That I had vowed with music loud
To clear yon wood from thing unblest,
530 Warned by a vision in my rest!
For in my sleep I saw that dove,
That gentle bird, whom thou dost love,
And call'st by thy own daughter's name—
Sir Leoline! I saw the same
535 Fluttering, and uttering fearful moan,
Among the green herbs in the forest alone.
Which when I saw and when I heard,
I wonder'd what might ail the bird;
For nothing near it could I see,
540 Save the grass and herbs underneath the old tree.

"And in my dream methought I went
To search out what might there be found;
And what the sweet bird's trouble meant,
That thus lay fluttering on the ground.
545 I went and peered, and could descry

No cause for her distressful cry;
But yet for her dear lady's sake
I stooped, methought, the dove to take,
When lo! I saw a bright green snake
Coiled around its wings and neck.
Green as the herbs on which it couched,
Close by the dove's its head it crouched;
And with the dove it heaves and stirs,
Swelling its neck as she swelled hers!
I woke; it was the midnight hour,
The clock was echoing in the tower;
But though my slumber was gone by,
This dream it would not pass away—
It seems to live upon my eye!
And thence I vowed this self-same day,
With music strong and saintly song
To wander through the forest bare,
Lest aught unholy loiter there."

Thus Bracy said: the Baron, the while,
Half listening heard him with a smile;
Then turned to Lady Geraldine,
His eyes made up of wonder and love;
And said in courtly accents fine,
"Sweet maid, Lord Roland's beauteous dove,
With arms more strong than harp or song,
Thy sire and I will crush the snake!"
He kissed her forehead as he spake,
And Geraldine in maiden wise,
Casting down her large bright eyes,
With blushing cheek and courtesy fine
She turned her from Sir Leoline;
Softly gathering up her train,
That o'er her right arm fell again;
And folded her arms across her chest,
And couched her head upon her breast,
And looked askance at Christabel—
Jesu, Maria, shield her well!

A snake's small eye blinks dull and shy;
And the lady's eyes they shrunk in her head,
Each shrunk up to a serpent's eye,
And with somewhat of malice, and more of dread,

At Christabel she looked askance!—
One moment—and the sight was fled!
But Christabel in dizzy trance
Stumbling on the unsteady ground
Shuddered aloud, with a hissing sound;
And Geraldine again turned round,
And like a thing, that sought relief,
Full of wonder and full of grief,
She rolled her large bright eyes divine
Wildly on Sir Leoline.

The maid, alas! her thoughts are gone,
She nothing sees—no sight but one!
The maid, devoid of guile and sin,
I know not how, in fearful wise,
So deeply had she drunken in
That look, those shrunken serpent eyes,
That all her features were resigned
To this sole image in her mind:
And passively did imitate
That look of dull and treacherous hate!
And thus she stood, in dizzy trance,
Still picturing that look askance
With forced unconscious sympathy
Full before her father's view—
As far as such a look could be
In eyes so innocent and blue!

And when the trance was o'er, the maid
Paused awhile, and inly prayed:
Then falling at the Baron's feet,
"By my mother's soul do I entreat
That thou this woman send away!"
She said: and more she could not say:
For what she knew she could not tell,
O'er-mastered by the mighty spell.

Why is thy cheek so wan and wild,
Sir Leoline? Thy only child
Lies at thy feet, thy joy, thy pride,
So fair, so innocent, so mild;
The same, for whom thy lady died!
O by the pangs of her dear mother

Think thou no evil of thy child!
For her, and thee, and for no other,
She prayed the moment ere she died:
630 Prayed that the babe for whom she died,
Might prove her dear lord's joy and pride!
   That prayer her deadly pangs beguiled,
      Sir Leoline!
   And wouldst thou wrong thy only child,
635   Her child and thine?

Within the Baron's heart and brain
If thoughts, like these, had any share,
They only swelled his rage and pain,
And did but work confusion there.
640 His heart was cleft with pain and rage,
His cheeks they quivered, his eyes were wild,
Dishonored thus in his old age;
Dishonored by his only child,
And all his hospitality
645 To the wronged daughter of his friend
By more than woman's jealousy
Brought thus to a disgraceful end—
He rolled his eye with stern regard
Upon the gentle minstrel bard,
650 And said in tones abrupt, austere—
"Why, Bracy! dost thou loiter here?
I bade thee hence!" The bard obeyed;
And turning from his own sweet maid,
The agéd knight, Sir Leoline,
655 Led forth the lady Geraldine!

THE CONCLUSION TO PART 2

A little child, a limber elf,
Singing, dancing to itself,
A fairy thing with red round cheeks,
That always finds, and never seeks,
660 Makes such a vision to the sight
As fills a father's eyes with light;
And pleasures flow in so thick and fast
Upon his heart, that he at last
Must needs express his love's excess
665 With words of unmeant bitterness.

Perhaps 'tis pretty to force together
Thoughts so all unlike each other;
To mutter and mock a broken charm,
To dally with wrong that does no harm.
670 Perhaps 'tis tender too and pretty
At each wild word to feel within
A sweet recoil of love and pity.
And what, if in a world of sin
(O sorrow and shame should this be true!)
675 Such giddiness of heart and brain
Comes seldom save from rage and pain,
So talks as it's most used to do.
—1801

Dejection: An Ode[1]

Late, late yestreen I saw the new Moon,
With the old Moon in her arms;
And I fear, I fear, my Master dear!
We shall have a deadly storm.
            "Ballad of Sir Patrick Spence"[2]

I

Well! If the Bard was weather-wise, who made
   The grand old ballad of Sir Patrick Spence,
   This night, so tranquil now, will not go hence
Unroused by winds, that ply a busier trade
5 Than those which mould yon cloud in lazy flakes,
Or the dull sobbing draft, that moans and rakes
Upon the strings of this Æolian lute,[3]
      Which better far were mute.
   For lo! the New-moon winter-bright!
10   And overspread with phantom light,
      (With swimming phantom light o'erspread
      But rimmed and circled by a silver thread)

---

[1] *Dejection: An Ode* Coleridge originally wrote this poem as a verse letter to Sara Hutchinson (Wordsworth's future sister-in-law), with whom he had fallen in love.

[2] *Ballad of Sir Patrick Spence* Anonymous; published in Thomas Percy's *Reliques of Ancient English Poetry* (1765).

[3] *Æolian lute* Musical instrument named after Æolus, Greek god of the winds; the music of the lute, or, rather, harp, is made by exposure to the wind passing through it.

I see the old Moon in her lap, foretelling
   The coming-on of rain and squally blast.
5 And oh! that even now the gust were swelling,
   And the slant night-shower driving loud and fast!
Those sounds which oft have raised me, whilst they awed,
    And sent my soul abroad,
Might now perhaps their wonted° impulse give,   *usual*
20 Might startle this dull pain, and make it move and live!

2

A grief without a pang, void, dark, and drear,
   A stifled, drowsy, unimpassioned grief,
   Which finds no natural outlet, no relief,
    In word, or sigh, or tear—
25 O Lady! in this wan and heartless mood,
To other thoughts by yonder throstle° woo'd,   *song-thrush*
   All this long eve, so balmy and serene,
Have I been gazing on the western sky,
   And its peculiar tint of yellow green:
30 And still I gaze—and with how blank an eye!
And those thin clouds above, in flakes and bars,
That give away their motion to the stars;
Those stars, that glide behind them or between,
Now sparkling, now bedimmed, but always seen:
35 Yon crescent Moon, as fixed as if it grew
In its own cloudless, starless lake of blue;
I see them all so excellently fair,
I see, not feel, how beautiful they are!

3

   My genial spirits fail;
40   And what can these avail
To lift the smothering weight from off my breast?
   It were a vain endeavour,
   Though I should gaze for ever
On that green light that lingers in the west:
45 I may not hope from outward forms to win
The passion and the life, whose fountains are within.

4

O Lady! we receive but what we give,
And in our life alone does Nature live:
Ours is her wedding-garment, ours her shroud!

50 And would we aught behold, of higher worth,
Than that inanimate cold world allowed
To the poor loveless ever-anxious crowd,
   Ah! from the soul itself must issue forth
A light, a glory, a fair luminous cloud
55   Enveloping the Earth—
And from the soul itself must there be sent
   A sweet and potent voice, of its own birth,
Of all sweet sounds the life and element!

5

O pure of heart! thou need'st not ask of me
60 What this strong music in the soul may be!
What, and wherein it doth exist,
This light, this glory, this fair luminous mist,
This beautiful and beauty-making power.
   Joy, virtuous Lady! Joy that ne'er was given,
65 Save to the pure, and in their purest hour,
Life, and Life's effluence, cloud at once and shower,
Joy, Lady! is the spirit and the power,
Which wedding Nature to us gives in dower
   A new Earth and new Heaven,
70 Undreamt of by the sensual and the proud—
Joy is the sweet voice, Joy the luminous cloud—
   We in ourselves rejoice!
And thence flows all that charms or ear or sight,
   All melodies the echoes of that voice,
75 All colours a suffusion from that light.

6

There was a time when, though my path was rough,
   This joy within me dallied with distress,
And all misfortunes were but as the stuff
   Whence Fancy made me dreams of happiness:
80 For hope grew round me, like the twining vine,
And fruits, and foliage, not my own, seemed mine.
But now afflictions bow me down to earth:
Nor care I that they rob me of my mirth;
   But oh! each visitation
85 Suspends what nature gave me at my birth,
   My shaping spirit of Imagination.
For not to think of what I needs must feel,
   But to be still and patient, all I can;

And haply by abstruse research to steal
90   From my own nature all the natural man—
         This was my sole resource, my only plan:
Till that which suits a part infects the whole,
And now is almost grown the habit of my soul.

                           7

Hence, viper thoughts, that coil around my mind,
95   Reality's dark dream!
I turn from you, and listen to the wind,
         Which long has raved unnoticed. What a scream
Of agony by torture lengthened out
That lute sent forth! Thou Wind, that rav'st without,
100   Bare crag, or mountain-tairn,[1] or blasted tree,
Or pine-grove whither woodman never clomb,
Or lonely house, long held the witches' home,
         Methinks were fitter instruments for thee,
Mad Lutanist! who in this month of showers,
105   Of dark-brown gardens, and of peeping flowers,
Mak'st Devils' yule, with worse than wintry song,
The blossoms, buds, and timorous leaves among.
         Thou Actor, perfect in all tragic sounds!
Thou mighty Poet, e'en to frenzy bold!
110   What tell'st thou now about?
          'Tis of the rushing of an host in rout,
         With groans, of trampled men, with smarting
                  wounds—
At once they groan with pain, and shudder with the cold!
But hush! there is a pause of deepest silence!
115   And all that noise, as of a rushing crowd,
With groans, and tremulous shudderings—all is over—
         It tells another tale, with sounds less deep and loud!
            A tale of less affright,
            And tempered with delight,
120   As Otway's[2] self had framed the tender lay,—

'Tis of a little child
          Upon a lonesome wild,
Not far from home, but she hath lost her way:
And now moans low in bitter grief and fear,
125   And now screams loud, and hopes to make her
          mother hear.

                           8

'Tis midnight, but small thoughts have I of sleep:
Full seldom may my friend such vigils keep!
Visit her, gentle Sleep! with wings of healing,
         And may this storm be but a mountain-birth,
130   May all the stars hang bright above her dwelling,
         Silent as though they watched the sleeping Earth!
            With light heart may she rise,
            Gay fancy, cheerful eyes,
         Joy lift her spirit, joy attune her voice;
135   To her may all things live, from the pole to pole,
Their life the eddying of her living soul!
      O simple spirit, guided from above,
Dear Lady! friend devoutest of my choice,
Thus mayest thou ever, evermore rejoice.
—1802

Phantom

All look and likeness caught from earth,
   All accident of kin and birth,
Had pass'd away. There was no trace
Of aught on that illumined face,
5   Upraised beneath the rifted° stone   *cracked*
But of one spirit all her own—
She, she herself, and only she,
Shone through her body visibly.
—1805

---

[1]   [Coleridge's note]   Tairn is a small lake, generally if not always
applied to the lakes up in the mountains and which are the feeders of
those in the valleys. This address to the Storm-wind will not appear
extravagant to those who have heard it at night and in a mountainous
country.

[2]   *Otway*   Thomas Otway (1652–85), English playwright known for
his tragedies.

Kubla Khan

Or, A Vision in a Dream. A Fragment[1]

In Xanadu did Kubla Khan
A stately pleasure-dome decree:
Where Alph, the sacred river, ran

Through caverns measureless to man
5   Down to a sunless sea.
So twice five miles of fertile ground
With walls and towers were girdled round:
And there were gardens bright with sinuous rills,° *brooks*
Where blossomed many an incense-bearing tree;
10   And here were forests ancient as the hills,
Enfolding sunny spots of greenery.

But oh! that deep romantic chasm which slanted
Down the green hill athwart a cedarn cover!
A savage place! as holy and enchanted
15   As e'er beneath a waning moon was haunted
By woman wailing for her demon-lover!
And from this chasm, with ceaseless turmoil seething,
As if this earth in fast thick pants were breathing,
A mighty fountain momently was forced:
20   Amid whose swift half-intermitted burst
Huge fragments vaulted like rebounding hail,
Or chaffy grain beneath the thresher's flail:
And 'mid these dancing rocks at once and ever
It flung up momently the sacred river.
25   Five miles meandering with a mazy° motion   *labyrinthine*
Through wood and dale the sacred river ran,
Then reached the caverns measureless to man,
And sank in tumult to a lifeless ocean:
And 'mid this tumult Kubla heard from far
30   Ancestral voices prophesying war!
      The shadow of the dome of pleasure
      Floated midway on the waves;
      Where was heard the mingled measure
      From the fountain and the caves.
35   It was a miracle of rare device,
A sunny pleasure-dome with caves of ice!

      A damsel with a dulcimer
      In a vision once I saw:
      It was an Abyssinian maid,
40   And on her dulcimer she played,
      Singing of Mount Abora.

[1] [Coleridge's note] The following fragment is here published at the request of a poet [Lord Byron] of great and deserved celebrity, and as far as the Author's own opinions are concerned, rather as a psychological curiosity, than on the ground of any supposed poetic merits.

In the summer of the year 1797, the Author, then in ill health, had retired to a lonely farmhouse between Porlock and Linton, on the Exmoor confines of Somerset and Devonshire. In consequence of a slight indisposition [dysentery], an anodyne [opium] had been prescribed, from the effects of which he fell asleep in his chair at the moment that he was reading the following sentence, or words of the same substance, in *Purchas's Pilgrimage* [i.e., *Purchas his Pilgrimage* (1613, 1614, 1617, 1626)]: "Here the Khan Kubla commanded a palace to be built, and a stately garden thereunto. And thus ten miles of fertile ground were inclosed with a wall." The author continued for about three hours in a profound sleep, at least of the external senses, during which time he has the most vivid confidence, that he could not have composed less than from two to three hundred lines, if that indeed can be called composition in which all the images rose up before him as things, with a parallel production of the correspondent expressions, without any sensation or consciousness of effort. On awaking he appeared to himself to have a distinct recollection of the whole, and taking his pen, ink, and paper, instantly and eagerly wrote down the lines that are here preserved. At this moment he was unfortunately called out by a person on business from Porlock, and detained by him above an hour, and on his return to his room, found to his no small surprise and mortification, that though he still retained some vague and dim recollection of the general purpose of the vision, yet, with the exception of some eight or ten scattered lines and images, all the rest had passed away like the images on the surface of a stream into which a stone has been cast, but, alas! without the after restoration of the latter!

         Then all the charm
Is broken—all that phantom-world so fair
Vanishes, and a thousand circlets spread,
And each mis-shape the other. Stay awhile,
Poor youth! who scarcely dar'st lift up thine eyes—
The stream will soon renew its smoothness, soon
The visions will return! And lo, he stays,
And soon the fragments dim of lovely forms
Come trembling back, unite, and now once more
The pool becomes a mirror.
[from Coleridge's "The Picture, or the Lover's Resolution" (1802) 69–78]

Yet from the still surviving recollections in his mind, the Author has frequently purposed to finish for himself what had been originally, as it were, given to him. Σαμερον αδιον ασω [from Theocritus's *Idyll*

1.145]: but the tomorrow is yet to come.

As a contrast to this vision, I have annexed a fragment of a very different character [Coleridge's poem "The Pains of Sleep"], describing with equal fidelity the dream of pain and disease.

Could I revive within me
Her symphony and song,
To such a deep delight 'twould win me,
45 That with music loud and long,
I would build that dome in air,
That sunny dome! those caves of ice!
And all who heard should see them there,
And all should cry, Beware! Beware!
50 His flashing eyes, his floating hair!
Weave a circle round him thrice,
And close your eyes with holy dread,
For he on honey-dew hath fed,
And drunk the milk of Paradise.
—1816 (WRITTEN 1798)

Limbo[1]

'Tis a strange place, this Limbo!—not a Place,
    Yet name it so—where Time and weary Space
Fettered from flight, with night-mare sense of fleeing,
Strive for their last crepuscular[2] half-being—
5 Lank Space, and scytheless Time with branny[3] hands
Barren and soundless as the measuring sands,
Not mark'd by flit of Shades—unmeaning they
As moonlight on the dial of the day!
But that is lovely—looks like human Time—
10 An old man with a steady look sublime,
That stops his earthly task to watch the skies;
But he is blind—a statue hath such eyes—
Yet having moonward turn'd his face by chance,
Gazes the orb with moon-like countenance,
15 With scant white hairs, with foretop bald and high,
He gazes still—his eyeless face all eye—
As 'twere an organ full of silent sight,
His whole face seemeth to rejoice in light!

Lip touching lip, all moveless, bust and limb—
20 He seems to gaze at that which seems to gaze on him!
    No such sweet sights doth Limbo den
        immure,°   *imprison*
Wall'd round, and made a spirit-jail secure,
By the mere horror of blank Naught-at-all,°   *nothingness*
Whose circumambience° doth these ghosts   *omnipresence*
    enthral.
25 A lurid thought is growthless, dull Privation,
Yet that is but a Purgatory[4] curse;
Hell knows a fear far worse,
A fear—a future state—'tis positive Negation!
—1817

Work without Hope

Lines Composed 21st February 1825

All Nature seems at work. Slugs leave their lair—
    The bees are stirring—birds are on the wing—
And Winter slumbering in the open air,
Wears on his smiling face a dream of Spring!
5 And I the while, the sole unbusy thing,
Nor honey make, nor pair, nor build, nor sing.

    Yet well I ken° the banks where   *recognize*
        amaranths[5] blow,
Have traced the fount whence streams of nectar flow.
Bloom, O ye amaranths! bloom for whom ye may,
10 For me ye bloom not! Glide, rich streams, away!
With lips unbrightened, wreathless brow, I stroll:
And would you learn the spells that drowse my soul?
Work without hope draws nectar in a sieve,
And Hope without an object cannot live.
—1828

---

[1] *Limbo* In some Christian thought, the location of souls that have been excluded from Heaven through no fault of their own (e.g., virtuous individuals who lived before the coming of Christ, or unbaptized infants). More generally, the word has come to indicate any place or state of nothingness.

[2] *crepuscular* Dim; of or like twilight.

[3] *branny* Resembling bran; scaly, coarse.

---

[4] *Purgatory* In Catholic thought, the state or place in which souls that are not banished permanently to Hell are instead sent to undergo suffering in order to become sufficiently purified to go to Heaven. The word has come to indicate, more generally, any place or state of waiting or of temporary suffering.

[5] *amaranths* Imaginary flowers, the blossoms of which never fade.

Epitaph

Stop, Christian passerby!—Stop, child of God,
And read with gentle breast. Beneath this sod
A poet lies, or that which once seem'd he.
O, lift one thought in prayer for S.T.C.;
5 That he who many a year with toil of breath
Found death in life, may here find life in death!
Mercy for praise—to be forgiven for[1] fame
He ask'd, and hoped, through Christ. Do thou the
     same!
—1833

On Donne's Poetry

With Donne,[2] whose muse on dromedary trots,
     Wreathe iron pokers into true-love knots,
Rhyme's sturdy cripple, fancy's maze and clue,
Wit's forge and fire-blast, meaning's press and screw.
—1836

from *Lectures and Notes on Literature*

[DEFINITION OF POETRY]

Readers may be divided into four classes:
  1. Sponges, who absorb all they read, and return it
nearly in the same state, only a little dirtied.
  2. Sand-glasses, who retain nothing, and are content
to get through a book for the sake of getting through
the time.
  3. Strain-bags, who retain merely the dregs of what
they read.
  4. Mogul diamonds, equally rare and valuable, who
profit by what they read, and enable others to profit by
it also.

from [NOTES ON *LEAR*]

Of all Shakespeare's plays *Macbeth* is the most rapid,
Hamlet the slowest, in movement. *Lear* combines length
with rapidity—like the hurricane and the whirlpool,
absorbing while it advances. It begins as a stormy day in
summer, with brightness; but that brightness is lurid,
and anticipates the tempest. ...

  It is well worth notice, that *Lear* is the only serious
performance of Shakespeare the interest and situations
of which are derived from the assumption of a gross
improbability; whereas Beaumont and Fletcher's tragedies are, almost all, founded on some out-of-the-way
accident or exception to the general experience of
mankind. But observe the matchless judgement of
Shakespeare! First, improbable as the conduct of Lear is,
in the first scene, yet it was an old story, rooted in the
popular faith—a thing taken for granted already, and
consequently without any of the *effects* of improbability.
Secondly, it is merely the canvas to the characters and
passions, a mere *occasion*—not (as in Beaumont and
Fletcher) perpetually recurring, as the cause and *sine qua
non*[3] of the incidents and emotions. Let the first scene of
Lear have been lost, and let it be only understood that a
fond father had been duped by hypocritical professions
of love and duty on the part of two daughters to disin-
herit a third, previously, and deservedly, more dear to
him, and all the rest of the tragedy would retain its
interest undiminished, and be perfectly intelligible. The
accidental is nowhere the groundwork of the passions,
but the κάθολου,[4] that which in all ages has been and
ever will be close and native to the heart of man—
parental anguish from filial ingratitude, the genuineness
of worth, tho' coffered in bluntness, the vileness of
smooth iniquity. ...

---

[1] [Coleridge's note] "For" in the sense of "instead of."

[2] *Donne* English poet John Donne (1572–1631).

[3] *sine qua non* Latin: literally, without which not; i.e., something
essential.

[4] κάθολου Greek: universal, general. Coleridge here contrasts the
idea of universal or general characteristics (common to all people) with
those that are "accidental," particular, or specific to certain people in
certain times and places. (Cf. Aristotle's *Poetics*, in which he discusses
the universal versus the accidental in history and poetry.)

from [On the English Language]

The language, that is to say the particular tongue, in which Shakespeare wrote, cannot be left out of consideration. It will not be disputed, that one language may possess advantages which another does not enjoy; and we may state with confidence, that English excels all other languages in the number of its practical words. The French may bear the palm in the names of trades, and in military and diplomatic terms. Of the German it may be said, that, exclusive of many mineralogical words, it is incomparable in its metaphysical and psychological force. … Italian is the sweetest and softest language; Spanish the most majestic. All these have their peculiar faults; but I never can agree that any language is unfit for poetry, although different languages, from the condition and circumstances of the people, may certainly be adapted to one species of poetry more than to another.

    Take the French as an example. It is, perhaps, the most perspicuous[1] and pointed language in the world, and therefore best fitted for conversation, for the expression of light and airy passion, attaining its object by peculiar and felicitous turns of phrase, which are evanescent, and, like the beautifully coloured dust on the wings of a butterfly, must not be judged by the test of touch. It appears as if it were all surface and had no substratum, and it constantly most dangerously tampers with morals, without positively offending decency. As the language for what is called modern genteel comedy all others must yield to French.

    … Italian, though sweet and soft, is not deficient in force and dignity. …

    But in English I find that which is possessed by no other modern language, and which, as it were, appropriates it to the drama. It is a language made out of many, and it has consequently many words, which originally had the same meaning; but in the progress of society those words have gradually assumed different shades of meaning. Take any homogeneous language, such as German, and try to translate into it the following lines:

But not to one, in this benighted age,
    Is that diviner inspiration given,
That burns in Shakespeare's or in Milton's page,
    The pomp and prodigality of heaven.
           Gray's "Stanzas to Bentley"[2]

In German it would be necessary to say "the pomp and *spend-thriftness* of heaven," because the German has not, as we have, one word with two such distinct meanings, one expressing the nobler, the other the baser idea of the same action.

    The monosyllabic character of English enables us, besides, to express more meaning in a shorter compass than can be done in any other language.

[Mechanic vs. Organic Form]

Are the plays of Shakespeare works of rude uncultivated genius, in which the splendour of the parts compensates, if aught can compensate, for the barbarous shapelessness and irregularity of the whole? … Or is the form equally admirable with the matter, the judgment of the great poet not less deserving of our wonder than his genius? Or to repeat the question in other words, is Shakespeare a great dramatic poet on account only of those beauties and excellencies which he possesses in common with the ancients, but with diminished claims to our love and honour to the full extent of his difference from them? Or are these very differences additional proofs of poetic wisdom, at once results and symbols of living power as contrasted with lifeless mechanism, of free and rival originality as contradistinguished from servile imitation, or more accurately, a blind copying of effects instead of a true imitation of the essential principles? Imagine not I am about to oppose genius to rules. No! the comparative value of these rules is the very cause to be tried. The spirit of poetry, like all other living powers, must of necessity circumscribe itself by rules, were it only to unite power with beauty. It must embody in order to reveal itself; but a living body is of necessity an organized one—and what is organization but the connection of parts to a whole, so that each part is at once end and

---

[1]   *perspicuous*   Transparent.

[2]   *Gray's … Bentley*   I.e., Thomas Gray's "Stanzas to Mr. Bentley."

means! This is no discovery of criticism; it is a necessity of the human mind—and all nations have felt and obeyed it, in the invention of meter and measured sounds as the vehicle and involucrum[1] of poetry, itself a fellow growth from the same life, even as the bark is to the tree.

No work of true genius dare want its appropriate form; neither indeed is there any danger of this. As it must not, so neither can it, be lawless! For it is even this that constitutes its genius—the power of acting creatively under laws of its own origination. How then comes it that ... whole nations have combined in unhesitating condemnation of our great dramatist, as a sort of African nature, fertile in beautiful monsters, as a wild heath where islands of fertility look greener from the surrounding waste, where the loveliest plants now shine out among unsightly weeds and now are choked by their parasitic growth, so intertwined that we cannot disentangle the weed without snapping the flower. ... The true ground of the mistake, as has been well remarked by a continental critic,[2] lies in the confounding mechanical regularity with organic form. The form is mechanic when on any given material we impress a predetermined form, not necessarily arising out of the properties of the material, as when to a mass of wet clay we give whatever shape we wish it to retain when hardened. The organic form, on the other hand, is innate; it shapes as it develops itself from within, and the fullness of its development is one and the same with the perfection of its outward form. Such is the life, such the form. Nature, the prime genial artist, inexhaustible in diverse powers, is equally inexhaustible in forms. Each exterior is the physiognomy of the being within, its true image reflected and thrown out from the concave mirror. And even such is the appropriate excellence of her chosen poet, of our own Shakespeare, himself a nature humanized, a genial understanding directing self-consciously a power and an implicit wisdom deeper than consciousness.

—1811–12

---

[1] *involucrum* Outer membrane.

[2] *a continental critic* German art and literary critic August Wilhelm Schlegel (1767–1845).

from *Biographia Literaria; or Biographical Sketches of My Literary Life and Opinions*

from CHAPTER 1
RECEPTION OF THE AUTHOR'S FIRST PUBLICATION

... In 1794, when I had barely passed the verge of manhood, I published a small volume of juvenile poems. They were received with a degree of favour, which young as I was, I well know was bestowed on them not so much for any positive merit, as because they were considered buds of hope, and promises of better works to come. The critics of that day, the most flattering, equally with the severest, concurred in objecting to them: obscurity, a general turgidness of diction, and a profusion of new coined double epithets.[3] ... From that period to the date of the present work I have published nothing, with my name, which could by any possibility have come before the board of anonymous criticism. Even the three or four poems, printed with the works of a friend, as far as they were censured at all, were charged with the same or similar defects, though I am persuaded not with equal justice: with an excess of ornament, in addition to strained and elaborate diction.

---

[3] [Coleridge's note] The authority of Milton and Shakespeare may be usefully pointed out to young authors. In the *Comus* and other early poems of Milton there is a superfluity of double epithets, while in the *Paradise Lost* we find very few, in the *Paradise Regained* scarce any. The same remark holds almost equally true of the *Love's Labour Lost*, *Romeo and Juliet*, *Venus and Adonis*, and *Lucrece*, compared with the *Lear*, *Macbeth*, *Othello*, and *Hamlet* of our great dramatist. The rule for the admission of double epithets seems to be this: either that they should be already denizens of our language, such as blood-stained, terror-stricken, self-applauding, or when a new epithet, or one found in books only, is hazarded, that it, at least, be one word, not two words made one by mere virtue of the printer's hyphen. A language which, like the English, is almost without cases, is indeed in its very genius unfitted for compounds. If a writer, every time a compounded word suggests itself to him, would seek for some other mode of expressing the same sense, the chances are always greatly in favour of his finding a better word. *Ut tanquam scopulum sic fugias insolens verbum* [avoid an unfamiliar word as you would a rocky promontory], is the wise advice of Caesar to the Roman orators, and the precept applies with double force to the writers in our own language. But it must not be forgotten that the same Caesar wrote a treatise for the purpose of reforming the ordinary language by bringing it to a greater accordance with the principles of logic or universal grammar.

(*Vide*[1] *the criticisms on the "Ancient Mariner" in the Monthly and Critical Reviews of the first volume of the* Lyrical Ballads.) May I be permitted to add, that, even at the early period of my juvenile poems, I saw and admitted the superiority of an austerer, and more natural style, with an insight not less clear, than I at present possess. My judgement was stronger, than were my powers of realizing its dictates; and the faults of my language, though indeed partly owing to a wrong choice of subjects, and the desire of giving a poetic colouring to abstract and metaphysical truths, in which a new world then seemed to open upon me, did yet, in part likewise, originate in unfeigned diffidence of my own comparative talent. …

THE EFFECT OF CONTEMPORARY WRITERS ON YOUTHFUL MINDS

… Among those with whom I conversed, there were, of course, very many who had formed their taste, and their notions of poetry, from the writings of Mr. Pope[2] and his followers: or to speak more generally, in that school of French poetry, condensed and invigorated by English understanding, which had predominated from the last century. I was not blind to the merits of this school, yet as from inexperience of the world and consequent want of sympathy with the general subjects of these poems, they gave me little pleasure, I doubtless undervalued the *kind*, and with the presumption of youth withheld from its masters the legitimate name of poets. I saw, that the excellence of this kind consisted in just and acute observations on men and manners in an artificial state of society, as its matter and substance: and in the logic of wit, conveyed in smooth and strong epigrammatic couplets, as its *form*. Even when the subject was addressed to the fancy, or the intellect, as in *The Rape of the Lock*, or *The Essay on Man*—nay, when it was a consecutive narration, as in that astonishing product of matchless talent and ingenuity, Pope's Translation of the *Iliad*—still a *point* was looked for at the end of each

second line, and the whole was as it were a sorites,[3] or, if I may exchange a logical for a grammatical metaphor, a *conjunction disjunctive*, of epigrams.[4] Meantime the matter and diction seemed to me characterized not so much by poetic thoughts, as by thoughts *translated* into the language of poetry.

… I was … led to a conjecture, which, many years afterwards was recalled to me from the same thought having been started in conversation, but far more ably, and developed more fully, by Mr. Wordsworth; namely, that this style of poetry, which I have characterised above, as translations of prose thoughts into poetic language, had been kept up by, if it did not wholly arise from, the custom of writing Latin verses, and the great importance attached to these exercises, in our public schools. Whatever might have been the case in the fifteenth century, when the use of the Latin tongue was so general among learned men, that Erasmus[5] is said to have forgotten his native language; yet in the present day it is not to be supposed, that a youth can *think* in Latin, or that he can have any other reliance on the force or fitness of his phrases, but the authority of the writer from whence he has adopted them. Consequently he must first prepare his thoughts, and then pick out, from Virgil, Horace, Ovid,[6] or perhaps more compendiously from his *Gradus*,[7] halves and quarters of lines, in which to embody them. …

BOWLES'S SONNETS

… Our genuine admiration of a great poet is a continuous *undercurrent* of feeling; it is everywhere present, but seldom anywhere as a separate excitement. I was wont boldly to affirm, that it would be scarcely more difficult

---

[1] *Vide* Latin: See.

[2] *Mr. Pope* British poet Alexander Pope (1688–1744). It is to his work that Coleridge proceeds to refer.

[3] *sorites* Type of argument in which the predicate of one thesis becomes the subject of the next.

[4] *conjunction disjunctive, of epigrams* Connecting and disconnecting, in poems that seem to lead up to one point and then turn at the end to make another.

[5] *Erasmus* Dutch author, priest, and scholar (1466?–1536), who translated many classics into Greek and Latin.

[6] *Virgil, Horace, Ovid* Roman poets.

[7] *Gradus* Latin dictionary of verse (*Gradus ad Parnassum*) used to aid in composition.

to push a stone out from the pyramids with the bare hand, than to alter a word, or the position of a word, in Milton or Shakespeare (in their most important works at least), without making the author say something else, or something worse, than he does say. One great distinction, I appeared to myself to see plainly, between, even the characteristic faults of our elder poets, and the false beauty of the moderns. In the former, from Donne to Cowley,[1] we find the most fantastic out-of-the-way thoughts, but in the most pure and genuine mother English; in the latter, the most obvious thoughts, in language the most fantastic and arbitrary. Our faulty elder poets sacrificed the passion, and passionate flow of poetry, to the subtleties of intellect, and to the starts of wit; the moderns to the glare and glitter of a perpetual, yet broken and heterogeneous imagery, or rather to an amphibious something, made up, half of image, and half of abstract meaning. The one sacrificed the heart to the head; the other both heart and head to point and drapery.

The reader must make himself acquainted with the general style of composition that was at that time deemed poetry, in order to understand and account for the effect produced on me by the *Sonnets*, the "Monody at Matlock," and the "Hope," of Mr. Bowles;[2] for it is peculiar to original genius to become less and less *striking*, in proportion to its success in improving the taste and judgement of its contemporaries. The poems of West indeed had the merit of chaste and manly diction, but they were cold, and, if I may so express it, only *dead-coloured*; while in the best of Warton's there is a stiffness, which too often gives them the appearance of imitations from the Greek. Whatever relation therefore of cause or impulse Percy's collection of ballads[3] may bear to the most *popular* poems of the present day; yet in the more sustained and elevated style, of the then living poets, Bowles and Cowper[4] were, to the best of my knowledge, the first who combined natural thoughts with natural diction; the first who reconciled the heart with the head. …

from CHAPTER 4
MR. WORDSWORTH'S EARLIER POEMS

… During the last year of my residence at Cambridge, I became acquainted with Mr. Wordsworth's first publication entitled *Descriptive Sketches*,[5] and seldom, if ever, was the emergence of an original poetic genius above the literary horizon more evidently announced. In the form, style, and manner of the whole poem, and in the structure of the particular lines and periods, there is an harshness and acerbity connected and combined with words and images all aglow, which might recall those products of the vegetable world, where gorgeous blossoms rise out of the hard and thorny rind and shell, within which the rich fruit was elaborating. The language was not only peculiar and strong, but at times knotty and contorted, as by its own impatient strength, while the novelty and struggling crowd of images, acting in conjunction with the difficulties of the style, demanded always a greater closeness of attention than poetry (at all events, than descriptive poetry) has a right to claim. It not seldom therefore justified the complaint of obscurity. In the following extract I have sometimes fancied that I saw an emblem of the poem itself, and of the author's genius as it was then displayed.

---

1 *Donne to Cowley* English poets of the early seventeenth century.

2 *Mr. Bowles* William Lisle Bowles (1762–1850), English poet and literary critic, who published a collection of his sonnets in 1789.

3 *Percy's collection of ballads* Reverend Thomas Percy's *Reliques of Ancient English Poetry* (1765).

4 [Coleridge's note] Cowper's *Task* was published some time before the *Sonnets* of Mr. Bowles; but I was not familiar with it till many years afterwards. The vein of satire which runs through that excellent poem, together with the somber hue of its religious opinions, would probably, *at that time*, have prevented its laying any strong hold on my affections. The love of nature seems to have led Thompson to a cheerful religion; and a gloomy religion to have led Cowper to a love of nature. The one would carry his fellow men along with him into nature; the other flies to nature from his fellow men. In chastity of diction, however, and the harmony of blank verse, Cowper leaves Thompson immeasurably below him; yet still I feel the latter to have been the *born poet*.

5 *Descriptive Sketches* Published 1793 and again in 1815 in an altered version.

'Tis storm; and hid in mist from hour to hour,
All day the floods a deepening murmur pour;
The sky is veiled, and every cheerful sight:
Dark is the region as with coming night;
And yet what frequent bursts of overpowering light!
Triumphant on the bosom of the storm,
Glances the fire-clad eagle's wheeling form;
Eastward, in long perspective glittering, shine
The wood-crowned cliffs that o'er the lake recline;
Wide o'er the Alps a hundred streams unfold,
At once to pillars turned that flame with gold;
Behind his sail the peasant strives to shun
The West, that burns like one dilated sun,
Where in a mighty crucible expire
The mountains, glowing hot, like coals of fire.[1]

The poetic psyche, in its process to full development, undergoes as many changes as its Greek namesake, the butterfly.[2] And it is remarkable how soon genius clears and purifies itself from the faults and errors of its earliest products; faults which, in its earliest compositions, are the more obtrusive and confluent, because as heterogeneous elements, which had only a temporary use, they constitute the very *ferment*, by which themselves are carried off. Or we may compare them to some diseases, which must work on the humours, and be thrown out on the surface, in order to secure the patient from their future recurrence. I was in my twenty-fourth year, when I had the happiness of knowing Mr. Wordsworth personally, and while memory lasts, I shall hardly forget the sudden effect produced on my mind, by his recitation of a manuscript poem, which still remains unpub-

lished,[3] but of which the stanza, and tone of style were the same as those of "The Female Vagrant" as originally printed in the first volume of the *Lyrical Ballads*. There was here, no mark of strained thought, or forced diction, no crowd or turbulence of imagery; and, as the poet hath himself well described in his lines "on revisiting the Wye,"[4] manly reflection, and human associations had given both variety, and an additional interest to natural objects, which in the passion and appetite of the first love they had seemed to him neither to need or permit. The occasional obscurities, which had risen from an imperfect control over the resources of his native language, had almost wholly disappeared, together with that worse defect of arbitrary and illogical phrases, at once hackneyed, and fantastic, which hold so distinguished a place in the *technique* of ordinary poetry, and will, more or less, alloy the earlier poems of the truest genius, unless the attention has been specifically directed to their worthlessness and incongruity.[5] I did not perceive anything particular in the mere style of the poem alluded to during its recitation, except indeed such difference as was not separable from the thought and manner; and the Spenserian stanza, which always, more or less, recalls to the reader's mind Spenser's own style, would doubtless have authorized, in my then

---

[1] *'Tis storm ... fire* From "Descriptive Sketches Taken During a Pedestrian Tour in the Alps" (1815).

[2] [Coleridge's note] The fact that in Greek Psyche is the common name for the soul, and the butterfly is thus alluded to in the following stanzas from an unpublished poem ["The Butterfly" (1817)] of the author:

The butterfly the ancient Grecians made
The soul's fair emblem, and its only name—
But of the soul, escaped the slavish trade
Of mortal life! For in this earthly frame
Our's is the reptile's lot, much toil, much blame,
Manifold motions making little speed,
And to deform and kill the things, whereon we feed.

[3] *manuscript ... unpublished* "Guilt and Sorrow; or, Incidents upon Salisbury Plain" (1842; written 1793–94).

[4] *his lines "on revisiting the Wye"* Wordsworth's "Lines Composed a Few Miles above Tintern Abbey"; see lines 77–94.

[5] [Coleridge's note] Mr. Wordsworth, even in his two earliest, "An Evening Walk" and the "Descriptive Sketches," is more free from this latter defect than most of the young poets his contemporaries. It may, however, be exemplified, together with the harsh and obscure construction, in which he more often offended, in the following lines:

'Mid stormy vapours ever driving by,
Where ospreys, cormorants, and herons cry;
Where hardly given the hopeless waste to cheer,
Denied the bread of life, the foodful ear,
Dwindles the pear on autumn's latest spray,
And *apple sickens* pale in summer's ray;
*Ev'n here content has fixed her smiling reign
With independence, child of high disdain.*

I hope, I need not say, that I have quoted these lines for no other purpose than to make my meaning fully understood. It is to be regretted that Mr. Wordsworth has not republished these two poems entire.

opinion, a more frequent descent to the phrases of ordinary life, than could without an ill effect have been hazarded in the heroic couplet. It was not however the freedom from false taste, whether as to common defects, or to those more properly his own, which made so unusual an impression on my feelings immediately, and subsequently on my judgement. It was the union of deep feeling with profound thought; the fine balance of truth in observing, with the imaginative faculty in modifying the objects observed; and above all the original gift of spreading the tone, the *atmosphere*, and with it the depth and height of the ideal world around forms, incidents, and situations, of which, for the common view, custom had bedimmed all the lustre, had dried up the sparkle and the dew drops. "To find no contradiction in the union of old and new; to contemplate the Ancient of days and all his works with feelings as fresh, as if all had then sprang forth at the first creative fiat;[1] characterizes the mind that feels the riddle of the world, and may help to unravel it. To carry on the feelings of childhood into the powers of manhood; to combine the child's sense of wonder and novelty with the appearances, which every day for perhaps forty years had rendered familiar;

> With sun and moon and stars throughout the year,
> And man and woman;[2]

this is the character and privilege of genius, and one of the marks which distinguish genius from talents. And therefore is it the prime merit of genius and its most unequivocal mode of manifestation, so to represent familiar objects as to awaken in the minds of others a kindred feeling concerning them and that freshness of sensation which is the constant accompaniment of mental, no less than of bodily, convalescence. Who has not a thousand times seen snow fall on water? Who has not watched it with a new feeling, from the time that he has read Burns' comparison of sensual pleasure

> To snow that falls upon a river
> A moment white—then gone for ever![3]

In poems, equally as in philosophic disquisitions, genius produces the strongest impressions of novelty, while it rescues the most admitted truths from the impotence caused by the very circumstance of their universal admission. Truths of all others the most awful and mysterious, yet being at the same time of universal interest, are too often considered as so true, that they lose all the life and efficiency of truth, and lie bedridden in the dormitory of the soul, side by side with the most despised and exploded errors."—The Friend,[4] p. 76, No. 5.

This excellence, which in all Mr. Wordsworth's writings is more or less predominant, and which constitutes the character of his mind, I no sooner felt, than I sought to understand. Repeated meditations led me first to suspect (and a more intimate analysis of the human faculties, their appropriate marks, functions, and effects matured my conjecture into full conviction) that fancy and imagination were two distinct and widely different faculties, instead of being, according to the general belief, either two names with one meaning, or, at furthest, the lower and higher degree of one and the same power. It is not, I own, easy to conceive a more apposite translation of the Greek *Phantasia* than the Latin *Imaginatio*; but it is equally true that in all societies there exists an instinct of growth, a certain collective, unconscious good sense working progressively to desynonymize[5] those words originally of the same

---

[1] *fiat* Command.

[2] *With sun … woman* Milton's sonnet "To Mr. Cyriack Skinner upon His Blindness" (1655) actually reads: "Of sun or moon or star throughout the year, / Or man or woman."

[3] *To snow … for ever!* Robert Burns's "Tam O'Shanter" (1791) reads: "Or like the snow falls in the river, / A moment white—then melts for ever."

[4] [Coleridge's note] As "The Friend" was printed on stampt sheets, and sent only by the poet to a very limited number of subscribers, the author has felt less objection to quote from it, though a work of his own. To the public at large indeed it is the same as a volume in manuscript.

[5] [Coleridge's note] This is effected either by giving to the one word a general, and to the other an exclusive use; as "to put on the back" and "to indorse;" or by an actual distinction of meanings as "naturalist," and "physician"; or by difference of relation as "I" and "Me"; (each of which the rustics of our different provinces still use in all the cases singular of the first personal pronoun). Even   [continued …]

meaning, which the conflux of dialects had supplied to the more homogeneous languages, as the Greek and German: and which the same cause, joined with accidents of translation from original works of different countries, occasion in mixed languages like our own. The first and most important point to be proved is, that two conceptions perfectly distinct are confused under one and the same word, and (this done) to appropriate that word exclusively to one meaning, and the synonym (should there be one) to the other. But if (as will be often the case in the arts and sciences) no synonym exists, we must either invent or borrow a word. In the present instance the appropriation has already begun, and been legitimated in the derivative adjective: Milton had a highly *imaginative*, Cowley a very *fanciful* mind. If therefore I should succeed in establishing the actual existences of two faculties generally different, the nomenclature would be at once determined. To the faculty by which I had characterized Milton, we should confine the term *imagination*; while the other would be contra-distinguished as *fancy*. Now were it once fully ascertained, that this division is no less grounded in nature, than that of delirium from mania, or Otway's

Lutes, lobsters, seas of milk, and ships of amber,[1]

from Shakespeare's

What! have his daughters brought him to this pass?[2]

or from the preceding apostrophe to the elements; the theory of the fine arts, and of poetry in particular, could not, I thought, but derive some additional and important light. It would in its immediate effects furnish a torch of guidance to the philosophical critic; and ultimately to the poet himself. In energetic minds, truth soon changes by domestication into power; and from directing in the discrimination and appraisal of the product, becomes influencive in the production. To admire on principle, is the only way to imitate without loss of originality. …

from CHAPTER 11
AN AFFECTIONATE EXHORTATION TO THOSE WHO IN EARLY LIFE FEEL THEMSELVES DISPOSED TO BECOME AUTHORS

… With no other privilege than that of sympathy and sincere good wishes, I would address an affectionate exhortation to the youthful literati, grounded on my own experience. It will be but short; for the beginning, middle, and end converge to one charge: NEVER PURSUE LITERATURE AS A TRADE. With the exception of one extraordinary man, I have never known an individual, least of all an individual of genius, healthy or happy without a *profession*, i.e., some *regular* employment, which does not depend on the will of the moment, and which can be carried on so far *mechanically* that an average quantum only of health, spirits, and intellectual exertion are requisite to its faithful discharge. Three hours of leisure, unannoyed by any alien anxiety, and looked forward to with delight as a change and recreation, will suffice to realize in literature a larger product

---

the mere difference, or corruption, in the *pronunciation* of the same word, if it have become general, will produce a new word with a distinct signification; thus "property" and "propriety"; the latter of which, even to the time of Charles II was the *written* word for all the senses of both. Thus too "mister" and "master" both hasty pronunciations of the same word "magister," "mistress," and "miss," "if," and "give," &c. &c. There is a sort of *minim immortal* among the *animalcula infusoria* which has not naturally either birth, or death, absolute beginning, or absolute end: for at a certain period a small point appears on its back, which deepens and lengthens till the creature divides into two, and the same process recommences in each of the halves now become integral. This may be a fanciful, but it is by no means a bad emblem of the formation of words, and may facilitate the conception, how immense a nomenclature may be organized from a few simple sounds by rational beings in a social state. For each new application, or excitement of the same sound, will call forth a different sensation, which cannot but affect the pronunciation. The after recollection of the sound, without the same vivid sensation, will modify it still further; till at length all trace of the original likeness is worn away.

1 *Lutes … amber* From Thomas Otway's play *Venice Preserved* (1682) 5.2.; Otway's version has the word "laurel" replacing "lobster."

2 *What! … pass?* From Shakespeare's *King Lear* 3.4.65.

of what is truly *genial*, than weeks of compulsion. Money, and immediate reputation form only an arbitrary and accidental end of literary labour. The *hope* of increasing them by any given exertion will often prove a stimulant to industry; but the *necessity* of acquiring them will in all works of genius convert the stimulant into a *narcotic*. Motives by excess reverse their very nature, and instead of exciting, stun and stupify the mind. For it is one contradistinction of genius from talent, that its predominant end is always comprized in the means; and this is one of the many points which establish an analogy between genius and virtue. Now though talents may exist without genius, yet as genius cannot exist, certainly not manifest itself, without talents, I would advise every scholar, who feels the genial power working within him, so far to make a division between the two, as that he should devote his *talents* to the acquirement of competence in some known trade or profession, and his genius to objects of his tranquil and unbiased choice; while the consciousness of being actuated in both alike by the sincere desire to perform his duty, will alike ennoble both. My dear young friend (I would say), "Suppose yourself established in any honourable occupation. From the manufactory or counting-house, from the law-court, or from having visited your last patient, you return at evening,

Dear tranquil time, when the sweet sense of home
Is sweetest[1]—

to your family, prepared for its social enjoyments, with the very countenances of your wife and children brightened, and their voice of welcome made doubly welcome, by the knowledge that, as far as *they* are concerned, you have satisfied the demands of the day by the labour of the day. Then, when you retire into your study, in the books on your shelves you revisit so many venerable friends with whom you can converse. Your own spirit scarcely less free from personal anxieties than the great minds, that in those books are still living for you! Even your writing desk with its blank paper and all its other implements will appear as a chain of flowers, capable of linking your feelings as well as thoughts to events and characters past or to come; not a chain of iron which binds you down to think of the future and the remote by recalling the claims and feelings of the peremptory present. But why should I say *retire*? The habits of active life and daily intercourse with the stir of the world will tend to give you such self-command, that the presence of your family will be no interruption. Nay, the social silence, or undisturbing voices of a wife or sister will be like a restorative atmosphere, or soft music which moulds a dream without becoming its object. If facts are required to prove the possibility of combining weighty performances in literature with full and independent employment, the works of Cicero and Xenophon among the ancients; of Sir Thomas Moore, Bacon, Baxter, or to refer at once to later and contemporary instances, Darwin and Roscoe,[2] are at once decisive of the question."

from CHAPTER 13
ON THE IMAGINATION, OR ESEMPLASTIC[3] POWER

The IMAGINATION then I consider either as primary, or secondary. The primary IMAGINATION I hold to be the living Power and prime Agent of all human Perception, and as a repetition in the finite mind of the eternal act of creation in the infinite I AM. The secondary I consider as an echo of the former, co-existing with the conscious will, yet still as identical with the primary in the *kind* of its agency, and differing only in *degree,* and in the *mode* of its operation. It dissolves, diffuses,

---

[1] *Dear … sweetest* From Coleridge's "To William Wordsworth" 96–97.

[2] *Cicero* Roman orator, philosopher, and political figure of the first century BCE; *Xenophon* Greek historian (c. 430 BCE–c. 355 BCE); *Sir Thomas Moore* Thomas More, humanist, philosopher, political figure, and writer (1478–1533) best known for *Utopia* (1516). He was eventually beatified by the Catholic Church; *Bacon* Francis Bacon (1561–1626), English philosopher and political figure; *Baxter* Clergyman Richard Baxter (1615–91); *Darwin* Erasmus Darwin (1731–1802), physician, botanist, and author of *The Botanic Garden* (1789); *Roscoe* William Rosco (1753–1831), English lawyer, historian, and MP. All of those mentioned are also authors.

[3] *ESEMPLASTIC* Word coined by Coleridge to mean "moulded into unity."

dissipates, in order to re-create; or where this process is rendered impossible, yet still at all events it struggles to idealize and to unify. It is essentially *vital*, even as all objects (as objects) are essentially fixed and dead.

FANCY, on the contrary, has no other counters to play with, but fixities and definites. The Fancy is indeed no other than a mode of Memory emancipated from the order of time and space; and blended with, and modified by that empirical phenomenon of the will, which we express by the word CHOICE. But equally with the ordinary memory it must receive all its materials ready made from the law of association.

Whatever more than this, I shall think it fit to declare concerning the powers and privileges of the imagination in the present work, will be found in the critical essay on the uses of the Supernatural in poetry and the principles that regulate its introduction, which the reader will find prefixed to the poem of *The Ancient Mariner*.

CHAPTER 14
OCCASION OF THE LYRICAL BALLADS

During the first year that Mr. Wordsworth and I were neighbours, our conversations turned frequently on the two cardinal points of poetry, the power of exciting the sympathy of the reader by a faithful adherence to the truth of nature, and the power of giving the interest of novelty by the modifying colours of imagination. The sudden charm, which accidents of light and shade, which moonlight or sunset diffused over a known and familiar landscape, appeared to represent the practicability of combining both. These are the poetry of nature. The thought suggested itself (to which of us I do not recollect) that a series of poems might be composed of two sorts. In the one, the incidents and agents were to be, in part at least, supernatural; and the excellence aimed at was to consist in the interesting of the affections by the dramatic truth of such emotions, as would naturally accompany such situations, supposing them real. And real in *this* sense they have been to every human being who, from whatever source of delusion, has at any time believed himself under supernatural agency. For the

second class, subjects were to be chosen from ordinary life; the characters and incidents were to be such, as will be found in every village and its vicinity, where there is a meditative and feeling mind to seek after them, or to notice them, when they present themselves.

In this idea originated the plan of the *Lyrical Ballads*, in which it was agreed, that my endeavours should be directed to persons and characters supernatural, or at least romantic; yet so as to transfer from our inward nature a human interest and a semblance of truth sufficient to procure for these shadows of imagination that willing suspension of disbelief for the moment, which constitutes poetic faith. Mr. Wordsworth, on the other hand, was to propose to himself as his object, to give the charm of novelty to things of every day, and to excite a feeling analogous to the supernatural, by awakening the mind's attention from the lethargy of custom, and directing it to the loveliness and the wonders of the world before us; an inexhaustible treasure, but for which in consequence of the film of familiarity and selfish solicitude we have eyes, yet see not, ears that hear not, and hearts that neither feel nor understand.[1]

With this view I wrote *The Ancient Mariner*, and was preparing among other poems, the "Dark Ladie," and the "Christabel," in which I should have more nearly realized my ideal, than I had done in my first attempt. But Mr. Wordsworth's industry had proved so much more successful, and the number of his poems so much greater, that my compositions, instead of forming a balance, appeared rather an interpolation of heterogeneous matter. Mr. Wordsworth added two or three poems written in his own character, in the impassioned, lofty, and sustained diction, which is characteristic of his genius. In this form the *Lyrical Ballads* were published; and were presented by him, as an *experiment*, whether subjects, which from their nature rejected the usual ornaments and extra-colloquial style of poems in general, might not be so managed in the language of ordinary life as to produce the pleasurable interest, which it is the peculiar business of poetry to impart. To

---

[1] *we have eyes … understand* Cf. Isaiah 6.9: "Hear ye indeed, but understand not; and see ye indeed, but perceive not." See also Matthew 13.13–14.

the second edition he added a preface of considerable length, in which notwithstanding some passages of apparently a contrary import, he was understood to contend for the extension of this style to poetry of all kinds, and to reject as vicious and indefensible all phrases and forms of style that were not included in what he (unfortunately, I think, adopting an equivocal expression) called the language of *real* life. From this preface, prefixed to poems in which it was impossible to deny the presence of original genius, however mistaken its direction might be deemed, arose the whole long continued controversy. For from the conjunction of perceived power with supposed heresy I explain the inveteracy[1] and in some instances, I grieve to say, the acrimonious passions, with which the controversy has been conducted by the assailants.

Had Mr. Wordsworth's poems been the silly, the childish things, which they were for a long time described as being; had they been really distinguished from the compositions of other poets merely by meanness of language and inanity of thought; had they indeed contained nothing more than what is found in the parodies and pretended imitations of them; they must have sunk at once, a dead weight, into the slough of oblivion, and have dragged the preface along with them. But year after year increased the number of Mr. Wordsworth's admirers. They were found too not in the lower classes of the reading public, but chiefly among young men of strong sensibility and meditative minds; and their admiration (inflamed perhaps in some degree by opposition) was distinguished by its intensity, I might almost say, by its *religious* fervour. These facts, and the intellectual energy of the author, which was more or less consciously felt, where it was outwardly and even boisterously denied, meeting with sentiments of aversion to his opinions, and of alarm at their consequences, produced an eddy of criticism, which would of itself have borne up the poems by the violence with which it whirled them round and round. With many parts of this preface in the sense attributed to them and which the words undoubtedly seem to authorise, I never concurred; but on the contrary objected to them as errone-

ous in principle, and as contradictory (in appearance at least) both to other parts of the same preface, and to the author's own practice in the greater number of the poems themselves. Mr. Wordsworth in his recent collection[2] has, I find, degraded this prefatory disquisition to the end of his second volume, to be read or not at the reader's choice. But he has not, as far as I can discover, announced any change in his poetic creed. At all events, considering it as the source of a controversy, in which I have been honoured, more than I deserve, by the frequent conjunction of my name with his, I think it expedient to declare once for all, in what points I coincide with his opinions, and in what points I altogether differ. But in order to render myself intelligible I must previously, in as few words as possible, explain my ideas, first, of a POEM; and secondly, of POETRY itself, in *kind*, and in *essence*.

The office of philosophical *disquisition* consists in just *distinction*; while it is the privilege of the philosopher to preserve himself constantly aware, that distinction is not division. In order to obtain adequate notions of any truth, we must intellectually separate its distinguishable parts; and this is the technical *process* of philosophy. But having so done, we must then restore them in our conceptions to the unity, in which they actually co-exist; and this is the *result* of philosophy. A poem contains the same elements as a prose composition; the difference therefore must consist in a different combination of them, in consequence of a different object proposed. According to the difference of the object will be the difference of the combination. It is possible, that the object may be merely to facilitate the recollection of any given facts or observations by artificial arrangement; and the composition will be a poem, merely because it is distinguished from prose by metre, or by rhyme, or by both conjointly. In this, the lowest sense, a man might attribute the name of a poem to the well known enumeration of the days in the several months;

Thirty days hath September,
April, June, and November, &c.

---

[1] *inveteracy* Deeply rooted prejudice.

[2] *recent collection* Wordsworth's collected edition *Poems* (1815); the Preface to *Lyrical Ballads* appears at the end of the second volume of the two-volume collection.

and others of the same class and purpose. And as a particular pleasure is found in anticipating the recurrence of sounds and quantities, all compositions that have this charm superadded, whatever be their contents, *may* be entitled poems.

So much for the superficial *form*. A difference of object and contents supplies an additional ground of distinction. The immediate purpose may be the communication of truths; either of truth absolute and demonstrable, as in works of science; or of facts experienced and recorded, as in history. Pleasure, and that of the highest and most permanent kind, may *result* from the *attainment* of the end; but it is not itself the immediate end. In other works the communication of pleasure may be the immediate purpose; and though truth, either moral or intellectual, ought to be the *ultimate* end, yet this will distinguish the character of the author, not the class to which the work belongs. Blest indeed is that state of society, in which the immediate purpose would be baffled by the perversion of the proper ultimate end; in which no charm of diction or imagery could exempt the Bathyllus even of an Anacreon, or the Alexis of Virgil,[1] from disgust and aversion! But the communication of pleasure may be the immediate object of a work not metrically composed; and that object may have been in a high degree attained, as in novels and romances. Would then the mere superaddition of metre, with or without rhyme, entitle *these* to the name of poems? The answer is, that nothing can permanently please, which does not contain in itself the reason why it is so, and not otherwise. If metre be superadded, all other parts must be made consonant with it. They must be such, as to justify the perpetual and distinct attention to each part, which an exact correspondent recurrence of accent and sound are calculated to excite. The final definition then, so deduced, may be thus worded. A poem is that species of composition, which is opposed to works of science, by proposing for its *immediate* object pleasure, not truth; and from all other species (having *this* object in common with it) it is discriminated by proposing to itself such delight from the *whole*, as is compatible with a distinct gratification from each component *part*.

Controversy is not seldom excited in consequence of the disputants attaching each a different meaning to the same word; and in few instances has this been more striking, than in disputes concerning the present subject. If a man chooses to call every composition a poem, which is rhyme, or measure, or both, I must leave his opinion uncontroverted. The distinction is at least competent to characterize the writer's intention. If it were subjoined, that the whole is likewise entertaining or affecting, as a tale, or as a series of interesting reflections, I of course admit this as another fit ingredient of a poem, and an additional merit. But if the definition sought for be that of a *legitimate* poem, I answer, it must be one, the parts of which mutually support and explain each other; all in their proportion harmonizing with, and supporting the purpose and known influences of metrical arrangement. The philosophic critics of all ages coincide with the ultimate judgment of all countries, in equally denying the praises of a just poem, on the one hand, to a series of striking lines or distichs,[2] each of which absorbing the whole attention of the reader to itself disjoins it from its context, and makes it a separate whole, instead of an harmonizing part; and on the other hand, to an unsustained composition, from which the reader collects rapidly the general result unattracted by the component parts. The reader should be carried forward, not merely or chiefly by the mechanical impulse of curiosity, or by a restless desire to arrive at the final solution; but by the pleasurable activity of mind excited by the attractions of the journey itself. Like the motion of a serpent, which the Egyptians made the emblem of intellectual power; or like the path of sound through the air; at every step he pauses and half recedes, and from the retrogressive movement collects the force which again carries him onward. *Præcipitandus est liber spiritus*,[3] says Petronius Arbiter most happily.

---

[1]   *Bathyllus … Virgil*   Coleridge disparagingly references passages in Virgil and Anacreon's work. During this period, many people held strong prejudice against sexuality between men, and "sodomy" was punishable by death.

[2]   *distichs*   Poetic couplets.

[3]   *Præcipitandus est liber spiritus*   Latin: The free spirit must be hurried along. From the *Satyricon*.

The epithet, *liber*,[1] here balances the preceding verb; and it is not easy to conceive more meaning condensed in fewer words.

But if this should be admitted as a satisfactory character of a poem, we have still to seek for a definition of poetry. The writings of Plato, and Bishop Taylor, and the *Theoria Sacra* of Burnet,[2] furnish undeniable proofs that poetry of the highest kind may exist without metre, and even without the contra-distinguishing objects of a poem. The first chapter of Isaiah (indeed a very large proportion of the whole book) is poetry in the most emphatic sense; yet it would be not less irrational than strange to assert, that pleasure, and not truth, was the immediate object of the prophet. In short, whatever *specific* import we attach to the word, poetry, there will be found involved in it, as a necessary consequence, that a poem of any length neither can be, or ought to be, all poetry. Yet if an harmonious whole is to be produced, the remaining parts must be preserved *in keeping* with the poetry; and this can be no otherwise effected than by such a studied selection and artificial arrangement, as will partake of *one*, though not a *peculiar*, property of poetry. And this again can be no other than the property of exciting a more continuous and equal attention, than the language of prose aims at, whether colloquial or written.

My own conclusions on the nature of poetry, in the strictest use of the word, have been in part anticipated in the preceding disquisition on the fancy and imagination. What is poetry? is so nearly the same question with, what is a poet? that the answer to the one is involved in the solution of the other. For it is a distinction resulting from the poetic genius itself, which sustains and modifies the images, thoughts, and emotions of the poet's own mind. The poet, described in *ideal* perfection, brings the whole soul of man into activity, with the subordination of its faculties to each other, according to their relative worth and dignity. He diffuses a tone, and spirit of unity, that blends, and (as it were) *fuses*, each into each, by that synthetic and magical power, to which we have exclusively appropriated the name of imagination. This power, first put in action by the will and understanding, and retained under their irremissive, though gentle and unnoticed, controul (*laxis effertur habenis*)[3] reveals itself in the balance or reconciliation of opposite or discordant qualities: of sameness, with difference; of the general, with the concrete; the idea, with the image; the individual, with the representative; the sense of novelty and freshness, with old and familiar objects; a more than usual state of emotion, with more than usual order; judgement ever awake and steady self-possession, with enthusiasm and feeling profound or vehement; and while it blends and harmonizes the natural and the artificial, still subordinates art to nature; the manner to the matter; and our admiration of the poet to our sympathy with the poetry. "Doubtless," as Sir John Davies observes of the soul (and his words may with slight alteration be applied, and even more appropriately to the poetic IMAGINATION):

Doubtless this could not be, but that she turns
Bodies to spirit by sublimation strange,
As fire converts to fire the things it burns,
As we our food into our nature change.

From their gross matter she abstracts their forms,
And draws a kind of quintessence from things;
Which to her proper nature she transforms
To bear them light, on her celestial wings.

Thus does she, when from individual states
She doth abstract the universal kinds;
Which then re-clothed in divers names and fates
Steal access through our senses to our minds.[4]

Finally, GOOD SENSE is the BODY of poetic genius, FANCY, its DRAPERY, MOTION its LIFE, and IMAGINATION the SOUL that is everywhere, and in each; and forms all into one graceful and intelligent whole.

[1] *liber* Latin: free.

[2] *Bishop Taylor* English theologian and author Jeremy Taylor (1613–67); *Burnet* English cleric and author Thomas Burnet (1635–1715), who wrote *Sacred Theory of the Earth*.

[3] *laxis effertur habenis* Latin: moved forward with loosened rein.

[4] *Doubtless … minds* Adapted from "Nosce Teipsum: Of Human Knowledge" (1599).

from CHAPTER 17
EXAMINATION OF THE TENETS PECULIAR TO
MR. WORDSWORTH

As far then as Mr. Wordsworth in his preface contended, and most ably contended, for a reformation in our poetic diction, as far as he has evinced the truth of passion, and the *dramatic* propriety of those figures and metaphors in the original poets, which stript of their justifying reasons, and converted into mere artifices of connection or ornament, constitute the characteristic falsity in the poetic style of the moderns; and as far as he has, with equal acuteness and clearness, pointed out the process in which this change was effected, and the resemblances between that state into which the reader's mind is thrown by the pleasurable confusion of thought from an unaccustomed bain[1] of words and images; and that state which is induced by the natural language of empassioned feeling; he undertook a useful task, and deserves all praise, both for the attempt and for the execution. …

My own differences from certain supposed parts of Mr. Wordsworth's theory ground themselves on the assumption, that his words had been rightly interpreted, as purporting that the proper diction for poetry in general consists altogether in a language taken, with due exceptions, from the mouths of men in real life, a language which actually constitutes the natural conversation of men under the influence of natural feelings. My objection is, first, that in *any* sense this rule is applicable only to *certain* classes of poetry; secondly, that even to these classes it is not applicable, except in such a sense, as hath never by any one (as far as I know or have read) been denied or doubted; and lastly, that as far as, and in that degree in which it is *practicable*, yet as a *rule* it is useless, if not injurious, and therefore either need not, or ought not to be practised. The poet informs his reader, that he had generally chosen *low and rustic* life; but not *as* low and rustic, or in order to repeat that pleasure of doubtful moral effect, which persons of elevated rank and of superior refinement oftentimes derive from a happy *imitation* of the rude unpolished manners and discourse of their inferiors. For the plea-

sure so derived may be traced to three exciting causes. The first is the naturalness, in *fact*, of the things presented. The second is the apparent naturalness of the *representation*, as raised and qualified by an imperceptible infusion of the author's own knowledge and talent, which infusion does, indeed, constitute it an *imitation* as distinguished from a mere *copy*. The third cause may be found in the reader's conscious feeling of his superiority awakened by the contrast presented to him; even as for the same purpose the kings and great barons of yore retained, sometimes *actual* clowns and fools, but more frequently shrewd and witty fellows in that *character*. These, however, were not Mr. Wordsworth's objects. *He* chose low and rustic life, "because in that condition the essential passions of the heart find a better soil, in which they can attain their maturity, are less under restraint, and speak a plainer and more emphatic language; because in that condition of life our elementary feelings coexist in a state of greater simplicity, and consequently may be more accurately contemplated, and more forcibly communicated; because the manners of rural life germinate from those elementary feelings; and from the necessary character of rural occupations are more easily comprehended, and are more durable; and lastly, because in that condition the passions of men are incorporated with the beautiful and permanent forms of nature."[2]

Now it is clear to me, that in the most interesting of the poems, in which the author is more or less dramatic, as the "Brothers," "Michael," "Ruth," the "Mad Mother," &c. the persons introduced are by no means taken *from low or rustic life* in the common acceptation of those words; and it is not less clear, that the sentiments and language, as far as they can be conceived to have been really transferred from the minds and conversation of such persons, are attributable to causes and circumstances not necessarily connected with "their occupations and abode." The thoughts, feelings, language, and manners of the shepherd-farmers in the vales of Cumberland and Westmoreland, as far as they are actually adopted in those poems, may be accounted for from causes, which will and do produce the same results

---

[1] *bain* Vessel for water.

[2] *because … nature* From Wordsworth's "Preface" to *Lyrical Ballads* (1800).

in *every* state of life, whether in town or country. As the two principal I rank that INDEPENDENCE, which raises a man above servitude, or daily toil for the profit of others, yet not above the necessity of industry and a frugal simplicity of domestic life; and the accompanying unambitious, but solid and religious EDUCATION, which has rendered few books familiar, but the Bible, and the liturgy or hymn book. To this latter cause, indeed, which is so far *accidental*, that it is the blessing of particular countries and a particular age, not the product of particular places or employments, the poet owes the shew of probability, that his personages might really feel, think, and talk with any tolerable resemblance to his representation. It is an excellent remark of Dr. Henry More's (*Enthusiasmus triumphatus*, Sec. xxxv) that "a man of confined education, but of good parts, by constant reading of the Bible will naturally form a more winning and commanding rhetoric than those that are learned; the intermixture of tongues and of artificial phrases debasing *their* style."

It is, moreover, to be considered that to the formation of healthy feelings, and a reflecting mind, *negations* involve impediments not less formidable, than sophistication intermixture. I am convinced, that for the human soul to prosper in rustic life, a certain vantage-ground is prerequisite. It is not every man, that is likely to be improved by a country life or by country labours. Education, or original sensibility, or both, must pre-exist, if the changes, forms, and incidents of nature are to prove a sufficient stimulant. And where these are not sufficient, the mind contracts and hardens by want of stimulants; and the man becomes selfish, sensual, gross, hard-hearted. Let the management of the POOR LAWS in Liverpool, Manchester, or Bristol be compared with the ordinary dispensation of the poor rates in agricultural villages, where the *farmers* are the overseers and guardians of the poor. ... [The] result would engender more than skepticism concerning the desirable influences of low and rustic life in and for itself. ...

If then I am compelled to doubt the theory, by which the choice of *characters* was to be directed, not only *a priori*,[1] from grounds of reason, but both from the few instances in which the poet himself *need* be supposed to have been governed by it, and from the comparative inferiority of those instances; still more must I hesitate in my assent to the sentence which immediately follows the former citation; and which can neither admit as particular fact, or a general rule. "The language too of these men is adopted (purified indeed from what appear to be its real defects, from all lasting and rational causes of dislike or disgust) because such men hourly communicate with the best objects from which the best part of language is originally derived; and because, from their rank in society, and the sameness and narrow circle of their intercourse, being less under the action of social vanity, they convey their feelings and notions in simple and unelaborated expressions."[2] To this I reply; that a rustic's language, purified from all provincialism and grossness, and so far reconstructed as to be made consistent with the rules of grammar which are in essence no other than the laws of universal logic, applied to psychological materials will not differ from the language of any other man of commonsense, however learned or refined he may be, except as far as the notions, which the rustic has to convey, are fewer and more indiscriminate. This will become still clearer, if we add the consideration (equally important though less obvious) that the rustic, from the more imperfect development of his faculties, and from the lower state of their cultivation, aims almost solely to convey *insulated facts*, either those of his scanty experience or his traditional belief; while the educated man chiefly seeks to discover and express those *connections* of things, or those relative *bearings* of fact to fact, from which some more or less general law is deducible. For *facts* are valuable to a wise man, chiefly as they lead to the discovery of the indwelling *law*, which is the true *being* of things, the sole solution of their modes of existence, and in the knowledge of which consists our dignity and our power. ...

Here let me be permitted to remind the reader, that the positions, which I controvert, are contained in the sentences—"*a selection of the* REAL *language of men*"—"*the language of these men* (i.e., men in low and rustic

---

[1] *a priori* Latin: without direct experience.

[2] *The language ... expressions* From Wordsworth's "Preface" to *Lyrical Ballads* (1800).

life) *I propose to myself to imitate, and as far as possible, to adopt the very language of men." "Between the language of prose and that of metrical composition, there neither is, nor can be any essential difference.*"[1] It is against these exclusively, that my opposition is directed.

I object, in the very first instance, to an equivocation in the use of the word "real." Every man's language varies, according to the extent of his knowledge, the activity of his faculties, and the depth or quickness of his feelings. Every man's language has, first, its *individualities*; secondly, the common properties of the *class* to which he belongs; and thirdly, words and phrases of *universal* use. The language of Hooker,[2] Bacon, Bishop Taylor, and Burke,[3] differ from the common language of the learned class only by the superior number and novelty of the thoughts and relations which they had to convey. The language of Algernon Sidney differs not at all from that, which every well educated gentleman would wish to write, and (with due allowances for the undeliberateness, and less connected train, of thinking natural and proper to conversation) such as he would wish to talk. Neither one or the other differ half as much from the general language of cultivated society, as the language of Mr. Wordsworth's homeliest composition differs from that of a common peasant. For "real" therefore, we must substitute *ordinary*, or *lingua communis*.[4] And this, we have proved, is no more to be found in the phraseology of low and rustic life, than in that of any other class. Omit the peculiarities of each, and the result of course must be common to all. And assuredly the omissions and changes to be made in the language of rustics, before it could be transferred to any species of poem, except the drama or other professed imitation, are at least as numerous and weighty, as would be required in adapting to the same purpose the ordinary language of tradesmen and manufacturers. Not to mention, that the language so highly extolled by Mr. Wordsworth varies in every county, nay in every village, according to the accidental character of the clergyman, the existence or non-existence of schools; or even, perhaps, as the exciseman, publican, or barber happen to be, or not to be, zealous politicians, and readers of the weekly newspaper *pro bono publico*.[5] Anterior to cultivation the lingua communis of every country, as Dante has well observed, exists everywhere in parts, and nowhere as a whole.

Neither is the case rendered at all more tenable by the addition of the words, "*in a state of excitement.*" For the nature of a man's words, when he is strongly affected by joy, grief, or anger, must necessarily depend on the number and quality of the general truths, conceptions and images, and of the words expressing them, with which his mind had been previously stored. For the property of passion is not to *create*; but to set in increased activity. At least, whatever new connections of thought or images, or (which is equally, if not more than equally, the appropriate effect of strong excitement) whatever generalizations of truth or experience, the heat of passion may produce; yet the terms of their conveyance must have pre-existed in his former conversations, and are only collected and crowded together by the unusual stimulation. It is indeed very possible to adopt in a poem the unmeaning repetitions, habitual phrases, and other blank counters, which an unfurnished or confused understanding interposes at short intervals, in order to keep hold of his subject which is still slipping from him, and to give him time for recollection; or in mere aid of vacancy, as in the scanty companies of a country stage the same player pops backwards and forwards, in order to prevent the appearance of empty spaces, in the procession of *Macbeth*, or *Henry VIII*. But what assistance to the poet, or ornament to the poem, these can supply, I am at a loss to conjecture. Nothing assuredly can differ either in origin or in mode more widely from the *apparent* tautologies[6] of intense and turbulent feeling, in which the passion is

---

[1]　*a selection … difference* From Wordsworth's "Preface" to *Lyrical Ballads* (1800).

[2]　*Hooker* English clergy member and theologian Richard Hooker (1554–1600).

[3]　*Burke* British politician and political writer Edmund Burke (1729–97).

[4]　*lingua communis* Latin: common language.

[5]　*pro bono publico* Latin: for the good of the public.

[6]　*tautologies* Repetitions.

greater and of longer endurance, than to be exhausted or satisfied by a single representation of the image or incident exciting it. Such repetitions I admit to be a beauty of the highest kind; as illustrated by Mr. Wordsworth himself from the song of Deborah. "*At her feet he bowed, he fell, he lay down; at her feet he bowed, he fell; where he bowed, there he fell down dead.*"[1]
—1817

from *Table Talk*

[On Various Shakespearean Characters]

Othello must not be conceived as a negro, but a high and chivalrous Moorish chief. Shakespeare learned the spirit of the character from the Spanish poetry, which was prevalent in England in his time. Jealousy does not strike me as the point in his passion; I take it to be rather an agony that the creature, whom he had believed angelic, with whom he had garnered up his heart, and whom he could not help still loving, should be proved impure and worthless. It was the struggle *not* to love her. It was a moral indignation and regret that virtue should so fall: "But yet the *pity* of it, Iago!—O Iago! the *pity* of it, Iago!" In addition to this, his honour was concerned: Iago would not have succeeded but by hinting that his honour was compromised. There is no ferocity in Othello; his mind is majestic and composed. He deliberately determines to die, and speaks his last speech with a view of showing his attachment to the Venetian state, though it had superseded him.

Schiller has the material sublime; to produce an effect, he sets you a whole town on fire, and throws infants with their mothers into the flames, or locks up a father in an old tower. But Shakespeare drops a handerchief, and the same or greater effects follow.

Lear is the most tremendous effort of Shakespeare as a poet; Hamlet as a philosopher or meditator; and Othello is the union of the two. There is something gigantic and unformed in the former two; but in the latter, everything assumes its due place and proportion, and the whole mature powers of his mind are displayed in admirable equilibrium.

I have often told you that I do not think there is any jealousy, properly so called, in the character of Othello. There is no predisposition to suspicion, which I take to be an essential term in the definition of the word. Desdemona very truly told Emilia that he was not jealous, that is, of a jealous habit, and he says so as truly of himself. Iago's suggestions, you see, are quite new to him; they do not correspond with any thing of a like nature previously in his mind. If Desdemona had, in fact, been guilty, no one would have thought of calling Othello's conduct that of a jealous man. He could not act otherwise than he did with the lights he had; whereas jealousy can never be strictly right. See how utterly unlike Othello is to Leontes, in *The Winter's Tale*, or even to Leonatus, in *Cymbeline*! The jealousy of the first proceeds from an evident trifle, and something like hatred is mingled with it; and the conduct of Leonatus in accepting the wager, and exposing his wife to the trial, denotes a jealous temper already formed.

Hamlet's character is the prevalence of the abstracting and generalizing habit over the practical. He does not want courage, skill, will, or opportunity; but every incident sets him thinking; and it is curious, and, at the same time, strictly natural, that Hamlet, who all the play seems reason itself, should be impelled, at last, by mere accident, to effect his object. I have a smack of Hamlet myself, if I may say so.

[The Ancient Mariner]

Mrs. Barbauld[2] once told me that she admired the Ancient Mariner very much, but that there were two faults in it—it was improbable, and had no moral. As for the probability, I owned that that might admit some question; but as to the want of a moral, I told her that in my own judgement the poem had too much; and that the only or chief fault, if I might say so, was the obtrusion[3] of the moral sentiment so openly on the reader as

---

[1] *At her feet ... dead* From Wordsworth's note to "The Thorn" (1798).

[2] *Mrs. Barbauld* Poet Anna Laetitia Barbauld (1743–1825).

[3] *obtrusion* Imposition.

a principle or cause of action in a work of such pure imagination. It ought to have had no more moral than the Arabian Nights' tale of the merchant's sitting down to eat dates by the side of a well, and throwing the shells aside, and lo! a genie starts up, and says he *must* kill the aforesaid merchant, *because* one of the date-shells had, it seems, put out the eye of the genie's son.

I took the thought of "*grinning for joy*," in that poem, from poor Burnett's remark to me, when we had climbed to the top of Plinlimmon, and were nearly dead with thirst. We could not speak from the constriction, till we found a little puddle under a stone. He said to me, "You grinned like an idiot!" He had done the same.

[On Borrowing]

A poet ought not to pick nature's pocket: let him borrow, and so borrow as to repay by the very act of borrowing. Examine nature accurately, but write from recollection; and trust more to your imagination than to your memory.

[On Metre]

Really, the metre of some of the modern poems I have read, bears about the same relation to metre properly understood, that dumb bells do to music; both are for exercise, and pretty severe too, I think.

[On Women]

"Most women have no character at all," said Pope,[1] and meant it for satire. Shakespeare, who knew man and woman much better, saw that it, in fact, was the perfection of woman to be characterless.

Every one wishes a Desdemona or Ophelia for a wife—creatures who, though they may not always understand you, do always feel you, and feel with you.

[On Corrupt Language]

I regret to see that vile and barbarous vocable *talented*, stealing out of the newspapers into the leading reviews and most respectable publications of the day. Why not *shillinged, farthinged, tenpenced*, &c.? The formation of a participle passive from a noun is a license that nothing but a very peculiar felicity can excuse. If mere convenience is to justify such attempts upon the idiom, you cannot stop till the language becomes, in the proper sense of the word, corrupt. Most of these pieces of slang come from America.

[On Keats]

A loose, slack, not well-dressed youth met Mr. —— and myself in a lane near Highgate. —— knew him, and spoke. It was Keats. He was introduced to me, and stayed a minute or so. After he had left us a little way, he came back and said: "Let me carry away the memory, Coleridge, of having pressed your hand!"—"There is death in that hand," I said to ——, when Keats was gone; yet this was, I believe, before the consumption showed itself distinctly.

[On Milton]

In the *Paradise Lost*—indeed, in every one of his poems—it is Milton himself whom you see; his Satan, his Adam, his Raphael, almost his Eve—are all John Milton; and it is a sense of this intense egotism that gives me the greatest pleasures in reading Milton's works. The egotism of such a man is a revelation of spirit.

[The Three Most Perfect Plots]

What a master of composition Fielding[2] was! Upon my word, I think the *Oedipus Tyrannus, The Alchymist*, and *Tom Jones* the three most perfect plots ever planned. And how charming, how wholesome, Fielding always is! To take him up after Richardson[3] is like emerging from a sick-room heated by stoves into an open lawn on a breezy day in May.

—1836

---

[1] *Most women ... Pope* From Alexander Pope's "Epistle II: To a Lady," 2.

[2] *Fielding* Henry Fielding, English novelist and playwright (1707–54).

[3] *Richardson* Samuel Richardson, English novelist (1689–1761).

MARY TIGHE
1772 – 1810

Mary Tighe's reputation rests primarily on a single long poem—*Psyche*—but that one poem exerted significant influence on the poetry of the Romantic period. Tighe's sonnets and shorter lyrics were also well-received, but *Psyche* was effusively admired by critics, who praised its "classical elegance," "powers of imagination," and "sublimity of sentiment," and on its strengths ranked Tighe's short career as highly as that of such prominent poets as Felicia Hemans and Joanna Baillie.

Daughter of Theodosia Tighe Blachford, an Irish aristocrat, and the Reverend William Blachford (who died shortly after her birth), Mary Tighe was born in Dublin on 9 October 1772. Her mother believed in advanced education for women and dedicated herself to the schooling of Mary and her brother, John. Tutors were retained for music and drawing; Mary and John copied out and memorized poems; they both learned to translate French authors. Mary eventually married her first cousin, Henry Tighe of Woodstock, County Wicklow. They spent their first eight years of marriage engaged in an active social life in London. The couple had no children, and their marriage is widely considered to have been unhappy. Henry did, however, fulfill her request for daily lessons in Latin—knowledge of which is reflected in the wide-ranging literary allusions that appear in her work.

In 1801, the Tighes returned to Ireland, where Mary composed *Psyche; or The Legend of Love*, a reworking of the myth of Cupid and Psyche based on Apuleius and written in Spenserian stanzas. Tighe professed to have "pictured innocent love, such as the purest bosom might confess," but the poem is a masterpiece of decorously sublimated Eros, sensual as well as sensuous in its lush imagery. The poem was printed privately in 1805, and it circulated quite widely considering that only fifty copies were made. When *Psyche* was formally published in 1811, a year after Tighe died, it was an immediate success. The poem went into a fourth edition within one year. Both Shelley and Keats were impressed by the poem, and the latter's "Ode to Psyche" (1819) clearly owes a debt of gratitude to Tighe's masterpiece; as Wordsworth observed, it is hard to imagine that Keats could have composed the "first of his great Odes … without [Tighe] coming to mind." Other admirers of Tighe's poem included Thomas Moore and Felicia Hemans, who was moved to write two poems about Tighe after visiting her grave. But Tighe's work was largely forgotten in the Victorian period, and remained so for most of the next hundred years; only in the late twentieth century did the very considerable aesthetic virtues of her poetry begin again to be acknowledged.

As early as 1804, Tighe began to show signs of tuberculosis. She died in Ireland on 24 March 1810, at the age of thirty-seven. A selection of her sonnets and lyrics was published after her death, some in *Psyche, with Other Poems*, and some in a second 1811 collection, *Mary, a Series of Reflections During Twenty Years*. Much of her writing, however, was not published until the twenty-first century. Among these literary remains is the courtship novel *Selena*, a tangled narrative of intrigue and vengeance that, when it was finally published in 2012, received approbation for its satirical critique of fashionable English society. It is chiefly for *Psyche*, however, that she continues to be remembered.

⌘ ⌘ ⌘

from *Psyche;*[1] *or The Legend of Love*

SONNET ADDRESSED TO MY MOTHER

Oh, thou! whose tender smile most partially
  Hath ever blessed thy child: to thee belong
  The graces which adorn my first wild song,
If aught of grace it knows: nor thou deny
5 Thine ever prompt attention to supply.
    But let me lead thy willing ear along,
    Where virtuous love still bids the strain prolong
His innocent applause; since from thine eye
    The beams of love first charmed my infant breast,
10 And from thy lip Affection's soothing voice
    That eloquence of tenderness expressed,
Which still my grateful heart confessed divine:
Oh! ever may its accents sweet rejoice
The soul which loves to own whate'er it has is thine!

PSYCHE

Let not the rugged brow the rhymes accuse,
  Which speak of gentle knights and ladies fair,
  Nor scorn the lighter labours of the muse,
  Who yet, for cruel battles would not dare
5 The low-strung chords of her weak lyre prepare:
  But loves to court repose in slumbery lay,
  To tell of goodly bowers and gardens rare,

Of gentle blandishments and amorous play,
And all the lore of love, in courtly verse essay.

10 And ye whose gentle hearts in thraldom held
  The power of mighty Love already own,
  When you the pains and dangers have beheld,
  Which erst your lord hath for his Psyche known,
  For all your sorrows this may well atone,
15 That he you serve the same hath suffered;
  And sure, your fond applause the tale will crown
  In which your own distress is pictured,
And all that weary way which you yourselves must tread.

  Most sweet would to my soul the hope appear,
20 That sorrow in my verse a charm might find,
  To smooth the brow long bent with bitter cheer,
  Some short distraction to the joyless mind
  Which grief, with heavy chain, hath fast confined
  To sad remembrance of its happier state;
25 For to myself I ask no boon more kind
  Than power another's woes to mitigate,
And that soft soothing art which anguish can abate.

  And thou, sweet sprite,° whose sway doth   *spirit*
    far extend,
  Smile on the mean historian of thy fame!
30 My heart in each distress and fear befriend,
  Nor ever let it feel a fiercer flame
  Than innocence may cherish free from blame,
  And hope may nurse, and sympathy may own;
  For, as thy rights I never would disclaim,
35 But true allegiance offered to thy throne,
So may I love but one, by one belov'd alone.

  That anxious torture may I never feel,
  Which, doubtful, watches o'er a wandering heart.
  Oh! who that bitter torment can reveal,
40 Or tell the pining anguish of that smart!

[1] *Psyche* Mortal daughter of royalty in Greek and Roman mythology. When Venus, goddess of beauty, saw that Psyche's beauty eclipsed her own, she ordered her son Cupid, winged god of love, to punish the beautiful virgin. Rather than obeying Venus's orders, Cupid became Psyche's anonymous lover, visiting her in the dark of night and ordering her not to investigate his identity. Psyche's sisters eventually persuaded her to unmask her lover. She lit a lamp but in doing so dropped some oil upon Cupid, wakening him, whereupon he abandoned her. She then wandered in search of him and was forced to perform daunting tasks for Venus. Eventually Cupid took pity upon her and made her his immortal wife.

In those affections may I ne'er have part,
Which easily transferred can learn to rove:
No, dearest Cupid! when I feel thy dart,
For thy sweet Psyche's sake may no false love
45 The tenderness I prize lightly from me remove!

from Canto 1

Much wearied with her long and dreary way,
And now with toil and sorrow well nigh spent,
Of sad regret and wasting grief the prey,
Fair Psyche through untrodden forests went,
5   To lone shades uttering oft a vain lament.
And oft in hopeless silence sighing deep,
As she her fatal error did repent,
While dear remembrance bade her ever weep,
And her pale cheek in ceaseless showers of sorrow steep.

10 'Mid the thick covert of that woodland shade,
A flowery bank there lay undressed by art,
But of the mossy turf spontaneous made;
Here the young branches shot their arms athwart,
And wove the bower so thick in every part,
15 That the fierce beams of Phœbus[1] glancing strong
Could never through the leaves their fury dart;
But the sweet creeping shrubs that round it throng,
Their loving fragrance mix, and trail their flowers along.

And close beside a little fountain played,
20 Which through the trembling leaves all joyous shone,
And with the cheerful birds sweet music made,
Kissing the surface of each polished stone
As it flowed past; sure as her favourite throne
Tranquillity might well esteem the bower,
25 The fresh and cool retreat have called her own,
A pleasant shelter in the sultry hour,
A refuge from the blast, and angry tempest's power.

Wooed by the soothing silence of the scene
Here Psyche stood, and looking round, lest aught
30 Which threatened danger near her might have been,
Awhile to rest her in that quiet spot

She laid her down, and piteously bethought
Herself on the sad changes of her fate,
Which in so short a space so much had wrought,
35 And now had raised her to such high estate,
And now had plunged her low in sorrow desolate.

Oh! how refreshing seemed the breathing wind
To her faint limbs! and while her snowy hands
From her fair brow her golden hair unbind,
40 And of her zone° unloose the silken bands,   *belt*
More passing bright unveiled her beauty stands;
For faultless was her form as beauty's queen,
And every winning grace that Love demands,
With mild attempered° dignity was seen   *balanced*
45 Play o'er each lovely limb, and deck her angel mien.[2] …

from Canto 2

… Illumined bright now shines the splendid dome,
Melodious accents her arrival hail:
But not the torches' blaze can chase the gloom,
165 And all the soothing powers of music fail;
Trembling she seeks her couch with horror pale,
But first a lamp conceals in secret shade,
While unknown terrors all her soul assail.
Thus half their treacherous counsel is obeyed,
170 For still her gentle soul abhors the murderous blade.

And now, with softest whispers of delight,
Love welcomes Psyche still more fondly dear;
Not unobserved, though hid in deepest night,
The silent anguish of her secret fear.
175 He thinks that tenderness excites the tear
By the late image of her parents' grief,
And half offended seeks in vain to cheer,
Yet, while he speaks, her sorrows feel relief,
Too soon more keen to sting from this suspension
brief! …

Allowed to settle on celestial eyes
Soft Sleep exulting now exerts his sway,
940 From Psyche's anxious pillow gladly flies

---

[1] *beams of Phœbus* Sunbeams. Phoebus is Phoebus Apollo, the god of the sun.

[2] *mien* Face.

To veil those orbs, whose pure and lambent ray
The powers of heaven submissively obey.
Trembling and breathless then she softly rose
And seized the lamp, where it obscurely lay,
945 With hand too rashly daring to disclose
The sacred veil which hung mysterious o'er her woes.

Twice, as with agitated step she went,
The lamp expiring shone with doubtful gleam,
As though it warned her from her rash intent:
950 And twice she paused, and on its trembling beam
Gazed with suspended breath, while voices seem
With murmuring sound along the roof to sigh;
As one just waking from a troublous dream,
With palpitating heart and straining eye,
955 Still fixed with fear remains, still thinks the danger nigh.

Oh, daring Muse! wilt thou indeed essay
To paint the wonders which that lamp could
          shew?°   *show*
And canst thou hope in living words to say
The dazzling glories of that heavenly view?
960 Ah! well I ween,° that if with pencil true   *think*
That splendid vision could be well exprest,
The fearful awe imprudent Psyche knew
Would seize with rapture every wondering breast,
When Love's all potent charms divinely stood confest.

965 All imperceptible to human touch,
His wings display celestial essence light,
The clear effulgence of the blaze is such,
The brilliant plumage shines so heavenly bright
That mortal eyes turn dazzled from the sight;
970 A youth he seems in manhood's freshest years;
Round his fair neck, as clinging with delight,
Each golden curl resplendently appears,
Or shades his darker brow, which grace majestic wears.

Or o'er his guileless front the ringlets bright
975 Their rays of sunny lustre seem to throw,
That front than polished ivory more white!
His blooming cheeks with deeper blushes glow
Than roses scattered o'er a bed of snow:

While on his lips, distilled in balmy dews,
980 (Those lips divine that even in silence know
The heart to touch) persuasion to infuse
Still hangs a rosy charm that never vainly sues.

The friendly curtain of indulgent sleep
Disclosed not yet his eyes' resistless sway,
985 But from their silky veil there seemed to peep
Some brilliant glances with a softened ray,
Which o'er his features exquisitely play,
And all his polished limbs suffuse with light.
Thus through some narrow space the azure day
990 Sudden its cheerful rays diffusing bright,
Wide darts its lucid beams, to gild the brow of night.

His fatal arrows and celestial bow
Beside the couch were negligently thrown,
Nor needs the god his dazzling arms, to show
995 His glorious birth, such beauty round him shone
As sure could spring from Beauty's self alone;
The bloom which glowed o'er all of soft desire,
Could well proclaim him Beauty's cherished son;
And Beauty's self will oft these charms admire,
1000 And steal his witching smile, his glance's living fire.

Speechless with awe, in transport strangely lost
Long Psyche stood with fixed adoring eye;
Her limbs immoveable, her senses tossed
Between amazement, fear, and ecstasy,
1005 She hangs enamoured o'er the Deity.
Till from her trembling hand extinguished falls
The fatal lamp—He starts—and suddenly
Tremendous thunders echo through the halls,
While ruin's hideous crash bursts o'er the affrighted walls.

1010 Dread horror seizes on her sinking heart,
A mortal chillness shudders at her breast,
Her soul shrinks fainting from death's icy dart,
The groan scarce uttered dies but half expressed,
And down she sinks in deadly swoon oppressed:
1015 But when at length, awaking from her trance,
The terrors of her fate stand all confessed,

In vain she casts around her timid glance,
The rudely frowning scenes her former joys enhance.

No traces of those joys, alas, remain!
A desert solitude alone appears.
No verdant shade relieves the sandy plain,
The wide spread waste no gentle fountain cheers,

1025

One barren face the dreary prospect wears;
Nought through the vast horizon meets her eye
To calm the dismal tumult of her fears,
No trace of human habitation nigh,
A sandy wild beneath, above a threatening sky.
—1805

JANE AUSTEN

1775 – 1817

Jane Austen is considered to be one of the finest novelists in the English language. Her six major novels, along with her shorter fictional works, juvenilia, and surviving correspondence, share a keenness of wit and irony of observation that have ensured her continued popularity among scholars and general readers alike into the twenty-first century. Her fiction scrutinizes human manners and behavior with particular attention to women of the emergent middle class in Georgian England who need to negotiate between feeling and duty, personal desire and social expectation. As Sir Walter Scott observed, her writing bears "that exquisite touch which renders ordinary commonplace things and characters interesting." Her life and work have for generations been the subject of what is often called an "industry," both scholarly and popular.

Jane Austen was born at Steventon, Hampshire, the sixth child in a family of seven, and the younger of two daughters. Her father, the Reverend George Austen, was a spirited and cultivated man who allowed his daughters free access to his extensive library. Educated mostly at home, she read broadly, including novels by Frances Burney, Laurence Sterne, Henry Fielding, and Samuel Richardson, whose *Sir Charles Grandison* was a particular favorite. Owing in part to the proximity of the boys' school run by Austen's parents from the Steventon Rectory, the household in which Austen grew up was busy and lively, and its members enjoyed and encouraged each others' literary and theatrical pursuits. The young Jane Austen's imagination was fed by family theatricals directed and performed by her elder siblings and cousins for friends and neighbors, possibly with Austen's participation. Most importantly, she was encouraged to read aloud from her early writing, and her family delighted in the comic stories and burlesques she produced in her teenage years. Fictions such as *Lesley Castle* and *Love & Freindship* (sic), the latter written when Austen was 14, are filled with impertinent and riotous humor, indecorous behavior on the part of young women, and an already astute sense of generic convention. Her father was particularly supportive of her writing: at the front of a notebook he had given her, in which she had composed her *History of England*, a juvenile parody of popular histories, George Austen inscribed the following appreciation: "Effusions of Fancy by a very Young Lady Consisting of Tales in a Style entirely new."

Austen lived a quiet country life among a wide network of relations, friends, and neighbors, an ideal context in which to hone the skills in social observation that informed her writing. She never married, although she had at least two admirers, and even accepted a proposal of marriage in 1802 (retracting her acceptance the following day). In 1795–96 she wrote an epistolary sketch called "Elinor and Marianne," which went through several rewrites in subsequent years before taking its final form as *Sense and Sensibility*. This became Austen's first published work (1811), selling out by 1813 and receiving positive reviews. Three other novels were published in quick succession: *Pride and Prejudice* in 1813, *Mansfield Park* in 1814, and *Emma* in 1816. *Pride and Prejudice*, whose first title was "First Impressions," had initially been rejected in 1797 by the publisher Thomas Cadell, who did not even read the manuscript before returning it. When it finally did appear, *Pride and Prejudice* was an instant hit, and it has since become one of the most widely read novels in the English language. Much of its success is due to the appeal of its heroine, Elizabeth Bennet, whose intelligence, feeling, and independence of thought Austen conveys through sparkling dialogue and pioneering use of narrative techniques that provide for flexibility of viewpoint.

The composition of Austen's major works can be divided into two distinct periods. By 1800 she had written three full-length novels, none of them published. Then followed a ten-year silence: the Austens' decision to quit the family home at Steventon and move to Bath, taking Jane and her elder sister Cassandra with them, meant a break in Austen's writing routine. The family moved often in the next several years, and with the death of several friends and family members in this period, most importantly her father in 1805, Austen seems to have experienced a depression that prevented her from writing. Austen's biographer Claire Tomalin points out how easily Austen's existing manuscripts in this decade could have been lost or destroyed. With her settlement at Chawton Cottage in Hampshire late in 1808 with her mother and sister, Austen again found the time and space to write, and it was here that she revised "Elinor and Marianne" into *Sense and Sensibility,* and wrote *Mansfield Park*, *Emma*, and *Persuasion*.

Two of Austen's six major novels were published posthumously in 1818. *Northanger Abbey* had been written under the title "Susan" in 1798–99 and sold to the publisher Richard Crosby in 1803 for the low sum of ten pounds. Although he placed advertisements for the book, he never printed it, and refused to turn over the manuscript or copyright at her request in 1809. *Persuasion*, written in 1815–16, was Austen's last completed novel. It is unique among her major works as the only novel for which any manuscript material survives. Many of her letters were also destroyed by her elder sister, Cassandra Austen, after her death. The Austen sisters were extremely close, sparing no confidence in their correspondence with each other. Many of Austen's surviving letters to her sister are characterized by harshly honest observations of others' foibles.

Lady Susan stands between Jane Austen's juvenilia and her major work in several respects. She probably wrote most of it in 1794–95, revising and adding its abrupt conclusion by 1805, thus putting its date of composition between her last known juvenile writing and her first draft of what would become *Sense and Sensibility* (1811). More importantly, *Lady Susan* seems to bring many of the impulses of Austen's juvenile writing to a head while displaying a sophistication that anticipates her mature work. Many critics have pointed out the novel's debt in both theme and form to the mid-eighteenth-century fiction and Restoration drama Austen grew up on, with its sexual frankness and cynical tone. The novel is in several respects anomalous in the Austen canon: it is her only mature fiction written in the epistolary form, and its eponymous heroine is a female rake—a sexual predator—who openly uses her sexual power to dominate others. Although Austen seems to have become frustrated with the limitations of the epistolary form, eventually abandoning it altogether in her adult writing, in *Lady Susan* it allows the author a moral detachment from the story's action: one is never quite sure whether Austen approved of or deplored her heroine's rebellion against accepted models of proper femininity. *Lady Susan* remained unpublished until 1871, when Austen's nephew James Austen-Leigh included it in his *Memoir of Jane Austen*.

Austen wrote fiction at a moment when women were getting their work into print in ever greater numbers, yet faced relentless pressure to think and behave in ways that militated against their attaining, or expressing, social power and authority. Although by 1816 Austen was a critical and popular success (whose most illustrious fan was the Prince Regent himself), she wore her success lightly, famously referring in a letter of that year to her nephew to the "little bit (two inches wide) of Ivory on which I work with so fine a brush." Perhaps the best known description of Austen's writing, the statement has been read by critics as both a disclaimer and a sly celebration of "women's" writing and the domestic novel. But perhaps not too much should be made of a comment made in a spirit of playful banter with a teenager.

Austen was already suffering from illness when she finished *Persuasion*. She began another novel—*Sanditon*—but it was never finished. Jane Austen died of an undetermined illness on 18 July 1817, and was buried at Winchester Cathedral.

⌘ ⌘ ⌘

Lady Susan

LETTER 1
LADY SUSAN VERNON TO MR. VERNON
December
Langford

My dear brother,

I can no longer refuse myself the pleasure of profiting by your kind invitation when we last parted, of spending some weeks with you at Churchill, and therefore if quite convenient to you and Mrs. Vernon to receive me at present, I shall hope within a few days to be introduced to a sister whom I have so long desired to be acquainted with. My kind friends here are most affectionately urgent with me to prolong my stay, but their hospitable and cheerful dispositions lead them too much into society for my present situation and state of mind; and I impatiently look forward to the hour when I shall be admitted into your delightful retirement. I long to be made known to your dear little children, in whose hearts I shall be very eager to secure an interest. I shall soon have occasion for all my fortitude, as I am on the point of separation from my own daughter. The long illness of her dear father prevented my paying her that attention which duty and affection equally dictated, and I have but too much reason to fear that the governess to whose care I consigned her, was unequal to the charge. I have therefore resolved on placing her at one of the best private schools in town, where I shall have an opportunity of leaving her myself, in my way to you. I am determined, you see, not to be denied admittance at Churchill. It would indeed give me most painful sensations to know that it were not in your power to receive me.

Your most obliged and affectionate sister,
Susan Vernon

LETTER 2
LADY SUSAN TO MRS. JOHNSON
Langford

You were mistaken, my dear Alicia, in supposing me fixed at this place for the rest of the winter. It grieves me to say how greatly you were mistaken, for I have seldom spent three months more agreeably than those which have just flown away. At present nothing goes smoothly. The females of the family are united against me. You foretold how it would be, when I first came to Langford; and Manwaring is so uncommonly pleasing that I was not without apprehensions myself. I remember saying to myself as I drove to the house, "I like this man; pray Heaven no harm come of it!" But I was determined to be discreet, to bear in mind my being only four months a widow, and to be as quiet as possible—and I have been so; my dear creature, I have admitted no one's attentions but Manwaring's, I have avoided all general flirtation whatever, I have distinguished no creature besides of all the numbers resorting hither, except Sir James Martin, on whom I bestowed a little notice in order to detach him from Miss Manwaring. But if the world could know my motive *there,* they would honour me. I have been called an unkind mother, but it was the sacred impulse of maternal affection, it was the advantage of my daughter that led me on; and if that daughter were not the greatest simpleton on earth, I might have been rewarded for my exertions as I ought. Sir James did make proposals to me for Frederica—but Frederica, who was born to be the torment of my life, chose to set herself so violently against the match, that I thought it better to lay aside the scheme for the present. I have more than once repented that I did not marry him myself, and were he but one degree less contemptibly weak I certainly should, but I must own myself rather romantic in that respect, and that riches only, will not satisfy me. The event of all this is very provoking. Sir James is gone, Maria highly incensed, and Mrs. Manwaring insupportably jealous; so jealous in short, and so enraged against me, that in the fury of her temper I should not be surprised at her appealing to her guardian if she had the liberty of addressing him—but there your husband stands my friend, and the kindest, most amiable action of his life was his throwing her off forever on her marriage. Keep up his resentment therefore I charge you. We are now in a sad state; no house was ever more altered; the whole family are at war, and Manwaring scarcely dares speak to me. It is time for me to be gone; I have therefore determined on leaving them, and shall spend I hope a comfortable day with you in town within this week. If I am as little in favour with Mr. Johnson as ever, you must come to me at No. 10, Wigmore St.—but I hope this may not be the case, for as Mr. Johnson with all his faults is a man to whom that great word "Respectable" is always given, and I am known to be so intimate with his wife, his slighting me has an awkward look. I take town in my way to that insupportable spot, a country village, for I am really going to Churchill. Forgive me my dear friend, it is my last resource. Were there another place in England open to me, I would prefer it. Charles Vernon is my aversion, and I am afraid of his wife. At Churchill, however, I must remain till I have something better in view. My young lady accompanies me to town, where I shall deposit her under the care of Miss Summers in Wigmore Street, till she becomes a little more reasonable. She will make good connections there, as the girls are all of the best families. The price is immense, and much beyond what I can ever attempt to pay.

Adieu. I will send you a line, as soon as I arrive in town.

Yours ever,
Susan Vernon

LETTER 3
MRS. VERNON TO LADY DE COURCY
Churchill

My dear mother,

I am very sorry to tell you that it will not be in our power to keep our promise of spending the Christmas with you; and we are prevented that happiness by a circumstance which is not likely to make us any amends. Lady Susan in a letter to her brother, has declared her intention of visiting us almost immediately—and as such a visit is in all probability merely an affair of convenience, it is impossible to conjecture its length. I was by no means prepared for such an event, nor can I now account for her ladyship's conduct. Langford appeared so exactly the place for her in every respect, as well from the elegant and expensive style of living there, as from her particular attachment to Mrs. Manwaring, that I was very far from expecting so speedy a distinction,[1] though I always imagined from her increasing friendship for us since her husband's death, that we should at some future period be obliged to receive her. Mr. Vernon I think was a great deal too kind to her, when he was in Staffordshire. Her behaviour to him, independent of her general character, has been so inexcusably artful[2] and ungenerous since our marriage was first in agitation, that no one less amiable and mild than himself could have overlooked it at all; and though as his brother's widow and in narrow circumstances it was proper to render her pecuniary assistance, I cannot help thinking his pressing invitation to her to visit us at Churchill perfectly unnecessary. Disposed however as he always is to think the best of every one, her display of grief, and professions of regret, and general resolutions of prudence were sufficient to soften his heart, and make him really confide in her sincerity. But as for myself, I am still unconvinced; and plausibly as her ladyship has now written, I cannot make up my mind, till I better understand her real meaning in coming to us. You may guess therefore my dear Madam, with what feelings I look forward to her arrival. She will have

---

[1] *from expecting so speedy a distinction* From expecting to be favored [by the announcement of an impending visit] so quickly.

[2] *artful* Crafty, deceitful.

occasion for all those attractive powers for which she is celebrated, to gain any share of my regard; and I shall certainly endeavour to guard myself against their influence, if not accompanied by something more substantial. She expresses a most eager desire of being acquainted with me, and makes very generous mention of my children, but I am not quite weak enough to suppose a woman who has behaved with inattention if not unkindness to her own child, should be attached to any of mine. Miss Vernon is to be placed at a school in town before her mother comes to us, which I am glad of, for her sake and my own. It must be to her advantage to be separated from her mother; and a girl of sixteen who has received so wretched an education would not be a very desirable companion here. Reginald has long wished I know to see this captivating Lady Susan, and we shall depend on his joining our party soon. I am glad to hear that my father continues so well, and am, with best love etc.,

Catherine Vernon

LETTER 4
MR. DE COURCY TO MRS. VERNON
Parklands

My dear sister,

I congratulate you and Mr. Vernon on being about to receive into your family, the most accomplished coquette in England. As a very distinguished flirt, I have always been taught to consider her; but It has lately fallen in my way to hear some particulars of her conduct at Langford, which prove that she does not confine herself to that sort of honest flirtation which satisfies most people, but aspires to the more delicious gratification of making a whole family miserable. By her behaviour to Mr. Manwaring, she gave jealousy and wretchedness to his wife, and by her attentions to a young man previously attached to Mr. Manwaring's sister, deprived an amiable girl of her lover. I learnt all this from a Mr. Smith now in this neighbourhood—I have dined with him at Hurst and Wilford—who is just come from Langford, where he was a fortnight in the house with her ladyship, and who is therefore well qualified to make the communication.

What a woman she must be! I long to see her, and shall certainly accept your kind invitation, that I may form some idea of those bewitching powers which can do so much—engaging at the same time and in the same house the affections of two men who were neither of them at liberty to bestow them—and all this, without the charm of youth. I am glad to find that Miss Vernon does not come with her mother to Churchill, as she has not even manners to recommend her, and according to Mr. Smith's account, is equally dull and proud. Where pride and stupidity unite, there can be no dissimulation worthy notice, and Miss Vernon shall be consigned to unrelenting contempt; but by all that I can gather, Lady Susan possesses a degree of captivating deceit which must be pleasing to witness and detect. I shall be with you very soon, and am

Your affectionate brother Reginald De Courcy

LETTER 5
LADY SUSAN TO MRS. JOHNSON
Churchill

I received your note, my dear Alicia, just before I left town, and rejoice to be assured that Mr. Johnson suspected nothing of your engagement the evening before; it is undoubtedly better to deceive him entirely; since he will be stubborn, he must be tricked. I arrived here in safety, and have no reason to complain of my reception from Mr. Vernon; but I confess myself not equally satisfied with the conduct of his lady. She is perfectly well bred indeed, and has the air of a woman of fashion, but her manners are not such as can persuade me of her being prepossessed in my favour. I wanted her to be delighted at seeing me—I was as amiable as possible on the occasion—but all in vain—she does not like me. To be sure, when we consider that I *did* take some pains to prevent my brother-in-law's marrying her, this want of cordiality is not very surprising—and yet it shows an illiberal and vindictive spirit to resent a project which influenced me six years ago, and which never succeeded at last. I am sometimes half disposed to repent that I did not let Charles buy Vernon Castle when we were obliged to sell it, but it was a trying circumstance, especially as the sale took place exactly at the time of his marriage—and everybody ought to respect the delicacy of those feelings, which could not endure that my husband's dignity should be lessened by his younger brother's having possession of the family estate. Could matters have been so arranged as to prevent the necessity of our leaving the Castle, could we have lived with Charles and kept him single, I should have been very far from persuading my husband to dispose of it elsewhere; but Charles was then on the point of marrying Miss De Courcy, and the event has justified me. Here are children in abundance, and what benefit could have accrued to me from his purchasing Vernon? My having prevented it, may perhaps have given his wife an unfavourable impression—but where there is a disposition to dislike a motive will never be wanting; and as to money-matters, it has not withheld him from being very useful to me. I really have a regard for him, he is so easily imposed on!

The house is a good one, the furniture fashionable, and everything announces plenty and elegance. Charles is very rich I am sure; when a man has once got his name in a banking house he rolls in money. But they do not know what to do with their fortune, keep very little company, and never go to town[1] but on business. We shall be as stupid as possible. I mean to win my sister-in-law's heart through her children; I know all their names already, and am going to attach myself with the greatest sensibility to one in particular, a young Frederic, whom I take on my lap and sigh over for his dear uncle's sake. Poor Manwaring! I need not tell you how much I miss him—how perpetually he is in my thoughts. I found a dismal letter from him on my arrival here, full of complaints of his wife and sister, and lamentations on the cruelty of his fate. I passed off the letter as his wife's, to the Vernons, and when I write to him, it must be under cover to you.

Yours ever, S.V.

---

[1] *to town* To London.

LETTER 6
MRS. VERNON TO MR. DE COURCY
Churchill

Well, my dear Reginald, I have seen this dangerous creature, and must give you some description of her, though I hope you will soon be able to form your own judgement. She is really excessively pretty. However you may choose to question the allurements of a lady no longer young, I must for my own part declare that I have seldom seen so lovely a woman as Lady Susan. She is delicately fair, with fine grey eyes and dark eyelashes; and from her appearance one would not suppose her more than five and twenty, though she must in fact be ten years older. I was certainly not disposed to admire her, though always hearing she was beautiful; but I cannot help feeling that she possesses an uncommon union of symmetry, brilliancy and grace. Her address to me was so gentle, frank and even affectionate, that if I had not known how much she has always disliked me for marrying Mr. Vernon, and that we had never met before, I should have imagined her an attached friend. One is apt I believe to connect assurance of manner with coquetry, and to expect that an impudent address will necessarily attend an impudent mind; at least I was myself prepared for an improper degree of confidence in Lady Susan; but her countenance is absolutely sweet, and her voice and manner winningly mild. I am sorry it is so, for what is this but deceit? Unfortunately, one knows her too well. She is clever and agreeable, has all that knowledge of the world which makes conversation easy, and talks very well, with a happy command of language, which is too often used I believe to make black appear white. She has already almost persuaded me of her being warmly attached to her daughter, though I have so long been convinced of the contrary. She speaks of her with so much tenderness and anxiety, lamenting so bitterly the neglect of her education, which she represents however as wholly unavoidable, that I am forced to recollect how many successive springs her ladyship spent in town, while her daughter was left in Staffordshire to the care of servants or a governess very little better, to prevent my believing whatever she says.

If her manners have so great an influence on my resentful heart, you may guess how much more strongly they operate on Mr. Vernon's generous temper. I wish I could be as well satisfied as he is, that it was really her choice to leave Langford for Churchill; and if she had not stayed three months there before she discovered that her friends' manner of living did not suit her situation or feelings, I might have believed that concern for the loss of such a husband as Mr. Vernon, to whom her own behaviour was far from unexceptionable, might for a time make her wish for retirement. But I cannot forget the length of her visit to the Manwarings, and when I reflect on the different mode of life which she led with them, from that to which she must now submit, I can only suppose that the wish of establishing her reputation by following, though late, the path of propriety, occasioned her removal from a family where she must in reality have been particularly happy. Your friend Mr. Smith's story however cannot be quite true, as she corresponds regularly with Mrs. Manwaring; at any rate it must be exaggerated; it is scarcely possible that two men should be so grossly deceived by her at once.

Yours etc., Catherine Vernon

LETTER 7
LADY SUSAN TO MRS. JOHNSON
Churchill

My dear Alicia,

You are very good in taking notice of Frederica, and I am grateful for it as a mark of your friendship; but as I cannot have a doubt of the warmth of that friendship, I am far from exacting so heavy a sacrifice. She is a stupid girl, and has nothing to recommend her. I would not therefore on any account have you encumber one moment of your precious time by sending her to Edward St., especially as every visit is so many hours deducted from the grand affair of education, which I really wish to be attended to, while she remains with Miss Summers. I want her to play and sing with some portion of taste, and a good deal of assurance, as she has my hand and arm, and a tolerable voice. I was so much indulged in my infant years that I was never obliged to attend to anything, and consequently am without those accomplishments which are necessary to finish a pretty woman. Not that I am an advocate for the prevailing fashion of acquiring a perfect knowledge in all the languages, arts, and sciences; it is throwing time away; to be mistress of French, Italian, German, music, singing, drawing etc., will gain a woman some applause, but will not add one lover to her list. Grace and manner after all are of the greatest importance. I do not mean therefore that Frederica's acquirements should be more than superficial, and I flatter myself that she will not remain long enough at school to understand anything thoroughly. I hope to see her the wife of Sir James within a twelvemonth. You know on what I ground my hope, and it is certainly a good foundation, for school must be very humiliating to a girl of Frederica's age; and by the bye, you had better not invite her any more on that account, as I wish her to find her situation as unpleasant as possible. I am sure of Sir James at any time, and could make him renew his application by a line. I shall trouble you meanwhile to prevent his forming any other attachment when he comes to town; ask him to your house occasionally, and talk to him about Frederica that he may not forget her.

Upon the whole I commend my own conduct in this affair extremely, and regard it as a very happy mixture of circumspection and tenderness. Some mothers would have insisted on their daughter's accepting so great an offer on the first overture, but I could not answer it to myself to force Frederica into a marriage from which her heart revolted; and instead of adopting so harsh a measure, merely propose to make it her own choice by rendering her life thoroughly uncomfortable till she does accept him. But enough of this tiresome girl.

You may well wonder how I contrive to pass my time here—and for the first week, it was most insufferably dull. Now however, we begin to mend; our party is enlarged by Mrs. Vernon's brother, a handsome young man, who promises me some amusement. There is something about him that rather interests me, a sort of sauciness, of familiarity which I shall teach him to correct. He is lively and seems clever, and when I have inspired him with greater respect for me than his sister's kind offices have implanted, he may be an agreeable flirt. There is exquisite pleasure in subduing an insolent spirit, in making a person pre-determined to dislike, acknowledge one's superiority. I have disconcerted him already by my calm reserve; and it shall be my endeavour to humble the pride of these self-important De Courcys still lower, to convince Mrs. Vernon that her sisterly cautions have been bestowed in vain, and to persuade Reginald that she has scandalously belied me. This project will serve at least to amuse me, and prevent my feeling so acutely this dreadful separation from you and all whom I love. Adieu.

Yours ever,
S. Vernon

LETTER 8
MRS. VERNON TO LADY DE COURCY
Churchill

My dear mother,

You must not expect Reginald back again for some time. He desires me to tell you that the present open weather induces him to accept Mr. Vernon's invitation to prolong his stay in Sussex that they may have some hunting together. He means to send for his horses immediately, and it is impossible to say when you may see him in Kent. I will not disguise my sentiments on this change from you, my dear Madam, though I think you had better not communicate them to my father, whose excessive anxiety about Reginald would subject him to an alarm which might seriously affect his health and spirits. Lady Susan has certainly contrived in the space of a fortnight to make my brother like her. In short, I am persuaded that his continuing here beyond the time originally fixed for his return, is occasioned as much by a degree of fascination towards her, as by the wish of hunting with Mr. Vernon, and of course I cannot receive that pleasure from the length of his visit which my brother's company would otherwise give me. I am indeed provoked at the artifice of this unprincipled woman. What stronger proof of her dangerous abilities can be given, than this perversion of Reginald's judgement, which when he entered the house was so decidedly

against her? In his last letter he actually gave me some particulars of her behaviour at Langford, such as he received from a gentleman who knew her perfectly well, which if true must raise abhorrence against her, and which Reginald himself was entirely disposed to credit. His opinion of her, I am sure, was as low as of any woman in England, and when he first came it was evident that he considered her as one entitled neither to delicacy nor respect, and that he felt she would be delighted with the attentions of any man inclined to flirt with her.

Her behaviour I confess has been calculated to do away with such an idea, I have not detected the smallest impropriety in it—nothing of vanity, of pretension, of levity—and she is altogether so attractive, that I should not wonder at his being delighted with her, had he known nothing of her previous to this personal acquaintance; but against reason, against conviction, to be so well pleased with her as I am sure he is, does really astonish me. His admiration was at first very strong, but no more than was natural; and I did not wonder at his being struck by the gentleness and delicacy of her manners; but when he has mentioned her of late, it has been in terms of more extraordinary praise, and yesterday he actually said, that he could not be surprised at any effect produced on the heart of man by such loveliness and such abilities; and when I lamented in reply the badness of her disposition, he observed that whatever might have been her errors, they were to be imputed to her neglected education and early marriage, and that she was altogether a wonderful woman.

This tendency to excuse her conduct, or to forget it in the warmth of admiration vexes me; and if I did not know that Reginald is too much at home at Churchill to need an invitation for lengthening his visit, I should regret Mr. Vernon's giving him any.

Lady Susan's intentions are of course those of absolute coquetry, or a desire of universal admiration. I cannot for a moment imagine that she has anything more serious in view, but it mortifies me to see a young man of Reginald's sense duped by her at all. I am etc.,

Catherine Vernon

LETTER 9
MRS. JOHNSON TO LADY SUSAN
Edward St.

My dearest friend,

I congratulate you on Mr. De Courcy's arrival, and advise you by all means to marry him; his father's estate is we know considerable, and I believe certainly entailed. Sir Reginald is very infirm, and not likely to stand in your way long. I hear the young man well spoken of, and though no one can really deserve you my dearest Susan, Mr. De Courcy may be worth having. Manwaring will storm of course, but you may easily pacify him. Besides, the most scrupulous point of honour could not require you to wait for his emancipation. I have seen Sir James—he came to town for a few days last week, and called several times in Edward Street. I talked to him about you and your daughter, and he is so far from having forgotten you, that I am sure he would marry either of you with pleasure. I gave him hopes of Frederica's relenting, and told him a great deal of her improvements. I scolded him for making love to Maria Manwaring; he protested that he had been only in joke, and we both laughed heartily at her disappointment, and in short were very agreeable. He is as silly as ever.—

Yours faithfully,
Alicia

LETTER 10 [1]
LADY SUSAN TO MRS. JOHNSON
Churchill

I am obliged to you, my dear friend, for your advice respecting Mr. De Courcy, which I know was given with the full conviction of its expediency, tho' I am not quite determined on following it. I cannot easily resolve on anything so serious as Marriage; especially as I am not at present in want of money, & might perhaps, till the old Gentleman's death, be very little benefited by the match. It is true that I am vain enough to beleive it within my reach. I have made him sensible of my power, & can now enjoy the pleasure of triumphing over a Mind prepared to dislike me, & prejudiced against all my past actions. His sister, too, is, I hope, convinced how little the ungenerous representations of any one to the disadvantage of another will avail when opposed to the immediate influence of Intellect & Manner. I see plainly that she is uneasy at my progress in the good opinion of her Brother, & conclude that nothing will be wanting on her part to counteract me; but having once made him doubt the justice of her opinion of me, I think I may defy her. It has been delightful to me to watch his advances towards intimacy, especially to observe his altered manner in consequence of my repressing by the calm dignity of my deportment his insolent approach to direct familiarity. My conduct has been equally guarded from the first, & I never behaved less like a Coquette in the whole course of my Life, tho' perhaps my desire of dominion was never more decided. I have subdued him entirely by sentiment & serious conversation, & made him, I may venture to say, at least *half* in Love with me, without the semblance of the most commonplace flirtation. Mrs. Vernon's consciousness of deserving every sort of revenge that it can be in my power to inflict for her ill-offices could alone enable her to perceive that I am actuated by any design in behaviour so gentle & unpretending. Let her think & act as she chuses, however. I have never yet found that the advice of a Sister could prevent a young Man's being in love if he chose it. We are advancing now towards some kind of confidence, & in short are likely to be engaged in a sort of platonic friendship. On *my* side you may be sure of its never being more, for if I were not already as much attached to another person as I can be to any one, I should make a point of not bestowing my affection on a Man who had dared to think so meanly of me.

---

[1]   *LETTER 10*   Though the manuscript of *Lady Susan* was completed circa 1805, it was not published until 1871, when it appeared as part of Edward Austen-Leigh's *Memoir* (Austen had left her manuscript untitled; the title was provided by Austen-Leigh). Not surprisingly, then, the original text is illustrative of spelling and punctuation practices that were common in the very late eighteenth and very early nineteenth centuries. Spelling had still not been regularized (particularly in such matters as "i before e"); something of the eighteenth century habit of capitalizing abstract nouns (such as "intellect" and "manner") remained; and the ampersand ("&") was frequently used in place of "and."

Reginald has a good figure, & is not unworthy the praise you have heard given him, but is still greatly inferior to our friend at Langford. He is less polished, less insinuating than Manwaring, & is comparatively deficient in the power of saying those delightful things which put one in good humour with oneself & all the world. He is quite agreable enough, however, to afford me amusement, & to make many of those hours pass very pleasantly which would otherwise be spent in endeavouring to overcome my sister-in-law's reserve, & listening to her Husband's insipid talk.

Your account of Sir James is most satisfactory, & I mean to give Miss Frederica a hint of my intentions very soon.—Yours, &c.,

S. VERNON.

LETTER 11
MRS. VERNON TO LADY DE COURCY

I really grow quite uneasy, my dearest mother, about Reginald, from witnessing the very rapid increase of Lady Susan's influence. They are now on terms of the most particular friendship, frequently engaged in long conversations together, and she has contrived by the most artful coquetry to subdue his judgement to her own purposes. It is impossible to see the intimacy between them, so very soon established, without some alarm, though I can hardly suppose that Lady Susan's views extend to marriage. I wish you could get Reginald home again, under any plausible pretence. He is not at all disposed to leave us, and I have given him as many hints of my father's precarious state of health, as common decency will allow me to do in my own house. Her power over him must now be boundless, as she has entirely effaced all his former ill-opinion, and persuaded him not merely to forget, but to justify her conduct. Mr. Smith's account of her proceedings at Langford, where he accused her of having made Mr. Manwaring and a young man engaged to Miss Manwaring distractedly in love with her, which Reginald firmly believed when he came to Churchill, is now he is persuaded only a scandalous invention. He has told me so in a warmth of manner which spoke his regret at having ever believed the contrary himself.

How sincerely do I grieve that she ever entered this house! I always looked forward to her coming with uneasiness—but very far was it, from originating in anxiety for Reginald. I expected a most disagreeable companion to myself, but could not imagine that my brother would be in the smallest danger of being captivated by a woman with whose principles he was so well acquainted, and whose character he so heartily despised. If you can get him away, it will be a good thing.

Yours affectionately,

Catherine Vernon

LETTER 12
SIR REGINALD DE COURCY TO HIS SON
Parklands

I know that young men in general do not admit of any enquiry even from their nearest relations, into affairs of the heart; but I hope my dear Reginald that you will be superior to such as allow nothing for a father's anxiety, and think themselves privileged to refuse him their confidence and slight his advice. You must be sensible that as an only son and the representative of an ancient family, your conduct in life is most interesting to your connections. In the very important concern of marriage especially, there is everything at stake; your own happiness, that of your parents, and the credit of your name. I do not suppose that you would deliberately form an absolute engagement of that nature without acquainting your mother and myself, or at least without being convinced that we should approve your choice; but I cannot help fearing that you may be drawn in by the lady who has lately attached you, to a marriage, which the whole of your family, far and near, must highly reprobate.[1]

Lady Susan's age is itself a material objection, but her want of character is one so much more serious, that the difference of even twelve years becomes in comparison of small account. Were you not blinded by a sort of fascination, it would be ridiculous in me to repeat the instances of great misconduct on her side, so very generally known. Her neglect of her husband, her encouragement of other

---

[1] *reprobate* Disapprove of.

men, her extravagance and dissipation were so gross and notorious, that no one could be ignorant of them at the time, nor can now have forgotten them. To our family, she has always been represented in softened colours by the benevolence of Mr. Charles Vernon; and yet in spite of his generous endeavours to excuse her, we know that she did, from the most selfish motives, take all possible pains to prevent his marrying Catherine.

My years and increasing infirmities make me very desirous, my dear Reginald, of seeing you settled in the world. To the fortune of your wife, the goodness of my own, will make me indifferent; but her family and character must be equally unexceptionable. When your choice is so fixed as that no objection can be made to either, I can promise you a ready and cheerful consent; but it is my duty to oppose a match, which deep art only could render probable, and must in the end make wretched.

It is possible that her behaviour may arise only from vanity, or a wish of gaining the admiration of a man whom she must imagine to be particularly prejudiced against her; but it is more likely that she should aim at something farther. She is poor, and may naturally seek an alliance which may be advantageous to herself. You know your own rights, and that it is out of my power to prevent your inheriting the family estate. My ability of distressing you during my life, would be a species of revenge to which I should hardly stoop under any circumstances. I honestly tell you my sentiments and intentions. I do not wish to work on your fears, but on your sense and affection. It would destroy every comfort of my life, to know that you were married to Lady Susan Vernon. It would be the death of that honest pride with which I have hitherto considered my son, I should blush to see him, to hear of him, to think of him.

I may perhaps do no good, but that of relieving my own mind, by this letter; but I felt it my duty to tell you that your partiality for Lady Susan is no secret to your friends, and to warn you against her. I should be glad to hear your reasons for disbelieving Mr. Smith's intelligence; you had no doubt of its authenticity a month ago.

If you can give me your assurance of having no design beyond enjoying the conversation of a clever woman for a short period, and of yielding admiration only to her beauty and abilities without being blinded by them to her faults, you will restore me to happiness; but if you cannot do this, explain to me at least what has occasioned so great an alteration in your opinion of her.

I am etc.,
Reginald De Courcy

LETTER 13
LADY DE COURCY TO MRS. VERNON
Parklands

My dear Catherine,

Unluckily I was confined to my room when your last letter came, by a cold which affected my eyes so much as to prevent my reading it myself, so I could not refuse your father when he offered to read it to me, by which means he became acquainted to my great vexation with all your fears about your brother. I had intended to write to Reginald myself, as soon as my eyes would let me, to point out as well as I could the danger of an intimate acquaintance with so artful a woman as Lady Susan, to a young man of his age and high expectations. I meant moreover to have reminded him of our being quite alone now, and very much in need of him to keep up our spirits these long winter evenings. Whether it would have done any good, can never be settled now; but I am excessively vexed that Sir Reginald should know anything of a matter which we foresaw would make him so uneasy. He caught all your fears the moment he had read your letter, and I am sure has not had the business out of his head since; he wrote by the same post to Reginald, a long letter full of it all, and particularly asking for an explanation of what he may have heard from Lady Susan to contradict the late shocking reports. His answer came this morning, which I shall enclose to you, as I think you will like to see it; I wish it was more satisfactory, but it seems written with such a determination to think well of Lady Susan, that his assurances as to marriage etc., do not set my heart at ease. I say all I can however to satisfy your father, and he is certainly less uneasy since Reginald's letter. How provoking it is, my dear

Catherine, that this unwelcome guest of yours, should not only prevent our meeting this Christmas, but be the occasion of so much vexation and trouble. Kiss the dear children for me.

Your affectionate mother,
C. De Courcy

LETTER 14
MR. DE COURCY TO SIR REGINALD
Churchill

My dear Sir,

I have this moment received your letter, which has given me more astonishment than I ever felt before. I am to thank my sister I suppose, for having represented me in such a light as to injure me in your opinion, and give you all this alarm. I know not why she should choose to make herself and her family uneasy by apprehending an event, which no one but herself, I can affirm, would ever have thought possible. To impute such a design to Lady Susan would be taking from her every claim to that excellent understanding which her bitterest enemies have never denied her; and equally low must sink my pretensions to common-sense, if I am suspected of matrimonial views in my behaviour to her. Our difference of age must be an insuperable objection, and I entreat you my dear Sir to quiet your mind, and no longer harbour a suspicion which cannot be more injurious to your own peace than to our understandings.

I can have no view in remaining with Lady Susan than to enjoy for a short time (as you have yourself expressed it) the conversation of a woman of high mental powers. If Mrs. Vernon would allow something to my affection for herself and her husband in the length of my visit, she would do more justice to us all; but my sister is unhappily prejudiced beyond the hope of conviction against Lady Susan. From an attachment to her husband which in itself does honour to both, she cannot forgive those endeavours at preventing their union, which have been attributed to selfishness in Lady Susan. But in this case, as well as in many others, the world has most grossly injured that lady, by supposing the worst, where the motives of her conduct have been doubtful.

Lady Susan had heard something so materially to the disadvantage of my sister, as to persuade her that the happiness of Mr. Vernon, to whom she was always much attached, would be absolutely destroyed by the marriage. And this circumstance, while it explains the true motive of Lady Susan's conduct, and removes all the blame which has been so lavished on her, may also convince us how little the general report of any one ought to be credited, since no character however upright, can escape the malevolence of slander. If my sister in the security of retirement, with as little opportunity as inclination to do evil, could not avoid censure, we must not rashly condemn those who living in the world and surrounded with temptation, should be accused of errors which they are known to have the power of committing.

I blame myself severely for having so easily believed the scandalous tales invented by Charles Smith to the prejudice of Lady Susan, as I am now convinced how greatly they have traduced her. As to Mrs. Manwaring's jealousy, it was totally his own invention; and his account of her attaching Miss Manwaring's lover was scarcely better founded. Sir James Martin had been drawn in by that young lady to pay her some attention, and as he is a man of fortune, it was easy to see that her views extended to marriage. It is well known that Miss Manwaring is absolutely on the catch for a husband, and no one therefore can pity her, for losing by the superior attractions of another woman, the chance of being able to make a worthy man completely miserable. Lady Susan was far from intending such a conquest, and in finding how warmly Miss Manwaring resented her lover's defection, determined, in spite of Mr. and Mrs. Manwaring's most earnest entreaties, to leave the family. I have reason to imagine that she did receive serious proposals from Sir James, but her removing from Langford immediately on the discovery of his attachment, must acquit her on that article, with every mind of common candour. You will, I am sure my dear Sir, feel the truth of this reasoning, and will hereby learn to do justice to the character of a very injured woman.

I know that Lady Susan in coming to Churchill was governed only by the most honourable and amiable intentions. Her prudence and economy are exemplary, her regard for Mr. Vernon equal even to *his* deserts, and her wish of obtaining my sister's good opinion merits a better return than it had received. As a mother she is unexceptionable.[1] Her solid affection for her child is shown by placing her in hands, where her education will be properly attended to; but because she has not the blind and weak partiality of most mothers, she is accused of wanting[2] maternal tenderness. Every person of sense however will know how to value and commend her well directed affection, and will join me in wishing that Frederica Vernon may prove more worthy than she has yet done, of her mother's tender care.

I have now my dear Sir, written my real sentiments of Lady Susan; you will know from this letter, how highly I admire her abilities, and esteem her character; but if you are not equally convinced by my full and solemn assurance that your fears have been most idly created, you will deeply mortify and distress me.—I am etc.,

R. De Courcy

LETTER 15
MRS. VERNON TO LADY DE COURCY

Churchill

My dear mother,

I return you Reginald's letter, and rejoice with all my heart that my father is made easy by it. Tell him so, with my congratulations, but between ourselves, I must own it has only convinced *me* of my brother's having no present intention of marrying Lady Susan—not that he is in no danger of doing so three months hence. He gives a very plausible account of her behaviour at Langford, I wish it may be true, but his intelligence must come from herself, and I am less disposed to believe it, than to lament the degree of intimacy subsisting between them, implied by the discussion of such a subject.

I am sorry to have incurred his displeasure, but can expect nothing better while he is so very eager in Lady

Susan's justification. He is very severe against me indeed, and yet I hope I have not been hasty in my judgement of her. Poor woman! though I have reasons enough for my dislike, I can not help pitying her at present as she is in real distress, and with too much cause. She had this morning a letter from the lady with whom she has placed her daughter, to request that Miss Vernon might be immediately removed, as she had been detected in an attempt to run away. Why, or whither she intended to go, does not appear; but as her situation seems to have been unexceptionable, it is a sad thing and of course highly afflicting to Lady Susan.

Frederica must be as much as sixteen, and ought to know better, but from what her mother insinuates I am afraid she is a perverse girl. She has been sadly neglected however, and her mother ought to remember it.

Mr. Vernon set off for town as soon as she had determined what should be done. He is if possible to prevail on Miss Summers to let Frederica continue with her, and if he cannot succeed, to bring her to Churchill for the present, till some other situation can be found for her. Her ladyship is comforting herself meanwhile by strolling along the shrubbery with Reginald, calling forth all his tender feelings I suppose on this distressing occasion. She has been talking a great deal about it to me, she talks vastly well, I am afraid of being ungenerous or I should say she talks too well to feel so very deeply. But I will not look for faults. She may be Reginald's wife. Heaven forbid it!—but why should I be quicker sighted than anybody else? Mr. Vernon declares that he never saw deeper distress than hers, on the receipt of the letter —and is his judgement inferior to mine?

She was very unwilling that Frederica should be allowed to come to Churchill, and justly enough, as it seems a sort of reward to behaviour deserving very differently. But it was impossible to take her any where else, and she is not to remain here long.

"It will be absolutely necessary," said she, "as you my dear sister must be sensible, to treat my daughter with some severity while she is here—a most painful necessity, but I will endeavour to submit to it. I am afraid I have been too often indulgent, but my poor Frederica's temper could never bear opposition well. You must

---

[1] *she is unexceptionable* It would be impossible to take exception to her behavior in this regard.

[2] *wanting* Lacking.

support and encourage me—you must urge the necessity of reproof, if you see me too lenient."

All this sounds very reasonable. Reginald is so incensed against the poor silly girl! Surely it is not to Lady Susan's credit that he should be so bitter against her daughter; his idea of her must be drawn from the mother's description.

Well, whatever may be his fate, we have the comfort of knowing that we have done our utmost to save him. We must commit the event to an Higher Power. Yours ever etc.,

Catherine Vernon

LETTER 16
LADY SUSAN TO MRS. JOHNSON
Churchill

Never my dearest Alicia, was I so provoked in my life as by a letter this morning from Miss Summers. That horrid girl of mine has been trying to run away.—I had not a notion of her being such a little devil before; she seemed to have all the Vernon milkiness; but on receiving the letter in which I declared my intentions about Sir James, she actually attempted to elope; at least, I cannot otherwise account for her doing it. She meant I suppose to go to the Clarkes in Staffordshire, for she has no other acquaintance. But she shall be punished, she shall have him. I have sent Charles to town to make matters up if he can, for I do not by any means want her here. If Miss Summers will not keep her, you must find me out another school, unless we can get her married immediately. Miss S. writes word that she could not get the young lady to assign any cause for her extraordinary conduct, which confirms me in my own private explanation of it.

Frederica is too shy I think, and too much in awe of me, to tell tales; but if the mildness of her uncle should get anything from her, I am not afraid. I trust I shall be able to make my story as good as hers. If I am vain of anything, it is of my eloquence. Consideration and esteem as surely follow command of language, as admiration waits on beauty. And here I have opportunity enough for the exercise of my talent, as the chief of my time is spent in conversation. Reginald is never easy unless we are by ourselves, and when the weather is tolerable, we pace the shrubbery for hours together. I like him on the whole very well, he is clever and has a good deal to say, but he is sometimes impertinent and troublesome. There is a sort of ridiculous delicacy about him which requires the fullest explanation of whatever he may have heard to my disadvantage, and is never satisfied till he thinks he has ascertained the beginning and end of everything.

This is *one* sort of love—but I confess it does not particularly recommend itself to me. I infinitely prefer the tender and liberal spirit of Manwaring, which impressed with the deepest conviction of my merit, is satisfied that whatever I do must be right; and look with a degree of contempt on the inquisitive and doubting fancies of that heart which seems always debating on the reasonableness of its emotions. Manwaring is indeed beyond compare superior to Reginald—a superior in everything but the power of being with me. Poor fellow! he is quite distracted by jealousy, which I am not sorry for, as I know no better support of love. He has been teasing me to allow of his coming into this country, and lodging somewhere near me *incog.*—but I forbid anything of the kind. Those women are inexcusable who forget what is due to themselves and the opinion of the world.

S. Vernon

LETTER 17
MRS. VERNON TO LADY DE COURCY
Churchill

My dear mother,

Mr. Vernon returned on Thursday night, bringing his niece with him. Lady Susan had received a line from him by that day's post informing her that Miss Summers had absolutely refused to allow of Miss Vernon's continuance in her Academy. We were therefore prepared for her arrival, and expected them impatiently the whole evening. They came while we were at tea, and I never saw any creature look so frightened in my life as Frederica when she entered the room.

Lady Susan who had been shedding tears before and showing great agitation at the idea of the meeting, received her with perfect self-command, and without betraying the least tenderness of spirit. She hardly spoke to her, and on Frederica's bursting into tears as soon as we were seated, took her out of the room and did not return for some time; when she did, her eyes looked very red, and she was as much agitated as before. We saw no more of her daughter.

Poor Reginald was beyond measure concerned to see his fair friend in such distress, and watched her with so much tender solicitude that I, who occasionally caught her observing his countenance with exultation, was quite out of patience. This pathetic representation lasted the whole evening, and so ostentatious and artful a display had entirely convinced me that she did in fact feel nothing.

I am more angry with her than ever since I have seen her daughter. The poor girl looks so unhappy that my heart aches for her. Lady Susan is surely too severe, because Frederica does not seem to have the sort of temper to make severity necessary. She looks perfectly timid, dejected and penitent.

She is very pretty, though not so handsome as her mother, nor at all like her. Her complexion is delicate, but neither so fair, nor so blooming as Lady Susan's—and she has quite the Vernon cast of countenance, the oval face and mild dark eyes, and there is peculiar sweetness in her look when she speaks either to her uncle or me, for as we behave kindly to her, we have of course engaged her gratitude. Her mother has insinuated that her temper is untractable, but I never saw a face less indicative of any evil disposition than hers; and from what I now see of the behaviour of each to the other, the invariable severity of Lady Susan, and the silent dejection of Frederica, I am led to believe as heretofore that the former has no real love for her daughter and has never done her justice, or treated her affectionately.

I have not yet been able to have any conversation with my niece; she is shy, and I think I can see that some pains are taken to prevent her being much with me. Nothing satisfactory transpires as to her reason for running away. Her kindhearted uncle you may be sure, was too fearful of distressing her, to ask many questions as they travelled. I wish it had been possible for me to fetch her instead of him; I think I should have discovered the truth in the course of a thirty mile journey.

The small pianoforte has been removed within these few days at Lady Susan's request, into her dressing room, and Frederica spends great part of the day there; *practising* it is called, but I seldom hear any noise when I pass that way. What she does with herself there I do not know, there are plenty of books in the room, but it is not every girl who has been running wild the first fifteen years of her life, that can or will read. Poor creature! the prospect from her window is not very instructive, for that room overlooks the lawn you know with the shrubbery on one side, where she may see her mother walking for an hour together, in earnest conversation with Reginald. A girl of Frederica's age must be childish indeed, if such things do not strike her. Is it not inexcusable to give such an example to a daughter? Yet Reginald still thinks Lady Susan the best of mothers—still condemns Frederica as a worthless girl! He is convinced that her attempt to run away, proceeded from no justifiable cause, and had no provocation. I am sure I cannot say that it *had,* but while Miss Summers declares that Miss Vernon showed no sign of obstinacy or perverseness during her whole stay in Wigmore St. till she was detected in this scheme, I cannot so readily credit what Lady Susan has made him and wants to make me believe, that it was merely an impatience of restraint, and a desire of escaping from the tuition of masters which brought on the plan of an elopement. Oh! Reginald, how is your judgement enslaved! He scarcely dares even allow her to be handsome, and when I speak of her beauty, replies only that her eyes have no brilliancy.

Sometimes he is sure that she is deficient in understanding, and at others that her temper only is in fault. In short when a person is always to deceive, it is impossible to be consistent. Lady Susan finds it necessary for her own justification that Frederica should be to blame, and probably has sometimes judged it expedient to accuse her of ill-nature and sometimes to lament her want of sense. Reginald is only repeating after her ladyship.

I am etc.,

Catherine Vernon

LETTER 18
FROM THE SAME TO THE SAME

Churchill

My dear Madam,

I am very glad to find that my description of Frederica Vernon has interested you, for I do believe her truly deserving of our regard, and when I have communicated a notion that has recently struck me, your kind impression in her favour will I am sure be heightened. I cannot help fancying that she is growing partial to my brother, I so very often see her eyes fixed on his face with a remarkable expression of pensive admiration! He is certainly very handsome—and yet more—there is an openness in his manner that must be highly prepossessing, and I am sure she feels it so. Thoughtful and pensive in general her countenance always brightens with a smile when Reginald says anything amusing; and let the subject be ever so serious that he may be conversing on, I am much mistaken if a syllable of his uttering, escape her.

I want to make him sensible of all this, for we know the power of gratitude on such a heart as his; and could Frederica's artless affection detach him from her mother, we might bless the day which brought her to Churchill. I think my dear Madam, you would not disapprove of her as a daughter. She is extremely young to be sure, has had a wretched education and a dreadful example of levity in her mother; but yet I can pronounce her disposition to be excellent, and her natural abilities very good.

Though totally without accomplishment, she is by no means so ignorant as one might expect to find her, being fond of books and spending the chief of her time in reading. Her mother leaves her more to herself now than she *did*, and I have her with me as much as possible, and have taken great pains to overcome her timidity. We are very good friends, and though she never opens her lips before her mother, she talks enough when alone with me, to make it clear that if properly treated by Lady Susan she would always appear to much greater advantage. There cannot be a more gentle, affectionate heart, or more obliging manners, when acting without restraint. Her little cousins are all very fond of her.

Yours affectionately,

Catherine Vernon

LETTER 19
LADY SUSAN TO MRS. JOHNSON

Churchill

You will be eager I know to hear something farther of Frederica, and perhaps may think me negligent for not writing before. She arrived with her uncle last Thursday fortnight, when of course I lost no time in demanding the reason of her behaviour, and soon found myself to have been perfectly right in attributing it to my own letter. The purport of it frightened her so thoroughly that with a mixture of true girlish perverseness and folly, without considering that she could not escape from my authority by running away from Wigmore Street, she resolved on getting out of the house, and proceeding directly by the stage to her friends the Clarkes, and had really got as far as the length of two streets in her journey, when she was fortunately missed, pursued, and overtaken.

Such was the first distinguished exploit of Miss Frederica Susanna Vernon, and if we consider that it was achieved at the tender age of sixteen we shall have room for the most flattering prognostics of her future renown. I am excessively provoked however at the parade of propriety which prevented Miss Summers from keeping the girl; and it seems so extraordinary a piece of nicety, considering what are my daughter's family connections, that I can only suppose the lady to be governed by the fear of never getting her money. Be that as it may, however, Frederica is returned on my hands, and having now nothing else to employ her, is busy in pursuing the plan of romance begun at Langford. She is actually falling in love with Reginald De Courcy. To disobey her mother by refusing an unexceptionable offer is not enough; her affections must likewise be given without her mother's approbation. I never saw a girl of her age bid fairer to be the sport of mankind. Her feelings are tolerably lively, and she is so charmingly artless in their display, as to afford the most reasonable hope of her being ridiculed and despised by every man who sees her.

Artlessness will never do in love matters, and that girl is born a simpleton who has it either by nature or affectation. I am not yet certain that Reginald sees what she is about; nor is it of much consequence; she is now an object of indifference to him, she would be one of contempt were he to understand her emotions. Her beauty is much admired by the Vernons, but it has no effect on him. She is in high favour with her aunt altogether—because she is so little like myself of course. She is exactly the companion for Mrs. Vernon, who dearly loves to be first, and to have all the sense and all the wit of the conversation to herself; Frederica will never eclipse her. When she first came, I was at some pains to prevent her seeing much of her aunt, but I have since relaxed, as I believe I may depend on her observing the rules I have laid down for their discourse.

But do not imagine that with all this lenity, I have for a moment given up my plan of her marriage; no, I am unalterably fixed on that point, though I have not yet quite resolved on the manner of bringing it about. I should not choose to have the business brought forward here, and canvassed by the wise heads of Mr. and Mrs. Vernon; and I cannot just now afford[1] to go to town. Miss Frederica must therefore wait a little.

Yours ever,
S. Vernon

LETTER 20
MRS. VERNON TO LADY DE COURCY
Churchill

We have a very unexpected guest with us at present, my dear mother. He arrived yesterday. I heard a carriage at the door as I was sitting with my children while they dined, and supposing I should be wanted left the nursery soon afterwards and was halfway down stairs, when Frederica as pale as ashes came running up, and rushed by me into her own room. I instantly followed, and asked her what was the matter. "Oh!" cried she, "he is come, Sir James is come—and what am I to do?" This was no explanation; I begged her to tell me what she meant. At that moment we were interrupted by a knock at the door; it was Reginald, who came by Lady Susan's direction to call Frederica down. "It is Mr. De Courcy," said she, colouring violently, "Mama has sent for me, and I must go."

We all three went down together, and I saw my brother examining the terrified face of Frederica with surprise. In the breakfast room we found Lady Susan and a young man of genteel appearance, whom she introduced to me by the name of Sir James Martin, the very person, as you may remember, whom it was said she had been at pains to detach from Miss Manwaring. But the conquest it seems was not designed for herself, or she has since transferred it to her daughter, for Sir James is now desperately in love with Frederica, and with full encouragement from Mama. The poor girl however I am sure dislikes him; and though his person and address are very well, he appears both to Mr. Vernon and me a very weak young man.

Frederica looked so shy, so confused, when we entered the room, that I felt for her exceedingly. Lady Susan behaved with great attention to her visitor, and yet I thought I could perceive that she had no particular pleasure in seeing him. Sir James talked a good deal, and made many civil excuses to me for the liberty he had taken in coming to Churchill, mixing more frequent laughter with his discourse than the subject required; said many things over and over again, and told Lady Susan three times that he had seen Mrs. Johnson a few evenings before. He now and then addressed Frederica, but more frequently her mother. The poor girl sat all this time without opening her lips; her eyes cast down, and her colour varying every instant, while Reginald observed all that passed, in perfect silence.

At length Lady Susan, weary I believe of her situation, proposed walking, and we left the two gentlemen

---

[1] *afford* Manage.

together to put on our pelisses.[1]

As we went upstairs Lady Susan begged permission to attend me for a few moments in my dressing room, as she was anxious to speak with me in private. I led her thither accordingly, and as soon as the door was closed she said, "I was never more surprised in my life than by Sir James's arrival, and the suddenness of it requires some apology to you my dear sister, though to me as a mother, it is highly flattering. He is so warmly attached to my daughter that he could no longer exist without seeing her. Sir James is a young man of an amiable disposition, and excellent character; a little too much of the rattle perhaps, but a year or two will rectify that, and he is in other respects so very eligible a match for Frederica that I have always observed his attachment with the greatest pleasure, and am persuaded that you and my brother will give the alliance your hearty approbation. I have never before mentioned the likelihood of its taking place to any one, because I thought that while Frederica continued at school, it had better not be known to exist; but now, as I am convinced that Frederica, is too old ever to submit to school confinement, and have therefore begun to consider her union with Sir James as not very distant, I had intended within a few days to acquaint yourself and Mr. Vernon with the whole business. I am sure my dear sister, you will excuse my remaining silent on it so long, and agree with me that such circumstances, while they continue from any cause in suspense, cannot be too cautiously concealed. When you have the happiness of bestowing your sweet little Catherine some years hence on a man, who in connection and character is alike unexceptionable, you will know what I feel now; though thank heaven! you cannot have all my reasons for rejoicing in such an event. Catherine will be amply provided for, and not like my Frederica indebted to a fortunate establishment for the comforts of life."

She concluded by demanding my congratulations. I gave them somewhat awkwardly I believe; for in fact, the sudden disclosure of so important a matter took from me the power of speaking with any clearness. She thanked me however most affectionately for my kind concern in the welfare of herself and her daughter, and then said,

"I am not apt to deal in professions,[2] my dear Mrs. Vernon, and I never had the convenient talent of affecting sensations foreign to my heart; and therefore I trust you will believe me when I declare that much as I had heard in your praise before I knew you, I had no idea that I should ever love you as I now do; and must farther say that your friendship towards me is more particularly gratifying, because I have reason to believe that some attempts were made to prejudice you against me. I only wish that they—whoever they are—to whom I am indebted for such kind intentions, could see the terms on which we now are together, and understand the real affection we feel for each other! But I will not detain you any longer. God bless you, for your goodness to me and my girl, and continue to you all your present happiness."

What can one say of such a woman, my dear mother?—such earnestness, such solemnity of expression!—and yet I cannot help suspecting the truth of everything she said.

As for Reginald, I believe he does not know what to make of the matter. When Sir James first came, he appeared all astonishment and perplexity. The folly of the young man and the confusion of Frederica entirely engrossed him; and though a little private discourse with Lady Susan has since had its effect, he is still hurt I am sure at her allowing of such a man's attentions to her daughter.

Sir James invited himself with great composure to remain here a few days; hoped we would not think it odd, was aware of its being very impertinent, but he took the liberty of a relation, and concluding by wishing with a laugh, that he might be really one soon. Even Lady Susan seemed a little disconcerted by this forwardness; in her heart I am persuaded, she sincerely wishes him gone.

But something must be done for this poor girl, if her feelings are such as both her uncle and I believe them to be. She must not be sacrificed to policy or ambition, she must not be even left to suffer from the dread of it. The girl, whose heart can distinguish Reginald De Courcy,

---

[1] *pelisses* Long cloaks.

[2] *professions* Declarations, whether true or false.

deserves, however he may slight her, a better fate than to be Sir James Martin's wife. As soon as I can get her alone, I will discover the real truth, but she seems to wish to avoid me. I hope this does not proceed from anything wrong, and that I shall not find out I have thought too well of her. Her behaviour before Sir James certainly speaks the greatest consciousness and embarrassment; but I see nothing in it more like encouragement.

Adieu my dear Madam,

Yours etc.,

Catherine Vernon

LETTER 21
MISS VERNON TO MR. DE COURCY

Sir,

I hope you will excuse this liberty, I am forced upon it by the greatest distress, or I should be ashamed to trouble you. I am very miserable about Sir James Martin, and have no other way in the world of helping myself but by writing to you, for I am forbidden ever speaking to my uncle or aunt on the subject; and this being the case, I am afraid my applying to you will appear no better than equivocation, and as if I attended only to the letter and not the spirit of Mama's commands, but if you do not take my part, and persuade her to break it off, I shall be half-distracted, for I cannot bear him. No human being but you could have any chance of prevailing with her. If you will therefore have the unspeakable great kindness of taking my part with her, and persuading her to send Sir James away, I shall be more obliged to you than it is possible for me to express. I always disliked him from the first, it is not a sudden fancy I assure you Sir, I always thought him silly and impertinent and disagreeable, and now he is grown worse than ever. I would rather work for my bread than marry him. I do not know how to apologize enough for this letter, I know it is taking so great a liberty, I am aware how dreadfully angry it will make Mama, but I must run the risk. I am Sir, your most humble servant,

F.S.V.

LETTER 22
LADY SUSAN TO MRS. JOHNSON
Churchill

This is insufferable! My dearest friend, I was never so enraged before, and must relieve myself by writing to you, who I know will enter into all my feelings. Who should come on Tuesday but Sir James Martin? Guess my astonishment and vexation—for as you well know, I never wished him to be seen at Churchill. What a pity that you should not have known his intentions! Not content with coming, he actually invited himself to remain here a few days. I could have poisoned him; I made the best of it however, and told my story with great success to Mrs. Vernon who, whatever might be her real sentiments, said nothing in opposition to mine. I made a point also of Frederica's behaving civilly to Sir James, and gave her to understand that I was absolutely determined on her marrying him. She said something of her misery, but that was all. I have for some time been more particularly resolved on the match, from seeing the rapid increase of her affection for Reginald, and from not feeling perfectly secure that a knowledge of that affection might not in the end awaken a return. Contemptible, as a regard founded only on compassion, must make them both, in my eyes, I felt by no means assured that such might not be the consequence. It is true that Reginald had not in any degree grown cool towards me; but yet he had lately mentioned Frederica spontaneously and unnecessarily, and once had said something in praise of her person.

He was all astonishment at the appearance of my visitor; and at first observed Sir James with an attention which I was pleased to see not unmixed with jealousy; but unluckily it was impossible for me really to torment him, as Sir James though extremely gallant to me, very soon made the whole party understand that his heart was devoted to my daughter.

I had no great difficulty in convincing De Courcy when we were alone, that I was perfectly justified, all things considered, in desiring the match; and the whole business seemed most comfortably arranged. They could none of them help perceiving that Sir James was no

Solomon, but I had positively forbidden Frederica's complaining to Charles Vernon or his wife, and they had therefore no pretence for interference, though my impertinent sister I believe wanted only opportunity for doing so.

Everything however was going on calmly and quietly; and though I counted the hours of Sir James's stay, my mind was entirely satisfied with the posture of affairs. Guess then what I must feel at the sudden disturbance of all my schemes, and that too from a quarter, whence I had least reason to apprehend it. Reginald came this morning into my dressing room, with a very unusual solemnity of countenance, and after some preface informed me in so many words, that he wished to reason with me on the impropriety and unkindness of allowing Sir James Martin to address my daughter, contrary to her inclination. I was all amazement. When I found that he was not to be laughed out of his design, I calmly required an explanation, and begged to know by what he was impelled, and by whom commissioned to reprimand me. He then told me, mixing in this speech a few insolent compliments and ill timed expressions of tenderness to which I listened with perfect indifference, that my daughter had acquainted him with some circumstances concerning herself, Sir James, and me, which gave him great uneasiness.

In short, I found that she had in the first place actually written to him, to request his interference, and that on receiving her letter he had conversed with her on the subject of it, in order to understand the particulars and assure himself of her real wishes!

I have not a doubt but that the girl took this opportunity of making downright love[1] to him; I am convinced of it, from the manner in which he spoke of her. Much good, may such love do him! I shall ever despise the man who can be gratified by the passion, which he never wished to inspire, nor solicited the avowal of. I shall always detest them both. He can have no true regard for me, or he would not have listened to her; and she, with her little rebellious heart and indelicate feelings

to throw herself into the protection of a young man with whom she had scarcely ever exchanged two words before. I am equally confounded at her impudence and his credulity. How dared he believe what she told him in my disfavour! Ought he not to have felt assured that I must have unanswerable motives for all that I had done! Where was his reliance on my sense or goodness then; where the resentment which true love would have dictated against the person defaming me, that person, too, a chit, a child, without talent or education, whom he had been always taught to despise?

I was calm for some time, but the greatest degree of forbearance may be overcome; and I hope I was afterwards sufficiently keen. He endeavoured, long endeavoured to soften my resentment, but that woman is a fool indeed who while insulted by accusation, can be worked on by compliments. At length he left me, as deeply provoked as myself, and he showed his anger more. I was quite cool, but he gave way to the most violent indignation. I may therefore expect it will sooner subside; and perhaps his may be vanished forever, while mine will be found still fresh and implacable.

He is now shut up in his apartment, whither I heard him go, on leaving mine. How unpleasant, one would think, must his reflections be! But some people's feelings are incomprehensible. I have not yet tranquillized myself enough to see Frederica. She shall not soon forget the occurrences of this day. She shall find that she has poured forth her tender tale of love in vain, and exposed herself forever to the contempt of the whole world, and the severest resentment of her injured mother.

Yours affectionately,

S. Vernon

LETTER 23
MRS. VERNON TO LADY DE COURCY
Churchill

Let me congratulate you, my dearest mother. The affair which has given us so much anxiety is drawing to a happy conclusion. Our prospect is most delightful; and since matters have now taken so favourable a turn, I am

---

[1] *making … love* Expressing romantic affection. (The phrase "making love" did not carry with it any suggestion of sexual activity until the 1960s.)

quite sorry that I ever imparted my apprehensions to you; for the pleasure of learning that the danger is over, is perhaps dearly purchased by all that you have previously suffered.

I am so much agitated by delight that I can scarcely hold a pen, but am determined to send you a few lines by James, that you may have some explanation of what must so greatly astonish you, as that Reginald should be returning to Parklands.

I was sitting about half an hour ago with Sir James in the breakfast parlour, when my brother called me out of the room. I instantly saw that something was the matter; his complexion was raised, and he spoke with great emotion. You know his eager manner, my dear Madam, when his mind is interested.

"Catherine," said he, "I am going home today. I am sorry to leave you, but I must go. It is a great while since I have seen my father and mother. I am going to send James forward with my hunters immediately, if you have any letter therefore he can take it. I shall not be at home myself till Wednesday or Thursday, as I shall go through London, where I have business. But before I leave you," he continued, speaking in a lower voice and with still greater energy, "I must warn you of one thing. Do not let Frederica Vernon be made unhappy by that Martin. He wants to marry her—her mother promotes the match— but she cannot endure the idea of it. Be assured that I speak from the fullest conviction of the truth of what I say. I know that Frederica is made wretched by Sir James' continuing here. She is a sweet girl, and deserves a better fate. Send him away immediately. He is only a fool—but what her mother can mean, Heaven only knows! Good bye," he added shaking my hand with earnestness—"I do not know when you will see me again. But remember what I tell you of Frederica; you must make it your business to see justice done her. She is an amiable girl, and has a very superior mind to what we have ever given her credit for."

He then left me and ran upstairs. I would not try to stop him, for I knew what his feelings must be; the nature of mine as I listened to him, I need not attempt to describe. For a minute or two I remained in the same spot, overpowered by wonder—of a most agreeable sort

indeed; yet it required some consideration to be tranquilly happy.

In about ten minutes after my return to the parlour, Lady Susan entered the room. I concluded of course that she and Reginald had been quarrelling, and looked with anxious curiosity for a confirmation of my belief in her face. Mistress of deceit however she appeared perfectly unconcerned, and after chatting on indifferent subjects for a short time, said to me, "I find from Wilson that we are going to lose Mr. De Courcy. Is it true that he leaves Churchill this morning?" I replied that it was. "He told us nothing of all this last night," said she laughing, "or even this morning at breakfast. But perhaps he did not know it himself. Young men are often hasty in their resolutions—and not more sudden in forming, than unsteady in keeping them. I should not be surprised if he were to change his mind at last, and not go."

She soon afterwards left the room. I trust however my dear mother, that we have no reason to fear an alteration of his present plan; things have gone too far. They must have quarrelled, and about Frederica too. Her calmness astonishes me. What delight will be yours in seeing him again, in seeing him still worthy your esteem, still capable of forming your happiness!

When next I write, I shall be able I hope to tell you that Sir James is gone, Lady Susan vanquished, and Frederica at peace. We have much to do, but it shall be done. I am all impatience to know how this astonishing change was effected. I finish as I began, with the warmest congratulations.

Yours ever,
Catherine Vernon

LETTER 24
FROM THE SAME TO THE SAME

Churchill

Little did I imagine my dear mother, when I sent off my last letter, that the delightful perturbation of spirits I was then in, would undergo so speedy, so melancholy a reverse! I never can sufficiently regret that I wrote to you at all. Yet who could have foreseen what has happened?

My dear mother, every hope which but two hours ago made me so happy, is vanished. The quarrel between Lady Susan and Reginald is made up, and we are all as we were before. One point only is gained; Sir James Martin is dismissed. What are we now to look forward to? I am indeed disappointed. Reginald was all but gone; his horse was ordered, and almost brought to the door! Who would not have felt safe?

For half an hour I was in momentary expectation of his departure. After I had sent off my letter to you, I went to Mr. Vernon and sat with him in his room, talking over the whole matter. I then determined to look for Frederica, whom I had not seen since breakfast. I met her on the stairs and saw that she was crying.

"My dear aunt," said she, "he is going, Mr. De Courcy is going, and it is all my fault. I am afraid you will be angry, but indeed I had no idea it would end so."

"My love," replied I, "do not think it necessary to apologize to me on that account. I shall feel myself under an obligation to anyone who is the means of sending my brother home; because (recollecting myself) I know my father wants very much to see him. But what is it that you have done to occasion all this?"

She blushed deeply as she answered, "I was so unhappy about Sir James that I could not help—I have done something very wrong, I know—but you have not an idea of the misery I have been in, and Mama had ordered me never to speak to you or my uncle about it,—and—" "You therefore spoke to my brother, to engage *his* interference," said I, wishing to save her the explanation. "No—but I wrote to him. I did indeed. I got up this morning before it was light—I was two hours about it—and when my letter was done, I thought I never should have the courage to give it. After breakfast, however, as I was going to my own room, I met him in the passage, and then as I knew that everything must depend on that moment, I forced myself to give it. He was so good as to take it immediately; I dared not look at him—and ran away directly. I was in such a fright that I could hardly breathe. My dear aunt, you do not know how miserable I have been."

"Frederica," said I, "you ought to have told me all your distresses. You would have found in me a friend always ready to assist you. Do you think that your uncle and I should not have espoused your cause as warmly as my brother?"

"Indeed I did not doubt your goodness," said she, colouring again, "but I thought that Mr. De Courcy could do anything with my mother; but I was mistaken; they have had a dreadful quarrel about it, and he is going. Mama will never forgive me, and I shall be worse off than ever." "No, you shall not," replied I.—"In such a point as this, your mother's prohibition ought not to have prevented your speaking to me on the subject. She has no right to make you unhappy, and she shall not do it. Your applying however to Reginald can be productive only of good to all parties. I believe it is best as it is. Depend upon it that you shall not be made unhappy any longer."

At that moment, how great was my astonishment at seeing Reginald come out of Lady Susan's dressing room. My heart misgave me instantly. His confusion on seeing me was very evident. Frederica immediately disappeared. "Are you going?" said I. "You will find Mr. Vernon in his own room." "No Catherine," replied he. "I am not going. Will you let me speak to you a moment?"

We went into my room. "I find," continued he, his confusion increasing as he spoke, "that I have been acting with my usual foolish impetuosity. I have entirely misunderstood Lady Susan, and was on the point of leaving the house under a false impression of her conduct. There has been some very great mistake—we have been all mistaken I fancy. Frederica does not know her mother—Lady Susan means nothing but her good—but Frederica will not make a friend of her. Lady Susan therefore does not always know what will make her daughter happy. Besides I could have no right to interfere—Miss Vernon was mistaken in applying to me. In short Catherine, everything has gone wrong—but it is now all happily settled. Lady Susan I believe wishes to speak to you about it, if you are at leisure." "Certainly"; replied I, deeply sighing at the recital of so lame a story. I made no remarks however, for words would have been in vain. Reginald was glad to get away, and I went to Lady Susan; curious indeed to hear her account of it.

"Did not I tell you," said she with a smile, "that your brother would not leave us after all?" "You did indeed," replied I very gravely, "but I flattered myself that you would be mistaken." "I should not have hazarded such an opinion," returned she, "if it had not at that moment occurred to me, that his resolution of going might be occasioned by a conversation in which we had been this morning engaged, and which had ended very much to his dissatisfaction from our not rightly understanding each other's meaning. This idea struck me at the moment, and I instantly determined that an accidental dispute in which I might probably be as much to blame as himself, should not deprive you of your brother. If you remember, I left the room almost immediately. I was resolved to lose no time in clearing up these mistakes as far as I could. The case was this. Frederica had set herself violently against marrying Sir James." "And can your ladyship wonder that she should?" cried I with some warmth. "Frederica has an excellent understanding, and Sir James has none." "I am at least very far from regretting it, my dear sister," said she; "on the contrary, I am grateful for so favourable a sign of my daughter's sense. Sir James is certainly under par—his boyish manners make him appear the worse—and had Frederica possessed the penetration, the abilities, which I could have wished in my daughter, or had I ever known her to possess so much as she does, I should not have been anxious for the match." "It is odd that you alone should be ignorant of your daughter's sense." "Frederica never does justice to herself; her manners are shy and childish. She is besides afraid of me; she scarcely loves me. During her poor father's life she was a spoilt child; the severity which it has since been necessary for me to show, has entirely alienated her affection; neither has she any of that brilliancy of intellect, that genius, or vigour of mind which will force itself forward." "Say rather that she has been unfortunate in her education." "Heaven knows, my dearest Mrs. Vernon, how fully I am aware of that; but I would wish to forget every circumstance that might throw blame on the memory of one, whose name is sacred with me."

Here she pretended to cry. I was out of patience with her. "But what," said I, "was your ladyship going to tell me about your disagreement with my brother?" "It originated in an action of my daughter's, which equally marks her want of judgement, and the unfortunate dread of me I have been mentioning. She wrote to Mr. De Courcy." "I know she did. You had forbidden her speaking to Mr. Vernon or me on the cause of her distress; what could she do therefore but apply to my brother?" "Good God," she exclaimed, "what an opinion you must have of me! Can you possibly suppose that I was aware of her unhappiness? That it was my object to make my own child miserable, and that I had forbidden her speaking to you on that subject, from a fear of your interrupting the diabolical scheme? Do you think me destitute of every honest, every natural feeling? Am I capable of consigning her to everlasting misery, whose welfare it is my first earthly duty to promote?" "The idea is horrible. What then was your intention when you insisted on her silence?" "Of what use my dear sister, could be any application to you, however the affair might stand? Why should I subject you to entreaties, which I refused to attend to myself? Neither for your sake, for hers, nor for my own, could such a thing be desirable. Where my own resolution was taken, I could not wish for the interference, however friendly, of another person. I was mistaken, it is true, but I believed myself to be right." "But what was this mistake, to which your ladyship so often alludes? From whence arose so astonishing a misapprehension of your daughter's feelings? Did not you know that she disliked Sir James?" "I knew that he was not absolutely the man she would have chosen. But I was persuaded that her objections to him did not arise from any perception of his deficiency. You must not question me however, my dear sister, too minutely on this point—" continued she, taking me affectionately by the hand. "I honestly own that there is something to conceal. Frederica makes me very unhappy. Her applying to Mr. De Courcy hurt me particularly." "What is it that you mean to infer," said I, "by this appearance of mystery? If you think your daughter at all attached to Reginald, her objecting to Sir James could not less deserve to be attended to, than if the cause of her objecting had been a consciousness of his folly. And why should your ladyship at any rate quarrel with my brother for an interference which you must know, it was not in his nature to refuse, when urged in such a manner?"

"His disposition you know is warm, and he came to expostulate with me, his compassion all alive for this ill-used girl, this heroine in distress! We misunderstood each other. He believed me more to blame than I really was; I considered his interference as less excusable than I now find it. I have a real regard for him, and was beyond expression mortified to find it as I thought so ill bestowed. We were both warm, and of course both to blame. His resolution of leaving Churchill is consistent with his general eagerness; when I understood his intention however, and at the same time began to think that we had perhaps been equally mistaken in each other's meaning, I resolved to have an explanation before it were too late. For any member of your family I must always feel a degree of affection, and I own it would have sensibly hurt me, if my acquaintance with Mr. De Courcy had ended so gloomily. I have now only to say farther, that as I am convinced of Frederica's having a reasonable dislike to Sir James, I shall instantly inform him that he must give up all hope of her. I reproach myself for having ever, though so innocently, made her unhappy on that score. She shall have all the retribution in my power to make; if she values her own happiness as much as I do, if she judge wisely and command herself as she ought, she may now be easy. Excuse me, my dearest sister, for thus trespassing on your time, but I owed it to my own character; and after this explanation I trust I am in no danger of sinking in your opinion."

I could have said "Not much indeed"—but I left her almost in silence. It was the greatest stretch of forbearance I could practise. I could not have stopped myself, had I begun. Her assurance, her deceit—but I will not allow myself to dwell on them; they will strike you sufficiently. My heart sickens within me.

As soon as I was tolerably composed, I returned to the parlour. Sir James's carriage was at the door, and he, merry as usual, soon afterwards took his leave. How easily does her ladyship encourage, or dismiss a lover!

In spite of this release, Frederica still looks unhappy, still fearful perhaps of her mother's anger, and though dreading my brother's departure jealous, it may be, of his staying. I see how closely she observes him and Lady Susan. Poor girl, I have now no hope for her. There is

not a chance of her affection being returned. He thinks very differently of her, from what he used to do, he does her some justice, but his reconciliation with her mother precludes every dearer hope.

Prepare my dear Madam, for the worst. The probability of their marrying is surely heightened. He is more securely hers than ever. When that wretched event takes place, Frederica must belong wholly to us.

I am thankful that my last letter will precede this by so little, as every moment that you can be saved from feeling a joy which leads only to disappointment is of consequence.

Yours ever,
Catherine Vernon

LETTER 25
LADY SUSAN TO MRS. JOHNSON
Churchill

I call on you, dear Alicia, for congratulations. I am again myself—gay and triumphant. When I wrote to you the other day, I was in truth in high irritation, and with ample cause. Nay, I know not whether I ought to be quite tranquil now, for I have had more trouble in restoring peace than I ever intended to submit to. This Reginald has a proud spirit of his own!—a spirit too, resulting from a fancied sense of superior integrity which is peculiarly insolent. I shall not easily forgive him I assure you. He was actually on the point of leaving Churchill! I had scarcely concluded my last, when Wilson brought me word of it. I found therefore that something must be done, for I did not choose to have my character at the mercy of a man whose passions were so violent and resentful. It would have been trifling with my reputation, to allow of his departing with such an impression in my disfavour; in this light, condescension[1] was necessary.

I sent Wilson to say that I desired to speak with him before he went. He came immediately. The angry emotions which had marked every feature when we last parted, were partially subdued. He seemed astonished at

---
[1] *condescension* Gracious and considerate behavior.

the summons, and looked as if half wishing and half fearing to be softened by what I might say.

If my countenance expressed what I aimed at, it was composed and dignified—and yet with a degree of pensiveness which might convince him that I was not quite happy. "I beg your pardon Sir, for the liberty I have taken in sending to you," said I, "but as I have just learnt your intention of leaving this place today, I feel it my duty to entreat that you will not on my account shorten your visit here, even an hour. I am perfectly aware that after what has passed between us, it would ill suit the feelings of either to remain longer in the same house. So very great, so total a change from the intimacy of friendship, must render any future intercourse the severest punishment; and your resolution of quitting Churchill is undoubtedly in unison with our situation and with those lively feelings which I know you to possess. But at the same time, it is not for me to suffer such a sacrifice, as it must be, to leave relations to whom you are so much attached and are so dear. My remaining here cannot give that pleasure to Mr. and Mrs. Vernon which your society must; and my visit has already perhaps been too long. My removal[1] therefore, which must at any rate take place soon, may with perfect convenience be hastened; and I make it my particular request that I may not in any way be instrumental in separating a family so affectionately attached to each other. Where I go is of no consequence to anyone; of very little to myself; but you are of importance to all your connections." Here I concluded, and I hope you will be satisfied with my speech. Its effect on Reginald justifies some portion of vanity, for it was no less favourable than instantaneous. Oh! How delightful it was, to watch the variations of his countenance while I spoke, to see the struggle between returning tenderness and the remains of displeasure. There is something agreeable in feelings so easily worked on. Not that I would envy him their possession, nor would for the world have such myself, but they are very convenient when one wishes to influence the passions of another. And yet this Reginald, whom a very few words from me softened at once into the utmost submission, and ren-

dered more tractable, more attached, more devoted than ever, would have left me in the first angry swelling of his proud heart, without deigning to seek an explanation!

Humbled as he now is, I cannot forgive him such an instance of pride; and am doubtful whether I ought not to punish him, by dismissing him at once after this our reconciliation, or by marrying and teasing him for ever. But these measures are each too violent to be adopted without some deliberation. At present my thoughts are fluctuating between various schemes. I have many things to compass.[2] I must punish Frederica, and pretty severely too, for her application to Reginald; I must punish him for receiving it so favourably, and for the rest of his conduct. I must torment my sister-in-law for the insolent triumph of her look and manner since Sir James has been dismissed—for in reconciling Reginald to me, I was not able to save that ill-fated young man—and I must make myself amends for the humiliations to which I have stooped within these few days. To effect all this I have various plans. I have also an idea of being soon in town, and whatever may be my determination as to the rest, I shall probably put that project in execution—for London will be always the fairest field of action, however my views may be directed, and at any rate, I shall there be rewarded by your society and a little dissipation for a ten weeks' penance at Churchill.

I believe I owe it to my own character, to complete the match between my daughter and Sir James, after having so long intended it. Let me know your opinion on this point. Flexibility of mind, a disposition easily biased by others, is an attribute which you know I am not very desirous of obtaining; nor has Frederica any claim to the indulgence of her whims, at the expense of her mother's inclination. Her idle love for Reginald too; it is surely my duty to discourage such romantic nonsense. All things considered therefore, it seems incumbent on me to take her to town, and marry her immediately to Sir James.

When my own will is effected, contrary to his, I shall have some credit in being on good terms with Reginald, which at present in fact I have not, for though he is still

---

[1] *removal* Departure.

[2] *compass* Contrive, devise.

in my power, I have given up the very article by which our quarrel was produced, and at best, the honour of victory is doubtful.

Send me your opinion on all these matters, my dear Alicia, and let me know whether you can get lodgings to suit me within a short distance of you.

Your most attached,
S. Vernon

LETTER 26
MRS. JOHNSON TO LADY SUSAN
Edward St.

I am gratified by your reference, and this is my advice; that you come to town yourself without loss of time, but that you leave Frederica behind. It would surely be much more to the purpose to get yourself well established by marrying Mr. De Courcy, than to irritate him and the rest of his family, by making her marry Sir James. You should think more of yourself, and less of your daughter. She is not of a disposition to do you credit in the world, and seems precisely in her proper place, at Churchill with the Vernons; but you are fitted for society, and it is shameful to have you exiled from it. Leave Frederica therefore to punish herself for the plague she has given you, by indulging that romantic tender-heartedness which will always ensure her misery enough; and come yourself to town, as soon as you can.

I have another reason for urging this.

Manwaring came to town last week, and has contrived, in spite of Mr. Johnson, to make opportunities of seeing me. He is absolutely miserable about you, and jealous to such a degree of De Courcy, that it would be highly unadvisable for them to meet at present; and yet if you do not allow him to see you here, I cannot answer for his not committing some great imprudence—such as going to Churchill for instance, which would be dreadful. Besides, if you take my advice, and resolve to marry De Courcy, it will be indispensably necessary for you to get Manwaring out of the way, and you only can have influence enough to send him back to his wife.

I have still another motive for your coming. Mr. Johnson leaves London next Tuesday. He is going for his health to Bath, where if the waters[1] are favourable to his constitution and my wishes, he will be laid up with the gout many weeks. During his absence we shall be able to choose our own society, and have true enjoyment.

I would ask you to Edward St. but that he once forced from me a kind of promise never to invite you to my house. Nothing but my being in the utmost distress for money, could have extorted it from me. I can get you however a very nice drawing-room-apartment in Upper Seymour St., and we may be always together, there or here, for I consider my promise to Mr. Johnson as comprehending only (at least in his absence) your not sleeping in the house.

Poor Manwaring gives me such histories of his wife's jealousy! Silly woman, to expect constancy from so charming a man! But she was always silly; intolerably so, in marrying him at all. She, the heiress of a large fortune, he without a shilling! *One* title I know she might have had, besides Baronet's. Her folly in forming the connection was so great, that though Mr. Johnson was her guardian and I do not in general share his feelings, I never can forgive her.

Adieu,
Yours, Alicia

LETTER 27
MRS. VERNON TO LADY DE COURCY
Churchill

This letter, my dear mother, will be brought you by Reginald. His long visit is about to be concluded at last, but I fear the separation takes place too late to do us any good. She is going to town, to see her particular friend, Mrs. Johnson. It was at first her intention that Frederica should accompany her for the benefit of masters, but we overruled her there. Frederica was wretched in the idea of going, and I could not bear to have her at the mercy of

[1] *waters* Since Roman times the hot mineral springs at Bath in southwestern Britain have been a destination for those seeking their supposed healing powers.

her mother. Not all the masters in London could compensate for the ruin of her comfort. I should have feared too for her health, and for everything in short but her principles; *there* I believe she is not to be injured, even by her mother, or all her mother's friends; but with those friends (a very bad set I doubt not) she must have mixed, or have been left in total solitude, and I can hardly tell which would have been worse for her. If she is with her mother, moreover, she must alas! in all probability, be with Reginald—and that would be the greatest evil of all.

Here we shall in time be at peace. Our regular employments, our books and conversation, with exercise, the children, and every domestic pleasure in my power to procure her, will, I trust, gradually overcome this youthful attachment. I should not have a doubt of it, were she slighted for any other woman in the world, than her own mother.

How long Lady Susan will be in town, or whether she returns here again, I know not. I could not be cordial in my invitation; but if she chooses to come, no want of cordiality on my part will keep her away.

I could not help asking Reginald if he intended being in town this winter, as soon as I found that her ladyship's steps would be bent thither; and though he professed himself quite undetermined, there was a something in his look and voice as he spoke, which contradicted his words. I have done with lamentation. I look upon the event as so far decided, that I resign myself to it in despair. If he leaves you soon for London, everything will be concluded.

Yours affectionately,
Catherine Vernon

LETTER 28
MRS. JOHNSON TO LADY SUSAN
Edward St.

My dearest friend,

I write in the greatest distress; the most unfortunate event has just taken place. Mr. Johnson has hit on the most effectual manner of plaguing us all. He had heard I imagine by some means or other, that you were soon to be in London, and immediately contrived to have such an attack of the gout, as must at least delay his journey to Bath, if not wholly prevent it. I am persuaded the gout is brought on, or kept off at pleasure; it was the same, when I wanted to join the Hamiltons to the Lakes;[1] and three years ago when I had a fancy for Bath, nothing could induce him to have a gouty symptom.

I have received yours, and have engaged the lodgings in consequence. I am pleased to find that my letter had so much effect on you, and that De Courcy is certainly your own. Let me hear from you as soon as you arrive, and in particular tell me what you mean to do with Manwaring. It is impossible to say when I shall be able to see you. My confinement must be great. It is such an abominable trick, to be ill here, instead of at Bath, that I can scarcely command myself at all. At Bath, his old aunts would have nursed him, but here it all falls upon me—and he bears pain with such patience that I have not the common excuse for losing my temper.

Yours ever,
Alicia

LETTER 29
LADY SUSAN TO MRS. JOHNSON
Upper Seymour St.

My dear Alicia,

There needed not this last fit of the gout to make me detest Mr. Johnson; but now the extent of my aversion is not to be estimated. To have you confined, a nurse in his apartment! My dear Alicia, of what a mistake were you guilty in marrying a man of his age!—just old enough to be formal, ungovernable and to have the gout—too old to be agreeable, and too young to die.

I arrived last night about five, and had scarcely swallowed my dinner when Manwaring made his appearance. I will not dissemble what real pleasure his sight afforded me, nor how strongly I felt the contrast between his person and manners, and those of Reginald, to the infinite disadvantage of the latter. For an hour or two, I was even staggered in my resolution of marrying him—

---

[1] *the Lakes* The Lake District in northwestern England, renowned for its scenery, and a popular holiday destination.

and though this was too idle and nonsensical an idea to remain long on my mind, I do not feel very eager for the conclusion of my marriage, or look forward with much impatience to the time when Reginald according to our agreement is to be in town. I shall probably put off his arrival, under some pretence or other. He must not come till Manwaring is gone.

I am still doubtful at times, as to marriage. If the old man would die, I might not hesitate; but a state of dependance on the caprice of Sir Reginald, will not suit the freedom of my spirit; and if I resolve to wait for that event, I shall have excuse enough at present, in having been scarcely ten months a widow.

I have not given Manwaring any hint of my intention—or allowed him to consider my acquaintance with Reginald as more than the commonest flirtation; and he is tolerably appeased. Adieu till we meet. I am enchanted with my lodgings.

Yours ever,
S. Vernon

LETTER 30
LADY SUSAN TO MR. DE COURCY
Upper Seymour St.

I have received your letter; and though I do not attempt to conceal that I am gratified by your impatience for the hour of meeting, I yet feel myself under the necessity of delaying that hour beyond the time originally fixed. Do not think me unkind for such an exercise of my power, or accuse me of instability, without first hearing my reasons. In the course of my journey from Churchill, I had ample leisure for reflection on the present state of our affairs, and every review has served to convince me that they require a delicacy and cautiousness of conduct, to which we have hitherto been too little attentive. We have been hurried on by our feelings to a degree of precipitance which ill accords with the claims of our friends, or the opinion of the world. We have been unguarded in forming this hasty engagement; but we must not complete the imprudence by ratifying it, while there is so much reason to fear the connection would be opposed by those friends on whom you depend.

It is not for us to blame any expectation on your father's side of your marrying to advantage; where possessions are so extensive as those of your family, the wish of increasing them, if not strictly reasonable, is too common to excite surprise or resentment. He has a right to require a woman of fortune in his daughter-in-law, and I am sometimes quarrelling with myself for suffering you to form a connection so imprudent. But the influence of reason is often acknowledged too late by those who feel like me.

I have now been but a few months a widow; and however little indebted to my husband's memory for any happiness derived from him during an union of some years, I cannot forget that the indelicacy of so early a second marriage, must subject me to the censure of the world, and incur what would be still more insupportable, the displeasure of Mr. Vernon. I might perhaps harden myself in time against the injustice of a general reproach; but the loss of his valued esteem, I am as you well know, ill fitted to endure; and when to this, may be added the consciousness of having injured you with your family, how am I to support myself? With feelings so poignant as mine, the conviction of having divided the son from his parents, would make me, even with you, the most miserable of beings.

It will surely therefore be advisable to delay our union, to delay it till appearances are more promising, till affairs have taken a more favourable turn. To assist us in such a resolution, I feel that absence will be necessary. We must not meet. Cruel as this sentence may appear, the necessity of pronouncing it, which can alone reconcile it to myself, will be evident to you when you have considered our situation in the light in which I have found myself imperiously obliged to place it. You may be, you must be well assured that nothing but the strongest conviction of duty, could induce me to wound my own feelings by urging a lengthened separation; and of insensibility to yours, you will hardly suspect me. Again therefore I say that we ought not, we must not yet meet. By a removal for some months from each other, we shall tranquillize the sisterly fears of Mrs. Vernon, who, accustomed herself to the enjoyment of riches, considers fortune as necessary every where, and whose sensibilities are not of a nature to comprehend ours.

Let me hear from you soon, very soon. Tell me that you submit to my arguments, and do not reproach me for using such. I cannot bear reproaches. My spirits are not so high as to need being repressed. I must endeavour to seek amusement abroad, and fortunately many of my friends are in town—among them, the Manwarings. You know how sincerely I regard both husband and wife.

I am ever, faithfully yours,
S. Vernon

LETTER 31
LADY SUSAN TO MRS. JOHNSON
Upper Seymour St.

My dear friend,

That tormenting creature Reginald is here. My letter, which was intended to keep him longer in the country, has hastened him to town. Much as I wish him away, however, I cannot help being pleased with such a proof of attachment. He is devoted to me, heart and soul. He will carry this note himself, which is to serve as an introduction to you, with whom he longs to be acquainted. Allow him to spend the evening with you, that I may be in no danger of his returning here. I have told him that I am not quite well, and must be alone—and should he call again there might be confusion, for it is impossible to be sure of servants. Keep him therefore I entreat you in Edward St. You will not find him a heavy companion, and I allow you to flirt with him as much as you like. At the same time do not forget my real interest; say all that you can to convince him that I shall be quite wretched if he remain here; you know my reasons—propriety and so forth. I would urge them more myself, but that I am impatient to be rid of him, as Manwaring comes within half an hour. Adieu.

S.V.

LETTER 32
MRS. JOHNSON TO LADY SUSAN
Edward St.

My dear creature,

I am in agonies, and know not what to do, nor what *you* can do. Mr. De Courcy arrived, just when he should not. Mrs. Manwaring had that instant entered the house, and forced herself into her guardian's presence, though I did not know a syllable of it till afterwards, for I was out when both she and Reginald came, or I would have sent him away at all events; but *she* was shut up with Mr. Johnson, while *he* waited in the drawing room for me. She arrived yesterday in pursuit of her husband; but perhaps you know this already from himself. She came to this house to entreat my husband's interference, and before I could be aware of it, everything that you could wish to be concealed, was known to him; and unluckily she had wormed out of Manwaring's servant that he had visited you every day since your being in town, and had just watched him to your door herself! What could I do? Facts are such horrid things! All is by this time known to De Courcy, who is now alone with Mr. Johnson. Do not accuse me; indeed, it was impossible to prevent it. Mr. Johnson has for some time suspected De Courcy of intending to marry you, and would speak with him alone, as soon as he knew him to be in the house.

That detestable Mrs. Manwaring, who for your comfort, had fretted herself thinner and uglier than ever, is still here, and they have been all closeted together. What can be done? If Manwaring is now with you, he had better be gone. At any rate I hope he will plague his wife more than ever. With anxious wishes,

Yours faithfully,
Alicia

LETTER 33
LADY SUSAN TO MRS. JOHNSON
Upper Seymour St.

This *éclaircissement* [1] is rather provoking. How unlucky that you should have been from home! I thought myself sure of you at seven. I am undismayed however. Do not torment yourself with fears on my account. Depend upon it, I can make my own story good with Reginald. Manwaring is just gone; he brought me the news of his wife's arrival. Silly woman! what does she expect by such manoeuvres? Yet, I wish she had stayed quietly at Langford.

Reginald will be a little enraged at first, but by tomorrow's dinner, everything will be well again. Adieu.

S.V.

LETTER 34
MR. DE COURCY TO LADY SUSAN
Hotel

I write only to bid you farewell. The spell is removed. I see you as you are. Since we parted yesterday, I have received from indisputable authority, such an history of you as must bring the most mortifying conviction of the imposition I have been under, and the absolute necessity of an immediate and eternal separation from you. You cannot doubt to what I allude; Langford—Langford—that word will be sufficient. I received my information in Mr. Johnson's house, from Mrs. Manwaring herself.

You know how I have loved you, you can intimately judge of my present feelings; but I am not so weak as to find indulgence in describing them to a woman who will glory in having excited their anguish, but whose affection they have never been able to gain.

R. De Courcy

LETTER 35
LADY SUSAN TO MR. DE COURCY
Upper Seymour St.

I will not attempt to describe my astonishment on reading the note, this moment received from you. I am bewildered in my endeavours to form some rational conjecture of what Mrs. Manwaring can have told you, to occasion so extraordinary a change in your sentiments. Have I not explained everything to you with respect to myself which could bear a doubtful meaning, and which the ill-nature of the world had interpreted to my discredit? What can you now have heard to stagger your esteem for me? Have I ever had a concealment from you? Reginald, you agitate me beyond expression. I cannot suppose that the old story of Mrs. Manwaring's jealousy can be revived again, or at least, be listened to again. Come to me immediately, and explain what is at present absolutely incomprehensible. Believe me, the single word of *Langford* is not of such potent intelligence, as to supersede the necessity of more. If we *are* to part, it will at least be handsome to take your personal leave. But I have little heart to jest; in truth, I am serious enough—for to be sunk, though but an hour, in your opinion, is an humiliation to which I know not how to submit. I shall count every moment till your arrival.

S.V.

LETTER 36
MR. DE COURCY TO LADY SUSAN
Hotel

Why would you write to me? Why do you require particulars? But since it must be so, I am obliged to declare that all the accounts of your misconduct during the life and since the death of Mr. Vernon which had reached me in common with the world in general, and gained my entire belief before I saw you, but which you by the exertion of your perverted abilities had made me resolve to disallow, have been unanswerably proved to me. Nay, more, I am assured that a connection, of which I had never before entertained a thought, has for some time existed, and still continues to exist between you and

1   *éclaircissement*   Clarification (of Lady Susan's behavior).

the man, whose family you robbed of its peace, in return for the hospitality with which you were received into it! That you have corresponded with him ever since your leaving Langford—not with his wife, but with him—and that he now visits you every day. Can you, dare you deny it? and all this at the time when I was an encouraged, an accepted lover! From what have I not escaped! I have only to be grateful. Far from me be all complaint, and every sigh of regret. My own folly has endangered me, my preservation I owe to the kindness, the integrity of another. But the unfortunate Mrs. Manwaring, whose agonies while she related the past, seemed to threaten her reason—how is she to be consoled?

After such a discovery as this, you will scarcely affect farther wonder at my meaning in bidding you adieu. My understanding is at length restored, and teaches me no less to abhor the artifices which had subdued me, than to despise myself for the weakness, on which their strength was founded.

R. De Courcy

LETTER 37
LADY SUSAN TO MR. DE COURCY
Upper Seymour St.

I am satisfied—and will trouble you no more when these few lines are dismissed. The engagement which you were eager to form a fortnight ago, is no longer compatible with your views, and I rejoice to find that the prudent advice of your parents has not been given in vain. Your restoration to peace will, I doubt not, speedily follow this act of filial obedience, and I flatter myself with the hope of surviving my share in this disappointment.

S.V.

LETTER 38
MRS. JOHNSON TO LADY SUSAN
Edward St.

I am grieved, though I cannot be astonished at your rupture with Mr. De Courcy; he has just informed Mr. Johnson of it by letter. He leaves London he says to-day.

Be assured that I partake in all your feelings, and do not be angry if I say that your intercourse even by letter must soon be given up. It makes me miserable—but Mr. Johnson vows that if I persist in the connection, he will settle in the country for the rest of his life—and you know it is impossible to submit to such an extremity while any other alternative remains.

You have heard of course that the Manwarings are to part; I am afraid Mrs. M. will come home to us again. But she is still so fond of her husband and frets so much about him that perhaps she may not live long.

Miss Manwaring is just come to town to be with her aunt, and they say, that she declares she will have Sir James Martin before she leaves London again. If I were you, I would certainly get him myself. I had almost forgot to give you my opinion of De Courcy, I am really delighted with him, he is full as handsome I think as Manwaring, and with such an open, good-humoured countenance that one cannot help loving him at first sight. Mr. Johnson and he are the greatest friends in the world. Adieu, my dearest Susan. I wish matters did not go so perversely. That unlucky visit to Langford! But I dare say you did all for the best, and there is no defying destiny.

Your sincerely attached,

Alicia

LETTER 39
LADY SUSAN TO MRS. JOHNSON
Upper Seymour St.

My dear Alicia,

I yield to the necessity which parts us. Under such circumstances you could not act otherwise. Our friendship cannot be impaired by it; and in happier times, when your situation is as independent as mine, it will unite us again in the same intimacy as ever. For this I shall impatiently wait; and meanwhile can safely assure you that I never was more at ease, or better satisfied with myself and everything about me, than at the present hour. Your husband I abhor—Reginald I despise—and I am secure of never seeing either again. Have I not reason to rejoice? Manwaring is more devoted to me than ever; and were he at liberty, I doubt if I could resist even matrimony offered by him. This event, if his wife live with you, it may be in your power to hasten. The violence of her feelings, which must wear her out, may be easily kept in irritation. I rely on your friendship for this. I am now satisfied that I never could have brought myself to marry Reginald; and am equally determined that Frederica never shall. Tomorrow I shall fetch her from Churchill, and let Maria Manwaring tremble for the consequence. Frederica shall be Sir James's wife before she quits my house. She may whimper, and the Vernons may storm; I regard them not. I am tired of submitting my will to the caprices of others—of resigning my own judgement in deference to those, to whom I owe no duty, and for whom I feel no respect. I have given up too much—have been too easily worked on; but Frederica shall now find the difference.

Adieu, dearest of friends. May the next gouty attack be more favourable. And may you always regard me as unalterably yours,

S. Vernon

Letter 40
Lady De Courcy to Mrs. Vernon

Parklands

My dear Catherine,

I have charming news for you, and if I had not sent off my letter this morning, you might have been spared the vexation of knowing of Reginald's being gone to town, for he is returned, Reginald is returned, not to ask our consent to his marrying Lady Susan, but to tell us that they are parted forever! He has been only an hour in the house, and I have not been able to learn particulars, for he is so very low, that I have not the heart to ask questions; but I hope we shall soon know all. This is the most joyful hour he has ever given us, since the day of his birth. Nothing is wanting but to have you here, and it is our particular wish and entreaty that you would come to us as soon as you can. You have owed us a visit many long weeks. I hope nothing will make it inconvenient to Mr. Vernon, and pray bring all my grandchildren, and

your dear niece is included of course; I long to see her. It has been a sad heavy winter hitherto, without Reginald, and seeing nobody from Churchill; I never found the season so dreary before, but this happy meeting will make us young again. Frederica runs much in my thoughts, and when Reginald has recovered his usual good spirits (as I trust he soon will), we will try to rob him of his heart once more, and I am full of hopes of seeing their hands joined at no great distance.

Your affectionate mother,

C. De Courcy

Letter 41
Mrs. Vernon to Lady De Courcy

Churchill

My dear Madam,

Your letter has surprised me beyond measure. Can it be true that they are really separated—and for ever? I should be overjoyed if I dared depend on it, but after all that I have seen, how can one be secure? And Reginald really with you! My surprise is the greater, because on Wednesday, the very day of his coming to Parklands, we had a most unexpected and unwelcome visit from Lady Susan, looking all cheerfulness and good humour, and seeming more as if she were to marry him when she got back to town, than as if parted from him for ever. She stayed nearly two hours, was as affectionate and agreeable as ever, and not a syllable, not a hint was dropped of any disagreement or coolness between them. I asked her whether she had seen my brother since his arrival in town—not as you may suppose with any doubt of the fact—but merely to see how she looked. She immediately answered without any embarrassment that he had been kind enough to call on her on Monday, but she believed he had already returned home—which I was very far from crediting.

Your kind invitation is accepted by us with pleasure, and on Thursday next, we and our little ones will be with you. Pray heaven! Reginald may not be in town again by that time!

I wish we could bring dear Frederica too, but I am sorry to add that her mother's errand hither was to fetch her away; and miserable as it made the poor girl, it was impossible to detain her. I was thoroughly unwilling to let her go, and so was her uncle; and all that could be urged, we *did* urge. But Lady Susan declared that as she was now about to fix herself in town for several months, she could not be easy if her daughter were not with her, for masters, etc. Her manner, to be sure, was very kind and proper—and Mr. Vernon believes that Frederica will now be treated with affection. I wish I could think so too!

The poor girl's heart was almost broke at taking leave of us. I charged her to write to me very often, and to remember that if she were in any distress, we should be always her friends. I took care to see her alone, that I might say all this, and I hope made her a little more comfortable. But I shall not be easy till I can go to town and judge of her situation myself.

I wish there were a better prospect than now appears, of the match, which the conclusion of your letter declares your expectation of. At present it is not very likely.

Yours etc.,

Catherine Vernon

CONCLUSION

This correspondence, by a meeting between some of the parties and a separation between the others, could not, to the great detriment of the Post Office revenue, be continued longer. Very little assistance to the state could be derived from the epistolary intercourse of Mrs. Vernon and her niece, for the former soon perceived by the style of Frederica's letters, that they were written under her mother's inspection, and therefore deferring all particular enquiry till she could make it personally in town, ceased writing minutely[1] or often.

Having learnt enough in the meanwhile from her open-hearted brother, of what had passed between him and Lady Susan to sink the latter lower than ever in her opinion, she was proportionably more anxious to get Frederica removed from such a mother, and placed under her own care; and though with little hope of success, was resolved to leave nothing unattempted that

might offer a chance of obtaining her sister-in-law's consent to it. Her anxiety on the subject made her press for an early visit to London; and Mr. Vernon, who, as it must have already appeared, lived only to do whatever he was desired, soon found some accommodating business to call him thither. With a heart full of the matter, Mrs. Vernon waited on Lady Susan, shortly after her arrival in town; and she was met with such an easy and cheerful affection as made her almost turn from her with horror. No remembrance of Reginald, no consciousness of guilt, gave one look of embarrassment. She was in excellent spirits, and seemed eager to show at once, by every possible attention to her brother and sister, her sense of their kindness, and her pleasure in their society.

Frederica was no more altered than Lady Susan; the same restrained manners, the same timid look in the presence of her mother as heretofore, assured her aunt of her situation's being uncomfortable, and confirmed her in the plan of altering it. No unkindness however on the part of Lady Susan appeared. Persecution on the subject of Sir James was entirely at an end—his name merely mentioned to say that he was not in London; and in all her conversation she was solicitous only for the welfare and improvement of her daughter, acknowledging in terms of grateful delight that Frederica was now growing every day more and more what a parent could desire.

Mrs. Vernon surprised and incredulous, knew now what to suspect, and without any change in her own views, only feared greater difficulty in accomplishing them. The first hope of anything better was derived from Lady Susan's asking her whether she thought Frederica looked quite as well as she had done at Churchill, as she must confess herself to have sometimes an anxious doubt of London's perfectly agreeing with her.

Mrs. Vernon encouraging the doubt, directly proposed her niece's returning with them into the country. Lady Susan was unable to express her sense of such kindness; yet knew not from a variety of reasons how to part with her daughter; and as, though her own plans were not yet wholly fixed, she trusted it would ere long be in her power to take Frederica into the country herself, concluded by declining entirely to profit by such unexampled attention. Mrs. Vernon however persevered

---

[1] *minutely* Thoroughly.

in the offer of it, and though Lady Susan continued to resist, her resistance in the course of a few days seemed somewhat less formidable.

The lucky alarm of an influenza, decided what might not have been decided quite so soon. Lady Susan's maternal fears were then too much awakened for her to think of anything but Frederica's removal from the risk of infection. Above all disorders in the world, she most dreaded influenza for her daughter's constitution. Frederica returned to Churchill with her uncle and aunt, and three weeks afterwards Lady Susan announced her being married to Sir James Martin.

Mrs. Vernon was then convinced of what she had only suspected before, that she might have spared herself all the trouble of urging a removal, which Lady Susan had doubtless resolved on from the first. Frederica's visit was nominally for six weeks; but her mother, though inviting her to return in one or two affectionate letters, was very ready to oblige the whole party by consenting to a prolongation of her stay, and in the course of two months ceased to write of her absence, and in the course of two more, to write to her at all.

Frederica was therefore fixed in the family of her uncle and aunt, till such time as Reginald De Courcy could be talked, flattered and finessed into an affection for her—which, allowing leisure for the conquest of his attachment to her mother, for his abjuring all future attachments and detesting the sex, might be reasonably looked for in the course of a twelvemonth. Three months might have done it in general, but Reginald's feelings were no less lasting than lively.

Whether Lady Susan was, or was not happy in her second choice—I do not see how it can ever be ascertained—for who would take her assurance of it, on either side of the question? The world must judge from probability. She had nothing against her, but her husband, and her conscience.

Sir James may seem to have drawn an harder lot than mere folly merited. I leave him therefore to all the pity that anybody can give him. For myself, I confess that I can pity only Miss Manwaring, who coming to town and putting herself to an expense in clothes, which impoverished her for two years, on purpose to secure him, was

defrauded of her due by a woman ten years older than herself.

—1871 (WRITTEN 1793–94, 1805)

Pride and Prejudice

Pride and Prejudice, first published in 1813, has remained Austen's most popular novel. The story turns on the marriage prospects of the five daughters of Mr. and Mrs. Bennet; on the affection between the eldest, Jane, and the charming Mr. Bingley; and on the prejudice formed by Jane's sister, Elizabeth, against the proud and distant Mr. Darcy. The novel's famous opening chapters set the tone; they also provide a sense of the characteristic style of Austen's major novels.

from *Pride and Prejudice*

CHAPTER I

It is a truth universally acknowledged, that a single man in possession of a good fortune must be in want of a wife.

However little known the feelings or views of such a man may be on his first entering a neighbourhood, this truth is so well fixed in the minds of the surrounding families that he is considered as the rightful property of some one or other of their daughters.

"My dear Mr. Bennet," said his lady to him one day, "have you heard that Netherfield Park is let at last?"

Mr. Bennet replied that he had not.

"But it is," returned she; "for Mrs. Long has just been here, and she told me all about it."

Mr. Bennet made no answer.

"Do not you want to know who has taken it?" cried his wife impatiently.

"*You* want to tell me, and I have no objection to hearing it."

This was invitation enough.

"Why, my dear, you must know, Mrs. Long says that Netherfield is taken by a young man of large fortune from the north of England; that he came down on Monday in a chaise and four[1] to see the place, and was so much delighted with it that he agreed with Mr. Morris immediately; that he is to take possession before Michaelmas,[2] and some of his servants are to be in the house by the end of next week."

"What is his name?"

"Bingley."

"Is he married or single?"

"Oh! single, my dear, to be sure! A single man of large fortune; four or five thousand a year. What a fine thing for our girls!"

"How so? how can it affect them?"

"My dear Mr. Bennet," replied his wife, "how can you be so tiresome! You must know that I am thinking of his marrying one of them."

"Is that his design in settling here?"

"Design! nonsense, how can you talk so! But it is very likely that he *may* fall in love with one of them, and therefore you must visit him as soon as he comes."

"I see no occasion for that. You and the girls may go, or you may send them by themselves, which perhaps will be still better, for as you are as handsome as any of them, Mr. Bingley might like you the best of the party."

"My dear, you flatter me. I certainly *have* had my share of beauty, but I do not pretend to be anything extraordinary now. When a woman has five grown up daughters, she ought to give over thinking of her own beauty."

"In such cases, a woman has not often much beauty to think of."

"But, my dear, you must indeed go and see Mr. Bingley when he comes into the neighbourhood."

"It is more than I engage for,[3] I assure you."

"But consider your daughters. Only think what an establishment it would be for one of them. Sir William and Lady Lucas are determined to go, merely on that account, for in general you know they visit no new-comers. Indeed you must go, for it will be impossible for *us* to visit him, if you do not."

"You are over scrupulous, surely. I dare say Mr. Bingley will be very glad to see you; and I will send a few lines by you to assure him of my hearty consent to his marrying which ever he chooses of the girls, though I must throw in a good word for my little Lizzy."

"I desire you will do no such thing. Lizzy is not a bit better than the others, and I am sure she is not half so handsome as Jane, nor half so good humoured as Lydia. But you are always giving *her* the preference."

"They have none of them much to recommend them," replied he; "they are all silly and ignorant like other girls, but Lizzy has something more of quickness than her sisters."

"Mr. Bennet, how can you abuse your own children in such a way? You take delight in vexing me. You have no compassion on my poor nerves."

"You mistake me, my dear. I have a high respect for your nerves. They are my old friends. I have heard you mention them with consideration these twenty years at least."

"Ah! you do not know what I suffer."

"But I hope you will get over it, and live to see many young men of four thousand a year come into the neighbourhood."

"It will be no use to us if twenty such should come, since you will not visit them."

"Depend upon it, my dear, that when there are twenty, I will visit them all."

Mr. Bennet was so odd a mixture of quick parts, sarcastic humour, reserve, and caprice, that the experience of three and twenty years had been insufficient to make his wife understand his character. *Her* mind was less difficult to develop. She was a woman of mean[4] understanding, little information, and uncertain temper. When she was discontented she fancied herself nervous. The business of her life was to get her daughters married; its solace was visiting and news.

---

[1]   *chaise and four*   Traveling carriage pulled by four horses.

[2]   *Michaelmas*   The feast of St. Michael, on 29 September.

[3]   *engage for*   Promise to perform.

[4]   *mean*   Modest.

CHAPTER 2

Mr. Bennet was among the earliest of those who waited on Mr. Bingley. He had always intended to visit him, though to the last always assuring his wife that he should not go; and till the evening after the visit was paid, she had no knowledge of it. It was then disclosed in the following manner. Observing his second daughter employed in trimming a hat, he suddenly addressed her with,

"I hope Mr. Bingley will like it, Lizzy."

"We are not in a way to know *what* Mr. Bingley likes," said her mother resentfully, "since we are not to visit."

"But you forget, mama," said Elizabeth, "that we shall meet him at the assemblies, and that Mrs. Long has promised to introduce him."

"I do not believe Mrs. Long will do any such thing. She has two nieces of her own. She is a selfish, hypocritical woman, and I have no opinion of her."[1]

"No more have I," said Mr. Bennet; "and I am glad to find that you do not depend on her serving you."

Mrs. Bennet deigned not to make any reply; but unable to contain herself, began scolding one of her daughters.

"Don't keep coughing so, Kitty, for heaven's sake! Have a little compassion on my nerves. You tear them to pieces."

"Kitty has no discretion in her coughs," said her father; "she times them ill."

"I do not cough for my own amusement," replied Kitty fretfully.

"When is your next ball to be, Lizzy?"

"Tomorrow fortnight."[2]

"Aye, so it is," cried her mother, "and Mrs. Long does not come back till the day before; so, it will be impossible for her to introduce him, for she will not know him herself."

"Then, my dear, you may have the advantage of your friend, and introduce Mr. Bingley to *her*."

"Impossible, Mr. Bennet, impossible, when I am not acquainted with him myself; how can you be so teazing?"

"I honour your circumspection. A fortnight's acquaintance is certainly very little. One cannot know what a man really is by the end of a fortnight. But if *we* do not venture, somebody else will; and after all, Mrs. Long and her nieces must stand their chance; and therefore, as she will think it an act of kindness, if you decline the office, I will take it on myself."

The girls stared at their father. Mrs. Bennet said only, "Nonsense, nonsense!"

"What can be the meaning of that emphatic exclamation?" cried he. "Do you consider the forms of introduction, and the stress that is laid on them, as nonsense? I cannot quite agree with you *there*. What say you, Mary? for you are a young lady of deep reflection I know, and read great books, and make extracts."

Mary wished to say something very sensible, but knew not how.

"While Mary is adjusting her ideas," he continued, "let us return to Mr. Bingley."

"I am sick of Mr. Bingley," cried his wife.

"I am sorry to hear *that*; but why did not you tell me so before? If I had known as much this morning, I certainly would not have called on him. It is very unlucky, but as I have actually paid the visit, we cannot escape the acquaintance now."

The astonishment of the ladies was just what he wished; that of Mrs. Bennet perhaps surpassing the rest; though when the first tumult of joy was over, she began to declare that it was what she had expected all the while.

"How good it was in you, my dear Mr. Bennet! But I knew I should persuade you at last. I was sure you loved your girls too well to neglect such an acquaintance. Well, how pleased I am! and it is such a good joke, too, that you should have gone this morning, and never said a word about it till now."

"Now, Kitty, you may cough as much as you choose," said Mr. Bennet; and, as he spoke, he left the room, fatigued with the raptures of his wife.

---

[1] *have no opinion of her* I.e., have no great opinion of her; regard her as unworthy.

[2] *Tomorrow fortnight* I.e., a fortnight (two weeks) from tomorrow.

"What an excellent father you have, girls," said she, when the door was shut. "I do not know how you will ever make him amends for his kindness; or me either, for that matter. At our time of life, it is not so pleasant, I can tell you, to be making new acquaintance every day; but for your sakes, we would do anything. Lydia, my love, though you *are* the youngest, I dare say Mr. Bingley will dance with you at the next ball."

"Oh!" said Lydia stoutly, "I am not afraid; for though I *am* the youngest, I'm the tallest."

The rest of the evening was spent in conjecturing how soon he would return Mr. Bennet's visit, and determining when they should ask him to dinner.

Chapter 3

Not all that Mrs. Bennet, however, with the assistance of her five daughters, could ask on the subject was sufficient to draw from her husband any satisfactory description of Mr. Bingley. They attacked him in various ways: with barefaced questions, ingenious suppositions, and distant surmises; but he eluded the skill of them all, and they were at last obliged to accept the second-hand intelligence of their neighbour Lady Lucas. Her report was highly favourable. Sir William had been delighted with him. He was quite young, wonderfully handsome, extremely agreeable, and to crown the whole, he meant to be at the next assembly with a large party. Nothing could be more delightful! To be fond of dancing was a certain step towards falling in love; and very lively hopes of Mr. Bingley's heart were entertained.

"If I can but see one of my daughters happily settled at Netherfield," said Mrs. Bennet to her husband, "and all the others equally well married, I shall have nothing to wish for."

In a few days Mr. Bingley returned Mr. Bennet's visit, and sat about ten minutes with him in his library. He had entertained hopes of being admitted to a sight of the young ladies, of whose beauty he had heard much; but he saw only the father. The ladies were somewhat more fortunate, for they had the advantage of ascertaining, from an upper window, that he wore a blue coat and rode a black horse.

An invitation to dinner was soon afterwards dispatched; and already had Mrs. Bennet planned the courses that were to do credit to her housekeeping, when an answer arrived which deferred it all. Mr. Bingley was obliged to be in town the following day, and consequently unable to accept the honour of their invitation, &c. Mrs. Bennet was quite disconcerted. She could not imagine what business he could have in town so soon after his arrival in Hertfordshire, and she began to fear that he might be always flying about from one place to another, and never settled at Netherfield as he ought to be. Lady Lucas quieted her fears a little by starting the idea of his being gone to London only to get a large party for the ball; and a report soon followed that Mr. Bingley was to bring twelve ladies and seven gentlemen with him to the assembly. The girls grieved over such a large number of ladies, but were comforted the day before the ball by hearing that, instead of twelve, he had brought only six with him from London, his five sisters and a cousin. And when the party entered the assembly room, it consisted of only five altogether; Mr. Bingley, his two sisters, the husband of the eldest, and another young man.

Mr. Bingley was good looking and gentlemanlike; he had a pleasant countenance, and easy, unaffected manners. His sisters were fine women, with an air of decided fashion. His brother-in-law, Mr. Hurst, merely looked the gentleman; but his friend Mr. Darcy soon drew the attention of the room by his fine, tall person, handsome features, noble mien,[1] and the report which was in general circulation within five minutes after his entrance, of his having ten thousand a year. The gentlemen pronounced him to be a fine figure of a man, the ladies declared he was much handsomer than Mr. Bingley, and he was looked at with great admiration for about half the evening, till his manners gave a disgust which turned the tide of his popularity; for he was discovered to be proud, to be above his company, and above being pleased; and not all his large estate in

---

[1] *mien* Bearing.

Derbyshire could then save him from having a most forbidding, disagreeable countenance, and being unworthy to be compared with his friend.

Mr. Bingley had soon made himself acquainted with all the principal people in the room; he was lively and unreserved, danced every dance, was angry that the ball closed so early, and talked of giving one himself at Netherfield. Such amiable qualities must speak for themselves. What a contrast between him and his friend! Mr. Darcy danced only once with Mrs. Hurst and once with Miss Bingley, declined being introduced to any other lady, and spent the rest of the evening in walking about the room, speaking occasionally to one of his own party. His character was decided. He was the proudest, most disagreeable man in the world, and everybody hoped that he would never come there again. Amongst the most violent against him was Mrs. Bennet, whose dislike of his general behaviour was sharpened into particular resentment by his having slighted one of her daughters.

Elizabeth Bennet had been obliged, by the scarcity of gentlemen, to sit down for two dances; and during part of that time, Mr. Darcy had been standing near enough for her to overhear a conversation between him and Mr. Bingley, who came from the dance for a few minutes to press his friend to join it.

"Come, Darcy," said he, "I must have you dance. I hate to see you standing about by yourself in this stupid manner. You had much better dance."

"I certainly shall not. You know how I detest it, unless I am particularly acquainted with my partner. At such an assembly as this, it would be insupportable. Your sisters are engaged, and there is not another woman in the room whom it would not be a punishment to me to stand up with."

"I would not be so fastidious as you are," cried Bingley, "for a kingdom! Upon my honour, I never met with so many pleasant girls in my life as I have this evening; and there are several of them you see uncommonly pretty."

"*You* are dancing with the only handsome girl in the room," said Mr. Darcy, looking at the eldest Miss Bennet.

"Oh! she is the most beautiful creature I ever beheld! But there is one of her sisters sitting down just behind you who is very pretty, and, I dare say, very agreeable. Do let me ask my partner to introduce you."

"Which do you mean?" and turning round, he looked for a moment at Elizabeth, till, catching her eye, he withdrew his own and coldly said, "She is tolerable; but not handsome enough to tempt *me*; and I am in no humour at present to give consequence to young ladies who are slighted by other men. You had better return to your partner and enjoy her smiles, for you are wasting your time with me." Mr. Bingley followed his advice. Mr. Darcy walked off, and Elizabeth remained with no very cordial feelings towards him. She told the story however with great spirit among her friends; for she had a lively, playful disposition, which delighted in anything ridiculous.

The evening altogether passed off pleasantly to the whole family. Mrs. Bennet had seen her eldest daughter much admired by the Netherfield party. Mr. Bingley had danced with her twice, and she had been distinguished by his sisters. Jane was as much gratified by this as her mother could be, though in a quieter way. Elizabeth felt Jane's pleasure. Mary had heard herself mentioned to Miss Bingley as the most accomplished girl in the neighbourhood; and Catherine and Lydia had been fortunate enough to be never without partners, which was all that they had yet learnt to care for at a ball. They returned therefore in good spirits to Longbourn, the village where they lived, and of which they were the principal inhabitants. They found Mr. Bennet still up. With a book he was regardless of time; and on the present occasion he had a good deal of curiosity as to the event of an evening which had raised such splendid expectations. He had rather hoped that all his wife's views on the stranger would be disappointed; but he soon found that he had a very different story to hear.

"Oh! my dear Mr. Bennet," as she entered the room, "we have had a most delightful evening, a most excellent ball. I wish you had been there. Jane was so admired, nothing could be like it. Everybody said how well she looked; and Mr. Bingley thought her quite beautiful, and danced with her twice. Only think of *that* my dear;

he actually danced with her twice, and she was the only creature in the room that he asked a second time. First of all, he asked Miss Lucas. I was so vexed to see him stand up with her; but, however, he did not admire her at all—indeed, nobody can, you know—and he seemed quite struck with Jane as she was going down the dance. So, he enquired who she was, and got introduced, and asked her for the two next. Then, the two third he danced with Miss King, and the two fourth with Maria Lucas, and the two fifth with Jane again, and the two sixth with Lizzy, and the Boulanger."[1]

"If he had had any compassion for *me*," cried her husband impatiently, "he would not have danced half so much! For God's sake, say no more of his partners. Oh! that he had sprained his ankle in the first dance!"

"Oh! my dear," continued Mrs. Bennet, "I am quite delighted with him. He is so excessively handsome! and his sisters are charming women. I never in my life saw anything more elegant than their dresses. I dare say the lace upon Mrs. Hurst's gown—"

Here she was interrupted again. Mr. Bennet protested against any description of finery. She was therefore obliged to seek another branch of the subject, and related, with much bitterness of spirit and some exaggeration, the shocking rudeness of Mr. Darcy.

"But I can assure you," she added, "that Lizzy does not lose much by not suiting *his* fancy; for he is a most disagreeable, horrid man, not at all worth pleasing. So high and so conceited that there was no enduring him! He walked here, and he walked there, fancying himself so very great! Not handsome enough to dance with! I wish you had been there, my dear, to have given him one of your set downs. I quite detest the man."

Chapter 4

When Jane and Elizabeth were alone, the former, who had been cautious in her praise of Mr. Bingley before, expressed to her sister how very much she admired him.

"He is just what a young man ought to be," said she, "sensible, good humoured, lively; and I never saw such happy manners!—so much ease, with such perfect good breeding!"

"He is also handsome," replied Elizabeth, "which a young man ought likewise to be, if he possibly can. His character is thereby complete."

"I was very much flattered by his asking me to dance a second time. I did not expect such a compliment."

"Did not you? *I* did for you. But that is one great difference between us. Compliments always take *you* by surprise, and *me* never. What could be more natural than his asking you again? He could not help seeing that you were about five times as pretty as every other woman in the room. No thanks to his gallantry for that. Well, he certainly is very agreeable, and I give you leave to like him. You have liked many a stupider person."

"Dear Lizzy!"

"Oh! you are a great deal too apt, you know, to like people in general. You never see a fault in anybody. All the world are good and agreeable in your eyes. I never heard you speak ill of a human being in my life."

"I would wish not to be hasty in censuring anyone; but I always speak what I think."

"I know you do; and it is *that* which makes the wonder. With *your* good sense, to be honestly blind to the follies and nonsense of others! Affectation of candour is common enough; one meets it everywhere. But to be candid without ostentation or design—to take the good of everybody's character and make it still better, and say nothing of the bad—belongs to you alone. And so, you like this man's sisters too, do you? Their manners are not equal to his."

"Certainly not, at first. But they are very pleasing women when you converse with them. Miss Bingley is to live with her brother and keep his house; and I am much mistaken if we shall not find a very charming neighbour in her."

Elizabeth listened in silence, but was not convinced; their behaviour at the assembly had not been calculated to please in general; and with more quickness of observation and less pliancy of temper than her sister, and with a judgment too unassailed by any attention to

---

[1] *Boulanger* French dance, performed by a circle of couples, in which each person dances briefly with each member of the opposite sex. The boulanger was the closing dance at balls.

herself, she was very little disposed to approve them. They were in fact very fine ladies; not deficient in good humour when they were pleased, nor in the power of being agreeable where they chose it; but proud and conceited. They were rather handsome, had been educated in one of the first private seminaries in town, had a fortune of twenty thousand pounds, were in the habit of spending more than they ought, and of associating with people of rank; and were therefore in every respect entitled to think well of themselves, and meanly of others. They were of a respectable family in the north of England, a circumstance more deeply impressed on their memories than that their brother's fortune and their own had been acquired by trade.

Mr. Bingley inherited property to the amount of nearly an hundred thousand pounds from his father, who had intended to purchase an estate, but did not live to do it. Mr. Bingley intended it likewise, and sometimes made choice of his county; but as he was now provided with a good house and the liberty of a manor, it was doubtful to many of those who best knew the easiness of his temper, whether he might not spend the remainder of his days at Netherfield, and leave the next generation to purchase.

His sisters were very anxious for his having an estate of his own; but though he was now established only as a tenant, Miss Bingley was by no means unwilling to preside at his table, nor was Mrs. Hurst, who had married a man of more fashion than fortune, less disposed to consider his house as her home when it suited her. Mr. Bingley had not been of age two years when he was tempted by an accidental recommendation to look at Netherfield House. He did look at it and into it for half an hour, was pleased with the situation and the principal rooms, satisfied with what the owner said in its praise, and took it immediately.

Between him and Darcy there was a very steady friendship, in spite of a great opposition of character. Bingley was endeared to Darcy by the easiness, openness, ductility of his temper—though no disposition could offer a greater contrast to his own, and though with his own he never appeared dissatisfied. On the strength of Darcy's regard Bingley had the firmest reliance, and of his judgment the highest opinion. In understanding, Darcy was the superior. Bingley was by no means deficient, but Darcy was clever. He was at the same time haughty, reserved, and fastidious, and his manners, though well bred, were not inviting. In that respect his friend had greatly the advantage. Bingley was sure of being liked wherever he appeared; Darcy was continually giving offence.

The manner in which they spoke of the Meryton assembly was sufficiently characteristic. Bingley had never met with pleasanter people or prettier girls in his life; everybody had been most kind and attentive to him, there had been no formality, no stiffness, he had soon felt acquainted with all the room; and as to Miss Bennet, he could not conceive an angel more beautiful. Darcy, on the contrary, had seen a collection of people in whom there was little beauty and no fashion, for none of whom he had felt the smallest interest, and from none received either attention or pleasure. Miss Bennet he acknowledged to be pretty, but she smiled too much.

Mrs. Hurst and her sister allowed it to be so—but still they admired her and liked her, and pronounced her to be a sweet girl, and one whom they should not object to know more of. Miss Bennet was therefore established as a sweet girl, and their brother felt authorised by such commendation to think of her as he chose.
—1813 (WRITTEN 1796–97)

IN CONTEXT

Austen's Letters

Though there is little in the correspondence that has come down to us that sheds direct light on Jane Austen's novels, Austen's letters are of considerable interest both in the impressions they give us of the daily life of the time and in comments Austen makes about writing—far more often the writing of others than her own work. The following sampling includes two letters to her sister Cassandra; one to her niece, Anna Austen Lefroy, the latter written in response to her niece having sent her a manuscript; and one to her nephew, James-Edward Austen, who later wrote *A Memoir of Jane Austen*.

Monday night [24 December 1798]
Steventon

My Dear Cassandra,[1]

I have got some pleasant news for you which I am eager to communicate, and therefore begin my letter sooner, though I shall not *send* it sooner than usual.

Admiral Gambier,[2] in reply to my father's application, writes as follows:—"As it is usual to keep young officers in small vessels, it being most proper on account of their inexperience, and it being also a situation where they are more in the way of learning their duty, your son has been continued in the 'Scorpion'; but I have mentioned to the Board of Admiralty his wish to be in a frigate, and when a proper opportunity offers and it is judged that he has taken his turn in a small ship, I hope he will be removed. With regard to your son now in the 'London' I am glad I can give you the assurance that his promotion is likely to take place very soon, as Lord Spencer has been so good as to say he would include him in an arrangement that he proposes making in a short time relative to some promotions in that quarter."[3]

There! I may now finish my letter and go and hang myself, for I am sure I can neither write nor do anything which will not appear insipid to you after this. *Now* I really think he will soon be made, and only wish we could communicate our foreknowledge of the event to him whom it principally concerns.[4] My father has written to Daysh[5] to desire that he will inform us, if he can, when the commission is sent. Your chief wish is now ready to be accomplished; and could Lord Spencer give happiness to Martha[6] at the same time, what a joyful heart he would make of yours!

I have sent the same extract of the sweets of Gambier to Charles, who, poor fellow, though he sinks into nothing but an humble attendant on the hero of the piece, will, I hope, be contented with the

---

[1] *Cassandra* Austen's elder sister and dear friend.

[2] *Admiral Gambier* James Gambier, first Baron Gambier, and Lord of the Admiralty. He was related by marriage to the Austens.

[3] *"As it is usual … in that quarter"* Two of Jane Austen's brothers, Francis-William ("Frank") and Charles-John ("Charles") served in the British Navy.

[4] *him whom it principally concerns* Frank.

[5] *Daysh* George Daysh of the Navy Office.

[6] *Martha* Martha Lloyd, whom Frank married thirty years later (a second marriage).

prospect held out to him. By what the Admiral says, it appears as if he had been designedly kept in the "Scorpion." But I will not torment myself with conjectures and suppositions; facts shall satisfy me.

Frank had not heard from any of us for ten weeks when he wrote to me on November 12 in consequence of Lord St. Vincent[1] being removed to Gibraltar. When his commission is sent, however, it will not be so long on its road as our letters, because all the Government despatches are forwarded by land to his lordship from Lisbon with great regularity.

I returned from Manydown[2] this morning, and found my mother certainly in no respect worse than when I left her. She does not like the cold weather, but that we cannot help. I spent my time very quietly and very pleasantly with Catherine. Miss Blackford[3] is agreeable enough. I do not want people to be very agreeable, as it saves me the trouble of liking them a great deal. I found only Catherine and her when I got to Manydown on Thursday. We dined together and went together to Worting to seek the protection of Mrs. Clarke, with whom were Lady Mildmay, her eldest son, and a Mr. and Mrs. Hoare.

Our ball was very thin, but by no means unpleasant. There were thirty-one people, and only eleven ladies out of the number, and but five single women in the room. Of the gentlemen present you may have some idea from the list of my partners—Mr. Wood, G. Lefroy, Rice, a Mr. Butcher (belonging to the Temples, a sailor and not of the 11th Light Dragoons), Mr. Temple (not the horrid one of all), Mr. Wm. Orde (cousin to the Kingsclere man), Mr. John Harwood, and Mr. Calland, who appeared as usual with his hat in his hand, and stood every now and then behind Catherine and me to be talked to and abused for not dancing. We teased him, however, into it at last. I was very glad to see him again after so long a separation, and he was altogether rather the genius and flirt of the evening. He inquired after you.

There were twenty dances, and I danced them all, and without any fatigue. I was glad to find myself capable of dancing so much, and with so much satisfaction as I did; from my slender enjoyment of the Ashford balls (as assemblies for dancing) I had not thought myself equal to it, but in cold weather and with few couples I fancy I could just as well dance for a week together as for half an hour. My black cap was openly admired by Mrs. Lefroy, and secretly I imagine by everybody else in the room.

Tuesday. [25 December 1798]—I thank you for your long letter, which I will endeavour to deserve by writing the rest of this as closely as possible. I am full of joy at much of your information; that you should have been to a ball, and have danced at it, and supped with the Prince,[4] and that you should meditate the purchase of a new muslin gown, are delightful circumstances. *I* am determined to buy a handsome one whenever I can, and I am so tired and ashamed of half my present stock, that I even blush at the sight of the wardrobe which contains them. But I will not be much longer libelled by the possession of my coarse spot; I shall turn it into a petticoat very soon. I wish you a merry Christmas, but *no* compliments of the season.

Poor Edward! It is very hard that he, who has everything else in the world that he can wish for, should not have good health too.[5] But I hope with the assistance of stomach complaints, faintnesses,

---

[1] *Lord St. Vincent*   Admiral John Jervis, 1st Earl of St. Vincent, commanded the British fleet in the Mediterranean.

[2] *Manydown*   The manor house of the Bigg-Wither family in Wooton St. Lawrence, Hants. Elizabeth, Catherine, and Alethea Bigg were friends of Jane and Cassandra Austen.

[3] *Miss Blackford*   The Blachfords (sic) were cousins of the Bigg-Withers'.

[4] *the Prince*   Prince William-Frederick, second Duke of Gloucester. Prince William-Frederick was also a Major-General and would have been in Kent because of his military duties.

[5] *Poor Edward! ... too*   Edward Austen, Jane's brother, was adopted by a cousin, Thomas Knight, and made heir to Knight's three estates.

and sicknesses, he will soon be restored to that blessing likewise. If his nervous complaint proceeded from a suppression of something that ought to be thrown out, which does not seem unlikely, the first of these disorders may really be a remedy, and I sincerely wish it may, for I know no one more deserving of happiness without alloy than Edward is.

I cannot determine what to do about my new gown; I wish such things were to be bought ready-made. I have some hopes of meeting Martha at the christening at Deane[1] next Tuesday, and shall see what she can do for me. I want to have something suggested which will give me no trouble of thought or direction.

Again I return to my joy that you danced at Ashford, and that you supped with the Prince. I can perfectly comprehend Mrs. Cage's distress and perplexity. She has all those kind of foolish and incomprehensible feelings which would make her fancy herself uncomfortable in such a party. I love her, however, in spite of all her nonsense. Pray give "t'other Miss Austen's" compliments to Edward Bridges when you see him again.

I insist upon your persevering in your intention of buying a new gown; I am sure you must want one, and as you will have 5*l.* due in a week's time, I am certain you may afford it very well, and if you think you cannot, I will give you the body-lining.

Of my charities to the poor since I came home you shall have a faithful account. I have given a pair of worsted stockings to Mary Hutchins, Dame Kew, Mary Steevens, and Dame Staples; a shift to Hannah Staples, and a shawl to Betty Dawkins; amounting in all to about half a guinea. But I have no reason to suppose that the *Battys* would accept of anything, because I have not made them the offer.

I am glad to hear such a good account of Harriet Bridges; she goes on now as young ladies of seventeen ought to do, admired and admiring, in a much more rational way than her three elder sisters, who had so little of that kind of youth.[2] I dare say she fancies Major Elkington as agreeable as Warren, and if she can think so, it is very well.

I was to have dined at Keane to-day, but the weather is so cold that I am not sorry to be kept at home by the appearance of snow. We are to have company to dinner on Friday: the three Digweeds and James. We shall be a nice silent party, I suppose. Seize upon the scissors as soon as you possibly can on the receipt of this. I only fear your being too late to secure the prize.

The Lords of the Admiralty will have enough of our applications at present, for I hear from Charles that he has written to Lord Spencer[3] himself to be removed. I am afraid his Serene Highness will be in a passion, and order some of our heads to be cut off.

My mother wants to know whether Edward has ever made the hen-house which they planned together. I am rejoiced to hear from Martha that they certainly continue at Ibthorp, and I have just heard that I am sure of meeting Martha at the christening.

You deserve a longer letter than this; but it is my unhappy fate seldom to treat people so well as they deserve … God bless you!

Yours affectionately,

Jane Austen

[1] *christening at Deane* That of James-Edward Austen-Leigh, son of Austen's brother James and author of *A Memoir of Jane Austen.*

[2] *Harriet Bridges … that kind of youth* Harriet Bridges' sisters married young, and two of them died young.

[3] *Lord Spencer* George John, second Earl Spencer, First Lord of the Admiralty 1794–1826.

Rolinda Sharples, *The Cloakroom, Clifton Assembly Rooms* (detail), c. 1815.
This painting conveys a vivid sense of the atmosphere of English social gatherings in the early nineteenth century.

Thomas Rowlandson, *Mrs. Siddons, Old Kemble, and Henderson Rehearsing in the Green Green*, 1789. The famous Mrs. Siddons (Sarah Kemble), whom Austen expresses regret at not having seen, is portrayed here in rehearsal, with her father, Roger Kemble.

Drawing attributed to Cassandra Austen (sister of Jane), of Austen's niece, Fanny Knight, painting a watercolor, c. 1814.

Thursday [25 April 1811]
Sloane St:[1]

My Dearest Cassandra,

I can return the compliment by thanking you for the unexpected pleasure of *your* letter yesterday, and as I like unexpected pleasure, it made me very happy; and, indeed, you need not apologise for your letter in any respect, for it is all very fine, but not *too* fine, I hope, to be written again, or something like it.

I think Edward will not suffer much longer from heat; by the look of things this morning I suspect the weather is rising into the balsamic north-east. It has been hot here, as you may suppose, since it was so hot with you, but I have not suffered from it at all, nor felt it in such a degree as to make me imagine it would be anything in the country. Everybody has talked of the heat, but I set it all down to London.

I give you joy of our new nephew,[2] and hope if he ever comes to be hanged it will not be till we are too old to care about it. It is a great comfort to have it so safely and speedily over. The Miss Curlings[3] must be hard worked in writing so many letters, but the novelty of it may recommend it to *them*; mine was from Miss Eliza, and she says that my brother[4] may arrive to-day.

No, indeed, I am never too busy to think of S. & S.[5] I can no more forget it than a mother can forget her sucking child; and I am much obliged to you for your inquiries. I have had two sheets to correct, but the last only brings us to Willoughby's first appearance.[6] Mrs. K.[7] regrets in the most flattering manner that she must wait *till* May, but I have scarcely a hope of its being out in June. Henry does not neglect it; he *has* hurried the printer, and says he will see him again to-day. It will not stand still during his absence, it will be sent to Eliza.[8]

The *Incomes* remain as they were, but I will get them altered if I can. I am very much gratified by Mrs. K's interest in it; and whatever may be the event of it as to my credit with her, sincerely wish her curiosity could be satisfied sooner than is now probable. I think she will like my Elinor, but cannot build on anything else.

Our party went off extremely well. There were many solicitudes, alarms, and vexations, beforehand, of course, but at last everything was quite right. The rooms were dressed up with flowers, &c., and looked very pretty. A glass for the mantlepiece was lent by the man who is making their own. Mr. Egerton and Mr. Walter came at half-past five, and the festivities began with a pair of very fine soals.

Yes, Mr. Walter—for he postponed his leaving London on purpose—which did not give much pleasure at the time, any more than the circumstance from which it rose—his calling on Sunday and being asked by Henry to take the family dinner on that day, which he did; but it is all smoothed over now, and she likes him very well.

----

[1] *Sloane St.*   Home of Austen's brother Henry-Thomas Austen, in London.

[2] *our new nephew*   Henry Edgar Austen, second son of Francis-William Austen (Frank).

[3] *Miss Curlings*   Cousins of Mary Gibson, Frank's wife.

[4] *my brother*   Frank Austen.

[5] *S. & S.*   Austen's novel *Sense and Sensibility*.

[6] *Willoughby's first appearance*   The character Willoughby first appears in *Sense and Sensibility* in Book 1, chapter 9.

[7] *Mrs. K.*   Catherine Knight, who adopted Austen's brother Edward with her husband, Thomas Knight.

[8] *Eliza*   Henry's wife Eliza.

At half-past seven arrived the musicians in two hackney coaches, and by eight the lordly company began to appear. Among the earliest were George and Mary Cooke, and I spent the greater part of the evening very pleasantly with them. The drawing-room being soon hotter than we liked, we placed ourselves in the connecting passage, which was comparatively cool, and gave us all the advantage of the music at a pleasant distance, as well as that of the first view of every new comer.

I was quite surrounded by acquaintances, especially gentlemen; and what with Mr. Hampson, Mr. Seymour, Mr. W. Knatchbull, Mr. Guillemarde, Mr. Cure, a Captain Simpson, brother to *the* Captain Simpson, besides Mr. Walter and Mr. Egerton, in addition to the Cookes, and Miss Beckford, and Miss Middleton, I had quite as much upon my hands as I could do.

Poor Miss B. has been suffering again from her old complaint, and looks thinner than ever. She certainly goes to Cheltenham the beginning of June. We were all delight and cordiality of course. Miss M. seems very happy, but has not beauty enough to figure in London.

Including everybody we were sixty-six—which was considerably more than Eliza had expected, and quite enough to fill the back drawing-room and leave a few to be scattered about in the other and in the passage.

The music was extremely good. It opened (tell Fanny) with "Prike de Parp pirs praise of Prapela"; and of the other glees I remember, "In peace love tunes," "Rosabelle," "The Red Cross Knight," and "Poor Insect." [1] Between the songs were lessons on the harp, or harp and pianoforte together; and the harp-player was Wiepart, whose name seems famous, though new to me. There was one female singer, a short Miss Davis, all in blue, bringing up for the public line, whose voice was said to be very fine indeed; and all the performers gave great satisfaction by doing what they were paid for, and giving themselves no airs. No amateur could be persuaded to do anything.

The house was not clear till after twelve. If you wish to hear more of it, you must put your questions, but I seem rather to have exhausted than spared the subject.

This said Captain Simpson told us, on the authority of some other Captain just arrived from Halifax, that Charles was bringing the "Cleopatra" home, and that she was probably by this time in the Channel; but, as Captain S. was certainly in liquor, we must not quite depend on it. It must give one a sort of expectation, however, and will prevent my writing to him any more. I would rather he should not reach England till I am at home, and the Steventon party gone.

My mother and Martha both write with great satisfaction of Anna's[2] behaviour. She is quite an Anna with variations, but she cannot have reached her last, for that is always the most flourishing and showy; she is at about her third or fourth, which are generally simple and pretty.

Your lilacs are in *leaf*, are in bloom, The horse-chestnuts are quite out, and the elms almost. I had a pleasant walk in Kensington Gardens on Sunday with Henry, Mr. Smith, and Mr. Tilson; everything was fresh and beautiful.

We *did* go to the play after all on Saturday. We went to the Lyceum, and saw the "Hypocrite,"[3] an old play taken from Molière's "Tartuffe," and were well entertained. Dowton and Mathews were the good actors; Mrs. Edwin was the heroine, and her performance is just what it used to be. I have no chance of seeing Mrs. Siddons; she *did* act on Monday, but, as Henry was told by the boxkeeper

---

[1] *"Prike de Parp"* "Strike the Harp," a chorus by Sir Henry Rowley Bishop; *"In peace love tunes"* A glee by J. Attwood; *"Rosabelle"* A glee by John Wall Callcott; *"The Red Cross Knight"* By Callcott; *"Poor Insect"* "The May Fly," by Calcott.

[2] *Anna* James Austen's eldest child, and recipient of the following letter.

[3] *"Hypocrite"* A play by Isaac Bickerstaffe.

that he did not think she would, the plans, and all thought of it, were given up. I should particularly have liked seeing her in "Constance,"[1] and could swear at her with little effort for disappointing me.

Henry has been to the Water-Colour Exhibition,[2] which opened on Monday, and is to meet us there again some morning. If Eliza cannot go (and she has a cold at present) Miss Beaty will be invited to be my companion. Henry leaves town on Sunday afternoon, but he means to write soon himself to Edward, and will tell his own plans.

The tea is this moment setting out.

Do not have your coloured muslin unless you really want it, because I am afraid I could not send it to the coach without giving trouble here.

Eliza caught her cold on Sunday in our way to the D'Entraigues.[3] The horses actually gibbed on this side of Hyde Park Gate: a load of fresh gravel made it a formidable hill to them, and they refused the collar; I believe there was a sore shoulder to irritate. Eliza was frightened and we got out, and were detained in the evening air several minutes. The cold is in her chest, but she takes care of herself, and I hope it may not last long.

This engagement prevented Mr. Walter's staying late—he had his coffee and went away. Eliza enjoyed her evening very much, and means to cultivate the acquaintance; and I see nothing to dislike in them but their taking quantities of snuff. Monsieur, the old Count, is a very fine-looking man, with quiet manners, good enough for an Englishman, and, I believe, is a man of great information and taste. He has some fine paintings, which delighted Henry as much as the son's music gratified Eliza; and among them a miniature of Philip V of Spain, Louis XIV's grandson, which exactly suited *my* capacity. Count Julien's performance is very wonderful.

We met only Mrs. Latouche and Miss East, and we are just now engaged to spend next Sunday evening at Mrs. L.'s, and to meet the D'Entraigues, but M. le Comte must do without Henry. If he would but speak English, *I* would take to him.

Have you ever mentioned the leaving off tea to Mrs. K.? Eliza has just spoken of it again. The *benefit* she has found from it in sleeping has been very great.

I shall write soon to Catherine to fix my day, which will be Thursday. We have no engagement but for Sunday. Eliza's cold makes quiet advisable. Her party is mentioned in this morning's paper. I am sorry to hear of poor Fanny's state.[4] From *that* quarter, I suppose, is to be the alloy of her happiness. I *will* have no more to say.

Yours affectionately,

J.A.

---

[1] *Mrs. Siddons … Constance*   I.e., Austen would have liked to have seen the famous actress, Sarah Siddons, in the role of Constance in Shakespeare's *King John*, one of Siddons's greatest triumphs.

[2] *Water-Colour Exhibition*   The annual exhibition of the Society of Painters in Watercolours, established in 1805.

[3] *the D'Entraigues*   The family of Comte Emmanuel-Lewis D'Antraigues, scholar, spy, forger, and double-agent for the French and English governments.

[4] *poor Fanny's state*   Austen's sister-in-law Fanny, wife of her brother Charles, was pregnant with her third child. Fanny would give birth four times within six years. She died, aged 24, in childbirth.

My Dear Anna,

I am quite ashamed to find that I have never answered some question of yours in a former note. I kept it on purpose to refer to it at a proper time and then forgot it. I like the name "Which is the Heroine" very well, and I daresay shall grow to like it very much in time; but "Enthusiasm" was something so very superior that my common title must appear to disadvantage. I am not sensible of any blunders about Dawlish;[1] the library was pitiful and wretched twelve years ago and not likely to have anybody's publications. … There is no such title as Desborough either among dukes, marquises, earls, viscounts, or barons. These were your inquiries. I will now thank you for your envelope received this morning. … Your Aunt Cass is as well pleased with St. Julian as ever, and I am delighted with the idea of seeing Progillian again.

Wednesday 17.—We have just finished the first of the three books I had the pleasure of receiving yesterday. *I* read it aloud and we are all very much amused, and like the work quite as well as ever. I depend on getting through another book before dinner, but there is really a good deal of respectable reading in your forty-eight pages. I have no doubt six would make a very good-sized volume. You must have been quite pleased to have accomplished so much. I like Lord Portman and his brother very much. I am only afraid that Lord P.'s good nature will make most people like him better than he deserves. The whole family are very good, and Lady Anne, who was your great dread, you have succeeded particularly well with. Bell Griffin is just what she should be. My corrections have not been more important than before; here and there we have thought the sense could be expressed in fewer words, and I have scratched out Sir Thos. from walking with the others to the stables, &c. the very day after breaking his arm; for, though I find your papa *did* walk out immediately after *his* arm was set, I think it can be so little usual as to *appear* unnatural in a book. Lyme will not do. Lyme is towards forty miles from Dawlish and would not be talked of there. I have put Starcross instead. If you prefer Exeter, that must be always safe.[2]

I have also scratched out the introduction between Lord Portman and his brother and Mr. Griffin. A country surgeon (don't tell Mr. C. Lyford) would not be introduced to men of their rank, and when Mr. P. is first brought in, he would not be introduced as the Honourable. That distinction is never mentioned at such times, at least I believe not. Now we have finished the second book, or rather the fifth. I *do* think you had better omit Lady Helena's postscript. To those that are acquainted with "Pride and Prejudice" it will seem an imitation. And your Aunt C. and I both recommend your making a little alteration in the last scene between Devereux F. and Lady Clanmurray and her daughter. We think they press him too much, more than sensible or well-bred women would do; Lady C., at least, should have discretion enough to be sooner satisfied with his determination of not going with them. I am very much pleased with Egerton as yet. I did not expect to like him, but I do, and Susan is a very nice little animated creature; but St. Julian is the delight of our lives. He is quite interesting. The whole of his break off with Lady Helena is very well done. Yes; Russell Square is a very proper distance from Berkeley Square.[3] We are reading the last book. They must be *two* days going from Dawlish to Bath. They are nearly 100 miles apart.

---

[1] *Dawlish*   On the south coast of Devon in southwest England.

[2] *Lyme … be always safe*   Lyme, Dawlish, Starcross, and Exeter are all in Devon, England.

[3] *Russell Square … Berkeley Square*   Addresses in London.

Thursday.— We finished it last night after our return from drinking tea at the Great House. The last chapter does not please us quite so well; we do not thoroughly like the play, perhaps from having had too much of plays in that way lately, and we think you had better not leave England. Let the Portmans go to Ireland; but as you know nothing of the manners there, you had better not go with them. You will be in danger of giving false representations. Stick to Bath and the Foresters. There you will be quite at home.

Your Aunt C. does not like desultory novels, and is rather afraid yours will be too much so, that there will be too frequently a change from one set of people to another, and that circumstances will be introduced of apparent consequence which will lead to nothing. It will not be so great an objection to *me* if it does. I allow much more latitude than she does, and think nature and spirit cover many sins of a wandering story, and people in general do not care so much about it, for your comfort.

I should like to have had more of Devereux. I do not feel enough acquainted with him. You were afraid of meddling with him I dare say. I like your sketch of Lord Clanmurray, and your picture of the two young girls' enjoyment is very good. I have not noticed St. Julian's serious conversation with Cecilia, but I like it exceedingly. What he says about the madness of otherwise sensible women on the subject of their daughters is worth its weight in gold.

I do not perceive that the language sinks. Pray go on.

J.A.

Monday, Dec. 16th [1816].
Chawton

My Dear E.,[1]—One reason for my writing to you now is, that I may have the pleasure of directing to you Esqre. I give you joy of having left Winchester.[2] Now you may own how miserable you were there; now it will gradually all come out, your crimes and your miseries—how often you went up by the Mail[3] to London and threw away fifty guineas at a tavern, and how often you were on the point of hanging yourself, restrained only, as some ill-natured aspersion upon poor old Winton has it, by the want of a tree within some miles of the city. Charles Knight and his companions passed through Chawton about 9 this morning; later than it used to be. Uncle Henry and I had a glimpse of his handsome face, looking all health and good humour. I wonder when you will come and see us. I know what I rather speculate upon, but shall say nothing. We think uncle Henry in excellent looks. Look at him this moment, and think so too, if you have not done it before; and we have the great comfort of seeing decided improvement in uncle Charles, both as to health, spirits, and appearance. And they are each of them so agreeable in their different way, and harmonise so well, that their visit is thorough enjoyment. Uncle Henry writes very superior sermons.[4] You and I must try to get hold of one or two, and put them into our novels: it would be a fine help to a volume; and we could make our heroine read it aloud on a Sunday evening, just as well as Isabella Wardour, in the "Antiquary,"[5] is made to read the "History of the Hartz Demon" in the ruins of St.

---

[1] *My Dear E.*   James-Edward Austen, Jane Austen's nephew and son of her brother James.

[2] *I may have … left Winchester*   I.e., having left Winchester, an English public school, Edward is now to be considered a man ("Esquire").

[3] *the Mail*   The Mail Coach.

[4] *Uncle Henry … sermons*   Henry Austen took Holy Orders and became curate of Chawton at this time.

[5] *"Antiquary"*   Sir Walter Scott's novel *The Antiquary* had been published earlier in 1816.

Ruth, though I believe, on recollection, Lovell is the reader. By the bye, my dear E., I am quite concerned for the loss your mother mentions in her letter. Two chapters and a half to be missing is monstrous! It is well that *I* have not been at Steventon lately, and therefore cannot be suspected of purloining them: two strong twigs and a half towards a nest of my own would have been something. I do not think however, that any theft of that sort would be really very useful to me. What should I do with your strong, manly, spirited sketches, full of variety and glow? How could I possibly join them on to the little bit (two inches wide) of ivory on which I work with so fine a brush, as produces little effect after much labour?

You will hear from uncle Henry how well Anna is. She seems perfectly recovered. Ben was here on Saturday, to ask uncle Charles and me to dine with them, as to-morrow, but I was forced to decline it, the walk is beyond my strength (though I am otherwise very well), and this is not a season for donkey-carriages; and as we do not like to spare uncle Charles, he has declined it too. *Tuesday.* Ah, ha! Mr. E., I doubt your seeing uncle Henry at Steventon to-day. The weather will prevent your expecting him, I think. Tell your father, with aunt Cass's love and mine, that the pickled cucumbers are extremely good, and tell him also—"tell him what you will." No, don't tell him what you will, but tell him that grandmamma begs him to make Joseph Hall pay his rent, if he can.

You must not be tired of reading the word *uncle*, for I have not done with it. Uncle Charles thanks your mother for her letter; it was a great pleasure to him to know that the parcel was received and gave so much satisfaction, and he begs her to be so good as to give *three shillings* for him to Dame Staples, which shall be allowed for in the payment of her debt here.

Adieu, Amiable! I hope Caroline behaves well to you.

Yours affectionately,

J. Austen

WILLIAM HAZLITT
1778 – 1830

William Hazlitt is often placed alongside the major authors of the Romantic era—a remarkable association in that Hazlitt was neither a poet nor a novelist nor a playwright. He was, however, among the most significant essayists of his time, writing with great facility and great energy on literature, on theater, on art, and on politics. Hazlitt won many admirers for the steadfastness of his moral stance and, even more so, for his lively and penetrating prose style; it has sometimes been claimed that he changed the nature of criticism, turning it into an art form in itself. His personality was less widely admired, however. With his critical essays and "portraits" of authors, many of them disparaging, many of them passionately argued, Hazlitt made scores of enemies, and was in turn often viciously attacked by the press. According to his contemporary Thomas De Quincey, he "wilfully placed himself in collision from the first with all the interests that were in the sunshine of the world, and of all the persons that were then powerful in England."

Hazlitt came by his rebellious nature honestly: he was born in Maidstone, Kent, into a family of Dissenters, a group of independent thinkers who disagreed with the tenets of the Church of England. His father was an Irish Unitarian minister who outspokenly supported the ideals of the French and American Revolutions and moved his family first to Ireland and then to the new republic of the United States of America in 1783, where he founded its first Unitarian church. In 1787 the family returned to England and settled in Shropshire. When he was 15, Hazlitt was sent to the New Unitarian College in London to train for the ministry, but he eventually realized he had no calling. For a time he followed in his brother John's footsteps and attempted a career as a painter; he ultimately recognized that he could not make a living painting portraits, but his eye for detail would later surface in the literary "portraits" for which he would become famous.

In 1798, Hazlitt made the acquaintance of Samuel Taylor Coleridge and William Wordsworth; years later the two would become the subjects of a charming essay, "My First Acquaintance with Poets" (1823). Hazlitt began to move in literary circles, also becoming friends (and sometimes enemies) with William Godwin, Leigh Hunt, Robert Southey, Percy Bysshe Shelley, Lord Byron, and Charles Lamb (Lamb was one of the few to remain a loyal companion). Hazlitt embarked on a career as a writer himself in 1805, publishing his first book, *An Essay on the Principles of Human Action*. It was followed by various political essays and pamphlets, and in 1808 (also the year in which he began an ill-fated marriage to Sarah Stoddart) Hazlitt began writing for *The Times*. Within a few years he was writing as well for the *Morning Chronicle* and for Leigh Hunt's journal *The Examiner*; in later years the *Edinburgh Review* and *London Magazine* were added to this list. It was for the *London Magazine* that he wrote *Table-Talk* (published in book form in 1821 and 1822), a series of brilliant and sparkling essays.

In 1824 *New Monthly Magazine* began publishing Hazlitt's next series of essays, *The Spirit of the Age*, in which he created memorably biting literary portraits of such contemporary writers as Byron ("he cares little what it is he says, so that he can say it differently from others") and Sir Walter Scott ("his speculative understanding is empty, flaccid, poor, and dead"). Hazlitt established himself as a leading art, literary, and drama critic, and, through his lectures and essays on William Shakespeare, helped spark a revival of Elizabethan theater.

Hazlitt stayed true to his radical roots, and remained an ardent supporter of Napoleon and the principles of the French Revolution (Hazlitt's four-volume *The Life of Napoleon Buonaparte* was published in 1828 and 1830). This spirit caused a rift with many of his fellow writers—most notably with Wordsworth, whose writing Hazlitt would praise, but whom he would publicly accuse of being an "apostate" to the French Revolution, saying that he "turned from his beliefs of his younger days and sold out to the establishment in accepting government jobs, pensions and laurels." For these convictions Hazlitt was blasted by the conservative press, whose recriminations were often scathing (Hazlitt was prompted to bring charges of libel against *Blackwood's Magazine* in 1818).

Hazlitt wrote about an enormous variety of subjects, telling the public, as J.B. Priestley put it in 1960, "what William Hazlitt thought and felt about everything," leaving a legacy of writing that spans 21 volumes. He died of cancer in 1830; although Hazlitt claimed on his death bed that he had led "a happy life," Charles Lamb was the only one of his old friends to attend his funeral. For Hazlitt, however, a life was made happy by the power of one's convictions and the zeal with which one lived out those convictions. "The love of life" was, according to Hazlitt, "the elect not of our enjoyment, but of our passions."

⌘ ⌘ ⌘

from *The Spirit of the Age; or Contemporary Portraits*

MR. COLERIDGE

The present is an age of talkers, and not of doers; and the reason is, that the world is growing old. We are so far advanced in the Arts and Sciences, that we live in retrospect, and dote on past achievements. The accumulation of knowledge has been so great, that we are lost in wonder at the height it has reached, instead of attempting to climb or add to it; while the variety of objects distracts and dazzles the looker-on. What *niche* remains unoccupied? What path untried? What is the use of doing anything, unless we could do better than all those who have gone before us? What hope is there of this? We are like those who have been to see some noble monument of art, who are content to admire without thinking of rivalling it; or like guests after a feast, who praise the hospitality of the donor "and thank the bounteous Pan"[1]—perhaps carrying away some trifling fragments; or like the spectators of a mighty battle, who still hear its sound afar off, and the clashing of armour and the neighing of the war-horse and the shout of victory is in their ears, like the rushing of innumerable waters!

Mr. Coleridge has "a mind reflecting ages past";[2] his voice is like the echo of the congregated roar of the "dark rearward and abyss" of thought. He who has seen a mouldering tower by the side of a crystal lake, hid by the mist, but glittering in the wave below, may conceive the dim, gleaming, uncertain intelligence of his eye: he who has marked the evening clouds unrolled (a world of vapours), has seen the picture of his mind, unearthly, unsubstantial, with gorgeous tints and ever-varying forms—

---

[1] *"and thank the bounteous Pan"* From John Milton's *A Mask Presented at Ludlow Castle* ("Comus"): "In wanton dance they praise the bounteous Pan" (Greek god of shepherds and flocks).

[2] *"a mind ... past"* In an 1818 lecture, Hazlitt also wrote of Shakespeare: "He had 'a mind reflecting ages past' and present."

That which was now a horse, even with a thought
The rack dislimns, and makes it indistinct
As water is in water.[1]

Our author's mind is (as he himself might express it) *tangential*. There is no subject on which he has not touched, none on which he has rested. With an understanding fertile, subtle, expansive, "quick, forgetive, apprehensive,"[2] beyond all living precedent, few traces of it will perhaps remain. He lends himself to all impressions alike; he gives up his mind and liberty of thought to none. He is a general lover of art and science, and wedded to no one in particular. He pursues knowledge as a mistress, with outstretched hands and winged speed; but as he is about to embrace her, his Daphne turns—alas! not to a laurel![3] Hardly a speculation has been left on record from the earliest time, but it is loosely folded up in Mr. Coleridge's memory, like a rich, but somewhat tattered piece of tapestry; we might add (with more seeming than real extravagance), that scarce a thought can pass through the mind of man, but its sound has at some time or other passed over his head with rustling pinions. On whatever question or author you speak, he is prepared to take up the theme with advantage—from Peter Abelard down to Thomas Moore,[4] from the subtlest metaphysics to the politics of the *Courier*. There is no man of genius, in whose praise he descants, but the critic seems to stand above the author, and "what in him is weak, to strengthen, what is low, to raise and support": nor is there any work of genius that does not come out of his hands like an illuminated Missal,[5] sparkling even in its defects. If Mr. Coleridge had not been the most impressive talker of his age, he would probably have been the finest writer; but

he lays down his pen to make sure of an auditor, and mortgages the admiration of posterity for the stare of an idler. If he had not been a poet, he would have been a powerful logician; if he had not dipped his wing in the Unitarian controversy,[6] he might have soared to the very summit of fancy. But in writing verse, he is trying to subject the Muse to *transcendental* theories: in his abstract reasoning, he misses his way by strewing it with flowers. All that he has done of moment, he had done twenty years ago: since then, he may be said to have lived on the sound of his own voice. Mr. Coleridge is too rich in intellectual wealth, to need to task himself to any drudgery: he has only to draw the sliders of his imagination, and a thousand subjects expand before him, startling him with their brilliancy, or losing themselves in endless obscurity—

And by the force of blear illusion,
They draw him on to his confusion.[7]

What is the little he could add to the stock, compared with the countless stores that lie about him, that he should stoop to pick up a name, or to polish an idle fancy? He walks abroad in the majesty of a universal understanding, eyeing the "rich strond,"[8] or golden sky above him, and "goes sounding on his way," in eloquent accents, uncompelled and free! Persons of the greatest capacity are often those, who for this reason do the least; for surveying themselves from the highest point of view, amidst the infinite variety of the universe, their own share in it seems trifling, and scarce worth a thought, and they prefer the contemplation of all that is, or has been, or can be, to the making a coil about doing what, when done, is no better than vanity. It is hard to concentrate all our attention and efforts on one pursuit, except from ignorance of others; and without this concentration of our faculties, no great progress can be made in any one effort; it does not think the effort

---

[1] *That which ... water* From Shakespeare's *Antony and Cleopatra* 4.14.9–11.

[2] *"quick, forgetive, apprehensive"* From Shakespeare's *2 Henry IV*, 4.3.98–99: "Apprehensive, quick, forgetive"; *forgetive* inventive.

[3] *Daphne ... laurel* In Greek mythology, a nymph who eluded her pursuer by transforming herself into a laurel tree.

[4] *Peter Abelard* French philosopher and theologian (1079–1142); *Thomas Moore* Irish poet and composer (1779–1852).

[5] *Missal* Roman Catholic prayerbook.

[6] *Unitarian controversy* Coleridge became a Unitarian preacher in 1798; Hazlitt wrote in praise of Coleridge's lay-sermon of 1798.

[7] *And by ... confusion* From Shakespeare's *Macbeth* 3.5.28–29.

[8] *"rich strond"* Beach; from Edmund Spenser's *The Faerie Queene* 3.4.2.

worth making. Action is one; but thought is manifold. He whose restless eye glances through the wide compass of nature and art, will not consent to have "his own nothings monstered";[1] but he must do this, before he can give his whole soul to them. The mind, after "letting contemplation have its fill," or

> Sailing with supreme dominion,
> Through the azure deep of air,[2]

sinks down on the ground, breathless, exhausted, powerless, inactive; or if it must have some vent to its feelings, seeks the most easy and obvious; is soothed by friendly flattery, lulled by the murmur of immediate applause, thinks as it were aloud, and babbles in its dreams! A scholar (so to speak) is a more disinterested and abstracted character than a mere author. The first looks at the numberless volumes of a library, and says, "All these are mine": the other points to a single volume (perhaps it may be an immortal one) and says, "My name is written on the back of it." This is a puny and groveling ambition, beneath the lofty amplitude of Mr. Coleridge's mind. No, he revolves in his wayward soul, or utters to the passing wind, or discourses to his own shadow, things mightier and more various!—Let us draw the curtain, and unlock the shrine.

Learning rocked him in his cradle, and while yet a child,

> He lisped in numbers, for the numbers came.[3]

At sixteen he wrote his *Ode on Chatterton*,[4] and he still reverts to that period with delight, not so much as it relates to himself (for that string of his own early promise of fame rather jars than otherwise) but as exemplifying the youth of a poet. Mr. Coleridge talks of himself, without being an egotist, for in him the indi-

vidual is always merged in the abstract and general. He distinguished himself at school and at the University by his knowledge of the classics, and gained several prizes for Greek epigrams. How many men are there (great scholars, celebrated names in literature) who having done the same thing in their youth, have no other idea all the rest of their lives but of this achievement, of a fellowship and dinner, and who, installed in academic honours, would look down on our author as a mere strolling bard! At Christ's Hospital,[5] where he was brought up, he was the idol of those among his school-fellows, who mingled with their bookish studies the music of thought and of humanity; and he was usually attended round the cloisters by a group of these (inspiring and inspired) whose hearts, even then, burnt within them as he talked, and where the sounds yet linger to mock ELIA[6] on his way, still turning pensive to the past! One of the finest and rarest parts of Mr. Coleridge's conversation, is when he expatiates on the Greek tragedians (not that he is not well acquainted, when he pleases, with the epic poets, or the philosophers, or orators, or historians of antiquity)—on the subtle reasonings and melting pathos of Euripides, on the harmonious gracefulness of Sophocles, tuning his love-laboured song, like sweetest warblings from a sacred grove; on the high-wrought trumpet-tongued eloquence of Æschylus,[7] whose Prometheus, above all, is like an Ode to Fate, and a pleading with Providence, his thoughts being let loose as his body is chained on his solitary rock, and his afflicted will (the emblem of mortality)

> Struggling in vain with ruthless destiny.[8]

---

[1] *"his own ... monstered"* From Shakespeare's *Coriolanus* 3.2.81.

[2] *Sailing ... air* From Thomas Gray's *The Progress of Poesy: A Pindaric Ode* 2.116–17.

[3] *He lisped ... came* From Alexander Pope's "An Epistle to Dr. Arbuthnot" 128: "I lisped in numbers, for the numbers came."

[4] *Ode on Chatterton* "Monody on the Death of Chatterton."

[5] *Christ's Hospital* Christ's Hospital School for poor boys, founded by Edward VI.

[6] *ELIA* Pen name of essayist Charles Lamb (1775–1834). Lamb's "Elia" essays included a piece on Christ's, where he had been to school with Coleridge.

[7] *Euripides* Greek tragedian (480?–406 BCE), author of *Medea*; *Sophocles* Greek tragedian (496?–406 BCE), author of *Oedipus Rex*; *Æschylus* The father of the Greek tragedy (525–456 BCE), author of *Prometheus Bound*.

[8] *Struggling ... destiny* From William Wordsworth's *The Excursion* (1814) 6.557.

As the impassioned critic speaks and rises in his theme, you would think you heard the voice of the Man hated by the Gods, contending with the wild winds as they roar, and his eye glitters with the spirit of Antiquity!

Next, he was engaged with Hartley's[1] tribes of mind, "etherial braid, thought-woven,"—and he busied himself for a year or two with vibrations and vibratiuncles[2] and the great law of association that binds all things in its mystic chain, and the doctrine of Necessity (the mild teacher of Charity) and the Millennium, anticipative of a life to come—and he plunged deep into the controversy on Matter and Spirit, and, as an escape from Dr. Priestley's Materialism,[3] where he felt himself imprisoned by the logician's spell, like Ariel in the cloven pine-tree,[4] he became suddenly enamoured of Bishop Berkeley's[5] fairy-world,[6] and used in all companies to build the universe, like a brave poetical fiction, of fine words—and he was deep-read in Malebranche, and in Cudworth's Intellectual System (a huge pile of learning, unwieldy, enormous) and in Lord Brook's hieroglyphic theories, and in Bishop Butler's Sermons, and in the Duchess of Newcastle's fantastic folios, and in Clark and South and Tillotson, and all the fine thinkers and masculine reasoners of that age—and

Leibnitz's[7] Pre-Established Harmony reared its arch above his head, like the rainbow in the cloud, covenanting[8] with the hopes of man—and then he fell plump, ten thousand fathoms down (but his wings saved him harmless) into the hortus siccus[9] of Dissent, where he pared religion down to the standard of reason and stripped faith of mystery, and preached Christ crucified and the Unity of the Godhead, and so dwelt for a while in the spirit with John Huss and Jerome of Prague and Socinus and old John Zisca,[10] and ran through Neal's History of the Puritans, and Calamy's Non-Conformists' Memorial,[11] having like thoughts and passions with them—but then Spinoza[12] became his God, and he took up the vast chain of being in his hand, and the round world became the centre and the soul of all things in some shadowy sense, forlorn of meaning, and around him he beheld the living traces and the sky-pointing proportions of the mighty Pan—but poetry redeemed him from this spectral philosophy, and he bathed his heart in beauty, and gazed at the golden light of heaven, and drank of the spirit of the universe, and wandered at eve by fairy-stream or fountain,

---

[1] *Hartley's* Referring to the theories of David Hartley (1705–57), English physician and materialist philosopher, who believed that all mental phenomena are functions of the brain; Hartley's ideas greatly influenced Coleridge.

[2] *vibratiuncles* Small vibrations.

[3] *Dr. Priestley's Materialism* Joseph Priestley's (1733–1804) philosophical theory: all things that exist are composed of matter.

[4] *Ariel … pine-tree* From Shakespeare's *The Tempest* 1.2.324; the evil witch Sycorax imprisoned the spirit Ariel in a cloven pine tree.

[5] *Bishop Berkeley's* Referring to the theories of George Berkeley (1685–1753), an Anglo-Irish clergyman and idealist philosopher who argued that God thinks everything into existence.

[6] [Hazlitt's note] Mr. Coleridge named his eldest son (the writer of some beautiful sonnets) after Hartley, and the second after Berkeley. The third was called Derwent, after the river of that name. Nothing can be more characteristic of his mind than this circumstance. All his ideas indeed are like a river, flowing on for ever, and still murmuring as it flows, discharging its still waters and still replenished—"And so by many winding nooks it strays, with willing sport to the ocean world!" [*"And so by … ocean world"* From Shakespeare's *The Two Gentlemen of Verona* 2.7.31–32.]

[7] *Malebranche* Nicolas Malebranche (1638–1715) was a French Cartesian philosopher who argued that mind and body are separate, but God coordinates the two; *Cudworth* Ralph Cudworth (1617–88) was an English philosopher who argued against atheism and determinism; *Lord Brook* Robert Greville, Lord Brooke (1608–43) was an English philosopher who proposed that all things are emanations from God; *Duchess of Newcastle* Margaret Cavendish (1623–73) was an English author and materialist philosopher who argued that nothing in nature is incorporeal; *Tillotson* John Tillotson (1630–94) was an Archbishop of Canterbury who argued against atheism; *Leibnitz* Gottfried Leibniz (1646–1716) was a German mathematician and rationalist philosopher who argued that there is a non-causal relationship between mind and body, and that there is a pre-existing harmony in the world established by God.

[8] *covenanting* Suiting; agreeing.

[9] *hortus siccus* Dry garden.

[10] *John Huss … John Zisca* Church reformers, most of whom died for their beliefs.

[11] *Neal's … Memorial* Daniel Neal (1678–1743), English historian; Edmund Calamy (1678–1732), English historian and dissenting minister.

[12] *Spinoza* Dutch determinist philosopher (1632–77) who argued that God and nature are one and the same.

—When he saw nought but beauty,

When he heard the voice of that Almighty One

In every breeze that blew, or wave that murmured[1]—

and wedded with truth in Plato's shade, and in the writings of Proclus and Plotinus saw the ideas of things in the eternal mind, and unfolded all mysteries with the Schoolmen and fathomed the depths of Duns Scotus and Thomas Aquinas, and entered the third heaven with Jacob Behmen, and walked hand in hand with Swedenborg through the pavilions of the New Jerusalem, and sung his faith in the promise and in the word in his *Religious Musings*[2]—and lowering himself from that dizzy height, poised himself on Milton's wings, and spread out his thoughts in charity with the glad prose of Jeremy Taylor,[3] and wept over Bowles's Sonnets,[4] and studied Cowper's[5] blank verse, and betook himself to Thomson's Castle of Indolence,[6] and sported with the wits of Charles the Second's days and of Queen Anne,

and relished Swift's[7] style and that of the John Bull (Arbuthnot's we mean, not Mr. Croker's),[8] and dallied with the British essayists and novelists, and knew all qualities of more modern writers with a learned spirit, Johnson, and Goldsmith, and Junius, and Burke, and Godwin, and the Sorrows of Werter, and Jean Jacques Rousseau, and Voltaire, and Marivaux, and Crebillon, and thousands more—now "laughed with Rabelais[9] in his easy chair" or pointed to Hogarth, or afterwards dwelt on Claude's classic scenes, or spoke with rapture of Raphael,[10] and compared the women at Rome to figures that had walked out of his pictures, or visited the Oratory of Pisa, and described the works of Giotto and Ghirlandaio and Masaccio,[11] and gave the moral of the picture of the Triumph of Death, where the beggars and the wretched invoke his dreadful dart, but the rich and mighty of the earth quail and shrink before it; and in that land of siren sights and sounds, saw a dance of peasant girls, and was charmed with lutes and gondolas,—or wandered into Germany and lost himself in the labyrinths of the Hartz Forest and of the Kantean philosophy, and amongst the cabalistic names of Fichte

---

1 *When ... murmered* From Coleridge's *Remorse* 4.2.100–02.

2 *Plato* Greek philosopher (428?–348? BCE) and author of *The Republic*, who argued that all we see in the world is a glimpse of what is ultimately a perfect "form" and that good art stimulates the passions, giving us a vision of the ideal form; *Proclus* Greek philosopher (411–85), whose Neoplatonic philosophy saw all things as emanating from the power of the One; *Plotinus* Egyptian philosopher (205–270), Neoplatonist, whose theories of emanation postulated the existence of one supreme source that creates the possibility of all other existences; *Duns Scotus* Scottish philosopher and theologian (c. 1266–1308), who argued for the "univocity" or commonality of being that provides our understanding of "essential truths"; *Thomas Aquinas* Italian priest (later made a saint) and philosopher (1225–74), who said that reason can prove the existence of God; *Jacob Behmen* Sometimes spelled Jakob Boehme (1575– 1634), German mystic who wrote of a Supreme reality and of humankind's struggle to choose good over evil; *Swedenborg* Emanuel Swedenborg, Swedish theologian, scientist, and philosopher (1688–1772), whose visionary writings gave rise to the Church of the New Jerusalem (or New Church); *Religious Musings* Coleridge's *Religious Musings: a Desultory Poem, written on Christmas Eve in the year of our Lord, 1794.*

3 *Jeremy Taylor* (1613 67), clergyman.

4 *Bowles's Sonnets* William Lyle Bowles's (1762–1850) influential *Fourteen Sonnets.*

5 *Cowper* Poet William Cowper (1731–1800).

6 *Thomson's Castle of Indolence* A poem by James Thomson (1700–48).

7 *Swift's* Jonathan Swift's (1667–1745) satiric style.

8 *John Bull ... Croker's* John Arbuthnot (1667–1735) wrote *The History of John Bull* (1727), a satire; John Wilson Croker (1780–1857), was a conservative MP, writer, and critic.

9 *Johnson ... Rabelais* *Johnson* Samuel Johnson (1709–84); *Goldsmith* Oliver Goldsmith (1728–74); *Junius* A pseudonym for the author of *The Letters of Junius* (1772), satirical polemics on English politics; *Burke* Edmund Burke (1729–97), statesman, orator, and author; *Godwin* William Godwin (1756–1836), radical philosopher; *Sorrows of Werter* *The Sorrows of Young Werther*, by Johann Wolfgang von Goethe (1749–1832); *Jean Jacques Rousseau* French philosopher (1712–78); *Voltaire* Author and philosopher (1694–1778); *Marivaux* Pierre Carlet de Marivaux (1688–1763), French dramatist; *Crebillon* P.J. de Crébillon (1674–1762), French dramatist; *Rabelais* François Rabelais (1494–1553), writer known for his humorous *La Vie de Gargantua and Pantagruel.*

10 *Hogarth ... Raphael* *Hogarth* English artist William Hogarth (1697–1764); *Claude's* Referring to the paintings of Claude Lorrain, Baroque painter (c. 1600–82); *Raphael* Raffaello Sanzi, Italian artist (1483–1520).

11 *Giotto ... Masaccio* *Giotto* Giotto di Bondone, Florentine painter and architect (1267–1337); *Ghirlandaio* Domenico Ghirlandaio, Florentine painter (1448–94); *Masaccio* Tommaso Cassai, Florentine painter (1401–28).

and Schelling and Lessing,[1] and God knows who—this was long after, but all the former while, he had nerved his heart and filled his eyes with tears, as he hailed the rising orb of liberty, since quenched in darkness and in blood, and had kindled his affections at the blaze of the French Revolution, and sang for joy when the towers of the Bastille[2] and the proud places of the insolent and the oppressor fell, and would have floated his bark, freighted with fondest fancies, across the Atlantic wave with Southey[3] and others to seek for peace and freedom—

In Philarmonia's undivided dale![4]

Alas! "Frailty, thy name is *Genius*!"[5]—What is become of all this mighty heap of hope, of thought, of learning, and humanity? It has ended in swallowing doses of oblivion and in writing paragraphs in the *Courier*.—Such, and so little is the mind of man!

It was not to be supposed that Mr. Coleridge could keep on at the rate he set off; he could not realize all he knew or thought, and less could not fix his desultory ambition; other stimulants supplied the place, and kept up the intoxicating dream, the fever and the madness of his early impressions. Liberty (the philosopher's and the poet's bride) had fallen a victim, meanwhile, to the murderous practices of the hag, Legitimacy. Proscribed by court-hirelings, too romantic for the herd of vulgar politicians, our enthusiast stood at bay, and at last turned on the pivot of a subtle casuistry to the *unclean side*: but his discursive reason would not let him tram-

mel himself into a poet-laureate or stamp-distributor,[6] and he stopped, ere he had quite passed that well-known "bourne from whence no traveller returns"[7]—and so has sunk into torpid, uneasy repose, tantalized by useless resources, haunted by vain imaginings, his lips idly moving, but his heart for ever still, or, as the shattered chords vibrate of themselves, making melancholy music to the ear of memory! Such is the fate of genius in an age, when in the unequal contest with sovereign wrong, every man is ground to powder who is not either a born slave, or who does not willingly and at once offer up the yearnings of humanity and the dictates of reason as a welcome sacrifice to besotted prejudice and loathsome power.

Of all Mr. Coleridge's productions, the *Ancient Mariner* is the only one that we could with confidence put into any person's hands, on whom we wished to impress a favourable idea of his extraordinary powers. Let whatever other objections be made to it, it is unquestionably a work of genius—of wild, irregular, overwhelming imagination, and has that rich, varied movement in the verse, which gives a distant idea of the lofty or changeful tones of Mr. Coleridge's voice. In the *Christabel*, there is one splendid passage on divided friendship. The *Translation of Schiller's Wallenstein* is also a masterly production in its kind, faithful and spirited. Among his smaller pieces there are occasional bursts of pathos and fancy, equal to what we might expect from him; but these form the exception, and not the rule. Such, for instance, is his affecting Sonnet to the author of the Robbers.

Schiller! that hour I would have wish'd to die,
  If through the shudd'ring midnight I had sent
  From the dark dungeon of the tower time-rent,
That fearful voice, a famish'd father's cry—

---

[1] *Kantean philosophy ... Lessing   Kantean philosophy* The theories of philosopher Immanuel Kant (1724–1804); *Fichte* J.G. Fichte (1762–1814), German philosopher and follower of Kant; *Schelling* Friedrich W.J. Schelling (1775–1854), German philosopher and follower of Kant; *Lessing* Gotthold Ephraim Lessing (1729–81), German critic and playwright.

[2] *towers of ... Bastille* The Bastille, a French prison, was stormed by the people of Paris on 14 July 1789.

[3] *Southey* Robert Southey (1774–1843) collaborated with Coleridge on political and creative works, and shared an interest in the egalitarian principles of the French Revolution.

[4] *In ... dale* From Coleridge's "Monody on the Death of Chatterton" 40.

[5] *"Frailty ... Genius"* From Shakespeare's *Hamlet* 1.2.146, "Frailty, thy name is woman!"

---

[6] *poet-laureate* Southey, who became British Poet Laureate in 1813, was thereafter frequently attacked for abandoning his earlier radical values; *stamp distributor* When William Wordsworth in 1813 took a position with the tax department as the Distributor of Stamps, many proponents of the reform came to believe that he had abandoned progressive causes.

[7] *"bourne ... returns"* From Shakespeare's *Hamlet* 3.1: "The undiscover'd country from whose bourne / No traveller returns."

>   That in no after-moment aught less vast
>   Might stamp me mortal! A triumphant shout
>   Black horror scream'd, and all her goblin rout
>   From the more with'ring scene diminsh'd pass'd.
>   Ah! Bard tremendous in sublimity!
>   Could I behold thee in thy loftier mood,
>   Wand'ring at eve, with finely frenzied eye,
>   Beneath some vast old tempest-swinging wood!
>   Awhile, with mute awe gazing, I would brood,
>   Then weep aloud in a wild ecstacy.[1]

His Tragedy, entitled *Remorse,* is full of beautiful and striking passages, but it does not place the author in the first rank of dramatic writers. But if Mr. Coleridge's works do not place him in that rank, they injure instead of conveying a just idea of the man, for he himself is certainly in the first class of general intellect.

If our author's poetry is inferior to his conversation, his prose is utterly abortive. Hardly a gleam is to be found in it of the brilliancy and richness of those stores of thought and language that he pours out incessantly, when they are lost like drops of water in the ground. The principal work, in which he has attempted to embody his general views of things, is the FRIEND,[2] of which, though it contains some noble passages and fine trains of thought, prolixity and obscurity are the most frequent characteristics.

No two persons can be conceived more opposite in character or genius than the subject of the present and of the preceding sketch. Mr. Godwin, with less natural capacity, and with fewer acquired advantages, by concentrating his mind on some given object, and doing what he had to do with all his might, has accomplished much, and will leave more than one monument of a powerful intellect behind him; Mr. Coleridge, by dissipating his, and dallying with every subject by turns, has done little or nothing to justify to the World or to posterity, the high opinion which all who have ever heard him converse, or known him intimately, with one accord entertain of him. Mr. Godwin's faculties have

kept at home, and plied their task in the workshop of the brain, diligently and effectually: Mr. Coleridge's have gossiped their time away, and gadded about from house to house, as if life's business were to melt the hours in listless talk. Mr. Godwin is intent on a subject, only as it concerns himself and his reputation; he works it out as a matter of duty, and discards from his mind whatever does not forward his main object as impertinent and vain. Mr. Coleridge, on the other hand, delights in nothing but episodes and digressions, neglects whatever he undertakes to perform, and can act only on spontaneous impulses, without object or method. "He cannot be constrained by mastery."[3] While he should be occupied with a given pursuit, he is thinking of a thousand other things; a thousand tastes, a thousand objects tempt him, and distract his mind, which keeps open house, and entertains all comers; and after being fatigued and amused with morning calls from idle visitors, finds the day consumed and its business unconcluded. Mr. Godwin, on the contrary, is somewhat exclusive and unsocial in his habits of mind, entertains no company but what he gives his whole time and attention to, and wisely writes over the doors of his understanding, his fancy, and his senses—"No admittance except on business." He has none of that fastidious refinement and false delicacy, which might lead him to balance between the endless variety of modern attainments. He does not throw away his life (nor a single half-hour of it) in adjusting the claims of different accomplishments, and in choosing between them or making himself master of them all. He sets about his task, (whatever it may be) and goes through it with spirit and fortitude. He has the happiness to think an author the greatest character in the world, and himself the greatest author in it. Mr. Coleridge, in writing an harmonious stanza, would stop to consider whether there was not more grace and beauty in a *Pas de trois,*[4] and would not proceed till he had resolved this question by a chain of metaphysical reasoning without end. Not

1   *Schiller! ... ecstacy* Coleridge's "Effusion" 20, from *Poems on Various Subjects* (1796).

2   *the* FRIEND   Coleridge's *The Friend* was first published in periodical form (1809–10).

3   *"He cannot be constrained by mastery"*   From Geoffrey Chaucer's *The Canterbury Tales,* "The Franklin's Tale" 764: "Love wol nat been constreyned by maistrye."

4   *Pas de trois*   Dance for three.

so Mr. Godwin. That is best to him, which he can do best. He does not waste himself in vain aspirations and effeminate sympathies. He is blind, deaf, insensible to all but the trump of Fame. Plays, operas, painting, music, ballrooms, wealth, fashion, titles, lords, ladies, touch him not—all these are no more to him than to the magician in his cell, and he writes on to the end of the chapter, through good report and evil report. *Pingo in eternitatem*[1]—is his motto. He neither envies nor admires what others are, but is contented to be what he is, and strives to do the utmost he can. Mr. Coleridge has flirted with the Muses[2] as with a set of mistresses: Mr. Godwin has been married twice, to Reason and to Fancy, and has to boast no short-lived progeny by each. So to speak, he has *valves* belonging to his mind, to regulate the quantity of gas admitted into it, so that like the bare, unsightly, but well-compacted steam-vessel, it cuts its liquid way, and arrives at its promised end: while Mr. Coleridge's bark, "taught with the little nautilus to sail,"[3] the sport of every breath, dancing to every wave,

Youth at its prow, and Pleasure at its helm,[4]

flutters its gaudy pennons[5] in the air, glitters in the sun, but we wait in vain to hear of its arrival in the destined harbour. Mr. Godwin, with less variety and vividness, with less subtlety and susceptibility both of thought and feeling, has had firmer nerves, a more determined purpose, a more comprehensive grasp of his subject, and the results are as we find them. Each has met with his reward: for justice has, after all, been done to the pretensions of each; and we must, in all cases, use means to ends!

It was a misfortune to any man of talent to be born in the latter end of the last century. Genius stopped the

way of Legitimacy, and therefore it was to be abated, crushed, or set aside as a nuisance. The spirit of the monarchy was at variance with the spirit of the age. The flame of liberty, the light of intellect was to be extinguished with the sword—or with slander, whose edge is sharper than the sword. The war between power and reason was carried on by the first of these abroad—by the last at home. No quarter was given (then or now) by the Government-critics, the authorised censors of the press, to those who followed the dictates of independence, who listened to the voice of the tempter, Fancy. Instead of gathering fruits and flowers, immortal fruits and amaranthine[6] flowers, they soon found themselves beset not only by a host of prejudices, but assailed with all the engines of power, by nicknames, by lies, by all the arts of malice, interest and hypocrisy, without the possibility of their defending themselves "from the pelting of the pitiless storm,"[7] that poured down upon them from the strong-holds of corruption and authority. The philosophers, the dry abstract reasoners, submitted to this reverse pretty well, and armed themselves with patience "as with triple steel"[8] to bear discomfiture, persecution, and disgrace. But the poets, the creatures of sympathy, could not stand the frowns both of king and people. They did not like to be shut out when places and pensions, when the critic's praises, and the laurel-wreath were about to be distributed. They did not stomach being *sent to Coventry*,[9] and Mr. Coleridge sounded a retreat for them by the help of casuistry, and a musical voice.—"His words were hollow, but they pleased the ear"[10] of his friends of the Lake School, who turned back disgusted and panic-struck from the dry desert of unpopularity, like Hassan the camel driver,

---

[1] *Pingo in eternitatem* Ceaselessly depict.

[2] *Muses* The nine goddesses of classical mythology who inspire learning and the arts.

[3] *"taught ... sail"* From Pope's *An Essay on Man: Epistle* (1733–34) 3.177: "Learn of the little Nautilus to sail."

[4] *Youth ... helm* From Thomas Gray's *The Bard: A Pindaric Ode* (1757) 2.2.12: "Youth on the prow, and Pleasure at the helm."

[5] *pennons* Banners.

[6] *amaranthine* Everlasting.

[7] *"from ... storm"* From Shakespeare's *King Lear* (1608) 3.4.28–29: "Poor naked wretches, whereso'er you are / That bide the pelting of this pitiless storm."

[8] *"as with triple steel"* From Milton's *Paradise Lost* (1667) 2.569.

[9] *sent to Coventry* Shunned.

[10] *"His words ... ear"* From Milton's *Paradise Lost* 2.112–17: "But all was false and hollow ... yet he pleas'd the ear."

And curs'd the hour, and curs'd the luckless day,
When first from Shiraz' walls they bent their way.[1]

They are safely enclosed there, but Mr. Coleridge did not enter with them; pitching his tent upon the barren waste without, and having no abiding place nor city of refuge.[2]

MR. WORDSWORTH

Mr. Wordsworth's genius is a pure emanation of the Spirit of the Age. Had he lived in any other period of the world, he would never have been heard of. As it is, he has some difficulty to contend with the hebetude[3] of his intellect, and the meanness of his subject. With him "lowliness is young ambition's ladder":[4] but he finds it a toil to climb in this way the steep of Fame. His homely Muse can hardly raise her wing from the ground, nor spread her hidden glories to the sun. He has "no figures nor no fantasies, which busy *passion* draws in the brains of men":[5] neither the gorgeous machinery of mythologic lore, nor the splendid colours of poetic diction. His style is vernacular: he delivers household truths. He sees nothing loftier than human hopes; nothing deeper than the human heart. This he probes, this he tampers with, this he poises, with all its incalculable weight of thought and feeling, in his hands; and at the same time calms the throbbing pulses of his own heart, by keeping his eye ever fixed on the face of nature. If he can make the life-blood flow from the wounded breast, this is the living colouring with which he paints his verse: if he can assuage the pain or close up the wound with the balm of solitary musing,

or the healing power of plants and herbs and "skyey influences,"[6] this is the sole triumph of his art. He takes the simplest elements of nature and of the human mind, the mere abstract conditions inseparable from our being, and tries to compound a new system of poetry from them; and has perhaps succeeded as well as any one could. "*Nihil humani a me alienum puto*"[7]—is the motto of his works. He thinks nothing low or indifferent of which this can be affirmed: every thing that professes to be more than this, that is not an absolute essence of truth and feeling, he holds to be vitiated, false, and spurious. In a word, his poetry is founded on setting up an opposition (and pushing it to the utmost length) between the natural and the artificial; between the spirit of humanity, and the spirit of fashion and of the world!

It is one of the innovations of the time. It partakes of, and is carried along with, the revolutionary movement of our age: the political changes of the day were the model on which he formed and conducted his poetical experiments. His Muse (it cannot be denied, and without this we cannot explain its character at all) is a levelling one. It proceeds on a principle of equality, and strives to reduce all things to the same standard. It is distinguished by a proud humility. It relies upon its own resources, and disdains external show and relief. It takes the commonest events and objects, as a test to prove that nature is always interesting from its inherent truth and beauty, without any of the ornaments of dress or pomp of circumstances to set it off. Hence the unaccountable mixture of seeming simplicity and real abstruseness in the *Lyrical Ballads*. Fools have laughed at, wise men scarcely understand them. He takes a subject or a story merely as pegs or loops to hang thought and feeling on; the incidents are trifling, in proportion to his contempt for imposing appearances; the reflections are profound, according to the gravity and the aspiring pretensions of his mind.

His popular, inartificial style gets rid (at a blow) of all the trappings of verse, of all the high places of poetry:

---

[1] *And curs'd ... way* From William Collins's *The Persian Eclogues* 11.3–4: "Eclogue the Second Hassan; or, The Camel Driver" (1742): "Sad was the hour and luckless was the day, / When first from Shiraz' walls I bent my way."

[2] *city of refuge* From Joshua 20.7–9.

[3] *hebetude* Dullness.

[4] *"lowliness ... ladder"* From William Shakespeare's *Julius Caesar* 2.1.22.

[5] *"no figures ... men"* From *Julius Caesar* 2.1.231–32; Hazlitt substitutes the word "passion" for "care."

[6] *"skyey influences"* Influences of the stars. From Shakespeare's *Measure for Measure* 3.1.9.

[7] *"Nihil ... puto"* From Roman playwright Terence (195–159 BCE), "Nothing human is alien to me."

"the cloud-capt towers, the solemn temples, the gorgeous palaces," are swept to the ground, and "like the baseless fabric of a vision, leave not a wreck behind."[1] All the traditions of learning, all the superstitions of age, are obliterated and effaced. We begin *de novo,* on a *tabula rasa*[2] of poetry. The purple pall, the nodding plume of tragedy are exploded as mere pantomime and trick, to return to the simplicity of truth and nature. Kings, queens, priests, nobles, the altar and the throne, the distinctions of rank, birth, wealth, power, "the judge's robe, the marshal's truncheon, the ceremony that to great ones 'longs,"[3] are not to be found here. The author tramples on the pride of art with greater pride. The Ode and Epode, the Strophe and the Antistrophe,[4] he laughs to scorn. The harp of Homer, the trump of Pindar and of Alcaeus[5] are still. The decencies of costume, the decorations of vanity are stripped off without mercy as barbarous, idle, and Gothic. The jewels in the crisped hair,[6] the diadem[7] on the polished brow are thought meretricious, theatrical, vulgar; and nothing contents his fastidious taste beyond a simple garland of flowers. Neither does he avail himself of the advantages which nature or accident holds out to him. He chooses to have his subject a foil to his invention, to owe nothing but to himself. He gathers manna in the wilderness, he strikes the barren rock for the gushing moisture. He elevates the mean by the strength of his own aspirations; he clothes the naked with beauty and grandeur from the stores of his own recollections. No cypress grove loads his verse with funeral pomp: but his imagination lends "a sense of joy"

> To the bare trees and mountains bare,
> And grass in the green field.[8]

No storm, no shipwreck startles us by its horrors: but the rainbow lifts its head in the cloud, and the breeze sighs through the withered fern. No sad vicissitude of fate, no overwhelming catastrophe in nature deforms his page: but the dew-drop glitters on the bending flower, the tear collects in the glistening eye.

> Beneath the hills, along the flowery vales,
> The generations are prepared; the pangs,
> The internal pangs, are ready; the dread strife
> Of poor humanity's afflicted will,
> Struggling in vain with ruthless destiny.[9]

As the lark ascends from its low bed on fluttering wing, and salutes the morning skies; so Mr. Wordsworth's unpretending Muse, in russet guise, scales the summits of reflection, while it makes the round earth its footstool, and its home!

Possibly a good deal of this may be regarded as the effect of disappointed views and an inverted ambition. Prevented by native pride and indolence from climbing the ascent of learning or greatness, taught by political opinions to say to the vain pomp and glory of the world, "I hate ye,"[10] seeing the path of classical and artificial poetry blocked up by the cumbrous ornaments of style and turgid *common-places,* so that nothing more could be achieved in that direction but by the most ridiculous

---

[1] *"the ... behind"* From Shakespeare's *The Tempest* 4.1.151–56: "And, like the baseless fabric of this vision, / The cloud-capp'd towers, the gorgeous palaces, / The solemn temples, the great globe itself, / Yea all which it inherit, shall dissolve / And, like this insubstantial pageant faded, / Leave not a rack behind."

[2] *de novo, on a tabula rasa* Anew, on a blank slate.

[3] *"the judge's robe ... 'longs"* From Shakespeare's *Measure for Measure* 2.2.59–61: "No ceremony that to great ones 'longs, / Not the king's crown, nor the deputed sword, / The marshal's truncheon, nor the judge's robe."

[4] *Ode* Rhymed lyric poem in the form of an address, with an irregular or varied meter; *Epode* Lyric poem composed of couplets, in which a long line is followed by a short line; *Strophe* Metrically-structured section of an ode; *Antistrophe* Response to strophe.

[5] *The harp ... Alcaeus* Homer: ancient Greek poet, author of the *Iliad* and the *Odyssey*; Pindar (518?–c. 438 BCE) and Alcaeus (c. 620–c. 580 BCE): Greek lyric poets.

[6] *jewels in the crisped hair* From William Collins's "The Manners: An Ode"; Hazlitt substitutes "the" for "his"; *crisped* Wavy.

[7] *diadem* Jeweled crown.

[8] *a sense ... field* From Wordsworth's "To My Sister" 6–8.

[9] *Beneath ... destiny* From *The Excursion* 6.553–57; the first line should read: "Amid the groves, under the shadowy hills."

[10] *vain pomp ... ye* From Shakespeare's *Henry VIII* 3.2.365: "Vain pomp and glory of this world, I hate ye!"

bombast or the tamest servility; he has turned back partly from the bias of his mind, partly perhaps from a judicious policy—has struck into the sequestered vale of humble life, sought out the Muse among sheep-cotes and hamlets and the peasant's mountain-haunts, has discarded all the tinsel pageantry of verse, and endeavoured (not in vain) to aggrandise the trivial and add the charm of novelty to the familiar. No one has shown the same imagination in raising trifles into importance: no one has displayed the same pathos in treating of the simplest feelings of the heart. Reserved, yet haughty, having no unruly or violent passions, (or those passions having been early suppressed,) Mr. Wordsworth has passed his life in solitary musing, or in daily converse with the face of nature. He exemplifies in an eminent degree the power of *association*; for his poetry has no other source or character. He has dwelt among pastoral scenes, till each object has become connected with a thousand feelings, a link in the chain of thought, a fibre of his own heart. Every one is by habit and familiarity strongly attached to the place of his birth, or to objects that recall the most pleasing and eventful circumstances of his life. But to the author of the *Lyrical Ballads*, nature is a kind of home; and he may be said to take a personal interest in the universe. There is no image so insignificant that it has not in some mood or other found the way into his heart: no sound that does not awaken the memory of other years.—

> To him the meanest flower that blows can give
> Thoughts that do often lie too deep for tears.[1]

The daisy looks up to him with sparkling eye as an old acquaintance: the cuckoo haunts him with sounds of early youth not to be expressed: a linnet's nest startles him with boyish delight: an old withered thorn is weighed down with a heap of recollections: a grey cloak, seen on some wild moor, torn by the wind, or drenched in the rain, afterwards becomes an object of imagination to him: even the lichens on the rock have a life and

being in his thoughts. He has described all these objects in a way and with an intensity of feeling that no one else had done before him, and has given a new view or aspect of nature. He is in this sense the most original poet now living, and the one whose writings could the least be spared: for they have no substitute elsewhere. The vulgar do not read them, the learned, who see all things through books, do not understand them, the great despise, the fashionable may ridicule them: but the author has created himself an interest in the heart of the retired and lonely student of nature, which can never die. Persons of this class will still continue to feel what he has felt: he has expressed what they might in vain wish to express, except with glistening eye and faultering tongue! There is a lofty philosophic tone, a thoughtful humanity, infused into his pastoral vein. Remote from the passions and events of the great world, he has communicated interest and dignity to the primal movements of the heart of man, and ingrafted his own conscious reflections on the casual thoughts of hinds[2] and shepherds. Nursed amidst the grandeur of mountain scenery, he has stooped to have a nearer view of the daisy under his feet, or plucked a branch of white-thorn from the spray: but in describing it, his mind seems imbued with the majesty and solemnity of the objects around him—the tall rock lifts its head in the erectness of his spirit; the cataract roars in the sound of his verse; and in its dim and mysterious meaning, the mists seem to gather in the hollows of Helvellyn, and the forked Skiddaw[3] hovers in the distance. There is little mention of mountainous scenery in Mr. Wordsworth's poetry; but by internal evidence one might be almost sure that it was written in a mountainous country, from its bareness, its simplicity, its loftiness and its depth!

His later philosophic productions have a somewhat different character. They are a departure from, a dereliction of his first principles. They are classical and courtly. They are polished in style, without being gaudy; dignified in subject, without affectation. They seem to have

---

[1] *To him … tears* From Wordsworth's "Ode: Intimations of Immortality from Recollections of Early Childhood" 11.203; Hazlitt substitutes "him" for "me."

[2] *hinds* Deer.

[3] *Helvellyn … Skiddaw* Mountains in England's Lake District.

THE SPIRIT OF THE AGE 677

been composed not in a cottage at Grasmere,[1] but among the half-inspired groves and stately recollections of Cole-Orton.[2] We might allude in particular, for examples of what we mean, to the lines on a Picture by Claude Lorraine,[3] and to the exquisite poem, entitled *Laodamia*. The last of these breathes the pure spirit of the finest fragments of antiquity—the sweetness, the gravity, the strength, the beauty and the languor of death—

> Calm contemplation and majestic pains.[4]

Its glossy brilliancy arises from the perfection of the finishing, like that of careful sculpture, not from gaudy colouring—the texture of the thoughts has the smoothness and solidity of marble. It is a poem that might be read aloud in Elysium,[5] and the spirits of departed heroes and sages would gather round to listen to it! Mr. Wordsworth's philosophic poetry, with a less glowing aspect and less tumult in the veins than Lord Byron's on similar occasions, bends a calmer and keener eye on morality; the impression, if less vivid, is more pleasing and permanent; and we confess it (perhaps it is a want of taste and proper feeling) that there are lines and poems of our author's, that we think of ten times for once that we recur to any of Lord Byron's.[6] Or if there are any of the latter's writings, that we can dwell upon in the same way, that is, as lasting and heart-felt sentiments, it is when laying aside his usual pomp and pretension, he descends with Mr. Wordsworth to the common ground of a disinterested humanity. It may be considered as characteristic of our poet's writings, that they either make no impression on the mind at all, seem mere *nonsense-verses*, or that they leave a mark behind them that never wears out. They either

Fall blunted from the indurated breast[7]—

without any perceptible result, or they absorb it like a passion. To one class of readers he appears sublime, to another (and we fear the largest) ridiculous. He has probably realised Milton's wish,—"and fit audience found, though few";[8] but we suspect he is not reconciled to the alternative. There are delightful passages in the EXCURSION, both of natural description and of inspired reflection (passages of the latter kind that in the sound of the thoughts and of the swelling language resemble heavenly symphonies, mournful *requiems* over the grave of human hopes); but we must add, in justice and in sincerity, that we think it impossible that this work should ever become popular, even in the same degree as the *Lyrical Ballads*. It affects a system without having any intelligible clue to one; and instead of unfolding a principle in various and striking lights, repeats the same conclusions till they become flat and insipid. Mr. Wordsworth's mind is obtuse, except as it is the organ and the receptacle of accumulated feelings; it is not analytic, but synthetic; it is reflecting, rather than theoretical. The EXCURSION, we believe, fell still-born from the press. There was something abortive, and clumsy, and ill-judged in the attempt. It was long and laboured. The personages, for the most part, were low, the fare rustic: the plan raised expectations which were not fulfilled, and the effect was like being ushered into a stately hall and invited to sit down to a splendid banquet in the company of clowns, and with nothing but successive courses of apple-dumplings served up. It was not even *toujours perdrix*![9]

Mr. Wordsworth, in his person, is above the middle size, with marked features, and an air somewhat stately and Quixotic. He reminds one of some of Holbein's heads,[10] grave, saturnine, with a slight indication of sly humour, kept under by the manners of the age or by the

---

Grasmere Wordsworth's home in the Lake District.

[2] *Cole-Orton* Coleorton, a village in Leicestershire.

[3] *Claude Lorraine* Baroque painter Claude Lorrain (c. 1600–82).

[4] *Calm … pains* From "Laodamia" 72: "Calm pleasures there abide—majestic pains."

[5] *Elysium* Paradise.

[6] *Byron's* The poems of George Gordon, Lord Byron (1788–1824).

[7] *Fall … breast* From Oliver Goldsmith's "The Traveller" 232: "Falls blunted from each indurated heart."

[8] *"and fit … few"* From Milton's *Paradise Lost* 7.30–31: "govern thou my Song, / Urania, and fit audience find, though few."

[9] *toujours perdrix* "Always partridge": too much of the same thing.

[10] *Holbein's heads* The portraits of Hans Holbein (1497–1543).

pretensions of the person. He has a peculiar sweetness in his smile, and great depth and manliness and a rugged harmony, in the tones of his voice. His manner of reading his own poetry is particularly imposing; and in his favourite passages his eye beams with preternatural lustre, and the meaning labours slowly up from his swelling breast. No one who has seen him at these moments could go away with an impression that he was a "man of no mark or likelihood."[1] Perhaps the comment of his face and voice is necessary to convey a full idea of his poetry. His language may not be intelligible, but his manner is not to be mistaken. It is clear that he is either mad or inspired. In company, even in a *tête-à-tête*,[2] Mr. Wordsworth is often silent, indolent, and reserved. If he is become verbose and oracular of late years, he was not so in his better days. He threw out a bold or an indifferent remark without either effort or pretension, and relapsed into musing again. He shone most (because he seemed most roused and animated) in reciting his own poetry, or in talking about it. He sometimes gave striking views of his feelings and trains of association in composing certain passages; or if one did not always understand his distinctions, still there was no want of interest—there was a latent meaning worth inquiring into, like a vein of ore that one cannot exactly hit upon at the moment, but of which there are sure indications. His standard of poetry is high and severe, almost to exclusiveness. He admits of nothing below, scarcely of any thing above himself. It is fine to hear him talk of the way in which certain subjects should have been treated by eminent poets, according to his notions of the art. Thus he finds fault with Dryden's description of Bacchus in the *Alexander's Feast*, as if he were a mere good-looking youth, or boon companion—

Flushed with a purple grace, He shows his honest face[3]—

instead of representing the God returning from the conquest of India, crowned with vine-leaves, and drawn by panthers, and followed by troops of satyrs, of wild

men and animals that he had tamed. You would think, in hearing him speak on this subject, that you saw Titian's picture of the meeting of *Bacchus and Ariadne*—so classic were his conceptions, so glowing his style. Milton is his great idol, and he sometimes dares to compare himself with him. His sonnets, indeed, have something of the same high-raised tone and prophetic spirit. Chaucer is another prime favourite of his, and he has been at the pains to modernize some of the Canterbury Tales. Those persons who look upon Mr. Wordsworth as a merely puerile writer, must be rather at a loss to account for his strong predilection for such geniuses as Dante and Michelangelo.[4] We do not think our author has any very cordial sympathy with Shakespeare. How should he? Shakespeare was the least of an egotist of any body in the world. He does not much relish the variety and scope of dramatic composition. "He hates those interlocutions between Lucius and Caius." Yet Mr. Wordsworth himself wrote a tragedy when he was young; and we have heard the following energetic lines quoted from it, as put into the mouth of a person smit with remorse for some rash crime:

—Action is momentary,
The motion of a muscle this way or that;
Suffering is long, obscure, and infinite![5]

Perhaps for want of light and shade, and the unshackled spirit of the drama, this performance was never brought forward. Our critic has a great dislike to Gray, and a fondness for Thomson and Collins. It is mortifying to hear him speak of Pope and Dryden,[6] whom, because they have been supposed to have all the possible excellences of poetry, he will allow to have none. Nothing, however, can be fairer, or more amusing, than the way in which he sometimes exposes the unmeaning

---

[1] *"man ... likelihood"* From Shakespeare's *1 Henry IV*, 3.2.45: "A fellow of no mark nor likelihood."

[2] *tête-à-tête* Private conversation between two people.

[3] *Flushed ... face* From John Dryden's "Alexander's Feast," 3.5–6.

[4] *Dante* Dante Alighieri (1265–1321); *Michelangelo* Michelangelo Buonarroti (1475–1564).

[5] *Action ... infinite!* From Wordsworth's play *The Borderers*: "Action is transitory—a step, a blow, / The motion of a muscle—this way or that— /... / Suffering is permanent, obscure and dark."

[6] *Gray ... Dryden* Poets Thomas Gray (1716–71), James Thomson (1700–48), William Collins (1721–59), Alexander Pope (1688–1744), John Dryden (1631–1700).

verbiage of modern poetry. Thus, in the beginning of Dr. Johnson's *Vanity of Human Wishes*—

> Let observation with extensive view
> Survey mankind from China to Peru[1]

he says there is a total want of imagination accompanying the words, the same idea is repeated three times under the disguise of a different phraseology: it comes to this—"let *observation*, with extensive *observation, observe mankind*"; or take away the first line, and the second,

> Survey mankind from China to Peru.

literally conveys the whole. Mr. Wordsworth is, we must say, a perfect Drawcansir[2] as to prose writers. He complains of the dry reasoners and matter-of-fact people for their want of *passion*; and he is jealous of the rhetorical declaimers and rhapsodists as trenching on the province of poetry. He condemns all French writers (as well of poetry as prose) in the lump. His list in this way is indeed small. He approves of Walton's Angler, Paley,[3] and some other writers of an inoffensive modesty of pretension. He also likes books of voyages and travels, and Robinson Crusoe.[4] In art, he greatly esteems Bewick's woodcuts, and Waterloo's[5] sylvan etchings. But he sometimes takes a higher tone, and gives his mind fair play. We have known him enlarge with a noble intelligence and enthusiasm on Nicolas Poussin's fine landscape-compositions, pointing out the unity of design that pervades them, the superintending mind, the imaginative principle that brings all to bear on the same end; and declaring he would not give a rush for any landscape that did not express the time of day, the climate, the period of the world it was meant to illustrate, or had not this character of *wholeness* in it. His eye

also does justice to Rembrandt's[6] fine and masterly effects. In the way in which that artist works something out of nothing, and transforms the stump of a tree, a common figure into an *ideal* object, by the gorgeous light and shade thrown upon it, he perceives an analogy to his own mode of investing the minute details of nature with an atmosphere of sentiment; and in pronouncing Rembrandt to be a man of genius, feels that he strengthens his own claim to the title. It has been said of Mr. Wordsworth, that "he hates conchology, that he hates the Venus of Medicis."[7] But these, we hope, are mere epigrams and *jeux-d'esprit*,[8] as far from truth as they are free from malice; a sort of running satire or critical clenches—

> Where one for sense and one for rhyme
> Is quite sufficient at one time.[9]

We think, however, that if Mr. Wordsworth had been a more liberal and candid critic, he would have been a more sterling writer. If a greater number of sources of pleasure had been open to him, he would have communicated pleasure to the world more frequently. Had he been less fastidious in pronouncing sentence on the works of others, his own would have been received more favourably, and treated more leniently. The current of his feelings is deep, but narrow; the range of his understanding is lofty and aspiring rather than discursive. The force, the originality, the absolute truth and identity with which he feels some things, makes him indifferent to so many others. The simplicity and enthusiasm of his feelings, with respect to nature, renders him bigotted and intolerant in his judgments of men and things. But it happens to him, as to others, that his strength lies in his weakness; and perhaps we have no right to complain. We might get rid of the cynic and the egotist, and find in his stead a common place man. We should "take the

---

[1] *Let ... Peru* "The Vanity of Human Wishes" 1–2.

[2] *Drawcansir* Bully, from a character in George Villiers's play *The Rehearsal*.

[3] *Walton's Angler* Izaak Walton's *The Compleat Angler* (1653); *Paley* William Paley (1743–1805), philosopher and theologian.

[4] *Robinson Crusoe* Novel by Daniel Defoe (1660–1731).

[5] *Bewick* Thomas Bewick (1753–1828); *Waterloo* Anthonie Waterloo (1610–90).

[6] *Rembrandt* Rembrandt Harmenszoon van Rijn (1606–69).

[7] *"he hates ... Medicis"* Referring to Sandro Botticelli's painting *The Birth of Venus*, in which Venus is standing on a scallop shell.

[8] *jeux-d'esprit* Witticisms.

[9] *Where ... time* From Samuel Butler's *Hudibras* 2.1.29–30: "For one for sense, and one for rhyme, / I think's sufficient at one time."

good the Gods provide us":[1] a fine and original vein of poetry is not one of their most contemptible gifts, and the rest is scarcely worth thinking of, except as it may be a mortification to those who expect perfection from human nature; or who have been idle enough at some period of their lives, to deify men of genius as possessing claims above it. But this is a chord that jars, and we shall not dwell upon it.

Lord Byron we have called, according to the old proverb, "the spoiled child of fortune":[2] Mr. Wordsworth might plead, in mitigation of some peculiarities, that he is "the spoiled child of disappointment." We are convinced, if he had been early a popular poet, he would have borne his honours meekly, and would have been a person of great *bonhommie*[3] and frankness of disposition. But the sense of injustice and of undeserved ridicule sours the temper and narrows the views. To have produced works of genius, and to find them neglected or treated with scorn, is one of the heaviest trials of human patience. We exaggerate our own merits when they are denied by others, and are apt to grudge and cavil[4] at every particle of praise bestowed on those to whom we feel a conscious superiority. In mere self-defence we turn against the world, when it turns against us; brood over the undeserved slights we receive; and thus the genial current of the soul is stopped, or vents itself in effusions of petulance and self-conceit. Mr. Wordsworth has thought too much of contemporary critics and criticism; and less than he ought of the award of posterity, and of the opinion, we do not say of private friends, but of those who were made so by their admiration of his genius. He did not court popularity by a conformity to established models, and he ought not to have been surprised that his originality was not understood as a matter of course. He has *gnawed too much on the bridle*; and has often thrown out crusts to the critics, in mere defiance or as a point of honour when he was challenged, which otherwise his own good sense would have withheld. We suspect that Mr. Wordsworth's feelings are a little morbid in this respect, or that he resents censure more than he is gratified by praise. Otherwise, the tide has turned much in his favour of late years—he has a large body of determined partisans—and is at present sufficiently in request with the public to save or relieve him from the last necessity to which a man of genius can be reduced—that of becoming the God of his own idolatry!

—1825

---

[1] *"take ... provide us"*   From Plautus's play *Rudens* 4.7.3: "If you are wise, be wise; keep what goods the gods provide you."

[2] *"spoiled child of fortune"*   From the Latin *"fortunae filius."* After Byron's death in 1824, Thomas Moore wrote: "[Byron] was truly a spoiled child, not merely the spoiled child of his parent, but the spoiled child of nature, the spoiled child of fortune, the spoiled child of fame, the spoiled child of society."

[3] *bonhommie*   Pleasant nature.

[4] *cavil*   Quibble.

THOMAS MOORE
1779 – 1852

Thomas Moore

Nicknamed "Melody Moore" by his admirers, Thomas Moore secured a central place in Irish poetic tradition through melodic rhythms, deceptively simple rhymes—and his ten-volume collection of *Irish Melodies* (1808–34). For much of his life he was also favored in society. A romantic figure, he loved "watching and pursuing / the light that lies / in Woman's eyes." Yet Moore was also deeply religious and highly political, and wrote passionately on a variety of subjects.

Moore was born a Catholic in Dublin to successful grocer John Moore and Anastasia Codd Moore, an intelligent woman who impressed upon her children an appreciation for the humanities. He entered Trinity College in 1795, after the Catholic Relief Act (1793) permitted the enrollment of Catholic students. The French Revolution and the struggle of the Irish against British oppression were the great issues of the time, and Moore was soon acquainted with politically-minded students who belonged to the "United Irishmen" society. Encouraged by his friends Robert Emmet and Edward Hudson, Moore began to try his hand at political writing though, unlike Emmet, he played no part in the 1798 and 1803 uprisings against British rule. (Moore's poem "Oh, Breathe Not His Name" was written in memory of Emmet, who was hanged for treason in 1803.) Upon completion of his B.A. at Trinity, Moore went on to study law, but left in order to complete *Odes of Anacreon* (1800), which was permitted a dedication to the Prince of Wales.

In 1803, Moore was appointed registrar to the Admiralty in Bermuda, but found the work boring, and soon left to take a grand tour of the United States and Canada. The North American landscape made a great impression on Moore, inspiring a number of poems (including "A Canadian Boat Song"). Moore was less enamored with the American political system, however; he publicly denounced slavery, and referred to America as "anti-democratic." Upon returning to Britain he summarized his tour in his next book, *Epistles, Odes, and Other Poems* (1806), a publication that sparked controversy in Britain as well as in America.

A sometime actor and playwright as well as a poet, Moore in 1811 married actress Elizabeth Dyke—an English woman and Protestant. (For some time he did not inform his parents of the union.) The couple would eventually have five children. In 1807 Moore was asked by a publisher to write lyrics for a number of Irish tunes; thus began a project that grew to 10 volumes of *Irish Melodies* (1808–34)—and that earned Moore close to £500 annually. His lyrics were for both traditional tunes and music newly written by some leading composers of the day, including Sir John Strenson; among the most popular were "'Tis the Last Rose of Summer," "The Minstrel Boy," and "The Harp That Once through Tara's Halls." In addition to his work as a balladeer, he also wrote a number of satires, including *The Sceptic: A Philosophical Satire* (1809), *The Fudge Family in Paris* (1818), *The Fudges in England* (1835), and *Odes upon Cash, Corn, Catholics, and Other Matters* (1828). Perhaps his most successful piece during his lifetime was *Lalla Rookh* (1817), an Orientalist romance about an intended bride who, while en-route to her betrothed, listens to stories told by a poet. *Lalla Rookh* was quickly translated into multiple languages and rivaled in popularity anything written by Moore's fellow Romantics.

Between 1818 and 1822, Moore lived in exile in France, held liable for the embezzlement of large sums by his deputy in Bermuda. One of Byron's closest friends, Moore at this time received Byron's memoirs and agreed to be Byron's literary executor. When Byron died in 1824, Moore unsuccessfully resisted a move by a group of Byron's other friends to have the memoirs destroyed. Eventually, he took it upon himself to pen Byron's biography, as he had done for another of his acquaintances, the dramatist and politician Richard Brinsley Sheridan.

In the 1830s and 1840s Moore suffered several personal tragedies (including the death and disgrace of one of his sons in Algeria); for the last years of his life he was afflicted with dementia. After his death in 1852 his wife continued to live in their cottage at Sloperton, Wiltshire, for another thirteen years.

Byron rated Moore's poetry very highly, writing that he had a "peculiarity of talent, or rather talents,—poetry, music, voice, all his own," and throughout most of the nineteenth century Moore's work remained popular in England as well as in Ireland.

⌘ ⌘ ⌘

A Canadian Boat Song
Written on the River St. Lawrence[1]

Et remigem cantus hortatur.[2]
QUINTILIAN[3]

Faintly as tolls the evening chime,
  Our voices keep tune and our oars keep time.
Soon as the woods on shore look dim,
We'll sing at St. Ann's[4] our parting hymn.
5 Row brothers, row, the stream runs fast,
The rapids are near and the day-light's past!

Why should we yet our sail unfurl?
There is not a breath the blue wave to curl!
But, when the wind blows off the shore,
10 Oh! sweetly we'll rest our weary oar.

Blow, breezes, blow, the stream runs fast,
The rapids are near and the day-light's past!

Utawa's[5] tide! this trembling moon,
Shall see us float over thy surges soon.
15 Saint of this green isle! hear our prayers,
Oh! grant us cool heavens and favouring airs.
Blow, breezes, blow, the stream run fast,
The rapids are near and the day-light's past.
  —1805

'Tis the Last Rose of Summer

'Tis the last rose of summer
  Left blooming all alone;
All her lovely companions
  Are faded and gone;
5 No flower of her kindred,
  No rose-bud is nigh,

---

[1] *Written ... Lawrence* The poem was written during a five-day boat journey between Niagara Falls and Montreal (part of Moore's tour of North America in 1804).

[2] *Et remigem cantus hortatur* Latin: Encouraging song of the oarsmen.

[3] *QUINTILIAN* Rhetorician and author of *Institutio Oratoria* (95 CE).

[4] *St. Ann* Settlement along the St. Lawrence and location of a Gothic church that is sacred to fur traders and voyageurs. St. Ann is also the patron saint of sailors.

---

[5] *Utawa* Tributary of the St. Lawrence River, the Uttawa (now Ottawa) River divided Upper and Lower Canada (now Ontario and Quebec), and was also the main route for fur traders from Montreal to the Northwest Territories.

To reflect back her blushes,
Or give sigh for sigh.

I'll not leave thee, thou lone one!
0   To pine on the stem;
Since the lovely are sleeping,
Go, sleep thou with them.
Thus kindly I scatter
Thy leaves o'er the bed,
5   Where thy mates of the garden
Lie scentless and dead.

So soon may *I* follow,
When friendships decay,
And from love's shining circle
20   The gems drop away.
When true hearts lie withered,
And fond ones are flown,
Oh! who would inhabit
This bleak world alone?
    —1813

Oh! Breathe Not His Name[1]

Oh! breathe not his name —let it sleep in the shade,
Where cold and unhonoured his relics are laid![2]
Sad, silent, and dark, be the tears that we shed,
As the night-dew that falls on the grass o'er his head!

5   But the night-dew that falls, though in silence it weeps,
Shall brighten with verdure[3] the grave where he sleeps;
And the tear that we shed, though in secret it rolls,
Shall long keep his memory green in our souls.
    —1821

The Harp That Once through Tara's[4] Halls

The harp that once through Tara's halls,
    The soul of music shed,
Now hangs as mute on Tara's walls
As if the soul were fled:
5   So sleeps the pride of former days,
So glory's thrill is o'er;
And hearts, that once beat high for praise,
Now feel that pulse no more!

No more to chiefs and ladies bright
10   The harp of Tara swells;
The chord, alone, that breaks at night,
Its tale of ruin tells:
Thus freedom now so seldom wakes,
The only throb she gives
15   Is when some heart indignant breaks,
To show that still she lives!
    —1821

The Minstrel Boy[5]

The Minstrel boy to the war is gone,
    In the ranks of death you'll find him;
His father's sword he has girded on,
And his wild harp slung behind him.
5   "Land of song!" said the warrior-bard,
"Though all the world betrays thee,
One sword, at least, thy rights shall guard,
One faithful harp shall praise thee!"

The Minstrel fell!—but the foreman's chain
10   Could not bring that proud soul under;
The harp he loved never spoke again,
For he tore its chords asunder;
And said, "No chains shall sully thee,
Thou soul of love and bravery!

---

[1]   *Oh! Breathe Not His Name*   In memoriam of Robert Emmet, who was hanged for treason in 1803. At his execution he famously requested that his epitaph be left unwritten until his country had taken "her place among the nations of the earth."

[2]   *unhonoured his relics are laid*   Emmet's burial site is unknown.

[3]   *verdure*   Greenness.

---

[4]   *Tara*   Seat of the high Celtic kings in ancient Ireland and location of battle between Irish rebels and British troops during the Irish Rebellion (1798).

[5]   *The Minstrel Boy*   Thought to have been composed in remembrance of friends who perished during the Irish Rebellion (1798).

15   Thy songs were made for the pure and free,
      They shall never sound in slavery."
                    —1821

The Time I've Lost in Wooing

The time I've lost in wooing,
      In watching and pursuing
The light that lies
In woman's eyes,
5   Has been my heart's undoing.
Though wisdom oft has sought me,
I scorned the lore she brought me;
My only books
Were woman's looks,
10   And folly's all they've taught me.

Her smile when beauty granted,
I hung with gaze enchanted,
Like him the sprite[1]
Whom maids by night
15   Oft meet in glen that's haunted.
Like him, too, beauty won me,
But, while her eyes were on me,
If once their ray
Was turned away.
20   O! winds could not outrun me.

And are those follies going?
And is my proud heart growing
Too cold or wise
For brilliant eyes
25   Again to set it glowing?
No—vain, alas! th' endeavour
From bonds so sweet to sever;

Poor wisdom's chance
Against a glance
30   Is now as weak as ever!
                    —1821

When Midst the Gay I Meet

When midst the gay I meet
      That gentle smile of thine,
Though still on me it turns most sweet,
I scarce can call it mine:
5   But when to me alone
Your secret tears you show,
Oh, then I feel those tears my own,
And claim them while they flow.
Then still with bright looks bless
10   The gay, the cold, the free;
Give smiles to those who love you less,
But keep your tears for me.

The snow on Jura's[2] steep
Can smile in many a beam.
15   Yet still in chains of coldness sleep,
How bright soe'er it seem.
But, when some deep-felt ray,
Whose touch is fire, appears,
Oh, then the smile is warmed away,
20   And, melting, turns to tears.
Then still with bright looks bless
The gay, the cold, the free;
Give smiles to those who love you less,
But keep your tears for me.
                    —1840–41

---

[1] *sprite* Irish fairy.

[2] *Jura* Mountain range on the border between France and Switzerland.

THOMAS DE QUINCEY
1785 – 1859

Because he published his first essay in 1821, Thomas De Quincey appears to be a contemporary of Byron, Shelley, and Keats. The sensational title of his most famous work, *Confessions of an English Opium-Eater*, adds to the case for associating him with these later Romantics. For his elegant and introspective style, however, De Quincey is better compared with Wordsworth and Coleridge, the earlier Romantics he so admired, as well as with other prominent essayists of his time such as Charles Lamb and William Hazlitt. Written in installments for one of the magazines popular in the day, *Confessions* was one of the first pieces De Quincey submitted, and it brought him immediate notoriety and success. Citing St. Augustine and Rousseau as predecessors of his autobiographical "impassioned prose," De Quincey at times wrote lovingly about his addiction: "If opium-eating be a sensual pleasure, and if I am bound to confess that I have indulged in it to an excess not yet *recorded* of any other man, it is no less true that I have struggled against this fascinating enthralment with a religious zeal, and have at length accomplished what I never yet heard attributed to any other man—have untwisted, almost to its final links, the accursed chain which fettered me." Whether he ever became unfettered is in question—De Quincey seems to have remained hopelessly addicted his entire adult life—but he went on to write hundreds of essays on subjects as diverse as German philosophy and literature, Shakespearean drama, the French Revolution, economics, Christianity, and the California gold rush.

De Quincey was born in Manchester in 1785 to Elizabeth Penson and Thomas Quincey, a successful linen merchant. One of eight children, he had already experienced the loss of two sisters by the time of his father's early death in 1793. Even though these events made for a troubled childhood, De Quincey gained a reputation as a precocious student and scholar. In 1796 he entered Bath Grammar School, where he became fluent in Latin and Greek despite what he considered his ineffectual teachers. He later wrote that a headmaster once said of his brilliance as a Greek scholar, "That boy could harangue an Athenian mob better than you and I could address an English one."

In 1802 De Quincey left the school with the thought of presenting himself to Wordsworth, whose *Lyrical Ballads* he had greatly admired. Instead he embarked on a tour of Wales and eventually arrived in London, hungry and destitute. These years, although difficult, were fodder for some of his most vivid recollections. In the *Confessions*, for example, De Quincey often recalls his relationship with a prostitute named Ann, who had befriended and housed him in London. A year later, he returned to his family and enrolled in Worcester College, Oxford, where he became known as a solitary but brilliant scholar. During his college years, he began taking laudanum—a drug derived from opium—for a toothache, and for a number of years his habit was kept under control. In 1807 he once again quit school, this time on the brink of examinations for which he had appeared to be extremely well-prepared.

De Quincey came to know Coleridge during his university years, and through Coleridge he met his idol, Wordsworth. The attraction was such that De Quincey settled in Grasmere in order to be near both poets, eventually moving into Dove Cottage, the Wordsworths' home, when Dorothy and William moved into a larger house. After years of close friendship, De Quincey became estranged from the Wordsworths when his addiction became uncontrollable and when he chose to live out of wedlock with Margaret Simpson, a local farmer's daughter. The couple married in 1816 after the birth of their son. They eventually had eight children together during their twenty-one years of marriage.

Again destitute, De Quincey moved his family to London and began publishing the *Confessions* anonymously in *The London Magazine*. His "spiritual autobiography" is in part a paean to the glories of opium—"Thou hast the keys of Paradise, oh just, subtle, and mighty opium!"—and in part a record of the nightmares and dream visions he experienced as a result of his addiction. (He influenced both Edgar Allan Poe and Charles Baudelaire, not only in their writing, but also in their use of the drug.)

De Quincey had a sense of the importance of dreams and the unconscious that was remarkable for his time. "I feel assured," he wrote in *Confessions*, "that there is no such thing as *forgetting* possible to the mind; a thousand accidents may, and will, interpose a veil between our present consciousness and the secret inscriptions on the mind. Accidents of the same sort will also rend away this veil; but alike, whether veiled or unveiled, the inscription remains forever." De Quincey later penned *Suspiria de Profundis* (1845), a sequel to the *Confessions* in which he wrote about his dreams with considerable psychological acuity; many regard his ideas as precursors to Freud's dream theories.

Although his lifestyle was anything but conservative, the political and moral conservatism of many of his ideas was deep-seated. He was also a talented humorist, as his 1827 essay "On Murder Considered as One of the Fine Arts" well illustrates. De Quincey delineates how "drinking and Sabbath-breaking" and eventual "incivility and procrastination" follows on the "downward path" from murder. "Many a man," De Quincey writes, "dated his ruin from some murder or other that perhaps he thought little of at the time."

In the 1850s De Quincey began compiling the fourteen-volume series *Selections Grave and Gay from Writings Published and Unpublished*, which was completed in 1860, a year after his death. In the words of a review written shortly afterward in London's *Quarterly Review*, "The position of De Quincey in the literature of the present day is remarkable. We might search in vain for a writer who, with equal powers, has made an equally slight impression upon the general public. His style is superb; his powers of reasoning are unsurpassed; his imagination is warm and brilliant, and his humor … delicate." The past few decades have seen a surge of interest in De Quincey and his *Confessions of an English Opium-Eater*, which has struck a chord with many who have similarly experienced isolation and alienation from society.

⌘ ⌘ ⌘

from *Confessions of an English Opium-Eater*

TO THE READER

I here present you, courteous reader, with the record of a remarkable period in my life; according to my application of it, I trust that it will prove not merely an interesting record, but in a considerable degree useful and instructive. In *that* hope it is that I have drawn it up; and *that* must be my apology for breaking through that delicate and honourable reserve which, for the most part, restrains us from the public exposure of our own errors and infirmities. Nothing, indeed, is more revolting to English feelings than the spectacle of a human being obtruding on our notice his moral ulcers or scars, and tearing away that "decent drapery"[1] which time or indulgence to human frailty may have drawn over them; accordingly, the greater part of *our* confessions (that is, spontaneous and extra-judicial confessions) proceed from demi-reps,[2] adventurers, or swindlers; and for any such acts of gratuitous self-humiliation from those who can be supposed in sympathy with the decent and self-respecting part of society, we must look to French literature, or to that part of the German which is tainted with the spurious and defective sensibility of the French. All this I feel so forcibly, and so nervously am I alive to reproach of this tendency, that I have for many months hesitated about the propriety of allowing this or any part of my narrative to come before the public eye until after my death (when, for many reasons, the whole will be published); and it is not without an anxious review of the reasons for and against this step that I have at last concluded on taking it.

Guilt and misery shrink, by a natural instinct, from public notice; they court privacy and solitude; and even in their choice of a grave will sometimes sequester themselves from the general population of the church-yard, as if declining to claim fellowship with the great family of man, and wishing (in the affecting language of Mr. Wordsworth)

—humbly to express
A penitential loneliness.[3]

It is well, upon the whole, and for the interest of us all, that it should be so; nor would I willingly in my own person manifest a disregard of such salutary feelings, nor in act or word do anything to weaken them; but, on the one hand, as my self-accusation does not amount to a confession of guilt, so, on the other, it is possible that, if it *did*, the benefit resulting to others

from the record of an experience purchased at so heavy a price might compensate, by a vast overbalance, for any violence done to the feelings I have noticed, and justify a breach of the general rule. Infirmity and misery do not of necessity imply guilt. They approach or recede from shades of that dark alliance, in proportion to the probable motives and prospects of the offender, and the palliations,[4] known or secret, of the offence, in proportion as the temptations to it were potent from the first, and the resistance to it, in act or in effort, was earnest to the last. For my own part, without breach of truth or modesty, I may affirm that my life has been, on the whole, the life of a philosopher; from my birth I was made an intellectual creature, and intellectual in the highest sense my pursuits and pleasures have been, even from my schoolboy days. If opium-eating be a sensual pleasure, and if I am bound to confess that I have indulged in it to an excess not yet *recorded*[5] of any other man, it is no less true that I have struggled against this fascinating enthralment with a religious zeal, and have at length accomplished what I never yet heard attributed to any other man —have untwisted, almost to its final links, the accursed chain which fettered me. Such a self-conquest may reasonably be set off in counterbalance to any kind or degree of self-indulgence. Not to insist that in my case the self-conquest was unquestionable, the self-indulgence open to doubts of casuistry,[6] according as that name shall be extended to acts aiming at the bare relief of pain, or shall be restricted to such as aim at the excitement of positive pleasure.

Guilt, therefore, I do not acknowledge; and if I did, it is possible that I might still resolve on the present act of confession in consideration of the service which I may thereby render to the whole class of opium-eaters. But who are they? Reader, I am sorry to say a very numerous class indeed. Of this I became convinced some years ago by computing at that time the number of those in one small class of English society (the class of men distin-

---

[1] *decent drapery* From Edmund Burke's *Reflections on the Revolution in France* (1790): "All the pleasing illusions ... are to be dissolved by this new conquering empire of light and reason. All the decent drapery of life is to be rudely torn off."

[2] *demi-reps* Women of dubious character.

[3] *humbly ... loneliness* From Wordsworth's "The White Doe of Rylstone, or The Fate of the Nortons" (176–77): "[G]uilt, that humbly would express / A penitential loneliness."

[4] *palliations* Concealment or alleviation of symptoms.

[5] [De Quincey's note] "Not yet *recorded*," I say; for there is one celebrated man of the present day, who, if all be true which is reported of him, has greatly exceeded me in quantity. [De Quincey is referring to Samuel Taylor Coleridge.]

[6] *casuistry* Specious rationalization used to determine morality.

guished for talents, or of eminent station) who were known to me, directly or indirectly, as opium-eaters; such, for instance, as the eloquent and benevolent ——,[1] the late Dean of ——, Lord ——, Mr. —— the philosopher, a late Under-Secretary of State (who described to me the sensation which first drove him to the use of opium in the very same words as the Dean of ——, viz.,[2] "that he felt as though rats were gnawing and abrading the coats of his stomach"), Mr. ——, and many others hardly less known, whom it would be tedious to mention. Now, if one class, comparatively so limited, could furnish so many scores of cases (and that within the knowledge of one single inquirer), it was a natural inference that the entire population of England would furnish a proportionable number. The soundness of this inference, however, I doubted, until some facts became known to me which satisfied me that it was not incorrect. I will mention two.

(1) Three respectable London druggists, in widely remote quarters of London, from whom I happened lately to be purchasing small quantities of opium, assured me that the number of amateur opium-eaters (as I may term them) was at this time immense; and that the difficulty of distinguishing those persons to whom habit had rendered opium necessary from such as were purchasing it with a view to suicide, occasioned them daily trouble and disputes. This evidence respected London only. But,

(2) —which will possibly surprise the reader more— some years ago, on passing through Manchester, I was informed by several cotton manufacturers that their workpeople were rapidly getting into the practice of opium-eating, so much so, that on a Saturday afternoon the counters of the druggists were strewed with pills of one, two, or three grains, in preparation for the known demand of the evening. The immediate occasion of this practice was the lowness of wages, which at that time would not allow them to indulge in ale or spirits, and wages rising, it may be thought that this practice would

cease; but as I do not readily believe that any man having once tasted the divine luxuries of opium will afterwards descend to the gross and mortal enjoyments of alcohol, I take it for granted

That those eat now who never ate before;
And those who always ate, now eat the more.

Indeed, the fascinating powers of opium are admitted even by medical writers, who are its greatest enemies. Thus, for instance, Awsiter, apothecary to Greenwich Hospital, in his "Essay on the Effects of Opium" (published in the year 1763), when attempting to explain why Mead[3] had not been sufficiently explicit on the properties, counteragents, &c., of this drug, expresses himself in the following mysterious terms (φωνάντα συνετοῖσ[4]): "Perhaps he thought the subject of too delicate a nature to be made common; and as many people might then indiscriminately use it, it would take from that necessary fear and caution which should prevent their experiencing the extensive power of this drug, *for there are many properties in it, if universally known, that would habituate the use, and make it more in request with us than with Turks themselves*, the result of which knowledge," he adds, "must prove a general misfortune." In the necessity of this conclusion I do not altogether concur; but upon that point I shall have occasion to speak at the close of my Confessions, where I shall present the reader with the moral of my narrative.

PRELIMINARY CONFESSIONS

These preliminary confessions, or introductory narrative of the youthful adventures which laid the foundation of the writer's habit of opium-eating in afterlife, it has been judged proper to premise, for three several reasons:

1. As forestalling that question, and giving it a satisfactory answer, which else would painfully obtrude itself in the course of the Opium Confessions—"How came any reasonable being to subject himself to such a

[1] *benevolent* —— De Quincey entered the full names in his 1856 revision to the *Confessions*, saying that the editor of the original version deleted the names.

[2] *viz.* I.e., *videlicet*. Latin: that is to say.

[3] *Mead* Dr. Richard Mead (1673–1754), said to be the leading physician of the age, whose patients included Queen Anne and Sir Isaac Newton.

[4] φωνάντα συνετοῖσ Greek: speaking to the wise.

yoke of misery; voluntarily to incur a captivity so servile, and knowingly to fetter himself with such a sevenfold chain?"—a question which, if not somewhere plausibly resolved, could hardly fail, by the indignation which it would be apt to raise as against an act of wanton folly, to interfere with that degree of sympathy which is necessary in any case to an author's purposes.

2. As furnishing a key to some parts of that tremendous scenery which afterwards peopled the dreams of the opium-eater.

3. As creating some previous interest of a personal sort in the confessing subject, apart from the matter of the confessions, which cannot fail to render the confessions themselves more interesting. If a man "whose talk is of oxen" should become an opium-eater, the probability is that (if he is not too dull to dream at all) he will dream about oxen; whereas, in the case before him, the reader will find that the opium-eater boasteth himself to be a philosopher, and accordingly, that the phantasmagoria of *his* dreams (waking or sleeping, daydreams or nightdreams) is suitable to one who in that character

Humani nihil a se alienum putat.[1]

For amongst the conditions which he deems indispensable to the sustaining of any claim to the title of philosopher is not merely the possession of a superb intellect in its *analytic* functions (in which part of the pretensions, however, England can for some generations show but few claimants; at least, he is not aware of any known candidate for this honour who can be styled emphatically *a subtle thinker*, with the exception of Samuel Taylor Coleridge, and in a narrower department of thought with the recent illustrious exception[2] of

David Ricardo[3]) but also on such a constitution of the *moral* faculties as shall give him an inner eye and power of intuition for the vision and the mysteries of our human nature: *that* constitution of faculties, in short, which (amongst all the generations of men that from the beginning of time have deployed into life, as it were, upon this planet) our English poets have possessed in the highest degree, and Scottish professors[4] in the lowest. ...

from PART 2

THE PLEASURES OF OPIUM

It is so long since I first took opium that if it had been a trifling incident in my life I might have forgotten its date; but cardinal events are not to be forgotten, and from circumstances connected with it I remember that it must be referred to the autumn of 1804. During that season I was in London, having come thither for the first time since my entrance at college. And my introduction to opium arose in the following way. From an early age I had been accustomed to wash my head in cold water at least once a day; being suddenly seized with toothache, I attributed it to some relaxation caused by an accidental intermission of that practice, jumped out of bed, plunged my head into a basin of cold water, and with hair thus wetted went to sleep. The next morning, as I need hardly say, I awoke with excruciating rheumatic pains of the head and face, from which I had hardly any respite for about twenty days. On the twenty-first day I think it was, and on a Sunday, that I went out into the streets, rather to run away, if possible, from my torments, than with any distinct purpose. By accident I met a college acquaintance, who recommended opium. Opium! dread agent of unimaginable

---

[1] *Humani ... putat* Latin: from Terence's *Heautontimorumenos* (163 BCE); translates to: He thinks that nothing that is human is alien to him.

[2] [De Quincey's note] A third exception might perhaps have been added; and my reason for not adding that exception is chiefly because it was only in his juvenile efforts that the writer whom I allude to [William Hazlitt] expressly addressed hints to philosophical themes; his riper powers having been all dedicated (on very excusable and very intelligible grounds, under the present direction of the popular mind in England) to criticism and the fine arts. This reason apart, however, I doubt whether he is not rather to be considered an acute thinker than a subtle one. It is, besides, a great drawback on his mastery over

philosophical subjects that he has obviously not had the advantage of a regular scholastic education: he has not read Plato in his youth (which most likely was only his misfortune), but neither has he read Kant in his manhood (which is his fault).

[3] *David Ricardo* British political economist, author of *On the Principles of Political Economy, and Taxation* (1819).

[4] [De Quincey's note] I disclaim any allusion to *existing* professors, of whom indeed I know only one.

pleasure and pain! I had heard of it as I had of manna or of ambrosia,[1] but no further. How unmeaning a sound was it at that time; what solemn chords does it now strike upon my heart! what heart-quaking vibrations of sad and happy remembrances! Reverting for a moment to these, I feel a mystic importance attached to the minutest circumstances connected with the place and the time and the man (if man he was) that first laid open to me the Paradise of Opium-eaters. It was a Sunday afternoon, wet and cheerless, and a duller spectacle this earth of ours has not to show than a rainy Sunday in London. My road homewards lay through Oxford Street; and near "the stately Pantheon"[2] (as Mr. Wordsworth has obligingly called it) I saw a druggist's shop. The druggist—unconscious minister of celestial pleasures!—as if in sympathy with the rainy Sunday, looked dull and stupid, just as any mortal druggist might be expected to look on a Sunday; and when I asked for the tincture of opium, he gave it to me as any other man might do, and furthermore, out of my shilling returned me what seemed to be real copper halfpence, taken out of a real wooden drawer. Nevertheless, in spite of such indications of humanity, he has ever since existed in my mind as the beatific vision of an immortal druggist, sent down to earth on a special mission to myself. And it confirms me in this way of considering him, that when I next came up to London I sought him near the stately Pantheon, and found him not; and thus to me, who knew not his name (if indeed he had one), he seemed rather to have vanished from Oxford Street than to have removed in any bodily fashion. The reader may choose to think of him as possibly no more than a sublunary[3] druggist; it may be so, but my faith is better—I believe him to have evanesced,[4] or evaporated. So unwillingly would I connect any mortal remembrances with that hour, and place, and creature, that first brought me acquainted with the celestial drug.

Arrived at my lodgings, it may be supposed that I lost not a moment in taking the quantity prescribed. I was necessarily ignorant of the whole art and mystery of opium-taking, and what I took I took under every disadvantage. But I took it—and in an hour—oh, heavens! what a revulsion! what an upheaving, from its lowest depths, of inner spirit! what an apocalypse of the world within me! That my pains had vanished was now a trifle in my eyes; this negative effect was swallowed up in the immensity of those positive effects which had opened before me—in the abyss of divine enjoyment thus suddenly revealed. Here was a panacea, a φαρμακον νήωενθες[5] for all human woes; here was the secret of happiness, about which philosophers had disputed for so many ages, at once discovered; happiness might now be bought for a penny, and carried in the waistcoat pocket; portable ecstacies might be had corked up in a pint bottle, and peace of mind could be sent down in gallons by the mail coach. But if I talk in this way the reader will think I am laughing, and I can assure him that nobody will laugh long who deals much with opium; its pleasures even are of a grave and solemn complexion, and in his happiest state the opium-eater cannot present himself in the character of L'Allegro; even then he speaks and thinks as becomes Il Penseroso.[6] Nevertheless, I have a very reprehensible way of jesting at times in the midst of my own misery; and unless when I am checked by some more powerful feelings, I am afraid I shall be guilty of this indecent practice even in these annals of suffering or enjoyment.

---

[1] *manna* Biblical food that saved the Jews in their escape from Egypt; *ambrosia* Food of the Greek gods.

[2] *the stately Pantheon* From Wordsworth's "Power of Music" (3); London's Pantheon was then a concert hall.

[3] *sublunary* Earthly.

[4] [De Quincey's note] *Evanesced*: this way of going off the stage of life appears to have been well known in the 17th century, but at that time to have been considered a peculiar privilege of blood-royal, and by no means to be allowed to druggists. For about the year 1686 a poet of rather ominous name (and who, by-the-hye, did ample justice to his name), viz., Mr. *Flat-man*, in speaking of the death of Charles II expresses his surprise that any prince should commit so absurd an act as dying, because, says he, "Kings should disdain to die, and only *disappear*." They should *abscond*, that is, into the other world. [Cf. Thomas Flatman's *On the Death of Our Late Sovereign Lord King Charles II of Blessed Memory: A Pindarique Ode* (1685): "*Princes* (like the wondrous *Enoch*) should be free / From death's unbounded tyranny, / And when their godlike race is run, / And nothing glorious left undone, / Never submit to fate, but only disappear."]

[5] φαρμακον νήωενθες Greek: soothing and healing drug.

[6] *L'Allegro ... Il Penseroso* Poems by Milton (1645), whose titles mean "The Happy Man" and "The Brooding Man" respectively.

The reader must allow a little to my infirm nature in this respect; and with a few indulgences of that sort I shall endeavour to be as grave, if not drowsy, as fits a theme like opium, so antimercurial as it really is, and so drowsy as it is falsely reputed.

And first, one word with respect to its bodily effects; for upon all that has been hitherto written on the subject of opium, whether by travellers in Turkey (who may plead their privilege of lying as an old immemorial right), or by professors of medicine, writing *ex cathedra*,[1] I have but one emphatic criticism to pronounce—Lies! lies! lies! I remember once, in passing a book stall, to have caught these words from a page of some satiric author: "By this time I became convinced that the London newspapers spoke truth at least twice a week, viz., on Tuesday and Saturday,[2] and might safely be depended upon for—the list of bankrupts." In like manner, I do by no means deny that some truths have been delivered to the world in regard to opium. Thus it has been repeatedly affirmed by the learned that opium is a dusky brown in colour; and this, take notice, I grant. Secondly, that it is rather dear, which also I grant, for in my time East Indian opium has been three guineas a pound, and Turkey eight. And thirdly, that if you eat a good deal of it, most probably you must do what is particularly disagreeable to any man of regular habits, viz., die.[3] These weighty propositions are, all and singular, true; I cannot gainsay them, and truth ever was, and will be, commendable. But in these three theorems I believe we have exhausted the stock of knowledge as yet accumulated by men on the subject of opium. And therefore, worthy doctors, as there seems to

be room for further discoveries, stand aside, and allow me to come forward and lecture on this matter.

First, then, it is not so much affirmed as taken for granted, by all who ever mention opium, formally or incidentally, that it does or can produce intoxication. Now, reader, assure yourself, *meo periculo*,[4] that no quantity of opium ever did or could intoxicate. As to the tincture of opium (commonly called laudanum) *that* might certainly intoxicate if a man could bear to take enough of it, but why? Because it contains so much proof spirit, and not because it contains so much opium. But crude opium, I affirm peremptorily, is incapable of producing any state of body at all resembling that which is produced by alcohol, and not in *degree* only incapable, but even in *kind*; it is not in the quantity of its effects merely, but in the quality, that it differs altogether. The pleasure given by wine is always mounting and tending to a crisis, after which it declines; that from opium, when once generated, is stationary for eight or ten hours: the first, to borrow a technical distinction from medicine, is a case of acute—the second, the chronic pleasure; the one is a flame, the other a steady and equable glow. But the main distinction lies in this, that whereas wine disorders the mental faculties, opium, on the contrary (if taken in a proper manner), introduces amongst them the most exquisite order, legislation, and harmony. Wine robs a man of his self-possession; opium greatly invigorates it. Wine unsettles and clouds the judgment, and gives a preternatural brightness and a vivid exaltation to the contempts and the admirations, the loves and the hatreds of the drinker; opium, on the contrary, communicates serenity and equipoise to all the faculties, active or passive, and with respect to the temper and moral feelings in general it gives simply that sort of vital warmth which is approved by the judgment, and which would probably always accompany a bodily constitution of primeval or antediluvian[5] health. Thus, for instance, opium, like wine, gives an expansion to the heart and the benevolent affections; but then, with this remarkable difference, that in the sudden development of kind-

---

[1] *ex cathedra* With authority (from the Latin, meaning, literally, "from the chair," i.e., of a teacher or religious leader).

[2] *Tuesday and Saturday* Days on which the newspaper would publish a list of bankruptcies.

[3] [De Quincey's note] Of this, however, the learned appear latterly to have doubted; for in a pirated edition of Buchan's *Domestic Medicine*, which I once saw in the hands of a farmer's wife, who was studying it for the benefit of her health, the doctor was made to say—"Be particularly careful never to take above five-and-twenty *ounces* of laudanum [the liquid form of opium] at once;" the true reading being probably five-and-twenty *drops*, which are held equal to about one grain of crude opium.

[4] *meo periculo* Latin: at my risk.

[5] *antediluvian* Before the biblical flood, hence primitive.

heartedness which accompanies inebriation there is always more or less of a maudlin character, which exposes it to the contempt of the bystander. Men shake hands, swear eternal friendship, and shed tears, no mortal knows why; and the sensual creature is clearly uppermost. But the expansion of the beniguer feelings incident to opium is no febrile access, but a healthy restoration to that state which the mind would naturally recover upon the removal of any deep-seated irritation of pain that had disturbed and quarrelled with the impulses of a heart originally just and good. True it is that even wine, up to a certain point and with certain men, rather tends to exalt and to steady the intellect; I myself, who have never been a great wine drinker, used to find that half a dozen glasses of wine advantageously affected the faculties—brightened and intensified the consciousness, and gave to the mind a feeling of being "*ponderibus librata suis*;"[1] and certainly it is most absurdly said, in popular language, of any man that he is *disguised* in liquor; for, on the contrary, most men are disguised by sobriety, and it is when they are drinking (as some old gentleman says in Athenaeus), that men ἑαυτοὺς ἐμφανίζουσιν οἵτινες εἰσίν—display themselves in their true complexion of character, which surely is not disguising themselves. But still, wine constantly leads a man to the brink of absurdity and extravagance, and beyond a certain point it is sure to volatilize and to disperse the intellectual energies, whereas opium always seems to compose what had been agitated, and to concentrate what had been distracted. In short, to sum up all in one word, a man who is inebriated, or tending to inebriation, is, and feels that he is, in a condition which calls up into supremacy the merely human, too often the brutal part of his nature; but the opium-eater (I speak of him who is not suffering from any disease or other remote effects of opium) feels that the diviner part of his nature is paramount; that is, the moral affections are in a state of cloudless serenity, and overall is the great light of the majestic intellect.

This is the doctrine of the true church on the subject of opium, of which church I acknowledge myself to be the only member—the alpha and the omega;[2] but then it is to be recollected that I speak from the ground of a large and profound personal experience, whereas most of the unscientific[3] authors who have at all treated of opium, and even of those who have written expressly on the *materia medica*, make it evident, from the horror they express of it, that their experimental knowledge of its action is none at all. I will, however, candidly acknowledge that I have met with one person who bore evidence to its intoxicating power, such as staggered my own incredulity, for he was a surgeon, and had himself taken opium largely. I happened to say to him that his enemies (as I had heard) charged him with talking nonsense on politics, and that his friends apologized for him by suggesting that he was constantly in a state of intoxication from opium. Now the accusation, said I, is not *prima facie*[4] and of necessity an absurd one; but the defence *is*. To my surprise, however, he insisted that both his enemies and his friends were in the right. "I will maintain," said he, "that I *do* talk nonsense; and secondly, I will maintain that I do not talk nonsense upon principle, or with any view to profit, but solely

---

[1] *ponderibus librata suis* Latin: from Ovid's *Metamorphoses* (1.16): "[the earth, not] poised, did on its own foundations lie."

[2] *the alpha and the omega* The beginning and the end; from the first and last letters of the Greek alphabet.

[3] [De Quincey's note] Amongst the great herd of travellers, &c., who show sufficiently by their stupidity that they never held any intercourse with opium, I must caution my readers specially against the brilliant author [Thomas Hope] of *Anastasius* [(1819)]. This gentleman, whose wit would lead one to presume him an opium-eater, has made it impossible to consider him in that character, from the grievous misrepresentation which he gives of its effects at pp. 215–17 of vol. 1. Upon consideration it must appear such to the author himself, for, waiving the errors I have insisted on in the text, which (and others) are adopted in the fullest manner, he will himself admit that an old gentleman "with a snow-white beard," who eats "ample doses of opium," and is yet able to deliver what is meant and received as very weighty counsel on the bad effects of that practice, is but an indifferent evidence that opium either kills people prematurely or sends them into a madhouse. But for my part, I see into this old gentleman and his motives: the fact is, he was enamoured of "the little golden receptacle of the pernicious drug" which Anastasius carried about him; and no way of obtaining it so safe and so feasible occurred as that of frightening its owner out of his wits (which, by the bye, are none of the strongest). This commentary throws a new light upon the case, and greatly improves it as a story; for the old gentleman's speech, considered as a lecture on pharmacy, is highly absurd; but considered as a hoax on Anastasius, it reads excellently.

[4] *prima facie* Latin: on first impression.

and simply," said he, "solely and simply—solely and simply (repeating it three times over), because I am drunk with opium, and *that* daily." I replied that, as to the allegation of his enemies, as it seemed to be established upon such respectable testimony, seeing that the three parties concerned all agree in it, it did not become me to question it; but the defence set up I must demur to. He proceeded to discuss the matter, and to lay down his reasons; but it seemed to me so impolite to pursue an argument which must have presumed a man mistaken in a point belonging to his own profession, that I did not press him even when his course of argument seemed open to objection, not to mention that a man who talks nonsense, even though "with no view to profit," is not altogether the most agreeable partner in a dispute, whether as opponent or respondent. I confess, however, that the authority of a surgeon, and one who was reputed a good one, may seem a weighty one to my prejudice; but still I must plead my experience, which was greater than his greatest by 7,000 drops a day; and though it was not possible to suppose a medical man unacquainted with the characteristic symptoms of vinous intoxication, it yet struck me that he might proceed on a logical error of using the word intoxication with too great latitude, and extending it generically to all modes of nervous excitement, instead of restricting it as the expression for a specific sort of excitement connected with certain diagnostics. Some people have maintained in my hearing that they had been drunk upon green tea; and a medical student in London, for whose knowledge in his profession I have reason to feel great respect, assured me the other day that a patient in recovering from an illness had got drunk on a beefsteak.

Having dwelt so much on this first and leading error in respect to opium, I shall notice very briefly a second and a third, which are, that the elevation of spirits produced by opium is necessarily followed by a proportionate depression, and that the natural and even immediate consequence of opium is torpor and stagnation, animal and mental. The first of these errors I shall content myself with simply denying, assuring my reader that for ten years, during which I took opium at intervals, the day succeeding to that on which I allowed myself this luxury was always a day of unusually good spirits.

With respect to the torpor supposed to follow, or rather (if we were to credit the numerous pictures of Turkish opium-eaters) to accompany the practice of opium-eating, I deny that also. Certainly opium is classed under the head of narcotics, and some such effect it may produce in the end; but the primary effects of opium are always, and in the highest degree, to excite and stimulate the system. This first stage of its action always lasted with me, during my noviciate, for upwards of eight hours, so that it must be the fault of the opium-eater himself if he does not so time his exhibition of the dose (to speak medically) as that the whole weight of its narcotic influence may descend upon his sleep. Turkish opium-eaters, it seems, are absurd enough to sit, like so many equestrian statues, on logs of wood as stupid as themselves. But that the reader may judge of the degree in which opium is likely to stupefy the faculties of an Englishman, I shall (by way of treating the question illustratively, rather than argumentatively) describe the way in which I myself often passed an opium evening in London during the period between 1804–1812. It will be seen that at least opium did not move me to seek solitude, and much less to seek inactivity, or the torpid state of self-involution ascribed to the Turks. I give this account at the risk of being pronounced a crazy enthusiast or visionary, but I regard *that* little. I must desire my reader to bear in mind that I was a hard student, and at severe studies for all the rest of my time; and certainly I had a right occasionally to relaxations as well as other people. These, however, I allowed myself but seldom. …

Thus I have shown that opium does not of necessity produce inactivity or torpor, but that, on the contrary, it often led me into markets and theatres. Yet, in candour, I will admit that markets and theatres are not the appropriate haunts of the opium-eater when in the divinest state incident to his enjoyment. In that state, crowds become an oppression to him; music even, too sensual and gross. He naturally seeks solitude and silence, as indispensable conditions of those trances, or profoundest reveries, which are the crown and consummation of what opium can do for human nature. I, whose disease it was to meditate too much and to observe too little, and who upon my first entrance at college was nearly falling into a deep melancholy, from brooding too much on the sufferings which I had witnessed in London, was sufficiently aware of the tendencies of my own thoughts to do all I could to counteract them. I was, indeed, like a person who, according to the old legend, had entered the cave of Trophonius;[1] and the remedies I sought were to force myself into society, and to keep my understanding in continual activity upon matters of science. But for these remedies I should certainly have become hypochondriacally melancholy. In after years, however, when my cheerfulness was more fully re-established, I yielded to my natural inclination for a solitary life. And at that time I often fell into these reveries upon taking opium; and more than once it has happened to me, on a summer night, when I have been at an open window, in a room from which I could overlook the sea at a mile below me, and could command a view of the great town of L——, at about the same distance, that I have sat from sunset to sunrise, motionless, and without wishing to move. …

INTRODUCTION TO THE PAINS OF OPIUM

… I remember about this time a little incident, which I mention because, trifling as it was, the reader will soon meet it again in my dreams, which it influenced more fearfully than could be imagined. One day a Malay[2] knocked at my door. What business a Malay could have to transact amongst English mountains I cannot conjecture, but possibly he was on his road to a seaport about forty miles distant.

The servant who opened the door to him was a young girl, born and bred amongst the mountains, who had never seen an Asiatic dress of any sort; his turban therefore confounded her not a little; and as it turned out that his attainments in English were exactly of the same extent as hers in the Malay, there seemed to be an impassable gulf fixed between all communication of ideas, if either party had happened to possess any. In this dilemma, the girl, recollecting the reputed learning of her master (and doubtless giving me credit for a knowledge of all the languages of the earth besides perhaps a few of the lunar ones), came and gave me to understand that there was a sort of demon below, whom she clearly imagined that my art could exorcise from the house. I did not immediately go down, but when I did, the group which presented itself, arranged as it was by accident, though not very elaborate, took hold of my fancy and my eye in a way that none of the statuesque attitudes exhibited in the ballets at the opera house, though so ostentatiously complex, had ever done. In a cottage kitchen, but panelled on the wall with dark wood that from age and rubbing resembled oak, and looking more like a rustic hall of entrance than a kitchen, stood the Malay—his turban and loose trousers of dingy white relieved upon the dark panelling. He had placed himself nearer to the girl than she seemed to relish, though her native spirit of mountain intrepidity contended with the feeling of simple awe which her countenance expressed as she gazed upon the tiger cat before her. And a more striking picture there could not be imagined than the beautiful English face of the girl, and its exquisite fairness, together with her erect and independent attitude, contrasted with the sallow and bilious skin of the Malay, enamelled or veneered with mahogany by marine air, his small, fierce, restless eyes, thin lips, slavish gestures and adorations. Half hidden by the ferocious-looking Malay was a little child from a neighbouring cottage who had crept in after him, and was now in the act of reverting its head and gazing upwards at the turban and the fiery eyes beneath it, whilst with one hand he caught at the dress of the young woman for protection. My knowledge of the Oriental tongues is not remarkably extensive, being indeed confined to two words—the Arabic word for barley and the Turkish for opium (*madjoon*), which I have learned from *Anastasius*; and as I had neither a Malay dictionary nor even Adelung's *Mithridates*,[3] which might have

---

[1] *cave of Trophonius*   State of despair: in Greek mythology, Trophonius, who had killed his brother, was buried in a cave that became famous for its oracle that would overwhelm with melancholy all those who consulted it.

[2] *Malay*   Member of a people that inhabits Malaysia, Brunei, and parts of Indonesia.

[3] *Adelung's Mithridates*   German scholar Johann Christoph Adelung's *Mithridates, or General Linguistics* (1806–17), the first volume of which focuses on Asian languages.

helped me to a few words, I addressed him in some lines from the *Iliad*, considering that, of such languages as I possessed, Greek, in point of longitude, came geographically nearest to an Oriental one. He worshipped me in a most devout manner, and replied in what I suppose was Malay. In this way I saved my reputation with my neighbours, for the Malay had no means of betraying the secret. He lay down upon the floor for about an hour and then pursued his journey. On his departure I presented him with a piece of opium. To him, as an Orientalist, I concluded that opium must be familiar, and the expression of his face convinced me that it was. Nevertheless, I was struck with some little consternation when I saw him suddenly raise his hand to his mouth, and, to use the schoolboy phrase, bolt the whole, divided into three pieces, at one mouthful. The quantity was enough to kill three dragoons[1] and their horses, and I felt some alarm for the poor creature, but what could be done? I had given him the opium in compassion for his solitary life, on recollecting that if he had travelled on foot from London it must be nearly three weeks since he could have exchanged a thought with any human being. I could not think of violating the laws of hospitality by having him seized and drenched with an emetic, and thus frightening him into a notion that we were going to sacrifice him to some English idol. No, there was clearly no help for it. He took his leave, and for some days I felt anxious, but as I never heard of any Malay being found dead, I became convinced that he was used to opium,[2] and that I must have done him the service I designed by giving him one night of respite from the pains of wandering. …

---

[1] *dragoons* Mounted soldiers.

[2] [De Quincey's note]   This, however, is not a necessary conclusion; the varieties of effect produced by opium on different constitutions are infinite. A London magistrate (Harriott's *Struggles through Life*, vol. iii. p. 391, third edition) has recorded that, on the first occasion of his trying laudanum for the gout he took *forty* drops, the next night *sixty*, and on the fifth night *eighty*, without any effect whatever, and this at an advanced age. I have an anecdote from a country surgeon, however, which sinks Mr. Harriott's case into a trifle; and in my projected medical treatise on opium, which I will publish provided the College of Surgeons will pay me for enlightening their benighted understandings upon this subject, I will relate it; but it is far too good a story to be published gratis.

The Pains of Opium

—as when some great painter dips
His pencil in the gloom of earthquake and eclipse.
Shelley's *Revolt of Islam*.

Reader, who have thus far accompanied me, I must request your attention to a brief explanatory note on three points:

1. For several reasons I have not been able to compose the notes for this part of my narrative into any regular and connected shape. I give the notes disjointed as I find them, or have now drawn them up from memory. Some of them point to their own date, some I have dated, and some are undated. Whenever it could answer my purpose to transplant them from the natural or chronological order, I have not scrupled to do so. Sometimes I speak in the present, sometimes in the past tense. Few of the notes, perhaps, were written exactly at the period of time to which they relate; but this can little affect their accuracy, as the impressions were such that they can never fade from my mind. Much has been omitted. I could not, without effort, constrain myself to the task of either recalling, or constructing into a regular narrative, the whole burden of horrors which lies upon my brain. This feeling partly I plead in excuse, and partly that I am now in London, and am a helpless sort of person, who cannot even arrange his own papers without assistance; and I am separated from the hands which are wont to perform for me the offices of an amanuensis.[3]

2. You will think perhaps that I am too confidential and communicative of my own private history. It may be so. But my way of writing is rather to think aloud, and follow my own humors, than much to consider who is listening to me; and if I stop to consider what is proper to be said to this or that person, I shall soon come to doubt whether any part at all is proper. The fact is, I place myself at a distance of fifteen or twenty years ahead of this time, and suppose myself writing to those who will be interested about me hereafter; and wishing to have some record of time, the entire history of which no one can know but myself, I do it as fully as I am able with the efforts I am now capable of making, because I

---

[3] *amanuensis* Latin: scribe or secretary.

know not whether I can ever find time to do it again.

3. It will occur to you often to ask, why did I not release myself from the horrors of opium by leaving it off or diminishing it? To this I must answer briefly: it might be supposed that I yielded to the fascinations of opium too easily; it cannot be supposed that any man can be charmed by its terrors. The reader may be sure, therefore, that I made attempts innumerable to reduce the quantity. I add, that those who witnessed the agonies of those attempts, and not myself, were the first to beg me to desist. But could not have I reduced it a drop a day, or, by adding water, have bisected or trisected a drop? A thousand drops bisected would thus have taken nearly six years to reduce, and that way would certainly not have answered. But this is a common mistake of those who know nothing of opium experimentally; I appeal to those who do, whether it is not always found that down to a certain point it can be reduced with ease and even pleasure, but that after that point further reduction causes intense suffering. Yes, say many thoughtless persons, who know not what they are talking of, you will suffer a little low spirits and dejection for a few days. I answer, no; there is nothing like low spirits; on the contrary, the mere animal spirits are uncommonly raised; the pulse is improved; the health is better. It is not there that the suffering lies. It has no resemblance to the sufferings caused by renouncing wine. It is a state of unutterable irritation of stomach (which surely is not much like dejection), accompanied by intense perspirations, and feelings such as I shall not attempt to describe without more space at my command. ...

I now pass to what is the main subject of these latter confessions, to the history and journal of what took place in my dreams, for these were the immediate and proximate cause of my acutest suffering.

The first notice I had of any important change going on in this part of my physical economy was from the reawakening of a state of eye generally incident to childhood, or exalted states of irritability. I know not whether my reader is aware that many children, perhaps most, have a power of painting, as it were upon the darkness, all sorts of phantoms. In some that power is simply a mechanical affection of the eye; others have a voluntary or semi-voluntary power to dismiss or to summon them, or, as a child once said to me when I questioned him on this matter, "I can tell them to go, and they go; but sometimes they come when I don't tell them to come." Whereupon I told him that he had almost as unlimited a command over apparitions as a Roman centurion over his soldiers. In the middle of 1817, I think it was, that this faculty became positively distressing to me: at night, when I lay awake in bed, vast processions passed along in mournful pomp; friezes of never-ending stories, that to my feelings were as sad and solemn as if they were stories drawn from times before Oedipus or Priam, before Tyre, before Memphis.[1] And at the same time a corresponding change took place in my dreams; a theater seemed suddenly opened and lighted up within my brain, which presented nightly spectacles of more than earthly splendour. And the four following facts may be mentioned as noticeable at this time:

1. That as the creative state of the eye increased, a sympathy seemed to arise between the waking and the dreaming states of the brain in one point—that whatsoever I happened to call up and to trace by a voluntary act upon the darkness was very apt to transfer itself to my dreams, so that I feared to exercise this faculty, for, as Midas turned all things to gold that yet baffled his hopes and defrauded his human desires,[2] so whatsoever things capable of being visually represented I did but think of in the darkness, immediately shaped themselves into phantoms of the eye; and by a process apparently no less inevitable, when thus once traced in faint and visionary colours, like writings in sympathetic[3] ink, they were drawn out by the fierce chemistry of my dreams into insufferable splendour that fretted my heart.

2. For this and all other changes in my dreams were accompanied by deep-seated anxiety and gloomy melancholy, such as are wholly incommunicable by words. I

---

[1] *Oedipus* King of Thebes, a city in ancient Egypt; *Priam* King of Troy, a city in ancient Greece; *Tyre* Ancient city of Phoenicia, now Lebanon; *Memphis* Capital of ancient Egypt.

[2] *Midas ... desires* The Greek god Dionysus granted King Midas his wish that everything he touched be turned to gold; the king was devastated when his food, wine, and eventually his daughter were all turned to gold.

[3] *sympathetic* Invisible.

seemed every night to descend, not metaphorically, but literally to descend, into chasms and sunless abysses, depths below depths, from which it seemed hopeless that I could ever re-ascend. Nor did I, by waking, feel that I *had* re-ascended. This I do not dwell upon because the state of gloom which attended these gorgeous spectacles, amounting at last to utter darkness, as of some suicidal despondency, cannot be approached by words.

3. The sense of space, and in the end the sense of time, were both powerfully affected. Buildings, landscapes, &c., were exhibited in proportions so vast as the bodily eye is not fitted to receive. Space swelled and was amplified to an extent of unutterable infinity. This, however, did not disturb me so much as the vast expansion of time; I sometimes seemed to have lived for 70 or 100 years in one night— nay, sometimes had feelings representative of a millennium passed in that time, or, however, of a duration far beyond the limits of any human experience.

4. The minutest incidents of childhood, or forgotten scenes of later years, were often revived; I could not be said to recollect them, for if I had been told of them when waking, I should not have been able to acknowledge them as parts of my past experience. But placed as they were before me, in dreams like intuitions, and clothed in all their evanescent circumstances and accompanying feelings, I *recognized* them instantaneously. I was once told by a near relative of mine, that having in her childhood fallen into a river, and being on the very verge of death but for the critical assistance which reached her, she saw in a moment her whole life, in its minutest incidents, arrayed before her simultaneously as in a mirror; and she had a faculty developed as suddenly for comprehending the whole and every part. This, from some opium experiences of mine, I can believe; I have indeed seen the same thing asserted twice in modern books, and accompanied by a remark which I am convinced is true, viz., that the dread book of account which the Scriptures speak of[1] is in fact the mind itself of each individual. Of this at least I feel assured, that there is no such thing as *forgetting* possible to the mind; a thousand accidents may and will interpose a veil between our present consciousness and the secret inscriptions on the mind; accidents of the same sort will also rend away this veil; but alike, whether veiled or unveiled, the inscription remains forever, just as the stars seem to withdraw before the common light of day, whereas in fact we all know that it is the light which is drawn over them as a veil, and that they are waiting to be revealed when the obscuring daylight shall have withdrawn. …

May 1818

The Malay has been a fearful enemy for months. I have been every night, through his means, transported into Asiatic scenes. I know not whether others share in my feelings on this point, but I have often thought that if I were compelled to forego England and to live in China, and among Chinese manners and modes of life and scenery, I should go mad. The causes of my horror lie deep, and some of them must be common to others. Southern Asia in general is the seat of awful images and associations. As the cradle of the human race, it would alone have a dim and reverential feeling connected with it. But there are other reasons. No man can pretend that the wild, barbarous, and capricious superstitions of Africa, or of savage tribes elsewhere, affect him in the way that he is affected by the ancient, monumental, cruel, and elaborate religions of Indostan, &c. The mere antiquity of Asiatic things, of their institutions, histories, modes of faith, &c., is so impressive, that to me the vast age of the race and name overpowers the sense of youth in the individual. A young Chinese seems to me an antediluvian man renewed. Even Englishmen, though not bred in any knowledge of such institutions, cannot but shudder at the mystic sublimity of *castes* that have flowed apart, and refused to mix, through such immemorial tracts of time; nor can any man fail to be awed by the names of the Ganges or the Euphrates.[2] It

---

[1]   *dread … speak of*   Cf. Revelation 20.12: "I saw the dead, small and great, stand before God; and the books were opened: and another book was opened, which is the book of life: and the dead were judged out of those things which were written in the books, according to their works."

[2]   *Ganges or the Euphrates*   Major rivers of Asia.

contributes much to these feelings that southern Asia is, and has been for thousands of years, the part of the earth most swarming with human life, the great *officina gentium*.[1] Man is a weed in those regions. The vast empires also in which the enormous population of Asia has always been cast, give a further sublimity to the feelings associated with all Oriental names or images. In China, over and above what it has in common with the rest of southern Asia, I am terrified by the modes of life, by the manners, and the barrier of utter abhorrence and want of sympathy placed between us by feelings deeper than I can analyse. I could sooner live with lunatics or brute animals. All this, and much more than I can say or have time to say, the reader must enter into before he can comprehend the unimaginable horror which these dreams of Oriental imagery and mythological tortures impressed upon me. Under the connecting feeling of tropical heat and vertical sunlights I brought together all creatures, birds, beasts, reptiles, all trees and plants, usages and appearances, that are found in all tropical regions, and assembled them together in China or Indostan. From kindred feelings, I soon brought Egypt and all her gods under the same law. I was stared at, hooted at, grinned at, chattered at, by monkeys, by parroquets,[2] by cockatoos. I ran into pagodas, and was fixed for centuries at the summit or in secret rooms. I was the idol; I was the priest; I was worshipped; I was sacrificed. I fled from the wrath of Brama through all the forests of Asia; Vishnu hated me. Seeva[3] laid wait for me. I came suddenly upon Isis and Osiris. I had done a deed, they said, which the ibis and the crocodile[4] trembled at. I was buried for a thousand years in stone coffins, with mummies and sphinxes, in narrow chambers at the heart of eternal pyramids. I was kissed, with cancerous kisses, by crocodiles, and laid, confounded with all unutterable slimy things, amongst reeds and Nilotic mud.[5]

[1] *officina gentium*   Latin: factory of nations.

[2] *parroquets*   I.e., parakeets.

[3] *Brama ... Seeva*   The Hindu triad: the gods Brahma, Vishnu, and Shiva.

[4] *Isis ... crocodile*   Isis and Osiris were deities of ancient Egypt; Thoth, in the shape of an ibis, and Sobek, a crocodile, were also Egyptian gods.

[5] *Nilotic mud*   I.e., mud of the river Nile.

I thus give the reader some slight abstraction of my Oriental dreams, which always filled me with such amazement at the monstrous scenery that horror seemed absorbed for a while in sheer astonishment. Sooner or later came a reflux of feeling that swallowed up the astonishment, and left me not so much in terror as in hatred and abomination of what I saw. Over every form, and threat, and punishment, and dim sightless incarceration, brooded a sense of eternity and infinity that drove me into an oppression as of madness. Into these dreams only it was, with one or two slight exceptions, that any circumstances of physical horror entered. All before had been moral and spiritual terrors. But here the main agents were ugly birds, or snakes, or crocodiles, especially the last. The cursed crocodile became to me the object of more horror than almost all the rest. I was compelled to live with him, and (as was always the case almost in my dreams) for centuries. I escaped sometimes, and found myself in Chinese houses, with cane tables, &c. All the feet of the tables, sofas, &c., soon became instinct with life; the abominable head of the crocodile, and his leering eyes, looked out at me, multiplied into a thousand repetitions, and I stood loathing and fascinated. And so often did this hideous reptile haunt my dreams that many times the very same dream was broken up in the very same way: I heard gentle voices speaking to me (I hear everything when I am sleeping), and instantly I awoke. It was broad noon, and my children were standing, hand in hand, at my bedside—come to show me their coloured shoes, or new frocks, or to let me see them dressed for going out. I protest that so awful was the transition from the damned crocodile, and the other unutterable monsters and abortions of my dreams, to the sight of innocent *human* natures and of infancy, that in the mighty and sudden revulsion of mind I wept, and could not forbear it, as I kissed their faces.

June 1819

I have had occasion to remark, at various periods of my life, that the deaths of those whom we love, and indeed the contemplation of death generally, is (*caeteris paribus*)[1] more affecting in summer than in any other season of the year. And the reasons are these three, I think: first, that the visible heavens in summer appear far higher, more distant, and (if such a solecism may be excused) more infinite; the clouds, by which chiefly the eye expounds the distance of the blue pavilion stretched over our heads, are in summer more voluminous, massed and accumulated in far grander and more towering piles. Secondly, the light and the appearances of the declining and the setting sun are much more fitted to be types and characters of the Infinite. And thirdly (which is the main reason), the exuberant and riotous prodigality of life naturally forces the mind more powerfully upon the antagonist thought of death, and the wintry sterility of the grave. For it may be observed generally, that wherever two thoughts stand related to each other by a law of antagonism, and exist, as it were, by mutual repulsion, they are apt to suggest each other. On these accounts it is that I find it impossible to banish the thought of death when I am walking alone in the endless days of summer; and any particular death, if not more affecting, at least haunts my mind more obstinately and besiegingly in that season. Perhaps this cause, and a slight incident which I omit, might have been the immediate occasions of the following dream, to which, however, a predisposition must always have existed in my mind; but having been once roused it never left me, and split into a thousand fantastic varieties, which often suddenly reunited, and composed again the original dream.

I thought that it was a Sunday morning in May, that it was Easter Sunday, and as yet very early in the morning. I was standing, as it seemed to me, at the door of my own cottage. Right before me lay the very scene which could really be commanded from that situation, but exalted, as was usual, and solemnized by the power of dreams. There were the same mountains, and the same lovely valley at their feet; but the mountains were raised to more than Alpine height, and there was interspace far larger between them of meadows and forest lawns; the hedges were rich with white roses, and no living creature was to be seen, excepting that in the green churchyard there were cattle tranquilly reposing upon the verdant graves, and particularly round about the grave of a child whom I had tenderly loved, just as I had really beheld them, a little before sunrise in the same summer, when that child died. I gazed upon the well-known scene, and I said aloud (as I thought) to myself, "It yet wants much of sunrise, and it is Easter Sunday; and that is the day on which they celebrate the first fruits of resurrection. I will walk abroad; old griefs shall be forgotten today, for the air is cool and still, and the hills are high and stretch away to heaven; and the forest glades are as quiet as the churchyard, and with the dew I can wash the fever from my forehead, and then I shall be unhappy no longer." And I turned as if to open my garden gate, and immediately I saw upon the left a scene far different, but which yet the power of dreams had reconciled into harmony with the other. The scene was an Oriental one, and there also it was Easter Sunday, and very early in the morning. And at a vast distance were visible, as a stain upon the horizon, the domes and cupolas of a great city—an image or faint abstraction, caught perhaps in childhood from some picture of Jerusalem. And not a bowshot[2] from me, upon a stone and shaded by Judean palms, there sat a woman, and I looked, and it was—Ann! She fixed her eyes upon me earnestly, and I said to her at length: "So, then, I have found you at last." I waited, but she answered me not a word. Her face was the same as when I saw it last, and yet again how different! Seventeen years ago, when the lamplight fell upon her face, as for the last time I kissed her lips (lips, Ann, that to me were not polluted), her eyes were streaming with tears; the tears were now wiped away; she seemed more beautiful than she was at that time, but in all other points the same, and not older. Her looks were tranquil, but with unusual solemnity of expression, and I now gazed upon her with some awe; but suddenly her countenance grew dim, and turning to the mountains I perceived vapours rolling between us. In a moment all had vanished, thick darkness came on, and in the twinkling of an eye I was far away from mountains, and by lamplight in Oxford Street, walking again with Ann—just as we walked seventeen years before, when we were both children.

---

[1] *caeteris paribus* Latin: other things being equal.

[2] *bowshot* Measurement of distance: the span an arrow will fly from the bow.

As a final specimen, I cite one of a different character, from 1820.

The dream commenced with a music which now I often heard in dreams—a music of preparation and of awakening suspense, a music like the opening of the Coronation Anthem, and which, like *that*, gave the feeling of a vast march, of infinite cavalcades filing off, and the tread of innumerable armies. The morning was come of a mighty day—a day of crisis and of final hope for human nature, then suffering some mysterious eclipse, and labouring in some dread extremity. Somewhere, I knew not where—somehow, I knew not how—by some beings, I knew not whom—a battle, a strife, an agony, was conducting, was evolving like a great drama or piece of music, with which my sympathy was the more insupportable from my confusion as to its place, its cause, its nature, and its possible issue. I, as is usual in dreams (where of necessity we make ourselves central to every movement), had the power, and yet had not the power, to decide it. I had the power, if I could raise myself to will it, and yet again had not the power, for the weight of twenty Atlantics was upon me, or the oppression of inexpiable guilt. "Deeper than ever plummet sounded,"[1] I lay inactive. Then like a chorus the passion deepened. Some greater interest was at stake, some mightier cause than ever yet the sword had pleaded, or trumpet had proclaimed. Then came sudden alarms, hurryings to and fro, trepidations of innumerable fugitives—I knew not whether from the good cause or the bad, darkness and lights, tempest and human faces, and at last, with the sense that all was lost, female forms, and the features that were worth all the world to me, and but a moment allowed—and clasped hands, and heartbreaking partings, and then—everlasting farewells! And with a sigh, such as the caves of Hell sighed when the incestuous mother uttered the abhorred name of death,[2] the sound was reverberated—everlasting farewells! And again and yet again reverberated—everlasting farewells!

And I awoke in struggles, and cried aloud—"I will sleep no more."[3]

But I am now called upon to wind up a narrative which has already extended to an unreasonable length. Within more spacious limits the materials which I have used might have been better unfolded, and much which I have not used might have been added with effect. Perhaps, however, enough has been given. It now remains that I should say something of the way in which this conflict of horrors was finally brought to a crisis. The reader is already aware (from a passage near the beginning of the introduction to the first part) that the opium-eater has, in some way or other, "unwound almost to its final links the accursed chain which bound him." By what means? To have narrated this according to the original intention would have far exceeded the space which can now be allowed. It is fortunate, as such a cogent reason exists for abridging it, that I should, on a maturer view of the case, have been exceedingly unwilling to injure, by any such unaffecting details, the impression of the history itself, as an appeal to the prudence and the conscience of the yet unconfirmed opium-eater—or even (though a very inferior consideration) to injure its effect as a composition. The interest of the judicious reader will not attach itself chiefly to the subject of the fascinating spells, but to the fascinating power. Not the opium-eater, but the opium, is the true hero of the tale, and the legitimate centre on which the interest revolves. The object was to display the marvellous agency of opium, whether for pleasure or for pain; if that is done, the action of the piece has closed.

However, as some people, in spite of all laws to the contrary, will persist in asking what became of the opium-eater, and in what state he now is, I answer for him thus: The reader is aware that opium had long ceased to found its empire on spells of pleasure; it was solely by the tortures connected with the attempt to abjure it that it kept its hold. Yet, as other tortures, no less it may be thought, attended the non-abjuration of such a tyrant, a choice only of evils was left; and *that*

---

[1] *Deeper ... sounded*   From Shakespeare's *The Tempest* 3.3.115.

[2] *incestuous ... death*   In Milton's *Paradise Lost* 2.787–89, Sin, the daughter of Satan, fled and: "cried out DEATH! / Hell trembled at the hideous name, and sighed / From all her caves, and back resounded, DEATH!"

[3] *I will sleep no more*   From Shakespeare's *Macbeth* 2.2.46, in which the guilt-ridden Macbeth says: "Methought I heard a voice cry 'Sleep no more!'"

might as well have been adopted which, however terrific in itself, held out a prospect of final restoration to happiness. This appears true, but good logic gave the author no strength to act upon it. However, a crisis arrived for the author's life, and a crisis for other objects still dearer to him—and which will always be far dearer to him than his life, even now that it is again a happy one. I saw that I must die if I continued the opium. I determined, therefore, if that should be required, to die in throwing it off. How much I was at that time taking I cannot say, for the opium which I used had been purchased for me by a friend, who afterwards refused to let me pay him, so that I could not ascertain even what quantity I had used within the year. I apprehend, however, that I took it very irregularly, and that I varied from about fifty or sixty grains to 150 a day. My first task was to reduce it to forty, to thirty, and as fast as I could to twelve grains.

I triumphed. But think not, reader, that therefore my sufferings were ended, nor think of me as of one sitting in a *dejected* state. Think of me as one, even when four months had passed, still agitated, writhing, throbbing, palpitating, shattered, and much perhaps in the situation of him who has been racked, as I collect the torments of that state from the affecting account of them left by a most innocent sufferer[1] of the times of James I. Meantime, I derived no benefit from any medicine, except one prescribed to me by an Edinburgh surgeon of great eminence, viz., ammoniated tincture of valerian. Medical account, therefore, of my emancipation I have not much to give, and even that little, as managed by a man so ignorant of medicine as myself, would probably tend only to mislead. At all events, it would be misplaced in this situation. The moral of the narrative is addressed to the opium-eater, and therefore of necessity limited in its application. If he is taught to

fear and tremble, enough has been effected. But he may say that the issue of my case is at least a proof that opium, after a seventeen years' use and an eight years' abuse of its powers, may still be renounced, and that *he* may chance to bring to the task greater energy than I did, or that with a stronger constitution than mine he may obtain the same results with less. This may be true. I would not presume to measure the efforts of other men by my own. I heartily wish him more energy. I wish him the same success. Nevertheless, I had motives external to myself which he may unfortunately want, and these supplied me with conscientious supports which mere personal interests might fail to supply to a mind debilitated by opium.

Jeremy Taylor[2] conjectures that it may be as painful to be born as to die. I think it probable; and during the whole period of diminishing the opium I had the torments of a man passing out of one mode of existence into another. The issue was not death, but a sort of physical regeneration; and I may add that ever since, at intervals, I have had a restoration of more than youthful spirits, though under the pressure of difficulties which in a less happy state of mind I should have called misfortunes.

One memorial of my former condition still remains—my dreams are not yet perfectly calm; the dread swell and agitation of the storm have not wholly subsided; the legions that encamped in them are drawing off, but not all departed; my sleep is still tumultuous, and, like the gates of Paradise to our first parents when looking back from afar, it is still (in the tremendous line of Milton)

With dreadful faces thronged, and fiery arms.[3]

—1821

[1] [De Quincey's note] William Lithgow. His book (*Travels*, &c.) is ill and pedantically written; but the account of his own sufferings on the rack at Malaga is overpoweringly affecting. [Lithgow was tortured in Malaga, Spain, after being accused of being a spy for King James I, who reigned from 1604 to 1625.]

[2] *Jeremy Taylor* English bishop, theologian, and author (1613–67).
[3] *With dreadful ... arms* From Milton's *Paradise Lost* (12.644).

MARY PRINCE
1788 – after 1833

"I will say the truth to the English people," declared the abolitionist Mary Prince, whose autobiography detailing her life in the West Indies is the earliest extant slave narrative by a woman. Published at a crucial moment in the campaign to end slavery in British possessions, *The History of Mary Prince* represents an important contribution to the abolitionist movement, as well as a work of historical and literary interest in its own right.

Mary Prince was born into bondage in the British colony of Bermuda, where for the first twelve years of her life she was, relatively speaking, spared the cruelty that dominated her adult years. Both her parents were also enslaved, the property of Charles Myners. After Myners died, Mary and her mother were sold to a Captain Williams, whose daughter Betsey treated Mary with racist condescension, but with relative compassion. Williams sold Prince to another family to raise money for his marriage, and in 1806 she was sent to work in the salt ponds of Turks Island: "This work was perfectly new to me. I was given a half barrel and shovel, and had to stand up to my knees in the water, from four o'clock in the morning till nine, when we were given some Indian corn boiled in water, which we were obliged to swallow as fast as we could for fear the rain should come on and melt the salt." In addition to these intolerable working conditions, Prince also endured physical and probably sexual abuse from her master.

In 1818, Prince was sold for three hundred dollars to John Wood, a plantation owner in Antigua, who beat, overworked, and otherwise abused her. By this time Prince had developed a serious skin problem, and while working for the Woods she became essentially crippled by severe rheumatism; her mistreatment would also eventually lead to damaged eyesight. Prince began attending meetings held at the Moravian Church, where various women taught her to read: "After we had done spelling, we tried to read in the Bible. After reading was over, the missionary gave out a hymn for us to sing." Prince was married in this church to Daniel Jones, a formerly enslaved man who had purchased his own freedom. Wood horsewhipped Prince when he discovered the marriage. In 1828 Wood took Prince to London as his servant. Abolitionist sympathizers helped her escape (which they were able to do because slavery was illegal in England), and she found employment as a domestic servant of Thomas Pringle, a Methodist and secretary of the Society for the Abolition of Slavery.

Pringle encouraged Prince to tell the story of her life and, in 1831, he arranged for the publication of her book, *The History of Mary Prince, a West Indian Slave, Related by Herself.* In his "Preface" to the work, Pringle wrote: "The idea of writing Mary Prince's history was first suggested by herself. She wished it to be done, she said, that good people in England might hear from a slave what a slave had felt and suffered." Mary Prince told her story to Susanna Strickland (later Moodie), who recorded it in writing. It seems improbable that Strickland—who would later come to be regarded as one of Canada's most accomplished writers in the nineteenth century—would not at a minimum have edited the dictated narrative for grammar and syntax, and some have suggested that Pringle may have had some hand in shaping the manuscript so as to better serve abolitionist ends. (His insistence that the rhetorical flourish at the end of Prince's first paragraph is "given verbatim as uttered by Mary Prince" has struck more than one reader as rather forced.) But most scholars have stopped short of suggesting that material was fabricated by Pringle and Strickland, or that this is not in essence Prince's own narrative. Strickland herself attested that she had "been writing Mr. Pringle's black Mary's life from her own dictation and for her benefit adhering to her own simple story and language without deviating to the paths of flourish or romance."

The book was a great success, and gave rise to considerable controversy. *Blackwood's Magazine* and *The Glasgow Courier* claimed it was fraudulent and propagandistic. A number of libel suits resulted, with Wood suing Pringle and Pringle counter-suing. Wood claimed that the book had "endeavored to injure the character of my family by the most vile and infamous falsehoods." Wood lost the case, and the libel scandal served only to make Prince's work more widely known. It reached a third edition in the same year it was published, and it has since that time retained its place as one of the most moving, detailed, and comprehensive narratives of the life of a slave.

Slavery was legally abolished in almost all British colonies in 1833. Little is known of Prince's life after the publication of her *History*, and we do not know when, where, or how she died.

⌘ ⌘ ⌘

The History of Mary Prince
A West Indian Slave
Related by Herself

PREFACE [BY THOMAS PRINGLE][1]

The idea of writing Mary Prince's history was first suggested by herself. She wished it to be done, she said, that good people in England might hear from a slave what a slave had felt and suffered; and a letter of her late master's, which will be found in the Supplement, induced me to accede to her wish without farther delay. The more immediate object of the publication will afterwards appear.

The narrative was taken down from Mary's own lips by a lady who happened to be at the time residing in my family as a visitor. It was written out fully, with all the narrator's repetitions and prolixities,[2] and afterwards pruned into its present shape; retaining, as far as was practicable, Mary's exact expressions and peculiar phraseology. No fact of importance has been omitted, and not a single circumstance or sentiment has been added. It is essentially her own, without any material alteration farther than was requisite to exclude redundances and gross grammatical errors, so as to render it clearly intelligible.

After it had been thus written out, I went over the whole, carefully examining her on every fact and circumstance detailed; and in all that relates to her residence in Antigua I had the advantage of being assisted in this scrutiny by Mr. Joseph Phillips, who was a resident in that colony during the same period, and had known her there.

The names of all the persons mentioned by the narrator have been printed in full, except those of Capt. I— and his wife, and that of Mr. D—, to whom conduct of peculiar atrocity is ascribed. These three individuals are now gone to answer at a far more awful tribunal than that of public opinion, for the deeds of which their former bondwoman accuses them; and to hold them up more openly to human reprobation could no longer affect themselves, while it might deeply lacerate the feelings of their surviving and perhaps innocent relatives, without any commensurate public advantage.

Without detaining the reader with remarks on other points which will be adverted to more conveniently in the Supplement, I shall here merely notice farther, that the Anti-Slavery Society have no concern whatever with this publication, nor are they in any degree responsible for the statements it contains. I have published the tract, not as their Secretary, but in my private capacity; and any profits that may arise from the sale will be exclusively appropriated to the benefit of Mary Prince herself.

THOMAS PRINGLE

---

[1] *THOMAS PRINGLE* Poet and abolitionist Thomas Pringle (1789–1834) was born in Scotland and lived in South Africa between 1820 and 1826, where he published a newspaper and a magazine. In 1826 he returned to England, where he devoted himself to the antislavery movement as secretary to the Society for the Abolition of Slavery.

[2] *prolixities* Instances of wordiness.

7, Solly Terrace, Claremont Square,
January 25, 1831

P.S. Since writing the above, I have been furnished by my friend Mr. George Stephen, with the interesting narrative of Asa-Asa, a captured African, now under his protection; and have printed it as a suitable appendix to this little history.

T.P.

The History of Mary Prince

I was born at Brackish-Pond, in Bermuda, on a farm belonging to Mr. Charles Myners. My mother was a household slave; and my father, whose name was Prince, was a sawyer[1] belonging to Mr. Trimmingham, a ship-builder at Crow-Lane. When I was an infant, old Mr. Myners died, and there was a division of the slaves and other property among the family. I was bought along with my mother by old Captain Darrel, and given to his grandchild, little Miss Betsey Williams. Captain Williams, Mr. Darrel's son-in-law, was master of a vessel which traded to several places in America and the West Indies, and he was seldom at home long together.

Mrs. Williams was a kind-hearted good woman, and she treated all her slaves well. She had only one daughter, Miss Betsey, for whom I was purchased, and who was about my own age. I was made quite a pet of by Miss Betsey, and loved her very much. She used to lead me about by the hand, and call me her little nigger. This was the happiest period of my life; for I was too young to understand rightly my condition as a slave, and too thoughtless and full of spirits to look forward to the days of toil and sorrow.

My mother was a household slave in the same family. I was under her own care, and my little brothers and sisters were my play-fellows and companions. My mother had us several fine children after she came to Mrs. Williams, three girls and two boys. The tasks given out to us children were light, and we used to play together with Miss Betsey, with as much freedom almost as if she had been our sister.

My master, however, was a very harsh, selfish man; and we always dreaded his return from sea. His wife was herself much afraid of him; and, during his stay at home, seldom dared to show her usual kindness to the slaves. He often left her, in the most distressed circumstances, to reside in other female society, at some place in the West Indies of which I have forgot the name. My poor mistress bore his ill-treatment with great patience, and all her slaves loved and pitied her. I was truly attached to her, and, next to my own mother, loved her better than any creature in the world. My obedience to her commands was cheerfully given: it sprung solely from the affection I felt for her, and not from fear of the power which the white people's law had given her over me.

I had scarcely reached my twelfth year when my mistress became too poor to keep so many of us at home; and she hired me out to Mrs. Pruden, a lady who lived about five miles off, in the adjoining parish, in a large house near the sea. I cried bitterly at parting with my dear mistress and Miss Betsey, and when I kissed my mother and brothers and sisters, I thought my young heart would break, it pained me so. But there was no help; I was forced to go. Good Mrs. Williams comforted me by saying that I should still be near the home I was about to quit, and might come over and see her and my kindred whenever I could obtain leave of absence from Mrs. Pruden. A few hours after this I was taken to a strange house, and found myself among strange people. This separation seemed a sore trial to me then; but oh! 'twas light, light to the trials I have since endured!—'twas nothing—nothing to be mentioned with them; but I was a child then, and it was according to my strength.

I knew that Mrs. Williams could no longer maintain me; that she was fain to part with me for my food and clothing; and I tried to submit myself to the change. My new mistress was a passionate woman; but yet she did not treat me very unkindly. I do not remember her striking me but once, and that was for going to see Mrs. Williams when I heard she was sick, and staying longer than she had given me leave to do. All my employment

---

[1] *sawyer* Worker whose job it is to saw timber.

at this time was nursing a sweet baby, little Master Daniel; and I grew so fond of my nursling that it was my greatest delight to walk out with him by the sea-shore, accompanied by his brother and sister, Miss Fanny and Master James.—Dear Miss Fanny! She was a sweet, kind young lady, and so fond of me that she wished me to learn all that she knew herself; and her method of teaching me was as follows:—Directly she had said her lessons to her grandmamma, she used to come running to me, and make me repeat them one by one after her; and in a few months I was able not only to say my letters but to spell many small words. But this happy state was not to last long. Those days were too pleasant to last. My heart always softens when I think of them.

At this time Mrs. Williams died. I was told suddenly of her death, and my grief was so great that, forgetting I had the baby in my arms, I ran away directly to my poor mistress's house; but reached it only in time to see the corpse carried out. Oh, that was a day of sorrow—a heavy day! All the slaves cried. My mother cried and lamented her sore; and I (foolish creature!) vainly entreated them to bring my dear mistress back to life. I knew nothing rightly about death then, and it seemed a hard thing to bear. When I thought about my mistress I felt as if the world was all gone wrong; and for many days and weeks I could think of nothing else. I returned to Mrs. Pruden's; but my sorrow was too great to be comforted, for my own dear mistress was always in my mind. Whether in the house or abroad, my thoughts were always talking to me about her.

I stayed at Mrs. Pruden's about three months after this; I was then sent back to Mr. Williams to be sold. Oh, that was a sad sad time! I recollect the day well. Mrs. Pruden came to me and said, "Mary, you will have to go home directly; your master is going to be married, and he means to sell you and two of your sisters to raise money for the wedding." Hearing this I burst out a crying,—though I was then far from being sensible of the full weight of my misfortune, or of the misery that waited for me. Besides, I did not like to leave Mrs. Pruden, and the dear baby, who had grown very fond of me. For some time I could scarcely believe that Mrs.

Pruden was in earnest, till I received orders for my immediate return.—Dear Miss Fanny! how she cried at parting with me, whilst I kissed and hugged the baby, thinking I should never see him again. I left Mrs. Pruden's, and walked home with a heart full of sorrow. The idea of being sold away from my mother and Miss Betsey was so frightful, that I dared not trust myself to think about it. We had been bought of Mrs. Myners, as I have mentioned, by Miss Betsey's grandfather, and given to her, so that we were by right *her* property, and I never thought we should be separated or sold away from her.

When I reached the house, I went in directly to Miss Betsey. I found her in great distress; and she cried out as soon as she saw me, "Oh, Mary! my father is going to sell you all to raise money to marry that wicked woman. You are *my* slaves, and he has no right to sell you; but it is all to please her." She then told me that my mother was living with her father's sister at a house close by, and I went there to see her. It was a sorrowful meeting; and we lamented with a great and sore crying our unfortunate situation. "Here comes one of my poor piccaninnies!"[1] she said, the moment I came in, "one of the poor slave-brood who are to be sold tomorrow."

Oh dear! I cannot bear to think of that day,—it is too much.—It recalls the great grief that filled my heart, and the woeful thoughts that passed to and fro through my mind, whilst listening to the pitiful words of my poor mother, weeping for the loss of her children. I wish I could find words to tell you all I then felt and suffered. The great God above alone knows the thoughts of the poor slave's heart, and the bitter pains which follow such separations as these. All that we love taken away from us—oh, it is sad, sad! and sore to be borne!—I got no sleep that night for thinking of the morrow; and dear Miss Betsey was scarcely less distressed. She could not bear to part with her old playmates and she cried sore and would not be pacified.

The black morning at length came; it came too soon for my poor mother and us. Whilst she was putting on

---

[1] *piccaninnies* Children, usually applied derogatively to Black children.

us the new osnaburgs[1] in which we were to be sold, she said, in a sorrowful voice, (I shall never forget it!) "See, I am *shrouding* my poor children; what a task for a mother!"—She then called Miss Betsey to take leave of us. "I am going to carry my little chickens to market," (these were her very words) "take your last look of them; may be you will see them no more." "Oh, my poor slaves! my own slaves!" said dear Miss Betsey, "you belong to me; and it grieves my heart to part with you."—Miss Betsey kissed us all, and, when she left us, my mother called the rest of the slaves to bid us good bye. One of them, a woman named Moll, came with her infant in her arms. "Ay!" said my mother, seeing her turn away and look at her child with the tears in her eyes, "your turn will come next." The slaves could say nothing to comfort us; they could only weep and lament with us. When I left my dear little brothers and the house in which I had been brought up, I thought my heart would burst.

Our mother, weeping as she went, called me away with the children Hannah and Dinah, and we took the road that led to Hamble Town, which we reached about four o'clock in the afternoon. We followed my mother to the market-place, where she placed us in a row against a large house, with our backs to the wall and our arms folded across our breasts. I, as the eldest, stood first, Hannah next to me, then Dinah; and our mother stood beside, crying over us. My heart throbbed with grief and terror so violently, that I pressed my hands quite tightly across my breast, but I could not keep it still, and it continued to leap as though it would burst out of my body. But who cared for that? Did one of the many bystanders, who were looking at us so carelessly, think of the pain that wrung the hearts of the negro woman and her young ones? No, no! They were not all bad, I dare say, but slavery hardens white people's hearts towards the blacks; and many of them were not slow to make their remarks upon us aloud, without regard to our grief—though their light words fell like cayenne on the fresh wounds of our hearts. Oh those white people have small hearts who can only feel for themselves.

At length the vendue[2] master, who was to offer us for sale like sheep or cattle, arrived, and asked my mother which was the eldest. She said nothing, but pointed to me. He took me by the hand, and led me out into the middle of the street, and, turning me slowly round, exposed me to the view of those who attended the vendue. I was soon surrounded by strange men, who examined and handled me in the same manner that a butcher would a calf or a lamb he was about to purchase, and who talked about my shape and size in like words—as if I could no more understand their meaning than the dumb beasts. I was then put up for sale. The bidding commenced at a few pounds, and gradually rose to fifty-seven, when I was knocked down to the highest bidder; and the people who stood by said that I had fetched a great sum for so young a slave.

I then saw my sisters led forth, and sold to different owners; so that we had not the sad satisfaction of being partners in bondage. When the sale was over, my mother hugged and kissed us, and mourned over us, begging of us to keep up a good heart, and do our duty to our new masters. It was a sad parting; one went one way, one another, and our poor mammy went home with nothing.

My new master was a Captain I—, who lived at Spanish Point. After parting with my mother and sisters, I followed him to his store, and he gave me into the charge of his son, a lad about my own age, Master Benjy, who took me to my new home. I did not know where I was going, or what my new master would do with me. My heart was quite broken with grief, and my thoughts went back continually to those from whom I had been so suddenly parted. "Oh, my mother! my mother!" I kept saying to myself, "Oh, my mammy and my sisters and my brothers, shall I never see you again!"

Oh, the trials! the trials! they make the salt water come into my eyes when I think of the days in which I was afflicted—the times that are gone; when I mourned and grieved with a young heart for those whom I loved.—It was night when I reached my new home. The house was large, and built at the bottom of a very high

[1] *osnaburgs* Clothes made of osnaburg, a coarse linen.

[2] *vendue* Sale.

hill; but I could not see much of it that night. I saw too much of it afterwards. The stones and the timber were the best things in it; they were not so hard as the hearts of the owners.

Before I entered the house, two slave women, hired from another owner, who were at work in the yard, spoke to me, and asked who I belonged to? I replied, "I am come to live here." "Poor child, poor child!" they both said; "you must keep a good heart, if you are to live here."—When I went in, I stood up crying in a corner. Mrs. I— came and took off my hat, a little black silk hat Miss Pruden made for me, and said in a rough voice, "You are not come here to stand up in corners and cry, you are come here to work." She then put a child into my arms, and, tired as I was, I was forced instantly to take up my old occupation of a nurse.—I could not bear to look at my mistress, her countenance was so stern. She was a stout tall woman with a very dark complexion, and her brows were always drawn together into a frown. I thought of the words of the two slave women when I saw Mrs. I—, and heard the harsh sound of her voice.

The person I took the most notice of that night was a French Black called Hetty, whom my master took in privateering from another vessel, and made his slave. She was the most active woman I ever saw, and she was tasked to her utmost. A few minutes after my arrival she came in from milking the cows, and put the sweet-potatoes on for supper. She then fetched home the sheep, and penned them in the fold; drove home the cattle, and staked them about the pond side; fed and rubbed down my master's horse, and gave the hog and the fed cow their suppers; prepared the beds, and undressed the children, and laid them to sleep. I liked to look at her and watch all her doings, for her's was the only friendly face I had as yet seen, and I felt glad that she was there. She gave me my supper of potatoes and milk, and a blanket to sleep upon, which she spread for me in the passage before the door of Mrs. I—'s chamber.

I got a sad fright, that night. I was just going to sleep, when I heard a noise in my mistress's room; and she presently called out to inquire if some work was finished that she had ordered Hetty to do. "No, Ma'am, not yet," was Hetty's answer from below. On hearing this, my master started up from his bed, and just as he was, in his shirt, ran down stairs with a long cow-skin in his hand. I heard immediately after, the cracking of the thong, and the house rang to the shrieks of poor Hetty, who kept crying out, "Oh, Massa! Massa! me dead. Massa! have mercy upon me—don't kill me outright."—This was a sad beginning for me. I sat up upon my blanket, trembling with terror, like a frightened hound, and thinking that my turn would come next. At length the house became still, and I forgot for a little while all my sorrows by falling fast asleep.

The next morning my mistress set about instructing me in my tasks. She taught me to do all sorts of household work; to wash and bake, pick cotton and wool, and wash floors, and cook. And she taught me (how can I ever forget it!) more things than these; she caused me to know the exact difference between the smart of the rope, the cart-whip, and the cow-skin, when applied to my naked body by her own cruel hand. And there was scarcely any punishment more dreadful than the blows I received on my face and head from her hard heavy fist. She was a fearful woman, and a savage mistress to her slaves.

There were two little slave boys in the house, on whom she vented her bad temper in a special manner. One of these children was a mulatto, called Cyrus, who had been bought while an infant in his mother's arms; the other, Jack, was an African from the coast of Guinea, whom a sailor had given or sold to my master. Seldom a day passed without these boys receiving the most severe treatment, and often for no fault at all. Both my master and mistress seemed to think that they had a right to ill-use them at their pleasure; and very often accompanied their commands with blows, whether the children were behaving well or ill. I have seen their flesh ragged and raw with licks.—Lick—lick—they were never secure one moment from a blow, and their lives were passed in continual fear. My mistress was not contented with using the whip, but often pinched their cheeks and arms in the most cruel manner. My pity for these poor boys was soon transferred to myself; for I was licked, and flogged, and pinched by her pitiless fingers in the neck and arms, exactly as they were. To strip me naked—to hang me up by the wrists and lay my flesh open with the cow-skin, was an ordinary punishment for even a slight offence. My mistress often robbed me too of the hours that belong to sleep. She used to sit up very late, frequently even until morning; and I had then to stand at a bench and wash during the greater part of the night, or pick wool and cotton and often I have dropped down overcome by sleep and fatigue, till roused from a state of stupor by the whip, and forced to start up to my tasks.

Poor Hetty, my fellow slave, was very kind to me, and I used to call her my Aunt; but she led a most miserable life, and her death was hastened (at least the slaves all believed and said so,) by the dreadful chastisement she received from my master during her pregnancy. It happened as follows. One of the cows had dragged the rope away from the stake to which Hetty had fastened it, and got loose. My master flew into a terrible passion, and ordered the poor creature to be stripped quite naked, notwithstanding her pregnancy, and to be tied up to a tree in the yard. He then flogged her as hard as he could lick, both with the whip and cow-skin, till she was all over streaming with blood. He rested, and then beat her again and again. Her shrieks were terrible. The consequence was that poor Hetty was brought to bed before her time, and was delivered after severe labour of a dead child. She appeared to recover after her confinement, so far that she was repeatedly flogged by both master and mistress afterwards; but her former strength never returned to her. Ere long her body and limbs swelled to a great size; and she lay on a mat in the kitchen, till the water burst out of her body and she died. All the slaves said that death was a good thing for poor Hetty; but I cried very much for her death. The manner of it filled me with horror. I could not bear to think about it; yet it was always present to my mind for many a day.

After Hetty died all her labours fell upon me, in addition to my own. I had now to milk eleven cows every morning before sunrise, sitting among the damp weeds; to take care of the cattle as well as the children; and to do the work of the house. There was no end to

my toils—no end to my blows. I lay down at night and rose up in the morning in fear and sorrow; and often wished that like poor Hetty I could escape from this cruel bondage and be at rest in the grave. But the hand of that God whom then I knew not, was stretched over me; and I was mercifully preserved for better things. It was then, however, my heavy lot to weep, weep, weep, and that for years; to pass from one misery to another, and from one cruel master to a worse. But I must go on with the thread of my story. One day a heavy squall of wind and rain came on suddenly, and my mistress sent me round the corner of the house to empty a large earthen jar. The jar was already cracked with an old deep crack that divided it in the middle, and in turning it upside down to empty it, it parted in my hand. I could not help the accident, but I was dreadfully frightened, looking forward to a severe punishment. I ran crying to my mistress, "O mistress, the jar has come in two." "You have broken it, have you?" she replied; "come directly here to me." I came trembling: she stripped and flogged me long and severely with the cow-skin; as long as she had strength to use the lash, for she did not give over till she was quite tired.—When my master came home at night, she told him of my fault; and oh, frightful! how he fell a swearing. After abusing me with every ill name he could think of, (too, too bad to speak in England,) and giving me several heavy blows with his hand, he said, "I shall come home tomorrow morning at twelve, on purpose to give you a round hundred." He kept his word—Oh sad for me! I cannot easily forget it. He tied me up upon a ladder, and gave me a hundred lashes with his own hand, and master Benjy stood by to count them for him. When he had licked me for some time he sat down to take breath; then after resting, he beat me again and again, until he was quite wearied, and so hot (for the weather was very sultry), that he sank back in his chair, almost like to faint. While my mistress went to bring him drink, there was a dreadful earthquake. Part of the roof fell down, and every thing in the house went –clatter, clatter, clatter. Oh I thought the end of all things near at hand; and I was so sore with the flogging, that I scarcely cared whether I lived or died. The earth was groaning and shaking; every thing tumbling about; and my mistress and the slaves were shrieking and crying out, "The earthquake! the earthquake!" It was an awful day for us all.

During the confusion I crawled away on my hands and knees, and laid myself down under the steps of the piazza, in front of the house. I was in a dreadful state— my body all blood and bruises, and I could not help moaning piteously. The other slaves, when they saw me, shook their heads and said, "Poor child! poor child"—I lay there till the morning, careless of what might happen, for life was very weak in me, and I wished more than ever to die. But when we are very young, death always seems a great way off, and it would not come that night to me. The next morning I was forced by my master to rise and go about my usual work, though my body and limbs were so stiff and sore, that I could not move without the greatest pain.—Nevertheless, even after all this severe punishment, I never heard the last of that jar; my mistress was always throwing it in my face.

Some little time after this, one of the cows got loose from the stake, and eat one of the sweet-potato slips. I was milking when my master found it out. He came to me, and without any more ado, stooped down, and taking off his heavy boot, he struck me such a severe blow in the small of my back, that I shrieked with agony, and thought I was killed; and I feel a weakness in that part to this day. The cow was frightened by his violence, and kicked down the pail and spilt the milk all about. My master knew that this accident was his own fault, but he was so enraged that he seemed glad of an excuse to go on with his ill usage. I cannot remember how many licks he gave me then, but he beat me till I was unable to stand, and till he himself was weary.

After this I ran away and went to my mother, who was living with Mr. Richard Darrel. My poor mother was both grieved and glad to see me; grieved because I had been so ill used, and glad because she had not seen me for a long, long while. She dared not receive me into the house, but she hid me up in a hole in the rocks near, and brought me food at night, after every body was asleep. My father, who lived at Crow-Lane, over the salt-water channel, at last heard of my being hid up in the cavern, and he came and took me back to my master. Oh I was loath, loath to go back; but as there was no remedy, I was obliged to submit.

When we got home, my poor father said to Capt. I—, "Sir, I am sorry that my child should be forced to run away from her owner; but the treatment she has received is enough to break her heart. The sight of her wounds has nearly broke mine.—I entreat you, for the love of God, to forgive her for running away, and that you will be a kind master to her in future." Capt. I— said I was used as well as I deserved, and that I ought to be punished for running away. I then took courage and said that I could stand the floggings no longer; that I was weary of my life, and therefore I had run away to my mother; but mothers could only weep and mourn over their children, they could not save them from cruel masters—from the whip, the rope, and the cow-skin. He told me to hold my tongue and go about my work, or he would find a way to settle me. He did not, however, flog me that day.

For five years after this I remained in his house, and almost daily received the same harsh treatment. At length he put me on board a sloop, and to my great joy sent me away to Turk's Island.[1] I was not permitted to see my mother or father, or poor sisters and brothers, to say good bye, though going away to a strange land, and might never see them again. Oh the Buckra[2] people who keep slaves think that black people are like cattle, without natural affection. But my heart tells me it is far otherwise.

We were nearly four weeks on the voyage, which was unusually long. Sometimes we had a light breeze, sometimes a great calm, and the ship made no way; so that our provisions and water ran very low, and we were put upon short allowance. I should almost have been starved had it not been for the kindness of a black man called Anthony, and his wife, who had brought their own victuals, and shared them with me.

---

[1] *sloop* Small ship; *Turk's Island* The southernmost and easternmost island of the Bahamas.

[2] *Buckra* White.

When we went ashore at the Grand Quay, the captain sent me to the house of my new master, Mr. D—, to whom Captain I— had sold me. Grand Quay is a small town upon a sandbank; the houses low and built of wood. Such was my new master's. The first person I saw, on my arrival, was Mr. D—, a stout sulky looking man, who carried me through the hall to show me to his wife and children. Next day I was put up by the vendue master to know how much I was worth, and I was valued at one hundred pounds currency.

My new master was one of the owners or holders of the salt ponds, and he received a certain sum for every slave that worked upon his premises, whether they were young or old. This sum was allowed him out of the profits arising from the salt works. I was immediately sent to work in the salt water with the rest of the slaves. This work was perfectly new to me. I was given a half barrel and a shovel, and had to stand up to my knees in the water, from four o'clock in the morning till nine, when we were given some Indian corn boiled in water, which we were obliged to swallow as fast as we could for fear the rain should come on and melt the salt. We were then called again to our tasks, and worked through the heat of the day; the sun flaming upon our heads like fire, and raising salt blisters in those parts which were not completely covered. Our feet and legs, from standing in the salt water for so many hours, soon became full of dreadful boils, which eat down in some cases to the very bone, afflicting the sufferers with great torment. We came home at twelve; ate our corn soup, called *blawly*, as fast as we could, and went back to our employment till dark at night. We then shovelled up the salt in large heaps, and went down to the sea, where we washed the pickle from our limbs, and cleaned the barrows and shovels from the salt. When we returned to the house, our master gave us each our allowance of raw Indian corn, which we pounded in a mortar and boiled in water for our suppers. We slept in a long shed, divided into narrow slips, like the stalls used for cattle. Boards fixed upon stakes driven into the ground, without mat or covering, were our only beds. On Sundays, after we had washed the salt bags, and done other work required of us, we went into the bush and cut the long soft grass, of

which we made trusses for our legs and feet to rest upon, for they were so full of the salt boils that we could get no rest lying upon the bare boards.

Though we worked from morning till night, there was no satisfying Mr. D—. I hoped, when I left Capt. I—, that I should have been better off, but I found it was but going from one butcher to another. There was this difference between them: my former master used to beat me while raging and foaming with passion; Mr. D— was usually quite calm. He would stand by and give orders for a slave to be cruelly whipped, and assist in the punishment, without moving a muscle of his face; walking about and taking snuff with the greatest composure. Nothing could touch his hard heart—neither sighs, nor tears, nor prayers, nor streaming blood; he was deaf to our cries, and careless of our sufferings.— Mr. D— has often stripped me naked, hung me up by the wrists, and beat me with the cow-skin, with his own hand, till my body was raw with gashes. Yet there was nothing very remarkable in this; for it might serve as a sample of the common usage of the slaves on that horrible island.

Owing to the boils in my feet, I was unable to wheel the barrow fast through the sand, which got into the sores, and made me stumble at every step; and my master, having no pity for my sufferings from this cause, rendered them far more intolerable, by chastising me for not being able to move so fast as he wished me. Another of our employments was to row a little way off from the shore in a boat, and dive for large stones to build a wall round our master's house. This was very hard work, and the great waves breaking over us continually, made us often so giddy that we lost our footing, and were in danger of being drowned.

Ah, poor me!—my tasks were never ended. Sick or well, it was work—work—work!—After the diving season was over, we were sent to the South Creek, with large bills, to cut up mangoes to burn lime with. Whilst one party of slaves were thus employed, another were sent to the other side of the island to break up coral out of the sea.

When we were ill, let our complaint be what it might, the only medicine given to us was a great bowl of hot salt water, with salt mixed with it, which made us very sick. If we could not keep up with the rest of the gang of slaves, we were put in the stocks,[1] and severely flogged the next morning. Yet, not the less, our master expected, after we had thus been kept from our rest, and our limbs rendered stiff and sore with ill usage, that we should still go through the ordinary tasks of the day all the same.—Sometimes we had to work all night, measuring salt to load a vessel; or turning a machine to draw water out of the sea for the salt-making. Then we had no sleep—no rest—but were forced to work as fast as we could, and go on again all next day the same as usual. Work—work—work—Oh that Turk's Island was a horrible place! The people in England, I am sure, have never found out what is carried on there. Cruel, horrible place!

Mr. D— had a slave called old Daniel, whom he used to treat in the most cruel manner. Poor Daniel was lame in the hip, and could not keep up with the rest of the slaves; and our master would order him to be stripped and laid down on the ground, and have him beaten with a rod of rough briar till his skin was quite red and raw. He would then call for a bucket of salt, and fling upon the raw flesh till the man writhed on the ground like a worm, and screamed aloud with agony. This poor man's wounds were never healed, and I have often seen them full of maggots, which increased his torments to an intolerable degree. He was an object of pity and terror to the whole gang of slaves, and in his wretched case we saw, each of us, our own lot, if we should live to be as old.

Oh the horrors of slavery!—How the thought of it pains my heart! But the truth ought to be told of it; and what my eyes have seen I think it is my duty to relate; for few people in England know what slavery is. I have been a slave—I have felt what a slave feels, and I know what a slave knows; and I would have all the good people in England to know it too, that they may break our chains, and set us free.

Mr. D— had another slave called Ben. He being very hungry, stole a little rice one night after he came in from work, and cooked it for his supper. But his master soon discovered the theft; locked him up all night; and kept him without food till one o'clock the next day. He then hung Ben up by his hands, and beat him from time to time till the slaves came in at night. We found the poor creature hung up when we came home; with a pool of blood beneath him, and our master still licking him, but this was not the worst. My master's son was in the habit of stealing the rice and rum. Ben had seen him do this, and thought he might do the same, and when master found out that Ben had stolen the rice and swore to punish him, he tried to excuse himself by saying that Master Dickey did the same thing every night. The lad denied it to his father, and was so angry with Ben for informing against him, that out of revenge he ran and got a bayonet, and whilst the poor wretch was suspended by his hands and writhing under his wounds, he run it quite through his foot. I was not by when he did it, but I saw the wound when I came home, and heard Ben tell the manner in which it was done.

I must say something more about this cruel son of a cruel father.—He had no heart—no fear of God; he had been brought up by a bad father in a bad path, and he delighted to follow in the same steps. There was a little old woman among the slaves called Sarah, who was nearly past work; and, Master Dickey being the overseer of the slaves just then, this poor creature, who was subject to several bodily infirmities, and was not quite right in her head, did not wheel the barrow fast enough to please him. He threw her down on the ground, and after beating her severely, he took her up in his arms and flung her among the prickly-pear[2] bushes, which are all covered over with sharp venomous prickles. By this her naked flesh was so grievously wounded, that her body swelled and festered all over, and she died in a few days after. In telling my own sorrows, I cannot pass by those of my fellow-slaves—for when I think of my own griefs, I remember theirs.

I think it was about ten years I had worked in the salt ponds at Turk's Island, when my master left off business, and retired to a house he had in Bermuda,

1 *stocks* Device for confining the ankles and sometimes the wrists.

2 *prickly-pear* Type of cactus.

leaving his son to succeed him in the island. He took me with him to wait upon his daughters; and I was joyful, for I was sick, sick of Turk's Island, and my heart yearned to see my native place again, my mother, and my kindred.

I had seen my poor mother during the time I was a slave in Turk's Island. One Sunday morning I was on the beach with some of the slaves, and we saw a sloop come in loaded with slaves to work in the salt water. We got a boat and went aboard. When I came upon the deck I asked the black people, "Is there any one here for me?" "Yes," they said, "your mother." I thought they said this in jest—I could scarcely believe them for joy; but when I saw my poor mammy my joy was turned to sorrow, for she had gone from her senses. "Mammy," I said, "is this you!" She did not know me. "Mammy," I said, "what's the matter?" She began to talk foolishly and said that she had been under the vessel's bottom. They had been overtaken by a violent storm at sea. My poor mother had never been on the sea before, and she was so ill, that she lost her senses, and it was long before she came quite to herself again. She had a sweet child with her—a little sister I had never seen, about four years of age, called Rebecca. I took her on shore with me, for I felt I should love her directly; and I kept her with me a week. Poor little thing! her's has been a sad life, and continues so to this day. My mother worked for some years on the island, but was taken back to Bermuda some time before my master carried me again thither.

After I left Turk's Island, I was told by some negroes that came over from it, that the poor slaves had built up a place with boughs and leaves, where they might meet for prayers, but the white people pulled it down twice, and would not allow them even a shed for prayers. A flood came down soon after and washed away many houses, filled the place with sand, and overflowed the ponds: and I do think that this was for their wickedness; for the Buckra men there were very wicked. I saw and heard much that was very very bad at that place.

I was several years the slave of Mr. D— after I returned to my native place. Here I worked in the grounds. My work was planting and hoeing sweet-potatoes, Indian corn, plaintains, bananas, cabbages, pumpkins, onions, &c. I did all the household work, and attended upon a horse and cow besides,—going also upon all errands. I had to curry the horse—to clean and feed him—and sometimes to ride him a little. I had more than enough to do—but still it was not so very bad as Turk's Island.

My old master often got drunk, and then he would get in a fury with his daughter, and beat her till she was not fit to be seen. I remember on one occasion, I had gone to fetch water, and when I was coming up the hill I heard a great screaming; I ran as fast as I could to the house, put down the water, and went into the chamber, where I found my master beating Miss D— dreadfully. I strove with all my strength to get her away from him; for she was all black and blue with bruises. He had beat her with his fist, and almost killed her. The people gave me credit for getting her away. He turned round and began to lick me. Then I said, "Sir, this is not Turk's Island." I can't repeat his answer, the words were too wicked—too bad to say. He wanted to treat me the same in Bermuda as he had done in Turk's Island.

He had an ugly fashion of stripping himself quite naked and ordering me then to wash him in a tub of water. This was worse to me than all the licks. Sometimes when he called me to wash him I would not come, my eyes were so full of shame. He would then come to beat me. One time I had plates and knives in my hand, and I dropped both plates and knives, and some of the plates were broken. He struck me so severely for this, that at last I defended myself, for I thought it was high time to do so. I then told him I would not live longer with him, for he was a very indecent man—very spiteful, and too indecent; with no shame for his servants, no shame for his own flesh. So I went away to a neighbouring house and sat down and cried till the next morning, when I went home again, not knowing what else to do.

After that I was hired to work at Cedar Hills, and every Saturday night I paid the money to my master. I had plenty of work to do there—plenty of washing; but yet I made myself pretty comfortable. I earned two dollars and a quarter a week, which is twenty pence a day.

During the time I worked there, I heard that Mr. John Wood was going to Antigua. I felt a great wish to go there, and I went to Mr. D—, and asked him to let me go in Mr. Wood's service. Mr. Wood did not then want to purchase me; it was my own fault that I came under him, I was so anxious to go. It was ordained to be, I suppose; God led me there. The truth is, I did not wish to be any longer the slave of my indecent master.

Mr. Wood took me with him to Antigua, to the town of St. John's, where he lived. This was about fifteen years ago. He did not then know whether I was to be sold; but Mrs. Wood found that I could work, and she wanted to buy me. Her husband then wrote to my master to inquire whether I was to be sold? Mr. D— wrote in reply, "that I should not be sold to any one that would treat me ill." It was strange he should say this, when he had treated me so ill himself. So I was purchased by Mr. Wood for 300 dollars (or £100 Bermuda currency).

My work there was to attend the chambers and nurse the child, and to go down to the pond and wash clothes. But I soon fell ill of the rheumatism, and grew so very lame that I was forced to walk with a stick. I got the Saint Anthony's fire,[1] also, in my left leg, and became quite a cripple. No one cared much to come near me, and I was ill a long long time; for several months I could not lift the limb. I had to lie in a little old out-house, that was swarming with bugs and other vermin, which tormented me greatly; but I had no other place to lie in. I got the rheumatism by catching cold at the pond side, from washing in the fresh water; in the salt water I never got cold. The person who lived in next yard, (a Mrs. Greene,) could not bear to hear my cries and groans. She was kind, and used to send an old slave woman to help me, who sometimes brought me a little soup. When the doctor found I was so ill, he said I must be put into a bath of hot water. The old slave got the bark of some bush that was good for pains, which she boiled in the hot water, and every night she came and put me into the bath, and did what she could for me; I don't know what I should have done, or what would have become of me, had it not been for her.—My mistress, it is true, did send me a little food; but no one

from our family came near me but the cook, who used to shove my food in at the door, and say, "Molly, Molly, there's your dinner." My mistress did not care to take any trouble about me; and if the Lord had not put it into the hearts of the neighbours to be kind to me, I must, I really think, have lain and died.

It was a long time before I got well enough to work in the house. Mrs. Wood, in the meanwhile, hired a mulatto woman to nurse the child; but she was such a fine lady she wanted to be mistress over me. I thought it very hard for a coloured woman to have rule over me because I was a slave and she was free. Her name was Martha Wilcox; she was a saucy woman, very saucy; and she went and complained of me, without cause, to my mistress, and made her angry with me. Mrs. Wood told me that if I did not mind what I was about, she would get my master to strip me and give me fifty lashes: "You have been used to the whip," she said, "and you shall have it here." This was the first time she threatened to have me flogged; and she gave me the threatening so strong of what she would have done to me, that I thought I should have fallen down at her feet, I was so vexed and hurt by her words. The mulatto woman was rejoiced to have power to keep me down. She was constantly making mischief; there was no living for the slaves—no peace after she came.

I was also sent by Mrs. Wood to be put in the Cage one night, and was next morning flogged, by the magistrate's order, at her desire; and this all for a quarrel I had about a pig with another slave woman. I was flogged on my naked back on this occasion; although I was in no fault after all; for old Justice Dyett, when we came before him, said that I was in the right, and ordered the pig to be given to me. This was about two or three years after I came to Antigua.

When we moved from the middle of the town to the Point, I used to be in the house and do all the work and mind the children, though still very ill with the rheumatism. Every week I had to wash two large bundles of clothes, as much as a boy could help me to lift; but I could give no satisfaction. My mistress was always abusing and fretting after me. It is not possible to tell all her ill language.—One day she followed me foot after

---

[1] *Saint Anthony's fire* Erysipelas or ergotism, diseases that cause intense redness, swelling of the skin, and severe pain.

foot scolding and rating me. I bore in silence a great deal of ill words: at last my heart was quite full, and I told her that she ought not to use me so;—that when I was ill I might have lain and died for what she cared; and no one would then come near me to nurse me, because they were afraid of my mistress. This was a great affront. She called her husband and told him what I had said. He flew into a passion: but did not beat me then; he only abused and swore at me; and then gave me a note and bade me go and look for an owner. Not that he meant to sell me; but he did this to please his wife and to frighten me. I went to Adam White, a cooper,[1] a free black who had money, and asked him to buy me. He went directly to Mr. Wood, but was informed that I was not to be sold. The next day my master whipped me.

Another time (about five years ago) my mistress got vexed with me because I fell sick and I could not keep on with my work. She complained to her husband, and he sent me off again to look for an owner. I went to a Mr. Burchell, showed him the note, and asked him to buy me for my own benefit; for I had saved about 100 dollars, and hoped with a little help, to purchase my freedom. He accordingly went to my master: "Mr. Wood," he said, "Molly has brought me a note that she wants an owner. If you intend to sell her, I may as well buy her as another." My master put him off and said that he did not mean to sell me. I was very sorry at this, for I had no comfort with Mrs. Wood, and I wished greatly to get my freedom.

The way in which I made my money was this.—When my master and mistress went from home, as they sometimes did, and left me to take care of the house and premises, I had a good deal of time to myself and made the most of it. I took in washing, and sold coffee and yams and other provisions to the captains of ships. I did not sit still idling during the absence of my owners; for I wanted, by all honest means, to earn money to buy my freedom. Sometimes I bought a hog cheap on board ship, and sold it for double the money on shore; and I also earned a good deal by selling coffee. By this means I by degrees acquired a little cash. A gentleman also lent me some to help to buy my freedom—but when I could not get free he got it back again. His name was Captain Abbot.

My master and mistress went on one occasion into the country, to Date Hill, for a change of air, and carried me with them to take charge of the children, and to do the work of the house. While I was in the country, I saw how the field negroes are worked in Antigua. They are worked very hard and fed but scantily. They are called out to work before daybreak, and come home after dark; and then each has to heave his bundle of grass for the cattle in the pen. Then, on Sunday morning, each slave has to go out and gather a large bundle of grass; and, when they bring it home, they have all to sit at the manager's door and wait till he comes out: often have they to wait there till past eleven o'clock without any breakfast. After that, those that have yams or potatoes, or fire-wood to sell, hasten to market to buy a dog's[2] worth of salt fish, or pork, which is a great treat for them. Some of them buy a little pickle out of the shad barrels, which they call sauce, to season their yams and Indian corn. It is very wrong, I know, to work on Sunday or go to market; but will not God call the Buckra men to answer for this on the great day of judgment—since they will give the slaves no other day?

While we were at Date Hill Christmas came; and the slave woman who had the care of the place (which then belonged to Mr. Roberts the marshal), asked me to go with her to her husband's house, to a Methodist meeting for prayer, at a plantation called Winthorps. I went; and they were the first prayers I ever understood. One woman prayed; and then they all sung a hymn; then there was another prayer and another hymn; and then they all spoke by turns of their own griefs as sinners. The husband of the woman I went with was a black driver. His name was Henry. He confessed that he had treated the slaves very cruelly; but said that he was compelled to obey the orders of his master. He prayed them all to forgive him, and he prayed that God would

---

[1] *cooper* Barrel- and tub-maker.

[2] *dog* Coin of low value.

forgive him. He said it was a horrid thing for a ranger to have sometimes to beat his own wife or sister; but he must do so if ordered by his master.

I felt sorry for my sins also. I cried the whole night, but I was too much ashamed to speak. I prayed God to forgive me. This meeting had a great impression on my mind, and led my spirit to the Moravian church; so that when I got back to town, I went and prayed to have my name put down in the Missionaries' book; and I followed the church earnestly every opportunity. I did not then tell my mistress about it; for I knew that she would not give me leave to go. But I felt I *must* go. Whenever I carried the children their lunch at school, I ran round and went to hear the teachers.

The Moravian ladies (Mrs. Richter, Mrs. Olufsen, and Mrs. Sauter) taught me to read in the class; and I got on very fast. In this class there were all sorts of people, old and young, grey headed folks and children; but most of them were free people. After we had done spelling, we tried to read in the Bible. After the reading was over, the missionary gave out a hymn for us to sing. I dearly loved to go to the church, it was so solemn. I never knew rightly that I had much sin till I went there. When I found out that I was a great sinner, I was very sorely grieved, and very much frightened. I used to pray God to pardon my sins for Christ's sake, and forgive me for every thing I had done amiss; and when I went home to my work, I always thought about what I had heard from the missionaries, and wished to be good that I might go to heaven. After a while I was admitted a candidate for the holy Communion.—I had been baptized long before this, in August 1817, by the Rev. Mr. Curtin, of the English Church, after I had been taught to repeat the Creed and the Lord's Prayer. I wished at that time to attend a Sunday School taught by Mr. Curtin, but he would not receive me without a written note from my master, granting his permission. I did not ask my owner's permission, from the belief that it would be refused; so that I got no farther instruction at that time from the English Church.

Some time after I began to attend the Moravian Church, I met with Daniel James, afterwards my dear husband. He was a carpenter and cooper to his trade; an honest, hard-working, decent black man, and a widower. He had purchased his freedom of his mistress, old Mrs. Baker, with money he had earned whilst a slave. When he asked me to marry him, I took time to consider the matter over with myself, and would not say yes till he went to church with me and joined the Moravians. He was very industrious after he bought his freedom; and he had hired a comfortable house, and had convenient things about him. We were joined in marriage, about Christmas 1826, in the Moravian Chapel at Spring Gardens, by the Rev. Mr. Olufsen. We could not be married in the English Church. English marriage is not allowed to slaves; and no free man can marry a slave woman.

When Mr. Wood heard of my marriage, he flew into a great rage, and sent for Daniel, who was helping to build a house for his old mistress. Mr. Wood asked him who gave him a right to marry a slave of his? My husband said, "Sir, I am a free man, and thought I had a right to choose a wife; but if I had known Molly was not allowed to have a husband, I should not have asked her to marry me." Mrs. Wood was more vexed about my marriage than her husband. She could not forgive me for getting married, but stirred up Mr. Wood to flog me dreadfully with his horsewhip. I thought it very hard to be whipped at my time of life for getting a husband—I told her so. She said that she would not have nigger men about the yards and premises, or allow a nigger man's clothes to be washed in the same tub where hers were washed. She was fearful, I think, that I should lose her time, in order to wash and do things for my husband: but I had then no time to wash for myself; I was obliged to put out my own clothes, though I was always at the wash-tub.

I had not much happiness in my marriage, owing to my being a slave. It made my husband sad to see me so ill-treated. Mrs. Wood was always abusing me about him. She did not lick me herself, but she got her husband to do it for her, whilst she fretted the flesh off my bones. Yet for all this she would not sell me. She sold five slaves whilst I was with her; but though she was always finding fault with me, she would not part with me. However, Mr. Wood afterwards allowed Daniel to have a place to live in our yard, which we were very thankful for.

After this, I fell ill again with the rheumatism, and was sick a long time; but whether sick or well, I had my work to do. About this time I asked my master and mistress to let me buy my own freedom. With the help of Mr. Burchell, I could have found the means to pay Mr. Wood; for it was agreed that I should afterwards serve Mr. Burchell a while, for the cash he was to advance for me. I was earnest in the request to my owners; but their hearts were hard—too hard to consent. Mrs. Wood was very angry—she grew quite outrageous—she called me a black devil, and asked me who had put freedom into my head. "To be free is very sweet," I said: but she took good care to keep me a slave. I saw her change colour, and I left the room.

About this time my master and mistress were going to England to put their son in school, and bring their daughters home; and they took me with them to take care of the child. I was willing to come to England: I thought that by going there I should probably get cured of my rheumatism, and should return with my master and mistress, quite well, to my husband. My husband was willing for me to come away, for he had heard that my master would free me,—and I also hoped this might prove true; but it was all a false report.

The steward of the ship was very kind to me. He and my husband were in the same class in the Moravian Church. I was thankful that he was so friendly, for my mistress was not kind to me on the passage; and she told me, when she was angry, that she did not intend to treat me any better in England than in the West Indies—that I need not expect it. And she was as good as her word.

When we drew near to England, the rheumatism seized all my limbs worse than ever, and my body was dreadfully swelled. When we landed at the Tower, I showed my flesh to my mistress, but she took no great notice of it. We were obliged to stop at the tavern till my master got a house; and a day or two after, my mistress sent me down into the wash-house to learn to wash in the English way. In the West Indies we wash with cold water—in England with hot. I told my mistress I was afraid that putting my hands first into the hot water and then into the cold, would increase the pain in my limbs. The doctor had told my mistress long before I came from the West Indies, that I was a sickly body and the washing did not agree with me. But Mrs. Wood would not release me from the tub, so I was forced to do as I could. I grew worse, and could not stand to wash. I was then forced to sit down with the tub before me, and often through pain and weakness was reduced to kneel or to sit down on the floor, to finish my task. When I complained to my mistress of this, she only got into a passion as usual, and said washing in hot water could not hurt any one;—that I was lazy and insolent, and wanted to be free of my work; but that she would make me do it. I thought her very hard on me, and my heart rose up within me. However I kept still at that time, and went down again to wash the child's things; but the English washerwomen who were at work there, when they saw that I was so ill, had pity upon me and washed them for me.

After that, when we came up to live in Leigh Street, Mrs. Wood sorted out five bags of clothes which we had used at sea, and also such as had been worn since we came on shore, for me and the cook to wash. Elizabeth the cook told her, that she did not think that I was able to stand to the tub, and that she had better hire a woman. I also said myself, that I had come over to nurse the child, and that I was sorry I had come from Antigua, since mistress would work me so hard, without compassion for my rheumatism. Mr. and Mrs. Wood, when they heard this, rose up in a passion against me. They opened the door and bade me get out. But I was a stranger, and did not know one door in the street from another, and was unwilling to go away. They made a dreadful uproar, and from that day they constantly kept cursing and abusing me. I was obliged to wash, though I was very ill. Mrs. Wood, indeed once hired a washerwoman, but she was not well treated, and would come no more.

My master quarrelled with me another time, about one of our great washings, his wife having stirred him up to do so. He said he would compel me to do the whole of the washing given out to me, or if I again refused, he would take a short course with me: he would either send me down to the brig in the river, to carry me back to Antigua, or he would turn me at once out of doors, and let me provide for myself. I said I would willingly go back, if he would let me purchase my own freedom. But this enraged him more than all the rest: he cursed and swore at me dreadfully, and said he would never sell my freedom—if I wished to be free, I was free in England, and I might go and try what freedom would do for me, and be d—d. My heart was very sore with this treatment, but I had to go on. I continued to do my work, and did all I could to give satisfaction, but all would not do.

Shortly after, the cook left them, and then matters went on ten times worse. I always washed the child's clothes without being commanded to do it, and any thing else that was wanted in the family; though still I was very sick—very sick indeed. When the great washing came round, which was every two months, my mistress got together again a great many heavy things, such as bed-ticks, bed-coverlets, &c. for me to wash. I told her I was too ill to wash such heavy things that day. She said, she supposed I thought myself a free woman, but I was not; and if I did not do it directly I should be instantly turned out of doors. I stood a long time before I could answer, for I did not know well what to do. I knew that I was free in England, but I did not know where to go, or how to get my living; and therefore, I did not like to leave the house. But Mr. Wood said he would send for a constable to thrust me out; and at last I took courage and resolved that I would not be longer thus treated, but would go and trust to Providence. This was the fourth time they had threatened to turn me out, and, go where I might, I was determined now to take them at their word; though I thought it very hard, after I had lived with them for thirteen years, and worked for them like a horse, to be driven out in this way, like a beggar. My only fault was being sick, and therefore unable to please my mistress, who thought she never could get work enough out of her slaves; and I told them so: but they only abused me and drove me out. This took place from two to three months, I think, after we came to England.

When I came away, I went to the man (one Mash) who used to black the shoes of the family, and asked his wife to get somebody to go with me to Hatton Garden to the Moravian Missionaries: these were the only persons I knew in England. The woman sent a young girl with me to the mission house, and I saw there a gentleman called Mr. Moore. I told him my whole story, and how my owners had treated me, and asked him to take in my trunk with what few clothes I had. The missionaries were very kind to me—they were sorry for my destitute situation, and gave me leave to bring my things to be placed under their care. They were very good people, and they told me to come to the church.

When I went back to Mr. Wood's to get my trunk, I saw a lady, Mrs. Pell, who was on a visit to my mistress. When Mr. and Mrs. Wood heard me come in, they set this lady to stop me, finding that they had gone too far with me. Mrs. Pell came out to me, and said, "Are you really going to leave, Molly? Don't leave, but come into the country with me." I believe she said this because she thought Mrs. Wood would easily get me back again. I replied to her, "Ma'am, this is the fourth time my master and mistress have driven me out, or threatened to drive me—and I will give them no more occasion to bid me go. I was not willing to leave them, for I am a stranger in this country, but now I must go—I can stay no longer to be used." Mrs. Pell then went up stairs to my mistress, and told that I would go, and that she could not stop me. Mrs. Wood was very much hurt and frightened when she found I was determined to go out that day. She said, "If she goes the people will rob her, and then turn her adrift." She did not say this to me, but she spoke it loud enough for me to hear; that it might induce me not to go, I suppose. Mr. Wood also asked me where I was going to. I told him where I had been, and that I should never have gone away had I not been driven out by my owners. He had given me a written paper some time before, which said that I had come with them to England by my own desire; and that was true. It said also that I left them of my own free will, because I was a free woman in England; and that I was idle and would not do my work—

which was not true. I gave this paper afterwards to a gentleman who inquired into my case.

I went into the kitchen and got my clothes out. The nurse and the servant girl were there, and I said to the man who was going to take out my trunk, "Stop, before you take up this trunk, and hear what I have to say before these people. I am going out of this house, as I was ordered; but I have done no wrong at all to my owners, neither here nor in the West Indies. I always worked very hard to please them, both by night and day; but there was no giving satisfaction, for my mistress could never be satisfied with reasonable service. I told my mistress I was sick, and yet she has ordered me out of doors. This is the fourth time; and now I am going out."

And so I came out, and went and carried my trunk to the Moravians. I then returned back to Mash the shoeblack's house, and begged his wife to take me in. I had a little West Indian money in my trunk; and they got it changed for me. This helped to support me for a little while. The man's wife was very kind to me. I was very sick, and she boiled nourishing things up for me. She also sent for a doctor to see me, and sent me medicine, which did me good, though I was ill for a long time with the rheumatic pains. I lived a good many months with these poor people, and they nursed me, and did all that lay in their power to serve me. The man was well acquainted with my situation, as he used to go to and fro to Mr. Wood's house to clean shoes and knives; and he and his wife were sorry for me.

About this time, a woman of the name of Hill told me of the Anti-Slavery Society, and went with me to their office, to inquire if they could do any thing to get me my freedom, and send me back to the West Indies. The gentlemen of the Society took me to a lawyer, who examined very strictly into my case; but told me that the laws of England could do nothing to make me free in Antigua. However they did all they could for me: they gave me a little money from time to time to keep me from want; and some of them went to Mr. Wood to try to persuade him to let me return a free woman to my husband; but though they offered him, as I have heard, a large sum for my freedom, he was sulky and obstinate, and would not consent to let me go free.

This was the first winter I spent in England, and I suffered much from the severe cold, and from the rheumatic pains, which still at times torment me. However, Providence was very good to me, and I got many friends—especially some Quaker ladies, who hearing of my case, came and sought me out, and gave me good warm clothing and money. Thus I had great cause to bless God in my affliction.

When I got better I was anxious to get some work to do, as I was unwilling to eat the bread of idleness. Mrs. Mash, who was a laundress, recommended me to a lady for a charwoman. She paid me very handsomely for what work I did, and I divided the money with Mrs. Mash; for though very poor, they gave me food when my own money was done, and never suffered me to want.

In the spring, I got into service with a lady, who saw me at the house where I sometimes worked as a charwoman. This lady's name was Mrs. Forsyth. She had been in the West Indies, and was accustomed to Blacks, and liked them. I was with her six months, and went with her to Margate. She treated me well, and gave me a good character when she left London.

After Mrs. Forsyth went away, I was again out of place, and went to lodgings, for which I paid two shillings a week, and found coals and candle. After eleven weeks, the money I had saved in service was all gone, and I was forced to go back to the Anti-Slavery office to ask a supply, till I could get another situation. I did not like to go back—I did not like to be idle. I would rather work for my living than get it for nothing. They were very good to give me a supply, but I felt shame at being obliged to apply for relief whilst I had strength to work.

At last I went into the service of Mr. and Mrs. Pringle, where I have been ever since, and am as comfortable as I can be while separated from my dear husband, and away from my own country and all old friends and connections. My dear mistress teaches me daily to read the word of God, and takes great pains to make me understand it. I enjoy the great privilege of being enabled to attend church three times on the Sunday; and I have met with many kind friends since I have been here, both clergymen and others. The Rev.

Mr. Young, who lives in the next house, has shown me much kindness, and taken much pains to instruct me, particularly while my master and mistress were absent in Scotland. Nor must I forget, among my friends, the Rev. Mr. Mortimer, the good clergyman of the parish, under whose ministry I have now sat for upwards of twelve months. I trust in God I have profited by what I have heard from him. He never keeps back the truth, and I think he has been the means of opening my eyes and ears much better to understand the word of God. Mr. Mortimer tells me that he cannot open the eyes of my heart, but that I must pray to God to change my heart, and make me to know the truth, and the truth will make me free.

I still live in the hope that God will find a way to give me my liberty, and give me back to my husband. I endeavour to keep down my fretting, and to leave all to Him, for he knows what is good for me better than I know myself. Yet, I must confess, I find it a hard and heavy task to do so.

I am often much vexed, and I feel great sorrow when I hear some people in this country say, that the slaves do not need better usage, and do not want to be free. They believe the foreign people, who deceive them, and say slaves are happy. I say, Not so. How can slaves be happy when they have the halter round their neck and the whip upon their back? and are disgraced and thought no more of than beasts?—and are separated from their mothers, and husbands, and children, and sisters, just as cattle are sold and separated? Is it happiness for a driver in the field to take down his wife or sister or child, and strip them, and whip them in such a disgraceful manner?—women that have had children exposed in the open field to shame! There is no modesty or decency shown by the owner to his slaves; men, women, and children are exposed alike. Since I have been here I have often wondered how English people can go out into the West Indies and act in such a beastly manner. But when they go to the West Indies, they forget God and all feeling of shame, I think, since they can see and do such

things. They tie up slaves like hogs—moor them up like cattle, and they lick them, so as hogs, or cattle, or horses never were flogged;—and yet they come home and say, and make some good people believe, that slaves don't want to get out of slavery. But they put a cloak about the truth. It is not so. All slaves want to be free—to be free is very sweet. I will say the truth to English people who may read this history that my good friend, Miss S—, is now writing down for me. I have been a slave myself—I know what slaves feel—I can tell by myself what other slaves feel, and by what they have told me. The man that says slaves be quite happy in slavery—that they don't want to be free—that man is either ignorant or a lying person. I never heard a slave say so. I never heard a Buckra man say so, till I heard tell of it in England. Such people ought to be ashamed of themselves. They can't do without slaves they say. What's the reason they can't do without slaves as well as in England? No slaves here—no whips—no stocks—no punishment, except for wicked people. They hire servants in England; and if they don't like them, they send them away; they can't lick them. Let them work ever so hard in England, they are far better off than slaves. If they get a bad master, they give warning and go hire to another. They have their liberty. That's just what *we* want. We don't mind hard work, if we had proper treatment, and proper wages like English servants, and proper time given in the week to keep us from breaking the Sabbath. But they won't give it; they will have work—work—work, night and day, sick or well, till we are quite done up; and we must not speak up nor look amiss, however much we be abused. And then when we are quite done up, who cares for us, more than for a lame horse? This is slavery. I tell it to let English people know the truth; and I hope they will never leave off to pray God, and call loud to the great King of England, till all the poor blacks be given free, and slavery done up for evermore.

—1831

‎‎———

IN CONTEXT

Mary Prince and Slavery

Mary Prince's Petition Presented to Parliament on 24 June 1829

A Petition of Mary Prince or James, commonly called Molly Wood, was presented, and read; setting forth, That the Petitioner was born a Slave in the colony of Bermuda, and is now about forty years of age; That the Petitioner was sold some years go for the sum of 300 dollars to Mr. John Wood, by whom the Petitioner was carried to Antigua, where she has since, until lately resided as a domestic slave on his establishment; that in December 1826, the Petitioner who is connected with the Moravian Congregation, was married in a Moravian Chapel at Spring Gardens, in the parish of Saint John's, by the Moravian minister, Mr. Ellesen, to a free Black of the name of Daniel James, who is a carpenter at Saint John's, in Antigua, and also a member of the same congregation; that the Petitioner and the said Daniel James have lived together ever since as man and wife; that about ten months ago the Petitioner arrived in London, with her master and mistress, in the capacity of nurse to their child; that the Petitioner's master has offered to send her back in his brig to the West Indies, to work in the yard; that the Petitioner expressed her desire to return to the West Indies, but not as a slave, and has entreated her master to sell her, her freedom on account of her services as a nurse to his child, but he has refused, and still does refuse; further stating the particulars of her case; and praying the House to take the same into their consideration, and to grant such relief as to them may, under the circumstances, appear right. Ordered, That the said Petition do lie upon the Table.

from Thomas Pringle, Supplement to *The History of Mary Prince* (1831)

It was through the auspices of Thomas Pringle that Mary Prince's narrative came to be published, and that Prince found employment in London. Pringle contributed a substantial *Supplement* to the *History* when it was first published; excerpts are reproduced below.

By the Original Editor, Thomas Pringle

Leaving Mary's narrative, for the present, without comment to the reader's reflections, I proceed to state some circumstances connected with her case which have fallen more particularly under my own notice, and which I consider it incumbent now to lay fully before the public.

About the latter end of November, 1828, this poor woman found her way to the office of the Anti-Slavery Society in Aldermanbury, by the aid of a person who had become acquainted with her situation, and had advised her to apply there for advice and assistance. After some preliminary examination into the accuracy of the circumstances related by her, I went along with her to Mr. George Stephen, solicitor, and requested him to investigate and draw up a statement of her case, and have it submitted to counsel, in order to ascertain whether or not, under the circumstances, her freedom could be legally established on her return to Antigua. On this occasion, in Mr. Stephen's presence and mine, she expressed, in very strong terms, her anxiety to return thither if she could go as a free person, and, at the same time, her extreme apprehensions of the fate that would probably await her if she returned as a slave. Her words were, "I would rather go into my grave than go back a slave to Antigua, though I wish to go back to my husband very much—very much—very much! I am much afraid my owners would separate me from my husband, and use me very hard, or perhaps sell me for a field negro;—and slavery is too too bad. I would rather go into my grave!"

The paper which Mr. Wood had given her before she left his house, was placed by her in Mr. Stephen's hands. It was expressed in the following terms:—

I have already told Molly, and now give it her in writing, in order that there may be no misunderstanding on her part, that as I brought her from Antigua at her own request and entreaty, and that she is consequently now free, she is of course at liberty to take her baggage and go where she pleases. And, in consequence of her late conduct, she must do one of two things—either quit the house, or return to Antigua by the earliest opportunity, as she does not evince a disposition to make herself useful. As she is a stranger in London, I do not wish to turn her out, or would do so, as two female servants are sufficient for my establishment. If after this she does remain, it will be only during her good behaviour; but on no consideration will I allow her wages or any other remuneration for her services.

JOHN A. WOOD
London, 18 August 1828

This paper, though not devoid of inconsistencies, which will be apparent to any attentive reader, is craftily expressed; and was well devised to serve the purpose which the writer had obviously in view, namely, to frustrate any appeal which the friendless black woman might make to the sympathy of strangers, and thus prevent her from obtaining an asylum, if she left his house, from any respectable family. As she had no one to refer to for a character in this country except himself, he doubtless calculated securely on her being speedily driven back, as soon as the slender fund she had in her possession was expended, to throw herself unconditionally upon his tender mercies; and his disappointment in this expectation appears to have exasperated his feelings of resentment towards the poor woman, to a degree which few persons alive to the claims of common justice, not to speak of Christianity or common humanity, could easily have anticipated. Such, at least, seems the only intelligible inference that can be drawn from his subsequent conduct.

The case having been submitted, by desire of the Anti-Slavery Committee, to the consideration of Dr. Lushington and Mr. Sergeant Stephen, it was found that there existed no legal means of compelling Mary's master to grant her manumission; and that if she returned to Antigua, she would inevitably fall again under his power, or that of his attorneys, as a slave. It was, however, resolved to try what could be effected for her by amicable negotiation; and with this view Mr. Ravenscroft, a solicitor, (Mr. Stephen's relative,) called upon Mr. Wood, in order to ascertain whether he would consent to Mary's manumission on any reasonable terms, and to refer, if required, the amount of compensation for her value to arbitration. Mr. Ravenscroft with some difficulty obtained one or two interviews, but found Mr. Wood so full of animosity against the woman, and so firmly bent against any arrangement having her freedom for its object, that the negotiation was soon broken off as hopeless. The angry slave-owner declared "that he would not move a finger about her in this country, or grant her manumission on any terms whatever; and that if she went back to the West Indies, she must take the consequences."

This unreasonable conduct of Mr. Wood, induced the Anti-Slavery Committee, after several other abortive attempts to effect a compromise, to think of bringing the case under the notice of Parliament. The heads of Mary's statement were accordingly engrossed in a Petition, which Dr.

Lushington offered to present, and to give notice at the same time of his intention to bring in a Bill to provide for the entire emancipation of all slaves brought to England with the owner's consent. But before this step was taken, Dr. Lushington again had recourse to negotiation with the master; and, partly through the friendly intervention of Mr. Manning, partly by personal conference, used every persuasion in his power to induce Mr. Wood to relent and let the bondwoman go free. Seeing the matter thus seriously taken up, Mr. Wood became at length alarmed,—not relishing, it appears, the idea of having the case publicly discussed in the House of Commons; and to avert this result he submitted to temporize—assumed a demeanour of unwonted civility, and even hinted to Mr. Manning (as I was given to understand) that if he was not driven to utter hostility by the threatened exposure, he would probably meet our wishes "in his own time and way." Having gained time by these manoeuvres, he adroitly endeavoured to cool the ardour of Mary's new friends, in her cause, by representing her as an abandoned and worthless woman, ungrateful towards him, and undeserving of sympathy from others; allegations which he supported by the ready affirmation of some of his West India friends, and by one or two plausible letters procured from Antigua. By these and like artifices he appears completely to have imposed on Mr. Manning, the respectable West India merchant whom Dr. Lushington had asked to negotiate with him; and he prevailed so far as to induce Dr. Lushington himself (actuated by the benevolent view of thereby best serving Mary's cause), to abstain from any remarks upon his conduct when the petition was at last presented in Parliament. In this way he dextrously contrived to neutralize all our efforts, until the close of the Session of 1829; soon after which he embarked with his family for the West Indies.

Every exertion for Mary's relief having thus failed; and being fully convinced from a twelve-month's observation of her conduct, that she was really a well-disposed and respectable woman; I engaged her, in December 1829, as a domestic servant in my own family. In this capacity she has remained ever since; and I am thus enabled to speak of her conduct and character with a degree of confidence I could not have otherwise done. …

I may here add a few words respecting the earlier portion of Mary Prince's narrative. The facts there stated must necessarily rest entirely,—since we have no collateral evidence,—upon their intrinsic claims to probability, and upon the reliance the reader may feel disposed, after perusing the foregoing pages, to place on her veracity. To my judgment, the internal evidence of the truth of her narrative appears remarkably strong. The circumstances are related in a tone of natural sincerity, and are accompanied in almost every case with characteristic and minute details, which must, I conceive, carry with them full conviction to every candid mind that this negro woman has actually seen, felt, and suffered all that she so impressively describes; and that the picture she has given of West Indian slavery is not less true than it is revolting.

But there may be some persons into whose hands this tract may fall, so imperfectly acquainted with the real character of Negro Slavery, as to be shocked into partial, if not absolute incredulity, by the acts of inhuman oppression and brutality related of Capt. I— and his wife, and of Mr. D—, the salt manufacturer of Turk's Island. Here, at least, such persons may be disposed to think, there surely must be *some* exaggeration; the facts are too shocking to be credible. The facts are indeed shocking, but unhappily not the less credible on that account. Slavery is a curse to the oppressor scarcely less than to the oppressed: its natural tendency is to brutalize both.

The Narrative of Ashton Warner

The History of Mary Prince was published in January of 1831. The following month Susanna Strickland recorded the narrative of the life of another slave, Ashton Warner, which was published March 1st. No doubt inevitably, there is some similarity in the descriptions of horrific abuse in the two narratives, but there is also a good deal to suggest that Strickland was not being disingenuous in her assertion that she was quite faithful in recording these narratives as they were related to her; certainly there are noticeable differences between the narrative style of Warner and that of Prince. (Strickland's note inviting readers to "see and converse with themselves" if they doubt that someone of Warner's background would be able to express himself so well is particularly interesting in this connection.)

Advertisement

In consequence of the unexpected decease of Ashton Warner, while this little volume was in the press, the profits that may arise from its sale will no longer be required, as was originally designed, for his personal benefit. But, in compliance with a wish expressed by the poor negro on his death-bed, it is now proposed to appropriate the proceeds to the benefit of his aged mother, and the enfranchisement (should the amount prove so considerable) of his enslaved wife and child. And I have the satisfaction of being authorized to add, for the information of benevolent individuals disposed to contribute liberally towards the objects now intimated—whether by the purchase of copies of this volume, or by pecuniary donations—that the little charitable fund thus contemplated, will be placed under the immediate management of George Stephen, Esq., Solicitor, 17, King's Arms Yard, Coleman Street, and Thomas Pringle, Esq., Secretary of the Anti-Slavery Society, 18, Aldermanbury, who have kindly undertaken to superintend its proper application.

S. STRICKLAND.

from Introduction

In writing Ashton's narrative, I have adhered strictly to the simple facts, adopting, wherever it could conveniently be done, his own language, which, for a person in his condition, is remarkably expressive and appropriate. Had I been inclined to give a recital of revolting cruelty, I should have chosen another case; and for such, unhappily, I had not far to seek. But those who wish to read such mournful narratives of human depravity will find enough for their information (far too many for the honour of human nature!) recorded in the publications of the Anti-Slavery Society.

The profits arising from the sale of this tract will be appropriated to the benefit of Ashton, who has been for the last three months in England, endeavouring to establish his claims to freedom; and who is at present suffering under severe illness, without any adequate means of subsistence.

With a view to render this Sketch of Colonial Slavery more complete, and to enable the reader to compare the details given by Ashton with those recorded by intelligent and conscientious eye-witnesses from England, I have subjoined, as an Appendix, the very important testimonies on this subject of three highly respectable clergymen of the established Church, and of an excellent Wesleyan Missionary—testimonies as yet but partially known to the public, and which comprise a mass of information equally recent and interesting.

Should this little tract assist, however feebly, in the diffusion of correct information in regard to the general condition and the feelings of the slaves, and thus tend to promote the great and good cause of justice and mercy, the writer's object will be fully accomplished. Like the widow's mite cast into the sacred treasury,[1] those who love the truth will not deem it unworthy because its value is but humble.

London, 19 February 1831
S.S.

NEGRO SLAVERY
DESCRIBED
BY A NEGRO:
BEING
THE NARRATIVE OF ASHTON WARNER,
A NATIVE OF ST. VINCENT'S.
With an Appendix,
CONTAINING THE
TESTIMONY OF FOUR CHRISTIAN MINISTERS,
RECENTLY RETURNED FROM THE COLONIES,
ON THE SYSTEM OF SLAVERY AS IT NOW EXISTS.
BY
S. STRICKLAND.

"And tears and toil have been my lot
Since I the white man's thrall became;
And sorer griefs I wish forgot—
Harsh blows and burning shame!
Oh, Englishman! thou ne'er canst know
The injured bondman's bitter woe,
When round his heart, like scorpions, cling
Black thoughts that madden while they sting!"

LONDON:
SAMUEL MAUNDER, NEWGATE STREET.
1831.

from The Narrative of Ashton Warner (1831)

I was born in the Island of St. Vincent's, and baptized by the name of Ashton Warner, in the parish church, by the Rev. Mr. Gildon. My father and mother, at the time of my birth, were slaves on Cane Grove estate, in Bucumar Valley, then the property of Mr. Ottley. I was an infant at the breast when Mr. Ottley died; and shortly after the estate was put to sale, that the property might be divided among his family. Before Cane Grove was sold, my aunt, Daphne Crosbie, took the opportunity of buying my mother and me of Mr. Ottley's trustees. My aunt had been a slave, but a favoured one. She had money left her by a coloured gentleman of the name of Crosbie, with whom she lived, and whose name she took. After his death she went to reside at Kingston. Finding it a good thing to be free, aunt Daphne wished to make all her friends free also, particularly the slaves on the estate where she was born, and with whom she had shared, in her early days, all the sorrows of negro servitude. She had a large heart, and felt great kindness for her own people; but her means were not equal to her

---

[1] *widow's ... treasury* See Luke 21.1–4.

good wishes. She bought her old parents of Mr. Jackson, Mr. Ottley's executor; and, as it was her earnest desire to make us all happy, she would have bought my uncle John Baptiste (my mother's brother) too; but Mr. Wilson, the gentleman who purchased the estate, would not sell him, His reason for refusing my aunt never knew, for my uncle was an old man then, and nearly past work. Mr. Wilson sent him away to the Island of St. Lucia, and it was some years before aunt Daphne heard any tidings of him. At last some persons, coming from St. Lucia to St. Vincent's, told her that he lay very sick on Mr. Grant's estate. My aunt was glad to find that he was still living, and she went herself to make him free. She had never crossed the water, or been on the great sea, but she overcame her fears, and hired a small boat, and went directly to St. Lucia. She found my poor uncle in a very miserable state, and in this condition she bought him of his master, and brought him back to St. Vincent's. He was ill a long, long time; it was many long weary months before he could even take up a broom to sweep the house. He was very grateful to aunt Daphne for all that she had done for him; and so were we all. She was a very good, kind woman, and a Christian, though a black woman; and we (her relations) all loved her very, very much. We had no one else to love—she was all the world to us.

Whilst I lived with my aunt at Kingston I was very happy. I had no heavy tasks to do; and she was as careful over me as if she had been my own mother, and used to keep me with her in the house, that I might not be playing about in the streets with bad companions. My mother made sausages and *souse*,[1] and I used to help her to carry them to gentlemen's houses for sale. This was light labour to her, for she had been a field slave, kept at hard work, and driven to it by the whip. I am sure our best days were spent with my dear aunt; nor did she make us alone happy; all the money she could save went to purchase the freedom of slaves who had formerly been her companions in bondage at Cane Grove, or to make their condition better. There was not a person upon the island who did not speak well of Daphne Crosbie; black or white it was all the same. She bore a good character until the day she died.

I lived with my aunt till I was ten years old, when I was claimed as a slave belonging to the Cane Grove estate, by Mr. Wilson. This was a hard and unjust claim; but Mr. Wilson said, that though my mother was sold I was not—that the best slaves had been sold off the estate—that I was *his* property, and he would claim me wherever I was to be found. Now, he was wrong in all this, and I can prove to you, in two short minutes, that I did not belong to him. When my aunt manumitted my mother and me, Mr. Wilson had not-yet bought the estate; and in the Island of St. Vincent's it has always been a customary rule that the young child at the breast is sold as one with its mother, and does not become separate property till it is five or six years old; so that Mr. Wilson's claim was very unjust and oppressive.[2]

When my aunt found Mr. Wilson bent on taking me away by force, she went to Mr. Jackson, the gentleman from whom she had purchased my mother, and told him the state of the case, and he gave her a written paper to take to the Chief Justice of the island, to prove that I belonged to Daphne Crosbie, should Mr. Wilson continue to claim me. My aunt went to the Governor and showed him this paper, and also the manumission paper she had received from Mr. Jackson. The Governor, after looking at it, said that Mr. Wilson had no legal right to claim me upon the estate, and he promised my aunt that he would write to him to that effect. But we never knew whether he did or not, for we never got an answer from him. It is of no use trusting to what the white people in the West Indies say; they always forget their promises to slaves. Before this happened, my aunt had bound me apprentice

---

[1] [Strickland's note] Slices of pig's head, salted and prepared in a particular manner, and sold in the markets by the slaves.

[2] [Strickland's note] This is poor Ashton's own statement. Whether the Colonial *Slave Law* will support his claim for freedom on this ground, is a question which remains to be determined.—S.S.

to a cooper, to learn his trade. I was bound for seven years, and had signed the indenture myself, as a free black, by making a cross for my name.

My master's name was Pierre Wynn. He was a kind good master, and I never ceased to lament the cause which parted me from him. I had been with him between two and three months, and was busy one morning at work in the cooper's yard, helping the journeyman to truss a molasses-cask, when Mr. Wilson's manager, Mr. Donald, with two coloured men, and a white named Newman, came into the yard. This man, Newman, had informed Mr. Wilson where I was, and he sent his people to take me away by force. When the manager came into the yard, he said, "Which is Ashton?" I answered, quite innocently, not suspecting any mischief, "I am Ashton." Directly I said so the manager caught hold of me by the back of my neck. I did not know why he held me. I did not know what to think—I could not get my breath to speak—I was dreadfully frightened, and trembled all over. The other men got hold of me, and held me fast. They then led me away to Mr. Dalzell, Mr. Wilson's attorney, and shut me up in his office till Mr. Wilson came. Mr. Dalzell was afraid that I would try to make my escape, and to make sure of me one man kept watch at the window and another at the door. When Mr. Wilson came in he did not know me, and asked who I was. One of the men told him that I was Ashton. He said, "Very well; keep him here till I am ready to send him down to the estate." He then came up to the place where I was standing, and examined me from head to foot; then turned to Mr. Dalzell, and began talking to him about me. I was too young, and too much frightened at being stolen away, to remember much of their discourse; but I am very sure that I shall never forget that day.

Before Mr. Wilson left the office, my mother and Daphne Crosbie came to hear what was to be done with me, and why I had been taken away. But all they said was of no use; they could do no good where there was no justice to be had. Mr. Wilson insisted that I was a slave, and *his* slave, and he would have it so, in spite of my mother's tears and my aunt's entreaties. My poor mother was greatly distressed, and cried very bitterly. She entreated Mr. Wilson, if he thought he had a just claim for me, to put me in gaol till the question as to my freedom could be fairly settled; but he refused to do this, and when she continued her entreaties he grew angry, and ordered her not to stop in the yard, but to go away directly. And she and aunt Crosbie, on finding that nothing could be done for me there, were obliged to leave me in his hands.

The manager then put me into a boat, and took me down to the estate. It was rather late in the afternoon when we got there. I had nothing given me to do that day. It was Saturday, and I was not set to work till the Monday morning. I was very sad, and wished very much to run away. I could not bear the thought of being a slave, and I was very restless and unhappy.

On the Monday morning, John, the head cooper, took me down to the sugar works to help him; but I had no heart to work—I did nothing but think how I might run away. I was not knowing enough, however, to make my escape; and, after consulting with myself a long time, I found it would be the best plan to make myself as patient as I could. But still I was always thinking of my mother and aunt, and of Pierre Wynn, and the home I had been taken from. The estate of Cane Grove was in the middle of a deep valley, near the sea shore. Mr. Wilson's house stood upon the brow of the hill, and overlooked the whole sugar plantation. He had about three hundred slaves, and was considered one of the severest masters in the whole island.

As I have spoken of the condition of the field negroes as being so much worse than that of the mechanics among whom I was ranked on the estate, I shall here endeavour to describe the manner in which the field gang were worked on Cane Grove estate. They were obliged to be in the field before five o'clock in the morning; and, as the negro houses were at the distance of from three to four miles from the cane pieces, they were generally obliged to rise as early as four o'clock, to be at their work in time. The driver is first in the field, and calls the slaves together by cracking the whip or blowing the conch shell. Before five o'clock the overseer calls over the roll; and if any of the slaves are so unfortunate as to be too late, even by a few minutes, which, owing to the distance, is often the case, the driver flogs them as they come in, with the cart-whip, or with a scourge of tamarind rods. When flogged with the whip, they are stripped and held down upon the ground, and exposed in the most shameful manner.

In the cultivation of the canes the slaves work in a row. Each person has a hoe, and the women are expected to do as much as the men. This work is so hard that any slave, newly put to it, in the course of a month becomes so weak that often he is totally unfit for labour. If he falls back behind the rest, the driver keeps forcing him up with the whip.

They work from five o'clock to nine, when they are allowed to sit down for half an hour in the field, and take such food as they have been able to prepare over night. But many have no food ready, and so fast till mid-day.

They go to work again directly after half an hour's respite, and labour till twelve o'clock, when they leave off for dinner. They are allowed two hours of mid-day intermission, out of crop time, and an hour and a half in crop time.

During this interval every slave must pick a bundle of grass to bring home for the cattle at night. The grass grows in tufts, often scattered over a great space of ground, and, when the season is dry, it is very scarce and withered, so that the slaves collect it slowly and with difficulty, and are often employed most of the time allowed them for mid-day rest, in seeking for it. I have frequently known them occupied the whole two hours in collecting it.

They work again in gang from two till seven o'clock. It is then dark. When they return home the overseer calls over the roll, and demands of every man and woman their bundles of grass. He weighs with his hand each bundle as it is given in, and, if it be too light, the person who presents it is either instantly laid down and flogged severely with the cart-whip, or is put into the stocks for the whole night. If the slaves bring home no grass, they are not only put into the stocks all night, but are more severely flogged the next morning. This grass-picking is a very sore grievance to the field slaves.

When they are manuring the ground, the slaves are forced to carry the wet manure in open baskets upon their heads. This is most unpleasant as well as severe work. It is a usual occupation for wet weather, and the moisture from the manure drips constantly down upon the faces, and over the body and clothes of the slaves. They are forced to run with their loads as fast as they can; and, if they flag, the driver is instantly at their heels with the cart-whip.

The crop-time usually commences in January and lasts till June, and, if the season is wet, till July. During this season every slave must bring in a bundle of cane-tops for the cattle, instead of a bundle of grass. They then go immediately to the sugar works, where they have to take up the *mogass* which was spread out at nine o'clock in the morning to dry for fuel to boil the sugar. This mogass is the stalks of the cane after the juice has been squeezed out by the mill. The slaves are employed till ten at night in gathering in the mogass, that it may not be wetted with the dew and rendered unfit for immediate use. The overseer then calls over the roll, and issues orders for a certain spell of them to be up and at the works at one o'clock in the morning. After this the slaves have to prepare their suppers; for, if they have no very aged parents or friends belonging to them, they must do this themselves, which occupies them another hour. Every creature that is capable of work must take a part in the labours of the crop; and no person remains at home but those who are totally unfit for work. Slaves who are too old and weak to go to the field have to make up bundles of mogass, cut grass for the stock, &c.

During this season all the mechanics on the estate are employed to pot the sugar; carpenters, coopers, masons, and rum-distillers, even the pasture-boys who tend the cattle, are called in to assist. To the little people are given small tubs to carry the sugar into the curing house; and the grown-up slaves have shovels to fill the tubs for them. When employed in potting the sugar, we did not leave off to get our breakfast till ten or eleven o'clock, and I have known it mid-day before we have tasted food.

The whole gang of field slaves are divided into spells, and every man and woman able to work has not only to endure during crop-time the severe daily labour, but to work half the night also, or three whole nights in the week. The work is very severe, and great numbers of the slaves, during this period, sink under it, and become ill; but if they complain, their complaints are not readily believed, or are considered only a pretence to escape from labour. If they are so very ill that their inability to work can be no longer doubted, they are at length sent to the sick house.

The sick-house is just like a pen to keep pigs in; if you wish to keep yourself clean and decent, you cannot. It is one of the greatest punishments to the slaves to be sent there. When we were hard pressed, and had much sugar to pot, the manager would often send to the sick-house for the people who were sick, or lame with sores, to help us. If they refused to come, and said that they were unable to work, they were taken down and severely flogged, by the manager's order, with the cart-whip. There is nothing in slavery harder to bear than this. When you are ill and cannot work, your pains are made light of, and your complaints neither listened to, nor believed. I have seen people who were so sick that they could scarcely stand, dragged out of the sick-house, and tied up to a tree, and flogged in a shocking manner; then driven with the whip to the work. I have seen slaves in this state crawl away, and lie down among the wet trash to get a little ease, though they knew that it would most likely cause their death.

The quantity of food allowed the slaves is from two pounds and a half to three pounds of salt-fish per week, for each grown person. They could easily eat this in two days, but they must make it last till they receive a fresh allowance from the overseer. The rest of their food they raise upon their provision grounds. The owner gives to each slave from thirty to forty feet square of ground; not the best ground, but such as has been over-cropped, and is no longer productive for canes. This is taken from them the next year, when, by manuring and planting with yams and other things, it has been brought round, and recovered strength for the cultivation of sugar. The slaves are likewise permitted to cultivate waste pieces of ground, and the headlands of fields, that are unfit for planting. They work this ground every Sunday. It is generally given to them in March or April, and it is taken away in December or January. Besides the Sunday, they get part of twenty-six Saturdays, out of crop-time, to cultivate their grounds. What I mean by saying they get only *part* of these Saturdays is this—that they are employed in their master's work, such as carrying out trash, &c., from five to ten o'clock in the forenoon; and in the evening they must bring each his bundle of grass to deliver as usual at the calling of the lists; so that about seven hours, even of the day which is called their own, is occupied with their owner's work. They are obliged to work on these days at the provision grounds, if they wish ever so much for a holiday. If they are absent when the overseer inspects the grounds, they are flogged, or put in the stocks. The grounds produce plantains, yams, potatoes, pumpkins, calabashes, &c. On the Sunday, at every town, a market is held, in which the slaves are allowed to sell the produce of their grounds. Those that can save a little money, buy a pig and fatten it, that, in case of any death happening among their friends, they may sell the pig to provide a few necessaries for the funeral. They bury the dead during the night, being allowed no time during the day for their funerals.

In building their houses, they are allowed as much board as will form a window and a door. They go to the woods and cut wild canes, to form the walls and roof. The huts are thatched with cane-trash or tops.

For clothing, the owner gives to each slave in the year six yards of blue stuff, called bamboo, and six yards of brown. The young people and children are given a less allowance, in proportion to their size and age; the young children getting only a small stripe to tie round the waist. For bed-clothing, they give them only a blanket once in four or five years; and they are obliged to wear this till it falls in pieces. If the slaves require other clothes, they must buy them out of their own little savings. Many of the field negroes are very badly off for clothing. A good many are always to be seen with only a rag of cloth round their loins in all weathers.

People so hardly, so harshly, treated, and so destitute of every comfort, cannot be supposed to work with a willing mind. They have no home which they can well call their own. They are worked beyond their strength, and live in perpetual fear of the whip. They are insulted, tormented, and indecently exposed and degraded; yet English people wonder that they are not contented. Some have even said that they are happy! Let such people place themselves for a few minutes under the same yoke, and see if they could bear it. Such bondage is ruin both to the soul and body of the slave; and I hope every good Englishman will daily pray to God, that the yoke of slavery may soon be broken from off the necks of my unfortunate countrymen for ever.[1]

What made me feel more deeply for the sad condition of the field slaves was the circumstance of my having taken a wife from among them, after I had resided several years on Cane Grove estate. When I was about twenty-one years of age, finding my condition lonely, because I had no friends to manage for me, as the other slaves had, I wished to marry, and have a home of my own, and a kind partner to do for me. Among the field slaves there was a very respectable young woman, called Sally, for whom I had long felt a great deal of regard. At last I asked her to be my wife; and we stood up in her father's house, before her mother, and her uncle, and her sisters, and, holding each other by the hand, pledged our troth as husband and wife, and promised before God to be good and kind to each other, and to love and help each other, as long as we lived.

And so we married. And though it was not as white folks marry, before the parson, yet I considered her as much my wife, and I loved her as well, as though we had been married in the church; and she was as careful, and managed as well for me, as if she had been my mother. I could not bear to see her work in the field. It is, as I have already said, a very sad and hard condition of slavery; and the more my wife suffered, the more I wished to be free, and to make her so. When she was with child, she was flogged for not coming out early enough to work, and afterwards, when far advanced in pregnancy, she was put into the stocks by the manager, because she said she was unable to go to the field. My heart was almost broken to see her so treated, but I could do nothing to help her; and it would have made matters worse if I had attempted to speak up for her. She was twice punished in this cruel manner, though the overseer must have known that she was in no condition to work. After our child was born, she was again repeatedly flogged for not coming sooner to the field, though she had stopped merely to attend and suckle the baby. But they had no feeling for the mother or for her child, they cared only for the work. It is a dreadful thing to be a field negro; and it is scarcely less dreadful, if one's heart is not quite hardened, to have a wife, or a husband, or a child, in that condition. On this account I was often grieved that I had taken poor Sally to be my wife; for it caused her more suffering as a mother, while her cruel treatment wrung my heart, without my being able to move a finger, or utter a word, in her behalf.

---

[1] [Strickland's note] Such is the impressive language in which Ashton speaks of slavery. The above are his own expressions; for, though an uneducated, he is a very intelligent negro, and speaks remarkably good English. Any reader, who wishes it, may see and converse with himself, by making application through the publisher.—S.S.

SLAVERY AND ITS ABOLITION

CONTEXTS

In the 1750s it was possible for John Newton, the author of the hymn "Amazing Grace," to write that neither he nor any of his friends had had any notion that "slavery could be considered unlawful and wrong." By 1807 the tide had turned sufficiently that the British Parliament (through the Slave Trade Act) prohibited British vessels from participating in the trading of humans. And in 1833 (through the Slavery Abolition Act) slavery in most British territory was ended.

What brought about such a vast change in such a relatively short time? In part the answer lies in the history of ideas; the Enlightenment gave birth to concepts of freedom and equality—of human rights which, as they were thought through, were widely recognized to apply to all humans, regardless of gender, regardless of race. These ideas, though not initially thought to apply to those enslaved by the world's empires, did lead to antislavery uprisings and revolutions, most notably (and successfully) in Haiti, between 1789 and 1804. But the abolition first of the slave trade and then of slavery itself in Britain and its colonies was also the result of concerted political pressure. Some have identified the birth of the modern political movement and modern political lobbying in the campaign to abolish slavery. Certainly the Society for Effecting the Abolition of the Slave Trade, formed in 1787 and led by Thomas Clarkson and Granville Sharp, among others, played a hugely important role in acquiring and disseminating information as to the actual conditions endured by enslaved people, and in pressuring the government to take action. In Parliament, William Wilberforce became the de facto leader of the antislavery movement: Wilberforce, the author of *Practical Christianity*, was tireless in his efforts. The Society of Friends (also known as the Quakers) also played a leading role, both within the Society for Effecting the Abolition of the Slave Trade and independently, in shaping public opinion and pressing for change. Former enslaved people, such as Olaudah Equiano and Mary Prince, testified to the inhumanity of slavery in persuasive works of autobiography. And a number of established authors—including William Wordsworth, Samuel Taylor Coleridge, Helen Maria Williams, Anna Laetitia Barbauld, and Mary Robinson—lent their voices to the cause.

The legal system too played an important role in the process. In a landmark 1772 case the owner of one James Somerset lost his legal suit to regain ownership of Somerset, who had run away from servitude while in England. Lord Mansfield, the Lord Chief Justice, ruled in Somerset's favor. The language he used stated only that there was no legal justification for forcibly transporting enslaved people out of England for sale, but the verdict was popularly interpreted to mean that, according to the established principles of English law, everyone in England was free. Despite Mansfield's *caveat* against taking his ruling to apply to British possessions overseas, the progressive decision also gave abolitionists some reason to feel confident that the law would eventually support their arguments universally and unequivocally, in Britain's colonies as well as within Britain itself.

⌘ ⌘ ⌘

from John Newton, *A Slave Trader's Journal* (1751)

John Newton (1725–1807) first went to sea at the age of ten, sailing with his father, the captain of the vessel. By the age of twenty-eight he had wide experience both of the sea and of the slave trade, and was for the first time commanding a vessel himself. The *Duke of Argyll* left England for Bassa in West Africa (in what is now Guinea Bissau) in 1750, made the "middle passage" from Bassa to Antigua in the West Indies between 22 May and 2 July, and returned to Liverpool with a cargo of sugar, arriving in November. The following excerpts are from Newton's journal of that voyage. In later life, Newton came to regret deeply his life as a slave trader (which he had given up for health reasons in 1754). He became a Christian minister and wrote that he would have left the slave trade sooner "had I considered it as I now do to be unlawful and wrong. But I never had a scruple upon this head at the time; nor was such a thought ever suggested to me by any friend." In 1770 Newton wrote the famous hymn "Amazing Grace." He became a strong advocate for the abolition of the slave trade.

Thursday 16 May

… [A] long boat came on board from Grande Bassa. I sent Billinge [the second mate] chiefly to satisfy myself of the state and price of slaves. He says the glut we heard so much of is entirely over, the Brittannia and Ranger having met very few. About Settra Crue there is still plenty (upon the account of a war very probably begun with that view) but extravagantly dear. … He brought me a sample of the prices in a woman slave he bought at Bassa, which upon costing up the goods I find cost 96 bars, and I ordered him to get one upon any terms for that reason. That I might not think he gave more than usual, he brought me a list of goods he saw Saunders pay for a man which amounts to 102 bars, and the farther to leeward the dearer still. I think I have sufficient reason not to go down, for setting aside the cost, the assortments in demand there would ruin me soon.

Tuesday 28 May

Secured the after bulkhead of the men's room, for they had started almost every stantient. Their plot was exceedingly well laid, and had they been let alone an hour longer, must have occasioned us a good deal of trouble and damage. I have reason to be thankful they did not make attempts upon the coast when we had often 7 or 8 of our best men out of the ship at a time and the rest busy. They still look very gloomy and sullen and have doubtless mischief in their heads if they could find every opportunity to vent it. But I hope (by the Divine Assistance) we are fully able to overawe them now. …

Wednesday 12 June

Got the slaves up this morn. Washed them all with fresh water. They complained so much that was obliged to let them go down again when the rooms were cleaned. Buryed a man slave (No. 84) of a flux, which he has been struggling with near 7 weeks. …

Saturday 22 June

Being pretty warm, got up the men and washed all the slaves with fresh water. I am much afraid of another ravage from the flux, for we have had 8 taken within these few days. Have seen 2 or 3 tropick birds and a few flying fish.

Monday 24 June

Buried a girl slave (No. 92). In the afternoon while we were off the deck, William Cooney seduced a woman slave down into the room and lay with her brutelike in view of the whole quarter deck, for which I put him in irons.[1] I hope this has been the first affair of the kind on board and I am determined to keep them quiet if possible. If anything happens to the woman I shall impute it to him, for she was big with child. Her number is 83. …

---

[1] *for which … irons* In contrast to Newton, some captains actively encouraged their crew to rape the enslaved women, since pregnant women could be sold at a higher price; mulatto children were especially highly valued as house servants.

Friday 28 June

By the favour of Divine Providence made a timely discovery today that the slaves were forming a plot for an insurrection. Surprised 2 of them attempting to get off their irons, and upon farther search in their rooms, upon the information of 3 of the boys, found some knives, stones, shot, etc., and a cold chissel. Upon enquiry there appeared 8 principally concerned to move in projecting the mischief and 4 boys in supplying them with the above instruments. Put the boys in irons and slightly in the thumbscrews to urge them to a full confession. We have already 36 men out of our small number. …

Friday 5 July

… [I]n the morning Mr. Guichard went off with me to view the slaves. When came on shore again, after comparing orders and intelligence, he judged it best for the concern to sell here, if I approved it, without which, he was pleased to say, he would do nothing, tho my letters from the owners referred me wholly to his direction. It seems by all I can learn that this is likely to prove as good a market as any of the neighbouring islands; and as for Jamaica or America, I should be extremely loth to venture so far, for we have had the men slaves so long on board that their patience is just worn out, and I am certain they would drop fast had we another passage to make. Monday is appointed for the sale.

from Quobna Ottobah Cugoano, *Thoughts and Sentiments on the Evil and Wicked Traffic of the Slavery and Commerce of the Human Species* (1787)

> Cugoano was kidnapped in West Africa in 1770 and sold into slavery in the West Indies. His owner traveled with him to England in 1772, and he declared himself a free man on English soil following the landmark Somerset case. His *Thoughts and Sentiments* is the first substantial antislavery work by a Black writer.

But why should total abolition, and an universal emancipation of slaves, and the enfranchisement of all the Black People employed in the culture of the Colonies, taking place as it ought to do, and without any hesitation, or delay for a moment, even though it might have some seeming appearance of loss either to government or to individuals, be feared at all? Their labour, as freemen, would be as useful in the sugar colonies as any other class of men that could be found; and should it even take place in such a manner that some individuals, at first, would suffer loss as a just reward for their wickedness in slave-dealing, what is that to the happiness and good of doing justice to others; and, I must say, to the great danger, otherwise, that must eventually hang over the whole community? It is certain, that the produce of the labour of slaves, together with all the advantages of the West-India traffic, bring in an immense revenue to government; but let that amount be what it will, there might be as much or more expected from the labour of an equal increase of free people, and without the implication of any guilt attending it, and which, otherwise, must be a greater burden to bear, and more ruinous consequences to be feared from it, than if the whole national debt was to sink at once, and to rest upon the heads of all that might suffer by it. Whereas, if a generous encouragement were to be given to a free people, peaceable among themselves, intelligent and industrious, who by art and labour would improve the most barren situations, and make the most of that which is fruitful; the free and voluntary labour of many, would soon yield to any government, many greater advantages than any thing that slavery can produce. And this should be expected, wherever a Christian government is extended, and the true religion is embraced, that the blessings of liberty should be extended likewise, and that it should diffuse its influences first to fertilize the mind, and then the effects of its benignity would extend, and arise with exuberant blessings and advantages from all its operations. Was this to be the case, every thing would increase and prosper at home and abroad, and ten thousand times greater and greater advantages would arise to the state, and more permanent and solid benefit to individuals from the service of freemen, than ever they can reap, or in any possible way enjoy, by the labour of slaves. …

from Alexander Falconbridge, *Account of the Slave Trade on the Coast of Africa* (1788)

Falconbridge sailed aboard slave trading vessels as a surgeon in the 1780s. The work from which the following excerpts are taken was given wide distribution by the Society for Effecting the Abolition of the Slave Trade. In 1789 Falconbridge also testified as to the horrors of the trade before the Parliamentary Committee investigating the issue.

The men negroes, on being brought aboard the ship, are immediately fastened together, two and two, by hand-cuffs on their wrists, and by irons rivetted on their legs. They are then sent down between the decks, and placed in an apartment partitioned off for that purpose. The women likewise are placed in a separate apartment between decks, but without being ironed. And an adjoining room, on the same deck, is besides appointed for the boys. Thus are they all placed in different apartments.

But at the same time, they are frequently stowed so close, as to admit of no other posture than lying on their sides. Neither will the height between decks, unless directly under the grating, permit them the indulgence of an erect posture; especially where there are platforms, which is generally the case. These platforms are a kind of shelf, about eight or nine feet in breadth, extending from the side of the ship towards the centre. They are placed nearly midway between the decks, at the distance of two or three feet from each deck. Upon these the negroes are stowed in the same manner as they are on the deck underneath.

In each of the apartments are placed three or four large buckets, of a conical form, being near two feet in diameter at the bottom, and only one foot at the top, and in depth about twenty-eight inches; to which, when necessary, the negroes have recourse. It often happens, that those who are placed at a distance from the buckets,

in endeavouring to get to them, tumble over their companions, in consequence of their being shackled. These accidents, although unavoidable, are productive of continual quarrels, in which some of them are always bruised. In this distressed situation, unable to proceed, and prevented from getting to the tubs, they desist from the attempt; and, as the necessities of nature are not to be repelled, ease themselves as they lie. This becomes a fresh source of broils and disturbances, and tends to render the condition of the poor captive wretches still more uncomfortable. The nuisance arising from these circumstances, is not unfrequently increased by the tubs being much too small for the purpose intended, and their being usually emptied but once every day. The rule for doing this, however, varies in different ships, according to the attention paid to the health and convenience of the slaves by the captain. …

The diet of the negroes, while on board, consists chiefly of horse-beans, boiled to the consistence of a pulp; of boiled yams and rice, and sometimes of a small quantity of beef or pork. The latter are frequently taken from the provisions laid in for the sailors. They sometimes make use of a sauce, composed of palm-oil, mixed with flour, water, and pepper, which the sailors call *slabber-sauce.* Yams are the favourite food of the Eboe, or Bight negroes, and rice or corn, of those from the Gold and Windward Coasts; each preferring the produce of their native soil. …

They are commonly fed twice a day, about eight o'clock in the morning and four in the afternoon. In most ships they are only fed with their *own food* once a day. Their food is served up to them in tubs, about the size of a small water bucket. They are placed round these tubs in companies of ten to each tub, out of which they feed themselves with wooden spoons. These they soon lose, and when they are not allowed others, they feed themselves with their hands. In favourable weather they are fed upon deck, but in bad weather their food is given them below. Numberless quarrels take place among them during their meals; more especially when they are put upon short allowance. … Their allowance of water is about half a pint each at every meal. It is handed round in a bucket, and given to each negroe in a panne-kin; a small utensil with a strait handle, somewhat similar to a sauce-boat. …

Upon the negroes refusing to take sustenance, I have seen coals of fire, glowing hot, put on a shovel, and placed so near their lips, as to scorch and burn them. And this has been accompanied with threats, of forcing them to swallow the coals, if they any longer persisted in refusing to eat. These means have generally had the desired effect. I have also been credibly informed, that a certain captain in the slave trade, poured melted lead on such of the negroes as obstinately refused their food.

Exercise being deemed necessary for the preservation of their health, they are sometimes obliged to dance, when the weather will permit their coming on deck. If they go about it reluctantly, or do not move with agility, they are flogged; a person standing by them all the time with a cat-o'-nine-tails[1] in his hand for that purpose. Their musick, upon these occasions consists of a drum, sometimes with only one head; and when that is worn out, they do not scruple to make use of the bottom of one of the tubs before described. The poor wretches are frequently compelled to sing also; but when they do so, their songs are generally, as may naturally be expected, melancholy lamentations of their exile from their native country. …

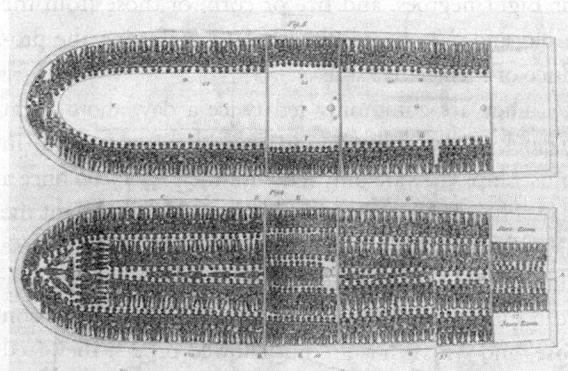

Diagram showing allotment of space for enslaved people on two decks of a late eighteenth-century sailing ship.

---

[1] *cat-o'-nine-tails* Switch with nine ropes attached, used as a beating implement.

On board some ships, the common sailors are allowed to have intercourse with such of the black women whose consent they can procure. And some of them have been known to take the inconstancy of their paramours so much to heart, as to leap overboard and drown themselves. The officers are permitted to indulge their passions among them at pleasure, and sometimes are guilty of such brutal excesses, as disgrace human nature.

William Cowper, "Sweet Meat Has Sour Sauce, or, The Slave-Trader in the Dumps"[2] (1788)

A trader I am to the African shore,
But since that my trading is like to be o'er,
I'll sing you a song that you ne'er heard before,
    Which nobody can deny, deny,
5   Which nobody can deny.

When I first heard the news it gave me a shock,
Much like what they call an electrical knock,
And now I am going to sell off my stock,
    Which nobody, &c.

10 'Tis a curious assortment of dainty regales,
To tickle the negroes with when the ship sails,
Fine chains for the neck, and a cat with nine tails,
    Which nobody, &c.

Here's supple-jack plenty, and store of rat-tan,[3]
15 That will wind itself round the sides of a man,
As close as a hoop round a bucket or can,
    Which nobody, &c.

Here's padlocks and bolts, and screws for the thumbs,
That squeeze them so lovingly till the blood comes,

---

[2] *Sweet Meat … Dumps* The poem is one of several antislavery poems by Cowper. The Society for Effecting the Abolition of the Slave Trade distributed his ballad "The Negro's Complaint" widely; both that poem and this were set to music and sung as well as read.

[3] *supple-jack* Climbing vine; *rat-tan* Palm stem. Both supple-jack and rattan were used for switches or canes.

20   They sweeten the temper like comfits or plums,[1]
    Which nobody, &c.

When a negro his head from his victuals withdraws,
And clenches his teeth and thrusts out his paws,
Here's a notable engine to open his jaws,
25   Which nobody, &c.

Thus going to market, we kindly prepare
A pretty black cargo of African ware,
For what they must meet with when they get there,
    Which nobody, &c.

30   'Twould do your heart good to see 'em below
Lie flat on their backs all the way as we go,
Like sprats on a gridiron,[2] scores in a row,
    Which nobody, &c.

But ah! if in vain I have studied an art
35   So gainful to me, all boasting apart,
I think it will break my compassionate heart,
    Which nobody, &c.

For oh! how it enters my soul like an awl![3]
This pity, which some people self-pity call,
40   Is sure the most heart-piercing pity of all,
    Which nobody, &c.

So this is my song, as I told you before;
Come buy off my stock, for I must no more
Carry Caesars and Pompeys[4] to Sugar-cane shore,
45   Which nobody can deny, deny,
    Which nobody can deny.

---

[1] *comfits or plums* Sweetmeats; sugarplums: fruits preserved with sugar.

[2] *sprats on a gridiron* Small fish on a griddle or broiling-pan.

[3] *awl* Tool for piercing holes in leather.

[4] *Caesars and Pompeys* Names commonly given to enslaved people from Africa.

from William Wilberforce, "Speech to the House of Commons," 13 May 1789

William Wilberforce began his long struggle to have the British Parliament abolish the slave trade with the speech excerpted below. In April of 1791, a bill put forward by Wilberforce was voted down by 163 votes to 88; not until 1807 were his efforts on this score successful. News of the passage of the Slavery Abolition Act reached Wilberforce on his deathbed in 1833.

A report has been made by his Majesty's Privy Council, which, I trust, every Gentleman has read, and which ascertains the Slave Trade to be just such in practice as we know, from theory, that it must be. What should we suppose must naturally be the consequence of our carrying on a Slave Trade with Africa? With a country, vast in its extent, not utterly barbarous, but civilized in a very small degree? Does any one suppose a Slave Trade would *help* their civilization? That Africa would *profit* by such an intercourse? Is it not plain, that she must *suffer* from it? That civilization must be checked; that her barbarous manners must be made more barbarous; and that the happiness of her millions of inhabitants must be prejudiced by her intercourse with Britain? Does not every one see, that a Slave Trade, carried on around her coasts, must carry violence and desolation to her very centre? That, in a Continent, just emerging from barbarism, if a Trade in Men is established—if her men are all converted into goods, and become commodities that can be bartered, it follows, they must be subject to ravage just as goods are; and this too, at a period of civilization, when there is no protecting Legislature to defend this their only sort of property, in the same manner as the rights of property are maintained by the legislature of every civilized country.

We see then, in the nature of things, how easily all the practices of Africa are to be accounted for. Her kings are never compelled to war, that we can hear of, by public principles,—by national glory—still less by the love of their people. In Europe it is the extension of commerce, the maintenance of national honor, or some great public object, that is ever the motive to war with every monarch; but, in Africa, it is the personal *avarice* and *sensuality* of their kings: these two vices of avarice and sensuality, (the most powerful and predominant in natures thus corrupt) we tempt, we stimulate in all these African Princes, and we depend upon these vices for the very maintenance of the Slave Trade. ...

Sir, the nature and all the circumstances of this trade are now laid open to us; we can no longer plead ignorance,—we cannot evade it,—it is now an object placed before us,—we cannot pass it; we may spurn it, we may kick it out of our way, but we cannot turn aside so as to avoid seeing it; for it is brought now so directly before our eyes, that this House must decide, and must justify to all the world, and to their own consciences, the rectitude of the grounds and principles of their decision.

A Society [the Society for Effecting the Abolition of the Slave Trade] has been established for the abolition of this trade, [in 1787] in which Dissenters, Quakers, Churchmen—in which the most conscientious of all persuasions have all united, and made a common cause in this great question. Let not Parliament be the only body that is insensible to the principles of national justice. Let us make reparation to Africa, so far as we can, by establishing a trade upon true commercial principles, and we shall soon find the rectitude of our conduct rewarded, by the benefits of a regular and a growing commerce.

Proponents of Slavery

It is often (and rightly) pointed out that appeals to Christian virtue were central to the abolitionist cause. As some of the following excerpts illustrate, appeals to Christian principles were also made on the other side of the argument—as were appeals of a variety of other sorts.

from Reverend Robert Boncher Nicholls, *Observations, Occasioned by the Attempts Made in England to Effect the Abolition of the Slave Trade* (1788)

[T he author] thought it incumbent on him first to search the scriptures, to learn whether slavery was inconsistent with the revealed will of the Deity. The result of his enquiry was perfectly satisfactory to himself, and he thought it but right to point out some few of the many passages, to be found in the sacred volumes, which justify that commerce. Since the following observations went to the press the author has the great satisfaction to find, that he might have pursued his original plan without any injury to the cause he has endeavoured to support, as he has seen a pamphlet by the Rev. Mr. Harris, of Liverpool, who has so clearly proved, from the scriptures, that slavery is neither contrary to the law nor gospel, that it is scarcely possible for the most conscientious believer, who reads that tract, to doubt in future; whether the man servant or the maid servant is not as much a man's property as "*his ox or his ass, or any thing that is his.*" ...

About the time of Lord Mansfield's determination in the case of Mr. Stuart's negro, [those in England who were attended by slaves] ... had every right to suppose they were authorised, by the laws of Great Britain, as well as those of the colonies, to consider those people as their property; and that they had a right to their services in Europe, or to send, or accompany them back to the colonies, as they judged proper: They found themselves mistaken, and that it was permitted to debauch their slaves, to encourage or entice them to run away, with impunity. The ideas of liberty, the charms of novelty, and an ignorance of the country they had got to; where they found themselves upon a perfect equality, at least, with the inferior white people, could not fail of having pernicious effects upon their minds, and great numbers ran away from their masters. They in general plunged into vice and debauchery, and many of them, who were desirous of returning to their masters and mistresses, were refused to be received. The whole of those thus lost to their owners, and as to every useful purpose, to the community, cannot have been less in number than from 15,000 to 20,000.—As most of them were prime, young, seasoned, or Creole slaves, the loss to their owners, the planters, have not been less than from 1,000,000 to 1,200,000 sterling. A large sum to be sacrificed, to the mere names of *liberty and humanity*! What has been the result of thus extending *the blessings of liberty* to so many *wretched slaves*. Let any body shew scarce a single instance of any one of these people being in so happy a situation as they were before. The greater part, it is known, died miserably, in a very short time. No parish was willing to receive them, so that the survivers, after begging about the streets of London, and suffering all those evils, and inconveniencies, consequent on idleness and poverty, famine, disease, and the inclemency of the weather; attracted the attention of the public, and government was prevailed upon to undertake the transportation of them to the country from whence they or their ancestors had been ravished *by the wicked traders* of London, Liverpool, and Bristol.

Equal unhappiness would be the lot of the slaves in the islands, if they were set free; what could they do to obtain a livelihood? To suppose they would hire themselves out to work, can only enter into the imagination of those who do not know the people, or the country: What has so lately passed in England is surely sufficient to shew that there can be no idea, they will, any of them, wish to return to their own country. Thousands of negroes have been made free by their masters in the colonies, and it may, with truth, be asserted, that, notwithstanding many of them were very capable of paying for a passage to any part of Africa they thought proper; scarce a single instance can be produced of any one of them desiring to return to the place of his nativity.

The present attempt to cram liberty down the throats of people who are incapable of digesting it, can with propriety, be resembled to nothing, so well as to the account of poor Gulliver, when he was carried out of his little cabinet to the top of the house, by the Brobdignag Monkey.

from Anonymous, *Thoughts on the Slavery of Negroes, as It Affects the British Colonies in the West Indies: Humbly Submitted to the Consideration of Both Houses of Parliament* (1788)

If I am able to shew that the blacks are really happy; that their condition (if the odious name of slave could be forgotten) is preferable to the lower orders of the people in Great Britain and Ireland; and that they enjoy the necessaries, and often the luxuries of life, I trust every honest man will feel a just indignation at any attempt to mislead his judgment, and to impose upon him an opinion of cruelty, which has no existence in any of the British West India islands. ...

Let us take a view of the situation of the Africans, the nature of their country, their climate and government, and the genius and disposition of its inhabitants. The appearance of the slave-coast of Africa, when it was first visited by the Europeans, strongly marked the barbarous state of the people; a rude, inhospitable country, susceptible indeed of cultivation, but almost every way covered with thick, impenetrable forests. The wild luxuriance of nature was here portrayed in rich attire. The pruning hand of man was hardly seen. The peaceful labours of agriculture were little known.

It has been observed, that those countries most favoured by nature, often make the slowest progress to civilization; and that the people always groan under the weight of a cruel despotism. "This is an effect which springs from a natural cause. Great heat enervates the strength and courage of men, while in cold climates they have a certain vigour of body and mind, which renders them capable of long, painful, great, and intrepid actions. We ought not, then, to be astonished, that the effeminacy of the people in hot climates has almost always rendered them slaves; and that the bravery of those in colder regions has enabled them to maintain their liberties."

In those countries between the tropics, and especially under the equator, "the excess of heat renders men so slothful and dispirited, that nothing but the most pressing necessity can induce them to perform any laborious duty." An unconquerable indolence is universally felt and acknowledged. Sunk into the most deplorable degeneracy, they feel no incitements beyond the present moment. In vain may we represent to them the happiness of others. In vain may we attempt to rouse them to a sense of their own weakness. The soul, unwilling to enlarge itself, becomes the prey of every ignoble passion. Strangers to every virtuous and magnanimous sentiment, they are without fame—they are without glory.

The Africans have been always represented as a cruel and perfidious people, lazy, lascivious, faithless in their engagements, innate thieves, without morals, and without any just notion of any one religious duty. Their laws are founded on such principles as naturally flow from so impure a source. The government of the slave-coast of Africa is despotic. The will of the Prince must be obeyed. There is no appeal upon earth from his awful decree. The lives and fortunes of every one are absolutely at his disposal. These tyrants have thought fit to distinguish a number of crimes, but have taken no care to proportionate their degrees of punishment. Every offence is there punished with loss of life or liberty. Captives in war are deliberately murdered, or sold as slaves, as may most indulge the sanguinary caprice of the conqueror. Those convicted of adultery or theft, lose their liberty. He who is in debt, and unable to pay must either sell himself or his children to satisfy the creditor. It may be said, that the loss of life, or liberty, only commences with the injury done to society. I answer, "that in Africa, the civil liberty is already destroyed by the political slavery." A country like this, doomed to bear the weight of human misery, will always present a history of the most shocking cruelties, and of the severest slavery upon earth.

After viewing this melancholy picture, we ought not to be surprised at the extent of the present intercourse between the Africans and Europeans. For want of proper consideration, and from the influence of certain prejudices, the slave-trade has long been considered the scandal and reproach of every nation who have been anywise engaged in it, but without sufficient reason.

Men who enjoy the benefits of civilization, and who are protected in life, liberty, and property, by the wisdom of humane and equal laws, feel that spirit of liberty, and enthusiastic love of their country, which freedom only can inspire. Talk to them of banishment, and it is more terrible than death. Not so the poor African—he has few motives for wishing any longer to behold the distresses of his country; he is, alas! perhaps, the last witness of the sad misfortunes of his house—Already deprived of family, friends, and every other tender endearment, he has no relief but in banishment or death.

It is pleasant to mark the progress of the barbarian, from the moment he is put on shore in an English colony, to the time he becomes the master of a family, and acquires property of his own. He is first of all clothed (a thing unknown to him in his own country) and then instructed in the necessity of cleanliness. When carried to the plantation, he is shewn how to work in common with others. In a little time he chooses himself a wife, and has a house given to him, much better, allowing for the difference of climate, than what the peasants have in this country. When he is sufficiently instructed in the management of ground, a certain portion is allotted to the exclusive use of himself and family, which, with a moderate share of industry, is not only sufficient to supply every personal want, but leave a considerable part to be sent to market, to be sold, or exchanged for either necessaries or luxuries. The African now, finding himself a family man, and in possession of house and land, he begins to rear hogs, poultry, and other small stock, and either sells them to his master at a fair price, or carries them to market, for which one day in the week is allowed him. …

The African, no longer remembering a country to which he owes nothing but birth, becomes attached to the soil which is so propitious to his wants, and having few cares, and few desires, that are not completely satisfied, there is nothing so terrible to him as a change of situation. The master is the steward, the faithful guardian of all his wants and necessities. In sickness and in health—in youth and in old age, his assiduities are undiminished. The reader will anticipate the happiness of these people—and happy they must be, while their labours are directed by equity and humanity, and not by avarice.

God forbid that I should be an advocate for slavery, or servitude of any description, that can anywise limit the extent of human happiness: at the same time let me caution my countrymen against the weakness and folly of believing that happiness can only be sought in a constitution as free as their own. The history of all nations shew how extremely improper the laws of one country would be for those of another.

from Gordon Turnbull, *An Apology of Negro Slavery; or, the West India Planters Vindicated from the Charge of Inhumanity* (1786)

As a contrast to the horrid and fictitious picture, which has been drawn of the state of the negroes in the West-Indies, I shall here exhibit a true and more pleasing representation, taken from the life.

To begin then with the period of the Guinea negroe's arrival in one of the islands.—As soon as the ship that brings them is at anchor, the master or surgeon goes on shore to procure fresh provisions, fruit, and vegetables of all kinds, which are immediately sent on board for the slaves. Parties of them are sent on shore at different times, and conducted a little way into the country, where they frequently meet with many natives of their own country, who speak the same language, and sometimes with near and dear relations, who all appear very cheerful and happy. These agreeable and unexpected meetings are truly affecting, and excite the most tender and pleasing sensations in the breasts of the bystanders. It is not uncommon for these newly arrived guests, to mingle in the dance, or to join in the song, with their country people. If any of them appear dull or desponding, the old negroes endeavour to enliven them, by the most soothing and endearing expressions, telling them, in their own tongue, not to be afraid of the white men; that the white men are very good; that they will get plenty of *yam, yam,* (their general name for victuals) and that their work will be of the easiest kind. By these means, they are perfectly reconciled to the white men, and to a change of country, and of situation, which many of them declare, to be far superior to that which they had quitted. When the day of sale arrives, they not only meet the planter's looks, and answer his enquiries, by means of an interpreter, with great firmness, but they try, by offering their stout limbs to his inspection, jumping to shew their activity, and other allurements, to induce those, whose appearance pleases them, to buy them, and to engage, if possible, a preference in their favour. …

As soon as the new negroes are brought home to the plantation, if a planter has purchased them they are properly clothed.—A sufficient quantity of wholesome food is prepared, and served to them three times a day. They are comfortably lodged in some room of the manager's own house, or in some other convenient place, where they can be immediately under his eye for a few days. During this time they are not put to any kind of labour whatever, but are regularly conducted to bathe in the river, or in the sea, if it is nigh, twice a day. In the evenings they sing and dance, after the manner of their own nation, together with the old negroes who happen to be from the same country, one or two of whom are commonly instrumental performers, in these very noisy, but very joyous assemblies. In a very short time, they are taken into the houses of the principal and best disposed negroes, who adopt one or two of these new subjects into each family, to assist them in all the little domestic offices of cookery, carrying water, wood, &c. This is almost the only work they are employed in for the first two or three months, at the expiration of which, they are put to the easiest kind of labour for some months more. …

John Bicknell and Thomas Day, "The Dying Negro, A Poem" (1775)

In his fiction and essays, Thomas Day (1748–89) often wrote about oppression and injustice; "The Dying Negro," which he co-authored with his life-long friend John Bicknell, is one of the first English poems to attack slavery directly. It was inspired by the true story of an enslaved man who escaped from his master to marry a white servant, but was captured and returned to his ship. Rather than allow himself to be transported to the New World, he shot himself. The poem was very popular, and its success prompted Bicknell and Day to publish two revised and expanded versions in two years; the following is the third edition text.

Armed with thy sad last gift—the pow'r to die,
Thy shafts, stern fortune, now I can defy;
Thy dreadful mercy points at length the shore,

Where all is peace, and men are slaves no more;
5   —This weapon, ev'n in chains, the brave can wield,
And vanquished, quit triumphantly the field:
—Beneath such wrongs let pallid Christians live,
Such they can perpetrate, and may forgive.

       Yet while I tread that gulf's tremendous brink,
10   Where nature shudders, and where beings sink,
Ere yet this hand a life of torment close,
And end by one determined stroke my woes,
Is there a fond regret, which moves my mind
To pause, and cast a ling'ring look behind?
15   —O my loved bride!—for I have called thee mine,
Dearer than life, whom I with life resign,
For thee ev'n here this faithful heart shall glow,
A pang shall rend me, and a tear shall flow.—
How shall I soothe thy grief, since fate denies
20   Thy pious duties to my closing eyes?
I cannot clasp thee in a last embrace,
Nor gaze in silent anguish on thy face;
I cannot raise these fettered arms for thee,
To ask that mercy heav'n denies to me;
25   Yet let thy tender breast my sorrows share,
Bleed for my wounds, and feel my deep despair.
Yet let thy tears bedew a wretch's grave,
Whom fate forbade thy tenderness to save.
Receive these sighs—to thee my soul I breathe—
30   Fond love in dying groans is all I can bequeath.

       Why did I, slave, beyond my lot aspire?
Why didst thou fan the inauspicious fire?
For thee I bade my drooping soul revive;
For thee alone I could have borne to live;
35   And love, I said, shall make me large amends,
For persecuting foes, and faithless friends:
Fool that I was! inured so long to pain,
To trust to hope, or dream of joy again.
Joy, stranger guest, my easy faith betrayed,
40   And love now points to death's eternal shade;
There while I rest from mis'ry's galling load,
Be thou the care of ev'ry pitying God!
Nor may that Demon's unpropitious° pow'r,   *malevolent*
Who shed his influence on my natal hour,

45   Pursue thee too with unrelenting hate,
And blend with mine the colour of thy fate.
For thee may those soft hours return again,
When pleasure led thee smiling o'er the plain,
Ere, like some hell-born spectre of dismay,
50   I crossed thy path, and darkened all the way.
Ye waving groves, which from this cell I view!
Ye meads° now glitt'ring with the morning dew!   *meadows*
Ye flowers, which blush on yonder hated shore,
That at my baneful step shall fade no more,
55   A long farewell!—I ask no vernal° bloom—   *of spring*
No pageant wreaths to wither on my tomb.
—Let serpents hiss and night-shade blacken there,
To mark the friendless victim of despair!

       And better in th'untimely grave to rot,
60   The world and all its cruelties forgot,
Than, dragged once more beyond the Western
    main,°   *sea*
To groan beneath some dastard planter's chain,
Where my poor countrymen in bondage wait
The slow enfranchisement° of ling'ring fate.   *liberation*
65   Oh! my heart sinks, my dying eyes o'erflow,
When mem'ry paints the picture of their woe!
For I have seen them, ere the dawn of day,
Roused by the lash, begin their cheerless way;
Greeting with groans unwelcome morn's return,
70   While rage and shame their gloomy bosoms burn;
And, chiding every hour the slow-paced sun,
Endure their toils 'till all his race was run;
No eye to mark their suff'rings with a tear,
No friend to comfort, and no hope to cheer;
75   Then like the dull unpitied brutes repair
To stalls as wretched, and as coarse a fare;
Thank heav'n one day of misery was o'er,
And sink to sleep, and wish to wake no more.—
Sleep on! ye lost companions of my woes,
80   For whom in death this tear of pity flows;
Sleep, and enjoy the only boon of heav'n
To you in common with your tyrants giv'n!
O while soft slumber from their couches flies,
Still may the balmy blessing steep your eyes;
85   In sweet oblivion lull awhile your woes,

And brightest visions gladden the repose!
Let fancy then, unconscious of the change,
Through our own fields, and native forests range;
Waft ye to each once-haunted stream and grove,
And visit every long-lost scene ye love!
—I sleep no more—nor in the midnight shade,
Invoke ideal phantoms to my aid;
Nor wake again, abandoned and forlorn,
To find each dear delusion fled at morn;
A slow-consuming death let others wait,
I snatch destruction from unwilling fate:—
Yon ruddy streaks the rising sun proclaim,
That never more shall beam upon my shame;
Bright orb! for others let thy glory shine,
Mature the golden grain and purple vine,
While fettered Afric still for Europe toils,
And nature's plund'rers riot on her spoils;
Be theirs the gifts thy partial rays supply,
Be mine the gloomy privilege to die.

And thou, whose impious avarice and pride
The holy cross to my sad brows denied,[1]
Forbade me nature's common rights to claim,
Or share with thee a Christian's sacred name;
Thou too farewell!—for not beyond the grave
Extends thy pow'r, nor is my dust thy slave.
In vain heav'n spread so wide the swelling sea,
Vast wat'ry barrier, 'twixt thy world and me;
Swift round the globe, by earth nor heav'n controlled,
Fly stern oppression, and dire lust of gold.
Where-e'er the hell-hounds mark their bloody way,
Still nature groans, and man becomes their prey.
In the wild wastes of Afric's sandy plain,
Where roars the lion through his drear domain,
To curb the savage monarch in the chase,
There too heav'n planted man's majestic race;
Bade reason's sons with nobler titles rise,
Lift high their brow sublime, and scan the skies.
What though the sun in his meridian blaze

Dart on their naked limbs his scorching rays?
What though no rosy tints adorn their face,
No silken tresses shine with flowing grace?
Yet of ethereal temper are their souls,
And in their veins the tide of honour rolls;
And valour kindles there the hero's flame,
Contempt of death, and thirst of martial fame:
And pity melts the sympathising breast,
Ah! fatal virtue!—for the brave distrest.

My tortured bosom, sad remembrance spare!
Why dost thou plant thy keenest daggers there?
And show me what I was, and aggravate despair?
Ye streams of Gambia,[2] and thou sacred shade!
Where in my youth's first dawn I joyful strayed,
Oft have I roused, amid your caverns dim,
The howling tiger, and the lion grim;
In vain they gloried in their headlong force,
My javelin pierced them in their raging course.
But little did my boding° mind bewray,°   *foreseeing | disclose*
The victor and his hopes were doomed a prey
To human brutes more fell,° more cruel   *evil, destructive*
    far than they.
Ah! what avails the conqu'ror's bloody meed,[3]
The gen'rous purpose, or the dauntless deed?
This hapless breast exposed on every plain,
And liberty preferred to life in vain?
Fall'n are my trophies, blasted is my fame,
Myself become a thing without a name,
The sport of haughty lords, and ev'n of slaves the shame.

Curst be the winds, and curst the tides which bore
These European robbers to our shore!
O be that hour involved in endless night,
When first their streamers met my wond'ring sight!
I called the warriors from the mountains steep,
To meet these unknown terrors of the deep;
Roused by my voice, their gen'rous bosoms glow,
They rush indignant, and demand the foe,

---

[1] *The holy ... brows denied* Slaveowners often prevented the people they enslaved from converting to Christianity for fear that this would give the impression that enslaved people and free people were spiritually equal (and therefore deserving of equal rights).

[2] *Gambia* Located in north western Africa, and occupied by the British in the middle of the eighteenth century.

[3] *meed* Reward of honor.

160 And poise the darts of death, and twang the bended bow:
When lo! advancing o'er the sea-beat plain,
I marked the leader of a warlike train.
Unlike his features to our swarthy race;
And golden hair played round his ruddy face.

165 While with insidious smile and lifted hand,
He thus accosts our unsuspecting band.
"Ye valiant chiefs, whom love of glory leads
To martial combats, and heroic deeds;
No fierce invader your retreat explores,

170 No hostile banner waves along your shores.
From the dread tempests of the deep we fly,
Then lay, ye chiefs, these pointed terrors by:
And O, your hospitable cares extend,
So may ye never need the aid ye lend!

175 So may ye still repeat to ev'ry grove
The songs of freedom, and the strains of love!"
Soft as the accents of the traitor flow,
We melt with pity, and unbend the bow;
With lib'ral hand our choicest gifts we bring,

180 And point the wand'rers to the freshest spring.
Nine days we feasted on the Gambian strand,
And songs of friendship echoed o'er the land.
When the tenth morn her rising lustre gave,
The chief approached me by the sounding wave.

185 "O, youth," he said, "What gifts can we bestow,
Or how requite the mighty debt we owe?
For lo! propitious to our vows, the gale
With milder omens fills the swelling sail.
Tomorrow's sun shall see our ships explore

190 These deeps, and quit your hospitable shore.
Yet while we linger, let us still employ
The numbered hours in friendship and in joy;
Ascend our ships, their treasures are your own,
And taste the produce of a world unknown."

195   He spoke; with fatal eagerness we burn,—
And quit the shores, undestined to return!
The smiling traitors with insidious care,
The goblet proffer, and the feast prepare,
'Till dark oblivion shades our closing eyes,

200 And all disarmed each fainting warrior lies.
O wretches! to your future evils blind!

O morn for ever present to my mind!
When bursting from the treach'rous bands of sleep,
Roused by the murmurs of the dashing deep,

205 I woke to bondage and ignoble pains,
And all the horrors of a life in chains.
Ye Gods of Afric! in that dreadful hour
Where were your thunders and avenging pow'r!
Did not my prayers, my groans, my tears invoke

210 Your slumb'ring justice to direct the stroke?
No pow'r descended to assist the brave,
No lightnings flashed, and I became a slave.
From lord to lord my wretched carcass sold,
In Christian traffic, for their sordid gold:

215 Fate's blackest clouds were gathered o'er my head;
And, bursting now, they mix me with the dead.

    Yet when my fortune cast my lot with thine,
And bade beneath one roof our labours join,
Surprised I felt the tumults of my breast

220 Lulled by thy beauties to unwonted rest.
Delusive hopes my changing soul enflame,
And gentler transports° agitate   *overpowering emotions*
    my frame.
What though obscure thy birth, superior grace
Shone in the glowing features of thy face.

225 Ne'er had my youth such winning softness seen,
Where Afric's sable beauties dance the green,
When some sweet maid receives her lover's vow,
And binds the offered chaplet[1] to her brow.
While on thy languid eyes I fondly gaze,

230 And trembling meet the lustre of their rays,
Thou, gentle virgin, thou didst not despise
The humble homage of a captive's sighs.
By heav'n abandoned, and by man betrayed,
Each hope resigned of comfort or of aid,

235 Thy gen'rous love could every sorrow end,
In thee I found a mistress and a friend;
Still as I told the story of my woes,
With heaving sighs thy lovely bosom rose;
The trickling drops of liquid crystal stole

240 Down thy fair cheek, and marked thy pitying soul:

---

1 *chaplet* Wreath worn on the head.

Dear drops! upon my bleeding heart, like balm
They fell, and soon my tortured mind grew calm;
Then my loved country, parents, friends forgot;
Heav'n I absolved, nor murmured at my lot;
5   Thy sacred smiles could every pang remove,
And liberty became less dear than love.

   —And I have loved thee with as pure a fire
As man e'er felt, or woman could inspire:
No pangs like these my pallid tyrants know,
0   Not such their transports, and not such their woe.
Their softer frames a feeble soul conceal,
A soul unused to pity or to feel;
Damped by base lucre,° and repelled by fear,   *money*
Each nobler passion faintly blazes here.
5   Not such the mortals burning Afric breeds,
Mother of virtues and heroic deeds!
Descended from yon radiant orb, they claim
Sublimer courage, and a fiercer flame.
Nature has there, unchilled by art, impressed
0   Her awful majesty on every breast.
Where'er she leads, impatient of control,
The dauntless Negro rushes to the goal;
Firm in his love, resistless in his hate,
His arm is conquest, and his frown is fate.

5   What fond affection in my bosom reigns!
What soft emotions mingle with my pains!
Still as thy form before my mind appears,
My haggard eyes are bathed in gushing tears;
Thy loved idea rushes to my heart,
0   And stern despair suspends the lifted dart——
O could I burst these fetters which restrain
My struggling limbs, and waft thee o'er the main,
To some far distant shore, where Ocean roars
In horrid tempests round the gloomy shores;
5   To some wild mountain's solitary shade,
Where never European faith betrayed;
How joyful could I, of thy love secure,
Meet every danger, every toil endure!
For thee I'd climb the rock, explore the flood,
0   And tame the famished savage of the wood;
When scorching summer drinks the shrinking streams,

My care should screen thee from its sultry beams;
At noon I'd crown thee with the fairest flowers,
At eve I'd lead thee to the safest bowers;[1]
285   And when bleak winter howled around the cave,
For thee his horrors and his storms I'd brave;
Nor snows nor raging winds should damp my soul,
Nor such a night as shrouds the dusky pole;
O'er the dark waves my bounding skiff I'd guide,
290   To pierce each mightier monster of the tide;
Through frozen forests force my dreadful way,
In their own dens to rouse the beasts of prey;
Nor other blessing ask, if this might prove
How fixed my passion, and how fond my love.
295   —Then should vain fortune to my sight display
All that her anger now has snatched away;
Treasures more vast than av'rice e'er designed
In midnight visions to a Christian's mind;
The Monarch's diadem,° the conqu'ror's meed,   *crown*
300   That empty prize for which the valiant bleed;
All that ambition strives to snatch from fate,
All that the Gods e'er lavished in their hate;
Not these should win thy lover from thy arms,
Or tempt a moment's absence from thy charms;
305   Indignant would I fly these guilty climes,
And scorn their glories as I hate their crimes!

   But whither does my wand'ring fancy rove?
Hence ye wild wishes of desponding love!
—Ah! where is now that voice which lulled my woes?
310   That angel-face, which soothed me to repose?
By nature tempted, and with passion blind,
Are these the joys hope whispered to my mind?
Is this the end of constancy like thine,
Are these the transports of a love like mine?
315   My hopes, my joys, are vanished into air,
And now of all that once engaged my care,
These chains alone remain, this weapon and despair!

   —So be thy life's gay prospects all o'ercast,
All thy fond hopes dire disappointment blast!
320   Thus end thy golden visions, son of pride!

---

1   *bowers* Sheltered places in the woods.

Whose ruthless ruffians tore me from my bride;
That beauteous prize heav'n had reserved at last,
Sweet recompense for all my sorrows past.
O may thy hardened bosom never prove
325 The tender joys of friendship or of love!
Yet may'st thou, doomed to hopeless flames a prey,
In unrequited passion pine away!
May every transport violate thy rest,
Which tears the jealous lover's gloomy breast!
330 May secret anguish gnaw thy cruel heart,
'Till death in all his terrors wing the dart;
Then, to complete the horror of thy doom,
A favoured rival smile upon thy tomb!

Why does my ling'ring soul her flight delay?
335 Come, lovely maid, and gild the dreary way!
Come, wildly rushing with disordered charms,
And clasp thy bleeding lover in thy arms;
Close his sad eyes, receive his parting breath,
And soothe him sinking to the shades of death!
340 O come—thy presence can my pangs beguile,
And bid th'inexorable tyrant smile;
Transported will I languish on thy breast,
And sink enraptured to eternal rest:
The hate of men, the wrongs of fate forgive,
345 Forget my woes, and almost wish to live.
—Ah! rather fly, lest aught of doubt control
The dreadful purpose lab'ring in my soul;
Tears must not bend me, nor thy beauties move,
This hour I triumph over fate and love.

350   —Again with tenfold rage my bosom burns,
And all the tempest of my soul returns;
Again the furies fire my madding° brain,   *agitated*
And death extends his shelt'ring arms in vain;
For unrevenged I fall, unpitied die,
355 And with my blood glut pride's insatiate eye!

Thou Christian God! to whom so late I bowed,
To whom my soul its new allegiance vowed,
When crimes like these thy injured pow'r profane,
O God of nature! art thou called in vain?
360 Didst thou for this sustain a mortal wound,

While heav'n, and earth, and hell, hung trembling round?
That these vile fetters might my body bind,
And agony like this distract my mind?
On thee I called with reverential awe,
365 Adored thy wisdom, and embraced thy law;
Yet mark thy destined convert as he lies,
His groans of anguish, and his livid eyes,
These galling chains, polluted with his blood,
Then bid his tongue proclaim thee just and good!
370 But if too weak thy vaunted power to spare,
Or suff'rings move thee not, O hear despair!
Thy hopes and blessings I alike resign,
But let revenge, let swift revenge be mine!
Be this proud bark,° which now triumphant rides,   *ship*
375 Tossed by the winds, and shattered by the tides!
And may these fiends, who now exulting view
The horrors of my fortune, feel them too!
Be theirs the torment of a ling'ring fate,
Slow as thy justice, dreadful as my hate;
380 Condemned to grasp the riven° plank in vain,   *broken*
And chased by all the monsters of the main;
And while they spread their sinking arms to thee,
Then let their fainting souls remember me!

—Thanks, righteous God!—Revenge shall yet be mine!
385 Yon flashing lightning gave the dreadful sign.
I see the flames of heav'nly anger hurled,
I hear your thunders shake a guilty world.
The time has come, the fated hour is nigh,
When guiltless blood shall penetrate the sky.
390 Amid these horrors, and involving night,
Prophetic visions flash before my sight;
Eternal justice wakes, and in their turn
The vanquished triumph, and the victors mourn;
Lo! Discord, fiercest of th'infernal band,
395 Fires all her snakes, and waves her flaming brand;[1]
No more proud Commerce courts the western gales,
But marks the lurid skies, and furls her sails;
War mounts his iron car, and at his wheels
In vain soft Pity weeps, and Mercy kneels;

---

[1] *Discord ... flaming brand* The Roman goddess Discord is here associated with the Furies, goddesses who avenge the dead and are sometimes depicted carrying torches and using snakes as weapons.

He breathes a savage rage through all the host,
And stains with kindred blood the impious coast;
Then, while with horror sick'ning Nature groans,
And earth and heav'n the monstrous race disowns,—
Then the stern genius° of my native land,   spirit
With delegated vengeance in his hand,
Shall raging cross the troubled seas, and pour
The plagues of Hell on yon devoted shore.
What tides of ruin mark his ruthless way!
How shriek the fiends exulting o'er their prey!
I see their warriors gasping on the ground,
I hear their flaming cities crash around.—
In vain with trembling heart the coward turns,
In vain with gen'rous rage the valiant burns.—
One common ruin, one promiscuous° grave, indiscriminate
O'erwhelms the dastard, and receives the brave—
For Afric triumphs!—his avenging rage
No tears can soften, and no blood assuage.
He smites the trembling waves, and at the shock
Their fleets are dashed upon the pointed rock.
He waves his flaming dart, and o'er their plains,
In mournful silence, desolation reigns—
Fly swift ye years!—Arise thou glorious morn!
Thou great avenger of thy race be born!
The conqu'ror's palm and deathless fame be thine!
One gen'rous stroke, and liberty be mine!
—And now, ye pow'rs! to whom the brave are dear,
Receive me falling, and your suppliant hear.
To you this unpolluted blood I pour,
To you that spirit which you gave restore!
I ask no lazy pleasures to possess,
No long eternity of happiness;—
But if unstained by voluntary guilt,
At your great call this being I have spilt,
For all the wrongs which innocent I share,
For all I've suffered, and for all I dare;
O lead me to that spot, that sacred shore,
Where souls are free, and men oppress no more!

from Mary Wollstonecraft, *A Vindication of the Rights of Men* (1790)

Wollstonecraft's more famous work, *A Vindication of the Rights of Woman*, was published two years after her much shorter work on the rights of men, which briefly discusses the issue of slavery.

Is it necessary to repeat, that there are rights which we received, at our birth, as men, when we were raised above the brute creation by the power of improving ourselves—and that we receive these not from our forefathers, but from God?

My father may dissipate his property, yet I have no right to complain;—but if he should attempt to sell me for a slave, or fetter me with laws contrary to reason; nature, in enabling me to discern good from evil, teaches me to break the ignoble chain. …

But on what principle Mr. Burke[1] could defend American independence, I cannot conceive; for the whole tenor of his … arguments settles slavery on an everlasting foundation. Allowing his servile reverence for antiquity, and prudent attention to self-interest, to have the force which he insists on, it ought never to be abolished; and, because our ignorant forefathers, not understanding the native dignity of man, sanctioned a traffic that outrages every suggestion of reason and religion, we are to submit to the inhuman custom, and term an atrocious insult to humanity the love of our country and a proper submission to those laws which secure our property.—Security of property! Behold, in a few words, the definition of English liberty. And to this selfish principle every nobler one is sacrificed. …

---

[1] *Mr. Burke* Edmund Burke (1729–97), Anglo-Irish political figure, author, and philosopher. Burke famously supported the right of the colonies to self-rule.

Anna Laetitia Barbauld, "Epistle to William Wilberforce, Esq., on the Rejection of the Bill for Abolishing the Slave Trade"[1] (1791)

Cease, Wilberforce, to urge thy generous aim!
    Thy country knows the sin, and stands the shame!
The preacher, poet, senator in vain
Has rattled in her sight the Negro's chain;
With his deep groans assailed her startled ear,   5
And rent the veil that hid his constant tear;
Forced her averted eyes his stripes[2] to scan,
Beneath the bloody scourge laid bare the man,
Claimed Pity's tear, urged Conscience's strong control,
And flashed conviction on her shrinking soul.   10
The Muse too, soon awaked, with ready tongue
At Mercy's shrine applausive paeans rung;
And Freedom's eager sons, in vain foretold
A new Astraean[3] reign, an age of gold:
She knows and she persists—Still Afric bleeds,   15
Unchecked, the human traffic still proceeds;
She stamps her infamy to future time,
And on her hardened forehead seals the crime.
    In vain, to thy white standard[4] gathering round,
Wit, Worth, and Parts° and Eloquence   *intelligence*   20
    are found:
In vain, to push to birth thy great design,
Contending chiefs, and hostile virtues join;
All, from conflicting ranks, of power possest
To rouse, to melt, or to inform the breast.
Where seasoned tools of Avarice prevail,   25
A nation's eloquence, combined, must fail:

Each flimsy sophistry by turns they try;
The plausive° argument, the daring lie,   *plausible*
The artful gloss,° that moral sense confounds,   *explanation*
Th'acknowledged thirst of gain that honour wounds: 30
Bane of ingenuous minds, th'unfeeling sneer,
Which, sudden, turns to stone the falling tear:
They search assiduous, with inverted skill,
For forms of wrong, and precedents of ill;
With impious mockery wrest the sacred page,   35
And glean up crimes from each remoter age:
Wrung Nature's tortures, shuddering, while you tell,
From scoffing fiends bursts forth the laugh of hell;
In Britain's senate, Misery's pangs give birth
To jests unseemly, and to horrid mirth[5]—   40
Forbear!—thy virtues but provoke our doom,
And swell th'account of vengeance yet to come;
For, not unmarked in Heaven's impartial plan,
Shall man, proud worm, condemn his fellow man?
And injured Afric, by herself redrest,   45
Darts her own serpents at her tyrant's breast.
Each vice, to minds depraved by bondage known,
With sure contagion fastens on his own;
In sickly languors melts his nerveless frame,
And blows to rage impetuous Passion's flame: 50
Fermenting swift, the fiery venom gains
The milky innocence of infant veins;
There swells the stubborn will, damps learning's fire,
The whirlwind wakes of uncontrolled desire,
Sears the young heart to images of woe,   55
And blasts the buds of Virtue as they blow.
    Lo! where reclined, pale Beauty courts the breeze,
Diffused on sofas of voluptuous ease;
With anxious awe, her menial train around,

---

[1] *William Wilberforce … Slave Trade* This poem appeared shortly after the bill put forward by Wilberforce (and supported both by the Prime Minister, William Pitt, and the leader of the opposition, Charles Fox) was defeated by a vote of 163 to 88.

[2] *stripes* Open wounds caused by the lash.

[3] *Astraea* Greek goddess of justice.

[4] *standard* Flag.

---

[5] *To jests … mirth* Barbauld refers to some Members of Parliament who laughed in the House of Commons upon hearing of the suffering of enslaved people.

Catch her faint whispers of half-uttered sound;
See her, in monstrous fellowship, unite
At once the Scythian, and the Sybarite;[1]
Blending repugnant vices, misallied,
Which frugal nature purposed to divide;
See her, with indolence to fierceness joined,
Of body delicate, infirm of mind,
With languid tones imperious mandates urge;
With arm recumbent wield the household scourge;
And with unruffled mien,° and placid sounds,   *appearance*
Contriving torture, and inflicting wounds.
Nor, in their palmy walks and spicy groves,
The form benign of rural pleasure roves;
No milkmaid's song, or hum of village talk,
Soothes the lone poet in his evening walk:
No willing arm the flail unwearied plies,
Where the mixed sounds of cheerful labour rise;
No blooming maids, and frolic swains are seen
To pay gay homage to their harvest queen:
No heart-expanding scenes their eyes must prove
Of thriving industry, and faithful love:
But shrieks and yells disturb the balmy air,
Dumb sullen looks of woe announce despair,
And angry eyes through dusky features glare.
Far from the sounding lash the Muses fly,
And sensual riot drowns each finer joy.
      Nor less from the gay East,° on   *India*
            essenced wings,
Breathing unnamed perfumes, Contagion springs;
The soft luxurious plague alike pervades
The marble palaces, and rural shades;
Hence, thronged Augusta° builds her rosy bowers,   *London*
And decks in summer wreaths her smoky towers;
And hence, in summer bow'rs, Art's costly hand
Pours courtly splendours o'er the dazzled land:
The manners melt—One undistinguished blaze
O'erwhelms the sober pomp of elder days;

Corruption follows with gigantic stride,
And scarce vouchsafes his shameless front to hide:
The spreading leprosy taints ev'ry part,
Infects each limb, and sickens at the heart.
100 Simplicity! most dear of rural maids,
Weeping resigns her violated shades:
Stern Independence from his glebe° retires,   *field*
And anxious Freedom eyes her drooping fires;
By foreign wealth are British morals changed,
105 And Afric's sons, and India's, smile avenged.
      For you, whose tempered ardour long has borne
Untired the labour, and unmoved the scorn;
In Virtue's fasti° be inscribed your fame,   *calendar*
And uttered yours with Howard's[2] honoured name,
110 Friends of the friendless—Hail, ye generous band!
Whose efforts yet arrest Heav'n's lifted hand,
Around whose steady brows, in union bright,
The civic wreath, and Christian's palm unite:
Your merit stands, no greater and no less,
115 Without, or with the varnish of success;
But seek no more to break a nation's fall,
For ye have saved yourselves—and that is all.
Succeeding times your struggles, and their fate,
With mingled shame and triumph shall relate,
120 While faithful History, in her various page,
Marking the features of this motley age,
To shed a glory, and to fix a stain,
Tells how you strove, and that you strove in vain.

William Blake, Images of Slavery

The engravings reproduced here are among sixteen plates prepared by William Blake in 1792–93 as illustrations for John Stedman's *Narrative of Five Years' Expedition against the Revolted Negroes of Surinam* (1796).

---

[1] *Scythian* Ancient nomadic Europeans: synonym for ferocity; *Sybarite* People from the ancient Greek city of Sybaris: synonym for pleasure-loving.

[2] *Howard* John Howard (1726–90), prison reformer and philanthropist.

from Samuel Taylor Coleridge, *On the Slave Trade* (1796)

The article from which these excerpts are taken was originally delivered as a lecture in Bristol in 1795. It was published the following year in Coleridge's magazine *The Watchman*; the excerpts included here comprise approximately one half of the full article.

At the time slavery—and various proposals for its abolition—were the subject of increasing controversy, with William Wilberforce having recently proposed in the House of Commons several (unsuccessful) bills to put an end to the slave trade.

Whence arise our miseries? Whence arise our vices? From *imaginary* wants. No man is wicked without temptation; no man is wretched without a cause. But if each among us confined his wishes to the actual necessaries and real comforts of life, we should preclude all the causes of complaint and all the motives to iniquity.[1] …

I have dwelt anxiously on this subject, with a particular view, to the slave-trade, which, I knew, has insinuated in the minds of many, uneasy doubts respecting the existence of a beneficent deity. And indeed the evils arising from the formation of *imaginary* wants, have in no instance been so dreadfully exemplified, as in this inhuman traffic. We receive from the West-India Islands sugars, rum, cotton, logwood, cocoa, coffee, pimento, ginger, indigo, mahogany, and conserves.[2] Not one of these articles are necessary; indeed with the exception of cotton and mahogany we cannot truly call them even useful: and not one of them is at

---

[1] *preclude* Prevent; *iniquity* Injustice.

[2] *West-India Islands* With the American colonies by this time independent of Britain, the largest number of enslaved people on British territory in the final decade of the eighteenth century were enslaved on plantations in the various British possessions in the West Indies—notably Barbados, Jamaica, and Trinidad; *logwood* Species of tree harvested in Central America, used as a dye; *pimento* Variety of chili pepper; *conserves* Preserved foods.

present attainable by the poor and labouring part of society. In return we export vast quantities of necessary tools, raiment, and defensive weapons, with great stores of provision. So that in this trade as in most others the poor are employed with unceasing toil first to raise, and then to send away the comforts, which they themselves absolutely want,[1] in order to procure idle superfluities for their masters. If this trade had never existed, no one human being would have been less comfortably clothed, housed, or nourished. Such is its value—they who would estimate the price which we pay for it, may consult the evidence delivered before the House of Commons. … It is my present purpose to consider the objections of[2] the abolition of this commerce—which may be reduced to the five following—First, that the abolition would be useless, since though *we* should not carry it on, other nations would. 2. That the Africans are better treated and more happy in the plantations than in their native country. 3. That the revenue would be greatly injured. 4. That the right of property would be invaded. 5. That this is not a fit opportunity.

1. That if England abolish the slave-trade, other nations will carry it on. The same argument has been adduced by the French planters:[3] a sufficient proof of its fallacy. Somebody must *begin*; and there is little reason to fear, that a wise and politic example will not be followed. As society is constituted, there will be always highway robberies: it is useless therefore to prevent any *one* man from committing them. Fortunately for travellers this logic will not hold good in law. But although it cannot operate in favour of little rogues, it

appears to possess wonderful power in the higher circles of villainy. …

2. That the slaves are more humanely treated and live more happily in the plantations than in their native country. If any incredulous person should entertain a doubt of this, the slave-merchants, slave-holders, and slave-drivers, together with the manufacturers of neck-collars and thumb-screws,[4] are ready and willing to take their bible oaths of it!! When treated with tolerable humanity the human race, as well as other animals, multiply. The Negroes multiply in their native country: they do *not* multiply in the West-India Islands; for if they did, the slave-trade would have been abolished long ago by its inutility. This is a fact which no perjury can overwhelm, which no sophistry[5] can undermine.

That tyranny of the African Chiefs[6] is in a great measure owing to the agency of Europeans, who flock to their courts, and seduce them by bribery, and madden them by intoxication. The Africans are not slaves in their native country; slavery is their highest punishment for the greatest crimes, which their chiefs now wantonly impute to the innocent for the sole purpose of making them slaves in order to sell them to the European merchants: and with the same views the chiefs make war with each other. Wadestrom,[7] a disinterested[8] and religious man, who has travelled into the interior parts of Africa, informs us that those Africans who are situated beyond the contagion of European vice are innocent and happy. The peaceful inhabitants of a fertile soil, they cultivate their fields in common, and reap the crop as the common property of all. Each family, like the peasants in some parts of Europe, spins, weaves, sews, hunts, fishes, and makes baskets, fishing-

---

[1] *want* Lack.

[2] *of* To.

[3] [Coleridge's note] "Very soon this society of Friends to the Negroes require an abolition of the slave-trade; that is to say, that the profits which may result from it to the French commerce should be transferred to foreigners. For never will their romantic philosophy persuade the other European Powers &c." See the address of the Planters of St. Domingo to the French Legislature. [This address was made in November 1791, months after the beginning of a revolution carried out by enslaved people. The Society of the Friends of the Blacks was created in Paris in 1788, lobbying for abolition.]; *planters* Owners of slave plantations.

[4] *incredulous* In the older sense of skeptical; *neck-collars and thumb-screws* Instruments used to punish and torture enslaved people.

[5] *sophistry* Persuasive but ultimately fallacious arguments.

[6] *tyranny of the African Chiefs* I.e., the tyranny of African rulers (with whom European traders had made agreements regarding the sale of enslaved people) over their own and nearby peoples.

[7] *Wadestrom* Carl Bernhard Wadström (1746–99), Swedish economist and abolitionist who traveled to western Africa in the late 1780s and early 1790s.

[8] *disinterested* Unbiased.

tackle, and the implements of agriculture: and this variety of employment gives an acuteness of intellect to the Negro which the mechanic whom the division of labour[1] condemns to one simple operation is precluded from attaining.

3. That the revenue would be injured.[2] To the friends of humanity this is indeed a cogent[3] argument against the abolition. They will doubtless reflect, how worthily this revenue has been employed for these last hundred years—they will review with delight waste-lands cultivated, sciences publicly protested and rewarded, and population increased, and the peasantry of England and Ireland instructed in useful learning, and humanized. The universal plenty, which this revenue has been applied to scatter and secure, they will recognize in every land, hamlet, and cottage. ... The friends of humanity may mourn that so excellent an end could not be effected by less calamitous means; but they will stifle their feelings, and lose[4] the miseries of the West-Indies in the contemplation of that paradisiacal state of their native country—for which it is indebted to this well-raised, well-applied Revenue, which while it remains in such *pure* hands, no friend of freedom and virtue can possibly wish diminished! ...

4. That the right of property would be injured. Yes perhaps, if immediate emancipation had been the object of Mr. Wilberforce's bill.[5] But how would the right of property be invaded by a law which should leave the estate and everything on it untouched and only prevent the owner from *forcing* men to work for him? From

forcing men to leave their friends and country, and live as slaves in a climate so unwholesome or beneath a usage so unnatural, that contrary to the universal law of life they annually diminish? Can a man possess a right to commit actual and virtual murder? To shorten and prevent existence? ...

5. This is not the time. This not the time? "The French," says Abbé Sieyès,[6] "hear with delight of the numerous armaments which England sends to certain death in the West-India islands. We make war there more effectually as well as economically by sending over a few adventurous officers to preach the rights of man to the negroes, and furnish them with weapons to assert those rights." What can prevent the success of these intrigues among the slaves, but the most active humanity on the part of their present masters?

Such have been the cosmetics with which our parliamentary orators have endeavoured to conceal the deformities of a commerce, which is blotched all over with one leprosy of evil. In the year 1786 its enormities became the subject of general conversation,[7] and in the following years petitions poured into parliament from various parts of the kingdom, requesting its abolition. The bill for that purpose passed the House of Commons mangled and mutilated by the amendments of Mr. Dundas,[8] and it has been dying ever since of a slow decline in the House of Lords. The jealous spirit of liberty placed the Elector of Hanover on the throne of Great Britain:[9] and the Duke of Clarence, one of his illustrious descendants, made his maiden speech in

---

[1] *division of labour* Assignment of different stages of production to different workers for the sake of efficiency.

[2] *the revenue would be injured* I.e., that government revenue would be reduced. The British government obtained substantial revenues from taxes on sugar, molasses, rum, and other products of slave labor.

[3] *cogent* Powerful and convincing.

[4] *lose* I.e., lose sight of.

[5] *if immediate ... Mr. Wilberforce's bill* Wilberforce proposed at this time only the abolition of the trade of enslaved people, and not an outright prohibition of slavery itself (which he then believed would naturally cease over time after the cessation of the trade).

[6] *Abbé Sieyès* Emmanuel Joseph Sieyès (1748–1836), French Catholic priest and political theorist.

[7] *In the year ... general conversation* Perhaps referring to the formation of the Society for the Abolition of the Slave Trade, which in fact occurred in May 1787. The society was very influential in raising awareness of the slave trade and its cruelties throughout England.

[8] *The bill ... Mr. Dundas* Wilberforce's antislavery bill in 1792 was passed only after amendments by Henry Dundas, then British Home Secretary; these amendments calling for a "gradual abolition" would in practice have had the effect of delaying abolition almost indefinitely.

[9] *Elector of Hanover ... Great Britain* George I (1660–1727), ruler of the Electorate of Hanover in the Holy Roman Empire since 1698, became king of Great Britain and Ireland in 1714 upon the death of his cousin, Queen Anne of Great Britain.

favour of the slave trade![1] ...

The Abbé Raynal computes that at the time of his writing,[2] nine millions of slaves had been consumed by the Europeans—add one million since (for it is near thirty years since his book was first published) and recollect, that for one procured ten at least are slaughtered, that a fifth die in the passage, and a third in the seasoning;[3] and the calculation will amount to one hundred and eighty million! Ye who have joined in this confederacy,[4] ask of yourselves this fearful question—"if the God of Justice inflict on us that mass only of anguish which we have wantonly heaped on our brethren, what must a state of retribution be?" But who are they who have joined in this tartarean[5] confederacy? Who are these kidnappers, and assassins? In all reasoning neglecting the intermediate links we attribute the final effect to the first cause. And what is the first and constantly acting cause of the slave-trade? That cause, by which it exists and deprived of which it would immediately cease? Is it not self-evidently the consumption of its products? And does not then the guilt rest on the consumers? And is it not an allowed axiom in morality, that wickedness may be multiplied, but cannot be divided; and that the guilt of all attaches to each one who is knowingly an accomplice? Think not of the slave-captains and slave-holders! These very men, their darkened minds, and brutalized hearts, will prove one part of the dreadful charge against you! They are more to be pitied than the slaves, because more depraved. I address myself to you who, independently of all political distinctions, profess yourself Christians! As you hope to live with Christ hereafter, you are commanded to do unto others as ye would that others should do unto you.[6] Would *you* choose that a slave merchant should incite an intoxicated chieftain to make war on your country, and murder your wife and children before your face, or drag them with yourself to the market? Would you choose to be sold? To have the hot iron hiss upon your breasts, after having been crammed into the hold of a ship with so many fellow-victims, that the heat and stench, arising from your diseased bodies, should rot the very planks? Would *you*, that others should do this unto *you*? And if you shudder with selfish horror at the bare idea, do you yet dare be the occasion of it to others? ... If only one tenth part among you who profess yourselves Christians; if one half only of the petitioners; instead of bustling about with ostentatious sensibility,[7] were to leave off—not *all* the West-India commodities—but only sugar and rum, the one useless and the other pernicious—all this misery might be stopped. Gracious Heaven! At your meals you rise up, and pressing your hands to your bosoms, you lift up your eyes to God, and say "O Lord! Bless the food which thou hast given us!" A part of that food among most of you, is sweetened with brothers' blood. "Lord! Bless the food which thou hast given us?" O blasphemy! Did God give food mingled with the blood of the murdered? Will God bless the food which is polluted with the blood of his own innocent children? ...

I have read and heard one argument in favour of the slave-trade, which I mention chiefly on account of its seditions and treasonable tendency. It has been asserted by more than one writer on the subject that the plantation slaves are at least as well off as the peasantry in England. Now I appeal to common sense, whether to affirm that the slaves are as well off as our peasantry, be not the same as to assert that our peasantry are as bad off

---

[1] *Duke of Clarence ... slave trade!* Son of George III (1738–1820), and later King of Great Britain as William IV, the Duke of Clarence in his early years as a politician spoke vehemently in the House of Lords against the abolition of the slave trade—and against Wilberforce.

[2] *Abbé Raynal ... his writing* Reference to *A Philosophical and Political History of the Settlement and Trade of the Europeans in the East and West Indies* (1770) by French Enlightenment writer Guillaume-Thomas Raynal; *computes* Calculates.

[3] *passage* The voyage known as the Middle Passage—the shipment of people from Africa to the Americas to be sold for the purpose of slavery; *seasoning* Period and process during which enslaved people were forcibly accustomed to the conditions of slavery.

[4] *confederacy* Evil scheme or alliance.

[5] *tartarean* Relating to Tartarus, realm of punishment in the afterlife in Greek mythology; infernal.

[6] *do unto others ... unto you* Cf. Matthew 7.12: "Therefore all things whatsoever ye would that men should do to you, do ye even so to them: for this is the law and the prophets."

[7] *ostentatious sensibility* Insincere emotional response meant only for show.

as negro-slaves? And whether, if our peasantry believed it, they would not be inclined to rebel?

from William Earle, *Obi; or, the History of Three-Fingered Jack* (1800)

Earle's novel is set against the background of an enslaved people's uprising in Jamaica; it is based on the true story of Jack Mansong, a man who had escaped slavery and who was said to have gained strength to lead the rebellion from the religion of "obeah," or "obi." The epistolary novel is for the most part made up of letters from one George Stanford, "a resident of Jamaica," to Charles, "his friend in England." The excerpt that appears here is from the letter with which the book opens.

Jack is a noble fellow, and in spite of every cruel hard-hearted planter, I shall repeat the same to the last hour of my life. "Jack is a Negro," say they. "Jack is a MAN," say I.

—"He is a slave."

—"MAN cannot be a slave to MAN."

—"He is my property."

—"How did you acquire that property?"

—"By paying for it."

—"Paying! Paying whom?"

—"Him who brought him from Africa."

—"How did he get possession of him?"

—"He caught him there."

—"Caught! what? Like a wild beast?"

—"No, but he contrived means to convey him into his ship."

—"Contrived! Then he brought him without his consent?"

—"Very likely."

—"And what is become of that robber?"

—"Robber! He is a very respectable man, who has left off trade, has married the daughter of a rich planter, and now lives very comfortably, after the fatigues of an industrious life."

—"What! Do they hang a poor hard-labouring man, who, driven by despair at the sight of his numerous family ready to starve for want of a bit of bread, takes advantage of a dark night, goes on the highway and frightens the traveller out of a few pieces of gold; and shall a daring ruffian, who is openly guilty of a crime more heinous in its nature and baneful in its effects, get respected by every body and pass his days in the peaceable enjoyment of riches acquired by such infamous means?"

—"I don't understand you; I never heard that the traffic was infamous. Is it not authorised by all the nations of Europe, Asia and America? Have not regulations been made concerning it by all governments?"

—"Very true, but that does not make it more honorable."

Mary Robinson, Poems on Slavery

Robinson, one of the best-known writers of the age, published a substantial number of works devoted in whole or in part to antislavery themes, including "Captivity: A Poem" (1777), "The African" (1798), and "The Negro Girl" (1800). "The African" was published initially in the *Morning Post*, 2 August 1798 and later incorporated into the long poem *The Progress of Liberty*. "The Negro Girl" appeared in Robinson's collection of *Lyrical Tales*.

The African (1798)

Shall the poor AFRICAN, the passive Slave,
Born in the bland effulgence of broad day,
Cherish'd by torrid splendours, while around
The plains prolific teem with honey'd stores,
Sink prematurely to a grave obscure,   5
No tear to grace his ashes? Or suspire
To wear Submission's long and goading chain,
To drink the tear that down his swarthy cheek
Flows fast, to moisten his toil-fever'd lip
Parch'd by the noon-tide blaze? Shall HE endure   10
The frequent lash, the agonizing scourge,
The day of labour, and the night of pain;

Expose his naked limbs to burning gales;
Faint in the sun, and wither in the storm;
Traverse hot sands, imbibe the morbid breeze,
Wing'd with contagion; while his blister'd feet,
Scorch'd by the vertical and raging beam,
Pour the swift life-stream? Shall his frenzied eyes,
Oh! worst of mortal miseries! behold
The darling of his heart, his sable love,
Selected from the trembling timid throng,
By the wan TYRANT, whose licentious touch
Seals the dark fiat of the SLAVE's despair!

OH LIBERTY! From thee the suppliant claims
The meed of retribution! Thy pure flame
Would light the sense opaque, and warm the spring
Of boundless ecstacy: while Nature's laws,
So violated, plead immortal tongu'd,
For her dark-fated children! Lead them forth
From bondage infamous! Bid Reason own
The dignities of MAN, whate'er his clime,
Estate, or colour. And, O sacred TRUTH!
Tell the proud Lords of traffic, that the breast
Thrice ebon-tinted, owns a crimson tide
As pure,—as clear, as Europe's Sons can boast.

The Negro Girl (1800)

1

Dark was the dawn, and o'er the deep
The boist'rous whirlwinds blew;
The Sea-bird wheel'd its circling sweep,
    And all was drear to view—
When on the beach that binds the western shore
The love-lorn ZELMA stood, list'ning the tempest's roar.

2

Her eager Eyes beheld the main,
    While on her DRACO dear
She madly call'd, but call'd in vain,
    No sound could DRACO hear,
Save the shrill yelling of the fateful blast,
While ev'ry Seaman's heart, quick shudder'd as it past.

3

White were the billows, wide display'd
    The clouds were black and low;
The Bittern shriek'd, a gliding shade
    Seem'd o'er the waves to go!
The livid flash illum'd the clam'rous main,
While ZELMA pour'd, unmark'd, her melancholy
    strain.

4

"Be still!" she cried, "loud tempest cease!
    O! spare the gallant souls:
The thunder rolls—the winds increase—
    The Sea, like mountains, rolls!
While, from the deck, the storm-worn victims leap,
And o'er their struggling limbs, the furious billows sweep.

5

"O! barb'rous Pow'r! relentless Fate!
    Does Heav'n's high will decree
That some should sleep on beds of state, –
    Some, in the roaring Sea?
Some, nurs'd in splendour, deal Oppression's blow,
While worth and DRACO pine—in Slavery and woe!

6

"Yon Vessel oft has plough'd the main
    With human traffic fraught;
Its cargo,—our dark Sons of pain—
    For worldly treasure bought!
What had they done?—O Nature tell me why—
Is taunting scorn the lot, of thy dark progeny?

7

"Thou gav'st, in thy caprice, the Soul
    Peculiarly enshrin'd;
Nor from the ebon Casket stole
    The Jewel of the mind!
Then wherefore let the suff'ring Negro's breast
Bow to his fellow, MAN, in brighter colours drest.

8

"Is it the dim and glossy hue
    That marks him for despair?—

45 While men with blood their hands embrue,
      And mock the wretch's pray'r?
Shall guiltless Slaves the Scourge of tyrants feel,
And, e'en before their GOD! unheard, unpitied kneel.

                        9
"Could the proud rulers of the land
50   Our Sable race behold;
Some bow'd by torture's Giant hand
      And others, basely sold!
Then would they pity Slaves, and cry, with shame,
Whate'er their TINTS may be, their SOULS are still
      the same!

                        10
55 "Why seek to mock the Ethiop's face?
      Why goad our hapless kind?
Can features alienate the race—
      Is there no kindred mind?
Does not the cheek which vaunts the roseate hue
60 Oft blush for crimes, that Ethiops never knew?

                        11
"Behold! the angry waves conspire
      To check the barb'rous toil!
While wounded Nature's vengeful ire—
      Roars, round this trembling Isle!
65 And hark! her voice re-echoes in the wind—
Man was not form'd by Heav'n, to trample on his kind!

                        12
"Torn from my Mother's aching breast,
      My Tyrant sought my love—
But, in the Grave shall ZELMA rest,
70   E'er she will faithless prove—
No DRACO!—Thy companion I will be
To that celestial realm, where Negroes shall be free!

                        13
"The Tyrant WHITE MAN taught my mind—
      The letter'd page to trace;—
75 He taught me in the Soul to find
      No tint, as in the face:

He bade my Reason, blossom like the tree—
But fond affection gave, the ripen'd fruits to thee.

                        14
"With jealous rage he mark'd my love;
80   He sent thee far away;—
And prison'd in the plantain grove—
      Poor ZELMA pass'd the day—
But ere the moon rose high above the main,
ZELMA, and Love contriv'd, to break the Tyrant's chain.

                        15
85 "Swift, o'er the plain of burning Sand
      My course I bent to thee;
And soon I reach'd the billowy strand
      Which bounds the stormy Sea.—
DRACO! my Love! Oh yet, thy ZELMA's soul
90 Springs ardently to thee,—impatient of controul.

                        16
"Again the lightning flashes white—
      The rattling cords among!
Now, by the transient vivid light,
      I mark the frantic throng!
95 Now up the tatter'd shrouds my DRACO flies—
While o'er the plunging prow, the curling billows rise.

                        17
"The topmast falls—three shackled slaves—
      Cling to the Vessel's side!
Now lost amid the madd'ning waves—
100   Now on the mast they ride—
See! on the forecastle my DRACO stands
And now he waves his chain, now clasps his bleeding
      hands.

                        18
"Why, cruel WHITE-MAN! when away
      My sable Love was torn,
105 Why did you let poor ZELMA stay,
      On Afric's sands to mourn?
No! ZELMA is not left, for she will prove
In the deep troubled main, her fond—her faithful LOVE."

19

The lab'ring Ship was now a wreck,
    The Shrouds were flutt'ring wide!
The rudder gone, the lofty deck
    Was rock'd from side to side—
Poor ZELMA's eyes now dropp'd their last big tear,
While, from her tawny cheek, the blood recoil'd with
    fear.

20

Now frantic, on the sands she roam'd,
    Now shrieking stop'd to view
Where high the liquid mountains foam'd,
    Around the exhausted crew—
'Till, from the deck, her DRACO's well known form
Sprung mid the yawning waves, and buffetted the Storm.

21

Long, on the swelling surge sustain'd
    Brave DRACO sought the shore,
Watch'd the dark Maid, but ne'er complain'd,
    Then sunk, to gaze no more!
Poor ZELMA saw him buried by the wave—
And, with her heart's true Love, plung'd in a wat'ry grave.

———————

from Dorothy Wordsworth, *The Grasmere Journal*

As the following excerpt from Dorothy Wordsworth's journals indicates, brutality on slave ships
could also be directed at members of the crew.

Monday Morning [15 March 1802] We sat reading the poems and I read a little German. … During W's[1] absence a sailor who was travelling from Liverpool to Whitehaven called. He was faint and pale when he knocked at the door, a young man very well dressed. We sat by the kitchen fire talking with him for 2 hours—he told us most interesting stories of his life. His name was Isaac Chapel—he had been at sea since he was 15 years old. He was by trade a sail-maker. His last voyage was to the coast of Guinea. He had been on board a slave ship the captain's name Maxwell where one man had been killed a boy put to lodge with the pigs & was half eaten, one boy set to watch in the hot sun till he dropped down dead. He had been cast away in North America and had travelled 30 days among the Indians where he had been well treated. He had twice swum from a king's ship in the night & escaped, he said he would rather be in hell than be pressed.[2] He was now going to wait in England to appear against Captain Maxwell—"Oh he's a rascal, sir, he ought to be put in the papers!" The poor man had not been in bed since Friday night—he left Liverpool at 2 o'clock on Saturday morning. He had called at a farm house to beg victuals and had been refused. The woman said she would give him noth-ing—"Won't you? Then I can't help it." He was exces-sively like my brother John.

from Thomas Clarkson, *The History of the Rise, Progress and Accomplishment of the Abolition of the African Slave Trade* (1808)

In 1785, Clarkson (1760–1846) was the author of a prize-winning essay at Cambridge University on "slavery and commerce of the human species, particularly the African." Thereafter he devoted enormous energy to the abolitionist cause. He played a leading role in founding the Society for Effecting the Abolition of the Slave Trade in 1787, and in pressing for the abolition of slavery itself after the halting of the slave trade in 1807.

Let us examine the state of the unhappy Africans, reduced to slavery in this manner, while on board the vessels, which are to convey them across the ocean to other lands. And here I must observe at once, that, as far as this part of the evil is concerned, I am at a loss to describe it. Where shall I find words to express properly their sorrow, as arising from the reflection of being parted for ever from their friends, their relatives, and

———————

[1] *W's* William Wordsworth's.

[2] *pressed* Forced into naval service. "Press gangs" were authorized to force men into the Navy at this period.

their country? Where shall I find language to paint in appropriate colours the horror of mind brought on by thoughts of their future unknown destination, of which they can augur nothing but misery from all that they have yet seen? How shall I make known their situation, while labouring under painful disease, or while struggling in the suffocating holds of their prisons, like animals inclosed in an exhausted receiver? How shall I describe their feelings as exposed to all the personal indignities, which lawless appetite or brutal passion may suggest? How shall I exhibit their sufferings as determining to refuse sustenance and die, or as resolving to break their chains, and, disdaining to live as slaves, to punish their oppressors? How shall I give an idea of their agony, when under various punishments and tortures for their reputed crimes? Indeed every part of this subject defies my powers, and I must therefore satisfy myself and the reader with a general representation, or in the words of a celebrated member of Parliament, that "Never was so much human suffering condensed in so small a space."

I now come to the evil, as it has been proved to arise in the third case; or to consider the situation of the unhappy victims of the trade, when their painful voyages are over, or after they have been landed upon their destined shores. And here we are to view them first under the degrading light of cattle. We are to see them examined, handled, selected, separated, and sold. Alas! relatives are separated from relatives, as if, like cattle, they had no rational intellect, no power of feeling the nearness of relationship, nor sense of the duties belonging to the ties of life! We are next to see them labouring, and this for the benefit of those, to whom they are under no obligation, by any law either natural or divine, to obey. We are to see them, if refusing the commands of their purchasers, however weary, or feeble, or indisposed, subject to corporal punishments, and, if forcibly resisting them, to death. We are to see them in a state of general degradation and misery. The knowledge, which their oppressors have of their own crime in having violated the rights of nature, and of the disposition of the injured to seek all opportunities of revenge, pro-

duces a fear, which dictates to them the necessity of a system of treatment by which they shall keep up a wide distinction between the two, and by which the noble feelings of the latter shall be kept down, and their spirits broken. We are to see them again subject to individual persecution, as anger, or malice, or any bad passion may suggest. Hence the whip—the chain—the iron-collar. Hence the various modes of private torture, of which so many accounts have been truly given. Nor can such horrible cruelties be discovered so as to be made punishable, while the testimony of any number of the oppressed is invalid against the oppressors, however they may be offences against the laws. And, lastly, we are to see their innocent offspring, against whose person liberty the shadow of an argument cannot be advanced, inheriting all the miseries of their parents' lot.

from Matthew Gregory Lewis, *Journal of a West India Proprietor* (1815–17)

Lewis (1775–1818), whose father was the absentee owner of sugar plantations in Jamaica and the Deputy Secretary of War, became well known with the publication of *The Monk*, a sensational Gothic novel written in a ten-week period when he was nineteen years old. Lewis inherited his father's property in 1812, and made two trips to Jamaica (in 1815–16 and 1817–18) with a view to ascertaining the condition of the plantations and ameliorating conditions for the people his family enslaved there. His journals were first offered for publication in 1817, but did not appear in print until 1834, sixteen years after Lewis's death from yellow fever, during the return voyage after his second residence in Jamaica.

Though Lewis was clearly considerably more humane than most plantation owners, he opposed any move to abolish slavery, on the grounds that it was necessary to the plantation economy.

15 January 1815

The offspring of a white man and black woman is a *mulatto*; the mulatto and black produce a *sambo*; from the mulatto and white comes the *quadroon*; from the quadroon and white the *mustee*; the child of a mustee by a white man is called a *musteefino*; while the children of a musteefino are free by law, and rank as white persons to all intents and purposes. I think it is Long who asserts, that two mulattoes will never have children; but, as far as the most positive assurances can go, since my arrival in Jamaica, I have reason to believe the contrary, and that mulattoes breed together just as well as blacks and whites; but they are almost universally weak and effeminate persons, and thus their children are very difficult to rear. On a sugar estate one black is considered as more than equal to two mulattoes. Beautiful as are their forms in general, and easy and graceful as are their movements (which, indeed, appear to me so striking, that they cannot fail to excite the admiration of any one who has ever looked with delight on statues), still the women of colour are deficient in one of the most requisite points of female beauty. When Oromases[1] was employed in the formation of woman, and said,—"Let her enchanting bosom resemble the celestial spheres," he must certainly have suffered the negress to slip out of his mind. Young or old, I have not yet seen such a thing as a *bosom*.

16 January 1815

I never witnessed on the stage a scene so picturesque as a negro village. I walked through my own to-day, and visited the houses of the drivers, and other principal persons; and if I were to decide according to my own taste, I should infinitely have preferred their habitations to my own. Each house is surrounded by a separate garden, and the whole village is intersected by lanes, bordered with all kinds of sweet-smelling and flowering plants; but not such gardens as those belonging to our English cottages, where a few cabbages and carrots just peep up and grovel upon the earth between hedges, in square narrow beds, and where the tallest tree is a

gooseberry bush: the vegetables of the negroes are all cultivated in their provision-grounds; these form their *kitchen*-gardens, and these are all for ornament or luxury, and are filled with a profusion of oranges, shaddocks, cocoa-nuts, and peppers of all descriptions: in particular I was shown the abba, or palm tree, resembling the cocoa-tree, but much more beautiful, as its leaves are larger and more numerous, and, feathering to the ground as they grow old, they form a kind of natural arbour. It bears a large fruit, or rather vegetable, towards the top of the tree, in shape like the cone of the pine, but formed of seeds, some scarlet and bright as coral, others of a brownish-red or purple. The abba requires a length of years to arrive at maturity: a very fine one, which was shown me this morning, was supposed to be upwards of an hundred years old; and one of a very moderate size had been planted at the least twenty years, and had only borne fruit once.

It appears to me a strong proof of the good treatment which the negroes on Cornwall have been accustomed to receive, that there are many very old people upon it; I saw to-day a woman near a hundred years of age; and I am told that there are several of sixty, seventy, and eighty. I was glad, also, to find, that several negroes who have obtained their freedom, and possess little properties of their own in the mountains, and at Savannah la Mar, look upon my estate so little as the scene of their former sufferings while slaves, that they frequently come down to pass a few days in their ancient habitations with their former companions, by way of relaxation. One woman in particular expressed her hopes, that I should not be offended at her still coming to Cornwall now and then, although she belonged to it no longer; and begged me to give directions before my return to England, that her visits should not be hindered on the grounds of her having no business there.

My visit to Jamaica has at least produced one advantage to myself. Several runaways, who had disappeared for some time (some even for several months), have again made their appearance in the field, and I have desired that no questions should be asked. On the other hand, after enjoying herself during the Saturday and Sunday, which were allowed for holidays on my

---

[1] *Oromases* The good principle, the god of light, in ancient Persian thought.

arrival, one of my ladies chose *to pull foot,* and did not return from her hiding-place in the mountains till this morning. Her name is Marcia; but so unlike is she to Addison's Marcia, that she is not only as black as Juba, (instead of being "fair, oh! how divinely fair!") but,— whereas Sempronius[1] complains, that "Marcia, the lovely Marcia, is left behind," the complaint against my heroine is, that "Marcia, the lovely Marcia" is always running away. In excuse for her disappearance she alleged, that so far was her husband from thinking that "she towered above her sex," that he had called her "a very bad woman," which had provoked her so much, that she could not bear to stay with him; and she assured me, that he was himself "a very bad man"; which, if true, was certainly enough to justify any lady, black or white, in making a little incognito excursion for a week or so; therefore, as it appeared to be nothing more than a conjugal quarrel, and as Marcia engaged never to run away any more (at the same time allowing that she had suffered her resentment to carry her too far, when it had carried her all the way to the mountains), I desired that an act of oblivion might be passed in favour of Cato's daughter, and away she went, quite happy, to pick hog's meat.

The negro houses are composed of wattles[2] on the outside, with rafters of sweet-wood, and are well plastered within and white-washed; they consist of two chambers, one for cooking and the other for sleeping, and are, in general, well furnished with chairs, tables, etc., and I saw none without a four-post bedstead and plenty of bedclothes; for, in spite of the warmth of the climate, when the sun is not above the horizon the negro always feels very chilly. I am assured that many of my slaves are very rich (and their property is inviolable), and that they are never without salt provisions, porter, and even wine, to entertain their friends and their visitors from the bay or the mountains. As I passed through their grounds, many little requests were preferred to me: one wanted an additional supply of lime for the whitewashing his house; another was building a new house for a superannuated wife (for they have all so much decency as to call their sexual attachments by a conjugal name), and wanted a little assistance towards the finishing it; a third requested a new axe to work with; and several entreated me to negotiate the purchase of some relation or friend belonging to another estate, and with whom they were anxious to be reunited: but all their requests were for additional indulgences; not one complained of ill-treatment, hunger, or over-work.

Poor Nicholas gave me a fresh instance of his being one of those whom Fortune pitches upon to show her spite: he has had four children, none of whom are alive; and the eldest of them, a fine little girl of four years old, fell into the mill-stream, and was drowned before any one was aware of her danger. His wife told me that she had had fifteen children, had taken the utmost care of them, and yet had now but two alive: she said, indeed, fifteen at the first, but she afterwards corrected herself, and explained that she had had "twelve whole children and three half ones"; by which she meant miscarriages.

Besides the profits arising from their superabundance of provisions, which the better sort of negroes are enabled to sell regularly once a week at Savannah la Mar to a considerable amount, they keep a large stock of poultry, and pigs without number; which latter cost their owners but little, though they cost me a great deal; for they generally make their way into the cane-pieces, and sometimes eat me up an hogshead of sugar in the course of the morning: but the most expensive of the planter's enemies are the rats, whose numbers are incredible, and are so destructive that a reward is given for killing them. During the last six months my agent has paid for three thousand rats killed upon Cornwall. Nor is the sugar which they consume the worst damage which they commit; the worst mischief is, that if, through the carelessness of those whose business it is to supply the mill, one cane which has been gnawed by the rats is allowed admittance, that single damaged piece is sufficient to produce acidity enough to spoil the whole sugar.

---

[1] *Addison's Marcia ... Sempronius* Marcia and Sempronius are characters in Joseph Addison's *Cato* (1713).

[2] *wattles* Woven branches.

24 February 1815

On the Sunday after my first arrival, the whole body of Eboe negroes came to me to complain of the attorney, and more particularly of one of the book-keepers. I listened to them, if not with unwearied patience, at least with unsubdued fortitude, for above an hour and a half; and finding some grounds for their complaint against the latter, in a few days I went down to their quarter of the village, told them that to please them I had discharged the book-keeper, named a day for examining their other grievances, and listened to them for an hour more. When the day of trial came, they sent me word that they were perfectly satisfied, and had no complaint to make. I was, therefore, much surprised to receive a visit from Edward, the Eboe, yesterday evening, who informed me, that during my absence his fellows had formed a plan of making a complaint *en masse* to a neighbouring magistrate; and that, not only against the attorney, but against myself "for not listening to them when they were injured"; and Edward claimed great merit with me for having prevented their taking this step, and convinced them, that while I was on the estate myself, there could be no occasion for applying to a third person. Now, having made me aware of my great obligations to him, here Edward meant the matter to rest; but being a good deal incensed at their ingratitude, I instantly sent for the Eboes, and enquired into the matter; when it appeared, that Edward (who is a clever fellow, and has great influence over the rest) had first goaded them into a resolution of complaining to a magistrate, had then stopped them from putting their plan into execution, and that the whole was a plot of Edward's, in order to make a merit with me for himself at the expense of his countrymen. However, as they confessed their having had the intention of applying to Mr. Hill as a magistrate, I insisted upon their executing their intention. I told them, that as Mr. Hill was the person whom they had selected for their protector, to Mr. Hill they should go; that they should either make their complaint to him against me, or confess that they had been telling lies, and had no complaint to make; and that, as the next day was to be a play-day given them by me, instead of passing it at home in singing and dancing, they should pass it at the Bay in stating their grievances.

This threw them into terrible confusion; they cried out that they wanted to make no complaint whatever, and that it was all Edward's fault, who had misled them. Three of them, one after the other, gave him the lie to his face; and each and all (Edward as well as the rest) declared that go to the Bay they absolutely would *not*. The next morning they were all at the door waiting for my coming out: they positively refused to go to Mr. Hill, and begged and prayed, and humbled themselves; now scraping and bowing to me, and then blackguarding Edward with all their might and main; and when I ordered the driver to take charge of them, and carry them to Mr. Hill, some of them fairly took to their heels, and ran away. However, the rest soon brought them back again, for they swore that if one went, all should go; and away they were marched, in a string of about twenty, with the driver at their head. When they got to the Bay, they told Mr. Hill that, as to their massa, they had no complaint to make against him, except that he had compelled them to make one; and what they said against the attorney was so trifling, that the magistrate bade the driver take them all back again. Upon which they slunk away to their houses, while the Creoles cried out "Shame! shame!" as they passed along.

Indeed, the Creoles could not have received a greater pleasure than the mortification of the Eboes; for the two bodies hate each other as cordially as the Guelphs and Ghibellines;[1] and after their departure for the Bay, I heard the head cook haranguing a large audience, and declaring it to be her fixed opinion, "that massa ought to sell all the Eboes, and buy Creoles instead." Probably, Mrs. Cook was not the less loud in her exclamations against the ingratitude of the Eboes, from her own loyalty having lately been questioned. She had found fault one day in the hospital with some women who feigned sickness in order to remain idle. "You no work willing for massa," said Mrs. Cook, "and him so vex, him say him go to Kingston to-morrow, and him wish him neber come back again!"—"What!" cried Philippa,

---

[1] *Guelphs and Ghibellines* Opposing factions in political struggles between papal and imperial powers during the later Middle Ages.

the mad woman, "you wish massa neber come back from Kingston?" So she gave Mrs. Cook a box on the ear with all her might; upon which Mrs. Cook snatched up a stick and broke the mad woman's pate with it. But though she could beat a hole in her head, she never could beat out of it her having said that she wished massa might never come back. And although Philippa has recovered her senses, in her belief of Mrs. Cook's disloyalty she continues firm; and they never meet without renewing the dispute.

To-day being a play-day, the gaiety of the negroes was promoted by a distribution of an additional quantity of salt-fish (which forms a most acceptable ingredient in their pepper-pots), and as much rum and sugar as they chose to drink. But there was also a dinner prepared at the house where the "white people" reside, expressly for none but the *piccaninny-mothers*; that is, for the women who had children living. I had taken care, when this play-day was announced by the head driver, to make him inform the negroes that they were indebted for it entirely to these mothers; and to show them the more respect, I went to them after dinner myself, and drank their healths. The most respectable blacks on the estate were also assembled in the room; and I then told them that clothes would wear out, and money would be spent, and that I wished to give them something more lasting than clothes or money. The law only allows them, as a matter of right, every alternate Saturday for themselves, and holidays for three days at Christmas, which, with all Sundays, forms their whole legal time of relaxation. I therefore granted them as a matter of right, and of which no person should deprive them on any account whatever, *every* Saturday to cultivate their grounds; and in addition to their holidays at Christmas, I gave them for play-days Good-Friday, the second Friday in October, and the second Friday in July. By which means, they will in future have the same number of holidays four times a year, which hitherto they have been allowed only once, *i.e.* at Christmas. The first is to be called "the royal play-day," in honour of that excellent Princess, the Duchess of York; and the negroes are directed to give three cheers upon the head driver's announcing "The health of our good lady, HRH the Duchess of York." And I told them, that before my leaving the island, I should hear them drink this health, and should not fail to let Her Royal Highness know, that the negroes of Cornwall drank her health every year. This evidently touched the right chord of their vanity, and they all bowed and courtesied down to the very ground, and said, that would do them much high honour. The ninth being my own birthday, the July play-day is to be called "the massa's"; and that in October is to be in honour of the piccaninny-mothers, from whom it is to take its name.

The poor creatures overflowed with gratitude; and the prospective indulgences which had just been announced, gave them such an increase of spirits, that on returning to my own residence, they fell to singing and dancing again with as much violence as if they had been a pack of French furies at the Opera. The favourite song of the night was, "Since massa come, we very well off"; which words they repeated in chorus, without intermission (dancing all the time), for hours together; till, at half-past three, neither my eyes nor my brain could endure it any longer, and I was obliged to send them word that I wanted to go to bed, and could not sleep till the noise should cease.

1 May 1815 (Friday)
This morning I signed the manumission of Nicholas Cameron, the best of my mulatto carpenters. He had been so often on the very point of getting his liberty, and still the cup was dashed from his lips, that I had promised to set him free, whenever he could procure an able negro as his substitute; although being a good workman, a single negro was by no means an adequate price in exchange. On my arrival this year I found that he had agreed to pay 150*l.* for a female negro, and the woman was approved of by my trustee. But on enquiry it appeared that she had a child, from which she was unwilling to separate, and that her owner refused to sell the child, except at a most unreasonable price. Here then was an insurmountable objection to my accepting her, and Nicholas was told to his great mortification, that he must look out for another substitute. The woman, on her part, was determined to belong to

Cornwall estate and no other: so she told her owner, that if he attempted to sell her elsewhere she would make away with herself, and on his ordering her to prepare for a removal to a neighbouring proprietor's, she disappeared, and concealed herself so well, that for some time she was believed to have put her threats of suicide into execution. The idea of losing his 150*l.* frightened her master so completely, that he declared himself ready to let me have the child at a fair price, as well as the mother, if she ever should be found; and her friends having conveyed this assurance to her, she thought proper to emerge from her hiding-place, and the bargain was arranged finally. The titles, however, were not yet made out, and as the time of my departure for Hordley was arrived, these were ordered to be got ready against my return, when the negroes were to be delivered over to me, and Nicholas was to be set free. In the meanwhile, the child was sent by her mistress (a free mulatto) to hide some stolen ducks upon a distant property, and on her return blabbed out the errand: in consequence the mistress was committed to prison for theft; and no sooner was she released, than she revenged herself upon the poor girl by giving her thirty lashes with the cattle-whip, inflicted with all the severity of vindictive malice. This treatment of a child of such tender years reduced her to such a state, as made the magistrates think it right to send her for protection to the workhouse, until the conduct of the mistress should have been enquired into. In the meanwhile, as the result of the enquiry might be the setting the girl at liberty, the joint title for her and her mother could not be made out, and thus poor Nicholas's manumission was at a stand-still again. The magistrates at length decided, that although the chastisement had been severe, yet (according to the medical report) it was not such as to authorise the sending the mistress to be tried at the assizes. She was accordingly dismissed from farther investigation, and the girl was once more considered as belonging to me, as soon as the title could be made out. But the fatality which had so often prevented Nicholas from obtaining his freedom, was not weary yet. On the very morning, when he was to sign the title, a person whose signature was indispensable, was thrown out of his chaise, the wheel of which

passed over his head, and he was rendered incapable of transacting business for several weeks. Yesterday, the titles were at length brought to me complete, and this morning put Nicholas in possession of the object, in the pursuit of which he has experienced such repeated disappointments. The conduct of the poor child's mulatto mistress in this case was most unpardonable, and is only one of numerous instances of a similar description, which have been mentioned to me. Indeed, I have every reason to believe, that nothing can be uniformly more wretched, than the life of the slaves of free people of colour in Jamaica; nor would any thing contribute more to the relief of the black population, than the prohibiting by law any mulatto to become the owner of a slave for the future. Why should not rich people of colour be served by poor people of colour, hiring them as domestics? It seldom happens that mulattoes are in possession of plantations; but when a white man dies, who happens to possess twenty negroes, he will divide them among his brown family, leaving (we may say) five to each of his four children. These are too few to be employed in plantation work; they are, therefore, ordered to maintain their owner by some means or other, and which means are frequently not the most honest, the most frequent being the travelling about as higglers, and exchanging the trumpery contents of their packs and boxes with plantation negroes for stolen rum and sugar. I confess I cannot see why, on such bequest being made, the law should not order the negroes to be sold, and the produce of the sale paid to the mulatto heirs, but absolutely prohibiting the mulattoes from becoming proprietors of the negroes themselves. Every man of humanity must wish that slavery, even in its best and most mitigated form, had never found a legal sanction, and must regret that its system is now so incorporated with the welfare of Great Britain as well as of Jamaica, as to make its extirpation an absolute impossibility, without the certainty of producing worse mischiefs than the one which we annihilate. But certainly there can be no sort of occasion for continuing in the colonies the existence of *domestic slavery*, which neither contributes to the security of the colonies themselves, nor to the opulence of the mother-country, the revenue of which derived from colonial duties would suffer no defalcation whatever, even if neither whites nor blacks in the West Indies were suffered to employ slaves, except in plantation labour.

from Elizabeth Heyrick, *Immediate, Not Gradual Abolition* (1824)

In 1823, Wilberforce and Clarkson established a new organization to lead the mainstream abolition campaign: the Society for the Mitigation and Gradual Abolition of Slavery Throughout the British Dominions, more commonly known as the Antislavery Society. The same year, an Antislavery Society member introduced a parliamentary motion to gradually secure the "extinction of slavery altogether, by rendering all the negro children, born after a certain day, free."

The more radical position—that emancipation should be immediate, not "gradual"—was at first advocated primarily by the members of women's abolitionist societies, and especially by the Quaker and reformer Elizabeth Heyrick, whose pamphlet on the issue is excerpted below. Despite resistance from Wilberforce, who opposed not only immediate emancipation but also the involvement of women in political matters, Heyrick and her associates pressured the Antislavery Society into removing "Gradual" from its official name and adopting immediate abolition as its stated goal.

... We that hear, and read, and approve, and applaud the powerful appeals, the irrefragable arguments against the Slave Trade, and against slavery—are we *ourselves* sincere, or hypocritical? Are *we* the true friends of justice, or do we only cant[1] about it? To which party do *we* really belong—to the friends of emancipation, or of perpetual slavery? Every individual belongs to one party or the other; not speculatively, or professionally merely, but practically. The perpetuation of slavery in our West India colonies is not an abstract question, to be settled between the Government and the Planters—it is a question in which we are *all* implicated; we are all guilty (with shame and compunction let us admit the opprobrious truth) of supporting and perpetuating slavery. The West Indian planter and the people of this country stand in the same moral relation to each other as the thief and the receiver of stolen goods. The planter refuses to set his wretched captive at liberty; treats him as a beast of burden; compels his reluctant unremunerated labour under the lash of the cart-whip—why?—because WE furnish the stimulant to all this injustice, rapacity, and cruelty, by PURCHASING ITS PRODUCE. Heretofore, it may have been thoughtlessly and unconsciously—but now this palliative is removed; the veil of ignorance is rent aside; the whole nation must now divide itself into the *active supporters*, and the *active opposers* of slavery; there is no longer any ground for a neutral party to stand upon. ...

... Are there no tests to prove our sincerity—no sacrifices to be offered in confirmation of our zeal? Yes, there is one—but it is in itself so small and insignificant that it seems almost burlesque to dignify it with the name of sacrifice—it is ABSTINENCE FROM THE USE OF WEST INDIAN PRODUCTIONS, sugar especially, in the cultivation of which slave labour is chiefly occupied. Small, however, and insignificant as the sacrifice may appear, it would at once give the death blow to West Indian slavery. When there is no longer a market for the productions of *slave labour*, then, and *not till then*, will the slaves be emancipated. ...

... It has been abundantly proved that voluntary labour is more productive, more advantageous to the employer, than compulsory labour. The experiments of the venerable and philanthropic Joshua Steele[2] have established the fact beyond all doubt. But the planter shuts his eyes to such facts, though clear and evident as the sun at noon day. None are so blind as those who *will* not see. The conviction then must be *forced* upon these infatuated[3] men. It is often asserted that slavery is

---

[1] *cant* Talk or argue in a way that involves insincere posturing.

[2] *Joshua Steele* British plantation owner who improved the productivity of his Barbados estates by treating the people he enslaved somewhat more justly; among other things, he paid them wages. His letters to Clarkson detailing the success of his reforms were published in 1814.

[3] *infatuated* Extremely foolish.

too deeply rooted an evil to be eradicated by the exertions of any principle less potent and active than *self-interest*: if so, the resolution to abstain from West Indian produce would bring this potent and active principle into the fullest operation—would *compel* the planter to set his slaves at liberty.[1] ...

"But (it will be objected) it is not an *immediate*, but a *gradual* emancipation, which the most enlightened and judicious friends of humanity call for; as a measure best calculated, in their judgment, to promote the real interests of the *slave*, as well as his master; the former not being in a condition to make a right use of his freedom, were it suddenly restored to him." This, it must be admitted, appears not only the general, but almost universal sentiment of the abolitionists; to oppose it, therefore, may seem a most presumptuous as well as hopeless attempt. But truth and justice are stubborn and inflexible; they yield neither to numbers or authority.

The history of emancipation in St. Domingo,[2] and of the conduct of the emancipated slaves for thirty years subsequent to that event (as detailed in Clarkson's admirable pamphlet,[3] on the necessity of improving the condition of our West Indian slaves), is a complete refutation of all the elaborate arguments which have been artfully advanced to discredit the design of *immediate* emancipation. No instance has been recorded in these important annals, of the emancipated slaves (not the *gradually*, but the *immediately* emancipated slaves) having abused their freedom. On the contrary, it is frequently asserted in the course of the narrative that the negroes continued to work upon all the plantations as quietly as before emancipation. ...

In the face of such a body of evidence, the detaining our West Indian slaves in bondage is a continued acting of the same atrocious injustice which first kidnapped and tore them from their kindred and native soil, and robbed them of that sacred unalienable right which no considerations, how plausible soever, can justify the withholding. We have no right, on any pretext of expediency or pretended humanity, to say—"because you have been made a slave, and thereby degraded and debased, therefore I will continue to hold you in bondage, until you have acquired a capacity to make a right use of your liberty." As well might you say to a poor wretch, gasping and languishing in a pest house,[4] "here will I keep you, till I have given you a capacity for the enjoyment of pure air." ...

... Thus, by a train of most exquisite reasoning, has [the father of lies] brought the abolitionists to the conclusion that the interest of the poor, degraded, and oppressed *slave*, as well as that of his master, will be best secured by his *remaining in slavery*. It has, indeed, been proposed to mitigate, in some degree, the miseries of his interminable bondage, but the blessings of *emancipation*, according to the propositions of the abolitionists in the last session of Parliament, were to be reserved for his *posterity* alone; and every idea of *immediate* emancipation is still represented, not only as impolitic, enthusiastic, and visionary, but as highly injurious to the slave himself; and a train of supposed apt illustrations is continually at hand to expose the absurdity of such a project. "Who (it is asked) would place a sumptuous banquet before a half-famished wretch, whilst his powers of digestion were so feeble that it would be fatal to partake of it? Who would bring a body, benumbed and half frozen with cold, into sudden contact with fervid heat? Who would take a poor captive from his dungeon, where he had been immured whole years, in total darkness, and bring him at once into the dazzling light of a meridian sun? No one in his senses, certainly. All these transitions from famine to plenty, from cold to heat, from darkness to light, must be gradual, in order to be salutary. But must it therefore follow, by any inductions of common sense, that emancipation out of the grip of a robber or an assassin, out of the jaws of a

---

[1] [Heyrick's note]   It has been ascertained that the abstinence of *one tenth* of the inhabitants of this country from West Indian sugar would abolish West Indian slavery.

[2] *St. Domingo*   St. Domingue became Haiti during the Haitian Revolution (1791–1804), through which the enslaved people of the nation freed themselves and obtained independence from France.

[3] *Clarkson's admirable pamphlet*   See Thomas Clarkson, *Thoughts on the Necessity of Improving the Condition of the Slaves in the British Colonies, with a View to Their Ultimate Emancipation* (1823).

[4] *pest house*   Literally, a hospital for the treatment of infectious disease; figuratively, any place where the air is infectious.

shark or a tiger, must be gradual? Must it therefore follow that the wretched victim of slavery must always remain in slavery—that emancipation must be so gradual that the blessings of freedom shall never be tasted by him who has endured all the curses of slavery, but be reserved for his posterity alone? ...

It is utterly astonishing, with such an object as West Indian slavery before us, rendered palpable, in all its horrors, almost to our very senses, by a multitude of indubitable facts, collected from various sources of the highest authority, all uniting in the same appalling evidence; with the sight of our fellow-creatures in bondage so rigorous, in moral and physical degradation so abject; under a tyranny so arbitrary, wanton, and barbarous; it is utterly astonishing that our compassion and sympathy should be so timid and calculating, so slow and cautious. ...

... Why then, in the name of humanity, of common sense, and common honesty, do we petition Parliament, year after year, for a gradual abolition of this horrid system, this complication of crime and misery? Why petition Parliament *at all*, to do that for us which, were they ever so well disposed, we can do more speedily and more effectually for ourselves? ...

Should the wretched African find the moment for *breaking his own chains, and asserting his own freedom*, he may well be expected to take terrible vengeance—to push the law of retaliation to its utmost extreme. But, when presented with his freedom—when the sacred rights of humanity are restored to him, would that be the moment for rage, for revenge and murder? To *polished* and *Christianized* Europeans, such abuses of liberty may appear natural and inevitable, since their own history abounds with them. But the history of negro emancipation abundantly proves that no such consequences are to be apprehended from the poor *uncultivated* and *despised* African. ...

The interests and prejudices of the West Indian planters have occupied much too prominent a place in the discussion of this great question. The abolitionists have shewn a great deal too much politeness and accommodation towards these gentlemen. With reference to them, the question is said to be a very *delicate* one. (Was

ever the word delicacy so preposterously misapplied!) It is said to be beset with difficulties and dangers. Yes, the parties interested—*criminally* interested—protest that the difficulties are insurmountable, the dangers tremendous. ... Must hundreds of thousands of human beings ... continue to be roused and stimulated to uncompensated labour, night as well as day, during a great part of the year, by the impulse of the cart whip, that a few *noble lords* and *honourable gentlemen* may experience no privation of expensive luxury—no contraction of profuse expenditure—no curtailment of state and equipage?[1] Must the scale in which is placed the just claims, the sacred rights of *eight hundred thousand British subjects*, be made to kick the beam[2] when weighed in the balance against pretensions so comparatively light and frivolous? ...

But if the West Indian gentlemen fail to obtain *protection* against the designs of the abolitionists, then they demand *compensation*, in the event of the emancipation of their slaves, to the immense amount of *sixty-four millions*. And is *compensation* demanded in no other quarter—or, if not demanded, is it no where else due? If compensation be demanded as an act of justice to the slave-holder, in the event of the liberation of his slaves, let justice take her free impartial course—let compensation be made in the first instance where it is most due—let compensation be first made to the *slave*, for his long years of uncompensated labour, degradation, and suffering. It is in *this* quarter that justice cries aloud for compensation—and if our attention is turned, but for a moment, to these two substantial and well authenticated claims, the demands of the *slave-holder* (even had they been couched in terms less arrogant and insulting) will become not a little questionable.

Experience has already sufficiently evinced the fallacy of the notion of the superior policy of aiming at gradual, instead of immediate emancipation, on the ground of its

[1] *equipage* Material markers of social status, such as domestic objects, clothing, and staff.

[2] *kick the beam* The beam of a pair of scales is the cross bar from which the scales hang; a scale is said to "kick the beam" when the weight of the opposing scale is so comparatively great that the lighter scale is lifted as high as it will go.

meeting with less opposition; for the planters have shewn themselves just as much enraged at the idea of *gradual* as of immediate emancipation. They appear, indeed, either incapable of perceiving or determined to confound all distinction between them; for, in the bitterness of their invectives, they accuse the *gradual* abolitionists of endeavouring to bring upon their heads all the calamities and destruction which they formerly deprecated as the inevitable consequence of *immediate* emancipation.

On this great question, the spirit of accommodation and conciliation has been a spirit of delusion. The abolitionists have lost, rather than gained ground by it; their cause has been weakened, instead of strengthened. The great interests of truth and justice are betrayed, rather than supported, by all softening qualifying concessions. Every iota which is yielded of their rightful claims, impairs the conviction of their rectitude, and, consequently, weakens their success. Truth and justice make their best way in the world when they appear in bold and simple majesty; their demands are most willingly conceded, when they are most fearlessly claimed.

The Haitian Revolution

The latter half of the eighteenth century saw numerous uprisings by enslaved people in colonial holdings throughout the West Indies and South America, notably in Panama, Jamaica, Surinam, and Guyana. But the only successful uprising took place in St. Domingue, the French colony that would become Haiti. Beginning in 1791 and ending in 1804, the Haitian Revolution spanned thirteen years and led to the foundation of a black state free from slavery.

In the decades leading up to the Revolution, the disdainful and violent treatment of the people enslaved on St. Domingue created a situation of barely contained hatred against the white masters—whom the enslaved people outnumbered by at least a 10 to 1 ratio. Enslaved people were treated with extreme cruelty; workdays as long as twenty hours were enforced by brutal supervision and corporal punishment.

In August 1791 the revolt began, and within ten days the rebels had gained control of the Northern provinces, killing the whites and burning the plantations. In the following years the rebel army confronted not only French forces, but also those sent by Britain to seize control of the lucrative colony. Britain's five-year attempt, beginning in 1793, was a costly disaster, with soldiers dying in great numbers from disease.

Toussaint Louverture, a plantation manager who had been emancipated from slavery decades earlier, began to take a leadership role in the rebel army in 1791, becoming commander-in-chief in 1796. By 1801 he controlled the entire island (St. Domingue as well as the Spanish colony Santo Domingo), and he created a new constitution that abolished slavery across the territory.

In 1802, French forces, now under the leadership of Napoleon, renewed efforts to retake the colony and reinstitute slavery. In June of that year Toussaint was captured, deported to France, and imprisoned, while the fighting continued, with the French perpetrating mass executions of captured soldiers. Toussaint died in prison in 1803; in November of the same year, the rebel army, now under the leadership of Jean-Jacques Dessalines, defeated the French, exacting their surrender and departure from the island. Dessalines declared independence for Haiti on 1 January 1804. He then ordered the massacre of the remaining white population.

In Britain, news of the Haitian Revolution elicited mixed responses. Most abolitionists were sympathetic to the Revolution and saw it as further proof that societies built on slavery were inherently unstable; few, however, were willing to support the Revolution outright, particularly as the bloodshed escalated. For plantation owners, sugar merchants, and many others in England, the violence of the Haitian Revolution was associated with the grisly scenes enacted in Revolutionary France, and compassion for the enslaved people was either absent or tempered by fear of civil unrest.

Nonetheless, the Haitian Revolution marked a turning point in the history of abolition. As Frederick Douglass later said in 1893, "Until [Haiti] spoke no Christian nation had abolished negro slavery. Until she spoke no Christian nation had given to the world an organized effort to abolish slavery. Until she spoke the slave ship, followed by hungry sharks, greedy to devour the dead and dying slaves flung overboard to feed them, ploughed in peace the South Atlantic, painting the sea with the Negro's blood."

from Baron de Wimpffen, *A Voyage to Saint Domingo, in the Years 1788, 1789, and 1790*[1] (1797)

Alexandre-Stanislas de Wimpffen (1748–1819), a German sea captain, soldier, and explorer, is best known for this account of his experiences in St. Domingue, in which he describes the social conditions that led to the 1791 uprising.

from LETTER 12 [MAY 1789]

I have determined, Sir, to give you a description of one of my days; it will be the simplest method of giving you, once for all, a summary idea of the manner of living at St. Domingo, in what is called a town. …

The cracking of whips, the smothered cries, and the indistinct groans of the negroes, who never see the day break but to curse it; who are never recalled to a feeling of their existence but by sufferings—this, Sir, is what takes place of the crowing of the early cock; and by the strains of this infernal harmony, was I awakened out of my first sleep at St. Domingo. I started, screamed, and fancied that I had waked in the gulf of Tartarus, between Prometheus and Ixion[2]—And I was among Christians! Among the worshippers of a God—who died to mitigate the sorrows of the afflicted! Custom has

already weakened the effect of the impression; it will never obliterate it altogether.

A walk of an hour served to dissipate the chagrin of this gloomy awakening. I came back in time to see a troop of male and female negroes lying against the wall, or squatting upon their heels, and waiting amidst a universal yawn, for the master's giving the signal of going to work, by loud cracks of the arceau,[3] on their back and shoulders—for, you will hardly conceive, and indeed it cost six months observation to convince me of the truth of it, there are negroes who must absolutely be beaten before they can be put in motion. The arceau is the true key of this species of watch—If I had chosen to take the word of the masters for it, I should have looked no farther for the cause of this singular disposition of the slaves, than to their natural sloth and inactivity: but on considering the matter a little more narrowly, I fancied I could see that these dispositions were marvelously seconded by the inactivity and sloth of their masters, who, for the greater part, too ignorant and too unindulgent to comprehend that the vices of education can only be subdued by time and patience, find the plan of beating more practicable than that of instructing! The natural consequence of which is, that the negro, once accustomed to this mode of treatment, can only be wrought on by rigour and severity. I have persisted, month after month, in lavishing on those who attended me, nothing but patience, gentleness, and good offices of every kind—all were in vain: the bent was taken, and nothing was left me, after all my endeavours, but the alternative of waiting on myself, or of having recourse to the arceau. …

---

[1] *A Voyage … 1790* Translated from the French by J. Wright, 1797.

[2] *gulf of Tartarus* In Greek mythology, an underworld prison associated with creative torture; *Prometheus and Ixion* Figures in Greek mythology who were subjected to extreme punishment. Prometheus's liver was eaten by an eagle (in some versions, a vulture) only to regrow and be eaten again; Ixion was strapped to an eternally revolving burning wheel.

---

[3] [Wimpffen's note] A kind of short-handled whip, so called in the colonies.

from LETTER 23 [MARCH 1790]

If this expedition has increased my local knowledge, and corrected some of my opinions, the alteration, Sir, has not always been favourable to the inhabitants of Saint Domingo. Amongst a variety of anecdotes, some of which may be exaggerated or untrue, there is one which the multiplicity, and respectability of the proofs do not permit me to call in doubt, in spite of its atrocity. A lady, whom I have seen, a young lady, and one of the handsomest in the island, gave a grand dinner. Furious at seeing a dish of pastry brought to the table overdone, she ordered her negro cook to be seized, and *thrown into the oven, yet glowing with heat*—And this horrible Magæra,[1] whose name I suppress out of respect to her family; this infernal fiend, whom public execration ought to drive with every mark of abhorrence from society; this worthy rival of the too famous Chaperon,[2] is followed, and admired—for she is rich and beautiful!

So much for what I have heard, and now for what I have seen.

The day after my return, I was walking before the casa of a planter with one of his neighbours, when we overheard him bid a negro go into the inclosure of this very neighbour, pull up two young trees which he pointed out to him, and re-plant them immediately on a terrace he was then forming.

The negro went: the neighbour followed him, surprised him in the fact, and brought him to his master, whom I had by this time joined, in the hope of witnessing a scene of confusion which promised to be amusing.

Conceive, Sir, what passed in my mind, when, on the complaint of the neighbour, I heard the master coldly order another of his negroes to tie the pretended culprit to a ladder, and give him an hundred lashes! We were both of us struck with such astonishment, that, stupefied, pale, and shuddering, while the unhappy negro received the barbarous chastisement in silence, we

looked at one another without being able to utter a single word—And he who ordered, he who thus punished his own crime on the blind instrument of his will; at once the dastardly perpetrator and the unfeeling witness of the most atrocious injustice, is here one of the first organs of the law, the official protector of innocence! Heavens! If a pitiful respect for decorum forbids me to devote the name of this monster to eternal infamy, let me at least be permitted to hope that Divine Justice will hear the cries of the sufferer, and sooner or later accumulate on the tyrants' head, all the weight of its vengeance! ...

from "Insurrection at St. Domingo: No. 1: Remarks on the Resolutions of the West-India Merchants and Planters, at the London Tavern, Nov. 3, and 8, 1791," *Star and Evening Advertiser* (18 November 1791)

The following article, from the British evening paper the *Star*, begins with a transcription of the resolutions made at a meeting of the London Society of West India Planters and Merchants, an organization founded in London in 1780 to lobby for the interests of sugar merchants and plantation owners in the West Indies. The meeting was held in response to the uprising in St. Domingue. Following the transcription of the meeting, the anonymous commentator of the *Star*, writing under the pseudonym "Common Sense," argues for a different interpretation of the causes of the Haitian Revolution.

RESOLUTION 1ST AND 3RD, PASSED NOV. 3

Resolved,

From the official papers now laid before this meeting, as well as from other accounts, it appears that the very alarming insurrection of the Negroes which has arisen, and is believed yet to exist in the French colony of St. Domingo, and which has already occasioned much bloodshed and destruction, originates not solely in political differences consequent on the late changes of government in France, but rather in

---

[1] *Magæra* One of the Furies, monstrous goddesses of vengeance in Greek mythology.

[2] [Wimpffen's note] A planter of Saint Domingo, who, in the same circumstances, seeing the heat shrivel and draw open the lips of the unhappy negro, exclaimed in a fury, "The rascal laughs."

a mutinous disposition recently discovered, though long dreaded among the Negroes, and which has been industriously promoted by communications between mischievous or misguided persons in this country and in France,[1] subversive of that subordination on which entirely depends the welfare of the Negroes themselves, and of every other inhabitant of the West-India Colonies.

Resolved,
That dreadful consequences may result from the insurrection in St. Domingo to the British West-India islands in general, and particularly to the Island of Jamaica, should the revolt be of long duration, or should it end (as, from the distractions prevailing, and from the small effective military force now in the Island, there is too much cause to fear) in the desertion of that colony by the Europeans. ...

Charged, as the West Indians have lately been, with upholding the most arbitrary principles and practices, it was natural to suppose that the insurrection in St. Domingo, though evidently arising out of the pernicious system of slavery, will be turned by them into an argument for their own side of the question.[2]

It is one of the evils of slavery and arbitrary power, that every new danger and insurrection is pleaded as a ground for still farther severity, and that serves only to increase the misery ... of those who have been already too much oppressed. Nay, it often happens, that the oppressor affects to blame himself for an overstrained lenity in times past, in order to justify the stricter measures he is about to pursue. Recrimination on every friend of freedom is another natural consequence of a man's finding himself in danger from his own injured slaves—Hence all the evil effects of slavery are transferred to the very people who, foreboding these effects, had been attempting to avert them.

Another evil of slavery is, that events in other countries insignificant, become dangerous and portentous in places where slavery exists; and that events carrying only a smaller degree of evil in them, threaten a land of slavery with total ruin and desolation. On this principle the French Revolution seems to have wrought ten-fold mischief in those parts of their empire where slavery is tolerated. The British West Indians, however, curiously enough discover, that this tremendous convulsion in the French Islands is not at all the effect of slavery itself, is not to be ascribed to the French Revolution, but rather, as they say, "to communications between mischievous or misguided persons in this country and France, subversive of that SUBORDINATION *on which entirely depends the safety of the Negroes themselves, and of every other inhabitant of the West-India Colonies.*"

It is here evidently implied, that certain questions which have been agitated in England are the cause of the insurrection in St. Domingo—A supposition which the French themselves do not seem to have made, but which, if true, would only serve to exhibit the *extreme insecurity* of countries subject to slavery, in the strongest light; for, if the mere discussion of the question of importing slaves, in a foreign and independent country, has been sufficient to cause a general insurrection in the French Islands, how wretched a system must it be which exposes men to dangers so trivial, ... and against which it is so impossible to provide! ...

COMMON SENSE.

William Wordsworth, "To Toussaint L'Ouverture" (1803)

Toussaint Louverture (1743–1803) was the leader of the Haitian Revolution from 1791 to 1802. In 1802, Toussaint was forced to resign by forces sent by Napoleon; he was deported to France, where he died in 1803. Wordsworth composed the sonnet during a trip to Calais in 1802; it was published in *The Morning Post* the following year. This sonnet represents one of very few works by Wordsworth to engage with slavery directly.

---

[1] *misguided ... in France* I.e., abolitionists.

[2] *the question* I.e., the debate surrounding abolition.

Toussaint, the most unhappy Man of Men!
    Whether the rural milk-maid by her cow
Sing in thy hearing, or thou liest now
Alone in some deep dungeon's earless den,
5   O miserable chieftain! where and when
Wilt thou find patience? Yet die not; do thou
Wear rather in thy bonds a cheerful brow:
Though fallen thyself, never to rise again,
Live, and take comfort. Thou hast left behind
10   Powers that will work for thee; air, earth, and skies;
There's not a breathing of the common wind
That will forget thee; thou hast great allies;
Thy friends are exultations, agonies,
And love, and Man's unconquerable mind.

from Jean-Jacques Dessalines, "Liberty or Death. Proclamation. Jean Jacques Dessalines, Governor General, to the People of Hayti"[1] (1804)

When Haiti became an independent country, Jean-Jacques Dessalines (1758–1806) declared himself the state's Governor General-for-life; he then ruled as Emperor of Haiti until his assassination in 1806. One of the earliest state documents printed by the new country was his "Liberty or Death" speech, excerpted below. In part, the speech is offered as a justification for a series of massacres of the remaining white population of Haiti that Dessalines had ordered in the early months of 1804.

Crimes, the most atrocious, such as were until then unheard of, and would cause nature to shudder, have been perpetrated. The measure was overheaped. At length the hour of vengeance has arrived, and the implacable enemies of the rights of man have suffered the punishment due to their crimes.

My arm, raised over their heads, has too long delayed to strike. At that signal, which the justice of God has urged, your hands, righteously armed, have brought the axe upon the ancient tree of slavery and prejudices. In vain had time, and more especially the infernal politics of Europeans, surrounded it with triple brass; you have stripped it of its armour; you have placed it upon your hearts, that you may become (like your natural enemies) cruel and merciless. Like an overflowing mighty torrent that tears down all opposition, your vengeful fury has carried away every thing in its impetuous course. Thus perish all tyrants over innocence, all oppressors of mankind!

What then? bent for many ages under an iron yoke; the sport of the passions of men, of their injustice, and of the caprice of fortune; mutilated victims of the cupidity of white Frenchmen? after having fattened with our toils these insatiate blood-suckers, with a patience and resignation unexampled, we should again have seen that sacrilegious horde make an attempt upon our destruction, without any distinction of sex or age; and we, men without energy, of no virtue, or no delicate sensibility, should not we have plunged in their breast the dagger of desperation? Where is that vile Haytian, so unworthy of his regeneration, who thinks he has not accomplished the decrees of the Eternal, by exterminating these bloody thirsty tigers! If there is one, let him fly; indignant nature discards him from our bosom; let him hide his shame far from hence; the air we breathe is not suited to his gross organs; it is the pure air of Liberty, august and triumphant.

Yes, we have rendered to these true cannibals war for war, crime for crime, outrage for outrage. Yes, I have saved my country—I have avenged America.[2] The avowal I make of it in the face of earth and heaven, constitutes my pride and my glory. Of what consequence to me is the opinion which contemporary and future generations will pronounce upon my conduct? I have performed my duty; I enjoy my own approbation; for me that is sufficient. But what do I say? The preservation of my unfortunate brothers, the testimony of my own conscience are not my only recompence: I have seen two classes of men, born to cherish, assist and

---

1 *Liberty or Death ... Hayti* This anonymous translation from the French appeared in 1804 in several American papers; it appears here as it did in the *Connecticut Herald*.

2 *America* I.e., the Americas (North, South, and Central).

succour one another—mixed, in a word, and blended together—crying for vengeance, and disputing the honour of the first blow. ...

... [S]ooner or later Divine Justice will unchain on earth some mighty winds, above the weakness of the vulgar, for the destruction and terror of the wicked; tremble, tyrants, usurpers, scourges of the new world! our daggers are sharpened; your punishment is ready! sixty thousand men, equipped, inured to war, obedient to my orders, burn to offer a new sacrifice to the manes of their assassinated brothers. Let that nation come who may be mad and daring enough to attack me. Already at its approach, the irritated genius[1] of Hayti, rising out of the bosom of the ocean, appears; his menacing aspect throws the waves into commotion, excites tempests, and with his mighty hand disperses ships, or dashes them in pieces; to his formidable voice the laws of nature pay obedience; diseases, plague, famine, conflagration, poison, are his constant attendants. But why calculate on the assistance of the climate and of the elements? Have I forgot that I command a people of no common cast, brought up in adversity, whose audacious daring frowns at the obstacles and increases by dangers? Let them come, then, these homicidal Cohorts! I wait for them with firmness and with a steady eye. I abandon to them freely the sea-shore, and the places where cities have existed; but woe to those who may approach too near the mountains! It were better for them that the sea received them into its profound abyss, than to be devoured by the anger of the children of Hayti

"War and Death to Tyrants!" this is my motto;
"Liberty! Independence!" this is our rallying cry

Generals, officers, soldiers, a little unlike him who has preceded me, the ex-general TOUSSAINT LOUVERTURE, I have been faithful to the promise which I made to you when I took up arms against tyranny, and whilst the last spark of life remains in me I shall keep my oath. Never again shall a colonist or an European set his foot upon this territory with the title of master or proprietor. This resolution shall henceforward form the fundamental basis of our constitution.

Should other chiefs, after me, by pursuing a conduct diametrically opposite to mine, dig their own graves and those of their species, you will have to accuse only the law of destiny which shall have taken me away from the happiness and welfare of my fellow-citizens. May my successors follow the path I shall have traced out for them! It is the system best adapted for consolidating their power; it is the highest homage they can render to my memory.

As it is derogatory to my character and my dignity to punish the innocent for the crimes of the guilty, a handful of whites, commendable by the religion they have always professed, and who have besides taken the oath to live with us in the woods, have experienced my clemency. I order that the sword respect them, and that they be unmolested.

I recommend anew and order to all the generals of department, &c. to grant succours, encouragement, and protection, to all neutral and friendly nations who may wish to establish commercial relations in this island.

The Governor-General
(Signed) DESSALINES
A true Copy. The Sec'y-General
JUSTE CHANLATTE

---

[1] *genius* Guardian spirit.

GEORGE GORDON, LORD BYRON
1788 – 1824

"If the finest poetry be that which leaves the deepest impression on the minds of its readers," the critic Francis Jeffrey wrote, "Lord Byron, we think, must be allowed to take precedence of all his distinguished contemporaries." The theatrical melancholy, incisive wit, and sometimes scandalous content of Byron's poetry undoubtedly evoked strong reactions, both of praise and condemnation. So did the poet himself: handsome, charming, sexually unconventional, and politically iconoclastic, Byron has been alternately celebrated and reviled from his own time to the present. His works—the long poems *Childe Harold's Pilgrimage* and *Don Juan* among them—were tremendous popular successes, and the "Byronic hero," a character type he developed and embodied throughout his career, remains a cultural icon.

Byron's beginnings were inauspicious. He was born in near-poverty on 22 January 1788, lame in one leg (probably the result of a form of cerebral palsy). His father, Captain John ("Mad Jack") Byron, a notorious spendthrift and rake, had married Byron's mother, the Scottish heiress Catherine Gordon, for her money. This he quickly squandered, afterward fleeing to France. Byron and his mother moved to Aberdeen. Here Byron lived out his first ten years, the object of his mother's capricious mixture of love and sudden overwhelming rages, deeply conscious of his lameness, and steeped in Calvinism. Here, too, at ten years old, he was regularly molested by his nursemaid.

In 1798 Byron's great-uncle, the fifth Lord Byron, died childless, and Byron inherited the title. He and his mother moved to the family's ancestral, debt-encumbered home, Newstead Abbey, in Nottinghamshire. Byron was sent to school, first to an academy in Dulwich, then to Harrow in 1801. Around 1801 he also met for the first time his half-sister Augusta, the product of an earlier marriage of his father's. In 1805 Byron entered Trinity College, Cambridge, where he made the most lasting friendships of his life. He also contracted huge debts to which he would only add in the future.

Byron took a degree from Cambridge in 1807. In the same year, he published his first poetry collection, *Hours of Idleness*. The book was excoriated in the press as pretentious and derivative; Byron responded in 1809 with the verse satire *English Bards and Scotch Reviewers*, in which he attacked the most notable of his critics and many of the leading poets of the day. In that same year, Byron came of age and took possession of Newstead Abbey, where he held riotous parties; as a result of carousing and redecorating, his mountain of debt grew larger. In March he made his first appearance in the House of Lords, and in July, after having incurred more debt to finance himself, he set off on a trip through Europe and the Near East, areas largely closed to the English as a result of the Napoleonic Wars. This journey began an intense attachment to Greece that would color the rest of Byron's life and writing and allowed him to fulfill the same-sex desires that were dangerous to explore in England (where sodomy was a capital crime). During this time he also began *Childe Harold's Pilgrimage*, the work that would make him a celebrity.

Featuring a journey almost identical to that which Byron himself had just completed, undertaken by a mysteriously gloomy hero, *Childe Harold's Pilgrimage*, Cantos I&II, launched both the figure of the "Byronic hero" and the association between that figure and Byron that the poet would alternately embrace and seek to evade for the remainder of his life. The poem cunningly managed to weave elements from familiar genres such as travel writing, Gothic novels, and sentimental literature with experiments in mood and tone. It enthralled its readers. Byron wrote in Spenserian stanzas, but as the poem progressed he began to bend this stiff form so that it became his own. (Harold's discoveries and the narrator's own growing observational and meditative abilities find their mirror in the rhythms of the verse.) With its panoramic focus, high-flown tone, and alluringly aloof protagonist, *Childe Harold's Pilgrimage* marked an important moment in English and European literature.

Now a celebrity, Byron played that role with gusto. He became a darling of Whig society and indulged in a series of affairs, most scandalously with Lady Caroline Lamb. In addition, some time in 1813 Byron became close with his half-sister Augusta. There is some evidence to suggest that this relationship may have been sexual in nature; in any case, it was one of Byron's deepest and most lasting attachments. He also continued writing, producing a collection of hugely popular works ranging from the short lyrics of *Hebrew Melodies* to the "Eastern Tales" produced in 1813 and 1814. In this series of long narrative poems, set in the Near East, he fleshed out the anti-heroic figure he had sketched in *Childe Harold's Pilgrimage*. The protagonists of the "Tales" stood aloof from those who surround them, tortured by a mysterious but deeply felt guilt. Brave, glamorous, and in each case devoted utterly to one woman (who herself was an idealized romantic heroine), they were nonetheless fated to be outcasts. Described most fully in the first of the "Eastern Tales," "The Giaour," the hero reached his final refinement in the last, "Lara." The public embraced this figure, and a literary type entered into the canon with a vengeance: the writing of the next hundred years would be crowded with Byronic heroes.

In January of 1815, Byron married Annabella Milbanke, a sheltered heiress. The marriage was based on a short courtship and false hopes, and the two participants were utterly unsuited. Byron was psychologically abusive to his wife, whose piety and conventionality were a constant irritant to him. Early in 1816, a few weeks after the birth of their daughter, Augusta Ada, Annabella left him. A public scandal followed, aided by the unauthorized publication of Byron's poems. Now a social outcast, Byron departed for Europe, never to return. He continued to communicate with his friends in England through a voluminous and revealingly frank series of letters that detailed his sexual adventures, his political and literary beliefs, and his continued involvement with affairs in England. Even if he had written no poetry, the letters would qualify Byron for a place as one of England's foremost authors: urbane, broad-ranging, dazzling, and hilarious, they make for riveting and delightful reading.

Landing in Belgium in April of 1816, Byron made his way through scenes—including a visit to Waterloo—which he would describe in the final two cantos of *Childe Harold*. At Geneva he met Mary and Percy Shelley. They had traveled to Switzerland accompanied by Mary's stepsister Claire Clairmont, who had had a brief sexual relationship with Byron in England. The two poets formed an intimate and intellectually rich friendship, and the four lived in close proximity during the summer. Byron resumed his involvement with Claire; she bore him a daughter, Allegra, in January of 1817.

When the Shelleys departed for England in August, Byron journeyed to Venice, where he lived for the next three years. Here he flung himself into a period of promiscuity (he estimated that he had sex with over two hundred women during this time), but continued to work as well, producing his verse drama *Manfred*, the fourth canto of *Childe Harold*, and the humorous *Beppo*, written in *ottava rima*. This colloquial Italian form was fiendishly ill-adapted to English, but Byron made it his own, also using it to produce his masterpiece, *Don Juan*, which he began in July of 1818.

Don Juan is the creation of an author who has found his *métier*. It is the longest satirical poem in English, a rollicking tale of a young hero who bears the same name as the seducer but resembles him in no other way. Juan, passive and sweet-natured, is seduced by women ranging from a family friend to Catherine the Great. His adventures take him on a journey from Spain to London by way of Greece and Russia. Byron was thus able to mock not only current social mores but also his own previous poems, Don Juan standing as a kind of anti-Byronic hero. He took as his model for the poem a slight satire in *ottava rima*, written in 1817 by John Hookham Frere, but *Don Juan* is also descended from Swift's *Gulliver's Travels*, and Sterne's *Tristram Shandy*. As with the latter, the focus of Byron's poem is not so much what is narrated as its narrator, a garrulous, easily distracted gentleman who at times bears a remarkable resemblance to the author. Byron's publisher, friends, and the critical establishment condemned *Don Juan* for its immorality, but he himself relished it, asserting that he had written it only "to giggle and make giggle"—a comment typically Byronic in its attempt to deny responsibility by invoking comedy. For all its author's disclaimers, *Don Juan* is no mere comic throwaway. It is a text of great cultural and political scope and a work of questing philosophy, arguably the best of its age.

In April of 1819 Byron met Countess Teresa Guiccioli, a young Italian woman married to a much older man. Almost immediately they began a socially sanctioned affair that would last, with reasonable fidelity, until the end of Byron's life. Through her family, Byron was drawn into nationalist schemes to free Italy from the Austrians When the family was exiled to Pisa in 1821 as a result of this plotting, Byron followed. The Shelleys were now based in Pisa, and Byron became one of their group. Soon, however, this "Pisan circle" fell apart, first because of Shelley's anger over Byron's callous treatment of Allegra (she had joined him in Venice in 1819, only for him first to neglect her and then send her to be brought up in a convent, where she died, unvisited by him, in 1822), then because of Byron's decision to follow the Countess's family to Genoa, and finally because of Shelley's own death in July 1822.

Despite these upheavals, Byron wrote at a furious pace. Between 1819 and 1823 he produced numerous works, including a series of closet dramas (such as *Sardanapalus*, *The Two Foscari*, and *Cain*), and his biting satire of England under George III, *The Vision of Judgment*. He also continued *Don Juan*, finishing sixteen cantos by the end of 1823.

In 1824 Byron organized an expedition to assist the Greeks in their fight for independence from the Turks. Settled in the marsh town of Missolonghi, he financed and trained soldiers. Exhausted and worn down, he contracted a fever and died on 19 April, aged thirty-six, his death hastened by copious bloodletting performed by his incompetent doctors.

The Giaour

The Giaour (pronounced, roughly, "jower") offered much of what an early nineteenth-century reader might hope for: a sensational story of a love triangle, murder, and revenge; a regretful and passionate Byronic hero; and a romanticized vision of Eastern people, places, and practices. It was also a new work by Byron, who had recently made himself famous with the publication of the first two cantos of *Childe Harold's Pilgrimage* (1812). Audiences responded with predictable enthusiasm when *The Giaour* was published in June 1813. New editions were released quickly, and Byron took advantage of the opportunity to write more material; by the time the seventh edition was published in December, the poem had almost doubled in length. Critics complained that before one version could be reviewed, the next was already being sold.

Part of *The Giaour*'s commercial success can be attributed to a popular fascination with the East. Interest in "the Orient" remained high in England throughout the late eighteenth and early nineteenth centuries. The poem draws inspiration from works such as William Beckford's novella *Vathek* (1786) and Robert Southey's epic poem *Thabala* (1801), fanciful stories whose major draw was the exoticized depiction of their Middle Eastern settings. For his own entries into Orientalist literature, Byron had the advantage of firsthand experience: he had spent the years 1809 to 1811 on a Grand Tour that had included Greece, Albania, and Turkey. In a letter, he described the inspiration his travels had provided:

> My head is full of Oriental names & scenes—it is my story & my East—(& here I am venturing with no one to contend against—from having seen what my contemporaries must copy from the drawings of others only) that I want to make palpable—and my skull is … crammed from having lived much with them & in their own way. …

Byron's experiences are reflected in the poem's footnotes explaining Ottoman terms and practices—notes that, in many cases, adopt a comic and satiric tone in contrast to the Gothic tone of the poem itself. But the sensational narrative, too, may have been shaped by Byron's time in the Middle East. Byron suggested that one of the poem's central plot points, the murder of the unfaithful slave-girl, had been inspired by a real incident; he claimed to have put a stop while he was in Athens to the execution of a woman whose situation in some ways paralleled that of the slave girl in the poem.

Byron's 1809–11 Grand Tour was the first time he visited Greece, and was a formative moment in the development of a lifelong passion for Greek independence from the Ottoman Empire (which occupied the area from 1543 to 1821). *The Giaour*, set in Greece in the 1770s, links the ongoing occupation to the wars fought between ancient Greece and ancient Persia thousands of years before; the poem casts both periods as part of an endless contest between Eastern tyranny and Western democracy. Many critics see a parallel embodiment of conflict between East and West in the clash between the poem's Muslim villain and its protagonist, the titular giaour (a derogatory term for a non-Muslim). Alongside this offensively Orientalist paradigm, the poem simultaneously reveals admiration and respect for Ottoman culture: Byron supplemented his direct observation with extensive research, striving to represent Ottoman practices accurately. At least to some extent, he provided a corrective to the Orientalist genre's tendencies (exemplified more fully in texts such as *Vathek*) to represent a generalized, imaginary view of "the East" divorced from specific historical context.

While it may strive for greater accuracy than most works of Orientalist literature, *The Giaour* also resembles many of these works in that it combines exoticism with the Gothic allure of secrets, romance, and shocking violence. (The poem includes one of the first mentions in Western European literature of the Eastern European folk figure known as a "vampire.") As one of Byron's most overtly Gothic works, and one whose protagonist is an early example of a Byronic hero, *The Giaour* also reveals the links between the Byronic hero and the conventional Gothic villain. The type of the Gothic villain, whose outline was shaped at the turn of the century by writers such as Ann Radcliffe and Matthew Lewis, was at first purely and immovably evil. Soon, however, Gothic literature began to depict "villains" who were more complex and sympathetic. Like many of these Gothic predecessors, the Giaour is plagued by regret, has an air of defiant individualism and fallen nobility, and even possesses an "evil eye."

The fragmented form in which *The Giaour* is presented is a characteristic of Gothic fiction; the Gothic fragment, a short story commencing in the midst of the action and ending suddenly before the climax is resolved, was a popular form in the late eighteenth and early nineteenth centuries. Even outside the Gothic genre, to present literature in fragmented form—either to conceive a work as such from the outset or simply to share one unfinished—was a popular approach during the period—one taken by contemporaries such as Coleridge (e.g., "Kubla Khan" [written 1797, published 1816]) and Wordsworth (e.g., "The Danish Boy" [1800]). Critical response to fragmentation in *The Giaour*, however, was mixed. Many reviewers found the effect to be confusing and suggested that it limits the reader's engagement in the story. Others, however, were impressed; Sir Walter Scott, for example, wrote to Byron that

> every real lover of the art is obliged to you for condensing the narrative, by giving us only those striking scenes which you have shown to be so susceptible of poetic ornament, and leaving to imagination the says I's and says he's, and all the minutiae of detail which might be proper in giving evidence before a court of justice.

Whatever concerns some critics might have had, *The Giaour*'s popular success set the stage for its author to publish three more "Eastern Tales": *The Bride of Abydos* (1813), *The Corsair* (1814), and *Lara* (1814). Taken together, these were among Byron's best-selling works in his lifetime.

⌘ ⌘ ⌘

The Giaour. A Fragment of a Turkish Tale[1]

ADVERTISEMENT

The tale which these disjointed fragments present, is founded upon circumstances now less common in the East than formerly; either because the ladies are more circumspect than in the "olden time"; or because the Christians have better fortune, or less enterprize. The story, when entire, contained the adventures of a female slave, who was thrown, in the Mussulman[2] manner, into the sea for infidelity, and avenged by a young Venetian, her lover, at the time the Seven Islands were possessed by the Republic of Venice,[3] and soon after the Arnauts[4] were beaten back from the Morea,[5] which they had ravaged for some time subsequent to the Russian invasion.[6] The desertion of the Mainotes, on being refused the plunder of Misitra,[7] led to the abandonment of that

---

[1] *The Giaour. A Fragment of a Turkish Tale*   After *The Giaour* was first published in June 1813, the text was gradually expanded over the course of several subsequent editions. The present text is that of the seventh edition, the last expansion, released in December 1813; *Giaour* Derogatory term for a non-Muslim, used especially by Muslims in the Ottoman Empire to refer to Christians.

[2] *Mussulman* Muslim.

[3] *the time ... of Venice*   The period indicated is near the end of the eighteenth century; the Seven Islands, on the western coast of Greece, were in Venetian possession from 1363 to 1797. They briefly became a republic in the first few years of the nineteenth century.

[4] *Arnauts* Ottoman Turkish term for Albanians, especially those serving in the Ottoman army.

[5] *Morea* Another term for the Peloponnese, a peninsula in southwestern Greece. Except for a few decades of Venetian rule in the seventeenth century, the Peloponnese was a possession of the Ottoman Empire from the mid-fifteenth to the early nineteenth century.

[6] *the Russian invasion* The Peloponnesian Uprising of 1770, a rebellion that involved both local Greeks and forces from Russia, which was at war with the Ottoman Empire at the time. Though this rebellion failed, guerilla fighters in the area continued to struggle for independence.

[7] *Mainotes* People of the southern part of the Peloponnese; *Misitra* Mystras, a town in the southern Peloponnese; *desertion ... Misitra* Byron's attribution of the uprising's failure to the greed of the Mainotes is unusual; most historians suggest [continued ...]

enterprize, and to the desolation of the Morea, during
which the cruelty exercised on all sides was unparalleled
even in the annals of the faithful.

No breath of air to break the wave
  That rolls below the Athenian's grave,
That tomb[1] which, gleaming o'er the cliff,
First greets the homeward-veering skiff,
5 High o'er the land he saved in vain—
When shall such hero live again?

*   *   *

    Fair clime! where every season smiles
Benignant o'er those blessed isles,[2]
Which seen from far Colonna's[3] height,
10 Make glad the heart that hails the sight,
And lend to loneliness delight.
There mildly dimpling—Ocean's cheek
Reflects the tints of many a peak
Caught by the laughing tides that lave
15 These Edens of the eastern wave;
And if at times a transient breeze
Break the blue chrystal of the seas,
Or sweep one blossom from the trees,
How welcome is each gentle air,
20 That wakes and wafts the odours there!
For there—the Rose o'er crag or vale,
Sultana of the Nightingale,[4]
The maid for whom his melody—
His thousand songs are heard on high,
25 Blooms blushing to her lover's tale;

His queen, the garden queen, his Rose,
Unbent by winds, unchill'd by snows,
Far from the winters of the west
By every breeze and season blest,
30 Returns the sweets by nature given
In softest incense back to heaven;
And grateful yields that smiling sky
Her fairest hue and fragrant sigh.
And many a summer flower is there,
35 And many a shade that love might share,
And many a grotto, meant for rest,
That holds the pirate for a guest;
Whose bark° in sheltering cove below   *boat*
Lurks for the passing peaceful prow,
40 Till the gay mariner's guitar[5]
Is heard, and seen the evening star;
Then stealing with the muffled oar,
Far shaded by the rocky shore,
Rush the night-prowlers on the prey,
45 And turn to groans his roundelay.°   *song*
Strange—that where Nature lov'd to trace,
As if for Gods, a dwelling-place,
And every charm and grace hath mixed
Within the paradise she fixed—
50 There man, enamour'd of distress,
Should mar it into wilderness,
And trample, brute-like, o'er each flower
That tasks not one laborious hour;
Nor claims the culture of his hand
55 To bloom along the fairy land,
But springs as to preclude his care,
And sweetly woos him—but to spare!
Strange—that where all is peace beside
There passion riots in her pride,
60 And lust and rapine wildly reign,
To darken o'er the fair domain.
It is as though the fiends prevail'd

---

that the Russians provided inadequate support.

[1] [Byron's note]   A tomb above the rocks on the promontory, by
some supposed the sepulchre of Themistocles. [Themistocles led the
Greek naval forces to a crucial victory against the invading Persians in
the legendary sea battle of Salamis in 480 BCE.]

[2] *blessed isles*   Also called "Fortunate Isles," the Isles of the Blessed
were both a real location and, in Greek mythology, an ideal place
where winter never occurred.

[3] *Colonna*   Cape Colonna, on the Italian coast across the sea from
Greece.

[4] [Byron's note]   The attachment of the nightingale to the rose is a
well-known Persian fable. If I mistake not, the "Bulbul of a thousand
tales" is one of his appellations.

[5] [Byron's note]   The guitar is the constant amusement of the Greek
sailor by night; with a steady fair wind, and during a calm, it is
accompanied always by the voice, and often by dancing.

Against the seraphs they assail'd,[1]
And fixed, on heavenly thrones, should dwell
5 The freed inheritors of hell—
So soft the scene, so form'd for joy,
So curst the tyrants that destroy!

    He who hath bent him o'er the dead,
Ere the first day of death is fled;
70 The first dark day of nothingness,
The last of danger and distress;
(Before Decay's effacing fingers
Have swept the lines where beauty lingers,)
And mark'd the mild angelic air—
75 The rapture of repose that's there—
The fixed yet tender traits that streak
The languor of the placid cheek,
And—but for that sad shrouded eye,
    That fires not—wins not—weeps not—now—
80   And but for that chill changeless brow,
Where cold Obstruction's[2] apathy
Appals the gazing mourner's heart,
As if to him it could impart
The doom he dreads, yet dwells upon—
85 Yes—but for these and these alone,
Some moments—aye—one treacherous hour,
He still might doubt the tyrant's power,
So fair—so calm—so softly seal'd
The first—last look—by death reveal'd![3]
90 Such is the aspect of this shore—
'Tis Greece—but living Greece no more!

So coldly sweet, so deadly fair,
We start—for soul is wanting there.
Hers is the loveliness in death,
95 That parts not quite with parting breath;
But beauty with that fearful bloom,
That hue which haunts it to the tomb—
Expression's last receding ray,
A gilded halo hovering round decay,
100 The farewell beam of Feeling past away!
Spark of that flame—perchance of heavenly birth—
Which gleams—but warms no more its cherish'd earth!

    Clime of the unforgotten brave!—
Whose land from plain to mountain-cave
105 Was Freedom's home or Glory's grave—
Shrine of the mighty! can it be,
That this is all remains of thee?
Approach thou craven crouching slave—
Say, is not this Thermopylae?[4]
110 These waters blue that round you lave
Oh servile offspring of the free—
Pronounce what sea, what shore is this?
The gulf, the rock of Salamis!
These scenes—their story not unknown—
115 Arise, and make again your own;
Snatch from the ashes of your sires
The embers of their former fires,
And he who in the strife expires
Will add to theirs a name of fear,
120 That Tyranny shall quake to hear,
And leave his sons a hope, a fame,
They too will rather die than shame;
For Freedom's battle once begun,
Bequeathed by bleeding Sire to Son,
125 Though baffled oft is ever won.
Bear witness, Greece, thy living page,
Attest it many a deathless age!
While kings in dusty darkness hid,

---

[1] *as though … assail'd* As though Satan and the rebel angels had won their war against God and the good angels; *seraphs* The highest of the nine orders of angels.

[2] [Byron's note] "Aye, but to die, and go we know not where; / To lie in cold obstruction?" *Measure for Measure* 3.1.115–16.

[3] [Byron's note] I trust that few of my readers have ever had an opportunity of witnessing what is here attempted in description; but those who have will probably retain a painful remembrance of that singular beauty which pervades, with few exceptions, the features of the dead, a few hours, and but for a few hours, after "the spirit is not there." It is to be remarked in cases of violent death by gun-shot wounds, the expression is always that of languor, whatever the natural energy of the sufferer's character; but in death from a stab the countenance preserves its traits of feeling or ferocity, and the mind its bias, to the last.

---

[4] *Thermopylae* Site of a famous battle between the invading Persians and the Greeks, who were vastly outnumbered yet held their ground for three days.

Have left a nameless pyramid,[1]
130 Thy heroes—though the general doom[2]
Hath swept the column from their tomb,
A mightier monument command,
The mountains of their native land!
There points thy Muse to stranger's eye,
135 The graves of those that cannot die!
'Twere long to tell, and sad to trace,
Each step from splendour to disgrace,
Enough—no foreign foe could quell
Thy soul, till from itself it fell,
140 Yes! Self-abasement pav'd the way
To villain°-bonds and despot-sway.   serf, slave

What can he tell who treads thy shore?
    No legend of thine olden time,
No theme on which the muse might soar,
145 High as thine own in days of yore,
    When man was worthy of thy clime.
The hearts within thy valleys bred,
The fiery souls that might have led
    Thy sons to deeds sublime;
150 Now crawl from cradle to the grave,
Slaves—nay, the bondsmen of a slave,[3]
    And callous, save to crime;
Stain'd with each evil that pollutes
Mankind, where least above the brutes;
155 Without even savage virtue blest,
Without one free or valiant breast.
Still to the neighbouring ports they waft
Proverbial wiles, and ancient craft,
In this the subtle Greek is found,
160 For this, and this alone, renown'd.
In vain might Liberty invoke
The spirit to its bondage broke,

Or raise the neck that courts the yoke:
No more her sorrows I bewail,
165 Yet this will be a mournful tale,
And they who listen may believe,
Who heard it first had cause to grieve.

* * *

    Far, dark, along the blue sea glancing,
    The shadows of the rocks advancing,
170 Start on the fisher's eye like boat
Of island-pirate or Mainote;
And fearful for his light caique°   boat
He shuns the near but doubtful creek,
Though worn and weary with his toil,
175 And cumber'd with his scaly spoil,
Slowly, yet strongly, plies the oar,
Till Port Leone's safer shore
Receives him by the lovely light
That best becomes an Eastern night.

* * *

180   Who thundering comes on blackest steed?
With slacken'd bit and hoof of speed,
Beneath the clattering iron's sound
The cavern'd echoes wake around
In lash for lash, and bound for bound;
185 The foam that streaks the courser's side,
Seems gather'd from the ocean-tide:
Though weary waves are sunk to rest,
There's none within his rider's breast,
And though to-morrow's tempest lower,
190 'Tis calmer than thy heart, young Giaour!
I know thee not, I loathe thy race
But in thy lineaments I trace
What time shall strengthen, not efface;
Though young and pale, that sallow front
195 Is scath'd by fiery passion's brunt,
Though bent on earth thine evil eye
As meteor like thou glidest by,
Right well I view, and deem thee one
Whom Othman's sons[4] should slay or shun.

---

1 *a nameless pyramid*   The reference is to the Egyptian pyramids, built for pharaohs whose names remain unknown.

2 *the general doom*   The passage of time.

3 [Byron's note]   Athens is the property of the Kislar Aga (the slave of the Seraglio [harem] and guardian of the women), who appoints the Waywode [Turkish governor of Athens]. A pander and eunuch—these are not polite, yet true appellations—now governs the governor of Athens!

---

4 *Othman's sons*   Muslims.

On—on he hastened—and he drew
My gaze of wonder as he flew:
Though like a demon of the night
He passed and vanished from my sight;
His aspect and his air impressed
A troubled memory on my breast;
And long upon my startled ear
Rung his dark courser's hoofs of fear.
He spurs his steed—he nears the steep,
That jutting shadows o'er the deep—
He winds around—he hurries by—
The rock relieves him from mine eye—
For well I ween unwelcome he
Whose glance is fixed on those that flee;
And not a star but shines too bright
On him who takes such timeless flight.
He wound along—but ere he passed
One glance he snatched—as if his last—
A moment checked his wheeling steed—
A moment breathed him from his speed—
A moment on his stirrup stood—
Why looks he o'er the olive wood?—
The crescent glimmers on the hill,
The Mosque's high lamps are quivering still;
Though too remote for sound to wake
In echoes of the far tophaike,[1]
The flashes of each joyous peal
Are seen to prove the Moslem's zeal.
To-night—set Rhamazani's sun—
To-night—the Bairam feast's[2] begun—
To-night—but who and what art thou
Of foreign garb and fearful brow?
And what are these to thine or thee,
That thou should'st either pause or flee?
He stood—some dread was on his face—
Soon Hatred settled in its place—
It rose not with the reddening flush

Of transient Anger's darkening blush,
But pale as marble o'er the tomb,
Whose ghastly whiteness aids its gloom.
240 His brow was bent—his eye was glazed—

He raised his arm, and fiercely raised;
And sternly shook his hand on high,
As doubting to return or fly;—
Impatient of his flight delayed
245 Here loud his raven charger neighed—
Down glanced that hand, and grasped his blade—
That sound had burst his waking dream,
As Slumber starts at owlet's scream.—
The spur hath lanced his courser's sides—
250 Away—away—for life he rides —
Swift as the hurled on high jerreed,[3]
Springs to the touch his startled steed,
The rock is doubled—and the shore
Shakes with the clattering tramp no more—
255 The crag is won— no more is seen
His Christian crest and haughty mien.°—   *bearing*
'Twas but an instant—he restrained
That fiery barb so sternly reined—
'Twas but a moment that he stood,
260 Then sped as if by death pursued;
But in that instant, o'er his soul
Winters of Memory seemed to roll;
And gather in that drop of time
A life of pain, an age of crime.
265 O'er him who loves, or hates, or fears,
Such moment pours the grief of years—
What felt *he* then—at once opprest
By all that most distracts the breast?
That pause—which pondered o'er his fate,
270 Oh, who its dreary length shall date!
Though in Time's record nearly nought,
It was Eternity to Thought!
For infinite as boundless space

[1] [Byron's note] "Tophaike," musket. The Bairam is announced by the cannon at sunset: the illumination of the mosques, and the firing of all kinds of small arms, loaded with ball, proclaim it during the night.

[2] *Rhamazani's sun … Bairam feast* References to the end of Ramadan, the Islamic month of fasting; a feast is celebrated to mark its conclusion.

[3] [Byron's note] Jerreed, or Djerrid, a blunted Turkish javelin, which is darted from horseback with great force and precision. It is a favourite exercise of the Mussulmans; but I know not if it can be called a manly one, since the most expert in the art are the Black Eunuchs of Constantinople. I think, next to these, a Mamlouk [slave] at Smyrna was the most skilful that came within my observation.

The thought that Conscience must embrace,
275   Which in itself can comprehend
Woe without name—or hope—or end.—

          The hour is past, the Giaour is gone,
And did he fly or fall alone?
Woe to that hour he came or went,
280   The curse for Hassan's sin was sent
To turn a palace to a tomb;
He came, he went, like the Simoom,[1]
That harbinger of fate and gloom,
Beneath whose widely-wasting breath
285   The very cypress[2] droops to death—
Dark tree—still sad, when others' grief is fled,
The only constant mourner o'er the dead!

          The steed is vanished from the stall,
No serf is seen in Hassan's hall;
290   The lonely Spider's thin grey pall
Waves slowly widening o'er the wall;
The Bat builds in his Haram bower;
And in the fortress of his power
The Owl usurps the beacon-tower;
295   The wild-dog howls o'er the fountain's brim,
With baffled thirst, and famine, grim,
For the stream has shrunk from its marble bed,
Where the weeds and the desolate dust are spread.
'Twas sweet of yore to see it play
300   And chase the sultriness of day—
As springing high the silver dew
In whirls fantastically flew,
And flung luxurious coolness round
The air, and verdure o'er the ground.—
305   'Twas sweet, when cloudless stars were bright,
To view the wave of watery light,
And hear its melody by night.—
And oft had Hassan's Childhood played
Around the verge of that cascade;
310   And oft upon his mother's breast
That sound had harmonized his rest;

And oft had Hassan's Youth along
Its bank been sooth'd by Beauty's song;
And softer seemed each melting tone
315   Of Music mingled with its own.—
But ne'er shall Hassan's Age repose
Along the brink at Twilight's close—
The stream that filled that font is fled—
The blood that warmed his heart is shed!—
320   And here no more shall human voice
Be heard to rage—regret—rejoice—
The last sad note that swelled the gale
Was woman's wildest funeral wail—
That quenched in silence—all is still,
325   But the lattice that flaps when the wind is shrill—
Though raves the gust, and floods the rain,
No hand shall close its clasp again.
On desart sands 'twere joy to scan
The rudest steps of fellow man,
330   So here the very voice of Grief
Might wake an Echo like relief—
At least 'twould say, "all are not gone;
There lingers Life, though but in one"—
For many a gilded chamber's there,
335   Which Solitude might well forbear;
Within that dome as yet Decay
Hath slowly worked her cankering way—
But Gloom is gathered o'er the gate,
Nor there the Fakir's[3] self will wait;
340   Nor there will wandering Dervise[4] stay,
For Bounty cheers not his delay;
Nor there will weary stranger halt
To bless the sacred "bread and salt."[5]
Alike must Wealth and Poverty
345   Pass heedless and unheeded by,
For Courtesy and Pity died
With Hassan on the mountain side.—
His roof—that refuge unto men—
Is Desolation's hungry den.—

---

1   [Byron's note]   The blast of the desert, fatal to everything living, and often alluded to in Eastern poetry.

2   *cypress*   Very long-lived tree traditionally planted in graveyards.

3   *Fakir*   Muslim ascetic.

4   *Dervise*   Dervish, similar to a fakir.

5   *sacred … and salt*   These are considered sacred because once a guest and a host eat together, the guest is protected from harm by the bonds of hospitality.

50 The guest flies the hall,[1] and the vassal from labour,
Since his turban was cleft by the infidel's sabre!

* * *

I hear the sound of coming feet,
But not a voice mine ear to greet—
More near—each turban I can scan,
55 And silver-sheathed ataghan;[2]
The foremost of the band is seen
An Emir[3] by his garb of green:[4]
"Ho! who art thou?"—"this low salam[5]
Replies of Moslem faith I am."
60 "The burthen ye so gently bear,
Seems one that claims your utmost care,
And, doubtless, holds some precious freight,
My humble bark would gladly wait."

"Thou speakest sooth, thy skiff unmoor,
65 And waft us from the silent shore;
Nay, leave the sail still furl'd, and ply
The nearest oar that's scatter'd by,
And midway to those rocks where sleep
The channel'd waters dark and deep.—
70 Rest from your task—so bravely done,
Our course has been right swiftly run,
Yet 'tis the longest voyage, I trow,
That one of"—

* * *

Sullen it plunged, and slowly sank,
375 The calm wave rippled to the bank;
I watch'd it as it sank, methought
Some motion from the current caught
Bestirr'd it more,—'twas but the beam
That chequer'd o'er the living stream—
380 I gaz'd, till vanishing from view,
Like lessening pebble it withdrew;
Still less and less, a speck of white
That gemm'd the tide, then mock'd the sight;
And all its hidden secrets sleep,
385 Known but to Genii[6] of the deep,
Which, trembling in their coral caves,
They dare not whisper to the waves.

* * *

As rising on its purple wing
The insect-queen[7] of eastern spring,
390 O'er emerald meadows of Kashmeer
Invites the young pursuer near,
And leads him on from flower to flower
A weary chase and wasted hour,
Then leaves him, as it soars on high
395 With panting heart and tearful eye:
So Beauty lures the full-grown child
With hue as bright, and wing as wild;
A chase of idle hopes and fears,
Begun in folly, closed in tears.
400 If won, to equal ills betrayed,
Woe waits the insect and the maid,
A life of pain, the loss of peace,
From infant's play, or man's caprice:
The lovely toy so fiercely sought
405 Has lost its charm by being caught,
For every touch that wooed its stay
Has brush'd the brightest hues away
Till charm, and hue, and beauty gone,
'Tis left to fly or fall alone.

---

[1] [Byron's note]   I need hardly observe, that Charity and Hospitality are the first duties enjoined by Mahomet; and to say truth, very generally practised by his disciples. The first praise that can be bestowed on a chief is a panegyric on his bounty; the next, on his valour.

[2] [Byron's note]   The ataghan, a long dagger worn with pistols in the belt, in a metal scabbard, generally of silver; and, among the wealthier, gilt, or of gold.

[3] *Emir*   Arabic title of office given to rulers or military commanders.

[4] [Byron's note]   Green is the privileged colour of the prophet's numerous pretended descendants; with them, as here, faith (the family inheritance) is supposed to supersede the necessity of good works: they are the worst of a very indifferent brood.

[5] *salam*   Customary bow, a gesture of greeting in some Islamic countries.

[6] *Genii*   Jinn, spirits mentioned in the Koran and in the folklore of some Muslim cultures.

[7] [Byron's note]   The blue-winged butterfly of Kashmeer, the most rare and beautiful of the species.

410 With wounded wing, or bleeding breast,
Ah! where shall either victim rest?
Can this with faded pinion° soar   *wing*
From rose to tulip as before?
Or Beauty, blighted in an hour,
415 Find joy within her broken bower?
No: gayer insects fluttering by
Ne'er droop the wing o'er those that die,
And lovelier things have mercy shewn
To every failing but their own,
420 And every woe a tear can claim
Except an erring sister's shame.

*   *   *

The Mind, that broods o'er guilty woes,
 Is like the Scorpion girt by fire,
In circle narrowing as it glows
425 The flames around their captive close,
Till inly search'd by thousand throes,
 And maddening in her ire,
One sad and sole relief she knows,
The sting she nourish'd for her foes,
430 Whose venom never yet was vain,
Gives but one pang, and cures all pain,
And darts into her desperate brain.[1]—
So do the dark in soul expire,
Or live like Scorpion girt by fire;
435 So writhes the mind Remorse hath riven,
Unfit for earth, undoom'd for[2] heaven,
Darkness above, despair beneath,
Around it flame, within it death!—

*   *   *

Black Hassan from the Haram flies,
440 Nor bends on woman's form his eyes,
The unwonted chase each hour employs,
Yet shares he not the hunter's joys.
Not thus was Hassan wont to fly
When Leila dwelt in his Serai.°   *palace*
445 Doth Leila there no longer dwell?
That tale can only Hassan tell:
Strange rumours in our city say
Upon that eve she fled away;
When Rhamazan's last sun was set,
450 And flashing from each minaret[3]
Millions of lamps proclaim'd the feast
Of Bairam through the boundless East.
'Twas then she went as to the bath,
Which Hassan vainly search'd in wrath,
455 But she was flown her master's rage
In likeness of a Georgian page;
And far beyond the Moslem's power
Had wrong'd him with the faithless Giaour.
Somewhat of this had Hassan deem'd,
460 But still so fond, so fair she seem'd,
Too well he trusted to the slave
Whose treachery deserv'd a grave:
And on that eve had gone to mosque,
And thence to feast in his kiosk.°   *pavilion*
465 Such is the tale his Nubians tell,
Who did not watch their charge too well;
But others say, that on that night,
By pale Phingari's[4] trembling light,
The Giaour upon his jet black steed
470 Was seen—but seen alone to speed
With bloody spur along the shore,
Nor maid nor page behind him bore.

*   *   *

Her eye's dark charm 'twere vain to tell,
But gaze on that of the Gazelle,
475 It will assist thy fancy well,

---

1 [Byron's note] Alluding to the dubious suicide of the scorpion, so placed for experiment by gentle philosophers. Some maintain that the position of the sting, when turned towards the head, is merely a convulsive movement; but others have actually brought in the verdict "Felo de se [suicide]." The scorpions are surely interested in a speedy decision of the question; as, if once fairly established as insect Catos, they will probably be allowed to live as long as they think proper, without being martyred for the sake of an hypothesis.

2 *undoom'd for* Not judged (fit) for.

---

3 *minaret* Tower (usually, one connected to a mosque).

4 [Byron's note] Phingari, the moon. φεγγάρι is derived from φεγγάριον, dim. of φέγγος.

As large, as languishingly dark,
But Soul beam'd forth in every spark
That darted from beneath the lid,
Bright as the jewel of Giamschid.[1]
Yea, *Soul*, and should our prophet say
That form was nought but breathing clay,
By Alla! I would answer nay;
Though on Al-Sirat's[2] arch I stood,
Which totters o'er the fiery flood,
With Paradise within my view,
And all his Houris[3] beckoning through.
Oh! who young Leila's glance could read
And keep that portion of his creed
Which saith, that woman is but dust,
A soulless toy[4] for tyrant's lust?
On her might Muftis[5] gaze, and own
That through her eye the Immortal shone—
On her fair cheek's unfading hue,

The young pomegranate's[6] blossoms strew
495 Their bloom in blushes ever new—
Her hair in hyacinthine[7] flow
When left to roll its folds below;
As midst her handmaids in the hall
She stood superior to them all,
500 Hath swept the marble where her feet
Gleamed whiter than the mountain sleet
Ere from the cloud that gave it birth,
It fell, and caught one stain of earth.
The cygnet[8] nobly walks the water—
505 So moved on earth Circassia's daughter—
The loveliest bird of Franguestan![9]
As rears her crest the ruffled Swan,
    And spurns the wave with wings of pride,
When pass the steps of stranger man
510   Along the banks that bound her tide;
Thus rose fair Leila's whiter neck:—
Thus armed with beauty would she check
Intrusion's glance, till Folly's gaze
Shrunk from the charms it meant to praise.
515 Thus high and graceful was her gait;
Her heart as tender to her mate—
Her mate—stern Hassan, who was he?
Alas! that name was not for thee!

                    * * *

    Stern Hassan hath a journey ta'en
520 With twenty vassals in his train,
Each arm'd as best becomes a man
With arquebuss° and ataghan;   *early firearm*
The chief before, as deck'd for war
Bears in his belt the scimitar
525 Stain'd with the best of Arnaut blood,

---

[1] [Byron's note] The celebrated fabulous ruby of Sultan Giamschid, the embellisher of Istakhar; from its splendour, named Schebgerag, "the torch of night;" also "the cup of the sun," etc. In the First Edition, "Giamschid" was written as a word of three syllables; so D'Herbelot has it; but I am told Richardson reduces it to a dissyllable, and writes "Jamshid." I have left in the text the orthography of the one with the pronunciation of the other.

[2] [Byron's note] Al-Sirat, the bridge of breadth narrower than the thread of a famished spider, and sharper than the edge of a sword, over which the Mussulmans must *skate* into Paradise, to which it is the only entrance; but this is not the worst, the river beneath being hell itself, into which, as may be expected, the unskilful and tender of foot contrive to tumble with a "facilis descensus Averni," not very pleasing in prospect to the next passenger. There is a shorter cut downwards for the Jews and Christians. [The Latin phrase, from Virgil's *Aeneid* 6.126, means roughly "the descent to hell is easy."]

[3] *Houris* Beautiful, perfect companions promised in the Koran to those who attain Paradise.

[4] [Byron's note] A vulgar error: the Koran allots at least a third of Paradise to well-behaved women; but by far the greater number of Mussulmans interpret the text their own way, and exclude their moieties from heaven. Being enemies to Platonics, they cannot discern "any fitness of things" in the souls of the other sex, conceiving them to be superseded by the Houris.

[5] *Muftis* Muslim legal officials, educated in Muslim law and religious texts.

[6] [Byron's note] An Oriental simile, which may, perhaps, though fairly stolen, be deemed "plus Arabe qu'en Arabie" [French: more Arabian than Arabia].

[7] [Byron's note] Hyacinthine, in Arabic "Sunbul;" as common a thought in the Eastern poets as it was among the Greeks.

[8] *cygnet* Baby swan.

[9] [Byron's note] "Franguestan," Circassia. [Circassian women were highly prized for their fair skin.]

When in the pass the rebels stood,
And few return'd to tell the tale
Of what befell in Parne's[1] vale.
The pistols which his girdle bore
530   Were those that once a pasha[2] wore,
Which still, though gemm'd and boss'd with gold,
Even robbers tremble to behold.—
'Tis said he goes to woo a bride
More true than her who left his side;
535   The faithless slave that broke her bower,
And, worse than faithless, for a Giaour!—

* * *

The sun's last rays are on the hill,
And sparkle in the fountain rill,°   stream
Whose welcome waters cool and clear,
540   Draw blessings from the mountaineer;
Here may the loitering merchant Greek
Find that repose 'twere vain to seek
In cities lodg'd too near his lord,
And trembling for his secret hoard—
545   Here may he rest where none can see,
In crowds a slave, in deserts free;
And with forbidden wine may stain
The bowl a Moslem must not drain.—

* * *

The foremost Tartar's[3] in the gap,
550   Conspicuous by his yellow cap,
The rest in lengthening line the while
Wind slowly through the long defile;
Above, the mountain rears a peak,
Where vultures whet the thirsty beak,
555   And theirs may be a feast to-night,
Shall tempt them down ere morrow's light.

Beneath, a river's wintry stream
Has shrunk before the summer beam,
And left a channel bleak and bare,
560   Save shrubs that spring to perish there.
Each side the midway path there lay
Small broken crags of granite gray,
By time or mountain lightning riven,
From summits clad in mists of heaven;
565   For where is he that hath beheld
The peak of Liakura[4] unveil'd?

* * *

They reach the grove of pine at last,
"Bismillah![5] now the peril's past;
For yonder view the opening plain,
570   And there we'll prick our steeds amain":[6]
The Chiaus[7] spake, and as he said,
A bullet whistled o'er his head;
The foremost Tartar bites the ground!
Scarce had they time to check the rein
575   Swift from their steeds the riders bound,
But three shall never mount again,
Unseen the foes that gave the wound,
The dying ask revenge in vain.
With steel unsheath'd, and carbine[8] bent,
580   Some o'er their courser's harness leant,
Half shelter'd by the steed,
Some fly behind the nearest rock,
And there await the coming shock,
Nor tamely stand to bleed
585   Beneath the shaft of foes unseen,
Who dare not quit their craggy screen.
Stern Hassan only from his horse
Disdains to light, and keeps his course,

1   *Parne*   Mount Parnitha, in southern Greece.
2   *pasha*   High-ranking Ottoman officer.
3   *Tartar*   Tatars (to use the modern spelling) are an ethnic group that originated in central Asia; some settled on the Crimean Peninsula, which became an Ottoman possession. The Crimean Tatars provided cavalry for the Ottoman army as part of its agreement with the empire.
4   *Liakura*   Mountain, also known as Parnassus, of great significance in Greek mythology; it is sacred to both Apollo and Dionysus, and is the home of the Muses.
5   [Byron's note]   "In the name of God"; the commencement of all the chapters of the Koran but one, and of prayer and thanksgiving.
6   *amain*   With full force.
7   *Chiaus*   Turkish military rank—a messenger or sergeant.
8   *carbine*   Early firearm.

Till fiery flashes in the van[1]
Proclaim too sure the robber-clan
Have well secur'd the only way
Could now avail the promis'd prey;
Then curl'd his very beard[2] with ire,
And glared his eye with fiercer fire.
"Though far and near the bullets hiss,
I've scaped a bloodier hour than this."
And now the foe their covert quit,
And call his vassals to submit;
But Hassan's frown and furious word
Are dreaded more than hostile sword,
Nor of his little band a man
Resign'd carbine or ataghan—
Nor raised the craven cry, Amaun![3]
In fuller sight, more near and near,
The lately ambush'd foes appear,
And issuing from the grove advance,
Some who on battle charger° prance.—   *war horse*
Who leads them on with foreign brand,
Far flashing in his red right hand?
"'Tis he— 'tis he—I know him now,
I know him by his pallid brow;
I know him by the evil eye[4]
That aids his envious treachery;
I know him by his jet-black barb,
Though now array'd in Arnaut garb,
Apostate from his own vile faith,
It shall not save him from the death;
'Tis he, well met in any hour,
Lost Leila's love—accursed Giaour!"

---

[1] *van* Foremost section.

[2] [Byron's note] A phenomenon not uncommon with an angry Mussulman. In 1809 the Capitan Pacha's whiskers at a diplomatic audience were no less lively with indignation than a tiger cat's, to the horror of all the dragomans; the portentous mustachios twisted, they stood erect of their own accord, and were expected every moment to change their colour, but at last condescended to subside, which, probably, saved more heads than they contained hairs.

[3] [Byron's note] "Amaun," quarter, pardon.

[4] [Byron's note] The "evil eye," a common superstition in the Levant, and of which the imaginary effects are yet very singular on those who conceive themselves affected.

620   As rolls the river into ocean,
In sable torrent wildly streaming;
     As the sea-tide's opposing motion
In azure column proudly gleaming,
Beats back the current many a rood,
625   In curling foam and mingling flood;
While eddying whirl, and breaking wave,
Roused by the blast of winter rave;
Through sparkling spray in thundering clash,
The lightnings of the waters flash
630   In aweful whiteness o'er the shore,
That shines and shakes beneath the roar;
Thus—as the stream and ocean greet,
With waves that madden as they meet—
Thus join the bands whom mutual wrong,
635   And fate and fury drive along.
The bickering sabres' shivering jar
     And pealing wide—or ringing near
     Its echoes on the throbbing ear
The deathshot hissing from afar—
640   The shock—the shout—the groan of war—
     Reverberate along that vale,
     More suited to the shepherd's tale:
Though few the numbers—theirs the strife,
That neither spares nor speaks for life!
645   Ah! fondly youthful hearts can press,
To seize and share the dear caress;
But Love itself could never pant
For all that Beauty sighs to grant,
With half the fervour Hate bestows
650   Upon the last embrace of foes,
When grappling in the fight they fold
Those arms that ne'er shall lose their hold;
Friends meet to part—Love laughs at faith;—
True foes, once met, are joined till death!

* * *

655   With sabre shiver'd to the hilt,
Yet dripping with the blood he spilt;
Yet strain'd within the sever'd hand
Which quivers round that faithless brand;
His turban far behind him roll'd,

660 And cleft in twain its firmest fold;
His flowing robe by falchion° torn,   *scimitar*
And crimson as those clouds of morn
That streak'd with dusky red, portend
The day shall have a stormy end;
665 A stain on every bush that bore
A fragment of his palampore,[1]
His breast with wounds unnumber'd riven,
His back to earth, his face to heaven,
Fall'n Hassan lies—his unclos'd eye
670 Yet lowering on his enemy,
As if the hour that seal'd his fate,
Surviving left his quenchless hate;
And o'er him bends that foe with brow
As dark as his that bled below.—

* * *

675   "Yes, Leila sleeps beneath the wave,
But his shall be a redder grave;
Her spirit pointed well the steel
Which taught that felon heart to feel.
He call'd the Prophet, but his power
680 Was vain against the vengeful Giaour:
He call'd on Alla—but the word
Arose unheeded or unheard.
Thou Paynim[2] fool!—could Leila's prayer
Be pass'd, and thine accorded there?
685 I watch'd my time; I leagu'd with these,
The traitor in his turn to seize;
My wrath is wreak'd, the deed is done,
And now I go—but go alone."

* * * *
* * *

      The browzing camels' bells are tinkling—
690 His Mother looked from her lattice high,
      She saw the dews of eve besprinkling
The pasture green beneath her eye,

      She saw the planets faintly twinkling,
"'Tis twilight—sure his train is nigh."—
695 She could not rest in the garden-bower,
But gazed through the grate of his steepest tower—
"Why comes he not? his steeds are fleet,
Nor shrink they from the summer heat;
Why sends not the Bridegroom his promised gift,
700 Is his heart more cold, or his barb less swift?
Oh, false reproach! yon Tartar now
Has gained our nearest mountain's brow,
And warily the steep descends,
And now within the valley bends;
705 And he bears the gift at his saddle bow—
How could I deem his courser slow?
Right well my largess shall repay
His welcome speed, and weary way."—
The Tartar lighted at the gate,
710 But scarce upheld his fainting weight;
His swarthy visage spake distress,
But this might be from weariness;
His garb with sanguine° spots was dyed,   *blood-red*
But these might be from his courser's side;—
715 He drew the token from his vest—
Angel of Death! 'tis Hassan's cloven crest!
His calpac[3] rent—his caftan red—
"Lady, a fearful bride thy Son hath wed—
Me, not from mercy, did they spare,
720 But this empurpled pledge to bear.
Peace to the brave! whose blood is spilt—
Woe to the Giaour! for his the guilt."

* * *

      A turban[4] carv'd in coarsest stone,
A pillar with rank weeds o'ergrown,
725 Whereon can now be scarcely read
The Koran verse that mourns the dead;

1 [Byron's note] The flowered shawls generally worn by persons of rank.

2 *Paynim* Non-Christian, especially Muslim.

3 [Byron's note] The calpac is the solid cap or centre part of the head-dress; the shawl is wound round it, and forms the turban.

4 [Byron's note] The turban, pillar, and inscriptive verse, decorate the tombs of the Osmanlies, whether in the cemetery or the wilderness. In the mountains you frequently pass similar mementos; and on inquiry you are informed that they record some victim of rebellion, plunder, or revenge.

Point out the spot where Hassan fell
A victim in that lonely dell.
There sleeps as true an Osmanlie°   *Ottoman Turk*
As e'er at Mecca[1] bent the knee;
As ever scorn'd forbidden wine,
Or pray'd with face towards the shrine,
In orisons° resumed anew   *prayers*
At solemn sound of "Alla Hu!"[2]
Yet died he by a stranger's hand,
And stranger in his native land—
Yet died he as in arms he stood,
And unaveng'd, at least in blood.
But him the maids of Paradise
      Impatient to their halls invite,
And the dark Heaven of Houri's eyes
      On him shall glance for ever bright;
They come—their kerchiefs green[3] they wave,
And welcome with a kiss the brave!
Who falls in battle 'gainst a Giaour,
Is worthiest an immortal bower.

                    *   *   *

      But thou, false Infidel! shalt writhe
Beneath avenging Monkir's[4] scythe;
And from its torment 'scape alone

To wander round lost Eblis'[5] throne;
And fire unquench'd, unquenchable—
Around—within—thy heart shall dwell,
Nor ear can hear, nor tongue can tell
The tortures of that inward hell!—
But first, on earth as Vampire[6] sent,
Thy corse° shall from its tomb be rent;   *corpse*
Then ghastly haunt thy native place,
And suck the blood of all thy race,
There from thy daughter, sister, wife,
At midnight drain the stream of life;
Yet loathe the banquet which perforce
Must feed thy livid living corse;
Thy victims ere they yet expire
Shall know the dæmon for their sire,
As cursing thee, thou cursing them,
Thy flowers are wither'd on the stem.
But one that for thy crime must fall—
The youngest—most belov'd of all,
Shall bless thee with a *father's* name—
That word shall wrap thy heart in flame!
Yet must thou end thy task, and mark
Her cheek's last tinge, her eye's last spark,
And the last glassy glance must view
Which freezes o'er its lifeless blue;
Then with unhallowed hand shalt tear
The tresses of her yellow hair,
Of which in life a lock when shorn,
Affection's fondest pledge was worn;
But now is borne away by thee,
Memorial of thine agony!
Wet with thine own best blood shall drip,

---

1 *Mecca* Holiest Muslim pilgrimage site.

2 [Byron's note] "Alla Hu!" the concluding words of the Muezzin's call to prayer from the highest gallery on the exterior of the Minaret. On a still evening, when the Muezzin has a fine voice, which is frequently the case, the effect is solemn and beautiful beyond all the bells in Christendom.

3 [Byron's note] The following is part of a battle-song of the Turks:—"I see—I see a dark-eyed girl of Paradise, and she waves a handkerchief, a kerchief of green; and cries aloud, 'Come, kiss me, for I love thee,'" etc.

4 [Byron's note] Monkir and Nekir are the inquisitors of the dead, before whom the corpse undergoes a slight noviciate and preparatory training for damnation. If the answers are none of the clearest, he is hauled up with a scythe and thumped down with a red-hot mace till properly seasoned, with a variety of subsidiary probations. The office of these angels is no sinecure; there are but two, and the number of orthodox deceased being in a small proportion to the remainder, their hands are always full.—See Relig. Ceremon., v. 290; vii. 59, 68, 118, and Sale's Preliminary Discourse to the Koran, p. 101.

5 [Byron's note] Eblis, the Oriental Prince of Darkness.

6 [Byron's note] The Vampire superstition is still general in the Levant. Honest Tournefort tells a long story, which Mr. Southey, in the notes on Thalaba, quotes about these "Vroucolochas," as he calls them. The Romaic term is "Vardoulacha." I recollect a whole family being terrified by the scream of a child, which they imagined must proceed from such a visitation. The Greeks never mention the word without horror. I find that "Broucolokas" is an old legitimate Hellenic appellation—at least is so applied to Arsenius, who, according to the Greeks, was after his death animated by the Devil. The moderns, however, use the word I mention.

Thy gnashing tooth and haggard lip;[1]
'Then stalking to thy sullen grave—
Go—and with Gouls and Afrits[2] rave;
785   Till these in horror shrink away
From spectre more accursed than they!

* * *

"How name ye yon lone Caloyer?[3]
   His features I have scann'd before
In mine own land—'tis many a year,
790   Since, dashing by the lonely shore,
I saw him urge as fleet a steed
As ever serv'd a horseman's need.
But once I saw that face—yet then
It was so mark'd with inward pain
795   I could not pass it by again;
It breathes the same dark spirit now,
As death were stamped upon his brow."

"'Tis twice three years at summer tide
   Since first among our freres he came;
800   And here it soothes him to abide
   For some dark deed he will not name.
But never at our vesper prayer,
Nor e'er before confession chair
Kneels he, nor recks° he when arise   *cares*
805   Incense or anthem to the skies,
But broods within his cell alone,
His faith and race alike unknown.
The sea from Paynim land he crost,
And here ascended from the coast,
810   Yet seems he not of Othman race,
But only Christian in his face:
I'd judge him some stray renegade,
Repentant of the change he made,
Save that he shuns our holy shrine,

815   Nor tastes the sacred bread and wine.
Great largess to these walls he brought,
And thus our abbot's favour bought;
But were I Prior, not a day
Should brook such stranger's further stay,
820   Or pent within our penance cell
Should doom him there for aye to dwell.
Much in his visions mutters he
Of maiden 'whelmed beneath the sea;
Of sabres clashing—foemen flying,
825   Wrongs aveng'd—and Moslem dying.
On cliff he hath been known to stand,
And rave as to some bloody hand
Fresh sever'd from its parent limb,
Invisible to all but him,
830   Which beckons onward to his grave,
And lures to leap into the wave."

* * *
* * *

Dark and unearthly is the scowl
That glares beneath his dusky cowl—
The flash of that dilating eye
835   Reveals too much of times gone by—
Though varying—indistinct its hue,
Oft will his glance the gazer rue—
For in it lurks that nameless spell
Which speaks—itself unspeakable—
840   A spirit yet unquelled and high
That claims and keeps ascendancy,
And like the bird whose pinions quake—
But cannot fly the gazing snake—
Will others quail beneath his look,
845   Nor 'scape the glance they scarce can brook.
From him the half-affrighted Friar
When met alone would fain retire—
As if that eye and bitter smile
Transferred to others fear and guile—
850   Not oft to smile descendeth he,
And when he doth 'tis sad to see
That he but mocks at Misery.
How that pale lip will curl and quiver!

---

[1] [Byron's note]   The freshness of the face and the wetness of the lip with blood, are the never-failing signs of a Vampire. The stories told in Hungary and Greece of these foul feeders are singular, and some of them most incredibly attested.

[2] *Gouls and Afrits*   Demon-like spirits in Arabian mythology.

[3] *Caloyer*   Greek Orthodox monk.

Then fix once more as if for ever—
55 As if his sorrow or disdain
Forbade him e'er to smile again.—
Well were it so—such ghastly mirth
From joyaunce° ne'er deriv'd its birth.—   *joy, amusement*
But sadder still it were to trace
50 What once were feelings in that face—
Time hath not yet the features fixed,
But brighter traits with evil mixed—
And there are hues not always faded,
Which speak a mind not all degraded
55 Even by the crimes through which it waded—
The common crowd but see the gloom
Of wayward deeds—and fitting doom—
The close observer can espy
A noble soul, and lineage high.
70 —Alas! though both bestowed in vain,
Which Grief could change—and Guilt could stain—
It was no vulgar tenement°   *dwelling*
To which such lofty gifts were lent,
And still with little less than dread
75 On such the sight is riveted.—
The roofless cot° decayed and rent,   *cottage*
    Will scarce delay the passer by —
The tower by war or tempest bent,
While yet may frown one battlement,
80   Demands and daunts the stranger's eye—
Each ivied arch—and pillar lone,
Pleads haughtily for glories gone!

"His floating robe around him folding,
    Slow sweeps he through the columned aisle—
85 With dread beheld—with gloom beholding
    The rites that sanctify the pile.
But when the anthem shakes the choir,
And kneel the monks—his steps retire—
By yonder lone and wavering torch
00 His aspect glares within the porch;
There will he pause till all is done—
And hear the prayer—but utter none.
See—by the half-illumin'd wall
His hood fly back—his dark hair fall—
05 That pale brow wildly wreathing round,

As if the Gorgon[1] there had bound
The sablest of the serpent-braid
That o'er her fearful forehead strayed.
For he declines the convent oath,
900 And leaves those locks unhallowed growth—
But wears our garb in all beside;
And—not from piety but pride
Gives wealth to walls that never heard
Of his one holy vow nor word.—
905 Lo!—mark ye—as the harmony
Peals louder praises to the sky—
That livid cheek—that stoney air
Of mixed defiance and despair!
Saint Francis! keep him from the shrine!
910 Else may we dread the wrath divine
Made manifest by awful sign.—
If ever evil angel bore
The form of mortal, such he wore—
By all my hope of sins forgiven
915 Such looks are not of earth nor heaven!"

To love the softest hearts are prone,
But such can ne'er be all his own;
Too timid in his woes to share,
Too meek to meet, or brave despair;
920 And sterner hearts alone may feel
The wound that time can never heal.
The rugged metal of the mine
Must burn before its surface shine,
But plung'd within the furnace-flame,
925 It bends and melts—though still the same;
Then tempered to thy want, or will,
'Twill serve thee to defend or kill;
A breast-plate for thine hour of need,
Or blade to bid thy foeman bleed;
930 But if a dagger's form it bear,
Let those who shape its edge, beware!
Thus passion's fire, and woman's art,
Can turn and tame the sterner heart;
From these its form and tone are ta'en,

---

[1] *the Gorgon* In Greek mythology, the Gorgons were three sisters—including, most famously, Medusa—with snakes for hair.

935 And what they make it, must remain,
But break- -before it bend again.

* * *
* * *

If solitude succeed to grief,
Release from pain is slight relief;
The vacant bosom's wilderness
940 Might thank the pang that made it less.
We loathe what none are left to share—
Even bliss—'twere woe alone to bear;
The heart once left thus desolate,
Must fly at last for ease—to hate.
945 It is as if the dead could feel
The icy worm around them steal,
And shudder, as the reptiles creep
To revel o'er their rotting sleep
Without the power to scare away
950 The cold consumers of their clay!
It is as if the desart-bird,[1]
    Whose beak unlocks her bosom's stream
    To still her famish'd nestlings' scream,
Nor mourns a life to them transferr'd;
955 Should rend her rash devoted breast,
And find them flown her empty nest.
The keenest pangs the wretched find
    Are rapture to the dreary void—
The leafless desart of the mind—
960   The waste of feelings unemploy'd—
Who would be doom'd to gaze upon
A sky without a cloud or sun?
Less hideous far the tempest's roar,
Than ne'er to brave the billows more—
965 Thrown, when the war of winds is o'er,
A lonely wreck on fortune's shore,
'Mid sullen calm, and silent bay,
Unseen to drop by dull decay;—
Better to sink beneath the shock
970 Than moulder piecemeal on the rock!

---

[1] [Byron's note] The pelican is, I believe, the bird so libelled, by the imputation of feeding her chickens with her blood.

* * *

"Father! thy days have pass'd in peace,
'Mid counted beads, and countless prayer;
To bid the sins of others cease,
    Thyself without a crime or care,
975 Save transient ills that all must bear,
Has been thy lot, from youth to age,
And thou wilt bless thee from the rage
Of passions fierce and uncontroul'd,
Such as thy penitents unfold,
980 Whose secret sins and sorrows rest
Within thy pure and pitying breast.
My days, though few, have pass'd below
In much of joy, but more of woe;
Yet still in hours of love or strife,
985 I've scap'd the weariness of life;
Now leagu'd with friends, now girt by foes,
I loath'd the languor of repose;
Now nothing left to love or hate,
No more with hope or pride elate;
990 I'd rather be the thing that crawls
Most noxious o'er a dungeon's walls,
Than pass my dull, unvarying days,
Condemn'd to meditate and gaze—
Yet, lurks a wish within my breast
995 For rest—but not to feel 'tis rest—
Soon shall my fate that wish fulfil;
    And I shall sleep without the dream
Of what I was, and would be still,
    Dark as to thee my deeds may seem—
1000 My memory now is but the tomb
Of joys long dead—my hope—their doom—
Though better to have died with those
Than bear a life of lingering woes—
My spirit shrunk not to sustain
1005 The searching throes of ceaseless pain;
Nor sought the self-accorded grave
Of ancient fool, and modern knave:
Yet death I have not fear'd to meet,
And in the field it had been sweet
1010 Had danger wooed me on to move
The slave of glory, not of love.

I've brav'd it—not for honour's boast;
I smile at laurels won or lost.—
To such let others carve their way,
For high renown, or hireling pay;
But place again before my eyes
Aught that I deem a worthy prize;—
The maid I love—the man I hate—
And I will hunt the steps of fate,
(To save or slay—as these require)
Through rending steel, and rolling fire;
Nor need'st thou doubt this speech from one
Who would but do—what he *hath* done.
Death is but what the haughty brave—
The weak must bear—the wretch must crave—
Then let Life go to him who gave:
I have not quailed to danger's brow—
When high and happy—need I *now*?

* * *
* * *

"I lov'd her, friar! nay, adored—
     But these are words that all can use—
I prov'd it more in deed than word—
There's blood upon that dinted sword—
     A stain its steel can never lose:
'Twas shed for her, who died for me,
     It warmed the heart of one abhorred:
Nay, start not—no—nor bend thy knee,
     Nor midst my sins such act record,
Thou wilt absolve me from the deed,
For he was hostile to thy creed!
The very name of Nazarene°   *Christian*
Was wormwood to his Paynim spleen,
Ungrateful fool! since but for brands,°   *swords*
Well wielded in some hardy hands;
And wounds by Galileans° given,   *Christians*
The surest pass to Turkish heav'n;
For him his Houris still might wait
Impatient at the prophet's gate.
I lov'd her—love will find its way
Through paths where wolves would fear to prey,
And if it dares enough, 'twere hard

If passion met not some reward—
No matter how—or where—or why,
I did not vainly seek—nor sigh:
Yet sometimes with remorse in vain
1055 I wish she had not lov'd again.
She died—I dare not tell thee how,
But look—'tis written on my brow!
There read of Cain[1] the curse and crime,
In characters unworn by time:
1060 Still, ere thou dost condemn me—pause—
Not mine the act, though I the cause;
Yet did he but what I had done
Had she been false to more than one;
Faithless to him—he gave the blow,
1065 But true to me—I laid him low;
Howe'er deserv'd her doom might be,
Her treachery was truth to me;
To me she gave her heart, that all
Which tyranny can ne'er enthrall;
1070 And I, alas! too late to save,
Yet all I then could give—I gave—
'Twas some relief—our foe a grave.
His death sits lightly; but her fate
Has made me—what thou well may'st hate.
1075 His doom was seal'd—he knew it well,
Warn'd by the voice of stern Taheer,
Deep in whose darkly boding ear[2]

---

[1] *Cain* Son of Adam and Eve who murdered his brother Abel and was cursed and marked by God (Genesis 4.1–15). Some have imagined Cain's mark as a literal writing on the forehead.

[2] [Byron's note] This superstition of a second-hearing (for I never met with downright second-sight in the East) fell once under my own observation. On my third journey to Cape Colonna, early in 1811, as we passed through the defile that leads from the hamlet between Keratia and Colonna, I observed Dervish Tahiri riding rather out of the path and leaning his head upon his hand, as if in pain. I rode up and inquired. "We are in peril," he answered. "What peril? We are not now in Albania, nor in the passes to Ephesus, Messalunghi, or Lepanto; there are plenty of us, well armed, and the Choriates have not courage to be thieves."—"True, Affendi, but nevertheless the shot is ringing in my ears."—"The shot. Not a tophaike has been fired this morning."—"I hear it notwithstanding—Bom—Bom—as plainly as I hear your voice."— "Psha!"—"As you please, Affendi; if it is written, so will it be."—I left this quick-eared predestinarian, and rode up to Basili, his Christian compatriot, whose ears, though not at all prophetic, by no means relished the intelligence. We all [continued …]

The deathshot peal'd of murder near—
As filed the troop to where they fell!
1080 He died too in the battle broil—
A time that heeds nor pain nor toil—
One cry to Mahomet for aid,
One prayer to Alla—all he made:
He knew and crossed me in the fray—
1085 I gazed upon him where he lay,
And watched his spirit ebb away;
Though pierced like Pard° by hunters' steel,   leopard
He felt not half that now I feel.
I search'd, but vainly search'd to find,
1090 The workings of a wounded mind;
Each feature of that sullen corse
Betrayed his rage, but no remorse.
Oh, what had Vengeance given to trace
Despair upon his dying face!
1095 The late repentance of that hour,
When Penitence hath lost her power

---

arrived at Colonna, remained some hours, and returned leisurely, saying a variety of brilliant things, in more languages than spoiled the building of Babel, upon the mistaken seer. Romaic, Arnaout, Turkish, Italian, and English were all exercised, in various conceits, upon the unfortunate Mussulman. While we were contemplating the beautiful prospect, Dervish was occupied about the columns. I thought he was deranged into an antiquarian, and asked him if he had become a "*Palaocastro*" man? "No," said he; "but these pillars will be useful in making a stand;" and added other remarks, which at least evinced his own belief in his troublesome faculty of *forehearing*. On our return to Athens we heard from Leoné (a prisoner set ashore some days after) of the intended attack of the Mainotes, mentioned, with the cause of its not taking place, in the notes to *Childe Harold*, Canto 2nd. I was at some pains to question the man, and he described the dresses, arms, and marks of the horses of our party so accurately, that, with other circumstances, we could not doubt of *his* having been in "villanous company" [*I Henry IV* 3.3.11] and ourselves in a bad neighbourhood. Dervish became a soothsayer for life, and I dare say is now hearing more musketry than ever will be fired, to the great refreshment of the Arnaouts of Berat, and his native mountains.—I shall mention one trait more of this singular race. In March, 1811, a remarkably stout and active Arnaout came (I believe the fiftieth on the same errand) to offer himself as an attendant, which was declined. "Well, Affendi," quoth he, "may you live!—you would have found me useful. I shall leave the town for the hills to-morrow; in the winter I return, perhaps you will then receive me."—Dervish, who was present, remarked as a thing of course, and of no consequence, "in the mean time he will join the Klephtes" (robbers), which was true to the letter. If not cut off, they come down in the winter, and pass it unmolested in some town, where they are often as well known as their exploits.

To tear one terror from the grave—
And will not soothe, and can not save!

* * *

"The cold in clime are cold in blood,
1100 Their love can scarce deserve the name;
But mine was like the lava flood
    That boils in Ætna's[1] breast of flame,
I cannot prate in puling° strain   whining
Of ladye-love, and beauty's chain;
1105 If changing cheek, and scorching vein—
Lips taught to writhe, but not complain—
If bursting heart, and mad'ning brain—
And daring deed, and vengeful steel—
And all that I have felt—and feel—
1110 Betoken love—that love was mine,
And shewn by many a bitter sign.
'Tis true, I could not whine nor sigh,
I knew but to obtain or die.
I die—but first I have possest,
1115 And come what may, I *have been* blest;
Shall I the doom I sought upbraid?
No—reft of all—yet undismay'd
But for the thought of Leila slain,
Give me the pleasure with the pain,
1120 So would I live and love again.
I grieve, but not, my holy guide!
For him who dies, but her who died;
She sleeps beneath the wandering wave,
Ah! had she but an earthly grave,
1125 This breaking heart and throbbing head
Should seek and share her narrow bed.
She was a form of life and light—
That seen—became a part of sight,
And rose—where'er I turned mine eye—
1130 The Morning-star of Memory!

"Yes, Love indeed is light from heaven—
    A spark of that immortal fire

---

[1] *Ætna*   Mount Etna, an active volcano.

With angels shar'd—by Alla given,
 To lift from earth our low desire.
35 Devotion wafts the mind above,
But Heaven itself descends in love—
A feeling from the Godhead caught,
To wean from self each sordid thought—
A Ray of him who form'd the whole—
40 A Glory circling round the soul!
I grant *my* love imperfect—all
That mortals by the name miscall—
Then deem it evil—what thou wilt—
But say, oh say, *hers* was not guilt!
45 She was my life's unerring light—
That quench'd—what beam shall break my night?
Oh! would it shone to lead me still,
Although to death or deadliest ill!—
Why marvel ye? if they who lose
50 This present joy, this future hope,
 No more with sorrow meekly cope—
In phrenzy then their fate accuse—
In madness do those fearful deeds
 That seem to add but guilt to woe.
55 Alas! the breast that inly bleeds
 Hath nought to dread from outward blow—
Who falls from all he knows of bliss,
Cares little into what abyss.—
Fierce as the gloomy vulture's now
60 To thee, old man, my deeds appear—
I read abhorrence on thy brow,
 And this too was I born to bear!
'Tis true, that, like that bird of prey,
With havock have I mark'd my way—
65 But this was taught me by the dove—
To die—and know no second love.
This lesson yet hath man to learn,
Taught by the thing he dares to spurn—
The bird that sings within the brake,°   *thicket*
70 The swan that swims upon the lake,
One mate, and one alone, will take.
And let the fool still prone to range,
And sneer on all who cannot change—

Partake his jest with boasting boys,
1175 I envy not his varied joys—
But deem such feeble, heartless man,
Less than yon solitary swan—
Far—far beneath the shallow maid
He left believing and betray'd.
1180 Such shame at least was never mine—
Leila—each thought was only thine!—
My good, my guilt, my weal,° my woe,   *happiness*
My hope on high—my all below.
Earth holds no other like to thee,
1185 Or if it doth, in vain for me—
For worlds I dare not view the dame
Resembling thee, yet not the same.
The very crimes that mar my youth
This bed of death—attest my truth—
1190 'Tis all too late—thou wert— thou art
The cherished madness of my heart!

"And she was lost—and yet I breathed,
 But not the breath of human life —
A serpent round my heart was wreathed,
1195 And stung my every thought to strife.—
Alike all time—abhorred all place,
Shuddering I shrunk from Nature's face,
Where every hue that charmed before
The blackness of my bosom wore:—
1200 The rest—thou do'st already know,
And all my sins and half my woe—
But talk no more of penitence,
Thou see'st I soon shall part from hence—
And if thy holy tale were true—
1205 The deed that's done can'st *thou* undo?
Think me not thankless—but this grief
Looks not to priesthood for relief.[1]
My soul's estate in secret guess—
But would'st thou pity more—say less—

---

[1] [Byron's note] The monk's sermon is omitted. It seems to have had so little effect upon the patient, that it could have no hopes from the reader. It may be sufficient to say that it was of a customary length (as may be perceived from the interruptions and uneasiness of the patient), and was delivered in the usual tone of all orthodox preachers.

1210 When thou can'st bid my Leila live,
      Then will I sue thee to forgive;
      Then plead my cause in that high place
      Where purchased masses proffer grace—
      Go—when the hunter's hand hath wrung
1215 From forest-cave her shrieking young,
      And calm the lonely lioness—
      But soothe not—mock not *my* distress!

      "In earlier days, and calmer hours,
          When heart with heart delights to blend,
1220 Where bloom my native valley's bowers—
          I had—Ah! have I now?—a friend!—
      To him this pledge I charge thee send—
      Memorial of a youthful vow;
      I would remind him of my end,—
1225   Though souls absorbed like mine allow
      Brief thought to distant friendship's claim,
      Yet dear to him my blighted name.
      'Tis strange—he prophesied my doom,
          And I have smil'd—(I then could smile—)
1230 When Prudence would his voice assume,
          And warn—I reck'd not what—the while—
      But now remembrance whispers o'er
      Those accents scarcely mark'd before.
      Say—that his bodings came to pass,
1235   And he will start to hear their truth,
          And wish his words had not been sooth.
      Tell him—unheeding as I was—
          Through many a busy bitter scene
          Of all our golden youth had been—
1240 In pain, my faultering tongue had tried
      To bless his memory ere I died;
      But heaven in wrath would turn away,
      If Guilt should for the guiltless pray.
      I do not ask him not to blame—
1245 Too gentle he to wound my name;
      And what have I to do with fame?
      I do not ask him not to mourn,
      Such cold request might sound like scorn;
      And what than friendship's manly tear
1250 May better grace a brother's bier?
      But bear this ring—his own of old—

And tell him—what thou dost behold!
The wither'd frame, the ruined mind,
The wrack by passion left behind—
1255 A shrivelled scroll, a scatter'd leaf,
Sear'd by the autumn blast of grief!

                    * * *

"Tell me no more of fancy's gleam,
No, father, no, 'twas not a dream;
Alas! the dreamer first must sleep,
1260 I only watch'd, and wish'd to weep;
But could not, for my burning brow
Throbb'd to the very brain as now.
I wish'd but for a single tear,
As something welcome, new, and dear;
1265 I wish'd it then—I wish it still,
Despair is stronger than my will.
Waste not thine orison—despair
Is mightier than thy pious prayer;
I would not, if I might, be blest,
1270 I want no paradise—but rest.
'Twas then, I tell thee, father! then
I saw her—yes—she liv'd again;
And shining in her white symar,[1]
As through yon pale grey cloud—the star
1275 Which now I gaze on, as on her
Who look'd and looks far lovelier;
Dimly I view its trembling spark—
To-morrow's night shall be more dark—
And I—before its rays appear,
1280 That lifeless thing the living fear.
I wander, father! for my soul
Is fleeting towards the final goal;
I saw her, friar! and I rose,
Forgetful of our former woes;
1285 And rushing from my couch, I dart,
And clasp her to my desperate heart;
I clasp—what is it that I clasp?
No breathing form within my grasp,
No heart that beats reply to mine,

---

[1] [Byron's note] "Symar," a shroud. [Normally, a symar is a long robe or dress.]

Eugène Delacroix, *The Combat of the Giaour and the Pasha*, 1835.

1290 Yet, Leila! yet the form is thine!
And art thou, dearest, chang'd so much,
As meet my eye, yet mock my touch?
Ah! were thy beauties e'er so cold,
I care not—so my arms enfold
1295 The all they ever wish'd to hold.
Alas! around a shadow prest,
They shrink upon my lonely breast;
Yet still—'tis there—in silence stands,
And beckons with beseeching hands!
1300 With braided hair, and bright-black eye—
I knew 'twas false—she could not die!
But he is dead—within the dell
I saw him buried where he fell;
He comes not—for he cannot break
1305 From earth—why then art thou awake!
They told me, wild waves roll'd above
The face I view, the form I love;
They told me—'twas a hideous tale!
I'd tell it—but my tongue would fail—
1310 If true—and from thine ocean-cave
Thou com'st to claim a calmer grave;
Oh! pass thy dewy fingers o'er
This brow that then will burn no more;
Or place them on my hopeless heart—
1315 But, shape or shade!—whate'er thou art,
In mercy, ne'er again depart—
Or farther with thee bear my soul,
Than winds can waft—or waters roll!—

* * *

"Such is my name, and such my tale,[1]
1320   Confessor—to thy secret ear,

I breathe the sorrows I bewail,
    And thank thee for the generous tear
This glazing eye could never shed.
Then lay me with the humblest dead,
1325 And save the cross above my head,
Be neither name nor emblem spread—
By prying stranger to be read,
Or stay the passing pilgrim's tread."
He pass'd—nor of his name and race
1330 Hath left a token or a trace,
Save what the father must not say
Who shrived him on his dying day;
This broken tale was all we knew
Of her he lov'd, or him he slew.
—1813

Sun of the Sleepless

Sun of the sleepless! melancholy star!
Whose tearful beam glows tremulously far,
    That show'st the darkness thou canst not dispel,
How like art thou to joy remembered well!
5 So gleams the past, the light of other days,

---

[1] [Byron's note]   The circumstance to which the above story relates was not very uncommon in Turkey. A few years ago the wife of Muchtar Pacha complained to his father of his son's supposed infidelity; he asked with whom, and she had the barbarity to give in a list of the twelve handsomest women in Yanina. They were seized, fastened up in sacks, and drowned in the lake the same night! One of the guards who was present informed me that not one of the victims uttered a cry, or showed a symptom of terror at so sudden a "wrench from all we know, from all we love." The fate of Phrosine, the fairest of this sacrifice, is the subject of many a Romaic and Arnaout ditty. The story in the text is one told of a young Venetian many years ago,

and now nearly forgotten. I heard it by accident recited by one of the coffee-house story-tellers who abound in the Levant, and sing or recite their narratives. The additions and interpolations by the translator will be easily distinguished from the rest, by the want of Eastern imagery, and I regret that my memory has retained so few fragments of the original. For the contents of some of the notes I am indebted partly to D'Herbelot, and partly to that most Eastern, and, as Mr. Weber justly entitles it, "sublime tale," the "Caliph Vathek." I do not know from what source the author of that singular volume may have drawn his materials; some of his incidents are to be found in the *Bibliothèque Orientale*; but for correctness of costume, beauty of description, and power of imagination, it far surpasses all European imitations, and bears such marks of originality that those who have visited the East will find some difficulty in believing it to be more than a translation. As an Eastern tale, even Rasselas must bow before it; his "Happy Valley" will not bear a comparison with the "Hall of Eblis." [*Vathek* (1786), a Gothic novel by William Beckford, details the morally degenerate activities of a Muslim official who renounces his faith and is finally trapped in Hell, ruled by the demon Eblis. The *Bibliothèque orientale* (1697), compiled by Barthélemy d'Herbelot, is a large French-language collection of Middle Eastern texts. *The History of Rasselas, Prince of Abissinia* (1759), by Samuel Johnson, tells the story of a prince of present-day Ethiopia who leaves behind his home in Happy Valley.]

Which shines, but warms not with its powerless rays;
A night-beam Sorrow watcheth to behold,
Distinct, but distant—clear—but, oh how cold!
—1814

Stanzas for Music[1]

I speak not—I trace not—I breathe not thy name,
There is grief in the sound—there were guilt in the
    fame;
But the tear which now burns on my cheek may impart
The deep thought that dwells in that silence of heart.

5 Too brief for our passion, too long for our peace,
Were those hours, can their joy or their bitterness cease?
We repent—we abjure—we will break from our chain;
We must part—we must fly to—unite it again.

Oh! thine be the gladness and mine be the guilt,
10 Forgive me, adored one—forsake if thou wilt;
But the heart which is thine shall expire undebased,
And man shall not break it—whatever thou may'st.

And stern to the haughty, but humble to thee,
My soul in its bitterest blackness shall be;
15 And our days seem as swift—and our moments more
    sweet,
With thee by my side—than with worlds at our feet.

One sigh of thy sorrow—one look of thy love,
Shall turn me or fix, shall reward or reprove;
And the heartless may wonder at all we resign,
20 Thy lips shall reply not to them—but to mine.
—1829 (WRITTEN 1814)

She walks in beauty

1

She walks in beauty, like the night
Of cloudless climes and starry skies;
    And all that's best of dark and bright
    Meet in her aspect and her eyes:
5 Thus mellow'd to that tender light
    Which heaven to gaudy day denies.

2

One shade the more, one ray the less,
    Had half impair'd the nameless grace
Which waves in every raven tress,
10   Or softly lightens o'er her face;
Where thoughts serenely sweet express
    How pure, how dear their dwelling place.

3

And on that cheek, and o'er that brow,
    So soft, so calm, yet eloquent,
15 The smiles that win, the tints that glow,
    But tell of days in goodness spent,
A mind at peace with all below,
    A heart whose love is innocent!
—1815 (WRITTEN 1814)

When we two parted [2]

1

When we two parted
    In silence and tears,
    Half broken-hearted
    To sever for years,
5 Pale grew thy cheek and cold,

---

[1] *Stanzas for Music* Byron's half-sister Augusta is generally considered to be the subject of this poem, which was unpublished during the poet's life.

[2] *When we two parted* This poem has a complex history, at least partially because Byron deliberately misdated its composition as 1816, in order to hide its true subject. In fact, the lines were written in 1815, and their subject is Lady Frances Wedderburn Webster, the wife of a friend of Byron's; Byron had heard gossip about her affair with the Duke of Wellington. Byron himself had had a brief "platonic" affair with Lady Webster in 1813: a heated and exciting chase, kept secret from her husband and ending without consummation.

Colder thy kiss;
Truly that hour foretold
   Sorrow to this.

2

The dew of the morning
10   Sunk chill on my brow—
It felt like the warning
   Of what I feel now.
Thy vows are all broken,
   And light is thy fame;
15 I hear thy name spoken,
   And share in its shame.

3

They name thee before me,
   A knell to mine ear;
A shudder comes o'er me—
20   Why wert thou so dear?
They know not I knew thee,
   Who knew thee too well:—
Long, long shall I rue thee,
   Too deeply to tell.

4

25 In secret we met—
   In silence I grieve,
That thy heart could forget,
   Thy spirit deceive.
If I should meet thee
30   After long years,
How should I greet thee!—
   With silence and tears.
—1816 (WRITTEN 1815)

Stanzas for Music [1]

1

There's not a joy the world can give like that it
   takes away,
   When the glow of early thought declines in
   feeling's dull decay;
'Tis not on youth's smooth cheek the blush alone,
   which fades so fast,
But the tender bloom of heart is gone, ere youth
   itself be past.

2

5 Then the few whose spirits float above the wreck
   of happiness,
Are driven o'er the shoals of guilt or ocean of excess:
The magnet of their course is gone, or only points
   in vain
The shore to which their shiver'd sail shall never
   stretch again.

3

Then the mortal coldness of the soul like death
   itself comes down;
10 It cannot feel for others' woes, it dare not dream its own;
That heavy chill has frozen o'er the fountain of our tears,
And tho' the eye may sparkle still, 'tis where the
   ice appears.

4

Tho' wit may flash from fluent lips, and mirth
   distract the breast,
Through midnight hours that yield no more their
   former hope of rest;
15 'Tis but as ivy-leaves around the ruin'd turret wreath,
All green and wildly fresh without but worn and
   grey beneath.

---

[1] *Stanzas for Music*   Byron wrote this poem in 1815 to commemorate
the death of one of the friends of his youth, the Duke of Dorset. He
referred to it in an 1816 letter as "the truest, though the most
melancholy, I ever wrote."

5

Oh could I feel as I have felt,—or be what I have been,
Or weep as I could once have wept, o'er many a
    vanished scene:
As springs in deserts found seem sweet, all
    brackish though they be,
So midst the wither'd waste of life, those tears
    would flow to me.
    —1816

from *Childe Harold's Pilgrimage*
Canto the Third

Byron began *Childe Harold III* immediately upon
leaving England in 1816 (on the manuscript he
wrote "Begun at sea"). Separated from his wife, the
subject of dark rumors, shunned by the society that
had once embraced him, Byron decided to travel to
Europe; he never returned to England. This third
canto of *Childe Harold* charts his journey through
Belgium, Germany, and Switzerland.

"Afin que cette application vous forçât à penser à autre
chose; il n'y a en vérité de remède que celui-là et le temps."[1]
    —*Lettre du Roi de Prusse à D'Alembert,*
    Sept. 7, 1776.

1

Is thy face like thy mother's, my fair child!
  Ada![2] sole daughter of my house and heart?
When last I saw thy young blue eyes they smiled,

---

[1] *Afin … le temps* French: So that this exercise forces you to think of
something else. There is, in truth, no other remedy than that and time.
Oeuvres de Fréderic le Grand (1846–57) 25.49–50. In the quoted
letters, Frederick II (the Great) of Prussia recommended "some
problem very difficult to solve" as a consolation for Jean le Rond
d'Alembert (1717–83), who was in mourning for the death of a
woman he loved.

[2] *Ada* Augusta Ada Byron was born on 10 December 1815. Lady
Byron left her husband on 15 January 1816, taking their child with
her. Byron never saw either of them again, although he continued to
display an interest in Ada's progress. In daguerreotypes, Ada fluctuates
between a striking resemblance to her mother and a striking resemblance to the Byron side of the family.

And then we parted,—not as now we part,
But with a hope.—
            Awaking with a start,
The waters heave around me; and on high
The winds lift up their voices: I depart,
Whither I know not; but the hour's gone by,
When Albion's lessening shores could grieve or glad
    mine eye.

2

Once more upon the waters! yet once more![3]
And the waves bound beneath me as a steed
That knows his rider. Welcome, to their roar!
Swift be their guidance, wheresoe'er it lead!
Though the strain'd mast should quiver as a reed,
And the rent canvas fluttering strew the gale,
Still must I on; for I am as a weed,
Flung from the rock, on Ocean's foam, to sail
Where'er the surge may sweep, the tempest's breath
    prevail.

3

In my youth's summer I did sing of One,
The wandering outlaw of his own dark mind;
Again I seize the theme, then but begun,
And bear it with me, as the rushing wind
Bears the cloud onwards: in that Tale I find
The furrows of long thought, and dried-up tears,
Which, ebbing, leave a sterile track behind,
O'er which all heavily the journeying years
Plod the last sands of life—where not a flower appears.

4

Since my young days of passion—joy, or pain,
Perchance my heart and harp have lost a string,
And both may jar: it may be, that in vain
I would essay as I have sung to sing.
Yet, though a dreary strain, to this I cling;
So that it wean me from the weary dream
Of selfish grief or gladness—so it fling
Forgetfulness around me—it shall seem
To me, though to none else, a not ungrateful theme.

---

[3] *yet once more* See Shakespeare's *Henry V* 3.1.1.

5

He, who grown aged in this world of woe,
In deeds, not years, piercing the depths of life,
So that no wonder waits him; nor below
40   Can love, or sorrow, fame, ambition, strife,
Cut to his heart again with the keen knife
Of silent, sharp endurance: he can tell
Why thought seeks refuge in lone caves, yet rife
With airy images, and shapes which dwell
45   Still unimpair'd, though old, in the soul's haunted cell.

6

'Tis to create, and in creating live
A being more intense, that we endow
With form our fancy, gaining as we give
The life we image, even as I do now.
50   What am I? Nothing: but not so art thou,
Soul of my thought! with whom I traverse earth,
Invisible but gazing, as I glow
Mix'd with thy spirit, blended with thy birth,
And feeling still with thee in my crush'd feelings' dearth.

7

55   Yet must I think less wildly: I *have* thought
Too long and darkly, till my brain became,
In its own eddy boiling and o'er-wrought,
A whirling gulf of phantasy and flame:
And thus, untaught in youth my heart to tame,
60   My springs of life were poison'd. 'Tis too late!
Yet am I chang'd; though still enough the same
In strength to bear what time can not abate,
And feed on bitter fruits without accusing Fate.

8

Something too much of this—but now 'tis past,
65   And the spell closes with its silent seal.
Long absent HAROLD re-appears at last;
He of the breast which fain no more would feel,
Wrung with the wounds which kill not, but ne'er
    heal,
Yet Time, who changes all, had alter'd him
70   In soul and aspect as in age: years steal
Fire from the mind as vigour from the limb;
And life's enchanted cup but sparkles near the brim,

9

His had been quaff'd[1] too quickly, and he found
The dregs were wormwood; but he fill'd again,
75   And from a purer fount, on holier ground,
And deem'd its spring perpetual; but in vain!
Still round him clung invisibly a chain
Which gall'd for ever, fettering though unseen,
And heavy though it clank'd not; worn with pain,
80   Which pined although it spoke not, and grew keen,
Entering with every step, he took, through many a scene.

10

Secure in guarded coldness, he had mix'd
Again in fancied safety with his kind,
And deem'd his spirit now so firmly fix'd
85   And sheath'd with an invulnerable mind,
That, if no joy, no sorrow lurk'd behind;
And he, as one, might 'midst the many stand
Unheeded, searching through the crowd to find
Fit speculation; such as in strange land
90   He found in wonder-works of God and Nature's hand.

11

But who can view the ripen'd rose, nor seek
To wear it? who can curiously behold
The smoothness and the sheen of beauty's cheek,
Nor feel the heart can never all grow old?
95   Who can contemplate Fame through clouds unfold
The star which rises o'er her steep, nor climb?
Harold, once more within the vortex, roll'd
On with the giddy circle, chasing Time,
Yet with a nobler aim than in his youth's fond prime.

12

100   But soon he knew himself the most unfit
Of men to herd with Man; with whom he held
Little in common; untaught to submit
His thoughts to others, though his soul was quell'd
In youth by his own thoughts; still uncompell'd,
105   He would not yield dominion of his mind
To spirits against whom his own rebell'd;

---

[1] *quaff'd* Drunk.

Proud though in desolation; which could find
A life within itself, to breathe without mankind.

13

Where rose the mountains, there to him were
    friends;
Where roll'd the ocean, thereon was his home;
Where a blue sky, and glowing clime, extends,
He had the passion and the power to roam;
The desert, forest, cavern, breaker's foam,
Were unto him companionship; they spake
A mutual language, clearer than the tome
Of his land's tongue, which he would oft forsake
For Nature's pages glass'd by sunbeams on the lake.

14

Like the Chaldean,[1] he could watch the stars,
Till he had peopled them with beings bright
As their own beams; and earth, and earth-born jars,
And human frailties, were forgotten quite:
Could he have kept his spirit to that flight
He had been happy; but this clay will sink
Its spark immortal, envying it the light
To which it mounts, as if to break the link
That keeps us from yon heaven which woos us to its
    brink.

15

But in Man's dwellings he became a thing
Restless and worn, and stern and wearisome,
Droop'd as a wild-born falcon with clipt wing,
To whom the boundless air alone were home:
Then came his fit again, which to o'ercome,
As eagerly the barr'd-up bird will beat
His breast and beak against his wiry dome
Till the blood tinge his plumage, so the heat
Of his impeded soul would through his bosom eat.

16

Self-exil'd Harold wanders forth again,
With nought of hope left, but with less of gloom;

The very knowledge that he lived in vain,
That all was over on this side the tomb,
Had made Despair a smilingness assume,
Which, though 'twere wild,—as on the plunder'd
    wreck
When mariners would madly meet their doom
With draughts intemperate on the sinking deck,
Did yet inspire a cheer, which he forbore to check.

17

Stop!—for thy tread is on an Empire's dust!
An Earthquake's spoil is sepulchred below!
Is the spot mark'd with no colossal bust?
Nor column trophied for triumphal show?
None; but the moral's truth tells simpler so,
As the ground was before, thus let it be;—
How that red rain hath made the harvest grow!
And is this all the world has gain'd by thee,
Thou first and last of fields! king-making Victory?

18

And Harold stands upon this place of skulls,
The grave of France, the deadly Waterloo![2]
How in an hour the power which gave annuls
Its gifts, transferring fame as fleeting too!
In "pride of place"[3] here last the eagle flew,
Then tore with bloody talon the rent plain,
Pierc'd by the shaft of banded nations through;
Ambition's life and labours all were vain;
He wears the shatter'd links of the world's broken
    chain.[4]

19

Fit retribution! Gaul may champ the bit
And foam in fetters:—but is Earth more free?
Did nations combat to make *One* submit;

---

1 *Chaldean* Native of Chaldea, i.e., proverbial for one who possessed occult learning and astrological knowledge.

2 *Waterloo* Site of Napoleon's great defeat by the British and Prussians on 18 June 1815. Byron visited on 4 May 1816.

3 [Byron's note] Pride of Place is a term of falconry, and means the highest pitch of flight. See *Macbeth* &c.
    "A Falcon towering in her pride of place
    Was by a mousing Owl hawked at and killed."

4 *Ambition's … chain* After his defeat, Napoleon was exiled to St. Helena.

Or league to teach all kings true sovereignty?
What! shall reviving Thraldom again be
The patch'd-up idol of enlighten'd days?
Shall we, who struck the Lion down, shall we
170 Pay the Wolf homage? proffering lowly gaze
And servile knees to thrones? No; *prove* before ye praise!

20

If not, o'er one fallen despot boast no more!
In vain fair cheeks were furrow'd with hot tears
For Europe's flowers long rooted up before
175 The trampler of her vineyards; in vain years
Of death, depopulation, bondage, fears,
Have all been borne, and broken by the accord
Of rous'd-up millions; all that most endears
Glory, is when the myrtle wreathes a sword
180 Such as Harmodius drew on Athens' tyrant lord.[1]

21

There was a sound of revelry by night,
And Belgium's capital[2] had gather'd then
Her Beauty and her Chivalry, and bright
The lamps shone o'er fair women and brave men;
185 A thousand hearts beat happily; and when
Music arose with its voluptuous swell,
Soft eyes look'd love to eyes which spake again,
And all went merry as a marriage bell;[3]
But hush! hark! a deep sound strikes like a rising knell!

22

190 Did ye not hear it?—No; 'twas but the wind,
Or the car rattling o'er the stony street;
On with the dance! let joy be unconfined;
No sleep till morn, when Youth and Pleasure meet
To chase the glowing Hours with flying feet—

195 But hark!—that heavy sound breaks in once more,
As if the clouds its echo would repeat;
And nearer, clearer, deadlier than before!
Arm! Arm! it is—it is—the cannon's opening roar!

23

Within a window'd niche of that high hall
200 Sate Brunswick's fated chieftain;[4] he did hear
That sound the first amidst the festival,
And caught its tone with Death's prophetic ear;
And when they smiled because he deem'd it near,
His heart more truly knew that peal too well
205 Which stretch'd his father on a bloody bier,[5]
And rous'd the vengeance blood alone could quell:
He rush'd into the field, and, foremost fighting, fell.

24

Ah! then and there was hurrying to and fro,
And gathering tears, and tremblings of distress,
210 And cheeks all pale, which but an hour ago
Blush'd at the praise of their own loveliness;
And there were sudden partings, such as press
The life from out young hearts, and choking sighs
Which ne'er might be repeated; who could guess
215 If ever more should meet those mutual eyes,
Since upon night so sweet such awful morn could rise?

25

And there was mounting in hot haste: the steed,
The mustering squadron, and the clattering car,
Went pouring forward with impetuous speed,
220 And swiftly forming in the ranks of war;
And the deep thunder peal on peal afar;
And near, the beat of the alarming drum
Roused up the soldier ere the morning star;
While throng'd the citizens with terror dumb,
225 Or whispering, with white lips—"The foe! they come! they come!"

---

[1] [Byron's note] See the famous song on Harmodius and Aristogiton.—The best English translation is in Bland's Anthology, by Mr. Denman. "With myrtle my sword will I wreathe," &c. [Harmodius and Aristogeiton were Athenian patriots who attempted to assassinate the tyrants Hippias and Hipparchus in 514 BCE.]

[2] *Belgium's capital* Brussels.

[3] [Byron's note] On the night previous to the action, it was said that a ball was given at Brussels. [The Duchess of Richmond gave a ball on 15 June 1815, the night before the inconclusive battle of Quatre Bras. Waterloo was fought on 18 June.]

[4] *Brunswick's fated chieftain* Frederick, Duke of Brunswick (1771–1815), brother of Caroline, Princess of Wales, and nephew of George III, was killed at the battle of Quatre Bras, the first engagement of the Waterloo campaign, 16 June 1815.

[5] *his father … bier* Brunswick's father, Charles, Duke of Brunswick (1735–1806) was killed at the battle of Auerstädt.

26

And wild and high the "Cameron's gathering"[1] rose!
The war-note of Lochiel, which Albyn's[2] hills
Have heard, and heard, too, have her Saxon foes:—
How in the noon of night that pibroch[3] thrills,
Savage and shrill! But with the breath which fills
Their mountain-pipe, so fill the mountaineers
With the fierce native daring which instils
The stirring memory of a thousand years,
And Evan's, Donald's fame rings in each clansman's ears![4]

27

And Ardennes waves above them her green leaves,[5]
Dewy with nature's tear-drops, as they pass,
Grieving, if aught inanimate e'er grieves,
Over the unreturning brave,—alas!
Ere evening to be trodden like the grass
Which now beneath them, but above shall grow
In its next verdure, when this fiery mass
Of living valour, rolling on the foe
And burning with high hope, shall moulder cold and
low.

28

Last noon beheld them full of lusty life,
Last eve in Beauty's circle proudly gay,
The midnight brought the signal-sound of strife,
The morn the marshalling in arms,—the day
Battle's magnificently-stern array!
The thunder-clouds close o'er it, which when rent
The earth is cover'd thick with other clay,
Which her own clay shall cover, heap'd and pent,
Rider and horse,—friend, foe,—in one red burial blent!

29

Their praise is hymn'd by loftier harps than mine:
Yet one I would select from that proud throng,
Partly because they blend me with his line,
And partly that I did his sire some wrong,
And partly that bright names will hallow song;
And his was of the bravest, and when shower'd
The death-bolts deadliest the thinn'd files along,
Even where the thickest of war's tempest lower'd,
They reach'd no nobler breast than thine, young,
gallant Howard![6]

30

There have been tears and breaking hearts for thee,
And mine were nothing had I such to give;
But when I stood beneath the fresh green tree,
Which living waves where thou didst cease to live,
And saw around me the wide field revive
With fruits and fertile promise, and the Spring
Come forth her work of gladness to contrive,
With all her reckless birds upon the wing,
I turn'd from all she brought to those she could not
bring.[7]

---

1 *Cameron's gathering* War song of the Scottish clan Cameron.

2 *Albyn* Scots Gaelic name for Scotland.

3 *pibroch* Song of war or mourning.

4 [Byron's note] Sir Evan Cameron, and his descendant Donald, the "gentle Lochiel" of the "forty-five." [Sir Evan Cameron (1629–1719) fought against Cromwell, and his grandson Donald Cameron (1695–1748) was a supporter of Charles Stuart, fighting with him at his defeat at Culloden Moor in 1745. His great-great-grandson, John Cameron (1771–1815), was killed at Quatre Bras. Byron was half Scots.]

5 [Byron's note] The wood of Soignies is supposed to be a remnant of the "forest of Ardennes," famous in Boiardo's Orlando, and immortal in Shakspeare's "As you like it." It is also celebrated in Tacitus as being the spot of successful defence by the Germans against the Roman encroachments.—I have ventured to adopt the name connected with nobler associations than those of mere slaughter. [Cf. Tacitus, *Annals* 1.60 and 3.42 and Boiardo, *Orlando Innamorato* 1.2.30. The forest of Ardennes is actually in Belgium and Luxembourg, but extends into Germany and France.]

6 *Their praise … Howard* In this stanza Byron refers to his cousin Frederick Howard (1785–1815), son of the Earl of Carlisle.

7 [Byron's note] My guide from Mont St. Jean over the field seemed intelligent and accurate. The place where Major Howard fell was not far from two tall and solitary trees (there was a third cut down, or shivered in the battle) which stand a few yards from each other at a pathway's side.—Beneath these he died and was buried. The body has since been removed to England. A small hollow for the present marks where it lay, but it will probably soon be effaced; the plough has been upon it, and the grain is.

After pointing out the different spots where Major Picton and other gallant men had perished, the guide said, "here Major Howard lay; I was near him when wounded." I told him my relationship, and he seemed then still more anxious to point out the particular spot and circumstances. The place is one of the most marked in the field from the peculiarity of the two trees above mentioned.   [continued …]

31

I turn'd to thee, to thousands, of whom each
And one as all a ghastly gap did make
In his own kind and kindred, whom to teach
Forgetfulness were mercy for their sake;
275 The Archangel's trump,[1] not Glory's, must awake
Those whom they thirst for; though the sound of
    Fame
May for a moment soothe, it cannot slake
The fever of vain longing, and the name
So honour'd but assumes a stronger, bitterer claim.

32

280 They mourn, but smile at length; and, smiling,
    mourn;
The tree will wither long before it fall;
The hull drives on, though mast and sail be torn;
The roof-tree sinks, but moulders on the hall
In massy hoariness; the ruin'd wall
285 Stands when its wind-worn battlements are gone;
The bars survive the captive they enthral;
The day drags through though storms keep out
    the sun;
And thus the heart will break, yet brokenly live on:[2]

33

Even as a broken mirror, which the glass
290 In every fragment multiplies; and makes
A thousand images of one that was,
The same, and still the more, the more it breaks;
And thus the heart will do which not forsakes,

Living in shatter'd guise; and still, and cold,
295 And bloodless, with its sleepless sorrow aches,
Yet withers on till all without is old,
Showing no visible sign, for such things are untold.

34

There is a very life in our despair,
Vitality of poison,—a quick root
300 Which feeds these deadly branches; for it were
As nothing did we die; but Life will suit
Itself to Sorrow's most detested fruit,
Like to the apples on the Dead Sea's shore,[3]
All ashes to the taste: Did man compute
305 Existence by enjoyment, and count o'er
Such hours 'gainst years of life,—say, would he name
    threescore?

35

The Psalmist[4] number'd out the years of man:
They are enough: and if thy tale be *true*,
Thou, who didst grudge him even that fleeting
    span,
310 More than enough, thou fatal Waterloo!
Millions of tongues record thee, and anew
Their children's lips shall echo them, and say—
"Here, where the sword united nations drew,
Our countrymen were warring on that day!"
315 And this is much, and all which will not pass away.

36

There sunk the greatest, nor the worst of men,
Whose spirit, antithetically mixt,
One moment of the mightiest, and again
On little objects with like firmness fixt;
320 Extreme in all things! hadst thou been betwixt,
Thy throne had still been thine, or never been;
For daring made thy rise as fall: thou seek'st

I went on horseback twice over the field, comparing it with my
recollection of similar scenes. As a plain, Waterloo seems marked out
for the scene of some great action, though this may be mere imagination: I have viewed with attention those of Platea, Troy, Mantinea,
Leuctra, Chaeronea, and Marathon; and the field around Mont St.
Jean and Hougoumont appears to want little but a better cause, and
that undefinable but impressive halo which the lapse of ages throws
around a celebrated spot, to vie in interest with any or all of these,
except perhaps the last mentioned.

1 *Archangel's trump* The trumpet that will sound at the end of the
world, to revive the dead; see 1 Corinthians 15.52.

2 *the heart ... live on* Cf. Robert Burton (1577–1640), *The Anatomy
of Melancholy* 2.3.5; and John Donne (1572–1631), "The Broken
Heart" 23–32.

3 [Byron's note] The (fabled) apples on the brink of the lake
Asphaltes were said to be fair without, and within ashes.—Vide
Tacitus Histor. 1.5.7. [These apples are mentioned in Deuteronomy
32.32.]

4 *The Psalmist* King David: see Psalm 90.10.

Even now to re-assume the imperial mien,
And shake again the world, the Thunderer of the
    scene!

37

Conqueror and captive of the earth art thou!
She trembles at thee still, and thy wild name
Was ne'er more bruited in men's minds than now
That thou art nothing, save the jest of Fame,
Who woo'd thee once, thy vassal, and became
The flatterer of thy fierceness, till thou wert
A god unto thyself; nor less the same
To the astounded kingdoms all inert,
Who deem'd thee for a time whate'er thou didst
    assert.

38

Oh, more or less than man—in high or low,
Battling with nations, flying from the field;
Now making monarchs' necks thy footstool, now
More than thy meanest soldier taught to yield;
An empire thou couldst crush, command, rebuild,
But govern not thy pettiest passion, nor,
However deeply in men's spirits skill'd,
Look through thine own, nor curb the lust of war,
Nor learn that tempted Fate will leave the loftiest star.

39

Yet well thy soul hath brook'd the turning tide
With that untaught innate philosophy,
Which, be it wisdom, coldness, or deep pride,
Is gall and wormwood to an enemy.
When the whole host of hatred stood hard by,
To watch and mock thee shrinking, thou hast
    smiled
With a sedate and all-enduring eye;—
When Fortune fled her spoil'd and favourite child,
He stood unbow'd beneath the ills upon him piled.

40

Sager than in thy fortunes; for in them
Ambition steel'd thee on too far to show
That just habitual scorn, which could contemn
Men and their thoughts; 'twas wise to feel, not so

To wear it ever on thy lip and brow,
And spurn the instruments thou wert to use
Till they were turn'd unto thine overthrow;
'Tis but a worthless world to win or lose,
So hath it proved to thee, and all such lot who choose.

41

If, like a tower upon a headland rock,
Thou hadst been made to stand or fall alone,
Such scorn of man had help'd to brave the shock;
But men's thoughts were the steps which paved thy
    throne,
Their admiration thy best weapon shone;
The part of Philip's son[1] was thine, not then
(Unless aside thy purple had been thrown)
Like stern Diogenes to mock at men;
For sceptred cynics earth were far too wide a den.[2]

42

But quiet to quick bosoms is a hell,
And *there* hath been thy bane; there is a fire
And motion of the soul which will not dwell
In its own narrow being, but aspire
Beyond the fitting medium of desire;
And, but once kindled, quenchless evermore,
Preys upon high adventure, nor can tire
Of aught but rest; a fever at the core,
Fatal to him who bears, to all who ever bore.

---

[1] *Philip's son* Alexander the Great (356–323 BCE), son of Philip of Macedon. He is reported to have said that if he had not been a king (kings traditionally wore purple), he would have liked to have been a philosopher like Diogenes (the founder of the Cynic School). Diogenes is said to have replied that if he had not been a philosopher, he would have liked to have been a king like Alexander.

[2] [Byron's note] The great error of Napoleon, "if we have writ our annals true" [Shakespeare, *Coriolanus* 5.6.112], was a continued obtrusion on mankind of his want of all community of feeling for or with them; perhaps more offensive to human vanity than the active cruelty of more trembling and suspicious tyranny.

Such were his speeches to public assemblies as well as individuals: and the single expression which he is said to have used on returning to Paris after the Russian winter had destroyed his army, rubbing his hands over a fire, "This is pleasanter than Moscow," would probably alienate more favour from his cause than the destruction and reverses which led to the remark.

43

This makes the madmen who have made men mad
380 By their contagion; Conquerors and Kings,
Founders of sects and systems, to whom add
Sophists, Bards, Statesmen, all unquiet things
Which stir too strongly the soul's secret springs,
And are themselves the fools to those they fool;
385 Envied, yet how unenviable! what stings
Are theirs! One breast laid open were a school
Which would unteach mankind the lust to shine or
rule.

44

Their breath is agitation, and their life
A storm whereon they ride, to sink at last,
390 And yet so nurs'd and bigoted to strife,
That should their days, surviving perils past,
Melt to calm twilight, they feel overcast
With sorrow and supineness, and so die;
Even as a flame unfed, which runs to waste
395 With its own flickering, or a sword laid by,
Which eats into itself, and rusts ingloriously.

45

He who ascends to mountain-tops, shall find
The loftiest peaks most wrapt in clouds and snow;
He who surpasses or subdues mankind,
400 Must look down on the hate of those below.
Though high *above* the sun of glory glow,
And far *beneath* the earth and ocean spread,
Round him are icy rocks, and loudly blow
Contending tempests on his naked head,
405 And thus reward the toils which to those summits led.

46

Away with these! true Wisdom's world will be
Within its own creation, or in thine,
Maternal Nature! for who teems like thee,
Thus on the banks of thy majestic Rhine?
410 There Harold gazes on a work divine,
A blending of all beauties; streams and dells,
Fruit, foliage, crag, wood, cornfield, mountain, vine,
And chiefless castles breathing stern farewells
From gray but leafy walls, where Ruin greenly dwells.

47

415 And there they stand, as stands a lofty mind,
Worn, but unstooping to the baser crowd,
All tenantless, save to the crannying wind,
Or holding dark communion with the cloud.
There was a day when they were young and proud;
420 Banners on high, and battles pass'd below;
But they who fought are in a bloody shroud,
And those which waved are shredless dust ere now,
And the bleak battlements shall bear no future blow.

48

Beneath these battlements, within those walls,
425 Power dwelt amidst her passions; in proud state
Each robber chief upheld his armed halls,
Doing his evil will, nor less elate
Than mightier heroes of a longer date.
What want these outlaws conquerers should have[1]
430 But history's purchased page to call them great?
A wider space, an ornamented grave?
Their hopes were not less warm, their souls were full
as brave.

49

In their baronial feuds and single fields,
What deeds of prowess unrecorded died!
435 And Love, which lent a blazon to their shields,
With emblems well devised by amorous pride,
Through all the mail of iron hearts would glide;
But still their flame was fierceness, and drew on
Keen contest and destruction near allied,
440 And many a tower for some fair mischief won,
Saw the discolour'd Rhine beneath its ruin run.

50

But Thou, exulting and abounding river!
Making thy waves a blessing as they flow

---

1 [Byron's note]
"What wants that knave
That a king should have?"
was King James's question on meeting Johnny Armstrong and his
followers in full accoutrements.—See the Ballad. [Johnnie Armstrong,
Laird of Gilnockie, surrendered to James V of Scotland in 1532. He
was so magnificently dressed that James hanged him for impudence.
The ballad is in Walter Scott, *Minstrelsy of the Scottish Border*.]

Through banks whose beauty would endure for
    ever
5 Could man but leave thy bright creation so,
Nor its fair promise from the surface mow
With the sharp scythe of conflict,—then to see
Thy valley of sweet waters, were to know
Earth paved like Heaven; and to seem such to me,
0 Even now what wants thy stream?—that it should
    Lethe[1] be.

51

A thousand battles have assail'd thy banks,
But these and half their fame have pass'd away,
And Slaughter, heap'd on high his weltering ranks;
Their very graves are gone, and what are they?
5 Thy tide wash'd down the blood of yesterday,
And all was stainless, and on thy clear stream
Glass'd, with its dancing light, the sunny ray;
But o'er the blackened memory's blighting dream
Thy waves would vainly roll, all sweeping as they
    seem.

52

0 Thus Harold inly said, and pass'd along,
Yet not insensible to all which here
Awoke the jocund birds to early song
In glens which might have made even exile dear:
Though on his brow were graven lines austere,
5 And tranquil sternness, which had ta'en the place
Of feelings fiercer far but less severe,
Joy was not always absent from his face,
But o'er it in such scenes would steal with transient
    trace.

53

Nor was all love shut from him, though his days
0 Of passion had consumed themselves to dust.
It is in vain that we would coldly gaze
On such as smile upon us; the heart must
Leap kindly back to kindness, though disgust
Hath wean'd it from all worldlings: thus he felt,
5 For there was soft remembrance, and sweet trust

In one fond breast, to which his own would melt,[2]
And in its tenderer hour on that his bosom dwelt.

54

And he had learn'd to love,—I know not why,
For this in such as him seems strange of mood,—
480 The helpless looks of blooming infancy,
Even in its earliest nurture; what subdued,
To change like this, a mind so far imbued
With scorn of man, it little boots to know;
But thus it was; and though in solitude
485 Small power the nipp'd affections have to grow,
In him this glow'd when all beside had ceased to glow.

55

And there was one soft breast, as hath been said,
Which unto his was bound by stronger ties
Than the church links withal; and, though unwed,
490 *That* love was pure, and, far above disguise,
Had stood the test of mortal enmities
Still undivided, and cemented more
By peril, dreaded most in female eyes;
But this was firm, and from a foreign shore
495 Well to that heart might his these absent greetings
    pour!

I

The castled crag of Drachenfels[3]
Frowns o'er the wide and winding Rhine,
Whose breast of waters broadly swells
Between the banks which bear the vine,
500 And hills all rich with blossom'd trees,
And fields which promise corn and wine,
And scatter'd cities crowning these,
Whose far white walls along them shine,

---

1 *Lethe* River of forgetfulness in the classical underworld.

2 *there was … melt* A coded reference to Byron's half-sister, Augusta Leigh.

3 [Byron's note] The castle of Drachenfels stands on the highest summit of "the Seven Mountains," over the Rhine banks; it is in ruins, and connected with some singular traditions: it is the first in view on the road from Bonn, but on the opposite side of the river; on this bank, nearly facing it, are the remains of another called the Jew's castle, and a large cross commemorative of the murder of a chief by his brother: the number of castles and cities along the course of the Rhine on both sides is very great, and their situations remarkably beautiful.

Have strew'd a scene, which I should see

505 With double joy wert *thou* with me.

2

And peasant girls, with deep blue eyes,
And hands which offer early flowers,
Walk smiling o'er this paradise;
Above, the frequent feudal towers

510 Through green leaves lift their walls of gray;
And many a rock which steeply lowers,
And noble arch in proud decay,
Look o'er the vale of vintage-bowers;
But one thing want these banks of Rhine,—

515 Thy gentle hand to clasp in mine!

3

I send the lilies given to me;
Though long before thy hand they touch,
I know that they must wither'd be,
But yet reject them not as such;

520 For I have cherish'd them as dear,
Because they yet may meet thine eye,
And guide thy soul to mine even here,
When thou behold'st them drooping nigh,
And know'st them gather'd by the Rhine,

525 And offer'd from my heart to thine!

4

The river nobly foams and flows,
The charm of this enchanted ground,
And all its thousand turns disclose
Some fresher beauty varying round:

530 The haughtiest breast its wish might bound
Through life to dwell delighted here;
Nor could on earth a spot be found
To nature and to me so dear,
Could thy dear eyes in following mine

535 Still sweeten more these banks of Rhine!

56

By Coblentz, on a rise of gentle ground,
There is a small and simple pyramid,
Crowning the summit of the verdant mound;

Beneath its base are heroes' ashes hid,

540 Our enemy's—but let not that forbid
Honour to Marceau![1] o'er whose early tomb
Tears, big tears, gush'd from the rough soldier's lid,
Lamenting and yet envying such a doom,
Falling for France, whose rights he battled to resume.

57

545 Brief, brave, and glorious was his young career,—
His mourners were two hosts, his friends and foes;
And fitly may the stranger lingering here
Pray for his gallant spirit's bright repose;
For he was Freedom's champion, one of those,

550 The few in number, who had not o'erstept
The charter to chastise which she bestows
On such as wield her weapons; he had kept
The whiteness of his soul, and thus men o'er him
wept.[2]

---

[1] *Marceau* François Séverin Desgravins Marceau (1769–96), French general, was killed in battle against the counter-revolutionary armies.

[2] [Byron's note] The monument of the young and lamented General Marceau (killed by a rifle-ball at Alterkirchen on the last day of the fourth year of the French republic) still remains as described.

The inscriptions on his monument are rather too long, and not required: his name was enough; France adored, and her enemies admired; both wept over him.—His funeral was attended by the generals and detachments from both armies. In the same grave General Hoche is interred, a gallant man also in every sense of the word, but though he distinguished himself greatly in battle, *he* had not the good fortune to die there; his death was attended by suspicions of poison.

A separate monument (not over his body, which is buried by Marceau's) is raised for him near Andernach, opposite to which one of his most memorable exploits was performed, in throwing a bridge to an island on the Rhine. The shape and style are different from that of Marceau's, and the inscription more simple and pleasing.
"The Army of the Sambre and Meuse
to its Commander-in-Chief
Hoche."
This is all, and as it should be. Hoche was esteemed among the first of France's earlier generals before Buonaparte monopolised her triumphs.—He was the destined commander of the invading army of Ireland. [General Lazare Hoche (1768–97) actually died of consumption. He performed his bridge exploit on 18 April 1797, at the battle of Neuwied.]

58

Here Ehrenbreitstein,[1] with her shatter'd wall
Black with the miner's blast, upon her height
Yet shows of what she was, when shell and ball
Rebounding idly on her strength did light:
A tower of victory! from whence the flight
Of baffled foes was watch'd along the plain:
But Peace destroy'd what War could never blight,
And laid those proud roofs bare to Summer's
       rain—
On which the iron shower for years had pour'd in
       vain.

59

Adieu to thee, fair Rhine! How long delighted
The stranger fain would linger on his way!
Thine is a scene alike where souls united
Or lonely Contemplation thus might stray;
And could the ceaseless vultures cease to prey
On self-condemning bosoms,[2] it were here,
Where Nature, nor too sombre nor too gay,
Wild but not rude, awful yet not austere,
Is to the mellow Earth as Autumn to the year.

60

Adieu to thee again! a vain adieu!
There can be no farewell to scene like thine;
The mind is colour'd by thy every hue;
And if reluctantly the eyes resign
Their cherish'd gaze upon thee, lovely Rhine!
'Tis with the thankful glance of parting praise;
More mighty spots may rise, more glaring shine,

580   But none unite in one attaching maze
The brilliant, fair, and soft,—the glories of old days.

61

The negligently grand, the fruitful bloom
Of coming ripeness, the white city's sheen,
The rolling stream, the precipice's gloom,
The forest's growth, and Gothic walls between,
585   The wild rocks shaped as they had turrets been,
In mockery of man's art; and these withal
A race of faces happy as the scene,
Whose fertile bounties here extend to all,
Still springing o'er thy banks, though Empires near
       them fall.

62

590   But these recede. Above me are the Alps,
The palaces of Nature, whose vast walls
Have pinnacled in clouds their snowy scalps,
And throned Eternity in icy halls
Of cold sublimity, where forms and falls
595   The avalanche,—the thunderbolt of snow!
All that expands the spirit, yet appals,
Gather around these summits, as to show
How Earth may pierce to Heaven, yet leave vain man
       below.

63

But ere these matchless heights I dare to scan,
600   There is a spot should not be pass'd in vain,—
Morat![3] the proud, the patriot field! where man
May gaze on ghastly trophies of the slain,
Nor blush for those who conquer'd on that plain;
Here Burgundy bequeath'd his tombless host,
605   A bony heap, through ages to remain,
Themselves their monument;—the Stygian coast[4]

---

1 [Byron's note] Ehrenbreitstein, i.e. "the broad Stone of Honour," one of the strongest fortresses in Europe, was dismantled and blown up by the French at the truce of Leoben.—It had been and could only be reduced by famine or treachery. It yielded to the former, aided by surprise. After having seen the fortifications of Gibraltar and Malta, it did not much strike by comparison, but the situation is commanding. General Marceau besieged it in vain for some time, and I slept in a room where I was shown a window at which he is said to have been standing observing the progress of the siege by moonlight, when a ball struck immediately below it. [The castle was in fact demolished not after the treaty of Leoben (1797), but that of Lunéville (1801).]

2 *And could ... bosoms* An allusion to the punishment of Prometheus. See Byron's "Prometheus," in this volume.

3 *Morat* Battlefield where the Swiss defeated the Burgundians on 14 June 1476. The Burgundian dead were placed in an ossuary, which was destroyed by the revolutionary French army in 1798.

4 *Stygian coast* Coast of the River Styx; in classical mythology, the souls crossed the Styx to enter the underworld.

Unsepulchred they roam'd, and shriek'd each
    wandering ghost.[1]

64

    While Waterloo with Cannae's[2] carnage vies,
    Morat and Marathon[3] twin names shall stand;
610   They were true Glory's stainless victories,
    Won by the unambitious heart and hand
    Of a proud, brotherly, and civic band,
    All unbought champions in no princely cause
    Of vice-entail'd Corruption; they no land
615   Doom'd to bewail the blasphemy of laws
Making kings' rights divine, by some Draconic[4] clause.

65

    By a lone wall a lonelier column rears
    A gray and grief-worn aspect of old days,
    'Tis the last remnant of the wreck of years,
620   And looks as with the wild-bewilder'd gaze
    Of one to stone converted by amaze,
    Yet still with consciousness; and there it stands
    Making a marvel that it not decays,

When the coeval pride of human hands,
625 Levell'd Aventicum,[5] hath strew'd her subject lands.

66

    And there—oh! sweet and sacred be the name!—
    Julia—the daughter, the devoted—gave
    Her youth to Heaven; her heart, beneath a claim
    Nearest to Heaven's, broke o'er a father's grave.
630   Justice is sworn 'gainst tears, and hers would crave
    The life she lived in; but the judge was just,
    And then she died on him she could not save.
    Their tomb was simple, and without a bust,
And held within their urn one mind, one heart, one
    dust.[6]

67

635 But these are deeds which should not pass away,
    And names that must not wither, though the earth
    Forgets her empires with a just decay,
    The enslavers and the enslaved, their death and
    birth;

---

1 [Byron's note]   The chapel is destroyed, and the pyramid of bones diminished to a small number by the Burgundian Legion in the service of France, who anxiously effaced this record of their ancestors' less successful invasions. A few still remain notwithstanding the pains taken by the Burgundians for ages, (all who passed that way removing a bone to their own country) and the less justifiable larcenies of the Swiss postillions, who carried them off to sell for knife-handles, a purpose for which the whiteness imbibed by the bleaching of years had rendered them in great request. Of these relics I ventured to bring away as much as may have made the quarter of a hero, for which the sole excuse is, that if I had not, the next passer by might have perverted them to worse uses than the careful preservation which I intend for them.

2 *Cannae*   Battle between the Romans and the Carthaginians, 216 BCE.

3 *Marathon*   Battle between the Greeks and the Persians, 490 BCE. Byron contrasts Morat and Marathon, battles where free peoples defeated imperialist aggressors, with Cannae (216 BCE) and Waterloo, battles between two imperial powers.

4 *Draconic*   Draco, an Athenian politician of the seventh century BCE, was notorious for the severity of his laws.

5 [Byron's note]   Aventicum (near Morat) was the Roman capital of Helvetia, where Avenches now stands. [The column is the only remaining relic.]

6 [Byron's note]   Julia Alpinula, a young Aventian priestess, died soon after a vain endeavour to save her father, condemned to death as a traitor by Aulus Caecina. Her epitaph was discovered many years ago;—it is thus—

Julia Alpinula
Hic jaceo
Infelicis patris, infelix proles
Deae Aventiae Sacerdos;
Exorare patris necem non potui
Male mori in fatis ille erat.
Vixi annos XXIII.

[Latin: Julia Alpinula: Here I lie, the unhappy child of an unhappy father. Priestess of the Goddess of Aventicum; I was unable to avert the death of my father: it was his fate to die badly. I lived 23 years.] I know of no human composition so affecting as this, nor a history of deeper interest. These are the names and actions which ought not to perish, and to which we turn with a true and healthy tenderness, from the wretched and glittering detail of a confused mass of conquests and battles, with which the mind is roused for a time to a false and feverish sympathy, from whence it recurs at length with all the nausea consequent on such an intoxication. [Julius Alpinus was put to death in 69 BCE; see Tacitus, *Historia* 1.67–68. There is no evidence that he had a daughter, but both her "history" and this epitaph appear in a collection of epitaphs published in 1707.]

The high, the mountain-majesty of worth
40   Should be, and shall, survivor of its woe,
And from its immortality look forth
In the sun's face, like yonder Alpine snow,[1]
Imperishably pure beyond all things below.

68

Lake Leman[2] woos me with its crystal face,
45   The mirror where the stars and mountains view
The stillness of their aspect in each trace
Its clear depth yields of their far height and hue:
There is too much of man here, to look through
With a fit mind the might which I behold;
50   But soon in me shall Loneliness renew
Thoughts hid, but not less cherish'd than of old,
Ere mingling with the herd had penn'd me in their
    fold.

69

To fly from, need not be to hate, mankind:
All are not fit with them to stir and toil,
55   Nor is it discontent to keep the mind
Deep in its fountain, lest it overboil
In the hot throng, where we become the spoil
Of our infection, till too late and long
We may deplore and struggle with the coil,
60   In wretched interchange of wrong for wrong
Midst a contentious world, striving where none are
    strong.

70

There, in a moment we may plunge our years
In fatal penitence, and in the blight
Of our own soul turn all our blood to tears,
65   And colour things to come with hues of Night;
The race of life becomes a hopeless flight
To those that walk in darkness: on the sea
The boldest steer but where their ports invite;

But there are wanderers o'er Eternity
670   Whose bark drives on and on, and anchor'd ne'er
    shall be.

71

Is it not better, then, to be alone,
And love Earth only for its earthly sake?
By the blue rushing of the arrowy Rhone,[3]
Or the pure bosom of its nursing lake,
675   Which feeds it as a mother who doth make
A fair but froward infant her own care,
Kissing its cries away as these awake;—
Is it not better thus our lives to wear,
Than join the crushing crowd, doom'd to inflict or
    bear?

72

680   I live not in myself, but I become
Portion of that around me; and to me
High mountains are a feeling, but the hum
Of human cities torture: I can see
Nothing to loathe in nature, save to be
685   A link reluctant in a fleshly chain,
Class'd among creatures, when the soul can flee,
And with the sky, the peak, the heaving plain
Of ocean, or the stars, mingle, and not in vain.

73

And thus I am absorb'd, and this is life:
690   I look upon the peopled desert past,
As on a place of agony and strife,
Where, for some sin, to sorrow I was cast,
To act and suffer, but remount at last
With a fresh pinion;° which I feel to spring,   wing
695   Though young, yet waxing vigorous as the blast
Which it would cope with, on delighted wing,
Spurning the clay-cold bonds which round our being
    cling.

---

1 [Byron's note]   This is written in the eye of Mont Blanc (June 3d,
1816) which even at this distance dazzles mine. (July 20th). I this day
observed for some time the distinct reflection of Mont Blanc and
Mont Argentiere in the calm of the lake, which I was crossing in my
boat; the distance of these mountains from their mirror is 60 miles.

2 *Lake Leman* Lake Geneva.

3 [Byron's note]   The colour of the Rhone at Geneva is *blue*, to a
depth of tint which I have never seen equalled in water, salt or fresh,
except in the Mediterranean and Archipelago.

74

And when, at length, the mind shall be all free
From what it hates in this degraded form,
700 Reft of its carnal life, save what shall be
Existent happier in the fly and worm,—
When elements to elements conform,
And dust is as it should be, shall I not
Feel all I see, less dazzling, but more warm?
705 The bodiless thought? the Spirit of each spot?
Of which, even now, I share at times the immortal lot?

75

Are not the mountains, waves, and skies, a part
Of me and of my soul, as I of them?
Is not the love of these deep in my heart
710 With a pure passion? should I not contemn
All objects, if compared with these? and stem
A tide of suffering, rather than forego
Such feelings for the hard and worldly phlegm
Of those whose eyes are only turn'd below,
715 Gazing upon the ground, with thoughts which dare
not glow?

76

But this is not my theme; and I return
To that which is immediate, and require
Those who find contemplation in the urn
To look on One, whose dust was once all fire,[1]
720 A native of the land where I respire
The clear air for a while—a passing guest,
Where he became a being,—whose desire
Was to be glorious; 'twas a foolish quest,
The which to gain and keep, he sacrificed all rest.

77

725 Here the self-torturing sophist, wild Rousseau,
The apostle of affliction, he who threw
Enchantment over passion, and from woe
Wrung overwhelming eloquence, first drew
The breath which made him wretched; yet he knew
730 How to make madness beautiful, and cast

O'er erring deeds and thoughts a heavenly hue
Of words, like sunbeams, dazzling as they past
The eyes, which o'er them shed tears feelingly and
fast.

78

His love was passion's essence—as a tree
735 On fire by lightning, with ethereal flame
Kindled he was, and blasted; for to be
Thus, and enamour'd, were in him the same.
But his was not the love of living dame,
Nor of the dead who rise upon our dreams,
740 But of ideal beauty, which became
In him existence, and o'erflowing teems
Along his burning page, distemper'd though it seems.

79

This breathed itself to life in Julie, *this*
Invested her with all that's wild and sweet;
745 This hallow'd, too, the memorable kiss[2]
Which every morn his fever'd lip would greet,
From hers, who but with friendship his would
meet;
But to that gentle touch through brain and breast
Flash'd the thrill'd spirit's love-devouring heat;
750 In that absorbing sigh perchance more blest
Than vulgar minds may be with all they seek possest.

80

His life was one long war with self-sought foes,
Or friends by him self-banish'd; for his mind
Had grown Suspicion's sanctuary, and chose,
755 For its own cruel sacrifice, the kind,
'Gainst whom he rag'd with fury strange and
blind.

---

1 *One ... all fire* Jean-Jacques Rousseau (1712–78), Genevan philosopher and novelist, author of *Du contrat social* (1762), *Julie; ou, la nouvelle Héloïse* (1761), and *Confessions* (1782–89).

2 [Byron's note]   This refers to the account in his *Confessions* (2.9) of his passion for the Comtesse d'Houdetot (the mistress of St. Lambert) and his long walk every morning for the sake of the single kiss which was the common salutation of French acquaintance.—Rousseau's description of his feelings on this occasion may be considered as the most passionate, yet not impure description and expression of love that ever kindled into words; which after all must be felt, from their very force, to be inadequate to the delineation: a painting can give no sufficient idea of the ocean.

But he was phrensied,—wherefore, who may
    know?
Since cause might be which skill could never find;
But he was phrensied by disease or woe,
To that worst pitch of all, which wears a reasoning
    show.

81

For then he was inspired, and from him came,
As from the Pythian's mystic cave of yore,[1]
Those oracles which set the world in flame,
Nor ceas'd to burn till kingdoms were no more:
Did he not this for France? which lay before
Bow'd to the inborn tyranny of years?
Broken and trembling to the yoke she bore,
Till by the voice of him and his compeers
Rous'd up to too much wrath, which follows
    o'ergrown fears?

82

They made themselves a fearful monument!
The wreck of old opinions—things which grew,
Breathed from the birth of time: the veil they rent,
And what behind it lay, all earth shall view.
But good with ill they also overthrew,
Leaving but ruins, wherewith to rebuild
Upon the same foundation, and renew
Dungeons and thrones, which the same hour
    refill'd
As heretofore, because ambition was self-will'd.

83

But this will not endure, nor be endured!
Mankind have felt their strength, and made it felt.
They might have used it better, but, allured
By their new vigour, sternly have they dealt
On one another; pity ceased to melt
With her once natural charities. But they,
Who in oppression's darkness caved had dwelt,
They were not eagles, nourish'd with the day;

What marvel then, at times, if they mistook their
    prey?

84

What deep wounds ever closed without a scar?
The heart's bleed longest, and but heal to wear
That which disfigures it; and they who war
With their own hopes, and have been vanquish'd,
    bear
Silence, but not submission: in his lair
Fix'd Passion holds his breath, until the hour
Which shall atone for years; none need despair:
It came, it cometh, and will come,—the power
To punish or forgive—in *one* we shall be slower.

85

Clear, placid Leman! thy contrasted lake,
With the wild world I dwelt in, is a thing
Which warns me, with its stillness, to forsake
Earth's troubled waters for a purer spring.
This quiet sail is as a noiseless wing
To waft me from distraction; once I loved
Torn ocean's roar, but thy soft murmuring
Sounds sweet as if a Sister's voice reproved,
That I with stern delights should e'er have been so
    moved.

86

It is the hush of night, and all between
Thy margin and the mountains, dusk, yet clear,
Mellow'd and mingling, yet distinctly seen,
Save darken'd Jura,[2] whose capt heights appear
Precipitously steep; and drawing near,
There breathes a living fragrance from the shore,
Of flowers yet fresh with childhood; on the ear
Drops the light drip of the suspended oar,
Or chirps the grasshopper one good-night carol more;

87

He is an evening reveller, who makes
His life an infancy, and sings his fill;
At intervals, some bird from out the brakes°   thickets

---

[1] *For then ... cave of yore* Byron compares Rousseau to the Pythia, the oracle of Apollo at Delphi.

[2] *Jura* Mountain range northwest of Lake Geneva.

Starts into voice a moment, then is still.
There seems a floating whisper on the hill,
820 But that is fancy, for the starlight dews
All silently their tears of love instil,
Weeping themselves away, till they infuse
Deep into nature's breast the spirit of her hues.

88

Ye stars! which are the poetry of heaven!
825 If in your bright leaves we would read the fate
Of men and empires,—'tis to be forgiven,
That in our aspirations to be great,
Our destinies o'erleap their mortal state,
And claim a kindred with you; for ye are
830 A beauty and a mystery, and create
In us such love and reverence from afar,
That fortune, fame, power, life, have named
     themselves a star.

89

All heaven and earth are still—though not in sleep,
But breathless, as we grow when feeling most;
835 And silent, as we stand in thoughts too deep:—
All heaven and earth are still: From the high host
Of stars, to the lull'd lake and mountain-coast,
All is concenter'd in a life intense,
Where not a beam, nor air, nor leaf is lost,
840 But hath a part of being, and a sense
Of that which is of all Creator and defence.

90

Then stirs the feeling infinite, so felt
In solitude, where we are *least* alone;
A truth, which through our being then doth melt,
845 And purifies from self: it is a tone,
The soul and source of music, which makes known
Eternal harmony, and sheds a charm
Like to the fabled Cytherea's zone,[1]
Binding all things with beauty;—'twould disarm
850 The spectre Death, had he substantial power to harm.

---

[1] *Cytherea's zone* The belt (zone, or girdle) of Venus (Cytherea) made its wearer irresistible.

91

Not vainly did the early Persian make
His altar the high places, and the peak
Of earth-o'ergazing mountains, and thus take[2]
A fit and unwall'd temple, there to seek
855 The Spirit, in whose honour shrines are weak,
Uprear'd of human hands. Come, and compare
Columns and idol-dwellings, Goth or Greek,
With Nature's realms of worship, earth and air,
Nor fix on fond abodes to circumscribe thy pray'r!

---

[2] [Byron's note] It is to be recollected, that the most beautiful and impressive doctrines of the divine Founder of Christianity were delivered, not in the *Temple*, but on the *Mount* (Matthew 6–7).

To waive the question of devotion, and turn to human eloquence,—the most effectual and splendid specimens were not pronounced within walls. Demosthenes addressed the public and popular assemblies. Cicero spoke in the forum. That this added to their effect on the mind of both orator and hearers, may be conceived from the difference between what we read of the emotions then and there produced, and those we ourselves experience in the perusal in the closet. It is one thing to read the *Iliad* at Sigaeum and on the tumuli, or by the springs with mount Ida above, and the plain and rivers and Archipelago around you: and another to trim your taper over it in a snug library—*this* I know.

Were the early and rapid progress of what is called Methodism to be attributed to any cause beyond the enthusiasm excited by its vehement faith and doctrines (the truth or error of which I presume neither to canvass nor to question) I should venture to ascribe it to the practice of preaching in the *fields*, and the unstudied and extemporaneous effusions of its teachers.

The Mussulmans [Muslims], whose erroneous devotion (at least in the lower orders) is most sincere, and therefore impressive, are accustomed to repeat their prescribed orisons and prayers where-ever they may be at the stated hours—of course frequently in the open air, kneeling upon a light mat (which they carry for the purpose of a bed or cushion as required); the ceremony lasts some minutes, during which they are totally absorbed, and only living in their supplication; nothing can disturb them. On me the simple and entire sincerity of these men, and the spirit which appeared to be within and upon them, made a far greater impression than any general rite which was ever performed in places of worship, of which I have seen those of almost every persuasion under the sun: including most of our own sectaries, and the Greek, the Catholic, the Armenian, the Lutheran, the Jewish, and the Mahometan [Muslim]. Many of the negroes, of whom there are numbers in the Turkish empire, are idolaters, and have free exercise of their belief and its rites: some of these I had a distant view of at Patras; and from what I could make out of them, they appeared to be of a truly Pagan description, and not very agreeable to a spectator.

92

The sky is changed!—and such a change! Oh
    night,[1]
And storm, and darkness, ye are wondrous strong,
Yet lovely in your strength, as is the light
Of a dark eye in woman! Far along,
From peak to peak, the rattling crags among
Leaps the live thunder! Not from one lone cloud,
But every mountain now hath found a tongue,
And Jura answers, through her misty shroud,
Back to the joyous Alps, who call to her aloud!

93

And this is in the night:—Most glorious night!
Thou wert not sent for slumber! let me be
A sharer in thy fierce and far delight,—
A portion of the tempest and of thee!
How the lit lake shines, a phosphoric sea,
And the big rain comes dancing to the earth!
And now again 'tis black,—and now, the glee
Of the loud hills shakes with its mountain-mirth,
As if they did rejoice o'er a young earth-quake's birth.

94

Now, where the swift Rhone cleaves his way
    between
Heights which appear as lovers who have parted
In hate, whose mining depths so intervene,
That they can meet no more, though broken-
    hearted;
Though in their souls, which thus each other
    thwarted,
Love was the very root of the fond rage
Which blighted their life's bloom, and then
    departed:—
Itself expired, but leaving them an age
Of years all winters,—war within themselves to wage.

95

Now, where the quick Rhone thus hath cleft his
    way,
The mightiest of the storms hath ta'en his stand:
For here, not one, but many, make their play,
And fling their thunder-bolts from hand to hand,
Flashing and cast around; of all the band,
The brightest through these parted hills hath fork'd
His lightnings,—as if he did understand,
That in such gaps as desolation work'd,
There the hot shaft should blast whatever therein lurk'd.

96

Sky, mountains, river, winds, lake, lightnings! ye!
With night, and clouds, and thunder, and a soul
To make these felt and feeling, well may be
Things that have made me watchful; the far roll
Of your departing voices, is the knoll
Of what in me is sleepless,—if I rest.
But where of ye, O tempests! is the goal?
Are ye like those within the human breast?
Or do ye find, at length, like eagles, some high nest?

97

Could I embody and unbosom now
That which is most within me,—could I wreak
My thoughts upon expression, and thus throw
Soul, heart, mind, passions, feelings, strong or weak,
All that I would have sought, and all I seek,
Bear, know, feel, and yet breathe—into *one* word,
And that one word were Lightning, I would speak;
But as it is, I live and die unheard,
With a most voiceless thought, sheathing it as a sword.

98

The morn is up again, the dewy morn,
With breath all incense, and with cheek all bloom,
Laughing the clouds away with playful scorn,
And living as if earth contain'd no tomb,—
And glowing into day: we may resume
The march of our existence: and thus I,
Still on thy shores, fair Leman! may find room
And food for meditation, nor pass by
Much, that may give us pause, if ponder'd fittingly.

---

[1] [Byron's note] The thunder-storms to which these lines refer occurred on the 13th of June, 1816, at midnight. I have seen among the Acroceraunian mountains of Chimari several more terrible, but none more beautiful.

99

Clarens![1] sweet Clarens, birthplace of deep Love!
Thine air is the young breath of passionate
    thought;
Thy trees take root in Love; the snows above,   925
The very Glaciers have his colours caught,
And sun-set into rose-hues sees them wrought[2]

By rays which sleep there lovingly: the rocks,
The permanent crags, tell here of Love, who
    sought
In them a refuge from the worldly shocks,   930
Which stir and sting the soul with hope that woos,
    then mocks.

100

Clarens! by heavenly feet thy paths are trod,—
Undying Love's, who here ascends a throne
To which the steps are mountains; where the god
Is a pervading life and light,—so shown   935
Not on those summits solely, nor alone
In the still cave and forest: o'er the flower
His eye is sparkling, and his breath hath blown,
His soft and summer breath, whose tender power
Passes the strength of storms in their most desolate   940
    hour.

101

All things are here of *him*;[3] from the black pines,
Which are his shade on high, and the loud roar
Of torrents, where he listeneth, to the vines
Which slope his green path downward to the
    shore,
Where the bow'd waters meet him, and adore,   945
Kissing his feet with murmurs; and the wood,
The covert of old trees, with trunks all hoar,
But light leaves, young as joy, stands where it
    stood,
Offering to him, and his, a populous solitude.

---

[1] *Clarens* Town on Lake Geneva, site of the main action of Rousseau's *Julie*. Byron and Percy Bysshe Shelley visited it on 26 June 1816.

[2] [Byron's note] Rousseau's *Heloise*, Letter 17, part 4, note. "Ces montagnes sont si hautes qu'une demi-heure après le soleil couché, leurs sommets sont encore éclairés de ses rayons; dont le rouge forme sur ces cimes blanches *une belle couleur de rose* qu'on aperçoit de fort loin." [These mountains are so high, that a half-hour after the sun sets, their summits are still lit up by its rays, whose redness creates on these white peaks a beautiful pink color, which can be seen from quite far away.] This applies more particularly to the heights over Meillerie. "J'allai à Vevay loger à la Clef; et pendant deux jours que j'y restai sans voir personne, je pris pour cette ville un amour qui m'a suivi dans tous mes voyages, et qui m'y a fait établir enfin les héros de mon roman. Je dirois volontiers à ceux qui ont du goût et qui sont sensibles: allez à Vevay—visitez le pays, examinez les sites, promenez-vous sur le lac, et dites si la Nature n'a pas fait ce beau pays pour une Julie, pour une Claire, et pour un St. Preux; mais ne les y cherchez pas."—*Les Confessions*, livre iv. page 306. Lyons ed. 1796. [1.4: I went to Vévay to stay at the Key, and during the two days that I stayed there without seeing anyone, I acquired for this town a love that has accompanied me in all my travels, and that made me place the heroes of my novel there. I would willingly say to anyone with taste and sensibility: Go to Vévay, visit the countryside, look at the locales, walk by the lake, and say whether Nature hasn't made this beautiful country for a Julie, for a Claire, and for a St. Preux, but don't look for them there.]

In July [actually 23–27 June], 1816, I made a voyage around the Lake of Geneva; and, as far as my own observations have led me in a not uninterested nor inattentive survey of all the scenes most celebrated by Rousseau in his "Heloise," I can safely say, that in this there is no exaggeration. It would be difficult to see Clarens (with the scenes around it, Vevay, Chillon, Bôveret, St. Gingo, Meillerie, Evian, and the entrances of the Rhone), without being forcibly struck with its peculiar adaptation to the persons and events with which it has been peopled. But this is not all; the feeling with which all around Clarens, and the opposite rocks of Meillerie is invested, is of a still higher and more comprehensive order than the mere sympathy with individual passion; it is a sense of the existence of love in its most extended and sublime capacity, and of our own participation of its good and of its glory: it is the great principle of the universe, which is there more condensed, but not less manifested; and of which, though knowing ourselves a part, we lose our individuality, and mingle in the beauty of the whole.

If Rousseau had never written, nor lived, the same associations would not less have belonged to such scenes. He has added to the interest of his works by their adoption; he has shewn his sense of their beauty by the selection; but they have done that for him which no human being could do for them.

I had the fortune (good or evil as it might be) to sail from Meillerie (where we landed for some time), to St. Gingo during a lake storm, which added to the magnificence of all around, although occasionally accompanied by danger to the boat, which was small and overloaded. By a coincidence which I could not regret, it was over this very part of the lake that Rousseau has driven the boat of St. Preux and Madame Wolmar to Meillerie for shelter during a tempest [*Julie* 4.7].

[3] *him* I.e., Love.

102

50 A populous solitude of bees and birds,
And fairy-form'd and many-colour'd things,
Who worship him with notes more sweet than
      words,
And innocently open their glad wings,
Fearless and full of life: the gush of springs,
55 And fall of lofty fountains, and the bend
Of stirring branches, and the bud which brings
The swiftest thought of beauty, here extend,
Mingling, and made by Love, unto one mighty end.

103

He who hath loved not, here would learn that
      lore,
60 And make his heart a spirit; he who knows
That tender mystery, will love the more;
For this is Love's recess, where vain men's woes,
And the world's waste, have driven him far from
      those,
For 'tis his nature to advance or die;
65 He stands not still, but or decays, or grows
Into a boundless blessing, which may vie
With the immortal lights, in its eternity!

104

'Twas not for fiction chose Rousseau this spot,
Peopling it with affections; but he found
70 It was the scene which Passion must allot
To the Mind's purified beings; 'twas the ground
Where early Love his Psyche's zone unbound,[1]
And hallow'd it with loveliness: 'tis lone,
And wonderful, and deep, and hath a sound,
75 And sense, and sight of sweetness; here the Rhone
Hath spread himself a couch, the Alps have rear'd a
      throne.

105

Lausanne! and Ferney! ye have been the abodes
Of names which unto you bequeath'd a name;[2]
Mortals, who sought and found, by dangerous
      roads,
980 A path to perpetuity of fame:
They were gigantic minds, and their steep aim
Was, Titan-like, on daring doubts to pile
Thoughts which should call down thunder, and
      the flame
Of Heaven again assail'd,[3] if Heaven the while
985 On man and man's research could deign do more
      than smile.

106

The one was fire and fickleness, a child
Most mutable in wishes, but in mind
A wit as various,—gay, grave, sage, or wild,—
Historian, bard, philosopher, combined;
990 He multiplied himself among mankind,
The Proteus[4] of their talents: But his own
Breathed most in ridicule,—which, as the wind,
Blew where it listed, laying all things prone,—
Now to o'erthrow a fool, and now to shake a throne.

107

995 The other, deep and slow, exhausting thought,
And hiving wisdom with each studious year,
In meditation dwelt, with learning wrought,
And shaped his weapon with an edge severe,
Sapping a solemn creed with solemn sneer;
1000 The lord of irony,—that master-spell,
Which stung his foes to wrath, which grew from
      fear,
And doom'd him to the zealot's ready Hell,
Which answers to all doubts so eloquently well.

---

[2] [Byron's note] Voltaire and Gibbon. [Edward Gibbon (1737–94), author of *The Decline and Fall of the Roman Empire* (1788), lived in Lausanne; Voltaire (1694–1778), author of *Candide*, lived in Ferney.]

[3] *They were gigantic … assail'd* In classical mythology, the Titans piled Mount Pelion on top of Mt. Ossa in the attempt to reach the top of Mount Olympus and overthrow the gods.

[4] *Proteus* Sea god, known for his ability to alter his shape.

---

[1] *Where … unbound* Allusion to the myth of Cupid and Psyche (Love and the Soul) in Apuleius, *The Golden Ass*.

108

Yet, peace be with their ashes,—for by them,
1005   If merited, the penalty is paid;
It is not ours to judge,—far less condemn;
The hour must come when such things shall be made
Known unto all, or hope and dread allay'd
By slumber, on one pillow, in the dust,
1010   Which, thus much we are sure, must lie decay'd;
And when it shall revive, as is our trust,
'Twill be to be forgiven, or suffer what is just.

109

But let me quit man's works, again to read
His Maker's, spread around me, and suspend
1015   This page, which from my reveries I feed,
Until it seems prolonging without end.
The clouds above me to the white Alps tend,
And I must pierce them, and survey whate'er
May be permitted, as my steps I bend
1020   To their most great and growing region, where
The earth to her embrace compels the powers of air.

110

Italia! too, Italia! looking on thee,
Full flashes on the soul the light of ages,
Since the fierce Carthaginian[1] almost won thee,
1025   To the last halo of the chiefs and sages
Who glorify thy consecrated pages;
Thou wert the throne and grave of empires; still,
The fount at which the panting mind assuages
Her thirst of knowledge, quaffing there her fill,
1030   Flows from the eternal source of Rome's imperial hill.

111

Thus far have I proceeded in a theme
Renew'd with no kind auspices:—to feel
We are not what we have been, and to deem
We are not what we should be, and to steel
1035   The heart against itself; and to conceal,
With a proud caution, love, or hate, or aught,—
Passion or feeling, purpose, grief or zeal,—

Which is the tyrant spirit of our thought,
Is a stern task of soul:—No matter,—it is taught.

112

1040   And for these words, thus woven into song,
It may be that they are a harmless wile,—
The colouring of the scenes which fleet along,
Which I would seize, in passing, to beguile
My breast, or that of others, for a while.
1045   Fame is the thirst of youth, but I am not
So young as to regard men's frown or smile,
As loss or guerdon[2] of a glorious lot;
I stood and stand alone,—remember'd or forgot.

113

I have not loved the world, nor the world me;
1050   I have not flatter'd its rank breath, nor bow'd
To its idolatries a patient knee,
Nor coin'd my cheek to smiles, nor cried aloud
In worship of an echo; in the crowd
They could not deem me one of such; I stood
1055   Among them, but not of them; in a shroud
Of thoughts which were not their thoughts, and
    still could,
Had I not filed my mind, which thus itself subdued.[3]

114

I have not loved the world, nor the world me,—
But let us part fair foes; I do believe,
1060   Though I have found them not, that there may be
Words which are things, hopes which will not
    deceive,
And virtues which are merciful, nor weave
Snares for the failing; I would also deem
O'er others' griefs that some sincerely grieve;[4]
1065   That two, or one, are almost what they seem,—
That goodness is no name, and happiness no dream.

---

2 *guerdon* Reward.

3 [Byron's note]   —"If it be thus,
For Banquo's issue have I *filed* my mind." *Macbeth.* [Cf. *Macbeth*
3.1.64–65.]

4 [Byron's note] It is said by Rochefoucault that "there is *always*
something in the misfortunes of men's best friends not displeasing to
them." [François, duc de la Rochefoucauld (1613–80), *Maximes.*]

---

1 *Carthaginian* Hannibal (247–183 BCE), a Carthaginian general,
crossed the Alps to invade Italy in 218 BCE, during the Second Punic
War.

115

My daughter! with thy name this song begun;
My daughter! with thy name thus much shall end;
I see thee not, I hear thee not, but none
Can be so wrapt in thee; thou art the friend
To whom the shadows of far years extend:
Albeit my brow thou never shouldst behold,
My voice shall with thy future visions blend,
And reach into thy heart, when mine is cold,
A token and a tone, even from thy father's mould.

116

To aid thy mind's development, to watch
Thy dawn of little joys, to sit and see
Almost thy very growth, to view thee catch
Knowledge of objects,—wonders yet to thee!
To hold thee lightly on a gentle knee,
And print on thy soft cheek a parent's kiss, –
This, it should seem, was not reserved for me;
Yet this was in my nature: as it is,
I know not what is there, yet something like to this.

117

Yet though dull Hate as duty should be taught,
I know that thou wilt love me; though my name
Should be shut from thee, as a spell still fraught
With desolation, and a broken claim:
Though the grave closed between us,—'twere the same,
I know that thou wilt love me; though to drain
My blood from out thy being were an aim,
And an attainment,—all would be in vain,—
Still thou wouldst love me, still that more than life retain.

118

The child of love, though born in bitterness,
And nurtured in convulsion. Of thy sire
These were the elements, and thine no less.
As yet such are around thee, but thy fire
Shall be more temper'd, and thy hope far higher.
Sweet be thy cradled slumbers! O'er the sea
And from the mountains where I now respire,
Fain would I waft such blessing upon thee,
As, with a sigh, I deem thou might'st have been to me.

from *Canto the Fourth*

In this final canto of *Childe Harold*, written in 1817–18, Byron at last abandoned any attempt to separate Harold from himself, declaring in the opening dedication that he was "weary of drawing a line which every one seemed determined not to perceive." The canto sees Byron traveling through Italy, drawing parallels between his experiences and Europe's civilization. The stanzas excerpted here are Byron's hymn to Venice, where he lived during the winter of 1816 and spring of 1817.

1

I stood in Venice, on the Bridge of Sighs;
A palace and a prison on each hand:[1]
    I saw from out the wave her structures rise
As from the stroke of the enchanter's wand:
A thousand years their cloudy wings expand
Around me, and a dying Glory smiles
O'er the far times, when many a subject land
Look'd to the winged Lion's marble piles,[2]
Where Venice sate in state, thron'd on her hundred isles!

2

She looks a sea Cybele,[3] fresh from ocean,
Rising with her tiara of proud towers
At airy distance, with majestic motion,
A ruler of the waters and their powers:
And such she was; her daughters had their dowers
From spoils of nations, and the exhaustless East
Pour'd in her lap all gems in sparkling showers.
In purple was she rob'd, and of her feast
Monarchs partook, and deem'd their dignity increas'd.

---

1 *A palace ... hand* Venice's Bridge of Sighs spans the water between the Doge's Palace and the state prison (the prison of San Marco). Traditionally, those who had been found guilty by the Doge of the crimes of which they were accused were taken immediately from his palace to the prison.

2 *the winged Lion's marble piles* St. Mark's Cathedral. The lion was the emblem of St. Mark, the patron saint of Venice.

3 *Cybele* Nature goddess, sometimes represented as wearing a crown of towers ("tiara").

3

In Venice Tasso's[1] echoes are no more,
20 And silent rows the songless gondolier;
Her palaces are crumbling to the shore,
And music meets not always now the ear:
Those days are gone—but Beauty still is here.
States fall, arts fade—but Nature doth not die,
25 Nor yet forget how Venice once was dear,
The pleasant place of all festivity,
The revel of the earth, the masque of Italy![2]

4

But unto us she hath a spell beyond
Her name in story, and her long array
30 Of mighty shadows, whose dim forms despond
Above the dogeless city's vanish'd sway;[3]
Ours is a trophy which will not decay
With the Rialto; Shylock and the Moor,
And Pierre,[4] cannot be swept or worn away—
35 The keystones of the arch! though all were o'er,
For us repeopl'd were the solitary shore.

5

The beings of the mind are not of clay;
Essentially immortal, they create
And multiply in us a brighter ray
40 And more belov'd existence: that which Fate
Prohibits to dull life, in this our state
Of mortal bondage, by these spirits supplied,
First exiles, then replaces what we hate;
Watering the heart whose early flowers have died,
45 And with a fresher growth replenishing the void.

---

[1] *Tasso* Torquato Tasso (1544–95), an important poet of the Italian Renaissance.

[2] *masque of Italy* Masques were lavish Renaissance entertainments, short plays heavy with symbolic meaning, involving elaborate costumes and staging and including songs and dances. Byron here also hints at Venice's abandonment to luxury and pleasure during Carnival time.

[3] *dogeless city's ... sway* The last Doge (Duke) had been deposed by Napoleon in 1797.

[4] *With the Rialto ... Pierre* The Rialto, the business district of Venice, was a setting in Shakespeare's *The Merchant of Venice* and *Othello* (which feature the characters Shylock and Othello the "Moor," respectively), as well as in Thomas Otway's *Venice Preserved*, the hero of which is named Pierre.

6

Such is the refuge of our youth and age,
The first from Hope, the last from Vacancy;
And this worn feeling peoples many a page,
And, maybe, that which grows beneath mine eye:
50 Yet there are things whose strong reality
Outshines our fairy-land; in shape and hues
More beautiful than our fantastic sky,
And the strange constellations which the Muse
O'er her wild universe is skilful to diffuse:

7

55 I saw or dream'd of such—but let them go;
They came like truth—and disappear'd like
      dreams;
And whatsoe'er they were—are now but so:
I could replace them if I would; still teems
My mind with many a form which aptly seems
60 Such as I sought for, and at moments found;
Let these too go—for waking Reason deems
Such overweening fantasies unsound,
And other voices speak, and other sights surround.

8

I've taught me other tongues, and in strange eyes
65 Have made me not a stranger; to the mind
Which is itself, no changes bring surprise;
Nor is it harsh to make, nor hard to find
A country with—ay, or without mankind;
Yet was I born where men are proud to be—
70 Not without cause; and should I leave behind
The inviolate island of the sage and free,
And seek me out a home by a remoter sea,

9

Perhaps I lov'd it well: and should I lay
My ashes in a soil which is not mine,
75 My spirit shall resume it—if we may
Unbodied choose a sanctuary. I twine
My hopes of being remember'd in my line
With my land's language: if too fond and far
These aspirations in their scope incline,
80 If my fame should be, as my fortunes are,
Of hasty growth and blight, and dull Oblivion bar

10

My name from out the temple where the dead
Are honour'd by the nations[1]—let it be—
And light the laurels on a loftier head!
And be the Spartan's epitaph on me—
"Sparta hath many a worthier son than he."[2]
Meantime I seek no sympathies, nor need;
The thorns which I have reap'd are of the tree
I planted: they have torn me, and I bleed:
I should have known what fruit would spring from
    such a seed.

11

The spouseless Adriatic mourns her lord;
And annual marriage now no more renew'd,
The Bucentaur lies rotting unrestor'd,
Neglected garment of her widowhood![3]
St. Mark yet sees his lion where he stood
Stand, but in mockery of his wither'd power,
Over the proud Place where an Emperor sued,
And monarchs gaz'd and envied in the hour
When Venice was a queen with an unequall'd dower.

12

The Suabian sued, and now the Austrian reigns—
An Emperor tramples where an Emperor knelt;[4]
Kingdoms are shrunk to provinces, and chains
Clank over sceptred cities, nations melt
From power's high pinnacle, when they have felt
The sunshine for a while, and downward go
Like lauwine° loosen'd from the   avalanche
    mountain's belt:

Oh, for one hour of blind old Dandolo,
Th' octogenarian chief, Byzantium's conquering foe![5]

13

Before St. Mark still glow his steeds of brass,
Their gilded collars glittering in the sun;
But is not Doria's menace come to pass?[6]
Are they not *bridled*?—Venice, lost and won,
Her thirteen hundred years of freedom done,
Sinks, like a sea-weed, into whence she rose!
Better be whelm'd beneath the waves, and shun,
Even in destruction's depth, her foreign foes,
From whom submission wrings an infamous repose.

14

In youth she was all glory, a new Tyre,[7]
Her very by-word sprung from victory,
The "Planter of the Lion,"[8] which through fire
And blood she bore o'er subject earth and sea;
Though making many slaves, herself still free,
And Europe's bulwark 'gainst the Ottomite;
Witness Troy's rival, Candia![9] Vouch it, ye
Immortal waves that saw Lepanto's fight![10]
For ye are names no time nor tyranny can blight.

---

[1] *My name ... nations* The Temple of Fame.

[2] *Sparta ... than he* In Plutarch's *Moralia*, the mother of a slain Spartan made this response to those who praised her son.

[3] *Neglected ... widowhood* Each Ascension Day, the Doge would throw a ring into the Adriatic from the state barge, the Bucentaur, symbolizing the marriage of the city to sea.

[4] *The Suabian ... knelt* Frederic Barbaross, a Suabian, submitted to the Pope in St. Mark's Plaza after losing the Battle of Legnano in 1176. Francis I of Austria, in contrast, ruled Venice from 1797–1805, and again after 1814.

[5] *Oh ... conquering foe* Enrico Dandolo became Doge of Venice in 1193. He was, according to legend, 85 years old and completely blind. He led at least two expeditions against the Byzantine Empire, and harbored a lasting hatred of the Byzantines.

[6] *Doria's menace come to pass* During the War of Chioggia between Venice and Genoa (1378–81), Luciano Doria, a Genoese admiral, defeated the Venetians at Pola and blockaded Venice. A battle followed, in which Doria was killed.

[7] *Tyre* Island city in ancient Phoenicia, famous in its time for its splendor and its maritime trade.

[8] *the Lion* I.e., lion of St. Mark.

[9] *Candia* The capital of Crete, which was under Venetian control until 1669, when it fell to the Turks.

[10] *Lepanto's fight* The Battle of Lepanto (1571) occurred in the Gulf of Lepanto (now the Gulf of Corinth) off the coast of Greece. The forces of the Ottoman Empire were defeated by those of the Holy League (an alliance including Genoa, Spain, and Venice, among others)—an outcome credited with preventing Ottoman expansion into the northwestern part of the Mediterranean coast.

15

Statues of glass—all shiver'd—the long file
Of her dead Doges are declin'd to dust;
But where they dwelt, the vast and sumptuous pile
130   Bespeaks the pageant of their splendid trust;
Their sceptre broken, and their sword in rust,
Have yielded to the stranger: empty halls,
Thin streets, and foreign aspects, such as must
Too oft remind her who and what enthralls,
135 Have flung a desolate cloud o'er Venice' lovely walls.

16

When Athens' armies fell at Syracuse,
And fetter'd thousands bore the yoke of war,
Redemption rose up in the Attic Muse,
Her voice their only ransom from afar:
140   See! as they chant the tragic hymn, the car
Of the o'ermaster'd victor stops, the reins
Fall from his hands—his idle scimitar
Starts from its belt—he rends his captive's chains,
And bids him thank the bard for freedom and his strains.

17

145   Thus, Venice! if no stronger claim were thine,
Were all thy proud historic deeds forgot,
Thy choral memory of the Bard divine,[1]
Thy love of Tasso, should have cut the knot
Which ties thee to thy tyrants; and thy lot
150   Is shameful to the nations—most of all,
Albion,[2] to thee: the Ocean queen should not
Abandon Ocean's children; in the fall
Of Venice think of thine, despite thy watery wall.

18

I loved her from my boyhood; she to me
155   Was as a fairy city of the heart,
Rising like water-columns from the sea,
Of joy the sojourn, and of wealth the mart;
And Otway, Radcliffe, Schiller, Shakespeare's art,[3]

Had stamp'd her image in me, and even so,
160   Although I found her thus, we did not part;
Perchance even dearer in her day of woe,
Than when she was a boast, a marvel, and a show.
—CANTO THE THIRD 1816, CANTO THE FOURTH 1818

Darkness[4]

I had a dream, which was not all a dream.
The bright sun was extinguish'd, and the stars
Did wander darkling in the eternal space,
Rayless, and pathless, and the icy earth
5 Swung blind and blackening in the moonless air;[5]
Morn came, and went—and came, and brought no day,
And men forgot their passions in the dread
Of this their desolation; and all hearts
Were chill'd into a selfish prayer for light:
10 And they did live by watchfires—and the thrones,
The palaces of crowned kings—the huts,
The habitations of all things which dwell,
Were burnt for beacons; cities were consumed,
And men were gathered round their blazing homes
15 To look once more into each other's face;
Happy were those who dwelt within the eye
Of the volcanos, and their mountain-torch:
A fearful hope was all the world contain'd;
Forests were set on fire—but hour by hour
20 They fell and faded—and the crackling trunks
Extinguish'd with a crash—and all was black.
The brows of men by the despairing light
Wore an unearthly aspect, as by fits

---

[1] *Bard divine* I.e., Tasso.

[2] *Albion* England.

[3] *And Otway ... art* References, again, to Otway's *Venice Preserved* and *The Merchant of Venice* and *Othello*, as well as to Friedrich von Schiller (1759–1805), German dramatist and poet whose unfinished

novel *The Ghost-Seer* is set in Venice, and to *The Mysteries of Udolpho*, by the Gothic novelist Ann Radcliffe (1764–1823), which contains famous descriptions of the city.

[4] *Darkness* The dust thrown into the atmosphere in 1815 by Mount Tamboro, an Indonesian volcano, made the summer of 1816 the coldest and wettest on record. Influenced by the weather, and perhaps by recent warnings by an Italian astronomer that sunspots might lead to the extinction of the sun, Byron produced this prescient poem, which he labeled "a Fragment."

[5] *icy earth ... moonless air* Cf. Ezekiel 32.7–8; Joel 2.31; Revelation 6.12.

The flashes fell upon them; some lay down
25 And hid their eyes and wept; and some did rest
Their chins upon their clenched hands, and smiled;
And others hurried to and fro, and fed
Their funeral piles with fuel, and looked up
With mad disquietude on the dull sky,
30 The pall of a past world; and then again
With curses cast them down upon the dust,
And gnash'd their teeth and howl'd: the wild
    birds shriek'd,
And, terrified, did flutter on the ground,
And flap their useless wings; the wildest brutes
35 Came tame and tremulous; and vipers crawl'd
And twined themselves among the multitude,
Hissing, but stingless—they were slain for food:
And War, which for a moment was no more,
Did glut himself again;—a meal was bought
40 With blood, and each sate sullenly apart
Gorging himself in gloom: no love was left;
All earth was but one thought—and that was death,
Immediate and inglorious; and the pang
Of famine fed upon all entrails—men
45 Died, and their bones were tombless as their flesh;
The meagre by the meagre were devoured,
Even dogs assail'd their masters, all save one,
And he was faithful to a corse,° and kept   corpse
The birds and beasts and famish'd men at bay,
50 Till hunger clung them, or the dropping dead
Lured their lank jaws; himself sought out no food,
But with a piteous and perpetual moan
And a quick desolate cry, licking the hand
Which answered not with a caress—he died.
55 The crowd was famish'd by degrees; but two
Of an enormous city did survive,
And they were enemies; they met beside
The dying embers of an altar-place
Where had been heap'd a mass of holy things
60 For an unholy usage; they raked up,
And shivering scraped with their cold skeleton hands
The feeble ashes, and their feeble breath
Blew for a little life, and made a flame
Which was a mockery; then they lifted up
65 Their eyes as it grew lighter, and beheld

Each other's aspects—saw, and shriek'd, and died—
Even of their mutual hideousness they died,
Unknowing who he was upon whose brow
Famine had written Fiend. The world was void,
70 The populous and the powerful was a lump,
Seasonless, herbless, treeless, manless, lifeless—
A lump of death—a chaos of hard clay.
The rivers, lakes, and ocean all stood still,
And nothing stirred within their silent depths;
75 Ships sailorless lay rotting on the sea,
And their masts fell down piecemeal; as they dropp'd
They slept on the abyss without a surge—
The waves were dead; the tides were in their grave,
The moon their mistress had expired before;
80 The winds were withered in the stagnant air,
And the clouds perish'd; Darkness had no need
Of aid from them—She was the universe.
—1816

Prometheus[1]

I

Titan! to whose immortal eyes
The sufferings of mortality,
    Seen in their sad reality,
Were not as things that gods despise;
5 What was thy pity's recompense?
A silent suffering, and intense;
The rock, the vulture, and the chain,
All that the proud can feel of pain,
The agony they do not show,
10 The suffocating sense of woe,
    Which speaks but in its loneliness,
And then is jealous lest the sky

---

[1] *Prometheus* The Titan Prometheus stole fire from heaven and gave it to humanity. To punish him, Jupiter, King of the gods, had him chained to a rock in the Caucasus, where a vulture (in some versions, an eagle) tore at his liver. Each night Prometheus's liver grew afresh, to be torn out the next day. Prometheus's story is the subject of the *Prometheia*, a trio of plays attributed to the ancient Greek playwright Aeschylus. Only the first play, *Prometheus Bound*, survives; Byron's poem represents itself as a chorus from the lost second play, *Prometheus Unbound*.

Should have a listener, nor will sigh
    Until its voice is echoless.

2

15 Titan! to thee the strife was given
    Between the suffering and the will,
    Which torture where they cannot kill;
And the inexorable Heaven,
And the deaf tyranny of Fate,
20 The ruling principle of Hate,
Which for its pleasure doth create
The things it may annihilate,
Refused thee even the boon to die:
The wretched gift eternity
25 Was thine—and thou hast borne it well.
All that the Thunderer[1] wrung from thee
Was but the menace which flung back
On him the torments of thy rack;
The fate thou didst so well foresee
30 But would not to appease him tell;
And in thy Silence was his Sentence,
And in his Soul a vain repentance,
And evil dread so ill dissembled
That in his hand the lightnings trembled.

3

35 Thy Godlike crime was to be kind,
    To render with thy precepts less
    The sum of human wretchedness,
And strengthen Man with his own mind;
But baffled as thou wert from high,
40 Still in thy patient energy,
In the endurance, and repulse
    Of thine impenetrable Spirit,
Which Earth and Heaven could not convulse,
    A mighty lesson we inherit:
45 Thou art a symbol and a sign
    To Mortals of their fate and force;
Like thee, Man is in part divine,

A troubled stream from a pure source;
And Man in portions can foresee
50 His own funereal destiny;
His wretchedness, and his resistance,
And his sad unallied existence:
To which his Spirit may oppose
Itself—an equal to all woes,
55 And a firm will, and a deep sense,
Which even in torture can descry
    Its own concentered recompense,
Triumphant where it dares defy,
And making Death a Victory.
—1816

Stanzas to ————[2]

1

Though the day of my destiny's over,
    And the star of my fate hath declined,
Thy soft heart refused to discover
    The faults which so many could find;
5 Though thy soul with my grief was acquainted,
    It shrunk not to share it with me,
And the love which my spirit hath painted
    It never hath found but in *thee*.

2

Then when nature around me is smiling
10   The last smile which answers to mine,
I do not believe it beguiling,
    Because it reminds me of thine;
And when winds are at war with the ocean,
    As the breasts I believed in with me,
15 If their billows° excite an emotion   *waves*
    It is that they bear me from *thee*.

3

Though the rock of my last hope is shiver'd,°   *shattered*
    And its fragments are sunk in the wave,

---

[1] *Thunderer* Jupiter.

[2] ———— In later editions of the poem this long dash is replaced with "Augusta," the name of Byron's half-sister.

Though I feel that my soul is deliver'd
20   To pain—it shall not be its slave.
There is many a pang to pursue me:
    They may crush, but they shall not contemn—
They may torture, but shall not subdue me—
    'Tis of *thee* that I think—not of them.

4

25 Though human, thou didst not deceive me,
    Though woman, thou didst not forsake,
Though loved, thou forborest to grieve me,
    Though slander'd, thou never couldst shake,—
Though trusted, thou didst not disclaim me,
30   Though parted, it was not to fly,
Though watchful, 'twas not to defame me,
    Nor, mute, that the world might belie.

5

Yet I blame not the world, nor despise it,
    Nor the war of the many with one—
35 If my soul was not fitted to prize it
    'Twas folly not sooner to shun:
And if dearly that error hath cost me,
    And more than I once could foresee,
I have found that, whatever it lost me,
40   It could not deprive me of *thee*.

6

From the wreck of the past, which hath perish'd,
    Thus much I at least may recall,
It hath taught me that what I most cherish'd
    Deserved to be dearest of all:
45 In the desert a fountain is springing,
    In the wide waste there still is a tree,
And a bird in the solitude singing,
    Which speaks to my spirit of *thee*.
—1816

So, we'll go no more a roving[1]

1

So, we'll go no more a roving
    So late into the night,
Though the heart be still as loving,
    And the moon be still as bright.

2

5 For the sword outwears its sheath,
    And the soul wears out the breast,
And the heart must pause to breathe,
    And love itself have rest.

3

Though the night was made for loving,
10   And the day returns too soon,
Yet we'll go no more a roving
    By the light of the moon.
—1817

When a man hath no freedom to fight for at home[2]

When a man hath no freedom to fight for at home,
    Let him combat for that of his neighbors;
Let him think of the glories of Greece and of Rome,
    And get knock'd on the head for his labours.

5 To do good to mankind is the chivalrous plan,
    And is always as nobly requited;
Then battle for freedom wherever you can,
    And, if not shot or hang'd, you'll get knighted.
—1820

---

[1] *So, we'll ... roving* Originally written as part of a letter from Byron to his friend Thomas Moore, 28 February 1817. Just before these lines Byron writes, "The Carnival ... knocked me up a little. But it is over—and it is now Lent, with all its abstinence and sacred music. The mumming closed with a masked ball ... and, though I did not dissipate much upon the whole, yet I find 'the sword wearing out the scabbard,' though I have but just turned the corner of twenty-nine."

[2] *When a man ... home* Byron first sent these lines in a letter to his friend Thomas Moore on 5 November 1820. They are based on Byron's activities with the Italian freedom-fighters, the Carbonari, and their abortive attempt to stage an uprising.

January 22nd 1824.
Missolonghi
On this day I complete my thirty sixth year[1]

1

'Tis time this heart should be unmoved
    Since others it hath ceased to move,
Yet though I cannot be beloved
        Still let me love.

2

5   My days are in the yellow leaf[2]
    The flowers and fruits of love are gone—
The worm—the canker, and the grief
        Are mine alone.

3

The fire that on my bosom preys
10   Is lone as some Volcanic Isle,
No torch is kindled at its blaze
        A funeral pile!

4

The hope, the fear, the jealous care
    The exalted portion of the pain
15 And power of Love I cannot share
        But wear the chain.

5

But 'tis not *thus*—and 'tis not *here*
    Such thoughts should shake my soul, nor *now*
Where Glory decks the hero's bier
20   Or binds his brow.

6

The Sword—the Banner—and the Field
    Glory and Greece around us see!
The Spartan borne upon his shield[3]
        Was not more free!

7

25 Awake! (not Greece—She *is* awake!)
    Awake my spirit—think through *whom*
Thy life-blood tracks its parent lake
        And then strike home!

8

Tread those reviving passions down
30   Unworthy Manhood;—unto thee
Indifferent should the smile or frown
        Of Beauty be.

9

If thou regret'st thy youth, why *live*?
    The land of honourable Death
35 Is here—up to the Field! and give
        Away thy Breath.

10

Seek out—less often sought than found,
    A Soldier's Grave—for thee the best,
Then look around and choose thy ground
40   And take thy Rest.
—1824

---

1 *On this ... year* This poem was until recently most commonly known by its subtitle, but the date and place are the correct title. Byron wrote it on his 36th birthday, in Greece. A companion who was with him at the time says, "January 22.—Lord Byron came from his bedroom into the apartment ... where some friends were assembled, and said, with a smile, 'You were complaining, the other day, that I never write any poetry now:—this is my birthday, and I have just finished something which, I think, is better than what I usually write.'" The poem is informed by Byron's relationship with two people, his young Greek companion of the time, Loukas Chalandritsanos, and a Turkish girl, Hataje, whom he had taken into his care. Byron's feelings for Chalandritsanos are commonly understood to be the stronger influence of the two.

2 *My days ... leaf* See Shakespeare's *Macbeth* 5.3.21–22.

3 [Byron's note] The slain were borne on their shields—witness the Spartan mother's speech to her son, delivered with his buckler—"Either *with* this or *on* this."

Epistle to Augusta[1]

1

My Sister—my sweet Sister—if a name
   Dearer and purer were—it should be thine.
Mountains and seas divide us—but I claim
   No tears, but tenderness to answer mine:
5 Go where I will, to me thou art the same—
   A loved regret which I would not resign—
There yet are two things in my destiny
A world to roam through—and a home with thee.

2

The first were nothing—had I still the last
10 It were the haven of my happiness—
But other claims and other ties thou hast—
   And mine is not the wish to make them less.
A strange doom is thy father's son's and past
   Recalling—as it lies beyond redress—
15 Reversed for him our grandsire's fate of yore
He had no rest at sea—nor I on shore.[2]

3

If my inheritance of storms hath been
   In other elements—and on the rocks
Of perils overlooked or unforeseen
20 I have sustained my share of worldly shocks
The fault was mine—nor do I seek to screen
   My errors with defensive paradox—
I have been cunning in mine overthrow
The careful pilot of my proper woe.

4

25 Mine were my faults—and mine be their reward—
   My whole life was a contest—since the day
That gave me being gave me that which marred
   The gift—a fate, or will that walked astray—
And I at times have found the struggle hard
30 And thought of shaking off my bonds of clay—

But now I fain would for a time survive
If but to see what next can well arrive.

5

Kingdoms and empires in my little day
   I have outlived, and yet I am not old—
35 And when I look on this, the petty spray
   Of my own years of trouble, which have rolled
Like a wild bay of breakers, melts away:—
   Something—I know not what—does still uphold
A spirit of slight patience;—not in vain,
40 Even for its own sake—do we purchase pain.

6

Perhaps—the workings of defiance stir
   Within me, or perhaps a cold despair—
Brought on when ills habitually recur,—
   Perhaps a kinder clime—or purer air—
45 For even to this may change of soul refer—
   And with light armour we may learn to bear—
Have taught me a strange quiet which was not
The chief companion of a calmer lot.

7

I feel almost at times as I have felt
50 In happy childhood—trees, and flowers, and brooks
Which do remember me of where I dwelt
   Ere my young mind was sacrificed to books—
Come as of yore upon me—and can melt
   My heart with recognition of their looks—
55 And even at moments I could think I see
Some living thing to love—but none like thee.

8

Here are the Alpine landscapes—which create
   A fund for contemplation;—to admire
Is a brief feeling of a trivial date—
60 But something worthier do such scenes inspire:
Here to be lonely is not desolate—
   For much I view which I could most desire—
And, above all a lake I can behold—
Lovelier—not dearer than our own of old.

---

[1] *Augusta* Byron's half-sister, Augusta Leigh (1783–1851).

[2] *He had no … on shore* Byron and Augusta's grandfather, Admiral John Byron, was renowned for never making a sea voyage without encountering a storm. He was known as "Foulweather Jack."

9

65 Oh that thou wert but with me!—but I grow
        The fool of my own wishes—and forget
    The solitude which I have vaunted so
        Has lost its praise in this but one regret—
    There may be others which I less may show—
70   I am not of the plaintive mood—and yet
    I feel an ebb in my philosophy
    And the tide rising in my altered eye.

10

    I did remind thee of our own dear lake
        By the old Hall which may be mine no more—
75 Leman's is fair—but think not I forsake
        The sweet remembrance of a dearer shore—
    Sad havoc Time must with my memory make
        Ere that or thou can fade these eyes before—
    Though like all things which I have loved—they are
80 Resigned° for ever—or divided far.   given up

11

    The world is all before me—I but ask
        Of Nature that with which she will comply—
    It is but in her Summer's sun to bask—
        To mingle with the quiet of her sky—
85 To see her gentle face without a mask
        And never gaze on it with apathy—
    She was my early friend—and now shall be
    My Sister—till I look again on thee.

12

    I can reduce all feelings but this one,
90   And that I would not—for at length I see
    Such scenes as those wherein my life begun
        The earliest—were the only paths for me.
    Had I but sooner learnt the crowd to shun
        I had been better than I now can be
95 The passions which have torn me would have slept—
    I had not suffered—and thou hadst not wept.

13

    With false Ambition what had I to do?
        Little with love, and least of all with fame!
    And yet they came unsought and with me grew,
100   And made me all which they can make—a Name.
    Yet this was not the end I did pursue—
        Surely I once beheld a nobler aim.
    But all is over—I am one the more
    To baffled millions which have gone before.

14

105 And for the future—this world's future may
        From me demand but little from my care;
    I have outlived myself by many a day,
        Having survived so many things that were—
    My years have been no slumber—but the prey
110   Of ceaseless vigils;—for I had the share
    Of life which might have filled a century
    Before its fourth in time had passed me by.

15

    And for the remnants which may be to come
        I am content—and for the past I feel
115 Not thankless—for within the crowded sum
        Of struggles—happiness at times would steal
    And for the present—I would not benumb
        My feelings farther—nor shall I conceal
    That with all this I still can look around
120 And worship Nature with a thought profound.

16

    For thee—my own sweet Sister—in thy heart
        I know myself secure—as thou in mine
    We were and are—I am—even as thou art—
        Beings who ne'er each other can resign
125 It is the same together or apart
        From Life's commencement to its slow decline—
    We are entwined—let death come slow or fast
    The tie which bound the first endures the last.
                —1830

Don Juan

Byron worked on *Don Juan* from 1818 until his death, publishing it piecemeal from 1819 to 1824. His immediate poetic inspiration for his satirical reworking of the *Don Juan* legend was *The Monks and the Giants* (1817), by his friend John Hookham Frere. In this, he said, he discovered the power of the *ottava rima* rhyme scheme (abababcc) that drives his own poem. His models for *Don Juan*'s rambling episodic format were the serio-comic romances of the fifteenth- and sixteenth-century Italian writers Pulci, Ariosto, and Berni. Byron, however, did more with these influences than anyone could have hoped or dreamed. The flexible structure allowed him to range widely, moving with ease from high-flown philosophical reflections to the most trivial minutiae, and back again—sometimes within the same stanza. In the guise of a garrulous raconteur, Byron was able to comment seriously on English and European politics, the hypocrisy of sexual mores, the falseness of conventional morals, and the often painful complexities of human emotions.

At the same time, *Don Juan* remains a comic goldmine. All forms of wit—satire, wordplay, parody, just plain silliness—confront the reader, and no cultural shibboleth escapes Byron's mockery. For this reason, the poem was met with outrage and horror upon its publication. Indeed, Byron's own mistress, Teresa Guiccioli, found it immoral, but although he stopped writing it at her request in 1821, he resumed again in 1822. Friends and critics alike lamented what they saw as Byron's lack of tact, his lack of taste, and his lack of decency. He was attacked for making his personal life public (the portrait of Juan's mother, Donna Inez, in the first canto was agreed to be a satirical picture of Lady Byron), and for writing a poem "not ... didactic of any thing but mischief." Byron himself famously insisted that he had written the poem only "to giggle and make giggle," and continued writing.

Byron's protagonist is a many-layered creation. The story of the great seducer was first told by Tirso de Molina (Gabriel Téllez) in *El Burlador de Sevilla y convidado di piedra* ("The Trickster of Seville and the Stone Guest," 1616?); it subsequently inspired such masterpieces as Molière's *Don Juan ou Le Festin de pierre* (1665), Thomas Shadwell's *The Libertine* (1676), and Mozart's *Don Giovanni* (1787). Apparently Byron first encountered the story in a pantomime (see Canto 1, line 7 below). But Byron's Don Juan (pronounced, in the English manner, Joo-an, with the stress on the first syllable), like his poem, is more than the sum of his sources. He is, first and foremost, a parody of the famous Don Juan, for he is a passive fellow, seduced and sweet-natured rather than seducing and ruthless. He is also a parodic version of the epic hero figure (including Byron's own most famous creation, Childe Harold), and by extension, of Byron himself; throughout the poem Byron uses Juan to play on the public notion of what it meant to be "Byron."

Don Juan incorporates three chronological levels: Byron wrote it from 1818 to 1824, using his memories of the England in which he moved from 1812 to 1816, but Juan lives in the late eighteenth century. The narrative voice is carefully constructed; it evidently both is and is not meant to be Byron. This subversion of certainty pervades the poem at every level. Yet paradoxically, the effect it creates is often naturalistic. "Confess—you dog!" Byron wrote to his friend Douglas Kinnaird about the poem in 1819, asking "is it not life?—is it not the thing?"

from *Don Juan*

"Difficile est proprie communia dicere."[1]

Horace, *Epistola ad Pisones*

DEDICATION[2]

1

Bob Southey! You're a poet—Poet Laureate,
      And representative of all the race;
Although 'tis true that you turned out a Tory[3] at
      Last—yours has lately been a common case:
5 And now, my epic renegade! what are ye at,
      With all the Lakers[4] in and out of place?
A nest of tuneful persons, to my eye
Like "four and twenty Blackbirds in a pye;[5]

2

"Which pye being opened they began to sing"
10   (This old song and new simile holds good),
"A dainty dish to set before the King,"

Or Regent,[6] who admires such kind of food;
And Coleridge, too, has lately taken wing,
      But like a hawk encumbered with his hood,
15 Explaining Metaphysics to the nation—
I wish he would explain his Explanation.[7]

3

You, Bob! are rather insolent, you know,
      At being disappointed in your wish
To supersede all warblers here below,
20   And be the only Blackbird in the dish;
And then you overstrain yourself, or so,
      And tumble downward like the flying fish
Gasping on deck, because you soar too high, Bob,
And fall, for lack of moisture quite a-dry, Bob![8]

4

25 And Wordsworth, in a rather long "Excursion"
      (I think the quarto holds five hundred pages),[9]
Has given a sample from the vasty version
      Of his new system to perplex the sages;
'Tis poetry—at least by his assertion,
30   And may appear so when the dog-star rages[10]—
And he who understands it would be able
To add a story to the Tower of Babel.

5

You—Gentlemen! by dint of long seclusion
      From better company, have kept your own
35 At Keswick,[11] and, through still continued fusion
      Of one another's minds, at last have grown

---

1 *Difficile … dicere* Latin: It is hard to treat in your own way what is common.

2 *DEDICATION* This Dedication is an attack on Robert Southey (1774–1843), then England's Poet Laureate, although Byron also makes jokes at the expense of other poets (especially Coleridge and Wordsworth). Southey had spread the rumor that Byron and Shelley participated in a "league of incest" when they were living in Switzerland (Byron was at that time conducting an affair with Mary Shelley's stepsister, Clair Clairmont. Southey believed them to be half-sisters, and further believed that both had sex with both men). Less personally, Byron felt that Southey had played the part of a traitor when he abandoned his early republican ideals and became a wholehearted supporter of the increasingly conservative government. Nonetheless, when he decided to publish the first two cantos anonymously, Byron had the Dedication omitted; he felt it was cowardly to attack Southey anonymously. The stanzas were first published in 1833.

3 *Tory* Supporter of the conservative group in Parliament; the Tories were opposed to a more republican political stance, which Southey once assumed.

4 *Lakers* The name applied by the *Edinburgh Review* to Coleridge, Southey, and Wordsworth, who all resided in the Lake District at one time or another.

5 *pye* Byron here makes a pun on the familiar nursery rhyme. Henry James Pye (1745–1813) had been Poet Laureate before Southey.

6 *Regent* The Prince of Wales (later George IV) was appointed Prince Regent in 1811, after his father, George III, had become permanently incapacitated for ruling.

7 *I wish … his Explanation* Coleridge's philosophical prose was notoriously vague and hard to follow.

8 *a-dry, Bob* Slang for sex without ejaculation.

9 *Wordsworth … pages* Byron here refers to Wordsworth's *The Excursion* (1814). It was presented as a portion of a projected philosophical love poem, *The Recluse*, which Wordsworth never completed.

10 *dog-star rages* Sirius, ascendant during the hottest days of the summer, was once believed to have a maddening influence.

11 *Keswick* Of the Lake Poets only Southey lived at Keswick; Coleridge had moved there with his family in 1800, but he was no longer living there in 1819. Wordsworth lived nearby, at Grasmere.

To deem as a most logical conclusion,
    That Poesy has wreaths for you alone:
There is a narrowness in such a notion,
40 Which makes me wish you'd change your lakes
     for Ocean.

6

I would not imitate the petty thought,
    Nor coin my self-love to so base a vice,
For all the glory your conversion brought,
    Since gold alone should not have been its price.
45 You have your salary; was't for that you wrought?
    And Wordsworth has his place in the Excise.[1]
You're shabby fellows—true—but poets still,
And duly seated on the Immortal Hill.

7

Your bays[2] may hide the baldness of your brows—
50   Perhaps some virtuous blushes—let them go—
To you I envy neither fruit nor boughs—
    And for the fame you would engross below,
The field is universal, and allows
    Scope to all such as feel the inherent glow:
55 Scott, Rogers, Campbell, Moore and Crabbe,[3] will try
'Gainst you the question with posterity.

8

For me, who, wandering with pedestrian Muses,
    Contend not with you on the winged steed,
I wish your fate may yield ye, when she chooses,
60   The fame you envy, and the skill you need;
And, recollect, a poet nothing loses

In giving to his brethren their full meed
Of merit, and complaint of present days
Is not the certain path to future praise.

9

65 He that reserves his laurels for posterity
    (Who does not often claim the bright reversion)
Has generally no great crop to spare it, he
    Being only injured by his own assertion;
And although here and there some glorious rarity
70   Arise like Titan[4] from the sea's immersion,
The major part of such appellants go
To—God knows where—for no one else can know.

10

If, fallen in evil days on evil tongues,
    Milton appealed to the Avenger, Time,
75 If Time, the Avenger, execrates his wrongs,
    And makes the word "Miltonic" mean "sublime,"
He deigned not to belie his soul in songs,
    Nor turn his very talent to a crime;
He did not loathe the Sire to laud the Son,
80 But closed the tyrant-hater he begun.

11

Think'st thou, could he—the blind Old Man—arise
    Like Samuel from the grave,[5] to freeze once more
The blood of monarchs with his prophecies
    Or be alive again—again all hoar
85 With time and trials, and those helpless eyes,
    And heartless daughters—worn—and pale—and
     poor;[6]

---

[1] *Wordsworth ... Excise* In 1813, Wordsworth had been appointed Distributor of Stamps for Westmoreland (a sinecure), through the influence of his patron Lord Lonsdale. In gratitude, he dedicated *The Excursion* to Lonsdale.

[2] *bays* Bay, or laurel, leaves were awarded both to military heroes and to poets (hence the term "poet laureate"). Julius Caesar was allegedly gratified with his because they hid the fact that he was bald. Southey was not bald, and this particular insult is striking, given that Byron himself had frequently commented on Southey's good looks.

[3] *Scott* Sir Walter Scott, poet and novelist (1771–1832); *Rogers* Samuel Rogers, poet (1763–1855); *Campbell* Thomas Campbell, poet (1777–1844); *Moore* Thomas Moore, poet (1779–1852); *Crabbe* George Crabbe, poet (1754–1832).

[4] *Titan* The Latin name for Helios, the Sun God.

[5] *Samuel from the grave* See 1 Samuel 28.13–14.

[6] [Byron's note] Pale, but not cadaverous:—Milton's two elder daughters are said to have robbed him of his books, besides cheating and plaguing him in the economy of his house, &c. His feelings on such an outrage, both as a parent and a scholar, must have been singularly painful. Hayley compares him to Lear. See part third, *Life of Milton*, by W. Hayley (or Hailey, as spelt in the edition before me).

Would *he* adore a sultan? *he* obey
The intellectual eunuch Castlereagh?[1]

12

Cold-blooded, smooth-faced, placid miscreant!
90   Dabbling its sleek young hands in Erin's gore,
And thus for wider carnage taught to pant,
    Transferred to gorge upon a sister shore,
The vulgarest tool that Tyranny could want,
    With just enough of talent, and no more,
95 To lengthen fetters by another fixed,
And offer poison long already mixed.

13

An orator of such set trash of phrase
    Ineffably—legitimately vile,
That even its grossest flatterers dare not praise,
100   Nor foes—all nations—condescend to smile,
Not even a sprightly blunder's spark can blaze
    From that Ixion grindstone's ceaseless toil,[2]
That turns and turns to give the world a notion
Of endless torments and perpetual motion.

14

105 A bungler even in its disgusting trade,
    And botching, patching, leaving still behind
Something of which its masters are afraid,
    States to be curbed, and thoughts to be confined,
Conspiracy or Congress to be made—
110   Cobbling at manacles for all mankind—
A tinkering slave-maker, who mends old chains,
With God and Man's abhorrence for its gains.

15

If we may judge of matter by the mind,
    Emasculated to the marrow *It*
115 Hath but two objects, how to serve, and bind,
    Deeming the chain it wears even men may fit,

Eutropius of its many masters,[3] blind
    To worth as freedom, wisdom as to Wit,
Fearless—because *no* feeling dwells in ice,
120 Its very courage stagnates to a vice.

16

Where shall I turn me not to *view* its bonds,
    For I will never *feel* them?—Italy!
Thy late reviving Roman soul desponds
    Beneath the lie this State-thing breathed o'er
        thee—
125 Thy clanking chain, and Erin's yet green wounds,
    Have voices—tongues to cry aloud for me.
Europe has slaves—allies—kings—armies still,
And Southey lives to sing them very ill.

17

Meantime—Sir Laureate—I proceed to dedicate,
130   In honest simple verse, this song to you,
And, if in flattering strains I do not predicate,
    'Tis that I still retain my "buff and blue";[4]
My politics as yet are all to educate:
    Apostasy's so fashionable, too,
135 To keep *one* creed's a task grown quite Herculean;
Is it not so, my Tory, ultra-Julian?[5]

Canto 1

1

I want a hero: an uncommon want,
    When every year and month sends forth a new one,
Till, after cloying the gazettes with cant,
    The age discovers he is not the true one;
5 Of such as these I should not care to vaunt,

---

1 *Castlereagh*   Robert Stewart, Lord Castlereagh (1769–1822), a politician widely reviled at this time as reactionary.

2 *Ixion ... toil*   For attempting to rape Hera, Ixion was bound to a wheel that rolled forever through Hades.

3 [Byron's note]   For the character of Eutropius, the eunuch and minister at the court of Arcadius, see Gibbon. [See Edward Gibbon, *The Decline and Fall of the Roman Empire*, ch. 32.]

4 *buff and blue*   The colors of the Whig Club, and of the cover of the leading Whig periodical, the *Edinburgh Review*.

5 [Byron's note]   I allude not to our friend Landor's hero, the traitor Count Julian, but to Gibbon's hero, vulgarly yclept "The Apostate." [The Emperor Julian was raised as a Christian, but returned to the worship of the Roman gods before becoming emperor in 361.]

I'll therefore take our ancient friend Don Juan—
We all have seen him in the pantomime,
Sent to the devil somewhat ere his time.

2

Vernon, the butcher Cumberland, Wolfe, Hawke,
    Prince Ferdinand, Granby, Burgoyne, Keppel, Howe,
Evil and good, have had their tithe of talk,
    And filled their sign posts then, like Wellesley[1] now;
Each in their turn like Banquo's monarchs stalk,
    Followers of fame, "nine farrow" of that sow:[2]
France, too, had Buonaparte and Dumourier
Recorded in the Moniteur and Courier.[3]

3

Barnave, Brissot, Condorcet, Mirabeau,
    Petion, Clootz, Danton, Marat, La Fayette,[4]
Were French, and famous people, as we know:
    And there were others, scarce forgotten yet,

Joubert, Hoche, Marceau, Lannes, Desaix, Moreau[5]
    With many of the military set,
Exceedingly remarkable at times,
    But not at all adapted to my rhymes.

4

Nelson was once Britannia's god of war,
    And still should be so, but the tide is turned;
There's no more to be said of Trafalgar,
    'T is with our hero quietly inurned;
Because the army's grown more popular,
    At which the naval people are concerned;
Besides, the prince is all for the land-service,
Forgetting Duncan, Nelson, Howe, and Jervis.[6]

5

Brave men were living before Agamemnon[7]
    And since, exceeding valorous and sage,
A good deal like him too, though quite the same none;
    But then they shone not on the poet's page,
And so have been forgotten:— I condemn none,
    But can't find any in the present age
Fit for my poem (that is, for my new one);
So, as I said, I'll take my friend Don Juan.

6

Most epic poets plunge "in medias res"[8]
    (Horace makes this the heroic turnpike road),
And then your hero tells, whene'er you please,
    What went before—by way of episode,
While seated after dinner at his ease,

[1] *Vernon* Admiral Edward Vernon (1684–1757); *Cumberland* William, Duke of Cumberland (1721–65), whose victory over the Young Pretender at Culloden (1746) was notorious for its brutality, and whose nickname was "Billy the Butcher"; *Wolfe* General James Wolfe (1726–59); *Hawke* Edward, Lord Admiral Hawke (1715–81); *Ferdinand* Ferdinand, Duke of Brunswick (1721–92); *Granby* John Manners, Marquess of Granby (1721–90); *Burgoyne* General John Burgoyne (d. 1792); *Keppel* Augustus, Lord Admiral Keppel (1725–86); *Howe* Richard, Lord Admiral Howe (1725–99); *Wellesley* Arthur Wellesley, Duke of Wellington. Wellington Street and Waterloo Bridge were both opened on the anniversary of Waterloo, in 1817.

[2] *Each in … sow* See Shakespeare's *Macbeth* 4.1.64–65, 112–24.

[3] *Dumourier* Charles-François Duperier Dumouriez (1739–1823), French general; *Moniteur and Courier* French newspapers.

[4] *Barnave* Antoine-Pierre-Joseph Barnave (1761–93); *Brissot* Jean-Pierre Brissot de Warville (1754–93); *Condorcet* Marie-Jean-Antoine, marquis de Condorcet (1743–94); *Mirabeau* Honoré-Gabriel Riquetti, comte de Mirabeau (1749–91); *Petion* Jérôme Petion de Villeneuve (1753–94); *Clootz* Jean-Baptiste, baron de Clootz (1755–94); *Danton* Georges-Jacques Danton (1759–94); *Marat* Jean-Paul Marat (1744–93); *La Fayette* Marie-Jean-Paul, marquis de La Fayette (1757–1834). All those listed were French Revolutionaries. Mirabeau died of natural causes, Marat was assassinated, and La Fayette was still alive; the rest all perished in the Terror that followed the French Revolution. Clootz, who changed his name to Anacharsis Clootz and nominated himself "l'orateur du genre humain," is a clue to Byron's plans for the conclusion of his unfinished epic: see his letter to John Murray on 16 February 1821 (below).

[5] *Joubert … Moreau* Barthélemi-Catherine Joubert (1769–99); Louis Lazare Hoche (1768–97); François Séverin Marceau-Desgraviers (1769–96); Jean Lannes, duc de Montebello (1769–1809); Louis-Charles-Antoine Desaix de Voygoux (1768–1800); and Jean-Victor Moreau (1763–1813), were generals in the French Revolutionary Army.

[6] *Duncan* Adam, Lord Admiral Duncan (1731–1804); *Nelson* Horatio, Lord Admiral Nelson (1758–1805), killed at Trafalgar; *Jervis* John, Lord Admiral Jervis (1735–1823); for Howe, see note to line 12.

[7] [Byron's note] "'Vixere fortes ante Agamemnona,' &c.— HORACE." [Agamemnon was the king of the Greeks and leader of the Greek expedition against Troy in Homer's *Iliad*.]

[8] *in medias res* Latin: in the middle of things.

Beside his mistress in some soft abode,
Palace, or garden, paradise, or cavern,
Which serves the happy couple for a tavern.

7

That is the usual method, but not mine—
50   My way is to begin with the beginning;
The regularity of my design
        Forbids all wandering as the worst of sinning,
And therefore I shall open with a line
        (Although it cost me half an hour in spinning)
55   Narrating somewhat of Don Juan's father,
And also of his mother, if you'd rather.

8

In Seville was he born, a pleasant city,
        Famous for oranges and women—he
Who has not seen it will be much to pity,
60   So says the proverb—and I quite agree;
Of all the Spanish towns is none more pretty,
        Cadiz[1] perhaps—but that you soon may see:
Don Juan's parents lived beside the river,
A noble stream, and called the Guadalquivir.

9

65   His father's name was Jóse[2]—Don,[3] of course,
        A true Hidalgo,[4] free from every stain
Of Moor or Hebrew blood, he traced his source
        Through the most Gothic gentlemen of Spain;
A better cavalier ne'er mounted horse,
70   Or, being mounted, e'er got down again,
Than Jóse, who begot our hero, who
Begot—but that's to come—Well, to renew:

10

His mother was a learned lady,[5] famed
        For every branch of every science known—
75   In every Christian language ever named,
        With virtues equalled by her wit alone,
She made the cleverest people quite ashamed,
        And even the good with inward envy groan,
Finding themselves so very much exceeded
80   In their own way by all the things that she did.

11

Her memory was a mine: she knew by heart
        All Calderon and greater part of Lopé,[6]
So that if any actor missed his part
        She could have served him for the prompter's copy;
85   For her Feinagle's were an useless art,[7]
        And he himself obliged to shut up shop—he
Could never make a memory so fine as
That which adorned the brain of Donna Inez.

12

Her favourite science was the mathematical,
90   Her noblest virtue was her magnanimity,
Her wit (she sometimes tried at wit) was Attic all,[8]
        Her serious sayings darkened to sublimity;
In short, in all things she was fairly what I call
        A prodigy—her morning dress was dimity,
95   Her evening silk, or, in the summer, muslin,
And other stuffs, with which I won't stay puzzling.

13

She knew the Latin—that is, "The Lord's Prayer,"
        And Greek—the alphabet—I'm nearly sure;
She read some French romances here and there,
100   Although her mode of speaking was not pure;

---

1. *Cadiz*   Byron anglicizes the pronunciations of his Spanish words, so that Seville is pronounced "SEVil"; Cadiz to rhyme with "ladies."

2. *Jóse*   Byron changes the stress, so that José is pronounced with the emphasis on the first syllable.

3. *Don*   Spanish title, denoting high rank.

4. *Hidalgo*   Gentleman, by birth.

5. *His mother … lady*   Although Byron denied that the character of Donna Inez was a satiric portrait of his wife, a perceived resemblance to her was one of the chief complaints his friends made against these cantos.

6. *Calderon … Lopé*   Calderón de la Barca (1600–81) and Lopé de Vega (1562–1635), Spanish dramatists.

7. *Feinagle's … art*   Gregor von Feinagle (1765?–1819) invented a new method of memorization.

8. *Her wit … Attic all*   Attic, that is, Grecian wit, refined and delicate.

For native Spanish she had no great care,
    At least her conversation was obscure;
Her thoughts were theorems, her words a problem,
As if she deemed that mystery would ennoble 'em.

14

105 She liked the English and the Hebrew tongue,
    And said there was analogy between 'em;
She proved it somehow out of sacred song,
    But I must leave the proofs to those who've seen 'em,
But this I heard her say, and can't be wrong,
110   And all may think which way their judgments lean
        'em,
"'Tis strange—the Hebrew noun which means 'I am,'
The English always used to govern d—n."[1]

15

Some women use their tongues—she *looked* a lecture,
    Each eye a sermon, and her brow a homily,
115 An all-in-all sufficient self director,
    Like the lamented late Sir Samuel Romilly,[2]
The Law's expounder, and the State's corrector,
    Whose suicide was almost an anomaly—
One sad example more, that "All is vanity"
120 (The jury brought their verdict in "Insanity").

16

In short, she was a walking calculation,
    Miss Edgeworth's novels stepping from their covers,
Or Mrs. Trimmer's books on education,
    Or "Cœlebs' Wife" set out in quest of lovers,[3]
125 Morality's prim personification,
    In which not Envy's self a flaw discovers,

To others' share let "female errors fall,"
For she had not even one—the worst of all.

17

Oh! she was perfect past all parallel—
130   Of any modern female saint's comparison;
So far above the cunning powers of hell,
    Her guardian angel had given up his garrison;
Even her minutest motions went as well
    As those of the best time-piece made by Harrison:[4]
135 In virtues nothing earthly could surpass her,
Save thine "incomparable oil," Macassar![5]

18

Perfect she was, but as perfection is
    Insipid in this naughty world of ours,
Where our first parents never learned to kiss
140   Till they were exiled from their earlier bowers,
Where all was peace, and innocence, and bliss
    (I wonder how they got through the twelve hours)
Don José, like a lineal son of Eve,
Went plucking various fruit without her leave.

19

145 He was a mortal of the careless kind,
    With no great love for learning, or the learned,
Who chose to go where'er he had a mind,
    And never dreamed his lady was concerned:
The world, as usual, wickedly inclined
150   To see a kingdom or a house o'erturned,
Whispered he had a mistress, some said *two*,
But for domestic quarrels *one* will do.

20

Now Donna Inez had, with all her merit,
    A great opinion of her own good qualities;
155 Neglect, indeed, requires a saint to bear it,
    And such, indeed, she was in her moralities;

---

[1] *d—n* Cf. Exodus 3.14. Byron is referring to "God damn."

[2] *Romilly* Sir Samuel Romilly (1757–1818), lawyer and legal reformer, represented Lady Byron during the separation proceedings, despite having previously accepted a retainer from Byron. Byron never forgave him. Romilly's wife died in October 1818, and he committed suicide. This stanza was censored in the first edition.

[3] *Miss Edgeworth's … lovers* Byron here refers to three female writers famous for their didactic and moral works: Maria Edgeworth (1767–1849), author of *Moral Tales* (1801) and other fiction; Sarah Trimmer (1741–1810), author of books for children and publisher of *Guardian to Education* (1802–06); and Hannah More, to whose *Coelebs in Search of a Wife* (1809) he alludes.

[4] *Harrison* John Harrison (1693–1776) invented a chronometer so accurate that it could be used to calculate longitude.

[5] [Byron's note] 'description des *vertus incomparables* de l'Huile de Macassar.'—See the Advertisement. [Macassor oil, a dressing for the hair named after an Indonesian location said to be the source of its ingredients, was very popular through the nineteenth century.]

But then she had a devil of a spirit,
    And sometimes mixed up fancies with realities,
And let few opportunities escape
160   Of getting her liege lord into a scrape.

21

This was an easy matter with a man
    Oft in the wrong, and never on his guard;
And even the wisest, do the best they can,
    Have moments, hours, and days, so unprepared,
165 That you might "brain them with their lady's fan;"[1]
    And sometimes ladies hit exceeding hard,
And fans turn into falchions° in fair hands,   *swords*
And why and wherefore no one understands.

22

'Tis pity learned virgins ever wed
170   With persons of no sort of education,
Or gentlemen, who, though well-born and bred,
    Grow tired of scientific conversation:
I don't choose to say much upon this head,
    I'm a plain man, and in a single station,
175 But—Oh! ye lords of ladies intellectual,
Inform us truly, have they not hen-pecked you all?

23

Don Jóse and his lady quarrelled—*why*,
    Not any of the many could divine,
Though several thousand people chose to try,
180   'Twas surely no concern of theirs nor mine;
I loathe that low vice curiosity,
    But if there's any thing in which I shine
'Tis in arranging all my friends' affairs,
Not having, of my own, domestic cares.

24

185 And so I interfered, and with the best
    Intentions, but their treatment was not kind;
I think the foolish people were possessed,
    For neither of them could I ever find,
Although their porter afterwards confessed—
190   But that's no matter, and the worst's behind,

---

1 *brain them … fan* Cf. Shakespeare, *1 Henry IV* 2.3.21.

For little Juan o'er me threw, down stairs,
A pail of housemaid's water unawares.

25

A little curly-headed, good-for-nothing,
    And mischief-making monkey from his birth;
195 His parents ne'er agreed except in doting
    Upon the most unquiet imp on earth;
Instead of quarrelling, had they been but both in
    Their senses, they'd have sent young master forth
To school, or had him soundly whipped at home,
200 To teach him manners for the time to come.

26

Don Jóse and the Donna Inez led
    For some time an unhappy sort of life,
Wishing each other, not divorced, but dead;
    They lived respectably as man and wife,
205 Their conduct was exceedingly well-bred,
    And gave no outward signs of inward strife,
Until at length the smothered fire broke out,
And put the business past all kind of doubt.

27

For Inez called some druggists and physicians,
210   And tried to prove her loving lord was *mad*,
But as he had some lucid intermissions,
    She next decided he was only *bad*;
Yet when they asked her for her depositions,
    No sort of explanation could be had,
215 Save that her duty both to man and God
Required this conduct—which seemed very odd.

28

She kept a journal, where his faults were noted,
    And opened certain trunks of books and letters,
All which might, if occasion served, be quoted;
220   And then she had all Seville for abettors,
Besides her good old grandmother (who doted);
    The hearers of her case became repeaters,

Then advocates, inquisitors, and judges,
Some for amusement, others for old grudges.[1]

29

25 And then this best and meekest woman bore
    With such serenity her husband's woes,
Just as the Spartan ladies did of yore,
    Who saw their spouses killed, and nobly chose
Never to say a word about them more—
30 Calmly she heard each calumny that rose,
And saw *his* agonies with such sublimity,
That all the world exclaimed, "What magnanimity!"

30

No doubt, this patience, when the world is damning us,
    Is philosophic in our former friends;
35 'Tis also pleasant to be deemed magnanimous,
    The more so in obtaining our own ends;
And what the lawyers call a "*malus animus*"[2]
    Conduct like this by no means comprehends:
Revenge in person's certainly no virtue,
40 But then 'tis not my fault, if *others* hurt you.

31

And if our quarrels should rip up old stories,
    And help them with a lie or two additional,
I'm not to blame, as you well know, no more is
    Any one else—they were become traditional;
45 Besides, their resurrection aids our glories
    By contrast, which is what we just were wishing all:
And science profits by this resurrection—
Dead scandals form good subjects for dissection.

32

Their friends had tried at reconciliation,
50 Then their relations, who made matters worse;
('Twere hard to tell upon a like occasion
    To whom it may be best to have recourse—
I can't say much for friend or yet relation):
    The lawyers did their utmost for divorce,

---

[1] *For Inez ... grudges* During the months leading up to their separation, Lady Byron did, or was suspected by her husband of doing, all the things attributed to Donna Inez in these two stanzas.

[2] *malus animus* Latin: bad spirit.

255 But scarce a fee was paid on either side
Before, unluckily, Don Jóse died.

33

He died: and most unluckily, because,
    According to all hints I could collect
From counsel learned in those kinds of laws
260   (Although their talk's obscure and circumspect)
His death contrived to spoil a charming cause;
    A thousand pities also with respect
To public feeling, which on this occasion
Was manifested in a great sensation.

34

265 But ah! he died; and buried with him lay
    The public feeling and the lawyers' fees:
His house was sold, his servants sent away,
    A Jew took one of his two mistresses,
A priest the other—at least so they say:
270   I asked the doctors after his disease,
He died of the slow fever called the tertian,
And left his widow to her own aversion.

35

Yet Jóse was an honourable man,
    That I must say, who knew him very well;
275 Therefore his frailties I'll no further scan,
    Indeed there were not many more to tell;
And if his passions now and then outran
    Discretion, and were not so peaceable
As Numa's (who was also named Pompilius),[3]
280 He had been ill brought up, and was born bilious.

36

Whate'er might be his worthlessness or worth,
    Poor fellow! he had many things to wound him,
Let's own, since it can do no good on earth;
    It was a trying moment that which found him
285 Standing alone beside his desolate hearth,
    Where all his household gods lay shivered round him;

---

[3] *Pompilius* The peaceable second king of Rome; see Plutarch, *Parallel Lives*.

No choice was left his feelings or his pride,
Save death or Doctors' Commons[1]—so he died.

37

Dying intestate, Juan was sole heir
290   To a chancery suit, and messuages, and lands,
Which, with a long minority and care,
      Promised to turn out well in proper hands:
Inez became sole guardian, which was fair,
      And answered but to nature's just demands;
295 An only son left with an only mother
Is brought up much more wisely than another.

38

Sagest of women, even of widows, she
      Resolved that Juan should be quite a paragon,
And worthy of the noblest pedigree:
300   (His sire was of Castile, his dam from Aragon).
Then for accomplishments of chivalry,
      In case our lord the king should go to war again,
He learned the arts of riding, fencing, gunnery,
And how to scale a fortress—or a nunnery.

39

305 But that which Donna Inez most desired,
      And saw into herself each day before all
The learned tutors whom for him she hired,
      Was, that his breeding should be strictly moral;
Much into all his studies she inquired,
310   And so they were submitted first to her, all,
Arts, sciences, no branch was made a mystery
To Juan's eyes, excepting natural history.

40

The languages, especially the dead,
      The sciences, and most of all the abstruse,
315 The arts, at least all such as could be said
      To be the most remote from common use,
In all these he was much and deeply read;
      But not a page of any thing that's loose,
Or hints continuation of the species,
320 Was ever suffered, lest he should grow vicious.

41

His classic studies made a little puzzle,
      Because of filthy loves of gods and goddesses,
Who in the earlier ages raised a bustle,
      But never put on pantaloons or boddices;
325 His reverend tutors had at times a tussle,
      And for their Æneids, Iliads, and Odysseys,
Were forced to make an odd sort of apology,
For Donna Inez dreaded the mythology.

42

Ovid's a rake, as half his verses show him,
330   Anacreon's morals are a still worse sample,
Catullus scarcely has a decent poem,
      I don't think Sappho's Ode a good example,
Although Longinus tells us there is no hymn
      Where the sublime soars forth on wings more ample;[2]
335 But Virgil's songs are pure, except that horrid one
Beginning with "*Formosum Pastor Corydon*."[3]

43

Lucretius' irreligion is too strong
      For early stomachs, to prove wholesome food;
I can't help thinking Juvenal was wrong,
340   Although no doubt his real intent was good,
For speaking out so plainly in his song,
      So much indeed as to be downright rude;
And then what proper person can be partial
To all those nauseous epigrams of Martial?[4]

---

1 *Doctors' Commons*   Divorce courts.

2 [Byron's note]   See Longinus, Section 10, "*hina me hen ti peri auten pathos phainetai, pathon de sunodos*." [See Ovid's *Amores* and *Ars Amatoria*; the erotic lyrics then attributed to Anacreon; the erotic lyrics of Catullus; and the poem by Sappho beginning "To me he seems a peer of the gods," praised by Longinus in *On the Sublime* 10.]

3 *Formosum ... Corydon*   This is the first line of Virgil's second Eclogue, which may be translated, "The shepherd Corydon [burned for] fair [Alexis, his master's darling]." The poem is about love between men.

4 *Lucretius' ... Martial*   Byron here refers to three classical works which Inez certainly would have considered dangerous: Lucretius, *On the Nature of Things*, a philosophical poem; Juvenal, *Satires*; and Martial's epigrams, which are notoriously scurrilous and obscene.

44

Juan was taught from out the best edition,
    Expurgated by learned men, who place,
Judiciously, from out the schoolboy's vision,
    The grosser parts; but fearful to deface
Too much their modest bard by this omission,
    And pitying sore his mutilated case,
They only add them all in an appendix,
Which saves, in fact, the trouble of an index.[1]

45

For there we have them all at one fell swoop,
    Instead of being scattered through the pages;
They stand forth marshalled in a handsome troop,
    To meet the ingenuous youth of future ages,
Till some less rigid editor shall stoop
    To call them back into their separate cages,
Instead of standing staring altogether,
Like garden gods—and not so decent either.

46

The Missal too (it was the family Missal)
    Was ornamented in a sort of way
Which ancient mass-books often are, and this all
    Kinds of grotesques illumined; and how they,
Who saw those figures on the margin kiss all,
    Could turn their optics to the text and pray
Is more than I know—but Don Juan's mother
Kept this herself, and gave her son another.

47

Sermons he read, and lectures he endured,
    And homilies, and lives of all the saints;
To Jerome and to Chrysostom[2] inured,
    He did not take such studies for restraints;
But how faith is acquired, and then insured,

So well not one of the aforesaid paints
    As Saint Augustine in his fine Confessions,
Which make the reader envy his transgressions.[3]

48

This, too, was a sealed book to little Juan—
    I can't but say that his mamma was right,
If such an education was the true one.
    She scarcely trusted him from out her sight;
Her maids were old, and if she took a new one
    You might be sure she was a perfect fright,
She did this during even her husband's life—
I recommend as much to every wife.

49

Young Juan waxed in goodliness and grace;
    At six a charming child, and at eleven
With all the promise of as fine a face
    As e'er to man's maturer growth was given:
He studied steadily, and grew apace,
    And seemed, at least, in the right road to heaven,
For half his days were passed at church, the other
Between his tutors, confessor, and mother.

50

At six, I said, he was a charming child,
    At twelve he was a fine, but quiet boy;
Although in infancy a little wild,
    They tamed him down amongst them; to destroy
His natural spirit not in vain they toiled,
    At least it seemed so; and his mother's joy
Was to declare how sage, and still, and steady,
Her young philosopher was grown already.

51

I had my doubts, perhaps I have them still,
    But what I say is neither here nor there:
I knew his father well, and have some skill

---

1 [Byron's note] Fact. There is, or was, such an edition, with all the obnoxious epigrams of Martial placed by themselves at the end. [The Delphin edition of Martial (Amsterdam, 1701) has an appendix entitled "Epigrammata Obscaena."]

2 *Jerome* St. Jerome (340?–420), translator of the Bible into Latin; *Chrysostom* St. John Chrysostom (347?–407); both were ascetics.

3 [Byron's note] See his *Confessions*, lib. i. cap. ix. By the representation which Saint Augustine gives of himself in his youth, it is easy to see that he was what we should call a rake. He avoided the school as the plague; he loved nothing but gaming and public shows; he robbed his father of everything he could find; he invented a thousand lies to escape the rod, which they were obliged to make use of to punish his irregularities.

In character—but it would not be fair
405 From sire to son to augur good or ill:
    He and his wife were an ill-sorted pair —
But scandal's my aversion—I protest
Against all evil speaking, even in jest.

52

For my part I say nothing—nothing—but
410   *This* I will say—my reasons are my own—
That if I had an only son to put
    To school (as God be praised that I have none)
'Tis not with Donna Inez I would shut
    Him up to learn his catechism alone,
415 No—no—I'd send him out betimes to college,
For there it was I picked up my own knowledge.

53

For there one learns—'tis not for me to boast,
    Though I acquired—but I pass over *that*,
As well as all the Greek I since have lost:
420   I say that there's the place—but "*Verbum sat.*"[1]
I think, I picked up too, as well as most,
    Knowledge of matters—but no matter *what*—
I never married—but, I think, I know
That sons should not be educated so.

54

425 Young Juan now was sixteen years of age,
    Tall, handsome, slender, but well knit; he seemed
Active, though not so sprightly, as a page;
    And every body but his mother deemed
Him almost man; but she flew in a rage,
430   And bit her lips (for else she might have screamed),
If any said so, for to be precocious
Was in her eyes a thing the most atrocious.

55

Amongst her numerous acquaintance, all
    Selected for discretion and devotion,
435 There was the Donna Julia, whom to call
    Pretty were but to give a feeble notion
Of many charms in her as natural

As sweetness to the flower, or salt to ocean,
    Her zone to Venus, or his bow to Cupid
440 (But this last simile is trite and stupid).

56

The darkness of her oriental eye
    Accorded with her Moorish origin;
(Her blood was not all Spanish, by the by;
    In Spain, you know, this is a sort of sin).
445 When proud Granada fell, and, forced to fly,
    Boabdil[2] wept, of Donna Julia's kin
Some went to Africa, some staid in Spain,
Her great great grandmamma chose to remain.

57

She married (I forget the pedigree)
450   With an Hidalgo, who transmitted down
His blood less noble than such blood should be;
    At such alliances his sires would frown,
In that point so precise in each degree
    That they bred *in and in*, as might be shown,
455 Marrying their cousins—nay, their aunts and nieces,
Which always spoils the breed, if it increases.[3]

58

This heathenish cross restored the breed again,
    Ruined its blood, but much improved its flesh;
For, from a root the ugliest in Old Spain
460   Sprung up a branch as beautiful as fresh;
The sons no more were short, the daughters plain:
    But there's a rumour which I fain would hush,
'Tis said that Donna Julia's grandmamma
Produced her Don more heirs at love than law.

59

465 However this might be, the race went on
    Improving still through every generation,
Until it centred in an only son,
    Who left an only daughter; my narration
May have suggested that this single one

---

[1] *Verbum sat*   Latin: A word [to the wise] is enough.

[2] *Boabdil*   Muhammed XI, the last Moorish king of Granada, defeated by the Spanish in 1492.

[3] *Marrying ... increases*   The Byron family frequently intermarried, cousins wedding cousins.

Could be but Julia (whom on this occasion
I shall have much to speak about), and she
Was married, charming, chaste, and twenty-three.

60

Her eye (I'm very fond of handsome eyes)
    Was large and dark, suppressing half its fire
Until she spoke, then through its soft disguise
    Flashed an expression more of pride than ire,
And love than either; and there would arise
    A something in them which was not desire,
But would have been, perhaps, but for the soul
Which struggled through and chastened down the
    whole.

61

Her glossy hair was clustered o'er a brow
    Bright with intelligence, and fair and smooth;
Her eyebrow's shape was like the aerial bow,
    Her cheek all purple with the beam of youth,
Mounting, at times, to a transparent glow,
    As if her veins ran lightning; she, in sooth,
Possessed an air and grace by no means common:
Her stature tall—I hate a dumpy woman.

62

Wedded she was some years, and to a man
    Of fifty, and such husbands are in plenty;
And yet, I think, instead of such a ONE
    'Twere better to have TWO of five-and-twenty,
Especially in countries near the sun:
    And now I think on't, "mi vien in mente,"[1]
Ladies even of the most uneasy virtue
Prefer a spouse whose age is short of thirty.

63

'Tis a sad thing, I cannot choose but say,
    And all the fault of that indecent sun,
Who cannot leave alone our helpless clay,
    But will keep baking, broiling, burning on,
That howsoever people fast and pray
    The flesh is frail, and so the soul undone:

What men call gallantry, and gods adultery,
Is much more common where the climate's sultry.

64

Happy the nations of the moral north!
    Where all is virtue, and the winter season
Sends sin, without a rag on, shivering forth;
    ('Twas snow that brought St. Anthony to reason);[2]
Where juries cast up what a wife is worth
    By laying whate'er sum, in mulct, they please on
The lover, who must pay a handsome price,
Because it is a marketable vice.

65

Alfonso was the name of Julia's lord,
    A man well looking for his years, and who
Was neither much beloved, nor yet abhorred;
    They lived together as most people do,
Suffering each other's foibles by accord,
    And not exactly either one or two;
Yet he was jealous, though he did not show it,
For jealousy dislikes the world to know it.

66

Julia was—yet I never could see why—
    With Donna Inez quite a favourite friend;
Between their tastes there was small sympathy,
    For not a line had Julia ever penned:
Some people whisper (but, no doubt, they lie,
    For malice still imputes some private end)
That Inez had, ere Don Alfonso's marriage,
Forgot with him her very prudent carriage.

67

And that still keeping up the old connexion,
    Which time had lately rendered much more chaste,
She took his lady also in affection,
    And certainly this course was much the best:
She flattered Julia with her sage protection,

---

[1] mi ... mente Italian: it comes into my mind.

[2] [Byron's note] For the particulars of St. Anthony's recipe for hot blood in cold weather, see Mr. Alban Butler's *Lives of the Saints*. [It was actually St. Francis of Assisi who was reported to have thrown himself naked into the snow to counteract the temptations of the flesh.]

And complimented Don Alfonso's taste;
535 And if she could not (who can?) silence scandal,
At least she left it a more slender handle.

68
I can't tell whether Julia saw the affair
　　With other people's eyes, or if her own
Discoveries made, but none could be aware
540 　　Of this, at least no symptom e'er was shown;
Perhaps she did not know, or did not care,
　　Indifferent from the first, or callous grown:
I'm really puzzled what to think or say,
She kept her counsel in so close a way.

69
545 Juan she saw, and, as a pretty child,
　　Caressed him often, such a thing might be
Quite innocently done, and harmless styled,
　　When she had twenty years, and thirteen he;
But I am not so sure I should have smiled
550 　　When he was sixteen, Julia twenty-three,
These few short years make wondrous alterations,
Particularly amongst sun-burnt nations.

70
Whate'er the cause might be, they had become
　　Changed; for the dame grew distant, the youth shy,
555 Their looks cast down, their greetings almost dumb,
　　And much embarrassment in either eye;
There surely will be little doubt with some
　　That Donna Julia knew the reason why,
But as for Juan, he had no more notion
560 Than he who never saw the sea of ocean.

71
Yet Julia's very coldness still was kind,
　　And tremulously gentle her small hand
Withdrew itself from his, but left behind
　　A little pressure, thrilling, and so bland
565 And slight, so very slight, that to the mind
　　'Twas but a doubt; but ne'er magician's wand

Wrought change with all Armida's[1] fairy art
Like what this light touch left on Juan's heart.

72
And if she met him, though she smiled no more,
570 　　She looked a sadness sweeter than her smile,
As if her heart had deeper thoughts in store
　　She must not own, but cherished more the while,
For that compression in its burning core;
　　Even innocence itself has many a wile,
575 And will not dare to trust itself with truth,
And love is taught hypocrisy from youth.

73
But passion most dissembles yet betrays
　　Even by its darkness; as the blackest sky
Foretells the heaviest tempest, it displays
580 　　Its workings through the vainly guarded eye,
And in whatever aspect it arrays
　　Itself, 'tis still the same hypocrisy;
Coldness or anger, even disdain or hate,
Are masks it often wears, and still too late.

74
585 Then there were sighs, the deeper for suppression,
　　And stolen glances, sweeter for the theft,
And burning blushes, though for no transgression,
　　Tremblings when met, and restlessness when left;
All these are little preludes to possession,
590 　　Of which young Passion cannot be bereft,
And merely tend to show how greatly Love is
Embarrassed at first starting with a novice.

75
Poor Julia's heart was in an awkward state;
　　She felt it going, and resolved to make
595 The noblest efforts for herself and mate,
　　For honour's, pride's, religion's, virtue's sake;
Her resolutions were most truly great,
　　And almost might have made a Tarquin[2] quake;

1　*Armida*　The enchantress in Torquato Tasso's *Jerusalem Delivered*.

2　*Tarquin*　Sextus Tarquinius raped Lucretia, a Roman matron, who subsequently stabbed herself.

She prayed the Virgin Mary for her grace,
As being the best judge of a lady's case.

76

She vowed she never would see Juan more,
    And next day paid a visit to his mother,
And looked extremely at the opening door,
    Which, by the Virgin's grace, let in another;
Grateful she was, and yet a little sore—
    Again it opens, it can be no other,
'Tis surely Juan now—No! I'm afraid
That night the Virgin was no further prayed.

77

She now determined that a virtuous woman
    Should rather face and overcome temptation,
That flight was base and dastardly, and no man
    Should ever give her heart the least sensation;
That is to say, a thought beyond the common
    Preference, that we must feel upon occasion,
For people who are pleasanter than others,
But then they only seem so many brothers.

78

And even if by chance—and who can tell?
    The devil's so very sly—she should discover
That all within was not so very well,
    And, if still free, that such or such a lover
Might please perhaps, a virtuous wife can quell
    Such thoughts, and be the better when they're over;
And if the man should ask, 'tis but denial:
I recommend young ladies to make trial.

79

And then there are such things as love divine,
    Bright and immaculate, unmixed and pure,
Such as the angels think so very fine,
    And matrons, who would be no less secure,
Platonic, perfect, "just such love as mine:"
    Thus Julia said—and thought so, to be sure,
And so I'd have her think, were I the man
On whom her reveries celestial ran.

80

Such love is innocent, and may exist
    Between young persons without any danger,
A hand may first, and then a lip be kist;
    For my part, to such doings I'm a stranger,
But *hear* these freedoms form the utmost list
    Of all o'er which such love may be a ranger:
If people go beyond, 'tis quite a crime,
But not my fault—I tell them all in time.

81

Love, then, but love within its proper limits,
    Was Julia's innocent determination
In young Don Juan's favour, and to him its
    Exertion might be useful on occasion;
And, lighted at too pure a shrine to dim its
    Ethereal lustre, with what sweet persuasion
He might be taught, by love and her together—
I really don't know what, nor Julia either.

82

Fraught with this fine intention, and well fenced
    In mail of proof —her purity of soul—
She, for the future of her strength convinced,
    And that her honour was a rock, or mole,[1]
Exceeding sagely from that hour dispensed
    With any kind of troublesome control;
But whether Julia to the task was equal
Is that which must be mentioned in the sequel.

83

Her plan she deemed both innocent and feasible,
    And, surely, with a stripling of sixteen
Not scandal's fangs could fix on much that's seizable,
    Or if they did so, satisfied to mean
Nothing but what was good, her breast was peaceable—
    A quiet conscience makes one so serene!
Christians have burnt each other, quite persuaded
That all the Apostles would have done as they did.

---

[1] *mole* Massive structure, such as a pier or breakwater.

84

665 And if in the mean time her husband died,
    But heaven forbid that such a thought should cross
Her brain, though in a dream! (and then she sighed)
    Never could she survive that common loss;
But just suppose that moment should betide,
670   I only say suppose it—*inter nos.*
(This should be *entre nous,*[1] for Julia thought
In French, but then the rhyme would go for nought.)

85

I only say suppose this supposition:
    Juan being then grown up to man's estate
675 Would fully suit a widow of condition,
    Even seven years hence it would not be too late;
And in the interim (to pursue this vision)
    The mischief, after all, could not be great,
For he would learn the rudiments of love,
680 I mean the seraph way[2] of those above.

86

So much for Julia. Now we'll turn to Juan,
    Poor little fellow! he had no idea
Of his own case, and never hit the true one;
    In feelings quick as Ovid's Miss Medea,
685 He puzzled over what he found a new one,
    But not as yet imagined it could be a
Thing quite in course, and not at all alarming,
Which, with a little patience, might grow charming.

87

Silent and pensive, idle, restless, slow,
690   His home deserted for the lonely wood,
Tormented with a wound he could not know,
    His, like all deep grief, plunged in solitude:
I'm fond myself of solitude or so,
    But then, I beg it may be understood,
695 By solitude I mean a sultan's, not
A hermit's, with a haram° for a grot.   *harem*

88

"Oh Love! in such a wilderness as this,
    Where transport and security entwine,
Here is the empire of thy perfect bliss,
700   And here thou art a god indeed divine."[3]
The bard I quote from does not sing amiss,
    With the exception of the second line,
For that same twining "transport and security"
Are twisted to a phrase of some obscurity.

89

705 The poet meant, no doubt, and thus appeals
    To the good sense and senses of mankind,
The very thing which every body feels,
    As all have found on trial, or may find,
That no one likes to be disturbed at meals
710   Or love.—I won't say more about "entwined"
Or "transport," as we knew all that before,
But beg "Security" will bolt the door.

90

Young Juan wandered by the glassy brooks,
    Thinking unutterable things; he threw
715 Himself at length within the leafy nooks
    Where the wild branch of the cork forest grew;
There poets find materials for their books,
    And every now and then we read them through,
So that their plan and prosody are eligible,
720 Unless, like Wordsworth, they prove unintelligible.

91

He, Juan (and not Wordsworth), so pursued
    His self-communion with his own high soul,
Until his mighty heart,[4] in its great mood,
    Had mitigated part, though not the whole
725 Of its disease; he did the best he could
    With things not very subject to control,

---

1 *inter nos* Latin: between us; *entre nous* French: between us.

2 *seraph way* I.e., angelic way.

3 [Byron's note] Campbell's *Gertrude of Wyoming,* (I think) the opening of Canto II; but quote from memory [Thomas Campbell, *Gertrude of Wyoming* 3.1.1–4.]

4 *so pursued … heart* See Wordsworth's "Composed upon Westminster Bridge" (1802), 14.

And turned, without perceiving his condition,
Like Coleridge, into a metaphysician.[1]

92

He thought about himself, and the whole earth,
    Of man the wonderful, and of the stars,
And how the deuce they ever could have birth;
    And then he thought of earthquakes, and of wars,
How many miles the moon might have in girth,
    Of air-balloons, and of the many bars
To perfect knowledge of the boundless skies;
And then he thought of Donna Julia's eyes.

93

In thoughts like these true wisdom may discern
    Longings sublime, and aspirations high,
Which some are born with, but the most part learn
    To plague themselves withal, they know not why:
'Twas strange that one so young should thus concern
    His brain about the action of the sky;
If *you* think 'twas philosophy that this did,
I can't help thinking puberty assisted.

94

He pored upon the leaves, and on the flowers,
    And heard a voice in all the winds; and then
He thought of wood nymphs and immortal bowers,
    And how the goddesses came down to men:
He missed the pathway, he forgot the hours,
    And when he looked upon his watch again,
He found how much old Time had been a winner—
He also found that he had lost his dinner.[2]

95

Sometimes he turned to gaze upon his book,
    Boscan, or Garcilasso;[3]—by the wind
Even as the page is rustled while we look,
    So by the poesy of his own mind

Over the mystic leaf his soul was shook,
    As if 'twere one whereon magicians bind
Their spells, and give them to the passing gale,
According to some good old woman's tale.

96

Thus would he while his lonely hours away
    Dissatisfied, nor knowing what he wanted;
Nor glowing reverie, nor poet's lay,
    Could yield his spirit that for which it panted,
A bosom whereon he his head might lay,
    And hear the heart beat with the love it granted,
With—several other things, which I forget,
Or which, at least, I need not mention yet.

97

Those lonely walks, and lengthening reveries,
    Could not escape the gentle Julia's eyes;
She saw that Juan was not at his ease;
    But that which chiefly may, and must surprise,
Is, that the Donna Inez did not tease
    Her only son with question or surmise;
Whether it was she did not see, or would not,
Or, like all very clever people, could not.

98

This may seem strange, but yet 'tis very common;
    For instance—gentlemen, whose ladies take
Leave to o'erstep the written rights of woman,
    And break the—Which commandment is't they break?[4]
(I have forgot the number, and think no man
    Should rashly quote, for fear of a mistake.)
I say, when these same gentlemen are jealous,
They make some blunder, which their ladies tell us.

99

A real husband always is suspicious,
    But still no less suspects in the wrong place,
Jealous of some one who had no such wishes,
    Or pandering blindly to his own disgrace

---

[1] *turned ... metaphysician* See Coleridge's "Dejection: An Ode" 87–93.

[2] *lost his dinner* I.e., was so late for dinner that he had missed it entirely.

[3] *Boscan* Spanish poet Juan Boscán (1500–44); *Garcilasso* Spanish poet Garcias Lasso or Garcilaso de la Vega (1503–36).

[4] *Which commandment ... break?* They break the commandment "Thou shalt not commit adultery."

By harbouring some dear friend extremely vicious;
790   The last indeed's infallibly the case:
And when the spouse and friend are gone off wholly,
He wonders at their vice, and not his folly.

100

Thus parents also are at times short-sighted;
    Though watchful as the lynx, they ne'er discover,
795   The while the wicked world beholds delighted,
    Young Hopeful's mistress, or Miss Fanny's lover,
Till some confounded escapade has blighted
    The plan of twenty years, and all is over;
And then the mother cries, the father swears,
800   And wonders why the devil he got heirs.[1]

101

But Inez was so anxious, and so clear
    Of sight, that I must think, on this occasion,
She had some other motive much more near
    For leaving Juan to this new temptation;
805   But what that motive was, I shan't say here;
    Perhaps to finish Juan's education,
Perhaps to open Don Alfonso's eyes,
In case he thought his wife too great a prize.

102

It was upon a day, a summer's day;—
810   Summer's indeed a very dangerous season,
And so is spring about the end of May;
    The sun, no doubt, is the prevailing reason;
But whatsoe'er the cause is, one may say,
    And stand convicted of more truth than treason,
815   That there are months which nature grows more
        merry in,
March has its hares, and May must have its heroine.

103

'Twas on a summer's day—the sixth of June:—
    I like to be particular in dates,
Not only of the age, and year, but moon;
820   They are a sort of post-house, where the Fates
Change horses, making history change its tune,

Then spur away o'er empires and o'er states,
Leaving at last not much besides chronology,
Excepting the post-obits[2] of theology.

104

825   'Twas on the sixth of June, about the hour
    Of half-past six—perhaps still nearer seven,
When Julia sat within as pretty a bower
    As e'er held hour in that heathenish heaven
Described by Mahomet, and Anacreon Moore,[3]
830   To whom the lyre and laurels have been given,
With all the trophies of triumphant song—
He won them well, and may he wear them long!

105

She sate, but not alone; I know not well
    How this same interview had taken place,
835   And even if I knew, I should not tell—
    People should hold their tongues in any case;
No matter how or why the thing befell,
    But there were she and Juan, face to face—
When two such faces are so, 'twould be wise,
840   But very difficult, to shut their eyes.

106

How beautiful she looked! her conscious heart
    Glowed in her cheek, and yet she felt no wrong.
Oh Love! how perfect is thy mystic art,
    Strengthening the weak, and trampling on the
        strong,
845   How self-deceitful is the sagest part
    Of mortals whom thy lure hath led along—
The precipice she stood on was immense,
So was her creed in her own innocence.

---

[1] got heirs I.e., begot children, heirs to his estate.

[2] post-obits Latin: after death; here, referring to a legacy, that which comes after a death.

[3] Anacreon Moore Byron's friend Thomas Moore was known as "Anacreon" Moore because he first became famous for translating the lyric poems then attributed to the Roman poet Anacreon. The reference is to "Paradise and the Peri," one of the tales in Moore's Lalla Rookh (1817).

107

She thought of her own strength, and Juan's youth
And of the folly of all prudish fears,
Victorious virtue, and domestic truth,
And then of Don Alfonso's fifty years:
I wish these last had not occurred, in sooth,
Because that number rarely much endears,
And through all climes, the snowy and the sunny,
Sounds ill in love, whate'er it may in money.

108

When people say, "I've told you *fifty* times,"
They mean to scold, and very often do;
When poets say, "I've written *fifty* rhymes,"
They make you dread that they'll recite them too;
In gangs of *fifty*, thieves commit their crimes;
At *fifty* love for love is rare, 'tis true,
But then, no doubt, it equally as true is,
A good deal may be bought for *fifty* Louis.[1]

109

Julia had honour, virtue, truth, and love
For Don Alfonso; and she inly swore,
By all the vows below to powers above,
She never would disgrace the ring she wore,
Nor leave a wish which wisdom might reprove;
And while she pondered this, besides much more,
One hand on Juan's carelessly was thrown,
Quite by mistake—she thought it was her own;

110

Unconsciously she leaned upon the other,
Which played within the tangles of her hair;
And to contend with thoughts she could not smother,
She seemed by the distraction of her air.
'Twas surely very wrong in Juan's mother
To leave together this imprudent pair,
She who for many years had watched her son so—
I'm very certain *mine* would not have done so.

111

The hand which still held Juan's, by degrees
Gently, but palpably confirmed its grasp,
As if it said, "detain me, if you please;"
Yet there's no doubt she only meant to clasp
His fingers with a pure Platonic squeeze;
She would have shrunk as from a toad, or asp,
Had she imagined such a thing could rouse
A feeling dangerous to a prudent spouse.

112

I cannot know what Juan thought of this,
But what he did, is much what you would do;
His young lip thanked it with a grateful kiss,
And then, abashed at its own joy, withdrew
In deep despair, lest he had done amiss,
Love is so very timid when 'tis new:
She blushed, and frowned not, but she strove to speak,
And held her tongue, her voice was grown so weak.

113

The sun set, and up rose the yellow moon:
The devil's in the moon for mischief; they
Who called her CHASTE, methinks, began too soon
Their nomenclature; there is not a day,
The longest, not the twenty-first of June,
Sees half the business in a wicked way
On which three single hours of moonshine smile—
And then she looks so modest all the while.

114

There is a dangerous silence in that hour,
A stillness, which leaves room for the full soul
To open all itself, without the power
Of calling wholly back its self-control;
The silver light which, hallowing tree and tower,
Sheds beauty and deep softness o'er the whole,
Breathes also to the heart, and o'er it throws
A loving languor, which is not repose.

115

And Julia sat with Juan, half embraced
And half retiring from the glowing arm,
Which trembled like the bosom where 'twas placed;

---

1 *Louis* French gold coin.

Yet still she must have thought there was no harm,
Or else 'twere easy to withdraw her waist;
But then the situation had its charm,
And then—God knows what next—I can't go on;
920 I'm almost sorry that I e'er begun.

116

Oh Plato! Plato! you have paved the way,
With your confounded fantasies, to more
Immoral conduct by the fancied sway
Your system feigns o'er the controlless core
925 Of human hearts, than all the long array
Of poets and romancers:—You're a bore,
A charlatan, a coxcomb—and have been,
At best, no better than a go-between.

117

And Julia's voice was lost, except in sighs,
930 Until too late for useful conversation;
The tears were gushing from her gentle eyes,
I wish, indeed, they had not had occasion,
But who, alas! can love, and then be wise?
Not that remorse did not oppose temptation,
935 A little still she strove, and much repented,
And whispering "I will ne'er consent"—consented.

118

'Tis said that Xerxes[1] offered a reward
To those who could invent him a new pleasure;
Methinks, the requisition's rather hard,
940 And must have cost His majesty a treasure:
For my part, I'm a moderate-minded bard,
Fond of a little love (which I call leisure);
I care not for new pleasures, as the old
Are quite enough for me, so they but hold.

119

945 Oh Pleasure! you're indeed a pleasant thing,
Although one must be damned for you, no doubt;
I make a resolution every spring
Of reformation, ere the year run out,
But, somehow, this my vestal vow takes wing,

950 Yet still, I trust, it may be kept throughout:
I'm very sorry, very much ashamed,
And mean, next winter, to be quite reclaimed.

120

Here my chaste Muse a liberty must take—
Start not! still chaster reader—she'll be nice
hence—
955 Forward, and there is no great cause to quake;
This liberty is a poetic licence,
Which some irregularity may make
In the design, and as I have a high sense
Of Aristotle and the Rules,[2] 'tis fit
960 To beg his pardon when I err a bit.

121

This licence is to hope the reader will
Suppose from June the sixth (the fatal day,
Without whose epoch my poetic skill
For want of facts would all be thrown away),
965 But keeping Julia and Don Juan still
In sight, that several months have passed; we'll say
'Twas in November, but I'm not so sure
About the day—the era's more obscure.

122

We'll talk of that anon.—'Tis sweet to hear
970 At midnight on the blue and moonlit deep
The song and oar of Adria's gondolier,
By distance mellowed, o'er the waters sweep;
'Tis sweet to see the evening star appear;
'Tis sweet to listen as the night winds creep
975 From leaf to leaf; 'tis sweet to view on high
The rainbow, based on ocean, span the sky.

123

'Tis sweet to hear the watch-dog's honest bark
Bay deep-mouthed welcome as we draw near home;
'Tis sweet to know there is an eye will mark
980 Our coming, and look brighter when we come;
'Tis sweet to be awakened by the lark,

---

[1] *Xerxes* Xerxes was king of Persia from 486 to 465 BCE.

[2] *Rules* I.e., rules for literary composition set out in Aristotle's *Poetics*.

Or lulled by falling waters; sweet the hum
Of bees, the voice of girls, the song of birds,
The lisp of children, and their earliest words.

124

Sweet is the vintage, when the showering grapes
  In Bacchanal profusion reel to earth
Purple and gushing: sweet are our escapes
  From civic revelry to rural mirth;
Sweet to the miser are his glittering heaps,
  Sweet to the father is his first-born's birth,
Sweet is revenge—especially to women,
Pillage to soldiers, prize-money to seamen.

125

Sweet is a legacy, and passing sweet
  The unexpected death of some old lady
Or gentleman of seventy years complete,
  Who've made "us youth" wait too—too long already
For an estate, or cash, or country-seat,
  Still breaking, but with stamina so steady,
That all the Israelites are fit to mob its
Next owner for their double-damned post-obits.[1]

126

'Tis sweet to win, no matter how, one's laurels
  By blood or ink; 'tis sweet to put an end
To strife; 'tis sometimes sweet to have our quarrels,
  Particularly with a tiresome friend;
Sweet is old wine in bottles, ale in barrels;
  Dear is the helpless creature we defend
Against the world; and dear the schoolboy spot
We ne'er forget, though there we are forgot.

127

But sweeter still than this, than these, than all,
  Is first and passionate love—it stands alone,
Like Adam's recollection of his fall;
  The tree of knowledge has been plucked—all's
    known—
And life yields nothing further to recall

Worthy of this ambrosial sin, so shown,
No doubt in fable, as the unforgiven
Fire which Prometheus filched for us from heaven.

128

Man's a strange animal, and makes strange use
  Of his own nature, and the various arts,
And likes particularly to produce
  Some new experiment to show his parts;
This is the age of oddities let loose,
  Where different talents find their different marts;
You'd best begin with truth, and when you've lost your
Labour, there's a sure market for imposture.

129

What opposite discoveries we have seen!
  (Signs of true genius, and of empty pockets.)
One makes new noses, one a guillotine,
  One breaks your bones, one sets them in their
    sockets;
But vaccination certainly has been
  A kind antithesis to Congreve's rockets,
With which the Doctor paid off an old pox,
By borrowing a new one from an ox.[2]

130

Bread has been made (indifferent) from potatoes;
  And galvanism has set some corpses grinning,
But has not answered like the apparatus
  Of the Humane Society's beginning
By which men are unsuffocated gratis:
  What wondrous new machines have late been
    spinning!
I said the small-pox has gone out of late;
Perhaps it may be followed by the great.

---

[1] *post-obits* Here, loans repayable after a death; that is, when the borrower comes into an inheritance.

[2] *new noses* Benjamin Charles Perkins, an American quack, alleged that his metallic "tractors" could cure toes afflicted with the gout, as well as broken legs, flatulence, and red noses; *Congreve's rockets* Sir William Congreve (1772–1828) invented the Congreve rocket, which terrified the French at the Battle of Leipzig (1813), although it did little actual harm; *old pox … ox* Edward Jenner (1749–1823) created a vaccine against smallpox in 1796, using the related cow-pox virus as his inoculant.

131

'Tis said the great came from America;
    Perhaps it may set out on its return,—
The population there so spreads, they say
    'Tis grown high time to thin it in its turn,
1045 With war, or plague, or famine,[1] any way,
    So that civilisation they may learn;
And which in ravage the more loathsome evil is—
Their real lues,° or our pseudo-syphilis?   *syphilis*

132

This is the patent age of new inventions
1050   For killing bodies, and for saving souls,[2]
All propagated with the best intentions;
    Sir Humphry Davy's lantern, by which coals
Are safely mined for in the mode he mentions,[3]
    Timbuctoo travels, voyages to the Poles,[4]
1055 Are ways to benefit mankind, as true,
Perhaps, as shooting them at Waterloo.[5]

133

Man's a phenomenon, one knows not what,
    And wonderful beyond all wondrous measure;
'Tis pity though, in this sublime world, that
1060   Pleasure's a sin, and sometimes sin's a pleasure;
Few mortals know what end they would be at,
    But whether glory, power, or love, or treasure,
The path is through perplexing ways, and when
The goal is gained, we die, you know—and then—

134

1065 What then?—I do not know, no more do you—
    And so good night.—Return we to our story:
'Twas in November, when fine days are few,
    And the far mountains wax a little hoary,
And clap a white cape on their mantles blue;
1070   And the sea dashes round the promontory,
And the loud breaker boils against the rock,
And sober suns must set at five o'clock.

135

'Twas, as the watchmen say, a cloudy night;
    No moon, no stars, the wind was low or loud
1075 By gusts, and many a sparkling hearth was bright
    With the piled wood, round which the family crowd;
There's something cheerful in that sort of light,
    Even as a summer sky's without a cloud:
I'm fond of fire, and crickets, and all that,
1080 A lobster salad, and champagne, and chat.

136

'Twas midnight—Donna Julia was in bed,
    Sleeping, most probably,—when at her door
Arose a clatter might awake the dead,
    If they had never been awoke before,
1085 And that they have been so we all have read,
    And are to be so, at the least, once more—
The door was fastened, but with voice and fist
First knocks were heard, then "Madam—Madam—hist!"[6]

137

"For God's sake, Madam—Madam—here's my master,
1090   With more than half the city at his back—
Was ever heard of such a curst disaster!
    'Tis not my fault—I kept good watch—Alack!
Do, pray undo the bolt a little faster—
    They're on the stair just now, and in a crack
1095 Will all be here; perhaps he yet may fly—
Surely the window's not so *very* high!"

---

[1] *war, or plague, or famine* Byron here refers to the theory propounded by Thomas Malthus in *An Essay on the Principle of Population* (1798–1817).

[2] *killing bodies … saving souls* The British and Foreign Bible Society was founded in 1804.

[3] *Sir Humphry … mentions* Sir Humphrey Davy (1778–1829) invented the safety lantern in 1815.

[4] *Timbuctoo … Poles* Byron here refers to voyages of exploration such as those recounted in James Grey Jackson, *An Account of the Empire of Marocco* (1809) and Sir John Ross (1777–1856), *A Voyage of Discovery … for the Purpose of Exploring Baffin's Bay* (1819).

[5] *Waterloo* I.e., the Battle of Waterloo, 18 June 1815.

[6] *hist!* I.e., listen!

138

By this time Don Alfonso was arrived,
    With torches, friends, and servants in great number;
The major part of them had long been wived,
    And therefore paused not to disturb the slumber
Of any wicked woman, who contrived
    By stealth her husband's temples to encumber:[1]
Examples of this kind are so contagious,
Were *one* not punished, *all* would be outrageous.

139

I can't tell how, or why, or what suspicion
    Could enter into Don Alfonso's head;
But for a cavalier of his condition
    It surely was exceedingly ill-bred,
Without a word of previous admonition,
    To hold a levee[2] round his lady's bed,
And summon lackeys, armed with fire and sword,
To prove himself the thing he most abhorred.

140

Poor Donna Julia, starting as from sleep!
    (Mind —that I do not say—she had not slept)
Began at once to scream, and yawn, and weep;
    Her maid Antonia, who was an adept,[3]
Contrived to fling the bed-clothes in a heap,
    As if she had just now from out them crept:
I can't tell why she should take all this trouble
To prove her mistress had been sleeping double.[4]

141

But Julia mistress, and Antonia maid,
    Appeared like two poor harmless women, who
Of goblins, but still more of men afraid,
    Had thought one man might be deterred by two,
And therefore side by side were gently laid,
    Until the hours of absence should run through,

And truant husband should return, and say,
"My dear, I was the first who came away."

142

Now Julia found at length a voice, and cried,
    "In heaven's name, Don Alfonso, what d'ye mean?
Has madness seized you? would that I had died
    Ere such a monster's victim I had been!
What may this midnight violence betide,
    A sudden fit of drunkenness or spleen?
Dare you suspect me, whom the thought would kill?
Search, then, the room!"—Alfonso said, "I will."

143

He searched, *they* searched, and rummaged every where,
    Closet and clothes'-press, chest and window-seat,
And found much linen, lace, and several pair
    Of stockings, slippers, brushes, combs, complete,
With other articles of ladies fair,
    To keep them beautiful, or leave them neat:
Arras[5] they pricked and curtains with their swords,
And wounded several shutters, and some boards.

144

Under the bed they searched, and there they found—
    No matter what— it was not that they sought;
They opened windows, gazing if the ground
    Had signs or footmarks, but the earth said nought;
And then they stared each others' faces round:
    'Tis odd, not one of all these seekers thought,
And seems to me almost a sort of blunder,
Of looking *in* the bed as well as under.

145

During this inquisition, Julia's tongue
    Was not asleep—"Yes, search and search," she cried,
"Insult on insult heap, and wrong on wrong!
    It was for this that I became a bride!
For this in silence I have suffered long
    A husband like Alfonso at my side;
But now I'll bear no more, nor here remain,
If there be law, or lawyers, in all Spain.

---

1   *temples to encumber* That is, to give him horns, the traditional
symbol of a cuckold.

2   *levee* Morning reception.

3   *adept* Skilled person.

4   *sleeping double* I.e., with Antonia.

---

5   *Arras* Wall-hangings.

146

"Yes, Don Alfonso! husband now no more,
 If ever you indeed deserved the name,
Is't worthy of your years?—you have threescore,
 Fifty, or sixty—it is all the same—
1165 Is't wise or fitting causeless to explore
 For facts against a virtuous woman's fame?
Ungrateful, perjured, barbarous Don Alfonso,
How dare you think your lady would go on so?

147

"Is it for this I have disdained to hold
1170 The common privileges of my sex?
That I have chosen a confessor so old
 And deaf, that any other it would vex,
And never once he has had cause to scold,
 But found my very innocence perplex
1175 So much, he always doubted I was married—
How sorry you will be when I've miscarried!

148

"Was it for this that no Cortejo¹ ere
 I yet have chosen from out the youth of Seville?
Is it for this I scarce went any where,
1180 Except to bull-fights, mass, play, rout, and revel?
Is it for this, whate'er my suitors were,
 I favoured none—nay, was almost uncivil?
Is it for this that General Count O'Reilly,
Who took Algiers, declares I used him vilely?²

149

1185 "Did not the Italian Musico° Cazzani   musician
 Sing at my heart six months at least in vain?
Did not his countryman, Count Corniani,³
 Call me the only virtuous wife in Spain?
Were there not also Russians, English, many?

---

¹ *Cortejo* The acknowledged lover of a married woman.

² [Byron's note] Donna Julia here made a mistake. Count O'Reilly did not take Algiers—but Algiers very nearly took him: he and his army and fleet retreated with great loss, and not much credit, from before that city in the year 17[75]. [Alexander O'Reilly (1722–94), Irish-born Spanish general.]

³ *Cazzani* From cazzo (penis); *Corniani* From cornuto (horned; i.e., cuckolded).

1190 The Count Strongstroganoff I put in pain,
And Lord Mount Coffeehouse, the Irish peer,
Who killed himself for love (with wine) last year.

150

"Have I not had two bishops at my feet?
 The Duke of Ichar, and Don Fernán Nunez?
1195 And is it thus a faithful wife you treat?
 I wonder in what quarter now the moon is:
I praise your vast forbearance not to beat
 Me also, since the time so opportune is—
Oh, valiant man! with sword drawn and cocked trigger,
1200 Now, tell me, don't you cut a pretty figure?

151

"Was it for this you took your sudden journey,
 Under pretence of business indispensible
With that sublime of rascals your attorney,
 Whom I see standing there, and looking sensible
1205 Of having played the fool? though both I spurn, he
 Deserves the worst, his conduct's less defensible,
Because, no doubt, 'twas for his dirty fee,
And not from any love to you nor me.

152

"If he comes here to take a deposition,
1210 By all means let the gentleman proceed;
You've made the apartment in a fit condition:—
 There's pen and ink for you, sir, when you need—
Let every thing be noted with precision,
 I would not you for nothing should be feed—
1215 But, as my maid's undrest, pray turn your spies out."
"Oh!" sobbed Antonia, "I could tear their eyes out."

153

"There is the closet, there the toilet, there
 The antechamber—search them under, over;
There is the sofa, there the great arm-chair,
1220 The chimney—which would really hold a lover.
I wish to sleep, and beg you will take care
 And make no further noise, till you discover
The secret cavern of this lurking treasure—
And when 'tis found, let me, too, have that pleasure.

154

"And now, Hidalgo! now that you have thrown
  Doubt upon me, confusion over all,
Pray have the courtesy to make it known
  Who is the man you search for? how d'ye call
Him? what's his lineage? let him but be shown—
  I hope he's young and handsome—is he tall?
Tell me—and be assured, that since you stain
My honour thus, it shall not be in vain.

155

"At least, perhaps, he has not sixty years,
  At that age he would be too old for slaughter,
Or for so young a husband's jealous fears—
  (Antonia! let me have a glass of water.)
I am ashamed of having shed these tears,
  They are unworthy of my father's daughter;
My mother dreamed not in my natal hour
That I should fall into a monster's power.

156

"Perhaps 'tis of Antonia you are jealous,
  You saw that she was sleeping by my side
When you broke in upon us with your fellows:
  Look where you please—we've nothing, sir, to hide;
Only another time, I trust, you'll tell us,
  Or for the sake of decency abide
A moment at the door, that we may be
Drest to receive so much good company.

157

"And now, sir, I have done, and say no more;
  The little I have said may serve to show
The guileless heart in silence may grieve o'er
  The wrongs to whose exposure it is slow:—
I leave you to your conscience as before,
  'Twill one day ask you *why* you used me so?
God grant you feel not then the bitterest grief!
Antonia! where's my pocket-handkerchief?"

158

She ceased, and turned upon her pillow; pale
  She lay, her dark eyes flashing through their tears,
Like skies that rain and lighten; as a veil,

Waved and o'ershading her wan cheek, appears
  Her streaming hair; the black curls strive, but fail,
To hide the glossy shoulder, which uprears
  Its snow through all;—her soft lips lie apart,
And louder than her breathing beats her heart.

159

The Senhor Don Alfonso stood confused;
  Antonia bustled round the ransacked room,
And, turning up her nose, with looks abused
  Her master, and his myrmidons,[1] of whom
Not one, except the attorney, was amused;
  He, like Achates,[2] faithful to the tomb,
So there were quarrels, cared not for the cause,
Knowing they must be settled by the laws.

160

With prying snub-nose, and small eyes, he stood,
  Following Antonia's motions here and there,
With much suspicion in his attitude;
  For reputations he had little care;
So that a suit or action were made good,
  Small pity had he for the young and fair,
And ne'er believed in negatives, till these
Were proved by competent false witnesses.

161

But Don Alfonso stood with downcast looks,
  And, truth to say, he made a foolish figure;
When, after searching in five hundred nooks,
  And treating a young wife with so much rigour,
He gained no point, except some self-rebukes,
  Added to those his lady with such vigour
Had poured upon him for the last half-hour,
Quick, thick, and heavy—as a thunder-shower.

162

At first he tried to hammer an excuse,
  To which the sole reply were tears and sobs,
And indications of hysterics, whose

---

[1] *myrmidons* Warriors led by Achilles to the siege of Troy.

[2] *Achates* Aeneas's companion in *The Aeneid*, famous for his faithfulness.

Prologue is always certain throes, and throbs,
Gasps, and whatever else the owners choose:—
   Alfonso saw his wife, and thought of Job's;[1]
1295 He saw too, in perspective, her relations,
And then he tried to muster all his patience.

163

He stood in act to speak, or rather stammer,
   But sage Antonia cut him short before
The anvil of his speech received the hammer,
1300   With "Pray, sir, leave the room, and say no more,
Or madam dies."—Alfonso muttered, "D—n her,"
   But nothing else, the time of words was o'er;
He cast a rueful look or two, and did,
He knew not wherefore, that which he was bid.

164

1305 With him retired his "*posse comitatus*,"[2]
   The attorney last, who lingered near the door,
Reluctantly, still tarrying there as late as
   Antonia let him—not a little sore
At this most strange and unexplained "*hiatus*"
1310   In Don Alfonso's facts, which just now wore
An awkward look; as he revolved the case,
The door was fastened in his legal face.

165

No sooner was it bolted, than—Oh shame!
   Oh sin! Oh sorrow! and Oh womankind!
1315 How can you do such things and keep your fame,
   Unless this world, and t'other too, be blind?
Nothing so dear as an unfilched good name!
   But to proceed—for there is more behind:
With much heart-felt reluctance be it said,
1320 Young Juan slipped, half-smothered, from the bed.

166

He had been hid—I don't pretend to say
   How, nor can I indeed describe the where—
Young, slender, and packed easily, he lay,

No doubt, in little compass, round or square;
1325 But pity him I neither must nor may
   His suffocation by that pretty pair;
'Twere better, sure, to die so, than be shut
With maudlin Clarence in his Malmsey butt.[3]

167

And, secondly, I pity not, because
1330   He had no business to commit a sin,
Forbid by heavenly, fined by human laws,
   At least 'twas rather early to begin;
But at sixteen the conscience rarely gnaws
   So much as when we call our old debts in
1335 At sixty years, and draw the accompts of evil,
And find a deuced balance with the devil.

168

Of his position I can give no notion:
   'Tis written in the Hebrew Chronicle,
How the physicians, leaving pill and potion,
1340   Prescribed, by way of blister, a young belle,
When old King David's blood grew dull in motion,[4]
   And that the medicine answered very well;
Perhaps 'twas in a different way applied,
For David lived, but Juan nearly died.

169

1345 What's to be done? Alfonso will be back
   The moment he has sent his fools away.
Antonia's skill was put upon the rack,
   But no device could be brought into play—
And how to parry the renewed attack?
1350   Besides, it wanted but few hours of day:
Antonia puzzled; Julia did not speak,
But pressed her bloodless lip to Juan's cheek.

---

1 *Job's* Job's (unnamed) wife criticizes him harshly at the moment when his suffering is most extreme.

2 *posse comitatus* Latin: literally, "the power of the county," a group of deputies.

3 *Clarence ... butt* According to rumors that passed into legend, King Richard III of England, when Duke of Gloucester, arranged for his elder brother the Duke of Clarence to be drowned in a barrel of Malmsey wine, thus moving Richard closer to the throne. A "butt" is a unit of measure used for a large quantity of wine.

4 *When old ... motion* See 1 Kings 1.1–4.

855

170

He turned his lip to hers, and with his hand
    Called back the tangles of her wandering hair;
Even then their love they could not all command,
    And half forgot their danger and despair:
Antonia's patience now was at a stand—
    "Come, come, 'tis no time now for fooling there,"
She whispered, in great wrath—"I must deposit
This pretty gentleman within the closet.

171

"Pray, keep your nonsense for some luckier night—
    Who can have put my master in this mood?
What will become on't—I'm in such a fright,
    The devil's in the urchin, and no good—
Is this a time for giggling? this a plight?
    Why, don't you know that it may end in blood?
You'll lose your life, and I shall lose my place,
My mistress all, for that half-girlish face.

172

"Had it but been for a stout cavalier
    Of twenty-five or thirty—(Come, make haste)
But for a child, what piece of work is here!
    I really, madam, wonder at your taste—
(Come, sir, get in)—my master must be near.
    There, for the present, at the least he's fast,
And if we can but till the morning keep
Our counsel—(Juan, mind, you must not sleep.)"

173

Now, Don Alfonso entering, but alone,
    Closed the oration of the trusty maid:
She loitered, and he told her to be gone,
    An order somewhat sullenly obeyed;
However, present remedy was none,
    And no great good seemed answered if she staid:
Regarding both with slow and sidelong view,
She snuffed the candle, curtsied, and withdrew.

174

Alfonso paused a minute—then begun
    Some strange excuses for his late proceeding;
He would not justify what he had done,

To say the best, it was extreme ill-breeding;
    But there were ample reasons for it, none
Of which he specified in this his pleading:
    His speech was a fine sample, on the whole,
Of rhetoric, which the learned call "*rigmarole*."

175

Julia said nought; though all the while there rose
    A ready answer, which at once enables
A matron, who her husband's foible knows,
    By a few timely words to turn the tables,
Which if it does not silence still must pose,
    Even if it should comprise a pack of fables;
'Tis to retort with firmness, and when he
Suspects with *one*, do you reproach with *three*.

176

Julia, in fact, had tolerable grounds,
    Alfonso's loves with Inez were well known;
But whether 'twas that one's own guilt confounds,
    But that can't be, as has been often shown,
A lady with apologies abounds;
    It might be that her silence sprang alone
From delicacy to Don Juan's ear,
To whom she knew his mother's fame was dear.

177

There might be one more motive, which makes two,
    Alfonso ne'er to Juan had alluded,
Mentioned his jealousy, but never who
    Had been the happy lover, he concluded,
Concealed amongst his premises; 'tis true,
    His mind the more o'er this its mystery brooded;
To speak of Inez now were, one may say,
Like throwing Juan in Alfonso's way.

178

A hint, in tender cases, is enough;
    Silence is best, besides there is a *tact*
(That modern phrase appears to me sad stuff,
    But it will serve to keep my verse compact)
Which keeps, when pushed by questions rather rough,
    A lady always distant from the fact—

The charming creatures lie with such a grace,
There's nothing so becoming to the face.

179

1425 They blush, and we believe them; at least I
        Have always done so; 'tis of no great use,
In any case, attempting a reply,
        For then their eloquence grows quite profuse;
And when at length they're out of breath, they sigh,
1430   And cast their languid eyes down, and let loose
A tear or two, and then we make it up;
And then—and then—and then—sit down and sup.

180

Alfonso closed his speech, and begged her pardon,
        Which Julia half withheld, and then half granted,
1435 And laid conditions, he thought, very hard on,
        Denying several little things he wanted:
He stood like Adam lingering near his garden,
        With useless penitence perplexed and haunted,
Beseeching she no further would refuse,
1440 When, lo! he stumbled o'er a pair of shoes.

181

A pair of shoes!—what then? not much, if they
        Are such as fit with lady's feet, but these
(No one can tell how much I grieve to say)
        Were masculine; to see them, and to seize,
1445 Was but a moment's act.—Ah! Well-a-day!
        My teeth begin to chatter, my veins freeze—
Alfonso first examined well their fashion,
And then flew out into another passion.

182

He left the room for his relinquished sword,
1450   And Julia instant to the closet flew.
"Fly, Juan, fly! for heaven's sake—not a word—
        The door is open—you may yet slip through
The passage you so often have explored—
        Here is the garden-key—Fly—fly—Adieu!
1455 Haste—haste!—I hear Alfonso's hurrying feet—
Day has not broke—there's no one in the street."

183

None can say that this was not good advice,
        The only mischief was, it came too late;
Of all experience 'tis the usual price,
1460   A sort of income-tax laid on by fate:
Juan had reached the room-door in a trice,
        And might have done so by the garden-gate,
But met Alfonso in his dressing-gown,
Who threatened death—so Juan knocked him down.

184

1465 Dire was the scuffle, and out went the light,
        Antonia cried out "Rape!" and Julia "Fire!"
But not a servant stirred to aid the fight.
        Alfonso, pommelled to his heart's desire,
Swore lustily he'd be revenged this night;
1470   And Juan, too, blasphemed an octave higher,
His blood was up; though young, he was a Tartar,
And not at all disposed to prove a martyr.

185

Alfonso's sword had dropped ere he could draw it,
        And they continued battling hand to hand,
1475 For Juan very luckily ne'er saw it;
        His temper not being under great command,
If at that moment he had chanced to claw it,
        Alfonso's days had not been in the land
Much longer.—Think of husbands', lovers' lives!
1480 And how ye may be doubly widows—wives!

186

Alfonso grappled to detain the foe,
        And Juan throttled him to get away,
And blood ('twas from the nose) began to flow;
        At last, as they more faintly wrestling lay,
1485 Juan contrived to give an awkward blow,
        And then his only garment quite gave way;
He fled, like Joseph, leaving it; but there,
I doubt, all likeness ends between the pair.[1]

---

[1] *He fled ... the pair* See the story of Joseph and Potiphar's wife,
Genesis 39.7–20.

187

Lights came at length, and men, and maids, who found
　　An awkward spectacle their eyes before;
Antonia in hysterics, Julia swooned,
　　Alfonso leaning, breathless, by the door;
Some half-torn drapery scattered on the ground,
　　Some blood, and several footsteps, but no more:
Juan the gate gained, turned the key about,
And liking not the inside, locked the out.

188

Here ends this canto.—Need I sing, or say,
　　How Juan, naked, favoured by the night,
Who favours what she should not, found his way,
　　And reached his home in an unseemly plight?
The pleasant scandal which arose next day,
　　The nine days' wonder which was brought to light,
And how Alfonso sued for a divorce,
Were in the English newspapers, of course.

189

If you would like to see the whole proceedings,
　　The depositions, and the cause at full,
The names of all the witnesses, the pleadings
　　Of counsel to nonsuit, or to annul,
There's more than one edition, and the readings
　　Are various, but they none of them are dull,
The best is that in short-hand ta'en by Gurney,[1]
Who to Madrid on purpose made a journey.

190

But Donna Inez, to divert the train
　　Of one of the most circulating scandals
That had for centuries been known in Spain,
　　At least since the retirement of the Vandals,
First vowed (and never had she vowed in vain)
　　To Virgin Mary several pounds of candles;
And then, by the advice of some old ladies,
She sent her son to be shipped off from Cadiz.

---

[1] *Gurney* William Brodie Gurney (1777–1855), official shorthand writer to the Houses of Parliament, also reported several notorious trials.

191

She had resolved that he should travel through
　　All European climes, by land or sea,
To mend his former morals, or get new,
　　Especially in France and Italy,
1525 (At least this is the thing most people do.)
　　Julia was sent into a convent; she
Grieved, but, perhaps, her feelings may be better
Shown in the following copy of her letter:

192

"They tell me 'tis decided; you depart:
1530　　'Tis wise—'tis well, but not the less a pain;
I have no further claim on your young heart,
　　Mine is the victim, and would be again;
To love too much has been the only art
　　I used;—I write in haste, and if a stain
1535 Be on this sheet, 'tis not what it appears,
My eyeballs burn and throb, but have no tears.

193

"I loved, I love you, for this love have lost
　　State, station, heaven, mankind's, my own esteem,
And yet can not regret what it hath cost,
1540　　So dear is still the memory of that dream;
Yet, if I name my guilt, 'tis not to boast,
　　None can deem harshlier of me than I deem:
I trace this scrawl because I cannot rest—
I've nothing to reproach, or to request.

194

1545 "Man's love is of man's life a thing apart,
　　'Tis woman's whole existence; man may range
The court, camp, church, the vessel, and the mart;
　　Sword, gown, gain, glory, offer in exchange
Pride, fame, ambition, to fill up his heart,
1550　　And few there are whom these cannot estrange;
Men have all these resources, we but one,
To love again, and be again undone.

195

"You will proceed in pleasure, and in pride,
　　Beloved and loving many; all is o'er
1555 For me on earth, except some years to hide

My shame and sorrow deep in my heart's core;
These I could bear, but cannot cast aside
    The passion which still rages as before,
And so farewell—forgive me, love me—No,
1560 That word is idle now—but let it go.

196

"My breast has been all weakness, is so yet;
    But still I think I can collect my mind;
My blood still rushes where my spirit's set,
    As roll the waves before the settled wind;
1565 My heart is feminine, nor can forget—
    To all, except one image, madly blind;
So shakes the needle, and so stands the pole,
As vibrates my fond heart to my fixed soul.

197

"I have no more to say, but linger still,
1570   And dare not set my seal upon this sheet,
And yet I may as well the task fulfil,
    My misery can scarce be more complete:
I had not lived till now, could sorrow kill;
    Death shuns the wretch who fain the blow would
        meet,
1575 And I must even survive this last adieu,
And bear with life, to love and pray for you!"

198

This note was written upon gilt-edged paper
    With a neat little crow-quill, slight and new;
Her small white hand could hardly reach the taper,
1580   It trembled as magnetic needles do,
And yet she did not let one tear escape her;
    The seal a sun-flower; "*Elle vous suit partout*,"[1]
The motto, cut upon a white cornelian;
The wax was superfine, its hue vermilion.

199

1585 This was Don Juan's earliest scrape; but whether
    I shall proceed with his adventures is
Dependent on the public altogether;
    We'll see, however, what they say to this,

Their favour in an author's cap's a feather,
1590   And no great mischief's done by their caprice;
And if their approbation we experience,
Perhaps they'll have some more about a year hence.

200

My poem's epic, and is meant to be
    Divided in twelve books; each book containing,
1595 With love, and war, a heavy gale at sea,
    A list of ships, and captains, and kings reigning,
New characters; the episodes are three:
    A panorama view of hell's in training,
After the style of Virgil and of Homer,
1600 So that my name of Epic's no misnomer.[2]

201

All these things will be specified in time,
    With strict regard to Aristotle's rules,
The *Vade Mecum*[3] of the true sublime,
    Which makes so many poets, and some fools;
1605 Prose poets like blank-verse, I'm fond of rhyme,
    Good workmen never quarrel with their tools;
I've got new mythological machinery,
And very handsome supernatural scenery.

202

There's only one slight difference between
1610   Me and my epic brethren gone before,
And here the advantage is my own, I ween;
    (Not that I have not several merits more,
But this will more peculiarly be seen)
    They so embellish, that 'tis quite a bore
1615 Their labyrinth of fables to thread through,
Whereas this story's actually true.

203

If any person doubt it, I appeal
    To history, tradition, and to facts,
To newspapers, whose truth all know and feel,
1620   To plays in five, and operas in three acts;

---

1 *Elle ... partout* French: She follows you everywhere.

2 *My poem's ... no misnomer* Byron lists the traditional elements of an epic poem. See also the letter to John Murray, 16 February 1821 (below).

3 *Vade Mecum* Latin: Go with me; i.e., a guidebook.

All these confirm my statement a good deal,
    But that which more completely faith exacts
Is, that myself, and several now in Seville,
    Saw Juan's last elopement with the devil.

204

25 If ever I should condescend to prose,
    I'll write poetical commandments, which
Shall supersede beyond all doubt all those
    That went before; in these I shall enrich
My text with many things that no one knows,
30   And carry precept to the highest pitch:
I'll call the work "Longinus o'er a Bottle,
Or, Every Poet his *own* Aristotle."[1]

205

 Thou shalt believe in Milton, Dryden, Pope;
    Thou shalt not set up Wordsworth, Coleridge,
        Southey;
35 Because the first is crazed beyond all hope,
    The second drunk, the third so quaint and mouthey:
With Crabbe it may be difficult to cope,
    And Campbell's Hippocrene[2] is somewhat
        drouthy:°   *dry*
Thou shalt not steal from Samuel Rogers, nor
40 Commit—flirtation with the muse of Moore.

206

Thou shalt not covet Mr. Sotheby's[3] Muse,
    His Pegasus, nor any thing that's his;
Thou shalt not bear false witness like "the Blues,"[4]
    (There's *one*, at least, is very fond of this);
45 Thou shalt not write, in short, but what I choose:
    This is true criticism, and you may kiss—
Exactly as you please, or not, the rod,
But if you don't, I'll lay it on, by G——d!

---

[1] *Longinus … Aristotle* Longinus, *On the Sublime,* and Aristotle, *Poetics*: two renowned works of literary theory.

[2] *Hippocrene* A fountain sacred to the Muses, which started flowing when the winged horse Pegasus (see line 1642) struck the ground with his hoof.

[3] *Sotheby* William Sotheby (1757–1833), poet.

[4] *Blues* Group of intellectual women commonly called the Bluestockings.

207

If any person should presume to assert
1650   This story is not moral, first, I pray,
That they will not cry out before they're hurt,
    Then that they'll read it o'er again, and say,
(But, doubtless, nobody will be so pert)
    That this is not a moral tale, though gay;
1655 Besides, in canto twelfth, I mean to show
The very place where wicked people go.

208

If, after all, there should be some so blind
    To their own good this warning to despise,
Led by some tortuosity of mind,
1660   Not to believe my verse and their own eyes,
And cry that they "the moral cannot find,"
    I tell him, if a clergyman, he lies;
Should captains the remark or critics make,
They also lie too—under a mistake.

209

1665 The public approbation I expect,
    And beg they'll take my word about the moral,
Which I with their amusement will connect,
    (So children cutting teeth receive a coral);[5]
Meantime, they'll doubtless please to recollect
1670   My epical pretensions to the laurel:
For fear some prudish readers should grow skittish,
I've bribed my grandmother's review—the British.[6]

210

I sent it in a letter to the editor,
    Who thanked me duly by return of post—
1675 I'm for a handsome article his creditor;
    Yet if my gentle Muse he please to roast,
And break a promise after having made it her,
    Denying the receipt of what it cost,
And smear his page with gall instead of honey,
1680 All I can say is—that he had the money.

---

[5] *coral* Teething rings were commonly made of coral.

[6] *British* William Roberts, editor of the *British Review*, took this accusation seriously and contradicted it in his review of *Don Juan*, prompting Byron to write "Letter to the Editor of my Grandmother's Review" (1822).

211

I think that with this holy *new* alliance
 I may ensure the public, and defy
All other magazines of art or science,
 Daily, or monthly, or three monthly; I
1685 Have not essayed to multiply their clients,
 Because they tell me 'twere in vain to try,
And that the Edinburgh Review and Quarterly
Treat a dissenting author very martyrly.

212

"*Non ego hoc ferrem calida juventa*
1690 *Consule Planco*,"[1] Horace said, and so
Say I; by which quotation there is meant a
 Hint that some six or seven good years ago
(Long ere I dreamt of dating from the Brenta)[2]
 I was most ready to return a blow,
1695 And would not brook at all this sort of thing
In my hot youth—when George the Third was King.

213

But now at thirty years my hair is gray—
 (I wonder what it will be like at forty?
I thought of a peruke° the other day)   *wig*
1700 My heart is not much greener; and, in short, I
Have squandered my whole summer while 'twas May,
 And feel no more the spirit to retort; I
Have spent my life, both interest and principal,
And deem not, what I deemed, my soul invincible.

214

1705 No more—no more—Oh! never more on me
 The freshness of the heart can fall like dew,
Which out of all the lovely things we see
 Extracts emotions beautiful and new,
Hived in our bosoms like the bag o' the bee:
1710 Think'st thou the honey with those objects grew?
Alas! 'twas not in them, but in thy power
To double even the sweetness of a flower.

215

No more—no more—Oh! never more, my heart,
 Canst thou be my sole world, my universe!
1715 Once all in all, but now a thing apart,
 Thou canst not be my blessing or my curse:
The illusion's gone for ever, and thou art
 Insensible, I trust, but none the worse,
And in thy stead I've got a deal of judgment,
1720 Though heaven knows how it ever found a lodgement.

216

My days of love are over, me no more[3]
 The charms of maid, wife, and still less of widow,
Can make the fool of which they made before,
 In short, I must not lead the life I did do;
1725 The credulous hope of mutual minds is o'er,
 The copious use of claret is forbid too,
So for a good old-gentlemanly vice,
I think I must take up with avarice.

217

Ambition was my idol, which was broken
1730 Before the shrines of Sorrow and of Pleasure;
And the two last have left me many a token
 O'er which reflection may be made at leisure:
Now, like Friar Bacon's brazen head,[4] I've spoken,
 "Time is, Time was, Time's past,"—a
  chymic° treasure   *counterfeit gold*
1735 Is glittering youth, which I have spent betimes—
My heart in passion, and my head on rhymes.

218

What is the end of Fame? 'tis but to fill
 A certain portion of uncertain paper:
Some liken it to climbing up a hill,
1740 Whose summit, like all hills, is lost in vapour;

---

1 *Non ... Planco* Latin: I would not have borne with this in the heat of my youth, when Plancus was consul. Horace, *Odes* 3.14.27–28.

2 *Brenta* River flowing into the Adriatic at Venice.

3 [Byron's note] 'Me nec femina, nec puer
    Jam, nec spes animi credula mutui,
   Nec certare juvat mero;
    Nec vincire novis tempora floribus.'
[Horace, *Odes* 4.1.30: "Now neither a woman nor a boy delights me, nor confident hope of love returned, nor drinking bouts, nor binding my temples with fresh flowers."]

4 *Friar Bacon's brazen head* See Robert Greene's *Friar Bacon and Friar Bungay* (c. 1589).

For this men write, speak, preach, and heroes kill,
    And bards burn what they call their "midnight
        taper,"
To have, when the original is dust,
A name, a wretched picture, and worse bust.[1]

219

What are the hopes of man? old Egypt's King
    Cheops erected the first pyramid
And largest, thinking it was just the thing
    To keep his memory whole, and mummy hid;
But somebody or other rummaging,
    Burglariously broke his coffin's lid:
Let not a monument give you or me hopes,
Since not a pinch of dust remains of Cheops.

220

But I, being fond of true philosophy,
    Say very often to myself, "Alas!
All things that have been born were born to die,
    And flesh (which Death mows down to hay) is grass;[2]
You've passed your youth not so unpleasantly,
    And if you had it o'er again—'twould pass—
So thank your stars that matters are no worse,
And read your Bible, sir, and mind your purse."

221

But for the present, gentle reader! and
    Still gentler purchaser! the bard—that's I—
Must, with permission, shake you by the hand,
    And so your humble servant, and good-bye!
We meet again, if we should understand
    Each other; and if not, I shall not try
Your patience further than by this short sample—
'Twere well if others followed my example.

222

"Go, little book, from this my solitude!
    I cast thee on the waters—go thy ways!
And if, as I believe, thy vein be good,

The world will find thee after many days."
When Southey's read, and Wordsworth, understood,
    I can't help putting in my claim to praise—
1775 The four first rhymes are Southey's every line:[3]
For God's sake, reader! take them not for mine.

Canto 2

1

Oh ye! who teach the ingenuous youth of nations,
    Holland, France, England, Germany, or Spain,
I pray ye flog them upon all occasions,
    It mends their morals; never mind the pain:
5 The best of mothers and of educations
    In Juan's case were but employed in vain,
Since in a way, that's rather of the oddest, he
Became divested of his native modesty.

2

Had he but been placed at a public school,
10   In the third form, or even in the fourth,
His daily task had kept his fancy cool,
    At least, had he been nurtured in the north;
Spain may prove an exception to the rule,
    But then exceptions always prove its worth—
15 A lad of sixteen causing a divorce
Puzzled his tutors very much, of course.

3

I can't say that it puzzles me at all,
    If all things be considered: first, there was
His lady-mother, mathematical,
20   A—never mind; his tutor, an old ass;
A pretty woman—(that's quite natural,
    Or else the thing had hardly come to pass);
A husband rather old, not much in unity
With his young wife—a time, and opportunity.

---

[1] *bust* Byron sat for a number of busts and disliked all the results; he also found fault with most of his portraits.

[2] *flesh ... grass* See Isaiah 40.6.

[3] *Southey's every line* From Southey, *The Lay of the Laureate* (1816), "L'Envoy."

4

25 Well—well, the world must turn upon its axis,
　　And all mankind turn with it, heads or tails,
And live and die, make love and pay our taxes,
　　And as the veering wind shifts, shift our sails;
The king commands us, and the doctor quacks us,
30 　　The priest instructs, and so our life exhales,
A little breath, love, wine, ambition, fame,
Fighting, devotion, dust,—perhaps a name.

5

I said that Juan had been sent to Cadiz—
　　A pretty town, I recollect it well—
35 'Tis there the mart of the colonial trade is,
　　(Or was, before Peru learned to rebel)[1]
And such sweet girls—I mean, such graceful ladies,
　　Their very walk would make your bosom swell;
I can't describe it, though so much it strike,
40 Nor liken it—I never saw the like.

6

An Arab horse, a stately stag, a barb
　　New broke, a camelopard,° a gazelle,　　　　　giraffe
No—none of these will do;—and then their garb!
　　Their veil and petticoat—Alas! to dwell
45 Upon such things would very near absorb
　　A canto—then their feet and ankles—well,
Thank Heaven I've got no metaphor quite ready,
(And so, my sober Muse—come, let's be steady—

7

Chaste Muse!—well, if you must, you must)—the veil
50 　　Thrown back a moment with the glancing hand,
While the o'erpowering eye, that turns you pale,
　　Flashes into the heart:—All sunny land
Of love! when I forget you, may I fail
　　To—say my prayers—but never was there planned
55 A dress through which the eyes give such a volley,
Excepting the Venetian Fazzioli.[2]

8

But to our tale: the Donna Inez sent
　　Her son to Cadiz only to embark;
To stay there had not answered her intent,
60 　　But why?—we leave the reader in the dark—
'Twas for a voyage the young man was meant,
　　As if a Spanish ship were Noah's ark,
To wean him from the wickedness of earth,
And send him like a dove of promise forth.

9

65 Don Juan bade his valet pack his things
　　According to direction, then received
A lecture and some money: for four springs
　　He was to travel; and though Inez grieved,
(As every kind of parting has its stings)
70 　　She hoped he would improve—perhaps believed:
A letter, too, she gave (he never read it)
Of good advice—and two or three of credit.[3]

10

In the mean time, to pass her hours away,
　　Brave Inez now set up a Sunday school
75 For naughty children, who would rather play
　　(Like truant rogues) the devil, or the fool;
Infants of three years old were taught that day,
　　Dunces were whipt, or set upon a stool:
The great success of Juan's education
80 Spurred her to teach another generation.

11

Juan embarked—the ship got under way,
　　The wind was fair, the water passing rough;
A devil of a sea rolls in that Bay,
　　As I, who've crossed it oft, know well enough;
85 And, standing upon deck, the dashing spray
　　Flies in one's face, and makes it weather-tough:
And there he stood to take, and take again,
His first—perhaps his last—farewell of Spain.

---

[1] *Peru learned to rebel* Peru rebelled against Spain in 1813, and would finally win its independence in 1824.

[2] [Byron's note] *Fazzioli*—literally, little handkerchiefs—the veils most availing of St. Mark.

---

[3] *letter … of credit* For presentation in order to procure funds.

12

I can't but say it is an awkward sight
    To see one's native land receding through
The growing waters; it unmans one quite,
    Especially when life is rather new:
I recollect Great Britain's coast looks white,
    But almost every other country's blue,
When gazing on them, mystified by distance,
We enter on our nautical existence.

13

So Juan stood, bewildered, on the deck:
    The wind sung, cordage strained, and sailors swore,
And the ship creaked, the town became a speck,
    From which away so fair and fast they bore.
The best of remedies is a beef-steak
    Against sea-sickness; try it, sir, before
You sneer, and I assure you this is true,
For I have found it answer—so may you.

14

Don Juan stood, and, gazing from the stern,
    Beheld his native Spain receding far:
First partings form a lesson hard to learn,
    Even nations feel this when they go to war;
There is a sort of unexpressed concern,
    A kind of shock that sets one's heart ajar:
At leaving even the most unpleasant people
And places, one keeps looking at the steeple.

15

But Juan had got many things to leave,
    His mother, and a mistress, and no wife,
So that he had much better cause to grieve
    Than many persons more advanced in life;
And if we now and then a sigh must heave
    At quitting even those we quit in strife,
No doubt we weep for those the heart endears—
That is, till deeper griefs congeal our tears.

16

So Juan wept, as wept the captive Jews
    By Babel's waters, still remembering Sion:[1]
I'd weep, but mine is not a weeping Muse,
    And such light griefs are not a thing to die on;
Young men should travel, if but to amuse
    Themselves; and the next time their servants tie on
Behind their carriages their new portmanteau,
Perhaps it may be lined with this my canto.

17

And Juan wept, and much he sighed and thought,
    While his salt tears dropped into the salt sea,
"Sweets to the sweet;" (I like so much to quote;
    You must excuse this extract, 'tis where she,
The Queen of Denmark, for Ophelia brought
    Flowers to the grave);[2] and, sobbing often, he
Reflected on his present situation,
And seriously resolved on reformation.

18

"Farewell, my Spain! a long farewell!" he cried,
    "Perhaps I may revisit thee no more,
But die, as many an exiled heart hath died,
    Of its own thirst to see again thy shore:
Farewell, where Guadalquivir's waters glide!
    Farewell, my mother! and, since all is o'er,
Farewell, too, dearest Julia!"—(Here he drew
Her letter out again, and read it through.)

19

"And, oh! if e'er I should forget, I swear—
    But that's impossible, and cannot be—
Sooner shall this blue ocean melt to air,
    Sooner shall earth resolve itself to sea,
Than I resign thine image, Oh, my fair!
    Or think of any thing excepting thee;
A mind diseased no remedy can physic—"
(Here the ship gave a lurch, and he grew sea-sick.)

---

[1] *Babel's waters ... Sion* See Psalm 137.1.

[2] *Sweets to ... the grave* See Shakespeare's *Hamlet* 4.3.

20

"Sooner shall heaven kiss earth—(here he fell sicker)
　Oh, Julia! what is every other woe?—
155　(For God's sake let me have a glass of liquor;—
　　Pedro, Battista, help me down below.)
Julia, my love!—(you rascal, Pedro, quicker)—
　　Oh Julia!—(this curst vessel pitches so)—
Beloved Julia, hear me still beseeching!"
160　(Here he grew inarticulate with retching.)

21

He felt that chilling heaviness of heart,
　Or rather stomach, which, alas! attends,
Beyond the best apothecary's art,
　The loss of love, the treachery of friends,
165　Or death of those we dote on, when a part
　　Of us dies with them as each fond hope ends:
No doubt he would have been much more pathetic,
But the sea acted as a strong emetic.

22

Love's a capricious power; I've known it hold
170　Out through a fever caused by its own heat,
But be much puzzled by a cough and cold,
　And find a quinsy very hard to treat;
Against all noble maladies he's bold,
　But vulgar illnesses don't like to meet,
175　Nor that a sneeze should interrupt his sigh,
Nor inflammations redden his blind eye.

23

But worst of all is nausea, or a pain
　About the lower region of the bowels;
Love, who heroically breathes a vein,
180　Shrinks from the application of hot towels,
And purgatives are dangerous to his reign,
　Sea-sickness death: his love was perfect, how else
Could Juan's passion, while the billows roar,
Resist his stomach, ne'er at sea before?

24

185 The ship, called the most holy "Trinidada,"[1]
　Was steering duly for the port Leghorn;
For there the Spanish family Moncada
　Were settled long ere Juan's sire was born:
They were relations, and for them he had a
190　Letter of introduction, which the morn
Of his departure had been sent him by
His Spanish friends for those in Italy.

25

His suite consisted of three servants and
　A tutor, the licentiate[2] Pedrillo,
195 Who several languages did understand,
　But now lay sick and speechless on his pillow,
And, rocking in his hammock, longed for land,
　His headache being increased by every billow;
And the waves oozing through the port-hole made
200 His berth a little damp, and him afraid.

26

'Twas not without some reason, for the wind
　Increased at night, until it blew a gale;
And though 'twas not much to a naval mind,
　Some landsmen would have looked a little pale,
205 For sailors are, in fact, a different kind:
　At sunset they began to take in sail,
For the sky showed it would come on to blow,
And carry away, perhaps, a mast or so.

27

At one o'clock the wind with sudden shift
210　Threw the ship right into the trough of the sea,
Which struck her aft, and made an awkward rift,
　Started the stern-post, also shattered the
Whole of her stern-frame, and, ere she could lift
　Herself from out her present jeopardy,

1　*Trinidada*　Spanish: Trinity.
2　*licentiate*　Graduate of a university.

15   The rudder tore away: 'twas time to sound
    The pumps, and there were four feet water found.[1]

28

    One gang of people instantly was put
        Upon the pumps, and the remainder set
    To get up part of the cargo, and what not,
20   But they could not come at the leak as yet;
    At last they did get at it really, but
        Still their salvation was an even bet:
    The water rushed through in a way quite puzzling,
    While they thrust sheets, shirts, jackets, bales of muslin,

29

25   Into the opening; but all such ingredients
        Would have been vain, and they must have gone
            down,
    Despite of all their efforts and expedients,
        But for the pumps: I'm glad to make them known
    To all the brother tars[2] who may have need hence,
30   For fifty tons of water were upthrown
    By them per hour, and they had all been undone,
    But for the maker, Mr. Mann, of London.

30

    As day advanced the weather seemed to abate,
        And then the leak they reckoned to reduce,
35   And keep the ship afloat, though three feet yet
        Kept two hand and one chain-pump still in use.
    The wind blew fresh again: as it grew late
        A squall came on, and while some guns broke loose,
    A gust—which all descriptive power transcends—
40   Laid with one blast the ship on her beam ends.

31

    There she lay motionless, and seemed upset;
        The water left the hold, and washed the decks,
    And made a scene men do not soon forget;

---

1   *At one o'clock … found*   Byron was proud of the verisimilitude of his
portrayal of a shipwreck, for which he drew many details from William
Bligh, *A Narrative of the Mutiny of the Bounty* (1790), Sir John G.
Dalyell, *Shipwrecks and Disasters at Sea* (1812), and Philip Aubin,
Remarkable Shipwrecks (1813).

2   *tars*   Sailors.

For they remember battles, fires, and wrecks,
245   Or any other thing that brings regret,
        Or breaks their hopes, or hearts, or heads, or necks:
    Thus drownings are much talked of by the divers
    And swimmers who may chance to be survivors.

32

    Immediately the masts were cut away,
250   Both main and mizzen; first the mizzen went,
    The main-mast followed: but the ship still lay
        Like a mere log, and baffled our intent.
    Foremast and bowsprit were cut down, and they
        Eased her at last (although we never meant
255   To part with all till every hope was blighted),
    And then with violence the old ship righted.

33

    It may be easily supposed, while this
        Was going on, some people were unquiet,
    That passengers would find it much amiss
260   To lose their lives as well as spoil their diet;
    That even the able seaman, deeming his
        Days nearly o'er, might be disposed to riot,
    As upon such occasions tars will ask
    For grog, and sometimes drink rum from the cask.

34

265   There's nought, no doubt, so much the spirit calms
        As rum and true religion; thus it was,
    Some plundered, some drank spirits, some sung psalms,
        The high wind made the treble, and as bass
    The hoarse harsh waves kept time; fright cured the
            qualms
270   Of all the luckless landsmen's sea-sick maws:
    Strange sounds of wailing, blasphemy, devotion,
    Clamoured in chorus to the roaring ocean.

35

    Perhaps more mischief had been done, but for
        Our Juan, who, with sense beyond his years,
275   Got to the spirit-room, and stood before
        It with a pair of pistols; and their fears,
    As if Death were more dreadful by his door
        Of fire than water, spite of oaths and tears,

Kept still aloof the crew, who, ere they sunk,
280   Thought it would be becoming to die drunk.

36

"Give us more grog," they cried, "for it will be
    All one an hour hence." Juan answered, "No!
'Tis true that death awaits both you and me,
    But let us die like men, not sink below
285 Like brutes;"—and thus his dangerous post kept he,
    And none liked to anticipate the blow;
And even Pedrillo, his most reverend tutor,
Was for some rum a disappointed suitor.

37

The good old gentleman was quite aghast,
290   And made a loud and pious lamentation;
Repented all his sins, and made a last
    Irrevocable vow of reformation;
Nothing should tempt him more (this peril past)
    To quit his academic occupation,
295 In cloisters of the classic Salamanca,[1]
To follow Juan's wake, like Sancho Panca.[2]

38

But now there came a flash of hope once more;
    Day broke, and the wind lulled: the masts were gone,
The leak increased; shoals round her, but no shore,
300   The vessel swam, yet still she held her own.
They tried the pumps again, and though before
    Their desperate efforts seemed all useless grown,
A glimpse of sunshine set some hands to bale—
The stronger pumped, the weaker thrummed a sail.

39

305 Under the vessel's keel the sail was past,
    And for the moment it had some effect;
But with a leak, and not a stick of mast,
    Nor rag of canvas, what could they expect?
But still 'tis best to struggle to the last,
310   'Tis never too late to be wholly wrecked:

[1] *Salamanca* Spanish university.

[2] *Sancho Panca* Don Quixote's page, in the novel by Miguel de Cervantes (often spelled Sancho Panza).

And though 'tis true that man can only die once,
'Tis not so pleasant in the Gulf of Lyons.

40

There winds and waves had hurled them, and from
    thence,
    Without their will, they carried them away;
315 For they were forced with steering to dispense,
    And never had as yet a quiet day
On which they might repose, or even commence
    A jurymast or rudder, or could say
The ship would swim an hour, which, by good luck,
320 Still swam—though not exactly like a duck.

41

The wind, in fact, perhaps was rather less,
    But the ship laboured so, they scarce could hope
To weather out much longer; the distress
    Was also great with which they had to cope
325 For want of water, and their solid mess
    Was scant enough: in vain the telescope
Was used—nor sail nor shore appeared in sight,
Nought but the heavy sea, and coming night.

42

Again the weather threatened,—again blew
330   A gale, and in the fore and after hold
Water appeared; yet, though the people knew
    All this, the most were patient, and some bold,
Until the chains and leathers were worn through
    Of all our pumps:—a wreck complete she rolled,
335 At mercy of the waves, whose mercies are
Like human beings during civil war.

43

Then came the carpenter, at last, with tears
    In his rough eyes, and told the captain, he
Could do no more; he was a man in years,
340   And long had voyaged through many a stormy sea,
And if he wept at length, they were not fears
    That made his eyelids as a woman's be,
But he, poor fellow, had a wife and children,
Two things for dying people quite bewildering.

44

The ship was evidently settling now
    Fast by the head; and, all distinction gone,
Some went to prayers again, and made a vow
    Of candles to their saints—but there were none
To pay them with; and some looked o'er the bow;
    Some hoisted out the boats; and there was one
That begged Pedrillo for an absolution,
Who told him to be damned—in his confusion.

45

Some lashed them in their hammocks, some put on
    Their best clothes, as if going to a fair;
Some cursed the day on which they saw the sun,
    And gnashed their teeth, and, howling, tore their
        hair;
And others went on as they had begun,
    Getting the boats out, being well aware
That a tight boat will live in a rough sea,
Unless with breakers close beneath her lee.

46

The worst of all was, that in their condition,
    Having been several days in great distress,
'Twas difficult to get out such provision
    As now might render their long suffering less:
Men, even when dying, dislike inanition;
    Their stock was damaged by the weather's stress:
Two casks of biscuit, and a keg of butter,
Were all that could be thrown into the cutter.

47

But in the long-boat they contrived to stow
    Some pounds of bread, though injured by the wet;
Water, a twenty-gallon cask or so;
    Six flasks of wine; and they contrived to get
A portion of their beef up from below,
    And with a piece of pork, moreover, met,
But scarce enough to serve them for a luncheon—
Then there was rum, eight gallons in a puncheon.

48

The other boats, the yawl and pinnace, had
    Been stove in the beginning of the gale;
And the long-boat's condition was but bad,
    As there were but two blankets for a sail,
And one oar for a mast, which a young lad
    Threw in by good luck over the ship's rail;
And two boats could not hold, far less be stored,
To save one half the people then on board.

49

'Twas twilight, for the sunless day went down
    Over the waste of waters; like a veil,
Which, if withdrawn, would but disclose the frown
    Of one whose hate is masked but to assail,
Thus to their hopeless eyes the night was shown,
    And grimly darkled o'er the faces pale,
And the dim desolate deep: twelve days had Fear
Been their familiar, and now Death was here.

50

Some trial had been making at a raft,
    With little hope in such a rolling sea,
A sort of thing at which one would have laughed,
    If any laughter at such times could be,
Unless with people who too much have quaffed,
    And have a kind of wild and horrid glee,
Half epileptical and half hysterical:—
Their preservation would have been a miracle.

51

At half-past eight o'clock, booms, hencoops, spars,
    And all things, for a chance, had been cast loose,
That still could keep afloat the struggling tars,
    For yet they strove, although of no great use:
There was no light in heaven but a few stars,
    The boats put off o'ercrowded with their crews;
She gave a heel, and then a lurch to port,
And, going down head foremost—sunk, in short.

52

Then rose from sea to sky the wild farewell,
    Then shrieked the timid, and stood still the brave,
Then some leaped overboard with dreadful yell,

As eager to anticipate their grave;
And the sea yawned around her like a hell,
    And down she sucked with her the whirling wave,
415 Like one who grapples with his enemy,
    And strives to strangle him before he die.

53

And first one universal shriek there rushed,
    Louder than the loud ocean, like a crash
Of echoing thunder; and then all was hushed,
420   Save the wild wind and the remorseless dash
Of billows; but at intervals there gushed,
    Accompanied with a convulsive splash,
A solitary shriek, the bubbling cry
Of some strong swimmer in his agony.

54

425 The boats, as stated, had got off before,
    And in them crowded several of the crew;
And yet their present hope was hardly more
    Than what it had been, for so strong it blew
There was slight chance of reaching any shore;
430   And then they were too many, though so few—
Nine in the cutter, thirty in the boat,
Were counted in them when they got afloat.

55

All the rest perished; near two hundred souls
    Had left their bodies; and what's worse, alas!
435 When over Catholics the ocean rolls,
    They must wait several weeks before a Mass
Takes off one peck of purgatorial coals,
    Because, till people know what's come to pass,
They won't lay out their money on the dead—
440 It costs three francs for every Mass that's said.

56

Juan got into the long-boat, and there
    Contrived to help Pedrillo to a place;
It seemed as if they had exchanged their care,
    For Juan wore the magisterial face
445 Which courage gives, while poor Pedrillo's pair
    Of eyes were crying for their owner's case:

Battista, though, (a name called shortly Tita)[1]
Was lost by getting at some aqua-vita.°   *spirits*

57

Pedro, his valet, too, he tried to save,
450   But the same cause, conducive to his loss,
Left him so drunk, he jumped into the wave
    As o'er the cutter's edge he tried to cross,
And so he found a wine-and-watery grave;
    They could not rescue him although so close,
455 Because the sea ran higher every minute,
And for the boat—the crew kept crowding in it.

58

A small old spaniel,—which had been Don Jóse's,
    His father's, whom he loved, as ye may think,
For on such things the memory reposes
460   With tenderness, stood howling on the brink,
Knowing, (dogs have such intellectual noses!)
    No doubt, the vessel was about to sink;
And Juan caught him up, and ere he stepped
Off, threw him in, then after him he leaped.

59

465 He also stuffed his money where he could
    About his person, and Pedrillo's too,
Who let him do, in fact, whate'er he would,
    Not knowing what himself to say, or do,
As every rising wave his dread renewed;
470   But Juan, trusting they might still get through,
And deeming there were remedies for any ill,
Thus re-embarked his tutor and his spaniel.

60

'Twas a rough night, and blew so stiffly yet,
    That the sail was becalmed between the seas,
475 Though on the wave's high top too much to set,
    They dared not take it in for all the breeze;
Each sea curled o'er the stern, and kept them wet,
    And made them bale without a moment's ease,

---

[1] *Tita*   Byron's own servant Giovanni Battista Lusieri (1798–1874) was nicknamed "Tita."

So that themselves as well as hopes were damped,
And the poor little cutter quickly swamped.

61

Nine souls more went in her: the long-boat still
    Kept above water, with an oar for mast,
Two blankets stitched together, answering ill
    Instead of sail, were to the oar made fast:
Though every wave rolled menacing to fill,
    And present peril all before surpassed,
They grieved for those who perished with the cutter,
And also for the biscuit casks and butter.

62

The sun rose red and fiery, a sure sign
    Of the continuance of the gale: to run
Before the sea, until it should grow fine,
    Was all that for the present could be done:
A few tea-spoonfuls of their rum and wine
    Were served out to the people, who begun
To faint, and damaged bread wet through the bags,
And most of them had little clothes but rags.

63

They counted thirty, crowded in a space
    Which left scarce room for motion or exertion;
They did their best to modify their case,
    One half sat up, though numbed with the
        immersion,
While t'other half were laid down in their place,
    At watch and watch; thus, shivering like the tertian
Ague° in its cold fit, they filled their boat,   *flu*
With nothing but the sky for a great coat.

64

'Tis very certain the desire of life
    Prolongs it; this is obvious to physicians,
When patients, neither plagued with friends nor wife,
    Survive through very desperate conditions,
Because they still can hope, nor shines the knife
    Nor shears of Atropos[1] before their visions:

Despair of all recovery spoils longevity,
And makes men's miseries of alarming brevity.

65

'Tis said that persons living on annuities
    Are longer lived than others,—God knows why,
Unless to plague the grantors,—yet so true it is,
    That some, I really think, *do* never die;
Of any creditors the worst a Jew it is,[2]
    And *that's* their mode of furnishing supply:
In my young days they lent me cash that way,
Which I found very troublesome to pay.

66

'Tis thus with people in an open boat,
    They live upon the love of life, and bear
More than can be believed, or even thought,
    And stand like rocks the tempest's wear and tear;
And hardship still has been the sailor's lot,
    Since Noah's ark went cruising here and there;
She had a curious crew as well as cargo,
Like the first old Greek privateer, the Argo.[3]

67

But man is a carnivorous production,
    And must have meals, at least one meal a day;
He cannot live, like woodcocks, upon suction,[4]
    But, like the shark and tiger, must have prey:
Although his anatomical construction
    Bears vegetables, in a grumbling way,
Your labouring people think beyond all question,
Beef, veal, and mutton, better for digestion.

---

1 *Atropos* One of the three Fates: Clotho spun the thread of life, Lachesis measured it, and Atropos cut it off.

2 *Of any … is* Since the Middle Ages European Christian society had condemned Jews for the practice of usury, or money-lending, which was in most European countries one of the few professions that Jews were allowed to follow. Discrimination against Jews was less severe in Britain than in many European jurisdictions, but, as Byron's casual slur here demonstrates, virulent anti-Semitism was common among the English as well. In his youth, Byron had borrowed from Jewish moneylenders; he did not pay these debts off for many years.

3 *Argo* The ship in which Jason and the Argonauts sailed.

4 *live … upon suction* Woodcocks feed by probing the grass with their beaks.

68

And thus it was with this our hapless crew;
　　For on the third day there came on a calm,
And though at first their strength it might renew,
540　　　And, lying on their weariness like balm,
Lulled them like turtles sleeping on the blue
　　Of ocean, when they woke they felt a qualm,
And fell all ravenously on their provision,
Instead of hoarding it with due precision.

69

545 The consequence was easily foreseen—
　　　They ate up all they had, and drank their wine,
In spite of all remonstrances, and then
　　　On what, in fact, next day were they to dine?
They hoped the wind would rise, these foolish men!
550　　　And carry them to shore; these hopes were fine,
But as they had but one oar, and that brittle,
It would have been more wise to save their victual.

70

The fourth day came, but not a breath of air,
　　And Ocean slumbered like an unweaned child:
555 The fifth day, and their boat lay floating there,
　　　The sea and sky were blue, and clear, and mild—
With their one oar (I wish they had had a pair)
　　　What could they do? and hunger's rage grew wild:
So Juan's spaniel, spite of his entreating,
560 Was killed, and portioned out for present eating.

71

On the sixth day they fed upon his hide,
　　And Juan, who had still refused, because
The creature was his father's dog that died,
　　　Now feeling all the vulture in his jaws,
565 With some remorse received (though first denied)
　　　As a great favour one of the fore-paws,
Which he divided with Pedrillo, who
Devoured it, longing for the other too.

72

The seventh day, and no wind—the burning sun
570　　Blistered and scorched, and, stagnant on the sea,
They lay like carcasses; and hope was none,
　　Save in the breeze that came not; savagely
They glared upon each other—all was done,
　　Water, and wine, and food,—and you might see
575 The longings of the cannibal arise
　　(Although they spoke not) in their wolfish eyes.

73

At length one whispered his companion, who
　　Whispered another, and thus it went round,
And then into a hoarser murmur grew,
580　　An ominous, and wild, and desperate sound,
And when his comrade's thought each sufferer knew,
　　'Twas but his own, suppressed till now, he found:
And out they spoke of lots for flesh and blood,
And who should die to be his fellow's food.

74

585 But ere they came to this, they that day shared
　　Some leathern caps, and what remained of shoes;
And then they looked around them, and despaired,
　　And none to be the sacrifice would choose;
At length the lots were torn up, and prepared,
590　　But of materials that much shock the Muse—
Having no paper, for the want of better,
They took by force from Juan Julia's letter.

75

The lots were made, and marked, and mixed, and
　　handed,
　　In silent horror, and their distribution
595 Lulled even the savage hunger which demanded,
　　Like the Promethean vulture,[1] this pollution;
None in particular had sought or planned it,
　　'Twas nature gnawed them to this resolution,
By which none were permitted to be neuter—
600 And the lot fell on Juan's luckless tutor.

76

He but requested to be bled to death:
　　The surgeon had his instruments, and bled
Pedrillo, and so gently ebbed his breath,

---

[1] *Promethean vulture* As a punishment for stealing fire from the gods, Prometheus was chained to a rock while a vulture (in some versions, an eagle) pecked at his liver.

You hardly could perceive when he was dead.
    He died as born, a Catholic in faith,
      Like most in the belief in which they're bred,
And first a little crucifix he kissed,
    And then held out his jugular and wrist.

77

The surgeon, as there was no other fee,
    Had his first choice of morsels for his pains;
But being thirstiest at the moment, he
    Preferred a draught from the fast-flowing veins:
Part was divided, part thrown in the sea,
    And such things as the entrails and the brains
Regaled two sharks, who followed o'er the billow—
The sailors ate the rest of poor Pedrillo.

78

The sailors ate him, all save three or four,
    Who were not quite so fond of animal food;
To these was added Juan, who, before
    Refusing his own spaniel, hardly could
Feel now his appetite increased much more;
    'Twas not to be expected that he should,
Even in extremity of their disaster,
Dine with them on his pastor and his master.

79

'Twas better that he did not; for, in fact,
    The consequence was awful in the extreme:
For they, who were most ravenous in the act,
    Went raging mad—Lord! how they did blaspheme!
And foam and roll, with strange convulsions racked,
    Drinking salt water like a mountain-stream,
Tearing, and grinning, howling, screeching, swearing,
And, with hyaena laughter, died despairing.[1]

80

Their numbers were much thinned by this infliction,
    And all the rest were thin enough, heaven knows;
And some of them had lost their recollection,
    Happier than they who still perceived their woes;

But others pondered on a new dissection,
    As if not warned sufficiently by those
Who had already perished, suffering madly,
For having used their appetites so sadly.

81

And next they thought upon the master's mate,
    As fattest; but he saved himself, because,
Besides being much averse from such a fate,
    There were some other reasons: the first was,
He had been rather indisposed of late;
    And that which chiefly proved his saving clause,
Was a small present made to him at Cadiz,
By general subscription of the ladies.[2]

82

Of poor Pedrillo something still remained,
    But was used sparingly,—some were afraid,
And others still their appetites constrained,
    Or but at times a little supper made;
All except Juan, who throughout abstained,
    Chewing a piece of bamboo, and some lead:
At length they caught two boobies, and a noddy,[3]
And then they left off eating the dead body.

83

And if Pedrillo's fate should shocking be,
    Remember Ugolino condescends
To eat the head of his arch-enemy
    The moment after he politely ends
His tale; if foes be food in hell, at sea
    'Tis surely fair to dine upon our friends,
When shipwreck's short allowance grows too scanty,
Without being much more horrible than Dante.[4]

84

And the same night there fell a shower of rain,
    For which their mouths gaped, like the cracks of
      earth

---

[1] *Went raging mad ... despairing* It was believed that cannibalism produced madness.

[2] *small present ... ladies* I.e., venereal disease.

[3] *boobies ... noddy* Birds.

[4] *Ugolino ... Dante* See Dante's *Inferno* 32–33, in which Ugolino is condemned to perpetually gnaw the head of the man who ordered his death by starvation.

When dried to summer dust; till taught by pain,
 Men really know not what good water's worth;
If you had been in Turkey or in Spain,
670 Or with a famished boat's-crew had your berth,
Or in the desert heard the camel's bell,
You'd wish yourself where Truth is—in a well.

85

It poured down torrents, but they were no richer
 Until they found a ragged piece of sheet,
675 Which served them as a sort of spongy pitcher,
  And when they deemed its moisture was complete,
They wrung it out, and though a thirsty ditcher
  Might not have thought the scanty draught so sweet
As a full pot of porter, to their thinking
680 They ne'er till now had known the joys of drinking.

86

And their baked lips, with many a bloody crack,[1]
 Sucked in the moisture, which like nectar streamed;
Their throats were ovens, their swol'n tongues were
 black,
  As the rich man's in hell, who vainly screamed
685 To beg the beggar, who could not rain back
  A drop of dew, when every drop had seemed
To taste of heaven—If this be true, indeed,
Some Christians have a comfortable creed.[2]

87

There were two fathers in this ghastly crew,
690 And with them their two sons, of whom the one
Was more robust and hardy to the view,
  But he died early; and when he was gone,
His nearest messmate told his sire, who threw
  One glance at him, and said, "Heaven's will be done!
695 I can do nothing," and he saw him thrown
Into the deep without a tear or groan.

88

The other father had a weaklier child,
 Of a soft cheek and aspect delicate;

But the boy bore up long, and with a mild
700 And patient spirit held aloof his fate;
Little he said, and now and then he smiled,
  As if to win a part from off the weight
He saw increasing on his father's heart,
With the deep deadly thought, that they must part.

89

705 And o'er him bent his sire, and never raised
 His eyes from off his face, but wiped the foam
From his pale lips, and ever on him gazed,
  And when the wished-for shower at length was come,
And the boy's eyes, which the dull film half glazed,
710 Brightened, and for a moment seemed to roam,
He squeezed from out a rag some drops of rain
Into his dying child's mouth—but in vain.

90

The boy expired—the father held the clay,
 And looked upon it long, and when at last
715 Death left no doubt, and the dead burthen lay
  Stiff on his heart, and pulse and hope were past,
He watched it wistfully, until away
  'Twas borne by the rude wave wherein 'twas cast;
Then he himself sunk down all dumb and shivering,
720 And gave no sign of life, save his limbs quivering.

91

Now overhead a rainbow, bursting through
 The scattering clouds, shone, spanning the dark sea,
Resting its bright base on the quivering blue;
  And all within its arch appeared to be
725 Clearer than that without, and its wide hue
  Waxed broad and waving, like a banner free,
Then changed like to a bow that's bent, and then
Forsook the dim eyes of these shipwrecked men.

92

It changed, of course; a heavenly chameleon,
730 The airy child of vapour and the sun,
Brought forth in purple, cradled in vermilion,
  Baptized in molten gold, and swathed in dun,
Glittering like crescents o'er a Turk's pavilion,
  And blending every colour into one,

---

[1] *And ... crack*   Cf. Coleridge's *The Rime of the Ancient Mariner* 3.157.

[2] *As the rich man's ... creed*   See Luke 16.19–25.

85 Just like a black eye in a recent scuffle,
(For sometimes we must box without the muffle.)

93

Our shipwrecked seamen thought it a good omen—
    It is as well to think so, now and then;
'Twas an old custom of the Greek and Roman,
    And may become of great advantage when
40 Folks are discouraged; and most surely no men
    Had greater need to nerve themselves again
Than these, and so this rainbow looked like hope—
Quite a celestial kaleidoscope.[1]

94

45 About this time a beautiful white bird,
    Webfooted, not unlike a dove in size
And plumage, (probably it might have erred
    Upon its course) passed oft before their eyes,
And tried to perch, although it saw and heard
50   The men within the boat, and in this guise
It came and went, and fluttered round them till
Night fell:—this seemed a better omen still.

95

But in this case I also must remark,
    'Twas well this bird of promise did not perch,
55 Because the tackle of our shattered bark
    Was not so safe for roosting as a church;
And had it been the dove from Noah's ark,
    Returning there from her successful search,
Which in their way that moment chanced to fall,
60 They would have eat[2] her, olive-branch and all.

96

With twilight it again came on to blow,
    But not with violence; the stars shone out,
The boat made way; yet now they were so low,
    They knew not where nor what they were about;
65 Some fancied they saw land, and some said "No!"
    The frequent fog-banks gave them cause to doubt—

---

1 *kaleidoscope* Sir David Brewster invented the kaleidoscope in 1817.
Byron's lawyer, John Hanson, brought him one in November 1818.

2 *eat* Pronounced "et," in certain segments of English society—the
past tense form of "eat."

Some swore that they heard breakers, others guns,
And all mistook about the latter once.

97

As morning broke the light wind died away,
770   When he who had the watch sung out, and swore
If 'twas not land that rose with the suns ray,
    He wished that land he never might see more;
And the rest rubbed their eyes, and saw a bay,
    Or thought they saw, and shaped their course for
        shore;
775 For shore it was, and gradually grew
Distinct, and high, and palpable to view.

98

And then of these some part burst into tears,
    And others, looking with a stupid stare,
Could not yet separate their hopes from fears,
780   And seemed as if they had no further care;
While a few prayed—(the first time for some years)—
    And at the bottom of the boat three were
Asleep; they shook them by the hand and head,
And tried to awaken them, but found them dead.

99

785 The day before, fast sleeping on the water,
    They found a turtle of the hawk's-bill kind,
And by good fortune, gliding softly, caught her,
    Which yielded a day's life, and to their mind
Proved even still a more nutritious matter,
790   Because it left encouragement behind:
They thought that in such perils, more than chance
Had sent them this for their deliverance.

100

The land appeared a high and rocky coast,
    And higher grew the mountains as they drew,
795 Set by a current, toward it: they were lost
    In various conjectures, for none knew
To what part of the earth they had been tost,
    So changeable had been the winds that blew;

Some thought it was Mount Ætna, some the highlands
800 Of Candia,[1] Cyprus, Rhodes, or other islands.

101

Meantime the current, with a rising gale,
    Still set them onwards to the welcome shore,
Like Charon's bark of spectres, dull and pale:[2]
    Their living freight was now reduced to four,
805 And three dead, whom their strength could not avail
    To heave into the deep with those before,
Though the two sharks still followed them, and dashed
The spray into their faces as they splashed.

102

Famine, despair, cold, thirst, and heat, had done
810   Their work on them by turns, and thinned them to
Such things a mother had not known her son
    Amidst the skeletons of that gaunt crew;
By night chilled, by day scorched, thus one by one
    They perished, until withered to these few,
815 But chiefly by a species of self-slaughter,
In washing down Pedrillo with salt water.

103

As they drew nigh the land, which now was seen
    Unequal in its aspect here and there,
They felt the freshness of its growing green,
820   That waved in forest-tops, and smoothed the air,
And fell upon their glazed eyes like a screen
    From glistening waves, and skies so hot and bare—
Lovely seemed any object that should sweep
Away the vast, salt, dread, eternal deep.

104

825 The shore looked wild, without a trace of man,
    And girt by formidable waves; but they
Were mad for land, and thus their course they ran,
    Though right ahead the roaring breakers lay:
A reef between them also now began
830   To show its boiling surf and bounding spray,

But finding no place for their landing better,
They ran the boat for shore,—and overset her.

105

But in his native stream, the Guadalquivir,
    Juan to lave° his youthful limbs was wont;   *wash*
835 And having learnt to swim in that sweet river,
    Had often turned the art to some account:
A better swimmer you could scarce see ever,
    He could, perhaps, have passed the Hellespont,
As once (a feat on which ourselves we prided)
840 Leander, Mr. Ekenhead, and I did.[3]

106

So here, though faint, emaciated, and stark,
    He buoyed his boyish limbs, and strove to ply
With the quick wave, and gain, ere it was dark,
    The beach which lay before him, high and dry:
845 The greatest danger here was from a shark,
    That carried off his neighbour by the thigh;
As for the other two they could not swim,
So nobody arrived on shore but him.

107

Nor yet had he arrived but for the oar,
850   Which, providentially for him, was washed
Just as his feeble arms could strike no more,
    And the hard wave o'erwhelmed him as 'twas dashed
Within his grasp; he clung to it, and sore
    The waters beat while he thereto was lashed;
855 At last, with swimming, wading, scrambling, he
Rolled on the beach, half-senseless, from the sea.

108

There, breathless, with his digging nails he clung
    Fast to the sand, lest the returning wave,
From whose reluctant roar his life he wrung,
860   Should suck him back to her insatiate grave:
And there he lay, full length, where he was flung,

---

[1] *Candia* Crete.

[2] *Charon's bark ... pale* Charon ferried the souls of the newly dead across the river Acheron in Hades.

[3] *Hellespont ... did* In imitation of the classical hero Leander, who swam across the Hellespont to reach his lover, Byron swam the Hellespont on 3 May 1810, accompanied by Lieutenant Ekenhead of the Marines. See Byron's "Written after Swimming from Sestos to Abydos."

Before the entrance of a cliff-worn cave,
With just enough of life to feel its pain,
And deem that it was saved, perhaps, in vain.

109

55 With slow and staggering effort he arose,
    But sunk again upon his bleeding knee
And quivering hand; and then he looked for those
    Who long had been his mates upon the sea,
But none of them appeared to share his woes,
70   Save one, a corpse from out the famished three,
Who died two days before, and now had found
An unknown barren beach for burial ground.

110

And as he gazed, his dizzy brain spun fast,
    And down he sunk; and as he sunk, the sand
75 Swam round and round, and all his senses passed:
    He fell upon his side, and his stretched hand
Drooped dripping on the oar, (their jury-mast)
    And, like a withered lily, on the land
His slender frame and pallid aspect lay,
80 As fair a thing as e'er was formed of clay.

111

How long in his damp trance young Juan lay
    He knew not, for the earth was gone for him,
And Time had nothing more of night nor day
    For his congealing blood, and senses dim;
85 And how this heavy faintness passed away
    He knew not, till each painful pulse and limb,
And tingling vein, seemed throbbing back to life,
For Death, though vanquished, still retired with strife.

112

His eyes he opened, shut, again unclosed,
90   For all was doubt and dizziness; methought
He still was in the boat, and had but dozed,
    And felt again with his despair o'erwrought,
And wished it death in which he had reposed,
    And then once more his feelings back were brought,
95 And slowly by his swimming eyes was seen
A lovely female face of seventeen.

113

'Twas bending close o'er his, and the small mouth
    Seemed almost prying into his for breath;
And chafing him, the soft warm hand of youth
900   Recalled his answering spirits back from death;
And, bathing his chill temples, tried to soothe
    Each pulse to animation, till beneath
Its gentle touch and trembling care, a sigh
To these kind efforts made a low reply.

114

905 Then was the cordial poured, and mantle flung
    Around his scarce-clad limbs; and the fair arm
Raised higher the faint head which o'er it hung;
    And her transparent cheek, all pure and warm,
Pillowed his death-like forehead; then she wrung
910   His dewy curls, long drenched by every storm;
And watched with eagerness each throb that drew
A sigh from his heaved bosom—and hers, too.

115

And lifting him with care into the cave,
    The gentle girl and her attendant,—one
915 Young, yet her elder, and of brow less grave,
    And more robust of figure,—then begun
To kindle fire, and as the new flames gave
    Light to the rocks that roofed them, which the sun
Had never seen, the maid, or whatsoe'er
920 She was, appeared distinct, and tall, and fair.

116

Her brow was overhung with coins of gold,
    That sparkled o'er the auburn of her hair,
Her clustering hair, whose longer locks were rolled
    In braids behind, and though her stature were
925 Even of the highest for a female mould,
    They nearly reached her heel; and in her air
There was a something which bespoke command,
As one who was a lady in the land.

117

Her hair, I said, was auburn; but her eyes
930   Were black as death, their lashes the same hue,
Of downcast length, in whose silk shadow lies

Deepest attraction, for when to the view
Forth from its raven fringe the full glance flies,
     Ne'er with such force the swiftest arrow flew;
935 'Tis as the snake late coiled, who pours his length,
And hurls at once his venom and his strength.

118

Her brow was white and low, her cheek's pure dye
     Like twilight rosy still with the set sun;
Short upper lip—sweet lips! that make us sigh
940   Ever to have seen such; for she was one
Fit for the model of a statuary
     (A race of mere impostors, when all's done—
I've seen much finer women, ripe and real,
Than all the nonsense of their stone ideal).

119

945 I'll tell you why I say so, for 'tis just
     One should not rail without a decent cause:
There was an Irish lady,[1] to whose bust
     I ne'er saw justice done, and yet she was
A frequent model; and if e'er she must
950   Yield to stern Time and Nature's wrinkling laws,
They will destroy a face which mortal thought
Ne'er compassed, nor less mortal chisel wrought.

120

And such was she, the lady of the cave;
     Her dress was very different from the Spanish,
955 Simpler, and yet of colours not so grave;
     For, as you know, the Spanish women banish
Bright hues when out of doors, and yet, while wave
     Around them (what I hope will never vanish)
The basquiña[2] and the mantilla, they
960 Seem at the same time mystical and gay.

121

But with our damsel this was not the case:
     Her dress was many-coloured, finely spun;
Her locks curled negligently round her face,

But through them gold and gems profusely shone;
965 Her girdle sparkled, and the richest lace
     Flowed in her veil, and many a precious stone
Flashed on her little hand; but, what was shocking
Her small snow feet had slippers, but no stocking.

122

The other female's dress was not unlike,
970   But of inferior materials; she
Had not so many ornaments to strike,
     Her hair had silver only, bound to be
Her dowry; and her veil, in form alike,
     Was coarser; and her air, though firm, less free;
975 Her hair was thicker, but less long; her eyes
As black, but quicker, and of smaller size.

123

And these two tended him, and cheered him both
     With food and raiment, and those soft attentions,
Which are (as I must own) of female growth,
980   And have ten thousand delicate inventions:
They made a most superior mess of broth,
     A thing which poesy but seldom mentions,
But the best dish that e'er was cooked since Homer's
Achilles ordered dinner for new comers.[3]

124

985 I'll tell you who they were, this female pair,
     Lest they should seem princesses in disguise;
Besides, I hate all mystery, and that air
     Of clap-trap, which your recent poets prize;
And so, in short, the girls they really were
990   They shall appear before your curious eyes,
Mistress and maid; the first was only daughter
Of an old man, who lived upon the water.

125

A fisherman he had been in his youth,
     And still a sort of fisherman was he;
995 But other speculations were, in sooth,
     Added to his connexion with the sea,
Perhaps not so respectable, in truth:

---

[1] *Irish lady* Perhaps a reference to Lady Adelaide Forbes (1798–1858), whom Byron compared to the Apollo Belvedere.

[2] *basquiña* Beautiful outer petticoat.

[3] *since Homer's … comers* See Homer, *Iliad* 9.

A little smuggling, and some piracy,
Left him, at last, the sole of many masters
00   Of an ill-gotten million of piastres.[1]

126

A fisher, therefore, was he—though of men,
    Like Peter the Apostle,[2]—and he fished
For wandering merchant-vessels, now and then,
    And sometimes caught as many as he wished;
05   The cargoes he confiscated, and gain
    He sought in the slave-market too, and dished
Full many a morsel for that Turkish trade,
By which, no doubt, a good deal may be made.

127

He was a Greek, and on his isle had built
10   (One of the wild and smaller Cyclades)
A very handsome house from out his guilt,
    And there he lived exceedingly at ease;
Heaven knows what cash he got, or blood he spilt,
    A sad old fellow was he, if you please;
15   But this I know, it was a spacious building,
Full of barbaric carving, paint, and gilding.

128

He had an only daughter, called Haidée,
    The greatest heiress of the Eastern Isles;
Besides, so very beautiful was she,
20   Her dowry was as nothing to her smiles:
Still in her teens, and like a lovely tree
    She grew to womanhood, and between whiles
Rejected several suitors, just to learn
How to accept a better in his turn.

129

25   And walking out upon the beach, below
    The cliff, towards sunset, on that day she found,
Insensible,—not dead, but nearly so,—
    Don Juan, almost famished, and half drowned;
But being naked, she was shocked, you know,
30   Yet deemed herself in common pity bound,

As far as in her lay, "to take him in,
A stranger" dying, with so white a skin.

130

But taking him into her father's house
    Was not exactly the best way to save,
1035   But like conveying to the cat the mouse,
    Or people in a trance into their grave;
Because the good old man had so much "*vous*,"[3]
    Unlike the honest Arab thieves so brave,
He would have hospitably cured the stranger,
1040   And sold him instantly when out of danger.

131

And therefore, with her maid, she thought it best
    (A virgin always on her maid relies)
To place him in the cave for present rest:
    And when, at last, he opened his black eyes,
1045   Their charity increased about their guest;
    And their compassion grew to such a size,
It opened half the turnpike-gates to heaven—
(St. Paul says, 'tis the toll which must be given).

132

They made a fire, but such a fire as they
1050   Upon the moment could contrive with such
Materials as were cast up round the bay,
    Some broken planks, and oars, that to the touch
Were nearly tinder, since so long they lay
    A mast was almost crumbled to a crutch;
1055   But, by God's grace, here wrecks were in such plenty,
That there was fuel to have furnished twenty.

133

He had a bed of furs, and a pelisse,
    For Haidée stripped her sables off to make
His couch; and, that he might be more at ease,
1060   And warm, in case by chance he should awake,
They also gave a petticoat apiece,
    She and her maid, and promised by day-break
To pay him a fresh visit, with a dish
For breakfast, of eggs, coffee, bread, and fish.

---

1   *piastres*   Pieces of eight.
2   *Like ... Apostle*   Cf. Matthew 4.18–19.
3   *vous*   Greek: intelligence, or, more cynically, cunning.

134

1065 And thus they left him to his lone repose:
      Juan slept like a top, or like the dead,
    Who sleep at last, perhaps, (God only knows)
      Just for the present; and in his lulled head
    Not even a vision of his former woes
1070   Throbbed in accursed dreams, which sometimes
          spread
    Unwelcome visions of our former years,
    Till the eye, cheated, opens thick with tears.

135

    Young Juan slept all dreamless:—but the maid,
      Who smoothed his pillow, as she left the den
1075 Looked back upon him, and a moment staid,
      And turned, believing that he called again.
    He slumbered; yet she thought, at least she said,
      (The heart will slip even as the tongue and pen)
    He had pronounced her name—but she forgot
1080 That at this moment Juan knew it not.

136

    And pensive to her father's house she went,
      Enjoining silence strict to Zoe, who
    Better than her knew what, in fact, she meant,
      She being wiser by a year or two:
1085 A year or two's an age when rightly spent,
      And Zoe spent hers, as most women do,
    In gaining all that useful sort of knowledge
    Which is acquired in Nature's good old college.

137

    The morn broke, and found Juan slumbering still
1090   Fast in his cave, and nothing clashed upon
    His rest; the rushing of the neighbouring rill,
      And the young beams of the excluded sun,
    Troubled him not, and he might sleep his fill;
      And need he had of slumber yet, for none
1095 Had suffered more—his hardships were comparative
    To those related in my grand-dad's Narrative.[1]

---

[1] *Narrative* Byron's grandfather, Admiral John Byron (1723–86),
was famous for encountering a storm each time he sailed, and hence
was nicknamed "Foulweather Jack." In 1768 he published *Narrative
of Great Distresses on the Shores of Patagonia.*

138

    Not so Haidée: she sadly tossed and tumbled,
      And started from her sleep, and, turning o'er,
    Dreamed of a thousand wrecks, o'er which she stumbled,
1100   And handsome corpses strewed upon the shore;
    And woke her maid so early that she grumbled,
      And called her father's old slaves up, who swore
    In several oaths—Armenian, Turk, and Greek—
    They knew not what to think of such a freak.

139

1105 But up she got, and up she made them get,
      With some pretence about the sun, that makes
    Sweet skies just when he rises, or is set;
      And 'tis, no doubt, a sight to see when breaks
    Bright Phoebus,[2] while the mountains still are wet
1110   With mist, and every bird with him awakes,
    And night is flung off like a mourning suit
    Worn for a husband, or some other brute.

140

    I say, the sun is a most glorious sight,
      I've seen him rise full oft, indeed of late
1115 I have sat up on purpose all the night,
      Which hastens, as physicians say, one's fate;
    And so all ye, who would be in the right
      In health and purse, begin your day to date
    From day-break, and when coffined at fourscore,
1120 Engrave upon the plate, you rose at four.

141

    And Haidée met the morning face to face;
      Her own was freshest, though a feverish flush
    Had dyed it with the headlong blood, whose race
      From heart to cheek is curbed into a blush,
1125 Like to a torrent which a mountain's base,
      That overpowers some Alpine river's rush,
    Checks to a lake, whose waves in circles spread;
    Or the Red Sea—but the sea is not red.

---

[2] *Phoebus* Phoebus Apollo, god of the sun; i.e., the sun.

142

And down the cliff the island virgin came,
  And near the cave her quick light footsteps drew, 30
While the sun smiled on her with his first flame,
  And young Aurora[1] kissed her lips with dew,
Taking her for a sister; just the same
  Mistake you would have made on seeing the two,
Although the mortal, quite as fresh and fair, 35
Had all the advantage, too, of not being air.

143

And when into the cavern Haidée stepped
  All timidly, yet rapidly, she saw
That like an infant Juan sweetly slept;
  And then she stopped, and stood as if in awe, 40
(For sleep is awful) and on tiptoe crept
  And wrapt him closer, lest the air, too raw,
Should reach his blood, then o'er him still as death
Bent, with hushed lips, that drank his scarce-drawn
  breath.

144

And thus like to an angel o'er the dying 45
  Who die in righteousness, she leaned; and there
All tranquilly the shipwrecked boy was lying,
  As o'er him lay the calm and stirless air:
But Zoe the meantime some eggs was frying,
  Since, after all, no doubt the youthful pair 50
Must breakfast, and betimes—lest they should ask it,
She drew out her provision from the basket.

145

She knew that the best feelings must have victual,
  And that a shipwrecked youth would hungry be;
Besides, being less in love, she yawned a little, 55
  And felt her veins chilled by the neighbouring sea;
And so, she cooked their breakfast to a tittle;
  I can't say that she gave them any tea,
But there were eggs, fruit, coffee, bread, fish, honey,
With Scio wine,—and all for love, not money. 60

146

And Zoe, when the eggs were ready, and
  The coffee made, would fain have wakened Juan;
But Haidée stopped her with her quick small hand,
  And without word, a sign her finger drew on
Her lip, which Zoe needs must understand; 1165
  And, the first breakfast spoilt, prepared a new one
Because her mistress would not let her break
That sleep which seemed as it would ne'er awake.

147

For still he lay, and on his thin worn cheek
  A purple hectic played like dying day 1170
On the snow-tops of distant hills; the streak
  Of sufferance yet upon his forehead lay,
Where the blue veins looked shadowy, shrunk, and
  weak;
  And his black curls were dewy with the spray,
Which weighed upon them yet, all damp and salt, 1175
Mixed with the stony vapours of the vault.

148

And she bent o'er him, and he lay beneath,
  Hushed as the babe upon its mother's breast,
Drooped as the willow when no winds can breathe,
  Lulled like the depth of ocean when at rest, 1180
Fair as the crowning rose of the whole wreath,
  Soft as the callow cygnet in its nest;
In short, he was a very pretty fellow,
Although his woes had turned him rather yellow.

149

He woke and gazed, and would have slept again, 1185
  But the fair face which met his eyes forbade
Those eyes to close, though weariness and pain
  Had further sleep a further pleasure made;
For woman's face was never formed in vain
  For Juan, so that even when he prayed 1190
He turned from grisly saints, and martyrs hairy,
To the sweet portraits of the Virgin Mary.

150

And thus upon his elbow he arose,
  And looked upon the lady, in whose cheek

---

1 *Aurora* Goddess of the dawn.

1195 The pale contended with the purple rose,
         As with an effort she began to speak;
     Her eyes were eloquent, her words would pose,
         Although she told him, in good modern Greek,
     With an Ionian accent, low and sweet,
1200 That he was faint, and must not talk, but eat.

                        151

     Now Juan could not understand a word,
         Being no Grecian; but he had an ear,
     And her voice was the warble of a bird,
         So soft, so sweet, so delicately clear,
1205 That finer, simpler music ne'er was heard;
         The sort of sound we echo with a tear,
     Without knowing why—an overpowering tone,
     Whence Melody descends as from a throne.

                        152

     And Juan gazed as one who is awoke
1210   By a distant organ, doubting if he be
     Not yet a dreamer, till the spell is broke
         By the watchman, or some such reality,
     Or by one's early valet's cursed knock;
         At least it is a heavy sound to me,
1215 Who like a morning slumber—for the night
     Shows stars and women in a better light.

                        153

     And Juan, too, was helped out from his dream,
         Or sleep, or whatso'er it was, by feeling
     A most prodigious appetite: the steam
1220   Of Zoe's cookery no doubt was stealing
     Upon his senses, and the kindling beam
         Of the new fire, which Zoe kept up, kneeling
     To stir her viands, made him quite awake
     And long for food, but chiefly a beef-steak.

                        154

1225 But beef is rare within these oxless isles;
         Goat's flesh there is, no doubt, and kid, and mutton;
     And, when a holiday upon them smiles,
         A joint upon their barbarous spits they put on:
     But this occurs but seldom, between whiles,
1230   For some of these are rocks with scarce a hut on;

Others are fair and fertile, among which
This, though not large, was one of the most rich.

                        155

     I say that beef is rare, and can't help thinking
         That the old fable of the Minotaur—
1235 From which our modern morals, rightly shrinking,
         Condemn the royal lady's taste who wore
     A cow's shape for a mask—was only (sinking
         The allegory) a mere type, no more,
     That Pasiphae promoted breeding cattle,
1240 To make the Cretans bloodier in battle.[1]

                        156

     For we all know that English people are
         Fed upon beef—I won't say much of beer,
     Because 'tis liquor only, and being far
         From this my subject, has no business here;
1245 We know, too, they are very fond of war,
         A pleasure—like all pleasures—rather dear;
     So were the Cretans—from which I infer
     That beef and battles both were owing to her.

                        157

     But to resume. The languid Juan raised
1250   His head upon his elbow, and he saw
     A sight on which he had not lately gazed,
         As all his latter meals had been quite raw,
     Three or four things, for which the Lord he praised,
         And, feeling still the famished vulture gnaw,[2]
1255 He fell upon whate'er was offered, like
     A priest, a shark, an alderman, or pike.

                        158

     He ate, and he was well supplied; and she,
         Who watched him like a mother, would have fed

---

[1] *Minotaur ... battle* Pasiphaë, Queen of Crete, lusted after a bull sent by Poseidon. To fulfill her desires, she had herself enclosed in a hollow model of a cow to mate with the bull. She gave birth to the Minotaur, a creature with the body of a man and the head of a bull. Her husband Minos imprisoned the monster in a labyrinth built by Daedalus.

[2] *feeling still ... gnaw* Jove sent a vulture (in some versions, an eagle) to gnaw the liver of Prometheus, chained to a mountainside.

Him past all bounds, because she smiled to see
Such appetite in one she had deemed dead;
But Zoe, being older than Haidée,
Knew (by tradition, for she ne'er had read)
That famished people must be slowly nurst,
And fed by spoonfuls, else they always burst.

159

And so she took the liberty to state,
Rather by deeds than words, because the case
Was urgent, that the gentleman, whose fate
Had made her mistress quit her bed to trace
The sea-shore at this hour, must leave his plate,
Unless he wished to die upon the place—
She snatched it, and refused another morsel,
Saying, he had gorged enough to make a horse ill.

160

Next they—he being naked, save a tattered
Pair of scarce decent trousers—went to work,
And in the fire his recent rags they scatterd,
And dressed him, for the present, like a Turk,
Or Greek—that is, although it not much mattered,
Omitting turban, slippers, pistols, dirk,—
They furnished him, entire except some stitches,
With a clean shirt, and very spacious breeches.[1]

161

And then fair Haidée tried her tongue at speaking,
But not a word could Juan comprehend,
Although he listened so that the young Greek in
Her earnestness would ne'er have made an end;
And, as he interrupted not, went eking
Her speech out to her protegé and friend,
Till pausing at the last her breath to take,
She saw he did not understand Romaic.[2]

162

And then she had recourse to nods, and signs,
And smiles, and sparkles of the speaking eye,
And read (the only book she could) the lines

Of his fair face, and found, by sympathy,
The answer eloquent, where the soul shines
And darts in one quick glance a long reply;
And thus in every look she saw exprest
A world of words, and things at which she guessed.

163

And now, by dint of fingers and of eyes,
And words repeated after her, he took
A lesson in her tongue; but by surmise,
No doubt, less of her language than her look:
As he who studies fervently the skies
Turns oftener to the stars than to his book,
Thus Juan learned his alpha beta better
From Haidée's glance than any graven letter.

164

'Tis pleasing to be schooled in a strange tongue
By female lips and eyes—that is, I mean,
When both the teacher and the taught are young,
As was the case, at least, where I have been;
They smile so when one's right, and when one's wrong
They smile still more, and then there intervene
Pressure of hands, perhaps even a chaste kiss;—
I learned the little that I know by this:

165

That is, some words of Spanish, Turk, and Greek,
Italian not at all, having no teachers;
Much English I cannot pretend to speak,
Learning that language chiefly from its preachers,
Barrow, South, Tillotson, whom every week
I study, also Blair,[3] the highest reachers
Of eloquence in piety and prose—
I hate your poets, so read none of those.

166

As for the ladies, I have nought to say,
A wanderer from the British world of fashion,
Where I, like other "dogs, have had my day,"[4]

---

1 *breeches* Pronounced "britches."

2 *Romaic* Modern Greek.

3 *Barrow* Isaac Barrow (1630–77); *South* Robert South (1634–1716); *Tillotson* John Tillotson (1630–94); *Blair* Hugh Blair (1718–1800); British preachers.

4 *dogs … day* See Shakespeare's *Hamlet* 5.1.279.

Like other men, too, may have had my passion—
1325 But that, like other things, has passed away,
And all her fools whom I *could* lay the lash on,
Foes, friends, men, women, now are nought to me
But dreams of what has been, no more to be.

167

Return we to Don Juan. He begun
1330   To hear new words, and to repeat them; but
Some feelings, universal as the sun,
    Were such as could not in his breast be shut
More than within the bosom of a nun:
    He was in love,—as you would be, no doubt,
1335 With a young benefactress—so was she,
Just in the way we very often see.

168

And every day by day-break—rather early
    For Juan, who was somewhat fond of rest—
She came into the cave, but it was merely
1340   To see her bird reposing in his nest;
And she would softly stir his locks so curly,
    Without disturbing her yet slumbering guest,
Breathing all gently o'er his cheek and mouth,
As o'er a bed of roses the sweet south.

169

1345 And every morn his colour freshlier came,
    And every day helped on his convalescence;
'Twas well, because health in the human frame
    Is pleasant, besides being true love's essence,
For health and idleness to passion's flame
1350   Are oil and gunpowder; and some good lessons
Are also learnt from Ceres and from Bacchus,[1]
Without whom Venus will not long attack us.

170

While Venus fills the heart (without heart really
    Love, though good always, is not quite so good),
1355 Ceres presents a plate of vermicelli,—
    For love must be sustained like flesh and blood,—

While Bacchus pours out wine, or hands a jelly:
    Eggs, oysters, too, are amatory food;
But who is their purveyor from above
1360 Heaven knows,—it may be Neptune, Pan, or Jove.

171

When Juan woke he found some good things ready,
    A bath, a breakfast, and the finest eyes
That ever made a youthful heart less steady,
    Besides her maid's, as pretty for their size;
1365 But I have spoken of all this already—
    And repetition's tiresome and unwise,—
Well—Juan, after bathing in the sea,
Came always back to coffee and Haidée.

172

Both were so young, and one so innocent,
1370   That bathing passed for nothing; Juan seemed
To her, as 'twere, the kind of being sent,
    Of whom these two years she had nightly dreamed,
A something to be loved, a creature meant
    To be her happiness, and whom she deemed
1375 To render happy; all who joy would win
Must share it,—Happiness was born a twin.

173

It was such pleasure to behold him, such
    Enlargement of existence to partake
Nature with him, to thrill beneath his touch,
1380   To watch him slumbering, and to see him wake:
To live with him forever were too much;
    But then the thought of parting made her quake:
He was her own, her ocean-treasure, cast
Like a rich wreck—her first love, and her last.

174

1385 And thus a moon rolled on, and fair Haidée
    Paid daily visits to her boy, and took
Such plentiful precautions, that still he
    Remained unknown within his craggy nook;
At last her father's prows put out to sea,
1390   For certain merchantmen upon the look,

---

[1] *Ceres* Ceres, or Demeter, was the goddess of agriculture; *Bacchus* God of wine.

Not as of yore to carry off an Io,[1]
But three Ragusan vessels, bound for Scio.

175

Then came her freedom, for she had no mother,
 So that, her father being at sea, she was
Free as a married woman, or such other
 Female, as where she likes may freely pass,
Without even the incumbrance of a brother,
 The freest she that ever gazed on glass:
I speak of Christian lands in this comparison,
Where wives, at least, are seldom kept in garrison.

176

Now she prolonged her visits and her talk
 (For they must talk), and he had learnt to say
So much as to propose to take a walk,—
 For little had he wandered since the day
On which, like a young flower snapped from the stalk,
 Drooping and dewy on the beach he lay,—
And thus they walked out in the afternoon,
And saw the sun set opposite the moon.

177

It was a wild and breaker-beaten coast,
 With cliffs above, and a broad sandy shore,
Guarded by shoals and rocks as by an host,
 With here and there a creek, whose aspect wore
A better welcome to the tempest-tost;
 And rarely ceased the haughty billow's roar,
Save on the dead long summer days, which make
The outstretched ocean glitter like a lake.

178

And the small ripple spilt upon the beach
 Scarcely o'erpassed the cream of your champagne,
When o'er the brim the sparkling bumpers reach,
 That spring-dew of the spirit! the heart's rain!
Few things surpass old wine; and they may preach
 Who please,—the more because they preach in
  vain,—

Let us have wine and woman, mirth and laughter,
Sermons and soda-water the day after.

179

1425 Man, being reasonable, must get drunk;
 The best of life is but intoxication:
Glory, the grape, love, gold, in these are sunk
 The hopes of all men, and of every nation;
Without their sap, how branchless were the trunk
1430 Of life's strange tree, so fruitful on occasion:
But to return,—Get very drunk; and when
You wake with headache, you shall see what then.

180

Ring for your valet—bid him quickly bring
 Some hock[2] and soda-water, then you'll know
1435 A pleasure worthy Xerxes the great king;
 For not the blest sherbet, sublimed with snow,
Nor the first sparkle of the desert-spring,
 Nor Burgundy in all its sunset glow,
After long travel, ennui, love, or slaughter,
1440 Vie with that draught of hock and soda-water.

181

The coast—I think it was the coast that I
 Was just describing—Yes, it *was* the coast—
Lay at this period quiet as the sky,
 The sands untumbled, the blue waves untost,
1445 And all was stillness, save the sea-bird's cry,
 And dolphin's leap, and little billow crost
By some low rock or shelve, that made it fret
Against the boundary it scarcely wet.

182

And forth they wandered, her sire being gone,
1450 As I have said, upon an expedition;
And mother, brother, guardian, she had none,
 Save Zoe, who, although with due precision
She waited on her lady with the sun,
 Thought daily service was her only mission,
1455 Bringing warm water, wreathing her long tresses,
And asking now and then for cast-off dresses.

---

[1] *Io* A nymph spirited away by Zeus.

[2] *hock* Wine from the area of Hochheim in Germany.

183

It was the cooling hour, just when the rounded
    Red sun sinks down behind the azure hill,
Which then seems as if the whole earth it bounded,
1460   Circling all nature, hushed, and dim, and still,
With the far mountain-crescent half surrounded
    On one side, and the deep sea calm and chill
Upon the other, and the rosy sky,
With one star sparkling through it like an eye.

184

1465 And thus they wandered forth, and hand in hand,[1]
    Over the shining pebbles and the shells,
Glided along the smooth and hardened sand,
    And in the worn and wild receptacles
Worked by the storms, yet worked as it were planned,
1470   In hollow halls, with sparry roofs and cells,
They turned to rest; and, each clasped by an arm,
Yielded to the deep twilight's purple charm.

185

They looked up to the sky, whose floating glow
    Spread like a rosy ocean, vast and bright;
1475 They gazed upon the glittering sea below,
    Whence the broad moon rose circling into sight;
They heard the wave's splash, and the wind so low,
    And saw each other's dark eyes darting light
Into each other—and, beholding this,
1480 Their lips drew near, and clung into a kiss;

186

A long, long kiss, a kiss of youth, and love,
    And beauty, all concentrating like rays
Into one focus, kindled from above;
    Such kisses as belong to early days,
1485 Where heart, and soul, and sense, in concert move,
    And the blood's lava, and the pulse a blaze,
Each kiss a heart-quake,—for a kiss's strength,
I think, it must be reckoned by its length.

---

[1]   *they wandered … hand* Cf. Milton's *Paradise Lost* 12.645–49.

187

By length I mean duration; theirs endured
1490   Heaven knows how long—no doubt they never
      reckoned;
And if they had, they could not have secured
    The sum of their sensations to a second:
They had not spoken; but they felt allured,
    As if their souls and lips each other beckoned,
1495 Which, being joined, like swarming bees they clung—
Their hearts the flowers from whence the honey sprung.

188

They were alone, but not alone as they
    Who shut in chambers think it loneliness;
The silent ocean, and the starlight bay,
1500   The twilight glow, which momently grew less,
The voiceless sands, and dropping caves, that lay
    Around them, made them to each other press,
As if there were no life beneath the sky
Save theirs, and that their life could never die.

189

1505 They feared no eyes nor ears on that lone beach,
    They felt no terrors from the night, they were
All in all to each other: though their speech
    Was broken words, they *thought* a language there,—
And all the burning tongues the passions teach
1510   Found in one sigh the best interpreter
Of nature's oracle—first love,—that all
Which Eve has left her daughters since her fall.

190

Haidée spoke not of scruples, asked no vows,
    Nor offered any; she had never heard
1515 Of plight and promises to be a spouse,
    Or perils by a loving maid incurred;
She was all which pure ignorance allows,
    And flew to her young mate like a young bird;
And, never having dreamt of falsehood, she
1520 Had not one word to say of constancy.

191

She loved, and was beloved—she adored,
    And she was worshipped; after nature's fashion,

Their intense souls, into each other poured,
    If souls could die, had perished in that passion,—
25 But by degrees their senses were restored,
    Again to be o'ercome, again to dash on;
And, beating 'gainst *his* bosom, Haidée's heart
Felt as if never more to beat apart.

192

Alas! they were so young, so beautiful,
30   So lonely, loving, helpless, and the hour
Was that in which the heart is always full,
    And, having o'er itself no further power,
Prompts deeds eternity can not annul,
    But pays off moments in an endless shower
35 Of hell-fire—all prepared for people giving
Pleasure or pain to one another living.

193

Alas! for Juan and Haidée! they were
    So loving and so lovely—till then never,
Excepting our first parents, such a pair
40   Had run the risk of being damn'd for ever;
And Haidée, being devout as well as fair,
    Had, doubtless, heard about the Stygian river,[1]
And hell and purgatory—but forgot
Just in the very crisis she should not.

194

45 They look upon each other, and their eyes
    Gleam in the moonlight; and her white arm clasps
Round Juan's head, and his around her lies
    Half buried in the tresses which it grasps;
She sits upon his knee, and drinks his sighs,
50   He hers, until they end in broken gasps;
And thus they form a group that's quite antique,
Half naked, loving, natural, and Greek.

195

And when those deep and burning moments passed
    And Juan sunk to sleep within her arms,
55 She slept not, but all tenderly, though fast,
    Sustained his head upon her bosom's charms;

---

[1] *Stygian river* River Styx, in Hades.

And now and then her eye to heaven is cast,
    And then on the pale cheek her breast now warms,
Pillowed on her o'erflowing heart, which pants
1560 With all it granted, and with all it grants.

196

An infant when it gazes on a light,
    A child the moment when it drains the breast,
A devotee when soars the Host in sight,
    An Arab with a stranger for a guest,
1565 A sailor when the prize has struck in fight,
    A miser filling his most hoarded chest,
Feel rapture; but not such true joy are reaping
As they who watch o'er what they love while sleeping.

197

For there it lies so tranquil, so beloved,
1570   All that it hath of life with us is living;
So gentle, stirless, helpless, and unmoved,
    And all unconscious of the joy 'tis giving;
All it hath felt, inflicted, passed, and proved,
    Hushed into depths beyond the watcher's diving;
1575 There lies the thing we love with all its errors
And all its charms, like death without its terrors.

198

The lady watched her lover—and that hour
    Of Love's, and Night's, and Ocean's solitude,
O'erflowed her soul with their united power;
1580   Amidst the barren sand and rocks so rude
She and her wave-worn love had made their bower,
    Where nought upon their passion could intrude,
And all the stars that crowded the blue space
Saw nothing happier than her glowing face.

199

1585 Alas! the love of women! it is known
    To be a lovely and a fearful thing;
For all of theirs upon that die is thrown,
    And if 'tis lost, life hath no more to bring
To them but mockeries of the past alone,
1590   And their revenge is as the tiger's spring,
Deadly, and quick, and crushing; yet, as real
Torture is theirs, what they inflict they feel.

200

They are right; for man, to man so oft unjust,
    Is always so to women; one sole bond
1595 Awaits them, treachery is all their trust;
    Taught to conceal, their bursting hearts despond
Over their idol, till some wealthier lust
    Buys them in marriage—and what rests beyond?
A thankless husband, next a faithless lover,
1600 Then dressing, nursing, praying, and all's over.

201

Some take a lover, some take drams or prayers,
    Some mind their household, others dissipation,
Some run away, and but exchange their cares,
    Losing the advantage of a virtuous station;
1605 Few changes e'er can better their affairs,
    Theirs being an unnatural situation,
From the dull palace to the dirty hovel:
Some play the devil, and then write a novel.[1]

202

Haidée was Nature's bride, and knew not this;
1610   Haidée was Passion's child, born where the sun
Showers triple light, and scorches even the kiss
    Of his gazelle-eyed daughters; she was one
Made but to love, to feel that she was his
    Who was her chosen: what was said or done
1615 Elsewhere was nothing—She had nought to fear,
Hope, care, nor love beyond, her heart beat *here*.

203

And oh! that quickening of the heart, that beat!
    How much it costs us! yet each rising throb
Is in its cause as its effect so sweet,
1620   That Wisdom, ever on the watch to rob
Joy of its alchymy, and to repeat
    Fine truths; even Conscience, too, has a tough job
To make us understand each good old maxim,
So good—I wonder Castlereagh don't tax 'em.

204

1625 And now 't was done—on the lone shore were plighted
    Their hearts; the stars, their nuptial torches, shed
Beauty upon the beautiful they lighted:
    Ocean their witness, and the cave their bed,
By their own feelings hallowed and united,
1630   Their priest was Solitude, and they were wed:
And they were happy, for to their young eyes
Each was an angel, and earth paradise.

205

Oh, Love! of whom great Caesar was the suitor,
    Titus the master, Antony the slave,[2]
1635 Horace, Catullus, scholars, Ovid tutor,[3]
    Sappho the sage blue-stocking, in whose grave
All those may leap who rather would be neuter[4]—
    (Leucadia's rock still overlooks the wave)
Oh, Love! thou art the very god of evil,
1640 For, after all, we cannot call thee devil.

206

Thou mak'st the chaste connubial state precarious,
    And jestest with the brows of mightiest men:
Caesar and Pompey, Mahomet, Belisarius[5]
    Have much employed the muse of history's pen;
1645 Their lives and fortunes were extremely various,
    Such worthies Time will never see again;
Yet to these four in three things the same luck holds,
They all were heroes, conquerors, and cuckolds.

---

1 *write a novel* Byron's former lover, Lady Caroline Lamb, published *Glenarvon*, a roman-à-clef about their relationship, in 1816. Byron's comment on the book was, "I read 'Glenarvon,' too, by Caro. Lamb / God damn!"

2 *great Caesar … slave* Caesar and Antony were lovers of Cleopatra. Titus mastered his passion for Berenice, sending her away.

3 *tutor* Ovid's works include a didactic poem, *Ars Amatoria* (*The Art of Love*).

4 *Sappho … neuter* An allusion to the legend of Sappho's suicide; neuter is a reference to her poetry expressing passion towards women.

5 *Caesar … Belisarius* Julius Caesar divorced his third wife, Pompeia, apparently for attempted adultery. Pompey divorced his third wife, Mucia, for committing adultery with Caesar. Mohammed's favorite wife, Ayesha, was suspected of impropriety, but he received a divine revelation of her purity. Antonina, the wife of Justinian's great general Belisarius, had several lovers before she married him.

207

Thou mak'st philosophers; there's Epicurus
    And Aristippus,[1] a material crew!
Who to immoral courses would allure us
    By theories quite practicable too;
If only from the devil they would insure us,
    How pleasant were the maxim, (not quite new)
"Eat, drink, and love, what can the rest avail us?"
So said the royal sage Sardanapalus.[2]

208

But Juan! had he quite forgotten Julia?
    And should he have forgotten her so soon?
I can't but say it seems to me most truly a
    Perplexing question; but, no doubt, the moon
Does these things for us, and whenever newly a
    Strong palpitation rises, 'tis her boon,
Else how the devil is it that fresh features
Have such a charm for us poor human creatures?

209

I hate inconstancy—I loathe, detest,
    Abhor, condemn, abjure the mortal made
Of such quicksilver clay that in his breast
    No permanent foundation can be laid;
Love, constant love, has been my constant guest,
    And yet last night, being at a masquerade,
I saw the prettiest creature, fresh from Milan,
Which gave me some sensations like a villain.

210

But soon Philosophy came to my aid,
    And whispered "think of every sacred tie!"
"I will, my dear Philosophy!" I said,
    "But then her teeth, and then, Oh heaven! her eye!
I'll just inquire if she be wife or maid,
    Or neither—out of curiosity."

"Stop!" cried Philosophy, with air so Grecian,
1680 (Though she was masqued then as a fair Venetian.)

211

"Stop!" so I stopped.—But to return: that which
    Men call inconstancy is nothing more
Than admiration due where nature's rich
    Profusion with young beauty covers o'er
1685 Some favoured object; and as in the niche
    A lovely statue we almost adore,
This sort of adoration of the real
Is but a heightening of the "beau ideal."[3]

212

'Tis the perception of the beautiful,
1690   A fine extension of the faculties,
Platonic, universal, wonderful,
    Drawn from the stars, and filtered through the skies,
Without which life would be extremely dull;
    In short, it is the use of our own eyes,
1695 With one or two small senses added, just
To hint that flesh is formed of fiery dust.

213

Yet 'tis a painful feeling, and unwilling,
    For surely if we always could perceive
In the same object graces quite as killing
1700   As when she rose upon us like an Eve,
'Twould save us many a heartache, many a shilling,
    (For we must get them any how, or grieve)
Whereas if one sole lady pleased for ever,
How pleasant for the heart, as well as liver!

214

1705 The heart is like the sky, a part of heaven,
    But changes night and day too, like the sky;
Now o'er it clouds and thunder must be driven,
    And darkness and destruction as on high:
But when it hath been scorched, and pierced, and riven,
1710   Its storms expire in water-drops; the eye
Pours forth at last the heart's-blood turned to tears,
Which make the English climate of our years.

---

[1] *Epicurus* Greek philosopher (341–270 BCE); *Aristippus* Philosopher (435–356 BCE) and pupil of Socrates. Byron thinks of them (unfairly in the case of Epicurus) as advocating the unrestrained pursuit of pleasure.

[2] *Sardanapalus* Legendary self-indulgent king of Assyria. Byron wrote a tragedy about him in 1821.

---

[3] *beau ideal* French: ideal beauty.

215

The liver is the lazaret[1] of bile,
　　But very rarely executes its function,
1715　For the first passion stays there such a while,
　　That all the rest creep in and form a junction,
Like knots of vipers on a dunghill's soil,
　　Rage, fear, hate, jealousy, revenge, compunction,
So that all mischiefs spring up from this entrail,
1720　Like earthquakes from the hidden fire called "central."

216

In the mean time, without proceeding more
　　In this anatomy, I've finished now
Two hundred and odd stanzas as before,
　　That being about the number I'll allow
1725　Each canto of the twelve, or twenty-four;
　　And, laying down my pen, I make my bow,
Leaving Don Juan and Haidée to plead
For them and theirs with all who deign to read.

from *Canto 3*

In this canto, Haidée takes Juan to the palace of her
absent father, the fierce pirate Lambro (see Canto
2.174–75, above). He returns home to find them
feasting, entertained by a bard. In the figure of the
bard (who "lied with such a fervour of intention /
There was no doubt he earned his laureate pension"),
Byron again parodies Robert Southey, but he also
mocks himself (see stanzas 84–85), and all poets.
Greece was then still part of the Ottoman Empire;
Byron's commitment to the cause of a free Greece
finds expression in the poet's song.

1

Hail, Muse! *et cetera.*—We left Juan sleeping,
　　Pillowed upon a fair and happy breast,
And watched by eyes that never yet knew weeping,
　　And loved by a young heart, too deeply blest
5　To feel the poison through her spirit creeping,

Or know who rested there; a foe to rest,
Had soiled the current of her sinless years,
And turned her pure heart's purest blood to tears!

2

Oh, Love! what is it in this world of ours
10　　Which makes it fatal to be loved? Ah why
With cypress[2] branches hast thou wreathed thy bowers,
　　And made thy best interpreter a sigh?
As those who dote on odours pluck the flowers,
　　And place them on their breast—but place to die—
15　Thus the frail beings we would fondly cherish
Are laid within our bosoms but to perish.

3

In her first passion woman loves her lover,
　　In all the others all she loves is love,
Which grows a habit she can ne'er get over,
20　　And fits her loosely—like an easy glove,
As you may find, whene'er you like to prove her:
　　One man alone at first her heart can move;
She then prefers him in the plural number,
Not finding that the additions much encumber.

4

25　I know not if the fault be men's or theirs;
　　But one thing's pretty sure; a woman planted—
(Unless at once she plunge for life in prayers)—
　　After a decent time must be gallanted;
Although, no doubt, her first of love affairs
30　　Is that to which her heart is wholly granted;
Yet there are some, they say, who have had *none,*
But those who have ne'er end with only *one.*

5

'Tis melancholy, and a fearful sign
　　Of human frailty, folly, also crime,
35　That love and marriage rarely can combine,
　　Although they both are born in the same clime;
Marriage from love, like vinegar from wine—
　　A sad, sour, sober beverage—by time

1　*lazaret* Hospital for those with infectious diseases, particularly
leprosy.

2　*cypress* Tree traditionally symbolic of mourning.

Is sharpened from its high celestial flavour
40 Down to a very homely household savour.

6

There's something of antipathy, as 'twere,
   Between their present and their future state;
A kind of flattery that's hardly fair
   Is used until the truth arrives too late—
45 Yet what can people do, except despair?
   The same things change their names at such a rate;
For instance—passion in a lover's glorious,
But in a husband is pronounced uxorious.

7

Men grow ashamed of being so very fond;
50   They sometimes also get a little tired
(But that, of course, is rare), and then despond:
   The same things cannot always be admired,
Yet 'tis "so nominated in the bond,"[1]
   That both are tied till one shall have expired.
55 Sad thought! to lose the spouse that was adorning
Our days, and put one's servants into mourning.

8

There's doubtless something in domestic doings
   Which forms, in fact, true love's antithesis;
Romances paint at full length people's wooings,
60   But only give a bust of marriages;[2]
For no one cares for matrimonial cooings,
   There's nothing wrong in a connubial kiss:
Think you, if Laura had been Petrarch's wife,
He would have written sonnets all his life?[3]

9

65 All tragedies are finished by a death,
   All comedies are ended by a marriage;

The future states of both are left to faith,
   For authors fear description might disparage
The worlds to come of both, or fall beneath,
70   And then both worlds would punish their
      miscarriage;
So leaving each their priest and prayer-book ready,
They say no more of Death or of the Lady.[4] …

70

Of all the dresses I select Haidée's:
   She wore two jelicks[5]—one was of pale yellow;
555 Of azure, pink, and white was her chemise—
   'Neath which her breast heaved like a little billow;
With buttons formed of pearls as large as peas,
   All gold and crimson shone her jelick's fellow,
And the striped white gauze baracan[6] that bound her,
560 Like fleecy clouds about the moon, flowed round her.

71

One large gold bracelet clasped each lovely arm,
   Lockless—so pliable from the pure gold
That the hand stretched and shut it without harm,
   The limb which it adorned its only mould;
565 So beautiful—its very shape would charm,
   And clinging as if loath to lose its hold,
The purest ore enclosed the whitest skin
That e'er by precious metal was held in.

72

Around, as princess of her father's land,
570   A like gold bar above her instep rolled
Announced her rank; twelve rings were on her hand;
   Her hair was starred with gems; her veil's fine fold
Below her breast was fastened with a band
   Of lavish pearls, whose worth could scarce be told;
575 Her orange silk full Turkish trousers furled
About the prettiest ankle in the world.

---

[1] *Yet … the bond* From Shakespeare's *The Merchant of Venice* 4.1.254. Byron here uses bond to mean marriage bond.

[2] *Romances … marriages* Romances detail all of courtship (as a full-length portrait does a person), but only mention marriage briefly (as a sculpted bust cuts off a person).

[3] *Think … life* Petrarch (Francesco Petrarca, 1304–74), the Italian poet, fell passionately in love with a woman named Laura, who was already married. He wrote a series of sonnets in praise of her.

---

[4] *Death … Lady* In the ballad *Death and the Lady*, Death demands the life of the Lady, despite her pleas. The ballad's conclusion asserts that the only hope for salvation is to have lived a moral life.

[5] *jelicks* Bodices worn by Turkish women.

[6] *baracan* Byron means a veil of delicate material, but he uses the word incorrectly. The actual definition is a wooly garment.

73

Her hair's long auburn waves down to her heel
    Flowed like an Alpine torrent which the sun
Dyes with his morning light,—and would conceal
580   Her person if allowed at large to run,
And still they seem resentfully to feel
    The silken fillet's° curb, and   *thin headband*
        sought to shun
Their bonds whene'er some Zephyr[1] caught began
To offer his young pinion as her fan.

74

585 Round her she made an atmosphere of life,
    The very air seemed lighter from her eyes,
They were so soft and beautiful, and rife
    With all we can imagine of the skies,
And pure as Psyche ere she grew a wife—
590   Too pure even for the purest human ties;
Her overpowering presence made you feel
It would not be idolatry to kneel.

75

Her eyelashes, though dark as night, were tinged
    (It is the country's custom), but in vain;
595 For those large black eyes were so blackly fringed,
    The glossy rebels mocked the jetty stain,
And in their native beauty stood avenged:
    Her nails were touched with henna; but again
The power of art was turned to nothing, for
600 They could not look more rosy than before.

76

The henna should be deeply dyed to make
    The skin relieved appear more fairly fair;
She had no need of this, day ne'er will break
    On mountain tops more heavenly white than her:
605 The eye might doubt if it were well awake,
    She was so like a vision; I might err,
But Shakespeare also says 'tis very silly
"To gild refined gold, or paint the lily."[2]

77

Juan had on a shawl of black and gold,
610   But a white baracan, and so transparent
The sparkling gems beneath you might behold,
    Like small stars through the milky way apparent;
His turban, furled in many a graceful fold,
    An emerald aigrette[3] with Haidée's hair in't
615 Surmounted, as its clasp, a glowing crescent,
Whose rays shone ever trembling, but incessant.

78

And now they were diverted by their suite,
    Dwarfs, dancing girls, black eunuchs, and a poet,
Which made their new establishment complete;
620   The last was of great fame, and liked to show it:
His verses rarely wanted their due feet—
    And for his theme—he seldom sung below it,
He being paid to satirise or flatter,
As the psalm says, "inditing a good matter."[4]

79

625 He praised the present, and abused the past,
    Reversing the good custom of old days,
An Eastern Anti-Jacobin[5] at last
    He turned, preferring pudding to *no* praise—
For some few years his lot had been o'ercast
630   By his seeming independent in his lays,
But now he sung the Sultan and the Pacha[6]
With truth like Southey, and with verse like Crashaw.[7]

80

He was a man who had seen many changes,
    And always changed as true as any needle;[8]

---

[1] *Zephyr* Wind. Zephyrus was the Greek god of the west wind.

[2] *To gild … the lily* See Shakespeare's *King John* 4.2.11.

[3] *aigrette* Ornament worn on the head, consisting of gems clasping a spray of feathers. In this case, it seems, the piece incorporates some of Haidée's hair.

[4] *As the psalm … matter* See Psalm 45.1.

[5] *Anti-Jacobin* The Anti-Jacobins fought against subversive thought brought into England after the French Revolution, urging the English to maintain conservative standards and institutions.

[6] *Pacha* In Turkey, a man of high rank or office. Usually spelled Pasha.

[7] *Crashaw* Richard Crashaw (1613–49), a poet then widely judged to have written verse of uneven quality.

[8] *needle* Compass needle.

35 His polar star being one which rather ranges,
　　And not the fixed—he knew the way to wheedle:
So vile he 'scaped the doom which oft avenges;
　　And being fluent (save indeed when fee'd ill),
He lied with such a fervour of intention—
40 There was no doubt he earned his laureate pension.

81

But he had genius,—when a turncoat has it,
　　The "Vates irritabilis"[1] takes care
That without notice few full moons shall pass it;
　　Even good men like to make the public stare:—
45 But to my subject—let me see—what was it?—
　　Oh!—the third canto—and the pretty pair—
Their loves, and feasts, and house, and dress, and mode
Of living in their insular abode.

82

Their poet, a sad trimmer, but no less
50 In company a very pleasant fellow,
Had been the favourite of full many a mess
　　Of men, and made them speeches when half mellow;
And though his meaning they could rarely guess,
　　Yet still they deigned to hiccup or to bellow
55 The glorious meed of popular applause,
Of which the first ne'er knows the second cause.

83

But now being lifted into high society,
　　And having picked up several odds and ends
Of free thoughts in his travels for variety,
60 　　He deemed, being in a lone isle, among friends,
That without any danger of a riot, he
　　Might for long lying make himself amends;
And singing as he sung in his warm youth,
Agree to a short armistice with truth.

84

65 He had travelled 'mongst the Arabs, Turks, and Franks,
　　And knew the self-loves of the different nations;
And having lived with people of all ranks,
　　Had something ready upon most occasions—

Which got him a few presents and some thanks.
670 　　He varied with some skill his adulations;
To "do at Rome as Romans do," a piece
Of conduct was which he observed in Greece.

85

Thus, usually, when he was asked to sing,
　　He gave the different nations something national;
675 'Twas all the same to him—"God save the King,"
　　Or "Ça ira,"[2] according to the fashion all:
His muse made increment of any thing,
　　From the high lyric down to the low rational:
If Pindar sang horse-races, what should hinder
680 Himself from being as pliable as Pindar?[3]

86

In France, for instance, he would write a chanson;[4]
　　In England a six canto quarto tale;
In Spain, he'd make a ballad or romance on
　　The last war—much the same in Portugal;
685 In Germany, the Pegasus he'd prance on
　　Would be old Goethe's—(see what says de Staël)[5]
In Italy he'd ape the "Trecentisti";[6]
In Greece, he'd sing some sort of hymn like this t'ye:

1

The isles of Greece, the isles of Greece!
690 　　Where burning Sappho loved and sung,
Where grew the arts of war and peace,—
　　Where Delos rose, and Phoebus sprung![7]
Eternal summer gilds them yet,
But all, except their sun, is set.

---

1 *Vates irritabilis* Latin: The irritability of men of genius.

2 *Ça ira* French: It will succeed (a song of the French Revolution).

3 *Pindar … Pindar* The Greek poet Pindar (c. 522–443 BCE), was famous for his Odes. His first Olympian Ode celebrates the winner of a horse race.

4 *chanson* French: song; possibly a reference to the *chansons de geste*, poems in Old French detailing legends about historical figures.

5 *de Staël* In *De l'Allemagne* (1818), Madame de Staël (1766–1817) writes that Goethe "will be able to represent the whole of German literature."

6 *Trecentisti* Italian poets of the fourteenth century.

7 *Delos … sprung* Delos, the mythical birthplace of Phoebus Apollo, was called out of the ocean by Poseidon.

2

695 The Scian and the Teian muse,[1]
　　　 The hero's harp, the lover's lute,
　　 Have found the fame your shores refuse;
　　　 Their place of birth alone is mute
　　 To sounds which echo further west
700 Than your sires' "Islands of the Blest."

3

　　 The mountains look on Marathon—
　　　 And Marathon looks on the sea;
　　 And musing there an hour alone,
　　　 I dreamed that Greece might still be free;
705 For standing on the Persians' grave,[2]
　　 I could not deem myself a slave.

4

　　 A king sat on the rocky brow
　　　 Which looks o'er sea-born Salamis;
　　 And ships, by thousands, lay below,
710 　　 And men in nations;—all were his!
　　 He counted them at break of day—
　　 And when the sun set where were they?[3]

5

　　 And where are they? and where art thou,
　　　 My country? On thy voiceless shore
715 The heroic lay is tuneless now—
　　　 The heroic bosom beats no more!
　　 And must thy lyre, so long divine,
　　 Degenerate into hands like mine?

6

　　 'Tis something, in the dearth of fame,
720 　　 Though linked among a fettered race,
　　 To feel at least a patriot's shame,
　　　 Even as I sing, suffuse my face;
　　 For what is left the poet here?
　　 For Greeks a blush—for Greece a tear.

7

725 Must we but weep o'er days more blest?
　　　 Must *we* but blush?—Our fathers bled.
　　 Earth! render back from out thy breast
　　　 A remnant of our Spartan dead!
　　 Of the three hundred grant but three,
730 To make a new Thermopylae![4]

8

　　 What, silent still? and silent all?
　　　 Ah! no;—the voices of the dead
　　 Sound like a distant torrent's fall,
　　　 And answer, "Let one living head,
735 But one arise,—we come, we come!"
　　 'Tis but the living who are dumb.

9

　　 In vain—in vain: strike other chords;
　　　 Fill high the cup with Samian wine![5]
　　 Leave battles to the Turkish hordes,
740 　　 And shed the blood of Scio's vine!
　　 Hark! rising to the ignoble call—
　　 How answers each bold Bacchanal!

10

　　 You have the Pyrrhic dance as yet,
　　　 Where is the Pyrrhic phalanx[6] gone?
745 Of two such lessons, why forget
　　　 The nobler and the manlier one?
　　 You have the letters Cadmus[7] gave—
　　 Think ye he meant them for a slave?

11

　　 Fill high the bowl with Samian wine!
750 　　 We will not think of themes like these!
　　 It made Anacreon's song divine:

[1] *Scian ... muse* Homer, primarily a poet of war and heroes, was born on Scio; Anacreon, famous for his poems of love, was born at Teos.

[2] *Persians' grave* The Greeks defeated the Persians at the Battle of Marathon in 490 BCE.

[3] *A king ... they* At the Battle of Salamis in 480 BCE, the Persian king Xerxes watched from a promontory as the Greeks, although vastly outnumbered, defeated his men in a sea battle.

[4] *Spartan ... Thermopylae* In 480 BCE the Persians slaughtered 300 Spartans in the narrow pass of Thermopylae. The Spartan sacrifice, however, halted the Persian advance into Greece.

[5] *Samian wine* The Greek island of Samos was famous for its Muscat wine.

[6] *Pyrrhic dance* In the Pyrrhic dance, armed men perform quick acrobatic movements of attack and defense; *Pyrrhic phalanx* The Pyrrhic phalanx was a close massing of soldiers, a maneuver responsible for many Greek victories.

[7] *Cadmus* Phoenician prince who reputedly introduced the use of letters in Greece.

He served—but served Polycrates[1]—
A tyrant; but our masters then
Were still, at least, our countrymen.

12

The tyrant of the Chersonese
 Was freedom's best and bravest friend;
That tyrant was Miltiades![2]
 Oh! that the present hour would lend
Another despot of the kind!
Such chains as his were sure to bind.

13

Fill high the bowl with Samian wine!
 On Suli's rock, and Parga's shore,[3]
Exists the remnant of a line
 Such as the Doric mothers bore;
And there, perhaps, some seed is sown,
The Heracleidan blood[4] might own.

14

Trust not for freedom to the Franks[5]—
 They have a king who buys and sells:
In native swords, and native ranks,
 The only hope of courage dwells;
But Turkish force, and Latin fraud,
Would break your shield, however broad.

15

Fill high the bowl with Samian wine!
 Our virgins dance beneath the shade—
I see their glorious black eyes shine;

But gazing on each glowing maid,
My own the burning tear-drop laves,
To think such breasts must suckle slaves.

16

Place me on Sunium's[6] marbled steep,
 Where nothing, save the waves and I,
May hear our mutual murmurs sweep;
 There, swan-like, let me sing and die:
A land of slaves shall ne'er be mine—
Dash down yon cup of Samian wine!

87

Thus sung, or would, or could, or should have sung,
 The modern Greek, in tolerable verse;
If not like Orpheus quite, when Greece was young,
 Yet in these times he might have done much worse:
His strain displayed some feeling—right or wrong;
 And feeling, in a poet, is the source
Of others' feeling; but they are such liars,
And take all colours—like the hands of dyers.

88

But words are things, and a small drop of ink,
 Falling like dew, upon a thought, produces
That which makes thousands, perhaps millions, think;
 'Tis strange, the shortest letter which man uses
Instead of speech, may form a lasting link
 Of ages; to what straits old Time reduces
Frail man, when paper—even a rag like this,
Survives himself, his tomb, and all that's his.

---

1 *Polycrates* Greek tyrant and ruler of Samos, the island to which Anacreon fled after Teos was captured by Persians in 510 BCE.

2 *tyrant … Miltiades* In the fifth century BCE, Miltiades became the ruler of Chersonesus, now the peninsula of the Dardanelles.

3 *Suli's rock … Parga's shore* The Suliotes were a fierce Albanian tribe; Parga is a town on the Ionian coast.

4 *Heracleidan blood* The Heracleidae, supposedly descendants of Hercules, conquered the Peloponnesus.

5 *Franks* Western Europeans.

---

6 *Sunium's* I.e., Cape Sounion's. Cape Sounion was the site of a temple of Poseidon.

from *Canto 7*

In Cantos 7 and 8 Byron describes the Siege of Ismail and Juan's participation in it. In December of 1790, Russian troops under the command of General Alexander Suvarov besieged and overpowered the Turkish fortress of Ismail in a quick, brutal attack. Byron's cantos vividly depict the action, confusion, brutality, and devastation of war.

78

... —The work of glory still went on
    In preparations for a cannonade
As terrible as that of Ilion,[1]
620   If Homer had found mortars ready made;
But now, instead of slaying Priam's son,[2]
    We only can but talk of escalade,
Bombs, drums, guns, bastions, batteries, bayonets, bullets;
Hard words, which stick in the soft Muses' gullets.

79

625 Oh, thou eternal Homer! who couldst charm
    All ears, though long; all ages, though so short,
By merely wielding with poetic arm
    Arms to which men will never more resort,
Unless gunpowder should be found to harm
630   Much less than is the hope of every court,
Which now is leagued young Freedom to annoy;
But they will not find Liberty a Troy:—

80

Oh, thou eternal Homer! I have now
    To paint a siege, wherein more men were slain,
635 With deadlier engines and a speedier blow,
    Than in thy Greek gazette of that campaign;
And yet, like all men else, I must allow,
    To vie with thee would be about as vain
As for a brook to cope with ocean's flood;
640 But still we moderns equal you in blood;

---

[1] *Ilion* I.e., Troy.

[2] *Priam's son* I.e., Hector, Trojan hero and prince of Troy.

81

If not in poetry, at least in fact;
    And fact is truth, the grand desideratum![3]
Of which, howe'er the Muse describes each act,
    There should be ne'ertheless a slight substratum.
645 But now the town is going to be attacked;
    Great deeds are doing—how shall I relate 'em?
Souls of immortal generals! Phoebus watches
To colour up his rays from your despatches.

from *Canto 11*

In Canto 11 Juan, having passed through a Turkish harem, the Siege of Ismail (above), and the court of Catherine the Great, establishes himself in London among the upper classes. Byron uses this canto to describe Juan's experiences and, in the excerpt below, to muse on the changes that have occurred in his own life in the years since he left England.

55

In twice five years the "greatest living poet,"
    Like to the champion in the fisty ring,[4]
435 Is called on to support his claim, or show it,
    Although 'tis an imaginary thing.
Even I—albeit I'm sure I did not know it,
    Nor sought of foolscap subjects to be king—
Was reckoned a considerable time,
440 The grand Napoleon of the realms of rhyme.[5]

56

But Juan was my Moscow,[6] and Faliero
    My Leipsic,[7] and my Mount Saint Jean seems Cain:

---

[3] *desideratum* Latin: something desired or believed to be essential.

[4] *the fisty ring* The boxing ring. Byron was a keen amateur boxer.

[5] *Even I ... rhyme* Byron frequently likens himself to Napoleon throughout his work. Here he makes ironic reference to both Napoleon's conspicuous success and his equally conspicuous fall.

[6] *Moscow* Napoleon attempted to conquer Russia by capturing Moscow, but was defeated by the Russian winter.

[7] *Leipsic* The battle of Leipzig in October 1813 effectively broke the power of the French army. Byron draws a mocking parallel between this and his play *Marino Faliero*, which failed when it was performed against his wishes in 1821.

"*La Belle Alliance*"[1] of dunces down at zero,
    Now that the Lion's fall'n, may rise again:
But I will fall at least as fell my hero;
    Nor reign at all, or as a *monarch* reign;
Or to some lonely isle of gaolers go,
With turncoat Southey for my turnkey Lowe.[2]

57

Sir Walter reigned before me; Moore and Campbell[3]
    Before and after; but now grown more holy,
The Muses upon Sion's hill must ramble
    With poets almost clergymen, or wholly;
And Pegasus hath a psalmodic amble
    Beneath the very Reverend Rowley Powley,[4]
Who shoes the glorious animal with stilts,
A modern Ancient Pistol[5]—"by these hilts!"

58

Still he excels that artificial hard
    Labourer in the same vineyard, though the vine
Yields him but vinegar for his reward,—
    That neutralised dull Dorus of the Nine;
That swarthy Sporus, neither man nor bard;
    That ox of verse, who *ploughs* for every line:—
Cambyses' roaring Romans beat at least
The howling Hebrews of Cybele's priest.[6]—

59

Then there's my gentle Euphues,[7] who, they say,
    Sets up for being a sort of *moral me*;
He'll find it rather difficult some day
    To turn out both, or either, it may be.
Some persons think that Coleridge hath the sway;
    And Wordsworth has supporters, two or three;
And that deep-mouthed Boeotian "Savage Landor"[8]
Has taken for a swan rogue Southey's gander.

60

John Keats, who was killed off by one critique,
    Just as he really promised something great,[9]
If not intelligible, without Greek
    Contrived to talk about the gods of late,
Much as they might have been supposed to speak.[10]
    Poor fellow! His was an untoward fate;
'Tis strange the mind, that very fiery particle,
Should let itself be snuffed out by an article.

61

The list grows long of live and dead pretenders
    To that which none will gain—or none will know
The conqueror at least; who, ere Time renders
    His last award, will have the long grass grow
Above his burnt-out brain, and sapless cinders.
    If I might augur, I should rate but low

---

[1] *Cain: / La Belle Alliance* Byron's *Cain* (1821), was condemned by critics for its blasphemy, and Byron likens it to Napoleon's defeat at Waterloo (crucial action occurred at Mont St. Jean). "La Belle Alliance" was the farmhouse in which the victors met after Waterloo; Byron is also punning on the alliance of England, Russia, Austria, and Prussia, which combined to rout Napoleon.

[2] *Lowe* Sir Hudson Lowe, governor of St. Helena during Napoleon's exile.

[3] *Sir Walter ... Campbell* Sir Walter Scott, Thomas Moore, and Thomas Campbell, contemporary poets.

[4] *Reverend Rowley Powley* The Reverend George Croly (1780–1860), a minor but prolific poet, fond of imitating Byron's work and known for his bombastic manner.

[5] *Pistol* In Shakespeare's *1 Henry IV*, Pistol is a blustering friend of Falstaff.

[6] *Cybele's priest* Byron here attacks Henry Milman (1791–1868), author of *The Fall of Jerusalem*, and a reviewer whose criticism he resented. He offers him several different insults. Dorus was a eunuch in Terence's *Eunuchus*; effeminate Sporus was castrated by the emperor Nero, who then married him; in the last two lines he suggests that the

"howling Hebrews" of Milman's *Fall* are inferior even to the "roaring Romans" of George Croly. In the final line, he calls Milman "Cybele's priest," alluding to followers of the Asiatic goddess Cybele: these followers were often castrated.

[7] *gentle Euphues* Bryan Waller Proctor (1787–1874), whose poem *Diego de Montilla* was said to resemble *Don Juan*, but without the satire of social mores. Euphues, who gave his name to the "Euphuistic" style, is the hero of a prose romance by the Elizabethan writer John Lyly.

[8] *Boeotian* The Athenians believed the Boeotians to be stupid and boorish; *Savage Landor* Walter Savage Landor (1775–1864), a poet and friend of Robert Southey. He joined Southey in propagating rumors about Byron.

[9] *John Keats ... great* It was commonly believed that Keats's death was hastened by a savage attack by John Wilson Croker in the *Quarterly Review*, a popular journal. This notion came from Shelley (see *Adonais*).

[10] *Contrived to talk ... speak* Referring to Keats's *Hyperion*, which Byron admired.

Their chances; they're too numerous, like the thirty
Mock tyrants,[1] when Rome's annals waxed but dirty.

62

This is the literary *lower* empire,
490   Where the prætorian bands[2] take up the matter;—
A "dreadful trade," like his who "gathers samphire,"[3]
        The insolent soldiery to soothe and flatter,
With the same feelings as you'd coax a vampire.
        Now, were I once at home, and in good satire,
495 I'd try conclusions with those Janizaries,[4]
And show them *what* an intellectual war is.

63

I think I know a trick or two, would turn
        Their flanks;—but it is hardly worth my while
With such small gear to give myself concern:
500   Indeed I've not the necessary bile;
My natural temper's really aught but stern,
        And even my Muse's worst reproof's a smile;
And then she drops a brief and modern curtsy,
And glides away, assured she never hurts ye.

64

505 My Juan, whom I left in deadly peril
        Amongst live poets and *blue* ladies, past
With some small profit through that field so sterile,
        Being tired in time, and, neither least nor last,
Left it before he had been treated very ill;
510   And henceforth found himself more gaily classed
Amongst the higher spirits of the day,
The sun's true son, no vapour, but a ray.

---

[1] *thirty ... tyrants* The thirty pretenders to the throne of Rome during the third century.

[2] *prætorian bands* The Roman emperor's guard, whose power was so strong during the Empire's decline that they had effective control over succession to the throne; in one case, they auctioned it off.

[3] *gathers samphire* Samphire is a European plant, used in cooking, that grows on rocks near the sea. In Shakespeare's *King Lear* 4.6.15–16, Edgar says that the man he pretends to see is engaged in a fearful trade because he must cling halfway down a cliff in order to gather samphire.

[4] *Janizaries* The sultan's guard.

65

His morns he passed in business—which, dissected,
        Was like all business a laborious nothing
515 That leads to lassitude, the most infected
        And Centaur Nessus garb[5] of mortal clothing,
And on our sofas makes us lie dejected,
        And talk in tender horrors of our loathing
All kinds of toil, save for our country's good—
520 Which grows no better, though 'tis time it should.

66

His afternoons he passed in visits, luncheons,
        Lounging and boxing; and the twilight hour
In riding round those vegetable puncheons[6]
        Called "Parks," where there is neither fruit nor flower
525 Enough to gratify a bee's slight munchings;
        But after all it is the only "bower"
(In Moore's phrase), where the fashionable fair
Can form a slight acquaintance with fresh air.

67

Then dress, then dinner, then awakes the world!
530   Then glare the lamps, then whirl the wheels, then
            roar
Through street and square fast flashing chariots hurled
        Like harnessed meteors; then along the floor
Chalk mimics painting;[7] then festoons are twirled;
        Then roll the brazen thunders of the door,
535 Which opens to the thousand happy few
An earthly paradise of ormolu.[8]

68

There stands the noble hostess, nor shall sink
        With the three-thousandth curtsy; there the waltz,
The only dance which teaches girls to think,
540   Makes one in love even with its very faults.
Saloon, room, hall, o'erflow beyond their brink,

---

[5] *Centaur Nessus garb* Hercules's wife gave him a garment dipped in the blood of the dying centaur Nessus, who told her it would win her back her husband's love. Instead, it killed Hercules.

[6] *puncheons* Large casks for liquids.

[7] *Chalk mimics painting* In ballrooms of the period, floors were decorated with elaborate chalk drawings.

[8] *ormolu* Gilded bronze decoration.

And long the latest of arrivals halts,
'Midst royal dukes and dames condemned to climb,
And gain an inch of staircase at a time.

69

45 Thrice happy he who, after a survey
    Of the good company, can win a corner,
A door that's *in* or boudoir *out* of the way,
    Where he may fix himself like small "Jack Horner,"
And let the Babel round run as it may,
50   And look on as a mourner, or a scorner,
Or an approver, or a mere spectator,
Yawning a little as the night grows later.

70

But this won't do, save by and by; and he
    Who, like Don Juan, takes an active share,
55 Must steer with care through all that glittering sea
    Of gems and plumes and pearls and silks, to where
He deems it is his proper place to be;
    Dissolving in the waltz to some soft air,
Or proudlier prancing with mercurial skill
60 Where Science marshals forth her own quadrille.

71

Or, if he dance not, but hath higher views
    Upon an heiress or his neighbour's bride,
Let him take care that that which he pursues
    Is not at once too palpably descried.
65 Full many an eager gentleman oft rues
    His haste: impatience is a blundering guide,
Amongst a people famous for reflection,
Who like to play the fool with circumspection.

72

But, if you can contrive, get next at supper;
70   Or, if forestalled, get opposite and ogle:—
Oh, ye ambrosial moments! always upper
    In mind, a sort of sentimental bogle,°   goblin
Which sits for ever upon memory's crupper,°   hindquarters
    The ghost of vanished pleasures once in vogue! Ill
75 Can tender souls relate the rise and fall
Of hopes and fears which shake a single ball.

73

But these precautionary hints can touch
    Only the common run, who must pursue,
And watch, and ward; whose plans a word too much
580   Or little overturns; and not the few
Or many (for the number's sometimes such)
    Whom a good mien, especially if new,
Or fame, or name, for wit, war, sense, or nonsense,
Permits whate'er they please, or *did* not long since.

74

585 Our hero, as a hero, young and handsome,
    Noble, rich, celebrated, and a stranger,
Like other slaves of course must pay his ransom,
    Before he can escape from so much danger
As will environ a conspicuous man. Some
590   Talk about poetry, and "rack and manger,"[1]
And ugliness, disease, as toil and trouble;—
I wish they knew the life of a young noble.

75

They are young, but know not youth—it is anticipated;
    Handsome but wasted, rich without a sou;[2]
595 Their vigour in a thousand arms is dissipated;
    Their cash comes *from*, their wealth goes *to* a Jew;
Both senates see their nightly votes participated
    Between the tyrant's and the tribunes' crew;[3]
And having voted, dined, drunk, gamed, and whored,
600 The family vault receives another lord.

76

"Where is the world?" cries Young, at *eighty*[4]—"Where
    The world in which a man was born?" Alas!
Where is the world of *eight* years past? 'Twas there—
    I look for it—'tis gone, a globe of glass!
605 Cracked, shivered, vanished, scarcely gazed on, ere
    A silent change dissolves the glittering mass.

---

[1] *rack and manger* Rack and ruin.

[2] *without a sou* Penniless.

[3] *Both … crew* The young noble does not express principles of his own, but simply votes the party line, a situation seen every night in both Houses of Parliament.

[4] *Where … eighty* Edward Young (1683–1765) was over eighty when he included this question in his poem, *Resignation*.

Statesmen, chiefs, orators, queens, patriots, kings,
And dandies, all are gone on the wind's wings.

77

Where is Napoleon the Grand? God knows.
610   Where little Castlereagh?[1] The devil can tell:
Where Grattan, Curran, Sheridan,[2] all those
      Who bound the bar or senate in their spell?
Where is the unhappy Queen, with all her woes?
      And where the Daughter,[3] whom the Isles loved well?
615 Where are those martyred saints the Five per Cents?[4]
And where—oh, where the devil are the rents?

78

Where's Brummel? Dished. Where's Long Pole
      Wellesley? Diddled.[5]
      Where's Whitbread?[6] Romilly? Where's George
      the Third?
Where is his will? (That's not so soon unriddled.)[7]

620   And where is "Fum" the Fourth, our "royal bird?"[8]
Gone down, it seems, to Scotland to be fiddled
      Unto by Sawney's[9] violin, we have heard:
"Caw° me, caw thee"—for six months   scratch
      hath been hatching
This scene of royal itch and loyal scratching.

79

625 Where is Lord This? And where my Lady That?
      The Honourable Mistresses and Misses?
Some laid aside like an old Opera hat,
      Married, unmarried, and remarried (this is
An evolution oft performed of late).
630   Where are the Dublin shouts—and London hisses?
Where are the Grenvilles? Turned as usual.[10] Where
My friends the Whigs? Exactly where they were.

80

Where are the Lady Carolines and Franceses?
      Divorced or doing thereanent.[11] Ye annals
635 So brilliant, where the list of routs and dances is,—
      Thou Morning Post, sole record of the panels
Broken in carriages, and all the phantasies
      Of fashion,—say what streams now fill those
      channels?
640 Some die, some fly, some languish on the Continent,
Because the times have hardly left them *one* tenant.

---

[1] *Castlereagh* Robert Stewart, Lord Castlereagh (1769–1822), Tory politician and Foreign Secretary during the Napoleonic Wars. Castlereagh committed suicide ("Where is little Castlereagh? The devil can tell").

[2] *Grattan* Henry Grattan (1746–1820), Whig statesman who supported Irish interests; *Curran* John Philpot Curran (1750–1814), who aided in the attempt to achieve Irish emancipation; *Sheridan* Richard Brinsley Sheridan (1751–1816), Whig MP, playwright, and wit.

[3] *Queen* Caroline of Brunswick (1768–1821), whom George IV (1762–1830) married and then immediately repudiated, always treating her with contempt. In 1820 he attempted to divorce her in a scandalous proceeding before the House of Lords; *the Daughter* Princess Charlotte (1796–1817), daughter of George IV and Caroline and heir to the throne, was extremely popular. She died in childbirth in 1817.

[4] *Five per Cents* Government bonds.

[5] *Brummel … Diddled* Dished and diddled both mean ruined. George "Beau" Brummel (1788–1840), the famous dandy, was forced to flee to Calais in 1816 because of his enormous debts; William Pole Tylney Wellesley (1788–1857) was notorious for spending his money with abandon.

[6] *Whitbread* Samuel Whitbread (1758–1815), who supported Queen Caroline against the Prince Regent, committed suicide in 1815.

[7] *Where … unriddled* King George III made two wills, one in 1770 and one in 1810. He left the later will unsigned. The earlier was thus official, although many of its provisions were outdated.

[8] *Fum … bird* George IV. The king's nickname was "Hum," while an apartment at the lavishly decorated and ruinously expensive Brighton Pavilion contained an ornament called "Fum, the Chinese Bird of Royalty." Byron here alludes also to Moore's satire, *Fum and Hum, the Two Birds of Royalty* (1818).

[9] *Sawney's* Scotsman's. Sawney was a contemptuous term for a Scot.

[10] *Where are … usual* George Grenville (1712–70) first supported Pitt, then later broke with him; his son William Wyndam, Baron Grenville (1759–1834), was first a social reformer, then a repressive Tory.

[11] *doing thereanent* Doing something related to that. After her affair with Byron, Lady Caroline Lamb was for some years estranged from her husband; Lady Frances Wedderburn Webster (d. 1837), with whom Byron had once carried on a nearly adulterous flirtation, left her husband in 1821; Byron helped to effect a reconciliation about the time that he wrote this canto.

81

Some who once set their caps¹ at cautious dukes,
  Have taken up at length with younger brothers:
Some heiresses have bit at sharpers' hooks:²
  Some maids have been made wives, some merely
      mothers;
5 Others have lost their fresh and fairy looks:
  In short, the list of alterations bothers.
There's little strange in this, but something strange is
The unusual quickness of these common changes.

82

Talk not of seventy years as age; in seven
  I have seen more changes, down from monarchs to
The humblest individual under heaven,
  Than might suffice a moderate century through.
I knew that nought was lasting, but now even
  Change grows too changeable, without being new:
5 Nought's permanent among the human race,
Except the Whigs *not* getting into place.

83

I have seen Napoleon, who seemed quite a Jupiter,
  Shrink to a Saturn. I have seen a Duke
(No matter which) turn politician stupider,
  If that can well be, than his wooden look.
But it is time that I should hoist my "blue Peter,"³
  And sail for a new theme:—I have seen—and shook
To see it—the king hissed, and then caressed;
But don't pretend to settle which was best.

84

5 I have seen the Landholders without a rap—
  I have seen Joanna Southcote⁴—I have seen—

The House of Commons turned to a tax-trap⁵—
  I have seen that sad affair of the late Queen—
I have seen crowns worn instead of a fool's cap—
670 I have seen a Congress doing all that's mean—
I have seen some nations like o'erloaded asses
Kick off their burthens, meaning the high classes.⁶

85

I have seen small poets, and great prosers, and
  Interminable—*not eternal*—speakers—
675 I have seen the funds at war with house and land⁷—
  I have seen the country gentlemen turn squeakers—
I have seen the people ridden o'er like sand
  By slaves on horseback—I have seen malt liquors
Exchanged for "thin potations"⁸ by John Bull—
680 I have seen John half detect himself a fool.—

86

But "*carpe diem*,"⁹ Juan, "*carpe, carpe!*"
  To-morrow sees another race as gay
And transient, and devoured by the same harpy.
  "Life's a poor player,"—then "play out the play,
685 Ye villains!" above all keep a sharp eye
  Much less on what you do than what you say:
Be hypocritical, be cautious, be
Not what you *seem*, but always what you *see*.

87

But how shall I relate in other cantos
690 Of what befell our hero in the land,

---

¹ *set their caps* Set out to attract, with the sense of attracting into a marriage proposal.

² *bit at sharpers' hooks* Been seduced into marriage by money-seeking rogues.

³ *blue Peter* A blue flag with a white square in the center, raised as a sign of immediate sailing.

⁴ *Southcote* Joanna Southcott (1750–1814), the founder of a fanatical sect, announced that she was about to give birth to the second messiah; in fact, she was suffering from dropsy and did not know it.

⁵ *tax-trap* To pay for the Napoleonic Wars, Parliament levied extremely high taxes.

⁶ *Congress* Probably the Congress of Vienna, which, after Napoleon's defeat, divided up Europe without regard for the wishes of the populace; *nations … classes* The recent revolts in Spain, Mexico, and South America.

⁷ *funds at … land* The National Debt and the Sinking Fund, which unsuccessfully attempted to reduce it.

⁸ *I have … horseback* Byron may be referring to scenes of political unrest he had witnessed in Italy or to the Peterloo Massacre in Manchester (1819), in which several peaceful protestors were murdered by the militia; *thin potations* Cf. Shakespeare's *2 Henry IV* 3.120–24. English brewers reduced the amount of malt they used in order to avoid the malt tax.

⁹ *carpe diem* Latin: seize the day.

Which 'tis the common cry and lie to vaunt as
    A moral country? But I hold my hand—
For I disdain to write an Atalantis;[1]
    But 'tis as well at once to understand,
695 You are *not* a moral people, and you know it
Without the aid of too sincere a poet.

88

What Juan saw and underwent shall be
    My topic, with of course the due restriction
Which is required by proper courtesy;
700   And recollect the work is only fiction,
And that I sing of neither mine nor me,
    Though every scribe, in some slight turn of diction,
Will hint allusions never *meant*. Ne'er doubt
This—when I speak, I *don't hint*, but *speak out*.

89

705 Whether he married with the third or fourth
    Offspring of some sage husband-hunting countess,

Or whether with some virgin of more worth
    (I mean in Fortune's matrimonial bounties)
He took to regularly peopling Earth,
710   Of which your lawful awful wedlock fount is,—
Or whether he was taken in for damages,
For being too excursive in his homages,—

90

Is yet within the unread events of time.
    Thus far, go forth, thou lay, which I will back
715 Against the same given quantity of rhyme,
    For being as much the subject of attack
As ever yet was any work sublime,
    By those who love to say that white is black.
So much the better!—I may stand alone,
720 But would not change my free thoughts for a throne.
    —1819–23

---

[1] *Atalantis*   Delarivier Manley (1663–1724) wrote *The New Atalantis, or Memoirs and Manners of Several Persons of Quality* (1709), a satire that was openly disrespectful toward important Whig politicians.

IN CONTEXT

Don Juan

"Remarks on *Don Juan*," from *Blackwood's Magazine*, August 1819

That Lord Byron has never written anything more decisively and triumphantly expressive of the greatness of his genius, will be allowed by all who have read this poem. That (laying all its manifold and grievous offences for a moment out of our view) it is by far the most admirable specimen of the mixture of ease, strength, gaiety, and seriousness extant in the whole body of English poetry, is a proposition to which, we are almost as well persuaded, very few of them will refuse their assent. With sorrow and humiliation do we speak it: the poet has devoted his powers to the worst of purposes and passions; and it increases his guilt and our sorrow, that he has devoted them entire. What the immediate effect of the poem may be on contemporary literature, we cannot pretend to guess—too happy could we hope that its lessons of boldness and vigour in language, and versification, and conception, might be attended to, as they deserve to be—without any stain being suffered to fall on the purity of those who minister to the general shape and culture of the public mind, from the mischievous insults against all good principle and all good feeling, which have been unworthily embodied in so many elements of fascination.

The moral strain of the whole poem is pitched in the lowest key, and if the genius of the author lifts him now and then out of his pollution, it seems as if he regretted the elevation, and made all haste to descend again. To particularize the offences committed in its pages would be worse than vain because the great genius of the man seems to have been throughout exerted to its utmost strength, in devising every possible method of pouring scorn upon every element of good or noble nature in the hearts of his readers. Love, honour, patriotism, religion, are mentioned only to be scoffed at and derided, as if their sole remaining resting-place were, or ought to be, in the bosoms of fools. It appears, in short, as if this miserable man, having exhausted every species of sensual gratification, having drained the cup of sin even to its bitterest dregs, were resolved to show us that he is no longer a human being, even in his frailties—but a cool unconcerned fiend, laughing with a detestable glee over the whole of the better and worse elements of which human life is composed; treating well nigh with equal derision the most pure of virtues, and the most odious of vices, dead alike to the beauty the one, and the deformity of the other; a mere heartless despiser of that frail but noble humanity, whose type was never exhibited in a shape of more deplorable degradation than in his own contemptuously distinct delineation of himself.

Personal Writings

Byron's letters and journals are valuable literary artifacts in their own right. Only Keats rivaled him for breadth of subject matter and depth of thought in his personal correspondence, and even Keats could not match his dazzling wit. The letters are filled with gossip and scandal, with the most intimate details of Byron's life and those of his friends, all recounted with great shrewdness and relish. At the same time, however, Byron was not afraid to place his most intimate thoughts, and accounts of his greatest anguish, on paper for others to read. The letters and journal entries record his minute observations on the foreign countries he passed through, his political beliefs, his growing involvement with revolutionary movements, his frank descriptions (and ratings) of his many sexual involvements, his sorrow and rage over the end of his marriage, his generosity and kindness toward both friends and strangers—all recounted with a dexterity of language that mirrors that of his poetical works.

TO CATHERINE GORDON BYRON
12 November 1809
Prevesa

My dear Mother,—I have now been some time in Turkey: this place is on the coast but I have traversed the interior of the province of Albania on a visit to the Pacha.[1]—I left Malta in the Spider a brig of war on the 21st of Septr. & arrived in eight days at Prevesa.—I thence have been about 150 miles as far as Tepaleen his highness's country palace where I staid three days.—The name of the Pacha is Ali,[2] & he is considered a man of the first abilities, he governs the whole of Albania (the ancient Illyricum) Epirus, & part of Macedonia, his Son *Velly* Pacha to whom he has given me letters governs the Morea & he has great influence in Egypt, in short he is one of the most powerful men in the Ottoman empire.—When I reached Yanina the capital after a journey of three days over the mountains through a country of the most picturesque beauty, I found that Ali Pacha was with his army in Illyricum besieging Ibraham Pacha[3] in the castle of Berat.—He had heard that an Englishman of rank was in his dominions & had left orders in Yanina with the Commandant to provide a house & supply me with every kind of necessary, *gratis*,[4] & though I have been allowed to make presents to the slaves &c. I have not been permitted to pay for a single article of household consumption.—I rode out on the viziers[5] horses & saw the palaces of himself & grandsons, they are splendid but much too ornamented with silk & gold.—I then went over the mountains through Zitza a village with a Greek monastery (where I slept on my return) in the most beautiful Situation (always excepting Cintra in Portugal) I ever beheld.—In nine days I reached Tepaleen,[6] our Journey was much prolonged by the torrents that had fallen from the mountains & intersected the roads. I shall never forget the singular scene on entering Tepaleen at five in the afternoon as the Sun was going down, it brought to my recollection (with some change of *dress* however) Scott's description of Branksome Castle in his lay,[7] & the feudal system.—The Albanians in their dresses (the most magnificent in the world, consisting of a long *white kilt*, gold worked cloak, crimson velvet gold laced jacket & waistcoat,

---

[1] *Pacha* High-ranking Turkish officer.

[2] *Ali* Ali Pasha of Yanina (1741–1822), known as "the Muslim Bonaparte" or the "Lion of Yanina," was ruler of the western European part of the Ottoman Empire (including what are now Greece and parts of Albania). He had been a leader of robber bandits, but raised himself to become absolute ruler over his own regions. While the town of Ioannina became a cultural and economic center during his rule, and while his rule was a relatively stable one, Ali Pasha was capable of great cruelty and perpetrated many infamous atrocities.

[3] *Illyricum* Illyricum, a region of the Balkan Peninsula bordering the Adriatic sea, was a province in the Roman Empire in the first and second centuries CE; the region comprised what are now northern Serbia, Croatia, and western Hungary; *Ibraham Pacha* Ruler of the Pashalik of Berat from 1787 to 1809. Ali defeated Ibrahim and incorporated his lands into the Pashalik of Yanina.

[4] *gratis* Latin: without charge.

[5] *vizier* High state official, here referring to Ali Pasha.

[6] *Tepaleen* Tepelenë is a town in southern Albania.

[7] *lay* Sir Walter Scott's poem *The Lay of the Last Minstrel*. See Canto 1, stanzas 1–5.

silver mounted pistols & daggers,) the Tartars[1] with their high caps, the Turks in their vast pelises[2] & turbans, the soldiers & black slaves with the horses, the former stretched in groupes in an immense open gallery in front of the palace, the latter placed in a kind of cloister below it, two hundred steeds ready caparisoned[3] to move in a moment, couriers entering or passing out with dispatches, the kettle drums beating, boys calling the hour from the minaret of the mosque, altogether, with the singular appearance of the building itself, formed a new & delightful spectacle to a stranger.—I was conducted to a very handsome apartment & my health enquired after by the vizier's secretary "a la mode de Turque."[4]—The next day I was introduced to Ali Pacha, I was dressed in a full suit of Staff uniform[5] with a very magnificent sabre &c.———The Vizier received me in a large room paved with marble, a fountain was playing in the centre, the apartment was surrounded by scarlet Ottomans, he received me *standing*, a wonderful compliment from a Mussulman,[6] & made me sit down on his right hand.—I have a Greek interpreter for general use, but a Physician of Ali's named [Seculario?] who understands Latin acted for me on this occasion.—His first question was why at so early an age I left my country? (the Turks have no idea of travelling for amusement) he then said the English Minister Capt. Leake[7] had told him I was of a great family, & desired his respects to my mother, which I now in the name of

Ali Pacha present to you. He said he was certain I was a man of birth because I had small ears, curling hair, & little white hands, and expressed himself pleased with my appearance & garb.—He told me to consider him as a father whilst I was in Turkey, & said he looked on me as his son.— Indeed he treated me like a child, sending me almonds & sugared sherbet, fruit & sweetmeats[8] 20 times a day.—He begged me to visit him often, and at night when he was more at leisure—I then after coffee & pipes retired for the first time. I saw him thrice afterwards.—It is singular that the Turks who have no hereditary dignities & few great families except the Sultan's pay so much respect to birth, for I found my pedigree more regarded than even my title.—His Highness is 60 years old, very fat & not tall, but with a fine face, light blue eyes & a white beard, his manner is very kind & at the same time he possesses that dignity which I find universal amongst the Turks.———He has the appearance of any thing but his real character, for he is a remorseless tyrant, guilty of the most horrible cruelties, very brave & so good a general, that they call him the Mahometan Buonaparte.—Napoleon has twice offered to make him King of Epirus, but he prefers the English interest & abhors the French as he himself told me, he is of so much consequence that he is much courted by both, the Albanians being the most warlike subjects of the Sultan, though Ali is only nominally dependent on the Porte.[9] He has been a mighty warrior, but is as barbarous as he is successful, roasting rebels &c. &c.—Buonaparte sent him a snuffbox with his picture[;] he said the snuffbox was very well, but the picture he could excuse, as he neither liked *it* nor the *original*.—His ideas of judging a man's birth from ears, hands, &c. were curious enough.—To me he was indeed a father, giving me letters, guards, & every possible accommodation.—Our next conversations were of war & travelling, politics & England.—He called my Albanian soldier who attends me, and told him to protect me at all hazards.—His name is Viscillie & like all the Albanians he is brave, rigidly honest, & faithful,

[1] *Tartars* Tatars (to use the modern spelling) are an ethnic group that originated in central Asia; some settled on the Crimean Peninsula, which became an Ottoman possession. The Crimean Tatars provided cavalry for the Ottoman army as part of its agreement with the empire.

[2] *pelises* Fur-lined cloaks.

[3] *caparisoned* Harnessed.

[4] *a la mode de Turque* French: in the fashion of the Turk.

[5] *Staff uniform* I.e., military uniform.

[6] *standing … Mussulman* The Prophet Mohammed would not permit his followers to stand when he entered a room, so it was not always customary for Muslims to stand when greeting someone. It was, however, considered a mark of respect and was not forbidden; *Mussulman* Muslim.

[7] *Captain Leake* William Martin Leake (1777–1860), British topographer and antiquarian; in 1807 he was assigned as British representative to Ali Pasha.

[8] *sweetmeats* Sugared pastries or fruit drops.

[9] *Porte* Sublime Porte of the Ottoman Empire; the term refers to the central government of the Ottoman Empire.

but they are cruel though not treacherous, & have several vices, but no meannesses.—They are perhaps the most beautiful race in point of countenance in the world, their women are sometimes handsome also, but they are treated like slaves, *beaten* & in short complete beasts of burthen, they plough, dig & sow, I found them carrying wood & actually repairing the highways, the men are all soldiers, & war & the chase their sole occupations, the women are the labourers, which after all is no great hardship in so delightful a climate, yesterday the 11th Nov. I bathed in the sea, today It is so hot that I am writing in a shady room of the English Consul's with three doors wide open no fire or even *fireplace* in the house except for culinary purposes.— The Albanians [11 lines crossed out[1]] Today I saw the remains of the town of *Actium* near which Anthony lost the world in a small bay where two frigates could hardly manouvre, a broken wall is the sole remnant.—On another part of the gulph stand the ruins of Nicopolis built by Augustus in honour of his victory.———Last night I was at a Greek marriage, but this & 1000 things more I have neither time or *space* to describe.—I am going tomorrow with a guard of fifty men to Patras in the Morea, & thence to Athens where I shall winter.—Two days ago I was nearly lost in a Turkish ship of war owing to the ignorance of the captain & crew though the storm was not violent.—Fletcher[2] yelled after his wife, the Greeks called on all the Saints, the Mussulmen on Alla, the Captain burst into tears & ran below deck telling us to call on God, the sails were split, the main-yard shivered, the wind blowing fresh, the night setting in, & all our chance was to make Corfu which is in possession of the French, or (as Fletcher *pathetically* termed it) "a *watery* grave."—I did what I could to console Fletcher but finding him incorrigible wrapped myself up in my Albanian capote (an immense cloak) & lay down on deck to wait the worst, I have learnt to philosophize on my travels, & if I had not, complaint was useless.—Luckily the wind abated &

only drove us on the coast of Suli[3] on the main land where we landed & proceeded by the help of the natives to Prevesa again; but I shall not trust Turkish Sailors in future, though the Pacha had ordered one of his own galleots[4] to take me to Patras, I am therefore going as far as Missolonghi by land & there have only to cross a small gulph to get to Patras.—Fletcher's next epistle will be full of marvels, we were one night lost for *nine* hours in the mountains in a *thunder* storm, & since nearly wrecked, in both cases Fletcher was sorely bewildered, from apprehensions of famine & banditti in the first, & drowning in the second instance.—His eyes were a little hurt by the lightning or crying (I dont know which) but are now recovered.—When you write address to me at Mr. *Strané's* English Consul, Patras, Morea.———I could tell you I know not how many incidents that I think would amuse you, but they crowd on my mind as much as would swell my paper, & I can neither arrange them in the one, or put them down on the other, except in the greatest confusion & in my usual horrible hand.—I like the Albanians much, they are not all Turks, some tribes are Christians, but their religion makes little difference in their manner or conduct; they are esteemed the best troops in the Turkish service.—I lived on my route two days at once, & three days again in a Barrack at Salora, & never found soldiers so tolerable, though I have been in the garrisons of Gibraltar & Malta & seen Spanish, French, Sicilian & British troops in abundance, I have had nothing stolen, & was always welcome to their provision & milk.—Not a week ago, an Albanian chief (every village has its chief who is called Primate) after helping us out of the Turkish Galley in her distress, feeding us & lodging my suite[5] consisting of Fletcher, a Greek, Two Albanians, a Greek Priest and my companion Mr. Hobhouse,[6] refused any

---

[1] *crossed out*   The deleted passage seems to have concerned a page of the household's love for an Albanian girl; there seems to have been a struggle to save her honour from Ali Pasha's son (noted in Marchand).

[2] *Fletcher*   Byron's valet.

---

[3] *Suli*   Souli, a region in northwestern Greece.

[4] *galleots*   Small sail boats; a term often applied to Mediterranean vessels.

[5] *suite*   Retinue of followers or servants.

[6] *Mr. Hobhouse*   John Cam Hobhouse (1786–1869) 1st Baron Broughton. A friend of Byron's from Cambridge, Hobhouse accompanied the poet on his travels to Greece and Turkey. Byron dedicated Canto IV of *Childe Harold's Pilgrimage* to Hobhouse.

compensation but a written paper stating that I was well received, & when I pressed him to accept a few sequins,[1] "no, he replied, I wish you to love me, not to pay me." These were his words.—It is astonishing how far money goes in this country, while I was in the capital, I had nothing to pay by the vizier's order, but since, though I have generally had sixteen horses & generally 6 or 7 men, the expence has not been *half* as much as staying only 3 weeks in Malta, though Sir A. Ball[2] the governor gave me a house for nothing, & I had only *one servant*.—By the bye I expect Hanson[3] to remit regularly, for I am not about to stay in this province for ever, let him write to me at Mr. Strané's, English Consul, Patras.——The fact is, the fertility of the plains are wonderful, & specie[4] is scarce, which makes this remarkable cheapness.—I am now going to Athens to study modern Greek which differs much from the ancient though radically similar.—I have no desire to return to England, nor shall I unless compelled by absolute want & Hanson's neglect, but I shall not enter Asia for a year or two as I have much to see in Greece & I may perhaps cross into Africa at least the Ægyptian part.—Fletcher like all Englishmen is very much dissatisfied, though a little reconciled to the Turks by a present of 80 piastres[5] from the vizier, which if you consider every thing & the value of specie here is nearly worth ten guineas English.—He has suffered nothing but from *cold*, heat, & vermin which those who lie in cottages & cross mountains in a wild country must undergo, & of which I have equally partaken with himself, but he is not valiant, & is afraid of robbers & tempests.—I have no one to be remembered to in England, & wish to hear nothing from it but that you are well, & a letter or two on business from Hanson, whom you may tell to write.——I will write when I can, & beg you to believe me,

yr affect. Son,
BYRON

P.S. *M* I have some very "magnifique"[6] Albanian dresses the only expensive articles in this country they cost 50 guineas each & have so much gold they would cost in England two hundred.—I have been introduced to Hussein Bey, & Mahmout Pacha both little boys grandchildren of Ali at Yanina. They are totally unlike our lads, have painted complexions like rouged dowagers, large black eyes & features perfectly regular. They are the prettiest little animals I ever saw, & are broken into the court ceremonies already, the Turkish salute is a slight inclination of the head with the hand on the breast, intimates always kiss, Mahmout is ten years old & hopes to see me again, we are friends without understanding each other, like many other folks, though from a different cause;—he has given me a letter to his father in the Morea, to whom I have also letters from Ali *Pacha*.—

from a letter TO FRANCIS HODGSON[7]
13 September 1811
Newstead Abbey

My dear Hodgson

… I won't dispute with you on the arcana of your new calling; they are bagatelles,[8] like the King of Poland's rosary.[9] One remark and I have done: the basis of your religion is *injustice*; the *Son of God*, the *pure*, the *immaculate*, the *innocent*, is sacrificed for the *guilty*. This proves *His* heroism; but no more does away with *man's* guilt than a schoolboy's volunteering to be flogged for

---

[1] *sequins*   Another name for Turkish coins called "sultanins."

[2] *Sir A. Ball*   British admiral Sir Alexander Ball (1757–1809) forced the capitulation of Malta in 1800. He afterwards served as governor of the island.

[3] *Hanson*   John Hanson (1755–1841), Byron's lawyer and business representative.

[4] *specie*   Coined money.

[5] *piastres*   Small coins of the Ottoman Empire.

[6] *magnifique*   French: magnificent.

[7] *HODGSON*   Francis Hodgson (1781–1832) was Provost of Eton College and one of Byron's closest friends.

[8] *bagatelles*   Toys, trifles.

[9] *King of Poland's rosary*   In 1683 the Ottoman Empire laid siege to Vienna. The city was saved by an army under the Polish king, John Sobieski, who was dedicated to the rosary. The king believed that the rosary, and this dedication, had been instrumental in his victory.

another would exculpate the dunce from negligence, or preserve him from the rod. You degrade the Creator, in the first place, by making Him a begetter of children, and in the next you convert Him into a tyrant over an immaculate and injured Being, who is sent into existence to suffer death for the benefit of some millions of scoundrels, who, after all, seem as likely to be damned as ever. As to miracles, I agree with Hume that it is more probable men should *lie* or be *deceived*, than that things out of the course of nature should so happen.[1] Mahomet wrought miracles, Brothers the prophet had *proselytes*, and so would Breslau the conjurer,[2] had he lived in the time of Tiberius.

Besides, I trust that God is not a *Jew*, but the God of all mankind; and, as you allow that a virtuous Gentile may be saved, you do away the necessity of being a Jew or a Christian.

I do not believe in any revealed religion, because no religion is revealed; and if it pleases the Church to damn me for not allowing a *nonentity*, I throw myself on the mercy of the "*Great First Cause, least understood*,"[3] who must do what is most proper; though I conceive He never made anything to be tortured in another life, whatever it may in this. I will neither read *pro* nor *con*. God would have made His will known without books, considering how very few could read them when Jesus of Nazareth lived, had it been His pleasure to ratify any peculiar mode of worship. As to your immortality, if people are to live, why die? And our carcases, which are to rise again, are they worth raising? I hope, if mine is, that I shall have a better *pair of legs* than I have moved on these two-and-twenty years, or I shall be sadly behind in the squeeze into Paradise. Did you ever read

"Malthus on Population?"[4] If he be right, war and pestilence are our best friends, to save us from being eaten alive, in this "best of all possible worlds."[5]

I will write, read, and think no more; indeed, I do not wish to shock your prejudices by saying all I do think. Let us make the most of life, and leave dreams to Emanuel Swedenborg.[6] ...

Yours ever,

BYRON

To LADY MELBOURNE[7]
21 September 1813
Aston Hall Rotherham

My dear Ly. M[elbourn]e—My stay at Cambridge was very short—but feeling feverish & restless in town I flew off & here I am on a visit to my friend Webster now married—& (according to ye.[8] Duke of Buckingham's curse—) "settled in ye. country."[9]—His bride Lady Frances[10] is a pretty pleasing woman—but in delicate health & I fear going—if not gone—into a

---

[1] *As to miracles ... happen* In his book, *An Enquiry Concerning Human Understanding* (1748), the Scottish philosopher David Hume (1711–76) argued that it was miraculous that so many believed in miracles.

[2] *Brothers* Richard Brothers (1757–1824) claimed that in 1795 he would be revealed as Prince of the Hebrews and ruler of the world; *Breslau the conjurer* Philip Breslaw was a German magician who performed in England in the 1760s. He wrote *Breslaw's Last Legacy; or, the Magical Companion* (1784).

[3] *Great First Cause ... understood* Cf. Alexander Pope's *The Universal Prayer*, st. 2.

[4] *Malthus on Population* Thomas Malthus (1766–1834) wrote in his *Essay on the Principle of Population* (1798) that plague, famine, and war were necessary means of reducing the population. See also *Don Juan*, Canto 11.131.

[5] *best of all possible worlds* Cf. Voltaire's *Candide*, chapter 30.

[6] *leave dreams ... Swedenborg* The Swedish philosopher and theologian Emanuel Swedenborg (1688–1772) believed that he had received messages from God and Jesus Christ in a series of vivid waking dreams.

[7] *LADY MELBOURNE* Viscountess Melbourne (1751–1818), wife of Peniston Lamb, 1st Viscount Melbourne. She was a celebrated hostess with considerable social influence.

[8] *ye* I.e., the, written in an approximation of the Old English manner; the "y" represents þ, the Old English letter carrying the sound "th."

[9] *Duke of Buckingham ... country* George Villiers, 2nd Duke of Buckingham (1628–87), was reported to have said to a dog who had annoyed him, "Ah, I wish you were married and settled in the country."

[10] *Lady Frances* Lady Frances Caroline Wedderburn Webster (1793–1837). She carried on flirtations with both Byron and the Duke of Wellington. Byron's poem "When We Two Parted" was written after he heard of Lady Frances's affair with Wellington.

decline—Stanhope & his wife[1]—pretty and pleasant too but not at all consumptive—left us today—leaving only ye. family—another single gentleman & your slave.— The sister Ly. Catherine[2] is here too—& looks very pale from a *cross* in her love for Lord Bury[3] (Ld. Alb[emarl]e's son) in short we are a society of happy wives and unfortunate maidens.—The place is very well & quiet & the children only scream in low voice—so that I am not much disturbed & shall stay a few days in tolerable repose.—W[ebster] don't want sense nor good nature but both are occasionally obscured by his suspicions & absurdities of all descriptions—he is passionately fond of having his wife admired—& at the same time jealous to jaundice of every thing & every body—I have hit upon the medium of praising her to him perpetually behind her back—& never looking at her before his face—as for her I believe she is disposed to be very faithful—& I don't think any one now here is inclined to put her to the test.—W[ebster] himself is with all his jealousy & admiration a little tired—he has been lately at Newstead[4]—& wants to go again—I suspected this sudden penchant & soon discovered that a foolish nymph[5] of the Abbey—about whom fortunately I care not—was the attraction—now if I wanted to make mischief—I could extract much good perplexity from a proper management of such events—but I am grown so good or so indolent—that I shall not avail myself of so pleasant an opportunity of tormenting mine host—though he deserves it for poaching.—I believe he has hitherto been unsuccessful—or rather it is too astonishing to be believed.—He proposed to me with great gravity to carry him over there—& I replied with equal candour that *he* might set out when he pleased but that I should remain here to take care of his household

in the interim—a proposition which I thought very much to the purpose—but which did not seem at all to his satisfaction—by way of opiate he preached me a sermon on his wife's good qualities concluding by an assertion that in all moral & mortal qualities she was very like "*Christ*!!!" I think the virgin Mary would have been a more appropriate typification—but it was the first comparison of the kind I ever heard & made me laugh till he was angry—& then I got out of humour too—which pacified him & shortened his panegyric—Ld. Petersham[6] is coming here in a day or two— who will certainly flirt furiously with Ly. F[rances]—& I shall have some comic Iagoism with our little Othello—I should have no chance with his Desdemona[7] myself—but a more lively & better dressed & formed personage might in an innocent way—for I really believe the girl is a very good well disposed wife & will do very well if she lives & he himself don't tease her into some dislike of her lawful owner.——I passed through Hatfield the night of your *ball*—suppose we had jostled at a turnpike!![8]—At Bugden I blundered on a Bishop— the Bishop put me in mind of ye Government—the Government of the Governed—& the governed of their *indifference* towards their governors which you must have remarked as to all *parties*—these reflections expectorated as follows—you know I *never* send you my scribblings & when you read these you will wish I never may.—

Tis said—*Indifference* marks the present time
Then hear the reason—though 'tis told in rhyme—
A King who *can't*—a Prince of Wales who *don't*—
Patriots who *shan't*—Ministers who *won't*—
What matters who are *in* or *out* of place
The *Mad*—the *Bad*—the *Useless*—or the *Base*?

---

[1] *Stanhope & his wife* Philip Henry Stanhope, 4th Earl Stanhope (1781–1855) and Catherine Lucy, daughter of the 1st Baron Carrington.

[2] *Ly. Catherine* Sister to Lady Frances.

[3] *Lord Bury* Son to the 4th Earl of Albemarle.

[4] *Newstead* Newstead Abbey was Lord Byron's ancestral home.

[5] *nymph* It is unclear who is being referred to here; it may be "one of the servant girls," according to Fiona MacCarthy in *Byron: Life and Legend* (Faber, 2003).

[6] *Ld. Petersham* Charles Stanhope (1780–1851), who became 4th Earl of Harrington.

[7] *Iagoism ... Desdemona* Iago is the villain of Shakespeare's *Othello*. Byron suggests he will conjure jealousy in Webster and Lady Frances's marriage as Iago does in Shakespeare's play. Iago drives Othello to murder his wife, Desdemona, out of jealousy; here, Webster is jokingly referred to as "Othello" and Lady Frances as "Desdemona."

[8] *jostled at a turnpike* A turnpike was a gate across a road that required travelers to pay a toll to pass (or at least to stop and wait while the barrier was lifted). Byron is saying that it is possible he and Lady Melbourne may have passed each other on the road.

You may read the 2d. couplet *so* if you like—

"A King who *cannot*—& a Prince who don't—
Patriots who *would not*—ministers who won't—"

I am asked to stay for the Doncaster races but I am not in plight[1]—& am a miserable beau at the best of times—so I shall even return to town or elsewhere—and in the mean time ever am

yrs. dear Ly. M[elbourn]e
B

P.S.—If you write address to B[enne]t Street, were I once gone—I should not wish my letters to travel *here* after me for fear of *accidents.*————There is a delightful epitaph on Voltaire in Grimm[2]—I read it coming down—the French I should probably misspell so take it only in bad English—"Here lies the spoilt child of *the*/*a* world which he spoiled."—It is good short & true.————

To Lady Byron

Byron's marriage was a disaster from the start, and his cruelty and bizarre behavior caused his wife to leave him after a year. He was at first devastated, then full of bitter rage. In the early weeks of their separation, he wrote her a number of letters expressing confusion at her, apologizing for his bad behavior, and pleading with her to return, or at least to meet with him. In the letter below he gives vent to both his sorrow and his rage.

8 February 1816

All I can say seems useless—and all I could say,—might be no less unavailing—yet I still cling to the wreck of my hopes,—before they sink forever.——Were you then *never* happy with me?—did you never at any times express yourself so?—have no marks of affection—of the warmest & most reciprocal attachment passed between us?—or did in fact hardly a day go down without some such on one side and generally on both?—do not mistake me—[two lines crossed out] I have not denied my state of mind—but you know it's causes—& were those deviations from calmness never followed by acknowledgment & repentance?—was not the last which occurred more particularly so?—& had I not—had we not—the days before & on the day when we parted——every reason to believe that we loved each other—that we were to meet again——were not your letters kind?—had I not acknowledged to you all my faults & follies, & assured you that some had not—& would not be repeated?—I do not require these questions to be answered to me—but to your own heart.—— The day before I received your father's letter—I had fixed a day for rejoining you—if I did not write lately—Augusta did—and as you had been my proxy in correspondence with her—so did I imagine—she might be the same for me to you.—Upon your letter to me—this day—I surely may remark, that it's expressions imply a treatment which I am incapable of inflicting—& you of imputing to me if aware of their latitude & the extent of the inferences to be drawn from them.—This is not just——but I have no reproaches—nor the wish to find cause for them.—Will you see me?—when & where you please—in whose presence you please:—the interview shall pledge you to nothing—& I will say & do nothing to agitate either—it is torture to correspond thus—& there are things to be settled & said which cannot be written.—— You say "it is my disposition to deem what I *have worthless*"—did I deem *you* so?—did I ever express myself to you—or of you—to others?——You are much changed within these twenty days or you would never have thus poisoned your own better feelings—and trampled on mine.——

ever yrs. most truly & affectionately
B

[1] *Doncaster races* Doncaster is a center for horse racing in Yorkshire, with races dating back to the 16th century; *plight* State of mind or mood.

[2] *Grimm* Baron von Grimm (1723–1807), critic and diplomat. The epitaph quoted here is drawn from the *Edinburgh Review* of July 1813, in which there is a review of Grimm's *Correspondance Littéraire, Philosophique et Critique.*

To Augusta Leigh

Byron's relationship with his half-sister was complex. He was closer to her than to any other woman in his life: she was for him the gentle mother he had never had, an ally against the world, possibly a lover, and a reflection of himself. The letters he wrote to her after they were separated by his departure from England in 1816 are among his most tender writings.

17 September 1816
Ouchy

My dearest Augusta,[1]—I am thus far on my way to the Bernese Alps & the Grindewald[2]—and the *Yungfrau*[3] (that is the "Wild woman" being interpreted —as it is so perverse a mountain that no other sex would suit it), which journey may occupy me eight days or so, and then it is my intention to return to Geneva, preparatory to passing the Simplon[4]—

Continue to direct as usual to Geneva.[5] I have lately written to you several letters (3 or 4 by post and two by hand) and I have received all yours very safely. I rejoice to have heard that you are well. You have been in London too lately, & H[obhouse][6] tells me that at your levée he generally found Ld. F. Bentinck[7]—pray why is that fool so often a visitor? is he in love with you? I have recently broken through my resolution of not speaking to you of Lady B[yron]—but do not on that account name her to me. It is a relief—a partial relief to me to talk of her sometimes to you—but it would be none to hear of her. *Of* her you are to judge for yourself, but do not altogether forget that she has destroyed your brother. Whatever my faults might or may have been—*She*—was not the person marked out by provi-

dence to be their avenger. One day or another her conduct will recoil on her own head; *not* through *me*, for my feelings towards her are not those of Vengeance, but—mark—if she does not end miserably *tot ou tard*.[8] She may think—talk—or act as she will, and by any process of cold reasoning and jargon of "duty & acting for the best" &c., &c., impose upon her own feelings & those of others for a time—but woe unto her—the wretchedness she has brought upon the man to whom she has been everything evil except in one respect: will flow back into its fountain. I may thank the strength of my constitution that has enabled me to bear all this, but those who bear the longest and most do not suffer the least. I do not think a human being could endure more mental torture than that woman has directly & indirectly inflicted upon me—within the present year.

She has (for a time at least) separated me from my child—& from you—but I turn from the subject for the present.

Tomorrow I repass Clarens & Vevey;[9] if in the new & more extended tour I am making, anything I think may please you occurs, I will detail it.

Scrope[10] has by this time arrived with my little presents for you and yours[11] & Ada. I still hope to be able to see you next Spring, perhaps you & one or two of the children could be spared some time next year for a little tour *here* or in France with me for a month or two. I think I could make it very pleasing to you, & it should be no expense to L[eigh][12] or to yourself. Pray think of this hint. You have no idea how very beautiful great part of this country is—and *women* and *children* traverse it with ease and expedition. I would return from any distance at any time to see you, and come to England for you; and when you consider the chances against our—but I won't relapse into the dismals and anticipate long absences—

---

1. *Augusta* Augusta Leigh, Byron's half-sister (1783–1851).

2. *Grindewald* Town in Switzerland.

3. *Yungfrau* I.e., Jungfrau, a mountain in the Alps.

4. *Simplon* Simplon Pass, in the Alps.

5. *Continue … Geneva* I.e., continue to send your letters to Geneva.

6. *Hobhouse* John Cam Hobhouse (1786–1869), Byron's best friend.

7. *Ld. F. Bentinck* Lord Frederick Cavendish-Bentinck (1781–1828), a friend of Augusta's husband.

8. *tot ou tard* French: sooner or later.

9. *Clarens & Vevey* Swiss towns.

10. *Scrope* Scrope Berdmore Davies (1782–1852), a charming and feckless, but very loyal, friend of Byron's. His first name is pronounced "Scroop."

11. *yours* Augusta's five children.

12. *Leigh* Augusta's first cousin and husband, Colonel George Leigh.

The great obstacle would be that you are so admirably yoked—and necessary as a housekeeper—and a letter writer—& a place-hunter to that very helpless gentleman your Cousin,[1] that I suppose the usual self-love of an elderly person would interfere between you & any scheme of recreation or relaxation, for however short a period.

What a fool I was to marry—and *you* not very wise—my dear—we might have lived so single and so happy—as old maids and bachelors; I shall never find any one like you—nor you (vain as it may seem) like me. We are just formed to pass our lives together, and therefore—we—at least—I—am by a crowd of circumstances removed from the only being who could ever have loved me, or whom I can unmixedly feel attached to.

Had you been a Nun—and I a Monk—that we might have talked through a grate[2] instead of across the sea—no matter—my voice and my heart are

ever thine—

B

from "*Alpine Journal*"[3]

20 September 1816

Up at 6—off at 8—the whole of this day's journey at an average of between from two thousand seven hundred to three thousand feet above the level of the Sea. This valley the longest—narrowest—& considered one of the finest of the Alps——little traversed by travellers—saw the Bridge of La Roche[4]—the bed of the river very low & deep between immense rocks & rapid as anger—a man & mule said to have tumbled over without damage—(the mule was lucky at any rate—un-

less I knew the *man* I should be loth to pronounce *him* fortunate).—The people looked free & happy and *rich* (which last implies neither of the former) the cows superb—a Bull nearly leapt into the Charaban[5]— "agreeable companion in a postchaise"[6]—Goats & Sheep very thriving—a mountain with enormous Glaciers to the right—the Klettersteig—further on—the Hockenhorn[7]—nice names—so soft—Hockenhorn I believe very lofty & craggy—patched with snow only— no Glaciers on it—but some good epaulettes[8] of clouds.—Past the boundaries—out of Vaud[9]—& into Bern Canton[10]—French exchanged for a bad German— the district famous for Cheese—liberty—property—& no taxes.—H.[11] went to fish—caught none—strolled to river—saw a boy [and] a kid[12]—kid followed him like a dog—kid could not get over a fence & bleated piteously—tried myself to help kid—but nearly overset both self & kid into the river.—Arrived here about six in the evening—nine o'clock—going to bed—H. in next room—knocked his head against the door—and exclaimed of course against doors—not tired to-day—but hope to sleep nevertheless—women gabbling[13] below—read a French translation of Schiller[14]—Good Night—Dearest Augusta.

---

[1] *that ... Cousin* In 1807, Augusta married her first cousin Colonel George Leigh (the Byrons frequently married their first cousins). Leigh's main activity was betting on horse-racing, and the marriage was not entirely happy.

[2] *grate* Cloistered monks and nuns spoke to visitors from behind a grate that separated the cloister from the rest of the world.

[3] *Alpine Journal* Addressed to his half-sister, Augusta Leigh (1783–1851), the *Alpine Journal* records Byron's trip to the Alps in the autumn of 1816 with John Hobhouse, Baron Broughton (1786–1869).

[4] *La Roche* Village in the Gruyère region of Switzerland.

[5] *the Charaban* Probably referring to the Serbache river, near La Roche.

[6] *agreeable companion in a postchaise* Perhaps an allusion to Samuel Johnson, as quoted by James Boswell in *Life of Johnson*: "If (said he,) I had no duties, and no reference to futurity, I would spend my life in driving briskly in a post-chaise with a pretty woman; but she should be one who could understand me, and would add something to the conversation."

[7] *Klettersteig* German for "climbing path," a traditional mountain pass with climbing aids; *Hockenhorn* Mountain in the Bernese Alps.

[8] *epaulettes* Shoulder ornaments indicating rank on military uniforms.

[9] *Vaud* Canton in western Switzerland, largely French-speaking.

[10] *Bern Canton* Second-largest canton in Switzerland, just east of Vaud, where Bernese German is widely spoken.

[11] *H.* John Hobhouse, Baron Broughton (1786–1869).

[12] *kid* I.e., a young goat.

[13] *gabbling* Chatting, talking incoherently.

[14] *Schiller* Friedrich von Schiller (1759–1805), German poet and philosopher.

21 September 1816

Off early—the valley of Simmenthal[1] as before—entrance to the plain of Thoun[2] very narrow—high rocks—wooded to the top—river—new mountains—with fine Glaciers—Lake of Thoun—extensive plain with a girdle of Alps—walked down to the Chateau de Schadau[3]—view along the lake—crossed the river in a boat rowed by women—*women* [went?] right for the first time in my recollection. Thoun a pretty town—the whole day's journey Alpine & proud.

22 September 1816

Left Thoun in a boat which carried us the length of the lake in three hours—the lake small—but the banks fine—rocks down to the water's edge. Landed at Neuhause—passed Interlachen[4]—entered upon a range of scenes beyond all description—or previous conception.—Passed a rock—inscription—2 brothers—one murdered the other[5]—just the place fit for it.—After a variety of windings came to an enormous rock—Girl with fruit—very pretty—blue eyes—good teeth—very fair—long but good features—reminded me of Fy.[6] Bought some of her pears—and patted her upon the cheek—the expression of her face very mild—but good—and not at all coquettish.—Arrived at the foot of the Mountain (the Yung-frau—i.e. the Maiden)

Glaciers—torrents—one of these torrents *nine hundred feet* in height of visible descent[7]—lodge at the Curate's[8]—set out to see the Valley—heard an Avalanche fall—like thunder—saw Glacier—enormous—Storm came on—thunder—lightning—hail—all in perfection—and beautiful—I was on horseback—Guide wanted to carry my cane—I was going to give it him when I recollected that it was a Swordstick[9] and I thought that the lightning might be attracted towards him—kept it myself—a good deal encumbered with it & my cloak—as it was too heavy for a whip—and the horse was stupid—& stood still every other peal.[10] Got in—not very wet—the Cloak being staunch[11]—H. wet through—H. took refuge in cottage—sent man—umbrella—& cloak (from the Curate's when I arrived—) after him.—Swiss Curate's house—very good indeed—much better than most English Vicarages—it is immediately opposite the torrent I spoke of—the torrent is in shape curving over the rock—like the *tail* of a white horse streaming in the wind—such as it might be conceived would be that of the "*pale* horse" on which *Death* is mounted in the Apocalypse.[12] It is neither mist nor water but a something between both—its immense height (nine hundred feet) gives it a wave—a curve—a spreading here—a condensation there—wonderful—& indescribable.—I think upon the whole—that this day has been better than any of this present excursion.

---

[1] *valley of Simmenthal* Valley which runs from the towns of Lenk to Boltigen in Bern Canton.

[2] *Thoun* Large Swiss town, located on the northern tip of an Alpine lake.

[3] *Chateau de Schadau* During Byron's time, a seventeenth-century manor house with a history dating to the middle ages; in its present form, the castle dates to 1852, several decades after Byron's death.

[4] *Neuhause* Town near the southern tip of Lake Thun; *Interlachen* Resort town just east of Neuhaus.

[5] *2 brothers … the other* Likely referring to the legendary Lord of Rothenfluh, who, some time prior to the seventeenth century, is said to have murdered his brother and then gone into exile, thus ending the Rothenfluh line.

[6] *Fy* Uncertain; perhaps referring to Fanny Webster, with whom Byron was reputed to have had an affair.

[7] *Arrived at … visible descent* This is the Staubbach Waterfall.

[8] *Curate* Leading clergyman of a given parish.

[9] *Swordstick* Hollow cane in which a metal sword or blade is concealed.

[10] *peal* I.e, of thunder.

[11] *staunch* Waterproof.

[12] *pale horse … the Apocalypse* Allusion to the four horsemen who are described as bringing about the Apocalypse in the New Testament (Cf. Revelation 6.8: "and behold a pale horse: and his name that sat on him was Death, and Hell followed him").

23 September 1816

Before ascending the mountain—went to the torrent (7 in the morning) again—the Sun upon it forming a *rainbow* of the lower part of all colours—but principally purple and gold—the bow moving as you move—I never saw anything like this—it is only in the Sunshine.——Ascended the Wengren [sic] Mountain[1]—at noon reached a valley near the summit—left the horses—took off my coat & went to the summit—7000 feet (English feet) above the level of the sea—and about 5000 above the valley we left in the morning—on one side our view comprized the *Yung frau* with all her glaciers—then the *Dent d'Argent*[2]—shining like truth—then the *little Giant* (the Kleine Elgher) & the great Giant (the Grosser Elgher) and last not least—the Wetterhorn.[3] The height of the Yung frau is 13000 feet above the sea—and 11000 above the valley—she is the highest of this range,—heard the Avalanches falling every five minutes nearly—as if God was pelting the Devil down from Heaven with snow balls—from where we stood on the *Wengren* [sic] Alp—we had all these in view on one side—on the other the clouds rose from the opposite valley curling up perpendicular precipices—like the foam of the Ocean of Hell during a Springtide[4]—it was white & sulphery—and immeasurably deep in appearance—the side we ascended was (of course) not of so precipitous a nature—but on arriving at the summit we looked down the other side upon a boiling sea of cloud—dashing against the crags on which we stood (these crags on one side quite perpendicular); staid a quarter of an hour—began to descend—quite clear from cloud on that side of the mountain—in passing the masses of snow—I made a snowball & pelted H. with it—got down to our horses again—eat something—remounted—heard the Avalanches still—came to a morass[5]—H. dismounted—H. got well over—I tried to pass my horse over—the horse sunk up [to] the chin—& of course he & I were in the mud together—bemired all over—but not hurt—laughed & rode on.—Arrived at the Grindenwald[6]—dined—mounted again & rode to the higher Glacier—twilight—but distinct—very fine Glacier—like a *frozen hurricane*—Starlight—beautiful—but a devil of a path—never mind—got safe in—a little lightning—but the whole of the day as fine in point of weather—as the day on which Paradise was made.— Passed *whole woods of withered pines—all withered*—trunks stripped & barkless—branches lifeless—done by a single winter—their appearance reminded me of me & my family.

To Douglas Kinnaird[7]

Don Juan created a sensation among Byron's friends before it was published and among the public after it appeared in print. Byron, however, refused to yield either to the pleas to neutralize the poem by those who knew him, or to the horrified condemnations of the reviewers: he remained proud of it and convinced of its ultimate value. The two letters and the review give some sense of the public reaction to the poem, and of Byron's own thoughts about it.

[1] *Wengren Mountain* I.e., the Wengen Jungfrau, a peak just north of its parent peak, the Jungfrau.
[2] *Dent d'Argent* I.e., the Silberhorn.
[3] *Kleine Elgher ... Grosser Elgher ... Wetterhorn* Peaks in the Bernese Alps.
[4] *Springtide* Period of highest tide levels.
[5] *morass* Marsh.
[6] *Grindenwald* Village in the Bernese Alps.
[7] *KINNAIRD* Douglas Kinnaird (1788–1830), Byron's friend and banker.

26 October 1818 [1819]
Venice

My dear Douglas—My late expenditure has arisen from living at a distance from Venice and being obliged to keep up two establishments, from frequent journeys—and buying some furniture and books as well as a horse or two—and not from any renewal of the EPICUREAN system as you suspect. I have been faithful to my honest liaison with Countess Guiccioli[1]—and I can assure you that *She* has never cost me directly or indirectly a sixpence—indeed the circumstances of herself and family render this no merit.— I never offered her but one present—a broach of brilliants—and she sent it back to me with her *own hair* in it (I shall *not* say of *what part*—but *that* is an Italian custom)[2] and a note to say that she was not in the habit of receiving presents of that value—but hoped that I would not consider her sending it back as an affront—nor the value diminished by the enclosure—I have not had a whore this half-year—confining myself to the strictest adultery.——Why should you prevent Hanson[3] from making a *peer* if he likes it—I think the "*Garretting*" would be far the best parliamentary privilege—I know of. Damn your delicacy. It is a low commercial quality, and very unworthy a man who prefixes "honourable" to his nomenclature. If you say that I must sign the bonds, I suppose that I must, but it is very iniquitous to make me pay my debts—you have no idea of the pain it gives one. Pray do three things—get my property out of the *funds*—get Rochdale[4] sold—get me some information from Perry[5] about *South America*—and 4thly. ask Lady Noel[6] not to live so very long.——As to Subscribing to Manchester—if I do that—I will write a letter to Burdett[7]—for publication—to accompany the Subscription—which shall be more radical than anything yet rooted—but I feel lazy.—I have thought of this for some time—but alas! the air of this cursed Italy enervates—nd disfranchises the thoughts of a man after nearly four years of respiration—to say nothing of emission.—As to "Don Juan"—confess—confess—you dog—and be candid—that it is the sublime of *that there* sort of writing—it may be bawdy—but is it not good English?—it may be profligate—but is it not *life*, is it not *the thing*?—Could any man have written it—who has not lived in the world?—and tooled in a post-chaise? in a hackney coach? in a Gondola? against a wall? in a court carriage? in a vis-a-vis?[8]—on a table?—and under it?—I have written about a hundred stanzas of a third Canto—but it is damned modest—the outcry has frightened me.—I had such projects for the Don—but the *Cant* is so much stronger than *Cunt*—now a days,—that the benefit of experience in a man who had well weighed the worth of both monosyllables—must be lost to despairing posterity.—After all what stuff this outcry is—Lalla Rookh and Little[9]—are more dangerous than my burlesque poem can be—Moore has been here—we got tipsy together—and were very amicable—he is gone on to Rome—I put my life (in M.S.) into his hands—(*not* for publication); you—or any body else may see it—at his return.[10]—It only comes up to 1816.—He is a noble fellow—and looks quite fresh and poetical—nine years (the age of a poem's education) my Senior—he looks younger—his comes of marriage and

---

[1] *Countess Guiccioli* Teresa Gamba Ghiselli (1800–79) married Count Alessandro Guiccioli in 1818; in 1819, she and Byron began a love affair that lasted until his death.

[2] *own hair ... custom* There seems to have been something about Byron that inspired women to send him their pubic hair; Lady Caroline Lamb had done the same.

[3] *Hanson* John Hanson (d. 1841), Byron's lawyer.

[4] *Rochdale* One of Byron's estates. He had been trying to sell it since 1809.

[5] *Perry* James Perry (1756–1821), editor of the Whig *Morning Chronicle*. Byron expected him to have an interest in the South American independence movements in which he was contemplating taking part.

[6] *Lady Noel* Lady Judith Milbanke Noel (1751–1822), Byron's mother-in-law.

[7] *Burdett* Sir Francis Burdett (1770–1844), radical political leader.

[8] *vis-a-vis* French: face-to-face. Here, referring to a light carriage in which two persons sit face-to-face.

[9] *Lalla ... Little* Two works by Thomas Moore: *Lalla Rookh* (1817) and *The Poetical Works of the Late Thomas Little* (1801).

[10] *I put ... return* After his death, Byron's memoirs were burned by his publisher, who had not read them, over the protests of Moore, who had.

being settled in the Country. I want to go to South America—I have written to Hobhouse all about it.—I wrote to my wife—three months ago—under care to Murray[1]—has she got the letter—or is the letter got into Blackwood's magazine?[2]——You ask after my Christmas pye—remit it any how—*Circulars* is the best—you are right about *income*—must have it all—how the devil do I know that I may live a year or a month?—I wish I knew that I might regulate my spending in more ways than one.—As it is one always thinks that there is but a span.—A man may as well break or be damned for a large sum as a small one—I should be loth to pay the devil or any other creditor more than sixpence in the pound.—

[scrawl for signature]

P.S.—I recollect nothing of "Davies's landlord"—but what ever Davies *says*—I will *swear* to—and *that's* more than *he* would.—So pray pay—has he a landlady too?—perhaps I may owe her something.——With regard to the bonds I will sign them but—it goes against the grain.——As to the rest—you *can't* err—so long as you *don't* pay.——Paying is executor's or executioner's work.——You may write somewhat oftener—Mr. Galignani's messenger[3] gives the outline of your public affairs—but I see no results—you have no man yet—(always excepting Burdett—& you & H[obhouse] and the Gentlemanly leaven of your two-penny loaf of rebellion) don't forget however my charge of horse—and commission for the Midland Counties and by the holies!—You shall have your account in decimals.—Love to Hobby[4]—but why leave the Whigs?——

17 May 1819
Venice

Dear Hobhouse—I return by this post the second proofs—the first went by the former post—if the Subsequent ones don't reach you by return of post—you need not wait for them but publish without—as I leave Venice next week—and have ordered my letters *not* to be sent after me—my stay being uncertain—as my plans are.—What you say may be all very right—but the die is cast—and I must (not figuratively—but *literally*) "pass the *Rubicon*"[6]—you know I believe that it is in my way,—The Adventure is so far past preventing—that we had consummated our unlawful union with all the proper rites four days and daily—previously to *her*[7] leaving Venice.—She was with child too—previous to this ingrafting——and to our connection but [three or four words crossed out] miscarried at Pomposa on the road to R[avenn]a in [sic] her return, and is now on her recovery—For any thing I know the affair may terminate in some such way as you hint at—for they are liberal with the knife in It[ali]a and the Cavalier Conte G[uiccioli] her respected Lord—is shrewdly suspected of two assassinations already—one of a certain Mazzoni—who had been the cause of Count G[uiccioli]'s being put in the Castle of Saint Angelo—for some dispute or other—the which Mazzoni soon after G[uiccioli]'s release was stabbed going to the theatre and killed upon the Spot—nobody knows by *whom*—and other of a Commissary[8] who had interfered

[1] *Murray*   John Murray II (1778–1843), Byron's publisher.

[2] *Blackwood's magazine*   The Tory publication always critical of Byron, had just published a savage review of *Don Juan*. See the extract following *Don Juan*.

[3] *Galignani's messenger*   An English-language periodical published in Paris and available in Venice.

[4] *Hobby*   I.e., John Cam Hobhouse.

[5] *JOHN CAM HOBHOUSE*   John Cam Hobhouse (1786–1869), 1st Baron Broughton. A friend of Byron's from Cambridge, Hobhouse accompanied the poet on his travels to Greece and Turkey. Byron dedicated Canto IV of *Childe Harold's Pilgrimage* to Hobhouse.

[6] *the die is cast*   Translation of the Latin "alea iacta est," the words spoken by Julius Caesar as he led his legion across the Rubicon river in 49 BCE, a move that broke the law and precipitated the ensuing civil war; *"pass the Rubicon"*   Phrase that has come to refer to any rebellious action with sure consequences; it is similar to the saying "pass the point of no return."

[7] *her*   Teresa, Contessa Guiccioli (1800–73); Byron's lover.

[8] *Commissary*   Delegate or deputy.

with him—these are but "dicerie"[1] & may be true or no—it is a place where proof is not particularly in request.—But be that as it may—every thing is to be risked for a woman one likes—and those are not the things I mind—but your miserable cutting—maiming —and robbing—where you are incommoded & ill used for the sake of paltry pence and baggage—on the highway—and forced to expose yourself & your life without any one of the motives which reconcile one to the chances of a conflict.—And then a man may not only lose his life but his tooth-brushes and dressing Case—and shirts—and other articles difficult to be replaced.——I have looked over the proofs—and *not* acquiesced in the Suggestions—by the way there is one line we will alter towards the close of Canto *1st.* instead of

"I thought of dying the other day"

(i.e. *hair*) put—

"I thought about a Wig the other day"[2]

What are you so anxious about Donna Inez[3] for? She is not meant for Clytemnestra[4]—and if She were—would you protect the fiend—of whom I may say like "Jacopo Rusticucci" in Dante—

"è certo
La *fiera Moglie più ch'altro mi Nuoce.*"[5]—

and was it not owing to that "Porca buzzerena"[6] that they tried to expose me upon Earth to the same stigma—which the said Jacopo is saddled with in hell?[7]—What—is a ludicrous character of a tiresome woman in a burlesque poem to be suppressed or altered because a contemptible and hypocritical wretch may be supposed to be pointed at?—Do you supposed that I will ever forgive—or forget—or lose sight of her or hers—till I am nothing?——You will talk to me of prudence—and give me good reasons for "ones own sake" &c. &c.—you will have the satisfaction of giving good advice—and I that of not taking it.—Excuse my warmth—it is the cursed subject which puts me out of temper.——Neither you nor Murray[8] say aught of *Canto second*—from whence I infer *your* disapprobation—and *his fear* to have *any opinion at all*—till he knows what the Public think—and the Douglas[9] has not written to me about "the fee" why the devil don't he make the (not Social) Contract?[10] Don't go to America—there are leagues enough between us already.—— What is all this about Dr. Polidori?—who I perceive has got into "the Magazine"?[11]—you may at least thank me for finding you always something to be done;—I thought it was a French imposition—and wrote to Galignani's[12] Editor— to beg of him to contradict "the

[1] *"dicerie"*   Italian: rumors.

[2] *proofs … day*   Byron is writing about the proofs of *Don Juan I* and *II* (published anonymously on 15 July 1819). The line he changes here eventually becomes "I thought of a peruke the other day" (see 1.213; "peruke" is an archaic term for a wig).

[3] *Donna Inez*   In *Don Juan I*, Donna Inez is the wife of Don José and the mother of Don Juan; she is a rather thinly disguised portrait of Bryon's wife, Annabella Byron (1792–1860).

[4] *Clytemnestra*   In Ancient Greek legend, Clytemnestra was the wife of Agamemnon, ruler of Argos. In Aeschylus's *Oresteia*, Clytemnestra murders Agamemnon in his bath upon his return from Troy, to avenge the sacrifice of their daughter Iphigenia. Here and in other letters, Byron uses the name in reference to his own wife.

[5] *"è certo … mi Nuoce"*   Italian: certainly, my savage wife, more than anything else, harms me. See Dante, *Inferno* 16.44–45.

[6] *"Porca buzzerena"*   Italian: Sodomite sow.

[7] *the said Jacopo … in hell*   In Dante's *Inferno*, Jacopo Rusticucci was relegated to the third ring of the seventh circle of hell, the ring reserved for sodomites.

[8] *Murray*   John Murray II (1778–1843), Byron's publisher.

[9] *Douglas*   Douglas James William Kinnaird (1788–1830) was an English banker and politician. He managed Byron's finances and negotiated his book contracts.

[10] *(not Social) Contract*   A play on the title of Rousseau's *The Social Contract* (1762). The "contract" referred to is likely the book contract with Murray to publish the second canto of *Don Juan*.

[11] *Dr. Polidori*   John William Polidori (1795–1821), English writer and physician, best known for his short story "The Vampyre"; *"the Magazine"*   "The Vampyre" was first published in *The New Monthly Magazine* in April 1819. The story was mistakenly attributed to Byron when it first appeared.

[12] *Galignani*   John Anthony Galignani (1796–1873) and William Galignani (1798–1882) were Parisian publishers. They published *Galignani's Messenger*, a progressive newspaper printed in English that circulated across Europe.

Vampire" and "a residence in Mitylene"[1]—Oons[2] what is this residence?——I saw Sir William Drummond[3] the other day;—the same evening he was robbed at an Inn by a Mr. Wraxall—(an English Gentleman) of Cash & trinkets—Wraxall has been taken and is "like to be troubled at Size"[4] about it—he hath since confessed—but is still in Custody; he was in the army and wears a Waterloo[5] ribbon—the theft was of various Coins—Napoleons &c. rings—jewels and what not—the young man is of amiable manners—excellent conduct and is son to a Baronet—he had previously cheated and lied a good deal in various cities—but this is his first overt attempt at the direct conversion of property.——There has been a splendid Opera lately at San Benedetto—by Rossini[6]—who came in person to play the Harpsichord—the People followed him about—crowned him—cut off his hair "for memory"; he was Shouted and Sonnetted and feasted——and immortalized much more than either of the Emperors.—In the words of my Romagnola[7] (speaking of Ravenna & the way of life there which is more licentious than most here) "Ciò ti mostri una Quadri morale del' Paese; e ti basta."[8]—

Think of a people frantic for a fiddler—or at least an inspirer of fiddles.——I doubt if they will do much in the Liberty line.—An Elephant went Mad here about two months ago—killed his keeper—knocked down a house—broke open a Church—dispersed all his assailants and was at last killed by a Shot in his *posteriore* from a field-piece brought from the *Arse*-nal on purpose.—I'll tell you a story which is beastly—but will make you laugh;—a young man at Ferrara detected his Sister amusing herself with a Bologna Sausage—he said nothing—but perceiving the same Sausage presented at table—he got up—made it a low bow—and exclaimed "*Vi riverisco mio Cognato.*"[9]—Translate—and expound this to Scrope[10]—and to "the Creature Dougal."[11]—Tell the "Dougal Creature" to write—and let me know about "the fee."——Write—whether I am to hear from you or no—write.—But don't wait for my further revision of proofs—I can't be gone for less than a moon—and it would be losing time.—Publish Juan anonymously— *without* the dedication—"Mazeppa" and "the Ode"[12] as you like but don't send the proofs here.——I sent Murray—a second copy of "Julia's letter"[13]—of which the first copy seems not to have arrived.—Perhaps this may be more fortunate.

yrs. ever

B

---

[1] *"a residence in Mitylene"* There was a rumor circulating at the time that Byron had a residence in Mitylene, the capital of the island of Lesbos in Greece.

[2] *Oons* Archaic expletive (a contraction of "zounds," itself a contraction of "God's wounds").

[3] *Sir William Drummond* Scottish diplomat, MP, poet, and philosopher (1770–1828).

[4] *at Size* At assize, the periodic criminal and civil law court of England and Wales.

[5] *Waterloo* The Battle of Waterloo was fought in June 1815; led by the Duke of Wellington, the battle resulted in the defeat of Napoleon and of the First French Empire.

[6] *Rossini* Gioachino Antonio Rossini (1792–1868) was an Italian composer of immensely popular operas.

[7] *Romagnola* Byron is referring to his lover, the Contessa Guiccioli, who was from Ravenna, a city in the Emilia-Romagna region of Italy.

[8] *"Ciò … basta"* Italian: This shows a moral picture of the country; it should be enough for you (tr. Valeria Vallucci, as noted in *Byron's European Impact* by Peter Cochran).

[9] *"Vi … Cognato"* Italian: I pay my respects, my brother-in-law.

[10] *Scrope* Scrope Berdmore Davies (1782–1852), a gambler and rake, was a close friend of Byron's.

[11] *"the Creature Dougal"* Cf. Sir Walter Scott's *Rob Roy*, ch. 31. The "Creature Dougal" in Scott's novel is a prison guard from the Highlands who has himself been taken prisoner; Byron is referring to his banker and friend Douglas Kinnaird.

[12] *"Mazeppa" … "Ode"* Byron's *Mazeppa* and "Ode on Venice" were published in June 1819.

[13] *"Julia's letter"* See *Don Juan* 1.192–97.

from a letter TO JOHN MURRAY

16 February 1821
Ravenna

Dear Moray[1]—In the month of March will arrive from Barcelona—*Signor Curioni*[2] engaged for the Opera.—He is an acquaintance of mine—and a gentlemanly young man—high in his profession.—I must request your personal kindness and patronage in his favour. Pray introduce him to such of the theatrical people, Editors of Papers—and others, as may be useful to him in his profession publicly and privately.—He is accompanied by the Signora Arpalice Taruscelli[3]—a Venetian lady of great beauty and celebrity and a particular friend of mine—your natural gallantry will I am sure induce you to pay her proper attention.—Tell Israeli[4]—that as he is fond of *literary* anecdotes—she can tell him some of your acquaintance abroad.—I presume that he speaks Italian.—Do not neglect this request, but do them and me a favour in their behalf.——I shall write to some others to aid you in assisting them with your countenance.

I agree to your request of leaving in abeyance the terms for the three D.J.s till you can ascertain the effect of publication.—If I refuse to alter— you have a claim to so much courtesy in return.—I had let you off your proposal about the price of Cantos, last year (the 3d. & 4th. always to reckon as *one* only—which they originally were) and I do not call upon you to renew it.—You have therefore no occasion to fight so shy of such subjects as I am not conscious of having given you occasion.——The 5th. is so far from being the last of D.J. that it is hardly the beginning.—I meant to take him the tour of Europe—with a proper mixture of siege— battle—and adventure—and to make him finish as *Anacharsis Cloots*[5] in the French revolution.—To how many cantos this may extend—I know not—nor whether (even if I live) I shall complete it—but this was my notion.—I meant to have made him a Cavalier Servente[6] in Italy and a cause for a divorce in England—and a Sentimental "Werther-faced man"[7] in Germany—so as to show the different ridicules of the society in each of those countries—and to have displayed him gradually gaté and blasé as he grew older—as is natural.— But I had not quite fixed whether to make him end in Hell—or in an unhappy marriage—not knowing which would be the severest.—The Spanish tradition says Hell,—but it is probably only an Allegory of the other state.——You are now in possession of my notions on the subject.—

… How came George Bankes[8] to quote English Bards in the House of Commons? all the World keep flinging that poem in my face.——Belzoni[9] is a grand traveller and his English is very prettily broken.——As for News—the Barbarians[10] are marching on Naples—and if they lose a single battle, all Italy will be up.—It will be like the Spanish war if they have any bottom.

---

[1] *Moray* Pun on Murray's name. A moray is a kind of eel.

[2] *Curioni* Alberico Curioni (1785–1875), an Italian tenor who sang in London from 1821 to 1832.

[3] *Arpalice Taruscelli* A woman with whom Byron had had a brief affair in Venice in 1818.

[4] *Israeli* British writer Isaac D'Israeli (1766–1848), a member of Murray's social circle.

[5] *Anacharsis Cloots* Jean Baptiste Clootz (1755–94) was a Prussian baron who became involved in the French Revolution. He took the name "Anacharsis" and described himself as "l'orateur de genre humain" ("the orator of the human race"). He was executed by guillotine in 1794, during the Reign of Terror. See *Don Juan*, Canto 1.3, above.

[6] *Cavalier Servente* Official lover of a married woman. Byron was himself Teresa Guiccioli's cavalier servente, and was often embarrassed by the servile nature of the position.

[7] *Werther-faced man* Byron here refers to the protagonist of Goethe's *The Sorrows of Young Werther* (1774), a depressive young man, but he borrows the phrase from Thomas Moore, who had first used it in his *Fudge Family in Paris* (1818).

[8] *George Bankes* George Bankes (1787–1856), an English Member of Parliament, quoted Byron's early satire, *English Bards and Scotch Reviewers*, in an address at the opening of Parliament in 1821.

[9] *Belzoni* Giovanni Battista Belzoni (1778–1823), an Italian explorer, insisted on writing his account of his travels in English, though he was far from a master of the language.

[10] *Barbarians* Germans.

——"*Letters opened* !"[1] to be sure they are—and that's the reason why I always put in my opinion of the German Austrian Scoundrels;—there is not an Italian who loathes them more than I do—and whatever I could do to scour Italy and the earth of their infamous oppression—would be done "con amore."[2]—

yrs. ever & truly
BYRON

Recollect that the *Hints*[3] must be printed with the *Latin* otherwise there is no sense.—

[1] *Letters opened* Because Byron was connected with the Gamba family, known for its devotion to the Italian national cause, his mail might be secretly opened and read by the authorities

[2] *con amore* Italian: with love.

[3] *Hints* *Hints from Horace*, originally to be published in 1811, but superseded by the first two cantos of *Childe Harold's Pilgrimage*. Byron's interest in publishing it was revived in 1820, but lapsed. It was finally issued in 1831.

PERCY BYSSHE SHELLEY
1792 – 1822

Percy Bysshe Shelley's progressive social and political ideas have been an inspiration to many readers, from nineteenth-century socialists such as Marx and Engels to radical thinkers of the 1960s. Although he was born into wealth and privilege, Shelley opposed the powerful, from those who teased and harassed him in school at Eton to the Tory government and press whom he believed were responsible for the oppression of the working classes. He collaborated on *The Necessity of Atheism* (1811), a pamphlet destined to alienate not only his father, but also the bishops and authorities at Oxford, to whom Shelley sent the piece. Antagonistic to kings, priests, judges, the conservative press, and aristocracy, he was called "Mad Shelley" at Oxford. He earned this sobriquet not only for his radicalism but also for his intense interest in science. These intellectual passions underwrite a body of remarkable visionary poetry characterized by an elegance and complexity that is at once very wonderful and very difficult.

Shelley was born in 1792 at Field Place in Sussex, the first of the six children of Elizabeth and Timothy Shelley, a Member of Parliament who became a baronet on the death of his father, Sir Bysshe Shelley. Percy grew up in the affluence befitting his role as heir to the estate and title of his father and grandfather. He spent his early years running free on the estate and entertaining his siblings, so he was unprepared for the rules of the boys' academy he attended, or the bullying he would suffer there. Shelley later attended Eton College, and there the teasing continued, further developing his allegiance to outcasts and the disenfranchised, and nurturing his rebellious spirit. He was still a student at Eton when he published *Zastrozzi* (1810), a Gothic romance novel. He continued to publish during his short stint at Oxford University, from which he and Thomas Jefferson Hogg, his friend and the co-author of *The Necessity of Atheism*, were expelled for writing the pamphlet.

In 1813 Shelley published his first important work: *Queen Mab*, a poetic dream-vision that vilified conventional morality and institutional religion in a utopian picture of humanity returned to a condition of innocence. Shelley's greatest utopian fantasy, *Prometheus Unbound* (1820), would essentially reprise the same picture, imagining a world grown young again as human beings learn to undo the curse of their acquired historical fears and hatreds and replace it with a program based on love, which he called "the great secret" of all morality.

Shelley's personal involvements with love, fueled by his ideals, were also fraught with that inherited curse. In 1811 Shelley married Harriet Westbrook, and the couple had a daughter born to them in 1813. But before long he would fall in love with another young woman, Mary Godwin, the daughter of the radical thinkers William Godwin and Mary Wollstonecraft.

In 1814 Shelley left Harriet to undertake a six-week tour of the continent with Mary and her half sister Claire Clairmont. When they returned to England, Shelley proposed that Harriet should live with Mary and himself as free lovers. When Harriet refused, Shelley, Mary, and Claire again traveled to Europe, where the three met Lord Byron in Switzerland in June of 1816. In the meantime, Harriet had given birth to Shelley's second child, a son, in late 1814, and at the end of 1816 she died by suicide. Mary and Percy were then married.

The summer of 1816 is one of the most famous in the history of English letters. Out of it came a series of stunning literary works: Mary's great novel *Frankenstein*; Byron's third canto of *Childe Harold* as well as various apocalyptic works, especially *Manfred*; and a series of key lyric poems by Shelley including "Mont Blanc" and "Hymn to Intellectual Beauty." Later (1818) Shelley would write "Julian and Maddalo: A Conversation," a verse dialogue representing the conversations that he and Byron had been having since they met in 1816.

Upon his return to England from Switzerland, his life bristling with personal and political scandals, Shelley was denied custody of his two children from his first marriage. In 1818 the Shelleys moved to the Continent with their baby girl Clara in the hope of joining Byron in Italy and avoiding the judgment of English society. Unfortunately, Clara died in September, and William, born in 1816, died the following year. The only child to survive would be Percy Florence, born in 1819.

The year 1819 was a productive one for Shelley. He composed his lyric masterpiece *Prometheus Unbound*, as well as the political tragedy *The Cenci*. During this prolific period Shelley also responded to the Peterloo Massacre—in which at least eleven workers were killed at what was meant to be a peaceful rally in Manchester—by writing "The Mask of Anarchy," "Song: To the Men of England," "A Philosophical View of Reform," and "Ode to the West Wind," a revolutionary lyric that recapitulates, in miniature, the argument and structure of *Prometheus Unbound*. Shelley hoped his verse would undermine the retrograde political institutions of his time and seed the future with a promise of rejuvenation. Enjoying scant fame or immediate influence, he nevertheless believed in the power of art to effect political change, however slowly, and he concluded his *Defence of Poetry* (1821), with the now-famous pronouncement that poets are "the unacknowledged legislators of the World."

In 1822 Shelley—who could not swim—went sailing on the Bay of Spezia in Italy with his friend Edward Williams. They were caught in a sudden squall and drowned. When Shelley's body washed up on the beach a few days later, a copy of Keats's poems was found in his pocket. A funeral pyre was hastily built and his corpse cremated—except for his heart, which was snatched from the pyre by his friend Edward Trelawney.

In a letter to some of his conservative English friends Byron famously declared: "You are all brutally mistaken about Shelley who was without exception—the *best* and least selfish man I ever knew." His ashes were placed near the recently buried Keats in the Protestant Cemetery in Rome. His inconsumable heart remained in Mary Shelley's possession, wrapped in the pages of *Adonais*, Shelley's elegy for Keats, until her death. It is buried with her in her tomb at St. Peter's Churchyard in Bournemouth.

⌘ ⌘ ⌘

To Wordsworth[1]

Poet of Nature, thou hast wept to know
That things depart which never may return:
Childhood and youth, friendship and love's first glow,
Have fled like sweet dreams, leaving thee to mourn.
5 These common woes I feel. One loss is mine
Which thou too feel'st, yet I alone deplore.
Thou wert as a lone star, whose light did shine
On some frail bark in winter's midnight roar:
Thou hast like to a rock-built refuge stood
10 Above the blind and battling multitude:
In honoured poverty thy voice did weave
Songs consecrate to truth and liberty—
Deserting these, thou leavest me to grieve,
Thus having been, that thou shouldst cease to be.
—1816

Alastor; or, The Spirit of Solitude

PREFACE

The poem entitled "Alastor" may be considered as allegorical of one of the most interesting situations of the human mind. It represents a youth of uncorrupted feelings and adventurous genius[2] led forth by an imagination inflamed and purified through familiarity with all that is excellent and majestic, to the contemplation of the universe. He drinks deep of the fountains of knowledge, and is still insatiate. The magnificence and beauty of the external world sinks profoundly into the frame of his conceptions, and affords to their modifications a variety not to be exhausted. So long as it is possible for his desires to point towards objects thus infinite and unmeasured, he is joyous, and tranquil, and self-possessed. But the period arrives when these objects cease to suffice. His mind is at length suddenly awakened and thirsts for intercourse with an intelligence similar to itself. He images to himself the Being whom he loves. Conversant with speculations of the sublimest and most perfect natures, the vision in which he embodies his own imaginations unites all of wonderful, or wise, or beautiful, which the poet, the philosopher, or the lover could depicture. The intellectual faculties, the imagination, the functions of sense, have their respective requisitions[3] on the sympathy of corresponding powers in other human beings. The Poet is represented as uniting these requisitions, and attaching them to a single image. He seeks in vain for a prototype of his conception. Blasted by his disappointment, he descends to an untimely grave.

The picture is not barren of instruction to actual men. The Poet's self-centred seclusion was avenged by the furies of an irresistible passion pursuing him to speedy ruin. But that Power which strikes the luminaries of the world with sudden darkness and extinction, by awakening them to too exquisite a perception of its influences, dooms to a slow and poisonous decay those meaner spirits that dare to abjure its dominion. Their destiny is more abject and inglorious as their delinquency is more contemptible and pernicious. They who, deluded by no generous error, instigated by no sacred thirst of doubtful knowledge, duped by no illustrious superstition, loving nothing on this earth, and cherishing no hopes beyond, yet keep aloof from sympathies with their kind, rejoicing neither in human joy nor mourning with human grief; these, and such as they, have their apportioned curse. They languish, because none feel with them their common nature. They are morally dead. They are neither friends, nor lovers, nor fathers, nor citizens of the world, nor benefactors of their country. Among those who attempt to exist without human sympathy, the pure and tender-hearted perish through the intensity and passion of their search after its communities, when the

---

[1] *To Wordsworth* As a young man, Wordsworth identified himself as a political radical, but as his career progressed he gradually became more conservative. His 1814 poem *The Excursion* showed a marked change in his political and religious thinking, and was received with disappointment by many of his early admirers, such as Shelley.

[2] *youth of ... genius* This protagonist is unnamed, although because of the poem's title he is often (incorrectly) assumed to be called Alastor. In his *Memoirs of Shelley*, Shelley's friend Thomas Love Peacock explains that Shelley was "at a loss for a title, and I proposed that which he adopted: Alastor, or the Spirit of Solitude. The Greek word *Alastor* is an evil genius."

[3] *requisitions* Claims.

vacancy of their spirit suddenly makes itself felt. All else, selfish, blind, and torpid, are those unforeseeing multitudes who constitute, together with their own, the lasting misery and loneliness of the world. Those who love not their fellow-beings live unfruitful lives, and prepare for their old age a miserable grave.

> "The good die first,
> And those whose hearts are dry as summer dust,
> Burn to the socket!"[1]

14 December 1815

Alastor; or, The Spirit of Solitude

Nondum amabam, et amare amabam, quaerebam quid amarem, amans amare.

—*Confess. St. August.*[2]

Earth, ocean, air, belovèd brotherhood!
If our great Mother[3] has imbued my soul
With aught of natural piety[4] to feel
Your love, and recompense the boon with mine;
5　If dewy morn, and odorous noon, and even,
With sunset and its gorgeous ministers,
And solemn midnight's tingling silentness;
If autumn's hollow sighs in the sere wood,
And winter robing with pure snow and crowns
10　Of starry ice the grey grass and bare boughs;
If spring's voluptuous pantings when she breathes
Her first sweet kisses, have been dear to me;
If no bright bird, insect, or gentle beast
I consciously have injured, but still loved
15　And cherished these my kindred; then forgive
This boast, belovèd brethren, and withdraw
No portion of your wonted favour now!

Mother of this unfathomable world!
Favour my solemn song, for I have loved
20　Thee ever, and thee only; I have watched
Thy shadow, and the darkness of thy steps,
And my heart ever gazes on the depth
Of thy deep mysteries. I have made my bed
In charnels[5] and on coffins, where black death
25　Keeps record of the trophies won from thee,
Hoping to still these obstinate questionings[6]
Of thee and thine, by forcing some lone ghost,
Thy messenger, to render up the tale
Of what we are. In lone and silent hours,
30　When night makes a weird sound of its own stillness,
Like an inspired and desperate alchemist
Staking his very life on some dark hope,
Have I mixed awful talk and asking looks
With my most innocent love, until strange tears
35　Uniting with those breathless kisses, made
Such magic as compels the charmèd night
To render up thy charge: … and, though ne'er yet
Thou hast unveiled thy inmost sanctuary,
Enough from incommunicable dream,
40　And twilight phantasms, and deep noon-day thought,
Has shone within me, that serenely now
And moveless, as a long-forgotten lyre
Suspended in the solitary dome
Of some mysterious and deserted fane,°　　*temple*
45　I wait thy breath, Great Parent, that my strain
May modulate with murmurs of the air,
And motions of the forests and the sea,
And voice of living beings, and woven hymns
Of night and day, and the deep heart of man.

50　There was a Poet whose untimely tomb
No human hands with pious reverence reared,
But the charmed eddies of autumnal winds
Built o'er his mouldering bones a pyramid
Of mouldering leaves in the waste wilderness:
55　A lovely youth—no mourning maiden decked

---

[1] *The … socket*　From Wordsworth's *Excursion*, 1.500–02.

[2] *Nondum … August.*　Latin: I was not yet in love, and I loved to love, I sought what I might love, loving to love. From St. Augustine's *Confessions* 3.1, in which he describes his youthful desire for sexual love, rather than the spiritual love of God that he later found.

[3] *our great Mother*　Cybele, goddess of the powers of nature and fertility.

[4] *natural piety*　From Wordsworth's "My Heart Leaps Up," line 9.

[5] *charnels*　Houses of death, mortuaries.

[6] *obstinate questionings*　From Wordsworth's "Ode: Intimations of Immortality," lines 144–45: "Those obstinate questionings / Of sense and outward things."

With weeping flowers, or votive cypress wreath,[1]
The lone couch of his everlasting sleep:
Gentle, and brave, and generous—no lorn° bard   *forlorn*
Breathed o'er his dark fate one melodious sigh:
60   He lived, he died, he sung, in solitude.
Strangers have wept to hear his passionate notes,
And virgins, as unknown he passed, have pined
And wasted for fond love of his wild eyes.
The fire of those soft orbs has ceased to burn,
65   And Silence, too enamoured of that voice,
Locks its mute music in her rugged cell.

      By solemn vision, and bright silver dream,
His infancy was nurtured. Every sight
And sound from the vast earth and ambient air,
70   Sent to his heart its choicest impulses.
The fountains of divine philosophy
Fled not his thirsting lips, and all of great,
Or good, or lovely, which the sacred past
In truth or fable consecrates, he felt
75   And knew. When early youth had passed, he left
His cold fireside and alienated home
To seek strange truths in undiscovered lands.
Many a wide waste and tangled wilderness
Has lured his fearless steps; and he has bought
80   With his sweet voice and eyes, from savage men,
His rest and food. Nature's most secret steps
He like her shadow has pursued, where'er
The red volcano overcanopies
Its fields of snow and pinnacles of ice
85   With burning smoke, or where bitumen° lakes   *pitch*
On black bare pointed islets ever beat
With sluggish surge, or where the secret caves
Rugged and dark, winding among the springs
Of fire and poison, inaccessible
90   To avarice or pride, their starry domes
Of diamond and of gold expand above
Numberless and immeasurable halls,
Frequent with crystal column, and clear shrines
Of pearl, and thrones radiant with chrysolite.[2]
95   Nor had that scene of ampler majesty

Than gems or gold, the varying roof of heaven
And the green earth lost in his heart its claims
To love and wonder; he would linger long
In lonesome vales, making the wild his home,
100   Until the doves and squirrels would partake
From his innocuous hand his bloodless food,
Lured by the gentle meaning of his looks,
And the wild antelope, that starts whene'er
The dry leaf rustles in the brake,° suspend   *thicket*
105   Her timid steps to gaze upon a form
More graceful than her own.
                                             His wandering step
Obedient to high thoughts, has visited
The awful ruins of the days of old:
Athens, and Tyre, and Balbec,[3] and the waste
110   Where stood Jerusalem,[4] the fallen towers
Of Babylon, the eternal pyramids,
Memphis and Thebes,[5] and whatsoe'er of strange
Sculptured on alabaster obelisk,
Or jasper tomb, or mutilated sphynx,
115   Dark Æthiopia in her desert hills
Conceals. Among the ruined temples there,
Stupendous columns, and wild images
Of more than man, where marble daemons[6] watch
The Zodiac's brazen mystery,[7] and dead men
120   Hang their mute thoughts on the mute walls around,
He lingered, poring on memorials
Of the world's youth, through the long burning day
Gazed on those speechless shapes, nor, when the moon
Filled the mysterious halls with floating shades
125   Suspended he that task, but ever gazed

---

[3] *Tyre* Ancient capital of Phoenicia, located in present-day Lebanon, a site of several battles during the Crusades. It fell to Muslim forces in 1291; *Balbec* Ancient Phoenician city in eastern Lebanon that is known for its Roman ruins.

[4] *Jerusalem* Destroyed by Emperor Titus in 70 CE.

[5] *Memphis and Thebes* Ancient cities of lower and upper Egypt, respectively.

[6] *daemons* Supernatural beings, or minor deities, of Greek mythology.

[7] *Zodiac's brazen mystery* Representations of the Zodiac decorate the ceiling of the temple of Isis (goddess of fertility) at Denderah, in Egypt.

---

[1] *cypress wreath* Worn to represent mourning.

[2] *chrysolite* Green gemstone.

And gazed, till meaning on his vacant mind
Flashed like strong inspiration, and he saw
The thrilling secrets of the birth of time.

     Meanwhile an Arab maiden brought his food,
130 Her daily portion, from her father's tent,
And spread her matting for his couch, and stole
From duties and repose to tend his steps—
Enamoured, yet not daring for deep awe
To speak her love—and watched his nightly sleep,
135 Sleepless herself, to gaze upon his lips
Parted in slumber, whence the regular breath
Of innocent dreams arose: then, when red morn
Made paler the pale moon, to her cold home
Wildered,° and wan, and panting, she returned. *bewildered*

140   The Poet wandering on, through Arabie
And Persia, and the wild Carmanian waste,[1]
And o'er the aërial mountains which pour down
Indus and Oxus[2] from their icy caves,
In joy and exultation held his way;
145 Till in the vale of Cashmire, far within
Its loneliest dell, where odorous plants entwine
Beneath the hollow rocks a natural bower,
Beside a sparkling rivulet he stretched
His languid limbs. A vision on his sleep
150 There came, a dream of hopes that never yet
Had flushed his cheek. He dreamed a veilèd maid
Sate near him, talking in low solemn tones.
Her voice was like the voice of his own soul
Heard in the calm of thought; its music long,
155 Like woven sounds of streams and breezes, held
His inmost sense suspended in its web
Of many-coloured woof[3] and shifting hues.
Knowledge and truth and virtue were her theme,
And lofty hopes of divine liberty,
160 Thoughts the most dear to him, and poesy,
Herself a poet. Soon the solemn mood

Of her pure mind kindled through all her frame
A permeating fire: wild numbers[4] then
She raised, with voice stifled in tremulous sobs
165 Subdued by its own pathos: her fair hands
Were bare alone, sweeping from some strange harp
Strange symphony, and in their branching veins
The eloquent blood told an ineffable tale.
The beating of her heart was heard to fill
170 The pauses of her music, and her breath
Tumultuously accorded with those fits
Of intermitted song. Sudden she rose,
As if her heart impatiently endured
Its bursting burthen: at the sound he turned,
175 And saw by the warm light of their own life
Her glowing limbs beneath the sinuous veil
Of woven wind, her outspread arms now bare,
Her dark locks floating in the breath of night,
Her beamy bending eyes, her parted lips
180 Outstretched, and pale, and quivering eagerly.
His strong heart sunk and sickened with excess
Of love. He reared his shuddering limbs and quelled
His gasping breath, and spread his arms to meet
Her panting bosom … she drew back a while,
185 Then, yielding to the irresistible joy,
With frantic gesture and short breathless cry
Folded his frame in her dissolving arms.
Now blackness veiled his dizzy eyes, and night
Involved and swallowed up the vision; sleep,
190 Like a dark flood suspended in its course,
Rolled back its impulse on his vacant brain.

     Roused by the shock he started from his trance—
The cold white light of morning, the blue moon
Low in the west, the clear and garish hills,
195 The distinct valley and the vacant woods,
Spread round him where he stood. Whither have fled
The hues of heaven that canopied his bower
Of yesternight? The sounds that soothed his sleep,
The mystery and the majesty of Earth,
200 The joy, the exultation? His wan eyes
Gaze on the empty scene as vacantly

---

[1] *Carmanian waste* Kerman Desert, in present-day Iran.

[2] *Indus and Oxus* Rivers which flow from opposite sides of the Hindu Kush mountains in Asia.

[3] *woof* Thread that crosses from side to side in a web of weaving.

[4] *wild numbers* Verses of irregular meter.

As ocean's moon looks on the moon in heaven.
The spirit of sweet human love has sent
A vision to the sleep of him who spurned
205 Her choicest gifts. He eagerly pursues
Beyond the realms of dream that fleeting shade;
He overleaps the bounds. Alas! Alas!
Were limbs, and breath, and being intertwined
Thus treacherously? Lost, lost, for ever lost,
210 In the wide pathless desert of dim sleep,
That beautiful shape! Does the dark gate of death
Conduct to thy mysterious paradise,
O Sleep? Does the bright arch of rainbow clouds,
And pendent mountains seen in the calm lake,
215 Lead only to a black and watery depth,
While death's blue vault, with loathliest vapours hung,
Where every shade which the foul grave exhales
Hides its dead eye from the detested day,
Conducts, O Sleep, to thy delightful realms?
220 This doubt with sudden tide flowed on his heart,
The insatiate hope which it awakened, stung
His brain even like despair.
                          While daylight held
The sky, the Poet kept mute conference
With his still soul. At night the passion came,
225 Like the fierce fiend of a distempered dream,
And shook him from his rest, and led him forth
Into the darkness. As an eagle, grasped
In folds of the green serpent, feels her breast
Burn with the poison, and precipitates
230 Through night and day, tempest, and calm, and cloud,
Frantic with dizzying anguish, her blind flight
O'er the wide aëry° wilderness: thus driven   *lofty*
By the bright shadow of that lovely dream,
Beneath the cold glare of the desolate night,
235 Through tangled swamps and deep precipitous dells,
Startling with careless step the moonlight snake,
He fled. Red morning dawned upon his flight,
Shedding the mockery of its vital hues
Upon his cheek of death. He wandered on
240 Till vast Aornos seen from Petra's steep[1]
Hung o'er the low horizon like a cloud;

Through Balk,[2] and where the desolated tombs
Of Parthian kings[3] scatter to every wind
Their wasting dust, wildly he wandered on,
245 Day after day a weary waste of hours,
Bearing within his life the brooding care
That ever fed on its decaying flame.
And now his limbs were lean; his scattered hair
Sered° by the autumn of strange suffering   *made dry*
250 Sung dirges in the wind; his listless hand
Hung like dead bone within its withered skin;
Life, and the lustre that consumed it, shone
As in a furnace burning secretly
From his dark eyes alone. The cottagers,
255 Who ministered with human charity
His human wants, beheld with wondering awe
Their fleeting visitant. The mountaineer,
Encountering on some dizzy precipice
That spectral form, deemed that the Spirit of wind
260 With lightning eyes, and eager breath, and feet
Disturbing not the drifted snow, had paused
In its career: the infant would conceal
His troubled visage in his mother's robe
In terror at the glare of those wild eyes,
265 To remember their strange light in many a dream
Of after-times; but youthful maidens, taught
By nature, would interpret half the woe
That wasted him, would call him with false names
Brother, and friend, would press his pallid hand
270 At parting, and watch, dim through tears, the path
Of his departure from their father's door.

     At length upon the lone Chorasmian shore[4]
He paused, a wide and melancholy waste
Of putrid marshes. A strong impulse urged
275 His steps to the sea-shore. A swan was there,
Beside a sluggish stream among the reeds.
It rose as he approached, and with strong wings
Scaling the upward sky, bent its bright course
High over the immeasurable main.

---

1 *Aornos* Mountain on the Indus; *Petra's steep* Probably the Rock of Soghdiana in Uzbekistan. ("Petra" is Latin for "rock.")

2 *Balk* Balkh, in present-day Afghanistan.

3 *Parthian kings* Rulers of northern Persia.

4 *Chorasmian shore* Shore of the Caspian sea.

His eyes pursued its flight—"Thou hast a home, 280
Beautiful bird; thou voyagest to thine home,
Where thy sweet mate will twine her downy neck
With thine, and welcome thy return with eyes
Bright in the lustre of their own fond joy.
And what am I that I should linger here, 285
With voice far sweeter than thy dying notes,
Spirit more vast than thine, frame more attuned
To beauty, wasting these surpassing powers
In the deaf air, to the blind earth, and heaven
That echoes not my thoughts?" A gloomy smile 290
Of desperate hope wrinkled his quivering lips.
For sleep, he knew, kept most relentlessly
Its precious charge, and silent death exposed,
Faithless perhaps as sleep, a shadowy lure,
With doubtful smile mocking its own strange charms. 295

    Startled by his own thoughts he looked around.
There was no fair fiend near him, not a sight
Or sound of awe but in his own deep mind.
A little shallop[1] floating near the shore
Caught the impatient wandering of his gaze. 300
It had been long abandoned, for its sides
Gaped wide with many a rift, and its frail joints
Swayed with the undulations of the tide.
A restless impulse urged him to embark
And meet lone Death on the drear ocean's waste; 305
For well he knew that mighty Shadow loves
The slimy caverns of the populous deep.

    The day was fair and sunny, sea and sky
Drank its inspiring radiance, and the wind
Swept strongly from the shore, blackening the waves. 310
Following his eager soul, the wanderer
Leaped in the boat, he spread his cloak aloft
On the bare mast, and took his lonely seat,
And felt the boat speed o'er the tranquil sea
Like a torn cloud before the hurricane. 315

    As one that in a silver vision floats
Obedient to the sweep of odorous winds
Upon resplendent clouds, so rapidly

Along the dark and ruffled waters fled
The straining boat. A whirlwind swept it on, 320
With fierce gusts and precipitating force,
Through the white ridges of the chafèd sea.
The waves arose. Higher and higher still
Their fierce necks writhed beneath the tempest's scourge
Like serpents struggling in a vulture's grasp. 325
Calm and rejoicing in the fearful war
Of wave ruining on wave, and blast on blast
Descending, and black flood on whirlpool driven
With dark obliterating course, he sate:
As if their genii were the ministers 330
Appointed to conduct him to the light
Of those belovèd eyes, the Poet sate
Holding the steady helm. Evening came on,
The beams of sunset hung their rainbow hues
High 'mid the shifting domes of sheeted spray 335
That canopied his path o'er the waste deep;
Twilight, ascending slowly from the east,
Entwined in duskier wreaths her braided locks
O'er the fair front and radiant eyes of day;
Night followed, clad with stars. On every side 340
More horribly the multitudinous streams
Of ocean's mountainous waste to mutual war
Rushed in dark tumult thundering, as to mock
The calm and spangled sky. The little boat
Still fled before the storm; still fled, like foam 345
Down the steep cataract of a wintry river;
Now pausing on the edge of the riven wave;
Now leaving far behind the bursting mass
That fell, convulsing ocean: safely fled—
As if that frail and wasted human form 350
Had been an elemental god.
                At midnight
The moon arose: and lo! the ethereal cliffs
Of Caucasus,[2] whose icy summits shone
Among the stars like sunlight, and around
Whose caverned base the whirlpools and the waves 355
Bursting and eddying irresistibly
Rage and resound for ever. Who shall save?
The boat fled on—the boiling torrent drove—

---

1 *shallop* Small open boat or dinghy.

2 *ethereal* Belonging to the upper air; *Caucasus* On the western shore of the Caspian sea, in present-day Georgia.

The crags closed round with black and jaggèd arms,
60 The shattered mountain overhung the sea,
And faster still, beyond all human speed,
Suspended on the sweep of the smooth wave,
The little boat was driven. A cavern there
Yawned, and amid its slant and winding depths
65 Ingulfed the rushing sea. The boat fled on
With unrelaxing speed. "Vision and Love!"
The Poet cried aloud, "I have beheld
The path of thy departure. Sleep and death
Shall not divide us long!"

            The boat pursued
70 The windings of the cavern. Daylight shone
At length upon that gloomy river's flow;
Now, where the fiercest war among the waves
Is calm, on the unfathomable stream
The boat moved slowly. Where the mountain, riven,
75 Exposed those black depths to the azure sky,
Ere yet the flood's enormous volume fell
Even to the base of Caucasus, with sound
That shook the everlasting rocks, the mass
Filled with one whirlpool all that ample chasm;
80 Stair above stair the eddying waters rose,
Circling immeasurably fast, and laved°   *bathed*
With alternating dash the gnarlèd roots
Of mighty trees, that stretched their giant arms
In darkness over it. I'the midst was left,
85 Reflecting, yet distorting every cloud,
A pool of treacherous and tremendous calm.
Seized by the sway of the ascending stream,
With dizzy swiftness, round, and round, and round,
Ridge after ridge the straining boat arose,
90 Till on the verge of the extremest curve,
Where, through an opening of the rocky bank,
The waters overflow, and a smooth spot
Of glassy quiet mid those battling tides
Is left, the boat paused shuddering. Shall it sink
95 Down the abyss? Shall the reverting stress
Of that resistless gulf embosom it?
Now shall it fall? A wandering stream of wind,
Breathed from the west, has caught the expanded sail,
And, lo! with gentle motion, between banks

400 Of mossy slope, and on a placid stream,
Beneath a woven grove it sails, and, hark!
The ghastly torrent mingles its far roar
With the breeze murmuring in the musical woods.
Where the embowering trees recede, and leave
405 A little space of green expanse, the cove
Is closed by meeting banks, whose yellow flowers[1]
For ever gaze on their own drooping eyes,
Reflected in the crystal calm. The wave
Of the boat's motion marred their pensive task,
410 Which nought but vagrant bird, or wanton wind,
Or falling spear-grass, or their own decay
Had e'er disturbed before. The Poet longed
To deck with their bright hues his withered hair,
But on his heart its solitude returned,
415 And he forbore. Not the strong impulse hid
In those flushed cheeks, bent eyes, and shadowy frame
Had yet performed its ministry: it hung
Upon his life, as lightning in a cloud
Gleams, hovering ere it vanish, ere the floods
420 Of night close over it.

            The noonday sun
Now shone upon the forest, one vast mass
Of mingling shade, whose brown° magnificence   *dark*
A narrow vale embosoms. There, huge caves,
Scooped in the dark base of their aëry rocks
425 Mocking its moans, respond and roar for ever.
The meeting boughs and implicated° leaves   *entwined*
Wove twilight o'er the Poet's path, as led
By love, or dream, or god, or mightier Death,
He sought in Nature's dearest haunt, some bank,
430 Her cradle, and his sepulchre. More dark
And dark the shades accumulate. The oak,
Expanding its immense and knotty arms,
Embraces the light beech. The pyramids
Of the tall cedar overarching, frame
435 Most solemn domes within, and far below,
Like clouds suspended in an emerald sky,
The ash and the acacia floating hang
Tremulous and pale. Like restless serpents, clothed

---

1 *yellow flowers* Narcissus flowers. According to Greek mythology,
the handsome youth Narcissus fell in love with his own reflection in
a pool of water and wasted away pining after his own image.

In rainbow and in fire, the parasites,
440   Starred with ten thousand blossoms, flow around
The grey trunks, and, as gamesome° infants' eyes,   *playful*
With gentle meanings, and most innocent wiles,
Fold their beams round the hearts of those that love,
These twine their tendrils with the wedded boughs
445   Uniting their close union; the woven leaves
Make net-work of the dark blue light of day,
And the night's noontide clearness, mutable
As shapes in the weird clouds. Soft mossy lawns
Beneath these canopies extend their swells,
450   Fragrant with perfumed herbs, and eyed with blooms
Minute yet beautiful. One darkest glen
Sends from its woods of musk-rose, twined with jasmine,
A soul-dissolving odour, to invite
To some more lovely mystery. Through the dell,
455   Silence and Twilight here, twin-sisters, keep
Their noonday watch, and sail among the shades,
Like vaporous shapes half seen; beyond, a well,
Dark, gleaming, and of most translucent wave,
Images[1] all the woven boughs above,
460   And each depending leaf, and every speck
Of azure sky, darting between their chasms;
Nor aught else in the liquid mirror laves
Its portraiture, but some inconstant star
Between one foliaged lattice twinkling fair,
465   Or, painted bird, sleeping beneath the moon,
Or gorgeous insect floating motionless,
Unconscious of the day, ere yet his wings
Have spread their glories to the gaze of noon.

      Hither the Poet came. His eyes beheld
470   Their own wan light through the reflected lines
Of his thin hair, distinct in the dark depth
Of that still fountain; as the human heart,
Gazing in dreams over the gloomy grave,
Sees its own treacherous likeness there. He heard
475   The motion of the leaves, the grass that sprung
Startled and glanced and trembled even to feel
An unaccustomed presence, and the sound

Of the sweet brook that from the secret springs
Of that dark fountain rose. A Spirit seemed
480   To stand beside him—clothed in no bright robes
Of shadowy silver or enshrining light,
Borrowed from aught the visible world affords
Of grace, or majesty, or mystery—
But, undulating woods, and silent well,
485   And leaping rivulet, and evening gloom
Now deepening the dark shades, for speech assuming,
Held commune with him, as if he and it
Were all that was,—only … when his regard
Was raised by intense pensiveness, … two eyes,
490   Two starry eyes, hung in the gloom of thought,
And seemed with their serene and azure smiles
To beckon him.

          Obedient to the light
That shone within his soul, he went, pursuing
The windings of the dell. The rivulet
495   Wanton and wild through many a green ravine
Beneath the forest flowed. Sometimes it fell
Among the moss with hollow harmony
Dark and profound. Now on the polished stones
It danced; like childhood laughing as it went:
500   Then, through the plain in tranquil wanderings crept,
Reflecting every herb and drooping bud
That overhung its quietness. "O stream!
Whose source is inaccessibly profound,
Whither do thy mysterious waters tend?
505   Thou imagest my life. Thy darksome stillness,
Thy dazzling waves, thy loud and hollow gulfs,
Thy searchless° fountain,° and   *undiscoverable* / *source*
    invisible course
Have each their type in me: and the wide sky,
And measureless ocean may declare as soon
510   What oozy cavern or what wandering cloud
Contains thy waters, as the universe
Tell where these living thoughts reside, when stretched
Upon thy flowers my bloodless limbs shall waste
I' the passing wind!"

---

1 *Images* Reflects; forms an image of.

Beside the grassy shore

5 Of the small stream he went; he did impress
On the green moss his tremulous step, that caught
Strong shuddering from his burning limbs. As one
Roused by some joyous madness from the couch
Of fever, he did move; yet, not like him,

20 Forgetful of the grave, where, when the flame
Of his frail exultation shall be spent,
He must descend. With rapid steps he went
Beneath the shade of trees, beside the flow
Of the wild babbling rivulet; and now

25 The forest's solemn canopies were changed
For the uniform and lightsome° evening sky.   *luminous*
Grey rocks did peep from the spare moss, and stemmed
The struggling brook: tall spires of windlestrae[1]
Threw their thin shadows down the rugged slope,

30 And nought but gnarled roots[2] of ancient pines,
Branchless and blasted, clenched with grasping roots
The unwilling soil. A gradual change was here,
Yet ghastly. For, as fast years flow away,
The smooth brow gathers, and the hair grows thin

35 And white, and where irradiate° dewy eyes   *illumined*
Had shone, gleam stony orbs: so from his steps
Bright flowers departed, and the beautiful shade
Of the green groves, with all their odorous winds
And musical motions. Calm, he still pursued

40 The stream, that with a larger volume now
Rolled through the labyrinthine dell; and there
Fretted a path through its descending curves
With its wintry speed. On every side now rose
Rocks, which, in unimaginable forms,

45 Lifted their black and barren pinnacles
In the light of evening, and, its precipice
Obscuring the ravine, disclosed above,
Mid toppling stones, black gulfs and yawning caves,
Whose windings gave ten thousand various tongues

50 To the loud stream. Lo! where the pass expands
Its stony jaws, the abrupt mountain breaks,
And seems, with its accumulated crags,
To overhang the world: for wide expand

Beneath the wan stars and descending moon
555 Islanded seas, blue mountains, mighty streams,
Dim tracts and vast, robed in the lustrous gloom
Of leaden-coloured even,° and fiery hills   *evening*
Mingling their flames with twilight, on the verge
Of the remote horizon. The near scene,

560 In naked and severe simplicity,
Made contrast with the universe. A pine,
Rock-rooted, stretched athwart the vacancy
Its swinging boughs, to each inconstant blast
Yielding one only response, at each pause

565 In most familiar cadence, with the howl
The thunder and the hiss of homeless streams
Mingling its solemn song, whilst the broad river,
Foaming and hurrying o'er its rugged path,
Fell into that immeasurable void

570 Scattering its waters to the passing winds.

Yet the grey precipice and solemn pine
And torrent, were not all— one silent nook
Was there. Even on the edge of that vast mountain,
Upheld by knotty roots and fallen rocks,

575 It overlooked in its serenity
The dark earth, and the bending vault of stars.
It was a tranquil spot, that seemed to smile
Even in the lap of horror. Ivy clasped
The fissured stones with its entwining arms,

580 And did embower with leaves for ever green,
And berries dark, the smooth and even space
Of its inviolated floor, and here
The children of the autumnal whirlwind bore,
In wanton sport, those bright leaves, whose decay,

585 Red, yellow, or ethereally pale,
Rivals the pride of summer. 'Tis the haunt
Of every gentle wind, whose breath can teach
The wilds to love tranquillity. One step,
One human step alone, has ever broken

590 The stillness of its solitude; one voice
Alone inspired its echoes—even that voice
Which hither came, floating among the winds,
And led the loveliest among human forms
To make their wild haunts the depository

---

[1] *windlestrae* Windlestraw; withered grass stalks.

[2] *roots* Believed to be a misprint for "trunks" or "knots."

595   Of all the grace and beauty that endued[1]
Its motions, render up its majesty,
Scatter its music on the unfeeling storm,
And to the damp leaves and blue cavern mould,
Nurses of rainbow flowers and branching moss,
600 Commit the colours of that varying cheek,
That snowy breast, those dark and drooping eyes.

    The dim and hornèd moon hung low, and poured
A sea of lustre on the horizon's verge
That overflowed its mountains. Yellow mist
605 Filled the unbounded atmosphere, and drank
Wan moonlight even to fulness: not a star
Shone, not a sound was heard; the very winds,
Danger's grim playmates, on that precipice
Slept, clasped in his embrace—O, storm of death!
610 Whose sightless speed divides this sullen night:
And thou, colossal Skeleton, that, still
Guiding its irresistible career
In thy devastating omnipotence,
Art king of this frail world, from the red field
615 Of slaughter, from the reeking hospital,
The patriot's sacred couch, the snowy bed
Of innocence, the scaffold and the throne,
A mighty voice invokes thee. Ruin calls
His brother Death. A rare and regal prey
620 He hath prepared, prowling around the world;
Glutted with which thou mayst repose, and men
Go to their graves like flowers or creeping worms,
Nor ever more offer at thy dark shrine
The unheeded tribute of a broken heart.

625   When on the threshold of the green recess
The wanderer's footsteps fell, he knew that death
Was on him. Yet a little, ere it fled,
Did he resign his high and holy soul
To images of the majestic past,
630 That paused within his passive being now,
Like winds that bear sweet music, when they breathe
Through some dim latticed chamber. He did place
His pale lean hand upon the rugged trunk
Of the old pine. Upon an ivied stone

635 Reclined his languid head, his limbs did rest,
Diffused and motionless, on the smooth brink
Of that obscurest chasm—and thus he lay,
Surrendering to their final impulses
The hovering powers of life. Hope and despair,
640 The torturers, slept; no mortal pain or fear
Marred his repose, the influxes of sense,
And his own being unalloyed by pain,
Yet feebler and more feeble, calmly fed
The stream of thought, till he lay breathing there
645 At peace, and faintly smiling—his last sight
Was the great moon, which o'er the western line
Of the wide world her mighty horn suspended,
With whose dun° beams inwoven darkness   *dusky*
    seemed
To mingle. Now upon the jaggèd hills
650 It rests, and still as the divided frame
Of the vast meteor[2] sunk, the Poet's blood,
That ever beat in mystic sympathy
With nature's ebb and flow, grew feebler still:
And when two lessening points[3] of light alone
655 Gleamed through the darkness, the alternate gasp
Of his faint respiration scarce did stir
The stagnate° night—till the minutest ray   *stagnant*
Was quenched, the pulse yet lingered in his heart.
It paused—it fluttered. But when heaven remained
660 Utterly black, the murky shades involved
An image, silent, cold, and motionless,
As their own voiceless earth and vacant air.
Even as a vapour° fed with golden beams   *cloud*
That ministered on sunlight, ere the west
665 Eclipses it, was now that wondrous frame—
No sense, no motion, no divinity—
A fragile lute, on whose harmonious strings
The breath of heaven did wander—a bright stream
Once fed with many-voicèd waves—a dream
670 Of youth, which night and time have quenched for ever,
Still, dark, and dry, and unremembered now.

---

[1] *endued* Were inherent in.

[2] *meteor* Formerly used to refer to any atmospheric phenomenon;
here, the moon.

[3] *two lessening points* The horns, or curved points, of the crescent
moon.

O, for Medea's wondrous alchemy,[1]
Which wheresoe'er it fell made the earth gleam
With bright flowers, and the wintry boughs exhale
75 From vernal blooms fresh fragrance! O, that God,
Profuse of poisons, would concede the chalice
Which but one living man has drained, who now,
Vessel of deathless wrath, a slave that feels
No proud exemption in the blighting curse
80 He bears, over the world wanders for ever,
Lone as incarnate death![2] O, that the dream
Of dark magician in his visioned[3] cave,
Raking the cinders of a crucible
For life and power, even when his feeble hand
85 Shakes in its last decay, were the true law
Of this so lovely world! But thou art fled
Like some frail exhalation; which the dawn
Robes in its golden beams—ah! thou hast fled!
The brave, the gentle, and the beautiful,
90 The child of grace and genius. Heartless things
Are done and said i'the world, and many worms
And beasts and men live on, and mighty Earth
From sea and mountain, city and wilderness,
In vesper[4] low or joyous orison,°   prayer
95 Lifts still its solemn voice—but thou art fled—
Thou canst no longer know or love the shapes
Of this phantasmal scene, who have to thee
Been purest ministers, who are, alas!
Now thou art not. Upon those pallid lips
100 So sweet even in their silence, on those eyes
That image sleep in death, upon that form
Yet safe from the worm's outrage, let no tear
Be shed—not even in thought. Nor, when those hues
Are gone, and those divinest lineaments,

705 Worn by the senseless° wind, shall live alone   unfeeling
In the frail pauses of this simple strain,
Let not high verse, mourning the memory
Of that which is no more, or painting's woe
Or sculpture, speak in feeble imagery
710 Their own cold powers. Art and eloquence,
And all the shows o'the world are frail and vain
To weep a loss that turns their lights to shade.
It is a woe too "deep for tears,"[5] when all
Is reft at once, when some surpassing Spirit,
715 Whose light adorned the world around it, leaves
Those who remain behind, not sobs or groans,
The passionate tumult of a clinging hope;
But pale despair and cold tranquillity,
Nature's vast frame, the web of human things,
720 Birth and the grave, that are not as they were.
—1816

Mutability

We are as clouds that veil the midnight moon;
    How restlessly they speed, and gleam, and
        quiver,
Streaking the darkness radiantly! Yet soon
Night closes round, and they are lost for ever:

5 Or like forgotten lyres,[6] whose dissonant strings
Give various response to each varying blast,
To whose frail frame no second motion brings
One mood or modulation like the last.

We rest—A dream has power to poison sleep;
10 We rise—One wandering thought pollutes the day;
We feel, conceive or reason, laugh or weep;
Embrace fond woe, or cast our cares away:

It is the same! For, be it joy or sorrow,
The path of its departure still is free:

---

[1] *Medea's wondrous alchemy* According to Greek myth, the sorceress Medea brewed a magic potion to restore youth to the dying Aeson. In Ovid's version of the tale (*Metamorphoses* 7.275ff), some of the potion spills on the ground and has the effect described in the following lines.

[2] *one living ... death* Reference to the legend of Ahasuerus, the Wandering Jew, who taunted Christ on the way to his crucifixion and as punishment was condemned to wander the earth until Christ's second coming.

[3] *visioned* I.e., in which he has visions.

[4] *vesper* Evening prayer.

---

[5] *deep for tears* From the last line of Wordsworth's "Ode: Intimations of Immortality": "Thoughts that do often lie too deep for tears."

[6] *lyres* Aeolian harps, stringed instruments that produce music when exposed to wind.

15 Man's yesterday may ne'er be like his morrow;
Nought may endure but Mutability.
—1816

Mont Blanc

Lines Written in the Vale of Chamouni [1]

1

The everlasting universe of things
Flows through the mind, and rolls its rapid waves,
Now dark—now glittering—now reflecting gloom—
Now lending splendour, where from secret springs
5 The source of human thought its tribute brings
Of waters—with a sound but half its own,
Such as a feeble brook will oft assume
In the wild woods, among the mountains lone,
Where waterfalls around it leap for ever,
10 Where woods and winds contend, and a vast river
Over its rocks ceaselessly bursts and raves.

2

Thus thou, Ravine of Arve—dark, deep Ravine—
Thou many-coloured, many-voicèd vale,
Over whose pines, and crags, and caverns sail
15 Fast cloud shadows and sunbeams: awful°   *awe-inspiring*
    scene,
Where Power in likeness of the Arve comes down
From the ice gulfs that gird his secret throne,
Bursting through these dark mountains like the flame
Of lightning through the tempest—thou dost lie,
20 Thy giant brood of pines around thee clinging,
Children of elder time, in whose devotion
The chainless winds still come and ever came
To drink their odours, and their mighty swinging
To hear—an old and solemn harmony;

25 Thine earthly rainbows stretched across the sweep
Of the etherial waterfall, whose veil
Robes some unsculptured [2] image; the strange sleep
Which when the voices of the desert fail
Wraps all in its own deep eternity—
30 Thy caverns echoing to the Arve's commotion,
A loud, lone sound no other sound can tame;
Thou art pervaded with that ceaseless motion,
Thou art the path of that unresting sound—
Dizzy Ravine! and when I gaze on thee
35 I seem as in a trance sublime and strange
To muse on my own separate fantasy,
My own, my human mind, which passively
Now renders and receives fast influencings,
Holding an unremitting interchange
40 With the clear universe of things around;
One legion of wild thoughts, whose wandering wings
Now float above thy darkness, and now rest
Where that or thou art no unbidden guest,
In the still cave of the witch Poesy,
45 Seeking among the shadows that pass by,
Ghosts of all things that are, some shade of thee,
Some phantom, some faint image; till the breast
From which they fled recalls them, thou art there!

3

Some say that gleams of a remoter world
50 Visit the soul in sleep—that death is slumber,
And that its shapes the busy thoughts outnumber
Of those who wake and live. I look on high;
Has some unknown omnipotence unfurled
The veil of life and death? or do I lie
55 In dream, and does the mightier world of sleep
Spread far around and inaccessibly
Its circles? For the very spirit fails,
Driven like a homeless cloud from steep to steep
That vanishes among the viewless° gales!   *invisible*
60 Far, far above, piercing the infinite sky,
Mont Blanc appears—still, snowy, and serene—
Its subject mountains their unearthly forms
Pile around it, ice and rock; broad vales between
Of frozen floods, unfathomable deeps,

---

[1] *Mont Blanc ... Chamouni* Mont Blanc, located near France's border with Italy, is the highest peak in the Alps. Shelley conceived the idea for the poem when standing on a bridge over the Arve River in the Valley of Chamonix in southeastern France. Of the poem, Shelley wrote, "It was composed under the immediate impression of the deep and powerful feelings excited by the objects which it attempts to describe; and, as an indisciplined overflowing of the soul, rests its claim to approbation on an attempt to imitate the untameable wildness and inaccessible solemnity from which those feelings sprang."

[2] *unsculptured* I.e., not shaped by humans.

55 Blue as the overhanging heaven, that spread
    And wind among the accumulated steeps;
    A desert peopled by the storms alone,
    Save when the eagle brings some hunter's bone,
    And the wolf tracks her there—how hideously
70 Its shapes are heaped around: rude, bare, and high,
    Ghastly, and scarred, and riven. Is this the scene
    Where the old Earthquake-daemon[1] taught her young
    Ruin? Were these their toys? or did a sea
    Of fire envelop once this silent snow?
75 None can reply—all seems eternal now.
    The wilderness has a mysterious tongue
    Which teaches awful doubt, or faith so mild,
    So solemn, so serene, that man may be
    But for such faith with nature reconciled;
80 Thou hast a voice, great Mountain, to repeal
    Large codes of fraud and woe; not understood
    By all, but which the wise, and great, and good
    Interpret, or make felt, or deeply feel.

4

    The fields, the lakes, the forests, and the streams,
85 Ocean, and all the living things that dwell
    Within the daedal[2] earth; lightning, and rain,
    Earthquake, and fiery flood, and hurricane,
    The torpor of the year when feeble dreams
    Visit the hidden buds, or dreamless sleep
90 Holds every future leaf and flower; the bound
    With which from that detested trance they leap;
    The works and ways of man, their death and birth,
    And that of him and all that his may be;
    All things that move and breathe with toil and sound
95 Are born and die; revolve, subside and swell.
    Power dwells apart in its tranquillity
    Remote, serene, and inaccessible:
    And *this*, the naked countenance of earth,
    On which I gaze, even these primeval mountains
100 Teach the adverting mind. The glaciers creep

    Like snakes that watch their prey, from their far
        fountains,
    Slow rolling on; there, many a precipice,
    Frost and the Sun in scorn of mortal power
    Have piled: dome, pyramid, and pinnacle,
105 A city of death, distinct with many a tower
    And wall impregnable of beaming ice.
    Yet not a city, but a flood of ruin
    Is there, that from the boundaries of the sky
    Rolls its perpetual stream; vast pines are strewing
110 Its destined path, or in the mangled soil
    Branchless and shattered stand; the rocks, drawn down
    From yon remotest waste, have overthrown
    The limits of the dead and living world,
    Never to be reclaimed. The dwelling-place
115 Of insects, beasts, and birds, becomes its spoil;
    Their food and their retreat for ever gone,
    So much of life and joy is lost. The race
    Of man flies far in dread; his work and dwelling
    Vanish, like smoke before the tempest's stream,
120 And their place is not known. Below, vast caves
    Shine in the rushing torrent's restless gleam,
    Which from those secret chasms in tumult welling[3]
    Meet in the vale, and one majestic River,
    The breath and blood of distant lands, for ever
125 Rolls its loud waters to the ocean waves,
    Breathes its swift vapours to the circling air.

5

    Mont Blanc yet gleams on high—the power is there,
    The still and solemn power of many sights
    And many sounds, and much of life and death.
130 In the calm darkness of the moonless nights,
    In the lone glare of day, the snows descend
    Upon that Mountain; none beholds them there,
    Nor when the flakes burn in the sinking sun,
    Or the star-beams dart through them. Winds contend
135 Silently there, and heap the snow with breath
    Rapid and strong, but silently! Its home
    The voiceless lightning in these solitudes
    Keeps innocently, and like vapour broods
    Over the snow. The secret strength of things

---

[1] *daemon* In Greek mythology, supernatural being or minor deity that controls some natural force.

[2] *daedal* Skillfully or intricately wrought. (From Daedalus of classical myth, who built the famous labyrinth in Crete.)

[3] *Which from … welling* Cf. Coleridge's *Kubla Khan*, lines 12–24.

140 Which governs thought, and to the infinite dome
Of heaven is as a law, inhabits thee!
And what were thou, and earth, and stars, and sea,
If to the human mind's imaginings
Silence and solitude were vacancy?
—1817

Hymn to Intellectual Beauty[1]

1

The awful shadow of some unseen Power
Floats though unseen amongst us, visiting
This various world with as inconstant wing
As summer winds that creep from flower to flower.
5   Like moonbeams that behind some piny mountain
shower,
It visits with inconstant glance
Each human heart and countenance;
Like hues and harmonies of evening,
Like clouds in starlight widely spread,
10   Like memory of music fled,
Like aught that for its grace may be
Dear, and yet dearer for its mystery.

2

Spirit of BEAUTY, that doth consecrate
With thine own hues all thou dost shine upon
15   Of human thought or form—where art thou gone?
Why dost thou pass away and leave our state,
This dim vast vale of tears, vacant and desolate?
Ask why the sunlight not forever
Weaves rainbows o'er yon mountain river,
20   Why aught should fail and fade that once is shown,
Why fear and dream and death and birth
Cast on the daylight of this earth
Such gloom—why man has such a scope
For love and hate, despondency and hope?

3

25   No voice from some sublimer world hath ever
To sage or poet these responses given—
Therefore the name of God, and ghosts, and Heaven,
Remain the records of their vain endeavour,
Frail spells—whose uttered charm might not avail to
sever,
30   From all we hear and all we see,
Doubt, chance, and mutability.
Thy light alone—like mist o'er mountains driven,
Or music by the night wind sent
Through strings of some still instrument,
35   Or moonlight on a midnight stream,
Gives grace and truth to life's unquiet dream.

4

Love, Hope, and Self-esteem, like clouds depart
And come, for some uncertain moments lent.
Man were° immortal, and omnipotent,   *would be*
40   Didst thou,[2] unknown and awful as thou art,
Keep with thy glorious train firm state within his heart.
Thou messenger of sympathies
That wax and wane in lovers' eyes—
Thou—that to human thought art nourishment,
45   Like darkness to a dying flame!
Depart not as thy shadow came,
Depart not—lest the grave should be,
Like life and fear, a dark reality.

5

While yet a boy I sought for ghosts, and sped
50   Through many a listening chamber, cave and ruin,
And starlight wood, with fearful steps pursuing
Hopes of high talk with the departed dead.
I called on poisonous names with which our youth is fed,
I was not heard—I saw them not—
55   When musing deeply on the lot
Of life, at that sweet time when winds are wooing
All vital things that wake to bring
News of buds and blossoming—
Sudden, thy shadow fell on me;
60   I shrieked, and clasped my hands in ecstasy!

---

[1] *Hymn ... Beauty* Composed during the summer of 1816, the same summer in which Shelley wrote "Mont Blanc." The concept of "intellectual beauty" is Platonic in origin and was a popular one in contemporary writing. It denotes a beauty of the soul, or the mind and its inventions, that cannot be perceived by the senses and therefore must be grasped intuitively.

[2] *Didst thou* I.e., if thou didst.

6

I vowed that I would dedicate my powers
   To thee and thine—have I not kept the vow?
   With beating heart and streaming eyes, even now
I call the phantoms of a thousand hours
65 Each from his voiceless grave: they have in visioned
     bowers
       Of studious zeal or love's delight
       Outwatched with me the envious night—
They know that never joy illumed my brow
       Unlinked with hope that thou wouldst free
70   This world from its dark slavery,
       That thou—O awful LOVELINESS,
Wouldst give whate'er these words cannot express.

7

The day becomes more solemn and serene
   When noon is past— there is a harmony
75   In autumn, and a lustre in its sky,
Which through the summer is not heard or seen,
As if it could not be, as if it had not been!
       Thus let thy power, which like the truth
       Of nature on my passive youth
80 Descended, to my onward life supply
       Its calm—to one who worships thee,
       And every form containing thee,
       Whom, SPIRIT fair, thy spells did bind
To fear° himself, and love all human kind.   *revere*
—1817

Ozymandias[1]

I met a traveller from an antique land
  Who said: Two vast and trunkless legs of stone
Stand in the desert ... Near them, on the sand,
Half sunk, a shattered visage lies, whose frown,
5 And wrinkled lip, and sneer of cold command,

Tell that its sculptor well those passions read
Which yet survive, stamped on these lifeless things,
The hand that mocked them, and the heart that fed:
And on the pedestal these words appear:
10 "My name is Ozymandias, king of kings:
Look on my works, ye Mighty, and despair!"
Nothing beside remains. Round the decay
Of that colossal wreck, boundless and bare
The lone and level sands stretch far away.
—1818

Ode to the West Wind[2]

I

O Wild West Wind, thou breath[3] of Autumn's
     being,
Thou, from whose unseen presence the leaves dead
Are driven, like ghosts from an enchanter fleeing,

Yellow, and black, and pale, and hectic° red,   *feverish*
5 Pestilence-stricken multitudes: O thou,
Who chariotest to their dark wintry bed

The winged seeds, where they lie cold and low,
Each like a corpse within its grave, until
Thine azure sister of the Spring shall blow

10 Her clarion[4] o'er the dreaming earth, and fill
(Driving sweet buds like flocks to feed in air)
With living hues and odours plain and hill:

Wild Spirit, which art moving everywhere;
Destroyer and Preserver; hear, oh, hear!

---

1 *Ozymandias* Greek name for King Ramses II of Egypt (1304–1237 BCE). First century BCE Greek historian Diodorus Siculus records the story of this monument (Ozymandias's tomb was in the shape of a male sphinx) and its inscription, which Diodorus says reads: "King of Kings am I, Ozymandias. If anyone would know how great I am and where I lie, let him surpass one of my exploits."

2 [Shelley's note] This poem was conceived and chiefly written in a wood that skirts the Arno, near Florence, and on a day when that tempestuous wind, whose temperature is at once mild and animating, was collecting the vapours which pour down the autumnal rains. They began, as I foresaw, at sunset with a violent tempest of hail and rain, attended by that magnificent thunder and lightning peculiar to the Cispaline regions.

3 *breath* The Latin word for wind, *spiritus*, also means "breath" and "soul," and is the root of the word "inspiration."

4 *clarion* High-pitched trumpet.

2

15 Thou on whose stream, 'mid the steep sky's commotion,
Loose clouds like earth's decaying leaves are shed,
Shook from the tangled boughs of Heaven and Ocean,

Angels° of rain and lightning: there are spread   *harbingers*
On the blue surface of thine aëry surge,
20 Like the bright hair uplifted from the head

Of some fierce Mænad,[1] even from the dim verge
Of the horizon to the zenith's height,
The locks of the approaching storm. Thou dirge

Of the dying year, to which this closing night
25 Will be the dome of a vast sepulchre,
Vaulted with all thy congregated might

Of vapours,° from whose solid atmosphere   *clouds*
Black rain, and fire, and hail will burst: oh, hear!

3

Thou who didst waken from his summer dreams
30 The blue Mediterranean, where he lay,
Lulled by the coil of his chrystàlline streams,[2]

Beside a pumice isle in Baiae's bay,[3]
And saw in sleep old palaces and towers
Quivering within the wave's intenser day,

35 All overgrown with azure moss and flowers
So sweet, the sense faints picturing them! Thou
For whose path the Atlantic's level powers

Cleave themselves into chasms, while far below
The sea-blooms and the oozy woods which wear
40 The sapless foliage of the ocean, know

Thy voice, and suddenly grow gray with fear,
And tremble and despoil themselves:[4] oh, hear!

4

If I were a dead leaf thou mightest bear;
If I were a swift cloud to fly with thee;
45 A wave to pant beneath thy power, and share

The impulse of thy strength, only less free
Than thou, O uncontrollable! If even
I were as in my boyhood, and could be

The comrade of thy wanderings over Heaven,
50 As then, when to outstrip thy skiey speed
Scarce seemed a vision; I would ne'er have striven

As thus with thee in prayer in my sore need.
Oh! lift me as a wave, a leaf, a cloud!
I fall upon the thorns of life! I bleed!

55 A heavy weight of hours has chained and bowed
One too like thee: tameless, and swift, and proud.

5

Make me thy lyre,[5] even as the forest is:
What if my leaves are falling like its own!
The tumult of thy mighty harmonies

60 Will take from both a deep, autumnal tone,
Sweet though in sadness. Be thou, Spirit fierce,
My spirit! Be thou me, impetuous one!

Drive my dead thoughts over the universe
Like withered leaves to quicken a new birth!
65 And, by the incantation of this verse,

---

1 *Mænad* Female attendant of Bacchus, the Greek god of wine.

2 *coil ... streams* Currents of the Mediterranean, the color of which are often different from the surrounding water.

3 *pumice* Porous stone made from cooled lava; *Baiae's bay* Bay west of Naples that contains the ruins of several imperial villas.

4 [Shelley's note] The phenomenon alluded to at the conclusion of the third stanza is well known to naturalists. The vegetation at the bottom of the sea, of rivers, and of lakes, sympathizes with that of the land in the change of seasons, and is consequently influenced by the winds which announce it.

5 *lyre* Here, an Aeolian harp, a stringed instrument that produces music when exposed to wind.

Scatter, as from an unextinguished hearth
Ashes and sparks, my words among mankind!
Be through my lips to unawakened Earth

70   The trumpet of a prophecy! O, Wind,
If Winter comes, can Spring be far behind?
—1820

The Cloud

I bring fresh showers for the thirsting flowers,
    From the seas and the streams;
I bear light shade for the leaves when laid
    In their noonday dreams.
5   From my wings are shaken the dews that waken
    The sweet buds every one,
When rocked to rest on their mother's breast,
    As she dances about the sun.
I wield the flail of the lashing hail,
10   And whiten the green plains under,
And then again I dissolve it in rain,
    And laugh as I pass in thunder.

I sift the snow on the mountains below,
    And their great pines groan aghast;
15   And all the night 'tis my pillow white,
    While I sleep in the arms of the blast,
Sublime on the towers of my skiey bowers,
    Lightning my pilot sits;
In a cavern under is fettered the thunder,
20   It struggles and howls at fits;[1]
Over earth and ocean, with gentle motion,
    This pilot is guiding me,
Lured by the love of the genii that move
    In the depths of the purple sea;
25   Over the rills, and the crags, and the hills,
    Over the lakes and the plains,
Wherever he dream, under mountain or stream,
    The Spirit he loves remains;

30   And I all the while bask in Heaven's blue smile,
    Whilst he is dissolving in rains.

The sanguine Sunrise, with his meteor eyes,
    And his burning plumes outspread,
Leaps on the back of my sailing rack,[2]
    When the morning star shines dead;
35   As on the jag of a mountain crag,
    Which an earthquake rocks and swings,
An eagle alit one moment may sit
    In the light of its golden wings.
And when Sunset may breathe, from the lit sea beneath,
40   Its ardours of rest and love,
And the crimson pall[3] of eve may fall
    From the depth of Heaven above,
With wings folded I rest, on mine aëry nest,
    As still as a brooding dove.

45   That orbèd maiden with white fire laden,
    Whom mortals call the Moon,
Glides glimmering o'er my fleece-like floor,
    By the midnight breezes strewn;
And wherever the beat of her unseen feet,
50   Which only the angels hear,
May have broken the woof° of my tent's   *weave*
    thin roof,
    The stars peep behind her and peer;
And I laugh to see them whirl and flee,
    Like a swarm of golden bees,
55   When I widen the rent in my wind-built tent,
    Till the calm rivers, lakes, and seas,
Like strips of the sky fallen through me on high,
    Are each paved with the moon and these.

I bind the Sun's throne with a burning zone,°   *belt*
60   And the Moon's with a girdle of pearl;
The volcanoes are dim, and the stars reel and swim,
    When the whirlwinds my banner unfurl.
From cape to cape, with a bridge-like shape,
    Over a torrent sea,

---

[1] *at fits* Fitfully.

[2] *rack* Mass of clouds in the upper air.

[3] *pall* Rich cloth or canopy.

65 Sunbeam-proof, I hand like a roof—
    The mountains its columns be.
The triumphal arch through which I march
    With hurricane, fire, and snow,
When the Powers of the air are chained to my chair,
70   Is the million-coloured bow;
The sphere-fire[1] above its soft colours wove,
    While the moist Earth was laughing below.

I am the daughter of Earth and Water,
    And the nursing of the Sky;
75 I pass through the pores of the ocean and shores;
    I change, but I cannot die.
For after the rain, when with never a stain
    The pavilion of Heaven is bare,
And the winds and sunbeams with their convex gleams
80   Build up the blue dome of air,
I silently laugh at my own cenotaph,[2]
    And out of the caverns of rain,
Like a child from the womb, like a ghost from the tomb,
    I arise and unbuild it again.
—1820

To a Skylark[3]

Hail to thee, blithe Spirit!
  Bird thou never wert,
That from Heaven, or near it,
    Pourest thy full heart
5 In profuse strains of unpremeditated art.

Higher still and higher
    From the earth thou springest
Like a cloud of fire;
    The blue deep thou wingest,
10 And singing still dost soar, and soaring ever singest.

In the golden lightning
    Of the sunken sun,
O'er which clouds are bright'ning,
    Thou dost float and run;
15 Like an unbodied joy whose race is just begun.

The pale purple even
    Melts around thy flight;
Like a star of Heaven,
    In the broad daylight
20 Thou art unseen, but yet I hear thy shrill delight,

Keen as are the arrows
    Of that silver sphere,[4]
Whose intense lamp narrows
    In the white dawn clear
25 Until we hardly see—we feel that it is there.

All the earth and air
    With thy voice is loud,
As, when night is bare,
    From one lonely cloud
30 The moon rains out her beams, and Heaven is
    overflowed.

What thou art we know not;
    What is most like thee?
From rainbow clouds there flow not
    Drops so bright to see
35 As from thy presence showers a rain of melody.

Like a Poet hidden
    In the light of thought,
Singing hymns unbidden,
    Till the world is wrought
40 To sympathy with hopes and fears it heeded not:

Like a high-born maiden
    In a palace-tower,
Soothing her love-laden

---

[1] *sphere-fire* I.e., sunlight.

[2] *cenotaph* Empty sepulcher; monument honoring a dead person whose body lies elsewhere.

[3] *Skylark* Small bird that sings only when in flight, and often flies so high that it cannot be easily seen.

[4] *silver sphere* I.e., the morning star.

Soul in secret hour
45 With music sweet as love, which overflows her bower:

Like a glow-worm golden
   In a dell of dew,
Scattering unbeholden
   Its aëreal hue
50 Among the flowers and grass, which screen it from the
      view:

Like a rose embowered
   In its own green leaves,
By warm winds deflowered,
   Till the scent it gives
55 Makes faint with too much sweet these heavy-wingèd
      thieves:

Sound of vernal° showers   *springtime*
   On the twinkling grass,
Rain-awakened flowers,
   All that ever was
60 Joyous, and clear, and fresh, thy music doth surpass:

Teach us, Sprite° or Bird,   *fairy*
   What sweet thoughts are thine:
I have never heard
   Praise of love or wine
65 That panted forth a flood of rapture so divine.

Chorus Hymeneal,[1]
   Or triumphal chaunt,°   *chant*
Matched with thine would be all
   But an empty vaunt,
70 A thing wherein we feel there is some hidden want.

What objects are the fountains
   Of thy happy strain?
What fields, or waves, or mountains?
   What shapes of sky or plain?
75 What love of thine own kind? what ignorance of pain?

With thy clear keen joyance
   Languor cannot be:
Shadow of annoyance
   Never came near thee:
80 Thou lovest—but ne'er knew love's sad satiety.

Waking or asleep,
   Thou of death must deem
Things more true and deep
   Than we mortals dream,
85 Or how could thy notes flow in such a crystal stream?

We look before and after,
   And pine for what is not:
Our sincerest laughter
   With some pain is fraught;
90 Our sweetest songs are those that tell of saddest thought.

Yet if we could scorn
   Hate, and pride, and fear;
If we were things born
   Not to shed a tear,
95 I know not how thy joy we ever should come near.

Better than all measures
   Of delightful sound,
Better than all treasures
   That in books are found,
100 Thy skill to poet were, thou scorner of the ground!

Teach me half the gladness
   That thy brain must know,
Such harmonious madness
   From my lips would flow
105 The world should listen then—as I am listening now.
   —1820

---

[1] *Hymeneal* Marital (Hymen is the Greek god of marriage).

Prometheus Unbound

Shelley's lyrical drama *Prometheus Unbound*, written between 1818 and 1820 and published in 1820, takes as its foundation two plays by Greek playwright Aeschylus: *Prometheus Bound* and its lost sequel (or what is known of it), *Prometheus Unbound*. In the first play, Aeschylus takes as his subject the mythological Prometheus, a Titan who stole fire from the gods and brought it to humankind. As punishment, Jupiter (Zeus), the king of the Olympian gods, chained Prometheus to a rock at Mount Caucasus, where a vulture would daily feed on his liver, which regenerated nightly. Aeschylus's sequel supposedly staged a reconciliation between Prometheus and the king of the gods, and the subsequent freeing of Prometheus.

With the morality, characters, and rich storylines of classical myth, Shelley combines biblical references and allusion to Milton's *Paradise Lost*'s epic battle of good and evil (among other sources) and a distinctly Romantic sense of the sublime to create his ideal vision of human freedom. *Prometheus Unbound* touches on the psychological nature of tyranny, slavery, and true freedom and happiness. In Prometheus's triumph over his hatred and anger at Jupiter, his desire for revenge, and his possible despair at the visions of humanity's errors shown to him by the terrible Furies, Shelley argues that successful revolution must come from within. It is not political, external revolution that will ultimately triumph, but a moral revolution of each citizen. His ideal of "moral excellence" shows, in the place of greed, vengeance, hatred, and contempt, the cultivation of selfless love, and the resulting potential for a truly reformed society.

Shelley originally planned his play as encompassing only the first three acts (included here), which deal with Prometheus and focus on individual reform. He returned to the play after a few months, however, to add a final act describing his vision of the new society, extending his idea of reform of the individual psyche to a cosmic level.

from *Prometheus Unbound, a Lyrical Drama in Four Acts*[1]

Audisne haec Amphiarae, sub terram adbite?[2]

PREFACE

The Greek tragic writers, in selecting as their subject any portion of their national history or mythology, employed in their treatment of it a certain arbitrary discretion. They by no means conceived themselves bound to adhere to the common interpretation or to imitate in story as in title their rivals and predecessors. Such a system would have amounted to a resignation of those claims to preference over their competitors which incited the composition. The Agamemnonian story[3] was exhibited on the Athenian theatre with as many variations as dramas.

I have presumed to employ a similar license. The "Prometheus Unbound" of Aeschylus supposed the reconciliation of Jupiter with his victim as the price of the disclosure of the danger threatened to his empire by the consummation of his marriage with Thetis. Thetis, according to this view of the subject, was given in marriage to Peleus, and Prometheus, by the permission of Jupiter, delivered from his captivity by Hercules. Had I framed my story on this model, I should have done no more than have attempted to restore the lost drama of Aeschylus; an ambition which, if my preference to this mode of treating the subject had incited me to cherish, the recollection of the high comparison such an attempt would challenge might well abate. But, in truth, I was averse from a catastrophe so feeble as that of reconciling the Champion with the Oppressor of mankind. The

---

[1] *Prometheus Unbound ... Acts*   The three-act version is presented here.

[2] *Audisne ... adbite*   Latin: Do you hear this, Amphiarus, hidden beneath the earth? This is a quotation from *Epigoni*, a lost drama by ancient Greek playwright Aeschylus. Amphiarus, a seer, was saved from his enemies by Zeus, who threw a lightning bolt that opened a crack in the earth, swallowing Amphiarus.

[3] *Agamemnonian story*   Aeschylus's play *Agamemnon* (written c. 458 BCE).

moral interest of the fable, which is so powerfully sustained by the sufferings and endurance of Prometheus, would be annihilated if we could conceive of him as unsaying his high language and quailing before his successful and perfidious[1] adversary. The only imaginary being resembling in any degree Prometheus, is Satan; and Prometheus is, in my judgement, a more poetical character than Satan, because, in addition to courage, and majesty, and firm and patient opposition to omnipotent force, he is susceptible of being described as exempt from the taints of ambition, envy, revenge, and a desire for personal aggrandisement, which, in the Hero of "Paradise Lost," interfere with the interest. The character of Satan engenders in the mind a pernicious casuistry[2] which leads us to weigh his faults with his wrongs, and to excuse the former because the latter exceed all measure. In the minds of those who consider that magnificent fiction with a religious feeling it engenders something worse. But Prometheus is, as it were, the type of the highest perfection of moral and intellectual nature, impelled by the purest and the truest motives to the best and noblest ends.

This Poem was chiefly written upon the mountainous ruins of the Baths of Caracalla, among the flowery glades, and thickets of odoriferous blossoming trees, which are extended in ever winding labyrinths upon its immense platforms and dizzy arches suspended in the air. The bright blue sky of Rome, and the effect of the vigorous awakening spring in that divinest climate, and the new life with which it drenches the spirits even to intoxication, were the inspiration of this drama.

The imagery which I have employed will be found, in many instances, to have been drawn from the operations of the human mind, or from those external actions by which they are expressed. This is unusual in modern poetry, although Dante and Shakespeare are full of instances of the same kind: Dante indeed more than any other poet, and with greater success. But the Greek poets, as writers to whom no resource of awakening the sympathy of their contemporaries was unknown, were

in the habitual use of this power; and it is the study of their works (since a higher merit would probably be denied me) to which I am willing that my readers should impute this singularity.

One word is due in candour to the degree in which the study of contemporary writings may have tinged my composition, for such has been a topic of censure with regard to poems far more popular, and indeed more deservedly popular, than mine. It is impossible that anyone who inhabits the same age with such writers as those who stand in the foremost ranks of our own, can conscientiously assure himself that his language and tone of thought may not have been modified by the study of the productions of those extraordinary intellects. It is true, that, not the spirit of their genius, but the forms in which it has manifested itself, are due less to the peculiarities of their own minds than to the peculiarity of the moral and intellectual condition of the minds among which they have been produced. Thus a number of writers possess the form, whilst they want the spirit of those whom, it is alleged, they imitate; because the former is the endowment of the age in which they live, and the latter must be the uncommunicated lightning of their own mind.

The peculiar style of intense and comprehensive imagery which distinguishes the modern literature of England has not been, as a general power, the product of the imitation of any particular writer. The mass of capabilities remains at every period materially the same; the circumstances which awaken it to action perpetually change. If England were divided into forty republics, each equal in population and extent to Athens, there is no reason to suppose but that, under institutions not more perfect than those of Athens, each would produce philosophers and poets equal to those who (if we except Shakespeare) have never been surpassed. We owe the great writers of the golden age of our literature to that fervid awakening of the public mind which shook to dust the oldest and most oppressive form of the Christian religion. We owe Milton to the progress and development of the same spirit: the sacred Milton was,

---

[1] *perfidious* Treacherous; faithless.

[2] *casuistry* Reasoning regarding morality.

let it ever be remembered, a republican,[1] and a bold inquirer into morals and religion. The great writers of our own age are, we have reason to suppose, the companions and forerunners of some unimagined change in our social condition or the opinions which cement it. The cloud of mind is discharging its collected lightning, and the equilibrium between institutions and opinions is now restoring, or is about to be restored.

As to imitation, poetry is a mimetic art. It creates, but it creates by combination and representation. Poetical abstractions are beautiful and new, not because the portions of which they are composed had no previous existence in the mind of man or in nature, but because the whole produced by their combination has some intelligible and beautiful analogy with those sources of emotion and thought, and with the contemporary condition of them: one great poet is a masterpiece of nature which another not only ought to study but must study. He might as wisely and as easily determine that his mind should no longer be the mirror of all that is lovely in the visible universe as exclude from his contemplation the beautiful which exists in the writings of a great contemporary. The pretence of doing it would be a presumption in any but the greatest; the effect, even in him, would be strained, unnatural and ineffectual. A poet is the combined product of such internal powers as modify the nature of others; and of such external influences as excite and sustain these powers; he is not one, but both. Every man's mind is, in this respect, modified by all the objects of nature and art; by every word and every suggestion which he ever admitted to act upon his consciousness; it is the mirror upon which all forms are reflected, and in which they compose one form. Poets, not otherwise than philosophers, painters, sculptors and musicians, are, in one sense, the creators, and, in another, the creations, of their age. From this subjection the loftiest do not escape. There is a similarity between Homer and Hesiod, between Aeschylus and Euripides, between Virgil and Horace, between Dante and Petrarch, between Shakespeare and Fletcher, between Dryden and Pope; each has a generic resemblance under which their specific distinctions are arranged. If this similarity be the result of imitation, I am willing to confess that I have imitated.

Let this opportunity be conceded to me of acknowledging that I have what a Scotch philosopher characteristically terms, "a passion for reforming the world":[2] what passion incited him to write and publish his book, he omits to explain. For my part I had rather be damned with Plato and Lord Bacon, than go to Heaven with Paley and Malthus.[3] But it is a mistake to suppose that I dedicate my poetical compositions solely to the direct enforcement of reform, or that I consider them in any degree as containing a reasoned system on the theory of human life. Didactic poetry is my abhorrence; nothing can be equally well expressed in prose that is not tedious and supererogatory in verse. My purpose has hitherto been simply to familiarise the highly refined imagination of the more select classes of poetical readers with beautiful idealisms of moral excellence; aware that until the mind can love, and admire, and trust, and hope, and endure, reasoned principles of moral conduct are seeds cast upon the highway of life which the unconscious passenger tramples into dust, although they would bear the harvest of his happiness. Should I live to accomplish what I purpose, that is, produce a systematical history of what appear to me to be the genuine elements of human society, let not the advocates of injustice and superstition flatter themselves that I should take Aeschylus rather than Plato as my model.

The having spoken of myself with unaffected freedom will need little apology with the candid; and let the uncandid consider that they injure me less than their own hearts and minds by misrepresentation. Whatever talents a person may possess to amuse and instruct others, be they ever so inconsiderable, he is yet bound to

---

[1] *republican* I.e., Milton advocated the overthrow of the monarchy and England's transition to a republic.

[2] *Scotch philosopher ... world* The Scottish philosopher is Robert Forsyth (1766–1845), and the quotation is the title of chapter 16 of his *Principles of Moral Science* (1805).

[3] *Paley and Malthus* William Paley (1743–1805), author of *The Principles of Moral and Political Philosophy* (1785), and Thomas Malthus (1766–1834), whose *Essay on the Principle of Population* (1798) argued that population increases would soon surpass increases in food supply, and that population checks were thus required. Shelley was not fond of either author's theories.

exert them: if his attempt be ineffectual, let the punishment of an unaccomplished purpose have been sufficient; let none trouble themselves to heap the dust of oblivion upon his efforts; the pile they raise will betray his grave, which might otherwise have been unknown.

DRAMATIS PERSONAE

Prometheus
Demogorgon
Jupiter
The Earth
Ocean
Apollo
Mercury
Hercules
Oceanides: Asia, Panthea, Ione
The Phantasme of Jupiter
The Spirit of the Earth
The Spirit of the Moon
Spirits of the Hours
Spirits, Echoes, Fauns, Furies

ACT 1

Scene: A Ravine of Icy Rocks in the Indian Caucus.[1] *Prometheus*[2] *is discovered bound to the Precipice. Panthea and Ione*[3] *are seated at his feet. Time, Night. During the Scene, Morning slowly breaks.*

PROMETHEUS. Monarch of Gods and Daemons,[4]
    and all Spirits
But One, who throng those bright and rolling worlds
Which Thou and I alone of living things
Behold with sleepless eyes! regard this Earth

---

1 *Indian Caucus* Said to be where civilization originated. Shelley has changed the location from that of the original Greek myth.

2 *Prometheus* In Greek myth, Prometheus, one of the Titans, took fire from the gods and gave it to humans.

3 *Panthea and Ione* These two and their third sister, Asia, are daughters of Oceanus.

4 *Monarch* I.e., Jupiter (also called Jove), king of the gods; *Daemons* Supernatural beings between gods and humans.

5 Made multitudinous with thy slaves, whom thou
Requitest for knee-worship, prayer, and praise,
And toil, and hecatombs[5] of broken hearts,
With fear and self-contempt and barren hope.
Whilst me, who am thy foe, eyeless° in hate,   *blind*
10 Hast thou made reign and triumph, to thy scorn,
O'er mine own misery and thy vain revenge.
Three thousand years of sleep-unsheltered hours,
And moments aye° divided by keen pangs   *ever*
Till they seemed years, torture and solitude,
15 Scorn and despair,—these are mine empire:—
More glorious far than that which thou surveyest
From thine unenvied throne, O Mighty God!
Almighty, had I deigned to share the shame
Of thine ill tyranny, and hung not here
20 Nailed to this wall of eagle-baffling mountain,
Black, wintry, dead, unmeasured; without herb,° *vegetation*
Insect, or beast, or shape or sound of life.
Ah me! alas, pain, pain ever, forever!

No change, no pause, no hope! Yet I endure.
25 I ask the Earth, have not the mountains felt?
I ask yon Heaven, the all-beholding Sun,
Has it not seen? The Sea, in storm or calm,
Heaven's ever-changing Shadow, spread below,
Have its deaf waves not heard my agony?
30 Ah me! alas, pain, pain ever, forever!

The crawling glaciers pierce me with the spears
Of their moon-freezing crystals; the bright chains
Eat with their burning cold into my bones.
Heaven's wingèd hound,[6] polluting from thy lips
35 His beak in poison not his own, tears up
My heart; and shapeless sights come wandering by,
The ghastly people of the realm of dream,
Mocking me: and the Earthquake-fiends are charged
To wrench the rivets from my quivering wounds
40 When the rocks split and close again behind:
While from their loud abysses howling throng
The genii° of the storm, urging the rage   *sprites*

---

5 *hecatombs* Large public sacrifices of many victims.

6 *Heaven's wingèd hound* Vulture sent by Jupiter to torture Prometheus daily.

Of whirlwind, and afflict me with keen hail.
And yet to me welcome is day and night,
45 Whether one breaks the hoar-frost of the morn,
Or starry, dim, and slow, the other climbs
The leaden-coloured east; for then they lead
The wingless, crawling Hours,[1] one among whom
—As some dark Priest hales° the reluctant victim—   *hauls*
50 Shall drag thee, cruel King, to kiss the blood
From these pale feet, which then might trample thee
If they disdained not such a prostrate slave.
Disdain! Ah, no! I pity thee. What ruin
Will hunt thee undefended through wide Heaven!
55 How will thy soul, cloven to its depth with terror,
Gape like a hell within! I speak in grief,
Not exultation, for I hate no more,
As then ere misery made me wise. The curse
Once breathed on thee I would recall.[2] Ye Mountains,
60 Whose many-voiced Echoes, through the mist
Of cataracts, flung the thunder of that spell!
Ye icy Springs, stagnant with wrinkling frost,
Which vibrated to hear me, and then crept
Shuddering through India! Thou serenest Air,
65 Through which the Sun walks burning without beams!
And ye swift Whirlwinds, who on poised wings
Hung mute and moveless o'er yon hushed abyss,
As thunder, louder than your own, made rock
The orbed world! If then my words had power,
70 Though I am changed so that aught evil wish
Is dead within; although no memory be
Of what is hate, let them not lose it now!
What was that curse? for ye all heard me speak.

FIRST VOICE (*from the Mountains*).
Thrice three hundred thousand years
75   O'er the Earthquake's couch we stood:
Oft, as men convulsed with fears,
We trembled in our multitude.

---

[1] *wingless, crawling Hours* Horae; the embodiments of the hours and
the seasons in classical mythology, were human figures with wings.

[2] *recall* Here, remember (although there is also the sense of "take
back" or "revoke").

SECOND VOICE (*from the Springs*).
Thunderbolts had parched our water,
We had been stained with bitter blood,
80 And had run mute, 'mid shrieks of slaughter,
Through a city and a solitude.

THIRD VOICE (*from the Air*).
I had clothed, since Earth uprose,
Its wastes in colours not their own,
And oft had my serene repose
85   Been cloven by many a rending groan.

FOURTH VOICE (*from the Winds*).
We had soared beneath these mountains
Unresting ages; nor had thunder,
Nor yon volcano's flaming fountains,
Nor any power above or under
90   Ever made us mute with wonder.

FIRST VOICE.
But never bowed our snowy crest
As at the voice of thine unrest.

SECOND VOICE.
Never such a sound before
To the Indian waves we bore.
95 A pilot asleep on the howling sea
Leaped up from the deck in agony,
And heard, and cried, "Ah, woe is me!"
And died as mad as the wild waves be.

THIRD VOICE.
By such dread words from Earth to Heaven
100 My still realm was never riven:°   *torn apart*
When its wound was closed, there stood
Darkness o'er the day like blood.

FOURTH VOICE.
And we shrank back: for dreams of ruin
To frozen caves our flight pursuing
105 Made us keep silence—thus—and thus—
Though silence is a hell to us.

THE EARTH.   The tongueless caverns of the craggy hills
   Cried, "Misery!" then; the hollow Heaven replied,
   "Misery!" And the Ocean's purple waves,
110   Climbing the land, howled to the lashing winds,
   And the pale nations heard it, "Misery!"

PROMETHEUS.   I hear a sound of voices: not the voice
   Which I gave forth. Mother,[1] thy sons and thou
   Scorn him, without whose all-enduring will
115   Beneath the fierce omnipotence of Jove,°   *Jupiter*
   Both they and thou had vanished, like thin mist
   Unrolled on the morning wind. Know ye not me,
   The Titan? He who made his agony
   The barrier to your else° all-conquering foe?   *otherwise*
120   Oh, rock-embosomed lawns, and snow-fed streams,
   Now seen athwart° frore° vapours,   *through | frosty*
     deep below,
   Through whose o'ershadowing woods I wandered once
   With Asia, drinking life from her loved eyes;
   Why scorns the spirit which informs ye, now
125   To commune with me? me alone, who checked,
   As one who checks a fiend-drawn charioteer,
   The falsehood and the force of him who reigns
   Supreme, and with the groans of pining slaves
   Fills your dim glens and liquid wildernesses:
130   Why answer ye not, still? Brethren!

THE EARTH.   They dare not.

PROMETHEUS.   Who dares? for I would hear that curse
    again.
   Ha, what an awful whisper rises up!
   'Tis scarce like sound: it tingles through the frame
   As lightning tingles, hovering ere it strike.
135   Speak, Spirit! from thine inorganic[2] voice
   I only know that thou art moving near
   And love. How cursed I him?

THE EARTH.   How canst thou hear
   Who knowest not the language of the dead?

---

[1] *Mother* I.e., Mother Earth.

[2] *inorganic* I.e., not coming from a physical body.

PROMETHEUS.   Thou art a living spirit; speak as they.

140 THE EARTH.   I dare not speak like life, lest Heaven's
    fell° King   *ruthless*
   Should hear, and link me to some wheel of pain
   More torturing than the one whereon I roll.
   Subtle thou art and good; and though the Gods
   Hear not this voice, yet thou art more than God,
145   Being wise and kind: earnestly hearken° now.   *listen*

PROMETHEUS.   Obscurely through my brain, like
    shadows dim,
   Sweep awful° thoughts, rapid and thick. I feel *awe inspiring*
   Faint, like one mingled in entwining love;
   Yet 'tis not pleasure.

THE EARTH.   No, thou canst not hear:
150   Thou art immortal, and this tongue is known
   Only to those who die.

PROMETHEUS.   And what art thou,
   O, melancholy Voice?

THE EARTH.   I am the Earth,
   Thy mother; she within whose stony veins,
   To the last fibre of the loftiest tree
155   Whose thin leaves trembled in the frozen air,
   Joy ran, as blood within a living frame,
   When thou didst from her bosom, like a cloud
   Of glory, arise, a spirit of keen joy!
   And at thy voice her pining sons uplifted
160   Their prostrate brows from the polluting dust,
   And our almighty Tyrant with fierce dread
   Grew pale, until his thunder chained thee here.
   Then, see those million worlds which burn and roll
   Around us: their inhabitants beheld
165   My sphered light wane in wide Heaven; the sea
   Was lifted by strange tempest, and new fire
   From earthquake-rifted mountains of bright snow
   Shook its portentous hair beneath Heaven's frown;
   Lightning and Inundation vexed the plains;
170   Blue thistles bloomed in cities; foodless toads
   Within voluptuous chambers panting crawled:

When Plague had fallen on man, and beast, and worm,
And Famine; and black blight on herb and tree;
And in the corn, and vines, and meadow-grass,
175 Teemed ineradicable poisonous weeds
Draining their growth, for my wan breast was dry
With grief; and the thin air, my breath, was stained
With the contagion of a mother's hate
Breathed on her child's destroyer; ay, I heard
180 Thy curse, the which, if thou rememberest not,
Yet my innumerable seas and streams,
Mountains, and caves, and winds, and yon wide air,
And the inarticulate people of the dead,
Preserve, a treasured spell. We meditate
185 In secret joy and hope those dreadful words,
But dare not speak them.

PROMETHEUS.   Venerable mother!
All else who live and suffer take from thee
Some comfort; flowers, and fruits, and happy sounds,
And love, though fleeting; these may not be mine.
190 But mine own words, I pray, deny me not.

THE EARTH.   They shall be told. Ere Babylon was dust,
The Magus Zoroaster,[1] my dead child,
Met his own image walking in the garden.
That apparition, sole of men, he saw.
195 For know there are two worlds of life and death:
One that which thou beholdest; but the other
Is underneath the grave, where do inhabit
The shadows of all forms that think and live
Till death unite them and they part no more;
200 Dreams and the light imaginings of men,
And all that faith creates or love desires,
Terrible, strange, sublime and beauteous shapes.
There thou art, and dost hang, a writhing shade,
'Mid whirlwind-peopled mountains; all the gods
205 Are there, and all the powers of nameless worlds,

Vast, sceptred[2] phantoms; heroes, men, and beasts;
And Demogorgon,[3] a tremendous gloom;
And he, the supreme Tyrant, on his throne
Of burning gold. Son, one of these shall utter
210 The curse which all remember. Call at will
Thine own ghost, or the ghost of Jupiter,
Hades or Typhon,[4] or what mightier Gods
From all-prolific Evil, since thy ruin,
Have sprung, and trampled on my prostrate sons.
215 Ask, and they must reply: so the revenge
Of the Supreme may sweep through vacant shades,
As rainy wind through the abandoned gate
Of a fallen palace.

PROMETHEUS.   Mother, let not aught
Of that which may be evil, pass again
220 My lips, or those of aught resembling me.
Phantasm° of Jupiter, arise, appear!   *phantom*

IONE.
My wings are folded o'er mine ears:
    My wings are crossed o'er mine eyes:
Yet through their silver shade appears,
225   And through their lulling plumes arise,
A Shape, a throng of sounds;
    May it be no ill to thee
O thou of many wounds!
    Near whom, for our sweet sister's sake,
230 Ever thus we watch and wake.

PANTHEA.
The sound is of whirlwind underground,
    Earthquake, and fire, and mountains cloven;
The shape is awful like the sound,
    Clothed in dark purple, star-inwoven.
235 A sceptre of pale gold

---

[2] *sceptred* I.e., carrying sceptres, ornamental rods symbolizing royal authority.

[3] *Demogorgon* Mysterious, great deity often associated with magic rites; also, a primordial god of classical mythology.

[4] *Hades* King of the underworld; *Typhon* Monstrous giant with a hundred fire-breathing heads who lay imprisoned under volcanic Mt. Etna.

---

[1] *Magus Zoroaster* Zoroaster, or Zarathustra, was a sixth- or seventh-century Persian king who founded a dualistic religion based on an opposition between fire and light (worshipped as good) and darkness and evil. A Priest of this religion was called a "Magus" (plural: Magi).

To stay steps proud, o'er the slow cloud
His veined hand doth hold.
Cruel he looks, but calm and strong,
Like one who does, not suffers wrong.

PHANTASM OF JUPITER.   Why have the secret powers
   of this strange world
  Driven me, a frail and empty phantom, hither
  On direst storms? What unaccustomed sounds
  Are hovering on my lips, unlike the voice
  With which our pallid race hold ghastly talk
245 In darkness? And, proud sufferer, who art thou?

PROMETHEUS.   Tremendous Image, as thou art must be
  He whom thou shadowest forth. I am his foe,
  The Titan. Speak the words which I would hear,
  Although no thought inform thine empty voice.

250 THE EARTH.   Listen! And though your echoes must be
   mute,
  Grey mountains, and old woods, and haunted springs,
  Prophetic caves, and isle-surrounding streams,
  Rejoice to hear what yet ye cannot speak.

PHANTASM.   A spirit seizes me and speaks within:
255 It tears me as fire tears a thunder cloud.

PANTHEA.   See, how he lifts his mighty looks, the Heaven
  Darkens above.

IONE.   He speaks! O shelter me!

PROMETHEUS.   I see the curse on gestures proud and cold,
  And looks of firm defiance, and calm hate,
260 And such despair as mocks itself with smiles,
  Written as on a scroll: yet speak! Oh, speak!

PHANTASM.   Fiend, I defy thee! with a calm, fixed mind,
  All that thou canst inflict I bid thee do;
  Foul Tyrant both of Gods and Humankind,
65   One only being shalt thou not subdue.
  Rain then thy plagues upon me here,
  Ghastly disease, and frenzying fear;

And let alternate frost and fire
Eat into me, and be thine ire
270 Lightning, and cutting hail, and legioned forms
Of furies, driving by upon the wounding storms.

Ay, do thy worst. Thou art omnipotent.
   O'er all things but thyself I gave thee power,
  And my own will. Be thy swift mischiefs sent
275   To blast mankind, from yon ethereal tower.
Let thy malignant spirit move
In darkness over those I love:
On me and mine I imprecate°   *invoke*
The utmost torture of thy hate;
280 And thus devote to sleepless agony,
This undeclining head while thou must reign on high.

But thou, who art the God and Lord: O, thou,
   Who fillest with thy soul this world of woe,
To whom all things of Earth and Heaven do bow
285   In fear and worship: all-prevailing foe!
I curse thee! let a sufferer's curse
Clasp thee, his torturer, like remorse;
Till thine Infinity shall be
A robe of envenomed agony;[1]
290 And thine Omnipotence a crown of pain,[2]
To cling like burning gold round thy dissolving brain.

Heap on thy soul, by virtue of this Curse,
   Ill deeds, then be thou damned, beholding good;
Both infinite as is the universe,
295   And thou, and thy self-torturing solitude.
An awful image of calm power
Though now thou sittest, let the hour
Come, when thou must appear to be
That which thou art internally;
300 And after many a false and fruitless crime
Scorn track thy lagging fall through boundless space
   and time.

---

[1] *robe of envenomed agony* Reference to the poison shirt of the centaur (half man, half horse) Nessus, which Heracles put on only to have it consume his flesh.

[2] *crown of pain* Reference to Christ's crown of thorns.

PROMETHEUS.   Were these my words, O Parent?

THE EARTH.   They were thine.

PROMETHEUS.   It doth repent me: words are quick
    and vain;
   Grief for awhile is blind, and so was mine.
305 I wish no living thing to suffer pain.

THE EARTH.
    Misery, Oh misery to me,
    That Jove at length should vanquish thee.
    Wail, howl aloud, Land and Sea,
    The Earth's rent heart shall answer ye.
310 Howl, Spirits of the living and the dead,
   Your refuge, your defence, lies fallen and vanquished.

FIRST ECHO.
    Lies fallen and vanquishèd!

SECOND ECHO.
    Fallen and vanquishèd!

IONE.
    Fear not: 'tis but some passing spasm,
315   The Titan is unvanquished still.
   But see, where through the azure chasm
    Of yon forked and snowy hill
   Trampling the slant winds on high
    With golden-sandalled feet, that glow
320 Under plumes of purple dye,
   Like rose-ensanguined[1] ivory,
    A Shape comes now,
   Stretching on high from his right hand
    A serpent-cinctured wand.[2]

325 PANTHEA.   'Tis Jove's world-wandering herald, Mercury.

IONE.
   And who are those with hydra[3] tresses
    And iron wings that climb the wind,
   Whom the frowning God represses
    Like vapours steaming up behind,
330 Clanging loud, an endless crowd—

PANTHEA.
    These are Jove's tempest-walking hounds,[4]
   Whom he gluts with groans and blood,
   When charioted on sulphurous cloud
    He bursts Heaven's bounds.

IONE.
335 Are they now led, from the thin dead
   On new pangs to be fed?

PANTHEA.   The Titan looks as ever, firm, not proud.

FIRST FURY.   Ha! I scent life!

SECOND FURY.   Let me but look into his eyes!

THIRD FURY.   The hope of torturing him smells like a heap
340 Of corpses, to a death-bird after battle.

FIRST FURY.   Darest thou delay, O Herald! take cheer,
  Hounds
Of Hell: what if the Son of Maia[5] soon
Should make us food and sport—who can please long
The Omnipotent?

MERCURY.   Back to your towers of iron,
345 And gnash, beside the streams of fire and wail,[6]
Your foodless teeth. Geryon, arise! and Gorgon,

---

[1] *rose-ensanguined* Stained rose-colored with blood.

[2] *serpent-cinctured wand* The staff, or caduceus, encircled by two facing snakes is the symbol of peace carried by Mercury, the messenger of the Gods.

[3] *hydra* Mythological many-headed snake.

[4] *tempest-walking hounds* Three Furies, avengers of crime.

[5] *Son of Maia* Mercury.

[6] *streams of fire and wail* A reference to the two rivers in Hades, the underworld. "Wail" here is a noun, referring to cries of lamentation, the sound of wailing.

Chimaera, and thou Sphinx,[1] subtlest of fiends
Who ministered to Thebes Heaven's poisoned wine,
Unnatural love, and more unnatural hate:
50 These shall perform your task.

FIRST FURY.   Oh, mercy! mercy!
We die with our desire: drive us not back!

MERCURY. Crouch then in silence.
                          Awful° Sufferer! *awe inspiring*
To thee unwilling, most unwillingly
I come, by the great Father's will driven down,
55 To execute a doom of new revenge.
Alas! I pity thee, and hate myself
That I can do no more: aye from thy sight
Returning, for a season, Heaven seems Hell,
So thy worn form pursues me night and day,
60 Smiling reproach. Wise art thou, firm and good,
But vainly wouldst stand forth alone in strife
Against the Omnipotent; as yon clear lamps
That measure and divide the weary years
From which there is no refuge, long have taught
65 And long must teach. Even now thy Torturer arms
With the strange might of unimagined pains
The powers who scheme slow agonies in Hell,
And my commission is to lead them here,
Or what more subtle, foul, or savage fiends
70 People the abyss, and leave them to their task.
Be it not so! there is a secret known
To thee, and to none else of living things,
Which may transfer the sceptre of wide Heaven,
The fear of which perplexes the Supreme:
75 Clothe it in words, and bid it clasp his throne
In intercession; bend thy soul in prayer,

---

[1] *Geryon* Three-headed, three-bodied mythological monster; *Gorgon* I.e., Medusa, one of the three Gorgons, mythological monsters with snakes for hair, whose gaze turned onlookers to stone; *Chimaera* Monster with the head of a lion, body of a goat, and tail of a snake (or sometimes said to have three heads—one goat, one lion, one serpent); *Sphinx* Monster with the head of a woman, wings, and the body of a lion. The following lines refer to the Sphinx's riddle, which she put to the citizens of Thebes, killing those who could not answer. Oedipus solved the riddle, prompting the Sphinx to kill herself, but this led to his unknowingly marrying his own mother, Jocasta, and, later, his cursing his two sons to kill each other.

And like a suppliant in some gorgeous fane,°   *temple*
Let the will kneel within thy haughty heart:
For benefits and meek submission tame
380 The fiercest and the mightiest.

PROMETHEUS.   Evil minds
Change good to their own nature. I gave all
He has; and in return he chains me here
Years, ages, night and day: whether the Sun
Split my parched skin, or in the moony night
385 The crystal-wingèd snow cling round my hair:
Whilst my belovèd race is trampled down
By his thought-executing ministers.
Such is the tyrant's recompense: 'tis just:
He who is evil can receive no good;
390 And for a world bestowed, or a friend lost,
He can feel hate, fear, shame; not gratitude:
He but requites me for his own misdeed.
Kindness to such is keen reproach, which breaks
With bitter stings the light sleep of Revenge.
395 Submission, thou dost know I cannot try:
For what submission but that fatal word,
The death-seal of mankind's captivity,
Like the Sicilian's hair-suspended sword,[2]
Which trembles o'er his crown, would he accept,
400 Or could I yield? Which yet I will not yield.
Let others flatter Crime, where it sits throned
In brief Omnipotence: secure are they:
For Justice, when triumphant, will weep down
Pity, not punishment, on her own wrongs,
405 Too much avenged by those who err. I wait,
Enduring thus, the retributive hour
Which since we spake is even nearer now.
But hark,° the hell-hounds clamour: fear delay: *listen*
Behold! Heaven lowers° under thy Father's frown.   *cowers*

410 MERCURY. Oh, that we might be spared; I to inflict
And thou to suffer! Once more answer me:

---

[2] *Sicilian's ... sword* Damocles, after commenting that Dionysius I of Syracuse, Sicily, was the happiest man on earth because of his wealth, was made to dine sitting on Dionysius's throne with a sword, dangling by a single horse hair, suspended above his head, thus illustrating the insecurity of a ruler's position.

Thou knowest not the period° of Jove's power? *conclusion*

PROMETHEUS.   I know but this, that it must come.

MERCURY.   Alas!
Thou canst not count thy years to come of pain?

415   PROMETHEUS.   They last while Jove must reign: nor
        more, nor less
Do I desire or fear.

MERCURY.   Yet pause, and plunge
Into Eternity, where recorded time,
Even all that we imagine, age on age,
Seems but a point, and the reluctant mind
420   Flags wearily in its unending flight,
Till it sink, dizzy, blind, lost, shelterless;
Perchance it has not numbered the slow years
Which thou must spend in torture, unreprieved?

PROMETHEUS.   Perchance no thought can count them,
        yet they pass.

425   MERCURY.   If thou might'st dwell among the Gods the
        while
Lapped in voluptuous joy?

PROMETHEUS.   I would not quit
This bleak ravine, these unrepentant pains.

MERCURY.   Alas! I wonder at, yet pity thee.

PROMETHEUS.   Pity the self-despising slaves of Heaven,
430   Not me, within whose mind sits peace serene.
As light in the sun, throned: how vain is talk!
Call up the fiends.

IONE.   O, sister, look! White fire
Has cloven to the roots yon huge snow-loaded cedar;
How fearfully God's thunder howls behind!

435   MERCURY.   I must obey his words and thine: alas!
Most heavily remorse hangs at my heart!

PANTHEA.   See where the child of Heaven, with
        wingèd feet,
Runs down the slanted sunlight of the dawn.

IONE.   Dear sister, close thy plumes over thine eyes
440   Lest thou behold and die: they come: they come
Blackening the birth of day with countless wings,
And hollow underneath, like death.

FIRST FURY.   Prometheus!

SECOND FURY.   Immortal Titan!

THIRD FURY.   Champion of Heaven's slaves!

PROMETHEUS.   He whom some dreadful voice invokes
        is here,
445   Prometheus, the chained Titan. Horrible forms,
What and who are ye? Never yet there came
Phantasms° so foul through monster-teeming Hell *spirits*
From the all-miscreative brain of Jove;
Whilst I behold such execrable shapes,
450   Methinks I grow like what I contemplate,
And laugh and stare in loathsome sympathy.

FIRST FURY.   We are the ministers of pain, and fear,
And disappointment, and mistrust, and hate,
And clinging crime; and as lean dogs pursue
455   Through wood and lake some struck and sobbing fawn,
We track all things that weep, and bleed, and live,
When the great King betrays them to our will.

PROMETHEUS.   Oh! many fearful natures in one name,
I know ye; and these lakes and echoes know
460   The darkness and the clangour of your wings.
But why more hideous than your loathèd selves
Gather ye up in legions from the deep?

SECOND FURY.   We knew not that: Sisters, rejoice,
        rejoice!

PROMETHEUS.   Can aught exult in its deformity?

SECOND FURY.   The beauty of delight makes lovers glad,
    Gazing on one another: so are we.
    As from the rose which the pale priestess kneels
    To gather for her festal° crown of flowers   *festive*
    The aereal crimson falls, flushing her cheek,
    So from our victim's destined agony
    The shade which is our form invests us round,
    Else we are shapeless as our mother Night.

PROMETHEUS.   I laugh your power, and his who sent
        you here,
    To lowest scorn. Pour forth the cup of pain.

FIRST FURY.   Thou thinkest we will rend thee bone
        from bone,
    And nerve from nerve, working like fire within?

PROMETHEUS.   Pain is my element, as hate is thine;
    Ye rend me now; I care not.

SECOND FURY.   Dost imagine
    We will but laugh into thy lidless eyes?

PROMETHEUS.   I weigh not what ye do, but what ye suffer,
    Being evil. Cruel was the power which called
    You, or aught else so wretched, into light.

THIRD FURY.   Thou think'st we will live through thee,
        one by one,
    Like animal life, and though we can obscure not
    The soul which burns within, that we will dwell
    Beside it, like a vain loud multitude
    Vexing the self-content of wisest men:
    That we will be dread thought beneath thy brain,
    And foul desire round thine astonished heart,
    And blood within thy labyrinthine veins
    Crawling like agony?

PROMETHEUS.   Why, ye are thus now;
    Yet am I king over myself, and rule
    The torturing and conflicting throngs within,
    As Jove rules you when Hell grows mutinous.

CHORUS OF FURIES.
From the ends of the earth, from the ends of the earth,
    Where the night has its grave and the morning its birth,
        Come, come, come!
    Oh, ye who shake hills with the scream of your mirth,
    When cities sink howling in ruin; and ye
    Who with wingless footsteps trample the sea,
    And close upon Shipwreck and Famine's track,
    Sit chattering with joy on the foodless wreck;
        Come, come, come!
    Leave the bed, low, cold, and red,
    Strewed beneath a nation dead;
    Leave the hatred, as in ashes
        Fire is left for future burning:
    It will burst in bloodier flashes
        When ye stir it, soon returning:
    Leave the self-contempt implanted
    In young spirits, sense-enchanted,
        Misery's yet unkindled fuel:
    Leave Hell's secrets half unchanted
        To the maniac dreamer; cruel
    More than ye can be with hate
        Is he with fear.
        Come, come, come!
    We are steaming up from Hell's wide gate
        And we burthen the blast of the atmosphere,
        But vainly we toil till ye come here.

IONE.   Sister, I hear the thunder of new wings.

PANTHEA.   These solid mountains quiver with the sound
    Even as the tremulous air: their shadows make
    The space within my plumes more black than night.

FIRST FURY.   Your call was as a wingèd car,
    Driven on whirlwinds fast and far;
    It rapped° us from red gulfs of war.   *seized*

SECOND FURY.   From wide cities, famine-wasted;

THIRD FURY.   Groans half heard, and blood untasted;

FOURTH FURY.   Kingly conclaves stern and cold,
530   Where blood with gold is bought and sold;

FIFTH FURY.   From the furnace, white and hot,
In which—

A FURY.   Speak not: whisper not:
I know all that ye would tell,
535   But to speak might break the spell
Which must bend the Invincible,
The stern of thought;
He yet defies the deepest power of Hell.

A FURY.   Tear the veil!

ANOTHER FURY.   It is torn.

CHORUS.
                              The pale stars of the morn
540   Shine on a misery, dire to be borne.
Dost thou faint, mighty Titan? We laugh thee to scorn.
Dost thou boast the clear knowledge thou waken'dst
    for man?
Then was kindled within him a thirst which outran
Those perishing waters; a thirst of fierce fever,
545   Hope, love, doubt, desire, which consume him for ever.
    One[1] came forth of gentle worth
    Smiling on the sanguine earth;
    His words outlived him, like swift poison
        Withering up truth, peace, and pity.
550   Look! where round the wide horizon
        Many a million-peopled city
    Vomits smoke in the bright air.
    Hark that outcry of despair!
    'Tis his mild and gentle ghost
555   Wailing for the faith he kindled:
    Look again, the flames almost
        To a glow-worm's lamp have dwindled:
    The survivors round the embers
        Gather in dread.
560   Joy, joy, joy!

Past ages crowd on thee, but each one remembers,
And the future is dark, and the present is spread
Like a pillow of thorns for thy slumberless head.

SEMICHORUS 1.
Drops of bloody agony flow
565   From his white and quivering brow.
Grant a little respite now:
See a disenchanted Nation[2]
Springs like day from desolation;
To Truth its state is dedicate,
570   And Freedom leads it forth, her mate;
A legioned band of linked brothers
Whom Love calls children—

SEMICHORUS 2.
                              'Tis another's:
See how kindred murder kin:
'Tis the vintage-time for death and sin:
575   Blood, like new wine, bubbles within:
        Till Despair smothers
The struggling world, which slaves and tyrants win.[3]

[All the Furies vanish, except one.]

IONE.   Hark, sister! what a low yet dreadful groan
Quite unsuppressed is tearing up the heart
580   Of the good Titan, as storms tear the deep,
And beasts hear the sea moan in inland caves.
Darest thou observe how the fiends torture him?

PANTHEA.   Alas! I looked forth twice, but will no more.

IONE.   What didst thou see?

PANTHEA.   A woful sight: a youth°   Christ
585   With patient looks nailed to a crucifix.

IONE.   What next?

_____

[1]   One   I.e., Christ.

_____

[2]   disenchanted Nation   France before the French Revolution.

[3]   See how ... win   After the bloody Reign of Terror and the Revolutionary and Napoleonic wars, the monarchy was restored in France.

PANTHEA.   The heaven around, the earth below
  Was peopled with thick shapes of human death,
  All horrible, and wrought by human hands,
  And some appeared the work of human hearts,
590 For men were slowly killed by frowns and smiles:
  And other sights too foul to speak and live
  Were wandering by. Let us not tempt worse fear
  By looking forth: those groans are grief enough.

FURY. Behold an emblem: those who do endure
595 Deep wrongs for man, and scorn, and chains, but heap
  Thousand-fold torment on themselves and him.

PROMETHEUS. Remit the anguish of that lighted stare;
  Close those wan lips; let that thorn-wounded brow
  Stream not with blood; it mingles with thy tears!
600 Fix, fix those tortured orbs in peace and death,
  So thy sick throes shake not that crucifix,
  So those pale fingers play not with thy gore.
  O, horrible! Thy name I will not speak,
  It hath become a curse. I see, I see
605 The wise, the mild, the lofty, and the just,
  Whom thy slaves hate for being like to thee,
  Some hunted by foul lies from their heart's home,
  An early-chosen, late-lamented home;
  As hooded ounces[1] cling to the driven hind;°   *female deer*
610 Some linked to corpses in unwholesome cells:
  Some—Hear I not the multitude laugh loud?—
  Impaled in lingering fire: and mighty realms
  Float by my feet, like sea-uprooted isles,
  Whose sons are kneaded down in common blood
615 By the red light of their own burning homes.

FURY. Blood thou canst see, and fire; and canst hear
    groans;
  Worse things unheard, unseen, remain behind.

PROMETHEUS. Worse?

FURY.   In each human heart terror survives

The ravin° it has gorged:° the loftiest fear   *prey / devoured*
620 All that they would disdain to think were true:
  Hypocrisy and custom make their minds
  The fanes of many a worship, now outworn.
  They dare not devise good for man's estate,
  And yet they know not that they do not dare.
625 The good want° power, but° to weep   *lack / except*
    barren tears.
  The powerful goodness want: worse need for them.
  The wise want love; and those who love want wisdom;
  And all best things are thus confused to ill.
  Many are strong and rich, and would be just,
630 But live among their suffering fellow-men
  As if none felt: they know not what they do.[2]

PROMETHEUS. Thy words are like a cloud of wingèd
    snakes;
  And yet I pity those they torture not.

FURY. Thou pitiest them? I speak no more!
[*Vanishes.*]

PROMETHEUS.   Ah woe!
635 Ah woe! Alas! pain, pain ever, for ever!
  I close my tearless eyes, but see more clear
  Thy works within my woe-illumèd mind,
  Thou subtle tyrant! Peace is in the grave.
  The grave hides all things beautiful and good:
640 I am a God and cannot find it there,
  Nor would I seek it: for, though dread revenge,
  This is defeat, fierce king, not victory.
  The sights with which thou torturest gird° my soul   *brace*
  With new endurance, till the hour arrives
645 When they shall be no types of things which are.

PANTHEA. Alas! what sawest thou more?

PROMETHEUS.   There are two woes:
  To speak, and to behold; thou spare me one.
  Names are there, Nature's sacred watchwords, they
  Were borne aloft in bright emblazonry;

---

1 *ounces* Medium-sized wild cats such as cheetahs or lynxes. Cheetahs were sometimes hooded (making them easier to control) and used for hunting.

2 *they know not what they do* Words spoken by Christ on the cross (see Luke 23.34) to beg his father to forgive those who torture him.

650 The nations thronged around, and cried aloud,
As with one voice, Truth, liberty, and love!
Suddenly fierce confusion fell from heaven
Among them: there was strife, deceit, and fear:
Tyrants rushed in, and did divide the spoil.
655 This was the shadow of the truth I saw.

THE EARTH.   I felt thy torture, son; with such mixed joy
As pain and virtue give. To cheer thy state
I bid ascend those subtle and fair spirits,
Whose homes are the dim caves of human thought,
660 And who inhabit, as birds wing the wind,
Its world-surrounding aether: they behold
Beyond that twilight realm, as in a glass,°   *mirror*
The future: may they speak comfort to thee!

PANTHEA.   Look, sister, where a troop of spirits gather,
665 Like flocks of clouds in spring's delightful weather,
Thronging in the blue air!

IONE.   And see! more come,
Like fountain-vapours when the winds are dumb,
That climb up the ravine in scattered lines.
And, hark! is it the music of the pines?
670 Is it the lake? Is it the waterfall?

PANTHEA.   'Tis something sadder, sweeter far than all.

CHORUS OF SPIRITS.
From unremembered ages we
Gentle guides and guardians be
Of heaven-oppressed mortality;
675 And we breathe, and sicken not,
The atmosphere of human thought:
Be it dim, and dank, and gray,
Like a storm-extinguished day,
Travelled o'er by dying gleams;
680   Be it bright as all between
Cloudless skies and windless streams,
    Silent, liquid, and serene;
As the birds within the wind,
    As the fish within the wave,
685 As the thoughts of man's own mind

Float through all above the grave;
We make there our liquid lair,
Voyaging cloudlike and unpent°   *unconfined*
Through the boundless element:
690 Thence we bear the prophecy
Which begins and ends in thee!

IONE.   More yet come, one by one: the air around them
Looks radiant as the air around a star.

FIRST SPIRIT.   On a battle-trumpet's blast
695 I fled hither, fast, fast, fast,
'Mid the darkness upward cast.
From the dust of creeds outworn,
From the tyrant's banner torn,
Gathering round me, onward borne,
700 There was mingled many a cry—
Freedom! Hope! Death! Victory!
Till they faded through the sky;
And one sound, above, around,
One sound beneath, around, above,
705 Was moving; 'twas the soul of Love;
'Twas the hope, the prophecy,
Which begins and ends in thee.

SECOND SPIRIT.   A rainbow's arch stood on the sea,
Which rocked beneath, immovably;
710 And the triumphant storm did flee,
Like a conqueror, swift and proud,
Between, with many a captive cloud,
A shapeless, dark and rapid crowd,
Each by lightning riven° in half: *split*
715 I heard the thunder hoarsely laugh:
Mighty fleets were strewn like chaff
And spread beneath a hell of death
O'er the white waters. I alit
On a great ship lightning-split,
720 And speeded hither on the sigh
Of one who gave an enemy
His plank, then plunged aside to die.

THIRD SPIRIT.   I sate beside a sage's bed,
And the lamp was burning red

25 Near the book where he had fed,
When a Dream with plumes of flame,
To his pillow hovering came,
And I knew it was the same
Which had kindled long ago
30 Pity, eloquence, and woe;
And the world awhile below
Wore the shade, its lustre made.
It has borne me here as fleet
As Desire's lightning feet:
35 I must ride it back ere morrow,
Or the sage will wake in sorrow.

FOURTH SPIRIT.   On a poet's lips I slept
Dreaming like a love-adept
In the sound his breathing kept;
40 Nor seeks nor finds he mortal blisses,
But feeds on the aereal kisses
Of shapes that haunt thought's wildernesses.
He will watch from dawn to gloom
The lake-reflected sun illume
45 The yellow bees in the ivy-bloom,
Nor° heed nor see, what things they be;   neither
But from these create he can
Forms more real than living man,
Nurslings° of immortality!   children
50 One of these awakened me,
And I sped to succour° thee.   help

IONE.   Behold'st thou not two shapes from the East
and West
Come, as two doves to one belovèd nest,
Twin nurslings of the all-sustaining air
55 On swift still wings glide down the atmosphere?
And, hark! their sweet sad voices! 'tis despair
Mingled with love and then dissolved in sound.

PANTHEA.   Canst thou speak, sister? all my words are
drowned.

IONE.   Their beauty gives me voice. See how they float
60 On their sustaining wings of skiey grain,

Orange and azure deepening into gold:
Their soft smiles light the air like a star's fire.

CHORUS OF SPIRITS.   Hast thou beheld the form of Love?

FIFTH SPIRIT.   As over wide dominions
I sped, like some swift cloud that wings the wide air's
wilderness,
765 That planet-crested shape[1] swept by on lightning-
braided pinions,°   wings
Scattering the liquid joy of life from his
ambrosial° tresses: divine
His footsteps paved the world with light; but as I
passed 'twas fading,
And hollow Ruin yawned behind: great sages bound
in madness,
And headless patriots, and pale youths who perished,
unupbraiding,°   unreproachful
770 Gleamed in the night. I wandered o'er, till thou, O
King of sadness,
Turned by thy smile the worst I saw to recollected
gladness,

SIXTH SPIRIT.   Ah, sister! Desolation is a delicate thing:
It walks not on the earth, it floats not on the air,
But treads with lulling footstep, and fans with silent wing
775 The tender hopes which in their hearts the best and
gentlest bear;
Who, soothed to false repose by the fanning plumes
above
And the music-stirring motion of its soft and busy feet,
Dream visions of aereal joy, and call the monster, Love,
And wake, and find the shadow Pain, as he whom
now we greet.

CHORUS.

780 Though Ruin now Love's shadow be,
Following him, destroyingly,
On Death's white and wingèd steed,
Which the fleetest cannot flee,
Trampling down both flower and weed,

---

[1] *planet-crested shape*   God of Love, who wears the crest of Venus and
is associated with lightning.

PERCY BYSSHE SHELLEY

785 Man and beast, and foul and fair,
Like a tempest through the air;
Thou shalt quell this horseman grim,
Woundless though in heart or limb.

PROMETHEUS.   Spirits! how know ye this shall be?

CHORUS.

790   In the atmosphere we breathe,
As buds grow red when the snow-storms flee,
    From Spring gathering up beneath,
Whose mild winds shake the elder-brake,°   bush
And the wandering herdsmen know
795 That the white-thorn soon will blow:
Wisdom, Justice, Love, and Peace,
When they struggle to increase,
    Are to us as soft winds be
    To shepherd boys, the prophecy
800   Which begins and ends in thee.

IONE.   Where are the Spirits fled?

PANTHEA.   Only a sense
Remains of them, like the omnipotence
Of music, when the inspired voice and lute
Languish, ere yet the responses are mute,
805 Which through the deep and labyrinthine soul,
Like echoes through long caverns, wind and roll.

PROMETHEUS.   How fair these airborn shapes! and yet
   I feel
Most vain all hope but love; and thou art far,
Asia! who, when my being overflowed,
810 Wert like a golden chalice to bright wine
Which else had sunk into the thirsty dust.
All things are still: alas! how heavily
This quiet morning weighs upon my heart;
Though I should dream I could even sleep with grief
815 If slumber were denied not. I would fain
Be what it is my destiny to be,
The saviour and the strength of suffering man,
Or sink into the original gulf of things:

There is no agony, and no solace left;
820 Earth can console, Heaven can torment no more.

PANTHEA.   Hast thou forgotten one who watches thee
The cold dark night, and never sleeps but when
The shadow of thy spirit falls on her?

PROMETHEUS.   I said all hope was vain but love: thou
   lovest.

825 PANTHEA.   Deeply in truth; but the eastern star[1] looks
   white,
And Asia waits in that far Indian vale,
The scene of her sad exile; rugged once
And desolate and frozen, like this ravine;
But now invested with fair flowers and herbs,
830 And haunted by sweet airs and sounds, which flow
Among the woods and waters, from the aether
Of her transforming presence, which would fade
If it were mingled not with thine. Farewell!

[*End of Act 1.*]

ACT 2, SCENE 1

Morning. A lovely vale in the Indian Caucus. Asia alone.

ASIA.   From all the blasts of heaven thou hast descended:
Yes, like a spirit, like a thought, which makes
Unwonted° tears throng to the horny[2] eyes,   *unaccustomed*
And beatings haunt the desolated heart,
5 Which should have learnt repose: thou hast descended
Cradled in tempests; thou dost wake, O Spring!
O child of many winds! As suddenly
Thou comest as the memory of a dream,
Which now is sad because it hath been sweet;
10 Like genius, or like joy which riseth up
As from the earth, clothing with golden clouds
The desert of our life.

---

[1] *eastern star* Venus.

[2] *horny* I.e., semi-opaque, as horn is.

This is the season, this the day, the hour;
At sunrise thou shouldst come, sweet sister mine,
15 Too long desired, too long delaying, come!
How like death-worms the wingless moments crawl!
The point of one white star¹ is quivering still
Deep in the orange light of widening morn
Beyond the purple mountains: through a chasm
20 Of wind-divided mist the darker lake
Reflects it: now it wanes: it gleams again
As the waves fade, and as the burning threads
Of woven cloud unravel in pale air:
'Tis lost! and through yon peaks of cloud-like snow
25 The roseate sunlight quivers: hear I not
The Aeolian² music of her sea-green plumes
Winnowing° the crimson dawn?   *flapping*
(*Panthea Enters.*)
                                        I feel, I see
Those eyes which burn through smiles that fade in tears,
Like stars half quenched in mists of silver dew.
30 Beloved and most beautiful, who wearest
The shadow of that soul by which I live,
How late thou art! the sphered sun had climbed
The sea; my heart was sick with hope, before
The printless air felt thy belated plumes.

35 PANTHEA. Pardon, great Sister! but my wings were
        faint
With the delight of a remembered dream,
As are the noontide plumes of summer winds
Satiate with sweet flowers. I was wont to sleep
Peacefully, and awake refreshed and calm
40 Before the sacred Titan's fall, and thy
Unhappy love, had made, through use and pity,
Both love and woe familiar to my heart
As they had grown to thine: erewhile° I slept   *formerly*
Under the glaucous³ caverns of old Ocean
45 Within dim bowers of green and purple moss,
Our young Ione's soft and milky arms

---

¹ *one white star* Venus, the morning, or eastern, star.

² *Aeolian* Borne on the wind. Asia is here referring to Panthea, the
"her" of this line.

³ *glaucous* Pale-green or grayish-blue color.

Locked then, as now, behind my dark, moist hair,
While my shut eyes and cheek were pressed within
The folded depth of her life-breathing bosom:
50 But not as now, since I am made the wind
Which fails beneath the music that I bear
Of thy most wordless converse; since dissolved
Into the sense with which love talks, my rest
Was troubled and yet sweet; my waking hours
55 Too full of care and pain.

ASIA.   Lift up thine eyes,
And let me read thy dream.

PANTHEA.   As I have said
With our sea-sister at his feet I slept.
The mountain mists, condensing at our voice
Under the moon, had spread their snowy flakes,
60 From the keen ice shielding our linked sleep
Then two dreams came. One, I remember not.
But in the other his pale wound-worn limbs
Fell from Prometheus, and the azure night
Grew radiant with the glory of that form
65 Which lives unchanged within, and his voice fell
Like music which makes giddy the dim brain,
Faint with intoxication of keen joy:
"Sister of her whose footsteps pave the world
With loveliness—more fair than aught but her,
70 Whose shadow thou art—lift thine eyes on me."
I lifted them: the overpowering light
Of that immortal shape was shadowed o'er
By love; which, from his soft and flowing limbs,
And passion-parted lips, and keen, faint eyes,
75 Steamed forth like vaporous fire; an atmosphere
Which wrapped me in its all-dissolving power,
As the warm aether of the morning sun
Wraps ere it drinks some cloud of wandering dew.
I saw not, heard not, moved not, only felt
80 His presence flow and mingle through my blood
Till it became his life, and his grew mine,
And I was thus absorbed, until it passed,
And like the vapours when the sun sinks down,
Gathering again in drops upon the pines,
85 And tremulous as they, in the deep night

My being was condensed; and as the rays
Of thought were slowly gathered, I could hear
His voice, whose accents lingered ere they died
Like footsteps of weak melody: thy name
90 Among the many sounds alone I heard
Of what might be articulate; though still
I listened through the night when sound was none.
Ione wakened then, and said to me:
"Canst thou divine what troubles me to-night?
95 I always knew, what I desired before,
Nor ever found delight to wish in vain.
But now I cannot tell thee what I seek;
I know not; something sweet, since it is sweet
Even to desire; it is thy sport, false sister;
100 Thou hast discovered some enchantment old,
Whose spells have stolen my spirit as I slept
And mingled it with thine: for when just now
We kissed, I felt within thy parted lips
The sweet air that sustained me, and the warmth
105 Of the life-blood, for loss of which I faint,
Quivered between our intertwining arms."
I answered not, for the Eastern star grew pale,
But fled to thee.

ASIA.   Thou speakest, but thy words
Are as the air: I feel them not: Oh, lift
110 Thine eyes, that I may read his written soul!

PANTHEA. I lift them though they droop beneath the
      load
Of that they would express: what canst thou see
But thine own fairest shadow imaged there?

ASIA. Thine eyes are like the deep, blue, boundless
      heaven
115 Contracted to two circles underneath
Their long, fine lashes; dark, far, measureless,
Orb within orb, and line through line inwoven.

PANTHEA. Why lookest thou as if a spirit passed?

ASIA. There is a change: beyond their inmost depth
120 I see a shade, a shape: 'tis He, arrayed

In the soft light of his own smiles, which spread
Like radiance from the cloud-surrounded moon.
Prometheus, it is thine! depart not yet!
Say not those smiles that we shall meet again
125 Within that bright pavilion which their beams
Shall build o'er the waste world? The dream is told.
What shape[1] is that between us? Its rude hair
Roughens the wind that lifts it, its regard
Is wild and quick, yet 'tis a thing of air,
130 For through its gray robe gleams the golden dew
Whose stars the noon has quenched not.

DREAM.   Follow! Follow!

PANTHEA. It is mine other dream.

ASIA.   It disappears.

PANTHEA. It passes now into my mind. Methought
As we sate here, the flower-infolding buds
135 Burst on yon lightning-blasted almond tree,[2]
When swift from the white Scythian wilderness
A wind swept forth wrinkling the Earth with frost:
I looked, and all the blossoms were blown down;
But on each leaf was stamped, as the blue bells
140 Of Hyacinth tell Apollo's written grief,[3]
O, FOLLOW, FOLLOW!

ASIA.   As you speak, your words
Fill, pause by pause, my own forgotten sleep
With shapes. Methought among these lawns together
We wandered, underneath the young gray dawn,
145 And multitudes of dense white fleecy clouds
Were wandering in thick flocks along the mountains
Shepherded by the slow, unwilling wind;
And the white dew on the new-bladed grass,
Just piercing the dark earth, hung silently;
150 And there was more which I remember not:

---

[1] *shape* This is Panthea's second dream.

[2] *almond tree* In Jeremiah 1, the almond tree is a symbol of hope.

[3] *Hyacinth ... grief* Hyacinth was loved by the god Apollo but killed by the jealous Zephyrus. Apollo turned her spilled blood to flowers marked with the Greek words for "woe" and "alas."

But on the shadows of the morning clouds,
Athwart the purple mountain slope, was written
FOLLOW, O, FOLLOW! as they vanished by;
And on each herb, from which Heaven's dew had fallen,
55 The like was stamped, as with a withering fire;
A wind arose among the pines; it shook
The clinging music from their boughs, and then
Low, sweet, faint sounds, like the farewell of ghosts,
Were heard: O, FOLLOW, FOLLOW, FOLLOW ME!
60 And then I said, "Panthea, look on me."
But in the depth of those belovèd eyes
Still I saw, FOLLOW, FOLLOW!

ECHO.   Follow, follow!

PANTHEA.   The crags, this clear spring morning, mock
       our voices
As they were spirit-tongued.

ASIA.   It is some being
65 Around the crags. What fine clear sounds! O, list!

ECHOES (Unseen).
Echoes we: listen!
    We cannot stay:
As dew-stars glisten
    Then fade away—
70   Child of Ocean!¹

ASIA.   Hark! Spirits speak. The liquid responses
Of their aereal tongues yet sound.

PANTHEA.   I hear.

ECHOES.
Oh, follow, follow,
    As our voice recedeth
75 Through the caverns hollow,
    Where the forest spreadeth;
[More Distant.]
    Oh, follow, follow!

Through the caverns hollow,
As the song floats thou pursue,
180 Where the wild bee never flew,
Through the noontide darkness deep,
By the odour-breathing sleep
Of faint night-flowers, and the waves
At the fountain-lighted caves,
185 While our music, wild and sweet,
Mocks thy gently falling feet,
    Child of Ocean!

ASIA. Shall we pursue the sound? It grows more faint
       and distant.

PANTHEA.   List! the strain floats nearer now.

ECHOES.
190 In the world unknown
    Sleeps a voice unspoken;
By thy step alone
    Can its rest be broken,
       Child of Ocean!

195 ASIA.   How the notes sink upon the ebbing wind!

ECHOES.
    Oh, follow, follow!
    Through the caverns hollow,
As the song floats thou pursue,
By the woodland noontide dew;
200 By the forests, lakes, and fountains,
Through the many-folded mountains;
To the rents, and gulfs, and chasms,
Where the Earth reposed from spasms,
On the day when He and thou
205 Parted, to commingle now;
       Child of Ocean!

ASIA. Come, sweet Panthea, link thy hand in mine,
And follow, ere the voices fade away.

---

¹ *Child of Ocean* Asia, Ione, and Panthea are daughters of the ocean god Oceanus; they are referred to as Oceanides.

ACT 2, SCENE 2

*A forest, intermingled with rocks and caverns. Asia and
Panthea pass into it. Two young fauns are sitting on a
rock listening.*

SEMICHORUS 1 OF SPIRITS.
The path through which that lovely twain°   pair
    Have passed, by cedar, pine, and yew,
    And each dark tree that ever grew,
    Is curtained out from Heaven's wide blue;
5 Nor sun, nor moon, nor wind, nor rain,
      Can pierce its interwoven bowers,
    Nor aught, save where some cloud of dew,
  Drifted along the earth-creeping breeze,
  Between the trunks of the hoar° trees,   bare, gray
10   Hangs each a pearl in the pale flowers
    Of the green laurel,[1] blown° anew,   blooming
  And bends, and then fades silently,
  One frail and fair anemone:[2]
  Or when some star of many a one
15 That climbs and wanders through steep night,
  Has found the cleft through which alone
  Beams fall from high those depths upon
  Ere it is borne away, away,
  By the swift Heavens that cannot stay,
20 It scatters drops of golden light,
  Like lines of rain that ne'er unite:
  And the gloom divine is all around,
  And underneath is the mossy ground.

SEMICHORUS 2.
There the voluptuous nightingales,
25   Are awake through all the broad noonday.
  When one with bliss or sadness fails,
      And through the windless ivy-boughs,
    Sick with sweet love, droops dying away
  On its mate's music-panting bosom;
30 Another from the swinging blossom,
      Watching to catch the languid close

---

[1] *laurel* Bay laurel, whose foliage was woven into crowns to honor
poets of distinction in ancient Greece.

[2] *anemone* Plant with brilliant flowers, also known as the windflower.

Of the last strain, then lifts on high
    The wings of the weak melody,
    Till some new strain of feeling bear
35   The song, and all the woods are mute;
  When there is heard through the dim air
  The rush of wings, and rising there
    Like many a lake-surrounded flute,
  Sounds overflow the listener's brain
40 So sweet, that joy is almost pain.

SEMICHORUS 1.
There those enchanted eddies play
    Of echoes, music-tongued, which draw,
    By Demogorgon's mighty law,
    With melting rapture, or sweet awe,
45 All spirits on that secret way;
    As inland boats are driven to Ocean
  Down streams made strong with mountain-thaw:
      And first there comes a gentle sound
      To those in talk or slumber bound,
50   And wakes the destined soft emotion,—
  Attracts, impels them; those who saw
    Say from the breathing earth behind
    There steams a plume-uplifting wind
  Which drives them on their path, while they
55   Believe their own swift wings and feet
  The sweet desires within obey:
  And so they float upon their way,
  Until, still sweet, but loud and strong,
  The storm of sound is driven along,
60   Sucked up and hurrying: as they fleet
    Behind, its gathering billows meet
  And to the fatal mountain bear
  Like clouds amid the yielding air.

FIRST FAUN.   Canst thou imagine where those spirits live
65 Which make such delicate music in the woods?
  We haunt within the least frequented caves
  And closest° coverts,° and we know   secluded / shelter
    these wilds,°   wilderness
  Yet never meet them, though we hear them oft:
  Where may they hide themselves?

SECOND FAUN.   'Tis hard to tell;
70 I have heard those more skilled in spirits say,
The bubbles, which the enchantment of the sun
Sucks from the pale faint water-flowers that pave
The oozy bottom of clear lakes and pools,
Are the pavilions where such dwell and float
75 Under the green and golden atmosphere
Which noontide kindles through the woven leaves;
And when these burst, and the thin fiery air,
The which they breathed within those lucent°   luminous
        domes,
Ascends to flow like meteors through the night,
80 They ride on them, and rein their headlong speed,
And bow their burning crests, and glide in fire
Under the waters of the earth again.[1]

FIRST FAUN. If such live thus, have others other lives,
Under pink blossoms or within the bells
85 Of meadow flowers, or folded violets deep,
Or on their dying odours, when they die,
Or in the sunlight of the sphèrèd dew?

SECOND FAUN. Ay, many more which we may well
        divine.
But should we stay to speak, noontide would come,
90 And thwart° Silenus[2] find his goats   cross
        undrawn,°   unmilked
And grudge to sing those wise and lovely songs
Of Fate, and Chance, and God, and Chaos old,
And Love, and the chained Titan's woful doom,
And how he shall be loosed, and make the earth
95 One brotherhood: delightful strains which cheer
Our solitary twilights, and which charm
To silence the unenvying nightingales.

---

[1] *The bubbles ... again* These lines describe the hydrogen cycle,
through which hydrogen, released by the pond plants, rises into the air
and ignites to form what is known as the will-o'-the-wisp (or ignis
fatuus), the appearance of phosphorescent light flitting over bogs or
marshes.

[2] *Silenus* Demi-god and tutor of Bacchus (Roman god of wine,
called Dionysus in Greek myth).

ACT 2, SCENE 3

A pinnacle of rock among mountains. Asia and Panthea.

PANTHEA.   Hither the sound has borne us—to the realm
Of Demogorgon, and the mighty portal,
Like a volcano's meteor-breathing chasm,
Whence the oracular vapour is hurled up
5 Which lonely men drink wandering in their youth,
And call truth, virtue, love, genius, or joy,
That maddening wine of life, whose dregs they drain
To deep intoxication; and uplift,
Like Maenads[3] who cry loud, Evoe! Evoe!
10 The voice which is contagion to the world.

ASIA.   Fit throne for such a Power! Magnificent!
How glorious art thou, Earth! And if thou be
The shadow of some spirit lovelier still,
Though evil stain its work, and it should be
15 Like its creation, weak yet beautiful,
I could fall down and worship that and thee.
Even now my heart adoreth: Wonderful!
Look, sister, ere the vapour dim thy brain:
Beneath is a wide plain of billowy mist,
20 As a lake, paving in the morning sky,
With azure waves which burst in silver light,
Some Indian vale. Behold it, rolling on
Under the curdling winds, and islanding
The peak whereon we stand, midway, around,
25 Encinctured° by the dark and blooming forests,   circled
Dim twilight-lawns, and stream-illumèd caves,
And wind-enchanted shapes of wandering mist;
And far on high the keen sky-cleaving mountains
From icy spires of sun-like radiance fling
30 The dawn, as lifted Ocean's dazzling spray,
From some Atlantic islet scattered up,
Spangles the wind with lamp-like water-drops.
The vale is girdled with their walls, a howl
Of cataracts from their thaw-cloven ravines,
35 Satiates the listening wind, continuous, vast,
Awful as silence. Hark! the rushing snow!

---

[3] *Maenads* Female followers of Bacchus. "Evoe!" was their cry.

The sun-awakened avalanche! whose mass,
Thrice sifted by the storm, had gathered there
Flake after flake, in heaven-defying minds
40 As thought by thought is piled, till some great truth
Is loosened, and the nations echo round,
Shaken to their roots, as do the mountains now.

PANTHEA.   Look how the gusty sea of mist is breaking
In crimson foam, even at our feet! it rises
45 As Ocean at the enchantment of the moon
Round foodless men wrecked on some oozy isle.

ASIA.   The fragments of the cloud are scattered up;
The wind that lifts them disentwines my hair;
Its billows now sweep o'er mine eyes; my brain
50 Grows dizzy; see'st thou shapes within the mist?

PANTHEA.   A countenance with beckoning smiles:
      there burns
An azure fire within its golden locks!
Another and another: hark! they speak!

SONG OF SPIRITS.
      To the deep, to the deep,
55   Down, down!
      Through the shade of sleep,
      Through the cloudy strife
      Of Death and of Life;
      Through the veil and the bar
60   Of things which seem and are
      Even to the steps of the remotest throne,
            Down, down!

      While the sound whirls around,
            Down, down!
65   As the fawn draws the hound,
      As the lightning the vapour,
      As a weak moth the taper;°   candle
      Death, despair; love, sorrow;
      Time both; to-day, to-morrow;

70 As steel obeys the spirit of the stone,[1]
            Down, down!

      Through the gray, void abysm,
            Down, down!
      Where the air is no prism,
75   And the moon and stars are not,
      And the cavern-crags wear not
      The radiance of Heaven,
      Nor the gloom to Earth given,
Where there is One pervading, One alone,
80   Down, down!

      In the depth of the deep,
            Down, down!
      Like veiled lightning asleep,
      Like the spark nursed in embers,
85   The last look Love remembers,
      Like a diamond, which shines
      On the dark wealth of mines,
A spell is treasured but for thee alone.
            Down, down!

90   We have bound thee, we guide thee;
            Down, down!
      With the bright form beside thee;
      Resist not the weakness,
      Such strength is in meekness
95   That the Eternal, the Immortal,
      Must unloose through life's portal
The snake-like Doom coiled underneath his throne
            By that alone.

ACT 2, SCENE 4

The cave of Demogorgon. Asia and Panthea.

PANTHEA.   What veiled form sits on that
      ebon° throne?   black

---
[1] *stone*   I.e., a lodestone, a magnet.

ASIA.   The veil has fallen.

PANTHEA.   I see a mighty darkness
  Filling the seat of power, and rays of gloom
  Dart round, as light from the meridian sun.
5 —Ungazed upon and shapeless; neither limb,
  Nor form, nor outline; yet we feel it is
  A living Spirit.

DEMOGORGON.   Ask what thou wouldst know.

ASIA.   What canst thou tell?

DEMOGORGON.   All things thou dar'st demand.

ASIA.   Who made the living world?

DEMOGORGON.   God.

ASIA.   Who made all
10 That it contains? thought, passion, reason, will,
  Imagination?

DEMOGORGON.   God: Almighty God.

ASIA.   Who made that sense which, when the winds of
      Spring
  In rarest visitation, or the voice
  Of one beloved heard in youth alone,
15 Fills the faint eyes with falling tears which dim
  The radiant looks of unbewailing flowers,
  And leaves this peopled earth a solitude
  When it returns no more?

DEMOGORGON.   Merciful God.

ASIA.   And who made terror, madness, crime, remorse,
20 Which from the links of the great chain of things,
  To every thought within the mind of man
  Sway and drag heavily, and each one reels
  Under the load towards the pit of death;
  Abandoned hope, and love that turns to hate;
25 And self-contempt, bitterer to drink than blood;

Pain, whose unheeded and familiar speech
Is howling, and keen shrieks, day after day;
And Hell, or the sharp fear of Hell?

DEMOGORGON.   He reigns.

ASIA.   Utter his name: a world pining in pain
30 Asks but his name: curses shall drag him down.

DEMOGORGON.   He reigns.

ASIA.   I feel, I know it: who?

DEMOGORGON.   He reigns.

ASIA.   Who reigns? There was the Heaven and Earth at
      first,[1]
  And Light and Love; then Saturn,[2] from whose throne
  Time fell, an envious shadow: such the state
35 Of the earth's primal spirits beneath his sway,
  As the calm joy of flowers and living leaves
  Before the wind or sun has withered them
  And semivital worms; but he refused
  The birthright of their being, knowledge, power,
40 The skill which wields the elements, the thought
  Which pierces this dim universe like light,
  Self-empire, and the majesty of love;
  For thirst of which they fainted. Then Prometheus
  Gave wisdom, which is strength, to Jupiter,
45 And with this law alone, "Let man be free,"
  Clothed him with the dominion of wide Heaven.
  To know nor faith, nor love, nor law; to be
  Omnipotent but friendless is to reign;
  And Jove now reigned; for on the race of man
50 First famine, and then toil, and then disease,
  Strife, wounds, and ghastly death unseen before,
  Fell; and the unseasonable seasons drove
  With alternating shafts of frost and fire,
  Their shelterless, pale tribes to mountain caves:

---

[1] *There was … first* Heaven and Earth, or Uranus and Gaia, were the
parents of the Titans.

[2] *Saturn* One of the Titans, whose reign was, in Greek myth, a
golden age of perpetual spring.

55 And in their desert° hearts fierce wants he sent,   *barren*
And mad disquietudes, and shadows idle
Of unreal good, which levied mutual war,
So ruining the lair wherein they raged.
Prometheus saw, and waked the legioned hopes
60 Which sleep within folded Elysian[1] flowers,
Nepenthe, Moly, Amaranth,[2] fadeless blooms,
That they might hide with thin and rainbow wings
The shape of Death; and Love he sent to bind
The disunited tendrils of that vine
65 Which bears the wine of life, the human heart;
And he tamed fire which, like some beast of prey,
Most terrible, but lovely, played beneath
The frown of man; and tortured to his will
Iron and gold, the slaves and signs of power,
70 And gems and poisons, and all subtlest forms
Hidden beneath the mountains and the waves.
He gave man speech, and speech created thought,
Which is the measure of the universe;
And Science struck the thrones of earth and heaven,
75 Which shook, but fell not; and the harmonious mind
Poured itself forth in all-prophetic song;
And music lifted up the listening spirit
Until it walked, exempt from mortal care,
Godlike, o'er the clear billows of sweet sound;
80 And human hands first mimicked° and then   *imitated*
    mocked,
With moulded limbs more lovely than its own,
The human form, till marble grew divine;
And mothers, gazing, drank the love men see
Reflected in their race, behold, and perish.
85 He told the hidden power of herbs and springs,
And Disease drank and slept. Death grew like sleep.
He taught the implicated° orbits woven   *entangled*
Of the wide-wandering stars; and how the sun
Changes his lair, and by what secret spell
90 The pale moon is transformed, when her broad eye

Gazes not on the interlunar[3] sea:
He taught to rule, as life directs the limbs,
The tempest-wingèd chariots of the Ocean,
And the Celt knew the Indian.[4] Cities then
95 Were built, and through their snow-like columns flowed
The warm winds, and the azure ether shone,
And the blue sea and shadowy hills were seen.
Such, the alleviations of his state,
Prometheus gave to man, for which he hangs
100 Withering in destined pain: but who rains down
Evil, the immedicable° plague, which, while   *untreatable*
Man looks on his creation like a God
And sees that it is glorious, drives him on,
The wreck of his own will, the scorn of earth,
105 The outcast, the abandoned, the alone?
Not Jove: while yet his frown shook Heaven ay, when
His adversary from adamantine° chains   *unbreakable*
Cursed him, he trembled like a slave. Declare
Who is his master? Is he too a slave?

110 DEMOGORGON.   All spirits are enslaved which serve
        things evil:
    Thou knowest if Jupiter be such or no.

ASIA.   Whom calledst thou God?

DEMOGORGON.   I spoke but as ye speak,
    For Jove is the supreme of living things.

ASIA.   Who is the master of the slave?

DEMOGORGON.   If the abysm
115 Could vomit forth its secrets … But a voice
    Is wanting, the deep truth is imageless;
    For what would it avail to bid thee gaze
    On the revolving world? What to bid speak
    Fate, Time, Occasion, Chance and Change? To these
120 All things are subject but eternal Love.

---

[1] *Elysian* I.e., heavenly, so called after Elysium, the idyllic world where virtuous Greeks spent the afterlife.

[2] *Nepenthe* In Homer's *Odyssey*, a drug said to banish grief or cares; *Moly* In Homer's *Odyssey*, the herb given to Odysseus to stop the effects of the witch Circe's potion; *Amaranth* Flower whose name in Greek means "unfading" or "everlasting."

---

[3] *interlunar* I.e., dark; between the old and new moons.

[4] *tempest-wingèd chariots of the Ocean* I.e., sailing ships; *Celt knew the Indian* I.e., when Europeans (of Celtic descent) were able to travel to India.

ASIA. So much I asked before, and my heart gave
  The response thou hast given; and of such truths
  Each to itself must be the oracle.
  One more demand; and do thou answer me
25 As my own soul would answer, did it know
  That which I ask. Prometheus shall arise
  Henceforth the sun of this rejoicing world:
  When shall the destined hour arrive?

DEMOGORGON.   Behold!

ASIA. The rocks are cloven, and through the purple
    night
30 I see cars° drawn by rainbow-wingèd steeds   *chariots*
  Which trample the dim winds: in each there stands
  A wild-eyed charioteer urging their flight.
  Some look behind, as fiends pursued them there,
  And yet I see no shapes but the keen stars:
35 Others, with burning eyes, lean forth, and drink
  With eager lips the wind of their own speed,
  As if the thing they loved fled on before,
  And now, even now, they clasped it. Their bright locks
  Stream like a comet's flashing hair; they all
40 Sweep onward.

DEMOGORGON. These are the immortal Hours,
  Of whom thou didst demand. One waits for thee.

ASIA. A Spirit with a dreadful countenance
  Checks its dark chariot by the craggy gulf.
  Unlike thy brethren, ghastly charioteer,
45 Who art thou? Whither wouldst thou bear me? Speak!

SPIRIT. I am the shadow of a destiny
  More dread than is my aspect: ere yon planet
  Has set, the darkness which ascends with me
  Shall wrap in lasting night heaven's kingless throne.[1]

150 ASIA. What meanest thou?

PANTHEA.   That terrible shadow floats
  Up from its throne, as may the lurid[2] smoke
  Of earthquake-ruined cities o'er the sea.
  Lo! it ascends the car; the coursers[3] fly
  Terrified: watch its path among the stars
155 Blackening the night!

ASIA.   Thus I am answered: strange!

PANTHEA. See, near the verge,° another   *horizon*
    chariot stays;
  An ivory shell inlaid with crimson fire,
  Which comes and goes within its sculptured rim
  Of delicate strange tracery; the young spirit
160 That guides it has the dove-like eyes of hope;[4]
  How its soft smiles attract the soul! as light
  Lures wingèd insects through the lampless air.

SPIRIT.
  My coursers are fed with the lightning,
    They drink of the whirlwind's stream,
165 And when the red morning is bright'ning
    They bathe in the fresh sunbeam;
    They have strength for their swiftness I deem;
  Then ascend with me, daughter of Ocean.

  I desire: and their speed makes night kindle;
170   I fear: they outstrip the Typhoon;
  Ere the cloud piled on Atlas[5] can dwindle
    We encircle the earth and the moon:
    We shall rest from long labours at noon:
  Then ascend with me, daughter of Ocean.

---

1 *I am … throne* This spirit is of the hour of revolution, the overthrow of the old order.

---

2 *lurid* Shining red in the dark.

3 *coursers* Chargers; powerful racing horses.

4 *hope* I.e., hope for the new order. This chariot will carry Asia to a reunion with Prometheus.

5 *Atlas* The Atlas mountains, located in northwestern Africa, are associated with the god Atlas who, according to classical mythology, was forced to hold up the sky forever.

ACT 2, SCENE 5

The Car pauses within a cloud on top of a snowy
mountain. Asia, Panthea, and the Spirit of the Hour.

SPIRIT.
  On the brink of the night and the morning
    My coursers are wont to respire;[1]
  But the Earth has just whispered a warning
    That their flight must be swifter than fire:
5   They shall drink the hot speed of desire!

ASIA.   Thou breathest on their nostrils, but my breath
  Would give them swifter speed.

SPIRIT.   Alas! it could not.

PANTHEA.   Oh Spirit! pause, and tell whence is the light
  Which fills this cloud? the sun is yet unrisen.

10 SPIRIT.   The sun will rise not until noon. Apollo
  Is held in heaven by wonder; and the light
  Which fills this vapour, as the aereal hue
  Of fountain-gazing roses fills the water,
  Flows from thy mighty sister.

PANTHEA.   Yes, I feel—

15 ASIA.   What is it with thee, sister? Thou art pale.

PANTHEA.   How thou art changed! I dare not look on
      thee;
  I feel but see thee not. I scarce endure
  The radiance of thy beauty. Some good change
  Is working in the elements, which suffer
20 Thy presence thus unveiled. The Nereids[2] tell

That on the day when the clear hyaline[3]
Was cloven at thine uprise, and thou didst stand
Within a veinèd shell, which floated on
Over the calm floor of the crystal sea,
25 Among the Aegean isles, and by the shores
Which bear thy name; love, like the atmosphere
Of the sun's fire filling the living world,
Burst from thee, and illumèd earth and heaven
And the deep ocean and the sunless caves
30 And all that dwells within them; till grief cast
Eclipse upon the soul from which it came:
Such art thou now; nor is it I alone,
Thy sister, thy companion, thine own chosen one,
But the whole world which seeks thy sympathy.
35 Hearest thou not sounds i' the air which speak the love
Of all articulate beings? Feelest thou not
The inanimate winds enamoured of thee? List!°   listen

[*Music.*]

ASIA.   Thy words are sweeter than aught else but his
  Whose echoes they are; yet all love is sweet,
40 Given or returned. Common as light is love,
  And its familiar voice wearies not ever.
  Like the wide heaven, the all-sustaining air,
  It makes the reptile equal to the God:
  They who inspire it most are fortunate,
45 As I am now; but those who feel it most
  Are happier still, after long sufferings,
  As I shall soon become.

PANTHEA.   List! Spirits speak.

VOICE (*in the Air, singing*).
  Life of Life! thy lips enkindle
    With their love the breath between them;
50 And thy smiles before they dwindle
    Make the cold air fire; then screen them
  In those looks, where whoso gazes
  Faints, entangled in their mazes.

---

1 *respire*   Stop to catch their breath.

2 *Nereids*   Sea nymphs, daughters of Nereus, the old god of the sea.
This story told by the Nereids, along with Asia's ivory-shell chariot,
associates Asia with Aphrodite (goddess of love) who was said to have
sprung from the foam of the Mediterranean Sea and been carried on
a shell to the island of Cythera. (This is the topic of Botticelli's famous
painting, *The Birth of Venus*, c. 1485.)

---

3 *hyaline*   Smooth, glass-like surface of the water.

Child of Light! thy limbs are burning
55   Through the vest which seems to hide them;
As the radiant lines of morning
      Through the clouds ere they divide them;
And this atmosphere divinest
Shrouds thee wheresoe'er thou shinest.

60 Fair are others; none beholds thee,
      But thy voice sounds low and tender
Like the fairest, for it folds thee
      From the sight, that liquid splendour,
And all feel, yet see thee never,
65 As I feel now, lost for ever!

Lamp of Earth! where'er thou movest
      Its dim shapes are clad with brightness,
And the souls of whom thou lovest
      Walk upon the winds with lightness,
70 Till they fail, as I am failing,
      Dizzy, lost, yet unbewailing!

ASIA.
      My soul is an enchanted boat,
      Which, like a sleeping swan, doth float
Upon the silver waves of thy sweet singing;
75   And thine doth like an angel sit
      Beside a helm conducting it,
Whilst all the winds with melody are ringing.
      It seems to float ever, for ever,
      Upon that many-winding river,
80   Between mountains, woods, abysses,
      A paradise of wildernesses!
Till, like one in slumber bound,
Borne to the ocean, I float down, around,
Into a sea profound, of ever-spreading sound:

85   Meanwhile thy spirit lifts its pinions°   *wings*
      In music's most serene dominions;
Catching the winds that fan that happy heaven.
      And we sail on, away, afar,
      Without a course, without a star,
90 But, by the instinct of sweet music driven;
      Till through Elysian garden islets

By thee most beautiful of pilots,
      Where never mortal pinnace[1] glided,
      The boat of my desire is guided:
95 Realms where the air we breathe is love,
Which in the winds on the waves doth move,
Harmonizing this earth with what we feel above.

      We have passed Age's icy caves,
      And Manhood's dark and tossing waves,
100 And Youth's smooth ocean, smiling to betray:
      Beyond the glassy gulfs we flee
      Of shadow-peopled Infancy,
Through Death and Birth, to a diviner day;
      A paradise of vaulted bowers,
105   Lit by downward-gazing flowers,
      And watery paths that wind between
      Wildernesses calm and green,
Peopled by shapes too bright to see,
And rest, having beheld; somewhat like thee;
110 Which walk upon the sea, and chant melodiously!

[End of Act 2.]

ACT 3, SCENE 1

Heaven. Jupiter on his throne; Thetis and the other deities assembled.

JUPITER. Ye congregated powers of heaven, who share
The glory and the strength of him ye serve,
Rejoice! henceforth I am omnipotent.
All else had been subdued to me; alone
5 The soul of man, like unextinguished fire,
Yet burns towards heaven with fierce reproach, and doubt,
And lamentation, and reluctant prayer,
Hurling up insurrection, which might make
Our antique empire insecure, though built
10 On eldest faith, and hell's coeval,° fear;   *contemporary*

---

[1] *pinnace* Small sailing or row boat, often a scout for a larger ship.

And though my curses through the
    pendulous° air,   *overhanging*
Like snow on herbless peaks, fall flake by flake,
And cling to it; though under my wrath's night
It climbs the crags of life, step after step,
15   Which wound it, as ice wounds unsandalled feet,
It yet remains supreme o'er misery,
Aspiring, unrepressed, yet soon to fall:
Even now have I begotten a strange wonder,
That fatal child,[1] the terror of the earth,
20   Who waits but till the destined hour arrive,
Bearing from Demogorgon's vacant throne
The dreadful might of ever-living limbs
Which clothed that awful spirit unbeheld,
To redescend, and trample out the spark.
25   Pour forth heaven's wine, Idaean Ganymede,[2]
And let it fill the Daedal cups[3] like fire,
And from the flower-inwoven soil divine
Ye all-triumphant harmonies arise,
As dew from earth under the twilight stars:
30   Drink! be the nectar circling through your veins
The soul of joy, ye ever-living Gods,
Till exultation burst in one wide voice
Like music from Elysian winds.
                 And thou
Ascend beside me, veilèd in the light
35   Of the desire which makes thee one with me,
Thetis,[4] bright image of eternity!
When thou didst cry, "Insufferable might!
God! Spare me! I sustain not the quick flames,
The penetrating presence; all my being,
40   Like him whom the Numidian seps[5] did thaw
Into a dew with poison, is dissolved,
Sinking through its foundations": even then

Two mighty spirits, mingling, made a third
Mightier than either, which, unbodied now,
45   Between us floats, felt, although unbeheld,
Waiting the incarnation, which ascends,
(Hear ye the thunder of the fiery wheels
Griding° the winds?) from Demogorgon's   *piercing*
    throne.
Victory! victory! Feel'st thou not, O world,
50   The earthquake of his chariot thundering up
Olympus?[6]
[*The car of the hour arrives. Demogorgon descends, and
moves towards the throne of Jupiter.*]
            Awful shape, what art thou? Speak!

DEMOGORGON.   Eternity. Demand no direr name.
Descend, and follow me down the abyss.
I am thy child, as thou wert Saturn's child;
55   Mightier than thee: and we must dwell together
Henceforth in darkness. Lift thy lightnings not.
The tyranny of heaven none may retain,
Or reassume, or hold, succeeding thee:
Yet if thou wilt, as 'tis the destiny
60   Of trodden worms to writhe till they are dead,
Put forth thy might.

JUPITER.   Detested prodigy!
Even thus beneath the deep Titanian prisons[7]
I trample thee! thou lingerest?
                Mercy! mercy!
No pity, no release, no respite! Oh,
65   That thou wouldst make mine enemy my judge,
Even where he hangs, seared by my long revenge,
On Caucasus! he would not doom me thus.
Gentle, and just, and dreadless, is he not
The monarch of the world? What then art thou?
70   No refuge! no appeal!
                Sink with me then,
We two will sink on the wide waves of ruin,
Even as a vulture and a snake outspent

---

[1] *That fatal child* Some power that will defeat Demogorgon and prevent the freeing of Prometheus, and mankind.

[2] *Ganymede* Jupiter's cup-bearer, an extremely beautiful youth who was seized from his home on Mount Ida by an eagle and brought to serve Jupiter.

[3] *Daedal cups* Cups made with the skill of the craftsman Daedalus.

[4] *Thetis* Sea nymph and the mother of Achilles.

[5] *Numidian seps* Venomous snake of Numidia whose poisonous bite was fabled to cause the bitten person to melt, or dissolve.

[6] *Olympus* Mount Olympus, home of the gods.

[7] *Titanian prisons* Tartarus, the deep underground prison where the Titans were imprisoned after their defeat by Jupiter and the other Olympian gods.

Drop, twisted in inextricable fight,
Into a shoreless sea. Let hell unlock
75   Its mounded oceans of tempestuous fire,
And whelm on[1] them into the bottomless void
This desolated world, and thee, and me,
The conqueror and the conquered, and the wreck
Of that for which they combated.
                  Ai, Ai!
80   The elements obey me not. I sink
Dizzily down, ever, for ever, down.
And, like a cloud, mine enemy above
Darkens my fall with victory! Ai, Ai!

ACT 3, SCENE 2

The mouth of a great river in the island of Atlantis.[2]
Ocean is discovered reclining near the shore; Apollo
stands beside him.

OCEAN.   He fell, thou sayest, beneath his conqueror's
     frown?

APOLLO.[3]   Ay, when the strife was ended which made
     dim
The orb I rule, and shook the solid stars,
The terrors of his eye illumèd heaven
5   With sanguine° light, through the thick   *blood-red*
     ragged skirts
Of the victorious darkness, as he fell:
Like the last glare of day's red agony,
Which, from a rent among the fiery clouds,
Burns far along the tempest-wrinkled deep.

10   OCEAN.   He sunk to the abyss? To the dark void?

APOLLO.   An eagle so caught in some bursting cloud
     On Caucasus, his thunder-baffled wings

Entangled in the whirlwind, and his eyes
Which gazed on the undazzling sun, now blinded
15   By the white lightning, while the ponderous hail
Beats on his struggling form, which sinks at length
Prone, and the aereal ice clings over it.

OCEAN.   Henceforth the fields of heaven-reflecting sea
Which are my realm, will heave, unstained with blood,[4]
20   Beneath the uplifting winds, like plains of corn
Swayed by the summer air; my streams will flow
Round many-peopled continents, and round
Fortunate isles; and from their glassy thrones
Blue Proteus[5] and his humid nymphs shall mark
25   The shadow of fair ships, as mortals see
The floating bark of the light-laden moon
With that white star,[6] its sightless° pilot's crest,   *invisible*
Borne down the rapid sunset's ebbing sea;
Tracking their path no more by blood and groans,
30   And desolation, and the mingled voice
Of slavery and command; but by the light
Of wave-reflected flowers, and floating odours,
And music soft, and mild, free, gentle voices,
And sweetest music, such as spirits love.

35   APOLLO.   And I shall gaze not on the deeds which make
My mind obscure with sorrow, as eclipse
Darkens the sphere I guide; but list, I hear
The small, clear, silver lute of the young Spirit
That sits i' the morning star.

OCEAN.   Thou must away;
40   Thy steeds will pause at even,° till when farewell: *evening*
The loud deep calls me home even now to feed it
With azure calm out of the emerald urns
Which stand for ever full beside my throne.
Behold the Nereids under the green sea,
45   Their wavering limbs borne on the wind-like stream,
Their white arms lifted o'er their streaming hair

---

[1]   *whelm on*   Submerge, sink.

[2]   *Atlantis*   Mythical island that figures in Plato's *Critias* as the scene
of the ideal commonwealth.

[3]   *APOLLO*   Greek god of the sun, medicine, and poetry.

[4]   *unstained with blood*   I.e., from battles at sea.

[5]   *Proteus*   Sea god, son of Oceanus.

[6]   *white star*   Venus (also called the morning star, 3.2.39).

With garlands pied° and starry   *of variegated colors*
    sea-flower crowns,
Hastening to grace their mighty sister's joy.
[*A sound of waves is heard.*]
It is the unpastured° sea hungering for calm.   *unfed*
50   Peace, monster; I come now. Farewell.

APOLLO.   Farewell.

ACT 3, SCENE 3

Caucasus. Prometheus, Hercules, Ione, the Earth, Spirits,
Asia, and Panthea, borne in the car with the Spirit of the
Hour. Hercules unbinds Prometheus, who descends.

HERCULES.   Most glorious among Spirits, thus doth
    strength
To wisdom, courage, and long-suffering love,
And thee, who art the form they animate,
Minister like a slave.

PROMETHEUS.   Thy gentle words
5   Are sweeter even than freedom long desired
And long delayed.
                            Asia, thou light of life,
Shadow of beauty unbeheld: and ye,
Fair sister nymphs, who made long years of pain
Sweet to remember, through your love and care:
10   Henceforth we will not part. There is a cave,
All overgrown with trailing odorous plants,
Which curtain out the day with leaves and flowers,
And paved with veined emerald, and a fountain
Leaps in the midst with an awakening sound.
15   From its curved roof the mountain's frozen tears
Like snow, or silver, or long diamond spires,
Hang downward, raining forth a doubtful light:
And there is heard the ever-moving air,
Whispering without from tree to tree, and birds,
20   And bees; and all around are mossy seats,
And the rough walls are clothed with long soft grass;
A simple dwelling, which shall be our own;
Where we will sit and talk of time and change,

As the world ebbs and flows, ourselves unchanged.
25   What can hide man from mutability?
And if ye sigh, then I will smile; and thou,
Ione, shalt chant fragments of sea-music,
Until I weep, when ye shall smile away
The tears she brought, which yet were sweet to shed.
30   We will entangle buds and flowers and beams
Which twinkle on the fountain's brim, and make
Strange combinations out of common things,
Like human babes in their brief innocence;
And we will search, with looks and words of love,
35   For hidden thoughts, each lovelier than the last,
Our unexhausted spirits; and like lutes
Touched by the skill of the enamoured wind,
Weave harmonies divine, yet ever new,
From difference sweet where discord cannot be;
40   And hither come, sped on the charmèd winds,
Which meet from all the points of heaven, as bees
From every flower aereal Enna[1] feeds,
At their known island-homes in Himera,[2]
The echoes of the human world, which tell
45   Of the low voice of love, almost unheard,
And dove-eyed pity's murmured pain, and music,
Itself the echo of the heart, and all
That tempers or improves man's life, now free;
And lovely apparitions,—dim at first,
50   Then radiant, as the mind, arising bright
From the embrace of beauty (whence the forms
Of which these are the phantoms) casts on them
The gathered rays which are reality—
Shall visit us, the progeny immortal
55   Of Painting, Sculpture, and rapt Poesy,
And arts, though unimagined, yet to be.
The wandering voices and the shadows these
Of all that man becomes, the mediators
Of that best worship love, by him and us
60   Given and returned; swift shapes and sounds, which grow
More fair and soft as man grows wise and kind,
And, veil by veil, evil and error fall:

---

[1]   *Enna* Meadow in Sicily and the site of Proserpine's abduction by
Hades, god of the underworld. Enna is here described as "aereal"
because it is above the underworld, in the open air.

[2]   *Himera* Town in Sicily.

Such virtue has the cave and place around.
[*Turning to the Spirit of the Hour.*]
For thee, fair Spirit, one toil° remains. Ione,   job
65 Give her that curved shell,[1] which Proteus old
Made Asia's nuptial boon, breathing within it
A voice to be accomplished, and which thou
Didst hide in grass under the hollow rock.

IONE.   Thou most desired Hour, more loved and lovely
70 Than all thy sisters, this is the mystic shell;
See the pale azure fading into silver
Lining it with a soft yet glowing light:
Looks it not like lulled music sleeping there?

SPIRIT.   It seems in truth the fairest shell of Ocean:
75 Its sound must be at once both sweet and strange.

PROMETHEUS.   Go, borne over the cities of mankind
On whirlwind-footed coursers: once again
Outspeed the sun around the orbèd world;
And as thy chariot cleaves the kindling air,
80 Thou breathe into the many-folded shell,
Loosening its mighty music; it shall be
As thunder mingled with clear echoes: then
Return; and thou shalt dwell beside our cave.
[*Kissing the ground.*]
And thou, O Mother Earth!—

THE EARTH.   I hear, I feel;
85 Thy lips are on me, and thy touch runs down
Even to the adamantine central gloom
Along these marble nerves; 'tis life, 'tis joy,
And, through my withered, old, and icy frame
The warmth of an immortal youth shoots down
90 Circling. Henceforth the many children fair
Folded in my sustaining arms; all plants,
And creeping forms, and insects rainbow-wingèd,
And birds, and beasts, and fish, and human shapes,
Which drew disease and pain from my wan bosom,
95 Draining the poison of despair, shall take
And interchange sweet nutriment; to me

Shall they become like sister-antelopes
By one fair dam, snow-white and swift as wind,
Nursed among lilies near a brimming stream.
100 The dew-mists of my sunless sleep shall float
Under the stars like balm: night-folded flowers
Shall suck unwithering hues in their repose:
And men and beasts in happy dreams shall gather
Strength for the coming day, and all its joy:
105 And death shall be the last embrace of her
Who takes the life she gave, even as a mother,
Folding her child, says, "Leave me not again."

ASIA.   Oh, mother! wherefore speak the name of death?
Cease they to love, and move, and breathe, and speak,
110 Who die?

THE EARTH.   It would avail not to reply:
Thou art immortal, and this tongue is known
But to the uncommunicating dead.
Death is the veil which those who live call life:
They sleep, and it is lifted; and meanwhile
115 In mild variety the seasons mild
With rainbow-skirted showers, and odorous winds,
And long blue meteors cleansing the dull night,
And the life-kindling shafts of the keen sun's
All-piercing bow, and the dew-mingled rain
120 Of the calm moonbeams, a soft influence mild,
Shall clothe the forests and the fields, ay, even
The crag-built deserts of the barren deep,
With ever-living leaves, and fruits, and flowers.
And thou! There is a cavern where my spirit
125 Was panted forth in anguish whilst thy pain
Made my heart mad, and those who did inhale it
Became mad too, and built a temple there,
And spoke, and were oracular, and lured
The erring nations round to mutual war,
130 And faithless faith, such as Jove kept with thee;
Which breath now rises, as amongst tall weeds
A violet's exhalation, and it fills
With a serener light and crimson air
Intense, yet soft, the rocks and woods around;
135 It feeds the quick growth of the serpent vine,

---

1   *that curved shell*   I.e., a conch shell.

And the dark linked ivy[1] tangling wild,
And budding, blown, or odour-faded blooms
Which star the winds with points of coloured light,
As they rain through them, and bright golden globes
140 Of fruit, suspended in their own green heaven,
And through their veinèd leaves and amber stems
The flowers whose purple and translucid bowls
Stand ever mantling with aereal dew,
The drink of spirits: and it circles round,
145 Like the soft waving wings of noonday dreams,
Inspiring calm and happy thoughts, like mine,
Now thou art thus restored. This cave is thine.
Arise! Appear!
[*A Spirit rises in the likeness of a wingèd child.*]
        This is my torch-bearer;
Who let his lamp out in old time with gazing
150 On eyes from which he kindled it anew
With love, which is as fire, sweet daughter mine,
For such is that within thine own. Run, wayward,
And guide this company beyond the peak
Of Bacchic Nysa,[2] Maenad-haunted mountain,
155 And beyond Indus and its tribute rivers,
Trampling the torrent streams and glassy lakes
With feet unwet, unwearied, undelaying,
And up the green ravine, across the vale,
Beside the windless and crystalline pool,
160 Where ever lies, on unerasing waves,
The image of a temple, built above,
Distinct with column, arch, and architrave,[3]
And palm-like capital, and over-wrought,
And populous with most living imagery,
165 Praxitelean[4] shapes, whose marble smiles
Fill the hushed air with everlasting love.
It is deserted now, but once it bore
Thy name, Prometheus; there the emulous youths

Bore to thy honour through the divine gloom
170 The lamp which was thine emblem;[5] even as those
Who bear the untransmitted torch of hope
Into the grave, across the night of life,
As thou hast borne it most triumphantly
To this far goal of Time. Depart, farewell.
175 Beside that temple is the destined cave.

ACT 3, SCENE 4

A forest. In the background a cave. Prometheus, Asia,
Panthea, Ione, and the Spirit of the Earth.[6]

IONE.   Sister, it is not earthly: how it glides
    Under the leaves! how on its head there burns
    A light, like a green star, whose emerald beams
    Are twined with its fair hair! how, as it moves,
5   The splendour drops in flakes upon the grass!
    Knowest thou it?

PANTHEA.   It is the delicate spirit
    That guides the earth through heaven. From afar
    The populous constellations call that light
    The loveliest of the planets; and sometimes
10 It floats along the spray of the salt sea,
    Or makes its chariot of a foggy cloud,
    Or walks through fields or cities while men sleep,
    Or o'er the mountain tops, or down the rivers,
    Or through the green waste wilderness, as now,
15 Wondering at all it sees. Before Jove reigned
    It loved our sister Asia, and it came
    Each leisure hour to drink the liquid light
    Out of her eyes, for which it said it thirsted
    As one bit by a dipsas,[7] and with her
20 It made its childish confidence, and told her
    All it had known or seen, for it saw much,
    Yet idly reasoned what it saw; and called her—

---

[1] *ivy*   Plant sacred to Bacchus, or Dionysus.

[2] *Bacchic Nysa*   Nysa was the name of several ancient cities, all
supposedly founded by or somehow associated with Bacchus. One, in
India, was said to be his birthplace.

[3] *architrave*   Architectural term referring to the main beam that rests
upon the capitals of columns.

[4] *Praxitelean*   Showing the characteristics of work by Praxiteles, a
Greek sculptor of the fourth century BCE.

[5] *once it bore … emblem*   In ancient Athens, a group annually
celebrated Prometheus's gift of fire with a race called the Lampa-
dephoria, in which young men ran with torches.

[6] *Spirit of the Earth*   Often thought to represent electricity.

[7] *dipsas*   Poisonous snake of classical myth whose bite caused its
victim to suffer from unquenchable thirst.

For whence it sprung it knew not, nor do I—
Mother, dear mother.

THE SPIRIT OF THE EARTH (*Running to Asia*).
              Mother, dearest mother;
25 May I then talk with thee as I was wont?°   *accustomed*
    May I then hide my eyes in thy soft arms,
    After thy looks have made them tired of joy?
    May I then play beside thee the long noons,
    When work is none in the bright silent air?

30 ASIA. I love thee, gentlest being, and henceforth
    Can cherish thee unenvied: speak, I pray:
    Thy simple talk once solaced, now delights.

SPIRIT OF THE EARTH. Mother, I am grown wiser,
      though a child
    Cannot be wise like thee, within this day;
35 And happier too; happier and wiser both.
    Thou knowest that toads, and snakes, and loathly worms,
    And venomous and malicious beasts, and boughs
    That bore ill berries in the woods, were ever
    An hindrance to my walks o'er the green world:
40 And that, among the haunts of humankind,
    Hard-featured men, or with proud, angry looks,
    Or cold, staid gait, or false and hollow smiles,
    Or the dull sneer of self-loved ignorance,
    Or other such foul masks, with which ill thoughts
45 Hide that fair being whom we spirits call man;
    And women too, ugliest of all things evil,
    (Though fair, even in a world where thou art fair,
    When good and kind, free and sincere like thee)
    When false or frowning made me sick at heart
50 To pass them, though they slept, and I unseen.
    Well, my path lately lay through a great city
    Into the woody hills surrounding it:
    A sentinel was sleeping at the gate:
    When there was heard a sound, so loud, it shook
55 The towers amid the moonlight, yet more sweet
    Than any voice but thine, sweetest of all;
    A long, long sound, as it would never end:
    And all the inhabitants leaped suddenly
    Out of their rest, and gathered in the streets,

60 Looking in wonder up to Heaven, while yet
    The music pealed along. I hid myself
    Within a fountain in the public square,
    Where I lay like the reflex° of the moon   *reflection*
    Seen in a wave under green leaves; and soon
65 Those ugly human shapes and visages
    Of which I spoke as having wrought me pain,
    Passed floating through the air, and fading still
    Into the winds that scattered them; and those
    From whom they passed seemed mild and lovely forms
70 After some foul disguise had fallen, and all
    Were somewhat changed, and after brief surprise
    And greetings of delighted wonder, all
    Went to their sleep again: and when the dawn
    Came, wouldst thou think that toads, and snakes,
      and efts,°   *newts*
75 Could e'er be beautiful? yet so they were,
    And that with little change of shape or hue:
    All things had put their evil nature off:
    I cannot tell my joy, when o'er a lake,
    Upon a drooping bough with nightshade twined,
80 I saw two azure halcyons[1] clinging downward
    And thinning one bright bunch of amber berries,
    With quick long beaks, and in the deep there lay
    Those lovely forms imaged as in a sky;
    So, with my thoughts full of these happy changes,
85 We meet again, the happiest change of all.

ASIA. And never will we part, till thy chaste sister
    Who guides the frozen and inconstant moon
    Will look on thy more warm and equal light
    Till her heart thaw like flakes of April snow
90 And love thee.

SPIRIT OF THE EARTH. What! as Asia loves
    Prometheus?

ASIA. Peace, wanton, thou art yet not old enough.
    Think ye by gazing on each other's eyes
    To multiply your lovely selves, and fill
    With spherèd fires the interlunar air?

---

[1] *halcyons* Kingfishers, which normally eat fish, here described as berry-eating.

SPIRIT OF THE EARTH.   Nay, mother, while my sister
    trims her lamp[1]
  'Tis hard I should go darkling.

ASIA.   Listen; look!

[*The Spirit of the Hour enters.*]

PROMETHEUS.   We feel what thou hast heard and
    seen: yet speak.

SPIRIT OF THE HOUR.   Soon as the sound had ceased
    whose thunder filled
  The abysses of the sky and the wide earth,
100 There was a change: the impalpable thin air
  And the all-circling sunlight were transformed,
  As if the sense of love dissolved in them
  Had folded itself round the sphered world.
  My vision then grew clear, and I could see
105 Into the mysteries of the universe:
  Dizzy as with delight I floated down,
  Winnowing° the lightsome° air with   *beating | light*
    languid plumes,
  My coursers sought their birthplace in the sun,
  Where they henceforth will live exempt from toil,
110 Pasturing flowers of vegetable fire;
  And where my moonlike car will stand within
  A temple, gazed upon by Phidian forms[2]
  Of thee, and Asia, and the Earth, and me,
  And you fair nymphs looking the love we feel,—
115 In memory of the tidings it has borne,—
  Beneath a dome fretted with graven flowers,
  Poised on twelve columns of resplendent stone,
  And open to the bright and liquid sky.
  Yoked to it by an amphisbaenic snake[3]
120 The likeness of those wingèd steeds will mock
  The flight from which they find repose. Alas,
  Whither has wandered now my partial° tongue   *biased*

When all remains untold which ye would hear?
  As I have said, I floated to the earth:
125 It was, as it is still, the pain of bliss
  To move, to breathe, to be. I wandering went
  Among the haunts and dwellings of mankind,
  And first was disappointed not to see
  Such mighty change as I had felt within
130 Expressed in outward things; but soon I looked,
  And behold, thrones were kingless, and men walked
  One with the other even as spirits do,
  None fawned, none trampled; hate, disdain, or fear,
  Self-love or self-contempt, on human brows
135 No more inscribed, as o'er the gate of hell,
  "All hope abandon ye who enter here";[4]
  None frowned, none trembled, none with eager fear
  Gazed on another's eye of cold command,
  Until the subject of a tyrant's will
140 Became, worse fate, the abject° of his own,   *outcast*
  Which spurred him, like an outspent° horse,   *exhausted*
    to death.
  None wrought his lips in truth-entangling lines
  Which smiled the lie his tongue disdained to speak;
  None, with firm sneer, trod out in his own heart
145 The sparks of love and hope till there remained
  Those bitter ashes, a soul self-consumed,
  And the wretch crept a vampire among men,
  Infecting all with his own hideous ill;
  None talked that common, false, cold, hollow talk
150 Which makes the heart deny the "yes" it breathes,
  Yet question that unmeant hypocrisy
  With such a self-mistrust as has no name.
  And women, too, frank, beautiful, and kind
  As the free heaven which rains fresh light and dew
155 On the wide earth, past; gentle radiant forms,
  From custom's evil taint exempt and pure;
  Speaking the wisdom once they could not think,
  Looking emotions once they feared to feel,
  And changed to all which once they dared not be,
160 Yet being now, made earth like heaven; nor°   *neither*
    pride,
  Nor jealousy, nor envy, nor ill shame,

---

[1] *trims her lamp* I.e., gets it ready to light, by trimming the wick.

[2] *Phidian forms* Forms resembling those sculpted by great Athenian sculptor Phidias of the fifth century BCE.

[3] *amphisbaenic snake* Snake with a head on each end.

[4] *All hope … here* See Dante's *Inferno* 3.9, in which this is the inscription written over the gate of hell.

The bitterest of those drops of treasured gall,
Spoiled the sweet taste of the nepenthe, love.

Thrones, altars, judgement-seats, and prisons; wherein,
65 And beside which, by wretched men were borne
Sceptres, tiaras, swords, and chains, and tomes
Of reasoned wrong, glozed° on by ignorance,   shone
Were like those monstrous and barbaric shapes,
The ghosts of a no-more-remembered fame,
70 Which, from their unworn obelisks, look forth
In triumph o'er the palaces and tombs
Of those who were their conquerors: mouldering[1] round,
These imaged to the pride of kings and priests
A dark yet mighty faith, a power as wide
75 As is the world it wasted, and are now
But an astonishment; even so the tools
And emblems of its last captivity,
Amid the dwellings of the peopled earth,
Stand, not o'erthrown, but unregarded now.
480 And those foul shapes, abhorred by god and man,—
Which, under many a name and many a form
Strange, savage, ghastly, dark and execrable,
Were Jupiter, the tyrant of the world;
And which the nations, panic-stricken, served
185 With blood, and hearts broken by long hope, and love
Dragged to his altars soiled and garlandless,
And slain among men's unreclaiming tears,
Flattering the thing they feared, which fear was hate,—
Frown, mouldering fast, o'er their abandoned shrines:
190 The painted veil, by those who were, called life,
Which mimicked, as with colours idly spread,
All men believed and hoped, is torn aside;
The loathsome mask has fallen, the man remains
Sceptreless, free, uncircumscribed, but man
195 Equal, unclassed, tribeless, and nationless,
Exempt from awe, worship, degree, the king
Over himself; just, gentle, wise; but man
Passionless?—no, yet free from guilt or pain,
Which were, for his will made or suffered them,
200 Nor yet exempt, though ruling them like slaves,
From chance, and death, and mutability,
The clogs of that which else might oversoar

---
[1] *mouldering* Decaying, crumbling.

The loftiest star of unascended heaven,
Pinnacled° dim in the intense inane.° *crowning | empty space*

[*End of Act 3.*]
—1820

Adonais

In this pastoral elegy for fellow poet John Keats, Shelley calls the young poet Adonais after Adonis, the beautiful youth of classical myth who was loved by Venus and killed by a wild boar. In some versions of the story Venus asks Persephone, Queen of the underworld, to allow Adonis to return above ground for four months of every year, while in others she transforms his blood into the bright red anemone, enabling him to live on in this ever-blooming flower.

Shelley had known Keats only casually, through their mutual acquaintance Leigh Hunt, the editor of the radical *Examiner*, but he admired his poetry and agreed with many of his political views. Hearing of Keats's serious illness in 1820, Shelley had invited Keats to spend the winter with him in Pisa. Keats did journey to Italy, but died in Rome in February of 1821, before he could reach Pisa.

The beast whom Shelley blames for Keats's death is the anonymous critic who ridiculed Keats's *Endymion* in *The Quarterly Review* (April 1818); Shelley thus gave force to a sentimental myth that Keats's illness and death were brought on by demoralizing reviews, both in *The Quarterly Review* and *Blackwood's Magazine*. For many years after his death, it was commonly maintained that, as Byron said, Keats was "snuffed out by an article." Until the late 1840s, Keats was better known by *Adonais* and the legend of his death than by his own poetry.

Adonais
An Elegy on the Death of John Keats

Αστήρ πρὶν μὲν ἐλαμπες ενι ζωοισιν εωος.
Νυν δε θανών, λαμπεις ἔοπερος εν φθίμενοις.

PLATO[1]

1

I weep for Adonais—he is dead!
O, weep for Adonais! though our tears
Thaw not the frost which binds so dear a head!
And thou, sad Hour, selected from all years
5   To mourn our loss, rouse thy obscure compeers,
And teach them thine own sorrow, say: with me
Died Adonais; till the Future dares
Forget the Past, his fate and fame shall be
An echo and a light unto eternity!

2

10   Where wert thou mighty Mother, when he lay,
When thy Son lay, pierced by the shaft which flies
In darkness? Where was lorn° Urania[2]   *forlorn*
When Adonais died? With veiled eyes,
'Mid listening Echoes, in her Paradise
15   She sate, while one, with soft enamoured breath,
Rekindled all the fading melodies,
With which, like flowers that mock the corse°   *body*
     beneath,
He had adorned and hid the coming bulk of death.

3

O, weep for Adonais—he is dead!
20   Wake, melancholy Mother, wake and weep!
Yet wherefore? Quench within their burning bed
Thy fiery tears, and let thy loud heart keep
Like his, a mute and uncomplaining sleep;
For he is gone, where all things wise and fair
25   Descend—oh, dream not that the amorous Deep°   *abyss*
Will yet restore him to the vital air;
Death feeds on his mute voice, and laughs at our
     despair.

4

Most musical of mourners, weep again!
Lament anew, Urania! He[3] died,
30   Who was the Sire of an immortal strain,
Blind, old, and lonely, when his country's pride,
The priest, the slave, and the liberticide,
Trampled and mocked with many a loathed rite
Of lust and blood; he went, unterrified,
35   Into the gulf of death; but his clear Sprite°   *spirit*
Yet reigns o'er earth; the third among the sons of light.

5

Most musical of mourners, weep anew!
Not all to that bright station dared to climb;
And happier they their happiness who knew,
40   Whose tapers yet burn through that night of time
In which suns perished; others more sublime,
Struck by the envious wrath of man or God,
Have sunk, extinct in their refulgent° prime;   *gleaming*
And some yet live, treading the thorny road,
45   Which leads, through toil and hate, to Fame's serene
     abode.

6

But now, thy youngest, dearest one, has perished,
The nursling of thy widowhood, who grew,
Like a pale flower by some sad maiden cherished,
And fed with true love tears, instead of dew;
50   Most musical of mourners, weep anew!
Thy extreme hope, the loveliest and the last,
The bloom, whose petals nipt before they blew,°   *bloomed*

---

[1] Αστήρ... PLATO [Shelley's translation] Thou wert the morning
star among the living, / Ere thy fair light had fled— / Now, having
died, thou art as Hesperus, giving / New splendour to the dead.
[Translation from the Greek of Plato's *Epigram on Aster*. The planet
Venus appears in the sky as both the morning star, Phosphorus, and
the evening star, Vesper.]

[2] *Urania* Muse who is invoked near the beginning of Milton's
Paradise Lost. Urania is also an epithet for the goddess Venus, who
loved Adonis.

[3] *He* Poet John Milton (1608–74), who served in Cromwell's
parliamentary government and, as a result, was imprisoned when the
monarchy was restored, although he was released quickly. At the end
of this stanza, Shelley places Milton in a triumvirate with the earlier
epic poets Homer and Dante ("the third among the sons of light").

Died on the promise of the fruit, is waste;
The broken lily lies—the storm is overpast.

7

55 To that high Capital,[1] where kingly Death
Keeps his pale court in beauty and decay,
He came; and bought, with price of purest breath,
A grave among the eternal. Come away!
Haste, while the vault of blue Italian day
60 Is yet his fitting charnel°-roof! while still   *mortuary*
He lies, as if in dewy sleep he lay;
Awake him not! surely he takes his fill
Of deep and liquid rest, forgetful of all ill.

8

He will awake no more, oh, never more!
65 Within the twilight chamber spreads apace,
The shadow of white Death, and at the door
Invisible Corruption waits to trace
His extreme way to her dim dwelling-place;
The eternal Hunger sits, but pity and awe
70 Soothe her pale rage, nor dares she to deface
So fair a prey, till darkness, and the law
Of mortal change, shall fill the grave which is her
    maw.°   *stomach*

9

O, weep for Adonais! The quick° Dreams,   *living*
The passion-winged Ministers of thought,
75 Who were his flocks, whom near the living streams
Of his young spirit he fed, and whom he taught
The love which was its music, wander not—
Wander no more, from kindling brain to brain,
But droop there, whence they sprung; and mourn their
    lot
80 Round the cold heart, where, after their sweet pain,
They ne'er will gather strength, or find a home again.

10

And one with trembling hands clasps his cold head,
And fans him with her moonlight wings, and cries,
"Our love, our hope, our sorrow, is not dead;

85 See, on the silken fringe of his faint eyes,
Like dew upon a sleeping flower, there lies
A tear some Dream has loosened from his brain."
Lost Angel of a ruined Paradise!
She knew not 'twas her own; as with no stain
90 She faded, like a cloud which had outwept its rain.

11

One from a lucid° urn of starry dew   *resplendent*
Washed his light limbs as if embalming them;
Another clipt her profuse locks, and threw
The wreath upon him, like an anadem,°   *garland*
95 Which frozen tears instead of pearls begem;
Another in her wilful grief would break
Her bow and winged reeds,° as if to stem   *arrows*
A greater loss with one which was more weak;
And dull the barbed fire against his frozen cheek.

12

100 Another Splendour on his mouth alit,
That mouth, whence it was wont to draw the breath
Which gave it strength to pierce the guarded wit,
And pass into the panting heart beneath
With lightning and with music: the damp death
105 Quenched its caress upon his icy lips;
And, as a dying meteor stains a wreath
Of moonlight vapour, which the cold night clips,°   *clasps*
It flushed through his pale limbs, and passed to its
    eclipse.

13

And others came … Desires and Adorations,
110 Winged Persuasions and veiled Destinies,
Splendours, and Glooms, and glimmering Incarnations
Of hopes and fears, and twilight Phantasies;
And Sorrow, with her family of Sighs,
And Pleasure, blind with tears, led by the gleam
115 Of her own dying smile instead of eyes,
Came in slow pomp—the moving pomp might seem
Like pageantry of mist on an autumnal stream.

14

All he had loved, and moulded into thought,
From shape, and hue, and odour, and sweet sound,

---

[1] *high Capital* Rome, where Keats died.

120 Lamented Adonais. Morning sought
Her eastern watchtower, and her hair unbound,
Wet with the tears which should adorn the ground,
Dimmed the aerial eyes that kindle day;
Afar the melancholy thunder moaned,
125 Pale Ocean in unquiet slumber lay,
And the wild winds flew round, sobbing in their dismay.

15

Lost Echo sits amid the voiceless mountains,
And feeds her grief with his remembered lay,°   song
And will no more reply to winds or fountains,
130 Or amorous birds perched on the young green spray,
Or herdsman's horn, or bell° at closing day;   church-bell
Since she can mimic not his lips, more dear
Than those for whose disdain she pined away
Into a shadow of all sounds[1]—a drear
135 Murmur, between their songs, is all the woodmen hear.

16

Grief made the young Spring wild, and she threw down
Her kindling buds, as if she Autumn were,
Or they dead leaves; since her delight is flown
For whom should she have waked the sullen year?
140 To Phoebus was not Hyacinth so dear[2]
Nor to himself Narcissus, as to both
Thou Adonais: wan they stand and sere°   withered
Amid the drooping comrades of their youth,
With dew all turned to tears; odour, to sighing ruth.°   pity

17

145 Thy spirit's sister, the lorn nightingale
Mourns not her mate with such melodious pain;

Not so the eagle, who like thee could scale
Heaven, and could nourish in the sun's domain
Her mighty youth with morning,[3] doth complain,
150 Soaring and screaming round her empty nest,
As Albion[4] wails for thee: the curse of Cain[5]
Light on his head who pierced thy innocent breast,
And scared the angel soul that was its earthly guest!

18

Ah woe is me! Winter is come and gone,
155 But grief returns with the revolving year;
The airs and streams renew their joyous tone;
The ants, the bees, the swallows reappear;
Fresh leaves and flowers deck the dead Seasons' bier;
The amorous birds now pair in every brake,°   thicket
160 And build their mossy homes in field and brere;°   briar
And the green lizard, and the golden snake,
Like unimprisoned flames, out of their trance awake.

19

Through wood and stream and field and hill and Ocean
A quickening life from the Earth's heart has burst
165 As it has ever done, with change and motion,
From the great morning of the world when first
God dawned on Chaos; in its steam immersed
The lamps of Heaven flash with a softer light;
All baser things pant with life's sacred thirst;
170 Diffuse themselves; and spend in love's delight,
The beauty and the joy of their renewed might.

20

The leprous corpse touched by this spirit tender
Exhales itself in flowers of gentle breath;
Like incarnations of the stars, when splendour
175 Is changed to fragrance, they illumine death
And mock the merry worm that wakes beneath;

---

1 *those for … sounds* Narcissus, whom the nymph Echo loved. Echo
had been robbed of her voice by the goddess Hera, and could only
repeat what others said. After falling in love with Narcissus, who
rejected her in favor of his own reflection, she pined away until only
her echoing voice remained.

2 *To Phoebus … dear* Phoebus Apollo, god of poetry and the sun,
loved the beautiful youth Hyacinthus. When Hyacinthus was
accidentally slain by a discus the god had thrown, Apollo caused the
hyacinth flower to spring up from his spilt blood. It was said that
Zephyrus (the west wind), a rejected suitor of Hyacinthus, blew the
discus off course so that it would strike the youth. "Zephyr" was also
the pen name of the reviewer of *Endymion*.

3 *nourish … morning* According to legend, the eagle could renew her
youth by flying toward the sun until its heat burnt off her old plumage
and cleared the film from her eyes.

4 *Albion* England.

5 *curse of Cain* For murdering his brother Abel, Cain was forced to
wander the earth as a vagabond, unable to farm because no land would
yield crops for him. See Genesis 4.

Nought we know, dies. Shall that alone which knows[1]
Be as a sword consumed before the sheath
By sightless[2] lightning?— th'intense atom glows
80   A moment, then is quenched in a most cold repose.

21

Alas! that all we loved of him should be,
But for our grief, as if it had not been,
And grief itself be mortal! Woe is me!
Whence are we, and why are we? of what scene
85   The actors or spectators? Great and mean
Meet massed in death, who lends what life must borrow.
As long as skies are blue, and fields are green,
Evening must usher night, night urge the morrow,
Month follow month with woe, and year wake year to
        sorrow.

22

90   *He* will awake no more, oh, never more!
"Wake thou," cried Misery, "childless Mother, rise
Out of thy sleep, and slake,° in thy heart's core,   *ease*
A wound more fierce than his with tears and sighs."
And all the Dreams that watched Urania's eyes,
95   And all the Echoes whom their sister's song
Had held in holy silence, cried: "Arise!"
Swift as a Thought by the snake Memory stung,
From her ambrosial rest the fading Splendour[3] sprung.

23

She rose like an autumnal Night, that springs
00   Out of the East, and follows wild and drear
The golden Day, which, on eternal wings,
Even as a ghost abandoning a bier,
Had left the Earth a corpse. Sorrow and fear
So struck, so roused, so rapt Urania;
05   So saddened round her like an atmosphere
Of stormy mist; so swept her on her way
Even to the mournful place where Adonais lay.

24

24
Out of her secret Paradise she sped,
Through camps and cities rough with stone, and steel,
210   And human hearts, which to her aery tread
Yielding not, wounded the invisible
Palms of her tender feet where'er they fell:
And barbed tongues, and thoughts more sharp than they
Rent the soft Form they never could repel,
215   Whose sacred blood, like the young tears of May,
Paved with eternal flowers that undeserving way.

25

25
In the death chamber for a moment Death,
Shamed by the presence of that living Might,
Blushed to annihilation, and the breath
220   Revisited those lips, and life's pale light
Flashed through those limbs, so late her dear delight.
"Leave me not wild and drear and comfortless,
As silent lightning leaves the starless night!
Leave me not!" cried Urania: her distress
225   Roused Death: Death rose and smiled, and met her
        vain caress.

26

26
"Stay yet awhile! speak to me once again;
Kiss me, so long but as a kiss may live;
And in my heartless breast and burning brain
That word, that kiss shall all thoughts else survive,
230   With food of saddest memory kept alive,
Now thou art dead, as if it were a part
Of thee, my Adonais! I would give
All that I am to be as thou now art!
But I am chained to Time, and cannot thence depart!

27

27
235   "Oh gentle child, beautiful as thou wert,
Why didst thou leave the trodden paths of men
Too soon, and with weak hands though mighty heart
Dare° the unpastured dragon in his den?   *challenge*
Defenceless as thou wert, oh where was then
240   Wisdom the mirrored shield,[4] or scorn the spear?

---

[1]   *that alone which knows*   I.e., the mind.

[2]   *sightless*   Invisible; blind.

[3]   *ambrosial*   Divine (ambrosia is the food of the gods); *the fading Splendour*   Urania.

[4]   *mirrored shield*   Because the stare of the Gorgon Medusa would turn men into stone, Perseus fought and defeated her by viewing her reflection in his shield.

Or hadst thou waited the full cycle, when
Thy spirit should have filled its crescent sphere,
The monsters of life's waste had fled from thee like deer.

28

"The herded wolves, bold only to pursue;
245 The obscene ravens, clamorous o'er the dead;
The vultures to the conqueror's banner true
Who feed where Desolation first has fed,
And whose wings rain contagion—how they fled,
When like Apollo, from his golden bow,
250 The Pythian of the age[1] one arrow sped
And smiled! The spoilers tempt no second blow,
They fawn on the proud feet that spurn them as they
        go.

29

"The sun comes forth, and many reptiles spawn;
He sets, and each ephemeral insect then
255 Is gathered into death without a dawn,
And the immortal stars awake again;
So is it in the world of living men:
A godlike mind soars forth, in its delight
Making earth bare and veiling heaven, and when
260 It sinks, the swarms that dimmed or shared its light
Leave to its kindred lamps the spirit's awful°   *awe-inspiring*
        night."

30

Thus ceased she: and the mountain shepherds came,
Their garlands sere, their magic mantles rent;
The Pilgrim of Eternity,[2] whose fame
265 Over his living head like Heaven is bent,
An early but enduring monument,
Came, veiling all the lightnings of his song
In sorrow; from her wilds Ierne° sent   *Ireland*
The sweetest lyrist of her saddest wrong,

270 And love taught grief to fall like music from his
        tongue.[3]

31

Midst others of less note, came one frail Form,[4]
A phantom among men; companionless
As the last cloud of an expiring storm
Whose thunder is its knell;° he, as I guess,   *funeral-bell*
275 Had gazed on Nature's naked loveliness,
Actæon-like,[5] and now he fled astray
With feeble steps o'er the world's wilderness,
And his own thoughts, along that rugged way,
Pursued, like raging hounds, their father and their prey.

32

280 A pardlike° Spirit beautiful and swift—   *leopard-like*
A Love in desolation masked—a Power
Girt round with weakness; it can scarce uplift
The weight of the superincumbent hour;
It is a dying lamp, a falling shower,
285 A breaking billow—even whilst we speak
Is it not broken? On the withering flower
The killing sun smiles brightly: on a cheek
The life can burn in blood, even while the heart may
        break.

33

His head was bound with pansies overblown,
290 And faded violets, white, and pied, and blue;
And a light spear topped with a cypress cone,
Round whose rude shaft dark ivy tresses grew[6]
Yet dripping with the forest's noonday dew,
Vibrated, as the ever-beating heart
295 Shook the weak hand that grasped it; of that crew

---

[1] *Pythian of the age* Byron, who attacked the unfavorable reviewers of his *Hours of Idleness* in his satire *English Bards and Scotch Reviewers* (1809). The epithet "Pythian" was given to the god Apollo when he slew the dragon Python.

[2] *Pilgrim of Eternity* Byron.

[3] *The sweetest … tongue* Poet Thomas Moore (1779–1852), whose *Irish Melodies* deals with the oppression of his native Ireland by England.

[4] *one frail Form* Shelley.

[5] *Actæon-like* Actaeon was a hunter who accidentally came upon Diana, goddess of chastity, bathing naked. Angered, she turned him into a stag, and his own hounds chased him down and tore him apart.

[6] *pansies overblown* Pansies (a symbol of sorrow) past their bloom; *violets* Representing death; *light spear … tresses grew* Thyrsus, staff borne by Dionysus, the god of fertility, and his followers.

He came the last, neglected and apart;
A herd-abandoned deer struck by the hunter's dart.

34

All stood aloof, and at his partial° moan   *sympathetic*
Smiled through their tears; well knew that gentle band
Who in another's fate now wept his own;
As in the accents of an unknown land,
He sung new sorrow; sad Urania scanned
The Stranger's mien, and murmured: "who art thou?"
He answered not, but with a sudden hand
Made bare his branded and ensanguined° brow,   *bloody*
Which was like Cain's or Christ's—Oh! that it should
          be so!

35

What softer voice is hushed over the dead?
Athwart what brow is that dark mantle thrown?
What form leans sadly o'er the white death-bed,
In mockery of monumental stone,
The heavy heart heaving without a moan?
If it be He, who, gentlest of the wise,
Taught, soothed, loved, honoured the departed one;[1]
Let me not vex, with inharmonious sighs
The silence of that heart's accepted sacrifice.

36

Our Adonais has drunk poison—oh!
What deaf and viperous murderer could crown
Life's early cup with such a draught of woe?
The nameless worm would now itself disown:
It felt, yet could escape the magic tone
Whose prelude held all envy, hate, and wrong,
But what was howling in one breast alone,
Silent with expectation of the song,
Whose master's hand is cold, whose silver lyre unstrung.[2]

---

[1] *He, who ... one* Radical journalist Leigh Hunt, to whom Keats dedicated his first volume.

[2] *silver lyre unstrung* On Keats's tomb is engraved the image of a Greek lyre with half its strings broken. According to his friend Joseph Severn, this symbolizes "his classical genius cut off by death before its maturity."

37

325 Live thou, whose infamy is not thy fame!
Live! fear no heavier chastisement from me,
Thou noteless blot on a remembered name!
But be thyself, and know thyself to be!
And ever at thy season be thou free
330 To spill the venom when thy fangs o'er flow:
Remorse and Self-contempt shall cling to thee;
Hot Shame shall burn upon thy secret brow,
And like a beaten hound tremble thou shalt—as now.

38

Nor let us weep that our delight is fled
335 Far from these carrion kites[3] that scream below;
He wakes or sleeps with the enduring dead;
Thou canst not soar where he is sitting now.
Dust to the dust! but the pure spirit shall flow
Back to the burning fountain whence it came,
340 A portion of the Eternal, which must glow
Through time and change, unquenchably the same,
Whilst thy cold embers choke the sordid hearth of
          shame.

39

Peace, peace! he is not dead, he doth not sleep—
He hath awakened from the dream of life—
345 'Tis we who lost in stormy visions keep
With phantoms an unprofitable strife,
And in mad trance, strike with our spirit's knife
Invulnerable nothings. *We* decay
Like corpses in a charnel; fear and grief
350 Convulse us and consume us day by day,
And cold hopes swarm like worms within our living
          clay.

40

He has outsoared the shadow of our night;
Envy and calumny° and hate and pain,   *slander*
And that unrest which men miscall delight,
355 Can touch him not and torture not again;
From the contagion of the world's slow stain
He is secure, and now can never mourn

---

[3] *kites* Falcon-like birds of prey.

A heart grown cold, a head grown grey in vain;
Nor, when the spirit's self has ceased to burn,
360   With sparkless ashes load an unlamented urn.

41

He lives, he wakes—'tis Death is dead, not he;
Mourn not for Adonais. Thou young Dawn
Turn all thy dew to splendour, for from thee
The spirit thou lamentest is not gone;
365   Ye caverns and ye forests, cease to moan!
Cease ye faint flowers and fountains, and thou Air
Which like a mourning veil thy scarf hadst thrown
O'er the abandoned Earth, now leave it bare
Even to the joyous stars which smile on its despair!

42

370   He is made one with Nature: there is heard
His voice in all her music, from the moan
Of thunder, to the song of night's sweet bird;[1]
He is a presence to be felt and known
In darkness and in light, from herb and stone,
375   Spreading itself where'er that Power may move
Which has withdrawn his being to its own;
Which wields the world with never wearied love,
Sustains it from beneath, and kindles it above.

43

He is a portion of the loveliness
380   Which once he made more lovely: he doth bear
His part, while the one Spirit's plastic° stress   *formative*
Sweeps through the dull dense world, compelling there,
All new successions to the forms they wear;
Torturing th'unwilling dross° that checks   *impure matter*
   its flight
385   To its own likeness, as each mass may bear;
And bursting in its beauty and its might
From trees and beasts and men into the Heaven's light.

44

The splendours of the firmament of time
May be eclipsed, but are extinguished not;

390   Like stars to their appointed height they climb
And death is a low mist which cannot blot
The brightness it may veil. When lofty thought
Lifts a young heart above its mortal lair,
And love and life contend in it, for what
395   Shall be its earthly doom,° the dead live there   *fate*
And move like winds of light on dark and stormy air.

45

The inheritors of unfulfilled renown
Rose from their thrones, built beyond mortal thought,
Far in the Unapparent. Chatterton[2]
400   Rose pale, his solemn agony had not
Yet faded from him; Sidney,[3] as he fought
And as he fell and as he lived and loved
Sublimely mild, a Spirit without spot,
Arose; and Lucan,[4] by his death approved:
405   Oblivion as they rose shrank like a thing reproved.

46

And many more, whose names on Earth are dark
But whose transmitted effluence cannot die
So long as fire outlives the parent spark,
Rose, robed in dazzling immortality.
410   "Thou art become as one of us," they cry,
"It was for thee yon kingless sphere has long
Swung blind in unascended majesty,
Silent alone amid an Heaven of song.
Assume thy winged throne, thou Vesper[5] of our
   throng!"

47

415   Who mourns for Adonais? Oh come forth
Fond° wretch! and know thyself and him aright.   *foolish*
Clasp with thy panting soul the pendulous Earth;

---

[1]   *night's sweet bird*   I.e., the nightingale, in reference to Keats's "Ode to a Nightingale."

[2]   *Chatterton*   Poet Thomas Chatterton, who died by suicide in 1770 at the age of 17.

[3]   *Sidney*   Sir Philip Sidney (1554–86), who was killed in battle when he was 31.

[4]   *Lucan*   First-century CE Roman poet Marcus Annaeus Lucan, who at the age of twenty-five killed himself to avoid being executed for conspiring against the tyrannical emperor Nero.

[5]   *Vesper*   The evening star.

As from a centre, dart thy spirit's light
Beyond all worlds, until its spacious might
20 Satiate the void circumference: then shrink
Even to a point within our day and night;
And keep thy heart light lest it make thee sink
When hope has kindled hope, and lured thee to the
    brink.

48

Or go to Rome, which is the sepulchre
25 O, not of him, but of our joy: 'tis nought
That ages, empires, and religions there
Lie buried in the ravage they have wrought;
For such as he can lend°—they borrow not   *bestow*
Glory from those who made the world their prey;
30 And he is gathered to the kings of thought
Who waged contention with their time's decay,
And of the past are all that cannot pass away.

49

Go thou to Rome—at once the Paradise,
The grave, the city, and the wilderness;
35 And where its wrecks like shattered mountains rise,
And flowering weeds, and fragrant copses° dress   *thickets*
The bones of Desolation's nakedness
Pass, till the Spirit of the spot shall lead
Thy footsteps to a slope of green access[1]
40 Where, like an infant's smile, over the dead,
A light of laughing flowers along the grass is spread.

50

And gray walls moulder round,[2] on which dull Time
Feeds, like slow fire upon a hoary° brand;[3]   *white*
And one keen pyramid with wedge sublime,
45 Pavilioning the dust of him who planned
This refuge for his memory, doth stand
Like flame transformed to marble; and beneath,

---

[1] *slope of green access* The Protestant Cemetery in Rome, where Keats is buried. Shelley's son William, who died at age three, is also buried there.

[2] *gray ... round* One of the boundaries of the cemetery incorporates the wall of ancient Rome, while another is formed by the pyramid-tomb of Roman tribune Caius Cestius.

[3] *brand* Burning log.

A field is spread, on which a newer band
Have pitched in Heaven's smile their camp of death
450 Welcoming him we lose with scarce extinguished
    breath.

51

Here pause: these graves are all too young as yet
To have outgrown the sorrow which consigned
Its charge to each; and if the seal is set,
Here, on one fountain of a mourning mind,
455 Break it not thou! too surely shalt thou find
Thine own well full, if thou returnest home,
Of tears and gall. From the world's bitter wind
Seek shelter in the shadow of the tomb.
What Adonais is, why fear we to become?

52

460 The One remains, the many change and pass;
Heaven's light forever shines, Earth's shadows fly;
Life, like a dome of many-coloured glass,
Stains the white radiance of Eternity,
Until Death tramples it to fragments. Die,
465 If thou wouldst be with that which thou dost seek!
Follow where all is fled! Rome's azure sky,
Flowers, ruins, statues, music, words, are weak
The glory they transfuse with fitting truth to speak.

53

Why linger, why turn back, why shrink, my Heart?
470 Thy hopes are gone before: from all things here
They have departed; thou shouldst now depart!
A light is past from the revolving year,
And man, and woman; and what still is dear
Attracts to crush, repels to make thee wither.
475 The soft sky smiles—the low wind whispers near:
'Tis Adonais calls! Oh, hasten thither,
No more let Life divide what Death can join together.

54

That Light whose smile kindles the Universe,
That Beauty in which all things work and move,
480 That Benediction which the eclipsing Curse
Of birth can quench not, that sustaining Love
Which through the web of being blindly wove

By man and beast and earth and air and sea,
Burns bright or dim, as[1] each are mirrors of
485   The fire for which all thirst; now beams on me,
Consuming the last clouds of cold mortality.

55

The breath whose might I have invoked in song
Descends on me; my spirit's bark is driven,
Far from the shore, far from the trembling throng
490   Whose sails were never to the tempest given;
The massy earth and sphered skies are riven!
I am borne darkly, fearfully, afar;
Whilst burning through the inmost veil of Heaven,
The soul of Adonais, like a star,
495   Beacons from the abode where the Eternal are.
—1821

from *Hellas*[2]

CHORUS[3]

Worlds on worlds are rolling ever
From creation to decay,
Like the bubbles on a river
Sparkling, bursting, borne away.
5   But they[4] are still immortal

Who, through birth's orient° portal   *eastern*
And death's dark chasm hurrying to and fro,
Clothe their unceasing flight
In the brief dust and light
10   Gathered around their chariots as they go;
New shapes they still may weave,
New gods, new laws receive,
Bright or dim are they as the robes they last
On Death's bare ribs had cast.

15   A power from the unknown God,[5]
A Promethean conqueror, came;
Like a triumphal path he trod
The thorns of death and shame.
A mortal shape to him
20   Was like the vapour dim
Which the orient planet[6] animates with light;
Hell, Sin, and Slavery came,
Like bloodhounds mild and tame,
Nor preyed, until their Lord had taken flight;
25   The moon of Mahomet[7]
Arose, and it shall set:
While blazoned as on Heaven's immortal noon
The cross leads generations on.[8]

Swift as the radiant shapes of sleep
30   From one whose dreams are Paradise

---

[1] *as*   I.e., to the extent that.

[2] *Hellas*   Classical name for Greece. Shelley's inspiration for the poem was the 1821 Greek revolt (against the Turks), which began their eleven-year war for independence. He uses as a model fifth century BCE playwright Aeschylus's *Persians*, which details the Greek defeat of Xerxes and the invading Persians at Salamis in 480 BCE. In his preface to the play, Shelley explains that his interest in Greece results from his belief that the culture, religion, and laws of his society all have their roots in Greece (a belief, common at the time, often referred to now as "Romantic Hellenism"). He also declares his wholehearted support for the Greek cause in an age characterized by "war of the oppressed against the oppressors."

[3] *CHORUS*   Shelley's chorus is composed of Greek women in Constantinople, the city founded by Roman Emperor Constantine the Great but conquered by the Ottoman Empire in 1453.

[4] *they*   "Living and thinking beings which inhabit the planets." In a note to *Hellas*, Shelley says that in this first stanza he contrasts the immortality of these beings with "the transience of the noblest manifestations of the external world." The following verses go on, he says, to "indicate a progressive state of more or less exalted existence, according to the degree of perfection which every distinct intelligence may have attained," and to "conjecture the condition of futurity towards which we are all impelled by an inextinguishable thirst for immortality."

[5] *unknown God*   God is here "unknown" because this is before the coming of Christ. Shelley goes on to compare Christ to Prometheus, the classical god who stole fire from Mount Olympus (home of the gods) and gave it to humans. For this, Zeus, King of the gods, chained him to a rock and had an eagle (in some versions, a vulture) eat out his liver, which grew back daily only to be devoured again.

[6] *orient planet*   Venus, which appears in the east as the morning star.

[7] *moon of Mahomet*   Crescent moon, the emblem of Islam (which was founded by the prophet Mohammed in the sixth century CE).

[8] *While blazoned ... on*   In 312 CE, Constantine is said to have beheld a flaming cross inscribed with the words "In this sign, thou shalt conquer." He converted to Christianity and won control of Rome.

Fly, when the fond° wretch° wakes   *foolish / mortal*
    to weep,
    And Day peers forth with her blank eyes;
      So fleet, so faint, so fair,
      The Powers of earth and air
35 Fled from the folding-star[1] of Bethlehem:
      Apollo, Pan, and Love,
      And even Olympian Jove[2]
Grew weak, for killing Truth had glared on them;
      Our hills and seas and streams,
40   Dispeopled of their dreams,
Their waters turned to blood, their dew to tears.
      Wailed for the golden years. ...

CHORUS[3]

The world's great age begins anew,
    The golden years return,
45 The earth doth like a snake renew
    Her winter weeds outworn:
Heaven smiles, and faiths and empires gleam,
Like wrecks of a dissolving dream.

A brighter Hellas rears its mountains
50   From waves serener far;
A new Peneus[4] rolls his fountains°   *waters*
    Against the morning star.

Where fairer Tempes bloom, there sleep
Young Cyclads[5] on a sunnier deep.

55 A loftier Argo[6] cleaves the main,°   *sea*
    Fraught with a later prize;
Another Orpheus[7] sings again,
    And loves, and weeps, and dies.
A new Ulysses leaves once more
60 Calypso for his native shore.[8]

Oh, write no more the tale of Troy,
    If earth Death's scroll must be!
Nor mix with Laian rage the joy
    Which dawns upon the free:
65 Although a subtler Sphinx renew
Riddles of death Thebes never knew.[9]

Another Athens shall arise,
    And to remoter time
Bequeath, like sunset to the skies,
70   The splendour of its prime;

[1] *folding-star*   I.e., star that appears as shepherds are herding their sheep back to the pen (fold).

[2] *Apollo ... Jove*   Greek and Roman gods.

[3] [From Shelley's note]   The final chorus is indistinct and obscure, as the event of the living drama whose arrival it foretells. Prophesies of wars, and rumours of wars, etc., may safely be made by poet or prophet in any age, but to anticipate however darkly a period of regeneration and happiness is a more hazardous exercise of the faculty which bards possess or feign.... [This chorus occurs after the Greek rebels have been defeated by the Turks.]

[4] *Peneus*   River in Thessaly, also known as the Salambria, which flows from Mount Pindus (one of the homes of the Muses) through the Tempe Valley; also, god of that river.

[5] *Cyclads*   Islands in the Aegean Sea off the southeast shore of Greece.

[6] *Argo*   Ship of classical myth in which Jason sailed in search of the Golden Fleece.

[7] *Orpheus*   Celebrated Thracian musician and poet of Greek mythology. When his beloved, Eurydice, was killed by a snake, he so charmed Hades with his lyre playing that Hades allowed him to lead Eurydice back with him, provided he not look at her on the journey from the underworld. When he could not resist making sure she was behind him, she was condemned to return to Hades forever. In his grief, Orpheus spent the rest of his life as a wandering recluse until the women of Thrace, enraged by his inattention, tore him to pieces.

[8] *A new ... shore*   Ulysses (Odysseus) in Homer's *Odyssey* is shipwrecked on the nymph Calypso's island on his voyage home from the Trojan War. He spends seven years with her, entranced by her charms, until finally leaving to continue his voyage home.

[9] *Nor mix ... knew*   Laius, King of Thebes, ordered the death of his son Oedipus after it was prophesied that the boy would later kill him. Oedipus was rescued and grew up in ignorance of his origin. As a grown man he became involved in a dispute with Laius, not knowing him to be his father, and killed him. He then married Laius's widow, similarly ignorant of her identity as his mother. When he discovered what he had done, he blinded himself, and his mother committed suicide. The Sphinx was a monster who challenged travelers on the road to Thebes with riddles. If they solved the riddle (as Oedipus did) they were allowed to pass. If they did not, they were slain.

And leave, if nought so bright may live,
All earth can take or Heaven can give.

Saturn and Love their long repose
    Shall burst, more bright and good
75 Than all who fell, than One who rose,
    Than many unsubdued:[1]
Not gold, not blood, their altar dowers,°   *dowries*
But votive tears and symbol flowers.

Oh, cease! must hate and death return?
    Cease! must men kill and die?
80 Cease! drain not to its dregs the urn
    Of bitter prophecy.
The world is weary of the past,
Oh, might it die or rest at last!
—1822

Julian and Maddalo
A Conversation

PREFACE

The meadows with fresh streams, the bees with thyme,
The goats with the green leaves of budding Spring,
Are saturated not—nor Love with tears.

                      VIRGIL, Ecl. X.

Count Maddalo[2] is a Venetian nobleman of ancient family and of great fortune, who, without mixing much in the society of his countrymen, resides chiefly at his magnificent palace in that city. He is a person of the most consummate genius, and capable, if he would direct his energies to such an end, of becoming the redeemer of his degraded country. But it is his weakness to be proud: he derives, from a comparison of his own extraordinary mind with the dwarfish intellects that surround him, an intense apprehension of the nothingness of human life. His passions and his powers are incomparably greater than those of other men; and, instead of the latter having been employed in curbing the former, they have mutually lent each other strength. His ambition preys upon itself, for want of objects which it can consider worthy of exertion. I say that Maddalo is proud, because I can find no other word to express the concentred and impatient feelings which consume him; but it is on his own hopes and affections only that he seems to trample, for in social life no human being can be more gentle, patient and unassuming than Maddalo. He is cheerful, frank and witty. His more serious conversation is a sort of intoxication; men are held by it as by a spell. He has travelled much; and there is an inexpressible charm in his relation of his adventures in different countries.

Julian[3] is an Englishman of good family, passionately attached to those philosophical notions which assert the power of man over his own mind, and the immense improvements of which, by the extinction of certain moral superstitions, human society may be yet susceptible. Without concealing the evil in the world he is forever speculating how good may be made superior. He is a complete infidel and a scoffer at all things reputed holy; and Maddalo takes a wicked pleasure in drawing out his taunts against religion. What Maddalo thinks on these matters is not exactly known. Julian, in spite of his heterodox opinions, is conjectured by his friends to possess some good qualities. How far this is possible the pious reader will determine. Julian is rather serious.

---

[1] [From Shelley's note] Saturn and Love were among the deities of a real or imaginary state of innocence and happiness. *All* those *who fell*, or the Gods of Greece, Asia and Egypt; the *One who rose*, or Jesus Christ …; and *the many unsubdued*, or the monstrous objects of the idolatry of China, India, the Antarctic islands, and the native tribes of America.

[2] *Count Maddalo* This character strongly resembles Lord Byron, with whom Shelley was close friends. The two regularly corresponded, visited each other, and spent much time in debate and philosophical discussion. Byron said to Thomas Medwin, Shelley's cousin and lifelong friend of Byron, that Shelley's portrayal of him in *Julian and Maddalo* did "not make [him] cut a good figure."

[3] *Julian* This character serves as a mirror of Shelley, enabling him to apply his own philosophies to the circumstances and contrast his ideals to those of Byron.

Of the Maniac[1] I can give no information. He seems, by his own account, to have been disappointed in love. He was evidently a very cultivated and amiable person when in his right senses. His story, told at length, might be like many other stories of the same kind. The unconnected exclamations of his agony will perhaps be found a sufficient comment for the text of every heart.

I rode one evening with Count Maddalo
  Upon the bank of land which breaks the flow
Of Adria[2] towards Venice: a bare strand
Of hillocks, heaped from ever-shifting sand,
5 Matted with thistles and amphibious weeds,
Such as from earth's embrace the salt ooze breeds,
Is this; an uninhabited sea-side,
Which the lone fisher, when his nets are dried,
Abandons; and no other object breaks
10 The waste, but one dwarf tree and some few stakes
Broken and unrepaired, and the tide makes
A narrow space of level sand thereon,
Where 'twas our wont to ride while day went down.
This ride was my delight. I love all waste°   *uninhabited*
15 And solitary places; where we taste
The pleasure of believing what we see
Is boundless, as we wish our souls to be:
And such was this wide ocean, and this shore
More barren than its billows; and yet more
20 Than all, with a remembered friend I love
To ride as then I rode—for the winds drove
The living spray along the sunny air
Into our faces; the blue heavens were bare,
Stripped to their depths by the awakening north;
25 And, from the waves, sound like delight broke forth
Harmonizing with solitude, and sent
Into our hearts aerial merriment.

So, as we rode, we talked; and the swift thought,
Winging itself with laughter, lingered not,
30 But flew from brain to brain—such glee was ours,
Charged with light memories of remembered hours,
None slow enough for sadness: till we came
Homeward, which always makes the spirit tame.
This day had been cheerful but cold, and now
35 The sun was sinking, and the wind also.
Our talk grew somewhat serious, as may be
Talk interrupted with such raillery
As mocks itself, because it cannot scorn
The thoughts it would extinguish—'twas forlorn,
40 Yet pleasing, such as once, so poets tell,
The devils held within the dales of Hell,
Concerning God, freewill and destiny;
Of all that earth has been or yet may be,
All that vain men imagine or believe,
45 Or hope can paint or suffering may achieve,
We descanted;° and I (for ever still   *discussed*
Is it not wise to make the best of ill?)
Argued against despondency, but pride
Made my companion take the darker side.
50 The sense that he was greater than his kind
Had struck, methinks, his eagle spirit blind
By gazing on its own exceeding light.
Meanwhile the sun paused ere it should alight,
Over the horizon of the mountains—Oh,
55 How beautiful is sunset, when the glow
Of Heaven descends upon a land like thee,
Thou Paradise of exiles, Italy!
Thy mountains, seas, and vineyards, and the towers
Of cities they encircle!—It was ours
60 To stand on thee, beholding it: and then,
Just where we had dismounted, the Count's men
Were waiting for us with the gondola.—
As those who pause on some delightful way
Though bent on pleasant pilgrimage,[3] we stood
65 Looking upon the evening, and the flood
Which lay between the city and the shore

---

[1] *the Maniac* This character does not seem to represent a specific individual. The maniac does have much in common, however, with many literary figures of the Romantic period, including a number in Byron's writings—notably Bonnivard of *The Prisoner of Chillon* and Tasso of *The Lament of Tasso*.

[2] *Adria* The Adriatic Sea, a body of water that lies between Italy and the Balkan Peninsula.

---

[3] *As ... pilgrimage* Italy and much of continental Europe was frequented by travelers from England, who often undertook the journeys in hope of finding artistic inspiration.

Paved with the image of the sky …[1] the hoar
And airy Alps towards the North appeared
Through mist, a heaven-sustaining bulwark reared
70   Between the East and West; and half the sky
Was roofed with clouds of rich emblazonry
Dark purple at the zenith, which still grew
Down the steep West into a wondrous hue
Brighter than burning gold, even to the rent
75   Where the swift sun yet paused in his descent
Among the many-folded hills: they were
Those famous Euganean hills,[2] which bear,
As seen from Lido[3] through the harbor piles,
The likeness of a clump of peakèd isles—
80   And then—as if the earth and sea had been
Dissolved into one lake of fire, were seen
Those mountains towering as from waves of flame
Around the vaporous sun, from which there came
The inmost purple spirit of light, and made
85   Their very peaks transparent. "Ere it fade,"
Said my companion, "I will show you soon
A better station"—So, o'er the lagoon
We glided; and from that funereal bark
I leaned, and saw the city, and could mark
90   How from their many isles, in evening's gleam,
Its temples and its palaces did seem
Like fabrics of enchantment piled to Heaven.
I was about to speak, when—"We are even
Now at the point I meant," said Maddalo,
95   And bade the gondolieri cease to row.
"Look, Julian, on the west, and listen well
If you hear not a deep and heavy bell."
I looked, and saw between us and the sun
A building on an island; such a one
100   As age to age might add, for uses vile,
A windowless, deformed and dreary pile;
And on the top an open tower, where hung
A bell, which in the radiance swayed and swung;
We could just hear its hoarse and iron tongue;

105   The broad sun sunk behind it, and it tolled
In strong and black relief.—"What we behold
Shall be the madhouse and its belfry tower,"
Said Maddalo; "and ever at this hour
Those who may cross the water hear that bell,
110   Which calls the maniacs, each one from his cell,
To vespers."[4]—"As much skill as need to pray
In thanks or hope for their dark lot have they
To their stern maker," I replied. "O ho!
You talk as in years past," said Maddalo.
115   'Tis strange men change not. You were ever still
Among Christ's flock a perilous infidel,
A wolf for the meek lambs—if you can't swim
Beware of Providence." I looked on him,
But the gay smile had faded in his eye.
120   "And such," he cried, "is our mortality,
And this must be the emblem and the sign
Of what should be eternal and divine!—
And, like that black and dreary bell, the soul,
Hung in a heaven-illumined tower, must toll
125   Our thoughts and our desires to meet below
Round the rent heart and pray—as madmen do
For what? they know not—till the night of death,
As sunset that strange vision, severeth
Our memory from itself, and us from all
130   We sought, and yet were baffled." I recall
The sense of what he said, although I mar
The force of his expressions. The broad star
Of day meanwhile had sunk behind the hill,
And the black bell became invisible,
135   And the red tower looked gray, and all between
The churches, ships and palaces were seen
Huddled in gloom—into the purple sea
The orange hues of heaven sunk silently.
We hardly spoke, and soon the gondola
140   Conveyed me to my lodgings by the way.

    The following morn was rainy, cold and dim:
Ere Maddalo arose, I called on him,
And whilst I waited with his child[5] I played;

---

[1]   … The ellipses throughout this poem appear in Shelley's original.

[2]   *Euganean hills* Volcanic hills that run along the Padovan-Venetian Plain, south of Padua. Shelley also wrote of them in "Lines Written Among the Euganean Hills."

[3]   *Lido* Venice Lido, a long island just south of Venice.

[4]   *vespers* Evening prayers.

[5]   *his child* Maddalo's child is thought to be modeled on Byron's daughter Allegra.

A lovelier toy sweet Nature never made,
45 A serious, subtle, wild, yet gentle being,
Graceful without design and unforeseeing,
With eyes—Oh, speak not of her eyes!—which seem
Twin mirrors of Italian Heaven, yet gleam
With such deep meaning as we never see
50 But in the human countenance: with me
She was a special favorite: I had nursed
Her fine and feeble limbs when she came first
To this bleak world; and she yet seemed to know
On second sight her ancient playfellow,
55 Less changed than she was by six months or so;
For after her first shyness was worn out
We sat there, rolling billiard balls about,
When the Count entered. Salutations past—
"The word you spoke last night might well have cast
60 A darkness on my spirit—if man be
The passive thing you say, I should not see
Much harm in the religions and old saws
(Though I may never own such leaden laws)
Which break a teachless nature to the yoke:
65 Mine is another faith"— thus much I spoke
And noting he replied not, added: "See
This lovely child, blithe, innocent and free;
She spends a happy time with little care,
While we to such sick thoughts subjected are
70 As came on you last night—it is our will
That thus enchains us to permitted ill—
We might be otherwise—we might be all
We dream of happy, high, majestical.
Where is the love, beauty, and truth we seek
75 But in our mind? and if we were not weak
Should we be less in deed than in desire?"
"Ay, if we were not weak—and we aspire
How vainly to be strong!" said Maddalo:
"You talk Utopia." "It remains to know,"
80 I then rejoined, "and those who try may find
How strong the chains are which our spirit bind;
Brittle perchance as straw … We are assured
Much may be conquered, much may be endured,
Of what degrades and crushes us. We know
85 That we have power over ourselves to do
And suffer—what, we know not till we try;

But something nobler than to live and die—
So taught those kings of old philosophy[1]
Who reigned, before Religion made men blind;
190 And those who suffer with their suffering kind
Yet feel this faith religion." "My dear friend,"
Said Maddalo, "my judgment will not bend
To your opinion, though I think you might
Make such a system refutation-tight
195 As far as words go. I knew one like you
Who to this city came some months ago,
With whom I argued in this sort, and he
Is now gone mad—and so he answered me
Poor fellow! but if you would like to go
200 We'll visit him, and his wild talk will show
How vain are such aspiring theories."
"I hope to prove the induction otherwise,
And that a want of that true theory, still,
Which seeks a 'soul of goodness' in things ill
205 Or in himself or others, has thus bowed
His being—There are some by nature proud,
Who patient in all else demand but this—
To love and be beloved with gentleness;
And, being scorned, what wonder if they die
210 Some living death? this is not destiny
But man's own wilful ill."
                          As thus I spoke
Servants announced the gondola, and we
Through the fast-falling rain and high-wrought sea
Sailed to the island where the madhouse stands.
215 We disembarked. The clap of tortured hands,
Fierce yells and howlings and lamentings keen,
And laughter where complaint had merrier been,
Moans, shrieks, and curses, and blaspheming prayers
Accosted us. We climbed the oozy stairs
220 Into an old courtyard. I heard on high,
Then, fragments of most touching melody,
But looking up saw not the singer there—
Through the black bars in the tempestuous air
I saw, like weeds on a wrecked palace growing,
225 Long tangled locks flung wildly forth, and flowing,
Of those who on a sudden were beguiled

---

[1] *kings of old philosophy* Philosophers of Ancient Greece.

Into strange silence, and looked forth and smiled
Hearing sweet sounds—Then I: "Methinks there were
A cure of these with patience and kind care,
230 If music can thus move … but what is he
Whom we seek here?" "Of his sad history
I know but this," said Maddalo: "he came
To Venice a dejected man, and fame
Said he was wealthy, or he had been so;
235 Some thought the loss of fortune wrought him woe;
But he was ever talking in such sort
As you do—far more sadly—he seemed hurt,
Even as a man with his peculiar wrong,
To hear but of the oppression of the strong,
240 Or those absurd deceits (I think with you
In some respects, you know) which carry through
The excellent impostors of this earth
When they outface detection—he had worth,
Poor fellow! but a humourist in his way."
245 "Alas, what drove him mad?" "I cannot say;
A lady came with him from France, and when
She left him and returned, he wandered then
About yon lonely isles of desert sand
Till he grew wild—he had no cash or land
250 Remaining—the police had brought him here—
Some fancy took him and he would not bear
Removal; so I fitted up for him
Those rooms beside the sea, to please his whim,
And sent him busts and books and urns for flowers,
255 Which had adorned his life in happier hours,
And instruments of music—you may guess
A stranger could do little more or less
For one so gentle and unfortunate:
And those are his sweet strains which charm the weight
260 From madmen's chains, and make this Hell appear
A heaven of sacred silence, hushed to hear."—
"Nay, this was kind of you—he had no claim,
As the world says"—"None—but the very same
Which I on all mankind were I as he
265 Fallen to such deep reverse—his melody
Is interrupted—now we hear the din
Of madmen, shriek on shriek, again begin;
Let us now visit him; after this strain
He ever communes with himself again,

270 And sees nor hears not any." Having said
These words we called the keeper, and he led
To an apartment opening on the sea—
There the poor wretch was sitting mournfully
Near a piano, his pale fingers twined
275 One with the other, and the ooze and wind
Rushed through an open casement, and did sway
His hair, and starred it with the brackish spray;
His head was leaning on a music book,
And he was muttering, and his lean limbs shook;
280 His lips were pressed against a folded leaf
In hue too beautiful for health, and grief
Smiled in their motions as they lay apart—
As one who wrought from his own fervid heart
The eloquence of passion, soon he raised
285 His sad meek face and eyes lustrous and glazed
And spoke—sometimes as one who wrote, and thought
His words might move some heart that heeded not,
If sent to distant lands; and then as one
Reproaching deeds never to be undone
290 With wondering self-compassion; then his speech
Was lost in grief, and then his words came each
Unmodulated, cold, expressionless—
But that from one jarred accent you might guess
It was despair made them so uniform:
295 And all the while the loud and gusty storm
Hissed through the window, and we stood behind
Stealing his accents from the envious wind
Unseen. I yet remember what he said
Distinctly: such impression his words made.

300 "Month after month," he cried, "to bear this load
And, as a jade urged by the whip and goad,
To drag life on, which like a heavy chain
Lengthens behind with many a link of pain!—
And not to speak my grief—O, not to dare
305 To give a human voice to my despair,
But live and move, and, wretched thing! smile on
As if I never went aside to groan,
And wear this mask of falsehood even to those
Who are most dear—not for my own repose—
310 Alas! no scorn or pain or hate could be
So heavy as that falsehood is to me—

But that I cannot bear more altered faces
Than needs must be, more changed and cold embraces,
More misery, disappointment, and mistrust
5 To own me for their father … Would the dust
Were covered in upon my body now!
That the life ceased to toil within my brow!
And then these thoughts would at the least be fled;
Let us not fear such pain can vex the dead.

20   "What Power delights to torture us? I know
That to myself I do not wholly owe
What now I suffer, though in part I may.
Alas! none strewed sweet flowers upon the way
Where wandering heedlessly, I met pale Pain,
25 My shadow, which will leave me not again—
If I have erred, there was no joy in error,
But pain and insult and unrest and terror;
I have not as some do, bought penitence
With pleasure, and a dark yet sweet offence,
30 For then—if love and tenderness and truth
Had overlived hope's momentary youth,
My creed should have redeemed me from repenting;
But loathèd scorn and outrage unrelenting
Met love excited by far other seeming
35 Until the end was gained … as one from dreaming
Of sweetest peace, I woke, and found my state
Such as it is.—

            "O Thou, my spirit's mate
Who, for thou art compassionate and wise,
Wouldst pity me from thy most gentle eyes
40 If this sad writing thou shouldst ever see—
My secret groans must be unheard by thee,
Thou wouldst weep tears bitter as blood to know
Thy lost friend's incommunicable woe.

    "Ye few by whom my nature has been weighed
45 In friendship, let me not that name degrade
By placing on your hearts the secret load
Which crushes mine to dust. There is one road
To peace and that is truth, which follow ye!
Love sometimes leads astray to misery.
50 Yet think not though subdued—and I may well

Say that I am subdued—that the full Hell
Within me would infect the untainted breast
Of sacred Nature with its own unrest;
As some perverted beings think to find
355 In scorn or hate a medicine for the mind
Which scorn or hate have wounded—O how vain!
The dagger heals not, but may rend again …
Believe that I am ever still the same
In creed as in resolve, and what may tame
360 My heart, must leave the understanding free,
Or all would sink in this keen agony—
Nor dream that I will join the vulgar cry;
Or with my silence sanction tyranny;
Or seek a moment's shelter from my pain
365 In any madness which the world calls gain,
Ambition or revenge or thoughts as stern
As those which make me what I am; or turn
To avarice or misanthropy or lust …
Heap on me soon, O grave, thy welcome dust!
370 Till then the dungeon may demand its prey,
And Poverty and Shame may meet and say,
Halting beside me on the public way—
'That love-devoted youth is ours—let's sit
Beside him— he may live some six months yet.'
375 Or the red scaffold, as our country bends,
May ask some willing victim, or ye friends
May fall under some sorrow which this heart
Or hand may share or vanquish or avert;
I am prepared—in truth, with no proud joy—
380 To do or suffer aught, as when a boy
I did devote to justice and to love
My nature, worthless now! …

                    "I must remove
A veil from my pent mind. 'Tis torn aside!
O, pallid as Death's dedicated bride,
385 Thou mockery which art sitting by my side,
Am I not wan like thee? at the grave's call
I haste, invited to thy wedding-ball,
To greet the ghastly paramour, for whom
Thou hast deserted me … and made the tomb
390 Thy bridal bed … But I beside your feet
Will lie and watch ye from my winding-sheet—

Thus … wide awake though dead … yet stay, O, stay!
Go not so soon—I know not what I say—
Hear but my reasons … I am mad, I fear,
395   My fancy is o'erwrought … thou art not here …
Pale art thou, 'tis most true … but thou art gone,
Thy work is finished … I am left alone.—

    "Nay, was it I who wooed thee to this breast
Which like a serpent, thou envenomest
400   As in repayment of the warmth it lent?
Didst thou not seek me for thine own content?
Did not thy love awaken mine? I thought
That thou wert she who said, 'You kiss me not
Ever, I fear you do not love me now'—
405   In truth I loved even to my overthrow
Her, who would fain forget these words: but they
Cling to her mind, and cannot pass away.

    "You say that I am proud—that when I speak
My lip is tortured with the wrongs which break
410   The spirit it expresses … Never one
Humbled himself before, as I have done!
Even the instinctive worm on which we tread
Turns, though it wound not—then with prostrate head
Sinks in the dust and writhes like me—and dies?
415   No: wears a living death of agonies!
As the slow shadows of the pointed grass
Mark the eternal periods, his pangs pass
Slow, ever-moving—making moments be
As mine seem—each an immortality!

420   "That you had never seen me—never heard
My voice, and more than all had ne'er endured
The deep pollution of my loathed embrace—
That your eyes ne'er had laid love in my face—
That, like some maniac monk, I had torn out
425   The nerves of manhood by their bleeding root
With mine own quivering fingers, so that ne'er
Our hearts had for a moment mingled there
To disunite in horror—these were not
With thee like some suppressed and hideous thought
430   Which flits athwart our musings, but can find
No rest within a pure and gentle mind …

Thou sealedst them with many a bare broad word,
And searedst my memory o'er them—for I heard
And can forget not … they were ministered
435   One after one, those curses. Mix them up
Like self-destroying poisons in one cup,
And they will make one blessing, which thou ne'er
Didst imprecate for on[1] me—death.

                        "It were
A cruel punishment for one most cruel,
440   If such can love, to make that love the fuel
Of the mind's hell; hate, scorn, remorse, despair:
But me—whose heart a stranger's tear might wear
As water-drops the sandy fountain-stone,
Who loved and pitied all things, and could moan
445   For woes which others hear not, and could see
The absent with the glance of fantasy,
And with the poor and trampled sit and weep,
Following the captive to his dungeon deep;
Me—who am as a nerve o'er which do creep
450   The else unfelt oppressions of this earth,
And was to thee the flame upon thy hearth,
When all beside was cold—that thou on me
Shouldst rain these plagues of blistering agony![2]
Such curses are from lips once eloquent
455   With love's too partial praise—let none relent
Who intend deeds too dreadful for a name
Henceforth, if an example for the same
They seek … for thou on me lookedst so, and so—
And didst speak thus … and thus … I live to show
460   How much men bear and die not!

                        "Thou wilt tell
With the grimace of hate, how horrible
It was to meet my love when thine grew less;
Thou wilt admire how I could e'er address
Such features to love's work … this taunt, though true,
465   (For indeed Nature nor in form nor hue
Bestowed on me her choicest workmanship)

---

1 *imprecate for on* Bestow upon. (The word *imprecate* is normally used in the context of curses rather than blessings.)

2 *plagues of blistering agony* Reference to the biblical plagues in Exodus (see Exodus 5.1–23.36).

Shall not be thy defence ... for since thy lip
Met mine first, years long past, since thine eye kindled
With soft fire under mine, I have not dwindled
Nor changed in mind or body, or in aught
But as love changes what it loveth not
After long years and many trials.

                                    "How vain
Are words! I thought never to speak again,
Not even in secret, not to mine own heart—
But from my lips the unwilling accents start,
And from my pen the words flow as I write,
Dazzling my eyes with scalding tears ... my sight
Is dim to see that charactered in vain
On this unfeeling leaf which burns the brain
And eats into it ... blotting all things fair
And wise and good which time had written there.
Those who inflict must suffer, for they see
The work of their own hearts, and this must be
Our chastisement or recompense—O child!
I would that thine were like to be more mild[1]
For both our wretched sakes ... for thine the most
Who feelest already all that thou hast lost
Without the power to wish it thine again;
And as slow years pass, a funereal train
Each with the ghost of some lost hope or friend
Following it like its shadow, wilt thou bend
No thought on my dead memory?

                                    "Alas, love!
Fear me not ... against thee I would not move
A finger in despite.° Do I not live   malice
That thou mayst have less bitter cause to grieve?
I give thee tears for scorn and love for hate;
And that thy lot may be less desolate
Than his on whom thou tramplest, I refrain
From that sweet sleep which medicines all pain.
Then, when thou speakest of me, never say
'He could forgive not.' Here I cast away
All human passions, all revenge, all pride;
I think, speak, act no ill; I do but hide

Under these words, like embers, every spark
Of that which has consumed me—quick and dark
The grave is yawning ... as its roof shall cover
My limbs with dust and worms under and over
So let Oblivion hide this grief ... the air
Closes upon my accents as despair
Upon my heart—let death upon despair!"

        He ceased, and overcome leant back awhile,
Then rising, with a melancholy smile
Went to a sofa, and lay down, and slept
A heavy sleep, and in his dreams he wept
And muttered some familiar name, and we
Wept without shame in his society.°   company
I think I never was impressed so much;
The man who were not, must have lacked a touch
Of human nature ... Then we lingered not,
Although our argument was quite forgot,
But calling the attendants, went to dine
At Maddalo's; yet neither cheer nor wine
Could give us spirits, for we talked of him
And nothing else, till daylight made stars dim;
And we agreed his was some dreadful ill
Wrought on him boldly, yet unspeakable,
By a dear friend; some deadly change in love
Of one vowed deeply which he dreamed not of;
For whose sake he, it seemed, had fixed a blot
Of falsehood on his mind which flourished not
But in the light of all-beholding truth;
And having stamped this canker° on his youth   blemish
She had abandoned him—and how much more
Might be his woe, we guessed not—he had store
Of friends and fortune once, as we could guess
From his nice habits and his gentleness;
These were now lost ... it were a grief indeed
If he had changed one unsustaining reed
For all that such a man might else adorn.
The colors of his mind seemed yet unworn;
For the wild language of his grief was high,
Such as in measure were called poetry;
And I remember one remark which then
Maddalo made. He said—"Most wretched men

---

[1] *I would that ... more mild* I would prefer your [sufferings] to be
more mild.

545 Are cradled into poetry by wrong,
They learn in suffering what they teach in song."

    If I had been an unconnected man
    I, from this moment, should have formed some plan
    Never to leave sweet Venice—for to me
550 It was delight to ride by the lone sea;
    And then the town is silent—one may write
    Or read in gondolas by day or night,
    Having the little brazen lamp alight,
    Unseen, uninterrupted; books are there,
555 Pictures, and casts from all those statues fair
    Which were twin-born with poetry, and all
    We seek in towns, with little to recall
    Regrets for the green country.[1] I might sit
    In Maddalo's great palace, and his wit
560 And subtle talk would cheer the winter night
    And make me know myself, and the firelight
    Would flash upon our faces, till the day
    Might dawn and make me wonder at my stay:
    But I had friends in London too: the chief
565 Attraction here, was that I sought relief
    From the deep tenderness that maniac wrought
    Within me—'twas perhaps an idle thought—
    But I imagined that if day by day
    I watched him, and but seldom went away,
570 And studied all the beatings of his heart
    With zeal, as men study some stubborn art
    For their own good, and could by patience find
    An entrance to the caverns of his mind,
    I might reclaim him from this dark estate:
575 In friendships I had been most fortunate—
    Yet never saw I one whom I would call
    More willingly my friend; and this was all
    Accomplished not; such dreams of baseless good
    Oft come and go in crowds and solitude
580 And leave no trace—but what I now designed
    Made, for long years, impression on my mind.
    The following morning, urged by my affairs,
    I left bright Venice.

                        After many years
    And many changes I returned; the name
585 Of Venice, and its aspect, was the same;
    But Maddalo was travelling far away
    Among the mountains of Armenia.
    His dog was dead. His child had now become
    A woman; such as it has been my doom
590 To meet with few—a wonder of this earth,
    Where there is little of transcendent worth—
    Like one of Shakespeare's women:[2] kindly she,
    And, with a manner beyond courtesy,
    Received her father's friend; and, when I asked
595 Of the lorn maniac, she her memory tasked,
    And told as she had heard the mournful tale:
    "That the poor sufferer's health began to fail
    Two years from my departure, but that then
    The lady who had left him, came again.
600 Her mien had been imperious, but she now
    Looked meek—perhaps remorse had brought her low.
    Her coming made him better, and they stayed
    Together at my father's—for I played,
    As I remember, with the lady's shawl—
605 I might be six years old—but after all
    She left him" … "Why, her heart must have been tough:
    How did it end?" "And was not this enough?
    They met—they parted"—"Child, is there no more?"
    "Something within that interval which bore
610 The stamp of *why* they parted, *how* they met;
    Yet if thine agèd eyes disdain to wet
    Those wrinkled cheeks with youth's remembered tears,
    Ask me no more, but let the silent years
    Be closed and cered[3] over their memory,
615 As yon mute marble where their corpses lie."[4]
    I urged and questioned still, she told me how
    All happened—but the cold world shall not know.
    —1824 (WRITTEN 1818)

---

[1]   *green country*   England.

[2]   *Shakespeare's women*   Shelley is evidently referring here to idealized women characters in Shakespeare's plays—not characters such as Lady Macbeth.

[3]   *cered*   Wrapped in a cerecloth (wax-treated burial cloth).

[4]   *As … lie*   Silent as the memorials that lie above the dead.

Mutability

1

The flower that smiles to-day
    To-morrow dies;
All that we wish to stay
    Tempts and then flies.
5   What is this world's delight?
Lightning that mocks the night,
    Brief even as bright.

2

Virtue, how frail it is!
    Friendship how rare!
10   Love, how it sells poor bliss
    For proud despair!
But we, though soon they fall,
Survive their joy, and all
    Which ours we call.

3

15   Whilst skies are blue and bright,
    Whilst flowers are gay,
Whilst eyes that change ere night
    Make glad the day;
Whilst yet the calm hours creep,
20   Dream thou—and from thy sleep
    Then wake to weep.
—1824

Stanzas

Written in Dejection—December 1818, near Naples

1

The sun is warm, the sky is clear,
    The waves are dancing fast and bright,
Blue isles and snowy mountains wear
    The purple noon's transparent might,
5   The breath of the moist earth is light,
    Around its unexpanded buds;

Like many a voice of one delight,
    The winds, the birds, the ocean floods,
The City's voice itself, is soft like Solitude's.

2

10   I see the Deep's untrampled floor
    With green and purple seaweeds strown;
I see the waves upon the shore,
    Like light dissolved in star-showers,[1] thrown:
    I sit upon the sands alone—
15   The lightning of the noontide ocean
    Is flashing round me, and a tone
Arises from its measured motion,
How sweet! did any heart now share in my emotion.

3

Alas! I have nor hope nor health,
20   Nor peace within nor calm around,
Nor that content surpassing wealth
    The sage in meditation found,
    And walked with inward glory crowned—
Nor fame, nor power, nor love, nor leisure.
25   Others I see whom these surround—
    Smiling they live, and call life pleasure;—
To me that cup has been dealt in another measure.

4

Yet now despair itself is mild,
    Even as the winds and waters are;
30   I could lie down like a tired child,
    And weep away the life of care
    Which I have borne and yet must bear,
Till death like sleep might steal on me,
    And I might feel in the warm air
35   My cheek grow cold, and hear the sea
Breathe o'er my dying brain its last monotony.

5

Some might lament that I were cold,
    As I, when this sweet day is gone,
Which my lost heart, too soon grown old,
40   Insults with this untimely moan;

---

[1] star-showers   Meteor showers.

They might lament—for I am one
Whom men love not—and yet regret,
   Unlike this day, which, when the sun
   Shall on its stainless glory set,
45 Will linger, though enjoyed, like joy in memory yet.
—1824

Sonnet [*Lift Not the Painted Veil*]

Lift not the painted veil which those who live
   Call Life: though unreal shapes be pictured there,
And it but mimic all we would believe
With colours idly spread—behind, lurk Fear
5 And Hope, twin Destinies; who ever weave
Their shadows, o'er the chasm, sightless and drear.
I knew one who had lifted it—he sought,
For his lost heart was tender, things to love,
But found them not, alas! nor was there aught
10 The world contains, the which he could approve.
Through the unheeding many he did move,
A splendour among shadows, a bright blot
Upon this gloomy scene, a Spirit that strove
For truth, and like the Preacher[1] found it not.
—1824

To Night

1

Swiftly walk o'er the western wave,
   Spirit of Night!
Out of the misty eastern cave,
Where, all the long and lone daylight,
5 Thou wovest dreams of joy and fear,
Which make thee terrible and dear,
   Swift be thy flight!

2

Wrap thy form in a mantle gray,
   Star-inwrought!
10 Blind with thine hair the eyes of Day;
Kiss her until she be wearied out,
Then wander o'er city, and sea, and land,
Touching all with thine opiate° wand—   *sleep-inducing*
   Come, long-sought!

3

15 When I arose and saw the dawn,
   I sighed for thee;
When light rode high, and the dew was gone,
And noon lay heavy on flower and tree,
And the weary Day turned to his rest,
20 Lingering like an unloved guest,
   I sighed for thee.

4

Thy brother Death came, and cried,
   Wouldst thou me?
Thy sweet child Sleep, thy filmy-eyed,
25 Murmured like a noontide bee,
Shall I nestle near thy side?
Wouldst thou me? And I replied,
   No, not thee!

5

Death will come when thou art dead,
30   Soon, too soon—
Sleep will come when thou art fled;
Of neither would I ask the boon
I ask of thee, beloved Night—
Swift be thine approaching flight,
35   Come soon, soon!
—1824

---

[1] *Preacher* Speaker of Ecclesiastes, who says, "I have seen all the works that are done under the sun; and, behold, all is vanity and vexation of spirit" (1.14).

To ——

Music, when soft voices die,
Vibrates in the memory—
Odours, when sweet violets sicken,
Live within the sense they quicken.°   *vivify*

5 Rose leaves, when the rose is dead,
Are heaped for the beloved's bed;
And so thy thoughts, when thou art gone,
Love itself shall slumber on.
—1824

The Mask of Anarchy

On 16 August 1819, roughly 80,000 men, women, and children, led by radical orator Henry Hunt, peaceably gathered on St. Peter's Field in Manchester in support of parliamentary reform and a repeal of the corn laws (restricting the import and export of grain). After ordering the meeting to disband, the magistrates sent out the militia to attack the crowd. Eleven people were killed and over four hundred injured. When the Home Office condoned this violent response, public outrage was widespread, and the radical journal *The Examiner* was filled with indignant reports on what became known as the "Peterloo Massacre," in mockery of the English victory at the Battle of Waterloo.

Though he was in Italy at the time, Shelley was inspired by the public outcry in *The Examiner* to write *The Mask of Anarchy*. He sent the poem to Leigh Hunt, editor of the journal, in September 1819, but Hunt thought its publication would be a risk to both Shelley's reputation and that of *The Examiner*. When Hunt did finally print the poem, in 1832, it was with the subtitle and the specific references to Jon Scott, Earl of Eldon and Lord Chancellor (who was responsible for depriving Shelley of access to his children with Harriet, his first wife) and Home Secretary Sidmouth removed. He gave the title as *The Masque of Anarchy*, which Shelley had called the poem in a letter to him, thus making explicit the reference to the literary genre of the masque, a courtly drama.

The Mask of Anarchy
Written on the Occasion of the
Massacre at Manchester

1

As I lay asleep in Italy
There came a voice from over the Sea,
And with great power it forth led me
To walk in the visions of Poesy.

2

5 I met Murder on the way—
He had a mask like Castlereagh[1]—
Very smooth he looked, yet grim;
Seven bloodhounds[2] followed him;

3

All were fat; and well they might
10 Be in admirable plight,
For one by one, and two by two,
He tossed them human hearts to chew
Which from his wide cloak he drew.

4

Next came Fraud, and he had on,
15 Like Eldon, an ermined gown;[3]
His big tears, for he wept well,
Turned to mill-stones as they fell.[4]

5

And the little children, who
Round his feet played to and fro,

---

[1] *Castlereagh* Robert Stuart Castlereagh, Foreign Secretary (1812–22), who was very unpopular with radicals such as Shelley. In 1815 he was responsible for Britain's joining with seven other European nations to postpone the final abolition of the slave trade.

[2] *bloodhounds* Faction of Parliament that supported war.

[3] *ermined gown* Traditional robe of office for the Lord Chancellor.

[4] *big tears … fell* Lord Chancellor John Scott, 1st Earl of Eldon (1751–1838), frequently shed tears during his public appearances.

20   Thinking every tear a gem,
     Had their brains knocked out by them.

6

     Clothed with the Bible, as with light,
     And the shadows of the night,
     Like Sidmouth, next, Hypocrisy
25   On a crocodile[1] rode by.

7

     And many more Destructions played
     In this ghastly masquerade,
     All disguised, even to the eyes,
     Like Bishops, lawyers, peers, or spies.

8

30   Last came Anarchy: he rode
     On a white horse, splashed with blood;
     He was pale even to the lips,
     Like Death in the Apocalypse.[2]

9

     And he wore a kingly crown;
35   And in his grasp a sceptre shone;
     On his brow this mark I saw—
     "I AM GOD, AND KING, AND LAW!"

10

     With a pace stately and fast,
     Over English land he passed,
40   Trampling to a mire of blood
     The adoring multitude.

11

     And a mighty troop around,
     With their trampling shook the ground,

     Waving each a bloody sword,
45   For the service of their Lord.

12

     And with glorious triumph, they
     Rode through England proud and gay,
     Drunk as with intoxication
     Of the wine of desolation.

13

50   O'er fields and towns, from sea to sea,
     Passed the Pageant swift and free,
     Tearing up, and trampling down;
     Till they came to London town.

14

     And each dweller, panic-stricken,
55   Felt his heart with terror sicken
     Hearing the tempestuous cry
     Of the triumph of Anarchy.

15

     For with pomp to meet him came,
     Clothed in arms like blood and flame,
60   The hired murderers, who did sing
     Thou art God, and Law, and King.

16

     "We have waited, weak and lone
     For thy coming, Mighty One!
     Our purses are empty, our swords are cold,
65   Give us glory, and blood, and gold."

17

     Lawyers and priests, a motley crowd,
     To the earth their pale brows bowed;
     Like a bad prayer not over loud,
     Whispering—"Thou art Law and God."

18

70   Then all cried with one accord,
     "Thou art King, and God, and Lord;
     Anarchy, to thee we bow,
     Be thy name made holy now!"

---

[1] *Clothed with ... light* Home Secretary Henry Addington, 1st
Viscount Sidmouth (1757–1844), invested in the construction of
several churches for the poor, but did nothing to improve their living
conditions; *crocodile* Animal often used to symbolize hypocrisy
because it was fabled to shed tears as it devoured its victims.

[2] *he rode ... Apocalypse* See Revelation 6, in which John the Divine
has a vision of the four horsemen of the Apocalypse. Of the fourth
horse he says, "and behold a pale horse: and his name that sat on him
was Death, and Hell followed him" (6.8).

19

And Anarchy, the Skeleton,
Bowed and grinned to every one,
As well as if his education
Had cost ten millions to the nation.

20

For he knew the Palaces
Of our Kings were rightly his;
His the sceptre, crown, and globe,[1]
And the gold-inwoven robe.

21

So he sent his slaves before
To seize upon the Bank and Tower,[2]
And was proceeding with intent
To meet his pensioned Parliament

22

When one fled past, a maniac maid,
And her name was Hope, she said:
But she looked more like Despair,
And she cried out in the air:

23

"My father Time is weak and gray
With waiting for a better day;
See how idiot-like he stands,
Fumbling with his palsied hands!

24

"He has had child after child,
And the dust of death is piled
Over every one but me—
Misery, oh, Misery!"

25

Then she lay down in the street,
Right before the horses' feet,

26

When between her and her foes
A mist, a light, an image rose,
Small at first, and weak, and frail
Like the vapour of a vale:

27

Till as clouds grow on the blast,
Like tower-crowned giants striding fast,
And glare with lightnings as they fly
And speak in thunder to the sky,

28

It grew—a Shape arrayed in mail°   *chain mail*
Brighter than the viper's scale,
And upborne on wings whose grain°   *texture*
Was as the light of sunny rain.

29

On its helm, seen far away,
A planet, like the Morning's,[3] lay;
And those plumes its light rained through
Like a shower of crimson dew.

30

With step as soft as wind it passed
O'er the heads of men—so fast
That they knew the presence there
And looked—but all was empty air.

31

As flowers beneath May's footstep waken,
As stars from Night's loose hair are shaken,
As waves arise when loud winds call,
Thoughts sprung where'er that step did fall.

32

And the prostrate multitude
Looked—and ankle-deep in blood,

Expecting, with a patient eye,
Murder, Fraud, and Anarchy.

---

1 *globe* Golden ball that, like the scepter, is an emblem of sovereignty.

2 *Bank* Bank of England, the national treasury; *Tower* Tower of London, where the crown jewels are kept.

3 *Morning* Venus, as the morning star.

Hope, that maiden most serene,
Was walking with a quiet mien:°   *countenance*

33

130 And Anarchy, the ghastly birth,
Lay dead earth upon the earth;
The Horse of Death tameless as wind
Fled, and with his hoofs did grind
To dust the murderers thronged behind.

34

135 A rushing light of clouds and splendour,
A sense awakening and yet tender
Was heard and felt—and at its close
These words of joy and fear arose

35

As if their own indignant Earth
140 Which gave the sons of England birth
Had felt their blood upon her brow,
And shuddering with a mother's throe

36

Had turnèd every drop of blood
By which her face had been bedewed
145 To an accent unwithstood—
As if her heart had cried aloud:

37

"Men of England, heirs of Glory,
Heroes of unwritten story,
Nurslings of one mighty Mother,
150 Hopes of her, and one another,

38

"Rise like Lions after slumber
In unvanquishable number,
Shake your chains to earth like dew
Which in sleep had fallen on you—
155 Ye are many, they are few.

39

"What is Freedom? Ye can tell
That which slavery is, too well—

For its very name has grown
To an echo of your own.

40

160 "'Tis to work and have such pay
As just keeps life from day to day
In your limbs, as in a cell
For the tyrants' use to dwell,

41

"So that ye for them are made
165 Loom, and plough, and sword, and spade,
With or without your own will bent
To their defence and nourishment.

42

"'Tis to see your children weak
With their mothers pine° and peak,°   *suffer | waste away*
170 When the winter winds are bleak—
They are dying whilst I speak.

43

"'Tis to hunger for such diet
As the rich man in his riot
Casts to the fat dogs that lie
175 Surfeiting beneath his eye;

44

"'Tis to let the Ghost of Gold[1]
Take from Toil a thousandfold
More than e'er its substance could
In the tyrannies of old.

45

180 "Paper coin—that forgery
Of the title-deeds, which ye
Hold to something of the worth
Of the inheritance of Earth.

---

1 *Ghost of Gold*   Paper money. At the time paper money was regarded as unreliable currency, and was not backed by any gold reserves. Paper money was often used to pay laborers' wages.

46

"'Tis to be a slave in soul
And to hold no strong control
Over your own wills, but be
All that others make of ye.

47

"And at length when ye complain
With a murmur weak and vain
'Tis to see the Tyrant's crew
Ride over your wives and you—
Blood is on the grass like dew.

48

"Then it is to feel revenge
Fiercely thirsting to exchange
Blood for blood—and wrong for wrong—
Do not thus when ye are strong.

49

"Birds find rest, in narrow nest
When weary of their wingèd quest;
Beasts find fare, in woody lair
When storm and snow are in the air.

50

"Asses, swine, have litter spread
And with fitting food are fed;
All things have a home but one—
Thou, Oh, Englishman, hast none![1]

51

"This is Slavery—savage men,
Or wild beasts within a den,
Would endure not as ye do—
But such ills they never knew.

52

"What art thou Freedom? O! could slaves
Answer from their living graves

This demand—tyrants would flee
Like a dream's dim imagery:

53

"Thou art not, as impostors say,
A shadow soon to pass away,
215   A superstition, and a name
Echoing from the cave of Fame.°   *rumor*

54

"For the labourer thou art bread,
And a comely table spread
From his daily labour come
220   In a neat and happy home.

55

"Thou art clothes, and fire, and food
For the trampled multitude—
No—in countries that are free
Such starvation cannot be
225   As in England now we see.

56

"To the rich thou art a check,
When his foot is on the neck
Of his victim, thou dost make
That he treads upon a snake.

57

230   "Thou art Justice—ne'er for gold
May thy righteous laws be sold
As laws are in England—thou
Shield'st alike the high and low.

58

"Thou art Wisdom—Freemen never
235   Dream that God will damn for ever
All who think those things untrue
Of which Priests make such ado.

59

"Thou art Peace—never by thee
Would blood and treasure wasted be

---

[1] *Asses … none* See Matthew 8.20, in which Jesus says, "The foxes have holes, and the birds of the air have nests; but the Son of man hath not where to lay his head."

240 As tyrants wasted them, when all
Leagued to quench thy flame in Gaul.[1]

60

"What if English toil and blood
Was poured forth, even as a flood?
It availed, Oh, Liberty,
245 To dim, but not extinguish thee.

61

"Thou art Love—the rich have kissed
Thy feet, and like him following Christ,
Give their substance to the free,
And through the rough world follow thee,[2]

62

250 "Or turn their wealth to arms, and make
War for thy belovèd sake
On wealth, and war, and fraud—whence they
Drew the power which is their prey.

63

"Science, Poetry, and Thought
255 Are thy lamps; they make the lot
Of the dwellers in a cot°   cottage
So serene, they curse it not.

64

"Spirit, Patience, Gentleness,
All that can adorn and bless
260 Art thou—let deeds, not words, express
Thine exceeding loveliness.

65

"Let a great Assembly be
Of the fearless and the free
On some spot of English ground
265 Where the plains stretch wide around.

66

"Let the blue sky overhead,
The green earth on which ye tread,
All that must eternal be
Witness the solemnity.

67

270 "From the corners uttermost
Of the bounds of English coast;
From every hut, village, and town
Where those who live and suffer moan
For others' misery or their own,

68

275 "From the workhouse[3] and the prison
Where pale as corpses newly risen,
Women, children, young and old
Groan for pain, and weep for cold—

69

"From the haunts of daily life
280 Where is waged the daily strife
With common wants and common cares
Which sows the human heart with tares°—   weeds

70

"Lastly from the palaces
Where the murmur of distress
285 Echoes, like the distant sound
Of a wind alive around

71

"Those prison halls of wealth and fashion,
Where some few feel such compassion
For those who groan, and toil, and wail
290 As must make their brethren pale—

72

"Ye who suffer woes untold,
Or° to feel, or to behold   either

---

[1] *Gaul* France.

[2] *like him ... thee* See Matthew 19.21, in which Jesus counsels a rich man to "go and sell that thou hast, and give to the poor, and thou shalt have treasure in heaven: and come and follow me."

[3] *workhouse* Institution established to provide work, shelter, and food for the parish poor; appalling conditions were the norm at most workhouses.

Your lost country bought and sold
With a price of blood and gold—

73

95　"Let a vast assembly be,
And with great solemnity
Declare with measured words that ye
Are, as God has made ye, free—

74

00　"Be your strong and simple words
Keen to wound as sharpened swords,
And wide as targes° let them be,　　　　　　shields
With their shade to cover ye.

75

"Let the tyrants pour around
With a quick and startling sound,
05　Like the loosening of a sea,
Troops of armed emblazonry.

76

"Let the charged artillery drive
Till the dead air seems alive
With the clash of clanging wheels,
10　And the tramp of horses' heels.

77

"Let the fixed bayonet
Gleam with sharp desire to wet
Its bright point in English blood
Looking keen as one for food.

78

15　"Let the horsemen's scimitars[1]
Wheel and flash, like sphereless stars
Thirsting to eclipse their burning
In a sea of death and mourning.

79

"Stand ye calm and resolute,
20　Like a forest close and mute,

With folded arms and looks which are
Weapons of unvanquished war,

80

"And let Panic, who outspeeds
The career of armèd steeds
325　Pass, a disregarded shade
Through your phalanx undismayed.

81

"Let the laws of your own land,
Good or ill, between ye stand
Hand to hand, and foot to foot,
330　Arbiters of the dispute,

82

"The old laws of England—they
Whose reverend heads with age are gray,
Children of a wiser day;
And whose solemn voice must be
335　Thine own echo—Liberty!

83

"On those who first should violate
Such sacred heralds in their state
Rest the blood that must ensue,
And it will not rest on you.

84

340　"And if then the tyrants dare
Let them ride among you there,
Slash, and stab, and maim, and hew—
What they like, that let them do.

85

"With folded arms and steady eyes,
345　And little fear, and less surprise,
Look upon them as they slay
Till their rage has died away,

86

"Then they will return with shame
To the place from which they came,

---

[1]　scimitars　Short curved swords.

350 And the blood thus shed will speak
In hot blushes on their cheek.

87

"Every woman in the land
Will point at them as they stand—
They will hardly dare to greet
355 Their acquaintance in the street.

88

"And the bold, true warriors
Who have hugged Danger in wars
Will turn to those who would be free,
Ashamed of such base company.

89

360 "And that slaughter to the Nation
Shall steam up like inspiration,
Eloquent, oracular;
A volcano heard afar.

90

"And these words shall then become
365 Like Oppression's thundered doom
Ringing through each heart and brain,
Heard again—again—again—

91

"Rise like Lions after slumber
In unvanquishable number—
370 Shake your chains to earth like dew
Which in sleep had fallen on you—
Ye are many, they are few."
—1832 (WRITTEN 1819)

Song to the Men of England [1]

1

Men of England, wherefore plough
For the lords who lay ye low?
Wherefore weave with toil and care
The rich robes your tyrants wear?

2

5 Wherefore feed, and clothe, and save,
From the cradle to the grave,
Those ungrateful drones who would
Drain your sweat—nay, drink your blood?

3

Wherefore, Bees of England, forge
10 Many a weapon, chain, and scourge,
That these stingless drones may spoil
The forced produce of your toil?

4

Have ye leisure, comfort, calm,
Shelter, food, love's gentle balm?
15 Or what is it ye buy so dear
With your pain and with your fear?

5

The seed ye sow, another reaps;
The wealth ye find, another keeps;
The robes ye weave, another wears;
20 The arms ye forge, another bears.

6

Sow seed—but let no tyrant reap;
Find wealth—let no impostor heap;
Weave robes—let not the idle wear;
Forge arms—in your defence to bear.

---

[1] *Song ... England* Composed in 1819, during a time of economic
depression and social turmoil following the end of the Napoleonic
Wars. In this song, which became a hymn for the British labor
movement, Shelley urges the proletariat to force change in the social
and economic order.

7

5 Shrink to your cellars, holes, and cells;
In halls ye deck another dwells.
Why shake the chains ye wrought? Ye see
The steel ye tempered glance on[1] ye.

8

10 With plough and spade, and hoe and loom,
Trace your grave, and build your tomb,
And weave your winding-sheet, till fair
England be your sepulchre.
—1839 (WRITTEN 1819)

England in 1819

An old, mad, blind, despised, and dying king,[2]
Princes, the dregs of their dull race, who flow
Through public scorn—mud from a muddy spring—
Rulers who neither see, nor feel, nor know,
5 But leech-like to their fainting country cling,
Till they drop, blind in blood, without a blow
A people starved and stabbed in the untilled field[3]—
An army, which liberticide and prey
Makes as a two-edged sword to all who wield—
10 Golden and sanguine laws[4] which tempt and slay;
Religion Christless, Godless—a book sealed;
A Senate, Time's worst statute, unrepealed,[5]
Are graves, from which a glorious Phantom[6] may
Burst, to illumine our tempestuous day.
—1839 (WRITTEN 1819)

---

1 *glance on* Strike obliquely.

2 *old, mad ... king* George III, who was declared insane in 1811. His sons were known for their corruption and their licentious behavior.

3 *A people ... field* Reference to the massacre at St. Peter's Field on 16 August 1819 (the Peterloo Massacre), when the militia attacked a crowd of people who were peacefully demonstrating for political reform. Eleven people were killed and hundreds more injured (see "The Mask of Anarchy").

4 *Golden ... laws* I.e., laws, bought with gold, that lead to bloodshed.

5 *Time's ... unrepealed* Laws against Catholics and Dissenters.

6 *a glorious Phantom* I.e., revolution.

The Triumph of Life

Swift as a spirit hastening to his task
Of glory and of good, the Sun sprang forth
Rejoicing in his splendour, and the mask

Of darkness fell from the awakened Earth—
5 The smokeless altars of the mountain snows
Flamed above crimson clouds, and at the birth

Of light, the Ocean's orison° arose,   *prayer*
To which the birds tempered their
    matin° lay,   *morning prayer*
All flowers in field or forest which unclose

10 Their trembling eyelids to the kiss of day,
Swinging their censers in the element,
With orient incense lit by the new ray

Burned slow and inconsumably, and sent
Their odorous sighs up to the smiling air;
15 And, in succession due, did continent,

Isle, ocean, and all things that in them wear
The form and character of mortal mould,
Rise as the Sun their father rose, to bear

Their portion of the toil, which he of old
20 Took as his own and then imposed on them:
But I, whom thoughts which must remain untold

Had kept as wakeful as the stars that gem[7]
The cone of night, now they were laid asleep
Stretched my faint limbs beneath the hoary stem

25 Which an old chestnut flung athwart the steep°   *slope*
Of a green Apennine:[8] before me fled
The night; behind me rose the day; the deep

---

7 *gem* Decorate (as with gems).

8 *Apennine* The Apennine Mountains extend 1200 km along the length of Italy.

Was at my feet, and Heaven above my head—
When a strange trance over my fancy grew
30 Which was not slumber, for the shade it spread

Was so transparent, that the scene came through
As clear as when a veil of light is drawn
O'er evening hills they glimmer; and I knew

That I had felt the freshness of that dawn
35 Bathe in the same cold dew my brow and hair,
And sate as thus upon that slope of lawn

Under the self same bough, and heard as there
The birds, the fountains and the ocean hold
Sweet talk in music through the enamoured air,
40 And then a Vision on my brain was rolled.

As in that trance of wondrous thought I lay,
This was the tenour° of my waking dream—   *meaning*
Methought I sat beside a public way

Thick strewn with summer dust, and a great stream
45 Of people there was hurrying to and fro,
Numerous as gnats upon the evening gleam,

All hastening onward, yet none seemed to know
Whither he went, or whence he came, or why
He made one of the multitude, and so

50 Was borne amid the crowd, as through the sky
One of the million leaves of summer's bier;
Old age and youth, manhood and infancy,

Mixed in one mighty torrent did appear,
Some flying from the thing they feared, and some
55 Seeking the object of another's fear;

And others, as with steps towards the tomb,
Pored on the trodden worms that crawled beneath,
      hers mournfully within the gloom

Of their own shadow walked, and called it death;
60 And some fled from it as it were a ghost,
Half fainting in the affliction of vain breath:

But more, with motions which each other crossed,
Pursued or shunned the shadows the clouds threw,
Or birds within the noonday ether° lost,   *sky*

65 Upon that path where flowers never grew—
And weary with vain toil and faint for thirst,
Heard not the fountains, whose melodious dew

Out of their mossy cells forever burst;
Nor felt the breeze which from the forest told
70 Of grassy paths, and wood lawns interspersed

With overarching elms and caverns cold,
And violet banks where sweet dreams brood, but they
Pursued their serious folly as of old.

And as I gazed methought that in the way
75 The throng grew wilder, as the woods of June
When the south wind shakes the extinguished day,

And a cold glare, intenser than the noon,
But icy cold, obscured with blinding light
The sun, as he the stars. Like the young moon—

80 When on the sunlit limits of the night
Her white shell trembles amid crimson air,
And whilst the sleeping tempest gathers might—

Doth, as a herald of its coming, bear
The ghost of her dead mother, whose dim form
85 Bends in dark ether from her infant's chair—

So came a chariot on the silent storm
Of its own rushing splendour, and a Shape
So sat within as one whom years deform,

Beneath a dusky hood and double cape,
90 Crouching within the shadow of a tomb;
And o'er what seemed the head, a cloud-like crape[1]

Was bent a dun and faint ethereal gloom
Tempering the light. Upon the chariot-beam
A Janus[2]-visaged° Shadow did assume   *faced*

95 The guidance of that wonder-wingèd team;
The shapes which drew it in thick lightnings
Were lost—I heard alone on the air's soft stream

The music of their ever-moving wings.
All the four faces of that Charioteer
100 Had their eyes banded; little profit° brings   *benefit*

Speed in the van° and blindness in the rear,   *front*
Nor then avail the beams that quench the sun—
Or that his banded eyes could pierce the sphere

Of all that is, has been or will be done;
105 So ill was the car° guided   but it passed   *chariot*
With solemn speed majestically on.

The crowd gave way, and I arose aghast,
Or seemed to rise, so mighty was the trance,
And saw, like clouds upon the thunder-blast,

110 The million with fierce song and maniac dance
Raging around—such seemed the jubilee
As when to greet some conqueror's advance

Imperial Rome poured forth her living sea
From senate-house, and forum,° and theatre   *public square*
115 When … upon[3] the free

Had bound a yoke which soon they stooped to bear.
Nor wanted° here the true similitude   *lacked*
Of a triumphal pageant, for where'er

The chariot rolled, a captive multitude
120 Was driven—all those who had grown old in power
Or misery—all who have their age subdued°   *overcome*

By action or by suffering, and whose hour
Was drained to its last sand in weal or woe,
So that the trunk survived both fruit and flower—

125 All those whose fame or infamy must grow
Till the great winter lay the form and name
Of this green earth with them forever low—

All but the sacred few who could not tame
Their spirits to the conquerors—but as soon
130 As they had touched the world with living flame,

Fled back like eagles to their native noon,
Of those who put aside the diadem°   *jeweled crown*
Of earthly thrones or gems …

Were there, of Athens or Jerusalem,
135 Were neither mid the mighty captives seen,
Nor 'mid the ribald crowd that followed them,

Nor those who went before fierce and obscene.
The wild dance maddens in the van, and those
Who lead it—fleet as shadows on the green,

140 Outspeed the chariot, and without repose
Mix with each other in tempestuous measure
To savage music, wilder as it grows,

They, tortured by their agonizing pleasure,
Convulsed and on the rapid whirlwinds spun
145 Of that fierce Spirit, whose unholy leisure

Was soothed by mischief since the world begun,
Throw back their heads and loose their streaming hair;
And in their dance round her who dims the sun

---

[1] *crape* Dark band, worn as a symbol of mourning.

[2] *Janus* Two-faced Roman god of transitions; Janus looked with one face into the past, with the other into the future.

[3] *When … upon* The poem was unfinished when Shelley died. At several points there are gaps in the manuscript (as here).

Maidens and youths fling their wild arms in air
150 As their feet twinkle; they recede, and now
Bending within each other's atmosphere,

Kindle invisibly—and as they glow,
Like moths by light attracted and repelled,
Oft to new bright destruction come and go,

155 Till like two clouds into one vale impelled,
That shake the mountains when their lightnings mingle
And die in rain—the fiery band which held

Their natures, snaps—while the shock still may tingle;
One falls and then another in the path
160 Senseless—nor is the desolation single,

Yet ere I can say *where*—the chariot hath
Past over them—nor other trace I find
But as of foam after the ocean's wrath

Is spent upon the desert shore—behind,
165 Old men and women foully disarrayed,
Shake their grey hairs in the insulting wind,

And follow in the dance, with limbs decayed,
Seeking to reach the light which leaves them still
Farther behind and deeper in the shade.

170 But not the less with impotence of will
They wheel, though ghastly shadows interpose
Round them and round each other, and fulfill

Their work, and in the dust whence they arose
Sink, and corruption veils them as they lie,
175 And past in these performs what in those.

Struck to the heart by this sad pageantry,
Half to myself I said—"And what is this?
Whose shape is that within the car? and why—"

I would have added—"is all here amiss?—"
180 But a voice answered—"Life!"—I turned, and knew
(O Heaven, have mercy on such wretchedness!)

That what I thought was an old root which grew
To strange distortion out of the hill side,
Was indeed one of those deluded crew,

185 And that the grass, which methought hung so wide
And white, was but his thin discoloured hair,
And that the holes it vainly sought to hide,

Were or had been eyes—"If thou canst, forbear
To join the dance, which I had well forborne!"
190 Said the grim Feature° (of my thought aware).[1]   creature

"I will unfold that which to this deep scorn
Led me and my companions, and relate
The progress of the pageant since the morn;

"If thirst of knowledge doth not then abate,
195 Follow it even to the night, but I
Am weary."—Then like one who with the weight

Of his own words is staggered, wearily
He paused; and ere he could resume, I cried,
"First, who art thou?"—"Before thy memory,

200 "I feared, loved, hated, suffered, did and died,
And if the spark with which Heaven lit my spirit
Had been with purer nutriment supplied,

"Corruption would not now thus much inherit
Of what was once Rousseau[2]—nor this disguise
205 Stain that within which ought to have disdained to
       wear it;

"If I have been extinguished, yet there rise
A thousand beacons from the spark I bore"—
"And who are those chained to the car?"—"The wise,

---

1   *Said the ... aware*   In some versions of the poem, this line is
punctuated as "said the grim feature of my thought: 'Aware,'"; *grim
Feature*   Phrase used in reference to Death in Milton's *Paradise Lost*
10.279.

2   *Rousseau*   Jean-Jacques Rousseau (1712–78), Genevan philosopher
whose political ideals were influential among those who sparked the
French Revolution.

"The great, the unforgotten—they who wore
10 Mitres° and helms and crowns, or wreaths of *bishop's hats*
     light,
     Signs of thought's empire over thought—their lore

"Taught them not this, to know themselves; their might
     Could not repress the mutiny within,
     And for the morn of truth they feigned, deep night

15 "Caught them ere evening."—"Who is he with chin
     Upon his breast, and hands crossed on his chain?"[1]—
     "The child of a fierce hour; he sought to win

"The world, and lost all that it did contain
     Of greatness, in its hope destroyed; and more
20 Of fame and peace than virtue's self can gain

"Without the opportunity which bore
     Him on its eagle pinions to the peak
     From which a thousand climbers have before

"Fallen as Napoleon fell."—I felt my cheek
25 Alter, to see the great form pass away,
     Whose grasp had left the giant world so weak

"That every pygmy kicked it as it lay;
     And much I grieved to think how power and will
     In opposition rule our mortal day,

30 And why God made irreconcilable
     Good and the means of good; and for despair
     I half disdained mine eyes' desire to fill

"With the spent vision of the times that were
     And scarce have ceased to be—"Dost thou behold,"
35 Said then my guide, "those spoilers spoiled, Voltaire,[2]

"Frederick, and Paul, Catherine, and Leopold,[3]
     And hoary anarchs, demagogues and sage—
     names which the world thinks always old,

"For in the battle Life and they did wage,
240 She remained conqueror. I was overcome
     By my own heart alone, which neither age,

"Nor tears, nor infamy, nor now the tomb
     Could temper to its object."—"Let them pass,"
     I cried, "the world and its mysterious doom

245 "Is not so much more glorious than it was,
     That I desire to worship those who drew
     New figures on its false and fragile glass

"As the old faded."—"Figures ever new
     Rise on the bubble, paint them how you may;
250 We have but thrown, as those before us threw,

"Our shadows on it as it passed away.
     But mark how chained to the triumphal chair
     The mighty phantoms of an elder day;

"All that is mortal of great Plato[4] there
255 Expiates the joy and woe his master knew not;
     That star that ruled his doom was far too fair,

"And life, where long that flower of Heaven grew not,
     Conquered the heart by love, which gold, or pain,
     Or age, or sloth, or slavery could subdue not.

---

1 *Who ... chain?* This and the following lines describe Napoleon
Bonaparte (1769–1821).

2 *Voltaire* French writer and philosopher (1694–1778).

---

3 *Frederick* Frederick II of Prussia (1712–86); *Paul* Paul I of
Russia (1754–1801); *Catherine* Catherine II of Russia (1729–96);
Leopold Leopold II, Grand Duke of Tuscany and Holy Roman
Emperor (1747–92).

4 *Plato* Greek philosopher (c. 427–347 BCE). According to legend,
he loved a boy named Aster (a name which means "star" and is also the
name of a type of flower).

"And near him walk the twain,
260 The tutor and his pupil, whom Dominion
Followed as tame as vulture in a chain.[1]

"The world was darkened beneath either pinion
Of him whom from the flock of conquerors
265 Fame singled as her thunder-bearing minion;

"The other long outlived both woes and wars,
Throned in new thoughts of men, and still had kept
The jealous keys of Truth's eternal doors,

"If Bacon's[2] eagle spirit had not leapt
270 Like lightning out of darkness—he compelled
The Proteus[3] shape of Nature, as it slept

"To wake, and to unbar the caves that held
The treasure of the secrets of its reign.
See the great bards of elder time, who quelled

275 "The passions which they sung, as by their strain
May well be known: their living melody
Tempers its own contagion to the vein

"Of those who are infected with it—I
Have suffered what I wrote, or viler pain!
280 And so my words were seeds of misery—

"Even as the deeds of others, not as theirs."
And then he pointed to a company,

Midst whom I quickly recognized the heirs
Of Caesar's crime, from him to Constantine;[4]
285 The anarch chiefs, whose force and murderous snares

Had founded many a sceptre-bearing line,
And spread the plague of blood and gold abroad:
And Gregory and John[5] and men divine,

Who rose like shadows between man and God;
290 Till that eclipse, still hanging under heaven,
Was worshipped by the world o'er which they strode,

For the true Sun it quenched—"Their power was given
But to destroy," replied the leader—"I
Am one of those who have created, even

295 "If it be but a world of agony."—
"Whence camest thou? and whither goest thou?
How did thy course begin?" I said, "and why?

"Mine eyes are sick of this perpetual flow
Of people, and my heart sick of one sad thought—
300 Speak!"—"Whence I am, partly I seem to know,

"And how and by what paths I have been brought
To this dread pass, methinks even thou mayst guess—
Why this should be, my mind can compass not;

"Whither the conqueror hurries me, still less—
305 But follow thou, and from spectator turn
Actor or victim in this wretchedness,

"And what thou wouldst be taught I then may learn
From thee. Now listen—In the April prime,
When all the forest-tips began to burn

---

[1] *And ... chain* This passage describes Aristotle (384–322 BCE), Greek philosopher and student of Plato, walking with Alexander the Great, whom Aristotle taught.

[2] *Bacon* Francis Bacon (1561–1626), English philosopher and political figure.

[3] *Proteus* Greek god known for his ability to take on other shapes and forms.

[4] *Caesar* Julius Caesar (100–44 BCE), Roman general and leader of the Roman Republic. His "crime" was making himself dictator, thus bringing about the end of the Roman Republic. His adopted heir, Octavian, became the first Roman emperor; *Constantine* Constantine I (272–337), the first Roman emperor to convert to Christianity.

[5] *Gregory* Saint Gregory (c. 540–604 CE), an important pope; *John* There are several saints with this name.

"With kindling green, touched by the azure clime
Of the young season, I was laid asleep
Under a mountain which from unknown time

"Had yawned into a cavern, high and deep;
And from it came a gentle rivulet,
Whose water, like clear air, in its calm sweep

"Bent the soft grass, and kept for ever wet
The stems of the sweet flowers, and filled the grove
With sounds, which all who hears must needs forget

"All pleasure and all pain, all hate and love,
Which they had known before that hour of rest;
A sleeping mother then would dream not of

"Her only child who died upon her breast
At eventide—a king would mourn no more
The crown of which his brow was dispossessed

"When the sun lingered o'er the ocean floor
To gild his rival's new prosperity.
Thou wouldst forget thus vainly to deplore

"Ills, which if ills can find no cure from thee,
The thought of which no other sleep will quell,
Nor other music blot from memory,

"So sweet and deep is the oblivious spell;
Whether my life had been before that sleep
The Heaven which I imagine, or a Hell

"Like this harsh world in which I wake to weep,
I know not. I arose and for a space
The scene of woods and waters seemed to keep,

"Though it was now broad day, a gentle trace
Of light diviner than the common sun
Sheds on the common earth, and all the place

"Was filled with many sounds woven into one
Oblivious melody, confusing sense
Amid the gliding waves and shadows dun;

"And as I looked the bright omnipresence
Of morning through the orient° cavern flowed,   *eastern*
345 And the Sun's image radiantly intense

"Burned on the waters of the well that glowed
Like gold, and threaded all the forest's maze
With winding paths of emerald fire; there stood

"Amid the sun, as he amid the blaze
350 Of his own glory, on the vibrating
Floor of the fountain, paved with flashing rays,

"A Shape all light, which with one hand did fling
Dew on the earth, as if she were the dawn,
And the invisible rain did ever sing

355 "A silver music on the mossy lawn;
And still before me on the dusky grass,
Iris[1] her many coloured scarf had drawn:

"In her right hand she bore a crystal glass,
Mantling with bright Nepenthe;[2] the fierce splendour
360 Fell from her as she moved under the mass

"Of the deep cavern, and with palms so tender,
Their tread broke not the mirror of its billow,
Glided along the river, and did bend her

"Head under the dark boughs, till like a willow
365 Her fair hair swept the bosom of the stream
That whispered with delight to be its pillow.

"As one enamoured is upborne in dream
O'er lily-paven lakes, mid silver mist,
To wondrous music, so this shape might seem

370 "Partly to tread the waves with feet which kissed
The dancing foam; partly to glide along
The airs that roughened the moist amethyst,

---

1 *Iris* Classical goddess associated with rainbows.

2 *Mantling* Foaming; *Nepenthe* Medicine that combated sorrow through forgetfulness.

"Or the faint morning beams that fell among
The trees, or the soft shadows of the trees;
375 And her feet, ever to the ceaseless song

"Of leaves, and winds, and waves, and birds, and bees,
And falling drops, moved in a measure new
Yet sweet, as on the summer evening breeze,

"Up from the lake a shape of golden dew
380 Between two rocks, athwart the rising moon,
Dances in the wind, where eagle never flew;

"And still her feet, no less than the sweet tune
To which they moved, seemed as they moved to blot
The thoughts of him who gazed on them; and soon

385 "All that was, seemed as if it had been not;
As all the gazer's mind was strewn beneath
Her feet like embers; and she, thought by thought,

"Trampled its sparks into the dust of death;
As day upon the threshold of the east
390 Treads out the lamps of night, until the breath

"Of darkness re-illumine even the least
Of heaven's living eyes—like day she came,
Making the night a dream; and ere she ceased

"To move, as one between desire and shame
395 Suspended, I said—if, as it doth seem,
Thou comest from the realm without a name

"Into this valley of perpetual dream,
Show whence I came, and where I am, and why—
Pass not away upon the passing stream.

400 "Arise and quench thy thirst, was her reply,
And as a shut lily, stricken by the wand
Of dewy morning's vital alchemy,

"I rose; and, bending at her sweet command,
Touched with faint lips the cup she raised,
405 And suddenly my brain became as sand

"Where the first wave had more than half erased
The track of deer on desert° Labrador;[1]   deserted
Whilst the wolf, from which they fled amazed,

"Leaves his stamp visibly upon the shore,
410 Until the second bursts—so on my sight
Burst a new vision never seen before,

"And the fair shape waned in the coming light,
As veil by veil the silent splendour drops
From Lucifer,[2] amid the chrysolite[3]

415 "Of sunrise, ere it strike the mountain-tops;
And as the presence of that fairest planet,
Although unseen, is felt by one who hopes

"That his day's path may end as he began it,
In that star's smile, whose light is like the scent
420 Of a jonquil[4] when evening breezes fan it,

"Or the soft note in which his dear lament
The Brescian[5] shepherd breathes, or the caress
That turned his weary slumber to content;

"So knew I in that light's severe excess
425 The presence of that Shape which on the stream
Moved, as I moved along the wilderness,

"More dimly than a day appearing dream,
The ghost of a forgotten form of sleep:
A light from Heaven, whose half-extinguished beam

430 "Through the sick day in which we wake to weep
Glimmers, forever sought, forever lost;
So did that shape its obscure tenour keep

---

1 *Labrador* Large area of land in northeastern Canada, running along the Atlantic coast and adjacent to Quebec and Newfoundland.

2 *Lucifer* The planet Venus, also called the morning star for its appearance in the early morning sky.

3 *chrysolite* Here, greenish yellow.

4 *jonquil* Fragrant flower.

5 *Brescian* From the area of Brescia, in northern Italy.

"Beside my path, as silent as a ghost;
But the new Vision, and its cold bright car,
35   With solemn speed and stunning music, crossed

"The forest, and as if from some dread war
Triumphantly returning, the loud million
Fiercely extolled the fortune of her star.

"A moving arch of victory, the vermilion
40   And green and azure plumes of Iris had
Built high over her wind-winged pavilion,

"And underneath ethereal glory clad
The wilderness, and far before her flew
The tempest of the splendour, which forbade

45   "Shadow to fall from leaf or stone; the crew
Seemed in that light, like atomies° to dance   *particles*
Within a sunbeam—some upon the new

"Embroidery of flowers that did enhance
The grassy vesture° of the desert, played,   *covering*
50   Forgetful of the chariot's swift advance;

"Others stood gazing, till within the shade
Of the great mountain its light left them dim;
Others outspeeded it; and others made

"Circles around it, like the clouds that swim
55   Round the high moon in a bright sea of air;
And more did follow, with exulting hymn,

"The chariot and the captives fettered there—
But all like bubbles on an eddying flood
Fell into the same track at last, and were

60   "Borne onward—I among the multitude
Was swept—me, sweetest flowers delayed not long;
Me, not the shadow nor the solitude;

"Me, not the falling stream's Lethean[1] song;
Me, not the phantom of that early Form
465   Which moved upon its motion—but among

"The thickest billows of the living storm
I plunged, and bared my bosom to the clime
Of that cold light, whose airs too soon deform.

"Before the chariot had begun to climb
470   The opposing steep of that mysterious dell,
Behold a wonder worthy of the rhyme

"Of him[2] whom from the lowest depths of hell
Through every paradise and through all glory,
Love led serene, and who returned to tell

475   "In words of hate and awe; the wondrous story
How all things are transfigured except Love;
For deaf as is a sea, which wrath makes hoary,

"The world can hear not the sweet notes that move
The sphere whose light is melody to lovers—
480   A wonder worthy of his rhyme. The grove

"Grew dense with shadows to its inmost covers,
The earth was grey with phantoms, and the air
Was peopled with dim forms, as when there hovers

"A flock of vampire-bats before the glare
485   Of the tropic sun, bringing, ere evening
Strange night upon some Indian isle—thus were

"Phantoms diffused around; and some did fling
Shadows of shadows, yet unlike themselves,
Behind them; some like eaglets on the wing

---

[1] *Lethean* In Greek mythology, Lethe is a river in Hades whose waters cause forgetfulness.

[2] *him* Dante Alighieri, whose fourteenth-century masterpiece *The Divine Comedy* describes a journey through Hell and Purgatory to Paradise.

490 "Were lost in the white day; others like elves
Danced in a thousand unimagined shapes
Upon the sunny streams and grassy shelves;

"And others sate chattering like restless apes
On vulgar hands, …
495 Some made a cradle of the ermined capes

"Of kingly mantles; some upon the tiar°   *crown*
Of pontiffs° sat like vultures; others played   *high priests*
Under the crown which girt with empire

"A baby's or an idiot's brow, and made
500 Their nests in it. The old anatomies[1]
Sat hatching their bare brood under the shade

"Of daemon wings, and laughed from their dead eyes
To reassume the delegated power,
Arrayed in which these worms did monarchize,

505 "Who make this earth their charnel.°   *burial house*
        Others more
Humble, like falcons, sate upon the fist
Of common men, and round their heads did soar;

"Or like small gnats and flies, as thick as mist
On evening marshes, thronged about the brow
510 Of lawyers, statesmen, priest and theorist—

"And others, like discoloured flakes of snow
On fairest bosoms and the sunniest hair,
Fell, and were melted by the youthful glow

"Which they extinguished; for like tears, they were
515 A veil to those from whose faint lids they rained
In drops of sorrow. I became aware

"Of whence those forms proceeded which thus stained
The track in which we moved. After brief space,
From every form the beauty slowly waned;

520 "From every firmest limb and fairest face
The strength and freshness fell like dust, and left
The action and the shape without the grace

"Of life. The marble brow of youth was cleft
With care; and in those eyes where once hope shone
525 Desire, like a lioness bereft

"Of her last cub, glared ere it died; each one
Of that great crowd sent forth incessantly
These shadows, numerous as the dead leaves blown

"In autumn evening from a popular tree.
530 Each like himself and like each other were
At first; but some distorted seemed to be

"Obscure clouds, moulded by the casual air;
And of this stuff the car's creative ray
Wrought all the busy phantoms that were there,

535 "As the sun shapes the clouds; thus on the way
Mask after mask fell from the countenance
And form of all; and long before the day

"Was old, the joy which waked like heaven's glance
The sleepers in the oblivious valley, died;
540 And some grew weary of the ghastly dance,

"And fell, as I have fallen, by the way side—
Those soonest from whose forms most shadows past,
And least of strength and beauty did abide.

"Then, what is Life? I cried."[2]
—1824

---

1 *anatomies*   Skeletons or withered corpses.

2 *Then, what … cried*   Shelley was in the midst of work on this poem at the time of his death. Though there are a few sentence fragments omitted here, this is the last complete sentence of the manuscript.

A Defence of Poetry

This essay, begun in 1822 and never completed, was written in response to an 1820 essay by Shelley's friend Thomas Love Peacock called "The Four Ages of Poetry." In this partially ironic essay, Peacock describes four cycles through which poetry passes: the first is an iron age of crude folk ballads, medieval romances, etc.; the second, the gold age, contains the great epics of Homer, Dante, and Milton; the silver age contains the "derivative" poetry of the Augustan poets (who included John Dryden and Alexander Pope); and the fourth stage, the age of brass, is that of Peacock's contemporaries, whom he claimed were markedly inferior. Criticizing Romantic poets such as Byron, Coleridge, and Wordsworth, Peacock urged the men of his generation to apply themselves to new sciences, such as astronomy, economics, politics, mathematics, or chemistry, instead of poetry. Though Shelley recognized Peacock's satirical humor, he also acknowledged that Peacock had put his finger on a common bias of the time—both in the theories of utilitarian philosophers and in general public opinion—in favor of economic growth and scientific progress over creativity and humanitarian concerns. It was this bias that he attempted to correct in his *Defence*.

from *A Defence of Poetry*,
or Remarks Suggested by an Essay Entitled "The Four Ages of Poetry"

According to one mode of regarding those two classes of mental action which are called reason and imagination, the former may be considered as mind contemplating the relations borne by one thought to another, however produced; and the latter, as mind acting upon those thoughts so as to colour them with its own light, and composing from them, as from elements, other thoughts, each containing within itself the principle of its own integrity. The one is the τὸ ποιεῖν,[1] or

the principle of synthesis, and has for its objects those forms which are common to universal nature and existence itself; the other is the τὸ λογίζειν[2] or principle of analysis, and its action regards the relations of things, simply as relations; considering thoughts, not in their integral unity, but as the algebraical representations which conduct to certain general results. Reason is the enumeration of quantities already known; imagination is the perception of the value of those quantities, both separately and as a whole. Reason respects the differences, and imagination the similitudes of things. Reason is to Imagination as the instrument to the agent, as the body to the spirit, as the shadow to the substance.

Poetry, in a general sense, may be defined to be "the expression of the Imagination": and poetry is connate with the origin of man. Man is an instrument over which a series of external and internal impressions are driven, like the alternations of an ever-changing wind over an Æolian lyre,[3] which move it by their motion to ever-changing melody. But there is a principle within the human being, and perhaps within all sentient beings, which acts otherwise than in the lyre, and produces not melody alone, but harmony, by an internal adjustment of the sounds or motions thus excited to the impressions which excite them. It is as if the lyre could accommodate its chords to the motions of that which strikes them, in a determined proportion of sound; even as the musician can accommodate his voice to the sound of the lyre. A child at play by itself will express its delight by its voice and motions; and every inflexion of tone and every gesture will bear exact relation to a corresponding antitype in the pleasurable impressions which awakened it; it will be the reflected image of that impression; and as the lyre trembles and sounds after the wind has died away, so the child seeks, by prolonging in its voice and motions the duration of the effect, to prolong also a consciousness of the cause. In relation to the objects which delight a child, these expressions are what poetry is to higher objects. The savage (for the savage is to ages what the child is to years) expresses the

---

[1] τὸ ποιεῖν Greek: making.

[2] τὸ λογίζειν Greek: reasoning.

[3] *Æolian lyre* Stringed instrument that produces music when exposed to wind.

emotions produced in him by surrounding objects in a similar manner; and language and gesture, together with plastic[1] or pictorial imitation, become the image of the combined effect of those objects, and of his apprehension of them. Man in society, with all his passions and his pleasures, next becomes the object of the passions and pleasures of man; an additional class of emotions produces an augmented treasure of expressions; and language, gesture, and the imitative arts become at once the representation and the medium, the pencil and the picture, the chisel and the statue, the chord and the harmony. The social sympathies, or those laws from which as from its elements society results, begin to develop themselves from the moment that two human beings coexist; the future is contained within the present as the plant within the seed; and equality, diversity, unity, contrast, mutual dependence, become the principles alone capable of affording the motives according to which the will of a social being is determined to action, inasmuch as he is social; and constitute pleasure in sensation, virtue in sentiment, beauty in art, truth in reasoning, and love in the intercourse of kind. Hence men, even in the infancy of society, observe a certain order in their words and actions, distinct from that of the objects and the impressions represented by them, all expression being subject to the laws of that from which it proceeds. But let us dismiss those more general considerations which might involve an enquiry into the principles of society itself, and restrict our view to the manner in which the imagination is expressed upon its forms.

In the youth of the world, men dance and sing and imitate natural objects, observing[2] in these actions, as in all others, a certain rhythm or order. And, although all men observe a similar, they observe not the same order, in the motions of the dance, in the melody of the song, in the combinations of language, in the series of their imitations of natural objects. For there is a certain order or rhythm belonging to each of these classes of mimetic representation, from which the hearer and the spectator receive an intenser and purer pleasure than from any

other: the sense of an approximation to this order has been called taste, by modern writers. Every man in the infancy of art observes an order which approximates more or less closely to that from which this highest delight results: but the diversity is not sufficiently marked, as that its gradations should be sensible, except in those instances where the predominance of this faculty of approximation to the beautiful (for so we may be permitted to name the relation between this highest pleasure and its cause) is very great. Those in whom it exists in excess are poets, in the most universal sense of the word; and the pleasure resulting from the manner in which they express the influence of society or nature upon their own minds, communicates itself to others, and gathers a sort of reduplication from that community. Their language is vitally metaphorical; that is, it marks the before unapprehended relations of things, and perpetuates their apprehension, until the words which represent them, become through time signs for portions or classes of thoughts instead of pictures of integral thoughts; and then if no new poets should arise to create afresh the associations which have been thus disorganized, language will be dead to all the nobler purposes of human intercourse. These similitudes or relations are finely said by Lord Bacon to be "the same footsteps of nature impressed upon the various subjects of the world"[3]—and he considers the faculty which perceives them as the storehouse of axioms common to all knowledge. In the infancy of society every author is necessarily a poet, because language itself is poetry; and to be a poet is to apprehend the true and the beautiful, in a word the good which exists in the relation, subsisting, first between existence and perception, and secondly between perception and expression. Every original language near to its source is in itself the chaos of a cyclic poem:[4] the copiousness of lexicography and the distinctions of grammar are the works of a later age, and are merely the catalogue and the form of the creations of Poetry.

---

[1] *plastic* Formative.

[2] *observing* Following.

[3] *the same ... world* From Francis Bacon's *Of the Advancement of Learning* (1605) 3.1.

[4] *cyclic poem* Set of poems dealing with the same subject (though not always by the same author). The "Arthurian Cycle," a series of poems about the court of King Arthur, is one example of the genre.

But Poets, or those who imagine and express this indestructible order, are not only the authors of language and of music, of the dance and architecture and statuary and painting: they are the institutors of laws, and the founders of civil society and the inventors of the arts of life and the teachers, who draw into a certain propinquity with the beautiful and the true that partial apprehension of the agencies of the invisible world which is called religion. Hence all original religions are allegorical, or susceptible of allegory, and like Janus have a double face of false and true.[1] Poets, according to the circumstances of the age and nation in which they appeared, were called in the earlier epochs of the world legislators or prophets:[2] a poet essentially comprises and unites both these characters. For he not only beholds intensely the present as it is, and discovers those laws according to which present things ought to be ordered, but he beholds the future in the present, and his thoughts are the germs of the flower and the fruit of latest time. Not that I assert poets to be prophets in the gross sense of the word, or that they can foretell the form as surely as they foreknow the spirit of events: such is the pretence of superstition which would make poetry an attribute of prophecy, rather than prophecy an attribute of poetry. A Poet participates in the eternal, the infinite, and the one; as far as relates to his conceptions, time and place and number are not. The grammatical forms which express the moods of time, and the difference of persons and the distinction of place, are convertible with respect to the highest poetry without injuring it as poetry, and the choruses of Æschylus, and the book of Job, and Dante's Paradise[3] would afford, more than any other writings, examples of this fact, if the limits of this essay did not forbid citation. The creations of sculpture, painting, and music are illustrations still more decisive.

Language, colour, form, and religious and civil habits of action are all the instruments and materials of poetry; they may be called poetry by that figure of speech which considers the effect as a synonym of the cause. But poetry in a more restricted sense expresses those arrangements of language, and especially metrical language, which are created by that imperial faculty whose throne is curtained within the invisible nature of man. And this springs from the nature itself of language, which is a more direct representation of the actions and passions of our internal being, and is susceptible of more various and delicate combinations, than colour, form, or motion, and is more plastic and obedient to the control of that faculty of which it is the creation. For language is arbitrarily produced by the Imagination and has relation to thoughts alone; but all other materials, instruments and conditions of art, have relations among each other, which limit and interpose between conception and expression. The former is as a mirror which reflects, the latter as a cloud which enfeebles, the light of which both are mediums of communication. Hence the fame of sculptors, painters and musicians, although the intrinsic powers of the great masters of these arts, may yield in no degree to that of those who have employed language as the hieroglyphic of their thoughts, has never equalled that of poets in the restricted sense of the term; as two performers of equal skill will produce unequal effects from a guitar and a harp. The fame of legislators and founders of religions, so long as their institutions last, alone seems to exceed that of poets in the restricted sense; but it can scarcely be a question whether, if we deduct the celebrity which their flattery of the gross opinions of the vulgar usually conciliates, together with that which belonged to them in their higher character of poets, any excess will remain.

We have thus circumscribed the meaning of the word Poetry within the limits of that art which is the most familiar and the most perfect expression of the faculty itself. It is necessary however to make the circle still narrower, and to determine the distinction between

---

[1] *like Janus ... true* Janus, the Roman god of doorways and of beginnings and endings (after whom the month of January is named) is generally depicted with two faces, one looking forward and one back.

[2] *were called ... prophets* Cf. Sir Philip Sidney's *Defence of Poesy* (1595), in which he points out that *vates*, the Latin word for poet, also means diviner or prophet.

[3] *Æschylus* Greek tragic dramatist (c. 525–456 BCE); *Dante's Paradise* Reference to Italian poet Dante Alighieri's fourteenth-century work, *The Divine Comedy*, which describes a journey from Hell, through Purgatory, to Paradise.

measured and unmeasured language; for the popular division into prose and verse is inadmissible in accurate philosophy. Sounds as well as thoughts have relation both between each other and towards that which they represent, and a perception of the order of those relations has always been found connected with a perception of the order of the relations of thoughts. Hence the language of poets has ever affected a certain uniform and harmonious recurrence of sound, without which it were not poetry, and which is scarcely less indispensable to the communication of its influence, than the words themselves, without reference to that peculiar order. …

A poem is the very image of life expressed in its eternal truth. There is this difference between a story and a poem, that a story is a catalogue of detached facts, which have no other bond of connection than time, place, circumstance, cause and effect; the other is the creation of actions according to the unchangeable forms of human nature, as existing in the mind of the creator, which is itself the image of all other minds. The one is partial, and applies only to a definite period of time, and a certain combination of events which can never again recur; the other is universal, and contains within itself the germ of a relation to whatever motives or actions have place in the possible varieties of human nature. …

Poetry is ever accompanied with pleasure: all spirits on which it falls open themselves to receive the wisdom which is mingled with its delight. In the infancy of the world, neither poets themselves nor their auditors are fully aware of the excellence of poetry: for it acts in a divine and unapprehended manner, beyond and above consciousness; and it is reserved for future generations to contemplate and measure the mighty cause and effect in all the strength and splendour of their union. Even in modern times, no living poet ever arrived at the fulness of his fame; the jury which sits in judgement upon a poet, belonging as he does to all time, must be composed of his peers: it must be impanelled by Time from the selectest of the wise of many generations. A Poet is a nightingale, who sits in darkness and sings to cheer its own solitude with sweet sounds; his auditors are as men entranced by the melody of an unseen musician, who feel that they are moved and softened, yet know not

whence or why. The poems of Homer and his contemporaries were the delight of infant Greece; they were the elements of that social system which is the column upon which all succeeding civilization has reposed. Homer embodied the ideal perfection of his age in human character; nor can we doubt that those who read his verses were awakened to an ambition of becoming like to Achilles, Hector and Ulysses:[1] the truth and beauty of friendship, patriotism, and persevering devotion to an object were unveiled to the depths in these immortal creations: the sentiments of the auditors must have been refined and enlarged by a sympathy with such great and lovely impersonations, until from admiring they imitated, and from imitation they identified themselves with the objects of their admiration. …

The whole objection, however, of the immorality of poetry[2] rests upon a misconception of the manner in which poetry acts to produce the moral improvement of man. Ethical science[3] arranges the elements which poetry has created, and propounds schemes and proposes examples of civil and domestic life: nor is it for want of admirable doctrines that men hate, and despise, and censure, and deceive, and subjugate one another. But Poetry acts in another and diviner manner. It awakens and enlarges the mind itself by rendering it the receptacle of a thousand unapprehended combinations of thought. Poetry lifts the veil from the hidden beauty of the world, and makes familiar objects be as if they were not familiar; it reproduces[4] all that it represents, and the impersonations clothed in its Elysian[5] light stand thenceforward in the minds of those who have once contemplated them, as memorials of that gentle and exalted content which extends itself over all

---

[1] *Achilles, Hector and Ulysses* Trojan and Greek heroes in Homer's *Iliad* and *Odyssey*.

[2] *immorality of poetry* An objection voiced by Plato in his *Republic*, in which he says that poetry often depicts characters who are morally imperfect and whose actions do not provide suitable examples for readers.

[3] *Ethical science* Moral philosophy.

[4] *reproduces* I.e., produces or creates anew.

[5] *Elysian* I.e., paradisical. From Elysium, the paradise where the blessed reside after death, according to Greek myth.

thoughts and actions with which it coexists. The great secret of morals is Love; or a going out of our own nature, and an identification of ourselves with the beautiful which exists in thought, action, or person not our own. A man, to be greatly good, must imagine intensely and comprehensively; he must put himself in the place of another and of many others; the pains and pleasures of his species must become his own. The great instrument of moral good is the imagination; and poetry administers to the effect by acting upon the cause. Poetry enlarges the circumference of the imagination by replenishing it with thoughts of ever new delight, which have the power of attracting and assimilating to their own nature all other thoughts, and which form new intervals and interstices whose void for ever craves fresh food. Poetry strengthens that faculty which is the organ of the moral nature of man, in the same manner as exercise strengthens a limb. A Poet therefore would do ill to embody his own conceptions of right and wrong, which are usually those of his place and time, in his poetical creations, which participate in neither. By this assumption of the inferior office of interpreting the effect, in which perhaps after all he might acquit himself but imperfectly, he would resign the glory in a participation in the cause. There was little danger that Homer, or any of the eternal poets, should have so far misunderstood themselves as to have abdicated this throne of their widest dominion. Those in whom the poetical faculty, though great, is less intense, as Euripides, Lucan, Tasso, Spenser,[1] have frequently affected a moral aim, and the effect of their poetry is diminished in exact proportion to the degree in which they compel us to advert to this purpose. …

The drama at Athens, or wheresoever else it may have approached to its perfection, coexisted with the moral and intellectual greatness of the age. The tragedies of the Athenian poets are as mirrors in which the spectator beholds himself, under a thin disguise of circumstance, stript of all but that ideal perfection and

energy which every one feels to be the internal type of all that he loves, admires, and would become. The imagination is enlarged by a sympathy with pains and passions so mighty that they distend in their conception the capacity of that by which they are conceived; the good affections are strengthened by pity, indignation, terror and sorrow; and an exalted calm is prolonged from the satiety of this high exercise of them into the tumult of familiar life; even crime is disarmed of half its horror and all its contagion by being represented as the fatal consequence of the unfathomable agencies of nature; error is thus divested of its wilfulness; men can no longer cherish it as the creation of their choice. In a drama of the highest order there is little food for censure or hatred; it teaches rather self-knowledge and self-respect. Neither the eye nor the mind can see itself, unless reflected upon that which it resembles. The drama, so long as it continues to express poetry, is as a prismatic and many-sided mirror, which collects the brightest rays of human nature and divides and reproduces them from the simplicity of these elementary forms, and touches them with majesty and beauty, and multiplies all that it reflects, and endows it with the power of propagating its like wherever it may fall.

But in periods of the decay of social life, the drama sympathizes with that decay. Tragedy becomes a cold imitation of the form of the great masterpieces of antiquity, divested of all harmonious accompaniment of the kindred arts; and often the very form misunderstood: or a weak attempt to teach certain doctrines, which the writer considers as moral truths; and which are usually no more than specious flatteries of some gross vice or weakness with which the author in common with his auditors are infected. …

The drama being that form under which a greater number of modes of expression of poetry are susceptible of being combined than any other, the connection of poetry and social good is more observable in the drama than in whatever other form: and it is indisputable that the highest perfection of human society has ever corresponded with the highest dramatic excellence; and that the corruption or the extinction of the drama in a nation where it has once flourished, is a mark of a

---

[1] *Euripides* Greek tragedian of the fifth century BCE; *Lucan* Roman poet of the first century CE; *Tasso* Torquato Tasso, Italian epic poet of the sixteenth century; *Spenser* Edmund Spenser, sixteenth-century epic poet, author of *The Faerie Queene*.

corruption of manners, and an extinction of the energies which sustain the soul of social life. But, as Machiavelli[1] says of political institutions, that life may be preserved and renewed, if men should arise capable of bringing back the drama to its principles. And this is true with respect to poetry in its most extended sense: all language, institution and form, require not only to be produced but to be sustained: the office and character of a poet participates in the divine nature as regards providence, no less than as regards creation.

… It is admitted that the exercise of the imagination is most delightful, but it is alleged that that of reason is more useful. Let us examine as the grounds of this distinction, what is here meant by Utility. Pleasure or good, in a general sense, is that which the consciousness of a sensitive and intelligent being seeks, and in which when found it acquiesces. There are two kinds of pleasure, one durable, universal, and permanent; the other transitory and particular. Utility may either express the means of producing the former or the latter. In the former sense, whatever strengthens and purifies the affections, enlarges the imagination, and adds spirit to sense, is useful. But the meaning in which the Author of the Four Ages of Poetry seems to have employed the word utility is the narrower one of banishing the importunity of the wants of our animal nature, the surrounding men with security of life, the dispersing the grosser delusions of superstition, and the conciliating such a degree of mutual forbearance among men as may consist with the motives of personal advantage.

Undoubtedly the promoters of utility in this limited sense have their appointed office in society. They follow the footsteps of poets, and copy the sketches of their creations into the book of common life. They make space, and give time. Their exertions are of the highest value so long as they confine their administration of the concerns of the inferior powers of our nature within the limits due to the superior ones. But whilst the sceptic destroys gross superstitions, let him spare to deface, as some of the French writers have defaced, the eternal truths charactered upon the imaginations of men. Whilst the mechanist abridges, and the political economist combines, labour, let them beware that their speculations, for want of correspondence with those first principles which belong to the imagination, do not tend, as they have in modern England, to exasperate at once the extremes of luxury and want. They have exemplified the saying, "To him that hath, more shall be given; and from him that hath not, the little that he hath shall be taken away."[2] The rich have become richer, and the poor have become poorer; and the vessel of the state is driven between the Scylla and Charybdis[3] of anarchy and despotism. Such are the effects which must ever flow from an unmitigated exercise of the calculating faculty.

It is difficult to define pleasure in its highest sense; the definition involving a number of apparent paradoxes. For, from an inexplicable defect of harmony in the constitution of human nature, the pain of the inferior is frequently connected with the pleasures of the superior portions of our being. Sorrow, terror, anguish, despair itself are often the chosen expressions of an approximation to the highest good. Our sympathy in tragic fiction depends on this principle; tragedy delights by affording a shadow of the pleasure which exists in pain. This is the source also of the melancholy which is inseparable from the sweetest melody. The pleasure that is in sorrow is sweeter than the pleasure of pleasure itself. And hence the saying, "It is better to go to the house of mourning, than to the house of mirth."[4] Not that this highest species of pleasure is necessarily linked with pain. The delight of love and friendship, the ecstasy of the admiration of nature, the joy of the perception and still more of the creation of poetry is often wholly unalloyed.

The production and assurance of pleasure in this highest sense is true utility. Those who produce and preserve this pleasure are Poets or poetical philosophers.

---

[1] *Machiavelli* Niccolò Machiavelli (1469–1527), author of the political treatise *The Prince*.

[2] *To him … away* Repeatedly said by Jesus (Matthew 25.29, Mark 4.25, Luke 8.18 and 19.26).

[3] *Scylla and Charybdis* A group of rocks and a whirlpool located at the Strait of Messina (between Sicily and mainland Italy).

[4] *It is … mirth* From Ecclesiastes 7.2.

The exertions of Locke, Hume, Gibbon, Voltaire, Rousseau,[1] and their disciples, in favour of oppressed and deluded humanity, are entitled to the gratitude of mankind. Yet it is easy to calculate the degree of moral and intellectual improvement which the world would have exhibited, had they never lived. A little more nonsense would have been talked for a century or two; and perhaps a few more men, women, and children, burnt as heretics. We might not at this moment have been congratulating each other on the abolition of the Inquisition in Spain.[2] But it exceeds all imagination to conceive what would have been the moral condition of the world if neither Dante, Petrarch, Boccaccio, Chaucer, Shakespeare, Calderon,[3] Lord Bacon, nor Milton, had ever existed; if Raphael and Michael Angelo[4] had never been born; if the Hebrew poetry had never been translated; if a revival of the study of Greek literature had never taken place; if no monuments of ancient sculpture had been handed down to us; and if the poetry of the religion of the ancient world had been extinguished together with its belief. The human mind could never, except by the intervention of these excitements, have been awakened to the invention of the grosser sciences, and that application of analytical reasoning to the aberrations of society, which it is now attempted to exalt over the direct expression of the inventive and creative faculty itself.

... The cultivation of those sciences which have enlarged the limits of the empire of man over the external world, has, for want of the poetical faculty, proportionally circumscribed those of the internal world; and man, having enslaved the elements, remains himself a slave. To what but a cultivation of the mechanical arts in a degree disproportioned to the presence of the creative faculty, which is the basis of all knowledge, is to be attributed the abuse of all invention for abridging and combining labour, to the exasperation of the inequality of mankind? From what other cause has it arisen that the discoveries which should have lightened, have added a weight to the curse imposed on Adam? Poetry, and the principle of Self, of which money is the visible incarnation, are the God and the Mammon of the world.[5]

The functions of the poetical faculty are two-fold; by one it creates new materials of knowledge, and power and pleasure; by the other it engenders in the mind a desire to reproduce and arrange them according to a certain rhythm and order which may be called the beautiful and the good. The cultivation of poetry is never more to be desired than at periods when, from an excess of the selfish and calculating principle, the accumulation of the materials of external life exceed the quantity of the power of assimilating them to the internal laws of human nature. The body has then become too unwieldy for that which animates it.

Poetry is indeed something divine. It is at once the centre and circumference of knowledge; it is that which comprehends all science, and that to which all science must be referred. It is at the same time the root and blossom of all other systems of thought: it is that from which all spring, and that which adorns all; and that which, if blighted, denies the fruit and the seed, and withholds from the barren world the nourishment and the succession of the scions[6] of the tree of life. It is the perfect and consummate surface and bloom of things; it is as the odour and the colour of the rose to the texture of the elements which compose it, as the form and the splendour of unfaded beauty to the secrets of anatomy and corruption. What were Virtue, Love, Patriotism, Friendship &c.—what were the scenery of this beautiful Universe which we inhabit—what were our consolations

[1] *Locke ... Rousseau* John Locke, David Hume, Edward Gibbon, François-Marie Arouet (Voltaire), and Jean-Jacques Rousseau, noted philosophers of the seventeenth and eighteenth centuries.

[2] *We might ... Spain* The Inquisition was suspended in 1820 (the year before Shelley wrote this essay) and abolished permanently in 1834.

[3] *Petrarch* Fourteenth-century Italian poet, famous for his love lyrics; *Boccaccio* Italian poet, author of the *Decameron* (c. 1349–53); *Calderon* Pedro Calderón de la Barca, seventeenth-century Spanish poet and dramatist.

[4] *Raphael and Michael Angelo* Italian Renaissance painters.

[5] *God and ... world* Cf. Matthew 6.24: "No man can serve two masters: for either he will hate the one, and love the other; or else he will hold to the one, and despise the other. Ye cannot serve God and Mammon," Mammon being the false idol of worldly possessions.

[6] *scions* Shoots.

on this side of the grave—and what were our aspirations beyond it—if Poetry did not ascend to bring light and fire from those eternal regions where the owl-winged faculty of calculation dare not ever soar? Poetry is not like reasoning, a power to be exerted according to the determination of the will. A man cannot say, "I will compose poetry." The greatest poet even cannot say it: for the mind in creation is as a fading coal which some invisible influence, like an inconstant wind, awakens to transitory brightness: this power arises from within, like the colour of a flower which fades and changes as it is developed, and the conscious portions of our natures are unprophetic either of its approach or its departure. ...

Poetry is the record of the best and happiest moments of the happiest and best minds. We are aware of evanescent visitations of thought and feeling sometimes associated with place or person, sometimes regarding our own mind alone, and always arising unforeseen and departing unbidden, but elevating and delightful beyond all expression: so that even in the desire and the regret they leave, there cannot but be pleasure, participating as it does in the nature of its object. It is as it were the interpenetration of a diviner nature through our own; but its footsteps are like those of a wind over a sea, which the coming calm erases, and whose traces remain only as on the wrinkled sand which paves it. These and corresponding conditions of being are experienced principally by those of the most delicate sensibility and the most enlarged imagination; and the state of mind produced by them is at war with every base desire. The enthusiasm of virtue, love, patriotism, and friendship is essentially linked with these emotions; and whilst they last, self appears as what it is, an atom to a Universe. Poets are not only subject to these experiences as spirits of the most refined organization, but they can colour all that they combine with the evanescent hues of this ethereal world; a word, a trait in the representation of a scene or a passion, will touch the enchanted chord, and reanimate, in those who have ever experienced these emotions, the sleeping, the cold, the buried image of the past. Poetry thus makes immortal all that is best and most beautiful in the world; it arrests the vanishing apparitions which haunt the inter-lunations[1] of life, and veiling them or in language or in form sends them forth among mankind, bearing sweet news of kindred joy to those with whom their sisters abide—abide, because there is no portal of expression from the caverns of the spirit which they inhabit into the universe of things. Poetry redeems from decay the visitations of the divinity in man.

Poetry turns all things to loveliness; it exalts the beauty of that which is most beautiful, and it adds beauty to that which is most deformed: it marries exultation and horror, grief and pleasure, eternity and change; it subdues to union under its light yoke all irreconcilable things. It transmutes all that it touches, and every form moving within the radiance of its presence is changed by wondrous sympathy to an incarnation of the spirit which it breathes; its secret alchemy turns to potable[2] gold the poisonous waters which flow from death through life; it strips the veil of familiarity from the world, and lays bare the naked and sleeping beauty which is the spirit of its forms.

All things exist as they are perceived: at least in relation to the percipient. "The mind is its own place, and of itself can make a heaven of hell, a hell of heaven."[3] But poetry defeats the curse which binds us to be subjected to the accident of surrounding impressions. And whether it spreads its own figured curtain or withdraws life's dark veil from before the scene of things, it equally creates for us a being within our being. It makes us the inhabitants of a world to which the familiar world is a chaos. It reproduces the common universe of which we are portions and percipients, and it purges from our inward sight the film of familiarity which obscures from us the wonder of our being. It compels us to feel that which we perceive, and to imagine that which we know. It creates anew the universe after it has been annihilated in our minds by the recurrence of impressions blunted by reiteration. ...

---

[1] *interlunations* Period between an old and a new moon; period of darkness.

[2] *potable* Drinkable. Alchemists sought a liquid form of gold that, when consumed, would be the elixir of life.

[3] *The mind ... heaven* From Satan's speech in Milton's *Paradise Lost* 1.254–55.

The first part of these remarks has related to Poetry in its elements and principles; and it has been shown, as well as the narrow limits assigned them would permit, that what is called poetry, in a restricted sense, has a common source with all other forms of order and of beauty according to which the materials of human life are susceptible of being arranged, and which is poetry in an universal sense.

The second part[1] will have for its object an application of these principles to the present state of the cultivation of Poetry, and a defence of the attempt to idealize the modern forms of manners and opinion, and compel them into a subordination to the imaginative and creative faculty. For the literature of England, an energetic development of which has ever preceded or accompanied a great and free development of the national will, has arisen as it were from a new birth. In spite of the low-thoughted envy which would undervalue contemporary merit, our own will be a memorable age in intellectual achievements, and we live among such philosophers and poets as surpass beyond comparison any who have appeared since the last national struggle for civil and religious liberty.[2] The most unfailing herald, companion, and follower of the awakening of a great people to work a beneficial change in opinion or institution, is Poetry. At such periods there is an accumulation of the power of communicating and receiving intense and impassioned conceptions respecting man and nature. The persons in whom this power resides, may often, as far as regards many portions of their nature, have little apparent correspondence with that spirit of good of which they are the ministers. But even whilst they deny and abjure, they are yet compelled to serve the Power which is seated upon the throne of their own soul. It is impossible to read the compositions of the most celebrated writers of the present day without being startled with the electric life which burns within their words. They measure the circumference and sound the depths of human nature with a comprehensive and all-penetrating spirit, and they are themselves perhaps the most sincerely astonished at its manifestations, for it is less their spirit than the spirit of the age. Poets are the hierophants[3] of an unapprehended inspiration, the mirrors of the gigantic shadows which futurity casts upon the present, the words which express what they understand not; the trumpets which sing to battle, and feel not what they inspire: the influence which is moved not, but moves.[4] Poets are the unacknowledged legislators of the World.

—1820

---

[1] *The second part* Shelley did not complete a second part.

[2] *the last ... liberty* I.e., the English Civil War of the 1640s.

[3] *hierophants* Interpreters of sacred mysteries.

[4] *is moved ... moves* Reference to Greek philosopher Aristotle's description of God as the "Unmoved Mover" of the universe.

IN CONTEXT

The Peterloo Massacre

Though Shelley's "The Mask of Anarchy" was not published until years after the Peterloo Massacre, many poems on the subject were published soon after the event—among them the four reprinted below. Robert Shorter's satire "The Bloody Fields of Peterloo! A New Song" appeared attributed to "R.S." in *The Theological and Political Comet*, which Shorter edited, as did the anonymous "A New Song," which in several respects takes an approach parallel to that of the "The Mask of Anarchy." "Stanzas Occasioned by the Manchester Massacre!" (the second stanza of which may be of particular interest in relation to Shelley's poem) and "The Peterloo Man" both appeared in *The Black Dwarf*, a radical weekly periodical, edited by Thomas Wooler, that was widely read among the laboring classes.

In stanza 87 of "The Mask of Anarchy" Shelley imagines that "Every woman in the land / Will point at" the tyrants in accusation. In fact, the role of women at St. Peter's Field and in the Radical Movement generally had already become substantial. In the first of the passages reprinted below from his biography, *Passages in the Life of a Radical*, Samuel Bamford (1788–1872), a prominent political radical, describes the part played by women in the Radical Movement at the time. Bamford led the Middleton contingent to St. Peter's Field the day of the Massacre, and was later charged with treason—though it was determined that his actions were peaceful and orderly, and he was only sentenced to a year in jail for inciting a riot. His account of the Massacre is also excerpted below, as is that of his wife, whose story he included in his biography.

Robert Shorter, "The Bloody Field of Peterloo! A New Song" (1819)

Heroes of Manchester, all hail!
    Your fame the astonished world shall know;
Th' immortalizing bard can't fail,
    To sing the *deeds* of Peterloo!

5   The Muse[1] shall soar on daring wing,
        And her ecstatic numbers flow;
But Pindar's[2] muse would fail to sing
        Your *glorious deeds* at Peterloo!

You all shall live in deathless fame,
10   For chivalry you there did show;
Children shall lisp the Yeomen's name,
    As Heroes all of Peterloo!

---

[1] *Muse* In Greek mythology, one of nine daughters of Zeus and Mnemosyne, each of whom presided over and provided inspiration for an aspect of learning or the arts.

[2] *Pindar* Fifth-century BCE Greek poet celebrated for his odes.

How on that memorable day,
    Ye did with martial ardor glow;
15   And such heroic zeal display,
    All on the plains of Peterloo!

How swelled your breasts with rapture high,
    To meet the *well armed*, bannered foe;
What courage teemed in Yeoman's eye,
20   When dashing on to Peterloo!

Methinks I see the mettled° steed,   *spirited*
    Trampling the mangled corses° low,   *corpses*
Whilst charging round, in furious speed,
    The *bloody field* of Peterloo!!

25   Methinks I hear the cries, the groans,
    (And view their fatal overthrow)
Heart-rending sighs, and piteous moans,
    Rise from the field of Peterloo!

Methinks I see the crimson flood,
30   And mark the well aimed fatal blow,
The Yeoman's sabre died in blood,
    Reeking° on far famed Peterloo!   *smeared*

Wives, mothers, children, on the plain,
    In one promiscuous heap, I view;
35   The husband, son, and father slain,
    Stretched on the field of Peterloo!

But Yeomen's hearts are formed of steel,
    Ardent to fields of blood they go;
Their gallant souls disdain to feel,
40   Whilst dealing death at Peterloo!

My muse the truth shall ne'er deny;
    The good, the wise, the just, we know,
Think you deserve promotion high,
    In *iron case* on Peterloo!!

Anonymous, "A New Song" (1819)

Rouse, rouse, loyal Britons, your fame to maintain
Nor tamely submit to wear Slavery's chain;
Like Britons stand firm in Humanity's cause,
Asserting with spirit your rights and your laws.

5   *Chor.*   Thus united and free,
                 May we ever agree;
                 And man view each other
                 As friend and as brother;
           And may Britons be happy, as happy can be!

10   By Justice supported, with rapturous eye,
     See the banners of Liberty waving on high;
     Her sons are all rallying round at her call,
     Resolved by her standard to stand or to fall.

           Chor.   Thus united, &c.

15   To the traitors' perdition, whose merciless plan
     Is, by Tyranny's force, to destroy Rights of Man,
     Your freedom to shackle, your rights to invade,
     And, by state-craft and trick, make religion a trade.

           Chor.   Thus united, &c.

20   Not long shall the demons o'er Britain have sway,
     Not long on her vitals these vultures shall prey;[1]
     United and firm all their efforts withstand,
     And Oppression and Anarchy chase from our land.

           Chor.   Thus united, &c.

25   While Nature, in plenty, her riches doth pour,
     And Providence kindly is blessing the store,
     With the feelings of Britons, how shall we endure
     To see Pride and Cruelty starving the poor?

           Chor.   Thus united, &c.

30   Old England, my country, may Heaven thee defend,
     On each patriot heart all thy blessings descend;

---

[1] *on her vitals ... prey*   Reference to the Greek myth of Prometheus, a Titan who stole fire from Olympus (the home of the gods) and gave it to humankind. As punishment Zeus chained him to a rock in Hades (the classical underworld), where a vulture (in some versions, an eagle) fed on his liver, which grew back daily.

Thy foes all confounded, thy triumphs secured,
That the sun of thy glory be never obscured!

   Chor.   Thus united, &c.

Hibernicus, "Stanzas Occasioned by the Manchester Massacre!" (21 August 1819)

Oh, weep not for those who are freed
   From bondage so frightful as ours!
Let *tyranny* mourn for the deed,
And howl o'er the prey she devours!

5   The mask for a century worn,
Has fallen from her visage at last;
Of all its sham attributes shorn,
Her reign of delusion is past.

   In native deformity now
10   Behold her, how shattered and weak!
With *murder* impressed on her brow,
And *cowardice* blanching her cheek.

   With guilt's gloomy terrors bowed down,
She scowls on the smile of the slave!
15   She shrinks at the patriot's frown;
She *dies* in the grasp of the brave.

   Then brief be our wail for the dead,
Whose blood has sealed tyranny's doom;
And the tears that affliction will shed,
20   Let vengeance, bright flashes illume.

   And shame on the passionless thing
Whose soul can *now* slumber within him!
To slavery still let him cling,
For liberty scorns to win him.

25   *Her* manlier spirits arouse
At the summons so frightfully given!
And glory exults in their vows,
While virtue records them in Heaven.

Anonymous, "The Peterloo Man" (1819)

You have heard of the far-renowned Waterloo plains,
    Where the sun, horror-struck at the slaughter, declined;
Where courage to frenzy abandoned the reins,
    And liberty fell 'midst the tears of mankind.

5 But a scene still more dreadful remains to the story,
        Where the blood of the helpless in wild torrents ran;
    When women, and children, and grandsires hoary,°   *grey-haired*
        Fell beneath the fierce sword of the *Peterloo Man!*

    How brave were the heroes, what muse can relate;
10   On the breast of its mother, he bade the babe bleed!
    And the mother herself would in vain shun the fate,
        That awaited her under the hoofs of his steed.

    Stained deep with their gore, how he dashed along,
        Of banditti° the first, since fell° murder began;   *bandits / savage*
15 How tremble the feeble among the scared throng,
        When they hear the fierce shout of the Peterloo Man!

    What groups there assemble, what ferment prevails!
        'Tis a nation in search of the savages base;
    And justice demands, in her still even scales,
20   To balance the wretches who Britain disgrace.

    Whether Yeomen, or Magistrates, forth be they brought,
        Their deeds which a nation indignantly scan,
    Well merit the doom to eternity fraught
        With the vengeance of God on the Peterloo Man.

from Samuel Bamford, *Passages in the Life of a Radical* (1843)

from CHAPTER 28

With the restoration of the Habeas Corpus Act, the agitation for reform was renewed.... Numerous meetings followed in various parts of the country; and Lancashire, and the Stockport borders of Cheshire, were not the last to be concerned in public demonstrations for reform. At one of these meetings, which took place at Lydgate, in Saddleworth, and at which Bagguley, Drummond, Fitton, Haigh, and others, were the principal speakers, I, in the course of an address, insisted on the right, and the propriety also, of females who were present at such assemblages voting, by show of hand, for or against the resolutions. This was a new idea; and the women, who attended numerously on that bleak ridge, were mightily pleased with it; and the men being nothing dissentient, when the resolution was put, the women held up their hands, amid much laughter; and ever from that time, females voted with the men at the radical meetings. I was not then aware that the new impulse thus given to political movement would in a short time be applied to charitable and religious purposes. But it was so; our females voted at every subsequent meetings; it became the practice—female political unions were formed, with their chair-women, committees, and other officials; and from us, the practice was soon borrowed, very judiciously no doubt, and applied in a greater or less degree to the promotion of religious and charitable institutions. ...

from CHAPTER 35 [At the St. Peter's Field meeting, 16 August 1819]

In about half an hour after our arrival at the meeting, the sounds of music, and reiterated shouts, proclaimed the near approach of Mr. Hunt and his party; and in a minute or two they were seen coming from towards Deansgate, preceded by a band of music, and several flags. ... Their approach was hailed by one universal shout from probably eighty thousand persons. They threaded their way slowly past us, and through the crowd, which Hunt eyed, I thought with almost as much of astonishment as satisfaction. This spectacle could not be otherwise in his view, than solemnly impressive. Such a mass of human beings he had never beheld till then. ... Mr. Hunt, stepping towards the front of the stage, took off his white hat, and addressed the people.

Whilst he was doing so, I proposed to an acquaintance, that, as the speeches and resolutions were not likely to contain anything new to us, and as we could see them in the papers, we should retire awhile, and get some refreshment, of which I stood in much need, being in not very robust health. He assented, and we had got to nearly the outside of the crowd, when a noise and strange murmur arose towards the church. Some persons said it was the Blackburn people coming; and I stood on tip-toe, and looked in the direction whence the noise proceeded, and saw a party of cavalry in blue and white uniform, come trotting sword in hand, round the corner of a garden-wall, and to the front of a row of new houses, where they reined up in a line.

"The soldiers are here," I said, "we must go back and see what this means." "Oh," some one made reply, "they are only come to be ready if there should be any disturbance in the meeting." "Well, let us go back," I said, and we forced our way towards the colours.

On the cavalry drawing up they were received with a shout, of good will, as I understood it. They shouted again, waving their sabres over their heads; and then, slackening rein, and striking spur into their steeds, they dashed forward, and began cutting the people.

"Stand fast," I said, "they are riding upon us, stand fast." And there was a general cry in our quarter of "Stand fast." The cavalry were in confusion: they evidently could not, with all the weight of man and horse, penetrate that compact mass of human beings; and their sabres were plied to hew a way through naked held-up hands, and defenceless heads; and then chopped limbs, and wound-gaping skulls were seen; and groans and cries were mingled with the din of that horrid confusion. "Ah! ah!" "For shame! for shame!" was shouted. Then, "Break! break! they are killing them in front, and they cannot get away"; and there was a general cry of "Break! break." For a moment the crowd held back as in a pause; then was a rush, heavy and resistless as a headlong sea; and a sound like low thunder, with screams, prayers, and imprecations from the crowd-moiled[1] and sabre-doomed, who could not escape.

---

[1] *crowd-moiled* Harassed by, or worn out with toiling in, the crowd.

By this time Hunt and his companions had disappeared from the hustings,[1] and some of the yeomanry, perhaps less sanguinarily disposed than others, were busied in cutting down the flag-staves, and demolishing the flags at the hustings.

On the breaking of the crowd, the yeomanry wheeled; and dashing wherever there was an opening, they followed, pressing and wounding. Many females appeared as the crowd opened; and striplings or mere youths also were found. Their cries were piteous and heart-rending; and would, one might have supposed, have disarmed any human resentment: but here, their appeals were vain. Women, white-vested maids, and tender youths were indiscriminately sabred or trampled; and we have reason for believing that few were the instances in which that forbearance was vouchsafed which they so earnestly implored.

In ten minutes from the commencement of the havoc, the field was an open and almost deserted space. The sun looked down through a sultry and motionless air. The curtains and blinds of the windows within view were all closed. A gentleman or two might occasionally be seen looking out from one of the new houses before-mentioned, near the door of which, a group of persons, (special constables) were collected, and apparently in conversation; others were assisting the wounded, or carrying off the dead. The hustings remained, with a few broken and hewed flag-staves erect, and a torn and gashed banner or two dropping; whilst over the whole field, were strewed caps, bonnets, hats, shawls, and shoes, and other parts of male and female dress; trampled, torn, and bloody. …

from CHAPTER 36

… A number of our people were driven to some timber which lay at the foot of the wall of the Quakers' meeting house. Being pressed by the yeomanry, a number sprung over the balks and defended themselves with stones which they found there. It was not without difficulty, and after several were wounded, that they were driven out. A heroine, a young married woman of our party, with her face all bloody, her hair streaming about her, her bonnet hanging by the string, and her apron weighted with stones, kept her assailant at bay until she fell backwards and was near being taken; but she got away covered with severe bruises. It was near this place, and about this time, that one of the yeomanry was dangerously wounded, and unhorsed, by a blow from the fragment of a brick; and it was supposed to have been flung by this woman. …

from CHAPTER 39 [The narrative of Bamford's wife, Jemima]

As a narrative collateral with these passages, the account given by my dear wife, of her attendance at the meeting on Saint Peter's Field, and of some incidents which befell her, may not be devoid of interest to the reader, and certainly will not be out of place, if introduced here. She says:

I was determined to go to the meeting, and should have followed, even if my husband had refused his consent to my going with the procession. From what I, in common with others, had heard the week previous, "that if the country people went with their caps of liberty, and their banners, and music, the soldiers would be brought to them," I was uneasy, and felt persuaded, in my own mind, that something would be the matter, and I had best go with my husband, and be near him; and if I only saw him I should be more content than in staying at home. I accordingly, he having consented after much persuasion, gave my little girl

---

[1]   *hustings* Platforms.

something to please her, and, promising more on my return, I left her with a careful neighbour woman, and joined some other married females at the head of the procession.

Every time I went aside to look at my husband, and that was often, an ominous impression smote my heart. He looked very serious, I thought, and I felt a foreboding of something evil to befall us that day.

I was dressed plainly as a countrywoman, in my second best attire. My companions were also neatly dressed as the wives of working men; I had seen Mr. Hunt before that time; they had not, and some of them were quite eager to obtain good places, that they might see and hear one of whom so much had been reported.

In going down Mosley Street, I lost sight of my husband. Mrs. Yates, who had hold of my arm, would keep hurrying forward to get a good place, and when the crowd opened for the Middleton procession, Mrs. Yates and myself, and some others of the women, went close to the hustings, quite glad that we had obtained such a situation for seeing and hearing all. My husband got on the stage, but when afterwards I saw him leap down, and lost sight of him, I began to be unhappy.

The crowd seemed to have increased very much, for we became insufferably pressed. We were surrounded by men who were strangers; we were almost suffocated, and to me the heat was quite sickening; but Mrs. Yates, being taller than myself, supported it better.

I felt I could not bear this long, and I became alarmed. I reflected that if there was any more pressure I must faint, and then what would become of me? and I begged of the men to open a way and let me go out, but they would not move. Every moment I became worse, and I told some other men then, who stood in a row, that I was sick, and begged they would let me pass them, and they immediately made a way, and I went down a long passage betwixt two ranks of these men, many of them saying, "Make way, she's sick, she's sick, let her go out," and I passed quite out of the crowd, and, turning to my right, I got on some high ground, on which stood a row of houses—This was Windmill Street.

I thought if I could get to stand at the door of one of those houses, I should have a good view of the meeting, and should perhaps see my husband again; and I kept going further down the row, until I saw a door open, and I stepped within it, the people of the house making no objections.

By this time Mr. Hunt was on the hustings, addressing the people. In a minute or two some soldiers came riding up. The good folks of the house, and some who seemed to be visitors, said, "the soldiers were only come to keep order; they would not meddle with the people"; but I was alarmed. The people shouted, and then the soldiers shouted, waving their swords. Then they rode amongst the people, and there was a great outcry, and a moment after, a man passed without hat, and wiping the blood off his head with his hand, and it ran down his arm in a great stream.

The meeting was all in a tumult; there were dreadful cries; the soldiers kept riding amongst the people, and striking with their swords. I became faint, and turning from the door, I went unobserved down some steps into a cellared passage; and, hoping to escape from the horrid noise, and to be concealed, I crept into a vault, and sat down, faint and terrified, on some fire-wood.

The cries of the multitude outside still continued, and the people of the house, up stairs, kept bewailing most pitifully. They could see all the dreadful work through the window, and their exclamations were so distressing that I put my fingers in my ears to prevent my hearing more; and, on removing them, I understood that a young man had just been brought past, wounded. The front door of the passage before-mentioned soon after opened, and a number of men entered, carrying the body of a decent, middle-aged woman, who had been killed. I thought they were going to put her beside me, and was about to scream, but they took her forward, and deposited her in some premises at the back of the house.

I had sat in my hiding place some time, and the tumult seemed abated, when a young girl, one of the family, came into the vault, and suddenly crouching, she bumped against my knee, and starting up, and seeing another dead woman, as she probably thought, she ran up stairs quite terrified, and told her mother. The good woman, Mrs. Jones, came down with the girl and several others, and, having ascertained that I was living, but sadly distressed, she spoke very kindly, and assisted me to a chair in her front room. …

from John Tyas, An Account of the Events Leading Up to the Massacre, *The Times* 19 August 1819

A club of Female Reformers, amounting in numbers, according to our calculations, 150 came from Oldham; and another, not quite so numerous, from Royton. The first bore a white silk banner, by far the most elegant displayed during the day, inscribed "Major Cartwright's Bill, Annual Parliaments, Universal Suffrage, and Vote by Ballot." The females of Royton bore two red flags, the one inscribed "Let us die like men, and not sold like slaves"; the other "Annual Parliaments and Universal Suffrage."

A group of women of Manchester, attracted by the crowd, came to the corner of the street where we had taken our post. They viewed the Oldham Female Reformers for some time with a look in which compassion and disgust was equally blended, and at last burst out into an indignant exclamation—"Go home to your families, and leave sike-like as these to your husbands and sons, who better understand them." The women who addressed them were of the lower order of life.

Peterloo Massacre (detail), 1819, a print published by Richard Carlile (publisher of the radical newspaper *The Republican* and a speaker at the St. Peter's Field Meeting). The banners read (from left to right) "Manchester Female Reform [Group]," "Universal Suffrage," "Liberty or Death," and "Universal Civil and Religious Liberty." The woman in white on the stage is thought to be Mary Fildes, a leading campaigner for the expansion of the Manchester Female Reform Group. Fildes was slashed by a cavalryman and seriously wounded during the attack, but survived to become an active participant in the Chartist Movement, a working-class movement for parliamentary democracy.

IN CONTEXT

Youth and Love

Thomas Jefferson Hogg was a close friend of Shelley (and later his biographer). They were students together at Oxford at the time the following correspondence between the two occurred. Both were expelled from the university later that same year, after the publication of Shelley's *Necessity of Atheism*. Also included below is a long letter by Shelley to William Godwin. Profoundly influenced by Godwin's *Enquiry Concerning Political Justice* (1793), Shelley sought out a correspondence with the author, who would later become his father-in-law.

Letter to T.J. Hogg

3 January 1811
Field Place

My Dear Friend,

Before we deny or believe the existence of anything, it is necessary that we should have a tolerably clear idea of what it is. The word "God," a vague word, has been, and will continue to be, the source of numberless errors, until it is erased from the nomenclature of philosophy. Does it not imply "the soul of the universe, the intelligent and *necessarily* beneficent, actuating principle"? This it is impossible not to believe in. I may not be able to adduce proofs; but I think that the leaf of a tree, the meanest insect on which we trample, are, in themselves, arguments more conclusive than any which can be advanced, that some vast intellect animates infinity. If we disbelieve *this*, the strongest argument in support of the existence of a future state instantly becomes annihilated. I confess that I think Pope's—

All are but parts of one stupendous whole,[1]

something more than poetry. It has ever been my favourite theory, for the immortal soul, "never to be able to die, never to escape from some shrine as chilling as the clay-formed dungeon which now it inhabits"; it is the future punishment which I can most easily believe in.

Love, love *infinite in extent*, eternal in duration, yet (allowing your theory in that point), perfectible, should be the reward; but can we suppose that this reward will arise, spontaneously, as a necessary appendage to our nature, or that our nature itself could be without cause—a first cause—a God? When do we see effects arise without causes? What causes are there without correspondent effects? Yet here, I swear—and as I break my oaths, may Infinity, Eternity blast me—here I swear that never will I forgive intolerance! It is the only point on which I allow myself to encourage revenge; every moment shall be devoted to my object, which I can spare; and let me hope that it will not be a blow which spends itself, and leaves the wretch at rest—but lasting, long revenge! I am convinced, too, that it is of great disservice to society—that it encourages prejudices, which strike at the root of the dearest, the tenderest of its ties. Oh! how I wish I were the avenger!—that it were mine to crush the demon; to hurl him to his native hell, never to rise again, and thus to establish for ever perfect and universal toleration. I expect to gratify some of this insatiable feeling in poetry. You shall see—you shall hear—how it has injured me. She[2] is no longer mine! she abhors me as a sceptic, as what *she* was

---

[1] *All are ... whole*   Alexander Pope's *Essay on Man* 1.267.

[2] *She*   Shelley's cousin Harriet Grove, with whom he was briefly in love.

before! Oh, bigotry! When I pardon this last, this severest of thy persecutions, may Heaven (if there be wrath in Heaven) blast me! Has vengeance, in its armoury of wrath, a punishment more dreadful? Yet forgive me, I have done; and were it not for your great desire to know *why* I consider myself as the victim of severer anguish, I could not have entered into this brief recital.

I am afraid there is selfishness in the passion of love, for I cannot avoid feeling every instant as if my soul was bursting; but I *will* feel no more! It is selfish. I would feel for others, but for myself—oh! how much rather would I expire in the struggle! Yes, that were a relief! Is suicide wrong? I slept with a loaded pistol and some poison, last night, but did not die. I could not come on Monday, my sister would not part with me; but I must—I will see you soon. My sister is now comparatively happy; she has felt deeply for me. Had it not been for her—had it not been for a sense of what I owed to her, to *you*, I should have bidden you a final farewell some time ago. But can the dead feel; dawns any day-beam on the night of dissolution?

Adieu, my dear friend. Your sincere,

P.B.S.

Letter to T.J. Hogg, 1811

[Undated]

My Dear Friend—

You will perhaps see me before you can answer this; perhaps not; Heavens knows! I shall certainly come to York, but *Harriet Westbrook*[1] will decide whether now or in three weeks. Her father has persecuted her in a most horrible way, by endeavouring to compel her to go to school. She asked my advice: resistance was the answer, at the same time that I essayed to mollify Mr. W. in vain! And in consequence of my advice *she* has thrown herself upon *my* protection. I set off for London on Monday. How flattering a distinction!—I am thinking of ten million things at once.

What have I said? I declare, quite *ludicrous*. I advised her to resist. She wrote to say that resistance was useless, but that she would fly with me, and threw herself upon my protection. We shall have £200 a year: when we find it run short, we must live, I suppose, upon love! Gratitude and admiration all demand that I should love her *for ever*. We shall see you at York. I will hear your arguments for matrimonialism, by which I am now almost convinced. I can get lodgings at York, I suppose. Direct[2] to me at Graham's, 18 Sackville Street, Piccadilly.

Your inclosure of £10 has arrived; I am now indebted to you £30. In spite of philosophy, I am rather ashamed of this unceremonious exsiccation[3] of your financial river. But indeed, my dear friend, the gratitude which I owe you for your society and attachment ought so far to over-balance this consideration as to leave me nothing but that. I must, however, pay you when I can. I suspect that the *strain* is gone for ever. This letter will convince you that I am not under the influence of a *strain*. I am thinking at once of ten million things. I shall come to live near you, as Mr. Peyton.

Ever your most faithful friend,

P.B.S.

I shall be at 18 Sackville Street; at least direct there. Do not send more cash; I shall raise supplies in London.

---

[1] *Harriet Westbrook*   With whom Shelley eloped on 28 August 1811.

[2] *Direct*   Send a message or letter.

[3] *exsiccation*   Complete drying out or absorption.

Joseph Severn, *Percy Bysshe Shelley* (detail), 1845.

Letter to William Godwin

10 January 1812
Keswick

Sir—

It is not otherwise to be supposed than that I should appreciate your avocations far beyond the pleasure or benefit which can accrue to me from their sacrifice. The time, however, will be small which may be mis-spent in reading this letter; and much individual pleasure as an answer might give me, I have not the vanity to imagine that it will be greater than the happiness elsewhere diffused during the time which its creation will occupy.

You complain that the generalizing character of my letter renders it deficient in interest; that I am not an individual to you. Yet, intimate as I am with your character and your writings, intimacy with *yourself* must in some degree precede this exposure of my peculiarities. It is scarcely possible, however pure be the morality which he has endeavoured to diffuse, but that generalization must characterize the uninvited address of a stranger to a stranger.

I proceed to remedy the fault. I am the son of a man of fortune in Sussex. The habits of thinking of my father and myself never coincided. Passive obedience was inculcated and enforced in my childhood. I was required to love, because it was *my duty* to love: it is scarcely necessary to remark, that coercion obviated its own intention. I was haunted with a passion for the wildest and most extravagant romances. Ancient books of Chemistry and Magic were perused with an enthusiasm of wonder, almost amounting to belief. My sentiments were unrestrained by anything within me; external impediments were numerous and strongly applied; their effect was merely temporary.

From a reader, I became a writer of romances; before the age of seventeen I had published two, *St. Irvyn* and *Zastrozzi*, each of which, though quite uncharacteristic of me as now I am, yet serves to mark the state of my mind at the period of their composition. I shall desire them to be sent to you: do not, however, consider this as any obligation to yourself to misapply your valuable time.

It is now a period of more than two years since first I saw your inestimable book of *Political Justice*; it opened to my mind fresh and more extensive views; it materially influenced my character, and I rose from its perusal a wiser and a better man. I was no longer the votary of romance; till then I had existed in an ideal world—now I found that in this universe of ours was enough to excite the interest of the heart, enough to employ the discussions of reason; I beheld, in short, that I had duties to perform. Conceive the effect which the *Political Justice* would have upon a mind before jealous of its independence, participating somewhat singularly in a peculiar susceptibility.

My age is now *nineteen*; at the period to which I allude I was at Eton. No sooner had I formed the principles which I now profess, than I was anxious to disseminate their benefits. This was done without the slightest caution. I was twice expelled,[1] but recalled by the interference of my father. I went to Oxford. Oxonian society was insipid to me, uncongenial with my habits of thinking. I could not descend to common life: the sublime interest of poetry, lofty and exalted achievements, the proselytism of the world, the equalization of its inhabitants, were to me the soul of my soul. You can probably form some idea of the contrast exhibited to my character by those with whom I was surrounded. Classical reading and poetical writing employed me during my residence at Oxford.

---

[1] *I was twice expelled* Shelley's friend Jefferson Hogg claimed that Shelley's letters "must be received with caution," not because he intended to deliberately tell falsehoods, but because "he was the creature, the unsuspecting and unresisting victim, of his irresistible imagination." According to Hogg, Shelley was never expelled from Eton, and he never published anything controversial there. He also states that the incident between Shelley and Mr. ——, described in the following paragraph, never occurred, and that Shelley's father never offered him a commission in the army.

In the meantime I became, in the popular sense of the word, a sceptic. I printed a pamphlet, avowing my opinion, and its occasion. I distributed this anonymously to men of thought and learning, wishing that Reason should decide on the case at issue: it was never my intention to deny it. Mr.——, at Oxford, among others, had the pamphlet; he showed it to the Master and the Fellows of University College, and *I* was sent for. I was informed, that in case I denied the publication, no more would be said. I refused, and was expelled.

It will be necessary, in order to elucidate this part of my history, to inform you that I am heir by entail to an estate of £6,000 per annum. My principles have induced me to regard the law of primogeniture as an evil of primary magnitude. My father's notions of family honour are incoincident with my knowledge of public good. I will never sacrifice the latter to any consideration. My father has ever regarded me as a blot, a defilement of his honour. He wished to induce me by poverty to accept of some commission in a distant regiment, and in the interim of my absence to prosecute the pamphlet, that a process of outlawry might make the estate, on his death, devolve to my younger brother. These are the leading points of the history of the man before you. Others exist, but I have thought proper to make some selection, not that it is my design to conceal or extenuate any part, but that I should by their enumeration quite outstep the bounds of modesty. Now, it is for you to judge whether, by permitting me to cultivate your friendship, you are exhibiting yourself more really useful than by the pursuance of those avocations, of which the time spent in allowing this cultivation would deprive you. I am now earnestly pursuing studious habits. I am writing "An inquiry into the causes of the failure of the French Revolution to benefit mankind." My plan is that of resolving to lose no opportunity to disseminate truth and happiness.

I am married to a woman whose views are similar to my own. To you, as the regulator and former of my mind, I must ever look with real respect and veneration.

Yours sincerely,

P.B. SHELLEY.

IN CONTEXT

Shelley and Keats

The unfinished letter excerpted below was written to the editor of the *Quarterly Review*, which had published unfavorable notices both of Shelley's own work and of that of Keats. It shows Shelley's conviction that Keats was of a fragile constitution, easily discouraged, and demoralized by criticism—a conviction that, after Keats's death, spurred his composition of *Adonais*. Also excerpted below is the response of Leigh Hunt, editor of the radical journal *The Examiner*, to Shelley's *Adonais*.

from Letter to the Editor of the *Quarterly Review*, 1820

Sir,

Should you cast your eye on the signature of this letter before you read the contents, you might imagine that they related to a slanderous paper which appeared in your *Review* some time since. I never notice anonymous attacks. ...

The case is different with the unfortunate subject of this letter, the author of *Endymion*, to whose feelings and situations I entreat you to allow me to call your attention. ...

Poor Keats was thrown into a dreadful state of mind by this review, which, I am persuaded, was not written with any intention of producing the effect, to which it has, at least, greatly contributed, of embittering his existence, and inducing a disease, from which there are now but faint hopes of his recovery. The first effects are described to me to have resembled insanity, and it was by assiduous watching that he was restrained from effecting purposes of suicide. The agony of his sufferings at length produced the rupture of a blood vessel in the lungs, and the usual process of consumption[1] appears to have begun. He is coming to pay me a visit in Italy; but I fear that, unless his mind can be kept tranquil, little is to be hoped from the mere influence of climate.

But let me not extort anything from your pity. I have just seen a second volume,[2] published by him evidently in careless despair. I have desired my bookseller to send you a copy, and allow me to solicit your especial attention to the fragment of a poem entitled *Hyperion*, the composition of which was checked by the Review in question.[3] The great proportion of this piece is surely in the very highest style of poetry. I speak impartially, for the canons of taste to which Keats has conformed in his other compositions are the very reverse of my own. I leave you to judge for yourself; if it would be an insult to you to suppose that, from motives however honourable, you would lend yourself to a deception of the public.

Leigh Hunt on "Mr. Shelley's New Poem Entitled *Adonais*" (1822)

Since I left London, Mr. Shelley's *Adonais, or Elegy on the Death of Mr. Keats*, has, I find, made its appearance. I have not seen the London edition; but I have an Italian one printed at Pisa, with which I must content myself at present. The other was to have had notes. It is not a poem calculated to be popular, any more than the *Prometheus Unbound*;[4] it is of too abstract and subtle a nature for that purpose; but it will delight the few, to whom Mr. Shelley is accustomed to address himself. Spenser would be pleased with it if he were living. A mere town reader and a Quarterly Reviewer will find it *caviare*.[5] *Adonais,* in short, is such an elegy as poet might be expected to write upon poet. The author has had before him his recollections of Lycidas, of Moschus and Bion, and of the doctrines of

---

[1] *consumption* I.e., tuberculosis.

[2] *second volume* Keats's *Lamia and Other Poems* (1820).

[3] *the composition ... question* This is not true. Keats had worked on *Hyperion* intermittently for several years and was having difficulty completing it. Shelley here greatly exaggerates the effects of the review on Keats, who did not attach much importance to the opinions of reviewers. He himself thought *Endymion* to be a mediocre and adolescent poetic attempt.

[4] *Prometheus Unbound* 1820 drama by Shelley.

[5] *caviare* Unpalatable. (Caviar is generally not appreciated by those who have not acquired a taste for it.)

Plato; and in the stanza of the most poetical of poets, Spenser, has brought his own genius, in all its etherial beauty, to lead a pomp of Loves, Graces, and Intelligences, in honour of the departed.

Nor is the Elegy to be considered less sincere, because it is full of poetical abstractions. Dr. Johnson would have us believe, that _Lycidas_[1] is not "the effusion of real passion." "Passion," says he, in his usual conclusive tone (as if the force of critic could no further go) "plucks no berries from the myrtle and ivy; nor calls upon Arethuse and Mincius nor tells of rough Satyrs and Fauns with cloven heel. Where there is leisure for fiction, there is little grief."[2] This is on a more genteel commonplace, brought in to put down a vulgar one. Dr. Johnson, like most critics, had no imagination; and because he found nothing natural to his own impulses in the associations of poetry, and saw them so often abused by the practice of versifiers inferior to himself, he was willing to conclude that on natural occasions they were always improper. But a poet's world is as real to him as the more palpable one to people in general. He spends his time in it as truly as Dr. Johnson did his in Fleet Street or at the club.[3] Milton felt that the happiest hours he had passed with his friend had been passed in the regions of poetry. He had been accustomed to be transported with him "beyond the visible diurnal sphere" of his fire-side and supper table, things which he could record nevertheless with a due relish. (See the _Epitaphium Damonis_.[4]) The next step was to fancy himself again among them, missing the dear companion of his walks; and then it is that the rivers murmur complainingly, and the flowers hang their heads—which to a truly poetical habit of mind, though to no other, they may literally be said to do, because such is the aspect which they present to an afflicted imagination. "I see nothing in the world but melancholy," is a common phrase with persons who are suffering under a great loss. With ordinary minds in this condition the phrase implies a vague feeling, but still an actual one. The poet, as in other instances, gives it a life and particularity. The practice has doubtless been abused; so much so, that even some imaginative minds may find it difficult at first to fall in with it, however beautifully managed. But the very abuse shows that it is founded in a principle in nature. And a great deal depends upon the character of the poet. What is mere frigidity and affectation in common magazine rhymers, or men of wit and fashion about town, becomes another thing in minds accustomed to live in the sphere I spoke of. It was as unreasonable in Dr. Johnson to sneer at Milton's grief in _Lycidas_ as it was reasonable in him to laugh at Prior and Congreve for comparing Chloe to Venus and Diana, and pastoralizing about Queen Mary.[5] Neither the turn of their genius, nor their habits of life, included this sort of ground. We feel that Prior should have stuck to V tuckers and bodices, and Congreve appeared in his proper Court-mourning.

Milton perhaps overdid the matter a little when he personified the poetical enjoyments of his friend and himself under the character of actual shepherds. Mr. Shelley is the more natural in this respect, inasmuch as he is entirely abstract and imaginative, and recalls his lamented acquaintance to

---

[1] _Lycidas_ Pastoral elegy by John Milton (1608–74).

[2] _Passion ... little grief_ From Samuel Johnson's "Life of Milton" (1779), in which he criticizes Milton's pastoral elegy _Lycidas_ for a lack of passion and for "remote allusions and obscure opinions," such as those quoted here. (Myrtle and ivy are used to crown poets; Arethuse, a spring on Ortygia, and Mincius, a river of Mantua, symbolize Greek and Latin pastoral poetry.)

[3] _Fleet Street_ Where Johnson lived; _the club_ Johnson's famous Literary Club, which included prominent writers and thinkers such as Edmund Burke, Oliver Goldsmith, and Charles Burney.

[4] _Epitaphium Damonis_ 1639 Latin poem by John Milton.

[5] _Prior_ Poet Matthew Prior (1664–1721). The poem referred to is "To Chloe Jealous"; _Congreve ... Queen Mary_ Poet and playwright William Congreve (1670–1729). The poem referred to is his "The Mourning Muse of Alexis," written upon the death of Queen Mary in 1694.

mind in no other shape than one strictly poetical. I say acquaintance, because such Mr. Keats was; and it happens, singularly enough, that the few hours which he and Mr. Shelley passed together were almost entirely of a poetical character. I recollect one evening in particular which they spent with the writer of these letters in composing verses on a given subject. But it is not as a mere acquaintance, however poetical, that Mr. Shelley records him. It is as the intimate acquaintance of all lovely and lofty thoughts, as the nursling of the Muse, the hope of her coming days, the creator of additional Beauties and Intelligences for the adornment and the inhabitation of the material world. …

FELICIA HEMANS
1793 – 1835

Among the most widely read poets in England during her lifetime, Felicia Hemans was seen, as an 1820s critic phrased it, as "the mistress-mind of the day." Her poetry in many ways reflected the ethos of the late Romantic era, deftly capturing its underlying values and intellectual concerns, but several of her poems—perhaps most notably "Casabianca" and "The Homes of England"— remained enormously popular well into the twentieth century. Adept at negotiating the gendered expectations of her readers, Hemans crafted a feminine literary persona that earned her a great deal of admiration; one reviewer, for example, praised her for a "purity of taste, a correctness of sentiment, and an elegance of expression truly feminine." (This is not to say that she escaped all sexist censure; Byron famously parodied her as "Mrs. Hewoman.") She achieved immense popular success and acclaim while addressing not only subjects deemed acceptable for women, from domesticity to the experience of women's writing and celebrity, but also subjects that were often taken to be the preserve of men—such as war, patriotism, history, and death.

Hemans was born Felicia Browne, the fifth of seven children of a Liverpool wine merchant and his wife, the daughter of a foreign diplomat. The failure of her father's business in 1799 caused the family to move to Wales; Felicia adored the country- side and it became the inspiration for much of her poetry. She learned several languages and a great deal about music from her mother, and benefited from a well-stocked family library. She loved Shakespeare as a child and was said to have had an excellent memory for reciting verse. Her own first published volume appeared in 1808, when she was only 14. Although *Poems* received some negative reviews, it sold 1,000 copies and she was encouraged to continue writing. Two of her brothers were then engaged in the British war against Spain, and many of the poems are patriotic depictions of Britain in battle. Her brothers passed the volume on to one of their colleagues, Captain Alfred Hemans; he later became Felicia's husband. Percy Bysshe Shelley also received her first volume and began a correspondence with the young poet.

Felicia Browne married in 1812, shortly after the publication of her third volume of poetry, *The Domestic Affections and Other Poems*. She and her husband initially lived in her mother's house in Wales, a situation that would eventually prove uncomfortable for Alfred. While Hemans continued to publish and become more popular, Alfred became disillusioned with Wales and moved to Italy in 1818 on grounds of "ill health," leaving his wife with their five young sons. From this point onwards she supported herself and her children solely by her writing.

Hemans was in the prime of her writing career in the 1810s and 1820s, occupying something of an uneasy position between the Romantics and the Victorians. Long after her death, her work retained a high degree of popularity, with Victorian critics perceiving her poetry as characterized by powerful rhythms and powerful passions. And certainly the strength of form and of feeling in poems of patriotic fervor such as "The Homes of England" and "Casabianca" (both of which were learnt by heart by English schoolchildren into the twentieth century) is unquestionable. Yet in her own day, seen against the backdrop of the extravagant passions of Byron and other poets associated with the Romantic movement, her poetry was praised for its formal and emotional restraint.

Though Hemans's most famous poems are short, she was also successful with longer works, notably the dramatic poem *The Siege of Valencia* (1823), which recounts the epic story of Elmira after her two sons are captured by a Moorish army. And she wrote innovative linked poems, such as those in *Records of Woman* (1828). Though she is often thought of as an important poet of domesticity, Hemans focused at least as much on women acting out their lives on a larger stage.

In 1821 Hemans was awarded the Royal Society of Literature's annual prize of £52.50 (a substantial amount at the time). She was then publishing regularly in British literary magazines, and from 1823 she was earning roughly £200 per year, enough to support herself and her children in some comfort. Her work was never out of print, and she was widely read in Britain and in America. The death of her mother in 1827 had a devastating effect on her, however, and from that point onwards she was plagued by poor health.

In her later years, she rivaled Byron in popularity, and was highly sought after by budding poets and autograph-seekers. She found herself caught, however, between the success she needed to support herself and the masculine characteristics attributed to it, a theme she explores in "Women and Fame." In 1831 Hemans moved to Dublin to live with one of her brothers. She died there in 1835, of a weak heart and the effects of rheumatic fever.

⌘ ⌘ ⌘

The Homes of England

Where's the coward that would not dare
To fight for such a land?
—MARMION[1]

The stately Homes of England,
   How beautiful they stand!
Amidst their tall ancestral trees,
   O'er all the pleasant land.
5 The deer across their greensward° bound   *turf*
   Thro' shade and sunny gleam,

And the swan glides past them with the sound
   Of some rejoicing stream.

The merry Homes of England!
10   Around their hearths by night,
What gladsome looks of household love
   Meet, in the ruddy° light!   *red-hued*
There woman's voice flows forth in song,
   Or childhood's tale is told,
15 Or lips move tunefully along
   Some glorious page of old.

The blessed Homes of England!
   How softly on their bowers°   *arbors*
Is laid the holy quietness
20   That breathes from Sabbath-hours!
Solemn, yet sweet, the church-bell's chime
   Floats thro' their woods at morn;
All other sounds, in that still time,
   Of breeze and leaf are born.

---

[1] MARMION Walter Scott's *Marmion: A Tale of Flodden Field* (1808), 4.30. When first published in *Blackwood's Magazine*, the poem had instead the following epigraph from Joanna Baillie, *Ethwald: A Tragedy* (1802) 2.1.2.76–82:

> A land of peace,
> Where yellow fields unspoil'd, and pastures green,
> Mottled with herds and flocks, who crop secure
> Their native herbage, nor have ever known
> A stranger's stall, smile gladly.
> See through its tufted alleys to Heaven's roof
> The curling smoke of quiet dwellings rise.

25 The Cottage Homes of England!
      By thousands on her plains,
They are smiling o'er the silvery brooks,
      And round the hamlet-fanes.[1]
Thro' glowing orchards forth they peep,
30   Each from its nook of leaves,
And fearless there the lowly sleep,
      As the bird beneath their eaves.

The free, fair Homes of England!
      Long, long, in hut and hall,
35 May hearts of native proof be rear'd
      To guard each hallow'd wall!
And green for ever be the groves,
      And bright the flowery sod,
Where first the child's glad spirit loves
40   Its country and its God![2]
         —1812

The Land of Dreams

      And dreams, in their development, have breath,
      And tears and tortures, and the touch of joy;
      They leave a weight upon our waking thoughts,
      They make us what we were not—what they will,
      And shake us with the vision that's gone by.
                              —BYRON.[3]

O h spirit land, thou land of dreams!
      A world thou art of mysterious gleams,
Of startling voices, and sounds at strife—
A world of the dead in the hues of life.

5 Like a wizard's magic-glass° thou art   *mirror*
When the wavy shadows float by, and part—
Visions of aspects, now loved, now strange,
Glimmering and mingling in ceaseless change.

Thou art like a city of the past
10 With its gorgeous halls into fragments cast,
Amidst whose ruins there glide and play
Familiar forms of the world's today.

Thou art like the depths where the seas have birth,
Rich with the wealth that is lost from earth—
15 All the sere° flowers of our days gone by,   *dry*
And the buried gems in thy bosom lie.

Yes, thou art like those dim sea-caves,
A realm of treasures, a realm of graves!
And the shapes through thy mysteries that come and go,
20 Are of beauty and terror, of power and woe.

But for me, oh thou picture-land of sleep,
Thou art all one world of affections deep—
And wrung from my heart is each flushing dye
That sweeps o'er thy chambers of imagery.

25 And thy bowers° are fair—even as Eden fair;   *arbors*
All the beloved of my soul are there!
The forms my spirit most pines to see,
The eyes whose love hath been life to me:

They are there, and each blessed voice I hear,
30 Kindly, and joyous, and silvery clear;
But undertones are in each, that say,
"It is but a dream; it will melt away!"

I walk with sweet friends in the sunset's glow;
I listen to music of long ago;
35 But one thought, like an omen, breathes faint through
      the lay[4]—
"It is but a dream; it will melt away!"

I sit by the hearth of my early days;
All the home-faces are met by the blaze,
And the eyes of the mother shine soft, yet say,
40 "It is but a dream; it will melt away!"

And away, like a flower's passing breath, 'tis gone,
And I wake more sadly, more deeply lone—

---

1 *hamlet-fanes* Weather vanes of the village.

2 [Hemans's note] Originally published in *Blackwood's Magazine*.
[1828.]

3 *And dreams ... BYRON* From "The Dream," by George Gordon,
Lord Byron (1788–1824).

---

4 *lay* Medieval narrative song or poem.

Oh, a haunted heart is a weight to bear!
Bright faces, kind voices, where are ye, where?

5   Shadow not forth, oh thou land of dreams,
The past, as it fled by my own blue streams!
Make not my spirit within me burn
For the scenes and the hours that may ne'er return!

Call out from the future thy visions bright,
10   From the world o'er the grave, take thy solemn light,
And oh! with the loved, whom no more I see,
Show me my home as it yet may be!

As it yet may be in some purer sphere,
No cloud, no parting, no sleepless fear;
15   So my soul may bear on through the long, long day,
Till I go where the beautiful melts not away!
—1821

Evening Prayer at a Girls' School

Now in thy youth, beseech of Him,
     Who giveth, upbraiding° not,   *sharply scolding*
That his light in thy heart become not dim,
     And his love be unforgot;
And thy God, in the darkest of days, will be
Greenness, and beauty, and strength to thee.[1]
                              BERNARD BARTON.

Hush! 'tis a holy hour—the quiet room
     Seems like a temple, while yon soft lamp sheds
A faint and starry radiance, through the gloom
     And the sweet stillness, down on bright young heads,
5   With all their clust'ring locks, untouch'd by care,
And bow'd, as flowers are bow'd with night—in prayer.

Gaze on,—'tis lovely!—childhood's lip and cheek,
     Mantling[2] beneath its earnest brow of thought—
Gaze—yet what seest thou in those fair, and meek,

10   And fragile things, as but for sunshine wrought?
—Thou seest what grief must nurture for the sky,
What death must fashion for eternity!

Oh! joyous creatures, that will sink to rest,
     Lightly, when those pure orisons° are done,   *prayers*
15   As birds with slumber's honey-dew oppress'd,
     'Midst the dim folded leaves, at set of sun—
Lift up your hearts!—though yet no sorrow lies
Dark in the summer-heaven of those clear eyes;

Though fresh within your breasts th'untroubled springs
20   Of hope make melody where'er ye tread;
And o'er your sleep bright shadows, from the wings
     Of spirits visiting but youth, be spread;
Yet in those flute-like voices, mingling low,
Is woman's tenderness—how soon her woe!°   *sorrow*

25   Her lot° is on you—silent tears to weep,   *fate*
     And patient smiles to wear through suffering's hour,
And sumless riches, from Affection's deep,
     To pour on broken reeds —a wasted shower!
And to make idols, and to find them clay,[3]
30   And to bewail that worship—therefore pray!

Her lot is on you —to be found untir'd,
     Watching the stars out by the bed of pain,
With a pale cheek, and yet a brow inspir'd,
     And a true heart of hope, though hope be vain.
35   Meekly to bear with wrong, to cheer decay,
And oh! to love through all things—therefore pray!

And take the thought of this calm vesper° evening prayer
     time,
     With its low murmuring sounds and silvery light,
Or through the dark days fading from their prime,
40   As a sweet dew to keep your souls from blight.
Earth will forsake—oh! happy to have given
Th'unbroken heart's first fragrance unto Heaven!
—1825

---

1 *Now in ... strength to thee* "The Ivy, Addressed to a Young Friend"
(1825), 43–48, by Bernard Barton (1784–1849).

2 *Mantling* Blushing, coloring from emotion.

3 *And to ... clay* See Daniel 2.31–45.

Casabianca[1]

The boy stood on the burning deck,
    Whence all but him had fled;
The flame that lit the battle's wreck,
    Shone round him o'er the dead.

5   Yet beautiful and bright he stood,
        As born to rule the storm;
A creature of heroic blood,
        A proud, though child-like form.

The flames roll'd on—he would not go,
10   Without his father's word;
That father, faint in death below,
        His voice no longer heard.

He call'd aloud—"Say, father, say
    If yet my task is done?"
15   He knew not that the chieftain lay
        Unconscious of his son.

"Speak, Father!" once again he cried,
    "If I may yet be gone!"
—And but the booming shots replied,
20   And fast the flames roll'd on.

Upon his brow he felt their breath,
    And in his waving hair;
And look'd from that lone post of death,
        In still, yet brave despair.

25   And shouted but once more aloud,
    "My father! must I stay?"

While o'er him fast, through sail and shroud,
    The wreathing fires made way.

They wrapt the ship in splendor wild,
30   They caught the flag on high,
And stream'd above the gallant child,
        Like banners in the sky.

There came a burst of thunder sound—
    The boy—oh! where was he?
35   —Ask of the winds that far around
        With fragments strew'd the sea!

With mast, and helm, and pennon[2] fair,
    That well had borne their part—
But the noblest thing that perish'd there,
40   Was that young faithful heart.
—1826

Corinne at the Capitol[3]

Les femmes doivent penser qu'il est dans cette carrière
bien peu de sorte qui puissent valoir la plus obscure vie
d'une femme aimée et d'une mère heureuse.[4]
        —MADAME DE STAËL.

Daughter of th'Italian heaven!
    Thou, to whom its fires are given,
Joyously thy car° hath roll'd   *chariot*
Where the conqueror's pass'd of old;
5   And the festal° sun that shone,   *festive*

---

1 [Hemans's note] Young Casabianca, a boy about thirteen years old, son to the admiral of the Orient, remained at his post (in the battle of the Nile), after the ship had taken fire, and all the guns had been abandoned; and perished in the explosion of the vessel, when the flames had reached the powder. [The British fleet, commanded by Horatio Nelson, defeated Napoleon's fleet, commanded by Louis de Casabianca, at the battle of the Nile on 1 August 1798. Among those killed when the French flagship, *L'Orient*, exploded were the Admiral and his son, Giacomo Jocante Casabianca (who in fact was only ten). Hemans's source is probably Southey, *Life of Horatio, Lord Nelson* (1813). The poem was first published in the *Monthly Magazine*.]

2 *pennon* Banner or flag.

3 *Corinne at the Capitol* Based on the novel *Corinne, ou l'Italie* (1807), by Germaine de Staël (1766–1817). Corinne is an Italian *improvisatrice*—a poet who improvises verses in public. The English Lord Nelvil first sees her when she is being honored at the Capitol, in Rome. They fall in love and he offers to marry her, but she declines, preferring her independence. When he marries her half-sister instead, she dies of a broken heart. The poem was first published in *The Literary Souvenir for 1827*, 189–91.

4 *Les femmes ... heureuse* French: Women must reflect that there are in this career [of glory] very few destinies that can equal in worth the most obscure life of a beloved wife and happy mother. See de Staël, *De l'Influence des passions sur le bonheur des individus et des nations* (1796) chapter 3.

O'er three hundred triumphs gone,[1]
Makes thy day of glory bright,
With a shower of golden light.

Now thou tread'st th'ascending road,
10 Freedom's foot so proudly trode;[2]
While, from tombs of heroes borne,
From the dust of empire shorn,
Flowers upon thy graceful head,
Chaplets[3] of all hues, are shed,
15 In a soft and rosy rain,
Touch'd with many a gemlike stain.

Thou hast gain'd the summit now!
Music hails thee from below;
Music, whose rich notes might stir
20 Ashes of the sepulchre;°   tomb
Shaking with victorious notes
All the bright air as it floats,
Well may woman's heart beat high
Unto that proud harmony!

25 Now afar it rolls—it dies,
And thy voice is heard to rise
With a low and lovely tone
In its thrilling power alone;
And thy lyre's deep silvery string,
30 Touch'd as by a breeze's wing,
Murmurs tremblingly at first,
Ere° the tide of rapture burst.   before

All the spirit of thy sky
Now hath lit thy large dark eye,
35 And thy cheek a flush hath caught
From the joy of kindled thought;
And the burning words of song
From thy lip flow fast and strong,

With a rushing stream's delight
40 In the freedom of its might.

Radiant daughter of the sun!
Now thy living wreath is won.
Crown'd of Rome!—Oh! art thou not
Happy in that glorious lot?°—   fate
45 Happier, happier far than thou,
With the laurel on thy brow,[4]
She that makes the humblest hearth
Lovely but to one on earth!
—1826

The Effigies[5]

Der rasche Kampf verewigt einen Mann:
Er falle gleich, so preiset ihn das Lied.
Allein die Thränen, die unendlichen
Der überbliebnen, der verluss'nen Frau,
Zählt keine Nachwelt.[6]
                              —GOETHE

Warrior! whose image on thy tomb,
    With shield and crested head,
Sleeps proudly in the purple gloom
    By the stain'd window shed;
5 The records of thy name and race
    Have faded from the stone,
Yet, through a cloud of years, I trace
    What thou hast been and done.

A banner, from its flashing spear,
10   Flung out o'er many a fight;
A war-cry ringing far and clear,
    And strong to turn the flight;
An arm that bravely bore the lance
    On for the holy shrine;

---

[1] [Hemans's note] The trebly hundred triumphs.—Byron. [See *Childe Harold's Pilgrimage* 4.82 (1818)]; *triumph* Ancient Roman celebration of a military victory; there were a total of 320.

[2] *trode* Archaic past tense of "tread."

[3] *Chaplets* Garlands of flowers worn on the head.

[4] *laurel on ... brow* Poets were traditionally honored with crowns of laurel, which was sacred to Apollo.

[5] *Effigies* Sculptural representations of people, often upon their tombs.

[6] *Der rasche ... Nachwelt* German: Rash combat oft immortalizes man. / If he should fall, he is renowned in song; / But after ages reckon not the tears / Which ceaseless the forsaken woman sheds. (Goethe, *Iphigenia in Tauris* 5.6. English translation by Anna Swanwick [1909–14].)

15   A haughty heart and a kingly glance—
          Chief! were not these things thine?

      A lofty place where leaders sate°   sat
          Around the council-board;°   table
      In festive halls a chair of state
20   When the blood-red wine was pour'd;
      A name that drew a prouder tone
          From herald, harp, and bard;°   court poet
      Surely these things were all thine own,—
          So hadst thou thy reward.

25   Woman! whose sculptur'd form at rest
          By the armed knight is laid,
      With meek hands folded o'er a breast
          In matron robes array'd;
      What was thy tale?—Oh! gentle mate
30   Of him, the bold and free,
      Bound unto his victorious fate,
          What bard hath sung of *thee*?

      He woo'd a bright and burning star—
          Thine was the void, the gloom,
35   The straining eye that follow'd far
          His fast-receding plume;
      The heart-sick listening while his steed
          Sent echoes on the breeze;
      The pang—but when did *Fame* take heed
40   Of griefs obscure as these?

      Thy silent and secluded hours
          Thro' many a lonely day,
      While bending o'er thy broider'd° flowers,   embroidered
          With spirit far away;
45   Thy weeping midnight prayers for him
          Who fought on Syrian plains,
      Thy watchings till the torch grew dim—
          These fill no minstrel strains.

      A still, sad life was thine!—long years
50   With tasks unguerdon'd° fraught,   unrewarded
      Deep, quiet love, submissive tears,
          Vigils of anxious thought;

      Prayer at the cross in fervour pour'd,
          Alms[1] to the pilgrim given—
55   Oh! happy, happier than thy lord,
          In that lone path to heaven!
                                        —1826

The Image in Lava[2]

Thou thing of years departed!
    What ages have gone by,
Since here the mournful seal was set
    By love and agony!

5   Temple and tower have moulder'd,
        Empires from earth have pass'd,—
    And woman's heart hath left a trace
        Those glories to outlast!

    And childhood's fragile image
10   Thus fearfully enshrin'd,
    Survives the proud memorials rear'd
        By conquerors of mankind.

    Babe! wert thou brightly slumbering
        Upon thy mother's breast,
15 When suddenly the fiery tomb
        Shut round each gentle guest?

    A strange, dark fate o'ertook you,
        Fair babe and loving heart!
    One moment of a thousand pangs—
20   Yet better than to part!

    Haply° of that fond bosom,   by chance
        On ashes here impress'd,

---

[1] *Alms*   Money given in charity to the poor.

[2] [Hemans's note]   The impression of a woman's form, with an infant clasped to the bosom, found at the uncovering of Herculaneum. [Herculaneum and Pompeii were destroyed by the eruption of Vesuvius in 79 CE. The image is one of the casts made during the excavations (1763–1820) by pouring plaster into the holes left in the lava by the victims' bodies. The poem was first published in the *New Monthly Magazine* in 1827.]

Thou wert the only treasure, child!
    Whereon a hope might rest.

5 Perchance all vainly lavish'd,
    Its other love had been,
And where it trusted, nought remain'd
    But thorns on which to lean.

Far better then to perish,
10   Thy form within its clasp,
Than live and lose thee, precious one!
    From that impassion'd grasp.

Oh! I could pass all relics
    Left by the pomps of old,
15 To gaze on this rude° monument,   *primitive*
    Cast in affection's mould.

Love, human love! what art thou?
    Thy print upon the dust
Outlives the cities of renown
20   Wherein the mighty trust!

Immortal, oh! immortal
    Thou art, whose earthly glow
Hath given these ashes holiness—
    It must, it must be so!
—1827

The Grave of a Poetess[1]

"Ne me plaignez pas—si vous saviez
Combien de peines ce tombeau m'a épargnées!"[2]

I stood beside thy lowly grave;—
    Spring-odours breath'd around,
And music, in the river-wave,
    Pass'd with a lulling sound.
5 All happy things that love the sun[3]
    In the bright air glanc'd by,
And a glad murmur seem'd to run
    Thro' the soft azure sky.
Fresh leaves were on the ivy-bough
10   That fring'd the ruins near;
Young voices were abroad—but thou
    Their sweetness couldst not hear.
And mournful grew my heart for thee,
    Thou in whose woman's mind
15 The ray that brightens earth and sea,
    The light of song was shrined.
Mournful, that thou wert slumbering low,
    With a dread curtain drawn
Between thee and the golden glow
20   Of this world's vernal° dawn.   *spring*
Parted from all the song and bloom
    Thou wouldst have lov'd so well,
To thee the sunshine round thy tomb
    Was but a broken spell.
25 The bird, the insect on the wing,
    In their bright reckless play,

---

1 [Hemans's note] Extrinsic interest has lately attached to the fine scenery of Woodstock, near Kilkenny, on account of its having been the last residence of the author of *Psyche*. Her grave is one of many in the churchyard village. The river runs smoothly by. The ruins of an ancient abbey, that have been partially converted into a church, reverently throw their mantle of tender shadow over it.—*Tales by the O'Hara Family*. [Passage adapted from "The Fetches" in John and Michael Banim's *Tales by the O'Hara Family*, 1825; the poetess is Mary Tighe (1772–1810), author of *Psyche; or The Legend of Love* (1805).]

2 *Ne me ... épargnées* French: Do not weep for me—if you only knew / How many pains this tomb has spared me. See Germaine de Staël's *Corinne, ou l'Italie*, 18.3.

3 *All happy ... love the sun* Cf. William Wordsworth's "Resolution and Independence," line 8.

Might feel the flush and life of spring,—
    And thou wert pass'd away!
But then, ev'n then, a nobler thought
30   O'er my vain sadness came;
Th' immortal spirit woke, and wrought
    Within my thrilling frame.
Surely on lovelier things, I said,
    Thou must have look'd ere now,
35 Than all that round our pathway shed
    Odours and hues below.
The shadows of the tomb are here,
    Yet beautiful is earth!
What see'st thou then where no dim fear,
40   No haunting dream hath birth?
Here a vain love to passing flowers
    Thou gav'st—but where thou art,
The sway is not with changeful hours,
    There love and death must part.
45 Thou hast left sorrow in thy song,
    A voice not loud, but deep!
The glorious bowers of earth among,
    How often didst thou weep!
Where couldst thou fix on mortal ground
50   Thy tender thoughts and high?—
Now peace the woman's heart hath found,
    And joy the poet's eye.
—1827

The Bride of the Greek Isle[1]

Fear!—I'm a Greek, and how should I fear death?
A slave, and wherefore should I dread my freedom?
    *   *   *   *   *   *
I will not live degraded.
              —*Sardanapalus.*[2]

Come from the woods with the citron-flowers,[3]
  Come with your lyres for the festal hours,
Maids of bright Scio![4] They came, and the breeze
Bore their sweet songs o'er the Grecian seas;—
5 They came, and Eudora[5] stood robed and crowned,
The bride of the morn, with her train around.
Jewels flashed out from her braided hair,
Like starry dews midst the roses there;
Pearls on her bosom quivering shone,
10 Heaved by her heart through its golden zone;°   *band*
But a brow, as those gems of the ocean pale,
Gleamed from beneath her transparent veil;
Changeful and faint was her fair cheek's hue,
Though clear as a flower which the light looks through;
15 And the glance of her dark resplendent eye,
For the aspect of woman at times too high,
Lay floating in mists, which the troubled stream
Of the soul sent up o'er its fervid beam.

She looked on the vine at her father's door,
20 Like one that is leaving his native shore;
She hung o'er the myrtle[6] once called her own,
As it greenly waved by the threshold stone;
She turned—and her mother's gaze brought back
Each hue of her childhood's faded track.
25 Oh! hush the song, and let her tears
Flow to the dream of her early years!
Holy and pure are the drops that fall
When the young bride goes from her father's hall;
She goes unto love yet untried and new,
30 She parts from love which hath still been true;
Mute be the song and the choral strain,
Til her heart's deep well-spring is clear again!
She wept on her mother's faithful breast,
Like a babe that sobs itself to rest;

---

1 [Hemans's note] Founded on a circumstance related in the Second Series of the *Curiosities of Literature*, and forming part of a picture in the "*Painted Biography*" there described.

2 *Sardanapalus* See Byron's *Sardanapalus* 1.2. Sardanapalus, the legendary last king of Assyria, was said to be self-indulgent and excessive in his behavior; when his empire fell, he had himself and many attendants burned to death.

3 *citron-flowers* See Byron's *The Bride of Abydos* 1.9. Orange blossoms are traditionally associated with weddings.

4 *Scio* Italian name for the Greek Island of Chios in the Aegean Sea, considered to be the island where Homer resided.

5 *Eudora* One of the Hyades, a sisterhood of nymphs from Greek mythology that bring rain.

6 *myrtle* Deciduous tree, sacred to Aphrodite, the Greek goddess of love, beauty, pleasure, and procreation.

She wept—yet laid her hand awhile
In *his* that waited her dawning smile,
Her soul's affianced,[1] nor cherished less
For the gush of nature's tenderness!
She lifted her graceful head at last—
The choking swell of her heart was past;
And her lovely thoughts from their cells found way
In the sudden flow of a plaintive lay.[2]

THE BRIDE'S FAREWELL

Why do I weep?—to leave the vine
    Whose clusters o'er me bend,—
The myrtle—yet, oh! call it mine!—
    The flowers I loved to tend.
A thousand thoughts of all things dear,
    Like shadows o'er me sweep,
I leave my sunny childhood here,
    Oh, therefore let me weep!

I leave thee, sister! we have played
    Through many a joyous hour,
Where the silvery green of the olive shade
    Hung dim o'er fount and bower.
Yes, thou and I, by stream, by shore,
    In song, in prayer, in sleep,
Have been as we may be no more—
    Kind sister, let me weep!

I leave thee, father! Eve's bright moon
    Must now light at other feet,
With the gathered grapes, and the lyre in tune,
    Thy homeward steps to greet.
Thou in whose voice, to bless thy child,
    Lay tones of love so deep,
Whose eye o'er all my youth hath smiled—
    I leave thee! let me weep!

Mother! I leave thee! on thy breast,
    Pouring out joy and woe,
I have found that holy place of rest
    Still changeless,—yet, I go!
Lips, that have lulled me with your strain,
    Eyes, that have watched my sleep!
Will earth give love like *yours* again?
    Sweet mother! let me weep!

And like a slight young tree, that throws
The weight of rain from its drooping boughs,
Once more she wept. But a changeful thing
Is the human heart, as a mountain spring,
That works its way, through the torrent's foam,
To the bright pool near it, the lily's home!
It is well!—the cloud, on her soul that lay,
Hath melted in glittering drops away.
Wake again, mingle, sweet lute and lyre!
She turns to her lover, she leaves her sire.
Mother! on earth it must still be so,
Thou rearest the lovely to see them go!

They are moving onward, the bridal throng,
Ye may track their way by the swells of song;
Ye may catch through the foliage their white robe's
    gleam,
Like a swan midst the reeds of a shadowy stream.
Their arms bear up garlands, their gliding tread
Is over the deep-veined violet's bed;
They have light leaves around them, blue skies above,
An arch for the triumph of youth and love!

2

Still and sweet was the home that stood
In the flowering depths of a Grecian wood,
With the soft green light o'er its low roof spread,
As if from the glow of an emerald shed,
Pouring through lime-leaves that mingled on high,
Asleep in the silence of noon's clear sky.
Citrons amidst their dark foliage glowed,
Making a gleam round the lone abode;
Laurels o'erhung it, whose faintest shiver
Scattered out rays like a glancing river;

---

[1] *affianced* Promised in marriage.

[2] [Hemans's Note] A Greek bride, on leaving her father's house, takes leave of her friends and relatives frequently in extemporaneous verse.—See Fauriel's *Chants Populaires de la Grèce Moderne*.

105 Stars of jasmine its pillars crowned,
Vine-stalks its lattice and walls had bound,
And brightly before it a fountain's play
Flung showers through a thicket of glossy bay,
To a cypress which rose in that flashing rain,
110 Like one tall shaft of some fallen fane.°   *temple*
And thither Ianthis[1] had brought his bride,
And the guests were met by that fountain-side;
They lifted the veil from Eudora's face,
It smiled out softly in pensive grace,
115 With lips of love, and a brow serene,
Meet for the soul of the deep wood-scene.—
Bring wine, bring odours!—the board is spread—
Bring roses! a chaplet for every head!
The wine-cups foamed, and the rose was showered,
120 On the young and fair from the world embowered,
The sun looked not on them in that sweet shade,
The winds amid scented boughs were laid;
But there came by fits, through some wavy tree,
A sounds and a gleam of the moaning sea.

125 Hush! be still!—was that no more
Than the murmur from the shore?
Silence!—did thick rain-drops beat
On the grass like trampling feet?—
Fling down the goblet, and draw the sword!
130 The groves are filled with a pirate-horde!
Through the dim olives their sabres shine;—
Now must the red blood stream for wine!

The youths from the banquet to battle sprang,
The woods with the shriek of the maidens rang;
135 Under the golden-fruited boughs
There were flashing poniards,° and   *small daggers*
    darkening brows,
Footsteps, o'er garland and lyre that fled;
And the dying soon on a greensward bed.

Eudora, Eudora! *thou* dost not fly!—
140 She saw but Ianthis before her lie,
With the blood from his breast in a gushing flow,

Like a child's large tears in its hour of woe,
And a gathering film in his lifted eye,
That sought his young bride out mournfully.—
145 She knelt down beside him, her arms she wound,
Like tendrils, his drooping neck around,
As if the passion of that fond grasp
Might chain in life with its ivy-clasp.
But they tore her thence in her wild despair,
150 The sea's fierce rovers—they left him there;
They left to the fountain a dark-red vein,
And on the wet violets a pile of slain,
And a hush of fear through the summer-grove,—
So closed the triumph of youth and love!

3

155 Gloomy lay the shore that night,
When the moon, with sleeping light,
Bathed each purple Sciote hill,—
Gloomy lay the shore, and still.
O'er the wave no gay guitar
160 Sent its floating music far;
No glad sound of dancing feet
Woke, the starry hours to greet.
But a voice of mortal woe,
In its changes wild or low,
165 Through the midnight's blue repose,
From the sea-beat rocks arose,
As Eudora's mother stood
Gazing o'er th'Egean flood,
With a fixed and straining eye—
170 Oh! was the spoilers' vessel nigh?
Yes! there, becalmed in silent sleep,
Dark and alone on a breathless deep,
On a sea of molten silver dark,
Brooding it frowned that evil bark!
175 There its broad pennon[2] a shadow cast,
Moveless and black from the tall still mast,
And the heavy sound of its flapping sail,
Idly and vainly wooed the gale.
Hushed was all else—had ocean's breast
180 Rocked e'en Eudora that hour to rest?

---

1 *Ianthis* Greek: Violet.

2 *pennon* Long pointed streamer or flag on a ship.

To rest?—the waves tremble!—what piercing cry
Bursts from the heart of the ship on high?
What light through the heavens, in a sudden spire,
Shoots from the deck up? Fire! 'tis fire!
There are wild forms hurrying to and fro,
Seen darkly clear on that lurid glow;
There are shout, and signal-gun, and call,
And the dashing of water,—but fruitless all!
Man may not fetter, nor ocean tame
The might and wrath of the rushing flame!
It hath twined the mast like a glittering snake,
That coils up a tree from a dusky brake;[1]
It hath touched the sails, and their canvas rolls
Away from its breath into shrivelled scrolls;
It hath taken the flag's high place in air,
And reddened the stars with its wavy glare,
And sent out bright arrows, and soared in glee,
To a burning mount midst the moonlight sea.
The swimmers are plunging from stern and prow—
Eudora, Eudora! where, where art thou?
The slave and his master alike are gone.—
Mother! who stands on the deck alone?
The child of thy bosom!—and lo! a brand
Blazing up high in her lifted hand!
And her veil flung back, and her free dark hair
Swayed by the flames as they rock and flare;
And her fragile form to its loftiest height
Dilated, as if by the spirit's might,
And her eye with an eagle-gladness fraught,—
Oh! could this work be of woman wrought?
Yes! 'twas her deed!—by that haughty smile
It was hers!—She hath kindled the funeral pile!
Never might shame on that bright head be,
Her blood was the Greek's, and hath made her free.

Proudly she stands, like an Indian bride,
On the pyre with the holy dead beside;[2]
But a shriek from her mother hath caught her ear,
As the flames to her marriage-robe draw near,

And starting, she spreads her pale arms in vain
To the form they must never infold again.

One moment more, and her hands are clasped,
Fallen is the torch they had wildly grasped,
Her sinking knee unto Heaven is bowed,
And her last look raised through the smoke's dim shroud,
And her lips as in prayer for her pardon move—
Now the night gathers o'er youth and love!
—1825

Properzia Rossi[3]

(Properzia Rossi, a celebrated female sculptor of Bologna, possessed also of talents for poetry and music, died in consequence of an unrequited attachment.—A painting, by Ducis, represents her showing her last work, a basso-relievo of Ariadne,[4] to a Roman knight, the object of her affection, who regards it with indifference.)

—Tell me no more, no more
Of my soul's lofty gifts! Are they not vain
To quench its haunting thirst for happiness?
Have I not lov'd, and striven, and fail'd to bind
One true heart unto me, whereon my own
Might find a resting-place, a home for all
Its burden of affections? I depart,
Unknown, tho' Fame goes with me; I must leave
The earth unknown. Yet it may be that death
Shall give my name a power to win such tears
As would have made life precious.[5]

I

One dream of passion and of beauty more!
And in its bright fulfilment let me pour
My soul away! Let earth retain a trace

---

[1] *brake* Thicket.

[2] *like an ... dead beside* Reference to sati, the Hindu practice (outlawed in India in the nineteenth century) of immolating a widow on her husband's funeral pyre.

[3] *Properzia Rossi* Properzia de'Rossi (c.1491–1530), Bolognese sculptor, painter, and poet.

[4] *Ducis* Louis Ducis (1775–1847), *Properzia de'Rossi and Her Last Bas-relief*; *basso-relievo* Relief sculpture; *Ariadne* Cretan princess who helped the hero Theseus find his way through the labyrinth that enclosed the Minotaur, which he killed. They eloped, but he abandoned her on the island of Naxos. See Ovid's *Heroides* 10.

[5] *Tell me ... precious* The epigraph is by Hemans herself.

Of that which lit my being, tho' its race
5   Might have been loftier far.—Yet one more dream!
From my deep spirit one victorious gleam
Ere I depart! For thee alone, for thee!
May this last work, this farewell triumph be,
Thou, loved so vainly! I would leave enshrined
10   Something immortal of my heart and mind,
That yet may speak to thee when I am gone,
Shaking thine inmost bosom with a tone
Of lost affection;—something that may prove
What she hath been, whose melancholy love
15   On thee was lavish'd; silent pang and tear,
And fervent song, that gush'd when none were near,
And dream by night, and weary thought by day,
Stealing the brightness from her life away,—
While thou—Awake! not yet within me die,
20   Under the burden and the agony
Of this vain tenderness,—my spirit, wake!
Ev'n for thy sorrowful affection's sake,
Live! in thy work breathe out!—that he may yet,
Feeling sad mastery there, perchance regret
25   Thine unrequited gift.

2

It comes,—the power
Within me born, flows back; my fruitless dower°   *dowry*
That could not win me love. Yet once again
I greet it proudly, with its rushing train
Of glorious images:—they throng—they press—
30   A sudden joy lights up my loneliness,—
I shall not perish all!¹

The bright work grows
Beneath my hand, unfolding, as a rose,
Leaf after leaf, to beauty; line by line,
I fix my thought, heart, soul, to burn, to shine,
35   Thro' the pale marble's veins. It grows—and now
I give my own life's history to thy brow,
Forsaken Ariadne! thou shalt wear
My form, my lineaments;² but oh! more fair,
Touch'd into lovelier being by the glow
40   Which in me dwells, as by the summer-light

All things are glorified. From thee my woe
Shall yet look beautiful to meet his sight,
When I am pass'd away. Thou art the mould
Wherein I pour the fervent thoughts, th'untold,
45   The self-consuming! Speak to him of me,
Thou, the deserted by the lonely sea,
With the soft sadness of thine earnest eye,
Speak to him, lorn° one! deeply, mournfully,   *forlorn*
Of all my love and grief! Oh! could I throw
50   Into thy frame a voice, a sweet, and low,
And thrilling voice of song! when he came nigh,
To send the passion of its melody
Thro' his pierced bosom—on its tones to bear
My life's deep feeling, as the southern air
55   Wafts the faint myrtle's³ breath,—to rise, to swell,
To sink away in accents of farewell,
Winning but one, one gush of tears, whose flow
Surely my parted spirit yet might know,
If love be strong as death!

3

Now fair thou art,
60   Thou form, whose life is of my burning heart!
Yet all the vision that within me wrought,
I cannot make thee! Oh! I might have given
Birth to creations of far nobler thought,
I might have kindled, with the fire of heaven,
65   Things not of such as die! But I have been
Too much alone;⁴ a heart whereon to lean,
With all these deep affections, that o'erflow
My aching soul, and find no shore below;
An eye to be my star, a voice to bring
70   Hope o'er my path, like sounds that breathe of spring,
These are denied me—dreamt of still in vain,—
Therefore my brief aspirings from the chain,
Are ever but as some wild fitful° song,   *irregular*

---

¹ *I shall ... all* Cf. Horace, *Odes* 3.30.6.

² *lineaments* Distinctive shapes.

³ *myrtle's* Belonging to the myrtle, a Mediterranean evergreen shrub bearing pink flowers and black berries.

⁴ *Too ... alone* Cf. Byron's *Mazeppa* 839.

Rising triumphantly, to die ere° long   *before*
75 In dirge-like[1] echoes.

4

        Yet the world will see
Little of this, my parting work, in thee,
    Thou shalt have fame! Oh, mockery! give the reed
From storms a shelter,—give the drooping vine
Something round, which its tendrils may entwine,—
80   Give the parch'd flower a rain-drop, and the
        meed°   *reward*
Of love's kind words to woman! Worthless fame!
That in *his* bosom wins not for my name
Th'abiding place it ask'd! Yet how my heart,
In its own fairy world of song and art,
85 Once beat for praise!—Are those high longings o'er?
That which I have been can I be no more?—
Never, oh! never more; tho' still thy sky
Be blue as then, my glorious Italy!
And tho' the music, whose rich breathings fill
90 Thine air with soul, be wandering past me still,
And tho' the mantle° of thy sunlight streams,   *cloak*
Unchang'd on forms, instinct with poet-dreams;
Never, oh! never more! Where'er I move,
The shadow of this broken-hearted love
95 Is on me and around! Too well *they* know,
    Whose life is all within, too soon and well,
When there the blight hath settled;—but I go
    Under the silent wings of peace to dwell;
From the slow wasting, from the lonely pain,
100 The inward burning of those words—"*in vain*,"
    Sear'd on the heart—I go. 'Twill soon be past.
Sunshine, and song, and bright Italian heaven,
    And thou, oh! thou, on whom my spirit cast
Unvalued wealth,—who know'st not what was given
105 In that devotedness,—the sad, and deep,
And unrepaid—farewell! If I could weep
Once, only once, belov'd one! on thy breast,
Pouring my heart forth ere I sink to rest!
But that were happiness, and unto me

110 Earth's gift is *fame*. Yet I was form'd to be
So richly blest! With thee to watch the sky,
Speaking not, feeling but that thou wert nigh;
With thee to listen, while the tones of song
Swept ev'n as part of our sweet air along,
115 To listen silently;—with thee to gaze
On forms, the deified of olden days,
This had been joy enough;—and hour by hour,
From its glad well-springs drinking life and power,
How had my spirit soar'd, and made its fame
120   A glory for thy brow!—Dreams, dreams!—the fire
Burns faint within me. Yet I leave my name—
    As a deep thrill may linger on the lyre[2]
When its full chords are hush'd—awhile to live,
And one day haply in thy heart revive
125 Sad thoughts of me:—I leave it, with a sound,
A spell o'er memory, mournfully profound,
I leave it, on my country's air to dwell,—
Say proudly yet—"'Twas hers who lov'd me well!"
—1828

Indian Woman's Death-Song

An Indian woman, driven to despair by her husband's desertion of her for another wife, entered a canoe with her children, and rowed it down the Mississippi towards a cataract. Her voice was heard from the shore singing a mournful death-song, until overpowered by the sound of the waters in which she perished. The tale is related in Long's Expedition[3] to the source of St. Peter's River.

Non, je ne puis vivre avec un coeur brisé. Il faut que je retrouve la joie, et que je m'unisse aux espirits libres de l'air.[4]

Bride of Messina
Translated by Madame de Staël[5]

---

[2] *lyre* Stringed instrument.

[3] *Long's Expedition* Stephen Harriman Long's account of this expedition was published in 1823.

[4] *Non … l'air* French: No, I cannot live with a broken heart. I must find joy, and unite myself to the free spirits of the air.

[5] *Madame de Staël* French-speaking Swiss author (1766–1817). *Bride of Messina* was originally published in German.

---

[1] *dirge-like* Like a funeral hymn, solemn and mournful.

1056   FELICIA HEMANS

> Let not my child be a girl, for very sad is the life of a
> woman.
>
> *The Prairie*[1]

Down a broad river of the western wilds,
    Piercing thick forest glooms, a light canoe
Swept with the current; fearful was the speed
Of the frail bark,° as by a tempest's wing   boat
5 Borne leaf-like on to where the mist of spray
Rose with the cataract's thunder.—Yet within,
Proudly, and dauntlessly, and all alone,
Save that a babe lay sleeping at her breast,
A woman stood: upon her Indian brow
10 Sat a strange gladness, and her dark hair waved
As if triumphantly. She pressed her child,
In its bright slumber, to her beating heart,
And lifted her sweet voice that rose awhile
Above the sound of waters, high and clear,
15 Wafting a wild proud strain, her song of death.

Roll swiftly to the Spirit's land, though mighty
    stream and free!
Father of ancient waters, roll! and bear our lives with
    thee!
The weary bird that storms have tossed, would seek
    the sunshine's calm,
And the deer that hath the arrow's hurt, flies to the
    woods of balm.

20 Roll on!—my warrior's eye hath looked upon
    another's face,
And mine hath faded from his soul, as fades a
    moonbeam's trace;
My shadow comes not o'er his path, my whisper to
    his dream,
He flings away the broken reed—roll swifter yet,
    though stream!

The voice that spoke of other days is hushed within
    his breast,
25 But *mine* its lonely music haunts, and will not let me
    rest;

It sings a low and mournful song of gladness that is
    gone,
I cannot live without that light—Father of waves!
    roll on!

Will he not miss the bounding step that met him
    from the chase?
The heart of love that made his home an ever sunny
    place?
30 The hand that spread the hunter's board, and decked
    his couch of yore?—
He will not!—roll, dark foaming stream, on to the
    better shore!

Some blessed fount amidst the woods of that bright
    land must flow,
Whose waters from my soul may lave the memory of
    this woe;
Some gentle wind must whisper there, whose breath
    may waft away
35 The burden of the heavy night, the sadness of the day.

And thou, my babe! though born, like me, for
    woman's weary lot,
Smile!—to that wasting of the heart, my own! I leave
    thee not;
Too bright a thing art *thou* to pine in aching love
    away,
Thy mother bears thee far, young Fawn! from sorrow
    and decay.

40 She bears thee to the glorious bowers where none are
    heard to weep,
And where th'unkind one hath no power again to
    trouble sleep;
And where the soul shall find its youth, as wakening
    from a dream,—
One moment, and that realm is ours—On, on, dark
    rolling stream!
—1828

---

[1] *The Prairie*   Novel by James Fenimore Cooper, published in 1827.

Joan of Arc in Rheims[1]

Jeanne d'Arc avait eu la joie de voir à Chalons quelques amis de son enfance. Une joie plus ineffable encore l'attendait à Rheims, au sein de son triomphe: Jacques d'Arc, son père, y se trouva, aussitôt que de troupes de Charles VII. y furent entrées; et comme les deux frères de notre Héroïne l'avaient accompagnés, elle se vit, pour un instant au milieu de sa famille, dans les bras d'un père vertueux.

Vie de Jeanne d'Arc[2]

Thou hast a charmed cup, O Fame!
    A draught that mantles° high,   *froths*
And seems to lift this earth born frame
    Above mortality:
Away! To me—a woman—bring
Sweet waters from affection's spring.[3]

That was a joyous day in Rheims of old,
    When peal on peal of might music rolled
Forth from her thronged cathedral; while around,
A multitude, whose billows made no sounds,
5 Chained to a hush of wonder, though elate
With victory, listened at their temple's gate.
And what was done within?—within, the light
    Through the rich gloom of pictured windows
       flowing,
Tinged with soft awfulness a stately sight,
10   The chivalry of France, their proud heads bowing

In martial vassalage![4]—while midst that ring,
And shadowed by ancestral tombs, a king
Received his birthright's crown. For this, the hymn
    Swelled out like rushing waters, and the day
15 With the sweet censer's[5] misty breath grew dim,
    As through long aisles it floated over th'array
Of arms and sweeping stoles. But who, alone
And unapproached, beside the altar-stone,
With the white banner, forth like sunshine streaming,
20 And the gold helm,° through clouds of   *helmet*
      fragrance gleaming,
Silent and radiant stood?—the helm was raised,
And the fair face revealed, that upward gazed,
    Intensely worshipping:—a still, clear face,
Youthful, but brightly solemn!—Woman's cheek
25 And brow were there, in deep devotion meek,
    Yet glorified with inspiration's trace
On its pure paleness; while, enthroned above,
The pictured virgin, with her smile of love,
Seemed bending o'er her votaress.[6]—That slight form!
30 Was that the leader through the battle storm?
Had the soft light in that adoring eye,
Guided the warrior where the swords flashed high?
'Twas so, even so!—and thou, the shepherd's child,
Joanne, the lowly dreamer of the wild!
35 Never before, and never since that hour,
Hath woman, mantled with victorious power,
Stood forth as *thou* beside the shrine didst stand,
Holy amidst the knighthood of the land;
And beautiful with joy and with renown,
40 Lift thy white banner o'er the golden crown,
Ransomed for France by thee!
               The rites are done.
Now let the dome with trumpet-notes be shaken,
And bid the echoes of the tombs awaken,
    And come thou forth, that Heaven's rejoicing sun
45 May give thee welcome from thine own blue skies,
    Daughter of victory!—A triumphant strain,
A proud rich stream of warlike melodies,

---

[1] *Rheims* City in the Champagne region of France, site of perhaps the greatest triumph of Joan of Arc. In 1424, in a vision, Joan had been told to drive the English occupying forces from France and to lead young Charles (heir to the throne) to Rheims, where he would be crowned king. In 1429, following a series of victories, she led her forces into the city on July 16; Charles was crowned the following day.

[2] *Jeanne d'Arc ... Jeanne d'Arc* French: Joan of Arc had the joy of seeing some childhood friends in Chalons. A still more ineffable joy was waiting for her in Rheims, at the heart of her triumph: Jacques d'Arc, her father, arrived there as soon as the troops of Charles VII had entered the town; and as the two brothers of our Heroine had accompanied them she saw herself for a moment amid her family, in the arms of a virtuous father. *Life of Joan of Arc.*

[3] *Thou hast ... affection's spring* Cf. Felicia Hemans's *Woman and Fame.*

[4] *vassalage* Servitude.

[5] *censer* Small vessel used to carry burning incense.

[6] *votaress* Woman devoted to religious life.

Gushed through the portals of the antique
    fane,°   *temple*
And forth she came.—Then rose a nation's sound—
50 Oh! what a power to bid the quick heart bound
The wind beats onward with the stormy cheer
Man gives to glory on her high career!
Is there indeed such power?—far deeper dwells
In one kind household voice, to reach the cells
55 Whence happiness flows forth!—The shouts that filled
The hollow heaven tempestuously, were stilled
One moment; and in that brief pause, the tone,
As of a breeze that o'er her home had blown,
Sank on the bright maid's heart.—"Joanne!"—Who
    spoke
60 Like those whose childhood with *her* childhood grew
Under one roof?—"Joanne!"—*that* murmur broke
    With sounds of weeping forth!—She turned!—she
    knew
Beside her, marked from all the thousands there,
In the calm beauty of his silver hair,
65 The stately shepherd: and the youth, whose joy
From his dark eye flashed proudly; and the boy,
The youngest-born, that ever loved her best:
"Father! and ye, my brothers!"—On the breast
Of that grey sire she sank—and swiftly back,
70 Ev'n in an instant, to their native track
Her free thoughts flowed.   She saw the pomp no
    more—
The plumes, the banners:—to her cabin-door,
And to the Fairy's fountain in the glade,[1]
Where her young sisters by her side had played,
75 And to her hamlet's chapel, where it rose
Harrowing the forest unto deep repose,
Her spirit turned.—The very wood-note, sung
    In early spring-time by the bird, which dwelt
Where o'er her father's roof the beech-leaves hung,
80   Was in her heart; a music heard and felt,
Winning her back to nature.—She unbound
    The helm of many battles from her head,
And with her bright locks bowed to sweep the ground,

Lifting her voice up, wept for joy, and said,—
85 "Bless me, my father, bless me! and with thee,
To the still cabin and the beechen-tree,
Let me return!"[2]
        Oh! never did thine eye
Through the green haunts of happy infancy
Wander again, Joanne!—too much of fame
90 Had shed its radiance on thy peasant-name;
And brought alone by gifts beyond all price,
The trusting heart's repose, the paradise
Of home with all its loves, doth fate allow
The crown of glory unto a woman's brow.
—1828

The American Forest Girl

A fearful gift upon thy heart is laid,
Woman!—a power to suffer and to love,
Therefore thou so canst pity.

Wildly and mournfully the Indian drum
    On the deep hush of moonlight forests broke;—
"Sing us a death song, for thine hour is come,"—
So the red warriors to their captive spoke.
5 Still, and amidst those dusky forms alone,
    A youth, a fair-haired youth of England stood,
Like a king's son; though from his cheek had flown
    The mantling crimson of the island-blood.
And his pressed lips looked marble.—Fiercely bright,
10 And high around him, blazed the fires of night,
Rocking beneath the cedars to and fro,
As the wind passed, and with a fitful glow
Lighting the victim's face:—But who could tell
Of what within his secret heart befell,
15 Known to heaven that hour?—Perchance a thought
Of his far home then so intensely wrought,
That its full image, pictured to his eye
On the dark ground of mortal agony,
Rose clear as day!—and he might see the band,
20 Of his young sisters wand'ring hand in hand,

---

1 [Hemans's Note] A beautiful fountain near Domremi, believed to be haunted by fairies, and a favorite resort of Jeanne d'Arc in her childhood.

2 *Bless me ... return* Cf. Luke 15.11–32 (the parable of the prodigal son).

Where the laburnums drooped; or happily binding
The jasmine, up the doors' low pillars winding;
Or, as day closed upon their gentle mirth,
Gathering, with braided hair, around the hearth
Where sat their mother;—and that mother's face
Its grave sweet smile yet wearing in the place
Where so it ever smiled!—Perchance the prayer
Learned at her knee came back on his despair;
The blessing from her voice, the very tone
Of her "Good night," might breathe from boy-
    hood gone!
He started and looked up;—thick cypress boughs
    Full of strange sound, waved o'er him, darkly red
In the broad stormy firelight;—savage brows,
    With tall plumes crested and wild hues o'erspread,
Girt him like feverish phantoms; and pale stars
Looked through the branches as through dungeon bars,
Shedding no hope.—He knew, he felt his doom—
Oh! what a tale to shadow with its gloom
That happy hall in England!—Idle fear!
Would the winds tell it?—who might dream or hear
The secrets of the forests?—To the stake
    They bound him; and that proud young soldier
        strove
His father's spirit in his breast to wake,
    Trusting to die in silence! He, the love
Of many hearts!—the fondly reared,—the fair,
Gladdening all eyes to see!—And fettered there
He stood beside his death-pyre, and the brand
Flamed up to light it, in the chieftain's hand.
He thought upon his God.—Hush! hark! a cry
Breaks on the stern and dread solemnity,—
A step hath pierced the ring!—Who dares intrude
On the dark hunters in their vengeful mood!—
A girl—a young slight girl—a fawn-like child

Of green savannas and the leafy wild,
55 Springing unmarked till then, as some lone flower,
Happy because the sunshine is its dower;
Yet one that knew how early tears are shed,—
For hers had mourned a playmate brother dead.

She had sat gazing on the victim long,
60 Until the pity of her soul grew strong;
And, by its passion's deepening swayed,
Even to the stake she rushed, and gently laid
His bright head on her bosom, and around
His form her slender arms to shield it round
65 Like close Liannes;[1] then raised her glittering eye
And clear-toned voice that said, "He shall not die!"

"He shall not die!"—the gloomy forest thrilled
    To that sweet sound. A sudden wonder fell
On the fierce throng; and heart and hand were stilled,
70   Struck down, as by the whisper of a spell.
They gazed,—their dark souls bowed before the maid,
She of the dancing step in wood and glade!

And, as her cheek flushed through its olive hue,
As her black tresses to the night wind flew,
75 Something o'ermastered them from that young mien[2]—
Something of heaven, in silence felt and seen;
And seeming, to their child-like faith, a token
That the Great Spirit by her voice had spoken.

They loosed the bonds that held their captive's breath;
80 From his pale lips they took the cup of death;
They quenched the brand beneath the cypress tree;
"Away," they cried, "young stranger, thou art free!"
    —1828

---

[1] *Liannes* French: Climbing and twining plants, abundant in some
tropical forests.

[2] *mien* Countenance.

Woman and Fame

Happy—happier far than thou,
With the laurel on thy brow;[1]
She that makes the humblest hearth,
Lovely but to one on earth.[2]

Thou hast a charmed cup, O Fame!
A draught that mantles[3] high,
And seems to lift this earthly frame
    Above mortality.
5 Away! to me—a woman—bring
Sweet waters from affection's spring.

Thou hast green laurel leaves, that twine
    Into so proud a wreath;
For that resplendent gift of thine,
10   Heroes have smiled in death:
Give *me* from some kind hand a flower,
The record of one happy hour!

Thou hast a voice, whose thrilling tone
    Can bid each life-pulse beat
15 As when a trumpet's note hath blown,
    Calling the brave to meet:
But mine, let mine—a woman's breast,
By words of home-born love be bless'd.

A hollow sound is in thy song,
20   A mockery in thine eye,
To the sick heart that doth but long
    For aid, for sympathy—
For kindly looks to cheer it on,
For tender accents that are gone.

25 Fame, Fame! thou canst not be the stay°   support
    Unto the drooping reed,
The cool fresh fountain in the day
    Of the soul's feverish need:
Where must the lone one turn or flee?—
30 Not unto thee—oh! not to thee!
—1829

---

[1] *laurel on ... brow* Poets were traditionally honored with crowns of laurel, which was sacred to Apollo.

[2] *Happy—happier ... earth* Paraphrased from Hemans's own "Corinne at the Capitol" (ll. 45–48).

[3] *mantles* Here, foams.

JOHN CLARE
1793 – 1864

Later in his life, John Clare recalled that, as a young aspiring poet, he had made a brief effort to master the rules of grammar; however, "finding a jumble of words classed together under this name, and that name and this such-a-figure of speech and that another-hard-worded figure, I turned from further notice of it in instant disgust." Clare, however, read widely, particularly the work of other poets, and he chose to concentrate on the rhythms and sounds of his poetry, honing his craft carefully and steeping his writing in the dialect of his home town.

Born in Northamptonshire, England, in 1793 to Parker Clare, a poor thresher, and Ann Stimson, daughter of the town shepherd, John Clare grew up in a house where his love for reading and writing

was an anomaly—though both his parents passed on to him numerous traditional hymns, ballads, and verses. While attempting to perfect the rhythms and meters of his first volume, *Poems Descriptive of Rural Life and Scenery* (1820), Clare would recite his poems to his parents for approval. When this volume was published, Clare was marketed as successor to Robert Burns: a poet shaped by the language and customs of rural life. The book enjoyed considerable success, and curious readers would often come to observe this "peasant poet" working in the fields.

With a keen eye for the natural world, Clare wrote several poems celebrating the niches in which various animals flourish. If Clare is frequently regarded as a nature poet, it is largely because of his evocation of these habitats. As he saw many of these animals hunted, their habitats destroyed, and what he observed to be the delicate balance between humanity and nature threatened, the mood of Clare's nature poems became darker and the tone more indignant. Of particular concern to Clare was the increasing division of the commons—the closing of public pathways, and the general enclosure of open land. Clare's home parish of Helpston was affected by the enclosures in 1809, and his protests against this can be seen in such poems as "Remembrances" and "The Lament of Swordy Well."

Building on the success of his debut, Clare published *The Village Minstrel* (1821), *The Shepherd's Calendar* (1827), and *The Rural Muse* (1835), but these works did not enjoy the popularity of Clare's first volume. The degree to which these successive disappointments, coupled with the pressures of providing for a steadily growing family, may have affected his mental health is unclear, but by 1830 Clare was unquestionably displaying symptoms of insanity. In that year, while watching a production of *The Merchant of Venice*, Clare became so incensed by the character Shylock demanding his pound of flesh that he began to upbraid the actor and had to be removed from the theater. He often imagined himself to be Lord Byron, and in that connection wrote "Don Juan: A Poem," a continuation of Byron's unfinished *Don Juan*. Clare also insisted that he was possessed of (or by) two wives—one his actual wife, and the other his dead childhood sweetheart and muse, Mary Joyce (the subject of "To Mary").

Clare was placed in a private asylum in 1837 and later in the Northampton general lunatic asylum, where he continued to write poems. He escaped from the first asylum in 1841 and walked eighty miles home, eating grass to survive, after which he was committed to the second institution, where he remained until his death some twenty-three years later.

Some of Clare's most interesting poems were written while he was institutionalized. In many of these later, "mad" lyrics, critics have found an inspired desolation; in others they have discerned interesting points of connection with his earlier work and with that of other poets. In "I Am," for example, Clare signals his increasing estrangement from the world; like some other Romantic poets, he sees in childhood an altogether different, and entirely blissful, form of asylum. Meanwhile, Clare's early "nesting" poems ("Mouse's Nest," for example) find analogues in later fantasies such as "Clock A Clay."

Clare died in May 1864 and was largely forgotten until the mid-twentieth century. Since that time, however, he has consistently been seen as one of the more important poetic voices of the first half of the nineteenth century. For many years his poems suffered at hands of editors who sought to standardize his spelling and punctuation and to remove his idiosyncratic use of dialect; recently, however, efforts have been made to restore the poems, enabling readers to experience them as Clare intended.

⌘⌘⌘

Written in November

Autumn I love thy latter end to view
In cold novembers[1] day so bleak & bare
When like lifes dwindld thread worn nearly thro
Wi lingering pottering° pace & head bleachd   *dawdling*
    bare
5 Thou like an old man bids the world adieu
I love thee well & often when a child
Have roamd the bare brown heath a flower to find
& in the moss clad vale & wood bank wild
Have cropt the little bell flowers paley blue
10 That trembling peept the sheltering bush behind
When winnowing north winds cold & blealy° blew *bleakly*
How have I joyd wi dithering° hands to find   *shivering*
Each fading flower & still how sweet the blast
Woud bleak novembers hour Restore the joy thats past
—1821

[*The Lament of Swordy Well*][2]

Petitioners are full of prayers
To fall in pitys way
But if her hand the gift forbears
Theyll sooner swear then pray
5 They're not the worst to want who lurch[3]
On plenty with complaints
No more then those who go to church
Are eer the better saints

I hold no hat to beg a mite°   *coin*
10 Nor pick it up when thrown
Nor limping leg I hold in sight
But pray to keep my own
Where profit gets his clutches in
Theres little he will leave

---

[1] *novembers* The usual practice of this anthology regarding modernization of spelling and punctuation has not been followed in the case of Clare; his idiosyncrasies have been retained.

[2] *Swordy Well* Area of land near Clare's home parish of Helpston. Once the site of a stone quarry, Swordy Well (also called Swaddy Well) was a common space used for grazing and other purposes until 1809, when it was made private by an act of enclosure. Part of the enclosed space was converted to farmland, and part was used again as a quarry.

[3] *lurch* Consume rapidly, so as to get as much as possible for oneself.

15 Gain stooping for a single pin
Will stick it on his sleeve

For passers bye I never pin
No troubles to my breast
Nor carry round some names to win
20 More money from the rest
Im swordy well a piece of land
Thats fell upon the town[1]
Who worked me till I couldnt stand
& crush me now Im down

25 In parish bonds I well may wail
Reduced to every shift[2]
Pity may grieve at troubles tale
But cunning shares the gift
Harvests with plenty on his brow
30 Leaves losses taunts with me
Yet gain comes yearly with the plough
& will not let me be

Alas dependence thou'rt a brute
Want° only understands   *privation*
35 His feelings wither branch & root
That falls in parish hands
The muck that clouts the ploughmans shoe
The moss that hides the stone
Now Im become the parish due
40 Is more then I can own

Though Im no man yet any wrong
Some sort of right may seek
& I am glad if een a song
Gives me the room to speak

45 Ive got among such grubbling° geer   *digging*
& such a hungry pack
If I brought harvests twice a year
They'd bring me nothing back

When war their tyrant prices got
50 I trembled with alarms
They fell & saved my little spot
Or towns had turned to farms
Let profit keep an humble place
That gentry may be known
55 Let pedigrees their honours trace
& toil enjoy its own

The silver springs grown naked dykes
Scarce own a bunch of rushes
When grain got high the tasteless tykes[3]
60 Grubbed up trees banks & bushes
& me they turned me inside out
For sand & grit & stones
& turned my old green hills about
& pickt my very bones

65 These things that claim my own as theirs
Where born but yesterday
But ere I fell to town affairs
I were as proud as they
I kept my horses cows & sheep
70 & built the town below
Ere they had cat or dog to keep
& then to use me so

Parish allowance gaunt & dread
Had it the earth to keep
75 Would even pine the bees to dead[4]
To save an extra keep
Prides workhouse is a place that yields
From poverty its gains
& mines a workhouse for the fields
80 A starving the remains

---

1 *Thats fell upon the town* That has become dependent on the town's charity. Before 1834, each parish administered its own relief for the poor, which might be provided in the form of a minimum allowance or via a workhouse, an institution in which the poor were given lodging and a minimal level of sustenance in exchange for work performed. After an 1834 act standardized the treatment of the poor across the country, allowances were discontinued; workhouses, the only remaining option, were designed to be as unpleasant as possible so as to discourage people from entering them.

2 *shift* I.e., inventive means of survival.

3 *tykes* Rustics, base people.

4 *pine the … dead* Cause the bees to suffer until they die.

The bees flye round in feeble rings
& find no blossom bye
Then thrum their almost weary wings
Upon the moss & die
85 Rabbits that find my hills turned oer
Forsake my poor abode
They dread a workhouse like the poor
& nibble on the road

If with a clover bottle° now   *flower*
90 Spring dares to lift her head
The next day brings the hasty plough
& makes me miserys bed
The butterflyes may wir° & come   *whir*
I cannot keep em now
95 Nor can they bear my parish home
That withers on my brow

No now not een a stone can lie
Im just what eer they like
My hedges like the winter flye
100 & leave me but the dyke
My gates are thrown from off the hooks
The parish thoroughfare
Lord he thats in the parish books
Has little wealth to spare

105 I couldnt keep a dust of grit
Nor scarce a grain of sand
But bags & carts claimed every bit
& now theyve got the land
I used to bring the summers life
110 To many a butterflye
But in oppressions iron strife
Dead tussocks bow & sigh

Ive scarce a nook to call my own
For things that creep or flye
115 The beetle hiding neath a stone
Does well to hurry bye
Stock° eats my struggles every day   *livestock*
As bare as any road

He's sure to be in somthings way
120 If eer he stirs abroad

I am no man to whine & beg
But fond of freedom still
I hing° no lies on pitys peg   *hang*
To bring a gris to mill[1]
125 On pitys back I neednt jump
My looks speak loud alone
My only tree they've left a stump
& nought remains my own

My mossy hills gains greedy hand
130 & more then greedy mind
Levels into a russet land
Nor leaves a bent[2] behind
In summers gone I bloomed in pride
Folks came for miles to prize
135 My flowers that bloomed no where beside
& scarce believe their eyes

Yet worried with a greedy pack
They rend & delve & tear
The very grass from off my back
140 Ive scarce a rag to wear
Gain takes my freedom all away
Since its dull suit I wore
& yet scorn vows I never pay
& hurts me more & more

145 Who ever pays me rent or takes it
Ive neither words or dates
One makes the law & others break it
& stop my mouth with rates[3]

& should the price of grain get high
150 Lord help & keep it low

---

[1] *bring a gris to mill* "To bring grist to the mill" (literally, "to bring grain to the flour mill for grinding") is a proverbial phrase meaning "to turn a situation to one's own advantage."

[2] *bent* Single reed or blade of grass.

[3] *Who ever … with rates* This partial verse is omitted in some versions of the poem.

I shant possess a single flye
Or get a weed to grow
I shant possess a yard of ground
To bid a mouse to thrive
5 For gain has put me in a pound[1]
I scarce can keep alive

Im not a man as some may think
Petitioning for loss
Of cow that dyed of ages drink
10 & spavin foundered horse[2]
For which some beg a list of pelf°   stolen riches
& seem on loss to thrive
But I perition for my self
& beg to keep alive

15 Theres folks that make a mort[3] of bother
& oer lost gainings whine
But lord of me Im this & tother
Theres no one cares for mine
They strip the grass from off my back
20 & take my things away
Im robbed by every outlaw pack
& nones to say em nay[4]

I own Im poor like many more
But then the poor mun° live   must
25 & many came for miles before
For what I had to give
But since I fell upon the town
They pass me with a sigh
Ive scarce the room to say sit down
30 & so they wander bye

But when a poor man is allowed
So to enslave another

Well may the worlds tongue prate aloud
How brother uses brother
185 I couldnt keep a bush to stand
For years but what was gone
& now I hant° a foot of land   haven't
To keep a rabbit on

They used to come & feed at night
190 When dangers day was gone
& in the morning out of sight
Hide underneath a stone
Im fain to shun the greedy pack
That now so tear & brag
195 They strip my coat from off my back
& scarcely leave a rag
That like the parish hurt & hurt
While gains new suit I wear
Then swear I never pay 'em for't
200 & add to my despair[5]

Though now I seem so full of clack°   noise
Yet when yer' riding bye
The very birds upon my back
Are not more fain° to flye   eager
205 I feel so lorn° in this disgrace   forlorn
God send the grains to fall
I am the oldest in the place
& the worst served of all

Lord bless ye I was kind to all
210 & poverty in me
Could always find a humble stall
A rest & lodging free
Poor bodys with an hungry ass
I welcomed many a day
215 & gave him tether room & grass
& never said him nay

There was a time my bit of ground
Made freemen of the slave

---

[1] *pound* Enclosure in which trespassing or lost livestock are kept until claimed.

[2] *spavin foundered horse* Horse unable to work because of a bone growth in a leg joint.

[3] *a mort* A lot.

[4] *Im not a man … say em nay* These verses are omitted in some versions of the poem.

---

[5] *But when … despair* These verses are omitted in some versions of the poem.

The ass no pindard[1] dare to pound°   impound
220 When I his supper gave
The gipseys camp was not affraid
I made his dwelling free
Till vile enclosure came & made
A parish slave of me

225 The gipseys further on sojourn
No parish bounds they like
No sticks I own & would earth burn
I shouldnt own a dyke
I am no friend to lawless work
230 Nor would a rebel be
& why I call a christian turk[2]
Is they are turks to me

& if I could but find a friend
With no deciet to sham
235 Who'd send me some few sheep to tend
& leave me as I am
To keep my hills from cart & plough
& strife of mongerel men
& as spring found me find me now
240 I should look up agen

& save his Lordships woods that past
The day of danger dwell
Of all the fields I am the last
That my own face can tell
245 Yet what with stone pits delving holes
& strife to buy & sell
My name will quickly be the whole
Thats left of swordy well
—1935 (WRITTEN 1821–24)

Remembrances

Summer pleasures they are gone like to visions
    every one
& the cloudy days of autumn & of winter cometh on
I tried to call them back but unbidden they are gone
Far away from heart & eye & for ever far away
5 Dear heart & can it be that such raptures meet decay
I thought them all eternal when by Langley bush[3] I lay
I thought them joys eternal when I used to shout & play
On its bank at "clink & bandy" "chock" & "taw" &
    ducking stone[4]
Where silence sitteth now on the wild heath as her own
10 Like a ruin of the past all alone

When I used to lie & sing by old east wells boiling
    spring[5]
When I used to tie the willow boughs together for a
    "swing"
& fish with crooked pins & thread & never catch a
    thing
With heart just like a feather—now as heavy as a stone
15 When beneath old lea close oak I the bottom
    branches broke
To make our harvest cart like so many working folk
& then to cut a straw at the brook to have a soak
O I never dreamed of parting or that trouble had a sting
Or that pleasures like a flock of birds would ever take
    to wing
20 Leaving nothing but a little naked spring

When jumping time away on old cross berry way
& eating awes like sugar plumbs ere they had lost the may
& skipping like a leveret° before the peep of day   young hare

---

[1] *pindard* Contraction meaning "pinder would." A pinder policed enclosures and impounded any livestock not belonging to the land's owners.

[2] *turk* I.e., cruel; "Turk" was at this time used to mean "Muslim" and carried connotations of brutality and barbarism that reflected prejudices commonly held in Britain.

[3] *Langley bush* An old whitethorn (a type of hawthorn with light-colored bark) tree that Clare claimed had stood for more than a century. It fell in 1823.

[4] *clink ... stone* Three children's games played with marbles or stones.

[5] *old east ... spring* Before the enclosures in Clare's home parish, Eastwell Spring was a popular place to meet on Sundays for sugared water.

On the rolly polly up & downs of pleasant swordy well[1]
25 When in round oaks narrow lane as the south got
        black again
We sought the hollow ash that was shelter from the rain
With our pockets full of peas we had stolen from the grain
How delicious was the dinner time on such a showry day
O words are poor receipts for what time hath stole away
30 The ancient pulpit trees & the play

When for school oer "little field" with its brook &
        wooden brig°   *bridge*
Where I swaggered like a man though I was not half
        so big
While I held my little plough though twas but a
        willow twig
& drove my team along made of nothing but a name
35 "Gee hep" & "hoit" & "woi"—O I never call to mind
These pleasant names of places but I leave a sigh behind
While I see the little mouldywharps[2] hang
        sweeing° to the wind   *swinging*
On the only aged willow that in all the field remains
& nature hides her face where theyre sweeing in their chains
40 & in a silent murmuring complains

Here was commons for their hills where they seek for
        freedom still
Though every commons gone & though traps are set
        to kill
The little homeless miners—O it turns my bosom chill
When I think of old "sneap green" puddocks°   *buzzard's*
        nook & hilly snow
45 Where bramble bushes grew & the daisy
        gemmed° in dew   *shone*
& the hills of silken grass like to cushions to the view
Where we threw the pissmire° crumbs when   *ants*
        we'd nothing else to do
All leveled like a desert by the never weary plough
All vanished like the sun where that cloud is passing now
50 & settled here for ever on its brow

O I never thought that joys would run away from boys
Or that boys would change their minds & forsake
        such summer joys
But alack I never dreamed that the world had other toys
To petrify first feelings like the fable into stone
55 Till I found the pleasure past & a winter come at last
Then the fields were sudden bare & the sky got over cast
& boyhoods pleasing haunts like a blossom in the blast
Was shrivelled to a withered weed & trampled down
        & done
Till vanished was the morning spring & set that
        summer sun
60 & winter fought her battle strife & won

By Langley bush I roam but the bush hath left its hill
On cowper green I stray tis a desert strange & chill
& spreading lea close oak ere decay had penned its will
To the axe of the spoiler & self interest fell a prey
65 & cross berry way & old round oaks narrow lane
With its hollow trees like pulpits I shall never see again
Inclosure like a Buonaparte let not a thing remain
It levelled every bush & tree & levelled every hill
& hung the moles for traitors—though the brook is
        running still
70 It runs a naker° brook cold & chill[3]   *more naked*

O had I known as then joy had left the paths of men
I had watched her night & day besure & never slept agen
& when she turned to [go] O I'd caught her mantle then
& wooed her like a lover by my lonely side to stay
75 Aye knelt & worshiped on as love in beautys bower
& clung upon her smiles as a bee upon a flower
& gave her heart my poesys all cropt in a sunny hour
As keepsakes & pledges all to never fade away
But love never heeded to treasure up the may
80 So it went the common road with decay
—1908 (WRITTEN C. 1832)

---

[1] *swordy well* An old stone quarry, also called Swaddy Well, where
Clare used to watch butterflies and collect ferns.

[2] *mouldywharps* Moles. Mole-catchers would hang the dead moles
they had caught from trees to prove they had done their jobs.

[3] *though the … chill* Round Oak Waters, which flowed from Round
Oak Spring, was surrounded by trees and meadows that were removed
during enclosure.

from *The Flitting*

I've left mine own old home of homes[1]
Green fields & every pleasant place
The summer like a stranger comes
I pause & hardly know her face
5 I miss the hazels happy green
The bluebells quiet hanging blooms
Where envys sneer was never seen
Where staring malice never comes

I miss the heath its yellow furze[2]
10 Molehills & rabbit tracts that lead
Through beesom ling[3] & teazle[4] burrs
That spread a wilderness indeed
The wood land oaks & all below
That their white powdered branches shield
15 The mossy paths—the very crow
Croaks music in my native field …

I dwell on trifles like a child
I feel as ill becomes a man
& still my thoughts like weedlings wild
20 Grow up to blossom where they can
They turn to places known so long
& feel that joy was dwelling there
So home fed pleasures fill the song
That has no present joys to heir° …   inherit

25 Strange scenes mere shadows are to me
Vague unpersonifying things
I love with my old home to be
By quiet woods & gravel springs
Where little pebbles wear as smooth
30 As hermits beads° by gentle floods   rosary beads
Whose noises doth my spirits sooth
& warms them into singing moods …

I love the verse that mild & bland
Breaths of green fields & open sky
35 I love the muse that in her hand
Bears wreaths of native poesy
Who walks nor skips the pasture brook
In scorn—but by the drinking horse
Leans oer its little brig° to look   bridge
40 How far the sallows° lean across   willows

& feels a rapture in her breast
Upon their root-fringed grains to mark
A hermit morehens° sedgy° nest   moorhen's / grassy
Just like a naiads summer bark
45 She counts the eggs she cannot reach
Admires the spots & loves it well
& yearns so natures lessons teach
Amid such neighbourhoods to dwell

I love the muse who sits her down
50 Upon the molehills little lap
Who feels no fear to stain her gown
& pauses by the hedgrow[5] gap
Not with that affectation praise
Of song to sing & never see
55 A field flower grow in all her days
Or een° a forests aged tree   even

Een here my simple feelings nurse
A love for every simple weed
& een this little "shepherds purse"[6]
60 Grieves me to cut it up—Indeed
I feel at times a love & joy
For every weed & every thing
A feeling kindred from a boy
A feeling brought with every spring

65 & why—this "shepherds purse" that grows
In this strange spot—In days gone bye
Grew in the little garden rows
Of my old home now left—And I

---

1 *Ive … homes* This was written after Clare had relocated from Helpston to Northborough.

2 *furze* Type of flowering evergreen shrub found throughout Europe.

3 *beesom ling* Besom-heather; heather used to make brooms ("besoms").

4 *teazle* Type of plant with prickly leaves.

5 *hedgrow* I.e., hedgerow.

6 *shepherds purse* A common type of weed.

Feel what I never felt before
70 This weed an ancient neighbour here
& though I own the spot no more
Its every trifle makes it dear

The Ivy at the parlour end
The wood bine[1] at the garden gate
75 Are all & each affections friend
That rendered parting desolate
But times will change & friends must part
& nature still can make amends
Their memory lingers round the heart
80 Like life whose essence is its friends

Time looks on pomp with careless moods
Or killing apathys disdain
—So where old marble citys stood
Poor persecuted weeds remain
85 She feels a love for little things
That very few can feel beside
& still the grass eternal springs
Where castles stood & grandeur died
—1908 (WRITTEN 1832)

The Badger

The badger grunting on his woodland track
With shaggy hide & sharp nose scrowed°   *marked*
   with black
Roots in the bushes & the woods & makes
A great hugh° burrow in the ferns & brakes° *huge | bracken*
5 With nose on ground he runs a awkard pace
& anything will beat him in the race
The shepherds dog will run him to his den
Followed & hooted by the dogs & men
The wood man when the hunting comes about
10 Go round at night to stop the foxes out
& hurrying through the bushes ferns & brakes
Nor sees the many hol[e]s the badger makes

& often through the bushes to the chin
Breaks the old holes & tumbles headlong in
15 When midnight comes a host of dogs & men
Go out & track the badger to his den
& put a sack within the hole & lye
Till the old grunting badger passes bye
He comes & hears they let the strongest loose
20 The old fox hears the noise & drops the goose
The poacher shoots & hurrys from the cry
& the old hare half wounded buzzes bye
They get a forked stick to bear him down
& clapt the dogs & bore him to the town
25 & bait him all the day with many dogs
& laugh & shout & fright the scampering hogs
He runs along & bites at all he meets
They shout & hollo down the noisey streets

He turns about to face the loud uproar
30 & drives the rebels to their very doors
The frequent stone is hurled where ere they go
When badgers fight & every ones a foe
The dogs are clapt & urged to join the fray
The badger turns & drives them all away
35 Though scar[c]ely half as big dimute° & small   *diminutive*
He fights with dogs for hours & beats them all
The heavy mastiff savage in the fray
Lies down & licks his feet & turns away
The bull dog knows his match & waxes cold
40 The badger grins & never leaves his hold
He drive[s] the crowd & follows at their heels
& bites them through the drunkard swears & reels

The frighted women takes the boys away
The blackguard[2] laughs & hurrys in the fray
45 He trys to reach the woods a awkard race
But sticks & cudgels quickly stop the chace
He turns agen & drives the noisey crowd
& beats the many dogs in noises loud
He drives away & beats them every one
50 & then they loose them all & set them on

---

1 *wood bine* Honeysuckle.

2 *blackguard* Scoundrel; a worthless or vicious character.

He falls as dead & kicked by boys & men
Then starts & grins & drives the crowd agen
Till kicked & torn & beaten out he lies
& leaves his hold & cackles groans & dies
—1920 (WRITTEN C. 1835–37)

Written in a Thunder Storm July 15th 1841[1]

The heavens are wrath—the thunders rattling peal
Rolls like a vast volcano in the sky
Yet nothing starts the apathy I feel
Nor chills with fear eternal destiny

5   My soul is apathy—a ruin vast
Time cannot clear the ruined mass away
My life is hell—the hopeless die is cast
& manhoods prime is premature decay

Roll on ye wrath of thunders—peal on peal
10   Till worlds are ruins & myself alone
Melt heart & soul cased in obdurate steel
Till I can feel that nature is my throne

I live in love sun of undying light
& fathom my own heart for ways of good
15   In its pure atmosphere day without night
Smiles on the plains the forest & the flood

Smile on ye elements of earth & sky
Or frown in thunders as ye frown on me
Bid earth & its delusions pass away
20   But leave the mind as its creator free

This twilight seems a veil of gause & mist
Trees seem dark hills between the earth & sky
Winds sob awake & then a gusty hist°   *hissing*
Fanns through the wheat like serpents gliding bye
25   I love to stretch my length 'tween earth & sky
& see the inky foliage oer me wave
Though shades are still my prison where I lie

---

[1]   *July 15th 1841*   Five days before Clare's escape from the asylum.

Long use grows nature which I easy brave
& think how sweet cares rest within the grave ...
—1949 (WRITTEN 1841)

Don Juan A Poem[2]

"Poets are born"—& so are whores—the trade is
Grown universal—in these canting days
Women of fashion must of course be ladies
& whoreing is the business—that still pays
5   Playhouses Ball rooms—there the masquerade is
—To do what was of old—& now adays
Their maids—nay wives so innocent & blooming
Cuckold[3] their spouses to seem honest women

Milton sung Eden & the fall of man[4]
10   Not woman for the name implies a wh—e
& they would make a ruin of his plan
Falling so often they can fall no lower
Tell me a worse delusion if you can
For innocence—& I will sing no more
15   Wherever mischief is tis womans brewing
Created from manself—to be mans ruin

The flower in bud hides from the fading sun
& keeps the hue of beauty on its cheek
But when full blown they into riot run
20   The hue turns pale & lost each ruddy streak
So 't'is with woman who pretends to shun
Immodest actions which they inly seek
Night hides the wh—e—cupboards tart & pasty
Flora was p-x-d—& womans quite as nasty

25   Marriage is nothing but a driveling hoax
To please old codgers when they're turned of forty
I wed & left my wife like other folks

---

[2]   *Don Juan A Poem*   After Byron's death in 1824, many poets experimented with writing continuations of his *Don Juan*. Parts of this poem demonstrate Clare's belief that he and Byron were one and the same person.

[3]   *Cuckold*   Commit adultery.

[4]   *Milton ... man*   See *Paradise Lost*.

But not untill I found her false & faulty
O woman fair—the man must pay thy jokes
Such makes a husband very often naughty
Who falls in love will seek his own undoing
The road to marriage is—"the road to ruin"

Love worse then debt or drink or any fate
It is the damnest smart of matrimony
A hell incarnate is a woman-mate
The knot is tied—& then we loose the honey
A wife is just the protetype to hate
Commons for stock° & warrens for the coney° *cattle / rabbit*
Are not more tresspassed over in rights plan
Then this incumberance on the rights of man

There's much said about love & more of women
I wish they were as modest as they seem
Some borrow husbands till their cheeks are blooming
Nor like the red rose blush—but yellow cream
Lord what a while those good days are in coming—
Routs[1] Masques & Balls—I wish they were a dream
—I wish for poor men luck –an honest praxis
Cheap food & cloathing—no corn laws[2] or taxes

I wish—but there is little got bye wishing
I wish that bread & great coats ne'er had risen
I wish that there was some such word as "pishun"
For ryhme sake for my verses must be dizen° *adorned*
With dresses fine—as hooks with baits for fishing
I wish all honest men were out of prison
I wish M.P.'s would spin less yarn—nor doubt
But burn false bills & cross bad taxes out

I wish young married dames were not so frisky
Nor hide the ring to make believe they're single
I wish small beer[3] was half as good as whiskey
& married dames with buggers would not mingle

There's some too cunning far & some too frisky
& here I want a ryhme—so write down "jingle"
& there's such putting in—in whores crim con[4]
Some mouths would eat forever & eat on

65 Childern are fond of sucking sugar candy
& maids of sausages—larger the better
Shopmen are fond of good sigars & brandy
& I of blunt°—& if you change the letter *money*
To C or K it would be quite as handy
70 & throw the next away—but I'm your debtor
For modesty—yet wishing nought between us
I'd hawl close to a she as vulcan did to venus[5]

I really cant tell what this poem will be
About—nor yet what trade I am to follow
75 I thought to buy old wigs[6]—but that will kill me
With cold starvation—as they're beaten hollow[7]
Long speeches in a famine will not fill me
& madhouse traps° still take me by the collar *warders*
So old wig bargains now must be forgotten
80 The oil that dressed them[8] fine has made them rotten

I wish old wigs were done with ere they're mouldy
I wish—but heres the papers large & lusty
With speeches that full fifty times they've told ye
—Noble Lord John to sweet Miss Fanny Fusty
85 Is wed[9]—a lie good reader I ne'er sold ye
—Prince Albert[10] goes to Germany & must he
Leave the queens snuff box where all fools are strumming
From addled eggs no chickens can be coming

---

[1] *Routs* Fashionable gatherings or evening parties, very popular in the late eighteenth and early nineteenth centuries.

[2] *corn laws* Series of British laws, repealed in 1846, regulating the trade of grain and restricting its import. One of the effects of these laws was to keep the price of bread very high.

[3] *small beer* Weak beer.

[4] *crim con* Criminal conversation (a legal term for adultery).

[5] *hawl close to* I.e., sleep with ("hawl" meaning "haul"); *as vulcan … venus* Vulcan, the Roman god of fire, was married to Venus, the goddess of love.

[6] *wigs* Slang for heads; also a pun on Whigs.

[7] *beaten hollow* The Whigs were defeated in the election of July 1841.

[8] *oil … them* Reference to the expression "to oil someone's wig," meaning to make them drunk.

[9] *Noble … wed* The marriage of Lord John Russell to Lady Fanny Elliott, daughter of the Earl of Minto, was announced in the papers in July 1841.

[10] *Prince Albert* Consort of Queen Victoria (1819–61).

Whigs strum state fiddle strings untill they snap
90 With cuckoo cuckold cuckoo year by year
The razor plays it on the barbers strap
—The sissars° grinder thinks it rather quere   scissors
That labour wont afford him "one wee drap"
Of ale or gin or half & half[1] or beer
95 —I wish prince Albert & the noble
    dastards°   despicable cowards
Who wed the wives—would get the noble bastards

I wish prince Albert on his german journey
I wish the Whigs were out of office &
Pickled in law books of some good atorney
100 For ways & speeches few can understand
They'll bless ye when in power—in prison scorn ye
& make a man rent his own house & land—
I wish prince Alberts queen was undefiled
—& every man could get his *wife* with child

105 I wish the devil luck with all my heart
As I would any other honest body
His bad name passes bye me like a f—t
Stinking of brimstone—then like whisky toddy[2]
We swallow sin which seems to warm the heart
110 —There's no imputing any sin to God—he
Fills hell with work—& is'n't it a hard case
To leave old whigs & give to hell the carcass

Me-b—ne may throw his wig to little Vicky[3]
& so resign his humbug & his power
115 & she with the young princess mount the dickey[4]
On ass milk diet[5] for her german tour
Asses like ministers are rather tricky
I & the country proves it every hour

W-ll—gt-n[6] & M-lb—n in their station
120 Coblers to queens—are phisic to the nation

These batch of toadstools on this rotten tree
Shall be the cabinet of any queen
Though not such coblers as her servants be
They're of Gods making—that is plainly seen
125 Nor red nor green nor orange—they are free
To thrive & flourish as the Whigs have been
But come tomorrow—like the Whigs forgotten
You'll find them withered stinking dead and rotten

Death is an awfull thing it is by God
130 I've said so often & I think so now
Tis rather droll to see an old wig nod
Then doze & die the devil don't know how
Odd things are wearisome & this is odd—
Tis better work then kicking up a row
135 I'm weary of old Whigs & old whigs heirs
& long been sick of teazing God with prayers

I've never seen the cow turn to a bull
I've never seen the horse become an ass
I've never seen an old brawn[7] cloathed in whool—
140 But I have seen full many a bonny lass
& wish I had one now beneath the cool
Of these high elms—Muse tell me where I was
O—talk of turning I've seen Whig & Tory
Turn imps of hell—& all for Englands glory

145 I love good fellowship & wit & punning
I love "true love" & God my taste defend
I hate most damnably all sorts of cunning—
I love the Moor & Marsh & Ponders end[8]—
I do not like the song of "cease your funning"[9]
150 I love a modest wife & trusty friend

---

[1] *half & half* Mixture of ale and porter, or any other two malt liquors.

[2] *whisky toddy* Whiskey mixed with warm water and sugar.

[3] *Me-b—ne* Lord Melbourne, who resigned as prime minister in August 1841; *little Vicky* Queen Victoria.

[4] *young princess* Victoria Adelaide, the Queen's first-born daughter; *dickey* Back seat of a carriage.

[5] *ass milk diet* Common diet for babies, asses' milk being the closest of all mammals' milk to that of humans.

[6] *W-ll—gt-n* Arthur Wellesley, Duke of Wellington, a former prime minister who became a cabinet minister in 1841 under Peel, and then commander-in-chief of the army.

[7] *brawn* Boar, also a male prostitute.

[8] *Ponders end* Ponders End is located three miles west of High Beach.

[9] *cease … funning* From John Gay's *Beggar's Opera* Air 19.2.13.

—Bricklayers want lime as I want ryhme for fillups
—So here's a health to sweet Eliza Phillips[1]

SONG

Eliza now the summer tells
Of spots where love & beauty dwells
55   Come & spend a day with me
Underneath the forest tree
Where the restless water flushes
Over mosses mounds & rushes
& where love & freedom dwells
60   With orchis° flowers & fox glove bells   *orchid*
Come dear Eliza set me free
& oer the forest roam with me

Here I see the morning sun
Among the beachtree's shadows run
65   That into gold the short sward° turns   *turf, grass*
Where each bright yellow blossom burns
With hues that would his beams out shine
Yet nought can match those smiles of thine
I try to find them all the day
70   But none are nigh when thou'rt away
Though flowers bloom now on every hill
Eliza is the fairest still

The sun wakes up the pleasant morn
& finds me lonely & forlorn
175   Then wears away to sunny noon
The flowers in bloom the birds in tune
While dull & dowie° all the year   *dreary*
No smiles to see no voice to hear
I in this forest prison lie
180   With none to heed my silent sigh
& underneath this beachen tree
With none to sigh for Love but thee

Now this new poem is entirely new
As wedding gowns or money from the mint
185   For all I know it is entirely true

For I would scorn to put a lie in print
—I scorn to lie for princes—so would you
& ere I shoot I try my pistol flint
—The cattle salesman—knows the way in trying
190   & feels his bullocks ere he thinks of buying

Lord bless me now the day is in the gloaming
& every evil thought is out of sight
How I should like to purchase some sweet woman
Or else creep in with my two wives[2] to night—
195   Surely that wedding day is on the comeing
Abscence like phisic poisons all delight—
Mary & Martha both an evil omen
Though both my own—they still belong to no man

But to our text again—& pray where is it
200   Begin as parsons do at the beginning
Take the first line friend & you cannot miss it
"Poets are born" & so are whores for sinning
—Here's the court circular—o Lord is this it
Court cards like lists of—not the naked meaning
205   Here's Albert going to germany they tell us
& the young queen down in the dumps & jealous

Now have you seen a tramper° on race courses   *vagrant*
Seeking an honest penny as his trade is
Crying a list of all the running horses
210   & showing handbills of the sporting ladies
—In bills of fare you'll find a many courses
Yet all are innocent as any maid is
Put these two dishes into one & dress it
& if there is a meaning—you may guess it

215   Don Juan was Ambassador from russia
But had no hand in any sort of tax
His orders hung like blossoms of the fushia
& made the ladies hearts to melt like wax
He knew Napoleon & the king of prusia
220   & blowed a cloud oer spirits wine or max°   *gin*

---

1 *Eliza Phillips* In a letter written after this poem, Clare dedicates "Don Juan" to Eliza, who has not been identified.

2 *my two wives* Reference to Clare's delusional belief that he possessed two wives—one being Martha ("Peggy"), his real wife, and the other being Mary, his dead childhood sweetheart.

But all his profits turned out losses rather
To save one orphan which he forced to father

Theres Docter Bottle imp who deals in urine
A keeper of state prisons for the queen
225 As great a man as is the Doge° of Turin   *Chief Magistrate*
& save in London is but seldom seen
Yclep'd° old A-ll-n[1]—mad brained ladies curing   *called*
Some p-x-d like Flora & but seldom clean
The new road oer the forest is the right one
230 To see red hell & further on the white one[2]

Earth hells or b-gg-r sh-ps or what you please
Where men close prisoners are & women ravished
I've often seen such dirty sights as these
I've often seen good money spent & lavished
235 To keep bad houses up for docters fees
& I have known a b-gg-rs tally travers'd[3]
Till all his good intents began to falter
—When death brought in his bill & left the halter°   *noose*

O glorious constitution what a picking
240 Ye've had from your tax harvest & your tythe[4]
Old hens which cluck about that fair young chicken
—Cocks without spurs[5] that yet can crow so
        blythe°   *cheerfully*
Truth is shut up in prison while ye're licking
The gold from off the gingerbread—be lythe
245 In winding that patched broken old state clock up
Playhouses open—but mad houses lock up

Give toil more pay where rank starvation lurches
& pay your debts & put your books to rights

Leave whores & playhouses & fill your churches
250 Old clovenfoot your dirty victory fights
Like theft he still on natures manor poaches
& holds his feasting on anothers rights
To show plain truth you act in bawdy farces
Men show their tools—& maids expose their arses

255 Now this day is the eleventh of July
& being sunday I will seek no flaw
In man or woman—but prepare to die
In two days more I may that ticket draw
& so may thousands more as well as I
260 To day is here—the next who ever saw
& In a madhouse I can find no mirth pay
—Next tuesday used to be Lord Byrons birthday[6]

Lord Byron poh—the man wot rites the werses
& is just what he is & nothing more
265 Who with his pen lies like the mist disperses
& makes all nothing as it was before
Who wed two wives[7] & oft the truth rehearses
& might have had some twenty thousand more
Who has been dead so fools their lies are giving
270 & still in Allens madhouse caged & living

If I do wickedness to day being sunday
Can I by hearing prayers or singing psalms
Clear off all debts twixt god & man on monday
& lie like an old hull that dotage calms
275 & is there such a word as Abergundy
I've read that poem called the "Isle of Palms"[8]
—But singing sense pray tell me if I can
Live an old rogue & die an honest man

---

[1] *A-ll-n* Dr. Matthew Allen, superintendent of the asylum. He would collect urine samples from patients, which were often used to diagnose venereal diseases.

[2] *To see … one* Reference to the two other houses of High Beach, the first for female patients and the second for male, which Clare could see from his residence.

[3] *tally travers'd* I.e., examined his list of wrong-doings or backslidings.

[4] *tythe* Tithe, tax amounting to one-tenth of one's income.

[5] *spurs* Back claws.

[6] *Next … birthday* 13 July was Clare's birthday, but Lord Byron was born on 22 January.

[7] *Who … wives* Byron married only once, though he was known for his sexual adventures.

[8] *Isle of Palms* Poem by John Wilson (published under the pseudonym Christopher North).

I wish I had a quire of foolscap paper
Hot pressed[1]—& crowpens°—how   *quill pens*
   I could endite
A silver candlestick & green wax taper
Lord bless me what fine poems I would write
The very tailors they would read & caper
& mantua[2] makers would be all delight
Though laurel wreaths[3] my brows did ne'er environ
I think myself as great a bard as Byron

I have two wives & I should like to see them
Both by my side before another hour
If both are honest I should like to be them
For both are fair & bonny as a flower
& one o Lord—now do bring in the tea mem°   *ma'am*
Were bards pens steamers[4] each of ten horse power
I could not bring her beautys fair to weather
So I've towed both in harbour blest together

Now i'n't this canto worth a single pound
From anybodys pocket who will buy
As thicves are worth a halter I'll be bound
Now honest reader take the book & try
& if as I have said it is not found
I'll write a better canto bye & bye
So reader now the money till unlock it
& buy the book & help to fill my pocket
—1949 (WRITTEN 1841)

Journey Out of Essex[5]

July 18—1841—Sunday—Felt very melancholly—went a walk on the forest in the afternoon—fell in with some gipseys one of whom offered to assist in my escape from the mad house by hideing me in his camp to which I almost agreed but told him I had no money to start with but if he would do so I would promise him fifty pounds and he agreed to do so before saturday

on friday I went again but he did not seem so willing so I said little about it—On sunday I went and they were all gone—an old wide awake hat[6] and an old straw bonnet of the plumb pudding sort was left behind—and I put the hat in my pocket thinking it might be usefull for another oppertunity—as good luck would have it, it turned out to be so

July 19—Monday—Did nothing

July 20—Reconnitered the rout[7] the Gipsey pointed out and found it a legible one to make a movement and having only honest courage and myself in my army I Led the way and my troops soon followed but being careless in mapping down the rout as the Gipsey told me I missed the lane to Enfield town and was going down Enfield highway till I passed "The Labour in vain" Public house where A person I knew comeing out of the door told me the way

I walked down the lane gently and was soon in Enfield Town and bye and bye on the great York Road where it was all plain sailing and steering ahead meeting no enemy and fearing none I reached Stevenage where being Night I got over a gate crossed over the corner of a green paddock where seeing a pond or hollow in the corner I forced to stay off a respectable distance to keep

[1] *Hot pressed*   Made smooth and shiny by being pressed between two hot plates.

[2] *mantua*   Type of fashionable, loose-fitting gown.

[3] *laurel wreaths*   Bestowed as a mark of honor upon poets, heroes, and victorious athletes in ancient Greece.

[4] *steamers*   Steam boats.

[5] *Journey Out of Essex*   The following journal documents Clare's four-day, eighty-mile journey home to Northborough after his escape from High Beach asylum. Five months following the events recounted here, Clare was committed to an asylum once again.

[6] *wide awake hat*   Wide-brimmed felt hat.

[7] *Reconnitered the rout*   I.e., investigated the route; "reconnoiter" suggests observation in advance of a military operation.

from falling into it for my legs were nearly knocked up[1] and began to stagger   I scaled some old rotten paleings[2] into the yard and then had higher pailings to clamber over to get into the shed or hovel which I did with difficulty being rather weak and to my good luck I found some trusses of clover piled up about 6 or more feet square which I gladly mounted and slept on   there was some trays in the hovel on which I could have reposed had I not found a better bed   I slept soundly but had a very uneasy dream   I thought my first wife[3] lay on my left arm and somebody took her away from my side which made me wake up rather unhappy   I thought as I awoke somebody said "Mary" but nobody was near—I lay down with my head towards the north to show myself the steering point in the morning

July 21—Daylight was looking in on every side and fearing my garrison might be taken by storm and myself be made prisoner I left my lodging by the way I got in and thanked God for his kindness in procureing it (for any thing in a famine is better than nothing and any place that giveth the weary rest is a blessing)   I gained the north road again and steered due north—on the left hand side the road under the bank like a cave I saw a Man and boy coiled up asleep which I hailed and they woke up to tell me the name of the next village

Some where on the London side the "Plough" Public house a Man passed me on horseback in a Slop frock[4] and said "here's another of the broken down haymakers" and threw me a penny to get a half pint of beer which I picked up and thanked him for and when I got to the plough I called for a half pint and drank it and got a rest and escaped a very heavy shower in the bargain by having a shelter till it was over—afterwards

I would have begged a penny of two drovers who were very saucey so I begged no more of any body meet who I would

—I passed 3 or 4 good built houses on a hill and a public house on the road side in the hollow below them

I seemed to pass the Milestones[5] very quick in the morning but towards night they seemed to be stretched further asunder   I got to a village further on and forgot the name   the road on the left hand was quite over shaded by some trees and quite dry so I sat down half an hour and made a good many wishes for breakfast but wishes was no hearty meal so I got up as hungry as I sat down—I forget here the names of the villages I passed through but reccolect at late evening going through Potton in Bedfordshire where I called in a house to light my pipe in which was a civil old woman and a young country wench makeing lace on a cushion as round as a globe and a young fellow all civil people—I asked them a few questions as to the way and where the clergyman and overseer lived but they scarcely heard me or gave me no answer[6]

I then went through Potton and happened with a kind talking country man who told me the Parson lived a good way from where I was or overseer I don't know which so I went on hopping with a crippled foot for the gravel had got into my old shoes one of which I had now nearly lost the sole   Had I found the overseers house at hand or the Parsons I should have gave my name and begged for a shilling to carry me home but I was forced to brush on pennyless and be thankfull I had

---

[1] *knocked up*   No longer functional due to exhaustion.

[2] *paleings*   Pieces of wood used to build a fence.

[3] *my first wife*   I.e., Mary Joyce, Clare's childhood sweetheart, whom he believed to be his wife. At the time of Clare's journey she had been dead for several years.

[4] *Slop frock*   Long, loose garment typically worn by a farm worker.

[5] *Milestones*   Roadside markers offering indications of distance and direction for travelers.

[6] [Clare's note]   On searching my pockets after the above was written I found part of a newspaper vide [see] "Morning Chronicle" on which the following fragments were pencilled soon after I got the information from labourers going to work or travellers journying along to better their condition as I was hopeing to do mine in fact I believed I saw home in every ones countenance which seemed so cheerfull in my own—"There is no place like home" the following was written by the Road side—1st Day—Tuesday—Started from Enfield and slept at Stevenage on some clover trusses—cold lodging
Wednesday—Jacks Hill is passed already consisting of a beer shop and some houses on the hill appearing newly built—the last Mile stone 35 Miles from London got through Baldeck and sat under a dry hedge and had a rest in lieu of breakfast

a leg to move on—I then asked him wether he could tell me of a farm yard any where on the road where I could find a shed and some dry straw and he said yes and if you will go with me I will show you the place—its a public house on the left hand side the road at the sign of the "Ram" but seeing a stone or flint heap I longed to rest as one of my feet was very painfull so I thanked him for his kindness and bid him go on—but the good natured fellow lingered awhile as if wishing to conduct me and then suddenly reccolecting that he had a hamper on his shoulder and a lock up bag in his hand cram full to meet the coach which he feared missing—he started hastily and was soon out of sight—I followed looking in vain for the country mans straw bed—and not being able to meet it I lay down by a shed side under some Elm trees between the wall and the trees being a thick row planted some 5 or 6 feet from the buildings   I lay there and tried to sleep but the wind came in between them so cold that I lay till I quaked like the ague[1] and quitted the lodging for a better at the Ram which I could hardly hope to find—It now began to grow dark apace and the odd houses on the road began to light up and show the inside tennants lots very comfortable and my outside lot very uncomfortable and wretched—still I hobbled forward as well as I could and at last came to the Ram   the shutters were not closed and the lighted window looked very cheering but I had no money and did not like to go in   there was a sort of shed or gighouse[2] at the end but I did not like to lie there as the people were up—so I still travelled on   the road was very lonely and dark in places being overshaded with trees   at length I came to a place where the road branched off into two turnpikes one to the right about and the other straight forward and on going bye my eye glanced on a mile stone standing under the hedge so I heedlessly turned back to read it to see where the other road led too and on doing so I found it led to London   I then suddenly forgot which was North or South and though I narrowly examined both ways I could see no tree or bush or stone

heap that I could reccolect I had passed so I went on mile after mile almost convinced I was going the same way I came and these thougts were so strong upon me that doubt and hopelessness made me turn so feeble that I was scarcely able to walk yet I could not sit down or give up but shuffled along till I saw a lamp shining as bright as the moon which on nearing I found was suspended over a Tollgate   before I got through the man came out with a candle and eyed me narrowly but having no fear I stopt to ask him wether I was going northward and he said when you get through the gate you are; so I thanked him kindly and went through on the other side and gathered my old strength   as my doubts vanished I soon cheered up and hummed the air of highland Mary as I went on   I at length fell in with an odd house all alone near a wood but I could not see what the sign was though the sign seemed to stand oddly enough in a sort of trough or spout   there was a large poach[3] over the door and being weary I crept in and glad enough I was to find I could lye with my legs straight   the inmates were all gone to roost for I could hear them turn over in bed as I lay at full length on the stones in the porch—I slept here till daylight and felt very much refreshed as I got up—I blest my two wives and both their familys when I lay down and when I got up and when I thought of some former difficultys on a like occasion I could not help blessing the Queen[4] Having passed a Lodge on the left hand within a mile and half or less of a town I think it might be St Ives but I forget the name[5] I sat down to rest on a flint heap where I might rest half an hour or more and while sitting here I saw a tall Gipsey come out of the Lodge gate and make down the road towards where I was sitting   when she got up to me on seeing she was a

---

1 *ague* Fever, especially one accompanied by shivering.

2 *gighouse* Shed for storing a carriage.

3 *poach* Porch.

4 [Clare's note] The man whose daughter is the queen of England is now sitting on a stone heap on the high way to bugden without a farthing in his pocket and without tasting a bit of food ever since yesterday morning—when he was offerd a bit of Bread and cheese at Enfield—he has not had any since but If I put a little fresh speed on hope too may speed to morrow—O Mary mary If you knew how anxious I am to see you and dear Patty with the childern I think you would come and meet me.

5 [Clare's note] It was St. Neots.

young woman with an honest looking countenance rather handsome I spoke to her and asked her a few questions which she answered readily and with evident good humour so I got up and went on to the next town with her—she cautioned me on the way to put something in my hat to keep the crown up and said in a lower tone "you'll be noticed" but not knowing what she hinted—I took no notice and made no reply   at length she pointed to a small tower church which she called Shefford Church and advised me to go on a footway which would take me direct to it and I should shorten my journey fifteen miles by doing so   I would gladly have taken the young womans advice feeling that it was honest and a nigh guess towards the truth but fearing I might loose my way and not be able to find the north road again I thanked her and told her I should keep to the road when she bade me "good day" and went into a house or shop on the left hand side the road   I have but a slight reccolection of my journey between here and Stilton for I was knocked up and noticed little or nothing—one night I lay in a dyke bottom from the wind and went sleep half an hour when I suddenly awoke and found one side wet through from the sock in the dyke bottom so I got out and went on—I remember going down a very dark road hung over with trees on both sides very thick which seemed to extend a mile or two   I then entered a town and some of the chamber windows had candle lights shineing in them—I felt so weak here that I forced to sit down on the ground to rest myself and while I sat here a[1] Coach that seemed to be heavy laden came rattling up and stopt in the hollow below me and I cannot reccolect its ever passing by me

I then got up and pushed onward seeing little to notice for the road very often looked as stupid as myself and I was very often half asleep as I went   on the third day I satisfied my hunger by eating the grass by the road side which seemed to taste something like bread   I was hungry and eat[2] heartily till I was satisfied and in fact the meal seemed to do me good   the next and last day

I reccollected that I had some tobacco and my box of lucifers[3] being exhausted I could not light my pipe so I took to chewing Tobacco all day and eat the quids[4] when I had done and I was never hungry afterwards—I remember passing through Buckden and going a length of road afterwards but I dont reccolect the name of any place until I came to stilton where I was compleatly foot foundered and broken down   when I had got about half through the town a gravel causeway invited me to rest myself so I lay down and nearly went sleep   a young woman (so I guessed by the voice) came out of a house and said "poor creature" and another more elderly said "O he shams" but when I got up the latter said "o no he don't" as I hobbled along very lame   I heard the voices but never looked back to see where they came from—when I got near the Inn at the end of the gravel walk I met two young women and I asked one of them wether the road branching to the right bye the end of the Inn did not lead to Peterborough and she said "Yes" it did so as soon as ever I was on it I felt myself in homes way and went on rather more cheerfull though I forced to rest oftener than usual   before I got to Peterborough a man and woman passed me in a cart and on hailing me as they passed I found they were neighbours from Helpstone where I used to live—I told them I was knocked up which they could easily see and that I had neither eat or drank any thing since I left Essex   when I told my story they clubbed together and threw me fivepence out of the cart   I picked it up and called at a small public house near the bridge were I had two half pints of ale and twopenn'orth[5] of bread and cheese when I had done I started quite refreshed only my feet was more crippled than ever and I could scarcely make a walk of it over the stones and being half ashamed to sit down in the street I forced to keep on the move and got through Peterborough better then I expected   when I got on the high road I rested on the stone heaps as I passed till I was able to go on afresh and bye and bye I passed Walton and soon reached Werrington and was

---

[1] [Clare's note] The Coach did pass me as I sat under some trees by a high wall and the lumps lasshed in my face and wakened me up from a doze when I knocked the gravel out of my shoes and started.

[2] *eat* Ate.

[3] *lucifers* Matches.

[4] *quids* Here, lumps of chewed tobacco.

[5] *twopenn'orth* Two pennies worth.

making for the Beehive[1] as fast as I could when a cart met me with a man and woman and a boy in it when nearing me the woman jumped out and caught fast hold of my hands and wished me to get into the cart but I refused and thought her either drunk or mad but when I was told it was my second wife Patty I got in and was soon in Northborough but Mary was not there neither could I get any information about her further then the old story of her being dead six years ago which might be taken from a bran new old Newspaper printed a dozen years ago but I took no notice of the blarney[2] having seen her myself about a twelvemonth ago alive and well and as young as ever—so here I am homeless at home and half gratified to feel that I can be happy any where

> May none those marks of my sad fate efface
> For they appeal from tyranny to God[3]
> BYRON

July 24th 1841 Returned home out of Essex and found no Mary—her and her family are as nothing to me now though she herself was once the dearest of all—and how can I forget
—1865 (WRITTEN 1841)

Sonnet
[*I am*]

I feel I am;—I only know I am,
And plod upon the earth, as dull and void:
Earth's prison chilled my body with its dram[4]
Of dullness, and my soaring thoughts destroyed,
5   I fled to solitudes from passions dream,
But strife persued—I only know, I am,
I was a being created in the race
Of men disdaining bounds of place and time:—

A spirit that could travel o'cr the space
10 Of earth and heaven,—like a thought sublime,
Tracing creation, like my maker, free,—
A soul unshackled—like eternity,
Spurning earth's vain and soul debasing thrall
But now I only know I am,—that's all.
—1932 (WRITTEN C. 1842–46)

To Mary[5]

I sleep with thee, and wake with thee,
And yet thou art not there:—
I fill my arms, with thoughts of thee,
And press the common air.—
5   Thy eyes are gazing upon mine,
When thou art out of sight;
My lips are always touching thine,
At morning, noon, and night.

I think, and speak of other things,
10 To keep my mind at rest:
But still to thee, my memory clings,
Like love in womans breast;—
I hide it from the worlds-wide eye;
And think, and speak contrary;
15 But soft, the wind comes from the sky,
And wispers tales of Mary.—

The night wind wispers in my ear,
The moon shines in my face;
A burden still of chilling fear,
20 I find in every place.—
The breeze is wispering in the bush;
And the dew-fall from the tree,
All; sighing on, and will not hush,
Some pleasant tales of thee.—
—1984 (WRITTEN C. 1844)

---

[1] *the Beehive* I.e., a nearby public house.

[2] *blarney* Gossip; nonsense.

[3] *May none ... to God* Paraphrased from Byron's "Sonnet on Chillon" (1816).

[4] *dram* Measurement of weight.

[5] *Mary* Clare's childhood sweetheart, who had died years earlier. Clare often believed that she was still alive and that he had married her.

I Am

I am—yet what I am, none cares or knows;
 My friends forsake me like a memory lost:—
I am the self-consumer of my woes;—
 They rise and vanish in oblivion's host,
5 Like shadows in love's frenzied stifled throes:—
And yet I am, and live—like vapours tost

Into the nothingness of scorn and noise,—
 Into the living sea of waking dreams,
Where there is neither sense of life or joys,
10 But the vast shipwreck of my lifes esteems;
Even the dearest, that I love the best
Are strange—nay, rather stranger than the rest.[1]

I long for scenes, where man hath never trod
 A place where woman never smiled or wept
15 There to abide with my Creator, God;
 And sleep as I in childhood, sweetly slept,
Untroubling, and untroubled where I lie,
The grass below—above the vaulted sky.
—1848

Clock A Clay [2]

In the cowslips peeps I lye[3]
Hidden from the buzzing fly
While green grass beneath me lies
Pearled wi' dew like fishes eyes
5 Here I lye a Clock a clay
Waiting for the time o' day[4]

While grassy forests quake surprise
And the wild wind sobs and sighs
My gold home rocks as like to fall
10 On its pillars green and tall
When the pattering rain drives bye
Clock a Clay keeps warm and dry

Day by day and night by night
All the week I hide from sight
15 In the cowslips peeps I lye
In rain and dew still warm and dry
Day and night and night and day
Red black spotted clock a clay

My home it shakes in wind and showers
20 Pale green pillar top't wi' flowers
Bending at the wild winds breath
Till I touch the grass beneath
Here still I live lone clock a clay
Watching for the time of day
—1873 (WRITTEN C. 1848)

An Invite to Eternity

Wilt thou go with me sweet maid
 Say maiden wilt thou go with me
Through the valley depths of shade
Of night and dark obscurity
5 Where the path hath lost its way
Where the sun forgets the day
Where there's nor life nor light to see
Sweet maiden wilt thou go with me

Where stones will turn to flooding streams
10 Where plains will rise like ocean waves
Where life will fade like visioned dreams
And mountains darken into caves
Say maiden wilt thou go with me
Through this sad non-identity
15 Where parents live and are forgot
And sisters live and know us not

---

[1] *Even the ... rest* Apparently Clare's family never came to visit him in the Northampton asylum.

[2] *Clock A Clay* Ladybug.

[3] *In ... lye* Cf. the spirit Ariel's song in Shakespeare's *The Tempest*, 5.1.88–89: "Where the bee sucks, there suck I: / In the cowslip's bell I lie"; *cowslips* Yellow primrose; *peeps* Pips; blossoms.

[4] *Waiting ... day* In a popular game, children would tell the time by counting the number of taps necessary to make the ladybug fly home.

Say maiden wilt thou go with me
In this strange death of life to be
To live in death and be the same
Without this life, or home, or name
At once to be, & not to be
That was, and is not—yet to see
Things pass like shadows—and the sky
Above, below, around us lie

25 The land of shadows wilt thou trace
And look—nor know each others face
The present mixed with reasons gone
And past, and present all as one
Say maiden can thy life be led
30 To join the living with the dead
Then trace thy footsteps on with me
We're wed to one eternity
—1984 (WRITTEN 1848)

JOHN KEATS
1795 – 1821

J ohn Keats has come to epitomize the popular conception of the Romantic poet as a passionate dreamer whose intense, sensuous poetry celebrates the world of the imagination over that of everyday life. Keats published only 54 poems in his short lifetime, but his work ranges across a number of poetic genres, including lyric, romance, and epic. In each of these genres his poetry seeks beauty and truth that will transcend the world of suffering, always questioning its own process of interpretation.

The eldest of four children, John Keats was born in London on 31 October 1795. He lost both his parents by the time he was fourteen—his father in a riding accident and his mother of tuberculosis (then commonly known as consumption). After his mother's death, Keats came under the care of two guardians. He continued to attend Enfield School, a liberal institution where he first became acquainted with Leigh Hunt's radical paper the *Examiner*, and where his interest in poetry grew, particularly after reading the poetry of Edmund Spenser. Keats's friend Charles Brown said it was *The Faerie Queene* that awakened Keats's talent for expressing the "acute sense of beauty" he possessed.

After a promising but incomplete schooling, Keats apprenticed himself in 1815 to a surgeon at Guy's Hospital in London. (He remained licensed as an apothecary until 1817.) Having befriended some of the most prolific artists and critics of his day, among them radical publisher Leigh Hunt, essayist Charles Lamb, painter Benjamin Haydon, and poets John Hamilton Reynolds and Percy Shelley (later to eulogize Keats in *Adonais*), Keats was spurred to further develop his own creative abilities. In 1816, after spending a night reading a translation of Homer with his school friend Cowden Clarke, Keats wrote "On First Looking into Chapman's Homer" (1816), a sonnet that presents a poet reflecting on poetic tradition and discovering his talent, as an explorer surveys "with a wild surmise" another, more literal ocean of possibility.

Shortly thereafter, Keats composed "Sleep and Poetry" (1817), a poetic manifesto of sorts in which he proclaims his devotion to a new type of poetry, one in the style of Wordsworth, devoted to nature and the human heart. By aligning himself with Wordsworth's naturalism, Keats ensured the condemnation of critics; nevertheless, that same year he chose to give up surgery and devote himself entirely to poetry. This decision was most likely sealed by Leigh Hunt's first "Young Poets" article (*Examiner*, December 1816), in which he identified Keats, Shelley, and Reynolds as the leaders of a new generation of poets.

Keats's first volume, *Poems* (1817), received little critical attention. The following year he published the long and ambitious romance *Endymion* (1818), about a shepherd-prince who pursues his elusive feminine ideal. The book was sharply criticized in a famous review published in the *Quarterly Review*, where Keats and his friend Hunt were ridiculed as representing "the Cockney school of poetry." Keats endured further criticism when he read "Hymn to Pan" from *Endymion* to the contemporary poet he most admired, Wordsworth; the elder poet ungenerously dismissed it as "a very pretty piece of paganism."

Despite such discouragement, Keats continued to pursue his poetic ideals. In a series of now-famous letters to Benjamin Bailey, he explored his aesthetic ideas and sought to define the purpose of literature for modern life. Keats's letters to his friends and family are justly acclaimed for their intuitions about life, suffering, and poetry. To Keats we owe the concepts of "negative capability," the "chameleon poet," and "the vale of Soul-making." He particularly admired what he saw as Shakespeare's chameleon-like ability to escape from his personality and enter fully into the being of his characters.

During this time, Keats fell in love with the lively and flirtatious Fanny Brawne, who became a kind of muse. Though they became engaged, Keats wanted to gain financial security before marrying. He had begun as well to be haunted by fears of his own early death. (Throat ulcers that had appeared during a walking tour in poor weather the previous summer had become chronic.) It was in this set of tumultuous emotional circumstances that Keats began one of the most extraordinary periods of creativity in the history of English literature. Between January and September of 1819 he composed all six of his "great Odes"—"Ode to Psyche," "Ode to a Nightingale," "Ode on a Grecian Urn," "Ode on Indolence," "Ode on Melancholy," and "To Autumn"—as well as "The Eve of St. Agnes," "La Belle Dame sans Merci," "Lamia," and a number of sonnets. Generations of readers have been seduced by the sensuous immediacy of this poetry.

Keats's largest poetic project was *Hyperion*, a blank-verse epic on Jupiter's dethroning of Saturn and Apollo's overthrow of Hyperion. An intense study of cultural loss, the poem is a self-consciously Miltonic exercise that Keats kept returning to but never completed. He began the poem in the autumn of 1818, but put the manuscript aside in April of the following year. (This first fragmentary version of the poem was published as "Hyperion: A Fragment" in the 1820 volume of his verse.)

In the summer he resumed work on the project, this time casting the story within the frame of a poet's dream vision, but he stopped for a second time in September. (This second version, also fragmentary, was finally published in 1856 as "The Fall of Hyperion.")

When Keats's extraordinary poetic outpouring of 1819 was coming to a close, he began to suspect himself inadequate to the task of undertaking a Miltonic epic. As he wrote to his friend John Reynolds on 21 September 1819:

> I have given up Hyperion … Miltonic verse cannot be written but in an artful or rather artist's humour. I wish to give myself up to other sensations. English ought to be kept up.

Keats wrote little after September of 1819, but he published his third volume of poetry, *Lamia, Isabella, The Eve of St. Agnes, and Other Poems*, in 1820—defiantly advertising himself on the cover as "the author of *Endymion*." Critics were gradually acquiring a taste for Keats's work, but by this time Keats was very ill, having contracted tuberculosis. With his lungs weakened and his throat still ulcerating, Keats received an invitation to join Shelley and his circle in Pisa, but went first to Rome, where he died in the house at the base of the Spanish Steps that is now the Keats-Shelley Memorial House. Keats was buried in the Protestant Cemetery in Rome.

In the generations since his death, many have wondered what Keats would have accomplished had he lived. Such thoughts, however, focus on the tragedy of the poet's death, rather than on the sustained richness of his achievement. Before his death, Keats asked that his epitaph be "Here lies one whose name was writ in water." (Though his friends complied, they added above, "This Grave contains all that was Mortal of a YOUNG ENGLISH POET, Who on his Death Bed in the

Bitterness of his Heart at the Malicious Power of his Enemies, Desired these Words to be incised on his Tomb Stone.") On visiting his gravesite in 1877, Oscar Wilde supplied another epitaph: "A Priest of Beauty slain before his time." But the last sentences of Keats's last letter to Charles Brown are perhaps more evocative: "I can scarcely bid you good bye even in a letter. I always made an awkward bow."

⌘ ⌘ ⌘

On First Looking into Chapman's Homer[1]

Much have I travell'd in the realms of gold,
  And many goodly states and kingdoms seen;
    Round many western islands have I been
Which bards in fealty to Apollo[2] hold.
5 Oft of one wide expanse had I been told
    That deep-brow'd Homer ruled as his demesne;
    Yet never did I breathe its pure serene,
Till I heard Chapman speak out loud and bold:
Then felt I like some watcher of the skies
10   When a new planet swims into his ken;[3]
Or like stout Cortez[4] when with eagle eyes
    He star'd at the Pacific—and all his men
Look'd at each other with a wild surmise—
    Silent, upon a peak in Darien.
—1816

On the Grasshopper and Cricket[5]

The poetry of earth is never dead:
  When all the birds are faint with the hot sun,
    And hide in cooling trees, a voice will run
From hedge to hedge about the new-mown mead;
5 That is the Grasshopper's—he takes the lead
    In summer luxury—he has never done
    With his delights; for when tired out with fun
He rests at ease beneath some pleasant weed.
The poetry of earth is ceasing never:
10   On a lone winter evening, when the frost
    Has wrought a silence, from the stove there shrills
The Cricket's song, in warmth increasing ever,
    And seems to one in drowsiness half lost,
    The Grasshopper's among some grassy hills.
—1817

Sleep and Poetry

As I lay in my bed slepe full unmete°   *unallotted*
Was unto me, but why that I ne might
Rest I ne wist,° for there n'as° erthly   *knew / was no*
  wight°   *creature*

---

[1] *On … Homer* Written in October 1816, on the morning after Keats and his friend and mentor Charles Cowden Clarke had stayed up all night reading the 1614 translation of Homer by George Chapman (1559–1634).

[2] *Apollo* Greek god of poetry

[3] *a new … ken* William Herschel had discovered Uranus in 1781.

[4] *Cortez* The first European to see the Pacific (from the Isthmus of Darien in Panama) was not actually Hernán Cortez (1485–1547), the conqueror of Mexico, but Vasco Nuñez de Balboa (1475–1519) in 1513.

[5] *On the Grasshopper and Cricket* This poem was composed on 30 December 1816, when Keats was visiting his friend Leigh Hunt (1784–1859) in Hampstead. The poets were reading Thomas Moore's English translation of the *Odes* of Anacreon; after reading Ode 34, which is in praise of a grasshopper, they noticed a cricket near the fireplace. Hunt spontaneously suggested a sonnet-writing contest on the subject of the grasshopper and the cricket, and he and Keats both wrote sonnets within a time limit of 15 minutes. Each poet modestly claimed that the other had won. Hunt's poem can be found on this anthology's companion website.

[As I suppose] had more of hertis ese°   *heart's ease*
Than I, for I n'ad° sicknesse nor disese.[1]   *had not*
CHAUCER

What is more gentle than a wind in summer?
 What is more soothing than the pretty hummer
That stays one moment in an open flower,
And buzzes cheerily from bower to bower?
5 What is more tranquil than a musk-rose
  blowing°   *blossoming*
In a green island, far from all men's knowing?
More healthful than the leafiness of dales?
More secret than a nest of nightingales?
More serene than Cordelia's[2] countenance?
10 More full of visions than a high romance?
What, but thee Sleep? Soft closer of our eyes!
Low murmurer of tender lullabies!
Light hoverer around our happy pillows!
Wreather of poppy buds, and weeping willows!
15 Silent entangler of a beauty's tresses!
Most happy listener! when the morning blesses
Thee for enlivening all the cheerful eyes
That glance so brightly at the new sun-rise.

But what is higher beyond thought than thee?
20 Fresher than berries of a mountain tree?
More strange, more beautiful, more smooth, more
  regal,
Than wings of swans, than doves, than dim-seen eagle?
What is it? And to what shall I compare it?
It has a glory, and naught else can share it:
25 The thought thereof is awful, sweet, and holy,
Chasing away all worldliness and folly;
Coming sometimes like fearful claps of thunder,
Or the low rumblings earth's regions under;
And sometimes like a gentle whispering
30 Of all the secrets of some wond'rous thing
That breathes about us in the vacant air;
So that we look around with prying stare,

Perhaps to see shapes of light, aërial limning,[3]
And catch soft floatings from a faint-heard hymning;
35 To see the laurel wreath,[4] on high suspended,
That is to crown our name when life is ended.
Sometimes it gives a glory to the voice,
And from the heart up-springs, "Rejoice! rejoice!"
Sounds which will reach the Framer of all things,
40 And die away in ardent mutterings.

No one who once the glorious sun has seen,
And all the clouds, and felt his bosom clean
For his great Maker's presence, but must know
What 'tis I mean, and feel his being glow:
45 Therefore no insult will I give his spirit,
By telling what he sees from native merit.

O Poesy! For thee I hold my pen
That am not yet a glorious denizen
Of thy wide heaven—Should I rather kneel
50 Upon some mountain-top until I feel
A glowing splendour round about me hung,
And echo back the voice of thine own tongue?
O Poesy! For thee I grasp my pen
That am not yet a glorious denizen
55 Of thy wide heaven; yet, to my ardent prayer,
Yield from thy sanctuary some clear air,
Smoothed for intoxication by the breath
Of flowering bays, that I may die a death
Of luxury, and my young spirit follow
60 The morning sun-beams to the great Apollo[5]
Like a fresh sacrifice; or, if I can bear
The o'erwhelming sweets, 'twill bring to me the fair
Visions of all places: a bowery nook
Will be elysium[6]—an eternal book
65 Whence I may copy many a lovely saying
About the leaves, and flowers—about the playing

---

1 *As … disese* From *The Floure and the Leafe* 17–21, which was then thought to have been written by Chaucer.

2 *Cordelia* Daughter of King Lear in Shakespeare's *King Lear*.

3 *limning* Painting.

4 *laurel wreath* Wreaths made of leaves of the bay laurel were traditionally bestowed upon those who distinguished themselves in poetry.

5 *Apollo* Greek god of poetry.

6 *elysium* State of perfect happiness. From the Elysium of Greek mythology, the place where the blessed reside after death.

Of nymphs in woods, and fountains; and the shade
Keeping a silence round a sleeping maid;
And many a verse from so strange influence
70 That we must ever wonder how, and whence
It came. Also imaginings will hover
Round my fire-side, and haply there discover
Vistas of solemn beauty, where I'd wander
In happy silence, like the clear Meander[1]
75 Through its lone vales; and where I found a spot
Of awfuller shade, or an enchanted grot,°   *grotto*
Or a green hill o'erspread with chequered dress
Of flowers, and fearful from its loveliness,
Write on my tablets all that was permitted,
80 All that was for our human senses fitted.
Then the events of this wide world I'd seize
Like a strong giant, and my spirit tease
Till at its shoulders it should proudly see
Wings to find out an immortality.

85 Stop and consider! Life is but a day;
A fragile dew-drop on its perilous way
From a tree's summit; a poor Indian's sleep
While his boat hastens to the monstrous steep
Of Montmorenci.[2] Why so sad a moan?
90 Life is the rose's hope while yet unblown;
The reading of an ever-changing tale;
The light uplifting of a maiden's veil;
A pigeon tumbling in clear summer air;
A laughing school-boy, without grief or care,
95 Riding the springy branches of an elm.

O for ten years, that I may overwhelm
Myself in poesy; so I may do the deed
That my own soul has to itself decreed.
Then will I pass the countries that I see
100 In long perspective, and continually
Taste their pure fountains. First the realm I'll pass
Of Flora, and old Pan:[3] sleep in the grass,

Feed upon apples red, and strawberries,
And choose each pleasure that my fancy sees;
105 Catch the white-handed nymphs in shady places,
To woo sweet kisses from averted faces,
Play with their fingers, touch their shoulders white
Into a pretty shrinking with a bite
As hard as lips can make it: till agreed,
110 A lovely tale of human life we'll read
And one will teach a tame dove how it best
May fan the cool air gently o'er my rest;
Another, bending o'er her nimble tread,
Will set a green robe floating round her head,
115 And still will dance with ever varied ease,
Smiling upon the flowers and the trees:
Another will entice me on, and on
Through almond blossoms and rich cinnamon;
Till in the bosom of a leafy world
120 We rest in silence, like two gems upcurl'd
In the recesses of a pearly shell.

And can I ever bid these joys farewell?
Yes, I must pass them for a nobler life,
Where I may find the agonies, the strife
125 Of human hearts: for lo! I see afar,
O'er sailing the blue cragginess, a car°   *chariot*
And steeds with streamy manes—the charioteer
Looks out upon the winds with glorious fear:
And now the numerous tramplings quiver lightly
130 Along a huge cloud's ridge; and now with sprightly
Wheel downward come they into fresher skies,
Tipt round with silver from the sun's bright eyes.
Still downward with capacious whirl they glide,
And now I see them on the green-hill's side
135 In breezy rest among the nodding stalks.
The charioteer with wond'rous gesture talks
To the trees and mountains; and there soon appear
Shapes of delight, of mystery, and fear,
Passing along before a dusky space
140 Made by some mighty oaks: as they would chase
Some ever-fleeting music on they sweep.
Lo! how they murmur, laugh, and smile, and weep:

---

[1] *Meander* Winding river in Asia Minor.

[2] *Montmorenci* Montmorency Falls near Québec City, Canada.

[3] *Flora ... Pan* In Greek mythology, the goddess of flowers and the shepherd god of nature, respectively. The realm of Flora and Pan is that of pastoral poesy, which, according to Virgil, should be the genre

---

with which the aspiring poet begins, eventually working his way up to the epic.

Some with upholden hand and mouth severe;
Some with their faces muffled to the ear
5 Between their arms; some, clear in youthful bloom,
Go glad and smilingly athwart the gloom;
Some looking back, and some with upward gaze;
Yes, thousands in a thousand different ways
Flit onward—now a lovely wreath of girls
10 Dancing their sleek hair into tangled curls;
And now broad wings. Most awfully intent
The driver of those steeds is forward bent,
And seems to listen: O that I might know
All that he writes with such a hurrying glow.

15 The visions all are fled—the car is fled
Into the light of heaven, and in their stead
A sense of real things comes doubly strong,
And, like a muddy stream, would bear along
My soul to nothingness: but I will strive
20 Against all doubtings, and will keep alive
The thought of that same chariot, and the strange
Journey it went.

            Is there so small a range
In the present strength of manhood, that the high
Imagination cannot freely fly
25 As she was wont of old? prepare her steeds,
Paw up against the light, and do strange deeds
Upon the clouds? Has she not shown us all?
From the clear space of ether, to the small
Breath of new buds unfolding? From the meaning
30 Of Jove's[1] large eyebrow, to the tender greening
Of April meadows? Here her altar shone,
E'en in this isle; and who could paragon
The fervid choir that lifted up a noise
Of harmony, to where it aye will poise
35 Its mighty self of convoluting sound,
Huge as a planet, and like that roll round,
Eternally around a dizzy void?
Ay, in those days the Muses[2] were nigh cloy'd

With honours; nor had any other care
180 Than to sing out and sooth their wavy hair.

Could all this be forgotten? Yes, a schism
Nurtured by foppery and barbarism,
Made great Apollo blush for this his land.
Men were thought wise who could not understand
185 His glories: with a puling infant's force
They sway'd about upon a rocking horse,
And thought it Pegasus.[3] Ah dismal soul'd!
The winds of heaven blew, the ocean roll'd
Its gathering waves—ye felt it not. The blue
190 Bared its eternal bosom, and the dew
Of summer nights collected still to make
The morning precious: beauty was awake!
Why were ye not awake? But ye were dead
To things ye knew not of—were closely wed
195 To musty laws lined out with wretched rule
And compass vile: so that ye taught a school
Of dolts to smooth, inlay, and clip, and fit,
Till, like the certain wands of Jacob's wit,[4]
Their verses tallied. Easy was the task:
200 A thousand handicraftsmen wore the mask
Of Poesy. Ill-fated, impious race!
That blasphemed the bright Lyrist[5] to his face,
And did not know it—no, they went about,
Holding a poor, decrepit standard out
205 Mark'd with most flimsy mottos, and in large
The name of one Boileau![6]

            O ye whose charge
It is to hover round our pleasant hills!
Whose congregated majesty so fills

---

[1] *Jove* Roman king of the gods.

[2] *Muses* In Greek mythology, nine daughters of Zeus and Mnemosyne, each of whom presided over and provided inspiration for an aspect of learning or the arts.

[3] *Pegasus* Great winged horse of Greek mythology. This line is a reference to William Hazlitt's essay "On Milton's Versification" (1815), in which he says, on the use of the heroic couplet by eighteenth-century poets, "Dr. Johnson and Pope would have turned [Milton's] vaulting Pegasus into a rocking-horse."

[4] *Jacob's wit* See Genesis 30.27–43, in which Jacob increases his wealth at the expense of Laban.

[5] *the bright Lyrist* I.e., Apollo.

[6] *Boileau* French literary critic Nicolas Boileau-Despréaux (1636–1711), whose *L'Art Poétique* (1674), a verse treatise on literary aesthetics, was extremely influential among English poets.

My boundly[1] reverence, that I cannot trace
210 Your hallowed names, in this unholy place,
So near those common folk; did not their shames
Affright you? Did our old lamenting Thames°   *river*
Delight you? Did ye never cluster round
Delicious Avon,° with a mournful sound,   *river*
215 And weep? Or did ye wholly bid adieu
To regions where no more the laurel grew?
Or did ye stay to give a welcoming
To some lone spirits[2] who could proudly sing
Their youth away, and die? 'Twas even so:
220 But let me think away those times of woe:
Now 'tis a fairer season; ye have breathed
Rich benedictions o'er us; ye have wreathed
Fresh garlands: for sweet music has been heard
In many places—some has been upstirr'd
225 From out its crystal dwelling in a lake,
By a swan's ebon bill;[3] from a thick brake,°   *thicket*
Nested and quiet in a valley mild,
Bubbles a pipe;[4] fine sounds are floating wild
About the earth: happy are ye and glad.

230 These things are doubtless: yet in truth we've had
Strange thunders from the potency of song;
Mingled indeed with what is sweet and strong,
From majesty: but in clear truth the themes
Are ugly clubs, the poets Polyphemes[5]
235 Disturbing the grand sea. A drainless shower
Of light is poesy; 'tis the supreme of power;
'Tis might half slumb'ring on its own right arm.
The very archings of her eye-lids charm
A thousand willing agents to obey,
240 And still she governs with the mildest sway:

But strength alone though of the Muses born
Is like a fallen angel: trees uptorn,
Darkness, and worms, and shrouds, and sepulchres
Delight it; for it feeds upon the burrs,
245 And thorns of life; forgetting the great end
Of poesy, that it should be a friend
To sooth the cares, and lift the thoughts of man.

     Yet I rejoice: a myrtle fairer than
E'er grew in Paphos,[6] from the bitter weeds
250 Lifts its sweet head into the air, and feeds
A silent space with ever sprouting green.
All tenderest birds there find a pleasant screen,
Creep through the shade with jaunty fluttering,
Nibble the little cupped flowers and sing.
255 Then let us clear away the choking thorns
From round its gentle stem; let the young fawns,
Yeaned° in after times, when we are flown,   *brought forth*
Find a fresh sward° beneath it, overgrown   *turf*
With simple flowers: let there nothing be
260 More boisterous than a lover's bended knee;
Nought more ungentle than the placid look
Of one who leans upon a closed book;
Nought more untranquil than the grassy slopes
Between two hills. All hail delightful hopes!
265 As she was wont, th'imagination
Into most lovely labyrinths will be gone,
And they shall be accounted poet kings
Who simply tell the most heart-easing things.
O may these joys be ripe before I die.

270 Will not some say that I presumptuously
Have spoken? that from hastening disgrace
'Twere better far to hide my foolish face?
That whining boyhood should with reverence bow
Ere the dread thunderbolt could reach? How!
275 If I do hide myself, it sure shall be
In the very fane, the light of Poesy:
If I do fall, at least I will be laid
Beneath the silence of a poplar shade;

---

[1] *boundly* Term coined by Keats, meaning either "boundless" or "bounden."

[2] *some lone spirits* Reference to poets Thomas Chatterton (1752–70), Henry White (1785–1806), and others, who died young, without receiving the critical attention their work deserved.

[3] *swan's ebon bill* Reference to William Wordsworth (1770–1850), who, along with Coleridge and Southey, was known as a "Lake Poet."

[4] *from a ... pipe* Reference to poet Leigh Hunt (1784–1859).

[5] *Polyphemes* Plural of Polyphemus, a one-eyed, club-wielding giant in Homer's *Odyssey*.

[6] *Paphos* City in Cyprus that is the site of a famous temple to Venus, goddess of love and beauty. Myrtle (line 248) is also associated with Venus.

And over me the grass shall be smooth shaven;
80 And there shall be a kind memorial graven.
But off Despondence! miserable bane!
They should not know thee, who athirst to gain
A noble end, are thirsty every hour.
What though I am not wealthy in the dower
85 Of spanning wisdom; though I do not know
The shiftings of the mighty winds that blow
Hither and thither all the changing thoughts
Of man: though no great minist'ring reason sorts
Out the dark mysteries of human souls
90 To clear conceiving: yet there ever rolls
A vast idea before me, and I glean
Therefrom my liberty; thence too I've seen
The end and aim of Poesy. 'Tis clear
As any thing most true; as that the year
95 Is made of the four seasons—manifest
As a large cross, some old cathedral's crest,
Lifted to the white clouds. Therefore should I
Be but the essence of deformity,
A coward, did my very eyelids wink
100 At speaking out what I have dared to think.
Ah! rather let me like a madman run
Over some precipice; let the hot sun
Melt my Dedalian wings,[1] and drive me down
Convuls'd and headlong! Stay! an inward frown
105 Of conscience bids me be more calm awhile.
An ocean dim, sprinkled with many an isle,
Spreads awfully before me. How much toil!
How many days! what desperate turmoil!
Ere I can have explored its widenesses.
110 Ah, what a task! upon my bended knees,
I could unsay those—no, impossible!
Impossible!

　　　　　For sweet relief I'll dwell
On humbler thoughts, and let this strange assay
Begun in gentleness die so away.

315 E'en now all tumult from my bosom fades:
I turn full hearted to the friendly aids
That smooth the path of honour; brotherhood,
And friendliness the nurse of mutual good.
The hearty grasp that sends a pleasant sonnet
320 Into the brain ere one can think upon it;
The silence when some rhymes are coming out;
And when they're come, the very pleasant rout:
The message certain to be done to-morrow.
'Tis perhaps as well that it should be to borrow
325 Some precious book from out its snug retreat,
To cluster round it when we next shall meet.
Scarce can I scribble on; for lovely airs
Are fluttering round the room like doves in pairs;
Many delights of that glad day recalling,
330 When first my senses caught their tender falling.
And with these airs come forms of elegance
Stooping their shoulders o'er a horse's prance,
Careless, and grand—fingers soft and round
Parting luxuriant curls—and the swift bound
335 Of Bacchus from his chariot, when his eye
Made Ariadne's cheek look blushingly.[2]
Thus I remember all the pleasant flow
Of words at opening a portfolio.

Things such as these are ever harbingers
340 To trains of peaceful images: the stirs
Of a swan's neck unseen among the rushes:
A linnet starting all about the bushes:
A butterfly, with golden wings broad parted,
Nestling a rose, convuls'd as though it smarted
345 With over° pleasure—many, many more,   *too much*
Might I indulge at large in all my store
Of luxuries: yet I must not forget
Sleep, quiet with his poppy coronet:[3]
For what there may be worthy in these rhymes

---

[1] *Dedalian wings* According to Greek mythology, the sculptor Daedalus built wings of wax and feathers so that he and his son Icarus could escape from the island of Crete, where they were imprisoned. Icarus flew too close to the sun, and his wings melted, causing him to fall into the sea.

[2] *Of Bacchus … blushingly* Ariadne, daughter of King Minos of Crete, was abandoned by her lover, Theseus, on the island of Naxos. Bacchus, god of wine, found her there, consoled her, and married her (Ovid, *Metamorphses* 8.172–82). Keats would also have been familiar with the painting *Bacchus and Ariadne* (1523) by Venetian painter Titian (c. 1488–1576).

[3] *poppy coronet* The seed capsules of some species of poppy contain opium, and therefore were associated with sleep.

350 I partly owe to him: and thus, the chimes
Of friendly voices had just given place
To as sweet a silence, when I 'gan retrace
The pleasant day, upon a couch at ease.
It was a poet's house who keeps the keys
355 Of pleasure's temple.[1] Round about were hung
The glorious features of the bards who sung
In other ages—cold and sacred busts
Smiled at each other. Happy he who trusts
To clear Futurity his darling fame!
360 Then there were fauns and satyrs taking aim
At swelling apples with a frisky leap
And reaching fingers, 'mid a luscious heap
Of vine leaves. Then there rose to view a fane°   temple
Of liny° marble, and thereto a train   veined
365 Of nymphs approaching fairly o'er the sward:
One, loveliest, holding her white hand toward
The dazzling sun-rise: two sisters sweet
Bending their graceful figures till they meet
Over the trippings of a little child:
370 And some are hearing, eagerly, the wild
Thrilling liquidity of dewy piping.
See, in another picture, nymphs are wiping
Cherishingly Diana's[2] timorous limbs;
A fold of lawny mantle dabbling swims
375 At the bath's edge, and keeps a gentle motion
With the subsiding crystal: as when ocean
Heaves calmly its broad swelling smoothness o'er
Its rocky marge,° and balances once more   edge
The patient weeds; that now unshent°   unharmed
    by foam
380 Feel all about their undulating home.

Sappho's[3] meek head was there half smiling down
At nothing; just as though the earnest frown
Of over thinking had that moment gone
From off her brow, and left her all alone.

385 Great Alfred's[4] too, with anxious, pitying eyes,
As if he always listened to the sighs
Of the goaded world; and Kosciusko's[5] worn
By horrid suffrance—mightily forlorn.

Petrarch, outstepping from the shady green,
390 Starts at the sight of Laura;[6] nor can wean
His eyes from her sweet face. Most happy they!
For over them was seen a free display
Of out-spread wings, and from between them shone
The face of Poesy: from off her throne
395 She overlook'd things that I scarce could tell.
The very sense of where I was might well
Keep Sleep aloof: but more than that there came
Thought after thought to nourish up the flame
Within my breast; so that the morning light
400 Surprised me even from a sleepless night;
And up I rose refresh'd, and glad, and gay,
Resolving to begin that very day
These lines; and howsoever they be done,
I leave them as a father does his son.
—1817

On Seeing the Elgin Marbles[7]

My spirit is too weak; mortality
Weighs heavily on me like unwilling sleep,
And each imagined pinnacle and steep
Of godlike hardship, tells me I must die
5 Like a sick Eagle looking at the sky.
    Yet 'tis a gentle luxury to weep,
    That I have not the cloudy winds to keep

---

[1] *It was … temple* Poet Leigh Hunt kept a bed for Keats in his study. Hunt's cottage was filled with busts and pictures, on which the following descriptions are probably based.

[2] *Diana* Roman goddess of chastity, childbirth, and the hunt.

[3] *Sappho* Greek lyric poet of the sixth century BCE.

[4] *Great Alfred* Alfred the Great, King of Wessex from 871 to 899.

[5] *Kosciusko* Polish patriot Tadeusz Kosciusko (1746–1817), who led his countrymen in an uprising against Russia, and also fought for the United States Army in the American struggle for independence.

[6] *Petrarch … Laura* Italian poet Petrarch (1304–74) wrote odes and sonnets in celebration of his beloved, Laura.

[7] *Elgin Marbles* In 1806 Lord Elgin brought friezes and other sculptures that had decorated the exterior of the Parthenon, in Athens, to England. In 1816 the government purchased them for display in the British Museum, where they remain today.

Fresh for the opening of the morning's eye.
Such dim-conceived glories of the brain
0   Bring round the heart an indescribable feud;
So do these wonders a most dizzy pain,
    That mingles Grecian grandeur with the rude
Wasting of old Time—with a billowy main,°   *sea*
    A sun, a shadow of a magnitude.
—1817

On Sitting Down to Read
King Lear Once Again

O golden tongued Romance, with serene lute!
    Fair plumed Syren![1] Queen of far-away!
    Leave melodizing on this wintry day,
Shut up thine olden pages, and be mute:
5   Adieu! for once again the fierce dispute
    Betwixt damnation and impassion'd clay
    Must I burn through; once more humbly assay
The bitter-sweet of this Shakespearian fruit.
Chief Poet! and ye clouds of Albion,[2]
0   Begetters of our deep eternal theme,
When through the old oak forest I am gone,
    Let me not wander in a barren dream,
But when I am consumed in the fire,
Give me new Phœnix[3] wings to fly at my desire.
—1838

When I Have Fears That I May Cease to Be

When I have fears that I may cease to be
    Before my pen has glean'd my teeming brain,
Before high piled books, in charact'ry,[4]
    Hold like rich garners the full-ripen'd grain;

5   When I behold, upon the night's starr'd face,
    Huge cloudy symbols of a high romance,
And think that I may never live to trace
    Their shadows, with the magic hand of chance;
And when I feel, fair creature of an hour!
10   That I shall never look upon thee more,
Never have relish in the fairy power
    Of unreflecting love—then on the shore
Of the wide world I stand alone, and think
Till love and fame to nothingness do sink.
—1848 (WRITTEN 1818)

Epistle to John Hamilton Reynolds[5]

Dear Reynolds! as last night I lay in bed,
    There came before my eyes that wonted thread
Of shapes, and shadows, and remembrances,
That every other minute vex and please:
5   Things all disjointed come from north and south—
Two witch's eyes above a cherub's mouth,
Voltaire with casque and shield and habergeon,[6]
And Alexander[7] with his night-cap on;
Old Socrates[8] a-tying his cravat,
10   And Hazlitt playing with Miss Edgeworth's[9] cat;
And Junius Brutus, pretty well so so,[10]
Making the best of's way towards Soho.[11]

    Few are there who escape these visitings—
Perhaps one or two whose lives have patent wings,

---

[1] *Syren* Monster of classical mythology who is half woman, half serpent, and whose enchanted singing lures sailors to their deaths.

[2] *Albion* England.

[3] *Phœnix* Mythical Egyptian bird that is consumed by fire, and then reborn, once every 500 years.

[4] *charact'ry* Symbols or characters.

[5] *John Hamilton Reynolds* Poet and lawyer (1794–1852) who was a close friend of Keats. Reynolds was ill at the time, and Keats sent him this verse letter to cheer him.

[6] *Voltaire* French philosopher (1694–1778); *casque* Helmet; *habergeon* Sleeveless jacket of chain mail.

[7] *Alexander* Poet Alexander Pope (1688–1744).

[8] *Socrates* Greek philosopher of the fifth century BCE.

[9] *Hazlitt* Painter and writer William Hazlitt (1778–1830); *Miss Edgeworth* Novelist Maria Edgeworth (1767–1849).

[10] *Junius Brutus* Actor Junius Brutus Booth (1796–1852); *so so* Tipsy.

[11] *Soho* Area in London, then rather disreputable.

15 And through whose curtains peeps no hellish nose,
No wild-boar tushes,° and no mermaid's toes;   *tusks*
But flowers bursting out with lusty pride,
And young Æolian harps[1] personified;
Some, Titian[2] colours touch'd into real life—
20 The sacrifice goes on; the pontiff knife
Gleams in the sun, the milk-white heifer lows,
The pipes go shrilly, the libation flows:
A white sail shows above the green-head cliff,
Moves round the point, and throws her anchor stiff;
25 The mariners join hymn with those on land.

      You know the Enchanted Castle[3]—it doth stand
Upon a rock, on the border of a lake,
Nested in trees, which all do seem to shake
From some old magic like Urganda's sword.[4]
30 O Phoebus![5] that I had thy sacred word
To show this Castle, in fair dreaming wise,
Unto my friend, while sick and ill he lies!

      You know it well enough, where it doth seem
A mossy place, a Merlin's Hall,[6] a dream;
35 You know the clear lake, and the little isles,
The mountains blue, and cold near neighbour rills,
All which elsewhere are but half animate;
There do they look alive to love and hate,
To smiles and frowns; they seem a lifted mound
40 Above some giant, pulsing underground.

      Part of the building was a chosen see,°   *dwelling-place*
Built by a banish'd Santon° of Chaldee;   *holy man*
The other part, two thousand years from him,

Was built by Cuthbert de Saint Aldebrim;[7]
45 Then there's a little wing, far from the sun,
Built by a Lapland witch[8] turn'd maudlin nun;
And many other juts of aged stone
Founded with many a mason-devil's groan.

      The doors all look as if they oped themselves,
50 The windows as if latched by fays° and elves,   *fairies*
And from them comes a silver flash of light,
As from the westward of a summer's night;
Or like a beauteous woman's large blue eyes
Gone mad through olden songs and poesies.

55   See! what is coming from the distance dim!
A golden galley all in silken trim!
Three rows of oars are lightening, moment whiles,
Into the verd'rous bosoms of those isles;
Towards the shade, under the Castle wall,
60 It comes in silence—now 'tis hidden all.
The clarion sounds, and from a postern-gate
An echo of sweet music doth create
A fear in the poor herdsman, who doth bring
His beasts to trouble the enchanted spring—
65 He tells of the sweet music, and the spot,
To all his friends, and they believe him not.

      O that our dreamings all, of sleep or wake,
Would all their colours from the sunset take:
From something of material sublime,
70 Rather than shadow our own soul's daytime
In the dark void of night. For in the world
We jostle—but my flag is not unfurl'd
On the admiral-staff—and to philosophise
I dare not yet! Oh, never will the prize,
75 High reason, and the lore of good and ill,
Be my award! Things cannot to the will
Be settled, but they tease us out of thought;
Or is it that imagination brought
Beyond its proper bound, yet still confin'd,
80 Lost in a sort of Purgatory blind,

---

[1] *Æolian harps*   Harps that produce sound when exposed to the wind or open air. From Æolus, the Greek god of the winds.

[2] *Titian*   I.e., rich; in the style of Titian, a Venetian Renaissance painter whose work was characterized by bold colors. The following lines most likely describe *Sacrifice to Apollo*, by French painter Claude Lorrain (1600–82).

[3] *the Enchanted Castle*   Painting by Claude Lorrain.

[4] *Urganda's sword*   Enchantress figure in *Amadis of Gaul*, a fifteenth-century romance.

[5] *Phoebus*   Apollo, Greek god of poetry and of the sun.

[6] *Merlin's Hall*   I.e., a hall built by magicians such as the sorcerer Merlin, from Arthurian legend.

[7] *Cuthbert … Aldebrim*   Character invented by Keats.

[8] *Lapland witch*   Lapland was supposed to be the dwelling-place of witches.

Cannot refer to any standard law
Of either earth or heaven? It is a flaw
In happiness, to see beyond our bourn—
It forces us in summer skies to mourn,
35   It spoils the singing of the nightingale.

Dear Reynolds! I have a mysterious tale,
And cannot speak it: the first page I read
Upon a lampit° rock of green sea-weed   limpet
Among the breakers; 'twas a quiet eve,
90   The rocks were silent, the wide sea did weave
An untumultuous fringe of silver foam
Along the flat brown sand; I was at home
And should have been most happy—but I saw
Too far into the sea, where every maw°   throat, gullet
95   The greater on the less feeds evermore.
But I saw too distinct into the core
Of an eternal fierce destruction,
And so from happiness I far was gone.
Still am I sick of it, and tho', to-day,
100   I've gather'd young spring-leaves, and flowers gay
Of periwinkle and wild strawberry,
Still do I that most fierce destruction see—
The shark at savage prey, the hawk at pounce,
The gentle robin, like a pard° or ounce,°   leopard / lynx
105   Ravening a worm—Away, ye horrid moods!
Moods of one's mind! You know I hate them well.
You know I'd sooner be a clapping bell
To some Kamschatkan[1] missionary church,
Than with these horrid moods be left i'the lurch.
110   Do you get health—and Tom the same—I'll dance,
And from detested moods in new romance[2]
Take refuge—Of bad lines a centaine[3] dose
Is sure enough—and so "here follows prose."[4]
—1848

---

[1] *Kamschatkan*   From the Kamchatka Peninsula in Siberia.

[2] *new romance*   Probably Keats's *Isabella* (1820), a romance based
on a tale from Italian poet Giovanni Boccaccio's *Decameron* (written
c. 1349–53).

[3] *centaine*   Company of one hundred.

[4] *here follows prose*   See Shakespeare's *Twelfth Night* 2.5.154.

To Homer[5]

S tanding aloof in giant ignorance,
    Of thee I hear and of the Cyclades,[6]
As one who sits ashore and longs perchance
    To visit dolphin-coral in deep seas.
5   So thou wast blind![7]—but then the veil was rent;
    For Jove[8] uncurtain'd Heaven to let thee live,
And Neptune[9] made for thee a spumy[10] tent,
    And Pan[11] made sing for thee his forest-hive;
Aye, on the shores of darkness there is light,
10   And precipices show untrodden green;
There is a budding morrow in midnight;
    There is a triple sight in blindness keen;
Such seeing hast thou, as it once befell
To Dian, Queen of Earth, and Heaven, and Hell.[12]
—1848 (WRITTEN C. 1818)

The Eve of St. Agnes[13]

I

S t. Agnes' Eve—Ah, bitter chill it was!
    The owl, for all his feathers, was a-cold;
The hare limp'd trembling through the frozen grass,

---

[5] *Homer*   Early Greek poet, believed to be the author of *The Iliad* and
Odyssey.

[6] *Cyclades*   Group of islands in the Aegean Sea, off the southeast coast
of Greece.

[7] *thou wast blind*   Homer was said to have been blind.

[8] *Jove*   Roman King of the gods.

[9] *Neptune*   Roman god of the sea.

[10] *spumy*   Covered in sea foam.

[11] *Pan*   Greek shepherd god of nature who was half goat and half
man. After the nymph Syrinx turned herself into a bed of reeds in
order to escape him, Pan created an instrument (the panpipe) out of
the reeds.

[12] *To Dian ... Hell*   Diana was sometimes envisioned as a multi-
figured goddess, presiding over the moon, childbirth, the hunt, and
hell.

[13] *St. Agnes*   Fourth-century Christian martyr, executed at the age of
thirteen, who is the patron saint of virgins. It was tradition that young
women could obtain a vision of their future husbands if they performed the proper rituals on 20 January, the night before St. Agnes's
Feast Day.

And silent was the flock in woolly fold:
5   Numb were the Beadsman's[1] fingers, while he told
His rosary, and while his frosted breath,
Like pious incense from a censer[2] old,
Seem'd taking flight for heaven, without a death,
Past the sweet Virgin's[3] picture, while his prayer he
    saith.

2

10   His prayer he saith, this patient, holy man;
Then takes his lamp, and riseth from his knees,
And back returneth, meagre, barefoot, wan,
Along the chapel aisle by slow degrees:
The sculptur'd dead, on each side, seem to freeze,
15   Emprison'd in black, purgatorial rails:
Knights, ladies, praying in dumb orat'ries,°   *chapels*
He passeth by; and his weak spirit fails
To think how they may ache in icy hoods and mails.

3

Northward he turneth through a little door,
20   And scarce three steps, ere Music's golden tongue
Flatter'd to tears this aged man and poor;
But no—already had his deathbell rung:
The joys of all his life were said and sung:
His was harsh penance on St. Agnes' Eve:
25   Another way he went, and soon among
Rough ashes sat he for his soul's reprieve,
And all night kept awake, for sinners' sake to grieve.

4

That ancient Beadsman heard the prelude soft;
And so it chanc'd, for many a door was wide,
30   From hurry to and fro. Soon, up aloft,
The silver, snarling trumpets 'gan to chide:
The level chambers, ready with their pride,
Were glowing to receive a thousand guests:
The carved angels, ever eager-eyed,
35   Star'd, where upon their heads the cornice rests,

With hair blown back, and wings put cross-wise on
    their breasts.

5

At length burst in the argent[4] revelry,
With plume, tiara, and all rich array,
Numerous as shadows haunting fairily
40   The brain, new stuff'd, in youth, with triumphs gay
Of old romance. These let us wish away,
And turn, sole-thoughted, to one Lady there,
Whose heart had brooded, all that wintry day,
On love, and wing'd St. Agnes' saintly care,
45   As she had heard old dames full many times declare.

6

They told her how, upon St. Agnes' Eve,
Young virgins might have visions of delight,
And soft adorings from their loves receive
Upon the honey'd middle of the night,
50   If ceremonies due they did aright;°   *arranged properly*
As, supperless to bed they must retire,
And couch supine their beauties, lily white;
Nor look behind, nor sideways, but require
Of Heaven with upward eyes for all that they desire.

7

55   Full of this whim was thoughtful Madeline:
The music, yearning like a God in pain,
She scarcely heard: her maiden eyes divine,
Fix'd on the floor, saw many a sweeping train
Pass by—she heeded not at all: in vain
60   Came many a tiptoe, amorous cavalier,
And back retir'd; not cool'd by high disdain,
But she saw not: her heart was otherwhere:
She sigh'd for Agnes' dreams, the sweetest of the year.

8

She danc'd along with vague, regardless eyes,
65   Anxious her lips, her breathing quick and short:
The hallow'd hour was near at hand: she sighs
Amid the timbrels,° and the throng'd resort   *tambourines*
Of whisperers in anger, or in sport;
'Mid looks of love, defiance, hate, and scorn,

---

[1] *Beadsman* Pensioner paid to say prayers for the souls of his benefactors. He "tells," or counts, the beads of his rosary, saying a prayer at each bead.

[2] *censer* Incense burner.

[3] *Virgin* I.e., Mary, virgin mother of Christ.

[4] *argent* Adorned with silver.

70 Hoodwink'd° with faery fancy; all   *blindfolded*
      amort,°   *dead*
   Save to St. Agnes and her lambs unshorn,[1]
   And all the bliss to be before to-morrow morn.

9

   So, purposing each moment to retire,
   She linger'd still. Meantime, across the moors,
75 Had come young Porphyro, with heart on fire
   For Madeline. Beside the portal doors,
   Buttress'd from moonlight, stands he, and implores
   All saints to give him sight of Madeline,
   But for one moment in the tedious hours,
80 That he might gaze and worship all unseen;
   Perchance speak, kneel, touch, kiss—in sooth such
      things have been.

10

   He ventures in: let no buzz'd whisper tell:
   All eyes be muffled, or a hundred swords
   Will storm his heart, Love's fev'rous citadel:
85 For him, those chambers held barbarian hordes,
   Hyena foemen, and hot-blooded lords,
   Whose very dogs would execrations howl
   Against his lineage: not one breast affords
   Him any mercy, in that mansion foul,
90 Save one old beldame,[2] weak in body and in soul.

11

   Ah, happy chance! the aged creature came,
   Shuffling along with ivory-headed wand,°   *staff*
   To where he stood, hid from the torch's flame,
   Behind a broad hall-pillar, far beyond
95 The sound of merriment and chorus bland:°   *soft*
   He startled her; but soon she knew his face,
   And grasp'd his fingers in her palsied hand,
   Saying, "Mercy, Porphyro! hie thee from this place;
   They are all here to-night, the whole blood-thirsty race!"

12

100 "Get hence! get hence! there's dwarfish Hildebrand;
   He had a fever late, and in the fit
   He cursed thee and thine, both house and land:
   Then there's that old Lord Maurice, not a whit
   More tame for his gray hairs—Alas me! flit!
105 Flit like a ghost away."—"Ah, Gossip[3] dear,
   We're safe enough; here in this arm-chair sit,
   And tell me how"—"Good Saints! not here, not here;
   Follow me, child, or else these stones will be thy bier."

13

   He follow'd through a lowly arched way,
110 Brushing the cobwebs with his lofty plume,
   And as she mutter'd "Well-a—well-a-day!"
   He found him in a little moonlight room,
   Pale, lattic'd, chill, and silent as a tomb.
   "Now tell me where is Madeline," said he,
115 "O tell me, Angela, by the holy loom
   Which none but secret sisterhood may see,
   When they St. Agnes' wool are weaving piously."

14

   "St. Agnes! Ah! it is St. Agnes' Eve—
   Yet men will murder upon holy days:
120 Thou must hold water in a witch's sieve,
   And be liege-lord of all the Elves and Fays,°   *fairies*
   To venture so: it fills me with amaze
   To see thee, Porphyro!—St. Agnes' Eve!
   God's help! my lady fair the conjuror plays
125 This very night: good angels her deceive!
   But let me laugh awhile, I've mickle° time   *much*
      to grieve."

15

   Feebly she laugheth in the languid moon,
   While Porphyro upon her face doth look,
   Like puzzled urchin on an aged crone
130 Who keepeth clos'd a wond'rous riddle-book,
   As spectacled she sits in chimney nook.
   But soon his eyes grew brilliant, when she told
   His lady's purpose; and he scarce could
      brook°   *prevent*

---

1 *St. Agnes ... unshorn* The Latin for lamb is *agnus*; thus the
traditional association of St. Agnes with lambs, which also carry
connotations of whiteness and purity.

2 *beldame* Grandmother, old woman, or elderly nurse.

3 *Gossip* Good friend; godmother.

Tears, at the thought of those enchantments cold
135 And Madeline asleep in lap of legends old.

16

Sudden a thought came like a full-blown rose,
Flushing his brow, and in his pained heart
Made purple riot: then doth he propose
A stratagem, that makes the beldame start:
140 "A cruel man and impious thou art:
Sweet lady, let her pray, and sleep, and dream
Alone with her good angels, far apart
From wicked men like thee. Go, go!—I deem
Thou canst not surely be the same that thou didst seem."

17

145 "I will not harm her, by all saints I swear,"
Quoth Porphyro: "O may I ne'er find grace
When my weak voice shall whisper its last prayer,
If one of her soft ringlets I displace,
Or look with ruffian passion in her face:
150 Good Angela, believe me by these tears;
Or I will, even in a moment's space,
Awake, with horrid shout, my foemen's ears,
And beard° them, though they be more   *oppose*
    fang'd than wolves and bears."

18

"Ah! why wilt thou affright a feeble soul?
155 A poor, weak, palsy-stricken, churchyard thing,
Whose passing-bell may ere the midnight toll;
Whose prayers for thee, each morn and evening,
Were never miss'd."—Thus plaining,°   *complaining*
    doth she bring
A gentler speech from burning Porphyro;
160 So woeful, and of such deep sorrowing,
That Angela gives promise she will do
Whatever he shall wish, betide her weal or woe.

19

Which was, to lead him, in close secrecy,
Even to Madeline's chamber, and there hide
165 Him in a closet, of such privacy
That he might see her beauty unespied,
And win perhaps that night a peerless bride,

While legion'd fairies pac'd the coverlet,
And pale enchantment held her sleepy-eyed.
170 Never on such a night have lovers met,
Since Merlin paid his Demon all the monstrous debt.[1]

20

"It shall be as thou wishest," said the Dame:
"All cates° and dainties shall be stored there   *delicacies*
Quickly on this feast-night: by the tambour frame[2]
175 Her own lute thou wilt see: no time to spare,
For I am slow and feeble, and scarce dare
On such a catering trust my dizzy head.
Wait here, my child, with patience; kneel in prayer
The while: Ah! thou must needs the lady wed,
180 Or may I never leave my grave among the dead."

21

So saying, she hobbled off with busy fear.
The lover's endless minutes slowly pass'd:
The dame return'd, and whisper'd in his ear
To follow her; with aged eyes aghast
185 From fright of dim espial. Safe at last,
Through many a dusky gallery, they gain
The maiden's chamber, silken, hush'd, and chaste;
Where Porphyro took covert, pleas'd amain.°   *completely*
His poor guide hurried back with agues°   *fever*
    in her brain.

22

Her falt'ring hand upon the balustrade,
190 Old Angela was feeling for the stair,
When Madeline, St. Agnes' charmed maid,
Rose, like a mission'd spirit, unaware:
With silver taper's light, and pious care,
She turn'd, and down the aged gossip led
195 To a safe level matting. Now prepare,
Young Porphyro, for gazing on that bed;
She comes, she comes again, like ring-dove
    fray'd° and fled.   *frightened*

---

1 *Since ... debt* Probably a reference to the episode in Arthurian legend in which the enchanter Merlin falls in love with the enchantress Vivien, or Nimue, who turns one of his spells against him and imprisons him in a cave.

2 *tambour frame* Circular frame for embroidery.

23

Out went the taper° as she hurried in;   *candle*
Its little smoke, in pallid moonshine, died:
She clos'd the door, she panted, all akin
To spirits of the air, and visions wide:
No uttered syllable, or, woe betide!
But to her heart, her heart was voluble,
Paining with eloquence her balmy side;
As though a tongueless nightingale should swell
Her throat in vain, and die, heart-stifled, in her dell.

24

A casement high and triple-arch'd there was,
All garlanded with carven imag'ries
Of fruits, and flowers, and bunches of knot-grass,
And diamonded with panes of quaint device,
Innumerable of stains and splendid dyes,
As are the tiger-moth's deep-damask'd wings;
And in the midst, 'mong thousand heraldries,[1]
And twilight saints, and dim emblazonings,
A shielded scutcheon blush'd with blood of queens
        and kings.[2]

25

Full on this casement shone the wintry moon,
And threw warm gules[3] on Madeline's fair breast,
As down she knelt for heaven's grace and boon;°   *blessing*
Rose-bloom fell on her hands, together prest,
And on her silver cross soft amethyst,
And on her hair a glory, like a saint:
She seem'd a splendid angel, newly drest,
Save wings, for heaven—Porphyro grew faint:
She knelt, so pure a thing, so free from mortal taint.

26

Anon his heart revives: her vespers° done,   *evening prayers*
Of all its wreathed pearls her hair she frees;
Unclasps her warmed jewels one by one;
Loosens her fragrant boddice; by degrees
Her rich attire creeps rustling to her knees:

Half-hidden, like a mermaid in sea-weed,
Pensive awhile she dreams awake, and sees,
In fancy, fair St. Agnes in her bed,
But dares not look behind, or all the charm is fled.

27

Soon, trembling in her soft and chilly nest,
In sort of wakeful swoon, perplex'd[4] she lay,
Until the poppied° warmth of sleep oppress'd   *narcotic*
Her soothed limbs, and soul fatigued away;
Flown, like a thought, until the morrow-day;
Blissfully haven'd both from joy and pain;
Clasp'd like a missal[5] where swart Paynims[6] pray;
Blinded alike from sunshine and from rain,
As though a rose should shut, and be a bud again.

28

Stol'n to this paradise, and so entranced,
Porphyro gazed upon her empty dress,
And listen'd to her breathing, if it chanced
To wake into a slumberous tenderness;
Which when he heard, that minute did he bless,
And breath'd himself: then from the closet crept,
Noiseless as fear in a wide wilderness,
And over the hush'd carpet, silent, stept,
And 'tween the curtains peep'd, where, lo!—how fast
        she slept.

29

Then by the bed-side, where the faded moon
Made a dim, silver twilight, soft he set
A table, and, half anguish'd, threw thereon
A cloth of woven crimson, gold, and jet—
O for some drowsy Morphean amulet![7]
The boisterous, midnight, festive clarion,°   *trumpet*
The kettle-drum, and far-heard clarinet,
Affray his ears, though but in dying tone—
The hall door shuts again, and all the noise is gone.

---

1 *heraldries* Emblems of rank and genealogy.

2 *scutcheon* I.e., escutcheon: shield; *blush'd ... kings* I.e., indicates she is of royal blood.

3 *gules* Red bars (a heraldic device).

4 *perplex'd* I.e., between sleep and waking.

5 *missal* Christian mass- or prayer-book.

6 *swart Paynims* Dark-skinned pagans.

7 *Morphean amulet* Sleep-inducing medicine or charm. (Morpheus is the god of dreams.)

30

And still she slept an azure-lidded sleep,
In blanched linen, smooth, and lavender'd,
While he from forth the closet brought a heap
265   Of candied apple, quince, and plum, and gourd;° *melon*
With jellies soother[1] than the creamy curd,
And lucent° syrops, tinct° with cinnamon; *clear / imbued*
Manna[2] and dates, in argosy[3] transferr'd
From Fez;[4] and spiced dainties, every one,
270   From silken Samarkand[5] to cedar'd Lebanon.

31

These delicates he heap'd with glowing hand
On golden dishes and in baskets bright
Of wreathed silver: sumptuous they stand
In the retired quiet of the night,
275   Filling the chilly room with perfume light.
"And now, my love, my seraph° fair, awake! *angel*
Thou art my heaven, and I thine eremite:° *hermit*
Open thine eyes, for meek St. Agnes' sake,
Or I shall drowse beside thee, so my soul doth ache."

32

280   Thus whispering, his warm, unnerved arm
Sank in her pillow. Shaded was her dream
By the dusk curtains—'twas a midnight charm
Impossible to melt as iced stream:
The lustrous salvers° in the moonlight gleam; *trays*
285   Broad golden fringe upon the carpet lies:
It seem'd he never, never could redeem
From such a stedfast spell his lady's eyes;
So mus'd awhile, entoil'd in woofed° phantasies. *woven*

33

Awakening up, he took her hollow lute—
290   Tumultuous—and, in chords that tenderest be,
He play'd an ancient ditty, long since mute,

---

[1]   *soother* A word of Keats's own invention, meaning more soothing, softer.

[2]   *Manna* Dried, sweet gum taken from various plants.

[3]   *argosy* Merchant vessels.

[4]   *Fez* City in Morocco.

[5]   *Samarkand* City in Uzbekistan.

In Provence call'd, "La belle dame sans mercy":[6]
Close to her ear touching the melody—
Wherewith disturb'd, she utter'd a soft moan:
295   He ceased—she panted quick—and suddenly
Her blue affrayed eyes wide open shone:
Upon his knees he sank, pale as smooth-sculptured stone.

34

Her eyes were open, but she still beheld,
Now wide awake, the vision of her sleep:
300   There was a painful change, that nigh expell'd
The blisses of her dream so pure and deep,
At which fair Madeline began to weep,
And moan forth witless words with many a sigh;
While still her gaze on Porphyro would keep;
305   Who knelt, with joined hands and piteous eye,
Fearing to move or speak, she look'd so dreamingly.

35

"Ah, Porphyro!" said she, "but even now
Thy voice was at sweet tremble in mine ear,
Made tuneable with every sweetest vow;
310   And those sad eyes were spiritual and clear:
How chang'd thou art! how pallid, chill, and drear!
Give me that voice again, my Porphyro,
Those looks immortal, those complainings° *lamentings*
   dear!
Oh leave me not in this eternal woe,
315   For if thou diest, my Love, I know not where to go."

36

Beyond a mortal man impassion'd far
At these voluptuous accents, he arose,
Ethereal, flush'd, and like a throbbing star
Seen mid the sapphire heaven's deep repose;
320   Into her dream he melted, as the rose
Blendeth its odour with the violet—
Solution sweet: meantime the frost-wind blows
Like Love's alarum° pattering the sharp sleet *warning bell*
Against the window-panes; St. Agnes' moon hath set.

---

[6]   *La belle ... mercy* French: The beautiful woman without pity. Title of a long poem by medieval poet Alain Chartier (c. 1385–1433); Keats had not yet written his own poem with this title.

37

325 'Tis dark: quick pattereth the flaw-blown°   *gust-driven*
  sleet:
"This is no dream, my bride, my Madeline!"
'Tis dark: the iced gusts still rave and beat:
"No dream, alas! alas! and woe is mine!
Porphyro will leave me here to fade and pine.
330 Cruel! what traitor could thee hither bring?
I curse not, for my heart is lost in thine,
Though thou forsakest a deceived thing—
A dove forlorn and lost with sick unpruned wing."

38

"My Madeline! sweet dreamer! lovely bride!
335 Say, may I be for aye° thy vassal blest?   *ever*
Thy beauty's shield, heart-shap'd and
  vermeil° dyed?   *vermilion (red)*
Ah, silver shrine, here will I take my rest
After so many hours of toil and quest,
A famish'd pilgrim, saved by miracle.
340 Though I have found, I will not rob thy nest
Saving of thy sweet self; if thou think'st well
To trust, fair Madeline, to no rude infidel.

39

"Hark! 'tis an elfin-storm from faery land,
Of haggard° seeming, but a boon indeed: *wild*
345 Arise—arise! the morning is at hand;
The bloated wassaillers° will never heed—   *drinkers*
Let us away, my love, with happy speed;
There are no ears to hear, or eyes to see—
Drown'd all in Rhenish and the sleepy mead:[1]
350 Awake! arise! my love, and fearless be,
For o'er the southern moors I have a home for thee."

40

She hurried at his words, beset with fears,
For there were sleeping dragons all around,
At glaring watch, perhaps, with ready spears—
355 Down the wide stairs a darkling[2] way they found.
In all the house was heard no human sound.

A chain-droop'd lamp was flickering by each door;
The arras,° rich with horseman, hawk, and   *tapestries*
  hound,
Flutter'd in the besieging wind's uproar;
360 And the long carpets rose along the gusty floor.

41

They glide, like phantoms, into the wide hall;
Like phantoms, to the iron porch, they glide;
Where lay the Porter, in uneasy sprawl,
With a huge empty flaggon by his side:
365 The wakeful bloodhound rose, and shook his hide,
But his sagacious eye an inmate owns:
By one, and one, the bolts full easy slide—
The chains lie silent on the footworn stones—
The key turns, and the door upon its hinges groans.

42

370 And they are gone: ay, ages long ago
These lovers fled away into the storm.
That night the Baron dreamt of many a woe,
And all his warrior-guests, with shade and form
Of witch, and demon, and large coffin-worm,
375 Were long be-nightmar'd. Angela the old
Died palsy-twitch'd, with meagre face deform;
The Beadsman, after thousand aves[3] told,
For aye unsought for slept among his ashes cold.
—1820

Bright Star

Bright star, would I were steadfast as thou art—
  Not in lone splendour hung aloft the night
And watching, with eternal lids apart,
  Like nature's patient, sleepless Eremite,°   *hermit*
5 The moving waters at their priestlike task
  Of pure ablution[4] round earth's human shores,
Or gazing on the new soft fallen mask
  Of snow upon the mountains and the moors—
No—yet still steadfast, still unchangeable,

---

[1] *Rhenish* Wine from the Rhine region; *mead* Alcoholic beverage made from fermented honey and water.

[2] *darkling* Obscure, gloomy.

[3] *aves* Latin: abbreviation for *Ave Marias*, or Hail Marys, prayers to the Virgin Mary.

[4] *ablution* Religious ritual washing of the body.

10   Pillow'd upon my fair love's ripening breast,
To feel for ever its soft fall and swell,
      Awake for ever in a sweet unrest,
Still, still to hear her tender-taken breath,
And so live ever—or else swoon to death.
—1838 (WRITTEN 1819)

La Belle Dame sans Merci[1]

O what can ail thee, knight-at-arms,
      Alone and palely loitering?
The sedge[2] has wither'd from the lake,
      And no birds sing.

5   O what can ail thee, knight-at-arms,
      So haggard, and so woe-begone?
The squirrel's granary is full,
      And the harvest's done.

I see a lily[3] on thy brow,
10   With anguish moist and fever dew
And on thy cheeks a fading rose
      Fast withereth too.

I met a lady in the meads,°   meadows
      Full beautiful—a faery's child,
15   Her hair was long, her foot was light,
      And her eyes were wild.

I made a garland for her head,
      And bracelets too, and fragrant zone;°   belt
She look'd at me as she did love,
20   And made sweet moan.

I set her on my pacing steed,
      And nothing else saw all day long,
For sidelong would she bend and sing
      A faery's song.

25   She found me roots of relish sweet,
      And honey wild, and manna dew,[4]
And sure in language strange she said
      "I love thee true."

She took me to her elfin grot,°   grotto
30   And there she wept and sigh'd full sore,
And there I shut her wild wild eyes
      With kisses four.

And there she lulled me asleep,
      And there I dream'd—Ah! woe betide!
35   The latest° dream I ever dream'd   last
      On the cold hill side.

I saw pale kings and princes too,
      Pale warriors, death-pale were they all;
They cried, "La belle dame sans merci
40   Hath thee in thrall!"°   captivity

I saw their starved lips in the gloam,°   twilight
      With horrid warning gaped wide,
And I awoke, and found me here,
      On the cold hill's side.

45   And this is why I sojourn here,
      Alone and palely loitering,
Though the sedge is wither'd from the lake,
      And no birds sing.
—1848 (WRITTEN 1819)

---

[1] *La Belle Dame sans Merci*   French: The beautiful lady without pity.
This original version of the poem, found in a journal letter to George
and Georgiana Keats, was first published in 1848. Keats's revised
version was published in 1820.

[2] *sedge* Rush-like grass.

[3] *lily* Flower traditionally symbolic of death.

---

[4] *manna dew* See Exodus 16, in which God provides the Israelites
with a food that falls from heaven, called manna.

La Belle Dame sans Mercy[1]

Ah, what can ail thee, wretched wight,°   *being*
　　Alone and palely loitering;
The sedge[2] is wither'd from the lake,
　　And no birds sing.

5　Ah, what can ail thee, wretched wight,
　　So haggard and so woe-begone?
The squirrel's granary is full,
　　And the harvest's done.

I see a lily[3] on thy brow,
10　With anguish moist and fever dew;
And on thy cheek a fading rose
　　Fast withereth too.

I met a lady in the meads°   *meadows*
　　Full beautiful, a fairy's child;
15　Her hair was long, her foot was light,
　　And her eyes were wild.

I set her on my pacing steed,
　　And nothing else saw all day long;
For sideways would she lean, and sing
20　A fairy's song.

I made a garland for her head,
　　And bracelets too, and fragrant zone:°   *belt*
She look'd at me as she did love,
　　And made sweet moan.

25　She found me roots of relish sweet,
　　And honey wild, and manna[4] dew;
And sure in language strange she said,
　　"I love thee true."

She took me to her elfin grot,°   *grotto*
30　And there she gaz'd and sighed deep.
And there I shut her wild sad eyes—
　　So kiss'd to sleep.

And there we slumber'd on the moss,
　　And there I dream'd, ah woe betide,
35　The latest dream I ever dream'd
　　On the cold hill side.

I saw pale kings, and princes too,
　　Pale warriors, death-pale were they all;
Who cry'd—"La belle dame sans mercy
40　Hath thee in thrall!"°   *captivity*

I saw their starv'd lips in the gloom
　　With horrid warning gaped wide,
And I awoke, and found me here
　　On the cold hill side.

45　And this is why I sojourn here
　　Alone and palely loitering,
Though the sedge is wither'd from the lake,
　　And no birds sing.
—1820 (WRITTEN 1819)

Incipit altera Sonneta[5]

I have been endeavouring to discover a better sonnet stanza than we have. The legitimate[6] does not suit the language over-well from the pouncing rhymes—the other kind appears too elegaiac—and the couplet at the end of it has seldom a pleasing effect—I do not pretend to have succeeded—it will explain itself—

If by dull rhymes our English must be chain'd
　　And, like Andromeda,[7] the Sonnet sweet

1　*La Belle … Mercy*   French: The beautiful lady without pity. This version of the poem, a revision of "La Belle Dame sans Merci," was published in 1820.

2　*sedge*   Rush-like grass.

3　*lily*   Flower traditionally symbolic of death.

4　*manna*   See Exodus 16, in which God provides the Israelites with a food that falls from heaven, called manna.

5　*Incipit altera Sonneta*   Latin: Another sonnet begins.

6　*The legitimate*   I.e., the Petrarchan sonnet. The "other kind" to which Keats refers is the Shakespearean sonnet.

7　*Andromeda*   In Greek myth, Andromeda is tied to a rock to be devoured by a sea serpent after her mother boasts that she is more beautiful than the sea nymphs. Perseus, on his winged horse Pegasus (a symbol of poetic inspiration), rescues her.

Fetter'd in spite of pained loveliness;
Let us find out, if we must be constrain'd
5   Sandals more interwoven & complete
To fit the naked foot of Poesy;
Let us inspect the Lyre,[1] & weigh the stress
Of every chord & see what may be gain'd
By ear industrious & attention meet;°   *fitting*
10   Misers of sound & syllable, no less
Than Midas of his coinage,[2] let us be
Jealous of dead leaves in the bay wreath Crown;[3]
So if we may not let the Muse[4] be free,
She will be bound with Garlands of her own.
—1836 (WRITTEN 1819)

Ode to Psyche[5]

O Goddess! hear these tuneless numbers, wrung
By sweet enforcement and remembrance dear,
And pardon that thy secrets should be sung
Even into thine own soft-conched[6] ear:
5   Surely I dreamt to-day, or did I see
The winged Psyche with awaken'd eyes?
I wander'd in a forest thoughtlessly,
And, on the sudden, fainting with surprise,
Saw two fair creatures, couched side by side
10   In deepest grass, beneath the whisp'ring roof
Of leaves and trembled blossoms, where there ran
A brooklet, scarce espied:

'Mid hush'd, cool-rooted flowers, fragrant-eyed,
Blue, silver-white, and budded Tyrian,[7]
15   They lay calm-breathing on the bedded grass;
Their arms embraced, and their pinions° too;   *wings*
Their lips touch'd not, but had not bade adieu,
As if disjoined by soft-handed slumber,
And ready still past kisses to outnumber
20   At tender eye-dawn of aurorean[8] love:
The winged boy° I knew;   *Cupid*
But who wast thou, O happy, happy dove?
His Psyche true!

O latest born and liveliest vision far
25   Of all Olympus'[9] faded hierarchy!
Fairer than Phœbe's[10] sapphire-region'd star,
Or Vesper,[11] amorous glow-worm of the sky;
Fairer than these, though temple thou hast none,
Nor altar heap'd with flowers;
30   Nor virgin-choir to make delicious moan
Upon the midnight hours;
No voice, no lute, no pipe, no incense sweet
From chain-swung censer° teeming;   *incense burner*
No shrine, no grove, no oracle, no heat
35   Of pale-mouth'd prophet dreaming.

O brightest! Though too late for antique vows,
Too, too late for the fond believing
lyre,°   *stringed instrument*
When holy were the haunted forest boughs,
Holy the air, the water, and the fire;
40   Yet even in these days so far retir'd
From happy pieties, thy lucent fans,°   *wings*
Fluttering among the faint Olympians,
I see, and sing, by my own eyes inspired.
So let me be thy choir, and make a moan

[1]   *Lyre*   Stringed instrument.

[2]   *Midas ... coinage*   In Ovid's *Metamorphoses*, King Midas of Phrygia gets his wish that everything he touches will turn to gold.

[3]   *bay wreath Crown*   Wreaths made of leaves of the bay laurel were traditionally bestowed upon those who distinguished themselves in poetry.

[4]   *Muse*   One of nine daughters of Zeus and Mnemosyne, each of whom presided over and provided inspiration for an aspect of learning or the arts.

[5]   *Psyche*   In classical mythology, a young woman who was beloved by Cupid, winged god of love and son of Venus. After winning over Venus, who was jealous of Psyche's beauty, Psyche was granted immortality by Jupiter. In Greek myth she is often a personification of the soul: her name in Greek means soul or mind as well as butterfly.

[6]   *soft-conched*   Shaped like a conch shell, but soft.

[7]   *Tyrian*   Purple. From the Phoenician city of Tyre, where purple or crimson dyes were made in ancient times.

[8]   *aurorean*   I.e., dawning. Aurora was the goddess of the dawn.

[9]   *Olympus*   Mount Olympus, home of the gods.

[10]   *Phœbe*   Diana, goddess of the moon.

[11]   *Vesper*   Venus, the evening star.

45   Upon the midnight hours;
Thy voice, thy lute, thy pipe, thy incense sweet
      From swinged censer teeming;
Thy shrine, thy grove, thy oracle, thy heat
      Of pale-mouth'd prophet dreaming.

50   Yes, I will be thy priest, and build a fane°   *temple*
      In some untrodden region of my mind,
      Where branched thoughts, new grown with pleasant
           pain,
      Instead of pines shall murmur in the wind:
Far, far around shall those dark-cluster'd trees
55   Fledge the wild-ridged mountains steep by steep;
And there by zephyrs,° streams, and birds,   *breezes*
        and bees,
      The moss-lain Dryads° shall be lull'd   *wood nymphs*
        to sleep;
And in the midst of quietness
A rosy sanctuary will I dress
60   With the wreath'd trellis of a working brain,
      With buds, and bells, and stars without a name,
With all the gardener Fancy e'er could feign,
      Who breeding flowers, will never breed the same:
And there shall be for thee all soft delight
65   That shadowy thought can win,
A bright torch, and a casement ope°   *window opened*
      at night,
To let the warm Love in!
      —1820

Ode to a Nightingale[1]

1

My heart aches, and a drowsy numbness pains
      My sense, as though of hemlock° I had   *poison*
           drunk,
Or emptied some dull opiate to the drains
      One minute past, and Lethe-wards[2] had sunk:
5   'Tis not through envy of thy happy lot,
      But being too happy in thine happiness—
        That thou, light-winged Dryad°   *wood-nymph*
        of the trees,
          In some melodious plot
      Of beechen green, and shadows numberless,
10   Singest of summer in full-throated ease.

2

O, for a draught of vintage! that hath been
      Cool'd a long age in the deep-delved earth,
Tasting of Flora[3] and the country green,
      Dance, and Provençal song,[4] and sunburnt mirth!
15   O for a beaker full of the warm South,
      Full of the true, the blushful Hippocrene,[5]
        With beaded bubbles winking at the brim,
          And purple-stained mouth;
      That I might drink, and leave the world unseen,
20   And with thee fade away into the forest dim:

---

[1] *Ode to a Nightingale* Written about 1 May 1819. Twenty years later, Keats's friend and housemate Charles Armitage Brown remembered the composition of the poem: "In the spring of 1819 a nightingale had built her nest near my house. Keats felt a tranquil and continual joy in her song; and one morning he took his chair from the breakfast-table to the grass-plot under a plum-tree, where he sat for two or three hours. When he came into the house, I perceived he had some scraps of paper in his hand, and these he was quietly thrusting behind the books. On enquiry, I found those scraps, four or five in number, contained his poetic feeling on the song of our nightingale."

[2] *Lethe-wards* Towards Lethe, the river of forgetfulness which, in classical mythology, the dead must cross to reach Hades, the underworld.

[3] *Flora* Roman goddess of flowers.

[4] *Provençal song* The region of Provence, in southern France, was known in the Middle Ages for its poet-singers, or troubadours.

[5] *Hippocrene* Fountain of the Muses (nine sister goddesses who presided over aspects of learning and the arts) located on the sacred Mount Helicon. Its waters were said to provide poetic inspiration.

3

Fade far away, dissolve, and quite forget
    What thou among the leaves hast never known,
The weariness, the fever, and the fret
    Here, where men sit and hear each other groan;
25 Where palsy shakes a few, sad, last gray hairs,
        Where youth grows pale, and spectre-thin, and dies;
            Where but to think is to be full of sorrow
                And leaden-eyed despairs,
        Where Beauty cannot keep her lustrous eyes,
30   Or new Love pine at them beyond to-morrow.

4

Away! away! for I will fly to thee,
    Not charioted by Bacchus and his pards,[1]
But on the viewless wings of Poesy,
    Though the dull brain perplexes and retards:
35 Already with thee! tender is the night,
        And haply° the Queen-Moon is on her throne,   *maybe*
            Cluster'd around by all her starry Fays;°   *fairies*
                But here there is no light,
        Save what from heaven is with the breezes blown
40   Through verdurous glooms and winding mossy ways.

5

I cannot see what flowers are at my feet,
    Nor what soft incense hangs upon the boughs,
But, in embalmed° darkness, guess each sweet   *fragrant*
    Wherewith the seasonable month endows
45 The grass, the thicket, and the fruit-tree wild;
        White hawthorn, and the pastoral eglantine;
            Fast fading violets cover'd up in leaves;
                And mid-May's eldest child,
        The coming musk-rose, full of dewy wine,
50   The murmurous haunt of flies on summer eves.

6

Darkling[2] I listen; and, for many a time
    I have been half in love with easeful Death,
Call'd him soft names in many a mused rhyme,
    To take into the air my quiet breath;

55 Now more than ever seems it rich to die,
    To cease upon the midnight with no pain,
        While thou art pouring forth thy soul abroad
            In such an ecstasy!
    Still wouldst thou sing, and I have ears in vain—
60   To thy high requiem[3] become a sod.

7

Thou wast not born for death, immortal Bird!
    No hungry generations tread thee down;
The voice I hear this passing night was heard
    In ancient days by emperor and clown:°   *rustic*
65 Perhaps the self-same song that found a path
        Through the sad heart of Ruth, when, sick for home,
            She stood in tears amid the alien corn;[4]
                The same that oft-times hath
        Charm'd magic casements, opening on the foam
70   Of perilous seas, in faery lands forlorn.

8

Forlorn! the very word is like a bell
    To toll me back from thee to my sole self!
Adieu! the fancy cannot cheat so well
    As she is fam'd to do, deceiving elf.
75 Adieu! adieu! thy plaintive anthem fades
        Past the near meadows, over the still stream,
            Up the hill-side; and now 'tis buried deep
                In the next valley-glades:
        Was it a vision, or a waking dream?
80   Fled is that music—Do I wake or sleep?
—1819

Ode on a Grecian Urn

1

Thou still unravish'd bride of quietness,
    Thou foster-child of silence and slow time,
Sylvan° historian, who canst thus express   *woodland*
    A flowery tale more sweetly than our rhyme:
5 What leaf-fring'd legend haunts about thy shape
        Of deities or mortals, or of both,

---

1 *Bacchus … pards* Bacchus, the god of wine, rides a chariot drawn by pards, or leopards.

2 *Darkling* In the dark.

3 *requiem* Mass sung for the dead.

4 *Ruth … corn* Widow in the Book of Ruth (1–4) who leaves Moab for Judah with her mother-in-law Naomi because of famine.

In Tempe or the dales of Arcady?[1]
What men or gods are these? What maidens loth?
    What mad pursuit? What struggle to escape?
10   What pipes and timbrels?° What   *tambourines*
        wild ecstasy?

2

Heard melodies are sweet, but those unheard
    Are sweeter; therefore, ye soft pipes, play on;
Not to the sensual° ear, but, more endear'd,   *physical*
    Pipe to the spirit ditties of no tone:
15 Fair youth, beneath the trees, thou canst not leave
    Thy song, nor ever can those trees be bare;
        Bold Lover, never, never canst thou kiss,
Though winning near the goal—yet, do not grieve;
    She cannot fade, though thou hast not thy bliss,
20   For ever wilt thou love, and she be fair!

3

Ah, happy, happy boughs! that cannot shed
    Your leaves, nor ever bid the Spring adieu;
And, happy melodist, unwearied,
    For ever piping songs for ever new;
25 More happy love! more happy, happy love!
    For ever warm and still to be enjoy'd,
        For ever panting, and for ever young;
All breathing human passion far above,
    That leaves a heart high-sorrowful and cloy'd,
30   A burning forehead, and a parching tongue.

4

Who are these coming to the sacrifice?
    To what green altar, O mysterious priest,
Lead'st thou that heifer lowing at the skies,
    And all her silken flanks with garlands drest?
35 What little town by river or sea shore,
    Or mountain-built with peaceful citadel,
        Is emptied of this folk, this pious morn?
And, little town, thy streets for evermore
    Will silent be; and not a soul to tell
40   Why thou art desolate, can e'er return.

5

O Attic[2] shape! Fair attitude! with brede°   *interwoven design*
    Of marble men and maidens overwrought,°   *overlaid*
With forest branches and the trodden weed;
    Thou, silent form, dost tease us out of thought
45 As doth eternity: Cold Pastoral!
    When old age shall this generation waste,
        Thou shalt remain, in midst of other woe
Than ours, a friend to man, to whom thou say'st,
    "Beauty is truth, truth beauty,"—that is all
50   Ye know on earth, and all ye need to know.[3]
—1820

Ode on Melancholy[4]

1

No, No, go not to Lethe,[5] neither twist
Wolf's-bane,[6] tight-rooted, for its poisonous
    wine;
Nor suffer thy pale forehead to be kiss'd

---

[1] *Tempe* Valley in ancient Greece renowned for its beauty; *Arcady* Ideal region of rural life, named for a mountainous district in Greece.

[2] *Attic* I.e., Greek. Attica was an ancient region of Greece that had Athens as its capital.

[3] *Beauty is … know* The quotation marks in line 49 are present in Keats's 1820 volume of poems, but are absent in transcripts of the poem made by Keats's friends and in the version of the poem published in *Annals of the Fine Arts* in 1820. As a result, their presence has engendered much critical debate. It is unclear whether Keats meant the last line and a half to be spoken by the poet, or whether the entire final two lines are the imagined declaration of the urn.

[4] *Ode on Melancholy* In the original manuscript version, the poem opened with the following stanza:
    Though you should build a bark of dead men's bones,
        And rear a phantom gibbet for a mast,
    Stitch creeds together for a sail, with groans
        To fill it out, bloodstained and aghast;
    Although your rudder be a Dragon's tail,
        Long sever'd, yet still hard with agony,
    Your cordage large uprootings from the skull
    Of bald Medusa; certes you would fail
        To find Melancholy, whether she
        Dreameth in any isle of Lethe dull.
(Medusa was one of the Gorgons, three monstrous, winged sisters who had snakes for hair.)

[5] *Lethe* River in Hades, the classical underworld, whose waters produce forgetfulness.

[6] *Wolf's-bane* Poisonous plant native to Europe.

By nightshade, ruby grape of Proserpine;[1]
5   Make not your rosary of yew-berries,[2]
     Nor let the beetle, nor the death-moth[3] be
       Your mournful Psyche,[4] nor the downy owl
A partner in your sorrow's mysteries;[5]
     For shade to shade will come too drowsily,
10   And drown the wakeful anguish of the soul.

2

But when the melancholy fit shall fall
     Sudden from heaven like a weeping cloud,
That fosters the droop-headed flowers all,
     And hides the green hill in an April shroud;
15   Then glut thy sorrow on a morning rose,
     Or on the rainbow of the salt sand-wave,
       Or on the wealth of globed peonies;
Or if thy mistress some rich anger shows,
     Emprison her soft hand, and let her rave,
20   And feed deep, deep upon her peerless eyes.

3

She dwells with Beauty—Beauty that must die;
     And Joy, whose hand is ever at his lips
Bidding adieu; and aching Pleasure nigh,
     Turning to poison while the bee-mouth sips:
25   Ay, in the very temple of Delight
     Veil'd Melancholy has her sovran° shrine,   *sovereign*

Though seen of none save him whose
     strenuous tongue
Can burst Joy's grape against his palate fine;°   *refined*
     His soul shall taste the sadness of her might,
30   And be among her cloudy trophies hung.
—1820

Ode on Indolence[6]

"They toil not, neither do they spin."[7]

1

One morn before me were three figures seen,
   With bowed necks, and joined hands, side-faced;
And one behind the other stepp'd serene,
     In placid sandals, and in white robes graced;
5   They pass'd, like figures on a marble urn,
     When shifted round to see the other side;
       They came again; as when the urn once more
Is shifted round, the first seen shades return;
     And they were strange to me, as may betide
10   With vases, to one deep in Phidian lore.[8]

2

How is it, shadows, that I knew ye not?
     How came ye muffled in so hush a masque?°   *play*
Was it a silent deep-disguised plot
     To steal away, and leave without a task
15   My idle days? Ripe was the drowsy hour;
     The blissful cloud of summer-indolence
       Benumb'd my eyes; my pulse grew less and less;
Pain had no sting, and pleasure's wreath no flower:

---

[1] *nightshade* Plants with poisonous berries; *Proserpine* Daughter of Demeter who was abducted by Pluto, god of the underworld, and made queen of Hades. Her mother, goddess of the harvest, mourned for her daughter and so caused an eternal winter until Pluto was prevailed upon to allow Proserpine to return to her mother six months of every year.

[2] *yew-berries* Poisonous berries of the yew tree, which is commonly planted in graveyards and is therefore often regarded as symbolic of death or sadness.

[3] *beetle* The scarab, a large black beetle that Egyptians placed in their tombs as a symbol of resurrection; *death-moth* Death's-head moth, whose wings carry a mark resembling a human skull.

[4] *Psyche* In classical mythology, a young woman who was beloved by Cupid, winged god of love and son of Venus. After winning over Venus, who was jealous of Psyche's beauty, Psyche was granted immortality by Jupiter. In Greek myth she is often a personification of the soul. Her name in Greek means butterfly as well as soul. Psyche was often represented as a butterfly flying out of a dying person's mouth.

[5] *mysteries* I.e., secret rites or ceremonies.

---

[6] *Ode on Indolence* See the 1819 letter to George and Georgiana Keats, reprinted below, in which Keats describes the bout of indolence that is thought to have inspired this poem.

[7] *They toil … spin* From Matthew 6.28–89: "Consider the lilies of the field, how they grow; they toil not, neither do they spin: And yet I say unto you, That even Solomon in all his glory was not arrayed like one of these."

[8] *Phidian lore* Lore concerning Phidias, the fifth-century Athenian sculptor of what were later named the Elgin Marbles, the marble sculptures that decorated the outside of the Parthenon and were brought to England by Lord Elgin.

O, why did ye not melt, and leave my sense
   Unhaunted quite of all but—nothingness?

3

A third time pass'd they by, and, passing, turn'd
   Each one the face a moment whiles to me;
Then faded, and to follow them I burn'd
   And ached for wings because I knew the three;
25 The first was a fair Maid, and Love her name;
   The second was Ambition, pale of cheek,
     And ever watchful with fatigued eye;
The last, whom I love more, the more of blame
   Is heap'd upon her, maiden most unmeek,
30   I knew to be my demon Poesy.

4

They faded, and, forsooth! I wanted wings:
   O folly! What is Love! and where is it?
And for that poor Ambition! It springs
   From a man's little heart's short fever-fit;
35 For Poesy! No—she has not a joy—
   At least for me—so sweet as drowsy noons,
     And evenings steep'd in honeyed indolence;
O, for an age so shelter'd from annoy,°   *harm*
   That I may never know how change the moons,
40   Or hear the voice of busy common sense!

5

A third time came they by—alas! wherefore?
   My sleep had been embroider'd with dim dreams;
My soul had been a lawn besprinkled o'er
   With flowers, and stirring shades, and baffled beams:
45 The morn was clouded, but no shower fell,
   Tho' in her lids hung the sweet tears of May;
     The open casement press'd a new-leav'd vine,
Let in the budding warmth and
   throstle's° lay;°   *thrush's / song*
   O shadows! 'twas a time to bid farewell!
50   Upon your skirts had fallen no tears of mine.

6

So, ye three ghosts, adieu! Ye cannot raise
   My head cool-bedded in the flowery grass;
For I would not be dieted with praise,

A pet-lamb in a sentimental farce!
55 Fade softly from my eyes, and be once more
   In masque-like figures on the dreamy urn;
     Farewell! I yet have visions for the night,
And for the day faint visions there is store;
   Vanish, ye phantoms! from my idle spright,°   *spirit*
60   Into the clouds, and never more return!
—1848 (WRITTEN 1819)

To Autumn

1

Season of mists and mellow fruitfulness,
   Close bosom-friend of the maturing sun;
Conspiring with him how to load and bless
   With fruit the vines that round the thatch-eves run;
5 To bend with apples the moss'd cottage-trees,
   And fill all fruit with ripeness to the core;
     To swell the gourd, and plump the hazel shells
With a sweet kernel; to set budding more,
   And still more, later flowers for the bees,
10   Until they think warm days will never cease,
     For Summer has o'er-brimm'd their clammy cells.

2

Who hath not seen thee oft amid thy store?
   Sometimes whoever seeks abroad may find
Thee sitting careless on a granary floor,
15   Thy hair soft-lifted by the winnowing wind;
Or on a half-reap'd furrow sound asleep,
   Drows'd with the fume of poppies, while thy hook[1]
     Spares the next swath and all its twined flowers:
And sometimes like a gleaner[2] thou dost keep
20   Steady thy laden head across a brook;
   Or by a cider-press, with patient look,
     Thou watchest the last oozings hours by hours.

3

Where are the songs of Spring? Ay, where are they?
   Think not of them, thou hast thy music too—

---

1 *hook* I.e., a reaping-hook or scythe.

2 *gleaner* One who gathers the grain left by the reaper.

25   While barred clouds bloom the soft-dying day,
    And touch the stubble-plains with rosy hue;
    Then in a wailful choir the small gnats mourn
      Among the river sallows,° borne aloft   *willows*
      Or sinking as the light wind lives or dies;
30   And full-grown lambs loud bleat from hilly bourn;° *realm*
    Hedge-crickets sing; and now with treble soft
    The red-breast whistles from a
      garden-croft;°   *enclosed garden*
    And gathering swallows twitter in the skies.
—1820

Lamia

Philostratus, in his fourth book *de Vita Apollonii*, hath a memorable instance in this kind, which I may not omit, of one Menippus Lycius, a young man of twenty-five years of age, that going betwixt Cenchreas and Corinth, met such a phantasm in the habit of a fair gentlewoman, which taking him by the hand, carried him home to her house, in the suburbs of Corinth, and told him she was a Phoenician by birth, and if he would tarry with her, he should hear her sing and play, and drink such wine as never any drank, and no man should molest him; but she, being fair and lovely, would live and die with him, that was fair and lovely to behold. The young man, a philosopher, otherwise staid and discreet, able to moderate his passions, though not this of love, tarried with her a while to his great content, and at last married her, to whose wedding, among other guests, came Apollonius; who, by some probable conjectures, found her out to be a serpent, a lamia; and that all her furniture was, like Tantalus' gold, described by Homer, no substance but mere illusions. When she saw herself descried, she wept, and desired Apollonius to be silent, but he would not be moved, and thereupon she, plate, house, and all that was in it, vanished in an instant: many thousand took notice of this fact, for it was done in the midst of Greece.[1]

---

[1] *Philostratus … midst of Greece*   In a footnote originally placed at the end of *Lamia*, Keats provides the above quotation from Robert Burton's *Anatomy of Melancholy* 3.2.1.1. (1621), his source for this narrative poem about a young man who falls in love with a lamia, a monster that has taken the form of a woman.

PART 1

Upon a time, before the faery broods
  Drove Nymph and Satyr from the prosperous
    woods,
Before King Oberon's bright diadem,°   *crown*
Sceptre, and mantle, clasp'd with dewy gem,
Frighted away the Dryads and the Fauns
From rushes green, and brakes,° and cowslip'd   *ferns*
    lawns,[2]
The ever-smitten Hermes[3] empty left
His golden throne, bent warm on amorous theft:
From high Olympus had he stolen light,
10 On this side of Jove's clouds,[4] to escape the sight
Of his great summoner, and made retreat
Into a forest on the shores of Crete.[5]
For somewhere in that sacred island dwelt
A nymph, to whom all hoofed Satyrs knelt;
15 At whose white feet the languid Tritons[6] poured
Pearls, while on land they wither'd and adored.
Fast by the springs where she to bathe was wont,
And in those meads° where sometime she   *meadows*
    might haunt,
Were strewn rich gifts, unknown to any Muse,[7]
20 Though Fancy's casket were unlock'd to choose.
Ah, what a world of love was at her feet!
So Hermes thought, and a celestial heat
Burnt from his winged heels to either ear,
That from a whiteness, as the lily clear,
25 Blush'd into roses 'mid his golden hair,
Fallen in jealous curls about his shoulders bare.

---

[2] *Before … lawns*   In classical mythology, nymphs, dryads (wood nymphs), and satyrs and fauns (half-men, half-goats) were all minor deities. Oberon, in Shakespeare's *A Midsummer Night's Dream*, is king of the fairies, who were immortal beings of a later period.

[3] *Hermes*   Wing-footed messenger of the gods (called Mercury in Roman mythology).

[4] *From high … clouds*   Jove is the King of the Roman gods, all of whom reside on Mt. Olympus.

[5] *Crete*   Island in the Aegean Sea.

[6] *Tritons*   Sea-gods, usually half-men and half-fish.

[7] *Muse*   One of nine daughters of Zeus and Mnemosyne, each of whom presided over and provided inspiration for an aspect of learning or the arts.

From vale to vale, from wood to wood, he flew,
Breathing upon the flowers his passion new,
And wound with many a river to its head,
30 To find where this sweet nymph prepar'd her secret bed:
In vain; the sweet nymph might nowhere be found,
And so he rested, on the lonely ground,
Pensive, and full of painful jealousies
Of the Wood-Gods, and even the very trees.
35 There as he stood, he heard a mournful voice,
Such as once heard, in gentle heart, destroys
All pain but pity: thus the lone voice spake:
"When from this wreathed tomb shall I awake!
When move in a sweet body fit for life,
40 And love, and pleasure, and the ruddy strife
Of hearts and lips! Ah, miserable me!"
The God, dove-footed, glided silently
Round bush and tree, soft-brushing, in his speed,
The taller grasses and full-flowering weed,
45 Until he found a palpitating snake,
Bright, and cirque-couchant[1] in a dusky brake.

    She was a gordian[2] shape of dazzling hue,
Vermilion°-spotted, golden, green, and blue;   *scarlet*
Striped like a zebra, freckled like a pard,°   *leopard*
50 Eyed like a peacock, and all crimson barr'd;
And full of silver moons, that, as she breathed,
Dissolv'd, or brighter shone, or interwreathed
Their lustres with the gloomier tapestries—
So rainbow-sided, touch'd with miseries,
55 She seem'd, at once, some penanced lady elf,
Some demon's mistress, or the demon's self.
Upon her crest she wore a wannish fire
Sprinkled with stars, like Ariadne's tiar:[3]
Her head was serpent, but ah, bitter-sweet!
60 She had a woman's mouth with all its pearls[4] complete:

---

[1] *cirque-couchant* French: lying in coils.

[2] *gordian* I.e., like the Gordian knot, tied by King Gordius of Phrygia and said to be impossible to untie. Alexander the Great eventually severed it with his sword.

[3] *Ariadne's tiar* According to myth, after Ariadne married the god Bacchus she was converted into a constellation. In his painting of her, Italian painter Titian (c. 1488–1576) shows Ariadne wearing a crown of seven stars.

[4] *pearls* I.e., teeth.

And for her eyes: what could such eyes do there
But weep, and weep, that they were born so fair?
As Proserpine still weeps for her Sicilian air.[5]
65 Her throat was serpent, but the words she spake
Came, as through bubbling honey, for Love's sake,
And thus; while Hermes on his pinions° lay,   *wings*
Like a stoop'd[6] falcon ere he takes his prey.

    "Fair Hermes, crown'd with feathers, fluttering
        light,
I had a splendid dream of thee last night:
70 I saw thee sitting, on a throne of gold,
Among the Gods, upon Olympus old,
The only sad one; for thou didst not hear
The soft, lute-finger'd Muses chaunting clear,
Nor even Apollo when he sang alone,
75 Deaf to his throbbing throat's long, long melodious
        moan.
I dreamt I saw thee, robed in purple flakes,
Break amorous through the clouds, as morning breaks,
And, swiftly as a bright Phoebean dart,[7]
Strike for the Cretan isle; and here thou art!
80 Too gentle Hermes, hast thou found the maid?"
Whereat the star of Lethe[8] not delay'd
His rosy eloquence, and thus inquired:
"Thou smooth-lipp'd serpent, surely high inspired!
Thou beauteous wreath, with melancholy eyes,
85 Possess whatever bliss thou canst devise,
Telling me only where my nymph is fled—
Where she doth breathe!" "Bright planet, thou hast said,"
Return'd the snake, "but seal with oaths, fair God!"
"I swear," said Hermes, "by my serpent rod,[9]
90 And by thine eyes, and by thy starry crown!"
Light flew his earnest words, among the blossoms
        blown.

---

[5] *As Proserpine … air* Hades, god of the underworld, abducted Proserpine from her home in Sicily to be his queen.

[6] *stoop'd* Swooping.

[7] *Phoebean dart* Sunbeam, after Phoebus Apollo, god of the sun.

[8] *star of Lethe* Hermes, who, like a star, guided the souls of the dead to the dark underworld (in which Lethe is a river).

[9] *my serpent rod* On Hermes's wand, or a caduceus, two serpents were entwined.

Then thus again the brilliance feminine:
"Too frail of heart! for this lost nymph of thine,
Free as the air, invisibly, she strays
95   About these thornless wilds; her pleasant days
She tastes unseen; unseen her nimble feet
Leave traces in the grass and flowers sweet;
From weary tendrils, and bow'd branches green,
She plucks the fruit unseen, she bathes unseen:
100   And by my power is her beauty veil'd
To keep it unaffronted, unassail'd
By the love-glances of unlovely eyes,
Of Satyrs, Fauns, and blear'd Silenus'[1] sighs.
Pale grew her immortality, for woe
105   Of all these lovers, and she grieved so
I took compassion on her, bade her steep
Her hair in weïrd° syrops, that would keep   magical
Her loveliness invisible, yet free
To wander as she loves, in liberty.
110   Thou shalt behold her, Hermes, thou alone,
If thou wilt, as thou swearest, grant my boon!"
Then, once again, the charmed God began
An oath, and through the serpent's ears it ran
Warm, tremulous, devout, psalterian.[2]
115   Ravish'd, she lifted her Circean head,[3]
Blush'd a live damask,[4] and swift-lisping said,
"I was a woman, let me have once more
A woman's shape, and charming as before.
I love a youth of Corinth—O the bliss!
120   Give me my woman's form, and place me where he is.
Stoop, Hermes, let me breathe upon thy brow,
And thou shalt see thy sweet nymph even now."
The God on half-shut feathers sank serene,
She breath'd upon his eyes, and swift was seen
125   Of both the guarded nymph near-smiling on the green.
It was no dream; or say a dream it was,
Real are the dreams of Gods, and smoothly pass
Their pleasures in a long immortal dream.

One warm, flush'd moment, hovering, it might seem
130   Dash'd by the wood-nymph's beauty, so he burn'd;
Then, lighting on the printless verdure, turn'd
To the swoon'd serpent, and with languid arm,
Delicate, put to proof the lithe Caducean charm.
So done, upon the nymph his eyes he bent
135   Full of adoring tears and blandishment,
And towards her stept: she, like a moon in wane,
Faded before him, cower'd, nor could restrain
Her fearful sobs, self-folding like a flower
That faints into itself at evening hour:
140   But the God fostering her chilled hand,
She felt the warmth, her eyelids open'd bland,°   soft
And, like new flowers at morning song of bees,
Bloom'd, and gave up her honey to the lees.°   dregs
Into the green-recessed woods they flew;
145   Nor grew they pale, as mortal lovers do.

Left to herself, the serpent now began
To change; her elfin blood in madness ran,
Her mouth foam'd, and the grass, therewith
    besprent,°   besprinkled
Wither'd at dew so sweet and virulent;
150   Her eyes in torture fix'd, and anguish drear,
Hot, glaz'd, and wide, with lid-lashes all sear,°   withered
Flash'd phosphor and sharp sparks, without one
    cooling tear.
The colours all inflam'd throughout her train,°   tail
She writh'd about, convuls'd with scarlet pain:
155   A deep volcanian yellow took the place
Of all her milder mooned[5] body's grace;
And, as the lava ravishes the mead,
Spoilt all her silver mail, and golden
    brede;°   interwoven pattern
Made gloom of all her frecklings, streaks and bars,
160   Eclips'd her crescents, and lick'd up her stars:
So that, in moments few, she was undrest
Of all her sapphires, greens, and amethyst,
And rubious-argent:° of all these bereft,   reddish-silver
Nothing but pain and ugliness were left.
165   Still shone her crown; that vanish'd, also she
Melted and disappear'd as suddenly;

---

[1]   *Silenus*   Foster-father of Bacchus, god of wine, who is typically portrayed drunk.

[2]   *psalterian*   Like the sound of a psaltery (a stringed instrument); or, possibly, like a psalm, which were printed in psalters.

[3]   *Circean head*   Like that of Circe, the enchantress who turns men into beasts in Homer's *Odyssey*, Book 10.

[4]   *damask*   Pink, like the color of a damask rose.

[5]   *milder-mooned*   I.e., of a milder, silver-moon color.

And in the air, her new voice luting soft,
Cried, "Lycius! gentle Lycius!" Borne aloft
With the bright mists about the mountains hoar°   *ancient*
70 These words dissolv'd: Crete's forests heard no more.

Whither fled Lamia, now a lady bright,
A full-born beauty new and exquisite?
She fled into that valley they pass o'er
Who go to Corinth from Cenchreas' shore;[1]
75 And rested at the foot of those wild hills,
The rugged founts of the Peraean rills,
And of that other ridge whose barren back
Stretches, with all its mist and cloudy rack,
South-westward to Cleone.[2] There she stood
80 About a young bird's flutter from a wood,
Fair, on a sloping green of mossy tread,
By a clear pool, wherein she passioned[3]
To see herself escap'd from so sore ills,
While her robes flaunted with the daffodils.

85 Ah, happy Lycius!—for she was a maid
More beautiful than ever twisted braid,
Or sigh'd, or blush'd, or on spring-flowered lea°   *pasture*
Spread a green kirtle° to the minstrelsy: *gown*
A virgin purest lipp'd, yet in the lore
90 Of love deep learned to the red heart's core:
Not one hour old, yet of sciential° brain   *knowledgeable*
To unperplex° bliss from its neighbour pain;   *extricate*
Define their pettish° limits, and estrange   *uncertain*
Their points of contact, and swift counterchange;
95 Intrigue with the specious° chaos, and   *seeming*
dispart°   *cleave*
Its most ambiguous atoms with sure art;
As though in Cupid's[4] college she had spent
Sweet days a lovely graduate, still unshent,°   *unspoiled*
And kept his rosy terms in idle languishment.

200 Why this fair creature chose so fairily
By the wayside to linger, we shall see;
But first 'tis fit to tell how she could muse
And dream, when in the serpent prison-house,
Of all she list,° strange or magnificent: *desired*
205 How, ever, where she will'd, her spirit went;
Whether to faint Elysium,[5] or where
Down through tress-lifting waves the Nereids fair
Wind into Thetis' bower[6] by many a pearly stair;
Or where God Bacchus drains his cups divine,
210 Stretch'd out, at ease, beneath a glutinous pine;
Or where in Pluto's[7] gardens palatine°   *palatial*
Mulciber's columns gleam in far piazzian line.[8]
And sometimes into cities she would send
Her dream, with feast and rioting to blend;
215 And once, while among mortals dreaming thus,
She saw the young Corinthian Lycius
Charioting foremost in the envious race,
Like a young Jove with calm uneager face,
And fell into a swooning love of him.
220 Now on the moth-time of that evening dim
He would return that way, as well she knew,
To Corinth from the shore; for freshly blew
The eastern soft wind, and his galley now
Grated the quaystones with her brazen prow
225 In port Cenchreas, from Egina isle
Fresh anchor'd; whither he had been awhile
To sacrifice to Jove, whose temple there
Waits with high marble doors for blood and incense
rare.
Jove heard his vows, and better'd his desire;
230 For by some freakful chance he made retire
From his companions, and set forth to walk,
Perhaps grown wearied of their Corinth talk:
Over the solitary hills he fared,
Thoughtless at first, but ere eve's star appeared
235 His phantasy was lost, where reason fades,

---

1 *Cenchreas' shore* Shore of Cenchrea, the eastern harbor of Corinth, in southern Greece.

2 *Cleone* Village between Corinth and Argos.

3 *passioned* Was moved by intense passion.

4 *Cupid* God of love.

5 *Elysium* Paradise of the classical underworld.

6 *Nereids ... bower* Thetis, the mother of Achilles, is a sea-nymph, or Nereid.

7 *Pluto* Another name for Hades, god of the underworld.

8 *Mulciber* Also called Vulcan, god of fire and metalworking; *piazzian line* Line of columns surrounding piazzas.

In the calm'd twilight of Platonic shades.°   *ghosts*
Lamia beheld him coming, near, more near—
Close to her passing, in indifference drear,
His silent sandals swept the mossy green;
240 So neighbour'd to him, and yet so unseen
She stood: he pass'd, shut up in mysteries,
His mind wrapp'd like his mantle, while her eyes
Follow'd his steps, and her neck regal white
Turn'd—syllabling thus, "Ah, Lycius bright,
245 And will you leave me on the hills alone?
Lycius, look back! and be some pity shown."
He did; not with cold wonder fearingly,
But Orpheus-like at an Eurydice;[1]
For so delicious were the words she sung,
250 It seem'd he had lov'd them a whole summer long:
And soon his eyes had drunk her beauty up,
Leaving no drop in the bewildering cup,
And still the cup was full—while he, afraid
Lest she should vanish ere his lip had paid
255 Due adoration, thus began to adore;
Her soft look growing coy, she saw his chain so sure:
"Leave thee alone! Look back! Ah, Goddess, see
Whether my eyes can ever turn from thee!
For pity do not this sad heart belie°—   *deceive*
260 Even as thou vanishest so I shall die.
Stay! though a Naiad° of the rivers, stay!   *water nymph*
To thy far wishes will thy streams obey:
Stay! though the greenest woods be thy domain,
Alone they can drink up the morning rain:
265 Though a descended Pleiad,[2] will not one
Of thine harmonious sisters keep in tune
Thy spheres, and as thy silver proxy shine?
So sweetly to these ravish'd ears of mine
Came thy sweet greeting, that if thou shouldst fade
270 Thy memory will waste me to a shade—
For pity do not melt!" "If I should stay,"
Said Lamia, "here, upon this floor of clay,
And pain my steps upon these flowers too rough,

What canst thou say or do of charm enough
275 To dull the nice remembrance of my home?
Thou canst not ask me with thee here to roam
Over these hills and vales, where no joy is—
Empty of immortality and bliss!
Thou art a scholar, Lycius, and must know
280 That finer spirits cannot breathe below
In human climes, and live: Alas! poor youth,
What taste of purer air hast thou to soothe
My essence? What serener palaces,
Where I may all my many senses please,
285 And by mysterious sleights a hundred thirsts appease?
It cannot be—Adieu!" So said, she rose
Tiptoe with white arms spread. He, sick to lose
The amorous promise of her lone complain,°   *complaint*
Swoon'd, murmuring of love, and pale with pain.
290 The cruel lady, without any show
Of sorrow for her tender favourite's woe,
But rather, if her eyes could brighter be,
With brighter eyes and slow amenity,
Put her new lips to his, and gave afresh
295 The life she had so tangled in her mesh:
And as he from one trance was wakening
Into another, she began to sing,
Happy in beauty, life, and love, and every thing,
A song of love, too sweet for earthly lyres,
300 While, like held breath, the stars drew in their panting
    fires.
And then she whisper'd in such trembling tone,
As those who, safe together met alone
For the first time through many anguish'd days,
Use other speech than looks; bidding him raise
305 His drooping head, and clear his soul of doubt,
For that she was a woman, and without
Any more subtle fluid in her veins
Than throbbing blood, and that the self-same pains
Inhabited her frail-strung heart as his.
310 And next she wonder'd how his eyes could miss
Her face so long in Corinth, where, she said,
She dwelt but half retir'd, and there had led
Days happy as the gold coin could invent
Without the aid of love; yet in content
315 Till she saw him, as once she pass'd him by,
Where 'gainst a column he leant thoughtfully

---

[1] *But ... Eurydice* The poet Orpheus won the right to lead his wife, Eurydice, back from the underworld on the condition that he not turn around to look at her on the journey back. When he could not resist doing so, she was forced to return to the underworld forever.

[2] *Pleiad* One of the seven stars, daughters of the Titan Atlas, that comprise the constellation Pleiades.

At Venus'[1] temple porch, 'mid baskets heap'd
Of amorous herbs and flowers, newly reap'd
Late on that eve, as 'twas the night before
20 The Adonian feast;[2] whereof she saw no more,
But wept alone those days, for why should she adore?
Lycius from death awoke into amaze,
To see her still, and singing so sweet lays;
Then from amaze into delight he fell
25 To hear her whisper woman's lore so well;
And every word she spake entic'd him on
To unperplex'd° delight and pleasure known.   certain
Let the mad poets say whate'er they please
Of the sweets of Fairies, Peris,[3] Goddesses,
30 There is not such a treat among them all,
Haunters of cavern, lake, and waterfall,
As a real woman, lineal indeed
From Pyrrha's pebbles[4] or old Adam's seed.
Thus gentle Lamia judg'd, and judg'd aright,
35 That Lycius could not love in half a fright,
So threw the goddess off, and won his heart
More pleasantly by playing woman's part,
With no more awe than what her beauty gave,
That, while it smote, still guaranteed to save.
40 Lycius to all made eloquent reply,
Marrying to every word a twinborn sigh;
And last, pointing to Corinth, ask'd her sweet,
If 'twas too far that night for her soft feet.
The way was short, for Lamia's eagerness
45 Made, by a spell, the triple league decrease
To a few paces; not at all surmised
By blinded Lycius, so in her comprized.°   absorbed
They pass'd the city gates, he knew not how,
So noiseless, and he never thought to know.

50   As men talk in a dream, so Corinth all,
Throughout her palaces imperial,

And all her populous streets and temples lewd,[5]
Mutter'd, like tempest in the distance brew'd,
To the wide-spreaded night above her towers.
355 Men, women, rich and poor, in the cool hours,
Shuffled their sandals o'er the pavement white,
Companion'd or alone; while many a light
Flared, here and there, from wealthy festivals,
And threw their moving shadows on the walls,
360 Or found them cluster'd in the corniced shade
Of some arch'd temple door, or dusky colonnade.

    Muffling his face, of greeting friends in fear,
Her fingers he press'd hard, as one came near
With curl'd gray beard, sharp eyes, and smooth bald
        crown,
365 Slow-stepp'd, and robed in philosophic gown:
Lycius shrank closer, as they met and past,
Into his mantle, adding wings to haste,
While hurried Lamia trembled: "Ah," said he,
"Why do you shudder, love, so ruefully?
370 Why does your tender palm dissolve in dew?"
"I'm wearied," said fair Lamia: "tell me who
Is that old man? I cannot bring to mind
His features—Lycius! wherefore did you blind
Yourself from his quick eyes?" Lycius replied,
375 "'Tis Apollonius sage, my trusty guide
And good instructor; but to-night he seems
The ghost of folly haunting my sweet dreams."

    While yet he spake they had arrived before
A pillar'd porch, with lofty portal door,
380 Where hung a silver lamp, whose phosphor glow
Reflected in the slabbed steps below,
Mild as a star in water; for so new,
And so unsullied was the marble hue,
So through the crystal polish, liquid fine,
385 Ran the dark veins, that none but feet divine
Could e'er have touch'd there. Sounds Æolian[6]
Breath'd from the hinges, as the ample span
Of the wide doors disclos'd a place unknown

---

[1] *Venus* Goddess of love.

[2] *Adonian feast* Festival in honor of Adonis, a beautiful young man who was loved by Venus and was killed when hunting a boar.

[3] *Peris* Beautiful women inhabiting the world of the Persian afterlife.

[4] *Pyrrha's pebbles* In classical myth, Jupiter exterminated humanity in a flood. Deucalion and his wife Pyrrha, the only two survivors, repopulated the earth by throwing pebbles, which turned into people.

[5] *temples lewd* Temples of Venus, goddess of love.

[6] *Sounds Æolian* Sounds resembling those of an Aeolian harp, which produces music when exposed to currents of air. Aeolus was god of the winds.

Some time to any, but those two alone,
390 And a few Persian mutes, who that same year
Were seen about the markets: none knew where
They could inhabit; the most curious
Were foil'd, who watch'd to trace them to their house:
And but the flitter-winged verse must tell,
395 For truth's sake, what woe afterwards befell,
'Twould humour many a heart to leave them thus,
Shut from the busy world of more incredulous.

PART 2

Love in a hut, with water and a crust,
Is—Love, forgive us!—cinders, ashes, dust;
Love in a palace is perhaps at last
More grievous torment than a hermit's fast—
5 That is a doubtful tale from faery land,
Hard for the non-elect to understand.
Had Lycius liv'd to hand his story down,
He might have given the moral a fresh frown,
Or clench'd it quite: but too short was their bliss
10 To breed distrust and hate, that make the soft voice hiss.
Besides, there, nightly, with terrific glare,
Love, jealous grown of so complete a pair,
Hover'd and buzz'd his wings, with fearful roar,
Above the lintel[1] of their chamber door,
15 And down the passage cast a glow upon the floor.

For all this came a ruin: side by side
They were enthroned, in the even tide,
Upon a couch, near to a curtaining
Whose airy texture, from a golden string,
20 Floated into the room, and let appear
Unveil'd the summer heaven, blue and clear,
Betwixt two marble shafts—there they reposed,
Where use had made it sweet, with eyelids closed,
Saving a tithe[2] which love still open kept,
25 That they might see each other while they almost slept;
When from the slope side of a suburb hill,
Deafening the swallow's twitter, came a thrill
Of trumpets—Lycius started—the sounds fled,

But left a thought, a buzzing in his head.
30 For the first time, since first he harbour'd in
That purple-lined palace of sweet sin,
His spirit pass'd beyond its golden bourn°   realm
Into the noisy world almost forsworn.
The lady, ever watchful, penetrant,
35 Saw this with pain, so arguing a want
Of something more, more than her empery°   empire
Of joys; and she began to moan and sigh
Because he mused beyond her, knowing well
That but a moment's thought is passion's passing bell.[3]
40 "Why do you sigh, fair creature?" whisper'd he:
"Why do you think?" return'd she tenderly:
"You have deserted me;—where am I now?
Not in your heart while care weighs on your brow:
No, no, you have dismiss'd me; and I go
45 From your breast houseless: ay, it must be so."
He answer'd, bending to her open eyes,
Where he was mirror'd small in paradise,
"My silver planet, both of eve and morn![4]
Why will you plead yourself so sad forlorn,
50 While I am striving how to fill my heart
With deeper crimson, and a double smart?
How to entangle, trammel up and snare
Your soul in mine, and labyrinth you there
Like the hid scent in an unbudded rose?
55 Ay, a sweet kiss—you see your mighty woes.
My thoughts! shall I unveil them? Listen then!
What mortal hath a prize, that other men
May be confounded and abash'd withal,
But lets it sometimes pace abroad majestical,
60 And triumph, as in thee I should rejoice
Amid the hoarse alarm of Corinth's voice.
Let my foes choke, and my friends shout afar,
While through the thronged streets your bridal car
Wheels round its dazzling spokes." The lady's cheek
65 Trembled; she nothing said, but, pale and meek,
Arose and knelt before him, wept a rain
Of sorrows at his words; at last with pain
Beseeching him, the while his hand she wrung,

---

1. *lintel* Horizontal support beam.

2. *tithe* I.e., a tenth, or very small part.

3. *passing bell* Bell tolled following a death.

4. *My silver … morn* I.e., my Venus (the planet that appears as both the morning and the evening star).

To change his purpose. He thereat was stung,
70　Perverse, with stronger fancy to reclaim
　　Her wild and timid nature to his aim:
　　Besides, for all his love, in self despite,
　　Against his better self, he took delight
　　Luxurious in her sorrows, soft and new.
75　His passion, cruel grown, took on a hue
　　Fierce and sanguineous as 'twas possible
　　In one whose brow had no dark veins to swell.
　　Fine was the mitigated fury, like
　　Apollo's presence when in act to strike
80　The serpent[1]—Ha, the serpent! certes,° she　　　*certainly*
　　Was none. She burnt, she lov'd the tyranny,
　　And, all subdued, consented to the hour
　　When to the bridal he should lead his paramour.
　　Whispering in midnight silence, said the youth,
85　"Sure some sweet name thou hast, though, by my truth,
　　I have not ask'd it, ever thinking thee
　　Not mortal, but of heavenly progeny,
　　As still I do. Hast any mortal name,
　　Fit appellation for this dazzling frame?
90　Or friends or kinsfolk on the citied earth,
　　To share our marriage feast and nuptial mirth?"
　　"I have no friends," said Lamia, "no, not one;
　　My presence in wide Corinth hardly known:
　　My parents' bones are in their dusty urns
95　Sepulchred, where no kindled incense burns,
　　Seeing all their luckless race are dead, save me,
　　And I neglect the holy rite for thee.
　　Even as you list° invite your many guests;　　　*desire to*
　　But if, as now it seems, your vision rests
00　With any pleasure on me, do not bid
　　Old Apollonius—from him keep me hid."
　　Lycius, perplex'd at words so blind and blank,
　　Made close inquiry; from whose touch she shrank,
　　Feigning a sleep; and he to the dull shade
05　Of deep sleep in a moment was betray'd.

　　　It was the custom then to bring away
　　The bride from home at blushing shut of day,
　　Veiled, in a chariot, heralded along

By strewn flowers, torches, and a marriage song,
110　With other pageants: but this fair unknown
　　Had not a friend. So being left alone
　　(Lycius was gone to summon all his kin),
　　And knowing surely she could never win
　　His foolish heart from its mad pompousness,
115　She set herself, high-thoughted, how to dress
　　The misery in fit magnificence.
　　She did so, but 'tis doubtful how and whence
　　Came, and who were her subtle servitors.
　　About the halls, and to and from the doors,
120　There was a noise of wings, till in short space
　　The glowing banquet-room shone with wide-arched
　　　grace.
　　A haunting music, sole perhaps and lone
　　Supportress of the faery-roof, made moan
　　Throughout, as fearful the whole charm might fade.
125　Fresh carved cedar, mimicking a glade
　　Of palm and plantain, met from either side,
　　High in the midst, in honour of the bride:
　　Two palms and then two plantains, and so on,
　　From either side their stems branch'd one to one
130　All down the aisled place; and beneath all
　　There ran a stream of lamps straight on from wall to
　　　wall.
　　So canopied, lay an untasted feast
　　Teeming with odours. Lamia, regal drest,
　　Silently paced about, and as she went,
135　In pale contented sort of discontent,
　　Mission'd her viewless servants to enrich
　　The fretted[2] splendour of each nook and niche.
　　Between the tree-stems, marbled plain at first,
　　Came jasper panels; then, anon, there burst
140　Forth creeping imagery of slighter trees,
　　And with the larger wove in small intricacies.
　　Approving all, she faded at self-will,
　　And shut the chamber up, close, hush'd and still,
　　Complete and ready for the revels rude,
145　When dreadful guests would come to spoil her solitude.

　　　The day appear'd, and all the gossip rout.
　　O senseless Lycius! Madman! wherefore flout

1　*Apollo's … serpent* Apollo killed a serpent, named Python, at
Delphi; when his oracle was established there, the priestess was known
as the Pythian.

2　*fretted* Adorned with elaborate carved patterns.

The silent-blessing fate, warm cloister'd hours,
And show to common eyes these secret bowers?
150 The herd approach'd; each guest, with busy brain,
Arriving at the portal, gaz'd amain,°   *intently*
And enter'd marveling: for they knew the sheet,
Remember'd it from childhood all complete
Without a gap, yet ne'er before had seen
155 That royal porch, that high-built fair demesne;°   *estate*
So in they hurried all, maz'd,° curious and keen: *bewildered*
Save one, who look'd thereon with eye severe,
And with calm-planted steps walk'd in austere;
'Twas Apollonius: something too he laugh'd,
160 As though some knotty problem, that had daft° *confounded*
His patient thought, had now begun to thaw,
And solve and melt—'twas just as he foresaw.

He met within the murmurous vestibule
His young disciple. "'Tis no common rule,
165 Lycius," said he, "for uninvited guest
To force himself upon you, and infest
With an unbidden presence the bright throng
Of younger friends; yet must I do this wrong,
And you forgive me." Lycius blush'd, and led
170 The old man through the inner doors broad-spread;
With reconciling words and courteous mien°   *manner*
Turning into sweet milk the sophist's°   *philosopher's*
   spleen.°   *ill-humor*

Of wealthy lustre was the banquet-room,
Fill'd with pervading brilliance and perfume:
175 Before each lucid panel fuming stood
A censer[1] fed with myrrh and spiced wood,
Each by a sacred tripod held aloft,
Whose slender feet wide-swerv'd upon the soft
Wool-woofed° carpets: fifty wreaths of smoke   *woven*
180 From fifty censers their light voyage took
To the high roof, still mimick'd as they rose
Along the mirror'd walls by twin-clouds odorous.
Twelve sphered tables, by silk seats ensphered,° *encircled*
High as the level of a man's breast rear'd
185 On libbard's° paws, upheld the heavy gold   *leopard's*
Of cups and goblets, and the store thrice told

Of Ceres' horn,[2] and, in huge vessels, wine
Come from the gloomy° tun° with merry   *dark / cask*
   shine.
Thus loaded with a feast the tables stood,
190 Each shrining in the midst the image of a God.

When in an antechamber every guest
Had felt the cold full sponge to pleasure press'd,
By minist'ring slaves, upon his hands and feet,
And fragrant oils with ceremony meet
195 Pour'd on his hair, they all mov'd to the feast
In white robes, and themselves in order placed
Around the silken couches, wondering
Whence all this mighty cost and blaze of wealth could
   spring.

Soft went the music the soft air along,
200 While fluent Greek a vowel'd undersong
Kept up among the guests, discoursing low
At first, for scarcely was the wine at flow;
But when the happy vintage touch'd their brains,
Louder they talk, and louder come the strains
205 Of powerful instruments—the gorgeous dyes,
The space, the splendour of the draperies,
The roof of awful richness, nectarous cheer,
Beautiful slaves, and Lamia's self, appear,
Now, when the wine has done its rosy deed,
210 And every soul from human trammels freed,
No more so strange; for merry wine, sweet wine,
Will make Elysian shades not too fair, too divine.
Soon was God Bacchus at meridian height;
Flush'd were their cheeks, and bright eyes double bright:
215 Garlands of every green, and every scent
From vales deflower'd, or forest-trees branch-rent,
In baskets of bright osier'd° gold were brought   *woven*
High as the handles heap'd, to suit the thought
Of every guest; that each, as he did please,
220 Might fancy-fit his brows, silk-pillow'd at his ease.

What wreath for Lamia? What for Lycius?
What for the sage, old Apollonius?

---

[1] *censer* Vessel for burning incense.

[2] *Ceres' horn* Ceres, goddess of grain and agriculture, is sometimes depicted with a horn of plenty, overflowing with produce.

Upon her aching forehead be there hung
The leaves of willow and of adder's tongue;[1]
25 And for the youth, quick, let us strip for him
The thyrsus,[2] that his watching eyes may swim
Into forgetfulness; and, for the sage,
Let spear-grass and the spiteful thistle wage
War on his temples. Do not all charms fly
30 At the mere touch of cold philosophy?[3]
There was an awful° rainbow once in heaven: *awe-inspiring*
We know her woof, her texture; she is given
In the dull catalogue of common things.
Philosophy will clip an angel's wings,
35 Conquer all mysteries by rule and line,
Empty the haunted air, and gnomed[4] mine—
Unweave a rainbow, as it erewhile made
The tender-person'd Lamia melt into a shade.

By her glad Lycius sitting, in chief place,
240 Scarce saw in all the room another face,
Till, checking his love trance, a cup he took
Full brimm'd, and opposite sent forth a look
'Cross the broad table, to beseech a glance
From his old teacher's wrinkled countenance,
245 And pledge him. The bald-head philosopher
Had fix'd his eye, without a twinkle or stir
Full on the alarmed beauty of the bride,
Brow-beating her fair form, and troubling her sweet
     pride.
Lycius then press'd her hand, with devout touch,
250 As pale it lay upon the rosy couch:
'Twas icy, and the cold ran through his veins;
Then sudden it grew hot, and all the pains
Of an unnatural heat shot to his heart.
"Lamia, what means this? Wherefore dost thou start?
255 Know'st thou that man?" Poor Lamia answer'd not.
He gaz'd into her eyes, and not a jot
Own'd they the lovelorn piteous appeal:
More, more he gaz'd: his human senses reel:

Some hungry spell that loveliness absorbs;
260 There was no recognition in those orbs.
"Lamia!" he cried—and no soft-toned reply.
The many heard, and the loud revelry
Grew hush; the stately music no more breathes;
The myrtle sicken'd in a thousand wreaths.
265 By faint degrees, voice, lute, and pleasure ceased;
A deadly silence step by step increased,
Until it seem'd a horrid presence there,
And not a man but felt the terror in his hair.
"Lamia!" he shriek'd; and nothing but the shriek
270 With its sad echo did the silence break.
"Begone, foul dream!" he cried, gazing again
In the bride's face, where now no azure vein
Wander'd on fair-spaced temples; no soft bloom
Misted the cheek; no passion to illume
275 The deep-recessed vision—all was blight;
Lamia, no longer fair, there sat a deadly white.
"Shut, shut those juggling° eyes, thou   *beguiling*
     ruthless man!
Turn them aside, wretch! or the righteous ban
Of all the Gods, whose dreadful images
280 Here represent their shadowy presences,
May pierce them on the sudden with the thorn
Of painful blindness; leaving thee forlorn,
In trembling dotage to the feeblest fright
Of conscience, for their long offended might,
285 For all thine impious proud-heart sophistries,
Unlawful magic, and enticing lies.
Corinthians! look upon that gray-beard wretch!
Mark how, possess'd, his lashless eyelids stretch
Around his demon eyes! Corinthians, see!
290 My sweet bride withers at their potency."
"Fool!" said the sophist, in an undertone
Gruff with contempt; which a death-nighing moan
From Lycius answer'd, as heart-struck and lost,
He sank supine beside the aching ghost.
295 "Fool! Fool!" repeated he, while his eyes still
Relented not, nor mov'd; "from every ill
Of life have I preserv'd thee to this day,
And shall I see thee made a serpent's prey?"
Then Lamia breath'd death breath; the sophist's eye,
300 Like a sharp spear, went through her utterly,
Keen, cruel, perceant,° stinging: she, as well   *piercing*

---

[1] *adder's tongue* Fern that bears spikes resembling a snake's tongue.

[2] *thyrsus* Staff tipped with a pine cone and wreathed with vine leaves; carried by the followers of Bacchus.

[3] *philosophy* I.e., science.

[4] *gnomed* I.e., inhabited by gnomes.

As her weak hand could any meaning tell,
Motion'd him to be silent; vainly so,
He look'd and look'd again a level—No!
305 "A serpent!" echoed he; no sooner said,
Than with a frightful scream she vanished:
And Lycius' arms were empty of delight,

As were his limbs of life, from that same night.
On the high couch he lay! His friends came round—
310 Supported him—no pulse, or breath they found,
And, in its marriage robe, the heavy body wound.
—1820

Hyperion: A Fragment

"If *Hyperion* be not grand poetry," Percy Shelley wrote in praise of John Keats's epic poem, "none has been produced by our contemporaries." One of the works that solidified Keats's reputation as an artist of importance, *Hyperion* retells the ancient narrative of the Titans' defeat at the hands of the Olympian gods. The resulting poem is both a lament and a celebration; it grapples with the suffering and renewal that accompany the forward motion of time—especially at moments of profound historical change.

Keats began work on *Hyperion* in the fall of 1818. This was a period of intense productivity and artistic exploration, following a summer Keats had spent gathering inspiration on a walking tour of Scotland and of England's Lake District. Late 1818 was also, however, a time of emotional difficulty, as Keats spent the last months of the year caring for his dying brother Thomas.

Keats worked on the poem until April 1819, and a year later included it in his collection *Lamia, Isabella, The Eve of St. Agnes, and Other Poems* (1820). It was printed as *Hyperion: A Fragment*, the title reflecting its unfinished form; this version of the epic includes two completed books but breaks off in the midst of the third.

Keats's poem retells a myth that was familiar to most of his readers: the story of the Titans. Keats would have encountered this story in ancient Greek and Roman mythological works such as Hesiod's *Theogony* (c. 700 BCE), as well as in Renaissance retellings and later educational texts including Andrew Tooke's *Pantheon* (1698), William Godwin's *Pantheon* (1806), and John Lemprière's *Classical Dictionary* (1788). Details vary between accounts, but the overarching narrative concerns three generations of gods: in the first we encounter the sky god Uranus, the first ruler of the universe; Uranus then conceives a second generation, the Titans, with the earth goddess Tellus; finally Saturn, the leader of the Titans, fathers a third generation, the Olympians. Saturn leads the Titans in a successful uprising against their father, but Saturn's own children—the Olympians, led by Jove—in turn rise against the Titans. Called the Titanomachy, the ten-year war waged between Titans and Olympians sees the younger deities emerge victorious and exile the Titans to Tartaros, a sunken pit guarded by the hundred-handed creatures known as Hecatonchires. Because Keats was able to assume that his readers would be familiar with this narrative, he was able to begin *Hyperion* near the end of the Titanomachy; he focuses far more on the emotional and philosophical implications of events, than on recounting the story itself.

In addition to its mythological sources, Keats's poem displays the influence of Shakespeare, Dante, Wordsworth, and Milton; Milton's *Paradise Lost* (1677) exerted a particularly powerful influence. *Hyperion* and *Paradise Lost* both vividly portray a loss of power and a struggle to accept the personal and political implications of such a change. Keats's poem also mirrors Milton's in specific narrative moments; the gathering of defeated Titans who try to make sense of their plight, for example, resembles the council Milton's fallen angels hold to discuss their exile from Heaven. And there are also echoes of Milton's style and phrasing throughout *Hyperion*.

Keats himself, in a September 1819 letter, criticized what he had come to see as his poem's excessive use of "Miltonic inversions"[1] and concluded that a Miltonic style "cannot be written [except] in an artful, or, rather, artist's humour," in contrast to "the true voice of feeling." According to the letter, his frustration with its Miltonic style was the major reason he chose not to finish his epic.

Though he looked to the past for sources and inspiration, in writing *Hyperion* Keats was concerned with shaping a new epic for his own time. In the years before Keats began work on *Hyperion*, Napoleon was defeated, the unstable King George III was removed from power and replaced by his son, and people throughout England pushed for political and social reform. Though he was saddened by the rise of Napoleon (whom he thought had "done more harm to the life of Liberty than anyone else could have done") in the wake of the French Revolution, Keats nonetheless hoped that political progress could really be achieved. "All civilized countries become gradually enlightened," he insisted in an 1819 letter, "and there should be a continual change for the better." Casting Hyperion, the last Titan to retain power, as the poem's central figure suggests a typically Romantic celebration of the fallen empires of the past, but the depiction of Hyperion's eventual usurper Apollo, a bringer of art and music, seems to anticipate with great hope the arrival of a new era.

It is thought that Keats intended to make *Hyperion* at least four books long—and perhaps as many as ten. By halting the narrative in the midst of the third book, as Apollo begins to "die into life" and take his place as a god, Keats leaves his poem in a moment of anticipation. Readers trying to imagine how the epic might have developed have paid close attention to statements by Keats's friends—notably Richard Woodhouse, who claimed that "the poem, if completed, would have treated of the dethronement of Hyperion, the former God of the Sun, by Apollo—and incidentally those of Oceanus by Neptune, of Saturn by Jupiter, etc., and of the war of the Giants for Saturn's reestablishment—with other events, of which we have but very dark hints in the mythological poets of Greece and Rome." Scholars have rightly approached these claims with caution, however, noting that Keats altered his plans frequently for a variety of reasons; we have no way of knowing what a four-book or a ten-book *Hyperion* would have looked like.

In the summer of 1819, Keats revisited *Hyperion* and reworked it significantly, this time giving a prominent place to a new character, a poet figure. The resulting poem, *The Fall of Hyperion*, was also left incomplete; it was not published until 1856.

---

[1] *Miltonic inversions*   The ways in which Milton inverts the normal order of words in English very often follow structures common in Latin; adjectives, for example, often follow the noun they modify ("darkness visible," "idols foul") and the verb often follows object and subject ("his speech he thus renews," "but long I sat not.")

Hyperion: A Fragment

BOOK I

Deep in the shady sadness of a vale°   *valley*
   Far sunken from the healthy breath of morn,
Far from the fiery noon, and eve's one star,
Sat gray-hair'd Saturn,[1] quiet as a stone,
5   Still as the silence round about his lair;
Forest on forest hung about his head
Like cloud on cloud. No stir of air was there,
Not so much life as on a summer's day
Robs not one light seed from the feather'd grass,
10   But where the dead leaf fell, there did it rest.
A stream went voiceless by, still deadened more
By reason of his fallen divinity
Spreading a shade: the Naiad° 'mid her reeds   *water nymph*
Press'd her cold finger closer to her lips.

15   Along the margin-sand large foot-marks went,
No further than to where his feet had stray'd,
And slept there since. Upon the sodden ground
His old right hand lay nerveless, listless, dead,
Unsceptred;[2] and his realmless eyes were closed;
20   While his bow'd head seem'd list'ning to the Earth,
His ancient mother,[3] for some comfort yet.

      It seem'd no force could wake him from his place;
But there came one, who with a kindred hand
Touch'd his wide shoulders, after bending low
25   With reverence, though to one who knew it not.
She was a Goddess of the infant world;
By her in stature the tall Amazon[4]
Had stood a pigmy's height: she would have ta'en
Achilles[5] by the hair and bent his neck;

30   Or with a finger stay'd Ixion's wheel.[6]
Her face was large as that of Memphian sphinx,[7]
Pedestal'd haply in a palace court,
When sages look'd to Egypt for their lore.
But oh! how unlike marble was that face:
35   How beautiful, if sorrow had not made
Sorrow more beautiful than Beauty's self.
There was a listening fear in her regard,
As if calamity had but begun;
As if the vanward[8] clouds of evil days
40   Had spent their malice, and the sullen rear
Was with its stored thunder labouring up.
One hand she press'd upon that aching spot
Where beats the human heart, as if just there,
Though an immortal, she felt cruel pain:
45   The other upon Saturn's bended neck
She laid, and to the level of his ear
Leaning with parted lips, some words she spake
In solemn tenour and deep organ tone:
Some mourning words, which in our feeble tongue
50   Would come in these like accents; O how frail
To[9] that large utterance of the early Gods!
"Saturn, look up!—though wherefore, poor old King?
I have no comfort for thee, no not one:
I cannot say, 'O wherefore sleepest thou?'
55   For heaven is parted from thee, and the earth
Knows thee not, thus afflicted, for a God;
And ocean too, with all its solemn noise,
Has from thy sceptre pass'd; and all the air
Is emptied of thine hoary° majesty.   *aged*
60   Thy thunder, conscious of the new command,[10]
Rumbles reluctant o'er our fallen house;
And thy sharp lightning in unpractised hands

---

1 *Saturn* Leader of the Titans and god of agriculture, liberation, and time.

2 *Unsceptred* Without a scepter.

3 *the Earth … mother* Tellus, the Earth, was the mother of Saturn and other Titans.

4 *Amazon* Member of a legendary race of warrior women whose attributes included exceptional height.

5 *Achilles* Trojan warrior; the hero of Homer's *Iliad*.

6 *Ixion's wheel* Ixion, a human king, was bound to an eternally spinning fiery wheel as a punishment.

7 *Memphian sphinx* This may simply mean "Egyptian sphinx," referring to Memphis, Egypt, but there is a specific alabaster statue known as the Sphinx of Memphis; it is similar in appearance to the Great Sphinx of Giza, though smaller.

8 *vanward* Advancing, as a vanguard, the part of a military force that leads a charge.

9 *To* I.e., compared to.

10 *Thy thunder … command* Jove, the leader of the rebel Olympians, obtained power over thunder and lightning in order to defeat Saturn.

Scorches and burns our once serene domain.
O aching time! O moments big as years!
65 All as ye pass swell out the monstrous truth,
And press it so upon our weary griefs
That unbelief has not a space to breathe.
Saturn, sleep on:—O thoughtless, why did I
Thus violate thy slumbrous solitude?
70 Why should I ope thy melancholy eyes?
Saturn, sleep on! while at thy feet I weep."

　　　As when, upon a tranced summer-night,
Those green-rob'd senators of mighty woods,
Tall oaks, branch-charmed by the earnest stars,
75 Dream, and so dream all night without a stir,
Save from one gradual solitary gust
Which comes upon the silence, and dies off,
As if the ebbing air had but one wave;
So came these words and went; the while in tears
80 She touch'd her fair large forehead to the ground,
Just where her falling hair might be outspread
A soft and silken mat for Saturn's feet.
One moon, with alteration slow, had shed
Her silver seasons four upon the night,[1]
85 And still these two were postured motionless,
Like natural sculpture in cathedral cavern;
The frozen God still couchant° on the earth,   *lying down*
And the sad Goddess weeping at his feet:
Until at length old Saturn lifted up
90 His faded eyes, and saw his kingdom gone,
And all the gloom and sorrow of the place,
And that fair kneeling Goddess; and then spake,
As with a palsied[2] tongue, and while his beard
Shook horrid with such aspen-malady:[3]
95 "O tender spouse of gold Hyperion,[4]
Thea,[5] I feel thee ere I see thy face;

Look up, and let me see our doom in it;
Look up, and tell me if this feeble shape
Is Saturn's; tell me, If thou hear'st the voice
100 Of Saturn; tell me, if this wrinkling brow,
Naked and bare of its great diadem,°   *crown*
Peers like the front° of Saturn. Who had power   *forehead*
To make me desolate? whence came the strength?
How was it nurtur'd to such bursting forth,
105 While Fate seem'd strangled in my nervous grasp?
But it is so; and I am smother'd up,
And buried from all godlike exercise
Of influence benign on planets pale,
Of admonitions to the winds and seas,
110 Of peaceful sway above man's harvesting,
And all those acts which Deity supreme
Doth ease its heart of love in.—I am gone
Away from my own bosom: I have left
My strong identity, my real self,
115 Somewhere between the throne, and where I sit
Here on this spot of earth. Search, Thea, search!
Open thine eyes eterne,° and sphere them round   *eternal*
Upon all space:[6] space starr'd, and lorn° of light;   *bereft*
Space region'd with[7] life-air; and barren void;
120 Spaces of fire, and all the yawn of hell.—
Search, Thea, search! and tell me, if thou seest
A certain shape or shadow, making way
With wings or chariot fierce to repossess
A heaven he lost erewhile: it must—it must
125 Be of ripe progress[8]—Saturn must be King.
Yes, there must be a golden victory;
There must be Gods thrown down, and trumpets blown
Of triumph calm, and hymns of festival
Upon the gold clouds metropolitan,
130 Voices of soft proclaim,° and silver stir   *speech*
Of strings in hollow shells;[9] and there shall be
Beautiful things made new, for the surprise
Of the sky-children; I will give command:
Thea! Thea! Thea! where is Saturn?"

---

[1] *One moon … the night*   I.e., the moon had passed through all of its phases.

[2] *palsied*   I.e., afflicted by tremors or weakness.

[3] *aspen-malady*   The aspen tree is also called the "quaking aspen" because it is easily shaken by even a mild breeze.

[4] *Hyperion*   God of light and the sun; one of the twelve Titans.

[5] *Thea*   Also a Titan; the sister and wife of Hyperion, with whom she conceived the sun, the moon, and the dawn.

[6] *sphere them … space*   I.e., look in all directions.

[7] *region'd with*   With regions of.

[8] *of ripe progress*   I.e., near to being achieved.

[9] *strings in hollow shells*   Lyres were sometimes made from tortoise shells.

135 This passion lifted him upon his feet,
And made his hands to struggle in the air,
His Druid locks to shake and ooze with sweat,
His eyes to fever out, his voice to cease.
He stood, and heard not Thea's sobbing deep;
140 A little time, and then again he snatch'd
Utterance thus.—"But cannot I create?
Cannot I form? Cannot I fashion forth
Another world, another universe,
To overbear and crumble this to nought?
145 Where is another chaos?[1] Where?"—That word
Found way unto Olympus,[2] and made quake
The rebel three.[3]—Thea was startled up,
And in her bearing was a sort of hope,
As thus she quick-voic'd spake, yet full of awe.

150 "This cheers our fallen house: come to our friends,
O Saturn! come away, and give them heart;
I know the covert,° for thence came I hither." *hiding place*
Thus brief; then with beseeching eyes she went
With backward footing through the shade a space:
155 He follow'd, and she turn'd to lead the way
Through aged boughs, that yielded like the mist
Which eagles cleave upmounting from their nest.

Meanwhile in other realms big tears were shed,
More sorrow like to this, and such like woe,
160 Too huge for mortal tongue or pen of scribe:
The Titans fierce, self-hid, or prison-bound,
Groan'd for the old allegiance once more,
And listen'd in sharp pain for Saturn's voice.
But one of the whole mammoth-brood still kept
165 His sov'reignty, and rule, and majesty;—
Blazing Hyperion on his orbed fire[4]
Still sat, still snuff'd the incense, teeming up

From man to the sun's God;[5] yet unsecure:
For as among us mortals omens drear
170 Fright and perplex, so also shuddered he—
Not at dog's howl, or gloom-bird's° hated screech, *owl's*
Or the familiar visiting of one
Upon the first toll of his passing-bell,[6]
Or prophesyings of the midnight lamp;[7]
175 But horrors, portion'd to a giant nerve,
Oft made Hyperion ache. His palace bright
Bastion'd with pyramids[8] of glowing gold,
And touch'd with shade of bronzed obelisks,
Glar'd a blood-red through all its thousand courts,
180 Arches, and domes, and fiery galleries;
And all its curtains of Aurorian clouds[9]
Flush'd angrily: while sometimes eagle's wings,
Unseen before by Gods or wondering men,
Darken'd the place; and neighing steeds were heard,
185 Not heard before by Gods or wondering men.
Also, when he would° taste the spicy wreaths *desired to*
Of incense, breath'd aloft from sacred hills,
Instead of sweets, his ample palate took
Savour of poisonous brass and metal sick:
190 And so, when harbour'd in the sleepy west,
After the full completion of fair day,—
For rest divine upon exalted couch
And slumber in the arms of melody,
He pac'd away the pleasant hours of ease
195 With stride colossal, on from hall to hall;
While far within each aisle and deep recess,
His winged minions in close clusters stood,
Amaz'd and full of fear; like anxious men
Who on wide plains gather in panting troops,
200 When earthquakes jar their battlements and towers.
Even now, while Saturn, rous'd from icy trance,

---

[5] *still snuff'd ... God* Still breathed the offerings of incense being burned for him by humans.

[6] *passing-bell* Bell rung for Christians when they are dying—a time when, according to folk wisdom, loved ones might see an apparition of the dying individual.

[7] *midnight lamp* I.e., candle, whose flame and wax might be interpreted for omens.

[8] *Bastion'd ... pyramids* With pyramids placed at the corners; bastions are defensive structures built at the corners of fortifications.

[9] *Aurorian clouds* Dawn clouds; Aurora is the goddess of dawn.

---

[1] *chaos* In Greek mythology, the world was formed out of Chaos, the void.

[2] *Olympus* Highest mountain in Greece; home to Jove and the other Olympian gods.

[3] *The rebel three* Jove, Neptune, and Pluto, Saturn's three Olympian sons who rebelled against him.

[4] *orbed fire* I.e., the sun.

Went step for step with Thea through the woods,
Hyperion, leaving twilight in the rear,
Came slope upon the threshold of the west;
205 Then, as was wont, his palace-door flew ope
In smoothest silence, save what solemn tubes,[1]
Blown by the serious Zephyrs,° gave of sweet   *west winds*
And wandering sounds, slow-breathed melodies;
And like a rose in vermeil° tint and shape,   *bright scarlet*
210 In fragrance soft, and coolness to the eye,
That inlet to severe magnificence
Stood full blown, for the God to enter in.

    He enter'd, but he enter'd full of wrath;
His flaming robes stream'd out beyond his heels,
215 And gave a roar, as if of earthly fire,
That scar'd away the meek ethereal Hours[2]
And made their dove-wings tremble. On he flared,
From stately nave to nave, from vault to vault,
Through bowers of fragrant and enwreathed light,
220 And diamond paved lustrous long arcades,[3]
Until he reach'd the great main cupola;°   *domed roof*
There standing fierce beneath, he stampt his foot,
And from the basements deep to the high towers
Jarr'd his own golden region; and before
225 The quavering thunder thereupon had ceas'd,
His voice leapt out, despite of godlike curb,[4]
To this result: "O dreams of day and night!
O monstrous forms! O effigies of pain!
O spectres busy in a cold, cold gloom!
230 O lank-eared Phantoms of black-weeded pools!
Why do I know ye? why have I seen ye? why
Is my eternal essence thus distraught
To see and to behold these horrors new?
Saturn is fallen, am I too to fall?
235 Am I to leave this haven of my rest,
This cradle of my glory, this soft clime,
This calm luxuriance of blissful light,
These crystalline pavilions, and pure fanes,°   *temples*

Of all my lucent° empire? It is left   *shining*
240 Deserted, void, nor any haunt of mine.
The blaze, the splendor, and the symmetry,
I cannot see—but darkness, death and darkness.
Even here, into my centre of repose,
The shady visions come to domineer,
245 Insult, and blind, and stifle up my pomp°—   *splendor*
Fall!—No, by Tellus and her briny robes![5]
Over the fiery frontier of my realms
I will advance a terrible right arm
Shall scare that infant thunderer, rebel Jove,
250 And bid old Saturn take his throne again."—
He spake, and ceas'd, the while a heavier threat
Held struggle with his throat but came not forth;
For as in theatres of crowded men
Hubbub increases more they call out "Hush!"
255 So at Hyperion's words the Phantoms pale
Bestirr'd themselves, thrice horrible and cold;
And from the mirror'd level[6] where he stood
A mist arose, as from a scummy marsh.
At this, through all his bulk an agony
260 Crept gradual, from the feet unto the crown,
Like a lithe serpent vast and muscular
Making slow way, with head and neck convuls'd
From over-strained might. Releas'd, he fled
To the eastern gates, and full six dewy hours
265 Before the dawn in season due should blush,
He breath'd fierce breath against the sleepy portals,
Clear'd them of heavy vapours, burst them wide
Suddenly on the ocean's chilly streams.
The planet orb of fire, whereon he rode
270 Each day from east to west the heavens through,
Spun round in sable curtaining of clouds;
Not therefore veiled quite, blindfold, and hid,
But ever and anon[7] the glancing spheres,
Circles, and arcs, and broad-belting colure,[8]

---

[1] *tubes* Parts of an organ or other wind instrument.

[2] *Hours* Horae, goddesses of the seasons or of the hours of the day; they are sometimes described as the handmaids or daughters of the sun.

[3] *arcades* Walkways covered by connected arches.

[4] *despite … curb* In spite of his godlike restraint.

[5] *Tellus … robes* The earth and the oceans.

[6] *the mirror'd level* I.e., the floor, which is so polished as to be reflective.

[7] *ever and anon* Every once in a while.

[8] *colure* Two circles traced around the celestial sphere, intersecting at the poles so as to divide the earth into quarters; one circle passes through the points of equinox, and the other through the points of solstice.

275 Glow'd through, and wrought upon the muffling dark
Sweet-shaped lightnings from the nadir[1] deep
Up to the zenith,[2]—hieroglyphics old,
Which sages and keen-eyed astrologers
Then living on the earth, with labouring thought
280 Won from the gaze of many centuries:
Now lost, save what we find on remnants huge
Of stone, or marble swart;° their import gone,   *dark*
Their wisdom long since fled—Two wings this orb
Possess'd for glory, two fair argent° wings,   *silver*
285 Ever exalted° at the God's approach: *lifted*
And now, from forth the gloom their plumes immense
Rose, one by one, till all outspreaded were;
While still the dazzling globe maintain'd eclipse,[3]
Awaiting for Hyperion's command.
290 Fain° would he have commanded, fain   *gladly*
      took throne
And bid the day begin, if but[4] for change.
He might not:—No, though a primeval God:
The sacred seasons might not be disturb'd.
Therefore the operations of the dawn
295 Stay'd° in their birth, even as here 'tis told.   *halted*
Those silver wings expanded sisterly,
Eager to sail their orb; the porches wide
Open'd upon the dusk demesnes° of night;   *domains*
And the bright Titan, phrenzied with new woes,
300 Unus'd to bend, by hard compulsion bent
His spirit to the sorrow of the time;
And all along a dismal rack[5] of clouds,
Upon the boundaries of day and night,
He stretch'd himself in grief and radiance faint.
305 There as he lay, the Heaven with its stars
Looked down on him with pity, and the voice
Of Coelus,[6] from the universal space,

Thus whisper'd low and solemn in his ear.
"O brightest of my children dear, earth-born
310 And sky-engendered, Son of Mysteries
All unrevealed even to the powers
Which met at thy creating; at whose joys
And palpitations sweet, and pleasures soft,
I, Coelus, wonder, how they came and whence;
315 And at the fruits thereof what shapes they be,
Distinct, and visible; symbols divine,
Manifestations of that beauteous life
Diffus'd unseen throughout eternal space:
Of these new-form'd art thou, oh brightest child!
320 Of these, thy brethren and the Goddesses!
There is sad feud among ye, and rebellion
Of son against his sire. I saw him fall,
I saw my first-born[7] tumbled from his throne!
To me his arms were spread, to me his voice
325 Found way from forth the thunders round his head!
Pale wox° I, and in vapours hid my face.   *became*
Art thou, too, near such doom? vague fear there is:
For I have seen my sons most unlike Gods.
Divine ye were created, and divine
330 In sad° demeanour, solemn, undisturb'd,   *serious*
Unruffled, like high Gods, ye liv'd and ruled:
Now I behold in you fear, hope, and wrath;
Actions of rage and passion; even as
I see them, on the mortal world beneath,
335 In men who die.—This is the grief, O Son!
Sad sign of ruin, sudden dismay, and fall!
Yet do thou strive; as thou art capable,
As thou canst move about, an evident God;
And canst oppose to each malignant hour
340 Ethereal presence:—I am but a voice;
My life is but the life of winds and tides,
No more than winds and tides can I avail:—
But thou canst.—Be thou therefore in the van° *vanguard*
Of circumstance; yea, seize the arrow's barb
345 Before the tense string murmur.—To the earth!
For there thou wilt find Saturn, and his woes.
Meantime I will keep watch on thy bright sun,
And of thy seasons be a careful nurse."—
Ere half this region-whisper had come down,

---

[1] *nadir* Lowest point on the celestial sphere directly beneath an object or observer.

[2] *zenith* Highest point in the celestial sphere directly above an object or observer.

[3] *maintain'd eclipse* Stayed hidden.

[4] *if but* If only.

[5] *rack* Fast-moving mass of clouds.

[6] *Coelus* Also called Uranus, god of the sky and father of Hyperion and the other Titans.

[7] *my first-born* I.e., Saturn (who, however, is usually considered the youngest of Uranus's Titan sons).

350 Hyperion arose, and on the stars
Lifted his curved lids, and kept them wide
Until it ceas'd; and still he kept them wide:
And still they were the same bright, patient stars.
Then with a slow incline of his broad breast,
355 Like to a diver in the pearly seas,
Forward he stoop'd over the airy shore,
And plung'd all noiseless into the deep night.

BOOK 2

Just at the self-same beat of Time's wide wings
Hyperion slid into the rustled air,
And Saturn gain'd° with Thea that sad place   *reached*
Where Cybele[1] and the bruised Titans mourn'd.
5 It was a den where no insulting light
Could glimmer on their tears; where their own groans
They felt, but heard not, for the solid roar
Of thunderous waterfalls and torrents hoarse,
Pouring a constant bulk, uncertain where.[2]
10 Crag jutting forth to crag, and rocks that seem'd
Ever as if just rising from a sleep,
Forehead to forehead held their monstrous horns;
And thus in thousand hugest phantasies
Made a fit roofing to this nest of woe.
15 Instead of thrones, hard flint they sat upon,
Couches of rugged stone, and slaty ridge
Stubborn'd° with iron. All were not assembled: *hardened*
Some chain'd in torture, and some wandering.
Coeus, and Gyges, and Briareüs,
20 Typhon, and Dolor, and Porphyrion,[3]

With many more, the brawniest in assault,
Were pent in regions of laborious breath;
Dungeon'd in opaque element,° to keep   *atmosphere*
Their clenched teeth still clench'd, and all their limbs
25 Lock'd up like veins of metal,[4] crampt and screw'd;
Without a motion, save of their big hearts
Heaving in pain, and horribly convuls'd
With sanguine° feverous boiling gurge°   *bloody / whirlpool*
    of pulse.
Mnemosyne[5] was straying in the world;
30 Far from her moon had Phoebe[6] wandered;
And many else, were free to roam abroad,
But for the main,[7] here found they covert drear.
Scarce images of life, one here, one there,
Lay vast and edgeways; like a dismal cirque°   *circle*
35 Of Druid stones, upon a forlorn moor,
When the chill rain begins at shut of eve,
In dull November, and their chancel vault,[8]
The Heaven itself, is blinded throughout night.
Each one kept shroud, nor to his neighbour gave
40 Or word, or look, or action of despair.
Creüs[9] was one; his ponderous iron mace
Lay by him, and a shatter'd rib of rock
Told of his rage, ere he thus sank and pined.
Iäpetus[10] another; in his grasp,
45 A serpent's plashy° neck; its barbed tongue   *slimy*
Squeez'd from the gorge,° and all its uncurl'd   *throat*
    length
Dead; and because the creature could not spit
Its poison in the eyes of conquering Jove.
Next Cottus:[11] prone he lay, chin uppermost,
50 As though in pain; for still upon the flint
He ground severe his skull, with open mouth

---

[1] *Cybele* Goddess of nature and fertility, sometimes considered equivalent to Ops, Saturn's Titan wife; she is referred to by this latter name elsewhere in the poem.

[2] *uncertain where* I.e., the waterfalls can be heard but not seen, and their location is difficult to determine.

[3] *Coeus ... Porphyrion* Only one of these divine beings, Coeus, is usually considered a Titan; here, however, they all appear to be presented as Titans or at least as Titan allies; *Gyges, and Briareüs* Powerful hundred-handed giants who were brothers of the Titans. They were trapped in the abyss of Tartarus until they were released by Jove, and are usually considered to have fought on the opposite side of this conflict, as Jove's allies; *Typhon* Tremendously powerful and horrifying monster, also imprisoned in Tartarus. He was a half-brother of the Titans; *Dolor* Spirit of pain; *Porphyrion* One of the Giants, half-brothers of the Titans. He is usually thought to have been destroyed by Jove.

[4] *like veins of metal* I.e., like veins of ore in rock.

[5] *Mnemosyne* Titan goddess of memory and mother of the muses.

[6] *Phoebe* Titan goddess of the moon.

[7] *for the main* For the most part.

[8] *chancel vault* Literally, vaulted temple roof; i.e., the sky.

[9] *Creüs* A Titan.

[10] *Iäpetus* Titan god of mortality.

[11] *Cottus* Another hundred-armed giant, brother to Gyges and Briareüs. Like his brothers, he is usually considered to have been an ally of Jove, not of the Titans, in this conflict.

And eyes at horrid working. Nearest him
Asia, born of most enormous Caf,[1]
Who cost her mother Tellus keener pangs,
55 Though feminine, than any of her sons:
More thought than woe was in her dusky face,
For she was prophesying of her glory;
And in her wide imagination stood
Palm-shaded temples, and high rival fanes,
60 By Oxus or in Ganges'[2] sacred isles.
Even as Hope upon her anchor[3] leans,
So leant she, not so fair, upon a tusk
Shed from the broadest of her elephants.
Above her, on a crag's uneasy shelve,
65 Upon his elbow rais'd, all prostrate else,
Shadow'd Enceladus;[4] once tame and mild
As grazing ox unworried in the meads;
Now tiger-passion'd, lion-thoughted, wroth,
He meditated, plotted, and even now
70 Was hurling mountains in that second war,[5]
Not long delay'd, that scar'd the younger Gods
To hide themselves in forms of beast and bird.
Not far hence Atlas;[6] and beside him prone
Phorcus, the sire of Gorgons.[7] Neighbour'd close
75 Oceanus, and Tethys,[8] in whose lap
Sobb'd Clymene[9] among her tangled hair.
In midst of all lay Themis,[10] at the feet

Of Ops the queen all clouded round from sight;
No shape distinguishable, more than when
80 Thick night confounds the pine-tops with the clouds:
And many else whose names may not be told.
For when the Muse's wings are air-ward spread,
Who shall delay her flight? And she must chaunt°   *sing*
Of Saturn, and his guide, who now had climb'd
85 With damp and slippery footing from a depth
More horrid still. Above a sombre cliff
Their heads appear'd, and up their stature grew
Till on the level height their steps found ease:
Then Thea spread abroad her trembling arms
90 Upon the precincts of this nest of pain,
And sidelong fix'd her eye on Saturn's face:
There saw she direst strife; the supreme God
At war with all the frailty of grief,
Of rage, of fear, anxiety, revenge,
95 Remorse, spleen,° hope, but most of all despair.   *ill will*
Against these plagues he strove in vain; for Fate
Had pour'd a mortal oil upon his head,
A disanointing poison:[11] so that Thea,
Affrighted, kept her still, and let him pass
100 First onwards in, among the fallen tribe.

     As with us mortal men, the laden heart
Is persecuted more, and fever'd more,
When it is nighing to the mournful house
Where other hearts are sick of the same bruise;
105 So Saturn, as he walk'd into the midst,
Felt faint, and would have sunk among the rest,
But that he met Enceladus's eye,
Whose mightiness, and awe of him, at once
Came like an inspiration; and he shouted,
110 "Titans, behold your God!" at which some groan'd;
Some started on their feet; some also shouted;
Some wept, some wail'd, all bow'd with reverence;
And Ops, uplifting her black folded veil,
Show'd her pale cheeks, and all her forehead wan,
115 Her eye-brows thin and jet, and hollow eyes.
There is a roaring in the bleak-grown pines
When Winter lifts his voice; there is a noise

[1] *Asia*   Titan goddess of Lydia, an ancient empire in present-day Turkey (though here she is linked with a larger portion of the Asian continent); *Caf*   Mountain that surrounds the world in Iranian myth.

[2] *Oxus*   Amu Darya, a sacred river in central Asia; *Ganges*   Sacred river in present-day India and Bangladesh.

[3] *Hope upon her anchor*   In Christian art, the personification of hope was often depicted with an anchor.

[4] *Enceladus*   A giant.

[5] *Was hurling ... second war*   Was planning how he would hurl mountains in the coming war between the Olympians and the Giants, which in mythological sources follows the war between the Olympians and the Titans.

[6] *Atlas*   Titan who held up the celestial sphere.

[7] *Phorcus*   Primordial sea god; *Gorgons*   Three sisters who had snakes for hair and whose appearance turned viewers to stone.

[8] *Oceanus, and Tethys*   Titan god and goddess of the sea.

[9] *Clymene*   Goddess of fame, the daughter of Oceanus and Tethys.

[10] *Themis*   Titan goddess of divine order, law, custom, and prophecy.

[11] *disanointing poison*   This image references the practice of anointing monarchs with oil as part of their coronation; here, the oil removes Saturn's power instead of granting it.

Among immortals when a God gives sign,
With hushing finger, how he means to load
20 His tongue with the full weight of utterless thought,
With thunder, and with music, and with pomp:
Such noise is like the roar of bleak-grown pines;
Which, when it ceases in this mountain'd world,
No other sound succeeds; but ceasing here,
25 Among these fallen, Saturn's voice therefrom
Grew up like organ, that begins anew
Its strain, when other harmonies, stopt short,
Leave the dinn'd[1] air vibrating silverly.
Thus grew it up—"Not in my own sad breast,
30 Which is its own great judge and searcher out,
Can I find reason why ye should be thus:
Not in the legends of the first of days,
Studied from that old spirit-leaved book
Which starry Uranus with finger bright
35 Sav'd from the shores of darkness, when the waves
Low-ebb'd still hid it up in shallow gloom;—
And the which book ye know I ever kept
For my firm-based footstool:—Ah, infirm!
Not there, nor in sign, symbol, or portent
40 Of element, earth, water, air, and fire,—
At war, at peace, or inter-quarreling
One against one, or two, or three, or all
Each several one against the other three,
As fire with air loud warring when rain-floods
45 Drown both, and press them both against earth's face,
Where, finding sulphur, a quadruple wrath
Unhinges the poor world;—not in that strife,
Wherefrom I take strange lore, and read it deep,
Can I find reason why ye should be thus:
50 No, no-where can unriddle, though I search,
And pore on Nature's universal scroll
Even to swooning, why ye, Divinities,
The first-born of all shap'd and palpable Gods,
Should cower beneath what, in comparison,
55 Is untremendous might. Yet ye are here,
O'erwhelm'd, and spurn'd, and batter'd, ye are here!
O Titans, shall I say 'Arise!'—Ye groan:
Shall I say 'Crouch!'—Ye groan. What can I then?
O Heaven wide! O unseen parent dear!

160 What can I? Tell me, all ye brethren Gods,
How we can war, how engine our great wrath![2]
O speak your counsel now, for Saturn's ear
Is all a-hunger'd. Thou, Oceanus,
Ponderest high and deep; and in thy face
165 I see, astonied,° that severe content   *astonished*
Which comes of thought and musing: give us help!"

So ended Saturn; and the God of the Sea,
Sophist and sage, from no Athenian grove,[3]
But cogitation° in his watery shades,   *thought*
170 Arose, with locks not oozy,[4] and began,
In murmurs, which his first-endeavouring tongue
Caught infant-like from the far-foamed sands.
"O ye, whom wrath consumes! who, passion-stung,
Writhe at defeat, and nurse your agonies!
175 Shut up your senses, stifle up your ears,
My voice is not a bellows unto ire.
Yet listen, ye who will, whilst I bring proof
How ye, perforce, must be content to stoop:
And in the proof much comfort will I give,
180 If ye will take that comfort in its truth.
We fall by course of Nature's law, not force
Of thunder, or of Jove. Great Saturn, thou
Hast sifted well the atom-universe;[5]
But for this reason, that thou art the King,
185 And only blind from sheer supremacy,[6]
One avenue was shaded from thine eyes,
Through which I wandered to eternal truth.
And first, as thou wast not the first of powers,
So art thou not the last; it cannot be:

---

[1] *dinn'd* Made to resonate with sound.

[2] *engine our great wrath* Make our wrath into an engine of war; or, provide means or tools with which to enact our wrath.

[3] *Sophist* Ancient Greek term for a wise and educated person; *from no ... grove* Two of the places an ancient Greek sophist might have studied—the Lyceum and Plato's Academy—were located in groves of trees.

[4] *locks not oozy* Hair not wet; this is notable because it is unusual for Oceanus to be on land.

[5] *atom-universe* The belief that matter is made of tiny indivisible particles called atoms had been held in some form by some British intellectuals since the late sixteenth century.

[6] *blind from sheer supremacy* I.e., blinded by his own great power.

190 Thou art not the beginning nor the end.[1]
From chaos and parental darkness came
Light, the first fruits of that intestine broil,[2]
That sullen ferment, which for wondrous ends
Was ripening in itself. The ripe hour came,
195 And with it light, and light, engendering
Upon its own producer, forthwith touch'd
The whole enormous matter into life.
Upon that very hour, our parentage,
The Heavens and the Earth, were manifest:
200 Then thou first-born, and we the giant-race,
Found ourselves ruling new and beauteous realms.
Now comes the pain of truth, to whom 'tis pain;
O folly! for to bear all naked truths,
And to envisage circumstance, all calm,
205 That is the top of sovereignty. Mark well!
As Heaven and Earth are fairer, fairer far
Than Chaos and blank Darkness, though once chiefs;
And as we show beyond that Heaven and Earth[3]
In form and shape compact and beautiful,
210 In will, in action free, companionship,
And thousand other signs of purer life;
So on our heels a fresh perfection treads,
A power more strong in beauty, born of us
And fated to excel us, as we pass
215 In glory that old Darkness: nor are we
Thereby more conquer'd, than by us the rule
Of shapeless Chaos. Say, doth the dull soil
Quarrel with the proud forests it hath fed,
And feedeth still, more comely than itself?
220 Can it deny the chiefdom of green groves?
Or shall the tree be envious of the dove
Because it cooeth, and hath snowy wings
To wander wherewithal and find its joys?
We are such forest-trees, and our fair boughs
225 Have bred forth, not pale solitary doves,
But eagles golden-feather'd, who do tower
Above us in their beauty, and must reign

In right thereof; for 'tis the eternal law
That first in beauty should be first in might:
230 Yea, by that law, another race may drive
Our conquerors to mourn as we do now.
Have ye beheld the young God of the Seas,[4]
My dispossessor? Have ye seen his face?
Have ye beheld his chariot, foam'd along
235 By noble winged creatures he hath made?[5]
I saw him on the calmed waters scud,°   *sail quickly*
With such a glow of beauty in his eyes,
That it enforc'd me to bid sad farewell
To all my empire: farewell sad I took,
240 And hither came, to see how dolorous fate
Had wrought upon ye; and how I might best
Give consolation in this woe extreme.
Receive the truth, and let it be your balm."

    Whether through poz'd[6] conviction, or disdain,
245 They guarded silence, when Oceanus
Left murmuring, what deepest thought can tell?
But so it was, none answered for a space,
Save one whom none regarded, Clymene;
And yet she answer'd not, only complain'd,
250 With hectic[7] lips, and eyes up-looking mild,
Thus wording timidly among the fierce:
"O Father, I am here the simplest voice,
And all my knowledge is that joy is gone,
And this thing woe crept in among our hearts,
255 There to remain for ever, as I fear:
I would not bode of evil; if I thought
So weak a creature could turn off the help
Which by just right should come of mighty Gods;[8]
Yet let me tell my sorrow, let me tell
260 Of what I heard, and how it made me weep,

---

[1] *Thou art … the end* See Revelation 1.8: "I am Alpha and Omega, the beginning and the ending, saith the Lord."

[2] *intestine broil* Civil war.

[3] *we … Earth* It is apparent that we are better than Heaven and Earth.

[4] *young God of the Seas* Neptune, the new Olympian god of the sea.

[5] *his chariot … hath made* Neptune drives a chariot pulled by seahorses.

[6] *poz'd* Probably confused, though the word is also used to mean "feigned."

[7] *hectic* Symptomatic of fever, and especially of fever associated with tuberculosis.

[8] *I would … mighty Gods* I would not speak of evil if I thought the words of someone as weak as I could prevent the help that justly should come from the mighty gods.

And know that we had parted from all hope.
I stood upon a shore, a pleasant shore,
Where a sweet clime° was breathed from a land   *atmosphere*
Of fragrance, quietness, and trees, and flowers.
65 Full of calm joy it was, as I of grief;
Too full of joy and soft delicious warmth;
So that I felt a movement in my heart
To chide, and to reproach that solitude
With songs of misery, music of our woes;
70 And sat me down, and took a mouthed shell
And murmur'd into it, and made melody—
O melody no more! for while I sang,
And with poor skill let pass into the breeze
The dull shell's echo, from a bowery strand
75 Just opposite, an island of the sea,
There came enchantment with the shifting wind,
That did both drown and keep alive my ears.
I threw my shell away upon the sand,
And a wave fill'd it, as my sense was fill'd
80 With that new blissful golden melody.
A living death was in each gush of sounds,
Each family of rapturous hurried notes,
That fell, one after one, yet all at once,
Like pearl beads dropping sudden from their string:
85 And then another, then another strain,
Each like a dove leaving its olive perch,
With music wing'd instead of silent plumes,
To hover round my head, and make me sick
Of joy and grief at once. Grief overcame,
90 And I was stopping up my frantic ears,
When, past all hindrance of my trembling hands,
A voice came sweeter, sweeter than all tune,
And still it cried, 'Apollo![1] young Apollo!
The morning-bright Apollo! young Apollo!'
95 I fled, it follow'd me, and cried 'Apollo!'
O Father, and O Brethren, had ye felt
Those pains of mine; O Saturn, hadst thou felt,
Ye would not call this too indulged tongue
Presumptuous, in thus venturing to be heard."

300   So far her voice flow'd on, like timorous brook
That, lingering along a pebbled coast,

Doth fear to meet the sea: but sea it met,
And shudder'd; for the overwhelming voice
Of huge Enceladus swallow'd it in wrath:
305 The ponderous syllables, like sullen waves
In the half-glutted° hollows of reef-rocks,   *half-filled*
Came booming thus, while still upon his arm
He lean'd; not rising, from supreme contempt.
"Or shall we listen to the over-wise,
310 Or to the over-foolish giant, Gods?
Not thunderbolt on thunderbolt, till all
That rebel Jove's whole armoury were spent,
Not world on world upon these shoulders piled,
Could agonize me more than baby-words
315 In midst of this dethronement horrible.
Speak! roar! shout! yell! ye sleepy Titans all.
Do ye forget the blows, the buffets vile?
Are ye not smitten by a youngling arm?
Dost thou forget, sham Monarch of the Waves,
320 Thy scalding in the seas? What, have I rous'd
Your spleens° with so few simple words as these?   *tempers*
O joy! for now I see ye are not lost:
O joy! for now I see a thousand eyes
Wide glaring for revenge!"—As this he said,
325 He lifted up his stature vast, and stood,
Still without intermission speaking thus:
"Now ye are flames, I'll tell you how to burn,
And purge the ether of our enemies;
How to feed fierce the crooked stings of fire,
330 And singe away the swollen clouds of Jove,
Stifling that puny essence in its tent.
O let him feel the evil he hath done;
For though I scorn Oceanus's lore,
Much pain have I for more than loss of realms:
335 The days of peace and slumberous calm are fled;
Those days, all innocent of scathing war,
When all the fair Existences of heaven
Came open-eyed to guess what we would speak:—
That was before our brows were taught to frown,
340 Before our lips knew else but solemn sounds;
That was before we knew the winged thing,
Victory,[2] might be lost, or might be won.
And be ye mindful that Hyperion,

---

[1] *Apollo* Olympian god whose associations include music, poetry, and knowledge.

[2] *winged ... Victory* Victoria, the Roman personification of victory, is depicted with wings.

Our brightest brother, still is undisgraced—
345 Hyperion, lo! his radiance is here!"

    All eyes were on Enceladus's face,
And they beheld, while still Hyperion's name
Flew from his lips up to the vaulted rocks,[1]
A pallid gleam across his features stern:
350 Not savage, for he saw full many a God
Wroth as himself. He look'd upon them all,
And in each face he saw a gleam of light,
But splendider in Saturn's, whose hoar° locks °gray / hair
Shone like the bubbling foam about a keel
355 When the prow sweeps into a midnight cove.
In pale and silver silence they remain'd,
Till suddenly a splendour, like the morn,
Pervaded all the beetling° gloomy steeps,   overhanging
All the sad spaces of oblivion,
360 And every gulf, and every chasm old,
And every height, and every sullen depth,
Voiceless, or hoarse with loud tormented streams:
And all the everlasting cataracts,°   waterfalls
And all the headlong torrents far and near,
365 Mantled before in darkness and huge shade,
Now saw the light and made it terrible.
It was Hyperion:—a granite peak
His bright feet touch'd, and there he stay'd to view
The misery his brilliance had betray'd°   revealed
370 To the most hateful seeing of itself.
Golden his hair of short Numidian curl,[2]
Regal his shape majestic, a vast shade
In midst of his own brightness, like the bulk
Of Memnon's image[3] at the set of sun
375 To one who travels from the dusking East:
Sighs, too, as mournful as that Memnon's harp[4]

---

[1] *vaulted rocks* Rocks that form a ceiling.

[2] *Numidian curl* I.e., short, dense curl. Numidia, an ancient kingdom in North Africa, later became a Roman province.

[3] *Memnon's image* The Colossus of Memnon, a sixty-foot-tall statue near Luxor, Egypt, famous for supposedly making a sound every dawn. Though its subject is actually the pharaoh Amenhotep III, the statue has long been associated with Memnon, a legendary Ethiopian warrior king. According to legend, Memnon was almost equal to the Trojan hero Achilles in skill and virtue, but was killed by him in battle.

[4] *Memnon's harp* Reference to the sound made by the statue, which was compared to that of a lyre string breaking.

He utter'd, while his hands contemplative
He press'd together, and in silence stood.
Despondence seiz'd again the fallen Gods
380 At sight of the dejected King of Day,
And many hid their faces from the light:
But fierce Enceladus sent forth his eyes
Among the brotherhood; and, at their glare,
Uprose Iäpetus, and Creüs too,
385 And Phorcus, sea-born, and together strode
To where he towered on his eminence.
There those four shouted forth old Saturn's name;
Hyperion from the peak loud answered, "Saturn!"
Saturn sat near the Mother of the Gods,
390 In whose face was no joy, though all the Gods
Gave from their hollow throats the name of "Saturn!"

BOOK 3

Thus in alternate uproar and sad peace,
    Amazed were those Titans utterly.
O leave them, Muse! O leave them to their woes;
For thou art weak to sing such tumults dire:
5 A solitary sorrow best befits
Thy lips, and antheming a lonely grief.
Leave them, O Muse! for thou anon° wilt find straightaway
Many a fallen old Divinity
Wandering in vain about bewildered shores.
10 Meantime touch piously the Delphic[5] harp,
And not a wind of heaven but will breathe
In aid soft warble from the Dorian[6] flute;
For lo! 'tis for the Father of all verse.
Flush every thing that hath a vermeil hue,
15 Let the rose glow intense and warm the air,
And let the clouds of even and of morn
Float in voluptuous fleeces o'er the hills;
Let the red wine within the goblet boil,
Cold as a bubbling well; let faint-lipp'd shells,
20 On sands, or in great deeps, vermilion turn
Through all their labyrinths; and let the maid
Blush keenly, as with some warm kiss surpris'd.

---

[5] *Delphic* Of Apollo, referring to Apollo's association with the Oracle at Delphi.

[6] *Dorian* One of the modes in which ancient Greek music was played; it was considered to be solemn and appropriate for war music.

Chief isle of the embowered Cyclades,[1]
Rejoice, O Delos, with thine olives green,
25 And poplars, and lawn-shading palms, and beech,
In which the Zephyr breathes the loudest song,
And hazels thick, dark-stemm'd beneath the shade:
Apollo is once more the golden theme!
Where was he, when the Giant of the Sun
30 Stood bright, amid the sorrow of his peers?
Together had he left his mother fair[2]
And his twin-sister[3] sleeping in their bower,
And in the morning twilight wandered forth
Beside the osiers° of a rivulet,°   willows / small stream
35 Full ankle-deep in lilies of the vale.
The nightingale had ceas'd, and a few stars
Were lingering in the heavens, while the thrush
Began calm-throated. Throughout all the isle
There was no covert, no retired cave
40 Unhaunted by the murmurous noise of waves,
Though scarcely heard in many a green recess.
He listen'd, and he wept, and his bright tears
Went trickling down the golden bow he held.
Thus with half-shut suffused[4] eyes he stood,
45 While from beneath some cumbrous° boughs obstructing
      hard by
With solemn step an awful° Goddess came, awe-inspiring
And there was purport in her looks for him,
Which he with eager guess began to read
Perplex'd, the while melodiously he said:
50 "How cam'st thou over the unfooted sea?
Or hath that antique mien° and robed form   bearing
Mov'd in these vales invisible till now?
Sure I have heard those vestments sweeping o'er
The fallen leaves, when I have sat alone
55 In cool mid-forest. Surely I have traced
The rustle of those ample skirts about
These grassy solitudes, and seen the flowers
Lift up their heads, as still the whisper pass'd.

Goddess! I have beheld those eyes before,
60 And their eternal calm, and all that face,
Or I have dream'd."—"Yes," said the supreme shape,
"Thou hast dream'd of me; and awaking up
Didst find a lyre all golden by thy side,
Whose strings touch'd by thy fingers, all the vast
65 Unwearied ear of the whole universe
Listen'd in pain and pleasure at the birth
Of such new tuneful wonder. Is't not strange
That thou shouldst weep, so gifted? Tell me, youth,
What sorrow thou canst feel; for I am sad
70 When thou dost shed a tear: explain thy griefs
To one who in this lonely isle hath been
The watcher of thy sleep and hours of life,
From the young day when first thy infant hand
Pluck'd witless the weak flowers, till thine arm
75 Could bend that bow heroic to all times.
Show thy heart's secret to an ancient Power
Who hath forsaken old and sacred thrones
For prophecies of thee, and for the sake
Of loveliness new born."—Apollo then,
80 With sudden scrutiny and gloomless eyes,
Thus answer'd, while his white melodious throat
Throbb'd with the syllables. "Mnemosyne!
Thy name is on my tongue, I know not how;
Why should I tell thee what thou so well seest?
85 Why should I strive to show what from thy lips
Would come no mystery? For me, dark, dark,
And painful vile oblivion seals my eyes:
I strive to search wherefore I am so sad,
Until a melancholy numbs my limbs;
90 And then upon the grass I sit, and moan,
Like one who once had wings.—O why should I
Feel curs'd and thwarted, when the liegeless° air free
Yields to my step aspirant?[5] why should I
Spurn the green turf as hateful to my feet?
95 Goddess benign, point forth some unknown thing:
Are there not other regions than this isle?
What are the stars? There is the sun, the sun!
And the most patient brilliance of the moon!
And stars by thousands! Point me out the way
100 To any one particular beauteous star,

---

[1] *Chief isle … Cyclades* Delos, Apollo's birthplace. It is one of the Cyclades, a group of Greek islands in the Aegean Sea.

[2] *his mother fair* Latona, who conceived Apollo with Jove.

[3] *his twin-sister* Diana, goddess of the hunt and of virginity and childbirth.

[4] *suffused* Covered with a film, i.e., of tears.

---

[5] *step aspirant* Ascending step.

And I will flit into it with my lyre,
And make its silvery splendour pant with bliss.
I have heard the cloudy thunder: Where is power?
Whose hand, whose essence, what divinity
105   Makes this alarum° in the elements,   disturbance
While I here idle listen on the shores
In fearless yet in aching ignorance?
O tell me, lonely Goddess, by thy harp,
That waileth every morn and eventide,
110   Tell me why thus I rave, about these groves!
Mute thou remainest—Mute! yet I can read
A wondrous lesson in thy silent face:
Knowledge enormous makes a God of me.
Names, deeds, gray legends, dire events, rebellions,
115   Majesties, sovran° voices, agonies,   sovereign
Creations and destroyings, all at once
Pour into the wide hollows of my brain,
And deify me, as if some blithe wine
Or bright elixir peerless I had drunk,
120   And so become immortal."—Thus the God,
While his enkindled eyes, with level glance
Beneath his white soft temples, stedfast kept
Trembling with light upon Mnemosyne.
Soon wild commotions shook him, and made flush
125   All the immortal fairness of his limbs;
Most like the struggle at the gate of death;
Or liker still to one who should take leave
Of pale immortal death, and with a pang
As hot as death's is chill, with fierce convulse
130   Die into life: so young Apollo anguish'd:
His very hair, his golden tresses famed
Kept undulation round his eager neck.
During the pain Mnemosyne upheld
Her arms as one who prophesied.—At length
135   Apollo shriek'd;—and lo! from all his limbs
Celestial. ...[1]
—1820

---

[1]   ...   Keats's poem was published unfinished. The text conludes here.

The Fall of Hyperion
A Dream

CANTO 1

Fanatics have their dreams, wherewith they weave
A paradise for a sect; the savage, too,
From forth the loftiest fashion of his sleep
Guesses at Heaven; pity these have not
5   Trac'd upon vellum° or wild Indian leaf   parchment
The shadows of melodious utterance.
But bare of laurel[2] they live, dream, and die;
For Poesy alone can tell her dreams—
With the fine spell of words alone can save
10   Imagination from the sable chain
And dumb enchantment. Who alive can say,
"Thou art no poet—may'st not tell thy dreams"?
Since every man whose soul is not a clod
Hath visions, and would speak, if he had lov'd
15   And been well nurtured in his mother tongue.
Whether the dream now purpos'd to rehearse
Be poet's or fanatic's will be known
When this warm scribe, my hand, is in the grave.

Methought I stood where trees of every clime,
20   Palm, myrtle, oak, and sycamore, and beech,
With plantane, and spice-blossoms, made a screen;
In neighbourhood of fountains, by the noise
Soft-showering in mine ears, and, by the touch
Of scent, not far from roses. Turning round,
25   I saw an arbour with a drooping roof
Of trellis vines, and bells, and larger blooms,
Like floral censers,[3] swinging light in air;
Before its wreathed doorway, on a mound
Of moss, was spread a feast of summer fruits,
30   Which, nearer seen, seemed refuse of a meal
By angel tasted or our Mother Eve;[4]
For empty shells were scatter'd on the grass,
And grape-stalks but half bare, and remnants more,

---

[2]   laurel   Wreaths made of leaves of the bay laurel were traditionally bestowed upon those who distinguished themselves in poetry.

[3]   censers   Vessels in which incense is burnt.

[4]   By angel ... Eve   See Milton's Paradise Lost 5.3, in which Eve serves a meal to Adam and the angel Raphael.

Sweet-smelling, whose pure kinds I could not know.
35 Still was more plenty than the fabled horn[1]
Thrice emptied could pour forth, at banqueting
For Proserpine[2] return'd to her own fields,
Where the white heifers low. And appetite,
More yearning than on earth I ever felt,
40 Growing within, I ate deliciously;
And, after not long, thirsted; for thereby
Stood a cool vessel of transparent juice,
Sipp'd by the wander'd bee, the which I took,
And, pledging all the mortals of the world,
45 And all the dead whose names are in our lips,
Drank. That full draught is parent of my theme.
No Asian poppy[3] nor elixir fine°   subtle
Of the soon-fading, jealous Caliphat,[4]
No poison gender'd in close monkish cell,
50 To thin the scarlet conclave[5] of old men,
Could so have rapt unwilling life away.
Among the fragrant husks and berries crush'd
Upon the grass, I struggled hard against
The domineering potion, but in vain.
55 The cloudy swoon came on, and down I sunk,
Like a Silenus[6] on an antique vase.
How long I slumber'd 'tis a chance to guess.
When sense of life return'd, I started up
As if with wings, but the fair trees were gone,
60 The mossy mound and arbour were no more:
I look'd around upon the carved sides
Of an old sanctuary with roof august,
Builded so high, it seem'd that filmed clouds
Might spread beneath, as o'er the stars of heaven.
65 So old the place was, I remember'd none

The like upon the earth: what I had seen
Of gray cathedrals, buttress'd walls, rent towers,
The superannuations of sunk realms,
Or Nature's rocks toil'd hard in waves and winds,
70 Seem'd but the faulture° of decrepit things   failing
To that eternal domed monument.
Upon the marble at my feet there lay
Store of strange vessels, and large draperies,
Which needs had been of dyed asbestos[7] wove,
75 Or in that place the moth could not corrupt,[8]
So white the linen, so, in some, distinct
Ran imageries from a sombre loom.
All in a mingled heap confus'd there lay
Robes, golden tongs, censer and chafing-dish,
80 Girdles, and chains, and holy jewelries.

Turning from these with awe, once more I rais'd
My eyes to fathom the space every way;
The embossed roof, the silent massy range
Of columns north and south, ending in mist
85 Of nothing; then to eastward, where black gates
Were shut against the sunrise evermore.
Then to the west I look'd, and saw far off
An image, huge of feature as a cloud,
At level of whose feet an altar slept,
90 To be approach'd on either side by steps
And marble balustrade, and patient travail
To count with toil the innumerable degrees.
Towards the altar sober-pac'd I went,
Repressing haste, as too unholy there;
95 And, coming nearer, saw beside the shrine
One minist'ring; and there arose a flame.
When in mid-May the sickening east wind
Shifts sudden to the south, the small warm rain
Melts out the frozen incense from all flowers,
100 And fills the air with so much pleasant health
That even the dying man forgets his shroud;
Even so that lofty sacrificial fire,

---

[1] *fabled horn* I.e., cornucopia, or horn of plenty, the symbol of Ceres, goddess of the harvest.

[2] *Proserpine* Daughter of Ceres who was kidnapped by Pluto, god of the underworld, and forced to become his queen. As a concession to Ceres, Pluto allows Proserpine to return to earth for half of every year. In the fall and winter, when Proserpine is in the underworld, the grief-stricken Ceres prevents crops from growing.

[3] *Asian poppy* I.e., opium poppy.

[4] *Caliphat* Council of Caliphs, or Muslim rulers.

[5] *scarlet conclave* College of Cardinals, which elects the Pope.

[6] *Silenus* Satyr (half-man, half-goat), a drunken companion of Bacchus, the wine god.

---

[7] *asbestos* Fibrous mineral that can be woven into incombustible fabric.

[8] *Which needs ... corrupt* See Matthew 6.20, in which Jesus instructs, "Lay up for yourselves treasures in heaven, where neither moth nor rust doth corrupt."

Sending forth Maian[1] incense, spread around
Forgetfulness of everything but bliss,
105 And clouded all the altar with soft smoke;
From whose white fragrant curtains thus I heard
Language pronounc'd: "If thou canst not ascend
These steps,[2] die on that marble where thou art.
Thy flesh, near cousin to the common dust,
110 Will parch for lack of nutriment—thy bones
Will wither in few years, and vanish so
That not the quickest eye could find a grain
Of what thou now art on that pavement cold.
The sands of thy short life are spent this hour,
115 And no hand in the universe can turn
Thy hourglass, if these gummed° leaves be burnt   *aromatic*
Ere thou canst mount up these immortal steps."
I heard, I look'd: two senses both at once,
So fine, so subtle, felt the tyranny
120 Of that fierce threat and the hard task proposed.
Prodigious seem'd the toil; the leaves were yet
Burning, when suddenly a palsied chill
Struck from the paved level up my limbs,
And was ascending quick to put cold grasp
125 Upon those streams that pulse beside the throat!
I shriek'd, and the sharp anguish of my shriek
Stung my own ears—I strove hard to escape
The numbness, strove to gain the lowest step.
Slow, heavy, deadly was my pace: the cold
130 Grew stifling, suffocating, at the heart;
And when I clasp'd my hands I felt them not.
One minute before death, my iced foot touch'd
The lowest stair; and, as it touch'd, life seem'd
To pour in at the toes: I mounted up,
135 As once fair angels on a ladder flew
From the green turf to heaven.[3] "Holy Power,"
Cried I, approaching near the horned shrine,[4]

"What am I that should so be saved from death?
What am I that another death come not
140 To choke my utterance, sacrilegious here?"
Then said the veiled shadow: "Thou hast felt
What 'tis to die and live again before
Thy fated hour; that thou hadst power to do so
Is thy own safety; thou hast dated on[5]
145 Thy doom." "High Prophetess," said I, "purge off,
Benign, if so it please thee, my mind's film."
"None can usurp this height," returned that shade,
"But those to whom the miseries of the world
Are misery, and will not let them rest.
150 All else who find a haven in the world,
Where they may thoughtless sleep away their days,
If by a chance into this fane° they come,   *temple*
Rot on the pavement where thou rotted'st half."
"Are there not thousands in the world," said I,
155 Encourag'd by the sooth° voice of the shade,   *truthful*
"Who love their fellows even to the death,
Who feel the giant agony of the world,
And more, like slaves to poor humanity,
Labour for mortal good? I sure should see
160 Other men here, but I am here alone."
"Those whom thou spak'st of are no visionaries,"
Rejoin'd that voice, "they are no dreamers weak;
They seek no wonder but the human face,
No music but a happy-noted voice—
165 They come not here, they have no thought to come—
And thou art here, for thou art less than they.
What benefit canst thou do, or all thy tribe,
To the great world? Thou art a dreaming thing,
A fever of thyself—think of the earth;
170 What bliss, even in hope, is there for thee?
What haven? Every creature hath its home;
Every sole man hath days of joy and pain,
Whether his labours be sublime or low—
The pain alone, the joy alone, distinct:
175 Only the dreamer venoms all his days,
Bearing more woe than all his sins deserve.
Therefore, that happiness be somewhat shar'd,
Such things as thou art are admitted oft
Into like gardens thou didst pass erewhile,

---

[1] *Maian incense* Incense burnt for Maia, Greek goddess of spring.

[2] *These steps* Cf. Dante's *Purgatory*, in which the poet must ascend to the seven terraces of the Mount of Purgatory, purging a deadly sin on each terrace.

[3] *As once ... heaven* See Genesis 28.12, in which Jacob dreams of a ladder from earth to heaven, with angels ascending and descending on it. Milton also alludes to this ladder in *Paradise Lost* 3.510–11.

[4] *horned shrine* Horns were often placed on ancient thrones. See Exodus 27.2.

[5] *dated on* Postponed.

80 And suffer'd° in these temples: for that cause   *allowed*
Thou standest safe beneath this statue's knees."
"That I am favour'd for unworthiness,
By such propitious parley medicin'd
In sickness not ignoble, I rejoice,
85 Aye, and could weep for love of such award."
So answered I, continuing, "If it please,
Majestic shadow, tell me: sure not all
Those melodies sung into the world's ear
Are useless: sure a poet is a sage;
90 A humanist, physician to all men.
That I am none I feel, as vultures feel
They are no birds when eagles are abroad.
What am I then: thou spakest of my tribe:
What tribe?" The tall shade veil'd in drooping white
95 Then spake, so much more earnest, that the breath
Moved the thin linen folds that drooping hung
About a golden censer from the hand
Pendent—"Art thou not of the dreamer tribe?
The poet and the dreamer are distinct,
100 Diverse, sheer opposite, antipodes.
The one pours out a balm upon the world,
The other vexes it." Then shouted I
Spite of myself, and with a Pythia's spleen,[1]
"Apollo! faded! O far-flown Apollo!
105 Where is thy misty pestilence[2] to creep
Into the dwellings, through the door crannies
Of all mock lyrists, large self-worshippers,
And careless hectorers[3] in proud bad verse?
Though I breathe death with them it will be life
110 To see them sprawl before me into graves.[4]
Majestic shadow, tell me where I am,
Whose altar this, for whom this incense curls;
What image this whose face I cannot see

For the broad marble knees; and who thou art,
215 Of accent feminine so courteous?"

Then the tall shade, in drooping linens veil'd,
Spake out, so much more earnest, that her breath
Stirr'd the thin folds of gauze that drooping hung
About a golden censer, from her hand
220 Pendent; and by her voice I knew she shed
Long-treasured tears. "This temple, sad and lone,
Is all spar'd from the thunder of a war
Foughten long since by giant hierarchy
Against rebellion: this old image here,
225 Whose carved features wrinkled as he fell,
Is Saturn's; I, Moneta,[5] left supreme,
Sole priestess of his desolation."
I had no words to answer, for my tongue,
Useless, could find about its roofed home
230 No syllable of a fit majesty
To make rejoinder to Moneta's mourn:
There was a silence, while the altar's blaze
Was fainting for sweet food. I look'd thereon,
And on the paved floor, where nigh were piled
235 Faggots of cinnamon, and many heaps
Of other crisped spicewood: then again
I look'd upon the altar, and its horns
Whiten'd with ashes, and its lang'rous flame,
And then upon the offerings again;
240 And so by turns—till sad Moneta cried:
"The sacrifice is done, but not the less
Will I be kind to thee for thy good will.
My power, which to me is still a curse,
Shall be to thee a wonder; for the scenes
245 Still swooning vivid through my globed brain,
With an electral changing misery,
Thou shalt with these dull mortal eyes behold
Free from all pain, if wonder pain thee not."
As near as an immortal's sphered words
250 Could to a mother's soften, were these last:
And yet I had a terror of her robes,
And chiefly of the veils, that from her brow
Hung pale, and curtain'd her in mysteries,

---

[1] *Pythia's spleen* The anger of a Pythia, the priestess and oracle of Apollo, god of poetry and the sun, at Delphi.

[2] *thy misty pestilence* In Homer's *Iliad*, Apollo is also the sender of plagues.

[3] *hectorers* Bullies; blusterers.

[4] *Majestic shadow … graves* Lines 187–210 were crossed out by Keats's friend Richard Woodhouse, who believed Keats intended to delete them. Some of the content of these lines is repeated in lines 211 and 216–20.

---

[5] *Saturn* King of the Titans who was overthrown by his son Jupiter; *Moneta* Mnemosyne (Greek: memory), mother of the nine Muses, patrons of learning and the arts.

That made my heart too small to hold its blood.
255 This saw that Goddess, and with sacred hand
Parted the veils. Then saw I a wan face,
Not pined by human sorrows, but bright-blanch'd
By an immortal sickness which kills not;
It works a constant change, which happy death
260 Can put no end to; deathwards progressing
To no death was that visage; it had pass'd
The lily and the snow; and beyond these
I must not think now, though I saw that face.
But for her eyes I should have fled away.
265 They held me back with a benignant light,
Soft mitigated by divinest lids
Half closed, and visionless entire they seem'd
Of all external things—they saw me not,
But, in blank splendour, beam'd like the mild moon,
270 Who comforts those she sees not, who knows not
What eyes are upward cast. As I had found
A grain of gold upon a mountain's side,
And, twing'd with avarice, strain'd out my eyes
To search its sullen entrails rich with ore,
275 So, at the view of sad Moneta's brow,
I ached to see what things the hollow brain
Behind enwombed: what high tragedy
In the dark secret chambers of her skull
Was acting, that could give so dread a stress
280 To her cold lips, and fill with such a light
Her planetary eyes, and touch her voice
With such a sorrow. "Shade of Memory!"
Cried I, with act adorant at her feet,
"By all the gloom hung round thy fallen house,
285 By this last temple, by the golden age,
By great Apollo, thy dear foster-child,
And by thyself, forlorn divinity,
The pale Omega[1] of a wither'd race,
Let me behold, according as thou saidst,
290 What in thy brain so ferments to and fro."
No sooner had this conjuration pass'd
My devout lips, than side by side we stood
(Like a stunt bramble by a solemn pine)

Deep in the shady sadness of a vale[2]
295 Far sunken from the healthy breath of morn,
Far from the fiery noon and eve's one star.
Onward I look'd beneath the gloomy boughs,
And saw what first I thought an image huge,
Like to the image pedestall'd so high
300 In Saturn's temple; then Moneta's voice
Came brief upon mine ear, "So Saturn sat
When he had lost his realms—" whereon there grew
A power within me of enormous ken,°   *range*
To see as a god sees, and take the depth
305 Of things as nimbly as the outward eye
Can size and shape pervade. The lofty theme
Of those few words hung vast before my mind
With half-unravell'd web. I sat myself
Upon an eagle's watch, that I might see,
310 And seeing ne'er forget. No stir of life
Was in this shrouded vale, not so much air
As in the zoning° of a summer's day   *course*
Robs not one light seed from the feather'd grass;
But where the dead leaf fell, there did it rest:
315 A stream went voiceless by, still deaden'd more
By reason of the fallen Divinity
Spreading more shade; the Naiad° 'mid   *water nymph*
    her reeds
Press'd her cold finger closer to her lips.

Along the margin sand large footmarks went
320 No farther than to where old Saturn's feet
Had rested, and there slept, how long a sleep!
Degraded, cold, upon the sodden ground
His old right hand lay nerveless, listless, dead,
Unsceptred, and his realmless eyes were clos'd;
325 While his bow'd head seem'd listening to the Earth,
His antient mother,[3] for some comfort yet.

It seem'd no force could wake him from his place;
But there came one who, with a kindred hand,
Touch'd his wide shoulders, after bending low
330 With reverence, though to one who knew it not.

---

1 *Omega* The last letter of the Greek alphabet.

2 *Deep in … vale* The opening line of the original *Hyperion*, of which the rest of the poem is a revision.

3 *Earth … mother* The Titans were the offspring of Heaven and Earth.

Then came the griev'd voice of Mnemosyne,
And griev'd I hearken'd. "That divinity
Whom thou saw'st step from yon forlornest wood,
And with slow pace approach our fallen king,
35 Is Thea,[1] softest-natur'd of our brood."
I mark'd the Goddess, in fair statuary°   stature
Surpassing wan Moneta by the head,
And in her sorrow nearer woman's tears.
There was a list'ning fear in her regard,
40 As if calamity had but begun;
As if the vanward clouds[2] of evil days
Had spent their malice, and the sullen rear
Was with its stored thunder labouring up.
One hand she press'd upon that aching spot
45 Where beats the human heart; as if just there,
Though an immortal, she felt cruel pain;
The other upon Saturn's bended neck
She laid, and to the level of his ear
Leaning with parted lips, some words she spoke
50 In solemn tenour and deep organ-tone;
Some mourning words, which in our feeble tongue
Would come in this like accenting; how frail
To that large utterance of the early Gods!

    "Saturn, look up! and for what, poor lost king?
55 I have no comfort for thee; no—not one;
I cannot cry, *Wherefore thus sleepest thou?*
For Heaven is parted from thee, and the Earth
Knows thee not, so afflicted, for a God.
The Ocean, too, with all its solemn noise,
60 Has from thy sceptre pass'd; and all the air
Is emptied of thine hoary majesty.
Thy thunder, captious° at the new command,   objecting
Rumbles reluctant o'er our fallen house;
And thy sharp lightning in unpractised hands
65 Scorches and burns our once serene domain.
With such remorseless speed still come new woes,
That unbelief has not a space to breathe.
Saturn! sleep on—Me thoughtless,[3] why should I
Thus violate thy slumbrous solitude?

---

[1] *Thea* Hyperion's wife and sister.

[2] *vanward clouds* I.e., the front line of clouds.

[3] *Me thoughtless* I.e., thoughtless me.

370 Why should I ope thy melancholy eyes?
Saturn! sleep on, while at thy feet I weep."

    As when upon a tranced summer night
Forests, branch-charmed by the earnest stars,
Dream, and so dream all night, without a noise,
375 Save from one gradual solitary gust
Swelling upon the silence; dying off;
As if the ebbing air had but one wave;
So came those words and went; the while in tears
She press'd her fair large forehead to the earth,
380 Just where her fallen hair might spread in curls,
A soft and silken mat for Saturn's feet.
Long, long these two were postured motionless,
Like sculpture builded up upon the grave
Of their own power. A long awful time
385 I look'd upon them: still they were the same;
The frozen God still bending to the earth,
And the sad Goddess weeping at his feet,
Moneta silent. Without stay or prop,
But my own weak mortality, I bore
390 The load of this eternal quietude,
The unchanging gloom and the three fixed shapes
Ponderous upon my senses, a whole moon;
For by my burning brain I measured sure
Her silver seasons shedded on the night,
395 And every day by day methought I grew
More gaunt and ghostly. Oftentimes I pray'd
Intense, that death would take me from the vale
And all its burthens—Gasping with despair
Of change, hour after hour I curs'd myself;
400 Until old Saturn rais'd his faded eyes,
And look'd around, and saw his kingdom gone,
And all the gloom and sorrow of the place,
And that fair kneeling Goddess at his feet.
As the moist scent of flowers, and grass, and leaves
405 Fills forest-dells with a pervading air,
Known to the woodland nostril, so the words
Of Saturn fill'd the mossy glooms around,
Even to the hollows of time-eaten oaks,
And to the windings in the foxes' holes,
410 With sad, low tones, while thus he spake, and sent

Strange musings to the solitary Pan.[1]
"Moan, brethren, moan; for we are swallow'd up
And buried from all godlike exercise
Of influence benign on planets pale,
415 And peaceful sway above man's harvesting,
And all those acts which Deity supreme
Doth ease its heart of love in. Moan and wail,
Moan, brethren, moan; for lo! the rebel spheres
Spin round, the stars their antient courses keep,
420 Clouds still with shadowy moisture haunt the earth,
Still suck their fill of light from sun and moon,
Still buds the tree, and still the sea-shores murmur.
There is no death in all the universe,
No smell of death—there shall be death—moan, moan;
425 Moan, Cybele,[2] moan, for thy pernicious babes
Have changed a god into a shaking palsy.
Moan, brethren, moan, for I have no strength left;
Weak as the reed—weak—feeble as my voice—
O, O, the pain, the pain of feebleness.
430 Moan, moan, for still I thaw—or give me help:
Throw down those imps, and give me victory.
Let me hear other groans; and trumpets blown
Of triumph calm, and hymns of festival,
From the gold peaks of heaven's high piled clouds;
435 Voices of soft proclaim, and silver stir
Of strings in hollow shells; and let there be
Beautiful things made new, for the surprise
Of the sky-children—" So he feebly ceas'd,
With such a poor and sickly-sounding pause,
440 Methought I heard some old man of the earth
Bewailing earthly loss; nor could my eyes
And ears act with that pleasant unison of sense
Which marries sweet sound with the grace of form,
And dolorous accent from a tragic harp
445 With large-limb'd visions. More I scrutinized.
Still fix'd he sat beneath the sable trees,

Whose arms spread straggling in wild serpent forms,
With leaves all hush'd; his awful presence there
(Now all was silent) gave a deadly lie
450 To what I erewhile heard: only his lips
Trembled amid the white curls of his beard.
They told the truth, though, round, the snowy locks
Hung nobly, as upon the face of heaven
A mid-day fleece of clouds. Thea arose,
455 And stretch'd her white arm through the hollow dark,
Pointing some whither: whereat he too rose
Like a vast giant seen by men at sea
To grow° pale from the waves at dull midnight.   arise
They melted from my sight into the woods:
460 Ere I could turn, Moneta cried, "These twain°   two
Are speeding to the families of grief,
Where, roof'd in by black rocks, they waste in pain
And darkness for no hope." And she spake on,
As ye may read who can unwearied pass
465 Onward from the antechamber of this dream,
Where even at the open doors awhile
I must delay, and glean my memory
Of her high phrase—perhaps no further dare.

CANTO 2

"Mortal, that thou mayst understand aright,
I humanize my sayings to thine ear,
Making comparisons of earthly things;[3]
Or thou might'st better listen to the wind,
5 Whose language is to thee a barren noise,
Though it blows legend-laden through the trees—
In melancholy realms big tears are shed,
More sorrow like to this, and such like woe,
Too huge for mortal tongue, or pen of scribe.
10 The Titans fierce, self-hid or prison-bound,
Groan for the old allegiance once more,
Listening in their doom for Saturn's voice.
But one of the whole eagle-brood still keeps

---

[1] *Pan* Greek shepherd god of nature who was half goat and half man. After the nymph Syrinx turned herself into a bed of reeds in order to escape him, Pan created an instrument (the panpipe) out of the reeds.

[2] *Cybele* Consort of Saturn and mother of the Olympian gods.

---

[3] *Mortal, that … things* Cf. Milton's *Paradise Lost* 5.571–76, in which Raphael likens "spiritual to corporeal forms" to explain the war in Heaven to Adam.

His sov'reignty, and rule, and majesty;
5 Blazing Hyperion on his orbed fire
Still sits, still snuffs the incense teeming up
From man to the Sun's God—yet unsecure,
For as upon the earth dire prodigies[1]
Fright and perplex, so also shudders he;
20 Nor at dog's howl, or gloom-bird's even screech,
Or the familiar visitings of one
Upon the first toll of his passing bell:[2]
But horrors, portion'd° to a giant nerve,   *proportioned*
Make great Hyperion ache. His palace bright,
25 Bastion'd with pyramids of glowing gold,
And touched with shade of bronzed obelisks,
Glares a blood-red through all the thousand courts,
Arches, and domes, and fiery galleries;
And all its curtains of Aurorian clouds[3]
30 Flush angerly; when he would taste the wreaths
Of incense breath'd aloft from sacred hills,
Instead of sweets, his ample palate takes
Savour of poisonous brass and metals sick.
Wherefore when harbour'd in the sleepy west,
35 After the full completion of fair day,
For rest divine upon exalted couch
And slumber in the arms of melody,
He paces through the pleasant hours of ease,
With strides colossal, on from hall to hall,
40 While, far within each aisle and deep recess,
His winged minions in close clusters stand
Amaz'd, and full of fear; like anxious men,
Who on a wide plain gather in sad troops,
When earthquakes jar their battlements and towers.
45 Even now while Saturn, roused from icy trance,
Goes, step for step, with Thea from yon woods,
Hyperion, leaving twilight in the rear,
Is sloping to the threshold of the west.
Thither we tend." Now in clear light I stood,
50 Relieved from the dusk vale. Mnemosyne
Was sitting on a square-edg'd polish'd stone,
That in its lucid depth reflected pure

Her priestess-garments. My quick eyes ran on
From stately nave[4] to nave, from vault to vault,
55 Through bowers of fragrant and enwreathed light,
And diamond-paved lustrous long arcades.
Anon rush'd by the bright Hyperion;
His flaming robes stream'd out beyond his heels,
And gave a roar, as if of earthly fire,
60 That scared away the meek ethereal hours,
And made their dove-wings tremble. On he flared.[5]
—1856 (WRITTEN 1819)

This Living Hand [6]

This living hand, now warm and capable
Of earnest grasping, would, if it were cold
And in the icy silence of the tomb,
So haunt thy days and chill thy dreaming nights
5 That thou would wish thine own heart dry of blood
So in my veins red life might stream again,
And thou be conscience calm'd—see here it is—
I hold it towards you—
—1898 (WRITTEN C. 1819)

Selected Letters

TO BENJAMIN BAILEY[7]
22 November 1817

My Dear Bailey,

… O I wish I was as certain of the end of all your troubles as that of your momentary start about the authenticity of the Imagination. I am certain of nothing but of the holiness of the Heart's affections and the truth of imagination—What the imagination seizes as Beauty must be truth—whether it existed before or

[4] *nave* Main body of a church.

[5] *On he flared* Keats's manuscript breaks off here.

[6] *This Living Hand* A fragment whose context is unknown.

[7] *BENJAMIN BAILEY* Undergraduate student in Divinity at Oxford University. Keats had stayed with him in September while he was working on *Endymion*.

---

[1] *dire prodigies* Ominous and unusual occurrences.

[2] *passing bell* Bell rung to announce a death.

[3] *Aurorian clouds* Clouds of the dawn (Aurora is goddess of the dawn).

not—for I have the same Idea of all our Passions as of Love they are all in their sublime, creative of essential Beauty—In a Word, you may know my favourite Speculation by my first Book and the little song I sent in my last[1]—which is a representation from the fancy of the probable mode of operating in these Matters—The Imagination may be compared to Adam's dream[2]—he awoke and found it truth. I am the more zealous in this affair, because I have never yet been able to perceive how any thing can be known for truth by consequitive[3] reasoning—and yet it must be—Can it be that even the greatest Philosopher ever arrived at his goal without putting aside numerous objections—However it may be, O for a Life of Sensations rather than of Thoughts! It is "a Vision in the form of Youth" a Shadow of reality to come—and this consideration has further convinced me for it has come as auxiliary to another favourite Speculation of mine, that we shall enjoy ourselves here after by having what we called happiness on Earth repeated in a finer tone and so repeated—And yet such a fate can only befall those who delight in sensation rather than hunger as you do after Truth—Adam's dream will do here and seems to be a conviction that Imagination and its empyreal[4] reflection is the same as human Life and its spiritual repetition. But as I was saying—the simple imaginative Mind may have its rewards in the repetition of its own silent Working coming continually on the spirit with a fine suddenness—to compare great things with small—have you never by being surprised with an old Melody—in a delicious place—by a delicious voice, felt over again your very speculations and surmises at the time it first operated on your soul—do you not remember forming to yourself the singer's face more beautiful [than] it was possible and yet with the elevation of the Moment you did not think so—even then you were mounted on the Wings of Imagination so high—that the Prototype must be here after—that delicious face you will see—What a time! I am continually running away from the subject—sure this cannot be exactly the case with a complex Mind—one that is imaginative and at the same time careful of its fruits—who would exist partly on sensation partly on thought—to whom it is necessary that years should bring the philosophic Mind[5]—such an one I consider yours and therefore it is necessary to your eternal Happiness that you not only have drink this old Wine of Heaven which I shall call the redigestion of our most ethereal Musings on Earth; but also increase in knowledge and know all things. I am glad to hear you are in a fair Way for Easter—you will soon get through your unpleasant reading and then!—but the world is full of troubles and I have not much reason to think myself pestered with many—I think Jane or Marianne has a better opinion of me than I deserve—for really and truly I do not think my Brother's illness connected with mine[6]—you know more of the real Cause than they do—nor have I any chance of being rack'd as you have been[7]—you perhaps at one time thought there was such a thing as Worldly Happiness to be arrived at, at certain periods of time marked out—you have of necessity from your disposition been thus led away—I scarcely remember counting upon any Happiness—I look not for it if it be not in the present hour—nothing startles me beyond the Moment. The setting sun will always set me to rights— or if a Sparrow come before my Window I take part in its existence and pick about the Gravel. The first thing that strikes me on hearing a Misfortune having befalled another is this. Well it cannot be helped.—he will have the pleasure of trying the resources of his spirit, and I beg now my dear Bailey that hereafter should you observe any thing cold in me not to [put] it to the account of heartlessness but abstraction—for I assure you I sometimes feel not the influence of a Passion or Affec-

---

[1] *my first Book* I.e., the first book of *Endymion*; *little song … last* The first five stanzas of "Ode to Sorrow," from Book 4 of *Endymion*, which Keats had enclosed with his previous letter.

[2] *Adam's dream* See Milton's *Paradise Lost* 8.460–90, in which Adam dreams about Eve and wakes to find she has been created.

[3] *consequitive* Consecutive and consequent: a word of Keats's invention.

[4] *empyreal* Celestial; pertaining to the highest heavens.

[5] *philosophic Mind* Cf. Wordsworth's *Ode: Intimations of Immortality*, line 186.

[6] *Jane or … mine* Jane and Marianne Reynolds, two friends of Keats, were afraid that his illness was a sign of tuberculosis, from which Keats's youngest brother, Tom, was suffering.

[7] *rack'd … been* Bailey was upset over a love affair that had recently ended.

tion during a whole week—and so long this sometimes continues I begin to suspect myself and the genuineness of my feelings at other times—thinking them a few barren Tragedy-tears—My Brother Tom is much improved—he is going to Devonshire—whither I shall follow him—at present I am just arrived at Dorking to change the Scene—change the Air and give me a spur to wind up my Poem, of which there are wanting 500 Lines. ...

Your affectionate friend
John Keats—

I want to say much more to you—a few hints will
    set me going
Direct Burford Bridge near dorking

To George and Thomas Keats
21, 27(?) December 1817
Hampstead Sunday

My Dear Brothers,

... I spent Friday evening with Wells[1] & went the next morning to see *Death on the Pale horse*. It is a wonderful picture, when West's[2] age is considered; But there is nothing to be intense upon; no women one feels mad to kiss; no face swelling into reality. the excellence of every Art is its intensity, capable of making all disagreeables evaporate, from their being in close relationship with Beauty & Truth—Examine *King Lear*[3] & you will find this exemplified throughout; but in this picture we have unpleasantness without any momentous depth of speculation excited, in which to bury its repulsiveness—The picture is larger than *Christ rejected*—I dined with Haydon[4] the sunday after you left, & had a very pleasant day, I dined too (for I have been out too much

lately) with Horace Smith[5] & met his two Brothers with Hill & Kingston & one Du Bois, they only served to convince me, how superior humour is to wit in respect to enjoyment—These men say things which make one start, without making one feel, they are all alike; their manners are alike; they all know fashionables; they have a mannerism in their very eating & drinking, in their mere handling a Decanter—They talked of Kean[6] & his low company—Would I were with that company instead of yours said I to myself! I know such like acquaintance will never do for me & yet I am going to Reynolds,[7] on Wednesday—Brown & Dilke[8] walked with me & back from the Christmas pantomime. I had not a dispute but a disquisition[9] with Dilke, on various subjects; several things dovetailed in my mind, & at once it struck me, what quality went to form a Man of Achievement especially in Literature & which Shakespeare possessed so enormously—I mean *Negative Capability*, that is when man is capable of being in uncertainties, Mysteries, doubts, without any irritable reaching after fact & reason—Coleridge, for instance, would let go by a fine isolated verisimilitude caught from the Penetralium[10] of mystery, from being incapable of remaining content with half knowledge. This pursued through Volumes would perhaps take us no further than this, that with a great poet the sense of Beauty overcomes every other consideration, or rather obliterates all consideration.

Shelley's poem[11] is out, & there are words about its being objected too, as much as Queen Mab was. Poor

---

1 *Wells* Charles Wells, a school friend of Tom Keats.

2 *West* American painter Benjamin West (1738–1820), who moved to England and became President of the Royal Academy. The painting *Christ Rejected*, mentioned later in this letter, is West's.

3 *King Lear* Painting by West that depicts the storm scene in Shakespeare's play.

4 *Haydon* Painter Benjamin Haydon (1786–1846).

5 *Horace Smith* Famous literary wit (1779–1849). The other men mentioned are all minor writers or literary critics.

6 *Kean* Shakespearean actor Edmund Kean (1787–1833).

7 *Reynolds* Lawyer and poet John Hamilton Reynolds (1796–1852).

8 *Brown & Dilke* Writers Charles Wentworth Dilke (1789–1864) and Charles Armitage Brown (1786–1842), a close friend and housemate of Keats's who cared for him after he first became ill and who later wrote his biography.

9 *disquisition* Systematic investigation.

10 *Penetralium* I.e., the innermost part. From the Latin *penetralia,* the innermost parts of a temple.

11 *Shelley's poem* Shelley's *Laon and Cythna* (*The Revolt of Islam*), which he was forced to withdraw because readers objected to the poem's description of incestuous love between its hero and heroine.

Benjamin West, *King Lear*, 1788.

Shelley I think he has his Quota of good qualities, in sooth la!![1] Write soon to your most sincere friend & affectionate Brother.

John

To JOHN HAMILTON REYNOLDS
3 February 1818
Hampstead

My Dear Reynolds,

I thank you for your dish of Filberts[2]—Would I could get a basket of them by way of dessert every day for the sum of two pence—Would we were a sort of ethereal Pigs, & turn'd loose to feed upon spiritual Mast[3] & Acorns—which would be merely being a squirrel & feeding upon filberts. For what is a squirrel but an airy pig, or a filbert but a sort of archangelical acorn. About the nuts being worth cracking, all I can say is that where there are a throng of delightful Images ready drawn simplicity is the only thing. The first is the best on account of the first line, and the "arrow—foil'd of its

---

[1] *in sooth la* In truth.

[2] *Filberts* Hazelnuts.

[3] *Mast* Fruit of certain woodland trees, such as beech, oak, and chestnut.

antler'd food"[1]—and moreover (and this is the only word or two I find fault with, the more because I have had so much reason to shun it as a quicksand) the last has "tender and true"—We must cut this, and not be rattle-snaked into any more of the like—It may be said that we ought to read our Contemporaries, that Wordsworth &c should have their due from us. But for the sake of a few fine imaginative or domestic passages, are we to be bullied into a certain Philosophy engendered in the whims of an Egotist—Every man has his speculations, but every man does not brood and peacock over them till he makes a false coinage and deceives himself—Many a man can travel to the very bourne[2] of Heaven, and yet want confidence to put down his halfseeing. Sancho[3] will invent a Journey heavenward as well as any body. We hate poetry that has a palpable design upon us—and if we do not agree, seems to put its hand in its breeches pocket.[4] Poetry should be great & unobtrusive, a thing which enters into one's soul, and does not startle it or amaze it with itself but with its subject.—How beautiful are the retired flowers! how would they lose their beauty were they to throng into the highway crying out, "admire me I am a violet! dote upon me I am a primrose!" Modern poets differ from the Elizabethans in this. Each of the moderns like an Elector of Hanover governs his petty state, & knows how many straws are swept daily from the Causeways in all his dominions & has a continual itching that all the Housewives should have their coppers well scoured: the antients were Emperors of vast Provinces, they had only heard of the remote ones and scarcely cared to visit them.—I will cut all this—I will have no more of Wordsworth or Hunt in particular—Why should we be of the tribe of Manasseh, when we can wander with Esau?[5] Why should we kick against the Pricks, when we can walk on Roses? Why should we be owls, when we can be Eagles? Why be teased with "nice Eyed wagtails," when we have in sight "the Cherub Contemplation"?[6]—Why with Wordsworths "Matthew with a bough of wilding in his hand" when we can have Jacques "under an oak &c"?[7]—The secret of the Bough of Wilding will run through your head faster than I can write it—Old Matthew spoke to him some years ago on some nothing, & because he happens in an Evening Walk to imagine the figure of the old man—he must stamp it down in black & white, and it is henceforth sacred—I don't mean to deny Wordsworth's grandeur & Hunt's merit, but I mean to say we need not be teazed with grandeur & merit—when we can have them uncontaminated & unobtrusive. Let us have the old Poets, & robin Hood Your letter and its sonnets gave me more pleasure than will the 4th Book of Childe Harold[8] & the whole of any body's life & opinions. In return for your dish of filberts, I have gathered a few Catkins, I hope they'll look pretty.[9]

Yr sincere friend and Coscribbler
John Keats

To John Taylor[10]
27 February 1818
Hampstead

My Dear Taylor,

Your alteration strikes me as being a great improvement—the page looks much better. And now I will attend to the Punctuations you speak of—the comma should be at *soberly,* and in the other passage the comma

[1] *arrow ... food* Keats is commenting on Reynolds's "Sonnet on Robin Hood 1," which Reynolds had sent to Keats.

[2] *bourne* Realm.

[3] *Sancho* Sancho Panza, squire of the naive and idealistic Don Quixote in Miguel de Cervantes's *Don Quixote.*

[4] *put its ... pocket* I.e., refuse to fight (by putting one's fists away).

[5] *Why should ... Esau* In the Old Testament, the tribe of Manasseh lived according to the old way of life, while in Genesis 25 Esau sold his birthright and became an outlaw.

[6] *nice Eyed wagtails* From Leigh Hunt's *The Nymphs* 2.170; *the Cherub Contemplation* From Milton's *Il Penseroso* 54.

[7] *Matthew ... hand* From Wordsworth's *The Two April Mornings* 57–60; *under ... &c* From Shakespeare's *As You Like It* 2.1.31.

[8] *4th ... Harold* Canto 4 of Byron's *Childe Harold's Pilgrimage,* whose publication was eagerly anticipated at the time.

[9] *In return ... pretty* In return for the sonnets on Robin Hood that Reynolds had sent, Keats enclosed two poems of his own, *Robin Hood* and *Lines on the Mermaid Tavern.*

[10] *JOHN TAYLOR* Partner in the publishing firm of Taylor and Hessey, who were publishing Keats's poem *Endymion* at this time.

should follow *quiet*.[1] I am extremely indebted to you for this attention and also for your after admonitions—It is a sorry thing for me that any one should have to overcome Prejudices in reading my Verses—that affects me more than any hyper-criticism on any particular Passage. In *Endymion* I have most likely but moved into the Gocart from the leading strings. In Poetry I have a few Axioms, and you will see how far I am from their Centre. 1st I think Poetry should surprise by a fine excess and not by Singularity—it should strike the Reader as a wording of his own highest thoughts, and appear almost a Remembrance—2nd Its touches of Beauty should never be half way thereby making the reader breathless instead of content: the rise, the progress, the setting of imagery should like the Sun come natural to him—shine over him and set soberly although in magnificence leaving him in the Luxury of twilight—but it is easier to think what Poetry should be than to write it—and this leads me on to another axiom. That if Poetry comes not as naturally as the Leaves to a tree it had better not come at all. However it may be with me I cannot help looking into new countries with "O for a Muse of fire to ascend!"[2]—If *Endymion* serves me as a Pioneer perhaps I ought to be content. I have great reason to be content, for thank God I can read and perhaps understand Shakespeare to his depths, and I have I am sure many friends, who, if I fail, will attribute any change in my Life and Temper to Humbleness rather than to Pride—to a cowering under the Wings of great Poets rather than to a Bitterness that I am not appreciated. I am anxious to get *Endymion* printed that I may forget it and proceed. I have copied the 3rd Book and have begun the 4th. On running my Eye over the Proofs—I saw one Mistake I will notice it presently and also any others if there be any—There should be no comma in "the raft branch down sweeping from a tall Ash top"[3]—I have besides made one or two alterations and also altered the 13 Line Page 32 to make sense of it as you will see. I will take care the Printer shall not trip

up my Heels—There should be no dash after Dryope in this Line "Dryope's lone lulling of her Child."[4] Remember me to Percy Street.

Your sincere and obliged friend
John Keats—

P. S. You shall have a short *Preface* in good time—

To BENJAMIN BAILEY
13 March 1818
Teignmouth

My dear Bailey,

… I have never had your Sermon[5] from Wordsworth but Mrs. Dilke lent it me—You know my ideas about Religion—I do not think myself more in the right than other people and that nothing in this world is proveable. I wish I could enter into all your feelings on the subject merely for one short 10 Minutes and give you a Page or two to your liking. I am sometimes so very sceptical as to think Poetry itself a mere Jack a lantern to amuse whoever may chance to be struck with its brilliance—As Tradesmen say every thing is worth what it will fetch, so probably every mental pursuit takes its reality and worth from the ardour of the pursuer—being in itself a nothing—Ethereal things may at least be thus real, divided under three heads—Things real—things semireal—and no things—Things real—such as existences of Sun Moon & Stars and passages of Shakespeare—Things semireal such as Love, the Clouds &c which require a greeting of the Spirit to make them wholly exist—and Nothings which are made Great and dignified by an ardent pursuit—Which by the by stamps the burgundy mark on the bottles of our Minds, insomuch as they are able to *"consecrate whate'er they look upon"*[6] I have written a Sonnet here of a somewhat collateral nature—so don't imagine it an a propos des

---

[1] *soberly … quiet*   References to *Endymion* 1.149 and 1.247.

[2] *O for … ascend*   Cf. Shakespeare's *Henry V* Prologue 1: "O for a Muse of fire, that would ascend / The brightest heaven of invention."

[3] *the raft … top*   From *Endymion* 1.334–35.

[4] *Dryope's … Child*   From *Endymion* 1.495.

[5] *your Sermon*   Bailey, like many clergymen at the time, had written a memorial sermon for Princess Charlotte, who died in childbirth in 1817.

[6] *consecrate … upon*   From Percy Shelley's *Hymn to Intellectual Beauty* 13–14.

bottes.[1]

[*The Human Seasons* is included here.]

Aye this may be carried—but what am I talking of—it is an old maxim of mine and of course must be well known that every point of thought is the centre of an intellectual world—the two uppermost thoughts in a Man's mind are the two poles of his World he revolves on them and every thing is southward or northward to him through their means—We take but three steps from feathers to iron. Now my dear fellow I must once for all tell you I have not one Idea of the truth of any of my speculations—I shall never be a Reasoner because I care not to be in the right, when retired from bickering and in a proper philosophical temper … My Brother Tom desires to be remember'd to you—he has just this moment had a spitting of blood poor fellow—Remember me to [Gleig] and Whitehead—

Your affectionate friend
John Keats—

To John Hamilton Reynolds

3 May 1818
Teignmouth

My dear Reynolds,

… **A**n extensive knowledge is needful to thinking people—it takes away the heat and fever; and helps, by widening speculation, to ease the Burden of the Mystery:[2] a thing I begin to understand a little, and which weighed upon you in the most gloomy and true sentence in your Letter. The difference of high Sensations with and without knowledge appears to me this—in the latter case we are falling continually ten thousand fathoms deep and being blown up again without wings and with all [the] horror of a bare shouldered Creature—in the former case, our shoulders are fledge,[3] and we go through the same air and space without fear. …

You may be anxious to know for fact to what sentence in your Letter I allude. You say "I fear there is little chance of any thing else in this life." You seem by that to have been going through with a more painful and acute zest the same labyrinth that I have—I have come to the same conclusion thus far. My Branchings out therefrom have been numerous: one of them is the consideration of Wordsworth's genius and as a help, in the manner of gold being the meridian Line of worldly wealth,[4] how he differs from Milton. And here I have nothing but surmises, from an uncertainty whether Milton's apparently less anxiety for Humanity proceeds from his seeing further or no than Wordsworth: And whether Wordsworth has in truth epic passion, and martyrs himself to the human heart, the main region of his song[5]—In regard to his genius alone—we find what he says true as far as we have experienced and we can judge no further but by larger experience—for axioms in philosophy are not axioms until they are proved upon our pulses: We have read fine ———— things but never feel them to the full until we have gone the same steps as the author. …

I will return to Wordsworth—whether or no he has an extended vision or a circumscribed grandeur—whether he is an eagle in his nest, or on the wing—And to be more explicit and to show you how tall I stand by the giant, I will put down a simile of human life as far as I now perceive it; that is, to the point to which I say we both have arrived at—Well—I compare human life to a large Mansion of Many Apartments,[6] two of which I can only describe, the doors of the rest being as yet shut upon me—The first we step into we call the infant or thoughtless Chamber, in which we remain as long as we do not think—We remain there a long while, and notwithstanding the doors of the second Chamber remain wide open, showing a bright appearance, we care not to hasten to it; but are at length imperceptibly impelled by the awakening of the thinking principle—

---

[1] *a propos des bottes*   French: on the subject of boots.

[2] *Burden of the Mystery*   From Wordsworth's "Lines Written a Few Miles above Tintern Abbey" (40).

[3] *fledge*   With developed feathers, capable of flight.

[4] *in the manner … wealth*   I.e., providing orienting information; the metaphor refers to the gold standard against which the values of currencies are measured, and to the prime meridian, the mark of 0° longitude.

[5] *main region of his song*   Paraphrased from Wordsworth's Prospectus (1799, 1814) to his unfinished long poem *The Recluse*.

[6] *Mansion … Apartments*   See John 14.2: "In my father's house are many mansions."

within us—we no sooner get into the second Chamber, which I shall call the Chamber of Maiden-Thought, than we become intoxicated with the light and the atmosphere, we see nothing but pleasant wonders, and think of delaying there for ever in delight: However among the effects this breathing is father of is that tremendous one of sharpening one's vision into the heart and nature of Man—of convincing ones nerves that the World is full of Misery and Heartbreak, Pain, Sickness and oppression—whereby This Chamber of Maiden Thought becomes gradually darkened and at the same time on all sides of it many doors are set open—but all dark—all leading to dark passages—we see not the balance of good and evil. We are in a Mist—*We* are now in that state—we feel the "burden of the Mystery." To this point was Wordsworth come, as far as I can conceive when he wrote "Tintern Abbey" and it seems to me that his genius is explorative of those dark Passages. Now if we live, and go on thinking, we too shall explore them. He is a Genius and superior [to] us, in so far as he can, more than we, make discoveries, and shed a light in them—Here I must think Wordsworth is deeper than Milton—though I think it has depended more upon the general and gregarious[1] advance of intellect, than individual greatness of Mind—From the *Paradise Lost* and the other Works of Milton, I hope it is not too presuming, even between ourselves to say, his Philosophy, human and divine, may be tolerably understood by one not much advanced in years. In his time Englishmen were just emancipated from a great superstition—and Men had got hold of certain points and resting places in reasoning which were too newly born to be doubted, and too much opposed by the Mass of Europe not to be thought ethereal[2] and authentically divine—who could gainsay his ideas on virtue, vice, and Chastity in *Comus*, just at the time of the dismissal of Cod-pieces[3] and a hundred

other disgraces? who would not rest satisfied with his hintings at good and evil in the *Paradise Lost*, when just free from the inquisition and burning in Smithfield?[4] The Reformation produced such immediate and great benefits, that Protestantism was considered under the immediate eye of heaven, and its own remaining Dogmas and superstition, then, as it were, regenerated, constituted those resting places and seeming sure points of Reasoning—from that I have mentioned, Milton, whatever he may have thought in the sequel,[5] appears to have been content with these by his writings—He did not think into the human heart, as Wordsworth has done—Yet Milton as a philosopher, had sure as great powers as Wordsworth—What is then to be inferred? O many things—It proves there is really a grand march of intellect, it proves that a mighty providence subdues the mightiest Minds to the service of the time being, whether it be in human Knowledge or Religion. ...

[T]he truth is there is something real in the World. Your third Chamber of Life shall be a lucky and a gentle one—stored with the wine of love—and the Bread of Friendship. ...

Your affectionate friend
John Keats

To BENJAMIN BAILEY

18 July 1818

My dear Bailey,

... I am certain I have not a right feeling towards Women—at this moment I am striving to be just to them but I cannot—Is it because they fall so far beneath my Boyish imagination? When I was a Schoolboy I thought a fair Woman a pure Goddess, my mind was a soft nest in which some one of them slept though she knew it not—I have no right to expect more than their reality. I thought them ethereal above Men—I find them perhaps equal. ... I do not like to think insults in

---

[1] *general and gregarious* I.e., applying to all.

[2] *ethereal* Heavenly.

[3] *Comus* 1634 masque in which Comus, a debauched god, kidnaps a woman and attempts to persuade her to abandon rational virtue; *Cod-pieces* Coverings that, in the fifteenth and sixteenth centuries, were commonly worn over male genitals, and often drew attention to the region with decoration or padding.

[4] *Smithfield* London site where many Protestants were executed, often via burning, during the reign of the Catholic queen Mary I (r. 1553–58).

[5] *in the sequel* I.e., in the end.

a Lady's Company—I commit a Crime with her which absence would have not known—is it not extraordinary? When among Men I have no evil thoughts, no malice, no spleen[1]—I feel free to speak or to be silent—I can listen and from every one I can learn—my hands are in my pockets I am free from all suspicion and comfortable. When I am among Women I have evil thoughts, malice spleen—I cannot speak or be silent—I am full of Suspicions and therefore listen to no thing—I am in a hurry to be gone—You must be charitable and put all this perversity to my being disappointed since Boyhood—Yet with such feelings I am happier alone among Crowds of men, by myself or with a friend or two— With all this trust me Bailey I have not the least idea that Men of different feelings and inclinations are more short sighted than myself—I never rejoiced more than at my Brother's Marriage[2] and shall do so at that of any of my friends—. I must absolutely get over this— but how? The only way is to find the root of evil, and so cure it "with backward mutters of dissevering Power."[3] That is a difficult thing; for an obstinate Prejudice can seldom be produced but from a gordian complication[4] of feelings, which must take time to unravell and care to keep unravelled—I could say a good deal about this but I will leave it in hopes of better and more worthy dispositions—and also content that I am wronging no one, for after all I do think better of Womankind than to suppose they care whether Mister John Keats five feet high likes them or not. …

Your affectionate friend
John Keats—

To Richard Woodhouse[5]
27 October 1818

My Dear Woodhouse,

Your Letter gave me a great satisfaction; more on account of its friendliness, than any relish of that matter in it which is accounted so acceptable in the "genus irritabile."[6] The best answer I can give you is in a clerklike manner to make some observations on two principle points, which seem to point like indices[7] into the midst of the whole pro and con, about genius, and views and achievements and ambition and coetera.[8] 1st As to the poetical Character itself, (I mean that sort of which, if I am any thing, I am a Member; that sort distinguished from the wordsworthian or egotistical sublime; which is a thing per se and stands alone) it is not itself—it has no self—it is every thing and nothing—It has no character—it enjoys light and shade; it lives in gusto, be it foul or fair, high or low, rich or poor, mean or elevated—It has as much delight in conceiving an Iago as an Imogen.[9] What shocks the virtuous philosopher delights the chameleon Poet. It does no harm from its relish of the dark side of things any more than from its taste for the bright one; because they both end in speculation. A Poet is the most unpoetical of any thing in existence; because he has no Identity—he is continually in for—and filling some other Body—The Sun, the Moon, the Sea and Men and Women who are creatures of impulse are poetical and have about them an unchangeable attribute—the poet has none; no identity—he is certainly the most unpoetical of all God's Creatures. If then he has no self, and if I am a Poet, where is the Wonder that I should

---

[1] *spleen* Irritability; ill-humor; melancholy.

[2] *my Brother's Marriage* Keats's brother George had recently married, as had Bailey.

[3] *with … Power* From Milton's *Comus* 816–17, in which the author describes the spells that will release a lady from the enchantment of Comus.

[4] *gordian complication* I.e., as difficult to undo as the intricate knot tied by King Gordias.

[5] *RICHARD WOODHOUSE* Young lawyer who worked with Keats's publishers. Woodhouse was struck by Keats's talent and preserved manuscript copies of many of his poems and letters.

[6] *genus irritabile* Latin: irritable tribe. The complete phrase, from Horace, *Epistles* 2.2.102, is "irritable race of poets."

[7] *indices* Pointers.

[8] *coetera* Latin: the following; the next.

[9] *gusto* Term used by William Hazlitt to describe expressive vitality in visual arts as well as in poetry. See Hazlitt's essay "On Gusto" (1816); *Iago* Villain of Shakespeare's *Othello*; *Imogen* Heroine of Shakespeare's *Cymbeline*.

say I would write no more? Might I not at that very instant [have] been cogitating on the Characters of Saturn and Ops?[1] It is a wretched thing to confess; but is a very fact that not one word I ever utter can be taken for granted as an opinion growing out of my identical nature—how can it, when I have no nature? When I am in a room with People if I ever am free from speculating on creations of my own brain, then not myself goes home to myself: but the identity of every one in the room begins [so] to press upon me that, I am in a very little time annihilated—not only among Men; it would be the same in a Nursery of children: I know not whether I make myself wholly understood: I hope enough so to let you see that no dependence is to be placed on what I said that day.[2]

In the second place I will speak of my views, and of the life I purpose to myself—I am ambitious of doing the world some good: if I should be spared that may be the work of maturer years—in the interval I will assay to reach to as high a summit in Poetry as the nerve bestowed upon me will suffer. The faint conceptions I have of Poems to come brings the blood frequently into my forehead—All I hope is that I may not lose all interest in human affairs—that the solitary indifference I feel for applause even from the finest Spirits, will not blunt any acuteness of vision I may have. I do not think it will—I feel assured I should write from the mere yearning and fondness I have for the Beautiful even if my night's labours should be burnt every morning and no eye ever shine upon them. But even now I am perhaps not speaking from myself; but from some character in whose soul I now live. I am sure however that this next sentence is from myself. I feel your anxiety, good opinion and friendliness in the highest degree, and am

Yours most sincerely
John Keats

To GEORGE AND GEORGIANA KEATS[3]
14 February–3 May 1819

My dear Brother & Sister—

... [19 March] **Y**esterday I got a black eye—the first time I took a Cricket bat—Brown who is always one's friend in a disaster applied a leech to the eyelid, and there is no inflammation this morning though the ball hit me directly on the sight—'t was a white ball—I am glad it was not a clout—This is the second black eye I have had since leaving school—during all my school days I never had one at all—we must eat a peck before we die[4]—This morning I am in a sort of temper indolent and supremely careless: I long after a stanza or two of Thomson's *Castle of indolence*[5]—My passions are all asleep from my having slumbered till nearly eleven and weakened the animal fibre all over me to a delightful sensation about three degrees on this side of faintness—if I had teeth of pearl and the breath of lilies I should call it langour—but as I am[6] I must call it Laziness—In this state of effeminacy the fibres of the brain are relaxed in common with the rest of the body, and to such a happy degree that pleasure has no show of enticement and pain no unbearable frown. Neither Poetry, nor Ambition, nor Love have any alertness of countenance as they pass by me: they seem rather like three figures on a greek vase—a Man and two women—whom no one but myself could distinguish in their disguisement. This is the only happiness; and is a rare instance of advantage in the body overpowering the Mind. I have this moment received a note from Haslam[7] in which he expects the death of his Father who has been for some time in a state of insensibility—his mother bears up he says very well—I shall go to [town]

---

1   *Saturn and Ops*   King and queen of the Titans in Keats's *Hyperion* (1820).

2   *what I ... day*   Keats had told Woodhouse that he felt preempted by great poets of the past.

3   *GEORGE AND GEORGIANA KEATS*   Keats's brother and sister-in-law, who had emigrated to America. Keats would compose long letters to them, each of which spanned several months, and in which he would include transcriptions of his poems.

4   *eat a peck ... die*   Proverbial: everyone must eat a peck of dirt before he or she dies.

5   *Thomson ... indolence*   James Thomson's *The Castle of Indolence*, in which a wizard named Indolence puts a spell of indolence on tired travelers who are lured into his castle.

6   [Keats's note]   Especially as I have a black eye.

7   *Haslam*   Keats's friend William Haslam, a businessperson.

tomorrow to see him. This is the world—thus we cannot expect to give way many hours to pleasure—Circumstances are like Clouds continually gathering and bursting—While we are laughing the seed of some trouble is put into the wide arable land of events—while we are laughing it sprouts [it] grows and suddenly bears a poison fruit which we must pluck—Even so we have leisure to reason on the misfortunes of our friends; our own touch us too nearly for words. Very few men have ever arrived at a complete disinterestedness[1] of Mind: very few have been influenced by a pure desire of the benefit of others—in the greater part of the Benefactors of & to Humanity some meretricious motive has sullied their greatness—some melodramatic scenery has fascinated them—From the manner in which I feel Haslam's misfortune I perceive how far I am from any humble standard of disinterestedness—Yet this feeling ought to be carried to its highest pitch, as there is no fear of its ever injuring society—which it would do I fear pushed to an extremity—For in wild nature the Hawk would loose his Breakfast of Robins and the Robin his of Worms. The Lion must starve as well as the swallow—The greater part of Men make their way with the same instinctiveness, the same unwandering eye from their purposes, the same animal eagerness as the Hawk—The Hawk wants a Mate, so does the Man—look at them both they set about it and procure one in the same manner—They want both a nest and they both set about one in the same manner—they get their food in the same manner—The noble animal Man for his amusement smokes his pipe—the Hawk balances about the Clouds—that is the only difference of their leisures. This it is that makes the Amusement of Life—to a speculative Mind. I go among the Fields and catch a glimpse of a stoat[2] or a fieldmouse peeping out of the withered grass—the creature hath a purpose and its eyes are bright with it—I go amongst the buildings of a city and I see a Man hurrying along—to what? The Creature has a purpose and his eyes are bright with it. But then as Wordsworth says, "we have all one human heart"[3]—there is an electric fire in human nature tending to purify—so that among these human creatures there is continually some birth of new hero-

ism—The pity is that we must wonder at it: as we should at finding a pearl in rubbish—I have no doubt that thousands of people never heard of have had hearts completely disinterested: I can remember but two—Socrates and Jesus—their Histories evince it—What I heard a little time ago, Taylor observe with respect to Socrates, may be said of Jesus—That he was so great a man that though he transmitted no writing of his own to posterity, we have his Mind and his sayings and his greatness handed to us by others. It is to be lamented that the history of the latter was written and revised by Men interested in the pious frauds of Religion. Yet through all this I see his splendour. Even here though I myself am pursuing the same instinctive course as the veriest human animal you can think of—I am however young writing at random—straining at particles of light in the midst of a great darkness—without knowing the bearing of any one assertion of any one opinion. Yet may I not in this be free from sin? May there not be superior beings amused with any graceful, though instinctive attitude my mind may fall into, as I am entertained with the alertness of a Stoat or the anxiety of a Deer? Though a quarrel in the streets is a thing to be hated, the energies displayed in it are fine; the commonest Man shows a grace in his quarrel—By a superior being our reasoning may take the same tone—though erroneous they may be fine—This is the very thing in which consists poetry; and if so it is not so fine a thing as philosophy—For the same reason that an eagle is not so fine a thing as a truth—Give me this credit—Do you not think I strive—to know myself? Give me this credit—and you will not think that on my own account I repeat Milton's lines

> How charming is divine Philosophy
> Not harsh and crabbed as dull fools suppose
> But musical as is Apollo's lute[4]—

No—no for myself—feeling grateful as I do to have got into a state of mind to relish them properly—Nothing ever becomes real till it is experienced—Even a Proverb is no proverb to you till your Life has illustrated it— …

[21 April] I have been reading lately two very different books Robertson's *America* and Voltaire's *Siecle De Louis*

---

[1] *disinterestedness* State unmotivated by self-interest.

[2] *stoat* Weasel-like animal.

[3] *we have ... heart* From *The Old Cumberland Beggar* 152–53.

[4] *How charming ... lute* See Milton's *Comus* 475–77.

xiv It is like walking arm and arm between Pizzarro and the great-little Monarch.[1] In How lamentable a case do we see the great body of the people in both instances: in the first, where Men might seem to inherit quiet of Mind from unsophisticated sense; from uncontamination of civilisation; and especially from their being as it were estranged from the mutual helps of Society and its mutual injuries—and thereby more immediately under the Protection of Providence—even there they had mortal pains to bear as bad; or even worse than Bailiffs, Debts and Poverties of civilised Life—The whole appears to resolve into this—that Man is originally "a poor forked creature"[2] subject to the same mischances as the beasts of the forest, destined to hardships and disquietude of some kind or other. If he improves by degrees his bodily accommodations and comforts—at each stage, at each accent there are waiting for him a fresh set of annoyances—he is mortal and there is still a heaven with its Stars above his head. The most interesting question that can come before us is, How far by the persevering endeavours of a seldom appearing Socrates Mankind may be made happy—I can imagine such happiness carried to an extreme—but what must it end in?—Death—and who could in such a case bear with death—the whole troubles of life which are now frittered away in a series of years, would then be accumulated for the last days of a being who instead of hailing its approach, would leave this world as Eve left Paradise—But in truth I do not at all believe in this sort of perfectibility—the nature of the world will not admit of it—the inhabitants of the world will correspond to itself—Let the fish philosophise the ice away from the Rivers in winter time and they shall be at continual play in the tepid delight of summer. Look at the Poles and at the sands of Africa, Whirlpools and volcanoes—Let men exterminate them and I will say that they may arrive at earthly Happiness—The point at which Man may arrive is as far as the parallel state in inanimate nature and no further—For instance suppose a rose to have sensation, it blooms on a beautiful morning it enjoys itself—but there comes a cold wind, a hot sun—it can not escape it, it cannot destroy its annoyances—they are as native to the world as itself: no more can man be happy in spite, the worldly elements will prey upon his nature—The common cognomen of this world among the misguided and superstitious is "a vale of tears" from which we are to be redeemed by a certain arbitrary interposition of God and taken to Heaven—What a little circumscribed straightened notion! Call the world if you Please "The vale of Soul-making" Then you will find out the use of the world (I am speaking now in the highest terms for human nature admitting it to be immortal which I will here take for granted for the purpose of showing a thought which has struck me concerning it) I say "*Soul making*" Soul as distinguished from an Intelligence—There may be intelligences or sparks of the divinity in millions—but they are not Souls till they acquire identities, till each one is personally itself. Intelligences are atoms of perception—they know and they see and they are pure, in short they are God—how then are Souls to be made? How then are these sparks which are God to have identity given them—so as ever to possess a bliss peculiar to each ones individual existence? How, but by the medium of a world like this? This point I sincerely wish to consider because I think it a grander system of salvation than the christian religion—or rather it is a system of Spirit-creation—This is effected by three grand materials acting the one upon the other for a series of years—These three Materials are the *Intelligence*—the *human heart* (as distinguished from intelligence or Mind) and the *World or Elemental space* suited for the proper action of *Mind and Heart* on each other for the purpose of forming the *Soul or Intelligence destined to possess the sense of Identity*. I can scarcely express what I but dimly perceive—and yet I think I perceive it—that you may judge the more clearly I will put it in the most homely form possible—I will call the world a School instituted for the purpose of teaching little children to read—I will call the *human*

---

1 *Robertson's ... Monarch* William Robertson's *History of the Discovery and Settlement of America* (1777) describes the Spanish conquistadors, including Francisco Pizarro, who conquered the Incas in the sixteenth century. French philosopher Voltaire's *Le Siècle de Louis XIV* (1751) describes the rule of Louis XIV, who was often called "The Great Monarch."

2 *a poor forked creature* From Shakespeare's *King Lear* 3.4.112–13, in which Lear looks at "Poor Tom" and says "Unaccommodated man is no more but such a poor, bare, forked animal as thou art."

heart the *horn Book*[1] used in that School—and I will call the *Child able to read, the Soul* made from that *school* and its *hornbook*. Do you not see how necessary a World of Pains and troubles is to school an Intelligence and make it a soul? A Place where the heart must feel and suffer in a thousand diverse ways! Not merely is the Heart a Hornbook, It is the Minds Bible, it is the Minds experience, it is the teat from which the Mind or intelligence sucks its identity—As various as the Lives of Men are—so various become their souls, and thus does God make individual beings, Souls, Identical Souls of the sparks of his own essence—This appears to me a faint sketch of a system of Salvation which does not affront our reason and humanity—I am convinced that many difficulties which christians labour under would vanish before it—there is one which even now Strikes me—the Salvation of Children—In them the Spark or intelligence returns to God without any identity—it having had no time to learn of, and be altered by, the heart—or seat of the human Passions—It is pretty generally suspected that the christian scheme has been copied from the ancient persian and greek Philosophers. Why may they not have made this simple thing even more simple for common apprehension by introducing Mediators and Personages in the same manner as in the heathen mythology abstractions are personified—Seriously I think it probable that this System of Soul-making—may have been the Parent of all the more palpable and personal Schemes of Redemption, among the Zoroastrians the Christians and the Hindus. For as one part of the human species must have their carved Jupiter; so another part must have the palpable and named Mediator and saviour, their Christ their Oromanes and their Vishnu[2]—If what I have said should not be plain enough, as I fear it may not be, I will but [put] you in the place where I began in this series of thoughts—I mean, I began by seeing how man was formed by circumstances—and what are circumstances?—but touchstones of his heart?—and what are touchstones?—but provings of his heart? and what are provings of his heart but fortifiers or alterers of his nature? and what is his altered nature but his soul?—and what was his soul before it came into the world and had These provings and alterations and perfectionings?—An intelligence—without Identity—and how is this Identity to be made? Through the medium of the Heart? And how is the heart to become this Medium but in a world of Circumstances?—There now I think what with Poetry and Theology you may thank your Stars that my pen is not very long winded— …

… [T]his is the 3rd of May & every thing is in delightful forwardness; the violets are not withered, before the peeping of the first rose; You must let me know every thing, how parcels go &. come, what papers you have, &. what Newspapers you want, & other things—God bless you my dear Brother & Sister

Your ever Affectionate Brother
John Keats—

To Fanny Brawne[3]

25 July 1819
Sunday Night
Isle of Wight

My Sweet Girl,

I hope you did not blame me much for not obeying your request of a Letter on Saturday: we have had four in our small room playing at cards night and morning leaving me no undisturb'd opportunity to write. Now Rice and Martin are gone I am at liberty. Brown to my sorrow confirms the account you give of your ill health. You cannot conceive how I ache to be with you: how I would die for one hour—for what is in the world? I say you cannot conceive; it is impossible you should look with such eyes upon me as I have upon you: it cannot be. Forgive me if I wander a little this evening, for I have been all day employ'd in a very

---

[1] *horn Book* Child's primer, originally made of a sheet of paper mounted on wood and protected by a thin sheet of transparent horn.

[2] *Oromanes* Ahriman, the chief evil spirit in Zoroastrianism, who is locked in perpetual struggle with Ahura Mazda; *Vishnu* Hindu deity who protects and preserves the world.

[3] *FANNY BRAWNE* Young woman whom Keats met in the summer of 1818, and to whom he was engaged by the end of the year (though the couple was waiting to marry until Keats felt he was financially secure). From October 1818 to May 1819 Keats stayed in his friend Charles Brown's apartment in Hampstead, which was next door to the Brawnes, who took care of him throughout the summer.

abstract Poem[1] and I am in deep love with you—two things which must excuse me. I have, believe me, not been an age in letting you take possession of me; the very first week I knew you I wrote myself your vassal; but burnt the Letter as the very next time I saw you I thought you manifested some dislike to me. If you should ever feel for Man at the first sight what I did for you, I am lost. Yet I should not quarrel with you, but hate myself if such a thing were to happen—only I should burst if the thing were not as fine as a Man as you are as a Woman. Perhaps I am too vehement, then fancy me on my knees, especially when I mention a part of your Letter which hurt me; you say speaking of Mr. Severn[2] "but you must be satisfied in knowing that I admired you much more than your friend." My dear love, I cannot believe there ever was or ever could be any thing to admire in me especially as far as sight goes—I cannot be admired, I am not a thing to be admired. You are, I love you; all I can bring you is a swooning admiration of your Beauty. I hold that place among Men which snubnos'd brunettes with meeting eyebrows do among women—they are trash to me—unless I should find one among them with a fire in her heart like the one that burns in mine. You absorb me in spite of myself—you alone: for I look not forward with any pleasure to what is call'd being settled in the world; I tremble at domestic cares—yet for you I would meet them, though if it would leave you the happier I would rather die than do so. I have two luxuries to brood over in my walks, your Loveliness and the hour of my death. O that I could have possession of them both in the same minute. I hate the world: it batters too much the wings of my self-will, and would I could take a sweet poison from your lips to send me out of it. From no others

would I take it. I am indeed astonish'd to find myself so careless of all charms but yours—remembering as I do the time when even a bit of ribband was a matter of interest with me. What softer words can I find for you after this—what it is I will not read. Nor will I say more here, but in a Postscript answer any thing else you may have mentioned in your Letter in so many words—for I am distracted with a thousand thoughts. I will imagine you Venus tonight and pray, pray, pray to your star like a Heathen.

> Yours ever, fair Star,
> John Keats

TO PERCY BYSSHE SHELLEY[3]
16 August 1820
Hampstead

My Dear Shelley,

I am very much gratified that you, in a foreign country, and with a mind almost over occupied, should write to me in the strain of the Letter beside me. If I do not take advantage of your invitation it will be prevented by a circumstance I have very much at heart to prophesy—There is no doubt that an english winter would put an end to me, and do so in a lingering hateful manner, therefore I must either voyage or journey to Italy as a soldier marches up to a battery. My nerves at present are the worst part of me, yet they feel soothed when I think that come what extreme may, I shall not be destined to remain in one spot long enough to take a hatred of any four particular bedposts. I am glad you take any pleasure in my poor Poem;[4]—which I would willingly take the trouble to unwrite, if possible, did I care so much as I have done about Reputation. I received a copy of the Cenci,[5] as from yourself from Hunt.

---

[1] *very abstract Poem*   Most likely *The Fall of Hyperion*.

[2] *Mr. Severn*   Joseph Severn, an artist and a friend of Keats. He cared for Keats during his final illness in Rome and was present when he died.

[3] *TO … SHELLEY*   This letter is written in response to one from Shelley, in which he, having learned of Keats's serious illness, invites Keats to stay with him in Pisa for the winter.

[4] *my poor Poem*   Keats's *Endymion*, which had received several negative reviews but which Shelley had praised in his letter.

[5] *Cenci*   Shelley's blank-verse tragedy (1820).

There is only one part of it I am judge of; the Poetry, and dramatic effect, which by many spirits now a days is considered the mammon.[1] A modern work it is said must have a purpose, which may be the God—*an artist* must serve Mammon—he must have "self concentration" selfishness perhaps. You I am sure will forgive me for sincerely remarking that you might curb your magnanimity and be more of an artist, and "load every rift" of your subject with ore.[2] The thought of such discipline must fall like cold chains upon you, who perhaps never sat with your wings furl'd for six Months together. And is not this extraordinary talk for the writer of *Endymion*? whose mind was like a pack of scattered cards—I am pick'd up and sorted to a pip.[3] My Imagination is a Monastry and I am its Monk—you must explain my [metaphysics] to yourself. I am in expectation of *Prometheus*[4] every day. Could I have my own wish for its interest effected you would have it still in manuscript—or be but now putting an end to the second act. I remember you advising me not to publish my first-blights, on Hampstead heath—I am returning advice upon your hands. Most of the Poems in the volume I send you[5] have been written above two years, and would never have been publish'd but from a hope of gain; so you see I am inclined enough to take your advice now. I must express once more my deep sense of your kindness, adding my sincere thanks and respects for Mrs. Shelley. In the hope of soon seeing you I remain

most sincerely yours,
John Keats—

To Charles Brown
30 November 1820
Rome

My Dear Brown,

'Tis the most difficult thing in the world to me to write a letter. My stomach continues so bad, that I feel it worse on opening any book,—yet I am much better than I was in Quarantine.[6] Then I am afraid to encounter the proing and conning of any thing interesting to me in England. I have an habitual feeling of my real life having past, and that I am leading a posthumous existence. God knows how it would have been—but it appears to me—however, I will not speak of that subject. I must have been at Bedhampton nearly at the time you were writing to me from Chichester—how unfortunate—and to pass on the river too! There was my star predominant! I cannot answer any thing in your letter, which followed me from Naples to Rome, because I am afraid to look it over again. I am so weak (in mind) that I cannot bear the sight of any hand writing of a friend I love so much as I do you. Yet I ride the little horse,[7]—and, at my worst, even in Quarantine, summoned up more puns, in a sort of desperation, in one week than in any year of my life. There is one thought enough to kill me—I have been well, healthy, alert &c, walking with her[8]—and now—the knowledge of contrast, feeling for light and shade, all that information (primitive sense) necessary for a poem are great enemies to the recovery of the stomach. There, you rogue, I put you to the torture,—but you must bring

---

[1] *mammon* Wealth and profit, regarded as a false god. Cf. Matthew 6.24, in which Jesus says, "Ye cannot serve God and Mammon."

[2] *load ... ore* Reference to Spenser's *Faerie Queene* 2.7.28, in which he describes the Palace of Mammon: "Embost with massy gold of glorious gift, / And with rich metal loaded every rift."

[3] *sorted to a pip* Put in order. Pips are the markings on playing cards.

[4] *Prometheus* Shelley's *Prometheus Unbound* (1820), a copy of which he had promised to send to Keats.

[5] *the volume ... you* Keats's 1820 volume, which Shelley had in his pocket when he drowned.

[6] *in Quarantine* Keats's ship was quarantined for ten days outside Naples, in extremely hot weather. Keats was writing this letter from Rome, where he was being cared for by Joseph Severn.

[7] *Yet ... horse* Recommended by Keats's doctor for exercise.

[8] *her* Fanny Brawne.

your philosophy to bear—as I do mine, really—or how should I be able to live? Dr Clarke is very attentive to me; he says, there is very little the matter with my lungs, but my stomach, he says, is very bad. I am well disappointed in hearing good news from George,—for it runs in my head we shall all die young. I have not written to * * * *[1] yet, which he must think very neglectful; being anxious to send him a good account of my health, I have delayed it from week to week. If I recover, I will do all in my power to correct the mistakes made during sickness; and if I should not, all my faults will be forgiven. I shall write to * * * * tomorrow, or next day. I will write to * * * * in the middle of next week. Severn

is very well, though he leads so dull a life with me. Remember me to all friends, and tell * * * * I should not have left London without taking leave of him, but from being so low in body and mind. Write to George as soon as you receive this, and tell him how I am, as far as you can guess; and also a note to my sister—who walks about my imagination like a ghost—she is so like Tom.[2] I can scarcely bid you good bye even in a letter. I always made an awkward bow.

God bless you!

John Keats.

---

1 * * * * Brown, whose transcription of this letter is the only surviving copy, deleted the names of Keats's friends in order to conceal their identities.

2 *my sister … Tom* Keats's sister Fanny closely resembled his youngest brother Tom, who had died of tuberculosis in December 1818.

IN CONTEXT

Politics, Poetry, and the "Cockney School Debate"

As literary journals and magazines of the time demonstrate, in the nineteenth century politics and literary theory were often inextricably intertwined. At the time, only a small minority of adult males had been granted the vote, and the political system was widely perceived to be corrupt. Leigh Hunt, John Keats, William Hazlitt, and Percy Bysshe Shelley were among those who pressed strongly for political reform. Leigh Hunt, with his brothers John and Robert, edited the *Examiner*, a liberal weekly journal that frequently riled the government. After offending the Prince of Wales, Leigh and John spent two years in prison (1813–15) for libel.

In August 1817 the *Edinburgh Review* began to refer to Wordsworth, Coleridge, and Robert Southey as "The Lake School"—all three had lived in and been inspired by England's Lake District. Those poets and some others—Lord Byron in particular—had been identified the previous year by Leigh Hunt as representative of a school of poets "who go directly to Nature for inspiration." Hunt had written his article "Young Poets" to bring to the attention of the public "three young writers [Shelley, Keats, and John Hamilton Reynolds] who appear to us to promise a considerable addition of strength to the new school." Hunt had not named himself as a member of this new group, but it was on him that John Gibson Lockhart focused in launching an attack on the group that was as much political as literary. Lockhart's series of articles on "The Cockney School of Poetry" appeared in *Blackwood's Edinburgh Magazine*, a conservative journal founded in response to the *Edinburgh Review*.

from Leigh Hunt, "Young Poets," *Examiner* (1 December 1816)

In sitting down to this subject, we happen to be restricted by time to a much shorter notice than we could wish: but we mean to take it up again shortly. Many of our readers however have perhaps observed for themselves, that there has been a new school of poetry rising of late, which promises to extinguish the French one that has prevailed among us since the time of Charles the 2d. It began with something excessive, like most revolutions, but this gradually wore away; and an evident aspiration after real nature and original fancy remained, which called to mind the finer times of the English Muse. In fact it is wrong to call it a new school, and still more so to represent it as one of innovation, its only object being to restore the same love of Nature, and of *thinking* instead of mere *talking*, which formerly rendered us real poets, and not merely versifying wits, and bead-rollers of couplets.

We were delighted to see the departure of the old school acknowledged in the number of the *Edinburgh Review* just published—a candour the more generous and spirited, inasmuch as that work has hitherto been the greatest surviving ornament of the same school in prose and criticism, as it is now destined, we trust, to be still the leader in the new.

We also felt the same delight at the third canto of Lord Byron's *Childe Harold*, in which, to our conceptions at least, he has fairly renounced a certain leaven of the French style, and taken his place where we always said he would be found—among the poets who have a real feeling for numbers,[1] and who go directly to Nature for inspiration. But more of this poem in our next.

The object of the present article is merely to notice three young writers, who appear to us to promise a considerable addition of strength to the new school. Of the first who came before us, we have, it is true, yet seen only one or two specimens, and these were no sooner sent us than we unfortunately mislaid them; but we shall procure what he has published, and if the rest answer to what we have seen, we shall have no hesitation in announcing him for a very striking and original thinker. His name is Percy Bysshe Shelley, and he is the author of a poetical work entitled *Alastor, or the Spirit of Solitude*.

The next with whose name we became acquainted was John Henry Reynolds, author of a tale called *Safie*, written, we believe, in imitation of Lord Byron, and more lately of a small set of poems published by Taylor and Hessey, the principal of which is called the *Naiad*. It opens thus:

> The gold sun went into the west,
> And soft airs sang him to his rest;
> And yellow leaves all loose and dry,
> Play'd on the branches listlessly:
> The sky wax'd palely blue, and high
> A cloud seem'd touch'd upon the sky—
> A spot of cloud—blue, thin, and still,
> And silence bask'd on vale and hill. ...

We shall give another extract or two in a future number. The author's style is too artificial, though he is evidently an admirer of Mr. Wordsworth. Like all young poets too, properly so called, his love of detail is too overwrought and indiscriminate; but still he is a young poet, and only wants a still closer attention to things as opposed to the seduction of words, to realize all that he promises. His nature seems very true and amiable.

The last of these young aspirants who we have met with, and who promise to help the new school to revive Nature and

> "To put a spirit of youth in every thing,"

is, we believe, the youngest of them all, and just of age. His name is John Keats. He has not yet published anything except in a newspaper; but a set of his manuscripts was handed us the other day, and fairly surprised us with the truth of their ambition, and ardent grappling with Nature. In the following sonnet there is one incorrect rhyme, which might be easily altered, but which shall serve in the mean time as a peace-offering to the rhyming critics. The rest of the composition, with the exception of a little vagueness in calling the regions of poetry "the realms of gold," we do not hesitate to pronounce excellent, especially the last six lines. The word *swims* is complete; and the whole conclusion is equally powerful and quiet

[Quotes "On First Looking into Chapman's Homer"]

We have spoken with the less scruple of these poetical promises, because we really are not in the habit of lavishing praises and announcements, and because we have no fear of any pettier vanity on the part of young men who promise to understand human nature so well.

---

[1] *numbers* I.e., metrical harmony, rhythm.

from John Lockhart ("Z."), "On the Cockney School of Poetry, No. 1," *Blackwood's Edinburgh Magazine* (October 1817)

> Our talk shall be (a theme we never tire on)
> Of Chaucer, Spenser, Shakespeare, Milton, Byron,
> (Our England's Dante)—Wordsworth—Hunt, and Keats,
> The Muses' son of promise; and of what feats
> He yet may do.
> —CORNELIUS WEBB

While the whole critical world is occupied with balancing the merits, whether in theory or in execution, of what is commonly called The Lake School, it is strange that no one seems to think it at all necessary to say a single word about another new school of poetry which has of late sprung up amongst us. This school has not, I believe, as yet received any name; but if I may be permitted to have the honour of christening it, it may henceforth be referred to by the designation of The Cockney School. Its chief Doctor and Professor is Mr. Leigh Hunt, a man certainly of some talents, of extravagant pretensions both in wit, poetry, and politics, and withal of exquisitely bad taste, and extremely vulgar modes of thinking and manners in all respects. He is a man of little education. He knows absolutely nothing of Greek, almost nothing of Latin, and his knowledge of Italian literature is confined to a few of the most popular of Petrarch's sonnets, and an imperfect acquaintance with Ariosto, through the medium of Mr. Hoole. As to the French poets, he dismisses them in the mass as a set of prim, precise, unnatural pretenders. The truth is, he is in a state of happy ignorance about them and all that they have done. …

With this stock of knowledge, Mr. Hunt presumes to become the founder of a new school of poetry, and throws away entirely the chance he might have had of gaining some true poetic fame, had he been less lofty in his pretensions. …

All the great poets of our country have been men of some rank in society, and there is no vulgarity in any of their writings; but Mr. Hunt cannot utter a dedication, or even a note, without betraying the *Shibboleth*[1] of low birth and low habits. He is the ideal of a Cockney Poet. He raves perpetually about "green fields," "jaunty streams," and "o'er-arching leafiness," exactly as a Cheapside shop-keeper does about the beauties of his box[2] on the Camberwell road. Mr. Hunt is altogether unacquainted with the face of nature in her magnificent scenes; he has never seen any mountain higher than Highgate-hill,[3] nor reclined by any stream more pastoral than the Serpentine River.[4] But he is determined to be a poet eminently rural, and he rings the changes—till one is sick of him, on the beauties of the different "high views" which he has taken of God and nature, in the course of some Sunday dinner parties, at which he has assisted in the neighbourhood of London. His books are indeed not known in the country; his fame as a poet (and I might almost say, as a politician too) is entirely confined to the young attorneys and embryo-barristers about town. In the opinion of these competent judges, London is the world—and Hunt is a Homer.

Mr. Hunt is not disqualified by his ignorance and vulgarity alone, for being the founder of a respectable sect in poetry. He labours under the burden of a sin more deadly than either of these. The two great elements of all dignified poetry, religious feeling and patriotic feeling, have no place in his

---

[1] *Shibboleth* Word distinguishing a certain class or party.

[2] *box* Boxwood.

[3] *Highgate-hill* Hill (and district) in the north of London.

[4] *Serpentine River* Lake in Hyde Park, in the center of London.

writings. His religion is a poor tame dilution of the blasphemies of the *Encyclopaedie*[1]—his patriotism a crude, vague, ineffectual, and sour Jacobinism.[2] His works exhibit no reverence either for God or man; neither altar nor throne have any dignity in his eyes. He speaks well of nobody but two or three great dead poets, and in so speaking of them he does well; but alas! Mr. Hunt is no conjurer τεχνη ὅ λανθανει.[3] He pretends, indeed, to be an admirer of Spenser and Chaucer, but what he praises in them is never what is most deserving of praise—it is only that which he humbly conceives bears some resemblance to the more perfect productions of Mr. Leigh Hunt; and we can always discover in the midst of his most violent ravings about the Court of Elizabeth, and the days of Sir Philip Sidney, and the Fairy Queen, that the real objects of his admiration are the Coterie of Hampstead and the Editor of the Examiner. When he talks about chivalry and King Arthur, he is always thinking of himself, and "*a small party of friends, who meet once a week at a Round Table, to discuss the merits of a leg of mutton, and of the subjects upon which we are to write.*"[4]—Mr. Leigh Hunt's ideas concerning the sublime, and concerning his own powers, bear a considerable resemblance to those of his friend Bottom, the weaver, on the same subjects; "I will roar, that it shall do any man's heart good to hear me."—"I will roar you an 'twere any nightingale."[5]

The poetry of Mr. Hunt is such as might be expected from the personal character and habits of its author. As a vulgar man is perpetually labouring to be genteel—in like manner, the poetry of this man is always on the stretch to be grand. He has been allowed to look for a moment from the antechamber into the salon, and mistaken the waving of feathers and the painted floor for the *sine qua non*'s[6] of elegant society. He would fain be always tripping and waltzing, and is sorry that he cannot be allowed to walk about in the morning with yellow breeches and flesh-coloured silk-stockings. He sticks an artificial rosebud into his button hole in the midst of winter. …

How such an indelicate writer as Mr. Hunt can pretend to be an admirer of Mr. Wordsworth, is to us a thing altogether inexplicable. One great charm of Wordsworth's noble compositions consists in the dignified purity of thought, and the patriarchal simplicity of feeling, with which they are throughout penetrated and imbued. We can conceive a vicious[7] man admiring with distant awe the spectacle of virtue and purity; but if he does so sincerely, he must also do so with the profoundest feeling of the error of his own ways, and the resolution to amend them. His admiration must be humble and silent, not pert and loquacious. Mr. Hunt praises the purity of Wordsworth as if he himself were pure, his dignity as if he also were dignified. …

The founder of the Cockney School would fain claim poetical kindred with Lord Byron and Thomas Moore.[8] Such a connection would be as unsuitable for them as for William Wordsworth. The days of Mr. Moore's follies are long since over; and, as he is a thorough gentleman, he must necessarily entertain the greatest contempt for such an under-bred person as Mr. Leigh Hunt. But

---

[1] *Encylopaedie*   Influential Enlightenment-era encyclopedia (1751) prepared by Denis Diderot and Jean le Rond d'Alembert.

[2] *Jacobinism*   Extreme democratic principles; belief in complete equality (after the practice of the French political sect the Jacobins).

[3] τεχνη ὅ λανθανει   Greek: his technique does not escape notice.

[4] *a small … write*   From a feature in the *Examiner*, initiated by Leigh Hunt, called "The Round Table."

[5] *I will … nightingale*   From Shakespeare's *A Midsummer Night's Dream* 1.2, in which Bottom the weaver (who is later transformed into an ass) desires to play the lion's part in a play.

[6] *sine qua non*   Latin: without which, not.

[7] *vicious*   Immoral.

[8] *Thomas Moore*   Irish poet (1779–1852).

Lord Byron! … We dare say Mr. Hunt has some fine dreams about the true nobility being the nobility of talent, and flatters himself, that with those who acknowledge only that sort of rank, he himself passes for being the *peer* of Byron. He is sadly mistaken. He is as completely a Plebeian[1] in his mind as he is in his rank and station in society. To that highest and unalienable nobility which the great Roman satirist styles "*sola atque unica*,"[2] we fear his pretensions would be equally unavailing.

The shallow and impotent pretensions, tenets, and attempts of this man—and the success with which his influence seems to be extending itself among a pretty numerous, though certainly a very paltry and pitiful, set of readers—have for the last two or three years been considered by us with the most sickening aversion. The very culpable manner in which his chief poem was reviewed in the *Edinburgh Review* (we believe it is no secret, at his own impatient and feverish request, by his partner in the Round Table[3]), was matter of concern to more readers than ourselves. The masterly pen which inflicted such signal chastisement on the early licentiousness of Moore, should not have been idle on that occasion. Mr. Jeffrey[4] does ill, when he delegates his important functions into such hands as those of Mr. Hazlitt. It was chiefly in consequence of that gentleman's allowing Leigh Hunt to pass unpunished through the scene of slaughter, which his execution might so highly have graced, that we came to the resolution of laying before our readers a series of essays on *the Cockney School*—of which here terminates the first.

from John Lockhart ("Z."), "On the Cockney School of Poetry, No. 4," *Blackwood's Edinburgh Magazine* (August 1818)

———Of Keats,
'The Muses' son of promise, and what feats
He yet may do, &c.
—CORNELIUS WEBB

Of all the manias of this mad age, the most incurable, as well as the most common, seems to be no other than the *Metromanie*.[5] The just celebrity of Robert Burns and Miss Baillie[6] has had the melancholy effect of turning the heads of we know not how many farm-servants and unmarried ladies; our very footmen compose tragedies, and there is scarcely a superannuated governess in the island that does not leave a roll of lyrics behind her in her band-box. To witness the disease of any human understanding, however feeble, is distressing; but the spectacle of an able mind reduced to a state of insanity is of course ten times more afflicting. It is with such sorrow as this that we have contemplated the case of Mr. John Keats. This young man appears to have received from nature talents of an excellent, perhaps even of a superior order—talents which, devoted to the purpose of any useful profession, must have rendered him a respectable, if not an eminent citizen. His friends, we understand, destined him to the career of medicine, and he was bound apprentice some years ago to

[1] *Plebeian*   In ancient Rome, a commoner, a person of low birth or rank.

[2] *sola atque unica*   Latin: alone and only. See Juvenal's *Satire* 8: "Virtue alone is the only true nobility."

[3] *partner … Table*   William Hazlitt, who contributed to both the *Examiner* and the *Edinburgh Review*. Hazlitt frequently wrote for the *Examiner* feature "The Round Table," and his first book-length collection of essays appeared in 1817 under that title.

[4] *Mr. Jeffrey*   Francis Jeffrey (1773–1850), founder and editor of the *Edinburgh Review*.

[5] *Metromanie*   Mania for writing poetry.

[6] *Miss Baillie*   Scottish poet and playwright Joanna Baillie (1762–1851).

a worthy apothecary in town. But all has been undone by a sudden attack of the malady to which we have alluded. Whether Mr. John had been sent home with a diuretic or composing draught to some patient far gone in the poetical mania, we have not heard. This much is certain, that he has caught the infection, and that thoroughly. For some time we were in hopes that he might get off with a violent fit or two; but of late the symptoms are terrible. The frenzy of the "Poems"[1] was bad enough in its way; but it did not alarm us half so seriously as the calm, settled, imperturbable drivelling idiocy of "Endymion." We hope, however, that in so young a person, and with a constitution originally so good, even now the disease is not utterly incurable. Time, firm treatment, and rational restraint, do much for many apparently hopeless invalids; and if Mr. Keats should happen, at some interval of reason, to cast his eye upon our pages, he may perhaps be convinced of the existence of his malady, which in such cases is often all that is necessary to put the patient in a fair way of being cured. …

[Keats's] Endymion is not a Greek shepherd, loved by a Grecian goddess;[2] he is merely a young Cockney rhymester, dreaming a fantastic dream at the full of the moon. Costume, were it worth while to notice such a trifle, is violated in every page of this goodly octavo. From his prototype Hunt, Keats has acquired a sort of vague idea that the Greeks were a most tasteful people, and that no mythology can be so finely adapted for the purposes of poetry as theirs. It is amusing to see what a hand the two Cockneys make of this mythology; the one confesses that he never read the Greek Tragedians, and the other knows Homer only from Chapman;[3] and both of them write about Apollo, Pan, Nymphs, Muses, and Mysteries, as might be expected from persons of their education. We shall not, however, enlarge at present upon this subject, as we mean to dedicate an entire paper to the classical attainments and attempts of the Cockney poets. As for Mr. Keats' "Endymion," it has just as much to do with Greece as it has with "old Tartary the fierce;" no man whose mind has ever been imbued with the smallest knowledge or feeling of classical poetry or classical history could have stooped to profane and vulgarise every association in the manner which has been adopted by this "son of promise." Before giving any extracts, we must inform our readers that this romance is meant to be written in English heroic rhyme. To those who have read any of Hunt's poems, this hint might indeed be needless. Mr. Keats has adopted the loose, nerveless versification and Cockney rhymes of the poet of *Rimini*;[4] but, in fairness to that gentleman, we must add that the defects of the system are tenfold more conspicuous in his disciple's work than in his own. Mr. Hunt is a small poet, but he is a clever man. Mr. Keats is a still smaller poet, and he is only a boy of pretty abilities, which he has done every thing in his power to spoil.

---

[1] *Poems* Keats's first volume of poetry, which was published in March 1817.

[2] *Endymion … goddess* "Endymion" retells the story of the goddess of the moon falling in love with a shepherd, as told by the Roman poet Ovid.

[3] *Homer … Chapman* Keats knew very little Greek, and read it only in translation. George Chapman's edition of Homer's *Iliad* appeared in 1612, and his edition of the *Odyssey* in 1616.

[4] *Rimini* Hunt's long poem *The Story of Rimini* (1816).

IN CONTEXT

The Death of Keats

Keats's friend Joseph Severn had accompanied him to Italy in September of 1820, and was with him when he died of tuberculosis on 23 February 1821.

Joseph Severn to Charles Brown

27 February 1821
Rome

My Dear Brown,

He is gone—he died with the most perfect ease—he seemed to go to sleep. On the 23rd, about 4, the approaches of death came on. "Severn—I—lift me up—I am dying—I shall die easy—don't be frightened—be firm, and thank God it has come!" I lifted him up in my arms. The phlegm seemed boiling in his throat, and increased until 11, when he gradually sunk into death—so quiet—that I still thought he slept. I cannot say now—I am broken down from four nights' watching, and no sleep since, and my poor Keats gone. Three days since, the body was opened; the lungs were completely gone. The Doctors could not conceive by what means he had lived these two months. I followed his poor body to the grave on Monday, with many English. They take such care of me here—that I must, else, have gone into a fever. I am better now—but still quite disabled.

The police have been. The furniture, the walls, the floor, everything must be destroyed by order of the law. But this is well looked to by Dr. C.

The letters I put into the coffin with my own hand.

I must leave off.

JOHN WILLIAM POLIDORI
1795 – 1821

Although other stories of the undead who feast on human blood have since become better known, John Polidori may be given credit for authoring the first English-language short story about vampires. The credit did not, however, come immediately: *The Vampyre*, first published in the *New Monthly Magazine* in 1819, was mistakenly attributed to Lord Byron, who quickly denied authorship, although he had provided both the pretext and the inspiration for the story. And while the issue of authorship has long since been put to rest, Polidori's own fate seemed, until recently, to remain in the shadow of his better-known Romantic peer and his famous literary acquaintances.

Born on 7 September 1795 in London, Polidori was the oldest son of an Italian scholar and an English governess. He was educated at the then recently established Ampleforth College, a private Catholic boarding school; he earned a medical degree at the age of 19, from the University of Edinburgh, writing a thesis on sleepwalking.

In 1816, too young to practice medicine in England, Polidori became Byron's personal physician and secretary, embarking on a European trip with his new employer, who had gone into self-imposed exile. At the behest of John Murray, the prominent publisher of Byron's work, Polidori kept a diary of his travels, which was posthumously edited by his nephew and published as *The Diary of Dr. John William Polidori* (1911). The association with Byron brought Polidori into contact with other writers who would soon become significant figures in English Romanticism, among them Percy Bysshe Shelley and his then-lover, Mary Godwin (who would shortly achieve fame as Mary Shelley). Polidori was present on the June night in 1816 when Byron suggested that the guests at his Lake Geneva house each write a ghost story inspired by the group's reading of a popular anthology of scary tales. Inspired by Byron's invitation, Polidori began work on what would eventually become *Ernestus Berchtold; or the Modern Oedipus* (published in 1819), a work whose title bears striking similarity to Mary Shelley's *Frankenstein; or, the Modern Prometheus*, a novel that famously had its origins in the same contest.

After being dismissed from his position in the fall of 1816—reputedly because of his temper, although Byron's and the Shelleys' evident contempt for Polidori, whose literary pretensions they often mocked, were perhaps also a factor—Polidori returned to England in 1817. He eventually settled in London, where he apparently began studying for admission to the bar, a goal perhaps fostered by disappointment at the fortunes of his practice as a physician in Norwich. He also worked on *The Vampyre*, a story based partly on a manuscript Byron quickly abandoned after the proposed competition. The work soon appeared in the *New Monthly Magazine*, where it was presented as a new work by Byron. Byron responded by publishing "Fragment of a Novel," the discarded story which Polidori had used as a starting point for his work, and Polidori publicly disputed the attribution and claimed authorship, but it is quite possible that Polidori had deliberately fostered the impression of Byron's authorship to attract attention to his tale; regardless of the protestations, the belief that *The*

Vampyre had been authored by Byron persisted, lending a certain celebrity to the work, particularly on the continent.

In the two years following *The Vampyre*'s appearance, Polidori succumbed to a prolonged depression after accruing massive gambling debts. Subsequent publications, now officially in his name, failed to make much impression on either the public or the critics. Polidori continued to implicitly associate himself with Byron, however, with the melodramatic *Ernestus Berchtold* capitalizing on the rumors of Byron's affair with his half-sister Augusta Leigh. *The Fall of the Angels*, a long epic poem concerned with the creation of the world and written in the style of Milton, was anonymously published—and harshly reviewed—shortly before his death on 24 August 1821. Although the coroner attributed the death to natural causes, there is ample evidence to suggest that Polidori had committed suicide.

The Vampyre had a tremendous influence on those vampire tales that followed, most notably in definitively transforming the vampire from a folklore figure to an aristocratic fiend who makes high society his prey. But this debt long went largely unacknowledged, and Polidori's audience essentially abandoned him; when he was mentioned, it was usually only as the sometime-companion of Byron and the uncle of the poet Christina Rossetti and her brother, the painter and poet Dante Gabriel Rossetti. Today, however, there is no doubt that the rich history of the vampire narrative in English literature begins with Polidori.

⌘ ⌘ ⌘

The Vampyre: A Tale

It happened in the midst of the dissipations attendant upon a London winter, that there appeared at the various parties of the leaders of the *ton*[1] a nobleman, more remarkable for his singularities, than for his rank. He apparently gazed upon the mirth around him, as if he could not participate therein. It seemed as if, the light laughter of the fair only attracted his attention, that he might by a look quell it, and throw fear into those breasts where thoughtlessness reigned. Those who felt this sensation of awe, could not explain whence it arose: some attributed it to the glance of that dead grey eye, which, fixing upon the object's face, seemed not to penetrate, and at one look to pierce through to the inward workings of the heart; but to throw upon the cheek a leaden ray that weighed upon the skin it could not pass. Some however thought that it was caused by their fearing the observation of one, who by his colourless cheek, which never gained a warmer tint from the blush of conscious shame or from any powerful emotion, appeared to be above human feelings and sympathies, the fashionable names for frailties and sins. His peculiarities caused him to be invited to every house; all wished to see him, and those who had been accustomed to violent excitement, and now felt the weight of *ennui*,[2] were pleased at having something in their presence capable of engaging their attention. Nay more in spite of the deadly hue of his finely turned head, many of the female hunters after notoriety attempted to win his attentions, and gain, at least, some marks of what they might term affection. Lady Mercer,[3] who had been the mockery of every monster shewn in drawing-rooms since her marriage, threw herself in his way, and did all

---

[1] *ton* French: people of fashion; fashionable society; the fashionable world.

[2] *ennui* French: the feeling of mental weariness and dissatisfaction produced by want of occupation, or by lack of interest in present surroundings or employments.

[3] *Lady Mercer* The character appears to be based on Lady Caroline Lamb (1785–1828), the aristocratic author of *Glenarvon* (1816), a popular Gothic novel based on her notorious affair with Byron. The name "Mercer" may also allude to Margaret Mercer Elphinstone (1788–1867), a prominent society hostess who had been especially kind to Byron when he was otherwise socially snubbed for the sexual scandals that eventually drove him into exile.

but put on the dress of a mountebank,[1] to attract his notice—but in vain—when she stood before him, though his eyes were apparently fixed upon her's, still it seemed as if they were unperceived; even her unappalled impudence was baffled, and she left the field. Yet though the common adultress could not influence even the guidance of his eyes, it was not that the sex was indifferent to him: but such was the caution with which he spoke to the virtuous wife and innocent daughter, that few knew he ever addressed himself to females. He had, however, the reputation of a winning tongue; and whether it was that this even overcame the dread of his singular character, or that they were moved by his apparent hatred of vice, he was as often among those females who adorn the sex by their domestic virtues, as among those who sully it by their vices.

About the same time, there came to London a young gentleman of the name of Aubrey: he was an orphan left with an only sister in the possession of great wealth, by parents who died whilst he was yet in childhood. Left also to himself by guardians, who thought it their duty merely to take care of his fortune, while they relinquished the more important charge of his mind to the care of mercenary and negligent subalterns, he cultivated more his imagination than his judgment. He had, hence, that high romantic feeling of honour and candour, which daily ruins so many milliners' apprentices. He believed all to sympathise with virtue, and thought that vice was thrown in by Providence as by authors in Romances merely for the picturesque[2] effect of the scene: he thought that the misery of a cottage merely consisted in the vesting of clothes, which were as warm, perhaps warmer than the thin naked draperies of a drawing room, but which were more pleasing to the painter's eye by their irregular folds and various coloured patches. He thought, in fine, that the dreams of poets were the realities of life. He was handsome, frank,

and rich: for these reasons, upon his entering into the gay circles, many mothers surrounded him, striving which should describe with least truth their languishing or romping favourites: many daughters at the same time, by their brightening countenances when he approached, and by their sparkling eyes, when he opened his lips, soon led him into false notions of his talents and his merit. Attached as he was to the romance of his solitary hours, he was startled at finding, that, except in the tallow and wax candles flickering, not from the presence of a ghost, but from a draught of air breaking through his golden leathered doors and felted floors, there was no foundation in real life for any of that congeries of pleasing horrors and descriptions contained in the volumes, which had formed the occupation of his midnight vigils. Finding, however, some compensation in his gratified vanity, he was about to relinquish his dreams, when the extraordinary being we have above described, crossed him in his career.

He watched him; the very impossibility of forming an idea of the character of a man entirely absorbed in himself, of one who gave few other signs of his observation of external objects, than the tacit assent to their existence, implied by the avoidance of their contact: at last allowed his imagination to picture some thing that flattered its propensity to extravagant ideas. He soon formed this person into the hero of a romance, and determined to observe the offspring of his fancy, rather than the individual before him. He became acquainted with him, paid him attentions, and so far advanced upon his notice, that his presence was always acknowledged. He gradually learnt that Lord Strongmore's affairs were embarrassed,[3] and soon found, from the notes of preparation in ——— Street, that he was about to travel. Desirous of gaining some information respecting

[1] *mountebank* Itinerant charlatan who sold supposed medicines and remedies, frequently using various entertainments to attract a crowd of potential customers. After the demise of her relationship with Byron (which she apparently refused to accept), Lady Caroline Lamb had visited him disguised as a page.

[2] *picturesque* Aesthetic category associated with the roughness and irregularity of nature as it is harmonized by deliberate composition.

[3] *Strongmore* The character's name was, originally—both in Byron's unfinished manuscript and Polidori's early drafts—"Ruthven." ("Ruthven" is also the name of the villain in Caroline Lamb's novel *Glenarvon*.) Polidori may have opted to rename his vampire "Strongmore" in order to avoid the Byronic reference as well as possible charges of libel, given the existence of an actual Lord Ruthven. The new name has the added bonus of connoting potency and virility; *affairs were embarrassed* Byron's own affairs—as Polidori would have well known—were in a grave state as he prepared to depart from England. Having been already forced to sell his books, he also found it necessary to evade the bailiffs.

this singular character, who, till now, had only whetted his curiosity, he hinted to his guardians, that it was time for him to perform the grand tour,[1] a tour which for many generations had been thought necessary to enable the young to take some important steps in the career of vice, put themselves upon an equality with the aged, and not allow them to appear as if fallen from the skies, whenever scandalous intrigues are mentioned as the subjects of pleasantry or of praise, according to the degree of skill shewn in their conduct. They consented: and Aubrey immediately mentioning his intentions to Lord Strongmore, was surprised to receive from him a proposal that they should travel together. Flattered by such a mark of esteem from him, who, apparently, had nothing in common with other men, he gladly accepted the invitation, and in a few days they had passed the circling waters.

Hitherto, Aubrey had had no opportunity of study-ing Lord Strongmore's character, and now he found, that, though many more of his actions were exposed to his view, the results offered different conclusions from the apparent motives to his conduct. His companion was profuse in his liberality; the idle, the vagabond, and the beggar, received from his hand more than enough to relieve their immediate wants. But Aubrey could not avoid remarking, that it was not upon the virtuous, reduced to indigence by the misfortunes attendant even upon virtue, that he bestowed his alms. These were sent from the door with hardly suppressed sneers; but when the profligate came to ask something, not to relieve his wants, but to allow him to wallow in his lust, or to sink him still deeper in his iniquity, he was sent away with rich charity. This was, however, attributed by him to the greater importunity of the vicious, which generally prevails over the retiring bashfulness of the virtuous indigent. There was one circumstance about the charity of his Lordship, which was however still more deeply impressed upon his mind: all those upon whom it was bestowed, inevitably found that there was a curse upon it, for they were all either led to the scaffold, or sunk to the lowest and the most abject misery. At Brussels and other towns through which they passed, Aubrey was surprized at the apparent eagerness, with which his companion sought for the centres of all fashionable vice; there he entered into all the spirit of the faro[2] table. He betted, and always gambled with success, except when the known sharper was his antagonist, and then he lost even more than he gained; but it was always with the same unchanging face, with which he generally watched the society around. It was not, however, so when he encountered the rash youthful novice, or the luckless father of a numerous family; then his very wish seemed fortune's law—his apparent abstractedness of mind was laid aside, and his eyes sparkled with vivid fire. In every town, he left the formerly affluent youth, torn from the circle he adorned, cursing, in the solitude of a dungeon, the fate that had drawn him within the reach of this fiend; whilst many a father sat frantic, amidst the speaking looks of mute hungry children, without a single florin of his late immense wealth, wherewith to buy even sufficient to satisfy their present craving. Yet he took no money from the gambling table; but imme-diately lost, to the ruiner of many, the last gilder he had just snatched from the convulsive grasp of the innocent. This might but be the result of a certain degree of knowledge, which was not, however, capable of combat-ing the cunning of the more experienced. Aubrey often wished to represent this to his friend, and beg him to resign that charity and pleasure which proved the ruin of all, and did not tend to his own profit;—but he delayed it—for each day he hoped his friend would give him some opportunity of speaking frankly and openly to him; this, however, never occurred. Lord Strongmore in his carriage, and amidst the various wild and rich scenes of nature, was always the same: his eye spoke less than his lip; and though Aubrey was near the object of his curiosity, he obtained no greater gratification from it than the constant excitement of vainly wishing to break that mystery, which to his exalted imagination began to assume the appearance of something supernat-ural.

---

[1] *grand tour* Tour of the principal cities and places of interest in Europe, formerly supposed to be an essential part of the education of young men of good birth or fortune.

[2] *faro* Gambling game of cards, in which the players bet on the order in which certain cards will appear when taken singly from the top of the pack.

They soon arrived at Rome, and Aubrey for a time lost sight of his companion; he left him in daily attendance upon the morning circle of an Italian countess, whilst he went in search of the memorials of another almost deserted city. Whilst he was thus engaged, letters arrived from England, which he opened with eager impatience; the first was from his sister, breathing nothing but affection; the others were from his guardians, these astonished him; if it had before entered into his imagination, that, there was an evil power resident in his companion, these seemed to give him almost sufficient reason for the belief. His guardians insisted upon his immediately leaving his friend, and urged, that such a character was to be dreaded, for the possession of irresistible powers of seduction, rendered his licentious habits too dangerous to society. It had been discovered, that his contempt for the adultress had not originated in hatred of her character; but that he had required, to enhance his gratification, that his victim, the partner of his guilt, should be hurled from the pinnacle of unsullied virtue, down to the lowest abyss of infamy and degradation: in fine, that all those females whom he had sought, apparently on account of their virtue, had, since his departure, thrown even the mask aside, and had not scrupled to expose the whole deformity of their vices to the public view.

Aubrey determined upon leaving one, whose character had not yet shown a single bright point on which to rest the eye. He resolved to invent some plausible pretext for abandoning him altogether, purposing, in the meanwhile, to watch him more closely, and to let no slight circumstances pass by unnoticed. He entered into the same circle, and soon perceived, that his Lordship was endeavouring to work upon the inexperience of the daughter of the lady whose house he chiefly frequented. In Italy, it is seldom that an unmarried female is met with in society; he was therefore obliged to carry on his plans in secret; but Aubrey's eye followed him in all his windings, and soon discovered that an assignation had been made, which would most likely end in the ruin of an innocent, though thoughtless girl. Losing no time, he entered the apartment of Lord Strongmore, and abruptly asked him his intentions with respect to the lady, informing him at the same time that he was aware of his

being about to meet her that very night. Lord Strongmore answered, that his intentions were such as he supposed all would have upon such an occasion; and upon being pressed whether he intended to marry her, merely laughed. Aubrey retired; and, immediately writing a note, to say, that from that moment he must decline accompanying his Lordship in the remainder of their purposed tour, he ordered his servant to seek other apartments, and calling upon the mother of the lady, informed her of all he knew, not only with regard to her daughter, but also with regard to the character of his Lordship. The meeting was prevented. Lord Strongmore next day merely sent his servant to notify his complete assent to a separation;[1] but did not hint any suspicion of his plans having been foiled by Aubrey's interposition.

Having left Rome, Aubrey directed his steps towards Greece, and crossing the Peninsula, soon found himself at Athens. He there fixed his residence in the house of a Greek; and was soon occupied in tracing the faded records of ancient glory upon monuments that apparently, ashamed of chronicling the deeds of freemen only before slaves, had hidden themselves beneath the sheltering soil or many coloured lichen. Under the same roof as himself, existed a being, so beautiful and delicate, that she might have formed the model for a painter, wishing to portray on canvass the promised hope of the faithful in Mahomet's paradise, save that her eyes spoke too much mind for anyone to think she could belong to those beings who had no souls.[2] As she danced upon the plain, or tripped along the mountain's side, one would have thought the gazelle a poor type of her beauties; for who would have exchanged her eye, apparently the eye of animated nature, for that sleepy luxurious look of the animal suited but to the taste of an epicure. The light step of Ianthe[3] often accompanied Aubrey in his search

---

[1] *separation* Byron's wife, Annabella (the cousin of Lady Caroline Lamb), left him in January 1816, taking their daughter Ada with her. In April of that year, Byron signed a Deed of Separation amid rumors of abuse, adultery, and incest with his half-sister.

[2] *those beings who had no souls* Byron notes, in *The Giaour* (1813), that the belief that Islam teaches that women have no souls is a Western misinterpretation.

[3] *Ianthe* "Flower of the Narcissus," the name—which recurs several times in Greek mythology—finds repeated use in the Romantic canon. The first two cantos of Byron's *Childe Harold's*   [continued ...]

after antiquities, and often would the unconscious girl, engaged in the pursuit of a Kashmere butterfly[1] show the whole beauty of her form, floating as it were upon the wind, to the eager gaze of him, who forgot, in the contemplation of her sylph-like figure, the letters he had just decyphered upon an almost effaced tablet. Often would her tresses falling, as she flitted around, exhibit in the sun's ray such delicately brilliant and swiftly fading hues, as might well excuse the forgetfulness of the antiquary, who let escape from his mind the very object he had before thought of vital importance to the proper interpretation of a passage in Pausanias.[2] But why attempt to describe charms which all feel, but none can appreciate? It was innocence, youth, and beauty, unaffected by crowded drawing-rooms and stifling balls. Whilst he drew those remains of which he wished to preserve a memorial for his future hours, she would stand by, and watch the magic effects of his pencil, in tracing the scenes of her native place; she would then describe to him the circling dance upon the open plain, would paint to him in all the glowing colours of youthful memory, the marriage pomp she remembered viewing in her infancy; and then, turning to subjects that had evidently made a greater impression upon her mind, would tell him all the supernatural tales of her nurse. Her earnestness and apparent belief of what she narrated, excited the interest even of Aubrey; and often as she told him the tale of the living vampyre, who had passed years amidst his friends, and dearest ties, forced every year, by feeding upon the life of a lovely female to prolong his existence for the ensuing months, his blood would run cold, whilst he attempted to laugh her out of such idle and horrible fantasies. But Ianthe cited to him the names of old men, who had at last detected one

living among themselves, after several of their near relatives and children had been found marked with the stamp of the fiend's appetite. When she found him incredulous, she begged of him to believe her, for it had been remarked, that those who had dared to question their existence, always had some proof given, which obliged them, with grief and heartbreaking, to confess its truth. She detailed to him the traditional appearance of these monsters, and his horror was increased, upon hearing a pretty accurate description of Lord Strongmore. He, however, still persisted in persuading her, that there could be no truth in her fears, though at the same time he wondered at the many coincidences which had all tended to excite a belief in the supernatural power of Lord Strongmore.

Aubrey began to attach himself more and more to Ianthe; her innocence, so contrasted with all the affected virtues of the women amongst whom he had sought for his vision of romance, won his heart; and while he ridiculed the idea of a young man of English habits, marrying an uneducated Greek girl, still he found himself more and more attached to the almost fairy form before him. He would tear himself at times from her, and, forming a plan for some antiquarian research, he would depart, determined not to return until his object was attained; but he always found it impossible to fix his attention upon the ruins around him, whilst in his mind he retained an image that seemed alone the rightful possessor of his thoughts. Ianthe was unconscious of his love, and was ever the same frank infantile being he had first known. She always seemed to part from him with reluctance; but it was because she had no longer anyone with whom she could visit her favourite haunts, to whom she could point out the beauties of the spots so dear to her infantile memory, whilst he was occupied in sketching or uncovering some fragment which had yet escaped the destructive hand of time. She had appealed to her parents on the subject of Vampyres, and they both, with several present, affirmed their existence, pale with horror at the very name. Soon after, Aubrey determined to proceed upon one of his excursions, which was to detain him for a few hours; when his hosts heard the name of the place, they all at once begged of him not to return at night, as he must neces-

Pilgrimage (1812) are dedicated to "Ianthe," Byron's nickname for Charlotte Harley, the daughter of his one-time lover Lady Oxford. In Percy Bysshe Shelley's Queen Mab: A Philosophical Poem (1813), the Queen visits a sleeping Ianthe, removing her soul to the Queen's celestial palace.

[1] Kashmere butterfly Cf. Byron's The Giaour, 388–99.

[2] Pausanias Second-century Greek geographer and renowned traveler, whose Description of Greece (a ten-volume work concerned with Greek history, culture, and topography) was often used as a guide by antiquarians, serving as a link between classical literature and archaeology.

sarily pass through a wood, where no Greek would ever remain, after the day had closed, upon any consideration. They described it as the resort of the vampyres in their nocturnal orgies, and denounced the most heavy evils as impending upon him who dared to cross their path. Aubrey made light of their representations, and tried to laugh them out of the idea; but when he saw them shudder at his daring thus to mock a superior, infernal power, the very name of which apparently made their blood freeze, he was silent.

Next morning Aubrey set off upon his excursion unattended; he was surprised to observe the melancholy face of his host, and was concerned to find that his words, mocking the belief of these horrible fiends, had inspired them with such terror. When he was about to depart, Ianthe came to the side of his horse, and earnestly begged of him to return, ere night allowed the power of these beings to be put in action; he promised. He was, however, so occupied in his research, that he did not perceive that day-light would soon end, and that in the horizon there was one of those specks which, in the warmer climates, so rapidly gather into a tremendous mass, and pour all their rage upon the devoted country. He at last, however, mounted his horse, determined to make up by speed for his delay: but it was too late. Twilight, in these southern climates, is almost unknown; immediately the sun sets, night begins: and ere he had advanced far, the power of the storm was above—its echoing thunders had scarcely an interval of rest—its thick heavy rain forced its way through the canopying foliage, whilst the blue forked lightning seemed to fall and radiate at his very feet. Suddenly his horse took fright, and he was carried with dreadful rapidity through the entangled forest. The animal at last, through fatigue, fell, and he found, by the glare of lightning, that he was in the neighbourhood of a hovel which hardly lifted itself up from the masses of dead leaves and brushwood surrounding it. Dismounting, he approached, hoping to find some one to guide him to the town, or at least trusting to obtain shelter from the pelting of the storm. When near the door, the thunders, for a moment silent, allowed him to hear the dreadful shrieks of a woman mingling with the stifled, exultant mockery of a laugh, continued in one almost unbroken sound; he was startled: but, roused by the thunder which again rolled over his head, he, with a sudden effort, forced open the door of the hut. He found himself in utter darkness: the sound, however, guided him. He was apparently unperceived; for, though he called, still the sounds continued, and no notice was taken of him. He found himself in contact with some one, whom he immediately seized; when a voice cried, "Again baffled!" to which a loud laugh succeeded; and he felt himself grappled by one whose strength seemed superhuman: determined to sell his life as dearly as he could, he struggled; but it was in vain: he was lifted from his feet and hurled with enormous force against the ground. His enemy threw himself upon him, and kneeling upon his breast, had placed his hands upon his throat—when the glare of many torches penetrating through the hole that gave light in the day, disturbed him. He instantly rose, leaving his prey, he rushed through the door, and in a moment the crashing of the branches, as he broke through the wood, was no longer heard. The storm was now still; and Aubrey, incapable of moving, was soon heard by those without. They entered; the light of their torches fell upon nothing but the mud walls, and the thatch loaded on every individual straw with heavy flakes of soot, though at this moment it was apparently untenanted. There was one spot slippery with blood but it was hardly visible on the black floor. No other trace was seen of human presence having disturbed its solitude for many years. At the desire of Aubrey they searched for her who had attracted him by her cries; he was again left in darkness; but what was his horror, when the light of the torches once more burst upon him, to perceive the airy form of his fair conductress brought in a lifeless corpse. He shut his eyes, hoping that it was but a vision arising from his disturbed imagination; but he again saw the same form, when he unclosed them, stretched by his side. There was no colour upon her cheek, not even upon her lip; yet there was a stillness about her face that seemed almost as attaching as the life that once dwelt there: upon her neck and breast was blood, and upon her throat were the marks of teeth having opened the vein of the neck: to this the men pointed, crying, simultaneously struck with horror, "A Vampyre! a Vampyre!"

A litter[1] was quickly formed, and Aubrey was laid by the side of her who had lately been to him the object of so many bright and fairy visions, now fallen with the flower of life that had died within her. He knew not what his thoughts were—his mind was benumbed and seemed to shun reflection, and take refuge in vacancy —he held almost unconsciously in his hand a naked dagger of a particular construction, which had been found in the hut. They were soon met by different parties who had been engaged in the search of her whom a mother had missed. Their lamentable cries, as they approached the city, forewarned the parents of some dreadful catastrophe. To describe their grief would be impossible; but when they ascertained the cause of their child's death, they looked at Aubrey, and pointed to the corpse. They were inconsolable; both died broken-hearted.

Aubrey being put to bed was seized with a most violent fever, and was often delirious; in these intervals he would call upon Lord Strongmore and upon Ianthe —by some unaccountable combination he seemed to beg of his former companion to spare the being he loved. At other times he would imprecate maledictions upon his head, and curse him as her destroyer. Lord Strongmore chanced at this time to arrive at Athens, and, from whatever motive, upon hearing of the state of Aubrey, immediately placed himself in the same house, and became his constant attendant. When the latter recovered from his delirium, he was horrified and startled at the sight of him whose image he had now combined with that of a Vampyre; but Lord Strongmore, by his kind words, implying almost repentance for the fault that had caused their separation, and still more by the attention, anxiety, and care which he showed, soon reconciled him to his presence. His lordship seemed quite changed; he no longer appeared that apathetic being who had so astonished Aubrey; but as soon as his convalescence began to be rapid, he again gradually retired into the same state of mind, and Aubrey perceived no difference from the former man, except that at times he was surprised to meet his gaze fixed intently upon him, with a smile of malicious

exultation playing upon his lips: he knew not why, but this smile haunted him. During the last stage of the invalid's recovery, Lord Strongmore was apparently engaged in watching the tideless waves raised by the cooling breeze, or in marking the progress of those orbs, circling, like our world, the moveless sun; indeed, he appeared to wish to avoid the eyes of all.

Aubrey's mind, by this shock, was much weakened, and that elasticity of spirit which had once so distinguished him now seemed to have fled for ever. He was now as much a lover of solitude and silence as Lord Strongmore; but much as he wished for solitude, his mind could not find it in the neighbourhood of Athens; if he sought it amidst the ruins he had formerly frequented, Ianthe's form stood by his side—if he sought it in the woods, her light step would sound wandering amidst the underwood, in quest of the modest violet; and often she would suddenly turning round, show, to his wild imagination, her pale face and wounded throat, while a meek smile played upon her lips. He determined to fly scenes, every feature of which created such bitter associations in his mind. He proposed to Lord Strongmore, to whom he held himself bound by the tender care he had taken of him during his illness, that they should visit those parts of Greece neither had yet seen. They travelled in every direction, and sought every spot to which a recollection could be attached: but though they thus hastened from place to place, yet they seemed not to heed what they gazed upon. They heard much of robbers,[2] but they gradually began to slight these reports, which they imagined were only the invention of individuals, whose interest it was to excite the generosity of those, whom they defended from pretended dangers. In consequence of thus neglecting the advice of the inhabitants, they travelled on one occasion with only a few guards, more to serve as guides than as a defence. Upon entering, however, a narrow defile, at the bottom of which was the bed of a torrent, with large masses of rock brought down from the neighbouring precipices, they had reason to repent their negligence; for scarcely were the whole of the party engaged in the narrow pass, when they were startled by the echoed report of several

---

[1] *litter* Framework supporting a bed or couch for the transport of the sick and wounded.

[2] *robbers* Byron had narrowly escaped robbers on a trip in Greece in December 1810, an incident documented in his journals.

guns, and by the whistling of bullets close to their heads. In an instant their guards had left them, and, placing themselves behind rocks, had begun to fire in the direction whence the report came. Lord Strongmore and Aubrey, imitating their example, retired for a moment behind the sheltering turn of the defile: but ashamed of being thus detained by a foe, who with insulting shouts bade them advance, and being exposed to unresisting slaughter, if any of the robbers should climb above and take them in the rear, they determined at once to rush forward in search of the enemy. Hardly had they lost the shelter of the rock, when Lord Strongmore received a shot in the shoulder, which brought him to the ground. Aubrey hastened to his assistance; and, no longer heeding the contest or his own peril, was soon surprised by seeing the robbers' faces around him—his guards having, upon Lord Strongmore's being wounded, immediately thrown up their arms and surrendered.

By promises of great reward, Aubrey soon induced them to convey his wounded friend to a neighbouring cabin; and having agreed upon a ransom, he was no more disturbed by their presence—they being content merely to guard the entrance until their comrade should return with the promised sum, for which he had an order. Lord Strongmore's strength rapidly decreased; in two days mortification ensued, and death seemed advancing with hasty steps. His conduct and appearance had not changed; he seemed as unconscious of pain as he had been of the objects about him: but towards the close of the last evening, his mind became apparently uneasy, and his eye often fixed upon Aubrey, who was induced to offer his assistance with more than usual earnestness—"Assist me! you may save me—you may do more than that—I mean not my life, I heed the death of my existence as little as that of the passing day; but you may save my honour, your friend's honour." "How? tell me how? I would do any thing," replied Aubrey. "I need but little—my life ebbs apace—I cannot explain the whole—but if you would conceal all you know of me, my honour were free from stain in the world's mouth—and if my death were unknown for some time in England—I—I—but life." "It shall not be known." "Swear!" cried the dying man, raising himself with exultant violence, "Swear by all your soul reveres, by all

your nature dreads, swear that for a year and a day you will not impart your knowledge of my crimes or death to any living being, in any way, whatever may happen, or whatever you may see." His eyes seemed bursting from their sockets: "I swear!" said Aubrey; he sunk laughing upon his pillow, and breathed no more.[1]

Aubrey retired to rest, but did not sleep; the many circumstances attending his acquaintance with this man arose upon his mind, and, he knew not why, when he remembered his oath a cold shivering came over him, as if from the presentiment of something horrible awaiting him. Rising early in the morning, he was about to enter the hovel, in which he had left the corpse, when a robber met him, and informed him that it was no longer there, having been conveyed by himself and comrades, upon his retiring, to the pinnacle of a neighbouring mount, according to a promise they had given his lordship, that it should be exposed to the first cold ray of the moon that rose after his death.[2] Aubrey was astonished, but taking several of the men, he determined to go and bury it upon the spot where it lay. When however he reached the summit he found no trace of the corpse, nor could he discover any remnant of the clothes, though the robbers assured him that they pointed out the identical rock on which they had laid the body. For a time his mind was bewildered in conjectures, but he at last returned, convinced that they had secretly buried his friend's remains for the sake of the dress in which he died.

Weary of a country in which he had met with such terrible misfortunes, and in which all apparently conspired to heighten that superstitious melancholy which had seized upon his mind, he resolved to leave it, and he soon arrived at Smyrna. While waiting for a vessel to

[1] *"I swear!" … breathed no more* Aubrey's oath closely parallels the fragment composed by Byron and later used by Polidori in writing *The Vampyre*, although in Byron's "Fragment of a Novel," the oath is less emphatic, less emotional, and less ritualized.

[2] *first cold ray … his death* In Byron's "Fragment," an elaborate ring ceremony is required for the resuscitation; in *The Vampyre*, only moonlight is necessary. Polidori's alteration of Byron's manuscript is particularly interesting in its reversal of the ancient Greek belief that moonlight quickened the decomposition of the dead body.

convey him to Otranto,[1] or to Naples, he occupied himself in arranging those effects he had with him belonging to Lord Strongmore. Amongst other things there was a case containing several weapons of offence, more or less adapted to ensure the death of the victim. There were several daggers and ataghans.[2] Whilst turning these over, and examining their curious forms, what was his surprise at finding a sheath apparently ornamented in the same style as the dagger discovered in the fatal hut—he shuddered—hastening to gain further proof, he found the weapon, and his horror may be imagined, when he discovered that it fitted, though peculiarly shaped, the sheath he held in his hand. His eyes seemed to need no further certainty—they seemed gazing to be bound to the dagger; yet still he wished not to believe his sight; but the particular form, the varying tints upon the haft and sheath were alike, and left no room for doubt; there were also drops of blood on each.

He left Smyrna, and on his way home, at Rome, he inquired concerning the lady he had attempted to snatch from Lord Strongmore's seductive arts. Her parents were in distress, their fortune ruined, and she had not been heard of since the departure of his lordship. Aubrey's mind became almost broken under so many repeated horrors; he was afraid that this lady had fallen a victim to the destroyer of Ianthe. He became morose and silent; and his only thought seemed to be how to urge the speed of the postilions,[3] as if he were hastening to save the life of some one he held dear. He arrived at Calais; a breeze, which seemed obedient to his will, soon wafted him to the English shores. He hastened to the mansion of his fathers, and there, for a moment, he appeared to lose, in the embraces and caresses of his sister, all memory of the past. If she before, by her infantine caresses, had gained his affection, now that the woman began to appear, she was still more attaching as a companion.

Miss Aubrey had not that winning grace which gains the gaze and applause of the drawing-room assemblies.

There was none of that ephemeral brilliancy which can only exist in the heated atmosphere of a crowded apartment. Her blue eye was never lit up by the levity of the mind beneath. There was a melancholy charm about it which did not seem to arise from misfortune, but from some feeling within, that appeared to indicate a soul conscious of a brighter realm. Her step was not that light footing, which strays where'er a butterfly or a colour may attract—it was sedate and pensive. When alone, her face was never brightened by the smile of joy; but when her brother breathed to her his affection, and would in her presence forget those griefs she knew destroyed his rest, who would have exchanged her smile for that of the voluptuary? It seemed as if those eyes, that face were then playing in the light of their own native sphere. She was yet only eighteen, and had not yet been presented to the world, her guardians having thought proper to delay her presentation at court until her brother's return from the continent, when he might be her protector. It was now, therefore, resolved that the next drawing-room,[4] which was fast approaching, should be the epoch of her entry into the "busy scene." Aubrey would rather have remained in the mansion of his fathers, to feed upon the melancholy which overpowered him. He could not feel interest about the frivolities of fashionable strangers, when his mind had been so torn by the events he had witnessed; but he determined to sacrifice his own comfort to the protection of his sister. They therefore soon arrived in town, and prepared for the day, which had been announced as the one on which a drawing-room was to be held.

The crowd was excessive—a drawing-room had not been held for a long time, and all who were anxious to bask in the smile of royalty, hastened thither. Aubrey was there with his sister. While he was standing in a corner by himself, heedless of all around him, engaged in the recollection that the first time he had seen Lord Strongmore was in this very place—he felt himself suddenly seized by the arm, and a voice he recognized too well, sounded in his ear—"Remember your oath." He had hardly courage to turn, fearful of seeing a

[1] *Otranto* Southern Italian port, which serves as the setting of the first Gothic novel, Horace Walpole's *The Castle of Otranto* (1764).

[2] *ataghans* Long daggers worn by Turks and Moors.

[3] *postilions* Guides or forerunners for the post, or for a messenger.

[4] *drawing-room* Levee held in a drawing-room; a formal reception by a king, queen, or person of rank; that at which ladies are "presented" at court.

spectre, that would blast him, when he perceived, at a little distance, the same figure which had attracted his notice on this spot upon his first entry into society. He gazed till his limbs almost refusing to bear their weight, he was obliged to take the arm of a friend, and forcing a passage through the crowd, to throw himself into his carriage, and be driven home. He paced the room with hurried steps, and fixed his hands upon his head, as if he were afraid his thoughts were bursting from his brain. Lord Strongmore again before him—circumstances started up in dreadful array—the dagger—his oath. He roused himself, he could not believe it possible—the dead rise again! He thought his imagination had conjured up the image his mind was resting upon. It was impossible that it could be real—he determined, therefore, to go again into society; for though he attempted to ask concerning Lord Strongmore, the name hung upon his lips, and he could not succeed in gaining information. He went a few nights after with his sister to the assembly of a near relation. Leaving her under the protection of a matron, he retired into a recess, and there gave himself up to his own devouring thoughts. Perceiving, at last, that many were retiring, he roused himself, and entering another room, found his sister surrounded by several gentlemen, apparently in earnest conversation; he attempted to pass and get near her, when one, whom he requested to move, turned round, and revealed to him those features he most abhorred. He sprang forward, seized his sister's arm, and, with a hurried step, forced her towards the street: at the door he found himself impeded by the crowd of servants, who were waiting for their lords; and while he was engaged in passing them, he again heard that voice whisper close to him—"Remember your oath!" He did not dare to turn, but, hurrying his sister, he soon reached home.

Aubrey became almost distracted. If before his mind had been absorbed by one subject, how much more completely was it engrossed now, that the certainty of the monster's living again pressed upon his thoughts. His sister's attentions were now unheeded, and it was in vain that she intreated him to explain to her what had caused his abrupt conduct. He only uttered a few words,

and those terrified her. The more he thought, the more he was bewildered. His oath startled him; was he then to allow this monster to roam, bearing ruin upon his breath, amidst all he held dear, and not avert its progress? His very sister might have been touched by him. But even if he were to break his oath, and disclose his suspicions, who would believe him? He thought of employing his own hand to free the world from such a wretch; but death, he remembered, had been already mocked. For days he remained in this state; shut up in his room, he saw no one, and eat[1] only when his sister came, who, her eyes streaming with tears, besought him, for her sake, to support nature. At last, no longer capable of bearing stillness and solitude, he left his house, roamed from street to street, anxious to fly that image which haunted him. His dress became neglected, and he wandered, as often exposed to the noon-day sun as to the mid-night damps. He was no longer to be recognized; at first he returned with the evening to his home; but at last he laid him down to rest wherever fatigue overtook him. His sister, anxious for his safety, employed people to follow him; but they were soon distanced by him, who fled from a pursuer swifter than any—from thought. His conduct, however, suddenly changed. Struck with the idea that he left by his absence the whole of his friends, with a fiend amongst them, of whose presence they were unconscious, he determined to enter again into society, and watch him closely, anxious to forewarn, in spite of his oath, all whom Lord Strongmore should approach with intimacy. But when he entered into a room, his haggard and suspicious looks were so striking, his inward shudderings so visible, that his sister was at last obliged to beg of him to abstain from seeking, for her sake, a society, which affected him so strongly. When, however, remonstrance proved unavailing, the guardians thought proper to interpose, and, fearing that his mind was becoming alienated, they thought it high time to resume again that trust, which had been before imposed upon them by Aubrey's parents.

---

[1] *eat*   In the early nineteenth century, this was the standard past tense of the verb; that is, "ate."

Desirous of saving him from the injuries and sufferings he had daily encountered in his wanderings, and of preventing him from exposing to the general eye those marks of what they considered folly, they engaged a physician to reside in the house, and take constant care of him. He hardly appeared to notice it, so completely was his mind absorbed by one terrible subject. His incoherence became at last so great, that he was confined to his chamber. There he would often lie for days, incapable of being roused. He had become emaciated, his eyes had attained a glassy lustre;[1] the only sign of affection and recollection remaining displayed itself upon the entry of his sister; then he would sometimes start, and, seizing her hands, with looks that severely afflicted her, he would desire her not to touch him. "Oh, do not touch him—if your love for me is aught, do not go near him!" When, however, she inquired to whom he referred, his only answer was, "True! true!" and again he sank into a state, whence not even she could rouse him. This lasted many months: gradually, however, as the year was passing, his incoherences became less frequent, and his mind threw off a portion of its gloom, whilst his guardians observed, that several times in the day he would count upon his fingers a definite number, and then smile.

The time had nearly elapsed, when, upon the last day of the year, one of his guardians entering his room, began to converse with his physician upon the melancholy circumstance of Aubrey's being in so awful a situation, when his sister was going next day to be married. Instantly Aubrey's attention was attracted; he asked anxiously to whom. Glad of this mark of returning intellect, of which they feared he had been deprived, they mentioned the name of the Earl of Marsden. Thinking this was a young Earl whom he had met with in society, Aubrey seemed pleased, and astonished them still more by expressing his intention to be present at the nuptials, and by desiring to see his sister. They answered not, but in a few minutes his sister was with him. He

was apparently again capable of being affected by the influence of her lovely smile; for he pressed her to his breast, and kissed her cheek, wet with tears, flowing at the thought of her brother's being once more alive to the feelings of affection. He began to speak with all his wonted warmth, and to congratulate her upon her marriage with a person so distinguished for rank and every accomplishment; but he suddenly perceived a locket upon her breast; having opened it, what was his surprise at beholding the features of the monster who had so long influenced his life. He seized the portrait in a paroxysm of rage, and trampled it under foot. Upon her asking him, why he thus destroyed the resemblance of her future husband, he looked as if he did not understand her—then seizing her hands, and gazing on her with a frantic expression of countenance, he bade her swear that she would never wed this monster, for he—But he could not continue—it seemed as if that voice again bade him remember his oath—he turned suddenly round, thinking Lord Strongmore was near him but he saw no one. In the meantime the guardians and physician, who had heard the whole, and thought this was but a return of his disorder, entered, and forcing him from Miss Aubrey, desired her to leave him. He fell upon his knees to them, he implored, he begged of them to delay but for one day. They, attributing this to the insanity, they imagined had taken possession of his mind, endeavoured to pacify him, and retired.

Lord Strongmore had called the morning after the drawing-room, and had been refused with everyone else. When he heard of Aubrey's ill health, he readily understood himself to be the cause of it; but, when he learned that he was deemed insane, his exultation and pleasure could hardly be concealed from those, among whom he had gained this information. He hastened to the house of his former companion, and, by constant attendance, and the pretence of great affection for her brother and interest in his fate, he gradually won the ear of Miss Aubrey. Who could resist his power? His tongue had dangers and toils to recount[2]—could speak of himself as

---

[1] *He had become ... glassy lustre*   After Byron ended their affair, Lady Caroline Lamb lost much weight and took to following him even though he had quickly begun other relationships. Her pursuits caused Byron to notoriously remark that he was being "haunted by a skeleton."

[2] *His tongue had ... to recount*   Cf. *Othello* (1.3.128–70). Othello courts Desdemona by recounting his military adventures: "She loved me for the dangers I had pass'd," he explains to those who accuse him of bewitching his new bride.

of an individual having no sympathy with any being on the crowded earth, save with her, to whom he addressed himself; could tell how, since he knew her, his existence had begun to seem worthy of preservation, if it were merely that he might listen to her soothing accents. In fine, he knew so well how to use the serpent's art,[1] or such was the will of fate, that he gained her affections. The title of the elder branch falling at length to him, he obtained an important embassy, which served as an excuse (in spite of her brother's deranged state), for hastening the marriage, which was to take place the very day before his departure for the continent.

Aubrey, when he was left by the physician and his guardians, attempted to bribe the servants, but in vain. He asked for pen and paper; it was given him; he wrote a letter to his sister, conjuring her, as she valued her own happiness, her own honour, and the honour of those now in the grave, who once held her in their arms as their hope and the hope of their house, to delay but for a few hours that marriage, on which he denounced the most heavy curses. The servants promised they would deliver it; but giving it to the physician, he thought it better not to harass any more the mind of Miss Aubrey by, what he considered, the ravings of a maniac. Night passed on without rest to the busy inmates of the house; and Aubrey heard, with a horror that may more easily be conceived than described, the notes of busy preparation. Morning came, and the sound of carriages broke upon his ear. Aubrey grew almost frantic. The curiosity of the servants at last overcame their vigilance, they gradually stole away, leaving him in the custody of an helpless old woman. He seized the opportunity, with one bound was out of the room, and in a moment

found himself in the apartment where all were nearly assembled. Lord Strongmore was the first to perceive him: he immediately approached, and, taking his arm by force, hurried him from the room, speechless with rage. When on the staircase, Lord Strongmore whispered in his ear—"Remember your oath, and know, if not my bride to day, your sister is dishonoured. Women are frail!" So saying, he pushed him towards his attendants, who, roused by the old woman, had come in search of him. Aubrey could no longer support himself; his rage not finding vent, had broken a blood-vessel,[2] and he was conveyed to bed. This was not mentioned to his sister, who was not present when he entered, as the physician was afraid of agitating her. The marriage was solemnized, and the bride and bridegroom left London.

Aubrey's weakness increased; the effusion of blood produced symptoms of the near approach of death. He desired his sister's guardians might be called, and, when the midnight hour had struck, he related composedly the substance of what the reader has perused—and died immediately after.

The guardians hastened to protect Miss Aubrey; but when they arrived, it was too late. Lord Strongmore had disappeared, and Aubrey's sister had glutted the thirst of a VAMPYRE![3]

—1819

---

[1] *serpent's art* Cf. Genesis 3.

[2] *broken a blood-vessel* Cf. Byron's *Don Juan* (1821): After rescuing the shipwrecked Don Juan and falling in love with him only to find that her father disapproves of the relationship, Haidée dies of the same cause when her father defeats Don Juan in a fight and has him put in chains.

[3] *The guardians … VAMPYRE* Polidori seems to have intended a sequel to *The Vampyre*, leaving the ending deliberately open. Nothing, however, came of his plan for a continuation.

MARY SHELLEY
1797 – 1851

As Mary Wollstonecraft Shelley wrote in her introduction to the second edition of *Frankenstein*, readers constantly asked her "How I, then a young girl, came to think of, and to dilate upon, so hideous an idea." At the age of nineteen, Shelley created one of the most extraordinary and powerful horror stories in Western literature, one that continues to pervade our popular culture. While *Frankenstein* is undoubtedly her most widely read and influential work, Shelley is also celebrated for a large body of fiction of vivid imaginative power that grapples in penetrating fashion with the political and social concerns of her day.

If Shelley's writing is extraordinary, neither is there anything ordinary in her parentage or her tumultuous life. She was born Mary Wollstonecraft Godwin in August of 1797. The only child of radical feminist Mary Wollstonecraft and the philosopher, author, and political journalist William Godwin, Shelley felt the weight of her parents' controversial reputations throughout her life. Her mother died just after giving birth, and Shelley came to know her only through her works— in particular the *Vindication of the Rights of Woman* (1792). Godwin, for whom Shelley later said she bore an "excess of attachment," raised Mary and her half-sister Fanny, educating them with the help of several friends and regular visitors—a group of supremely qualified teachers that included poet Samuel Taylor Coleridge, painter Thomas Lawrence, novelist Maria Edgeworth, and scientist Humphrey Davy. Godwin's novels and philosophical works, particularly his *Enquiry Concerning Political Justice* (1793), were formative influences on his daughter's thought.

After her father married Mary Jane Clairmont in 1801, Mary Godwin, who did not get along with her stepmother, spent extended periods of time with family friends in Scotland. On a visit home in 1814, she became acquainted with Percy Bysshe Shelley, a radical poet and admirer of Godwin's principles, who had become a regular visitor to the Godwin home. Although Percy was married at the time, within months the two declared their love for each other, meeting in secret by the grave of Mary's mother. The two then eloped to France, taking Mary's stepsister Claire Clairmont with them. Godwin disowned his daughter upon her elopement and was only slightly mollified when the two married in 1816, following the suicide of Percy's first wife, Harriet.

The couple toured France, Switzerland, and Germany (a trip described in Mary Shelley's first publication, *History of a Six Weeks' Tour*, 1817) before eventually settling in Italy near Lord Byron. The subsequent years in Italy were turbulent ones. Two of Shelley's children died in infancy, and her three-year-old son William died in 1819. A life-threatening miscarriage that same year plunged Shelley into severe depression, and she and her husband became increasingly distant. When Percy drowned with his friend Edward Williams in July of 1822, her sorrow at his death was further augmented by her guilt at their estrangement.

Although she wrote some poetry and verse dramas, Shelley's only publication during these years was *Frankenstein; or, The Modern Prometheus*, first published in 1818 and revised for a new edition in 1831. The novel was conceived in the summer of 1816, when the Shelleys were in Switzerland with Lord Byron and John Polidori, Byron's resident physician. The summer was rainy and miserable, so the friends spent much time around a fire indoors, reading ghost stories. Byron suggested that they amuse themselves by each writing a ghost story to share with the others, and he proceeded to begin a vampire horror story later published as "A Fragment" (1819). Polidori began work on his *Ernestus Berchtold; or, The Modern Oedipus* (1819). According to Mary Shelley's own account in her 1831 introduction to *Frankenstein*, she found inspiration for her contribution after listening to Byron and Percy discuss the work of Erasmus Darwin on galvanism and the possibility of reanimating corpses. That night, she fell asleep and had a "waking dream," of "the pale student of unhallowed arts kneeling beside the thing he had put together … the hideous phantasm of a man stretched out, and then, on the working of some powerful engine, show signs of life, and stir with an uneasy, half vital motion." This vision of horror, which "mock[ed] the stupendous mechanism of the Creator of the world," became the seed of her ghost story, which she eventually expanded into the novel *Frankenstein*.

As a result of the scandalous events in her past, as well as the radical views of her parents and husband—not to mention her own often radical opinions—Shelley felt exiled from society. After the deaths of Percy in 1822 and of Byron in 1824, she found herself without friendship or support. She had a small allowance from her father-in-law, but it was hardly enough to support her, so she turned to writing for income. She returned to London and began producing book reviews, essays, and short biographies while continuing to write novels. *The Last Man* (1826) presents a view of humanity in which a plague destroys the earth, leaving only one man, Lionel Verney. Shelley's novels *Valperga* (1823) and *The Fortunes of Perkin Warbeck: A Romance* (1830) experiment with the genre of historical fiction—a mode that had recently been made popular by Walter Scott—combining romance and fiction with historical and political analysis. In these novels, as well as in *The Last Man*, critics found evidence of the "unsavory politics" they expected from one of the Godwin circle. Critics and readers alike preferred Shelley's more traditional domestic fictions, such as *Lodore* (1835) and *Falkner* (1837).

Percy's father, Sir Timothy Shelley, for many years prevented Mary Shelley from publishing editions of her husband's work, but he eventually reconsidered, and in 1839 she released his four-volume *Poetical Works*, as well as his *Essays and Letters from Abroad, Translations and Fragments*. In writing about her husband, Shelley endeavored to rationalize his radical attitudes and behavior—particularly his atheism and sedition—in order to mediate his poetry for his audience and redeem his public image. Although she has been accused of altering his manuscripts and misrepresenting his politics, she succeeded in her goal of bringing his work to public notice.

In 1844 the concerns that had plagued Shelley since the death of her husband were relieved by the death of his father, whose title and estate her son, Percy Florence, inherited. Shelley spent her final years traveling with Percy Florence and helping him manage the estate. In 1848 he married Jane St. John, a widow and friend of Shelley. Jane nursed Shelley in the months before her death from a brain tumor in 1851.

⌘ ⌘ ⌘

The Last Man

Other than *Frankenstein*, Mary Shelley's 1826 novel *The Last Man* is the work that has excited the greatest critical interest and enjoyed the most attention from her readership over the past generation. In part this may relate to increased interest in apocalyptic visions around the turn of the millennium; it may also speak to humanity's perpetual fascination with the idea of its own extinction. Additional interest may stem from the parallels between the lives of Shelley and her companions and those of the characters in the novel—the circumstances of Percy Shelley's death are strikingly similar to those surrounding the drowning of Lionel Verney's companions. While Shelley's novel can be seen as a depiction of her own grief on a universal scale, her wistful look back at an idealized, but ultimately untenable, past may also be read as a political critique, and a disillusioned examination of Romanticism.

Shelley's protagonist, Lionel Verney, is the last man in the world, looking back on human history from 2100. During the final years of the twenty-first century the world has been devastated by plague. In its wake, humans have descended into brutality: American survivors have attacked Ireland; the Irish have invaded England; and, finally, small bands of English survivors have been wandering the now-ruined continent of Europe. Lionel Verney and his party suspect themselves to be the last of these groups of survivors. As the final two chapters open, Verney has two remaining companions, Adrian and Clara, the latter distraught after the death of her child. The party has been staying in an abandoned villa at Lake Como in the Alps.

---

from *The Last Man*

CHAPTER 29

Now—soft awhile—have I arrived so near the end? Yes! it is all over now—a step or two over those new-made graves, and the wearisome way is done. Can I accomplish my task? Can I streak my paper with words capacious of the grand conclusion? Arise, black Melancholy! quit thy Cimmerian solitude![1] Bring with thee murky fogs from hell, which may drink up the day; bring blight and pestiferous exhalations, which, entering the hollow caverns and breathing places of earth, may fill her stony veins with corruption, so that not only herbage may no longer flourish, the trees may rot, and the rivers run with gall—but the everlasting mountains be decomposed, and the mighty deep putrify, and the genial atmosphere which clips the globe, lose all powers of generation and sustenance. Do this, sad visaged power, while I write, while eyes read these pages.

And who will read them? Beware, tender offspring of the re-born world—beware, fair being, with human heart, yet untamed by care, and human brow, yet unploughed by time—beware, lest the cheerful current of thy blood be checked, thy golden locks turn grey, thy sweet dimpling smiles be changed to fixed, harsh wrinkles! Let not day look on these lines, lest garish day waste, turn pale, and die. Seek a cypress grove, whose moaning boughs will be harmony befitting; seek some cave, deep embowered in earth's dark entrails, where no light will penetrate, save that which struggles, red and flickering, through a single fissure, staining thy page with grimmest livery of death.

There is a painful confusion in my brain, which refuses to delineate distinctly succeeding events. Sometimes the irradiation of my friend's gentle smile comes before me; and methinks its light spans and fills eternity—then, again, I feel the gasping throes—

---

[1] *Cimmerian solitude* Referring to the Cimmerians, mythical people of Homer's *Odyssey* who inhabit the dark, misty fringes of the world.

We quitted Como, and in compliance with Adrian's earnest desire, we took Venice in our way to Rome. There was something to the English peculiarly attractive in the idea of this wave-encircled, island-enthroned city. Adrian had never seen it. We went down the Po and the Brenta[1] in a boat; and, the days proving intolerably hot, we rested in the bordering palaces during the day, travelling through the night, when darkness made the bordering banks indistinct, and our solitude less remarkable; when the wandering moon lit the waves that divided before our prow, and the night-wind filled our sails, and the murmuring stream, waving trees, and swelling canvass, accorded in harmonious strain. Clara, long overcome by excessive grief, had to a great degree cast aside her timid, cold reserve, and received our attentions with grateful tenderness. While Adrian with poetic fervour discoursed of the glorious nations of the dead, of the beauteous earth and the fate of man, she crept near him, drinking in his speech with silent pleasure. We banished from our talk, and as much as possible from our thoughts, the knowledge of our desolation. And it would be incredible to an inhabitant of cities, to one among a busy throng to what extent we succeeded. It was as a man confined in a dungeon, whose small and grated rift at first renders the doubtful light more sensibly obscure, till, the visual orb having drunk in the beam, and adapted itself to its scantiness, he finds that clear noon inhabits his cell. So we, a simple triad on empty earth, were multiplied to each other, till we became all in all. We stood like trees, whose roots are loosened by the wind, which support one another, leaning and clinging with increased fervour while the wintry storms howl.

Thus we floated down the widening stream of the Po, sleeping when the cicale[2] sang, awake with the stars. We entered the narrower banks of the Brenta, and arrived at the shore of the Laguna[3] at sunrise on the sixth of September. The bright orb slowly rose from behind its cupolas and towers, and shed its penetrating light upon the glassy waters. Wrecks of gondolas, and some few uninjured ones, were strewed on the beach at Fusina.[4] We embarked in one of these for the widowed daughter of ocean,[5] who, abandoned and fallen, sat forlorn on her propping isles, looking towards the far mountains of Greece. We rowed lightly over the Laguna, and entered Canale Grande.[6] The tide ebbed sullenly from out the broken portals and violated halls of Venice: sea weed and sea monsters were left on the blackened marble, while the salt ooze defaced the matchless works of art that adorned their walls, and the sea gull flew out from the shattered window. In the midst of this appalling ruin of the monuments of man's power, nature asserted her ascendancy, and shone more beauteous from the contrast. The radiant waters hardly trembled, while the rippling waves made many sided mirrors to the sun; the blue immensity, seen beyond Lido,[7] stretched far, unspecked by boat, so tranquil, so lovely, that it seemed to invite us to quit the land strewn with ruins, and to seek refuge from sorrow and fear on its placid extent.

We saw the ruins of this hapless city from the height of the tower of San Marco, immediately under us, and turned with sickening hearts to the sea, which, though it be a grave, rears no monument, discloses no ruin. Evening had come apace. The sun set in calm majesty behind the misty summits of the Apennines, and its golden and roseate hues painted the mountains of the opposite shore. "That land," said Adrian, "tinged with the last glories of the day, is Greece." Greece! The sound had a responsive chord in the bosom of Clara. She vehemently reminded us that we had promised to take her once again to Greece, to the tomb of her parents. Why go to Rome? what should we do at Rome? We might take one of the many vessels to be found here, embark in it, and steer right for Albania.

---

[1] *the Po and the Brenta*   Both rivers flow from the Alps down into the Venetian plain.

[2] *cicale*   Cicada.

[3] *the Laguna*   The Laguna Veneta, which surrounds Venice.

[4] *Fusina*   Located on the coast of the mainland, south of Venice.

[5] *widowed daughter of ocean*   I.e., Venice. In an ancient ceremony, the ruler of Venice threw a ring into the sea each Ascension Day to symbolize the marriage of Venice and the ocean.

[6] *Canale Grande*   Canal that runs through Venice.

[7] *Lido*   Island that forms a breakwater between the sea and the Laguna Veneta.

I objected the dangers of ocean, and the distance of the mountains we saw, from Athens; a distance which, from the savage uncultivation of the country, was almost impassable. Adrian, who was delighted with Clara's proposal, obviated these objections. The season was favourable; the north-west that blew would take us transversely across the gulph; and then we might find, in some abandoned port, a light Greek caique,[1] adapted for such navigation, and run down the coast of the Morea, and, passing over the Isthmus of Corinth, without much land-travelling or fatigue, find ourselves at Athens. This appeared to me wild talk; but the sea, glowing with a thousand purple hues, looked so brilliant and safe; my beloved companions were so earnest, so determined, that, when Adrian said, "Well, though it is not exactly what you wish, yet consent, to please me"—I could no longer refuse. That evening we selected a vessel, whose size just seemed fitted for our enterprize; we bent the sails and put the rigging in order, and, reposing that night in one of the city's thousand palaces, agreed to embark at sunrise the following morning.

When winds that move not its calm surface, sweep
The azure sea, I love the land no more;
The smiles of the serene and tranquil deep
Tempt my unquiet mind—

Thus said Adrian, quoting a translation of Moschus's poem, as, in the clear morning light, we rowed over the Laguna, past Lido, into the open sea—I would have added in continuation,

But, when the roar
Of ocean's gray abyss resounds, and foam
Gathers upon the sea, and vast waves burst[2]—

But my friends declared that such verses were evil augury; so in cheerful mood we left the shallow waters, and, when out at sea, unfurled our sails to catch the favourable breeze. The laughing morning air filled them while sun-light bathed earth, sky and ocean—the placid waves divided to receive our keel, and playfully kissed the dark sides of our little skiff, murmuring a welcome; as land receded, still the blue expanse, most waveless, twin sister to the azure empyrean, afforded smooth conduct to our bark.[3] As the air and waters were tranquil and balmy, so were our minds steeped in quiet. In comparison with the unstained deep, funereal earth appeared a grave, its high rocks and stately mountains were but monuments, its trees the plumes of a hearse, the brooks and rivers brackish with tears for departed man. Farewell to desolate towns—to fields with their savage intermixture of corn and weeds—to ever multiplying relics of our lost species. Ocean, we commit ourselves to thee—even as the patriarch of old[4] floated above the drowned world, let us be saved, as thus we betake ourselves to thy perennial flood.

Adrian sat at the helm; I attended to the rigging, the breeze right aft filled our swelling canvas, and we ran before it over the untroubled deep. The wind died away at noon; its idle breath just permitted us to hold our course. As lazy, fair weather sailors, careless of the coming hour, we talked gaily of our coasting voyage, of our arrival at Athens. We would make our home of one of the Cyclades,[5] and there in myrtle-groves, amidst perpetual spring, fanned by the wholesome sea-breezes —we would live long years in beatific union—Was there such a thing as death in the world?—

The sun passed its zenith and lingered down the stainless floor of heaven. Lying in the boat, my face turned up to the sky, I thought I saw on its blue white, marbled streaks, so slight, so immaterial, that now I said—"They are there"—and now, "It is a mere imagination." A sudden fear stung me while I gazed; and, starting up, and running to the prow—as I stood, my hair was gently lifted on my brow—a dark line of ripples appeared to the east, gaining rapidly on us—my breathless remark to Adrian was followed by the flapping of the canvas, as the adverse wind struck it, and our boat lurched—swift as speech, the web of the storm thickened overhead, the sun went down red, the dark sea was

1 caique Small row-boat or sail-boat.
2 When winds ... burst From Percy Shelley's sonnet "Translated from the Greek of Moschus" (1816), 2.1–6.
3 bark Boat.
4 the patriarch of old I.e., Noah.
5 Cyclades Group of islands in the Aegean Sea.

strewed with foam, and our skiff rose and fell in its increasing furrows.

Behold us now in our frail tenement, hemmed in by hungry, roaring waves, buffeted by winds. In the inky east two vast clouds, sailing contrary ways, met; the lightning leapt forth, and the hoarse thunder muttered. Again in the south, the clouds replied, and the forked stream of fire, running along the black sky, showed us the appalling piles of clouds, now met and obliterated by the heaving waves. Great God! And we alone—we three—alone—alone—sole dwellers on the sea and on the earth, we three must perish! The vast universe, its myriad worlds, and the plains of boundless earth which we had left—the extent of shoreless sea around—contracted to my view—they and all that they contained, shrunk up to one point, even to our tossing bark, freighted with glorious humanity.

A convulsion of despair crossed the love-beaming face of Adrian, while with set teeth he murmured, "Yet they shall be saved!" Clara, visited by a human pang, pale and trembling, crept near him—he looked on her with an encouraging smile—"Do you fear, sweet girl? O, do not fear, we shall soon be on shore!"

The darkness prevented me from seeing the changes of her countenance; but her voice was clear and sweet, as she replied, "Why should I fear? Neither sea nor storm can harm us, if mighty destiny or the ruler of destiny does not permit. And then the stinging fear of surviving either of you is not here—one death will clasp us undivided."

Meanwhile we took in all our sails, save a jib;[1] and, as soon as we might without danger, changed our course, running with the wind for the Italian shore. Dark night mixed everything; we hardly discerned the white crests of the murderous surges, except when lightning made brief noon, and drank the darkness, showing us our danger, and restoring us to double night. We were all silent, except when Adrian, as steersman, made an encouraging observation. Our little shell obeyed the rudder miraculously well, and ran along on the top of the waves as if she had been an offspring

of the sea, and the angry mother sheltered her endangered child.

I sat at the prow, watching our course; when suddenly I heard the waters break with redoubled fury. We were certainly near the shore—at the same time I cried, "About there!" and a broad lightning, filling the concave, showed us for one moment the level beach ahead, disclosing even the sands, and stunted, ooze-sprinkled beds of reeds, that grew at high water mark. Again it was dark, and we drew in our breath with such content as one may, who, while fragments of volcano-hurled rock darken the air, sees a vast mass plowing the ground immediately at his feet. What to do we knew not—the breakers here, there, everywhere, encompassed us—they roared, and dashed, and flung their hated spray in our faces. With considerable difficulty and danger we succeeded at length in altering our course, and stretched out from shore. I urged my companions to prepare for the wreck of our little skiff, and to bind themselves to some oar or spar which might suffice to float them. I was myself an excellent swimmer—the very sight of the sea was wont to raise in me such sensations as a huntsman experiences when he hears a pack of hounds in full cry; I loved to feel the waves wrap me and strive to overpower me; while I, lord of myself, moved this way or that, in spite of their angry bufferings. Adrian also could swim—but the weakness of his frame prevented him from feeling pleasure in the exercise, or acquiring any great expertness.

But what power could the strongest swimmer oppose to the overpowering violence of ocean in its fury? My efforts to prepare my companions were rendered nearly futile—for the roaring breakers prevented our hearing one another speak, and the waves that broke continually over our boat obliged me to exert all my strength in lading the water out, as fast as it came in. The while darkness, palpable and rayless, hemmed us round, dissipated only by the lightning; sometimes we beheld thunderbolts, fiery red, fall into the sea, and at intervals vast spouts stooped from the clouds, churning the wild ocean, which rose to meet them; while the fierce gale bore the rack[2] onwards, and they were lost in

1 *jib* Triangular sail to the fore of a ship.

2 *rack* Mass of clouds.

the chaotic mingling of sky and sea. Our gunwales had been torn away, our single sail had been rent to ribbands[1] and borne down the stream of the wind. We had cut away our mast, and lightened the boat of all she contained—Clara attempted to assist me in heaving the water from the hold, and, as she turned her eyes to look on the lightning, I could discern by that momentary gleam that resignation had conquered every fear. We have a power given us in any worst extremity, which props the else feeble mind of man, and enables us to endure the most savage tortures with a stillness of soul which in hours of happiness we could not have imagined. A calm, more dreadful in truth than the tempest, allayed the wild beatings of my heart—a calm like that of the gamester, the suicide, and the murderer, when the last die is on the point of being cast—while the poisoned cup is at the lips, as the death-blow is about to be given.

Hours passed thus—hours which might write old age on the face of beardless youth, and grizzle the silky hair of infancy—hours, while the chaotic uproar continued, while each dread gust transcended in fury the one before, and our skiff hung on the breaking wave, and then rushed into the valley below, and trembled and spun between the watery precipices that seemed most to meet above her. For a moment the gale paused, and ocean sank to comparative silence—it was a breathless interval; the wind which, as a practised leaper, had gathered itself up before it sprung, now with terrific roar rushed over the sea, and the waves struck our stern. Adrian exclaimed that the rudder was gone—"We are lost," cried Clara, "Save yourselves—O save yourselves!" The lightning showed me the poor girl half buried in the water at the bottom of the boat; as she was sinking in it Adrian caught her up, and sustained her in his arms. We were without a rudder—we rushed prow foremost into the vast billows piled up ahead—they broke over and filled the tiny skiff; one scream I heard—one cry that we were gone, I uttered; I found myself in the waters; darkness was around. When the light of the tempest flashed, I saw the keel of our upset boat close to me—I clung to this, grasping it with clenched hand and nails, while I endeavoured during

each flash to discover any appearance of my companions. I thought I saw Adrian at no great distance from me, clinging to an oar; I sprung from my hold, and with energy beyond my human strength, I dashed aside the waters as I strove to lay hold of him. As that hope failed, instinctive love of life animated me, and feelings of contention, as if a hostile will combated with mine. I breasted the surges, and flung them from me as I would the opposing front and sharpened claws of a lion about to enfang my bosom. When I had been beaten down by one wave, I rose on another, while I felt bitter pride curl my lip.

Ever since the storm had carried us near the shore, we had never attained any great distance from it. With every flash I saw the bordering coast; yet the progress I made was small, while each wave, as it receded, carried me back into ocean's far abysses. At one moment I felt my foot touch the sand, and then again I was in deep water; my arms began to lose their power of motion; my breath failed me under the influence of the strangling waters—a thousand wild and delirious thoughts crossed me: as well as I can now recall them, my chief feeling was, how sweet it would be to lay my head on the quiet earth, where the surges would no longer strike my weakened frame, nor the sound of waters ring in my ears—to attain this repose, not to save my life, I made a last effort—the shelving shore suddenly presented a footing for me. I rose, and was again thrown down by the breakers—a point of rock, to which I was enabled to cling, gave me a moment's respite; and then, taking advantage of the ebbing of the waves, I ran forwards—gained the dry sands, and fell senseless on the oozy reeds that sprinkled them.

I must have lain long deprived of life; for when first, with a sickening feeling, I unclosed my eyes, the light of morning met them. Great change had taken place meanwhile: grey dawn dappled the flying clouds, which sped onwards, leaving visible at intervals vast lakes of pure ether. A fountain of light arose in an increasing stream from the east, behind the waves of the Adriatic, changing the grey to a roseate hue, and then flooding sky and sea with aerial gold.

A kind of stupor followed my fainting; my senses were alive, but memory was extinct. The blessed respite was short—a snake lurked near me to sting me into life. On the first retrospective emotion I would have started up, but my limbs refused to obey me; my knees trembled, the muscles had lost all power. I still believed that I might find one of my beloved companions cast like me, half alive, on the beach; and I strove in every way to restore my frame to the use of its animal functions. I wrung the brine from my hair; and the rays of the risen sun soon visited me with genial warmth. With the restoration of my bodily powers, my mind became in some degree aware of the universe of misery, henceforth to be its dwelling. I ran to the water's edge, calling on the beloved names. Ocean drank in and absorbed my feeble voice, replying with pitiless roar. I climbed a near tree: the level sands bounded by a pine forest, and the sea clipped round by the horizon, was all that I could discern. In vain I extended my researches along the beach; the mast we had thrown overboard, with tangled cordage, and remnants of a sail, was the sole relic land received of our wreck. Sometimes I stood still, and wrung my hands. I accused earth and sky—the universal machine and the Almighty power that misdirected it. Again I threw myself on the sands, and then the sighing wind, mimicking a human cry, roused me to bitter, fallacious hope. Assuredly if any little bark or smallest canoe had been near, I should have sought the savage plains of ocean, found the dear remains of my lost ones, and, clinging round them, have shared their grave.

The day passed thus; each moment contained eternity; although when hour after hour had gone by, I wondered at the quick flight of time. Yet even now I had not drunk the bitter potion to the dregs; I was not yet persuaded of my loss; I did not yet feel in every pulsation, in every nerve, in every thought, that I remained alone of my race—that I was the LAST MAN.

The day had clouded over, and a drizzling rain set in at sunset. Even the eternal skies weep, I thought; is there any shame then, that mortal man should spend himself in tears? I remembered the ancient fables, in which human beings are described as dissolving away through weeping into ever-gushing fountains. Ah! that so it were; and then my destiny would be in some sort akin to the watery death of Adrian and Clara. Oh! grief is fantastic; it weaves a web on which to trace the history of its woe from every form and change around; it incorporates itself with all living nature; it finds sustenance in every object; as light, it fills all things, and, like light, it gives its own colours to all.

I had wandered in my search to some distance from the spot on which I had been cast, and came to one of those watch-towers, which at stated distances line the Italian shore. I was glad of shelter, glad to find a work of human hands, after I had gazed so long on nature's drear barrenness; so I entered, and ascended the rough winding staircase into the guard-room. So far was fate kind, that no harrowing vestige remained of its former inhabitants; a few planks laid across two iron tressels, and strewed with the dried leaves of Indian corn, was the bed presented to me; and an open chest, containing some half mouldered biscuit, awakened an appetite, which perhaps existed before, but of which, until now, I was not aware. Thirst also, violent and parching, the result of the sea-water I had drank, and of the exhaustion of my frame, tormented me. Kind nature had gifted the supply of these wants with pleasurable sensations, so that I—even I!—was refreshed and calmed as I ate of this sorry fare, and drank a little of the sour wine which half filled a flask left in this abandoned dwelling. Then I stretched myself on the bed, not to be disdained by the victim of shipwreck. The earthy smell of the dried leaves was balm to my sense after the hateful odour of sea-weed. I forgot my state of loneliness. I neither looked backward nor forward; my senses were hushed to repose; I fell asleep and dreamed of all dear inland scenes, of hay-makers, of the shepherd's whistle to his dog when he demanded his help to drive the flock to fold; of sights and sounds peculiar to my boyhood's mountain life, which I had long forgotten.

I awoke in a painful agony—for I fancied that ocean, breaking its bounds, carried away the fixed continent and deep rooted mountains, together with the streams I loved, the woods, and the flocks—it raged around, with that continued and dreadful roar which had accompanied the last wreck of surviving humanity. As my waking sense returned, the bare walls of the guard room closed round me, and the rain pattered against the single window. How dreadful it is to emerge from the oblivion of slumber and to receive as a good morrow the mute wailing of one's own hapless heart—to return from the land of deceptive dreams to the heavy knowledge of unchanged disaster!—Thus was it with me, now, and for ever! The sting of other griefs might be blunted by time; and even mine yielded sometimes during the day, to the pleasure inspired by the imagination or the senses; but I never look first upon the morning-light but with my fingers pressed tight on my bursting heart, and my soul deluged with the interminable flood of hopeless misery. Now I awoke for the first time in the dead world—I awoke alone—and the dull dirge of the sea, heard even amidst the rain, recalled me to the reflection of the wretch I had become. The sound came like a reproach, a scoff—like the sting of remorse in the soul—I gasped—the veins and muscles of my throat swelled, suffocating me. I put my fingers to my ears, I buried my head in the leaves of my couch, I would have dived to the centre to lose hearing of that hideous moan.

But another task must be mine—again I visited the detested beach, again I vainly looked far and wide, again I raised my unanswered cry, lifting up the only voice that could ever again force the mute air to syllable the human thought.

What a pitiable, forlorn, disconsolate being I was! My very aspect and garb told the tale of my despair. My hair was matted and wild, my limbs soiled with salt ooze; while at sea, I had thrown off those of my garments that encumbered me, and the rain drenched the thin summer-clothing I had retained—my feet were bare, and the stunted reeds and broken shells made them bleed—the while, I hurried to and fro, now looking earnestly on some distant rock which, islanded in the sands, bore for a moment a deceptive appearance—now with flashing eyes reproaching the murderous ocean for its unutterable cruelty.

For a moment I compared myself to that monarch of the waste—Robinson Crusoe.[1] We had been both thrown companionless—he on the shore of a desolate island: I on that of a desolate world. I was rich in the so-called goods of life. If I turned my steps from the near barren scene, and entered any of the earth's million cities, I should find their wealth stored up for my accommodation—clothes, food, books, and a choice of dwelling beyond the command of the princes of former times. Every climate was subject to my selection, while he was obliged to toil in the acquirement of every necessary, and was the inhabitant of a tropical island, against whose heats and storms he could obtain small shelter. Viewing the question thus, who would not have preferred the Sybarite[2] enjoyments I could command, the philosophic leisure, and ample intellectual resources, to his life of labour and peril? Yet he was far happier than I: for he could hope, nor hope in vain—the destined vessel at last arrived to bear him to countrymen and kindred, where the events of his solitude became a fire-side tale. To none could I ever relate the story of my adversity; no hope had I. He knew that, beyond the ocean which begirt his lonely island, thousands lived whom the sun enlightened when it shone also on him: beneath the meridian sun and visiting moon, I alone bore human features; I alone could give articulation to thought; and, when I slept, both day and night were unbeheld of any. He had fled from his fellows, and was transported with terror at the print of a human foot. I would have knelt down and worshipped the same. The wild and cruel Caribbee, the merciless Cannibal[3]—or worse than these, the uncouth, brute, and remorseless veteran in the vices of civilization, would have been to me a beloved companion, a treasure dearly prized. His nature would be kin to mine; his form cast in the same mould; human blood would flow in his veins; a human sympathy must link us for ever. It cannot be that I shall never behold a fellow being more!—never!—never!—not in the course of years!—Shall I wake, and speak to none, pass the interminable hours, my soul, islanded in the world, a solitary point, surrounded by vacuum? Will day follow day endlessly thus? No! no! a God rules the

---

[1] *Robinson Crusoe* Shipwrecked protagonist of Daniel Defoe's *The Life and Adventures of Robinson Crusoe* (1719).

[2] *Sybarite* Luxurious; from the Greek city of Sybaris, noted for its luxury.

[3] *Caribbee* Caribs, inhabitants of the southern West Indies; *Cannibal* Originally also a form of the word "Carib." The fierce inhabitants of this region were rumored to eat human flesh; thus the evolution of the word "cannibal" to its present meaning.

world—providence has not exchanged its golden sceptre for an aspic's[1] sting. Away! let me fly from the ocean-grave, let me depart from this barren nook, paled in,[2] as it is, from access by its own desolateness; let me tread once again the paved towns; step over the threshold of man's dwellings, and most certainly I shall find this thought a horrible vision—a maddening, but evanescent, dream.

I entered Ravenna[3] (the town nearest to the spot whereon I had been cast) before the second sun had set on the empty world; I saw many living creatures: oxen, and horses, and dogs, but there was no man among them. I entered a cottage, it was vacant; I ascended the marble stairs of a palace, the bats and the owls were nestled in the tapestry; I stepped softly, not to awaken the sleeping town. I rebuked a dog, that by yelping disturbed the sacred stillness; I would not believe that all was as it seemed—The world was not dead, but I was mad; I was deprived of sight, hearing, and sense of touch; I was labouring under the force of a spell, which permitted me to behold all sights of earth, except its human inhabitants; they were pursuing their ordinary labours. Every house had its inmate; but I could not perceive them. If I could have deluded myself into a belief of this kind, I should have been far more satisfied. But my brain, tenacious of its reason, refused to lend itself to such imaginations—and though I endeavoured to play the antic to myself, I knew that I, the offspring of man, during long years one among many—now remained sole survivor of my species.

The sun sank behind the western hills; I had fasted since the preceding evening, but, though faint and weary, I loathed food, nor ceased, while yet a ray of light remained, to pace the lonely streets. Night came on, and sent every living creature but me to the bosom of its mate. It was my solace to blunt my mental agony by personal hardship—of the thousand beds around, I would not seek the luxury of one; I lay down on the pavement—a cold marble step served me for a pil-

low—midnight came; and then, though not before, did my wearied lids shut out the sight of the twinkling stars, and their reflex on the pavement near. Thus I passed the second night of my desolation.

CHAPTER 30

I awoke in the morning, just as the higher windows of the lofty houses received the first beams of the rising sun. The birds were chirping, perched on the window sills and deserted thresholds of the doors. I awoke, and my first thought was, Adrian and Clara are dead. I no longer shall be hailed by their good-morrow, or pass the long day in their society. I shall never see them more. The ocean has robbed me of them—stolen their hearts of love from their breasts, and given over to corruption what was dearer to me than light, or life, or hope.

I was an untaught shepherd-boy when Adrian deigned to confer on me his friendship. The best years of my life had been passed with him. All I had possessed of this world's goods, of happiness, knowledge, or virtue, I owed to him. He had, in his person, his intellect, and rare qualities, given a glory to my life, which without him it had never known. Beyond all other beings he had taught me that goodness, pure and single, can be an attribute of man. It was a sight for angels to congregate to behold, to view him lead, govern, and solace the last days of the human race.

My lovely Clara also was lost to me—she who, last of the daughters of man, exhibited all those feminine and maiden virtues which poets, painters, and sculptors have in their various languages strove to express. Yet, as far as she was concerned, could I lament that she was removed in early youth from the certain advent of misery? Pure she was of soul, and all her intents were holy. But her heart was the throne of love, and the sensibility her lovely countenance expressed was the prophet of many woes, not the less deep and drear because she would have for ever concealed them.

These two wondrously endowed beings had been spared from the universal wreck to be my companions during the last year of solitude. I had felt, while they were with me, all their worth. I was conscious that every other sentiment, regret, or passion had by degrees

---

[1] *aspic* Asp, a poisonous snake.

[2] *paled in* Fenced in.

[3] *Ravenna* Town on the Adriatic Sea, approximately 80 miles south of Venice.

merged into a yearning, clinging affection for them. I had not forgotten the sweet partner of my youth, mother of my children, my adored Idris; but I saw at least a part of her spirit alive again in her brother;[1] and after, that by Evelyn's[2] death I had lost what most dearly recalled her to me; I enshrined her memory in Adrian's form, and endeavoured to confound the two dear ideas. I sound the depths of my heart, and try in vain to draw thence the expressions that can typify my love for these remnants of my race. If regret and sorrow came athwart me, as well it might in our solitary and uncertain state, the clear tones of Adrian's voice, and his fervent look, dissipated the gloom; or I was cheered unaware by the mild content and sweet resignation Clara's cloudless brow and deep blue eyes expressed. They were all to me—the suns of my benighted soul, repose in my weariness, slumber in my sleepless woe. Ill, most ill, with disjointed words, bare and weak, have I expressed the feeling with which I clung to them. I would have wound myself like ivy inextricably round them, so that the same blow might destroy us. I would have entered and been a part of them—so that

If the dull substance of my flesh were thought,[3]

even now I had accompanied them to their new and incommunicable abode.

Never shall I see them more. I am bereft of their dear converse—bereft of sight of them. I am a tree rent by lightning; never will the bark close over the bared fibres—never will their quivering life, torn by the winds, receive the opiate of a moment's balm. I am alone in the world—but that expression as yet was less pregnant with misery than that Adrian and Clara are dead.

The tide of thought and feeling rolls on for ever the same, though the banks and shapes around, which govern its course, and the reflection in the wave, vary. Thus the sentiment of immediate loss in some sort decayed, while that of utter, irremediable loneliness grew on me with time. Three days I wandered through Ravenna—now thinking only of the beloved beings who slept in the oozy caves of ocean, now looking forward on the dread blank before me; shuddering to make an onward step, writhing at each change that marked the progress of the hours.

For three days I wandered to and fro in this melancholy town. I passed whole hours in going from house to house, listening whether I could detect some lurking sign of human existence. Sometimes I rang at a bell; it tinkled through the vaulted rooms, and silence succeeded to the sound. I called myself hopeless, yet still I hoped; and still disappointment ushered in the hours, intruding the cold, sharp steel, which first pierced me, into the aching festering wound. I fed like a wild beast, which seizes its food only when stung by intolerable hunger. I did not change my garb, or seek the shelter of a roof, during all those days. Burning heats, nervous irritation, a ceaseless but confused flow of thought, sleepless nights, and days instinct with a frenzy of agitation, possessed me during that time.

As the fever of my blood increased, a desire of wandering came upon me. I remember that the sun had set on the fifth day after my wreck when, without purpose or aim, I quitted the town of Ravenna. I must have been very ill. Had I been possessed by more or less of delirium, that night had surely been my last; for, as I continued to walk on the banks of the Mantone,[4] whose upward course I followed, I looked wistfully on the stream, acknowledging to myself that its pellucid waves could medicine my woes for ever, and was unable to account to myself for my tardiness in seeking their shelter from the poisoned arrows of thought that were piercing me through and through. I walked a considerable part of the night, and excessive weariness at length conquered my repugnance to the availing myself of the deserted habitations of my species. The waning moon, which had just risen, showed me a cottage, whose neat entrance and trim garden reminded me of my own England. I lifted up the latch of the door and entered. A kitchen first presented itself, where, guided by the moon beams, I found materials for striking a light. Within this was a bed room; the couch was furnished with sheets of

1 *her brother* I.e., Adrian.

2 *Evelyn* Lionel and Idris's youngest son.

3 *If … thought* From Shakespeare's Sonnet 44, line 1.

4 *Mantone* River that flows through Ravenna and into the Adriatic.

snowy whiteness; the wood piled on the hearth, and an array as for a meal might almost have deceived me into the dear belief that I had here found what I had so long sought—one survivor, a companion for my loneliness, a solace to my despair. I steeled myself against the delusion; the room itself was vacant: it was only prudent, I repeated to myself, to examine the rest of the house. I fancied that I was proof against the expectation; yet my heart beat audibly as I laid my hand on the lock of each door, and it sunk again, when I perceived in each the same vacancy. Dark and silent they were as vaults; so I returned to the first chamber, wondering what sightless host had spread the materials for my repast, and my repose. I drew a chair to the table and examined what the viands were of which I was to partake. In truth it was a death feast! The bread was blue and mouldy; the cheese lay a heap of dust. I did not dare examine the other dishes; a troop of ants passed in a double line across the table cloth; every utensil was covered with dust, with cobwebs, and myriads of dead flies. These were object each and all betokening the fallaciousness of my expectations. Tears rushed into my eyes; surely this was a wanton display of the power of the destroyer. What had I done, that each sensitive nerve was thus to be anatomized? Yet why complain more now than ever? This vacant cottage revealed no new sorrow—the world was empty; mankind was dead—I knew it well—why quarrel therefore with an acknowledged and stale truth? Yet, as I said, I had hoped in the very heart of despair, so that every new impression of the hard-cut reality on my soul brought with it a fresh pang, telling me the yet unstudied lesson, that neither change of place nor time could bring alleviation to my misery, but that, as I now was, I must continue, day after day, month after month, year after year, while I lived. I hardly dared conjecture what space of time that expression implied. It is true, I was no longer in the first blush of manhood; neither had I declined far in the vale of years—men have accounted mine the prime of life: I had just entered my thirty-seventh year; every limb was as well knit, every articulation as true, as when I had acted the shepherd on the hills of Cumberland; and with these advantages I was to commence the train of solitary life. Such were the reflections that ushered in my slumber on that night.

The shelter, however, and less disturbed repose which I enjoyed, restored me the following morning to a greater portion of health and strength than I had experienced since my fatal shipwreck. Among the stores I had discovered on searching the cottage the preceding night, was a quantity of dried grapes; these refreshed me in the morning as I left my lodging and proceeded towards a town which I discerned at no great distance. As far as I could divine, it must have been Forli. I entered with pleasure its wide and grassy streets. All, it is true, pictured the excess of desolation; yet I loved to find myself in those spots which had been the abode of my fellow creatures. I delighted to traverse street after street, to look up at the tall houses, and repeat to myself, once they contained beings similar to myself—I was not always the wretch I am now. The wide square of Forli, the arcade around it, its light and pleasant aspect, cheered me. I was pleased with the idea, that, if the earth should be again peopled, we, the lost race, would, in the relics left behind, present no contemptible exhibition of our powers to the newcomers.

I entered one of the palaces and opened the door of a magnificent saloon. I started—I looked again with renewed wonder. What wild-looking, unkempt, half-naked savage was that before me? The surprise was momentary.

I perceived that it was I myself whom I beheld in a large mirror at the end of the hall. No wonder that the lover of the princely Idris should fail to recognize himself in the miserable object there portrayed. My tattered dress was that in which I had crawled half alive from the tempestuous sea. My long and tangled hair hung in elf locks on my brow; my dark eyes, now hollow and wild, gleamed from under them; my cheeks were discoloured by the jaundice, which (the effect of misery and neglect) suffused my skin, and were half hid by a beard of many days' growth.

Yet why should I not remain thus, I thought; the world is dead, and this squalid attire is a fitter mourning garb than the foppery of a black suit. And thus, methinks, I should have remained, had not hope, without which I do not believe man could exist, whispered to me that in such a plight I should be an object of fear and aversion to the being, preserved I knew not where, but, I fondly trusted, at length to be found by me. Will my readers scorn the vanity that made me attire myself with some care, for the sake of this visionary being? Or will they forgive the freaks of a half crazed imagination? I can easily forgive myself—for hope, however vague, was so dear to me, and a sentiment of pleasure of so rare occurrence, that I yielded readily to any idea that cherished the one, or promised any recurrence of the former to my sorrowing heart.

After such occupation, I visited every street, alley, and nook of Forli. These Italian towns presented an appearance of still greater desolation than those of England or France. Plague had appeared here earlier—it had finished its course and achieved its work much sooner than with us. Probably the last summer had found no human being alive in all the track included between the shores of Calabria and the northern Alps. My search was utterly vain, yet I did not despond. Reason methought was on my side; and the chances were by no means contemptible that there should exist in some part of Italy a survivor like myself—of a wasted, depopulate land. As therefore I rambled through the empty town, I formed my plan for future operations. I would continue to journey on towards Rome. After I should have satisfied myself, by a narrow search, that I left behind no human being in the towns through which I passed, I would write up in a conspicuous part of each, with white paint, in three languages, that "Verney, the last of the race of Englishmen, had taken up his abode in Rome."

In pursuance of this scheme, I entered a painter's shop and procured myself the paint. It is strange that so trivial an occupation should have consoled and even enlivened me. But grief renders one childish, despair fantastic. To this simple inscription, I merely added the adjuration, "Friend, come! I wait for thee!—*Deh, vieni! ti aspetto!*"

On the following morning, with something like hope for my companion, I quitted Forli on my way to Rome. Until now, agonizing retrospect and dreary prospects for the future had stung me when awake, and cradled me to my repose. Many times I had delivered myself up to the tyranny of anguish—many times I resolved a speedy end to my woes; and death by my own hands was a remedy whose practicability was even cheering to me. What could I fear in the other world? If there were a hell, and I were doomed to it, I should come an adept to the sufferance of its tortures—the act were easy, the speedy and certain end of my deplorable tragedy. But now these thoughts faded before the new-born expectation. I went on my way, not as before, feeling each hour, each minute, to be an age instinct with incalculable pain.

As I wandered along the plain, at the foot of the Appennines—through their valleys, and over their bleak summits—my path led me through a country which had been trodden by heroes, visited and admired by thousands. They had, as a tide, receded, leaving me blank and bare in the midst. But why complain? Did I not hope?—so I schooled myself, even after the enlivening spirit had really deserted me, and thus I was obliged to call up all the fortitude I could command, and that was not much, to prevent a recurrence of that chaotic and intolerable despair that had succeeded to the miserable shipwreck, that had consummated every fear, and dashed to annihilation every joy.

I rose each day with the morning sun, and left my desolate inn. As my feet strayed through the unpeopled country, my thoughts rambled through the universe, and I was least miserable when I could, absorbed in reverie, forget the passage of the hours. Each evening, in spite of weariness, I detested to enter any dwelling, there to take up my nightly abode—I have sat, hour after hour, at the door of the cottage I had selected, unable to lift the latch and meet face to face blank desertion within. Many nights, though autumnal mists were spread around, I passed under an ilex[1]—many times I have supped on arbutus berries and chestnuts, making a fire, gypsy-like, on the ground—because wild natural scenery reminded me less acutely of my hopeless state of loneliness. I counted the days, and bore with me a peeled willow-wand, on which, as well as I could remember, I had notched the days that had elapsed since my wreck, and each night I added another unit to the melancholy sum.

[1] *ilex* Evergreen oak.

I had toiled up a hill which led to Spoleto. Around was spread a plain, encircled by the chestnut-covered Apennines. A dark ravine was on one side, spanned by an aqueduct, whose tall arches were rooted in the dell below and attested that man had once deigned to bestow labour and thought here, to adorn and civilize nature. Savage, ungrateful nature, which in wild sport defaced his remains, protruding her easily renewed and fragile growth of wild flowers and parasite plants around his eternal edifices. I sat on a fragment of rock and looked round. The sun had bathed in gold the western atmosphere, and in the east the clouds caught the radiance, and budded into transient loveliness. It set on a world that contained me alone for its inhabitant. I took out my wand—I counted the marks. Twenty-five were already traced—twenty-five days had already elapsed since human voice had gladdened my ears or human countenance met my gaze. Twenty-five long, weary days, succeeded by dark and lonesome nights, had mingled with foregone years and had become a part of the past—the never to be recalled—a real, undeniable portion of my life—twenty-five long, long days.

Why this was not a month!—Why talk of days—or weeks—or months—I must grasp years in my imagination, if I would truly picture the future to myself—three, five, ten, twenty, fifty anniversaries of that fatal epoch might elapse—every year containing twelve months, each of more numerous calculation in a diary, than the twenty-five days gone by—Can it be? Will it be?—We had been used to look forward to death tremulously—wherefore, but because its place was obscure? But more terrible, and far more obscure, was the unveiled course of my lone futurity. I broke my wand; I threw it from me. I needed no recorder of the inch and barley-corn growth of my life, while my unquiet thoughts created other divisions than those ruled over by the planets—and, in looking back on the age that had elapsed since I had been alone, I disdained to give the name of days and hours to the throes of agony which had in truth portioned it out.

I hid my face in my hands. The twitter of the young birds going to rest, and their rustling among the trees, disturbed the still evening-air—the crickets chirped, the aziolo cooed at intervals. My thoughts had been of death—these sounds spoke to me of life. I lifted up my eyes—a bat wheeled round—the sun had sunk behind the jagged line of mountains, and the paly[1] crescent moon was visible, silver white amidst the orange sunset, and accompanied by one bright star, prolonged thus the twilight. A herd of cattle passed along in the dell below, untended, towards their watering place—the grass was rustled by a gentle breeze, and the olive-woods, mellowed into soft masses by the moonlight, contrasted their sea-green with the dark chestnut foliage. Yes, this is the earth; there is no change, no ruin, no rent made in her verdurous expanse; she continues to wheel round and round, with alternate night and day, through the sky, though man is not her adorner or inhabitant. Why could I not forget myself like one of those animals, and no longer suffer the wild tumult of misery that I endure? Yet, ah! what a deadly breach yawns between their state and mine! Have not they companions? Have not they each their mate—their cherished young, their home, which, though unexpressed to us, is, I doubt not, endeared and enriched, even in their eyes, by the society which kind nature has created for them? It is I only that am alone—I, on this little hilltop, gazing on plain and mountain recess; on sky, and its starry population, listening to every sound of earth, and air, and murmuring wave—I only cannot express to any companion my many thoughts, nor lay my throbbing head on any loved bosom, nor drink from meeting eyes an intoxicating dew that transcends the fabulous nectar of the gods. Shall I not then complain? Shall I not curse the murderous engine which has mowed down the children of men, my brethren? Shall I not bestow a malediction on every other of nature's offspring, which dares live and enjoy, while I live and suffer?

Ah, no! I will discipline my sorrowing heart to sympathy in your joys; I will be happy, because ye are so. Live on, ye innocents, nature's selected darlings; I am not much unlike to you. Nerves, pulse, brain, joint, and flesh, of such am I composed, and ye are organized by the same laws. I have something beyond this, but I will call it a defect, not an endowment, if it leads me to misery, while ye are happy. Just then, there emerged

---

[1] *paly* Pale.

from a near copse two goats and a little kid, by the mother's side; they began to browze[1] the herbage of the hill. I approached near to them without their perceiving me; I gathered a handful of fresh grass and held it out; the little one nestled close to its mother, while she timidly withdrew. The male stepped forward, fixing his eyes on me: I drew near, still holding out my lure, while he, depressing his head, rushed at me with his horns. I was a very fool; I knew it, yet I yielded to my rage. I snatched up a huge fragment of rock; it would have crushed my rash foe. I poised it—aimed it—then my heart failed me. I hurled it wide of the mark; it rolled clattering among the bushes into dell. My little visitants, all aghast, galloped back into the covert of the wood; while I, my very heart bleeding and torn, rushed down the hill, and by the violence of bodily exertion sought to escape from my miserable self.

No, no, I will not live among the wild scenes of nature, the enemy of all that lives. I will seek the towns—Rome, the capital of the world, the crown of man's achievements. Among its storied streets, hallowed ruins, and stupendous remains of human exertion, I shall not, as here, find every thing forgetful of man; trampling on his memory, defacing his works, proclaiming from hill to hill, and vale to vale—by the torrents freed from the boundaries which he imposed, by the vegetation liberated from the laws which he enforced, by his habitation abandoned to mildew and weeds—that his power is lost, his race annihilated for ever.

I hailed the Tiber, for that was, as it were, an unalienable possession of humanity. I hailed the wild Campagna,[2] for every rood[3] had been trod by man; and its savage uncultivation, of no recent date, only proclaimed more distinctly his power, since he had given an honourable name and sacred title to what else would have been a worthless, barren track. I entered Eternal Rome by the Porta del Popolo,[4] and saluted with awe its time-honoured space. The wide square, the churches

near, the long extent of the Corso, the near eminence of Trinita de' Monti[5] appeared like fairy work, they were so silent, so peaceful, and so very fair. It was evening, and the population of animals which still existed in this mighty city had gone to rest; there was no sound, save the murmur of its many fountains, whose soft monotony was harmony to my soul. The knowledge that I was in Rome soothed me; that wondrous city, hardly more illustrious for its heroes and sages than for the power it exercised over the imaginations of men. I went to rest that night; the eternal burning of my heart quenched, my senses tranquil.

The next morning I eagerly began my rambles in search of oblivion. I ascended the many terraces of the garden of the Colonna Palace,[6] under whose roof I had been sleeping; and, passing out from it at its summit, I found myself on Monte Cavallo. The fountain sparkled in the sun; the obelisk above pierced the clear dark-blue air. The statues on each side, the works, as they are inscribed, of Phidias and Praxiteles, stood in undiminished grandeur, representing Castor and Pollux,[7] who with majestic power tamed the rearing animal at their side. If those illustrious artists had in truth chiselled these forms, how many passing generations had their giant proportions outlived! and now they were viewed by the last of the species they were sculptured to represent and deify. I had shrunk into insignificance in my own eyes, as I considered the multitudinous beings these stone demigods had outlived, but this after-thought restored me to dignity in my own conception. The sight of the poetry eternized in these statues, took the sting from the thought, arraying it only in poetic ideality.

I repeated to myself—I am in Rome! I behold, and, as it were, familiarly converse with the wonder of the world, sovereign mistress of the imagination, majestic

---

[1] *browze* Feed on.

[2] *Campagna* Plain to the north of Rome through which the Tiber River flows before entering the city.

[3] *rood* Measure of land, varying from six to eight yards.

[4] *Porta del Popolo* Italian: Gate of the People.

[5] *Corso* Via del Corso, main street of central Rome; a fashionable promenade in Shelley's time; *Trinita de' Monti* Church located at the top of the Spanish Steps.

[6] *Colonna Palace* Located on Monte Cavallo (also called Quirinal Hill), it contains an art gallery of sixteenth- and seventeeth-century paintings.

[7] *The statues ... Pollux* The statues of Castor and Pollux, the twin sons of Zeus and Leda, were then commonly (but incorrectly) ascribed to the fifth- and sixth-century BCE Greek sculptors Phidias and Praxiteles.

and eternal survivor of millions of generations of extinct men. I endeavoured to quiet the sorrows of my aching heart by even now taking an interest in what in my youth I had ardently longed to see. Every part of Rome is replete with relics of ancient times. The meanest streets are strewed with truncated columns, broken capitals—Corinthian and Ionic—and sparkling fragments of granite or porphyry. The walls of the most penurious dwellings enclose a fluted pillar or ponderous stone, which once made part of the palace of the Caesars; and the voice of dead time, in still vibrations, is breathed from these dumb things, animated and glorified as they were by man.

I embraced the vast columns of the temple of Jupiter Stator,[1] which survives in the open space that was the Forum, and leaning my burning cheek against its cold durability, I tried to lose the sense of present misery and present desertion by recalling to the haunted cell of my brain vivid memories of times gone by. I rejoiced at my success, as I figured Camillus, the Gracchi, Cato, and last the heroes of Tacitus,[2] which shine meteors of surpassing brightness during the murky night of the empire; as the verses of Horace and Virgil, or the glowing periods of Cicero,[3] thronged into the opened gates of my mind, I felt myself exalted by long forgotten enthusiasm. I was delighted to know that I beheld the scene which they beheld—the scene which their wives and mothers, and crowds of the unnamed, witnessed, while at the same time they honoured applauded, or

wept for these matchless specimens of humanity. At length, then, I had found a consolation. I had not vainly sought the storied precincts of Rome—I had discovered a medicine for my many and vital wounds.

I sat at the foot of these vast columns. The Coliseum,[4] whose naked ruin is robed by nature in a verdurous and glowing veil, lay in the sunlight on my right. Not far off, to the left, was the Tower of the Capitol.[5] Triumphal arches, the falling walls of many temples, strewed the ground at my feet. I strove, I resolved, to force myself to see the Plebeian multitude and lofty Patrician forms congregated around; and, as the diorama of ages passed across my subdued fancy, they were replaced by the modern Roman: the Pope, in his white stole, distributing benedictions to the kneeling worshippers; the friar in his cowl; the dark-eyed girl, veiled by her mezzera;[6] the noisy, sun-burnt rustic, leading his herd of buffaloes and oxen to the Campo Vaccino.[7] The romance with which, dipping our pencils in the rainbow hues of sky and transcendent nature, we to a degree gratuitously endow the Italians, replaced the solemn grandeur of antiquity. I remembered the dark monk, and floating figures of "The Italian," and how my boyish blood had thrilled at the description.[8] I called to mind Corinna ascending the Capitol to be crowned,[9] and, passing from the heroine to the author, reflected how the Enchantress Spirit of Rome held sovereign sway over the minds of the imaginative, until it rested on me—sole remaining spectator of its wonders.

I was long wrapt by such ideas; but the soul wearies of a pauseless flight; and, stooping from its wheeling circuits round and round this spot, suddenly it fell ten

[1] *Jupiter Stator* Three large Corinthian columns remain of this temple, which is now thought to belong to Castor, rather than to Jupiter Stator (Jupiter the Stayer, or the Steadfast). The Forum, in which these columns stand, was the location of the marketplace and the center for political, economic, and religious activities.

[2] *Camillus* Roman statesman and general of the fourth century BCE; *the Gracchi* Brothers Tiberius and Caius Gracchus, second-century BCE supporters of the plebian cause; *Cato* Either Cato the Elder (234–149 BCE), a famous politician and orator, or Cato the Younger (95–46 BCE), a Roman statesman who committed suicide rather than submit to the tyranny of Julius Caesar; *Tacitus* Roman historian (c. 55–115 CE) whose heroes include Alexander, Julius Caesar, Mithridates, and Seneca.

[3] *Horace ... Cicero* Horace and Virgil were two famous Roman poets of the first century BCE, famous for, respectively, *Odes* and *The Aeneid*. Cicero was a great orator, statesman, and prose writer who was assassinated in 43 BCE.

[4] *Coliseum* Great amphitheater completed in 80 CE and used for gladiatorial combat.

[5] *Tower of the Capitol* Citadel located on Mons Capitolinus, one of the seven hills of Rome.

[6] *mezzera* Mesèro (Italian), a shawl worn by women over the head and shoulders.

[7] *Campo Vaccino* Italian: "Cattle Pasture," the original function of the Roman Forum.

[8] *I remembered ... description* References to the novel *The Italian* (1797), by Ann Radcliffe.

[9] *Corinna ... crowned* Reference to the heroine of Anne-Louise-Germaine de Staël's novel *Corinne, ou l'Italie* (1807).

thousand fathom deep, into the abyss of the present—into self-knowledge—into tenfold sadness. I roused myself—I cast off my waking dreams; and I, who just now could almost hear the shouts of the Roman throng, and was hustled by countless multitudes, now beheld the desert ruins of Rome sleeping under its own blue sky. The shadows lay tranquilly on the ground; sheep were grazing untended on the Palatine, and a buffalo stalked down the Sacred Way[1] that led to the Capitol. I was alone in the Forum; alone in Rome; alone in the world. Would not one living man—one companion in my weary solitude, be worth all the glory and remembered power of this time-honoured city? Double sorrow—sadness, bred in Cimmerian caves, robed my soul in a mourning garb. The generations I had conjured up to my fancy contrasted more strongly with the end of all—the single point in which, as a pyramid, the mighty fabric of society had ended, while I, on the giddy height, saw vacant space around me.

From such vague laments I turned to the contemplation of the minutiae of my situation. So far, I had not succeeded in the sole object of my desires, the finding a companion for my desolation. Yet I did not despair. It is true that my inscriptions were set up, for the most part, in insignificant towns and villages; yet, even without these memorials, it was possible that the person who, like me, should find himself alone in a depopulate land, should, like me, come to Rome. The more slender my expectation was, the more I chose to build on it, and to accommodate my actions to this vague possibility.

It became necessary, therefore, that for a time I should domesticate myself at Rome. It became necessary that I should look my disaster in the face—not playing the school-boy's part of obedience without submission; enduring life, and yet rebelling against the laws by which I lived.

Yet how could I resign myself? Without love, without sympathy, without communion with any, how could I meet the morning sun, and with it trace its oft repeated journey to the evening shades? Why did I continue to live—why not throw off the weary weight of time, and with my own hand let out the fluttering prisoner from my agonized breast? It was not cowardice that withheld me; for the true fortitude was to endure, and death had a soothing sound accompanying it that would easily entice me to enter its demesne. But this I would not do. I had, from the moment I had reasoned on the subject, instituted myself the subject to fate, and the servant of necessity, the visible laws of the invisible God—I believed that my obedience was the result of sound reasoning, pure feeling, and an exalted sense of the true excellence and nobility of my nature. Could I have seen in this empty earth, in the seasons and their change, the hand of a blind power only, most willingly would I have placed my head on the sod and closed my eyes on its loveliness for ever. But fate had administered life to me when the plague had already seized on its prey—she had dragged me by the hair from out the strangling waves. By such miracles she had bought me for her own; I admitted her authority, and bowed to her decrees. If, after mature consideration, such was my resolve, it was doubly necessary that I should not lose the end of life, the improvement of my faculties, and poison its flow by repinings without end. Yet how cease to repine, since there was no hand near to extract the barbed spear that had entered my heart of hearts? I stretched out my hand, and it touched none whose sensations were responsive to mine. I was girded, walled in, vaulted over, by seven-fold barriers of loneliness. Occupation alone, if I could deliver myself up to it, would be capable of affording an opiate to my sleepless sense of woe. Having determined to make Rome my abode, at least for some months, I made arrangements for my accommodation—I selected my home. The Colonna Palace was well adapted for my purpose. Its grandeur—its treasure of paintings, its magnificent halls were objects soothing and even exhilarating.

I found the granaries of Rome well stored with grain, and particularly with Indian corn; this product, requiring less art in its preparation for food, I selected as my principal support. I now found the hardships and lawlessness of my youth turn to account. A man cannot throw off the habits of sixteen years. Since that age, it is true, I had lived luxuriously, or at least surrounded by all the conveniences civilization afforded. But before

---

[1] *Palatine* Most important of the seven hills of Rome, it was the location of the earliest Roman settlement; *Sacred Way* Sacra Via (Latin), the oldest street in Rome.

that time, I had been "as uncouth a savage as the wolf-bred founder of old Rome"[1]—and now, in Rome itself, robber and shepherd propensities, similar to those of its founder, were of advantage to its sole inhabitant. I spent the morning riding and shooting in the Campagna; I passed long hours in the various galleries; I gazed at each statue, and lost myself in a reverie before many a fair Madonna or beauteous nymph. I haunted the Vatican, and stood surrounded by marble forms of divine beauty. Each stone deity was possessed by sacred gladness and the eternal fruition of love. They looked on me with unsympathizing complacency, and often in wild accents I reproached them for their supreme indifference—for they were human shapes, the human form divine was manifest in each fairest limb and lineament. The perfect moulding brought with it the idea of colour and motion; often, half in bitter mockery, half in self-delusion, I clasped their icy proportions, and, coming between Cupid and his Psyche's lips,[2] pressed the unconceiving marble.

I endeavoured to read. I visited the libraries of Rome. I selected a volume, and, choosing some sequestered, shady nook on the banks of the Tiber, or opposite the fair temple in the Borghese Gardens, or under the old pyramid of Cestius,[3] I endeavoured to conceal me from myself, and immerse myself in the subject traced on the pages before me. As if in the same soil you plant nightshade and a myrtle tree, they will each appropriate the mould, moisture, and air administered, for the fostering their several properties—so did my grief find sustenance, and power of existence, and growth, in what else had been divine manna, to feed radiant meditation. Ah! while I streak this paper with the tale of what my so-named occupations were—while I shape the skeleton of my days—my hand trembles, my heart pants, and my brain refuses to lend expression, or phrase, or idea, by which to image forth the veil of unutterable woe that clothed these bare realities. O worn and beating heart, may I dissect thy fibres, and tell how in each unmitigable misery, sadness dire, repinings, and despair, existed? May I record my many ravings—the wild curses I hurled at torturing nature, and how I have passed days shut out from light and food, from all except the burning hell alive in my own bosom?

I was presented, meantime, with one other occupation, the one best fitted to discipline my melancholy thoughts, which strayed backwards, over many a ruin, and through many a flowery glade, even to the mountain recess from which in early youth I had first emerged.

During one of my rambles through the habitations of Rome, I found writing materials on a table in an author's study. Parts of a manuscript lay scattered about. It contained a learned disquisition on the Italian language; one page an unfinished dedication to posterity, for whose profit the writer had sifted and selected the niceties of this harmonious language—to whose everlasting benefit he bequeathed his labours.

I also will write a book, I cried—for whom to read?—to whom dedicated? And then with silly flourish (what so capricious and childish as despair?) I wrote,

DEDICATION
TO THE ILLUSTRIOUS DEAD.
SHADOWS, ARISE, AND READ YOUR FALL!
BEHOLD THE HISTORY OF THE
LAST MAN.

Yet, will not this world be re-peopled, and the children of a saved pair of lovers, in some to me unknown and unattainable seclusion, wandering to these prodigious relics of the ante-pestilential race, seek to learn how beings so wondrous in their achievements, with imaginations infinite, and powers godlike, had departed from their home to an unknown country?

I will write and leave in this most ancient city, this "world's sole monument,"[4] a record of these things. I will leave a monument of the existence of Verney, the Last Man. At first I thought only to speak of plague, of

---

[1] *as ... Rome* Romulus, the founder of Rome, and his brother Remus were said to have been reared by a she-wolf. Lionel quotes a statement made earlier by himself, in Chapter 1.

[2] *Cupid ... lips* Cupid, god of love, and his mortal lover, Psyche.

[3] *old ... Cestius* Tomb of Praetor Gaius Cestius Epulo (d. 12 BCE), next to which is the Protestant cemetery in which Percy Shelley was buried.

[4] *world's sole monument* From Edmund Spenser's *Ruins of Rome* (1591): "Rome living, was the world's sole ornament, / And dead, is now the world's sole monument" (lines 405–06).

death, and last, of desertion; but I lingered fondly on my early years, and recorded with sacred zeal the virtues of my companions. They have been with me during the fulfilment of my task. I have brought it to an end—I lift my eyes from my paper—again they are lost to me. Again I feel that I am alone.

A year has passed since I have been thus occupied. The seasons have made their wonted round, and decked this eternal city in a changeful robe of surpassing beauty. A year has passed; and I no longer *guess* at my state or my prospects—loneliness is my familiar, sorrow my inseparable companion. I have endeavoured to brave the storm—I have endeavoured to school myself to fortitude—I have sought to imbue myself with the lessons of wisdom. It will not do. My hair has become nearly grey—my voice, unused now to utter sound, comes strangely on my ears. My person, with its human powers and features, seem to me a monstrous excrescence of nature. How express in human language a woe human being until this hour never knew! How give intelligible expression to a pang none but I could ever understand!—No one has entered Rome. None will ever come. I smile bitterly at the delusion I have so long nourished, and still more when I reflect that I have exchanged it for another as delusive, as false, but to which I now cling with the same fond trust.

Winter has come again; and the gardens of Rome have lost their leaves—the sharp air comes over the Campagna, and has driven its brute inhabitants to take up their abode in the many dwellings of the deserted city. Frost has suspended the gushing fountains, and Trevi[1] has stilled her eternal music. I had made a rough calculation, aided by the stars, by which I endeavoured to ascertain the first day of the new year. In the old outworn age, the Sovereign Pontiff[2] was used to go in solemn pomp, and mark the renewal of the year by driving a nail in the gate of the temple of Janus.[3] On that day I ascended St. Peter's, and carved on its topmost stone the aera 2100, last year of the world!

My only companion was a dog, a shaggy fellow, half water- and half shepherd's-dog, whom I found tending sheep in the Campagna. His master was dead, but nevertheless he continued fulfilling his duties in expectation of his return. If a sheep strayed from the rest, he forced it to return to the flock, and sedulously kept off every intruder. Riding in the Campagna I had come upon his sheep-walk, and for some time observed his repetition of lessons learned from man, now useless, though unforgotten. His delight was excessive when he saw me. He sprung up to my knees; he capered round and round, wagging his tail, with the short, quick bark of pleasure: he left his fold to follow me, and from that day has never neglected to watch by and attend on me, showing boisterous gratitude whenever I caressed or talked to him. His pattering steps and mine alone were heard when we entered the magnificent extent of nave and aisle of St. Peter's.[4] We ascended the myriad steps together when on the summit I achieved my design, and in rough figures noted the date of the last year. I then turned to gaze on the country, and to take leave of Rome. I had long determined to quit it, and I now formed the plan I would adopt for my future career, after I had left this magnificent abode.

A solitary being is by instinct a wanderer, and that I would become. A hope of amelioration always attends on change of place, which would even lighten the burden of my life. I had been a fool to remain in Rome all this time: Rome noted for malaria, the famous caterer for death. But it was still possible, that, could I visit the whole extent of earth, I should find in some part of the wide extent a survivor. Methought the sea-side was the most probable retreat to be chosen by such a one. If left alone in an inland district, still they could not continue in the spot where their last hopes had been extinguished; they would journey on, like me, in search of a partner for their solitude, till the watery barrier stopped their further progress.

To that water—cause of my woes—perhaps now to be their cure I would betake myself. Farewell, Italy!—farewell, thou ornament of the world, matchless Rome, the retreat of the solitary one during long

---

[1] *Trevi* Fountain on the Quirinal Hill, built in 1762 by Nicola Salvi.

[2] *Sovereign Pontiff* I.e., the Pontifex Maximus, the Roman High Priest, a title later given to the pope.

[3] *Janus* Roman god of gates, of doorways, and of the new year.

[4] *nave* Main body of a church; *St. Peter's* Basilica of the Vatican.

months!—to civilized life—to the settled home and succession of monotonous days, farewell! Peril will now be mine; and I hail her as a friend— death will perpetually cross my path, and I will meet him as a benefactor; hardship, inclement weather, and dangerous tempests will be my sworn mates. Ye spirits of storm, receive me! ye powers of destruction, open wide your arms, and clasp me for ever! if a kinder power have not decreed another end, so that after long endurance I may reap my reward, and again feel my heart beat near the heart of another like to me.

Tiber, the road which is spread by nature's own hand, threading her continent, was at my feet, and many a boat was tethered to the banks. I would with a few books, provisions, and my dog, embark in one of these and float down the current of the stream into the sea; and then, keeping near land, I would coast the beauteous shores and sunny promontories of the blue Mediterranean, pass Naples, along Calabria,[1] and would dare the twin perils of Scylla and Charybdis;[2] then with fearless aim, (for what had I to lose?) skim ocean's surface towards Malta and the further Cyclades. I would avoid Constantinople, the sight of whose well-known towers and inlets belonged to another state of existence from my present one; I would coast Asia Minor, and Syria, and, passing the seven-mouthed Nile, steer northward again, till, losing sight of forgotten Carthage and deserted Lybia, I should reach the pillars of Hercules.[3] And then, no matter where—the oozy caves and soundless depths of ocean may be my dwelling before I accomplish this long-drawn voyage, or the arrow of disease find my heart as I float singly on the weltering Mediterranean; or, in some place I touch at, I may find what I seek—a companion; or, if this may not be, to endless time, decrepit and grey headed—youth already in the grave with those I love—the lone wanderer will still unfurl his sail, and clasp the tiller, and, still obeying the breezes of heaven, for ever round another and another promontory, anchoring in another and another bay, still ploughing seedless ocean, leaving behind the verdant land of native Europe, adown the tawny shore of Africa, having weathered the fierce seas of the Cape,[4] I may moor my worn skiff in a creek, shaded by spicy groves of the odorous islands of the far Indian ocean.

These are wild dreams. Yet since, now a week ago, they came on me, as I stood on the height of St. Peter's, they have ruled my imagination. I have chosen my boat, and laid in my scant stores. I have selected a few books; the principal are Homer and Shakespeare—but the libraries of the world are thrown open to me, and in any port I can renew my stock. I form no expectation of alteration for the better; but the monotonous present is intolerable to me. Neither hope nor joy are my pilots—restless despair and fierce desire of change lead me on. I long to grapple with danger, to be excited by fear, to have some task, however slight or voluntary, for each day's fulfilment. I shall witness all the variety of appearance that the elements can assume—I shall read fair augury in the rainbow, menace in the cloud, some lesson or record dear to my heart in everything. Thus around the shores of deserted earth, while the sun is high, and the moon waxes or wanes, angels, the spirits of the dead, and the ever-open eye of the Supreme, will behold the tiny bark, freighted with Verney—the LAST MAN.

THE END

—1826

---

[1] *Calabria* Region of southern Italy.

[2] *Scylla and Charybdis* From Greek mythology, a sea monster, later turned into rock cliffs, and a whirlpool, located in the Straits of Messina.

[3] *the pillars of Hercules* The Rock of Gibraltar and the Hill of Ceuta, two promontories flanking the eastern end to the Strait of Gibraltar, which were considered in ancient times to mark the ends of the earth.

[4] *Cape* Cape of Good Hope.

IN CONTEXT

The "Last Man" Theme in the Nineteenth Century

The theme of "the last man" was one that captured a great many imaginations in the 1820s and 1830s. Shelley's 1826 novel followed on the heels of Thomas Campbell's 1823 poem of the same name (to which, according to Campbell, Byron's poem "Darkness" owes its inspiration). Also in 1826 a number of magazine pieces were published on the same theme, including "The Last Man" (*Blackwood's*) and "The Death of the World" (*European Magazine*). That same year the painter John Martin, whose work often focused on apocalyptic visions, painted an initial study (now lost) of "The Last Man," a watercolor of which he completed in 1832, and an oil painting in 1849. The Campbell poem and the Martin painting are reproduced below; both envisage the end of the world occurring as a result of the sun's light being extinguished, rather than as a result of plague or other natural disaster.

Thomas Campbell, "The Last Man," *New Monthly Magazine* 8 (1823)

> All worldly shapes shall melt in gloom,
>   The Sun himself must die,
> Before this mortal shall assume
>   Its Immortality!
> 5   I saw a vision in my sleep,
> That gave my spirit strength to sweep
>   Adown the gulf of Time!
> I saw the last of human mould,
> That shall Creation's death behold,
> 10   As Adam saw her prime!
>
> The Sun's eye had a sickly glare,
>   The Earth with age was wan,
> The skeletons of nations were
>   Around that lonely man!
> 15   Some had expir'd in fight—the brands
> Still rusted in their bony hands;
>   In plague and famine some!
> Earth's cities had no sound nor tread;
> And ships were drifting with the dead
> 20   To shores where all was dumb!

Yet, prophet like, that lone one stood,
    With dauntless words and high,
That shook the sere° leaves from the wood   *withered*
    As if a storm pass'd by,
25   Saying, we are twins in death, proud Sun,
Thy face is cold, thy race is run,
    'Tis Mercy bids thee go.
For thou ten thousand thousand years
Hast seen the tide of human tears,
30   That shall no longer flow.

What though beneath thee man put forth
    His pomp, his pride, his skill;
And arts that made fire, flood, and earth,
    The vassals of his will—
35   Yet mourn I not thy parted sway,
Thou dim discrownèd king of day:
    For all those trophied arts
And triumphs that beneath thee sprang,
Heal'd not a passion or a pang
40   Entail'd on human hearts.

Go, let oblivion's curtain fall
    Upon the stage of men,
Nor with thy rising beams recall
    Life's tragedy again.
45   Its piteous pageants bring not back,
Nor waken flesh, upon the rack
    Of pain anew to writhe;
Stretch'd in disease's shapes abhorr'd,
Or mown in battle by the sword,
50   Like grass beneath the scythe.

Ev'n I am weary in yon skies
    To watch thy fading fire;
Test of all sumless agonies,
    Behold not me expire.
55   My lips that speak thy dirge of death—
Their rounded gasp and gurgling breath
    To see thou shalt not boast.
The eclipse of Nature spreads my pall—
The majesty of Darkness shall
60   Receive my parting ghost!

This spirit shall return to Him
   That gave its heavenly spark;
Yet think not, Sun, it shall be dim
   When thou thyself art dark!
65   No! it shall live again, and shine
In bliss unknown to beams of thine,
   By Him recall'd to breath,
Who captive led captivity,
Who robb'd the grave of Victory—
70   And took the sting from Death!

Go, Sun, while Mercy holds me up
   On Nature's awful waste
To drink this last and bitter cup
   Of grief that man shall taste—
75   Go, tell the night that hides thy face,
Thou saw'st the last of Adam's race,
   On Earth's sepulchral clod,
The dark'ning universe defy
To quench his Immortality,
80   Or shake his trust in God!

from Thomas Campbell's letter to the editor of the *Edinburgh Review*, 28 February 1825

… You say that my poem, "The Last Man," seems to have been suggested by Lord Byron's poem "Darkness." Now the truth is, that fifteen, or it may be more, years ago, I called on Lord Byron, who at that time had lodgings near St. James's Street; and we had a long, and to me a very memorable, conversation, from which I have not a doubt that his Lordship imbibed those few ideas in the poem "Darkness" which have any resemblance to mine in "The Last Man." I remember my saying to him that I thought the idea of a being witnessing the extinction of his species and of the Creation, and of his looking, under the fading eye of nature, at desolate cities, ships floating at sea with the dead, would make a striking subject for a poem. I met those very ideas, many years afterwards, when I read Lord Byron's poem "Darkness."

John Martin, *The Last Man* (1849).

IN CONTEXT

Shelley's Life and *The Last Man*

Many critical discussions of *The Last Man* touch on the connections between its images of waste and desolation and the extraordinary series of losses that Shelley herself suffered—including the deaths of three of her children, a life-threatening miscarriage, and the drowning of her husband in Italy in 1822. The selections from her letters reprinted below convey Shelley's impressions of Italy as well as of these tragic events, and highlight some of the connections between her own life and the plot of *The Last Man* (which Shelley began soon after returning to England in 1823). In her diary entry for 14 May 1824, she makes the connection between her own situation and that portrayed in the novel explicit: "The last man! Yes, I may well describe that solitary being's feelings, feeling myself as the last relic of a beloved race, my companions extinct before me."

Selected Letters

To THOMAS JEFFERSON HOGG[1]
13 Arabella Road, Pimlico
6 March 1815

My dearest Hogg my baby is dead[2]—will you come to me as soon as you can—I wish to see you—It was perfectly well when I went to bed—I awoke in the night to give it suck it appeared to be sleeping so quietly that I would not awake it—it was dead then but we did not find that out till morning— from its appearance it evidently died of convulsions—

Will you come—you are so calm a creature & Shelley is afraid of a fever from the milk—for I am no longer a mother now.

Mary

To THOMAS JEFFERSON HOGG
Windmill Inn, Salt Hill
25 April 1815

My Dear Jefferson

... Do you mean to come down to us—I suppose not, Prince Prudent; well, as you please, but remember I should be *very* happy to see you. If you had not been a lawyer you might have come with us.[3]

Rain has come after a mild beautiful day but Shelley & I are going to walk as it is only showery.

How delightful it is to read poetry among green shades. "Tintern Abbey"[4] thrilled me with delight—

But Shelley calls me to come for
The sun it is set
And night is coming

I will write perhaps by a night coach or at least early tomorrow—

I shall return soon & remain till then an affectionate but

Runaway Dormouse

To MARIA GISBORNE[5]
Este
2 November 1818

My Dear Mrs. Gisborne

I have not heard from you since we parted—but I hope that nothing has occasioned this, except your dislike of letter writing—Several events have occurred to us since then, and the principal one, the death of my little Clara—I wrote to tell you of her illness, and the dreadful state of weakness that succeeded to it—In this state she began to cut all her teeth at once—pined a few weeks, and died.

Soon after this, William[6] grew rather ill, and as we were now soon frightened, and there is no good doctor at Este, Shelley and I took him to Venice, where we stayed about a fortnight. It is a pleasant town to visit—its appearance is so new and strange—but the want of walks and variety must render it disagreeable for a continuous residence. The Hoppners find it so—they have lived between four and five years here, and are heartily sick of it. We liked almost everything—however I must here except three things, as the disagreements of

1 *THOMAS JEFFERSON HOGG*   Hogg (1792–1862) was a close friend of both Mary and Percy Shelley. He attended Oxford with Percy, and was introduced to Mary after the two had eloped.

2 *my baby is dead*   The name of this child, who was a few weeks old, and the cause of her death are unknown. Percy Shelley had recorded in his journal, however, that she was not expected to live.

3 *If you ... us*   Percy Shelley's grandfather had recently died, leaving his estate to his son and grandson, and Shelley was in the midst of negotiating an agreement with his father, in which he would sell his part of the estate in exchange for an annual income.

4 *Tintern Abbey*   1798 poem by William Wordsworth entitled "Lines Composed a Few Miles Above Tintern Abbey, On Revisiting the Banks of the Wye During a Tour. July 13, 1798."

5 *MARIA GISBORNE*   Friend of Mary Shelley's who had been visiting her at Bagni to Lucca and who had accompanied Shelley as far as Lucca when Shelley set out to join her sister, Claire Clairmont, and Percy at Este.

6 *William*   The Shelleys' son, who was two at the time.

the city—1st its inhabitants, 2nd its streets to walk in, 3rd its canals at low water. These are tolerable deductions, and yet there is enough to like without liking these. The inhabitants I dislike, because they are some of the worst specimens of Italians, and to you, who have lived so long in the country, and know their characteristics, this is saying everything. The streets I dislike because they are narrow and dirty, and above all because they carry zucche[1] about to sell, the sight of which always makes me sick, and I dislike the canals at low water, because they are never cleaned, and the horrid smell makes my head ache, and so now, I daresay, you will think me reasonable enough in all my dislikes—

Well; tomorrow, God permitting, we set out for Naples—but having been forced to delay our journey so long, we must give up the hope of seeing you until next June, when we think of coming north again. ...

Yours affectionately and
Sincerely,
M.W.S.

To Maria Gisborne
Naples
c. 3 December 1818

My Dear Mrs. Gisborne

I hasten to answer your kind letter as soon as we are a little recovered from the fatigue of our long journey, although I still feel wearied and overcome by it—so you must expect a very stupid letter. We set out from Este the day after I wrote to you—we remained one day at Ferrara & two at Bologna looking at the memorials preserved of Tasso and Ariosto[2] in the former town and at the most exquisite pictures in the latter. Afterwards we proceeded along the Coast Road by Rimini, Fano, Fossombrone, &c—We saw the divine (aqueduct) waterfall of Terni[3]—And arrived safely at Rome. We

performed this journey with our own horses, with Paolo[4] to drive us, which we found a very economical & a very disagreeable way so we shall not attempt it again—To you who have seen Rome I need not say how enchanted we were with the first view of Rome and its antiquities—one drawback they have at present, which I hope will be fully compensated for in the future—The ruins are filled with galley slaves at work—They are propping the Coliseum & making very deep excavations in the Forum.[5] We remained a week at Rome and our fears for the journey to Naples were entirely removed; they said there that there had not been a robbery on the road for 8 months—This we found afterwards to be an exaggeration, but it tranquillized us so much that Shelley went on first to secure us lodgings and we followed a day or two after—We found the road guarded, and the only part of the road where there was any talk of fear was between Terracina and Fondi, where it was not thought advisable that we should set out from the former place before daylight—Shelley travelled with a Lombard merchant & a Neapolitan priest—he remained only two nights on the road—and he went veterino,[6] so you may guess he had to travel early & late—The priest, a great strong muscular fellow, was almost in convulsions with fear to travel before daylight along the Pomptine Marshes—There was talk of two bishops murdered & that touched him nearly—The robbers spare foreigners but never Neapolitan men if they are young & strong, so he was the worst off of the party—the merchant did not feel very comfortable & they were both surprised at Shelley's quietness—That quiet was disturbed however between Capua & Naples by an assassination committed in broad daylight before their eyes—a young man ran out of a shop on the road followed by a woman armed with a great stick & a man

---

[1] *zucche* Gourds.

[2] *Tasso* Italian poet Torquato Tasso (1544–95); *Ariosto* Ludovico Ariosto, poet; author of *Orlando Furioso* (1474–1533).

[3] *aqueduct ... Terni* The Marmore Falls, located approximately four miles outside of Terni, is an artificial waterfall, constructed in 290 BCE by the Romans, who dug a canal from the stagnant Velino River to the

Marmore cliff. From the cliff the water falls 540 feet into the bed of the river Nera.

[4] *Paolo* Paolo Foggi, the Shelleys' Italian servant.

[5] *Coliseum* Great amphitheater completed in 80 CE and used for gladiatorial combat; *Forum* Public square and marketplace of ancient Rome.

[6] *veterino* Owner of a coach who could be contracted to drive passengers a certain distance and also to provide food and accommodation.

with a great knife—the man overtook him & stabbed him in the nape of the neck so that he fell down instantly stone dead—The fearful priest laughed heartily at Shelley's horror on the occasion— …

Use our little purse in paying for our letters & parcels—William is very well—S. & Claire send their kindest remembrances—Excuse this stupid scrawl.

Ever yours affectionately,

Mary W. Shelley

To Maria Gisborne

Rome
9 April 1819

My Dear Mrs. Gisborne,

You will have received Shelley's letter inviting you to Naples—but you will not come—I wish you would; but how many things do I wish as uselessly as I do this. We shall stay all the summer and perhaps the autumn somewhere on the shores of the bay—I am with child—and an eminent English surgeon will be there—that is one reason for going, for we have no faith in the Italians.

We are delighted with Rome, and nothing but the malaria would drive us from it for many months—It is very busy now with the funzioni[1] of the holy week, and the arrival of the Emperor of Austria,[2] who goes about to see these things preceded by an officer, who rudely pushes the people back with a drawn sword, a curious thing that a fellow, whose power only subsists through the supposed conveniences of the state of the complaisance of his subjects, should be thus insolent—Of course, we keep out of his track; for our English blood, would, I am afraid, boil over at such insolence.

The place is full of English, rich, noble—important and foolish. I am sick of it—I am sick of seeing the world in dumb show, and but that I am in Rome, in the city where stocks and stones defeat a million of times over my father's quoted maxim, "that a man is better

than a stock or a stone,"[3] who could see the Apollo, and a dandy spying at it, and not be of my opinion—Our little Will is delighted with the goats and the horses and the men rotti, and the ladies' white marble feet.

We saw the illuminated cross in St Peter's last night, which is very beautiful; but how much more beautiful is the Pantheon[4] by moonlight! As superior, in my opinion, as is the ancient temple to the modern church! I don't think much of S. Peter's after all—I cannot—it is so cut up—it is large—and not simple. …

Affectionately yours,

MWS

To Marianne Hunt[5]

Leghorn
29 June 1819

My dear Marianne

Although we have not heard from you or of you for some time I hope you are going on well—that you enjoy [y]our health and see your children lively about you—

You see by our hap[6] how blind we mortals are when we go seeking after what we think our good—We came to Italy thinking to do Shelley's health good—but the climate is not any means warm enough to be of benefit to him & yet it is that that has destroyed my two children[7]—We went from England comparatively prosperous & happy—I should return broken hearted & miserable—I never know one moment's ease from the wretchedness & despair that possesses me—May you my dear Marianne never know what it is to lose two

---

[1] *funzioni*   Italian: functions.

[2] *Emperor of Austria*   Francis I, Emperor of Austria from 1804 to 1835, and Holy Roman Emperor (as Francis II) from 1792 to 1806.

[3] *a stock or a stone*   Here, sacred images, such as statues of gods (like the Apollo).

[4] *St. Peter's*   St. Peter's Basilica, in the Vatican; *Pantheon*   Circular temple in Rome, constructed in 27 BCE in dedication to all the gods.

[5] *MARIANNE HUNT*   Wife of poet and essayist, Leigh Hunt. A close friend of Percy Shelley, Leigh Hunt was also co-owner of the weekly newspaper *The Examiner*.

[6] *hap*   Luck; chance.

[7] *my two children*   Clara Everina Shelley, born in September 1817, died in Venice in September 1818. William Shelley, born in January 1816, died in Rome on 7 June 1819.

only & lovely children in one year—to watch their dying moments—& then at last to be left childless & for ever miserable.

It is useless complaining & I shall therefore only write a short letter, for as all my thoughts are nothing but misery it is not kind to transmit them to you— Since Shelley wrote to Hunt we have taken a house in the neighbourhood of Leghorn; be so kind as to inform Peacock[1] of this—and that he must direct to us Ferma in Posta, Livorno, & to let us know whether he has sent any letter to Florence—I am very anxious to know whether or not I am to receive the clothes[2] I wrote to you about—for if we do not I must provide others and although that will be a great expense & trouble yet it would be better for me to know as soon as possible if anyone can or will send them— …

I am sorry to write to you all about these petty affairs, yet if I would write anything else about myself it would be a list of hours spent in tears and grief—Hunt used to call me serious what would he say to me now?—I feel that I am not fit for anything & therefore not fit to live, but how must that heart be moulded which would not be broken by what I have suffered—William was so good so beautiful so entirely attached to me—To the last moment almost he was in such abounding health & spirits—and his malady appeared of so slight a nature—and as arising simply from worms inspired no fear of danger that the blow was as sudden as it was terrible—Did you ever know a child with a fine colour—wonderful spirits—breeding worms (and those of the most innocent kind) that would kill him in a fortnight—we had a most excellent English surgeon to attend him and he allowed that these were the fruits of this hateful Italy—

But all this is all nothing to anyone but myself & I wish that I were incapable of feeling that or any other sorrow—Give my love to Hunt keep yourselves well and happy.

Yours—MW Shelley

---

1 *Peacock* Percy Shelley's friend Thomas Love Peacock.

2 *clothes* For the baby Mary Shelley was expecting in November.

To Maria Gisborne

Casa Magni, presso a Lerici
2 June 1822

My Dear Mrs. Gisborne

We received a letter from Mr. G.[3] the other day, which promised one from you—It is not yet come, and although I think that you are two or three in my debt, yet I am good enough to write to you again, and thus to increase your debit—nor will I allow you, with one letter, to take advantage of the Insolvent act,[4] and thus to free yourself from all claims at once. …

About a month ago Claire came to visit us at Pisa, and went, with the Williamses,[5] to find a house in the Gulf of Spezia; when, during her absence, the disastrous news came of the death of Allegra[6]—She died of a typhus fever, which had been raging in the Romagna;[7] but no one wrote to say it was there—she had no friends, except the nuns of the convent, who were kind to her, I believe, but you know Italians—If half of the convent had died of the plague, they would never have written to have had her removed, and so the poor child fell a sacrifice. Lord B—felt the loss, at first, bitterly—he also felt remorse, for he felt that he had acted against everybody's councils and wishes, and death had stamped with truth the many and often urged prophecies of Claire, that the air of the Romagna, joined to the ignorance of the Italians, would prove fatal to her. Shelley wished to conceal the fatal news from her, as long as possible, so when she returned from Spezia, he resolved to remove thither without delay—with so little delay, that he packed me off with Claire and Percy the very next day. She wished to return to Florence, but he persuaded her to accompany me—The next day, he packed up all our goods and chattels (for a furnished house was not to be found in this part of the world), and like a torrent, hurrying everything in its course, he

---

3 *Mr. G.* I.e., Mr. Gisborne.

4 *Insolvent act* I.e., for bankrupts.

5 *the Williamses* Edward and Jane Williams, both of whom had been close friends of the Shelleys for many years.

6 *Allegra* Daughter of Claire and Lord Byron, born in January 1817.

7 *the Romagna* Region in north-central Italy.

persuaded the W's to do the same. They came here—but one house was to be found for us all—It is beautifully situated on the seashore, under a woody hill. But such a place as this is! The poverty of the people is beyond anything—Yet, they do not appear unhappy, but go on in dirty content, or contented dirt, while we find it hard work to purvey, miles around for a few eatables—We were in wretched discomfort at first, but now we are in a kind of disorderly order, living from day to day as we can—After the first day or two, Claire insisted on returning to Florence—so S. was obliged to disclose the truth—You may judge of what was her first burst of grief, and despair—however she reconciled herself to her fate, sooner than we expected; and although, of course, until she forms new ties, she will always grieve, yet she is now tranquil—more tranquil than, when prophesying her disaster, she was forever forming plans for getting her child from a place she judged, but too truly, would be fatal to her. She has now returned to Florence, and I do not know whether she will join us again. …

I have not even heard of the arrival of my novel;[1] but I suppose, for his own sake, Papa will dispose of it to the best advantage—If you see it advertised, pray tell me—also its publisher, &c &c. We have heard from Hunt the day he was to sail, and anxiously and daily now await his arrival—S—will go over to Leghorn to him, and I also, if I can so manage it—We shall be at Pisa next winter, I believe—fate so decrees—Of course you have heard that the lawsuit went against my father. This was the summit and crown of our spring misfortunes—but he writes in so few words, and in such a manner, that any information that I could get, through anyone, would be a great benefit to me.

Adieu—Pray write now, and at length—remember both S. and I to Hogg—Did you get *Matilda*[2] from Papa?

Yours ever,

Mary W. Shelley

---

[1] *my novel* Shelley's novel *Valperga*, which William Godwin was publishing for his daughter. He withheld the book from publishers until February 1823, fearing that news of his financial problems (the result of a legal decision against him) would cause booksellers to offer less than its real value.

[2] *Matilda* I.e., *Mathilda*, novella by Shelley.

To Maria Gisborne

Pisa
15 August 1822

I said in a letter to Peacock, my dear Mrs. Gisborne, that I would send you some account of the last miserable months of my disastrous life. From day to day I have put this off, but I will now endeavour to fulfill my design. The scene of my existence is closed, & though there be no pleasure in retracing the scenes that have preceded the event which has crushed my hopes, yet there seems to be a necessity in doing so, and I obey the impulse that urges me. I wrote to you either at the end of May or the beginning of June. I described to you the place we were living in—Our desolate house, the beauty yet strangeness of the scenery and the delight Shelley took in all this—he never was in better health or spirits than during this time. I was not well in body or mind. My nerves were wound up to the utmost irritation, and the sense of misfortune hung over my spirits. No words can tell you how I hated our house & the country about it. Shelley reproached me for this—his health was good & the place was quite after his own heart—What could I answer—that the people were wild & hateful, that though the country was beautiful yet I liked a more countrified place, that there was great difficulty in living—that all our Tuscans would leave us, & that the very jargon of these Genovese was disgusting—This was all I had to say but no words could describe my feelings—the beauty of the woods made me weep & shudder—so vehement was my feeling of dislike that I used to rejoice when the winds & waves permitted me to go out in the boat so that I was not obliged to take my usual walk among tree shaded paths, alleys of vine festooned trees—all that before I doted on—& that now weighed on me. My only moments of peace were on board that unhappy boat, when lying down with my head on his knee I shut my eyes & felt the wind & our swift motion alone. My ill health might account for much of this—bathing in the sea somewhat relieved me—but on the 8th of June (I think it was) I was threatened with a miscarriage, & after a week of great ill health on Sunday the 16th this took place at eight in the morning. I was so ill that for seven hours I lay nearly lifeless—kept from fainting by brandy, vinegar, eau de cologne, &c—at length ice was brought to our solitude—it came before the doctor so Claire & Jane[1] were afraid of using it but Shelley overruled them & by an unsparing application of it I was restored. They all thought & so did I at one time that I was about to die—I hardly wish that I had, my own Shelley could never have lived without me, the sense of eternal misfortune would have pressed to heavily upon him, & what would have become of my poor babe? My convalescence was slow and during it a strange occurence happened to retard it. ... As I said Shelley was at first in perfect health, but having over-fatigued himself one day, & then the fright my illness gave him caused a return of nervous sensations & visions as bad as in his worst times. I think it was the Saturday after my illness, while yet unable to walk I was confined to my bed—in the middle of the night I was awoke by hearing him scream & come rushing into my room; I was sure that he was asleep & tried to waken him by calling on him, but he continued to scream which inspired me with such a panic that I jumped out of bed & ran across the hall to Mrs. W.'s room, where I fell through weakness, though I was so frightened that I got up again immediately—she let me in & Williams went to S. who had been wakened by my getting out of bed—he said that he had not been asleep & that it was a vision that he saw that had frightened him—But as he declared that he had not screamed it was certainly a dream & no waking vision—What had frightened him was this—He dreamt that lying as he did in bed Edward & Jane came into him, they were in the most horrible condition, their bodies lacerated—their bones starting through their skin, the faces pale yet stained with blood, they could hardly walk, but Edward was the weakest & Jane was supporting him—Edward said—"Get up, Shelley, the sea is flooding the house & it is all coming down." S. got up, he thought, & went to his window that looked on the terrace & the sea & thought he saw the sea rushing in. Suddenly his vision changed & he saw the figure of himself strangling me, that had made him rush into my room, yet fearful of frightening me he dared not

approach the bed, when my jumping out awoke him, or as he phrased it, caused his vision to vanish. ...

Well, we thought no more of these things & I slowly got better. Having heard from Hunt that he had sailed from Genoa, on Monday July 1st, S., Edward, & Captain Roberts (the gent. who built our boat) departed in our boat for Leghorn to receive him—I was then just better, had begun to crawl from my bedroom to the terrace; but bad spirits succeeded to ill health, and this departure of Shelley's seemed to add insufferably to my misery. I could not endure that he should go—I called him back two or three times, & told him that if I did not see him soon I would go to Pisa with the child—I cried bitterly when he went away. They went, & Jane, Claire, & I remained alone with the children—I could not walk out, & though I gradually gathered strength it was slowly & my ill spirits increased; in my letters to him I entreated him to return—"the feeling that some misfortune would happen," I said, "haunted me": I feared for the child, for the idea of danger connected with him never struck me—When Jane & Claire took their evening walk I used to patrol the terrace, oppressed with wretchedness, yet gazing on the most beautiful scene in the world. This Gulf of Spezia is subdivided into many small bays of which ours was far the most beautiful—the two horns of the bay (so to express myself) were wood-covered promontories crowned with castles—at the foot of these on the furthest was Lerici, on the nearest San Arenzo—Lerici being above a mile by land from us & San Arenzo about a hundred or two yards—trees covered the hills that enclosed this bay, & then beautiful groups were picturesquely contrasted with the rocks, the castle, and the town—the sea lay far extended in front while to the west we saw the promontory & islands which formed one of the extreme boundaries of the gulf—to see the sun set upon this scene, the stars shine & the moon rise was a sight of wondrous beauty, but to me it added only to my wretchedness—I repeated to myself all that another would have said to console me, & told myself the tale of love peace & competence which I enjoyed—but I answered myself by tears—did not my William die? & did I hold my Percy by a firmer tenure?—Yet I thought when he, when my Shelley returns I shall be happy—he will comfort me, if my boy be ill he will restore him & encourage me. I had a letter or two from Shelley mentioning the difficulties he had in establishing the Hunts, & that he was unable to fix the time of his return. Thus a week past. On Monday 8th Jane had a letter from Edward, dated Saturday; he said that he waited at Leghorn for S. who was at Pisa. That S.'s return was certain, "but" he continued, "if he should not come by Monday I will come in a felucca,[1] & you may expect me Tuesday evening at furthest." This was Monday, the fatal Monday, but with us it was stormy all day, & we did not at all suppose that they could put to sea. At twelve at night we had a thunderstorm; Tuesday it rained all day & was calm—the sky wept on their graves—on Wednesday the wind was fair from Leghorn & in the evening several feluccas arrived thence—one brought word that they had sailed Monday, but we did not believe them—Thursday was another day of fair wind & when twelve at night came & we did not see the tall sails of the little boat double the promontory before us we began to fear not the truth, but some illness—some disagreeable news for their detention. Jane got so uneasy that she determined to proceed the next day to Leghorn in a boat to see what was the matter—Friday came & with it a heavy sea & bad wind—Jane however resolved to be rowed to Leghorn (since no boat could sail) and busied herself in preparations—I wished her to wait for letters, since Friday was letter day—she would not—but the sea detained her, the swell rose so that no boat would venture out—At 12 at noon our letters came—there was one from Hunt to Shelley, it said—"pray write to tell us how you got home, for they say that you had bad weather after you sailed Monday & we are anxious"—the paper fell from me—I trembled all over—Jane read it—"Then it is all over!" she said. "No, my dear Jane," I cried, "it is not all over, but this suspense is dreadful—come with me, we will go to Leghorn, we will post to be swift & learn our fate." We crossed to Lerici, despair in our hearts; they raised our spirits there by telling us that no accident had been heard of & that it must have been known &c—but still our fear was great—& without resting we posted to Pisa.

It must have been fearful to see us—two poor, wild, aghast creatures—driving (like Matilda[2]) towards the sea to learn if we were to be for ever doomed to misery. I knew that Hunt was at Pisa at Lord Byron's house but I thought that L.B. was at Leghorn. … L.B. was in Pisa—Hunt was in bed, so I was to see L.B. instead of him—This was a great relief to me; I staggered upstairs—the Guiccioli[3] came to meet me smiling while I could hardly say—"Where is he—Sapete alcuna cosa di Shelley?"—They knew nothing—he had left Pisa on Sunday—on Monday he had sailed—there had been bad weather Monday afternoon—more they knew not. Both L.B. & the lady have told me since—that on that terrific evening I looked more like a ghost than a woman—light seemed to emanate from my features, my face was very white. I looked like marble—Alas. I had risen almost from a bed of sickness for this journey—I had travelled all day—it was now 12 at night—& we, refusing to rest, proceeded to Leghorn—not in despair—no, for then we must have died; but with sufficient hope to keep up the agitation of the spirits which was all my life. It was past two in the morning when we arrived—They took us to the wrong inn—neither Trelawny[4] or Capn. Roberts were there nor did we exactly know where they were so we were obliged to wait until daylight. We threw ourselves dressed on our beds & slept a little but at 6 o'clock we went to one or two inns to ask for one or the other of these gentlemen. We found Roberts at the Globe. He came down to us with a face which seemed to tell us that the worst was true, and here we learned all that had occurred during the week they had been absent from us, & under what circumstances they had departed on their return —Shelley had passed most of the time at Pisa—arranging the affairs of the Hunts—& screwing L.B.'s mind to

---

1 *felucca* Small Mediterranean vessel propelled by oars or sails.

2 *Matilda* I.e., Mathilda, the protagonist of Mary Shelley's novella of that name; in an attempt to prevent her father's suicide, she follows his rush "towards the sea."

3 *the Guiccioli* Count Alessandro Guiccioli and Countess Teresa Guiccioli, who was Byron's lover.

4 *Trelawny* Edward Trelawny, friend of the Shelleys and a former navy midshipman who lived in Pisa.

the sticking place about the journal.[1] He had found this a difficult task at first but at length he had succeeded to his heart's content with both points. Mrs. Mason said that she saw him in better health and spirits than she had ever known him, when he took leave of her Sunday July 7th. His face burnt by the sun, & his heart light that he had succeeded in rendering the Hunts tolerably comfortable. Edward had remained at Leghorn. On Monday July 8th during the morning they were employed in buying many things—eatables &c for our solitude. There had been a thunderstorm early but about noon the weather was fine & the wind right fair for Lerici—They were impatient to be gone. Roberts said, "Stay until tomorrow to see if the weather is settled; & S. might have stayed but Edward was in so great an anxiety to reach home—saying they would get there in seven hours with that wind—that they sailed! S. being in one of those extravagant fits of good spirits in which you have sometimes seen him. Roberts went out to the end of the mole[2] & watched them out of sight—they sailed at one & went off at the rate of about 7 knots—About three—Roberts, who was still on the mole—saw wind coming from the gulf—or rather what the Italians call a temporale—anxious to know how the boat would weather the storm, he got leave to go up the tower & with the glass discovered them about ten miles out at sea, off Via Reggio, they were taking in their topsails—"The haze of the storm," he said, "hid them from me & I saw them no more—when the storm cleared I looked again fancying that I should see them on their return to us—but there was no boat on the sea."—This then was all we knew, yet we did not despair—they might have been driven over to Corsica & not knowing the coast & gone god knows where. Reports favoured this belief—it was even said that they had been seen in the gulf—We resolved to return with all possible speed—We sent a courier to go from tower to tower along the coast to know if anything had been seen or found, & at 9 a.m. we quitted Leghorn—stopped but one moment at Pisa & proceeded towards Lerici. When at 2 miles from Via Reggio we rode down to that town to know if they knew anything—here our calamity first began to break on us—a little boat[3] & a water cask had been found five miles off— … We journeyed on and reached the Magra about ½ past ten p.m. I cannot describe to you what I felt in the first moment when, fording this river, I felt the water splash about our wheels—I was suffocated—I gasped for breath—I thought I should have gone into convulsions, & I struggled violently that Jane might not perceive it—looking down the river I saw two great lights burning at the *foce*—A voice from within me seemed to cry aloud that is his grace. After passing the river I gradually recovered. Arriving at Lerici we were obligated to cross our little bay in a boat—… we landed; nothing had been heard of them. This was Saturday July 13. & thus we waited until Thursday July 25th thrown about by hope & fear. We sent messengers along the coast towards Genoa & to Via Reggio—nothing had been found more than the *lancetta*; reports were brought us—we hoped—& yet to tell you all the agony we endured during those 12 days would be to make you conceive a universe of pain—each moment intolerable & giving place to one still worse. … On Thursday 25th Trelawny left us to go to Leghorn to see what was doing or what could be done. On Friday I was very ill but as evening came on I said to Jane—"If anything had been found on the coast Trelawny would have returned to let us know. He has not returned so I hope." About 7 o'clock p.m. he did return—all was over—all was quiet now, they had been found washed on shore—Well all this was to be endured.

Well what more have I to say? The next day we returned to Pisa. And here we are still—days pass away—one after another—& we live thus. We are all together—we shall quit Italy together. Jane must proceed to London—if letters do not alter my views I shall remain in Paris. Thus we live—Seeing the Hunts now & then. Poor Hunt has suffered terribly as you may guess. Lord Byron is very kind to me & comes with the Guiccioli to see me often.

---

[1] *the journal* Percy Shelley and Byron had agreed to start a liberal periodical, which would be owned by Shelley and Hunt, and to which Byron, Hunt, and Shelley would contribute.

[2] *mole* Pier.

[3] *a little boat* The small vessel (the "lancetta") of thin planks which had been constructed to allow the Shelleys to get from their boat (which drew four feet of water) to shore.

Today—this day—the sun shining in the sky—they are gone to the desolate sea coast to perform the last offices to their earthly remains. Hunt, L.B. & Trelawny. The quarantine laws would not permit us to remove them sooner—& now only on condition that we burn them to ashes. That I do not dislike—His rest shall be at Rome beside my child—where one day I also shall join them—"Adonais"[1] is not Keats's, it is his own elegy—he bids you there go to Rome. I have seen the spot where he now lies—the sticks that mark the spot where the sands cover him—he shall not be there it is too near Via Reggio—They are now about this fearful office—& I live! …

Well here is my story—the last story I shall have to tell—all that might have been bright in my life is now despoiled—I shall live to improve myself, to take care of my child, & render myself worthy to join him. Soon my weary pilgrimage will begin—I rest now—but soon I must leave Italy—& then—there is an end of all despair. Adieu I hope you are well & happy. I have an idea that while he was at Pisa that he received a letter from you that I have never seen—so not knowing where to direct I shall send this letter to Peacock—I shall send it open—he may be glad to read it—

Yours ever truly, Mary WS.—Pisa

I shall probably write to you soon again.

I have left out a material circumstance—A fishing boat saw them go down—It was about 4 in the afternoon—they saw the boy at mast head, when baffling winds struck the sails, they had looked away a moment & looking again the boat was gone—This is their story but there is little doubt that these men might have saved them, at least Edward who could swim. They could not they said get near her—but 3 quarters of an hour after passed over the spot where they had seen her—they protested no wreck of her was visible, but Roberts going on board their boat found several spars belonging to her—perhaps they let them perish to obtain these. Trelawny thinks he can get her up, since another fisherman thinks that he has found the spot where she lies, having drifted near shore. T. does this to

know perhaps the cause of her wreck—but I care little about it.

The Mortal Immortal

16th July 1833.—This is a memorable anniversary for me; on it I complete my three hundred and twenty-third year!

The Wandering Jew?—certainly not. More than eighteen centuries have passed over his head. In comparison with him, I am a very young Immortal.

Am I, then, immortal? This is a question which I have asked myself, by day and night, for now three hundred and three years, and yet cannot answer it. I detected a gray hair amidst my brown locks this very day—that surely signifies decay. Yet it may have remained concealed there for three hundred years—for some persons have become entirely white-headed before twenty years of age.

I will tell my story, and my reader shall judge for me. I will tell my story, and so contrive to pass some few hours of a long eternity, become so wearisome to me. For ever! Can it be? to live for ever! I have heard of enchantments, in which the victims were plunged into a deep sleep, to wake, after a hundred years, as fresh as ever: I have heard of the Seven Sleepers—thus to be immortal would not be so burthensome: but, oh! the weight of never-ending time—the tedious passage of the still-succeeding hours! How happy was the fabled Nourjahad![2]—But to my task.

All the world has heard of Cornelius Agrippa.[3] His memory is as immortal as his arts have made me. All the

---

[1] *Adonais* Percy Shelley's "Adonais: An Elegy on the Death of John Keats" (1821).

[2] *Nourjahad* A character in Frances Sheridan's *The History of Nourjahad* (1796). The "Oriental tale" tells of the young Persian sultan Schemzeddin's attempt to teach Nourjahad the vanity of his desires for boundless riches and endless life by tricking him into believing that he has achieved both, only to realize that his immortality is an illusion, the result of drugs and performance.

[3] *Cornelius Agrippa* German magician, theologian, astrologer, and writer on the occult who is perhaps best known as a practitioner of alchemy, the philosophy whose aim is the achievement of ultimate wisdom and immortality. In Shelley's *Frankenstein* (1818), Victor Frankenstein connects his misfortune to his early reading of Agrippa's work.

world has also heard of his scholar,[1] who, unawares, raised the foul fiend[2] during his master's absence, and was destroyed by him. The report, true or false, of this accident, was attended with many inconveniences to the renowned philosopher. All his scholars at once deserted him—his servants disappeared. He had no one near him to put coals on his ever-burning fires while he slept, or to attend to the changeful colours of his medicines while he studied. Experiment after experiment failed, because one pair of hands was insufficient to complete them: the dark spirits laughed at him for not being able to retain a single mortal in his service.

I was then very young—very poor—and very much in love. I had been for about a year the pupil of Cornelius, though I was absent when this accident took place. On my return, my friends implored me not to return to the alchymist's abode. I trembled as I listened to the dire tale they told; I required no second warning; and when Cornelius came and offered me a purse of gold if I would remain under his roof, I felt as if Satan himself tempted me. My teeth chattered—my hair stood on end—I ran off as fast as my trembling knees would permit.

My failing steps were directed whither for two years they had every evening been attracted,—a gently bubbling spring of pure living waters, beside which lingered a dark-haired girl, whose beaming eyes were fixed on the path I was accustomed each night to tread. I cannot remember the hour when I did not love Bertha; we had been neighbours and playmates from infancy—her parents, like mine, were of humble life, yet respectable—our attachment had been a source of pleasure to them. In an evil hour, a malignant fever carried off both her father and mother, and Bertha became an orphan. She would have found a home beneath my paternal roof, but, unfortunately, the old lady of the near castle, rich, childless, and solitary, declared her intention to adopt her. Henceforth Bertha was clad in silk—inhabited a marble palace—and was looked on as being highly favoured by fortune. But in her new situation among her new associates, Bertha remained true to the friend of her humbler days; she often visited the cottage of my father, and when forbidden to go thither, she would stray towards the neighbouring wood, and meet me beside its shady fountain.

She often declared that she owed no duty to her new protectress equal in sanctity to that which bound us. Yet still I was too poor to marry, and she grew weary of being tormented on my account. She had a haughty but an impatient spirit, and grew angry at the obstacles that prevented our union. We met now after an absence, and she had been sorely beset while I was away; she complained bitterly, and almost reproached me for being poor. I replied hastily,—"I am honest, if I am poor!—were I not, I might soon become rich!"

This exclamation produced a thousand questions. I feared to shock her by owning the truth, but she drew it from me; and then, casting a look of disdain on me, she said—"You pretend to love, and you fear to face the Devil for my sake!"

I protested that I had only dreaded to offend her;—while she dwelt on the magnitude of the reward that I should receive. Thus encouraged—shamed by her—led on by love and hope, laughing at my late fears, with quick steps and a light heart, I returned to accept the offers of the alchymist, and was instantly installed in my office.

A year passed away. I became possessed of no insignificant sum of money. Custom had banished my fears. In spite of the most painful vigilance, I had never detected the trace of a cloven foot; nor was the studious silence of our abode ever disturbed by demoniac howls. I still continued my stolen interviews with Bertha, and Hope dawned on me—Hope—but not perfect joy; for Bertha fancied that love and security were enemies, and her pleasure was to divide them in my bosom. Though true of heart, she was somewhat of a coquette in manner; and I was jealous as a Turk.[3] She slighted me in a thousand ways, yet would never acknowledge herself to be in the wrong. She would drive me mad with anger, and then force me to beg her pardon. Sometimes she

---

[1] *his scholar* Cf. Robert Southey's poem, "Cornelius Agrippa" (1798), which relates the story of the alchemist's disobedient apprentice.

[2] *foul fiend* The devil.

[3] *jealous as a Turk* The expression derives from the belief that Turkish men were more passionate than the English, and thus more prone to experiencing intense jealousy.

fancied that I was not sufficiently submissive, and then she had some story of a rival, favoured by her protectress. She was surrounded by silk-clad youths—the rich and gay. What chance had the sad-robed scholar of Cornelius compared with these?

On one occasion, the philosopher made such large demands upon my time, that I was unable to meet her as I was wont. He was engaged in some mighty work, and I was forced to remain, day and night, feeding his furnaces and watching his chemical preparations. Bertha waited for me in vain at the fountain. Her haughty spirit fired at this neglect; and when at last I stole out during the few short minutes allotted to me for slumber, and hoped to be consoled by her, she received me with disdain, dismissed me in scorn, and vowed that any man should possess her hand rather than he who could not be in two places at once for her sake. She would be revenged! And truly she was. In my dingy retreat I heard that she had been hunting, attended by Albert Hoffer. Albert Hoffer was favoured by her protectress, and the three passed in cavalcade[1] before my smoky window. Methought that they mentioned my name; it was followed by a laugh of derision, as her dark eyes glanced contemptuously towards my abode.

Jealousy, with all its venom, and all its misery, entered my breast. Now I shed a torrent of tears, to think that I should never call her mine; and, anon, I imprecated a thousand curses on her inconstancy. Yet, still I must stir the fires of the alchymist, still attend on the changes of his unintelligible medicines.

Cornelius had watched for three days and nights, nor closed his eyes. The progress of his alembics[2] was slower than he expected: in spite of his anxiety, sleep weighed upon his eyelids. Again and again he threw off drowsiness with more than human energy; again and again it stole away his senses. He eyed his crucibles wistfully. "Not ready yet," he murmured; "will another night pass before the work is accomplished? Winzy,[3] you are vigilant—you are faithful—you have slept, my boy—you slept last night. Look at that glass vessel. The liquid it contains is of a soft rose-colour: the moment it begins to change its hue, awaken me—till then I may close my eyes. First, it will turn white, and then emit golden flashes; but wait not till then; when the rose-colour fades, rouse me." I scarcely heard the last words, muttered, as they were, in sleep. Even then he did not quite yield to nature. "Winzy, my boy," he again said, "do not touch the vessel—do not put it to your lips; it is a philter[4]—a philter to cure love; you would not cease to love your Bertha—beware to drink!"

And he slept. His venerable head sunk on his breast, and I scarce heard his regular breathing. For a few minutes I watched the vessel—the rosy hue of the liquid remained unchanged. Then my thoughts wandered—they visited the fountain, and dwelt on a thousand charming scenes never to be renewed—never! Serpents and adders were in my heart as the word "Never!" half formed itself on my lips. False girl!—false and cruel! Never more would she smile on me as that evening she smiled on Albert. Worthless, detested woman! I would not remain unrevenged—she should see Albert expire at her feet—she should die beneath my vengeance. She had smiled in disdain and triumph—she knew my wretchedness and her power. Yet what power had she?—the power of exciting my hate—my utter scorn—my—oh, all but indifference! Could I attain that—could I regard her with careless eyes, transferring my rejected love to one fairer and more true, that were indeed a victory!

A bright flash darted before my eyes. I had forgotten the medicine of the adept; I gazed on it with wonder: flashes of admirable beauty, more bright than those which the diamond emits when the sun's rays are on it, glanced from the surface of the liquid; an odour the most fragrant and grateful stole over my sense; the vessel seemed one globe of living radiance, lovely to the eye, and most inviting to the taste. The first thought, instinctively inspired by the grosser sense, was, I will—I must drink. I raised the vessel to my lips. "It will cure me of love—of torture!" Already I had quaffed half of the most delicious liquor ever tasted by the palate of

---

[1] *cavalcade* I.e., riding on horseback.

[2] *alembics* Apparatus formerly used in distilling.

[3] *Winzy* According to the *OED*, a "winze" is "an imprecation, a curse." The name "Winzy" then may suggest the curse of immortality.

[4] *philter* Potion, drug, or charm supposed to be capable of exciting sexual attraction or love, especially toward a particular person; a love potion.

man, when the philosopher stirred. I started—I dropped the glass—the fluid flamed and glanced along the floor, while I felt Cornelius's gripe[1] at my throat, as he shrieked aloud, "Wretch! you have destroyed the labour of my life!"

The philosopher was totally unaware that I had drunk any portion of his drug. His idea was, and I gave a tacit assent to it, that I had raised the vessel from curiosity, and that, frighted at its brightness, and the flashes of intense light it gave forth, I had let it fall. I never undeceived him. The fire of the medicine was quenched—the fragrance died away—he grew calm, as a philosopher should under the heaviest trials, and dismissed me to rest.

I will not attempt to describe the sleep of glory and bliss which bathed my soul in paradise during the remaining hours of that memorable night. Words would be faint and shallow types of my enjoyment, or of the gladness that possessed my bosom when I woke. I trod air—my thoughts were in heaven. Earth appeared heaven, and my inheritance upon it was to be one trance of delight. "This it is to be cured of love," I thought; "I will see Bertha this day, and she will find her lover cold and regardless: too happy to be disdainful, yet how utterly indifferent to her!"

The hours danced away. The philosopher, secure that he had once succeeded, and believing that he might again, began to concoct the same medicine once more. He was shut up with his books and drugs, and I had a holiday. I dressed myself with care; I looked in an old but polished shield, which served me for a mirror; methought my good looks had wonderfully improved. I hurried beyond the precincts of the town, joy in my soul, the beauty of heaven and earth around me. I turned my steps towards the castle—I could look on its lofty turrets with lightness of heart, for I was cured of love. My Bertha saw me afar off, as I came up the avenue. I know not what sudden impulse animated her bosom, but at the sight, she sprung with a light fawn-like bound down the marble steps, and was hastening towards me. But I had been perceived by another person. The old high-born hag, who called herself her

protectress, and was her tyrant, had seen me, also; she hobbled, panting, up the terrace; a page, as ugly as herself, held up her train, and fanned her as she hurried along, and stopped my fair girl with a "How, now, my bold mistress? whither so fast? Back to your cage—hawks are abroad!"

Bertha clasped her hands—her eyes were still bent on my approaching figure. I saw the contest. How I abhorred the old crone who checked the kind impulses of my Bertha's softening heart. Hitherto, respect for her rank had caused me to avoid the lady of the castle; now I disdained such trivial considerations. I was cured of love, and lifted above all human fears; I hastened forwards, and soon reached the terrace. How lovely Bertha looked! her eyes flashing fire, her cheeks glowing with impatience and anger, she was a thousand times more graceful and charming than ever—I no longer loved—Oh no! I adored—worshipped—idolized her!

She had that morning been persecuted, with more than usual vehemence, to consent to an immediate marriage with my rival. She was reproached with the encouragement that she had shown him—she was threatened with being turned out of doors with disgrace and shame. Her proud spirit rose in arms at the threat; but when she remembered the scorn that she had heaped upon me, and how, perhaps, she had thus lost one whom she now regarded as her only friend, she wept with remorse and rage. At that moment I appeared. "O, Winzy!" she exclaimed, "take me to your mother's cot; swiftly let me leave the detested luxuries and wretchedness of this noble dwelling—take me to poverty and happiness."

I clasped her in my arms with transport. The old lady was speechless with fury, and broke forth into invective only when we were far on our road to my natal cottage. My mother received the fair fugitive, escaped from a gilt cage to nature and liberty, with tenderness and joy; my father, who loved her, welcomed her heartily; it was a day of rejoicing, which did not need the addition of the celestial potion of the alchymist to steep me in delight.

Soon after this eventful day, I became the husband of Bertha. I ceased to be the scholar of Cornelius, but I continued his friend. I always felt grateful to him for

---

[1] *gripe* I.c., grip.

having, unawares, procured me that delicious draught of a divine elixir, which, instead of curing me of love (sad cure! solitary and joyless remedy for evils which seem blessings to the memory), had inspired me with courage and resolution, thus winning for me an inestimable treasure in my Bertha.

I often called to mind that period of trance-like inebriation with wonder. The drink of Cornelius had not fulfilled the task for which he affirmed that it had been prepared, but its effects were more potent and blissful than words can express.

They had faded by degrees, yet they lingered long—and painted life in hues of splendour. Bertha often wondered at my lightness of heart and unaccustomed gaiety; for, before, I had been rather serious, or even sad, in my disposition. She loved me the better for my cheerful temper, and our days were winged by joy.

Five years afterwards I was suddenly summoned to the bedside of the dying Cornelius. He had sent for me in haste, conjuring my instant presence. I found him stretched on his pallet, enfeebled even to death; all of life that yet remained animated his piercing eyes, and they were fixed on a glass vessel, full of a roseate liquid.

"Behold," he said, in a broken and inward voice, "the vanity of human wishes! a second time my hopes are about to be crowned, a second time they are destroyed. Look at that liquor—you remember five years ago I had prepared the same, with the same success;—then, as now, my thirsting lips expected to taste the immortal elixir—you dashed it from me! and at present it is too late."

He spoke with difficulty, and fell back on his pillow. I could not help saying,—

"How, revered master, can a cure for love restore you to life?"

A faint smile gleamed across his face as I listened earnestly to his scarcely intelligible answer. "A cure for love and for all things—the Elixir of Immortality. Ah! if now I might drink, I should live for ever!"

As he spoke, a golden flash gleamed from the fluid; a well-remembered fragrance stole over the air; he raised himself, all weak as he was—strength seemed miraculously to re-enter his frame—he stretched forth his hand—a loud explosion startled me—a ray of fire shot up from the elixir, and the glass vessel which contained it was shivered[1] to atoms! I turned my eyes towards the philosopher; he had fallen back—his eyes were glassy—his features rigid—he was dead!

But I lived, and was to live for ever! So said the unfortunate alchymist, and for a few days I believed his words. I remembered the glorious drunkenness that had followed my stolen draught. I reflected on the change I had felt in my frame—in my soul. The bounding elasticity of the one—the buoyant lightness of the other. I surveyed myself in a mirror, and could perceive no change in my features during the space of the five years which had elapsed. I remembered the radiant hues and grateful scent of that delicious beverage—worthy the gift it was capable of bestowing—I was, then, IMMORTAL!

A few days after I laughed at my credulity. The old proverb, that "a prophet is least regarded in his own country," was true with respect to me and my defunct master. I loved him as a man—I respected him as a sage—but I derided the notion that he could command the powers of darkness, and laughed at the superstitious fears with which he was regarded by the vulgar. He was a wise philosopher, but had no acquaintance with any spirits but those clad in flesh and blood. His science was simply human; and human science, I soon persuaded myself, could never conquer nature's laws so far as to imprison the soul for ever within its carnal habitation. Cornelius had brewed a soul-refreshing drink—more inebriating than wine—sweeter and more fragrant than any fruit: it possessed probably strong medicinal powers, imparting gladness to the heart and vigour to the limbs; but its effects would wear out; already were they diminished in my frame. I was a lucky fellow to have quaffed health and joyous spirits, and perhaps long life, at my master's hands; but my good fortune ended there: longevity was far different from immortality.

I continued to entertain this belief for many years. Sometimes a thought stole across me—Was the alchymist indeed deceived? But my habitual credence was, that I should meet the fate of all the children of Adam at my appointed time—a little late, but still at a natural age. Yet it was certain that I retained a wonderfully

---

[1] *shivered* Broken, shattered.

youthful look. I was laughed at for my vanity in consulting the mirror so often, but I consulted it in vain—my brow was untrenched—my cheeks—my eyes—my whole person continued as untarnished as in my twentieth year.

I was troubled. I looked at the faded beauty of Bertha—I seemed more like her son. By degrees our neighbours began to make similar observations, and I found at last that I went by the name of the Scholar bewitched. Bertha herself grew uneasy. She became jealous and peevish, and at length she began to question me. We had no children; we were all in all to each other; and though, as she grew older, her vivacious spirit became a little allied to ill-temper, and her beauty sadly diminished, I cherished her in my heart as the mistress I had idolized, the wife I had sought and won with such perfect love.

At last our situation became intolerable: Bertha was fifty—I twenty years of age. I had, in very shame, in some measure adopted the habits of a more advanced age; I no longer mingled in the dance among the young and gay, but my heart bounded along with them while I restrained my feet; and a sorry figure I cut among the Nestors[1] of our village. But before the time I mention, things were altered—we were universally shunned; we were—at least, I was—reported to have kept up an iniquitous acquaintance with some of my former master's supposed friends. Poor Bertha was pitied, but deserted. I was regarded with horror and detestation.

What was to be done? we sat by our winter fire — poverty had made itself felt, for none would buy the produce of my farm; and often I had been forced to journey twenty miles, to some place where I was not known, to dispose of our property. It is true we had saved something for an evil day—that day was come.

We sat by our lone fireside—the old-hearted youth and his antiquated wife. Again Bertha insisted on knowing the truth; she recapitulated all she had ever heard said about me, and added her own observations. She conjured me to cast off the spell; she described how much more comely grey hairs were than my chestnut

locks; she descanted[2] on the reverence and respect due to age—how preferable to the slight regard paid to mere children: could I imagine that the despicable gifts of youth and good looks outweighed disgrace, hatred, and scorn? Nay, in the end I should be burnt as a dealer in the black art, while she, to whom I had not deigned to communicate any portion of my good fortune, might be stoned as my accomplice. At length she insinuated that I must share my secret with her, and bestow on her like benefits to those I myself enjoyed, or she would denounce me—and then she burst into tears.

Thus beset, methought it was the best way to tell the truth. I revealed it as tenderly as I could, and spoke only of a very long life, not of immortality—which representation, indeed, coincided best with my own ideas. When I ended, I rose and said—

"And now, my Bertha, will you denounce the lover of your youth?—You will not, I know. But it is too hard, my poor wife, that you should suffer from my ill-luck and the accursed arts of Cornelius. I will leave you—you have wealth enough, and friends will return in my absence. I will go; young as I seem, and strong as I am, I can work and gain my bread among strangers, unsuspected and unknown. I loved you in youth; God is my witness that I would not desert you in age, but that your safety and happiness require it."

I took my cap and moved towards the door; in a moment Bertha's arms were round my neck, and her lips were pressed to mine. "No, my husband, my Winzy," she said, "you shall not go alone—take me with you; we will remove from this place, and, as you say, among strangers we shall be unsuspected and safe. I am not so very old as quite to shame you, my Winzy; and I dare say the charm will soon wear off, and, with the blessing of God, you will become more elderly-looking, as is fitting; you shall not leave me."

I returned the good soul's embrace heartily. "I will not, my Bertha; but for your sake I had not thought of such a thing. I will be your true, faithful husband while you are spared to me, and do my duty by you to the last."

The next day we prepared secretly for our emigration. We were obliged to make great pecuniary sacrifices—it could not be helped. We realized a sum sufficient, at least, to maintain us while Bertha lived; and, without saying adieu to any one, quitted our native country to take refuge in a remote part of western France.

It was a cruel thing to transport poor Bertha from her native village, and the friends of her youth, to a new country, new language, new customs. The strange secret of my destiny rendered this removal immaterial to me; but I compassionated her deeply, and was glad to perceive that she found compensation for her misfortunes in a variety of little ridiculous circumstances. Away from all tell-tale chroniclers, she sought to decrease the apparent disparity of our ages by a thousand feminine arts—rouge, youthful dress, and assumed juvenility of manner. I could not be angry. Did not I myself wear a mask? Why quarrel with hers, because it was less successful? I grieved deeply when I remembered that this was my Bertha, whom I had loved so fondly, and won with such transport—the dark-eyed, dark-haired girl, with smiles of enchanting archness and a step like a fawn—this mincing, simpering, jealous old woman. I should have revered her grey locks and withered cheeks; but thus!—It was my work, I knew; but I did not the less deplore this type of human weakness.

Her jealousy never slept. Her chief occupation was to discover that, in spite of outward appearances, I was myself growing old. I verily believe that the poor soul loved me truly in her heart, but never had woman so tormenting a mode of displaying fondness. She would discern wrinkles in my face and decrepitude in my walk, while I bounded along in youthful vigour, the youngest looking of twenty youths. I never dared address another woman. On one occasion, fancying that the belle of the village regarded me with favouring eyes, she bought me a grey wig. Her constant discourse among her acquaintances was, that though I looked so young, there was ruin at work within my frame; and she affirmed that the worst symptom about me was my apparent health. My youth was a disease, she said, and I ought at all times to prepare, if not for a sudden and awful death, at least to awake some morning white-headed, and bowed down with all the marks of advanced years. I let her talk—I often joined in her conjectures. Her warnings chimed in with my never-ceasing speculations concerning my state, and I took an earnest, though painful, interest in listening to all that her quick wit and excited imagination could say on the subject.

Why dwell on these minute circumstances? We lived on for many long years. Bertha became bedrid and paralytic: I nursed her as mother might a child. She grew peevish, and still harped upon one string—of how long I should survive her. It has ever been a source of consolation to me, that I performed my duty scrupulously towards her. She had been mine in youth, she was mine in age, and at last, when I heaped the sod over her corpse, I wept to feel that I had lost all that really bound me to humanity.

Since then how many have been my cares and woes, how few and empty my enjoyments! I pause here in my history—I will pursue it no further. A sailor without rudder or compass, tossed on a stormy sea—a traveller lost on a wide-spread heath, without landmark or star to him—such have I been: more lost, more hopeless than either. A nearing ship, a gleam from some far cot, may save them; but I have no beacon except the hope of death.

Death! mysterious, ill-visaged friend of weak humanity! Why alone of all mortals have you cast me from your sheltering fold? Oh, for the peace of the grave! the deep silence of the iron-bound tomb! that thought would cease to work in my brain, and my heart beat no more with emotions varied only by new forms of sadness!

Am I immortal? I return to my first question. In the first place, is it not more probable that the beverage of the alchymist was fraught rather with longevity than eternal life? Such is my hope. And then be it remembered that I only drank half of the potion prepared by him. Was not the whole necessary to complete the charm? To have drained half the Elixir of Immortality is but to be half immortal—my For-ever is thus truncated and null.

But again, who shall number the years of the half of eternity? I often try to imagine by what rule the infinite may be divided. Sometimes I fancy age advancing upon me. One grey hair I have found. Fool! Do I lament? Yes, the fear of age and death often creeps coldly into my heart; and the more I live, the more I dread death, even while I abhor life. Such an enigma is man—born to perish—when he wars, as I do, against the established laws of his nature.

But for this anomaly of feeling surely I might die: the medicine of the alchymist would not be proof against fire—sword—and the strangling waters. I have gazed upon the blue depths of many a placid lake, and the tumultuous rushing of many a mighty river, and have said, peace inhabits those waters; yet I have turned my steps away, to live yet another day. I have asked myself, whether suicide would be a crime in one to whom thus only the portals of the other world could be opened. I have done all, except presenting myself as a soldier or duellist, an object of destruction to my—no, *not* my fellow-mortals, and therefore I have shrunk away. They are not my fellows. The inextinguishable power of life in my frame, and their ephemeral existence, place us wide as the poles asunder. I could not raise a hand against the meanest or the most powerful among them.

Thus I have lived on for many a year—alone, and weary of myself—desirous of death, yet never dying—a mortal immortal. Neither ambition nor avarice can enter my mind, and the ardent love that gnaws at my heart, never to be returned—never to find an equal on which to expend itself—lives there only to torment me.

This very day I conceived a design by which I may end all—without self-slaughter, without making another

man a Cain[1]—an expedition, which mortal frame can never survive, even endued with the youth and strength that inhabits mine. Thus I shall put my immortality to the test, and rest for ever—or return, the wonder and benefactor of the human species.[2]

Before I go, a miserable vanity has caused me to pen these pages. I would not die, and leave no name behind. Three centuries have passed since I quaffed the fatal beverage: another year shall not elapse before, encountering gigantic dangers—warring with the powers of frost in their home—beset by famine, toil, and tempest—I yield this body, too tenacious a cage for a soul which thirsts for freedom, to the destructive elements of air and water; or, if I survive, my name shall be recorded as one of the most famous among the sons of men; and, my task achieved, I shall adopt more resolute means, and, by scattering and annihilating the atoms that compose my frame, set at liberty the life imprisoned within, and so cruelly prevented from soaring from this dim earth to a sphere more congenial to its immortal essence.

—1833

---

[1] *Cain* The son of Adam and Eve, Cain committed the first murder, killing his brother Abel after God rejected his sacrifice but accepted that of his brother. Cain was condemned to wander the earth as punishment.

[2] *the wonder ... of the human species* Cf. *Frankenstein*. Winzy's statement echoes Robert Walton's plan to gain fame by exploring the North Pole.

LETITIA ELIZABETH LANDON
1802 – 1838

When Letitia Elizabeth Landon began publishing poetry she did so under her initials, L.E.L., and these "three magic letters" (as one admirer referred to them) soon attracted a reputation and a following all their own. Her melancholy verses described dark and passionate young heroines, usually forsaken by the ones they loved, and earned L.E.L. the epithet "the Byron of our poetesses"; like Byron she chose love and sorrow as her topics, and intimately detailed her characters' emotions. But the passivity and the distinctively feminine insights of her heroines as they observe the society around them—"cold spectators of a cold spectacle repeatedly masked in the warm colors of dissimulating love" (as Jerome McGann has memorably put it)—sets Landon's work apart from that of Byron or of any other poet of the time.

Readers constructed a romantic image of L.E.L. as a delicate, love-sick woman, but behind this highly idealized conception was an intelligent literary mind and a hard-working woman who knew how to please her audience. Landon was a great success as a professional writer; her work supported her family and enabled her brother to attend Oxford.

Letitia Elizabeth Landon was the daughter of John Landon and Catherine Bishop. Landon had little formal schooling, but her education was closely supervised by her older cousin, Elizabeth Landon. From an early age she began composing stories and verses that were highly influenced by the popular work of Sir Walter Scott. When the Landons moved from East Barnet to Old Brompton in 1815 one of their new neighbors was William Jerdan, editor of the new weekly journal *The Literary Gazette*. Jerdan, impressed with Landon's poetry, provided her with helpful advice and criticism and eventually published her poem "Rome" in the March 1818 issue of his journal. In the following months Landon (then only 18) published increasing amounts of verse in the *Gazette*, and in 1821 she released her first volume of poetry, *The Fate of Adelaide: A Swiss Tale of Romance*.

Amidst a favorable critical reception and increasing public attention, Landon followed her first verse collection with five others—*The Improvisatrice* (1824), *The Troubadour* (1825), *The Golden Violet* (1827), *The Venetian Bracelet* (1828), and *The Vow of the Peacock* (1835)—in each case signing herself L.E.L. Though the centerpieces of many of these collections were long poems, such as "The Improvisatrice" and "The Golden Violet" (each appearing in volumes of the same title), Landon's shorter works were also appreciated; soon the editors of nearly every gift book and annual anthology (two increasingly popular literary forms) sought L.E.L. as a regular contributor. Landon produced an almost unprecedented amount of poetry during these years. She was able to compose her poems quickly and she rarely revised or edited; her writing, as a result, has a distinctive style in which punctuation and grammar vary widely, and the organization of verses often emphasizes moods and moments of passion rather than narrative structure. But her eloquent plainness of diction and lyrical intensity convey a sense of emotions pouring unbidden and unobstructed onto the page, and this unique style was soon the height of fashion.

In addition to the poetry of L.E.L., Landon published under her own name a children's book called *Traits and Trials of Early Life* (1836) and three novels, *Romance and Reality* (1831), *Francesca Carrara* (1834), and *Ethel Churchill* (1837); the latter in particular established her as a gifted writer of romantic fiction. Writing anonymously, Landon also tackled other literary genres, including essays on the history of poetry and critical reviews. In fact, from the age of twenty Landon was the primary reviewer for *The Literary Gazette*, thus wielding an enormous amount of influence.

Landon was skilled at adapting her style to suit the demands of these various forms, but the place of a female writer in nineteenth-century London society was a precarious one, and much of the appeal of L.E.L.'s verses lay in the perceived authenticity of the dark and passionate emotions they expressed. As Landon became known, her gaiety and wit shocked and disillusioned former admirers of L.E.L. Public opinion gradually turned against Landon, and her detailed poetic examinations of female passion came to be seen as more indecorous than romantic. The literary community was further disconcerted when Landon was discovered to be Jerdan's reviewer; several male authors whose work she had criticized were particularly outraged.

Malicious gossip began to circulate concerning the nature of Landon's association with Jerdan and with several other young men, and her engagement to John Forster, editor of the *Daily News* and future biographer of Dickens, was broken off as a result. Though Landon had unconventional habits that fueled the gossip—including calling male friends by their first names and receiving them alone in private—she maintained, as she wrote to a friend, that the root of these allegations was "envy, malice, and all uncharitableness—these are the fruits of a successful literary career for a woman." No doubt there was some envy and uncharitableness, but recent scholarship has also established that there was some truth to the rumors. Landon, it turns out, had three illegitimate children by Jerdan.

Landon was eventually married in 1838 to George Maclean, governor of the British settlement at Cape Coast, West Africa. She sailed to Africa with him that July, planning to continue her writing career away from the merciless public scrutiny to which she had been subject. Landon arrived in Africa in August and died in October of an overdose of prussic acid. Such a sudden death, strange in any circumstances, was doubly mysterious when coupled with the already sensational rumors surrounding Landon's life. Suicide and murder have both been suggested, but the truth has never been uncovered. The coroner's report stated the cause of death as accidental overdose.

⌘ ⌘ ⌘

Lines Written under a Picture of a Girl Burning a Love Letter

The lines were filled with many a tender thing,
All the impassioned heart's fond communing.

I took the scroll: I could not brook
  An eye to gaze on it, save mine;
I could not bear another's look
  Should dwell upon one thought of thine.
5 My lamp was burning by my side,

I held thy letter to the flame,
  I marked the blaze swift o'er it glide,
It did not even spare thy name.
Soon the light from the embers past,
10 I felt so sad to see it die,
So bright at first, so dark at last,
  I feared it was love's history.
—1824

A Child Screening a Dove from a Hawk

By Stewardson[1]

Ay, screen thy favourite dove, fair child,
   Ay, screen it if you may,—
Yet I misdoubt° thy trembling hand   *doubt*
   Will scare the hawk away.

5 That dove will die, that child will weep—
   Is this their destiny?
Ever amid the sweets of life
   Some evil thing must be.

Ay, moralize—is it not thus
10   We've mourned our hope and love?
Alas! there's tears for every eye,
   A hawk for every dove!
—1825

Love's Last Lesson

"Teach it me, if you can,—forgetfulness![2]
  I surely shall forget, if you can bid me;
I who have worshipped thee, my god on earth,
I who have bowed me at thy lightest word.
5 Your last command, 'Forget me,' will it not
Sink deeply down within my inmost soul?
Forget thee!—ay, forgetfulness will be
A mercy to me. By the many nights
When I have wept for that I dared not sleep,
10 A dream had made me live my woes again,
Acting my wretchedness, without the hope
My foolish heart still clings to, though that hope
Is like the opiate which may lull a while,
Then wake to double torture; by the days
15 Passed in lone watching and in anxious fears,

---

[1] *By Stewardson* This poem was written in response to a painting by British artist Thomas Stewardson (1781–1859).

[2] *Teach … forgetfulness* One of the many echoes in this poem of Byron's *Manfred*. Cf. 1.1.135–36, in which Manfred is asked, "What wouldst thou with us, son of mortals, say?" to which he replies, "Forgetfulness."

When a breath sent the crimson to my cheek,
Like the red gushing of a sudden wound;
By all the careless looks and careless words
Which have to me been like the scorpion's stinging;
20 By happiness blighted, and by thee, forever;
By thy eternal work of wretchedness;
By all my withered feelings, ruined health,
Crushed hopes, and rifled heart, I will forget thee!
Alas! my words are vanity. Forget thee!
25 Thy work of wasting is too surely done.
The April shower may pass and be forgotten,
The rose fall and one fresh spring in its place,
And thus it may be with light summer love.
It was not thus with mine: it did not spring,
30 Like the bright colour on an evening cloud,
Into a moment's life, brief, beautiful;
Not amid lighted halls, when flatteries
Steal on the ear like dew upon the rose,
As soft, as soon dispersed, as quickly passed;
35 But you first called my woman's feelings forth,
And taught me love ere I had dreamed love's name.
I loved unconsciously, your name was all
That seemed in language, and to me the world
Was only made for you; in solitude,
40 When passions hold their interchange together,
Your image was the shadow of my thought;
Never did slave, before his Eastern lord,
Tremble as I did when I met your eye,
And yet each look was counted as a prize;
45 I laid your words up in my heart like pearls
Hid in the ocean's treasure-cave. At last
I learned my heart's deep secret: for I hoped,
I dreamed you loved me; wonder, fear, delight
Swept my heart like a storm; my soul, my life,
50 Seemed all too little for your happiness;
Had I been mistress of the starry worlds
That light the midnight, they had all been yours,
And I had deemed such boon but poverty.
As it was, I gave all I could—my love,
55 My deep, my true, my fervent, faithful love;
And now you bid me learn forgetfulness:
It is a lesson that I soon shall learn.
There is a home of quiet for the wretched,

A somewhat dark, and cold, and silent rest,
60 But still it is rest, for it is the grave."

    She flung aside the scroll, as it had part
In her great misery. Why should she write?
What could she write? Her woman's pride forbade
To let him look upon her heart and see
65 It was an utter ruin; and cold words,
And scorn and slight, that may repay his own,
Were as a foreign language, to whose sound
She might not frame her utterance. Down she bent
Her head upon an arm so white that tears
70 Seemed but the natural melting of its snow,
Touched by the flushed cheek's crimson; yet life-blood
Less wrings in shedding than such tears as those.

    And this then is love's ending! It is like
The history of some fair southern clime.
75 Hot fires are in the bosom of the earth,
And the warmed soil puts forth its thousand flowers,
Its fruits of gold, summer's regality,
And sleep and odours float upon the air.
At length the subterranean element
80 Breaks from its secret dwelling-place, and lays
All waste before it; the red lava stream
Sweeps like the pestilence, and that which was
A garden in its colours and its breath,
Fit for the princess of a fairy tale,
85 Is as a desert in whose burning sands,
And ashy waters, who is there can trace
A sign, a memory of its former beauty?
It is thus with the heart; love lights it up
With hopes like young companions, and with joys
90 Dreaming deliciously of their sweet selves.

    This is at first, but what is the result?
Hopes that lie mute in their own sullenness,
For they have quarrelled even with themselves;
And joys indeed like birds of Paradise:[1]
95 And in their stead despair coils scorpion-like,
Stinging itself; and the heart, burnt and crushed

With passion's earthquake, scorched and withered up,
Lies in its desolation,—this is love.

    What is the tale that I would tell? Not one
100 Of strange adventure, but a common tale
Of woman's wretchedness; one to be read
Daily in many a young and blighted heart.
The lady whom I spake of rose again
From the red fever's couch, to careless eyes
105 Perchance the same as she had ever been.
But oh, how altered to herself! She felt
That bird-like pining for some gentle home
To which affection might attach itself,
That weariness which hath but outward part
110 In what the world calls pleasure, and that chill
Which makes life taste the bitterness of death.

    And he she loved so well,—what opiate
Lulled consciousness into its selfish sleep?—
He said he loved her not; that never vow
115 Or passionate pleading won her soul for him;
And that he guessed not her deep tenderness.

    Are words, then, only false? are there no looks,
Mute but most eloquent; no gentle cares
That win so much upon the fair weak things
120 They seem to guard? And had he not long read
Her heart's hushed secret in the soft dark eye
Lighted at his approach, and on the cheek
Colouring all crimson at his lightest look?
This is the truth; his spirit wholly turned
125 To stern ambition's dream, to that fierce strife
Which leads to life's high places, and recked not
What lovely flowers might perish in his path.

    And here at length is somewhat of revenge:
For man's most golden dreams of pride and power
130 Are vain as any woman-dreams of love;
Both end in weary brow and withered heart,
And the grave closes over those whose hopes
Have lain there long before.
    —1827

---

[1] [Landon's note]   In Eastern tales, the bird of Paradise never rests on the earth.

Lines of Life

Orphan in my first years, I early learnt
To make my heart suffice itself, and seek
Support and sympathy in its own depths.

———

Well read my cheek and watch my eye—
    Too strictly schooled are they
One secret of my soul to show,
    One hidden thought betray.

5 I never knew the time my heart
    Looked freely from my brow;
It once was checked by timidness,
    'Tis taught by caution now.

I live among the cold, the false,
10   And I must seem like them;
And such I am, for I am false
    As those I most condemn.

I teach my lip its sweetest smile,
    My tongue its softest tone;
15 I borrow others' likeness, till
    Almost I lose my own.

I pass through flattery's gilded sieve,
    Whatever I would say;
In social life, all, like the blind,
20   Must learn to feel their way.

I check my thoughts like curbed steeds
    That struggle with the rein;
I bid my feelings sleep, like wrecks
    In the unfathomed main.

25 I hear them speak of love, the deep,
    The true, and mock the name;
Mock at all high and early truth,
    And I too do the same.

I hear them tell some touching tale,
30   I swallow down the tear;

I hear them name some generous deed,
    And I have learnt to sneer.

I hear the spiritual, the kind,
    The pure, but named in mirth;
35 Till all of good, ay, even hope,
    Seems exiled from our earth.

And one fear, withering ridicule,
    Is all that I can dread;
A sword hung by a single hair
40   Forever o'er the head.

We bow to a most servile faith
    In a most servile fear,
While none among us dares to say
    What none will choose to hear.

45 And if we dream of loftier thoughts,
    In weakness they are gone;
And indolence and vanity
    Rivet our fetters on.

Surely I was not born for this!
50   I feel a loftier mood
Of generous impulse, high resolve,
    Steal o'er my solitude!

I gaze upon the thousand stars
    That fill the midnight sky;
55 And wish, so passionately wish,
    A light like theirs on high.

I have such eagerness of hope
    To benefit my kind,
And feel as if immortal power
60   Were given to my mind.

I think on that eternal fame,
    The sun of earthly gloom,
Which makes the gloriousness of death,
    The future of the tomb—

65   That earthly future, the faint sign
  Of a more heavenly one;
A step, a word, a voice, a look—
  Alas! my dream is done.

And earth, and earth's debasing stain,
70   Again is on my soul;
And I am but a nameless part
  Of a most worthless whole.

Why write I this? Because my heart
  Towards the future springs,
75   That future where it loves to soar
  On more than eagle wings.

The present, it is but a speck
  In that eternal time,
In which my lost hopes find a home,
80   My spirit knows its clime.

Oh! not myself, for what am I?
  The worthless and the weak,
Whose every thought of self should raise
  A blush to burn my cheek.

85   But song has touched my lips with fire,
  And made my heart a shrine;
For what, although alloyed,[1] debased
  Is in itself divine.

I am myself but a vile link
90   Amid life's weary chain;
And I have spoken hallowed words,
  O do not say in vain!

My first, my last, my only wish—
  Say, will my charmed chords
95   Wake to the morning light of fame,
  And breathe again my words?

Will the young maiden, when her tears
  Alone in moonlight shine

(Tears for the absent and the loved),
100   Murmur some song of mine?

Will the pale youth by his dim lamp,
  Himself a dying flame,
From many an antique scroll beside,
  Choose that which bears my name?

105   Let music make less terrible
  The silence of the dead;
I care not, so my spirit last
  Long after life has fled.
 —1828

Revenge

Ay, gaze upon her rose-wreathed hair,
  And gaze upon her smile;
Seem as you drank the very air
  Her breath perfumed the while;

5   And wake for her the gifted line,
  That wild and witching lay,
And swear your heart is as a shrine,
  That only holds her sway.

'Tis well: I am revenged at last,
10   Mark you that scornful cheek—
The eye averted as you passed
  Spoke more than words could speak.

Ay, now by all the bitter tears
  That I have shed for thee,
15   The racking doubts, the burning fears,
  Avenged they well may be—

By the nights passed in sleepless care,
  The days of endless woe;
All that you taught my heart to bear,
20   All that yourself will know.

I would not wish to see you laid
  Within an early tomb;

---

[1]   *alloyed*   Mixed with a base metal.

I should forget how you betrayed,
    And only weep your doom:

25 But this is fitting punishment,
    To live and love in vain—
O my wrung heart, be thou content,
    And feed upon his pain.

Go thou and watch her lightest sigh,
30   Thine own it will not be;
And bask beneath her sunny eye,
    It will not turn on thee.

'Tis well: the rack, the chain, the wheel,
    Far better had'st thou proved;
35 Even I could almost pity feel,
    For thou art not beloved.
    —1828

The Little Shroud

She put him on a snow-white shroud,
    A chaplet° on his head;   *garland*
And gathered early primroses
    To scatter o'er the dead.

5 She laid him in his little grave—
    'Twas hard to lay him there,
When spring was putting forth its flowers,
    And every thing was fair.

She had lost many children—now
10   The last of them was gone;
And day and night she sat and wept
    Beside the funeral stone.

One midnight, while her constant tears
    Were falling with the dew,
15 She heard a voice, and lo! her child
    Stood by her, weeping too!

His shroud was damp, his face was white;
    He said, "I cannot sleep,
Your tears have made my shroud so wet;
20   Oh, mother, do not weep!"

Oh, love is strong! the mother's heart
    Was filled with tender fears;
Oh, love is strong! and for her child
    Her grief restrained its tears.

25 One eve a light shone round her bed,
    And there she saw him stand—
Her infant, in his little shroud,
    A taper° in his hand.   *candle*

"Lo! mother, see my shroud is dry,
30   And I can sleep once more!"
And beautiful the parting smile
    The little infant wore.

And down within the silent grave
    He laid his weary head;
35 And soon the early violets
    Grew o'er his grassy bed.
    —1832

Corinne at the Cape of Misena[1]

How much of mind is in this little scroll,
Whereon the artist's skill has bodied forth
The shapes which genius dreamed!—The quiet sea
Sleeps in the distance, with that happy sleep
5 Which, in the human world, but childhood knows—
Childhood, whose hope is present! Pale with light,
For colour has departed with the sun,
The moon has risen in the faint grey sky,
Bearing a clear young beauty on her brow,
10 Which has been turned to earth too short a while
To wear its shadow. With a darker hue
Than when the sun is on their shining leaves
The myrtles spread their branches to the night,
Whose dews are falling. By the moonlight touched
15 With silvery softness and with gentle shade,
The fair city seems as if repose
And sleep alone were in its quiet walls.
Silence was made for such a night, or song,
And song has just been floating o'er the waves;
20 The lute is yet within its mistress' hand,
Though now the music from its chords is gone
To wander o'er the waters, and to perish:
Ay, perished long the music of those chords,
They had but life from sweetness, so they died.
25 Not so the words!—for, even as the wind,
That wafts the seeds which afterwards spring up

In a perpetual growth, and then subsides,
The song was only minister to words
Which have the immortality of pain.

30 A lady leans upon that silent lute,
With large dark eyes, like the eternal night,
So spiritual and so melancholy—
The exquisite Corinne!

There is a power
Given to some minds to fashion and create,
35 Until the being present on the page
Is actual as our life's vitality!
Such was Corinne—and such the mind that gave
Its own existence to its work. Corinne
Is but another name for her who wrote,
40 Who felt, and poured her spirit on her lay.° *poem, or song*
What are the feelings but her own? The hope
Which in the bleak world finds no resting-place,
And, like the dove, returns unsatisfied,
But bringing no green leaf, it seeks its ark[2]
45 With wearied wing, and plumes whose gloss is gone.
Here, too, is traced that love which hath too much
Of heaven in its fine nature for the earth—
Where love pines for a home and finds a grave;
The eagerness which turns to lassitude;
50 The thirst of praise which ends in bitterness;
Those high aspirings which but rise to find
What weight is on their wings; and that keen sense
Of the wide difference between ourselves
And those who are our fellows; and which marks
55 A withered ring around all confidence:
We cannot soothe the pain we do not know.

The heart is sacrificed upon the shrine
Of mental power—at least its happiness.
A whole life's bitterness is in the song
60 Whose words, too truly, are the singer's own.
—1832

[1] *Corinne at the Cape of Misena* Landon, like many poets of her era, wrote several poems reimagining Corinne, the heroine of the French writer Anne Louise Germaine de Staël's novel *Corinne, or Italy* (1807). Germaine de Staël's Corinne is a young half-English, half-Italian poet who becomes famous. She struggles with the conflict between her desire for independence and artistic success—associated with the Italian portion of her background—and the expectations of her lover, Oswald, who is unable to accept her refusal to conform with English gender roles. After Oswald rejects Corinne and marries her more conventional, fully English half-sister, Corinne dies in Italy of a broken heart. The following poem focuses on a scene from Book 13, Chapter 4 of the novel, in which Corinne performs for a gathering at Cape Miseno in Naples, Italy. The performance takes place the night before Corinne plans to tell Oswald a secret that she correctly suspects will lead him to forsake her: that she fled her English family to live independently in Italy under an assumed name. "Corinne at the Cape of Misena" was initially published with an engraving of François Gérard's portrait of Madame de Staël dressed and posing as Corinne (see color insert); the poem's first two stanzas make reference to the image.

[2] *the dove … its ark* In Genesis 8.8–12, part of the story of Noah's ark, Noah periodically sends a dove out of the ark as the flood waters are receding. The first time, the dove finds "no rest for the sole of her foot" and returns with nothing; the second time, it returns with a leaf in its mouth.

Fragment of Corinne's Song at Naples[1]

"Thus, shrinking from the desert spread around,
 Doth Genius wander through the world,
 and finds
No likeness to himself—no echo given
By Nature: and the common crowd but hold
5 As madness that desire of the rapt soul
Which finds not in this world enough of air,
Of high enthusiasm, or of hope!
For Destiny compels exalted minds;
The poet whose imagination draws
10 Its power from loving and from suffering,
They are the banished of another sphere:
For the Almighty goodness might not frame
All for a few—th' elect or the proscribed.
Why spoke the ancients with such awe of Fate?
15 What had this terrible Fate to do with them,
The common and the quiet, who pursue
The seasons, and do follow timidly
The beaten track of ordinary life?
But she, the priestess of the oracle,
20 Shook with the presence of a cruel power.
I know not what the Involuntary force
That plunges Genius into misery.
Genius doth catch that music of the spheres[2]
Which mortal ear was never meant to know;
25 Genius can penetrate the mysteries
Of feeling all unknown to other hearts;—
A Power hath entered in his inmost soul,
Whose presence he may not contain."[3]

Such were the words of one who felt those words
30 With all the truth of sorrow. In this world,
Grief and life go together; 'neath the tent,
The palace, and the cottage, woe is heard,
Speaking with suffering's universal voice.
But of the many who at night are glad
35 To lay their common burden down and rest,
Surely the mind endowed with gifts from heaven
Must be most glad, for it foresees its home,
And saith, in its rejoicing orison,°   *prayer*
Thank God, thank God, there is a grave; and hope
40 That looks beyond to heaven!
—1832

---

[1] *Corinne's Song at Naples* I.e., the song Corinne performs at Cape Miseno in de Staël's novel.

[2] *music of the spheres* Music said to be made by the planets, audible only to angels.

[3] [Landon's note] The part marked as quotation is translated literally from Corinne's song. Its only merit is its exactness, for I have scarcely permitted myself to alter a word. This brief passage is chosen as having less reference to the story than other parts equally beautiful. There occurs, soon afterwards, one of those almost startling remarks which give such peculiarity of thoughtfulness to Madame de Staël's writings. Corinne says, "Perhaps it is what we shall do tomorrow that will decide our fate; perhaps even yesterday have we said some word that nothing can recall." I know not what may be the effect on others, but I could never read this short, but true, remark without a feeling of terror.—L.E.L.

François Gérard, *Corinne au Cap Misène*, 1819. The subject of this painting is a scene from Germaine de Staël's novel *Corinne, ou l'Italie* (1807). The novel focuses on a love affair between Corinne, a successful poet, and her lover, Oswald; he eventually rejects her and she dies of a broken heart. The painting draws on Book 13, Chapter 4, in which Corinne pauses in the midst of a performance:

> All her assembled hearers threw laurels and myrtle at her feet. The soft pure moonlight fell on her brow, and the breeze wantoned with her ringlets as if nature delighted to adorn her: she was so overpowered as she looked on the enchanting scene, and on Oswald, who shared this delicious eve with her, yet might not be thus near forever, that tears flowed from her eyes. Even the crowd, who had just applauded her so tumultuously, respected her emotion, and mutely awaited her words, which they trusted would make them participators in her feelings. …

Gérard's painting is also a posthumous portrait of de Staël, whose features are used in the depiction of Corinne.

READING POETRY

WHAT IS A POEM?

Most of us know what a poem is when we see one. Still, even poets find it difficult to define a poem, or poetry. In a lecture on "The Name and Nature of Poetry" (1933), the English poet A.E. Housman stated that he could "no more define poetry than a terrier can define a rat"; however, he added, "we both recognize the object by the symptoms which it provokes in us." Housman knew he was in the presence of poetry if he experienced a shiver down the spine, or "a constriction of the throat and a precipitation of water to the eyes." Implicit in Housman's response is a recognition that we have to go beyond mere formal characteristics—stanzas, rhymes, rhythms—if we want to know what poetry is, or why it differs from prose. Poetry both represents and *creates* emotions in a highly condensed way. Therefore, any definition of the genre needs to consider, as much as possible, the impact of poetry on us as readers or listeners.

Worth consideration too is the role of the listener or reader not only as passive recipient of a poem, but also as an active participant in its performance. Poetry is among other things the locus for a communicative exchange. A section below deals with the sub-genre of performance poetry, but in a very real sense all poetry is subject to performance. Poems are to be read aloud as well as on the page, and both in sensing meaning and in expressing sound the reader plays a vital role in bringing a poem to life, no matter how long dead its author may be; as W.H. Auden wrote memorably of his fellow poet W.B. Yeats, "the words of a dead man / Are modified in the guts of the living."

For some readers, poetry is, in William Wordsworth's phrase, "the breath and finer spirit of all knowledge" ("Preface" to the *Lyrical Ballads*). They look to poetry for insights into the nature of human experience, and expect elevated thought in carefully wrought language. In contrast, other readers distrust poetry that seems moralistic or didactic. "We hate poetry that has a palpable design upon us," wrote John Keats to his friend J.H. Reynolds; rather, poetry should be "great & unobtrusive, a thing which enters into one's soul, and does not startle it or amaze it with itself but with its subject." The American poet Archibald MacLeish took Keats's idea a step further: in his poem "Ars Poetica" he suggested that "A poem should not mean / But be." MacLeish was not suggesting that a poem should lack meaning, but rather that meaning should inhere in the poem's expressive and sensuous qualities, not in some explicit statement or versified idea.

Whatever we look for in a poem, the infinitude of forms, styles, and subjects that make up the body of literature we call "poetry" is, in the end, impossible to capture in a definition that would satisfy all readers. All we can do, perhaps, is to agree that a poem is a discourse that is characterized by a heightened attention to language, form, and rhythm, by an expressiveness that works through figurative rather than literal modes, and by a capacity to stimulate our imagination and arouse our feelings.

THE LANGUAGE OF POETRY

To speak of "the language of poetry" implies that poets make use of a vocabulary that is somehow different from the language of everyday life. In fact, all language has the capacity to be "poetic," if by poetry we understand a use of language to which some special importance is attached. The ritualistic utterances of religious ceremonies sometimes have this force; so do the skipping rhymes of children in the schoolyard. We can distinguish such uses of language from the kind of writing we find in, say, a computer user's manual: the author of the manual can describe a given function in a variety of ways, whereas the magic of the skipping rhyme can be invoked only by getting the right words in the right order. So with the poet: he or she chooses particular words in a particular order; the *way* the poet speaks is as important to our understanding as what is said. This doesn't mean that an instruction manual couldn't have poetic qualities—indeed, modern poets have created "found" poems from even less likely materials—but it does mean that in poetry there is an intimate relation amongst language, form, and meaning, and that the writer deliberately structures and manipulates language to achieve very particular ends.

THE BEST WORDS IN THE BEST ORDER

Wordsworth provides us with a useful example of the way that poetry can invest quite ordinary words with a high emotional charge:

> No motion has she now, no force,
> She neither hears nor sees;
> Rolled round in earth's diurnal course
> With rocks, and stones, and trees.

To paraphrase the content of this stanza from "A Slumber Did My Spirit Seal," "she" is dead and buried. But the language and structures used here give this prosaic idea great impact. For example, the regular iambic meter of the two last lines conveys something of the inexorable motion of the earth and of Lucy embedded in it; the monosyllabic last line is a grim reminder of her oneness with objects in nature; the repeated negatives in the first two lines drive home the irreparable destructiveness of death; the alliteration in the third and fourth lines gives a tangible suggestion of roundness, circularity, repetition in terms of the earth's shape and motion, suggesting a cycle in which death is perhaps followed by renewal. Even the unusual word "diurnal" (which would not have seemed so unusual to Wordsworth's readers) seems "right" in this context; it lends more weight to the notion of the earth's perpetual movement than its mundane synonym "daily" (which, besides, would not scan here). It is difficult to imagine a change of any kind to these lines; they exemplify another attempted definition of poetry, this time by Wordsworth's friend Samuel Taylor Coleridge: "the best words in the best order" (*Table Talk*, 1827).

POETIC DICTION AND THE ELEVATED STYLE

Wordsworth's diction in the "Lucy" poem cited above is a model of clarity; he has chosen language that, in its simplicity and bluntness, conveys the strength of the speaker's feelings far more strongly than an elaborate description of grief in more conventionally "poetic" language might have done. Wordsworth, disturbed by what he felt was a deadness and artificiality in the poetry of his day, sought to "choose incidents and situations from common life" and to describe them in "a selection of language really used by men" ("Preface" to *Lyrical Ballads*). His plan might seem an implicit reproach of the "raised" style, the elevated diction of epic poetry we associate with John Milton's *Paradise Lost*:

> Anon out of the earth a fabric huge
> Rose like an exhalation, with the sound
> Of dulcet symphonies and voices sweet,
> Built like a temple, where pilasters round
> Were set, and Doric pillars overlaid
> With golden architrave; nor did there want
> Cornice or frieze, with bossy sculptures graven;
> The roof was fretted gold.
>
> (*Paradise Lost* I.710–17)

At first glance this passage, with its Latinate vocabulary and convoluted syntax, might seem guilty of inflated language and pretentiousness. However, Milton's description of the devils' palace in Hell deliberately seeks to distance us from its subject in order to emphasize the scale and sublimity of the spectacle, far removed from ordinary human experience. In other words, language and style in *Paradise Lost* are well adapted to suit a particular purpose, just as they are in "A Slumber Did My Spirit Seal," though on a wholly different scale. Wordsworth criticized the poetry of his day, not because of its elevation, but because the raised style was too often out of touch with its subject; in his view, the words did not bear any significant relation to the "truths" they were attempting to depict.

"PLAIN" LANGUAGE IN POETRY

Since Wordsworth's time, writers have been conscious of a need to narrow the apparent gap between "poetic" language and the language of everyday life. In much of the poetry of the past century, especially free verse, we can observe a growing approximation to speech—even to conversation—in the diction and rhythms of poetry. This may have something to do with the changed role of the poet, who today has discarded the mantle of teacher or prophet that was assumed by poets of earlier times, and who is ready to admit all fields of experience and endeavor as appropriate for poetry. The modern poet looks squarely at life, and can often find a provoking beauty in even the meanest of objects.

We should not assume, however, that a greater concern with the "ordinary," with simplicity, naturalness, and clarity, means a reduction in complexity or suggestiveness. A piece such as Stevie Smith's "Mother, Among the Dustbins," for all the casual and playful domesticity of some of its lines, skillfully evokes a range of emotions and sense impressions defying simple paraphrase.

IMAGERY, SYMBOLISM, AND FIGURES OF SPEECH

The language of poetry is grounded in the objects and phenomena that create sensory impressions. Sometimes the poet renders these impressions quite literally, in a series of *images* that seek to recreate a scene in the reader's mind:

> Only a man harrowing clods
> In a slow silent walk
> With an old horse that stumbles and nods
> Half asleep as they stalk.

> Only thin smoke without flame
> From the heaps of couch-grass;
> Yet this will go onward the same
> Though Dynasties pass.
>
> Yonder a maid and her wight
> Come whispering by:
> War's annals will cloud into night
> Ere their story die.
>
>   (Thomas Hardy, "In Time of 'The Breaking of Nations'")

Here, the objects of everyday life are re-created with sensory details designed to evoke in us the sensations or responses felt by the speaker viewing the scene. At the same time, the writer invests the objects with such significance that the poem's meaning extends beyond the literal to the symbolic: that is, the images come to stand for something much larger than the objects they represent. Hardy's poem moves from the presentation of stark images of rural life to a sense of their timelessness. By the last stanza we see the ploughman, the burning grass, and the maid and her companion as symbols of recurring human actions and motives that defy the struggles and conflicts of history.

IMAGISM

The juxtaposition of clear, forceful images is associated particularly with the Imagist movement that flourished at the beginning of the twentieth century. Its chief representatives (in their early work) were the American poets H.D. and Ezra Pound, who defined an image as "that which represents an intellectual and emotional complex in an instant of time." Pound's two-line poem "In a Station of the Metro" provides a good example of the Imagists' goal of representing emotions or impressions through the use of concentrated images:

> The apparition of these faces in the crowd,
> Petals on a wet, black bough.

As in a Japanese *haiku*, a form that strongly influenced the Imagists, the poem uses sharp, clear, concrete details to evoke both a sensory impression and the emotion or the atmosphere of the scene. Though the Imagist movement itself lasted only a short time (from about 1912 to 1917), it had a far-reaching influence on modern poets such as T.S. Eliot and William Carlos Williams.

FIGURES OF SPEECH

Imagery often works together with figurative expression to extend and deepen the meaning or impact of a poem. "Figurative" language means language that is metaphorical, not literal or referential. Through "figures of speech" such as metaphor and simile, metonymy, synecdoche, and personification, the writer may alter the ordinary, denotative meanings of words in order to convey greater force and vividness to ideas or impressions, often by showing likenesses between unlike things.

With *simile*, the poet makes an explicit comparison between the subject (called the *tenor*) and another object or idea (known as the *vehicle*), using "as" or "like":

> It is a beauteous evening, calm and free,
> The holy time is quiet as a Nun
> Breathless with adoration. …

In this opening to a sonnet, Wordsworth uses a visual image of a nun in devout prayer to convey in concrete terms the less tangible idea of evening as a "holy time." The comparison also introduces an emotional dimension, conveying something of the feeling that the scene induces in the poet. The simile can thus illuminate and expand meaning in a compact way. The poet may also extend the simile to elaborate at length on any points of likeness.

In *metaphor*, the comparison between tenor and vehicle is implied: connectives such as "like" are omitted, and a kind of identity is created between the subject and the term with which it is being compared. Thus in John Donne's "The Good-Morrow," a lover asserts the endless joy that he and his beloved find in each other:

> My face in thine eye, thine in mine appears,
> And true plain hearts do in the faces rest;
> Where can we find two better hemispheres,
> Without sharp north, without declining west?

Here the lovers are transformed into "hemispheres," each of them a half of the world not subject to the usual natural phenomena of wintry cold ("sharp north") or the coming of night ("declining west"). Thus, they form a perfect world in balance, in which the normal processes of decay or decline have been arrested. Donne renders the abstract idea of a love that defies change in pictorial and physical terms, making it more real and accessible to us. The images here are all the more arresting for the degree of concentration involved; it is not merely the absence of "like" or "as" that gives the metaphor such direct power, but the fusion of distinct images and emotions into a new idea.

Personification is the figure of speech in which the writer endows abstract ideas, inanimate objects, or animals with human characteristics. In other words, it is a type of implied metaphorical comparison in which aspects of a non-human subject are compared to the feelings, appearance, or actions of a human being. In the second stanza of his ode "To Autumn," Keats personifies the concept of autumnal harvesting in the form of a woman, "sitting careless on a granary floor, / Thy hair soft-lifted by the winnowing wind." Personification may also help to create a mood, as when Thomas Gray attributes human feelings to a hooting owl in "Elegy Written in a Country Churchyard"; using such words as "moping" and "complain," Gray invests the bird's cries with the quality of human melancholy:

> … from yonder ivy-mantled tow'r
> The moping owl does to the moon complain
> Of such, as wand'ring near her secret bow'r,
> Molest her ancient solitary reign.

In his book *Modern Painters* (1856), the English critic John Ruskin criticized such attribution of human feelings to objects in nature. Calling this device the "pathetic fallacy," he objected to what he saw as an irrational distortion of reality, producing "a falseness in all our impressions of external things." Modern criticism, with a distrust of any notions of an objective "reality," tends to use Ruskin's term as a neutral label simply to describe instances of extended personification of natural objects.

Apostrophe, which is closely related to personification, has the speaker directly addressing a non-human object or idea as if it were a sentient human listener. Blake's "The Sick Rose," Shelley's "Ode to the West Wind," and his ode "To a Skylark" all employ apostrophe, personifying the object addressed. Keats's "Ode on a Grecian Urn" begins by apostrophizing the urn ("Thou still unravish'd bride of quietness"), then addresses it in a series of questions and reflections through which the speaker attempts to unravel the urn's mysteries.

Apostrophe also appeals to or addresses a person who is absent or dead. W.H. Auden's lament "In Memory of W.B. Yeats" apostrophizes both the earth in which Yeats is to be buried ("Earth, receive an honoured guest") and the dead poet himself ("Follow, poet, follow right / To the bottom of the night …"). Religious prayers offer an illustration of the usefulness of apostrophe, since they are direct appeals from an earth-bound supplicant to an invisible god. The suggestion of strong emotion associated with such appeals is a common feature of apostrophe in poetry also, especially poetry with a religious theme, like Donne's "Holy Sonnets" (e.g., "Batter My Heart, Three-Personed God").

Metonymy and *synecdoche* are two closely related figures of speech that further illustrate the power of metaphorical language to convey meaning more intensely and vividly than is possible with prosaic statement. *Metonymy* (from the Greek, meaning "change of name") involves referring to an object or concept by substituting the name of another object or concept with which it is usually associated: for example, we might speak of "the Crown" when we mean the monarch, or describe the US executive branch as "the White House." When the writer uses only part of something to signify the whole, or an individual to represent a class, we have an instance of *synecdoche*: T.S. Eliot provides an example in "The Love Song of J. Alfred Prufrock" when a crab is described as "a pair of ragged claws." Similarly, synecdoche is present in Milton's contemptous term "blind mouths" to describe the "corrupted clergy" he attacks in "Lycidas."

Dylan Thomas employs both metonymy and synecdoche in his poem "The Hand That Signed the Paper":

The hand that signed the paper felled a city;
Five sovereign fingers taxed the breath,
Doubled the globe of dead and halved a country;
These five kings did a king to death.

The mighty hand leads to a sloping shoulder,
The finger joints are cramped with chalk;
A goose's quill has put an end to murder
That put an end to talk.

The hand that signed the treaty bred a fever,
And famine grew, and locusts came;

> Great is the hand that holds dominion over
> Man by a scribbled name.
>
> The five kings count the dead but do not soften
> The crusted wound nor stroke the brow;
> A hand rules pity as a hand rules heaven;
> Hands have no tears to flow.

The "hand" of the poem is evidently a synecdoche for a great king who enters into treaties with friends and foes to wage wars, conquer kingdoms, and extend his personal power—all at the expense of his suffering subjects. The "goose quill" of the second stanza is a metonymy, standing for the pen used to sign the treaty or the death warrant that brings the war to an end.

Thomas's poem is an excellent example of the power of figurative language, which, by its vividness and concentrated force, can add layers of meaning to a poem, make abstract ideas concrete, and intensify the poem's emotional impact.

THE POEM AS PERFORMANCE: WRITER AND PERSON

Poetry is always dramatic. Sometimes the drama is explicit, as in Robert Browning's monologues, in which we hear the voice of a participant in a dialogue; in "My Last Duchess" we are present as the Duke reflects on the portrait of his late wife for the benefit of a visitor who has come to negotiate on behalf of the woman who is to become the Duke's next wife. Or we listen with amusement and pity as the dying Bishop addresses his venal and unsympathetic sons and tries to bargain with them for a fine burial ("The Bishop Orders His Tomb at St. Praxed's"). In such poems, the notion of a speaking voice is paramount: the speaker is a personage in a play, and the poem a means of conveying plot and character.

Sometimes the drama is less apparent, and takes the form of a plea, or a compliment, or an argument addressed to a silent listener. In Donne's "The Flea" we can infer from the poem the situation that has called it forth: a lover's advances are being rejected by his beloved, and his poem is an argument intended to overcome her reluctance by means of wit and logic. We can see a similar example in Marvell's "To His Coy Mistress": here the very shape of the poem, its three-paragraph structure, corresponds to the stages of the speaker's argument as he presents an apparently irrefutable line of reasoning. Much love poetry has this kind of background as its inspiration; the yearnings or lamentations of the lover are part of an imagined scene, not merely versified reflections about an abstraction called "love."

Meditative or reflective poetry can be dramatic too. Donne's "Holy Sonnets" are pleas from a tormented soul struggling to find its god; Tennyson's "In Memoriam" follows the agonized workings of a mind tracing a path from grief and anger to acceptance and renewed hope.

We should never assume that the speaker, the "I" of the poem, is simply a voice for the writer's own views. The speaker in W.H. Auden's "To an Unknown Citizen," presenting a summary of the dead citizen's life, appears to be an official spokesperson for the society which the citizen served ("Our report on his union"; "Our researchers …" etc.). The speaker's words are laudatory, yet we perceive immediately that Auden's own views of this society are anything but approving. The speaker seems satisfied with the highly regimented nature of his society, one in which every aspect of the individual's life is under scrutiny and subject to correction. The only things necessary to the happiness of the

"Modern Man," it seems, are "A phonograph, a radio, a car, and a frigidaire." The tone here is subtly ironic, an irony created by the gap between the imagined speaker's perception and the real feelings of the writer.

PERFORMANCE POETRY

Poetry began as an oral art, passed on in the form of chants, myths, ballads, and legends recited to an audience of listeners rather than readers. Even today, the dramatic qualities of a poem may extend beyond written text. "Performance poets" combine poetry and stagecraft in presenting their work to live audiences. Dramatic uses of voice, rhythm, body movement, music, and sometimes other visual effects make the "text" of the poem multi-dimensional. For example, Edith Sitwell's poem-sequence *Façade* (1922) was originally set to music: Sitwell read from behind a screen, while a live orchestra played. This performance was designed to enhance the verbal and rhythmic qualities of her poetry:

> Beneath the flat and paper sky
> The sun, a demon's eye
> Glowed through the air, that mask of glass;
> All wand'ring sounds that pass
>
> Seemed out of tune, as if the light
> Were fiddle-strings pulled tight.
> The market-square with spire and bell
> Clanged out the hour in Hell.

By performing their poetry, writers can also convey cultural values and traditions. The cultural aspect of performance is central to Black poetry, which originates in a highly oral tradition of folklore and storytelling. From its roots in Africa, this oral tradition has been manifested in the songs and stories of slaves, in spirituals, in the jazz rhythms of the Twenties and the Thirties and in the rebelliousness of reggae and of rap. Even when it remains "on the page," much Black poetry written in the oral tradition has a compelling rhythmic quality. The lines below from Linton Kwesi Johnson's "Mi Revalueshanary Fren," for example, blur the line between spoken poetry and song. Johnson often performs his "dub poetry" against reggae musical backings.

> yes, people powa jus a showa evry howa
> an evrybady claim dem democratic
> but some a wolf an some a sheep
> an dat is problematic

The chorus of Johnson's poems, with its constant repetitions, digs deeply into the roots of African song and chant. Its performance qualities become clearer when the poem is read aloud:

> I Husak
> e ad to go
> Honnicka
> e ad to go

Chowcheskhu
e ad to go
Just like apartied
will av to go

To perform a poem is one way to see and hear poetry as multi-dimensional, cultural, historical, and often also political. Performance is also another way to discover how poetic "meaning" can be constructed in the dynamic relation between speaker and listener.

TONE: THE SPEAKER'S ATTITUDE

In understanding poetry, it is helpful to imagine a poem as having a "voice." The voice may be close to the poet's own, or that of an imagined character, a *persona* adopted by the poet. The tone of the voice will reveal the speaker's attitude to the subject, thus helping to shape our understanding and response. In speech we can indicate our feelings by raising or lowering our voices, and we can accompany words with physical actions. In writing, we must try to convey the tonal inflections of the speaking voice through devices of language and rhythm, through imagery and figures of speech, and through allusions and contrasts.

THE IRONIC TONE

Housman's poem "Terence, This Is Stupid Stuff" offers a useful example of ways in which manipulating tone can reinforce meaning. When Housman, presenting himself in the poem as "Terence," imagines himself to be criticized for writing gloomy poems, his response to his critics takes the form of an ironic alternative: perhaps they should stick to drinking ale:

Oh, many a peer of England brews
Livelier liquor than the Muse,
And malt does more than Milton can
To justify God's ways to man.

The tone here is one of heavy scorn. The speaker is impatient with those who refuse to look at the realities of life and death, and who prefer to take refuge in simple-minded pleasure. The ludicrous comparisons, first between the brewers who have been made peers of England and the classical Muse of poetry, then between malt and Milton, create a sense of disproportion and ironic tension; the explicit allusion to *Paradise Lost* ("To justify God's ways to man") helps to drive home the poet's bitter recognition that his auditors are part of that fallen world depicted by Milton, yet unable or unwilling to acknowledge their harsh condition. The three couplets that follow offer a series of contrasts: in each case, the first line sets up a pleasant expectation and the second dashes it with a blunt reminder of reality:

Ale, man, ale's the stuff to drink
For fellows whom it hurts to think:
Look into the pewter pot

> To see the world as the world's not.
> And faith, 'tis pleasant till 'tis past:
> The mischief is that 'twill not last.

These are all jabs at the "sterling lads" who would prefer to lie in "lovely muck" and not think about the way the world is. Housman's sardonic advice is all the more pointed for its sharp and ironic tone.

POETIC FORMS

In poetry, language is intimately related to form, which is the structuring of words within identifiable patterns. In prose we speak of phrases, sentences, and paragraphs; in poetry, we identify structures by lines, stanzas, or complete forms such as the sonnet or the ode (though poetry in complete or blank verse has paragraphs of variable length, not formal stanzas: see below).

Rightly handled, the form enhances expression and meaning, just as a frame can define and enhance a painting or photograph. Unlike the photo frame, however, form in poetry is an integral part of the whole work. At one end of the scale, the term "form" may describe the *epic*, the lengthy narrative governed by such conventions as division into books, a lofty style, and the interplay between human and supernatural characters. At the other end lies the *epigram*, a witty and pointed saying whose distinguishing characteristic is its brevity, as in Alexander Pope's famous couplet,

> I am his Highness' dog at Kew;
> Pray tell me sir, whose dog are you?

Between the epic and the epigram lie many other poetic forms, such as the sonnet, the ballad, or the ode. "Form" may also describe stanzaic patterns like *couplets* and *quatrains*.

"FIXED FORM" POEMS

The best-known poetic form is probably the sonnet, the fourteen-line poem inherited from Italy (the word itself is from the Italian *sonetto*, little song or sound). Within those fourteen lines, whether the poet chooses the "Petrarchan" rhyme scheme or the "English" form (see below in the section on "Rhyme"), the challenge is to develop an idea or situation that must find its statement and its resolution within the strict confines of the sonnet frame. Typically, there is an initial idea, description, or statement of feeling, followed by a "turn" in the thought that takes the reader by surprise, or that casts the situation in an unexpected light. Thus in Sonnet 130, "My Mistress' Eyes Are Nothing Like the Sun," William Shakespeare spends the first three quatrains apparently disparaging his lover in a series of unfavorable comparisons—"If snow be white, why then her breasts are dun"—but in the closing couplet his point becomes clear:

> And yet, by heaven, I think my love as rare
> As any she belied with false compare.

In other words, the speaker's disparaging comparisons have really been parodies of sentimental clichés which falsify reality; his mistress has no need of the exaggerations or distortions of conventional love poetry.

Other foreign forms borrowed and adapted by English-language poets include the *ghazal* and the *pantoum*. The *ghazal*, strongly associated with classical Urdu literature, originated in Persia and Arabia and was brought to the Indian subcontinent in the twelfth century. It consists of a series of couplets held together by a refrain, a simple rhyme scheme (a/a, b/a, c/a, d/a…), and a common rhythm, but only loosely related in theme or subject. Some English-language practitioners of the form have captured the epigrammatic quality of the ghazal, but most do not adhere to the strict pattern of the classical form.

The *pantoum*, based on a Malaysian form, was imported into English poetry via the work of nineteenth-century French poets. Typically it presents a series of quatrains rhyming *abab*, linked by a pattern of repetition in which the second and fourth lines of a quatrain become the first and third lines of the stanza that follows. In the poem's final stanza, the pattern is reversed: the second line repeats the third line of the first stanza, and the last line repeats the poem's opening line, thus creating the effect of a loop.

Similar to the pantoum in the circularity of its structure is the *villanelle*, originally a French form, with five *tercets* and a concluding *quatrain* held together by only two rhymes (aba, aba, aba, aba, aba, abaa) and by a refrain that repeats the first line at lines 6, 12, and 18, while the third line of the first tercet reappears as lines 9, 15, and 19. With its interlocking rhymes and elaborate repetitions, the villanelle can create a variety of tonal effects, ranging from lighthearted parody to the sonorous and earnest exhortation of Dylan Thomas's "Do Not Go Gentle into That Good Night."

STANZAIC FORMS

Recurring formal groupings of lines within a poem are usually described as "stanzas." Both the recurring and the formal aspects of stanzaic forms are important; it is a common misconception to think that any group of lines in a poem, if it is set off by line spaces, constitutes a stanza. If such a group of lines is not patterned as one of a recurring group sharing similar formal characteristics, however, then it may be more appropriate to refer to such irregular groupings in the way we do for prose—as paragraphs. A ballad is typically divided into stanzas; a prose poem or a poem written in free verse, on the other hand, will rarely be divided into stanzas.

A stanza may be identified by the number of lines and the patterns of rhyme repeated in each grouping. One of the simpler traditional forms is the *ballad stanza*, with its alternating four- and three-foot lines and its *abcb* rhyme scheme. Drawing on this form's association with medieval ballads and legends, Keats produces the eerie mystery of "La Belle Dame sans Merci":

> I saw pale kings and princes too,
> Pale warriors, death-pale were they all;
> They cried—"La Belle Dame sans Merci
> Hath thee in thrall!"

Such imitations are a form of literary allusion; Keats uses a traditional stanza form to remind us of poems like "Sir Patrick Spens" or "Barbara Allen" to dramatize the painful thralldom of love by placing it within a well-known tradition of ballad narratives with similar forms and themes.

The four-line stanza, or *quatrain*, may be used for a variety of effects: from the elegiac solemnity of Gray's "Elegy Written in a Country Churchyard" to the apparent lightness and simplicity of some of Emily Dickinson's poems. Tennyson used a rhyming quatrain to such good effect in *In Memoriam* that the form he employed (four lines of iambic tetrameter rhyming *abba*) is known as the "In Memoriam stanza."

Other commonly used forms of stanza include the *rhyming couplet, terza rima, ottava rima, rhyme royal*, and the *Spenserian stanza*. Each of these is a rhetorical unit within a longer whole, rather like a paragraph within an essay. The poet's choice among such forms is dictated, at least in part, by the effects that each may produce. Thus the *rhyming couplet* often expresses a complete statement within two lines, creating a sense of density of thought, of coherence and closure; it is particularly effective where the writer wishes to set up contrasts, or to achieve the witty compactness of epigram:

> Of all mad creatures, if the learn'd are right,
> It is the slaver kills, and not the bite.
> A fool quite angry is quite innocent:
> Alas! 'tis ten times worse when they repent.

> (from Pope, "Epistle to Dr. Arbuthnot")

Ottava rima, as its Italian name implies, is an eight-line stanza, with the rhyme scheme *abababcc*. Like the sonnet, it is long enough to allow the development of a single thought in some detail and complexity, with a concluding couplet that may extend the central idea or cast it in a wholly unexpected light. W.B. Yeats uses this stanza form in "Sailing to Byzantium" and "Among School Children." Though much used by Renaissance poets, it is particularly associated with George Gordon, Lord Byron's *Don Juan*, in which the poet exploits to the full its potential for devastating irony and bathos. It is long enough to allow the development of a single thought in some detail and complexity; the concluding couplet can then, sonnet-like, turn that thought upon its head, or cast it in a wholly unexpected light:

> Sagest of women, even of widows, she
>   Resolved that Juan should be quite a paragon,
> And worthy of the noblest pedigree
>   (His sire was of Castile, his dam from Aragon).
> Then for accomplishments of chivalry,
>   In case our lord the king should go to war again,
> He learned the arts of riding, fencing, gunnery,
> And how to scale a fortress—or a nunnery.

> (*Don Juan* I.38)

FREE VERSE

Not all writers want the order and symmetry—some might say the restraints and limitations—of traditional forms, and many have turned to *free verse* as a means of liberating their thoughts and feelings. Deriving its name from the French "vers libre" made popular by the French Symbolistes at the end of the nineteenth century, free verse is characterized by irregularity of meter, line length, and rhyme. This does not mean that it is without pattern; rather, it tends to follow more closely than other forms the unforced rhythms and accents of natural speech, making calculated use of spacing, line breaks, and "cadences," the rhythmic units that govern phrasing in speech.

Free verse is not a modern invention. Milton was an early practitioner, as was Blake; however, it was the great modern writers of free verse—first Walt Whitman, then Pound, Eliot, and William Carlos Williams (interestingly, all Americans, at least originally)—who gave this form a fluidity and flexibility that could free the imagination to deal with any kind of feeling or experience. Perhaps because it depends so much more than traditional forms upon the individual intuitions of the poet, it is the form of poetic structure most commonly found today. The best practitioners recognize that free verse, like any other kind of poetry, demands clarity, precision, and a close connection between technique and meaning.

PROSE POETRY

At the furthest extreme from traditional forms lies poetry written in prose. Contradictory as this label may seem, the two have much in common. Prose has at its disposal all the figurative devices available to poetry, such as metaphor, personification, or apostrophe; it may use structuring devices such as verbal repetition or parallel syntactical structures; it can draw on the same tonal range, from pathos to irony. The difference is that prose poetry accomplishes its ends in sentences and paragraphs, rather than lines or stanzas. First given prominence by the French poet Charles Baudelaire (*Petits Poèmes en prose*, 1862), the form is much used to present fragments of heightened sensation, conveyed through vivid or impressionistic description. It draws upon such prosaic forms as journal entries, lists, even footnotes. Prose poetry should be distinguished from "poetic prose," which may be found in a variety of settings (from the King James Bible to the fiction of Jeanette Winterson); the distinction—which not all critics would accept—appears to lie in the writer's intention.

Christan Bök's *Eunoia* is an interesting example of the ways in which a writer of prose poetry may try to balance the demands of each medium. *Eunoia* is an avowedly experimental work in which each chapter is restricted to the use of a single vowel. The text is governed by a series of rules described by the author in an afterword; they include a requirement that all chapters "must allude to the art of writing. All sentences must accent internal rhyme through the use of syntactical parallelism. The text must exhaust the lexicon for each vowel, citing at least 98% of the available repertoire...." Having imposed such constraints upon the language and form of the work, Bök then sets himself the task of showing that "even under such improbable conditions of duress, language can still express an uncanny, if not sublime, thought." The result is a surrealistic narrative that blends poetic and linguistic devices to almost hypnotic effect.

THE POEM AS A MATERIAL OBJECT

Both free verse and prose poetry pay attention in different ways to the poem as a living thing on the printed page. But the way in which poetry is presented in material form is an important part of the existence of almost any form of poetry. In the six volumes of this anthology the material form of the poem is highlighted by the inclusion of a number of facsimile reproductions of poems of other eras in their earliest extant material form.

RHYTHM AND SCANSION

When we read poetry, we often become aware of a pattern of rhythm within a line or set of lines. The formal analysis of that rhythmic pattern, or "meter," is called *scansion*. The verb "to scan" may carry different meanings, depending upon the context: if the *critic* "scans" a line, he or she is attempting to determine the metrical pattern in which it is cast; if the *line* "scans," we are making the observation that the line conforms to particular metrical rules. Whatever the context, the process of scansion is based on the premise that a line of verse is built on a pattern of stresses, a recurring set of more or less regular beats established by the alternation of light and heavy accents in syllables and words. The rhythmic pattern so distinguished in a given poem is said to be the "meter" of that poem. If we find it impossible to identify any specific metrical pattern, the poem is probably an example of free verse.

QUANTITATIVE, SYLLABIC, AND ACCENTUAL-SYLLABIC VERSE

Although we owe much of our terminology for analyzing or describing poetry to the Greeks and Romans, the foundation of our metrical system is quite different from theirs. They measured a line of verse by the duration of sound ("quantity") in each syllable, and by the combination of short and long syllables. Such poetry is known as *quantitative* verse.

Unlike Greek or Latin, English is a heavily accented language. Thus poetry of the Anglo-Saxon period, such as *Beowulf*, was *accentual*: that is, the lines were based on a fixed number of accents, or stresses, regardless of the number of syllables in the line:

> Oft Scyld Scefing   sceapena þreatum
>   monegum maegþum   meodosetla ofteah.

Few modern poets have written in the accentual tradition. A notable exception was Gerard Manley Hopkins, who based his line on a pattern of strong stresses that he called "sprung rhythm." Hopkins experimented with rhythms and stresses that approximate the accentual quality of natural speech; the result is a line that is emphatic, abrupt, even harsh in its forcefulness:

> I caught this morning morning's minion, kingdom of daylight's dauphin, dapple-dawn-drawn
>   Falcon, in his riding
> Of the rolling level underneath him steady air ....
>
> (from "The Windhover")

Under the influence of French poetry, following the Norman invasion of the eleventh century, English writers were introduced to *syllabic* prosody: that is, poetry in which the number of syllables is the determining factor in the length of any line, regardless of the number of stresses or their placement. A few modern writers have successfully produced syllabic poetry.

However, the accentual patterns of English, in speech as well as in poetry, were too strongly ingrained to disappear. Instead, the native accentual practice combined with the imported syllabic conventions to produce the *accentual-syllabic* line, in which the writer works with combinations of stressed and unstressed syllables in lines of equal syllabic length. Geoffrey Chaucer was the first great writer to employ the accentual-syllabic line in English poetry:

> x   / / x x /   x /x / x
> Ther was also a Nonne, a Prioresse,

```
x   /  x   /x   x  /  x    x    /
```
That of hir smiling was ful simple and coy.
```
x   /  x   /   x   /  x  / x /
```
Hir gretteste ooth was but by saintè Loy,
```
x   /   x   / x   / x   /  x /  x
```
And she was clepèd Madame Eglantine.

(from The Canterbury Tales)

The fundamental pattern here is the ten-syllable line (although the convention of sounding the final "e" at the end of a line in Middle English verse sometimes produces eleven syllables). Each line contains five stressed syllables, each of which alternates with one or two unstressed syllables. This was to become the predominant meter of poetry in English until the general adoption of free verse in the twentieth century.

IDENTIFYING POETIC METER

Conventionally, meter is established by dividing a line into roughly equal parts, based on the rise and fall of the rhythmic beats. Each of these divisions, conventionally marked by a bar, is known as a "foot," and within the foot there will be a combination of stressed and unstressed syllables, indicated by the prosodic symbols / (stressed) and x (unstressed).

```
x   /     x   /  x    /   x  /
```
I know | that I | shall meet | my fate
```
/     x   x  /   x    /     x /
```
Somewhere | among | the clouds | above …

(from Yeats, "An Irish Airman Foresees His Death")

To describe the meter used in a poem, we must first determine what kind of foot predominates, and then count the number of feet in each line. To describe the resultant meter we use terminology borrowed from classical prosody. In identifying the meter of English verse we commonly apply the following labels:

iambic (x /): a foot with one weak stress followed by one strong stress

```
  x     /    x     /  x  /    x  /   x   /
```
("Look home | ward, Ang | el, now, | and melt | with ruth")

trochaic (/ x): strong followed by weak

```
 /  x    /  x   /  x    /
```
("Ty-ger! | Ty-ger! | burning | bright")

anapaestic (x x /): two weak stresses, followed by a strong

```
  x  x    /    x   x  /   x  x   /
```
("I have passed | with a nod | of the head")

dactylic (/ x x): strong stress followed by two weak

```
 /   x  x  /  x x    /
```
("Hickory | dickory | dock")

spondaic (/ /): two strong stresses

<pre>
       /   /   /   x   /   x   /   x
("If hate | killed men,| Brother | Lawrence,

      /   /   /   /   x   /
  God's blood,| would not | mine kill | you?")
</pre>

We also use classical terms to describe the number of feet in a line. Thus, a line with one foot is *monometer*; with two feet, *dimeter*; three feet, *trimeter*; four feet, *tetrameter*; five feet, *pentameter*; and six feet, *hexameter*.

Scansion of the two lines from Yeats's "Irish Airman" quoted above shows that the predominant foot is iambic (x /), that there are four feet to each line, and that the poem is therefore written in *iambic tetrameters*. The first foot of the second line, however, may be read as a trochee ("Somewhere"); the variation upon the iambic norm here is an example of *substitution*, a means whereby the writer may avoid the monotony that would result from adhering too closely to a set rhythm. We very quickly build up an expectation about the dominant meter of a poem; the poet will sometimes disturb that expectation by changing the beat, and so through substitution create a pleasurable tension in our awareness.

The prevailing meter in English poetry is iambic, since the natural rhythm of spoken English is predominantly iambic. Nonetheless, poets may employ other rhythms where it suits their purpose. Thus W.H. Auden can create a solemn tone by the use of a trochaic meter (/ x):

<pre>
  /   x   / x /   x   /
Earth, receive an honoured guest;
  /   x   /   x   / x   /
William Yeats is laid to rest:
  /   x / x   / x /
Let the Irish vessel lie
  /   x   /   x / x xx
Emptied of its poetry.
</pre>

The same meter may be much less funereal, as in Ben Jonson's song "*To Celia*":

<pre>
  /   x   / x   / x   /
Come, my Celia, let us prove,
   /   x   /   x   / x   /
While we may, the sports of love.
  /   x /   x   /   x / x
Time will not be ours forever;
  /   x   /   x   /   x / x
He, at length, our good will sever.
</pre>

The sense of greater pace in this last example derives in part from the more staccato phrasing, and also from the greater use of monosyllabic words. A more obviously lilting, dancing effect is obtained from anapaestic rhythm (x x /):

<pre>
  x   /   x x   / x   x / x x   /
I sprang to the stirrup, and Joris, and he;
  x / x   x   / x   x / x x   /
I galloped, Dirck galloped, we galloped all three.
   /   /   x x   /   x x / x x   /
"Good speed!" cried the watch, as the gatebolts undrew;
   /   / x   x / x x / x x   /
</pre>

"Speed!" echoed the wall to us galloping through.
    (from Browning, "How They Brought the Good News from Ghent to Aix")

Coleridge wittily captured the varying effects of different meters in "Metrical Feet: Lesson for a Boy," which the poet wrote for his sons, and in which he marked the stresses himself:

> /   x   /   x   /   x   /
> Trochee trips from long to short;
> x   /   x   /   x   /   x   /
> From long to long in solemn sort
> /   / x   /   /   /   x / / x
> Slow Spondee stalks; strong foot! yet ill able
> / x x   /   x x   / x   x / x x
> Ever to come up with Dactyl trisyllable.
> x / x   /   x   /   x /
> Iambics march from short to long:—
> x x /   x x /   x   x / x x   /
> With a leap and a bound the swift Anapaests throng....

A meter which often deals with serious themes is unrhymed iambic pentameter, also known as *blank verse*. This is the meter of Shakespeare's plays, notably his great tragedies; it is the meter, too, of Milton's *Paradise Lost*, to which it lends a desired sonority and magnificence; and of Wordsworth's "Lines Composed a Few Miles above Tintern Abbey," where the flexibility of the meter allows the writer to move by turns from description, to narration, to philosophical reflection.

RHYME, CONSONANCE, ASSONANCE, AND ALLITERATION

Perhaps the most obvious sign of poetic form is rhyme: that is, the repetition of syllables with the same or similar sounds. If the rhyme words are placed at the end of the line, they are known as *end-rhymes*. The opening stanza of Housman's "To an Athlete Dying Young" has two pairs of end-rhymes:

> The time you won your town the *race*
> We chaired you through the market-*place*;
> Man and boy stood cheering *by*,
> And home we brought you shoulder-*high*.

Words rhyming within a line are *internal rhymes*, as in the first and third lines of this stanza from Coleridge's "The Rime of the Ancient Mariner":

> The fair breeze *blew*, the white foam *flew*
> The furrow followed free;
> We were the *first* that ever *burst*
> Into that silent sea.

When, as is usually the case, the rhyme occurs in a stressed syllable, it is known as a *masculine rhyme*; if the rhyming word ends in an unstressed syllable, it is referred to as *feminine*. The difference is apparent in the opening stanzas of Alfred Tennyson's poem "The Lady of Shalott," where the first stanza establishes the basic iambic meter with strong stresses on the rhyming words:

On either side the river *lie*
Long fields of barley and of *rye*,
That clothe the wold and meet the *sky*;
And through the field the road runs *by*
To many-towered Camelot ...

In the second stanza Tennyson changes to trochaic lines, ending in unstressed syllables and feminine rhymes:

Willows whiten, aspens *quiver*,
Little breezes dusk and *shiver*
Through the wave that runs *forever*
By the island in the *river*
Flowing down to Camelot.

Not only does Tennyson avoid monotony here by his shift to feminine rhymes, he also darkens the mood by using words that imply a contrast with the bright warmth of day—"quiver," "dusk," "shiver"—in preparation for the introduction of the "silent isle" that embowers the Lady.

NEAR RHYMES

Most of the rhymes in "The Lady of Shalott" are exact, or "*perfect*" rhymes. However, in the second of the stanzas just quoted, it is evident that "forever" at the end of the third line is not a "perfect" rhyme; rather, it is an instance of "*near*" or "*slant*" rhyme. Such "*imperfect*" rhymes are quite deliberate; indeed, two stanzas later we find the rhyming sequence "early," "barley," "cheerly," and "clearly," followed by the rhymes "weary," "airy," and "fairy." As with the introduction of feminine rhymes, such divergences from one dominant pattern prevent monotony and avoid a too-mechanical sing-song effect.

More importantly, near-rhymes have an oddly unsettling effect, perhaps because they both raise and frustrate our expectation of a perfect rhyme. Their use certainly gives added emphasis to the words at the end of these chilling lines from Wilfred Owen's "Strange Meeting":

For by my glee might many men have laughed,
And of my weeping something had been left,
Which must die now. I mean the truth untold,
The pity of war, the pity war distilled.
Now men will go content with what we spoiled,
Or, discontent, boil bloody, and be spilled.

CONSONANCE AND ASSONANCE

In Owen's poem, the near-rhymes "laughed / left" and "spoiled / spilled" are good examples of *consonance*, which pairs words with similar consonants but different intervening vowels. Other examples from Owen's poem include "groined / groaned," "hall / Hell," "years / yours," and "mystery / mastery."

Related to consonance as a linking device is *assonance*, the echoing of similar vowel sounds in the stressed syllables of words with differing consonants (lane/hail, penitent/reticence). A device favored particularly by descriptive poets, it appears often in the work of the English Romantics, especially Shelley and Keats, and their great Victorian successor Tennyson, all of whom had a good ear for the musical quality of language. In the following passage, Tennyson makes effective use of repeated "o" and "ow" sounds to suggest the soft moaning of the wind as it spreads the seed of the lotos plant:

> The Lotos blooms below the barren peak,
> The Lotos blows by every winding creek;
> All day the wind breathes low with mellower tone;
> Through every hollow cave and alley lone
> Round and round the spicy downs the yellow Lotos dust is blown.
>
> (from "The Lotos-Eaters")

ALLITERATION

Alliteration connects words which have the same initial consonant. Like consonance and rhyme, alliteration adds emphasis, throwing individual words into strong relief, and lending force to rhythm. This is especially evident in the work of Gerard Manley Hopkins, where alliteration works in conjunction with the heavy stresses of *sprung rhythm*:

> Brute beauty and valour and act, oh, air, pride, plume, here
> Buckle! AND the fire that breaks from thee then, a billion
> Times told lovelier, more dangerous, O my chevalier!
>
> (from "The Windhover")

Like assonance, alliteration is useful in descriptive poetry, reinforcing an impression or mood through repeated sounds:

> Thou on whose stream, 'mid the steep sky's commotion,
> Loose clouds like Earth's decaying leaves are shed,
> Shook from the tangled boughs of Heaven and Ocean ....
>
> (from Percy Shelley, "Ode to the West Wind")

The repetition of "s" and "sh" sounds conveys the rushing sound of a wind that drives everything before it. This effect is also an example of *onomatopoeia*, a figure of speech in which the sound of the words seems to echo the sense.

RHYME AND POETIC STRUCTURE

Rhyme may play a central role in the structure of a poem. This is particularly apparent in the *sonnet* form, where the expression of the thought is heavily influenced by the poet's choice of rhyme-scheme. The "English" or "Shakespearean" sonnet has three quatrains rhyming *abab, cdcd, efef,* and concludes with a rhyming couplet, *gg.* This pattern lends itself well to the statement and restatement of an idea, as we find, for example, in Shakespeare's sonnet "That time of year thou mayst in me behold." Each of the quatrains presents an image of decline or decay—a tree in winter, the coming of night, a dying fire; the closing couplet then relates these images to the thought of an impending separation and attendant feelings of loss.

The organization of the "Italian" or "Petrarchan" sonnet, by contrast, hinges on a rhyme scheme that creates two parts, an eight-line section (the *octave*) typically rhyming *abbaabba,* and a concluding six-line section (the *sestet*) rhyming *cdecde* or some other variation. In the octave, the writer describes a thought or feeling; in the sestet, the writer may elaborate upon that thought, or may introduce a sudden "turn" or change of direction. A good example of the Italian form is Donne's "Batter My Heart, Three-Personed God."

The rhyming pattern established at the beginning of a poem is usually followed throughout; thus the opening sets up an expectation in the reader, which the poet may sometimes play on by means of an unexpected or surprising rhyme. This is especially evident in comic verse, where peculiar or unexpected rhymes can contribute a great deal to the comic effect:

> I shoot the Hippopotamus
> with bullets made of platinum,
>   Because if I use leaden ones
> his hide is sure to flatten 'em.
>   (Hilaire Belloc, "The Hippopotamus")

Finally, one of the most obvious yet important aspects of rhyme is its sound. It acts as a kind of musical punctuation, lending verse an added resonance and beauty. And as anyone who has ever had to learn poetry by heart will testify, the sound of rhyme is a powerful aid to memorization and recall, from helping a child to learn numbers—

> One, two,
> Buckle my shoe,
> Three, four,
> Knock at the door—

—to selling toothpaste through an advertising jingle in which the use of rhyme drives home the identity of a product:

> You'll wonder where the yellow went,
> When you brush your teeth with Pepsodent.

OTHER FORMS WITH INTERLOCKING RHYMES

Other forms besides the sonnet depend upon rhyme for their structural integrity. These include the *rondeau*, a poem of thirteen lines in three stanzas, with two half lines acting as a refrain, and having only two rhymes. The linking effect of rhyme is also essential to the three-line stanza called *terza rima*, the form chosen by Shelley for his "Ode to the West Wind," where the rhyme scheme (*aba, bcb, cdc*, etc.) gives a strong sense of forward movement. But a poet need not be limited to particular forms to use interlocking rhyme schemes.

THE POET'S TASK

The poet's task, in Sir Philip Sidney's view, is to move us to virtue and well-doing by coming to us with

> words set in delightful proportion, either accompanied with, or prepared for, the well-enchanting skill of music; and with a tale forsooth he cometh unto you, with a tale which holdeth children from play, and old men from the chimney corner; and pretending no more, doth intend the winning of the mind from wickedness to virtue: even as the child is often brought to take most wholesome things by hiding them in such other as have a pleasant taste.
>
> (*The Defence of Poesy*, 1593)

Modern poets have been less preoccupied with the didactic or moral force of poetry, its capacity to win the mind to virtue; nonetheless, like their Renaissance counterparts, they view poetry as a means to understanding, a point of light in an otherwise dark universe. To Robert Frost, a poem "begins in delight and ends in wisdom":

> It begins in delight, it inclines to the impulse, it assumes direction with the first line laid down, it runs a course of lucky events, and ends in a clarification of life—not necessarily a great clarification, such as sects and cults are founded on, but in a momentary stay against confusion.
>
> ("The Figure a Poem Makes," *Collected Poems*, 1939)

Rhyme and meter are important tools at the poet's disposal, and can be valuable aids in developing thought as well as in creating rhythmic or musical effects. However, the technical skills needed to turn a good line or create metrical complexities should not be confused with the ability to write good poetry. Sidney wryly observes in his *Defence of Poesy* that "there have been many excellent poets that never versified, and now swarm many versifiers that need never answer to the name of poets. ... [I]t is not rhyming and versing that maketh a poet, no more than a long gown maketh an advocate." Technical virtuosity may arouse our admiration, but something else is needed to bring that "constriction of the throat and ... precipitation of water to the eyes" that A.E. Housman speaks about. What that "something" is will always elude definition, and is perhaps best left for readers and listeners to determine for themselves through their own encounters with poetry.

Maps

COUNTIES
OF BRITAIN
AND IRELAND

THE BRITISH ISLES

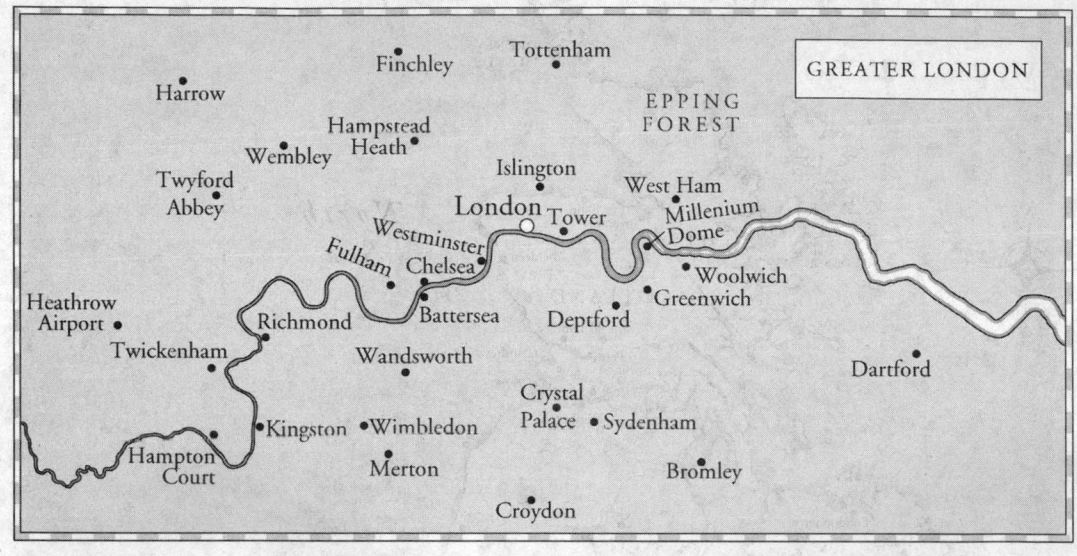

GREATER LONDON

Tottenham
Finchley
Harrow
EPPING FOREST
Hampstead Heath
Wembley
Islington
Twyford Abbey
London   Tower
West Ham
Millenium Dome
Westminster
Chelsea
Fulham
Woolwich
Greenwich
Heathrow Airport
Richmond   Battersea
Deptford
Twickenham
Wandsworth
Dartford
Kingston   Wimbledon
Crystal Palace   Sydenham
Hampton Court
Merton
Bromley
Croydon

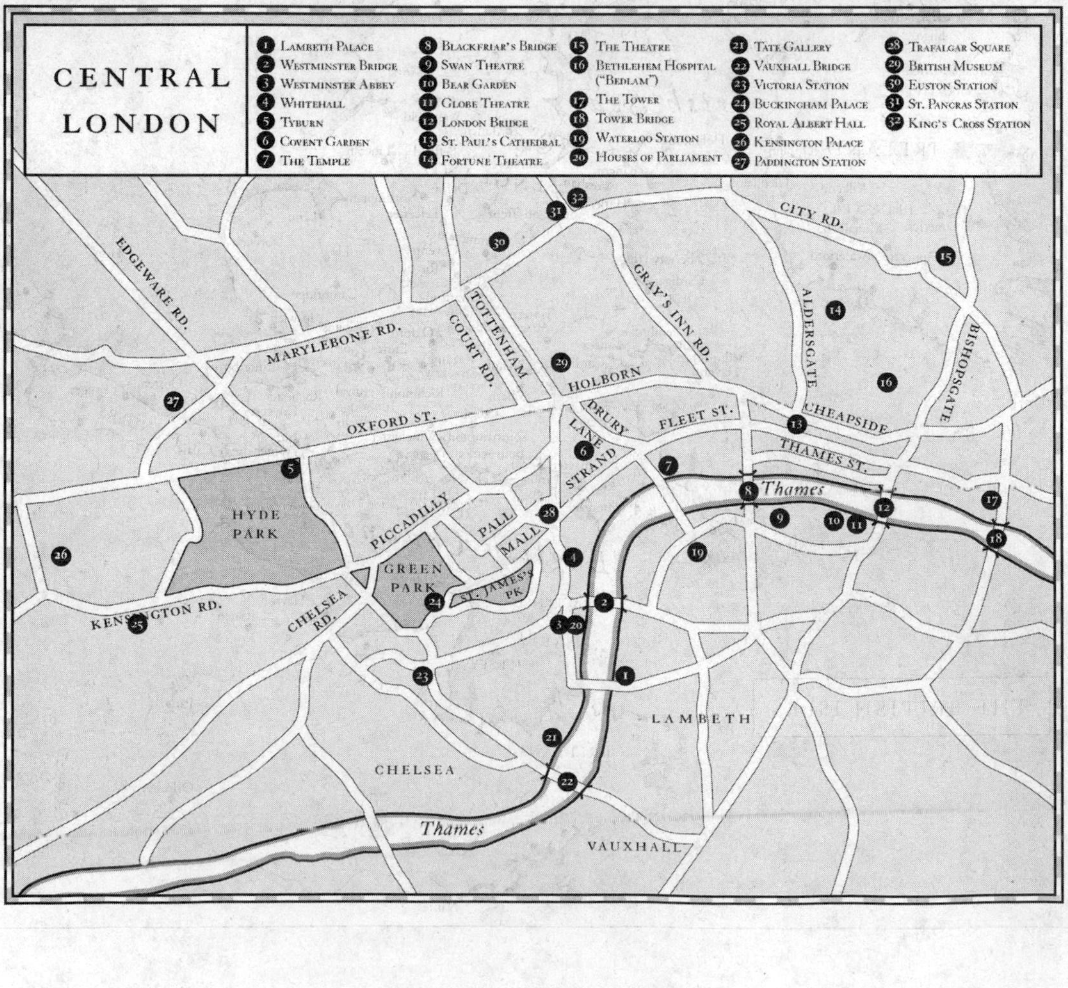

CENTRAL LONDON

1 LAMBETH PALACE
2 WESTMINSTER BRIDGE
3 WESTMINSTER ABBEY
4 WHITEHALL
5 TYBURN
6 COVENT GARDEN
7 THE TEMPLE

8 BLACKFRIAR'S BRIDGE
9 SWAN THEATRE
10 BEAR GARDEN
11 GLOBE THEATRE
12 LONDON BRIDGE
13 ST. PAUL'S CATHEDRAL
14 FORTUNE THEATRE

15 THE THEATRE
16 BETHLEHEM HOSPITAL ("BEDLAM")
17 THE TOWER
18 TOWER BRIDGE
19 WATERLOO STATION
20 HOUSES OF PARLIAMENT

21 TATE GALLERY
22 VAUXHALL BRIDGE
23 VICTORIA STATION
24 BUCKINGHAM PALACE
25 ROYAL ALBERT HALL
26 KENSINGTON PALACE
27 PADDINGTON STATION

28 TRAFALGAR SQUARE
29 BRITISH MUSEUM
30 EUSTON STATION
31 ST. PANCRAS STATION
32 KING'S CROSS STATION

EDGEWARE RD.
CITY RD.
MARYLEBONE RD.
TOTTENHAM COURT RD.
GRAY'S INN RD.
ALDERSGATE
BISHOPSGATE
OXFORD ST.
HOLBORN
DRURY LANE
FLEET ST.
CHEAPSIDE
THAMES ST.
HYDE PARK
Thames
PICCADILLY
STRAND
PALL MALL
GREEN PARK
ST. JAMES'S PK.
CHELSEA RD.
KENSINGTON RD.
LAMBETH
CHELSEA
Thames
VAUXHALL

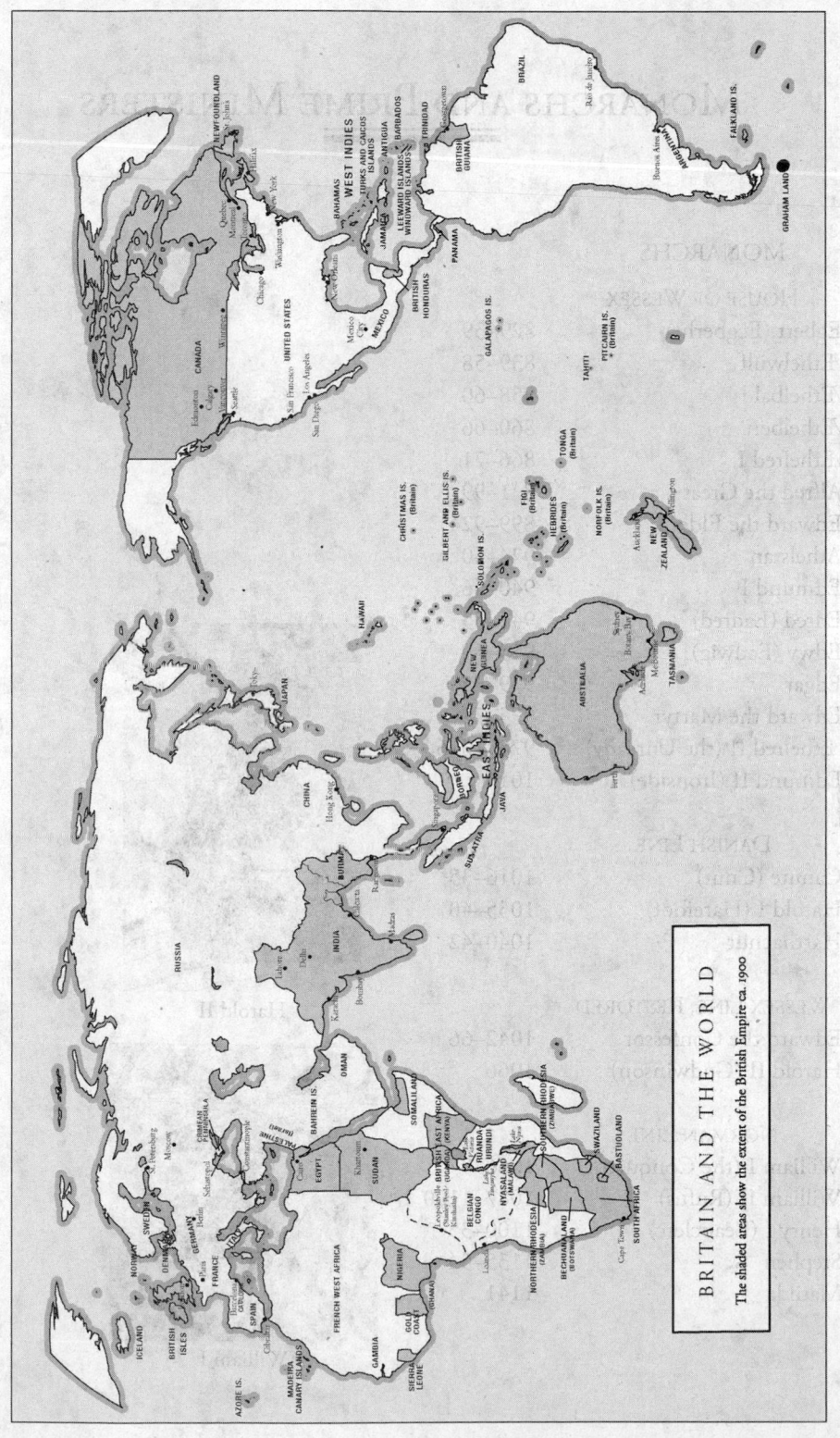

BRITAIN AND THE WORLD

The shaded areas show the extent of the British Empire ca. 1900

Monarchs and Prime Ministers

MONARCHS

HOUSE OF WESSEX

Egbert (Ecgberht)	829–39
Æthelwulf	839–58
Æthelbald	858–60
Æthelbert	860–66
Æthelred I	866–71
Alfred the Great	871–99
Edward the Elder	899–924
Athelstan	924–40
Edmund I	940–46
Edred (Eadred)	946–55
Edwy (Eadwig)	955–59
Edgar	959–75
Edward the Martyr	975–78
Æthelred II (the Unready)	978–1016
Edmund II (Ironside)	1016

DANISH LINE

Canute (Cnut)	1016–35
Harold I (Harefoot)	1035–40
Harthacnut	1040–42

WESSEX LINE, RESTORED

Edward the Confessor	1042–66
Harold II (Godwinson)	1066

NORMAN LINE

William I (the Conqueror)	1066–87
William II (Rufus)	1087–1100
Henry I (Beauclerc)	1100–35
Stephen	1135–54
Matilda	1141

Harold II

William I

MONARCHS

PLANTAGENET, ANGEVIN LINE

Henry II	1154–89
Richard I (Coeur de Lion)	1189–99
John (Lackland)	1199–1216
Henry III	1216–72
Edward I (Longshanks)	1272–1307
Edward II	1307–27
Edward III	1327–77
Richard II	1377–99

PLANTAGENET, LANCASTRIAN LINE

Henry IV	1399–1413
Henry V	1413–22
Henry VI	1422–61; 1470–71

PLANTAGENET, YORKIST LINE

Edward IV	1461–70; 1471–83
Edward V	1483
Richard III	1483–85

HOUSE OF TUDOR

Henry VII	1485–1509
Henry VIII	1509–47
Edward VI	1547–53
Jane	1553
Mary I	1553–58
Elizabeth I	1558–1603

HOUSE OF STUART

James I/VI	1603–25
Charles I	1625–49

(The Commonwealth)	1649–60
Oliver Cromwell	1649–58
Richard Cromwell	1658–59

Henry VIII

Mary I

MONARCHS		PRIME MINISTERS	
HOUSE OF STUART, RESTORED			
Charles II	1660–85		
James II	1685–89		
HOUSE OF ORANGE AND STUART			
William III and Mary II	1689–94		
William III	1694–1702		
HOUSE OF STUART			
Anne	1702–14		
HOUSE OF BRUNSWICK, HANOVER LINE			
George I	1714–27	Sir Robert Walpole (Whig)	1721–42
George II	1727–60	Earl of Wilmington (Whig)	1742–43
		Henry Pelham (Whig)	1743–54
		Duke of Newcastle (Whig)	1754–56
		Duke of Devonshire (Whig)	1756–57
George III	1760–1820	Duke of Newcastle (Whig)	1757–62
		Earl of Bute (Tory)	1762–63
		George Grenville (Whig)	1763–65
		Marquess of Rockingham (Whig)	1765–66
		William Pitt the Elder (Earl of Chatham) (Whig)	1766–68
		Duke of Grafton (Whig)	1768–70
		Frederick North (Lord North) (Tory)	1770–82
		Marquess of Rockingham (Whig)	1782
		Earl of Shelburne (Whig)	1782–83
		Duke of Portland (Whig)	1783
		William Pitt the Younger (Tory)	1783–1801
		Henry Addington (Tory)	1801–04
		William Pitt the Younger (Tory)	1804–06
		William Wyndham Grenville (Baron Grenville) (Whig)	1806–07

George III

George, Prince of Wales, Prince Regent

MONARCHS

George, Prince of Wales, Prince Regent	1811–20
George IV	1820–30
William IV	1830–37
Victoria	1837–1901

Victoria

HOUSE OF SAXE-COBURG-GOTHA

Edward VII	1901–10

HOUSE OF WINDSOR

George V	1910–36

PRIME MINISTERS

Duke of Portland (Tory)	1807–09
Spencer Perceval (Tory)	1809–12
Earl of Liverpool (Tory)	1812–27
George Canning (Tory)	1827
Viscount Goderich (Tory)	1827–28
Duke of Wellington (Tory)	1828–30
Earl Grey (Whig)	1830–34
Viscount Melbourne (Whig)	1834
Duke of Wellington (Tory)	1834
Sir Robert Peel (Tory)	1834–35
Viscount Melbourne (Whig)	1835–41
Sir Robert Peel (Tory)	1841–46
Lord John Russell (later Earl) (Whig)	1846–52
Earl of Derby (Con.)	1852
Earl of Aberdeen (Tory/Peelite)	1852–55
Viscount Palmerston (Lib.)	1855–58
Earl of Derby (Con.)	1858–59
Viscount Palmerston (Lib.)	1859–65
Earl Russell (Liberal)	1865–66
Earl of Derby (Con.)	1866–68
Benjamin Disraeli (Con.)	1868
William Gladstone (Lib.)	1868–74
Benjamin Disraeli (Con.)	1874–80
William Gladstone (Lib.)	1880–85
Marquess of Salisbury (Con.)	1885–86
William Gladstone (Lib.)	1886
Marquess of Salisbury (Con.)	1886–92
William Gladstone (Lib.)	1892–94
Earl of Rosebery (Lib.)	1894–95
Marquess of Salisbury (Con.)	1895–1902
Arthur Balfour (Con.)	1902–05
Sir Henry Campbell-Bannerman (Lib.)	1905–08
Herbert Asquith (Lib.)	1908–16

MONARCHS		PRIME MINISTERS	
		David Lloyd George (Lib.)	1916–22
		Bonar Law (Con.)	1922–23
		Stanley Baldwin (Con.)	1923–24
		Ramsay MacDonald (Labour)	1924
		Stanley Baldwin (Con.)	1924–29
		Ramsay MacDonald (Labour)	1929–35
Edward VIII	1936	Stanley Baldwin (Con.)	1935–37
George VI	1936–52	Neville Chamberlain (Con.)	1937–40
		Winston Churchill (Con.)	1940–45
		Clement Attlee (Labour)	1945–51
Elizabeth II	1952–	Sir Winston Churchill (Con.)	1951–55

Winston Churchill

		Sir Anthony Eden (Con.)	1955–57
		Harold Macmillan (Con.)	1957–63
		Sir Alec Douglas-Home (Con.)	1963–64
		Harold Wilson (Labour)	1964–70
		Edward Heath (Con.)	1970–74
		Harold Wilson (Labour)	1974–76
		James Callaghan (Labour)	1976–79
		Margaret Thatcher (Con.)	1979–90
		John Major (Con.)	1990–97
		Tony Blair (Labour)	1997–2007
		Gordon Brown (Labour)	2007–10
		David Cameron (Con.)	2010–16
		Theresa May (Con.)	2016–19
		Boris Johnson (Con.)	2019–

GLOSSARY OF TERMS

Accent: the natural emphasis (stress) speakers place on a syllable.

Accentual Verse: poetry in which a line is measured only by the number of accents or stresses, not by the number of syllables.

Accentual-Syllabic Verse: the most common metrical system in traditional English verse, in which a line is measured by the number of syllables and by the pattern of accented (stressed) and unaccented (unstressed) syllables.

Aesthetes: members of a late nineteenth-century movement that valued "art for art's sake"—for its purely aesthetic qualities, as opposed to valuing art for the moral content it may convey, for the intellectual stimulation it may provide, or for a range of other qualities.

Alexandrine: a line of verse that is 12 syllables long. In English verse, the alexandrine is always an iambic hexameter: that is, it has six iambic feet. The most-often quoted example is the second line in a couplet from Alexander Pope's "Essay on Criticism" (1711): "A needless Alexandrine ends the song / That, like a wounded snake, drags its slow length along." See also *Spenserian stanza*.

Allegory: a narrative with both a literal meaning and secondary, often symbolic meaning or meanings. Allegory frequently employs personification to give concrete embodiment to abstract concepts or entities, such as feelings or personal qualities. It may also present one set of characters or events in the guise of another, using implied parallels for the purposes of satire or political comment, as in John Dryden's poem "Absalom and Achitophel."

Alliteration: the grouping of words with the same initial consonant (e.g., "break, blow, burn, and make me new"). The repetition of sound acts as a connector. See also *assonance* and *consonance*.

Alliterative Verse: poetry that employs alliteration of stressed syllables in each line as its chief structural principle.

Allusion: a reference, often indirect or unidentified, to a person, thing, or event. A reference in one literary work to another literary work, whether as to its content or its form, also constitutes an allusion.

Ambiguity: an "opening" of language created by the writer to allow for multiple meanings or differing interpretations. In literature, ambiguity may be deliberately employed by the writer to enrich meaning; this differs from any unintentional, unwanted, ambiguity in non-literary prose.

Amphibrach: a metrical foot with three syllables, the second of which is stressed: x / x (e.g., sensation).

Analogy: a broad term that refers to our processes of noting similarities among things or events. Specific forms of analogy in poetry include *simile* and *metaphor* (see below).

Anapaest: a metrical foot containing two unstressed syllables followed by one stressed syllable: xx/ (e.g., underneath, intervene).

Anglican Church / Church of England: formed after Henry VIII's break with Rome in the 1530s, the Church of England had acquired a permanently Protestant cast by the 1570s. There has remained considerable variation within the Church, however, with distinctions often drawn among High Church, Broad Church, and Latitudinarian. At one extreme High Church Anglicans (some of whom prefer to be known as "Anglo-Catholics") prefer relatively elaborate church rituals not dissimilar in form to those of the Roman Catholic Church and place considerable emphasis on church hierarchy, while in the other direction Latitudinarians prefer relatively informal religious services and tend far more towards egalitarianism.

Antistrophe: from Greek drama, the chorus's countermovement or reply to an initial movement (strophe). See *ode* below.

Apostrophe: a figure of speech (a trope; see *figures of speech* below) in which a writer directly addresses an object—or a dead or absent person—as if the imagined audience were actually listening.

Archetype: in literature and mythology, a recurring idea, symbol, motif, character, or place. To some scholars and psychologists, an archetype represents universal human thought-patterns or experiences.

Assonance: the repetition of identical or similar vowel sounds in stressed syllables in which the surrounding consonants are different: for example, "shame" and "fate"; "gale" and "cage"; or the long "i" sounds in "Beside the pumice isle."

Aubade: a lyric poem that greets or laments the arrival of dawn.

Ballad: a folk song, or a poem originally recited to an audience, which tells a dramatic story based on legend or history.

Ballad Stanza: a quatrain with alternating four-stress and three-stress lines, rhyming *abcb*. A variant is "common measure," in which the alternating lines are strictly iambic, and rhyme *abab*.

Ballade: a fixed form most commonly characterized by only three rhymes, with an 8-line stanza rhyming *ababbcbc* and an envoy rhyming *bcbc*. Both Chaucer and Dante Gabriel Rossetti ("Ballad of the Dead Ladies") adopted this form.

Baroque: powerful and heavily ornamented in style. "Baroque" is a term from the history of visual art and of music that is sometimes also used to describe certain literary styles, such as that of Richard Crashaw.

Bathos: an anticlimactic effect brought about by a writer's descent from an elevated subject or tone to the ordinary or trivial.

Benedictine Rule: set of instructions for monastic communities, composed by Saint Benedict of Nursia (died c. 457).

Bildungsroman: from the German for *bildunge* (to shape) and *Roman* ("novel"), a narrative (often a novel) of personal development as a young or innocent person grows through a series of social, sexual, and political experiences, among others.

Blank Verse: unrhymed lines written in iambic pentameter, a form introduced to English verse by Henry Howard, Earl of Surrey, in his translation of parts of Virgil's *Aeneid* in 1547.

Bombast: inappropriately inflated or grandiose language.

Broadside: individual sheet of paper printed on only one side. From the sixteenth through to the eighteenth centuries broadsides of a variety of different sorts (e.g., ballads, political tracts, short satires) were sold on the streets.

Broken Rhyme: in which a multi-syllable word is split at the end of a line and continued onto the next, to allow an end-rhyme with the split syllable.

Burlesque: satire of a particularly exaggerated sort, particularly that which ridicules its subject by emphasizing its vulgar or ridiculous aspects.

Caesura: a pause or break in a line of verse occurring where a phrase, clause, or sentence ends, and indicated in scansion by the mark //. If it occurs in the middle of the line, it is known as a "medial" caesura.

Canon: in literature, those works that are commonly accepted as possessing authority or importance. In practice, "canonical" texts or authors are those that are discussed most frequently by scholars and taught most frequently in university courses.

Canto: a sub-section of a long (usually epic) poem.

Canzone: a short song or poem, with stanzas of equal length and an envoy.

Carpe Diem: Latin (from Horace) meaning "seize the day." The idea of enjoying the moment is a common one in Renaissance love poetry. See, for example, Marvell's "To His Coy Mistress."

Catalexis: the omission of unstressed syllables from a line of verse (such a line is referred to as "catalectic"). In iambic verse it is usually the first syllable of the line that is omitted; in trochaic, the last. For example, in the first stanza of Housman's "To an Athlete Dying Young" the third line is catalectic: i.e., it has dropped the first, unstressed syllable called for by the poem's iambic tetrameter form: "The time you won your town the race / We chaired you through the market-place; / Man and boy stood cheering by, / And home we brought you shoulder-high."

Catharsis: the arousal through the performance of a dramatic tragedy of "emotions of pity and fear" to a point where "purgation" or "purification" occurs and the feelings are released or transformed. The concept was developed by Aristotle in his *Poetics* from an ancient Greek medical concept, and adapted by him into an aesthetic principle.

Chiasmus: a figure of speech (a scheme) that reverses word order in successive parallel clauses. If the word order is A-B-C in the first clause, it becomes C-B-A in the second: for example, Donne's line "She is all states, and all princes, I" ("The Sun Rising") incorporates this reversal (though with an ellipsis).

Classical: originating in or relating to ancient Greek or Roman culture. As commonly conceived, *classical* implies a strong sense of formal order. The term *neoclassical* is often used with reference to literature of the Restoration and eighteenth century that was strongly influenced by ancient Greek and Roman models.

Closet Drama: a play (typically in verse) written for private performance. The term came into use in the first half of the nineteenth century.

Colored Narrative: alternative term for *free indirect discourse*.

Comedy: as a literary term, used originally to denote that class of ancient Greek drama in which the action ends happily. More broadly the term has been used to describe a wide variety of literary forms of a more or less light-hearted character.

***Commedia dell'arte*:** largely improvised comic performances conducted by masked performers and involving considerable physical activity. The genre of *commedia dell'arte* originated in Italy in the sixteenth century; it was influential throughout Europe for more than two centuries thereafter.

Commonwealth: from the fifteenth century, a term roughly equivalent to the modern "state," but tending to emphasize the commonality of interests among all citizens. In the seventeenth century Britain was named a commonwealth under Oliver Cromwell. In the twentieth century, the term came to be applied to associations of many nations; the British Commonwealth became the successor to the British Empire.

Conceit: an unusually elaborate metaphor or simile that extends beyond its original tenor and vehicle, sometimes becoming a "master" analogy for the entire poem (see, for example, Donne's "The Flea," and Robert Frost's sonnet "She is as in a field a silken tent"). Ingenious or fanciful images and comparisons were especially popular with the metaphysical poets of the seventeenth century, giving rise to the term "metaphysical conceit."

Concrete Poetry: an experimental form, most popular during the 1950s and 60s, in which the printed type itself forms a visual image of the poem's key words or ideas. See also *pattern poetry, assonance*.

Connotation: the implied, often unspoken meaning(s) of a given word, as distinct from its denotation, or literal meaning. Connotations may have highly emotional undertones and are usually culturally specific.

Conservative Party: See *Political Parties*.

Consonance: the pairing of words with similar initial and ending consonants, but with different vowel sounds (live/love, wander/wonder). See also *alliteration*.

Convention: aesthetic approach, technique, or practice accepted as characteristic and appropriate for a particular form. It is a convention of certain sorts of plays, for example, that the characters speak in blank verse, of other sorts of plays that characters speak in rhymed couplets, and of still other sorts of dramatic performances that characters frequently break into song to express their feelings.

Couplet: a pair of rhyming lines, usually in the same meter. If they form a complete unit of thought and are grammatically complete, the lines are known as a closed couplet. See also *heroic couplet* below.

Dactyl: a metrical foot containing one strong stress followed by two weak stresses: / xx (e.g., muttering, helplessly). A minor form known as "double dactyls" makes use of this meter for humorous purposes, e.g., "Jiggery pokery" or "Higgledy piggledy."

Denotation: See *connotation* above.

Devolution: process through which a degree of political power was transferred in the late twentieth and early twenty-first centuries from the British government to assemblies in Scotland and in Wales.

Dialogue: words spoken by characters to one another. (When a character is addressing him or her self or the audience directly, the words spoken are referred to as a *monologue*.)

Diction: word choice. Whether the diction of a literary work (or of a literary character) is colloquial, conversational, formal, or of some other type contributes significantly to the tone of the text as well as to characterization.

Didacticism: aesthetic approach emphasizing moral instruction.

Dimeter: a poetic line containing two metrical feet.

Dirge: a song or poem that mourns someone's death. See also *elegy* and *lament* below.

Disestablishmentarianism: movement opposing an official state-supported religion, in particular the Church of England in that role.

Dissonance: harsh, unmusical sounds or rhythms which poets may use deliberately to achieve certain effects.

Dramatic Irony: this form of irony occurs when the audience's reception of a speech by a character on the stage is affected by the possession by the audience of information not available to the character.

Dramatic Monologue: a lyric poem that takes the form of an utterance by a single person addressing a silent listener. The speaker may be an historical personage (as in some of Robert Browning's dramatic monologues), a figure drawn from myth or legend (as in some of Tennyson's), or an entirely imagined figure, as in Webster's "A Castaway."

Dub Poetry: a form of protest poetry originating in Jamaica, with its roots in dance rhythms, especially reggae, and often accompanied in performance by drums and music. See also *rap*.

Duple Foot: a duple foot of poetry has two syllables. The possible duple forms are iamb (in which the stress is on the second of the two syllables), trochee (in which the stress is on the first of the two syllables), spondee (in which both are stressed equally), and pyrrhic (in which both syllables are unstressed).

Eclogue: now generally used simply as an alternative name for a pastoral poem. In classical times and in the early modern period, however, an *eclogue* (or *idyll*) was a specific type of pastoral poem—a dialogue or dramatic monologue involving rustic characters. (The other main sub-genre of the pastoral was the *georgic*.)

Elegiac Stanza: a quatrain of iambic pentameters rhyming *abab*, often used in poems meditating on death or sorrow. The best-known example is Thomas Gray's "Elegy Written in a Country Churchyard."

Elegy: a poem which formally mourns the death of a particular person (e.g., Tennyson's "In Memoriam") or in which the poet meditates on other serious subjects (e.g., Gray's "Elegy"). See also *dirge*.

Elision: omitting or suppressing a letter or an unstressed syllable at the beginning or end of a word, so that a line of verse may conform to a given metrical scheme. For example, the three syllables at the beginning of Shakespeare's sonnet 129 are reduced to two by the omission of the first vowel: "Th' expense of spirit in a waste of shame." See also *syncope*.

Ellipsis: the omission of a word or words necessary for the complete grammatical construction of a sentence, but not necessary for our understanding of the sentence.

End-Rhyme: See *rhyme*.

End-Stopped: a line of poetry is said to be end-stopped when the end of the line coincides with a natural pause in the syntax, such as the conclusion of a sentence; e.g., in this couplet from Pope's "Essay on Criticism," both lines are end-stopped: "A little learning is a dangerous thing; / Drink deep, or taste not the Pierian spring." Compare this with *enjambement*.

Enjambement: the "running-on" of the sense from one line of poetry to the next, with no pause created by punctuation or syntax. (The more commonly found alternative is referred to as an *end-stopped line*.)

Envoy (Envoi): a stanza or half-stanza that forms the conclusion of certain French poetic forms, such as the *sestina* or the *ballade*. It often sums up or comments upon what has gone before.

Epic: a lengthy narrative poem, often divided into books and sub-divided into cantos. It generally celebrates heroic deeds or events, and the style tends to be lofty and grand. Examples in English include Spenser's *The Faerie Queene* and Milton's *Paradise Lost*.

Epic Simile: an elaborate simile, developed at such length that the vehicle of the comparison momentarily displaces the primary subject with which it is being compared.

Epigram: a very short poem, sometimes in closed couplet form, characterized by pointed wit.

Epigraph: a quotation placed at the beginning of a discourse to indicate or foreshadow the theme.

Epiphany: a moment at which matters of significance are suddenly illuminated for a literary character (or for the reader), typically triggered by something small and seemingly of little import. The term first came into wide currency in connection with the fiction of James Joyce.

Episodic Plot: plot comprising a variety of episodes that are only loosely connected by threads of story material (as opposed to plots that present one or more continually unfolding narratives where successive episodes build one on another).

Epithalamion: a poem celebrating a wedding. The best-known example in English is probably Edmund Spenser's "Epithalamion" (1595).

Eulogy: text expressing praise, especially for a distinguished person recently deceased.

Euphemism: mode of expression through which aspects of reality considered to be vulgar, crudely physical, or unpleasant are referred to indirectly rather than named explicitly. A variety of euphemisms exist for the processes of urination and defecation; *passed away* is often used as a euphemism for *died*. (The word *euphemism* has the same root as *Euphuism* (see below), but has taken on a different meaning.)

Euphony: pleasant, musical sounds or rhythms—the opposite of dissonance.

Euphuism: In the late sixteenth century John Lyly published a prose romance, *Euphues*, which employed a style that featured long sentences filled with balanced phrases and clauses, many of them adding little to the content. This highly mannered style was popular in the court of Elizabeth I for a few years following the publication of Lyly's famous work, and the style became known as *Euphuism*.

European Union (EU): group of nations formed in 1993 as the successor to the European Economic Community (Common Market). Britain first applied for membership in the latter in 1961; at first its efforts to join were blocked by the French government, but in 1973 Prime Minister Edward Heath successfully negotiated Britain's entry into the group. Britain resisted some moves towards full integration with the European community, in particular retaining its own currency when other European nations adopted the Euro on 1 January 2002. In 2016, a referendum was held and the UK voted to leave the EU altogether.

Exchequer: in earlier eras, the central royal financial office, responsible for receiving and keeping track of crown revenues. In later eras, part of the bureaucracy equivalent to the Ministry of Finance in Canada or the Treasury in the United States (the modern post of Chancellor of the Exchequer is equivalent to the American post of Secretary of the Treasury, the Canadian post of Minister of Finance, or the Australian post of Treasurer).

Exposition: the setting out of material in an ordered form, either in speech or in writing. In a play those parts of the action that do not occur on stage but are rather recounted by the characters are frequently described as being presented in exposition. Similarly, when the background narrative is filled in near the beginning of a novel, such material is often described as having been presented in exposition. Somewhat confusingly, however, the term "expository prose" is usually used with reference not to fiction but to the setting forth of arguments or descriptions in the context of essays or other works of prose non-fiction.

Eye-Rhyme: See *rhyme* below.

Feminine Ending: the ending of a line of poetry on an "extra," and, especially, on an unstressed syllable. See, for example, the first line of Keats's "Ode on a Grecian Urn": "A thing of beauty is a joy forever," a line of iambic pentameter in which the final foot is an amphibrach rather than an iamb.

Feminine Rhyme: See *rhyme* below.

Figures of Speech: deliberate, highly concentrated uses of language to achieve particular purposes or effects on an audience. There are two kinds of figures: schemes and tropes. Schemes involve changes in word-sound and word-order, such as *alliteration* and *chiasmus*. Tropes play on our understandings of words to extend, alter, or transform meaning, as in *metaphor* and *personification*.

First-Person Narrative: narrative recounted using *I* and *me*. See also *narrative perspective*.

Fixed Forms: the term applied to a number of poetic forms and stanzaic patterns, many derived from French models, such as *ballade*, *rondeau*, *sestina*, *triolet*, and *villanelle*. Other "fixed forms" include the *sonnet*, *rhyme royal*, *haiku*, and *ottava rima*.

Folio: largest of several sizes of book page commonly used in the first few centuries after the introduction of the printing press. A folio size results from sheets of paper of at least 14 inches by 20 inches being folded in half (a folio page size will thus be at least 7 inches by 10 inches). When the same sheet is folded twice a quarto is produced, and when it is folded 3 times an octavo.

Foot: a unit of a line of verse which contains a particular combination of stressed and unstressed syllables. Dividing a line into metrical feet (*iambs*, *trochees*, etc.), then counting the number of feet per line, is part of *scansion*. See also *meter*.

Franklin: in the late medieval period, a landholder of free status, but ranking below the gentry.

Free Indirect Discourse: in prose fiction, commentary in which a seemingly objective and omniscient narrative voice assumes the point of view of one or more characters. When we hear through the third person narrative voice of Jane Austen's *Pride and Prejudice*, for example, that Mr. Darcy "was the proudest, most disagreeable man in the world, and every body hoped that he would never come there again," the narrative voice has assumed the point of view of "every body" in the community; we as readers are not meant to take it that Mr. Darcy is indeed the most disagreeable man in the world. Similarly, in the following passage from the same novel, we are likely to take it as being the view of the character Charlotte that marriage is "the only honourable provision for well-educated young women of small fortune," not to take it to be an objective statement of perceived truth on the part of the novel's third person narrative voice:

> [Charlotte's] reflections were in general satisfactory. Mr. Collins to be sure was neither sensible nor agreeable; his society was irksome, and his attachment to her must be imaginary. But still he would be her husband. Without thinking highly either of men or of matrimony, marriage had always been her object; it was the only honourable provision for well-educated young women of small fortune, and however uncertain of giving happiness, must be their pleasantest preservative from want.

The term free indirect discourse may also be applied to situations in which it may not be entirely clear if the thoughts expressed emanate from the character, the narrator, or some combination of the two. (In the above-quoted passage expressing Charlotte's thoughts, indeed, some might argue that the statement concerning marriage should be taken as the expression of a belief that the narrative voice shares, at least in part.)

Free Verse: poetry that does not follow any regular meter, line length, or rhyming scheme. In many respects, though, free verse follows the complex natural "rules" and rhythmic patterns (or cadences) of speech.

Gaelic: Celtic language, variants of which are spoken in Ireland and Scotland.

Genre: a particular literary form. The concept of genre may be used with different levels of generality. At the most general, poetry, drama, and prose fiction are distinguished as separate genres. At a lower level of generality various sub-genres are frequently distinguished, such as (within drama) comedy and tragedy, or, at a still lower level of generality, Elizabethan domestic tragedy, Edwardian drawing-room comedy, and so on.

Georgic: (from Virgil's *Georgics*) a poem that celebrates the natural wealth of the countryside and advises how to cultivate and live in harmony with it. Pope's *Windsor Forest* and James Thomson's *Seasons* are classed as georgics. They were often said to make up, with eclogues, the two alliterative forms of pastoral poetry.

Ghazal: derived from Persian and Indian precedents, the ghazal presents a series of thoughts in closed couplets joined by a simple rhyme-scheme: *aa ba ca da*, etc.

Gothic: in architecture and the visual arts, a term used to describe styles prevalent from the twelfth to the fourteenth centuries, but in literature a term used to describe work with a sinister or grotesque tone that seeks to evoke a sense of terror on the part of the reader or audience. Gothic literature originated as a genre in the eighteenth century with works such as Horace Walpole's *The Castle of Otranto*. To some extent the notion of the medieval itself then carried with it associations of the dark and the grotesque, but from the beginning an element of intentional exaggeration (sometimes verging on self-parody) attached itself to the genre. The Gothic trend of youth culture that began in the late twentieth century is less clearly associated with the medieval, but shares with the various forms of Gothic literature (from Walpole in the eighteenth century, to Bram Stoker in the early twentieth, to Stephen King and Anne Rice in the late twentieth) a fondness for the sensational and the grotesque, as well as a propensity to self-parody.

Guilds: non-clerical associations that arose in the late Anglo-Saxon period, devoted both to social purposes (such as the organization of feasts for the members) and to piety. In the later medieval period guilds developed strong associations with particular occupations.

Haiku: a Japanese form, using three unrhymed lines of five, seven, and five syllables. Conventionally, it uses precise, concentrated images to suggest states of feeling.

Heptameter: a line containing seven metrical feet.

Heroic Couplet: a pair of rhymed iambic pentameters, so called because the form was much used in seventeenth- and eighteenth-century poems and plays on heroic subjects.

Hexameter: a line containing six metrical feet.

Home Rule: movement dedicated to making Ireland politically independent from Britain.

Horatian Ode: inspired by the work of the Roman poet Horace, an ode that is usually calm and meditative in tone, and homostrophic (i.e., having regular stanzas) in form. Keats's odes are English examples.

House of Commons: elected legislative body, in Britain currently consisting of six hundred and fifty members of Parliament. See also *Parliament*.

House of Lords: the "Upper House" of the British Houses of Parliament. Since the nineteenth century the House of Lords has been far less powerful than the elected House of Commons. The House of Lords is currently made up of both hereditary peers (Lords whose title is passed on from generation to generation) and life peers. As a result of legislation enacted by the Labour government of Tony Blair, the role of hereditary peers in Parliament is being phased out.

Humors: The four humors were believed in until the sixteenth and seventeenth centuries to be elements in the makeup of all humans; a person's temperament was thought to be determined by the way in which the humors were combined. When the *choleric* humor was dominant, the person would tend towards anger; when the *sanguine* humor was dominant, towards pleasant affability; when the *phlegmatic* humor was dominant, towards a cool and calm attitude and/or a lack of feeling or enthusiasm; and when the *melancholic* humor was dominant, towards withdrawal and melancholy.

Hymn: a song whose theme is usually religious, in praise of divinity. Literary hymns may praise more secular subjects.

Hyperbole: a *figure of speech* (a trope) that deliberately exaggerates or inflates meaning to achieve particular effects, such as the irony in A.E. Housman's claim (from "Terence, This Is Stupid Stuff") that "malt does more than Milton can / To justify God's ways to man."

Iamb: the most common metrical foot in English verse, containing one unstressed syllable followed by a stressed syllable: x / (e.g., between, achieve).

Idyll: traditionally, a short pastoral poem that idealizes country life, conveying impressions of innocence and happiness.

Image: the recreation in words of objects perceived by the senses, sometimes thought of as "pictures," although senses other than sight are usually involved. The term also refers more generally to the descriptive effects of figurative language, especially in *metaphor* and *simile*.

Imagism: a poetic movement that was popular mainly in the second decade of the twentieth century. The goal of Imagist poets (such as H.D. and Ezra Pound in their early work) was to represent emotions or impressions through highly concentrated imagery.

Incantation: a chant or recitation of words that are believed to have magical power. A poem can achieve an "incantatory" effect through a compelling rhyme scheme and other repetitive patterns.

In Memoriam Stanza: a four-line stanza in iambic tetrameter, rhyming *abba*: the type of stanza used by Tennyson in *In Memoriam*.

Interlocking Rhyme: See *rhyme*.

Internal Rhyme: See *rhyme*.

Irony: a subtle form of humor in which a statement is understood to convey a quite different (and often entirely opposite) meaning. A writer achieves this by carefully making sure that the statement occurs in a context which undermines or twists the statement's "literal" meaning. *Hyperbole* and *litotes* are often used for ironic effect. *Sarcasm* is a particularly strong or crude form of irony (usually spoken), in which the meaning is conveyed largely by the tone of voice adopted; something said sarcastically is meant clearly to imply its opposite.

Künstlerroman: from the German for *Künstler* (artist) and *Roman* (novel), a narrative (often in novel form) about the personal and aesthetic growth of an artist, as he or she apprentices in an art form (music, literature, painting, or sculpture).

Labour Party: See *Political Parties*.

Lament: a poem which expresses profound regret or grief either because of a death, or because of the loss of a former, happier state.

Language Poetry: a movement that defies the usual lyric and narrative conventions of poetry, and that challenges the structures and codes of everyday language. Often seen as both politically and aesthetically subversive, its roots lie in the works of modernist writers like Ezra Pound and Gertrude Stein.

Liberal Party: See *Political Parties*.

Litotes: a *figure of speech* (a trope) in which a writer deliberately uses understatement to highlight the importance of an argument, or to convey an ironic attitude.

Liturgical Drama: drama based on and/or incorporating text from the liturgy—the text recited during religious services.

Lollard: member of the group of radical Christians that took its inspiration from the ideas of John Wyclif (c. 1330–84). The Lollards, in many ways precursors of the Protestant Reformation, advocated making the Bible available to all, and dedication to the principles of evangelical poverty in imitation of Christ.

Luddites: protestors against the mechanization of industry on the grounds that it was leading to the loss of employment and to an increase in poverty. In the years 1811 to 1816 there were several Luddite protests in which machines were destroyed.

Lyric: a poem, usually short, expressing an individual speaker's feelings or private thoughts. Originally a song performed with accompaniment on a lyre, the lyric poem is often noted for musicality of rhyme and rhythm. The lyric genre includes a variety of forms, including the *sonnet*, the *ode*, the *elegy*, the *madrigal*, the *aubade*, the *dramatic monologue*, and the *hymn*.

Madrigal: a lyric poem, usually short and focusing on pastoral or romantic themes. A madrigal is often set to music.

Masculine Ending: a metrical line ending on a stressed syllable. *Masculine Rhyme*: see *rhyme*.

Masque: an entertainment typically combining music and dance, with a limited script, extravagant costumes and sets, and often incorporating spectacular special effects. Masques, which were performed before court audiences in the early seventeenth century, often focused on royal themes and frequently drew on classical mythology.

Mass: within Christianity, a church service that includes the sacrament of the Eucharist (Holy Communion), in which bread and wine are consumed which are believed by those of many Christian denominations to have been transubstantiated into the body and blood of Christ. Anglicans (Episcopalians) are more likely to believe the bread and wine merely symbolize the body and blood.

Melodrama: originally a term used to describe nineteenth-century plays featuring sensational story lines and a crude separation of characters into moral categories, with the pure and virtuous pitted against evil villains. Early melodramas employed background music throughout the action of the play as a means of heightening the emotional response of the audience. By extension, certain sorts of prose fictions or poems are often described as having melodramatic elements.

Metaphor: a *figure of speech* (in this case, a trope) in which a comparison is made or identity is asserted between two unrelated things or actions without the use of "like" or "as." The primary subject is known as the *tenor*; to illuminate its nature, the writer links it to wholly different images, ideas, or actions referred to as the *vehicle*. Unlike a *simile*, which is a direct comparison of two things, a metaphor "fuses" the separate qualities of two things, creating a new idea. For example, Shakespeare's "Let slip the dogs of war" is a metaphorical statement. The tenor, or primary subject, is "war"; the vehicle of the metaphor is the image of hunting dogs released from their leash. The line fuses the idea of war with the qualities of ravening bloodlust associated with hunting dogs.

Metaphysical Poets: a group of seventeenth-century English poets, notably Donne, Cowley, Marvell, and Herbert, who employed unusual difficult imagery and *conceits* (see above) in order to develop intellectual and religious themes. The term was first applied to these writers to mark as far-fetched their use of philosophical and scientific ideas in a poetic context.

Meter: the pattern of stresses, syllables, and pauses that constitutes the regular rhythm of a line of verse. The meter of a poem written in the English accentual-syllabic tradition is determined by identifying the stressed and unstressed syllables in a line of verse, and grouping them into recurring units known as feet. See *accent*, *accentual-syllabic*, *caesura*, *elision*, and *scansion*. For some of the better known meters, see *iamb*, *trochee*, *dactyl*, *anapaest*, and *spondee*. See also *monometer*, *dimeter*, *trimeter*, *tetrameter*, *pentameter*, and *hexameter*.

Methodist: Protestant denomination formed in the eighteenth century as part of the religious movement led by John and Charles Wesley. Originally a movement within the Church of England, Methodism entailed enthusiastic evangelism, a strong emphasis on free will, and a strict regimen of Christian living.

Metonymy: a *figure of speech* (a trope), meaning "change of name," in which a writer refers to an object or idea by substituting the name of another object or idea closely associated with it: for example, the substitution of "crown" for monarchy, "the press" for journalism, or "the pen" for writing. *Synecdoche* (see below) is a kind of metonymy.

Mock-heroic: a style applying the elevated diction and vocabulary of epic poetry to low or ridiculous subjects. An example is Alexander Pope's "The Rape of the Lock."

Monologue: words spoken by a character to him or herself or to an audience directly.

Monometer: a line containing one metrical foot.

Mood: This can describe the writer's attitude, implied or expressed, towards the subject (see *tone* below); or it may refer to the atmosphere that a writer creates in a passage of description or narration.

Motif: an idea, image, action, or plot element that recurs throughout a literary work, creating new levels of meaning and strengthening structural coherence. The term is taken from music, where it describes recurring melodies or themes. See also *theme*.

Narrative Perspective: in fiction, the point of view from which the story is narrated. A first-person narrative is recounted using *I* and *me*, whereas a third person narrative is recounted using *he, she, they*, and so on. When a narrative is written in the third person and the narrative voice evidently "knows" all that is being done and thought, the story is typically described as being recounted by an "omniscient narrator."

Neoclassical: adapted from or substantially influenced by the cultures of ancient Greece and Rome. The term *neoclassical* is often used to describe the ideals of Restoration and eighteenth-century writers and artists who looked to ancient Greek and Roman civilization for models.

Nobility: privileged class, the members of which are distinguished by the holding of titles. Dukes, Marquesses, Earls, Viscounts, and Barons (in that order of precedence) are all holders of hereditary titles—that is to say, in the British patrilineal tradition, titles passed on from generation to generation to the eldest son. The title of Baronet, also hereditary, was added to this list by James I. Holders of non-hereditary titles include Knights and Dames.

Nonconformist: general term used to describe one who does not subscribe to the Church of England.

Nonsense Verse: light, humorous poetry which contradicts logic, plays with the absurd, and invents words for amusing effects. Lewis Carroll is one of the best-known practitioners of nonsense verse.

Octave: also known as "octet," the first eight lines in an Italian/Petrarchan sonnet, rhyming *abbaabba*. See also *sestet* and *sonnet*.

Octosyllabic: a line of poetry with eight syllables, as in iambic tetrameter.

Ode: originally a classical poetic form, used by the Greeks and Romans to convey serious themes. English poetry has evolved three main forms of ode: the Pindaric (imitative of the odes of the Greek poet Pindar); the Horatian (modeled on the work of the Roman writer Horace); and the irregular ode. The Pindaric ode was an irregular stanza in English, has a tripartite structure of "strophe," "antistrophe," and "epode" (meaning turn, counterturn, and stand), and is modeled on the songs and movements of the Chorus in Greek drama. The Horatian ode is more personal, reflective, and literary, and employs a pattern of repeated stanzas. The irregular ode, as its name implies, avoids a recurrent stanza pattern, and is sometimes irregular in line length also (see, for example, Wordsworth's "Ode: Intimations of Immortality").

Onomatopoeia: a *figure of speech* (a scheme) in which a word "imitates" a sound, or in which the sound of a word seems to reflect its meaning.

Ottava Rima: an eight-line stanza, usually in iambic pentameter, with the rhyme scheme *abababcc*. For an example, see Byron's *Don Juan*, or Yeats's "Sailing to Byzantium."

Oxymoron: a *figure of speech* (a trope) in which two words whose meanings seem contradictory are placed together, a paradox: for example, the phrase "darkness visible," from Milton's *Paradise Lost*.

Paean: a triumphant, celebratory song, often associated with a military victory.

Pale: in the medieval period, term for a protective zone around a fortress. As of the year 1500 three of these had been set up to guard frontiers of territory controlled by England—surrounding Calais in France, Berwick-upon-Tweed on the Scottish frontier, and Dublin in Ireland. The Dublin Pale was the largest of the three, and the term remained in use for a longer period there.

Pantoum: a poem in linked quatrains that rhyme *abab*. The second and fourth lines of one stanza are repeated as the first and third lines of the stanza that follows. In the final stanza the pattern is reversed: the second line repeats the third line of the first stanza, the fourth and final line repeats the first line of the first stanza.

Parliament: in Britain, the legislative body, comprising both the House of Commons and the House of Lords. Since the eighteenth century, the most powerful figure in the British government has been the Prime Minister rather than the monarch, the House of Commons has been the dominant body in Parliament, and members of the House of Commons have been organized in political parties. Since the mid-nineteenth century the effective executive in the British Parliamentary system has been the Cabinet, each member of which is typically in charge of a department of government. Unlike the American system, the British parliamentary system (sometimes called the "Westminster system," after the location of the Houses of Parliament) brings together the executive and legislative functions of government, with the Prime Minister leading the government party in the House of Commons as well as directing the Cabinet. By convention it is understood that the House of Lords will not contravene the wishes of the House of Commons in any fundamental way, though the "Upper House," as it is often referred to, may sometimes modify or reject legislation.

Parody: a close, usually mocking imitation of a particular literary work, or of the well-known style of a particular author, in order to expose or magnify weaknesses. Parody is a form of satire—that is, humor that may ridicule and scorn its object.

Pastiche: a discourse which borrows or imitates other writers' characters, forms, style, or ideas. Unlike a parody, a pastiche is usually intended as a compliment to the original writer.

Pastoral: in general, pertaining to country life; in prose, drama, and poetry, a stylized type of writing that idealizes the lives and innocence of country people, particularly shepherds and shepherdesses. See also *eclogue, georgic, idyll*, above.

Pastoral Elegy: a poem in which the poet uses the pastoral style to lament the death of a friend, usually represented as a shepherd. Milton's "Lycidas" provides a good example of the form, including its use of such conventions as an invocation of the muse and a procession of mourners.

Pathetic Fallacy: a form of personification in which inanimate objects are given human emotions: for example, rain clouds "weeping." The word "fallacy" in this connection is intended to suggest the distortion of reality or the false emotion that may result from an exaggerated use of personification.

Pathos: the emotional quality of a discourse; or the ability of a discourse to appeal to our emotions. It is usually applied to the mood conveyed by images of pain, suffering, or loss that arouse feelings of pity or sorrow in the reader.

Pattern Poetry: a predecessor of modern concrete poetry, in which the shape of the poem on the page is intended to suggest or imitate an aspect of the poem's subject. George Herbert's "Easter Wings" is an example of pattern poetry.

Penny Dreadful: Victorian term for a cheap and poorly produced work of short fiction, usually of a sensational nature.

Pentameter: a line of verse containing five metrical feet.

Performance Poetry: poetry composed primarily for oral performance, often very theatrical in nature. See also *dub poetry* and *rap*.

Persona: the assumed identity or "speaking voice" that a writer projects in a discourse. The term "persona" literally means "mask." Even when a writer speaks in the first person, we should be aware that the attitudes or opinions we hear may not necessarily be those of the writer in real life.

Personification: a *figure of speech* (a trope), also known as "prosopopoeia," in which a writer refers to inanimate objects, ideas, or animals as if they were human, or creates a human figure to represent an abstract entity such as Philosophy or Peace.

Petrarchan Sonnet: the earliest form of the sonnet, also known as the Italian sonnet, with an 8-line octave and a six-line sestet. The Petrarchan sonnet traditionally focuses on love and descriptions of physical beauty.

Phoneme: a linguistic term denoting the smallest unit of sound that it is possible to distinguish. The words *fun* and *phone* each have three phonemes, though one has three letters and one has five. (Each makes up a single syllable.)

Pindaric: See *ode*.

Plot: the organization of story materials within a literary work. The order in which story material is presented (especially causes and consequences); the inclusion of elements that allow or encourage the reader or audience to form expectations as to what is likely to happen; the decision to present some story material through exposition rather than in more extended form as part of the main action of the narrative—all these are matters of plotting.

Political Parties: The party names "Whig" and "Tory" began to be used in the late seventeenth century; before that time members of the House of Commons acted individually or through shifting and very informal factions. At first the Whigs and Tories had little formal organization either, but by the mid-eighteenth century parties had acknowledged leaders, and the leader of the party with the largest number of members in the House of Commons had begun to be recognized as the Prime Minister. The Tories evolved into the modern Conservative Party, and the Whigs into the Liberal

Party. In the late nineteenth century the Labour Party was formed in an effort to provide better representation in Parliament for the working class, and since the 1920s Labour and the Conservatives have alternated as the party of government, with the Liberals reduced to third-party status. (Since 1988, when the Liberals merged with a breakaway faction from Labour known as the Social Democrats, this third party has been named the Liberal Democrats.)

Pre-Raphaelites: originally a group of Victorian artists and writers, formed in 1848. Their goal was to revive what they considered the simpler, fresher, more natural art that existed before Raphael (1483–1520). The poet Dante Gabriel Rossetti was one of the founders of the group.

Presbyterian: term applied to a group of Protestants (primarily English and Scottish) who advocated replacing the traditional hierarchical church in which bishops and archbishops governed lower level members of the clergy with a system in which all presbyters (or ministers) would be equal. The Presbyterians, originally led by John Knox, were strongly influenced by the ideas of John Calvin.

Prose Poem: a poetic discourse that uses prose formats (e.g., it may use margins and paragraphs rather than line breaks or stanzas) yet is written with the kind of attention to language, rhythm, and cadence that characterizes verse.

Prosody: the study and analysis of meter, rhythm, rhyme, stanzaic pattern, and other devices of versification.

Protagonist: the central character in a literary work.

Prothalamion: a wedding song; a term coined by the poet Edmund Spenser, adapted from "epithalamion" (see above).

Public School: See *schools* below.

Pun: a play on words, in which a word with two or more distinct meanings, or two words with similar sounds, may create humorous ambiguities. Also known as *paranomasia*.

Puritan: term, originally applied only in a derogatory fashion but later widely accepted as descriptive, referring to those in England who favored religious reforms that went beyond those instituted as part of the Protestant Reformation, or, more generally, who were more forceful and uncompromising in pressing for religious purity both within the Church and in society as a whole.

Pyrrhic: a metrical foot containing two weak stresses: xx.

Quadrivium: group of four academic subjects (arithmetic, astronomy, geometry, and music) that made up part of the university coursework in the Middle Ages. They were studied after the more basic subjects of the *trivium*.

Quantitative Meter: a metrical system used by Greek and Roman poets, in which a line of verse was measured by the "quantity," or length of sound of each syllable. A foot was measured in terms of syllables classed as long or short.

Quantity: duration of syllables in poetry. The line "There is a Garden in her face" (the first line from the poem of the same name by Thomas Campion) is characterized by the short quantities of the syllables. The last line of Thomas Hardy's "During Wind and Rain" has the same number of syllables as the line by Campion, but the quantities of the syllables are much longer—in other words, the line takes much longer to say: "Down their carved names the rain drop ploughs."

Quatrain: a four-line stanza, usually rhymed.

Quintet: a five-line stanza. Sometimes given as *quintain*.

Rap: originally coined to describe informal conversation, "rap" now usually describes a style of performance poetry in which a poet will chant rhymed verse, sometimes improvised and usually with musical accompaniment that has a heavy beat.

Realism: as a literary term, the presentation through literature of material closely resembling real life. As notions both of what constitutes "real life" and of how it may be most faithfully represented in literature have varied widely, "realism" has taken a variety of meanings. The term *naturalistic* has sometimes been used as a synonym for *realistic*; *naturalism* originated in the nineteenth century as a term denoting a form of realism focusing in particular on grim, unpleasant, or ugly aspects of the real.

Refrain: one or more words or lines repeated at regular points throughout a poem, often at the end of each stanza or group of stanzas. Sometimes a whole stanza may be repeated to create a refrain, like the chorus in a song.

Reggae: a style of heavily rhythmic music from the West Indies with lyrics that are colloquial in language and often anti-establishment in content and flavor. First popularized in the 1960s and 1970s, reggae has had a lasting influence on performance poetry and rap and is a progenitor of dub.

Rhetoric: in classical Greece and Rome, the art of persuasion and public speaking. From the Middle Ages onwards, the study of rhetoric gave greater attention to style, particularly figures of speech. Today in poetics, the term rhetoric may encompass not only figures of speech, but also the persuasive effects of forms, sounds, and word choices.

Rhyme: the repetition of identical or similar sounds, usually in pairs and generally at the ends of metrical lines.

  End-Rhyme: a rhyming word or syllable at the end of a line.

  Eye-Rhyme: rhyming that pairs words whose spellings are alike but whose pronunciations are different: for example, though/slough.

  Feminine Rhyme: a two-syllable (also known as "double") rhyme. The first syllable is stressed and the second unstressed. For example, hasty/tasty. See also *triple rhyme* below.

  Interlocking Rhyme: the repetition of rhymes from one stanza to the next, creating links that add to the poem's continuity and coherence. Examples may be found in Shelley's use of *terza* *rima* in "Ode to the West Wind" and in Dylan Thomas's villanelle "Do Not Go Gentle into That Good Night."

Internal Rhyme: the placement of rhyming words within lines so that at least two words in a line rhyme with each other.

Masculine Rhyme: a correspondence of sound between the final stressed syllables at the end of two or more lines, as in grieve/leave, arr-ive/sur-vive.

Slant Rhyme: an imperfect or partial rhyme (also known as "near" or "half" rhyme) in which the final consonants of stressed syllables match but the vowel sounds do not. E.g., spoiled/spilled, taint/stint.

Triple Rhyme: a three-syllable rhyme in which the first syllable of each rhyme-word is stressed and the other two unstressed (e.g., lottery/coterie).

True Rhyme: a rhyme in which everything but the initial consonant matches perfectly in sound and spelling.

Rhyme Royal: a stanza of seven iambic pentameters, with a rhyme-scheme of *ababbcc*. This is also known as the Chaucerian stanza, as Chaucer was the first English poet to use this form. See also *septet*.

Rhythm: in speech, the arrangement of stressed and unstressed syllables creates units of sound. In song or verse, these units usually form a regular rhythmic pattern, a kind of beat, described in prosody as *meter*.

Romanticism: a major social and cultural movement, originating in Europe, that shaped much of Western artistic thought in the late eighteenth and nineteenth centuries. Opposing the ideal of controlled, rational order of the Enlightenment, Romanticism emphasizes the importance of spontaneous self-expression, emotion, and personal experience in producing art. In Romanticism, the "natural" is privileged over the conventional or the artificial.

Rondeau: a fifteen-line poem, generally octosyllabic, with only two rhymes throughout its three stanzas, and an unrhymed refrain at the end of the ninth and fifteenth lines, repeating part of the opening line.

Sarcasm: See *irony*.

Satire: literary work designed to make fun of or seriously criticize its subject. According to many literary theories of the Renaissance and neoclassical periods, the ridicule through satire of a certain sort of behavior may function for the reader or audience as a corrective of such behavior.

Scansion: the formal analysis of patterns of rhythm and rhyme in poetry. Each line of verse will have a certain number of fairly regular "beats" consisting of alternating stressed and unstressed syllables. To "scan" a poem is to count the beats in each line, to mark stressed and unstressed syllables and indicate their combination into "feet," to note pauses, and to identify rhyme schemes with letters of the alphabet.

Scheme: See *figures of speech*.

Schools: In the sixteenth and seventeenth centuries the different forms of school in England included Cathedral schools (often founded with a view to the education of members of the choir); grammar schools (often founded by towns or by guilds, and teaching a much broader curriculum than the modern sense of "grammar" might suggest); private schools, operated by private individuals out of private residences; and public schools, which (like the private schools and the grammar schools) operated independent of any church authority, but unlike the grammar schools and private schools were organized as independent charities, and often offered free education. Over the centuries certain of these public schools, while remaining not-for-profit institutions, began to accept fee-paying students and to adopt standards that made them more and more exclusive. In the eighteenth and nineteenth centuries, attendance at such prestigious public boarding schools as Eton, Westminster, and Winchester had become almost exclusively the preserve of the upper classes; by the nineteenth century such "public" schools were the equivalent of private schools in North America. A few girls attended some early grammar schools, but the greater part of this educational system was for boys only. Though a number of individuals of earlier periods were concerned to increase the number of private schools for girls, the movement to create a parallel girls' system of public schools and grammar schools dates from the later nineteenth century.

Septet: a stanza containing seven lines.

Serf: in the medieval period, a person of unfree status, typically engaged in working the land.

Sestet: a six-line stanza that forms the second grouping of lines in an Italian/Petrarchan sonnet, following the octave. See *sonnet* and *sestina*.

Sestina: an elaborate unrhymed poem with six six-line stanzas and a three-line envoy.

Shire: originally a multiple estate; since the late medieval period a larger territory forming an administrative unit—also referred to as a county.

Simile: a *figure of speech* (a trope) which makes an explicit comparison between a particular object and another object or idea that is similar in some (often unexpected) way. A simile always uses "like" or "as" to signal the connection. Compare with *metaphor* above.

Sonnet: a highly structured lyric poem, which normally has fourteen lines of iambic pentameter. We can distinguish four major variations of the sonnet.

Italian/Petrarchan: named for the fourteenth-century Italian poet Petrarch, has an octave rhyming *abbaabba*, and a sestet rhyming *cdecde*, or *cdcdcd* (other arrangements are possible here). Usually, a turn in argument takes place between octave and sestet.

Miltonic: developed by Milton and similar to the Petrarchan in rhyme scheme, but eliminating the turn after the octave, thus giving greater unity to the poem's structure of thought.

Shakespearean: often called the English sonnet, this form has three quatrains and a couplet. The quatrains rhyme internally but do not interlock: *abab cdcd efef gg*. The turn may occur after the second quatrain, but is usually revealed in the final couplet. Shakespeare's sonnets are the best-known examples of this form.

Spenserian: after Edmund Spenser, who developed the form in his sonnet cycle *Amoretti*. This sonnet form has three quatrains linked through interlocking rhyme, and a separately rhyming couplet: *abab bcbc cdcd ee*.

Speaker: in the late medieval period, a member of the Commons in Parliament who spoke on behalf of that entire group. (The Commons first elected a Speaker in 1376.) In later eras the role of Speaker became one of chairing debates in the House of Commons and arbitrating disputes over matters of procedure.

Spenserian Stanza: a nine-line stanza, with eight iambic pentameters and a concluding alexandrine, rhyming *ababbcbcc*.

Spondee: a metrical foot containing two strong stressed syllables: // (e.g., blind mouths).

Sprung Rhythm: a modern variation of accentual verse, created by the English poet Gerard Manley Hopkins, in which rhythms are determined largely by the number of strong stresses in a line, without regard to the number of unstressed syllables. Hopkins felt that sprung rhythm more closely approximated the natural rhythms of speech than did conventional poetry.

Stanza: any lines of verse that are grouped together in a poem and separated from other similarly structured groups by a space. In metrical poetry, stanzas share metrical and rhyming patterns; however, stanzas may also be formed on the basis of thought, as in irregular odes. Conventional stanza forms include the *tercet*, the *quatrain*, *rhyme royal*, the *Spenserian stanza*, the *ballad stanza*, and *ottava rima*.

Stream of Consciousness: narrative technique that attempts to convey in prose fiction a sense of the progression of the full range of thoughts and sensations occurring within a character's mind. Twentieth-century pioneers in the use of the stream of consciousness technique include Dorothy Richardson, Virginia Woolf, and James Joyce.

Stress: See *accent*.

Strophe: the first stanza in a Pindaric ode. This is followed by an *antistrophe* (see above), which presents the same metrical pattern and rhyme scheme, and finally by an *epode*, differing in meter from the preceding stanzas. Upon completion of this "triad," the entire sequence can recur. *Strophe* may also describe a stanza or other subdivision in other kinds of poem.

Sublime: a concept, most popular in eighteenth-century England, of the qualities of grandeur, power, and awe that may be inherent in or produced by undomesticated nature or great art. The sublime was thought of as higher and loftier than something that is merely beautiful.

Subplot: a line of story that is subordinate to the main storyline of a narrative. (Note that properly speaking a subplot is a category of story material, not of plot.)

Substitution: a deliberate change from the dominant pattern of stresses in a line of verse to create emphasis or variation. Thus the first line of Shakespeare's sonnet "'Shall I compare thee to a summer's day?'" is decidedly iambic in meter (x / x / x / x / x /), whereas the second line substitutes a trochee (/ x) in the opening foot: "Thou art more lovely and more temperate."

Subtext: implied or suggested meaning of a passage of text, or of an entire work.

Syllabic Verse: poetry in which the length of a line is measured solely by the number of syllables, regardless of accents or patterns of stress.

Syllable: vocal sound or group of sounds forming a unit of speech; a syllable may be formed with a single effort of articulation. Some syllables consist of a single phoneme (e.g., the word *I*, or the first syllable in the word *u*-ni-ty) but others may be made up of several phonemes (as with one-syllable words such as *lengths*, *splurged*, and *through*). By contrast, the much shorter words *ago*, *any*, and *open* each have two syllables.

Symbol: a word, image, or idea that represents something more, or other, than for what it at first appears to stand. Like metaphor, the symbol extends meaning; but while the tenor and vehicle of metaphor are bound in a specific relationship, a symbol may have a range of connotations. For example, the image of a rose may call forth associations of love, passion, transience, fragility, youth, and beauty, among others. Depending upon the context, such an image could be interpreted in a variety of ways, as in Blake's lyric, "The Sick Rose." Though this power of symbolic representation characterizes all language, poetry most particularly endows the concrete imagery evoked through language with a larger meaning. Such meaning is implied rather than explicitly stated; indeed, much of the power of symbolic language lies in the reader's ability to make meaningful sense of it.

Syncope: in poetry, the dropping of a letter or syllable from the middle of a word, as in "trav'ler." Such a contraction allows a line to stay within a metrical scheme. See also *catalexis* and *elision*.

Synecdoche: a kind of *metonymy* in which a writer substitutes the name of a part of something to signify the whole: for example, "sail" for ship or "hand" for a member of the ship's crew.

Tercet: a group, or stanza, of three lines, often linked by an interlocking rhyme scheme as in *terza rima*. See also *triplet*.

Terza Rima: an arrangement of tercets interlocked by a rhyme scheme of *aba bcb cdc ded*, etc., and ending with a couplet that rhymes with the second-last line of the final tercet (for example, *efe, ff*). See, for example, Percy Shelley's "Ode to the West Wind."

Tetrameter: a line of poetry containing four metrical feet.

Theme: the governing idea of a discourse, conveyed through the development of the subject, and through the recurrence of certain words, sounds, or metrical patterns. See also *motif*.

Third-Person Narrative: See *narrative perspective*.

Tone: the writer's attitude toward a given subject or audience, as expressed through an authorial persona or "voice." Tone can be projected through particular choices of wording, imagery, figures of speech, and rhythmic devices. Compare *mood*.

Tories: See *Political Parties*.

Tragedy: in the traditional definition originating in discussions of ancient Greek drama, a serious narrative recounting the downfall of the protagonist. More loosely, the term has been applied to a wide variety of literary forms in which the tone is predominantly a dark one and the narrative does not end happily.

Transcendentalism: a philosophical movement that influenced such Victorian writers as Thomas Carlyle and Robert Browning. Also a mode of Romantic thought, Transcendentalism places the supernatural and the natural within one great Unity and believes that each individual person embodies aspects of the divine.

Trimeter: a line of poetry containing three metrical feet.

Triolet: a French form in which the first line appears three times in a poem of only eight lines. The first line is repeated at lines 4 and 7; the second line is repeated in line 8. The triolet has only two rhymes: *abaaabab*.

Triple Foot: poetic foot of three syllables. The possible varieties of triple foot are the anapest (in which two unstressed syllables are followed by a stressed syllable), the dactyl (in which a stressed syllable is followed by two unstressed lines), and the mollossus (in which all three syllables are stressed equally). English poetry tends to use duple rhythms far more frequently than triple rhythms.

Triplet: a group of three lines with the same end-rhyme, much used by eighteenth-century poets to vary or punctuate the flow of couplets. See also *tercet*.

Trivium: group of three academic subjects (dialectic, grammar, and rhetoric) that were part of the university curriculum in the Middle Ages. Their study precedes that of the more advanced subjects of the *quadrivium*.

Trochee: a metrical foot containing one strong stress followed by one weak stress: / x (heaven, lover).

Trope: any figure of speech that plays on our understandings of words to extend, alter, or transform "literal" meaning. Common tropes include *metaphor*, *simile*, *personification*, *hyperbole*, *metonymy*, *oxymoron*, *synecdoche*, and *irony*. See also *figures of speech*, above.

Turn (Italian "volta"): the point in a *sonnet* where the mood or argument changes. The turn may occur between the octave and sestet, i.e., after the eighth line, or in the final couplet, depending on the kind of sonnet.

Unities: Many literary theorists of the late sixteenth through late eighteenth centuries held that a play should ideally be presented as representing a single place, and confining the action to a single day and a single dominant event. They disapproved of plots involving gaps or long periods of time, shifts in place, or subplots. These concepts, which came to be referred to as the unities of space, time, and action, were based on a misreading of classical authorities (principally of Aristotle).

Vers de societé: literally, "verse about society." The term originated with poetry written by aristocrats and upper-middle-class poets that specifically disavows the ambition of creating "high art" while treating the concerns of their own group in verse forms that demonstrate a high degree of formal control (e.g., artful rhymes, surprising turns of diction).

Vers libre: See *free verse* above.

Verse: a general term for works of poetry, usually referring to poems that incorporate some kind of metrical structure. The term may also describe a line of poetry, though more frequently it is applied to a stanza.

Villanelle: a poem usually consisting of 19 lines, with five 3-line stanzas (tercets) rhyming *aba*, and a concluding quatrain rhyming *abaa*. The first and third lines of the first tercet are repeated at fixed intervals throughout the rest of the poem. See, for example, Dylan Thomas's "Do Not Go Gentle into That Good Night."

Whigs: See *Political Parties*.

Workhouse: public institution in which the poor were provided with a minimal level of sustenance and with lodging in exchange for work performed. Early workhouses were typically administered by individual parishes. In 1834 a unified system covering all of England and Wales was put into effect.

Zeugma: a *figure of speech* (trope) in which one word links or "yokes" two others in the same sentence, often to comic or ironic effect. For example, a verb may govern two objects, as in Pope's line "Or stain her honour, or her new brocade."

PERMISSIONS ACKNOWLEDGMENTS

Clare, John. "The Lament for Swordy Well," from *John Clare: Poems of the Middle Period, Volume V: 1822–1837*. General Editor, Eric Robinson. Reprinted with the permission of Oxford University Press.

Wordsworth, William. Manuscript D of "The Ruined Cottage," from *The Ruined Cottage* and *The Pedlar*, edited by James A. Butler. Copyright @ 1978 by Cornell University. Used by permission of the publisher, Cornell University Press.

ILLUSTRATION CREDITS

Color Insert: *Mountain Landscape*, n.d. Elizabeth Leveson-Gower, Duchess-Countess of Sutherland 1765–1830. Photo © Tate, London 2017.

Color Insert: *A Stoppage to a Stride Over the Globe*, published by Piercy Roberts. Copyright © Trustees of the British Museum.

Page 1: Reproduced by permission of the National Portrait Gallery, London. [Macpherson]

Page 26: Reproduced by permission of the National Portrait Gallery, London. [Barbauld]

Page 45: Reproduced by permission of the National Portrait Gallery, London. [C. Smith]

Page 127: Reproduced by permission of the National Portrait Gallery, London. [Robinson]

Page 137: Reproduced by permission of the National Portrait Gallery, London. [Wollstonecraft]

Page 409: "I Wandered Lonely as a Cloud" facsimile: The Wordsworth Trust.

Page 556: Reproduced by permission of the National Portrait Gallery, London. [Coleridge]

Page 609: Reproduced by permission of the National Portrait Gallery, London. [Tighe]

Page 685: Reproduced by permission of the National Portrait Gallery, London. [De Quincey]

Page 771: Reproduced by permission of the National Portrait Gallery, London. [Byron]

Page 919: Reproduced by permission of the National Portrait Gallery, London. [P. Shelley]

Page 1162: Reproduced by permission of the National Portrait Gallery, London. [Polidori]

Page 1175: Reproduced by permission of the National Portrait Gallery, London. [M. Shelley]

Page 1215: Reproduced by permission of the National Portrait Gallery, London. [Landon]

Information on all translations used is provided in footnotes at the beginning of selections. Copyright permission to reproduce material translated or edited for this anthology and material reproduced or adapted here that originally appeared in other books published by Broadview Press may be sought from Broadview.

The publisher has endeavored to contact rights holders of all copyright material and would appreciate receiving any information as to errors or omissions.

INDEX OF FIRST LINES

INDEX OF AUTHORS AND TITLES

From the Publisher

A name never says it all, but the word "Broadview" expresses a good deal of the philosophy behind our company. We are open to a broad range of academic approaches and political viewpoints. We pay attention to the broad impact book publishing and book printing has in the wider world; for some years now we have used 100% recycled paper for most titles. Our publishing program is internationally oriented and broad-ranging. Our individual titles often appeal to a broad readership too; many are of interest as much to general readers as to academics and students.

Founded in 1985, Broadview remains a fully independent company owned by its shareholders—not an imprint or subsidiary of a larger multinational.

For the most accurate information on our books (including information on pricing, editions, and formats) please visit our website at www.broadviewpress.com. Our print books and ebooks are also available for sale on our site.

broadview press
www.broadviewpress.com